ABLE OF ORWEGIAN PHONEMES ND THEIR PPROXIMATE NGLISH EQUIVALENTS

honemic ymbols	Int. Phon. Alphabet	Norwegian keyword	English keyword	Phonemic symbols	Int. Phon. Alphabet	Norwegian keyword	English keyword
]	[ɑ]	katt	cut	[o]	[ɷ]	bukk	book
·]	[ɑ:]	far	far =			[bokk]	
i]	[ɑi]	hai	high	[o·]	[ɷ:]	mo	moo/mow
u]	[æʉ]	haus	house	[oi]	[ɔi]	koie	coya
			(Southern)	[p]	[p]	pappa	papa —
]	[b]	bi	bee =	[r]	[r]	reis	race
]	[d]	du	do =	[s]	[s]	si	see =
]	[ɛ]	tenn	ten =	[sj]	[ṡ]	sju	shoe =
] weak	[ə]	lettes	lettuce	[t]	[t]	tenn	ten =
·]	[e:]	ben	bane	[u]	[ʉ]	futt	foot/Fr. fute
i]	[æi, ɛi]	nei	nay	[u·]	[u:]	ku	coo/Fr. cue
	[f]	fet	fate =	[ui]	[ʉi]	hui	hooey
]	[g]	gå	go =	[v]	[v]	vett	vet =
]	[h]	ha	ha =	[y]	[y]	sydd	Sid/Fr. sud
	[i]	bitt	bit	[y·]	[y:]	sy	see/Fr. su
]	[i:]	bit	beat =	[æ]	[æ]	lærd	laird
	[j]	jett	yet =	[æ·]	[æ:]	lær	lair
]	[k]	kul	cool =	[ø]	[ø]	trøst	trust
i]	[ç]	kjemi	Chemie	[ø·]	[ø:]	bød	bird
			(Ger.)				(Eastern)
	[l]	li	lee	[øy]	[øy]	bøyd	buoyed
]	[m]	mai	my =	[å]	[ɔ]	gått	got
]	[n]	nei	nay =				(Eastern)
g]	[ŋ]	seng	sang =	[å·]	[ɔ:]	kåt	caught/coat

y the sounds marked = can be said to have a fairly exact English equivalent.

NORSK
ENGELSK
ORDBOK

NORWEGIAN
ENGLISH
DICTIONARY

NORSK ENGELSK ORDBOK

Norsk [bokmål og nynorsk] rettskrivnings- og uttaleordbok
med oversettelser til amerikansk engelsk.
Med en historisk
og grammatisk innledning.

EINAR HAUGEN, Ph. D.
Hovedredaktør

Kenneth G. Chapman, Ph. D.
Dag Gundersen, Cand. Philol.
Jørgen Rischel, Mag. Art.
Medredaktører

Nytt amerikansk opplag med tillegg og rettelser

UNIVERSITETSFORLAGET - OSLO
UNIVERSITY OF WISCONSIN PRESS - MADISON

NORWEGIAN ENGLISH DICTIONARY

A Pronouncing and Translating Dictionary
of Modern Norwegian [Bokmål and Nynorsk]
With a Historical
and Grammatical Introduction

EINAR HAUGEN, Ph. D.
Editor-in-Chief

Kenneth G. Chapman, Ph. D.
Dag Gundersen, Cand. Philol.
Jørgen Rischel, Mag. Art.
Associate Editors

New and Enlarged American Printing

UNIVERSITETSFORLAGET - OSLO
UNIVERSITY OF WISCONSIN PRESS - MADISON

The University of Wisconsin Press
1930 Monroe Street
Madison, Wisconsin 53711

3 Henrietta Street
London WC2E 8LU, England

www.wisc.edu\wisconsinpress

In Norway
Universitetsforlaget
Postboks 2977, Tøyen
Oslo, Norway

17 16 15 14 13

Printed in the United States of America

ISBN 0-299-03874-2; LC 72-11462

TABLE OF CONTENTS

STAFF, NORWEGIAN-ENGLISH DICTIONARY

Editor-in-Chief

Einar Haugen, Vilas Professor of Scandinavian and Linguistics, University of Wisconsin (after July 1, 1964, Harvard University). Ph. D. (University of Illinois). Direction, editing (1961—1964).

Associates

Kenneth G. Chapman, Associate Professor of Scandinavian Languages, University of California, Los Angeles. Ph. D. (University of Wisconsin). Editing, glossing (July 1, 1962—February 1, 1963).

Dag Gundersen, Lexicographer, Oslo, Norway. Cand. philol. (University of Oslo). Selection, pronunciation, glossing, proofreading (October, 1961—September, 1962 in Madison); editing, proofreading (1962—1964 in Oslo).

Jørgen Rischel, Instructor in Phonetics, University of Copenhagen, Denmark. Mag. art. (University of Copenhagen). Selection, grammar, editing (September, 1961—June, 1962).

Assistants

A. Gerald Anderson, University of Wisconsin. B. A. (University of Wisconsin). Excerpting, editing, proofreading (September, 1961—August, 1962).

Eva Lund Haugen, Madison, Wisconsin. B. A. (University of Wisconsin). Glossing, proofreading (part time, 1961—1963).

Kenneth A. Hoem, University of Washington, Seattle, Washington. M. A. (University of Washington). Glossing, typing (September, 1962—August, 1963).

Lars Kindem, Minneapolis, Minn. B. A. (St. Olaf College). Selection (summer, 1961).

Lully Lund, Madison, Wisconsin. Proofreading, editing (1963—64).

Anne Margrete Manner, Oslo, Norway. Card punching, secretarial work, proofreading, typing, editing (May, 1963—June, 1964).

Barbara G. Morgridge, Everett Junior College, Everett, Wash. M. A. (University of Washington). Glossing, editing, proofreading (June, 1963—August, 1963).

Paul H. Overton, University of California, Los Angeles, Cal. B. A. (U. C. L. A.). Glossing, checking, proofreading (June, 1962—July, 1963).

Anne-Helene Rødland, Oslo, Norway. Proofreading, typing, editing (July, 1963—June, 1964).

Wenche M. Sandsten, Oslo, Norway. Card punching, secretarial work, pronunciation, typing (September, 1962—May, 1963).

Janice Stewart, Madison, Wisconsin. M. A. (University of Wisconsin). Glossing, proofreading, secretarial work (September, 1961—May, 1963).

Inger Astrid Ullestad, Voss, Norway. Card punching (September, 1961—May, 1962).

Consultant

Martin Joos, Professor of German, University of Wisconsin. Ph. D. (University of Wisconsin).

PREFACE

The present work is intended primarily as a tool for the learning of Norwegian by American students. For advanced students it will serve also as an introduction to a scientific description of the Norwegian language. These purposes have dictated the inclusion of some novel features suggested by the editor's experience as an American teacher of Norwegian. (*a*) It is the first dictionary in any language to include both forms of Norwegian, *Bokmål* (*Riksmål*, Dano-Norwegian) and *Nynorsk* (*Landsmål*, New Norwegian) in one alphabet, and the first Norwegian-English dictionary to include *Nynorsk*.[1] (*b*) It is the first Norwegian-English dictionary to give the pronunciation of the Norwegian words. (*c*) It is the first such dictionary to label areas of usage and to include quotations from Norwegian authors. Some useful features that are not as common in bilingual dictionaries as they might be are the inclusion of common abbreviations, of important place and proper names, and of cultural features. The grammatical information is fuller than in any previous work of its kind. Norwegian-English dictionaries prepared in Norway are oriented towards the Norwegian learner of English and are, therefore, very sparing in their information on Norwegian. It is hoped that the present dictionary will serve as a desk handbook for anyone interested in reading modern Norwegian, and in learning to use it in speaking and writing.

The orientation to American users will be apparent in the English glosses, which are in American English instead of the British English that has characterized most previous Norwegian-English dictionaries. However, the emphasis has been on a standard English such as is used by the best American writers and speakers, with slang specifically labeled as (*pop.*). Norwegians learning English are likely to find American English increasingly useful to them. More English synonyms have been included than strictly necessary, and they have been organized in such a way that the user should be able to decide which English word to use in a given context. The Norwegian user will also find that the information given on his native language is more copious than in any one-volume dictionary available to him in Norway. Here he will find all the spellings of any word that have been in use since 1917, within the limits of space available, for both languages and the manifold varieties of each down through the Textbook Norm of 1959.

The idea of preparing such a dictionary was first suggested to the Editor by his friend and then colleague, the late Dr. Sverre Kjeldstadli. The Editor had already been concerned over

[1] Note that the names of these languages are here everywhere capitalized, following English usage for language names, but contrary to Norwegian usage. For the most part they will be abbreviated as Bm and Nn, respectively.

many years with the problems of teaching and analyzing Norwegian. His textbooks (*Beginning Norwegian* 1937, *Reading Norwegian* 1939, and *Spoken Norwegian* 1944, revised edition 1964) could do no more than start the learner on his path. Beyond this the learner was on his own, with the dictionary as his only crutch. The dictionaries were either out-dated, inaccurate, or limited in their vocabulary selection. The students' need could be met for a time by the preparation of a number of page-by-page glossaries to current Norwegian books. But the only long-term solution was a dictionary which would be comprehensive enough to meet the students' need. The Editor had at his disposal a large body of materials in the form of more than two million vocabulary slips collected in the 1930's from the writings of certain classic Norwegian authors (published in part in 1942 as *Norwegian Word Studies*, 2 volumes). But he hesitated to undertake a dictionary until he could envisage a possibility of financing the project. In 1958 the National Defense Education Act began to make funds available for the preparation of materials in "neglected languages," a category for which Norwegian qualified. An application for funds was honored by the Office of Education in the Department of Health, Education, and Welfare in Washington, D.C., resulting in a contract between that office and the University of Wisconsin. It was estimated that the basic work should be completed in two and a half years, which proved to be feasible. Space was provided at the University of Wisconsin from June 1961 to June 1964, with most of the work being done between September 1961 and September 1963. During the latter period the Editor worked full time on the dictionary (except for teaching one class), directing and coordinating the efforts of a staff which averaged five full-time workers.

The Editor hereby expresses his gratitude to the Office of Education and the director of its Language Section, A. Bruce Gaarder, for their readiness to support this project. Above all he is grateful to Mr. James E. Alatis, Specialist for Research, and Mrs. Julia A. Petrov, Research Assistant, in the Bureau of Educational Assistance Programs, who were his immediate contacts and constant counselors. He is deeply grateful to the University of Wisconsin Graduate School and its Dean, John E. Willard, who provided funds for one Project Associate and two Project Assistants throughout the duration of the project; to The University of Wisconsin College of Letters of Science and its Dean, Mark H. Ingraham, who, with the assistance of the Trustees of the William F. Vilas Trust Estate, made it possible for the Editor to be freed from teaching for this project; to the University of Wisconsin Press and its director, Thompson Webb, Jr., who accepted the dictionary for publication and provided numerous services in the form of advice and editing; to Universitetsforlaget i Oslo (the University of Oslo Press) and its director, Tønnes Andenæs, who accepted the dictionary for publication in Norway and helped to get it printed in the best possible form; and to the director and staff of the Center for Advanced Study in the Behavioral Sciences, Stanford, California, where the writing was completed.

The Editor is particularly grateful to the members of his staff, whose names are listed above (p. 7), for their willingness to take time to assist in the planning and preparation of a book which in many ways has consumed time without yielding adequate returns in the form of personal satisfactions. Their work as "harmless drudges" (in Samuel Johnson's phrase) has at least made possible the reduction of drudgery for those who will have occasion to use the book. Mrs. Lully Lund merits special mention for her faithful proofreading of the entire book. Many thanks are due to the Editor's Norwegian colleagues in the Department of Scandinavian Studies at the University of Wisconsin, Professors Harald S. Næss and H. P. Krosby, who patiently answered his many questions on Norwegian usage; likewise to Alf Hellevik and Professor Alf Sommerfelt, of the University of Oslo, both of whom read and criticized an early version of the Introduction. Tape recordings of pronunciation were made by Ann Mari Næss, H. P. Krosby, Ragnhild Grevstad, Anne Margrete Manner, Dr. Samuel Abrahamsen, Prof. Alf Sommerfelt, and Aimée Sommerfelt. Thanks go to these and to many others who will have to remain unnamed.

Special thanks go to William T. Evjue, editor of Madison's *Capital Times*, who made a donation of $1,000 in memory of his Norwegian-born parents, Nils and Martha Evjue, to aid in defraying the costs of publication.

Finally, he wishes to single out for mention his wife, Eva Lund Haugen, whose share in the dictionary extends far beyond the work she did as a part-time member of the staff.

Harvard University,
May, 1965.

E. H.

INTRODUCTION

1 Instructions to the User

The reader is advised to study this section carefully so that he may derive maximum benefit from the use of the Dictionary. Each dictionary entry contains some or all of the following items of information, which are briefly explained below. More detailed treatment is given to some of them in the rest of the Introduction.

1.1 The Main Entry
1.2 Language Membership
1.3 Pronunciation
1.4 Grammar
1.5 Cross References
1.6 Secondary Entries
1.7 Usage Labels
1.8 English Glosses
1.9 Supplementary Notes
1.10 Idiomatic Phrases
1.11 Literary Illustrations

1.1 THE MAIN ENTRY.

1.1.1 *Types.* Each of the approximately 60,000 main entries begins a new line and is printed in boldface type. The entries are mostly *single words*, *abbreviations*, or *affixes;* phrases are entries only if they are foreign and consist of words not otherwise used in the language (**à vista**). Words are not capitalized unless they are proper nouns. The latter include place names likely to occur in Norwegian writing (including all the townships or *herreder*), as well as some common given names. Affixes are either prefixes (ending in a hyphen, e.g. **an-**) or suffixes (beginning with a hyphen, e.g. **-dom**). Idiomatic phrases are listed under their main word or words, as described below (**1.10**). Abbreviations are followed by an equals sign and their spelled-out equivalents (**d. e.** = **det er**), occasionally by a comparable English abbreviation (which in this case would be i.e.). Usually, however, they are listed only as idiomatic phrases under their appropriate headword.

1.1.2. *Order.* The main entries are arranged alphabetically, with the letters **æ ø å** at the end, in that order. Entries containing hyphens, periods, or slants as part of their spelling follow entries without such marks (e.g. **al, -al, a/l, a.l.**). Phrases are ordered as if they were printed solid (e.g. **al, à la**). Capitalized entries follow uncapitalized ones (**alf, Alf**).

1.1.3 *Form.* Any word that can have more than one grammatical form is entered in its *lexical* form: the singular indefinite *(sg if)* of *nouns*, the positive singular indefinite masculine *(pos sg if m)* of *adjectives*, the masculine singular *(m sg)* of *pronouns*, and the infinitive *(inf)* of *verbs*. Other forms are entered only if there is no lexical form or if they deviate in some irregular way from the lexical form, in which case there is a cross-reference to the latter (below, **1.5.3**).

1.1.4 *Headword.* Each word is normally entered in all spellings that have been accepted as official since 1917, plus some common dialect forms. Whenever the same word is entered in more than one form, these are cross-referenced to one that is currently official, which is selected as the headword. The translation is always listed under the headword (below, **1.5.2**).

1.1.5 *Homonyms.* Identically spelled entries are distinguished by small raised numbers to the right of the entry (**akt**[1] **akt**[2]). Capitalized and punctuated entries are not regarded as homonyms of otherwise identical uncapitalized or unpunctuated entries. Homonyms of different parts of speech are arranged so that nouns come first, then verbs, then the other parts of speech alphabetically.

1.2 LANGUAGE MEMBERSHIP. (See also Section **2**, esp. **2.1**).

1.2.1 All entries and their grammatical forms have been marked for official language membership. Any item preceded by a plus (+) is usually limited to Bm, while one preceded by a star (*) is usually limited to Nn. Any item preceded by a degree mark (°) is dialectal, i.e. not officially accepted in either Bm or Nn (e.g. °**hu** she = +**hun,** ***ho**). Unmarked items are presumed to be admissible in either language, though they are not necessarily equally common in both. Note that in the glosses dialectal usage is often marked by the abbreviation *dial.* instead of the degree mark. No systematic distinction of the two languages has been made in the glosses. Marking as + or * does not always imply official status.

1.3 PRONUNCIATION.

1.3.1 *Respelled Words.* If an entry word is followed immediately by a respelling in square brackets, pronounce it exactly as spelled in the brackets. Give each letter and diacritic mark the usual Norwegian value, as described in the *Guide to Pronunciation* below. For quick reference see the list of symbols in **3.2** and in the end papers. The diacritics are also listed at the foot of each right-hand page.

1.3.2 *Words not Respelled.* Most words are not respelled, but are only marked with diacritics which are not part of their spelling. Silent letters are marked by a subscript dot (in the case of **d g h t**). In order to save respellings, certain conventions have been adopted for letters or combinations of letters that are nearly always pronounced with a different sound than that used in the respelling. These are listed below as "Special Rules for Pronunciation."

1.3.3 *Partial Respelling.* If only part of an entry is included in the respelling bracket, read the rest of the word according to the Special Rules below. Example: **analog** [-lå'g], read [analå'g]; **agn/skjell** [ang`n/], read [ang`n/sjell·].

1.3.4 *Alternative Pronunciations.* If a word has more than one pronunciation, one will be marked on the entry, if possible, while the other will be entered in brackets, preceded by the word "also". The order of the two pronunciations has no significance; both are acceptable. Example: **Ag`der** [also ag'-], read that Agder can be pronounced either [ag`der] or [ag'der].

1.3.5 *No Marking.* If a compound is neither marked nor respelled, look for the next preceding word with the same first member and apply the same pronunciation. Example: **wiener/vals**, read [vi'ner/val·s] from the word **wiener** [vi'ner].

1.3.6 *Special Rules for Pronunciation.* If a word is not respelled, the following rules will apply: (1) Read all vowels and consonants short unless they are followed *immediately* by one of the accent marks (' ` ·). If there is no accent mark in the syllable, the vowels and consonants will be called "unaccented." *Exception:* the secondary accent mark (·) has been regularly omitted in the first syllable following a slant line, when the number of consonants clearly indicates the length of the vowel, e.g. **hu's/mann,** read [hu's/mann·]; **hu's/tak,** read [hu's/ta·k]; but **kris'ten/dom·**, read [kris'ten/dåmm·] (cf rule for short **o** below). (2) Read all vowels and consonants with the usual Norwegian values assigned them in the respelling, omitting any that have dots below. *Exceptions:* the following combinations are always pronounced as here shown in brackets, unless there is a respelling to the contrary. The respellings included below are omitted in the dictionary.

bs [ps]: **absolutt'**=[apsolutt']

c [s] before **e, i, y, æ, ø**: **cøliba't**=[søliba't]

[k] before all other letters: **cre'do**=[kre'do]

ds [ts]: **god's**=[got's]

dt [tt]: **godt'**=[gått']

er [ær] when **e** is short and accented: **ver'den**=[vær'den]

gi [ji]: **gi'**=[ji']

gj [j]: **gjes't**=[jes't]

gs [ks]: **slag's**=[slak's]

gt [kt]: **lag't**=[lak't]

gy [jy]: **gy'se**=[jy'se]

hj [j]: **hjel'm**=[jel'm]

hv [v]: **hva'**=[va']

ki [kji]: **kinn'**=[kjinn']

ky [kjy]: **kyss'**=[kjyss']

nk [ngk]: **ben'k**=[beng'k] (but not in ***nkj**, e.g. **ten'kje**=[ten'kje])

o [å] short accented, or unaccented before two or more consonants: **kom'me**=[kåm'me]; **fro'/kost**=[fro'/kås·t]; **morfi'n**=[mårfi'n]

qu [kv]: **qua'**=[kva']

sce [se]: **sce'ne**=[se'ne]

ski [sji]: **ski'p**=[sji'p]

skj [sj]: **skjæ'r**=[sjæ'r]

sky [sjy]: **skyss'**=[sjyss']

vs [fs]: **liv's**=[lif's]

vt [ft]: **la'vt**=[la'ft]

w [v]: **watt'**=[vatt']

x [ks]: **sex'**=[sek's]

z [s]: **zu'lu**=[su'lu]

1.4 GRAMMAR. (See also **2.13**).

1.4.1 *Parts of Speech.* Each entry is marked for part of speech right after its respelling (if there is one). Nouns are marked by their inflections only (**1.4.2**), unless they are incapable of appearing with an article, when *N* is used. Other parts of speech are marked by italicized abbreviations beginning with a capital letter, e.g. *A* (adjective), *Art* (article), *Av* (adverb) etc. For the complete list see the Table of Abbreviations (p. 47).

1.4.2 *Inflections.* Only such inflections are listed as are necessary for the user to produce the complete paradigm. This requires that he apply the grammatical rules given below for each part of speech (**1.4.3-7**). As an additional aid, complete sample paradigms are given in **2.13**. Whenever possible, only suffixes are listed; irregular forms are listed in full. Different inflections are separated by commas, e.g. **stå** *V stod, stått,* read: **stå** inf., **stod** past, **stått** perfect participle. Inflected compounds are marked in the same way, except that a few complicated strong verbs are referred back to their uncompounded forms. Alternate forms for the same inflection are separated by slants, e.g. *-en/-et,* read: this noun may take either *-en* or *-et* in the definite singular. If any alternate differs in language membership from other alternates or from the entry itself, this will be marked, e.g. *-a/+-et/*-te,* read: this verb forms its past by adding *-et* in Bm, *-te* in Nn, *-a* in both.

1.4.3 *Nouns.* These are primarily identified for gender by the suffixed def. sg. article, which most frequently determines the plural form also. If a noun cannot take a definite article, the indefinite is used instead (e.g. *en* instead of *-en,* or *ei* instead of *-a* etc.). If neither article can be used, it is marked *N* (e.g. **celsius** *N*). Suffixes are to be added directly to the entry form, unless the latter ends in unstressed *-e,* and one of the suffix alternatives is *-a,* in which case the suffix replaces the final *-e,* e.g. **vise** *-a/+-en,* read: the def. sg. of **vise** is **visen** in Bm, **visa** in both languages; but **hane** *-n,* read: the def. sg. of **hane**

is **hanen** (in both languages). The final unstressed syllables *-el*, *-en*, and *-er* are repeated with the article in those words where the *-e-* must be dropped when the suffix is added, e.g. **alter** *-eret/-ret*, read: the def. sg. of **alter** is either **alteret** or **altret**. Irregular plurals are entered after the abbreviation *pl*, e.g. **bok** *-a, pl bøker*, read: the def. sg. of **bok** is **boka**, the indef. pl. **bøker**.

1.4.4 *Adjectives*. These are left unmarked for inflection if they add the regular *-t* of the neuter singular, the *-e* of the def. sg. and indef. and def. pl. If they do not add *-t*, the *A* will be followed by a short dash, e.g. **stille** *A* -, read: the neuter sg. of **stille** is **stille**. The comparative form (if there is one) is assumed to be *+-ere/*-are*, the superlative *+-est/*-ast*. Other forms will be listed and appropriately identified.

1.4.5 *Adverbs*. Inflected adverbs are derived from adjectives, as a rule, and are not separately listed in the Dictionary. Their inflections are limited to comparison and are identical with those of the corresponding adjectives.

1.4.6 *Pronouns*. The headword for each pronoun is the masculine singular subjective *(m sg sb)*, where these forms are distinguished, so that e.g. **det** and **de** must be sought under **den**, **meg** under **jeg**. Since all of these are more or less irregular, nearly all forms are listed and appropriately identified.

1.4.7 *Verbs*. These are normally identified by the past suffix (*pt*); if two suffixes are listed, the second is the perfect participle (*pp*). Other needed forms are labeled, e.g. *pr* (present), *imp* (imperative) etc. Note that verbs (contrary to nouns) add all suffixes to the stem, i.e. after subtraction of any unstressed *-e* or *-a*, e.g. **kaste** *-a/+-et*, read: the past of **kaste** is Bm **kastet**, both languages **kasta**.

1.5 CROSS REFERENCES.

1.5.1 *Types*. All entries which are not themselves headwords (above, **1.1.4**) end with a cross reference. There are two different kinds of references, one in the case of deviant spellings (**1.5.2**), the other in the case of non-lexical forms (**1.5.3**). Entries are fully marked for language membership, pronunciation, and grammar.

1.5.2 *Deviant Spellings*. All the spellings of one word are cross-referenced to a single headword entry, where the gloss is to be found. Whenever there is a spelling which is common to the two languages according to the Textbook Norm of 1959, this is used as headword. Only forms listed as obligatory (**obligatoriske**) or alternative (**jamstelte**) have been used in this way; optional (**tillatte**) forms have not been considered. If there is no spelling common to the two languages, but there are two distinct spellings of what is obviously the same word, the Bm spelling has been made headword. Words which may mean the same thing but are not historically related (e.g. **anledning** and **høve**) are not cross-referenced. The form of deviant-spelling cross references is to follow the spelling with cf and the headword, e.g. **an\`de/laus** *A* cf **ånde/løs**, read: the gloss of **andelaus** will be found under **åndeløs**. To save space only one part of compounds is given, with its slash, if the other part is identical with that of the headword, e.g. **an\`de/drag** *-et* cf **ånde/**, read: the gloss of **andedrag** will be found under **åndedrag**. If there is no slant, a hyphen is used for the same purpose.

1.5.3 *Non-lexical Forms*. These are listed as entries only if they are in some way irregular, to the extent of having to be listed three or more entries away from the lexical form. To give the user as much help as possible, irregularity has been quite liberally interpreted. Compounds are abbreviated by hyphens (not slants), e.g. **an'/gikk** *pt of* **-gå**, read: **angikk** is the past of **angå**, where the gloss will be found. In these cross references the form is identified as an inflection *of* the headword.

1.5.4 *Omitted Spellings.* Space has been conserved by omitting deviations which involve regular and predictable relationships between the two languages in their system of suffixes. (1) *Infinitives:* all infinitives have been listed as ending in *-e*, as permitted in both languages by the Textbook Norm of 1959. (2) *Adjectives:* all adjectives that are common to the two languages are listed under their Bm endings *-et(e)*, *-ig*, and *-lig* and not under their Nn endings *-ut*, *-ug*, and *-leg*. (3) *Mediopassives:* all verbs that are common to the two languages are listed under their Bm endings *-s* and not under their Nn endings *-st*. Note that the agent suffix *-ar* of Nn is not suppressed in favor of Bm *-er*, but is included as a secondary entry, e.g. **+ar'v/taker** *-en, pl -e* (= ***-ar**), read: the Bm form **arvtaker** corresponds to Nn **arvtakar**. The reason is that some words have *-er* in both languages, e.g. **skipper.**

1.6 SECONDARY ENTRIES.

1.6.1 *Types.* After the grammatical information some entries include within parentheses other spellings than the one chosen as headword. These are preceded by an equals sign, are in boldface type, and are marked for language membership, sometimes for grammar. Like the cross references they may be abbreviated with either slants or hyphens. The secondary entries are of two types, being added either to provide additional spellings **(1.6.2)** or reverse references **(1.6.3)**.

1.6.2 *Additional Spellings.* If an alternative spelling would appear within three entries of its headword, it is often combined with the latter as a secondary entry, e.g. **a'v/kastning** *-a/+-en* (= ***/kasting**), read: **avkastning** is usable in both languages, while the form **avkasting** is limited to Nn.

1.6.3 *Reverse References.* While all non-headword spellings are cross-referenced to their headword, the reverse is not usually true. But a number of exceptions have been made to this rule, where it might conceivably serve some purpose. An example is the entry **au'st/frå** *Av* (= **+øst/fra**), read: the spelling **austfrå** is available in both languages and is therefore headword, but the better-known form in Bm is **østfra.** The latter is also an entry in its proper place, with a cross-reference to **austfrå.** There are no reverse references to officially unacceptable forms, e.g. from **sju** to **syv.**

1.7 USAGE LABELS.

1.7.1 *Types.* Usage labels appear in italics, usually abbreviated, immediately before the English gloss. When they apply to the entire word, they appear before all glosses; when only to a single gloss, then before that gloss. There are two types, subject labels and status labels.

1.7.2 *Subject Labels.* These designate the specialized field of activity within which a word or a meaning is normally or basically used. There is a large number of such labels (see Table of Abbreviations, p. 47), e.g., *anat.* (anatomical), *bot.* (botanical), *jur.* (legal), *naut.* (nautical), etc. The labels pinpoint a meaning, e.g. **aksep't** *-en merc.* acceptance, read: **aksept** is a mercantile word and the gloss "acceptance" is to be taken only in that sense. Some fields (e.g. sports) are written out in full and are not abbreviated. The label *hist.* (historical) is applied to institutions or customs no longer current, e.g. **spåmann** in the sense of 'soothsayer'.

1.7.3 *Status Labels.* These designate the kind of social or literary contexts in which a term is likely to occur. They are limited to the following: *archaic*, *obs.* (obsolete), *lit.* (literary), *fam.* (familiar), *hum.* (humorous), *pop.* (popular), and *dial.* (dialectal). The following brief statements indicate approximately what is meant by each of these. *Archaic* (= archaizing): not in current use, but may appear in writings intended to have an old-fashioned flavor, e.g. the historical novels of Sigrid Undset. *Obsolete:* entirely out of use, found only in older writings. *Literary:* used in formal or even journalistic writing, but not in speech to any extent. *Familiar:* favored in informal usage, as among friends or within the family. *Humorous:* found in jesting contexts, not to be applied seriously. *Popular:* used chiefly by uneducated people, or humorously by others. *Dialectal:* geographically or socially limited, usually to rural speakers, and unacceptable in the standard language, except in imaginative literature and for purposes of characterization.

1.7.4 *Evaluation.* It must not be thought that failure to apply a usage label means that a word could not have been so designated; there are anatomical terms that could have been labeled *anat.* and dialectal usages not labeled *dial.* The cue for the labeling often came from *Norsk Riksmålsordbok* (folk. = *pop.*, fam. = *fam.*), but it was impossible within the framework of this project to review the entire labeling system of that dictionary. The labels overlap and are to be regarded as suggestive, not exhaustive. Note that American slang usage, when included, has been labeled *(pop.)*, in parentheses, to advise the non-native user of its status.

1.8 ENGLISH GLOSSES.

1.8.1 *Problem.* The glosses, or translations, constitute the main body of the dictionary and are its chief *raison d'être.* Because of their complexity, they are also the most difficult to prepare and the least likely to meet with the user's approval. Except in the case of scientific terms with precise, mathematical definitions, it is not possible to speak of exact equivalents between two languages. The vocabulary of any language reflects in its network of meanings the culture and outlook of its users.

1.8.2 *Sequence.* Instead of just presenting for each word or phrase an unorganized list of possible translations the editors have attempted to organize the glosses into a meaningful sequence. This should simplify the use of the book and at the same time display the ramifications of each term. There are three kinds of glosses, which we will call "simple," "complex," and "multiple."

1.8.3 *Simple Glosses.* These consist of one, two, or three English words, arranged alphabetically and separated by commas (**lodd**[1] . . . fate, lot). When there is more than one word, it is intended that they be synonyms of one another, and that their overlap shall show the central meaning of the Norwegian term. Thus "fate" and "lot" overlap and mutually define one another, showing that "lot" is here to be taken in the meaning of "fate," not e.g., of a piece of property.

1.8.4 *Complex Glosses.* These consist of two or more simple glosses, set off by semicolons (**lodd**[2] . . . lot (as in cast lots); lottery ticket; lottery prize). The glosses in this example do not overlap in meaning, but they have in common a general association with gambling. The only requirement for a complex gloss is thus that its members have a semantic feature in common.

1.8.5 *Multiple Glosses.* These consist of two or more glosses, simple or complex, each of which is given a distinct number (**1**, **2**, **3**, etc. in boldface type) and set off by periods. Each numbered gloss is sufficiently distinct from the others so that it may to all intents and purposes be thought of as a different word. The multiple glosses of one word have little in common beyond their historical origin. Thus the meanings of **lodd**[2] referring to gambling have been numbered **1**, while those that refer to various kinds of weights are numbered 2.

1.8.6 *Order.* In arranging the complex and multiple glosses, emphasis has been given to placing the most common or general meanings first, followed by the more specialized or literary meanings.

1.9 SUPPLEMENTARY NOTES.

1.9.1 *Cultural Features.* Parentheses are used before and after the glosses to introduce additional explanation and comment beyond the bare gloss itself. This includes brief descriptions of Norwegian cultural features, such as foods, folklore, education, history, and geography, especially when these might not easily be available in American works of reference. Others are introduced in order to save the student the labor of looking up obscure technical terms and allusions. English equivalents are regularly given for metric terms. Latin botanical and zoological terms are included for the sake of precision.

1.9.2 *Prepositions.* An important service to the user who wishes to employ a given Norwegian word correctly or to understand shades of usage is the inclusion of prepositions and other connectives wherever these are called for. Thus "**akte** . . . **1** heed, pay attention (**på** to)" is to be read: **akte,** in the sense of "heed, pay attention," requires the preposition **på** in those contexts which in English require *to.* The preposition is usually placed after the last gloss to which it applies; it always appears in parentheses, with the Norwegian word preceding its English gloss. In some cases there may be more than one of either.

1.10 IDIOMATIC PHRASES.

1.10.1 *Meaning.* Idioms are important lexical items, which must be listed because it is not possible to discover their meanings by combining the meanings of their parts. The expression **i dag** is an idiom only because its parts **i** 'in' and **dag** 'day' do not in English add up to its meaning 'today'.

1.10.2 *Form.* Idioms are printed in boldface type, but are not listed as main entries. They are preceded by colons, and separated by semicolons. If a word occurs in idioms only, it will be followed immediately by a colon and its idioms and will have no other gloss.

1.10.3 *Location.* Idioms are listed under their most important member, usually the one of lowest frequency and greatest stress. Thus **i dag** is listed under **dag,** while the verb phrase **finne på** is listed under **finne.** In some cases idioms are listed under more than one member. Idioms are never interspersed within simple or complex glosses, but are gathered at the end of each multiple (numbered) gloss. Verb phrases (whether with prepositions or reflexive pronouns) are often collected under a separate number. The order of idioms within a gloss is roughly alphabetical.

1.10.4 *Abbreviation.* Idioms are abbreviated whenever possible. Necessary subjects or objects are represented by Norwegian **en, noen, noe** and by English sby (for somebody) or sth (for something). When the main entry word, or any of its glosses, occurs in the idiom or its gloss, it is represented by its first letter and a dash (plus possible suffixes), e.g. **aktorat** . . . prosecution: **fra a-ets side** on behalf of the p-, read: **fra aktoratets side** on behalf of the prosecution. Glosses are abbreviated only within one numbered gloss, when there can be no confusion.

1.11 LITERARY ILLUSTRATIONS.

1.11.1 A number of full sentences are listed together with the idioms and in the same format, though they are not precisely idioms, but merely illustrations of literary uses of certain words. These include popular proverbs, which often defy translation, biblical quotations with their exact references, and a number of well-known literary allusions. There are also sentences from *Norsk Riksmålsordbok* (uncredited) and from writings excerpted for this dictionary (see the Reference Bibliography, p. 43 ff.), usually identified by author only.

2 Historical Background of Norwegian

2.1 *What is Norwegian?* In our day any dictionary that presents itself as "*Norwegian*" must begin by answering this question, which is not as easy as one might expect. Within Norway there is sharp disagreement, stemming from a century-old conflict over the problem of providing Norway with a written language which should be at once distinctively and representatively Norwegian. The conflict is not purely linguistic, but runs through the entire fabric of Norwegian social life, and has found frequent and vigorous expression in Norwegian politics. The government officially recognizes the existence of two major types of Norwegian, *Bokmål* (literally "Book Language") and *Nynorsk* (literally "New Norwegian"). The former continues a Danish tradition of writing, which has been greatly modified under the influence of Norwegian speech habits, and is sometimes referred to as Dano-Norwegian. The latter was constructed as a purely Norwegian form of writing about a century ago, based on those modern dialects which most faithfully preserved the forms of Old Norwegian. Either one is admissible in the schools and in government offices, as determined by local and national political authorities. All pupils are required to learn to read both, but individual adults are free to choose their own medium. *Bokmål* is predominant in urban usage in all parts of the country, while *Nynorsk* has its strongholds in the rural areas of western and midland Norway. Both languages have a vigorous literary tradition, though *Bokmål* is overwhelmingly predominant in terms of quantity and variety of writing.

The differences between Bm and Nn (as we here abbreviate them) are not great from an outsider's point of view. In speech, users of either language communicate easily with those of the other, and the obstacles to reading are not insuperable. In modern times the differences have been decreasing, in part through natural development and in part through deliberate reform by government action. There are many today who envisage as a future goal the fusion of the two languages into one so-called *Samnorsk* (literally "Common Norwegian") language. Previous Norwegian-English dictionaries have all been dictionaries of Bm alone. It is no longer fair to the student of Norwegian to exclude the body of Nn literature from his reading, and give the impression that only Bm really exists. At the same time the large area of common ground between the two languages makes it wasteful to prepare two separate dictionaries for them.

The place of Norwegian in a larger scheme of things is given by its close neighborhood to Swedish on the east and Danish on the south. The contact between these three has never been entirely broken, and their mutual relationships through the centuries have been crucial in determining their present-day form. Even today they communicate without interpreters in most situations, each speaker using his own language in a kind of pan-Scandinavian harmony. Together with the more remote and archaic Faroese and Icelandic they constitute the Scandinavian group of languages, which all stem from Old Scandinavian. This was the northern branch of the Germanic family of languages, which includes also modern Dutch, English, and German. These, in turn, are members of the Indo-European stock of languages, extending from Iceland to India, and in modern times throughout the greater part of the world.

2.2 *Norwegian and its Neighbors.* Norway came into existence as a political entity in the 9th Century A.D., united according to tradition by King Harald the Fairhaired in 872. The only written monuments from this period are inscriptions on rock and other permanent objects in a highly inadequate alphabet known as the Younger Runes. Runes had been in use for magic and monumental writing since at least the 3rd Century, and it is clear from these that the language of Norway in the prehistoric period was a Common Nordic which did not differ essentially from that of Denmark and Sweden.

Christianity was permanently established in Norway soon after 1030 A.D. by the Roman Catholic Church, which brought with it the Latin alphabet and the practice of writing on parchment. The earliest manuscripts in Norwegian are from around 1150. These show a Norwegian language which in some respects was different from contemporary Danish and Swedish. At about the same time as Harald united Norway, a predominantly Norwegian population had established an independent settlement in Iceland, where the Norwegian language flourished in a form that gradually differed more and more from that of the mother country and eventually became modern Icelandic. Exposed as Norway was to constant influence and even domination from her continental neighbors, her language was also more liable to change, especially in grammar and vocabulary. Politically the kingdom of Norway prospered in the 12th and 13th Centuries, and the royal court did much to encourage the writing of Norwegian, primarily through the translation of medieval European writings.

2.3 *The Extinction of Norwegian.* Down to about 1300 written Old Norwegian remained substantially similar to Old Icelandic, to the extent that many have used the term "West Scandinavian" to include both, in order to distinguish them from "East Scandinavian," which included Old Danish and Old Swedish. In speech, however, the local communities were beginning to develop differentiated dialects, which formed a gradual transition throughout the North.

As long as there were three kingdoms, there were three courts, where most of the élite were congregated and most of the writing in each country was done. But in the 14th Century a series of dynastic unions between the three royal families resulted in a concentration of power in the hands of a single royal family. From about 1385 there was no longer an independent Norwegian king, and in 1397 the Union of Calmar brought all three countries under the rule of the Danish Queen Margaret. Sweden revolted in 1521 and achieved an independence in 1523 that has never since been lost. Norway did not have the strength to do the same and remained part of a United Kingdom of Denmark and Norway, in which Norway inevitably became the weaker member. This condition lasted until 1814.

During this period the writing of Norwegian gradually disappeared, since Norway had no court or government offices which could maintain the tradition. The writing that was necessary was done in Danish, which was not so different from Norwegian that any great obstacle seemed to stand in the way of its adoption. The process was similar to that which led to the adoption of High German in northern Germany during the same period.

2.4 *The Effects of Independence.* Political independence came to Norway in 1814, at a time when Denmark had been defeated by Sweden, and Norway had been promised to Sweden as part of the latter's reward for supporting the Allies against Napoleon. The stimulus of the American and French Revolutions inspired the Norwegians to adopt a democratic constitution and defy the powers in behalf of their own rights as citizens of a sovereign nation. Although the Norwegians were eventually compelled to submit to a dynastic union with Sweden, it was on terms that assured them internal self-government—and a future prospect for complete freedom, which was realized in 1905. The task of the intervening years was one of creating or restoring organs and functions of government atrophied for four centuries. In an age of awakening nationalism and incipient democracy the course was clear: a new nation like Norway had to build her culture on the resources of her own people. Norway had a weak tradition of aristocracy, and pride in the new-won democracy even led to the abolition of nobility in 1821. The traditions of Norway had to be found in the surviving literary sources from the Middle Ages, the Old Norwegian writings, and in the living tradition of oral literature among the common people, who had preserved much of the older culture, untouched by many continental movements. This dual source was tapped for art, music, literature, and language. In language it became the inspiration of vigorous efforts to shape a genuinely Norwegian language. Out of a union of Old Norwegian writing with dialectal Norwegian speech sprang a New Norwegian which became one of the explosive factors in the linguistic life of Norway.

In 1831 Henrik Wergeland (1808—1845), the first great poet-patriot of the new nation, declared in a famous essay that "an independent language of writing" must come into being in Norway "before the century draws to its close." The Constitution had declared that the official language of the country should be Norwegian, but it had not specified just what this meant. Although all Norwegians wrote Danish at this time, many thought of it as being also Norwegian, thanks to their active partnership during the recent union. But there was also a feeling of Norwegian's being different from Danish. This feeling built on the striking difference in pronunciation, which raised a gulf even between the most literate Norwegians and their Danish friends. It took a generation of agitation and research before some clarity could be achieved as to just how the two did differ and policies could be formulated on the method for bringing out Norwegian individuality in language.

The most vigorous forces in Norwegian intellectual life during this period were *nationalism* and *democracy*. The new-found pride of nationality called for a language distinctive of the nation, so that the blot on the national scutcheon from the days of political subjection might be removed. The surge of democracy under the new revolutionary constitution called for a language that would impose a lesser burden on the children than did Danish and thereby smooth the path of the people to greater educational opportunities. Both movements combined to push the language away from Danish in the direction of the spoken language of Norway. But four centuries had passed since Norway had had a written language of her own, and in the meanwhile the country had developed a great variety of dialectal usage. The rural population had no nation-wide language, only a vast variety of local dialects. The nearest approach to a nation-wide Norwegian was the speech of the bureaucracy and the bourgeoisie, a compromise between Norwegian speech and Danish writing. Norway at this time was a country with an overwhelmingly rural population, ruled by a small upper class which constituted less than ten per cent of the population.

Within the first generation of liberty, two solutions emerged and won adherents, one based on the speech of the upper class and one on that of the common people. The former called for Norwegianization of the Danish writing, the latter for a brand new start.

2.5 *The Dano-Norwegian Language.* The earlier and easier of the two solutions to be put into practice was that of a gradual but deliberate changeover from Danish to Norwegian. Writers like Wergeland, especially in his writings for the people, and Asbjørnsen and Moe in their folktales (1841ff.), made a point of employing Norwegian words which were not previously a part of the Danish tradition. These were mostly words characteristic of Norwegian scenery and folk life, used to give local color. At the same time they reflected a conscious effort to break with the Danish vocabulary.

The theoretician and indefatigable agitator for this policy was schoolmaster and grammarian Knud Knudsen (1812—1895), who in the early 1840's began advocating that Danish spelling, grammar, and vocabulary should be gradually Norwegianized. Although some of his reforms went further than this, his point of departure was cultivated speech, which he was the first to identify as a norm. His most famous disciple was the writer Bjørnstjerne Bjørnson (1832—1910), whose poems, plays, and novels became for half a century the most widely read vehicles of the new national ideas and of the reformed Dano-Norwegian language. No other writer of the classic age of modern Norwegian literature went as far in this respect as did Bjørnson. The dramatist Henrik Ibsen (1828—1906) was more cautious in his Norwegianizing, but each in his way contributed to the cutting of Danish linguistic moorings.

The full break did not come, however, until 1907, two years after Norway's political separation from Sweden, when a new orthography was adopted which, in effect, declared Norway's independence from Denmark in linguistic matters. In 1917 a further step was taken, which gave Danish in Norway not only a new look, but also an entirely new feel. While leaving most of the Danish vocabulary undisturbed, these new orthographies had respelled the words in terms of their urban Norwegian pronunciation and given them a different grammar. We are therefore justified in thinking of this language as no longer Danish, but Norwegian, albeit we may call it *Dano-Norwegian*, to distinguish it from the language we shall describe in the next section. In Norway the name *Riksmål*, or Official Language, was applied to it by its supporters, beginning in 1899, a name that is still in wide use. But in 1929 the Parliament renamed it *Bokmål* or Book Language, an inept term which has gradually superseded *Riksmål*, especially in reference to the government-sponsored form adopted in 1938.

2.6 *The New Norwegian Language.* While the gradualistic solution was still in its infancy, a more revolutionary approach was launched by Ivar Aasen (1813 1896), a self-taught genius of the people. Only 22 years old he set himself the goal of creating a purely Norwegian language, and with a single-mindedness and purposefulness virtually unparalleled he carried through his plan. His idea was to construct from the materials furnished by the spoken dialects of Norway a new language equal in dignity and range to Danish and Swedish. This would fill the gap left by the extinction of written Norwegian in the Middle Ages, and bring into being a modern Norwegian which would be related to Old Norwegian as modern Danish and Swedish are to Old Danish and Old Swedish.

The old language of Norway had only recently become an object of scholarly study, and Aasen set himself to learning what was known about it. The modern dialects had not been systematically studied at all, and Aasen's first major effort had to be the exploration of their nature. He performed single-handedly the laborious task of traveling about the countryside to collect the vocabulary and grammar of the major Norwegian dialects, using his familiarity with his own dialect of

Sunnmøre as a starting point. Aasen had a genius for systems, and the result of his researches was the establishment of an "overall pattern" (to use a term of modern linguistics) for the rural Norwegian dialects, especially those of the areas least "corrupted" by urban or Danish influence. He presented his first research results in a grammar of 1848 and a dictionary of 1850. In 1853 he published a little book containing specimens of the dialects he had investigated, together with some passages written in a generalized dialect which he called "det norske Landsmål," or "the Norwegian national language."

In popular usage the term *Landsmål* henceforth came to be associated with Aasen's language as its proper name. He himself did not continue to use it, but titled his definitive grammar of 1864 and dictionary of 1873 simply *Norsk*, or Norwegian. In these works he presented the grammar and the lexicon of his new language. The grammar was a masterpiece of normalization within the framework of his ideology. What he presented was not a dialect, but a completely codified written language. He had fitted the overall pattern of the dialects into a structure of systematic relationships, in which the pronunciation was of less consequence than the inner system of the phonology and the grammar. He did not hesitate to write silent letters to show the etymological identity of different but related word stems. He produced what modern linguists would call a morphophonemic orthography, which displayed at once the unity of the dialects, the continuity with Old Norwegian, and the parity with its nearest neighbors, Danish and Swedish. In his dictionary he displayed a complete stock of words drawn from the dialects, excluding as far as possible Danish and German loan words, and recommending the creation from Norwegian materials of as many terms for the phenomena of modern culture as possible.

If Norway had been an illiterate nation in 1864, without an upper class and a prestige language, there is no reason to believe that Aasen's language would not have been accepted, with some minor modifications. As it was, it broke too sharply with the established habits of the literate portions of the nation. Its norms were based on speech forms that differed widely from those of the urban upper class throughout the country, and even from those of the rural and lower class urban population in southeastern Norway, the most populous and prestigious part of the country. Nevertheless, it filled a need which was recognized by many patriots, and before long there was a small but respectable body of literature, beginning with the verse and prose of Aasen himself. Classic writers of western and midland rural origin like Arne Garborg and A. O. Vinje showed its possibilities as a medium of literary and polemical expression. As modified by these writers, it achieved official recognition in 1885, when the national parliament, the *Storting*, passed a resolution recognizing it as an alternate medium of public instruction and official usage, alongside the traditional Dano-Norwegian.

By the end of the century *Landsmål* had begun to spread in the rural schools, vigorous organizations had sprung into being to promote it, and from now on the battle was joined between "*Landsmål*" and "*Riksmål*." In 1901 *Landsmål* achieved a firm orthography along the lines laid down by Aasen, after a period of considerable anarchy and experimentation. In the years that followed, it was modernized step by step and made somewhat more palatable in other parts of the country. In 1929 the parliament rebaptized the language as *Nynorsk*, or New Norwegian, a name that has gradually replaced *Landsmål* in the usage of most Norwegians.

2.7 *The Twentieth Century*. The first

generation of Norwegian independence following 1905 proved to be a fertile one for spread and growth of Nn. Following each of the new orthographies of Bm there was a surge of communities which voted the language into their schools. By the outbreak of World War II approximately one-third of the children of Norway were being taught to write Nn, while everyone was required to learn to read it. Students entering the university had to write an essay in Nn as part of their entrance examination. The users of Nn were legally entitled to full equality in relation to users of Bm, e.g., when filling out government forms or writing to government offices; the latter were required to reply in the language in which they were addressed. Government subsidies were made available to authors, theaters, and publications in Nn, on the same basis as to those in Bm.

In spite of such assistance, however, it remained in all practical affairs a secondary language. The school children who were being taught Nn were all rural, and they were concentrated in western Norway and those internal mountain valleys upon whose language Aasen had primarily built his norm. To farsighted men it appeared clear that Nn had no chance of becoming what its advocates wished, the only official language of Norway. At the same time, its position was too firmly entrenched, and its value as a symbol of Norwegian independence too unquestioned for anyone to imagine that it would just shrivel up and die. It had a strength of expression and a poetry of the native sod which gave it a special warmth and musical quality. Its appeal was not unlike that of Robert Burns' Scottish to the people of Scotland. But it was evident that the adaptations to Norwegian habits which had been made by Bm had helped to keep that language dominant. It was still the only one that could be said to flow easily as a medium of public and commercial life. It accounted for the overwhelming majority of the newspapers, magazines, and books that appeared under private auspices, and in its spoken form had a reasonably firm norm, which was regarded by most people as having the greatest social prestige. Instead of becoming a symbol of national unity, Nn had become one of national division, and the controversy between the two kinds of Norwegian threatened to settle down into a cold war between East and West, between City and Country. From an economic point of view it seemed unprofitable to print double sets of schoolbooks and government forms, not to speak of the confusion entailed in requiring pupils to learn two closely similar forms of their own language.

2.8 *An Approach to Fusion.* The success of the spelling reforms in Bm of 1907 and 1917 gave impetus to an idea that had been proposed more than once, especially from 1900 on. It was eloquently formulated in 1906 by the folklorist Moltke Moe, who had concerned himself greatly with the reform of Bm: "Neither language can choke off the other or cast it out of the country. We cannot slash away either our old history or our later history; we cannot exclude either city or country. Both must participate, each from its own side, in reaching the great goal: a *samnorsk* ('Common Norwegian') language, grown out of the living dialects in the cities as well as in the country . . . What we need is a mingling of blood, a flowing together." The term "Samnorsk" which was to be used and abused much later, became a slogan for a trend to harmonization and amalgamation of the two language forms. The concept of synthesis was implicit in all the language planning that had been done in Norway so far, and it did not seem impossible that a united Norwegian might be created by purposeful effort. There were supporters of this idea in both language camps, people who were willing to yield a point here and there in their own language in order to bring it closer to the other. Most of its advocates envisaged a gradual fusion brought about by natural development, but there were also some who proposed practical steps toward closer cooperation between the languages.

There were many leading scholars on both sides of the language issue who supported this move, including such distinguished men as the linguist Didrik Arup Seip and the folklorist Knut Liestøl. But the impetus to a vigorous step in this direction had to come from the growing Labor Party, which up to this time had been uncommitted in the struggle. The man who more than any other succeeded in enlisting its support was the historian Halvdan Koht, who combined socialism and nationalism in his personal philosophy. He reinterpreted the language struggle as a class conflict between the rural folk and the urban bourgeoisie, with Nn as the symbol of the former and Bm as the symbol of the latter. The Labor Party, which drew its core support from the urban lower classes, was urged to join the rural folk in their struggle on behalf of the "folk language," which in its essential traits was theirs as well. However, Koht recognized that Nn in its most puristic form was not well adapted to the uses of urban life, and he therefore proposed a rapprochement of the two languages on the basis of the most widespread rather than the most purely Norwegian forms. He was influential in getting this principle incorporated into the so-called "optional forms" of the 1917 reform of Bm. One of the most typical examples of this was the introduction of the feminine singular (and neuter plural) definite article *-a* in both languages in place of the *-i* which Aasen had used and the masculine *-en* which was characteristic of Bm. The form became obligatory in 1917 in the two words *kua* 'the cow' and *barna* 'the children,' taking the place of Aasen's *kui* and *borni* in Nn and Danish *koen* and *børnene* in Bm, which were purely literary forms. This opened the way to its further extension to words where it was much less common in cultivated speech.

2.9 *The Orthography of 1938.* Socialism was a new factor in Norwegian life of the 20th Century, following the rise of industry and the rapid growth of a politically conscious working class. Tendencies to splintering in the direction of Communism were overcome in the 1920's, and a strong, united Labor Party came into power in 1935, with Halvdan Koht as its Minister of Foreign Affairs. The Labor Party had accepted as its policy the promotion of linguistic fusion along lines suggested by Koht. It was definitely a nationalistic rather than an international party and found in the language a plank which would unite laborer with farmer against the privileged commercial and bureaucratic classes. Labor Party support ensured that the committee for a new reform of the languages which had been appointed by the preceding *Venstre*, or Liberal, cabinet would survive the change of government and win recognition for its work. Koht was a member of the Committee, which put into practice the principles he had long advocated. The Orthography of 1938 won approval of the *Storting* thanks to support from Labor, Agrarians, and Liberals, over the opposition of the Conservatives, who by this time were a small and rather insignificant party (31 of 150 members). The major mandate of the Committee had been to prepare a proposal which would "bring the two languages closer together with respect to spelling, word forms, and inflections, on the basis of the Norwegian Folk Language *(på norsk folkemåls grunn)*." This was more drastic than the preceding reforms in the extent to which it emphasized two principles: *(a)* its inclusion of "word forms" and "inflections" in the mandate, both of which are clearly structural, and (*b*) its specification of the basis for the written language as being not the cultivated norm of the educated classes, but the speech of the common people. For both languages it represented a considerable departure from well-established traditions. Folk forms like the feminine gender, the diphthongs *au*, *ei*, and *øy*, and the suffix *-a* in the past tense of weak verbs, all of which had been optional in Bm, were now made obligatory in a long list of words. The full implementation of this reform and the consequent angry reactions were delayed by the outbreak of war and the German invasion of 1940, which gave Norwegians other things to think about.

2.10 *The Language Commission.* Constitutional government was restored at the end of the war, and before long the language controversy was again in full swing. Textbooks which embodied the new "radical" forms of the Orthography of 1938 stirred the animosity of many urban parents, who felt them to be vulgar in tone and inorganic in the Bm language. The opposition, widely publicized in the press, was led by distinguished authors like Arnulf Øverland and Sigurd Hoel, both Labor Party supporters. But most of the solid following came from politically conservative circles, which had the finances to mount a vigorous campaign of resistance to reform. Under the ægis of *Riksmålsforbundet* (The *Riksmål* League), various movements were started, including *Foreldreaksjonen* (The Parents' Action), in opposition to the introduction of folk forms in written Bm. This group regarded itself as a spearhead on behalf of the true *Riksmål*, which they distinguished from *Bokmål*, the official term for the same language. They used the term *Bokmål* as a derisive name, and poured scorn on it as a "Book Language" created and imposed by government bureaucrats. In spite of their opposition the *Storting* in 1951 passed, by an overwhelming majority (126 against 22 Conservative Party members and two Labor Party mavericks), a resolution to establish a Language Commission. This Commission was to serve the Ministry of Church and Education as an advisory body in matters of language, thus replacing the individual experts and *ad hoc* committees previously used. One of the directives given it by the *Storting* was to "promote the approach of the two written languages on the basis of the Norwegian folk language." This reaffirmation of the basic doctrine of the Orthography of 1938 awakened a lengthy and acrimonious controversy.

The Language Commission began its work in 1952. It consisted of 30 members, one half of them representing each language, and a permanent secretariat consisting of one secretary for each language. Among the functions so far performed by the Commission we may note the supervision of the language in textbooks authorized for use in the schools, the collection of research materials on the language problem, cooperation with similar commissions in Sweden and Denmark, advising private persons on language usage, and most importantly, the preparation of a so-called *Læreboknormal* (Textbook Norm), which was completed and officially adopted in 1959. This norm is held to be only a regulation of the Orthography of 1938, but on some points it rescinds the more far-reaching parts of the latter. It provides a scale of values for the variant forms of that orthography, establishing each one as either *obligatory* or *alternative* for the schools, with a further *optional* class of forms which cannot be used in textbooks, but may be accepted in the pupils' own written work.

2.11 *The Present Situation.* In spite of all attempts at fusion, there are still two forms of written Norwegian which are sufficiently distinct in structure and lexicon to be labeled as different languages. The languages are closer together than they ever were, and it may be expected that in the long run Norwegians will find it impossible and unprofitable to maintain both. Bm is still the dominant language of writing, in which at least 85 % of the books published are printed; it is the editorial language of all daily newspapers, though most of these accept contributions in Nn as well. It is the language of virtually all translations of foreign books, and all commercial transactions of any size. It is less predominant in the grade schools, where local option prevails, but even here the postwar years have shown a remarkable reversal of attitude. While Nn grew steadily during the prewar period to a high mark of 34 % of all pupils in 1943—44, it has fallen equally steadily in the postwar years to a new low of 21.5 % in 1962—63. The loss was chiefly in those areas which were newly converted to Nn in the 1930's, especially in northern Norway, but also in rural areas which the new urbanization has turned into suburbs or small towns. Army recruits who were queried in 1950 expressed a nearly 3 to 1 preference for Bm; only 22 % chose the Nn version of a psychological test given them. Only in the four western counties (Møre og Romsdal, Sogn og Fjordane, Hordaland, Rogaland) are a majority of the children learning Nn. At the same time Nn has shown its vigor especially in poetry and on the stage, and a number of young writers and scholars continue to make use of it in their writings. The norms for each language are fairly stable, but one can detect considerable variations from writer to writer, according to the norm which he or his publishers impose on his writing.

2.12 *Treatment of the Languages in this Dictionary.* In view of the fluid situation which prevails in Norway, it seemed advisable to make a broader selection of words and forms than that normally found in Norwegian-English dictionaries. The solid position of Nn, even though it is a minority one, called for its inclusion. The efforts of the government to encourage a more folk-oriented form of the language can hardly fail to have its effect in the years to come, if only in the shape of a less rigid adherence to the urban norm. Any future changes made by official action are almost certain to be drawn in either language from the other. It is therefore likely that such forms will be found in this dictionary, even if they may be differently evaluated. There is the possibility of further phonetic spellings, but there appears to be less fervor for this kind of reform than there once was. A realization is growing that stability of spelling may be at least as important as its phonetic accuracy.

The markings for language membership (see above, **1.2.1**) proved to be more difficult than had been anticipated and occasioned many discussions within the staff. Our general policy was to follow *Norsk Riksmålsordbok* and include as Bm any word contained in it, or in Sverdrup and Sandvei, *Norsk Rettskrivningsordbok.* But it was discovered that these books contained a great many local terms, which are marked "dialect" in the former and are not acceptable as part of the standard norm of Bm, although they can and do occur in Bm writers. Many of these have accordingly been marked *dial.* here to indicate their limitations in this respect. Conversely, our chief sources for Nn, the newly initiated *Norsk Ordbok*, Hellevik's *Nynorsk Ordliste*, and Skard's *Nynorsk Ordbok* proved to contain a number of terms which have previously been forbidden in Nn and are still avoided by the best Nn writers. It has therefore been impossible to lay down hard and fast rules about the usage of many words in the respective languages. For the idioms and glosses the attempt to distinguish the languages was largely abandoned, due chiefly to the scarcity of accurate information about Nn literary usage.

2.13 *Comparative Paradigms.* In order to show in detail how the grammatical forms of the entries are to be expanded, the possibilities of regular and irregular inflections in both languages are displayed below in the form of paradigms (see above **1.4**). The inflections are those of the obligatory, "moderate" norms of the 1959 Textbook Norm, as they are listed in this Dictionary. At the head of each paradigm is the dictionary entry. Forms that are common to the two languages are listed only once.

2.13.1 *Nouns.* The inflections shown are the singular indefinite *(sg if)*, the singular definite *(sg df)*, the plural indefinite *(pl if)*, and the plural definite *(pl df)*. The English equivalents for the first example are: *horse, the horse, horses,* and *the horses.* In Bm a possessive is formed by adding *-s* to any of the forms listed, e.g. **hes'ts, hes'tens, hes'ters, hes'tenes.**

(*a*) Regular.

Entry:	**hes't** *-en*	**ti'me** *-n*	**dø'r** *-a*	**ga'te** *-a*
Lang.:	Bm Nn	Bm Nn	Bm Nn	Bm Nn
sg if	**hes't**	**ti'me**	**dø'r**	**ga'te**
sg df	**hes'ten**	**ti'men**	**dø'ra**	**ga'ta**
pl if	**hes'ter hes'tar**	**ti'mer ti'mar**	**dø'rer**	**ga'ter**
pl df	**hes'tene hes'tane**	**ti'mene ti'mane**	**dø'rene**	**ga'tene**
Entry:	**kro'** *-a/⁺-en*	**da'me** *-a/⁺-en*	**hu's** *-et*	**ep'le** *-t*
sg if	**kro'**	**da'me**	**hu's**	**ep'le**
sg df	**kro'a, kro'a** **kro'en**	**da'ma, da'ma** **da'men**	**hu'seţ**	**ep'leţ**
pl if	**kro'er**	**da'mer**	**hu's**	**ep'ler ep'le**
pl df	**kro'ene**	**da'mene**	**hu'sene hu'sa**	**ep'lene ep'la**

(*b*) Irregular.

Entry:	**gjes't** *-en, pl *-er*	**bon'de** *-n, pl bøn'der*	**å'ker** *-eren, pl -rer*	**⁺ba'ker** *-en, pl -e* **(*-ar)**
sg if	**gjes't**	**bon'de**	**å'ker**	**ba'ker ba'kar**
sg df	**gjes'ten**	**bon'den**	**å'keren**	**ba'keren ba'karen**
pl if	**gjes'ter**	**bøn'der**	**å'krer å'krar**	**ba'kere ba'karar**
pl df	**gjes'tene**	**bøn'dene**	**å'krene å'krane**	**ba'kerne ba'karane**
Entry:	**el'v** *-a, pl *-ar*	**gei't** *-a, pl gei'ter*	**klo'** *-a, pl klør*	**tre'** *-et, pl ⁺trær*
sg if	**el'v**	**gei't**	**klo'**	**tre'**
sg df	**el'va**	**gei'ta**	**klo'a**	**tre'eţ**
pl if	**el'ver el'var**	**gei'ter**	**klø'r**	**træ'r træ'**
pl df	**el'vene el'vane**	**gei'tene**	**klø'rne**	**træ'rne tre'a**
Entry:	**⁺øy'e** *-t, pl øyne* ***au'ga** *nt df -a, pl augo*	**ban'ner** *-et, pl -/⁺-e*	**tem'pel** *-elet/-let pl -el/⁺-ler*	**stu'dium** *-iet, pl ⁺-ier/*-ium*
sg if	**øy'e au'ga**	**ban'ner**	**tem'pel**	**stu'dium**
sg df	**øy'eţ au'ga**	**ban'nereţ**	**tem'peleţ,** **tem'pleţ**	**stu'dieţ**
pl if	**øy'ne au'go**	**ban'ner, ban'ner** **ban'nere**	**tem'pler, tem'pel** **tem'pel**	**stu'dier stu'dium**
pl df	**øy'nene au'go**	**ban'nerne ban'nera**	**tem'plene tem'pla**	**stu'diene stu'dia**

Notes. **Øye** can also have the plural **øyer**, a dialectal form. **Auga** can also have the form **auge,** with the same inflections as **eple.** Some other members of this paradigm are **hjarta** and **øyra.** The Nn masculines in *pl -er* and feminines in *pl -ar* are small, limited classes, as are the ones with vowel change in the plural in both languages. The larger and more productive classes are the ones called "regular". A small group of distinctively Norwegian neuter nouns are supposed to have the Nn pl df *-a* in Bm: **barn, bein, beist, dyr, garn, hol, kje, kol, krøtter, naut, reis, segl, troll.** In Nn **barn** may have vowel change in the plural: **born.** "Side forms" not included above are: Nn *-i* for *-a*; Nn *-or* for *-er* in weak *f* nouns (type **ga'te, da'me** above); Bm *-er* for *-e* in masculines of the type **ba'ker;** Bm *-a* for *-ene* in masculines of the type **hes't.** Nn *f* nouns in **-ing** have the *pl -ar*.

2.13.2 *Adjectives.* The inflections shown are positive *(pos)*, comparative *(cp)*, and superlative *(sp)*, some of which are further marked as indefinite *(if)* or definite *(df)*, singular *(sg)* or plural *(pl)*, and masculine *(m)*, feminine *(f)*, or neuter *(nt)*. The English equivalents for the *pos*, *cp*, and *sp*, as applied to the first example, are: *pretty*, *prettier*, *prettiest*. The other inflections have no equivalents in English.

(*a*) Regular.

Entry:	pe'n *A*		venn'lig *A* -		ny' *A -tt*	
Language:	Bm	Nn	Bm	Nn	Bm	Nn
pos sg if m, f	pe'n		venn'lig	venn'leg	ny'	
nt	pe'nt				nytt'	
sg df, pl	pe'ne		venn'lige	venn'lege	ny'e	
cp	pe'nere	pe'nare	venn'ligere	venn'legare	ny'ere	ny'are
sp if	pe'nest	pe'nast	venn'ligst	venn'legast	ny'est	ny'ast
df	pe'neste	pe'naste	venn'ligste	venn'legaste	ny'este	ny'aste

(*b*) Irregular.

Entry:	na'ken *A -ent, pl -ne*		li'ten *A nt -e, df vesle, pl små*		sto'r *A, cp større, sp størst*
pos sg if m	na'ken		li'ten		sto'r
f			li'ten, li'ta	li'ta	
nt	na'kent	na'ke, -i	li'te		sto'rt
sg df	na'kne		lil'le	lit'le	sto're
pl			små'		
cp	na'knere	na'knare	min'dre		stør're
sp if	na'knest	na'knast	min'st		stør'st
df	na'kneste	na'knaste	min'ste		stør'ste

Notes. The *df sg* of **liten** is also **vesle** in both languages; **lisle** alternates with **litle** in Nn. "Side forms" not listed are: *nt -tt* for *-t* after diphthongs in Bm (**greitt**); *nt -ent* for *-e* or *-i* in Nn (**opent**); *f -i* or *-a* for *-en* in Nn (**naki, naka**).

2.13.3 *Pronouns.* These may have both nominal forms, with subjective *(sb)*, possessive *(po)*, and objective *(ob)* inflections, and adjectival forms, with masculine *(m)*, feminine *(f)*, neuter *(nt)*, singular *(sg)*, and plural *(pl)*.

(1) Nominal forms.

(*a*) Personal pronouns. These alone can have all three cases.

Case:	*subjective*		*objective*		*possessive*	
Language:	Bm	Nn	Bm	Nn	Bm	Nn
1st p sg	jeg	eg	meg		min	
2nd p sg	du		deg		din	
2nd p formal	De		Dem	Dykk	Deres	Dykkar
3rd p m	han		ham, han	han, honom	hans	
3rd p f	hun	ho	henne	ho, henne	hennes	hennar
3rd p common	den		den		dens	
3rd p nt	det		det		dets	
1st p pl	vi		oss		vår	
2nd p pl	dere	de	dere	dykk	deres	dykkar
3rd p pl	de	dei	dem	dei	deres	deira
3rd p refl	—		seg		sin	

An obsolete Bm form of the *2nd p pl* is **I** *(sb)*, **eder** *(ob)*, **eders** *(po)*.

(*b*) Other pronouns. These have no objective case and a possessive only in Bm.

sb (ob)	+**der**	**ein**/+**en**	+**hinannen**/***einannan**	+**hva**/***kva**	+**hvem**/***kven**
po	—	+**ens**	+**hinannens**	—	+**hvis**

sb (ob)	+**hverandre**/***kvarandre**	+**man**	**samme**	**sjølv**/+**selv**	**som**
po	+**hverandres**	—	—	—	—

Notes. A more popular form than +**hvis** is the phrase +**hvem sin** (***kven sin**); **sjølv** can form a similar possessive, ***sjølv sin.** Of the pronouns which may also be used adjectivally and are therefore listed below under (2), the following have possessive forms in Bm when they are used nominally (all formed by adding *-s*): **den, det, denne, disse, hin; alle, begge; annen, andre, hvilken, ingen, mangen, mange, noen; annenhver, enhver.**

(2) Adjectival forms.

(*a*) Possessives

<table>
<tr><th>Lang.:</th><th>Bm</th><th>Nn</th><th>Bm</th><th>Nn</th><th>Bm</th><th>Nn</th><th>Bm</th><th>Nn</th></tr>
<tr><td>m sg</td><td colspan="2">min</td><td colspan="2">din</td><td colspan="2" rowspan="2">vår</td><td colspan="2">sin</td></tr>
<tr><td>f sg</td><td>min, mi</td><td>mi</td><td>din, di</td><td>di</td><td>sin, si</td><td>si</td></tr>
<tr><td>nt sg</td><td colspan="2">mitt</td><td colspan="2">ditt</td><td colspan="2">vårt</td><td colspan="2">sitt</td></tr>
<tr><td>pl</td><td colspan="2">mine</td><td colspan="2">dine</td><td colspan="2">våre</td><td colspan="2">sine</td></tr>
</table>

(*b*) Demonstratives

<table>
<tr><td>m sg</td><td colspan="2" rowspan="2">den</td><td colspan="2" rowspan="2">denne</td><td colspan="2">hin</td></tr>
<tr><td>f sg</td><td>hin, hi</td><td>hi</td></tr>
<tr><td>nt sg</td><td colspan="2">det</td><td colspan="2">dette</td><td>hint</td><td>hitt</td></tr>
<tr><td>pl</td><td>de</td><td>dei</td><td>disse</td><td>desse</td><td colspan="2">hine</td></tr>
</table>

(*c*) Numeratives: (1) Plain.

<table>
<tr><td>m sg
f sg</td><td>all</td><td colspan="2"></td><td>hver</td><td>kvar</td><td>slik</td><td>*som</td><td>sånn,+sådan</td></tr>
<tr><td>nt sg</td><td>alt</td><td colspan="2"></td><td>hvert</td><td>kvart</td><td>slikt</td><td>somt</td><td>sånt,+sådant</td></tr>
<tr><td>pl</td><td>alle</td><td>begge</td><td>båe</td><td colspan="2"></td><td>slike</td><td>somme</td><td>sånne, sådanne</td></tr>
</table>

(2) Ending in *-on.*

<table>
<tr><td>m sg</td><td>annen</td><td>annan</td><td rowspan="2">+hvilken</td><td colspan="2">ingen</td><td rowspan="2">mangen</td><td>mang ein</td><td rowspan="2">noen</td><td>nokon</td></tr>
<tr><td>f sg</td><td colspan="2">anna</td><td colspan="2">inga</td><td>mang ei</td><td>noka</td></tr>
<tr><td>nt sg</td><td>annet</td><td>anna</td><td>+hvilket</td><td>intet</td><td>inkje</td><td>mangt et</td><td>mangt eit</td><td>noe</td><td>noko</td></tr>
<tr><td>pl</td><td colspan="2">andre</td><td>+hvilke</td><td colspan="2">ingen</td><td colspan="2">mange</td><td>noen</td><td>nokon</td></tr>
</table>

(3) Compounds.

<table>
<tr><td>m sg</td><td rowspan="2">annenhver</td><td>annankvar</td><td rowspan="2">enhver</td><td>einkvar</td><td>*einkvar</td></tr>
<tr><td>f sg</td><td>annakvar</td><td>eikvar</td><td>*eikor</td></tr>
<tr><td>nt seg</td><td>annethvert</td><td>annakvart</td><td>ethvert</td><td>eitkvart</td><td>*einkvart</td></tr>
<tr><td>pl</td><td></td><td></td><td></td><td></td><td></td></tr>
</table>

Notes. Another *pl* of **nokon** is **nokre.** In place of **hvilken** Nn uses **kva for ein** (+**hva for en**). In place of +**intet**/***inkje** it is common to use +**ikke noe**/***ikkje noko** and for **ingen** to use +**ikke noen**/***ikkje nokon.** Side forms not listed: Nn **onnor** *f* for **anna, nokor** *f* for **noka, ingi** *f* for **inga.**

2.13.4 *Verbs.* All suffixes are thought of as being added to the stem, which is the infinitive (or name form) minus its final *-e*, where there is one (the *-e* of **be, le, se** is part of the stem). For most verbs the crucial form is the past *(pt)*; only when they are irregular, are the present *(pr)* and the past participle *(pp)* listed. The non-paradigmatic inflections are: imperative no ending, e.g. **kast** (*-e* after some consonant clusters, e.g. **ergre**); also *-a* in Nn verbs of the *a*-class (**kast/kasta**); subjunctive *-e* (**kongen leve** 'long live the king'); present participle *+-ende/*-ande*; mediopassive *+-es/*-ast*, **-est*. The infinitive *(inf)* in *-e* is used for both languages here, although Nn more commonly uses *-a*. Similarly the mediopassive *-es* subsumes Nn *-ast*, unless the verb is peculiar to Nn. For irregular paradigms all the examples are listed. Verbs having a past suffix are called "weak", while those that do not are called "strong."

WEAK VERBS: (*a*) Regular

Entry:	**kas'te** *-a/+-et*		**+a'v/lede** *-et*		**sen'ḍe** *-te*		**sø'ke** *-te* (=*-je)	
Lang.:	Bm	Nn	Bm	Nn	Bm	Nn	Bm	Nn
inf	**kas'te**		**a'v/lede**		**sen'ḍe**		**sø'ke**	**sø'kje**
pr	**kas'ter**	**kas'tar**	**a'v/leder**		**sen'ḍer**		**sø'ker**	**sø'kjer**
pt	**kas'tet, -a**	**kas'ta**	**a'v/ledet**		**sen'ḍte**	**sen'de**	**sø'kte**	
pp	**kas'tet, -a**	**kas'ta**	**a'v/ledet**		**sen'ḍt**	**sen'd**	**sø'kt**	
Entry:	**+glem'me** *glemte* ***gløy'me** *gløym'de*		**tru'** *-dde*		**le've** *-de*		**bi'e** *-dde/*-a*	
inf	**glem'me**	**gløy'me**	**tru'**		**le've**		**bi'e**	
pr	**glem'mer**	**gløy'mer**	**tru'r**		**le'ver**		**bi'er**	**bi'er, bi'ar**
pt	**glem'te**	**gløym'de**	**trud'de**		**lev'de**		**bid'de,*bi'a**	
pp	**glem't**	**gløy'md, gløy'mt**	**trudd'**	**trudd', trutt'**	**lev'd**		**bidd'**	**bidd', bitt'**

(*b*) Irregular.

Entry:	**+tel'le** *talte/telte* ***tel'je** *tel, talde, talt*		**+set'te** *satte, satt* ***set'je** *set, sette, sett*		**+sel'ge** *solgte, solgt* ***sel'je** *sel, selde, selt*	
Lang.:	Bm	Nn	Bm	Nn	Bm	Nn
inf	**tel'le**	**tel'je**	**set'te**	**set'je**	**sel'ge**	**sel'je**
pr	**tel'ler**	**te'l**	**set'ter**	**se't**	**sel'ger**	**se'l**
pt	**tal'te, tel'te**	**tal'de**	**sat'te**	**set'te**	**sol'gte**	**sel'de**
pp	**tal't, tel't**	**tal't**	**satt'**	**sett'**	**sol'gt**	**sel't**

STRONG VERBS: These are characterized by having no suffix in the past, except for a few verbs which end in *+-t* (**binde, brenne, falle, holde, vinde, vinne, svinne**) or *-kk* (**få, gå, *hange**). They may be classified according to the nature of the vowel change from the stem of the infinitive to that of the past. The change differs for long and short vowels. Within the long vowels it differs according to the vowel of the infinitive. But there are many irregular forms, so that most verbs have to be memorized individually. The following rules apply quite generally: (1) *Present* is formed in Bm by adding *'-er*, in Nn by changing the stem vowel as follows:

a > **e**
å > **æ**
u > **y**
o > **ø** or **e**
(e.g. **sove** > **søv**; **kome** > **kjem**)

This alternation results from the historical sound change known as *umlaut*.

(2) *Past* is formed by changing the stem vowel as follows:

(*a*) long vowels

i > ei/+e
y (jo, ju, u) > au/+ø
e (æ) > a
a > o
å > *e or no change

(*b*) short vowels
any vowel > a (o)

This alternation results from the historical sound change known as *ablaut*. The less common alternatives are given in parentheses.

(3) *Perfect participle* is formed by adding the suffix *+-et/*-e/*-i* to the stem, which in most cases has the same stem vowel as the infinitive. Exceptions are found particularly in the long vowel stems with y and in some of the short vowel stems, where the participle has its own vowel, different from either the infinitive or the past. In Bm many participles have adopted the suffix of weak verbs, either *-t* or *-d*. Most strong verbs are listed in the dictionary with all their principal parts, e.g., **bi`te** *V beit/+bet, +bitt/*bite/*-i*. These are some sample paradigms:

(*a*) Long vowels.

<table>
<tr><td>Lang.:</td><td>(1) Bm</td><td>Nn</td><td>(2) Bm</td><td>Nn</td><td>(3) Bm</td><td>Nn</td></tr>
<tr><td>inf</td><td colspan="2">bi`te</td><td colspan="2">fly`te</td><td colspan="2">be'</td></tr>
<tr><td>pr</td><td>bi'ter</td><td>bi't</td><td>fly'ter</td><td>fly't</td><td>be'r</td><td>be'd, be'r</td></tr>
<tr><td>pt</td><td>be't, bei't</td><td>bei't</td><td>flø't, flau't</td><td>flau't</td><td colspan="2">ba'ḍ</td></tr>
<tr><td>pp</td><td>bit't</td><td>bi`te</td><td>flytt'</td><td>flo`te</td><td>bedt'</td><td>be`de</td></tr>
<tr><td></td><td>(4) Bm</td><td>Nn</td><td>(5) Bm</td><td>Nn</td><td>(6) Bm</td><td>Nn</td></tr>
<tr><td>inf</td><td colspan="2">fa`re</td><td colspan="2">grå`te</td><td colspan="2">so`ve</td></tr>
<tr><td>pr</td><td>fa'rer</td><td>fe'r</td><td>grå'ter</td><td>græ't</td><td>so'ver</td><td>sø'v</td></tr>
<tr><td>pt</td><td colspan="2">fo'r</td><td>grå't, gre't</td><td>gre't</td><td colspan="2">so'v</td></tr>
<tr><td>pp</td><td>fa`ret, fa'rt</td><td>fa`re</td><td>grått'</td><td>grå`te</td><td>so`vet</td><td>so`ve</td></tr>
</table>

(*b*) Short vowels.

<table>
<tr><td></td><td>Bm</td><td>Nn</td><td>Bm</td><td>Nn</td><td>Bm</td><td>Nn</td></tr>
<tr><td>inf</td><td colspan="2">tig`ge</td><td colspan="2">skvet`te</td><td colspan="2">drik`ke</td></tr>
<tr><td>pr</td><td>tig'ger</td><td>tigg'</td><td>skvet'ter</td><td>skvett'</td><td>drik'ker</td><td>drikk'</td></tr>
<tr><td>pt</td><td colspan="2">tagg'</td><td colspan="2">skvatt'</td><td colspan="2">drakk'</td></tr>
<tr><td>pp</td><td>tig`get</td><td>tig`ge</td><td>skvet`tet</td><td>skvot`te</td><td>druk`ket</td><td>druk`ke</td></tr>
</table>

There are approximately 200 strong verb bases in Norwegian. The following alphabetical list is not complete, but should include most of them: ***ake, *ale, be, *bide, binde, bite, bli, blåse, +brekke, brenne, breste/+briste, bryte, by/byde, bære, dette, dra/drage, drepe, drikke, drite, drive, *drype, ete, falle, fare, finne, fise, +fly/+flyve/flyge, flyte, +fornemme, fryse, fyke, få, gale, gi/*gje/*gjeve, +gidde, *gine, gjelde, *gjete, gleppe, *glette, gli/glide, +glippe, gnage, gnelle, *gneste, *gnette, gni/gnide, grave, grine, gripe, gråte, gyse, gyte, gyve, gå, +henge/*hange, +hete/ *heite, *hevje, hive, +hjelpe, hogge, +holde/*halde, +hvine/kvine, klinge, klive, +klype, klyve** (two verbs), **knekke, *knette, knipe, komme, kreke, krype, kvede, kvekke, *kvelve, kveppe, kverve, la/late, le, *leke, *lese, li/lide, +ligge/*liggje, lite, +lyde, lyge/+lyve/*ljuge, *lyte/*ljote, +løpe, *låst, låte, male, *mete, mige, nyse, nyte, +overvære, pipe, reke, rekke, renne, ri/ride, *rine, +rinne, *rise, rive, ryke, ryte, +se/*sjå, si, sige, +sitte/*sitje, *sive, *sjode/*syde, skake, *skave, +skinne/*skine, skite, skjelve, +skjære/*skjere, skli/*sklide, skrelle, skri/skride, skrike, skrive,**

+skryte, skvette, skyte, skyve, slenge, sleppe/+slippe, slite, slå, slåss, smelle, smette, smyge, snike, +snyte, sove, spinne, sprekke, sprette, springe, stige, stikke, *stinge, +stjele/*stele, strekke, stri/stride, stryke, *støkke, stå, suge, *supe, svelle, svelte, +sverge/*sverje, svi/*svide, svike, +svinge, svinne, svive, synge, søkke/+synke, ta/*take, tigge, +treffe, +trekke, *trengje, trive, tryte, +tvinge, *två, *tyggje, tyte, *vege, +vekke, *vekse, velte, verpe, *verte, veve, vike, vinde, vinne, vri/*vride, +være/*vere.

3 A Guide to Pronunciation

3.1 *Standards of Pronunciation.* There is no official or private organization that attempts to dictate standards of pronunciation in Norway. Nevertheless there is considerable agreement, at least for Bm, on what may be called a "standard pronunciation" (SP), which is comparable to the Received Pronunciation of British English or the *Bühnenaussprache* of German. This does not cover the precise sound quality of each phoneme, but it does regulate with relatively little variation the phonemes used in each word, including the prosodic ones, and their arrangement. SP is a rather literary pronunciation, used in circumstances where some formality is called for, as in reading, lecturing, or serious discussion. It will be used by those persons who have had implanted in them a striving for "correct" pronunciation. Deviations from it may occur in informal or intimate speech, and each region has its own particular variations which are recognized by others as marking one's regional origin. In general, SP tends to remain more closely tied to the spelling than informal pronunciation, and in part reflects such personal achievements as literacy, education, and social status.

In Norway, as in other countries, standards of cultivated pronunciation have been set by the privileged classes and have radiated from urban centers. In the period of the Danish union, when education was centered in Copenhagen, Danish pronunciation represented an ideal for most Norwegians. This tradition persisted into the 19th Century, when the most Danish-sounding kind of Norwegian, that of Kristiansand, had high prestige. The importance of Bergen as an international seaport and a seat of theatrical art also gave its pronunciation a prestige which only faded with the growing predominance of Oslo in the second half of the century. Oslo, as the capital city, is today the center of most cultural activities and its speech therefore a model to many speakers. For this reason it is customary in manuals of pronunciation to take the speech of "educated Oslo speakers" as the norm of correctness, although in actual fact each city has its own educated norm, which often deviates markedly from that of Oslo. Since Oslo is in Eastern Norway, its phonetic base is East Norwegian, though the pronunciation of cultivated speakers is clearly differentiated, not only from that of the surrounding countryside, but also from that of the man in the street.

Nn does not, in the strictest sense, have an SP, since there is no one region, social class, or urban center in which it is the prevailing spoken language. Nearly all who speak it have learned it in school or from reading and follow in their use of it a compromise between the spelling and their own basic dialect. Since its grammar and vocabulary are most congenial to those who have grown up in a Midland or West Norwegian dialect, the most commonly heard pronunciations are also based on these. It is generally felt that the most pleasing Nn pronunciation is from regions like Telemark, which has a Midland dialect with many East Norwegian traits.

The policy followed in marking pronunciations in the present dictionary was to establish at least one pronunciation for each word which would be both comprehensible and socially acceptable. When our sources vigorously disagreed, the situation was saved by adding a second, or rarely a third, pronunciation in brackets, preceded by the word "also." There is no intention of suggesting that the latter is either more or less acceptable than the other. For Bm such written sources as Alnæs, *Norsk Uttaleordbok* (ed. 1924), *Norsk Riksmålsordbok*, and Popperwell, *Norwegian Pronunciation* were considered, but not always followed. The first marking was made by a native of Eastern Norway (Hedmark), Dag Gundersen, and checked by a native of Oslo, Wenche Sandsten. Where these disagreed, a panel of six other East Norwegian speakers was consulted (by having their pronunciations recorded on tape). For Nn the sources were far less adequate, consisting largely of the markings found in Hellevik's *Ordliste*, which are limited to so-called "foreign" words.

A special problem arose when Bm and Nn words were combined into single entries, since the pronunciations are not necessarily identical even with the same spelling. In a few cases, separate pronunciations are indicated, but for the most part the two have been harmonized. It is assumed e.g. that final **g** (e.g. in **-leg**) may be pronounced in Nn, but not in Bm **-lig.** Combinations of **r** and following dental consonant form alveolars (supradentals) in East Norwegian speech, but are kept apart in West Norwegian.

The general principle followed has been to provide for American users the simplest possible guide to formal Norwegian pronunciation. It is a familiar fact of language learning that a foreigner is not expected to talk a dialect or an informal variety of a language. If he does, he imperils his status as a foreigner and risks being taken for an uneducated native.

3.2 *The Phonemes of Norwegian.* SP can be fully described by the assumption of nine vowels, six diphthongs, eighteen consonants, and four prosodemes (length, stress, tone, and juncture). This leaves out the factor of (sentence) intonation, which is of less importance in a lexical pronunciation. It also disregards certain marginal phonemes: (1) The vowel [œ], replacing [ø] before [r] in the speech of older persons, e.g. in **dør** 'door'; (2) the consonant [l], often called "thick l," technically a cacuminal flap, used in Eastern Norway for [l] or [rd] in certain positions in informal speech; (3) the alveolar clusters of [r] plus dental of East Norwegian, discussed below **(3.10)**.

The symbols used in this dictionary to identify each of these phonemes are listed in the table below. For the most part they are letters or combinations of letters taken from the Norwegian alphabet, to each of which has been assigned one of the values which it normally has in Norwegian pronunciation. This will be its most usual value, and whenever it is used in this value, it will be said to be "phonemic." If all or part of a word is placed between brackets, the letters within the brackets are all phonemic. The values here given to them can only be learned by hearing them pronounced. As an aid to the reader who does not have immediate access to a speaker of Norwegian, we have here listed in the second column some symbols of the International Phonetic Alphabet which approach those of Norwegian. In the third column are Norwegian keywords containing the phonemes in question. In the fourth column are English (or other language) words having a rough phonetic resemblance to the Norwegian keywords. The reader is expressly warned that except for the ones marked =, the resemblance is quite inexact and does no more than give a vague idea of the quality. The reader should get a Norwegian to pronounce the keywords and note the marked difference in phonetic quality. Where the fourth column has two words separated by a slant, the Norwegian sound is intermediate between the two.

Table of Norwegian Phonemes and their Approximate English Equivalents

Phonemic symbols	Int. Phon. Alphabet	Norwegian keyword	English keyword	Phonemic symbols	Int. Phon. Alphabet	Norwegian keyword	English keyword
[a]	[ɑ]	katt	cut	[o]	[ω]	bukk	book
[a·]	[ɑ:]	far	far =			[bokk]	
[ai]	[ɑi]	hai	high	[o·]	[ω:]	mo	moo/mow
[au]	[æʉ]	haus	house	[oi]	[ɔi]	koie	coya
			(Southern)	[p]	[p]	pappa	papa =
[b]	[b]	bi	bee =	[r]	[r]	reis	race
[d]	[d]	du	do =	[s]	[s]	si	see =
[e]	[ɛ]	tenn	ten =	[sj]	[ʃ]	sju	shoe =
[e] weak	[ə]	lettes	lettuce	[t]	[t]	tenn	ten =
[e·]	[e:]	ben	bane	[u]	[ʉ]	futt	foot/Fr.fute
[ei]	[æi, ɛi]	nei	nay	[u·]	[ʉ:]	ku	coo/Fr. cue
[f]	[f]	fet	fate =	[ui]	[ʉi]	hui	hooey
[g]	[g]	gå	go =	[v]	[v]	vett	vet =
[h]	[h]	ha	ha =	[y]	[y]	sydd	Sid/Fr. sud
[i]	[i]	bitt	bit	[y·]	[y:]	sy	see/Fr. su
[i·]	[i:]	bit	beat =	[æ]	[æ]	lærd	laird
[j]	[j]	jett	yet =	[æ·]	[æ:]	lær	lair
[k]	[k]	kul	cool =	[ø]	[ø]	trøst	trust
[kj]	[ç]	kjemi	Chemie	[ø·]	[ø:]	bød	bird
			(Ger.)				(Eastern)
[l]	[l]	li	lee	[øy]	[øy]	bøyd	buoyed
[m]	[m]	mai	my =	[å]	[ɔ]	gått	got
[n]	[n]	nei	nay =				(Eastern)
[ng]	[ŋ]	seng	sang =	[å·]	[ɔ:]	kåt	caught/coat

Only the sounds marked = can be said to have a fairly exact English equivalent. For discussion of phonemes see **3.8** and **3.9.** For prosodic diacritics see **3.4—3.7.** For rules of respelling entries see **1.3.** "Southern" and "Eastern" refer to American dialects.

While vowels and consonants are represented by letters, the prosodemes are represented by diacritics: [·] length, ['] stress (with length), [`] tone (with stress and length), [/] juncture.

The vowels constitute syllabic nuclei and are either simple or complex. The simple vowels are: [a e i o u y æ ø å]. The complex vowels, or diphthongs, are: [ai au ei oi ui øy].

The consonants constitute syllabic margins. They are: [b d f g h j k kj l m n ng p r s sj t v].

The system for marking pronunciation which is used here is substantially the same as that found in Einar Haugen and Kenneth G. Chapman, *Spoken Norwegian, Revised Edition* (New York: Holt, Rinehart and Winston, 1964).

3.3 *Syllabic Structure.* Any word is immediately divisible into syllables, each with a nucleus that is usually vocalic, and a potential consonantal margin. Vowels have a quality which we may call "syllabicity," the capacity of acting as syllabic nuclei. Any long vowel or diphthong may constitute a syllable by itself; short vowels require a following consonant unless they are unstressed. Sonorous continuants like [l n r] may also have syllabicity, though only when they are unstressed (aside from interjections). There is a centralized vowel usually written **e** in the Norwegian alphabet ([ə] in IPA), which may consist of little more than pure syllabicity. In such words as **fengsel** 'prison', **alen** 'ell', **lærer** 'teacher' it is hard to be sure whether there is any vowel at all where the **e** is written. When preceded by **d** or **t,** as in **middel** 'means' or **enten** 'either', it is certain that no vowel is actually pronounced, thereby making the consonants syllabic. In our respelling no attempt will be made to reflect this variation from zero to an obscure vowel, most of which is either automatic or free. It will be a rule that an unstressed **e** which follows the stressed syllable in a word is normally weakened to [ə] and may disappear entirely (as a vowel, but not as syllabicity) when preceded and followed by homorganic consonants.

3.4 *Juncture.* Within and between words there are often potential breaking points, known as *junctures.* In English juncture may distinguish a unitary word like *nitrate* from a compound like *night rate* because of the juncture in the latter between [t] and [r]. A corresponding Norwegian example is [u`/tøy·] 'vermin' and [u`t/øy·] 'remote island', both spelled **utøy.** In the former the [t] is aspirated as are other initial t's, so that it goes with the second part of the compound, while in the latter it is unaspirated like other final or medial t's. The first [u] is slightly longer than the second. The fact that Norwegian spelling mostly does not mark this difference has led to our division of such compounds by a slant whenever the first part is stressed. It is possible for a word to lose its juncture; this appears to be the case in such words as **altså, smørbrød.**

3.5 *Length and Gemination.* As the table in **3.2** shows, each vowel comes in two varieties, one unmarked and usually called "short," another marked by a raised dot [·] and usually called "long." In Bm the diphthongs function as long vowels, while in Nn they may also have short counterparts, e.g. in words like **greitt** *nt* or **nøydd** *pp*. If we regard the short vowels as basic, the long can be said to consist of the corresponding short vowels plus a factor of length, or quantity. Length not only gives the vowel greater duration (as much as double), but also makes it tenser, less central, and mildly diphthongal. Short vowels are crisper and shorter than English vowels, while the long are steadier and less diphthongal than the English.

In Norwegian, vowel length is linked to the gemination (doubling) of consonants, which may also be regarded as a kind of length. The effect is somewhat different, however, for geminated consonants are not appreciably different from the simple in quality, only in quantity. In weakly stressed position and before other consonants even the length is often hard to detect, e.g. in the second part of **hus/katt** 'house cat' or **all/visst** 'most certainly.' The one constant feature is that *before long consonants the vowel must be short*; long vowels and long consonants cannot coexist in the same syllable.

Since the spelling is not consistent about writing geminated consonants, a raised dot has occasionally been resorted to in our respelling to mark the presence of length. The dot is used only when there is neither stress (primary) nor tone (Accent 2) in the syllable and the spelling fails to make it clear which sound is long. It is used when a single consonant is to be pronounced long, as in **ei'en/dom·** 'property', or when a consonant cluster does not cause shortening of the vowel, as in **små'/pe·nt** 'pretty' *nt*, or when the length is on a later syllable than the first, as in **gra'ds/forskjell·** 'difference of degree.'

While length has here been marked only on the second members of compounds with stress on the first, it can occur elsewhere also, in syllables two or more syllables removed from the stress: **u·bestem'melig** 'indeterminate', **sub'jekti·v** 'subjective'.

3.6 *Stress (with Length).* Stress in Norwegian is phonetically similar to that of English and performs much the same function. It gives prominence to at least one syllable in each independent utterance, e.g. a single word pronounced in isolation. Other syllables in the same word are then weaker and may be said to be unstressed. Since we are dealing here only with individual words, there is no need to consider the stresses of connected discourse. We shall therefore assume only one kind of stress, that which for English is called *loud*, or *primary*. Weak stress will here be considered as absence of stress. The important thing about stress is its placement: e.g. **positiv** 'positive' is pronounced [po'siti·v], while **positiv** 'grind-organ' is pronounced [po·siti'v]. As these examples show, the symbol for stress is ['], an acute accent.

It is a rule of Norwegian that *every stressed syllable must contain either a long vowel or a long consonant*, in other words, one and only one long element. For this reason it is possible to use the stress mark to represent length also, by placing it either after the vowel (when it is long) or after the consonant (when it should be geminated). In the preceding examples, the location of the acute accents shows that the vowels are long. Such a word will not ordinarily be respelled in brackets, since its pattern is sufficiently indicated by writing the acute accent on the regular spelling: **po'sitiv** vs. **positi'v.** The same is true of gemination when it appears in the spelling, e.g. **kat'ten** 'the cat', **prosess'** 'process'. As these examples show, the mark is placed between geminated consonants medially, but after them finally. Often, however, there are words whose spelling is ambiguous or misleading, e.g. **tam'** [tamm'] 'tame', **fi'nt** 'fine' *nt* vs. **sin't** [sinn't] 'angry'. For consistency's sake, every entry has been marked for stress and length in this way, either on the spelling or a respelling.

In rapid speech the geminated consonant tends to be somewhat shortened, but is still distinctly different from the simple, e.g. before other consonants, as in **visst** 'certainly', or in trisyllables where the spelling has only one consonant, as in **an'anas** 'pineapple', **min'imum** 'minimum', **neg'ativ** 'negative'. The placing of the mark here shows that the consonants are long. In a few interior dialects (Gudbrandsdalen) there are stressed syllables with short vowels followed by short consonants (as in English), e.g. in the place name

Vågå. Speakers from other parts of the country are here likely to say either [vå`gå] or [våg`gå].

3.7 *Tone (with Stress and Length).* Each stressed syllable is accompanied by some kind of pitch movement, usually one which deviates either up or down from the median or normal pitch of the utterance. In North, West, and South Norway the usual pitch of a stressed syllable is *high*, as in English; the pitch in the rest of the utterance rises to this high and then falls away from it to a low conclusion. Any variation in emphasis or in emotional attitude can change this basic melody in a number of ways which we cannot discuss here. In East Norway and Trøndelag the usual pitch of a stressed syllable is *low*, so that the unemotional intonation pattern is the opposite of the English: the pitch falls to the stress, and then rises to a high at the end. This is often misunderstood by foreigners as a question intonation, which it is not. In lexical pronunciation, as when reading a list of words, Norwegians from East Norway are most likely to end each word on a high pitch, rising from a low point in the stressed syllable. In a whole sentence pronounced with only one major stress, the pitch rise may span as much as an octave.

In most Norwegian speech there is an additional phenomenon of pitch which is peculiar to Norwegian and its immediate neighbors, Swedish and (some dialects of) Danish. This is the use of lexical pitch to distinguish otherwise identical words (reminiscent of a phenomenon well known from Chinese and many African languages; in Europe it is found e.g. in Lithuanian and Serbo-Croatian). In Norwegian it occurs only in connection with stressed syllables and only in words which have at least one syllable following the stress. We shall call this phenomenon "tone" and say that *tone* is a feature that may be added to words of this type. Words that do not have tone, as here defined, are usually said to have Accent 1, or monosyllabic tone. Since the stress of Accent 1 words may be accompanied by a variety of pitches, as we have seen, one cannot for Norwegian as a whole speak of any particular pitch as characteristic of Accent 1. This so-called accent is simply stress with whatever tonal pattern is normal for the dialect in question. The high or low pitch deviation coincides with the stress and is limited to it. No stress can occur without it.

Accent 2, or polysyllabic tone, is different. As noted, it requires at least two syllables, of which the first is stressed, to develop. The pitch pattern is more complex than that of Accent 1 and its most characteristic phase comes later, usually developing on the second syllable. In North, West, and South Norway it rises to a peak, like that of Accent 1, but the peak comes later in the word, so that it is still rising when the other is falling, and only falls later. In East Norway and Trøndelag it does not immediately fall, but rises to a peak and then falls, with the fall coming in part on the second syllable. In all parts of the country except North Norway there is often a second rise and fall which may sound like a new stress.

It is possible to speak Norwegian without tone (as is done e.g. for Swedish in Finland), since most of the pairs of words that are distinguished by tone are not likely to be confused in context. But natural and correct Norwegian speech requires that it be applied. We have therefore marked tone for all words by the use of the grave accent [`]. Like the acute accent, this implies both stress and length, as previously noted.

In summarizing the preceding three sections, we note that the symbols [· ′ `] are all used to mark length of vowels and, on occasion, gemination of consonants. [·] is pure length ("secondary stress"), [′] length plus stress ("primary stress, accent 1"), [`] length plus stress plus tone ("primary stress, accent 2").

3.8 *The Vowels.* The nine simple vowels are distinguished from each other by features of *tongue height, advancement,* and *lip rounding.* In some dialects of the Midland and West Norway an older Norwegian system is preserved, which is similar to that of Danish (or German). This is often used by speakers of Nn, but sounds odd or foreign when used in Bm. The pattern formed by its features is as follows (rounding is shown by circles, the others are unround or spread):

	Front		Back
High	i	(y)	(u)
Higher mid	e	(ø)	(o)
Lower mid	æ		(å)
Low		a	

In comparison with this system, the typical East Norwegian (Oslo) system is markedly skewed (in the same direction as Swedish): [e æ] are lowered, [a] is retracted, [å] and [o] are raised, [u] is advanced, [y ø] are partially unrounded. In addition, [o u] are "overrounded," i. e. pronounced with a narrow, puckered rounding which is quite different from the rather relaxed rounding of [y ø å]. The whole system has undergone a counterclockwise movement, leaving only [i] constant. It may be represented as follows (overrounding is shown by a double circle):

	Front				Back
High	i	(y)		((u))	((o))
Mid	e		(ø)		(å)
Low	æ				a

For English speakers the rounded vowels are particularly difficult, since they coincide neither with any English sound, nor precisely with those of German or French. [å] seems intermediate between *aw* and *oh,* [o] between *oh* and *oo,* while [u] is sometimes misheard as *yew.* [u] is reminiscent of French *u* or German *ü,* but so is [y]; the former is more *oo*-like, the latter more *ee*-like than these, since [u] is overrounded and [y] is underrounded in comparison with them.

In general the short and long vowels fit into the same pattern, even though the short vowels are slightly more centralized than the long. When the long vowels are emphasized, they are lengthened and slightly diphthongized: the high vowels are *narrowed* near the end so that [i y] almost end in a [j], [u o] in a [w]; the mid vowels are *lowered* so that [e] sounds like [eæ], [ø] like [øö], and [å] like [åa]. Exaggerated diphthongization of the long vowels is considered dialectal or slovenly.

3.9 *The Diphthongs.* Each of the six diphthongs consists of two short vowels which function as a single syllabic nucleus. The second member is always a high vowel, [i y u]. This is shown in the respellings used to represent the diphthongs in this dictionary: [ai au ei oi ui øy]. As far as the first member is concerned, these respellings are not always accurate, since they are identical with the regular spelling. The first members of [au] and [ei] are usually [æ], while that of [oi] is [å], so that these would be more accurately written [æu æi åi]. They are here treated as unit symbols. As compared with similar English diphthongs, they have a shorter first member and a more sharply articulated vocalic second member. The crisper pronunciation of the Norwegian diphthongs is clearly heard by comparing English *neigh* to Norwegian **nei.** There is a common Oslo pronunciation of [au] as [æv], which should be avoided. According to their origin and function the diphthongs can be divided into a *central* group [au ei øy] and a *marginal* group [ai oi ui]. The former are important because many words alternate between a traditional Bm form without diphthong and a Nn (or recently introduced Bm) form with, e.g. **ben** vs. **bein** 'bone', **død** vs. **daud** 'dead', **mø** vs. **møy** 'maiden'. The marginal diphthongs are mostly found in words of foreign origin or in exclamations, e.g. **kai** 'quay', **koie** 'hut', **hui** 'whee'.

3.10 *The Consonants.* The consonants are distinguished from each other by the features of *oral closure*, *nasality*, *voice*, and four *points of articulation* (labial, dental, alveolar, palato-velar), plus some special features for [l r h]. Except for the alveolars, the consonant system differs little from one part of the country to the other. The pattern formed by the features is as follows:

Manner of articulation		Points of articulation			
		Labial	Dental	Alveolar	Palato-velar
Stops	Voiced Voiceless	b p	d t	rd rt	g k
Nasals	Voiced	m	n	rn	ng
Spirants	Voiced Voiceless	v f	 s	 rs/sj	j kj
Laterals	Voiced		l	rl	
Trill	Voiced			r	
Breathed	Voiceless				h

Most of these have reasonably close counterparts in English; special discussion will be given only to those that differ markedly from the nearest English equivalents.

Points of articulation. The *labials* correspond closely to English bilabial [p b m] and labiodental [v f]. The *dentals* are articulated farther forward than English apicals, at the lower edge of the gums. The acoustic difference is most noticeable with [l], which is "lighter" than in English. In East Norwegian the [l] is somewhat darker after [a å o] than the other vowels, but in West Norwegian it is light everywhere. The *alveolars* are retroflex, r-like consonants, discussed below under "r-clusters." The *palato-velars* include palatal spirants, velar and pre-velar stops (depending on the following vowel), and the glottal [h]. Northern dialects (including *trøndsk*) have a palatalized series corresponding to the dentals (except for [s]).

Manner of articulation. The *stops* are articulated as in English, the voiced being lax and unaspirated (with initial and final tendency to slight devoicing), the voiceless tense and aspirated, except after [s] and postvocalically. Along the coastal strip of southern Norway the voiced stops are extensively devoiced, as in Danish. The *nasals* are like their English counterparts; but they are not followed by [g] in East Norwegian, as they are in English words like *finger, linger*. Only in some West Norwegian dialects will one hear the [g] sounded. Although [ng] is a unit phoneme, it functions like a geminated consonant and is preceded by short vowels. The *spirants* [v f] are like English [v f], and [j] is like English consonantal [y] except for being slightly more tense and fricative. Its voiceless counterpart [kj] is strange to English, but familiar to anyone who knows German *ch* in *ich*. It is like a very strong [h], esp. in words like *hue, human,* but with a narrower and definitely palatal opening. In some dialects it is an affricate not unlike English *ch,* but this pronunciation is not to be recommended. The sibilants [s sj] are close to English *s* and *sh.* Norwegian conspicuously lacks *z* and *zh* (as in *rose* and *erosion*), so that one must guard against pronouncing these in Norwegian words. The *lateral* differs from that of English in being pronounced with a flat tongue, which helps to produce the "light" effect mentioned above. The *trill* [r] of most Norwegians is produced by vibrating the tip of the tongue against the gums. In Oslo it rarely gets more than a single tap, except when it is geminated. In Bergen and in the coastal cities from Stavanger to Risør, as well as the shoreline that joins the latter, the [r] is uvular, i.e. pronounced in the throat, with or without active participation of the uvula. This is similar to the standard [r] of Danish, German, and French. Concerning the [r]-clusters see below. The *breathed* consonant [h] is like English *h.*

The r-clusters. In East Norwegian (as in much Swedish) the tap of the [r] is lost before dentals, while these are changed into alveolars, producing a new series of retroflex consonants. In phonetic transcriptions these usually appear with dots under them. In our respelling we have left them as they are in the orthography, since the assimilation is in most cases predictable. They sound like the corresponding English consonants, with an r-coloring somewhat weaker than that of American [r] in the same position. The exception is [rs], which in many people's speech has coincided with [sj]; for this reason the word **æsj** 'ish' is sometimes misspelled **ærs.** The same speakers who assimilate these clusters usually give this sound also to s before **l,** e.g. in **slå** [sjlå']; while this is considered acceptable in initial position, it is held to be vulgar after vowels, e.g. in **Oslo** [os'lo, *not* osj'lo]. Coalescence of [r] and [d] fails to take place in Bm in some literary words, e.g. **ferd** [fær'd] 'journey', **verden** [vær'den] 'the world', **verdig** [vær'di] 'worthy'; but it does occur in **ferdig** [fær'di] 'ready', **verdi** [værdi'] 'value', **far din** [fa'r-din] 'your father'. As the last example shows, the assimilation also takes place across word boundaries. It is not heard in the speech of West and South Norwegians, whether they use tongue-tip or uvular [r].

Silent consonants. A great deal of respelling has been avoided by placing dots under certain consonants (esp. **ḍ** **g̣** **ṭ**) that are spelled but not pronounced. For words that are common to both languages the Bm rules have been followed; Nn pronounces some that are silent in the former, though many speakers follow the same rules. Length is not affected by silencing: **søl'ṿ** = [søll'], **lan'ḍ** = [lann'], **jo'rḍ** = [jo'r].

Special Rules. It is important to keep in mind that certain letters and letter sequences are not respelled even though they are unphonemic by the preceding rules. This is done only when they invariably (or nearly so) are pronounced in a certain way, so that it would be wasteful of space to keep respelling them. Thus **g, k,** and **sk** are nearly always "soft" (palatalized) before **i, j,** and **y,** i. e. they are pronounced [j kj sj] respectively. For this reason they are here respelled only when they do not have these pronunciations. Similarly the vowels **e** and **o** are pronounced [æ å] respectively in certain positions, unless the respelling shows the contrary. The complete list was given above in **1.3.6** and should be memorized by the user.

4 Reference Bibliography

The following books were used in the preparation of this Dictionary:

A: Dictionaries and Word Lists of Norwegian

1 Both Languages

Nordiske språkspørsmål. Oslo: Norsk Språknemnd, 1955, 1956, 1957—58, 1959—60 [Contain lists of new words in Norw.].

Ny læreboknormal 1959. Bokmål, Nynorsk. Oslo: Olaf Norli, 1959. 86pp.

Iversen, Ragnvald and Bakken, Ove. *Bokmål—nynorsk, nynorsk—bokmål. Damms Lommeordbøker.* Oslo: Damm, 1958. 421pp.

Teknisk ordliste, Bokmål—nynorsk. Ved Ingeniørmållaget. Oslo: Noregs Boklag, 1956. 178pp.

Haugen, Einar. *Norwegian Word Studies.* Madison, Wis.: Univ. of Wis. Press, 1942. 2 vols. (Complete word indices of Ivar Aasen, *Skrifter;* Sigrid Undset, *Samlede Romaner og Fortællinger fra Nutiden;* Sigrid Undset, *Middelalderromaner;* Henrik Wergeland, vols. 1 and 2 of *Skrifter*).

2 *Bokmål* (Dano-Norwegian)

Abel, Georges. *2500 forkortelser i norsk.* Oslo: Aschehoug, 1953. 54pp.

Abel, Georges. *Skikk og bruk i dagligtalen. Riksmål.* Oslo: Dreyer, n.d. 124pp.

Alnæs, Ivar. *Norsk Uttale-ordbok.* Oslo: Aschehoug, 2nd ed. 1925. 270pp.

Berg, Josef and Fremming, Dag. *Aftenpostens billedordbok.* Oslo: Chr. Schibsted, 1955. 472pp.

Berulfsen, Bjarne. *Fremmedordbok.* Oslo: Gyldendal, 1943. 270pp.

Berulfsen, Bjarne and Lundeby, Einar. *Bokmål 1. Fullstendig liste.* Oslo: Aschehoug, 1961. 120pp.

Berulfsen, Bjarne. *Bokmål 2. Med tradisjonelle ("moderate") former.* Oslo: Aschehoug, 1961. 126pp.

Christiansen, Hallfrid and Nielsen, Niels Åge. *Norsk-dansk ordbog.* Oslo: Gyldendal, 1955. 481pp.

Knudsen, Trygve and Sommerfelt, Alf. *Norsk Riksmålsordbok.* Oslo: Aschehoug, 1937—57. 2 vols. (in 4 parts).

Popperwell, R. G. *The Pronunciation of Norwegian.* Cambridge: University Press, 1963. 229pp.

Sverdrup, Jakob and Sandvei, Marius. *Norsk rettskrivningsordbok.* Bokmål. Oslo: Tanum, 1st ed. 1940, 2nd ed. 1953, 3rd ed. (entitled *Tanums store rettskrivningsordbok*) 1961. 460pp.

Riksmålsordliste til daglig bruk. Utg. av Riksmålsforbundet. Oslo: Dreyer, 1958. 111pp.

3 *Nynorsk* (New Norwegian)

Aasen, Ivar. *Norsk Ordbog med dansk Forklaring.* Oslo: P. T. Malling, 1873. 976pp.

Eskeland, Ivar and Torvik, Ingvald. *Nynorsk A. Fullstendig Liste.* Oslo: Aschehoug, 1959. 108pp.

Eskeland, Ivar. *Nynorsk 2, med tradisjonelle former.* Oslo: Aschehoug, 1961. 114pp.

Hellevik, Alf. *Norsk ordbok. Ordbok over det norske folkemålet og det nynorske skriftmålet.* Oslo: Det norske Samlaget, 1950— (Hefte 1—5, A-buver, 1963. 560pp.).

Hellevik, Alf. *Nynorsk ordliste. Større utgåve.* Oslo: Det norske Samlaget, 1962. 160pp.

Hellevik, Alf and Breidsvoll, Einar. *Nynorsk ordliste. Utvida utgåve, Læreboknormalen 1959.* Oslo: Det norske Samlaget, 1959. 110pp.

Ross, Hans, *Norsk Ordbog.* Oslo: Cammermeyer, 1895. 997pp.

Skard, Matias. *Nynorsk ordbok for rettskriving og litteraturlesnad.* 5th ed. by Vemund Skard. Oslo: Aschehoug, 1954. 209pp. (6th ed. 1962, 285pp, in prepublication form).

4 Encyclopedias and Technical Word Lists

Aschehougs Konversasjons-Leksikon. Ed. Arthur Holmesland, Alf Sommerfelt, Leif Størmer. Oslo: Aschehoug, 1954—61. 18 vols.

Norsk Allkunnebok. Ed. Arnulv Sudmann. Oslo: Fonna, 1948— (9 vols. by 1959).
Aasen, Ivar. *Norsk Navnebog.* Oslo: P. T. Malling, 1878. 107pp.
Anker, Øyvind and Gurvin, Olav. *Musikk-leksikon.* Rev. ed. Oslo: Dreyer, 1959. 452pp.
Bru, Ludvig. *Norske Folkenamn.* Oslo: Norli, 1913. 102pp.
Gulbransen, Egil and Hoffmann, Johan. *Norsk juridisk ordbok.* Oslo: Tanum, 1948. 248pp.
Havin, Henry. *Psykologisk ordbok.* Oslo: Tanum, 1950. 153pp.
Lid, Johannes. *Norsk flora.* 2nd ed. Oslo: Det norske Samlaget, 1952. 771pp.

B: Dictionaries and Word Lists from Norwegian or Danish to English

Askim, Per. *Norsk-engelsk maritimteknisk ordbok.* 3rd printing. Oslo: Grøndahl, 1947. 219pp.
Brynildsen, John. *Norsk-engelsk ordbok.* 3rd ed. Oslo: Aschehoug, 1927. 1228pp.
Elektroteknisk ordliste. *Norsk, fransk, engelsk, tysk.* Pub. by Norsk Elektroteknisk Komité. Oslo, 1947. 304pp.
Farmand, Bjørn. *Merkantil ordbok. Norsk-engelsk, engelsk-norsk.* Høvik, 1948. 271pp.
Follestad, Sverre. *Engelske idiomer.* Oslo: Fabritius, 1962. 512pp.
Guy, Walter. *Norsk-engelsk ordbok for det praktiske liv.* Oslo: Gyldendal, 1953. 292pp.
Haugen, Einar (and associates). Glossaries to
Asbjørnsen, P. Chr., and Moe, Jørgen. *Norske folkeeventyr.* Oslo: Mittet, 1936. 96pp.
Bang-Hansen, Odd. *Mette og Tom i fjellet.* Oslo: Tiden, 1948. 152pp.
Bojer, Johan. *Den siste viking.* Oslo: Gyldendal, 1921. 272pp.
Boo, Sigrid. *Vi som går kjøkkenveien.* Oslo: Aschehoug, 1931. 175pp.
Evensmo, Sigurd. *Englandsfarere.* Oslo: Gyldendal, 1947. 289pp.
Falkberget, Johan. *Den fjerde nattevakt.* Oslo: Aschehoug, 1939. 240pp.
Ibsen, Henrik. *Vildanden.* Oslo: Gyldendal, 1950. 102pp.
Sturlason, Snorre. *Kongesagaer.* Ved D. A. Seip. Oslo: Gyldendal, 1935. 119pp.
Undset, Sigrid. *Kristin Lavransdatter: Kransen.* Skoleutg. ved F. Grimnes. Oslo: Aschehoug, 1939. 227pp.
Jorgenson, Theodore and Galdal, Peder. *Norwegian-English School Dictionary.* Revised ed. Northfield, Minn.: The St. Olaf College Press, 1955. 448pp.
Larsen, A. *Dansk-norsk-engelsk Ordbog.* 3rd ed. Copenhagen: Gyldendal, 1897. 687pp.
Magnussen, Johs., Madsen, Otto and Vinterberg, Hermann. *Dansk-engelsk Ordbog.* 3rd ed. Copenhagen: Gyldendal, 1927. 329pp.
Oppegaard, Sven. *Teknisk ordliste. Tysk-norsk-engelsk.* Trondheim: Bruns bokhandel, 1945. 211pp.
Scavenius, H. *Norsk-engelsk.* Oslo: Gyldendal, 1933. 338pp. 4th ed., 1945. 5th ed. pub. as McKay's *Modern Norwegian-English, English-Norwegian Dictionary* (with Berulfsen's, see below).
Vinterberg, Hermann and Bodelsen, C. A. *Dansk-engelsk Ordbog.* Copenhagen: Gyldendal, 1954. 2 vols.

Special excerpting:

Joos, Martin. Hoel, Sigurd. *Møte ved milepelen.* Oslo: Gyldendal, 1947. 472pp.
Anderson, A. Gerald. Vesaas, Tarjei. *Dei svarte hestane.* 2nd ed. Oslo: Norli, 1928. 349pp.

C: Dictionaries and Word Lists from English to Norwegian or Danish

Berulfsen, Bjarne. *Engelsk-norsk.* Oslo: Gyldendal, 1938. 344pp. Revised ed.

pub. as part of McKay's *Norwegian-English English-Norwegian Dictionary.*

Brynildsen, John. *A Dictionary of the English and Dano-Norwegian Languages.* Copenhagen: Gyldendal, 1902. 2 vols.

Farmand, Bjørn (see above).

Gleditsch, Th. *Engelsk-norsk ordbok.* 2nd ed. Oslo: Aschehoug, 1948. 855pp. (Reissued by George Allen and Unwin, London, 1950, and by Macmillan, New York, 1953, as *English-Norwegian Dictionary.*)

Raknes, Ola. *Engelsk-norsk ordbok.* [Nynorsk] Oslo: Aschehoug, 1927. 1049pp.

D: Dictionaries and Word Lists of English

The American College Dictionary. New York: Random House, 1947. 1432pp.

Roget's College Thesaurus. New York: The New American Library (Signet), 1958. 414pp.

Sears Fall and Winter Catalogue, 1962. Minneapolis, Minn.: Sears, Roebuck and Co.

Webster's Third New International Dictionary of the English Language Unabridged. Editor in chief, Philip B. Gove. Springfield, Mass.: G. and C. Merriam Co., 1963. 2662pp.

E: Grammars and Histories of the Language

Aasen, Ivar. *Norsk Grammatik.* Christiania, 1864. 399pp.

Burgun, Achille. *Le développement linguistique en Norvège depuis 1814.* 2 vols. Kristiania, 1919—21.

Haugen, Einar. *Language Conflict and Language Planning: The Case of Modern Norwegian.* Cambridge, Mass., 1966.

Haugen, Einar. *The Norwegian Language in America.* 2 vols. Philadelphia, Pa. 1953.

Haugen, Einar and Kenneth G. Chapman. *Spoken Norwegian, Revised Edition.* New York: Holt, Rinehart and Winston, 1964. 447pp.

Hellevik, Alf, and Einar Lundeby. *Skriftspråk i utvikling.* Oslo: Cappelen, 1964. 262pp.

Indrebø, Gustav. *Norsk målsoga.* Ed. Per Hovda and Per Thorson. Bergen, 1951. 504pp.

Knudsen, Knud. *Haandbog i Dansk-norsk Sproglære.* Christiania, 1856.

Seip, Didrik Arup. *Grunnlaget for det norske riksmål.* Kristiania, 1916. (revised in *Norsk og nabospråkene,* 1959).

Seip, Didrik Arup. *Norsk språkhistorie til omkring 1370.* Oslo, 1931; 2nd ed 1955.

Western, August. *Norsk Riksmålsgrammatikk.* Kristiania, 1921. 572pp.

A section of additions and corrections to the entries in the main body of the Dictionary may be found on book pages 500 ff.

TABLE OF ABBREVIATIONS

A	adjective
ab.	about
adj.	adjectival
admin.	administrative
adv.	adverbial
agr.	agricultural
anat.	anatomical
anthro.	anthropological
approx.	approximately
arch.	architectural
archeol.	archeological
Art	article
astron.	astronomical
Av	adverb
bibl.	biblical
biol.	biological
Bm	Bokmål
bot.	botanical
Brit.	British (English)
C	conjunction
carp.	carpentry
cf	see
chem.	chemical
comp.	comparative
conj.	conjunctional
cp	comparative
cpd.	compound
def.	definite
derog.	derogatory
df	definite
dial.	dialectal
dipl.	diplomatic
eccl.	ecclesiastical
econ.	economic
educ.	educational
elec.	electrical
eng.	engineering
esp.	especially
f	feminine
fam.	familiar
fem.	feminine
fig.	figurative
folk.	folklore
forest.	forestry
geog.	geographical
geol.	geological
gram.	grammatical
gymn.	gymnastics
hist.	historical
hort.	horticultural
hum.	humorous
I	interjection
if	indefinite
imp	imperative
indef.	indefinite
inf.	infinitive
ip	imperative
IPA	International Phonetic Alphabet
journ.	journalistic
jur.	legal
lit.	literally
lit.	literary
m	masculine
masc.	masculine
math.	mathematical
med.	medical
merc.	mercantile
meteor.	meteorological
mil.	military
mus.	musical
myth.	mythological
N	noun
naut.	nautical
neg.	negative
Nn	Nynorsk
nt	neuter
Num	numeral
ob	objective (case)
obs.	obsolete
odont.	odontological
ON	Old Norse (Norwegian)
opp.	opposite
P	preposition
p.	page
pers.	personal
Pf	prefix
pharm.	pharmacological
philos.	philosophical
photog.	photographic
phys.	physics
physiol.	physiological
pl	plural
Pln	place name
Pn	pronoun
po	possessive (case)
poet.	poetic
pol.	political
pop.	popular (folkelig)
(pop.)	slang (American)
pos	positive
poss.	possessive
pp	perfect participle
pr	present (tense)
prep.	preposition
Prn	proper name
pron.	pronoun
prp	present participle
psych.	psychological, psychiatric
pt	past, preterite
pv	passive
refl.	reflexive
sb	subjective (case)
sby	somebody
sg	singular
sp	superlative
SP	standard pronunciation
sth	something
sup.	superlative
tech.	technological
teleg.	telegraphy
theo.	theological
twp	township
typog.	typographical
usu.	usually
V	verb
vet.	veterinary
wk	weak
zool.	zoological

Note: for technical reasons some words are abbreviated differently in the italicized grammatical identifications after the entry than they are in the rest of the text.

a'[1] *-en* (letter, *mus.* note) A, a: **fra a til å** from A to Z; **har en sagt a, får en også si b** if you start something, you had better finish it.
a'[2] *I* 1 ah, oh. 2 (with following *meg*): **gid a meg (=gid); isj a meg (=isj),** etc.
°**a**[3] *Pn* unstressed form of +**hun**/***ho, henne: har du sett a?** have you seen her?; **hels a Berit** say hello to Berit.
à' *P* 1 of: **2 kartonger à 12 bokser** 2 cartons of 12 cans. 2 at (price): **2 pakker à kr 4,—** 2 packs at 4 *kroner* each. 3 or: **5 à 6 dager** 5 or 6 days.
A=+**Arbeiderpartiet/*Arbeidar-t Aust**
AB=aktiebolag
abandone're *V -te jur.* abandon (insured property).
ab'bed *-en* abbot.
abbedi' *-et, pl -/+-er* abbey.
abbedis'se *-a/+-en* abbess.
+**ab'bor** *-en* cf **åbor**
abc [abese'] *-a/+-en* 1 primer. 2 *fig.* the rudiments: **politikkens ABC** the ABC's of politics.
abc/bok [abese'/] *-a, pl -bøker* primer.
abdikasjo'n *-en* abdication.
abdise're *V -te* abdicate.
a'ber *en/et* drawback; catch, snag: **det eneste a- ved saken** the only c- in the affair.
+**abessi'nier** *-en, pl -e* **(=*-ar)** (an) Abyssinian.
abessi'nsk *A* - Abyssinian.
ablegøy'er *pl* jokes, pranks, tricks: **gjøre a-** cut up, frolic.
abnor'm *A* abnormal.
abnormite't *-en* abnormity; abnormality.
abonnement [abonnemang'] *-et, pl -/+-er* subscription **(på** to).
abonnements/billett' *-en* season ticket.
abonnen't *-en* 1 subscriber **(på** to). 2 season-ticket holder.
abonnen't/tal *-et* **(=+/tall)** circulation.
abonne're *V -te* subscribe **(på** to).
abor't *-en* abortion; miscarriage.
aborte're *V -te* have a miscarriage.
abrakada'bra *-et* abracadabra, gibberish, mumbo-jumbo.
abrup't *A* - abrupt.
abs.=absolutt
abscess' *-en* abscess.
abscis'se *-n* abscissa.
absente're *V -te*: **a- seg** absent oneself; abscond, leave (hurriedly).
absin't *-en* absinthe (liqueur).
absolusjo'n *-en* absolution.
absolutis'me *-n* absolutism.
absolutt'[1] *-et* absolute.
absolutt'[2] *A* - absolute; *(adv.)* certainly, definitely, by all means: **han vil a- gjøre det** he insists on doing it.
absolve're *V -te* 1 absolve (from sin). 2 *obs.* pass, take (exam or degree).
absorbe're *V -te* absorb: **a-ende evne** absorption capacity; **a-ende stoff** absorbent.
absorpsjo'n *-en* absorption.
abstinen's *-en* abstinence **(fra** from).
abstrahe're *V -te* abstract, make abstraction **(fra** from).
abstraksjo'n *-en* abstraction.
abstrak't[1] *-et* abstract noun.
abstrak't[2] *A* - abstract.
absur'd *A* - absurd: **redusere ad a-um** reduce to an absurdity.
absurdite't *-en* absurdity.
acetyle'n *-en* acetylene.
+**a'd**[1] *P* (*obs.* except in idioms; often replaced by **av**) 1 toward, in the direction of: **(han er sin far) opp ad dage** (he is) the spitting image (of his father); **(en) ad gangen** (one) at a time; **(det går) ad helvete til** (things are going) to hell; **ad omveier** indirectly; **inn ad (døren)** in through (the door). 2 re: **ad: Deres søknad,** re: your application.
+**a'd**[2] *Av* cf **at**[1]
+**ad-** *Pf* cf **at-, åt-**
+**-ad** *P* -ward(s), e.g. **henad, nedad, oppad**
a'dam *-en* Adam, man: **den gamle a-** the old A-=unregenerate man.
a'dams/eple *-t* Adam's apple
adden'd *-en* addend.
adde're *V -te math.* add, add up.
addisjo'n *-en math.* addition.
adekva't *A* - adequate.
a'del *-en* nobility, peerage: **(han er) av a-** (he is) of noble birth.
a'delig *A* - noble, of noble birth.
a'del/skap *-en/+-et* nobility: **a- forplikter** noblesse oblige.
a'dels/brev *-et* patent of nobility.
a'dels/mann *-en, pl -menn/*-menner* noble, nobleman, peer.
a'dels/stand *-en/*et* nobility, peerage.
+**a'd/ferd** *-en* cf **åt/**
+**a'd/gang** *-en* 1 access, approach; admission, admittance **(til** to): **a- forbudt** no admittance, keep out; **ha fri a- til** have the run of. 2 opportunity, permission: **a- (til) kjøkken** kitchen privileges; **gi a- til** allow, provide an opportunity for; **det er a- til å bade** swimming is permitted.
+**a'dgangs/tegn** [/tein] *-et* admission card, ticket.
adhesjo'n *-en phys.* adhesion.
adia'fora *pl* adiaphora.
ad'jektiv [also ad'-] *-et, pl -/+-er* adjective.
adjun'kt *-en* teacher (in secondary school) holding title of **cand. mag.**
adjun'kt/eksa'men *-en* university degree examination giving the title of **cand. mag.** and qualifying for a position as **adjunkt** (about=Am. B.A.).
adjutan't *-en* adjutant, aide-de-camp.
adjø' *et* good-bye.
+**a'd/komst** *-en* cf **at/**
a'dle *V -a/+-et.* 1 knight, raise to the peerage. 2 dignify, ennoble: **arbeidet a-er mannen** labor dignifies the man.
+**a'd/lyde** *V -lød, -lydt* obey.
adm.=administrasjon, -ativ, -erende; admiral
administrasjo'n *-en* administration: **sette (en) under a-** place (one) under a-=declare (sby) bankrupt.
Administrasjo'ns/rådet *Prn* council which administered Norway April 15—Sept. 25, 1940.
adminis'trativ *A* administrative.
administra'tor *-en, pl -to'rer* administrator.
administre're *V- te* administer, manage.
admira'l *-en* admiral.
admiralite't *-et* admiralty.
admira'l/stab *-en* admiralty staff.
ad no'tam: ta noe a- make note of sth, bear sth in mind; **ta dette a-** keep this in mind.
adopsjo'n *-en* adoption (of children) **(av** of).
adopte're *V -te* adopt.
adopti'v/ba'rn *-et, pl -/*-born* adopted child.
adr.=adresse
adressan't *-en merc.* shipper.
adressa't *-en* addressee.
adres'se *-a/+-en* 1 address: **a- hr. X** c/o Mr. X. 2 scroll (inscribed with appropriate sentiments for special occasions).
Adres'se/avi'sen *Prn* name of Trondheim newspaper (Norway's oldest, founded 1767).
adres'se/bok *-a, pl -bøker* (city) directory.
adres'se/kalen'der *-eren, pl -rer* (city) directory.
adresse're *V -te* address (letter); consign (goods).
+**adrett'** *A* - *lit.* agile.
A'dria/havet *Pln* (=+**Adria'ter/**) the Adriatic.
+**a'd/skille** *V -skilte* cf **at/**
+**adskil'lig** *Av* cf **at-**
+**a'd/splitte** *V -et* cf **at/**
+**a'd/spre(de)** *V -dde/-dte* cf **at/**
+**a'd/spredelse** *-n* cf **at/**
+**adsta'dig** *A* - cf **at-**
ad un'das: gå a- go to pot.
adv.=adverb(ium); advokat
+**a'd/vare** *V -te* cf **åt/**
+**a'd/varsel** *-elen, pl -ler* cf **åt/varing**
ad'vent *-en* Advent.
adventis't *-en* Adventist.
adver'b *-et, pl -/+-er* (=+**adverbium)** adverb.
adverbia'l *A* cf **adverbiell**
adverbiell' *A -elt* adverbial.
+**adver'bium** *-iet, pl -ier* cf **adverb**
advi's *-en merc.* (letter of) advice.
advise're *V -te merc.* advise (e.g. **bill**), give notice.
advoka't *-en* 1 lawyer. 2 lawyer qualified to plead before the Appellate Court (as diff. from **sakfører**); attorney(-at-law), *(Brit.)* barrister, solicitor. 3 advocate (of a cause).
advokatu'r *-en* examination for title of **advokat 2.**
aerogram' *-met, pl -/+-mer* aerogram, air letter.
afasi' *-en* aphasia.
affeksjo'ns/verdi' *-en* **(=*/verd)** sentimental value.
affek't *-en* anger, excitement: **komme i a-** lose one's temper.
affektasjo'n *-en* affectation.
affekte're *V -te* affect; pretend.
affekte'rt *A* - affected=unnatural.
af'fektiv *A* emotional.
affik's *-et gram.* affix.
affinite't *-en chem.* affinity.
affise're *V -te* affect: **ikke la deg a- av været** don't let the weather bother you (get you down).
affæ're *-n* affair: **andres a-r** the a-s of others; **ta a-** take action; **det er ingen lett a-** it is no easy matter.

+ Bokmål; * Nynorsk; ° Dialect.
After letter: ' stress (Acc. 1);
' tone, stress (Acc. 2); · length.
Below letter: . not pronounced.

+afgha'ner *-en, pl -e* (=***afgha'n, -ar**) Afghan.
afgha'nsk *A* - Afghan; (of the language, also) Pashto.
aforis'me *-n* aphorism.
aforis'tisk *A* - aphoristic.
a'-form *-a/+-en gram.* Norw. fem. def. article in *-a* (contrastive with the older Nn. form in *-i* or the Bm. form in *-en*).
A'frika *Pln* Africa.
***afrika'n** *-en* cf **afrikaner**
+afrikan'der *-en, pl -e* (=***afrikan'd**) native of South Africa.
+afrika'ner *-en, pl -e* (=***-ar, *afrikan**) African.
afrika'nsk *A* - African.
***af'tan** *-en, pl aftnar* cf **aften**
+af'ten *-en* (=***aftan**) 1 evening: **god a-** good evening (either greeting or leavetaking); **i a-** this evening. 2 eve: **ju'l/** Christmas eve.
+af'ten/nummer [/nommer] *-et* evening edition.
Af'ten/posten *Prn* daily newspaper in Oslo.
+af'ten/røde *-n* evening sky, sunset glow.
+af'tens *en* evening meal, supper (usu. 8-9 PM).
+af'ten/sang *-en* evening services, vespers.
+af'tens/mat *-en* evening meal, supper (usu. 8-9 PM).
+af'ten/svermer *-en zool.* hawkmoth (Sphingidae).
+af'tes *Av*: **i a-** (earlier) this evening; **i går a-** [af'tes] yesterday evening, last night.
af'tning *-en pop.* evening.
aga't *-en* agate.
Ag'de/nes *Pln* twp, Sør-Trøndelag.
Ag'der [also Ag'-] *Pln* bishopric comprising Vest-Agder and Aust-Agder.
a'ge[1] *-n* 1 respect (**for** for); fear. 2 discipline: **holde i a-** keep in check; ***der det ikkje er age, er det heller ikkje ære** where there is no order, there is also no honor.
a'ge[2] *V -a/+-et* cow, overawe.
a'ge/laus *A* (=**+/løs**) undisciplined; disrespectful, wild.
***a'geleg** *A* - 1 fearsome, frightening. 2 impressive.
***a'ge/løyse** *-a* 1 wildness, lack of respect. 2 undisciplined person.
agen't *-en* 1 agent. 2 salesman.
agentu'r *-et merc.* agency.
age're *V -te* 1 act, play. 2 pretend (to be), play a part, sham: **a- doktor** act as doctor (without being one).
agg' *-et* bitterness, resentment: **bære (et) a- (i sinnet)** nourish r- (in one's heart).
***agg'/full** *A* resentful.
aggrega't *-et, pl -/+-er* aggregate; *tech.* unit (esp. of turbine and dynamo).
aggresjo'n *-en* aggression.
ag'gressiv *A* aggressive.
agio [a'dsjo] *-en merc.* agio=allowance (or premium) for difference in exchange value between two currencies.
agitasjo'n *-en* agitation.
agita'tor *-en, pl -to'rer* agitator.
agitato'risk *A* - agitatory, propagandistic.
agite're *V -te* agitate, propagandize (**for** for).
agn[1] [ang'n] *-a* (=**+agne**) 1 hull, husk (on ear of grain). 2 chaff.
agn[2] [ang'n] *-et* bait: **sette a- på kroken** bait the hook.
Agnar [ang'nar] *Prn(m)*.
agna't *-en* agnate=relative on male side.
agna'tisk *A* - agnate, agnatic.
+agne[1] [ang'ne] *-a* cf **agn**[1]
+agne[2] [ang'ne] *V -a/-et* bait: **a- kroken** b- the hook; **a- etter noe** fish for sth. (e.g. favor).
Agnes [ang'nes] *Prn(f)*.
°agnestei' *-et* cf **agnus dei**
***agn/hald** [ang'n/] *-et* barb (on fish hook).
agnor [ang'nor] *-a* barb (on fish hook or harpoon).
+agnos'tiker *-en, pl -e* (=***-ar**) agnostic.
agnostisis'me *-n* agnosticism.
+agn/skjell [ang'n/] *-et* (=***/skjel**) mussel (used as bait, esp. Mytilus modiola).
ag'nus de'i *et* lamb of God, religious pendant or medal with picture of lamb, etc.
agra'r *-en pol.* agrarian.
agra'r/parti' *-et* agrarian (farmers') party.
agrono'm *-en* agronomist.
agronomi' *-en* agronomy.
agur'k *-en* 1 cucumber; gherkin. 2 pickled cucumber(s). 3 *fig.* sour, disagreeable person.
agur'k/sala't *-en* cucumber salad.
a'h *I* ah.
aha' *I* aha.
ai' *I* ah (expressing surprise and satisfaction).
air [æ'r] *-en*: **en viss a-** a certain air.
°aje're *V -te* cf **agere**
à jour [asju'r] up to date: **à- med betalingen** on time with the payments; **føre à-** bring up to date; **holde seg à- med** keep abreast with.
+ajour/føre [asju'r/] *V -te* bring (accounts) up to date.
ajournere [asjurne're] *V -te pol.* adjourn.
akademi' *-et, pl -/+-er* academy.
+akade'miker *-en, pl -e* (=***-ar**) academician; college graduate.
akade'misk *A* - academic: **a- borger** "citizen of the a- community"= university student or graduate.
akan't *-en* cf **akantus**
akan'tus *-en* (=**akant**) 1 *bot.* acanthus. 2 *arch.* ornamentation based on acanthus vine.
aka'sie *-n bot.* acacia.
***a'ke**[1] *V ek, ok, eke/eki* cf **ake**[2]
a'ke[2] *V +-te/*-a* (=***ake**[1]) 1 ride (esp. in sleigh). 2 slide, go sliding (sledding); go tobogganing. 3 slide (e.g. on banister): **a- på ryggen** s- on one's back; **a- seg framover** edge one's way forward.
a'ke/bakke *-n* sliding hill; toboggan slide.
°akede're *V -te* cf **akkedere**
a'ke/føre *-t* (good, bad) sledding (=snow conditions).
akelei'e *-a/+-en bot.* columbine (Aquilegia vulgaris).
+a'ker *-eren, pl -rer* cf **åker**
A'ker *Pln* part of Oslo, formerly separate twp.
+a'ker/bruk *-et* cf **åker/**
Akershu's *Pln* 1 fortress in Oslo. 2 county surrounding (but not including) Oslo.
akevitt' *-en* aquavit (distilled drink, usu. flavored with caraway).
akil'les/hæl *-en* Achilles heel=vulnerable spot.
akil'les/sene *-a* (=***/sen**) Achilles' tendon (joining calf muscles to heelbone).
akk' *I* alas: **a- ja** oh dear.
***ak'kar** *-en* octopus.
ak'ke *V -a/+-et*: **a- seg** cry alas, sigh (over about)
akkeda's *-en pop.* dispute, quarrel.
akkede're *V -te* 1 bargain, haggle (**med** with); dispute. 2 **a- bort** let on contract.
akklamasjo'n *-en* acclamation: **velge ved a-** elect by a-.
akklimatise're *V -te* acclimate: **a- seg** adapt, adjust oneself.
akkomode're *V -te* accommodate: **a- seg** adapt oneself (**til** to).
akkompagnatrise [-panjatri'se] *-a/-en* (female) accompanist.
akkompagnatør [-panjatø'r] *-en* (male) accompanist.
akkompagnement [-panjemang'] *-et* accompaniment.
akkompagnere [-panje're] *V -te mus.* accompany.
akkor'd *-en* 1 *mus.* chord: **i a-** in harmony. 2 *jur.* agreement; arrangement, composition (of debts): **han fikk a-** a settlement was made. 3 contract: **arbeide på a-** work under a c- (i.e. not for hourly wages), do piece work. 4 compromise: **gå på a- (med)** compromise (with); **a-ens ånd** the spirit of c- (Ibsen).
akkor'd/arbeid *-et* job work, piece work; work done on contract.
akkor'd/beta'ling *-a/+-en* payment on contract (cf **akkord** 3).
akkorde're *V -te* 1 dispute, haggle. 2 reach agreement: **a- bort** let on contract. 3 *jur.* go into bankruptcy; compound (with creditors).
akkredite're *V -te* 1 *pol.* accredit (e.g. ambassador). 2 *merc.*: **a- noen (hos)** open an account for sby (with).
akkrediti'v *-et, pl -/+-er* 1 credentials. 2 *merc.* letter of credit.
akkumulasjo'n *-en* accumulation.
akkumula'tor *-en phys.* accumulator; storage battery.
akkumule're *V -te* accumulate, store (energy).
akkura't [also ak'kora't as *I*] *A* - 1 *lit.* accurate, precise. 2 *(adv.)* exactly, just: **a- slik** j- so; **a- som (om)** j- as (if).
akkus'ativ *-en gram.* accusative.
akkviesce're *V -te lit.* acquiesce (**ved** in).
akkvisisjo'n *-en* acquisition, gain.
akkvisitø'r *-en merc.* agent, salesman (esp. of advertising and insurance).
a kon'to *merc.* on account.
akroba't *-en* acrobat.
akrobatikk' *-en* acrobatics.
akroba'tisk *A* - acrobatic.
ak's *-et bot.* ear, head, spike (of grain): **sanke a-** glean; **skyte a-** head out, form spikes.
ak's/blomstra *A* - (=**+-et**) *bot.* spicate, spiked.
ak'se *-n* axis.
ak'sel[1] *-elen, pl -ler* 1 axle; shaft. 2 *bot.* axil.
ak'sel[2] *-la, pl -'ler* shoulder: **på a- gevær** s- arms.
Ak'sel *Prn(m)* Axel.
ak'sel/bein *-et* shoulder bone.
ak'sel/brei *A -tt* (=**+/bred**) broad-shouldered.
akselerasjo'n *-en* acceleration.
akselere're *V -te* accelerate.
aksent *-en* 1 [aksen't] accent (=symbol over letter marking pitch or stress; also ref. to the pitch or stress). 2 [aksang'] accent (=manner of pronunciation): **han har god a-** he has a good a-.
+aksen't/tegn [/tein] *-et* accent (=aksent 1).
aksentue're *V -te* 1 accent (e.g. syllable, note). 2 accentuate, emphasize.
aksep't *-en merc.* acceptance (=promise to pay draft or bill of exchange); accepted draft etc.
aksepta'bel *A -t, pl -le* acceptable.
akseptan't *-en merc.* acceptor.
aksepte're *V -te* 1 accept. 2 *merc.* accept, honor (bill of exchange).
aksiden's *-en* 1 *philos.* accident. 2 incidental work, or income, esp. in printing.
aksiden's/arbeid *-et* job printing.
aksiden's/trykkeri' *-et, pl +-er/*-* job printer, general printshop.
aksio'm *-et, pl -/+-er* axiom.
aksi'se *-n obs.* excise.
ak'sje *-n merc.* share; (*pl* also) stock: **hans a-r stiger** *fig.* his stock is rising; **han tegnet a-r i x** he bought stock in x.
ak'sje/bank *-en* joint-stock bank (as distinguished, in Europe, from government bank).
ak'sje/brev *-et* stock certificate.
ak'sje/bø'rs *-en* stock exchange.
+ak'sje/eier *-en, pl -e* (=***/eigar**) stockholder.
ak'sje/kapita'l *-en* share capital.
+ak'sje/leilighet *-en* apartment owned

by occupant (who takes stock in building).
+ak'sje/mekler *-en, pl -e* (=***-ar**) stockbroker.
ak'sje/selskap *-et* corporation, stock company; abbrev. **A/S**=Inc. (*Brit.* Ltd.).
+ak'sje/tegning [/teining] *-a/-en* stock subscription.
+ak'sje/utbyt'te *-t* stock dividend(s).
aksjo'n[1] *-en* 1 action: **bokhandlerne går til a-** the book dealers take a-; **reise en a- (mot)** start a movement (against). 2 *jur.* criminal prosecution.
°aksjo'n[2] *-en* cf **auksjon.**
aksjo'ns/radius *-radien, pl -radier* range of operation, radius.
aksjonæ'r *-en* shareholder, stockholder.
ak'sle *V -a/+-et* 1 *obs.* take sth on one's shoulder: *hum.* **a- sitt skinn** gird up one's loins (for battle). 2: **a- (på) seg** straighten up, stretch; elbow one's way.
ak'sling *-en* axle, shaft.
***ak'ster** *-en* riding (in vehicle).
ak't[1] *+-en/*-a* 1 attention; *care (of cattle): **gi a- på** pay heed to; **giv a-!** a-!; **ta seg i a- (for)** watch out (for). 2 respect: **holde en i a- og ære** honor and respect sby. 3 *archaic* intention: **det er ikke min a- at vi skal sette oss ned på Formo** it is not my i- that we should settle at Formo (Undset).
ak't[2] *-a/+-en* 1 act, ceremony. 2 act (in play). 3 nude (model), painting of nude. 4 *(pl)* documents: **sakens a-er** the d-s in the case. 5 *obs.* **ban: i rikets a-** outlawed.
ak'te *V -a/+-et* 1 heed, pay attention (**på** to); *take care of (cattle): **a- seg (for)** watch out (for). 2 respect: **en a-et familie** a r-ed family; **et a-et navn** a r-ed name. 3 *lit.* intend (**å** to): **a- seg** plan (to go); **han a-er seg hit** he is planning to come here.
+ak'telse *-n* honor, respect: **ha a- for** have r- for; **med a-** respectfully yours; **med all a-** with all due r-.
+ak'ten/for' *P* to the rear (of); *naut.* astern.
+ak'ten/fra *P naut.* from astern.
+ak'ten/om' *P naut.* astern of, behind.
ak'ter *Av* (=***atter**) aft, astern: **a- på skipet** in the stern of the ship; **fra for til a-** from stem to stern; **a-st** aftmost, farthest aft.
ak'ter/dekk *-et* afterdeck, quarterdeck.
ak'ter/ende *-n* stern.
ak'ter/over [/åver] *Av* aft, astern, towards the rear.
+ak'ters *Av* (=***atters**): **det går til a- (med)** things are going down hill (with).
ak'ter/skott *-et* aft bulkhead.
+ak'ter/speil *-et* stern; *hum.* posterior (of person).
+ak'ter/stavn *-en* sternpost; *obs.* stern.
ak'ter/ut *Av* aft, astern: **sakke a-** fall behind.
+ak'terut/seile *V -te* beat (in competition), leave (one) behind.
+-ak'tig [also -akti] *A* - -ish, -ive, as in **fordel-, løgn-, narr-,** etc.
ak'tiv *A* active: **i a- tjeneste** on a-duty.
ak'tiva *pl of* **aktivum.**
aktive're *V -te* activate.
aktivise're *V -te* activate.
aktivis't *-en* activist.
aktivite't *-en* activity: **sette seg i a-** take action, get busy.
ak'tivum *-umet, pl aktiva/+aktiver* asset.
***ak't/laus** *A* careless.
ak'tor *en* counsel for the prosecution.
aktora't *-et* prosecution: **fra a-ets side** on behalf of the p-.
+ak't/pågi'vende *A* - attentive, watchful.
+ak'tpågiven/het *-en* attention, watchfulness.
aktri'se *-a/-en obs.* actress.
***ak't/sam** *A* cf **/som**
***ak't/semd** *-a* attention, care.
+ak't/som *A -t, pl -me* attentive, careful.
+ak'tsom/het *-a/-en* attention, care.
ak't/stykke *-t, pl +-r/*-* document.
aktualise're *V -te* bring up to date, make (sth) current, revive (e.g. an old plan).
aktualite't *-en* current interest: **det har ingen a-** it is of no interest, has no relevance.
aktua'r *-en* actuary.
aktua'r/fag *-et* actuarial science.
aktuell' *A -elt* up to the minute, of current interest, topical: **et a-t spørsmål** a current problem; **det blir ikke a-t** the question won't arise.
ak't/verdig [also /ver'di] *A* - worthy of respect, (highly) respected.
aktø'r *-en obs.* actor; participant.
akustikk' *-en* (the science of) acoustics: **a -en er god (dårlig)** the acoustics are good (bad).
akus'tisk *A* - acoustic.
akutt'[1] *-en* acute (accent)=´.
akutt'[2] *A* - acute.
akvarell' *-en* (painting in) water color.
akva'rie/fisk *-en* fish for aquariums.
akva'rium *-iet, pl +-ier/*-ium* aquarium.
akveduk't *-en* aqueduct.
a'l[1] *-en* 1 duramen, heart, heartwood. 2 *geol.* hardpan.
a'l[2] *-et* breeding (of animals).
-al *A* as in **atal, frostal, gamal, gøyal, tagal.**
+A/L=**andelslag**
à la *P (Fr.)* according to, in the manner of: **biff à la lapskaus** beef hash.
alabas't *-en* alabaster.
alar'm *-en* 1 alarm: **rope (slå) a-** give (sound) the a; **blind a-** false a-. 2 hubbub, racket, uproar: **det ble voldsom a- etter talen** there was a great u- after the speech.
alarme're *V -te* 1 alarm: **a-ende nyheter** a-ing news. 2 call (police, fire department), warn; alert.
+alba'ner *-en, pl -e* (=***-ar, *alban**) Albanian.
alba'nsk *A* - Albanian.
al'batross *-en zool.* albatross (Diomedea culminata).
albi'no *-en, pl -er/-s* albino.
al'/boge[1] [/båge] *-n* (=+**/bu(e)**) elbow (on arms, sleeves, pipes): **ha spisse a-r** have sharp e-s (=be pushy).
al'/boge[2] [/båge] *V -a/+-et* (=+**/bue**) nudge (with elbow): **a- seg fram** elbow one's way, push one's way ahead.
alboge/støyt [al'båge/] *-en* (=+**/støt**): **han fikk en a-** he hit his elbow; **enkemannssorg er som a-en** the widower's grief is like hitting one's elbow (=the pain is short-lived).
+al'bu(e)[1] *-(e)n* cf **/boge**[1]
+al'/bue[2] *V -et* cf **/boge**[2]
al'bum *-et, pl -/+-er* album.
albumi'n *-et* albumin.
***al'de**[1] *-a* (ocean) wave.
***al'de**[2] *-a* fruit (esp. from trees).
alde'les *Av* completely, exactly, wholly: **a- gal** quite mad; **a- ikke** not at all; **a- som om** just as i ; **du tar a- feil** you are absolutely wrong.
al'der[1] *-eren, pl +-rer* 1 age: **liten (stor) for sin a-** small (big) for one's a-; **(han døde) i en a- av** (he died) at the a- of; **i en tidlig (sen) a-** early (late) in life; **i hans a-** at his a-; **i sin beste a-** in the prime of life; **(hun er) på min a-, på a- med meg** (she is) my a-. 2 (old) age: **a-en trykker ham** old a- weighs upon him; **det kommer med a-en** it comes with the years; **i høy a-** in advanced years; **han bærer sin a- godt** he doesn't look his a-.
°al'der[2] *Av* cf **aldri**
al'der/dom' *-men* (old) age: **vise respekt for a-men** show respect for old a-.
+alderdom'melig *A* - (=***al'derdomleg**) oldfashioned (e.g. clothing); conservative (e.g. grammatical forms).
+al'derdoms/svakhet *-en* senility.
al'derdoms/trygd *-a* cf **alders/**
al'ders/grense *-a/+-en*: **falle for a-n** reach retirement age.
al'ders/heim *-en* old peoples' home.
al'ders/klasse *-a/-en* age class: **i min a-** in my a-.
+al'der/stegen *A -ent, pl -ne* aged, ancient, hoary.
al'ders/tillegg *-et* increase in salary (due to age); *hum.* avoirdupois.
+al'ders/trin(n) *-et* age level: **på dette a-** at this age (level).
al'ders/trygd *-a/+-en* old age pension (social security).
al'drende *A* - elderly.
+al'dres *V -es pt -edes, pp -es* (=***aldrast**) age, grow old.
al'dri *Av* 1 never: **a- i evighet (livet, verden)** n-, n-; n- in my life; **a- mer** n- again; **bedre sent enn a-** better late than n-; **en skal a- si a-** n- say n-; **nesten a-** hardly ever; **nå eller a-** now or n-. 2 not: **a- det slag** nothing at all, n- a bit; **det var da vel a- (min bror)** surely it wasn't (my brother); **du skulle vel a- ha glemt det** surely you haven't forgotten it; **du tror da vel a- at** surely you don't think that... 3(intensively=no matter how): **a- så snart** no sooner; **a- så stor** no matter how big; **ikke for a- det** not for anything, not on your life; **ikke på a- den tid** for I don't know how long; **på a- så lang tid** for ever so long; **a- så lite** ever so little.
***al'drig**[1] *A* - elderly.
+al'drig[2] *Av* cf **aldri**
a'le *V -er/el, -te/ol, -t/*-e/*-i* breed: **a- opp** b-; bring up, raise, rear.
***a'le/dyr** *-et* cf **avls/**
alei'ne *Av* (=+**alene**) 1 alone, by oneself: **bli a-** be left b-; **en ulykke kommer sjelden a-** it never rains but it pours; **helt a-** all a-; **stå a-** be on one's own; **du er ikke a- om det** you are not the only one. 2 only: **ene og a-** solely; **ikke a- ... men også** not o- . . . but also.
+aleksandri'ner *-en, pl -e* (=***-ar**) Alexandrian; (of verse) alexandrine.
+aleman'ner *pl* (=***-ar**) Alemanni (ancient tribes in so. Germany).
a'len *-na, pl -en/-ner* ell, old unit of measure=0.6275 m or 2 feet (and ¾ in.): *bibl.* **legge en a- til sin vekst** add one cubit to his stature (Matt. 6,27); **to a- av samme stykke** two of a kind; **vi små en a- lange** we little ones no bigger than your arm (Wergeland).
+ale'ne *Av* cf **aleine**
a'len/mål *-et* 1 *obs.* ell-measure. 2 *fig.* yardstick.
+al'f *-en* cf **alv**
Al'f *Prn (m).*
al'fa *-en* 1 alpha (Greek letter). 2 *bot.* esparto grass.
alfabe't *-et* alphabet.
alfabetise're *V -te* alphabetize.
alfabe'tisk *A* - alphabetical.
al'fa/stråle *-n* alpha ray.
alfon's *-en* pimp.
alfonseri' *-et* pimping.
***al'/fort** [/fort] *Av* cf **all/**
+alfres'ko/maleri' *-et* fresco painting.
a'l/furu *-a* pine with high percentage of heartwood.
al'ge *-n bot.* alga, *(pl)* algae; seaweed.
al'gebra *-en* algebra (subject, also book).

+ Bokmål; * Nynorsk; ° Dialect.
After letter: ' stress (Acc. 1); ` tone, stress (Acc. 2); · length.
Below letter: . not pronounced.

algebra'isk *A* - algebraic.
Alger [alsje'] *Pln* Algiers.
Algerie [alsjeri'] *Pln* Algeria.
al'ge/sopp *-en bot.* fungus resembling the algae (Phycomycetes).
+algirer [alsji'rer] *-en, pl -e* (=***-ar**) (an) Algerian.
algirsk [alsji'rsk] *A* - Algerian.
***a'l/goḍ** *A* (of a tree) having a core of fresh heartwood.
a'lias *Av* alias=also known as.
alibi' *-et, pl -/+-er* alibi: **bevise sitt a-** establish an a-
alka'li *-et, pl +-er/*- chem.* alkali.
alka'lisk *A - chem.* alkaline.
al'ke *-a zool.* auk, esp. the razorbill (Alca torda): **full som ei a-** drunk as a coot.
al'ke/jakt *-a/+-en* auk hunt.
al'ke/konge *-n zool.* little auk, dovekie (Plantus alle).
alkoho'l *-en* alcohol.
alkoho'l/fri *A -tt* non-alcoholic.
+alkoho'l/holdig *A* - (=***/haldig**) alcoholic (=containing alcohol).
+alkoho'liker *-en, pl -e* (=***-ar**) (an) alcoholic.
alkoholise're *V -te* alcoholize: **han var sterkt a-t** he was soaked in alcohol.
alkoholis'me *-n* alcoholism.
alkoho'lisk *A* - alcoholic: **a-e drikker** a- drinks.
alkoholis't *-en* (an) alcoholic.
alkoho'l/misbruk *-en/-et* misuse of alcohol.
+alkoho'l/nytelse *-n* (=***-ing**) use of alcohol.
alkoho'l/prøve *-a/+-en* sobriety test.
alkoho'l/svak *A* with low alcohol content (ab. 0.5-2.5 %).
alkove [-å'-] *-n* alcove (usu. containing bed).
alkymi' *-en* alchemy.
alkymis't *-en* alchemist.
all' *A alt, pl alle* **1** *(adj.)* all: **a- den stund** inasmuch as, whereas; **han hadde a- (mulig) grunn** he had every (possible) reason; **a- verden** everybody, Tom, Dick, and Harry; **a- ære verdt** worthy of every honor; **a-e mann** everybody; **a- sin dag** his whole life; **en gang for a-e** once and for all; **for a- del** by all means, whatever you do; ***han var ikkje a- der dei såg han** he was not entirely to be trusted; **i a- hast** in great haste; **i a-e fall** in any case; **i a- korthet** in brief; **i a- stillhet** quietly; **(hva) i a- verden** what in the world; **(det går) over a- forstand** (it is) quite incomprehensible; **til alt hell** fortunately. **2** *(pron.)* **alle** everybody, everyone, all: **a-e andre** everybody else; **a-e i hop** everybody; **a-e og enhver** anybody and everybody; **a-e sammen** everybody; **a-e som en** one and all, to a man, with one voice; **a-es** everybody's, of all: **a-es øyne vokter på deg** *bibl.* all eyes are on you; **alt** everything: **alt annet enn (dum)** anything but (stupid); **alt det (han strevet)** no matter how (hard he worked); **(jeg ønsker Dem) alt godt** (I wish you) every happiness; **alt i alt** all in all, all told; **framfor alt** above all; **i alt** altogether, in sum; **alt i ett** constantly; **alt i hop** everything, the whole business; **alt skal en prøve og velge det beste** try all things and choose the best (*bibl.*, Ibsen); **i ett og alt** in every respect, entirely; **i stand til alt** capable of anything; **ikke for alt i verden** not for the world; **når alt kommer til alt** when all is said and done, after all; **alt sammen** all, everything.
***-all** *-alt* cf **-al**
allé *-en* avenue (of trees); trees lining an avenue.
al'le *pl of* **all**
allegori' *-en* allegory.
allego'risk *A* - allegorical.
***allehan'de[1]** *-t* cf **-hånde[1]**
***al'le/hande[2]** *A pl* cf **/hånde[2]**
allehel'gens/dag *-en* All Saints' Day (November 1).
+allehån'de[1] *-t* (=***-hande[1]**) allspice.
+al'le/hånde[2] *A pl* (=***/hande[2]**) all kinds of (things): **det gikk a- sagn om ham** many were the tales told about him.
***al'le/leis** *Av* in every way.
***al'le/mannen** *df* every man, the common man; most people.
***al'lemanns/bate** *-n* (the) general good.
+al'lemanns/eie *et* (=***/eige**) common (public) property.
al'ler[1] *Av* (intensifying a following superlative form, often written together with the following word, see also that word) by far, of all, very: **a- best som (vi satt og drakk kaffe)** just as (we were drinking coffee); **a- helst** preferably, above all; **ikke det a- bitterste** not the least bit; **med det a- første** at the (very) first opportunity; **en a- helvetes kar** a devil of a fellow; **noe a- helvetes (noe)** sth perfectly ghastly; **som a- snarest** for just a moment.
°al'ler[2] *Av* cf **aldri**
+al'le/rede [also allere'de, al'le/] *Av* (=***al'le/reiḍe**) **1** already, by now: **han skulle a- vært her** he ought to have arrived b-. **2** as early as: **a- i mellomalderen** as early as the Middle Ages. **3** even: **a- nå** e- now; **a- samme dag** the very same day; **a- av den grunn** for that reason alone.
allergi' *-en* allergy.
aller'gisk *A* - allergic.
al'ler/helst *Av* cf **aller[1]**
+allerkjæ'reste *-n*: **a-n min** my sweetheart.
+al'lesam'men *Pn* cf **all**
+al'le/steḍs *Av* everywhere, in all places.
+al'lesteḍs/nærvæ'renḍe *A* - omnipresent, ubiquitous.
+allevegne [-vei'ne] *Av* cf **vegne**
all'/fader *-en* (the) Father of All (one of the names of the Norse god Odin).
***all'/fares** *Av* altogether.
all'far/veg *-en* (=**+/vei**) highway, main road.
***all'/folkeleg** *A* - international.
***all'/fort** [/fort] *Av* constantly.
***all'/gilḍ** *A* of universal validity.
all'/goḍ *A* infinitely good.
***all'/gyldig** *A* - of universal validity.
***all'/heim** *-en* universe.
allianse [aliang'se] *-n* alliance.
allie're *V -te* ally (**seg med** oneself with): **de a-te** the Allies (in World War I or II).
alliga'tor *-en* alligator.
+alli'ke/vel' [also /vel'] *Av* cf **likevel**
allitterasjo'n *-en* alliteration.
allittere're *V -te* alliterate (**med** with).
***all'/jamt** *Av* always, constantly.
***all'kunne/bok** *-a, pl -bøker* encyclopedia.
all'/makt *-a/+-en* omnipotence.
***all'/mann** *-en* everybody, the public.
all'manna/mote *-t* general meeting.
***all'mann/veg** *-en* highway, main road.
allmek'tig *A* - almighty, all-powerful, omnipotent: **den a-e** the Almighty.
all'/menn *A -ment* common, general, public, universal: **det a-e beste, det a-e vel** the c- good.
+all'menn/befin'nenḍe *-t* general condition, state of health.
+all'menn/dannelse *-n* (=***-ing, */daning**) general, liberal education.
all'menn/dannenḍe *A* - (=***/danande**) educational (=broadening, liberal).
all'menn/gyldig *A* - of general validity, universal: **en a- sannhet** a u- truth.
+all'menn/het *-en*: **a-en** the public; **den store a-** the general public.
all'/menning *-en* **1** common (land). **2** square, wide street (esp. in Bergen). **3** *hist.* levy consisting of all men in a district.
all'menn/menneskelig *A* - (=***/menneskjeleg**) universal; human.
all'menn/nyttig *A* - of public utility; beneficial to all; public-spirited.
all'menn/skole *-n*: **den høgre (høyere) a-** *obs.* school between grammar school and university (=**realskole** and **gymnasium**).
all'menn/tilstanḍ *-en/*-et* general condition.
+all'mue/aktig *A* - narrow-minded; petty.
all'/muge *-n* (=**+/mue**) (the) common people; plebeians.
all'/natur *-en poet.* Nature.
alloke're *V -te* allocate (**til** to).
all right [å'l rai't] *A* - all right, O.K.: **han er a- igjen** he is a- now.
+all/rounder [ålrau'nder] *-en, pl -e* (-***ar**) all-round athlete.
+all'/sang *-en* community singing.
all'/sidig [also -si'd-] *A* - versatile; comprehensive; all-round: **en a- mann** a v- man; **a- utdannelse** a well-rounded education (training).
***all'/skrivar** *-en* one who writes about everything.
all'/slags *A* - (=**all slags, alle slags**) of all kinds: **det kommer a- mennesker dit** all kinds of people come there.
***all'/song** *-en* cf **/sang**
***all'/staḍ** *Av* cf **alle/steds**
***all'/støtt** *Av* for ever; steadily: **du sig a- djupare og djupare** you are sinking deeper and deeper all the time.
all'/tiḍ [also /tid] *Av* **1** always: **a- siden** ever since; **evig og a-** a-, perpetually; **du skal da a- ødelegge det hele** you a- spoil everything; **det kan vi a- gjøre** we can do that at any time (later on). **2** at least, always: **noe kan vi (da) a- gjøre** at least we can do something. **3** *lit.* (before comparative only) steadily: **larmen ble a- høyere** the din was s- increasing.
°all'/tiḍs *Av* cf **/tid**
all'/ting[1] *-et* **1** legislature of Iceland. **2** *hist.* popular assembly functioning as legislative body and supreme court of Iceland (founded A.D. 930).
all'/ting[2] *Pn* everything: **hvorom a- er** however that may be, anyhow; **når enden er god, er a- godt** all's well that ends well; **dermed er a- sagt** that is all there is to be said about that.
allude're *V -te* allude (**til** to).
***all'/veldig** *A - lit.* almighty, all-powerful, omnipotent.
+allver'den *N* cf **all**
***all'/vetande** *A* - cf **/vitende**
+allvi'denḍe *A* - cf **-vitende**
***all'/visst** *Av* at least, especially, to be sure.
+allvi'tenḍe *A* - (=***-vitande**) omniscient.
+allvi'ten/het *-en* omniscience.
al'm *-en* elm (Ulmus montana).
+alm.=alminnelig, almen
almanakk' *-en* almanac.
+al'/men *A* cf **all/menn**
al'me/tre *-et, pl -/+-trær* elm (tree).
+almin'delig *A* - cf **alminnelig**
+almin'nelig *A* - **1** common=general, universal (e.g. opinion, conscription, suffrage, error, theory, rule): **til a- forbauselse** to everyone's surprise; **den hellige, a-e kirke** The Holy Catholic (=Universal) Church. **2** common = ordinary, usual (e.g. people, words): **a- brød** light rye bread; **a- forstand** c- sense; **a-e talemåter** phrases, commonplaces. **3** *(adv.)* commonly, in general, universally, usually: **a- kjent** generally known.
+almin'nelig/het *-en* **1** generality: **i (sin) a-** in general, as a rule, generally speaking. **2** banality.
al'/misse *-a/+-en* alms; *(pl)* charity.
+al'/mue *-n* cf **all/muge**
***a'lnaḍ** *-en* breeding, raising: **hesten**

er hans eigen a- he has bred the horse himself.
°**a'lnakke** *-a* cf **almanakk**
***a'lne/mål** *-et* cf **alen/**
***a'lo** *-en* racket, uproar.
a'loe *-n bot.* aloe.
alpak'ka *-en* alpaca (animal; its wool; garments made from the wool).
al'pe/fio'l *-en bot.* cyclamen.
al'pe/lanḍskap *-et* alpine landscape.
al'pe/lue *-a* beret.
+**Al'pene** *Pln* **(=*Alpane)** the Alps.
al'pe/rose *-a/+-en bot.* rhododendron.
alpi'n *A* alpine.
alpi'nsk *A* - alpine.
al'/run(e) *-(e)n bot.* mandrake, mandragora (root used for magic purposes).
***a'ls/dyr** *-et* cf **avls/**
***a'ls/garḍ** *-en* cf **avls/**
al'sike/kløver *-en bot.* alsike clover (Trifolium hybridum).
al'skens *A* - all kinds of.
Al'sta/haug *Pln* twp, Nordland.
al't[1] *-en* **1** contralto (singer). **2** alto (part, instrument): **synge a-** sing a-.
al't[2] *-et lit.* universe: **a-ets midtpunkt** center of the u-.
al't[3] *Av* **1** already: **skal du a- gå igjen?** are you leaving a-?; **han hadde a- gjort det** he had a- done it. **2** all the way, clear: **der kom folk a- fra Bø** people came all the way from Bø; ***a- fram** all the way; ***a- ifrå han var fødd** all the time from his birth; **a- siden** ever since; ***a- til kvelds** c- till evening. **3** (intensifier, often omitted in transl.): **a- etter (som)** according to; **a- i ett** constantly; **a- imellom** now and then; **a- mens (*med, medan)** while; **a- mer** ever more; ***a- om** if; although; **a- som** while; **det kommer a- an på** it all depends. **4** no matter how (much): **a- hun skjente** no matter how she scolded; **a- det kongsdatteren ropte og gråt** no matter how the princess screamed and wept (Asbjørnsen).
al't[4] *nt of* **all**
Al'ta *Pln* twp, Finnmark.
alta'n *-en* balcony (on house), porch.
***al'tar** *-et* cf **alter**
+**al'ter** *-eret/-ret, pl -/-ere* **(=*altar)** altar; shrine: **a-ets sakramente** the Lord's supper, the Blessed Sacrament; **gå til a-s** go to communion.
+**al'ter/bok** *-a, pl -bøker* **(=*-ar/)** prayer book; Book of Common Prayer.
+**al'ter/duk** *-en* **(=*-ar/)** altar cloth.
altere'rt *A* - startled, upset: **Fru Kathrine ble sterkt a-** *Fru* K- was greatly u- (Falkberget).
+**al'ter/gang** *-en* **(=*-ar/)** communion.
+**al'ter/kalk** *-en* **(=*-ar/)** chalice.
alter'nativ[1] *-et, pl -/+-er* alternative.
alter'nativ[2] *A* alternative: **a- avstemning** voting on a- proposals.
alterne're *V -te* alternate (**med** with).
+**al'ter/ring** *-en* **(=*-ar/)** altar railing.
+**al'ter/tavle** *-a* **(=*-ar/)** altar piece; (with wings) triptych.
al't/etenḍe *A* - omnivorous.
al't/for' *Av* too, much too: **a- snill** far too kind.
+**altmulig/mann** [al't mu'li/] *-en, pl -menn* **(=*altmog(e)leg/)** handyman; jack of all trades.
+**al't/omfat'tenḍe** *A* - all-inclusive, universal.
+**al't/omspen'nenḍe** *A* - all-embracing, universal.
+**al't/oppslu'kenḍe** *A* - absorbing, engrossing (interest).
altruis'me *-n* altruism.
altruis'tisk *A* - altruistic.
+**altsammen** [al't sam'men] *Pn* cf **all**
***al'tso** *Av* cf **altså**
al'tså *Av* **1** so=accordingly: **det er a- ikke i dag** so it's not today; **a- kommer han i morgen** so he'll be coming tomorrow. **2** *pop.* (emphatic, usu. finally): **han er så kjekk a-** he is so nice; **han der Johnsen er gærn a-!** that J- is *crazy!*

alumi'nium *-en/-et* aluminum.
alu'n *-en/-et* alum.
al'v *-en* elf, elfin, fairy.
Al'v *Prn(m)*
***al'v/blåst(er)** *-en* cf **alve/**
Al'v/dal *Pln* twp, Hedmark.
al've/blåst *-en* hives, nettlerash (urticaria).
a'l/veḍ *-en* heartwood (cf **al**[1]).
al've/dans *-en* **1** elfin dance. **2** fairy ring (formed in grass by a mushroom growth).
al've/lanḍ *-et* fairyland; mirage: ***det stig av hav eit a-** a f- rises from the sea (Garborg).
Al'ver/sunḍ *Pln* twp, Hordaland.
al'v/kone *-a* fairy woman.
***al'v/never** *-nevra* lichen (esp. Lobaria or Peltigera), used in folk medicine against hives etc.
alvor [all'/vår] *-et* **1** seriousness, gravity: **en a-ets mann** a serious man; **nå blir det a- av** things are coming to a head; **stillingens a-** the g- of the situation. **2** sincerity, earnestness: **er det (ditt) a-?** do you mean it?; **for a-** seriously, in earnest; **gjøre a- av (noe)** carry out (one's plans); **(det er ment) i a-** (it is) seriously (intended); **i fullt a-** seriously; **i ramme a-** in full seriousness.
alvorlig [alvå'rli] *A* - **1** serious= grave, solemn: **holde seg a-** keep a straight face; **en a- fare** a g- danger; **en a- sak** a s- matter; **a- syk** s-ly ill. **2** serious=earnest; conscientious: **a- talt** s-ly speaking; **mene det a-** have s- intentions, mean business; **ta en a-** take one at his word; **på det a-ste** most e-ly.
***al'vor/sam** *A* serious, grave.
al'vors/mann *-en, pl -menn/*-menner* serious person, sobersides.
al'vors/o'rḍ *-et* word of warning: **han sa ham et a-** he gave him a piece of his mind.
al'vors/tung [/tong] *A* serious, solemn.
al'v/skott *-et* elf-shot (one of various diseases supposed to be caused by elves, esp. in cattle).
amalga'm *-et* amalgam.
amalgame're *V -te* amalgamate.
amanuen'sis *-ensen, pl +-enser* research assistant (e.g. in libraries, museums, laboratories).
amaso'ne *-a/+-en* amazon.
+**amaso'ne/aktig** *A* - amazonian, mannish.
amatø'r *-en* amateur.
+**amatø'r/aktig** *A* - amateurish.
+**amatø'r/messig** *A* - amateurish.
am'bar *-en, pl *ambrar* wooden vessel (usu. with handle on lid, for carrying butter, porridge, etc.).
ambassa'de *-n* embassy (chancery or residence).
ambassa'de/råd *-en* counsellor of embassy.
ambassadø'r *-en* ambassador.
ambisjo'n *-en* ambition: **honnett a-** social ambitiousness (Holberg).
ambivalen's *-en* ambivalence.
***am'boḍ** *-a* tools.
am'/bolt *-en* anvil (also *anat.*, bone in the ear).
am'bra *-en* **1** ambergris. **2** *bot.* southernwood (Artemisia abrotanum), European wormwood with aromatic leaves.
***am'brar** *pl of* **ambar**
ambulanse [ambulang'se] *-n* ambulance.
ambule're *V -te* rotate, wander: **a-ende** movable, ambulatory; touring (circus).
***a'me** *V -a* **1** irritate, rub (e.g. wound). **2** hurry, press: **a- på en** h- sby; **a- seg** h-.
am'en [also a'-, ame'n] *et* amen: **si ja og a-** give assent (**til** to); **så sikkert som a- i kjerka** sure as shooting.
Ame'rika *Pln* America (often of U.S.A. only).
ame'rika/båt *-en* transatlantic liner.

ame'rika/feber *-en hum.* "America fever" (used of the mass emigration from Europe in the 19th and 20th centuries).
+**amerika'ner** *-en, pl -e* **(=*-ar)** American (esp. from U.S.A.).
+**amerikanerin'ne** *-a/-en* **(=*-ar-)** American woman.
amerikanise're *V -te* Americanize.
amerikanis'me *-n* Americanism: **et folk som ... lever ... i tåpelig heseblest av modernitet og a-** a people living in an inane breathlessness of modernity and A- (Kjær).
amerika'nsk *A* - American: **a- olje** castor oil.
ametys't *-en* amethyst.
amfi' =**amfiteater**
amfi'bie/fly *-et* amphibian plane.
amfi'bisk *A* - amphibian.
amfi'bium *-iet, pl +-ier* amphibian.
amfi'/tea'ter *-eret/-ret, pl -er/*-re* **1** amphitheater. **2** last rows in theater gallery.
°**a'/minnels(e)** *-(e)n* memorial: **til a-** in remembrance.
***am'le** *V -a* putter, struggle (**med** with): **a- seg inn (på)** pick a quarrel (with).
***am'/loḍ** *-en/-et* fool, scamp.
am'me[1] *-a/+-en* wet nurse.
am'me[2] *V -a/+-et* breastfeed, suckle (a baby): **a- opp** foster, nourish, rear.
+**am'mestue/fortel'ling** *-a/-en* old wives' tale.
ammoniakk' *-en* ammonia.
ammunisjo'n *-en* ammunition.
amneste're *V -te* grant amnesty to, pardon.
amnesti' *-et, pl +-er/*-* amnesty, pardon: **alminnelig a-** general a-.
am'ning *-en naut.* draught, trim: **på god a-** in good t-.
amok' *Av*: **løpe a-** run amuck.
A'mor *Prn(m)* Cupid.
a'/moralsk *A* - amoral.
+**a'mor/bue** *-n* **(=/boge)** Cupid's bow.
amor'f *A* amorphous.
amori'n *-en* cupid (statuette, picture
amortisasjo'n *-en* amortization.
amortise're *V -te* amortize.
amorø's *A* amorous.
***am'pe**[1] *-n* bother, trouble; care.
***am'pe**[2] *V -a* bother, urge (sby) on: **ampast med** struggle with.
am'pel *-elen, pl -ler* hanging fixture, used as lamp or flower pot: **lyset fra a-en** the light of the lamp.
am'per *A -ert, pl -re* **1** fretful, irritable (esp. children). ***2** energetic, impatient, restless.
ampère [ampæ'r] *-n* ampere.
ampèremeter [ampærme'ter] *-eret* ammeter.
***am'pe/sam** *A* (of children or old people) demanding, troublesome.
amplity'de *-n* amplitude.
ampul'le *-n* **1** *eccl.* ampulla (sacred vessel). **2** *med.* ampule.
amputasjo'n *-en* amputation.
ampute're *V -te* amputate.
***am'stre** *V -a* complain, struggle, work.
am't *-et, pl +-er/*-* county (in Denmark; in Norway 1662-1918, now **fylke**).
am't/mann *-en, pl -menn/*menner* chief administrative officer in **amt**, about = county prefect, district governor; since 1918 called **fylkesmann.**
amulett' *-en* amulet.
A'munḍ *Prn(m)*
amø'be *-n* amoeba.
a'-mål *-et* (Norwegian) language form using the suffix *-a* for the fem. sg. and neut. pl. def. article.
an' *Av* **1** to (on bills to indicate charge

+ Bokmål; * Nynorsk; ° Dialect.
After letter: ' stress (Acc. 1); ` tone, stress (Acc. 2); · length.
Below letter: . not pronounced.

made): an 2 skjorter à kr 30,- two shirts at 30 *kroner* each. 2 on etc., in combination with verbs like gå, se, slå (see these).
an- *Pf* 1 (from German) on, to (used esp. with verbs, often separable, as in anlegge, leggean). 2 (from Greek) non-, a- (e.g. analfabet).
*-an *Av* from (e.g. austan, heiman).
anakoluti' *-en* anacoluthon.
anakronis'me *-n* anachronism.
anakronis'tisk *A* - anachronistic.
ana'l *A* anal.
an'/alfabe't *-en* illiterate.
analfabetis'me *-n* illiteracy.
analog [-lå'g] *A* analogous (med to).
analogi' *-en* analogy: i a- med in a- to.
analogisk [-lå'gisk] *A* - analogical.
analy'se *-n* analysis (av of).
analyse're *V -te* analyze.
+analy'tiker *-en, pl -e* (=*-ar) analyst.
analyt'isk *A* - analytical.
analytt' *-en* 1 *chem.* solution to be analyzed. 2 *math.* problem in analysis.
an'anas *-en* pineapple.
anapes't *-en* anapest (⏑⏑´).
anarki' [-ki'] *-et* anarchy.
anar'kisk [-kisk] *A* - anarchical.
anarkis'me [-kis'me] *-n* anarchism.
anarkis't [-kis't] *-en* anarchist.
anarkis'tisk [-kis'tisk] *A* - anarchistic.
anate'ma *-et* anathema.
anato'm *-en* anatomist.
anatomi' *-en* anatomy.
anato'misk *A* - anatomical.
an'/befa'le *V -te* recommend (til to): *obs.* jeg a-er meg I take my leave.
+an'befa'lelses/verdig *A* - worth recommending; commendable.
+an'/befa'ling *-en* recommendation (for for); (=letter of r.) reference.
+an'/bringe *V -brakte, -brakt* 1 locate, place: han visste ikke hvor han skulle a- sine lange ben he didn't know where he should find room for his long legs; han fikk a-t et kraftig slag he managed to land a powerful blow; barnet ble a-t på et hjem the child was p-d in a home. 2 invest (money etc.).
+an'/bringelse *-n* 1 location, placement (av of). 2 investment.
+an'/bud *-et* bid; estimate (på of, on): gi a- på submit an e- on.
+an'buds/innby'delse *-n* advertising for bids.
an'd[1] *-a, pl ender* duck.
*an'd[2] *-a* cf ånde[1]
an'd- *Pf* against, counter-.
an'dakt *-a/+-en* 1 devotions, prayers: holde a- lead d-. 2 piety, solemnity: med a- i sinnet piously; *hum.* spis det med a- eat it with respect.
an'dakts/full *A* devout, pious; solemn.
an'dakts/stund *-a/+-en* devotions, prayers.
*an'dast *V -ast* cf ånde[2]
*an'd/bakkes *Av* uphill.
*an'd/blæst *A* - out of breath: ho vart reint a- she was quite o-.
*an'de[1] *-n* cf ånde[1], ånd
*an'de[2] *V -a* cf ånde[2]
*-ande *A* - cf -ende
An'de/bu *Pln* twp, Vestfold.
an'de/dam' *-men* duck pond; *hum.* about narrow environment: det ble røre i a-men there was a stir in the henhouse (a flurry in the dovecote).
*an'de/drag *-et* cf ånde/
andek'tig *A* - devout, solemn: lytte a- listen d-ly.
+an'/del *-en* share (i in, of): arbeiderne bør ha a- i fortjenesten the workers should share in the profits.
*an'de/laus *A* cf ånde/løs
+an'dels/lag *-et* cooperative society.
+an'dels/selskap *-et* cooperative society.
an'de/mat *-en* 1 duck food. 2 *bot.* duckweed (Lemna).
An'de/nes *Pln* twp, Nordland.
+an'der/ledes *Av* cf ann/leis
An'ders *Prn (m)* =Andrew (from Andreas).
an'de/stegg *-en* (=*and/) drake.
*an'de/tak *-et* breath, esp. a difficult one.
*an'd/fanges *Av* face to face, clasped in embrace.
*an'd/farast *V -ferst, -forst, -farest/-ist* pass without meeting, miss each other (on the road).
*an'd/fares *Av* altogether; without a break: hogge skog a- cut down every tree.
an'dføttes *Av* (of two persons) (lie, sit) with feet in opposite directions.
an'd/let *-et* face; expression: lang i a-et with a disappointed e-.
*an'dlets/bragd *-a* (facial) expression.
an'dlets/drag *-et* (facial) feature.
*an'd/løgd *A -/-løgt* 1 inclined to laugh: eg vart så a- I wanted to burst out laughing. 2 amusing, funny.
*an'd/låt *-et* dying moments: liggje i a-om be about to die; a-s/dag day of death.
*an'd/marke *-n* herd (of cattle).
*an'd/mot(t) *A* - 1 out of breath, wearied; choking. 2 difficult, inconvenient, unpleasant.
*an'dov *-et* 1 stopping a boat (in midcurrent). 2 difficulty, trouble, worry.
an'd/pusten *A +-ent, pl -ne* out of breath: han blir lett a- he gets o- easily.
+an'/dra *V -drog, -dradd/-dratt* 1 apply (om for), petition 2 amount (til to).
+an'/dragende *-t* application, petition (om for).
+an'/dratt *pp of* -dra
an'dre *df and pl of* annen, annan
Andre'as *Prn (m)* Andrew.
+andre'as/kors *-et* (=*/kross) St. Andrew's cross.
andre'as/messe *-a* St. Andrew's mass (Nov. 30).
+an'drik *-en* drake (=male duck).
An'd/rimne *Prn* 1 *myth.* name of cook in Valhalla. 2 name of satirical periodical (pub. 1851 by Ibsen and others).
+an'/drog *pt of* -dra
an'd/ror *-en* 1 rowing against the wind. 2 headwind; opposition.
an'd/sjø *-en* currents, opposing wave.
*an'd/skræme *-a* frightful person; terror.
*an'd/sloppen *A -e/-i, pl -slopne* out of breath.
*an'd/stemne *V -de* reply (to); oppose.
*an'd/stev *-et* refrain; saying.
*an'd/svævd *A -/-svævt* sleepless.
an'd/synes *P* face to face (med with); *opposite; *in relation to: vi står her a- eit alvorleg spørsmål we are faced with a serious problem; ansvar a- banken responsibility to the bank.
*an'd/søles *Av* counter-clockwise.
*an'd/teppe *-t* headcold.
*an'duge[1] *-n* care, disquiet, worry (for for).
*an'duge[2] *V -a* care, worry (på about).
an'd/unge [/onge] *-n* duckling.
*an'd/vake *-a* cf /voke
*an'd/vaken *A -e/-i, pl -ne* sleepless.
*an'd/varpe *V -a* groan, sigh.
*an'd/ver *-et* contrary weather; headwind.
*an'd/vig *A* 1 contrary, stubborn. 2 difficult, heavy (work).
*an'd/vind *-en* head wind.
*an'd/voke [/våke] *-a* (=/vake) insomnia.
*an'd/æres *Av* backwards; contrary.
an'd/øve *V -de* 1 handle, manage (also *refl.*). 2 keep (boat) steady (in current), usu. by rowing.
An'd/øya *Pln* island in Vesterålen.
a'ne[1] *-n* (distinguished) ancestor (usu. *pl*).
a'ne[2] *V -te/*-a* suspect, have an (uneasy) feeling, think, dimly perceive (at that): a- fred og ingen fare be unsuspecting; a- uråd have misgivings, smell a rat; det a-er meg (at) *lit.* I have a notion (that); intet ondt a-ende unsuspecting; jeg a-te ikke (at) I had no idea, I didn't dream (that).
+a'ne/galleri' *-et* gallery of ancestors.
anekdo'te *-n* anecdote.
+a'nelse *-n* cf aning
anemi' *-en* anemia.
ane'misk *A* - anemic.
anemo'ne *-n* 1 poppy anemone (Anemone coronaria). 2 (genus) Anemone.
+an'/erkjen'ne *V -kjente* 1 recognize (e.g. state); acknowledge (e.g. claim); approve (e.g. person): a-te ideer accepted ideas. 2 praise, express approval of: en a-t forsker a celebrated scholar.
+an'/erkjen'nelse *-n* 1 acceptance, acknowledgement, recognition (av of, ved by). 2 appreciation, credit, praise, recognition (av of): nyte alminnelig a- enjoy general r-; han fikk a- for sin innsats he won p- for his contribution.
+an'/erkjen'nende *A* - appreciative, complimentary: et a- brev a letter of praise.
+an'/erkjen't *A* - accepted, acknowledged, respected (authority, principles, etc.).
+an'/fall *-et* 1 attack (of disease), fit, seizure (av of). 2 outburst, paroxysm (e.g. of rage).
+an'/falle *V -falt* assault, attack.
+an'/fekte *V -et* (usu. *neg.*): det a-er ham ikke it does not disturb him; han lot seg ikke a- (av det) he was not bothered (by it).
+an'/fektelse *-n* (=*-ing) 1 (religious) scruple, obsession. 2 temptation, troubled mind (esp. *pl*): leve i angst og a- live in an anxious and troubled state.
+an'/føre *V -te* 1 *lit.* command, head, lead. 2 adduce (e.g. examples), advance (e.g. an excuse), allege, cite: a- til sin unnskyldning (at) plead as one's excuse (that). 3 *merc.* enter: a- til ens debet enter to one's debit.
+an'/fører *-en, pl -e* chief. leader; ringleader (av of).
+an'/førsel *-elen, pl -ler* 1 command: under a- av commanded by. 2 citation, quotation: med a- av dag og dato citing the exact date. 3 statement: hans a-ler holdt ikke stikk his s-s did not hold water.
+an'førsels/tegn [/tein] *-et* quotation mark, quote.
+ang. =angående
+an'/gav *pt of* -gi
ang'e[1] *-n* fragrance, odor: *tung av a- heavy with f-.
ang'e[2] *V -a/+-et* smell (fragrantly).
+ang'el *-elen, pl -ler* (=*ongul) (fish) hook.
*ang'eleg *A* contrary, difficult, troublesome.
+angelsak'ser *-en, pl -e* (=*-saksar, -sakse) Anglo-Saxon.
angelsak'sisk *A* - Anglo-Saxon, Old English (language).
ang'er *-en* 1 regret, remorse, repentance (over for): a- og bot contrition and penitence. *2 sorrow (for loss).
-ang'er *Pln* (orig.) =fjord, narrow inlet, e.g. in Hardanger, Stavanger.
ang'er/full *A* contrite, penitent.
+ang'er/given *A -ent, pl -ne* (=*/gjeven) contrite, penitent.
ang'er/laus *A* (=+/løs) untroubled; blameless, without reproach: det kan du a-t gjøre you can do it with a clear conscience.
*ang'est *-en* cf angst[1]
+an'/gi *V -gav, -gitt* 1 state; give information about; report: a- kilde give one's source; a- som grunn give as (one's) reason. 2: a- tonen *mus.* give the pitch; *fig.* set the tone, strike the keynote. 3 inform against, report; denounce (a criminal), squeal (on).
+an'/gikk *pt of* -gå
angina [anggi'na] *-en* angina.
+an'/gitt *pp of* -gi
+angivelig [anji'-] *A* - ostensible, reported, supposed.

+an'/givelse -n 1 statement: **uten nærmere a-** without specification; **uten a- av kilde** without specifying the source. 2 declaration (of duty); tax return (cf **selv/**). 3 denunciation (of criminal), information.
+an'/giver -en, pl -e informer, stool pigeon.
+an'/giveri· [also -eri'] -et informing, squealing.
+an'/gjeldende A - (the person) concerned, (the party) in question: **a- var ikke til stede** the accused was not present.
ang'le V -a/+-et (=***ongle**) angle, fish (**etter** for): **a- etter stemmer** f- for votes.
anglika'nsk A - Anglican.
anglise're V -te anglicize.
anglisis'me -n anglicism (in language).
anglis't -en specialist in English.
ang'lo/amerika'nsk A - Anglo-American.
angora/geit [anggo'ra/] -a angora goat.
ango'ra/ull -a angora (wool).
ang're V -a/+-et 1 repent, be sorry for: **a- på** regret, be sorry about; **a- sine synder** repent one's sins; **a-ende** repentant, regretful. 2: **- seg** feel regret, be repentant; **han a-et seg med det samme** he was sorry immediately. *3 grieve (**på** for).
+an'/grep¹ -et attack, charge; assault (**på** on): **blåse til a-** sound the c-; **gå til a-** take the offensive; attack.
+an'/grep² pt of **-gripe**
+an'greps/krig -en war of offense (aggression).
+an'greps/vis Av: **gå a- til verks** take the offensive.
+an'/gripe V -grep, -grepet assault, attack; affect (e.g. by disease): **den a-ende part** the attacker.
+angri'pelig A - vulnerable, open to attack: **et a- punkt** a weak point.
+an'/griper -en, pl -e aggressor, assailant, attacker.
ang'st¹ -en (=***angest**) anxiety, dread, fear, terror (**for** of): **a- og beven** f- and trembling; **føle dødsens a-** be in mortal f-; **gå i a- (for)** be in t- (of).
+ang'st² A - afraid, anxious, fearful (**for** about, for).
+ang'st/biter -en, pl -e (=***-ar**) neurotic.
ang'st/full A anxious, uneasy; agonizing.
ang'st/skrik -et cry of terror.
+an'/gå V -gikk, -gått concern, refer to, relate to: **det a-r ikke meg** it does not concern me, is none of my business; **hva a-r X=hva X a-r** as for X, as far as X is concerned; **hva det a-r** as far as that goes, for that matter.
+an'/gående P about, as for, concerning, *re*, with regard to.
+an'/hang -et appendix, supplement.
+an'/holde V -holdt, -holdt 1 arrest, take into custody; seize, sequester (a ship). 2 make application (**om** for): **a- om ens hånd** ask formally for sby's hand (in marriage).
+an'/holdelse -n arrest, seizure (**av** of).
anili'n -en/-et aniline.
anili'n/farge -n aniline dye.
anima'lsk A - animal (opp. to vegetable).
anime're V -te 1 animate, encourage, stimulate. 2: **a-t** animated, lively (usu. due to alcoholic spirits).
animosite't -en animosity (**mot** against).
a'ning -a/+-en (=**+anelse**) 1 idea, inkling, notion; hunch, suspicion: **bange a-er** misgivings; **jeg har ingen (ikke den minste) a- (om)** I have no (not the faintest) idea (about). 2 hint, soupçon, touch (**av** of).
an'is -en *bot.* anise (Pimpinella anisum); anise-seed, aniseed.
an'is/drops -en/-et anise candy.
an'is/likø·r -en anisette.
an'k -en 1 anxiety, feeling of uneasiness (**for** about): **ligge på a-** be uneasy (to a point of sleeplessness). *2 complaint, nagging.
***an'kar** -en *jur.* appellant.
an'ke¹ -n 1 complaint, criticism (**mot** of). 2 *jur.* appeal (**til** to).
an'ke² V -a/+-et 1 complain (**over, på** about): **a- seg** lament. 2 *jur.* appeal (a case): **den a-ende part** the a-ing party. 3 worry (**på** about).
an'ke/dom·stol -en *jur.* appellate court, court of appeals.
an'ke/frist -en *jur.* time within which an appeal must be made.
an'ke/full A anxious.
an'ke/instan·s -en *jur.* court of appeals
+an'kel -elen, pl -ler (=***okle**) ankle.
+an'kel/djup A (=**/dyp**) ankle deep.
an'ke/mål -et complaint, criticism.
an'ke/nemnd [/nemd] -a board of appeals (for complaints at administrative decisions).
An'ke/nes *Pln* twp, Nordland.
an'ke/punkt [/pongt] -et complaint, grievance.
an'ker -et, pl -/+-e 1 anchor: **kaste a-** drop a-; **lette a-** weigh a-; **ligge for a-** ride at a-. 2 (in dynamo) armature. 3 barrel, cask: **et a- vin** a c- of wine (orig. ab. 10 gals.).
an'ker/botn -en (=**+/bunn**) anchorage.
an'ker/gang -en (in clocks) anchor escapement.
an'ker/mann -en, pl -menn/*-menner anchor man.
+an'ker/spill -et (=***/spel**) windlass.
+an'/klage¹ -n 1 accusation (**for** of; **mot** against): **a-n lød på (at)** the charge was (that); **rette sterke a-r (mot)** bring serious a-s (against). 2 *jur.* arraignment, charge, indictment.
+an'/klage² V -de/+-et accuse (**for** of): **han er a-et for mord** he is charged with murder.
+an'klage/benk -en: **sitte på a-en** be accused (lit. sit in the dock).
+an'/klagede df (the) accused, (the) prisoner, (the) defendant.
+an'klage/punkt [/pongt] -et count (of an indictment).
+an'/klager -en, pl -e 1 accuser. 2 *jur.* prosecutor; district attorney.
+an'/klang -en: **vinne a- (hos)** win support (of), gain sympathy (of).
+an'/komme V -kom, -kommet arrive (**til** at, in), get (**til** to): **a-ende tog** incoming train(s); **de først a-ne** the first arrivals.
+an'/komst -en arrival (**til** at, in).
an'kre V -a/+-et anchor: **a- opp** a-, cast a-.
+an'krings/avgift -en anchorage.
an'krings/plass -en anchorage (ground).
***an'k/sam** A anxious.
+an'/la pt of **-legge**
+an'/lagt A - 1 fitted, inclined, prone (**for** to): **han er pessimistisk a-** he is given to pessimism (pessimistically i-). 2 intended, planned (**på** to): **a- på å skremme ham** aimed to frighten him; **stort a-** p-ed on a large scale.
+anle'dning -en 1 cause, reason (**til** for): **gi a- til** give rise to; **i a- av** in connection with, on account of, in reference to (e.g. your letter); **i den a-** for this purpose (r-); **uten a-** without provocation. 2 chance, opportunity (**til** to, of): **gi en a- til å velge** give sby the c- of choosing. 3 event, occasion: **for a-en** for the o-; **i a- av** on the o- of; **i dagens a-** in honor of the day; **en stor a-** a great day; **ved lignende a-er** on such o-s.
an'/legg -et 1 (process of) construction, founding, start (**av** of); *jur.* bringing suit (esp. **saks/**). 2 (object of) construction, e.g. building (under construction); factory, plant, works; garden, grounds, layout, park. 3 inclination, proneness, receptivity (**for** to); aptitude, gift, talent, turn (**for** for): **a- for fedme** tendency to stoutness; **a- for musikk** musical talent; **gode a-** a good head, a gift (for sth). 4 *arch., eng.* gradient, incline. 5 *mil.* rest: **skyte fra a-** shoot from a position of r-; **i a-** (of a gun) cocked; **med pistolen i a-** with the pistol cocked.
an'/legge V -la, -lagt 1 construct (according to plan), establish, start, e.g. found or open (a business), build (a factory), lay out (a park). 2 *jur.*: **a- sak** bring suit, start an action. 3 adopt (a new costume or appearance), e.g. put on (a wig), change to (a new hairdo), start wearing (glasses), grow (a beard), assume (airs); adopt (a point of view, apply (standards).
an'leggs/arbeid -et construction work (on roads or railroads).
+an'leggs/arbei·der -en, pl -e (=***-ar**) construction worker.
+an'leggs/gartner -en, pl -e (=***-ar**) landscape gardener.
an'leggs/kapita·l -en investment capital.
+an'/liggende -t affair, business, concern: **et viktig a-** a matter of importance; **offentlige a-** public a-s.
+an'/løp -et (ship's) call (**av** of).
+an'/løpe V -løp, -løpet 1 *naut.* call at (a port), touch at. 2 (of silver etc.) oxidize, tarnish; cf **anløpen**. 3 (of metals) harden, temper.
+an'/løpen A -ent, pl -ne 1 (of metals) oxidized, tarnished; (of other substances, and of people) corrupted, decayed. 2 (slightly) drunk, "high".
+an'løps/havn -a/-en *naut.* port of call.
+an'løps/sted -et *naut.* place of call, stopping place.
an'/marsj: **i a-** approaching, on the way (esp. of sth threatening): **en storm er i a-** a storm is blowing up.
+an'/masse V -et: **a- seg (noe)** usurp (sth), arrogate (sth) to oneself; **a-ende** arrogant, demanding.
+an'/masselse -n usurpation (**av** of); arrogance.
+an'/melde V -te 1 review (book etc.). 2 report (e.g. crime); inform against (**til** to); announce (univ. lectures); apply for (patent).
+an'/meldelse -n 1 critique, review (of book etc.). 2 report (to police); notification. 3 entry (e.g. in contest).
+an'/melder -en, pl -e 1 critic, reviewer. 2 informer.
+an'melder/eksempla·r -et review copy.
+an'/merke V -et 1 note, make an annotation. 2 object; criticize: **er det noe å a-?** is there any objection?
+an'/merkning [also /mer'k-] -en 1 notation, note: **få a-** get a demerit. 2 annotation, footnote.
+an'/mode V -et request; ask (**om** for).
+an'/modning -en request (**om** for): **jeg rettet en a- til ham** I made a r- of him.
***ann'** A ant 1 active, busy, eager (**på** for). 2 (*nt.*): **han har ant om tida** he is short of time; **eg er så ant om det** I am eager for it.
***an'na¹** C 1 except: **ingen a- næraste skyldingane** no one but the nearest of kin. 2 but (on the contrary): **han klarte ikkje å gå, a- han kraup** he couldn't walk, b- he crept.
an'na² f, nt of ***annan**, f of **+annen**
An'na *Prn(f)*
anna'l -en annal (usu. *pl.*).
annam'me V -a/+-et 1 *lit.* accept, receive (e.g. the word of God): **djeve-**

+ Bokmål; * Nynorsk; ° Dialect.
After letter: ' stress (Acc. 1); ' tone, stress (Acc. 2); · length.
Below letter: . not pronounced.

len a-! *archaic* damn it! 2 *forest.* accept and mark (timber) on the buyer's behalf.

***an'nan** *A f anna, nt anna, df andre, pl andre* cf **annen**

***an'nan/dag** *-en* cf **annen/**

***an'nan/kvar** *A f anna/kvar, nt anna/kvart* cf **annen/hver**

***an'nan/manns** *po* cf **annen/**

***an'nan/stad** *Av* elsewhere, somewhere else (often preceded by **ein** or **einkvan**).

***an'nar/leis** *Av* cf **ann/leis**

***an'nars** *Av* if not, otherwise: **eg måtte skunda meg, for a- fór han ifrå meg** I had to hurry, for o- he would get ahead of me (Krohn).

***an'nast** *V -ast* be busy (**med** with), have responsibility for: **han hadde mykje å a- med** he had a lot to take care of.

***an'ne** *V -a* 1: **a- på** hurry, press (on) 2: **a- seg** hurry, make an effort; **i morgon lyt vi a- oss ut** tomorrow we have to get out.

An'ne *Prn (f)*

annek's *-et, pl -/+-er* 1 annex (of building). 2 section of parish having a church (chapel) of its own (usu. smaller and less frequently served than the main church).

anneksjo'n *-en* annexation.

+annek's/kirke *-n* (=***/kyrkje**) (secondary) church, chapel; cf **anneks 2.**

annekte're *V -te* annex, take possession of.

annen [a'en] *A m +-en/*-an, f -a/+-en, nt +-et/*-a; df sg andre/+-en, -et; pl andre, po andres* 1 other, *(pl)* others: (with articles) **en a-en (et a-et)** another; **den a-e** the other (one); **det a-e** the other (thing(s)); **de a-e** the others, the rest; (with *conj.*) **en eller a-en** sby or other; **ett eller a-et** sth or other; **en og a-en** some, a few; **ett og a-et** sth, a few, this and that; **det ene og det a-e** this and that; (with *prep.*) **+blant a-et/*mellom a-a** among other things, inter alia; **det ene med det a-e** one thing after another; **år om a-et** year after year; in most years; **fra det ene til det a-e** from one thing to another (used when changing topic); **fra ende til a-en** from beginning to end; **ord til a-et** word for word; **fra tid til a-en** from time to time; (with nouns) **bli et a-et menneske** become another (a better, changed) person; **det var ikke a-en råd** there was no other remedy (way out); **det er en a-en sak** that's another matter; **komme på a-e tanker** think better of it. 2 else: **noen a-en** sby else (**enn** but); **noe a-et** sth else; **ingen a-en** nobody else; **ikke (noe) a-et** nothing else, no other; **om ikke a-et** if nothing else; **alt a-et enn** anything (else) but, not at all; **ikke a-et enn** nothing (else) but, only; **ikke snakk (tale) om a-et** I won't hear of anything else; **det er ikke a-et for** there's nothing else to do; **det må a-et til** sth else is needed; ***han er ikkje a-a til** he isn't good for anything else; **han er a-et til kar** he's something else, more of a man. 3 (in comparisons) a, any: **han gråt som en a-en jente** he cried like any girl; ***han rota som ein a-an gris** he rooted around like any pig. 4 (as numeral, usu. *df sg +-en, -et*) second: **a-en september** September s-; **Fredrik den a-en** F- the S-; **a-en hver** every second, every other; **a-en juledag** the day after Christmas; **det a-et bud** the Third Commandment (the First and Second are combined); **for det a-e/a-t** secondly, in the second place; **selv a-en** with one companion. 5 following, next: **a-e dagen** the next day; ***anna kveld** tomorrow evening.

an'nen/dag *-en* the day after (one of the major church holidays): **a- jul** December 26.

+an'nengrads/likning *-a/-en* (=**+/ligning**) quadratic equation.

+an'nen/hver [/vær] *A annet/hvert* every other (=second).

+an'nen/hånds *A* - secondhand, indirect (information).

+an'nen/klasses *A* - second class (on railway etc.); second-rate.

an'nen/manns *po* other people's (goods).

an'nen/rangs *A* - second-rate.

+an'nen/steds *Av* elsewhere, somewhere else.

+an'nen/stemme *-n mus.* second part.

+an'ner/ledes *Av* cf **ann/leis**

+an'nerledes/tenkende *en* person(s) holding a different opinion.

+an'net *nt of* **annen**

+an'net/steds *Av* cf **annen/**

***an'nig** *A* - cf **onnig**

ann'/leis *Av* (=**+anner/ledes**) different: **det er a- enn jeg hadde tenkt** it is d- from what I had imagined.

an'no *(et)*: **a- 1962** in (the year) 1962; **pro a-** per annum.

annonse [anång'se] *-n* ad, advertisement: **rykke inn en a-** insert an a- (i in).

annonse/avde'ling *-a/+-en* advertising department.

annonse're [-ång-] *V -te* 1 advertise. 2 announce (e.g. piece of news).

annonsø'r [-ång-] *-en* advertiser.

***ann'/sam** *A* busy (person, time, etc.): **ha (det) a-t** be b- (**med** with).

***ann'/semd** *-a* activity, haste; hurry: **det var i a-a gjort** it was done in haste.

ann's/leis *Av* cf **ann/**

***ann's/manns** *po of* **annan/mann**

annuite't *-en* 1 annuity. 2 *math.* problem in annuities.

annuite'ts/lån *-et* loan repayable in annuities.

annulle're *V -te* annul, cancel (debt, order, etc.).

ann'/vinn *A -vint* 1 heavy, laborious. 2 busy: **ha det a-t** be b-.

ano'de *-n elec.* anode; plate (in electron tube).

ano'de/batteri' *-et, pl +-er/*-* anode battery.

anoma'l *A* anomalous.

anomali' *-en* anomaly.

anony'm *A* anonymous.

anonymite't *-en* anonymity.

anorakk' *-en* parka (ski jacket), windbreaker.

+an'/ordne *V -et* 1 decree, ordain. 2 prescribe (medicine).

+an'/ordning *-en jur.* decree, edict, ordinance.

an'/orga'nisk *A* - inorganic.

an'/retning *-en* 1 table setting, food served (esp. for a party): **kold a-** cold spread (=smørgåsbord). 2 [-ret'-] (butler's) pantry, service area (between kitchen and dining room).

an'retnings/bo'rd [also -ret'-] *-et* buffet, serving table, sideboard; tea wagon.

+an'/rette *V -et* 1 arrange, place, serve (food on platters or table). 2 cause, do (damage).

+an'/rop *-et* 1 *mil.* challenge. 2 *naut.* hail. 3 *teleg.* call.

+an'/rope *V -te* 1 challenge (to stop). 2 hail (a boat). 3 implore, invoke (e.g. God).

+an'rops/signa'l [/singna'l] *-et teleg.* call signal, CQ.

an's *-en/+-et* attention: **gi a- på** give a- to; **ha a- for** take an interest in.

+an'/samling *-en* collection; crowd, gathering (**av** of).

***an'sande** *A* - (usu. *neg.*): **ikkje a-** not worthy of attention.

an'/sats *-en* 1 disposition, tendency (**til** to); rudiments (**til** of): **a- til mage** beginnings of a paunch. 2 *mus.* lip, lipping; attack. 3 edge (filed or hammered on metal object).

+an'/satte *pt of* **-sette**

+an'/se¹ *V -så, -sett* 1 consider, regard (**for, som** as): **jeg a-r det for (som) min plikt** I r- it as my duty; **hun anså seg berettiget til dette** she c-ed herself entitled to this. 2 *jur.* sentence: **a- på mildeste måte** give the lightest possible sentence.

an'se² *V -a/+-te* cf **ense**

+an'/seelse [also -se'-] *-n* esteem, regard, respect, reputation: **uten persons a-** without fear or favor; **loven kjenner ingen persons a-** the law is no respecter of persons.

+anse'lig *A* - considerable, impressive, respectable, sizable (e.g. quantity, distance, size, person, object).

***an'sen** *A -e/-i, pl -ne* attentive.

+an'/sett¹ *pp of* **-se**

+an'/sett² *A* - distinguished, esteemed, honored, well regarded: **en a- familie** a highly respected family.

+an'/sette *V -satte, -satt* 1 appoint (**som** as), employ, hire: **de ansatte** the employees; **fast ansatt** permanently employed. 2 calculate (**til** at), estimate, value; assess (for tax purposes): **lavt ansatt** conservatively e-d. 3 *tech.* set up (the rigging); ram home (projectile in cannon); attack (a musical note).

+an'/settelse *-n* 1 appointment, employment. 2 *lit.* estimate; assessment.

ansiennite't *-en* seniority (rights).

an'sikt *-et, pl +-er/*-* face: **a- til a- med** f- to f- with, confronted by; **arbeide i sitt a-s sved** work in the sweat of one's brow; **han ble lang i a-et** his f- fell; **rett (like) opp i a-et på en** right to one's f-; **skjære a-er** make f-s; **et slag i a-et** a slap in the f-, an insult; **vise sitt sanne a-** show one's true colors.

an'sikts/drag *-et* (usu. *pl*) (facial) features.

an'sikts/farge *-n* complexion.

+an'sikts/trekk *-et* (usu. *pl*) (facial) features.

an'sikts/uttrykk *-et* (facial) expression.

ansjo's *-en* 1 anchovy (Engraulis encrasicholus). 2 (in Norway also used of) brisling canned with salt, sugar, and spices.

+an'/skaffe *V-et* obtain, procure, secure: **a- seg** o-, p-, s- (for oneself).

+an'/skaffelse *-n* procurement (**av** of).

+an'/skrevet *A* -: **(dårlig, godt) a- hos en** (badly, well) regarded by sby, (out of, in) favor with sby.

+an'/skrik *-et*: **gjøre a-** give the alarm, raise an outcry.

+an'/skue *V -et* perceive.

+ansku'elig *A* - clear, lucid; graphic: **en a- stil** a g- style.

+ansku'elig/gjøre *V -gjorde, -gjort* make clear, graphic; elucidate, illustrate.

+ansku'elig/het *-a/-en* lucidity, perspicuity.

+an'/skuelse [also -sku'-] *-n* 1 opinion, view (e.g. political, religious): **jeg deler ikke hans a-r** I do not share his v-s. 2 *philos.* (immediate) perception; intuition.

+ansku'elses/undervi'sning *-en* object lesson (Pestalozzian method of teaching by direct perception of objects); visual instruction.

+an'/slag *-et* 1 estimate, evaluation: **et løselig a-** a rough e-. 2 *mus.* touch; striking of a note, esp. the opening one. 3 impact (of machine, projectile, etc.); reaction (from vaccination). 4 plot (**mot** against): **a- mot hans liv** a design on his life. 5 *tech.* rest (of gun); edge, ledge (of tool); stop (of machine).

+an'slags/vis *Av* at an estimate.

***an's/laus** *A* inattentive; careless.

***an'sle** *V -a* work, keep busy (**med** with).

***an's/leis** *Av* cf **ann/**

+an'/slå *V -slo, -slått* 1 estimate, value (**til** at): **jeg a-r ham til å være femti år** I judge him to be fifty years old. 2 strike (a note), sound: **a-tonen** give the pitch; set the tone.

+an'/spenne *V -spente* exert, strain

(one's powers): **a- seg** do one's utmost, strain every nerve.

+**an'/spennelse** *-n* effort, exertion, strain: **med a- av sine siste krefter** exerting oneself to the utmost.

+**an'/spent** *A* - tense: **lytte a-** listen intently.

+**an'/spore** *V -te* goad, spur, stimulate (**til** to).

an'/stalt *-en* 1 institution, home (esp. for those needing public care). 2 *(pl)* arrangements, preparations: **gjøre a-er** make a fuss.

+**an'stalt/maker** *-en, pl -e* projector, schemer (derog. of one who is always thinking up new schemes).

+**an'stalt/makeri'** *-et* foolish schemes, needless activity; fuss.

an'/stand *-en* 1 decorum, dignity: **oppføre seg med a-** behave with dignity. 2 chaperone.

an'stands/dame *-a/+-en* (lady) chaperone.

ansten'dig *A* - decent, proper, respectable (citizen, girl, price, wages, clothes, etc.).

+**ansten'dig/het** *-en* decency, propriety, respectability.

+**ansten'dighets/følelse** *-n* (sense of) decency.

+**ansten'dig/vis** *Av* decently, in (all) decency.

+**an'/stifte** *V -et* cause, foment, stir up: **a- ildebrann** commit arson.

+**an'/stigende** *A* -: **komme a-** arrive (in an unexpected or comical way).

+**an'/stille** *V -stilte* 1 initiate, perform, undertake (usu. with *nouns*): **a- forsøk** experiment; **a- undersøkelser** investigate. 2: **a- seg** act, feign, pretend to be.

+**an'/stod** *pt of* **-stå**

+**an'/strenge** *V -te* 1 exert, strain: **a- seg** e- oneself, make an effort; **a- sin hjerne** rack one's brains; **a-t** strained, tense. 2 tire, tax: **a-ende** exhausting, fatiguing, strenuous; tiring, trying.

+**an'/strengelse** *-n* effort, exertion, strain: **gjøre seg a-r** take the trouble.

+**an'/strøk** *-et* tinge, touch (**av** of); dash, suspicion.

+**an'/strøken** *A -ent, pl -ne* tinged: **kommunistisk a-** tainted by communism.

+**an'/støt** *-et* offence: **gi (vekke) a-** offend; **ta a- av** take offence at.

+**anstø'telig** *A* - objectionable, offensive (action, word).

+**an'støts/ste(i)n** *-en* stumbling block (stone); cause of offense (Romans 9,33).

+**an'/stå** *V -stod, -stått* 1 (usu. *refl.*) **a- seg** be proper, become: **det a-r seg ikke for ham** it is beneath him. 2 (of metals) appear (on the surface).

an'/svar *-et* responsibility (**for** for; **overfor** to); blame, liability: **på eget a-** on one's own r-; **et tungt a-** a grave r-; **et a- på tre millioner** a l- of three millions; **dra (trekke) til a-** call to account; **frihet under a-** freedom with r-; **ha a- for** be responsible for; **stå til a- for** answer for, be called to account for; **ta på seg a-et** assume the r-.

ansva'rlig *A* - responsible (**for** for; **overfor** to); liable: **gjøre (holde) noen a-** make sby l-, blame sby.

+**an'svars/beviss't** *A* - conscientious, responsible.

+**an'svars/forsik'ring** *-a/-en* liability insurance.

an'svars/fri *A -tt* free from responsibility.

an'svars/full *A* responsible; bringing responsibility.

+**an'svars/følelse** *-n* sense of responsibility.

an'svars/havende *en* person having legal responsibility: **a- redaktør** editor-in-chief.

an'svars/kjensle *-a* sense of responsibility.

an'svars/laus *A* (=+**/løs**) irresponsible.

+**an'svars/løshet** *-en* cf **/løyse**

an'svars/løyse *-a* irresponsibility, lack of responsibility.

+**an'/søke** *V -te* apply to (**om** for), petition: **a- kongen om audiens** petition the king for an audience.

+**an'/søkning** *-en* application (**om** for, **til** to) cf **søknad**

+**an'/så** *pt of* **-se**

***an't** *nt of* **ann**

+**an'/ta** *V -tok, -tatt* 1 assume, presume, suppose: **a- for givet** take it for granted; **alminnelig a-tt** generally s-d. 2 accept, approve (offer, proposal, scheme); honor (check). 3 adopt, embrace (idea, religion); assume (name, shape), take on (character, expression): **a- seg en sak** take up a cause. 4 employ, sign on (employee); accept (for military service).

+**anta'gelig** *A* - cf **-takelig**

+**an'/tagelse** [also -ta'-] *-n* cf **/takelse**

antagonis'me *-n* antagonism.

+**anta'kelig** *A* - (=+**-tagelig**) 1 acceptable, satisfactory. 2 *(adv.)* presumably, probably; I suppose.

+**an'/takelse** *-n* (=+**/tagelse**) 1 assumption, guess, supposition. 2 acceptance (**av** of).

+**an'/tall** *-et* number (**av** of): **i et a- av** to the n- of.

Antar'ktis *Pln* the Antarctic.

antar'ktisk *A* - antarctic.

+**an'/taste** *V -et* assault, attack; force one's attention on.

+**an'/tatt** *pp of* **-ta**

antedate're *V -te* antedate (by placing at too early a period).

+**an'/tegnelse** *-n* (/teinelse) notation (esp. by auditor of accounts).

antemensa'le *-n* altar frontal, antependium.

***an'ten** *C* cf **enten**

anten'ne[1] *-a/+-en* aerial, antenna (also *zool.*).

+**an'/tenne**[2] *V -tente* ignite, kindle, set fire to.

+**anten'nelig** *A* - combustible, inflammable (now also "flammable").

+**an'/tennelse** *-n* igniting, kindling.

antesipe're *V -te* anticipate.

an'ti- *Pf* anti-.

antibio'tikum *-umet, pl -a* antibiotic.

antikk'[1] *-en*: **a-en** Antiquity.

antikk'[2] *A antikt* antique.

an'ti/klimaks *-en* anticlimax.

an'ti/krist *en* Antichrist.

antik'va *-en* Roman (type).

antikva'r *-en* 1 antiquary, antiquarian (esp. **riks/**). 2 *fam.* second-hand bookdealer.

antikva'r/bokhandel *-elen, pl -ler* second-hand bookstore.

antikvaria't *-et, pl -/+-er* second-hand bookstore.

antikva'risk *A* - 1 second-hand (of books). 2 *hum.* antiquated, old-fashioned.

antikve'rt *A* antiquated, obsolete, out of date.

antikvite't *-en* antique (object).

antikvite'ts/handel *-elen, pl -ler* antique shop.

+**antikvite'ts/handler** *-en, pl -e* (=***-ar**) antique dealer.

antilo'pe *-n* antelope.

an'ti/luftskyts *-et* anti-aircraft.

antimo'n *-et* antimony.

antipati' *-en* antipathy, aversion.

antipa'tisk *A* - antipathetic.

antipo'de *-n* 1 antipode (=person living on other side of globe). 2 contrast; antithesis: **de er rene a-r** they are absolute contrasts.

antisemitt' *-en* anti-Semite.

antisemit'tisk *A* - anti-Semitic.

antisemittis'me *-n* anti-Semitism.

antisep'tisk *A* - antiseptic.

an'ti/stoff *-et, pl +-er/*-* antibody.

antite'se *-n* antithesis.

antite'tisk *A* - antithetic.

+**an'/tok** *pt of* **-ta**

antologi' *-en* anthology.

An'ton *Prn(m)*

antrasitt' *-en* anthracite.

antrasitt'/kol [/kål] *-et* (=+**/kull**) anthracite coal.

***an'tra(st)** *V -a(st)* dispute, quarrel (**med** with).

+**an'/trekk** *-et* attire, dress: **daglig a-** business suit; **fest/** formal dress; **hva er a-et?** what do we wear?

antropolog [lå'g] *-en* anthropologist.

antropologi' *-en* anthropology.

antroposo'f *-en* anthroposophist.

antroposofi' *-en* anthroposophy (branch of theosophy founded by the Austrian Rudolph Steiner, which has a number of adherents in Norway).

+**an'/trukken** [/trokken] *A -et, pl -trukne* dressed: **fint a-** elegantly d-.

An't/werpen *Pln* Antwerp.

+**an'/tyde** *V -et* hint, intimate, suggest: **som navnet a-er** as the name implies.

+**an'/tydning** *-en* 1 hint, intimation, suggestion (**til** of): **komme med a-er** drop h-s. 2 hint, pinch, touch (**til** of): **en a- til nordlys** a faint gleam of northern lights.

+**an'/vende** *V -te* 1 use, utilize; make use of: **a- sin innflytelse (krefter)** exert one's influence (strength). 2 apply (a theory); employ (a word): **a-t** applied (art, mathematics, etc.).

+**anven'delig** *A* - 1 usable, of use (**til** for): **a- til alle anledninger** u- for all occasions; **lett a-** easy to use. 2 (of principle, theory, word) applicable (**på** to).

+**an'/vendelse** *-n* 1 use, making use (**av** of): **få a- for** find use for; **finne a-** be put to use. 2 application (**på** to): **loven finner ingen a- her** the law does not apply here.

+**an'/vise** *V -te* 1 indicate, point out, show: **a- (noen) plass** usher (sby) to his seat; **ekspedisjonen a-er** the business office will give further information. 2 allot, assign: **a- (noen) arbeid** assign work (to sby); **han fikk a-t værelse** he was given a room; **a- tømmer** select timber (to be logged). 3 *merc.*: **a- et beløp (en regning)** order payment of an amount (a bill); **a- på en bank** issue a draft on a bank.

+**an'/viser** *-en, pl -e* indicator, pointer; usher.

+**an'/visning** [also -vi's-] *-en* 1 directions, instructions (**på** about). 2 allotment, assignment. 3 [-vi's-] *merc.* draft, money order (**på** on, of).

AOF = **Arbeidernes Opplysningsforbund**

***a'p**[1] *-en* jester, teaser.

a'p[2] *-et* jesting, teasing: **drive (*gjere, *halde) ap med** make fun of, tease.

AP = **Arbeidernes Pressekontor, Associated Press**

a'pal *-en, pl +-er/*aplar* *apple (genus); apple tree (esp. wild).

a'pal/grå *A -tt, pl -/*-e* (of horses) dapple gray.

apana'sje *-n* appanage (annual grant for support of a royal person).

***apar'ta** *A* - cf **aparte**

apar'te *A* - 1 odd, queer, strange. 2 extraordinary, outstanding, unusual; extra special.

apa'sje *-n* 1 Apache (Indian). 2 apache (Parisian criminal).

***a'past** *V -ast/-test* cf **ape**[2]

apati' *-en* apathy.

apa'tisk *A* - apathetic.

a'pe[1] *-n* 1 ape, monkey. 2 fool.

a'pe[2] *V -a/+-te* 1 ape, imitate: **a- etter noen** a- sby. 2 joke, tease: **a- med noen** t- sby; *(refl.)* +*-es*/**-ast* joke.

a'pe/fant *-en* joker, tease.

+ Bokmål; * Nynorsk; ' Dialect.
After letter: ' stress (Acc. 1); ` tone, stress (Acc. 2); · length.
Below letter: . not pronounced.

a'pe/katt *-en* 1 monkey. 2 imitator, one who apes.
a'pekatt/strek *-en* monkeyshines.
***a'peleg** *A* absurd, foolish.
+**Apenni'nene** *Pln* (=***-ane**) the Apennines.
a'peri *-et* joking; nonsense.
aperitiff' *-en* aperitif (=appetizer drink).
***a'pe/sam** *A* jesting, teasing.
+**a'pe/spill** *-et* (=***/spel,** +**/spell**) foolish behavior: **drive a- med** play tricks on.
a'pe/strek *-en* monkeyshines, trick.
aplom'b *-en* aplomb, self-assurance.
apo- [apo-] *Pf*
apokalyp'se *-n* apocalypse.
apokalyp'tisk *A* - apocalyptic.
apoko'pe *-n* apocope.
apokry'f[1] [also -yff'] *-en* an apocryphal work, *pl* Apocrypha.
apokry'f[2] *A* apocryphal.
apokry'fisk [also -yf'fisk] *A* - apocryphal.
apologe't [-loge't] *-en* apologist (=defender of Christianity).
apologi' [-logi'] *-en* apologia.
apopleksi' *-en* apoplexy.
apoplek'tisk *A* - apoplectic.
apos'tel *-elen, pl* +*-ler* apostle.
aposto'lisk *A* - apostolic.
apostro'f *-en* apostrophe.
apote'k *-et, pl -/*+*-er* pharmacy.
+**apote'ker** *-en, pl -e* (=***-ar**) pharmacist.
apoteo'se *-n* apotheosis.
appara't *-et, pl -/*+*-er* 1 apparatus, instrument: **sette i gang et stort a-** start extensive preparations. 2 (short for **fotografi/**) camera.
apparatu'r *-en* apparatus (collectively).
apparisjo'n *-en* appearance.
appell' *-en* 1 appeal (**om** for): **a- til en høyere domstol** a- to a higher court; **rette en a- til noen** appeal to sby. 2 *mil.* assembly; roll call: **a-/plassen** the parade ground.
appella'bel *A -elt, pl -le jur.* which can be appealed.
appellan't *-en jur.* appellant.
appelle're *V -te* appeal (**til** to).
appelsi'n *-en* orange.
appen'diks *-et, pl -/*+*-er* appendix.
appetitt' *-en* appetite (**på** for): **god a-** good a-; **miste a-en** lose one's a-.
appetitt'lig *A* - appetizing, delicious.
+**appetitt'/vekkende** *A* - appetizing; which stimulates one's appetite.
+**appetitt'/vekker** *-en, pl -e* appetizer.
applaude're *V -te* applaud.
applau's *-en* applause.
applikasjo'n *-en* 1 application (**av** of). 2 appliqué embroidery.
+**applikasjo'ns/søm·** *-men* (=***/saum**) appliqué embroidery.
applikatu'r *-en mus.* 1 fingering. 2 higher position(s) (on string instrument).
applike're *V -te* appliqué (**på** to).
applise're *V -te* apply (e.g. rule).
apporte're *V -te* fetch, retrieve (game).
apposisjo'n [-pos-] *-en* apposition.
apposisjonell' [-pos-] *A -elt* appositional.
appretu'r *-en* finishing (of cloth after weaving).
approbasjo'n [-pro-] *-en* approbation, approval, sanction.
approbe're [-pro-] *V -te* approve, sanction.
apriko's *-en* apricot.
apri'l *en* April: **narre a-** play an A-fools' trick; **jeg velger meg a-** I choose A- as my own (Bjørnson).
apri'ls/narr *-en* April fool.
apri'l/spøk *-en* April fools' trick.
a prio'ri a priori (=in advance).
aprio'risk [also -o'-] *A* - a priori (e.g. theory).
apropos [apropo'] *Av* 1 apropos; at the right moment. 2 *(interj.)* by the way, speaking of.
a'r *-et* are (metric unit of land=100 sq. meters=119.6 sq. yards=ab. 4 sq. rods).
***-ar** *-en* cf **-er**
+**ara'ber** *-en, pl -e* (=***-ar**) Arab.
arabes'k *-en* arabesque.
ara'bisk *A* - Arabian, Arabic.
a'rak *-en* arrack (alcoholic beverage).
***a'ralds** *po* cf **arilds**
arame'isk *A* - Aramaic.
ar'beid [*-bei] *-et* 1 employment, job, work (being done): **gå på a-** go to w- (=place of employment); **i a- (med)** at w- (on); **i fullt a-** hard at w-; **sette i a-** put to w-; **det er under a-** it is being prepared; **uten a-** without a j-. 2 labor, task, work (completed): **Vigelands a-er** V-'s w-s (of sculpture); **et godt stykke a-** a good piece of w-, a good job; **norsk a-** made in Norway; **et fint a-** a piece of fine craftsmanship.
***arbei'dar/rørsle** *-a* labor movement.
***arbei'dar/ungdomsla·g** [-ong-] *-et* Young People's Society for Workers.
ar'beide [also -bei'-, *-beie] *V -dde/*+*-et* 1 labor, toil, work (**for** for; **på** at): **a- i** w- in, at; **a- på (en bok)** w- on (a book). 2 function, operate, work (hard): **hjertet a-er tungt** the heart is laboring; **vinen a-er** the wine is fermenting. 3 prepare, produce, work: **hun a-er småting av sølv** she makes little objects of silver; **a- jorda** cultivate the soil (intensely). 4 *(refl.)* **a- seg fram (opp)** work one's way up, make good; **a- seg over** work one's way across; **a- seg ut** extricate oneself, get loose.
+**arbei'der** *-en, pl -e* (=***-ar**) laborer, workman, worker: **a-ne** the working people; labor; *bibl.* **en a- er sin lønn verd** a l- is worthy of his hire; **A-nes Faglige Landsorganisasjon** National Federation of Labor.
+**arbei'der/beve·gelse** *-n* labor movement.
arbei'der/blad *-et* labor newspaper: **A-et** daily newspaper in Oslo.
+**arbei'der/klasse** *-a/-en* (=***-ar/**) laboring class.
+**arbei'der/parti·** *-et* (=***-ar/**) labor party.
+**arbei'der/regje·ring** *-a/-en* (=***-ar/**) labor government.
+**arbei'dervern/lovgi·vning** *-en* (=***-ar, -gjevning**) laborers' protective legislation.
***ar'beid/sam** *A* cf **/som**
+**ar'beids/bespa·rende** *A* - laborsaving.
***ar'beids/bolk** *-en* work term: **budsjettet for komande a-** the budget for the coming w-.
ar'beids/dag *-en* 1 working day, everyday; working hours. 2 workday: **midt i travle a-en** right in the middle of his w-.
ar'beids/deling *-a/*+*-en* division of labor.
+**ar'beids/dyktig** *A* - able-bodied, able to work.
ar'beids/evne *-a/*+*-en* working capacity.
ar'beids/folk *-et* workers; working people: **vi har a- i huset** we have workmen in the house.
ar'beids/forde·ling *-a/*+*-en* division of labor.
ar'beids/formann *-en, pl -menn/ *-menner* foreman.
+**ar'beids/formid·ling** *-a/-en* employment agency, service.
ar'beids/før *A* able-bodied, able to work.
+**ar'beids/giver** *-en, pl -e* (=***/gjevar**) employer.
+**ar'beidsgiver/fore·ning** *-a/*+*-en* employers' association.
ar'beids/glede *-a/*+*-en* enthusiasm for, pleasure in one's work, zest.
ar'beids/hest *-en* draft horse, work horse; *fig.* drudge.
ar'beids/hjelp *-a/*+*-en* 1 employee; servant. 2 help.
ar'beids/hypote·se *-n* working hypothesis.
ar'beids/kamera·t *-en* fellow worker.
ar'beids/kar *-en* 1 worker, working man. 2 hard worker: **han er riktig en a-** he's really a h-.
ar'beids/kledd *A -/***-kledt* dressed in working clothes.
+**ar'beids/klær** *pl* (=***/klede**) working clothes.
ar'beids/konto·r [/kon-] *-et* employment agency.
ar'beids/kraft *-a/*+*-en* 1 ability to work, working capacity. 2 labor, labor force, manpower: **mangel på a-** lack of m-. 3 person with great working capacity.
ar'beids/lag *-et* 1 working crew, gang. 2 skill in working: **han har godt a-** he works well.
ar'beids/laus *A* (=+**/løs**) out of work, unemployed.
ar'beids/ledig *A* - out of work, unemployed.
ar'beids/liv *-et* 1 life of hard work. 2 economic life (of community or nation): **gå ut i a-et** start working, take a job.
ar'beids/lyst *-a/*+*-en* eagerness, zest (for work): **jeg har ingen a-** I don't feel like working.
ar'beids/lønn *-a/*+*-en* wages.
+**ar'beids/løs** *A* cf **/laus**
+**ar'beids/løshet** *-en* cf **/løyse**
ar'beids/løyse *-a* unemployment.
ar'beids/mann *-en, pl -menn/***-menner* working man.
ar'beids/mark *-a* field of activity (or action), sphere.
ar'beids/maur *-en* 1 *zool.* worker (ant). 2 *fig.* work horse, diligent (but uninspired) worker.
ar'beids/måte *-n* method of work.
ar'beids/nemnd [/nemd] *-a* working (or executive) committee (of larger body).
+**ar'beid/som·** *A -me* (=***/sam**) diligent, hard-working, industrious; strenuous.
ar'beids/press *-et* pressure of work: **hardt a-** heavy work load.
ar'beids/rett *-en* 1 right to work. 2 labor law. 3 labor court.
ar'beids/ro *-a/*+*-en* 1 absence of labor unrest. 2 opportunity to work undisturbed: **la meg få a-** don't disturb me at my work.
ar'beids/rom [/romm] *-met* study; workroom.
ar'beids/skole *-n* 1 vocational school; reform school, school of correction (for young offenders). 2 activity school (child-centered method of education which emphasizes independent activity by the pupils, sometimes called "progressive" schools).
ar'beids/sky *A* - lazy, work-shy.
ar'beids/stokk *-en* labor force, workmen (on a job, in a factory).
ar'beids/styrke *-n* labor force, workmen; manpower.
+**ar'beids/taker** *-en, pl -e* (=***-ar**) employee, worker.
+**ar'beids/tegning** [/teining] *-a/-en* (=***/teikning**) blueprint, working drawing.
ar'beids/terapeu·t [also -pøy·t] *-en* occupational therapist.
ar'beids/terapi· *-en* occupational therapy.
ar'beids/tid *-a/*+*-en* 1 time for working. 2 working hours: **kort a-** short hours.
ar'beids/tilsyn *-et* (local) labor commission (to enforce labor laws).
+**ar'beids/trell** *-en* (=***/træl**) drudge, slave, toiler.
ar'beids/tvist *-en* labor conflict.
+**ar'beids/udyk·tig** *A* - disabled, incapacitated.
ar'beids/ufør *A* disabled, incapacitated.
+**ar'beids/utvalg** *-et* (=***/utval**) working committee.
ar'beids/vilkår *pl* working conditions.
ar'beids/villig *A* - (=***/viljug**) 1 willing to work. 2 *(noun)* strike breaker.
+**ar'beids/værelse** *-t* study, workroom.

arbitræ'r *A* arbitrary.
°a'r/bøst *-en* cf **arm/brøst**
a'rd *-en* primitive plow (wooden, with hoe-like blade).
a'rde *V -a/+-et* plow (with **ard**).
a're *-n* eagle.
area'l *-et, pl -/+-er* area (**på** of): **50 mål i a-** with an a- of 50 *mål*.
A're/mark *Pln* twp, Østfold.
are'na *-en* arena: **den politiske a-** the political a- (scene).
A'ren/dal *Pln* city, Aust-Agder.
arendalitt' *-en* person from Arendal.
ar'g *A* 1 angry (**over** about). 2 bad (esp. *superl.*): **den a-este løgn** the most arrant lie; **min a-este fiende** my bitterest enemy.
ar'ge *V -a/+-et*: **a- seg** be angry, irritated.
***ar'g(e)leg** *A* - annoying, irritating.
+argenti'ner *-en, pl -e* (=***-ar**) Argentine, Argentinian.
argenti'nsk *A* - Argentinian.
ar'g/skap [also ar'g/] *-en* 1 anger, fury; irritation. 2 badness, evil.
argumen't *-et, pl -/+-er* argument: **et slående a-** a striking a- (*hum.* about physical force).
argumentasjo'n *-en* argumentation.
argumente're *V -te* argue, reason (**for** for; **imot** against).
+ar'gus/øyne *pl* (=***/auge, */augo**) Argus eyes (sharp look-out, constant vigilance).
a'rie *-n mus.* aria.
a'rier** *-en, pl -e* (=-ar**) Aryan.
+a'rilds *po*: **fra a- tid** from time immemorial.
a'risk *A* - Aryan.
aristokra't *-en* aristocrat.
aristokrati' *-et* aristocracy.
aristokra'tisk *A* - aristocratic.
aritmetikk' *-en* arithmetic.
aritme'tisk *A* - arithmetical.
ar'k[1] *+-en/*-a bibl.* ark: **Noas a-** Noah's a-; **paktens a-** a- of the Covenant.
ar'k[2] *-en/*-a arch.* dormer.
ar'k[3] *-et* 1 sheet (of paper): **et a- papir** a s- of paper. 2 gathering, quire, sheet (unit of usu. 16 pages in a book, bearing a signature): **en bok på ti a-** a book of ten sheets.
arka'de *n* arcade.
arkaise're *V -te* archaize: **a-ende stil** a-ing (=deliberately old-fashioned) style.
arka'isk *A* - archaic.
arkais'me *-n* archaism.
arkeolog [-lå'g] *-en* archeologist.
arkeologi [-gi'] *-en* archeology.
arkipe'l [-ki-] *-et, pl +-er/*-* archipelago.
arkipela'g *-et, pl +-er/*-* archipelago.
arkitek't *-en* architect.
arkitekto'nisk *A* - architectonic.
arkitektu'r *-en* architecture.
arki'v *-et, pl -/+-er* archive(s), file: **legg det i a-et** put it in the f-s.
+arkiva'lier *pl* (=***arkiva'lia**) documents, records.
arkiva'r *-en* archivist.
arkive're *V -te* file; put in the archives.
+arki'v/skap *-et* (=***/skåp**) file, filing cabinet.
ar'k/skrivning *-en obs.* copying work.
Ar'ktis *Pln* the Arctic.
ar'ktisk *A* - arctic.
***a'rle** *V -a* move restlessly (of animals, people, sea, etc.).
ar'm[1] *-en* 1 arm (of person, ape, chair, etc.): **hun kastet seg i a-ene på meg** she threw herself into my a-s; **de sov i a-ene på hverandre** they slept in each other's a-s; **(løfte noe) på strak a-** (lift sth) at a-'s length; **(gå med en dame) under a-en** (walk) a- in a- (with a lady); **slå a-ene om en** embrace sby. 2 *pop.* sleeve.
ar'm[2] *A* 1 miserable, poor, unfortunate: **a-e mann!** p- man!; **(hun) vet ikke sin a-e råd** (she) doesn't know where to turn, what to do; **jeg a-e synder** a p- sinner like me. 2 impecunious, impoverished, poor: **a-e riddere** *lit.* p- knights (a kind of French toast).
-ar'ma *A* - (=**+-armet**) -armed.
arma'da *-en* armada.
armatu'r *-en tech.* fittings, mountings (of boiler, machine, electrical equipment).
ar'm/band *-et* (=**+/bånd**) bracelet.
ar'mbands/ur *-et* (=**+-bånds/**) wristwatch.
ar'm/bind *-et* 1 armband. 2 bandage, sling (for arm).
ar'm/brøst *-en* crossbow.
+ar'm/bøyning *-en* (=***/bøy(gn)ing**) bending, flexing of the arm; push-up.
+ar'm/bånd *-et* cf **/band**
armé *-en* army.
ar'me *V -a/+-et*: **a- (seg) ut** impoverish (oneself); overwork (oneself).
***ar'meleg** *A* - miserable.
+arme'ner *-en, pl -e* (=***-ar**) Armenian.
arme'nsk *A* - Armenian.
arme're *V -te* 1 arm (**med** with); armor. 2 reinforce (concrete): **a-t betong** r-d concrete.
arme'ring *-a/+-en* 1 armament, armor. 2 reinforcement (of concrete).
+-ar'met *A* - cf **-arma**
ar'm/gang *-en gymn.* traveling (on beam, suspended by arms).
ar'm/hol *-et* (=**+/hull**) armhole (for sleeve).
ar'm/hole *-a* (=**+/hule**) armpit, axilla.
ar'ming *-en* wretch; beggar.
ar'm/krok *-en* crook of the elbow.
+ar'm/lene *-t* arm, armrest (of chair).
+ar'm/lengde *-n* (=**/lengd**) arm's length: **i a-s avstand** at a-.
ar'mod *-a/+-en* 1 destitution, poverty: ***det er berre a-a** it is just bleak penury. *2 effort, trouble.
ar'mods/dom' *-men/*-en* misery, poverty.
ar'mod/skap *-en* misery, poverty.
ar'modslig *A* - miserable, poverty-stricken.
ar'm/ring *-en* bracelet.
ar'm/slag *-et* elbow room.
ar'm/stø *+-et/*-a* armrest.
***a'rne** *-n* hearth (usu. *fig.* or *poet.*): **hjemmets a-** h- and home; **ved a-n** by the fireside.
A'rne *Prn (m)*
+a'rne/sted *-et* 1 fireplace, hearth. 2 *fig.* center, focus, hotbed (**for** of).
A'rn/finn *Prn (m)*
A'rn/ljot' *Prn (m)*: **A- Gelline** follower of St. Olof; character in poem by Bjørnson.
Ar'nt *Prn (m)*
aro'ma *-en* aroma.
aroma'tisk *A* - aromatic.
arr' *-et* +1 scar. 2 stigma (of flower).
arrangement [arangsjemang'] *-et, pl -/+-er* arrangement (**av** of): **et vellykket a-** a successful occasion.
arrangere [arangsje're] *V -te* arrange: **a- seg** make an arrangement, a deal; make the best of a situation.
arrangør [arangsjø'r] *-en* arranger: **festens a-** the one who arranged the party.
arres't *-en* 1 detention, seizure (of goods): **holde i a-** keep in custody. 2 arrest, seizure (of person): **ta en i a-** arrest sby; **ti dagers a-** ten days in jail. 3 jail, prison: **sitte i a-en** stay in j-.
arrestan't *-en* prisoner.
arrestasjo'n *-en* arrest, detention.
arreste're *V -te* arrest, detain; seize (person or goods).
arres't/ordre *-n* warrant (for arrest).
+ar'ret(e) *A* - scarred.
+ar'rig *A* - *archaic* angry, ill-tempered.
+ar'rig/skap *-en archaic* bad temper.
arrive're *V -te archaic* 1 arrive. 2 occur.
arrogan'se *-n* arrogance.
arrogan't *A* - arrogant.
arronde're *V -te* round out (piece of property by buying intervening land).
ar's *-en* arse, podex.
arsena'l *-et, pl -/+-er* arsenal.
arsenikk' *-en* arsenic.
ar't *-a/-en* 1 (inborn) character, nature. 2 kind, nature: **et verk av samme a-** a work of the same k-; **jeg kjenner a-en** I know that k- (=type); **det er en a- religion** it's a k- of religion. 3 *biol.* species: **en slekt med mange a-er** a genus with many s-; **+Artenes opprinnelse/ *Opphavet åt artane** Origin of Species (Darwin).
art. =**artikkel; artilleri**
-arta *A* - (=**+-artet**) having a character or quality, e.g. **god-, van-**.
ar'te *V -a/+-et* 1: **a- seg** develop, turn out; **a- seg vel** behave well, be promising; **slik forholdene a-et seg** as conditions were. 2: **a- ut** degenerate (**til** into).
arte'rie *-n* artery.
arte'sisk *A* - artesian.
+-artet *A* - cf **-arta**
+artianer [artsia'ner] *-en, pl -e* (=***-ar**) candidate for the **artium** examination.
ar'tig *A* - 1 amusing, funny; interesting: **det var mangt a- å se** there were lots of i- things to see. 2 *lit.* courteous; well-behaved: **vær så a-** if you please (now usu. **vær så god**); **et a- bukk** a polite bow.
+ar'tig/het *-en lit.* 1 compliment. 2 courtesy, favor.
artik'kel *-elen, pl artikler* article (of faith; in periodical; grammatical; commercial).
artikulasjo'n *-en* articulation.
artikule're *V -te* articulate.
artilleri' *-et* artillery.
artilleris't *-en* artilleryman, gunner.
artisjokk' *-en* artichoke.
artis't *-en* 1 performer (in circus, variety, or vaudeville). 2 *lit.* artist (=**kunstner**).
artisteri' *-et* (exaggerated, self-conscious) artistry.
artis'tisk *A* - artistic.
artium [ar'tsium] *-en* degree conferred on students passing university entrance examination: **ta a-** get the *a-* degree; **hun er oppe til a-** she is taking the *a-* examination; **stå (stryke) til a-** pass (fail) the *a-* examination.
artiums/kamera't *-en* classmate (in same graduating class from gymnasium).
artiums/kull *-et* class of (expected) graduates from gymnasium in any one year.
artiums/stil *-en* examination paper in Norwegian composition for **artium** examination.
artiums/vitnemål *-et* diploma (testimonial) conferred on students receiving **artium** degree.
ar'ts/merke *-t, pl +-r/*- bot., zool.* characteristic trait (of a species).
ar'v *-en* 1 inheritance; bequest, legacy: **en a- på tusen kroner** a l- of 1,000 *kroner*; **få (ta) noe i a-** inherit sth, be left sth; **gi noe i a-** pass sth on; **det går i a-** it is passed on, descends (**til** to); **ta a- etter** inherit from; **til a- og eie** as one's very own property. 2 *fig.* heritage; inherited trait: **a- av anlegg** inheritance of abilities; **a-en fra fortida** the h- of the past; **løfte a-en etter en** carry on sby's work, assume the mantle, take up the torch.
***ar'v/boren** [/båren] *A -e/-i, pl -ne jur.* legitimate heir (**til** to).
ar've[1] *-n bot.* chickweed (esp. Cerastium caespitosum).

+ Bokmål; * Nynorsk; ° Dialect.
After letter: ' stress (Acc. 1); ` tone, stress (Acc. 2); · length.
Below letter: . not pronounced.

ar've[2] *V* *-a/+-et* **(=*erve)** inherit (property, personal traits, etc.) (**etter** from): **han a-a bestefar sin** he got his grandfather's estate; **han har a-a** *hum.* he has come into some money.
Ar've *Prn (m)*
ar've/anlegg *-et biol.* gene.
ar've/brev *-et* testament, will.
ar've/fall *-et jur.* succession of property (to heirs).
ar've/feste *-t jur.* heritable lease.
ar've/fiende *-n* archenemy: **a-n** Satan; **Englands a-** E-'s traditional enemy.
+ar've/følge *-n* **(=*/følgje)** order of succession (on the part of heirs).
ar've/gods [/gots] *-et* heirloom, inheritance; inherited estate: **Guds ord det er vårt a-** the word of God is our heritage (hymn).
+ar've/later *-en, pl -e* **(=*-ar)** *jur.* person giving inheritance (bequeather, testator).
ar'velig *A-* hereditary, (in)heritable: **a- belastet** having a hereditary taint.
+ar'velig/het *-en* heredity.
ar'velighets/forsker *-en, pl -e* geneticist.
+ar've/lodd *-en* cf **/lott**
+ar've/lott *-en* **(=*/lut)** (one's) share of an inheritance; heritage, legacy.
ar've/lov [/låv] *-en/*-a* law of succession; law of heredity.
***ar've/lut** *-en* cf **/lott**
+ar've/løs *A* **(=/laus)** disinherited: **gjøre a-** disinherit, cut off.
ar've/onkel *-elen, pl -ler* uncle whom one hopes to inherit.
ar've/o'rd *-et* native word (inherited from oldest known mother tongue).
ar've/prins *-en* heir presumptive (to the throne).
ar've/rett *-en jur.* **1** law of inheritance. **2** right of succession (**til** to).
ar've/skatt *-en* inheritance tax.
ar've/skifte *-t* partition of an inheritance.
ar've/stykke *-t, pl +-r/*-* heirloom.
ar've/synd *-a/+-en* original sin: **stygg som a-en** ugly as sin.
ar've/sølv [/søll] *-et* family silver, silver heirlooms.
Ar'vid *Prn (m)*
ar'ving *-en* **(=*erving)** heir, heiress (**til** to).
***ar'v/laus** *A* cf **arve/løs**
***ar'v/lut** *-en* cf **arve/lott**
+ar'v/tager *-en, pl -e* cf **/taker**
+ar'v/taker *-en, pl -e* **(=*-ar)** heir; successor (**til** to).
a's *-et* **1** toil: **et as og et mas** t- and trouble. **2** fermentation. **3** hubbub, racket.
A/S=aksjeselskap
a'sal *-en bot.* mountain ash (Sorbus, esp. hybrida and rupicola).
asbes't *-en* asbestos.
As'/bjørg *Prn (f)*
As'/bjørn *Prn (m)*
Aschehoug [as'ke/hau] *Prn* (name of publisher).
***a'se**[1] *V es, os, ase/-i* cf **ese**
a'se[2] *V -a/+-te* **1** toil: **a- og mase** t- and struggle. **2: a- seg ut** wear oneself out. **3** make an uproar.
a'sen[1] *-enet, pl -/+-ner* **1** ass, donkey. **2** *derog.* ass, fool.
***a'sen**[2] *A -e/-i, pl -ne* fermented, swelled up.
+asenin'ne *-a/-en* female donkey, jenny, she-ass.
asep'tisk *A -* aseptic.
***a'set** *A -* rackety; fatiguing.
as'falt *-en* asphalt.
asfalte're *V -te* asphalt.
+as'falt/traver *-en, pl -e* **(=*/tråvar)** pavement pounder (=city dweller).
***a'si** *pp of* **ase**[1]
asia't *-en* Asian.
asia'tisk *A -* Asian, Asiatic.
asjett' *-en* (dessert) plate.
as'k[1] *-en* ash (tree) (Fraxinus).
as'k[2] *-en* **1** (wooden) box (usu. round). **2** container (for butter, milk).
+as'ke *-a* cf **oske**
+as'ke/beger *-eret, pl -er/-re* ashtray.
+as'ke/blond *A* ash blonde.
+as'ke/grå *A -tt* ashen (color).
+as'ke/haug *-en* heap of ashes.
+as'ke/ladd *-en* folk tale hero (usu. *prn.*): **A-en** the Ashlad (because he idly pokes the ashes and is scorned by his older brothers — a male Cinderella).
+as'ke/onsdag *-en* Ash Wednesday.
+As'ke/pott *Prn* Cinderella.
As'ker *Pln* twp and village, Akershus.
aske'se *-n* asceticism.
aske't *-en* (an) ascetic.
aske'tisk *A -* ascetic.
Askim [asj'im] *Pln* twp, Østfold.
As'k/voll *Pln* twp, Sogn og Fjordane.
As'k/øy *Pln* twp, Hordaland.
As'lak *Prn (m)*
As'/laug *Prn (f)*
As'/mund *Prn (m)*
***a'sn** *-et* **1** crowding together, tumult. **2** hot-tempered person.
***a'sne** *V -a* crowd together, rush on.
+Aso'rene *Pln* **(=*-ane)** the Azores.
a'/sosia'l *A* asocial.
+as'p *-en* cf **osp**
aspar'ges *-en* asparagus.
aspek't *-en* **1** *astron.* aspect, configuration (of stars). **2** *pop. (pl)* omens, prospects (esp. for weather): **himmelens a-er** the looks of the heavens. **3** *gram.* aspect.
aspik' *-en* aspic.
aspiran't *-en* aspirant (**til** to), candidate.
aspirasjo'n *-en* aspiration (all meanings).
aspire're *V -te* **1** aspire (**til** to). **2** *gram.* aspirate.
aspiri'n *-en/-et* aspirin.
ass'[1] *en mus.* A flat.
***ass'**[2] *I* ish, ugh.
asses'sor *-en obs.* judge (in higher courts; **dommer** since 1927).
assimilasjo'n *-en gram.* assimilation.
assimilato'risk *A - gram.* assimilatory.
assimile're *V -te* assimilate.
assistanse [-ang'se] *-n* assistance (**til** to).
assisten't *-en* assistant, helper (used as title in laboratories, libraries, etc.).
assiste're *V -te* assist (**med** with).
assonans [-ang's] *-en* assonance.
assorte're *V -te* assort.
assortiment [-mang'] *-et merc.* assortment.
assosiasjo'n *-en* association (esp. *psych.*).
assosie're *V -te* associate (esp. *psych.*).
assurandø'r *-en* insurer, insurance agent (company), underwriter.
assuranse [-ang'se] *-n* insurance (**på** on).
assure're *V -te* insure (**mot** against).
+assy'rer *-en, pl -e* **(=*-ar)** Assyrian.
As'ta/fjo'rd *Pln* twp, Troms.
asteroide [astero-i'de] *-n* asteroid.
as'ters *-en* aster.
as'tma *-en* asthma.
astma'tisk *A -* asthmatic.
as'trakan *-en* astrakhan.
astra'l *A* astral.
+astra'l/legeme *-t* **(=*/lekam)** astral body.
As'trid *Prn (f)*
astrofysikk' *-en* astrophysics.
astrofy'sisk *A -* astrophysical.
astrolog [-olå'g] *-en* astrologer.
astrologi [-ologi'] *-en* astrology.
astronom [-ono'm] *-en* astronomer.
astronomi [-onomi'] *-en* astronomy.
astronomisk [-ono'-] *A -* astronomical.
asu'r/blå *A -tt, pl -/*-e* azure blue.
asy'l *-et, pl -/+-er* asylum (**1** institution. **2** refuge).
asy'l/rett *-en pol.* right of asylum (for political refugees).
+a't'[1] *Av*: **bære seg at** act, behave, go about it; **følges at** accompany one another, go together; **hjelpes at** help one another; **skilles at** part, separate.
at'[2] *C* **1** that. **2** (omitted, esp. after *prep.* or *conj.*): **jeg forstod det uten at hun sa noe** I understood it without her saying anything; **følgen av at han kom** the result of his coming; **fordi (at) han hadde sagt dette** because he had said this. **3** (introducing an exclamation) how, why: **at du kunne si noe slikt!** how could you say anything like that, why did you.... **4** (after **så**, implying a strong comparison in the omitted clause) **han er så snill at** he's so nice; **det er så sant at** it's absolutely true.
at'[3] *Inf Marker* cf **å**[5]
+at- *Pf* **(=*åt-)** (formerly **ad-**) sometimes separable, as in **-skille** vs. **skille at.**
a'tal *A* **1** derisive, teasing. **2** annoying, troublesome.
atavis'me *-n* atavism (reversion to type).
atavis'tisk *A -* atavistic.
ateisme [ate-is'me] *-n* atheism.
ateist [ate-is't] *-en* atheist.
atelier [atelje'] *-et, pl +-er/*-* (artist's, photographer's) studio: **på a-et** in the s-.
Ate'n *Pln* **(=Athen)** Athens.
+ate'ner *-en, pl -e* **(=*-ar, +athener)** Athenian.
ate'nsk *A -* **(=athensk)** Athenian.
+a't/ferd *-a/-en* cf **åt/**
+a'tferds/mønster *-mønstret* cf **åtferds/**
at'/geir *-en hist.* halberd (combination spear and battle-ax).
+a't/komst *-en* **1** access, approach. **2** claim, right, title (**til** to).
Atlan'ter/havet *Pln* the Atlantic Ocean.
+atlan'terhavs/pakten *df* the Atlantic Pact.
atlan'tisk *A -* Atlantic.
at'las *-et, pl -/+-er* atlas.
atlas'k *-en* satin.
At'le *Prn (m)*
atle't *-en* athlete.
atle'tisk *A -* athletic.
atmosfæ're *-n* atmosphere.
atmosfæ'risk *A -* atmospheric.
ato'm *-et pl -/+-er* atom.
ato'm/bombe *-a/+-en* atom(ic) bomb.
ato'm/energi' *-en* atomic energy.
ato'm/kjerne *-n* atomic nucleus.
ato'm/kraft *-a/+-en* atomic power.
ato'm/mile *-a* atomic pile.
ato'm/reak'tor [-tor] *-en* atomic reactor.
+ato'm/spalt(n)ing *-en* atom splitting.
ato'm/vekt *-a/+-en* atomic weight.
ato'm/våpen *-et* atomic weapon.
atona'l *A* atonal.
+a't/skille *V -skilte* **1** part, separate: **hva Gud har sammenføyet, skal mennesket ikke a-** what God has joined together, let no man put asunder. **2** divide, separate: **en elv a-er landene** a river d-s (s-s) the countries. **3** distinguish, tell apart: **a- seg (fra)** differ (from), distinguish itself, stand out, be different.
+a't/skillelse *-n* separation (**fra** from): **til a- fra** in distinction from, in contrast to.
atskil'lig *A -* **1** *(sg)* a good deal of, quite a bit of: **det kunne sies a-** a great deal could be said. **2** (with *comp.*) considerably, a good deal; several. **3** *(pl)* several, quite a few, a good many.
+a't/skilt *A -* apart, distinct, separate: **bo a-** live apart.
+a't/splitte *V -et* scatter, split.
+a't/spre(de) *V -dde/-dte* **1** distract (sby's thoughts), divert. **2** amuse, entertain: **a- seg** amuse oneself.
+a't/spredelse *-n* **1** distraction, diversion (of thoughts). **2** amusement, entertainment, recreation. **3: a-n** the Diaspora.
+a't/spredt *A -* absentminded, distracted, preoccupied.
+atsta'dig *A -* sedate, stodgy.
att' *Av* **1** back (direction): **a- og fram** b- and forth; **legge seg a- å bak** lie on one's back; (in many *prep.* and

adv., e.g. **atti, attmed, attpå**). 2 back (return): (of ghosts) **gå a-** haunt; **komme a-** come b-; **heim a-** b-home; **få noe a-** get sth b-. *3 left, behind: **er det noko a-** is anything l-; **det står ikkje mykje a-** not much is l- standing, there's not much l-.
attaché *-en* attaché.
attache're *V -te* attach (to an embassy).
***at'ta/for·** *P* cf **attan/**
attakk' *-et, pl -/+-er obs.* attack.
***at'tan** *Av and P* from behind.
***at'tan/for·** *P* (=**atta/**) behind.
***at'tan/om·** *P* behind.
***at'ta(n)/på** *P* on the back of.
***at'tan/til·** *Av* 1 in the back of. 2 from behind.
***at'tare** *A* - cf **attre**[2]
***at'tarst** *A* - farthest back, at the end.
at'ten *Num* eighteen.
atten'de[1] *Av* back.
+**at'tende**[2] *Num* (=***-ande**) eighteenth.
at'ten/del *-en* (an) eighteenth.
attenta't *-et, pl -/+-er* attack (**på** on), esp. an attempted assassination (e.g. of a ruler).
at'ter *Av* 1 *lit.* again, once more: **a- en** one more; **a- og a-** a- and a-; **tusen og a- tusen** thousands upon thousands. 2=**att: a- og fram er like langt** back and forth are the same distance (Ibsen). *3=**akter.**
+**at'ter/bud** *-et* (=*/**bod**): **sende a-** cancel a previous engagement, send regrets.
***at'ter/dekk** *-et* cf **akter/**
***at'ter/døypar** *-en* Anabaptist.
***at'ter/fall** *-et* relapse.
***at'ter/føde** *V -de* bear again; renew, revitalize; **a-/fødd** reborn, saved.
***at'ter/føding** *-a* rebirth.
***at'ter/gangar** *-en* apparition, ghost.
***at'ter/gav** *pt of* **-gieve**
***at'ter/gjeld** *-a* repayment: **gjera a-** return a favor; **til a-** in return.
***at'ter/gjeve** *V -gav, gjeve/-i* give back; imitate, reproduce.
***at'ter/gløyme** *-a* old maid.
at'ter/hald *-et* *1 holding back, restraint; modesty; conservatism, moderation. 2 condition, reservation: **ta a- om noe** make a r- for sth; **uten a-** unreservedly.
***at'ter/halden** *A -e/-i, pl -ne* 1 modest, restrained; conservative, moderate. 2 niggardly (**med** with).
***at'terhald/sam** *A*=**atterhalden.**
***at'ter/hand** *-a*=**bak/: sitje i a-** get into sth late; be the last.
***at'ter/kjøp** *-et* buying back, repurchase.
***at'ter/klang** *-en* 1 echo. 2 *fig.* response.
***at'ter/lit** *-et* care, concern; regret, sorrow (**for** for).
***at'ter/lite** *V -a* 1 look back (at). 2 regret: **eg a-er på det** I am sorry about that. 3 expect, plan, wish.
at'ter/ljom *-en* echo, response: **det gav a-** it reechoed.
***at'ter/løyst** *A* - redeemed.
***at'ter/over** *Av* backwards.
***at'ter/reise** *V -te* raise up, rebuild, restore (to former glory): **a- det norske målet** raise up again the Norwegian language.
***at'ter/rom** *-(m)et* 1 last seat (in rowboat). 2 rear (of boat).
***at'ters** *Av* cf **akters**
***at'ter/skape** *-te* re-create.
***at'ter/skin** *-et* reflection.
***at'ter/slag** *-et* 1 reaction: **no kom a-et** then the r- came. 2 return; retrogression; worsening.
***at'ter/spegel** *-en* cf **akter/speil**
***at'ter/steg** *-et* backward step; regression.
at'ter/sting *-et* backstitch.
***at'ter/støde** *-a* 1 remains, remnant (**av** of). 2 one who remains behind.
***at'ter/syn** *-a/-et* 1 seeing again, reunion: **på a-** see you again. 2 retrospect, survey: **A-** Looking Back (Anders Hovden).
***at'ter/ut** *Av* cf **akter/**
***at'ter/vende** *V -e* return.
attes't *-en* recommendation (**for** for), reference, testimonial (esp. written); certificate (e.g. **dåps/, vielses/**): **han har gode a-er** he is well recommended, he has good references; **utstede en a-** issue a certificate (etc.)
attestasjo'n *-en* attestation, witnessing.
atteste're *V -te* attest to, certify (a document).
***att'/etter** *P* 1 after. 2 *(adv.)* back, backwards.
***att'/for** *P* cf **attan/**
***att'/fortel'jing** *-a* retelling (esp. in school, of text read aloud).
attfram [att' fram'] *Av* backside front, awkwardly.
***att'/fylt** *A* - filled in.
att'/føre[1] *V -te* 1 lead back; bring back. 2 rehabilitate (handicapped persons).
***att'/føre**[2] *P* cf **attan/for**
att'førings/institutt· *-et* school (institute) for (workers') rehabilitation.
***att'/gift** *A* - remarried.
at'ti *P* 1 in the back (of), in the rear (of): **a- kyrkja** in the rear of the church. 2 back in (to): **langt a- tida** way back in time; **a- baksetet** back in the rear seat; **de kom a- heimbygda** they came back to the home community; **han er komen a- barndommen** he is in his second childhood. 3 into, next to: **blanda a-** mix i-; **kome (ta) a-** touch; **nå a-** catch up with. *4=**att: skjenke a-** fill up again; **så a-** resow; **ta a-** take hold of again.
***att'/imel'lom** *Av* here and there, now and then.
at'tisk *A* - Attic: **a- salt** A- salt, wit.
attity'de *-n* attitude (esp. of affected manner), posture.
att'/keik *A* bent backward (in posture); *fig.* proud: **han spankulerte a- i ryggen... trappen nedover** he strutted proudly down the stairs (Jølsen).
***att'/kjennande** *A* - recognizable.
***att'/knept** *A* - buttoned up (clothing); *fig.* (about face) closed, not revealing feelings.
***att'/kommen** *A -e/-i, pl -komne* returned.
***att'/lagd** *A -/-lagt* left behind.
***att'/laten** *A -e/-i, pl -ne* closed, shut.
att'/lege *-a* fallow field.
***att'/leies** *Av* back, on the way back.
***att'/leng(e)s** *Av* backwards.
***att'/levande** *A* - surviving.
att'/med *P* near to, next to; in addition to: ***likne a-** compare with.
att'/om· *P* behind, in back of.
***att'/over** [/åver] *P* backwards; to the rear of.
att'/på *P* 1 behind, in (on the) back of: **komme a- en** come up behind sby; **han hang seg a- lasset** he hung onto the back of the load; ***gå a- sine ord** renege, go back on a promise; ***tale a- seg** contradict oneself. 2 following: ***a- striden** after the battle. 3 in addition to, on top of: **han skjenket hver og en en dram a-maten** he poured everyone a drink along with the food (Bojer); **a-kjøpet** in the bargain.
att'på/sleng *-en* straggler; *hum.* child born long after its siblings.
att'på/til· *Av* besides, in addition.
attrahe're *V -te* attract.
attraksjo'n *-en* attraction.
***at'trast** *V -ast* fail, retrogress (in health); go back on one's word.
at'tre[1] *V -a* 1 move back. 2: **a- seg** have misgivings, renege; **a- seg på** regret.
at'tre[2] *A* -: **den a-** the hind, rear.
attrib'utiv *A* attributive.
attributt' *-et, pl -/+-er* attribute, characteristic.
+**at'trå**[1] *-en* desire, longing (**etter** for).
+**at'trå**[2] *V -dde* desire, yearn for.
+**at'trå/verdig** *A* - desirable.
***att'/ståande** *A* - remaining.
***att'/til·** *P* 1 alongside: **stolen din står a- min** your chair is next to mine. 2 in addition to: **drikke øl a- maten** drink beer with one's food.
***att'/under** *P* below, under.
***att'/val** *-et* reelection.
***att'/vald** *A* - reelected.
att'/ved *P* alongside, beside; in addition to.
att'/åt *P* 1 alongside, close by, close up to. 2 in addition to, with: ***ete brød a- kjøtet** eat bread w- one's meat; ***leggje a-** add, brag.
***at'tåt/brend** *A -brent* burned, scorched (esp. of porridge).
***at'tåt/forte'neste** *-a* extra profit or earnings.
au'[1] *Av* cf **og**[2]
au'[2] *I* 1 ouch, ow. 2 oh.
***au'd** *A* deserted, desolate; empty: **garden var a- for folk** the farm was deserted; **det er a-t for fisk i vatnet** there are no fish in the lake.
Au'd *Prn (f)*
***au'd-** [au'(d)-] *Pf* easily (cf **-kjend**).
audien's *-en* audience, hearing (usu. before a king).
audito'rium *-iet, pl -ium/+-ier* 1 auditorium. 2 audience: **a-iet sov under forelesningen** the a- slept through the lecture.
***au'd/kjend** *A -kjent* easily recognizable.
***au'd/mjuk** *A* humble.
***au'd/mykje** *V -te* humble, humiliate.
***au'd/mykt** *-a* humbleness, humility.
***au'dn** *-a* desolate condition or state.
***au'd/sett** *A* - evident, obvious.
***au'dsleg** *A* - cf **ødslig**
***au'd/synleg** *A* evident, obvious.
***au'd/synt** *A* - evident, obvious.
Au'dun *Prn (m)*
°**au'e**[1] *-t* cf **auge**
au'e[2] *V -a*: **a- seg** moan.
aug.=**august**
***au'ga** *nt df -a, pl augo* cf **auge**
au'ge** *-t, pl -* (=auga**) eye: **få a- på** catch sight of; **ha a-o med seg** keep one's e-s open; **lata upp a-o** open one's e-s.
***au'ge-** *Pf* cf **augne-, øye-**
***au'ger** *-en* cf **uer**
***au'g/fare** *V -fer, -for, -fare/-i* (=**augne/**) inspect, observe sth closely.
au'gias/stall *-en* Augean stable.
***au'g/leite** *-t* cf **augne/**
***au'gne**[1] *V -a* (=**øygne**) catch sight of.
***au'gne**[2] *A*: **a- grann** a little (bit).
***au'gne/blink** *-en* cf **øye/blikk**
***au'gne/bragd** *-a* expression (in sby's eyes).
***au'gne/brun** *-a* cf **øye/bryn**
***au'gne/bryn** *-et* cf **øye/**
***au'gne/fare** *V -for, -fare/-i* cf **aug/**
***au'gne/feste** *V -e* stare intently, fix with gaze.
***au'gne/for** *pt of* **-fare**
***au'gne/kast** *-et* cf **øye/**
***au'gne/kvarm** *-en* edge of the eyelid.
***au'gne/leite** *-t* (=**aug(e)/**) horizon.
***au'gne/med** *-et* landmark; *fig.* purpose, goal.
***au'gne/mål** *-et* cf **øye/**
***au'gne/stein** *-en* cf **øye/**
***au'gne/syn** *-a/-et* cf **øye/**
***au'go** *pl of* **auga**
au'gs/burgsk *A* - pertaining to Augsburg: **den a-e konfesjon** the Confession of Augsburg.
augu'r *-en* augur; *fig.* chief, bigwig.
augus't *en* August.
August [also Au'-] *Prn (m)*
+**augusti'ner** *-en, pl -e* (=***-ar**) Augustinian.
***au'g/vitne** *-t* cf **øye/**
au'k *-en* increase.
***au'kar** *-en* amplifier.
au'ke[1] *-n* growth, increase.

+ Bokmål; * Nynorsk; ° Dialect.
After letter: ' stress (Acc. 1); ` tone, stress (Acc. 2); · length.
Below letter: . not pronounced.

au'ke[2] *V -a/+-te* (=**+øke**) increase; amplify: **vinden a-er på** the wind is freshening.
***au'ke/glas** *-et* reading glass.
au'ke/monn** *-en* (=/mon**) (degree of) increase.
au'king *-a* (=***-ning**) growth, increase.
***au'knad** *-en* growth, increase.
auksjo'n *-en* auction.
auksjona'rius *en, pl *-ariar* auctioneer.
auksjone're *V -te* auction.
AUL=**arbeidarungdomslag**
au'la *-en* auditorium, hall used for festive occasions (esp. in university).
au'le *V -a/+-et/+-te* swarm, teem.
***au'mleg** *A* frail, infirm; wretched.
au'r *-en* soil consisting of a mixture of gravel and coarse sand.
Au'ra *Pln* water course, with power station and village, in Sunndal.
au'r/bakke *-n* river sandbank.
Au'r/dal *Pln* twp, Oppland.
au're[1] *-n* (=**+ørret**) trout.
***au're**[2] *V -a* 1 muddy. 2 erode. 3 mix, fill with gravel.
Au're *Pln* twp, Møre og Romsdal.
aureomyci'n *-et* (a trademark).
au'ret(e) *A* - (=***auren**) gravelly.
au'r/helle *-a geol.* hardpan.
aurik'kel *-elen, pl aurikler bot.* auricula, bear's ear (Primula auricula).
Au'r/land *Pln* twp, Sogn og Fjordane.
au'rlands/sko *-en, pl -r/+-* type of loafers.
au'r/lendt *A* - (pertaining to a tract of land) hard, gravelly.
Au'r/skog *Pln* twp, Akershus.
Au'r/sunden *Pln* lake northwest of Røros.
au'se[1] *-a* (=**+øse**) dipper, ladle, scoop.
au'se[2] *V -te* (=**+øse**[2]) 1 bail, dip, ladle: **a- opp suppen** l- out the soup; **a- lens** b- out (a boat). 2 *fig.* draw (av from, upon). 3 pour: **regnet a-te ned** the rain p-ed down; **a- ut penger** squander money.
+au'se/kar' *-et* bailer (for boat), dipper, ladle.
***au'sel** *-en* ladle, scoop (with handle).
***au's/fat** *-et* bailer (for boat).
***au's/kår** *-et* cf **ause/**
***au's/kjer** *-et* cf **ause/kar**
auspi'sier *pl* auspices: **under lovende a-** in auspicious circumstances.
au's/regn *-et* (=**+øs/**) downpour (of rain).
au's/regne *-a/+-et/+-te/*-de* (=**+øs/**) pour down, rain in torrents.
au'st *Av* (also *N*) (=**+øst**) east: **a- for** e- of; **i a-** in the e-; **mot a-** to the e- (cf **Østen**).
au'sta- *Pf* (=**+østa-**, ***austan-**) from the east.
Au'/stad *Pln* twp, Vest-Agder.
au'sta/drag *-et* breeze, wind from the east.
au'sta/fjells *Av* east of the mountain range dividing Norway, in eastern Norway.
au'sta/fjelsk *A* - East Norwegian.
au'sta/for *P* east of: **slottet a- sol og vestafor måne** the castle east of the sun and west of the moon (Asbjørnsen and Moe).
au'sta/frå *P* cf **aust/**
Au'st-Agder *Pln* most easterly of the two southern Norwegian counties.
***au'stan/etter** *P* from the east.
***au'stan/om'** *P* cf **østen/**
***au'sta(n)/til'** *Av* from the east; on the east side of.
***au'starleg** *A* - eastward.
au'sta/vind *-en* east wind.
+au'sta/vær *-et* (=***/ver**) easter (=storm or gale coming from the east).
au'st/blokk *-a/-en* (=**+øst/**) eastern bloc, coalition (ref. esp. to the Soviet Union and its allies).
au'ster *-en* 1 bailing out (of boat). 2 water to be bailed out (of boat).
***au'ster-** *Pf* cf **øster-**
***Au'ster/land** *Pln* cf **Øster/**
***au'ster/landsk** *A* - cf **øster/**
***au'ster/lending** *-en* cf **øster/**
***au'ster/riking** *-en* cf **øster/riker**
***au'ster/riksk** *A* - cf **øster/**
***Au'ster/sjøen** *Pln* cf **Øster/**
***au'ster/veg** *-en hist.* the east, esp. the eastern Baltic, Russia.
au'st/etter *P* eastwards.
au'st/europe'isk *A* - East European.
Au'ste/voll *Pln* twp, Hordaland.
au'st/frå *Av* (=**+øst/fra**) from the east.
au'st/gående *A* - eastward bound (ship, train, etc.).
Au'st/isen *Pln* the Barents Sea.
***Au'st/landet** *Pln* cf **Øst/**
***au'st/landsk** *A* - cf **øst/**
au'stlig *A* - (=**+østlig**) 1 eastern: **det a-e Canada** e- Canada; **a- lengd/+lengde** longitude east. 2 oriental: **den a-e verden** the o- world. 3 easterly; (from the) east: **i a- retning** in an e- direction; **a- bris** east wind.
***au'st/lending** *-en* cf **øst/**
au'st/mann *-en, pl -menn/*-menner* 1 (in Norway) easterner. 2 *hist.* (in Iceland and the Orkneys) man from Norway.
***au'st/med** *P* in the east by.
Au'st-Norge *Pln* East Norway.
au'st/norsk *A* - East Norwegian.
au'st/om' *P* eastward of.
au'st/over [/åver] *P* eastwards, to the east.
au'st/på *P* eastward, towards the east, farther east.
+austra'lier *-en, pl -e* (=***-ar**) Australian.
austra'l/neger *-eren, pl +-ere/+-rer/*-rar* Australian aborigine.
Austra'l-samban'det *Pln* Commonwealth of Australia.
austra'lsk *A* - Australian.
au'stre *A* - (=**+østre**) eastern.
Au'str/heim *Pln* twp, Hordaland.
***au'st/røn** *A* coming from the east.
***au'st/vend** *A* (of field) facing, sloping eastwards.
autarki' *-et* autarchy.
auten'tisk *A* - authentic.
autodafé *-en* auto-da-fé (*hist.* burning of heretics at stake).
autodidak't *-en* self-educated person.
autoge'n *A* autogenous, self-generated: **a-/sveisning** oxyacetylene welding
autogra'f *-en* autograph.
+autogra'f/samler *-en, pl -e* (=***-ar**) autograph collector.
autokra't *-en* autocrat.
autokrati' *-et* autocracy.
autokra'tisk *A* - autocratic.
automasjo'n *-en* automation.
automa't *-en* 1 vending machine (e.g. for candy, cigarettes); slot machine. 2 automat (=self-service restaurant). 3 *derog.* automaton.
automatise're *V -te* automate.
automatise'ring *-a/+-en* (conversion to) automation.
automa'tisk *A* - automatic.
automobi'l *-en* automobile.
autono'm *A* autonomous, independent.
au'tor *-en obs.* author.
autorisasjo'n *-en* authorization.
autorise're *V -te* authorize, empower.
autoritativ [-tor'-] *A* authoritative: **fra a- kilde** from an a- source.
autorite't *-en* authority: **skriftens a-** the a- of Scripture; **en a- i fysikk** an a- on physics; **de kommunale a-er** the municipal a-ies.
autoritæ'r *A* authoritarian.
autostra'da *-en* freeway. superhighway, turnpike.
a'v *P* 1 by (subject of action): **tatt av vinden** caught by the wind, (title) Gone with the Wind; **av navn** by name; **en bok av Ibsen** a book by I-. 2 because of, for (cause): **av frykt for** for fear of; **av denne grunn** for this reason; **av kjærlighet** for love. 3 from (source, origin): **ikke rør deg av flekken** don't move from the spot; **av jord er du kommet** from earth art thou come; **få en gave av noen** get a present from sby; **svart av sot** black from soot. 4 of (material, membership, possession): **bygd av eik** built of oak; **en av de verste** one of the worst; **en venn av meg** a friend of mine; **det er snilt av deg** that's kind of you; **en av hundre** one in a hundred; **ni av ti** nine out of ten. 5 (other idioms): **av hele mitt hjerte** with all my heart; **en av gangen** one at a time; **det har du godt av** that's good for you, that serves you right. 6 (*adv.*) away, off: **beinet er av** the leg is off; **fra den dagen av** from that day on; **fra barn av** from childhood on; **av og til** now and then; **av med hatten** hats off. (For uses with verbs, e.g. **stikke av**, see these entries).
a/v=**a vista**
A'valds/nes *Pln* twp, Rogaland.
avanse [avang'se] *-n* profit: **ta en ublu a-** profiteer.
avansement [avangsemang'] *-et, pl -/+-er* advancement, promotion.
avansere [avangse're] *V -te* 1 advance: **vi a-te ikke en tomme** we didn't a- an inch. 2 be promoted: **han a-te hurtig i gradene** he advanced rapidly in rank.
avan't/garde *-n mil.* vanguard; *fig.* avant-garde.
a'v/art *-a/-en bot., zool.* inferior species, variety.
a'v/baklig *A* - inaccessible; (of persons) contrary, unapproachable.
a'v/balanse're [-ang-] *V -te* balance (evenly), stabilize.
+a'v/benyt'te *V -et* have use of.
+a'v/benyt'telse *-n*: **etter a-n** when done with.
+a'v/bestil'le *V -bestilte* cancel, countermand.
a'v/beta'le *V -te* pay off: **a- mannskapet** pay off the crew; discharge (debt, loan): **han a-te på lånet** he was paying off the loan.
a'v/beta'ling *-a/+-en* instalment; liquidation (debt, loan): **kjøpe noe på a-** buy sth on the i- plan.
+a'v/bikt *-en* apology: **gjøre a- hos en for** apologize to sby for.
+a'v/bilde *V -et* depict, portray.
+a'vbiter/tang *-a, pl -tenger* (=***-ar/tong**) pincers.
a'v/bleikt *A* - bleached out, faded; discolored
+a'v/bleket *A* - cf **/bleikt**
a'v/blomstre *V -a/+-et* shed blossoms, wither: **hun var en a-et skjønnhet** she was a faded beauty, had seen her best years.
+a'v/blåse *V -te* 1 blow off: **de a-te øde skjærene** the desolate windblown skerries. 2 *mil.* sound the call for a cease fire. 3 *fig.* call off, cancel: **a- streiken** call off the strike.
***a'v/bod** [/bå] *-et* cf **/bud**
***a'v/bragsleg** *A-* strange, unusual.
+a'v/brekk *-et* 1 detriment; injury, loss. 2 interruption.
a'v/brenne *V +-te/*-de* burn down, burn off (land); discharge (firearms), set off (fireworks).
***a'v/brigde**[1] *-t* deviation, variation.
***a'v/brigde**[2] *V -a* deviate, diverge, vary.
***avbri'kjeleg** *A* - strange, unusual.
***a'v/broten** [/bråten] *A -e/-i, pl -ne* broken, fragmentary; abrupt; interrupted.
a'v/brott *-et* interruption: **uten a-** uninterruptedly.
+a'v/brudd *-et* cf **/brott**
a'v/bryte *V -brøt, -brutt* 1 break (off), stop: **a- forbindelsen** b- the connection; **a- kampen** s- the match; **en avbrutt stav** a broken stick. 2 interrupt: **du skal ikke a- meg** you mustn't i- me.
+a'v/brytelse *-n* (=***-ing**) breaking off; intermission, interruption: **med a-r** intermittently.
+a'v/brøt *pt of* **-bryte**

***a'v/brøyte** -t change, deviation; intermission, interruption.

+a'v/bud -et (=*/**bod**) rejection of originally accepted invitation: **han gav a-** he sent word he wasn't coming.

a'v/bøte V -te relieve, remedy: **a- nøden** relieve distress.

***a'v/bøying** -a deflection, turning.

+avd.=**avdeling**

***a'v/dagast** V -ast cf **/dage**

***a'v/dage** V -a (only refl. **-ast** or pp. **-a**) grow dark.

a'v/dal -en out-of-the-way valley.

a'v/danka A - (=+**-et**) cast off, superannuated: hum. **en a- professor** retired p-.

***a'v/deild** -a cf **/deling**

+a'v/dekke V +-et/-dekte (=*/**dekkje**) 1 unveil (e.g. statue). 2 merc.: **a- en risiko** reinsure. 3: **bordet er a-et** the table is cleared.

a'v/dele V -te divide, partition off: **et a-t rom** a room p-ed off,

avde'ling -a/+-en division, partition, section; branch (e.g. of bank), department (e.g. of firm), ward (e.g. of hospital); mil. detachment, unit.

a'v/drag -et instalment: **pianoet kan betales ved 12 månedlige a-** the piano can be paid for in 12 monthly i-s.

a'vdrags/fri A -tt: **det er a-tt til august** there is no payment until August.

a'v/drift -a/+-en deviation, drift; mil. (of projectile) deflection; naut. leeway.

a'v/drått -en yield from domestic animals (esp. cows).

a'v/duke V -a/+-et unveil (e.g. statue).

+a'v/død A - (=/**døydd**) dead, deceased: **den a-e** the departed.

***a'v/dømme** V -dømde condemn, denounce.

***a'v/døyvd** A - restrained, temperate; weakened.

a've et eccl. a "Hail Mary" (=Roman Catholic prayer).

***a'v/elde** -a: **i a-a** in decay, decline; in a tight fix.

***aventa's** -en/-et chance, opportunity.

aveny' -en avenue.

aver's -en front, obverse.

aversjo'n en antipathy, aversion, dislike.

averte're V -te advertise: **a- noe til salgs** a- sth for sale.

avertissement [avertissemang'] -et, pl -/+-er advertisement.

a'v/fall -et 1 refuse, scraps, waste; chem. residue. 2 geol. slope. 3 naut. falling off.

+a'v/fant pt of **-finne**

***a'vfar/dag** -en day of parting; deathday.

+a'v/farge V -a/+-et discolor, fade.

+a'v/fatte V -et compose, draw up.

+a'v/feie V -de brush aside, treat cavalierly: **han a-de utsagnet med et par intetsigende ord** he dismissed the statement in an offhand way.

a'v/feldig [also -fel'di] A - (of people) decrepit, infirm; dilapidated, tumbledown (e.g. house).

+a'vfeldig/het [also -fel'di/] -en decrepitude, dilapidation.

a'v/ferd [*/fær] -a/+-en departure; death.

+a'v/ferdige V -et brush aside, dismiss brusquely.

+a'v/finne V -fant, -funnet adapt to, put up with: **a- seg med** come to terms with; **han avfant seg med sine kreditorer** he made arrangements with his creditors; **han måtte a- seg med hennes lettferdighet** he had to live with her frivolity.

a'v/folke V -a/+-et depopulate.

+a'v/fordre V -a/+-et demand: **a- en noe** d- sth from sby.

+a'v/funnet pp of **-finne**

+a'v/fyre V -te discharge (firearms).

+a'v/føde V -te foster, give rise to.

a'v/føring -a/+-en 1 bowel movement. 2 excrement, stool.

a'vførings/middel -elet/-midlet, pl +-midler/*-el cathartic, laxative.

a'v/gang -en 1 departure (**fra** from). 2 decline, decrease; retirement. 3 sale (**på** of).

a'vgangs/eksa'men -en final examination (at end of schooling).

+avga'rde Av cf **garde**[3]

+a'v/gav [/ga'] pt of **-gi**

+a'v/gi V -gav, -gitt 1 give, make (statement, declaration): **a- bevis** furnish proof; **a- forklaring** make a deposition; **a- rapport** (make a) report. 2 emit, give off (e.g. odor); yield (e.g. profits).

a'v/gift -a/+-en fee (for license etc.); duty (on imports); (excise) tax (on luxuries); royalty (on books, patents); toll (on road).

a'vgifts/fri A -tt duty-free, tax-exempt.

a'vgifts/pliktig A - dutiable, taxable.

+a'v/gikk pt of **-gå**

a'v/gjerd [/jær] -a decision.

***a'v/gjere** V -gjorde, -gjort cf **/gjøre**

***a'v/gjersle** -a cf **/gjerd**

+a'v/gjo'rde pt of **-gjøre**

a'v/gjort [/jort] A - certain, decided: **det er en a- sak** that is c-; **en a- fordel** a d- advantage; **han sa det i en a- tone** he said it in an unmistakable tone.

+a'v/gjøre V -gjorde, -gjort 1 decide, settle: **a- en trette** s- a dispute; **det avgjør saken** that s-s it; **det er opp- og avgjort** it's all been s-d, straightened out. 2 ascertain, make out: **ikke kunne a- noe med bestemthet** not know for sure.

+a'v/gjørelse -n decision, settlement: **treffe en a-** decide, make a d-.

+a'v/gjørende A - conclusive, decisive, final: **a- beviser** c- evidence; **forholdet var av a- betydning** the matter was of vital importance; **i det a- øyeblikk** at the crucial moment; **si noe i en a- tone** say sth in a f- (peremptory) tone.

a'v/glans -en image, reflection.

***a'v/gløymd** A -gløymt forgotten.

***a'v/greie** V -dde 1 merc. liquidate (a business). 2 settle: **saka er a-dd** the matter is resolved.

a'v/grense V -a/+-et bound, limit: **landet er a-et av høye fjell** the country is b-ed by high mountains; **et a-et område** a l-ed area.

a'v/grunn -en abyss: **være på a-ens rand** be on the edge of the a-; **en a- av uvitenhet** abysmal ignorance; **det er en a- mellom dem** they are poles apart; **a-en** the bottomless pit.

a'vgrunns/djup A (=+/**dyp**) abysmal.

+a'v/grøde -n yield.

a'v/gud -en idol.

+a'v/guderi' -et idolatry.

a'vguds/dyrking -a/+-en idolatry.

+a'v/gå V -gikk, -gått 1 depart (**fra** from), leave. 2: **a- ved døden** die. 3: **a-tt** retired.

+a'v/gående A - departing.

+avgå'rde Av cf **garde**[3]

***a'v/hald** -et cf **/hold**

***a'v/halden** A -e/-i, pl -ne cf **/holdende**

***a'vhalds/mann** -en, pl -menn(er) cf **avholds/**

a'v/handling -a/+-en dissertation, monograph, thesis (**om** on).

+a'v/hang pt of **-henge**

***a'v/heidre** V -a disparage, run down; dishonor.

a'v/hende V -a/+-et/*- dispose of, sell; jur. alienate (e.g. property, title).

+a'v/henge V -hang: **det a-er av** that depends on.

a'v/hengig A - dependent: **være a- av** be d- on.

+a'vhengig/het -en dependence (**av** on).

+a'v/hente V -a/+-et call for, fetch.

a'v/herding -a tempering.

a'v/hjelpe V infl as **hjelpe** remedy, set right: **a- et savn** supply a need.

a'v/hol [/hål] -et (=+/**hull**) hicksville, hole of a place.

+a'v/hold -et (=*/**hald**) 1 abstinence. 2 abstinence from alcohol: **pliktmessig a-** compulsory a-.

+a'v/holde V -holdt, -holdt 1 restrain: **a- seg fra noe** r- oneself from (doing) sth. 2 hold (e.g. meeting).

+a'v/holdende A - abstinent.

+a'vholden/het -en abstinence.

+a'vholds/kafé -en temperance café, "family restaurant".

+a'vholds/mann -en, pl -menn teetotaler.

+a'vholds/sak -a/-en temperance cause.

+a'v/holdt A - beloved, popular.

+a'v/hopper -en, pl -e (=*-**ar**) defector (esp. from communist country).

***a'v/huga** A - who has lost all desire (to do sth); disinclined.

+a'v/hull -et cf **/hol**

+a'v/hør -et (=*/**høyring**) hearing, interrogation: **foreta a- av vitne** take testimony from witness.

+a'v/høre V -te (=*/**høyre**) interrogate, quiz.

***a'vig** A - 1 backward; turned the wrong way. 2 upside down. 3 (adv.) clumsily. 4 difficult; arduous.

+a'vind -en cf **avund**

+a'vinds/mann -en, pl -menn cf **avunds/**

+a'vind/syk A cf **avund/sjuk**

+a'vind/syke -n cf **avund/sjuke**

a'ving -en (usu. pl) warp ends, thrums.

avi's -a/+-en newspaper.

avi's/and -a, pl -ender canard, false (newspaper) report.

+avi's/bud -et (=*/**bod**) paper boy (carrier).

avi's/debatt' -en discussion conducted in columns of a newspaper.

avi's/ekspedisjo'n -en newspaper office.

+avi's/feide -n polemic conducted in columns of a newspaper.

avi's/stykke -t, pl +-r/*- newspaper article.

+a vis'ta merc. at sight: **a- veksel** sight draft.

a'v/kall -et renunciation, waiver: **gi a- på** disclaim, renounce, waive (right, claim).

+a'vkaste V -a/-et 1 throw off (a yoke). 2 yield (returns).

a'v/kastning -a/+-en (=*/**kasting**) income, yield.

a'v/kjøle V -te cool.

+a'v/kjøler -en, pl -e cooler.

a'v/kjølt A - cooled.

***a'v/kjøme** -t cf **/kom**

+a'v/klare V -te clarify: **situasjonen har a-t seg** the situation has cleared up.

+a'v/klar(e)t A (=*/**klåra**) clarified, clear: **en a- stil** a clear style.

a'v/klaring -a/+-en (=*/**klåring**) clarification.

a'v/kle V -dde lay bare, strip; undress: **a- seg** u- (oneself).

+a'vklednings/rom [/romm] -met (=***avkledings/**) dressing room, locker, (shower) room.

a'v/kok -et decoction.

a'v/kokt A - boiled (cod, flounder).

a'v/kom' -met (=*/**kome**) issue, offspring, progeny.

a'v/kopling -a/+-en diversion; relaxation.

a'v/korte V -a/+-et reduce, shorten: **a-et** truncated (e.g. cone, pyramid = frustum).

a'v/korting -a (=+-**ning**) curtailment, reduction; abbreviation, abridgement.

a'v/krefta A - (=+-**et**) invalidated; weakened.

+a'v/krefte V -et 1 enfeeble, weaken. 2 invalidate (argument, testimony).

+a'v/kreve V -de demand: **de a-de ham en forklaring** they d-ed an explanation from him.

+ Bokmål; * Nynorsk; ° Dialect.
After letter: ' stress (Acc. 1); ' tone, stress (Acc. 2); · length.
Below letter: . not pronounced.

a'v/kristne *V -a/⁺-et* dechristianize.

a'v/krok *-en* out-of-the-way place.

av'l[1] *-en* agricultural production; breeding.

av'l[2] *-en* forge.

***av'l**[3] *-en* physical strength.

⁺a'v/la *pt of* **-legge**

⁺a'v/lad *-en* cf **/lat**

***a'v/laga** *A* - **1** agreed upon, arranged; well-made. **2** disturbed, out of order; ill-humored.

***a'v/lagd** *-/-lagt* cf **/lagt**

a'v/la'gring *-a/⁺-en* **1** storing. **2** aging, maturing by storing.

⁺a'v/lagt *A* - cast-off: **a-e klær** c-clothes.

a'v/lang *A* oblong.

***av'lar** *-en* **1** person who acquires property, amasses wealth. **2** producer (e.g. of farm products, goods).

a'v/laste *V -a/⁺-et* relieve (**for** of): **han ble a-et for en del av arbeidet** part of the work was taken off his hands.

a'v/lat *-en* **1** *eccl.* indulgence. **2: uten a-** incessantly.

a'v/late *V infl as* **late**[1] cease.

⁺a'v/latelse *-n*: **uten a-** incessantly.

***a'v/laup** *-et* cf **/løp**

***a'v/laus** *A* **1** free, vacant. **2** not needed, superfluous. **3** (of horse) runaway.

***av'le**[1] *-n* **1** physical strength. **2** acquisition, obtaining. **3** production (esp. of farm products). **4** produce, yield; acquired property.

av'le[2] *V -a/⁺-et* **1** cultivate, raise (e.g. grain). **2** beget, breed: **a- barn** beget children. **3** *fig.* create, produce: **hans tyranni a-et hat** his tyranny begot hatred.

⁺a'v/lede *V -et* (=***/leide**) **1** divert: **en a-ende manøver** a diversionary maneuver; **a-ende sa hun** changing the subject, she said. **2** *gram.* derive (**av** from).

⁺a'v/ledning *-en* cf **/leiing**

***a'v/legen** *A -e/-i, pl -ne* out-of-the-way.

⁺a'v/legge *V -la, -lagt* (=***/leggje**) **1** lay aside, put down (e.g. burden). **2** *bibl.* cast off. **3** pay: **en godt avlagt stilling** *archaic* a well-paying position. **4: a- visitt** pay a call; **a- rapport** give a report; **a- eksamen** take an examination.

⁺a'v/legger *-en, pl -e* (=***/leggjar**) **1** *hort.* cutting, slip; runner. **2** *hum.* offspring.

a'v/leggs *A* - **1** antiquated, out of date. **2** *obs.* decrepit, doddering.

⁺a'v/legs *A* - cf **/leggs**

a'v/leie *V -de* cf **/lede**

***a'v/leies** *A* - out-of-the-way.

a'v/leiing *-a* derivation; derivative.

⁺a'v/leire *V -et geol.* deposit.

a'v/lese *V -te* read (an instrument).

a'v/lesse *V -te* unload.

***a'v/leta** *A* - **1** conspicuous in color; which has a color other than white (or: other than white, black or grey); multicolored. **2** faded.

***a'v/lette** *-a* thin round cooky.

⁺a'v/leve're *V -te* deliver, hand over: **a- et brev** d- a letter; **a- et dypt bukk** bow deeply.

***a'v/liden** *A -e/-i, pl -ne* **1** expired. **2** (of person) dead, passed away.

av'ling *-a/⁺-en* crop.

a'v/live *V -a/⁺-et* put to death (esp. animal): **a- et rykte** scotch a rumor.

***a'v/ljod** *-en* cf **/lyd**

⁺a'v/lot *pt of* **-late**

av'ls/dyr *-et* (=***ale/**, ***als/**) breeder.

av'ls/ga'rd *-en* subsidiary farm (usu. without dwellings).

av'ls/stasjo'n *-en* breeding station.

⁺a'v/lukke *-t* booth, enclosure.

⁺a'v/lure *V -te* learn by watching secretly: **a- en en hemmelighet, et knep** pick up a secret, a trick, from sby.

a'v/lyd *-en gram.* ablaut, gradation.

a'v/lyse *V -te* cancel, call off (e.g. meeting).

⁺a'v/lytte *-et* **1** learn by listening. **2** listen in on, monitor.

***a'v/læte** *-t* cessation.

⁺a'v/lønne *V -a/-te* pay (salary, wages).

⁺a'v/løp *-et* **1** outlet (**for** for), vent: **finne a- for sin energi** find an o- for one's energy. **2** drain, drainage; outlet pipe; water course.

⁺a'vløps/kana'l *-en* drain, drainage canal or ditch.

⁺a'v/løse *V -te* cf **/løyse**

⁺a'v/løser *-en, pl -e* (=***/løysar**) relief worker.

⁺a'v/lø's(n)ing *-a/-en* cf **/løysing**

a'v/løyse *V -te* **1** relieve, spell (**i arbeidet** at, in the work); succeed; replace: **regnet ble a-t av solskinn** the rain was succeeded by sunshine; **bilen har a-t hesten** cars have replaced horses. **2** absolve (of sin).

a'v/løysing *-a* (=**⁺/løsning**) **1** relief: **han fikk a-** he was spelled in his work. **2** absolution (**fra** from).

⁺a'v/ma'gre *V -a/-et* reduce (weight of body); emaciate.

a'v/ma'gring *-a/⁺-en* reducing, reduction (of weight of body).

a'v/makt *-en* **1** debility, weakness. **2** unconsciousness: **falle i a-** faint. **3** *fig.* impotence, powerlessness.

a'v/marsj *-en* marching off.

a'v/mektig *A* - **1** weak. **2** unconscious. **3** helpless, impotent, powerless.

a'v/melding *-a/⁺-en mil.* report, roll-call.

⁺a'v/merke *V -a/-et* (=***/merkje**) indicate, mark off (e.g. on map).

a'v/mønstre *V -a/⁺-et* **1** pay off (seaman). **2** (of seaman) leave ship.

a'v/må'lt *A* - measured; formal, reserved, withdrawn.

***a'v/måte** *V -a* adapt, adjust, regulate.

a'v/neitte** *V -e* (=/nekte**) deny.

a'v/norske *V -a/⁺-et* make less characteristically Norwegian.

⁺a'v/passe *V -et* adapt, adjust, fit (**etter, til** to).

***a'v/prent** *-et* **1** imprint. **2** offprint.

a'v/pussing *-a/⁺-en* (final) polishing.

***a'v/rak** *-et* **1** waste. **2** sth discardable, discarded, worthless. **3** dregs, scum (of society).

a'v/reage're *V -te* work off (e.g. anger, resentment).

⁺a'v/regning [/reining] *-a/-en* (=**/rekning**) **1** settlement (of account). **2** statement (of bank balance).

***a'v/reie** *V -dde* **1** unharness. **2** damage, injure; dirty. **3** scold.

a'v/reise[1] *-a/⁺-en* departure: **ved a-n** at (sby's) d-.

⁺a'v/reise[2] *V -te* depart, set out (**fra** from; **til** for).

***a'v/reisle** *-a* **1** rough treatment; damage, injury; dirtying. **2** scolding.

a'v/rette *V -a/⁺-et* **1** train (e.g. animal to do trick). ***2** execute (a criminal).

⁺a'v/rigge *V -a/⁺-et* (of ship) strip.

a'v/ringing *-a/⁺-en* (on older telephones) ringing off (by turning the crank).

a'v/riss *-et* outline, sketch.

⁺a'v/rive *V -rev, -revet* tear off.

⁺a'v/ri'vning *-a/-en* (=***/riving**): **kald a-** cold shower.

⁺a'vri'vnings/blokk *-a/-en* pad, tablet (of paper).

a'v/runde *V -a/⁺-et* round off.

⁺a'v/ruste *V -a/-et* disarm.

***a'v/røysting** *-a* ballot, election: **halde a-** ballot, vote.

***a'v/rå(de)** *V -dde* **1** advise against (**frå**): **han vart a-dd** he changed his mind. **2: a- seg** make a decision. **3** agree on.

⁺a'v/sa *pt of* **-si**

⁺a'v/sang *pt of* **-synge**

a'v/sanne *V -a/⁺-et* refute; deny, reject.

a'v/sats *-en* ledge, terrace (in terrain); landing (on staircase).

⁺a'v/satte *pt of* **-sette**

⁺a'v/savn *-et jur.* loss by being illegally deprived of property or right of use.

⁺a'v/se *V -så, -sett* (=***/sjå**) afford, be able to spare: **kan du a- fem minutter?** can you spare me five minutes?

***a'v/seie** *V -sa, -sagt* cf **/si**

⁺a'v/sende *V -te merc.* consign, dispatch, ship.

⁺a'v/sender *-en, pl -e* (=***-ar**) sender (e.g. of letter).

***a'v/sete** *-a* warp ends.

a'v/setning *-a/⁺-en* (=***/setnad**) **1** *jur.* sequestration. **2** sale: **forretningen har stor a- på verktøy** the store sells a lot of tools.

⁺a'v/sette *V -satte, -satt* (=***/setje**) **1** amputate. **2** remove from office. **3** *geol.* deposit. **4** leave (mark, spot). **5** mark off (esp. on map). **6** earmark, reserve, set aside. **7** be able to sell, find a market for.

⁺a'v/settelig [also -sett'-] *A* - (=***/setjande**) **1** who can be removed from office. **2** marketable, saleable.

⁺a'v/settelse *-n* (=***/setjing**) removal from office.

⁺a'v/si *V -sa, -sagt* (=***/seie**) pass, pronounce (sentence).

a'v/sides *A* - **1** out-of-the-way, remote. **2** apart, by itself.

⁺a'vsides/liggende *A* - (=***/liggjande**) out-of-the-way, remote.

a'v/sig *-et* seepage.

⁺a'v/sindig [also -sin'di] *A* - beside oneself, insane (**av** from).

⁺a'v/sinn *-et* insanity, madness.

⁺a'v/sjelet *A* - (=***-a**) dead, lifeless: **et a- legeme** a l- body.

a'v/skaffe *V -a/⁺-et* abolish, do away with.

a'v/skaling *-a* (=**⁺/skalling**) shedding: **en a- av Venstre** a splinter of the *Venstre* party.

***a'v/skape** *V -a/-te* disfigure, distort; **a-t** misshapen.

***a'v/skapleg** *A* - **1** disfigured, distorted, misshapen; ugly. **2** *(adv.)* awfully.

⁺a'v/skar *pt of* **-skjære**

***a'v/skil** *-et* **1** boundary; boundary marker. **2** departure, leave-taking. **3** resignation; discharge, dismissal: **søkje a-** tender one's r-; **få a-** be discharged.

⁺a'v/skipe[1] *V -a/-et merc.* send by ship.

***a'v/skipe**[2] *V -a* abolish (by law, proclamation).

⁺a'v/skjed [/sje(d)] *-en* **1** departure, leave-taking: **ta a- med en** take leave of sby. **2** resignation: **søke (ta) a- fra en stilling** resign from a position; **få a- i nåde** be honorably discharged (from civil service, by the King); **få a- på grått papir** be fired, get the sack.

⁺a'v/skjedige [also -skje'-] *V -et* discharge, fire.

⁺a'v/skjedigelse *-n* discharge, dismissal.

⁺a'v/skjære *V -skar, -skåret* **1** cut off, sever; cut short, interrupt: **a- en tilbaketoget** cut off sby's retreat; **a- diskusjonen** cut short the discussion; **avskårne blomster** cut flowers. **2** bar, preclude: **han var avskåret fra å forklare seg** he was not in a position to give an explanation.

⁺a'v/skjæring *-en* **1** tub made from a sawed-off barrel. **2** cut-down boot.

⁺a'v/skoge *V -a/-et* deforest, denude, strip.

a'v/skoging *-a/⁺-en* deforestation, denudation.

***a'v/skoren** [/skåren] *A -e/-i, pl -ne, pp of* **skjere av** cf **av/skjære**

⁺a'v/skrekke *V -et* discourage: **han lar seg ikke a- av vanskeligheter** he is not d-d by difficulties.

⁺a'v/skrekkende *A* - deterrent, discouraging, forbidding: **et a- eksempel** a horrible example; **jeg liker bilen, men prisen er a-** I like the car, but the price is exorbitant; **virke a-** have a deterrent effect.

⁺a'v/skrev *pt of* **-skrive**

a'v/skrift *-a/⁺-en* copy, transcript: **ta en a- av noe** make a c- of sth; **bekreftet a-** certified c-.

⁺a'v/skrive *V -skrev, -skrevet* **1** depreciate; write off: **a- en fordring** w- a debt. **2** *fig.* give up, not count on.

a'v/skriving *-a/+-en* (=**+/skrivning**) **1** copying, transcription. **2** writing off; depreciation.

***a'v/skræmeleg** *A* - frightening.

a'v/skum [/skomm] *-met derog.* scum.

a'v/sky[1] *-en* aversion, disgust, loathing (**for** for).

a'v/sky[2] *V -dde* detest, loathe.

avsky'elig *A* - abominable, detestable, loathsome, odious.

+a'v/skygning *-en* (=***/skygging**) nuance, shade: **livet i alle dets a-er** life in all its phases.

+a'v/skåret *pp of* **-skjære**

+a'v/skårne *A pl* cf **/skjære**

a'v/slag *-et* **1** discount, reduction (**i prisen** in price, **på varene** on the goods). **2** refusal: **få a- på en søknad** have one's application turned down; **få blankt a-** meet with a flat r-.

a'v/slapping *-a* (=**+/slapning**) relaxation, relaxing.

***a'v/slegen** *A -e/-i, pl -ne* **1** broken, cut off. **2** mown: **ein a- voll** a m- field. **3** refused, turned down: **ein a- søknad** a rejected application.

+a'v/slepet *A* - (=***/slipt**) polished, refined: **han snakker et a- språk** he has a cultivated speech.

a'v/slo *pt of* **-slå**

a'v/slutning *-en/*-a* conclusion, end, finish: **skolen holdt en fest ved a-en av kurset** the school gave a celebration at the e- of the term; **hopperen hadde en fin a-** the ski jumper rounded off his flight nicely; **a-en av en kontrakt** the signing of a contract.

a'v/slutte *V -a/+-et* bring to an end, conclude, finish: **møtet ble a-et med bønn** the meeting was c-ed with a prayer; **en a-ende bemerkning** a c-ing (final) remark; **a- et regnskap** balance (close) an account; **a- en traktat** c- a treaty; **danne et a-et hele** form a complete entity.

a'v/sløre *V -te* **1** unveil (e.g. statue). **2** disclose, reveal, uncover; expose, unmask: **a- en intrige** uncover a conspiracy; **ansiktet a-te hans frykt** his face showed his fright; **han sa noe som var ganske a-ende** he said something rather r-ing; **a- seg** show one's true nature; **han a-te seg som en tyrann** he showed himself to be a tyrant.

a'v/sløring *-a/+-en* **1** unveiling (**av** of). **2** disclosure, exposure, revelation.

a'v/slå *V -slo, -slått/*-slege/-i* **1** repel (e.g. attack). **2** deny, refuse, reject: **a- et tilbud** reject an offer; **han avslo å låne meg pengene** he refused to lend me the money.

a'v/smak *-en* distaste; dislike: **få a- for noe** develop a d- for sth.

a'v/snitt *-et* **1** period (of history). **2** paragraph. **3** section (e.g. of book).

+a'v/sondre *V -a/-et* **1** isolate, separate: **leve a-et** lead a secluded life. **2** secrete (fluid).

a'v/sone *V -a/+-te* serve (a sentence).

***a'v/spaning** *-a* cf **/spenning**

a'v/spark *-et* kickoff (in soccer game).

+a'v/speile *V -et/-te* (=***/spegle**) reflect (image, emotion): **a- seg i** be r-ed in.

a'v/spenning *+-en/*-a* relaxation (of tension).

+a'v/sperre *V -a/-et* block: **en a-et gate** a blocked-off street.

a'v/sperring *-a/+-en* (road) block; barricade, fence.

+a'v/spise *V -te* put off: **han ble a-t med en ussel pensjon** he was p- with a meagre pension.

+a'v/spore *V -a/-et/-te* derail.

***avsta'ḍ/kome** [/kåme] *-kom, -kome/-i* cf **avsted/komme**

+a'v/stamning *-en* (=***/stamming**) descent (**fra** from), extraction: **være av god a-** be of good e-.

a'v/stanḍ *-en/*-et* distance: **på lang a-** at a great d-; **jeg så fjellet på a-** I saw the mountain in the d-; **holde seg på tilbørlig a- fra noe** give sth a wide berth; **få noe på a-** get a better perspective of sth; **den siste krigen er kommet mer på a-** we can now view the last war with more detachment; **ta a- fra noe** disagree with sth, disassociate oneself from sth; **han holder alltid folk på a-** he always keeps people at a d-.

+a'vstanḍs/måler *-en, pl -e* (=***-ar**) range finder, telemeter.

+avste'ḍ *Av* cf **sted**

+avste'ḍ/komme *V -kom, -kommet* bring about, cause, give rise to.

a'v/stemme *V -stemte* **1** harmonize: **fargene var godt avstemt** the colors h-d well with each other. **2** *mus.* attune, tune (instrument); tune in (radio).

+a'v/stemning *-en* ballot, vote: **sette under a-** put to a v-.

***a'v/stengd** *A -/-stengt* cf **/stengt**

+a'v/stenge *V -te* close off: **holde et rom a-t** keep a room closed off.

***a'v/stengsle** *-a* closing off; isolation.

+a'v/stengt *A* - isolated: **en a- bygd** an i- community.

a'v/stigenḍe *A* -: **a- passasjerer** (=**de a-**) passengers leaving.

a'v/stikkenḍe *A* - conspicuous, eccentric; garish, gaudy: **han har et a- ytre** he has an e- appearance.

+a'v/stikker *-en, pl -e* (=***-ar**) side trip (**til** to): **gjøre en a-** make a s-.

+a'v/stive *V -a/-et* shore up; buttress.

+a'v/stiver *-en, pl -e* (=***-ar**) buttress, piling, prop, stay.

a'v/stoḍ *pt of* **-stå**

+a'v/straffe *V -et* punish (**for** for).

+a'v/straffelse *-n, pl -r* punishment.

+a'v/stumpet [/stom-] *A* - (=***-a**) **1** blunted, dull: **a-ede følelser** b- feelings. **2** short, shortened; docked.

***a'v/styggje** *V -stygde* scare off; antagonize.

***avstyg'g(j)eleg** *A* - frightening, horrible; loathsome.

***a'v/styre** *V -de* **1** keep (sby) on the straight and narrow; prevent (sby) from committing an impropriety. **2** avert, prevent (e.g. accident).

***a'v/stytte** *V -a/-e* abbreviate.

***a'v/stytting** *-a* abbreviation.

+a'v/støpning *-en* (=***/støyping**) **1** casting. **2** cast: **ta en a-** make a c-.

a'v/stå *V -stod, -stått* **1**: **a- fra noe** abstain, desist from doing sth. **2** cede, relinquish.

+a'v/ståelse *-n* (=***-ing**) cession, relinquishment.

a'v/stått *pp of* **-stå**

+a'v/sunget *pp of* **-synge**

+a'v/svekke *V -a/-et* invalidate (e.g. testimony).

+a'v/sverge *V -et/-svor, -et/-svoret* (=***/sverje**) abjure.

+avsy'ne *Av* cf **syne[1]**

***a'v/synes** *Av* out of sight.

+a'v/synge *V -sang, -sunget* (=***/syngje**) sing: **a- fedrelandssangen** s- the national anthem.

***a'v/søles** *Av* cf **/sølt**

***a'v/sølt** *A* - (=**/søles**) shady.

+a'v/så *pt of* **-se**

+a'v/ta *V -tok, -tatt* **1** *merc.* purchase (wholesale). **2** decrease, diminish: **kreftene a-r** (his) strength decreases; **lyden avtok i styrke** the sound diminished.

+a'v/tagende *A* decreasing, diminishing (e.g. strength); waning (moon).

+a'v/tager *-en, pl -e* cf **/taker**

a'v/tak *-et* **1** decrease, reduction. **2** hindrance. **3** part which has been removed. **4** disposal (of merchandise, product).

+a'vtak/bar *A* removable.

+a'v/taker *-en, pl -e* (=***-ar**) purchaser (wholesale).

***a'v/talde** *pt of* **-telje**

a'v/tale[1] *-n* agreement; appointment, date: **inngå (slutte, treffe) en a-** make an agreement, reach an understanding (**med** with; **om** about); **bryte en a-** break an agreement (appointment).

a'v/tale[2] *V -a/-te* agree upon, arrange: **a- et møte** arrange to meet; **de a-te å møtes klokken 8** they agreed to meet at 8; **a-t spill** a put-up job.

***a'v/talt** *pp of* **-telje** (also **/tale**)

+a'v/tegne [/teine] *V -et* delineate, draw: **a- seg** be silhouetted, be reflected.

***a'v/teikning** *-a* drawing, picture, sketch.

***a'v/telje** *V -talde, -talt* dissuade.

***a'v/tinge** *V -a* cancel (e.g. agreement).

+a'v/tjene *V -te*: **a- sin verneplikt** serve required time in armed forces.

+a'v/tok *pt of* **-ta**

+a'v/trede *-t* toilet.

a'v/trekk *-et* **1** clearing away; hood, outlet (for gases, air). **2** pull of a trigger: **geværet er lett i a-et** the gun is easy to fire; **være sein i a-et** be slow on the uptake.

+a'v/trekker *-en, pl -e* (=***/trekkjar**) trigger: **være rask på a-en** be quick on the t-.

a'v/trykk *-et* **1** impression, imprint (**av** of). **2** copy, print; proof.

+a'v/tvinge *V -tvang, -tvunget* exact (e.g. promise); **en handlemåte som a-er respekt** conduct that commands respect.

a'vunḍ *+-en/*-a* envy.

a'vunḍe *V -a/+-et* envy.

***a'v/undre** *V -a* admire.

a'vunḍ/sjuk *A* envious, jealous.

a'vunḍ/sjuke *-n* envy, jealousy.

a'vunḍs/mann *-en, pl -menn/*-menner* (bitter, personal) enemy.

***a'v/vande** *pt of* **-venje**

a'v/veg *-en* (=**+/vei**): **på a-e(r)** astray, on the wrong path.

+a'v/veie *V -de* (=**/vege**) balance, weigh: **a- mulighetene** w- the possibilities.

***a'v/veiking** *-a* weakening.

+a'v/vek *pt of* **-vike**

a'v/vekslenḍe *A* - **1** changing, varied (e.g. life). **2** *(adv.)* alternately, by turns.

a'v/veksling *-a/+-en* change (**fra** from), variation: **til en a-** for a c-.

a'v/venḍe *V -te* avert (e.g. danger, wrath).

***a'v/venje** *V -vande, -vant* cf **/venne**

+a'v/venne *V -vente* (=***/venje**) wean.

+a'v/vente *V -a/-et* **1** await: **a- begivenhetenes gang** a- the course of events. **2** expect: **a-ende** expectantly, in expectation.

+a'v/verge *V -et* (=***/verje**) avert, prevent, ward off: **a- en ulykke** p- an accident; **gjøre en a-ende bevegelse** make a deprecating gesture.

***a'v/verke** *V -a* cf **/virke**

a'v/vik *-et* deviation (**fra** from); aberration.

+a'v/vike *V -vek, -veket* (=***/vikje**) deviate (**fra** from), diverge: **ha et a-ende syn på noe** have a divergent view of sth.

+a'v/vikelse *-n* deviation; aberration.

+a'v/vikenḍe *A* - divergent, deviant.

a'v/vikle *V -a/+-et* liquidate, wind up: **a- en forretning** l- a business; **programmet ble greit a-et** the program was carried out smoothly.

a'v/vikling *-a/+-en* liquidation (e.g. of a business); performance (e.g. of program).

+a'v/virke *V -a/-et* (=***/verke**) produce (timber).

a'v/vise *V -te* refuse, turn away: **han ble a-t ved inngangen** he was turned away at the entrance; **a- et angrep** repulse an attack; **a- en tilnærmelse** reject advances.

a'v/visenḍe *A* - averse, opposed, unwilling: **innta en a- holdning til noe** take a negative position towards sth; **stille seg a- til noe** reject sth, turn sth down.

+ Bokmål; * Nynorsk; ° Dialect.
After letter: ' stress (Acc. 1); ' tone, stress (Acc. 2); · length.
Below letter: . not pronounced.

+**a'v/viser** *-en, pl -e* detour sign.
a'v/væpne *V -a/+-et* disarm: **et a-ende smil** a d-ing smile.
***a'v/øyde** *V -de* **1** destroy, exterminate, kill. **2** prevent (sby from doing sth).
***a'v/åt** *-et* **1** stripping of pasture (esp. by stray cattle). **2** pasture. **3** expenses: **det gjekk opp i a- e-** ate up the profit. **4** vermin. **5** freeloader, parasite. **6** lean creature.

B

b [be'] *-en* (letter) B, b; *mus.* B flat.
+**ba'** *pt of* **be**
babb' *n* cf **klabb**
bab'bel *-et* babble.
ba'bel *et* babel, confusion: **B-s tårn** the tower of Babel.
ba'belsk *A* -: **b- forvirring** general confusion.
***bab'l** *-et* cf **babbel**
bab'le *V -a/+-et* babble: **b- i veg** chatter away.
bab'let(e) *A* - babbling.
ba'/bo'rd *N* port (side of ship): **om b-** on the port side.
baby [bei'bi] *-en* baby.
+**baby/kurv** *-en* bassinette.
babylo'n(i)sk *A* - Babylonian.
baby/pose *-n* bunting (baby's bag of cloth or fur, for outdoor use esp. in cold weather).
bacala'o *-en* Spanish dish of dried cod, boiled with onions, tomatoes etc.
bacil'le *-n* cf **basill**
back [bekk'] *-en* back (football, soccer etc.).
back/fisch [bakk /fisj] *-en obs.* teenage girl.
bacon [bei'ken] *-et* bacon.
ba'd[1] *-et* **1** (cleansing) bath: **ta et b-** take a bath; **varmt b-** hot bath. **2** (recreational) swim, dip: **ta (seg) et b-** have a swim, go swimming. **3** bathroom, bath: **på b-et** in the bathroom. **4** bathing resort, baths, spa: **ligge ved b-** stay at a bath. **5** *chem.* (solution) bath.
ba'd[2] *pt of* **be(de)**
ba'de *V -a/+-et* **1** bathe: **b- i kaldt vann** b- in cold water; +**b-et i sol** flooded with sunlight; +**b-et i sved** bathed in sweat; **b- seg i** bathe in, bask in, enjoy (e.g. sun, fragrance, popularity). **2** go swimming: **b- i sjøen** swim in the sea.
ba'de/bukse [/bokse] *-a* trunks, (men's) swimming suit.
ba'de/drakt *-a/+-en* swimming suit.
ba'de/gjest *-en* guest at a bathing resort.
ba'de/hette *-a* shower cap; swimming cap.
ba'de/kar' *-et* bathtub.
ba'de/kåpe *-a* bathrobe.
+**ba'de/sted** *-et* bathing resort.
ba'de/strand *-a, pl -strender* bathing beach.
ba'de/vatn *-et* (=+/**vann**) bath water.
+**ba'dning** *-en* (=***-ing**) bathing: **B- forbudt** No B-.
ba'd/stove [/ståve] *-a* cf /**stue**
bads'tu/bad *-et* steam bath.
bad/stue [bas'tu] *-a* **1** small building or room for hot steam baths. **2** building for drying grain.
bag [bægg'] *-en* bag (esp. for shopping, carrying etc.).
baga'sje *-n* baggage, *(Brit.)* luggage.
baga'sje/brett *-et* carrier, rack (on bicycle).
baga'sje/hylle *-a* baggage rack.
baga'sje/rom [/romm] *-met* baggage compartment.
bagatell' *-en* trifle: **en ren b-** a mere t-.
bagatellise're *V -te* minimize.
+**bagatell'/messig** *A* - infinitesimal, petty, trifling.
bag'ge *-n* heavy, clumsy person.
+**bag'ler** *-en, pl -e* (=***-ar**) *hist.* adherent of clerical party in 13th century Norwegian Civil Wars.
Bagn [Bang'n] *Pln* parish, Sør-Aurdal twp, Oppland.
+**bai'er** *-en* cf **bayer**
baisse [bess'] *-n* fall (of stock market values).
bajas [bai'as] *-en* clown.
bajonett' *-en* bayonet.
ba'k[1] *+-en/*-et* baking.
ba'k[2] *-en/*-et* **1** rear, posterior: **falle på b-en** fall on one's seat. **2** seat (of trousers=**bukse/**). **3** back (of hand=**hand/**).
ba'k[3] *P* behind, in the rear (of): **b- fram** backwards; **det ligger noe b- (dette)** there is something behind (this); **folket står b- ham** the people are behind him.
ba'ka/for· *P* (=***bakan/**) behind.
***ba'kan/om·** *P* cf **baken/**
***ba'ka(n)/til·** *Av* cf **bak/**
ba'k/bein *-et* hind leg: **sette seg på b-a** make stubborn resistance.
ba'k/beist *-et*: **ditt b-** you mule.
ba'k/binde *V +-bandt/*-batt, +-bundet/*-e/*-i*: **de b-er ham** they tie his hands behind him.
ba'k/bo'rd *N* cf **ba/**
ba'k/del *-en* **1** hindpart, rear. **2** *fam.* disadvantage (opp. of **fordel**).
ba'ke *V -a/-te* bake.
+**ba'k/efter** *P* cf /**etter**
bakelitt' *-en* bakelite.
ba'k/ende *-n* rear (end).
+**ba'ken/for·** *P* cf **baka/**
+**ba'ken/om·** *P* (=***bakan/**) behind.
ba'ke/plate *-a/-en* baking sheet.
ba'ke/pulver *-et* baking powder.
+**ba'ker** *-en, pl -e* (=***-ar**) baker: **gi b-ens barn brød** carry coals to Newcastle; **rette smed for b-** make the innocent suffer for the guilty (from a poem by Wessel, where it runs **rette b- for smed.**)
bakeri' *-et, pl -/+-er* bakery, bakeshop.
+**ba'ker/lære** *-a/-en* (=***-ar/**) baker's apprenticeship: **gå i b-** learn the baker's trade.
+**ba'ker/ovn** *-en* (=***bakar/omn**) baking oven: **varmt som i en b-** hot as blazes.
+**ba'kerst** *sp of* **bakre** (=***-ast, *-arst**)
ba'k/etter *P* after, afterwards, behind.
ba'k/evje *-a* backwater, eddy: **komme (være) i en b-** get into (be in) a rut, be at a standstill.
ba'k/fot *-en, pl +-føtter/*-føter* hind foot.
+**ba'k/frå** *Av* (=+/**fra**) from behind.
ba'k/gate *-a* back street.
ba'k/grunn *-en* **1** background. **2** (in the theater) upstage: **holde seg i b-en** stay in the background.
ba'kgrunns/figu·r *-en* minor character.
ba'k/gå'rd *-en* rear court, service area (of apartment building).
***ba'k/hald** *-et* cf /**hold**
ba'k/hand *-a* (=+/**hånd**) **1: ha noe i b-** have sth in reserve, to fall back on, up one's sleeve. **2** (in card playing): **sitte (være) i b-** be the fourth hand, last player.
ba'k/hjul *-et* rear wheel.
+**ba'k/hode** *-t* (=*/**hovud**) back of the head.
+**ba'k/hol'd** *-et* (=*/**hald**): **ligge i b-** lie in ambush, in wait.
ba'k/hun *-en* (=/**hon**) slab (outside piece of sawed log).
+**ba'k/hånd** *-a/-en* cf /**hand**
ba'k/i *P* (=**bak i**) in the back (of).
Ba'k-India *Pln geog.* (peninsula including Burma, Thailand etc.).
bakk'[1] *-en naut.* forecastle.
bakk'[2] *-en naut.* food tray; group of men eating at the same table, messmates.
bakk'[3] *Av*: **slå b-** reverse (a motor, a sail).
bakkana'l *-et, pl -/+-er* bacchanalia, drunken revel.
bakkan't *-en* bacchant, reveller.
bak'ke[1] *-n* **1** hill: **b- opp og b- ned** up one hill and down the next; **opp b-n** up the hill; **oppover b-** uphill; **det går nedover b- med ham** things are going downhill for him. **2** ground: **han falt i b-n** he fell on the ground; **han lå på b-n** he was lying on the ground; **han måtte i b-n** he had to bite the dust; **stå (komme) på bar b-** be (become) destitute.
bak'ke[2] *-n* cf **bakk**[2]
bak'ke[3] *V -a/+-et* back (ship, sail, motor).
bak'ke[4] *V -a/+-et* take on the shape of a hill.
Bak'ke *Pln* twp, Agder.
bak'ke/bryn *-et* (=*/**brun**) crest of hill.
bak'ke/drag *-et* range of hills.
bak'ke/hell *-et* (=*/**hall**) hillside.
bak'ke/kam· *-men* crest of hill.
bak'ke/kneik *-a* steep part of hill.
bakkels(e) [bak'kels, bak'kelse] *-(e)n/*-(e)t* cooky (usu. homemade), cf **fattigmanns/**
bak'ke/mannskap *-et* ground crew.
bak'ken/bart *-en* sideburns.
bak'ke/rekor'd *-en* record jump at a particular ski hill.
bak'ke/stjerne *-a/+-en bot.* fleabane (Erigeron acer).
bak'ket(e) *A* - hilly.
bak'ke/topp *-en* hilltop.
ba'k/klok *A* hindsighted.
ba'k/kropp *-en* hind part of body, hindquarters.
bakk'/sag *-a* backsaw (short saw with reinforced back).
Bak'kus *Prn* Bacchus.
+**ba'k/lader** *-en, pl -e* (=***-ar**) breechloader.
ba'k/lasta *A* - (=+**-et**) heavily loaded in the rear.
ba'k/leies *Av* backwards.
ba'k/lekse *-a*: **komme (være, ligge) i b-a** fall behind, be backward.
ba'k/lengs *A* - (=*/**lenges**) backwards: **falle b-** fall over b-; **gå b-** back away.
ba'k/li *-a* shady side of a valley.
ba'k/lomme *-a* rear pocket.
ba'k/lur *-en/-et* ambush: **stå på b-** lie in a-.
ba'k/lykt *-a* taillight.
ba'k/lås *N*: **døra gikk i b-** the door lock jammed; **det gikk i b- for ham** things went wrong.
ba'k/meis *-en/*-a* knapsack made of willow.
ba'k/ol *-a* (=+/**ole**, */**ore**) crupper.
ba'k/om· *P* behind: **B- synger skogene** Beyond Sing the Woods (Gulbransen).
ba'k/over [/åver] *P* back, backwards: **gå b-** back up, walk backwards; **legge seg b-** lean back, lie back.

ba'k/på *P* on the back (of): **henge (seg) b-** hang on behind, hook a ride.
ba'kre *A* -, *sp* +*-erst*/**-a(r)st* rear: **de b- stolene** the seats in the back; *(sup.)* farthest back, hindmost, last; rear.
ba'k/rom [/romm] *-met* back room; aft seat (in rowing shell).
ba'k/rus *-en/-et*: **han er i b-** he has a hangover.
bak's[1] *-en naut.* (coal) box.
bak's[2] *-en geol.* (polar) ice.
bak's[3] *-et* 1 struggle, toil. 2 heavy flapping of wings.
bak'se *V* *-a/+-et* struggle, maneuver (a boat) with difficulty: **b- med noe** struggle with sth; **b- seg fram** fight one's way forward.
ba'k/sele *-n* rear part of harness (from bellyband back).
ba'k/sete *-t* back seat, rear seat.
ba'k/sett *A* - overloaded in the rear.
ba'k/side [*/si·e] *-a/+-en* 1 rear: **på b-a av huset** at the back of the house. 2 reverse: *fig.* **medaljens b-** the seamy side; the drawbacks, disadvantages. 3 *hum.* drawback.
ba'k/skott *-en* (**=/skut**) rear (section of boat).
ba'k/slag *-et* 1 (of gun) recoil; rebound. 2 *fig.* repercussions; reaction.
ba'k/smekk *-en* (**=*/smikk**) 1 sudden push or slap from behind. 2 *fig.* repercussions.
ba'k/smell *-en* repercussions; reaction causing unpleasant surprise.
ba'k/snakke *V* *-a/+-et* slander, speak ill of.
+**ba'k/spiller** *-en, pl -e* (**=*/spelar**) kibitzer.
bak'st *-en* (**=*-er**) 1 baking. 2 batch (e.g. of cookies); **jule/** Christmas cookies.
bak'ste/fjøl *-a* (**=+/fjel**) bread board, pastry board.
bak'ste/helle *-a* large griddle for baking **flatbrød** or **lefse**.
bak'ste/kone [*/kåne] *-a* woman who bakes for others (esp. **flatbrød** and **lefse**).
***bak'ster** *-en* cf **bakst**
bak'ster/kone [*/kåne] *-a* cf **bakste/**
bak'ste/ved *-en* (long, finely split) firewood for baking.
ba'k/strev *-et* reaction, ultra-conservatism.
+**ba'k/strever** *-en, pl -e* (**=*-ar**) reactionary.
ba'k/stuss *-en pop.* rump.
ba'k/tale *V* *-a/-te* defame, slander, speak ill of.
ba'k/tanke *-n* ulterior motive.
bakte'rie *-n* germ, microbe.
bakte'rie/kultu'r *-en* bacteria culture.
bakteriolog [-lå'g] *-en* bacteriologist.
bakteriologi [-gi'] *-en* bacteriology.
ba'k/til· *Av* behind, in back.
baktr. = **bakteriologi, bakteriologisk**
ba'k/tropp *-en* rear guard.
ba'k/tung [/tong] *A* back-heavy; (of sth flying) tail-heavy.
ba'k/ut *Av* behind; to the rear: **sakke b-** lag behind; **slå, sparke b-** kick (of a horse); become unmanageable.
ba'k/vaske *V* *-a/+-et* slander; libel.
ba'k/ved *P* (close) behind: **det ligger noe b-** there is sth behind (at the bottom of) this.
ba'k/veg *-en* 1 rear entrance. 2 secret path or passage: **gå b-er** use underhanded means.
ba'k/vendt *A* - (**=*/vend**) 1 backwards, turned the wrong way: **han tok på seg buksa b-** he put his trousers on backwards. 2 awkward, impractical: **en b- framgangsmåte** an impractical procedure; **snakke b-** get one's tongue tangled up; make a Spoonerism.
ba'k/verk *-et* cakes and cookies.
ba'l *-et* struggle: **det var et b- å få dette gjort** it was a tough job getting this done.
balalai'ka *-en* balalaika.

balanse [balang'se] *-n* 1 scales. 2 balance: **holde b-n** keep one's balance; **miste b-n** lose one's balance; **ute av b-** out of balance, off balance; **være ute av b-** be upset.
balanse/kunst *-en* balancing act.
balansere [balangse're] *V -te* balance; keep one's balance: **regnskapet b-er med kr 100,—** there is a b- of 100 *kroner*.
°**balbe're** *V -te* cf **barbere**
***bal'd** *A* bold, brave.
baldaki'n *-en* baldachin, canopy.
***bal'der** *-et* 1 din, noise. 2 confusion.
Bal'der *Prn (m) myth.* god of light, son of **Odin**.
bal'der/brå *-a/+-en bot.* corn mayweed (Matricaria inodora).
***bal'dre** *V -a* din, make a noise; speak unclearly.
bal'drian *-en bot.* valerian (Valeriana).
baldy're *V -te* embroider, esp. with gold or silver thread.
ba'le *V* *-a/+-te* struggle (**med** with): **vi b-er nå med det** we are struggling along.
+**Balea'rene** *Pln* (**=*-ane**) the Balearic Islands.
***ba'len** *A -e/-i, pl -ne* strenuous.
bale're *V -te* 1 struggle, work hard. 2 behave noisily.
***ba'le/sam·** *A* strenuous.
Ba'le/strand *Pln* twp and resort, Sogn og Fjordane.
bal'g *-en* sheath.
bal'je *-a/-en* (**=balj**) (wash) tub.
balkong' *-en* balcony.
ball'[1] *-en* ball: **spille, kaste b-** play ball.
ball'[2] *-et* ball, formal dance.
°**ball'**[3] *-et* 1 struggle, hard work. 2 chore. 3 tangle, mess: **komme i b-** become entangled; *fig.* **det går i b- for'n** he becomes confused, incoherent.
balla'de *-n* 1 ballad. 2 confusion, racket: **det ble stor b-** there was a big fuss.
Bal'langen *Pln* twp, Nordland.
ballas't [also bal'-] *-en* ballast: **gå i b-** (of a ship) sail with ballast (= without cargo); **han mangler b-** he lacks character.
ballas'te [also bal'-] *V* *-a/+-et* ballast.
ball'/blom [+/blåmm] + *men*/* *en bot.* globeflower (Trollius europaeus).
bal'le[1] *-n* bale.
bal'le[2] *V* *-a/+-et* wrap: **b- sammen** roll into a ball, bundle together.
ballett' *-en* ballet.
ballong' *-en* balloon.
ball'/sal *-en* ballroom.
bal'sam *-en* balm: **gyte b- på sårene** apply balm to the wounds.
balsame're *V -te* embalm.
balsami'ne *-n bot.* garden balsam (Impatiens balsamina).
balsa'misk *A* - fragrant.
Bal's/fjo'rd *Pln* twp, Troms.
bal'/styrig *A* - unruly, ungovernable.
+**bal'ter** *-en, pl -e* (**=*-ar**) Balt.
bal'tisk *A* - Baltic.
balustra'de *-n* balustrade.
Bamble [bam'le] *Pln* twp, Telemark.
bamble/sjuke *-n* (**=+/syke, */sykje**) infectious, flu-like disease (Myalgia epidemica).
bam'bus *-en* bamboo.
bam'bus/stav *-en* bamboo stick.
bam'se *-n* bruin, bear.
°**ba'n** *-et* cf **barn**
bana'l *A* banal.
banalite't *-en* banality.
bana'n *-en* banana.
+**bana'n/flue** *-a* (**=*/fluge**) *zool.* fruitfly (Drosophila melanogaster).
+**bana'n/skal** *-et* (**=+/skall**) banana peel
+**bana'n/stikker** *-en, pl e-* (**=*-ar**) banana plug (e.g. on radio).
ban'd[1] *-et* (**=+bånd**) 1 band, ribbon; stripe (on trousers); (dog) leash; (barrel) hoop: **holde hunden i b-** keep the dog on a leash. 2 *fig.* bond, tie: **blodets b-** blood ties; **bryte alle b-** break all bonds (ties); **legge b- på seg** restrain oneself.

band[2] [bæ'nd] *-et mus.* jazz band.
Ban'dak *Pln* lake in Telemark.
banda'sje *-n* bandage: **legge en b- på et sår** bandage a wound.
bandasje're *V -te* bandage.
bandasjis't *-en* maker or seller of surgical appliances.
ban'de[1] *-n* gang, mob.
***ban'de**[2] *V -a* put hoops on (barrel).
+**ban'de/fører** *-en, pl -e* (**=*-ar**) gang leader.
ban'd/hake *-n* hook used to squeeze hoop on barrel.
ban'd/hund *-en* bandog (angry watchdog, usu. tied).
banditt' *-en* bandit.
ban'd/jern *-et* strap iron.
ban'd/kniv *-en* drawknife.
***ban'd/mark** *-en* (**=*/makk**) tapeworm.
bandolæ'r *-et, pl +-er/*-* bandolier, Sam Browne belt.
***ban'd/oppta·kar** *-en* cf **bånd/opptaker**
ban'd/sag *-a* band saw.
ban'd/stokk *-en* key log in a logjam.
+**ban'dt** *pt of* **binde**
ban'd/vevnad *-en* band-weaving.
bandy [bæ'ndi] *-en* bandy (*Brit.* type of hockey).
bandy/kølle *-a/+-en* bandy stick.
ba'ne[1] *-n archaic* 1 violent death: **det ble to manns b-** it was the finish of two men. 2 slayer.
ba'ne[2] *-n* 1 path, track; (**=kjøre/**) (traffic) lane: **bringe et emne på b-** broach, bring up a subject; **i lange b-r** a lot, plenty, freely. 2 railroad (**=jern/**). 3 course, field, ground (used in sports and sports contests), (tennis) court, (skating) rink, (bowling) alley, (shooting) range. 4 trajectory, orbit, track. 5 career, course: **bryte seg en b-** make a career for oneself.
ba'ne[3] *V* *-a/+-te* clear, pave, smooth: **b- vei for noe(n)** smooth, clear the way for sth, sby.
ba'ne/brytende *A* - pioneering; trailbreaking.
ba'ne/hogg *-et* death blow (by battleax).
+**ba'ne/legeme** *-t* (**=*/lekam**) roadbed (of railroad).
ba'ne/mann *-en, pl -menn/*-menner* slayer.
ba'ne/rekor'd *-en* track record.
ba'ne/sår *-et* fatal wound.
+**ba'ne/vokter** *-en, pl -e* (**=*/vaktar**) railroad watchman, signalman.
°**ba'n/fostre** [/fostre] *-a* cf **barn/**
bang'[1] *-et* bang.
***bang'**[2] *-en* fright; anxiety.
+**bang'e** *A* - (**=*bang', *bang'en**) 1 afraid, frightened, scared (**for** of): **jeg er b- for at det er for sent** I am afraid it is too late. 2 anxious, apprehensive: **b- anelser** apprehensions, misgivings.
ban'jer *-en naut.* mess on orlop deck (cf next word).
ban'jer/dekk *-et naut.* orlop (deck below lower deck).
ban'jo *-en* banjo.
ban'k[1] *-en* bank: **sette penger i b-en** deposit money in the bank; **sprenge b-en** (in gambling) break the bank.
ban'k[2] *-et* 1 knock. 2 spanking; beating: **få, gi b-** receive, give a spanking, beating.
ban'k[3] *-en* cf **banke**[1]
ban'k/bok *-a/+-en, pl -bøker* bankbook, passbook.
ban'k/boks *-en* safe-deposit box.
ban'ke[1] *-n* (**=bank**[3]) bank (of clouds; fishing banks).
ban'ke[2] *V* *-a/+-et* 1 knock, beat; rap, tap; throb: **b- i bordet** knock on wood; **det b-er på døren** there is a knock on the door; **hjertet b-er** the

+ Bokmål; * Nynorsk; ° Dialect.
After letter: ' stress (Acc. 1); ' tone, stress (Acc. 2); · length.
Below letter: . not pronounced.

heart beats; **b-ende puls** throbbing pulse. **2** work on; shape by beating, knocking: **b- kjøtt** pound meat; **b- tepper** beat carpets; **b- ut en bulk** pound out a dent. **3** spank; beat: **b- en opp** beat sby up.

ban'ke/biff *-en* beef tenderized by pounding and served ab. like Swiss steak.

ban'ke/fiske *-t* fishing on banks such as those off the coast of Norway.

ban'ke/kjøtt *-et* **(=*/kjøt)** same as **b-/biff.**

+ban'ker *-en, pl -e* **(=*-ar)** rug beater.

bankerott'[1] *-en* bankruptcy: **gjøre b-, spille b-** go bankrupt.

+bankerott'[2] *A* - bankrupt.

ban'ke/tre *-et, pl -/+-trær* paddle for beating the dirt out of clothes when washing them in a stream.

bankett' *-en* banquet.

ban'ke/ånd *+-en/*-a* poltergeist.

ban'k/giro [/sjiro] *-en* bank exchange system: **betale en regning pr. b-** pay a bill by bank draft.

bankier [-kie'] *-en* banker.

bankier/firma *-et, pl +-er/*-* banking firm.

ban'k/konto *-en* bank account.

ban'ko *-en* the sending of cash through registered mail.

ban'ko/brev *-et, pl -/+-er* (registered) letter containing cash.

ban'ko/konvolutt' *-en* strong envelope used for sending money.

ban'k/sjef *-en* bank manager.

ban'k/styre *-t* board of directors of a bank.

bann' *-et* church ban, excommunication: **lyse i b-** excommunicate.

***ban'nast** *V -ast* cf **banne**

bann'/bulle *-n* (papal) bull of excommunication.

ban'ne *V -a/banle* **1** *archaic* forbid: **b- en adgangen til noe** deny one access to sth. **2** curse; swear: **b- på** swear to; **b- så det lyser** swear a blue streak.

ban'ner *-et, pl -/+-e* banner, ensign.

ban'ning *-a* cursing, swearing.

bann'/lyse *V -te* **1** excommunicate. **2** ban, forbid: **krig burde være b-t** war ought to be banned.

+bann'/satt *A* - **(=*/sett)** banned; cursed.

bann'/skap *-en* cursing, swearing.

bann'/stråle *-n* anathema: **slynge b-n mot** excommunicate, fulminate against.

°ba'ns/unge [/onge] *-n* cf **barns/**

ban'tam/vekt *-a/+-en* bantamweight.

°ba'n/taus *-a* nursemaid.

ban'te *pt of* **banne**

baptis't *-en* Baptist.

ba'r[1] *-en* bar: **gå på b-** go to a b-.

ba'r[2] *-et* evergreen (branches): **strø med b-** strew evergreens.

+ba'r[3] *A* **(=*berr) 1** bare, naked; open, uncovered: **gå b-** go without wraps; **med b-e ben** barelegged; **med b-t hår, med b-t hode** bareheaded; **et b-t landskap** an unforested district; **stå, bli satt på b- bakke** be left penniless, destitute. **2** (mostly in *df*) sheer; only: **hun er b-e barnet** she is a mere child; **stå i b-e skjorten** be dressed only in one's shirt; **hun gråt av b-e sinne** she wept from sheer anger; **blott og b-t vrøvl** sheer nonsense. **3** (with a swearword): **de skjøt som b-e fanden** they were shooting like the very devil. **4**: **løpe for b-e livet** run for one's life, for dear life; **jeg kan ikke for mitt b-e liv forstå . . .** for the life of me I cannot understand.

ba'r[4] *pt of* **bære, bere**

-bar *A* **1** -ful: **fruktbar** fruitful; **underbar** wonderful. **2** -able: **merkbar** noticeable; **stillbar** adjustable; **brennbar** inflammable.

barak'ke *+-n/*-a* cf **brakke**

barba'r *-en* barbarian.

barbari' *-et* **1** barbarism. **2** barbarity.

barbarise're *V -te* barbarize.

barba'risk *A* - **1** barbarian, barbaric. **2** barbarous.

+ba'r/beint *A* - barefoot; bare-legged.

barbe'r *-en* barber.

barbe'r/blad *-et, pl -/+-er* razor blade.

barbe're *V -te* shave.

+barbe'rer *-en, pl -e* **(=*-ar)** cf **barber**

barbe'r/høv'el *-elen, pl -ler* safety razor.

barbe'r/kniv *-en* (straight) razor.

barbe'r/kost [/kost] *-en* shaving brush.

barbe'r/maski'n *-en* shaver, electric razor.

barbe'r/saker *pl* shaving kit.

barbe'r/salong' *-en* barber shop.

barbe'r/stell *-et* shaving kit.

Bar'bro *Prn(f)* Barbara.

***ba'rd**[1] *-en* **(=*barde**[4]**)** outer edge; rim.

***bar'd**[2] *pp of* **berje**

ba'r/dage *-n archaic* fight; battle.

bar'de[1] *-n* bard (Celtic poet).

bar'de[2] *-n* whalebone, baleen.

bar'de[3] *-n* type of viking ship (with high, iron-clad prow).

***ba'rde**[4] *-n* cf **bard**[1]

***bar'de**[5] *pt of* **berje**

bar'de/kval *-en* **(=+/hval)** *zool.* baleen whale, whalebone whale (Mysticeti).

ba'r/disk *-en* bar counter.

Bar'du *Pln* twp, Troms.

bardu'n *-en* stay, guy wire; tent rope; *naut.* backstay.

bardu's *Av* suddenly; slam bang: **det kom b- på ham** it hit him suddenly; **falle b-** fall flat.

ba're[1] *V -a/+-et*: **b- seg for** help, keep from, resist; **jeg kunne ikke b- meg for å le** I could not help laughing.

***ba're**[2] *V -a* **1** strew evergreens. **2** beat.

+ba're[3] *Av* **(=*berre**[3]**) 1** just, merely, only: **b- gå** by all means go; **b- vent** just you wait; **b- for moro** just for fun; **det er b- det at . . .** the only trouble is that . . . **det blir b- verre** it just gets worse; **jeg kan b- ikke forstå . . .** what I can't understand is . . .; **jeg skulle b-** I was only going to; **b- så vidt** just barely. **2** if only: **du kan når du b- vil** you can if you only want to; **den som b- hadde penger** if only one had money; **b- jeg var voksen** if only I were grown up; **b- han ser på meg, blir jeg redd** I get scared when he just looks at me. **3** (intensifier, often omitted) **det skulle b- mangle** (see **mangle**); **der kan du b- se** there you see; **jeg skynder meg så mye jeg b- kan** I hurry all I possibly can; **du kan bare våge** just you try; **han løp som b- det (som b- fanden)** he ran like everything (like the devil).

barett' *-en* beret.

+ba'r/frost *-en* frost while the ground is still bare.

ba'r/frø *-en/-et* two-story section forming the entrance of an old-fashioned type of farmhouse.

ba'rfrø/stue *-a* **(=*/stove)** farmhouse with a **barfrø.**

+ba'r/føtt *A* - barefoot.

+ba'r/hodet *A* - bareheaded.

ba'r/hytte *-a* lean-to built from evergreen branches.

ba'rium *-et* barium.

bar'k[1] *-en* barque (ship).

+bar'k[2] *-en* **(=*bork)** bark: **komme mellom b-en og veden** get into a difficult position, be caught in a squeeze between two contending parties (be between the devil and the deep blue sea).

barkaro'le *-n* barcarole.

barkas's(e) *-(e)n* launch.

bar'ke[1] *-n* throat.

bar'ke[2] *V -a/+-et* bark (=strip the bark from), ross.

bar'ke[3] *V -a/+-et* rush: **b- i hop** rush one another, start fighting.

bar'ke/brød *-et* bread made from bark flour and rye.

***bar'ke/knute** *-n* Adam's apple.

bar'ke/mjøl *-et* **(=+/mel)** flour of ground bark (used, with rye, for bread).

bar'ke/spade *-n* barking iron, bark spud.

+bar'ket *A* - **1** tanned; bronzed, weather-beaten. **2** callous, horny.

ba'r/lind *-a bot.* yew (Taxus).

+ba'r/låg *-en* **(=*/log)** water in which grain has been soaked to be made into malt.

bar'm *-en* **1** bosom, breast, chest: **det har du ikke suget av din egen b-** you have not thought this up yourself; **nære en slange ved sin b-** nourish a viper in one's bosom; **gripe i sin egen b-** look nearer home. **2** corner of a sail.

***bar'me** *V -a* pity: **b- seg** groan, moan; complain.

+barmhjer'tig *A* **-(=*-hjartig)** merciful; kind.

+barmhjer'tig/het *-en* mercy.

+barmhjer'tighets/gjerning *-en* act of mercy.

ba'rn *-et, pl -/*born* [*bånn] child; baby, infant; descendant: **Israels b-** children of Israel; **få b-** have a baby; **bli med b-** become pregnant; **sette b- i verden** have children; **sette b- på en pike** get a girl with child; **ta i b-s sted** adopt; **han er et stort b-** (of adult) he is a big baby; **være et b- av sin tid** be a child of the times; **et Guds b-** a child of God; **være uskyldig som b- i mors liv** be innocent as a babe; **han er ikke mors beste b-** he is no angel; **slå b-et ut med badevannet** throw the baby out with the bath water; **brent b- skyr ilden** a burnt child dreads the fire (once bitten twice shy); **kjært b- har mange navn** a pet child gets many names (=call it what you like); **små b- har små gleder** small children have small pleasures (=little things please little minds).

ba'rn/aktig *A* - childish, infantile.

ba'rn/dom' *-men/*-en* childhood; infancy: **fra b-men av** from childhood; **flyvningens b-** the infancy of flying; **gå i b-men** be in one's second childhood.

ba'rndoms/heim *-en* **(=+/hjem)** childhood home.

***ba'rn/døme** *-t* childhood.

***ba'rne** *V -a* make pregnant.

ba'rne/ba'rn *-et, pl -/*-born* grandchild.

+ba'rne/bidrag *-et* child support payment.

ba'rne/billett' *-en* child's ticket.

ba'rne/blad *-et* children's magazine.

ba'rne/dåp *-en* baptism; christening.

ba'rne/far *-en* alleged father (of illegitimate child): **bli utlagt som b-** be pointed out as the father.

ba'rne/god *A* good to children; fond of children.

ba'rne/hage *-n* day nursery; playschool.

ba'rne/heim *-en* **(=+/hjem)** home for children; orphanage.

ba'rne/hug *-en* child's mind.

***ba'rn/eign** *-a* childbirth.

ba'rne/jente *-a* nursemaid.

ba'rne/kjær *A* fond of children.

ba'rne/kopper *pl* smallpox.

+ba'rne/krybbe *-a/-en* **(=*/krubbe)** day nursery.

ba'rne/kår *-et* status as a child (esp. *eccl.*: as God's child).

+ba'rne/lammelse *-n* polio (formerly infantile paralysis).

ba'rne/lærdom' *-(m)en* religious training (in childhood); *fig., hum.* elementary knowledge: **kan du ikke din b-?** don't you know your ABC's?; **det hører til min b-** I learned that at my mother's knee.

ba'rne/mat *-en* **1** baby food. **2** *fig.* child's play: **det var b- for ham** it was just child's play for him.

ba'rne/park *-en* (supervised) playground.

+**ba'rne/pike** *-a/-en* nursemaid.
ba'rne/pleie *-a/+-en* (professional) child care, nursing.
ba'rne/pleierske *-a/+-en* (trained) children's nurse.
ba'rne/regle *-a* nursery rhyme; chant.
ba'rne/rik *A* having many children: **b-e familier** large families.
ba'rne/rim *-et* nursery rhyme.
ba'rne/rumpe [/rompe] *-a*: **glatt i fjeset som en b-** smooth in the face as a baby's bottom.
ba'rne/seng *-a* crib.
ba'rne/sinn *-et*: **b-et** the mind of a child; innocence.
ba'rne/sjukdom *-men/*-en* 1 children's disease. 2 *fig.* growing pains.
ba'rne/skei *-a* child's spoon.
+**ba'rne/sko** *pl*: **han har trådt sine b-** he is no child; he is experienced.
+**ba'rne/strek** *-en* childish prank.
ba'rne/tekke *-t*: **ha b-** have a way with children, be liked by children.
ba'rne/time *-n* children's hour (on the radio, etc.).
ba'rne/tog [/tåg] *-et* children's procession (esp. on May 17).
ba'rne/tru *-a* (=+**/tro**) childhood faith.
ba'rne/trygd *-a/+-en* family allowance (given by the state for each child after the first one).
+**ba'rne/tøy** *-et* (=***/ty**) children's clothing.
ba'rne/vakt *-a/+-en* 1 baby-sitter. 2: **sitte b-** baby-sit.
ba'rne/vern [/væ'rn] *-et* child welfare (as a field for legislation, authorities and private effort).
ba'rneverns/akademi· *-et, pl +-er/*-* school that trains child welfare workers, esp. nursery school teachers.
ba'rneverns/nemnd [/nemd] *-a* child welfare council.
ba'rne/vis *N*: **på b-** like a child; as a child does.
ba'rne/vogn [/vång'n] *-a* baby carriage.
+**ba'rne/værelse** *-t* nursery.
ba'rn/fostre [/fostre] *-a* 1 nursemaid. 2 wet-nurse.
***ba'rn/kone** [/kåne] *-a* pregnant woman.
ba'rn/laus *a* childless.
ba'rnlig *A* childlike, innocent, naive.
+**barnlill′** *N poet* (of Jesus) little child.
ba'rns/bein *N* (=+**/ben**): **fra b- (av)** from childhood.
ba'rn/seng *-a* childbed.
***ba'rnsken** *A -e/-i, pl -ne* childish.
ba'rnslig *A* - 1 childish; childlike: **b- henrykkelse** childish delight. 2 childish; infantile: **oppføre seg b-** act like a baby.
ba'rns/nød *-a/+-en* (=***/naud**) labor; pains of childbirth.
ba'rns/unge [/onge] *-n* (=**barn/**) child.
***ba'rns/øl** *-et* cf **barsel**
ba'rn/unge [/onge] *-n* cf **barns/**
ba'r/nål *-a* needle of an evergreen.
barokk′[1] *-en* baroque style or period.
barokk′[2] *A barokt* 1 baroque. 2 fantastic, grotesque: **b-e ideer** queer ideas.
barome′ter *-eret/-ret, pl -er/+-re* barometer.
barome′ter/stanḍ *-en/*-et* barometric reading.
baro′n *-en* baron.
barones′se *-a/+-en* baroness.
baroni′ *-et, pl +-er/*-* barony.
bar′re *-n* bar (of a precious metal).
barriere [bariæ're] *-n* barrier.
barrika′de *-n* barricade.
barrikade′re *V -te* barricade.
bar'sel [also bar'-] *-elet/-let, pl -el/+-ler* (=***barns/øl**) 1 confinement. 2 christening celebration.
bar'sel/feber *-en* childbed fever.
bar'sel/graut *-en* mush of wheatflour boiled in cream, brought when visiting a woman after childbirth.
bar'sel/kone [*/kåne] *-a* woman in confinement.
bar'sel/krampe *-n med.* eclampsia.
bar'sel/seng *-a/+-en* childbed: **hun ligger i** (or: **på**) **b-** she is having a baby.
bar'sels/kone [*/kåne] *-a* cf **barsel/**
bar'sk *A* 1 (of climate, country) grim, inclement, severe. 2 (of person, behavior, voice) gruff, harsh, stern: **b- stemme** gruff voice. 3 *fam.* rough, tough; manly, robust.
+**bar'sk/het** *-en* 1 grimness, inclemency, severity. 2 gruffness, harshness, sternness.
ba'r/skog *-en* forest of conifers, evergreens.
bar'sle *V -a/+-et* have a baby.
ba'rsok *en* St. Bartholomew's Day, August 24th.
bar′t[1] *-en* moustache.
***bar′t**[2] *pp of* **berje**
ba'r/tender *-en, pl +-e* bartender.
ba'r/tre *-et, pl -/+-trær* evergreen.
bar'yton *-en* baritone.
ba's[1] *-en* 1 leading person within a group; headman, master: **spille b-lord it; du er nå b-en** you're tops. 2 boss (of a crew, gang), foreman.
***ba's**[2] *-et* 1 underbrush. 2 effort; elaborate party.
basal′t *-en* basalt.
basa′r *-en* bazaar (market place; sale for a charitable purpose).
basa′r/hall *+-en/*-a* arcade, bazaar (row of small shops under one roof).
ba'se[1] *-n* (military) base.
ba'se[2] *-n chem.* base.
ba'se[3] *V -a/+-te* 1 struggle, work hard. 2 romp, roll (in play): **b- i snøen** romp in the snow.
base′re *V -te* base: **være b-t på** be based upon; **vi må b- oss på å leve billig** we will have to live cheaply.
basi′lika *-en, pl -er* basilica.
basilis′k *-en* basilisk.
basill′ *-en* bacillus.
+**basill′/bærer** *-en, pl -e* (=***/berar**) carrier (of the bacteria of a disease).
ba′sis *-en* basis, base: **på bred b-** on a broad basis.
ba′sisk *A - chem.* basic.
ba′sis/år *-et* base year (in statistical comparison).
bas'k[1] *-en/-et* 1 slap: **barnet fikk b-** the child got a spanking. 2 struggle.
***bas′k**[2] *A* 1 competent, good (**til å** at). 2: **ikkje (så) bask(en)** not bad at all.
bas'ke *V -a/+-et* 1 slap. 2 flap: **fuglen b-et med vingene** the bird flapped its wings. 3 struggle: **b- med et arbeid** struggle with a job; **b- seg fram gjennom snøen** fight one's way through the snow.
+**bas'ker** *-en, pl -e* (=***-ar**) Basque.
+**bas'ker/lue** *-a* (=***-ar/**) beret.
bas'ke/tak *-et* scuffle: **det var et b- å få laksen på land** it was a struggle to land the salmon.
bas'kisk *A* - Basque.
bas'me[1] *-a/-en* a group of warp threads on a loom.
bas'me[2] *V -a/+-et* divide a warp into groups of threads.
bas/relieff [ba'/relief·] *-et, pl -/+-er* bas-relief.
bass′ *-en* bass; basso.
bass′/bar′yton *-en* bass baritone.
bas'se *-n* 1 big animal (orig. male bear); big specimen. 2 big, strong man. 3 unruly person (cf **vill/**). 4 (endearing word) boy, man, used in address: **b-n min** darling.
basseng′ *-et, pl -/+-er* basin (outdoor water tank or pool; topographical formation).
+**basseral'le** *-n* gay party.
bassis′t *-en* bass singer, player.
bas't *+-en/*-et* vegetable fibers such as cocoa, flax, hamp, raffia.
bas'ta *I* (to stop further argument) enough, period: **og dermed b-** and that's that.
bastan′t *A* - hefty, solid, strong: **et b- måltid** a h- meal.
bastar′d *-en* hybrid, mongrel.
bas'te *V -a/+-et* bind, tie: **b-et og bundet** tied and bound, trussed up.
bastio′n *-en* bastion.
°**bas'tu** *-a* cf **bad/stue**
basu′n *-en* trombone; (in bibl. language) trumpet: **blåse, støte i b- for en** toot the horn for sby; **blåse i b- for seg selv** blow one's own horn.
basu′n/engel *-elen, pl -ler* cherub (often depicted, e.g. on tombstones, blowing a trumpet).
basune′re *V -te*: **b- ut en hemmelighet** broadcast a secret.
basu′n/røst *-a/+-en* (=***/røyst**) clarion voice, stentorian voice.
batal'je *-n* brawl, fight.
bataljo′n *-en* battalion.
bataljo′ns/sjef *-en* battalion commander.
ba'te[1] *-n* advantage, benefit, good.
ba'te[2] *V -a/+-et* avail: ***det b-a ikkje stort** it didn't do much good.
***ba'teleg** *A* - useful.
batis′t *-en* batiste.
ba'tne *V -a/+-et* 1 become better, improve. 2 avail, have the desired effect.
batong′ *-en* billy club, night stick.
***batt′** *pt of* **binde**
bat′tens/tømmer *-et* logs ready for processing.
batteri′ *-et, pl +-er/*-* battery (**av** of).
batteris′t *-en* percussionist, drummer (in a band).
°**bau′** *-en* cf **baug**
bau′ḍ *pt of* **byde**
bau′/fil *-a* hacksaw.
bau′g̣ *-en* bow (of a ship).
+**bau′g̣/spryd** *-et* (=***/spryt**) bowsprit.
***bau'ke** *V -a* 1 (of animal) burrow, dig. 2 (of waters, sea) run high. 3 (of boat, ship) be tossed; **ride** rough sea. 4 work in a rough, noisy manner; roll, romp (e.g. of children playing in snow).
bauksitt′ *-en* bauxite.
***bau'le** *V -a* (esp. of cattle) bellow, low.
baun(e)[1] [bau'n, bau'ne] *-(e)n* beacon fire to warn of an approaching enemy.
***bau'ne**[2] *-a* cf **bønne**
***bau's** *A* 1 burly, stalwart; nimble. 2 proud; impetuous, inconsiderate.
bau'se[1] *-n* 1 burly, stalwart person. 2 important, proud person.
bau'se[2] *V -a/+-et/*-te dial* 1 make one's way recklessly, inconsiderately, regardless of obstacles: **b- på** rush (blindly) on. 2 speak openly and roughly, without mincing words: **b- ut med noe** blurt sth out.
bau′t *-en naut.* tack: **gå b-, gjøre (en) b-** come about.
bau'ta *-en* =**bautastein**
bau'ta/stein *-en* tall, roughly cut stone monument.
bau'te *V -a/+-et naut.* tack; come about.
bauxitt′ *-en* cf **bauksitt**
bavia′n *-en* baboon.
bav'l *-et* stupid talk; nonsense.
bav'le *V -a/+-et* talk stupidly; babble.
bay'er *-en* bottle of lager beer (=**b-/øl**).
Bay'ern *Pln* Bavaria.
bay'ersk *A* - Bavarian.
bay'er/øl *-et* lager beer (half-dark).
+**bay'rer** *-en, pl -e* (=***-ar**) Bavarian.
bd. =**bind**/***band**
be′ *V bad, bedt* (=***bede**) 1 ask (**om** for) beg, implore, request: **be en om noe** ask sby for sth; **be en (om å) gjøre noe** ask, tell sby to do sth; **be tynt** beg, implore; **be for seg** ask for mercy, for peace; **be om godt vær** ask to make up; **be om lov** ask for permission; **be om ordet** ask

+ Bokmål; * Nynorsk; ° Dialect.
After letter: ′ stress (Acc. 1); ' tone, stress (Acc. 2); · length.
Below letter: . not pronounced.

permission to speak; **be om unnskyldning** apologize; **(å) jeg ber** not at all, it is quite all right, you are welcome; please; **han lot seg ikke be to ganger** he did not need to be asked twice; **hvem har bedt deg om å ...** who asked you to ...; **bedende** entreating(ly), imploring(ly). 2 pray: **be til Gud** pray, say one's prayers; **be bordbønn** say grace. 3 ask, invite: **bli bedt** (or: **buden) i selskap hos en** be invited to sby's home for a party; **jeg er bedt ut** I have been invited out. 4: **be farvel** take leave.

+**be'/arbeide** [also -bei'de] *V -de/-et* 1 work, work up; process (e.g. raw material, data). 2 adapt (a book), arrange (music). 3 try to persuade: **b- en kunde** work on a customer (to buy sth).

+**be'/arbei'delse** [also -bei'-] *-n* 1 processing. 2 adaptation.

°**be'ar/mann** *-en, pl -menn/*-menner* person whose function it was to invite people e.g. to christenings, weddings, and funerals.

beatri'se *-n* portable kerosene burner for cooking.

+**bebo'** *V -dde* inhabit.

+**bebo'elig** *A* - habitable.

+**bebo'elses/hus** *-et* dwelling house.

+**bebo'er** *-en, pl -e* dweller; occupant.

+**bebrei'de** *V -et* reproach, upbraid; blame: **b-ende** reproachful.

+**bebrei'delse** *-n* reproach: **rette b-r mot en** direct criticism at sby.

+**bebril'let** *A* - bespectacled.

+**bebu'de** *-et* announce, herald, proclaim.

+**bebu'delse** *-n* announcement: **Maria b-** the Annunciation of the Virgin Mary.

+**bebyg'ge** *V -bygde* 1 build up: **b- et distrikt** build up an area. 2 colonize.

+**bebyg'gelse** *-n* 1 building(s). 2 built-up area; **byens gamle b-** the old part of the town. 3 colonization.

+**bebyr'de** *-et* burden.

***be'd**[1] *-en* bed, layer; (earthen) floor; (straw) mattress.

bed'[2] *-et* flowerbed.

***be'd**[3] *pr of* **bede**

+**beda'ge** *-et*: **b- seg** (of weather) clear.

+**beda'gelig** *A* - calm, unruffled; slow: **røyken steg b- opp av pipa** the smoke rose lazily from the chimney; **et b- tempo** an easy tempo.

+**beda'get** *A* - aged, elderly.

***be'd(ar)/lag** *-et* 1 circle of farms who invite each other, esp. to weddings and funerals. 2 country dance for which invitations are sent.

***bedd'** *pp of* **be**

bed'ding *-a/+-en naut.* berth, (building) slip, slipway.

be'de [*be'e] *V bad, bedt/*bede/*-i* cf **be**

be'de/dag *-en* Day of Prayer (Sunday before All Saints' Day).

be'de/hus *-et* (religious) meeting house.

+**bedek'ke** *V -et/-dekte* (=*-je) (of male animals) cover, mount, service.

bedek'ning *-a/+-en* 1 service, servicing (of a female animal). 2 cover, covering.

***be'del** *-en* 1 person whose function it is to invite to a party. 2 suitor. 3 engaged man who is soon to marry.

be'de/mann *-en, pl -menn/*-menner* 1 person whose function it was to deliver invitations to social functions, and to arrange funerals. 2 gloomy, unctuous person.

be'demanns/ansikt *-et* lugubrious face; funereal countenance.

+**be'dende** *A* - cf **be**

+**beder'velig** *A* - perishable.

+**beder'vet** *A* - (=-a) (of food) spoiled.

be'de/skammel *-elen, pl -skamler* prayer stool.

***be'ding** *-a* asking; praying; inviting.

***be'd/lag** *-et* cf **bedar/**

bedra' *V -drog, -dradd/-dratt* (=*-drage) deceive, defraud, swindle: **b- en for penger** s- sby out of money; **b- sin kone** be unfaithful to one's wife; **skinnet b-r** appearances are deceiving; **verden vil b-s** a sucker always comes back for more.

bedra'g *-et* 1 deceit, fraud, swindle. 2 illusion.

***bedra'ge** *V -drog, -drege/-i* cf **bedra**

+**bedra'ger** *-en, pl -e* (=*-ar) swindler.

+**bedrageri'** *-et* deceit, fraud, swindle.

+**bedra'gerske** *-n* female swindler.

+**be'dre**[1] *V -a/-et* (=*betre[2]) 1 better, improve: **b- sine kår** b- one's condition; **Gud b-** Lord help us; worse luck, unfortunately. 2: **b-es** get better, get well.

+**be'dre**[2] *cp of* **god** (=*betre[3])

***bedre'ge** *pp of* **-drage** (=-i)

+**bedre(i)'v** *pt of* **-drive**

+**be'dre/stil(le)t** *A* -: **de b-te** the moneyed classes, the well-to-do.

+**bedre'vet** *pp of* **-drive**

bedrif't *+-en/*-a* 1 achievement, accomplishment; noble deed: **øve store b-er** perform great deeds. 2 (industrial) concern.

bedrif'ts/lege *-n* company doctor.

bedrif'ts/råd *-et* workers' council in an industrial concern.

+**bedrif'ts/utval'g** *-et* (=*/utval) workers' committee.

bedrif'ts/økonomi' *-en* study of business economics.

+**be'dring** *-en* (=*betring) betterment; improvement: **god b-** (wishing you) a speedy recovery, get well soon; **i b-** getting better, recovering.

+**bedri've** *V -dre(i)v, -drevet* commit (an act): **b- hor** commit adultery.

bedro'g *pt of* **-dra**

+**bedrø've** *-et* grieve, sadden: **b-t** grieved; **et b-t ansikt** a sad face.

+**bedrø'velig** *A* - 1 sad, deplorable: **en b- situasjon** a deplorable situation; **en b- historie** a sad story. 2 miserable, sorry: **et b- syn** a sorry sight.

+**bedrø'velse** *-n* grief, sadness.

bedt' *pp of* **be(de)**

+**bedug'get** *A* - (=+-a) inebriated, tipsy.

bedui'n *-en* Bedouin.

+**bedy're** *V -et/-te* assert: **b- sin uskyld** declare one's innocence.

+**bedøm'me** *V -dømte* appraise, judge: **b- eksamensoppgaver** grade exams; **b- en situasjon** a- a situation.

+**bedøm'melse** *-n* appraisal, evaluation; grading (of examination papers).

bedø've *V -de/+-et* 1 numb, stun, stupefy. 2 anesthetize.

bedø'ving *-a/+-en* (=+-else) anesthetization: **få b-** get an anesthetic, be anesthetized.

bedø'vings/middel *-elet/-midlet, pl +-midler/*-el* anesthetic.

+**bedå're** *V -et* charm, fascinate: **b-ende** charming, delightful.

+**bee'dige** *V -et* swear to: **en b-et erklæring** a sworn statement.

befa'l *-et* 1 junior officers and noncommissioned officers. 2 all leaders of any given military unit.

befa'le *V -te* 1 command, order: **b- en å gjøre noe** o- sby to do sth; **b- over store ressurser** have c- of great resources. 2 commit (to sby's care): **b- sin sjel til Gud** c- one's soul to God.

+**befa'l/havende** *A* - commanding (officer).

befa'ling *-a/+-en* command, order: **ha b- over en avdeling** c- a unit; **gi en b-** give an o-.

befa'lings/mann *-en, pl -menn/*-menner* military officer.

befa'ls/ele'v *-en* trainee of a military academy working towards rank of sergeant.

befa'ls/skole *-n* (=*/skule) military academy for non-commissioned officers.

+**befan't** *pt of* **-finne**

+**befa're** *V -te* inspect.

+**befa'ring** *-a/-en* inspection.

+**befat'ning** *-en* concern, connection, involvement: **ha b- med** have dealings with.

+**befat'te** *V -et*: **b- seg med noe** be concerned with sth; **jeg b-er meg ikke med denslags** I stay clear of such things.

+**befeng't** *A* - infested (**med** with).

+**befer'det** *A* - frequented; crowded: **en b- gate** a crowded street.

+**befes'te** *V -et* fortify, make secure, strengthen: **b- sin posisjon** assure, fortify one's position; **b- en by** fortify a town.

+**befes'tet** *A* - 1 clarified, made definite: **et b- inntrykk** a definite impression. 2 fortified.

+**befes'tning** *-en* fortification.

+**befin'ne** *V -fant, -funnet* 1 *obs.* find: **b-es** be found (to be). 2 *(refl.)* **b- seg** be; feel: **jeg b-er meg vel** I am well, I feel fine; **vi b-er oss i et hus** we are (find ourselves) in a house.

+**befin'nende** *et* state of health: **spørre om ens b-** ask about the state of one's health.

+**befip'pelse** *-n* disconcertion, perplexity.

+**befip'pet** *A* - flustered, perplexed.

+**befiit'te** *V -et*: **b- seg på noe** try, make an effort to be (do) sth.

+**befol'ke** *V -a/-et* populate.

+**befol'kning** *-en* populace, population.

+**befol'knings/lag** *-et* stratum of the population; class level.

+**befol'knings/tetthet** *-en* density of population.

+**befor'dre** *V -et* 1 send, transport. 2 *obs.* promote (e.g. a cause): **b-ende** beneficial.

+**befor'dring** *-a/-en* 1 transportation. 2 means of transportation.

+**befor'drings/middel** *-elet/-midlet, pl -midler* means of conveyance.

+**befra'kte** *V -a/-et* charter.

+**befrak'ter** *-en, pl -e* charterer (of a ship).

+**befrak'tning** *-en* chartering (of a ship).

+**befri'** *V -dde* free, liberate, release: **en b-ende følelse** feeling of relief.

+**befri'else** *-n* liberation, release (**fra** from): **det kom som en b-** it came as a relief.

+**befri'er** *-en, pl -e* liberator.

+**befruk'te** *V -a/-et* 1 fertilize, inseminate. 2 stimulate: **virke b-ende** have a stimulating effect.

+**befruk'tning** *-en* fertilization, insemination.

+**befruk'tnings/hindrende** *A* - contraceptive.

+**befryk'te** *V -et* be apprehensive, fear: **det er å b-** it is to be feared.

+**befullmek'tiget** *A* - empowered.

+**befun'net** *pp of* **-finne**

+**beføy'else** *-n* grounds, justification.

begav [bega'] *pt of* **-gi**

+**bega'velse** *-n* 1 gift, talent. 2 gifted person: **han er en stor b-** he is brilliant.

+**bega'vet** *A* - gifted.

+**begei'stre** *V -a/-et* inspire: **b-et** enthusiastic (**for** about).

+**begei'string** *-a/-en* enthusiasm: **vekke b-** arouse e-.

be'ger *-eret, pl -er/+-re* (=*bekar) 1 beaker; chalice: **svinge b-et** carouse, celebrate; **dette var dråpen som fikk b-et til å flyte over** this was the last straw. 2 *bot.* calyx. 3 cup (trophy).

+**be'ger/blad** *-et bot.* sepal.

be'ger/klang *-en* clinking of glasses; sounds of drinking.

+**be'ger/svinger** *-en, pl -e* (=*-ar) beerslinger, elbow bender, heavy drinker.

beg'ge *Pn* 1 both: **b- deler** both; **b- to** both; **vi (de) begge** both of us (them); **skal vi komme b- to?** shall we b- come? 2 either: **i b- tilfelle** in either case; **de kan b- ha gjort det** either of them could have done it.

begi' *V -gav, -gitt* (=***-gje(ve)**) +1 *naut.* leave, quit: **b- sjøen** leave the sea. 2: **b- seg** abate, quiet down (of a storm). 3 *bibl.* come to pass: **og det begav seg i de dager** and it came t- p- in those days (Luke 2,1). 4 go, proceed: **b- seg av sted (på vei)** set out, start out.
+**begikk'** *pt of* **-gå**
+**begi'ven/het** *-en* event, occurrence: **en lykkelig b-** a happy e-; **avvente b-enes gang** suspend judgment, wait and see.
+**begi'venhets/løs** *A* uneventful.
***begje'(ve)** *V -gav, -gjeve/-i* cf **-gi**
+**begjæ'r** *-et* strong desire; lust.
+**begjæ're** *V -te* 1 desire, want strongly. 2 covet: **du skal ikke b- din nestes hus** thou shalt not c- thy neighbor's house. 3 request: **b- ordet** ask for the floor; **b- utkastelse** start eviction proceedings.
+**begjæ'ring** *-a/-en* demand; request.
+**begjæ'rlig** *A* - desirous: **være b- etter** to want, desire; **drikke b-** drink avidly, eagerly.
+**begjæ'rlig/het** *-en* avidity, greed; eagerness.
+**beglo'** *V -dde* gape at, stare at.
bego'nia *-iaen, pl -ier bot.* begonia.
+**begra've** *V infl as* **grave** bury.
+**begra'velse** *-n* funeral.
+**begra'velses/byrå·** *-et* funeral home.
+**begre'delig** *A* - mournful.
+**begren'se** *V -a/-et* bound, limit, restrict: **b-ede midler** limited means.
+**begren'sning** *-en* limit, limitation; restriction: **kjenne sin (egen) b-** know one's (own) limitations.
+**begre'p**[1] *-et, pl -/-er* 1 concept, conception; idea, notion: **b-et synd** the concept of sin; **danne seg et b- om noe** form an idea of sth; **jeg har ikke b- om hvor han er** I have no idea where he is. 2: **stå, være i b- med å gjøre noe** be on the point of doing sth.
+**begre'p**[2] *pt of* **-gripe**
+**begre'ps/forvir'ring** *-en* confusion of ideas.
+**begri'pe** *V -grep, -grepet* grasp, understand: **jeg b-er ikke noe av dette** I can't make head or tail of this; **b- seg på noe** have an understanding of sth.
+**begri'pelig** *A* - comprehensible: **gjøre en noe b-** make sth clear to sby.
+**begri'pelig/vis** *Av* certainly, of course; obviously.
+**begri'pelse** *-n* comprehension: **det går over min b-** it is beyond my c-; **være langsom i b-n** be slow-witted.
+**begrodd'** *A* - overgrown; (of ships) barnacled.
+**begro'v** *pt of* **-grave**
+**begrun'delse** *-n* cf **begrunnelse**
+**begrun'ne** *V -et* 1 state the reasons for, give the grounds for; justify. 2 base on: **vel b-et** well-founded; **b- sin mening på** base one's opinion on.
+**begrun'nelse** *-n* basis; grounds, justification: **med den b- at** on the g- that.
+**begun'stige** *V -et* show favor to.
+**begun'stigelse** *-n* favor, preferential treatment.
begyn'ne *V -gynte* begin, start (**å** to); commence, initiate, open: **b- med (på) noe** start (on) sth; **til å b- med** to begin with, at the start; **b- på fabrikk** start working in a factory; **b- på nytt** start over again; **b- på skolen** start school; **det b-er å bli mørkt** it's getting dark; **vel b-t er halvt fullendt** well begun is half done.
+**begyn'nelse** *-n* (=***-ing**) beginning, start (**av, til** of): **all b- er vanskelig** the first step is the hardest; **fra b-n (av)** from the outset; **i b-n var ordet** in the b- was the Word (St. John 1:1); **helt i b-n** right at first; **b-n til enden** the b- of the end.
+**begyn'ner** *-en, pl -e* (=***-ar**) beginner.
+**begyn'ner/lønn** *-a/-en* (=***-ar/**) beginning salary.

+**begå'** *V infl as* **gå** commit: **b- en feil, et mord** c- an error, a murder.
+**beha'g** *-et* pleasure: **etter b-** according to taste; **smak og b- kan ikke disputeres** there is no accounting for tastes.
+**beha'ge** *V -et* 1 please, win favor: **kunsten å b-** the art of p-ing; **det b-er meg ikke** it does not p- me; (with **å**) I do not choose to. 2 please to, choose to, deign to (do sth): **behag å sitte ned** p- sit down; **hva b-er?** I beg your pardon (when asking sby to repeat).
+**beha'gelig** *A* - comfortable; pleasant: **gjøre seg livet b-** make oneself c-.
***behal'd** *en* cf **-hold**
***behal'dar** *-en* cf **-holder**
***behal'de** *V infl as* **halde** cf **-holde**
behan'dle *V -a/+-et* handle; deal with, treat: **du må b- boka pent** you must h- the book carefully; **b- en med silkehansker** h- sby with kid gloves; **b- en sykdom, en pasient** treat a disease, a patient.
behan'dling *-a/+-en* treatment; handling: **ta under b-** treat (medically); take (a matter) up for consideration.
behan'dlings/måte *-n* treatment; therapy.
+**behe'fte** *V -et* burden, encumber; mortgage.
***behe'ldt** *pt of* **-halde**
+**behen'dig** *A* - agile, deft, nimble; ingenious.
+**behen'dig/het** *-en* agility, deftness, nimbleness; ingenuity.
+**beher'ske** *V -a/-et* 1 govern, rule; control: **b- seg** control oneself. 2 have a command of, master: **b- situasjonen** be master of the situation; **han b-er språket** he has a good command of the language.
+**beher'skelse** *-n* control; restraint, self-control.
+**behers'ket** *A* - controlled; restrained, self-controlled.
+**behjel'pelig** *A* -: **være en b- med (å gjøre) noe** be of assistance to sby in (doing) sth.
+**behjer'tet** *A* - (=+**-a**) brave, courageous.
+**behol'd** *en* (=***-hald**): **i b-** intact; **i god b-** safe and sound; **jeg har mine ord i b-** what I said still stands.
+**behol'de** *V -holdt* (=***-halde**) keep, retain: **la en b- livet** spare sby's life; **b- seieren** win the battle, gain the day.
+**behol'der** *-en, pl -e* (=***-haldar**) container, receptacle, vessel.
+**behol'dning** *-en* 1 stock; supply, supplies; holdings. 2 balance, cash: **kontant b-** cash on hand. 3 remainder.
beho'v *-et* need, necessity, requirement: **dekke b-et** meet the needs; **etter b-** as required.
beho'vs/prøve *-a/+-en* investigation of need.
+**behø'rig** *A* - due, proper: **vise b- respekt** show due respect.
+**behø've** *V -de* need: **du b-er ikke å gå** you don't have to leave; **dette b-er ikke å være tilfelle** this is not necessarily so; **det b-es ikke** it is not necessary.
°**behø'velig** *A* - necessary.
be'/hå *-en* bra (abbr. for **bysteholder** brassiere).
Bei'arn *Pln* twp, Nordland.
***bei'd** *pt of* **bide**
beige [be'sj] *A* - beige.
+**bei'le** *V -et* (=***bele**) 1 court, woo. 2 propose marriage.
+**bei'ler** *-en, pl -e* (=***belar**) suitor.
bei'n[1] *-et* 1 bone: **han har b- i nesen** he has plenty of backbone, a will of his own. 2 foot, leg: **hele byen er på b-a** the whole town is astir; **komme med (sette) det gale b-et ut av sengen** get out on the wrong side of bed; **komme ned på b-a** land on one's feet, come out smelling like a rose; **komme seg på b-a** get to (on) one's feet; **pengene fikk b- å gå på** the money took wings; **spenne b- for en** trip sby, place obstacles in sby's path; **stille en armé på b-a** raise an army; **stå på egne b-** stand on one's own two feet; **være dårlig til b-s** have difficulty walking; **være rask (lett) til b-s** be quick-footed; **være våt på b-a** have wet feet.
+**bei'n**[2] *A* straight; direct: **b-t fram** absolute, out and out; **gå b-este veien** take the shortest road; **gå b-t på** go s- ahead; **gå b-t på sak** not beat around the bush; **si b-t ut** put bluntly, plainly; **han svarte b-t nei** he gave a flat no.
°**bei'naug** *A* - cf **beinig**
bei'n/brott *-et* leg fracture.
bei'n/bygning *-a/+-en* (=+**ben/**, ***/bygnad**) bone structure.
bei'ne[1] *-a* help: **han gjorde meg ei b-** he did me a service.
***bei'ne**[2] *V -a* smooth, level.
bei'net(e) *A* - bony.
bei'n/fly *V infl as* **fly** dash, run.
bei'n/fri *A -tt* boned, boneless.
bei'n/grind *-a* skeleton.
bei'n/grov [+/gråv] *A* heavy-boned.
bei'n/ha·rd *A* hard as bone.
bei'nig** *A* - (=-ug**) helpful.
bei'ning *-a* 1 help, service; good turn. 2 *(pl)* gift.
bei'nke[1] *-a* (=+**benke**[1]) good turn.
bei'nke[2] *V -a/+-et* (=+**benke**[2]) straighten out.
bei'n/kløyvd *A* /* *kløyvd* (of wood) clean-splitting.
bei'n/laus *A* boned, boneless: **b-e (benløse) fugler** veal birds (using beef).
bei'n/leies *Av* the direct way.
bei'n/lim *-et* animal glue.
bei'n/mjøl *-et* bone meal.
bei'n/pipe *-a* shaft of the bone.
bei'n/rad *-a/+-en* skeleton.
bei'n/rangel *-elet/-let, pl +-ler/*-el* skeleton.
***bei'n/sam** *A* helpful.
+**bei'n/skinne** *-a* (=***/skjene**) splint.
bei'n/skjør *A* (=***/skøyr**) brittle-boned.
***bei'nsleg** *A* - direct, straight; straightforward.
***bei'n/styren** *A -e/-i, pl -ne* 1 going on a straight course. 2 (of persons) hard-driving, single-minded; straightforward.
bei'nt/fram *Av* (=**beint fram**) 1 straight (ahead); direct (e.g. of course). 2 letter-perfect. 3 frankly. 4 easy: **det var ikke alltid så b- for ham** it was not always e- for him. 5 absolutely: **det er b- kriminelt** it is a- criminal.
***bei'nug** *A* - cf **beinig**
bei'n/ved *-en bot.* holly; (Ilex aquifolium).
bei'n/veg *-en* (=+**/vei**) short-cut.
bei'n/veges *Av* directly.
bei's *-en* stain.
bei'se *V -a/-et/+-te* stain (wood).
***bei'sel** *-elet/-let* cf **beksel**
bei'sk *A* (=+**besk**) (of taste) bitter, sharp; *fig.* biting, cutting, scornful.
°**bei'skede** *I* (=**beiskade**) by gosh, goldarn.
***bei'skleg** *Av* bitterly; awfully.
bei'sk/leik *-en* bitterness.
bei'skne *V -a* (=+**beskne**) grow bitter, sharp.
***bei'sle** *V -a* cf **beksle**
bei'st *-et* animal, beast.
bei't[1] *-a/+-en* groove (esp. on underside of ski).
bei't[2] *-a* difficulty, dilemma: **være i b- for noe** be in need of sth; **gå b-** lose out.
bei't[3] *-a* 1 pasture. 2 twigs cut for animal fodder.

+ Bokmål; * Nynorsk; ° Dialect.
After letter: ' stress (Acc. 1); ` tone, stress (Acc. 2); · length.
Below letter: . not pronounced.

bei't[4] pt of bite[3]
bei'te[1] -a bait.
bei'te[2] -t, pl +-r/*- pasture.
bei'te[3] V -a/+-et/-te graze.
bei'tel -elen, pl -ler chisel.
bei'te/land -et (=beites/) pasture.
bei'te/mark[1] -en (=/makk) night crawler used for bait.
bei'te/mark[2] -a (=beites/) pasture.
bei'te/rett -en pasture rights.
bei'tes/land -et cf beite/
bei'tes/mark -a cf beite/[2]
bei'ting -a pasturing.
bei't/ski(e) -a plank used to frame door or window and support log ends.
Bei't/stad Pln twp, Nord-Trøndelag.
*beitt' A - 1 (of tool) sharp. 2 (of fish) biting; fig. eager (for sth).
be'k -et pitch.
*be'kar -en cf beger
*be'kar/blad -et cf beger/
be'k/blende -n/*-a pitchblende.
be'ke V -a/+-et/+-te apply pitch to.
be'kende Av pitch (dark, black).
be'ket(e) A - pitch-stained.
+bekjem'pe V -et combat, fight against.
+bekjem'pelse -n combat, struggle: b-n av kreft the combatting of cancer.
+bekjen'delse -n cf bekjennelse
+bekjen'ne V -kjente confess; admit.
+bekjen'nelse -n confession.
+bekjen'nelses/tro A - strictly orthodox
+bekjen'ner -en, pl -e true believer.
+bekjen't A - 1 famous, noted, well-known (for for): som b- as everyone knows; du kan ikke være b- av den hatten you can't be seen with that hat. 2 acquainted, familiar (med with): gjøre seg b- med familiarize oneself with; må jeg gjøre Dem b- med may I introduce you to. 3 (noun) acquaintance: en god b- a close a-; mange b-e many a-s.
+bekjen't/gjøre V -gjorde, -gjort announce.
+bekjen't/skap -et acquaintance (med with); gjøre, stifte b- med get acquainted with; ved nærmere b- on closer a-.
+bekjen'tskaps/krets -en circle of acquaintances.
bekk' -en, pl *-er brook, creek.
bekkasi'n -en zool. snipe (Capella).
bek'ke/blom [+/blåmm] +-men/*-en bot. marsh marigold, cowslip (Caltha palustris).
bek'ke/far -et creek bed.
bek'ken -et, pl -/+-er 1 basin; bedpan. 2 anat. pelvis. 3 mus. cymbal.
bek'ken/bein -et pelvis.
bek'ket(e) A - cf beket(e)
+bekla'ge V -de/-et 1 pity, (be) sorry for. 2 regret, (be) sorry (about). 3 (refl.) b- seg complain (til to; over about): tro ikke at jeg b-er meg don't think I'm c-ing.
+bekla'gelig A - deplorable, regrettable.
+bekla'gelse -n regret.
+bekla'gelses/verdig A - pitiable.
+bekle' V -dde/-dte 1 cover; line. 2 occupy: b- et embete o- an official position.
+bekle'de V -de cf bekle
+bekle'dning -en clothing; planking.
+bekle'dnings/gjenstand -en garment.
+beklem'mende A - depressing, disheartening, oppressive.
+beklem't A - anxious, uneasy.
+beklip'pe V -klipte cut; trim; abridge.
be'k/mørk A pitch-dark.
be'k/mørke -t (=*/mørker) pitch-darkness.
bekni'p et (=*-knep) pinch, tight spot: være i b- be in a jam.
+bekom'me V -kom, -kommet 1: b- en vel (e.g. of food) agree with sby; b- en ille disagree with sby; vel b- you are welcome (only as reply to takk for maten after meals); (ironically) take it and welcome, much good may it do you. 2 archaic receive.
+bekom'st en: han fikk sin b- he got what he had coming to him.
+bekos'te V -et assume the costs of, pay for.
+bekos'tning -en expense: på vår b- at our e-.
+bekran'se V -et crown with a wreath, wreathe: b- en grav lay a wreath at a grave.
bek're[1] -n ram.
bek're[2] V -a bleat.
+bekref'te V -et confirm: b-ende affirming, c-ing; affirmative.
+bekref'telse -n affirmation, confirmation, corroboration.
*be'k/saum -en cf /søm
bek'sel -elet/-let, pl -el/+-ler bit; bridle.
bek'sle V -a/+-et bridle (a horse).
be'k/svart A - pitch-black.
+bek'søm' -men (=*/saum) method of fastening the sole of a boot with cobbler's thread, without using pegs.
+bek'søm/sko -en, pl -/-r (=*-saum) heavy sport shoe, ski boot.
+bek'søm/støvel -elen, pl -ler (=*-saum/) ski boot.
be'k/tråd -en cobbler's thread (thread treated with pitch).
+bekvem' A -t, pl -me 1 comfortable: gjøre seg det b-t make oneself c-. 2 convenient.
+bekvem'me V -et: b- seg til å gjøre noe bring oneself to do sth.
+bekvem'melig/het -en comfort, convenience: moderne b-er modern c-s (facilities).
+bekvem'meligһets/hensyn -et consideration of convenience.
+bekym're V -a/-et trouble, worry: det skal du (bare) ikke b- deg om do not w- about it, that is none of your concern; b-et worried; jeg er b-et for ham I am concerned about him.
+bekym'ring -a/-en anxiety, worry.
+bekym'rings/full A 1 troubled (e.g. expression). 2 worrisome.
+bekym'rings/løs A carefree, untroubled; (adv.) without a care.
*be'l[1] -en cf beiler
be'l[2] -et dial. while: et lite b- a little w-.
bela' pt of -legge
+bela'ge V -et: b- seg på noe prepare for sth.
*be'lar -en cf beiler
+belas'te V -a/-et 1: være arvelig b-et med en sykdom have an inherited tendency toward a disease; han er arvelig b-et it runs in his family. 2 charge, debit (e.g. an account); load (e.g. a circuit).
+belas'tning -en (=*-ing) 1: arvelig b- hereditary weakness. 2 charge, debit; load, loading.
*be'le[1] -n cf beiler
*be'le[2] V -a cf beile
*be'le[3] V -a 1 fail. 2 suffice, be enough.
belegg' -et 1 coating, covering: ha b- på tungen have a coated tongue. 2 instance, occurrence (e.g. of a word): ha b- for have examples of. 3 binding, trimming. 4 number of persons: hotellet (sykehuset) har fullt b- the hotel (hospital) is filled to capacity.
+beleg'ge V -la, -lagt (=*-je) 1 coat, cover. 2 occupy; reserve: b- en plass save a place. 3 make fast (boat). 4 document: ordet er ikke belagt før 1500 the word is not found prior to 1500. 5: b- sine ord choose one's words.
+belei'lig A - convenient, opportune; at the right moment.
+belei're V -et besiege.
+belei'ring -a/-en siege.
+belem're V -et 1 clutter. 2 burden.
+beles'se V -et/-te load down.
+bele'st A - widely read.
+bele'ven A -ent, pl -ne courteous, polite.
+bele'ven/het -en courtesy, consideration.
bel'g -en, pl *-er 1 bot. pod. 2 bellows. 3 unsplit animal skin (e.g. of fox). 4 big belly.
*bel'ge V -a cf belgje
+bel'gende Av: b- mørkt pitch-dark.
°bel'ge/spell -et accordion.
+bel'ge/treder -en, pl -e (=*-ar, */trøar) person who pumps the bellows of an organ.
bel'g/flå V -dde skin an animal without splitting the skin.
bel'g/frukt -a/+-en legume.
Bel'gia Pln Belgium.
+bel'gier -en, pl -e (=*-ar) Belgian.
bel'gisk A - Belgian.
*bel'gje V -a (=*belge, +belje[2]) guzzle.
bel'g/mørk A pitch-dark.
bel'g/plante -a/+-en legume, leguminous plant.
bel'g/vott -en mitten.
+belig'gende A - located, situated.
+belig'gen/het -en location, site.
+beli'vet A - lively: et b- selskap a l- party.
bel'j -et/+-en bellow, roar.
bel'je[1] V -a/+-et bellow, roar.
+bel'je[2] V -a/+-et cf belgje
°bel'je/spell -et cf belge/
*bell' -en clapper.
*bel'le V belte 1 hold out, tolerate. 2 manage, be able to.
bel'ling -en 1 skin of the lower leg of an animal (esp. of moose or reindeer). 2 leg of boot or stocking.
bel'me V -a/+-et guzzle.
bel't -et sound, strait.
bel'te -t, pl +-r/*- belt.
bel'te/bil -en caterpillar (tractor); weasel.
bel'te/dyr -et zool. armadillo (Dasypus sexcinatus).
bel'te/spenne -a/+-en/-et belt buckle.
bel'te/spenning -a/+-en hist. duel with knives between two men strapped together.
+bel'te/sted -et (=*/stad) waist: under b-et below the belt.
+belu're V -te spy upon, watch secretly.
+bely'se V -te 1 illuminate. 2 elucidate, illustrate.
+bely'sning -en 1 lighting, illumination. 2 elucidation, illustration.
+belæ're V -te instruct, teach.
+belæ'rende A - instructive: et b- foredrag an i- talk; snakke i en b- tone speak in a didactic manner.
+beløn'ne V -et/-lønte reward; remunerate.
+beløn'ning -en reward: gutten fikk en kake som b- the boy got a cooky as a r-.
+belø'p -et amount of money.
+belø'pe V -løp, -løp(e)t: b- seg til amount to, total.
+belå'ne V -te mortgage, raise a loan on: huset er sterkt b-t the house is heavily m-d.
+beman'ne V -a/-et man.
+bemek'tige V -et: b- seg noe take possession of sth.
+bemer'ke V -a/-et 1 notice; become aware of: bemerk tidene note (opening, closing) hours; gjøre seg b-et draw attention to oneself. 2 remark: har De noe å b-? do you have any comment?
+bemer'kelses/verdig A - remarkable.
+bemer'kning -en remark.
+bemid'let A - well-off: en b- mann a man of means.
*bem'le V -a guzzle.
+bemyn'dige V -et authorize, empower.
+bemyn'digelse -n 1 authorization: ha b- til be authorized to; etter b- (in official letter) as authorized. 2 authority, power of attorney.
+bemøy'e V -de/-et: b- seg med noe take the trouble to do sth; take pains doing sth.
+be'n[1] -et cf bein[1]
+be'n[2] A cf bein[2]
+benau'et A - 1 uneasy, nervous. 2 sheepish.
+be'n/bygning -en cf bein/
ben'd -et: stå i b- be in a bent position.
*ben'de[1] -t 1 jerk. 2 bent position

(=**bend**). 3 tension; uncertainty (as to which side will win).

ben'de[2] *V -te* 1 to bend. 2 pry: **b- fra hverandre** p- apart; **b- med spettet** p- with the pry bar.

ben'del *-elen, pl -ler* 1=**bendelband.** 2 handful of straw for binding a sheaf of grain.

ben'del/band *-et* (twill)tape.

ben'del/orm *-en* tapeworm.

ben'dsel *-elet/-let, pl -el/+-ler naut.* seizing.

ben'dsle *V -a/+-et naut.* seize.

+**benedikti'ner** *-en, pl -e* (=***-tin(ar)**) 1 Benedictine. 2=**benediktiner-likør.**

+**benedikti'ner/likø'r** *-en* Benedictine (a liqueur orig. made at the Benedictine monastery of Fécamp).

+**benedikti'ner/munk** [/mongk] *-en* Benedictine monk.

+**benedikti'ner/ordenen** *df* the Order of St. Benedict.

benefi'se *-n* benefit performance.

benefise'rt *A -*: **b- gods** land assigned to a clergyman who received the profit from it as part of his salary; *jur.* **b- sak** case in which free legal aid has been granted.

+**benek'te** *V -a/-et* deny: **b- faktum** deny a fact.

+**benek'telse** *-n* denial.

+**benek'tende** *A -* negative: **svare b-** answer in the n-.

+**be'net(e)** *A -* cf **beinet(e)**

+**benev'ne** *V -te* 1 call, name; designate. 2: **b-t tall** number qualified as to its referent (e.g. $5, 7 lb.).

+**benev'ning** *-en* denomination: **omgjøre brøker til felles b-** change fractions to a common denominator.

benga'lsk *A -* Bengal: **b- belysning** Bengal light; **Den b-e bukt** the Bay of Bengal.

beng'el *-elen, pl -ler* lout, rascal, rogue: **din b-** you rascal.

***beng'le** *V -a* 1 work in an awkward, impractical manner. 2 walk unsteadily. 3 get in the way; create obstacles. 4 squabble.

ben'k *-en, pl *-er* bench (for sitting on, working at); pew, row: **første b-** first r-.

°**ben'ke**[1] *-a* cf **beinke**[1]

°**ben'ke**[2] *V -a/-et* cf **beinke**[2]

+**ben'ke**[3] *V -a/-et* (=***-je**) seat: **de b-et seg rundt bordet** they sat down around the table.

ben'ke/forslag *-et* esp. *pol.* motion from the floor.

+**ben'ke/gave** *-a/-en* (=***/gåve**) *hist.* gift fixed by negotiation and given by a bridegroom to his bride in her home previous to the marriage.

ben'ke/rad *-a/+-en* row of benches.

***ben'kje** *V -a* cf **benke**[3]

+**be'n/klær** *pl* trousers; panties: **lange b-** slacks.

+**be'n/løs** *A* cf **bein/laus**

+**be'n/pipe** *-n* cf **bein/**

+**be'n/rad** *-en* skeleton.

bensi'n *-en* gasoline.

bensi'n/stasjo'n *-en* gas station.

+**be'n/skjør** *A* cf **bein/**

ben'soe/syre *-a* benzoic acid.

benso'l *-en* benzene; benzol.

Ben't *Prn(m)*

Ben'te *Prn(f)*

+**be'n/vei** *-en* cf **bein/veg**

+**benyt'te** *V -et* make use of, use: **b- eksperter til arbeidet** employ experts for the job; **b- anledningen** take the opportunity; **b- seg av en** take advantage of sby.

+**benå'de** *V -et* pardon.

+**benå'dning** *-en* pardon, reprieve.

+**beor'dre** *V -et* assign; order: **b- en til å komme** order sby to come.

+**beplan'te** *V -et* plant (**med** with).

+**beplan'tning** *-en* 1 planting. 2 forest plantation; planted area.

***ber**[1] [bæ'r] *-et* cf **bær**

***ber**[2] [bæ'r] *pr of* **bere**[2]

***ber**[3] [bæ'r] *pr of* **berje**

+**beram'me** *V -et* assign, set: **b- en tid for møtet** fix a time for the meeting.

***berar** [bæ'rar] *-en* cf **bærer**

ber'ber *-en, pl +-e* Berber.

ber'beriss *-en bot.* barberry (Berberis vulgaris).

***bere**[1] [bæ're] *-a* 1 female bear. 2 big, rough woman.

***bere**[2] [bæ're] *V bar, bore/-i* cf **bære**[1]

°**be're**[3] *V* cf **bedre**[1]

°**be're**[4] *cp of* **god**

***bere/bår(e)** [bæ're/] *-a* cf **bære/**

+**bere'de** *V -te* 1 process: **b- huder** tan hides. 2 cause: **de b-te ham vanskeligheter** they c-d trouble for him. 3 prepare (sby) for death: **presten b-er den døende** the minister p-s the dying one for death.

+**bere'dning** *-en* processing; tanning (of leather).

+**bere'd/skap** *-en/-et* preparedness: **holde noe, seg i b-** keep sth, oneself in a state of p-; **militært b-** military p-.

+**bere'dskaps/lov** [/lå'v] *-en* defense law.

+**bere'dskaps/tjeneste** *-n* emergency military service.

+**beredt'** *A -* prepared: **han er b- til å gjøre det** he is p- to do it; **være b- på døden** be p- for death.

+**bere'd/villig** *A -* prompt, ready, willing: **b- imøtekommenhet** ready willingness.

+**bere'dvillig/het** *-en* promptness, readiness, willingness.

***bere/evne** [bæ're/] *-a* cf **bære/**

+**beregne** [-rei'ne] *V -a/-et* (=***-rek'ne**) 1 calculate=compute, figure: **b- omkostningene** c- the expenses. 2 calculate=estimate, expect: **b-et ankomst** estimated arrival; **b- virkningene av noe** calculate the effect of sth; **når b-er du å være framme** when do you expect to arrive. 3 intend for, take into account: **varene er b-et på eksport** the goods are intended for export; **b- sitt publikum** take one's audience into account. 4 *(refl.)* **b- seg** charge: **b- seg stor avanse** charge a high profit.

+**beregnende** [-rei'nene] *A -* calculating; scheming.

+**beregning** [-rei'ning] *-a/-en* (=***-rek'-ning**) 1 calculation; estimate: **b- av avanse** e- of profit; **ta med i b-en** take into consideration. 2 calculation, ingenuity: **han gjorde det bare av b-** he did it calculatedly, from ulterior motives.

+**berei'st** *A -* widely traveled.

***bere/stol** [bæ're/] *-en* cf **bære/**

***bere/stong** [bæ're/] *-a, pl -stenger* cf **bære/stang**

+**beret'ning** *-en* 1 account, report: **b- om rikets tilstand** state of the nation r-; **avlegge b-** present (e.g. annual) r-. 2 account, narrative.

+**beret'te** *V -et* narrate, relate, tell: **han visste å b- at de skulle skilles** according to him they were going to be divorced.

+**beret'ter** *-en, pl -e* narrator.

+**beret'tige** *V -et* justify, warrant: **skandalen b-er offentlig undersøkelse** this scandal w-s official investigation; **stillingen b-er til pensjon** the position entitles one to a pension.

+**beret'tigelse** *-n* justification: **anklagen var uten b-** the accusation was without j-.

ber'g *-et* 1 mountain: **over b- og dal** over hill and dale; **her på b-et** even out here in the sticks; **ta en i b-** (of mountain troll) lure sby into the m-. 2 rock: **grave seg ned på b-et** dig down to solid r-.

Ber'g *Pln* twps, Troms and Østfold.

bergamott' *-en bot.* bergamot (Citrus bergamia).

+**ber'g/arbei'der** *-en, pl -e* (=***-ar**) miner.

ber'g/blom [+/blåmm] *+-men/*-en bot.* mountain flower, esp. bergfrue (Saxifraga cotyledon).

***ber'g/drag** *-et* low mountain range.

ber'ge *V -a/+-et* 1 bring (crops etc.) into safekeeping: **b- høyet** bring in the hay; **b- et seil** take a sail in. 2 rescue, save: **b- skip** r- a ship; **b- livet** s- one's life. 3 *(refl.)* **b- seg** get along, manage: **han kunne ikke b- seg for å** he couldn't help.

ber'gelig *A -* 1 (of ship, cargo) which can be salvaged. 2 passable: **et b-utkomme** a p- living.

ber'ge/lønn *-a/+-en* (=***/løn**) salvage money.

ber'ge/mellom *Av* among the mountains; from one mountain to the next.

Ber'gen *Pln* city in Western Norway.

+**bergen'ser** *-en, pl -e* (=***-ar**) man from Bergen.

+**bergenserin'ne** *-a/-en* (=***-arinne**) woman from Bergen.

ber'gensk *A -* of, from, relating to Bergen.

ber'g/fast *A -* 1 (of rock projection) immovable because it is part of a rock stratum. 2 firm as a rock.

ber'g/flette *-a bot.* ivy (Hedera helix).

ber'g/folk *-et* 1 subterranean spirits living in the mountain. 2 miners.

ber'g/frue *-a bot.* mountain plant (Saxifraga cotyledon).

ber'g/gylte *-a zool.* ballan wrasse (Labrus berggylta).

ber'g/hammar *-en, pl -hamrer* cliff, crag.

ber'g/imel'lom *Av* cf **berge/mellom**

ber'ging *-a* 1 gathering; salvaging; rescue, salvation. 2 solution, way out: ***han såg inga b-** he couldn't see any w- o-. 3 food and means needed to survive; livelihood.

ber'gings/lønn *-a/+-en* cf **berge/**

ber'gings/mannskap *-et, pl -/+-er* salvage crew.

ber'gings/selskap *-et* salvage company.

ber'gings/von *-a* hope of rescue, salvation.

+**ber'g/kjede** *-n* mountain chain.

ber'g/kløft *-a/+-en* cleft in a mountain.

ber'g/knapp *-en bot.* sedum.

ber'g/knatt *-en* knoll.

ber'g/knaus *-en* knoll.

ber'g/krystall' *-en* rock crystal.

ber'g/lendt *A -* mountainous; rocky.

Ber'g/liot *Prn(f)*

ber'g/mann *-en, pl -menn/*-menner* miner.

+**ber'g/mester** *-eren, pl -ere/-rer* (=***/meister**) superintendent of mines.

ber'g/nabb *-en* crag.

ber'g/nebbe *-a zool.* a species of wrasse (Labrus rupestris).

+**ber'g/prekenen** *df* (=***/preika**) the Sermon on the Mount.

berg- og [å] **da'l/bane** *-n* roller coaster.

ber'g/rabb(e) *-(e)n* barren mountain ridge.

ber'g/rygg *-en* ridge of a mountain.

***ber'g/sam** *A* 1 thrifty. 2 helpful. 3 (of circumstances, object, place) adequate.

ber'g/sildre *-a bot.* saxifrage (Saxifraga).

ber'g/skort(e) [/skort(e)] *-a* canyon, defile; gulch, gully.

ber'g/skurd *-en* rock carving(s).

ber'g/stad *-en* mining town; **B-en Røros.**

ber'g/sugge *-a zool.* a species of wrasse (Labrus berggylta)=**berg-gylte.**

ber'g/ta *V -tok, -tatt* 1 (of mountain troll) lure into the mountain. 2 bewitch, cast a spell over: **han var b-tt av henne** he was under her spell.

+ Bokmål; * Nynorsk; ° Dialect.
After letter: ' stress (Acc. 1); ` tone, stress (Acc. 2); · length.
Below letter: . not pronounced.

ber'g/topp *-en* peak of a hill or a mountain.
ber'g/troll *-et* mountain troll.
ber'g/ugle *-a zool.* eagle owl (bubo bubo).
ber'g/vegg *-en, pl* ***-er** rock face of a cliff or a mountain.
ber'g/verk *-et* mine.
ber'gverks/drift *-a/-en* mining; mining industry.
be'ri-be'ri *N* beriberi.
+**beri'der** *-en, pl -e* circus rider.
+**beri'derske** *-a/-en* female circus rider.
+**beri'ke** *V -et* enrich: **b- seg på andres bekostning** e- oneself at other's expense; **føle seg b-et ved noe** feel e-ed by sth.
+**beri'kelse** *-n* enrichment.
+**berik'tige** *V -et* correct; rectify: **b- en feil** r- an error.
+**berik'tigelse** *-n* correction; rectification.
Be'rit *Prn (f)*
***ber'je** *V ber, barde, bart* **1** beat, pummel. **2** thresh with a flail. **3: b- på** work hard.
***ber'kje** *V -te* remove bark from log.
Ber'le/våg *Pln* twp, Finnmark.
berli'ner *-en, pl -e* (=***-ar**) inhabitant of Berlin.
+**berli'ner/blått** *et* (=***-ar/**) Prussian blue.
+**berli'ner/krans** *-en* (=***-ar/**) a kind of cooky ("butter rings").
ber'me *-n* (=***berm**) **1** dregs. **2** *fig.* dregs (of society), coarse people.
Ber'nt *Prn (m)*
+**bero'**[1] *N*: **sette, stille en sak i b-** suspend a matter, table a motion.
+**bero'**[2] *V -dde* **1** rest, wait; remain: **la saken b-** let the matter rest; **vi får la det b- med dette** this will have to do; **manuskriptet b-r hos forleggeren** the manuscript is being held by the publisher. **2** (with *prep.*) **det hele b-r på en misforståelse** the whole thing is due to a misunderstanding; **det b-r på været** it depends on the weather.
+**bero'lige** *V -et* calm down, quiet, soothe: **b- seg** set one's mind at rest; **b-ende middel** sedative.
+**bero'ligelse** *-n* reassurance, relief: **det er en b- å ha deg hjemme igjen** it is a relief to have you home again; **det er en b- å vite** it is a comfort to know.
+**bero'pe** *V -te*: **b- seg på noe** give sth as one's reason or excuse.
***berr'** *A bert* cf **bar**[3]
***berr'/baka** *A* - bareback.
***ber're**[1] *-a* bare spot in snow-covered ground; bare ground (when the snow is gone).
***ber're**[2] *V -a* bare.
***ber're**[3] *Av* cf **bare**[3]
***berr'/frost** *-en* cf **bar/**
***berr'/føtt** *A* - cf **bar/**
***berr'/hogg** *-et* **1: stå i b-(et)** be in a vulnerable position; be in danger. **2** deforested area; bare ground.
berr'/hovda** *A* - (=/hovud**) bareheaded.
***berr'/målug** *A* - outspoken.
***berr'/synleg** *A* - clear, evident, obvious.
***berr'/synt** *A* - **1** easily seen, obvious; open. **2** (of air, light) clear, light. **3** easy to understand.
ber'se[1] *-n* bear.
ber'se[2] *-n* miner.
berserk [bæ'r-] *-en* berserker (wild warrior, originally dressed in bear skins).
berserk/gang *-en* (=+**berserks/**, +**berserker/**): **gå b-** go berserk.
ber'te *V -a/+-et* honk, toot.
Ber'te *Prn (f)*
+**beru'se** *V -te* intoxicate: **b-ende drikke** i-ing beverages; **bli b-et av** get drunk on (e.g. beer); **dengang vi gikk og var b-te og trodde at det bare var to mennesker i hele verden** those days when we went around in a daze and thought there were only two people in the whole world (Heiberg).
+**beru'selse** *-n* intoxication.
+**beru'set** *A* - drunk, intoxicated: **kjøre i b- tilstand** drive under the influence of liquor; **b- av sin egen makt** d- with power.
+**beryk'tet** *A* - infamous, notorious: **en b- person** a bad character.
beryll' *-en* beryl.
+**berøm'me** *V -et/-rømte* praise: **de b-et ham for hans mot** they p-ed him for his courage; **b- seg av noe** brag about sth.
+**berøm'melig** *A* - famous, illustrious: **en b- dåd** a glorious feat.
+**berøm'melse** *-n* **1** celebrity, fame. **2** praise.
+**berøm't** *A* - famous.
+**berøm't/het** *-en* **1** fame. **2** famous person; celebrity.
+**berø're** *V -te* **1** touch. **2** affect, involve: **streiken b-er ikke vår fabrikk** the strike does not a- our factory; **føle seg ille b-t (av, ved noe)** be unpleasantly impressed (by sth). **3** mention, touch upon: **saken ble ikke b-t med et ord** not a word was said about the matter.
+**berø'ring** *-a/+-en* contact, touch: **b- av ledningen er livsfarlig** Danger. High Voltage; **jeg kom først i b- med ham i fjor** I first came into c- with him last year.
+**berø've** *V -de/-et*: **b- en (for) noe** deprive, rob sby of sth.
berå' *V -dde (refl.)* **b- seg** consider, think it over: **b- seg med** consult with; provide oneself with. **2** *(pp.)*: **han er b-dd på å reise** he is prepared to go; **jeg gjør det med b-dd hu** I'm doing it deliberately.
berå'd *-et*: **være i b- med noe, om noe** be doubtful, be of two minds about sth.
+**besatt'**[1] *A* - (=***-sett**) **1** occupied: **b- område** occupied area, territory; **stillingen er b-** the position has been filled. **2** possessed (**av en ond ånd** by an evil spirit): **han skrek som b-** he was yelling like mad. **3** obsessed (**av en idé** by an idea). **4** damned: **det er b- kaldt her** it's damned cold here.
+**besatt'**[2] *pp of* **-sette**
+**besatt'**[3] *pt of* **-sitte**
+**besat'te** *pt of* **-sette**
+**bese'**[1] *V -så, -sett* inspect; visit: **varene kan b-s** the merchandise may be i-ed; **b- seg på et sted** v- a place (as a sightseer); **rett b-tt** all things considered.
***be'se**[2] *V -a* **1** chatter, prattle; tattle. **2** humor, indulge, spoil.
+**besegle** [-sei'le] *V -et* seal: **b- en pakt** s- a treaty; **vår skjebne er b-et** our fate is s-ed.
+**besei're** *V -et* conquer, defeat, vanquish.
+**beset'ning** *-en* **1** decoration sewn e.g. on a dress, a hat; trim. **2** crew. **3** livestock; herd.
besett'[1] *A* - cf **-satt**[1]
+**besett'**[2] *pp of* **-se**[1]
+**beset'te** *V -satte, -satt* **1** occupy (a territory). **2** fill (a vacancy); take (a seat): **salen var fullt besatt** the hall was filled. **3** obsess, possess. **4** deck, stud, trim: **hendene var besatt med smykker** her hands were studded with jewels; **b- med skinn** trim with fur. **5** *naut.* fasten (ends of a seizing).
+**beset'telse** *-n* **1** occupation (of a territory). **2** filling (of a position). **3** obsession: **spillet var blitt en b- for ham** gambling had become an o- with him.
+**besid'de** *V -sad, -siddet* cf **besitte**
+**besid'delse** *-n* cf **besittelse**
+**besik'te** *V -et* inspect (the building or state of a ship).
+**besik'telse** *-n* inspection (of a ship).
+**besik'tige** *V -et* inspect, survey.
+**besik'tigelse** *-n* inspection, survey: **foreta en b- av tomten** inspect the site.
+**besin'delse** *-n* cf **besinnelse**
+**besin'dig** *A* - level-headed, sensible, steady.
+**besin'dig/het** *-en* level-headedness, steadiness.
+**besin'ne** *V -et (refl.)* **1** collect one's wits; restrain oneself. **2** think twice; change one's mind.
+**besin'nelse** *-n* composure: **komme til b-** regain one's c-; **tape b-n** lose one's head.
+**besit'te** *V -satt, -sittet* have, hold, possess.
+**besit'telse** *-n* **1** possession: **sette seg i b- av noe, ta noe i b-** take p- of sth; **være i b- av** possess. **2** dependency, possession: **Englands b-r i Afrika** England's p-s in Africa.
+**besje'le** *V -te* animate, inspire; fill one's soul: **være b-et av idealisme** be i-ed by idealism.
+**bes'k** *A* cf **beisk**
+**beska'dige** *V -et* damage, injure.
+**beska'digelse** *-n* damage, injury.
+**beskaf'fen** *A -ent, pl -skafne* constituted: **hvordan er dette stoffet b-t?** *lit.* what is the nature of this substance?
+**beskaf'fen/het** *-en* character, composition, nature; quality: **sakens b-** the nature of the matter; **av god b-** of good q-.
+**beska'r** *pt of* **-skjære**
+**beskat'ning** *-en* **1** assessment, levy, taxation. **2** controlled reduction (esp. of a species of animal, by killing a certain number per year).
+**beskat'te** *V -a/-et* **1** tax. **2** utilize (esp. a species of animal): **hvalen blir hardt b-et** whales are heavily hunted.
+**beskik'ke** *V -et* **1** allot: **han er blitt lite b-et** he has been a-ted little. **2** appoint: **bli b-et til et embete** be a-ed to an office. **3: b- sitt hus** put one's house in order.
+**beskik'kelse** *-n* appointment.
beskje'd *-en* information, instructions; answer; message: **få grei b-** get clear instructions; **det er ikke mulig å få b- av ham** it's impossible to get a straight answer from him; **han fikk b- om å komme** he was told to come; **gi b- om noe** give orders about sth; **hun gav ham ren b-** she really told him off; **overbringe en b-** deliver a message; **vente på nærmere b-** wait for further instructions.
+**beskje'den** *A -ent, pl -ne* modest.
+**beskje'den/het** *-en* modesty.
+**beskjef'tige** *V -et* **1** employ, give work to: **fabrikken b-er 100 mann** the factory employs 100 men. **2** concern, engage, occupy: **være b-et med noe** be o-ed with sth; **holde en b-et** keep sby busy; **b- seg med noe** have sth as one's main work or interest.
+**beskjef'tigelse** *-n* **1** employment: **finne b-** find e-; **være uten b-** be without a job, unemployed. **2** business, occupation, work: **en hederlig b-** an honest o-, honest work.
+**beskjem'me** *V -et* **1** disgrace, humiliate: **føle seg b-et** feel h-ed; **b-ende** humiliating. **2** disappoint: **hans håp om forfremmelse ble b-et** he was d-ed in his hope of promotion.
+**beskjem'melse** *-n* **1** disgrace, humiliation, shame. **2** disappointment.
+**beskjen'ke** *V -et/-te* give liquor to **b-et** intoxicated.
+**beskjer'me** *V -et* protect (**mot** against).
+**beskjæ're** *V -skar, -skåret* **1** cut trim; prune. **2** curtail; cut (down) reduce. **3** allot: **jeg er fornøyd med det som skjebnen har beskåret meg** I am satisfied with what fate has a-ted me.
+**beskjæ'ring** *-a/-en* **1** cutting, trimming; pruning. **2** abridgement; curtailment; reduction: **b- av et budsjett** t- of a budget.
+**beskjø't** *pt of* **-skyte**
+**bes'kne** *V -a/-et* cf **beiskne**

+**beskri've** *V -skrev, -skrevet* 1 write upon; fill with writing: **en beskreven side** a page filled with writing. 2 describe: **det var ikke til å b-** it could not be d-ed, it was indescribable; **steinen beskrev en bue gjennom luften** the stone d-ed an arc through the air; **b-ende** descriptive.

+**beskri'velse** *-n* description: **gi en b- av** give a d- of; **over all b-** beyond d-.

+**besku'e** *V -et* behold, contemplate, view; **b- sin egen navle** c- one's navel; *fig.* be concerned only with oneself; **b-ende** c-tive, meditative.

+**besku'else** *-n* contemplation (**av** of).

+**beskutt'** *pp of* **-skyte**

+**beskyl'de** *V -te*: **b- en for noe** accuse sby of sth.

+**beskyl'dning** *-en* accusation, allegation, charge.

+**besky'te** *V -skjøt, -skutt* fire at, into, on: **b- med granater** shell.

+**beskyt'te** *V -a/-et* 1 protect; shelter (**mot** against). 2 be patron of, patronize; **b-ende** protective.

+**beskyt'telse** *-n* protection; shelter (**mot** against): **stille seg under ens b-** place oneself under the p- of sby; **ta en under sin b-** become sby's patron.

+**beskyt'telses/farge** *-n* protective coloration.

+**beskyt'ter** *-en, pl -e* protector; patron: **kongen er utstillingens høye b-** the King is the patron of the exposition.

beskøy't *-en* sea biscuit.

+**beskå'ret** *pp of* **-skjære**

besla'g *-et* 1 fittings; mounting; metal ornamentation. 2 confiscation: **legge b- på noe** confiscate sth; occupy, take up; **legge b- på en plass** lay claim to a seat; **får jeg legge b- på Dem et øyeblikk** may I have your attention for a moment.

†**besla'g/legge** *V -la, -lagt* (=*-je) 1 confiscate, impound; requisition. 2 occupy: **arbeidet b-er hele hans tid** the work takes up all his time.

+**besla'g/leggelse** *-n* confiscation; attachment, impounding; requisitioning (**av** of).

+**beslek'tet** *A* - related (**med** to); kindred.

beslo' *pt of* **-slå**

+**beslut'ning** *-en* decision, resolution: **fatte, komme til, ta, treffe en b-** reach a d-; **det er min faste b- å gå av** I have definitely decided to resign.

+**beslut'nings/dyktig** *A* - (of assembly, meeting) having the necessary number to pass a resolution: **være b-** have a quorum.

+**beslut'te** *V -a/-et* decide, resolve: **b- seg til (å gjøre) noe** d-, make up one's mind to do sth.

+**beslutt'/som'** *A -t, pl -me* determined, resolute.

+**beslutt'som/het** *-en* resolution, resoluteness.

beslå' *V infl as* **slå** 1 furnish with fittings; mount; shoe; stud. 2 *naut.* stow (sails). 3: **være godt b-tt (med penger)** be well-heeled.

+**besmit'te** *V -et* contaminate, defile, pollute; sully: **b-et** sullied, unclean.

+**besmit'telse** *-n* contamination, defilement, pollution.

bes'ne *V -a/+-et* improve; grow better, recover.

+**besnæ're** *V -et/-te* allure, captivate, infatuate; lead astray: **et b-ende blikk** an alluring (seductive) glance.

+**bespa'relse** *-n* saving (**av** of).

+**bespa'rende** *A* - economical, saving: **en b- ordning** an arrangement that saves time, effort, or money.

+**bespi'se** *V -te* feed: **b- de fattige** f- the poor.

+**bespot'telig** *A* - blasphemous, profane: **det er b- å høre på** it's horrible to listen to.

+**bespot'telse** *-n* 1 blasphemy, profanity. 2 blasphemous act or utterance.

Bess'/eggen *Pln* (=*/eggi) mountain in Jotunheimen.

+**bes't**[1] *-et* cf **beist**

bes't[2] *sp of* **god**

best.=**bestemt, bestemt form**

+**bestakk'** *pt of* **-stikke**

+**bestal'ling** *-en* (royal) commission, license.

bestan'd *-en* stock (of animals); stand (of trees).

+**bestan'd/del** *-en* component, element; constituent; ingredient.

bestan'dig *A* - 1 continuous; incessant: **b- skiftende fargespill** continuously changing play of colors. 2 *(adv.)* always, forever: **for b-** for good.

+**bestan'dig/het** *-en* constancy.

bes'te[1] *-a* grandmother.

bes'te[2] *-n* grandfather.

bes'te[3] *et* advantage, benefit, good: **det allmenne b-** the public weal; **det er til ditt eget b-** it's for your own good; **gi en historie til b-** oblige with a story; **ha en til b-** pull one's leg, make a fool out of sby; **til felles b-** for the common good.

+**bes'te/borger** *-en, pl -e* (=*-ar) bourgeois, philistine, pillar of society.

+**bes'te/borgerlig** *A* - (=*/borgarleg) bourgeois, philistine.

bes'te/far *-en, pl +-fedre/*-fedrar* grandfather.

bes'te/forel'dre *pl* grandparents.

+**beste'g** *pt of* **-stige**

bes'te/mann *-en* 1 the best person within a group competing at sth: **han er b- i klassen** he is at the top of his class. 2 *naut.* (substitute) second mate (on a boat having only one mate).

bestem'me *V -stemte* 1 appoint, fix: **b- dagen for bryllupet** set the day for the wedding. 2 decide, decree; destine: **bestemt ved lov** decreed by law; **b- seg** make up one's mind; **jeg har bestemt meg for denne** I have decided in favor of this one, I have decided to take this one; **b- seg til å gjøre noe** decide to do sth; **dette kom til å b- (or: dette ble b-ende for) hans handlemåte** it was this that determined his course of action; **han var bestemt til å dø ung** he was destined to die young; **faren hadde bestemt ham til prest** his father had decided that he should be a minister. 3 determine: **b- grensene** d- the limits; **b- en plante** identify a plant; **verb b-es av adverb** verbs are modified by adverbs.

+**bestem'melse** *-n* 1 decision, resolution; destiny: **fatte, ta en b-** reach a decision; **oppfylle sin b-** fulfill one's destiny. 2 determination (of a value); identification (of a plant); modification (in grammar).

+**bestem'melses/havn** *-en* port of destination.

+**bestem'melses/sted** *-et* destination: **nå fram til b-et** reach one's d-.

bes'te/mor *-a/-en, pl -mødrer/ +-mødre* grandmother.

bestem't *A* - 1 certain, definite, fixed: **i en b- hensikt** for a d- purpose; **jeg kan ikke si noe b-** I can't say anything d-; **med b-e mellomrom** at f- intervals; **på b-e steder** at c- places; **til b-e tider** at f- times. 2 determined, firm, sure: **det vil b- bli den beste løsning** that will surely be the best solution; **et b- avslag** a categorical refusal; **jeg vil b- motsette meg det** I will strongly oppose it; **opptre fast og b-** act in a f- and d- manner; **snakke i en b- tone** speak in a f- tone of voice; **protestere på det b-este** protest very firmly; **vite noe b-** know sth for sure; **være b- på (å gjøre noe)** be d- (to do sth). 3 *gram.* definite: **b- form** d- form; **b- artikkel** d- article. 4 bound for, intended: **b- for New York** bound for N.Y.

+**bestem't/het** *-en* 1 certainty: **si noe med b-** say sth with c-. 2 determination, firmness: **han sa det med stor b-** he said it with great f-.

bes'te/stue *-a* (=*/stove) parlor.

bes'te/venn *-en* best friend: **de er b-er** they are great friends.

bes'te/vennin'ne *-a* best friend (used between women or girls).

bestia'lsk *A* - bestial.

+**besti'ge** *V -steg, -steget* mount: **b- en hest** m- a horse; **b- et fjell** climb a mountain.

bestikk'[1] *-en naut.* chart house (=**b-/lugar**).

bestikk'[2] *-et* 1 *naut.* dead reckoning: **gjøre opp b-et** work out the r-. 2: **gjøre opp sitt b-** chart one's position; **det var ikke etter mitt b-** it was not what I expected.

bestikk'[3] *-et* 1 case, set of instruments. 2 set of knife, fork and spoon.

+**bestik'ke** *V -stakk, -stukket* bribe.

+**bestik'kelig** *A* - corrupt, open to bribery.

+**bestik'kelse** *-n* bribe; bribery, corruption.

bestikk'/luga'r *-en* chart house.

+**bestil'le** *V -stilte* 1 order: **b- time** make an appointment; **b- billetter** reserve tickets. 2 do: **hva b-er du her?** what are you doing here?; **det er snart bestilt** that's soon done; **ha med en, noe å b-** have to do with sby, sth; **hva har du med det å b-** what business is it of yours; **du skal få med meg å b-** you'll have me to reckon with.

+**bestil'ling** *-en* 1 order: **etter b-** to o-; **oppta b-er** take o-s. 2 office, position; job.

+**bestil'lings/mann** *-en, pl -menn/ *-menner* (subordinate) official.

+**bestil'lings/seddel** *-elen, pl -sedler* order form, order slip.

+**bestje'le** *V -stjal, -stjålet* steal from, rob (**for** of).

besto'd *pt of* **-stå**

+**bestor'me** *V -et* assail; pester: **b- en med spørsmål** p- sby with questions.

+**bestre'be** *V -et/-te*: **b- seg for (på)** endeavor, strive (for), try hard (for).

+**bestri'de** *V -stred, -stridd/-stridt* 1 deny, question: **b- riktigheten av en påstand** q- the correctness of an assertion; **det kan ikke b-es** there is no denying it. 2 defray, pay.

+**bestry'ke** *V -strøk, -strøket* 1 rub, stroke. 2 coat, paint. 3 rake, sweep (with bullets).

+**bestrå'le** *V -te* 1 illumine, shine upon. 2 irradiate.

+**bes't/seller** *-en, pl -e* (=+/**selger**, */**seljar**) bestseller.

+**bestukket** [-stok'ket] *pp of* **-stikke**

+**bestyk'ning** *-en* armament.

+**besty'r** *-et* 1 occupation, tasks, work: **det daglige b-** the daily w-. 2 struggle; trouble. 3 commotion; noise.

+**besty're** *V -te* administer, be in charge of, manage.

+**besty'relse** *-n* management.

+**besty'rer** *-en, pl -e* 1 administrator, executor, manager, supervisor (**av** of). 2 (in school) principal, *(Brit.)* headmaster.

+**bestyrerin'ne** *-a/-en* woman administrator, cf **bestyrer**.

+**bestyr'ke** *V -et* bear out, confirm; corroborate; strengthen: **han ble b-et i sin mistanke** he had his suspicion confirmed; **dette b-et ham i hans forsett** this strengthened him in his resolution.

+**bestyr'telse** *-n* alarm, consternation, dismay.

+**bestyr'tet** *A* - alarmed, startled; dismayed.

+**bestø've** *V -et* pollinate.

+**bestø'vning** *-en* pollination.

bestå' *V -stod, -stått* 1 live through,

+ Bokmål; * Nynorsk; ° Dialect.
After letter: ' stress (Acc. 1); ` tone, stress (Acc. 2); ˙ length.
Below letter: . not pronounced.

undergo: **b- prøvelser** l- t- hardships; pass (an exam). **2** pay: **b- utgiftene** foot the bill. **3** continue, last: **så lenge verden b-r** as long as the world l-s; **hans ry vil b-** his fame will endure; **de b-ende forhold** the existing conditions. **4: b- av (i)** consist of; **arbeidet b-r i å punsje kort** the work consists of punching cards.

+bestå'en *en* existence; continuance.

+besud'le *V -et* soil, sully, tarnish.

+besvang're *V -et* make pregnant.

+besva're *V -te* answer, reply to: **b- et spørsmål** a- a question; **b- en hilsen** return a greeting; **b- fiendtlig ild** return enemy fire.

+besva'relse *-n* examination paper.

+besver'ge *V -et/-svor, -et/-svoret* **1** exorcise. **2** beseech, implore: **be og b-** ask and pray.

+besvi'me *V -te* faint.

+besvi'melse *-n* fainting.

+besvogret [-svå'gret] *A* - related by marriage (**med** to).

+besvo'r *pt of* **-sverge**

+besvæ'r *-et* **1** difficulties; troubles: **livets byrder og b-** life's burdens and t- (Ibsen). **2** difficulty; inconvenience: **ha b- med noe** have d- with sth; **være til b-** cause i-; **jeg kommer vel ikke til b-?** I hope I'm not intruding.

+besvæ're *V -et* **1** inconvenience; trouble: **b- en med spørsmål** bother sby with questions; **hun var b-et av varmen** she was oppressed by the heat; **b- seg med noe** worry about sth. **2: b- seg over** complain about.

+besvæ'ring *-a/-en* complaint.

+besvæ'rlig *A* - difficult, hard, strenuous; tiresome, troublesome.

+besvæ'rlig/het *-en* discomfort, hardship, inconvenience: **han pustet med b-** he breathed with difficulty.

+besyn'derlig *A* - curious, odd, strange: **en b- framtoning** (esp. of a person) a s- sight; **b- nok** s-ly enough.

+besy'v *N*: **gi sitt b- med i laget** put one's oar in, chime in.

besø'k *-et* **1** visit: **avlegge (et) b- hos en** pay a v- to sby; **få b- av** be v-ed by; **komme på b- til** v-. **2** attendance: **utstillingen hadde godt b-** the exposition was well attended.

+besø'ke *V -te* (=***-je**) **1** visit. **2** attend: **en godt b-t konsert** a well attended concert.

+besø'kelses/tid *-a/-en*: **kjenne sin b-** know the time of one's visitation (Luke 19:44); recognize an opportunity.

+besø'kende *en, pl* - visitor.

besø'ks/tid *-a/+-en* visiting hours.

+besør'ge *V -a/-et* take care of; take charge of: **det skal jeg b-** I'll t- care of that; **det er b-et** it has been t-n care of; **b- et ærend** run an errand; **b- en pakke** send a package.

+besø' *pt of* **-se[1]**

+be't[1] *-en*: **gå b-, gå 2 b-er** (in bridge) go down, be set 2 tricks.

+be't[2] *pt of* **bite[3]**

+bet.=**betydning; betegnelse; betalt**

+beta' *V -tok, -tatt* **1** rob, take away from: **synet betok meg appetitten** the sight robbed me of my appetite. **2** captivate: **hun betok ham** she captivated him. **3** impress; move; thrill: **beretningen betok dem sterkt** the tale moved them greatly.

+beta'gende *A* - moving, thrilling: **et b- syn** a t- sight.

+betak'ke *V -et*: **b- seg for** decline with thanks; **jeg b-er meg for din hjelp** (ironically) thanks all the same.

+beta'l/bar *A* payable.

beta'le *V -te/*-a* pay: **b- for sin dumhet** pay for one's stupidity; **dette skal du få b- for** you'll have to pay for this; *(refl.)* **det b-er seg alltid å være ærlig** honesty always pays.

+beta'ler *-en, pl -e* (=***-ar**) payer: **en dårlig, god, langsom b-** a bad, good, slow p-.

beta'ling *-a/+-en* pay, payment, salary: **kontant b-** cash payment; **innstille b-ene** suspend payments, go bankrupt; **han fikk god b-** he was paid well; **jeg vil ikke gjøre det for god b-** I won't do it for anything in the world.

beta'lings/balanse [/balang'se] *-n* balance of payment.

beta'lings/dyktig *A* - capable of paying, solvent.

beta'lings/middel *-elet/-midlet, pl +-midler/*-el* means of payment.

beta'lings/stans *-en* suspension of payment.

beta'lings/termi'n *-en* time of payment.

+betatt' *A* - impressed, moved, thrilled: **hun så b- på ham** she looked enraptured at him; **være b- av** be taken with, like very much.

be'te[1] *-n* **1** (small) piece: **en b- sukker** a lump of sugar. **2** mouthful.

be'te[2] *-n* crossbeam.

be'te[3]-*a/+-en bot.* beet (Beta vulgaris).

***be'te[4]** *V -a* cut, divide into pieces: **b- opp eit papir** tear a paper (into e.g. sections).

+betegne [-tei'ne] *V -et* **1** put a mark on: **b- med korsets tegn** mark with the sign of the cross. **2** characterize, designate: **jeg b-er boken som uanstendig** I would c- the book as indecent. **3** mean, signify; symbolize: **oppfinnelsen b-er noe nytt på området** the invention signifies sth new in this field; **kunstneren lar et tre b- livet selv** the artist lets a tree symbolize life itself.

+betegnelse [tei'nelse] *-n* designation; indication.

+betegnende [-tei'nene] *A* - **1** characteristic, typical: **svaret var b- for ham** the answer was t- of him. **2** to the point: **et b- uttrykk** an expression that hits the mark.

+beten'delse *-n* cf **betennelse**

+beten'ke *V -te* **1** bear in mind; consider; remember: **man må b- hans unge alder** you have to c- his youth; **rett b-t** all things considered. **2** *(refl.)* consider, reflect, think over: **han b-te seg både en og to ganger før han gjorde det** he gave it much thought before doing it; **jeg b-er meg på å gjøre det** I hesitate to do it. **3: b- en med (penger)** remember sby with (money).

+beten'kelig *A* - **1** critical, serious; dangerous, risky: **situasjonen er b-** the situation is c-; **et b- foretagende** a risky operation. **2** *(adv.)*: **han kom b- nær kanten** he came dangerously close to the edge. **3** anxious, uneasy; doubtful, hesitant.

+beten'kelig/het *-en* doubt, hesitation, misgivings, scruples: **få b-er** have second thoughts, get cold feet; **jeg nærer ingen b-er ved å si det** I have no hesitation about saying it.

+beten'kning *-en* **1** consideration, deliberation, reflection: hesitation: **etter et øyeblikks b-** after a moment's reflection; **han tar ikke i b- å sette livet på spill** he doesn't hesitate to risk his life. **2** (written) recommendation, report: **skrive en b- over et spørsmål** write an opinion on a question.

+beten'knings/tid *-a/-en* time to think it over; respite: **ta b-** *jur.* ask for a stay of execution.

+beten'k/som' *A -t, pl -me* **1** circumspect, deliberate; quiet; soberminded. **2** considerate, thoughtful: **det var lite b-t gjort av ham** that was inconsiderate of him.

+beten'kt *A* - **1: være b- på noe** *lit.* have a mind to do sth. **2** *lit.* deliberate, thoughtful; quiet; sober: **vel (ille) b-** well- (ill-)advised. **3** doubtful; hesitant: **han var blitt sterkt b-** he had developed strong doubts.

beten'nelse *-n* inflammation.

beten't *A* - **1** infected, inflamed. **2** depraved (e.g. imagination, morals).

+betids' *Av*: **b-, i b-** in time; **i god b-** in good time.

+beti'melig *A* - opportune, timely: **i b- tid** in good time.

+beting'e *V -et* **1** *(refl.)* give as condition; insist on, stipulate: **b- seg 50 %** demand a 50% cut. **2** determine: **prisene er b-et av etterspørselen** prices are contingent upon demand; **være b-et av** depend upon; **noten b-er et skarpt svar** the note invites a sharp answer.

+beting'else *-n* condition, term: **på b- av** on the c- that; **sette (stille) som b- at** stipulate that.

+betin'gelses/løs *A* unconditional.

+beting'et *A* - **1** conditional: **b- dom** suspended sentence. **2** qualified: **planen møtte b- tilslutning** the plan received q- support.

+betje'ne *V -te* **1** attend, serve: **b- seg selv** serve oneself. **2: b- en stilling** serve in an office; **b- en maskin** operate a machine. **3: b- seg av** make use of, utilize.

betje'ning *-a/+-en* **1** service: **rask b-** fast s-. **2** staff of attendants, clerks, servants.

betjen't *-en* minor public servant; (police or court) officer; clerk; messenger.

+bet'le *V -et* beg, panhandle.

+bet'ler *-en, pl -e* beggar, panhandler.

+bet'leri *-et* begging, panhandling.

+bet'lerske *-a/-en* woman beggar.

+beto'k *pt of* **-ta**

+beto'ne *V -te* accentuate, stress (e.g. a syllable); emphasize.

betong' *-en* concrete: **armert b-** reinforced c-.

betong'/bygg *-et* concrete structure.

+beto'ning *-a/-en* accent; emphasis, stress.

+betraff' *pt of* **-treffe**

+betrak'te *V -et* contemplate, look at, regard: **b- en** look (closely) at sby; **som fenomen b-et** viewed as a phenomenon.

+betrak'telig *A* - considerable.

+betrak'tning *-en* **1** consideration, contemplation: **hensunket i b-er** deep in meditation; **komme i b-** be considered; **sette ut av b-** drop from consideration; **ta i b-** take into consideration. **2** written meditation.

+betrak'tnings/måte *-n* point of view.

+betre'[1] *V -trådte, -trådt* set foot on, tread on; enter (on).

***bet're[2]** *V -a* cf **bedre[1]**

***bet're[3]** *cp of* **god** cf **bedre[2]**

+betref'fe *V -traff, -truffet*: **hva x b-er** *lit.* as to x, as regards x.

+betrekk' *-et* cover, upholstery.

+betreng't *A* - hard pressed; in distress.

***bet'ring** *-a* cf **bedring**

+betro' *V -dde* **1** entrust: **jeg b-r ham til din omsorg** I e- him to your care; **jeg ville ikke b- ham fem øre** I wouldn't trust him with a nickel. **2** confide: **b- seg til** c- in.

+betrodd' *A* - **1** entrusted: **b-e midler** trust funds. **2** responsible, trusted: **en b- stilling** a position of trust.

+betro'else *-n* confidence: **hun plager meg med sine b-r** she is pestering me with her c-s.

***betru'** *V -dde* cf **betro**

+betruffet [-trof'fet] *pp of* **-treffe**

+betryg'gelse *-n* reassurance; protection.

+betryg'gende *A* - **1** reassuring: **det er b- å ha ham her** it's r- to have him here. **2** adequate, satisfactory: **b- sikringstiltak** a- protective measures.

+betrådt'e *pt of* **-tre[1]**

°bet'terde *I* cf **bitter/død**

+betut'tet *A* - (=**+-a**) dumbfounded, nonplussed, taken aback.

+bety' *V -dde, -dd* mean, signify: **hva skal dette b-** what's the meaning of this; **et feiltrinn b-r døden** a false step m-s death; **firkløver b-r lykke** a four-leaf clover m-s luck; **han b-r ikke stort** he is not important.

+**bety'de** *V -et lit.* give to understand, make plain to.
+**bety'delig** *A* - considerable: **en b- formue** a c- fortune; **en b- mann** a man of consequence.
+**bety'dning** *-en* 1 meaning: **b-en av dette er** ... the m- of this is ...; **han er en helt i ordets rette b-** he is a hero in the true sense of the word. 2 importance; influence: **en sak av b-** a matter of importance; **en mann av b-** an important, influential man; **det er av b- for oss** it's important to us.
+**bety'dnings/full** *A* 1 meaningful (e.g. look). 2 important: **en b- avgjørelse** an i- decision.
+**bety'dnings/innhold** *-et* content, significance (of a word or a context).
+**bety'dnings/løs** *A* unimportant.
beun'dre *V -a/+-et* admire.
+**beun'drer** *-en, pl -e* (=***-ar**) admirer (**av** of).
+**beundrerin'ne** *-a/-en* (woman) admirer.
beun'dring *-a/+-en* admiration (**for** for).
+**beun'drings/verdig** *A* - admirable.
+**bevan'dret** *A* - conversant, versed (**i** in).
beva're *V -te* keep, preserve, save: **b- en fra alt ondt** p- one from all evil; **b- i minnet** cherish in one's memory; **du er ikke (riktig) vel b-t** you are out of your senses; **Gud b- kongen** God save the King; **Gud b- meg fra å si noe slikt,** (or:) **Gud b- min munn** Lord help me from saying that; **Gud b- oss,** (also:) **Gud b-es, Gud bevare, Gubbevars, bevares, bevars,** cf **bevares.**
+**beva'relse** *-n* (=**-ing**) keeping, preservation (**av** of).
+**beva'res** *I* (=**bevars**) (see also **bevare**) 1 dear me, good grief, good heavens: **b- (vel) så svart du er** good grief how dirty you are. 2 of course, to be sure: **ja b-** sure: **du burde ikke gjøre det, men b-, hvis du endelig vil, så** ... you ought not to do it, but of course, if you insist...
be've *V -de/+-et/*-a* tremble (**av** with).
+**beve'ge** *V -de/-et* 1 move=stir: **b- seg** move; **jorden b-er seg om sin egen akse** the earth turns on its own axis. 2 move=affect; agitate. 3 persuade (**til å** to).
+**beve'gelig** *A* - movable, mobile; (of person) agile; excitable.
+**beve'gelse** *-n* 1 motion, movement; gesture, move: **gjøre en b-** move, make a move; **en b- av tropper** a movement of troops; **det ble b- i mengden** there was a stir in the crowd; **sette seg i b-** start off; **være i b-** be in motion; **en politisk b-** a political movement. 2 agitation, emotion: **indre b-** inner a-. 3 movement (for a cause).
+**beve'gelses/frihet** *-en* freedom of movement.
+**beve'gelses/krig** *-en* mobile warfare.
+**beve'gelses/retning** *-en* direction of motion.
+**beve'gelses/verbum** *-(um)et, pl -/-er* verb denoting motion.
+**beve'get** *A* - agitated, moved, stirred; moving, stirring: **de tok en b- avskjed** they had a tearful farewell; **et b- møte** a stormy meeting; **en b- tilværelse** a checkered career; **et b- øyeblikk** a stirring moment.
+**beve'g/grunn** *-en* motivation, motive.
+**be'ven** *en* trembling: **frykt og b-** fear and t-.
+**beven'dt** *A* -: **det var dårlig b- med ham** he was not much good, was in poor shape.
be'ver *-eren, pl -rer/+-ere zool.* beaver (Castor fiber).
be'ver/gjel *-et* 1 castor gland in beaver; castor(eum). *2 rare or valuable object; sth that is impossible, that cannot be done.

be'ver/rotte *-a zool.* coypu, nutria (Myocastor coypus).
+**bever'te** *V -et* entertain, treat (**med** with).
+**bever'tning** *-en* entertainment (with food and drink): **etter møtet var det b-** there were refreshments after the meeting.
+**bevid'ne** *V -et* cf **-vitne**
+**bevil'ge** *-et* appropriate, grant: **Stortinget har b-ende myndighet** the Parliament has budgetary powers; *hum.* **jeg har b-et meg nye sko** I have treated myself to a new pair of shoes.
+**bevil'gning** *-en* appropriation (granting; funds granted).
+**bevil'ling** *-en* license: **søke om b- til å selge alkoholholdige drikker** apply for a liquor license.
+**beving'et** *A* - winged: **bevingede ord** familiar quotations.
+**bevir'ke** *V -et* cause, effect, lead to: **en gift som b-er døden** a poison that causes death.
+**bevi's** *-et* evidence, proof: **føre b- for sin uskyld** produce e- of one's innocence; **bli frikjent på grunn av b-ets stilling** be acquitted for lack of e-; **fellende b-** conclusive proof; **være (et) b- på noe** be proof of sth.
+**bevi's/byrde** *-n* burden of proof.
+**bevi'se** *V -te* 1 prove. 2 demonstrate, show: **hun b-te ham sin takknemlighet** *lit.* she s-ed him her appreciation.
+**bevi's/førsel** *-en* argumentation, demonstration, proof.
+**bevi's/kraft** *-en* weight as evidence.
+**bevi'slig** *A* - demonstrable, provable: **han er b- kommunist** he is a proven communist.
+**bevi's/materia'le** *-t jur.* evidence, proof.
+**bevis'st** *A* - conscious; deliberate: **han var seg ikke b- å ha gjort noe galt** he was not c- of having done anything wrong; **en b- løgn** a d- lie.
+**bevis'st/het** *-en* consciousness: **morderen hadde nedsatt b- i gjørningsøyeblikket** the murderer was temporarily insane at the moment of the crime; **komme til b-** regain c-; **miste b-en** lose c-.
+**bevis'st/løs** *A* unconscious.
+**bevit'ne** *V -et* 1 testify (to): **jeg kan b- at vi var sammen** I can t- that we were together. 2 express: **tillat meg å b- Dem min dypeste deltakelse** *lit.* allow me to e- my deepest sympathy.
+**bevit'nelse** *-n* 1 attestation; certificate. 2 expression (e.g. of sympathy).
+**bevok's(e)t** *A* - covered; overgrown: **området er b- med skog** the area is c- by forest.
+**bevok'te** *V -et* guard, watch.
+**bevok'tning** *-en* guard, watch; surveillance: **fangen ble holdt under streng b-** the prisoner was kept under strict s-.
+**bev're** *V -a/-et* cf **bivre**
+**bev're/osp** *-a bot.* aspen (Populus tremula).
+**bevæpne** [-ve'pne] *V -et* arm: **en b-et ransmann** an a-ed robber; **tungt b-et** heavily a-ed; **b- seg med tålmod** a- oneself with patience.
+**bevæpning** [-ve'pning] *-a/-en* arming; armament, arms.
+**bevå'gen** *A -ent, pl -ne lit.* favorable to: **han er meg b-** he is f-ly disposed towards me.
+**beæ're** *V -et* honor: **b- en med sitt nærvær** h- sby with one's presence; **føle seg b-et** feel h-ed.
+**beån'de** *V -et* animate, inspire: **et b-et foredrag** an i-ed lecture.
BH=**behå**
+**bi'**[1] *-en* cf **bie**[1]
bi'[2] *imp of* **bie**[2]
+**bi'**[3] *Av* by: **legge bi** lay by; **stå en bi (i nøden)** stand by sby (in time of need).
bi-[1] *Pf* by- (secondary).
bi-[2] *Pf* bi- (double).

+**bi'/avl** *-en* bee culture.
+**bi'/behold** *-et* retention: **med b- av alle rettigheter** retaining all rights.
bi'bel *-elen, pl -ler* Bible: **få b- til konfirmasjonen** receive a B- at confirmation; **Baedeker var den reisendes b-** Baedeker was the traveler's B-.
Bi'belen *Prn* the Bible: **lese i B-** read the B-.
bi'bel/fast *A* - 1 well versed in the Bible. 2 as strongly as (one believes in) the Bible: **han tror b- på almanakken** he believes in the almanac as he believes in the Bible.
bi'bel/histo'rie *-a/+-en* (collection of) Bible stories (part of religious instruction in school).
bi'bel/o'rd *-et* Bible verse.
bi'belsk *A* - biblical: **Isak er et b- navn** Isaac is a b- name.
+**bi'bel/sprengt** *A* - (=***/sprengd**) Bible-spouting (person).
+**bi'bel/sted** *-et* Bible passage, Bible verse.
bibliote'k *-et, pl -/+-er* library.
biblioteka'r *-en* librarian.
***bib're** *V -a* tremble.
+**bi'/bringe** *V -brakte, -brakt* administer, give: **b- en forståelsen av noe** convey to sby the understanding of sth; **b- en et sår** inflict a wound upon sby.
***bi'de** *V beid, bide/-i* 1 be, exist. 2 become. 3: **kvar b-ande kveld** every single evening; **det hjelpte ikkje det b-ande grann** it didn't help the least bit.
bi'de/vind *Av naut.* close-hauled.
bi'dig *A* -: **hver(t) b-e** every single.
***bi'd/lund** *-a* 1 patience; perseverance. 2 grace period.
***bid'ne** *-t* container (esp. a small one, e.g. bucket, cup, box).
+**bi'/dra** *V -drog, -dradd/-dratt* contribute (**til** to).
+**bi'/drag** *-et* contribution (**til** to).
+**bi'drags/yter** *-en, pl -e* contributor.
+**bi'/drog** *pt of* **-dra**
+**bi'/dronning** *-a* queen bee.
bi'e[1] *-a* (*as pf* +**bi-**, ***bie-**) bee.
bi'e[2] *V -dde/*-a* 1 wait (**på** for): **bi litt** w- a little; ***du lyt b- på meg** you must w- for me. *2 keep, last: **denne maten er ikkje mykje å b- på** this food won't hold you long.
***bi'e/al** *-et* cf **bi/avl**
***bi'e/folk** *-et* cf **bi/**
***bi'e/kube** *-n* cf **bi/**
***bi'e/pest** *-en* cf **bi/**
bi'/fag *-et* minor subject (in university course).
+**bi'/fall** *-et* 1 approbation, approval: **planen vant b-** the plan won a-; **med hans b-** with his concurrence. 2 applause, praise: **høste b-** win a-.
+**bi'/falle** *V -falt, -falt* approve: **foreldrene b-t giftermålet** the parents a-d the marriage.
+**bi'falls/rop** *-et* shout of applause.
+**bi'falls/tegn** *-et* applause, expression of approval.
biff'[1] *-en* 1 beef, esp. when prepared by braising or frying: **b- med løk** beef fillet with onions. 2: **greie b-en** manage (a difficult assignment).
+**biff'**[2] *A* - *pop.*: **saken er b-** all set; it's O.K.
+**biff'/banker** *-en, pl -e* (=***-ar**) meat pounder.
+**bi'/folk** *-et* community of bees.
bigami' *-et* bigamy.
bigamis't *-en* bigamist.
bigott' *A* - bigoted; *(noun)* bigot.
bigotteri' *-et* bigotry.
+**bi'/hensik't** *-en* subsidiary motive.
+**bi'/hensy'n** *-et* secondary consideration.

+ Bokmål; * Nynorsk; ° Dialect.
After letter: ' stress (Acc. 1); ` tone, stress (Acc. 2); · length.
Below letter: . not pronounced.

bi'/hole [/håle] -a (=+/hule) sinus.
bihole/beten'nelse -n (=+-hule/) sinus infection.
+bi'/inntek't -a/-en side income, supplementary income.
bijouteri [bisjuteri'] -et, pl +-er/*- 1 costume jewelry. 2 jeweler's shop.
bikk' -en: stå, være på b-(en) be on the point of tipping over.
bik'ke V -a/+-et 1 teeter. 2 cause to teeter. 3 shift, tilt (e.g. heavy stone) to the balancing point.
bikkj'e -a dog; mutt.
bikkj'e/kald A beastly cold.
bikkj'e/leven -et hullaballoo.
bikkj'e/slit -et (hard, unrewarding) struggle.
bik'se -n 1 peg; plug. 2 pop. big wheel.
°bik'sel -et cf beksel
°bik'sle V -a cf beksle
+bik'te V -et confess (one's sins).
+bi'/kube -n beehive.
bi'l -en automobile, car (also of truck); (=drosje) taxi.
+bi'/la pt of -legge
+bi'/lag -et 1 enclosure (e.g. in a letter). 2 voucher. 3 supplement: b- 1 exhibit 1.
bi'l/bransje [/brang'sje] -n automobile business.
+bil'de -t (=*bilete, as pf =+billed-, *bilet-) 1 picture (av of); illustration: ta et b- take a p-; male et b- paint a p-; danne seg et b- av situasjonen form a p- of the situation; hun var et b- på den dypeste elendighet she was a p- of the deepest misery. 2 image: se sitt b- i vannflaten see one's i- reflected in the water; Gud skapte mennesket i sitt b- God created man in his i-; sin fars uttrykte b- the spit and i- of his father. 3 metaphor; symbol: for å bruke et b- to use a m-.
+bil'de/band -et (=+/bånd, *bilet/) film strip (esp. educational).
+bil'de/bok -a/-en, pl- bøker cf billed/
bi'l/dekk -et tire (on car).
+bil'dende A -: b- kunst pictorial art.
bi'le[1] -a broad ax.
bi'le[2] V -te drive, go by car, motor.
+bi'/legge V -la, -lagt 1 settle (a dispute). 2 enclose (in a letter).
*bi'let/bok -a, pl -bøker cf billed/
*bi'lete -t cf bilde
*bi'let/hoggar -en cf billed/hogger
*bi'let/kort -et cf billed/
*bi'let/kunst -en cf billed/
*bi'letleg A - cf billedlig
biling'v A - bilingual.
bilingva'l A - bilingual.
bilis't -en motorist.
biljard [bilja'r] -en billiards.
biljard/kø -en billiard cue.
biljard/salong' -en billiard room.
bil'le[1] +-n/*-a beetle.
+bil'le[2] V bille: b- inn lead to believe; bamboozle, dupe; b- seg inn imagine, suppose.
+bil'led/band -et cf bilde/
+bil'led/bok -a, pl -bøker (=*bilet/) picture book.
+bil'lede -t cf bilde
+bil'led/gåte -a/-en (=*bilet/) rebus (=picture riddle).
+bil'led/hogger -en, pl -e (=*bilet/hoggar, +/hugger) sculptor.
+bil'led/kort -et picture card (in playing cards).
+bil'led/kunst -en pictorial art.
+bil'ledlig A - (=*biletleg) metaphorical.
+bil'led/skjønn A -skjønt beautiful as a picture=strikingly b-.
+bil'led/skrift -a/-en picture writing.
+bil'led/språk -et figurative language.
+bil'led/stormer -en, pl -e iconoclast, idol smasher.
+bil'led/teppe -t tapestry.
+bil'led/vevning -en tapestry weaving.
billetri'se -a/+-en ticket taker (fem.).
billett' -en, pl -er 1 note, small letter: (in want ad) b- mrk. reply at office counter. 2 ticket: kjøpe b- buy a t- til to, for).

billett'/konto'r -et box office, ticket office.
billett'/kø -en ticket line.
billett'/luke -a box office, ticket window.
billettø'r -en ticket taker.
bil'lig A - 1 cheap: være b- i drift be cheap to run; kjøpe noe for en b- penge buy sth for a song; slippe b- fra det get off cheaply; hun så temmelig b- ut she looked rather c-. 2 reasonable: han fant det b- he thought it fair, r-.
+bil'lige V -et approve: han b-et mitt valg he a-d of my choice.
+bil'ligelse -n approval (av of).
+bil'lig/het -en 1 fairness. 2 cheapness.
+bil'lig/salg -et (=*/sal) sale (e.g. spring s-).
bil'lig/vis Av in all fairness.
billio'n -en trillion.
billio'n/del -en trillionth.
bill. mrk.=billett merket
bi'l/park -en car population (e.g. of a country or area).
bi'l/reparatø'r -en automobile mechanic.
bi'l/ring -en (car) tire; hum. roll of fat, "spare tire".
bi'l/sakkyn'dig A - (=*/sakkunnig): Statens b- , state official who examines applicants for driver's licenses and checks the condition of motor vehicles.
bi'l/veg -en motor road.
+bi'l/verkste'd -et (=*-stad) auto repair (shop).
bin'd -et 1 bandage; sanitary napkin; truss: gå med armen i b- have one's arm in a sling. 2 blindfold. 3 binding (of a book). 4 volume (book): første b- volume 1.
Bin'/dal Pln twp, Nordland.
bin'/døling -en person from Bindal.
bin'de V +bandt/*batt, +bundet/*bunde/*-i 1 tie, tie up; chain: b- en hest tie up a horse; bundet på hender og føtter tied hand and foot; b- en en skrøne på ermet lie to sby; bunden kapital tied-up capital; sykdommen bandt ham til senga the sickness chained him to his bed; limet b-er dårlig the glue sticks badly; b- sammen tie together, unite. 2 bind: bundet av sitt løfte bound by one's promise; ingenting som b-er nothing to hold one; b- inn en bok bind a book; b- seg (for et år) commit oneself (for a year). 3 knit; weave: b- hoser knit stockings; b- kurver weave baskets. 4: b- an med take on (an opponent, a task).
+bin'de/gal A (=/galen) 1 fit to be tied, infuriated. 2 completely crazy.
+bin'de/ledd -et (=*/led) connecting link.
bin'de/middel -elet, pl /midler binder.
bin'dende A - binding: et b- løfte a b- promise.
bin'de/o'rd -et conjunction.
+bin'der -en, pl -e (=*-ar) binder (machine, object, person).
bin'ders -en, pl - paper clip.
bin'de/strek -en hyphen.
bin'de/vev -et connective tissue.
bin'ding[1] -en/*-a psych. fixation.
bin'ding[2] -a/-en 1 binding, fastening (on skis). 2 joining.
bin'dings/verk -et half-timber (construction).
bin'dsel -elet/-let, pl +-ler/*-el 1 bandage. 2 thin chain for tying up cow: løse kua av b-let untie the cow.
+bin'd/såle -n (=*/sole) welt.
bing'e -n (=*bing') bin.
bing'e/fjøs -et barn without separate cow stalls.
bing'se -a she-bear.
bin'ne -a she-bear.
bi'/nyre -a/+-en/-et adrenal gland.
bi'/næring -a/+-en subsidiary source of income.
biogra'f -en 1 biographer. 2 cinema, movie house.
biografi' -en biography.
biogra'fisk A - biographical.

biolog [-lå'g] -en biologist.
biologi' -en biology.
biolo'gisk A - biological.
+bi'/person -en minor character (e.g. in plot).
+bi'/pest -en foulbrood (bee disease).
+bi'/produkt -et by-product.
Bir'ger Prn (m)
Bir'git Prn (f)
+birgitti'ner -en, pl -e (=*birgittin(ar)) Brigittine (monastic order).
Bi'ri Pln twp, Oppland.
+bir'k -en cf bjørk
*bir'ke/bein -en, (=+/beiner) Birch leg, member of party in 12th and 13th century civil wars in Norway.
+bi'/rolle -a/-en minor part.
+bi'/røkt -en beekeeping.
+bi'/røkter -en, pl -e beekeeper.
+bi'/sak -a/-en minor matter, side issue.
bi'sam -en 1 zool. musk. 2 muskrat fur.
bi'sam/pels -en muskrat coat.
bi'sam/rotte -a zool. muskrat (Fiber zibethicus).
bisarr' A bisart bizarre.
+bi'/satte pt of -sette
+bi'/setning -en subordinate clause.
+bi'/sette V -satte, -satt bury, inter.
+bi'/settelse -n funeral service.
+bi'/sitter -en, pl -e archaic member of a higher court (approx. equivalent to State Supreme Court).
bis'k[1] -en doggie: snill b- nice d-.
*bis'k[2] -en 1 mouthful. 2 breakfast.
bis'k[3] A 1 (of dog) snappish. 2 (of person) gruff.
+bi'/skjøtsel -en beekeeping.
bis'kop -en bishop.
biskop'pelig A - episcopal: b- verdighet rank of bishop.
bi'/slag -et entry, entryway (of farm).
+bis'le V -a/-et cf beksle
+bis'ler pl of bissel
bi'/smak -en off taste; tang, tinge (esp. of a taste not supposed to be present, e.g. of decay).
+bis'mer -en (=*-ar) steelyard (old type of scales).
+bis'mer/pund -et (=*-ar/) obs. weight unit of ab. 12 lb.
bis'n -et/*-a dial. wonder, wondrou sight.
bis'ne V -a/+-et dial. gape at.
*bis'neleg A - amazing.
bison/okse [bi'sånn/okse] -n (=*/ukse) zool. bison.
bis'p[1] -en bishop: ha b-en til morbror have good connections.
bis'p[2] -en a hot drink made of claret, sugar, etc.
bis'pe/dømme -t, pl +-r/*- bishopric, diocese.
*bis'peleg A - as a bishop, like a bishop, episcopal.
bis'pe/sete -t, pl +-r/*- bishop's see; cathedral city.
bis'pe/stav -en crosier.
bis'pe/stol -en bishop's chair; bishopric.
bispin'ne -a/-en bishop's wife (used as title).
+bis'sel -elet/bislet, pl -el/bisler cf beksel
+bis'se/vov' -ven bow-wow, doggie.
+bi'/stand -en aid, assistance: yte b- aid.
bis'ter A -ert, pl -re fierce, forbidding, grim.
bis'trende Av: b- kald(t) bitter cold.
+bi'/tanke -n: han hadde en b- med å si det he had an ulterior motive for saying it.
bi't[1] -en 1 piece (av of). 2 bite, mouthful: få seg en b- mat have a bite to eat.
*bi't[2] -et bite (e.g. of mosquito).
bi'te[1] -n 1 bit, piece. 2 bite, mouthful.
bi'te[2] -n cf bete[2]
bi'te[3] V beit/+bet, +bitt/*bite/*-i 1 bite: fisken b-er the fish is b-ing; b- en av silence, interrupt sby; b- fra seg fight back; b- hodet av all skam lay aside all scruples; b- i noe take a bite of sth; b- i det sure eple swallow the bitter pill, take one's

punishment; **b- i graset** bite the dust; **b- (noe) i seg** hold back, suppress (e.g. angry words); **b- merke i noe** take note of sth; **b- negler** bite one's nails; **b- på (kroken)** bite (of fish; also *fig.*); **b- seg fast** clamp onto sth, take firm hold of; **b- tennene sammen (i hop)** clench (grit) one's teeth. 2 cut, have an effect: **ljåen b-er godt** the scythe cuts well; **kulden b-er** it is biting cold; **ingenting b-er på ham** nothing bothers him. 3: **b-es** fight, quarrel (cf **krybbe**).

bi‘tenḍe *Av* biting, cutting: **b- kulde** b- cold.

°**bi‘te/ti** *-et* snack.

bi‘te/vis *Av* piecemeal.

+**bi'/ting** *-en* side issue; matter of secondary importance.

bi‘t/jern *-et* sharp-edged tool (e.g. chisel, knife).

+**bi'/tone** *-n mus.* secondary tone, overtone.

bit‘re *pl of* **bitter**

+**bitt'**[1] *-et* 1 bite (e.g. of snake, mosquito): **dårlig b- i dag** (of fish) nothing biting today; **godt b- i ljåen** the scythe has a good (biting) edge. 2 bite mark or wound. 3 *odont.* relative position of upper and lower teeth (esp. in *comps*: **over/, under/**). 4: **ikke det b-** not a bit.

***bitt'**[2] *imp of* **binde**

bit'te *Av*: **b- liten, b- små** tiny little.

bit‘te/konvall· *-en bot.* plant of the lily family, related to the lily of the valley (Maianthemum bifolium).

bit‘te/li‘ten *A -lite, pl -små* cf **bitte**

bit‘tenḍe *Av*: **b- liten, b- små** little bitty, tiny.

bit‘ter *A -ert, pl bitre* bitter (e.g. almonds, pills; *fig.* of enemy, tears, etc.): **b- nød** dire distress; **det var b-t for ham** it was a b- disappointment to him.

bit'ter/dø'ḍ *I* (oath) by golly, by gosh.

+**bit‘ter/het** *-en* bitterness.

***bit‘ter/leik** *-en* bitterness.

bit‘terlig *Av* bitterly: **b- kaldt** bitter cold; **angre (gråte) b-** regret (weep) b-.

+**bit‘terste** *A* (=***-arste**) least, smallest, tiniest: **det hjalp ikke det b- (grann)** it didn't help the least bit.

bit‘ter/søt *A* bittersweet.

bit‘te/små *pl of* **/liten**

***bi‘v** *-en/-et* 1 shiver. 2 fright.

biv‘re *V -a/+-et* (=+**bevre**) tremble.

biv‘re/gras *-et bot.* quaking grass (Briza media).

bivuakk' *-en* bivouac.

bivuakke‘re *V -te* bivouac.

+**bi‘/våne** *V -et/-te* attend, be present at (esp. of person of rank, at solemn occasion).

Bjar‘k/øy *Pln* twp, Troms.

bjar‘køy/rett *-en hist.* laws governing trade matters and social behavior in old Scandinavian market towns and fishing settlements.

Bja‘rne *Prn (m)*

bjar‘t *A* - bright, clear, shining.

Bjar‘te *Prn (m)*

***bjar‘t/leik** *-en* brightness, clearness, light.

***bjar‘t/syn** *-a/-et* optimism.

***bjar‘t/sy‘nt** *A* - optimistic.

bjeff' *-et/*-en* bark, yelp.

bjef‘fe *V -a/+-et* bark, yelp.

bjel‘ke *-n* 1 beam. 2 *mus.* crossbar.

bjel‘ke/verk *-et* beams, timberwork.

Bjel'/lanḍ *Pln* twp, Vest-Agder.

+**bjel‘le** *-a* cf **bjølle**

+**bjer‘k** *-en* cf **bjørk**

Bjer‘k/reim *Pln* twp, Rogaland.

***bjo‘ḍe** *V byd, baud, bode/-i* cf **by(de)**[2]

bjo'r[1] *-en dial.* beaver.

bjo'r[2] *+-et/*-en* (of Old Norse times) beer, esp. of foreign type.

***bjo‘r/dam·** *-men* beaver dam.

bjo're *-n* wedge-shaped or triangular piece, esp. of upper leather in a shoe.

bju'g *A* bent, bow-shaped.

Bjugn [bjung'n] *Pln* twp, Sør-Trøndelag.

bjøl‘le *-a* (=+**bjelle**) bell: **henge b-a på katten** bell the cat; **en lydende malm og en klingende b-** sounding brass, or a tinkling cymbal (1. Corinthians 13:1).

bjøl‘le/kolv *-en* bell clapper.

bjøl‘le/ku *-a* bell cow.

bjøl‘le/sau *-en* bell sheep.

°**bjønn'** *-en* cf **bjørn**

***bjør'g** *-a* support; supplies, esp. of food.

Bjør'g *Prn (f)*

Bjør'g/vin *Pln* 1 the town Bergen (unofficial name sometimes used in nynorsk, taken from Icelandic and Old Norse name forms). 2 official name of the Bergen region used in administration, esp. of the Bergen diocese.

bjør'k *-a bot.* birch (Betula).

bjør‘ke/hage *-en* enclosed pasture area covered with young birch.

Bjør‘ke/langen *Pln* lake, crossroads and railway station in Nordre Høland twp, Akershus.

bjør‘ke/lauv *-et* (=+**/løv**) birch foliage: **pynte med b-** decorate with b- f-.

bjør‘ke/ris *-et* 1 twigs of birch, used e.g. for brooms. 2 birch rod, switch.

bjør‘ke/skog *-en* birch forest.

bjø'rn *-en* 1 bear: **sterk som en b-** strong as a b-; **selge skinnet før b-en er skutt** sell the hide before one has shot the b-, count one's chickens before they are hatched. 2 big strong man: **en b- av en kar** a b- of a fellow. 3 *astron.*: **Store B-** the Big Dipper; **Lille B-** the Little Dipper. 4 hook used for tightening the chain around a sledgeload of logs.

Bjø'rn *Prn (m)*

bjø'rne/bær *-et bot.* blackberry (Rubus).

bjø‘rne/grav *-a* bear pit (for catching bears or for keeping bears in a zoo).

bjø‘rne/ham· *+-men/*-en* bear's disguise; bearhide.

bjø‘rne/hi *-et* bear's lair.

bjø‘rne/mose *-n bot.* bear moss, haircap moss (Polytrichum).

bjø‘rneskinns/pels *-en* bearskin coat.

+**bjø‘rne/tjeneste** *-n* (=***/tenest(e)**) disservice (meant for sby's good), (unintentional) ill turn.

+**bjø‘rne/trekker** *-en, pl -e* bear trainer.

bjø‘rne/vok [/våk] *en* May 22nd, in popular belief the day when a bear will leave his den.

Bjø‘rn/skinn *Pln* twp, Nordland.

bjø‘rn/unge *-n* bear cub.

Bjø‘rn/øya *Pln* Bear Island (Norwegian possession between Norway and Spitzbergen).

***bjå'** *V -dde* 1 be fitting, suitable. 2 augur, portend, promise: **b- for** (the same).

bl.=**blad**

bla' *V -dde* flip, turn pages; thumb through (e.g. cards, bills): **b- i (gjennom) en bok** page (leaf) through a book; **b- om** turn the page; **b- opp en pengeseddel** peel off a bill; **b- opp på side 20** open to page 20.

+**bl. a.**=**blant annet**

bla'ḍ *-et, pl -/+-er* 1 leaf: **ta b-et fra munnen** speak out. 2 blade (e.g. of knife, saw, propeller). 3 page; sheet: **et b- papir** a s- of paper; **et ubeskrevet b-** a blank page; **han er et ubeskrevet b-** he is an unknown quantity; **b-et har vendt seg** things have changed; **spille, synge fra b-et** sight-read (music). 4 newspaper; periodical: **det står i b-et** it says in the paper. 5 playing card: **han fikk noen elendige b-** he got a wretched hand; **mala b-** (or: **malablad**) face card, honor. 6 print (of art).

***bla‘d/bu** *-a* newsstand; kiosk.

***bla‘de** *V -de* cf **bla**

bla‘ḍ/grønt *et* chlorophyll.

bla‘ḍ/gull *-et* gold leaf.

bla‘ḍ/lus *-a zool.* plant louse, aphid.

bla‘d/mage *-n zool.* omassum (part of the stomach of ruminant).

bla‘ḍ/mann *-en, pl -menn/*-menner* newspaperman.

+**bla‘ḍ/penger** *pl* (=***-ar**) subscription price of newspaper or periodical.

+**bla‘ḍ/smører** *-en, pl -e* (=***-jar**) *derog.* journalist; pulpwriter.

+**bla‘ḍ/styrer** *-en, pl -e* (=***-ar**) editor of newspaper or periodical.

bla‘ḍ/vott *-en* mitten.

blaff' *-et* 1 breath, puff (of wind); flapping (e.g. of flag or sail). 2 flash, flicker (of fire, emotion).

blaf‘fe *V -a/+-et* flap (of sail etc.); flash: **b- opp** flare (of fire, light etc.).

blaf‘fen *df fam.* **jeg gir b- i det** I couldn't care less.

blaf‘re *V -a/+-et* flutter; flicker.

***bla‘ge** *V -a* 1 flame, flash, flicker. 2 shine, look striking.

***bla‘ke** *V -a* 1 flap (e.g. of flag, sail). 2: **det b-ar** it is sheltered.

Bla‘ker *Pln* twp, Akershus.

blakk'[1] *A blakt* 1 faded, pale: opaque (e.g. of liquid). 2 (of horses) dun (yellowish or grayish brown). 3 broke, without money.

***blakk'**[2] *pr of* **blekke**[2]

Blak‘ka *df* name given dun mare.

blak‘ke *V -a/+-et* 1 make (a liquid) opaque. 2 cause (sby) to spend all his money: **han ble b-a i poker** he was cleaned out at poker; **b- seg** spend all one's cash.

Blak‘ken *df* name given dun horse.

blak‘ne *V -a/+-et* fade, pale (of color or sth colored).

blak‘re *V -a/+-et* rustle; twitch: **hesten b-er med ørene** the horse twitches his ears.

blama'sje *-n* disgrace, shame.

blame're *V -te* place in an unfortunate light: **b- seg** disgrace oneself, make a fool of oneself.

blan‘ḍe[1] *-a* liquid mixture, esp. **drink** of whey and water.

blan‘ḍe[2] *V -a/+-et* 1 mix (**med** with); blend, mingle: **b- blod** seal a friendship with blood (old Norse custom); **b- i** pour into, dilute with; **b- opp** mix, dilute; **b- en opp i** get sby mixed into; **b- sammen** confuse, mix up; **b-et** mixed (e.g. chorus, marriage, pleasure). 2 shuffle (cards): **b- kortene for en** confuse, trick sby. 3 *(refl.)*: **b- seg** mix; **b- seg (opp, inn) i** mix into, stick one's nose into; **b- seg med** associate with, mingle with, fraternize with.

+**blan‘ḍer** *-en, pl -e* (=***-ar**) mixer (e.g. concrete, food).

+**blan‘ḍet** *A* - (=***-a**) mixed (e.g. chorus, marriage, pleasure, train).

blan‘ḍing *-a/+-en* mixture; alloy: **en b- av godt og ondt** a m- of good and evil.

+**blan‘ḍings/forholḍ** *-et* ratio of mixture.

blan‘ḍings/rase *-n* mixed race.

blan‘ḍings/skog *-en* mixed forest.

blan‘ḍ/ko'rn *-et* 1 a mixture of two or more grains, esp. of barley and oats. 2 a publication consisting of a mixture of minor writings.

blan'k *A* 1 bright, clear; glittering, sunny. 2 glossy, shining, shiny: **b- nese** shiny nose; **b-e øyne, b- i øynene** eyes shining through tears, moistened eyes; **kjempe med b-e våpen** fight fairly. 3 plain: **b- løgn** a plain lie; **b-t nei** a flat no; **gi b-t opp** give up completely. 4 blank (check, page). 5 singleton (cards). 6 *fam.* broke.

blan‘ke *V -a/+-et* 1 polish, shine. 2 bare, empty: **b- en for penger** clean sby out of money; **b- seg** spend all one's cash.

+ Bokmål; * Nynorsk; ° Dialect.
After letter: ' stress (Acc. 1); ‘ tone, stress (Acc. 2); · length.
Below letter: . not pronounced.

blankett' *-en* blank, form.
blan'k/is *-en* ice that is clear and uncovered by snow.
blan'ko *Av*: **in b-** in blank.
blanko/endossement [blang'ko/angdåsemang'] *-et, pl -/+-er merc.* blank endorsement.
blan'ko/fullmakt *-a/+-en* plenipotentiary power; carte blanche; power of attorney.
blan'ko/veksel *-elen, pl -ler merc.* blank note.
blan'k/pusse *V -a/+-et* polish.
+blan'k/slitt *A* - worn smooth, shiny from wear.
blan'k/sverte *-a* blacking, black shoe-polish.
+blan'k/øyd *A* - (=***/øygd**) with shining (misty) eyes.
blan'k/ål *-en zool.* silver eel (Anguilla anguilla).
blan't *P* among: **være ute b- folk** be out a- people; **b- annet** a- other things, for one thing.
blase'rt *A* - blasé, cynical, sophisticated.
blasfemi' *-en* blasphemy.
blasfe'misk *A* - blasphemous.
blas'k *-et* cf **plask**
+blass' *A blast* colorless, pale, yellowish white.
blau't *A* (=**+bløt**) **1** wet: **han er b- på beina** his feet are wet. **2** (usu. **bløt**) soft; gentle: **b-t stål** mild steel; *fam.* **b- (på hjernen)** crazy, "nuts", softheaded; **en b- vits** a corny joke. **3** weak; cowardly: **de b- daner** the effeminate Danes. **4** *gram.* (of consonants) lenis.
+blau't/fengen *A -e/-i, pl -ne* effeminate, soft.
blau't/fisk *-en* effeminate, soft, weak person; coward.
***blau't/hjarta** *A* - soft-hearted.
blau'ting *-en* coward, softie.
***blau't/kake** *-a* cf **bløt/**
***blau't/koke** *V -a/-te* cf **bløt/**
blau't/lendt *A* - swampy.
blau't/myr *-a* bog.
blau't/mørje *-a* soggy mass.
***blau'tne** *V -a* **1** become soft. **2** (of person) be moved, soften; yield.
+blau't/råt(e) *-(e)n* (=***/rot, */rote**) black rot (a disease e.g. in potatoes).
+blau't/vær *-et* (=***/ver**) wet weather.
***ble'**[1] *V -dde* **1** leaf (through a book). **2** choose, select.
+ble'[2] *pt of* **bli**[1]
bled'nings/hogst *-en* selective cutting (of trees).
+blegne [blei'ne] *V -et* cf **bleikne**
blei'[1] *-en* (=**bleig**) **1** wedge. **2** difficult, unpleasant person: **en hoven b-** a stuck-up fellow.
blei'[2] *pt of* **bli**[1]
blei'e *-a* diaper.
blei'g *-en* cf **blei**[1]
***blei'gje** *V -de* split (wood) by using wedges.
blei'k[1] *-a/-en* **1** thin layer of clouds. **2** bleaching (of clothes). **3** place where clothes are laid out to bleach in the sun.
blei'k[2] *A* (=**+blek**) pale, pallid, sallow: **b-e stjerner** pale stars; **b- av skrekk** pale with fright; **b- om nebbet** pale around the gills; **et b-t smil** a wan smile.
***blei'k/andlet** *-et* paleface.
blei'k/ansikt *-et* paleface.
***blei'k/dæmd** *A -dæmt* of pale complexion.
+blei'ke[1] *-a* (=***bleikje**[1]) *zool.* whiting (Gadus merlangus).
+blei'ke[2] *V -te* (=***bleikje**[2]) bleach.
+blei'ke/middel *-elet/-midlet, pl -midler* (=***-je/**) bleach, bleaching powder.
+blei'ke/plass *-en* (=***-je/**) place where clothes are laid out to bleach in the sun.
+blei'ke/voll *-en* (=***-je/**) grass patch where clothes are laid out to bleach in the sun.
blei'k/feit *A* flabby.
blei'k/fis *-en* pale, sickly-looking person.
***blei'kje**[1] *-a* cf **bleike**[1]
***blei'kje**[2] *V -te* cf **bleike**[2]
blei'kne *V -a/+-et* (=**+blekne**) blanch, bleach, fade; turn pale.
blei'k/nebb *-en hum., derog.* paleface.
blei'k/nebba *A* - white-faced (e.g. from fear).
blei'k/sott *-a/+-en med.* anemia.
Blei'kvass/lia *Pln* mining village in Korgen twp, Nordland.
blei'v *pt of* **bli**[2], **blive**
+ble'k *A* cf **bleik**[2]
+ble'k/ansikt *-et* cf **bleik/**
+ble'ke *V -te* cf **bleike**[2]
+ble'k/fet *A* cf **bleik/feit**
***blekk'**[1] *-en* **1** blaze on a tree. **2** valve. **3** breath of wind.
blekk'[2] *-et* (=**+blikk**) **1** tin, tinplate. **2** sheet metal, sheet iron.
blekk'[3] *-et* ink.
blekk'/boks *-en* tin, tin can.
+blek'ke[1] *-a* (=***blekkje**[1]) **1** leaf (esp. dry leaf). **2** small unimportant news paper. **3** playing card of low value: **han fikk noen elendige b-r** he got a poor hand.
***blek'ke**[2] *V blakk, blokke/-i* **1** blow gently (of wind) or in breaths. **2** cf **blekke**[4].
blek'ke[3] *V -a/+-et* stain with ink: **b- seg til på fingrene** get ink on one's fingers.
+blek'ke[4] *V blekte* (=***blekkje**[2]) hit: **b- til en** hit sby.
blek'ket(e) *A* - ink-stained.
blekk'/hus *-et* inkwell.
***blek'kje**[1] *-a* cf **blekke**[1]
***blek'kje**[2] *V blekte* **1** flicker. **2** mark (tree) with a blaze. **3** hit.
***blek'kje**[3] *V blekte* look opaque (e.g. of liquid).
blekk'/klatt *-en* blot of ink, inkblot.
blekk'/plate *-a/+-en* tin plate; piece of tin.
***blekk'/slagar** *-en* cf **blikken/slager**
blekk'/smed *-en* tinsmith.
blekk'/sopp *-en bot.* inky cap (Coprinus).
blekk'/sprut *-en* (=***/sprute**) octopus, squid.
+blekk'/tøy *-et* (=***/ty**) sheetmetal articles (kitchen utensils), tin articles.
+ble'kne *V -a/-et* cf **bleikne**
+ble'k/nebb *-en* cf **bleik/**
+ble'k/sott *-a/-en* cf **bleik/**
***blek'te**[1] *V -a* bleat.
***blek'te**[2] *pt of* **bleke, blekke**[4], **blekkje**[2,3]
blem'me *-a* blister.
blen'de[1] *-n/*-a geol.* blende.
blen'de[2] *V -a/+-et* **1** blind; dazzle: **bli b-et av lyset** be b-ed by the light; **han ble b-et av hennes skjønnhet** he was d-ed by her beauty. **2** cover (lantern), dim (light), black-out (windows).
blen'dende *A* - blinding; brilliant, dazzling (e.g. light, beauty, genius).
+blen'der *-en, pl -e* (=***-ar**) shutter (e.g. in camera).
blen'ding *-a/+-en* blackout, dimming (of lights).
blen'd/lykt *-a* dark lantern.
+blen'd/verk *-et* delusion, mirage, phantom.
bleng' *-en* **1** whey. **2** drink of whey and water.
blen'k *-en* **1** blaze (marking tree for cutting). ***2** sparkle.
+blen'ke *V -te* (=**+blinke**[2], ***blenkje**) mark tree for cutting: **b- opp** blaze.
***blen'kje** *V -te* cf **blenke**
ble's[1] *-et* blaze (on horse's head); also as horse's name: **B-a, B-en.**
***ble's**[2] *pt of* **blåse**[2]
ble's/and *-a, pl -ender zool.* European type of widgeon (Mareca penelope).
ble'se[1] *-a* cf **bles**[1]
+ble'se[2] *V -te* cf **blåse**[2]
ble'set(e) *A* - (of animal) that has a blaze.
+bless' *-et* cf **bles**[1]
blesse're *V -te* wound.
blessure [blessy'r, -sy're] *-n* wound.
+bles't *-en* **1** cf **blåst. 2** fuss: **gjøre b- av noe** make a f- about sth, play sth up; **det stod b- om ham** he made himself noticed, he was a vigorous personality.
bles'tre *-t, pl +-r/*-* hollow dug in ground, used in smelting bog iron.
+ble'v *obs pt of* **bli**[1,2]
bli'[1] *V blei/vart/+ble, blitt/*vorte/*-i* **1** remain, stay: **b- sittende** remain seated; **han ble (værende) der i to år** he stayed there for two years; **det får b- med dette** this will have to be all; **det ble med den ene** that one was the last (Hoel); **han arbeidet i to dager og dermed ble det** he worked for two days and that was all; **b- ved det gamle** remain unchanged; **han ble ved sitt** he stuck to his guns. **2** will be; take place, turn out (to be): **det b-r tre kroner** that will be three *kroner*; **det b-r vanskelig** that will be difficult; **jeg b-r borte i morgen** I will be gone (won't be in) tomorrow; **du er og b-r en tosk** you are a fool and always will be; **jeg b-r atten år** I'll be eighteen; **(det) skal b-** it will be done; **det ble en stor suksess** it turned out to be a great success. **3** become, get (to be): **b- gal** go mad; **b- gift** get married; **b- lys!** let there be light!; **b- sint** get angry; **b- student** graduate (from *gymnasium*); **b- voksen** grow up; **hva vil han b-?** what does he want to be?; **han vil b- lærer** he wants to be a teacher; **det kunne b-tt til noe mellom oss** sth might have come of our relationship; **det var b-tt til at...** the upshot of it was that ... **4** be, get (with *pp.*): **han b-r ofte tatt for sin bror** he is often mistaken for his brother; **kalken b-r så blandet med vann** the lime is then mixed with water. **5** (with *adv.*): **b- av** become (of); **det b-r ikke noe av møtet** the meeting is off; **det b-r det ikke noe av** that will not be; **hva skal det b- av ham?** what will become of him?; **hvor b-r det av ham?** what's keeping him?; **b- av med** get rid of; **b- borte** disappear, get lost; **b- med** come (go) along, join (i in); **b- til** come into being; **hvordan ble verden til?** how was the world created? **b- ved** go on (e.g. speaking).
+bli'[2] *V bleiv, blitt* (=**blive**) be lost at sea, drown.
bli'd *A* gentle, mild; good-natured: **være b- på en** feel kindly towards sby; **vi får være like b-e for det** we'll have to take it with a smile; **han var ikke b-** he was angry; **et b-t landskap** a sunny, idyllic landscape; **det ble ikke sett på med b-e øyne** it was frowned upon.
***bli'de**[1] *-a* gentleness, a good temper.
bli'de[2] *-n* catapult (medieval war machine).
+bli'd/gjøre *V -gjorde, -gjort* pacify, soften (sby).
***bli'dke** *V -a* pacify, soften (sby).
bli'dne *V -a/+-et* **1** regain one's good temper. **2** pacify, soften (sby).
***bli'd(s)leg** *A* - friendly, good-humored, good-natured.
***bli'd/voren** [/våren] *A -e/-i, pl -ne* friendly, good-humored.
***bli'd/vær** *A* having a friendly, happy disposition.
***bli'k** *-et* cf **blikk**[2]
bli'kande** *Av* (=-ende**) cf **blikkende**
***bli'ke** *V -a* **1** have a pale or white appearance (e.g. of sea reflecting clouds). **2** sparkle. **3** mark with white spot(s), blaze(s).
blikk'[1] *-et* **1** glance, look: **kaste et b- på noe** take a (quick) look at sth; **han så det med ett b-** he saw it (took it in) at a glance; **kjærlighet ved første b-** love at first sight; **et sint b-** an angry look. **2** eye, understanding: **ha et åpent b- for noe** have a keen eye for sth; appreciate.
+blikk'[2] *-et* cf **blekk**[2]

+blikk'[3] *-et* (=***blik**) a pale light or shimmer.
blikk'[4] *Av* = **blikkende**
+blikk'/blåser *-en, pl -e* brass player.
+blikk'/boks *-en* cf **blekk/**
+blik'kende *Av* (=***blikande**): **b- stille** dead calm, dead still.
+blik'ken/slager *-en, pl -e* tinsmith.
blikk'/fang *-et* (=**+/fanger**) eye-catcher (advertisement or advertising sign, designed to catch eye).
+blikk'/plate *-n* cf **blekk/**
+blikk'/stille *A* - (=***blik/still**) dead calm.
+blikk'/tøy *-et* cf **blekk/**
***bli'k/still** *A -stilt* cf **blikk/stille**
***blik't** *-et* flash, glimpse, shadow.
***blik'te** *V -a* flash, glint.
blin'ḍ *A* **1** blind: **b- høne finner også et korn** even a stupid person can come up with sth good; **b- av røyken** blinded by the smoke; **b- på det ene øye** b- in one eye. **2** blind = uncritical: **lystre b-t** obey blindly; **stole b-t på en** have b- faith in sby; **b- for mulighetene** b- to the possibilities; **stirre (se) seg b- på noe** get so wrapped up in sth that one loses critical perspective. **3** hidden, unseen: **b-t skjær** underwater reef; **få fire kort b-t** get four cards face down. **4** blind = false: **gata ender b-t** it is a dead-end street; **b- alarm** false alarm.
blin'ḍe[1] *-a* blindness: **i b-** blindly; **jeg kunne gjøre det i b-** I could do it blindfolded.
blin'ḍe[2] *V -a/+-et* put (sby's) eyes out; blind.
blin'ḍe/alfabe't *-et, pl +-er/*-* Braille.
blin'ḍe/bukk [/bokk] *-en* **1** blindman's buff. **2** the blindfolded person in blindman's buff.
blin'ḍe/mann *-en* dummy (bridge).
Blin'ḍern *Pln* post office and university site in Oslo.
blin'ḍe/skrift *-a/+-en* Braille writing.
blin'ḍ/gate *-a* blind alley; cul-de-sac; dead-end street.
+blin'ḍ/gjenger *-en, pl -e* (=***/gangar**) projectile that fails to explode (=dud).
+blin'ḍ/het *-en* blindness.
blin'ḍing *-en* cf **blind/klegg**
blin'ḍ/klegg *-en* (=**blinding**) *zool.* a type of deerfly (Chrysops caecutiens).
blin'ḍ/passasje'r *-en* stowaway.
blin'ḍ/ramme *-a* stretcher (frame on which an artist's canvas is stretched).
***blin'ḍ/skap** *-en* blindness.
+blin'ḍ/skjær *-et* (=***/skjer**) underwater reef, hidden rock.
blin'ḍ/spor *-et* dead end.
blin'ḍ/tarm *-en anat.* appendix: **ta b-en** remove the a-.
blin'ḍ/veg *-en* (=**+/vei**) dead-end road.
+blin'ḍ/vindu *-et* blind (=false) window.
bling's[1] *-en* squint-eyed person.
bling's[2] *-en pop.* thick slice, chunk (of bread).
bling'se[1] *-a* squint-eyed woman.
bling'se[2] *V -a/+-et* squint.
bling'set(e) *A* - squint-eyed.
blin'k[1] *-en* **1** target; bull's-eye: **skyte på b-** shoot at a t-; **treffe midt i b-en** hit the bull's-eye, *fig.* hit the mark. **2** blaze (on tree to be cut).
+blin'k[2] *-et* **1** flash, gleam (e.g. from an oscillating beacon); twinkle, wink: **ha et b- i øyet** have a t- in one's eye. **2** glimpse; moment, second: **i et b-** in a flash.
blin'ke[1] *V -a/+-et* **1** emit flashes, sparkle; twinkle, wink: **b-ende stjerner** twinkling stars. **2** blink (one's eyes).
+blin'ke[2] *V -a/-et/-te* cf **blenke**
+blin'ker *-en, pl -e* (=***-ar**) person who marks trees for cutting.
blin'ke/øks *-a* pole stamp ax.
blin'k/fyr *-et* flashing beacon.
blis'tre *V -a/+-et* cf **plystre**

blitt' *pp of* **bli, blive**
blit'z/lampe *-a/-en* flash attachment, flashgun.
bli've *V bleiv, +blitt/*blive/*-i* cf **bli**[2]
+bli'vende *A* - lasting, permanent (e.g. value); **her er ikke (noe) b- sted** we can't stay here, let us move on.
blo'ḍ *-et* blood: **av kongelig b-** of royal b-; **blått b-** blue b-; **få b- på tann** taste b- = get excited about doing sth; **gå en i b-et** become second nature to sby; **sette ondt b- mellom noen** cause enmity between sby.
blo'ḍ/appelsi'n *-en* blood orange (with reddish pulp).
blo'ḍ/bad *-et* bloodbath.
blo'ḍ/bank *-en* blood bank.
blo'ḍ/bøk *-en bot.* copper beech (Fagus silvatica purpurea).
blo'ḍ/dråpe *-n* (=***/drope**) cf **blods/**
+blo'ḍ/dryppende *A* - (=***/drypande**) blood-curdling.
blo'ḍ/dåd *-en* killing, murder.
blo'ḍe *V -a/+-et* soil, stain with blood: **b- seg til på hendene** get one's hands bloody.
blo'ḍet(e) *A* - bloody, stained with blood.
blo'ḍ/fattig *A* - anemic.
blo'ḍ/fersk *A* fresh-killed (esp. of game).
+blo'ḍ/forgif'tning *-en* (=***/forgifting**) blood poisoning.
blo'ḍ/full *A* **1** full of blood, plethoric. **2** full of life; hot-blooded, temperamental.
***blodge** [blåg'ge] *V -a* **1** wound. **2** cut (newly caught fish) to make the blood flow away.
+blo'ḍ/giver *-en, pl -e* (=***/gjevar**) blood donor.
+blo'ḍ/hevn *-en* (=***/hemn**) blood vengeance.
blo'ḍ/hund *-en* bloodhound.
blo'dig *A* - **1** bloody (e.g. nose, revenge): **b- i ansiktet** having blood on one's face; **en b- kamp** a b- battle. **2** cruel, rank: **en b- urett** a r- injustice; **en b- pris** an unreasonable price, highway robbery.
blo'ḍ/igle *-a/-en* **1** leech (Hirudo medicinalis). **2** extortioner; usurer.
blo'ḍ/kar *-et* blood vessel.
blo'ḍ/klubb *-en* type of food shaped like a meatball, made of blood, flour, potatoes, etc.
***blo'ḍ/krinslaup** *-et* circulatory system of the blood; blood stream.
blo'ḍ/laus *A* (=**+/løs**) anemic.
+blo'ḍ/legeme *-t* (=***/lekam**) blood corpuscle.
+blo'ḍ/løs *A* cf **/laus**
blo'ḍ/mangel *-en* anemia.
blo'ḍ/mat *-en* food made from blood.
+blo'ḍ/omlø'p *-et* (=***/omlaup**) circulatory system of the blood; bloodstream.
blo'ḍ/overfø'ring *-a/+-en* blood transfusion.
+blo'ḍ/penger *pl* (=***-ar**) blood money.
blo'ḍ/plasma *-et* plasma.
blo'ḍ/propp *-en* blood clot; coronary thrombosis.
blo'ḍ/prøve *-a/+-en* blood test; blood sample.
blo'ḍ/pudding *-en* blood pudding.
blo'ḍ/pølse *-a* blood sausage.
+blo'ḍ/rød *A* (=***/raud**) blood-red.
blo'ds/dråpe *-en* (=**blod/**, ***/drope**) drop of blood: **slåss til siste b-** fight to the end; *bot.* **Kristi b-** fuchsia.
blo'ds/frende *-n* blood relation.
blo'ds/hest *-en* thoroughbred.
blo'ḍ/sinne *-t* mad, uncontrollable rage.
blo'ḍ/skam· *-ma/-men* incest.
+blo'ḍ/skutt *A* - bloodshot.
blo'ḍ/slit *-et* grueling toil.
blo'ḍ/sott *-a/+-en archaic* abnormal loss of blood during illness (e.g. dysentery).
+blo'ḍ/sprengt *A* - red in the face; (of eyes) bloodshot.
blo'ḍ/sprut *-en* jet, spurt of blood: **han skar seg så b-en stod** he cut himself so that the blood spurted.
blo'ḍ/stansing *-a/+-en* stanching the blood flow.
+blo'ḍ/stenkt *A* - blood-spattered.
blo'ḍ/stillende *A* - blood-stopping, styptic.
+blo'ḍ/styrtning *-en* hemorrhage (esp. hemoptysis).
+blo'ḍ/suger *-en, pl -e* (=***-ar**) bloodsucker.
+blo'ds/utgy'telse *-en* bloodshed.
blo'ḍ/tap *-et* loss of blood.
blo'ḍ/trykk *-et* blood pressure.
blo'ḍ/type *-n* blood group, blood type.
+blo'ḍ/tørstig *A* - bloodthirsty.
+blo'ḍ/underlø'pen *A -ent, pl -ne* bloodshot.
+blo'ḍ/uttre'delse *-n* effusion (extravasation) of blood.
blo'ḍ/varm *A* (of body) still warm.
blo'ḍ/vatn *-et* (=**+/vann**) blood serum.
***blo'ḍ/vekkje** *V -vekte* wound.
blo'ḍ/vitne *-et, pl +-r/*-* martyr.
blo'ḍ/ørn *-a/-en*: **riste b- på ryggen av en** "draw a bloody eagle on sby's back", kill sby by cutting his ribs loose from the spine and pulling out the lungs (said to have been practiced by the vikings).
blo'ḍ/åre *-a/+-en* (=***/år**) blood vein.
°**blog'ge** *V -a* cf **blodge**
bloka'de *-n* blockade.
+bloka'de/bryter *-en, pl -e* (=***-ar**) blockade-runner (of person, ship).
***blo'ke** *-a* **1** thin plate or segment. **2** corner of a garment; a small apron. **3** valve.
bloke're *V -te* cf **blokkere**
blokk' *-a/-en* **1** block (of wood, stone, etc.): **legge hodet på b-en** put one's head on the executioner's b-. **2** ingot. **3** (writing) pad. **4** bloc (in politics). **5** apartment house.
blok'ke[1] *-a* **1** leaf. **2** flap; patch.
blok'ke[2] *V -a/+-et* block, stretch by blocking (e.g. hats, gloves).
***blok'ke**[3] *pp of* **blekke**[2]
blok'ke/bær *-et bot.* type of blueberry (Vaccinium uliginosum).
blok'kende *Av*: **b- fast** sticking completely, not to be budged.
blokke're *V -te* **1** blockade. **2** block (e.g. entrance). **3** *typog.* reverse type (to show that a different type will be inserted later).
***blok'ket(e)** *A* - *bot.* **1** (of leaf) lacimiate. **2** (of tree) leafy.
blokk'/fløyte *-a* recorder (wooden flute).
blokk'/hus *-et* blockhouse.
***blo'kki** *pp of* **blekke**[2]
blokk'/kalen'der *-eren, pl -rer* desk calendar.
Blokk's/berg *Pln* Brocken (a mountain in Germany, where witches were thought to assemble): **dra til B-** go to hell.
blokk'/skrift *-a/+-en* block printing.
blo'm [+blåmm'] *+-men/*-en* flower: ***i b-** blooming.
Blom' *Prn*: **fru B-** *hum.* (tag added to repetition of a word to show mild disagreement), e.g. X: **"Maten er god"**. Y: **"God og god, fru B-."** X: "The food is good." Y: "Yes and no."
***blo'me** *-n* cf **blom**
blom'/karse *-n bot.* nasturtium (Tropaeolum).
blom'/kål *-en bot.* cauliflower (Brassica oleracea capitata).
+blom'me *-n* cf **blom**
+blom'st *-en, pl -er* cf **blomster**
blom'ster *-eren, pl -rer* (=**+blomst**) blossom, flower.
blom'ster/bed· *-et* flower bed.
blom'ster/botn *-en* (=**+/bunn**) *bot.* receptacle, torus.

+ Bokmål; * Nynorsk; ° Dialect.
After letter: ' stress (Acc. 1); ` tone, stress (Acc. 2); · length.
Below letter: . not pronounced.

blom'ster/bukett' *-en* bouquet.
blom'ster/dekke *-t bot.* perianth.
blom'ster/ert *-a* (=***/erter**) *bot.* sweet pea.
blom'ster/flor *-et* carpet of flowers; floral decoration.
blom'ster/glas *-et* (=**+/glass**) glass flower vase.
blom'ster/kasse *-a/-en* window box.
blom'ster/lauk *-en* bulb.
blom'ster/potte *-a* flowerpot.
blom'ster/stand *-en* cluster of flowers; *bot.* inflorescence.
blom'ster/støv *-et bot.* pollen.
blom'stre *V -a/+-et* **1** blossom, flower. **2** flourish, prosper: **b-ende handel** f-ing trade.
blom'stret(e) *A* - flowered.
blom'string *-a/+-en* bloom, flowering; flourishing.
blond' [also blån'd] *A* blond(e).
blon'de *+-n/*-a* lace.
blon'de/krage *-n* lace collar.
blondi'ne *-a/+-en* blond(e).
blo't[1] *-et* sacrifice to heathen (Norse) gods.
***blot[2]** [blå't] *-et* soaking: **leggje i b-** put to soak.
blo't/bolle *-n* bowl to collect blood at the **blot**.
***blote[1]** [blå'te] *-n* **1** mud. **2** wet weather (rain, thawing).
blo'te[2] *V -a/+-et* sacrifice (to heathen Norse gods).
***blote[3]** [blå'te] *V -a* become soaked, soft.
***blot'ne** *V -a* **1** become soaked, soft. **2** (of a person) soften, yield.
+blott' *A* - **1** bare, naked: **det b-e øye** the n- eye; **b- og bar** mere. **2** *(adv.)* merely, only, simply: **det er en saga b-** it has become a memory, it isn't any more; **b- og bart** merely.
+blot'te *V -a/-et* **1** expose, lay bare, uncover: **b- tennene** bare one's teeth; **stå med b-et hode** stand with bared head; **han er b-et for fantasi** he hasn't any imagination. **2: b- seg** betray oneself, make a blunder; lower one's guard; expose oneself indecently.
+blot'tende *Av*: **b- ung** quite young, in her first bloom.
+blot'ter *-en, pl -e* exhibitionist.
+blott'/legge *V -la, -lagt* expose, lay bare; betray.
+blott'/stille *V -stilte*: **b- seg** betray, expose oneself, leave oneself open (to attack, criticism).
+blott'/stillelse *-n* exposure.
+blu'es *V -edes, -es* cf **blyges**
+blufer'dig *A* - bashful; chaste, modest.
+blufer'dig/het *-en* bashfulness; chastity, modesty.
blund' *-en* doze, nap: **ta seg en b-** have a nap; **jeg fikk ikke b- på øynene i natt** I couldn't sleep a wink last night; **Jon b-** the sandman.
blun'de *V -a/+-et* doze, take a nap: **b- av** drop off.
blunder [bløn'der] *-en, pl +-e* blunder.
blunk [blong'k] *-en/+-et* **1** wink. **2** flash, moment: **på et b- var rommet fullt** in a m- the room was crowded.
blunke [blong'ke] *V -a/+-et* blink, wink: **b- med øynene** b- one's eyes, wink; **uten å b-** without batting an eye.
blu'se *-a/-en* blouse.
+blus'el *-en* cf **blygsel**
blu'se/liv *-et* blouse.
bluss' *-et* blaze, flame; flare; light; torch: *pop.* **ha b- på lampen** be lit (slightly drunk).
blus'se *V -a/+-et* blaze, flame, flare; blush, flush: **b- opp** flare up (of fire, anger); **kinnene b-et** (her) cheeks flushed.
blus'sende *A* - flushed: **b- rød** burning red, flaming red.
bly' *-et* lead.
bly'ant *-en* pencil.
+bly'ant/spisser *-en, pl -e* (=***-ar**) pencil sharpener.
bly'ant/stubb *-en* pencil stub.
bly'/farga *A* - (=**+-et**) leaden-hued.
bly'g *A* bashful, shy.
***blyg'd** *a* bashfulness, shyness.
***bly'gdest** *pt of* **blygjast**
+bly'ges *V -des/-es* (=**+blues, *blygjast**) be bashful, shy; feel embarrassed.
+bly'g/het *-en* bashfulness, shyness.
***bly'gjast** *V blygjest, blygdest, blygst* cf **blyges**
bly'/glans *-en geol.* galena.
bly'/grå *A -tt* grey as lead, leaden.
***bly'g/sam** *A* **1** bashful, shy. **2** which causes or would cause embarrassment.
bly'gsel *-la/+-elen* (=**+blusel, *blygsle**) bashfulness, shyness; embarrassment, feeling of shame.
***bly'g/skap** *-en* **1** bashfulness, shyness. **2** modesty.
***bly'gsle** *-a* cf **blygsel**
***bly'gst** *pp of* **blygjast**
bly'/hatt *-en* "leaden hat": **ha b-** be drunk.
+bly'/holdig *A* - (=***/haldig**) (of mineral) containing lead.
+bly'/hvitt *-et* white lead.
+bly'/innfat'tet *A* - leaded (of window pane).
bly'/svart *A* - leaden, black as lead: **en b- himmel** a l- sky.
bly'/tung *A* heavy as lead.
bly'/vatn *-et* (=**+/vann**) liquid solution of lead subacetate (used on bruises).
***blæ'je** *V -a* cf **bleie**
blæ're[1] *-a* **1** bladder. **2** blister. **3** bubble. **4** conceited person.
blæ're[2] *V -a/+-et* blister; **b- seg** put on airs; **seglet b-et seg ut** the sail filled (Bojer).
blæ're/rot *-a bot.* bladderwort (Utricularia).
blæ're/tang *-et/+-en bot.* bladder wrack (Fucus vesiculosus).
blæ'ret(e) *A* - **1** blistery, bubbly. **2** conceited, puffed up.
***blæ's** *pr of* **blåse[1]**
blø' *V -dde* (=**bløde**) **1** bleed, lose blood: **b- neseblod** have a nosebleed; **få b- for noe** have to b- for sth. **2** secrete a liquid, weep (e.g. of a tree that is cut).
blø'de *V -de* cf **blø**
blø'dende *A* - bleeding: **med b- hjerte** with a b- heart.
+blø'der *-en, pl -e* (=***-ar**) bleeder.
+blød'me *-n* pun; corny joke.
+blø'dning *-en* (=***bløding**) bleeding, hemorrhage.
bløff' *-en/-et* bluff (=deceit).
bløf'fe *V -a/+-et* bluff (=deceive).
***bløk'te** *V -a* **1** waft. **2** pulsate.
***blø'me[1]** *-a* flower.
***blø'me[2]** *V -de* **1** blossom. **2** flourish, prosper.
***blø'ming** *-a* **1** bloom, blossoming. **2** flourishing.
+blø't[1] *A* cf **blaut**
+blø't[2] *N* cf **bløyt**
+blø't/aktig *A* - effeminate, soft.
+blø't/dyr *-et* (=**blaut/**) mollusk.
+blø'te *V -te* cf **bløyte[2]**
+blø'te/kum [/komm] *-men* laundry tray, laundry tub.
+blø't/gjøre *V -gjorde, -gjort* mollify.
+blø't/het *-en* softness.
+blø't/hjertet *A* - (=***blaut/hjarta**) soft-hearted.
+blø't/kake *-a* (=***blaut/**) layer cake.
+blø't/koke *V -te* (=***blaut/**) soft boil (eggs).
+bløt'ne *V -a/-et* **1** become soaked, soft(er). **2** soften, make soft(er).
+bløt'te *pt of* **bløyte[2]**
***bløy'g** *-en* cf **bleig**
bløy't *n* (=**+bløt**): **legge klær i b-** put clothes to soak.
bløy'te[1] *-a* soaking; heavy rainfall.
bløy'te[2] *V -te/+bløtte* (=**+bløte**) soak: **b- opp noe** soften sth by soaking it.
+bløy'te/vær *-et* (=***/ver**) sopping wet (soppy) weather.
blå' *A -tt, pl -/*-e* **1** blue: **b- i ansiktet** b- in the face; **b- øyne** b- eyes; **b-tt blod** b- blood (aristocratic); **b- av kulde** b- with cold; **bak skyen er himmelen alltid b-** every cloud has a silver lining; **det brenner et b-tt lys over ham** he is in trouble. **2 det b-** the sky: **stirre ut i det b-** gaze into space; **det er i det b-** it's quite uncertain. **3** (of bruises) black: **et b-tt øye** a black eye; **jeg er gul og b- over det hele** I am black and blue all over. **4: det skal du bli b- for** you won't get your way. ***5** (blue) horizon: **fare frå b- til b-** travel from horizon to horizon.
blå'/aktig *A* - bluish.
blå'/bok *-a, pl -bøker* blue book: **1** an official publication. **2** a soldier's manual.
blå'/bær *-et bot.* blueberry (Vaccinium).
blå'/dress *-en* dark blue or black suit; best suit.
***blå'e** *-n* bluish color; blue horizon.
blå'/fjør *-a bot.* polygala.
+blå'/frossen *A -ent, pl -frosne* (=***/frosen**) blue with cold.
blå'/fryse *V infl as* **fryse** be blue with cold.
+blå'/holde *V -holdt, -holdt* (=***/halde**) hold on to (sth) with all one's might.
blå'/is *-en* blue ice (esp. in glaciers).
blå'/klokke *-a bot.* bluebell (Campanula rotundifolia).
blå'/knapp *-en bot.* blue scabious (Succisa pratensis).
blå'/knute *-n* (=***/knut**) a double knot, pulled hard and difficult to untie.
blå'/koll *-en bot.* self-heal (Prunella vulgaris).
blå'/kvit *A* bluish white.
blå'/leire *-a* (***/leir -et**) blue clay, potter's clay.
blå'lig *A* - bluish.
blå'/lys *-et* will o' the wisp (in popular belief a supernatural light showing in the dark and leading people astray).
Blå'/man *Pln* name of several mountains in Norway, e.g. near Bergen and near Tromsø.
+blå'/mandag *-en* (=***/måndag**) *fam.* the day after (esp. of a working day following a gay celebration).
blå'/mann *-en, pl -menn/*-menner* **1** "darkman", Old Norse term for negro and esp. Arab (Moor, Saracen). **2** *(prn.)* used of billygoat that is white with dark patches.
blå'/myra *df* "the blue moor", ocean, esp. the Atlantic: **dra over b-** go to America (as immigrant).
***blå'nad** *-en* blue color.
blå'ne[1] *-n* **1** faraway point on the horizon that has a bluish appearance; horizon. **2** blue spot in a cloudy sky.
blå'ne[2] *V -a/+-et/+-te* have a blue, bluish appearance.
blå'/nekte *V -a/+-et* deny (esp. an accusation) vigorously.
blå'/nøye *A* - **1** particular (in a petty, narrowminded manner, e.g. about detail or small amounts of money). **2** all-important: **det er ikke så b- med de ørene** don't bother with those few pennies.
blå'/papir *-et* carbon paper.
blå'/prikket(e) *A* - blue-dotted.
blå'/pugge *V -a/+-et* learn, memorize with great energy.
+blå'r *N* tow: **kaste en b- i øynene** pull the wool over sby's eyes.
blå'/raud *A* (=**+/rød**) bluish red, purple.
blå'/rev *-en* blue fox.
blå'/russ *-en* student of a commercial college, who wears a blue cap for some weeks around the time of his final examination.
blå'/rutet(e) *A* - blue-checked.
blå'se[1] *-a* **1** bladder (that can be inflated). **2** whistle.
***blå'se[2]** *V blæs, bles, blåse/-i* cf **blåse[3]**
blå'se[3] *V -te* **1** blow (of wind): **b-ende** windy; **det b-er opp** the wind is

coming up. 2 blow; puff, snort (of person): **b- glass** b- glass; **b- i fløyte** b- a whistle; **b- på horn (fløyte)** b- a horn (a flute); **b- opp en ballong** b- up a balloon; **b- seg opp** strut, put on airs; **han b-te da han kom opp av vannet** he snorted (puffed) when ge got out of the water; **vel b-t** well done. 3 sniff, scorn: **å blås** pooh-pooh; **det b-er jeg i** I couldn't care less; **b- en lang marsj (et langt stykke) i noe (noen)** not give a hang about sth (sby). 4: **rommet var b-t** the room was tidy; **plassen var b-t for folk** the square was deserted.

blå'se/belg *-en* bellows: **pusten gikk som en b- på ham** he was puffing like a b-.

blå'se/instrumen·t *-et, pl -/+-er* wind instrument.

blå'se/maski·n *-en* blower.

+**blå'/skjell** *-a/-et* (=*/**skjel**) *zool.* (common, edible) mussel (Mytilus edulis).

blå's/mess(e) *en* St. Blasius's Day (February 3rd).

blås't *-en* (=+**blest,** ***blåster**) wind; windy weather.

blå'/stein *-en* 1 bluish stone. 2 blue vitriol.

blås'ter *-en* 1 *dial.* =**blåst.** 2 smelting of bog iron ore.

blås'ter/jern [/jæ'rn] *-et* bog iron.

blå'/strømpe *-a/+-en* bluestocking.

blå'/sur *A* (of milk) that has gone sour and has a bluish color.

blå'/svart *A* - blue black, black and blue.

blå'/symre *-a bot.* blue anemone, hepatica (Anemone hepatica).

blå'/syre *-a* hydrocyanic acid, Prussic acid.

blå'/topp *-en bot.* moorgrass (Molinia coerulea).

blått' *et* blue color; blue material: **være kledd i b-** be dressed in blue.

+**blå'/tøy** *-et* (=*/**ty**) colored (often blue) and patterned cotton cloth.

blå'/veis *-en* 1 *bot.* blue anemone, hepatica (Anemone hepatica). 2 *pop.* black eye: **få seg en b-** receive a b- e-.

+**blå'/øyd** *A* - (=*/**øygd**) 1 blue-eyed. 2 gullible, naive.

bm.=**bokmål**

+**bo'**[1] *-et* 1 abode; home: **sette bo** settle down (after marriage), set up housekeeping, **feste bo** establish a home. 2 estate: **sitte i uskiftet bo** (of widow or widower) retain the common estate without dividing any of it among the heirs.

***bo'**[2] *N*: **ha bo å gjøre noe** need, ought to do sth.

+**bo'**[3] *V -dde* cf **bu**[3]

+**-bo** *-en* cf **-bu**

bo'a *-en* boa.

+**bob'le**[1] *-a/-en* (=***buble**[1]) bubble.

+**bob'le**[2] *V -a/-et* (=***buble**[2]) bubble.

+**bo'd**[1] *-en* cf **bot**[2]

+**bo'd**[2] *-en* 1 shack, shanty. 2 shop, stall, stand.

***bod**[3] [bå'] *-et* cf **bud**

***bode**[1] [bå'e] *V -a* 1 forebode. 2 send word.

***bode**[2] [bå'e] *pp of* **byde**

bode'ga *-en* bodega (wine shop).

+**bodfer'dig** *A* - cf **botferdig**

***bodi** [bå'i] *pp of* **byde**

Bo'dil *Prn (f)*

Bodin [bå'din] *Pln* twp, Nordland.

+**bod/o'rd** [bå'/] *-et* cf **bud/**

+**bod's/fengsel** *-elet/-let* cf **bots/**

***bod/skap** [bå'/] *-en* cf **bud/**

***bod/stikke** [bå'/] *-a* cf **bud/**

Bo'd/ø *Pln* town, Nordland.

bo'er *-en, pl +-e* (=***bur**) Boer.

+**-bo'er** *-en, pl -e* (=+**-buer,** ***-buar**) -dweller (e.g. **hule-** cave-).

boffe [bof'fe] *V -a/+-et* (of dog) woof.

bo'g *-en* shoulder of larger animal, esp. dressed for market (e.g. of sheep).

boge [bå'ge] *-n* (=+**bue**) 1 *mil., mus.* bow (usu. **bue** in idioms): **spenne b-n** bend the b-; **spenne b-n for høyt** aim too high, set one's ambitions too high. 2 arc; circle, curve: **gå i (en) b-, beskrive en b-** describe an a-, a c-; **gå i b- utenom, gjøre en b- forbi** make a wide c- in passing. 3 arch (e.g. supporting bridge); wicket (e.g. croquet).

boge/lampe *-n* (=+**bue/**) arc lamp.

***bogen** [bå'-] *A -e/-i, pl -ne* arched; bent.

boge/sag [bå'ge/] *-a* bow saw.

***boge/skyttar** *-en* cf **bue/skytter**

boge/streng *-en* (=+**bue/**) bowstring.

***boget(e)** [bå'-] *A* - arched, curved.

bog'gi *-en* bogie (a swiveling axle or truck on a railroad car).

bog'gi/vogn [/vångn] *-a* railroad car with bogie-type truck.

bogne [bong'ne] *V -a/+-et* (=+**bugne**) bend (from heavy load); bulge: **treet b-er av frukt** the tree is heavy with fruit; **et b-ende bord** a table loaded (groaning) with food.

bo'g/ring *-en* ring-shaped pad put around horse's neck to protect from chafing.

bo'g/tre *-et, pl -/+-trær* hame (wooden part of horse's collar).

+**bo'/have** *-t* furniture, furnishings.

bohe'm *-en* Bohemian (only of artists and authors, esp. in the 1880's, living an unconventional life).

boi [båi'] *-en* baize (a coarse, loose woolen fabric).

boikott [båi'-] *-en* boycott.

boikotte [båi'-] *V -a/+-et* boycott.

boja'r *-en* boyar.

bo'k[1] *-a, pl bøker* 1 book: **b-a kom ut til jul** the b- appeared before Christmas; **det står ikke i b-a** it isn't in the b-; **det står ikke i b-a** it isn't in the b-; **ha lyst til b-en** (usu. not **b-a**) want to study; **føre bøker** keep b-s; **ta (varer) på b-** buy (goods) on credit. 2 quire (of paper).

bo'k[2] *-a* cf **bøk**

+**bo'k/anmel·delse** *-n* book review.

bo'k/avl *-en* output of books (in a given period, by a country).

+**bo'k/binder** *-en, pl -e* (=***-ar**) bookbinder.

***bo'k/bu** *-a* bookstore.

bo'k/fink *-en zool.* chaffinch (Fringilla coelebs).

+**bo'k/flom·** *-men* deluge, flood of books, esp. the concentration of books published before Christmas in Norway.

bo'k/form *N*: **utgi i b-** publish in book form.

bo'k/føre *V -te* enter in the books, keep account of.

bo'k/føring *-a/+-en* bookkeeping (esp. as a school discipline).

+**bo'k/førsel** *-en* cf **/føring** (=*/**førsle**)

***bo'k/haldar** *-en* cf **/holder**

bo'k/handel *-elen, pl -ler* bookstore.

+**bo'k/handler** *-en, pl -e* (=***-ar**) bookseller.

***bo'k/heim** *-en* literature.

+**bo'k/holder** *-en, pl -e* (=*/**haldar**) bookkeeper.

+**bokholderi'** *-et* 1 bookkeeping: **dobbelt b-** double entry b-. 2 bookkeeping office.

+**bo'k/hvete** *-n* cf **/kveite**

bo'k/hylle *-a* bookshelf.

bokk [bokk'] *-en* bottle of bock beer.

***bok'ke** *-n* 1 bigwig, important person. 2 ghost; supernatural being (esp. subterranean).

bo'k/kveite *-n* (=+/**hvete**) *bot.* buckwheat (Fagopyrum).

bokk/øl· [bokk'/] *-et* bock beer.

+**bo'k/lade** *-n* bookstore.

bo'klig *A* - relating to books, bookish; literary: **b- lærdom** book learning.

bo'k/lærd *A* - learned.

bo'k/lærdom *-men/*-en* book learning.

bo'k/lært *A* - 1 literate. 2 educated.

bo'k/magasi·n *-et* stacks (in library).

bo'k/mann *-en, pl -menn/*-menner* author; man of letters.

bo'k/melding *-a/+-en* book review.

bo'k/merke *-t, pl +-r/*-* bookmark.

bo'k/mål *-et* "book language", one of the two official languages of Norway (formerly called **riksmål**).

Bok'n *Pln* twp, Rogaland.

Bok'na/fjorden *Pln* fjord in Rogaland, north of Stavanger.

bo'k/orm *-en* bookworm.

***bo'k/prentar** *-en* printer, typographer.

***bo'k/reiar** *-en* publisher.

***bo'k/reiing** *-a* publishing.

bo'k/reo·l *-en* bookcase, bookshelf.

bok's *-en* (metal) box; (safe deposit) box; (telephone) booth; (witness) box; (tin) can; locker.

bo'k/samling *-a/+-en* collection of books, library.

bok'se *V -a/+-et* box (=fight).

bok'se/kamp *-en* boxing match.

bok'se/mat *-en* canned food.

+**bok'ser** *-en, pl -e* (=***-ar**) boxer, pugilist.

bok's/kalv *-en* box calf.

+**bo'k/skap** *-et* (=*/**skåp**) bookcase.

***bo'k/soge** [/så·ge] *-a* history of literature.

bo'k/språk *-et* book language, stilted, unnatural language.

boksta'v *-en* letter: **store b-er** capitals (upper case l-s); **små b-er** small l-s (lower case l-s); **etter lovens b-** according to the l- of the law.

boksta'velig *A* - (=***bokstavleg**) literal, to the letter: **b- talt** literally.

bokstave're *V -te* spell.

boksta'v/gåte *-a/+-en* logogriph (a riddle involving anagrams).

boksta'v/læ·rdom *-men/*-en* rote learning.

boksta'v/rekning *-a* (=+/**regning**) algebra.

boksta'v/rett *A* - letter-perfect (e.g. rendering), letter by letter.

boksta'v/rim *-et* alliteration.

bo'k/støtte *-a* bookend.

bo'k/sy·nt *A* - able to read.

bo'k/trykk *-et* letterpress.

+**bo'k/trykker** *-en, pl -e* (=***-jar**) printer, typographer.

bo'k/vogn [/vångn] *-a* book truck.

+**bo'l**[1] *-en* (=***bul**) trunk; torso.

bo'l[2] *-et* 1 dwelling-place; farm. 2 (wasp) hive; lair.

+**bol'd** *A* (=***bald**) brave: **en b- ridder** a b- knight.

***bol'de** *-n* abscess.

***bo'le**[1] *-a* 1 bubble; bulge. 2 camber (on broach). 3 smallpox.

+**bo'le**[2] *V -et* whore.

***bo'len** *A -e/-i, pl -ne* swollen, tumid.

bole'ro *-en* bolero.

***bo'le/sott** *-a* smallpox.

+**bo'lig** *-en* abode, dwelling.

+**bo'lig/blokk** *-en* apartment building.

+**bo'lig/lån** *-et* housing loan.

+**bo'lig/nød** *-en* housing shortage.

bo'lig- og spa're/lag *-et* (cooperative) building and savings association.

+**bo'lig/selskap** *-et* housing cooperative.

bo'/line *-a* bowline.

+**bolivia'ner** *-en, pl -e* (=***-ar**) Bolivian.

bolivia'nsk *A* - Bolivian.

bol'k *-en* 1 partition; stall (in barn). 2 section (esp. in a book). 3 period, spell (of weather).

bol'ke *V -a/+-et* partition (**av** off).

bol'ket(e) *A* - uneven, patchy.

bol'le[1] *-n* (sweet) bun, roll; (fish, meat) ball: **nå skal det bli andre b-r** now things are going to be different.

bol'le[2] *-n* bowl (**med** of).

bol'le/fjes *-et* chubby, round-cheeked face.

bol'le/kinn *-et* chubby, round cheek.

bol'let(e) *A* - chubby, pudgy.

bo'lne[1] *V -a/+-et* swell, become tumid.

***bo'lne**[2] *pl of* **bolen**

bol'sjevik *-en* Bolshevik.

bolsjevis'me *-n* Bolshevism.

+ Bokmål; * Nynorsk; ° Dialect.
After letter: ' stress (Acc. 1); ' tone, stress (Acc. 2); · length.
Below letter: . not pronounced.

bo'lsok· *en* (**=botolvsok**) St. Botolv's Day (June 17th).
bol'ster *-eret/-ret, pl -er/+-re* **1** ticking. **2** bolster; heavy quilt.
Bo'ls/øy *Pln* twp, Møre og Romsdal.
bol't[1] *-en* bolt.
bol't[2] *-en* reinforcing in a sail.
bol'te *V -a/+-et* bolt, secure by bolts.
bol'tre *V -a/+-et* **1** caracole (a horse); play (**med** with). **2: b- seg** caper, frolic, romp.
***bo'lung** *-en* cf **bulung**
bol'/verk *-et* **1** bulwark. **2** breakwater, seawall, wharf.
Bolæ'rne *Pln* group of islands in the Oslo fjord.
bo'l/øks *-a* woodman's ax.
bom[1] [bom'] *-men* bar; barrier, hindrance; beam; boom, derrick: **sette b- for noe** prevent or stop sth.
bom[2] [bom'] *-men* miss: **skyte b-** miss one's shot, not hit the mark.
bom[3] [bom'] *-men*: **gå på b-men** go on the bum.
bom[4] [bom'] *Av* absolutely, completely: **tie b- stille** (also ***teie b-**) be a- silent; **sitte b- fast** be stuck c-.
bombardement [bombardemang'] *-et, pl -/+-er* bombardment, bombing.
bombarde're *V -te* bombard, bomb.
bombas't *-en* bombast.
bombas'tisk *A* - bombastic.
bombe[1] [bom'be] *-a/+-en* bomb, bombshell.
bombe[2] [bom'be] *V -a/+-et* bomb.
bombe/fly *-et* bomber.
bombe/sikker *A -ert, pl -sikre* **1** bombproof. **2** absolutely certain, sure.
bom/fast [bom'/] *A* - very firm, secure; certain.
bomme[1] [bom'me] *-a* round or oval box with lid, used for carrying food.
bomme[2] [bom'me] *V -a/+-et* miss, not hit the mark; fail to solve correctly: **b- på blinken** miss the target; **b- på en oppgave** foul up an exam question.
bomme[3] [bom'me] *V -a/+-et* beg from, bum from, touch.
+bommende [bom'mene] *Av* absolutely; completely: **sitte b- fast** be stuck c-.
bommert [bom'mert] *-en* blunder.
bommesi' *-en* Canton flannel.
bom/olje [bom'/] *-a/+-en* olive oil (as lubricant).
+bom/penger [bom'/] *pl* (**=*-ar**) toll.
boms[1] [bom's] *-en* bum.
boms[2] [bom's] *Av* cf **bums**[1]
+boms[3] [bom's] *I* cf **bums**[2]
bom/skott [bom'/] *-et* (**=+/skudd**) shot that misses the target.
bom/sterk *A* very strong.
bom/ull *-a* cotton.
bomulls/dott *-en* wad of cotton.
bomulls/fløyel *-elen* velveteen.
bomulls/ga'rn *-et* cotton yarn.
bon [bång'] *Av*: **ha det b-, leve b-** live comfortably.
bonbon [bångbång'] *-en* bonbon.
bonde [+bon'ne, *bon'de] *-n, pl bønder* **1** farmer, peasant; freeholder, yeoman. **2** *archaic* husband; master. **3** pawn (in chess).
bonde/anger [+bon'ne/, *bon'de/] *-en* contriteness, esp. over stupidities one has committed when drunk.
bonde/fange *V -a/+-et* con, sucker.
bonde/fangeri· *-et* conning, confidence trick.
+bonde/fortel'ling *-a/-en* (**=*/forteljing**) novel, story dealing with peasants and country life.
bonde/ful *A* shrewd, like a peasant.
bonde/ga'rd *-en* farm.
bonde/heim *-en* "farmer's hotel", frequently used as prn. of hotel or restaurant done up in country style and catering to country people.
bonde/kone *-a* farmer's wife.
bonde/kultu'r *-en* rural (peasant) culture.
bonde/lag *-et* farmer's association; grange.
bonde/rose *-a/+-en* **1** *bot.* peony. **2** ornamental rose in **rosemaling.**

bonde/sed *-en* country ways, rural customs.
bonde/studen't *-en* student from the country.
bondeungdoms/laget *df* Society of Farm Youth.
bonde/vis *N*: **på b-** in the rural way, according to rural custom.
bondsk [bon'sk] *A* - boorish, rustic.
bo'ne *V -te/*-a* polish, wax (floors).
bo'ne/voks *-et* floor wax.
bong' *-en* check, ticket; sales slip.
bonite're *V -te* analyze (soil).
bonite't *-en* quality (of soil).
bonjour [bångsju'r] *-en* redingote (men's coat).
bonmot [bångmå'] *-et* bon mot (witticism).
°**bonn'**[1] *-en* cf **botn**
°**bonn'**[2] *pl of* **barn**
°**bon'ne** *V -a* cf **botne**
Bon'ne/fjord(en) *Pln* arm of the Oslo fjord nearest Oslo.
bo'nus *-en* bonus.
+bo'/oppgjø'r *-et* settlement of an estate.
+bo'/pel *-en* dwelling, residence.
bor[1] [bårr'] *-en/-et* bit, drill.
bo'r[2] *-et/+-en chem.* boron.
+bo'r[3] *-et* (**=*bore**[1]) nostril.
bo'raks *-et/+-en* borax.
+bor'd[1] *-en* (**=*borde**[1]) border (on a garment), edging.
bo'rd[2] *-et, pl -/+-er* **1** table: **dekke b-et** set the t-; **ta av b-et** clear the t-; **gå til b-s** sit down to a meal; **ha en til b-s** have sby as one's table companion; **sitte til b-s** be seated at table; **Herrens b-** the Lord's supper, communion; **gjøre rent b-** make a clean sweep of it; come clean; **slå i b-et til en** (pound the t-) tell sby off in an angry manner; **bank i b-et** knock on wood; **du er inne på b-et** (in bridge) you're on the board; **legge pengene på b-et** pay cash; **b-et fanger** the card is played; a deal is a deal. **2** board, plank; (of a ship): **om b-** onboard; **(gå) over b-** (go) by the b-; **mann over b-** man overboard.
***bo'rd/bunad** *-en archaic* tableware.
+bo'rd/bønn *-en* (**=*/bøn**) grace: **be b-** say g-.
bo'rd/dame *-a/+-en* (female) dinner partner.
bo'rd/dans *-en* table tilting (in a spiritualistic séance).
bo'rd/duk *-en* tablecloth.
***bor'de**[1] *-a* border.
bo'rde[2] *V -a/+-et* board (a ship).
bordell' *-en/-et* brothel.
bo'rd/ende *-n* **1** end of a table. **2** plank end.
+bo'rd/felle *-n* table companion.
bo'rd/gang *-en* length of planking from stem to stern of a ship's side.
bo'rd/kalen·der *-eren, pl *-rer/+-ere* desk calendar.
bo'rd/kapp *-en* sawed-off plank ends.
bo'rd/kavale·r *-en* (male) dinner partner.
bo'rd/kle *V -dde* side (a house).
bo'rd/kledning *-en/*-a* board siding.
bo'rd/kniv *-en* table knife.
bo'rd/kort *-et* place card.
bo'rd/lampe *-a/-en* table lamp.
bo'rd/pane·l *-et, pl -/+-er* paneling.
bo'rd/plate *-a/+-en* tabletop.
+bo'rd/sang *-en* (**=*/song**) song to be sung at table during a party (e.g. at a wedding).
***bo'rds/ende** *-n* end of a table.
bo'rd/skikk *-en* table manners: **holde b-** remain seated at table until everybody has finished.
bo'rd/tak *-et* plank roof.
bo'rd/tennis *-en* ping-pong, table tennis.
bo'rd/teppe *-t* tablecloth.
bo'rd/tomt *-en* lumberyard.
bor'd/vin *-en* table wine.
***bo're**[1] *-a* cf **bor**[3]
bo're[2] *V -a/+-et* **1** bore, drill; penetrate: **b- blikket inn i en** look penetratingly at sby; **b- etter olje** d- for oil; **b- et skip i senk** sink a ship; **b- seg fast i noe** go into sth deeply, stick to sth. **2: b- seg fram** elbow one's way through.
***bore**[3] [bå're] *pp of* **bere**[2]
bo're/bille *+-n/*-a zool.* deathwatch beetle (Anobiidae).
+bo're/hull *-et* (**=*/hol**) borehole, drill hole.
bo're/maski'n *-en* machine drill.
+bo'retts/lag *-et* housing cooperative, organized for one particular project.
bor'g[1] *-a/+-en* castle, fortress; fortification, stronghold: **Vår Gud han er så fast en b-** A mighty fortress is our God (hymn).
bor'g[2] *N* credit: **ta (varer) på b-** buy (goods) on c-.
-bor'g *Prn (f)* e.g. **Ingeborg.**
***bor'garleg** *A* - cf **borgerlig**
***bor'gar/meister** *-eren, pl -rar* cf **borger/mester**
Bor'gar/syssel *Pln* in Old Norse times the name of an administrative district around Sarpsborg in southeastern Norway.
bor'ge *V -a/+-et* **1: b- for** guarantee. **2** buy on credit. **3** allow (sby) to buy on credit.
Bor'ge *Pln* twp. **1** Nordland. **2** Østfold.
+bor'gen *N* guarantee: **gå i b- for en** vouch for sby.
+bor'ger *-en, pl -e* (**=*-ar**) citizen: **akademisk b-** person who has received his certificate of admittance to a university.
+bor'ger/bevæ'pning *-en* citizens' militia.
+bor'ger/brev *-et* (**=*-ar/**) citizenship (papers): **akademisk b-** (see **borger**).
+bor'gerdåds/medal'je *-n* (**=*borgardåd/**) medal for outstanding civic service (given by the king).
+bor'ger/klasse *-n* (**=*-ar/**) bourgeoisie.
+bor'ger/krig *-en* (**=*-ar/**) civil war.
+bor'gerlig *A* - (**=*borgarleg**) **1** bourgeois, civil, middle-class: **b-e partier** non-socialist parties; **b-e rettigheter** c- rights; **det b-e samfunn** middle-class society; **b- vielse** c- ceremony. **2** decent, modest, simple; dull, trivial: **leve b-** lead a simple life; **komme hjem i b- tid** get home at a decent hour.
+bor'ger/mester *-en, pl -e* (**=*borgar/meister**) mayor.
+bor'ger/plikt *-a/-en* (**=*-ar/**) civic duty: **gjøre sin b-** do one's duty.
+bor'ger/rett *-en* (**=*-ar/**) right as citizen.
+bor'ger/sinn *-et* (**=*-ar/**) public spirit.
+bor'ger/skap[1] *-et/*-en* (**=*-ar/**) citizenship, nationality.
+bor'ger/skap[2] *-et* (**=*-ar/**) citizenry; bourgeoisie.
+bor'ger/stand *-en* (**=*-ar/**) bourgeoisie; middle class.
+bor'ger/tog [/tåg] *-et* (**=*-ar/**) civic parade (part of May 17th celebration).
+bor'ger/ånd *-en* (**=*-ar/**) public spirit.
+bor'g/gård *-en* courtyard.
Bor'g/hild *Prn (f)*
bor'gis *en typog.* bourgeois (type size).
Bor'gny *Prn (f)*
bor'g/stue *-a* (**=*/stove**) *hist.* servants' hall.
Bor'gund *Pln* twp, **1** Møre og Romsdal. **2** Sogn og Fjordane.
bor'/hylse *-a tech.* chuck (on drill).
***bori** [bå'ri] *pp of* **bere**[2]
bor'k[1] *-en* horse of a reddish yellow color.
***bor'k**[2] *-en* cf **bark**[2]
bor'ke/blakk *A -blakt* (of horses) dun, tawny.
***bor'ke/brød** *-et* cf **barke/**
Bor'ken *df* name given to a horse of a **borket** color.
bor'ket(e) *A* - (of horses) dun, sorrel (palish yellow, gray, or brown).
***bor'n** [bånn'] *pl of* **barn**

borne'rt *A* - narrow-minded.
bor're *-n/*-a* 1 burr: **henge på som en b-** cling like a b-. 2 *bot.* burdock (Arctium).
Bor're *Pln* twp, Vestfold.
bor'/sveiv *-a* brace (for drilling).
bo'r/syre *-a* boric acid.
bort [bor't] *Av* away, off (motion; cf **borte**): **b- med det** take it away; **jeg kommer b- (til deg) i aften** I'll come over tonight; **det er b- i veggene** it is beyond reason, quite wild.
borta/for· [bor'ta/] *P* (=***bortan/**) beyond, on the other side (of).
***bortan** [bor'tan] *P* from a more remote point to a nearer; from the other side of; from across.
***bortan/for·** *P* cf **borta/**
***bortan/frå** *Av* from afar, from a distance.
***bortan/om·** *P* cf **borten/**
***bort(a)re** [bor't-] *A* - farther, remoter (of two).
***bortast** [bor'tast] *A* - cf **borterst**
+**bort/bestil't** [bor't/] *A* - booked, taken: **alle plasser var b-** all seats were sold out.
borte [bor'te] *Av* away, off (place; cf **bort**): **der b-** over there; **bli b-** disappear, be lost, vanish; die; faint; be gone, stay away; **den var ikke b-** that was a good one; **han er ikke b- som maler** he is not a bad painter; **b- bra, men hjemme best** east, west, home is best.
+**borten/for·** [bor'ten/] *P* cf **borta/**
+**borten/om·** *P* out around; beyond.
+**borterst** [bor'terst] *sp of* **bortre** (=***bortast**)
bort/etter [bor't/] *P* along: **gå b- gata** walk along the street; ***og så b-** and so forth (**osb.** etc.).
bort/fall [bor't/] *-et* disappearance, disuse (**av** of).
+**bort/falle** [bor't/] *V -falt* disappear, go out of use: **det b-er** it no longer applies.
bort/ferd [bor't/,*/fær] *-a/+-en* departure, going away.
+**bort/forkla're** [bor't/] *V -te* explain away.
bort/føre *V -te* abduct, carry off; kidnap.
bort/gang [bor't/] *-en* death, passing.
bort/hefta [bor't/] *A* - (=+**et**) held up; having wasted time.
borti [bor'ti] *P* (=**bort i**) 1 against: **komme b- noe** brush against sth; get into sth; **han har vært b- alt mulig** he has given everything a try; **legge seg b- noe** meddle with sth, poke one's nose into sth. 2 over at, over in: **han holder på b- fjøset** he is working over in the cow-shed.
bort/igjen·nom [bor't/] *P* along, through, throughout.
bort/imo·t *P* (=**bort imot**) 1 toward. 2 almost, approximately, close to: **slik, eller noe b- kunne du selv bli** you yourself might get to be that way, or sth like it (Hoel).
bort/kasta *A* - (=+**et**) 1 thrown away. 2 futile, in vain.
+**bort/kommen** *A -ent/-et, pl -komne* (=***/komen**) gone astray; lost: **bortkomne saker** l- things; **han stod ganske b-** he was standing quite l-.
bort/med [bor't/] *P* 1 along. 2 over by: **hun satt b- veggen** she was sitting over by the wall.
bort/om· *P* 1 beyond. 2 around: **stikk b-** come a-, drop over.
bort/over [bor't/åver] *P* 1 along: **gå b- veien** walk a- the road. 2 across: **vinden feide b- markene** the wind swept a- the fields.
bort/på [bor't/] *P* over at (in, on).
bortre [bor'tre] *A* -, *sp* +*borte(r)st/* **bortast* further, more remote: **b-siden av vannet** the far side of the lake.
+**bort/satte** [bor't/] *pt of* **-sette**
+**bort/sett** *A* - (=***/sedd**): **b- fra** aside from, not considering; except.
+**bort/sette** *V -satte, -satt* farm out, lodge (e.g. orphans, lunatics).
bort/side [bor't/] *-a/+-en* far side.
+**bort/skjemt** [bor't/] *A* - (=***/skjemd**) spoiled (e.g. a child).
bort/til· [bor't/] *P* over to, up to: **sette seg b- bordet** sit up to the table.
bort/under *P* over (there), under.
bort/ved *P* over at, over by.
+**bort/vendt** [bor't/] *A* - (=***/vend**) averted, turned away (e.g. face).
+**bort/vise** *V -te* dismiss; expel.
bort/åt [bor't/] *P* over to, up to.
bo'r/vatn *-et* (+**/vann**) boric acid solution.
bor'/vinde *-a* brace (for drilling).
***bos** [bå's] *-et* cf **boss**
+**bo'/satt** *A* - cf **bu/**
+**bo'/satte** *pt of* **-sette**
***bose**[1] [bå'se] *-a* cf **boso**
***bose**[2] [bå'se] *V -a* strew.
***boset(e)** [bå'-] *A* - cf **bosset**
+**bo'/setning** *-en* cf **bu/setting**
+**bo'/sette** *V -satte, -satt* cf **bu/**
+**bo'/sittende** *A* - cf **bu/**
bos'nisk *A* - Bosnian.
bo'so *-a* bed of straw; animal's lair.
boss' *-et* (=+**bøss**) 1 straw used in beds. 2 sweepings of chaff, straw. 3 small bit, e.g. of a leaf, a straw: **ikke det bøss** not a bit.
bos'set(e) *A* - dusty, dirty from straw ends, sweepings.
***boste**[1] [bos'te] *-n* cf **børste**[1]
***boste**[2] [bos'te] *V -a* cf **børste**[2]
+**bo'/sted** *-et* abode, residence.
bos'ton *-en* boston (card game).
bo't[1] *-a, pl bøter* patch: **sette en b- over hullet** patch up the hole; blaze, marking (on a surface, e.g. animal's hide).
bo't[2] *-a/+-en, pl bøter* 1 fine. 2 damages. 3 amends, remedy: **råde b- på noe** set sth right. 4 penance; penitence, repentance: **gjøre b-** do penance; **love b- og bedring** promise to behave, to better one's ways.
bot. — **botanikk, botanisk**
+**bota'niker** *-en, pl -e* (=***-ar**) botanist.
botanikk' *-en* botany.
botanise're *V -te* botanize.
botanise'r/kasse *-a/-en* vasculum (for collecting plants).
bota'nisk *A* - botanical.
bo'te/middel *-elet/-midlet, pl +-midler/*-el* remedy.
bo'te/råd *+-et/*-a* remedy.
bo'te/von *-a* cf **bot/**
bo't/ferdig [also -fær'-] *A* - penitent, repentant.
+**botfer'dig/het** *-en* penitence, repentance.
botfor [båttfå'r] *-en* 1 big, sockshaped boot to pull over an ordinary boot. 2 man's snow boot.
***bo't/laus** *A* irreparable.
bot'n *-en* (=+**bunn**) (+**bunn** preferred, esp. in idioms) 1 (of glass, lake, ship, etc.) bottom (**av** of), floor: **b-en er nådd** this is the end (the worst); **være på b-en** have reached the b-, be down (or downhearted); **ta b-en** touch b-; **dobbelt b-** double meanings, (intentional) ambiguity; **i b- og grunn** essentially, when you get right down to it; **til b-s** (of ship) to the bottom; thoroughly, to the end. 2 (back)ground: **hvite figurer på blå b-** white figures on a blue ground. 3 (of fjord or valley) end. 4 (of forest) floor, ground, soil: **god b- (for)** good s- (for).
bot'ne *V +-et/*-a* (=+**bunne**) 1 put a bottom on (sth). 2 reach bottom. 3 be enough: **det b-er ikke i ham** he never gets enough. 4: **det b-er i (at)** it is caused by, has its basis in.
Bot'ne *Pln* twp, Vestfold.
bot'n/fall *-et* deposit, dregs, sediment.
bot'n/farge *-n* ground color.
bot'n/fast *A* - firm, solid: **b- is** s- ice.
bot'n/felle *V -felte* deposit, settle.
bot'n/fryse *V infl as* **fryse** freeze solid (e.g. of shallow lake).
bot'n/ga'rn *-et* ground net.
***bot'ning** *-en zool.* abomasum (part of the digestive system of a ruminant).
botn'/laus *A* bottomless.
bot'n/skrape *V -te* scrape the bottom of, empty.
bot'n/tilje *-a* bottom boards (in boat).
bot'n/tømmer *-et* deadheads (sunken logs).
bot'n/vatn *-et* bilge water.
bo'tolvsok *en* cf **bolsok**
***bo't/sam** *A* useful; invigorating, wholesome.
bo'ts/fengsel *-elet/-let, pl +-ler/*-el* penitentiary.
bo'ts/gang *-en* penitential journey.
+**bo'ts/øvelse** *-n* (=***/øving**) penance.
Bot'ten/vika *Pln* the Gulf of Bothnia (innermost part of the Baltic Sea).
bo't/von *-a dial.* hope of improvement: **det er ikke b- i disse skoene** these shoes are beyond repair.
bourgeois [bursjoa'] *-en* bourgeois.
bourgeoisi [bursjoasi'] *-et* bourgeoisie.
Bouvet/øya [buve'/] *Pln* Bouvet Island (Norwegian island in the Antarctic).
br. = **brei, breidd; bruk**[2]
bra' *A* 1 good; well: **ha det b-** (as greeting) take care of yourself; **jeg har det (bare) b-** I'm fine; **ha b- med penger** be well-heeled; **jeg er ikke b-** I'm not well; **synes b- om** like; **b- mørkt** rather dark. 2 decent, nice, respectable: **b- folk** d- people; **en b- pike** a good girl.
***bradd'** *-a* cf **bredd**
***bradd'/full** *A* cf **bredd/**
***bra'g** *-et* northern lights, aurora borealis.
brag'd *+-en/*-a* 1 method, way (of doing sth). 2 shape, state; behavior. 3 pattern (in a woven fabric). 4 flash, glint. 5 feat; fine deed.
***brag'det(e)** *A* - patterned; striped.
***bra'ge**[1] *-n* shape; state: **han var i sin beste b-** he was in his prime.
***bra'ge**[2] *V -a* 1 flare; flicker; glint. 2 dazzle, show off.
Bra'ge *Prn(m)* god of poetry in Norse mythology.
bra'ge/løfte *-t, pl +-r/*-* vow; a daring promise, a promise which may be difficult to fulfill.
Bra'ger/nes *Pln* area in the city of Drammen.
***brag'l** *-et* tinsel.
***brag'le** *V -a* 1 flare; flicker; glint. 2 dazzle, show off.
+**bragte** [brak'te] *pt of* **bringe**[3]
brahma'n *-en* cf **brahmin**
brahmi'n *-en* (=**brahman**) Brahman (Brahmin).
bra'k *-et* bang, crash.
bra'kal *-en bot.* buckthorn (Rhamnus frangula).
bra'kar *N* good fellow: **Bamse b-** Bruin the bear.
bra'ke[1] *-n* juniper,
bra'ke[2] *V -a/-et/+-te* bang, crack; crash, thunder: **det b-et løs** things started with a bang; **b-ende applaus** thundering applause; **en b-ende latter** roaring laughter; **det b-er i isen** you can hear the ice crack; **b- opp** crash open.
brakk'[1] *A brakt* 1 fallow (field). 2 brackish (water).
+**brakk'**[2] *pt of* **brekke**[2]
brak'ke *-a* (=+**barakke**) barracks.
brak'ke/baro'n *-en* "barracks baron", person who profited by building (esp. barracks) for the Germans in Norway during World War II.
brakk'/land *-et* fallow land.
brakk'/mark *-a* fallow field.
+**brakk'/nese** *-n* flat nose.
brakk'/vatn *-et* (=+**/vann**) brackish water.

+ Bokmål; * Nynorsk; ° Dialect.
After letter: ' stress (Acc. 1); ` tone, stress (Acc. 2); · length.
Below letter: . not pronounced.

+**brak'te** *pt of* **bringe**[3]
braktea't *-en hist.* bracteate (thin chased gold or silver coin or medal).
bram' *N* bragging, ostentation: **opptre med brask og b-** act ostentatiously, put on a big show.
***bra'me** *V -a* cf **bramme**
bram'/fri *A -tt* unostentatious.
brami'n *-en* cf **brahmin**
+**bram'me** *V -et* (=***brame**) brag: **b- med noe** display, parade sth.
bram'/rå *-a, pl -rær naut.* topgallant yard.
bram'/segl *-et* (=+**/seil**) *naut.* topgallant sail.
bran'd[1] *-en* 1 beam, log. 2 beam with carved ornaments, on a gable or in the stem of a ship. 3 (in ballads) sword. 4 big burly fellow; daredevil.
brand'[2] *-en* cf **brann**[1]
Brand'/bu *Pln* twp, Oppland.
***bran'de** *-n* 1 big burly man. 2 *zool.* moose ox.
+**bran'der** *-en, pl -e* 1 *hist.* ship fired in order to damage the enemy. 2 pun.
+**bran'det(e)** *A* - cf **brannet(e)**
Brand'/val *Pln* twp, Hedmark.
brank' *-en/-et dial.* 1 chafing. 2 chafed, worn part of a rope.
bran'ke *V -a/+-et dial.* break, injure, sprain.
brann'[1] *-en* 1 burning: **true med bål og b-** threaten (sby) with b- at the stake. 2 fire; glow; heat: **sette, stikke (noe) i b-** set (sth) afire; **stå i b-** be afire; **slokke en b-** put out a f-. 3 surf: **brott og b-** heavy s-. 4 brand, firebrand. 5 inflammation; burning pain; fever: **b- i blodet** fire in one's veins, passion, torment.
°**brann'**[2] *pt of* **brenne**[3]
brann'/bil *-en* fire engine, fire truck.
brann'/bombe [bom'be] *-a/+-en* incendiary bomb.
bran'net(e) *A* - brindled, spotted.
brann'/fakkel *-en, pl -fakler* torch: **kaste en b-** announce or publish sth that sets emotions afire, causes a commotion.
brann'/fare *-n* danger of fire.
brann'/farlig *A* - inflammable.
brann'/gul *A* fiery yellow.
brann'/kasse *-a/-en* fire insurance company.
brann'/korps *-et* fire department, *(Brit.)* fire brigade.
brann'/lidd *A -/*-litt* (=+**/lidt**) burned out, damaged by fire.
brann'/mann *-en, pl -menn/*-menner* fireman.
brann'/mur *-en* fire wall (protective brick or concrete wall behind a fireplace or stove in a wooden house).
brann'/rør *-et/*-a* (=***/røyr**) fuse in a projectile.
brann'/sjef *-en* fire chief.
brann'/skatte *V -a/+-et* extort heavy contributions; levy heavy taxes.
+**brann'/skudd** *-et* (=**/skott**) a cannon shot to announce that a fire has broken out.
brann'/slange *-n* fire hose.
+**brann'sloknings/appara't** *-et* fire extinguisher.
brann'/sprøyte *-a* a pump used for extinguishing fires.
***brann'/stell** *-et* fire department.
+**brann'/stiftelse** *-n* arson.
+**brann'/stifter** *-en, pl -e* arsonist.
brann'/sår *-et* burn.
brann'/tau *-et* rope for escape from a burning building.
brann'/tomt *-a* site of a fire.
brann'/trygd *-a* fire insurance.
+**brann'/vesen** *-et* fire department.
brann'/øks *-a, pl *-ar* fireman's ax.
bransje [brang'sje] *-n* (a particular line of) business; industry, trade.
bransje/kunnskap *-en* business knowledge.
bransje/råd *-et* council appointed by the king and made up of representatives for a line of business or an industry and for the state, in order to further cooperation within the business and between it and the state.
+**bran't** *pt of* **brenne**[3]
bra's[1] *-en* 1 *naut.* brace (a rope). 2: **klare b-ene** overcome the difficulties, manage (the situation).
bra's[2] *-et* 1 crackling sound. 2 crackling fire. 3 knotty firewood (that crackles when burning).
bra'se[1] *V -a/+-te* 1 *naut.* brace. 2 move noisily, crash.
bra'se[2] *V -a/+-te* fry; (of sth frying) splutter, sputter.
Brasi'l *Pln* Brazil.
+**brasilia'ner** *-en, pl -e* cf **brasilier**
+**brasilia'nsk** *A* - cf **brasilsk**
+**brasi'lier** *-en, pl -e* (=***-ar,** +**brasilianer**) Brazilian.
brasi'lsk *A* - (=+**brasiliansk**) Brazilian.
brask'[1] *N* : **med b- og bram** with hustle and bustle, ostentatiously.
brask'[2] *-et* small twigs.
bras'ke *V -a/+-et* 1 crackle (of wood); **b-ende** noisy. 2 brag.
bras'me *-a/+-en zool.* bream (Abramis brama).
brast'[1] *N* : **stå last og b- med en** stand shoulder to shoulder with sby; **vi skal stå last og b-** we'll stick together.
brast'[2] *pt of* **breste**[2], **briste**[1]
brat'ne *V -a/+-et* become steep(er).
bratsj' *-en mus.* viola.
bratsjis't *-en mus.* viola player, violist.
bratt' *A* - 1 steep; (of a person) curt, abrupt. 2 sudden: **hans glede fikk en b- ende** his joy was suddenly ended.
brat'te *-a* steep slope.
bratt'/lendt *A* - (of relatively large area) steep, with many steep inclines.
Bratt'/vær *Pln* twp, Møre og Romsdal.
brau't[1] *-a* 1 road. 2 edge (of a hill or a road).
brau't[2] *pt of* **bryte**
brau'te *V -a/+-et* bluster, swagger.
+**bra'v** *A* 1 *obs.* good, cf **bra.** 2 *obs.* brave.
brava'de *-n* bravado.
bravis'simo *I* superlative of bravo.
bra'vo *I* bravo.
bravu'r *-en* bravura.
bravu'r/nummer [/nommer] *-eret, pl -er/+-numre mus.* bravura number (daring, difficult number).
bre'[1] *-en* (=***brede**) glacier.
bre'[2] *V -dde* (=***brede**[2]) tar.
+**bre'**[3] *V -dde/-dte* cf **breie**
+**bre'd** *A* cf **brei**
bredd' *-a/+-en* (=***bradd**) bank, shore; brink.
+**bred'de** *-n* cf **breidd**
+**bred'de/grad** *-en* (=***breidde/**) degree of latitude: **på disse b-er** in these parts.
+**bredd'/full** *A* brimful, brimming.
***bre'de**[1] *-n* cf **bre**[1]
***bre'de**[2] *V -de* cf **bre**[2]
Bre'de *Prn(m)*
+**bred'sel** *-elet, -ler* blanket; spread; throw.
+**bre'd/side** *-a/-en* cf **brei/**
+**bre'd/sporet** *A* - cf **brei/**
***breg'de** *V -a* 1 change. 2 resemble. 3 braid (bands).
bregne [+brei'ne, *breng'ne] *-en/+-a* bracken; fern.
bre'/grøn *A* (=+**/grønn**) 1 green like the appearance of glacial ice. 2 (of water) greenish like glacier water or from having been mixed with glacial water.
brei' *A +-t/*-tt* (=+**bred**) 1 broad, wide: **vidt og b-dt** far and wide; **en b- rygg** a strong back; *bibl.* **den b-e veg** the broad path. 2 extensive: **i det vide og brede** at great length; **en b- framstilling** a comprehensive report. 3 common, ordinary: **de b-e lag** the lower classes; **et b-t språk** unpolished speech. 4 boastful, demanding: **han gjorde seg b-** he demanded attention, boasted.
brei'/bremmet *A* - wide-brimmed.
brei'/bygd *A -/*-bygt* broadly built, heavy-set.
brei'/bygda *df, pl -ene* the open country (esp. in East Norway).
Brei'da/blik' *Pln* name of the abode of the Norse god Balder.
breidd' *-a* (=+**bredde**) 1 breadth, width. 2 latitude.
***breid'de/grad** *-a/-en* cf **bredde/**
***breidd'/med** *P* alongside, beside, next to.
brei'e *V +-de/*-dde* (=+**bre**) spread: **b- høy** s- hay to dry; **b- over seg et teppe** cover oneself with a quilt; **b- seg** spread; puff oneself up, swagger; **landskapet b-dde seg ut** the landscape opened out; **b- ut (en duk)** spread (a table cloth).
brei'/flabb *-en zool.* angler (Lophius piscatorius).
brei'/fokk *-a naut.* square foresail.
brei'/føtt *A* - 1 who has broad feet. 2 with feet apart.
brei'/hakke *-a* broad-bladed pickax.
brei'/kjeft *-en* cf **brei/flabb**
***brei'/lagd** *A -/-lagt* broadly built, heavy-set.
***brei'/leitt** *A* - broad-faced.
Brei'm *Pln* twp, Sogn og Fjordane.
***brei'ne** *V -a* broaden.
bre'/is *-en* glacier ice.
brei'/side *-a* (=+**bred/**) broadside.
brei'/skuldra *A* - (=+**-et**) broad-shouldered.
brei'sle *-a* cf **bredsel**
brei'/slede *-n* sleigh that is broad enough to seat two.
brei'/spora *A* - (=+**-et**) broad-gaged (railway track).
brei'/tang *a, pl -tenger* wide-mouthed tong.
+**brei'/voksen** *A -ent, -ne* (=***/vaksen**) broadly built, heavy-set.
brei'/øks *-a* broadax.
bre'k *-et* baa, bleat.
bre'ke *V -a/+-te* baa, bleat.
***bre'kje** *V -te* cf **breke**
brekk'[1] *-et* brake.
+**brekk'**[2] *-et* 1 breakage. 2 breaker.
brekka'sje *-n* breakage.
brek'ke[1] *-a* steep hill; steep part of a hill.
+**brek'ke**[2] *V brakk, brukket* 1 (transitive) break: **b- beinet** b- a leg; **b- nakken** b- one's neck; **han brakk en kvist av treet** he broke a twig off the tree; **b- en farge** tint a color; *typog.* **b- om** make up; **b- opp en kasse** b- open a box; **brukken** broken: **en brukken linje** a broken line. 2 (intransitive) break, snap: **isen b-er** the ice is b-ing. 3: **b- seg** vomit; **det er til å b- seg av (or: over)** it makes me sick.
Brek'ke *Pln* twp, Sogn og Fjordane.
Brek'ken *Pln* twp, Sør-Trøndelag.
brekk'/jern [/jæ'rn] *-et* pinch bar, wrecking bar.
brekk'/middel *-elet/-midlet, pl +-midler/*-el* emetic.
+**brekk'/stang** *-a, pl -stenger* (=***/stong**) lever, pry bar.
brekk'/vogn [/vång'n] *-a* baggage car.
+**brek'ning** *-en* 1 vomiting: **få, ha b-er** throw up, vomit. 2 breaker.
+**brek'nings/fornem'melse** *-n* desire to vomit.
+**brem'** *-men, pl -mer* brim; edge.
Bremang'er *Pln* twp, Sogn og Fjordane.
+**brem'me** *V -et* edge, ridge: **kåpen var b-et med skinn** the coat was e-d with fur.
Brem'nes *Pln* twp, Hordaland.
brem's[1] *-en zool.* botfly, warble fly (Oestrus).
+**brem's**[2] *-en* cf **bremse**[1]
brem'se[1] *-a* (=+**brems**) brake: **virke som en b-** have a braking effect.
brem'se[2] *V -a/+-et/+-te* brake, put on the brakes; slow down: **nå får du b-** you'd better go slow; that's enough; take it easy.

Brem's/nes *Pln* twp, Møre og Romsdal.

***bren'de** *pt of* **brenne**[4]

***breng'** *-en* 1 jerk. 2 bend, twist (on wire etc.). 3 difficulty.

***breng'je** *V -a* bend, twist.

***breng'le** *V -a* bend, twist.

brenn'/bar *A* combustible: **b-e stoffer** combustibles; **et b-t spørsmål** an incendiary question.

***bren'ne**[1] *-a* burned area (e.g. where the forest has been burned to clear the land for cultivation).

bren'ne[2] *-t* 1 firewood. *2 hydrogen.

bren'ne[3] *V +brant/*brann, +brent/*brunne/*-i (intransitive,* can be replaced by **brenne**[4]) burn: **det b-er** it is b-ing; the house is on fire; **det b-er godt i ovnen** the fire is b-ing nicely; **han b-er for denne saken** he is passionately devoted to this cause; **halsen b-er** my throat is b-ing; **jorden b-er under meg** "the earth is b-ing under me" I'm in a hurry to get away; **tampen b-er** you're getting warm; **veden b-er ikke** this wood won't b-; **b- inne** b- to death while inside (in a house); **b- inne med noe** be unable to find an outlet for sth; **huset brant ned til grunnen** the house burned to the ground; **b- opp** b- up; **pæren er brent ut** the bulb is b-ed out.

bren'ne[4] *V +brente/*brende* 1 *(transitive)* burn, set fire to: **b- sine skip, b- alle broer (bak seg)** b- one's bridges; **b- en inne** murder sby by arson; **b- opp noe** b- sth completely; **den brente jords taktikk** scorched earth strategy; **brent barn skyr ilden** "a burned child shuns the fire", once bitten twice shy. 2: **b- seg på noe** b- oneself on sth; get one's fingers b-ed on sth; **b- seg fast** scorch; **det hadde brent seg fast i minnet** it was burned into his memory. 3 fire: **b- av et skudd** f- a shot; **b- løs** start shooting. 4 burn, use as fuel: **denne ovnen b-er koks** this stove b-s coke. 5 burn, give off intense heat; cause a burning pain: **b-ende sol** b-ing sun; **det varme vannet b-er på huden** the hot water b-s my skin. 6 burn, roast: **b- kaffe** r- coffee; **b- maten** b- the food; **brente mandler** r-ed almonds. 7 distill: **b- brennevin** d- brandy.

***bren'ne/fang** *-et* solid fuel; firewood.

+**bren'ne/merke**[1] *-t* (=***/merkje**) brand (e.g. on cattle).

+**bren'ne/merke**[2] *V -a/-et/-te* brand; stigmatize.

bren'nende *A* - 1 burning, consuming, intense: **b- begjær** a b- desire; **b- interesse** a c- interest; **et b- spørsmål** a b- question. 2 *(adv.)* intensely, very: **b- rød** flaming red; **b- snar** quick as lightning; **b- varm** piping hot.

bren'(ne)/nesle *-a bot.* small nettle (Urtica urens).

+**bren'ner** *-en, pl -e* (=***-ar**) burner (e.g. part of a kerosene lamp).

brenneri' *-et, pl +-er/*-* distillery, still.

***bren'ne/stein** *-en* sulphur.

bren'ne/vin *-et* brandy; (hard) liquor.

brenn'/fort *A* - very fast.

brenn'/glas *-et* (=+**/glass**) burning glass, magnifying glass.

brenn'/hast *+-en/*-a* big hurry.

brenn'/heit *A* burning hot.

brenn'/hug *-en* enthusiasm, passion.

+**bren'ning**[1] *-en* breakers, surf.

bren'ning[2] *-a/+-en* 1 burning, firing; combustion; cremation. 2 distilling.

brenn'/kald *A* biting cold.

brenn'/kulde *-a/-en* biting cold.

brenn'/mane't *-a/+-en zool.* sea nettle (stinging jellyfish).

brenn'/olje *-a/-en* fuel oil.

brenn'/punkt [/pong't] *-et math., phys., fig.* focus: **i begivenhetenes b-** in the focus of events.

brenn'/sikker *A -ert, pl -sikre* absolutely positive, sure.

brenn'/snar *A* very quick.

brenn'/sterk *A* very strong (esp. of sth tasted).

brenn'/stoff *-et* fuel.

brenn'/torv *-a/+-et* peat used for fuel.

brenn'/travel *A -elt, pl -le* very busy.

brenn'/varm *A* burning hot.

brenn'/vidd(e) *-a/+-en phys.* focal distance.

bren'sel *-elet/-let* fuel; firewood.

***bren'sle** *-a* burning.

***bre'se** *V -te* fry; prepare rich food.

bres'je *-n* breach: **gå, stille seg i b-n for en** step into the b- for sby.

°**bresk'** *-en* cf **brisk**[1]

°**bres'ke** *V -a/-et* cf **briske**

brest' *-en, pl *-er* (=+**brist**) 1 crack. 2 cracking, popping sound. *3 defect, flaw.

bres'te[1] *-a* curdled milk.

bres'te[2] *V brast, +brestet/*broste/*-i* (=+**briste**[1]) (in most idioms +**briste**) 1 burst, crack *(intransitive)*: **knoppene b-er** the buds are b-ing; **med b-ende stemme** in a breaking, faltering voice; **hans hjerte brast** his heart broke; **det brast for ham** he could not contain himself; **brustne øyne** the eyes of a dead creature; **det får b- eller bære** come hell or high water, let come what may. 2 fail: **et håp som brast** a hope that f-ed; **brustne illusjoner** broken illusions; **hans resonnement bygde på b-ende forutsetninger** his reasoning was based on faulty assumptions. 3 break forth; be blurted out: **det brast ut av ham** he blurted it out. 4 (of milk) curdle, turn.

bres'te[3] *V -a/+-et/*-e* 1 cause to burst. 2 curdle, turn (milk).

brett'[1] *-en* 1 crease, fold; cuff (of trousers). 2: **legge b- på noe** emphasize, give weight to sth.

brett'[2] *-et, pl -/+-er* 1 board; (wooden) nameplate. 2 tray: **på ett b-** at once, at one stroke; **sette alt på ett b-** risk everything in one throw. 3 diving board (=**stupe/**). 4 (baggage) rack (e.g. on bicycle). 5 *obs., naut.* bridge.

bret'te *V -a/+-et/*-e* fold, roll, wrap: **b- ned kraven** fold down the collar; **b- opp** roll up, turn up.

bret'te/mess(e) *en* St. Britiva's Day (January 11th).

+**brett'/spill** *-et* (=***/spel**) 1 game board. 2 board game (e.g. checkers, chess).

bre'v *-et, pl -/+-er* 1 letter: **skrive (et) b- til en** write a l- to sby; **åpent b-** an open l-; **ha b- på noe** have title to sth; be guaranteed sth. 2 package (of needles).

bre'v/ark *-et* sheet of (writing) paper.

bre'/vatn *-et* (=+**/vann**) glacial water.

bre'v/brott *-et* (=+**/brudd**) unauthorized opening of mail.

+**bre'v/bytte** *-t* (=***/byte**) exchange of letters; correspondence.

bre'v/due *-a* carrier pigeon.

+**bre'v/hode** *-t* letterhead.

+**bre'v/holder** *-en* (=***/haldar**) letter rack.

Bre'/vik *Pln* town in Telemark.

bre'v/kort *-et* postcard: **dobbelt b-** reply paid postcard.

+**bre'v/ordner** *-en, pl -e* (=***-ar**) letter file; letter holder.

bre'v/papi'r *-et* stationery.

bre'v/skap *-et* document.

bre'v/skifte *-t* exchange of letters; correspondence.

bre'v/skole *-n* correspondence school.

bre'v/sy'nt *A* - able to read, literate.

bre'v/veksle *V -a/+-et* exchange letters; correspond (**med** with).

bre'v/veksling *-a/+-en* exchange of letters; correspondence.

bre'v/vekt *-a* postage scale.

***bre'v/vær** *-et* envelope.

bridge [brid'sj] *-n* bridge (card game).

bridge/parti' *-et* bridge game.

briga'de *-n* brigade.

brigade'r *-en* brigadier.

***brig'de**[1] *-t* 1 change. 2 habit, trait that is typical for a country or an area. 3 dislocation, sprain.

***brig'de**[2] *V -a* 1 change. 2 roll or turn back. 3 dislocate, sprain.

brigg' *-en naut.* brig.

***brig'sle** *V -a* 1 reprove, upbraid. 2 bother.

***bri'k** *-a, pl *-ar* 1 counter; railing. 2 low plank wall, e.g. in a barn. 3 short bench.

***bri'ke** *V -te* cf **brikje**

***bri'ken** *A -e/-i, pl -ne* 1 splendid. 2 fresh, lively, pretty.

brikett' *-en* briquet.

***bri'kje** *V -te* 1 have a splendid appearance. 2 rear up, tower.

brik'ke *-a/+-en* 1 counter, man, piece (in a board game): **flytte en b-** make a move; **han er bare en b- i spillet** he is only a pawn in the game. 2 small (esp. wooden) tray. 3 doily.

brik's *-en* bed, bunk.

briljan't[1] *-en* brilliant (a decorative stone).

briljan't[2] *A* - radiant; splendid.

brilje're *V -te* shine, show off: **b- med sine kunnskaper** show off one's knowledge.

bril'le *-a/+-en* (esp. in *pl*) eyeglasses, glasses.

bril'le/futtera'l *-et, pl -/+-er* glasses case.

bril'le/glas *-et* (=+**/glass**) lens of eyeglasses.

bril'le/hus *-et* glasses case.

***bril'le/orm** *-en zool.* cobra.

***bril'le/slange** *-n zool.* cobra.

+**bril'le/stang** *-a, pl -stenger* (=***/stong**) bow (on eyeglasses).

bri'm *-et* surf.

bring'e[1] *-a* breast, chest: **bred om b-n** broadchested (J. S. Welhaven); **ha vondt for b-a** have a pain in one's c-; ***det gjer godt i b-a** it feels good inside.

***bring'e**[2] *-n* moose ox.

+**bring'e**[3] *V brakte, brakt* 1 bring (to the speaker), fetch: **b- hjelp** come with help; **bring meg brevet** get me the letter. 2 take (from the speaker), deliver, convey, put: **b- varer** deliver goods; **tøy hentes og b-es** clothing picked up and delivered; **b- noe i sikkerhet** b- sth to safety; **b- et emne på bane** b- up a subject; **b- hyllest** pay homage; **b- et offer** make a sacrifice; **b- på det rene** find (sth) out, clarify. 3 bring about, cause, produce: **b- forretningen på fote** put the business back on its feet; **b- orden i noe** set sth in order; **b- det over seg** get oneself to do sth; **ikke b- det til noe** not amount to anything; **b- ulykke** bring about misfortune; **b- en i ulykke** get sby into trouble; **b- det vidt** go far. 4 carry (=print, publish): **avisen brakte hans bilde** the paper carried his picture.

bring'e/bær *-et* raspberry.

bring'e/duk *-en* plastron.

bring'e/klut *-en* plastron.

bring'e/sjuk *A* tuberculous.

bring'e/sølv [/søll'] *-et* silver brooch(es).

bring'e/verk *-en* chest pain.

+**brin'k** *-en obs.* cliff; bluff.

bri's[1] *-en* breeze (wind velocities 3-5 on the Beaufort wind scale).

bri's[2] *-en* bonfire, glow.

***bri's**[3] *-et anat.* sweetbread (Thymus gland).

+**bri'se**[1] *V -te* (of wind) blow gently: **b- opp** begin to b-.

***bri'se**[2] *V -a* flare up; glow, give light.

***bri's/eld** *-en* bonfire.

***bri'sen** *A -e/-i, pl -ne* splendid.

bri'sing *-en* bonfire.

bris'k[1] *-en bot.* juniper.

+ Bokmål; * Nynorsk; ° Dialect.
After letter: ' stress (Acc. 1); ' tone, stress (Acc. 2); · length.
Below letter: . not pronounced.

bris'k[2] *-en* bed, bunk.
bris'ke *V -a/+-et*: **b- seg** puff oneself up, strut; **b- seg av noe** brag about sth, show off sth.
bris'ke/bar *-et* juniper twigs.
+**bris'ke/låg** *-en* (=***/log**) water boiled with juniper, used for cleaning (e.g. wooden containers).
bris'ling *-en* brisling, sprat (Clupea sprattus).
bris'sel *-elen, pl brisler anat.* sweetbread (Thymus gland).
+**bris't** *-en* 1 cf **brest.** 2 defect, flaw: **han har en b- i karakteren** there is a flaw in his character.
+**bris'te**[1] *V brast, bristet/brustet* cf **breste**[2]
+**bris'te**[2] *V -a/+-et* cf **breste**[3]
+**bris'te/ferdig** *A* - fit, ready to burst, at the bursting point.
+**bris'te/punkt** [/pong't] *-et* bursting point.
Bri'ta *Prn (f)*
Britan'nia *Pln obs.* Britain.
brit'e *-n* Briton.
brit'isk *A* - British.
Brit(t) *Prn (f)*
***brjos't** *-et* cf **bryst**
***brjo'te** *V bryt, braut, brote/-i* cf **bryte**
+**bro'** *-en* cf **bru**
brodd' *-en* 1 point (of stick, arrow etc.); stinger. 2 goad: **stampe mot b-en** kick against the pricks (Acts 9:5) = resist the inevitable. 3 calk, creeper (a plate with points, fastened to the shoe to protect against slipping). 4: **i b-en for** at the head of. 5 sting: **død, hvor er din b-** Death where is thy sting (1. Cor. 15:55).
+**brod'den** *A -ent, pl brodne* broken, damaged: **det er brodne kar i alle land** "there are broken pots in any country", there is a black sheep in every flock.
bro'der *-en, pl +brødre/*brødrar* cf **bror**
brode're *V -te* embroider.
+**bro'der/folk** *-et* sister nation.
brode'r/ga'rn *-et* embroidery cotton (silk, wool).
broderi' *-et, pl +-er/*-* embroidery.
+**bro'der/kjærlighet** *-en* brotherly love.
+**bro'der/krets** *-en eccl.* fellowship, society of fellow believers: **B- på havet** (religious society for sailors, cf Gideons in U.S.).
+**bro'der/land** *-et* sister country.
bro'derlig *A* - brotherly: **dele b-** share like brothers.
+**bro'der/mord** [/mor'd] *-et* fratricide.
bro'der/ring *-en eccl.* fellowship (see **/krets).**
+**brod'ne** *pl of* **brodden**
+**broget** [brå'get] *A* - cf **broket(e)**
+**bro'/hode** *-t* cf **bru/**
bro'k *-a, pl brøker* 1 *pop.* pants. 2 *naut.* any of various pieces of tackle.
broka'de *-n* brocade.
bro'k/band *-et archaic* drawstring in pants (used as belt).
bro'ket(e) *A* - 1 multicolored; speckled; (of one color) gaudy, gay. 2 motley, varied; confused, tangled: **en b- blanding** a medley. 3 complicated, difficult, intricate: **da det ble for b- for ham, rømte han** when things got too c-, he ran away.
brokk' *-en/-et med.* hernia, rupture.
brokk'/bind *-et med.* truss (for hernia).
+**brok'ke** *-n* fragment, piece: **b- av murverk** masonry debris; **kunne noen b-r norsk** know a few scraps of Norwegian.
+**brok'ke/vis** *Av* piecemeal.
brokk'/fugl [+/fu'l] *-en zool.* plover.
brom[1] [brom'] *-met/+-men chem.* bromine.
brom[2] [brom'] *-et* pieces, scraps of old metal.
brom/bær [brom'/] *-et obs.* blackberry.
bromkalium [bromka'lium] *-et chem.* potassium bromide (a sedative).
bron'kie *-n* bronchus: **b-ne** the bronchial tubes.
bronkitt' *-en* bronchitis.
bronse [brång'se] *-n* bronze.
bronse/alder *-en* Bronze Age.
bronse/medal'je *-n* bronze medal.
bronsere [brångse're] *V -te* bronze.
bro'r *-en, pl +brødre/*brør* brother (**til** of): **brødre i ånden** b-s in spirit; **en hul b-** hypocrite, undependable person; **en lystig b-** a gay dog.
+**bro'r/datter** *-en, pl -døtre* (=***/dotter**) brother's daughter, niece.
bro'r/part *-en* better part, most (of sth); lion's share.
bro'r/skap *-en* brotherhood: **intet b- i kjærlighet og kortspill** all's fair in love and war.
+**bro'r/sønn** *-en* (=***/son**) brother's son, nephew.
***brose** [brå'se] *-a* gust of wind, sudden storm.
bros'je *-a/-en* brooch.
brosjy're *-n* brochure, leaflet, pamphlet.
bros'me *+-a/*-en zool.* cusk (Brosmius brosme).
bros'te** *pp of* **breste** (=brosti**)
***brot** [brå't] *-et* cf **brott**
***brote**[1] [brå'te] *-n* cf **bråte**
***brote**[2] [brå'te] *V -a* 1 brake (flax). 2 throw together, heap up. 3 act noisily.
***brote**[3] [brå'te] *pp of* **bryte, brjote**
***brot/hest** [brå't/] *-en* a slambang worker.
***broti** [brå'ti] *pp of* **bryte, brjote**
brot'ne *V -a/+-et* begin to break, burst, crack.
***brotsleg** [brå'ts-] *A* - criminal.
brott' *-et* (=+**brudd,** ***brot**) 1 break; fracture, rupture. 2 violation; crime. 3 (stone) quarry. 4 reef. 5 surf. 6 breaking, cracking sound. 7 fragment, piece (of sth broken).
brott'/harv *-a* a type of harrow with big, stiff teeth.
brott'/sjø *-en* breaker.
brott'/skavl *-en* breaker.
brott's/mann *-en, pl -menn/*-menner* criminal, delinquent.
brott's/verk *-et* crime, criminal act.
BRT = **brutto-registertonn**
bru' *-a* 1 bridge. 2 jetty, pier. 3 *anat.* pons (in brain).
+**bru'/bygger** *-en, pl -e* (=***/byggjar**) bridge builder.
bru'd *+-en/*-a* (=**brur**) bride.
+**brudd'** *-et* cf **brott**
+**brud'den** *A -ent, pl brudne* fractional: **b-t tall** fraction; **b- brøk** complex fraction.
+**brudd'/flate** *-a/-en* fracture, fracture surface.
+**brudd'/stykke** *-t* fragment.
bru'de/bukett' *-en* bridal bouquet.
bru'de/ferd [*/fær] *-a/+-en* 1 a bride's journey to or from church. 2 bridal procession, bridal train.
bru'de/folk *pl* bridal couple.
bru'de/følgje *-t* (=+**/følge**) bridal procession.
bru'de/kjole *-n* bridal gown, wedding dress.
bru'de/krone *-a/+-en* bridal crown (ornament worn by a bride).
bru'de/lys *-et bot.* flowering rush (Butomus umbellatus).
bru'de/par' *-et* bridal couple.
+**bru'de/pike** *-n* bridesmaid, flower girl.
bru'de/seng *-a archaic* bridal bed: **komme i b-** (of woman) *hum.* get married.
bru'de/slør *-et* 1 bridal veil. 2 *bot.* baby's breath (Gypsophila paniculata).
bru'de/svein *-en* 1 page, train bearer (at wedding). 2 *bibl. (pl)* children of the bridechamber (Matt. 9,15).
+**bru'de/vie** *V -et/-gde* (=***brud/**) (of person performing marriage ceremony) marry.
+**bru'de/vielse** *-n* wedding.
brud'/gom' *-men/*-en* bridegroom.
***brud'/laup** *-et* cf **bryllup**
brudul'je *-n* 1 confused noise; hullabaloo. 2 roughhousing.
brug'de[1] *-a* bundle (esp. of flax) that one can grip in one hand.
brug'de[2] *-a zool.* basking shark (Cetorhinus maximus).
brug'de[3] *-a* raised edge or rim (on chair, sled, etc.).
brug'de/stol *-en archaic* chair with high back (used in church).
+**bru'/hode** *-t* (=***/hovud**) bridgehead.
bru'k[1] *-en/-et* 1 use: **b- av alkohol** u- of alcohol; **gjøre b- av** make u- of; **gå av b-** go out of u-; **ha b- for** need; **få b- for** be going to need; **det blir nok b- for det** it's going to come in handy; **være i b-** be in u-. 2 custom, practice, usage: **skikk og b-** common usage, what is commonly done.
bru'k[2] *-et* 1 (small) farm (once part of a larger farm). 2 industrial undertaking (e.g. mill, sawmill) located in the country. 3 outfit, gear (nets and other tackle used in fisheries).
***bru'kande** *A* - fit for use: **kniven er godt b-** the knife can very well be used.
bru'/kar *-et* (bridge) pier.
bru'k/bar *A* fit for use; passable, fairly good: **den er b- til mangt** it has many uses; **en b- løsning** a passable solution; **en ganske b- prestasjon** a pretty good performance.
bru'ke *V -te/*-a* 1 use (**til for**): **b- bena** use one's legs, hurry; **b-er De fløte?** do you take cream? **b- fornuft(en), vett(et)** use sense; **b- en gard** run a farm; **b- munn på en** scold. abuse sby; **la seg b-** allow oneself to be used; **b-t** secondhand, used; **den kan b-es til mangt** it has many uses. 2 consume, spend, use (**på** on): **b- penger** spend money; **de b-te av veden** they used some of the wood; **b- opp noe** use up sth. 3 do habitually, usually: **han b-er ikke å lyve** he doesn't usually lie; **det b-es ikke her** that isn't done here. 4 *(refl.)* complain, scold: **b- seg på en** abuse, scold sby; **b- seg over noe** complain about sth.
bru'kelig *A* - 1 usable. 2: **b- pant** forfeited collateral operated for the benefit of the creditor. 3 common, in use: **det er ikke b-** it isn't common; it isn't done; **det er b- å ta av seg hatten inne** people take off their hats indoors.
+**bru'ker** *-en, pl -e* (=***-ar**) person who operates, runs sth (often of the present owner of a farm).
+**brukket** [brok'ket] *pp of* **brekke**[2]
+**bruk's/anvi'sning** *-en* directions (for use).
bruk's/båt *-en* solid boat that will stand heavy use.
+**bruk's/eier** *-en, pl -e* (=***/eigar**) proprietor of an operation (e.g. sawmill) located in the country.
+**bruk's/gjenstand** *-en* article for everyday use, home furnishings.
bruk's/kunst *-en* arts and crafts.
bruk's/rett *-en* right of use.
bruk's/ting *-en* article for everyday use, home furnishings.
bruk's/verdi' *-en* (=***/verd(e)**) utility value.
+**bru'/legge** *V -la, -lagt* (=***/leggje**) pave.
+**bru'/legning** *-a/-en* (=***/legging**) paving, pavement.
brum[1] [brom'] *-met* (bear's) growl.
brum[2] [brom'] *+-met/*-et* 1 buds. 2 fresh twigs (for cattle feed).
brum/bass [brom'/] *-en* (=**/basse**) growler, grumbler.
***bru'me** *V -a* 1 (of tree) bud. 2 collect fresh twigs for cattle feed.
brumle [brom'le] *V -a/+-et* 1 growl, rumble. 2 buzz, drone.
brumme [brom'me] *V -a/+-et* 1 growl; grumble; grunt. 2 buzz, drone, hum.
Brum'und/dal *Pln* industrial village on Lake Mjøsa, Hedmark.
***bru'n**[1] *-a* 1 edge. 2 eyebrow. 3 brink.
bru'n[2] *A* 1 brown. 2 *pop.* drunk.

Bru'na *df* "Brownie", *prn.* given to a brown mare.
+**bru'n/aktig** *A* - brownish.
bru'n/barka *A* - (=+**-et**) tanned brown (of complexion).
brun'd *-en* heat, rut (in animals).
bru'ne[1] *-n* 1 burning. 2 fire. 3 burning sensation or pain.
bru'ne[2] *V -a/+-te* brown; bronze, tan.
Bru'nen *df* "Brownie", *prn.* given to a brown horse.
brunett' *A* - brunet.
brunet'te *-a/+-en* brunette.
***brun'ke** *V -a* look, turn brown.
bru'n/kol [/kål] *-et* (=+**/kull**) brown coal, lignite.
Brun'la/nes' *Pln* twp, Vestfold.
bru'nlig *A* - brownish.
***brunn'** *-en* cf **brønn**
brun'ne** *pp of* **brenne**[3] (=brunni**)
***brunn'/hus** *-et* cf **brønn/**
***brunn'/karse** *-n* cf **brønn/**
***brunn'/lokk** *-et* cf **brønn/**
***brunn'/vippe** *-a* cf **brønn/**
bru'n/rot *-a bot.* figwort (Scrophularia).
+**bru'nske** *V -a/-et* turn brownish.
brun'st *-en* heat, rut (in animals).
bru'n/stein *-en chem., geol.* pyrolusite.
brun'stig *A* - in heat, rutting (of animal).
bru'nt *et* brown (color or material): **være kledd i b-** be dressed in b-.
+**bru'n/øyd** *A* - (=***/øygd**) browneyed.
bru'r *-a* cf **brud**
bru'r(e)/ferd [*/fær] *-a* cf **brude/**
bru's[1] *-en* pop, soda.
bru's[2] *-et* 1 roar, rushing sound (esp. of water or wind); echo, swelling (of music). 2 effervescence, fizz; foam, froth, gush. 3 profusion, shock (e.g. of flowers, curly hair).
bru'se[1] *-n* 1 *bot.* juniper. 2 hairy tuft on the forehead of an animal: **Bukken B-** name of a billygoat in a fairytale.
bru'se[2] *V -te/*-a* 1 roar, rush, sound; (of music) swell. 2 babble, effervesce, fizz, foam. 3 swish, wave; stand out; (of feathers) be ruffled. 4: **b- opp** flare up (in anger), fly up.
bru's/hane *-n* 1 *zool.* ruff (Machetes pugnans). 2 *fig.* hothead.
+**bru's/hode** *-t* hothead.
brus'k *-en* cartilage.
bru'/spenn *-et* bridge span.
Brussel [brys'sel] *Pln* Brussels.
bru'/stein *-en* cobblestone.
+**brus'ten** *A -ent/-et, pl -ne* 1 broken (e.g. voice); dimmed, dulled by death (of eyes, look). 2 broken, failed (e.g. hopes).
bruta'l *A* brutal.
brutalise're *V -te* brutalize.
brutalite't *-en* brutality.
+**brutt'** *pp of* **bryte**
brut'to[1] *-en* gross (price, weight).
brut'to[2] *Av* gross.
brut'to/vekt *-a/+-en* gross weight.
Bru'/vik *Pln* twp, Hordaland.
bry'[1] *-et* bother, trouble: **gjøre seg b- med noe** take pains about sth; **komme til b-** arrive at an inopportune moment; **være til b-** be a lot of t-.
bry'[2] *V -dde* 1 bother, trouble: **b- en med noe** t- sby about sth; (polite phrase) **tør jeg b- Dem med å ...** may I t- you to ..., would you be kind enough to ...; **vil De være b-dd med å lukke vinduet** may I t- you to close the window. 2: **b- seg om** care for, like; bother with; be interested in, mind (usu. *neg.*); **jeg b-r meg ikke om fisk** I don't care for fish; **ikke b- deg om det** don't b- about it, don't mind. 3: **b- seg** act importantly, meddle: **ikke b- deg** stay out of this; **b- seg med en** take sby's affairs to heart; **b- seg med noe** meddle with sth, *(pop.)* butt in.
brydd' *A* - embarrassed, shamefaced.
bryd'de *V -a/+-et/*-e* sprout.
+**bryderi'** *-et* bother, trouble (**med** with): **det er da ikke noe b-** it's no trouble at all.
bry'e *-a* wooden trough, esp. for feed or water.
bryg'de *pt of* **brygge**[2]
brygg' *-et* brew.
+**bryg'ge**[1] *-a* (=***bryggje**[1]) boat landing, dock, wharf; jetty, pier: **arbeide på b-a** work on the dock, as a stevedore.
+**bryg'ge**[2] *V -a/-et/brygde* (=***bryggje**[2]) brew.
+**bryg'ge/kar'** *-et* brewing vat.
+**bryg'ge/panne** *-a* wash boiler.
+**bryg'ger** *-en, pl -e* (=***-jar**) brewer.
+**bryg'ger/hus** *-et* (=***-jar/**) 1 washhouse (on a farm). 2 laundry room.
+**bryggeri'** *-et, pl -er* (=***bryggjeri**) brewery.
+**bryg'ge/sjauer** *-en, pl -e* (=***bryggje/sjauar**) longshoreman, stevedore.
bryg'ging *-a* brewing.
***brygg'jar** *-en* cf **brygger**
***brygg'je**[1] *-a* cf **brygge**[1]
***brygg'je**[2] *V -a/brygde* cf **brygge**[2]
***bryggjeri'** *-et* cf **bryggeri**
***bryl'laup** *-et* cf **bryllup**
+**bryl'lup** *-et, pl -/-er* (=***bryllaup**) wedding.
+**bryl'lups/dag** *-en* 1 wedding day. 2 anniversary.
+**bryl'lups/fest** *-en* wedding celebration.
+**bryl'lups/ga'rd** *-en* farm, place where a wedding is going on.
+**bryl'lups/gave** *-a/-en* wedding present.
+**bryl'lups/kake** *-a* wedding cake.
+**bryl'lups/kledning** *-en bibl.* wedding garment (Matt. 22,11).
+**bryl'lups/klokke** *-a (pl)* wedding bells.
+**bryl'lups/marsj** [/mars] *-en* bridal march.
+**bryl'lups/natt** *-a/-en* bridal night.
+**bryl'lups/reise** *-a/-en* honeymoon.
bry'n *-et* 1 edge, outline, rim. 2 brow, eyebrow: **rynke b-ene, ha rynkede b-** knit one's b-s.
+**bryn'de** *-n* sexual desire: *bibl.* **lide b-** burn (1. Cor. 7,9).
bry'ne[1] *-t, pl +-r/*-* whetstone.
bry'ne[2] *V -te* sharpen, whet.
bry'ne/stein *-en* whetstone.
bry'ne/stokk *-en* container for whetstone and water.
bry'ning *-a/-en* 1 whetting. *2 edging (on a garment); rim (of mountain).
bryn'je *-a* coat of mail.
bryn'je/kledd *A -/*-kledt* clad in a coat of mail.
***bryn'ne** *V -te* cf **brønne**
-**bry'nt** *A* - -browed.
***bry'/sam'** *A* cf **/som**
brys'k *A* brusque.
brys'ke *V -a/+-et*: **b- seg** act brusquely; strut, swagger.
+**bry'/som'** *A -t, pl -me* (=***/sam**) troublesome.
+**brys'seler/knipling** *-en* (=***bryssel/**) Brussels lace.
+**brys'seler/teppe** *-t* (=***bryssel/**) Brussels carpet.
brys't *-et, pl -/+-er* 1 chest; *bibl.* breast: **være bred over b-et** be broad-chested; **slå seg for sitt b-** smite upon one's b- (Luke 18,13); give ostentatious expression to one's innocence or good conscience, protest one's innocence. 2 (woman's) breast: **få b-** be breast-fed; **gi b-** breast-feed. 3 breast, bosom: **hun puttet brevet inn på b-et** she hid the letter in her bosom. 4 front part, head (e.g. of boat, house).
brys't/ba'rn *-et, pl -/*-born* nursing child.
brys't/bein *-et* breastbone.
+**brys't/bilde** *-t* (=***/bilete**) half-length picture.
brys't/duk *-en* dickey, plastron (decorated breast piece on bodice).
brys'te *V -a/+-et*: **b- seg** strut, swagger; **b- seg av noe, over noe** brag, be proud of take pride in sth.
brys't/finne *-n* pectoral fin.
brys't/hinne *-a anat.* pleura, pleural sac.
+**brys't/holder** *-en, pl -e* (=***/haldar**) bra, brassiere.
brys't/hole [/håle] *-a* (=+**/hule**) *anat.* thoracic cavity.
brys't/høgd *-a* breastheight.
+**brys't/høyde** *-n* cf **/høgd**
brys't/kasse *-a/-en* chest, thorax.
brys't/knapp *-en* shirt stud.
brys'tning *-en arch.* parapet (low wall); front panel (of altar); window back.
brys't/nål *-a* brooch.
brys't/sjuk *A* tuberculous.
brys't/sukker [/sokker] *-et* (mostly crystallized) hard candy.
+**brys't/svømning** *-en* (=***/symjing**) breast stroke.
brys't/tone *-n* deep, full tone, chest tone.
brys't/vern [/væ'rn] *-et* breastwork, parapet.
brys't/vorte [/vorte] *-a* nipple.
bry'te *V brautt/+brøt, +brutt/*brote/*-i* 1 break (e.g. bread, a commandment, the ice, the law, one's promise, relations, etc.): **b- alle bruer bak seg** burn one's bridges; **b- en lanse for en** come to sby's defense; **b- staven over en** condemn sby. 2 disconnect; discontinue, stop: **tre minutter, vi må b-** your three minutes are up, we must disconnect you; **b- løpet** abandon, break off a race. 3 clear (land); mine, quarry (stone); dig, make (a hole); crack (a code); open (a letter). 4 overcome, weaken; **b- ens makt** b- sby's power, **motstanden er brutt** resistance has been broken; **med brutt stemme** with broken voice. 5 beat, press (of waves, *fig.* of emotions): **bølgene b-er (mot stranden)** the waves are breaking (against the shore); **gråten brøt på hos henne** she struggled to keep back her sobs. 6 struggle; wrestle: **han brøt og brøt for å få steinen løs** he kept struggling to get the stone loose; **han b-er i gresk-romersk stil** he wrestles in Greco-Roman style: **b-es (med)** wrestle (with); **guttene b-es** the boys are wrestling. 7 *(refl.)*: **b- seg igjennom** break through, win through; **b- seg så små (som å)** lower oneself (to); **b- seg vei** make one's way, succeed. 8 (with *adv.* and *prep.*): **b- av** b- off, interrupt (others or oneself); **b- fram** b-, b- forth, b- out, begin (shining); **b- igjennom** b- through; make a name for oneself, **b- inn** b- in, b- into (house, conversation); **b- løs** pry loose; break out, b- loose, begin (applause, rain); **b- med** b- with (friends); **b- ned** b- down (*trans.* and *intrans.*); **b- opp** b- open, force; get b- up (of ice); b- up, depart, leave; get up to leave; **b- over tvert (med)** stop abruptly, b- off (with); **b- på (svensk)** have a (Swedish) accent; **b- sammen** b- down, collapse; **b- ut** b- out (of jail), escape; burst out (laughing); break out, burst (of buds etc.).
bry'te/kamp *-en* wrestling match.
+**bry'ter** *-en, pl -e* (=***-ar**) 1 wrestler. 2 big, hulking fellow. 3 electric switch.
bry'ting *-a* wrestling.
***bryt'je** *V-a* 1 chop (meat) finely. 2 work hard.
+**bry'tning** *-en* 1 conflict, struggle: **en b-s/tid** an age of conflict. 2 convulsion, shudder. 3 breaking (e.g. of a vowel). 4 extraction (of ore).
bræ' *V -dde* cf **bre**[2]

+ Bokmål; * Nynorsk; ° Dialect.
After letter: ' stress (Acc. 1); ' tone, stress (Acc. 2); · length.
Below letter: . not pronounced.

***bræ'ḍe** *V -de* cf **bre**[2]

bræ'ke *V -te/+-et* cf **breke**

***bræ'kje** *V -te* cf **breke**

***bræ'le** *V -a* 1 hurry. 2 act up.

***bræ'se** *V -te* cf **brese**

brø'ḍ *-et* 1 bread: **alminnelig b-** light rye b-; **fint b-** white b-; **grovt b-** dark b-; **gammelt b-** stale b-; **ha smør på b-et** butter one's b-; **vi har bare det tørre b-** we have only dry b- to eat, only the bare necessities to live on; **vann og b-** b- and water; **gi en stener for b-** (Matt. 7,9, Luke 11,11) give sby stones instead of b-; **den enes død den annens b-** one man's loss is another man's gain. 2 loaf of bread: **to b-** two loaves. 3 living: **tjene sitt b-** earn one's l-. 4 employment: **ha, ta en i sitt b-** have, take sby into one's e-; **være i ens b-** be employed by sby.

brø'ḍ/bakk *-en* (=+**/bakke**) bread tray, bread basket.

brø'ḍ/boks *-en* bread box.

+brø'de *-n* offense; sin.

+brø'de/full *A* guilty, having a guilty conscience.

brø'ḍ/frukt *-a/+-en* breadfruit.

brø'ḍ/fø *V -dde* support: **Norge kan ikke b- seg selv med korn** Norway doesn't produce enough grain for its own needs.

brø'ḍ/kniv *-en* breadknife.

brø'ḍ/ko'rn *-et* food grain; cereals.

brø'ḍ/laus *A* (=+**/løs**) 1 out of bread. 2 unemployed. 3 unprofitable: **b-t arbeid** useless work.

brø'ḍ/leiv *-en* 1 whole piece of a very thin type of bread (e.g. **flatbrød**). 2 thick slice of bread.

+brø'ḍ/løs *A* cf **/laus**

brø'ḍ/mose [*/måse] *-n bot.* Iceland moss (Cetraria islandica), in earlier times mixed into flour used for bread.

brø'ḍ/nid' *-et* professional jealousy.

+brø'dre/menighet *-en* Moravian church.

+brø'ds/brytelse *-n bibl.* breaking of bread (Acts 2, 42).

brø'ḍ/skalk *-en* crust of bread; heel of a loaf.

brø'ḍ/skive *-a* slice of bread.

brø'ḍ/skorpe *-a* bread crust.

brø'ḍ/studium *-iet* vocational study.

brø'k [also **brøkk'**] *-en* fraction: **alminnelig b-** common f-; **ekte b-** proper f-; **uekte b-** improper f-; **forkorte en b-** reduce a f-.

brø'k/del *-en* fraction: **han måtte selge huset for en b- av verdien** he had to sell the house at a f- of its worth; **b-en av et sekund** a split second.

brø'ker *pl of* **brok, brøk**

brøk'/strek *-en/*-et* fraction line.

brø'l *-et* roar: **utstøte et b-** let out a r-.

brø'le *V -te/*-a* bellow, roar; yell: **b- av full hals** shout at the top of one's lungs.

brø'l(e)/ape *-n* 1 *zool.* howler (Alouatta). 2 person who uses a very loud voice in talking or singing.

+brø'ler *-en, pl -e* 1 sby who roars. 2 bad mistake, howler.

°brøl'lop *-et* cf **bryllup**

+brønn' *-en* (=***brunn**) well.

+brønn'/boring *-a/-en* well-boring.

+brønn'/båt *-en* well boat.

+brøn'ne *V -a/-et* (=***brynne**) water (animals).

+brønn'/gjest *-en* guest at a spa.

+brønn'/hus *-et* well house.

+brønn'/karse *-n bot.* well cress (Nasturtium).

+brønn'/kur *-en* cure consisting in taking the waters at a spa.

+brønn'/lokk *-et* well cover.

+brønn'/vippe *-a* well sweep.

Brønn'/øy *Pln* twp, Nordland.

Brøn'nøy/sunḍ *Pln* town in Nordland.

+brøs't[1] *-en/-et* defect, flaw, imperfection: **vår moders b- vi hylle til** our mother's flaws we keep concealed (Wergeland).

°brøs't[2] *-et* cf **bryst**

+brøs't/feldig [also -fel'-] *A* - dilapidated, ramshackle.

+brøs't/holden *A -ent, pl -ne* aggrieved, hurt, wronged.

+brø't *pt of* **bryte**

°brø'ten *A -ent/-e/-i, pl -ne* (of horse) wounded from chafing by the harness.

***brøys'k** *A* brittle, fragile.

brøy'te *V -te/+-a/+-et* 1 clear away (e.g. snow): **b- vei** clear a road; **b- vei for noe** prepare the way for sth; **b- seg fram** break a path. 2 break (new land). 3 struggle (**med** with).

brøy'te/bil *-en* truck with a snowplow attachment.

brøy'te/kant *-en* snowbank (thrown up along the roadside by trucks clearing the road).

***brå'**[1] *-a, pl brær* eyelash.

***brå'**[2] *V -dde* 1 flash, glint. 2 call out: **b- ved åt nokon** c- to sby. 3 look like: **b- på nokon** resemble sby. 4 be urgent: **det b-r ikkje med dette** there is no rush with this.

brå'[3] *A -tt, pl -/*-e* 1 abrupt, sudden; sharp: **en b- beslutning** a sudden decision; **det ble b-tt stille** it suddenly grew quiet; **en b- sving** a sharp turn. 2 impatient: **være b- av seg** have an impatient disposition. 3 *dial.* **ikke b-tt** nowhere near.

brå'/bremse *V -a/+-et/+-te* apply brakes suddenly.

***brå'ḍen** *A -e/-i, pl -ne* molten.

brå'/ḍjup *A* (=+**/dyp**) (of bottom of water) dropping off suddenly.

brå'/fang *-et* quick, successful move: **gjøre b-** seize a (sudden) opportunity.

brå'/fart *-en* high, sudden speed; mad rush.

brå'/fly *V infl as* **fly**[4] rush off.

brå'/hast *en* big hurry: **det har ingen b-** there is no rush about it.

+brå'/het *-en* suddenness.

brå'/hug *-en*: **ha b- etter noe** be impatient for sth; want sth badly.

brå'k *-et* 1 noise: **hold opp med det b-et** stop that n-. 2 difficulty; fuss, trouble: **gjøre, lage b- for en** make t- for sby; **få b- med noe** have d-ies, t- with sth; **jeg vil ikke ha noe b-** I don't want any t-.

brå'/kast *-et* sudden bolt, jump, turn; sudden gust of wind: **gjøre et b- (på seg)** start.

brå'ke *V -a/+-et/+-te* 1 be noisy: **b- seg fram** advance noisily. 2 make fuss, make trouble. 3 brake, scutch (flax, by beating).

brå'ket(e) *A* - noisy.

brå'/kjekk *A -kjekt* cocky.

+brå'k/maker *-en, pl -e* (=***-ar**) 1 noisy person. 2 troublemaker.

brå'/leik *-en* suddenness.

brå'/lynt *A* - (=***/lyndt**) quick-tempered.

brå'/mett *A* - suddenly unable to eat any more.

brå'ne *V -a/+-te* dissolve, melt (e.g. of snow).

brå'/sinne *-t* sudden anger.

brå'/sint *A* - easily angered.

brå'/snu *V -dde* turn around sharply.

brå'/stans *-en* sudden stop.

brå'/stanse *V -a/+-et/+-te* (=***/stane**) stop abruptly; stop short.

brå'/stoppe *V -a/+-et* stop abruptly; stop short.

brå'/sving *-en* sharp, sudden turn.

brå'te *-n* (=***brote**[1]) 1 burned clearing in a forest. 2 pile (of wood and leaves, for burning): **brenne b-** burn brush. 3: **en b- (med)** a lot (of), a great many.

brå'te/brann *-en* bonfire from a heap of brush.

brå'te/brenning *-a/+-en* burning of garden debris, brush.

brå'te/bruk *-et* farming method consisting in burning down a patch of forest and sowing rye in the ashes.

brå'te/vis *Av* lots, scads, stacks: **b- med folk** l- of people.

brått' *Av* suddenly.

brå'/vakker *A -t, pl -vakre* strikingly beautiful.

brå'/vakne *V -a/+-et* wake up suddenly.

brå'/venḍing *-a/+-en* sharp turn: **i en b-** in a hurry; in a pinch.

bu'[1] *-a* 1 hut, shack, shanty. 2 storeroom; storehouse. 3 general merchandise store in the country.

bu'[2] *-et* (=+**bo**) 1 abode, home. 2 household: ***setje bu** start a home. 3 estate, fortune, property. 4 cattle. 5 cattle population on a farm.

bu'[3] *V -dde* (=+**bo**[2]) 1 dwell, live; remain, stay. 2 be: **det bur mye godt i han** there is much good in him.

bu'[4] *V -dde* make ready, prepare: **bu seg til noe** prepare for sth.

-bu *-en* (=+**-bo, *-bue**) -dweller.

***bub'le**[1] *-a* cf **boble**[1]

***bub'le**[2] *V -a* cf **boble**[2]

+bu'd *-et* (=***bod**[3]) 1 command, order; commandment: **det ble gjort på hans b-** it was done at his c-; **de ti b-** the ten c-s. 2 message (**til** to): **lerken bringer b- om våren** the skylark is the harbinger of spring; **sende b- etter en, på en** send for sby. 3 tidings, word. 4 offer; bid: **gi b-, gjøre (et) b- (på)** make a b- (for), an o-. 5 messenger; delivery boy (man).

Bu'd *Pln* twp, Møre og Romsdal.

Bu'/dal *Pln* twp, Sør-Trøndelag.

bu'dals/stol *-en* light spindle-backed chair first made in Budal twp.

+bu'd/bringer *-en, pl -e* messenger; harbinger.

+bu'd/bærer *-en, pl -e* messenger; harbinger.

***budd'** *A* - prepared, ready.

buddhis'me *-n* Buddhism.

buddhis't *-en* Buddhist.

budei'e *-a* dairy maid, milkmaid.

+bu'den *A -ent, pl -ne* invited.

budoa'r *-et* boudoir.

+bu'd/orḍ *-et* commandment.

bu'/drått *-en* the output of milk products (butter, cheese) on a farm.

+bu'd/senḍe *V -te* send for.

budsjett' *-et, pl -/+-er* budget.

budsjette're *V -te* budget.

+bu'd/skap *-et, pl -/-er* message.

***bud'/stikke** *-a* 1 (in Norse times) a stick sent from farm to farm to call people together, e.g. for defense. 2 important message. 3 name given to a newspaper, e.g. **Asker og Bærums b-**, corresponding to "Messenger".

+buḍt' *pp of* **byde**

+bu'e *-n* cf **boge**

***-bu'e** *-n* cf **-bu**

+bu'e/føring *-a/+-en mus.* bowing.

+bu'e/gang *-en* 1 arcade; archway. 2 *anat.* semicircular canal.

+bu'e/korps *-et* boys' drill corps (in Bergen).

+bu'e/minutt' *-et* minute of an arc.

***bu'en** *A -e/-i, pl -ne* 1 prepared, ready. 2 ripe.

+bu'e/parentes [/parangte's] *-en* parenthesis.

+bu'e/sag *-a* cf **boge/**

+bu'e/skytter *-en, pl -e* archer.

+bu'e/streng *-en* cf **boge/**

+bu'et *A* - curved; arched, domed.

bu'far/dag *-en* day when the cattle are moved from the summer dairy back to the farm (or vice versa).

bu'/fast *A* - resident, settled.

bu'/fe *-et* cattle.

bu'/ferd [*/fær] *-a/+-en* journey home with the cattle from the summer dairy.

buf'fer *-en* buffer, shock absorber.

buf'fer/stat *-en* buffer state.

buffet [bufe'] *-en* buffet: **stående b-** b- meal.

bu'/føre *V -te* move (the cattle) to or from summer dairy.

***bu'g** *-en* 1 lengthy curve. 2 (shallow) bay.

*__bu`ge__ *V -a* bend, bow.
+__bugne__ [bong'ne] *V -a/-et* cf **bogne**
*__bu`/hage__ *V -a* make cheese; esp. wind up the cheesemaking at a summer dairy.
bu`/hund *-en* 1 Norwegian type of farm dog (relatively small, yellowish, with erect ears, thick coat and curly tail) used as watchdog and for tending cattle. 2 *dial.* whelk (a marine snail, Buccinum undatum).
*__bu`ing__ *-a* preparation (mostly last part of compounds).
bu`k *-en* abdomen; belly; stomach.
bukett' *-en* bouquet.
bu`k/finne *-n* ventral fin.
bu`k/gjord *-a* bellyband (of horse's harness).
bu`k/hinne *-a anat.* peritoneum.
+__bu`khinne/beten·nelse__ *-en* peritonitis.
bu`k/hole [/håle] *-a* (=+**/hule**) abdominal cavity.
bu`/kjær *A* (of domestic animals) not inclined to stray from the flock.
bukk[1] [bokk'] *-en* 1 male of certain horned and clovenhoofed animals (e.g. billygoat, buck, ram). 2 (of person) goat: **han er en gammel b-** he is an old g-. 3 trestle; sawbuck, sawhorse. 4 person that one leaps over in playing leapfrog; (in gymnastics) a short vaulting horse: **hoppe b-** play leapfrog; **hoppe b- over noe** (also:) skip sth, leave sth out. 5 driver's seat (of horse-drawn vehicle). 6 one of a pair of short sledges (**b- og geit**) used for hauling timber. 7 blunder, mistake.
bukk[2] [bokk'] *-et/*-en* bow: **gjøre et dypt b-** make a low b-.
bukke [bok`ke] *V -a/+-et* 1 bend: **b- seg ned etter noe** bend over to pick sth up. 2 bow. 3: **b- under** go under, succumb (**for** to).
bukke/bein [bok`ke/] *-et* leg of a billygoat: **sette b-** stand stiff-legged, be obstinate.
bukke/blad *-et bot.* buckbean (Menyanthes trifoliata).
bukke/ho·rn *-et* billygoat's horn (sometimes made into a trumpet).
bukkel [bok'kel] *-elen, pl bukler* 1 bump. 2 (woman's) roll of hair. 3 (on a shield) boss.
bukke/skjegg [bok`ke/] *-et* goat's beard; goatee.
bukke/sprang *-et* caper.
bu`k/landing *-a/+-en* belly landing.
bukle [bok`le] *V -a/+-et* form or produce a bump, dent.
buklet(e) [bok`let(e)] *A* - bumpy.
bu`k/ol *-a* (=+**/ole**, */**ore**) bellyband (of horse's harness).
buk's/bom [/bom'] *-men bot.* box.
bukse [bok'se] *-a* trousers, pants: **skjelve i b-ne** shiver in one's boots.
bukse/bak *-en* seat of trousers.
bukse/bjø·rn *-en* sleeper (child's nightwear).
bukse/press *-en* crease in trousers.
bukse'r/båt [bok-] *-en* tugboat.
bukse're [bok-] *V -te* 1 tow. 2 maneuver.
bukse/sele [bok'se/] *-n* suspender.
bukse/skjørt *-et* divided skirt.
bukse/smekk *-en* fly (of trousers).
Buks/nes [bok's/] *Pln* twp, Nordland.
bu`kspytt/kjertel *-en anat.* pancreas.
bukt [bok't] *-a* 1 bend, curve. 2 coil, loop; fold, wave; bight: **ormen slår b-er på seg** the snake slithers, undulates. 3 bay, gulf: **den Persiske bukt** The Persian Gulf. 4: **få b- med** get the upper hand with, manage, overcome; **ha b-en og begge endene** be in full control, have the upper hand.
+__bu`k/taler__ *-en, pl -e* (=***-ar**) ventriloquist.
bukte [bok`te] *V -a/+-et*: **b- seg** describe a wavy line; (of road) curve; (of landscape) roll, undulate; (of reptile) crawl, slither (**fram, framover** along).
buktet(e) [bok`tet(e)] *A* - curvy; wavy.
bukt(n)ing [bok`t-] *-a* curve, wave (in a line or in sth describing a line).
*__bu'l__ *-en* cf **bol[1]**
BUL = **Bondeungdomslag(et)**
bul'der *-et* din, roar, rumble.
bul'dre *V -a/-et* boom, rattle, roar; rumble: **b- løs** bellow out.
bul'dre/basse *-n* blusterer.
+__bu'le[1]__ *-n* bulge; bump, lump; dent.
+__bu'le[2]__ *-a/-en* dive, joint.
+__bu'le[3]__ *V -a/-et/-te* bulge (out).
+__bu'le/hatt__ *-en* soft broadbrimmed felt hat with dents pressed into it.
+__bu'let(e)__ *A* - bumpy, dented.
bulevar'd *-en* boulevard.
bulga'r *-en* Bulgarian.
Bulga'ria *Pln* Bulgaria.
bulga'rsk *A* - Bulgarian.
buljong' *-en* bouillon, consommé.
buljong'/terning *-en* bouillon cube.
bul'k *-en* dent, lump.
bul'ke *-a* dent (e.g. car).
bul'ket(e) *A* - dented; rough, irregular (of surface).
+__bull'/biter__ *-en, pl -e* (=***-ar**) 1 big fierce dog. 2 short-tempered, truculent person.
bull'/dogg *-en* bulldog.
+__bull'/doser__ *-en, pl -e* (=***-ar**) bulldozer.
bul'le[1] *-n* (papal) bull.
+__bul'le[2]__ *-a* small round loaf of bread.
bulletin [buleteng'] *-en* bulletin.
bul'me/urt *-a/-en bot.* henbane (Hyoscyamus niger).
bul't *-en* chunk of wood.
bul'te *V -a/+-et* 1 beat (e.g. of heart). 2 stomp, walk heavily.
*__bu'lung__ [-ong] *-en* 1 trunk (of body). 2 shirt.
bu'/mann *-en, pl -menn/*-menner* person who has a fixed residence (usu. as different from nomadic Lapps).
*__bumbe__ [bom'me] *-a* cf **bomme[1]**
bumerang' *-en* boomerang.
bu'/merke *-t, pl +-r/*-* mark used as signature by an illiterate person.
bump [bom'p] *-et* 1 bang, thud. 2 click, light noise. 3 bump, jolt.
bums[1] [bom's] *Av* slap-bang.
bums[2] [bom's] *I* crash, wham.
bumse [bom'se] *V -a/+-et* 1 fall with a bang. 2: **b- ut med noe** blurt sth out.
bumset(e) [bom'set(e)] *A* - awkward, clumsy, ungainly.
bu'nad *-en, pl *-er* 1 equipment, gear; decoration. 2 [also -nad] costume, dress, esp. national costume.
*__bun'de[1]__ *pt of* **bynje**
*__bun'de[2]__ *pp of* **binde**
bun'del *-elen, pl +-ler* bundle.
bun'den [+bun'nen] *A +-et, pl -ne* bound, tied; latent, potential: **b-et mandat** limited mandate; **b-et stil** rhymed style, verse; **b-ne krefter** l- powers, unused strength.
+__bun'det__ *pp of* **binde**
*__bun'di__ *pp of* **binde**
bun'ding *-en* knitting.
bun'dings/stikke *-a* knitting needle.
+__bun'ds/forvan·dt__ *en, pl -e* ally.
*__bu'ne__ *-a* bone (in body).
*__bu'ner__ *pl* 1 extremities, limbs. 2 bone structure.
bun'galow [-låv·] *-en* (=***-lov**) bungalow.
bunk [bong'k] *-en* bulge, bump, dent.
bunke[1] [bong'ke] *-n* bundle, heap pile: **en b- papir** a p- of paper.
bunke[2] [bong'ke] *-n* pudding bowl, esp. for junket.
bunke[3] [bong'ke] *V -a/+-et*: **b- seg** pile up.
bunker [bong'ker] *-en, pl +-e naut.* bunker.
+__bunker/kull__ [bong'ker/] *pl* bunker coal.
bunkers [bong'kers] *-en, pl - mil.* bunker.
bunkre [bong'kre] *V -a/+-et naut.* fill a bunker.
+__bunn'[1]__ *-en* cf **botn**
+__bunn'[2]__ *Av, Pf* thoroughly, utterly.
+__bun'ne__ *V -et* cf **botne**
Bun'ne/fjorden *Pln* cf **Bonne/**
+__bunn'/fall__ *-et* cf **botn/**
+__bunn'/falsk__ *A* utterly false, hypocritical.
+__bunn'/farge__ *-n* cf **botn/**
+__bunn'/fast__ *A* - cf **botn/**
+__bunn'/felle__ *V -felte* cf **botn/**
+__bunn'/forder·vet__ *A* - utterly corrupt, depraved.
+__bunn'/fryse__ *V infl as* **fryse** cf **botn/**
+__bunn'/ga·rn__ *-et* cf **botn/**
+__bunn'/hederlig__ *A* - honest clear through; thoroughly honorable.
+__bunn'/løs__ *A* cf **botn/laus**
+__bunn'/rekor·d__ *-en* record low.
+__bunn'/skrape__ *V -te* cf **botn/**
+__bunn'/tilje__ *-a* cf **botn/**
+__bunn'/tømmer__ *-et* cf **botn/**
+__bunn'/ulyk·kelig__ *A* - terribly unhappy.
+__bunn'/vann__ *-et* cf **botn/vatn**
+__bun'sen/brenner__ *-en, pl -e* (=***-ar**) Bunsen burner.
bun't[1] *-en* bunch, bundle: **heile b-en** the whole bunch.
*__bun't[2]__ *pp of* **bynje**
bun'te *V -a/+-et* bunch, bundle (**sammen** together).
bun't(e)/vis *Av* in bunches, bundles.
+__bun't/maker__ *-en, pl -e* (=***-ar**) furrier.
*__bu'/nøyte__ *-t* herd.
bu'/orm *-en* a nonvenomous snake (Tropidonotus natrix) of the Colubridae.
*__bu'r[1]__ *-en* cf **boer**
bu'r[2] *-en* bellow, roar.
bu'r[3] *-et* 1 storehouse. 2 storeroom. 3 farm building with sleeping rooms, esp. for guests. 4 bower; a maiden's room (e.g. in ballads). 5 cage: **sitte i b-** be caged.
*__bur'd__ *-en* 1 birth; extraction: **vere av høg b-** be of high b-. 2 embryo, esp. calf.
+__bur'de[1]__ *V bør, burde, burdet* 1 ought to, should: **vi bør (burde) gå nå** we ought to leave now; **vi burde (ha) gått** we should have left. 2 be proper, seemly: **som (det) seg hør og bør** as is meet and proper.
bur'de[2] *pt of* **burde, byrje[1]**
bu're *V -a/+-te* bellow, roar.
+__bu'/reiser__ *-en, pl -e* (=***-ar**) person who starts a farm on new land; pioneer, settler.
bu'/reising *-a* farming of new land.
+__burgun'der__ *-en, pl -e* (=***-ar**) 1 Burgundy (wine or color). 2 Burgundian.
bur'kne *-n* 1 bracken, fern. 2 spleenwort (Asplenium).
burles'k *A* burlesque.
bur'nus *-en* burnoose.
bursjiko's *A* free and easy (of student life and manners).
+__bursjoa'__ *-en* cf **bourgeois**
+__bursjoasi'__ *-et* cf **bourgeoisi**
bu'rs/loft *-et* loft room in farm storehouse.
*__bur't[1]__ *pp of* **byrje[1]**
*__bur't[2]__ *Av* cf **bort**
*__bur'te__ *Av* cf **borte**
*__bur't/yver__ *P* cf **bort/over**
*__bu's[1]__ *-en* cf **buss[2]**
bu's[2] *Av* 1 madly, violently. 2 head on, straight: **gå b- på noe** wade into sth.
bu'/satt *A* - cf **/sette**
+__bu'/satte__ *pt of* **-sette**
bu'se[1] *-n* 1 big brute of a man. 2 boogeyman.
bu'se[2] *V -a/+-et/-te* barge, rush: **b- på** rush on; **b- ut med noe** blurt sth out.
bu'se/mann *-en, pl -menn/*-menner* boogeyman.
*__bu'/setjing__ *-a* cf **/setting**
+__bu'/sette__ *V -satte, -satt* (=+**bo/**, */**setje**) settle: **han er busatt på Hamar** he lives at Hamar; **b- seg** settle down, take up residence.

+ Bokmål; * Nynorsk; ° Dialect.
After letter: ' stress (Acc. 1); ` tone, stress (Acc. 2); · length.
Below letter: . not pronounced.

+bu'/setting *-a/-en* settlement.
***bu'/sitjande** *A* - cf **/sittende**
bu'/sittende *A* - dwelling, living, resident.
bus'k *-en* (=**buske**[1]) bush, shrub.
+bus'k/aktig *A* - bushy, shrubby.
bu'/skap *-en* cattle, stock; herd.
***bu'/skape** *V -a* settle down, get set in a new residence.
+buska's *-et, pl -/-er* brush; shrubbery; thicket.
bus'ke[1] *-a* cf **busk**
bus'ke[2] *V -a/+-et*: **b- seg** bush out.
bus'ke/bjø'rn *-en hum.* squirrel ("bush bear").
Bus'ke/rud *Pln* county **(fylke)** in southern Norway.
bus'ket(e) *A* - bushy, shaggy.
bus'k/mann *-en, pl -menn/*-menner* Bushman.
***bu'/slag** *-et* cattle breed.
***bu'/slit** *-et* **1** big property loss. **2** bankruptcy.
buss'[1] *-en* bus.
***buss'**[2] *-en* baggy, swelling middle part of sail or net.
buss'[3] *-en* small piece, esp. a chew of tobacco.
bus'se[1] *-n* **1** *dial.* man. **2** *pop.* pal: **være gode b-r** be pals.
bus'se[2] *V -a/+-et* go by bus.
busserull' [also bus'-] *-en* work blouse.
buss'/rute *-a/+-en* **1** bus route. **2** bus schedule.
buss'/sjåfø'r *-en* bus driver.
bus't *-a* bristle; bristling hair: **slåss så b-a fyker** tear each other's hair out; **reise b-** (of dog, *fig.* of person) raise one's hackles, grumble.
bu'/stad *-en* (=+**bo/sted**) residence.
bus'te *V -a/+-et* tousle: **b- en til** muss up sby's hair; **b- seg til på håret** get one's hair mussed up; **b- seg** (of hair) be unruly, stand up like bristles.
+bu'/sted *-et* cf **/stad**
+bus'te/hue *-t* **1** tousled head. **2** person who has tousled hair.
bus't(e)/leiv *-a* piece of shoemaker's thread, covered with pitch and with a pig's bristle fastened to one end (to make it go through holes easily).
bus'tet(e) *A* - **1** uncombed, unkempt. **2** covered with chaff or straw.
***bu'/styrar** *-en* manager of an estate.
bus't/yvel *-elen, pl -ler* hedgehog.
***bu'tel** *-elen, pl -lar* bottle.
+butel'je *-n* bottle.
butikk' *-en* shop, store: **gå i b-er** (in the country often: **på b-en**) go shopping; **gjøre b- på noe** make a profit out of sth.
butikk'/jomfru *-/+-en obs.* female store clerk.
butikk'/loka'le *-t* salesroom.
butikk'/tjuv *-en* (=+**/tyv**) shoplifter.
+butikk'/vindu *-et* (=***/vindauge**) store window.
butt'[1] *-en* log end.
butt'[2] *-en* open wooden container.
butt'[3] *A* - **1** blunt. **2** chubby, plump.
but'te *V -a/+-et* ram **(mot** against).
?but'tel *-elen, pl butler* cf **butel**
but'ter/deig *-en* puff paste.
+but'tet(e) *A* - chubby, plump.
***bu've** *-n* boogeyman.
Bu'/vik *Pln* twp, Sør-Trøndelag.
by'[1] *-en* city, town: **by og bygd** town and country (often used meaning: the whole country); **Oslo by** the city of Oslo; **gå på byen** be out on the t-; **reise til byen** go to t-.
by'[2] *V -dde* (=**byde**) **1** command, order; bid, decree: **hun bød ham (å) gå** she o-ed him to leave; **loven byr det** the law d-s it; *archaic* **by opp, by ut** mobilize, summon (soldiers). **2** command, be the master of: **han byr over hundre mann** he has a hundred men at his command. **3** bid (welcome), greet: **by en velkommen** welcome sby; *archaic* **han bød Guds fred** he offered a greeting ("the peace of God"); **by farvel** take one's farewell. **4** offer: **hun bød ham sin hånd** she o-ed him her hand; **by en penger** o- sby money; **by en en dram** o- sby a drink; **by en juling** *pop.* o- to fight sby; **takk som byr** I don't mind if I do; **ikke la seg by noe** not allow, put up with sth; **det byr seg en sjanse** a chance is o-ed; **når anledningen byr seg** when the opportunity presents, o-s itself. **5** bid, make a bid: **by på noe** make a bid for sth (at an auction); **fem kroner er budt, hvem byr ti?** (said by an auctioneer:) I have a bid for five *kroner*, do I hear ten?; **by over en** outbid sby. **6** ask, invite: **by gjester** i- guests; **by en dame opp til en dans** a- a lady to dance. **7** (with *adv.* or *prep.*): **by fram** offer; **by seg fram** offer oneself; **by en imot** be repulsive, make one sick; **det byr meg imot** it is repulsive to me; **by på (en drink)** offer (a drink); **prosjektet bød på store vanskeligheter, men også på fordeler** the project involved great difficulties, but also offered possibilities; **hva har du å by på?** what do you have to offer? what do you have there?; **by rundt konfekt** pass candy around; **by seg til** offer (to do sth).
by'/dame *+-n/*-a* city girl, lady.
by'de *V baud/+bød, +budt/*bode/*-i* cf **by**[2]
by'de/form *-a/+en gram.* imperative.
by'/del *-en* area, district, part, section (of a city).
by'dende *A* - commanding, imperious, masterful, peremptory (e.g. of gesture, voice).
by'de/setning *+en/*-a gram.* imperative sentence.
by'e[1] *-a* (=+**byge, bøye**) shower (of hail, rain, snow); strong gusts of wind.
+by'e[2] *-a* bed (in children's language).
+by'e[3] *V -a/-et* lull (a child to sleep).
by'/fant *-en* "city feller", city slicker, person from town; (collectively:) people from town (*derog.* used in the country).
+by'/fogd [/fogd] *-en* (=***/fut**) (city) judge, justice of the peace: **gå til b-en** get married in a civil ceremony.
byg'd *-a* **1** country settlement that forms a topographical and usu. administrative unit (parish, township). **2** the countryside: **i by og b-** in town and country; **på b-ene** in the country.
byg'de/borg *-a/+-en archeol.* hill fort (prehistoric fortress, used as a refuge for the people in a settlement).
byg'de/by *-en* unincorporated town grown up around an industry or esp. a railroad station.
+byg'de/dikter *-en, pl -e* (=***-ar**) "parish poet", author or poet who usu. writes about his home community.
byg'de/folk *-et* **1** the people of a **bygd.** **2** country people, farmers.
byg'de/lag *-et* **1** districts within a given part of the country. **2** the people of a parish or township. **3** association of people who came from the same district (founded e.g. in the capital or among emigrants).
byg'de/mellom *Av* (=**bygd/imellom**) from one parish to another: **han reker b-** he goes around from one parish to the next.
byg'de/mål *-et* rural dialect (of a parish); local dialect.
byg'de/veg *-en* (=+**/vei**) parish road; country road; secondary road.
byg'd/imel'lom *Av* cf **bygde/mellom**
Byg'd/øy *Pln* a peninsula in Oslo.
+by'ge *-a/-en* cf **bye**[1]
***by'gen** *A -e/-i, pl -ne* grouchy, morose; obstinate.
+by'get(e) *A* - showery.
bygg'[1] *-et* barley.
bygg'[2] *-et* building project; building under construction.
-bygg' *-en, pl *-er* -dweller.
+byg'ge *V bygde* (=***-je**) **1** build, construct (a house, a wall, an organ etc.): **b- opp** b- up, rebuild; **b- på, b- til** build an addition, add to; **b- rede** nest; **en godt b-et mann** a well-built man. **2** *fig.* build **(på on),** be based on, depend: **mitt syn b-er på fakta** my view is built on facts. **3** dwell, settle down on: **b- og bo** live (in a place). **4** cultivate, develop: **jeg vil b- mitt land** I will build my country (Bjørnson).
+byg'ge/fang *-et* (=***byggje/**) building materials.
+byg'ge/fond *-et* (=***byggje/**) building fund.
+byg'ge/kloss *-en* (toy) building block.
+byg'ge/plass *-en* construction site.
+byg'ger *-en, pl -e* builder **(av** of).
bygg'/gryn *-et* pearl barley.
bygg'/herre *-n* builder (=owner of house).
byg'ging *-a/+-en* building activity.
***byg'gjar** *-en* cf **bygger**
***byg'gje/fang** *-et* building materials.
+bygg'/mester *-en* (=***/meister**) building contractor: **B- Solness** The Master Builder (play by Ibsen).
bygg'/verk *-et* building; structure.
Byg'/land *Pln* twp, Aust-Agder.
***byg'nad** *-en, pl -er* **1** building activity; building method. **2** building.
byg'ning *-en* **1** building, house. **2** structure. **+3** building activity, construction.
+byg'nings/arbei'der *-en, pl -e* (=***-ar**) carpenter, construction worker.
byg'nings/ingeniø'r [/insj-] *-en* civil engineer.
byg'nings/komplek's *-et* block, group of buildings.
byg'sel *+-elen/*-la, pl -ler* lease: **ta jord på b-** lease a farm (usually for life).
byg'sel/brev *-et* (=***bygsle/**) lease.
byg'sle *V -a/+-et* lease.
***byg'sle/brev** *-et* cf **bygsel/**
+by'/gutt *-en* (=***/gut**) city boy.
by'/gård *-en* **1** apartment house. **2** *hist.* town house.
by'/kar *-en* city fellow.
Byk'le *Pln* twp, Aust-Agder.
by'/kledd *A -/*-kledt* **1** wearing city clothes. **2** dressed (up) to go to town.
byk's *-et* bound, leap; jerk.
byk'se *V -te* bound, leap; jerk.
+byl'd *-en* cf **byll**
***byl'gje**[1] *-a* cf **bølgje**[1]
***byl'gje**[2] *V -a* cf **bølgje**[2]
+byll' *-en* abscess, boil: **der gikk det hull på b-en** *fig.* now it's out in the open; **røre ved en b-** *fig.* touch upon a sore spot, a sore subject.
+byl'le/pest *-en* bubonic plague.
byl't *-en* bundle.
byl'te *V -a/+-et* bundle: **b- sammen** b- up.
by'/mann *-en, pl -menn/*-menner* city dweller, townsman.
by'/mark *-a* common, park area (around a town, esp. Trondheim).
+by'/messig *A* - urban: **b- bebyggelse** u- area.
by'/mur *-en* city wall.
by'/mål *-et* urban dialect.
By'/nes'et *Pln* twp, Sør-Trøndelag.
***byn'je** *V byn, bunde, bunt* boom, rattle, rumble; work noisily.
by'/nytt *N* news from town, local news.
by'/port [/port] *-en* city gate.
***byr'd**[1] *-a* cf **bør**[2]
+byr'd[2] *-en* birth, descent.
byr'de *+-n/*-a* cf **bør**[2]
+byr'de/full *A* cumbersome, onerous.
by'/rett[1] *-en* municipal court.
byrett'[2] *-en chem.* burette.
byr'g *A* haughty, proud, sure of oneself.
byr'g/skap *-en* haughtiness, pride.
***byr'je**[1] *V bør, burde, burt* ought to, should (cf also **burde**[1]).
***byr'je**[2] *V -a* begin: **han b-ar pusse hestane** he starts to groom the horses (Vesaas).
***byr'jing** *-a* beginning.
***byr'ke** *-t* birch thicket.

***byr'n/skap** *-en* cf **børn/**
***byr'te** *V -a/-e* 1 make (a light) shine clearer by cleaning it. 2: **b- seg** brag, show off.
***byr'ten** *A -e/-i, pl -ne* boasting, gloating.
byrå' *-et, pl* +*-er/**- agency, bureau, office.
byråkra't *-en* bureaucrat.
byråkrati' *-et* bureaucracy, officialdom.
byråkra'tisk *A* - bureaucratic, red tape.
byrå'/sjef *-en* head of a government office.
bysanti'nsk *A* - Byzantine.
Bysan'ts *Pln* Byzantium.
by's/ba'rn *-et, pl -/*-born* fellow townsman.
+**by'/selger** *-en, pl -e* (=***/seljar**) salesman for a firm in its own city.
***bys'je** *V -a* cf **bysse**[3]
by'/skatt *-en* municipal tax.
***bys'ke** *-t* thicket.
byss' *I* "hush", "bye bye" (word spoken to a child to lull it to sleep).
bys'se[1] *-a* bed (in children's language).
+**bys'se**[2] *-a* caboose, galley (ship's kitchen).
bys'se[3] *V -a/*+*-et* lull (**i søvn** to sleep).
bys'te[1] *-a/-en* bust (=statue, bosom, tailor's dummy).
***bys'te**[2] *V -a/-e* brush, sweep.
+**bys'te/holder** *-en, pl -e* (=*/**haldar**) bra, brassiere.
by'/styre *-t* city council.
***by'te**[1] *-t* cf **bytte**[2]
***by'te**[2] *V -te* cf **bytte**[3]
***by'ting**[1] *-en* cf **bytting**[1]
***by'ting**[2] *-a* cf **bytting**[2]
by'/ting[3] *-et* municipal court session.
***byt'te**[1] *-a* cf **bøtte**[1]
+**byt'te**[2] *-t* (= ***byte**[1]) 1 changing; exchange, trade: **han gjorde et godt b-** he did well in the e-. 2 sth that one gets by exchange: **et dårlig b-** a poor exchange. 3 booty, loot, plunder, spoil: **de gjorde et rikt b-** they got a rich b-. 4 prey, quarry, victim: **katten leker med sitt b-** the cat plays with its p-; **han er dødens sikre** (or: **visse**) **b-** he is doomed to die; **hun var et b- for sterk sinnsbevegelse** she was a p- to strong emotions.
+**byt'te**[3] *V -a/*+*-et* (=***byte**[2]) change, exchange, interchange; swap, trade: **b- klokke** s- watches; **vil du b- plass med meg?** will you c- seats with me?; **jeg ville ikke b- (plass) med ham for alt i verden** I wouldn't t- places with him for the world; **han b-et bort kua, fikk fela igjen** he traded off his cow for the fiddle; **b- inn** trade in; **b- om** change around; **b- (om)** (also:) change clothes; **b- til seg noe** acquire sth by exchange; **b- ut noe** get rid of sth in exchange for sth better; **vi får b- ut Hansen med en yngre mann** we'll have to get a younger man in H-'s place.
+**byt'te/handel** *-en* barter, trade in kind.
+**byt'te/låne** *V -te* exchange (sth) as a loan.
+**byt'te/objek't** *-et* object offered for exchange, in trade.
+**byt'ting**[1] *-en* (=***byting**[1]) changeling.
byt'ting[2] *-a/*+*-en* (=* **byting**[2]) changing (**av** of); exchange, trade.
by'/tur *-en* trip to town.
by'/våpen *-et* city emblem.
bæ' *I* baa: **æ bæ** call that goes with thumbing one's nose at sby.
***bæ'gje**[1] *-t* obstacle.
***bæ'gje**[2] *V -de* obstruct; constitute an obstacle.
bæ'r *-et* berry.
-bær *A* (of cow) calving, freshening (**vår-** next spring, **høst-** next autumn).
+**bæ'r/bar** *A* portable.
bæ'r/busk *-en* berry bush.
+**bæ're**[1] *V bar, båret* (=***bere**[2]) 1 carry (an object); bear (a weight): **b- et barn til dåpen** hold a child at baptism; **b- om post** deliver mail; **b- på noe** be carrying sth (around), be weighed down (obsessed) by sth; **båten b-er ikke mer** the boat won't hold any more; **det var så vidt båten bar** we (etc.) made it by a hair's breadth. 2 *fig.* bear, bring; endure, suffer: **b- ansvaret for** bear the responsibility for; **b- bud om** bear (bring) a message; **b- følgene av** suffer the consequences of; **b- hodet høyt** hold one's head high; **b- julen ut** "carry Christmas out" =visit sby's house during Christmas and leave without being treated; **de b-ende krefter** the constructive forces; **b- nag til en** bear sby a grudge; **b- spor av** show traces of; **b- straffen** endure punishment. 3 bear, carry, wear (e.g. clothes, name): **b- et stolt navn** b- a proud name; **b- sorg** wear mourning; **b- uniform** wear a uniform; **b- våpen** bear arms. 4 bear, bring forth, yield: **kua skal b-** the cow is about to calve; **treet b-er godt** the tree has a good yield; **hans arbeid bar frukt** his work was fruitful. 5 (impersonal, with **det** as subject) begin, start, take a course: **det bar av sted (med en)** sby started off; **hvor b-er det hen?** where are we going?; **det bar i hop med dem** they began fighting; **det bar løs** it started, broke out; **det bar over ende** (he) fell over; **det bar slik til at** it so happened that, as luck would have it; **det bar utfor (med ham)** he started (plunged) down the hill (incline, slope). 6 (with *adv.*) **b- fram** convey (greetings, thanks): **b- fram ei sak** introduce a topic; take up a cause (and carry it through); **b- over med en** be patient with sby; **b- over sitt hjerte å** bring oneself to (do sth). 7 *(refl.)*: **det b-es meg for** *obs* it seems to me; **b- seg** (of a person) carry on, complain, cry out; (of a business) pay, show a profit; **b- seg at/åt (med noe)** act; do, go about, manage (sth); **b- seg ille (over noe)** moan (about sth).
°**bæ're**[2] *V* 1 cf **bedre**[1]. 2: **b- meg** heaven help me.
+**bæ're/bølge** *-a/-en* carrier wave.
+**bæ're/bår** *-a* (=***bere/**) handbarrow.
+**bæ're/evne** *-a/-en* (=***bere/**) carrying capacity; bearing capacity.
+**bæ're/nett** *-et* string (shopping) bag.
+**bæ'rer** *-en, pl -e* (=***berar**) bearer; carrier; porter, redcap.
+**bæ're/stang** *-a, pl -stenger* (=***bere/-stong**) carrying pole.
+**bæ're/stol** *-en* (=***bere/**) sedan chair.
+**bæ're/stykke** *-t* yoke (on clothes).
bæ'ring *-en* person from Bærum twp.
bæ'r/korg *-a* (=+**/kurv**) berry basket.
+**bæ'r/plukker** [/plokker] *-en, pl -e* (=***-ar**) berry picker.
°**bær're** *Av* cf **bare**[3]
bæ'r/skog *-en* woods where one goes to pick berries.
bæ'r/tur *-en* berry-picking trip.
Bæ'rum *Pln* twp, Akershus.
bø'[1] *-en* 1 *hist.* farm. 2 (fenced-in) meadow (surrounding farm houses).
bø'[2] *I* boo (used for frightening sby).
Bø' *Pln* twp, 1 Nordland. 2 Telemark.
+**bø'd** *pt of* **byde**.
bød'del *-elen, pl bødler* executioner, hangman.
+**bødt'ker** *-en, pl -e* cf **bøkker**
bøf'fel *-elen, pl bøfler* 1 buffalo; b-leather. 2 boorish person.
+**bøf'fel/aktig** *A* - boorish.
+**bø'hmer** *-en, pl -e* (=***-ar**) Bohemian.
bø'k *-en* (=**bok**[2]) beech.
bø'ke/skog *-en* beech forest.
***bø'kje** *V -te* half-dry.
+**bøk'ker** *-en, pl -e* (=***-ar**) cooper.
bøk'ling *-en* a type of smoked herring.
bø'le[1] *-a* (=**børe**) big chest used for storing grain or flour.
bø'le[2] *-t* 1 *hist.* dwelling place. 2 lair. 3 brood (**av** of).
+**bøl'ge**[1] *-a/-en* cf **bølgje**[1]
+**bøl'ge**[2] *V -a/-et* cf **bølgje**[2]
+**bøl'ge/beve'gelse** *-n* undulation; wave motion.
+**bøl'ge/blikk** *-et* cf **bølgje/blekk**
+**bøl'ge/bryter** *-en, pl -e* breakwater.
+**bøl'ge/lengde** *-n* cf **bølgje/lengd**
+**bøl'ge/vender** *-en, pl -e* cf **bølgje/**
bøl'gje[1] *-a* (=+**bølge**[1]) wave: **seile på bølgen den blå** sail the seas; **b-ene går høgt** the seas (=passions) run high; **gjøre b-r** make a splash.
bøl'gje[2] *V -a/*+*-et* (=+**bølge**[2]) billow, undulate, wave: **b-ende hår** flowing, wavy hair; **kampen b-et fram og tilbake** the battle swung back and forth.
bøl'gje/blekk *-et* corrugated iron.
bøl'gje/dal *-en* trough of a wave, between two waves: **være en b-** (also:) feel low; be in the dumps; be in a slump.
bøl'gje/forma *A* - (=+**-et**) waving, wavy, undulating.
bøl'gje/gang *-en* 1 wave action; rough sea. 2 fluctuations.
bøl'gje/kam' *-men* crest of a wave.
bøl'gje/lengd *-a* (=+**bølge/lengde**) wave length.
bøl'gje/linje *-a/*+*-en* wavy line.
bøl'gje/papp *-en* corrugated cardboard.
bøl'gje/rygg *-en* crest of a wave.
bøl'gje/slag *-et* wash of waves.
bøl'g(j)et(e) *A* - wavy.
bøl'gje/topp *-en* crest of a wave.
+**bøl'gje/vender** *-en, pl -e* (=***-ar**) wave length control, dial.
bø'ling *-en* 1 herd. 2 usu. *hum.* crew, gang.
°**bøl'j** *-et* cf **helj**
°**bøl'je** *V -a* cf **belje**[1]
bøl'le *-n* uncouth man; boor; hooligan, rowdy.
bøl'let(e) *A* - boorish, uncouth.
Bøm'lo *Pln* island in Hordaland.
***bø'n** *-a* cf **bønn**
bøn'der *pl of* **bonde**
+**bønn'** *-a/-en* (=***bøn**) 1 prayer: **be en b-** say a p-. 2 appeal, entreaty; plea, request: **rette en b- til en** make an a- to sby; **på min b-** at my r-; **en b- om hjelp** a p-, r- for help.
bøn'ne *-a* (=**baune**[1]) bean.
+**bøn'ne/bok** *-a/-en, pl bøker* (=***bøne/**) prayer book.
+**bøn'ne/møte** *-t* (=***bøne/**) prayer meeting.
+**bønn'/falle** *V -fall, -fall* beseech, implore.
+**bønn'/høre** *V -te* (=***bøn/høyre**) grant, hear a prayer.
+**bønn'/hørelse** *-n* (=***bøn/høyring**) granting of a prayer; answer to prayer.
+**bønn'lig** *A* - (=***bønleg**) beseeching, imploring, pleading.
+**bønn'/skrift** *-et* (=***bøn/**) petition.
bø'r[1] *-en* wind for sailing; favorable wind.
bø'r[2] *-a* (=**byrde**, ***byrd**[1]) burden, load (**med** of).
+**bør'**[3] *pr of* +**burde**, ***byrje**[1]
bø're *-a* cf **bøle**[1]
***bø'rel** *-elen, pl -lar* carrying handle.
bø'rn/skap *-en* fishing equipment for a boat, esp. nets.
Bør're *Prn (m)*
bø'rs *-en* stock exchange.
Bør'sa *Pln* twp, Sør-Trøndelag.
bør'se[1] *-a* (hunting) gun.
***bør'se**[2] *-a* cf **bøsse**
bø'rse[3] *V -a/*+*-et* buy or sell at black market prices.
+**bør'se/løp** *-et* gun barrel.
+**bør'se/maker** *-en, pl -e* (=***-ar**) gunsmith.
bør'se/munning *-en* muzzle of a gun.

+ Bokmål; * Nynorsk; ° Dialect.
After letter: ' stress (Acc. 1); ` tone, stress (Acc. 2); · length.
Below letter: . not pronounced.

bør'se/pipe *-a* gun barrel.
***bør'sing** *-en* cf **bøssing**
+bø'rs/mekler *-en, pl -e* (=***-ar**) stockbroker.
bø'rs/melding *-a/-en* stock market quotation.
bø'rs/note'ring *-a/+-en* quotation on the stock exchange.
bør'st *-en* 1 brushing. 2 beating, thrashing: **få b-** get a b-. 3 *fam.* (hard) liquor.
bør'ste[1] *-n* (=***boste[1]**) 1 brush. 2 active, energetic person.
+bør'ste[2] *-n* bristle: **reise b-r** *obs.* get one's hackles up, bristle (with indignation).
bør'ste[3] *V -a/+-et* (=***boste[2]**) 1 brush. 2 beat, thrash.
+bør'ste/binder *-en, pl -e* (=***-ar**) brush maker.
+bør'sten *A -ent, pl -ne* drunk.
+bør'sten/binder *-en, pl -e* cf **børste/**
bør't *-en* 1 duty. 2 chance, turn: **det er din b-** it's your t-.
bø's *A* angry, gruff, rough.
+bøss' *-et* cf **boss**
+bøs'se *-a* (=***børse[2]**) a small container; (salt)cellar; (piggy)bank.
+bøs'sing *-en* (=***børsing**) *tech.* bushing (=box, bush, thimble, etc.).
+bø'te[1] *-n* cf **bot[2]**
bø'te[2] *V -te* 1 fix, mend, repair. 2 pay (fines); atone: **han måtte b- for sin dumhet** he paid for his stupidity; **vi får b- på det** we'll have to make amends.
+bø'te/legge *V -la, -lagt* fine.
bø'ter *pl of* **bot**
+bøt'te[1] *-a* (=***bytte[1]**) bucket, pail: **en b- vann** a b- of water; **det var døden i b-a** *pop.* it was an ordeal, it was very bad.
+bøt'te[2] *pl of* **bøte[1]**
+bøt'te/kott *-et* broom closet.
+bøt'te/papi'r *-et* handmade paper.
Bøv'er/dalen *Pln* valley in Jotunheimen.
bøy' *-en* bend; bent part of sth: **veien gjorde en b- på seg** the road made a b-.
bøy'e[1] *-n* buoy.
bøy'e[2] *-a* cf **bye[1]**
bøy'e[3] *V +-de/*-gde* 1 bend (knee), bow (head), flex (muscles): **b- kne for en** knuckle under to sby; **alderdommen har b-et ham** he is bent with age; **en b-et rygg** a bent back. 2 curve, turn: **vegen b-er til venstre** the road t-s to the left; **b- om hjørnet** t- the corner. 3 master, subdue: **b- ens sinn** soften sby's heart. 4 *gram.* inflect (=conjugate, decline). 5 (with *adv.*): **b- av, b- unna** turn aside (off); change topics, back down. 6 *(refl.)* **b- seg** bend over; yield (in an argument): **jeg b-er meg for logikken** I yield to (your) logic; **b- seg ned** bend down; **b- seg over en** bend over sby; **b- seg unna et slag** duck a blow.
***bøy'el** *-elen, pl -lar* cf **bøyle**
bøy'elig *A* - flexible.
bøy'e/muskel *-elen, pl -ler physiol.* flexor muscle.
bøy'g *-en* ***1** bend, bow; curve, turn. 2 (in folklore) an enormous, invisible, serpentine being; (since Ibsen's "Peer Gynt":) obstacle (that can be felt but is hard to identify): **han støtte på en b- av uvitenhet** he was obstructed by a sea of ignorance.
***bøy'gje** *V -de* cf **bøye[3]**
***bøy'gning** *-a* cf **bøyning**
bøy'ing *-a/+-en* 1 bend. 2 *gram.* inflection.
+bøy'le *-n* (=***bøyel**) sth that has been given a bent shape: hoop, loop, ring; shackle; stirrup; strap.
+bøy'le/hest *-en* vaulting horse (with saddle).
+bøy'ning *-en* (=***bøygning**) 1 bend (in a path). 2 inclination (of the head), nod. 3 *gram.* inflection (declension, conjugation).
+bå'de[1] *-n obs.* benefit.
+bå'de[2] *V -et obs.* be of benefit to (sby): **det b-et ham ille** it boded him ill.
bå'de[3] *C* both: **b- . . . og b- . . .** and; **det er b- og** "both and", some good and some bad; so-so; **b- det ene og det andre** this and that; lots of things; **b- sent og tidlig** at all hours.
bå'e[1] *-n* (underwater) reef.
***bå'e[2]** *Pn* cf **begge**
***bå'g** *A* deterrent, troublesome.
bå'ke *-n* (=**+båk**) beacon.
bå'l *-et* open fire; bonfire: **brenne b-** have a fire; **lide døden på b-et** suffer death at the stake.
bå'l/ferd [*/fær] *-a/+-en* cremation by funeral pyre.
°bå'n *-et* cf **barn**
+bån'd *-et* cf **band[1]**
+bån'd/oppta'ker *-en, pl -e* tape recorder.
+bån'd/tvang *-en* legally enforced duty to keep one's dog leashed.
bå'n/sull *-en* lullaby.
bå'r *-a* handbarrow.
Bå'rd *Prn(m)*
bå're[1] *-a* billow, wave.
bå're[2] *-a/+-en* litter; stretcher.
bå're[3] *V -a/+-et* billow, break (of sea).
bå're/dal *-en* trough of a wave, between two waves.
bå're/gang *-en* rough sea.
+bå'ren *A -et, pl -ne* born: **være født og b- til (å bli) konge** be b- to the crown; **han er en kunstner født og b-** he is a b- artist.
+bå'ret *pp of* **bære[1]**
bå'ret(e) *A* - (of sea) wavy; rough.
°bå'r/stue *-a* servants' quarters on a farm.
bå's *-en* booth; cubicle; stall: **sette kua på b-en** tie the cow up in her stall; **han har ti kyr på b-en** he has a herd of ten cows; **komme, stå, være i b- med en** *hum.* be placed together with sby, share quarters with sby; **han er ikke grei å stå i b- med** he is difficult to get along with.
bå's/foring *-a/+-en* stall feeding.
bå't *-en* 1 boat (row/, sail/): **være i samme b- som en** be in the same b- with sby; **gi en på b-en** let sby go by the board. 2 ship, vessel: **Amerikalinjens nye b-** the new ship of the Norwegian America Line.
bå't/bru *-a* temporary bridge that has boats for pontoons.
bå't/kvelv *-et/+-en* (=**+/hvelv**) hull of a capsized boat: **ri, sitte på b-et** cling to the upturned boat.
bå't/ladning *-en* boatload.
bå't/lag *-et* fishing boat's crew.
bå't/naust *-et* boathouse.
bå't/rip *-a* (=**+/ripe**) gunwale.
bå'ts/hake *-n* boat hook.
bå'ts/mann *-en, pl -menn/*-menner* boatswain.
bå'tsmanns/knop *-en* square knot.
bå'tsmanns/mat *-en* boatswain's mate.
bå'tsmanns/pipe *-a* boatswain's pipe.
bå't/stø *-a* place on shore where boats can be pulled up.

C

c [se'] *-en* (letter, *mus.* note) C, c: **ta den høye c** sing a high C.
C =**Celsius**
ca. = **cirka**
cabin [kæb'bin] *-en* cf **kabin**
campe [kæ'mpe] *V -a/+-et* camp.
camping [kæ'mping] *+-en/*-a* camping.
camping/plass *-en* campground.
camping/tur *-en* camping trip.
cand. =**candidatus** university degree qualifying for position: **c- jur(is)** bachelor of law; **c- mag(isterii)**, ab. =M.A. (cf **adjunkteksamen**); **c- med(icinae)** doctor of medicine; **c- oecon(omiae)** graduate in economics; **c- pharm(aciae)** graduate in pharmacy; **c- philol(ogiae)** graduate in arts, ab. =Ph.D. (cf **lektoreksamen**); **c- psychol(ogiae)** graduate in psychology; **c- real(ium)** graduate in science, ab. =Ph.D. (cf **lektoreksamen**); **c- theol(ogiae)** graduate in theology.
cape [ke'p] *-n* cape (garment).
CD =**Corps Diplomatique**
cele'ber *A -ert, pl -re* celebrated, famous; notorious: **c-t besøk** distinguished visitor(s).
celebrite't *-en* celebrity.
cel'le *-a/+-en* cell.
cellis't *-en* cellist.
cel'lo *-en* cello.
cellofa'n *+-en/*-et* cellophane.
cell'/ull *-a* rayon staple fibre, spun rayon.
celluloid [-åi'd, -o-i'd] *-en* celluloid.
cellulo'se *-n* cellulose.
cellulo'se/fabrikk' *-en* pulp mill.
cel'sius *N* centigrade: **20° C(elsius)** 20° c-.
cel'sius/grad *-en/*-a* degree centigrade.
cel'sius/skala *-en, pl *-er* centigrade scale.
cen't *-en, pl* - cent.
cen'ti/gram' *-met* centigram (=0.154 grains).
cen'ti/liter *-en, pl* - centiliter (=0.61 cubic inches).
cen'ti/meter *-en, pl* - centimeter (= 0.3937 inches).
cen'tner *-en, pl +-e obs.* centner, hundredweight (=100 lbs.).
cerebra'l *A* cerebral: **c- parese** c- palsy.
certeparti' *-et, pl +-er/*-* charter, charter party (contract leasing a ship).
cess' *en mus.* C flat.
cesu'r *-en* caesura.
ceylon/te [sei'lånn/] *-en* Ceylon tea.
cg =**centigram**
champagne [sjampan'je] *-n* champagne.
champignon [sjampinjong'] *-en* champignon (common meadow mushroom).
champion [sjæ'mpien] *-en* champion.
changeant [sjangsjang'] *A* - (of color) changeable.
changere [sjangsje're] *V -te* (of color change, be changeable.
chanse [sjang'se] *-n* cf **sjanse**
chargé d'affaires [sjarsje' dafæ'r] *en* chargé d'affaires.
charmant [sjarmang't] *A* - cf **sjarmant**
charmantisere [sjarman(g)tise're] *V -te:* **c- seg** make oneself beautiful.
charme [sjar'm] *-n* cf **sjarm**

charmere [sjarme're] *V* *-te* cf **sjarmere**
charmør [sjarmø'r] *-en* cf **sjarmør**
charpi [sjarpi'] *-en* lint for bandages.
charter [sja'rter] *-eret/-ret, pl -er/+-re* charter (lease of a ship).
chartre [sja'rtre] *V -a/+-et* charter (a ship).
chassis [sjasi'] *-et, pl +-er/*-* chassis.
Chat Noir [sjanoa'r] *Prn* popular music hall and vaudeville theater in Oslo.
chauffør [sjåfø'r] *-en* cf **sjåfør**
chaussé [sjåse'] *-en* (paved) highway.
chemise [sjemi'se] *-n* chemise.
chevaleres'k [sje-] *A* - chivalrous.
chic [sjikk'] *A* chic, attractive.
chiffon [sjifång'] *-en* chiffon.
chiffoniere [sjifåniæ'r] *-n* chiffonier, chest of drawers.
chignon [sjinjång'] *-en* chignon, hair knot.
Chile [tsji'le] *Pln* Chile.
+chilener [tsjile'ner] *-en, pl -e* (=***ar**) Chilean.
chilensk [tsjile'nsk] *A* - Chilean.
chile/salpe'ter [tsji'le/] *-en* Chile saltpeter.
China [kji'na] *Pln* China.
chinchilla [sjinsjil'la] *-en* chinchilla.
choke [sjå'k] *-n* (car) choke.
Christia'nia [kris-] *Pln* former name of Oslo, used from 1624 to 1925.
ci'cero *-en typog.* pica.
cicero'ne *-n* cicerone, guide.
ci'der *-en* cf **sider**
cir'ka *Av* circa, about.
cirkumflek's *-en* circumflex.
ciss' *en* C sharp.
+cistercien'ser *-en, pl -e* (=***-ar**) Cistercian.
cister'ne *-a/+-en* cistern.
citadell' *-et* citadel.
cl=**centiliter**
clairvoyance [klærvoajang's] *-n* clairvoyance.
clairvoyant [klærvoajang'] *A* - clairvoyant.
clearing [kli'ring] *+-en/*-a* clearing (as applied in banking and in international trade).
clou [klu'] *-en/+-et* chief attraction, highlight, high spot.
clutch [kløt'sj] *-en* clutch (coupling, pedal).
cm = **centimeter**
+c-nøkkel [se'] *-en mus.* C clef.
c/o=**care of**
cockpit [kåkk'/pitt] *-en* cockpit.
cocktail [kåkk'/teil] *-en* cocktail.
cocktail/party [kåkk'teil/pa'rti] *-et* cocktail party.
college [kål'lidsj] *-t, pl -s/+-r/*-* college.
colora'do/bille *+-n/*-a zool.* potato bug (Leptinotarsa decemlineata).
combination [kåmbinei'sjen] *-en* combinations, union suit.
copy/right [kåp'irait] *-en* copyright.
corner [kå'rner] *-en, pl +-e* corner (in soccer, market etc.).
cos=**cosinus**
co'/sinus *-en* cosine.
co'/tangens *-en* cotangent.
cotg=**cotangens**
cowboy [kau'båi,kåv'båi] *-en, pl -s/+-er/*-ar* cowboy.
crash [kræsj'] *-en* cf **krasj**
crashe [kræsj'e] *V -a/+-et* cf **krasje**
crawl [krå'l] *-en* crawl (speed swimming).
crawle [krå'le] *V -a/+-et/+-te* craw (swim).
cruise [kru's] *-t naut.* cruise.
ctr.=**contra**
Cuba [ku'ba] *Pln* Cuba.
cup [køpp'] *-en* **1** cup (offered as prize); cup match. **2** (sports) tournament (e.g. in soccer).
cup/fina'le *-n* final game in tournament.
curaçao [kyraså'] *-en* curaçao (liqueur).
cutting [køt'ting] *-en* bob (hair style).
cyanka'lium *-et* cyanide of potassium.
cyklotro'n *-en* cyclotron.
Cæsar [se'sar] *Prn* Caesar.
cæsarisk [sesa'risk] *A* - Caesarean.

D

d [de'] *-en* (letter, *mus.* note) D, d.
d.=**død**[2]
da'[1] *Av* (=***då**[3]) **1** (stressed) then; at, by that time; in that case: **da begynte det å regne** then it began to rain; **vent til i morgen - da blir det moro** wait till tomorrow - then we'll have fun; **da kan det bli det samme** in that case it makes no difference; **nå og da** now and then; **det hendte han lo, men da gjerne når vi andre ikke syntes det fantes noe å le av** it happened that he laughed, but in that case when the rest of us didn't see anything to laugh about (Hoel); ***då og då** now and then, at any moment, frequently; ***då noko og då noko** gradually, little by little. **2** (unstressed) anyway, certainly, surely (often used to give an untranslatable emphasis): **god natt da** (well,) good night; **ja da** yes indeed, all right; **det var da godt du kom** it's certainly good, it's wonderful that you came; **det var da rart** that's very strange; **det tror jeg da** at least I think so; **det var stridt, men vi kom da fram** it was tough, but we got here anyway; **hva var det som hendte da?** what happened, anyway?; **hvem er han da?** who's he, anyway?
da'[2] *C* (=***då**[3]) **1** when (at one time in the past); by the time that: **da jeg kom, hadde han alt gått** when (by the time) I arrived, he had already left; **akkurat da jeg kom** just as I arrived; **det regnet da vi gikk** it was raining when we left. **+2** since: **da jeg ikke hadde flere penger igjen** since I had no money left.
d. a.=**dicto anno** in the said year.
dab'be *V -a/+-et* **1** shuffle, walk slowly and heavily. **2 d- av** die down, slow up: **interessen har d-et av** the interest has died down.
dachs [dak's] *-en* dachshund.
dadais'me *-n* dadaism.
+dad'da *-en* nurse (for children in a family, and living as a family member).
dad'del[1] *-elen, pl dadler bot.* date.
+dad'del[2] *-en* **1** blame, criticism. **2** defect, flaw: **uten frykt og d-** without fear and without reproach.
+dad'del/løs *A* blameless.
+dad'del/verdig *A* - blameworthy.
+dad'le *V -et* blame, censure, criticize: **han kan ikke d-es for dette** he is not to blame for this.
daf'fe *V -a/+-et* drag one's feet; loaf, saunter.
da'g *-en* **1** day: **d- for d-** d- by d-; **d- ut og d- inn** d- after d-; **d-ens navn** *journ.* names in the news; **d-en derpå** the d- after; **d-en lang, den lange d-** all day long; **den d- i d-** to this very d-, even today; **den d- i morgen** the coming d-; **en d-** (of an indefinite time) one d-, some d-; **en av d-ene** one of these d-s; **all sin d-** all one's d-s, one's whole life; **god d-(en)** hello; **jeg gir en god d- i ham** I don't give a hang about him; **hele d-en** all d- long; **i d-** today; **i d- for et år (en uke, osv.) siden** a year (week, etc.) ago today; **i disse d-er** at present, currently; **Mot Dag** "Toward Daybreak" (=radical political and social movement during the 1920's; also the organ published by the movement); **om d-en** per d-; during the d-; **om åtte (14) d-er** in a week (two weeks); **her om d-en** recently, a few d-s ago; **nå om d-en, nå til d-s** nowadays; **på d-en** to the d-; **(tidlig, seint) på d-en** (early, late) in the d-; **langt på d-** late in the d-; **ut på d-en** later in the d-; **siden d-enes morgen** from the beginning of time; **ha gode d-er** be well-off; **komme av d-e** die, meet one's end; **leve for d-en** live for today; **se d-ens lys** be born, come into being; **det er sikkert som d-en** it's dead-sure. **2** (day)light: **oppe i d-en** aboveground, in the light of day; **ved høylys d-** in broad daylight; **bringe (komme) for d-en** bring (come) to light; **legge for d-en** demonstrate, display, show; **ligge klart i d-en** be obvious, be easy to see.
Da'g *Prn(m)*
Da'ga/li *Pln* parish in Hol twp, Buskerud.
***da'gast** *V -ast* cf **dages**
da'g/bergart *-a/-en* volcanic rock.
da'g/blad *-et* daily newspaper: **D-et** daily newspaper in Oslo.
da'g/bok *-a, pl -bøker* diary.
+da'g/brekning *-en* daybreak.
+da'g/driver *-en, pl -e* (=***-ar**) idler, loafer.
+da'g/driveri *-et* idling, loafing.
+da'g/drøm' *-men* (=***/draum**) daydream.
+da'g/drømmer *-en, pl -e* (=***/drøymar**) daydreamer.
+da'ge[1] *N*: **ta av d-** kill, do away with; **han er faren opp ad (av) d-** he is the spitting image of his father.
***da'ge**[2] *V -a* dawn.
+da'ges *V -edes, -es* (=***-ast**) dawn.
da'ge/vis *Av*: **i d-** for days.
Da'g/finn *Prn(m)*
dag'gert *-en* dagger.
dag'/gry *-et* dawn, daybreak.
***da'g/havar** *-en mil.* duty officer.
da'g/havende *A* - *mil.* (of officer) on duty, duty officer.
da'g/heim *-en* (=**+/hjem**) crèche, day nursery, nursery school.
da'g/hjelp *-a/+-en* maid (not living in); domestic who works by the day.
+da'g/hjem *-met* cf **/heim**
da'g/laus *A* run out, having no more days to run: **kua er d- på fredag** from Friday on the cow can be expected to calve any time.
da'glig *A* - **1** daily: **gi oss i dag vårt d-e brød** give us this day our d- bread; **til d-** every day, usually; **to ganger d-** twice a day. **2** everyday: **d- antrekk** ordinary clothes.

+ Bokmål; * Nynorsk; ° Dialect.
After letter: ' stress (Acc. 1); ' tone, stress (Acc. 2); · length.
Below letter: . not pronounced.

da'glig/dags [/dak's] *A* - everyday.
da'glig/liv *-et* daily life, everyday life.
da'glig/stue *-a* living room.
da'glig/tale *-n/*-a* everyday language, speech.
da'g/lønn *-a/+-en* **(=*/løn)** day's wages; wages paid by the day.
Da'gmar *Prn (f)*
***da'gne** *V -a* dawn: **det d-er** the day is breaking.
da'gning *+-en/*-a* dawn, daybreak.
Dag'ny *Prn (f)*
+da'g/penger *pl* **(=*-ar)** per diem (e.g. for certain officials when traveling).
da'g/renning *-a* dawn, daybreak.
Da'g/run *Prn (f)*
dag's/aktuell· *A -elt* of current significance.
dag's/avi·s *-a/+-en* daily newspaper.
+dag's/befa·ling *-en* order of the day.
dag'sens *po* daily; today's: **d- strev** the toil of daily life.
+da'g/sette *V -satte, -satt* **(=*/setje)** date (a letter).
***dag's/lei** *-a* day's journey.
dag's/lys *-et* daylight.
dag's/marsj [/mars] *-en* day's march.
dag's/nytt *et* latest news (esp. on radio).
dag's/orden *-en* agenda (of a meeting): **til d-** back to the a-; **stå på d-en** be on the a-.
dag's/ordre *-n* order of the day.
dag's/presse *-a/+-en* daily press.
da'g/sprett *-en* sunrise.
dag's/pris *-en* current price.
dag's/reise *-a/+-en* **(=/reis)** day's journey.
da'g/stött *Av* every day; day after day.
dag's/verk *-et* day's work.
da'g/tinge *V -a/+-et* negotiate.
daguerreotypi [dagærotypi'] *-en/+-et* daguerreotype.
da'g/verd *-en* cf **dugurd**
da'g/vill *A -vilt* not knowing which day it is.
da'hlia *-en, pl *-er bot.* dahlia.
daka'po *Av mus.* da capo, encore.
daka'po/nummer [/nommer] *-eret, pl -er/+-numre mus.* encore.
dakty'l *-en* dactyl.
da'l *-en* valley: **dødsskyggens d-** the v- of the shadow of death (Psalms 23,4).
dal=**dekaliter**
Da'lane *Pln* mountainous region east of Jæren in Rogaland.
***da'lar** *-en, pl -/-ar* cf **daler**
da'la/sau *-en* "valley sheep", a Norwegian breed of large sheep.
da'l/botn *-en*: **i d-en** on the floor of the valley.
da'l/bu *-en* **(=*/bue),** dalesman, inhabitant of a valley, mountaineer.
+da'l/bunn *-en* cf **/botn**
da'le *V -te/*-a* **1** fall, sink slowly through the air. **2** decrease, sink: **d-ende aktelse** declining esteem.
***da'le/mann** *-en, pl -menn(er)* inhabitant of a valley, mountaineer.
+da'ler *-en, pl -e* **(=*-ar) 1** *obs.* Norwegian money unit, banknote and coin previous to 1875, ab. =a dollar. **2** (in American Norwegian) dollar.
da'l/føre *-t, pl +-r/*-* (extended) valley.
dal'ke *V -a/+-et dial.* fondle, handle: **sitt ikke og dalk med maten** don't dawdle over your food.
dall' *-en* round wooden container.
+da'l/senkning *-en* (wide) valley.
Da'ls/fjo'rd *Pln* twp, Møre og Romsdal.
da'l/side [*/sie] *-a* hillside, mountain slope.
da'l/søkk *-et* (little round, short) valley.
dal't *-en* person (esp. boy) who clings to sby, trails sby (e.g. mother, girls); sissy.
dal'te *V -a/+-et*: **d- etter en** follow in sby's wake, cling to sby.

dam'[1] *-men* **1** pool; pond: **over d-men** across the Atlantic. **2** dam.
dam'[2] *N* checkers.
dam'[3] *Av*: **d- stille** (of weather at sea) dead calm.
+damasce'ner/klinge *-n* sword (blade) made from Damascus steel.
+damasce'ner/stål *-et* **(=*damascen/)** Damascus steel.
damasce're *V -te* damascene.
damas'k *-en* damask.
damas'k/duk *-en* damask tablecloth.
dam'/brett *-et* checkerboard.
da'me *-a/+-en* **1** lady; woman; (female) dinner partner: **mine d-er og herrer** ladies and gentlemen. **2** (in cards) queen.
+da'me/aktig *A* - **1** ladylike. **2** *derog.* effeminate.
+da'me/bekjen'tskap *-et* usu. *derog.* female acquaintance.
da'me/bridge [/bridsj] *-n* ladies' bridge party.
da'me/frisø·r *-en* (ladies') hairdresser.
da'me/konfeksjo·n *-en* ladies' ready-to-wear.
da'me/selskap *-et* **1** ladies' party. **2** the company of a lady, of ladies: **historien passer ikke i d-** the story can't be told in the presence of ladies.
da'me/tekke *-t*: **ha d-** be a ladies' man, attractive to women.
da'me/toalett· *-et, pl -/+-er* ladies' restroom.
da'me/venn *-en* **(=*/ven)** ladies' man.
dam'/luke *-a* sluice gate.
dam'mende *Av* cf **dam[3]**
damok'les/sverd *-et* sword of Damocles.
dam'p *-en* **1** steam: **gå med d-** run on s-; **for full d-** (of ship) at full speed; **ha d-en oppe** have s- up. **2** fume, vapor. **3** *fig.* energy, steam.
dam'p/bad *-et* steam bath.
dam'p/båt *-en* steamboat, steamer.
dam'pe *V -a/+-et* **1** steam. **2** puff: **d- på pipa** p- on one's pipe.
+dam'per *-en, pl -e* **(=*-ar)** steamer, steamship.
dam'p/fløyte *-n* steam whistle.
dam'p/hammar *-en, pl +-hamrer/*-hamrar* steam hammer.
dam'p/kjel(e) *-(e)n* steam boiler.
dam'p/koke *V -te/*-a* steam (e.g. vegetables).
dam'p/maski·n *-en* steam engine.
dam'p/skip *-et* steamship.
dam'pskips/ekspeditø·r *-en* shipping agent.
dam'p/trykk *-et* steam pressure.
+dam'p/veival·s *-en* **(=/veg-)** steamroller.
°da'n *A* **(=°dann[1])** eager, feeling like: **hunden er d- på kjøttbein** the dog just loves bones.
+-dan· *Av* of what structure, in what way formed e.g. **hvordan** how, **sådan** such, thus.
dande're *V -te* arrange.
dandy [dæ'ndi] *-en* dandy.
da'ne[1] *-n, pl *-r* Dane.
***da'ne[2]** *V -a* cf **danne**
dang'el *-elen, pl -ler* sth that dangles (e.g. jewelry, esp. *derog.* of imitation jewelry).
dang'le *V -a/+-et* dangle.
***da'ning** *-a* cf **danning**
danis'me *-n* Danicism, Danism.
dan'k[1] *N*: **drive d-** idle, be inactive.
dan'k[2] *-en* coin of little value (often of copper coins).
dan'ke[1] *V -a/+-et* idle, loaf, be inactive.
dan'ke[2] *V -a/+-et* **1** fire (employee). **2** beat (in competition): **d- en (ut)** beat sby.
Dan'/mark *Pln* Denmark.
°dann'[1] *A* dant cf **dan**
+dann'[2] *Av*: **d- og vann** now and then, sometimes.
dan'ne *V -a/+-et* **(=*dane[2]) 1** form, make, shape: **d- et ord** create a word; **d- regjering** form a government; **d- en forening** organize a society; **d- seg** form, take shape. **2** cultivate, educate, refine (esp. as *pp*, cf **dannet**). **3** constitute, form: **d- en unntagelse** c- an exception; **d-es av** consists of.
Dan'ne/brog [/bråg] *Prn* Dannebrog (name of the Danish flag).
+dan'nelse *-n* **1** development, formation (**av** of). **2** breeding, culture, education: **mangel på d-** lack of breeding.
dan'ne/mann *-en, pl -menn/*-menner* **1** *obs.* good, honest man. **2** *hum.* recipient of Cross of the Order of Dannebrog.
+dan'net *A* - **(=*-a, *dana)** well-bred, well-mannered; cultured, educated.
dan'ning *-a/+-en* **(=*daning) 1** development, formation (**av** of). **2** breeding, culture, good manners.
danoma'n *-en derog.* Danophile.
dan's *-en* dance, dancing: **en d- på roser** *fig.* a bed of roses; **være ute (gå ut) av d-en** be out (step out) of the limelight, be (become) inactive, out of the running; **da blir det en annen d-** then things will be different; **det skal gå som en d-** there'll be nothing to it.
dan'sar/slått *-en* dance tune (folk dancing).
dan'sar/voll *-en* flat, grassy meadow used for folk dancing.
dan'se *V -a/+-et* dance; (of horses) prance: **d- etter ens pipe** dance to the piper, dance to sby's tune; **d- opp (ut)** lead off a dance; **d- på line** walk on a tightrope; **de d-ende** the dancers.
dan'se/golv *-et* dance floor.
dan'se/moro [/morro] *-a* dance (party).
+dan'ser *-en, pl -e* **(=*-ar)** dancer.
danserin'ne *-a/+-en* female dancer.
dan'se/sal *-en* dance hall.
+dan'se/trinn *-et* dance step.
dan'sk *A* - Danish.
dan'ske[1] *-n* Dane.
dan'ske[2] *V -a/+-et* (of Norwegians) speak like a Dane, use Danish-derived forms in one's language.
dan'ske/tid *-a/+-en hist.* period of Norwegian history (1450—1814) when Norway and Denmark were united.
dan'sk/norsk *-en* Dano-Norwegian, esp. of Norwegian language based upon Danish.
dar're[1] *-a* **1** stone that helps keep the lower end of a seine to the bottom. **2** pin in a door hinge.
dar're[2] *V -a/+-et* shake, tremble.
darwinis't *-en* Darwinian.
das'k *-en/+-et* slap: **få d-** (of children) be s-ped.
das'ke *V -a/+-et* **1** pat, slap; beat, flap, pound (e.g. tail). **2** move, trot (slowly). **3**: **d- med** flirt with.
dass' *-en/-et pop.* (vulgar) toilet.
da'ta *pl* data.
date're *V -te* date.
da'tiv *-en* dative.
da'to *-en* date: **dags d-** this day, today; **av gammel (ny) d-** ancient (recent); **til d-** to date.
da'to/parke·ring *-a/+-en* parking permitted on alternate days.
da'to/stempel *-(e)let, pl -ler/*-el* dater; date stamp.
da'to/stemple *V -a/+-et* date-stamp.
datt'[1] *pt of* **dette[1]**
datt'[2] *Pn*: **ditt og d-** this and that; all sorts of things.
+dat'ter *-a/-en, pl døtre(r)* **(=*dotter)** daughter (**av** of).
+dat'ter/datter *-a/-en, pl -døtre(r)* **(=*dotter/dotter)** granddaughter (=daughter's daughter).
+dat'terlig *A* - daughterly, filial.
+dat'ter/selskap *-et* subsidiary (company).
+dat'ter/sønn *-en* grandson (=daughter's son).
da'tum *-umen/-umet, pl -a* date.
da'tum/grense *-a/+-en* date line.
+dau' *A* cf **daud**

dau'd *A -t/+-daut* (=+**dau**) 1 (of animals) dead. 2 flat (taste); dull, insipid (person).
+**dau'd/biter** *-en, pl -e* (=*-**ar**) stick-in-the-mud.
dau'd/blod *-et* blood blister (causing a bluish discoloration).
*__dau'de__[1] *-n* cf **død**[1]
dau'de[2] *V -a/+-et* (=+**daue**) (of animals) die (vulgar if used of people).
*__Dau'de/havet__ *Pln* The Dead Sea.
*__dau'd/gang__ *-en* cf **død/**
dau'd/gjødsle *V -a/+-et* over-fertilize.
dau'd/hogge *V infl as* **hogge** (=+**dau/**) cut a tree so that the damage caused to it will make it dry up gradually.
dau'ding *-en* dead man; ghost.
dau'd/jo'rd *-a* (=+**dau/**) "dead soil", soil that doesn't yield.
dau'd/kjøtt *-et* (=*/**kjøt**, +**dau/**) 1 dead tissue (e.g. around a wound that won't heal), proud flesh. 2 *fig.* deadwood (e.g. in an organization).
dau'd/lendt *A* - (=+**dau/**) (of soil) poor.
dau'd/mann *-en, pl -menn/*-menner* dead man; ghost.
dau'd/nesle *-a* (=+**dau/**) *bot.* dead nettle (Lamium).
*__dau'd/punkt__ [/pong·t] *-et* cf **død/**
dau'd/skrott *-en* (=+**dau/**) 1 corpse; body of dead animal. 2 lazybones.
dau'd/stokk *-en* (=+**dau/**) (of person) lazybones.
*__dau'd/vatn__ *-et* cf **død/vann**
*__dau'd/vekt__ *-a* cf **død/**
+**dau'e** *V -a/-et* cf **daude**[2]
+**dau'ing** *-en* cf **dauding**
dauphin [dåfeng'] *-en* dauphin.
dau'v *A* cf **døv**
*__dau'v/heitt__ *A* - blunt.
*__dau'v/høyrd__ *A -høyrt* cf **døv/hørt**
*__dau'vleg__ *A* - dull, trivial.
*__dau'v/stum·__ *A -t, pl -me* cf **døv/**
Da'/vik *Pln* twp, Sogn og Fjordane.
da'vit *-en* davit.
+**da'/værende** *A* - then: **d- statsminister** the t- prime minister.
d. d.=**dags dato** cf **dato.**
+**de**[1] [di'] *Pn ob dem, po deres* (=*__dei__) they, them, their(s); *dial.* **dem (dom)** used for **de.**
*__de__[2] [di'] *Pn ob dykk, po dykkar* cf **dere**
+**de**[3] [di'] *Pn pl of* **den**[1,2] (=*__dei__)
De [di'] *Pn ob +Dem/*Dykk, po +Deres/*Dykkar* you, your(s) (non-intimate form).
d. e. = **det er** i.e.
deb.=**debet; debitor**
debacle [debak'kel] *-t* débacle.
debatt' *-en* debate, discussion: **sette noe under d-** take sth up as a topic for discussion.
debattan't *-en* debater, discussant.
debatte're *V -te* debate, discuss.
de'bet *-en* debit.
debi'l *A med.* feeble-minded.
debilite't *-en* debility; feeble-mindedness.
debite're *V -te* debit.
de'bitor *-en, pl -to'rer merc.* debtor.
debut [deby'] *-en* début.
debutan't *-en* beginner, debutant (on stage, in literature etc.).
debute're *V -te* make one's début (as artist etc.).
+**debut/opptre·den** [deby'/] *-en* (actor's) début.
decen'nium *-iet, pl +-ier/*-ium* decade.
dechiffrere [desjifre're] *V -te* decipher.
dedikasjo'n *-en* dedication (in a book).
dedise're *V -te* dedicate.
deduksjo'n *-en* deduction, deductive method.
de'duktiv *A* deductive.
deduse're *V -te* deduce.
defaitisme [defetis'me] *-n* defeatism.
defaitist [defetis't] *-en* defeatist.
defek't[1] *-en* defect.
defek't[2] *A* - defective.
defensiv[1] [def'angsiv] *-en* defensive.
defensiv[2] *A* defensive.
defen'sor *-en, pl -so'rer* defense counsel; defender.
defensora't *-et* defense (in court).
de'ficit *-en* deficit.
defile're *V -te mil.* defile, file (in line).
define're *V -te* define.
definisjo'n *-en* definition.
defin'itiv *A* definitive.
deflasjo'n *-en merc.* deflation.
deflate're *V -te merc.* deflate.
deflore're *V -te* deflower.
defor'm *A* deformed.
deforme're *V -te* deform.
deformite't *-en* deformity.
de'g [+dei'] *Pn ob of* **du**[2]
degenerasjo'n *-en* degeneration.
degenerere're *V -te* degenerate: **d-t** degenerate.
de'ger(e)n *I* cf **dæger(e)n**
De'ger/nes *Pln* twp, Østfold.
de'gerten *I* cf **dæger(e)n**
+**deg'ge** *V -a/-et* (=*-**je**): **d- for** pet, spoil; *fig.* wet-nurse.
*__deg'gje__ *V degde* cf **degge**
+**degn** [dei'n] *-en* (=*__dekn__) deacon.
degradasjo'n *-en mil.* degradation.
degrade're *V -te mil.* degrade.
*__dei'__ *pn ob dei, po deira* cf **de**[1,4]
dei'e *-a* maid.
dei'g *-en* dough; doughy mass: **slå opp for stor d-** make too much d-; *fig.* start on too high a scale.
dei'get(e) *A* - doughy.
*__dei'gle__ *-a* cf **digel**
*__dei'gne__ *V -a* soften, get a consistency like dough.
dei'g/trau *-et* kneading trough.
*__dei'ld__ *-a* 1 part, portion, section. 2 border, boundary, marker.
dei'lde/gast *-en* ghost of a person who cannot rest because he moved land markers illegally.
*__dei'lde/stein__ *-en* boundary marker, demarcation stone.
*__dei'le__ *V -te* cf **dele**[2]
+**dei'lig** *A* - beautiful, lovely; delicious, delightful.
+**dei'lig/het** *-en* 1 delightfulness; loveliness. 2 (a) beauty.
*__dei'ra__ *po of* **dei**
dei's *-en* 1 tumble. 2 blow.
dei'se *V -a/+-et/-te* 1 topple, tumble; fall heavily. 2: **d- til en** hit sby.
deisme [de-is'me] *-n* deism.
deist [de-is't] *-en* deist.
dejeuner [desjøne'] *-en* lunch.
dejeunere [desjøne're] *V -te* lunch.
dekadanse [dekadang'se] *-n* decadence.
deka'de *-n* decade.
dekaden't *A* - decadent.
deka'disk [also -ka'-] *A* - decadic.
de'ka/gram· *-met* decagram (10 g).
de'ka/liter *-en, pl* - decaliter (10 l).
deka'n *-en* dean (of a university college).
dekante're *V -te* decant.
deka'nus *-usen, pl -er* cf **dekan**
de'kar *-et* decare (measure of land), ab. ¼ acre.
de'kel(e)n *I* cf **dæger(e)n**
de'ken *I* cf **dæger(e)n**
de'ker(e)n *I* cf **dæger(e)n**
de'kerten *I* cf **dæger(e)n**
dekk' *-et* 1 *naut.* deck. 2 tire: **slangeløst d-** tubeless t-.
dekk'/blad *-et* 1 *bot.* bract. 2 wrapper (on cigar).
dek'ke[1] *-t, pl +-r/*-* 1 covering; protective layer: **et d- av asfalt** a layer of asphalt. 2 cover, protection: **under d- av mørket** under c- of darkness; **spille under d- med en** have a secret connection, understanding with sby. 3 shelter.
+**dek'ke**[2] *V -et/dekte* (=*-**je**) 1 cover; (of bills, debts, expenses) meet, pay: **d- for** conceal, hide; **d- hverandre** cover the same ground, be identical (e.g. geometric objects, meanings of words, expressions, etc.); **d- over, d- til** cover up; **d- seg** take cover; cover, protect oneself (e.g. against loss, retaliation); **d-et av** c-ed by, under cover of. 2 set (a table): **d -opp med** serve (food). 3 (*imperative*): **dekk!** down! (to dog). 4 *journ.* cover (a story).
dek'ken *-et, pl -/+-er* horse blanket.
+**dek'kende** *A* - adequate, exact, precise.
*__dek'ker__ *pl of* **dokk**[2]
+**dek'ke/taller·ken** *-en* service plate.
+**dek'ke/tøy** *-et* 1 table linen. 2 *fam.* table service.
dekk'/farge *-n* protective coloring.
*__dekk'/frøing__ *-en bot.* angiosperm.
*__dek'kje__ *V dekte* cf **dekke**[2]
+**dekk'/navn** *-et* alias.
dekk's/båt *-en naut.* small craft with a full length deck and one mast.
dekk's/folk *pl* deckhands.
+**dekk's/gutt** *-en* (=*/**gut**) deck boy, ship's boy (apprentice sailor).
dekk's/last *-a/-en* deck cargo.
dekk's/passasje'r *-en* steerage passenger.
dekk's/plass *-en* steerage.
+**dekk'/vinge** *-n zool.* elytron, wing case, wing cover.
deklamasjo'n *-en* declamation; recital.
deklamato'risk *A* - declamatory.
deklame're *V -te* recite, declaim.
deklarasjo'n *-en pol.* declaration.
deklare're *V -te* 1 declare (goods in customs). 2 announce (esp. engagement).
deklinasjo'n *-en* 1 *astron.* declination. 2 *gram.* declension.
dekline're *V -te gram.* decline.
*__dek'n__ *-en* cf **degn**
dek'ning *+-en/*-a* 1 cover, covering; hiding: **gå i d-** go into hiding; **søke d-** seek cover; *fig.* **ha d- for sine ord** have sth to back up one's words with. 2 *merc.* payment (of bills, debts); security: **til d- av** in payment of, to pay.
dekok't *-et* decoction.
dekollete'rt *A* - decolleté, low-necked.
dekor [dekå'r] *-en* décor.
dekorasjo'n *-en* 1 decoration. 2 centerpiece (on table).
dek'orativ *A* decorative.
dekoratø'r *-en* decorator.
dekore're *V -te* decorate.
dekor't *-en merc.* deduction, discount, rebate.
deko'rum *et* decorum.
dekre't *-et, pl -/+-er* decree.
dekrete're *V -te* decree.
dek'sel *-elet/-let, pl -el/+-ler* cap, cover, lid; housing.
de'l *-en* 1 part, section; share: **en d-** a few, some; (used *substantivally*) a bit; **en god (hel) d-** a lot, quite a bit, a good deal; **for all d-** by all means; **for en (stor) d-** to a (large) degree, in (great) part; **(jeg) for min d-** as far as I'm concerned, for my part; **for største d-en** mostly, for the most part; **i alle d-er** in all things, in all ways; **til d-s** in part, partially, partly; **bli en til d-** fall to sby's lot, share; **få d- i** participate in, share; **ha d- i** have a share in, be a part of; **ta d- i** participate in, take part in. 2 (as *noun substitute*): **begge d-er** both; **en av d-ene** one or the other, either; **ingen av d-ene** neither.
del.=**deleatur**
+**de'l/aktig** [also -ak't-] *A* - 1 concerned (i in), involved: **være d- (i en forbrytelse)** be party to (a crime). 2 informed (about), sharing (in): **bli d- i** share.
+**delak'tig/gjøre** *V -gjorde, -gjort* share: **d- en i sine planer** tell sby one's plans.
+**delak'tig/het** *-en* participation (i in); part.
+**de'l/bar** *A* divisible.
del'd *-a* dell.
de'le[1] *-t, pl +-r/*-* border marker (e.g. stone); borderline.

+ Bokmål; * Nynorsk; ° Dialect.
After letter: ' stress (Acc. 1); ` tone, stress (Acc. 2); · length.
Below letter: . not pronounced.

de'le[2] *V -te* divide, partition; share: **d- av** partition off; **d- på** dole out; divide, share; **d- ut** dole, parcel out, distribute; **d- halvt med** go halves with; **d- seg** branch off, divide, split; **d- skjebne** share the same fate with sby; **d-es om** share (e.g. work); **d-t** divided, partial (**det du er, vær fullt og helt, ikke stykkevis og delt** that which you are, be all out, not partially and half-baked (Ibsen)).
delea'tur *V* delete; *typog.* dele.
delegasjo'n *-en* delegation.
delega't *-en* delegate.
delege're *V -te* delegate.
delege'rt *en, pl -e* delegate.
de'lelig *A* - divisible (**med** by).
+**de'ler** *-en, pl -e* (=***-ar**) divider (on a harvester).
+**-de'les** *Av* old *po.* of **del** part, in **aldeles, fremdeles, særdeles,** etc.
de'le/vegg *-en, pl *-er* partition.
delfi'n *-en* dolphin.
delika't *A* - **1** delicious; tasty: **d- anrettet** (of food) arranged in a d-, t- way. **2** delicate, requiring delicacy.
delikate're *V -te*: **d- seg** enjoy; **d- seg med et eple** enjoy eating an apple.
delikates'se *-n* **1** delicacy, a delicious piece of food. **2** (=**d-/forretning**) delicatessen.
de'ling *-a/+-en* **1** division, partition: **(gjøre noe) på d-** go halves, divide up (work, profits, etc.); on shares. **2** pitch (of the teeth of a gear).
delinkven't *-en* delinquent.
deli'rium *+-iet/*-iumet, pl +-ier/*-ium* delirium: **d- tremens** d.t.'s.
del'j *-en* **1** powerful blow. **2** big, strong fellow.
del'je *V -a/+-et*: **d- til** hit hard.
+**del'jer** *-en, pl -e* (=***-ar**) big, strong fellow.
de'ls *Av* partly.
de'l/stat *-en* state (in a confederation).
del'ta[1] *-et, pl +-er/*-* delta.
+**de'l/ta**[2] *V -tok, -tatt* join, participate, share, take part (**i** in).
+**de'l/tagelse** *-n* cf **/taking**
+**de'l/tagende** *A* - **1** concerned; sympathetic; sympathizing. **2: de d-** the participants (**i** in).
+**de'l/tager** *-en, pl -e* cf **/taker**
+**de'l/takelse** *-n* cf **/taking**
+**de'l/taker** *-en, pl -e* (=***-ar**) **1** member, participant (**i** in); a party (**i** to). **2** (in contest) competitor, entrant.
de'l/taking *-a/+-en* (=+**-else**, +**/tagelse**) **1** participation (**i** in). **2** concern, sympathy (**for** for): **vise d-** show one's c-, s-.
de'l/vis *Av* in part, partly; to some extent, up to a point: **de gamle husene som delvis ligger der ennå** the old houses, some of which are still there (Bang-Hansen).
+**dem**[1] *Pn ob of* **de**[1]
°**dem**[2] *Pn* cf **de**[1]
+**Dem** *Pn ob of* **De**[2]
demago'g *-en* demagogue.
demagogi' *-en* demagoguery.
demago'gisk *A* - demagogic.
demaske're *V -te* unmask: **d- seg** take off one's mask.
***dem'be**[1] *-a* haze.
***dem'be**[2] *V damb, dumbe/-i* **1** be dusty. **2** raise dust.
demente're *V -te* deny, disclaim, disavow (a rumor etc.).
dementi' *-et, pl +-er/*-* denial, disclaimer, disavowal (**av** of).
demimonde [-mång'd] *+-n/*-a* demimonde.
demisjo'n *-en pol.* resignation.
demisjone're *V -te pol.* resign.
demisjo'ns/søknad *-en, pl *-er* resignation (esp. of cabinet member).
***dem'me**[1] *-a* puddle.
dem'me[2] *-a* sluice gate.
dem'me[3] *V +demte/*demde* **1** dam, dike, stem: **d- inn** dike, embank; **d- opp** dam up; **d- opp for vannet** s- the flow of the water. **2** repress, restrain, stem (the tide of): **d-opp for propagandaen** stem the flow of propaganda.

dem'ning *+-en/*-a* **1** dike, embankment. **2** dam.
de'/mobilise're *V -te* demobilize.
demokra't *-en* democrat.
demokrati' *-et, pl +-er/*-* democracy.
demokratise're *V -te* democratize.
demokra'tisk *A* - democratic.
demole're *V -te* demolish.
demo'n *-en* demon.
demo'nisk *A* - demonic.
demonstran't *-en* demonstrator.
demonstrasjo'n *-en* demonstration (e.g., public protest; show of feeling).
demonstrasjon's/tog [/tåg] *-et* demonstration march.
demon'strativ[1] *-et* demonstrative (pronoun).
demon'strativ[2] *A* demonstrative: **hun snudde seg d-t bort** she turned her back pointedly.
demonstre're *V -te* demonstrate: **d- sin forakt** show one's contempt; **d- mot atomvåpen** d- against nuclear weapons.
demonte're [also de'-] *V -te* dismantle.
demoralisasjo'n *-en* demoralization.
demoralise're *V -te* demoralize.
dem'pe *V -a/+-et* lessen, lower; muffle (a sound, a voice), soften (colors, light), subdue (a fire), suppress (an emotion, a revolt): **d- (på) en** calm sby down; **d- ens begeistring** put a damper on sby's enthusiasm; **d- bølgene med olje** pour oil on troubled waters; **en d-et samtale** a hushed (subdued) conversation.
+**dem'per** *-en, pl -e* (=***-ar**) **1** *mus.* mute. **2** damper; silencer. **3** *fig.* damper: **sjefens død la en d- på (or: over) jubileet** the death of the head of the firm put a d- on the jubilee.
dem're *V -a/+-et* **1** give a faint light; shimmer. **2** be outlined, show up. **3** dawn: **det d-er** dawn is breaking; **det d-er for ham** *fig.* it d-s on him.
dem'ring *+-en/*-a* dawn: **i d-en** at d-; **Norges Dæmring** The Dawn of Norway (sonnet cycle by J. S. Welhaven).
den'[1] *Art nt det, pl +de/*dei* the (before adjectives).
den'[2] *Pn nt det, pl +de/*dei* **1** *(pers. pron.)* it, they (them); *(poss.)* **dens** its: **vil du ha den?** do you want it? (referring to an *en*-noun); **her har du det** here it is (referring to an *et*-noun); **det er meg** it is I; **det regner** it's raining; **det banker** sby's knocking; **det er ingenting igjen** there is nothing left; **de har ikke kommet ennå** they haven't arrived yet; **har du sett dem?** have you seen them? **2** *(demonstrative pron.)* that (one), those (ones); he, she, they (who): **jeg tar den boka** I'll take that book; **den var god!** that was rich! **den går ikke!** oh, no you don't, you can't fool me; **den og den** such and such (a person, price, etc.); **den som** he (she) who (that one who); **han bor i det huset** he lives in that house; **det at han kommer** the fact that he is coming; **det er det jeg sier** that's what I'm saying; **det å spise (gå, sove, osv.)** eating (walking, sleeping, etc.); **det må du gjerne** you certainly may; **det som** that which; (with **det** translated as 'so': **hvorfor det?** why (so)? **det synes jeg, jeg tror det** I think so; **du sier ikke det** you don't say so; **hun er rik og det er han også** she is rich and so is he; **gå vekk med deg og det fort** go away and be quick about it (lit. and do so quickly); **så mange som bare det** as many as you please; **de menneskene er forferdelige** those people are terrible; **de som** they who (those who); **de tilstedeværende** those who were (are) present.
dena't *-en pop.* denatured alcohol.
denature're *V -te* denature (alcohol).
den'g *-en* thrashing, whipping.

+**den'/gang** *Av, C* (=**den gang,** ***den gongen**) **1** (at the time) when: **d- da jeg var pike** when I was a girl. **2** at the time, then; that time: **"d- ei" sa Tordenskjold** "not that time" said T-= I caught you that time.
+**deng'e** *V -te* (=***-je**) give (sby) a beating; thrash, whip.
***deng'je** *V -de* cf **denge**
***deng'sle** *-a* thrashing, whipping.
den'ne *Pn nt dette, pl +disse/*desse, +po -s* **1** this (one), these. **2** the latter. **3: d-s** this month.
+**dennes** *Pn po of* **denne**
+**den'ne/sidig** *A* - on this side: **vår d-e tilværelse** our life here on earth.
+**den's** *po of* **den**[2]
+**den'/slags** [/slaks] *Pn* cf **slags**
denta'l[1] *-en* dental.
denta'l[2] *A* dental.
departement [departemang'] *-et, pl -/+-er* **1** department. **2** ministry (a department of the government): **d-et** the government (office); **D-et for familie- og forbrukersaker** M- of Family and Consumer Affairs.
departementa'l *A* departmental (ref. esp. to government offices); bureaucratic.
***de'pel** *-elen, pl -lar* mud hole, puddle.
depe'sje *-n* dispatch.
deplasement [deplasemang'] *-et naut.* displacement.
***dep'let(e)** *A* - (of road) muddy.
depone're *V -te* deposit (**hos** with).
deportasjo'n *-en* deportation.
deporte're *V -te* deport.
depo'situm *-umet, pl +-a/*-um* deposit: **et d- på 50 kr** a d- of 50 *kroner.*
depo't *-et, pl +-er/*-* cache, depot, dump.
depresjo'n *-en* depression.
deprime're *V -te* depress: **d-ende vær** d-ing weather.
+**deprime'rt/het** *-en* depression, melancholy.
dep't *-et pop.* government office (cf **departement**).
deputasjo'n *-en* deputation.
depute'rt *en, pl -e* deputy (member of a chamber of deputies).
depute'rt/kammer *-et, pl -/+-e* chamber of deputies.
der[1] [dæ'r] *Av* **1** there, at that place: **der borte** over there; **der inn(e)** in there; **der ned(e)** down there; **der opp(e)** up there; **der ut(e)** out there; **der har vi det!** that's it! **der har du et eple** here's an apple for you; **der kan du se** see, I told you; **hvem der?** who's that, who's there?; (with demonstrative force) **han der** that (fellow); **den boka der, den der boka** that book; **der i landet** in that country. **2** *archaic* **der er (var)=det er (var)** there is (was).
+**der**[2] [dær] *Pn archaic* (=**som**) who: **den der** he (she) who, whoever.
derangert [derangsje'rt] *A* - **1** deranged. **2** disarranged.
der'/av *Av* from this (cause): **sterk varme med d- følgende tørke** hot weather and the drought caused by it; **d- forstår du nok at . . .** from this you will realize that. . . .
derborte [-bor'te] *Av* cf **der**[1]
+**de're** *Pn po deres* (=***de**[2]) **1** you *(pl)*: **nei nå tar vi en sang, dere** how about a song, people. **2** *pop.* (used erroneously in *sg* as "polite" address, instead of **De**).
+**de'res** *Pn po of* **de**[1]
+**De'res** *Pn po of* **De**
+**der'/etter** *Av* **1** after that, afterwards; then, thereafter: **d- gikk vi hjem** then we went home. **2** accordingly, as expected: **resultatet ble d-** the result was what might be expected.
der'/for' *Av* (=***di/**) **1** therefore. **2** all the same, still: **de kan jo d- ha et hjem** they may still have a home (Ibsen).
+**der'/fra** *Av* (=***/ifrå**) **1** from there, from that point; thence. **2** from that, because of that; as a result.

+der'/hen· *Av* (over, up, down) there; thither.
+der'/i *Av* therein; in that: **d- tar De feil** you are wrong there.
+der'/iblan't *Av* among these (those, them); including: **det var mange som så det, (og) d- jeg** many people saw it, and I was one of them.
***der'/ifrå·** *Av* cf **/fra**
der'/imo't *Av* on the other hand; however.
derinn' *Av* cf **der[1]**
derin'ne *Av* cf **der[1]**
derive're *V -te* derive; *math.* **den d-te** the derivative (of a function).
der'/med *Av* at that, so, with that: **d- var det gjort** that did it.
derne'd *Av* cf **der[1]**
derne'de *Av* cf **der[1]**
der'/nest *Av* (=***di/**) 1 next, subsequently, then: **d- sa han** then he said. 2 further, furthermore: **d- må du huske at...** furthermore you've got to remember that...
+der'/om· *Av* about that, on that point: **d- torde meningene være delte** opinions seem to differ on that point.
der'/omkring· *Av* 1 around there: **ingen hadde hørt om ham d-** nobody had heard of him in those parts. 2 thereabouts: **tusen eller d-** a thousand or t-.
deropp' *Av* cf **der[1]**
derop'pe *Av* cf **der[1]**
der'/over [/åver] *Av* 1 [also -å'ver] over there; over that; because of that. 2 above, beyond (that); upwards; more: **de på 40 og d-** those of 40 (years of age) and up.
+der'/på *Av* thereupon; afterwards; then: **dagen d-** [-på'] the day after.
der're *Av fam.* there (only used with a personal or demonstrative pronoun in 3rd person): **han, hun, den, det d-** that there; **de d-** those there, them there.
der'/som· *C* if, in case.
+der'/steds *Av* there; of that place: **myndighetene d-** the local authorities.
der't *-en* dandy, fop.
der'te *V -a/+-et* dress like a dandy, fop.
der'/til· *Av* 1 *archaic* to that, there. 2 for that (purpose): **men d- trengs det penger** but that takes money; **en d- skikket aften** a suitable evening. 3 besides (that), in addition: **d- kommer at** add to this the fact that; **han spiste biff og drakk øl d-** he ate a steak and drank beer with it.
+der'/under *Av* 1 below it (that), under it (that), under there. 2 below, less: **de på 40 og d-** those of 40 (years of age) and less.
deru't *Av* cf **der[1]**
deru'te *Av* cf **der[1]**
+der'/ved *Av* thereby; by that means; with that.
der'visj *-en* dervish.
+der'/værende *A* - there, of that place: **det d- politi** the local police.
des. =**desember**
desavue're *V -te* disavow, repudiate.
desem'ber *en* December.
de'/sentralise're *V -te* decentralize.
deserte're *V -te* desert (**fra** from).
desertø'r *-en* deserter.
de'si- *Pf* deci-.
deside'rt *A* - decided, definite: **han er d- den beste av dem** he is d-ly the best of them.
de'si/gram' *-met* decigram (= 1.54 grains).
de'si/liter *-en, pl* - deciliter (=0.21 pints).
desillusjone're *V -te* disillusion.
desima'l *-en* decimal.
desima'l/brøk *-en* decimal fraction.
desima'l/komma *-et, pl -/+-er* decimal point.
desime're *V -te* decimate.
de'si/meter *-en, pl* - decimeter (=3.94 in.).
desinfeksjo'n *-en* disinfection.
desinfeksjo'ns/middel *-elet/-midlet, pl +-midler/*-el* disinfectant.
desinfise're *V -te* disinfect.
desisjo'n *-en jur.* decision (concerning accounts).
des'kriptiv *A* descriptive.
+des'mer/urt *-a/-en bot.* moschatel (Adoxa moschatellina).
des'/organise're *V -te* disorganize.
des'/oriente'rt *A* - bewildered, confused.
despera'do *-en, pl -s/+-er* desperado.
desperasjo'n *-en* desperation.
despera't *A* - desperate (**av** from).
despo't *-en* despot.
despoti' *-et* despotism.
despo'tisk *A* - despotic.
dess'[1] *en mus.* D flat.
dess'[2] *Av* 1 (with a single comparative) all the, so much the: **d- bedre** all the better; **d- mer (meir)** all the more. 2 (with two comparatives) **dess ... dess ...** the ... the ...; **jo ... dess ...** the ... the. 3 ***d-heller (dessheller), d- meir (dessmeir)** either, even: **han kan knapt lese, d- heller** he can hardly even read.
***dess'[3]** *po of* **den**
+dess'/angå'ende *Av* as regards that; as far as that is concerned; on that subject.
+dessbe'dre *Av* cf **dess[2]**
***des'se** *pl of* **denne**
dessert [desæ'r] *-en* dessert.
dessert/bo'rd *-et* buffet table (for desserts).
dessert/skei *-a* dessert spoon.
dessert/skål *-a/+-en* compote (bowl).
+dess'/forme'delst *Av* because of that: **d- at ...** owing to the fact that...
+dess'/foru'ten *Av* (=***/forutan**) besides, furthermore, moreover.
***desshel'ler** *Av* cf **dess[2]**
***dess'/imel'lom** *Av* at times, now and then; meanwhile.
dessin [deseng'] *-en* design, pattern (in cloth).
+dessli'ke *A* - such, the like: **og d-** etc.
***dessmei'r** *Av* cf **dess[2]**
+dessme'r *Av* cf **dess[2]**
+dess'/uak'tet *Av* all the same, nevertheless.
+dess'/uten [also -u'-] *Av* (=***/utan**) besides, in addition, moreover.
+dessver're *Av* (=***dess verre**) unfortunately: **jeg kan d- ikke komme** I am sorry (to say) I can't come.
+dess'/årsak *Av archaic* for that reason.
destillasjo'n *-en* distillation.
destilla't *-et, pl -/+-er* distillate.
destillatø'r *-en* distiller.
destille're *V -te* distill.
+des'to *Av* the (with comparatives): **jo ... desto ...** the ... the ...; **så mye d- bedre** so much the better; **ikke d- mindre** nevertheless; **d- mer** all the more.
destrue're *V -te tech.* destroy.
destruksjo'n *-en* destruction.
des'truktiv *A* destructive.
+des'/uten *Av* cf **dess/**
de't *nt of* **den[1], den[2]**
detal'j *-en* 1 detail: **gå i d-(er)** go into d-. 2: **i d-** retail.
detalje'rt *A* - detailed.
detal'j/handel *-elen, pl -ler* retail trade.
detaljis't *-en* retailer.
detal'j/pris *-en* retail price.
detasjement [detasjemang'] *-et, pl +-er/*- mil.* detachment.
detasje're *V -te mil.* detach.
Det brit'iske sam'/velde *Prn* The British Commonwealth.
det'ektiv *-en* detective.
det'ektiv/roma'n *-en* detective story, mystery.
detek'tor *-en* detector.
determine'rt *A* - determined.
determinis'me *-n* determinism.
determinis't *-en* determinist.
detonasjo'n *-en* detonation.
detone're *V -te* detonate.
detronise're *V -te* dethrone.
+det's *po of* **det**
***dett'** *-en* fall.
det'te[1] *V datt, +-et/*dotte/*-i* fall: **d-ned, d- over ende** f- down; **d- fra hverandre** f- apart; **hopperen datt** the skijumper took a fall.
det'te[2] *nt of* **denne**
devalue're *V -te* devaluate.
°de'vel *-elen, pl -ler* devil.
deviasjo'n *-en* deviation.
devi'se *+-n/*-a* motto, slogan (usu. on a heraldic shield).
dev'on/tida *df geol.* the Devonian period.
devo't *A* - devout; sanctimonious.
***di[1]** *C* 1 the (with comparatives): **di før di betre** the sooner the better. 2 (this, that): **av (etter, for, med) di** because, since.
di'[2] *f of* **din**
+diabe'tiker *-en, pl -e* (=***-ar**) diabetic.
diabo'lsk *A* - diabolic.
diade'm *-et, pl +-er/*-* tiara; *hist.* diadem.
diagno'se *-n* diagnosis: **stille en d-** make a d-.
+diagnos'tiker *-en, pl -e* (=***-ar**) diagnostician.
diagnostise're *V -te* diagnose.
diagona'l[1] *-en* diagonal.
diagona'l[2] *A* diagonal.
diagona'l/gang *-en* "diagonal walk", a technique in cross-country skiing.
diagram' *-met, pl -/+-mer* diagram.
diako'n *-en* 1 deacon. 2 male nurse.
diakonis'se *-a/+-en* nurse, esp. one who works in collaboration with the minister of a parish.
dialek't *-en* dialect.
dialekta'l *A* dialectal.
+dialek'tiker *-en, pl -e* (=***-ar**) dialectician.
dialektikk' *-en* dialectic(s).
dialek'tisk *A* - 1 dialectic. 2 dialectal.
dialog [-lå'g] *-en* dialogue.
dialo'gisk *A* - dialogic(al).
diaman't *-en* diamond.
+diaman't/bryllup *-et* (=***/bryllaup**) diamond wedding, 60th wedding anniversary.
diaman't/nål *-a* diamond pin.
di'a/meter *-eren, pl +-ere/+-rer/*-rar* diameter.
diametra'l *A* - diametrical; complete: **de er d-e motsetninger** they are c-ly different natures.
diaré *-en* diarrhea.
didaktikk' *-en* didactics.
didak'tisk *A* - didactic.
***did're** *V -a* tremble.
Did'rik *Prn (m)*
+di'e[1] *-n*: **få d-** suckle; **gi d-** nurse.
+di'e[2] *V -et* 1 (of baby) suckle. 2 (of mother) nurse.
+di'e/ba'rn *-et* suckling, unweaned child.
diesel [di'sel] *-en* diesel (fuel).
diesel/motor *-en* diesel engine.
diesel/olje *-a/+-en* diesel oil.
+die't *-en* cf **diett**
diete'tisk *A* - dietary; dietetic.
diett' *-en* 1 diet. 2 per diem.
differanse [-ang's(e)] *-n* (=**+differen's**) difference.
differensia'l[1] *-en* (in car) differential.
differensia'l[2] *-et math.* differential.
differensia'l/rekning *-a* (=**+/regning**) differential calculus.
differensie're *V -te* differentiate.
differe're *V -te* differ.
diffu's *A -t* diffuse.
diffusjo'n *-en* diffusion.
***di'/for·** *Av* cf **der/**
difteri' *-en* (=**+difteritt'**) diphtheria.
difteri'/farang *-en* diphtheria epidemic.
diftong' *-en* diphthong.
diftonge're *V -te* diphthongize.
diftongise're *V -te* diphthongize.

+ Bokmål; * Nynorsk; ° Dialect.
After letter: ' stress (Acc. 1); ' tone, stress (Acc. 2); · length.
Below letter: . not pronounced.

+dig [dei'] *ob of* **du**[2] cf **deg**

di'gel *-elen, pl -ler* crucible, (melting) pot.

di'ger *A -ert, pl -re* big, enormous, heavy; thick: **et d-t best** a huge beast.

***dig'ne** *V -a* 1 bend, be heavy, be full (e.g. of load, fruit). 2 swell (up).

dignita'r *-en* dignitary.

dignitæ'r *-en* dignitary.

digresjo'n *-en* digression.

***dihel'ler** *Av* (with *neg.*) either, even: **han kan ikkje norsk d-** he doesn't even know Norwegian.

di'ke *-t, pl +-r/*-* 1 dike. 2 ditch. 3 mud hole, swamp.

di'ket(e) *A* - full of mud holes, marshy.

+dik'ke *V -et* chuck (under chin).

+dikkeda'rer *pl* fuss, nonsense: **gjøre d-** make a fuss; make trouble, be difficult.

dikkedikk' *I* cootchie-cootchie (to children when chucking under chin).

diksjo'n *-en* diction.

dik't[1] *-et, pl -* 1 poem; poetry: **skrive d-** write poetry. 2 invention, lie: **løgn og forbannet d-** lies and damnable romancing (Ibsen).

+dikt[2] *Av dial.* close (**ved** by).

diktafo'n *-en* Dictaphone (trademark).

dikta'men *-et* dictamen, pronouncement.

***dik'tarleg** *A* - poetic: **d- fridom** p- license.

dikta't *-en* dictation.

dikta'tor *-en, pl +diktato'rer/*-ar* dictator.

diktato'risk *A* - dictatorial.

diktatu'r *-et, pl -/+-er* dictatorship.

dik'te[1] *V -a/+-et* 1 compose, write (belles lettres, esp. poetry): **å d- — det er å holde dommedag over seg selv** to write is to pass judgment on oneself (Ibsen). 2 fabricate, invent, make up; envision: **d- i hop (opp, sammen)** make up (a lie, a story, etc.); **d- og drømme** dream dreams; **d- seg (bort fra virkeligheten)** delude oneself, lie to oneself.

+dik'te[2] *V -a/+-et* caulk.

dik'te/kunst *-en* art of poetry; art of literary creation.

+dik'ter *-en, pl -e* (=***-ar**) poet; author, writer.

dikte're *V -te* dictate: **d- til protokolls** d- a record of proceedings.

+dik'ter/ga'sje *-en* (=***-ar/**) author's stipend (annual lifetime grant awarded a writer by the State).

+dik'terisk *A* - poetic: **d- begavelse** p- talent; **d- frihet** p- license.

+dik'ter/verk *-et* (=***-ar/**) literary work; poetic work.

dik'ting *-a/+-en* (=**+-ning**) 1 writing; literary creation. 2 literary work; poetic work; literature.

dik't/samling *-a/+-en* collection of poems; anthology.

dilem'ma *-et, pl +-er/*-* dilemma.

dilettan't *-en* dilettante.

dilettanteri' *-et* dilettantism.

dilettan'tisk *A* - dilettante.

diligence [dilisjang'se] *-n* stagecoach.

***di'/lik** *A* similar; such: **... og d-t ...** and the like.

dill'[1] *-en* dill.

dill'[2] *-et* nonsense.

dil'le[1] *-a pop.*: **d-a** delirium, d. t.'s.

dil'le[2] *V -a/+-et* 1 dangle; wag. 2 talk nonsense, rubbish.

dil't[1] *-en* copycat, yesman.

dil't[2] *-et* canter, trot.

dil'te *V -a/+-et* 1 canter, trot. 2 straggle, toddle: **d- etter t-** after; *fig.* imitate, take the lead from.

dim'[1] *N* dimmed (lowered) lights.

dim'[2] *A -t, pl -me* 1 dim; hazy, unclear. 2: **d- på synet** having failing eyesight.

dim. = **diminuendo; diminutiv**

***dim'dest** *pt of* **dimmast**

***dimei'r** *Av* even: **eg har gard d-** I even have my own farm.

dimensjo'n *-en* dimension.

dimensjone're *V -te* dimension: **galt d-t** having been given wrong dimensions.

dimin'utiv[1] *-et* diminutive.

dimin'utiv[2] *A* diminutive.

dimisjo'n *-en mil.* discharge.

+dimiss'/preken *-en* (=***/preike**) probational sermon.

dimitte're *V -te mil.* discharge.

***dim'mast** *V dimdest, dimst* grow dim: **d- på synet** have failing eyesight.

dim'me[1] *-a* dimness, dusk.

dim'me[2] *V +-a/+-et/*-de* dim (headlights).

***dim'st** *pp of* **dimmast**

dim'/synt *A* - having failing eyesight.

+dim'/øyd *A* - (=***/øygd**) having failing eyesight.

di'n *Pn f di/+din, nt ditt, pl dine* 1 your(s): **boka di** your book; **boka er di** the book is yours. 2 (in terms of abuse) you: **din tufs** you fool; **ditt kjøtthue** you meathead.

diner [dine'] *-en* (formal) dinner.

dine're *V -te* dine.

***di'/nest** *Av* cf *der/*

ding'el/dangel *-et derog.* bangles, baubles.

ding'le *V -a/+-et* dangle, hang, swing.

ding's *-en fam.* thingumabob, what-you-may-call-it.

***din'se** *V -a* rock, shake.

diop'ter *-eret/-ret, pl +-ere/+-rer/*-* diopter.

diplo'm *-et, pl -/+-er* 1 diploma. 2 *hist.* official document, e.g. deed.

diploma't *-en* diplomat.

diplomata'risk *A* - diplomatic (copy).

diplomata'rium *-iet, pl +-ier/*-ium* collection of historical documents.

diploma't/frakk *-en* frock coat, Prince Albert.

diplomati' *-et* 1 diplomacy. 2 (the) foreign service. 3 the diplomatic corps.

diploma'tisk *A* - diplomatic.

diploma't/lo'sje *-n* diplomat's gallery.

diplo'm/eksa'men *-en* (German) degree examination (esp. in engineering).

diplo'm/ingeniør [/insjeniø'r] *-en* graduate engineer (from the Norwegian Technical College in Trondheim).

direksjo'n *-en* 1 board of directors, managers. 2 direction, management; conductorship.

direk'te *A* - 1 direct (method, route, tax, etc.). 2 immediate (consequence, result). 3 absolute, downright; forthright: **det er d- umulig** it's absolutely impossible; **en d- løgn** an outright lie.

direkti'v *-et, pl -/+-er* directive.

direktora't *-et, pl -/+-er* directorate (State office headed by a director).

direktri'se *-a/+-en* (woman) director.

direktø'r *-en admin.* director (head of a large office or institution).

dirigen't *-en mus.* conductor.

dirige're *V -te* 1 direct, guide; route (e.g. the mail, a train). 2 *mus.* conduct.

dir'ik *-en* cf **dirk**

dir'k *-en* picklock.

dir'ke *V -a/+-et*: **d- opp en lås** pick a lock.

dir'ke/fri *A -tt* (of lock, door) burglar-proof.

dirr' *-en/+-et* tremor.

dir're *V -a/+-et* quiver, tremble, vibrate.

di's[1] *-a/+-en myth.* (minor) goddess (Norse).

di's[2] *-en* haze, mist.

di's[3] *Av* on formal terms, addressing one another with **"De"**.

dis'- *Pf* dis-.

-dis *Prn (f)* e.g. in **Hjørdis, Vigdis.**

disagio [dissa'dsjo] *N merc.* discount.

di'sen *A +-ent, pl -ne* cf **disig**

di'set(e) *A* - hazy, misty.

dis'/favø'r *-en merc.* disfavor.

dis'/harmoni' *-en* disharmony, dissonance.

dis'/harmo'nisk *A* - disharmonious.

di'sig *A* - hazy, misty.

disipli'n *-en* discipline (=field, subject; order).

disipline're *V -te* discipline.

disiplinæ'r *A* disciplinary.

disip'pel *-elen, pl disipler* disciple.

dis'k *-en* 1 counter: **over d-en** across the c-; **selge under d-en** sell below the c-, secretly, on the black market. 2 *obs.* table: **holde d- og duk** have one's own household. 3 *dial.* dish.

diskan't *-en mus.* descant (upper voice); treble; high pitch: **oppe i d-en** in a falsetto voice.

dis'ke[1] *V -a/+-et*: **d- opp med** dish out, serve; **løperen d-et opp med ny rekord** the runner delighted us with a new record; **d- opp med en historie** tell a story with relish.

dis'ke[2] *V -a/+-et* (in sports) disqualify.

dis'ke/dame *-a/+-en* saleslady.

dis'ke/mann *-en, pl -menn/*-menner* clerk.

+dis'ken/springer *-en, pl -e* (=***-ar**) *derog.* sales clerk ("counterjumper").

diskonte're *V -te merc.* discount.

diskon'to *-en merc.* discount rate.

dis'kos *-en* discus.

+dis'kos/kaster *-en, pl -e* (=***-ar**) discus thrower.

diskredite're *V -te* discredit.

diskresjo'n *-en* discretion.

diskre't *A* - discreet; tactful.

diskrimine're *V -te* discriminate: **d- en d-** against sby; **d-ende bestemmelser** discriminatory rules.

diskur's *-en lit.* discourse.

diskusjo'n *-en* discussion: **innlede til d-** introduce the subject of d-.

diskusjo'ns/innlegg *-et* contribution to a discussion.

diskuta'bel *A -elt, pl -le* debatable.

diskute'r/bar *A* - debatable.

diskute're *V -te* discuss.

diskvalifise're *V -te* disqualify.

dispa'sje *-a/+-en* average adjustment (in marine insurance).

dispasjø'r *-en* average adjuster (in marine insurance).

dispensasjon [dispangsasjo'n] *-en* exemption (**fra** from).

dispensere [dispangse're] *V -te* exempt (**fra** from).

disponen't *-en* manager, managing director (**for, i** of).

dispone're *V -te* 1 have the use of, have at one's disposal; command, be master of: **han d-er (over) store midler** he has great means at his command; **vi d-er rommet hver fredag** we have the use of the room every Friday. 2 make use of, manage, use: **hvordan skal midlene d-es?** in what way is the money to be used?; **første etasje skal d-es til butikklokaler** the first floor will be used for stores. 3 organize, outline: **en godt d-t stil** a well organized paper. 4 predispose: **d-t (for)** inclined, susceptible (to).

disponi'bel *A -elt, pl -le* available, at hand, at one's disposal: **d-le midler** (the) means at hand.

disposisjo'n *-en* 1 disposition, nature. 2 *(pl)* measures, steps; plans: **treffe sine d-er** take steps. 3 organization, outline (of a paper etc.). 4 disposal: **stå til d- for en** be at sby's d-.

disputa's *-en* disputation (doctoral).

dispute're *V -te* 1 dispute. 2 defend a doctoral thesis.

disputt' *-en* dispute.

diss' *en mus.* D sharp.

dis'se[1] *-a* swing.

dis'se[2] *V -a/+-et* 1 quiver, shake (esp. of fat tissue). 2 swing.

+dis'se[3] *pl of* **denne**

disseke're *V -te* dissect.

disseksjo'n *-en* dissection.

dissen's *-en jur.* dissent: **under d-** with dissenting votes.

+dissen'ter *-en, pl -e* (=***-ar**) *eccl.* dissenter (from the State church).

dissente're *V -te* dissent.

disserta's *-en* dissertation.

dissonan's *-en* dissonance.

distanse [distang'se] *-n* (long) distance.
distanse/flyging *-a/+-en* long-distance flying.
+distanse/løper *-en, pl -e* long-distance runner.
distansere [distangse're] *V -te* outdistance, outrun.
distingve'rt *A* - distinguished(-looking).
distinksjo'n *-en* 1 distinction, discrimination. 2 *mil.* mark (of rank), chevron.
distinkt [-ting't] *A* - distinct.
distrahe're *V -te* distract.
distraksjo'n *-en* distraction.
distré *A* - absentminded.
distribue're *V -te* distribute.
distribusjo'n *-en* distribution.
distrik't *-et, pl -/+-er* district.
distrik'ts/komman'do *-en mil.* regional command.
distrik'ts/lege *-n* (=*/lækjar) "district physician", State-appointed physician in a rural district.
di't *Av* (to) there, thither: **er det langt d-?** is it far (from here to there)?; **dithen** (to) there, to that place, point; **d- inn** in (to) there; **d- ut** out (to) there.
di't/hen' *Av* cf **dit**
dityram'be *-n* dithyramb.
ditt'[1] *nt of* **din**
ditt'[2] *Pn*: **d- og datt, d-en og datten** this and that, one thing and another.
dit'to (do.) ditto, the same.
div. =**diverse; divisjon**
di'va *+-en/*ei* diva, prima donna.
diva'n *-en* couch, divan.
divergen's *-en* divergence.
diverge're *V -te* deviate, diverge: **d-ende oppfatninger** differing views.
***diver're** *Av* cf **dessverre**
diver'se *A* - 1 divers, sundry, various. 2 *merc.* incidentals; petty cash.
diverte're *V -te* amuse, divert.
dividen'd *-en math.* dividend.
dividen'de *-n* dividend: **boet er oppgjort med en d- til de uprioriterte kreditorer på 25 %** the estate has been liquidated by payment of a 25 % d- to the unsecured creditors.
divide're *V -te* 1 divide (**med** by). 2 puzzle, rack one's brains.
divisjo'n *-en* 1 *math.* division. 2 *mil., naut.* division.
divisjo'ns/musikk' *-en* military band.
divi'sor *-en math.* divisor.
djer'v *A* 1 audacious, daring; bold, fearless. 2 bluff, outspoken; frank, racy.
***djer'vast** *V -dest* risk, venture.
+djer'v/het *-en* 1 audacity, fearlessness. 2 frankness.
djer'v/skap *-en* 1 boldness, daring. 2 impudence.
dje'vel *-elen, pl -ler* demon, devil: **en stakkars d-** an unfortunate person, poor devil; **drive ut d-er** cast out demons, exorcise; **være en (ren) d- til å** have an uncanny skill at; **det var som d-en** well, I'll be damned; **hva d-en skulle jeg gjøre** what the hell was I supposed to do; (in oaths often in the forms **develen, devern, dekern, degeren, dægeren, jævelen**).
dje'velsk *A* - devilish, diabolical, fiendish.
dje'vel/skap *-en* 1 deviltry. 2 nuisance, unpleasantness.
+dje'vle/besatt' *A* - possessed (by demons, devils).
dje'vle/lue *-a* close-fitting knit hood.
+dje'vle/maner *-en, pl -e* (=*-ar) exorcist.
+dje'vler *pl of* **djevel**
dje'vle/tru *-a* (=+/tro) demonism; belief in the devil.
djunke [dsjong'ke] *-n* (Chinese) junk.
dju'p[1] *-et* (=+dyp[1]) deep; depth: **d-et** the deep; **komme ut på d-et** get beyond one's depth, get into deep water.
dju'p[2] *A* (=+dyp[2]) deep (water, snow, a voice, a hole, a color, etc.); intense (disappointment, joy, etc.); profound (thoughts, regrets, respect, etc.): **i d-e tanker** lost in thought; **d- tallerken** soup plate; **beklage d-t** be extremely sorry; **kikke for d-t i glasset** drink too much; **puste d-t** draw a deep breath; **sitte d-t i det** be deeply involved (**med** in).
dju'p/blå *A -tt, pl -/*-e* deep blue.
dju'p/fryse *V -te* deep-freeze, quick-freeze.
dju'p/lendt *A* - having deep soil.
dju'p/line *-a* fishline (used in deep water).
***djup'n** *-a* depth; profundity.
dju'ps/agn [/angn] *-a* (=**juks/, jukse**) hand line (used to fish in deep water).
dju'p/snø *-en* (=+**dyp/**) deep snow.
***dju'ps/ogn** [/ångn] *-a* cf **/agn**
dju'pt *nt of* **djup[2]**
dju'p/tenkt *A* - (=+**dyp/**) contemplative, meditative, profound.
dju'p/ål *-en* deepest channel in the bottom of a deep (river or sea).
***dju'v** *-et* cf **juv**
dl=**desiliter**
dm=**desimeter**
d.m.=**denne måneden**
DNA=**Det norske Arbeiderparti**
DNL=**Det Norske Luftfartsselskap**
do' *-et/+-en pop.* outhouse, privy; toilet: **gå på do** go to the bathroom.
+do.=**ditto**
dob'be *-a/+-en* float (on a fishline).
+dob'bel *-en: obs.* **d- og drikk** gambling and drinking, loose living.
+dob'belt *A* - (=***dobbel**) double; twice, twofold: **d- så (mye, mange)** twice as (much, many); **det d-e** double, twice as much; **i d- forstand** in both senses (of the word); **bli d- så stor** double in size.
+dob'belt/bunn *-en* 1 *naut.* false bottom; double bottom. 2 *fig.* ambiguity, ambivalence: **det er d- i ham** there are hidden depths in him (also: **d- bunn**).
+dob'belt/dør *-a* double door; Dutch door; folding door.
+dob'belt/gjenger *-en* double; doubleganger, fetch.
+dob'belt/grep *-et mus.* double stop (stopping).
+dob'belt/hake *-a/-en* double chin.
+dob'belt/knappet *A* - double-breasted.
+dob'belt/liv *-et* double existence.
+dob'belt/løpet *A* - double-barreled (gun).
+dob'belt/navn *-et* double surname.
+dob'belt/renset *A* - (grain alcohol) distilled twice.
+dob'belt/seng *-a* double bed.
+dob'belt/sidig *A* - bilateral, twosided; (of pneumonia) double.
+dob'belt/spent *A* - double-breasted (suit).
+dob'belt/spill *-et* double-dealing: **han driver et d-** he's playing a double game.
+dob'belt/stemme *-n* extra vote, tie breaking vote.
+dob'belt/strøk *-et mus.* double stop.
+dob'belt/værelse *-t* double (in a hotel, motel, etc.), double room.
dob'le *V -a/+-et* double (a bid in bridge).
+dog [då'g] *Av archaic* nevertheless, still, yet: (=**da[4]**): **en stund, så glad, og dog så vemoddryssende** an hour, so happy, and yet so tinged with sadness (Ibsen); **hva ville dog banksjefen i dag** what did the bank director want today, anyway (Kielland).
doge [då'dsje] *-n* doge.
dogg' *-a/+-en* 1 dew: **forsvinne som d- for sola** vanish suddenly and completely. 2 (on glass) steam.
***dog'gast** *V -ast* become damp from dew; steam up.
dog'ge *V -a/+-et* bedew, dew; become misted, condense, gather dew: **det d-er** the dew is falling; **d-es av tårer** become moist with tears.
Dog'ger/bank *Pln* Dogger Bank.
dog'get(e) *A* - dewy; steamy; moist (with tears).
dogg'/frisk *A* - dewy, fresh as the morning dew.
dogg'/sko *-en, pl -r/+-* cf **dopp/**
dogg'/slått *A* - dewy.
dogg'/våt *A* moist with dew.
+dogma'tiker *-en, pl -e* (=*-ar) dogmatist.
dogmatikk' *-en* dogmatics.
dogma'tisk *A* - dogmatic.
dog'me *-t, pl +-r/*-* dogma.
dokk'[1] *-a/+-en* dock: **skipet trenger til å komme i d-** the ship has to put into dock (for repairs).
dokk'[2] *-a, pl dekker/+-er* 1 depression, hollow (in the ground). 2 dimple.
+dokk'[3] *Pn* cf **dere**
Dok'ka *Pln* 1 post office, Valdresbanen. 2 river, Vestre Gausdal.
+dokk'/arbei'der *-en, pl -e* (=*-ar) dock worker, longshoreman.
dok'ke[1] *-a* 1 doll; dummy, marionette, puppet. 2 skein (of yarn).
dok'ke[2] *V -a/+-et naut.* dock.
dok'ke/ansikt *-et* baby face.
dok'ke/mann *-en, pl -menn/*-menner* doll, puppet (in the form of a man).
°dok'ker *Pn* cf **dere**
dok'ke/stue *-a* doll's house.
dok'ket(e) *A* - doll-like.
dok'ke/tea'ter *-eret/-ret* marionette theater; puppet show: **spille d-** put on a p- s-.
dok'ter[1] *-en* Irish coffee.
***dok'ter[2]** *-en* doctor, physician.
dokte're *V -te* (=+**doktorere**) doctor, heal, (attempt to) cure: **d- på en** doctor sby.
dok'tor *-en* 1 doctor, physician. 2 doctor (academic degree).
doktoran'd *-en* candidate for a doctor's degree.
dok'tor/avhan'dling *-a/+-en* doctor's thesis.
dok'tor/disputa's *-en* doctoral defense (occasion when a thesis is attacked by officially appointed opponents and defended by the candidate).
+doktore're *V -te* cf **doktere**
dok'tor/grad *-en* doctor's degree.
dok'tor/promosjo'n *-en* conferring of the doctor's degree.
doktri'ne *-n* (=+**doktri'n**) doctrine.
doktrinæ'r *A* doctrinaire.
dokumen't *-et, pl -/+-er* document; deed, instrument.
dokumenta'r/film *-en* documentary film.
dokumentasjo'n *-en* documentation, substantiation.
dokumente're *V -te* document, prove, substantiate; **d- seg** produce evidence of one's identity.
+dokumen't/falsk *en* use of falsified or forged documents.
dokumen't/mappe *-a* brief case.
dol'k *-en* dagger: **dreie d-en i såret** rub it in.
dol'ke *V -a/+-et* stab: **han ble d-et bakfra** he was stabbed in the back.
dol'ke/stikk *-et* dagger thrust, wound.
+dol'ke/støt *-et* (=*/støyt) dagger thrust.
dol'lar *-en, pl -/-s* dollar.
dol'lar/glis *-et hum.* postwar type of American car, especially one with an exaggerated grill.
dol'lar/prinses'se *-a/+-en* (wealthy) American heiress.
doll'/bo'rd *-et naut.* gunwale, planksheer.
dol'p *-a* depression, hollow (in the earth).
do'm[1] *-en* 1 cathedral. 2 dome (on locomotive).
dom'[2] *-men/*-en* 1 *jur.* judgment, sentence: **D-mens Dag** the Day of

+ Bokmål; * Nynorsk; ° Dialect.
After letter: ' stress (Acc. 1); ` tone, stress (Acc. 2); · length.
Below letter: . not pronounced.

J-; **d-men falt** j- was delivered, sentence was passed; *fig.* **betale i dyre d-mer** pay through the nose. 2 judgment, opinion: **holde d- over** pass j- on; **sitte til d-s over** sit in j- on; **ett vet jeg som aldri dør: d- om hver en død** one thing I know which never dies: the j- passed on each mortal man (Poetic Edda).

°**dom'**[3] *Pn* cf **de**[1]

-dom *-men/*-en* (used in e.g.) **fattigdom** (-ty), **hedendom** (-ism), **kristendom** (-ity), **helligdom** (-ness), **spådom** (-cy), etc.

***do'mar** *-en* cf **dommer**

dom/bjølle [domm'/] *-a* (=+/**bjelle**) sleigh bell.

Domb/ås [Domm'/] *Pln* twp, Oppland.

***do'me/dag** *en* cf **domme/**

dome'ne *-n* 1 *hist.* crown land. 2 domain, sphere (of authority, operations, etc.).

dom'/felle *V -felte* pass sentence upon, sentence.

dom'/herre *-en* 1 *eccl.* canon. 2 *zool.* bullfinch (Pyrrhula pyrrhula).

dominan't[1] *-en* 1 dominant. 2 *mus.* fifth tone of a scale: **d-/akkorden** the dominant chord.

dominan't[2] *A - genet.* dominant.

domine're *V -te* 1 command, dominate, predominate. 2 be overbearing; bluster, roar.

domine'rende *A -* 1 commanding, dominant, predominant. 2 domineering, overbearing.

+**dominika'ner** *-en, pl -e* (=***-ar**, ***dominikan**) Dominican.

dom'ino *-en* 1 domino (costume and the wearer). 2 dominoes.

domisi'l *-et, pl +-er/*-* domicile, place of residence.

domisilia't *-en merc.* person to whom a domiciled bill is made payable.

dom'/kapit'tel *-elet/-kapitlet, pl -el/ +-kapitler eccl.* chapter; chapter house (of cathedral).

+**dom'/kirke** *-a/-en* (=*/**kyrkje**) cathedral.

dom'me/dag *-en* the Day of Judgment, Doomsday: **holde d- over seg selv** pass judgment on oneself (Ibsen).

dom'medags/basu'n *-en* the last trumpet (summoning the dead to judgment on Doomsday).

dom'medags/mine *-a/+-en hum.* deadly serious expression.

+**dom'medags/preken** *-en* (=*/**preike**) fire and brimstone sermon.

+**dom'mer** *-en, pl -e* (=***-ar**) 1 judge (in court, of an exhibition, etc.), justice (of the Supreme Court): **d- over** judge of; *bibl.* **D-nes Bok** the Book of Judges. 2 (in sports competitions) referee, umpire.

+**dom'mer/fløyte** *-a* (=***-ar/**) referee's whistle (e.g. football, soccer).

+**dom'mer/fullmek'tig** *-en* (=***-ar/**) deputy judge.

dom'mer/kappe *-a* judge's robe.

dom/pap [domm'/papp] *-en* 1 blockhead, fool. 2 *zool.* bullfinch (Pyrrhula pyrrhula).

dom'/prost [/prost] *-en eccl.* dean (at a cathedral).

dom's/mann *-en, pl -menn/*-menner jur.* lay judge.

dom's/nemnd [/nemd] *-a* panel of judges.

dom'/sokn *-a/+-et jur.* judicial district.

dom'/stol *-en* 1 court of law, tribunal. 2 *bibl.* judgment seat.

***do'n**[1] *-et* 1 baggage, luggage. 2 tools.

°**do'n**[2] *-et* crash; roar.

donasjo'n *-en* donation, gift (usu. charitable or educational).

dona'tor *-en* donor.

Do'nau *Pln* the Danube.

do'ne[1] *-a* snare, trap.

°**do'ne**[2] *V -te* bang, crash; roar.

done're *V -te* donate.

dong'eri *-en* dungaree; blue denim.

+**dong'eri/klær** *pl* (=*/**klede**) blue jeans, dungarees, overalls.

do'ning[1] *-a/+-en* 1 implement, tool. 2 (light) carriage, rig.

°**do'ning**[2] *-en* voluntary labor, e.g. barn raising, husking bee.

Don Juan [dånnsjuang'] *-en* Don Juan; rake, roué, seducer.

donkey [dång'ki] *-en* donkey engine.

donkey/kjel *-en* boiler of donkey engine.

donkey/mann *-en, pl -menn/*-menner* donkeyman (operator of a donkey engine).

do'n/kraft *-a* jack.

don'na *+-en/*ei* 1 donna, lady. 2 *(pop.)* broad, dame, skirt.

don't *-en* business, job, task: *hum.* **passe sin d-** mind one's own business.

do'/papi'r *-et pop.* toilet paper.

+**dopp'** *-en* 1 boss, knob. 2 bushing, ferrule, metal protective tip (e.g. on a fencing foil).

+**dopp'/sko** *-en, pl -r/+-* (=**dogg/**) ferrule, tip.

do'r *-en* punch (tool).

-dor *Prn (m)* e.g. **Halldor.**

Dordei [dor'dei] *Prn (f)* Dorothy.

do're *V -a/+-et/+-te* enlarge a hole (by means of a punch).

+**do'rer** *-en, pl -e* (=***-ar**) Dorian.

dor'g *-a/+-en* trolling line.

dor'ge *V -a/+-et* troll.

dor'gende *Av* cf **dørgende**

do'risk *A -* Dorian, Doric.

dor'm *-en* nap.

dor'me *V -a/+-et* doze, nap: **d- av (bort, til)** doze off.

+**dor'sk** *A* apathetic, indolent, sluggish.

+**dor'sk/het** *-en* apathy, lethargy, sluggishness.

Dor'te *Prn (f)* Dorothy.

dor'y *-en* dory.

***dos** [då's] *-a* skirt.

do'se *-n* (=**dosis**) dosage, dose.

dosen't *-en* docent (university lecturer, ab.=associate professor).

dosentu'r *-et, pl -/+-er* position of docent.

dose're *V -te* 1 lecture (on), teach: **han d-te organisk kjemi** he lectured on organic chemistry. 2 hold forth, speak about sth in a didactic tone.

do'sis *-en* cf **dose**

+**dos'mer** *-en, pl -e* (=***-ar**) blockhead, dunce, nitwit.

+**dos'mer/aktig** *A -* slow-witted, stupid.

dosse're *V -te* bank (a road).

dosse'ring *-a/+-en* bank, embankment, slope.

dossier [dåssie'] *-et* dossier, file.

dotasjo'n *-en* donation, endowment.

dote're *V -te* donate, endow.

do't/sup *-en* drink, toast (partaken of in celebration of the kill in a hunt).

dott' *-en* 1 handful, wad: **en d- høy** a wisp of hay; **få d-er i ørene** be partially deafened, have one's ears plugged up. 2 small herd (e.g. of reindeer). 3 spineless person, weakling; fool.

***dot'te** *pp of* **dette**[1]

***dot'ter** *-a, pl døtrer* cf **datter**

dot'tet(e) *A -* 1 dotted, specked. 2 pliable, spineless.

***dot'ti** *pp of* **dette**[1]

double [døb'bel] *en* 1 doubles (in tennis). 2 understudy (movies, theater).

+**dov** [då'v] *A* deadened, muffled.

***dove** [då've] *V -a* 1 abate, calm. 2 alleviate, mitigate. 3: **d- seg** loaf.

doven [då'ven] *A +-ent, pl -ne* 1 lazy, sluggish. 2 (of limbs) numb: **foten min er d-** my foot's asleep. 3 (of drinks) flat, stale.

doven/dyr *-et* 1 *zool.* sloth (family Bradypodidae). 2 lazybones, sluggard.

doven/la'rs *-en* lazy, slothful person, sluggard.

doven/skap *-en* indolence, laziness, sloth.

dov'ne *V -a/+-et* 1 become flat, stale (of drinks): **d- av** abate, slacken; **d- bort** become numb, go to sleep (of limbs). 2: **d- seg** loaf.

dov'ning[1] *-en* (husking, quilting) bee, barn raising.

dov'ning[2] *-en* indolent, lazy, slothful person, sluggard.

Dovre [då'vre] *Pln* twp, Oppland.

Dovre/banen *Prn* railroad from Oslo to Trondheim via Dovrefjell.

Dovre/fjell *Pln* the Dovre mountain range.

Dovre/gubben *Prn* 1 troll king (of the Dovre mountains, in Ibsen's Peer Gynt). 2 *pop.* name of largest Norwegian type of steam locomotive, first built in the 1930's.

doyen [doajeng'] *-en* dean, senior member (esp. of a diplomatic corps).

dr.=**doktor, doctor, *dokter: dr. agr.** Ph. D. in agriculture; **dr. ing.** Ph. D. in engineering; **dr. jur.** doctor of laws; **dr. med.** Ph. D. in medicine; **dr. med. vet.** Ph. D. in veterinary science; **dr. odont.** Ph. D in dentistry; **dr. philos.** Ph. D. (in arts and sciences; more advanced than our Ph. D.); **dr. techn.** Ph. D. in engineering; **dr. theol.** Doctor of Sacred Theology.

+**dra'** *V drog, -dd/-tt* (=***dra(ge)**[2]) 1 drag, pull; attract, draw: **d- fisk** haul in fish; **d- fordel (nytte) av** benefit from, profit by; **d- kjensel på** recognize; **d- (hele) lasset** bear the brunt, the full load; **d- pusten (været, ånde)** breathe, draw a breath; **d- et sukk** heave a sigh. 2 (with *prep.* or *adv.*): **d- noe etter seg** have sth as a consequence, bring sth on; **det d-r etter med ham** sth occurs to him, a new thought strikes him; **d- i tvil** question, cast doubt on; **d- noe med seg** carry sth along; **d- på** carry, drag along; **d- på det** hem and haw; **d- på seg** put on (e.g. clothes); **d- på smilebåndet** smile; **d- på skulderen** hunch up, shrug one's shoulders; **d- på årene** be getting along in years; **d- til en** hit sby; **d- til seg** attract; **d- noe ut** drag sth out, take a long time with sth. 3 go, leave: **når d-r du?** when are you leaving?; **d- av gårde (sted)** leave, set out; **d- av gårde med** make off with; **d- bort (inn, hjem, til helvete, osv)** go away (in, home, to hell, etc.); **d- etter en** follow sby; **d- i krigen** go to war; **d- innpå en** gain on, overtake sby; **d- pokker i vold (nord og ned)** go to hell; **d- på landet** go to the country. 4 (*refl.*): **d- seg** crawl, move slowly; hang around, be idle, loaf.

draban't *-en* 1 *hist.* yeoman of the (royal) guard. 2 *hum.* follower, henchman. 3 satellite.

draban't/by *-en* "satellite city" (suburban development of homes and apartments with own shopping center).

+**dra'belig** *A -* 1 awe-inspiring, formidable. 2 *hum.* colossal, prodigious, tremendous: **en d- porsjon** a whopping portion.

dradd' *pp of* **dra**

+**dra'es** *V droges, drages* cf **dras**

draf't *-et, pl -/+-er naut.* (large scale) navigational chart.

dra'g *-et* 1 pull (at sth); breath of air (with which one fills one's lungs); puff (at a cigar, etc.); twitch (of the face muscles): **i ett d-** without pause; **han tømte flaska i ett d-** he emptied the bottle in one pull (draft, swig); **nyte i fulle d-** enjoy to the utmost. 2 shaft (of a plow, wagon). 3 groove in the ground up or along which a boat is pulled; keel guard (to protect a boat's keel when it is dragged along the ground); runner guard (on a sled). 4 motion (of air masses, clouds, waves). 5 stretch (of terrain); vein (of metal or rock). 6 characteristic, feature. line (in a face, the terrain, etc.); expression: **et trassig d-** a stubborn e-. 7 blow, rap. *8 note of hesitation in the voice; postponement.

***dra'gast** *V dregst, drogst, dregest/-ist* 1 wrestle. 2 be burdened, troubled (**med** with). 3: **d- ut** get late.

dra'g/dokke *-a* 1 *folk.* tutelary spirit in human or animal form which attracts wealth and good fortune to a dwelling. 2 *pop.* hooker (prostitute used by pimp as come-on).

+**dra'ge**[1] *-n* cf **drake**

***dra'ge**[2] *V dreg, drog, drege/-i* cf **dra**

+**dra'gelse** *-n* 1 attraction, fascination (**til** for). 2 strong reprimand: **få seg en d-** get one's ears pinned back.

+**dra'gende** *A* - compelling, fascinating.

+**dra'ger** *-en, pl -e* (=***-ar**) 1 porter, redcap. 2 girder; lintel.

+**dra'ges** *V droges,* - cf **dras**

+**dra'get** *A - archaic* attracted, drawn: **med d- sverd** *hum.* with sword unsheathed.

dra'g/kamp *-en* tug-of-war.

dra'g/kiste *-a* bureau, chest of drawers.

dra'g/kjerre *-a* handcart, pushcart.

***dra'gnad** *-en, pl -er* attraction, fascination.

dra'gning *-a/-en* 1 muscle spasm, twitch. 2 attraction, fascination; bent, inclination.

drago'n *-en mil.* dragoon.

dragse [drak'se] *V -a/+-et* drag (along): **d- på noe** drag sth along.

dra'gs/mål *-et* brawl, fight.

***dra'g/sog** *-et* cf **/su**

+**dra'g/spill** *-et* (=***/spel,** +**/spell**) accordion, concertina.

dragster [drak'ster] *-en* drawing, pulling.

dra'g/su *-a* (=+**/sug**) backwash, undertow.

+**dra'g/sug** *-et* cf **/su**

dra'ke *-n* 1 dragon (fabled animal; lizard; sailboat; severe woman, etc). 2 kite.

+**dra'ke/hode** *-t* 1 *archeol.* ornamental prow in the shape of a dragon's head, found on Viking ships. 2 *bot.* dragonhead (Dracocephalum ruyschianum).

dra'ke/stil *-en* 1 zoomorphic ornamentation (esp. as found on Norwegian stave churches). 2 florid architectural and furniture style, c. 1850 in Norway (dragon style).

+**dra'ke/sæd** [/sed] *-en* dragon's teeth: **så d-** cause discord, dissension.

drakk' *pt of* **drikke**[2]

drak't *-a/+-en* 1 attire, clothes, garb; suit, tailored suit; costume. 2 coat (e.g. of feathers, fur, etc.). 3 *vet.* back of a horse's hoof. 4: **en d-pryl** a thrashing.

drak't/pose *-n* moth proof bag (for clothes).

dram' *-men, pl -mer* drink, nip, shot (usu. of aquavit or brandy).

dra'ma *-et, pl -/+-er* drama.

+**drama'tiker** *-en, pl -e* (=***-ar**) dramatist.

dramatikk' *-en* drama, dramatic literature.

dramatise're *V -te* adapt for the stage; dramatize.

drama'tisk *A* - dramatic; spectacular, thrilling.

dramatur'g *-en* 1 drama critic. 2 dramaturge (=adviser to the producer in European theaters).

***dram'b** *-et* ostentation, splendor.

***dram'be/dros** *-a* exceptionally beautiful woman.

dram'me/glas *-et* (=+**/glass**) shot glass, "schnapps" glass.

Dram'men *Pln* city, Buskerud.

+**drammen'ser** *-en, pl -e* (=***-ar**) native of Drammen.

+**dram'me/sluker** *-en, pl -e* (=***-ar**) heavy drinker.

Drang'e/dal *Pln* twp, Telemark.

dran'k *-en* dregs, lees, sediment (from distillation).

+**dran'ker** *-en, pl -e* (=***-ar**) alcoholic, drunkard, sot; *(pop.)* lush.

dra'p[1] *-et* homicide, manslaughter, murder (**på** of).

dra'p[2] *pt of* **drepe**

+**dra'pelig** *A* - cf **drabelig**

drape're *V -te* deck, drape, hang with draperies.

draperi' *-et, pl +-er/*-* drapery.

drapp' *-en* beige cloth, material.

dra'ps/mann *-en, pl -menn/*-menner* homicide, murderer.

dra'ps/sak *-a/+-en* trial for homicide.

+**dra's** *V droges, drages* (=+**dra(g)es,** ***dragast**) 1: **d- med** contend, struggle with; be tormented by; **d- med døden** be dying, in one's death throes. 2: **d- mot en** be attracted, drawn towards sby.

drass *-et* (heavy) burden, nuisance.

dras'se *V -a/+-et* drag (**på** along); **komme d-ende med noe** come dragging sth.

dras'tisk *A* - drastic; brutal, crass.

dratt' *pp of* **dra**

drat'te *V -a/+-et* fall suddenly, flop: **d- av pinnen** fall off one's perch; **d- ned** flop down; **komme d-ende** plop down; drop in.

drau'g *-en* 1 *archaic* ghost, specter. 2 *folk.* apparition of a headless man (often in a half-boat) which appears to sby destined to die soon, esp. by drowning.

***drau'm** *-en* cf **drøm**

Drau'm/kvædet *Prn* "the Dream Ballad" (medieval Norwegian religious ballad).

***drau'p** *pt of* **drype**[1]

dra'v *-et* dregs, lees, sediment (from distillation).

drava't *-en* 1 test of endurance; severe reprimand. 2 push, shove (causing one to stumble).

drav'le *-n* simmered curds and whey.

draw/back [drå'/bækk] *-en/-et* drawback.

dread/nought [dredd'/nåt] *-en naut.* dreadnought.

***dre'g** *pr of* **drage**[2]

***dre'ge** *pp of* **drage**[2]

***dre'gest** *pp of* **dragast**

dregg' *-en naut.* grapnel (small anchor): **legge skipet for d-** anchor the ship.

+**dreg'ge** *V -a/-et* (=***-je**) *naut.* drag, dredge: **d- opp** throw out the grapnel; **d- etter** dredge, grapple for.

***dre'gi** *pp of* **drage**[2]

***dre'gst** *pr of* **dragast**

drei' *-en* 1 turn (**av, med** of); curve, turning. *2 blow.

drei'/bar *A* revolving, rotating; adjustable.

drei'e *V +-de/+-et/*-a* 1 rotate, turn, twist: **vinden d-er til** the wind is shifting to. 2 turn (on a lathe). 3 (with *adv.*:) **d- av** turn aside, veer off; **d- om på** turn, twist; **d- rundt** turn around; *naut.* **d- til** come about, heave to. 4 *(refl.)*: **d- seg** revolve, turn (**om** around); *fig.* concern: **det d-er seg om** it's a question, a matter of; **hva d-er det seg om?** what's it all about?

drei'e/benk *-en* lathe.

drei'e/bok *-a, pl -bøker* scenario.

drei'el *-en/+-et* drill (a tightly woven patterned cloth of linen and cotton, chiefly used for tablecloths).

+**drei'er** *-en, pl -e* (=***-ar**) 1 lathe operator, turner. 2 *naut.* heaver.

drei'e/scene *-n* revolving stage.

drei'l *-en/-et* cf **dreiel**

+**drei'ning** *-en* rotation, turn, turning.

drei't *pt of* **drite**

drei'v *pt of* **drive**[2]

drek't *-a* 1 capacity (esp. of a ship). 2 speed: **i full d-** at top s-.

drek'tig *A* - 1 pregnant, with young (of animals). 2 *naut.*: **d- 200 tonn** of 200 tons burden.

+**drek'tig/het** *-a/-en* 1 pregnancy (of animals). 2 *naut.* ship's burden.

***drem'be** *V -de*: **d- seg** exert oneself; **d- til** strike.

dre'n *-en* drain, drainpipe.

dre'ne *V -te* drain.

drene're *V -te* drain.

dreng' *-en* 1 hired man (on a farm). 2 *dial.* bachelor. 3 *archaic* half-grown boy. 4 *archaic* brave, daring man.

Dreng' *Prn(m)*

dreng'e/stue *-a* (=**/stove**) servants' quarters.

dreng'/kall *-en* aging bachelor.

dre'ns/rør *-et/*-a* (=***/røyr**) drainpipe.

dre'pe *V drap/+-te, +-t/*-e/*-i* kill, put to death, slay: **d-ende** deadly, fatal; boring.

+**dre'per** *-en, pl -e* (=***-ar**) 1 killer. 2 (explosive) harpoon.

dresi'n *-en* (RR) handcar, velocipede car.

dress' *-en* suit (of clothes).

dres'se *V -a/+-et*: **d- opp** dress up.

dresse're *V -te* break, train (animals, *hum.* people).

dressu'r *-en* (animal) training.

dressø'r *-en* (animal) trainer.

+**dre't** *pt of* **drite**

+**drett'** *-et* catch, haul (of fish).

dret'te[1] *-t, pl +-r/*-* drag (e.g. heavy harrow, or a stout sled).

+**dret'te**[2] *V -a/+-et* breed, raise (e.g. cattle).

dre'v[1] *-et* 1 chase, hunting. 2 drift, mist, shower (e.g. of sand, snow). 3 fishing with drift nets. 4 cogwheel pinion. 5 oakum.

+**dre'v**[2] *pt of* **drive**[1]

+**dre've** *V -a/-et* 1 calk. 2 dawdle, loiter.

+**dre'ven** *A -ent, pl -ne* (=***driven**) astute, experienced, shrewd.

+**dre'vende** *A* - poky, slow-paced, sluggish.

+**dre'vet** *pp of* **drive**[1]

drev'je *-a* mash (crushed malt, meal of grain) for cattle, horses.

drib'le *V -a/+-et* dribble (a ball, as in soccer).

drif't *-a/+-en* 1 management; operation (e.g. of a business, factory, farm, machine, etc.): **billig (dyr) i d-** cheap (expensive) to run, operate; **i full d-** in full swing, working at full capacity; **ute av d-** not operating, idle; **være i d-** be operating, in operation. 2 bent, inclination: **av egen d-** of one's own accord, on one's own initiative. 3 desire, instinct, urge (esp. of a sexual nature). 4 energy, enterprise: **det er d- i ham** he is enterprising. 5 drove, herd (of animals being driven). 6 *geol.* drift (=horizontal mine shaft). 7 drift, drifting (e.g. of ice, clouds, a ship, timber).

***drif'te** *V -a* be busy, occupied (**med** with).

drif'te/kar *-en* cattle dealer, drover.

drif'tig *A* - active, enterprising.

drif'ts/bygning *-en* factory, mill.

drif'ts/kapita'l *-en* working capital.

drif'ts/måte *-n* method of working.

+**drif'ts/omkos'tning** *-en* operating cost.

drif'ts/overskott [/åver-] *-et* net profit.

drif'ts/sikker *A -ert, pl -sikre* (of machine) in running, working order; dependable, reliable.

drif'ts/spenning *-a/+-en* load, voltage (electricity).

drikk' *-en, pl *-er* 1 drink; beverage, liquor: **en besk (bitter) d-** a bitter draught, sorrow; **sterke d-er** hard liquor. 2 drinking: **bli forfallen til d-, slå seg på d-** take to drink, *(pop.)* hit the bottle.

***drik'kar** *-en* drinker, drunkard.

drik'ke[1] *N* drink: **mat og d-** food and drink.

+ Bokmål; * Nynorsk; ° Dialect.
After letter: ' stress (Acc. 1); ' tone, stress (Acc. 2); · length.
Below letter: . not pronounced.

drik'ke[2] V *drakk*, +*drukket*/**drukke*/**-i* 1 drink: **d- dus med en** d- with sby as part of the ceremony of discarding the formal pronoun of address **(De)** for the informal **(du)**; **d- en full** get sby drunk; **d- ens minne** d- to sby's memory; **d- ens skål, d- for en** d- to sby's health, d- a toast to sby; **d- jul** celebrate Christmas. 2 (with *adv., prep.*): **d- av (flaska)** d- from (the bottle); **d- opp (penger)** spend (money) on liquor; **d- på noe** d- to sth; **d- en til** d- to sby; **d- ut** d- up, empty the glass; **d- en ut (av ungkarslaget)** hold a bachelor party for sby. 3 *(refl.)*: **d- seg fra sans og samling** get blind drunk; **d- seg full** get drunk; **d- seg i hjel** d- oneself to death; **d- seg mot til** get up Dutch courage.

drik'ke/bror *-en, pl* +*-brødre*/**-brør* drinking companion, fellow boozer, souse.

drik'ke/gilde *-t, pl* +*-r*/**-* drinking bout; beer bust, bottle party.

drik'ke/ho'rn *-et hist.* drinking horn.

drik'ke/kar' *-et* drinking vessel.

drik'ke/lag *-et* drinking bout; beer bust, bottle party.

drik'kelig *A* - drinkable, fit to drink.

drik'kende *A* - 1 drinkable: **vannet er ikke d-(s)** the water is not fit to drink. 2: **d-s** sth to drink.

+**drik'ke/penger** *pl* (=***-ar**) gratuity, tip.

drik'ke/skilling *-en* gratuity, tip.

drik'ke/vare *-a*/+*-en*: **d-r** (alcoholic) beverages, drinks.

drik'ke/vatn *-et* drinking water.

drik'ke/vise *-a*/+*-en* drinking song.

+**drikk'/feldig** [also -fel'-] *A* - addicted to drinking.

+**drikkfel'dig/het** *-en* alcoholism, intemperance.

drik'king *-a* drinking.

drik's *-en* gratuity, tip (term used by hotel personnel).

drill' *-en* drill (tool; small furrow; exercise).

drill'/bor' *-en*/*-et* drill.

+**dril'le**[1] V *-a*/*-et* 1 bore, drill. 2 sow in rows.

dril'le[2] V *-a*/+*-et archaic* tease.

drin'k *-en* drink (of hard liquor).

dris'le V *-a*/+*-et* fall, sift down.

dris'te V *-a*/+*-et*: **d- seg til** dare, presume, venture to; **d- seg fram** venture forth.

dris'tig *A* - 1 bold, daring: **overgå de d-ste forventninger** exceed one's wildest expectations. 2 brazen, impudent: **en d- sang** a risqué song.

+**dris'tig/het** *-en* 1 boldness, daring. 2 (act of) effrontery, impudence.

dri'te V *dreit*/+*dret*, +*-et*/**-e*/**-i vulg.* defecate.

dritt' *-en* 1 *vulg.* excrement, filth. 2 *pop.*: **hele d-en** the whole mess, miserable, paltry lot. 3 *(pop.)* crumbum, louse.

dritt'/sekk *-en* louse, stinker.

dritt'/vær *-et* (=***/ver**) foul weather.

dri'v *-et*/+*-en* 1 drift, shower (of sand, snow). 2 enterprise, initiative.

dri'v/aksel *-elen, pl -ler* drive shaft.

dri'v/anker *-eret, pl -er*/+*-ere*/+*-re* sea anchor.

dri'v/benk *-en agr.* hotbed.

Dri'v/dalen *Pln* valley, Oppdal twp, Sør-Trøndelag.

dri've[1] *-a* drift (of sand, snow).

dri've[2] V *dreiv*/+*drev*, +*drevet*/**drive*/**-i* 1 drive, force: **d- en fra vettet** drive sby mad; **d- en hardt** work sby hard; **d- en i vei** force sby on, ahead. 2 drift, float, wander; loaf, loiter, saunter: **gå og d-** hang, loiter around; **d- om** drift (around), loaf; **d- opp og ned** walk back and forth; **d- til havs** drift out to sea. 3 operate, run (a business, factory, farm, machine, etc.); carry on, pursue (an activity, a trade, etc.): **d- dank** goof off, loaf; **d- gjøn med** make fun of; **d- fiske (jakt)** fish (hunt); **d- idrett** participate in sports; **d- studier** study (=engage in a course of study). 4 (with *verb*) be engaged in doing: **han d-er og bygger hus** he's (busy) building a house. 5 (of liquids) pour, rush; (of loose objects) drift, float; fly: **gulvet drev av papir** paper floated all over the floor; **snøen drev inn** the snow drifted in; **svetten drev av ham** the sweat poured off him. 6 (of metals) chase. 7 *naut.* caulk. 8 (with *adv.*) **d- fram** propel, (of plants) force; **d- igjennom** carry, force through; **d- inn** collect (money); **d- det langt** go far in the world; **d- med en** court sby; make a fool of sby, tease sby; **d- med noe** be engaged in doing sth, work with sth; **hva d-er du med om dagen?** what are you doing these days? **d- over** go away, pass (e.g. bad weather); **d- på** be busy, keep at it, work hard; **d- på en** hurry sby up; **d- på med** be busy with; **d- det til noe** get somewhere; **d- det til å** manage to; **d- til en** hit sby; **d- ut djevler** cast out devils; **d- noe (for) vidt** carry sth (too) far, overdo sth.

***dri'ven** *A* *-e*/*-i, pl -ne* cf **dreven**

dri'vende[1] *A* - 1 energetic, enterprising: **en d-s kar** a hard worker. 2 (of climate, weather) favorable (to plant growth), propitious.

dri'vende[2] *Av*: **d- drukken, full** dead drunk; **d- våt** wringing wet.

dri'v/fjør *-a* (=+**/fjær**) 1 mainspring (of watch). 2 *fig.* incentive, motive.

dri'v/ga'rn *-et* drift net.

dri'v/gods [/gots] *-et* driftwood, flotsam.

dri'v/hjul [/jul] *-et* driving wheel; *fig.* motive force.

dri'v/hus *-et* greenhouse, hothouse.

dri'vhus/plante *-a*/*-en* hothouse plant.

dri'v/is *-en* drift ice, floating ice.

dri'v/kraft *-a*/+*-en* motive power; incentive, motive.

dri'v/kvit *A* dazzling white.

***dri'vnad** *-en* impulse, stimulus.

dri'v/reim *-a* (=+**/rem**) drive belt.

dri'v/tømmer *-et* driftwood.

dri'v/verdig *A* - productive, profitable (e.g. ore).

dri'v/våt *A* wringing wet.

***drju'g** *A* cf **dryg**

°**dro'g**[1] *-a* 1 sledge. 2 small valley.

+**dro'g**[2] *-et* cf **dråk**[2]

dro'g[3] *pt of* **dra,** ***drage**[2]

droge[1] [drå'ge] *-n* drug.

droge[2] [drå'ge] *-a* 1 heavy burden. 2 lengthy, straggling procession.

drogeri [drågeri'] *-et, pl* +*-er*/**-* 1 *(pl)* drugs. 2 drug store, pharmacy.

***dro'gst** *pt of* **dragast**

+**dro'len** *df archaic* the devil.

dromeda'r *-en* dromedary.

dro'ne *-n* drone (bee; idler, sluggard).

dron'ning *-a*/+*-en* queen: **ballets d-** queen of the ball; *naut.* **d-ens kvarter** the port watch; *bot.* **nattens d-** nightblooming cereus (Cereus grandiflorus); **spille d-** act like a queen, put on airs.

***drop** [drå'p] *-et* drip, drop.

***drope**[1] [drå'pe] *-n* cf **dråpe**[1]

drope**[2] [drå'pe] *pp of* **drype**[1] (=dropi**)

drop'le[1] *-n* marking, spot (on animals, e. g. cows).

***drop'le**[2] V *-a*/+*-et* dribble, drip, leak.

drop'let(e) *A* - marked, spotted (e.g. cow).

drop'pe V *-a*/+*-et* drop, let go.

drop's *-en*/*-et* hard candy, (lemon) drop.

***drop/stein** [drå'p/] *-en* stalactite.

***dro's** *-a* (fine) lady.

***drose** [drå'se] *-n* 1 flock, herd. 2 heap, pile.

dros'je *-a*/*-en* taxi.

dros'je/sjåfø'r *-en* taxi driver.

+**dros't** *-en hist.* (grand) seneschal (Denmark).

drott' *-en archaic, poet.* king, prince.

drot'ten *en archaic* king, prince: **D-** the Lord.

drott'/kvætt *A* - *hist., poet.* (in Old Norse) court meter.

drott'/sete *-n hist.* (grand) seneschal (medieval Scandinavia).

dru'e *-a*/+*-en* 1 grape; *poet.* wine. 2 *mil.* cascabel (cannon).

dru'e/blod *-et poet.* grape juice; (red) wine.

dru'e/brennevin *-et* cognac, grape brandy.

dru'e/klase *-n* cluster of grapes.

dru'e/saft *-a* grape juice.

dru'e/sukker [/sokker] *-et* dextrose, glucose, grape sugar.

°**dru'g** *A* cf **dryg**

drukken [drok'ken] *A* +*-ent, pl* **drukne** 1 drunk, intoxicated; *(pop.)* plastered. 2 *poet.* overcome, overwhelmed **(av** by) (e.g. with joy).

+**drukken/bolt** *-en* drunkard, *(pop.)* boozer.

drukken/skap *-en* drunkenness, intoxication.

+**drukket** [drok'ket] *pp of* **drikke**[2]

drukne[1] [drok'ne] V *-a*/+*-et* drown (also in all English *fig.* meanings): **den d-er ei som henges skal** he that is born to be hanged will never drown (the devil looks after his own); **d- i arbeid** be snowed under with work.

drukne[2] [drok'ne] *pl of* **drukken**

druknings/ulykke [drok'-] *-a*/+*-en* (=***/ulukke**) drowning accident.

***drun'de** *pt of* **drynje**

***drun'se** V *-a* fritter away time.

drun't[1] *-en* drone, sluggard.

***drun't**[2] *pp of* **drynje**

drun'te V *-a*/+*-et* dawdle, loiter.

***dru'pe** V *-te* hang; bend, lean forward.

dru's *A* 1 copious, overflowing, plentiful: **leve d-t** live high. 2 liberal, open-handed.

dru'se V *-te* 1 rage, storm: **d- på** plunge, rush headlong at, in. 2 fling, throw in profusion.

drus't *-a* pomp, splendor: **i dramb og d-** in the grand manner.

***drus'te** *pt of* **drysje**

drus'telig *A* - 1 copious, plentiful. 2 magnificent, splendid.

***dry'e** V *-gde* cf **dryge**

***dry'en** *A* *-e*/*-i, pl -ne* which makes sth last; poky.

dry'g *A* (=**drøy**) 1 economical (in use), going a long way, lasting. 2 demanding, tough; stiff: **et d-t arbeid** a tough job; **en d- pris** a stiff price. 3 bulky, heavy, substantial; powerful, violent. 4 coarse, crude: +**en drøy ed** a lurid oath; +**en drøy spøk** a drastic joke; ***d-e sogor** racy stories; 5: **i drøyeste laget** rather excessive; **for drøye hundre år siden** a good hundred years ago.

***dryg'd** *-a* durability; extent.

dry'ge V *-de* (=**drøye**) 1 make sth go a long way, last longer: **d- på, d- ut** eke out, make it last. 2 delay; hesitate; put off: **d- med noe** put sth off.

***dry'g/leik** *-en* durability, economy.

dry'gsel *-la*/+*-elen* durability, permanence: **det er ikke d- i pengene** the money doesn't go far.

***dry'gsle** *-a* 1 admixture (to make sth last longer). 2 adjournment, delay.

***drykk'** *-en, pl -er* cf **drikk**

***dryk'kje** *-a* banquet, feast.

***dry'n**[1] *-et* cf **drønn**

***dry'n**[2] *pr of* **drynje**

***dryn'je** V *dryn, drunde, drunt* cf **drønne**

***dry'pe**[1] V *draup, drope*/*-i* cf **dryppe**

***dry'pe**[2] V *-te* cf **dryppe**

+**drypp'** *-et* drip, drop; dripping.

+**dryp'pe** V *-et*/*drypte* (=***drype** [1,2]) 1 drip **(av** from), leak, trickle; (of nose) run; **d- av** drain, run off: **når det regner på presten, så d-er det på klokkeren** (ref. to custom of giving sexton small holiday offering at same time as minister) ab. = when a person gets sth good, some of it will trickle down to his friends and family. 2 drop, apply drops: **d- i øynene** put drops in one's eyes; **d- steken** baste the roast. 3 *naut.* drop (anchor).

+**dryp'pende** *Av*: **hans ansikt var d- rødt** he blushed like a rose; **det var d- stille i værelset** it was so quiet in the room you could hear a pin drop.

dryp'pert *-en* gonorrhea; *(pop.)* clap.

+**drypp'/stein** *-en* stalactite.

***drys'je** *V drys, druste, drust* cf **drysse**

dryss' *-et* (=**drøss**) gentle fall, powder, shower: **et d- av blomster** a shower of blossoms.

+**drys'se** *V -et/dryste* (=***drysje**) 1 scatter, sprinkle, strew. 2 drift, fall, sift down; lose petals. 3: **d-ende full av** loaded with (e.g. a tree with blossoms).

dryss'/regn [+/rein] *-et* gentle rain; drizzle.

***dræ'ker** *pl of* **dråk**[1]

Drøb'ak' *Pln* city, Akershus.

+**drø'bel** *-en* cf **drøpel**

drøf'te *V -a/+-et/*-e* 1 debate, discuss, talk over. 2 *agr.* winnow grain.

+**drøf'telse** *-n* debate, discussion.

***drø'gje** *-t* small burden, load.

drø'le *V -te* dawdle, delay.

+**drøm'** *-men* (=***draum**) dream: **i d-me** in one's dreams.

+**drøm'me** *V drømte* (=***drøyme**) 1 dream (**om** of); **d- seg vekk** daydream. 2: **d-ende** absorbed, engrossed.

+**drøm'me/aktig** *A* - dreamlike.

+**drøm'mer** *-en, pl -e* dreamer.

+**drømmeri'** *-et* daydream, reverie.

+**drøm'me/slott** *-et* castle in the air, castle in Spain.

+**drøm'me/syn** *-et* vision.

+**drøm'me/tyder** *-en, pl -e* interpreter of dreams.

drønn' *-et* (=***drøn**) bang, boom, roar.

+**drøn'ne** *V -et/drønte* (=***drynje**) 1 boom, thunder. 2 (of cattle) low.

drø'pel *-elen, pl -ler* uvula.

+**drø's** *-et* chatter; gossip.

drø'se *V -te* jabber, prattle; gossip.

drøss' *-en/-et* (=**dryss**) crowd, number, throng: **han har en d- med penger** he has a lot of money, *(pop.)* he's loaded with dough.

+**drø'v** *N*: **tygge d-** chew the cud; *fig.* **tygge d- på noe** ponder about sth, hash sth over.

+**drø'vel** *-elen, pl -ler* cf **drøpel**

+**drø'v/tygge** *V -tygde, -tygd* chew the cud; *fig.* hash (sth) over and over.

+**drø'v/tygger** *-en* 1 *zool.* ruminant. 2 one who hashes things over interminably.

+**drøy'** *A* cf **dryg**

+**drøy'e** *V -de* cf **dryge**

***drøy'me** *V -de* cf **drømme**

***drøy'msken** *A -e/-i, pl -ne* absorbed, dreamy, preoccupied.

drøy'pe *V -te* drop, put drops (**i** in).

***drå'k**[1] *-a, pl drœker dial.* girl.

+**drå'k**[2] *-et* idler, loafer.

***drå'p** *-et* cf **drap**[1]

+**drå'pa** *-en* (=***dråpe**[2]) *hist.* Old Norse laudatory poem (in honor of a king or chieftain).

drå'pe[1] *-n* (=***drope**[1]) 1 drop: **de likner hverandre som to d-r vann** they are alike as two peas in a pod; **det er som en d- i havet** it is a drop in the bucket; **d-n som fikk begeret til å flyte over** the straw that broke the camel's back. 2 *arch.* drop, gutta.

***drå'pe**[2] *-a* cf **dråpa**

+**drå'pe/teller** *-en, pl -e* (=*/**teljar**) eyedropper, (medicine) dropper.

drå'pe/vis *Av* drop by drop.

drått' *-en* 1 current of air, draft. 2 dairy products. 3 tracebearer (on a harness).

+**ds.** =**dennes**

D/S =**dampskip**

d. s. s. =**den/det** +**samme**/***same som**

+**du'**[1] *V -dde* cf **duge**

du'[2] *Pn ob deg* you (used to address children, relatives, and close friends): **du, Arne** say, Arne; **du gode Gud!** good heavens!; **si du til en** address sby with "du", be close friends.

dualis'me *-n* dualism.

dubb' *-en* forty winks, nap.

dub'be *V -a/+-et* doze, nap.

dubiø's *A* 1 of dubious, questionable reputation. 2 *merc.*: **d-e fordringer** spurious claims, demands.

dublé *-en* 1 doublet (=two birds killed in the air at the same time with a double-barreled shotgun). 2 double (billiards). 3 filled gold.

duble're *V -te* 1 understudy (in movies, theater). 2 coat, plate (metal). 3 kill two birds in the air by shots fired in rapid succession from a double-barreled shotgun. 4 double (in billiards). 5 *mil.* launch an attack from two flanks. 6: **d- et tog** run an extra train (along with the regularly scheduled one).

dublett' *-en* 1 duplicate. 2 doublet (hunting). 3 double-barreled shotgun.

du'e[1] *-a* 1 dove, pigeon: **holde d-r** keep pigeons; *bibl.* **vær kloke som slanger og enfoldige som d-r** (Matthew 10,16) be as wise as serpents and harmless as doves. 2 *astron.* Columba, Noah's Dove (constellation). 3 clay target (skeet shooting).

+**du'e**[2] *V -dde* cf **duge**

+**du'elig** *A* - cf **dugelig**

duell' *-en* duel.

duellan't *-en* duelist.

duelle're *V -te* duel, fight a duel.

du'e/slag *-et* dovecote.

du'e/stegg *-en* male dove.

duett' *-en* duet.

duf's *-en* tassel, tuft.

+**duf't** *-en* 1 fragrance, odor, perfume. 2 *dial.* dust: **ikke en d-** not the slightest amount, bit.

+**duf'te** *V -a/-et* emit a fragrance; smell.

du'g *-en* ability, capacity, fitness.

***du'gande** *A* - 1 capable, clever. 2 abundant; plenty (**med** of).

du'ge *V -de* be fit, good, suitable (**til noe** for sth); amount (to sth): **det d-er ikke til noe** it's no good, not good for anything; **alt som d-de** everything that was worth anything, *fig.* everybody who was anybody; **han d-er ikke** he's not suitable (**til** for), no good (at); **hva d-er han til** what can he do, what's he good for?

du'gelig *A* - 1 able, capable, clever: **d- til** capable of, fit for. 2 goodly, substantial: **et d- verk** a real piece of work. 3 **d- med** lots of: **det kommer d- med regn** there'll be plenty of rain.

+**dugg'** *-en* cf **dogg**

+**dug'ge** *V -et* cf **dogge**

du'g/laus *A* incapable, unqualified.

***du'gleg** *A* - cf **dugelig**

***du'g/leik** *-en* ability, fitness (**til** for).

du'gnad *-en* collective work on a project (e.g. barn raising, husking bee); community project.

du'gurd *-en* morning meal, (second) breakfast.

du'gurds/økt *-a* period of work between first and second breakfast.

du'k *-en* 1 tablecloth: **holde disk og d-** maintain a separate residence. 2 cloth (esp. in *cpds*): **flagg/** etc. 3 canvas, sailcloth. 4 mesh, screen.

duka't *-en* ducat.

du'ke *V -a/+-et* 1 lay a tablecloth, set a table: **d- av** clear a table. 2 *naut.*: **d- opp på et seil** reef a sail.

dukk' *-en/-et* dip; ducking.

***duk'kar** *-en* cf **dykker**

+**duk'ke**[1] *-n* cf **dokke**[1]

duk'ke[2] *V -a/+-et* 1 *(intrans.)* dip, dive, duck: **d- fram (opp)** appear, pop up, turn up; **d- ned i noe** *fig.* immerse oneself in, try to get to the bottom of; **d- opp (av)** appear, loom out (of); **d- under** dive under the surface, *fig.* fail, go to the bottom. 2 bend, duck: **d- en** duck sby (in water); **d- (med) hodet (nakken)** duck, bow one's head; **d- seg** duck; bow one's head (in shame); stoop. 3 *fig.* put sby in his place, squelch.

duk'kert *-en* dip, dive; ducking: **gi en en d-** give sby a ducking; *fig.* take sby down a peg or two.

+**dukk'/nakket** *A* - bent, stooped.

duk's *-en* top student in a class.

***du'l** *-et* hiding: **leggje d- på** conceal sth.

***dul'd**[1] *-a* cover, shelter; silence: **i d-a** quietly, secretly.

***dul'd**[2] *A dult* concealed, hidden.

***dul'de** *pt of* **dylje**

+**dul'gte** *pt of* **dølge**

***dull'** *-et* puttering; coddling.

dul'le *V -a/+-et* 1 putter around (with): **d- med, om en** coddle, pamper sby. 2 *dial.* trot. 3 *dial.* dangle, swing.

+**dul'me** *V -a/-et* allay, relieve, soothe: **det virket d-ende på hans nerver** it soothed his nerves.

dul'p *-en* depression, hollow.

dul'pe *V -a/+-et* pulsate, throb.

***du'l/ram'** *A* reliable, trustworthy (in keeping secrets).

***du'l/sam'** *A* reserved, reticent.

***dul's/mål** *-et* secrecy, secret.

dul't[1] *-en* jab, poke (as a friendly means of directing sby's attention to sth).

+**dul't**[2] *A* - concealed, secret (cf **dølge**).

dul'te[1] *V -a/+-et* 1: **d- til en** bump, jab, poke sby. 2 *dial.* jog along, trot.

+**dul'te**[2] *pt of* **dølge**

dum [dom'] *A -t, pl -me* dumb, stupid: **det er d-t at** it's too bad that; **det var d-t gjort (sagt)** that was a stupid thing to do (say); **det var d-t av ham (meg) å** he (I) was a fool to; **det var ikke så d-t** that's a good idea; not bad; **jeg var d- nok til å** like a fool I; **være d- av seg** be stupid, on the stupid side; **være d- til å** be poor at (doing sth); **se, det fikk fanden fordi han var d-, og ikke beregnet sitt publikum** that's what the devil got because he was stupid, and didn't take his audience into account (Ibsen).

***dum'be**[1] *-a* dust.

dum'be**[2] *pp of* **dembe**[2] (=dumbi**)

***dum'bet(e)** *A* - dusty.

+**dum/dristig** [dom'/] *A* - foolhardy, rash.

+**dumdristig/het** [dom'-] *-en* foolhardiness, rashness.

dum'dum/kule *-a* dumdum bullet.

+**dum/het** [dom'/] *-en* dullness, foolishness, stupidity: **mot d-en kjemper selv gudene forgjeves** against stupidity the gods themselves struggle in vain (Schiller); **si en d-** put one's foot in one's mouth.

dumme [dom'me] *V -a/+-et*: **d- seg ut** make a fool of oneself.

dumme/petter [dom'me/] *-en* (=+/**peter**) buffoon, clown.

dumming [dom'ming] *-en* 1 *dial.* deaf-mute. 2 blockhead, fool.

dump[1] [dom'p] *-a/+-en* 1 hollow, depression; (hole in road) bump. 2 (of a sled, wagon) bottom, lower portion.

+**dump**[2] [dom'p] *+-et/*-en* dull sound, thud.

+**dump**[3] [dom'p, dum'p] *A* dull, hollow, muffled.

dumpe[1] [dom'pe] *V -a/+-et* 1 fall heavily, tumble. 2: **d- opp i noe** come, stumble across sth unexpectedly. 3 fail, flunk an examination.

+ Bokmål; * Nynorsk; ° Dialect.
After letter: ' stress (Acc. 1); ` tone, stress (Acc. 2); · length.
Below letter: . not pronounced.

dumpe[2] [døm'pe] V -a/+-et merc. dump (goods on the market).

dumpet(e) [dom'pet(e)] A - (of a road) bumpy, full of ruts.

dumping [døm'ping] -a/+-en dumping (of goods).

dumping/vare -a/+-en goods, merchandise dumped on the market.

dumrian [dom'-] -en blockhead, fool, simpleton.

dum/snill [dom'/] A -snilt kind to a fault.

dum/stolt A - pompous, stuck-up.

***du'n**[1] -en explosion, noise.

du'n[2] -a/+-et down: **ha d- på haken** fuzzy-cheeked.

***dun'de** pt of **dynje**

dun'der[1] -en 1 (kind of) card game. 2 mixture of denatured alcohol etc. concocted for drinking by derelicts.

dun'der[2] -eret/-ret/*-eren 1 roar, thunder. 2 the devil: **gå til d-s** go to blazes.

Dun'derlands/dalen Pln valley at the lower end of Ranafjord, Nordland.

dun'dre[1] -a pop. old bag, slob (woman).

dun'dre[2] V -a/+-et 1 boom, roar, thunder; bang, hammer: **d- løs** blaze, fire away. 2: **en d-ende fiasko** a colossal fiasco, a complete flop; **et d-ende kalas** a roaring party.

dun'dre/børse -a blunderbuss.

***du'ne** V -a boom, rumble.

du'net(e) A - downy, fluffy.

dunge[1] [dong'e] -n dial heap (**av** of); manure pile.

dunge[2] [dong'e] V -a/+-et dial. heap, pile (**opp** up).

dunk[1] [dong'k] -en can, jar, (small) keg.

dunk[2] [dong'k] -et/+-en knock, pound, thump; bump: **d- i d-** thud upon thud.

dunke [dong'ke] V -a/+-et 1 knock, pound, thump: **d- løs** hammer away. 2 beat, throb.

dunkel [dong'kel] A -elt, pl -le 1 (half)dark, dim; (of sound) dull, faint. 2 (of feelings, ideas, thoughts, etc.) obscure, unclear, vague: **en d- fornemmelse (erindring) av** an unclear, vague feeling (recollection) of; **en d- hentydning** a veiled hint.

+**dunkel/het** -en 1 darkness, dimness, obscurity. 2 abstruseness, vagueness; mysteriousness.

du'n/kjevle -t, pl +-r/*- bot. cattail, reed mace (Typha latifolia).

du'n/lerret -et (=*/**lereft**) cambric.

dun's[1] -en 1 thud, thump. 2 jab, push.

dun's[2] -en 1 steam, vapor. 2 (oppressive) feeling of distress.

dun'st -en/*-a (heavy) smell, reek, stench: **vinens d-er** the fumes of the wine.

dun'ste V -a/+-et 1 reek, stink. 2: **d- bort, vekk** evaporate, fade away.

***dun't** pp of **dynje**

du'n/unge [/onge] -n fledgling.

du'n/vær -et place where eiderdown is gathered.

dupe're V -te deceive, take in: **la seg d- av noen** allow oneself to be taken in by sby.

duplika't -et, pl -/+-er duplicate.

duplika'tor -en duplicator, mimeograph machine.

duplikk' -en jur. counter affidavit, rejoinder, surrejoinder.

duplise're V -te 1 duplicate. 2 jur. rejoin.

dup'lo N: **in d-** in duplicate.

dupp' -en 1 float (fishing). 2 (+-et) bob; nod.

dup'pe[1] -a fat (used to dip food in).

dup'pe[2] V -a/+-et 1 bob; doze, nod. 2 dip (sth).

du'r[1] -en boom, roar (e.g. of the sea); hum, noise.

du'r[2] en mus. major: **i samme d-** in the same key, and so on and so forth.

dura'bel A -elt, pl -le big, huge.

du'r/alumi'nium -en/-et duralumin.

du're V -te/*-a boom, roar (e.g. the sea), rumble.

+**dur'k/dreven** A -ent, pl -ne (=*/**driven**) crafty, cunning, shrewd.

dur'ra -en bot. durra, Guinea corn (Andropogon sorghum).

du's[1] -et/+-en dial. apathy, lethargy.

du's[2] N: **leve i sus og d-** live a riotous life, (pop.) really live it up.

du's[3] A using the informal pronoun "du": **drikke d- med en** drink a toast with sby symbolizing the discarding of the formal "De" for "du"; **bli d-** agree to discard "De" for "du".

du's[4] A - mellow, soft, subdued.

du's/bror -en, pl +-brødre/*-brør bosom friend; boon companion.

du'se V -te 1 doze. 2 carouse.

+**dusement** [dussemang'] A - pop. ailing, ill; dejected, depressed.

dusi'n -et, pl - dozen: **han er av dem som det går tolv av på d-et** people like him are a dime a dozen.

dusi'n/vare -a/+-en cheap goods, trash.

dusi'n/vis Av: **i d-** by the dozen; in great quantities.

dusj' -en shower (bath; apparatus).

dusj'/bad -et shower (bath).

dusj'e V -a/+-et 1 (take a) shower. 2 spray.

dus'k -en 1 bunch, cluster (of flowers, fruit). 2 tassel, tuft.

dus'ke V -a/+-et drizzle.

dus'ke/lue -a (=/**luve**) tasselled cap (esp. of cap worn by Norwegian university students).

dus'k/regn [+/rein, */rengn] -et gentle rain, light drizzle.

dusk/regne V infl as **regne** drizzle, mist.

dus't[1] -en nitwit, numskull.

***dus't**[2] -en cf **dyst**

dus't[3] -a/+-et dust; bit, particle: **ikke en (et) d-, ikke det d-, ikke d-a** not the slightest.

dus'te[1] V -a/+-et 1 dust, powder. 2: dial. **det d-er ikke** it's of no use, it's no good; **du d-er ikke mot ham** you don't begin to compare with him.

***dus'te**[2] pt of **dysje**

+**dus'te/forbund** -et: **Norsk D-** Norwegian League of Nitwits (hum. creation by Stabel in Dagbladet).

dus'tet(e) A - 1 dusty. 2 foolish, stupid.

dus'ting -en blockhead, nitwit.

dusø'r -en reward.

dut'te[1] V -a/+-et address sby as "du" before being invited to do so.

+**dut'te**[2] V -a/-et: **d- noe på en** try to blame sth on sby; push sth on sby.

***duv'de** pt of **dyvje, duve**

du've V -a/+-et/+-de 1 bob, rock; sway, wave. 2 naut. reef sail.

duv'l -et float.

***dval'de** pt of **dvelje**

dva'le -n 1 lethargy, torpor, trance. 2 hibernation: **ligge i d-** hibernate.

dva'le/drikk -en (=*/**drykk**) magic potion.

dva'le/tilstand -en/*-et hibernation.

***dval't** pp of **dvelje**

+**dvas'k** A inert, supine, torpid.

dvei'l -en naut. swab.

***dve'l** pr of **dvelje**

+**dve'le** V -te (=*-**je**) linger, tarry; pause: **d- ved** dwell on (a subject, a thought, etc.): **se d-ende på noe** let one's glance rest on sth.

***dvel'je** V dvel, dvalde, dvalt cf **dvele**

Dver'/berg Pln twp, Nordland.

dver'g -en dwarf; midget, pygmy.

dver'g/bjørk -a bot. dwarf birch (Betula nana).

dver'g/høne -a bantam (chicken).

dver'g/mål -et poet. echo.

dver'g/smie -t folk. piece of iron rubbed over abscesses and boils to cure them.

dver'g/stein -en rock crystal, quartz (transparent).

dvs. =**det vil** +**si**/***seie** i.e.

dy'[1] -et mire, mud.

dy'[2] V -dde: **d- seg** contain, restrain oneself, forbear: **hun kunne ikke d- seg for å si** she couldn't keep from saying.

d. y. =**den yngre**

+**dyb'de** -n depth(s); fig. profundity: **på 10 meters d-** at a depth of 10 meters; **lodde d-n av** sound the depth(s) of, fig. go to the bottom of; fig. **ikke gå i d-n** merely scratch the surface; **øyne d-n** see to the bottom, understand fully (Ibsen).

+**dyb'de/psykologi'** [/syk-] -en depth psychology.

dy'd -en 1 advantage, good point, merit. 2 chastity; virtue: **en d- av nødvendighet** a virtue of necessity; **sant for d-en** (expressing surprise) of all things; well, if it isn't . . .; I declare; (emphatic) certainly: take it from me.

dy'dig A - virtuous (incl. in the ironic sense); demure, prudish.

+**dy'dig/het** -en virtue; prudery.

+**dy'd/siret** A - virtuous (ironic); priggish, prudish, smug.

dy'ds/mønster -eret/-ret, pl -er/+-re paragon of virtue.

***dy'e** -a mire, mud.

dy'ende Av: **d- våt** wringing wet.

***dy'et(e)** A - muddy.

dyf'fel -en/+-et duffel (=coarse woolen cloth).

***dyg'd** -a 1 moral excellence, virtue. 2 strength.

***dyg'de/full** A good; virtuous.

***dyg'd/laus** A unprincipled; worthless.

***dygg'** A dygt solid, sound, substantial.

***dykk** Pn ob of **de**[3]

***Dykk** Pn ob of **De**

***dykkar** Pn po of **de**[3]

***Dyk'kar** Pn po of **De**

+**dyk'ke** V -a/-et dive, plunge.

+**dyk'ker** -en, pl -e (=***dukkar**) 1 (professional) diver; skin diver. 2 zool. bird that habitually dives, e.g. great crested grebe (Colymbus cristatus).

+**dyk'ker/klokke** -a diving bell.

+**dyk'ker/syke** -n the bends.

dyk'kert -en brad.

dyk'tig A - 1 able, capable, proficient. 2 goodly, substantial: **et d- spark** a healthy kick. 3 (adv.) extremely, very; lots of: **d- våt** soaking wet; **det var d- (med) mat** there was plenty to eat.

+**dyk'tig/gjøre** V -gjorde, -gjort: **d- seg for en stilling** prepare, qualify oneself for a position.

+**dyk'tig/het** -en 1 ability, competence, proficiency. 2 capable, competent person.

***dyl'je** V -dulde cf **dølje**

dyl'le -a bot. sow thistle (Sonchus oleraceus).

***dy'n**[1] -et cf **dønn**[1]

***dy'n**[2] pr of **dynje**

dynamikk' -en dynamics.

dyna'misk A - dynamic.

dynamitt' -en dynamite.

dynamitt'/patro'n +-en/*-a stick of dynamite.

dyna'mo -en dynamo, generator.

dynasti' -et, pl +-er/*- dynasty.

dynas'tisk A - dynastic.

+**dyn'd** -et cf **dynn**

dy'ne[1] -a feather quilt, eiderdown coverlet: **komme fra d-a i halmen** jump from the frying pan into the fire.

dy'ne[2] +-n/*-a dune.

Dy'ne/kilen Pln fjord in Sweden (between Iddefjord and Strømstad).

dy'ne/trekk -et bedtick, ticking (on a dyne).

dy'ne/var -et bedtick, ticking (on a dyne).

+**dyng'e**[1] -a (=*-**je**) heap, mass, pile: **bære i d-** collect, gather together; **en hel d-** a whole lot.

+**dyng'e**[2] V -a/-et (=*-**je**) heap, pile: **d- ned** (med) bury, overwhelm (with); **d- (seg) opp, sammen** accumulate, amass, p- up.

***dyng'je**[1] -a cf **dynge**[1]

***dyng'je**[1] *V -de* cf **dynge**[1]

***dyn'je** *V dyn, dunde, dunt* cf **dønne**

dyn'ke *V -a/+-et* 1 spray, sprinkle. 2 duck (sby) in snow.

dyn'ke/kost [/kost] *-en* sprinkling brush.

+**dynn'** *-et* mire, mud; ooze.

+**dy'p**[1] *-et* cf **djup**[1]

+**dy'p**[2] *A* cf **djup**[2]

+**dy'p/blå** *A -tt* cf **djup/**

+**dy'pere/liggenḍe** *A* - (more) profound.

+**dy'p/fryse** *V -te* cf **djup/**

dypp' *-et* dip, dipping.

dyp'pe *V -a/+-et* dip: **d- seg** take a dip.

+**dy'p/røḍ** *A* deep red.

+**dy'p/sindig** [also -sin'-] *A* - penetrating, profound.

+**dy'p/sinn** *-et* depth of insight, profundity.

+**dy'p/snø** *-en* cf **djup/**

***dyp't**[1] *-a* depth, profundity.

+**dyp't**[2] [also dy'pt] *nt of* **dyp**[2]

+**dy'p/tenkt** *A* - cf **djup/**

+**dyp't/fø'lt** *A* - heartfelt, sincere.

+**dyp't/gåenḍe** *A* - 1 *naut.* deep draft (vessel). 2 profound, searching, thorough.

+**dyp't/liggenḍe** *A* - deepset; *fig.* deepseated, profound.

+**dy'p/trykk** *-et typog.* copperplate (photogravure, rotogravure) printing.

+**dy'pvanns/fisk** *-en* deep-sea fish.

Dy'p/våg *Pln* twp, Aust-Agder.

dy'r[1] *-et* 1 animal, beast, brute. 2 deer, hart, stag; *hum.* lice, vermin. 3 *derog.* beast, brute (person); **gjøre til d-** bestialize. 4 creature: **et rart d-** *pop.* a strange bird.

dy'r[2] *A* 1 dear, expensive; precious: **en d- pris** a high price; **et d-t kjøp** a costly purchase; **mitt d-este eie** my most precious possession; **betale d-t for noe** pay dearly for sth; **selle sitt liv d-t** go down fighting; **være d- på noe** ask a high price for sth; **det blir en d- historie** it's going to cost a lot; **det ble en d- fornøyelse** it turned out to be an expensive business; **dette skal komme ham d-t å stå** *lit.* he'll pay dearly for this; **vi lever i d-e tider** everything is expensive nowadays. 2 (of an oath) solemn: **sverge høyt og d-t** take a solemn oath.

Dy're *Prn(m)*

+**dy're/bar** *A* dear, precious, priceless.

+**dy're/beskyt'telse** *-n* prevention of cruelty to animals.

dy're/goḍ *A* kind to animals.

+**dy're/kjøpt** *A* - (=***dyr/**) dearly bought, hard earned.

+**dy're/krets** *-en* (=***/krins**) zodiac.

dy're/rikeṭ *df* the animal kingdom.

dy're/skjelv *-en* buck fever.

dy're/steik *-a* roast venison.

+**dy're/temmer** *-en* (=***/temjar**) animal tamer, trainer.

dy're/venn *-en* (=***/ven**) animal lover.

dy're/vern [/væ'rn] *-et* prevention of cruelty to animals.

***dy'r/grip** *-en* costly, precious object.

dy'risk *A* - animal; bestial, brutish, swinish.

+**dyr'k/bar** *A* arable, cultivable.

dyr'ke *V -a/+-et* 1 cultivate (the earth, the mind, sby's acquaintance, etc.); grow, raise (crops, plants); till (the soil): **d- opp** cultivate (the earth). 2 (of activities) go in for, practice, pursue. 3 worship (a god); *fig.* idolize.

+**dyr'ker** *-en, pl -e* (=***-ar**) 1 cultivator, grower, tiller. 2 devotee, student. 3 votary, worshipper.

dyr'kings/lanḍ *-et* arable, tillable land; cultivated land.

***dy'r/kjøpt** *A* - cf **dyre/**

dy'r/lege *-n* (=***/lækjar**) veterinarian.

***dy'rne** *V -a* become more expensive.

+**dy'r/plager** *-en, pl -e* (=***-ar**) tormentor of animals.

+**dy'r/plageri'** *-et* (=***/plaging**) cruelty to animals.

+**dy'r/skue** *-t* animal fair.

dy'r/tid *-a/+-en* period, time of high prices, high cost-of-living.

dy'rtids/tillegg *-et* cost-of-living allowance.

dy'r/verdig *A* - dear, precious, valuable.

Dy'r/øy *Pln* twp, island, Troms.

***dy's**[1] *-a, pl -jar* small cairn, heap of stones.

***dy's**[2] *pr of* **dysje**

dy'se *-n* jet, nozzle.

dysenteri' *-en* dysentery.

***dys'je** *V dys, duste, dust* spray, sprinkle (very fine).

+**dys'se**[1] *-n archeol.* cromlech, dolmen (esp. as found in Denmark).

dys'se[2] *V -a/+-et* lull, soothe: **d- en inn i** lull sby into believing sth; **d- sin samvittighet i søvn** put one's conscience to sleep: **d- noe ned** hush up, suppress (e.g. a scandal).

+**dys't** *-en* (=***dust**[2]) 1 combat, fight; brawl. 2 dispute, polemics. 3 *hist.* joust, passage of arms, tilt.

dys'te *V -a/+-et/*-e* powder, sprinkle.

dys'ter *A -ert, pl -re* bleak, gloomy; depressing, melancholy, sombre.

dytt' *-en* jab, nudge, shove.

dyt'te *V -a/+-et/*-te* 1 jab, nudge; push, shove (e.g. a car): **d- noe på en** saddle sth on sby. 2 chink, plug up; tuck (**om** around).

***dy'v** *pr of* **dyvje**

dy'vels/drek *-en bot.* asafetida (genus Ferula; used extensively in folk medicine).

***dyv'je** *V dyv, duvde, duvt* 1 tremble, vibrate. 2 resound, thump.

dy'/våt *A* soaked (clear through), (dripping, sopping) wringing wet.

dæ'ger(e)n *I* (=**dæker(e)n**) darn it, heck (=**djevelen**).

***dæl'd** *-a* cf **deld**

***dæ'le** *-a* conduit, pipe.

***-dæmd** *A -dæmt* having the characteristic of; cf **god/**, **mørk/**.

***dæ'me**[1] *-t* appearance, color.

***dæ'me**[2] *V -de* color, give a certain appearance, aspect to.

***dæ'se** *V -te* grow faint, languish.

°**dæ'vel** *-en* devil (e.g. in exclamations and oaths): **d-en rive!** the d-!

+**dø'** *V -de/-dde, dødd* (=***døy**) die (**av** of): **dø bort (hen)** die down, (of sound) fade out; **dø for egen hånd** commit suicide; **dø ut** become extinct, die out; ***det fyrste du hever å gjera, mann, det er å døy når ikkje lenger du elska kan den fagre møy** the first thing for you to do, my man, is to die when you no longer can love a beautiful girl (Vinje).

dø'ḍ[1] *-en* (=***daude**[1]) death: **d- hvor er din brodd?** d- where is thy sting? (1 Cor. 15,55); **(guds) d- og pine (helvete, plage, piske, salte, sylte), pine (piskende) d-, guds d-** mild oaths; **d-sens trett** dead tired, (*pop.*) bushed; **på d- og liv, liv og d-** absolutely, definitely **(han vil på liv og d- gjøre det** he insists on doing it); **den visse d-** certain d-; **det blir min d-** it will be the d- of me; **den enes d- (er) den annens brød** one man's meat is another man's poison; **gi d-en og djevelen i noe** not give a damn about sth; **gå i d-en for en** die for sby; **kjede seg til d-e** be bored to d-; **ligge for d-en** be on one's last, on one's deathbed; **se ut som d-en i Lübeck (i Åpenbaringen)** look pale as d-, like a corpse.

dø'ḍ[2] *A* (=***daud**) dead, lifeless; (of the eyes, face) expressionless, (of parts of the body) numb: **d- for verden** d- to the world; *naut.* (of a ship) **d- på roret** unresponsive; (of a sail) **henge d-t** hang loose; (n sports) **hoppe (trå) d-t** commit a foul (by stepping over a limiting line, e.g. in broad jumping); **la de d-e begrave sine d-e** let the d- bury their d- (Matthew 8, 22); **legge ballen d-** stop the ball (with the feet in soccer); **legge en d- hånd på** hinder, put a damper on; **stå opp fra de d-e** rise from the d-; **Når vi d-e våkner** When We Dead Awaken (play by Ibsen).

+**dø'd/bringenḍe** *A* - deadly, fatal, mortal.

dø'ḍ/drukken [/drokken] *A +-ent, pl /drukne* dead drunk; *(pop.)* out cold.

+**dø'de**[1] *N* cf **død**[1]

+**dø'de**[2] *V -et* (=***døyde**) *archaic* slay; repress (emotions, urges, etc.): **å være seg selv er: seg selv å døde** to be oneself is to slay oneself (Ibsen).

dø'delig *A* - (=***døyeleg**) deadly, fatal, mortal: **d- forelsket** head over heels in love; **d- fornærmet** mortally offended; **med d- utgang** fatal.

+**dø'delig/het** *-en* mortality; mortality rate.

dø'ḍ/føḍt *A -/*-fødd* stillborn.

dø'ḍ/gang *-en* (=***daud/**) backlash (in machinery); play (in steering wheel).

+**dø'd/lignenḍe** *A* - deathlike; catatonic.

+**dø'dning** *-en* cf **dauding**

+**dø'dning(e)/hode** *-et* 1 death's-head, skull. 2 *zool.* death's-head moth (Acherontia atropos).

+**dø'dning(e)/ur** *-et zool.* deathwatch beetle (Anobium striatum).

dø'ḍ/punkt [/pongt] *-et, pl -/-er* (=***daud/**) dead center; *fig.* impasse: **komme til et d- i forhandlingene** reach a deadlock in the negotiations.

døds/angst [døt's/] *-en* (=***/angest**) fear of death; mortal dread, fear.

døds/annonse [døt's/annång'se] *-n* death notice, obituary.

+**døds/bo** *-et* (=***/bu**) *jur.* decedent estate.

døds/dag *-en* day of one's death: **til min d-** until my dying day.

døds/dom' *-men/*-en* death sentence: **felle d- over en** sentence sby to death.

døds/dømme *V -te* (=***/døme**) 1 sentence to death. 2: **dødsdømt** condemned to death; doomed, ill-fated.

+**dødsens** [døt'sens] *Av* 1 deadly, mortally: **være d-** be certain to lose one's life, doomed. 2 extremely, terribly: **han er d- alvorlig** he is in dead earnest; **være d- trett** be dead tired.

døds/fall [døt's/] *-et* death.

døds/fiende *-en* mortal enemy.

+**døds/forak't** *-en* utter disregard of personal safety: **gå på med d-** tackle sth with unflinching courage.

døds/kamp *-en* death agony, throes.

døds/leie *-t* deathbed: **ligge på d-t** lie at death's door.

døds/maske *-a/-en* death mask.

+**døds/merket** *A* - (=***/merkt**) doomed, marked (for death).

døds/messe *-a/+-en* mass for the dead, requiem.

døds/rike *-t* realm of the dead.

+**døds/seiler** *-en, pl -e* (=***/seglar, */siglar**) 1 phantom ship = the Flying Dutchman. 2 doomed, sinking ship: **det er en d-** it (an enterprise) is foredoomed to failure.

døds/sjuk *A* mortally ill.

døds/sprang *-et* death leap.

+**døds/stille** *A* - deathly still, quiet as the grave.

døds/straff *-en* capital punishment, death penalty.

+**døds/syk** *A* cf **/sjuk**

døds/synḍ *-a/+-en* mortal sin.

+**døds/trett** *A* - dog-tired, exhausted.

+ Bokmål; * Nynorsk; ° Dialect.
After letter: ' stress (Acc. 1); ' tone, stress (Acc. 2); · length.
Below letter: . not pronounced.

døds/ulyk'ke -a/⁺-en (=*/ulukke) fatal accident.
⁺dø'd/vann -et (=*daud/vatn) 1 naut. dead water, slack water. 2 fig. backwater, stagnation: ligge i d-e stagnate.
dø'd/vekt -a/⁺-en (=*daud/) 1 naut. dead weight. 2 sports handicap. 3 fig. any heavy, oppressive burden.
⁺dø'ende A - dying; (as noun) (a) dying person, one who is dying.
⁺dø'ge/nikt [also dø'-] -en good-for-nothing, worthless bum.
dø'ger -eret/-ret cf døgn
dø'ger/vill A -vilt 1 having lost track of the time (or of the day). 2 confused, lost.
døgn [⁺døy'n, *døng'n] -et (=døger) 1 twenty-four hours, day and night: d-et rundt around the clock; til alle d-ets tider at all hours. 2 d-ets ephemeral: d-ets smak fashion of the day.
⁺døgn/flue [døy'n/] -a (=*/fluge) 1 zool. May fly (order Ephemerida). 2 ephemera, passing fashion.
døgn/liv -et ephemeral, transitory life.
døgn/vill A -vilt cf døger/
døkk' A døkt dark, gloomy, murky.
***døk'kast** V -ast become dark, gloomy.
dø'l[1] -en 1 dalesman, mountaineer. 2 awkward, clumsy person; (pop.) hick, square.
***dø'l[2]** pr of dølje
dø'le/hest -en large, sturdy horse bred in Eastern Norway.
dø'le/mål -et upland mountain dialect (used only of the dialects of the East Norwegian valleys).
⁺døl'g N: legge d- på noe conceal sth, make a secret of sth.
⁺døl'ge V dulte, dult (=*dølje) conceal, hide (emotion, feeling): d- for attempt to conceal, deny sth; jeg kan ikke d- for at I can't conceal the fact that; dult secret; (half) concealed, repressed.
⁺døl'gs/mål -et cf døls/
***døl'je** V døl, dulde, dult cf dølge
dø'lsk A 1 indigenous, native. 2 boorish, rustic, uncouth; (pop.) hick, square.
⁺døl's/mål -et concealment, secret: uten d- without trying to conceal anything; fødsel i d- jur. c- of birth; ikke legge d- på make no c- of.
dø'me[1] -t, pl - example, illustration: *til d-s for example.
***dø'me[2]** V -de cf dømme
***-døme** -t cf -dømme
døm'me V ⁺dømte/*dømde (=*døme[2]) 1 jur. convict, pass judgment, sentence; condemn: d- en fra livet condemn sby to death; d- en skyldig find sby guilty, convict sby; d- en til å betale fine sby; bli d-t skyldig i be convicted of, found guilty of. 2 evaluate, judge: d- om express an opinion about; etter alt å d- to all appearances, apparently; etter det å d- according to, judging by that. 3 (in sports) referee, umpire: d- frispark award a free kick (in soccer). 4 d-t condemned, doomed: planen er d-t til å mislykkes the plan is doomed to failure.
-døm'me -t, pl ⁺-r/*- (=*-døme) suffix denoting authority or the limits thereof; cf herre/, konge/.
døm'me/evne -a/⁺-en judgment.
døm'me/kraft -a/⁺-en judgment.
døm'mende A - judicial: d- myndighet judicial power, the judiciary.
døm'me/sjuk A carping, censorious, faultfinding.
døm'me/sjuke -n carping, censoriousness, faultfinding.
dønn'[1] -et (=*døn) boom, rumble; echo, (hollow) thump.
⁺dønn'[2] Av fam. completely, quite, right: det er d- umulig it's completely impossible.
Døn'na Pln large island, Nordland.
⁺døn'ne V -et/dønte boom, rumble; echo, resound.
Døn'nes Pln twp, Nordland.
døn'ning -en breaker(s), roller(s), wave; ground swell, swell.
⁺dø'pe V -te (=*døype) 1 baptize, christen: han ble d-t Per he was christened P-. 2 fig. name.
⁺dø'pe/font -en (=*døype/) baptismal font.
⁺dø'pe/navn -et (=*døype/namn) Christian name, given name.
⁺dø'per -en, pl -e (=*døypar) 1 baptist: Johannes d-en John the Baptist. 2: d-e Anabaptists.
dø'r -a door: for lukkede d-er in secret, secretly; for åpne d-er in public, publicly; på d- med ham! out with him!; bo d- i d- med live right next door to; gå stille i d-ene be (make oneself) inconspicuous; jage (kaste) en på d- turn (throw) sby out; renne på d-ene hos en pester sby (with too frequent visits); sette på d- dash out, rush away; stå for d-en be at hand, be imminent.
dø'r/fylling -a door panel.
⁺dør'g(ende) Av (=dorgende): d- stille stock-still.
***dør'gje** V -de fish by trolling.
dø'r/gløtt -en door opening: Randi stakk hodet inn i d-en R- stuck her head in the door (Falkberget).
⁺dø'r/hammer -en, pl -hamrer (=/hammar) knocker.
dør'k -en naut. deck.
dø'r/karm -en door frame.
dør'/slag -et 1 punch (tool). 2 colander.
dø'r/sprekk -en 1 chink, crack, narrow opening of a door. 2 slit (in door, for mail).
dø'r/stokk -en doorstep, sill, threshold.
dø'rstokk/mil -a: d-a er alltid lengst the first step is always the hardest (hum. of slow leave-takings).
⁺dø'r/terskel -elen, pl -ler (=*/treskel) doorstep, sill, threshold.
⁺dø'r/trinn -et doorstep, sill, threshold.
dø'r/vakt -a/⁺-en doorman, guard.
⁺dø'r/vokter -en (=*/vaktar) doorman, guard.
⁺dø'r/vrier -en (=*/vridar) doorknob.
dø's -en doze, drowsiness; apathy, lethargy; coma, stupor: falle i en d- doze off; ligge i en d- be in a coma.
dø'se V -te 1 doze (av off); be apathetic, lethargic: d- tiden hen loaf away the time. 2 (of lamp, light) burn dimly.
dø'sen A ⁺-ent, pl -ne 1 drowsy, somnolent; indolent, sluggish. 2 (of lamp, light) burning dimly.
⁺dø'sig A - =døsen.
⁺døt're pl of datter
døt'rer pl of datter, dotter
dø'v A (=*dauv) deaf: d- for deaf to, heedless of; han vendte det d-e øre til meg my words fell on deaf ears.
⁺dø've V -de/-et cf døyve
⁺dø'v/het -en deafness.
dø'v/hø'rt A - (=*dauv/høyrd) hard of hearing.
dø'v/stum' A -t, pl -me (=*dauv/) deaf and dumb; (a) deaf-mute.
***døy'** V -dde cf dø
***døy'ande** A - dying: til sin d- dag to his d- day.
***døyd'de** pt of døy, døyde
***døy'de** V -dde cf døde[2]
⁺døy'e V -de/-et endure, put up with, suffer: hun kunne ikke d- ham she couldn't stand him.
***døy'eleg** A - cf dødelig
***døy'par** -en cf døper
***døy'pe** V -te cf døpe
***døy'pe/font** -en cf døpe/
døy't en: ikke en d- not a bit, not the slightest; jeg gir ikke en d- for alle dine argumenter I don't care two hoots for all your arguments.
døy've V -de (=⁺døve) 1 deaden, mute, soften (pain); dull (an edge); d- sin samvittighet calm, appease one's conscience. 2 humble, overpower; curb, restrain: d- seg control oneself; ingen hadde d-et ham i en diskusjon no one had gotten the better of him in a discussion.
⁺då'[1] -en zool. fallow deer (Cervus dama).
då'[2] -en (=dåe) bot. hemp nettle (Galeopsis tetrahit).
***då'[3]** Av, C cf da[1,2]
d. å. =dette år
⁺då'b -en cf dåp
då'd -en (heroic) act, deed; achievement, exploit: i råd og d- in word and deed; endelig engang en d- action at last (Ibsen).
⁺då'd/løs A (=*/laus) inactive, inert; unheroic.
då'd/rik A poet. glorious, heroic.
då'ds/kraft ⁺-en/*-a heroic force.
då'ds/lyst -a/⁺-en ambition, urge to action.
⁺då'ds/trang -en ambition, urge to action.
då'ds/verk -et (heroic) action, deed.
då'/dyr -et zool. fallow deer (Cervus dama).
då'e -n cf då[2]
***då'en** A -e/-i, pl -(e)ne deceased.
***då'/fu'rde** V -a be thunderstruck.
***då'leg** A - cf dårlig
då'm -en 1 aspect, color. 2 flavor, tang, taste.
***då'm/laus** A colorless, odorless.
***då'ne[1]** pl of dåen
då'ne[2] V -a/⁺-te 1 faint (av, bort, hen away), swoon. 2 decline, fade (bort, hen, vekk away).
då'p -en baptism, christening: bære et barn til d-en act as godmother to a child.
då'ps/attes't -en baptismal, birth certificate.
då'ps/ba'rn -et, pl -/*-born child to be baptized, christened.
då'ps/dag -en day of baptism, christening.
då'ps/kjole -n baptismal, christening dress.
då'ps/pakt -a/⁺-en eccl. baptismal covenant.
⁺dårak'tig A - archaic foolish.
då're[1] -n fool, simpleton: en d- kan spørre mer enn ti vise kan svare a fool can ask more questions than ten wise men can answer; Vårherre er alle d-rs formynder the Lord looks out for fools.
då're[2] V -a/⁺-et charm, ensnare, fascinate; deceive, dupe; archaic seduce.
då're/kiste a/⁺-en archaic insane asylum, madhouse.
då'rlig A - 1 ill: føle seg d- feel sick; se d- ut not look well. 2 bad (weather, food, mood, etc.); of low quality, poor (book, sight, memory, etc.), low (grade): ha d- hjerte (øyne, bein, osv.) have a bad heart (eyes, legs, etc.); ha d- tid (råd) have little time (money); være d- til beins be poor at walking; være d- til å be poor, not good at; det var ikke d- that's not bad, that's pretty good. 3 bad (=immoral): d- selskap bad company; leve et d- liv live immorally; det var d- gjort that was a mean trick.
⁺då'rlig/het -en 1 folly, vanity. 2 depravity, evil, wickedness.
då'r/skap -en folly, piece of folly.
då'se -n small box, case (e.g. for needles, pins, powder, etc.); tin.
då'se/mat -en fam. canned food.
då'se/mikkel -elen, pl -mikler blockhead, nitwit; (pop.) dope.
då'set(e) A - bungling, stupid.
***dått'** Av: eg vart so d- ved I got a real start.
***dåt'teleg** A - sudden, unexpected.

E

e *-en* (letter, *mus.* note) E, e.

eau de cologne [ådøkålån'je] *-n* Eau de Cologne.

eau de vie [ådøvi'] *-en* type of brandy.

+**eb'be**[1] *-n* ebb, ebb tide: **e- og flod** ebb and flow; *fam.* **det var e- i kassa** the funds were running low.

+**eb'be**[2] *V -a/+-et* ebb; *fig.* (of strength, life, etc.) diminish: **e- ut** fade away.

ebonitt' *-en* ebonite.

+**e'd** *-en* (=***eid**[1]) oath: **avlegge ed** take an o- (**på** on); **gi (gjøre) sin ed på at** swear that; **falsk ed** perjury; **ta en i ed** swear sby in.

+**eda'mer** *-en, pl -e* Edam (cheese).

+**eda'mer/ost** [/ost] *-en* (=***e'dam/**) Edam cheese.

Ed'da *Prn* Edda: **den eldre E-** the Elder (Poetic) E- (collection of Old Norwegian poems of gnomic, heroic, and mythical content); **den yngre E-** the Younger (Prose) E-, (textbook in poetics by Snorri Sturluson, ab. 1122).

ed'da/dikt *-et* Eddic poem.

+**ed'der/kopp** *-en* spider.

ed'dik *-en* vinegar: *fig.* **han er sur som e-** he's a real sourpuss.

ed'dik/krukke [/krokke] *-a* vinegar pitcher: **være sur som en e-** be a sourpuss.

ed'dik/sur *A* vinegary; *chem.* acetic.

ed'dik/syre *-a* acetic acid.

e'del *A -elt, pl -le* noble: **e- dåd** heroic deed; **e- vin** fine wine; **edle metaller** precious metals; *(comp.)* **de e-ere deler** the vital parts (of the body); **e-ere følelser** gentler emotions, one's better self.

e'del/gass *-en* inert gas.

+**e'del/gran** *-a bot.* silver fir (Abies pectinata).

e'delig *A -* under oath: **e- forklaring, utsagn** affidavit, deposition.

e'del/metall' *-et* precious metal.

e'del/mod *-et* nobility (of spirit); magnanimity.

e'del/modig *A -* noble-minded; generous, magnanimous.

e'del/stein *-en* (=+**/sten**) gem, precious stone.

e'den *et* Eden.

+**e'der** *Pn ob of* **I**[3]

+**ed'er/dun** *-a/-et* eiderdown.

+**e'ders** *Pn po of* **I**[3]

+**e'd/feste** *V -a/-et* (=***eid/**) put under oath, swear in.

edik't *-et, pl +-er/*-* edict.

e'dru *A - pl +-/*-e* sober: **han hadde nytt en del, men han var helt e-** he had been imbibing a bit, but he was completely s-.

edru'elig *A -* sober; abstemious, temperate.

+**edru'elig/het** *-en* sobriety; abstemiousness, temperance.

e'dru/skap *-en* sobriety; abstemiousness, temperance.

+**e'ds/formula'r** *-en* (=***eids/**) (prescribed) formula for an oath.

+**e'd/svoren** *A -ent, pl -ne* (=***eid/**) sworn: **e- translatør** (also:) authorized translator.

E'd/øy *Pln* twp, Møre og Romsdal.

efeme'r *A -* ephemeral.

effek't *-en* 1 effect; sensation: **gjøre e-** create a s-; **jage etter e-** strain for an e-. 2 *tech.* output, power. 3 *(pl)* chattels, effects; negotiable stocks and bonds.

effek't/full *A* impressive, striking; effective.

ef'fektiv *A* effective, efficient; actual: **forbudet var helt e-t** the ban was totally effective; **gjøre noe e-t** do sth efficiently; **e-e hestekrefter** a- horsepower.

effektivise're *V -te* make more efficient.

effektivite't *-en* effectiveness, efficiency.

+**effek't/jageri'** *-et* sensationalism; straining for effect.

effektue're *V -te* execute, put into effect; *merc.* fill (an order).

°**ef'ta** *-en* afternoon.

***ef'tan** *-en* cf **aftan**

ef'tas/verd [/vær] *-en* (=***eftans/**) (about rural conditions) afternoon meal, eaten between 3 and 4 o'clock.

+**ef'ter** *P* cf **etter**

+**ef'terat** *C* cf **etter**

+**efterdi'** *C* because, inasmuch as.

+**ef'ter/følger** *-en, pl +-e* cf **etter/**

+**ef'tergiven/het** *-en* cf **ettergiven/**

+**efterhver't** *Av* cf **etter**

+**efterhån'den** *Av* cf **etter-**

+**ef'ter/ligne** *V -et* cf **etter/likne**[1,2]

+**ef'ter/nøler** *-en* cf **etter/**

+**ef'ter/retning** [also -ret'-] *-en* cf **etter/**

+**efterrett'telig** *A -* cf **etter-**

+**ef'ter/som'** *C* cf **etter/**

e'føy *-en* ivy (Hedera helix).

***e'g**[1] *-et* cf **jeg**[1]

***e'g**[2] *Pn ob meg, po min* cf **jeg**[2]

ega'l *A* 1 (of persons) calm, even-tempered. 2 *mus.* even, smooth (of the execution of a passage).

egalite't *-en mus.* evenness, smoothness of execution.

eg'd *-en* (=**egde**) person from Agder.

+**Ege'er/havet** *Pln* (=***Ege/**) Aegean Sea.

+**e'gen**[1] *A nt egent/eget, df sg egne, pl egne* distinctive, peculiar, strange: **geitost har en e- smak** goat cheese has a d- taste; **han er en e- skrue** he's an oddball; **være e- av seg** be a bit p-; **det var noe eget ved ham** there was sth unusual about him.

+**e'gen**[2] *A nt eget, df sg egen, pl egne* own cf **eigen**

+**e'gen/art** *-a/-en* peculiarity; distinctive quality.

+**e'gen/artet** *A -* peculiar, singular.

+**e'gen/hendig** *A -* cf **eigen/**

+**e'gen/het** *-en* peculiarity; oddness.

+**e'gen/interes'se** *-n* self-interest.

+**e'gen/kjærlig** *A -* egotistic(al), selfish.

+**e'gen/mektig** *A -* arbitrary, despotic, (of methods) high-handed.

+**e'gen/navn** *-et* proper name.

+**e'gen/nytte** *-n* egotism, self-interest, selfishness.

+**e'gen/rådig** *A -* headstrong, obstinate, self-willed.

+**e'gen/sindig** *A -* headstrong, obstinate, self-willed.

+**e'gensindig/het** *-en* obstinacy, pigheadedness, wilfulness.

+**e'gen/skap** *-en* characteristic, property, quality; qualification: **min svigermor har vel mange gode e-er også** I suppose my mother-in-law has many good qualities too; **han har den e- at** it is characteristic of him that; **i e- av statsråd snakket han for folket** in his capacity as cabinet member he spoke for the people.

+**e'gentlig** *A -* (=***eigen(t)leg**) 1 actual, proper, real, true: **i ordets e-e betydning** in the t- sense of the word; **i e- forstand** in the p- sense (of the word); **det er ikke noe e- nederlag** it is not an a- defeat; **denne krigen er forspillet til den store, e-e striden** this war is the prelude to the great struggle p- (Evensmo). 2 *(adv.)* actually, in reality: **tror du e- det?** do you really think so?; **e- burde jeg gå hjem, men—** strictly speaking I should go home, but—; **hvor gammel er du e-?** how old are you, anyway?.

+**e'gen/vekt** *-a/-en phys.* specific weight.

Egersun'd *Pln* town, Rogaland.

+**e'get** *nt of* **egen**[1,2]

***e'g/form** *-a* **first person: i e-a** in the first person.

egg'[1] *-a/-en* 1 edge (of knife, sharp stone, etc.). 2 sharp, narrow mountain ridge (also on island or reef): **langsmed e-en han (bukken) og jeg skar oss gjennom været vei** along the ridge he (the buck) and I cut through the thin air (Ibsen).

egg'[2] *-et* egg.

***-egga** *A -* cf **-egget**[1]

egg'/celle *-a/+-en* egg cell.

+**eg'ge** *V -a/-et* (=***eggje**) 1 egg on, incite, urge (often with **opp**): **e- seg opp** work oneself up. 2 edge, put an edge on (ax, knife, etc.).

Eg'ge *Pln* twp, Nord-Trøndelag; postoffice, Lier twp, Buskerud.

Eg'ge/dal *Pln* parish, Buskerud.

eggedo'sis *-en* yolks of egg beaten together with sugar.

eg'ge/glas *-et* (=+**/glass**) egg cup.

+**eg'ge/hvite** *-n* cf **/kvite**

eg'ge/krem *-en* soft custard (for filling, topping, etc.).

eg'ge/kvite *-n* (=+**/hvite**) albumen, egg white.

eg'gekvite/stoff *-et* albumen.

eg'ge/plomme *-a/-en* egg yolk.

eg'ge/røre *-a* scrambled eggs.

eg'ge/sjuk *A* (about hen) restless, trying to find a place to lay an egg; *fam.* impatient (e.g. to say sth), restless: **hun gjeter ham som en e-høne** she keeps an eye on him like a fidgety hen (Aanrud).

eg'ge/skal *-et* (=+**/skall**) egg shell.

+**-egget**[1] *A -* (=***-egga**) zygotic (e.g. monozygotic, dizygotic twins).

+**-egget**[2] *A -* (=***-eggja**) -edged (e.g. two-edged sword).

+**eg'ge/varmer** *-en, pl -e* (=***-ar**) cf **egg/**

egg'/forma *A -* (=+**-et**) egg-shaped, ovoid.

+**egg'/formig** *A -* egg-shaped, ovoid.

eg'ging *-a/+-en* egging on, incitement, urging.

***-eggja** *A -* cf **-egget**[2]

***eg'gje** *V -a* cf **egge**

egg'/jern [/jæ'rn] *-et* (=***/ja'rn**) edged tool.

+**egg'/leder** *-en, pl -e* (=***/leiar**) Fallopian tube, oviduct.

egg'/stokk *-en* ovary.

egg'/stål *-et* edged tool.

+**egg'/varmer** *-en, pl -e* (=+**egge/**, ***-ar**) egg coddler, egg warmer; *hum.* fur cap.

egg'/vær *-et* bird rock (where the eggs of seabirds are gathered).

E'gil *Prn (m)*

eg'le *V -a/+-et* bait, goad, heckle: **e- opp** b-, egg on; **e- seg inn på** pick a quarrel with.

eg'let(e) *A -* cantankerous, quarrelsome.

+**egn** [ei'n] *-en* district, region; neighborhood: **en mann her fra e-en** a man from these parts.

+**egne**[1] [ei'ne] *V -a/-et*: **e- seg** 1 be fit, suited (**til** for); lend itself (**til** to); **han e-er seg ikke til å være lærer** he's not cut out to be a teacher; **den slags musikk e-er seg ikke til kirkebruk** that sort of music isn't suitable for use in church; **e-et til** suited for; likely to; **bemerkningen var e-et til å vekke mistanke** the remark was liable to arouse sus-

+ Bokmål; * Nynorsk; ° Dialect. After letter: ' stress (Acc. 1); ` tone, stress (Acc. 2); · length. Below letter: . not pronounced.

picion. 2 be congenial, suitable (for for, to): det e-er seg ikke for meg it doesn't appeal to me, doesn't suit me.
egne[2] [eng'ne] V -a/+-te/*-de bait (fishing line).
+e'gne[3] pl of egen[1,2]
egois'me -n ego(t)ism.
egois't -en egotist.
egois'tisk A - egotistic(al).
egosen'trisk A - egocentric.
*eg'se[1] -t agitation(of nimd),excitement.
*eg'se[2] V -a incite, stir up.
Egyp't Pln Egypt.
+egyp'ter -en, pl -e (=*-ar) Egyptian.
egyp'tisk A - Egyptian.
ei'[1] Av archaic not: Peer, du lyver! Nei, jeg gjør ei. Peer, you're lying! No, I'm not. (Ibsen); «den gang ei,» sa Tordenskjold you didn't succeed that time (see under dengang); (hva) enten han vil eller ei whether he likes it or not.
ei'[2] Art, Num f of ein[1,2], en[1,2]
ei'[3] I hey, oh (in surprise or amazement).
+ei'a I archaic ah (in great joy or exhilaration): e- var vi der would that we were there (hymn).
*ei'd[1] -en cf ed
ei'd[2] -et isthmus.
Ei'd Pln twp, Sogn og Fjordane; twp, Møre og Romsdal.
Eidang'er Pln twp, Telemark.
Ei'de Pln twp, Aust-Agder; twp, Møre og Romsdal.
*ei'd/feste V -a cf ed/
Ei'd/fjo'rd Pln twp, Hordaland.
Ei'ds/berg [also æs'ber] Pln twp, Østfold.
Ei'dsiva/ting -et jurisdictional district comprising at present Oslo, Akershus, Østfold, Hedmark, Oppland and Buskerud counties, but covering in earlier periods of Norwegian history a smaller and varying area.
Ei'd/skog Pln twp, Hedmark.
Ei'ds/voll Pln town and twp, Akershus, site of the signing of the Norwegian Constitution in 1814.
*ei'd/svoren A -e/-i, pl -ne cf ed/
+ei'e[1] et (=*eige[1]) ownership, possession: få noe til e- acquire (gain p- of) sth; ta i e- take p- of; gå i arv og e- be handed down from generation to generation.
+ei'e[2] V -de/åtte, -d/ått (=*eige[2]) have, own, possess: han eier ikke en øre he hasn't got a red cent; hun eier ikke skam she has no sense of shame; dial. ha til eiendes own.
*ei'e[3] V -a: e- seg complain, lament.
*ei'e[4] I: e- meg woe is me.
+ei'e/form -a/-en gram. genitive.
+ei'e/god A extremely good, kindhearted.
*ei'end -a/-et grain sprouts.
+ei'en/del -en piece of property, possession; (pl) belongings, effects: jordiske e-er worldly goods.
+ei'en/dom' -men (=*eige/) possession(s), property; estate, grounds: fast e- real e-; en stor e- a large e-.
+eiendom'melig A - peculiar, remarkable, strange.
+eiendom'melig/het -en peculiarity; distinctive feature, special trait.
+ei'endoms/besitter -en, pl -e land owner, proprietor.
+ei'endoms/løs A unpropertied.
+ei'endoms/megler -en, pl -e real estate agent.
+ei'endoms/prono'men -et possessive pronoun.
+ei'endoms/rett -en 1 ownership (til of); rights, title (til to). 2 jur. (law of) property: avskaffe e-en abolish private property.
+ei'endoms/skatt -en property tax.
+ei'er -en, pl -e (=*eigar) owner: skifte e- change hands.
+eierin'ne -a/-en owner, proprietress.
+ei'er/mann -en, pl -menn owner.
*ei'g pr of eige[2]
ei'ga f of eigen
*ei'gar -en cf eier
*ei'gar/mann -en, pl -menn(er) cf eier/
*ei'ge[1] -a/-et cf eie[1]
*ei'ge[2] V eig, åtte, ått cf eie[2]
ei'ge[3] nt of eigen
*ei'ge/dom -(m)en cf eien/
*ei'gedoms/skatt -en cf eiendoms/
*ei'geleg A - worth owning.
ei'gen A f eiga, nt eige, pl eigne (=+egen[2]) own, private, separate: i eget navn in one's o- name; på e-hånd independently, of one's o- accord; til +eget/*eige bruk for personal use; det er din e- skyld it's your o- fault; jeg har sett det med mine egne øyne I've seen it with my o- eyes; det er av sine egne en skal ha det one's o- family is one's best critic, the hardest blows come from one's o- family; være sin e- herre be on one's o-.
ei'gen/hendig A - by (one's own) hand: underskrive e- sign personally.
*ei'gen/interes'se -a cf egen/
*ei'genleg A - cf egentlig
*ei'gen/skap -en cf egen/
*ei'gentleg A - cf egentlig
*ei'gen/vekt -a cf egen/
Ei'ger/sund Pln twp, Rogaland.
Ei'gil Prn(m)
*ei'gn -a possession, property.
*ei'gne[1] V -a: e- til seg appropriate, claim as one's own.
ei'gne[2] pl of eigen
*ei'gne/lut -en, pl -er (=/lott) piece of property, possession; (pl) belongings.
ei'k[1] -a oak (tree).
+ei'k[2] -en cf eike[1]
ei'ke[1] -a (=+eik[2]) spoke (of wheel).
+ei'ke[2] -a (=*eikje) narrow flat-bottomed boat, punt.
Ei'ke/fjo'rd Pln twp, Sogn og Fjordane.
ei'ke/lauv -et oak leaf.
Ei'ken Pln twp, Vest-Agder.
ei'ke/nøtt -a (=*/not) acorn.
Ei'ker Pln: Nedre E- twp, Buskerud; Øvre E- twp, Buskerud.
Ei'keren Pln lake, Buskerud.
Ei'kes/dalen Pln valley, Eresfjord twp, Møre og Romsdal.
ei'ke/skog -en oak forest.
ei'ke/tre' -et, pl +-trær/*- oak (tree).
ei'ke/tres A - oaken.
*ei'kje -a cf eike[2]
*ei'kor f of einkvan
*ei'kor/leis Av in one way or another.
*ei'/leis Av in one way or another.
Ei'lif' (-liv) Prn(m)
ei'm -en 1 steam, vapor. 2 fragrance, odor.
ei'me V -a/+-et 1 steam. 2 smell.
*ei'n[1] Art f ei, nt eit cf en[1]
*ei'n[2] Num f ei, nt eitt cf en[2]
*ei'n[3] Pn cf en[3]
ein- Pf mono-, one-.
Ei'na Pln twp, Oppland.
*ei'n/aktar -en cf en/akter
einan'nan Pn (=-annen) cf hinannen
*ei'nar -en cf ener[1]
Ei'nar Prn(m)
*ei'n/arving -en cf ene/
*ei'nast(e) A - cf eneste
*ei'n/boren [/båren] A -e/-i, pl -ne cf en/båren
*ei'n/bue -n (=ein(e)/buar) cf ene/boer
ei'n/bøle -t isolated, out-of-the-way farm.
ei'n/bø'lt A - (of farm) isolated, remote.
*ei'n/cella A - cf en/cellet
*ei'n/celling -en one-celled organism.
*ei'ne[1] -n cf einer
*ei'ne[2] V -a/-te combine, join, unite.
ei'ne/busk -en juniper bush.
ei'ne/bær -et juniper berry.
*ei'n/egga A - cf en/egget
+ei'ne/låg -en (=*/log) water boiled with juniper, used in cleaning (e.g. wooden containers).
ei'ner -en, pl +-e (=*eine) bot. juniper (Juniperus vulgaris).
+ei'ner/busk -en cf eine/
+ei'ner/bær -et cf eine/
*ei'ne/rett -en cf ein/
+ei'ner/låg -en cf eine/
*ei'ne/tale -n cf ene/
*ei'ne/velde -t cf ein/
*ei'n/felde -t plainness, simplicity.
ei'n/felt A - plain, simple; (of person) straightforward.
*ei'n/gifte -t cf en/
*ei'n/gong Av cf engang
ei'n/herje -n (in Scandinavian mythology) fallen warrior dwelling in Valhalla.
*ei'n/huga A - adamant, single-minded.
*ei'n/hyrning -en cf en/hjørning
*ei'nig A - cf enig
*ei'ning -a 1 totality; unit. 2: i e-a continually.
*ei'n/kjønna A - cf en/kjønnet
ei'n/kom' Av (=+en/) expressly, for that express purpose.
*ei'n/kvan' Pn f eikor, nt eitkvart one or another, some (person, thing): e- dagen some day, one of these days; e- gongen some time or other; eikor leid in one way or another, somehow; eitkvart slag something or other, some kind or other; e- stad somewhere, someplace or other.
*ei'nleg A - single, solitary.
*ei'n/leik -en similarity, uniformity.
*ei'n/leta A - of one color, single-colored.
*ei'nmanns/post -en mil. outpost manned by one man.
*ei'n/menne -t individual.
*ei'no N: i e- continually, incessantly.
*ei'n/rett -en (=*eine/) cf ene/
*ei'n/rom [/romm] -et cf en/
*ei'n/rådig A - (=*eine/) cf ene/
*ei'ns A - cf ens[1]
*ei'n/sam A cf en/som
*ei'ns/arta A - cf ens/artet
*ei'n/semd -a isolation, loneliness: stig da i meg e-, storm mitt jordlivs siste skanse rise up within me, l-, storm the last bastion of this my earthly life (Tor Jonsson).
*ei'nsemd/kjensle -a feeling of loneliness.
*ei'ns/formig A - cf ens/
*ei'n/sidig A - cf en/
*ei'nsidig/skap -en onesidedness, partiality.
*ei'n/skap -en similarity; unanimity, unity.
*ei'n/skild A -skilt distinct, individual, separate.
*ei'nskild/mann -en, pl -menn(er) (the) individual.
*ei'n/skils Av individually, singly.
*ei'nskils/hus -et single family dwelling.
*ei'nsleg A - cf enslig
*ei'ns/leis Av 1 in one way or another, somehow. 2 expressly, for that express purpose.
*ei'n/slungen A -e/-i, pl -ne simple, uncomplicated.
*ei'n/staka A - alone, isolated; single.
ei'n/stape -n bot. bracken, fern (Pteridium aquilinum).
+ei'n/stirre V -a/-et (=*/stire) stare intently.
*ei'n/strengt A - continually, without pause.
*ei'ns/tydig A - cf en/
ei'n/stø'ing -en hermit, lone wolf; eccentric.
*ei'n/sy'nt A - onesided, partial; one-eyed.
*ei'n/tal -et cf en/
*ei'n/tom A empty, unloaded.
*ei'n/toms A - cf en/
*ei'n/tydig A - cf en/
*ei'nvalds/konge -n cf enevolds/
ei'n/velde -t (=*eine/, +ene/) autocracy, absolute monarchy; absolutism.
ei'n/veldig A - (=*eine/, +ene/) absolute, autocratic.
*ei'n/vis A cf en/
*ei'n/øygd A -/-øygt cf en/øyd
ei'r -et (=+irr) copper rust, verdigris.
ei're V -a/+-et (=+irre[1]) (of copper) rust, become coated with verdigris.

ei'ret(e) *A* - (=+**irret**) (of copper) rusted, coated with verdigris.
ei'r/grøn *A* (=+**irr/**) (of copper) green with verdigris; dark green.
Ei'rik *Prn (m)*
***ei'smal** *A* alone, lonely: **e- sit ho att under busk** she is left sitting a-under a bush (Garborg).
***eit'** *Art nt of* **ein**[1] cf **en**[1]
ei'tel *-elen, pl -ler* (=+**itle**) 1 lymph gland. 2 small lump in meat. 3 hard bit of stone in surrounding softer stone.
ei'ter *-eret/-ret* venom.
ei'ter/maur *-en* poisonous ant.
ei'ter/orm *-en* poisonous snake, viper.
***eit'/kvart** *nt of* **einkvan**
ei'trende *Av*: **e- sint** extremely angry; **e- kaldt** biting cold.
***eitt'** *Num nt of* **ein**[2] cf **en**[2]
***eitt'/tal** *-et* cf **ett/**
***eitt'/årig** *A* - cf **ett/**
***eitt'/åring** *-en* cf **en/**
Ei'vind *Prn (m)*
Ei'vind/vik *Pln* postoffice, Gulen twp, Sogn og Fjordane.
ejek'tor *-en* ejector.
ejise're *V -te* eject (e.g. shell from gun).
+**e'k**[1] *-en* cf **eik**[1]
***e'k**[2] *pr of* **ake**[1]
+**e'ke**[1] *-n* cf **eike**[1]
e'ke**[2] *pp of* **ake**[1] (=eki**)
°**e'ke**[3] *V -a*: **e- seg fram** edge, inch forward; **e- seg inn på** edge closer to.
+**e'ke/løv** *-et* cf **eike/lauv**
ek'kel *A -elt, pl ekle* disgusting, revolting (e.g. smell, bug, etc.); (of person) nasty, repulsive; (of problem, situation) difficult, unpleasant.
***ek'kje** *-a* cf **enke**
ek'ko *-et, pl -/+-er* echo: **gi e-** produce an e-, re-echo.
ek'ko/lodd *-et* echo sounder, sonar; echo sounding.
eklatan't *A* - resounding, startling, striking: **et e- bevis** a striking proof; **en e- seier** an overwhelming victory.
ek'le[1] *V -a/+-et* disgust, revolt: **e-s** feel disgust, revulsion.
ek'le[2] *pl of* **ekkel**
ek'ling *-en* disgusting person.
eklip'se *-n* eclipse.
ekliptikk' *-en* (the) ecliptic.
ek'orn *-et/+-en* (=**ikorn**) squirrel.
e. Kr.=**etter Kristus, etter Kristi fødsel**
e'kre *-a* meadowland formerly under cultivation.
eks- *Pf* ex-, former(ly).
eksak't *A* - exact.
+**eksak't/het** *-en* exactitude, precision.
eksaltasjo'n *-en* exaltation, state of high excitement.
eksalte'rt *A* - overexcited, overwrought; fantastic, wild.
eksa'men *-en* 1 examination: **gå opp (være oppe) til e-** take an e-. 2 degree (received as the result of taking an examination): **han har en god e-** he took his d- with honors.
+**eksa'mens/besva'relse** *-n* (written) answer to an examination.
+**eksa'mens/bevi's** *-et* diploma.
eksa'mens/bo'rd *-et*: **han kommer like fra e-et** he has just finished his exams.
eksa'mens/feber *-en* nervousness before an examination.
+**eksa'mens/oppgave** *-a/-en* (=***/oppgåve**) examination paper in a given subject.
+**eksa'mens/vitnesbyr'd** *-et* diploma.
eksaminan'd *-en* candidate for a degree, examinee.
eksaminasjo'n *-en* examining, process of examination.
eksamina'tor *-en, pl -to'rer* examiner.
eksaminato'rium *-iet, pl +-ier/*-* class conducted by question and answer method.
eksamine're *V -te* examine.
***ek'se** *V -te* (of grain) ear.
eksege'se *-n* exegesis.
eksege'tisk *A* - exegetic.
eksekusjo'n *-en* 1 execution (of criminal). 2 *jur.* execution (against property): **gjøre e-** levy e- (i on); **det går tett med falliter og e-er** bankruptcies and e-s are coming thick and fast (Kielland).
eksekusjo'ns/pelotong' *-en* firing squad.
eksekuti'v[1] *-et* executive council.
eksekuti'v[2] *A* executive.
eksekuti'v/nemnd [/nemd] *-a* executive committee.
ekseku'tor *-en, pl -to'rer* executor.
eksekutø'r *-en* performing artist (esp. musician).
eksekve're *V -te jur.* execute (judgment), carry out (sentence).
eksellen'se *-n* (title) Excellency: **Deres E-** Your E-.
eksellere *V -te* excel (**i** in).
ekse'm *-en/-et* eczema.
eksem'pel *-elet/-let, pl -el/+-ler* 1 example, instance (**på** of): **for (til) e-** for e-, for i-; **jeg kan ikke komme på et godt e-** I can't think of a good e-. 2 example, precedent: **gi et godt e-** set a good e-; **ta en til e-** take sby as an e-; **e-ets makt** the power of e-.
+**eksem'pel/løs** *A* unexampled, unparalleled, unprecedented.
eksem'pel/vis *Av* as an example, for example.
eksempla'r *-et, pl -/+-er* 1 copy (of book etc.); specimen (plant, animal, etc.). 2 model, paragon.
eksempla'risk *A* - exemplary, model.
eksentrisite't *-en* eccentricity.
eksen'trisk *A* - eccentric.
eksepsjonell' *A -elt* exceptional.
°**ekse're** *V -te* cf **eksersere**
ekserpe're *V -te* excerpt (e.g. book).
ekser'pt *-et, pl -/+-er* excerpt.
eksersere *V -te mil.* drill; exercise strict command over; *fam.* boss, lord it over.
eksersé'r/plass *-en* drill grounds.
eksersi's *-en* (=**eksis**) *mil.* drill, training (of soldiers).
eksess' *-en* excess: **begå e-er** commit outrages.
ekshaust [ekso's] *-en* cf **eksos**
ekshibisjonis'me *-n* exhibitionism.
ekshibisjonis't *-en* exhibitionist.
eksi'l *-et* exile: **leve i e-** live in e-.
eksi'l/regje ring *-a/+-en* government in exile.
Ek'singe/dalen *Pln* postoffice, Modalen twp, Hordaland.
eksi's *-en* cf **eksersis**
eksisten's *-en* 1 existence: **kamp for e-en** struggle for survival. 2 *(pl)* beings: **løse e-er** drifters; **tvilsomme e-er** suspicious characters.
+**eksisten's/beret'tigelse** *-n* raison d'être.
eksistensialis'me *-n* existentialism.
eksistensiell' *A -elt* existential.
eksisten's/minimum *-et* subsistence level.
+**eksisten's/mulighet** *-en* possibility of making a living.
eksisten's/rett *-en* right to exist.
eksiste're *V -te* exist.
ekskłude're *V -te* exclude (from membership or participation in a group).
ek'sklusiv *A* exclusive.
ek'sklusive *Av* exclusive of, excluding: **boka koster 30 kroner e- porto** the cost of the book is 30 *kroner* plus postage.
eksklusjo'n *-en* exclusion (from participation in the activities of a group).
ekskommunise're *V -te* excommunicate.
ek's/konge *-n* ex-king.
ekskremen't *-et, pl -/+-er* excrement.
ekskur's *-et* digression, excursus.
ekskursjo'n *-en* excursion, field trip.
eksli'bris *-et* Ex Libris (book plate).
ekso's *-en* (=**ekshaust**) exhaust.
ekso's/rype *-a fam.* "exhaust-chick" (=girl who sits behind the driver of a motorcycle).
ekso's/rør *-et/*-a* (=***/røyr**) exhaust pipe.
ekso'tisk *A* - exotic.
ekspandere [ekspangde're] *V -te* expand (esp. of gas, etc.).
ekspansiv [ek'spangsiv] *A* expansive, expanding.
ekspansjon [ekspangsjo'n] *-en* expansion.
ekspede're *V -te* 1 dispatch, send (trunks etc.); *fig., fam.* kill: **jeg må e- bagasjen** I have to s- my luggage; **to ulver ble e-t på kort tid** two wolves were k-ed (polished off) in a short time. 2 attend to, take care of: **departementet har ennå ikke e-t saken** the matter has not yet been handled by the Department. 3 wait on (in store etc.): **blir De e-t?** are you being waited on?
ekspedisjo'n *-en* 1 attendance to, handling of (business etc.): **e-en av saken tok lang tid** the handling of the matter took a long time. 2 office (where business is transacted); counter (in large business office); **min bror arbeider i Aftenpostens e-** my brother works in the business office of A-; **e-en er på den andre siden av perrongen** the window is on the other side of the platform. 3 (scientific or military) expedition.
ekspedisjo'ns/sjef *-en* department head (in business or government office).
ekspedisjo'ns/tid *-a/+-en* office hours (of a business).
ekspeditri'se *-a/+-en* (female) clerk, saleswoman.
ekspeditt' *A* - businesslike, expeditious, prompt (service etc.).
ekspeditø'r *-en* clerk, salesman (in store); agent (for shipping company).
ekspektanse [-tang'se] *-n*: **stå på e-** be on a waiting list, wait for an opening.
ekspektanse/liste *-a* waiting list: **stå på e-** be on the w-.
eksperimen't *-et, pl -/+-er* experiment.
eksperimenta'tor *-en* experimentalist, experimenter.
eksperimentell' *A -elt* experimental.
eksperimente're *V -te* experiment.
eksper't *-en* expert (**i** in).
ekspertí'se *-n* expert opinion; expertise, expertness.
+**eksper't/utval'g** *-et* (=***/utval**) committee of experts.
ek'splisitt *A* - explicit.
eksploate're *V -te* exploit.
eksplode're *V -te* explode: **e- med** burst out with.
ek'splosiv *A* explosive.
eksplosjo'n *-en* explosion.
+**eksplosjo'ns/aktig** *A* - explosive.
eksplosjo'ns/moto'r *-en* internal combustion engine.
eksponen't *-en* exponent.
ekspone're *V -te* expose (e.g. film).
ekspor't *-en* 1 export(s), exportation: **Norges årlige e-** Norway's annual e-; **drive e-** carry on e- trade. 2 =**e-/øl.**
eksporte're *V -te* export.
ekspor't/øl' *-et* export beer: **lyst, mørkt e-** pale, dark e-.
eksportø'r *-en* exporter.
eksposé *-et, pl +-er/*-* summary presentation (e.g. of a case, matter).
ekspresjonis'me *-n* expressionism.
ekspresjonis't *-en* expressionist.
ekspress'[1] *-en* express, express train.
ekspress'[2] *A* - express.
ek'spressiv *A* expressive.
ekspress'/tog [/tåg] *-et* express train.
ekspropriasjo'n *-en* expropriation.
eksproprie're *V -te* expropriate.
eksta'se *-n* ecstasy.
eksta'tisk *A* - ecstatic.

+ Bokmål; * Nynorsk; ° Dialect.
After letter: ' stress (Acc. 1); ' tone, stress (Acc. 2); · length.
Below letter: . not pronounced.

ekstempora'l *A* extemporaneous.
ekstempore're *V -te* extemporize.
ek'stensiv *A* extensive.
eksteriø'r *-et, pl -/+-er* exterior.
ekster'n *A* external.
eksterritoria'l *A* extraterritorial.
eksterritoria'l/rett *-en* right of extraterritoriality.
ek'stra *A* - extra (additional, exceptional, supplementary): **arbeide e-** work overtime; **vinen er e- god** the wine is exceptionally good, superior; **tjene litt e-** make a little on the side.
ek'stra/blad *-et, pl -/+-er* extra, special edition (of newspaper).
+ek'stra/forplei'ning *-en* special food, diet.
ekstrahe're *V -te* extract; summarize (e.g. book, case).
ekstrak't *-en* extract; summary.
ek'stra/nummer [/nommer] *-eret, pl -er/+-numre* 1 special edition (of newspaper). 2 encore (in concert).
ek'stra/ordinæ'r *A* extraordinary.
ek'stra/skilling *-en* extra wages; earnings on the side.
ek'stra/tog [/tåg] *-et* special, unscheduled train.
ekstravagan'se *-n* extravagance.
ekstravagan't *A* - extravagant.
ekstre'm[1] *-et, pl +-er/*- extreme.
ekstre'm[2] *A* extreme.
ekstremite't *-en* extremity (i.e. limb).
ek'te[1] *N*: **gi til e-** give in marriage; **ta til e-** take as wife (husband).
ek'te[2] *V -a/+-et* marry.
ek'te[3] *A* - 1 (of children) legitimate. 2 genuine, real, true: **e- brøk** proper fraction; **det er en e- Rembrandt** it is a g- (painting by) R-; **han er en e- jeger** he is a t- hunter; **fargene i stoffet er e-** the cloth is colorfast; **det er e- varer** it's the r- thing.
+ek'te/felle *-n* spouse.
ek'te/folk *pl* husband and wife: **leve som e-** live together as husband and wife (without necessarily being so); **jeg erklærer dere for rette e- å være** I pronounce you man and wife.
ek'te/fødd *A -/-født* (=+/**født**) legitimate (=born in wedlock).
+ek'te/hustru *-en* wife.
ek'te/make *-n* spouse.
ek'te/mann *-en, pl -menn/*-menner* husband.
ek'te/pakt *-a/+-en* marriage contract, marriage settlement.
ek'te/par' *-et* married couple.
ek'te/seng *-a* conjugal bed; double bed.
ek'te/skap *-et, pl -/+-er* marriage: **inngå e- (med)** marry; **født utenfor e-** illegitimate.
+ekteska'pelig *A* - (=*-**skapleg**) conjugal, marital, matrimonial.
ek'teskaps/brott *-et* (=+/**brudd**) adultery.
ek'teskaps/byrå' *-et, pl +-er/*-* matrimonial agency, marriage bureau.
ek'teskaps/kandida't *-en hum.* eligible bachelor.
+ek'teskaps/løfte *-t* (=*/**lovnad**) 1 promise of marriage. 2 marriage vow.
+ek'teskaps/tilbud *-et* (=*-**bod**) proposal of marriage.
ek'te/stand *-en/*-et* matrimony, wedlock: **den hellige e-** holy m-; **han har fått mere enn nok av e-en** he's had more than enough of marriage (Ibsen).
ek'te/vie *V -vigde/+-et* marry, unite in wedlock.
+ek't/het *-a/-en* authenticity, genuineness; (of color) fastness.
ekva'tor *-en* equator: **under e-** on the e-.
ekvidistanse [-ang'se] *-n* equidistance.
ekvilibris't *-en* equilibrist.
ekvilibris'tisk *A* - equilibristic.
ekvipa'sje *-n* 1 carriage (and horses), equipage. 2 *hist., naut., mil.* naval shipyard.
ekvipe're *V -te* equip (esp. for journey), fit out.
ekvipe'ring *-a/+-en* 1 equipment; outfitting. 2 haberdashery, (men's) clothing store.
ekvivalen't[1] *-en* equivalent.
ekvivalen't[2] *A* - equivalent (**med** to).
ekvivale're *V -te* be equivalent (**med** to), balance out.
ekvivokk' *A -vokt* 1 ambiguous, equivocal. 2 off-color, risqué, suggestive.
e'l[1] *-et* flurry, shower (of rain or snow).
***e'l**[2] *pr of* **ale**
el- *Pf* electro- (e.g. **el-verk**).
el. =**eller**
e. l. =**eller liknende**
elan [elang'] *-en* élan (spirit, vigor, zest).
elastikk' *-en* elastic, elastic band.
elastisite't *-en* elasticity.
elas'tisk *A* - elastic, flexible (also *fig.*)
el'ḍ *-en* (=+**ild**) 1 fire, flame: **den evige i-/e-** hellfire; **gjøre/gjere opp i-/e-** light a fire; **gå gjennom i-/e- og vann/vatn** do one's utmost; **det var gått i-/e- i det** it had caught fire; **forskjellige som i-/e- og vann/vatn** different as night and day; **mange jern i i-en/e-en** many irons in the fire; **mellom i-/e- og vann/vatn** between the devil and the deep blue sea; **puste til i-en/e-en** fan the flames; **sette/setje i-/e- på** set fire to; ***sitje mellom to e-ar** be in a tight spot; **slå i-/e-** strike a light. 2 fire (of gun): **gi/gjeva i-/e-** fire (a gun); **mellom dobbelt/dobbel i-/e-** in a cross-f-; **være i i-en** be under f-; **åpne i-/e-** open f-. 3 *fig.* ardor, fire, heat, passion: **feberens i-** feverish h-; **vinens i-** warmth of the wine; **hans tale hadde makt og i-** he spoke with force and a-.
el'ḍbjørg/dag *-en* 13th day of Christmas (January 7), originally a day of pagan fire worship.
el'ḍ/dåp *-en* baptism of fire.
el'de[1] *-n* old age: **høy e-** advanced old age; **med år og e-** in due course of time.
***el'de**[2] *-t* 1 fostering, raising of young. 2 offspring. 3 litter.
el'de[3] *V -a/+-et* age, make old: **det siste året har e-et ham** this last year has a-d him; **e-es** become old, grow old; **e-et** aged.
el'de[4] *V -a/+-et* (=+**ilde**) 1 make, maintain a fire. 2 heat. *3 ache: **e- opp** have heartburn.
el'ḍenḍe *Av* (=***eldande, +ildende**) fiery: **en e- rød blomst** a bright red flower; **hun ble e-rød** she blushed crimson.
+el'des *V -edes, -es* (=*-**ast**) become, grow old.
el'ḍ/fast *A* - (=+**ild/**) fireproof, fireresistant; oven-proof.
***el'ḍ/fengd** *A -/-fengt* flammable.
***el'ḍ/fengen** *A -e/-i, pl -ne* flammable.
el'ḍ/full *A* (=+**ild/**) ardent, fiery, passionate: **en i- kvinne** a p- woman; **en mann med mitt i-e gemytt** a man of my f- temperament (Ibsen).
el'ḍ/gammal *A -t, pl -gamle* (=+/**gammel**) extremely old, old as the hills; ancient.
el'ḍ/hug *-en* ardor, enthusiasm.
el'ḍ/huga *A* - ardent, enthusiastic.
el'ḍ/hus *-et* "cookhouse" (separate building on farm used for baking, brewing, washing).
***el'ding** *-en* lightning.
el'ḍ/ja'rn *-et* (=/**jern**) steel (for striking sparks from flint).
el'ḍ/mørje *-a* live embers; flaming mass.
eldora'do *-et* Eldorado.
el'ḍ/prøve *-a/+-en* ordeal, trial by fire.
el'ḍ/rake *-a* poker.
el'ḍ/rauḍ *A* (=+**ild/rød**) fiery red; scarlet.
el'dre *cp of* **gammal**
el'ḍs/farlig *A* - combustible, flammable.
el'ḍ/sikker *A -t, pl -sikre* fire-resistant, incombustible.
el'ḍ/sjel *-a/+-en* dedicated soul; enthusiast, fanatic, zealot.
el'ḍs/lys *-et* light of a fire; artificial light.
***el'ḍs/mæle** *-t* bonfire, open fire.
***el'ḍs/mål** *-et* cf /**mæle**
el'ḍ/sprutenḍe *A* - (about dragons) fire-breathing; (about eyes) flashing: **e- berg** active volcano.
el'ḍst *sp of* **gammal**
el'ḍste/mann *-en* person with seniority in a group; senior partner.
el'ḍ/tunge [/tonge] *-a/+-en* tongue of flame.
***e'le** *-a* look like rain: **det e-er vesti** it looks like rain in the west.
elefan't *-en* elephant: **gjøre en mygg til en e-** make a mountain out of a molehill.
+elefan't/aktig *A* - elephantlike.
elefan't/jakt *-a/+-en* elephant hunt (hunting).
elefan't/sjuke *-n* (=+/**syke**, */**sykje**) *med.* elephantiasis.
elegan'se *-n* elegance.
elegan't *A* - elegant.
elegi' *-en* elegy (**over** on).
ele'gisk *A* - elegiac.
elektrifise're *V -te* electrify (esp. railroad).
+elek'triker *-en, pl -e* (=*-**ar**) electrician.
elektrise're *V -te* electrify.
elektrise'r/maski'n *-en* electrostatic generator.
elektrisite't *-en* electricity.
elektrisite'ts/verk *-et* power plant, power station.
elek'trisk *A* - electric(al).
elektro'de *-n* electrode.
elektrokje'misk *A* - electrochemical.
elektroly'se *-n* electrolysis.
elektrolyt'isk *A* - electrolytic.
elektrolytt' *-en* electrolyte.
elek'tro/mo'tor *-en* electric motor.
elektromoto'risk *A* - electromotive: **e- kraft** e- force, E.M.F.
elektro'n *-en/-et* electron.
elektronikk' *-en* electronics.
elektro'nisk *A* - electronic.
elektro'n/rør *-et/*-a* (=*/**røyr**) electron tube, vacuum tube.
elemen't *-et, pl -/+-er* 1 element: **han er i sitt rette e-** he's in his e-; **de kristne begreper har opptatt hedenske e-er** Christian concepts have incorporated heathen e-s; **latinens e-er** the e-s of Latin; **trosse e-ene** brave the e-s. 2: **galvanisk e-** galvanic cell.
elementæ'r *A* elementary; primary.
elementæ'r/bok *-a, pl -bøker* (=+**elementar/**) primer.
elen'de *-t* misery, wretchedness.
elen'dig *A* - miserable, unhappy, wretched; terrible; (in mild oath) accursed, confounded.
+elen'dig/het *-en* misery, wretchedness; squalor: **det fører ut i den rene e-** it will lead to utter ruin.
ele'v *-en* pupil (**av** of); apprentice, student.
elevasjo'n *-en* elevation.
eleva'tor *-en* elevator.
eleve're *V -te mil.* increase the elevation (of gun, cannon).
eleve'rt *A* - cultivated, cultured, refined: **en e- samtale** a polite conversation; **han fører et e- språk** he speaks in a r- manner.
ele'v/heim *-en* (=+/**hjem**) dormitory (usu. at boarding school).
ele'v/råd *-et* student council.
el'fen/bein *-et* (=+/**ben**) ivory.
+el'fenbens/aktig *A* - ivory.
el'g *-en* European moose (Alces alces, Alces machlis, slightly smaller than the American moose, Alces americanus; NB: not to be confused with the American elk, Cervus canadensis, which is most closely related to the European deer or hart, Cervus elaphus).
El'ge/seter *Pln hist.* Augustinian cloister, Trøndelag.
el'g/hunḍ *-en* Norwegian elkhound.

*el'gjen *A -e/-i, pl elgne* nauseous, sickening.
el'g/kolle *-a* cow moose (cf **elg**).
el'g/ku *-a* cow moose (cf **elg**).
el'g/okse *-n* bull moose (cf **elg**).
el'gs/blakk *A -blakt* (of horse) grayish tan (resembling **elg**).
E'li [also e'-] *Prn (f)*
eliksi'r *-en* elixir.
elimine're *V -te* eliminate.
Eli'ne *Prn (f)*
e'ling *-en* (=+**iling**) shower, squall.
Eli'se *Prn (f)*
eli'te *-n* elite, flower, pick.
eli'te/mannskap *-et* picked crew.
el'le *V -a/+-et* count out (as in children's games): **e- melle** eenie meenie.
El'len *Prn (f)*
el'ler *C* or: **nå e- aldri** now or never; **en dag e- to** a day or two; **et e- annet** something or other; **hverken . . . e-** neither . . . nor.
+**el'lers** *Av* (=***elles**) 1 otherwise; or (else); if not: **maten er dårlig, men e- er det et hyggelig sted** the food is bad, but otherwise it's a nice place; **jeg kommer hvis han blir bedt, men ikke e-** I'll come if he's invited, but not otherwise; **du må gjøre hva jeg sier, e- kan jeg ikke hjelpe deg** you have to do what I say, or (otherwise) I can't help you; **kom deg nå ut, e- slår jeg til deg** get out of here or (else) I'll knock your block off. 2 else, in addition: **var det e- noe?** was there anything e-?; **vi så oss litt om i byen, men e- gjorde vi ingenting** we looked around town a bit, but we didn't do anything e-. 3 usual, usually: **hun var uheldig som e-** she was unlucky as u-; **våren kom senere enn e- i år** spring came later than u- this year; **han var litt sur i dag, men han er e- hyggelig nok** he was a bit grumpy today, but he's u-ly quite pleasant. 4 anyway, by the way; really: **hva synes du e- om ham?** what do you think of him, a-?; **nei, e- takk** no but thanks a- (usu. ironic), nothing doing.
***el'les** *Av* cf **ellers**
elleve [el've] *Num* eleven.
elleve/del *-en* (one) eleventh.
+**el'le/vill** *A -vilt* wild, beside oneself (with joy, enthusiasm, etc.).
ellevte [el'lefte] *Num* eleventh.
el'levte/del *-en* cf **elleve/**
El'ling *Prn (m)*
ellip'se *-n* 1 *math.* ellipse. 2 *gram.* ellipsis.
ellip'tisk *A* - elliptic(al).
el'ms/eld *-en* (=+/**ild**) St. Elmo's fire.
elokse're *V -te* electropolish.
°**el's/blakk** *A -blakt* cf **elgs/**
El'se (Elsa) *Prn (f)*
El's/fjo'rd *Pln* twp, Nordland.
el'sk *-en* 1 great concern, interest: **legge sin e- på** take a great i- in, be taken by. 2 *dial.* love: **en lever ikke lenge av e- og sønnavind** one can't live long on l- and breezes (Asbjørnsen).
el'ske *V -a/-et* 1 love=be in love with: **du er den eneste kvinne jeg noen gang har e-et** you're the only woman I've ever l-d; **min e-ede** my beloved. 2 love=be devoted to: **han e-er sine barn** he l-s his children; **ja, vi e-er dette landet** yes, we l- this land (Bjørnson); **gjøre seg e-et av** endear oneself to, win the devotion of. 3 love=make love: **et e-ende par** a l-ing couple.
el'skelig *A* - endearing, lovable.
+**el'sker** *-en, pl -e* (=***-ar**) lover: **en e- av kunst** an art l-; **ta seg en e-** take a l-.
+**elskerin'ne** *-a/-en* (=***elskarinne**) mistress.
el'sk/hug *-en* love.
el'skling *-en* darling, sweetheart.
+**el'skov** *-en* love: **kom, la oss beruse oss i kjærlighet inntil morgenen, la oss forlyste oss i e-** come, let us take our fill of l- until the morning, let us solace ourselves with l- (Prov. 7,18).
+**el'skovs/full** *A* amorous.
+**el'skovs/syk** *A* lovesick.
elskver'dig *A* - 1 amiable, charming, gracious. 2 helpful, kind, obliging: **vil De være så e-** please (be so k-); **det var meget e- av Dem** that was very k- of you; **et e- tilbud** a k- offer.
+**elskver'dig/het** *-en* 1 amiability, charm: **si e-er** pay compliments. 2 helpfulness, kindness.
el'te[1] *-a* mass, mess; quagmire.
el'te[2] *V -a* knead (dough); form (figure from clay etc.); *fam.* **e- en i snøen** rub sby's face in the snow; roll sby in the snow.
el'te[3] *V -a/+-et/*-e* chase, hunt (usu. of predatory animals).
el'v *-a, pl *-ar* river, stream.
el've/bakke *-n* (grassy) riverbank, slope down to river.
***el've/bard** *-en* riverbank.
+**el've/blest** *-en* hives, urticaria.
el've/bredd *-en* riverbank.
el've/drag *-et* course of a river, river basin.
el've/far *-et* riverbed.
el've/kant *-en* riverbank.
el've/leie *-t, pl +-r/*-* riverbed.
+**el've/løp** *-et* course of a river.
el've/mel *-en* (sandy) riverbank, sandbank.
el've/munning *-en* mouth of a river.
el've/os *-en/-et* mouth of a river.
el'-verk *-et* power plant, power station.
El've/rum' *Pln* village, twp, Hedmark.
el'v/os *-en/-et* cf **elve/**
ely'sisk *A* - Elysian.
+**e'm** *-en* cf **eim**
EM=europamesterskap(et)
em.=emeritus; ettermiddag
emal'je *-n* enamel.
emal'je/lakk *-en* enamel lacquer.
emalje're *V -te* enamel: **e-t** enameled.
emanasjo'n *-en* emanation; *jur.* drawing up (of a law).
emane're *V -te* emanate; *jur.* draw up (a law).
emansipasjo'n *-en* emancipation.
emansipe're *V -te* emancipate.
emballa'sje *-n* packaging, packing, wrapping: **kostbar e- fordyrer varene** expensive packaging increases the cost of the goods.
emballe're *V -te* package, pack, wrap: **varene må e-es forsvarlig** goods must be properly packaged, packed.
embar'go *-en* embargo: **legge e- på** embargo, place an e- on; **være belagt med e-** be under e-.
+**em'bede** *-t* cf **embete**
em'bete *-t, pl +-r/*-* 1 office, (government) position: **i embeds medfør, på embeds vegne** in an official capacity, officially; **tiltre et e-** take up one's duties in a government office. 2 *fig.* duty: **forsømme sitt e-** neglect one's d-ies.
em'bets/aristokrati' *-et hist.* aristocracy of officialdom.
+**em'bets/bolig** *-en* official residence (provided for the use of a government official).
em'bets/eksa'men *-en* University degree.
+**em'bets/forta'pelse** *-n* loss of office (by dismissal).
em'bets/mann *-en, pl -menn/*-menner* government official, civil servant (appointed by the king).
em'bets/verk *-et* bureaucracy, officialdom.
emble'm *-et, pl -/+-er* badge, emblem; *mil.* insignia.
embonpoint [angbångpoeng'] *-et* plumpness, stoutness.
Em'bret *Prn (m)*
emb'ryo *-et, pl -/+-o'ner* embryo.
emende're *V -te* emend (a text).
emfa'se *-n* emphasis.
emfa'tisk *A* - emphatic.
emigran't *-en* emigrant.
emigrasjo'n *-en* emigration.
emigre're *V -te* emigrate.
eminen'se *-n* eminence: **Deres E-** Your E-; **grå e-** gray e- (person who exercises power behind the scenes).
eminen't *A* - eminent: **i e- grad** e-ly.
emi'r *-en* amir, emir.
emisjo'n *-en merc.* issue (of stock, currency).
emissæ'r *-en* (traveling) lay preacher.
emitte're *V -te merc.* issue (stock, currency).
***em'je** *V -a* bellow, howl, wail.
EMK=elektromotorisk kraft
em'men *A +-ent, pl emne* 1 cloying, sickeningly sweet or bittersweet (taste, e.g. of fruit). 2 heavy, pungent, suffocating (e.g. fragrance of flowers).
em'ne[1] *-t, pl -/+-r* 1 subject, topic: **det er et godt e- for en bok** that's a good s- for a book; **dagens e-r** current t-s (of discussion); **skifte e-** change the s-. 2 raw or half finished material out of which a finished product is to be made; material out of which something is made: **leire er et bra e- å arbeide med** clay is a good material to work with; **det var godt e- i eggen** there was good material in the blade; (of person) **det er e- til en stor idrettsmann (kunstner) i den gutten** that boy has the stuff to become a great athlete (artist). 3 (of person) candidate, prospect: **han er et lovende e-** he's a likely p- (e.g. for a political position).
em'ne[2] *V -a/+-et* form, prepare (for later finishing), roughcast: **e- på noe** be working on sth; **være e-et til** be qualified, suited for; *dial.* **e- seg til** get (oneself) ready to; **han e-er seg hit** he intends to come here.
em'ne[3] *pl of* **emmen**
***em'neleg** *A* - fitting, promising, suitable.
em'ne/regis'ter *-(e)ret, pl -/+-re* subject index.
em'ning *-a* development, preparation: **være i e-** be developing, be under p-; **hva er i e- her** what's going on here?
em'nings/tre *-et, pl -/+-trær* roughcast lumber.
emosjonell' *A -elt* emotional.
empire [angpi'r] *-n* Empire (style).
+**empi'riker** *-en, pl -e* (=***-ar**) empiricist.
empi'risk *A* - empiric(al).
emploi' *-en* employment.
+**em'sig** *A* - officious.
emulge're *V -te* emulsify.
emulsjo'n *-en* emulsion.
+**en**[1] *Art f ei/en, nt et* (=***ein**[1]) 1 a, an: **ei god bok** a good book. (Often omitted, e.g. when referring to names of professions: **Min far er lege** My father is a doctor; or to a general classification of items: **Er det spisevogn på toget?** Is there a diner on the train?). 2 one: **det hendte en dag at** it happened o- day that. 3 about, approximately, some: **om en tre fire dager** in about three or four days; **det kommer til å koste en ti tolv kroner** it will cost around ten or twelve *kroner*; **for en syv åtte år siden** s- seven or eight years ago. 4 a certain: **var ikke den damen en fru Linde?** wasn't that lady a certain Mrs. Linde? (Ibsen); **jeg traff en herr Smith i går** I met a (certain) Mr. Smith, a man named Smith yesterday.
+**e'n**[2] *Num f ei/en, nt ett* (=***ein**[2]) one: **ett er det å kritisere en ordbok,**

+ Bokmål; * Nynorsk; ° Dialect.
After letter: ' stress (Acc. 1); ` tone, stress (Acc. 2); · length.
Below letter: . not pronounced.

noe annet å skrive en it's o- thing to criticize a dictionary, another thing to write o-; **klokka er ett** it's o- o'clock; **Norge er ett av de vakreste land i verden** Norway is o- of the most beautiful countries in the world; **hun er hans ett og alt** she is everything to him; **du kan gjøre ett av to** you have two choices; **gå (løpe) i ett (med)** run together (with); **i ett og alt** in everything, in every respect; **i ett kjør (sett, vekk)** constantly, continuously; **med ett** right away, suddenly; **alle som en** everyone, to a man; **det kommer ut på ett** it's all the same, there's no difference; **under ett** collectively, together; **være ett med** be the same as, indistinguishable from; **være nummer en** be first; **det ene ... det andre ..** one thing ... the other...; +**det ene med det andre** all things considered, considering everything; **den ene hånden min** o- of my hands; **blind på det ene øyet** blind in o- eye.

+**en**[3] *Pn* (=***ein**[3]) 1 one, people, they, you: **en skal høre mye før ørene faller av** you'll hear a lot before your ears fall off, if you live long enough you'll hear everything; **en kan jo aldri vite** you never know, there's no telling; **en kan bare håpe at** one can only hope that; **han er hva en kaller en gentleman** he's what's called (what people call) a gentleman; **en sier at** they (people) say, I heard that; **som en sier** as the saying goes. 2 somebody, someone: **det er en nede som vil snakke med deg** there's sby downstairs who wants to talk to you; **en eller annen** sby or other; **hva er han for en?** who's that character?; **hver og en** everybody, everyone; **det var en som kunne spille!** he (she) can really play, what a player!; **en liten en** a small one (e.g. a drink); **hun har fått en liten** she's had a baby.

+**e'n/akter** *-en, pl -e* (=***ein/aktar**) one-act play; curtain raiser.

en bloc [angblåkk'] en bloc, together.

+**e'n/båren** *A -et, pl -ne* (=***ein/boren**) only begotten: **Gud gav sin e-ne sønn** God gave his only begotten son.

+**e'n/cellet** *A* (=***ein/cella**) *biol.* one-celled, unicellular.

encyklopedi [angsyklopedi'] *-en* encyclopedia.

encyklopedisk [angsyklope'disk] *A* - encyclopedic.

encyklopedist [angsyklopedis't] *-en* encyclopedist.

en'da[1] *Av* (=***endå**) 1 (before comparatives) still: **det blir e- varmere i morgen** it's going to be s- hotter tomorrow; **fløyel er e- dyrere** velvet is s- more expensive. 2 (before numerals and expressions of quantity) more: **gi meg e- en** give me one m-; **e- en gang bad Kristin et Ave** once m- K- offered an Ave (Undset); **han har e- mange igjen** he has many m- left. 3 (=**ennå**) still, yet: **er han ikke kommet e-** hasn't he come y-; **han er her e-** he's s- here. 4 *(adv.)*: **det er e- ikke det verste** that's not the worst of it either; **det kunne jeg e- gå med på** I wouldn't even balk at that; **jeg hadde e- spurt ham to ganger** I even asked him twice; **dersom jeg e- ikke var så sikker i min sak** if only I weren't so sure about it (Ibsen); **du er ikke så dårlig smed e- du** you're not such a bad blacksmith after all (Asbjørnsen); **men e- så vondt det gjorde, rørte han seg ikke** but no matter how much it hurt, he didn't move (Asbjørnsen).

en'da[2] *C* (=***endå**) although, even though: **han er sterk, e- så liten han er** he's strong e- he's small; **e- allting gikk fortere i dag enn ellers, syntes Sidsel det ble lenge a-** everything went more quickly today than usual, Sidsel thought it was taking a long time (Aanrud).

en'da/til' *Av* besides, in addition, too: **jo, så minsanten er det blåveis! En stor, svær bukett e-** yes, by George, it's hepatica! And a great big bouquet at that (Obstfelder).

en'de[1] *-n* 1 end=delimiting part: **for (ved) e-n av bordet** at the e- of the table; **fra e- til annen** from one e- to the other; **i (på) alle e-r (og kanter)** everywhere; **sette noe på e-** set sth on e-, *fig.* turn topsy-turvy. 2 posterior(s), rump: **sitte på e-n** sit on one's fanny; **få en på e-n** get a licking; **ha bly (kvikksølv) i e-n** have lead (ants) in your pants. 3 (piece of) rope: **gi (en båt) en e-** tow (a boat); **gå utenbords i en e-** be lowered over the side; **spinne en e-** spin a yarn. 4 end=termination; result: **fra begynnelsen til e-n** from the beginning to the e-; **det var ingen e- på** there was no e- to; **når e-n er god, er allting godt** all's well that ends well; **få (ha, ta) en e-** come to and e-, stop, terminate; **gjøre e- på** make an e- of, put an e- to (also=destroy, kill); **være (gå) til e-** be (be close to) the end. 5: **over e-** topsy-turvy, (usu.) down; **(fare) gå over e-** fall flat; **slå en over e-** knock sby down; **sette seg over e-** sit up(right).

en'de[2] *V* +*-te*/**-a* end, finish, terminate (**på** in); bring to an end: **det e-te med at** the result (end) was that.

en'de[3] *Av* straight (up or down): **e- til værs (*i veret)** s- up in the air; **e- opp (ned)** s- up (down); *fig.* **snakke e- ut** speak bluntly.

+**-ende** *A* - (=***-ande**) *(prp.)* -ing.

en'de/fram' *A -t, pl -me* direct, straightforward; *(adv.)* simply; bluntly.

+**ende'l** *A* - cf **del**

en'de/laus *A* (=+**/løs**) endless, interminable, unending.

en'delig *A* - 1 final, ultimate: **den e-e avgjørelse** the f- decision; *(adv.)* **e- er han kommet** he's f-ly arrived. 2 finite, limited: **universet er e-** the universe is f-; *math.* **en e- størrelse** a f- quantity. 3 *(adv.)* by all means, definitely: **du må e- ikke glemme det** be sure not to forget it; **hvis du e- vil** if you insist.

+**en'de/likt** *-et* (=***/lykt**) *lit.* death, end: **han fikk et sørgelig e-** he came to a sad e-.

+**en'delse** *-n* cf **ending**

***en'de/lykt** *-a* cf **/likt**

+**en'de/løs** *A* cf **/laus**

en'de/løyse *-a* endlessness, interminability.

en'de/punkt [/pongt] *-et* end point, terminus.

***en'der** *Av*: **e- og då, e- og gong** occasionally, now and then.

en'de/rim *-et* end rhyme.

en'de/stasjo'n *-en* terminus.

en detail [angdetai'] retail.

en'de/tarm *-en* rectum.

en'de/til' *A* - direct, straightforward; (of people) easy to get along with.

en'de/vende *V* +*-te*/**-e* turn upside down.

en'ding *-a*/+*-en* (=+**-else**) ending, termination; *gram.* ending, suffix.

+**en'dog** *Av* even: **lide store smerter, ja, e- døden for sine meningers skyld** suffer great pain, yes, e- death, for one's convictions (Ibsen).

endossa't [ang-] *-en* endorsee.

endossement [angdåssemang'] *-et, pl -/+-er* endorsement.

endossen't [ang-] *-en* endorser.

endosse're [ang-] *V -te* endorse.

en'dre *V -a*/+*-et* alter, change: **gjort gjerning står ikke til å e-** what's done is done.

En'dre *Prn(m)*

+**e'n/drektig** *A* - harmonious, in agreement.

+**endrek'tig/het** *-en* concord, harmony.

en'dring *-a*/+*-en* alteration, change.

en'drings/framlegg *-et* amendment: **stille et e-** move an a-.

en'd/skap *-en* conclusion, end: **få (en) e- på** bring to an e-; **lange bølger som gled til havs uten e- og mål** long waves that slid out to sea without e- or purpose (Kinck).

***en'då** *Av, C* cf **enda**[1,2]

+**e'ne**[1] *V -te* join, unite: **e-es** agree **(om** on).

+**e'ne**[2] *A* - alone: **e- og alene for å** for the sole purpose of; **være e- om** be a- at, in (work, opinion, etc.).

+**e'ne**[3] *df of* **en**[2]

+**e'ne/arving** *-en* sole heir.

E'ne/bakk *Pln* twp, Akershus.

+**e'ne/ba'rn** *-et* only child.

+**e'ne/beret'tiget** *A* -: **være e- til** have the exclusive rights to, have a monopoly on.

+**e'ne/boer** *-en, pl -e* hermit, recluse.

+**e'ne/bolig** *-en* single-family house.

+**e'ne/bær** *-et* cf **eine/**

+**e'ne/forhan'dler** *-en, pl -e merc.* sole agent.

+**e'n/egget** *A* -: **e-de tvillinger** identical twins.

+**e'ne/herskende** *A* universal (e.g. opinion).

+**e'ne/hersker** *-en, pl -e* absolute monarch.

+**e'ne/merker** *pl* domain, preserves (used of person's exclusive field of activity).

+**e'ne/pike** *-n* maid (in house where there are no other servants).

+**e'ner**[1] *-en, pl -e* (=***einar**) 1 one, number one. 2 champion, number one. 3 individualist, nonconformist, unique individual; loner.

+**e'ner**[2] *-en* cf **einer**

+**e'ne/rett** *-en* exclusive right, monopoly: **med e-** with all rights reserved.

energi [enærgi'] *-en* energy.

energi/kjelde [enærgi'/] *-a* (=+**/kilde**) source of energy.

energisk [enær'gisk] *A* - energetic.

enerve'rende *A* - nerve-racking, trying: **det virket e-** it got on (my, our, etc.) nerves.

+**e'ne/rådende** *A* - 1 absolute (in authority). 2 universal (e.g. opinion).

+**e'ne/rådig** *A* - autocratic, independent, stubborn.

+**e'nes** *V -tes* agree (**om** on).

+**e'ne/celle** *-a*/*-en* solitary confinement.

+**e'neste** *A* - (=***einaste**) only, single: **e- i sitt slag** unique; **en (et) e-** just one; **ikke en e-** not a single one; **han er den e-** he's the o- one; **hver e-** each, every; **hver e- en** every single one.

+**e'ne/stående** *A* - exceptional, unique; marvellous, wonderful.

+**e'ne/tale** *-n* monologue, soliloquy.

+**e'n/eta'sjes** *A* - one-story.

+**e'ne/velde** *-t* cf **ein/**

+**e'ne/veldig** *A* - cf **ein/**

+**e'nevolds/konge** *-n* (=***einvalds/**) absolute king, monarch.

en face [angfass'] full face.

+**e'n/faset** *A* - single phase (electric current).

enfin [angfeng'] *Av* in that case, oh well, so.

+**e'n/fold** *-et* naiveté, innocence, simplicity.

+**enfol'dig** *A* - 1 naive, innocent, unsophisticated. 2 simple: **en e- stakkar** a poor fool.

+**enfol'dig/het** *-en* naiveté, innocence, simplicity: **i all e-** in all i-.

+**e'n/frøbla'det** *A* - monocotyledonous.

eng'[1] *-a* meadow, pasture.

+**eng'**[2] *A* 1 limited, narrow: **i e-ere forstand** in a l- sense. 2 close, intimate: **e-ere kretser** select circles.

+**engang'** [also e'n/gang] *Av* (=***ein-gong**) 1 once, at one time (in the past): **det var e-** once upon a time; **e- (da) jeg var i Oslo** once when

I was in Oslo; **når jeg e- har lovet noe, så gjør jeg det** once I've promised something, I do it. 2 one day, some day, sometime (in the future): **e- kommer han** some day he'll come; **e- imellom** once in a while, sometimes; **da sees vi e- i kveld** be seeing you sometime this evening. 3: **ikke e-** not even; **kan du ikke gjøre meg den lille tjenesten e-** can't you even do me that little favor; **det var ingen som så ham e-** he wasn't even seen by anyone. 4 (emphatic, usu. with **nå**) after all, simply: **sånn er det nå e-** that's the way things are, you know; **det var nå e- meg som kom på det** after all, it was my idea.

+e'ngangs/skatt *-en* postwar assessment on capital gains made during World War II.

engasjement [anggasjemang'] *-et, pl -/+-er* 1 contract, engagement (for actor, artist, etc.). 2 *merc.* financial commitment. 3 *mil.* action, contact (between opposing troops); engagement (in fencing).

engasjere [anggasje're] *V -te* 1 engage (actor, artist, etc.). 2 *merc.*: **være e-t** be under financial commitments. 3 *mil.* engage (the enemy). 4 ask (for a dance): **e- en dame** ask a lady for a dance. 5: **e- seg** commit oneself, take up (a cause); **e-t (i)** committed (to), taken up (with).

eng'el *-elen, pl -ler* angel (also *fig.* of person): **det gikk en e- gjennom værelset** lit. an a- passed through the room (said when there is a sudden lull in the conversation).

eng'elsk *A* - English: **e- syke** rickets.

eng'elsk/mann *-en, pl -menn/*-menner* 1 Englishman. 2 blackwall hitch (a knot).

eng'elsk/vennlig *A* - anglophile, pro-British.

Eng'er/dal *Pln* twp, Hedmark.

+e'n/gifte *-t* (=***ein/**) monogamy.

eng'/kall *-en bot.* rattle (Rhinanthus major, minor).

+eng'le/aktig *A* - angelic.

eng'le/ba'rn *-et, pl -/*-born* little angel, little darling (often ironic); (teacher's) pet.

eng'le/hår *-et* angel's hair (Christmas tree decoration).

eng'/lende *-t* meadow land, prairie.

+englen'der [also eng'-] *-en* (=***-ar**) Englishman.

+englenderin'ne *-a/-en* (=***-ar-**) Englishwoman.

eng'le/røst *-en* (=***/røyst**) angelic voice.

+eng'le/tålmo'dighet *-en* patience of an angel, a saint.

+eng'le/ving(e) *-(e)n* (=***/veng**) angel's wing.

eng'/mark *-a* meadow land.

en gros [anggro'] wholesale.

engros/pris [anggro'] *-en* wholesale price.

eng'/solei'e *-a* buttercup (Ranunculus acris).

eng'/sprette *-a* (=**+/sprett** *-en*) grasshopper.

eng'ste *V -a/-et* frighten: **e- seg (e-es)** be alarmed, anxious (for about).

eng'stelig *A* - anxious, apprehensive, worried (for about).

+eng'stelse *-n* anxiety, worry (**for** about).

+e'n/het *-en* unit; unity: **de tre e-er** the three (dramatic) unities; **gå opp i en høyere e-** combine into a higher unity, form a unity.

+e'nhetlig *A* - uniform.

+e'nhets/pris *-en* unit price.

+e'nhets/skole *-n* comprehensive school (system adopted in recent years substituting single secondary school for parallel schools at ages 14-16).

+e'n/hjørning *-en* (=**+/horning, *ein/-hyrning**) unicorn.

+enhver [envæ'r] *Pn* 1 every (-one, -body): **e- er seg selv nærmest** e- man for himself, everyone looks out for number one; **spillet om E-** the play Everyman; **i e- henseende** in e- respect, in all respects; **gi e- sitt** give everyone his due; **det er ikke e- gitt å** it's not for everyone to; **det er noe e- vet** everybody knows that; **noe for e- smak** sth for everyone; **kall e- ting ved sitt rette navn** call a spade a spade. 2 any (-one, -body): **e- annen** a- other, anybody else; **alle og e-** just anybody; each and everybody; **det er ikke e-s sak å** it's not for just anybody to; **for e- pris** at a- cost; **til e- tid** at a- time.

+e'nig *A* - (=***einig**) agreed, in agreement: **bli e-** reach an agreement, agree (**om** about, on); **være e- med en** agree with sby (**i, om noe** about sth).

+e'nig/het *-en* agreement, unanimity: **e- gjør sterk** there is strength in numbers; **komme til e-** reach an a-; **det hersker e- om at** there is general a- that.

+en'ke *-a/-en* (=***enkje**) widow (**etter** of).

+en'ke/dronning *-a/-en* queen dowager.

+en'ke/fru(e) *-a/-en* widow (title).

+en'ke/kasse *-a/-en* widow's pension fund.

en'kel *A -elt, pl -le* plain, simple: **e- av vesen** unpretentious; **han gjorde det helt e-t fordi** he did it s-y because; **en e- oppgave** a s- problem.

+en'kel/het *-en* plainness, simplicity: **i all e-** informal(ly), simple (simply); potluck.

en'kelt *A* - 1 single; individual, separate: **en e- (bok, gang)** one single (book, time); **hver(t) e-** each single, separate one; **den e-e, det e-e menneske** the individual. 2 simple (in contrast to compound): **e- blad** s- leaf; **e- dør** single door; **legge et teppe e-** spread a blanket unfolded. 3 (*pl*, often with **noen**): a few, several, some (people): **e-e mener at** some people think that; **e-e av dem** some of them; **i (noen) e-e tilfelle** in a few cases; **de e-e deler av noe** the several (component) parts of sth.

en'kelt/billett' *-en* one-way ticket.

+en'kelt/het *-en* (usu. *pl*) detail(s), particulars: **i e-er** in detail; **e-er om ulykken foreligger ikke ennå** the d-s of the accident are not yet available.

en'kelt/knappa *A* - (=**+-et**) single-breasted.

en'kelt/spent *A* - single-breasted.

en'kelt/stående *A* - detached, isolated: **fordømme en mann for en e- handlings skyld** condemn a man on account of an i- act.

en'kelt/vis *Av* individually, one by one, singly.

+en'kelt/værelse *-t* single room.

+en'ke/mann *-en, pl -menn* widower.

+en'kemanns/støt *-et fam.* blow on the funny bone (cf **alboge/**).

***en'kje** *-a* cf **enke**

***en'kje/mann** *-en, pl -menn(er)* cf **enke/**

+e'n/kjønnet *A* - unisexual; *bot.* dioecious.

enklit'isk *A* - enclitic.

+e'n/kom' *Av* cf **ein/**

+e'nlig *A* - single, solitary: **den e-e** stand celibacy.

+e'nmanns/bolig *-en* single-family dwelling.

+e'nmanns/luga'r *-en* single cabin (on boat).

en masse [angmass'] in great numbers; aplenty, galore.

en miniature [angminiaty'r] in miniature, on a small scale.

enn'[1] *Av* 1 (before comparatives) still (=**enda[1]**): **e- mere** s- more; **e- si** let alone, s- less; **e- videre** besides, further(more), in addition. 2 (with interrogatives etc.) even if, no matter what: **hva som e- skjer** no matter what happens, whatever happens; **hvem som e- gjør det** no matter who does it, whoever does it; **hvor hardt jeg e- arbeider** no matter how hard I work; **hvordan han e- sier det** no matter how he says it; **om han e- gav meg tusen kroner** even if he gave me a thousand *kroner*; **det er fint om e- kjølig vær** it's nice weather though cool. 3: **e- ikke** not even.

enn[2] *C* 1 (after comparatives and **annen**) than: **var øynene større e- magen?** were your eyes bigger t- your stomach?; **jeg kysset henne mer e- en gang** I kissed her more t- once; **det var noe annet e- å sitte og arbeide** that was a lot better t- sitting and working. 2 (after **annen**) but: **det er ikke annet å gjøre e- å vente** there's nothing to do b- wait; **jeg kan ikke si annet e- godt om ham** I can say nothing b- good about him, only good about him; **hun så ingen annen e- ham** she saw nobody b- him, only him. 3 and, what about (in answer to question about one's state or condition): **e- du da?** and you, what about you?; **e- om** supposing, what if, what about; **e- om vi kledde fjellet, sa eneren** what about covering (let's cover) the mountain, said the juniper (Bjørnson); **e- å si slikt da!** just think of saying something like that!.

***en'ne** *-t* brow, forehead.

***en'no** *Av* cf **ennå**

+enn'/også [also -ås'så] *Av obs.* even.

ennsi' *Av* cf **enn[1]**

+en'nu *Av* cf **ennå**

ennvi'dere *Av* cf **enn[1]**

en'nå *Av* (=***enno**) 1 still, yet: **det er tid e-** there's s- time; **jeg har ikke sett ham e-** I haven't seen him y-. 2 (before comparatives) still (=**enda[1]**): **hun var e- vakrere enn søsteren** she was s- more beautiful than her sister. 3 (before numerals and expressions of quantity) more (=**enda[2]**): ***enno ein gong fekk eg våren å sjå** one m- time I was permitted to see the spring (Vinje).

enor'm *A* enormous, huge.

en passant [angpassang'] by the way, incidentally, in passing.

enquete [angke't] *-n* (newspaper) survey (usu. of expert opinion).

+e'n/rom [/romm] *N* (=***ein/**) privacy: **i e-** in private, privately.

+e'ns[1] *A* - (=***eins**) alike, similar, the same: **like e-** just the same; **være e- mot alle** treat everybody the same.

+e'ns[2] *po of* **en[3]**

+e'ns/artet *A* - homogeneous, uniform.

+e'nsartet/het *-en* homogeneity, uniformity.

+e'ns/bety'dende *A* - synonymous: **være e- med** be the same as, tantamount to.

en'se *V -te/*-a* (=**anse[2]**) heed, pay attention to, take notice of; *dial.* molest, touch.

ensemble [angsam'bel] *-t, pl -/+-r* ensemble.

+e'n/seter *-en, pl -e* one-seater, single-seater.

+e'ns/farget *A* - solid-colored.

+e'ns/formig [also -får'-] *A* - (=***eins/**) dull, monotonous.

+e'nsformig/het [also -får'-] *-en* monotony.

+e'n/sidig *A* - (=***ein/**) one-sided, partial; unilateral.

+e'nsidig/het *-en* one-sidedness, partiality.

ensila'sje *-n* silage.

ensile're *V -te* ensile.

en'ske *A* - *dial.* only, pure; nothing but: **hele jordet var e- kløveren** the meadow was all clover.

+ Bokmål; * Nynorsk; ° Dialect.
After letter: ' stress (Acc. 1); ` tone, stress (Acc. 2); ˙ length.
Below letter: . not pronounced.

+**enskjøn't** *A* - although, though.

+**e'nslig** *A* - (=***einsleg**) alone, single, solitary: **en e- gård** an isolated farm.

+**e'nslig/stil(le)t** *A* - alone (without friends or relatives).

+**e'ns/lydende** *A* - (=***eins/lydande**) homonymous, sounding alike.

+**e'n/som'** *A -t, pl -me* (=***ein/sam**) lonely, lonesome, solitary.

+**e'nsom/het** *-en* loneliness, solitude.

+**e'n/sporet** *A* - (=***ein/spora**) one-track, single-track (e.g. railroad, way of thinking).

+**e'ns/retning** *-en* 1 standardization (of opinion, thought). 2 *tech.* rectification (of electric current).

+**e'ns/rette** *V -a/-et* (=***eins/**) 1 direct into one channel, standardize (opinion, thought). 2 *tech.* rectify (electric current).

+**e'nstavings/o'rd** *-et* (=**enstavelses/**) monosyllable, monosyllabic word.

+**ensteds** [-stess'] *Av* (=**etsteds**) someplace, somewhere.

+**e'n/stemmig** *A* - 1 unanimous. 2 *mus.* (in) unison.

+**e'ns/tonig** *A* - (=***eins/**) (of sound) monotonous.

+**e'n/strøken** *A -ent, pl -ne: mus.* **den e-ne oktav** the one-line octave (beginning with middle C); **e- tone** any of the notes in the one-line octave.

en suite [angsvitt'] in a row, in succession.

+**e'n/tal(l)** *-et gram.* singular.

+**e'nte** *Num*: **hundre og e-** *math.* hundred and first.

+**en'ten** *C*: **enten ... eller ...** 1 either ... or ... 2 (in dependent clauses) whether ... or (not) ...: **e- han kommer eller ikke** whether he comes or not; **e- det er riktig eller galt** whether it's right or wrong.

entente [angtang'te] *-n* alliance, entente: **e-n** the Allies (during World War I).

+**entle'dige** *-et* dismiss, remove from office.

entomolog [-lå'g] *-en* entomologist.

entomologi' *-en* entomology.

+**e'n/toms** *A* - one-inch (boards, nails).

en'tre *V -a/+-et* 1 *naut.* board (a ship). 2 *naut.* climb, go aloft: **e- opp (til værs)** c- aloft; **e- ned** c- down; **e- inn (ut)** go midships, man stations; **e- inn (ut) på en rå** haul sail in, let sail out on a yard. 3 enter.

entré [angtre'] *-en* 1 entry, hall, vestibule. 2: **gjøre sin e-** make one's entrance, appear for the first time. 3 price of admission.

entré/dør [angtré/] *-a* entrance; (hallway) door, front door.

entré/klokke *-a* front doorbell.

entreprenø'r [ang-] *-en* contractor.

entreprise [angtrepri'se] *-n* contract: **sette bort i e-** let on c-.

entusias'me *-n* enthusiasm.

entusias't *-en* enthusiast.

entusias'tisk *A* - enthusiastic.

+**e'n/tydig** *A* - 1 unambiguous. 2 *math.* unique (e.g. solution).

+**e'nveis/kjøring** *-a/-en* one-way driving; (signs) one-way street.

+**e'n/virkes** *A* - (=***ein/**) one-man (e.g. farm).

+**e'n/vis** *A* (=***ein/**) obstinate, stubborn.

envoyé [angvoaje'] *-en* envoy.

enzy'm *-et* enzyme.

+**e'n/øring** *-en* (=***ein/**) one-øre coin.

+**e'n/øyd** *A* - (=**+/øyet**) one-eyed.

+**e'n/åring** *-en* yearling.

e'ols/harpe *-a/-en* Aeolian harp.

epak't *-en astron.* epact.

epidemi' *-en* epidemic.

epide'misk *A* - epidemic.

epigo'n *-en* epigone, imitator (of works of artist, writer, etc.).

epigram' *-met, pl -/+-mer* epigram.

epigramma'tisk *A* - epigrammatic.

+**e'piker** *-en, pl -e* (=***-ar**) epic poet.

epikk' *-en* epic poetry.

+**epikure'er** *-en, pl -e* (=***-ar**) epicurean.

epikure'isk *A* - epicurean.

epilepsi' *-en* epilepsy.

+**epilep'tiker** *-en, pl -e* (=***-ar**) epileptic

epilep'tisk *A* - epileptic.

epilog [-lå'g] *-en* epilogue.

e'pisk *A* - epic.

episkopa'l *A* episcopal.

episo'de *-n* episode, incident.

episo'disk [also -o'-] *A* - episodic.

epis'tel *-elen, pl -ler* epistle.

epite'l *-et, pl -/+-er med.* epithelium.

epite't *-et, pl -/+-er* epithet.

ep'le *-t, pl +-r/*-* apple: **e-t faller ikke langt fra stammen** he's a chip off the old block; **et stridens e-** an apple of discord, a bone of contention; **bite i det sure e-t** swallow a bitter pill.

ep'le/kart *-en* apple nubbin, green apple.

ep'le/mos *-en* applesauce.

ep'le/slang *-en* apple stealing.

ep'le/vin *-en* apple wine.

epo'ke *-n* epoch.

+**epo'ke/gjørende** *A* - (=***/gjerande**) epoch-making, history-making.

e'pos *-et, pl -/+-er* 1 epic poem, poetry. 2 narrative literature.

epålett' *-en* epaulet.

er [æ'r] *pr of* +**være[2]**, ***vere[3]**

+**-er** *-en, pl -e* (=***-ar**) -er (agent, instrument).

+**erak'te** *V -et* 1 *jur.* find, rule. 2 consider, deem.

-ere *Sf* verbal suffix, e.g. **avertere, spasere.**

eremitt' *-en* hermit.

eremitt'/kreps *-en* hermit crab.

E'res/fjo'rd og [å] **Vis't/dal** *Pln* twp, Møre og Romsdal.

+**erfa're** *V -te* experience; find out, learn (by experience).

+**erfa'ren** *A -ent, pl -ne* experienced (i in).

+**erfa'ren/het** *-en* experience, state of being experienced.

+**erfa'ring** *-a/-en* experience: **av egen e-** from personal e-; **gjøre e-er** gain e-, learn by e-; **tale av e-** speak from e-.

+**erfa'rings/bevi's** *-et* empirical proof.

+**erfa'rings/messig** *A* - empirical: **e- er det** experience has shown that there is.

E'r/fjo'rd *Pln* twp, Rogaland.

***er'ge** *V -a* cf **ergre**

er'ge(r)lig *A* - 1 annoying, irritating (matter). 2 annoyed, irritated: **være (bli) e- over noe** be (become) a- at sth; **være (bli) e- på en** be (become) a- with sby.

er'go *Av* ergo, therefore.

er'gre *V -a/+-et* annoy, irritate: **e- seg over** be a-ed (vexed) at.

+**er'grelse** *-n* annoyance, irritation.

+**erhol'de** *V -holdt, -holdt* get, obtain.

+**er/hverv** [æ'r/værv] *-et* cf **erverv**

+**erhver've** *V -et* cf **erverve**

-eri *-et* noun suffix, e.g. **bakeri, svineri.**

+**erin'dre** *V -et* 1 bear in mind, remember. 2 *archaic* remind (**en om** sby about).

+**erin'dring** *-en* 1 memory, reminiscence; remembrance; **til e- om** in m- of; **vekke e-er om** awaken m-ies of. 2 memoirs.

er'ke- *Pf* arch-.

er'ke/biskop *-en* (=**/bisp**) archbishop.

er'ke/engel *-elen, pl -ler* archangel.

er'ke/fiende *-n* archenemy.

er'ke/sludder *-et* pure hogwash, utter nonsense.

er'ke/slyngel *-elen, pl -ler* utter scoundrel.

+**erkjen'ne** *V -kjente* 1 acknowledge, admit. 2 perceive, realize.

+**erkjen'nelse** *-n* 1 acknowledgment, admission. 2 cognition, perception, realization: **komme til e- (av)** gain understanding (of).

+**erkjen'tlig** *A* - grateful: **vise seg e-** show one's gratitude.

+**erkjen'tlig/het** *-en* gratitude.

+**erklæ're** *V -te* declare, proclaim: **e- seg enig med** express one's agreement with.

+**erklæ'ring** *-a/-en* declaration, statement: **avgi e- om** make a s- about.

+**erkyn'dige** *V -et*: **e- seg om** make inquiries about.

er'le *-a zool.* wagtail (Motacilla).

+**erleg'ge** *V -la, -lagt* pay (fee, fine): **mot å e-** on payment of.

Erlend (-land) [æ'r-] *Prn(m)*

Erling [æ'r-] *Prn(m)*

***er'm** *-a, pl -ar* cf **erme**

+**er'me** *-t* (=***erm**) sleeve: **binde en noe på e-t** try to convince sby of sth, try to pull sby's leg.

er'me/forkle *-et, pl +-klær/*-* smock.

er'me/hol [/hål] *-et* (=**+/hull**) armhole.

+**ernæ're** *V -te* 1 feed, nourish: **nordmenn e-er seg hovedsakelig av fisk** Norwegians live for the most part on fish. 2 support: **e- en familie** s- a family; **e- seg av s-** oneself by, make a living from.

+**ernæ'ring** *-a/-en* nourishment; nutrition.

+**ernæ'rings-** *Pf* nutritional (e.g. **e-sykdom** nutritional disease).

+**ernæ'rings/fysiologi'** *-en* nutritional physiology.

+**ero'bre** *V -a/-et* capture, conquer.

+**ero'brer** *-en, pl -e* conqueror (**av** of).

+**ero'bring** *-a/-en* capture, conquest (**av** of).

erosjo'n *-en* erosion.

erotikk' *-en* eroticism, sex.

ero'tisk *A* - erotic, sexual.

+**erstat'ning** *-en* 1 compensation, damages (**for** for): **forlange i e-** claim as d-; **til e-** by way of c-. 2 replacement, substitute, substitution.

+**erstat'nings/krav** *-et* claim for damages: **reise e- (mot)** file a damage suit (against).

+**erstat'nings/plikt** *-en* liability.

+**erstat'te** *V -a/-et* 1 compensate, make compensation for, make good. 2 replace: **det kan ikke e-es** it is irreplaceable.

+**erstat'telig** *A* - replaceable.

***er'så** *C* if, in the case that.

er't[1] *N*: **gjøre noe på e-** do sth for the purpose of teasing.

er't[2] *-a* pea: **det renner av ham som e-er ut av en sekk** he talks a blue streak.

***er'tar** *-en* tease.

er'te *V -a/+-et* tease: **e- en med noe** t- sby with sth; **han kunne e- en stein på seg** he could try the patience of a saint; **e- seg opp** get oneself all worked up.

+**er'te/blomst** *-en* 1 pea flower. 2 sweet pea (Lathyrus odoratus).

er'te/krok *-en* tease: **han er riktig en e-** he's a big t-.

er'ten *A +-ent, pl -ne* teasing, inclined to tease.

***er'ter** *-ra, pl -er* cf **ert[2]**

***er'ter/blom** *-en* cf **erte/blomst**

+**er'te/ris** *-et* (=***erter/**) peavine: **de henger sammen som e-** they're inseparable.

er'ter/suppe *-a* cf **erte/**

er'te/skolm *-a/-en* (=***erter/**) pea pod.

er'te/stikke *-a* tease (=**ertekrok).**

er'te/suppe *-a* (=**erter/**) pea soup.

er'tet(e) *A* - teasing, inclined to tease.

er'ts *-en* ore.

erupsjo'n *-en* eruption.

er'uptiv *A* eruptive: **e-e bergarter** (also) igneous rocks.

***er've** *V -de* cf **arve[1]**

+**er/verv** [æ'r/] *-et* 1 occupation, trade; industry. 2 acquisition.

+**erver've** *V -et* acquire, gain, obtain: **e- seg a-**, earn.

+**erver'velse** *-n* acquisition (**av** of).

+**ervervs/dyktig** [æ'r-] *A* - ablebodied, able to work.

+**ervervs/messig** [æ'r-] *A* - commercial, occupational, professional.

***er'ving** *-en* cf **arving**

***e's** *pr of* **ase[1]**

ES =**etterskrift**

eschatologi' *-en* cf **eskatologi**

e'se *V -te* (of liquids) ferment; (of dough etc.) rise, spread, swell.

e'sel *-elet/-let, pl +-ler/*-* ass, donkey; *fig.* idiot, jackass.

+**e'sel/aktig** *A -* asinine, donkeyish.

e'sel/spark *-et* kick of a donkey: *fig.* **gi en et e-** kick a man when he's down (after Aesop's fable).

+**e'sel/øre** *-t* (=***/øyra**, ***/øyre**) 1 donkey's ear. 2 *naut.* cap eyebolt. 3 dog-ear (in book).

e'sing *-a/-en naut.* gunwale.

es'j *I* cf **æsj**

es'je[1] *-a* 1 fry (i.e. young of fish). 2 soapstone, talc.

***es'je**[2] *V -a* (of liquids) ferment; (of dough) rise.

eska'dre *-n naut.* squadron.

eska'dre/sjef *-en naut.* squadron commander.

eskadro'n *-en mil.* squadron (of cavalry).

eskapa'de *-n* escapade.

eskatologi' *-en* eschatology.

es'ke[1] *-a/+-en* box (usu. of cardboard), carton.

+**es'ke**[2] *-et archaic* ask, demand: **e-ens mening** ask sby's opinion.

es'ke/ost [/ost] *-en* cream cheese, processed cheese.

eskimo' *-en* Eskimo.

eskimo'isk *A -* Eskimoan.

eskor'te [also -or'te] *-n* escort.

eskorte're *V -te* escort.

es'le *V -a/-et* (=**etle**) 1 intend, think of: **jeg hadde e-et å si** I was thinking of saying. 2 assign, portion out (sth): **det er e-et (til) deg** it's meant for you.

espalier [espalje'] *-et, pl +-er/*-* 1 espalier, trellis. 2: **danne e-** make a lane, line a route; form a cordon.

esperantis't *-en* esperantist.

esperan'to *-en* Esperanto.

esplana'de *-n* esplanade.

espri't *-en* esprit.

ess'[1] *+-et/*-en* (in cards) ace: **kløver e-** the a- of clubs.

ess'[2] *et*: **være i sitt e-** be in one's element; be in high spirits.

ess'[3] *-et mus.* E flat.

essay [es'sei] *-et, pl -/-s* essay.

essayist [esseiis't] *-en* essayist.

+**es'se** *-n* forge.

essen's *-en* essence.

essensiell' *A -elt* essential.

+**es't** *pr of* **være**[2]

es'ter[1] *-en, pl -e* (=***-ar**) Estonian.

es'ter[2] *-en, pl +-e chem.* ester.

+**este'tiker** *-en, pl -e* (=***-ar**) esthete.

estetikk' *-en* esthetics.

este'tisk *A -* esthetic(al).

estime're *V -te* esteem.

es'tisk *A -* Estonian (language).

Es't/land *Pln* Estonia.

es't/landsk *A -* Estonian.

es't/lending *-en* Estonian.

+**es'tnisk** *A -* cf **estisk**

estra'de *-n* dais, platform.

+**et**[1] *Art nt of* **en**[1]

***e't**[2] *pr of* **ete**

etable're *V -te* establish: **e- seg** e- oneself, set oneself up (in business etc.).

etablissement [etablissemang'] *-et, pl -/+-er* establishment (i.e. business, hotel, etc.).

etagère [etasjæ'r] *-n* cf **etasjere**

***e'tande** *A -* edible.

etap'pe [also -p'pe] *-n* 1 stage, step; leg, stretch: **dele arbeidet i fem e-r** divide the work into five steps; **første e-** first leg. 2 *mil.* post, station.

e'tar/sekk *-en fam.* glutton.

eta'sje *-n* floor, story: **i annen e-** on the second f-; **ha noe i øverste (øvre) e-** have something upstairs (i.e. some brains).

etasjere [etasjæ'r] *-n* whatnot (bric-a-brac case); instrument cabinet.

eta'sje/seng *-a* bunk bed.

eta't *-en* (government) department, service.

eta'ts/råd *-en hist.* Councillor of State (title formerly granted by king).

e'te *V åt, +-t/*-e/*-i* 1 eat (usu. of animals, *derog.*, *dial.*, or *hum.* in connection with people). 2 corrode, eat away: **rusten åt seg inn i jernet** the rust ate away at the iron; **e- seg fram** move forward slowly.

-et(e) *A -* (=***-ut**) adj. suffix, e.g. **steinete** stony.

+**e'ter**[1] *-en, pl -e* (=***-ar**) eater (usu. glutton).

e'ter[2] *-en poet., chem., phys.* ether.

ete'risk *A -* ethereal.

eternitt' *-en* asbestos cement (fireproof building material usu. in the form of plates or sheets).

***e'te/sjokola'de** *-n* (eating) chocolate.

+**ethver't** *nt of* **enhver**

+**e'tiker** *-en, pl -e* (=***-ar**) ethician, student of ethics.

etikett' *-en* label: **forsyne med e-** label.

etiket'te *-n* etiquette.

etikette're *V -te* label.

etikk' *-en* ethics.

e'ting *-a* eating (usu. gluttony).

Etio'pia *Pln* Ethiopia.

+**etio'pier** *-en, pl -e* (=***etiop**, ***-ar**) Ethiopian.

etio'pisk *A -* Ethiopian.

e'tisk *A -* ethical.

et'le *V -a/+-et* cf **esle**

Et'ne *Pln* twp, Hordaland.

Et'ne/dal *Pln* twp, Oppland.

et'nisk *A -* ethnic.

etnogra'f *-en* ethnographer.

etnografi' *-en* ethnography.

etnolog [-olå'g] *-en* ethnologist.

etnologi' *-en* ethnology.

+**etrus'ker** *-en, pl -e* (=***-ar**) Etruscan.

etrus'kisk *A -* Etruscan.

et'se *V -a/+-et* corrode, etch: **e-ende** caustic, corrosive.

***et'sel** *-et* cf **åtsel**

et's/middel *-elet/-midlet, pl +-midler/*-el* corrosive, etchant.

+**etsteds'** *Av* cf **ensteds**

ett'[1] *pp of* **ete**

+**ett'**[2] *Num nt of* **en**[2]

et'ter *P* (=+**efter**) 1 (of time) after: **e- at (han gikk)** a- (he left); **e- krigen** a- the war; **e- å ha ventet** a- having waited; **dag e- dag** day a- day; **en e- en, den ene e- den andre** one a- the other; *(adv.)* **året e-** the year a-; **et år e-** a year later, **kort e-** a short time later. 2 (of order) following, succeeding: **b er bokstaven e- a** b is the letter f- a; **e- Oslo er Bergen Norges største by** next to Oslo Bergen is the largest city in Norway; **si e-** repeat (after sby); **enke e-** widow of. 3 (of position) after, behind: **følge e-** follow along b-, **stå e- hverandre** stand in line; *(adv.)* **bli e-** stay b-; **komme e-** follow; **ligge e-** be b- (the times.) 4 after, in pursuit of: **politiet er e- ham** the police are on his trail; **hun er stadig e- gutten** she is always a- the boy, nagging him. 5 along, alongside: **han gikk e- vegen** he walked along the road; **det vokser blomster e- bekken** flowers are growing beside the creek. 6 by: **trekke en e- håret** drag sby by the hair; **litt e- litt** little by little. 7 according to, on the basis of: **e- det jeg har hørt** according to what I've heard; **e- min mening** in my opinion; **alt e- som** according to whether; **kledt e- siste mote** dressed according to the latest fashion; **tegne e- modell** draw from a model. 8 as a result of, from: **trett e- reisen** tired f- the trip; **ikke spor e- ham** he left no traces; **nesen har han e- faren** he has his father's nose. 9 for: **han skulle til byen e- øl** he was going to town f- some beer; **har han vært (gått) e- doktoren?** has he gone f- the doctor? 10 (other idioms): ***e- di** as, since; ***e- hand**, **e-** +**hvert**/***kvart** gradually; **gjøre noe så det står e-** do sth with a vengeance. (For uses with other verbs see under these.)

+**et'ter/ape** *V -a/-te* ape, mimic.

et'ter/aping *-a/-en* aping, mimicry.

et'ter/behan'dling *-a/+-en* medical treatment during a period of convalescence, postoperative care.

et'ter/dønning *-a/+-en* reverberation; *fig.* repercussion.

+**et'ter/forske** *V -a/-et* investigate.

+**et'ter/følge** *V -fulgte, -fulgt* 1 follow (=succeed). 2 comply with (e.g. an order). 3 *archaic* imitate, take as a model.

+**et'ter/følgelse** *-n*: *archaic* **Kristi E-** Imitation of Christ (title); **et eksempel til e-** (let this be) an example (to you).

+**et'ter/følger** *-en* (=***-jar**) successor.

+**et'ter/gi** *V -gav, -gitt* annul, waive (debt, sentence, etc.).

et'ter/givende *A -* accommodating, compliant, yielding: **en e- far** an indulgent father.

+**et'tergiven/het** *-a/-en* compliance, indulgence.

+**et'ter/gjøre** *V -gjorde, -gjort* copy, imitate; counterfeit, falsify, simulate: **e-t** counterfeit, imitation; **e-te sedler** counterfeit bills, **e-t skinn** imitation leather; **e-t underskrift** forged signature.

+**et'ter/glemt** *A -* forgotten, left behind: **e-e saker** lost and found.

et'ter/heng *-et* hanger(s)-on.

+**etterhver't** *Av* cf **hver**

+**et'ter/høst** *-en* 1 late autumn. 2 *archaic* aftercrop.

+**etterhån'den** *Av* (=***etter hand**) gradually, little by little; **e- som** as.

et'terjuls/vinter *-eren, pl -rer* the part of winter following Christmas.

et'ter/klang *-en* resonance; echo.

et'ter/klok *A*: **være e-** have hindsight.

+**et'ter/komme** *V -kom, -kommet* comply with (a request), fulfill (a wish), obey (an order).

+**et'ter/kommer** *-en, pl -e* (=***-ar**, ***/komar**) descendant.

et'ter/krav *-et* 1 *jur.* additional claim. 2: **sende mot e-** send C.O.D.

et'ter/krigs *A -* postwar.

+**et'ter/late** *V -lot -latt* leave (behind): **e- seg** leave (by one's death).

+**et'ter/latende** *A -* careless, negligent.

+**et'terlaten/skap** *-en (pl)* deceased person's property and effects; *fig.* remains (after sth); *fam.* excrement: **e-er etter hunden** traces after the dog.

+**et'ter/latt** *A -*: **de e-e** the bereaved; **e-e skrifter** posthumous works.

+**et'ter/lengtet** *A -* (=***-a**) desired, longed-for.

+**et'ter/leve** *V -de* comply with, live by, obey: **e- Guds bud** o- the commandments of God.

et'ter/levende *A -*: **de e-** the survivors, surviving family.

et'ter/likne[1] *V -a/+-et* (=+**/ligne**) copy, imitate.

et'ter/likne[2] *V -a/+-et* (=+**/ligne**) assess for additional tax.

et'ter/likning *-a/+-en* (=+**/ligning**) 1 copy, imitation. 2 supplementary assessment.

+**et'ter/lot** *pt of* **-late**

et'ter/lyse *V -te* advertise for (e.g. lost property); institute a search for (e.g. missing person or criminal): **e-t** wanted (by the police).

et'ter/lysing *-a/+-en* (=+**/lysning**) advertisement (for lost property); police bulletin (for wanted criminal or missing person).

et'ter/mann *-en, pl -menn/*-menner* successor.

et'ter/middag *-en* late afternoon and early evening (period from about 4 P.M. to 8 or 9 P.M.); (in the country), afternoon.

+ Bokmål; * Nynorsk; ° Dialect.
After letter: ' stress (Acc. 1); ` tone, stress (Acc. 2); · length.
Below letter: . not pronounced.

et'ter/mo'dne *V -a/+-et* afterripen, ripen after picking.

et'ter/mæle *-t* posthumous fame, reputation: **ens e-**the name one leaves behind.

+**et'ter/navn** *-et* (=*/namn) family name, surname.

+**et'ter/nevnte** *A* - (=*/nemnde) mentioned (named) below; *jur.* the hereinafter named.

+**et'ter/nøler** *-en, pl -e* latecomer, straggler.

et'ter/o'rd *-et* postscript.

et'ter/prøve *V -de* check, run a final test on.

et'ter/på *Av* after, afterwards.

et'terpå/klok *A*: **være e-** have hindsight.

et'terpå/klokskap *-en* hindsight.

et'ter/rakster *-en* (=+/rakst) 1 reraking, second raking (of hay). 2 addendum, supplement(s).

+**et'ter/retning** [also -ret'-] *-en* (piece of) information, news; *(pl)* information, news: **gode e-er** good n-; **få e-om** at be informed that; **ta noe til e-** take cognizance, note of sth; **være til e- for en** be for one's i-.

+**et'terretnings/tjeneste** *-n mil.* intelligence service.

et'ter/rett *-en* dessert, final course.

+**etterret'telig** *A* -: **holde seg noe e-** comply with, observe sth (law, custom, etc.).

***et'ter/røkje** *V -te* investigate.

***et'ter/røknad** *-en, pl -er* investigation.

+**et'ter/se** *V -så, -sett* check, examine, look over.

+**et'ter/sittende** *A* - tight fitting.

et'ter/sju'kdom *-men* (=+/sykdom) *med.* sequela.

et'ter/skott *-et* (=*/skot, +/skudd): **være (stå) i e-** be in arrears.

et'terskotts/vis *Av* (=*-skots/, +-skudds/) (payable) at the end of the month.

et'ter/skrift *-a/+-en* postscript, P.S.

et'ter/slekt *-a/+-en* posterity.

et'ter/sleng *-en* 1 latecomer, straggler. 2 refrain of a ballad.

+**et'ter/slett** *-en* 1 aftercrop, second cutting. 2 *fig.* aftermath; addendum.

+**et'ter/slokke** *V -slokte, -slokt* extinguish (the remains of a fire).

et'ter/slått *-en* second cutting (of hay).

et'ter/smak *-en* aftertaste.

+**et'ter/som'** *C* (=**etter som**) 1 as, according to whether (how), depending on whether (how): **det er alt e- en tar det** it depends on how you look at it; **han sorterte eplene e- de var store eller små** he sorted the apples according to whether they were large or small. 2 as, because, inasmuch as, since.

+**et'ter/sommer** *-eren, pl -somrer* (=*/sommar) late summer: **ut på e-en** late in the summer.

+**et'ter/spill** *-et* (=*/spel) epilogue, postlude; *fig.* result, sequel: **ja, nå har vi e-et. Gråt og jammer.** Well, now we see the results. Weeping and wailing (Ibsen).

+**et'ter/spore** *V -a/-et/-te* track down.

+**et'ter/spu'rt** *A* - (=*/spurd) in demand, popular.

+**et'ter/spørsel** *-elen, pl -ler* (=*/spurnad) demand (etter for): **prisene bestemmes av forholdet mellom tilbud og e-** prices are subject to the law of supply and d-.

+**et'ter/strebe** *V -a/-et* 1 covet, pursue: **rødhåret og e-et var hun og** she was red-headed and sought after too (Hamsun). 2 attack, persecute: **e- ens liv** make an attempt on sby's life.

et'ter/syn *-et/*-a* examination, inspection: **ved nærmere e-** on closer scrutiny.

+**et'ter/søke** *V -te* search for, seek: **e-t av politiet** wanted by the police.

+**et'ter/så** *pt of* **-se**

et'ter/tanke *-n* reflection: **med e-** with due consideration; **stoff til e-** food for thought; **ved nærmere e-** on second thought; **vekke til e-** give food for thought.

+**et'ter/telle** *V infl as telle* recount (money for the purpose of checking a sum).

+**et'ter/tenksom** [also -ten'k-] *A -t, pl -me* (=*sam) pensive, thoughtful.

et'ter/tid *-a/+-en* 1 future: **for e-en** in (the) f-. 2 posterity.

+**et'ter/trakte** *V -et* covet, desire.

+**et'tertraktelses/verdig** *A* - desirable.

et'ter/tropp *-en* rear guard.

et'ter/trykk *-et* 1 emphasis, stress: **legge e- på** emphasize, place s- on; **med e-** emphatically. 2 reprinting (of book): **e- forbudt** all rights reserved.

+**ettertryk'kelig** *A* - emphatic, forcible.

+**et'ter/veer** *pl med.* afterpains (following childbirth); *fig.* aftereffects, repercussions: **føle e- etter** feel, suffer from the aftereffects of.

et'ter/vekst *-en* (=*/vokster) aftergrowth (of trees etc.).

+**et'ter/verden** *-en* posterity.

et'ter/vern [/væ·rn] *-et* court custody (esp. in connection with juvenile delinquents).

+**et'ter/virkning** *-en* (=*/verking, */verknad) aftereffect; repercussion.

+**et'ter/vise** *V -te* demonstrate, show.

+**et'ter/år** *-et* autumn, fall.

***et'ter/åt** *Av* after, afterwards.

+**ett'/tal(l)** *-et* (=*eitt/) (the number) one.

+**ett'/øring** *-en* (=*eitt/) cf **en/**

+**ett'/årig** *A* - (=*eitt/) one-year (in age or duration).

etui' *-et, pl -/+-er* case (for cigarettes, silverware, jewelry, etc).

ety'de *-n* étude.

etyll' *-et chem.* ethyl.

etyll'/alkoho'l *-en* ethyl alcohol.

etymolog [-olå'g] *-en* etymologist.

etymologi' *-en* etymology.

etymolo'gisk *A* - etymological.

eufemis'me *-n* (=**evfemisme**) euphemism.

Eufrat [au'fratt] *Pln* the Euphrates.

eunukk' [au-] *-en* (=**evnukk**) eunuch.

+**eurasier** [aura'sier] *-en, pl -e* (=*-ar) Eurasian.

eurasisk [aura'sisk] *A* - Eurasian.

Europa [auro'pa] *Pln* Europe.

+**europe'er** [au-] *-en, pl -e* (=*-ar) European.

europe'isk [au-] *A* - European.

***e'v** *-et* doubt, uncertainty.

E'va *Prn (f)*

+**e'va/datter** *-en* (=*/dotter) daughter of Eve (=very feminine woman).

evakue're *V -te* evacuate (troops or civilian population).

evakue'ring *-a/+-en* evacuation (of troops or civilian population).

evalue're *V -te psych.* evaluate (the results of a test or series of tests).

evange'lisk *A* - evangelical.

evangelis't *-en* evangelist.

evange'lium *-iet, pl +-ier/*-ium* gospel: **tro på noe som på e-et** take sth as the g- truth.

Evang'er *Pln* twp, Hordaland.

***e've**[1] *-n* doubt, uncertainty.

***e've**[2] *V -a/-et*: **e- seg** be uncertain about, be in doubt about.

E've/nes' *Pln* twp, Nordland.

event. =**eventuelt**

eventualite't *-en* eventuality, possibility: **være beredt på alle e-er** be ready for anything.

eventuell' *A -elt* 1 (any) possible, prospective: **e-t** (on agenda) miscellaneous, other business; **e-e kjøpere** prospective buyers; **for å unngå e-e misforståelser** in order to avoid any possible misunderstandings; **ved e-t krigsutbrudd** in the case of the outbreak of war; **han er ansvarlig for e-e overskridelser av budsjettet** he is responsible in case the budget is exceeded. 2 *(adv.)* possibly: **hvis han e-t skulle komme** in case he comes, if he should happen to come; **jeg kunne e-t hjelpe deg** I might (possibly) be able to help you; **jeg skal til Oslo neste sommer, og e-t til Bergen** I am going to Oslo next summer, and perhaps also to Bergen.

e'ventyr *-et* 1 adventure: **gå (dra) ut på e-** seek a-s (often of an erotic nature); **mitt liv har vært et eneste e-** my life has been one long a-. 2 fairytale, folktale: **Asbjørnsen og Moe samlet norske e-** A- and M- collected Norwegian folktales; **snipp snapp snute, så er e-et ute** one two three, that's the end of the tale.

+**e'ventyr/aktig** *A* - fanciful, unreal.

+**e'ventyrer** [also -ty'-] *-en, pl -e* (=*-ar) adventurer.

+**e'ventyrerske** [also -ty'-] *-a/-en* adventuress (often one who seeks erotic adventures).

e'ventyr/land *-et* fairyland, land of make-believe.

eventy'rlig *A* - 1 adventurous, daring. 2 fantastic, unbelievable. 3 *fig.* marvelous, tremendous.

e'ventyr/lysten *A +-ent, pl -ne* adventurous.

evfemis'me *-n* cf **eufemisme**

eviden's *-en*: **til e-** conclusively, obviously.

e'vig *A* - eternal, everlasting, perpetual: **e- og alltid** constantly, everlastingly; **e- snø** perpetual snow; **for e-** always, forever; **fra e-e tider** from time immemorial; **hver e-e** every single (one, day, time, etc.); **til e- tid** eternally, to all eternity; **den e-e hvile** everlasting peace; **den e-e jøde** the Wandering Jew; **den e-e stad** the Eternal City; **det e-e liv** life eternal; **det skal du ha e- takk for** I'll never be able to thank you enough; *fam.* **e- glad** very glad; **det har du e- rett i** you're most certainly right about that; **det tar en e- tid** it takes forever; **vente (vare) e-** wait (last) for ages.

e'vig/grøn *A* (=+/grønn) evergreen (e.g. tree).

+**e'vig/het** *-en* eternity: **fra e- til e-** for ever and ever; **aldri i e-!** not on my life, never in my life!; **for tid og e-** for ever; *fam.* **det er en e- siden jeg så deg sist** it's been ages since I last saw you.

+**e'vighets/blomst** *-en bot.* cudweed (Gnaphalium).

+**e'vighets/maski'n** *-en* perpetual motion machine.

e'vig/varende *A* - everlasting, perpetual.

+**evin'nelig** *A* - everlasting, perpetual: **i det e-e** to all eternity, without end.

ev'je *-a* 1 marshy bay. 2 calm part of a river. 3 (=**bak/**) backwater, eddy.

Ev'je *Pln* portion of Evje og Hornnes twp, Aust-Agder.

***e'v/laust** *Av* certainly, undoubtedly.

***ev'le**[1] *-t* might, power, strength.

ev'le[2] *V -a/+-et dial.* 1 be able (**med** to), be capable of, manage. 2 strive, work hard (at sth).

***ev'lug** *A* - capable; powerful, strong.

ev'ne[1] *-a/+-en* 1 ability, faculty; power: **etter e-** according to one's a-; **(gjøre noe) etter beste e-** (do sth) as well as one can; **etter fattig e-** as well as one can (though that might not be very good); **ha e- til å** have the f- of; **Over E-** Beyond Human Power (play by Bjørnson). 2 *(pl)* gift, talent: **ha store e-r** be very gifted. 3 *archaic*=**emne.** 4 (financial) means: **leve over e-** live beyond one's m-.

ev'ne[2] *V -a/+-et* be able (**å** to), be capable of.

ev'ne/laus *A* (=+/løs) incapable; untalented.

+**ev'neløs/het** *-en* incapability; lack of talent.

ev'ne/løyse *-a* cf **-løs/het**

ev'ne/prøve *-a/+-en* test of ability; intelligence test.

ev'ne/rik *A* capable; gifted, talented.

ev'ne/veik *A* mentally retarded.
evnukk' *-en* cf **eunukk**
evolusjo'n *-en* evolution.
examen artium [eksa'men ar'tsium] 1 final examination in the Norwegian secondary school **(gymnasium)**, serving also as entrance examination to the University. 2 degree awarded upon successful completion of the final secondary school examination: **han har e-** he has graduated from secondary school **(gymnasium)**.
ex audito'rio from the audience, unofficial(ly): **opponent e-** unofficial examiner, critic (during a Norwegian doctoral examination).
ex li'bris *en* bookplate.
Ey- *Prn* cf **Øy-**

F

f [eff'] *-en* (letter, *mus.* note) F, f.
f. =**følgende; for; fot; født**
fa. =**firma**
fa'bel *-elen, pl -ler* 1 fable, story, tale. 2 falsehood, fiction. 3 plot.
fa'bel/aktig *A* - fabulous, fantastic; exceptional, unusual.
fa'bel/dyr *-et* fabulous, supernatural monster.
fa'ble *V -a/+-et* rave, talk wildly: **f- om** daydream.
fabrikan't *-en* factory owner; manufacturer (**av** of).
fabrikasjo'n *-en* making, manufacture.
fabrika't *-et, pl -/+-er* goods, product; make, manufacture.
fabrike're *V -te* cf **fabrikkere**
fabrikk' *-en* factory, mill, works.
fabrikke're *V -te* 1 make, manufacture. 2 fabricate, fake.
fabrikk'/merke *-t, pl +-r/*-* trademark.
fabrikk'/pipe *-a* smokestack.
fabule're *V -te* 1 give one's imagination free rein; narrate, tell (fiction). 2 *psych.* pass off invented experiences as reality.
fad'der *-en, pl +-e/*fadrar* godparent, sponsor.
fad'der/skap *+-et/*-en* sponsorship.
fad'der/sladder *-en, pl +-e obs.* gossip; balderdash, nonsense.
fade [fei'de] *V -a/+-et elec.* fade.
fa'der *-en, pl +fedre/*fedrar* cf **far**[1]
fa'derlig *A* - 1 fatherly, paternal. 2 *fam.* powerful, tremendous: **vi hadde det f- moro** we enjoyed ourselves immensely; **f- fort** instantly, right away; at breakneck speed.
+fa'derlig/het *-en* fatherly manner; paternalism.
+fa'der/løs *A* cf **far/laus**
+fa'der/morder [/morder] *-en, pl -e* **(=*-ar)** 1 parricide, patricide. 2 *hum., hist.* high, tight collar (worn ab. 1850).
fa'der/vår *-et* the Lord's prayer: **kunne mer enn sitt f-** know a great deal (orig. about occult matters).
fade'se *-n* blunder, faux pas: **begå f-r** put one's foot in one's mouth.
fading [fei'ding] *-a/+-en* (of radio) fading.
fa'en *en* cf **fanden**
fa'en/skap *-en* cf **fanden/**
fa'g *-et* 1 line, profession, trade; field, subject: **det er ikke mitt f-** it's not in my l-; **og alt til f-et henhørende** with all the trimmings. 2 section (of wall); bay; window; pair of curtains. 3 compartment, pigeonhole; *typog.* box.
fa'g- og [å] **for'/skole** *-n* vocational and professional school.
+fa'g/arbei'der [also fa'g/] *-en, pl -e* **(=*-ar)** skilled worker.
+fa'g/beve'gelse *-n* labor, trade union movement.
fa'g/blad *-et* scientific, technical journal; trade journal.
fa'g/bok *-a, pl -bøker* (usu. *pl*) professional, technical book.
+fa'g/dommer *-en, pl -e* **(=*-ar)** *jur.* judge (i.e. one who has had legal training, in contrast to a lay judge).
fa'ger *A -ert, pl -re poet.* beautiful, fair, handsome: **lokke en med f-re ord og løfter** talk sby into doing sth (with false promises).
°fa'geren *df* cf **fanden**
fa'ger/gås *-a zool.* sheldrake (Tadorna tadorna).
Fa'ger/nes *Pln* town, Nord-Aurdal twp, Oppland.
fa'g/felle *-n* colleague, fellow worker.
fa'g/folk *pl* experts, professionals, specialists.
+fa'g/forbund *-et* federation of trade unions, ab. =AFL-CIO.
+fa'g/fore'ning *-a/-en* **(=*-eining)** labor union, trade union.
fa'g/idio't *-en derog.* one who limits his interest entirely to his specialty.
fa'g/krets *-en* **(=*/krins)** domain, field, sphere; range of subjects.
fa'g/kunnska'p *-en* technical knowledge.
fa'glig *A* - professional, technical.
fa'g/litteratu'r *-en* scientific, technical literature.
+fa'g/lært *A* - **(=*-lærd)** skilled; trained.
fa'g/mann *-en, pl -menn/*-menner* expert, specialist.
fa'g/messig *A* - professional, technical.
fa'gna *A* - excellent, worthy; promising; skillful: **eit f- kast** a great catch.
fa'gnad *-en* delight, joy, pleasure.
fa'gna/folk *-et* fine people.
***fa'gna/mann** *-en, pl -menn(er)* eminent, worthy man.
fa'gne *V -a/+-et* welcome sby cordially, with good cheer.
fa'g/organise'rt *A* - organized: **de f-e o-** labor.
fagott' *-en mus.* bassoon.
fa'g/skole *-n* trade, vocational school; technical school.
fa'g/språk *-et* technical language, terms.
fa'g/uttrykk *-et* technical term, trade term.
***fa'g/voren** *A -e/-i, pl -ne* professional, technical.
fair [fæ'r] *A* - fair (play).
fajanse [fajang'se] *-n* faience (porcelain).
faki'r *-en* fakir.
fak'ke *V -a/+-et* 1 catch, lay hold of, seize. 2 bow (felt).
fak'kel *-elen, pl fakler* 1 torch. 2 *astron.* solar prominence.
fak'kel/tog [/tåg] *-et* torchlight parade, procession.
fak'ler *pl of* **fakkel**
fak's *-et* 1 mane, shock of hair. 2 *bot.* brome grass (genus Bromus).
fak'set(e) *A* - -maned; e.g. **hvit/** white-maned.
faksi'mile *-t, pl +-r/*-* facsimile.
fak'ta 1 *pl of* **faktum.** 2 *(adv.) fam.* actually, as a matter of fact.
fak'te *-a/+-en* 1 antic, gesture: **gjøre f-r** gesticulate. 2 caprice, whim.
fak'tisk *A* - 1 factual; actual, matter-of-fact, real: **de f-e forhold** the facts of the case; **det er f-** it's a fact. 2 *(adv.)* actually, as a matter of fact.
fak'tor[1] *-en* printing shop foreman.
fak'tor[2] *-en, pl fakto'rer* 1 *math.* factor. 2 element, factor.
fakto'tum *-et, pl +-er/*-* factotum; jack-of-all-trades.
fak'tum *-et, pl fakta* circumstance, fact: **f- er** as a matter of fact, the fact of the matter is.
faktu'ra *-en, pl *-er merc.* invoice.
fakture're *V -te merc.* invoice.
fakul'tativ *A* facultative, optional.
fakulte't *-et, pl -/+-er educ.* college, faculty (=both department of learning and the teaching body).
fa'l[1] *-en* 1 socket (for shaft of spear etc.). 2 film, membrane.
fa'l[2] *A* for sale, to be bought; available.
falan'ks *-en, pl falanger* phalanx.
fal'/by *V infl as* **by**[2] offer for sale.
fal'd *-en* 1 hem. 2 *hist.* covering for the head (women).
***-fald** *Av* cf **-fold**
fal'de *V -a/+-et* hem.
fa'le *V -a/+-et* bargain, dicker, haggle.
°fa'lig *A* - cf **farlig**
fal'k *-en zool.* falcon (family Falconidae).
fal'ke/blikk *-et* eagle eye.
+fal'ke/fenger *-en, pl -e* falconer.
fal'ke/jakt *-a/+-en* falconry, hawking.
fal'k/unge [/onge] *-n* young falcon, young hawk.
fall'[1] *-et* 1 drop (e.g. in prices, temperature, etc.; height difference), fall, falling: **et f- på** a d- of (e.g. 5 feet); **stå for f-** be on the point of falling, be doomed; **hovmod står for f-** pride goeth before a fall. 2 waterfall. 3 wave (in hair). 4 *naut.* halyard. 5 case: **i f-** in c-, in the event: **i alle (alt) f-, i hvert f-** in any c-, at any rate, anyhow; **i beste (verste) f-** at best (worst); **i motsatt f-** on the other hand, if not; **i så f-** in that c-, if so.
***fall'**[2] *pt of* **falle**
fal'le *V +-er/*fell, +falt/*fall, +falt/*-e/*-i* 1 fall; (of judgment in a legal case) be handed down, pronounced; (of words) be spoken, dropped; (of materials) hang: **ta det som det f-er (seg)** take things as they come; **la f-** drop (e.g. object, hint, etc.); **det f-er meg tungt å si dette** it's difficult for me to say this. 2 decrease, drop (e.g. prices, temperature, etc.). 3 be killed (in action). 4 (of terrain) slope; (of river) run (in a given direction). 5 (with *prep.* and *adv.*): **f- av** fall off (also *naut.*); decline, decrease; **f- av seg selv** come naturally; **det f-er av seg selv** it's obvious; **f- bort** cease, die out; **f- for** fall by (e.g. the sword); fall for (sby), succumb to (a temptation); **f- fra** die, pass away; desert, drop off; **f- i** fall into, through (e.g. ice), drop off (to sleep); join in (singing etc.); **f- i ens smak** be to one's liking; **f- i fisk** fall through, go to pot; **f- i øynene** catch the eye; **f- igjennom** fail, fall through; **f- inn**

+ Bokmål; * Nynorsk; ° Dialect.
After letter: ' stress (Acc. 1); ` tone, stress (Acc. 2); · length.
Below letter: . not pronounced.

chime in, join in; **f- en inn** occur to sby, strike sby; **f- inn under** come under (a classification); **f- en lett (vanskelig)** be easy (difficult) for one; **f- om** fall over, topple; **f- en om halsen** throw one's arms around sby's neck; **f- på** dream up, hit on, think of; fall on (e.g. a day), fall to (e.g. sby); (of darkness) fall, close in; **f- sammen** collapse; coincide; **f- en til byrde** be a burden to sby; **f- til ro** calm down, grow quiet; **f- ut** fall out; turn out, work out; (of rivers) **f- ut i** flow into. 6 *(refl.)*: **f- seg** happen, turn out; **det falt seg slik (sånn) at** it so happened, turned out that.

fal'le/ferdig *A* - ramshackle, tumbledown.

fal'le/kniv *-en* jackknife.

fal'len *A* *+-ent, pl falne* fallen: **f- kvinne** f- woman.

fallen't *-en merc.* bankrupt.

fallera' *I* tralala (=refrain of meaningless syllables in old songs).

falle're *V -te merc.* fail (in business), go bankrupt; *(pop.)* go broke.

+fal'le/syke *-n* **(=*fall/sykje)** *med.* epilepsy.

fall'/gruve *-a* **(=+/grube)** pitfall.

+fall'/hastighet *-en phys.* velocity of falling bodies.

fall'/høgd *-a* **(=+/høyde)** *phys.* drop, height of a fall.

fallitt'[1] *-en merc.* bankruptcy, business failure.

fallitt'[2] *A* - *merc.* bankrupt.

+fallitt'/bo *-et* **(=*/bu)** *jur.* estate in bankruptcy.

+fallitt'/erklæ'ring *-a/-en* 1 declaration of bankruptcy. 2 admission of failure.

fall'/lem' *-men* trap door.

fal'los *-en* phallus.

fall'/reip *-et* **(=+/rep)** *naut.* gangway: **på f-et** on the point of leaving, when saying farewell.

fall'/skjerm *-en* parachute.

***fall'/sykje** *-a* cf **falle/syke**

fal'me *V -a/+-et* fade.

fal'ne *A pl of* **fallen**

fal's[1] *+en/*eit obs.* deceit, falsehood, guile: **f- slår sin egen herre på hals** dishonesty never pays.

fal's[2] *-en* 1 fold; groove, notch; rabbet (for doors and windows). 2 (of book) hinge, joint.

fal's[3] *N*: **til f-** for sale, to be bought.

fal'se *V -a/+-et* fold; notch; rabbet.

falsett' *-en* falsetto.

+fal'sk[1] *-en* 1 deceit, falsehood, guile. 2 *jur.* forgery.

fal'sk[2] *A* false: **f- ed** perjury; **komme i en f- stilling** be placed in a f- position; **synge f-t** sing out of tune.

***fal'skar** *-en* cf **falskner**

***fal'ske[1]** *-n* fine ashes.

fal'ske[2] *V -a/+-et* falsify; counterfeit, fake, forge.

+fal'sk/het *-en* 1 falsity. 2 duplicity, falsehood, guile.

+fal'sk/myntner *-en, pl -e* counterfeiter, forger.

+fal'sk/myntneri' *-et* counterfeiting, forgery.

+fal'skner *-en, pl -e* **(=*falskar)** counterfeiter, forger.

falskneri' *-et, pl +-er/*-* forgery: **begå f-** commit f-.

+fal'sk/spiller *-en, pl -e* **(=*/spelar)** cheat; (professional) cardsharp.

fal'sum *-et* fake, forgery; deceit; fabrication.

+fal't *pt, pp of* **falle**

fami'lie *-n* family: **f-ns sorte får** the black sheep of the f-; **stifte f-** start a f-; **være i f- med en** be related to sby.

fami'lie/bibel *-elen, pl -ler* family Bible.

fami'lie/drama *-et, pl -/+-er* domestic drama, tragedy.

fami'lie/far *-en, pl +-fedre/*-fedrar* head of the family, paterfamilias.

+fami'lie/forsør'ger *-en, pl -e* **(=*-jar)** breadwinner, family provider.

fami'lie/liv *-et* domestic life, home life.

+fami'lie/navn *-et* **(=*/namn)** family name, surname.

+fami'lie/overho'de *-t* head of the family.

fami'lie/tillegg *-et mil.* quarters and allowance; family allowance.

fami'lie/vennlig *A* -: **f- skattepolitikk** fiscal policy for the benefit of the family.

familiæ'r *A* 1 familiar, informal; bold, forward, intrusive. 2 *lit.* familial.

+fam'le *V -a/-et* fumble, grope, reach **(etter** for): **f- etter ordene** search for words; **f- i mørke** be groping in the dark; **f- seg fram** grope one's way; **f-ende** clumsily.

fam'n *-en* **(=+favn)** 1 arms, embrace: **ta en i sin f-** embrace sby. 2 *naut.* fathom: **på seks f-er** in six f-s of water. 3: **en f- ved** (ab.) a cord of wood.

fam'ne *V -a/+-et* **(=+favne)** 1 embrace, hug: *fig.* **han f-er vidt** he has broad interests, a broad grasp. 2 *naut.*: **f- opp** sound.

fam'ne/ved *-en* cf **famn/**

fam'n/tak *-et* embrace, hug.

fam'n/ved *-en* (=**famne/**) cord wood.

famø's *A* infamous, notorious.

fa'n *en* cf **fanden**

Fa'na *Pln* twp, Hordaland.

Fa'na/råken *Pln* cf **Fanna/råki**

+fana'tiker *-en, pl -e* **(=*-ar)** fanatic, zealot.

fana'tisk *A* - fanatic.

fanatis'me *-n* fanaticism.

fandango [fandang'go] *-en* fandango.

fan'den [*pop.* fa'en] *en* **(=faen, fan)** 1 the devil: **f- er løs** there'll be hell to pay; **lese noe som f- leser bibelen** twist the meaning of sth for one's own purposes; **før f- får sko på** at the crack of dawn; **male f- på veggen** raise bugbears, paint a dark picture of things. 2 (used as intensifier and in oaths): **f- ta (gale, hakke, hente, skjære, etc.) meg** (humorous oaths, ab.=) well, I'll be -; **for f-** (oath); **f- til kar** a helluva guy; **f- vet** damned if I know; **fy f-** (strong oath); **gi f- i** not give a damn about; **gå f- i vold** go to hell; **hva f- vil du** what the hell do you want; **som (bare) f-** like hell; **det var som f-** damn it all, that's a helluva note; **en f-s fyr** a helluva guy; **det blir en f-s historie** there'll be hell to pay.

+fanden/ivoldsk [fa'n/ivål'sk] *A* - devil-may-care, madcap, reckless.

fanden/skap [fa'n/skap] *-en* deviltry; the devil.

fandens/makt [fa'ns/makt] *-a/+-en* deviltry; the devil.

°fa'ne[1] *-a* cf **fonn**

fa'ne[2] *-a/+-en* 1 banner, ensign, standard; colors: **heise den hvite f-** indicate one's willingness to discuss terms of surrender; **med flyvende f-r og klingende spill** with flags flying and drums beating. 2 *zool.* (of feather) vane, web. 3 *mus.* hook.

+fa'ne/bærer *-en, pl -e* **(=*/berar)** standard-bearer.

fa'ne/flukt *-a/+-en* desertion (of a cause).

fa'ne/junker [/jongker] *-en, pl +-e mil.* (until 1927) highest non-commissioned officer (cf U.S. Army master sergeant).

fa'ne/tog [/tåg] *-et* parade (with the colors).

fanfa're *-n mus., fig.* fanfare, flourish.

fang'[1] *-et* 1 arms, embrace: **ta en i f-** hug sby. 2 knees, lap: **han tok barnet på f-et** he put the child on his lap. 3 *dial.* epilepsy.

fang'[2] *-et* (=**fange[2]**) 1 armful, armload: **et f- ved** an armful of wood. 2 materials, supply.

***fang'an** *-et* armful, armload.

fang'/arm *-en zool.* tentacle.

fang'e[1] *-n* convict; prisoner; captive, prisoner of war: **ta til f-** capture.

fang'e[2] *-t* cf **fang[2]**

fang'e[3] *V -a/+-et* capture, take prisoner; catch, trap (birds, wild animals): **f- ens blikk, oppmerksomhet** catch sby's eye, attract sby's attention; **f- ens interesse** engage one's interest; **f- i garnet** entangle in one's toils; **f- inn** catch, take in; **med alle sanser f-er du inn livet** with all your senses you drink in life (Evensmo).

+fang'e[4] *V -et archaic* get, receive; contract, encur.

fang'e/hol *-et* **(=+/hull)** dungeon.

fang'e/leir *-en mil.* prisoner-of-war camp.

fang'en/skap *-et* captivity, imprisonment.

+fang'er *-en, pl -e* **(=*-ar)** hunter; sealer; whaler.

fang'e/tå'rn *-et hist.* donjon, keep.

+fang'e/vokter *-en, pl -e* **(=*/vaktar)** jailer, warder (turnkey); prison guard.

fang'/hund *-en* lap dog.

fang'/line *-a naut.* painter.

fang'/skinn *-et* (leather) apron (used e.g. by carpenters).

fang'st *-en* 1 catching, taking (e.g. fish, seals, whales): **dra på f-** go (deep-sea) fishing. 2 bag, catch, haul; booty.

fang'st/båt *-en naut.* longboat, whaleboat.

fang'ste *V -a/+-et* hunt, take seals and whales.

fang'st/mann *-en, pl -menn/*-menner* sealer; whaler.

fang'st/plass *-en* fishing (sealing, whaling) ground.

fang'st/tid *-a/+-en* fishing (sealing, whaling) season.

fang'/ta *V infl as* **ta** 1 curb, tame. 2: **f-s** wrestle. 3 embrace, hug.

fang'/tak *-et* 1 wrestling. 2 embrace, hug.

fan'ken *I* cf **fanden**

***fann'** *pt of* **finne[5]**

Fan'na/råki *Pln* mountain in Jotunheimen.

+fan's *pt of* **finnes**

fa'ns/makt *-a/+-en* cf **fandens/**

***fan'st** *pt of* **finnast**

fan't[1] *-en* 1 gypsy; tramp, vagabond; *(pop.)* bum, hobo: **gjøre en til f-** ruin sby; **gjøre som f-en** leave as soon as one has been fed. 2 *hum.* rascal, scoundrel.

+fan't[2] *pt of* **finne[5]**

fantase're *V -te* 1 give free rein to one's imagination, indulge in fancies, reveries: **f- om** dream about. 2 *med.* be delirious, rave. 3 *mus.* improvise.

fantasi' *-en* 1 imagination; fantasy, figment; *med.* hallucination. 2 *mus.* fantasia.

+fantasi'/forestil'ling *-en* **(=*/førestelling)** *philos.* idea, image (i.e. concept formed in the mind not in close connection with sense perception).

fantasi'/foster [/foster] *-eret/-ret, pl -er/+-re* chimera, figment.

fantasi'/full *A* imaginative.

fantasi'/laus *A* **(=+/løs)** dull, unimaginative.

fantas't *-en* dreamer, visionary.

fantasteri' *-et, pl -/-er* fancy,vagary; dreams, ravings.

fantas'tisk *A* - fanciful, fantastic.

fan'te *V -a/+-et*: **f- bort** fritter away, squander (money, time).

fan'te/ferd [*/fær] *-a* knavery, rascally tricks, shenanigans.

+fan'te/følge *-t* **(=*/følgje)** gang of gypsies, tramps; *(pop.)* bums.

fan'te/gå *V +-gikk/*-gjekk, -gått obs.* 1 roam around like a gypsy, tramp; *(pop.)* ride the rods. 2 leave, quit one's job without prior notice, walk out on the job.

fan'teri *-et* 1 tricks; foolishness, nonsense: **gjøre noe på f-** play a trick; do sth as a joke; **slikt f-** such nonsense. 2 witchcraft; trolls.

+fan'tes *pt of* **finnes**

fan'te/strek *-en* dirty trick, mean act; practical joke.

fan'te/stykke *-t, pl +-r/*-* dirty trick, mean act; practical joke.

fan'te/vis *-a/-en/-et*: **på f-** like a tramp.

fanto'm *-et, pl -/+-er* phantom: **F-et** Superman (comic strip).

fan't/o'rd *-et* cutting, sarcastic remark; *(pop.)* nasty crack.

fa'r[1] *-en, pl +fedre/*fedrar* (=**fader**) 1 father; *(pop.)* dad: **Faderen** God the F-; **sjuende f- i huset** the seventh grandfather (from folk tale). 2 *(pl)* ancestors, forefathers: *bibl.* **gå til sine f-e** be gathered unto one's f-. 3=**farr** *(interj.) pop.* old man, old thing: **nei farr!** no sirree!

fa'r[2] *-et* 1 track, trail. 2 course (of brook, river).

***fa'rande** *A* - navigable, passable.

fa'rang *-en* epidemic.

fa'rao *-nen, pl -o'ner* 1 *hist.* Pharaoh. 2 faro (card game).

+fa'r/bar *A* navigable, passable.

far'/bror *-en, pl +-brødre/*-brør* uncle (father's brother).

fa're[1] *-n* danger; hazard, risk (**for** to): **bringe i f-** endanger, jeopardize; **det er f- for** there's a d- (r-) of; **med f- for sitt liv** at the r- of his life; **stå, være i f- for å** be in d-, run the r- of; **f-n over** all clear.

fa're[2] *V +-er/*fer, fór, +-(e)t/*-e/*-i* 1 go, travel; wander: **la noe f-** abandon sth, give up sth, let sth go, **stå, være på f-ende fot** be about to leave. 2 dash, rush; leap, run; flash: **f- som et lyn** dart, d- madly; **komme f-ende** come running, rush along; **det fór gjennom meg** it f-ed through my mind. 3 (with *prep., adv.*) **f- av sted** dash off; **f- fram** act, behave, deal (**med** with); **f- gjennom** read through quickly, rush through; **f- hen til** rush over to; *bibl.* **f- i fred** depart in peace; **f- ille** turn out badly; be injured, (of women) miscarry; **f- løs på en** fly at, go after sby; **f- med** deal with, treat (a person in a given way); be engaged in, do: **f- med løgn** lie, **f- med sladder** gossip, **f- med knep** be up to tricks; **ha lite (ikke mye) å f- med** not be very talented, have little to offer; **f- om halsen på en** throw oneself around sby's neck; **f- opp** start up, jump up; snap open; become angry, flare up; **f- over** do sth superficially, run over, through; stroke lightly (e.g. with the hand); **f- over med øynene** scan; **f- over ende** fall over; sit up suddenly; **f- på** go after, rush at; **f- sammen** start up, be startled; ***f- til** jump, start; ***f- til å** begin to; **f- vel** turn out well, have good fortune; ***f- åt** act, behave.

fa're/dag *-en* moving day.

fa're/fri *A -tt* free from danger, safe.

fa're/full *A* dangerous, perilous, risky.

fa're/momen't *-et, pl -/+-er* element of risk.

fa'ren *A +-ent, pl -ne* situated: **ille f-** in a bad way.

+-farer *-en, pl -e* (=***-ar**) explorer, traveler: e.g. **sydpolsf-** Antarctic explorer.

fa're/signal [/singna'l] *-et, pl -/+-er* danger signal.

fa're/sone *-a/+-en* danger zone.

+fa'ret *pp of* **fare[2]**

+fa're/truende *A* - ominous.

far'/far *-en, pl +-fedre/*-fedrar* (paternal) grandfather.

***far'g** *-et* heavy, severe pressure.

far'ge[1] *-n* 1 color, hue; shade, tint; dye, paint, pigment: **male med sterke f-r** lay on the colors too thickly (exaggerate); **skifte f-** turn pale (with fright) or red (with shame); **vise f-** show one's hand. 2 suit (in cards). 3 *typog.* ink.

far'ge[2] *V -a/+-et* color, dye, stain: **det f-er av** the color runs.

far'ge/band *-et* (=**+/bånd**) (typewriter) ribbon.

far'ge/blind *A* color-blind.

far'ge/blyant *-en* colored pencil, crayon.

far'ge/ekte *A* - fast, permanent (colors).

far'ge/film *-en* color film.

far'ge/glad *A* - delighting in colors; colorful.

far'ge/handel *-elen, pl -ler* paint store.

far'ge/la *pt of* **-legge**

far'ge/laus *A* (=**+/løs**) colorless; dull.

+far'ge/legge *V -la, -lagt* (=***-je**) color, tint.

far'ge/plante *-a/-en* plant yielding dyes, e.g. dyeweed (Genista tinctoria).

far'ge/prakt *-a/+-en* glowing, rich colors.

+far'ger *-en, pl -e* (=***-ar**) dyer.

fargeri' *-et, pl -/+-er* dyehouse.

far'ge/rik *A* colorful, richly colored.

+far'ge/sammenset'ning *-a/-en* color scheme.

far'ge/sans *-en* sense of color.

far'ge/skrin *-et* paint box.

+far'ge/spill *-et* (=***/spel**) play of colors; iridescence, opalescence.

far'ge/stoff *-et, pl -/+-er* dye, dyestuff.

far'ge/strålende *A*- brilliantly, gaily colored.

far'ge/tone *-n* shade, tint.

fari'n *-et/+-en* (granulated) sugar.

+farise'er *-en, pl -e* (=***-ar**) Pharisee.

farise'isk *A* - pharisaical.

far'k[1] *-en* tramp, vagabond; bum, hobo; undependable, unreliable person.

far'k[2] *-et* rabble, riffraff: **f- og fant** ne'er-do-wells; bums.

far'ke *V -a/+-et* botch, bungle.

far'ke/ferd [*/fær] *-a* dirty tricks, mean action.

°far'ken *N* the devil (used as intensifier and in oaths): **det er da f- til skrål** there's a hell of a racket.

far'ke/skap *-en* knavery, rascally tricks, shenanigans.

far'ket(e) *A* - tricky, underhanded.

fa'r/kost *-en* (small) boat, vessel.

fa'r/laus *A* fatherless.

fa'r/lei *-a* coastal channel, waterway.

fa'rlig *A* - 1 dangerous, hazardous, perilous; **det er ikke så f-** it doesn't matter. 2 awful, frightful, terrible: **et f- spetakkel** a fearful racket.

+fa'r/løs *A* cf **/laus**

far'm[1] *-en* farm.

***far'm[2]** *-en archaic* cargo, load.

farmakolog [-olå'g] *-en* pharmacologist.

farmakologi' *-en* pharmacology.

farmakopé' *-en* pharmacopoeia.

fa'r/mann *-en, pl -menn/*-menner archaic* traveling merchant: **Farmand** a magazine.

farmasi' *-en* pharmacy.

farmasøy't *-en* pharmacist.

+far'mer *-en, pl -e* (=***-ar**) farmer.

far'/mor *-a/-en, pl -mødrer/+-mødre* (paternal) grandmother.

farr' *N* cf **far[1]**

***far're** *-n* tramp, vagrant; gypsy.

Far'ris *Pln* lake, Brunlanes twp, Vestfold.

fa'rs/arv *-en* patrimony.

far'se *-n* 1 farce, forcemeat, mincemeat. 2 farce (comedy): **det var en ren f-** it was a complete f-.

+far'se/aktig *A* - farcical.

farse're *V -te* stuff with forcemeat, mincemeat.

fa'rs/ga'rd *-en* ancestral estate, home (farm).

fa'r/skap *+-et/*-en* fatherhood, paternity.

fa'rskaps/sak *-a/+-en jur.* paternity suit.

fa'r/sott *-a/+-en* endemic disease; epidemic.

fa'rs/side *-a/+-en*: **på f-n** on the father's side, paternal.

Far'/sund *Pln* seaport, Vest-Agder.

far't[1] *-en* 1 motion, speed: **det er f- på dem** they are in a hurry, moving fast; **for (i) full f-** at top s-; **i f-** in m-, (of elevator) busy; **i en f-** quickly, in a hurry; **i f-en** at the moment, offhand; **på f-en** in m-, on the go, on the move; **få, sette f- i** speed up; **sette f-en opp (ned)** increase (reduce) s-, accelerate (decelerate); **skyte en f- av** go at a s- of; **stå på f-en** be about to go, leave; **det er f- over ham (noe)** he is full of go (sth moves along briskly, is lively). 2 trade (by ship); voyage: **f-en på** the t- with (a port); **sette et skip i f-** put a ship into service.

+fa'rt[2] *pp of* **fare[2]**

far'te *V -a/+-et*: **f- om, rundt** wander from place to place; *(pop.)* knock about.

Far'/tein *Prn (m)*

far't/plan *-en* schedule, timetable.

far'ts/grense *-a/+-en* speed limit.

+far'ts/måler *-en, pl -e* (=***-ar**) speedometer; air speed indicator.

far'ts/tid *-a/+-en naut.* sea duty (total time for which a seaman signed on).

+far'/tøy *-et* (=***/ty**) boat, craft, vessel.

fa'r/vatn *-et* (=**+/vann**) seas, waters; channel, fairway: **f-et er klart** it's clear sailing; *fig.* the coast is clear; **han er i f-et** he can be expected (any time).

+far've[1] *-n* cf **farge[1]**

+far've[2] *V -et* cf **farge[2]**

farvel' *-let* (=**far vel**) goodbye; *(poet.)* farewell.

fasa'de *-n* 1 façade, front (e.g. of house). 2 *fig.* front, outward bearing, surface.

fasa'n *-en* pheasant.

fascine're *V -te* fascinate.

fascis'me *-n* fascism.

fascis't *-en* fascist.

fa'se *-n* phase.

+-faset *A* - (=***-fasa**) *elec.* phase, -phased: **enf-, tof-** single, double phase; **flerf-** polyphase.

fasett' *-en* facet.

fasette're *V -te* bevel, facet.

+fasett'/øye *-t, pl -r/-øyne* (=***/auga, */auge**) *zool.* compound eye (of arthropod).

fa'sit *-en* 1 answer, result, total. 2 *fam.* answer book, key.

fa'sit/bok *-a, pl -bøker* answer book, key.

fasjona'bel *A -elt, pl -le* fashionable, stylish.

faskin [fasji'n] *-en hist., mil.* fascine.

***fas'l** *-et* (=**fatl**) shoulder knot.

fas'le[1] *-n* (=**fatle[1]**) sling.

fas'le[2] *V -a/+-et* (=**fatle[2]**) carry one's arm in a sling.

fasong' *-en* 1 (of clothes) cut, style; shape. 2 custom, manners. 3 *archaic* manner, way (of doing sth).

fas't[1] *A* - 1 firm; fixed, solid; stable, steady: **f- bestemt på** firmly resolved to; **f- som fjell** as firm as a rock; **f-e legemer** solids; **med f- hånd** with a firm hand; **slå f-** ascertain, establish; **det står f- at** the fact remains that. 2 permanent (e.g. position), regular (e.g. customer, work): **f- eiendom** real property; **ha f- følge** go steady. 3 adhering, attached, stuck: **gripe f-ere om noe** tighten one's grip on sth; **henge f-** get s-; **hold f-** hold tight; **holde f- ved** adhere, stick to (an opinion); insist on; **sette f-** imprison; stump; **sette seg f-** get s-; get a foothold; **sitte, stå f-** be s- (also *fig.*). 4 *(adv.) obs.* almost.

+fas't[2] *C obs.* although.

+fas't/boende *A* - (=***/buande**) resident.

fas'te[1] *-a/+-en* 1 fast. 2 *eccl.* Lent.

fas'te[2] *V -a/+-et* fast (cf **fastende**).

+ Bokmål; * Nynorsk; ° Dialect.
After letter: ' stress (Acc. 1); ' tone, stress (Acc. 2); · length.
Below letter: . not pronounced.

Fas'te Prn(m)
fas'te/dag -en fast day.
fastela'vn -en eccl. Shrovetide; Mardi Gras.
fastela'vns/bolle -n cross bun (baked for Shrovetide).
fastela'vns/ris -et birch twigs (with which people playfully strike each other during Shrovetide).
fas'tende A - fasting: jeg er f- I haven't eaten anything yet; hum. I'm sober; på f- hjerte on an empty stomach.
fas'ter -ra/+-eren pl -rer/+re archaic (paternal) aunt.
+fas't/het -en 1 firmness, solidity. 2 determination, firmness.
+fas't/holde V -holdt, -holdt insist upon, maintain, stick to.
fas't/land -et mainland; continent: det mørke f- the Dark C- (orig. of Africa; used by Garborg of SW Norway).
fas't/lønt A - (=+/lønnet) salaried (employee).
fas'tne V -a/+-et 1 become, get stuck. 2 become compact, firm.
*fas't/rådd A - decided, determined: han er f- på å gå he's made up his mind to go.
*fas't/setje V -te cf /sette
+fas't/sette V -satte, -satt (=*/setje) decide on, fix, stipulate.
+fas't/settelse -n appointment; fixing, stipulation (av of).
+fas't/slå V -slo, -slått 1 assert, maintain. 2 demonstrate, establish, prove.
fa't -et, pl -/+-er 1 dish. 2 barrel, cask.
fa'ta pl of fatum
fata'l A unfortunate: det f-e er the tragic thing is.
fatalis'me -n fatalism.
fatalis't -en fatalist.
fatalite't -en calamity, misfortune.
fatamorga'na -et, pl +-er/*- mirage.
fa'te V -a/+-et cf fatte
fa'ting -a body (of carriage or sleigh).
*fat'l -et cf fasl
fat'le[1] -n cf fasle[1]
fat'le[2] V -a/+-et cf fasle[2]
fat'ne V -a/+-et catch fire, ignite.
+fat'ning -en 1 composure, selfpossession: bringe ut av f- disconcert; uten å miste f-en calmly, composedly. 2 mounting, setting.
fatt'[1] N: få f- i get hold of; ta f- (på) set to work (on), tackle (a problem).
fatt'[2] A -: det er galt f- med ham there's sth wrong with him, he's in a bad way; hva er f-? what's wrong?
fat'te V -a/+-et (=*fate) 1 grasp, seize: f- om clasp, grab hold of. 2 catch fire, ignite. 3 (=*fatte) comprehend, grasp, understand. 4 get, make: f- en beslutning come to a decision, make up one's mind; f- interesse for g- interested in; f- kjærlighet til be filled with love for; f- mot muster up courage. 5 (refl.) collect oneself; express oneself: f- seg i korthet be brief.
fat'te/evne -a/+-en comprehension, faculty of understanding.
fat'telig A - comprehensible, intelligible.
fat'ter -en hum. the old man, papa.
+fat'tet A - calm, cool, collected: blek, men f- pale but resolute.
fat'tig A - poor (på in); humble, mean; miserable, pitiful: de f-e the poor; de f-e i ånden the poor in spirit (Matt. 5,3); etter f- evne (leilighet) to the best of my (poor) ability.
fat'tig/dom' -men/*-en poverty.
fat'tig/kasse -a/-en poor relief: komme på f-en go on relief.
fat'tig/kvarte'r -et slum.
fat'tig/lem' +-met/*-en archaic pauper.
fat'tig/mann -en, pl -menn/*-menner 1 poor man. 2 =f-s/bakkels.
fat'tigmanns/bakkels(e) -(e)n/*-(e)t a deep-fried diamond-shaped Christmas cooky.
fat'tigslig A - mean, poor, wretched: en f- trøst cold comfort.
fat'tig/styre -t committee administering poor relief in a community.
+fat'tig/vesen -et poor relief (entire system).
fa'tum -et, pl fata destiny, fate.
fa't/øl' -et draft beer.
fau'k pt of fyke
fau'n -en faun.
fau'na -en fauna.
fau'sk -en touchwood.
Fau'ske Pln twp, Nordland.
°fau't -en cf fogd
+fav'n -en cf famn
+fav'ne V -a/-et cf famne
favorise're V -te favor, give preference to.
favoritt' -en favorite.
favø'r -en favor: i ens f- to sby's advantage, credit.
fayanse [fajang'se] -n cf fajanse
+fe'[1] -en fairy.
fe'[2] -et 1 cattle: folk og fe men and animals. 2 derog. blockhead, dunce, lunkhead.
+f. e. =for eksempel
+fe'/aktig A - bovine, stupid.
fe'/al -en (=+/avl) cattle breeding.
fe'ber -en fever: ha f- run a temperature.
+fe'ber/aktig A - feverish: f- travelhet f- activity.
fe'ber/fantasi'er pl delirium.
fe'ber/fri A -tt without a fever.
fe'ber/heit A burning with fever, feverish.
febr. =februar
febri'l A febrile, feverish.
febri'lsk A - agitated, excited: f- travelhet feverish activity.
februa'r en February.
Fe'da Pln twp, Vest-Agder.
fedd' -et skein (of yarn).
+fed'me -n corpulence, obesity.
*fe'drar pl of far[1]
+fe'dre pl of far[1]
fe'dre/heim -en ancestral home.
fe'dre/land -et fatherland, native country, native land: Amerika ble hans annet f- America became his second home (homeland).
+fe'drelands/sang -en (=*/song) national anthem, patriotic song.
fe'drelands/venn -en, pl *-er (=*/ven) patriot.
+fe'drene A -: på f- side on the father's side, paternal.
+fe'drene/jo'rd -a native soil.
fe'/drift -a/-en 1 cattle breeding, grazing. 2 herd (of cattle).
fe'/fot -en: legge for f- allow land to lie fallow, become pasture.
*fe'gen A -e/-i, pl -ne glad, happy.
*feg'nast V -ast be happy, pleased; rejoice.
fe'/hirde -n hist. royal treasurer (Medieval Norway).
+fe'/hode -t blockhead, lunkhead, simpleton.
fei' en: i en (fykende) f- in a jiffy, before you can say Jack Robinson.
+fei'de[1] -n 1 feud, quarrel; hist. private war. 2 controversy, polemic.
+fei'de[2] V -et 1 carry on a feud, quarrel; hist. engage in private warfare. 2 engage in controversy.
fei'e V -a/+-et/+-de 1 brush, clean, sweep: f- alt foran seg s- the board; f- bort, til side b-, s- aside; f- for egen dør put one's own house in order (before criticizing others); f- rent s- out. 2 dash, sweep: f- av sted s- along.
fei'e/brett -et dustpan.
fei'e/kost [/kost] -en broom; whiskbroom.
fei'ende A - dashing, sweeping: det gikk f- it went swimmingly.
fei'er -en, pl -e (=*-ar) 1 chimney sweep; street sweeper. 2 pop. fellow, guy.
fei'g A 1 cowardly, dastardly; (pop.) yellow. 2 archaic doomed, fey.
*fei'gd -a imminent death.
+fei'g/het -en cowardice.
fei'ging -en coward.
*fei'g/skap -en cowardice.
fei'l[1] -en, pl -/*-ar 1 defect, fault, flaw (ved in): finne f- hos en find fault with sby. 2 blunder, error, mistake: det er hans egen f- it is his own fault.
+fei'l[2] A - erroneous, incorrect, wrong: gå en f- vei take the w- road; han tok f- hatt he took sby else's hat; slå f- fail, go wrong; ta f- be mistaken.
+fei'l/aktig [also -ak'-] A - defective, faulty; erroneous, incorrect.
+fei'l/bar A - fallible.
fei'le V -a/+-et/+-te 1 lit. err, go astray: å f- er menneskelig to e- is human. 2 fail; make mistakes. 3 be wrong with: hva er det som f-er ham? what ails him?
fei'l/fri A -tt faultless, flawless.
fei'l/grep -et error, mistake, slip; error of judgment, misjudgment.
fei'l/kjelde -a (=+/kilde) source of error.
fei'l/slått A - (=+/slagen) abortive, unsuccessful.
+fei'l/tagelse [also /ta'-] -n error, erroneous assumption, mistake: ved en f- by m-.
fei'l/trekk -et erroneous move.
+fei'l/trinn -et false step, lapse, slip.
fei'l/vare -a/+-en defective merchandise.
*fei'men A -e/-i, pl -ne adhesive, sticky; unclear.
feinschmecker [fai'n/sjmekker] -en, pl +-e epicure, gourmet.
fei're V -a/+-et 1 celebrate. 2 pay homage to; lionize: et f-et navn a celebrated name.
Fei'ring Pln twp, Akershus.
fei'sel -elen, pl -ler mallet.
fei't A -t/+fett 1 fat (=greasy, oily; rich); fig. pompous, self-satisfied, smug: f-e ord big words, empty words. 2 fat (=obese). 3 fat (=fertile; profitable): en f- forretning fam. a good deal. 4 typog. boldface. 5: det er meg ett f-t, like f-t it's all the same to me.
fei'te[1] -a 1 fat, oil. 2 fatness, corpulence, obesity.
fei'te[2] V -a/+-et fatten (up): f- seg f- oneself.
fei'te/kur -en fattening diet.
fei'te/varer pl meats.
fei't/furu -a resinous pine.
*fei't/lagd A -/-lagt buxom; plump.
fei'tne V -a/+-et become fatter.
fei't/sild -a fat herring (3-4 yrs. old, 6-12 in. long).
*feitt' -et cf fett
*feit'tet(e) A - greasy.
fei't/ved -en resinous wood (full of pitch).
fe'/kar -en cattleman, cattle dealer.
*fekk' pt of få[1]
+f. eks. =for eksempel
fek'te V -a/+-et 1 fence; fight: f- seg fram fight one's way through. 2 gesticulate, wave: f- med armene w- one's arms.
fek'te/hanske -n fencing gauntlet.
+fek'ter -en, pl -e (=*-ar) fencer, swordsman.
+fek'tning -en (=*fekting) 1 fencing, fighting. 2 mil. engagement, skirmish.
*fe'/lage -n comrade, companion.
+fel'd -en cf fell[1]
fe'le -a fiddle.
fe'le/boge [/båge] -n (=+/bue) fiddle bow.
fe'le/slått -en composition, piece for the fiddle.
fel'g -en (of a wheel) felly, rim: være helt på f-en be down and out; være på f-en etter en fam. be crazy about sby.
fell'[1] -en 1 fur, pelt. 2 fur coverlet (usu. of sheepskin): duggen lå grå som en f- på gresset the dew lay gray as a sheepskin on the grass (Undset).
*fell'[2] pr of falle
°fell'[3] Av cf fulla
fel'lah -en fellah.

fel'le[1] *-n* associate, companion.

+**fel'le**[2] *-a/+-en* pitfall, trap: **lokke en i f-n** trap sby; **sette f- for en** set a t- for sby.

fel'le[3] *V felte* 1 moult, shed (e.g. feathers, tears); cut (teeth): (of knitting) **f- av** cast off; **f- masker** decrease (stitches). 2 cut down, fell (trees); knock over. 3 overthrow (a government); kill, slay. 4 *jur.* convict, damn: **f- en dom** pronounce judgment, sentence. 5 *chem.*: **f- ut** precipitate. 6 *mil.*: **f- bajonett** charge bayonets. 7 (of woodwork): **f- inn, sammen** join.

***fel'leleg** *A* - appropriate, convenient, suitable.

fel'lende *A* - damning (e.g. evidence).

fel'les *A* - common, collective, joint; mutual, reciprocal: **gjøre f- sak med** join forces with, make common cause with; **ha noe (til) f- med** have sth in common with.

+**fel'les/betegnelse** [/-tei·n-] *-n* collective term.

fel'les/bu *-et* (=+**/bo**) *jur.* joint estate.

+**fel'les/eie** *-t jur.* community property.

fel'les/ferie *-n* general holiday (for all the employees in one shop).

fel'les/grav *-a/-en* mass grave.

fel'les/kjønn *-et gram.* common gender.

+**fel'les/navn** *-et* (=***/namn**) 1 collective name. 2 *gram.* common noun.

+**fel'les/nevner** *-en, pl -e* (=***/nemnar**) common denominator.

fel'les/skap *+-et/*-en* 1 joint activity, efforts; joint ownership: **i f-** in common, jointly. 2 (sense of) common interests, solidarity.

fel'les/skule *-n* coeducational school.

fel't[1] *-en mil.* field: **dra i f-en** go to war; **dra til f-s mot en** open a campaign against sby.

fel't[2] *-et, pl -/+-er* 1 field; area, space; square. 2 province, sphere: **det er ikke mitt f-** that's not my field. 3 (tennis) court; (chess) square; (magnetic) field; fishing grounds.

***-felt** *A* - being of a certain quality, e.g. in **ein-, mang-, stor-.**

fel't/flaske *-a mil.* canteen.

fel't/fot *-en mil.*: **på f-** on a war footing.

fel't/herre *-n mil.* commander in chief; commanding general.

fel't/kjøkken *-et mil.* field kitchen.

fel't/marskal'k *-en mil.* field marshal (=general of the army, U.S. Army).

fel't/post *-en mil.* army mail.

fel't/prest *-en mil.* army chaplain.

fel't/rop *-et mil.* password.

fel't/seng *-a* camp cot, folding cot.

fel't/skjær *-en hist., mil.* barber-surgeon.

fel't/spat *-en geol.* feldspar.

fel't/stol *-en* camp stool.

fel't/tog [/tåg] *-et* campaign; (military) expedition.

fe'/læger *-et* (outdoor) cow pen; corral.

fem' *Num* five: **han er ikke ved sine fulle f-** he's not all there; *fam.* **gå f- på** miss the boat; **la f- være like** let tomorrow take care of itself.

fem'/børing *-en* Nordland boat with five pairs of rowers (when the mast was up, otherwise six).

fem'/del *-en* fifth, fifth part.

+**fem'/dobbelt** *A* - (=***/dobbel**) fivefold, quintuple.

femini'n *A* feminine; effeminate.

femini'num *-umet, pl -a/+-er/*-um gram.* feminine gender; feminine word.

fem'/kamp *-en* pentathlon.

fem'/kant *-en* pentagon.

fem'/kanta *A* - (=+**-et**) pentagonal.

fem'/kort *-et* Newmarket (=a kind of card game).

fem'/krone *-a* (=**/kroning**) five-*kroner* (bill, coin).

fem'ling *-en* quintuplet.

+**fem'mer** *-en, pl -e* (=***-ar**) 1 five (of any card suit). 2 fiver, five-*kroner* (bill, coin). 3 number five (e.g. streetcar).

***fem'ne** *V -a/-de* clasp, embrace.

fem'te *Num* fifth: **være f- hjul på vognen** be in the way, not wanted.

fem'te/del *-en* cf **fem/**

fem'te/kolon·ne *N* fifth column.

fem'ten *Num* fifteen.

fem'tende *Num* fifteenth.

fem'ten/del *-en* fifteenth, fifteenth part.

fem'ti *Num* fifty.

fem'ti/del *-en* fiftieth, fiftieth part.

fem'tiende *Num* fiftieth.

Fe'munden *Pln* lake, Østerdalen.

fem'/øre *-n* (=**/øring**) five-øre (coin.)

***fe'n** *-et* bog, fen.

***fe'nad** *-en* herd (of cattle).

fe'nad/knok *-en* (=+**/knoke,** +**fena/**) cured leg of mutton.

fe'nad/lår *-et* (=+**fena/**) cured leg of mutton.

fen'der *-en, pl +-e naut.* fender.

***fe'ne** *-a* cf **fen**

***fe'net(e)** *A* - marshy.

***feng'd** *-a* catching, taking (e.g. sealing, whaling); catch, haul.

-fengd *A -/*-fengt*: **lett-** easy to catch; **sjeld-** rarely, seldom caught.

+**feng'e**[1] *V -et/-te* (=***fengje**) 1 catch fire, kindle: **kruttet f-et** the powder ignited. 2 catch on; enthuse, inflame: **en f-ende tale** a rousing speech.

***feng'e**[2] *pp of* **få**[1]

***feng'en** *A -e/-i, pl -ne* inflammable.

***-feng'en** *A -e/-i, pl -ne*: **lett-** easy to catch; frivolous.

feng'/hette *-a* detonator.

***feng'i** *pp of* **få**[1]

***feng'je** *V -de* cf **fenge**[1]

feng'sel *-elet/-let, pl -ler/*-* 1 jail, penitentiary, prison. 2 imprisonment: **dømme til f-** sentence to prison.

+**feng'sels/aktig** *A* - prisonlike.

feng'sels/betje'nt *-en* prison guard.

feng'sle *V -a/+-et* 1 commit to prison, imprison; confine. 2 captivate, enthrall, fascinate.

feng'slende *A* - absorbing, captivating, enthralling.

+**feng'slings/kjennelse** *-n jur.* order of commitment (to prison).

***fen'ne** *V fente* drift, form snowdrifts.

***fen'ner** *pl of* **fonn**

fen'nikel *-en bot.* fennel (Fenniculum officinale).

fennoma'n *-en hist.* Fennoman (Finnish nationalist, advocating use of Finnish language).

fenome'n *-et, pl -/+-er* phenomenon.

fenomena'l *A* phenomenal.

fen'rik *-en mil.* Second Lieutenant (Army, Air Force); *naut.* Lieutenant junior grade (Navy).

Fen'ris/ulven *Prn myth.* Fenris wolf (son of Loki, slayer of Odin).

fen'te *-a* woman gypsy; *fam.* tramp.

***fer** [fæ'r] *pr of* **fare**[2]

fer'd [*fæ'r] *-a/+-en* 1 expedition, journey, voyage: *poet.* **fare den siste f-** die. 2 activity, movement: **fra første f-** from the very outset; **gi seg i f- med** start sth; **være i f- med** be on the point of; be busy at. 3 behavior, conduct: **ærlig f-** honest dealings.

ferda/budd [fæ'ra/] *A* - ready to depart, leave.

ferda/folk *-et* travelers.

***ferda/gods** [/gots] *-et* baggage, luggage.

ferda/mann *-en, pl -menn/*-menner* traveler.

***ferda/minne** *-t* travel recollection, travelogue (title of book by A. O. Vinje).

***ferdast** [fæ'rast] *V -ast* cf **ferdes**

ferde[1] [fæ're] *N*: **på f-**, e.g. **galt på f-** sth amiss; **hva er (det) på f-?** what's the matter?, what's up?; **tidlig på f-** up early.

***fer'de**[2] [fæ're] *V -a* 1 prepare, ready: **f- på reiskapen** fix up the tools. 2: **f- seg til** get ready.

+**fer'dedes** *pt of* **ferdes**

Fer'der *Pln* lighthouse on island at entrance to Oslo Fjord.

+**fer'des** *V -edes, -es* (=***ferdast**) 1 travel, voyage. 2 frequent, have one's daily round: **f- med** associate with.

fer'des/mann [*fæ'res/] *-en, pl -menn/*-menner* cf **ferda/**

fer'dig *A* - 1 prepared, ready (**til** for, **til å** to): **gjøre seg f-** get r-, make r-; **være f- til å gjøre noe** be r- to do sth. 2 completed, finished; through (**med** with): **f- med det** so much for that, that's that; **han er f-** he's finished, done for. 3 *archaic* accomplished, dexterous.

+**fer'dig/het** *-en* accomplishment; dexterity, proficiency, skill.

+**fer'dighets/fag** *-et educ.* subject requiring physical dexterity, skill (e.g. gymnastics, sloyd, etc.).

fer'dig/hus *-et* prefabricated dwelling ("prefab").

fer'dig/laga *A* - (=+**-et**) ready-made, ready-to-wear (e.g. clothes).

fer'dig/sydd *A -/*-sytt* ready-made, ready-to-wear (e.g. clothes).

ferdsel [fær'sel] *-elen/-la* traffic.

ferdsels/åre *-a* traffic artery.

***ferdsle** [fær'sle] *-a* cf **ferdsel**

***fe're** *-n* narrow strip (e.g. of land).

+**fer'ge**[1] *-n* cf **ferje**[1]

+**fer'ge**[2] *V -a/-et* cf **ferje**[2]

***fer'gje** *V -de* subject to pressure.

fe'rie *-n* holidays, vacation: **reise på f-** go on v-, go somewhere for the h-.

fe'rie/koloni· *-en* summer camp (for city children).

+**fe'rie/penger** *pl* (=***-ar**) holiday allowance, vacation allowance.

ferie're *V -te* vacation: **f- ved sjøen, på fjellet, på landet** go on vacation, spend the holidays at the seashore, in the mountains, in the countryside.

fe'rie/reis(e) *-a/+-en* holiday, vacation trip.

fe'/rist *-a* cattle guard (=grating in road to prevent cattle from crossing).

fer'je[1] *-a* ferry, ferryboat.

fer'je[2] *V -a/+-et* ferry (**over** across).

fer'je/anløp *-et* ferry station.

fer'je/mann *-en, pl -menn/*-menner* ferryman.

fer'm *A* (esp. of women) healthy, well-built; capable, energetic, firm.

fer'me *V -a/+-et hist., eccl.* confirm.

fermen't *-et, pl -/+-er* ferment.

fermente're *V -te* ferment.

ferniss' *-en* 1 varnish. 2 veneer: **en f- av dannelse** a v- of culture.

fernisse're *V -te* varnish.

fer'ro/lege'ring *-a/+-en* ferro-alloy.

fer'sk *A* 1 fresh, new, recent: **gripe på f- gjerning** catch red-handed. 2 (of food, esp. fish, meat) unsalted.

fer'sken *-en* peach.

fer'sken/hud [*/hu] *-a/+-en* skin like a peach.

fer'sk/fisk *-en* fresh (i.e. unsalted) fish.

fer'sk/mat *-en* fresh meat (or fish).

fer'sk/vatn *-et* (=+**/vann**) fresh water.

fer't *-en* scent: **få f-en av noe** get wind of sth.

ferti'l *A* fertile.

fertilite't *-en* fertility.

fe'/sjå *-et* cattle show.

fes'l(e)[1] *-(e)t* (=**fetl(e)**[1]) *dial.* bandage.

fes'le[2] *V -a/+-et* (=**fetle**[2]) *dial.* bandage.

fess' *-en* fez.

fes't[1] *-en* 1 banquet, celebration, party; fun: **hele byen var i f-** the whole town was celebrating. 2 *eccl.* feast, festival.

+ Bokmål; * Nynorsk; ° Dialect.
After letter: ' stress (Acc. 1); ` tone, stress (Acc. 2); · length.
Below letter: . not pronounced.

fes't[2] -a (=*fester) naut. painter.
+**fes't/antrekk** -et evening (formal) dress.
***fes'tar/mann** -en, pl -menn(er) cf feste/
***fes'tar/møy** -a cf feste/
***fes'tar/mål** -et cf feste/
fes't/dag -en 1 holiday; day of rejoicing. 2 eccl. feast day.
fes'te[1] -t 1 grip, hold; foothold: få f- catch hold. 2 (of a sword) handle, hilt. 3 naut. mooring line. 4 archaic, hist. citadel, fortress, stronghold.
fes'te[2] V -a/+-et 1 attach, fasten, secure: f- bo settle down, set up housekeeping; f- lit til have, place confidence in; f- oppmerksomheten på noe fix one's attention on sth, concentrate on sth; f- sine tanker på papiret put one's thoughts down on paper. 2 (refl.) be fixed: f- seg i hukommelsen sink in, lodge in one's mind; f- seg i minnet be engraved on one's memory; f- seg ved noe notice sth, take notice of sth. 3 hire, hire out: f- seg bort enter sby's service. 4 archaic betroth.
fes'te[3] V -a/+-et celebrate, have a party: feste til langt på natt make a night of it.
fes'te/konto'r -et, pl -/+-er employment office for domestic help.
+**fes'te/mann** -en, pl -menn archaic betrothed, fiancé.
+**fes'te/møy** -a archaic betrothed, fiancée.
+**fes'te/mål** -et archaic betrothal, engagement.
+**fes'te/penger** pl (=*-ar) hist., jur. earnest money.
***fes'ter** -tra cf fest[2]
fes'te/tau -et naut. mooring line.
+**fes't/forestil'ling** -a/-en special (gala) performance (in a theater).
fes't/humø'r -et festive, holiday atmosphere, mood.
festi'vitas -en festivity; festive atmosphere, mood.
festivite't -en festivity.
fes't/komité -en organizing committee for a banquet, social function.
fes'tlig A - 1 ceremonious, festive. 2 amusing, diverting: det var f- it was fun. 3 delightful, nice, pleasant.
+**fes'tlig/het** -en festiveness; celebration, festive occasion.
+**fes'tlig/holde** V -holdt, -holdt celebrate.
fes't/middag -en (special) banquet, feast.
fes'tne V -a/+-et: f- seg harden; be fixed; f- seg i hukommelsen stick in one's memory.
fes'tning +-en/*-a citadel, fort, fortress.
fes'tnings/verk -et, pl -/+-er: f-er fortifications.
fes'tnings/voll -en rampart.
festong' -en festoon; ruffle (curtain).
fes't/sal -en auditorium.
fes't/skrift -et memorial publication (=one in honor of a prominent scholar, etc.).
+**fes't/spill** -et (=*/spel) festival play (on special occasions).
fes't/stemning -a/-en festive, holiday mood, high spirits.
fes't/tale -n/*-a (principal) speech in honor of the occasion; after-dinner speech.
fes't/telegram' -met, pl -/+-mer greetings telegram.
***fe't**[1] -et step; track (e.g. of chicken).
+**fe't**[2] A cf feit
Fet' Pln twp, Akershus.
***fe'te**[1] -n strands of thread, yarn.
+**fe'te**[2] V -et cf feite[2]
***fe'te**[3] V -a step out, stride along.
+**fe'te/kur** -en cf feite/
fete're V -te lionize, make much of: en f-t kunstner a celebrated artist.
+**fe'te/varer** pl cf feite/
+**fe't/furu** -a cf feit/
fe'tisj -en fetish.
+**fe'tisj/dyrker** -en, pl -e (=*-ar) fetishist.
***fet'l(e)**[1] -(e)t cf fesl(e)[1]
fet'le[2] V -a/+-et cf fesle[2]
fet'ling -en hide, skin (of animal's hoof or shank).
+**fe't/sild** -a cf feit/
+**fett'** -et (=*feitt) fat, grease, lard: bli stekt i sitt eget f- stew in one's own juice; be hoist with one's own petard; det er meg ett f- it's all the same to me.
+**fet'te** V -et grease: f- til grease, spot.
+**fet'ter** -en, pl -e (male) cousin.
+**fet'tet(e)** A - (=*feittet(e)) greasy, slippery; dirty, stained.
+**fett'/gehal't** -en fat content.
+**fett'/lær** -et oil-tanned leather.
+**fett'/stoff** -et, pl -/-er fat, fatty substance: f-er oils and acids.
+**fett'/syre** -a chem. sebacic acid.
feudal [føyda'l] A cf føydal
ff. = (og) følgende sider
+**fhv.** = forhenværende
fiasko [fjass'ko] -en failure, fiasco; (fam.) flop.
fi'ber -eren, pl +-rer/+-re/*-rar fiber.
fi'bret(e) A - fibrous.
fideikomiss' -et, pl +-er/*- jur. settlement, trust; entailed property.
fi'dibus -en archaic pipe lighter (strip of paper).
fi'dus -en confidence, trust: ha f- til noe have c-, faith in sth.
fi'ende -n enemy, foe (av of): eccl. f-n the devil.
fi'ende/land -et enemy, hostile country.
fiendsk A - hostile, unfriendly.
fi'end/skap -en/+-et enmity, hostility (mot to).
***fi'endsleg** A - cf fiendtlig
+**fi'endtlig** A - enemy, hostile (mot to).
+**fi'endtlig/het** -en antagonism; hostility.
+**fi'endtlig/sinnet** A - antagonistic, hostile.
fiff'[1] -en 1 hum. elegant, stylish dress: i full f- (fam.) all dolled up, dressed fit to kill. 2 hum. (the) upper ten, (the) hoity-toity.
fiff'[2] -et dodge, trick.
fif'fe V -a/+-et: f- opp dress up, fix up; f- seg opp (fam.) doll up.
fif'fig A - clever, shrewd.
figu'r -en 1 figure: gjøre en dårlig f- cut a poor f-; portrett i hel f- full-length portrait. 2 figure of speech. 3 character (e.g. in play): en underlig f- a strange c-.
figure're V -te appear, figure.
figu'r/frakk -en tight-fitting coat.
figu'rlig A - figurative, metaphorical: i egentlig og f- betydning literally and f-ly.
fi'k -en box, cuff on the ear.
fi'ke[1] V -a/+-et/-te: f- til en box sby's ears.
fi'ke[2] V -a/+-et: f- etter desire, want; have a yearning for.
fi'ken[1] -en fig (genus Ficus).
fi'ken[2] A +-ent, pl -ne avid, desirous, eager (etter for).
fi'ken/tre -et, pl -/+-trær fig tree.
+**fikk'** pt of få[1]
fik'ke -a pocket.
fik'l -et fumbling, puttering around.
fik'le V -a/+-et fiddle, fumble around (med with).
fik's A - 1 handy; nimble, quick. 2 chic, smart. 3: f- (og) ferdig quite ready, pat (e.g. an answer). 4 fixed: f- idé idée fixe, obsession.
fiksati'v -et fixative; wave set.
fik'se V -a/+-et arrange, fix up; doctor, falsify (e.g. books, records): f- opp, på noe spruce sth up.
fikse'r/bad -et photog. fixing bath, hypo.
+**fikse'r/bilde** -t (=*/bilete) puzzle picture (in which a figure is concealed in the lines of the drawing).
fikse're V -te 1 establish, fix: merc. f- en pris set a price. 2: f- en stare hard at sby, (fam.) stare holes through sby. 3 psych. fixate, have a fixation. 4 photog. fix.
fiksfakseri' [also fik's/] -et, pl +-er/*- hanky-panky.
fiksjo'n -en fiction.
fik's/stjerne -a/+-en fixed star.
fik'te V -a/+-et: f- med armene gesticulate, wave one's arms wildly.
fikti'v A fictitious, imaginary.
fi'l[1] -a file: bruke f-en på fig. polish, put the finishing touches to.
fi'l[2] -a jack (cards).
fi'l[3] -en (traffic) lane.
filantro'p -en philanthropist.
filantropi' -en philanthropy.
filantro'pisk A - philanthropic.
filateli' -en philately.
filatelis't -en philatelist.
°**fil'e**[1] -n cream floating on top of milk.
fi'le[2] V -a/-te 1 file (av, over off). 2: f- på rasp, scrape (e.g. a fiddle); f- på ett og det samme harp continually on the same thing. 3 naut. hug the wind too closely. 4 fig. put the finishing touches to sth.
fil'e/bunk(e) [/bongk(e)] -(e)n dish of clabbered milk (with cream on top).
Fi'le/fjell Pln cf Fille/
file're V -te 1 make mesh, netting; net. 2 filet (lace). 3 filet (e.g. fish). 4 mus.: f- tonen filar il tuono (play without crescendos).
file't -en 1 filet (of fish or meat). 2 net work, netting.
filete're V -te fillet.
filharmo'nisk A - philharmonic.
filia'l -en merc. branch, branch office.
filigra'n -et filigree.
+**filigra'n/aktig** A - filigreed.
filigra'ns/arbeid -et filigree work.
filipen's -en pimple.
filipi'ne en fillipeen, philopena (game of forfeits involving the kernel of a nut, usu. almond).
Filippi'nene Pln the Philippines.
+**filis'ter** -eren, pl -ere/-rer (=*-ar) 1 hist. Philistine. 2 philistine, Babbitt.
filistrø's A philistine.
fi'l/kjøring -a/+-en (=*/køyring) driving in lanes.
Fil'lan Pln twp, Sør-Trøndelag.
fil'le[1] -a rag, shred, tatter: ikke f-a not the least bit, not the slightest; rive i f-r tear to pieces.
fil'le[2] A - good-for-nothing, worthless.
fil'le/fant -en tattered tramp; bum, hobo.
Fil'le/fjell Pln mountain between Valdres and Lærdal.
fil'le/haug -en bundle of rags: han forsvant som en ånd i en f- he vanished into thin air.
fil'le/onkel [/ongkel] -elen, pl -ler father's or mother's cousin (male).
+**fil'le/peller** -en, pl -e 1 ragpicker. 2 pop. (drink, bottle of) booze.
fil'leri -et trifle, anything valueless, worthless.
+**fil'lern** I shaw, shucks.
fil'le/rye -a rag rug.
fil'le/tante -a/+-en father's or mother's cousin (female).
fil'let(e) A - ragged, tattered; torn.
fil'm -en 1 film (celluloid; layer). 2 film, movie: innspille, oppta en f- make, produce a m-.
filmatise're V -te film, make a screen version of (a drama, novel).
filma'tisk A - cinematic.
fil'me V -a/+-et 1 act in the movies. 2 make, produce a movie. 3 pop. feign, sham.
fil'm/helt -en movie hero.
fil'm/stjerne [/stjæ'rne] -a/+-en movie star.
filolog [-olå'g] -en 1 philologist. 2 holder of the degree filologisk embetseksamen (q.v.).
filologi' -en 1 philology. 2 humanistic subjects at university.
filologisk [-olå'gisk] A - philological: f- embetseksamen (=språklig-historisk e-) degree in humanistic subjects (history, language, literature, etc.).
filoso'f -en philosopher.
filosofe're V -te philosophize.
filosofi' -en philosophy.

filoso'fisk *A* - 1 philosophical. 2 *educ.*: **den f-e doktorgrad** Ph.D.
fi'ls/bein *-et archaic* ivory.
fi'l/spon *-en* filings.
fil't *-en/*-et* felt.
fil'te *V -a/+-et* felt, mat or press together into felt.
fil'ter *-eret/-ret, pl -er/+-re* filter.
fil'tre *V -a/+-et* mat, tangle: **f- seg i hop (sammen)** become confused; **f-t** snarled, tangled.
filtre're *V -te* filter, strain.
Fi'l/tvet *Pln* post office, Hurum twp, Buskerud.
filu'r *-en* sly dog, slyboots.
filureri' *-et* mischievous pranks; trickery.
***fi'm** *A* quick, sudden, swift.
fim'bul/vinter *-eren, pl -rer* awful, terrible winter.
fi'n *A* 1 fine (=of good quality); choice, excellent, first-rate: **en f- utsikt** a fine view; (ironically) **f-e greier** a fine state of affairs, a pretty kettle of fish; **ha det f-t** enjoy oneself, have a good time. 2 fine (=upper-class); cultivated, genteel, refined; chic, fashionable: **de f-e** the hoity-toity, the swells; **den f-e verden** society, the world of fashion; **være for f- til noe** be too good for sth. 3 fine (=delicate); sensitive, subtle: **f-e hender** delicate hands; **en f- hentydning** a delicate hint; **på en f- måte** in a discreet way; **ha en f- nese for** have a flair (a nose) for; **ha en f- smak (for)** be a connoisseur (of); **fare f-t med** be careful with. 4 fine (=pure), **unalloyed.**
fina'le *-n* finale; finals (in sports); *hum.* posteriors.
fina'le/kamp *-en* finals (in sports).
finalis't *-en* finalist.
finan's [also finang's] *-en* 1 financial circles, the financial world. 2 *(pl)* finances.
finan's/departementet [-mang·e] *df* Ministry of Finance.
+**finan'ser** *pl* (=*-**ar**) finances.
finan's/geni [/sjeni·] *-et, pl +-er/*-* financial wizard.
finansiell' *A -elt* financial.
finansie're *V -te* finance.
finan's/mann *-en, pl -menn/*-menner* financier.
finan's/minis'ter *-eren, pl -rer/+-ere* Minister of Finance.
Finan's- og [å] **toll'/departementet** [-mang·e] *df* Ministry of Finance and Customs.
finan's/rådmann *-en, pl -menn/*-menner admin.* commissioner of finances (in a city government).
fi'n/brød *-et* bread made of sifted rye and wheat.
fi'n/bygd *A -/*-bygt* delicately built, fine featured.
fi'n/dele *V -te tech.* subdivide; (of food) cut into small bits.
fi'ne *V -te*: **f- seg** (of weather) improve, take a turn for the better; spruce up, *(fam.)* doll up.
finér *-en* veneer; (=**kryss/**) plywood.
fine're *V -te* veneer.
finér/plate *-a/+-en* plywood, sheet of veneer.
fines'se *-n* fine point; finesse, nicety, subtlety: **ta f-n** finesse (in bridge).
fi'n/fin *A* extra fine, superfine, tops.
+**fi'n/følelse** *-n* delicacy, tact.
+**fi'n/følenḍe** *A* - cf **fint/**
°**fing'** *-en* cf **finger**
fing'er *-eren, pl -rer* finger: **f-rene av fatet!** hands off!; **få f-rene i** get one's hands on; **gi fanden en f-** give the devil an inch; **ha en f- med i spillet** have a hand in the game; **ha et øye på hver f-** have one's eyes about one; **ha lange f-rer** be light-fingered, thieving; **holde f-rene vekk** keep one's hands off; **klø i f-rene etter** be itching to; **kunne noe på f-rene** have sth at one's fingertips; **ikke legge f-rene imellom** not spare sby, speak one's mind; **ikke løfte (røre) en f-** not raise a f-; **peke f-rer av** thumb one's nose at; **se gjennom f-rene med noe** wink at sth; **sette f-en på** put one's f- on; **slå en på f-rene** rap sby over the knuckles; **stikke f-en i jorda (og lukte hvor en er)** *derog.* trim one's sails to the wind.
fing'er/avtrykk *-et* fingerprint.
***fing'er/bjørg** *-a* cf **/bøl**
+**fing'er/bøl** *-et* thimble.
fingere [fingge're] *V -te* 1 feign, pretend, simulate. 2: **f-t navn** assumed name, pseudonym; *merc.* **f-t regning** pro forma invoice (indicating goods are ready for shipment).
+**fingere're** *V -te* cf **fingre**
+**fing'er/ferdig** *A* - deft, dexterous.
+**fing'erferdig/het** *-en* deftness, dexterity; keyboard technique.
fing'er/gull *-et* gold ring.
fing'er/klåe *-n* (=+**/kløe**) itch, restless desire.
fing'er/kyss *-en/+-et* blown kiss: **sende en et f-** blow sby a kiss.
+**fing'er/nem'** *A -t, pl -me* (=***/næm**) deft, dexterous.
+**fing'er/pek** *-et* (=***/peik**) pointing; *fig.* clue, hint; warning.
+**fing'er/setning** *-en* (=***/setjing** *-a*) *mus.* fingering.
fing'er/spiss *-en* fingertip: **til f-ene** every inch (e.g. a gentleman).
fing'er/språk *-et* dactylology, sign language.
fing'er/tupp *-en* fingertip.
fing'er/vante *-n* (woolen) glove.
fing'er/vott *-en* (woolen) glove.
fing're *V -a/+-et* 1 finger: **f- etter** try to lay hands on; **f- med (på, ved)** f-; fiddle with, pick at. 2: **f- seg** branch out.
+**fing'rer** *pl of* **finger**
fi'n/hakke *V -a/-et* chop up fine.
+**fi'n/het** *-en* fineness (=excellence, perfection, quality; elegance, refinement, style; delicacy, subtlety; purity).
finish [fin'isj] *-en* finish (on furniture).
finitt' *A - gram.* finite.
fi'n/kam' *-men* fine-toothed comb.
fin'ke *-n* (=**fink**) *zool.* finch (family Fringillidae).
fin'kel *-en* fusel, inferior liquor, *(fam.)* rotgut.
fin'ke/nett *-et naut.* hammock netting.
fi'n/kjemme *V +-kjemte/*-kjemde* comb (with a fine-toothed comb); *fig.* comb, search (e.g. an area); give a final checking.
fi'n/kjensle *-a* finesse, tact.
fi'n/ko'rna *A* - (=+**-et**) fine-grained.
***fi'n/leik** *-en* fineness (cf **finhet**).
+**fi'n/ma'lt** *A* - (finely) ground, pulverized.
fi'n/maska *A* - (=+**-et**) fine meshed.
+**fi'n/meka'niker** *-en, pl -e* (=***-ar**) precision mechanic.
finn'[1] *-en* 1 Lapp. 2 *zool.* finback, rorqual (Balaenoptera physalus).
***finn'**[2] *-en bot.* matgrass (Nardus stricta).
***finn'**[3] *-en* cf **finne**[3]
Finn' *Prn (m)*
***fin'nast** *V finst, fanst, funnest/-ist* cf **finnes**
fin'ne[1] *-n* 1 Finlander. 2 *archaic* Lapp.
fin'ne[2] *-n* fin (on fish).
+**fin'ne**[3] *-n* (=***finn**[3]) pimple, spot.
***fin'ne**[4] *-t* wasteland: **på fly og f-** in the highlands.
fin'ne[5] *V +fant/*fann, +funnet/*funne/*-i* 1 find (discover, locate): **f- døden** meet one's death; **f- olje** strike oil; **f- sted** take place; **jeg f-er ikke det uttrykket i ordboka** I can't f- that expression in the dictionary. 2 find (think): **jeg f-er det best å** I think it would be best to; **f- en skyldig** *jur.* find sby guilty. 3 (with *adv.* and *prep.*): **f- for godt** think fit, consider right; **f- fram** bring forth, get out; find one's way (**til** to); **f- igjen** find, recover; **f- opp** devise, invent; **f- på** think up, hit on; **f- ut** discover, find out; decide, figure out; **f- ut av** figure out, make out; solve, find a way out of (a problem, difficulty); **f- verken ut eller inn av noe** not be able to make head nor tail of sth. 4 *(refl.)*: **f- seg i** bear, put up with, tolerate; **f- seg til rette** feel at home, comfortable; become accustomed, reconcile oneself (**med** to); **f- seg vel ved** be satisfied with. 5 *(refl.)* cf **finnes.**
fin'ne/lønn *-a/-en* cf **finner/**
+**fin'ner** *-en, pl -e* (=***-ar**) finder.
+**fin'ner/lønn** *-a/-en* (=***-ar/**) reward.
+**fin'nes** *V fins, fan(te)s, funnes* (=***finnast**) be, be found, exist, occur: **f- det mange kommunister i Norge?** are there many communists in Norway?
fin'net(e) *A* - 1 finlike, finny. 2 *bot.* pinnate. 3 pimply.
finn'/ganḍ *-en* Lapp shamanism, witchcraft.
finn'/gras *-et bot.* matgrass (Nardus stricta).
finn'/kval *-en* (=+**/hval**) *zool.* finback, rorqual (Balaenoptera physalus).
Finn'/lanḍ *Pln* Finland.
finn'/lanḍsk *A* - Finnish.
finn'lanḍs/svenske *-n* Swedish-speaking Finn.
finn'/lenḍing *-en* Finn.
Finnm.=Finnmark
Finn'/mark *Pln* Finnmark (Norwegian county).
finn'/marking *-en* person from Finnmark.
finn'marks/fiske *-t* codfish fishing (off Finnmark from April to June)
finn'/mudd *-en* (=**/mut**) (Lapp's) fur coat (of reindeer skin).
finn'/skjegg *-et bot.* matgrass (Nardus stricta).
Finn'/skogene *Pln* stretch of forest east of Glomma.
finn'/skott *-et* sudden illness attributed to a spell cast by a Lapp shaman.
finn'/tått *-en bot.* matweed (Nardus stricta).
Finn'/øy *Pln* twp, Rogaland.
fi'n/puss *-en* plaster, stucco; *fig.* final polishing.
fi'n/pusse *V -a/+-et* plaster, stucco; *fig.* **f- et manuskript** polish, put the finishing touches on a manuscript.
+**fin's** *pr of* **finnes**
Fin'se *Pln* station on Bergen-Oslo RR., Hordaland.
+**fi'n/sikte** *V -a/-et* sift finely (e.g. flour).
fin'sk *A* - Finnish.
Fin's/lanḍ *Pln* twp, Vest-Agder.
***fi'nsleg** *A* - neat, nice.
***fin'st** *pr of* **finnast**
fin'te[1] *-a/+-en* 1 feint (in boxing, soccer). 2 gibe, sarcastic remark, taunt: **gi en f-r** tease, twit sby.
fin'te[2] *V -a/+-et* 1 feint (in boxing, soccer). 2 tease, twit.
+**fi'n/telling** *-a/+-en* (***/teljing**) final (vote) count.
+**fi'nt/følenḍe** *A* - delicate, sensitive, tactful.
+**fi'nt/merkenḍe** *A* - delicate, sensitive (esp. of measuring instrument).
fio'l[1] *-en bot.* violet (genus Viola).
+**fio'l**[2] *-en mus., obs.* violin.
fiolett' *A* - violet.
fioli'n *-en mus.* violin: **spille annen f-** play second fiddle.
fiolinis't *-en mus.* violinist.
fiolonsell' *-en mus.* cello, violoncello.
fipp' *-en* goatee.
fipp'/skjegg *-et* goatee.
fi'r/beint *A* - four-legged, quadruped.
fi'r/blaḍ *-et bot.* herb Paris (Paris quadrifolia).
+**fi'r/dobbelt** *A* - (=***/dobbel**) **fourfold,** quadruple.

+ Bokmål; * Nynorsk; ° Dialect.
After letter: ' stress (Acc. 1); ` tone, stress (Acc. 2); · length.
Below letter: . not pronounced.

fi're[1] *V -a/-te* 1 *naut.* let down, lower; ease off, pay out (e.g. a line): **f- ned, vekk** lower away; **f- på et tau** ease off a rope. 2 *fig.* give way, yield.

fi're[2] *Num* four: **f- lange** (in poker) f- of a kind; **på alle f-** on all f-s; **under f- øyne** confidentially, *(fam.)* between you and me and the gatepost.

fi're/del *-en* (=**fjerde/**) fourth, a fourth part: **fjerdedels note** quarter note (crotchet).

+**fi'remanns/bolig** *-en* four-family house.

fi'remanns/telt *-et* tent designed to accommodate four persons.

+**fi'rer** *-en, pl -e* (=***-ar**) 1 four (of any suit in cards). 2 four-oared boat. 3 number four (e.g. streetcar).

fi'retakts/motor *-en* (=**firtakts/**) four-cycle engine.

fi'r/fisle *-a zool.* (common) lizard (Lacerta vivipara).

fi'r/fota *A* - (=+**-et**) four-footed, quadruped.

fi'r/foting *-en* quadruped.

fi'r/føtt *A* - four-footed, quadruped.

+**fi'r/hendig** *A* - (=***/hendt**) *mus.* for four hands: **spille f-** play a piano duet.

fi'r/kant *-en* 1 rectangle, square. 2 *naut.*: **brase en rå f-** square a yard.

fi'r/kanta *A* - (=+**-et**) 1 rectangular, square. 2 mechanical, wooden; schematic.

fi'r/kløver *-en/+-et* 1 four-leaf clover. 2 quartet (**av** of).

fi'r/kort *-et* card game in which each player is dealt four cards.

***fi'r/lagd** *A -/-lagt* fourfold, quadruple.

fi'rling *-en* quadruplet.

fir'ma *-et, pl +-er/*-* firm: **oppta en i f-et** take a partner into the f-.

firmamen't *-et, pl +-er/*-* firmament.

fi'r/menning *-en* third cousin.

+**fir's** *Num obs.* eighty.

+**fi'r/seter** *-en, pl -e* automobile accommodating four persons.

+**fi'r/skåren** *A -ent, pl -ne* (=***/skoren**) 1 square, square cut. 2 stocky, thickset (person). 3 *naut.*: **f- talje** fourfold purchase, tackle.

fi'r/spann *-et* four-in-hand (team).

fi'r/sprang *-et*: **i fullt f-** at full tilt, at top speed, *(fam.)* hell-bent for election.

+**fi'r/strøken** *A -ent, pl -ne* (=***/stroken**) *mus.*: **den f-ne oktav** the four-line octave; **f- tone** any of the notes in the four-line octave.

fi'rtakts/motor *-en* cf **firetakts/**

+**fir'ti** *Num* cf **førti**

fi'r/toms *A* - four-inch.

+**fi'rtoms/spiker** *-eren, pl -/-rer* (=***/spikar**) four-inch nail.

fi'r/årig *A* - four year old.

fi's *-en vulg.* fart.

fi'se *V feis/+fes/+-te, +feset/+-t/*-e/*-i vulg.* break wind, fart.

fi'sen *A +-ent, pl -ne pop.* lousy, terrible.

fi'se/fin *A* pseudocultured, pseudo-elegant; *fam.* phony.

fis'k *-en* 1 fish: **fast i f-en** firm (of texture); **det er verken fugl eller f-** that is neither f- nor fowl; **frisk som en f-** fit as a fiddle, sound as a dollar; **en fæl f-** a horrid fellow; **ha det som f-en i vannet** feel completely at home, completely in one's element; **stum som en f-** silent as the grave; **ta noe for god f-** accept sth as genuine, at face value. 2 *typog.* pi(e): **falle i f-** collapse (in disorder, confusion), fail.

fiska'l *A* fiscal.

fiska'l/toll *-en* revenue tariff.

***fis'kar/lag** *-et* 1 fishing party. 2 fishermen's association.

fis'ke[1] *-t* fishing: **ute på f-** out f-.

fis'ke[2] *V -a/+-et* angle, catch (fish), fish (**etter** for): **f- etter komplimenter** f- for compliments; **f- i rørt vann** f- in troubled waters; **f- opp** f- out, up; **f- stemmer** solicit votes.

fis'ke/bein *-et* 1 fishbone. 2 whalebone (used in corsets). 3 herringbone (pattern, e.g. in skiing).

+**fis'ke/bestan'd** *-en* stock of fish (e.g. in lake).

fis'ke/bil *-en* fish truck.

+**fis'ke/bitt** *-et* (=***/bit**) (fish) bite.

fis'ke/bolle *-n* fish ball.

fis'ke/bu *-a* fisherman's shelter.

fis'ke/båt *-en* fishing boat.

fis'ke/drett *-et* (=***/drette**) *bibl.* draft, haul: **Peters f-** Peter's d- of fishes (Luke 5,9).

fis'ke/fangst *-en* 1 catch (of fish). 2 fishing: **dra ut på f-** go out f-.

fis'ke/felt *-et* fishing grounds.

fis'ke/ga'rn *-et* fishing net, seine.

+**fis'ke/handler** *-en, pl -e* (=***-ar**) dealer in fish; (chiefly *Brit.*) fishmonger.

fis'ke/hermetikk' *-en* canned fish.

fis'ke/jo *-en zool.* fish hawk, osprey (Pandion haliaetus).

fis'ke/kake *-a* fish cake.

fis'ke/krok *-en* fishhook.

fis'ke/lykke *-a/+-en* fisherman's luck, success.

fis'ke/mat *-en* fish products (e.g. fishballs, fish cakes, fish pudding, etc.).

fis'ke/pudding *-en* pudding of shredded fish.

+**fis'ker** *-en, pl -e* (=***-ar**) fisherman; angler.

+**fis'ker/båt** *-en* (=***-ar/**) fishing boat.

+**fis'ke/redskap** *-en* fishing gear, tackle.

fis'ke/rett *-en* 1 fish course. 2 fishing rights.

fiskeri' *-et, pl +-er/*-* fishing: **Norges f-er** the f- industry of Norway.

fiskeri'/departementet [-mang'e] *df* Ministry of Fisheries.

fis'ke/rik *A* rich in fish, well-stocked.

fiskeri'/minis'ter *-eren, pl -rer/+-ere* Minister of Fisheries.

+**fis'ker/kjelke** *-n* (=***-ar/**) long, light toboggan.

fis'ke/skitt *N* (=***/skit**): **bli f-** *pop.* have bad luck fishing.

fis'ke/slo *-et* fish entrails.

fis'ke/snøre *-t* fishline.

fis'ke/spade *-n* spatula (used in serving up fish).

+**fis'ke/stang** *-a, pl -stenger* (=***/stong**) fishing rod, fish pole.

fis'ke/suppe *-a* fish soup.

fis'ke/tur *-en* fishing trip: **dra på f-** go fishing.

fis'ke/vatn *-et* (=+**/vann**) good fishing lake.

fis'ke/vær[1] *-et* fishing station (from which fishermen set out).

+**fis'ke/vær**[2] *-et* (=***/ver**) good weather for fishing.

fis'ke/yngel *-en* small fry.

fis'ke/ø'rn *-a/-en zool.* fish hawk, osprey (Pandion haliaetus).

***fiskj'e** *-a* cf **fiske**[1]

fis'le *V -a/+-et*: **f- for** sweet-talk; ingratiate oneself with, lickspittle; *(fam.)* butter up.

fis'le/tut *-en* gossip, scandalmonger.

fiss' *-en mus.* F sharp: **f-/dur** F sharp major.

fis'te *V -a/+-et* punch (a ball, as by keeper in soccer).

fis'tel *-elen, pl -ler* 1 *med.* fistula. 2 *mus.* falsetto.

Fis'ter *Pln* twp, Rogaland.

***fi't** *-a, pl fitjar* meadow (near water).

Fit'jar *Pln* twp, Hordaland.

***fit'le** *V -a* fool around with, putter around; bungle, muddle through.

fi'vel *-elen, pl -ler* 1 *bot.* dandelion (Taraxacum officinale). 2 *bot.* cotton grass (genus Eriophorum).

fiv'reld(e) *-(e)t* butterfly.

Fja'ler *Pln* twp, Sogn og Fjordane.

fjam's *-en* fussbudget.

fjam'se[1] *-a* fussbudget (f.).

fjam'se[2] *V -a/+-et* flutter, fuss.

fjam'set(e) *A* - all atwitter, excited, flustered.

fjan'te *V -a/+-et* act and talk foolishly and frivolously.

fjan'tet(e) *A* - foolish, frivolous, silly.

fja's *-et* nonsense, tomfoolery, twaddle.

fja'se *V -a/+-et* act frivolously; flirt, play around, trifle: **f- bort tiden** fool away one's time.

fja'set(e) *A* - flighty, giddy, silly.

+**fje'd** *-et lit.* (foot) step.

+**fje'l** *-en* cf **fjøl**

Fjel'/berg *Pln* twp, Hordaland.

fjel'g *A* clean, nice, orderly.

fjel'ge *V -a/-et* clean up, put in order, straighten up.

fjell' *-et* 1 mountain: **Norges beste vern og feste er dets gamle f-** Norway's best protection and security are its ancient peaks (Wergeland). 2 bedrock, rock (also *fig.*): **fast som f-** solid as a r-. 3 *(sg def.)* the mountains: **reise på f-et i påsken** spend Easter in the m-.

Fjell' *Pln* twp, Hordaland.

fjell'/band *-et* area around timber line.

fjell'/bjørk *-a bot.* mountain birch (Betula odorata).

fjell'/brun *-a dial.* edge of mountain.

fjell'/bu *-en* (=***/bue**) mountaineer.

fjell'/bygd *-a* mountain community.

fjell'/bygg *-en, pl *-er* mountaineer.

fjell'/flokk *-en bot.* Jacob's ladder (Polemonium caeruleum).

fjell'/ga'rd *-en* 1 mountain range. 2 mountain farm.

fjell'/kam' *-men* crest of a mountain.

+**fjell'/kjede** *-n* mountain range.

+**fjell'/klatrer** *-en, pl -e* (=***-ar**) mountain climber.

fjell'/klatring *-a/+-en* mountain climbing.

fjell'/land *-et* mountainous country.

fjell'/masse *-n* mountain range, massif.

fjell'/ras *-et* landslide, rockslide.

fjell'/ris *-et bot.* dwarf birch (Betula nana).

fjell'/rygg *-en, pl *-er* mountain ridge.

fjell'/rype *-a zool.* ptarmigan (Lagopus mutus).

fjell'/stue *-a* mountain hostel.

fjell'/vatn *-et* (=+**/vann**) mountain lake.

fjell'/veg *-en* mountain road.

fjell'/vegg *-en* rock wall.

fjell'/vidde *-a* mountain plateau.

fjell'/våk *-en zool.* rough-legged hawk, roughleg (Buteo lagopus).

-fjelsk *A* - e.g. **det nordenf-e Norge** Norway north of the Dovre mts.

fjerde [fjæ're] *Num* fourth: **den f- juni** the f- of June; **det f- bud** the fifth commandment; **for det f-** in the f- place; **hvert f- år** quadrennially.

fjerde/del [fjæ're/] *-en* cf **fire/**

fjerde/mann [fjæ're/] *-en, pl -menn/*-menner* (the) fourth: **være f-** make a f- (e.g. at bridge).

fjerding [fjæ'ring] *-en hist.* 1 quarter of a pound (e.g. of butter, meat). 2 quarter of a Norwegian mile (=2½ kilometers or 1.5625 miles). 3 (of a city) district, quarter. 4 quarter of a county, parish (Vestlandet).

fjerding/år *-et* quarter of a year, three months.

***fje're** *-a* cf **fjære**[1]

fjer'n [also fjæ'rn] *A* 1 far; distant, faroff, remote; unapproachable: **en f- likhet** a d- resemblance; **fra f- og nær** from far and near; **i det f-e** in the distance; **ikke den f-este idé** not the r-st idea. 2 *(adv.)*: **det ligger meg f-t å** far be it from me to; **minne f-t om** remind one slightly of.

fjer'ne [also fjæ'rne] *V -a/+-et* 1 remove; dismiss, eliminate: **f- alle spor** cover up one's tracks; **f- en vanske** obviate a difficulty. 2 alienate, estrange. 3: **f- seg** retire, withdraw, move away; **f- seg fra** draw away from.

+**fjer'nelse** *-n* removal (**av** of); dismissal, elimination.

+**fjer'n/het** *-en* remoteness.

+**fjer'n/seer** *-en, pl -e* (=***/sjåar**) televiewer.

+**fjer'n/skriver** *-en, pl -e* (=***-ar**) teleprinter.

fjer'n/styre *V +-te/*-de*: **f-t** remote controlled.

fjer'n/syn *-et* television, TV.
fjer'n/syne *V -te* televise.
fjer'n/trafikk' *-en* long distance traffic (railroad), usu. =express.
***fjer're** *Av* about, nearly: **så f- stor at** a- big enough to.
fjer't *-en* fart.
fjer'te *V -a/+-et* break wind, fart.
fje's *-et* face; *(fam.)* mug, puss.
fje'sing *-en zool.* greater weever (Trachinus draco).
fjes'k *-et* fawning, obsequiousness, soft-soaping.
fjes'ke *V -a/+-et*: **f- for en** fawn on sby, sweet-talk sby.
fjet're[1] *-a* wooden peg (on sled).
fjet're[2] *V -a/+-et* bewitch, cast a spell over, spellbind.
fjoll' *-et* nonsense, tommyrot.
fjol'le *V -a/+-et* behave like an idiot, nincompoop.
fjol'leri [also -ri'] *-et* nonsense, rubbish, tommyrot.
fjol'let(e) *A -* idiotic, silly, stupid.
fjol's *-et* idiot, nincompoop, numskull.
***fjo'm** *-et* mote, speck.
+fjompe/nisse [fjom'pe/] *-n fam.* fool, sap.
fjo'n *+-et/*-a/*-en* 1 mote, speck. 2 tuft, wisp.
fjong' *A* chic, dashing, stylish: **gjøre seg f-** doll up, dress up.
fjo'r *N*: **i f-** last year; **i forf-** year before last.
fjo'rḍ *-en* 1 fjord, inlet (usu. long and narrow). 2 (in E. Norway) long, narrow lake. 3 region bordering a fjord: **Inne i fjordene** In the Fjords (novel by Egge).
Fjo'rḍane *Pln* northern part of Sogn og Fjordane county (incl. Nordfjord and Sunnfjord).
fjo'rḍ/botn *-en* (=+/**bunn**) 1 bottom of a fjord. 2 area surrounding innermost part of a fjord.
fjo`rḍ/gap *-et* mouth of a fjord, inlet.
fjo`rḍ/hest *-en* (western) Norwegian pony, small horse.
fjo`rḍing *-en* 1 person from a fjord region (esp. in W. Norway). 2 (western) Norwegian pony, small horse.
***fjo'r/føtle** *-a* cf **fir/fisle**
fjo'r/gammal *A -t, pl -gamle* (=+/**gammel**) year-old; yearling (e.g. a horse).
fjorten [fjor'ten] *Num* fourteen: **f- dager** two weeks, *(Brit.)* fortnight.
fjorten/dagliġ *A -* every two weeks, *(Brit.)* fortnightly.
fjortende [fjor'tene] *Num* fourteenth.
fjorten/del [fjor'ten/] *-en* one fourteenth, a fourteenth part.
fjo'r/åreṭ *df* last year.
Fjot'/lanḍ *Pln* twp, Vest-Agder.
fjott' *-en* nitwit, numskull, simpleton.
+fjæ'r *-a* cf **fjør**
+fjæ'r/ball' *-en* cf **fjør/**
+fjæ'r/busk *-en* crest, plume (on helmet).
+fjæ'r/drakt *-en* plumage.
+fjæ'r/dusk *-en* plume.
fjæ're[1] *-a* (=***fjøre**[1]) 1 ebb tide, low tide: **flo og f-** high and low tide. 2 beach, shore (esp. the part covered at high tide).
fjæ're[2] *V -a/+-et* (=**fjøre**[2]) ebb.
+fjæ're[3] *V -a/+-et* cf **fjøre**[3]
Fjæ're *Pln* twp, Aust-Agder.
fjæ're/mål *-et* low tide, low-water mark.
fjæ're/stein *-en* beach rock.
+fjæ're/strøm' *-men* (=*/**straum**) falling tidal current.
+fjæ'r/harv *-a* spring-tooth harrow.
+fjæ'ring *-a* spring suspension: **god f-** good springs.
+fjæ'r/kre *-et* poultry.
+fjæ'r/sky *-en* cirrus cloud.
+fjæ'r/vekt *-a* cf **fjør/**
fjø'l *-a* (thin) board, plank.
***fjøl'd** *-a* cf **fjølde**
***fjøl'de** *-n* crowd, multitude.
fjø'l/ende *-n* piece, remnant of a (thin) board, slab.
***fjøl'g** *A* numerous.
***fjøl'ge** *V -a* increase, multiply.
***fjøl'/ment** *A -* numerous; a crowd.

fjø'r *-a* (=**fjær**) 1 feather, plume. 2 spring, hairspring (e.g. in a watch). 3 tongue (on a board).
***fjø'ral** *A* resilient, springy; agile.
fjø'r/ball *-en* 1 shuttlecock. 2 badminton.
***fjø're**[1] *-a* cf **fjære**[1]
fjø're[2] *V -a/+-et* cf **fjære**[2]
fjø're[3] *V -a/+-et* (=+**fjære**[3]) 1 furnish with springs; be elastic, springy, yield. 2: **f-ende** elastic, resilient, springy. 3 tongue (boards).
fjø're/koll *-en bot.* thrift (Statice armeria).
***fjø'ren** *A -e/-i, pl -ne* resilient, springy; agile.
fjø'ret(e) *A -* feathered, plumed.
fjø'r/fe *-et* poultry.
fjø'r/ham' *+-men/*-en* plumage.
***fjø'r/harv** *-a* cf **fjær/**
***fjø'ring** *-a* cf **fjæring**
fjø'r/krage *-n* ruff.
fjø'r/penn *-en* (goose)quill pen.
***fjø'rug** *A -* lively, spirited.
fjø'r/vekt *-a/+-en* 1 spring scale. 2 featherweight (boxer).
fjø's *-et* cow barn.
+fjø's/mester *-eren, pl -ere/-rer* (=*/**meister**) manager of a dairy barn.
fjø's/stell *-et* (barn) chores.
fjå'g *A dial.* happy, joyful, pleased.
f. Kr. = **før Kristus**
fl. = +**flertall,** +**flere**/***fleirtal,** ***fleire**
flabb' *-en* 1 (of animal) chops, jaws. 2 *derog.* foolish, insolent person.
flab'bet(e) *A - derog.* foolish, impudent, *(pop.)* fresh.
°fla/brød [flab'brø] *-et* cf **flat/**
fla'ge[1] *-a* 1 gust of wind; squall. 2 chill; sharp pain.
***fla'ge**[2] *V -a* move by fits and starts, spasmodically.
flagellan't *-en* flagellant.
flagella't *-en zool.* flagellate (i.e. any of the Flagellata).
flageolett [flasjolett'] *-en* flageolet.
flagg' *-et* flag; colors, ensign: **hilse med f-et** dip the f-; **tone f-** show one's true c-s, speak out; **det rene f-** *hist.* "the pure flag" (Norway's red, white, and blue, without the blue and yellow mark of union with Sweden (before 1905)).
flagg'/duk *-en* bunting.
flag'ge *V -a/+-et* display, fly, hang out the flag: **f- på halv stang f-** the flag at half mast; **Det f-er i byen og på havnen** Flags are flying in town and harbor (novel by Bjørnson).
flag'ger/mus *-a zool.* bat (order Chiroptera).
flagg'/line *-a* 1 *naut.* signal halyard. 2 rope on flagpole.
flagg'/skip *-et* flagship.
+flagg'/stang *-a, pl -stenger* (=*/**stong**) flagpole, flagstaff.
flag're *V -a/+-et* flit, flutter.
fla'k[1] *-et* 1 flake. 2 (ice) floe.
fla'k[2] *-et* shirttail.
fla'ke[1] *-a* 1 shaft, streak (e.g. of light), strip. 2 hatch; foundation (of boards).
fla'ke[2] *V -a/+-et dial.* 1 (of clothes) flap, flutter. 2 rip, tear.
fla'ke[3] *V -a/+-et*: **f- seg** crack, flake, form floes.
flak'ke *V -a/+-et* 1: **f- (omkring)** ramble, roam, rove (around). 2 flicker, waver: **f-ende øyne** shifty eyes.
flak'ne *V -a/+-et* become split, torn, crack open; flake off.
flakong' *-en* flacon, flask, (perfume) bottle.
flak're *V -a/+-et* flicker, waver (e.g. a light).
flak's[1] *-en* (run of) luck: **ha f-** be lucky, make out well.
flak's[2] *-et* flap, flutter.
flak'se *V -a/+-et* flap (arms, wings), flutter; *fig., pop.* run around like a chicken with its head cut off.
Flak'/staḍ *Pln* twp, Nordland.
***flak'te** *pt of* **flekkje**
flamingo [flaming'go] *-en zool.* flamingo (family Phoenicopteridae).

flam'/lenḍing *-en* (= +/**lender**) Fleming.
flam'me[1] *+-n/*-a* 1 blaze, flame, glow; love, passion; sweetheart: **en ny f-** a new f- (girl friend); **komme i fyr og f-** be enthusiastic, rave about; **stå i f-r** be in f-s. 2 streak, vein, wave (in metal, wood).
flam'me[2] *V -a/+-et* 1 blaze, flame: **f- opp** flare up, leap into flame. 2 do flame embroidery.
flam'me/bjørk *-a* wavy-grained birchwood.
flam'me/hav *-et* sea of flames.
+flam'me/kaster *-en, pl -e* (=***-ar**) *mil.* flamethrower.
flam'me/skjær *-et* light from a fire, flame.
flam'met(e) *A -* streaked, veined, wavy; shot (e.g. shot silk); blotched, mottled (complexion).
flam'sk *A -* Flemish.
Flan'dern *Pln* Flanders.
fla'ne *-a/+-en* flirt.
flanell' *-en* flannel.
flane're *V -te lit.* promenade, stroll; loaf, lounge.
flan'ke *-n mil.* flank.
flanke're *V -te mil.* enfilade, outflank.
flanø'r *-en lit.* idler, lounger, man about town.
fla're *V -a/+-et/+-te* blaze up, burst into flame.
***fla's** *-et* cf **flass**
***fla'se** *V -a* cf **flasse**
flas'k *-en* flat (side): **kløve på f-en** split sth (e.g. a piece of wood) along the grain.
flas'ke[1] *-a* bottle, flask, phial; baby's bottle: **gi f-** give a baby its bottle; **på f-** bottled; **slå seg på f-a** take to the bottle, start drinking heavily.
flas'ke[2] *V -a/+-et*: **f- opp** raise a baby on the bottle; *fig.* **bli f-et opp med noe** be raised on sth from infancy (e.g. socialism).
flas'ke[3] *V -a/+-et*: **f- seg** pan out, work out.
flas'ke/brott *-et* (=*/**brot**) bits, pieces of broken bottles, shards.
flas'ke/for *-et* 1 *obs.* case in which to carry bottles, cellaret. 2 *hum.* (supply of) bottle goods.
flas'ke/hals *-en* bottleneck.
flas'ke/post *-en* message in a bottle (thrown into the sea).
+flas'ke/skår *-et* bits, pieces of broken bottles, shards.
flass' *-et* (=***flas**) dandruff.
flas'se *V -a/+-et* (=***flasa**) flake, peel (off); form dandruff.
flas'set(e) *A -* full of dandruff.
fla't[1] *-en/+-a* flat field.
fla't[2] *A* 1 flat, level: **f- tallerken** dinner plate. 2 crestfallen, embarrassed. 3 banal, commonplace, insipid.
Fla't/anger *Pln* twp, Nord-Trøndelag.
fla't/brysta *A -* (=+**-et**) flat-chested.
flat'brøḍ *-et* "flatbread" (very thin, crisp unleavened bread).
flat'brøḍ/soll *-en* mixture of milk or cream and crumbled **flatbrød.**
fla't/bygd *-a* rural community located in flat country.
fla'te[1] *-a/+-en* expanse, surface; level, plain; flat (e.g. of the hand, a sword).
fla'te[2] *V -a/+-et*: **f- ut** flatten.
+fla'te/innholḍ *-et* area.
fla'te/mål *-et* unit of area measurement.
fla't/fele *-a* (ordinary) violin.
fla't/lanḍ *-et* plain.
fla't/lenḍt *A -* flat, level (ground, land).
fla't/lus *-a, pl -/*-lyser zool.* crab louse (Phthirus pubis).

+ Bokmål; * Nynorsk; ° Dialect.
After letter: ' stress (Acc. 1); ` tone, stress (Acc. 2); ˙ length.
Below letter: . not pronounced.

fla'tne *V -a/⁺-et* become flatter, more level.

fla't/seng *-a* bed made up on floor.

flatte're *V -te* present in a flattering way: **en f-ende belysning** a flattering light.

flau' *A* 1 flat, insipid, stale; distasteful. 2 embarrassed, shamefaced: **gjøre en f-** embarrass sby. 3 embarrassing, humiliating. 4 *merc.* dull, slack (market).

°**flau'(g)**[1] *-et* cf **flog**

flau'g[2] *pt of* **fly**[4]

***flau'm** *-en* cf **flom**

flau'se *-n* 1 platitude, trite remark. 2 blunder, faux pas.

flau't *pt of* **flyte,** *nt of* **flau**

fleg'ma *-et* impassiveness, indifference.

⁺**flegma'tiker** *-en, pl -e* (=***-ar**) phlegmatic person.

flegma'tisk *A* - phlegmatic.

***flei'n**[1] *-et* bare spot.

flei'n[2] *pt of* **fline**

***flei'ne** *-a* (=**flein** *-en*) bare place, spot.

flei'n/skalla *A* - (=⁺**-et**) baldheaded.

flei'n/skalle *-n* bald head.

flei'p *-en* 1 cocky, insolent person, *(pop.)* smart aleck. 2 (also *-et*) flippant, pert remark(s).

flei'pe *V -a/⁺-et/-te* talk flippantly, pertly; make fun of sby, ridicule sby.

flei'pet(e) *A* - disrespectful, flippant, *(pop.)* fresh.

***flei'r/** *Pf* cf **fler/**

***flei're** *A cp* cf **flere**

***flei'r/farga** *A* - cf **fler/farga**

***flei'r/tal** *-et* cf **fler/tall**

flei's *-en pop.* mug, puss.

flekk' *-en, pl *-er* smudge, speck, spot; patch, plot; *fig.* blot, stain: **fjerne f-er** remove stains; **ikke kunne komme av f-en** not to be able to make any progress at all; **på (flyende) f-en** at once, immediately.

⁺**flek'ke**[1] *V flekte* (=***flekkje**) peel, skin, slit; lay bare, strip; cleave; split (fish): **f- av** peel off (e.g. paint), reveal; **f- tenner** show one's teeth.

flek'ke[2] *V -a/⁺-et* 1 smudge, spot, stain; *fig.* stain, sully (e.g. one's honor). 2 patch, spot (with cement, paint, plaster).

Flek'ke/fjo'rd *Pln* city, Vest-Agder.

flek'ke/kniv *-en* cleaver.

flek'ket(e) *A* - 1 spotted, stained. 2 speckled (e.g. trout); spotted (e.g. dog).

***flek'kje** *V flakte* cf **flekke**[1]

flekk'/tyfus *-en med.* spotted fever, typhus; tick fever.

flekk'/vatn *-et* (=⁺**/vann**) spot remover.

fleksi'bel *A -elt, pl -le* flexible.

fleksjo'n *-en gram.* inflection.

⁺**flek'te** *pt of* **flekke**[1]

flekte're *V -te gram.* inflect.

fleng' *N:* **i f-** at random, haphazardly; aplenty, galore, in abundance: **skylde penger i f-** owe everybody money.

⁺**fleng'e**[1] *-a* (=***flengje**[1]) rent, rift, tear; gash, slash; slit.

⁺**fleng'e**[2] *V -te* (=***flengje**[2]) rip, tear; gash, slash.

⁺**fleng'ende** *A* - ripping, slashing: **en f- kritikk** acid, caustic criticism.

***fleng'je**[1] *-a* cf **flenge**[1]

***fleng'je**[2] *V -de* cf **flenge**[2]

flen's *-en* flange.

flen'se *V -a/⁺-et* 1 flense (a whale). 2 put a flange on (a sheet of metal).

flen'se/kniv *-en* flensing knife.

fle'pe *V ⁺-te/*-a* blubber, snivel.

fle'pet(e) *A* - blubbering, sniveling.

⁺**fle'r** *A* - cf **flere**

⁺**fle'r/dobbelt** *A* - (=***fleir/dobbel**) manifold, multiple.

⁺**fle're** *A cp of* **mange** (=***fleire**) 1 more (in number): **det var f- kvinner enn menn** there were m- women than men; **jeg har ingen f- penger** I don't have any m- money. 2 several, various: **en av f-** one of s- **og f- andre** and s- others; **med f-** and others, et alia.

⁺**fle'r/farga** *A* - (=⁺**-et,** ***fleir/**) multicolored.

⁺**fle'r/faset** *A* - *elec.* polyphase.

⁺**flerfol'dig** *A* - (=***fleir/faldig**) manifold, many.

⁺**fle'r/gifte** *-t* (=***fleir/**) polyandry, polygamy.

⁺**fle'r/guderi** *-et* polytheism.

⁺**fle'r/het** *-en* majority, plurality (**av** of).

⁺**fle'r/koneri** *-et* polygamy.

fler're[1] *-a* (=⁺**flære**) rip, slash, tear.

fler're[2] *V -a/⁺-et* rip, slash, tear.

⁺**fle'r/sidig** *A* - (=***fleir/**) many-sided, versatile.

⁺**fle'rstavings/o'rd** *-et* (=⁺**-stavelses/**) *gram.* polysyllabic word.

⁺**fle'r/stemmig** *A* - polyphonic, sung in parts.

⁺**fle'r/tall** *-et* (=***fleir/tal**) 1 majority: **f-et har alltid retten på sin side** the m- is always right (Ibsen). 2 *gram.* plural.

⁺**fle'r/tydig** *A* - (=***fleir/**) having various meanings; ambiguous.

⁺**fle'r/årig** *A* - (=***fleir/**) 1 *bot.* perennial. 2 lasting for several years.

fle's *-a* low lying reef, skerry.

Fles'/berg *Pln* twp, Buskerud.

fles'k *-et* pork; (of person) corpulence, obesity: **gi grisen f-** carry coals to Newcastle; **det koster f-** it costs plenty (blood, a fortune).

⁺**fles'ke/fett** *-et* (=***/feitt**) pork drippings, fat: **store ord og f-** *(pop.)* hot air.

fles'ke/sentra'l *-en* cf **kjøtt- og fleske/sentral**

fles'ke/skinke *-a* ham.

fles'ke/svor *-en* bacon rind.

fles'ket(e) *A* - fat, flabby.

fle'st *A sp of* **mange** most (in number): **de f-e** m- people; **de f-e (av) bøkene mine** m- of my books; **i de f-e tilfelle** in m- cases; **folk f-** m- people, ordinary people.

***fles'talle** *Pn* cf **flest**

fles'te/part *-en:* **f-en** the majority (**av** of).

flet'ning *-en* 1 braid, plait. ⁺2 braiding, plaiting.

flet'te[1] *-a* braid, pigtail, plait.

flet'te[2] *V -a/⁺-et* braid, plait; twine, weave (e.g. baskets): **f- inn** w- in, work in (e. g. anecdotes in a speech).

flet'te[3] *V -a/⁺-et/*-e* flay, skin; peel, strip.

flet'te/band (=⁺**/bånd**) *-et* hair ribbon.

flett'/verk *-et* basketry, tracery, wickerwork.

fli'[1] *-a* disk, plate (esp. *naut.* in **anker/**).

fli'[2] *V -dde* 1 straighten up, tidy: **f- seg** make oneself presentable. 2 hand, pass to.

fli'd *-en* (=***flit**) application, diligence, industry: **gjøre seg f- med noe** take pains with sth.

fli'k *-en* 1 (of material, paper) corner, flap: **løfte en f- av sløret** reveal part of the mystery. 2 *bot.* lobe. 3 *naut.* (of an anchor) fluke.

⁺**fli'ke** *V -te* (=***-je**) (of clothes) gape, open as a gap.

fli'ket(e) *A* - (=***flika**) *bot.* laciniate.

***fli'kje** *V -te* cf **flike**

flikk' *-en* patch, scrap (e.g. of leather).

flik'ke *V -a/⁺-et* mend, patch; cobble: **f- opp, sammen** patch up.

⁺**flik'ker** *-en, pl -e* (=***-ar**) mender, patcher.

flikk'/flakk *N:* **slå f-** slap one's shoulders with the opposite hands (in order to keep warm).

***flik're** *V -a* flirt with sby, make up to sby.

flim'mer *-et* flicker, shimmer.

flim'mer/hår *-et zool.* cilium.

flim're *V -a/⁺-et* flicker, flutter, shimmer: **det f-er for øynene** my eyes are swimming.

fli'n *-en* giggling, tittering.

***fli'nad** *-en* arrangement, management.

***flin'dre** *-a* piece, splinter (e.g. of stone): **f-r** flinders.

fli'ne *V flein/⁺-te, ⁺flint/*-e/*-i* giggle, titter.

fling're[1] *-a* chip, splinter (e.g. of stone); snowflake.

fling're[2] *V -a/⁺-et* (of snow, snowflakes) fall thickly.

flin'k *A* able, clever, competent; bright, good at, quick to learn: **f- i matlagning** a good cook; **han er f- i språk** he's good at languages.

flin't[1] *-en/*-a* 1 flint. 2 chip, fragment (e.g. of stone, wood): **fly i f- fly** into a rage, fly off the handle.

⁺**flin't**[2] *pp of* **fline**

⁺**flin'te/børse** *-a* (=***flint/**) *hist.* flintlock.

⁺**flin'te/stein** *-en* (=***flint/**) flint, flint stone.

flin't/skalla *A* - (=⁺**-et**) baldheaded.

⁺**flipp'** *-en archaic* man's collar.

fli'r *-en/⁺-et* (derisive, scornful) laughter, sneer; (foolish) smile.

fli're *V -te* laugh, smile (usu. derisively, scornfully, or foolishly), sneer: **f- det hen** laugh it off; **f- fjollet** grin foolishly.

fli're/mikkel *-elen, pl -mikler derog.* grinning ape.

fli'ret(e) *A* - derisive, jeering.

fli's *-a* 1 chip, sliver, splinter: **f-er** flinders. 2 tile; flagstone.

Fli'sa [also Fli'sa] *Pln* post office, Åsnes twp, Hedmark.

⁺**fli'se**[1] *-n* flagstone, tile.

fli'se[2] *V -a/⁺-te:* **f- opp** chip, splinter.

⁺**fli'se/legge** *V -la, -lagt* pave with flagstones; cover with tiles, tile.

⁺**fli'se/spikker** *-en, pl -e* (=***-ar**) hairsplitter, quibbler.

⁺**fli'se/spikkeri'** *-et* (=***/spikking**) hairsplitting.

fli'set(e) *A* - 1 unraveled. 2 stringy, wispy (hair).

***fli't** *-en* cf **flid**

flit'ter *-et* spangle, tinsel; cheap, gaudy finery.

flit'tig *A* - assiduous, diligent, industrious: **gjøre f- bruk av** make d- use of, use frequently; **smake f- på øllet** guzzle the beer; *archaic* **f- hilsen** many greetings; *bot.* **F-e Lise** garden balsam, impatience (Impatiens sultana).

***fljo't** *A* cf **fløt**[2]

⁺**flo'**[1] *-a* (=***flod**[2]) flood tide, high tide, rising tide; heavy shower: **f- og fjære** high tide and low tide.

***flo'**[2] *-a, pl -er/flør* layer, stratum.

flo'd[1] *-en* 1 flood, inundation; deluge, torrent. ⁺2 *archaic* river.

***flo'd**[2] *-a* cf **flo**[1]

flo'd/bølgje *-a* (=⁺**/bølge**) tidal wave; *fig.* flood, wave (e.g. of indignation).

⁺**flo'd/båt** *-en* river boat.

⁺**flo'd/hest** *-en* hippopotamus.

***flo'd/mål** *-et* cf **flo/**

flo'e *-n* (small) pool, puddle in a bog, marsh.

flog [flå'g] *-et* 1 steep bluff. *2 flying, soaring; flight.

flog/bratt *A* - unscalable.

***floge**[1] [flå'ge] *-a* cf **flage**[1]

***floge**[2] [flå'ge] *V -a* 1 run around, be on a spree. 2 run forth, stream.

***floge**[3] [flå'ge] *pp of* **fly(ge)**[2]

flog/havre [flå'g/] *-n bot.* wild oat (Avena fatua).

***flogi** [flå'gi] *pp of* **fly(ge)**[2]

***flog's** *-et* coquette, flirt.

flog/sand [flå'g/] *-en* shifting sands.

***flog'se**[1] *-a* cf **flokse**[1]

***flog'se**[2] *V -a* cf **flokse**[2]

***flog/skrift** [flå'g/] *-et* brochure, pamphlet.

flog/vett** *-et* (=/vit**) genius.

flo'ing *-en* sudden, short shower.

flo'ke[1] *-n* knot, tangle; *fig.* complication, difficulty, problem.

flo'ke[2] *-n* snowflake.

flo'ke[3] *N:* **slå f-** flap one's arms (to keep warm).

flo'ke[4] *V -a/⁺-et* entangle, ravel, tangle; *fig.* complicate: **f- seg**

sammen become complicated, muddled.

flo'ket(e) *A* - ravelled, tangled; *fig.* complicated, difficult.

flokk' *-en* body, crowd, throng; (of geese, sheep) flock; (of cattle) herd; (of wolves) pack: **en f- mennesker** a group of people; **følge f-en** follow the herd, go with the crowd; **i f- og følge** in a body; in great numbers; **løfte i f-** join hands, pull together.

***flok'kast** *V -ast* cf **flokkes**

flok'ke *V -a/+-et* collect, gather: **f- seg rundt** crowd, swarm around; **f- seg sammen** crowd, gather, throng.

+flok'kes *V -edes, -es* (=***flokkast**) crowd, flock, gather: **f- om** crowd round.

flok'ke/vis *Av* in crowds, in flocks; by groups.

flok's *-en bot.* phlox (genus Phlox).

+flok'se^1 *-a* (=***flogse^1**) coquette, flirt.

+flok'se^2 *V -a/-et* (=***flogse^2**) flirt, play around.

+flok'set(e) *A* - coquettish, giddy.

+flom' *-men* (=***flaum**) flood, inundation: **en f- av sollys** a f- of sunshine.

+flom'me *V -a/-et* cf **flømme**

+flo'/mål *-et* (=***flod/**) high-water mark.

flo'r^1 *-en* 1 cow barn. 2 barn floor.

flo'r^2 *-et* bloom, flowering; (of flowers) profusion (**av** of): **i fullt f-** in full b-.

flo'r^3 *-et* crepe (used for mourning band, veil).

flo'ra *-en, pl *-er bot.* flora (book; plant life).

flo're *-a* ice floe; layer.

flore're *V -te* flourish, thrive; be rampant, rife.

florett' *-en* (fencing) foil.

+florett'/fektning *-a/-en* (=**/fekting**) fencing with foils.

florisant [-sang't] *A* - flourishing, prosperous.

flo'r/lett *A* - gauzy, gossamery.

flo'r/melis *-en* powdered sugar.

Flo'r/ø *Pln* seaport, Sogn og Fjordane.

***flo'se** *V -a* peel, scale off.

flos'kel *-elen, pl -ler* empty phrase, rhetorical phrase; platitude.

floss'^{1} *-en* 1 nap, shag. 2 (tall) silk hat, stovepipe, top hat.

floss'^{2} *-en naut.* inflatable raft; Carley raft.

flos'se *V -a/+-et*: **f- seg** fray.

flos'set(e) *A* - frayed, raveled, tattered; fleeced, napped.

floss'/hatt *-en* (tall) silk hat, stovepipe, top hat.

Flosta [flos'ta] *Pln* twp, Aust-Agder.

+flo'/strøm *-men* rising tide.

***flot^1** [flå't] *-a* level, grassy area.

***flot^2** [flå't] *-et* cf **flott^2**

***flote^1** [flå'te] *-n* cf **flåte^1**

***flote^2** [flå'te] *V -a* float (e.g. timber).

flote^3** [flå'te] *pp of* **flyte** (=floti**)

flotil'je *-n* flotilla.

flot'ne *V -a/+-et*: **f- opp** float up (to the surface).

***flott'^{1}** *-a* (mountain) meadow; treeless plain.

+flott'^{2} *-et* (=***flot^2**) 1 floating: **på f-** afloat. 2 float, floater. 3 (floating) fat.

flott'^{3} *A* - 1 generous, liberal, openhanded; extravagant, lavish. 2 grand, superb; elegant, smart, stylish; dashing, jaunty: **en f- prestasjon** a splendid performance. 3 reckless, sweeping (e.g. statements). 4 *naut.* afloat: **komme f-** be floated; float.

flot'tas *-en* show-off, spendthrift.

flot'te *V -a/+-et*: **f- seg** live in an extravagant, lavish fashion; **f- seg med** display ostentatiously, sport.

flot'ten/heimer *-en, pl +-e* show-off, spendthrift.

+flott'/het *-en* 1 generosity; extravagance. 2 elegance, ostentation. 3 recklessness.

flot'ting *-en* show-off, spendthrift.

flottø'r *-en* float.

flu'^{1} *-a* rock, skerry exposed at half tide.

flu'^{2} *V -dde* toss out bait for fish.

Flu'/berg *Pln* twp, Oppland.

+flu'e *-a* (=***fluge**) 1 fly, esp. common housefly (Musca domestica): **ha f-r i hodet** have a bee in one's bonnet; **sette f-r i hodet på en** turn sby's head; **slå to f-er i ett smekk** kill two birds with one stone. 2 fly (fishhook designed to resemble an insect).

+flu'e/fanger *-en, pl -e* 1 flycatcher, flypaper, flytrap. 2 *bot.* Venus's-flytrap (Dionaea muscipula).

+flu'e/fiske *-t* flyfishing.

+flu'e/lort [/lort] *-en* flyspeck.

+flu'e/smekker *-en, pl -e* flyswatter.

+flu'e/sopp *-en bot.*: **rød f-** fly agaric (Amanita muscaria); **grønn f-** death cup (genus Amanita).

+flu'e/vekt *-a/-en* flyweight.

***flu'ge** *-a* cf **flue**

***flu'ge/fiske** *-t* cf **flue/**

flu'idum' *-et, pl +fluida/*-* fluid, liquid; hard liquor (e.g. brandy).

+fluk's(ens) *Av* at once, immediately, straightway.

fluk't *-a/+-en* escape, flight: **gripe i f-en** seize by the forelock; **i f- med** flush, in line with; **jage på f-** put to flight, rout; **ta f-en** flee, fly.

fluk't/stol *-en* deck chair, folding chair.

fluktue're *V -te* fluctuate.

°flun'dre *-a* cf **flyndre**

+flunkende [flong'kene] *Av*: **f- ny** brand-new.

flu'or *-en* fluorine.

fluorescen's *-en* fluorescence.

fluoresce're *V -te* fluoresce.

fluorise're *V -te* add fluorine to (e.g. water).

flu'r *-en* shaggy, unkempt hair.

***flu's^1** *-et* dandruff, scale.

flu's^2 *A* 1 liberal, openhanded. 2: **det er f-t med penger** money is plentiful.

flus'k *-en* forelock.

fluss'/syre *-a chem.* hydrofluoric acid.

***flus't^1** *pp of* **flysje**

flus't^2 *nt of* **flus^2**

***flus'te** *pt of* **flysje**

***flut'ning** *-en* cf **flytning**

***flut'te** *pt of* **flytje**

fly'^{1} *-a* flat, level mountain plateau.

fly'^{2} *-et* flying insect, e.g. fly, gnat.

fly'^{3} *-et* (air)plane, aircraft: **sende med f-** send by air.

fly'^{4} *V flaug/+fløy, +flydd/+fløyet/*floge/*-i* (=**flyge^2**) fly; leave, run, rush: **f-ende** (see entry), **flygende, flyvende** flying; **f- av sted** rush off; **f- beina av seg for noen** run one's legs off for sby; **f- i flint** fly into a rage, fly off the handle; be maddened; **f- opp** (of door) fly open; **f- opp i sinne** flare up, (*pop.*) fly off the handle; **f- over** cross, fly across; **f- på en** fly at sby; **f- som et pisket skinn** run around like a madman.

fly'^{5} *V -dde* flee; avoid, shun.

fly'/alar'm *-en* air raid warning.

fly'/base *-n* air base.

+fly'/båren *A -ent, pl -ne* (=***/boren**) airborne.

flydd' *pp of* **fly^{4,5}**

+fly'ende *Av* flying: **på f- flekken** at once, immediately, posthaste; **f- fort** at breakneck speed; **f- sint** furiously angry.

+fly'/fille *-a* flighty girl (*derog.*, of one who is always running after boys).

fly'/fotografi' *-et, pl +-er/*-* aerial photograph.

***fly'ge^1** *-t* flying insects, e.g. fly, gnat.

fly'ge^2 *V flaug, +fløyet/*floge/*-i* cf **fly^4**

fly'ge/blad *-et* leaflet, pamphlet.

+fly'ge/dyktig *A* - able to, capable of flying.

***fly'ge/før** *A* fit for flying.

fly'ge/idé *-en* passing whim; fancy, notion.

***fly'gel^1** *-elen, pl -lar* flail.

fly'gel^2 *-elet/-let, pl +-ler/*-el* grand piano.

fly'ge/maski'n *-en* aircraft; airplane, plane.

+fly'ger *-en, pl -e* (=***-ar**) flier, pilot.

fly'ge/sand *-en* shifting sands.

fly'ge/skrift *-et* pamphlet.

fly'ge/tanke *-n* passing fancy, whim.

flygg' *-et naut.* fluke of an anchor.

flyk'te *V -a/+-et* flee, fly, run away (**fra** from): **f- for fienden** flee the enemy; **f- over hals og hode** flee head over heels, in confusion and disorder.

flyk'tig *A* - 1 cursory, hasty: **f- undersøkelse** superficial examination. 2 fleeting, transitory: **han smilte f-** he smiled slightly. 3 (of person) fickle; flighty, giddy. 4 *chem.* volatile.

flyk'tning *-en* fugitive, refugee.

flyk'tning/hjelp *-a/-en* (=**+flyktninge/**) assistance for displaced persons, refugees.

flyn'dre *-a* 1 *zool.* flounder (Pleuronectes flesus). 2 *fam.* flat stone: **kaste f-** skip stones.

fly'/plass *-en* airfield, airport.

fly'/post *-en* airmail: **med f-** by a-.

***fly's** *pr of* **flysje**

***flys'je** *V flys, fluste, flust* peel (off).

fly't *-en* movement: **det er (ikke) f- i trafikken** traffic is (not) flowing smoothly.

fly'te *V flaut/+fløt, +flytt/*flote/*-i* 1 flow, run: **f-ende** (see entry); **f- over** overflow; **det var dette som fikk begeret til å f- over** that was the last straw; **f- med melk og honning** be f-ing with milk and honey; **f- sammen** mingle, unite; **alt f-er** everything is in flux. 2 float: **f- opp** come to the surface; **f- på sin berømmelse** live on one's reputation. 3 be cluttered up, be littered, be in a mess: **f- overalt** be all over the place.

+fly'te/bru *-a* pontoon bridge.

fly'te/dokk *-a/+-en* floating dock.

fly'te/evne *-a/+-en* buoyancy.

fly'tende *A* 1 fluid, liquid, molten: **gjøre f-** liquefy. 2 *fig.* in flux (e.g. opinions), mobile. 3 fluent: **tale f- fransk** speak French f-ly.

***flyt'je** *V flutte* cf **flytte**

flyt'ning *-en* moving; move, removal, transfer.

***flytt'** *-en/-et* moving; move, removal, transfer.

+flytt'/bar *A* movable, portable; removable.

flytt'/blokk *-en* erratic boulder (block).

flyt'te *V -a/+-et/*-e* (=***flytje**) move (change place or position, shift; change one's residence, employment; remove; transfer): **f- på noe** m- sth (slightly); **f- på seg** m- over, make room; **f- seg** edge, m- up; **f- seg hit og dit** fidget, shift about.

flyt'te/dag *-en* moving day.

flyt'te/folk *pl* movers.

flyt'te/fot *-en*: **stå på f-** be about to move; **være på f-** be on the move.

flyt'te/lass *-et* load of furniture, vanful of furniture.

flyt'te/vogn [/vångn] *-a* moving van.

flytt'/fugl [+/ful] *-en* bird of passage, migratory bird.

flytt'/mann *-en, pl -menn/*-menner* ferryman.

flytt'/same *-n* Lapp nomad.

+fly've *V fløy, fløyet* cf **fly^4**

+fly've/grille *-a/-en* passing fancy, whim.

+fly've/idé *-en* cf **flyge/**

+fly'ver *-en* cf **flyger**

fly'/vertin'ne *-a/+-en* stewardess.

+fly've/sand *-en* cf **flyge/**

+fly'/vesen *-et* aviation.

+fly've/tanke *-n* cf **flyge/**

+fly'vning *-en* (=**flyging** *-a*) flying.

fly'/våpen *-et mil.* air force.

+ Bokmål; * Nynorsk; ° Dialect.
After letter: ' stress (Acc. 1); ` tone, stress (Acc. 2); · length.
Below letter: . not pronounced.

***flæ'r** *pl of* **flå**[1]

flæ're *-a* cf **flerre**[1]

flø' *V -dde* (=***fløde**) flow, run; rise with the tide.

***flø'de** *V -de* cf **flø**

***flø'kje** *V -te* ravel, tangle; complicate.

+fløm'me *V flømte* (=**+flomme**/ ***fløyme**) flow, stream: **det f-er med (brev)** (letters) are pouring in; **f- inn** rush in; **f- over** run over; **f- utover** gush out.

flø'rt *-en* flirtation; flirt.

flø'rte *V -a*/*+-et* flirt.

+flø't[1] *pt of* **flyte**

***flø't**[2] *A* (=**fljot**) **1** quick, swift. **2** fiery, high-spirited.

+flø'te[1] *-n* cf **fløyte**[1]

+flø'te[2] *V -te* cf **fløyte**[3]

+flø'te/fjes *-et* **1** effeminate face. **2** milksop.

+flø'te/grøt *-en* cream porridge.

+flø'ter *-en, pl -e* cf **fløyter**

+flø'ter/hake *-n* picaroon, pike pole (lumbering).

+flø'tning *-en* (=**+fløting, fløyting**) floating, rafting logs.

+fløtt' *-en*/*-et* **1** flotage; water transport. **2** float (used in fishing).

+fløtt'/mann *-en, pl -menn*/**-menner* cf **flytt/**

fløy'[1] *-a*/*+-en* **1** vane. **2** (of building) wing. **3** (of table) leaf; part of a double door. **4** wing (on a nut). **5** *mil.* flank, wing.

+fløy'[2] *-a*/*-en* (=***fløyg**) peel (stick for turning bread).

+fløy'[3] *pt of* **fly**[4]

fløy'/dør *-a* double door.

fløy'el *-en*/*-et* velvet.

fløy'els/blaut *A* (=**+/bløt**) soft as velvet, velvety.

fløy'els/graut *-en* (=**+/grøt**) pudding made of butter, flour, and milk.

fløy'els/hanske *-n* velvet glove: **bruke f-r på en** give sby the kid glove treatment.

+fløy'et *pp of* **fly**[4]

***fløy'g** *-en* cf **fløy**[2]

***fløy'gje** *V -de* let sth drop, slip (from one's hands); speed up.

fløy'/mann *-en, pl -menn*/**-menner* *mil.* pivot (man).

***fløy'me** *V -de* cf **flømme**

fløy't *-en* **1** flotage. **2** floating logs. **3** float. ***4** bringing to the surface, raising.

fløy'te[1] *-n* (=**+fløte**[1]) cream: **ha munnen full av f-** talk as though butter wouldn't melt in one's mouth.

fløy'te[2] *-a* **1** *mus.* flute. **2** pipe, whistle (e.g. a bosun's whistle).

fløy'te[3] *V -te* (=**+fløte**[2]) float logs (downstream); raft (logs).

fløy'te[4] *V -a*/*+-et* warble; whistle.

fløy'te/mugge *-a* cream pitcher.

fløytenis't *-en mus.* flutist.

+fløy'ter *-en, pl -e* (=**+fløter, *fløytar**) lumberjack, raftsman.

fløytis't *-en mus.* flutist.

flå'[1] *-a, pl +-er*/**flær* flat, level mountain plateau.

flå'[2] *V -dde* **1** flay, skin: **f- av** strip off (e.g. bark). **2** *fig.* bleed, fleece: **f- til skinnet** clean sby out completely (of money, property).

***flå'**[3] *A -tt* wide; flat, level.

Flå' *Pln* **1** twp, Buskerud. **2** twp, Sør-Trøndelag.

+flå'er *-en, pl -e* (=***-ar**) extortionist, robber, a Scrooge.

+flåeri' *-et* extortion, fleecing.

flå'/kjefta *A -* (=**+-et**) flapjawed, loose-mouthed; flippant.

Flåm' *Pln* post office, Aurland twp, Sogn og Fjordane.

flå's[1] *-en* flippant person, smart aleck.

flå's[2] *-et*/*+-en* disrespectful, flippant conduct, speech: **f- og flir** jokes and prattle.

flå'se *V +-te*/**-a* talk disrespectfully, flippantly.

+flå'seri [also -ri'] *-et* disrespect, flippancy.

flå'set(e) *A -* disrespectful, flippant; loose-mouthed.

flå'te[1] *-n* (=***flote**[1]) **1** float, raft (of logs). **2** fleet, flotilla, squadron. **3** merchant marine; navy.

flå'te[2] *V -a*/*+-et* float, raft (logs).

flå'te/hamn *-a* (=**+/havn**) naval base.

flått' *-en zool.* tick (Ixodes ricinus).

+f. m.=**forrige måned**

+FN=**De forente nasjoner** (=***SN**) UN.

fnatt' *-et* itch, scabies.

fnat'tet(e) *A -* itchy, scabious.

fni's *-et* giggle, snicker, titter.

fni'se *V -te* giggle, snicker, titter.

+fnokk' *-en bot.* pappus.

+fnugg' *-et* **1** (of dust) mote, speck. **2** (snow) flake. **3: ikke et (det) f-** not the slightest, not a shred.

+fny's *-et* snort.

+fny'se *V -te*/*fnøs, -t*/*fnøset* (=***fnøse**) snort: **f- av raseri** s- with rage.

+fnø's *pt of* **fnyse**

***fnø'se** *V -te* cf **fnyse**

foajé *-en* foyer, lobby.

fobi' *-en med.* phobia.

+fogd [fog'd] *-en* (=**+foged, *fut**) **1** bailiff. **2** (to 1894) tax collector in a rural district.

***fo'ge** *V -a* **1** fill joints. **2** stuff sausages.

+fo'ged *-en* cf **fogd**

***fok** [få'k] *-et* cf **fokk**[2]

foke** [få'ke] *pp of* **fyke** (=foki**)

fokk'[1] *-a naut.* foresail.

fokk'[2] *-et* (=***fok**) drift (of anything); drifting, whirling snow: **rokk og f-** snow and storm.

fok'ke/mast *-a naut.* foremast.

fok'ke/stag *-et naut.* forestay.

fok's/terrier *-en, pl +-e* fox terrier.

Fok'/stua *Pln* RR station, Dovre twp, Oppland.

fo'la *I* (call used to quiet horses): **F- f- Blakken** (children's verse).

fol'd[1] *-en* crease, fold, wrinkle, pleat; *geol.* fold: **legge ansiktet i de rette f-er** keep a straight face; **legge f-er i** pleat; **komme i de vante f-er igjen** settle back in the old groove, rut; **strømpene ligger i f-er** her stockings are sagging around her ankles.

+fol'd[2] *et* cf **foll**

+-fold *Av* (=***-fald**) -fold: e.g. **treff-** threefold; **tusenf-** thousandfold.

Fol'da *Pln* **1** open fjord between Sør- and Nord-Trøndelag. **2** open fjord in Nordland.

Fol'/dal *Pln* cf **Foll/**

fol'de[1] *V -a*/*+-et* fold: **f- opp, f- (seg) ut** unfold; **f- (seg) sammen** f- up.

+fol'de[2] *V -a*/*-et* cf **folle**

fol'der *-en, pl +-e* folder.

Fol'der/eid *Pln* twp, Nord-Trøndelag.

fol'de/rik *A* flowing (e.g. draperies), full (e.g. skirt).

fol'de/skjørt *-et* pleated skirt.

+-fol'dig *A -* (=***-faldig**) -fold: e.g. **mangf-** manifold.

fo'le[1] *-n* foal (colt, filly).

fo'le[2] *V -a*/*+-et* foal.

°fo'le[3] *V -a*/*-et* move: **fol deg ut** get out of here.

***fol'ge** *-a* allowance, pension (=support provided by the new owner of landed property for its previous owner, esp. by a son for his father).

Fol'ge/fonni *Pln* glacier in Hardanger.

folian't *-en* folio.

fo'lie *-n* foil.

folie're *V -te* foliate (number leaves of manuscript).

fo'lio *-en* **1** folio (book format). **2** foolscap. **3** *merc.* **f-/konto** current account.

fo'lio/ark *-et* **1** folio sheet. **2** foolscap.

fol'k *-et* **1** nation, people: **det norske f-** the Norwegian p-; **Folkenes Forbund** the League of Nations: **Norge var et rike, det skal bli et f-** Norway was a kingdom, it must become a n- (Ibsen). **2** (common) people; the masses: **en f-ets venn** a friend of the p-; **F-ets Hus** People's House (Labor Party headquarters). **3** people, persons: **mange f- i byen i dag** many people in town today; **f- sier** people say; **av godt f-** of a good family; **f- flest** most people; **bedre f-s barn** privileged children; **bli f- av noen** learn to behave, grow up; **han ser ut som f-** he looks like a decent fellow (Evensmo); **vil du være f-?** will you behave yourself? **4** servants; workers; staff; *naut.* crew, hands; *mil.* men: **vi har for få f-** we are understaffed.

fol'ke *V -a*/*+-et*: **f- seg** become a proper, well behaved person; grow up, reform.

+fol'ke/avstem'ning *-en* (=***/avrøysting**) plebiscite.

fol'ke/bok *-a, pl -bøker* widely read book, book for the masses.

fol'ke/dans *-en* folk dance.

fol'ke/eventy'r *-et* folktale.

fol'ke/ferd[1] [*/fær] *-a*/*+-en* order, proper behavior.

+fol'ke/ferd[2] *-et* race, sort, type (of people).

fol'ke/fiende *-n* public enemy: **En f-** An Enemy of the People (Ibsen).

+Fol'ke/forbundet *df hist.* the League of Nations.

fol'ke/helse *-a* public health.

fol'ke/høgsko'le *-n* "folk high school", people's college (having general cultural courses not leading to any degree).

fol'ke/karakte'r *-en* national character.

fol'ke/kjær *A* **1** beloved by the people, popular. **2** (of animals) fond of people.

fol'ke/le'sning *-en* popular literature.

fol'kelig *A -* **1** democratic, homely, plain; of the folk; popular. **2** decent, proper: **været ble f-** the weather became bearable.

fol'ke/liv *-et* **1** crowds, street life: **et yrende f-** a busy scene, a motley crowd. **2** *(def.)* everyday life, life of the people.

fol'kelivs/skildring *-a*/*+-en* story of folk life.

fol'ke/lynne *-t* national character.

+fol'ke/mengde *-n* (=**/mengd**) **1** crowd, mob. **2** population: **Norges f-** the p- of Norway.

fol'ke/minne *-et, pl +-r*/**-* folklore.

fol'ke/munne *N* **1: i (på) f-** in oral tradition. **2: komme i (på) f-** get oneself talked about, be the subject of gossip.

fol'ke/muse'um *-museet, pl -museer*/**-* museum of folk art and architecture.

fol'ke/musikk' *-en* folk music.

fol'ke/mål *-et* **1** folk speech; dialect. **2** *pol. (def.)* the language of the (Norwegian) people (used as a term of reference in language planning).

+fol'kens *pl hum.* folks.

fol'ke/opply'sning *-a*/*+-en* popular education.

fol'ke/parti' *-et* people's party: **Sosialistisk F-** Socialistic People's Party.

fol'ke/regis'ter *-eret*/*-ret* directory of residents; census rolls.

fol'ke/rett *-en* international law.

fol'ke/rik *A* populous.

fol'ke/røysting** *-a* (=/røsting**) plebiscite.

***fol'ke/setnad** *-en* population.

fol'ke/skikk *-en* (good) manners: **utenfor f-en** outside civilization.

fol'ke/skole *-n* elementary (grade, grammar) school.

fol'ke/sky *A -* retiring, shy, wary.

fol'ke/slag *-et* people, race.

fol'ke/snakk *-et* gossip, slander.

fol'ke/stamme *-n* tribe.

fol'ke/stue *-a* servants' quarters.

***fol'ke/stygg** *A -stygt* retiring, shy, wary.

fol'ke/styre *-t* democracy.

fol'ke/tal *-et* (=**+/tall**) population.

+fol'ke/taler *-en, pl -e* (=***-ar**) popular orator, speaker.

+fol'ke/telling *-a*/*-en* (=***/teljing**) national census.

fol'ke/tett *A -* densely populated.

fol'ke/tone *-n* folk tune.

fol'ke/tru *-a* (=**+/tro**) popular belief, superstition.

+fol'ke/utga've *-a*/*-en* popular edition, reprint.

+fol'ke/valgt *A* - **(=*/vald)** elected by popular vote.
fol'ke/vandring *-a/+-en* migration of nations, e.g. the migration of the Germanic tribes during the fourth to the sixth centuries.
fol'ke/vis *-a/-en/-et*: **på f-** decently, properly.
fol'ke/vise *-a* ballad, folk song.
fol'kevise/dans *-en* dance accompanying singing of ballads.
+fol'ke/vittighet *-en* popular wit; folk humor.
fol'ke/vond *A* dangerous, fierce (e.g. a bull, a dog).
fol'k/lore [/lår] *-n* folklore.
folkloris't *-en* folklorist.
+fol'k/som· *A -t, pl -me* **(=*/sam)** crowded, populous; much frequented.
foll' *-et* (of crop) yield: **gi tre f-** yield threefold.
Foll'/dal *Pln* twp, Hedmark.
fol'le *V -a/+-et* yield.
+fol'le/kniv *-en* cf **falle/**
***fol'lug** *A* - abundant, rich (yield).
fol'ne *V -a/+-et* fade, wither.
fo'l/unge [/onge] *-n* (newborn) foal (colt).
f. o. m. = **+fra/*frå og med**
fomle [fom'le] *V -a/+-et* be clumsy, bungle; fumble (**med** with).
fommel [fom'mel] *-elen, pl fomler* bungler, clumsy dolt.
fon'd[1] *-en* background, backdrop.
fon'd[2] *-et, pl -s* **1** fund, stock, store (**av** of). **2** fund, legacy; reserve. **3** *(pl)* securities, stocks.
fon'ds/lov [/låv] *-en/*-a merc.* law governing sale of securities and stocks (passed in 1918 in Norway, revised in 1937; cf Securities and Exchange Commission).
fon'ds/skatt *-en merc.* tax on reserve fund.
fone'm *-et, pl -/+-er* phoneme.
fonemikk' *-en* phonemics.
+fone'tiker *-en, pl -e* **(=*-ar)** phonetician.
fonetikk' *-en* phonetics.
fone'tisk *A* - phonetic.
fonn' *-a, pl -er/*fenner* snowdrift; snowfield.
fon'ne *V -a/+-et* form snowdrifts; drift.
fon'net(e) *A* - full of snowdrifts; drifted.
fonogra'f *-en* phonograph.
fonologi' *-en* phonology; phonemics.
fonologisk [-lå'gisk] *A* - phonological; phonemic.
fon't *-en* (baptismal) font.
fontanell' *-en med.* fontanel.
fonte'ne *-n* fountain.
***for**[1] [få'r] *-a* cf **får**[1]
fo'r[2] *-et* **1** feed, fodder. **2** lining: **sette f- i en jakke** line a coat.
fo'r[3] *pt of* **fare**[2]
for'[4] *Av* **1** too: **f- mye** t- much. **2** before, in front: **fra f- til akter** *naut.* from stem to stern; **spenne hestene f-** hitch up the horses; **trekke gardinene for** draw the curtains. **3**: **ta' seg f-** do, undertake; **ta' seg for** feel one's way; **det er ikke annet f-** there's nothing else to do. (For use with other verbs see these).
for'[5] *C* because, for.
for'[6] *P* **1** before, in front of: **ha dagen f- seg** have the day b- you; **skygge f- øynene** shade one's eyes; **sove f- åpne vinduer** sleep with the windows open; **f- lukkede dører** behind closed doors; **f- åpen scene** in public. **2** for: **f- så vidt** f- that matter; **f- tiden** f- the time being; **en gang f- alle** once and f- all; **jeg skal gjøre det f- deg** I'll do it f- you. **3** because of, on account of: **hun tør ikke f- mannen** she doesn't dare because of her husband; **vi ser ikke f- røyken** we can't see because of (for) the smoke; **ikke f- det** not (because of) that, just the same. **4** at: **f- en pris av** at a price of; **f- full fart** at top speed; **f- hånden** at hand. **5** in: **f- alvor, spøk** in earnest, in fun; **f- det første (annet, osv.)** in the first (second, etc.) place. **6** by: **f- seg** by itself (oneself), separately; **dag f- dag** day by day; **dø f- sverdet** die by the sword. **7** from, of, out of: **fri f-** free f-, of; **redd f-** afraid of; **til høyre, venstre f-** to the right, left of; **skjule noe f- en** hide sth f- sby; **være i veien f-** be in the way of. **8** to: **f- en stor del** to a great extent; **f- å** to, in order to; **felles f- dem** common to them; **være fremmed f-** be a stranger to; be unfamiliar with. **9** (in expressions of time): **f- fem år siden** five years ago. **10** (other expressions): **f- at** so that; **f- det** for all that, just the same; **men hun kom jo ikke f- det** but she didn't come anyway (Hoel); **kan ikke f- det** can't help it; (in exclamations) **f- en (et)** what a; **f- noe tull!** what nonsense! **f- min del (mitt vedkommende)** as far as I'm concerned; **gjerne f- meg** O. K. by me; **ha' f- seg** be up to; have at hand; **hva f- noe?** what? (For uses in other phrases with adjectives, nouns and verbs see these).
for'- *Pf* **1** (stressed) fore-, foremost, front; pre- (with nouns, adjectives, or verbs). **2** (unstressed) away, non-, dis-, over-; (as causative) e.g. **forgylle, fornorske** (usu. with verbs).
+forak't *-en* contempt, disdain, scorn (**for** for, of): **nære f- for en** feel c- for, despise sby.
+forak'te *V -a/-et* despise, scorn: **ikke å f-** not to be d-d.
+forak'telig *A* - **1** (of person) contemptible, despicable. **2** (of speech) contemptuous, disdainful.
+forak'ter *-en, pl -e* despiser, scorner (**av** of).
***foral'dra** *A* - cf **-elda**
+foran [får'ran] *P* before, in front of, ahead of; *(adv.)* ahead, before, in front: **gå f-** walk ahead, show the way, take the lead; **sitte f-** sit up front (e.g. in a car); **være f-** be ahead, out front. (For use with other verbs see these.)
+foran'derlig *A* - changeable, mutable; fickle, unstable, unsteady.
foran'dre *V -a/+-et* change; alter, modify: **det f-er saken** that a-s the case, *(pop.)* that's a horse of a different color; **det ville ikke ha f-et saken** it wouldn't have made any difference; **f- mening** c- one's mind, opinion; **f- samtaleemne** c- the subject; **f- seg (til det bedre)** c- (for the better); **f- tonen** c- one's tune; **f-et** c-d, different.
foran'dring *-a/+-en* change; alteration, modification: **f- fryder** variety is the spice of life.
foran'kre *V -a/+-et* anchor, moor: **f-et i et kristent livssyn** founded on a Christian view of life.
+for'/anle'dige *V -et* bring about, cause, occasion; lead to.
+for'/anle'dning *-en* cause, occasion (**til** for).
+for'an/nevnt *A* - already noted, already referred to (e.g. a matter): **f-e** the above.
+for'/anstal'te *V -et* arrange, bring about, cause to be done.
+for'/anstal'tning *-en* arrangement, preparation: **treffe f-er** take steps; **på min f-** on my initiative.
+for'an/stående *A* - the above, the foregoing (e.g. remarks).
+for'/arbei'd *-et* **(=*føre/)** preliminary, preparation, spade work: **f-er** preliminary studies.
+for'/arbei'de *V -et/-de* manufacture; prepare, work up.
forar'ge *V -a/+-et* outrage, scandalize, shock; *bibl.* offend (Matthew 18,6): **f-et** angry, indignant, shocked (**over** at).
forar'gelig *A* - scandalous, shocking; annoying, disgusting, irritating.
+forar'gelse *-n* **(=*-ing)** (moral) indignation, offence: **til f- for** offensive to; **vekke f-** cause o-.
+forar'gerlig *A* - cf **forargelig**
+forar'me *V -et* impoverish.
+For'-Asia *Pln* the Near East.
+for'at *C* (=**for at**) **1** in order that, so that. **2** *fam.* because.
for'/band *-et* **1** *arch.* bond (masonry): **legge i f-** bond. **2** *mil.* (army, navy) unit composed of different smaller units for special maneuvers.
+forban'dt *pt of* **forbinde**
+forban'na *A* - **(=+-et)** **1** accursed, cursed; confounded, damnable, damned. **2** bound, obligated: **det er hans f-ede plikt** it's no more than his duty. **3** angry, furious (**på at**).
forban'ne *V -a/+-et/bante* **1** curse (sby): **f- seg på** assert (usu. profanely); **det kan du f- deg på** you can be dead sure about that. **2** *bibl.* ban, banish, curse.
+forban'nelse *-n* **(=*-ing)** curse, imprecation: **han var sin norsklærers f-** he was the bane of his Norwegian teacher; **det hviler en f- over arbeidet** a c- rests on this work.
+forbar'me *V -a/-et*: **f- seg over** have mercy, pity on, pity.
forbas'ka *A* - **(=+-et)** confounded, infernal; doggone.
forbau'd *pt of* **forby(de)**
+forbau'se *V -a/-et* amaze, astonish, surprise.
+forbau'selse *-n* amazement; astonishment; surprise.
+forbe'dre *V -a/-et* improve: **f- seg** mend one's ways, reform; **f- sin stilling** i- one's position
+forbe'dring *-a/-en* betterment, improvement (**av** of).
+forbe'drings/anstal't *-en* reformatory.
+for'/behol'd *-et* proviso, reservation; caution, guardedness (e.g. in one's speech): **uten f-** unconditionally, unreservedly.
+for'/behol'de *V -holdt, -holdt*: **f- seg** reserve, stipulate; **f- seg retten til** reserve the right to; **f-t** reserved for, earmarked for.
+for'/behol'den *A -ent, pl -ne* guarded, reserved.
+for'beholden/het *-en* caution, reserve.
+forbe'net *A* - *fig.* fossilized, ossified.
+for'/bere'de *V -te* get ready, prepare: **f- seg på, til** p- for, p- oneself to; **f- seg til timen** p- one's lessons.
+for'/bere'delse *-n* arrangement, preparation.
+for'/bere'dende *A* - preparatory, preliminary.
+for'/beredt· *A* - prepared.
for'/berg *-et* promontory.
forbi' *P* **1** past; beyond, by: **det er ikke til å komme f-** there's no getting around the fact; **like f-** right by (past). **2** all over, finished: **det er f- med ham** he's done for, f-; **f- for bestandig** f- forever.
forbi'/fart *-en*: **i f-en** in passing.
+forbi'/gå *V -gikk, -gått* fail to promote, pass over in silence; pass over, slight.
+forbi'/gåelse *-n* neglect, passing over, slight (**av** of); failure to promote.
+forbi'/gående *A* - passing, temporary: **de f-** passers-by; **i f-** incidentally, in passing.
+forbi'/kjøring *-a/-en* passing.
+for'/bilde *-t* **(=*føre/bilete)** ideal, model, pattern (**for** of).
+for'/billede *-t* cf **/bilde**
+for'/billedlig *A* - ideal, model.
***forbi'na** *A* - astonished, amazed.
forbin'de *V infl as* **binde** **1** combine, connect, join; link, unite. **2** bandage, bind up, dress. **3** *fig.* associate, con-

+ Bokmål; * Nynorsk; ° Dialect.
After letter: ' stress (Acc. 1); ` tone, stress (Acc. 2); · length.
Below letter: . not pronounced.

nect: **f-er du noe med (navnet)?** does (the name) mean anything to you? 4 *(refl.)*: **f- seg til å** *lit.* obligate oneself to.

+forbin'ḍelse *-n* 1 connection (=association, contact; affair, liaison; communication, service; relations, etc.): **i f- med** in c- with; **komme (stå) i f- med** get (be) in touch with; **gode f-er** good c-s, pull; **inngå en f- med** join an alliance with; get engaged to. 2 *chem.* combination, compound.

+forbin'ḍelses/offise'r *-en* liaison officer.

forbin'ḍing *-a/+-en* bandage, dressing.

+forbin'ḍtlig *A* - courteous, obliging.

+forbin'ḍtlig/het *-en jur., merc.*: **uten f-** without prejudice.

+forbi'/passe'renḍe *en* passerby.

forbis'tra *A* - (=+**-et**) confounded, doggone.

+forbit're *V -a/-et* embitter: **f-et** furious, indignant (**på** at).

+forbit'relse *-n* indignation, resentment (**mot** towards).

***forbjo'ḍe** *V -byd, -baud, -bode/-i* cf **-by**

+forbli' *V -ble, -blitt* remain: **f- taus** keep silent; **f- tro mot** r- faithful to, stick by.

+forblin'ḍe *V -a/-et* blind, dazzle.

+forblom'met *A* - (of speech) disguised, veiled.

forblø' *V -dde* bleed to death: **f- seg** (the same).

+forblø'dning *-en* bleeding to death, hemorrhage.

+forbløf'fe *V -a/-et* disconcert, flabbergast, nonplus, take aback: **ikke la seg f-** not be overawed, remain unperturbed; **f-ende** astonishing(ly).

forbløf'felse *-n* amazement, bewilderment.

forblå'st *A* - windblown, windswept.

***for'/bod** [/bå] *-et* cf **/bud[1]**

forbode** [fårbå'e] *pp of* **-by(de)** (=-bodi**)

+for'/boksta'v *-en* initial (letter): **store f-er** capital letters.

+forbor'gen *A -ent, pl -ne* clandestine, secret: **et f-ent smil** an enigmatic smile.

+forbren'ne *V -brente, -brent* burn, consume; scorch: **han ble stygt f-t** he was badly b-ed.

forbren'ning *-a/+-en* 1 *chem.* combustion. 2 *med.* burn.

forbren'nings/motor *-en* internal-combustion engine.

for'/bruk *-et* consumption: **ha stort f- av noe** use large quantities of sth.

+forbru'ke *V -te* consume, use (up); spend.

+forbru'ker [also fårr'/] *-en, pl -e* (=***-ar**) consumer.

+for'bruker/råd *-et* (=***-ar/**) consumers' council.

+for'bruks/artik'kel *-elen, pl -artikler* article of consumption.

+forbrutt' *pp of* **forbryte**

+forbry'delse *-n* cf **forbrytelse**

+forbry'der *-en* cf **forbryter**

+forbry'te *V -brøt, -brutt* 1 *archaic* forfeit: **ha sitt liv forbrutt** f- one's life. 2: **f- seg mot** commit a crime against.

+forbry'telse *-n* crime, offence; *jur.* felony, misdemeanor: **begå en f-** commit a c-.

+forbry'ter *-en, pl -e* criminal.

+forbry'ter/bane *-n* career of crime: **komme inn på f-n** launch a career of crime.

+forbry'tersk *A* - criminal, felonious.

+forbry'ter/spire *-a/-en* budding criminal.

+forbrø'dring *-en* fraternization.

+forbrø't *pt of* **forbryte**

+for'/bud[1] *-et* (=***/bod**) ban (**mot** on), embargo, prohibition; veto; *jur.* injunction: **nedlegge f- mot noe** ban, prohibit; place an embargo against; *jur.* issue an injunction.

+for'/bud[2] *-et* (=***føre/bod**) harbinger, portent (**på** of).

+forbu'den *A* - forbidden: **f- frukt smaker best** f- fruit is sweet; **f-ne varer** contraband.

+for'buds/tiden *df* Prohibition (period).

+forbuḍt' *pp of* **forby(de)**

+for'/bunḍ *-et* alliance, pact; confederation, federation, league: **Folkenes F-** L- of Nations.

+forbun'ḍen *A -ent, pl -ne* indebted, obliged: **jeg ville være Dem f- om** I would be grateful if; **Deres f-ne** gratefully yours.

+forbun'ḍet *pp of* **forbinde**

+for'bunḍs/felle *-n* ally, support.

+for'bunḍs/stat *-en* 1 constituent state (e.g. the individual states of the United States). 2 federal state, federation.

+forbus'ke *V -a/-et*: **f- seg** 1 bush. 2 *hum.* hide in the bushes.

forby'(de) *V infl as* **by(de)** ban, forbid, prohibit: **det f-r seg selv** it's a moral impossibility, it's simply impossible; **f- kjøp (salg) av** lay an embargo on; **strengt forbudt** strictly p-ed.

+forbyg'ge *V -de/-et* 1 brace, prop, shore up (e.g. a wall). 2 build badly, confusedly. 3: **f- seg** build beyond one's means, overbuild.

forbyg'ning *-en* prop, retaining wall.

+forbyt'ning *-en* exchange (by mistake).

+forbyt'te *V -a/-et* (=***-byte**) 1 exchange (by mistake): **jeg har fått min hatt f-et** I have gotten the wrong hat. 2: **f- seg** make a bad bargain. 3: **f-et** (radically) transformed.

+forbø'd *pt of* **forby(de)**

+for'/bønn *-a/-en* (=***/bøn**) intercession: **gå i f- for en** intercede for sby, plead sby's case.

force majeure [fårs masjø'r] superior force; *jur.* act of God.

fordam'pe *V -a/+-et* evaporate, cause to evaporate; *fig.* vanish into thin air.

+for'/danser *-en, pl -e* (=***-ar**) leading, principal dancer; dance leader.

+for'/dekk *-et naut.* foredeck.

+fordek't *A* - 1 face downwards (cards). 2 *fig.* crafty, underhanded; **spille f-** play an u- game.

+fordek'tig *A* - questionable, suspicious; shady.

+for'/del[1] *-en* advantage (**over** over), benefit, interest; gain, profit: **dra f- av noe** profit by, turn to account; **forandre seg til sin f-** change for the better; **ha f- av noe** b-, p- by; **selge med f-** sell at a p-; **ta seg ut til sin f-** appear to a-, look its, one's best; **tale til ens f-** be to sby's credit, speak well for sby; **til f- for** for the b- of; in favor of; to the a- of.

+for'/del[2] *-en* forepart, front part (**av** of).

+for'del/aktig *A* - advantageous, beneficial; favorable; lucrative, profitable: **et f- tilbud** a good offer; **et f- ytre** a prepossessing appearance.

forde'le *V -te* 1 apportion, distribute, divide: *merc.* **f- på** spread the loss over (a number of years); **f- roller** assign parts, cast (a play). 2 disperse, scatter: **f- seg** s-, separate.

forde'ling *-a/+-en* 1 distribution (**av** of). 2 dispersion.

forde'lings/boks *-en elec.* distribution box, switchbox.

forder'v *-et* destruction, ruin, undoing.

forder'va *A* - (=+**-et**) 1 spoiled, tainted (food). 2 *fig.* corrupt, depraved.

forder've *V -a/+-et* 1 destroy, hurt; damage, spoil. 2 *fig.* corrupt.

forder'velig *A* - demoralizing, pernicious; *fam.* "blasted".

+forder'velse *-n* destruction, ruin; depravity, (moral) turpitude: **føre i f-** ruin.

fordi' *C* (=**for di**) because: **f- at** b-; **f- om** even if; **om ikke for annet så f-...** if only b-...

fordob'le *V -a/+-et* double: **f- sine anstrengelser** redouble one's efforts; **f- seg** d-.

fordob'ling *-a/+-en* 1 doubling. 2 *naut.* tabling (sail). 3 *gram.* gemination; reduplication.

for'/dom[1] *-men/*-en* bias, prejudice: **nære f-er mot** be biased, prejudiced against.

***for'/dom[2]** *Av* cf **fordum**

for'doms/fri *A -tt* unbiased, unprejudiced.

for'doms/full *A* biased, prejudiced; narrowminded.

fordra' *V -drog, -dradd/-dratt* bear, endure, stand: **jeg kan ikke f- te** I hate tea.

fordra'gelig *A* - tolerant.

+fordra'gelig/het *-en* tolerance.

+for'dre *V -a/-et* claim, demand; exact, require.

+fordrei'e *V -de* sprain, twist, wrench; *fig.* distort, misrepresent, pervert: **f- sin håndskrift** disguise one's handwriting; **f- hodet på en** turn sby's head.

fordrei'v *pt of* **fordrive**

+fordre'v *pt of* **fordrive**

+for'dring *-en* claim (**på** to), demand; requirement: **den ideale f-** the c- of the ideal (Ibsen); **gjøre f- på noe** claim sth, lay c- to; **stille store f-er til** make heavy d-s on.

+for'drings/full *A* demanding, exacting.

+for'drings/haver *-en, pl -e* creditor.

+for'drings/løs *A* modest, unassuming.

+fordris'te *V -et*: **f- seg til noe** make so bold as to, venture to.

fordri've *V infl as* **drive[1]** banish, dispel, drive away: **f- et foster** cause, produce an abortion; **f- tiden** pass, while away the time; **ondt skal ondt f-** fight fire with fire.

+fordri'ver *-en, pl -e* soft, flat painter's brush.

fordro'g *pt of* **fordra**

fordrukken [-drok'ken] *A -ent, pl fordrukne* (habitually) drunken; dipsomaniac.

+forduf'te *V -a/-et* evaporate, *hum.* vanish into thin air, make oneself scarce, pull a disappearing act.

+fordul'gt *pp of* **-dølge**

+for'/dum' *Av* (=***fordom[2]**) of old, in (the) days of yore.

fordumme [-dom'me] *V -a/+-et* reduce to stupidity, stupefy.

+fordummelse [-dom'melse] *-n* reduction to a state of stupidity, stupefaction.

+for'/dums *A* - former, previous: **i f- dager** in (the) days of yore, in times gone by.

+fordunkle [-dong'kle] *V -et* obscure; eclipse, outshine, surpass.

+fordun'ste *V -et* evaporate; *hum.* vanish into thin air.

+fordy'pe *V -et*: **f- seg i** become absorbed, engrossed in, lose oneself in: **f-et i** absorbed in.

+fordy'pelse *-n* absorption, preoccupation.

+fordy'pning *-en* depression, hollow.

fordy're *V -a/+-et* increase the cost (of), make more expensive.

+fordy'relse *-n* (=***-ing**) increase, rise in cost, price.

+fordøl'ge *V -dulgte, -dulgt* conceal (**for** from).

+fordøm'made *A* - cf **-dømt**

fordøm'me *V* *+-dømte/*-dømde* (=***-døme**) blame, condemn, denounce; *bibl.* damn (Mark 16,16).

fordøm'melig *A* - heinous, reprehensible.

+fordøm'melse *-n* (=***-døm(m)ing**) 1 condemnation, denunciation; *bibl.* eternal damnation. 2 curse.

+fordøm't *A* - (=***-dømd**) 1 condemned, doomed; *bibl.* damned: **f- til å mislykkes** doomed to failure. 2 confounded, damned: **f-e jåleri** infernal idiocy.

for'/dør *-a* storm door, outer door.

+fordøy'e *V -de/-et* 1 digest; *fig.*

absorb, take in. 2 *hum.* come to terms with: **f- den tort** accept the humiliation of.

+**fordøy'elig** *A* - digestible; *fig.* acceptable (**for** to).

+**fordøy'else** *-n* digestion: **dårlig f-** indigestion.

+**fordøy'elses/besvæ'rlighet** *-en* indigestion.

fo're[1] *V -a/+-et* line (e.g. with fur); *tech.* bush.

fo're[2] *V -a/+-et/+-te* feed: **f- opp kreaturer** raise cattle; *fig.* **f- med** cram, prime with (e.g. gossip).

***fore**[3] [få're] *V -a* make furrows.

+**fore**[4] [få're] *Av* cf **føre**[3]

+**fore/bringe** [få're/] *V -brakte, -brakt* report, submit (a matter) to (sby).

+**fore/bygge** *V -bygde, -bygd* avert, prevent; preclude.

+**fore/byggelse** *-n* prevention: **til f- av** for the p- of.

+**fore/byggende** *A* - preventive: *med.* **et f- middel mot** a prophylactic for.

fore'dle *V -a/+-et* 1 bring to great perfection, ennoble. 2 improve (e.g. a breed of horses). 3 convert, finish, refine (raw materials).

+**fore/dra** [få're/] *V -drog, -dradd/-dratt* 1 *admin., pol.* bring (up), present (a proposal). 2 *mus.* execute, render.

fore/drag *-et* 1 address, lecture: **holde f- om noe** deliver a l- on sth. 2 delivery; diction, execution.

+**foredrags/holder** *-en, pl -e* (=*/**haldar**) lecturer, speaker.

foredrags/turne *-en* lecture tour.

+**fore/dratt** *pp of* **-dra** (=+/**dradd**)

+**fore/drog** *pt of* **-dra**

+**fore/falle** *V -falt, -falt* happen, occur, take place: **gjøre f-ende arbeid** do whatever chores there are, work as a handyman.

+**fore/finne** *V -fant, -funnet*: **f-s** be, be found, exist.

+**foregangs/mann** *-en, pl -menn* (=***føre-**) forerunner, pioneer.

+**fore/gi** *V -gav, -gitt* feign, pretend, profess.

+**fore/gikk** *pt of* **-gå**

+**fore/givende** *-t* pretense, pretext: **under f- av** on the pretext of.

+**fore/gripe** *V -grep, -grepet* (=***føre/**) anticipate, forestall: **f- begivenhetenes gang** a- the course of events.

+**fore/gå** *V -gikk, -gått* 1 go on, happen, take place: **f- bak kulissene** go on behind the scene; **slik foregikk jakten i gamle dager** this is how hunting used to be done. 2: **f- med et godt eksempel** set a good example. 3 cf **f-ende**.

+**fore/gående** *A* - (=***føre/gåande**) preceding, previous: **det f-** the foregoing.

+**fore/havende** *-t* (=***føre/havande**) intention, purpose; project.

+**fore/holde** *V -holdt, -holdt* remonstrate with: **f- en noe** point out sth to sby.

***forei'ning**[1] *-a* cf **-ening**

***fo'r/eining**[2] *-a* cf **/enhet**

+**fore/komme** [få're/] *V -kom, -kommet* 1 happen, occur, take place. 2 be found, be met with. 3 appear, seem: **f- en underlig** strike sby as odd, strange.

+**fore/kommende** *A* - courteous, kind, obliging (**overfor, mot** to).

+**forekommen/het** *-en* courtesy, graciousness.

+**fore/komst** *-en* 1 occurrence (**av** of). 2 deposit (of ore).

+**fore/la** *pt of* **-legge**

forel'da *A* - (=+**-eldet**, ***-aldra**) antiquated, obsolete, out of date.

+**forel'des** *V -edes, -es* become antiquated, obsolete, outdated.

forel'dre *pl* parents.

forel'dre/laus *A* (=+/**løs**) orphan.

+**forel'dre/myndighet** *-en* custody.

+**fore/legg** [få're/] *-et* (=***føre/**) 1 model, original (e.g. of a manuscript). 2 *jur.* option of a fine in lieu of prosecution (for a misdemeanor).

+**fore/legge** *V -la, -lagt* lay, place before, submit to: **f- en noe** submit sth to sby; **f- en noe til avgjørelse** submit sth to sby for his decision.

+**fore/lese** *V -te* (=***føre/**) lecture (**over** on), teach (at university).

+**fore/leser** *-en, pl -e* (=***føre/lesar**) (university) lecturer.

***fore/lesing** *-a* cf **/lesning**

fore/lesning *-a/-en* (=***føre/les(n)ing**) (university) lecture.

+**forelesnings/rekke** *-a/-en* course, series of lectures.

+**fore/ligge** *V -lå, -ligget* 1 be at hand, lie before one for action, discussion: **f- til behandling** come up for consideration. 2 (of book): **f- trykt** be in print, be out.

forel'ske *V -a/+-et*: **f- seg i** fall in love with; take a fancy to.

+**forel'skelse** *-n* infatuation, love (affair): **f- ved første blikk** love at first sight.

+**forel'sket** *A* - (=**-a**) in love (**i** with).

+**fore/løbig** [få're/] *A* - cf **/løpig**

+**fore/løpig** *A* - preliminary, provisional, temporary; *(adv.)* for the time being.

+**fore/lå** *pt of* **-ligge**

+**for'/ende** *-n* front end; *naut.* bow.

+**fore'ne** *V -te* combine, join, unite; *fig.* reconcile: **f- med** c- with; **f- seg med** j-, u- with; **f- seg med hverandre** j- forces, j- together; **f-et i en og samme person** rolled into one; **la seg f- med** be compatible, consistent with.

+**fore'nelig** *A* - cf **forenlig**

+**fo'r/enhet** *-en* (=*/**eining**) unit used in calculating food value of fodder (food value contained in one kilogram of barley).

+**fore'ning** *-a/-en* 1 combination, union: **i f-** combined, jointly. 2 association, club, society: **stå i en f-** be a member of an a-.

foren'kle *V -a/+-et* simplify.

foren'kling *-a/+-en* simplification (**av** of).

+**fore'nlig** *A* - (=+**forenelig**) compatible, consistent (**med** with).

+**foren/om** [få'ren/] *P naut.* ahead of, on the foreside of.

+**fore'nte nasjo'ner, De** [di] *Prn* the United Nations.

+**fore'nte sta'ter, De** [di] *Prn* the United States.

+**fore/satt** [få're/] *A* - (=***føre/sett**) superior; (as noun, also:) authority, guardian.

+**fore/sette** *V -satte, -satt*: **f- seg** decide, make up one's mind, resolve.

+**fore/skrive** *V -skrev, -skrevet* prescribe.

+**fore/slå** *V -slo, -slått* propose, suggest; move (parliamentary procedure): **f- en skål for en** p- a toast in honor of sby.

+**fore/speile** *V -te*: **f- en noe** hold out expectations, false hopes to sby.

+**fore/spørre** *V -spurte* ask, inquire (**om** about, after): **f- hos et firma om** i- of a firm about.

+**fore/spørsel** *-elen, pl -ler* (=***føre-spurnad**) inquiry: **rette en f- til** address an i- to.

+**fore/stille** *V -stilte* 1 introduce, present: **f- en for** i- sby to. 2 depict, represent: **hva f-er dette?** what is this supposed to be? 3: **f- seg** conceive, imagine.

+**fore/stilling** *-a/-en* (=***føre/stelling**) 1 performance, show. 2 protest, remonstrance: **gjøre f-er** remonstrate. 3 conception, idea, notion: **gjøre seg en f- om** form a c- of.

+**forestillings/krets** *-en* horizon, intellectual range.

+**fore/stå** *V -stod, -stått* 1 be in charge of, direct, manage. 2 be at hand, be imminent.

+**fore/stående** *A* - approaching, imminent: **f- begivenheter** coming events.

+**fore/sveve** *V -de/-et*: **det f-er meg** I have a notion (a vague idea).

+**fore/ta** *V -tok, -tatt* carry out, do, make, undertake (an expedition, investigation, test, etc.): **f- seg noe** do sth.

+**fore/tagende** *-t* 1 undertaking, venture. 2 *merc.* industrial enterprise, project.

+**fore/tak** *-et* (=***føre/**) undertaking, venture.

+**foretak/som'** *A -t, pl -me* ambitious, enterprising.

+**foretaksom/het** *-en* enterprise, initiative.

+**fore/tatt** *pp of* **-ta**

fore'te *V -åt, -ett*: **f- seg** overeat.

+**fore/teelse** [få're/] *-n* phenomenon: **appelsiner etter aftens er blitt en hyppig f-** oranges after supper have become a common p- (Boo).

+**fore/tok** *pt of* **-ta**

+**fore/trakk** *pt of* **-trekke**

+**fore/trede** *-t* audience, interview.

+**fore/trekke** *V -trakk, -trukket* prefer: **f- det ene framfor det andre** p- sth to sth else; **f- å** p- to.

fore'vige *V +-et/*-a* 1 immortalize, perpetuate. 2 *hum.* preserve for posterity by photographing.

+**fore/vise** [få're/] *V -te* exhibit, show; present, produce.

+**fore/visning** *-en* presentation, showing (**av** of).

forf.=**forfatning; forfatter**

for'/fall *-et* 1 date of maturity, due date: **ved f-** on the due date, when due. 2 decadence, decay, decline: **komme i f-** fall into decay.

forfal'le *V infl as* **falle** 1 *merc.* be payable, fall due, mature. 2 fall into decay, disrepair; fall to pieces, go to rack and ruin. 3: **f- til** become addicted to.

forfal'len *A -ent, pl -falne* 1 *merc.* due, payable; overdue. 2 dilapidated, ramshackle. 3 addicted (**til** to).

for'falls/dag *-en* date of maturity, date of expiration.

forfal'ske *V -a/+-et* adulterate; counterfeit; falsify, forge.

forfal'skning *-a/+-en* adulteration; counterfeiting; falsification, forgery.

+**forfal't** *pt, pp of* **forfalle**

for'/fang *N*: **være til f- for en** be injurious to one's interests.

***forfa'rast** *V -ferst, -forst, -farest* decay, go to rack and ruin.

forfa'ren *A -ent, pl -ne* experienced, skilled (**i** in).

+**forfat'ning** *-en* 1 condition, state; plight. 2 *jur.* constitution.

+**forfat'nings/messig** *A* - constitutional.

+**forfat'nings/stridig** *A* - unconstitutional.

forfat'te *V -a/+-et* compose, write; draw up.

+**forfat'ter** *-en, pl -e* (=***-ar**) author, writer.

+**forfat'ter/honora'r** *-et* (=***-ar/**) author's royalty; author's fee.

+**forfatterin'ne** *-a/-en* (=***-ar-**) woman author, writer.

+**forfat'ter/skap** *-et* (=***-ar/**) authorship.

+**for'/fedre** *pl* (=***-ar**) ancestors.

+**forfei'le** *V -et/-te* miss: **f- sin hensikt** fail to produce a desired result, miss its goal; **f-et** a failure, wasted.

+**forfek'te** *V -et* defend, stand up for (e.g. a viewpoint).

+**forfeng'elig** *A* - 1 vain (=futile, unavailing, in vain; conceited). 2 *bibl.* fleeting, transitory, vain (II Kings, 17,15); disrespectful, irreverent: **ta Guds navn f-** take God's name in vain.

+**forfeng'elig/het** *-en* vanity (=hollowness; conceit): *bibl.* **alt er f-** all is v- (Eccl. 1,2).

+**forfer'de** *V -a/-et* appall, dismay: **f-et** aghast, dismayed; **f-et over** appalled at.

forfer'delig *A* - 1 dreadful, horrible, terrible. 2 *(adv.)* awfully, frightfully: **f- gjerne** love to, very much.
+forfer'delse *-n* fright, horror, terror; consternation, dismay: **det tok en ende med f-** it ended in disaster.
+forfer'dige *V -et lit.* make, manufacture: **f-et** wrought.
***forferst** [-fæ'rst] *pr of* **-farast**
+forfi'net *A* - (= **-a**) delicate, refined.
forfjam'set *A* - (= **-a**) bewildered, confused.
+forfjam'selse *-n* bewilderment, confusion.
for'/fjor *N*: **i f-** the year before last.
forfla'te *V -a/+-et* make (sth) banal, vulgarize.
***forflogen** [-flå'gen] *A -e/-i, pl -ne* cf **-fløyen**
forflyt'ning *-a/ +-en* removal, transfer (**til** to).
forflyt'te *V -a/+-et/*-e* transfer (e.g. to a new place or position).
+forfløy'en *A -ent, pl -ne* (=***-flogen**) (e.g. of women) flighty, frivolous; wild.
for'/forde'le *V -te* give (sby) less than his fair share, *(pop.)* give (sby) a raw deal.
***forfo'rst** *pt of* **-farast**
+for'/fra *Av* from the front; from the beginning: **begynne f-** make a fresh start.
+forfrem'me *V -a/-et* promote.
+forfrem'melse *-n* promotion
+forfris'kende *A* - cooling, refreshing.
forfris'kning *-a/+-en* refreshment.
+forfros'sen *A -ent, pl -frosne* (=***-frosen**) frostbitten, frozen, numb with cold; *fig.* cold, frozen (personality): **være f- av seg** be sensitive to cold.
forfry'se *V infl as* **fryse**[1] 1 be frostbitten, frozen, numb with cold. 2 damage by frost.
+forfry'sning *-en* frostbite; frost damage.
+forfulgte [-ful'kte] *pt of* **forfølge**
+forfus'ke *V -a/-et* botch, bungle; confuse (an issue), fail (a cause).
+forfyl'let *A* - (habitually) drunken, sodden.
forfæ'ld** *A -fælt* (=-færd**) frightened, terrified; dismayed.
+forføl'ge *V -fulgte* (=***-je**) 1 follow, hunt (down), pursue: **f- til ens skjulested** track sby down. 2 continue, follow up: **f- en suksess** follow up a success. 3 persecute, prosecute: **f- en** haunt sby, trouble the mind continually; **f-es av uhell** be dogged by bad luck.
+forføl'gelse *-n* (=***-ing**) 1 pursuit (**av** of). 2 following up, pressing home. 3 persecution.
+forføl'gelses/vanvidd *-et med.* persecution complex, mania.
+forføl'ger *-en, pl -e* (=***-jar**) pursuer; persecutor.
***forføl'ging** *-a* cf **forfølgelse**
***forføl'gje** *V -fulgte* cf **forfølge**
+forføl'gning *-en* prosecution: **han er under f- for tyveri** he is being prosecuted for theft.
forfø're *V -te* 1 lead astray, seduce; corrupt. 2 *bibl.* beguile (Genesis 3,13).
+forfø'relse *-n* (=***-ing**) seduction (**av** of).
forfø'rende *A* - alluring, seductive.
+forfø'rer *-en, pl -e* (=***-ar**) seducer; tempter.
+forfø'rerisk *A* - alluring, seductive; tempting.
***forfø'ring** *-a* cf **forførelse**
+forføy'e *V -et/-de* 1: **f- over** command, have at one's disposal. 2: **f- seg** betake oneself, go to; **f- seg hjem** go home.
+forføy'ning *-en* disposal; measure: **treffe f-er** take action, steps.
fo'r/gang *-en* feeding passage (in barn).
+forgang'en *A -ent, pl -ne* gone, past.
forgap'e *V -te*: **f- seg i** fall in love with, *(pop.)* be crazy about, fall for.

forgap't *A* - infatuated, *(pop.)* stuck on.
***for'/ga'rd** *-en* cf **/gård**
+forgas'ser *-en, pl -e* (=***-ar**) carburetor.
forgi' *V -gav, -gitt* (=***-gje(ve)**) dose to excess, poison.
+forgif't *-en* poison.
forgif'te *V -a/+-et* poison.
forgif'tning *-a/+-en* poisoning.
+forgikk' *pt of* **-gå**
***forgje'** *V -gjev, -gav, -gjeve/-i* cf **/gi**
***forgjekk'** *pt of* **-gå**
+forgjel'det *A* - deeply in debt, encumbered.
forgjeng'elig *A* - fleeting, transitory; perishable.
+forgjeng'elig/het *-en* transitoriness; perishability.
+for'/gjenger *-en, pl -e* predecessor.
***forgjere** [-jæ're] *V -gjorde, -gjord* cf **-gjøre**
***forgje've** *V -gjev, -gav, -gjeve/-i* cf **-gi**
+forgje'ves *Av* fruitless, in vain, to no purpose.
forgjo'rde *pt of* **-gjere, -gjøre**
+forgjø're *V -gjorde, -gjort* (=***-gjere**) 1 bewitch, cast a spell over: **forgjort etter** *(pop.)* crazy about. 2: **forgjort** confounded. 3 change, transform.
+forglem'me *V -glemte* forget: **ikke å f-** last but not least; **f- seg** make a faux pas, misstep.
+forglemmeg/ei [fårglem'mi/ei'] *-en bot.* forget-me-not (Myosotis palustris).
+forglem'melse *-n* 1 forgetfulness, oblivion. 2 omission, oversight.
+forgodt'/befin'nende *et*: **etter eget f-** at one's own discretion, pleasure.
forgrei'ne *V -a/+-te*: **f- seg** branch, branch out, ramify.
forgrei'ning *-a/+-en* ramification.
+forgrem'met *A* - careworn.
+forgre'ne *V -et/-te* cf **-greine**
+forgre'ning *-en* cf **-greining**
forgri'pe *V infl as* **gripe**: **f- seg på** assault, lay violent hands on; make free with, misappropriate; seize wrongly, steal.
+forgrove [-grå've] *V -et* coarsen, vulgarize.
for'/grunn *-en* foreground: **komme, trenge i f-en** come to the fore.
for'grunns/figu'r *-en* prominent figure.
+forgrått' *A* - red-eyed (with weeping); tearstained.
forgu'de *V -a/+-et* adore, idolize.
+forgu'delse *-n* (=***-ing**) adoration, idolatry.
forgyl'le *V -gylte* gild: **f-t** g-ed, gilt.
forgyl'ling *-a* (=**+-gylning**) gilding.
forgå' *V infl as* **gå**[1] 1 come to an end, perish. 2 be consumed (**av** with). 3: **f- seg** misbehave; **f- seg mot loven** violate the law.
+forgå'else *-n* transgression, trespass (**mot** against).
+for'/gå'rd *-en* 1 outer court; vestibule (e.g. of a church). 2 *anat.* vestibule (e.g. of the ear). 3 *bibl.* (of the tabernacle) court (Exodus 25,9).
for'/gå'rs *N*: **i f-** day before yesterday.
forhak'kende *Av*: **f- sint** furious, in a towering rage.
***forhal'de** *V -held, -heldt, -halde/-i* cf **-holde**
+forha'le *V -te* 1 delay, retard; procrastinate. 2 *naut.* shift berth.
for'/hall *+-en/*-a* entrance hall, vestibule.
forhan'dle *V -a/+-et* 1 discuss, negotiate (**med** with). 2 distribute, handle, sell.
+forhan'dler *-en, pl -e* (=***-ar**) 1 negotiator. 2 dealer, distributor (**av** of).
forhan'dling *-a/+-en* 1 discussion, negotiation, proceedings. 2 distribution, sale.
forhan'dlings/protokoll' *-en* minutes (of the proceedings).
forhas'ta *A* - (=**+-et**) hasty, premature: **trekke f-de slutninger** jump to conclusions.
forhas'te *V -a/+-et*: **f- seg** be too hasty, too much in a hurry; **ikke f- seg** take one's time.
+forhatt' *A* - despised, hated; hateful, odious.
+forhek'se *V -a/-et* bewitch, cast a spell over.
***forhel'd** *pr of* **-halde**
***forhel'dt** *pt of* **-halde**
+for'/hen' *Av* at one time, formerly.
for'/heng *-et* curtain.
+for'hen/værende *A* - 1 former, late. 2 antiquated, passé.
forher'de *V -a/+-et* 1 harden: **f- sitt hjerte** steel one's heart. 2: **f-et** callous, hardened, inveterate.
+forher'lige *V -et* extol, glorify.
+forher'ligelse *-n* glorification.
+forhin'dre *V -a/-et* hinder, obstruct, prevent (**fra** from).
+forhin'dring *-en* prevention; obstacle.
forhip'pen *A +-ent, pl -hipne*: **f- på** eager to, keen on, *(pop.)* dying to (do sth).
for'/histo'rie *-a/+-en* 1 antecedents, previous history (**til** of). 2 prehistory; archeology.
for'/histo'risk [also fårr'/] *A* - (=**før/**) prehistoric; archaic.
+for'/hjul *-et* front wheel.
+forhog'ning *-a/-en mil.* abatis (defense barrier of trees).
for'/hold *-et* 1 relation(s), relationship (**til** with, to): **stå i et godt f- til en** be on good terms with sby; **stå i (et) f- til** be having an affair with. 2 proportion, ratio: **i f- til** compared to, in p- to; **stå i omvendt f- til** be inversely proportional to. 3 circumstances, situation, state of affairs: **etter f-ene** according to, under the c-. 4 behavior, conduct.
+forhol'de *V -holdt, -holdt* 1 *obs.* (improperly) withhold: **f- en sannheten** keep the truth from sby. 2: **f- seg** (of people) behave, conduct oneself; (of a situation) be; (of numbers) be in a proportion, a ratio; **f- seg taus** keep silent; **hvis det f-er seg slik** if that's the case; **hvordan f-er det seg med** what's the situation with; **3 f-er seg til 6 som 4 til 8** the ratio between 3 and 6 is the same as that between 4 and 8.
+for'holds/messig *A* - proportionate, proportional.
+for'holds/ordre *-n, pl -r* directions, instructions.
+for'holds/regel *-elen, pl -ler* measure, precaution.
+forholds/tall *-et math.* proportional.
+for'holdstalls/valg *-et* proportional representation.
+for'holds/vis *Av* proportionately; comparatively, relatively.
for'/hud [*/hu] *-a/+-en anat.* foreskin, prepuce.
forhu'ding *-a/+-en* (=**+-hudning**) *naut.* sheathing.
+forhut'let *A* - down at the heels, shabby, seedy.
forhy're *V -te/*-a naut.* sign on.
for'/hør *-et* (=***/høyr**) examination, hearing, interrogation.
forhø're *V -te* (=***-høyre**) examine, interrogate: **f- seg** inquire (**om** about).
+for'hørs/dommer *-en, pl -e* (=***-ar**) *jur.* examining magistrate.
for'hørs/rett *-en jur.* magistrate's court.
+forhøy'e *V -de/-et* 1 elevate, raise aloft. 2 enhance, heighten (an effect); increase (prices, wages). 3 *mus.* sharpen (a note). 4 *math.* raise (to nth power).
+forhøy'else *-n* elevation (**av** of); enhancement; advance, increase.
+forhøy'ning *-en* elevation; platform.
***for'/høyr** *-et* cf **-hør**
***forhøy're** *V -de* cf **-høre**
+forhå'bentlig *Av* cf **forhåpentlig**
+for'/hånd *-en* (=**føre/hand**) 1 first hand (in bridge): **ha f-, sitte i f-**

have the lead. 2 *naut.*: **gå, stå, være i f-** be ahead of the reckoning. 3: **på f-** beforehand, in advance.

+forhån'den *Av* (=**+for hånden**) at hand, available.

+forhån'den/værende *A* - 1 at one's disposal, available. 2 existing, present.

+for'hånds/melding *-a/-en* 1 opening bid (cards). 2 prior notice.

+for'hånds/salg *-et* advance sale.

+forhå'ne *V -et/-te* deride, mock; insult.

+forhå'nelse *-n* derision (**av** of), mockery; insult.

+forhå'pentlig *Av* I hope, let us hope that.

+forhå'pentlig/vis *Av* I hope, let us hope that.

+forhå'pning *-en* expectation, hope.

+forhå'pnings/full *A* hopeful, optimistic.

For'-India *Pln obs.* India, Pakistan (opp. to **Bak-India**).

fo'ring *-a/+-en* lining, packing.

+forin'nen *P* before, beforehand, previous to.

+fori'vre *V -a/-et*: **f- seg** allow oneself to be carried away, go too far.

+forja'get *A* - harassed, worried.

+forjet'te *V -et poet.* promise: **det f-ede land** the p-d land.

+forjet'telse *-n poet.* promise.

for'k *-en* fork, forked branch.

+fork.=forkorting, forkortet

forkal'ke *V -a/+-et* calcify.

forkal'king *-a/+-en* calcification; hardening.

+for'/kammer *-eret, pl -er/-kamre anat.* auricle.

+for'/kant *-en* 1 front edge, leading edge. 2 *naut.*: **i, på f- av** forward of.

forkas'te *V -a/+-et* 1 reject, turn down. 2 *bibl.* condemn, repudiate (I Samuel 15,23). 3 *geol.* dislocate.

forkas'telig *A* - objectionable, reprehensible, vicious.

forka'va *A* - (=**+-et**) breathless, out of breath; in a bustle, flurried.

+for'/kim *-en/-et bot.* prothallium.

+for'/kjemper *-en, pl -e* advocate, champion.

forkjet're *V +-et/*-a* condemn, denounce (as a heretic); backbite.

forkjæ'le *V -te* pamper, spoil.

+for'/kjærlighet *-en* predilection, preference (**for** for).

+forkjæ'rt *A* - wrong; inconvenient; absurd: **gripe en sak f- an** go at sth the w- way.

forkjø'le *V +-a/+-et/-te*: **f- seg** catch a cold; **være f-(e)t** have a cold.

+forkjø'lelse *-n* (=***-ing**) cold.

for'/kjøp *-et*: **komme en i f-et** forestall sby, steal a march on sby.

forkjø'pe *V -te*: **f- seg** overbuy, pay more than one can afford.

for'kjøps/rett *-en* option, right of preemption.

for'kjørs/rett *-en* right-of-way.

forkla're *V -te/*-a* (=***-klåre**) 1 explain; expound, interpret; account for: **f- seg** clarify (to oneself), understand; speak, testify (e.g. in court); **f- seg nærmere** be more specific. 2 illuminate, light up, transfigure: **slettene lå blendende f-et** the plains were brilliantly sunlit (Olaf Bull).

+forkla'relse *-n* illumination, transfiguration.

forkla'rende *A* - explanatory.

forkla'ring *-a/+-en* 1 explanation (**på** of): **F-en** the E- (of the Catechism); **til f-** by way of explanation. 2. *jur.* deposition, statement: **avgi f-** make a d-, s-.

forkla'rlig *A* - explicable, intelligible; understandable.

for'/kle[1] *-et, pl +-klær/*-* (=***/klede**) 1 apron. 2 *fam.* chaperon, duenna.

forkle'[2] *V -dde* disguise.

forkledd' *A -/*-kledt* disguised.

***for'/klede** *-t* cf **/kle[1]**

***forkle'dnad** *-en* cf **-kledning**

forkle'dning *-en* disguise.

+forklei'nelse *-n* belittlement, disparagement: **til f- for** in d- of.

+forklei'nende *A* - belittling, disparaging.

for'kle/snipp *-en* corner of an apron.

+forklud're *V -a/-et* botch, bungle, make a mess of.

+for'/klæ *-et, pl -r* cf **/kle[1]**

***forklå're** *V -a* cf **-klare**

forknytt' *A* - fainthearted, timorous; dispirited, downhearted.

+forkom'me *V infl as komme[2]* be destroyed, decay, go to ruin.

+forkom'men *A -ent, pl -komne* (=***/komen**) exhausted, half dead, worn out (with cold, hunger); down-and-out.

+forkor'te *V -a/-et* cut short, shorten; abbreviate, abridge; foreshorten: **f-et for, f-ing av** abbreviation of.

+forkor'telse *-n* abbreviation.

+forkor'tning *-en* foreshortening.

+forkren'kelig *A* - *bibl.* corruptible, perishable.

forkromme [-krom'me] *V -a/+-et* chrome.

+forkrøp'le *V -a/-et* cripple, dwarf, stunt.

forku'e *V -a/+-et* cow, repress.

+forkul'le *V -a/-et* carbonize, char.

***for'/kunn** *A -kunt* 1 covetous; lustful: **være f- på noe** be greedy for sth. 2 appetizing, delicious.

***for'kunn/mat** *-en* appetizing, delicious food.

+for'/kunnska'per *pl* previous knowledge, training: **gode f-** a good grounding (**i** in).

forkvak'le *V -a/+-et* bungle, make a mess of; cripple: **f-et** (mentally) twisted, warped.

forkyn'ne *V -kynte* 1 announce, proclaim. 2 *eccl.* preach (the gospel). 3 *jur.*: **f- en stevning** serve a summons or writ (**for** on).

+forkyn'nelse *-n* (=***-ing**) 1 announcement, proclamation (**av** of). 2 *eccl.* preaching. 3 *jur.* service.

+forkyn'ner *-en, pl -e* (=***-ar**) preacher; advocate: **ordets f-** minister of the gospel.

forla' *pt of* **-legge**

+forla'delse *-n* cf **-latelse**

+for'/ladning *-en* wad, wadding (used in muzzle-loading gun).

+for'ladnings/gevæ'r *-et* muzzle-loader (cannon, gun).

for'/lag *-et* 1 (firm of) publishers, publishing house: **på eget f-** (published) at one's own expense. 2 *chem.* condenser. 3 *tech.* transmission.

for'lags/rett *-en* copyright, publishing rights.

for'lags/sjef *-en* head of a publishing firm, publisher.

forlag't *pp of* **-legge**

+forlang'e *V -te* ask for, demand, insist upon; order (e.g. at restaurant): **f- ordet** ask for the floor.

+forlang'ende *-t* demand, request; stipulation (in a contract).

forla'te *V +-er/*-let, +-lot/*-let, +-t/*-e/*-i* 1 leave; abandon, desert, forsake. 2 forgive (Matthew 6,12): **forlat oss vår skyld f-** us our trespasses; **Gud f- min sjel** God help my soul (Evensmo). 3: **f- seg på** depend, rely upon.

+forla'telse *-n* (=***-ing**) pardon; (of sins) forgiveness, remission: **om f-** I beg your pardon.

+forlatt' *A* - abandoned, deserted; desolate, forlorn: **en f- teori** a discarded theory; **et f- skip** a derelict.

+forlatt'/het *-en* abandonment, forsakenness; desolation, emptiness.

+forle'de *V -a/-et* lead astray, mislead: **f- en til (å tro)** delude sby into (believing).

+forle'den *A* - (=***-liden**) 1 the other (day, evening, etc.). 2 *(adv.)* recently, the other day. *3 gone, past: **dagen er f-** it is too late in the day.

+forle'gen *A -ent, pl -ne* 1 at a loss (**for** for): **aldri f- for svar** never at a loss for an answer. 2 bashful, embarrassed, shy.

+forle'gen/het *-en* 1 difficulty: **i f- for** in need of (e.g. money). 2 embarrassment, shyness.

+forleg'ge *V -la, -lagt* (=***-je**) 1 remove, transfer. 2 mislay. 3 publish.

+for'/legger[1] *-en, pl -e* (=***jar**) publisher.

+for'/legger[2] *-en pl -e* (=***-jar**) (bedroom) carpet, mat, rug.

***forleg'gje** *V -la(gde), -lagt* cf **-legge**

+forle'ne *V -te hist.* enfeoff (**med** with); *archaic* endow with, grant.

+forlen'ge *V -a/-et* (=***-je**) lengthen; extend, prolong; increase (length of): **f- fristen** extend the time limit; *anat.* **den f-ede ryggmarg** medulla oblongata.

+forleng'else *-n* (=***-ing**) continuation, extension (**av** of).

***forleng'je** *V -de* cf **-lenge**

+for'/lengs *Av* (face) forward: **kjøre f-** face the engine.

+forleng'st *Av* cf **lenge**

forle'se *V infl as* **lese**: **f- seg** read too much; **f- seg på Freud** (also:) swallow F- whole.

+forle'st *A* - (=***-lesen**) having read too much; bookish, dried-up.

***forle't** *pr, pt of* **forlate**

forli'be *V -te*: *hum.* **f- seg i** fall in love with, take a fancy to.

+forli'belse *-n* infatuation; love.

forlib't *A* - infatuated (**i** with).

for'/lik [also -li'k] *-et* agreement, conciliation, settlement: **inngå, slutte f- med** come to terms with, reach an a- with; *jur.* **et magert f- er bedre enn en fet prosess** a bad s- beats a good lawsuit any day.

forli'ke *V -te* conciliate, reconcile; compromise, settle: **f-es (med)** be r-d (with), agree, make peace; get on well together, *(pop.)* hit it off; **f- seg med** be r-d to, come to terms with; **han har f-t seg med sine kreditorer** he has made an arrangement with his creditors.

forli'kelig *A* - reconcilable.

for'liks/klage *-a/+-en jur.* complaint (to a **forliksnemnd**).

for'liks/nemnd [/nemd] *-a* commission of arbitration.

for'liks/råd *-et jur.* (local) arbitration, mediation board (for civil cases).

forlik't *A* - agreed: **bli f- om** agree on.

forli's *-et* (of ship) loss, shipwreck.

forli'se *V -te* be lost (at sea), be shipwrecked, founder.

+for'/lodds *Av* beforehand, in advance.

***for'/loge** [/låge] *-a* destiny, fate, fortune.

+forlok'ke *V -et* entice, lure, seduce; **f-ende** alluring, seductive.

forlo'ren *A +-ent, pl -ne* 1 false; artificial, mock: **f-ent egg** poached egg; **f- skilpadde** m- turtle. 2 *bibl.* (morally) lost; depraved: **den f-ne sønn** the prodigal son.

+forlo't *pt of* **-late**

for/lov [/lå'v] *N obs.*: **med f-** excuse me, with your permission.

forlove [-lå've] *V -a/+-et* 1: **f- seg** become engaged; **min f-ede** my fiancé(e). 2 *fam.* promise more than one can deliver.

+forlovelse [-lå'velse] *-n* (=***-ing**) engagement.

+forlovelses/tid *-a/-en* (duration of an) engagement.

+for'/lover [/låver] *-en, pl -e* (=***-ar**) 1 best man, maid of honor. 2 *jur.* sponsor, surety.

+forly'de *V -lød, lydt*: **det f-er at** it's rumored, it's said that; **la seg f- med** let it be understood.

+forly'dende *-t* hearsay, rumor: **det går et f- om** it's rumored that.

+ Bokmål; * Nynorsk; ° Dialect.
After letter: ' stress (Acc. 1); ` tone, stress (Acc. 2); · length.
Below letter: . not pronounced.

+**forlys'te** *V -et* amuse, entertain.
+**forlys'telse** *-n* amusement, entertainment, recreation.
+**forlø'd** *pt of* **-lyde**
+**for'/løfte**[1] *-t jur.* security, surety.
+**forløf'te**[2] *V -a/-et*: **f- seg** overstrain oneself by lifting; *fig.* overreach oneself in a task, *(pop.)* bite off more than one can chew.
+**for'/løp**[1] [also -lø'p] *-et* 1 expiration, lapse: **etter et års f-** at the end of a year. 2 course, progress: **sykdommens f-** the c- of the illness.
+**forlø'p**[2] *pt of* **-løpe**
+**forlø'pe** *V -løp, -løpt* (=*-**laupe**) 1 elapse, expire, pass: **i det f-ne år** during the past year. 2 follow a normal course; go off (badly, well). 3: **f- seg** commit a faux pas, forget oneself; pocket one's own ball (pool).
+**for'/løper** *-en, pl -e* 1 forerunner, precursor; harbinger, herald. 2 *naut.* strayline.
+**forlø'se** *V -te* deliver, release; *eccl.* redeem; *med.* deliver (a child): **bli f-t med en sønn** be d-ed of a son; **det f-ende ord** a timely word; **du har f-t min bundne tanke** you took the very words out of my mouth.
+**forlø'sning** *-en* deliverance, release; *eccl.* redemption; *med.* birth, delivery.
+**forløy'et** *A* - lying, mendacious.
fo'r/løyse *-a* scarcity of fodder.
for'm *-a/+-en* form, shape; mold, tin; formality: **en f- for** a form of; **for f-ens skyld** as a matter of form; **ha f- av** be shaped like; **holde på f-ene** insist on the formalities; **i f- av** in the s- of; **i flytende f-** in a fluid state; **ta f-** take s-.
+**forma'le** *V -te* grind exceedingly fine.
forma'lia *pl* formalities.
formalite't *-en* form, formality, *(pop.)* red tape.
forma'ne *V -a/+-te* admonish, exhort; correct.
forma'nende *A* - admonitory.
fo'r/mangel *-en* scarcity of fodder.
forma'ning *-a/+-en* (=+**-else**) admonition, exhortation.
for'/mann *-en, pl -menn/*-menner* 1 chairman; foreman. 2 *jur.* **rettens f-** presiding magistrate, judge.
for'mann/skap *-et* 1 chairmanship, presidency. 2 executive committee (of parish or town council).
+**fo'rmarg/kål** *-en* (=*-**merg/**) pithy kind of cabbage used for fodder.
formasjo'n *-en* formation.
+**for'/mast** *-a* foremast.
+**formas'telig** *A* - blasphemous; presumptuous.
forma't *-et, pl -/+-er* size; (of a book) format.
for'me *V -a/+-et* form, shape: **f- etter** mold after; model upon; **f- seg** take shape.
+**forme'delst** *P archaic* because of, on account of.
***formei'r** *A* - better.
***formei're** *V -a* cf **-mere**[1]
for'mel[1] *-elen, pl -ler* formula: **en stående f-** a set phrase.
+**fo'r/mel**[2] *-et* cf **/mjøl**
for'melig *A* - actual, regular, veritable; *(adv.)* actually, positively.
formell' *A -elt* formal, stiff; ostensible: **en f- feil** a technicality.
+**forme'ne** *V -te* 1 assume, suppose. 2 *archaic* forbid, prevent.
+**forme'ning** *-en* judgment, opinion: **etter min f-** in my o-.
+**forme'ntlig** *A* - alleged, presumed, reputed.
+**for'mer** *-en, pl -e* (=*-**ar**) molder.
+**forme're**[1] *V -te* (=*-**meire**): **f- seg** breed, propagate.
forme're[2] *V -te* 1 *mil.* organize into formations (e.g. battle groups, battalions, etc.). 2 *typog.* make up into pages.
+**for'm/fullen'dt** *A* - elegant, finished, flawless.
+**for'm/giver** *-en, pl -e* (=*/**gjevar**) (industrial) designer.
+**for'm/gi'vning** *-en* (=*/**gjeving**) fashioning, molding; industrial design.
formida'bel *A -elt, pl -le* formidable; prodigious, stupendous.
for'/middag *-en* (=***føre/**) forenoon; morning (now usu. until dinnertime ab. 3 PM): **i f-** this m-; **om f-en** in the m-.
+**for'middags/antrekk** *-et* morning dress.
+**for'middags/bryllup** *-et* (=*/**bryllaup**) wedding ceremony followed by a breakfast reception.
+**formid'le** *V -a/-et* arrange, effect; act as an intermediary, mediate.
+**-formig** *A* - (in compounds) -formed, -shaped.
formil'de *V -a/+-et* 1 mollify, pacify; alleviate: *jur.* **f- en straff** mitigate a sentence. 2: **f-ende** extenuating.
+**formin'ske** *V -a/-et* decrease, diminish; lessen, reduce.
+**formin'skelse** *-n* decrease; reduction (av of).
fo'r/mjøl *-et* (ground) feed, fodder.
for'm/kake *-a* loaf cake (e.g. pound cake).
for'm/laus *A* (=+**/løs**) 1 formless, shapeless; amorphous. 2 free and easy, informal.
for'm/lære *-n gram.* morphology.
+**formo'de** *V -et* assume, presume, suppose; **f-et** expected.
+**formo'dentlig** *Av* presumably, probably; I dare say, presume.
+**formo'dning** *-en* conjecture, presumption, supposition.
+**for'/monn** [/monn] *-en* cf **føre/**
for'm/sak *-a/+-en* formality, mere matter of form, routine.
for'm/sans *-en* feeling, sense for beauty of form, style.
for'm/språk *-et* 1 (artistic) style. 2 *gram.* language with many inflectional forms, e.g. Latin.
for'm/tre *-et* 1 molding wood. 2 *naut.* template.
+**for'/mue** *-n* 1 fortune; assets, capital: **tjene en f- på** make a f- on. 2: **over f-** beyond one's ability, strength.
+**formu'ende** *A* - wealthy, well-off.
+**for'mues/fellesskap** *-et jur.* community property.
+**for'mues/forhold** *pl* financial circumstances, means.
+**for'mues/skatt** *-en* capital levy.
formula'r *-en/-et* form, formula.
formula'r/bok *-a, pl -bøker* book of formulas, formulary.
formule're *V -te* formulate, word.
formule'ring *-a/+-en* formulation.
+**formum'met** *A* - disguised, masked.
+**formyn'der** *-en, pl -e* (=*-**ar**) guardian.
+**formyn'der/skap** *-et* (=*-**ar/**) 1 guardianship. 2 regency.
+**formæ'le** *V -te archaic*: **bli f-t med** marry.
+**formør'ke** *V -a/-et* (=*-**je**) cloud, darken.
+**formør'kelse** *-n* (=*-**ing**) clouding, darkening; eclipse.
***formør'kje** *V -te* cf **-mørke**
formå' *V -dde* 1 be able to do, be capable of doing: **ta til takke med det huset f-r** be content with what the house (i.e. the hostess) can produce, *fam.* take potluck. 2 induce, prevail on, persuade (**til å** to).
+**formå'ende** *A* - influential.
for'/mål *-et* (=***føre/**) aim, object, purpose: **f-et med** the a- of; **et godt f-** a good cause.
+**for'måls/tje'nlig** *A* - (=*/**tenleg**) appropriate, suitable.
***for'n**[1] [for'n] *-a* gift (esp. of food for party).
for'n[2] *A* ancient, old; old-fashioned.
for'naldar/saga *+-en/*ei* legendary saga (dealing with heroes of the period prior to 800 A.D.).
+**fornam'** *pt of* **-nemme**
+**for'/navn** *-et* (=*/**namn**) first name, given name.
Forne/bu [få'rne/] *Pln* Oslo airport.
+**forne'den** *Av* at the bottom, at the foot, below.
+**forne'dre** *V -et* debase, degrade, humiliate: **f- seg** humble oneself.
+**forne'drelse** *-n* debasement, humiliation.
fornek'te *V -a/+-et* 1 deny, renounce, repudiate. 2: **f- seg** deny oneself (sth).
+**fornek'ter** *-en, pl -e* (=*-**ar**) atheist, freethinker; denier.
for'/nem' *A -t, pl -me* 1 aristocratic, highborn; distinguished, noble, proud; dignified, stately; elegant, exclusive, select. 2 **f-st** first in rank, foremost.
+**for'nem/het** *-en* aristocracy; distinction, nobility; stateliness; exclusiveness.
+**fornem'me** *V -et/-nam, -nummet* notice, perceive.
+**fornem'melig** *Av* especially, principally.
+**fornem'melse** *-n* feeling, perception, sensation (av of): **ha noe på f-n** have a f- in one's bones.
***for'nem/skap** *-en* cf **/het**
for'n/funn *-et* discovery, find of antiquities.
fornik'le *V -a/+-et* nickelplate.
for'n/kvede *-t* ancient lay, poem.
fornor'ske *V -a/+-et* Norwegianize, make more Norwegian (esp. of language).
for'n/tid *-a/+-en* antiquity.
fornuf't *+-en/*-a* (common) sense, intelligence, reason; judgment, understanding: **sunn f-** common s-; **ta imot f-** listen to r-; **tale f-** talk s-.
fornuf'tig *A* - rational, reasonable, sensible: **intet f- menneske ville** no one in his senses would.
fornuf'tig/vis *Av* it stands to reason, obviously.
+**fornuf't/messig** *A* - rational.
+**fornuf't/stridig** *A* - irrational.
+**fornuf'ts/vesen** *-et, pl -/-er* rational being.
+**fornummet** [-nom'met] *pp of* **-nemme**
forny'e *V -a/+-et* renew (=renovate, repair, replace; revive, restore; repeat, resume): **ta under f-et overveielse** reconsider.
+**forny'else** *-n* (=*-**ing**) renewal (=renovation; revival; repetition) (**av** of).
+**forny'elses/veksel** *-elen, pl -ler merc* promissory note whose maturity date has been extended through a second note.
+**forny'er** *-en, pl -e* (=*-**ar**) *renovator*, restorer.
fornær'me *V -a/+-et* insult, offend: **f-et** (also:) sulky; **føle seg f-et over** take offence at; **f-et på** o-ed at.
fornær'melig *A* - insulting, offensive.
+**fornær'melse** *-n* (=*-**ing**) affront, insult (**mot** to).
+**fornø'den** *A -ent, pl -ne lit.* necessary, required: **nekte seg det f-ne** deny oneself the necessities of life.
+**fornø'den/het** *-en* necessity (of life).
fornøg'd *A -/*-nøgt* (=+-**nøyd**) content, gratified, satisfied; delighted, pleased (**over** at).
+**fornøy'd** *A* - cf **-nøgd**
+**fornøy'e** *V -de* amuse, make glad, happy: **f- seg** a-, enjoy oneself, have a good time.
+**fornøy'elig** *A* - amusing, delightful, enjoyable.
+**fornøy'else** *-n* gratification, pleasure; amusement, diversion, entertainment: **med f-** I'll be glad to; **betale f-n** foot the bill.
for'/o'rd *-et* (=***føre/**) foreword, preface.
+**foror'dne** *V -et* decree, ordain; prescribe.
+**foror'dning** *-en* decree, ordinance.
+**foroven** [fårå'ven] *Av* above, at the head, at the top.
+**for'/over** [/åver] *Av* forward; *naut.* full speed ahead.
forpak'te *V -a/+-et*: **f- en gård** rent,

take a lease on a farm; **f- bort** lease, rent (**til** to).

+forpak'ter *-en, pl -e* (=***-ar**) lessee, tenant.

+forpak'tning *-en* 1 lease; tenancy. 2 rent.

forpes'te *V -a/+-et* infect, poison.

+forˋ/pigg *-en naut.* forepeak.

forpi'nt *A -* anguished, harassed; racked with pain, suffering.

+forpjus'ket *A -* disheveled, tousled; unkempt (person).

fo'r/plante[1] *-a/-en* plant used for fodder.

forplan'te[2] *V -a/+-et* propagate, reproduce: **f- seg** be transmitted, spread.

+forplan'tning *-en* propagation; spread, transmission.

+forplan'tnings/lære *-a/-en* genetics.

+forplei'e *V -de mil.* provision (an army).

+forplei'ning *-en* provisions; provisioning.

+forplik'te *V -a/-et* 1 oblige: **adel f-er** noblesse o-; **f- en** bind sby, put sby under an obligation; **være f-et til** be under obligation to. **2: f- seg til å** commit oneself to.

+forplik'telse *-n* commitment, obligation; debt, liability (**mot** to; **til** for).

+forplik'tende *A -* binding (**for** on).

forˋ/post *-en* outpost; advanced position.

+forˋpost/fektning *-en* (=***/fekting**) *mil.* outpost skirmish; *fig.* preliminary skirmish.

forpup'pe *V -a/+-et: zool.* **f- seg** change into a chrysalis.

+forpur're *V -a/-et* frustrate: **f- ens planer** spoil sby's plans, *(pop.)* throw a monkey wrench into the works.

forpus'ta *A -* (=**+-et**) breathless, out of breath.

forˋ/rang *-en* precedence: **ha f-en for** take p- over.

forrang'la *A -* (=**+-et**) dissipated, dissolute; *(pop.)* hung over.

+forregne [-rei'ne] *V -a/-et*: **f- seg** make a mistake, miscalculate.

+forren'te *V -a/-et merc.* pay interest on: **f- seg med 5%** bear interest at the rate of 5 %.

+forren'tning *-en* accrual of interest.

+for'rest *A -* foremost, front, leading; *(adv.)*: **gå f-** lead the way.

forres'ten *Av* (=**for resten**) anyway, besides, moreover; however, it remains to be said; as a matter of fact; for that matter.

forret'ning *-a/+-en* 1 business; bargain, deal, transaction: **en fin f-** a good d-, a coup; **drive f-** carry on business; **gjøre en dårlig f-** make a bad bargain; **løpende f-er** current business. 2 place of business (premises, shop, store, etc).

+forret'nings/anlig·gende *-t*: **f-r** business affairs.

forret'nings/drivende *en* businessman, shopkeeper.

forret'nings/folk *pl* businessmen.

+forret'nings/forbin'delse *-n* business connection: **tre i f- med** enter into a business relationship with.

+forret'nings/fører *-en* (=***-ar**) (business) manager.

forret'nings/konvolutt· *-en* business envelope.

forret'nings/kvarte·r *-et, pl -/+-er* business district.

forret'nings/mann *-en, pl -menn/ *-menner* businessman.

+forret'nings/messig *A -* business, commercial; businesslike.

forret'nings/ministe·rium *df -iet, pl +-ier/*-* caretaker government.

forret'nings/papi·r *-et, pl +-er/*-* 1 business, commercial stationary. 2 material mailed at a special rate.

orret'nings/stand *-en/*-et* business circles, business community.

forˋ/rett[1] *-en* prerogative, privilege.

forˋ/rett[2] *-en* first course.

+forret'te *V -et* 1 function, serve (**som** as). 2 *eccl.* conduct, officiate at, perform (a service).

+forˋ/rettighet *-en* prerogative, privilege.

+forre'ven *A -ent, pl -ne* ragged, tattered; scratched, torn.

+forˋ/rider *-en, pl -e* (=***-ar**) outrider.

+for'rige *A df* (the) former, preceding, previous; last: **i f- måned** l- month; **onsdag i f- uke** l- Wednesday.

+forring'e *V -et* lessen, reduce; depreciate; disparage: **f-es** depreciate, deteriorate.

+forring'else *-n* debasement, depreciation, deterioration (**av** of).

forˋ/rom [/romm] *-met* 1 *hist.* front room. 2 *naut.* forehold.

+forry'kende *A -* furious, tremendous (e.g. speed): **f- storm** howling gale.

+forryk'ke *V -et* dislocate, disturb, upset.

+forryk't *A -* crazy, mad, *(pop.)* cracked, nuts.

+forræ'der *-en, pl -e* (=***-ar, *forrådar**) traitor (**mot** to).

forræderi' *-et, pl +-er/*-* treachery; treason.

forræ'dersk *A -* treacherous; treasonable.

***forrøy'ne** *V -de*: **f- seg** overexert oneself.

forˋ/råd *-et* stock, store, supply (**av** of): **ta inn f-** lay in s-ies.

***forrå'dar** *-en* cf **-ræder**

forrå'de *V +-te/*-de* 1 betray. 2 manifest, reveal.

forrå'e *V -a/+-et* brutalize, coarsen.

+forråt'nelse *n* decay, decomposition, putrefaction: **gå i f-** decay, decompose.

+forsa'ge *V -et* cf **forsake**

+forsa'gelse *-n* cf **forsakelse**

+forsagt [-sak't] *A -* discouraged, dispirited; timid, withdrawn.

+forsagt/het *-en* despondency.

forsa'ke *V -a/+-et* 1 give up, renounce. 2 *mil.* fail to go off, misfire.

+forsa'kelse *-n* (=***-ing**) renunciation, self-denial.

+forˋ/salg *-et* advance sale, reservation (of tickets).

+forsam'le *V -a/-et* assemble: **f-es** gather, meet; **f-et** a-d, g-d.

forsam'ling *-a/+-en* 1 assembly, gathering, meeting; audience, crowd: **lovgivende f-** legislature. 2 *bibl.* congregation, convocation; *eccl.* prayer meeting.

forsam'lings/loka·le *-t, pl +-r/*-* assembly, meeting room.

Forˋ/sand *Pln* twp, Rogaland.

+forˋ/sanger *-en, pl -e* 1 cantor, precentor. 2 (choir) leader, leading performer.

forˋ/sats *-en* end papers.

forˋsats/papi·r *-et* flyleaf.

forˋse[1] *-n* forte, strong point: **han har sin f- i det** that's his s-.

forse'[2] *V -så, -sett* (=***-sjå'**) **1: f- seg mot** offend, transgress against (e.g. the law); violate, wrong (sby). **2: f- seg på** fall blindly in love with, get on one's brain.

+forse'else *-n* offence (**mot** against); *jur.* misdemeanor.

+forˋseg/gjort [-sei/] *A -* (=***/gjord**) carefully, painstakingly made.

forseg'le [+fårsei'le] *V -a/-et* seal.

***forsei'nke** *V -a* cf **-sinke**[2]

+forsen'de *V -te* dispatch, forward, send; mail, ship.

+forsen'delse *-n* 1 dispatch, forwarding (**av** of). 2 consignment, shipment; letter.

+forsen'ke *V -a/-et* countersink.

+forsen'kning *-en* depression, hollow; countersink.

+forse'nt *Av* cf **sein**[2]

forse're *V -te* 1 force, strain. 2 hasten, speed up: **f- tempoet** force the pace. 3 force an entrance into.

forse'rt *A -* forced, unnatural (e.g smile).

forˋ/sete *-t, pl +-r/*-* 1 front seat. 2 chairmanship, presidency.

forˋ/sett[1] *-et, pl -/+-er* intention, purpose; *jur.* **gjøre noe med f-** do sth deliberately, wilfully, with malice aforethought.

forsett'[2] *A - dial.* confounded; difficult, too bad.

forset'tlig *A -* intentional, wilful.

+forˋ/side *-a/-en* front (**av** of); face, obverse (of medal); front page (of newspaper).

+forsik're *V -a/-et* 1 assure (**en om** sby of), reassure; assert, maintain: **f- seg om** assure oneself of. 2 insure (**hos** with; **mot** against).

+forsik'ring *-a/-en* 1 assurance; affirmation. 2 insurance.

+forsik'rings/selskap *-et* insurance company.

+forsik'rings/taker *-en, pl -e* insured, policyholder.

+forsik'tig *A -* careful, cautious, prudent; circumspect, discreet: **et f- svar** a guarded answer; **være f-** beware, take care.

+forsik'tig/het *-en* caution, discretion, prudence.

+forsik'tighets/regel *-elen, pl -ler* precaution: **ta sine f-ler** take p-s.

forsim'ple *V -a/+-et* debase, vulgarize.

forsin'ke[1] *V -a/+-et* galvanize.

+forsin'ke[2] *V -a/-et* delay: **være f-et** be behind schedule, d-ed, overdue.

+forsin'kelse *-n* delay (**på** of).

forsin'na *A -* enraged, infuriated.

+forsi're *V -et* adorn, decorate, embellish.

+forsi'ring *-en* 1 adornment, ornament: **f-er** ornamentation. 2 *mus.* appoggiatura, grace note.

***forsjå'** *V -ser, -såg, -sedd/-sett* cf **-se**[2]

forska'ling *-a/+-en* (=**+forskal'ling**) *tech.* 1 lathwork (for plastering). 2 formwork (for cement).

forska'lings/bo·rd *-et* (=**+forskallings/**) *tech.* 1 lath (used to support plastering). 2 lumber for forms (for cement).

forskan'se *V -a/-et* 1 *mil.* barricade, fortify. **2: f- seg** ensconce, entrench oneself.

+forskan'sning *-a/-en* (=***-ing**) barricade; entrenchment.

forska'r *pt of* **-skjere, -skjære**

forˋske *V -a/+-et* 1 carry on (do) research, investigate: **f- etter noe** search for sth. **2: f-ende** critical, inquiring.

+forˋsker *-en, pl -e* (=***-ar**) investigator, research worker, scientist.

+forˋ/skinn *-et* (blacksmith's, shoemaker's) apron.

+forˋ/skip *-et naut.* bow, forepart of a ship.

+forˋ/skjell *-en* difference (**i, på** in), disparity, distinction: **det gjør ingen f-** it makes no difference; **gjøre f- på** differentiate between, discriminate between; **uten f-** indiscriminately, without distinction.

+forskjel'lig *A -* 1 different, unlike; distinct: **på f- måte** differently; **være f-** differ. 2 assorted, several, various: **det er f-** it varies; **jeg så på f-e** I looked at s-.

+forskjel'lig/artet *A -* diversified, heterogeneous, varied.

+forskjel'lig/farget *A -* varicolored.

+forskjel'lig/heter *pl* differences, distinctions.

***forskjere** [-sjæ're] *V -skar, -skore/-i* cf **-skjære**

***forˋskjer/kniv** *-en* cf **forskjær/**

forˋ/skjerm *-en* front fender.

+forskjer'tse *V -et* forfeit; fritter, throw away.

+forskjæ're *V -skar, -skåret* 1 spoil in cutting: **f- seg** be distorted; go wrong. 2 *tech.* blend (wine).

+forˋskjær/kniv *-en* carving knife.

+ Bokmål; * Nynorsk; ° Dialect.
After letter: ' stress (Acc. 1); ˋ tone, stress (Acc. 2); · length.
Below letter: . not pronounced.

+forskjøn'ne *V -et* beautify, improve the appearance of; embellish.
+forskjøn'nelse *-n* beautification, improvement (of appearance).
+forskjø't *pt of* **-skyte**
+for'skning *-en* investigation, research.
for'/skole *-n* **1** preparatory school. **2** preparation (**til** for).
forskore** [-skå're] *pp of* **-skjere** (=-skori**)
for'/skott *-et* (=**+/skudd, */skot**) advance: **på f-** in a-; **ta noe på f-** anticipate (e.g. a triumph).
forskotte're *V -te* (=**+-skuttere, *-skotere**) advance money on, pay in advance.
for'skotts/vis *Av* in advance: **som erlegges f-** payable i-.
+forskrek'ke *V -a/-et* frighten: **f-et** alarmed (**over** at), f-ed, terrified.
+forskrek'kelig *A* - awful, frightful, terrible.
+forskrek'kelse *-n* fright, terror.
+forskrem't *A* - alarmed, fearful, frightened.
+forskre'v *pt of* **-skrive**
for'/skrift *-a/+-en* (=***føre/**) **1** precept, rule, regulation. **2** copy, sample (in writing book).
+for'skrifts/messig *A* - regular, regulation (e.g. uniform); *(adv.)* according to regulations.
forskri've *V infl as* **skrive 1** order; contract. **2** bind, pledge oneself to do sth: **f- seg til fanden** sell one's soul to the devil.
+forskrudd' *A* - (=**+-skruet**) hysterical; high-flown.
+for'/skudd *-et* cf **/skott**
+for'skudds/vis *Av* cf **-skotts/**
+forskutte're *V -te* cf **-skottere**
forskyl'de *V +-te/*-a/*-e* **1** deserve: **få lønn som f-t** get one's just deserts, serve one right. **2** *dial.* repay, return (a service).
+forsky'te *V -skjøt, -skutt* cast off, disown, reject.
forsky've *V infl as* **skyve: f- seg** be dislocated, displaced; shift.
+forsky'vning *-en* (=***-skyving**) dislocation, displacement; shift, shifting.
+forskå'ne *V -a/-te* spare (**for** from).
+forskå'ret *pp of* **-skjære**
+for'/slag¹ *-et* proposal, proposition, suggestion; bill, motion: **gjøre f- om** propose; **på f- av** on the recommendation of; **stille f- om** move that.
+for'/slag² *-et* anacrusis; *mus.* appoggiatura, grace note.
forsla'g³ *-et*: **det er ikke f- i pengene nå** *lit.* money has little purchasing power nowadays.
+forsla'gen *A -ent, pl -ne* crafty, cunning, sly.
+for'slags/stiller *-en, pl -e* (=***-ar**) author (of a bill, motion), mover.
+forslitt' *A* - (=***-sliten**) shabby, threadbare, worn-out; *fig.* hackneyed, trite.
forslo' *pt of* **-slå¹·²**
+forslu'ken *A -ent, pl -ne* greedy, gluttonous.
forslå'¹ *V -slo, -slått* avail, be sufficient, suffice: **så det f-r** so it does some good, in a high degree.
forslå'² *V -slo, -slått* hurt, injure: **f-tt** battered, bruised.
for'/smak *-en* foretaste (**på** of).
+forsme'delig *A* - disgraceful, ignominious; insulting.
+forsme'delse *-n* disgrace, ignominy, insult: **jeg måtte bite f-n i meg** I had to swallow my pride (Boo).
+forsmek'te *V -et* be dying (e.g. of thirst); *fig.* languish, pine away (**etter** for).
forsmå' *V -dde* disdain, reject, scorn: **ikke la seg f-** not hold back, step right up; **ikke å f-** not to be sneezed at.
forsnak'ke *V -a/+-et*: **f- seg** make a slip of the tongue; let the cat out of the bag; **han f-et seg og sa bisken istedenfor bispen** he misspoke and said "bisken" instead of "bispen".
+forsnak'kelse *-n* (=***-ing**) misspeaking, slip of the tongue.
forsnev'ring *-a/+-en* contraction; *med.* obstruction, stricture.
+forsof'fen *A -ent, pl forsofne* drunken; dissipated, dissolute.
+for'/sommer *-en* early summer.
forso'ne *V -te* **1** conciliate, reconcile: **f- seg med en** make up with sby; **f- seg med noe** resign oneself to sth. **2** mollify, placate.
forso'nende *A* - conciliatory; redeeming: **et f- trekk** a r- feature; a saving grace.
forso'ning *-a/-en* **1** reconciliation. **2** *eccl.* atonement.
forso'nlig *A* - conciliatory, forgiving.
+forso'nlig/het *-en* conciliatory spirit.
+forso'ren *A -ent, pl -ne* devil-may-care, jaunty.
for'/sorg *-a/+-en* **1** *archaic* care: **f- for fremtiden** c- for the future. **2** public assistance, poor relief.
forsove [-så've] *V infl as* **sove: f- seg** oversleep.
for'/spann *-et* team (e.g. of horses).
***for'/spel** *-et* cf **/spill**
+for'/spent [also fårr'/] *A* - (=***føre/**) drawn (**med** by); harnessed (**for** to).
+for'/spill *-et* (=***/spel, *føre/spel**) prelude (**til** to), prologue; curtain raiser.
forspil'le *V -spilte* **1** forfeit, lose; throw away, waste. **2** mar, spoil (**for** for).
+forspi'se *V -te*: **f- seg** overeat.
+forspi'st *A* - overfed, surfeited.
for'/sprang *-et* advantage, (head) start (**på** on), lead: **ha f-** have a head start, the lead.
+forspør're *V -spurte, -spurt* (=***-spørje**): **f- seg** be always asking questions; **en kan aldri f- seg** it never hurts to ask.
for'/stad *-en, pl +-steder/*-stader* suburb.
***forsta'den** *A -e/-i, pl -ne*: **f- åker** overripe field.
for'stads/bane *-n* suburban railway.
+forstakk' *pt of* **-stikke**
forstan'd *-en/*-et* **1** intellect, mind, reason: **gå (være) fra f-en** go (be) out of one's m-; **ha f- på** be a judge of, know about; **være ved full f-** have one's full (mental) powers; **det går over all (min) f-** it's beyond all understanding, *(pop.)* it's beyond me; **slå seg på f-en** affect one's m-. **2** meaning, sense: **i egentlig (bokstavelig) f-** in the real (literal) s- (of the word), literally.
+forstan'der *-en, pl -e* (=***-ar**) director, superintendent (**for** of).
+forstanderin'ne *-a/-en* (=***-ar-**) (female) director, superintendent (**for** of).
+forstan'der/skap *-et* (=***-ar/**) direction, management; directors (collectively).
forstan'dig *A* - reasonable, sensible, wise.
+for'/stavelse *-n* *gram.* prefix.
+for'/stavn *-en* *naut.* prow, stem.
+for'/steder *pl of* **-stad**
forstei'ne *V -a/+-et* petrify, turn to stone: **f-et** *fig.* paralyzed, stony.
forstei'ning *+-en/*-a* fossil; fossilization, petrifaction.
for'/stell *-et* front (of an automobile).
+forstem'melse *-n* dejection, gloom.
+forstem'mende *A* - depressing, discouraging: **det virker f-** it has a disheartening effect.
+forstem't *A* - dejected, depressed, discouraged, *(pop.)* blue.
+forstem't/het *-en* dejection, gloom.
+forste'net *A* - cf **-steine**
forster'ke *V -a/+-et* reinforce, strengthen; heighten, intensify; amplify.
+forster'ker *-en, pl -e* (=***-ar**) (radio) amplifier; *chem.* intensifier.
+forster'kning *-en* reinforcement (**av** of), strengthening; intensification; *mil. (pl)* reinforcements.
+forstik'ke *V -stakk, -stukket*: **f- seg** conceal, hide oneself.
+forstil'le *V -stilte* **1: f- seg** feign, pretend. **2: f-t** hypocritical, simulated.
+forstil'lelse *-n* dissimulation.
+for'/stilling *-a/-en* forecarriage; *mil.* limber (of a field gun).
for'st/kandida't *-en* graduate in forestry.
for'st/mann *-en, pl -menn/*-menner* forester.
+for'st/messig *A* - forestal, forestry.
forsto'd *pt of* **-stå**
fo'r/stoff¹ *-et* material for lining.
fo'r/stoff² *-et* fodder.
forstok'ka *A* (=**+-et**) hardened; obdurate, stubborn: **en f- konservativ** a hidebound conservative.
+forstop'pelse *-n* (=***-ing**) constipation.
for'/stove [/ståve] *-a* cf **/stue¹**
+forstrek'ke *V -strakk/-strakte, -strukket/-strakt* **1: f- en med** advance, loan sby (money). **2** overstrain, sprain, strain.
for'/stue¹ *-a* (entrance) hall; lobby.
forstu'e² *V -a/+-et* **1** sprain, strain. **2** *naut.*: **f- seg** (of cargo) shift.
+forstukket [-stok'ket] *pp of* **-stikke**
+forstum'me *V -a/-et* be silenced; become, fall silent; die down; cease.
forstu've *V -a/+-et* cf **-stue²**
for'st/vesen *-et* forestry.
+for'/stykke *-t* front (e.g. of a dress).
forstyr'ra *A* - (=**+-et**) distracted, flustered, upset; crazy, deranged.
forstyr're *V -a/+-et* disturb, interrupt; confuse, distract, upset: **virke f-ende på** have a distracting effect on; **jeg håper jeg ikke f-er** I hope I'm not intruding.
+forstyr'relse *-n* disturbance; confusion, upset.
forstøk't *A* - astounded; frightened.
forstør're *V -a/+-et* enlarge; magnify.
+forstør'relse *-n* (=***-ing**) enlargement (**av** of); magnification.
+forstør'relses/glass *-et* magnifying glass.
+forstø'te *V -te* disown, repudiate.
forstå' *V -stod, -stått* **1** understand (=comprehend, grasp, realize, see): **f- det slik** gather that; **f- på en** gather from sby; **det f-r seg** of course, to be sure; **det f-r seg av seg selv** that's self-evident. **2: f- seg på** be a connoisseur, judge of, know something about; **f- seg på tingene** know one's way around, know the ropes.
forstå'elig *A* - comprehensible, understandable; pardonable: **gjøre seg f-** make oneself understood.
+forstå'else *-n* (=***-ing**) **1** comprehension (**av** of), understanding; appreciation: **gi en f- av** bring home to sby, make sby realize. **2** response, sympathy; agreement: **vise f- for** sympathize with; **leve i god f- med** live on good terms with.
+forstå'elses/full *A* sympathetic, understanding.
+forstå'seg/påer [-sei/] *-en, pl -e* (=***-ar**) *hum.* selfappointed expert.
+forsul'ten *A -ent, pl -ne* famished, starved.
+forsum'pe *V -et* stagnate, *(pop.)* go to the dogs.
+forsu're *V -et*: **f- livet, tilværelsen** embitter, take the joy out of one's life.
+forsvan't *pt of* **-svinne**
for'/svar *-et* defense: **ta en i f-** defend sby; **tale til ens f-** stick up for sby; **til f- for** in d- of.
forsva're *V -te/*-a* defend; justify: **f- seg tappert** put up a good fight; **f- å be** j-ed in (doing, saying sth).
+forsva'rer *-en, pl -e* (=***-ar**) *jur.* counsel for the defense.
forsva'rlig *A* - **1** defensible, justifiable, reasonable. **2** safe, secure, sound: **i f- stand** in good condition (repair). **3** goodly, huge: **en f- bit** an enormous bite.
For'svars/departementet [-mang'e] *df* Ministry of Defense.

+**for'svars/fiendtlig** *A* - pacifistic.
for'svars/laus *A* (=+/**løs**) defenseless.
for'svars/minis'ter *-eren, pl -rer/+-ere* Minister of Defense.
for'svars/stab *-en mil.* general staff.
for'svars/stilling *-a/+-en* defensive position (attitude).
+**forsver'ge** *V -et/-svor, -et/-svoret* 1 forswear, renounce: **en skal aldri f- noe** stranger things have happened, you never can tell. **2: f- seg** swear falsely; **f- seg på** swear (that); **f- seg til fanden** sell one's soul to the devil.
***forsver'je** *V -sver, -svor, svore/-i* cf **-sverge**
+**forsvin'ne** *V -svant, -svunnet* disappear, fade away, vanish: **forsvinn!** get out, *(pop.)* scram!; **i lengst forsvunne dager** in days of long ago.
+**forsvin'nende** *A* - imperceptible, negligible; infinitesimal.
forsvin'nings/nummer [/nommer] *-et, pl -/+-numre*: **lage et f-** do a disappearing act.
forsvo'r *pt of* **-sverge, -sverje**
+**forsvun'net** *pp of* **-svinne**
for'/syn[1] *-et* fate, providence; Divine Providence, God.
+**for'/syn**[2] *-et* (=*/**synd** *-a*) snell (on fish line).
forsyn'de *V -a/+-et*: **f- seg** sin, transgress (**mot** against); offend.
forsy'ne *V -te* 1 furnish, provide, supply: **f- med varer** stock; **f- seg av** help oneself; **f- seg med** help oneself to; **f- seg rikelig av noe** take one's fill of sth. **2: f- meg** (mild oath); **f- meg om jeg gjør** I'll be hanged if I'll do it.
forsy'ning *-a/+-en* 1 stock, supply (**av** of). **2** supplier, e.g. **melke/f-en** dairy.
forsy'nlig *A* - farseeing, provident.
***forsyr'gjar** *-en* cf **-sørger**
***forsy'te** *V -te* maintain, provide for, support.
***for'/sæte** *-t* cf **/sete**
for'/søk *-et* attempt (**på** at); test, trial; (scientific) experiment: **det er et f- verdt** it's worth trying.
+**forsø'ke** *V -te* attempt, try: **f- en gang til** have another try at it; **f- seg** have a stab, try at sth; **f- seg fram** feel one's way; **f- seg på** t- one's hand at.
for'søks/drift *-a/+-en* experimental stage, work.
for'søks/dyr *-et* animal used in scientific experiments; guinea pig.
for'søks/kani'n *-en* guinea pig.
for'søks/perso'n *-en* subject (of an experiment); *fam.* guinea pig.
for'søks/stasjo'n *-en* experiment station.
for'søks/vis *Av* experimentally, tentatively.
forsølve [+-søl'le] *V -a/+-et* silver; electroplate with silver, silver-plate.
forsøm'me *V +-sømte/*-sømde* (=***-søme**) neglect, omit; miss: **f- en leilighet** let an opportunity pass; **f- skolen** miss school, play truant.
forsøm'melig *A* - negligent; remiss (e.g. in payments).
+**forsøm'melig/het** *-en* negligence, remissness.
+**forsøm'melse** *-n* (=***-søm(m)ing**) 1 neglect, negligence (**av** of). **2** absence (**fra** from).
+**forsøm't** *A* - neglected: **innhente, ta igjen det f-e** make up for lost time.
+**forsør'ge** *V -a/-et/-de* (=***-je**) 1 provide for support: **f- seg selv** be self-supporting. **2** (as mild oath): **f- meg** heaven help me (him).
+**forsør'gelse** *-n* provision, support (**av** of).
+**forsør'gelses/byrde** *-n* dependents, family responsibilities.
+**forsør'ger** *-en, pl -e* (=***-jar**) breadwinner, provider.
+**forsø'te** *V -et* sweeten: **f- tilværelsen for en** brighten sby's existence.
+**forså'** *pt of* **forse**[2]
forså'vidt cf **vid**

for't[1] *-et, pl -/+-er mil.* fort.
fort[2] [for't] *A* - fast, quick: **f-e skritt** q- steps; **flyende f-** at breakneck speed; **f- og galt** haste makes waste; **f- vekk** constantly, continually.
forta' *V -tok, -tatt*: **f- seg** 1 overtax oneself: ***det var lett å vete at far fortok seg** it was easy to see that father was overworking himself (Vesaas). **2** wear off (e.g. pain, anger).
***fortal'de** *pt of* **-telja**
for'/tale *-en/*-a* introduction, preface (**til** to).
forta'lt *pp of* **-telle, -telje**
+**forta'lte** *pt of* **-telle**
+**for'/tann** *-a, pl -tenner* front tooth, incisor.
forta'pe *V -te* 1 lose: **f- sin rett** forfeit one's right. **2: f-es** *bibl.* be doomed, perish. **3: f- seg i drømmerier** be daydreaming; **f- seg i noe** be absorbed, lost in sth.
+**forta'pelse** *-n* (=***-ing**) 1 *archaic* forfeiture, loss (**av** of). **2** *bibl.* damnation, perdition. **3** absorption (**i** in).
fortap't *A* - 1 lost; helpless, resigned: **gå f-** be l-. **2** *bibl.* lost; doomed: **den f-e sønn** the prodigal son. **3** absorbed: **han er helt f- i henne** he's completely wrapped up in her.
fortatt' *pp of* **-ta**
for'/tau *-et* sidewalk.
***for'/taum** *-en* cf **/tom**
for'taus/kant *-en* curb, edge of sidewalk.
forte [for'te] *V -a/+-et*: **f- seg** hurry; (e.g. of watch) gain.
+**for'/tegn** [/tein] *-et* (=*/**teikn**) 1 *math.* sign (plus, minus): **med omvendt f-** with reversed s-s, *fig.* the exact opposite. **2** *mus.* key signature; accidental.
+**fortegne** [-tei'ne] *V -a/-et* draw incorrectly; *fig.* distort.
+**fortegnelse** [-tei'nelse] *-n* catalog, inventory, list (**over** of): **oppta f- over** make an i- of.
***for'/teikn** *-et* cf **/tegn**
***fortel'jar** *-en* cf **-teller**
***fortel'je** *V -tel, -talde, -talt* cf **-telle**
***fortel'jing** *-a* cf **-telling**
+**fortel'le** *V -talte* (=***-telje**) 1 tell (a story) (**om** about); narrate, relate: **det er blitt meg fortalt** I have been told; **det f-es at** the story goes that; **etter hva det blir fortalt** according to all accounts; **f- godt** t- a good story; be a good narrator; **f- historier** spin yarns, t- stories; **f- i øst og vest** spread a rumor around. **2: f-ende** epic, narrative: **f- måte** *gram.* indicative mood, **f- nåtid** *gram.* historical present.
+**fortel'ler** *-en, pl -e* (=***-teljar**) narrator; storyteller.
+**fortel'ling** *-a/-en* (=***-teljing**) narrative; story, tale; novel.
***forte'ne** *V -te* cf **-tjene**
***forte'nest(e)** *-a* cf **-tjeneste**
+**forten'ke** *V -te* (=***-tenkje**): **det kan jeg ikke f- ham i** I can't blame him for doing it.
forten'kt *A* - absorbed, thoughtful; puzzled.
+**forter'sket** *A* - (=+**-a**) hackneyed, trite.
+**fortet'ning** *-en* (=***-tetting** *-a*) concentration, condensation, liquefaction.
fortet'te *V -a/+-et* concentrate, condense, liquefy; *fig.* concentrate, focus (e.g. one's attention, energy): **f- seg** condense.
+**for't/gang** *-en*: **gjøre all mulig f-** use all possible dispatch, speed.
for'/tid *-a/+-en* 1 past: **det hører f-en til** it's a thing of the p-. **2** *gram.* imperfect, past, preterite.
+**for'tids/levning** *-en* antiquity, relic of the past.
for'tids/minne *-t* antiquity, monument of the past.
+**forti'e** *V -dde* conceal, keep secret, suppress (**for** from); hush up.

+**forti'else** *-n* concealment, suppression (**av** of).
+**for'/til'** *Av* in front.
fortin'ne *V -a/+-et* tin-plate.
+**fortje'ne** *V -te* (=***-tene**) 1 deserve, merit: **det f-er å merkes** it's worthy of notice. **2** *archaic* earn (cf **fortjent**).
+**fortje'neste** *-a/-en* (=***-tenest(e)**) 1 earnings; profit: **gi f-** yield a p-; **ha f- på** make a p- on. **2** desert, merit: **etter f-** according to one's, its m-s; **innlegge seg f-r av** merit gratitude for, render services to.
+**fortje'nst/full** *A* deserving; meritorious.
+**fortje'nst/medal'je** *-n* medal of honor.
+**fortje'nt** *A* - 1 earned: **surt f-e penger** hard-earned money. **2** well-deserved, well-earned; deserving: **få lønn som f-** get what's coming to one, what one deserves.
***fortjo'ne** *V -a* harm, injure.
+**fort/løpende** [for't/] *A* - consecutive, running.
fortne [for'tne] *V -a/+-et* hurry: **f- seg** (of watch) gain.
forto'k *pt of* **-ta**
+**fortol'ke** *V -a/-et* expound, interpret; construe.
+**fortol'kning** *-en* interpretation; construction (**av** of).
fortol'le *V -a/+-et* declare, pay duty on (goods).
fortol'ling *-a/+-en* duty (on goods); declaration (of duty).
+**for'/tom'** *-men* (=*/**taum**) snell (in fishing).
forto'ne *V +-et/+-te/*-a* **1: f- seg** appear dimly, in vague outline; appear, seem. **2** *poet.* fade away; harmonize. **3** *lit.* set to music.
+**for'/topp** *-en naut.* foretop.
+**fortrakk'** *pt of* **-trekke**
***fortrau't** *pt of* **-tryte**
+**fortre'd** *-en* annoyance, vexation; harm, injury: **han gjør ingen katt f-** he is a harmless person.
+**fortre'delig** *A* - annoying, troublesome; cross, out of sorts, *(pop.)* crabby.
+**fortre'dige** *V -et* annoy, vex; harm, injure.
+**fortref'felig** *A* - excellent, first-class, splendid.
+**fortref'felig/het** *-en* excellence.
+**fortrek'ke** *V -trakk, -trukket* 1 clear out, go away. **2** distort, twist: **f- ansiktet** make a (wry) face; **ikke f- en mine** keep a straight face; **f- seg** be distorted.
+**for'trekks/gardi'n** *-a/-en/-et* draw curtain.
+**fortreng'e** *V -te* (=***-je**) 1 repress, suppress. **2** displace, oust, supplant.
+**fortreng'sel** *-en* (=***-le**) displacement: **til f- for** to the neglect of.
+**for'/trinn** *-et* 1 precedence, priority. **2** advantage (**framfor** over), merit; good point.
+**fortrinn'lig** *A* - excellent, first-rate, splendid.
+**for'trinns/beret'tiget** *A* - privileged.
+**for'trinns/rett** *-en jur.* preferred claim.
+**for'trinns/vis** *Av* above all, especially; preferably.
+**fortro'lig** *A* - (=***-truleg**) 1 confidential: **f- samtale** heart-to-heart talk. **2** conversant, familiar, well-acquainted (**med** with): **gjøre seg f- med** familiarize oneself with; resign oneself to. **3** familiar, intimate: **stå på en f- fot med** be on i- terms with; **hans f-e** his confidant(e).
+**fortro'lig/het** *-en* 1 confidence, trust: **i all f-** in strict c-. **2** familiarity (**med** with). **3** intimacy.

+ Bokmål; * Nynorsk; ° Dialect.
After letter: ' stress (Acc. 1); ` tone, stress (Acc. 2); ˙ length.
Below letter: . not pronounced.

fortrol'le *V* *-a*/⁺*-et* bewitch, transform.
for'/tropp *-en mil.* vanguard.
fortrote** [-trå'te] *pp of* **-tryte** (=-troti**)
***fortru'** *V* *-dde* confide: **f- seg til ein** c- in sby.
⁺**fortrudt'** *pp of* **-tryde**
⁺**fortrukket** [-trok'ket] *pp of* **-trekke**
⁺**fortrutt'** *pp of* **-tryte**
⁺**fortry'de** *V* *-trød, -trudt* cf **-tryte**
⁺**fortry'delig** *A* - cf **-trytelig**
⁺**fortryk't** *A* - cowed, intimidated, suppressed.
fortryl'le *V* *-trylte*/⁺*-et*/**-a** 1 bewitch, transform. 2 charm, fascinate: **en f-ende naivitet** a c-ing naiveté.
⁺**fortryl'lelse** *-n* (=***-ing**) spell; enchantment, fascination.
fortry'te *V* ⁺*-trøt*/**-traut*, ⁺*-trutt*/**trote*/**-i* be sorry for, regret, rue.
fortry'telig *A* - displeased, irritated (**over** at): **ta noe f- opp** take exception to, resent.
⁺**fortrø'd** *pt of* **-tryde**
⁺**fortrøs'te** *V* *-a*/*-et*: **f- seg til** put confidence in, trust; dare, trust oneself to.
⁺**fortrøs'tning** *-en* confidence (**til** in), reliance (**til** on).
⁺**fortrøs'tnings/full** *A* confident, hopeful, trusting.
⁺**for't/satt** *A*- continued, constant(ly).
⁺**for't/sette** *V* *-satte* continue, carry on; keep on, proceed with, resume: **f- i den gamle tralten** continue in the same old rut; **f- i det uendelige** go on forever; **f- med å gjøre** keep on doing; **fortsatt side fire** continued on page four.
⁺**for't/settelse** *-n* continuation: **f- følger** to be continued.
fortul'la *A* - (=⁺**-et**) bewildered, confused.
fortumla [-tom'la] *A* - (=⁺**-et**) bewildered, confused, dazed: **være f- i hodet** be out of one's mind, be beside oneself.
For'/tun *Pln* village, Luster twp, Sogn og Fjordane.
fortu'ra *A* - (=⁺**-et**) confused; depressed; dissipated.
⁺**for'/turner** *-en, pl -e* (=***-ar**) leader of a gymnastic group (performance).
***fortus'ta** *A* - astonished, surprised.
⁺**fortvekk** [for't vekk'] *Av* cf **fort²**
fortvi'le *V* *-te*/**-a* despair, despond, lose heart: **det er til å f- over** it's enough to drive a person out of his mind; **man skal aldri f-** never say die.
⁺**fortvi'lelse** *-n* (=***-ing**) despair, desperation: **bringe til f-** drive to desperation.
fortvi'lt *A* - (=⁺**-et**, ***-a**) despairing, in despair; desperate: **f-ede forhold** hopeless conditions.
⁺**fortyk'ning** *-en* thickening; callosity (e.g. of the skin).
⁺**fortyn'ne** *V* *-a*/*-et* dilute, thin out; rarefy (a gas); reduce the thickness (of a metal plate).
fortæ're *V* *-te* 1 consume, devour. 2 eat away; corrode (metals). 3: **f-ende sinne** furious anger; *(adv.)* **f-ende langsom** terribly slow.
fortæ'ring *-a*/⁺*-en* consumption (of food and drink): **ha fri f-** have free board; **til f- på stedet** to be consumed on the premises.
fortør'ka *A*- (=⁺**-et**) dried up, withered.
⁺**fortø'rne** *V* *-a*/*-et* anger, exasperate: **f-es** become angry; **f-et** exasperated (**over** at).
⁺**fortø'rnelse** *-n* anger, resentment (**over** at).
fortøy'e *V* ⁺*-de*/**-a*/**-dde* make fast, moor (a boat).
⁺**fortøy'ning** *-a*/*-en* (=***-tøying**) mooring.
⁺**fortøy'nings/plass** *-en* (ship's) berth.
⁺**for'/ulempe** *V* *-a*/*-et* annoy, molest.
⁺**for'/ulyk'ke** *V* *-a*/*-et* 1 lose one's life in an accident, perish. 2 (of ship) be lost, wrecked. 3: **f-et** casualty, injured person, victim; **den f-ede** the victim.
fo'rum *-et* forum.
forun'derlig *A* - odd, singular, strange: **f- nok** strange to say.
⁺**for'/underso'kelse** *-n jur.* preliminary investigation (of offences).
forun'dre *V* *-a*/⁺*-et* astonish, surprise: **f- seg over** be s-d, marvel at.
forun'dring *-a*/⁺*-en* astonishment, surprise; wonder (**over** at).
forun'drings/pakke *-a*/*-en* package with unknown contents (e.g. from a grab bag).
⁺**forun'ne** *V* *-unte* grant: **det ble meg f-t å** it was my privilege to.
⁺**for'/uren'se** *V* *-et* contaminate, pollute.
⁺**for'/uren'sning** *-en* contamination, pollution; impurity.
⁺**for'/uret'te** *V* *-et* do an injustice to, wrong; mistreat: **den f-ede** the injured party; **et f-et uttrykk** an injured expression.
⁺**for'/uro'lige** *V* *-et* alarm, disquiet, make uneasy.
⁺**for'/ut** *Av* 1 before, beforehand, in advance: **gå f- for** precede, usher in; **ha noe f- for en annen** have an advantage over sby else. 2 *naut.* ahead, forward: **f- og akter** fore and aft.
***foru'tan** *P* cf **-uten**
⁺**for'ut/anelse** *-n* presentiment.
⁺**for'ut/bestem'melse** *-n* predestination, predetermination.
⁺**for'ut/bestem't** *A* - predestined, predetermined, preordained.
⁺**for'ut/bestil'le** *V* *-bestilte* order, reserve in advance.
⁺**foru'ten** *P* (=***-utan**) 1 besides, in addition to, not counting. 2 without: **kan han leve dem f-?** can he live w- them? 3 *archaic* outside.
⁺**for'ut/fattet** *A* - preconceived.
⁺**for'ut/gående** *A* - previous, prior.
⁺**for'ut/inntatt** *A* - biased, prejudiced (**for** in favor of; **mot** against).
⁺**for'ut/sa** *pt of* **-si**
⁺**for'ut/satt** *pp of* **-sette**
⁺**for'ut/se** *V* *-så, -sett* anticipate, foresee.
⁺**for'ut/seende** *A* - foresighted, provident.
⁺**for'utseen/het** *-en* foresight.
⁺**for'ut/setning** *-en* 1 assumption, supposition: **under f- av** on the a- that. 2 condition, qualification (**for** of): **det var en stilltiende f- at** it was tacitly understood that.
⁺**for'ut/sette** *V* *-satte, -satt* assume, presuppose: **forutsatt at** assuming, provided that.
⁺**for'ut/si** *V* *-sa, -sagt* forecast, predict, prophesy.
⁺**for'ut/sigelse** *-n* forecast, prediction.
⁺**for'ut/skikke** *V* *-et* preface: **f- en bemerkning** make a preliminary remark.
⁺**for'ut/så** *pt of* **-se**
***forvak'sen** *A* *-e*/*-i*, *pl -ne* cf **-vokst**
***forva'kt** *A* - cf **-våkt**
⁺**forval'te** *V* *-a*/*-et* administer, conduct, manage.
⁺**forval'ter** *-en, pl -e* (=***-ar**) agent, manager.
⁺**forval'tning** *-en* administration, management.
***forvan'd** *A* *-vant* cf **-vent**
⁺**forvan'dle** *V* *-a*/*-et* change, transform; convert, turn (**til** into).
⁺**forvan'dling** *-en* change, transformation; *zool.* metamorphosis: **f-ens lov** the law of c- (Ibsen).
⁺**forvan'dlings/nummer** [/nommer] *-eret, pl -er*/*-numre* (of theater) quick-change act; transformation.
***forvann'** *pt of* **-vinne**
forvan'ske *V* *-a*/⁺*-et* distort, garble; corrupt, mutilate (e.g. a text).
⁺**forvan'skning** *-en* (=***-vansking**) distortion, corruption (**av** of).
⁺**forvan't** *pt of* **-vinne**
forva'r *-et* custody, safekeeping.
forva're *V* *-te*/**-a* keep, protect: **vel f-t** well p-ed, in safekeeping.
forva'ring *-a*/⁺*-en* custody, safekeeping: **bringe i f-** place in s-; **ta i fengslig f-** take into c-.
⁺**for'/varsel** *-elet*/*-let, pl -el*/*-ler* 1 alert (e.g. of an air raid). 2 *archaic* omen, portent.
⁺**for'/vegen** *df* (=⁺**/veien**): **i f-** beforehand, in advance, previously; already; **gå i f-** go ahead, precede.
⁺**forvek'sle** *V* *-a*/*-et* confuse, mistake: **f- en med** m- sby for; **f- årsak med virkning** c- cause and effect.
⁺**forvek'sling** *-a*/*-en* confusion, mistake, mix-up.
***forve'l** *Av* entirely, quite: **han er ikkje f- vaken enno** he isn't completely awake yet.
forvel'le *V* *-velte*/⁺*-et* parboil.
***forven'je** *V* *-de* cf *-venne*
⁺**forven'ne** *V* *-vente* (=***-venje**) pamper, spoil.
⁺**forven't** *A* - (=***-vand**) spoiled; fastidious, pampered.
⁺**forven'tning** *-en* expectation: **i f- om** in e- of; **over all f-** beyond all e-s.
⁺**forven'tnings/full** *A* expectant.
fo'r/verk¹ *-et* fur.
for'/verk² *-et mil.* outwork.
forver're *V* *-a*/⁺*-et* worsen: **f- seg** deteriorate, go from bad to worse, take a turn for the worse.
forver'ring *-a*/⁺*-en* turn for the worse, worsening.
°**forve'ten** *A* *-ent, pl -ne* cf **-viten**
⁺**forvik'ling** *-en* complication.
forvil'le *V* *-a*/⁺*-et*/**-te* 1 bewilder, confuse: **f-et** delinquent, erring, wild; bewildered, perplexed; *zool.* reverted to a wild state, running wild. 2: **f- seg** get lost, go astray, lose one's way.
⁺**forvil'lelse** *-n* (=***-ing**) aberration, moral lapse.
forvin'ne *V* *infl as* **vinne** get over, recover from (illness, sorrow).
forvir're *V* *-a*/⁺*-et* bewilder, confuse.
forvir'ring *-a*/⁺*-en* 1 confusion: **bringe i f-** throw into c-. 2 *med.* amentia, derangement.
⁺**forvi'se** *V* *-te* banish, deport, exile (**fra** from, **til** to).
⁺**forvi'sning** *-en* banishment, deportation, exile.
⁺**forvis'se** *V* *-a*/*-et*: **f- seg om** assure oneself, make sure of sth; **f-et** certain (**om** of).
⁺**forviss'ning** *-en* assurance, conviction (**om** about).
forviss't *Av* cf **visst³**
***forvi'ten** *A* *-e*/*-i*, *pl -ne* curious, inquisitive.
***forvi'ten/skap** *-en* curiosity, inquisitiveness.
***forvit'nast** *V* *-ast* be curious, inquisitive.
***forvit'ne** *-a* curiosity, inquisitiveness.
***forvit'neleg** *A* - interesting.
forvit're *V* *-a*/⁺*-et* crumble, disintegrate, weather.
⁺**forvok'st** *A* - (=***-vaksen**) deformed, overgrown.
⁺**forvol'de** *V* *-te* bring about, cause (damage, grief, etc.).
⁺**forvor'pen** *A* *-ent, pl -ne* corrupted, depraved: **enda var ikke Inger her aldeles f- og gudsforgåen** still I- was not entirely d- and debased (Hamsun).
⁺**forvoven** [-vå'ven] *A* *-ent, pl -ne* daring, venturesome; fool-hardy, rash.
⁺**forvre'den** *A* *-ent, pl -ne* distorted, twisted; dislocated, sprained.
⁺**forvreng'e** *V* *-te* distort, misrepresent, twist.
⁺**forvreng'ning** *-en* distortion, misrepresentation (**av** of).
forvri' *V* *infl as* **vri** dislocate, sprain; distort, twist.
⁺**forvri'dning** *-en* dislocation, sprain; distortion.
⁺**forvrøv'le** *V* *-et* confuse, jumble, muddle (by foolish talk): **f-et** maundering, muddleheaded.
⁺**forvun'net** *pp of* **-vinne** (=***-vunne**/**-i**)

+for'/værelse -t anteroom, waiting room.

+forvå'gen A -ent, pl -ne cf -voven

+forvå'kt A - (=*-vakt) exhausted (from lack of sleep), sleepless.

forward [få'rvard] -en forward (on soccer team).

+foryng'e V -a/-et rejuvenate: f-es take a new lease on life; f- seg (of forestry) propagate, transmit.

+foryng'else -n rejuvenation (av of); (of forestry) propagation.

+foræ're V -te give, present with: f- en noe make a present of sth to sby.

foræ'ring -a/+-en gift, present (til to): gi en i f- make sby a present of sth.

+forø'de V -te squander, waste.

+forø'ke V -et/-te increase.

+forø'kelse -n increase (av of).

+forøn'sket A - desired, wished for.

+forø've V -de/-et commit, perpetrate (e.g. a crime).

+forøv'rig Av cf øvrig

+for'/år -et poet. spring, springtime.

+for'/årsa'ke [also fårr'/] V -et bring about, cause.

+forå't pt of -ete

*fo'sen A -e/-i, pl -ne porous.

Fo'sen Pln 1 district in Sør-Trøndelag (on both sides of Trondheim Fjord). 2 peninsula between Trondheim Fjord and the sea. 3 island, Avaldsnes twp, Rogaland.

fosfa't -et, pl -/+-er phosphate.

fos'for -en/-et phosphorus.

fosforescen's -en phosphorescence.

fosforesce're V -te phosphoresce.

*fo'sne V -a become porous.

Fo's/nes Pln twp, Nord-Trøndelag.

foss' -en fall(s), waterfall; rapids: sjøen stod inn som en f- the seawater poured in like a flood (Ibsen); en f- av ord a torrent of words.

fos'se V -a/+-et cascade, gush; foam, pour, rush: f- ned pour down; f- opp well up.

fos'se/fall -et cascade, (water) fall.

fos'se/grim -en folk. (violin playing) supernatural being believed to dwell beneath waterfalls.

fos'se/kall -en zool. dipper, water ouzel (Cinclus cinclus).

fos'se/vell -et poet. cascade, (water) fall.

fossi'l[1] -et, pl +-er/*- fossil.

fossi'l[2] A fossil.

foss'/koke V -te/*-a boil furiously.

fost/bror [fos't/] -en, pl +-brødre/*-brør cf foster/

fostbror/skap -en/+-et hist. foster-brotherhood, sworn brotherhood (sealed by the mingling of the participants' blood).

foster [fos'ter] -eret/-ret, pl -er/+-re 1 zool. embryo, fetus. 2 fig. phantom (e.g. of one's imagination). *3 fostering.

foster/bror [fos'ter/] -en, pl +-brødre/*-brør foster brother; hist. sworn brother.

foster/far -en, pl +-fedre/*-fedrar foster father.

+foster/fordri'velse [fos'ter/] -n induced (criminal) abortion.

foster/forel'dre [fos'ter/] pl foster parents.

fostre[1] [fos'tre] -a/+-en hist. foster (brother, sister; mother, father; son, daughter).

fostre[2] [fos'tre] V -a/+-et 1 archaic bring up, rear. 2 nurture, produce.

fo't -en, pl +føtter/*føter 1 foot (of person, page, mountain, line of verse, etc.): for ens føtter at one's feet; fra f- til isse from tip to toe; på stående f- off hand, on the spur of the moment; til f-s on f-; lett (rask) til f-s light- (quick-) f-ed; få f- (in hunting) find a scent; få føtter (å gå på) get a move on; (of money) be quickly spent; komme på fri f- be set free, at liberty; komme seg på f-e get on one's feet, recover; leve på en stor f- live on a grand scale; slå (hugge osv.) ned for f-e strike down without mercy; tre under føtter trample under f-. 2 base, foundation; leg (of table); stem (of glass); heel (of mast). 3 footing, terms: stå på (en) god (dårlig) f- med be on good (bad) t- with; stå på like f- med be on an equal footing with. 4 (pl fot) archaic unit of measure (=0.31374 meters = 1.03 English feet). 5 standard (of coinage): cf gull/, mynt/.

fot.=fotografert av, fotograf

fot'/ball -en 1 soccer. 2 soccer ball.

fot'ball/bane -n soccer field.

+fot'ball/dommer -en, pl -e (=*-ar) soccer referee.

fo't/balle -n anat. ball of the foot.

fot'ball/kamp -en soccer match.

fot'ball/lag -et soccer team.

fo't/blad -et anat. sole of the foot.

*fo't/breidd -a cf fots/bredd

fo't/brett -et floorboard.

+fo'te N cf fot

fo'te/far -et footprint, tracks: i hans f- in his footsteps.

fo't/ende -n foot (of bed, table).

fo't/feste -t foothold: få f- gain a f-.

fo't/folk -et mil. infantry.

+fo't/gjenger -en, pl -e (=*/gangar) pedestrian; walker.

+fo'tgjenger/overgang [/åver-] -en (=*fotgangar/) pedestrian crossing, safety zone.

fo't/lag -et pace, step, (manner of) walk(ing).

fo't/ledd -et anat. ankle joint.

fo't/note -n footnote.

fo'to -et, pl -/+-s photo, photograph.

fo'to/celle -a/+-en photoelectric cell.

fotoge'n A 1 zool. photogenic (=phosphorescent). 2 petroleum.

fotogra'f -en photographer.

fotografe're V -te photograph, take a photograph of; be a photographer.

fotografi' -et, pl +-er/*- photograph.

fotografi'/appara't -et camera.

fotogra'fisk A - photographic.

fotogravy'r -en photogravure.

fo'to/monta'sje -n photomontage.

fo't/pleie -n chiropody; pedicure.

fo't/pose -n archaic foot warmer (muff for the feet).

+fo'ts/bredd -en breadth of a foot: ikke vike en f- not budge an inch.

fo't/sid A of floor length, reaching to the ground.

fo't/slag -et footfall; footstep: holde f- med en keep in step with sby.

*fo't/sole -n cf /såle

fo't/sopp -en foot fungus (pedomycosis).

fo't/spor -et footprint, tracks: gå i hans f- follow in his footsteps.

fo't/stykke -t, pl +-r/*- 1 base, foot, pedestal. 2 foot (of bed), footboard.

+fo't/såle -n sole.

+fo't/trinn -et 1 footfall; footstep. 2 footprint.

+fo't/tur -en hike: gå f- go on a h-.

fo't/turis't -en hiker.

foyer [foaje'] -en, pl +-e cf foajé

fp.=forsøksperson

fr.[1]=franc; fransk

fr.[2]=fru eller frøken[1]

+fra' P cf frå

+fra'/be V -bad, -bedt: blomster f-(de)s no flowers (at a funeral) by request; det skal jeg meget ha meg f-dt I'll have none of that (nonsense); jeg må f- meg enhver innblanding I'll thank you to stay out of this.

+fraborde [-bo're] Av cf borde

+fra'/drag -et (=frå/) allowance, deduction (på on); discount.

+fra'/dømme V -dømte jur. sentence to be deprived of (forfeit, lose).

+fra'/fall -et (=*frå/) 1 defection, desertion (fra from); secession. 2 eccl. apostasy. 3 jur. withdrawal (of a charge).

+fra'/falle V -falt, -falt give up, relinquish, waive (e.g. a claim): f- ordet yield the floor.

+fra'/fallen A -ent, pl -falne (=*frå/) eccl. apostate: Julian den f-ne J- the Apostate.

+fra'/flytte V -et leave, vacate.

+fra'/gikk pt of -gå

fragmen't -et, pl -/+-er fragment (av of).

fragmenta'risk A - fragmentary.

+fra'/gå V -gikk, -gått: av dette beløp f-r 100 kroner from this sum 100 kroner are to be deducted.

fra'k A cf frakk[2]

+fra'/kjenne V -kjente 1 deny sby's having: f- en enhver dyktighet deny sby's ability. 2 jur. sentence to be deprived of, forfeit, lose.

frakk'[1] -en overcoat; topcoat.

frakk'[2] A frakt (=frak) dial. capable; excellent; in good condition.

frak'ke/oppslag -et (coat) lapel.

+frak'ke/skjøt -et coattail.

fraksjo'n -en (of a political party) section, wing.

frak't -a/+-en 1 cargo, freight. 2 (freight) rate. 3 carriage, transportation.

*frak'tar -en charterer.

frak't/brev -et bill of lading; freight bill, waybill (railroad).

+frak't/damper -en, pl -e (=*-ar) freighter; tramp steamer.

frak'te V -a/+-et haul, transport (by railway, ship); carry, move.

frak'te/mann -en, pl -menn/*-menner carrier.

frak't/fart -en freight trade: gå i f- (of ship) be in the f-, engage in carrying.

frak't/gods [/got's] -et cargo, freight.

fraktu'r -en 1 typog. black letter, Gothic character. 2 med. fracture.

fraktu'r/skrift -a/+-en typog. black letter, Gothic character.

+fra'/la pt of -legge

+fra'lands/vind -en offshore breeze.

+fra'/legge V -la, -lagt: f- seg disavow, disclaim; f- seg alt ansvar disclaim all responsibility.

fram' A cp fremre, sp fremst (=+frem) ahead, forth, forward: f- for cf framfor; f- med det! out with it!; f- til våre dager down to our time; f- og tilbake back and forth; snakke f- og tilbake om discuss at length; beint f- straight a-; forthrightly; lenger f- further on; by f- offer; finne f- find one's way; gå rett f- go straight a-; komme f- arrive; get a-; nå f- arrive (at a destination); ta f- bring forth, take out; vise f- display. (For use with other verbs see these).

*fra'mand A cf fremmed

*fra'mandsleg A alien, strange; exotic.

*fram'a(n)/for' P cf fram/

*fram'a(n)/på P cf fram/

*fram'a(n)/til' P cf fram/

+fram'/bringe V -brakte, -brakt (=+frem/) bring about, cause, produce.

+fram'/bringelse -n (=+frem/) generation, production; product.

fram'/brott -et (=*/brot, +/brudd) outbreak: dagens f- dawn, daybreak; vårens f- coming of spring.

*fram'/burd -en delivery, presentation (e.g. of errand, speech).

+fram'/by V infl as by offer, present; entail, involve: f- til salg o- for sale; f- seg p- itself (e.g. an opportunity).

*fram'/bærleg A - frank, plainspoken.

fram'/djerv A aggressive, bold; frank, outspoken.

fram'/drift -a/+-en 1 tech. forward thrust. 2 fig. enterprise, initiative (pop.) get up and go, go.

fram'/dør -a front door.

fram'/ende -n front end.

fram'/etter P forward; along: de

+ Bokmål; * Nynorsk; ° Dialect. After letter: ' stress (Acc. 1); ` tone, stress (Acc. 2); · length. Below letter: . not pronounced.

gikk f- veien they walked a- the road; ***og så f-** and so forth (**osfr.** etc.).
fram'/faren *A* +-*ent, pl* -*ne* dead, deceased: *archaic* **i de lengst f-ne dager** in days of yore, long ago.
fram'/ferd [*/fæ·r] -*a* 1 enterprise, initiative, *(pop.)* go, push. 2 conduct; proceeding.
fram'/for· *P* 1 before, in front; ahead *of*: **f- seg** before one. 2 in preference to, rather than: **f- alt** above all; **ha noe f- en** have an advantage over sby.
fram'/fot -*en, pl* +-*føtter*/*-*føter* foreleg.
***fram'/fus** *A* headlong, impetuous.
+**fram'/fusende** *A* - headlong, impetuous.
+**fram'/føre**[1] *V* -*te* (=+**frem/**) 1 present, put on (e.g. a new play). 2 offer, tender (e.g. one's apologies, congratulations).
***fram'/føre**[2] *P* cf **/for**
fram'/føring -*a* presentation (e.g. of a play).
+**fram'/føtter** *pl of* **-fot** (=***/føter**)
fram'/gang -*en* advancement, progress; success: **ha f-** prosper, succeed.
fram'gangs/måte -*n* course of action, procedure.
fram'gangs/rik *A* prosperous.
+**fram'/gå** *V* -*gikk*, -*gått* (=+**frem/**) be a result of, result from; appear from, be evident from.
fram'/hald -*et* continuation, sequel.
***fram'halds/fortel'jing** -*a* continued story, serial.
fram'halds/skole -*n* (=***/skule**) "continuation school" (non-vocational school usu. of one year, following the grammar school).
+**fram'/heve** *V* -*de*/-*et* (=+**frem/**) call attention to; emphasize, stress; accentuate, set off, throw into relief.
fram'/hjelp -*a*/+-*en* encouragement, promotion (**av** of).
***fram'/huga** *A* - bold, courageous.
fram'/i *P* in (the) front of: **legge seg f-** meddle, put in one's oar.
fram'/ifrå· [also fram'/] *A* - 1 exceptional, unusual. 2 *(adv.)* exceedingly; very well.
fram'/kalle *V* +-*kalte*/*-*a* (=+**frem/**) 1 call forth, evoke. 2 cause, produce: **f- virkning** p- an effect. 3 develop (a negative). 4: **bli f-t** take (one's) curtain calls.
fram'/kalling -*a*/+-*en* (=+**frem/**) 1 development (of negatives). 2 curtain call (**av** of).
***fram'/kjøm** *A* passable (e.g. road); navigable, open (e.g. channel).
***fram'/kjømd** -*a* 1 appearance, arrival. 2 enterprise, initiative.
framkom'melig *A* - passable (e.g. road); navigable, open (e.g. channel).
fram'/komst -*en* (=+**frem/**) 1 advancement, forward movement; navigable, passable route. 2 appearance, arrival: **ved f-en** on arrival.
fram'komst/middel -*elet*/-*midlet, pl* +-*midler*/*-*el* conveyance; means of communication.
fram'/legg -*et* (written) proposal; bill, motion.
+**fram'/leie** -*a*/-*en* (=***/leige**) sublease, subletting.
+**fram'/leier** -*en, pl* -*e* sublessor.
fram'/leis *Av* still.
fram'/lengs *Av* (=***/lenges**) forwards.
***fram'/lut**[1] -*en* forepart, front end.
fram'/lut[2] *A* - bent forward, stooping.
fram'/lån -*et* loan by a borrower to a third person: **f- av bøker er forbudt** lending of books to a third party is forbidden.
fram'/marsj -*en* advance, forward movement, progress.
fram'me *Av* 1 ahead, in front: **jeg så ham langt f-** I saw him far a-. 2 in view, out: **ligge, stå f-** be exposed to view. 3 (of a subject) under consideration, discussion. 4 at a destination, there: **vi er f- kl. 2** we'll be there, we'll arrive at two o'clock.
fram'/med *P* up by.
fram'/møte -*t* attendance; turnout (**av** of).
fram'/om· *P* past.
fram'/over [/åver] *P* 1 ahead, forward: **gå f-** make progress, progress. 2 in the future: **et år f-** for the coming year.
fram'/part -*en* forepart, front part.
fram'/på *P* 1 in front of, on to, out in: **f- dagen** later in the day. 2 *(adv.)*: ***halde seg f-** thrust oneself forward; ***komme f-** come in, enter; ***legge seg f-** lie down (for a short rest); **snakke, slå f-** hint, throw out a hint.
fram'/rom [/romm] -*met*/*-*et naut.* forehold.
+**fram'/rykning** -*en* (=***/rykking** -*a*) esp. *mil.* advance (**av** of).
fram'/sete -*t, pl* +-*r*/*- front seat.
+**fram'/sette** *V* -*satte*, -*satt* (=+**frem/**) advance, propose, put forward: **f- et forslag** make a motion; **f- et krav** file, put in a claim; **f- et lovforslag** bring in a bill.
fram'/side -*a*/+-*en* (=+**frem/**) front side.
+**fram'/skap** -*et* large cupboard (hutch) standing near the front door of a farmhouse.
***fram'/skoten** [/skå·ten] *A* -*e*/-*i, pl* -*ne* cf **/skutt**
fram'/skott -*en* cf **/skut**
+**fram'/skritt** -*et* (=+**frem/**) advance, headway, progress; development, improvement, step in the right direction: **gjøre (gode) f-** make (good) progress (**i** in).
fram'skritts/vennlig *A* - progressive.
fram'/skut -*en naut.* bow.
+**fram'/skutt** *A*- (=***/skoten**) advanced; protruding; prominent.
***fram'/skuv** -*en* push; *fig.* impetus, stimulus.
+**fram'/skynde** *V* -*te* accelerate, expedite, speed up.
***fram'/skåp** -*et* cf **/skap**
+**fram'/slenge** -*a* (=***-je**) teen-ager (girl).
fram'/slenging -*en* teen-ager (boy), youngster.
***fram'/slengje** -*a* cf **/slenge**
fram'slengs/alder -*en* teen age, teens.
fram'/spring -*et* projection, salient.
fram'/springende *A* - jutting, projecting.
***fram'/stamn** -*en naut.* bow, prow, stem.
fram'/steg -*et* advance, headway, progress; development, improvement.
***fram'/stemne** -*a* direction, tendency, trend.
+**fram'/stille** *V* -*stilte*, -*stilt* (=+**frem/**) 1 depict, represent; act, play, portray; give an account, a version of: **f- for svakt** understate; **f- saken på den måten** put the matter in that light. 2 make, manufacture, produce. 3 present: *jur.* **f- for retten** bring before the court; **f- seg for noen** p- oneself before sby (e.g. a medical board).
+**fram'/stilling** -*a*/-*en* (=+**frem/**) 1 depiction, representation; portrayal; account. 2 manufacture (**av** of).
fram'/stup(e)s *Av* headlong.
+**fram'/støt** -*et* (=***/støyt**) drive, push; campaign, offensive (**mot** against).
fram'/stående *A* - protruding, prominent; *fig.* outstanding, prominent.
fram'/syn -*et*/*-*a* 1 foresight. 2 clairvoyance.
fram'/syning -*a* 1 demonstration, showing. 2 (theatrical) performance.
fram'/sy'nt *A* - 1 farsighted. 2 clairvoyant, having second sight.
fram'/tak -*et* enterprise, initiative.
fram'/tann -*a, pl* -*tenner* front tooth, incisor.
fram'/tenkt *A* - foresighted, provident.
fram'/tid -*a*/+-*en* (=+**frem/**) future; *gram.* future tense: **engang i f-en** at some future date; **i en ikke fjern f-** in a not too distant future.
fram'/tidig *A* - (=+**frem/**) future, prospective; *(adv.)* in the future.
fram'tids/musikk· -*en*: **det er f- it** belongs to the future, it is in the lap of the gods.
fram'tids/von -*a* hope for the future; future prospect(s).
***fram'/til·** *P* forward; up to.
fram'/toning -*a*/+-*en* (=+**frem/**) 1 phenomenon. 2 *derog.* figure, sight: **en komisk (uhyggelig) f-** a comical (sinister) f-.
+**fram'/tre** *V* -*trådte*, -*trådt* (=+**frem/**) 1 appear, manifest itself. 2: **f-dende** conspicuous, striking; distinguished, eminent, prominent.
fram'/tung [/tong] *A* (e.g. **of** car, ship) (too) heavy in front.
fram'/tur -*en* trip out (to a particular place); cf **tilbaketur.**
***fram'/tøk** *A* enterprising, having initiative; go-getting.
***fram'/vaksen** *A* -*e*/-*i, pl* -*ne* full-grown.
fram'/ved *P* in front of.
fram'/vekst -*en* development, growth (**av** of).
***fram'/vekstring** -*en* teen-ager (boy), youngster, youth.
fram'/vis *A* farsighted, provident.
***fram'/vogn** [/vångn] -*a mil.* forecarriage.
fram'/åt *P* up to: **sett deg f- bordet** sit down at the table.
+**fra'/narre** *V* -*a*/-*et*: **f- en noe** trick sby out of sth.
fran'k *A*: **fri og f-, f- og fri** free as the breeze, without any restraint whatsoever.
+**fran'ker** -*en, pl* -*e* (=***-ar**) *hist.* Frank.
franke're *V* -*te* stamp.
fran'kisk *A* - 1 Frankish. 2 Franconian (language).
fran'ko *Av* postpaid.
Fran'k/rike *Pln* France.
franktirø'r -*en mil.* franctireur (=guerilla, sniper).
franse'se -*n* quadrille.
+**fransiska'ner** -*en, pl* -*e* (=***fransiskan(ar)**) Franciscan.
fran'sk *A* - French: **f- hæl** Louis XV heel.
fran'sk/brød -*et* white bread.
fran'sk/mann -*en, pl* -*menn*/*-*menner* Frenchman.
franso's -*en hist. med.* syphilis.
frappan't *A* - striking, surprising.
frappe're *V* -*te* astonish, surprise: **bli f-t over** be s-d at; **en f-ende ferdighet** an uncanny ability.
+**fra'/regne** [/reine] *V* -*et* deduct, leave out of consideration: **omkostningene f-et** exclusive of costs.
+**fra'/rå(de)** *V* -*dde*: **f- en noe** advise sby against sth, deprecate.
+**fra'/sa** *pt of* **-si**
+**fra'/sagn** [/sangn] -*et* legend, story, tale: **det går f- om det** many's the t- that has been told about it.
+**fra'/sagt** *pp of* **-si**
fra'se[1] -*n* 1 cliché; empty, trite phrase. 2 *mus.* phrase.
fra'se[2] *V* -*a*/+-*te* crackle, rustle.
+**fra'/se**[3] *V* -*så*, -*sett* disregard: **f-tt (at)** apart from (the fact that).
fra'se/helt -*en* (empty, pretentious) talker, *(pop.)* windbag.
+**fra'se/maker** -*en, pl* -*e* (=***-ar**) phrasemaker, -monger; *(pop.)* windbag.
fraseologi' -*en* phraseology.
frase're *V* -*te mus.* phrase.
+**fra'/si** *V* -*sa*, -*sagt*: **f- seg** relinquish, renounce, waive; refuse.
+**fra'/skilt** *A* - divorced.
+**fra'/skrive** *V* -*skrev*, -*skrevet* 1 call into question, deny. 2 renounce: **f- seg ansvaret for** disclaim all responsibility for, wash one's hands of; **f- seg retten til noe** r-, sign away all right to sth.

+fra'/sorte·rt A - discarded, rejected (goods, merchandise).
+fra`/spark -et kick (in swimming).
+fra`/stand -en: i, på f- at a distance.
+fra'/støte V -te repel: f-ende forbidding, repulsive; elec. repellant.
+fra'/ta V -tok, -tatt deprive of: f- en lysten til noe take the edge off sby's anticipation.
*fra`te V -a/+-et crackle, rustle.
fraternise're V -te fraternize (med with).
+fra'/tok pt of -ta
+fra'/tre V -trådte, -trådt resign from (a position), retire.
+fra'/tredelse -n resignation; retirement.
+fra`/trekk -et deduction.
+fra'/trådte pt of -tre
frau' -a/+-en 1 foam, froth. 2 dung, manure.
*frau`dig A cf frodig
frau`e V -a 1 foam, froth. 2 dung, manure.
frau's pt of fryse[1]
+fra'/vike V -vek, -veket depart, deviate from.
+fra'/vriste V -a/-et wrest, wring from.
+fra`/vær -et absence (fra from).
+fra'/værende A - 1 absent. 2 absent-minded, preoccupied.
fre'd -en peace: f- for enhver pris p- at any price; f- i sinnet p- of mind; archaic Guds f- "God's p-" (greeting); hold f- shut up; la en i f- let sby alone; man har ikke f- lenger enn naboen vil a person can live in p- only as long as his neighbhor will let him; slutte f- make p-, conclude a p- treaty.
-fred Prn(m) e.g. in Hallfred.
fre'/dag -en Friday: forrige (sist) f- last F-; F- Man F- (Defoe).
fre`de V -a/+-et preserve, protect (by law) (e.g. fish, game, historical monuments, natural resources): f-et (also:) sacred.
fre`delig A - peaceful; pacific, peaceable.
+fre`d/hellig A - (=*/heilag) sacred, sacrosanct: et f- sted a sanctuary.
*fre`ding -a cf fredning
*fre`d/kjær A peaceable, peace loving.
fre`d/laus A (=+/løs) 1 hist. outlawed: gjøre en f- outlaw sby. 2 poet. restless, unhappy.
fre`d/lyse V -te dedicate, set apart (as inviolate): et f-t sted a hallowed spot.
+fre`d/løs A cf /laus
fre`d/løyse -a outlawry.
+fre`dning -en (=*freding) conservation, preservation (e.g. of historical monuments, natural resources, wild life).
Fred`rik/stad Pln city, Østfold.
Fredrikste'n Pln fortress in Halden (city, Østfold).
*fre`d/sam· A peaceful; peaceable.
fre`ds/brott -et (=*/brot, +/brudd) jur. breach of the peace.
+fre`ds/elskende A - peaceable, peace loving.
+fre`ds/forstyr·rer -en, pl -e (=*-ar) disturber of the peace.
+fredsom'melig A - peaceful; peaceable.
fre`ds/pipe -a peace pipe.
fre`ds/pris -en (Nobel) peace prize.
fre`ds/sak -a/+-en: f-en the cause of peace, the peace movement.
*fre`ds/semje -a (conclusion of) peace.
fre`ds/slutning *-a/+-en (conclusion of) peace.
fre`d/sæl [+/sel] A peaceable, peace loving.
fregatt' -en naut. frigate.
fre`ge V -a/+-et archaic, dial. ask, inquire.
+fregne [frei'ne] -a/-en (=*frekne) freckle.
+fregnet(e) [frei'net(e)] A - (=*freknet(e)) freckled.
Frei' Pln twp, Møre og Romsdal.
+frei`dig A - 1 audacious, bold; unabashed. 2 irresponsible, rash: en f- påstand a r- statement. 3 bluff, free and easy, outspoken: en f- fyr a brazen fellow.
+frei`dig/het -en assurance, boldness, confidence.
*frei`star -en cf frister
*frei`ste[1] V -a cf freste
*frei`ste[2] V -a cf friste[1]
*frei`sting -a cf fristelse
*frei`stnad -en, pl -er attempt, experiment, trial.
*fre'k A 1 greedy, voracious. 2 sharp, strong (smell, taste).
frekk' A frekt bold, impudent; brazen, shameless.
frek'kas -en bold, impudent person (pop.) smart aleck.
+frekk'/het -en audacity, impudence, insolence, (pop.) nerve.
*frek`ne -a cf fregne
*frek`net(e) A - cf fregnet(e)
frekven's -en frequency.
frekven't A - frequent.
frekvente're V -te lit. frequent, patronize: f- en skole attend a school.
frel`se[1] -a/+-en 1 deliverance, rescue. 2 bibl. redemption, salvation: f-ns hær S- Army.
frel`se[2] V -te 1 rescue, save (fra from). 2 bibl. redeem, save.
+frel`ser -en, pl -e (=*-ar) savior: F-en our Savior, the Redeemer.
frel`ses/armé -en Salvation Army.
+frem' Av cf fram
+frem'/ad Av ahead, forward, onward: f- marsj f- march
+frem'ad/skridende A - advancing (e.g. old age), progressive.
+frem'ad/strebende A - ambitious, up and coming.
+frem'/bar pt of -bære
+frem'/bringe V -brakte, -brakt cf fram/
+frem'/bringelse -n cf fram/
+frem`/brudd -et cf fram/brott
+frem'/by V -bød, -budt cf fram/
+frem'/bære V -bar, -båret express, offer (e.g. apologies, regrets), state (e.g. errand).
+frem'/bød pt of -by
+frem'/båret pp of -bære
*frem`de V -a encourage, further: f- seg make progress.
+fremde'les Av still.
+frem'/føre V -te cf fram/[1]
+frem'/førelse -n cf fram/føring
+frem'/gang -en cf fram/
+frem'/gå V -gikk, -gått cf fram/
+frem'/herskende A - predominant, prevailing.
+frem'/heve V -de/-et cf fram/
+frem`/hjelp -en cf fram/
+frem'/hjelpe V -hjalp, -hjulpet encourage, promote.
+frem'/holde V -holdt, -holdt call attention to, emphasize, point out.
*frem`je V -a cf fremme[2]
*frem`jing -a cf fremme[1]
+frem'/kalle V -kalte cf fram/
+frem'/kaste V -et: bring up, raise, suggest (an idea, a question).
+frem'/komme V -kom, -kommet 1 appear, come to light; be published. 2: f- med offer a suggestion, put forward a proposal. 3: f- ved result from. 4: f-n advanced to, reached (a certain stage of development); arrived.
+frem`/komst -en cf fram/
+frem'/legge V -la, -lagt produce, submit (esp. evidence in court).
+frem'/mane V -te call up, evoke.
+frem`me[1] N (=*fremjing) encouragement, promotion: til f- av for the p- of.
+frem`me[2] V -a/-et (=*fremje) advance, encourage, promote: f- sine egne mål further one's own private ambitions, interests.
+frem`me[3] Av cf framme
+frem`med A - (=fremmend, *framand) alien, foreign; strange, unfamiliar (for to): bli f- for en become a stranger to sby; det er f- for min natur it's (completely) contrary to my nature; en f- a foreigner, stranger, visitor; f-e guests; han har aldri f-e he never entertains.
+frem`med/artet A - exotic, outlandish, strange.
+frem`med/konto·r -et Office of Alien Affairs; Department of Immigration.
+frem`med/legeme -t foreign body, substance.
+frem`med/legio'n -en the (French) Foreign Legion.
+frem`med/lo'sje -n private box (in theater).
+frem`med/o·rd -et foreign (unassimilated) word, (pop.) big word.
+frem`med/o·rdbok -a, pl -bøker dictionary of foreign words and phrases.
+frem`melig A - advanced, forward; precocious.
frem`mend A cf fremmed
frem`mend/folk -et strangers, visitors.
+frem'/møte -t cf fram/
+frem'/ragende A - 1 exceptional, outstanding. 2 (adv.) remarkably.
frem're A - foremost, front: mil. f- bånd band (on gun).
+frem'/sette V -satte, -satt cf fram/
+frem'/side -n cf fram/
+frem'/skaffe V -et obtain, procure.
+frem'/skreden A -ent, pl -ne advanced (e.g. age).
+frem`/skritt -et cf fram/
+frem'/skynde V -te cf fram/
frem'st A - foremost: først og f- above all, first and foremost, primarily.
+frem'/stille V -stilte cf fram/
+frem'/stilling -en cf fram/
+frem`/tid -en cf fram/
+frem`/tidig A cf fram/
+frem`tids/musikk· -en cf framtids/
+frem'/toning -en cf fram/
+frem'/tre V -trådte, -trådt cf fram/
+frem`/treden en 1 appearance (e.g. on the stage). 2 behavior, manners: pen f- nice m-.
+frem'/tredende A - 1 conspicuous, striking. 2 distinguished, eminent, prominent.
+frem'/trådte pt of -tre
+frem'/ture V -et persevere, persist (med in).
+frem'/tvinge V -tvang, -tvunget compel, enforce.
+frem`/vis A cf fram/
+frem'/vise V -te display, exhibit, show.
fren`de -n archaic kinsman, relative; (pl) kindred.
fren`de/laus A without relatives.
fren`d/skap -en/+-et family ties, kinship.
frene'tisk A - frenetic, frenzied.
fren`ke -a/+-en archaic kinswoman.
frenolog [-olå'g] -en phrenologist.
frenologi' -en phrenology.
fre's -et/-en 1 speed: for full f- at top s-; det er f- i ham he has plenty of vim. 2 tech. (milling) cutter.
fre'se[1] V -te 1 (of fire, flames) crackle, sputter. 2 snarl, spit like a cat.
fre'se[2] V -te tech. cut, mill.
+fre'ser -en, pl -e (=*-ar) tech. 1 milling cutter. 2 milling machine operator.
fres`ke -n fresco.
fres`ko -en, pl -er/fresker fresco.
+fres`ko/maling -a/-en (=*/måling) fresco painting.
+fres`te V -a/-et (=*freiste[1]) 1 attempt, try (å to): f- lykken t- one's luck. 2 endure, experience.
*fret`nad -en information, news, report.
*fret`te V -a/-e cf fritte
fri'[1] V -dde propose (til to), (pop.) pop the question; court, flatter: f-

+ Bokmål; * Nynorsk; ° Dialect. After letter: ' stress (Acc. 1); ` tone, stress (Acc. 2); · length. Below letter: . not pronounced.

til publikum pander to the public.
fri'[2] *V -dde* (=*frie) free, set free (fra from): f- oss fra det onde deliver us from evil; f- seg clear oneself; Gud f- meg God help me.
fri'[3] *A -tt* free (for from, of) (= at liberty; exempt; unoccupied, vacant; unrestricted): f-tt for (noe) dibs on (sth); i det f-(e) out of doors, in the open air; på f- fot at large; gi f-tt løp til give vent, free rein to, let go; gå f- get off scot-free; ha (få, ta seg) f- have (get, take) a day off, a holiday; snakke f-tt speak openly; stå f-tt (of a building) be isolated, exposed; (of person) remain independent (neutral, unbiased); det står en f-tt å one is at liberty, is welcome to; det er ikke f-tt (for) at it can't be denied (that), it must be admitted (that), it does happen, there's a good chance (that); må jeg være så f- å may I take the liberty to; ordet er f-tt the meeting (floor) is open for discussion.
*fri'ar/mål *-et* courting, wooing.
fri'/billett' *-en* complimentary, free ticket; *(pop.)* Annie Oakley.
fri'/bo'rd *-et naut.* freeboard.
*fri'/boren [/båren] *A -e/-i, pl -ne* cf /båren
+fri'/bry'tning *-en* (=*/bryting *-a*) free style wrestling (catch-as-catch-can).
+fri'/bytter *-en, pl -e* buccaneer, freebooter.
+fri'/båren *A -ent, pl -ne* freeborn.
*fri'd *A* beautiful, lovely.
-frid *Prn (f)* e.g. in Hall/, Mål/, Magn/, Malm/.
Fri'da *Prn (f)*
fri'/dag *-en* holiday; day (night) off.
fri'/dom' *-men/*-en* freedom, independence, liberty.
Fridt'jof *Prn (m)*
*fri'e *V -a* cf fri[2]
+fri'/eksempla'r *-et* complimentary copy, free copy.
+fri'er *-en, pl -e* (=*-ar) suitor.
+fri'er/brev *-et* (=*-ar/) letter of proposal.
+fri'er/føtter *Pl* (=*friar/føter): gå på f- go courting.
frieri' *-et* courting, wooing.
fri'/finne *V infl as finne jur.* acquit, find not guilty: bli frifunnet i alle tiltalens punkter be acquitted on all counts; påstå seg frifunnet plead not guilty.
+fri'/finnelse *-n* (=*-ing) *jur.* acquittal.
fri'/fot *N*: på f- at large, at liberty.
+fri'/funnet *pp of* -finne
Frigg' *Prn myth.* Old Norse goddess, wife of Odin.
+fri'/gi [/ji] *V -gav, -gitt* liberate, release, set free: f- mot løsepenger hold for ransom; f- varer, hus osv. decontrol goods, rents, etc.
frigi'd *A* - frigid.
frigidite't *-en* frigidity.
+fri'/givelse [/jivelse] *-n* release, setting free; decontrol (av of).
+fri'/gjort [/jort] *A* - (=*/gjord) 1 emancipated. 2 *merc.* decontrolled, unrestricted.
+fri'/gjøre [/jøre] *V -gjorde, -gjort* (=*/gjere) emancipate, liberate: f- seg fra free oneself from, get rid of.
+fri'/gjøring *-a/-en* (=*/gjering *-a*) emancipation, liberation.
fri'/hamn *-a* (=+/havn) free port.
fri'/hand *N*: på f- freehand (e.g. drawing).
fri'/handel *-elen* free trade.
fri'/herre *-n hist.* baron.
+fri'/het *-en* 1 freedom, independence, liberty: f- for Loke så vel som for Tor f- of speech (for all opinions, even the unacceptable ones) (Grundtvig). 2 exemption (for from); privilege. 3 liberty (=improper act): ta seg f-er overfor take l-ies with; poetisk f- poetic license.
+fri'hets/dag *-en* Independence Day.
fri'/hjul *-et* freewheel (on bicycle).
fri'hjuls/bremse *-n* coaster brake.
+fri'/hånd *N* cf /hand
fri'/idrett' *-en* track (sports).
frikadel'le *+-en/*-a* (=+frikadell) meatball.
fri'/kar *-en* (unchallenged) champion.
frikassé *-en* fricassée.
+fri'/kirke *-a/-en* free church (= not state church).
fri'/kjenne *V +-kjente/*-kjende jur.* acquit, exonerate (for of).
*fri'/kjenning *-a jur.* acquittal, exoneration.
friksjo'n *-en* friction; *fig.* conflict, friction.
fri'/kvarte'r *-et* break, interval (between classes): det store f- (noon) recess (usu. 20 min.).
*fri'/kyrkje *-a* cf /kirke
fri'/land *-et*: dyrke på f- grow (e.g. vegetables) outdoors.
fril'le *-a/+-en hist.* mistress.
fri'/luft *N* open air, outdoors (chiefly in cpds.).
fri'lufts/liv *-et* outdoor life.
fri'lufts/tea'ter *-eret/-ret, pl -er/+-re* open air theater.
*fri'/lynne *-t* (=/lynde) broad-mindedness, liberalism.
fri'/lynt *A* - (=*/lyndt) broad-minded, liberal: f- ungdom (religiously) l- youth groups.
fri'/merke *-t, pl +-r/*-* (postage) stamp.
fri'/minutt' *-et/*-en* (school) recess (cf /kvarter).
frimo'dig *A* - cheerful, confident; frank, outspoken: f-e ytringer plain talk.
+fri'/murer *-en, pl -e* (=*-ar) Freemason.
+fri'/mureri' *-et* Freemasonry.
fri'/plass *-en* tuition scholarship.
fri'/postig *A* - bold, forward.
fri'/rådig *A* - free, independent.
+fri'rådig/het *-en* (=*/skap) freedom, independence.
fri'se *-n/*-a* frieze.
+fri'ser *-en, pl -e* (=*-ar) Frisian.
frise'r/dame *-a/+-en* hairdresser, hair stylist.
frise're *V -te* do, set sby's hair.
frise'r/salong' *-en* beauty parlor, beauty shop.
fri'/sinn *-et* broad-mindedness, liberalism.
+fri'/sinnet *A* - (=*/sinna) broad-minded, liberal.
fri'sisk *A* - Frisian.
fris'k[1] *en*: på ny f- afresh, anew.
fris'k[2] *A* 1 healthy, well; hale, hearty: f- som en fisk fit as a fiddle. 2 fresh, new, unspoiled: f-t fra fatet freshly tapped. 3 cooling, refreshing: et f-t bad a r- bath. 4 cheerful, lively, vigorous: f- bris fresh breeze (19-24 mi. per hr.); f-t mot good cheer; f-e farger cheerful colors.
fris'ke *V -a/+-et* 1 refresh, revive; enliven, stimulate: f- opp brush up, jog one's memory; f- på ilden stir up the fire. 2 (of wind) blow more briskly, freshen; f- på (the same).
fris'k/fyr *-en* jaunty, sprightly fellow.
fris'kne *V -a/+-et* (of wind) blow more briskly, freshen.
fris'kus *-en* daring, devil-may-care person.
fri'/spark *-et* free kick, penalty kick (in soccer).
fri'/språk *-et* (=+/sprog): han har f- he can say what he likes.
fris't *-en* 1 deadline, time limit: 15. mai er siste f- May 15th is the final date. 2 extension, grace (period); delay, reprieve: fem minutters f- five-minute delay (warning).
*fri'/stad *-en* cf /sted
fri'/stat *-en* free state: Den irske f- the Irish F- S-.
+fris'te[1] *V -a/-et* (=*freiste[1]) tempt; coax: f- til kritikk invite criticism; f-es til å be t-ed to.
+fris'te[2] *V -et* cf freste
+fri'/sted *-et* (=*/stad) asylum, place of refuge, sanctuary.
+fris'telse *-n* temptation: falle i f- succumb to t-.
+fris'ter *-en, pl -e* tempter: f-en the devil.
frisy're *-n* hair style.
frisø'r *-en* barber; hairdresser.
fri'/ta *V infl as* ta excuse, exempt, release (for from).
+fri'/tagelse *-n* cf /taking
fri'/taing *-a/-en* cf /taking
*fri'/take *V infl as take* cf /ta
fri'/taking *-a/+en* exemption (for from).
fri'/talende *A* - blunt, plainspoken.
*fri'/teke *pp of* -ta (=*/teki)
+fri'/tenker *-en, pl -e* (=*-jar) freethinker.
fri'/tid *-a/+-en* leisure time, spare time.
fri'/tok *pt of* -ta
fritt' *nt of* fri[3]
+frit'te *V -a/-et* (=*frette) *archaic*: f- ut question; cross-examine.
fritt'/stående *A* - detached, isolated.
frity'r *N* shortening (grease, lard).
+frity'r/steike *V -te* (=*-je) fry in shortening (grease, lard).
fri'/vakt *-a/+-en naut.* off duty watch, watch below.
°friv'il *-en poet.* butterfly.
fri'/villig *A* - (=*/viljug) 1 of one's free will; voluntary. 2 *mil.* en f- volunteer; gå i krigen som f- enlist; f- hjelpemannskap civilian volunteers.
frivo'l *A* frivolous; immoral.
frivolite't *-en* frivolity; immorality.
frk. = frøken[1]
+fro' *A* - *archaic* cheerful, joyous.
fro'd *A* *archaic* learned, well-informed.
*fro'de[1] *-a* cf fråde[1]
fro'de[2] *V -a* cf fråde[2]
Fro'de *Prn (m)*
fro'dig *A* - lush, luxuriant, vigorous (growth); fertile, lively, prolific (e.g. imagination); buxom, full-blooded, full-bosomed.
+fro'dig/het *-en* lushness; fertility; buxomness: f- på ideer inventiveness, originality.
Frogn [frång'n] *Pln* twp, Akershus.
+fro'/kost *-en* (=*fru/) breakfast.
Fro'l *Pln* twp, Nord-Trøndelag.
Fro'/land *Pln* twp, Aust-Agder.
from' *A -t, pl -me* pious; gentle, meek: et f-t bedrag a pious fraud; et f-t ønske a vain wish.
froma'sj *-en* mousse.
fro'/messe *-a/+-en eccl.* early service.
+from'/het *-en* piety; gentleness, meekness.
+from'me *N*: på lykke og f- at random, haphazardly, hit or miss.
Fro'n *Pln* two twps in Oppland (cf Nord/, Sør/).
fron't *-en meteor., mil.* front: gjøre f- imot *fig.* unite against.
fronta'l *A* frontal.
fron't/glas *-et* (=+/glass) windshield.
fron't/lo'sje *-n* front box (in theater).
fron't/rute *-a/+-en* windshield.
+fro'/preken *-en eccl.* early service; matins.
*frose [frå'se] *pp of* fryse[1]
*frosen [frå'sen] *A -e/-i, pl -ne* cf frossen
*frosi [frå'si] *pp of* fryse[1]
fros'k *-en* 1 *zool.* frog (genus Rana). 2 *mus.* frog.
fros'ke/mann *-en, pl -menn/*-menner* frogman.
+fros'sen *A -ent, pl frosne* (=*frosen) frozen; frostbitten: f- av seg chilly, unable to keep warm.
+fros'sen/pinn *-en* cf fryse/
+fros'set *pp of* fryse[1]
fros't *-en* frost, cold; chill, frostbite.
Fros'ta *Pln* twp, Nord-Trøndelag.
fros'tal *A* sensitive to cold.
fros't/fri *A -tt* frostless; frostproof.

fros't/lenḍt *A* - exposed (to damage from frost).
fros'/rose *-a/⁺-en* ice flower (formed on a windowpane).
fros't/røyk *-en* frost mist.
⁺**fros't/vær** *-et* (=***/ver**) frosty weather.
frotté *-en* terry cloth.
frotté- *Pf* cf **frottér-**
frotte're *V -te* rub (down).
⁺**frottér/håndkle** [/hångkle] *-et* (=***/handḳle(de)**) bath towel.
fru *N* Mrs.; *hist.* Lady.
fru'e *-a/⁺-en* 1 married woman, wife: **Deres f-** your wife. 2 lady, mistress (of the house): **er f-n hjemme?** is the l- of the house in? 3 *hist.* lady: **vår f-** Our L-.
fru'e/kjole *-n* wife's dress (esp. of maternity dress).
⁺**fru'en/timmer** *-eret, pl -er/-timre hum.* female, woman.
⁺**fru'er/stue** *-n hist.* women's quarters in a castle.
***fru'/kost** *-en* cf **fro/**
fruk't *-a/⁺-en* fruit; *fig.* fruit, product, result (av of).
***fruk'tast** *V -ast* cf **frukte**
fruk't/bar *A* fertile, productive, rich: **f-t samarbeid** fruitful cooperation.
⁺**fruk'tbar/het** *-en* fertility, productivity.
⁺**fruk't/bringenḍe** *A* - productive, profitable.
⁺**fruk'te** *V -a/-et* (=***-ast**) avail, be of use.
⁺**fruk'tes/løs** *A* fruitless, futile, unavailing.
fruk't/graut *-en* (=⁺**/grøt**) stewed fruit.
fruk't/hage *-n* orchard.
fruk't/kniv *-en* fruit knife.
fruk't/sala·t *-en* fruit salad.
⁺**fruktsom'melig** *A* - pregnant: **gjøre f-** get with child.
fruk't/tre *-et, pl -/⁺-trær* fruit tree.
***fru'm** *A* 1 excellent, superior. 2 primitive.
***fru'me** *-n* benefit, gain: **på lukke og f-** at random, haphazardly, hit or miss.
***frun'se**[1] *-a* cf **frynse**[1]
***frun'se**[2] *V -a* cf **frynse**[2]
fry'd *-en* (=***frygd**) delight, joy, rapture.
fry'de *V -a/⁺-et* (=***frygde**) delight, gladden: **forandring f-er** variety is the spice of life; **f- seg (over, ved)** rejoice (in), delight, revel in; **det f-er meg** I'm delighted.
fry'de/full *A* joyful, joyous.
fry'de/rop *-et bibl.* cry of exultation, joy.
***fryg'd** *-a* cf **fryd**
***fryg'de** *V -a* cf **fryde**
fry'gisk *A* - Phrygian.
fryk't ⁺*-en*/**-a* apprehension, fear (for of): **nære f- for** be anxious about, have f- for.
⁺**fryktak'tig** *A* - timid.
⁺**fryk't/blanḍet** *A* - (=***-a**) apprehensive, fearful.
fryk'te *V -a/⁺-et* be afraid of, fear: **f- for** f- that.
fryk'telig *A* - 1 dreadful, horrible, terrible. 2 awfully, frightfully: **f- ensom** f- lonely.
⁺**fryk't/inngy'tenḍe** *A* - awe-inspiring, awesome.
fryk't/laus *A* (=⁺**/løs**) fearless, unafraid.
⁺**fryk't/som'** *A -t, pl -me* (=***/sam**) timid, timorous.
fryn'se[1] *-a* 1 fringe. 2 frayed edge.
fryn'se[2] *V -a/⁺-et* fray: **f- seg** get f-ed; **f- opp** f- (cloth to make a fringe).
fryn'set(e) *A* - 1 fringed. 2 frayed: **f- i kanten** f- edge.
fry'se[1] *V fraus/⁺frøs, ⁺frosset/*frose/*-i* be, feel cold; freeze: **jeg f-er** I'm cold; **f- fast** be frozen in (e.g. in the ice); f- up; **f- inne** be frozen in; **f- i hjel** f- to death; **f- på** form ice, f- over; **f- på hendene** have cold hands; **f- som en hund** be chilled clear through; **f- til f-** over, up.
⁺**fry'se**[2] *V -te* deepfreeze.
fry'se/boks *-en* freezer.
fry'se/disk *-en* display case (for frozen foods).
⁺**fry'se/pinn** *-en derog.* person who has trouble keeping warm.
fry'se/punkt [/pongt] *-et* freezing point.
⁺**fry'ser** *-en, pl -e* (=***-ar**) freezer.
fryseri' *-et, pl ⁺-er/*-* cold storage plant.
fry'se/rom [/romm] *-met/*-et* cold storage locker, refrigerator (e.g. in a meat packing plant or ship).
fry'se/væske *-a/⁺-en* antifreeze.
⁺**fry'sning** *-en* 1 freezing. 2 shiver, shudder.
°**fryv'il** *-en* cf **frivil**
fræ'g *A* 1 famed, renowned. 2 *dial.* excellent, first-rate.
fræg'd *-a* fame, renown; glory.
⁺**fræ'ge** *V -et* cf **frege**
Fræ'na *Pln* twp, Møre og Romsdal.
fræ'se *V -te* cf **frese**[1, 2]
***fræ'v** *A* germinative, productive.
***fræ've** *V -a* fecundate, fertilize: **f-seg** go to seed.
frø'[1] *-et* seed: **gå i f-** go to s-.
frø'[2] *V -dde*: **f- seg** (of seed) scatter, spread.
frø'/brøḍ *-et* white bread with poppy seed.
frø'/hus *-et bot.* pericarp.
frø'ken[1] *-na/⁺-enen, pl -ner* 1 unmarried woman, young lady; miss. 2 *fam.* (lady) teacher: **vår f- er frue** our teacher is married. 3 (often used in address) waitress.
frø'ken[2] *A -ent, pl -ne* 1 *hist.* dauntless, intrepid: **Fridtjof den f-ne** F- the Bold. 2 *dial.* plump; having a good appetite.
frø's[1] *-et* (esp. of horse) snort.
⁺**frø's**[2] *pt of* **fryse**[1]
frø'se *V -te* 1 (esp. of horse) snort. 2 spit like a cat. 3 (of whale) blow water.
⁺**frø'sen** *A -ent, pl -ne* 1 chilled, numbed with cold. 2 apprehensive, timid. 3 embarrassed, self-conscious.
frø'/tre *-et, pl -/⁺-trær* seed tree.
Frøy' *Prn myth.* ON god of fertility.
Frøy'a[1] *Pln* 1 island at the entrance of Trondheim Fjord. 2 island at the entrance of Nordfjord.
Frøy'a[2] *Prn myth.* ON goddess of love.
***frøy'e** *V -dde* foam, froth; lather.
***frøy'ne** *V -te* (esp. of horse) snort.
***frøy'se** *V -te* freeze, frostbite; be numb with cold.
frå' *P* (=⁺**fra**) 1 from: **f- for til akter** f- stem to stern; **f- grunnen av** radically, thoroughly; **f- Herodes til Pilatus** f- pillar to post; **f- neden (oven)** f- below (above); **f- seg** beside oneself, out of one's mind; **f- (min) side** on (my) part; **det gjør verken f- eller til** it makes no difference; **en øre f- eller til** an *øre* more or less; **langt f-** far f- it, not at all. 2 (of time) from, since: **f- (jeg kom)** f- the time when, s- (I came); **f- første stund** f- the very first; **f- i dag (av)** f- this day (on); **f- og med** as of, on and after; **f- tid til annen** f- time to time; **f- x av** f- x on (e.g. **f- da av** f- then on; **f- først av** f- the outset; **f- gammelt av** for a very long time); **like f-** ever s-. (For idioms with verbs: see these).
***frå-** *Pf* also cf **fra-**
⁺**frå'de**[1] *-n* foam, froth: **f-n står om munnen på ham** he's foaming at the mouth.
⁺**frå'de**[2] *V -a/-et* foam.
frå'/drag *-et* cf **fra/**
frå'/fall *-et* cf **fra/**
***frå'/halḍ** *-et* abstinence.
***frå'/halḍen** *A -e/-i, pl -ne* abstinent.
***frå'halḍs/mann** *-en, pl -menn(er)* teetotaler.
***frå'seg/gjord** [/jo'rd] *A -gjort* finished, terminated.
***frå'/segn** *-a* account, report.
frås'se *V -a/⁺-et* gorge, overeat: **f- i** revel in.
⁺**frås'ser** *-en, pl -e* (=***-ar**) glutton.
frås'sing *-a* gluttony, gorging oneself.
***frå'/stanḍ** *-en/-et* distance.
⁺**fråt'se** *V -a/-et* cf **fråsse**
⁺**fråt'ser** *-en, pl -e* cf **fråsser**
⁺**fråtseri'** *-et* cf **fråssing**
***frå'/verande** *A* - cf **fra/værende**
***frå'/vere** *-a* cf **fra/vær**
f. t. = **for tida/⁺tiden**
fu'ga *-en* cf **fuge**[2]
fu'ge[1] *-n* joint: **løsne i f-ne** get out of joint.
fu'ge[2] *-n mus.* fugue.
fu'ge[3] *V -a/⁺-et* fit together, join.
fug'l [*fug'l] *-en* bird; fowl: **det er verken f- eller fisk** it's neither fish nor f-; **det smaker av f-** it's better than nothing (of an imitation); **en sjelden f-** a rare person; **en fremmed f-** a stranger, strange creature.
fug'le/berg *-et* nesting cliff, rookery (esp. of seabirds).
fug'le/bryst *-et* 1 breast of fowl; bird's breast. 2 birdlike chest (on person).
fug'le/bur *-et* birdcage.
fug'le/fjell *-et* nesting cliff, rookery (esp. of seabirds).
fug'le/hunḍ *-en* bird dog.
fug'le/konge *-n zool.* golden-crested kinglet, wren (Regulus regulus).
fug'le/perspekti'v *-et* bird's-eye view.
fug'le/reir (=⁺**/rede**) *-et* bird's nest.
fug'le/skremme *-a* cf **/skremsel**
fug'le/skremsel *-elet/-let, pl ⁺-ler/*-el* scarecrow.
fug'le/unge [/onge] *-n* fledgling, nestling.
fug'le/vær *-et* rookery.
fuk's *-en* 1 bay, sorrel horse. 2 *archaic* dunce.
fuk'sia *-en bot.* fuchsia (genus Fuchsia).
fukt [fok't] *-a/⁺-en* humidity, moisture.
fukte [fok'te] *V -a/⁺-et* dampen, moisten: *hum.* **f- strupen** wet one's whistle; **hennes øyne f-es** *lit.* her eyes fill with tears.
fuktig [fok'ti] *A* - damp, humid, moist; dank.
⁺**fuktig/het** *-en* dampness, humidity; moisture.
fu'l *A* cunning, sly.
fu'las *-en* sly, wily person; malicious person.
⁺**ful'gte** *pt of* **følge**[3]
fu'ling *-en* sly, wily person; malicious person.
full' *A* 1 full; complete, replete: **f-storm** whole gale; **f-e to år** a f- two years; **den f- sannhet** the whole truth; **f-t opp (av)** f- (of); plenty (of); **av f-t hjerte** with all one's heart; **for f- hals** at the top of one's lungs; **i f-t mål** f-ly, in f-; **ta munnen for f-** exaggerate, overstate; *(adv.)* **f-t** completely, fully; **ikke f-t (så)** not quite (as); **like f-t** anyway, just the same; **f-t ut** f-y, in f-; all out, full steam. 2 (of persons) drunk: **drikke seg (en) f-** get (sby) d-.
***ful'la** *Av* surely, undoubtedly; I suppose.
⁺**full'/befa'ren** *A -ent, pl -ne* able-bodied (seaman); experienced (person).
full'/blods [/blot's] *A* - 1 full-blooded; thoroughbred: **f-/hest** thoroughbred (horse). 2 *fig.* inveterate, out-and-out.
⁺**full'/bringe** *V -brakte, -brakt*: **fullbrakt** accomplished; *bibl.* **det er fullbrakt** it is finished (John 19,30).

⁺ Bokmål; * Nynorsk; ° Dialect.
After letter: ' stress (Acc. 1); ` tone, stress (Acc. 2); · length.
Below letter: . not pronounced.

+full'/byrde V -et accomplish, complete, consummate: dommen er f-et the sentence has been carried out.

+full'/båren A -ent/-et, pl -ne (=*/boren) fully developed.

+ful'le N: til f- fully, in full.

full'/enḍe V +-te/*-a complete, finish.

+full'/enḍt A - complete, perfect; thorough: vel begynt er halv f- well begun is half done.

*ful'les N cf fulle

full'/før A thoroughly qualified; completely suitable.

full'/føre V -te carry out, execute, see (sth) through; complete: f- et løp stay the route (as in a long distance race); f- en setning finish one's sentence.

+full'/førelse -n (=*-ing) accomplishment; completion (av of).

*full'/gilḍ A valid.

full'/goḍ A adequate, convincing, satisfactory: f- med on a par with.

full'/kommen [also -kåm'-] A +-ent, pl -komne (=*/komen) complete, perfect; absolute, utter: f- frisk p-ly well.

+full'kommen/het -en (=*/skap) perfection.

full'/lasta A (=+-et) fully loaded, loaded to the brim.

full'/makt -a/+-en power of attorney, proxy; credentials: gi f- til authorize, empower; ha f- be authorized.

fullmek'tig -en 1 agent, proxy. 2 (administrative) assistant; jur. law clerk.

full'/moden A -ent, pl -ne fully ripened; mature.

full'/måne -n full moon.

*full'nad -en adequacy, sufficiency: til f-s fully, in full.

*full'/nøye V -nøgde, -nøgt gratify, satisfy.

full'/pakka A - (=+-et) crammed, packed.

+full'/rigger -en, pl -e (=*-ar) naut. full-rigged ship.

*full'/rådd A - : f- på (firmly) decided on.

+full'/satt A - (=*/sett) fully occupied, jammed (av by); covered, decked (med by).

full'/skap -en drunkenness, intoxication.

+full'/skjegg -et (full) beard.

°full'/sku(v)enḍes A - (=°/skurende(s)) 1 sufficient; ample. 2 able-bodied, vigorous.

full'/stappa A - (=+-et) cram-full, overflowing.

fullsten'dig̣ A - complete, entire; perfect.

+fullsten'dig̣/gjøre V -gjorde, -gjort complete, make complete.

full'/takke V -a/+-et: kan ikke f- can't thank enough.

+full'/tallig̣ A - complete; attended by all members (e.g. of a committee).

+full'/tegnet [/teinet] A - (=*/teikna) merc. fully subscribed.

+full'/treffer -en, pl -e (=*-ar) mil. bull's-eye; direct hit.

*full'/vaksen A -e/-i, pl -ne cf /voksen

*full'/vel Av fully, in full.

full'/verdig̣ A - of full value, sterling.

+full'/voksen A -ent, pl -ne full-grown.

*fu'l/skap -en cunning, slyness.

fumle [fom'le] V -a/+-et cf fomle

fummel [fom'mel] -elen, pl -ler cf fommel

fun'ḍ -et cf funn

fundamen't -et, pl -/+-er foundation, base; fig. basis.

fundamenta'l A basic, fundamental.

fundamente're V -te lay the foundation (for a building).

funda's -en charter; articles of incorporation.

funde're V -te 1 base, found, ground: en dårlig f-t påstand an ill-founded assertion. 2 merc. consolidate, fund: f-t gjeld f-ed (permanent) debt. 3 meditate, ponder: f- på intend to, reflect on; mull over.

funde'ring -a/+-en meditation, pondering, speculation.

fungere [fungge're] V -te act, officiate (som as); function, work: f-ende sekretær a-ing secretary.

+fun'ke -n spark.

fun'kis -en arch. functionalistic (architecture), functionalism = modernistic, modernism.

fun'kis/hus -et modernistic house.

+fun'kis/møbler pl (=*-lar) modernistic furniture.

fun'kis/stil -en functionalistic, modernistic style.

+fun'kle V -et glitter, sparkle.

funksjo'n -en function (av of): i f- at work, operating.

funksjonalis'me -n arch., psych. functionalism.

funksjonell' A -elt functional.

funksjone're V -te function.

funksjonæ'r -en employee; functionary; officer, official (i of).

funn' -et discovery, find (av of): gjøre et f- make a f-; boka er et f- the book is a f- (a treasure).

*fun'ne pp of finne[5]

fun'nen A +-et, pl -e: kontor for f-e saker lost and found department.

+fun'nes pp of finnes

*fun'nest pp of finnast

+fun'net pp of finne[5]

*fun'ni pp of finne[5]

*fun'nist pp of finnast

fura'sje -n fodder, forage.

furasje're V -te secure forage.

*fu'rḍe[1] -a astonishment, surprise.

*fu'rḍe[2] V -a be astonished, surprised (på at): f-ast (the same).

*fu'rḍeleg A - astonishing, singular, strange.

+fu're[1] -n 1 furrow. 2 groove, track. 3 line, wrinkle (in the face).

*fu're[2] -a cf furu

+fu're[3] V -a/-et/-te furrow; groove.

°fu're[4] V -a/-te cf furde[2]

furér -en hist., mil. quartermaster sergeant.

+fu'ret(e) A - furrowed; deeply lined, wrinkled (face): f-, værbitt f-, weathered (of Norway, in national anthem by Bjørnson).

fu'rie -a/+-en 1 myth. Fury. 2 shrew, virago.

furne're V -te furnish (med with).

Fu'r/nes Pln twp, Hedmark.

furo're -n furore: gjøre f- be all the rage, cause a sensation.

fur'te V -a/+-et pout, sulk.

fur'te/krok -en 1 corner in which sulking children are made to stand. 2 pouting, sulky person.

fur'ten A +-ent, pl -ne pouting, sulky.

fu'ru -a (=*fure[2]) pine, esp. Scotch pine (Pinus silvestris); pinewood.

fu'ru/bar -et pine needles.

fu'ru/mo -en pine barren.

fu'runåls/bad -et med. bath to which an extract of pine needles is added (used medicinally in dermatology).

fu'ru/skog -en pine forest.

fu'ru/tre -et pine (tree): f-s bord table of pinewood.

fu's A eager, keen.

Fu'sa Pln twp, Hordaland.

fu'se V -te be impetuous: f- på storm along.

fu'sel -en raw (inferior) spirits, (pop.) rotgut; fusel oil.

fu'sen/tast -en derog. enthusiast, fantast, visionary.

fusjo'n -en merc. merger.

fus'k -et 1 bungling; dabbling, tinkering. 2 cheating (at cards, in an examination): f- og fanteri hanky-panky, trickery.

fus'ke V -a/+-et 1 botch, bungle: f- i, med dabble in; f- i faget be a jack of all trades (and master of none). 2 cheat (at cards, in an examination).

+fus'ker -en, pl -e (=*-ar) 1 bungler; dabbler. 2 cheat; cardsharp.

fusta'sje -n cask: en f- vin a c- of wine.

fu't -en cf fogd

futt' -en life, sparkle (e.g. in champagne); animation, energy, (pop.) go, spunk (i in).

fut'te V -a/+-et crackle; sparkle.

futtera'l -et, pl -/+-er case, cover.

*fu'tul -en fetter, hobble.

futuris'me -n futurism.

futuris'tisk A - futuristic.

futu'rum -et gram. future.

fy' I ugh!, whew! (what a smell); fie, shame (reproach): fy da for shame; fy fan (strong oath); fy skamme deg shame on you.

*fy'k[1] -en 1 =fyk[2]. 2 dial. horse-drawn hay rake.

fy'k[2] -et 1 haste, hurry: få f- be rushed away; i et (en) f- og fei in a jiffy. 2 drift (of anything); drifting, whirling snow; spray.

fy'ke V fauk/+føk, +føket/*foke/*-i 1 (of wind) blow, sweep; (of e.g. sand, snow, sparks) fly: f- i vei dash off; f- opp flare up, (pop.) fly off the handle. 2: f-ende dashing, flying, rushing; i f-ende fart with lightning speed, (pop.) like greased lightning; (adv.) f-ende sint furious, in a towering rage.

+fyl'de -n cf fylle[1]

+fyl'dest -en cf fyllest

fyl'dig A - 1 copious, complete, full; buxom, plump, well-rounded, (pop.) stacked. 2 full-bodied, rich (e.g. wine). 3 naut. bluff-bowed.

+fyl'dig/het -en 1 copiousness; plumpness. 2 body.

*fyl'gd -a cf følgd

fyl'gje[1] -a folk. attendant spirit in animal form; female guardian spirit.

*fyl'gje[2] -a cf følge[1]

*fyl'gje[3] -t cf følgje[2]

*fyl'gje[4] V -de cf følgje[3]

fyl'ke[1] -t, pl +-r/*- 1 county (called amt before 1918). 2 hist. (tribal) district.

fyl'ke[2] V -a/+-et/-te hist. array, draw up (in battle array): f- seg array oneself for battle; f- seg (rundt) rally (round).

fyl'kes/mann -en, pl -menn/*-menner 1 chief administrative officer of a fylke (about=county prefect, district governor). 2 hist. native of a county, district.

+fyl'kes/orḍfører -en, pl -e (=*-ar) chairman of the fylkesting.

fyl'kes/ting -et chief administrative body of a fylke (consisting of township mayors, meeting annually for tax and fiscal purposes), ab.= county board.

fyl'king -a/+-en hist., mil. battle line, phalanx: fig. en hel f- a whole army.

*fyl'kje V -te cf fylke[2]

fyll'[1] -a drinking, drunkenness: på f-a on a spree; f- er ikke fest drinks don't make a party (slogan of temperance movement).

fyll'[2] -a/+-et 1 fill, rubble. 2 padding, stuffing, filling.

fyl'le[1] +-n/*-a (=+fylde) 1 abundance, copiousness, wealth (av of). 2 fullness; plumpness; body. 3 bibl.: i tidens f- in the fullness of time (Gal. 4,4).

fyl'le[2] V fylte, fylt 1 fill (e.g. a bag, a tooth); cram, stuff; blow up, inflate; fill up, take up room (space): f- ens plass fill (take) sby's place; f- noe igjen refill sth; f- igjen et hull fill up a hole; f- i sekker bag (e.g. potatoes); f- med inflate, fig. imbue with; f- med redsel frighten half to death, out of one's wits; f- opp clutter up; pad out (e.g. an essay, a speech); f- på fill up (e.g. gasoline); f- ut fill in (a form; the details of a story). 2 complete (a certain age): f- tyve år reach twenty, turn twenty.

fyl'le[3] V -a/+-et drink and carouse, (pop.) booze it up, go barhopping.

fyl'le/arres't -en cell for drunks, (pop.) cooler, drunk tank.

+fyl'le/bøtte -a (=*/bytte) drunkard, (pop.) boozer, guzzler, souse.
fyl'le/fant -en drunkard, sot.
fyl'le/kalk -en filler, padding (esp. fig.).
+fyl'le/kjører -en, pl -e (=*-ar, */køyrar) drunken driver.
fyl'le/penn -en fountain pen.
+fyl'leri -et drinking, drunkenness.
fyl'le/sjuk A hung over.
+fyl'lest [also fyl'-] -en satisfaction: **gjøre f-** be satisfactory, meet (satisfy) all requirements; **gjøre god f- for seg** acquit oneself well.
+fyl'lest/gjørende A - adequate, satisfactory.
fyl'lik -en drunkard, sot.
fyl'ling -a 1 filling, padding; (of a tooth) filling. 2 tech. cut-off (in engine). 3 panel (in door or cupboard). 4 (in road-building) fill; (garbage) dump.
***fyl'lug** A - cf **fyldig**
fyl'te pt of **fylle**[2]
Fy'n Pln Funen (island in Southern Denmark).
fyn'd +-en/+-et/*-a pith, vigor: **med f- og klem** powerfully, with a will.
***fyn'de/heim** -en: **frå f-en** from time immemorial.
fyn'dig A - pithy, terse, to the point.
fyn'd/o'rd -et aphorism, terse, pointed expression.
fy'r[1] -en 1 fire: **sette f- på** set f- to; **ta f-** catch f-; fig. **være f- og flamme** be all enthusiasm. 2 naut., tech. furnace: **friske på f-en(e)** stoke the fire(s).
fy'r[2] -en fellow, (pop.) guy; fam. boy friend.
fy'r[3] +-et/*-en lighthouse; (traffic) light.
fy'r/aben -en (=+/abend) free time: **arbeide på f-** work on one's own time; have work on the side.
fy'raben(d)s/arbeid -et work on the side; leisure time occupation.
+fy'r/bøter -en, pl -e (=*-ar) fireman, stoker.
fy're V -te 1 fire, light; stoke: **f- opp** l- a fire; **f- under** add fuel, stoke. 2 fire (off) a gun: **f- løs på** f- rapidly at, pepper; fig. **f- løs** f- away.
***fy're-** Pf cf **føre-**
Fy'res/dal Pln twp, Telemark.
fy'r/fat -et brazier, chafing dish.
fy'rig [also fyr'ri] A - ardent, fervent, fiery; frisky, spirited.
+fy'rig/het -en ardor, fervor, spirit.
fy'rings/olje -a/-en fuel oil.
fy'r/liste -a naut. lighthouse list.
***fyrr'** P, C cf **før**[2]
fy'r/rom [/romm] -met/*-et boiler room, furnace room, naut. stokehold.
fy'r/skip -et lightship.
fyr'st[1] N prince (as title): **f- Rainier av Monaco** p- R- of M-.
***fyr'st**[2] A - cf **først**
fyr'ste -n prince; sovereign: bibl. **denne verdens f-** the p- of this world (=the devil) (John 16,11).
***fyr'ste-** Pf cf **første-**
fyr'ste/dømme -t (=*/døme, +fyrsten/) principality.
fyr'ste/kake -a (confectioners') cake with macaroon filling.
fyr'stelig A - 1 princely, royal. 2 lavish, sumptuous: **more seg f-** have a grand time.
***fyr'sten** N cf **førsten**
fyr'/stikke -a (=+/stikk) match: **har De en f-?** can you give me a light?.
fyr'stikk/eske -a/+-en matchbox.
fyrstin'ne -a/+-en princess: **f- Grace** p- G-.
***fyr'stning** -a cf **førstning**
***fyr'/stundes** Av at first, in the beginning.
fy'r/stål -et hist. steel (used with flint to start a fire).
+fy'r/tøy -et hist. tinderbox.
fy'r/tå'rn -et lighthouse.
***fy'rug** A - cf **fyrig**
***fy'r/vaktar** -en cf **/vokter**
***fy'r/verk** -et cf **/verkeri**
fy'r/verkeri' [also -ri'] -et, pl +-er/*- (=*/verk) fireworks, fireworks display.
+fy'r/vesen -et lighthouse service of the Coast Guard.
+fy'r/vokter -en, pl -e (head) lighthouse keeper.
fy'sak -en derog., hum. fellow, man, (pop.) guy.
***fy'se**[1] -a desire; delight, pleasure.
fy'se[2] V -te desire, have a desire for.
fy'se/mat -en delicacy, tidbit.
fy'sen A +-ent, pl -ne eager, hungry, longing (**på** for).
fysika'lsk A - physical: **f- kjemi** p- chemistry.
+fy'siker -en, pl -e (=*-ar) physicist.
fysikk' -en physics.
fy'sikus -en city health officer, city medical officer.
fysiognomi' -en/+-et physiognomy.
fysiokra't -en physiocrat.
fysiokra'tisk A - physiocratic.
fysiolog [-olå'g] -en physiologist.
fysiologi' -en physiology.
fysiologisk [-olå'g-] A - physiological.
fy'sio/terapi' -en physiotherapy.
fy'sisk A - bodily, physical: **i f- henseende** in a p- sense, p-ly.
fysj' I hum. fie, shame; whew.
***fy'sne** -a bliss, transport of joy.
***fys'se** V -te cascade, gush.
fæ'l [usu. +fe'l] A awful, terrible; disgusting, horrid, nasty: **være f- i munnen** talk dirty; **f- mot** mean to (sby); **f-t til vær** awful weather; **f- til å** (overly) given to, inclined to; **f-t** (adv.) awfully, terribly; **f-t ubehagelig** very unpleasant.
fæ'le[1] -a fear; terror: ***ta f-** be horror-struck, terrified; take fright.
fæ'le[2] V -te be afraid, frightened (**for** at).
fæ'len A +-ent, pl -ne alarmed, frightened; creepy, scary.
fæ'lende Av: **f- fort** at breakneck speed.
fæ'lske -a/-en fright, horror, terror.
fæ'lslig A - awful, fearful; creepy, frightening: ***ein slik f- klump i bringa** such an a- lump in one's breast (Vesaas).
***fæ'r** pr of **få**[1]
Fær'der Pln cf **Ferder**
fæ'ring -en 1 (four- or six-oared) boat. 2 Faroese.
fær're cp of **få**[3]
fær'rest sp of **få**[3]
°fæ'rt A nt of **fæl**
+Fæ'r/øyene Pln (=*-ane) The Faroe Islands.
fæ'r/øying -en Faroese.
fæ'r/øysk A - Faroese.
fø' V -dde (=føde[1]) 1 feed, nourish; maintain, support: **f- fram, på** keep, raise, rear (esp. animals). 2 (usu. **føde**) bear, give birth to; bring forth: **man fødes dikter** poets are born, not made.
fø'de[1] [*fø'e] -a/+-en food, nourishment: **arbeide for f-n** work for a living; **fast f-** solid food, nourishment.
fø'de[2] [*fø'e] V -de/+-te cf **fø**
fø'de/bygd -a birthplace, home community (rural).
***fø'de/flekk** -en cf **fø/**
+fø'de/hjem [/jem'] -met maternity home.
fø'de/middel -elet/-midlet, pl +-midler/*-el foodstuff.
føderasjo'n -en federation; federal state.
fød'erativ A federal.
fø'de/råd -et pension paid to owner of estate, farm (after cession to heirs).
fø'deråds/bygning -en pensioner's cottage, house.
+fø'de/vann -et tech. feedwater.
fø'de/venti'l -en tech. check valve.
-føding -en e.g. **heimf-**.
***fø'dnad** -en winter feeding.
fød'sel [føt'sel] -elen, pl -ler birth: **kvele i f-en** nip in the bud; **norsk av f-** born in Norway.
fød'sels/dag -en birthday.
fød'selsdags/ba'rn -et person whose birthday is being celebrated.
fød'sels/hjelp -a/+-en 1 obstetric aid; midwifery. 2 obstetrician; midwife.
+fød'sels/tang -a, pl -tenger (=*/tong) obstetric forceps.
fød'sels/år -et birth date, year of birth.
***føds'le** -a cf **fødsel**
født' pp of **fø**
fø'/flekk -en, pl *-er birthmark.
+fø'k pt of **fyke**
fø'l -et (=+føll) colt, foal.
+fø'l/bar A noticeable, perceptible.
+fø'le V -te 1 feel; perceive, sense: **f- avsky** detest, be disgusted, f- aversion (**for** at, to); **f- trang** f- like, f- inclined (**til** to); **få å f-** find, learn to one's cost; **f-es varm** f-s hot (to the touch). 2 (with prep. and adv.): **f- det på seg** have a feeling, have a hunch; **f- en på tennene** sound sby out, (pop.) give sby the once over; **f- for, med en** f- (sorry) for sby, sympathize with sby; **f- på noe** f- sth (e.g. the pulse). 3 (refl.): **f- seg** feel; **f- seg bra** f- fine; **f- seg ferdig** f- all done in, completely exhausted; **f- seg fram (for)** f-, grope one's way; **f- seg heime** f- at home; **f- seg liten** f- cheap, (pop.) f- like thirty cents; **f- seg litt rar** have a funny feeling; **f- seg nedfor** f- depressed, (pop.) have the blues; **f- seg trygg** f- safe; **f- seg uvel** f- ill.
+fø'le/ho'rn -et zool. antenna, feeler, tentacle: hum. **trekke f-ene til seg** pull in one's horns.
+fø'lelig A - 1 noticeable, perceptible. 2 serious, severe (e.g. loss).
+fø'lelse -n feeling (=sensation, touch; emotion, sentiment) (**av** of): **ha det på f-n** have a hunch; **med f-** feelingly; **f- for** a f- for (e.g. art).
+fø'lelses/beto'nt A - emotional, with emotional overtones.
+fø'lelses/liv -et emotional makeup; emotional life.
+fø'lelses/løs A insensible, numb; callous, unfeeling.
+fø'lelses/messig A - emotional, sentimental.
+fø'lelses/sak -a/-en emotional matter, matter of feeling.
+fø'ler -en, pl -e 1 zool. antenna, feeler. 2 fig. feeler, hint.
+fø'leri -et derog. emotionalism, sentimentality.
***føl'gd** -a 1 company: **halde f- med** keep pace with. 2 consequence (**av** of). 3 order, succession: **i same f-** respectively.
+føl'ge[1] -n consequence, result (**av** of): **ha til f-** entail, result in; **ta f-ne** take the c-s.
+føl'ge[2] -t cf **følgje**[2]
+føl'ge[3] V fulgte, fulgt cf **følgje**[3]
+føl'ge/brev -et cf **følgje/**
+føl'gelig Av accordingly, consequently, therefore.
+følgende A - following, next: **i (under) det f-** after that, then; **jeg foreslår f-** I propose the f-; **side 25 ff. (=f-)** page 25 ff. (and following).
+føl'ge/riktig A - consistent, logical.
+føl'ge/skap -et company: **i f- med** together with.
+føl'ge/skriv -et (=+/skrivelse) cf **følgje/**
+føl'ge/svenn -en attendant, companion, follower; archaic squire.
***føl'gje**[1] -a cf **følge**[1]
føl'gje[2] -t (=+følge[2]) company; (funeral) cortege; escort, retinue: **gjøre en f-, gi seg i f- med en, slå f- med en** accompany sby, go with; **holde f- med** keep up with; **i f- (med)** together (with).
føl'gje[3] V +-te/*-de (=+følge[3]) 1 fol-

+ Bokmål; * Nynorsk; ° Dialect.
After letter: ' stress (Acc. 1); ` tone, stress (Acc. 2); · length.
Below letter: . not pronounced.

low, succeed: **f- en politikk** pursue a policy; **f- ens råd** take sby's advice; **f- forelesninger** attend lectures (at a university); **f- som en skygge** shadow, trail; **det f-er av at** it is the result of; **det f-er av seg selv** it's a matter of course, it goes without saying. 2 accompany, go with: **f- en hjem** see sby home; **f- en til døra (ut)** see sby out; **f-es (at)** go together, keep company. 3 (with *prep.* and *adv.*): **f- etter** follow, succeed; **f- med** be attentive, listen carefully; keep up, keep pace with; keep informed, well posted; be included, go with; result from, attend on; accompany.

føl'gje/brev *-et* blank accompanying packages in mail, containing sender's and addressee's names and addresses.

føl'gje/rett *A* - logical, consistent.

***føl'gje/skap** *-en* cf **følge/**

føl'gje/skriv *-et* accompanying (covering) letter.

***føl'gje/streng** *A* logical, consistent.

+**fø'ling** *-en* 1 *mil.* contact (**med** with): *fig.* **få (ha) f- med** get (have) contact with; experience. 2 communion, sympathy.

føljetong' *-en* serial.

+**føll'** *-et* cf **føl**

+**føl'le** *V -a/-et* foal.

+**fø'l/som'** *A -t, pl -me* sensitive; emotional, sentimental.

fø'n *-en* 1 *meteor.* foehn (dry thaw wind). 2 (process of) hand drying and waving (hair).

fø'ne *V -te* hand-dry and wave (hair).

+**føni'ker** *-en, pl -e* (=*-**ar**) Phoenician.

Føni'kia *Pln* Phoenicia.

føni'kisk *A* - Phoenician.

fø'niks *-en* phoenix.

fø'n/vind *-en meteor.* foehn (dry thaw wind).

fø'r[1] *A* 1 able, capable (**til** of). 2 corpulent, plump, stout. *3 (of a road) passable.

fø'r[2] *P, C* 1 *(adv.* and *prep.)* before; previous(ly), prior (to): **f- eller senere** sooner or later; **f- i tiden** formerly; **jo f- jo heller (bedre)** the sooner the better; **f- hadde jeg** I used to have; **ikke f- var han kommet, så** no sooner had he come, than. 2 *(adv.)* rather: (in contrasting statements) **f- vil jeg . . . enn** I'd sooner . . . than. 3 *(conj.)* before: **f- jeg kom** b- I came.

***fø'r/dagen** *df* day before yesterday.

***fø'r/dags** *Av* up to now: **i f-** day before yesterday.

Før'de *Pln* 1 twp, Sogn og Fjordane. 2 post office, Vikebygd twp, Hordaland.

fø're[1] *-t* (condition of) roads; snow conditions (for skiing etc.): **glatt f-** slippery road; **godt f-** good skiing; **tungt f-** heavy going.

fø're[2] *V -te* 1 conduct, guide, lead; drive (a car); command (e.g. a regiment); lead (partner in dance). 2 bring, carry, transport (goods); move (e.g. one's hand): **f- sverd** bear a sword. 3 *merc.* carry, stock (a brand, goods); keep (books etc.): **f- dagbok** k- a diary. 4 carry on, lead (e.g. one's life, negotiations). 5 (idioms with nouns): **f- bevis** furnish proof (**for** of); **f-bøker** keep books; **f- dannet tale** speak in a cultivated way; **f- hus** keep house; **f- klage** lodge a complaint; **f- kontroll med** check, exercise control over; **f- krig** wage war; **f- ordet** speak, be the spokesman; **f- pennen** wield the pen; **f- sak (mot)** bring suit (against); **f- en samtale** carry on a conversation; **f- det store ord** lay down the law; **f- vitner** call witnesses. 6 (with *prep.* and *adv.*): **f- à jour** bring up to date; **f- an** lead the way, take the initiative, set (fashions); **f- bort** take away, remove; **f- for vidt** go too far; lead too far afield; **f- inn** bring; lead in; enter (in a ledger etc.); **f- med seg** cause, entail, lead to; **f- opp (på)** enter (on) (e.g. a bill, an account); **f- sammen** bring together; **f- til** lead to, result in; **f- tilbake til** lead, trace back to. 7 *(refl.)*: **f- seg** behave, conduct oneself.

fø're[3] *Av* (=+**fore**[4]) 1 before; in front: **bedre f- var enn etter snar** look before you leap, a stitch in time saves nine; **ha noe f-** have sth to do, be at work on sth. 2 (with *refl. verbs*): **gjøre seg f- (med)** put on airs, take special pains (with); **legge seg f- (på et sted)** settle down, stay (at a place); **se seg f-** be careful, cautious; **sette seg noe f-** take sth on; **spørre seg f-** ask for directions, make inquiries.

fø're[4] *P* before: **f- jul** b- Christmas.

føre- *Pf* before, fore-, pre-.

***fø're/arbeid** *-et* cf **for/**

***fø're/be'ls** *Av* preliminary, provisional.

***fø're/bilete** *-t* cf **for/bilde**

***fø're/bod** [/bå] *-et* cf **for/bud**[2]

***fø're/bu** *V -dde* prepare; make preparations for.

fø're/dugurd *-en* (early) breakfast.

***fø're/døme** *-t* example, model (**på** of).

fø're/fall *-et* bad road (snow) conditions (due to spring thaw).

***fø're/falle** *V infl as* **falle** cf **fore/**

***fø're/ferd** [/fær] *-a* omen, portent.

***fø'regangs/mann** *-en, pl -menn(er)* cf **fore-**

***fø're/gjerd** [/jær] *-a* preparation; precaution, prevention.

***fø're/gripe** *V -greip, -gripe/-i* cf **fore/**

***fø're/gåande** *A* - cf **fore/gående**

fø're/hand *-a* cf **for/hånd**

***fø're/havande** *-t* cf **fore/havende**

fø'rejuls/vinter *-eren, pl -rer* early winter (prior to Christmas).

***fø're/kjensle** *-a* presentiment.

***fø're/legg** *-et* cf **fore/**

***fø're/lesar** *-en* cf **fore/leser**

***fø're/lese** *V -las, -lese/-i* cf **fore/**

***fø're/les(n)ing** *-a* cf **fore/**

***fø're/loge** [/låge] *-a* duty, task; problem.

***fø're/mann** *-en, pl -menn(er)* cf **for/**

***fø're/middag** *-en* cf **for/**

fø're/monn *-en* (=*/**mon**, +**for/monn**) advantage, benefit, profit.

***fø're/mæling** *-a* 1 recommendation; reference. 2 preface.

***fø're/mål** *-et* cf **for/**

fø'r/enn *C* before.

***fø're/o'rd** *-et* cf **for/**

+**fø'rer** *-en, pl -e* (=*-**ar**) 1 chief, commander, leader; (of a ship) captain, skipper; chauffeur, driver. 2 guide; guidebook: **F- for Oslo og omegn** G- to Oslo and Surroundings.

***fø're/rett**[1] *-en* cf **for**[1]/

***fø're/rett**[2] *-en* cf **for**[2]/

+**fø'rer/hus** *-et* (=*-**ar/**) driver's cab (on train, truck).

***fø're/rit** *-et* blank, form.

+**fø'rer/kort** *-et* (=*-**ar/**) driver's license.

+**fø'rer/skap** *-et* (=*-**ar/**) leadership.

+**fø'rer/stilling** *-a/-en* position of leadership.

***fø're/segn** [/sengn] *-a* regulation, rule.

***fø're/setnad** *-en* cf **forut/setning**

***fø're/sett** *ein* cf **fore/satt**

***fø're/slå** *V infl as* **slå** cf **fore/**

***fø're/songar** *-en* cf **for/sanger**

***fø're/spel** *-et* cf **for/spill**

***fø're/spurnad** *-en, pl -er* cf **fore/-spørsel**

***fø're/stelling** *-a* cf **fore/stilling**

***fø're/sviv** *-et* vague idea.

***fø're/tak** *-et* cf **fore/**

***fø're/teljing** *-a* persuasion.

***fø're/tenkt** *A* - considerate, thoughtful; foresighted.

***fø're/veg** *-en* cf **for/vegen**

***fø're/vis** *A* clairvoyant, having previous knowledge of.

***fø're/åt** *Av* ahead; beforehand, in advance.

fø'r/histo'risk [also **fø'r/**] *A*- (=+**for/**) prehistoric.

***fø'rig** *A* - able-bodied, well.

fø'ring *-a/+-en* 1 handling, transport (**av** of). 2 cargo, load. 3 *tech.* guide, regulator. 4 *dial.* gift.

fø'rings/båt *-en naut.* (small) cargo vessel, lighter.

fø'rjuls/vinter *-eren, pl -rer* cf **føre/**

før'kje *-a derog.* or *dial.* girl.

fø'r/krigs *A* - prewar.

+**fø'r/laten** *A -ent, pl -ne* stout.

***fø'r/leik** *-en* 1 fitness, health, vigor. 2 ability, skill. 3 stoutness.

fø'r/lemma *A* - (=+**-et**) heavy-limbed.

fø'rlig *A* - able-bodied, fit, sound.

+**fø'rlig/het** *-en* 1 health, vigor; (full) use of one's limbs. 2 size, thickness.

***fø'rnad** *-en* baggage, luggage.

+**fø'r/nevnt** *A* - above mentioned, referred to above.

før're *A* - former, previous; last.

før'sel *-elen, pl -ler* (=***førsle**[1]) hauling, supply; transport (usu. in *cpds*: **inn/, til/, ut/**).

før'sels/skute *-a* (=***førsle/**) supply ship.

før'sels/veg *-en* (=+**/vei**, ***førsle/**) supply route.

***før'sle**[1] *-a* cf **førsel**

før'sle[2] *V -a/+-et* transport (esp. by means of pack animals).

***før'sle/veg** *-en* cf **førsels/**

før'st *A* - (=***fyrst**[2]) 1 first, initial; *(adv.)* first(ly), at first, initially: **f- på dagen (sommeren, i juni osv.)** early in the day (summer, June, etc.); **for det f-e** in the first place; for the time being; **fra f- av** from the outset, originally; **fra f- til sist** from beginning to end; **med det f-e** shortly, soon; **det (den) f-e, det (den) beste** any old thing (person), the first that comes along; **en av de f-e dagene** one of the next few days. 2 not until; only: **f- nå** o- now; **f- når** not until, o- when; **når f-** now that; **han kom f- i går** he didn't come until (only got here) yesterday; **han kommer f- i morgen** he's not coming until tomorrow.

første- *Pf* (the) first.

før'stedags/stempel *-elet/-let, pl -el/+-ler* first-day cover.

før'ste/fioli'n *-en* (=***fyrste/**) first violin.

før'stefødsels/rett *-en* (right of) primogeniture.

+**før'ste/født** *A* - (=*/**fødd**) first-born, oldest.

+**før'ste/grøde** *-a/-en* first fruits (cf Deut. 18,4).

før'ste/hands *A* - direct, firsthand.

før'ste/hjelp *-a/+-en* first aid.

+**før'ste/hånds** *A* - cf **/hands**

før'ste/klasses *A* - first-class.

før'ste/mann *-en* first man (e.g. to fly the Atlantic); firstcomer; best, most capable person: **f- i klassen** top student in the class.

før'sten *N* (=***fyrsten**): **i f-** at the outset, from the beginning.

før'ste/rangs *A* - first-class, first-rate.

+**før'stereis/gutt** *-en* (=*/**gut**) *naut.* seaman making his first voyage.

før'ste/rett *-en* first (prior) claim, priority (**til** to).

før'ste/styrmann *-en naut.* first mate.

før'st/kommende *A* - (=*/**komande**) next.

+**før'st/nevnte** *A* - (of two) first mentioned, former.

før'stning *-a/+-en* (=***fyrstning**): **i f-en** at first.

før'ti *Num* forty.

før'ti/del *-en* one fortieth, a fortieth part.

før'tiende *Num* fortieth.

***fø'te** *V -a*: **f- seg** advance step by step.

***fø'ter** *pl of* **fot**

-føtt *A* - -footed (e.g. **bar/, lett/, snar/**).

+**føt'ter** *pl of* **fot**

føy' *I* ugh!; whew! (expression of disgust).

føyda'l *A* feudal.

føydalis'me *-n* feudalism.

+føy'e[1] *N* **1: med f-** justly, with reason. **2: falle til f-** submit, yield.

føy'e[2] *V +-de/*-dde* **1** give in to (sby), humor: **f- seg** comply, give in, obey; **f- seg etter** comply with, give in to. **2** join: **f- inn, sammen** connect, j-, put together; **f- seg sammen** j- together. **3: f- til** add.

+føy'e[3] *A* - *lit.*: **om f- tid** in a short while, soon.

føy'elig *A* - accommodating, agreeable; obedient; favorable (weather, wind).

føy'k *-en* (snow) shower; drifting, whirling (e.g. of sand, snow); grain, mote: **i en f-** in a jiffy.

+føy'ke[1] *-a* (=***føykje**[1]) (snow) shower; drifting, whirling (e.g. of sand, snow).

***føy'ke**[2] *-t* cf **føyk**

+føy'ke[3] *V -a/-et* (of sand, snow) blow, drift.

***føy'kje**[1] *-a* cf **føyke**[1]

***føy'kje**[2] *V -te* cf **føyke**[3]

***føy'rast** *V -ast* become porous.

***føy're** *-a* **1** crevice, hole. **2** marrow.

***føy'ret(e)** *A* - porous.

føy'se *V -te* brush, sweep aside; send packing: **f- en på dør** kick sby out of the house.

få'[1] *V +fikk/*fekk, fått* **1** get = acquire, obtain, receive: **helten får heltinnen** the hero marries the heroine; **en vet hva en har, men ikke hva en får** a bird in the hand is worth two in the bush; **få det godt** be comfortable, in good circumstances; **få det med å** get into the habit of; **nå skal du få** now you're going to get (catch) it; **snart fått er snart gått** easy come, easy go; **det er å få i butikkene** it can be bought in the stores; **få fatt i (på), tak i** get hold of. **2** get = accomplish, manage to get (sth done): **jeg har ikke fått gjort det ennå** I haven't been able to get it done yet. **3** get = cause, make: **få en (noe) til å gjøre noe** make sby (sth) do sth; **få seg til å** bring oneself to; **få slutt på** make an end of. **4** have: **få barn** have a child (children); **få brev** have (get) a letter; **hva får vi til middag i dag?** what are we going to have for dinner today? **5** shall, will (expressing futurity): **det får komme som det vil** let come what may (Evensmo); **vi får se** we'll see; **du får hilse ham fra meg** please give him my regards. **6** better, (will) have to: **det får være** let it go; it can't be helped; **du får skynde deg** you'd better hurry; **jeg får gjøre det selv** I'd better (I'll have to) do it myself. **7** may (=get permission): **får jeg (kan jeg få, må jeg få) gjøre det?** may I do it?; **få se!** let me see! **8** (often untranslated): **jeg vil gjerne få høre om det** I'd like to hear about it; **hvor kan jeg få kjøpt?** where can I buy?; **9** (with *prep.* and *adv.*): **få noe for seg** get sth into one's head; **få en fra noe** dissuade sby from doing sth; **få i seg** swallow; **få igjen på** get change for; **få noe igjen** get sth back; **få med** fit in, include; bring along, take with one; **få med noe å gjøre** have to take care of, do sth; **få med seg** take along; **få ned** down (food); **få opp** get (sth) open; increase (e.g. production); **få til** accomplish, manage; **jeg får det ikke til** I can't do it, can't manage; **få til overs for** grow fond of. **10** (*refl.*): **få seg** get (oneself); **jeg må få meg litt mat** I have to get sth to eat; **få seg til å** bring oneself to. (For use with nouns and other prep. see these).

***få'**[2] *V fådde* ret (soak, flax, hemp).

få'[3] *A pl, cp færre, sp færrest* few: **f- eller ingen** f-, if any; **ikke f-** quite a f-; **med f- ord** briefly; **noen f-** a f-; **noen ganske f-** a very f-; **de færreste** very f-.

f.å.=**forrige år**

Få'/berg *Pln* twp, Oppland.

***få'/fengd**[1] *-a* futility; hollowness, worthlessness.

***få'/fengd**[2] *A -/-fengt* cf **/fengt**

***få'/fengleg** *A* - futile, unavailing; hollow, worthless.

+få'/fengt *A* - (=***/fengd**[2]) futile, unavailing; fruitless, in vain.

***få'/gjeten** *A -e/-i, pl -ne* obscure, unknown.

***få'/kunne** *-a* ignorance.

***få'/kunnig** *A* - ignorant.

***få'me** *-n* fool, simpleton.

***få'men** *A -ent, pl -ne* idiotic, stupid.

få'/ment *A* - few in number.

få'ming *-en* bungler, clumsy fool; idiot.

få'/mælt [/me'lt] *A* - silent, taciturn.

***få'n** *-et* dust, (fine) ash.

***få'ne** *V -a* fade, turn grey.

få'/nytte *N*: **i f-, til f-s** in vain, uselessly.

+få'r[1] *-a* (=**+fure, *for**) furrow.

+få'r[2] *-et* mutton; *archaic* sheep: **det fortapte f-** the lost s-; **sort f-** black s- (only *fig.*).

***få're** *-n* cf **fare**[1]

+få're/aktig *A* - sheeplike, stupid.

°få're/hue *-t, pl -r* blockhead, ninny.

+få're/kjøtt *-et* mutton.

+få're/klær *pl*: **en ulv i f-** a wolf in sheep's clothing.

+få're/sopp *-en bot.* bracket fungus, mushroom (Polyporus ovinus).

+få'ret(e) *A* - sheeplike, stupid.

få'ri/kål *-en* mutton and cabbage stew.

***få'rleg** *A* - cf **farlig**

***få'st** *V fekst, fåst*: **f- i** try; **f- med (ved)** have to do with, concern oneself with; wrestle with.

***få'/sy'nt** *A* - rarely seen.

få'/tal *-et* (=**+/tall**) (a) few, (a) minority (av of).

+få'/tallig *A* - few (in number).

få'/tenkt *A* - shortsighted, simpleminded.

få'/vett *-et* (=***/vit**) ignorance, stupidity.

få'/vettig *A* - ignorant, stupid.

få'/vis *A* foolish, stupid.

***få'/vit** *-et* cf **/vett**

***få'/vitug** *A* - cf **/vettig**

G

g[1] [ge'] *-en* (letter, *mus.* note) G, g.

g[2]=**gram**[2]

g.=**gift**[2]

gabardi'n *-en* gabardine.

gabb' *-en* (drifting, whirling) dust.

***gab'be** *V -a* be dusty, blow.

gab'bro *-en geol.* gabbro.

+gad' *pt of* **gide**

gadd'[1] *-en* **1** point, prick, spike. **2** packed down earth; narrow track. **3** *bot.* Norway spruce (Picea abies).

gadd'[2] *pt of* **gidde**[1]

gaf'fel *-elen, pl gafler* **1** fork; cradle (on telephone). **2** *mus.* tuning fork. **3** *naut.* crutch; gaff; oarlock.

gaf'fel/bit *-en* fillet of pickled herring.

gaf'fel/segl *-et* (=**+/seil**) *naut.* trysail.

gaf'fel/truck [/trøkk] *-en* fork lift.

gaf'le *V -a/+-et* **1: g- i seg** eat voraciously, *(pop.)* shovel it in with both hands. **2** bifurcate, fork.

***ga'g** *A* bent backward.

***ga'ge** *V -a* bend backward.

gag'l *-a zool.* graylag (Anser anser).

***gag'le** *V -a* strut, swagger.

gagn [gang'n] *-et* benefit, good; advantage, gain: **gjøre g-** do good; **gjøre mer skade enn g-** do more harm than good; **til g- for** for the benefit of; **til g-s** effectually, to good purpose; in earnest, in full measure; **være til g- for** benefit.

gagne [gang'ne] *V -a/+-et* benefit, be good for; be of use: **hva g-er det?** what good does it do?

gagnlig [gang'nli] *A* - advantageous, beneficial; useful.

gagns/verk [gang'ns/] *-et* useful work.

gakk'[1] *-et* quack (esp. of a duck).

gakk'[2] *ip of* **gå**[1]

gakk'[3] *I* quack.

gak'ke *V -a/+-et* quack.

ga'l[1] *-et* crow.

+ga'l[2] *A* **1** crazy, demented, insane; mad; *(pop.)* nuts: **bli g-** go mad, out of one's mind; **er du g-?** are you crazy? (often = you are mistaken); **jo g-ere desto bedre** the crazier the better; **være splitter g-** be stark, raving mad. **2** angry, furious (på at); frenzied: **det er til å bli g- over** it's enough to drive a person crazy, out of his mind. **3** madcap, wild: **være g- etter** be crazy, mad about, *(pop.)* be nuts about. **4** wrong, incorrect, mistaken: **aldri så g-t at det ikke er godt for noe** it's an ill wind that blows nobody any good; **bære seg g-t at med noe** set about sth in the wrong way; **det er g-t fatt med ham** there's sth wrong with him, *(pop.)* he has a screw loose; **det hadde nær gått ham g-t** he almost came to grief, he had a close shave; **gjøre g-t verre** make matters worse; **gjøre noe g-t** make a mistake; **gå g-t** take the wrong road; *fig.* fail, go wrong, miscarry; **komme g-t av sted** come to grief; (of a woman) get into trouble; **nå har jeg aldri hørt så g-t!** well, I never! **om g-t skal være** if worst comes to worst. **5** bad, improper; morally wrong: **det var g-t gjort av meg** that was wrong of me; **ikke så g-t** not bad, quite good.

+gala'n *-en* paramour.

galan't *A* - attentive, chivalrous, courteous.

galanteri' *-et, pl +-er/*-* chivalry, courtesy.

galanteri'/varer *pl* fancy articles, luxuries; gift shop.

+gala'ter *-en, pl -e* (=***-ar**) Galatian.

gal'd *-en dial.* **1** packed down earth. **2** steep path (down a mountain side).

+gal'de[1] *-n* cf **galle**[1]

***gal'de**[2] *V -a* cull (male) hemp.

gal'der[1] *-eren, pl -rer folk.* magic charm, song; sorcery, witchcraft.

gal'der[2] *-eret/+-ret/*-eren vet.* windgall.

Gal'dhø/piggen *Pln* mountain in Jotunheimen (highest in Norway).

gal'dre *V -a/+-et folk.* chant magic charms, songs; conjure: **g- til live** bring to life by a magic spell (Undset).

+gal'dre/sang -*en* (=***/song**) *folk.* magic charm, song.

gal'dt *pt of* **gjelde**[1]

ga'le *V* +-*er*/**gjel, gol*/+-*te*, +-*t*/*-*e*/*-*i* 1 crow. 2 *folk.* chant magic charms, songs over one; "bewitch" (now used only in oaths): **fanden g- meg om jeg vil** I'll be damned if I will.

galea's -*en naut.* ketch (kind of sailboat); hermaphrodite brig.

ga'le/hus -*et* (=***galne/**) madhouse.

galei' -*en hist.* galley: **hva ville han på den g-?** he asked for it (he had only himself to blame).

galei'/slave -*n* galley slave.

ga'len *A* +-*ent, pl -ne* 1 crazy, mad (often in *dial.* form **gæern, gæren,** etc.). 2 angry, furious; frenzied: ***han vart g- på oss** he got mad at us. 3 madcap, wild: **g- etter** wild after; **g- ungdom** wild youth. *4 wrong; incorrect, mistaken; foolish: **på g- veg** on the wrong road; **en stakkar, som støtt har kjørt gali og rangt velta** a wretch who always has driven wrong and tipped badly (Falkberget).

ga'len/skap -*en* cf **gal/**

gal'ge -*n* 1 gallows: **dømme til g-n** sentence to be hanged. 2 *naut.* gallows bitts. 3 *tech.* filming (mobile) boom.

gal'ge/bakke -*n* gallows hill.

gal'gen/frist -*en* (short) reprieve.

gal'gen/fugl [+/ful] -*en* gallows bird, rascal.

gal'gen/humor -*en* grim, sardonic humor.

Galile'a *Pln* Galilee.

+galile'er -*en, pl -e* (=***-ar**) Galilean.

galile'isk *A* - Galilean.

galimati'as -*et* gibberish, nonsense; *(pop.)* balderdash.

***gall'**[1] -*et* cf **galle**[1]

***gall'**[2] *pt of* **gjelle**[2]

gal'la -*en* full dress: **kledd i g-** in evening dress.

+gal'la/antrekk -*et* evening dress; evening gown.

gal'la/middag -*en* gala banquet.

gal'la/unifor'm -*a*/+-*en* full-dress uniform.

***gall'/blære** -*a* cf **galle/**

+gal'le[1] -*n* (=***gall**[1]) bile, gall: **utøse sin g-** vent one's spleen.

gal'le[2] -*n* 1 *bot.* gall nut. 2 *vet.* windgall.

+gal'le/blære -*a* (=***gall/**) *anat.* gall bladder.

gall'/eple -*t, pl* +-*r*/*- *bot.* gall.

+gal'ler[1] -*en, pl -e* (=***-ar**) Gaul.

+gal'ler[2] -*et* cf **galder**[2]

galleri' -*et, pl* +-*er*/*- gallery (theater; museum); balcony: **sitte på g-et** sit in the b-; **spille for g-et** play to the grandstand.

+gal'le/stein -*en* (=***gall/**) *med.* gallstone.

gallio'n -*en* 1 *hist.* galleon. 2 *naut.* (figure) head.

gallio'ns/figu'r -*en naut.* figurehead (also *fig.*).

gallisis'me -*n* Gallicism.

gal'lisk *A* - Gallic.

***gall'/kvefs** -*en* cf **/veps**

gall'/sjuk *A* bitter, rancorous.

gall'/sott -*a med.* jaundice.

***gall'/stein** -*en* cf **galle/**

+gal'lup/undersø'kelse -*n* (=***/undersøking**) Gallup Poll.

gall'/veps -*en* (=***/kvefs**) *zool.* gall wasp (family Cynipidae).

+ga'lmanns/ferd -*a*/-*en* actions, behavior of a madman.

+ga'lmanns/verk -*et* act of a madman; a mad idea.

***ga'lnast** *V* -*ast* be frivolous, dally.

ga'lne/heie -*a* wild girl.

***ga'lne/hus** -*et* cf **gale/**

ga'lning -*en* madcap.

galo'n -*en* galloon (braid, trimming).

galone're *V* -*te* trim with braid, lace.

galopp' -*en* gallop: **i g-** at a gallop.

galoppa'de -*n* 1 *hum.* gallop. 2 *archaic, mus.* gallopade.

galoppe're *V* -*te* gallop; canter, lope.

ga'l/skap -*en* (=**galen/**) 1 insanity, lunacy; frenzy, rage: **det er metode i g-en** there's method in his madness. 2 folly, madness: **det er den rene g-** it is the height of folly; **jeg er oppsatt på g-er** I'm in the mood for devilry.

gal'te -*n* (=**gal't**) 1 *zool.* boar, hog (family Suidae). 2 *zool.* wild boar (Sus scrofa).

galvanise're *V* -*te* galvanize; electroplate.

galva'nisk *A* - galvanic.

***ga'mal** *A* -*t, pl gamle* cf **gammal**

***ga'man** -*et* cf **gammen**

***ga'man(s)/ferd** [/fær] -*a* pleasure trip.

gamasj'e -*n* legging; spat.

gam'bit -*en* gambit (chess).

game[1] [gei'm] -*t* game.

***ga'me**[2] *V* -*a*: **g- seg** have fun, have a good time.

game[3] [gei'm] *A* - game: **være g- for noe** be game to do or try sth.

game't -*en biol.* gamete.

gamin [gameng'] -*en* gamin.

gam'la *df* the old lady.

Gam'la/byen *Pln* the old city (oldest part of Oslo).

+Gam'le/erik *Prn* (=***/eirik**) Old Nick (the devil).

gam'le/far -*en* grandfather; the old man.

gam'le/heim -*en* (=**+/hjem**) home for the aged.

+gam'le/kjæreste -*n* cf **gammal/**

gam'le/landet *df* the old country, i.e. Norway.

gam'le/mor -*a* grandmother; the old lady.

gam'len [also: gam'mærn] *df* the old man.

gam'ling -*en* old man.

gam'mal *A* -*t, pl gamle* (=**+gammel, *gamal**) 1 old; aged, ancient, antique; second-hand, stale, used: **alt ble ved det g-e** everything went on as before, there were no changes made; **fra g- tid** from time immemorial; **g- jomfru** old maid; **g- og velbrukt** old and time-honored (e.g. a custom); **g-t skrap** old rubbish; **han var og ble den g-e Georg** he was still the same old George; **han ble g- før tiden** he was old before his time; **på sine g-e dager** in his old age; **være g- i tjenesten** grown old in the service (e.g. of a company or firm). 2 *(comp.)* **eldre** elder, older: **min e- bror** my elder brother; **Alexander Dumas d.e.** (=**den e-**) A- D-, senior; **en e- herre** an elderly gentleman; **de e-** older people; one's elders; **den e- jernalder** the Early Iron Age; **den e- steinalder** the Paleolithic; **ikke e- enn jeg var** young as I was (even at my tender age). 3 *(sup.)* **eldst** eldest, oldest; earliest: **de e-e** the Elders; **de e-e kristne** the earliest Christians; **jeg er e- av oss to** I am the older of us two, your senior.

gam'mal/dags *A* - old-fashioned, out of date.

+gam'mal/kjent *A* - (=***/kjend**) familiar, of long acquaintance.

+gam'mal/kjæreste -*n* (=***/kjærast(e)**) *hum.* old flame.

gam'mal/klok *A* knowing, precocious.

gam'malmanns/snakk -*et* senile twaddle.

gam'mal/modig *A* - 1 knowing, precocious. 2 oldish.

gam'mal/norsk *A* - Old Norwegian (loosely used for Old Norse, Old Icelandic).

gam'mal/ost [/ost] -*en* fully matured, highly pungent sour milk cheese (light brown in color).

gam'mal/voren *A* +-*ent, pl -ne* elderly, oldish.

gam'ma/stråler *pl phys.* gamma rays.

gam'ma/stråling -*a phys.* gamma radiation.

gam'me -*n* (Lapp) turf hut.

+gam'mel *A* -*elt, pl gamle* cf **gammal**

+gam'mel/dags *A* - cf **gammal/**

+gam'mel/klok *A* cf **gammal/**

+gam'melmanns/aktig *A* - senile.

+gam'mel/modig *A* - cf **gammal/**

+gam'mel/norsk *A* - cf **gammal/**

+gam'mel/ost [/ost] -*en* cf **gammal/**

+gam'mel/testamen'tlig *A* - (of the) Old Testament.

+gam'men -*et* (=***gaman**) delight, joy, pleasure: **leve i fryd og g-** live in joy and delight, in merriment.

°gam'mern *df* cf **gamlen**

gam'p -*en* horse, jade, nag.

***gam's** -*et* frivolity, giddiness.

***gam'se** *V* -*a* banter, jest, joke.

Gam'/vik *Pln* twp, Finnmark.

ga'n -*et* (of a fish) gill; entrails, head.

gan'd -*en folk.* Lapp magic, sorcery.

gan'de *V* -*a*/+-*et folk.* place under a Lapp spell; practice sorcery.

gan'd/finn -*en* Lapp shaman.

+gan'd/flue -*a* (=***/fluge**) *folk.* fly sent by a Lapp shaman to bring misfortune to a person.

+ga'ne[1] -*n* 1 *anat.* palate, roof of the mouth: **fukte sin g-** wet one's whistle; **åpen g-** cleft palate. 2 *bot.* palate.

ga'ne[2] *V* -*a*/-*te* gut (a fish).

ga'ne/jente -*a* girl who guts fish.

ga'ne/segl -*et* (=**+/seil**) *anat.* soft palate, velum.

gang'[1] -*en* 1 gait, going, walk(ing); movement (e.g. of the stars, planets): **gå en en høy g-** give sby a run for his money; **ha sin g- i huset** come and go freely; **kjenne en på g-en** recognize sby by his walk. 2 course, passage (e.g. of time), way; plot, sequence: **all kjødets g-** the way of all flesh; **g-en i fortellingen** the plot of the story; **gå sin g-** take its course; **verdens g-** the way of the world. 3 operation, running, working: **i g-** in motion, in operation, under way; **i full g-** in full swing; **få, sette i g-** set going, start; **gå i g- med** start on; **komme i g-** get started; **være i g- med å** be in the process of, be at work with. 4 aisle, corridor; entry, hallway. 5 *med.* duct, tube. 6 lode, vein (of metal).

gang'[2] -*en* occasion, time: **en g-** once; someday, sometime; **en g- for alle** once and for all; **en g- imellom** once in a while; **en g- til** again, once more; **en av (ad) g-en** one at a time; **en og annen g-** occasionally, once in a while; **en sjelden g-** rarely; **den g-** that time; (as *conj.*) when; **for en g-s skyld** for once; **g- på g-** again and again, time after time; **ikke en g-** not even; **med en g-** at once, right away, suddenly; **noen g-** ever (**har du noen g-** have you ever); sometime; **på en g-** at once, at one time; **to g-er** twice; **tre g-er tre er ni** three times three is nine; **et lite hus på fire g-er seks meter** a little house four by six meters in size (Hoel).

gang'ar -*en* Norwegian country dance (similar to a roundel, but slower in tempo); folk tune in 6/8 time used for such a dance.

+gang'/art -*a*/-*en* (of a horse) pace; (of a person) gait, walk.

gang'/bar *A* 1 passable. 2 current; customary: **g- mynt** coin of the realm; **g-e varer** marketable, saleable merchandise. 3 prevailing (e.g. expression).

gang'/bru -*a* foot bridge.

gang'/dag -*en eccl. hist.* procession day: **store g-en** April 25.

gang'/dør -*a* front door.

+gang'e[1] -*a*/-*en* (=***gonge**[1]) gait, walk; walking.

+gang'e[2] *V* -*a*/-*et* (=***gonge**[2]) multiply.

***gang'e**[3] *V gjeng, gjekk, gjenge*/-*i* cf **gå**[1]

+gang'er -*en, pl -e* (=***-ar**) 1 Norwegian folk dance (cf **gangar**). 2 *poet.* steed.

gang'/før *A* able to walk.

gang'/jern [/jæ'rn] -*et* (=***/jarn**) hinge.

+**gang'/klær** *pl* (=*/**klede**) clothing, wearing apparel.
gang'/lag *-et* gait, walk; walking.
gang'lie *-t, pl* +*-r*/**-* (=**-lion**, ***-lien**) *anat.* ganglion.
gang'lie/celle *-a/-en anat.* nerve cell.
gang'lion *-et* cf **ganglie**
***gang'/spel** *-et* cf **/spill**
gang'/sperre *-a* soreness, stiffness from walking.
+**gang'/spill** *-et* (=+**/spell**, ***/spel**) *naut.* capstan.
gang'ster *-en, pl* +*-e* gangster.
+**gang'/sti** *-en* (=***/stig**) (foot) path.
gang'/syn *-et*/**-a*: **ha g-** see well enough to walk.
***gang'/sy'nt** *A* - seeing well enough to walk.
gang'/veg *-en* (foot) path.
gang'/verk *-et* movement (in a watch).
gan'ske *Av* 1 quite; entirely, wholly: **det er g- visst så at** it is true that; **en g- annen sak** quite a different matter, a horse of a different color; **g- enkelt** pure and simple; **g- riktig** right you are, sure enough; **ikke g-** not quite; **jeg er g- enig med ham** I quite agree with him. 2 fairly, pretty, very: **en g- stor ordre** a fairly (pretty) large order; **g- god** pretty good.
+**gan'tes** *V -edes, gantes* (=***-ast**) dally, trifle; jest.
ga'p[1] *-en* yawn.
ga'p[2] *-en* chatterbox, joker; fool, *(pop.)* jackass.
ga'p[3] *-et* jaws, (wide open) mouth; chasm, gap, opening: **døra stod på vidt g-** the door was wide open; **på g-** ajar.
°**ga'pa/trast** *-en* big talker, chatterer.
ga'pe *V -a/-te* gape, open one's mouth wide; yawn: **g- over for myc** bite off more than one can chew.
ga'pen *A* +*-ent, pl -ne* flap-jawed; foolish, silly.
+**ga'peri** *-et* nonsense; *(pop.)* balderdash, flapdoodle; tomfoolery.
ga'pe/stokk *-en* pillory: **stå i g-en** be the laughing stock, an object of derision.
ga'pe/stykke *-t, pl* +*-r*/**-* foolish prank, tomfoolery.
ga'pet(e) *A* - flippant, foolish.
ga'p/le *V infl as* **le**[3] guffaw, laugh derisively.
***ga'pleg** *A* - foolish, silly.
ga'p/skratte *V -a*/+*-et* laugh uproariously (derisively).
garan't *-en* co-signer, guarantor, surety.
garante're *V -te* guarantee, warrant: **g- et lån** co-sign for a loan.
garanti' *-en* guarantee, warranty.
garantis't *-en* co-signer, guarantor, surety.
gara'sje *-n* garage.
ga'rd *-en* (=+**gård**) 1 farm, farmstead; estate, manor: **til g-s** to the farm. 2 barrier, fence, hedge. 3 yard (courtyard, farmyard); court, quadrangle: **gå i g-en** go to the toilet. 4 (only in form **gård**) apartment, office building. 5 **(ingenting i veien) der i g-en** (nothing wrong) with him (her, them).
Gar'da/rike *Pln hist.* Russia (kingdom of Novgorod, ON Holmgarðr, founded by Swedish Vikings, ca. 850 A.D.).
+**ga'rd/bruker** *-en, pl -e* (=***-ar**) farmer.
gar'de[1] *-n* bodyguard, guard; *mil.* crack, elite fighting group: **den gamle g-** the old guard.
garde[2] [gar'd]: **en g-** [ang gar'd] on guard (fencing).
ga'rde[3] *N* (=+**gårde**): **av g-** away, off (**se en av g-** see sby off).
gar'de/kaser'ne *-n mil.* Guards' barracks.
ga'rde/mellom *Av* cf **gard/imellom**
garde're *V -te* guard: **g- seg mot noe** guard against sth.
Gar'der/moen *Pln* village, Ullensaker twp, Akershus; nearby military air base and drill grounds.
gardero'be *-n* 1 checkroom, cloakroom. 2 wardrobe (personal, theatrical).
gardero'be/dame *-a*/+*-en* 1 cloakroom attendant. 2 wardrobe mistress (theater).
+**gardero'be/skap** *-et* (=***/skåp**) clothespress, locker, wardrobe.
+**ga'rd/gutt** *-en* (=***/gut**) heir to a farm.
ga'rd/imel'lom *Av* from farm to farm.
gardi'n *-a*/+*-en/-et* curtain; blind, drape.
+**gardi'n/preken** *-en* (=***/preike**) curtain lecture (private scolding, esp. by a wife to her husband).
gardi'n/trapp *-a* stepladder.
gardis't *-en* guardsman.
ga'rd/jente *-a* heiress to a farm.
ga'rd/mann *-en, pl -menn*/**-menner* farmer.
ga'rds/bruk *-et* farm; farming.
ga'rds/drift *-a* farming, farm work, running a farm.
+**ga'rds/gutt** *-en* (=***/gut**) farm hand.
ga'rds/hund *-en* (farm) watchdog.
ga'rds/kar *-en* farm hand.
ga'rds/led *-et* yard gate.
ga'rds/rom [/romm] *-met*/**-et* cf **gårds/**
ga'rd/staur *-en* fence picket.
ga'rds/veg *-en* road leading to a farm or group of farms.
ga'rd/vo'rd *-en folk.* brownie (believed to live on a farm and protect it against misfortune).
°**ga're** *-n* cf **garde**[2]
ga'rn *-et* 1 yarn. 2 net, seine: *fig.* **fanget i sitt eget g-** caught in his own trap; **legge sine g- ut etter** set one's cap for.
ga'rn/bruk *-et* seine fishing; fishing gear, nets.
garne're *V -te* 1 trim. 2 garnish.
garne'ring *-a*/+*-en* 1 flounce, trimming. 2 garnish. 3 *naut.* ceiling (=inner lining).
ga'rn/fisk *-en* fish caught in a net.
ga'rn/hespel *-elen, pl -ler* skein (of yarn).
garniso'n *-en* garrison: **ligge i g-** be stationed.
garnity'r *-et* 1 set (e.g. of forks, knives, etc.). 2 trimming.
ga'rn/lag *-et* seine gang.
+**ga'rn/lenke** *-a/-en* (=+**/lenk**, ***/lenkje**) number of nets (10-30) tied together.
ga'rn/vinde *-n* yarn reel.
gar'p *-en hist.* nickname for a Hanseatic merchant in Bergen; any ruffian.
***gar'pe** *V -a* act like a brutal bully, ruffian.
***gar'te** *V -a* banter, jest; dally, trifle.
+**gar'tner** *-en, pl -e* (=***-ar**) gardener.
gartneri' *-et, pl* +*-er*/**-* nursery; truck garden.
gar've *V -a*/+*-et* 1 curry, dress, tan (leather). 2 tilt (steel). 3 *fig.* treat roughly, give sby a hard time.
+**gar'ver** *-en, pl -e* (=***-ar**) tanner.
garveri' *-et, pl* +*-er*/**-* tannery.
gar've/syre *-a* tannic acid, tannin.
***gar've/verk** *-et* tannery.
ga's[1] *-en* gauze.
+**ga's**[2] *pt of* **gis** cf **gi**
ga's/bind *-et* (=***/band**) bandage.
gasell' *-en* 1 *zool.* gazelle. 2 ghazel (Persian poem).
ga'sje *-n* salary, wages: **heve sin g-** draw one's salary.
ga'sje/pålegg *-et* salary raise.
gasje're *V -te* pay: **høyt g-t** highly paid (e.g. official).
gasoli'n *-en* gasoline
gass' *-en* gas.
gas'se[1] *-n* gander.
gas'se[2] *V -a*/+*-et*: **g- seg i** luxuriate, revel in; **g- seg med** feast on, regale oneself with.
gas'se[3] *V -a*/+*-et* 1 produce gas. 2 disinfect with gas. 3 (expose to) gas, kill with gas.
+**gas'ser** *-en, pl -e* (=***-ar**) native of Madagascar.
gas'sisk *A* - of, or pertaining to Madagascar.
gass'/kammer *-et, pl -*/+*-kamre* gas chamber.
gass'/maske *-a*/+*-en* gas mask.
gass'/peda'l *-en* accelerator, gas pedal.
gass'/verk *-et* gasworks.
gas't[1] *-en* 1 *naut.* hand, sailor. 2 *dial.* brutal bully, ruffian.
gas't[2] *-en folk.* spook, troll; supernatural being in the form of a bird with a bloodcurdling shriek.
gas'ta *A* large; first-rate, splendid.
***gas'teleg** *A* - exceedingly large, powerful.
gastere're *V -te fam.* 1 go calling, visiting. 2 live extravagantly.
***gas't/givar** *-en* cf **gjest/giver**
***gas't/gjevar** *-en* cf **gjest/giver**
gastrono'm *-en* epicure, gourmet.
gastronomi' *-en* gastronomy.
gastrono'misk *A* - gastronomical.
***ga't**[1] *-et* cf **gatt**
***ga't**[2] *pt of* **gjete**[1]
ga'te[1] *-a* street; thoroughfare; avenue, boulevard: **gå over g-a** cross the street; **i samme g-** in the same vein; **kaste på g-a** evict; **mannen fra g-a** man in the street, *(pop.)* John Q. Public; **på g-a** in the street.
***ga'te**[2] *V -a* drill, pierce with a knife.
+**ga'te/bely'sning** *-en* street lighting.
+**ga'te/bilde** *-t* street scene.
ga'te/dør *-a* entrance door, front door, main entrance.
+**ga'te/feier** *-en, pl -e* (=***-ar**) street sweeper.
+**ga'te/gutt** *-en* (=***/gut**) street urchin.
ga'te/hjørne [/jø'rne] *-t, pl* +*-r*/**-* intersection, street corner.
ga'te/jente *-a* prostitute, streetwalker.
ga'te/kamp *-en mil.* house-to-house fighting; street fighting.
ga'te/kryss *-et* (street) crossing, intersection.
ga'te/langs *Av* up and down the street.
+**ga'te/legeme** *-t* roadway.
ga'te/liv *-et* street life.
ga'te/musikan't *-en* strolling musician.
+**ga'te/pike** *-a/-en* prostitute, streetwalker.
ga'te/stein *-en* paving stone.
ga'te/uor'den *-en* disturbance of the peace.
+**gatt'** *-et* (=+**gat**[1]) 1 *naut.* hole, vent; locker, storeroom. 2 *zool.* anus.
+**gatt'/finne** *-n zool.* anal fin.
gau'da *-en* Gouda (Holland) cheese.
gau'da/ost [/ost] *-en* Gouda (Holland) cheese.
***gau'e** *V -a* bark, yelp; scream, yell.
gau'k[1] *-en* (=+**gjøk**) *zool.* cuckoo (Cuculus canorus).
gau'k[2] *-en* joker, rogue; bootlegger, moonshiner.
gau'ke *V -a*/+*-et* 1 bootleg. *2 prattle.
gau'ke/syre *-a bot.* wood sorrel (Oxalis acetosella).
gau'ks/mess(e) *en eccl. hist.* May 1st.
gau'k/syre *-a* cf **gauke/**
gau'k/unge [/onge] *-n* young cuckoo.
gau'l *-et* bellow, howl, yell.
Gau'la *Pln* 1 river in Trøndelag. 2 river in Sunnfjord.
Gau'lar *Pln* twp, Sogn og Fjordane.
Gau'l/dalen *Pln* valley extending some 80 miles from Aursunden (Ålen) to Trondheim Fjord.
gau'le *V -a/-te* bellow, howl, yell.
***gau'm** *-en* attention: **gje g- (etter)** pay a- (to).
***gau'me** *V -a*: **g- på** pay attention to, heed.
***gau'm/sam'** *A* attentive, observant.
***gau'm/semd** *-a* attention, attentiveness.
gau'pe *-a zool.* lynx (Lynx lynx).

+ Bokmål; * Nynorsk; ° Dialect.
After letter: ' stress (Acc. 1); ' tone, stress (Acc. 2); · length.
Below letter: . not pronounced.

***gau'pn** *-a* hand used as a scoop (e.g. for water).
***gau'pne** *V -a* scoop (e.g. water) with the hands.
***gau's**[1] *-en* current of air: **soli gyv mot stogeveggen og blir kasta i g-ar kring i tunet** the sun beats against the house wall and is tossed around the yard in waves (Vesaas).
***gau's**[2] *pt of* **gjose**
Gau's/dal *Pln* valley in Gudbrandsdal.
gau's/døl *-en* person from Gausdal.
Gau'sta *Pln* mountain, Tinn twp, Telemark.
gau'stad/kandida't *-en* candidate for the asylum (Gaustad is a mental institution near Oslo).
***gau't** *pt of* **gyte**
gau'te *V -a* boast, talk big.
Gau't(e) *Prn (m)*
gau'/tjuv [/kjuv] *-en* joker, rascal, rogue.
gau'v[1] *-en* (drifting, whirling) dust, snow.
gau'v[2] *pt of* **gyve**
***gau've** *-n* important man, *(pop.)* big shot, VIP.
ga'v *pt of* **gi, gje(ve)**
+ga've *-a/-en* (=***gåve**) **1** gift, present; contribution, donation: **Guds g-r** gifts of God, usu. of food. **2** gift= aptitude, bent, talent: **talens g-** *(pop.)* gift of gab.
+ga've/bo'rd *-et* gift table.
+ga've/brev *-et jur.* deed of conveyance (for a gift).
+ga've/kort *-et* gift certificate (redeemable e.g. in a department store).
gav'l *-en* gable.
+ga'v/mild *A* generous, liberal, openhanded.
+ga'vmild/het *-en* generosity, magnanimity.
gavott' *-en* gavotte.
+ga'v/tyv *-en* cf **gau/tjuv**
gear [gi'r] *-et* cf **gir**[2]
+geber'de[1] *-n* gesture.
+geber'de[2] *V -et*: **g- seg** behave (esp. foolishly, unproperly), carry on.
+gebe't *-et, pl -/+-er* territory; *fig.* domain, province: **det faller utenfor mitt g-** that's not in my line.
gebiss' *-et, pl -/+-er* (set of) false teeth.
+gebrek'kelig *A* - frail, infirm (person); rickety (object).
+gebrok'ken *A -ent, pl gebrokne* (of pronunciation) broken: **g-t engelsk** broken English.
+geburts/dag [jebu'rs/] *-en* birthday.
+geburtsdags/ba'rn *-et* person whose birthday is being celebrated.
geby'r *-et, pl -/+-er* fee.
+gedi'gen *A -ent, pl -ne* (of metals) pure, solid, sterling; *fig.* excellent, genuine: **et g-t verk** a solid piece of work.
gehal't *-en* substance, (intrinsic) value.
geheng' *-et* sword belt.
gehø'r *-et* **1** *mus.* musical ear: **absolutt g-** perfect pitch; **spille etter g-** play by ear. **2**: **finne g- for** get sympathy (support) for; **gi g-** lend an ear to (e.g. to sby's complaints).
gei'ger/teller [gai'-] *-en, pl +-e* (=***/teljar**) Geiger counter.
geil[1] [jei'l] *-a/+-en* lane (between hedges or houses).
+gei'l[2] *A* (of animals) in heat, ruttish; *derog.* (of persons) lascivious, lustful.
+gei'le *V -a/-et*: **g- opp** excite sexually.
Geilo [jei'lo] *Pln* tourist center, Hol twp, Buskerud.
gein [jei'n] *-a naut.* heavy tackle.
***geine** [jei'ne] *V -a* **1** run obliquely. **2** chime in (a conversation). **3** sneer at, taunt.
gein(e)/tau *-et* cable fastened to a seine.
geip [jei'p] *-en/+-et* grimace, (mocking) grin, pout: **dra på g-en** make a face (at sth unpleasant), screw up one's face (ready to cry); **sette opp en g-** pull a long face.
geipe [jei'pe] *V -a/+-te* curl one's lips in a sneer, make faces, pout: **g- av, til** make fun of, ridicule.
geipet(e) [jei'pet(e)] *A* - flippant, mocking; disagreeable.
gei'r *-en hist.* javelin, spear.
Gei'r *Prn (m)*
Gei'r/anger [also jei'r/] *Pln* parish and village, Sunnylven, Møre og Romsdal.
gei'r/fugl *-en zool.* great auk (extinct) (Alca impennis).
***geis** [jei's] *-en* steam, vapor.
geisha [gei'sja] *+-en/*ei* geisha.
***geisle** [jei'sle] *-n* beam, ray.
***geisp** [jei'sp] *-en* cf **gjesp**
***geispe** [jei'spe] *V -a* cf **gjespe**
gei'st *-en* **1** *obs.* spirit, spirituality. **2** (of champagne, wine) effervescence, fizz; bouquet.
gei'stlig *A* - **1** clerical. **2**: **en g-** cleric, clergyman.
+gei'stlig/het *-en* clergy.
geit [jei't] *-a* **1** goat; nanny goat. **2** affected, foolish woman.
Geita/strand [jei'ta/] *Pln* twp, Sør-Trøndelag.
geite [jei'te] *-a* sapwood; alburnum.
geite/bukk [jei'te/bokk] *-en* (male) goat (billy goat, buck).
geite/klokke *-a bot.* lily of the valley (Convallaria majalis).
+geite/rams *-en* cf **geit/**
geit/fivel [jei't/] *-elen, pl -ler bot.* pasqueflower (Anemone pulsatilla).
geit/kje *-et* kid.
geit/ost [jei't/ost] *-en* "goat cheese" (sweet, brown cheese made of goat's milk).
geit/rams *-en bot.* willow herb (Epilobium angustifolium).
***geivle** [jei'vle] *V -a* munch.
gelatin [sjelati'n] *-en* gelatin.
gelé [sjele'] *-en* jelly.
gelé/aktig *A* - gelatinous, jelly-like.
geledd' *-et, pl -/+-er mil.* line, rank: **på g-** lined up.
+gelei'de *V -et archaic* accompany, escort.
gelen'der *-eret/-ret, pl -er/+-re* banister, handrail, railing.
+gelen'k *-en* (of a foot) arch; (of a shoe) shank.
+geliker [jeli'ker] *-en* cf **gjeliker**
gemakk' *-et, pl -/+-er* apartment, room.
gema'l *-en* consort; *hum.* husband.
gemalin'ne *-a/+-en* consort; *hum.* wife.
+geme'n *A* **1** base, mean, vile. **2** *archaic* common, ordinary, public: **det g-e beste** the common good; **den g-e mann** the common man.
+geme'n/het *-en* baseness, vileness; base, vile act.
+geme'nslig [also jeme'nsli] *A* - plain, simple; convivial, friendly.
gemine're *V -te* geminate.
gem'se *-n zool.* chamois (Rupicapra rupicapra).
gemytt' *-et* **1** disposition, temperament; character, nature. **2** person (of a given temperament): **han var et uroligt g-** he was temperamentally restless.
gemytt'lig *A* - cheerful, congenial, genial; convivial, jovial.
ge'n *-en/-et biol.* gene.
+genanse [sjenang'se] *-n* cf **sjenanse**
gendarm [sjangdar'm] *-en* gendarme.
gendarmeri [sjangdarmeri'] *-et* gendarmerie.
gêne [sje'ne] *-n* embarrassment, inconvenience: **være til g-** be a nuisance.
genealog [-lå'g] *-en* genealogist.
genealogi' *-en* genealogy.
+gene'gen *A -ent, pl -ne lit.* inclined.
ge'nera *pl of* **genus**
genera'l *-en mil.* general.
genera'l/agentu'r *-et* general agency.
genera'l/direktø'r *-en* **1** *admin.* director general. **2** *merc.* managing director.
genera'l/forsam'ling *-a/+-en* **1** *admin.* general assembly (e.g. of UN). **2** *merc.* board meeting; stockholders' meeting.
generalin'ne *-a/+-en* general's wife.
generalisasjo'n *-en* generalization.
generalise're *V -te* generalize, make sweeping statements.
generalis'simus *-en* generalissimo.
genera'l/konsul *-en* consul general.
genera'l/løytnant *-en* lieutenant general.
genera'l/majo'r *-en* major general.
genera'l/prøve *-a/+-en* (final) dress rehearsal.
genera'l/sekretæ'r *-en* secretary general.
genera'l/stab *-en mil.* general staff.
genera'l/streik *-en* general strike.
generasjo'n *-en* generation.
gen'erativ *A* generative.
genera'tor *-en, pl -to'rer* generator (gas, electric).
genera'tor/gass *-en* producer gas.
+genere [sjene're] *V -te* cf **sjenere**
generell [sjenerell'] *A -elt* general: **g-t sett** g-ly speaking.
gene'risk *A* - generic.
+genert [sjene'rt] *A* - cf **sjenert**
generøs [sjenerø's] *A* generous, liberal.
generøsitet [sjenerøsite't] *-en* generosity.
ge'nesis *-en* genesis, origin.
genetikk' *-en* genetics.
gene'tisk *A* - genetic.
Genève [sjene'v] *Pln* Geneva (Switzerland).
genever [sjene'ver] *-en, pl +-e* cf **sjenever**
+gen'fer- *Pf* cf **genf-**
gen'f/konvensjo'nen *-en* (=**+-er/**) the Geneva Convention.
+gen'f/kors *-et* (=**+-er/**, ***/kross**) Geneva cross, red cross.
geni [sjeni'] *-et, pl +-er/*-* **1** genius, natural ability. **2** genius (person).
genia'l *A* highly gifted, of genius; brilliant, ingenious: **han er g-** he is a genius; **en g- idé** a brilliant idea.
genialite't *-en* genius; brilliance.
ge'nier *pl of* **genius**
geni/strek [sjeni'/] *-en* stroke of genius.
genita'lia *pl* (=**+-ier**) *anat.* genitalia.
ge'nitiv *-en gram.* genitive.
ge'nius *-ien, pl -ier myth.* guardian spirit.
genre [sjang'er] *-n* genre: **noe i den g-** sth like that, of that kind.
+genre/bilde *-t* (=***/bilete**) genre painting.
gen'ser *-en, pl +-e* (pullover) sweater.
gentil [sjangti'l] *A* gentlemanly, magnanimous.
gentleman [dsjen'telmæn] *-en, pl -men* gentleman.
genui'n *A* genuine.
ge'nus *+-en/-et, pl +genera gram.* gender.
geode't *-en* geodesist; (land) surveyor.
geofysikk' *-en* geophysics.
geofy'sisk *A* - geophysical.
geogra'f *-en* geographer.
geografi' *-en* geography.
geogra'fisk *A* - geographical.
geolog [geolå'g] *-en* geologist.
geologi' *-en* geology.
geologisk [geolå'g-] *A* - geological.
geometri' *-en* geometry.
geome'trisk *A* - geometrical.
Ge'org *Prn (m)* George.
georgi'ne *-a/+-en bot.* dahlia (Dahlia).
geosen'trisk *A* - geocentric.
gera'nium *-ien, pl -ier bot.* geranium (Pelargonium).
Ger'd(a) *Prn (f)*
geril'ja *-en* guerrilla.
geril'ja/krig *-en* guerrilla war.
germ. =**germansk**
+germa'ner *-en, pl -e* (=***-ar, *german**) Teuton; speaker of Old Germanic.
germa'nsk *A* - Germanic, Teutonic.
+gerå'de *V -et*: **g- en til ære** redound to one's credit; **g- (ut) i raseri** fall into a rage.
gesan'dt *-en* ambassador, envoy.
gesan'dt/skap *-et* embassy, legation.

gesell' *-en* 1 *hist.* merchant's ablest foreman (at Tyskebryggen in Bergen). 2 *hist.* journeyman. 3 tramp; fellow.

gesim's *-en* cornice.

geskjef't *-en derog.* business.

+**geskjef'tig** *A* - bustling, zealous; *derog.* officious: **en g- dame** a busybody.

+**gespen'st** *-et, pl* +*-er*/*** ghost.

gess' *-en mus.* g flat.

ges't [also sjes't] *-en* gesture: **en smukk g-** a handsome g-.

+**gestal't** *-en* 1 form, outline, shape. 2 *psych.* Gestalt.

gestal't/psykologi' *-en* Gestalt psychology.

gestapis't *-en* Gestapo agent.

+**ges'ter** *pl of* **gestus**

gestikule're *V -te* gesticulate, gesture.

ges'tus *-en, pl -/gester* gesture.

+**gesvin't** *A* - *archaic* fast, quick, swift.

°**gett'** *I* cf **gitt**[2]

get'to *-en* cf **ghetto**

gevan't *-et, pl -/*+*-er* drapery, loosely hanging clothes.

+**gevek'st** *-en* excrescence.

+**gevin'st** *-en* 1 gain, profit. 2 prize.

+**gevin'st- og** [å] **ta'ps/konto** *-en* profit and loss (account).

gevi'r *-et, pl -/*+*-er* antler.

gevær [gevæ'r] *-et, pl -/*+*-er* gun, rifle: **presentere g-** present arms; **på aksel g-** right shoulder arms; **(vakt) i g-** to arms.

gevær/kule *-a* rifle bullet.

gevær/pipe *-a* gun barrel.

geysir [gei'sir] *-en* geyser.

Gha'na *Pln* Ghana.

ghana'nsk *A* - Ghanian.

ghet'to *-en* (=***getto**) ghetto.

gi' *V gav, gitt* (=***gje(ve)**) 1 give, present; bestow, grant: **det er ikke enhver gitt (å)** it is not for everybody (to); **Gud gi (at)** may God grant (that); **hva gir du meg!** (in surprise, indignation) how do you like that! can you beat that! 2 produce, yield (e.g. crops); result in: **gi mening** make sense; **gi svar** answer. 3 (in cards) deal. 4 (with *prep.* and *adv.*): **giv akt!** attention!; **gi av seg** produce, yield; **gi etter** give in; **gi fra seg** hand over, part with, surrender up; **gi igjen** hand back, return; make change; get back at, pay back; **gi opp** give up; **gi slipp på** give up; **gi til kjenne** display, make known; express; **gi tål** be patient; **gi ut** publish; **gi noe ut for å være** try to pass sth off as (sth else); **gi videre** pass on. 5 *(refl.)*: **gi seg** give in (up), surrender (**gi deg nå** aw, cut it out); bend, give, stretch; (of a storm, etc.) diminish, subside; **gi seg god tid** take one's time; **gi seg hen (til)** abandon oneself (to), give oneself over (to), become addicted (to); **gi seg i kast med** grapple with, tackle (e.g. a problem), embark on (e.g. a project, task); **gi seg i snakk med** enter into a conversation with; **gi seg i vei** start off, set out; **gi seg tid** take one's time; **gi seg til å** start to; **gi seg under en** accept sby's leadership, submit to sby; **gi seg ut for å være** pretend to be, try to pass oneself off as. 6 (passive) **gives (gis)** is, are, exist(s): **der gives visse krav** there are certain demands (Ibsen).

+**gid**[1] [gi'd] *C* (=***gjev**[2]) may, would that: **g- det var så vel** I hope so, that would be good news; **g- hun ville** if she only would; **g- jeg var** I wish, if only I were.

+**gid**[2] [gi'd] *I* dear me, good grief, good heavens (usu. *fem.*).

gidde[1] [gid'de] *V gadd,* +*-et*/**-e*/**-i* 1 bother to, take the trouble to: **jeg g-er ikke** it's too much trouble, I can't be bothered. 2 care to, feel disposed, inclined to: **(jeg) gadd vite om** (I) wonder if.

***gid'de**[2] *V -a* quiver, vibrate.

gid'der *-eret/gidret* quivering, vibration; shimmering.

+**gide** [gid'de] *V gad, -et* cf **gidde**[1]

***gid'n** *-a* (of light) shimmering.

gid're *V -a* (of light) quiver, shimmer.

+**gi'ende(s)** *N*: **få til g-** be made a present of; get for nothing; be handed on a silver platter.

gif't[1] *-a/*+*-en* poison: **det kan du ta g- på** *(pop.)* you bet your sweet life; **spy g-** vent one's spleen.

gif't[2] *A* - married (**med** to): **bli g-** get married.

gif't/blanding *-a/*+*-en* 1 preparation of a poison. 2 poison.

+**gif't/blomst** *-en* (=***/blome)** poisonous flower.

gif't/brodd *-en* 1 *zool.* sting, stinger. 2 *fig.* malice, spite.

***gif'te**[1] *-a* spouse.

gif'te[2] *-t* 1 marriage; match. 2 spouse.

gif'te[3] *V -a/*+*-et/***-e* 1 marry: **g- bort** marry off. 2: **g- seg** marry; **g- seg inn i en familie** marry into a family; **g- seg med en** marry sby; **g- seg til penger** marry a fortune.

gif'te/ferdig *A* - marriageable.

gif'te/kniv *en*: **Kirsten g-** matchmaker (Holberg).

gif'te/ring *-en* wedding ring.

+**gif'ter/mål** *-et* (=***-ar/**) marriage.

+**gif'te/tanker** *pl* (=***-ar): gå i g-** be daydreaming; contemplate matrimony.

gif'tig *A* - poisonous, venomous (also *fig.*); toxic, virulent.

+**gif'tig/het** *-en* poisonousness; toxicity, virulence.

+**gif't/slange** *-n* (=***/orm)** poisonous snake.

gif't/tann *-a, pl -tenner zool.* (poison) fang (e.g. of a rattlesnake).

gigant [gigan't] *-en* 1 giant. 2 *myth.* Titan.

gigantisk [gigan'tisk] *A* - gigantic, giant.

gi'ge *-n hist.* fiddle.

gigg' *-en* 1 *naut.* gig. 2 *mus.* jig.

gigolo [sji'golo] *-en* gigolo.

+**gikk'** *pt of* **gå**[1]

gik't *-a* 1 *med.* arthritis, rheumatism. 2 *tech.* (of a blast furnace) mouth.

+**gik't/brudden** *A -ent, pl -brudne* (=***/broten)** arthritic, rheumatic.

gik't/feber *-en med.* rheumatic fever.

gik'tisk *A* - arthritic, rheumatic.

gik't/kroket(e) *A* - crippled, doubled over (with arthritis, rheumatism).

***gi'l** *-et* cf **gjel**[2]

gil'd *A* excellent, fine, splendid; dashing, elegant, stylish: **ha det g-t, leve g-t** live in the lap of luxury, *(pop.)* live the life of Riley.

gil'de[1] *-t* celebration, party: **betale g-t** foot the bill; **holde g- på** devour.

***gil'de**[2] *V -a* 1 accept at face value. 2: **g- seg** strut, swagger about.

gil'de/hall +*-en/***-a* guildhall.

gil'der *-eret/-ret* cf **gildre**[1]

gil'de/skrå +*-en/***-a hist.* laws, rules of order for a guild.

Gil'de/skål *Pln* twp, Nordland.

gil'dre[1] *-a* 1 (animal) snare, trap. 2 *tech.* stick holding a box trap in position.

gil'dre[2] *V -a/*+*-et* 1 set (animal) snares, traps. 2: **g- opp** *dial.* pile up loosely, rickety.

***gil'd/skap** *-en* validity, worth.

***gil'dsleg** *A* - competent; satisfactory.

gil'je *V -a/*+*-et archaic* lead astray, seduce.

+**giljotin** [giljoti'n] *-en* (=***-e)** guillotine.

giljotinere [giljotine're] *V -te* guillotine.

***gim'ber** *-ra, pl -rar* cf **gimmer**

***gim'ling** *-en* partition (in a house).

gim'mer *gimra, pl* +*gimrer/***gimrar* (=***gimber**) ewe (which has not yet lambed).

***gim'sen** *A -e/-i, pl -ne* capricious, whimsical.

Gim's/øy *Pln* large island, twp Nordland.

gin[1] [dsjin'] *-en* (English) gin.

***gi'n**[2] *-et* narrow opening.

Gin'nunga/gap [-ongga/] *Pln* (Norse) *myth.* primeval chaos (before Midgard was created).

gip's *-en* gypsum, plaster of Paris.

gip'se *V -a/*+*-et* plaster (e.g. a wall); put in a cast (e.g. a leg).

gi'r[1] *-en naut.* yaw.

***gi'r**[2] *-en* desire, enthusiasm, excitement: **dei fekk ein g- i seg** they grew eager (for sth) (Aasen).

gir[3] [gi'r] *-et* gear.

+**giraff** [sjiraff'] *-en* cf **sjiraff**

***gi're**[1] *V -te*: **g- etter** aspire to, desire, long for.

gi're[2] [gi're] *V* +*-te/***-a* shift gears.

gire[3] *V* +*-te/***-a naut.* yaw.

girere [sjire're] *V -te merc.* transfer (from one account to another) by endorsement.

girlande [girlan(g)'d] *-n* festoon, garland.

giro [sji'ro] *-en* 1 kind of money order by which the money is paid to the "postal check account" of the payee. 2 *merc.* transfer (from one account to another) by endorsement.

giro/konto *-en* postal check account.

giro/nummer [/nommer] *-eret, pl -er/*+*-numre* postal check account number.

+**gir/stang** [gi'r/] *-a, pl -stenger* (=***/stong)** gearshift lever.

+**gi's** *pt of* **gi**

***gi'sen** *A -e/-i, pl -ne* cf **gissen**

Gis'ke[1] *Pln* 1 twp, Møre og Romsdal. 2 island, Giske twp.

Gis'ke[2] [gi-] *Prn (f)*

Gis'le [gi-] *Prn (m)*

gisler [gis'ler] *pl of* **gissel**

gis'ne[1] *V -a/*+*-et* (of wood) shrink; crack open; *naut.* be leaky, unseaworthy.

gis'ne[2] *pl of* **gissen**

+**gis'ning** *-en* guess, guesswork.

+**gis'p** *-et* gasp.

+**gis'pe** *V -a/-et* 1 gasp: **g- etter luft** gasp for air. 2 yawn (=**gjespe**).

giss[1] [giss'] *en mus.* g sharp: **g- moll** g sharp minor.

giss[2] [giss'] *I* here piggy piggy; sooey (used for hogs).

gis'se *V -a/*+*-et* cf **gjette**

gissel [gis'sel] *-elen/*+*-elet/*+*gislet, pl gisler* hostage.

gis'sen *A* +*-ent, pl gisne* (=***gisen**) cracked, not tight; open, shrunk; *naut.* leaky, unseaworthy.

gis'ten *A* +*-ent, pl -ne* cf **gissen**

+**gis'tne** *V -a/-et* cf **gisne**[1]

gitar [gita'r] *-en* guitar.

gitarist [gitaris't] *-en* guitarist.

gi'/tau *-et naut.* clew line; clew garnet; brail.

git're *V -a/*+*-et naut.* skeet.

gitt'[1] *pp of* **gi**

°**gitt**[2] [gitt'] *I* (=**gett**) *fam.* boy, fellow, kid: **god tur g-!** good trip, kid! (Evensmo); **så moro det var da, g-!** boy, that sure was fun!

gitter [git'ter] *-eret/gitret, pl -er/*+*gitre* grating, grille; (prison) bars; lattice (work), trellis; (wire) netting; (fence) railing; (radio) grid.

gitter/verk [git'ter/] *-et* grating, latticework, trelliswork.

+**givak't** *en* cf **akt**[1]

+**gi've** *V gav, givet* cf **gi**

+**gi'ven** *A -et, pl -ne* given: **anse det for g-et** take it for granted; **det er ikke g-et at** it does not (necessarily) follow that; **en g- sak** a foregone conclusion.

+**gi'vende** *A* - (=***gjevande**) 1 helpful, productive (of ideas, etc.): **en g- diskusjon** a valuable discussion. 2: **få til g-(s)** be made a present of; get for nothing; be handed on a silver platter.

+ Bokmål; * Nynorsk; ° Dialect. After letter: ' stress (Acc. 1); ' tone, stress (Acc. 2); · length. Below letter: . not pronounced.

+**gi'ver** _-en, pl -e_ (=*-ar, *gjevar) donor, giver: _bibl._ **Gud elsker en glad g-** God loveth a cheerful giver (II Corinth. 9,7).

***giv'nad** _-en, pl -er_ aptitude, gift, talent (**til å** for): **g- til å gledjast av alt som er fagert** the ability to enjoy everything beautiful (Aasen).

+**gjal'dt** _pt of_ **gjelde**[1]

Gjal'lar/ho'rn _Prn_ (Norse) _myth._ Heimdal's horn (the blowing of which proclaims the end of the world).

gjal'le _V -a/+-et_ (=***gjelle**[2]) reverberate, resound, ring.

***gje'** _V gjev, gav, gjeve/-i_ cf **gi**

gjed'de _-a zool._ (northern) pike (Esox lucius).

***gjegn** [jeng'n] _A_ 1 straight. 2 comfortable, convenient.

***gjegne** [jeng'ne] _V -de_ 1 meet. 2 dispel, drive away. 3 answer, refute.

***gjegn/veg** [jeng'n/] _-en_ cf **gjen/**

°**gjei'p** _-en/-et_ cf **geip**

gjekk'[1] _-en_ fool, silly person: **drive g- med** make a fool of; **slå g-en løs** act with complete abandon, wantonly.

***gjekk'**[2] _pt of_ **gå**[1]

gjek'ke _V -a/+-et archaic_ fool, hoax; fool around with, tease.

gje'l[1] _-et/+-en_ (=**bever/g-**) castor, castoreum (used by professional trappers to scent bait).

gje'l[2] _-et_ (narrow) canyon, pass, ravine.

***gje'l**[3] _pr of_ **gale**

gjel'ḍ[1] _-a/+-en_ debt, indebtedness: **stifte g-** contract debts; **stå i g- til en** owe sby money, _fig._ be indebted to sby.

gjel'ḍ[2] _-et archaic, eccl._ clerical district, parish (=**preste/g-**).

gjel'ḍ[3] _A_ 1 castrated, emasculated. 2 barren, sterile; dry (e.g. a cow).

gjel'ḍ/bukk [/bokk] _-en_ castrated billy goat (or ram).

gjel'ḍ/bunḍen _A +-ent, pl -ne_ encumbered with debts, heavily indebted.

gjel'de[1] _V galdt/+gjaldt, +-t/*golde/*-i_ 1 be considered, be worth, count (**for, som** as); matter, be important: **han g-er ikke stort utafor bygda** he doesn't much count outside his community; **steinene gjaldt for (som) penger** the stones counted as money. 2 apply, be in force, be valid, hold good: **denne loven g-er ikke lenger** this law is no longer in force, valid. 3 be a matter, question of; be necessary, be needed; be intended for: **det g-er** (_fam._ **gjelds om**) it's a question of; it's necessary to; **det g-er livet** it's a question of life (and death); **her g-er det å ha mot** here (in this) one has to have courage; **nå g-er det** now's the time, the critical moment (to do one's best, put forth one's energies, etc.); **skuddet gjaldt oss** the shot was intended for us. 4 apply to, concern; relate to, refer to: **diskusjonen gjaldt ikke dette spørsmålet** the discussion didn't concern this question. (Cf **gjeldende.**)

gjel'ḍe[2] _V -a/+-et/+-te/*-e_ castrate, emasculate.

gjel'ḍenḍe _A_ - in force, valid: **bli g-** come into force, take effect; **gjøre g-** claim, contend, maintain; **gjøre sin innflytelse g- på** exert one's influence on; **gjøre seg g-** assert oneself (person), be in evidence, manifest itself.

gjel'ḍ/fri _A -tt_ free from (out of) debt, unencumbered.

gjel'ḍing _-en_ eunuch.

gjel'ḍ/ku _-a_ barren, sterile cow; dry cow.

+**gjel'ḍs/bevi's** _-et_ any written acknowledgment of debt (e.g. IOU, promissory note, etc.).

gjel'ḍs/brev _-et_ any written acknowledgment of debt (e.g. bond, debenture, IOU, promissory note, etc.).

gjel'ḍs/post _-en merc._ debit, item of debt.

+**gjeli'ker** _-en, pl -e/*gjelikar_ equal.

gjell' _A gjelt_ piercing, sharp, shrill.

gjel'le[1] _-a zool._ gill.

***gjel'le**[2] _V gall, golle/-i_ cf **gjalle**

gjel'le/blaḍ _-et zool._ gill lamella.

***gje'm** _-en_ steam, vapor; odor, smell.

***gje'me** _V -a_ steam; smell.

+**gjem'me**[1] _-t_ (=***gøyme**[1]) 1 custody, keeping. 2 hiding place; repository.

+**gjem'me**[2] _V gjemte_ (=+**gjømme**, ***gøyme**[2]) 1 keep, preserve; put, set aside, save: **g- på noe** keep sth; _fig._ treasure sth (e.g. a memory); **g- til senere** defer, hold over; **g-t er ikke glemt** unmentioned but not forgotten; **la g-t være glemt** let bygones be bygones. 2 conceal, hide: **g- seg bort** be a recluse; **g- unna** put out of sight; save for later.

+**gjem'me/sted** _-et_ hiding place; repository.

+**gjem'sel** _-elet/-let, pl -ler_ (=+**gjømsel**, ***gøymsle**) hiding place: **leke g-** play hide and seek.

+**gjen'-** _Pf_ re-.

+**gjen'/bo** _-en_ (=**/boer**) neighbor across the street, across the way.

Gjen'de _Pln_ lake, Jotunheimen.

+**gjen'/drive** _V -drev, -drevet_ disprove, refute.

+**gjen'/døper** _-en, pl -e_ Anabaptist.

+**gjen'/ero'bre** _V -et_ recapture, reconquer.

+**gjen'/ferd** _-et_ apparition, ghost, spectre.

+**gjen'/fortel'le** _V -fortalte_ repeat, retell.

+**gjen'/fortel'ling** _-en_ retelling (e.g. of a story in a foreign language class); transcription (e.g. of an oral narrative).

+**gjen'/føde** _V -te theol._ regenerate (spiritually): **g-s** be born again (spiritually).

gjeng'[1] _-en_ gang, work crew; gang (e.g. of bootleggers, hoodlums): **hele g-en** the whole lot of them.

***gjeng'**[2] _pr of_ **gange**[3]

+**gjen'/ganger** _-en, pl -e_ apparition, ghost, revenant: **Ibsens G-e** Ibsen's _Ghosts_ (play, 1881).

+**gjen'/gav** [/ga] _pt of_ **-gi**[1]

***gjeng'd** _A -/-gjengt_ walking; able to walk; convenient (for walking).

+**gjeng'e**[1] _N_ course, progress: **alt var i beste g-** everything was going as well as could be expected; **i den gamle g-** in the old groove; **saken er i god g-** the matter is well in hand.

gjeng'e[2] _-t/+-n_ 1 _tech._ thread: **gå over g-** (of a screw) fail to catch, hold. 2 _dial._ (of a lock or key) ward. 3 _dial._ hinge.

gjeng'e[3] _V -a/+-et tech._ cut threads.

***gjeng'e**[4] _pp of_ **gange**[3]

***gjeng'eleg** _A_ - current, prevailing.

***gjeng'en** _A -e/-i, pl -ne_ 1 gone; past. 2 skilled.

+**gjen'/gi**[1] _V -gav, -gitt_ 1 _archaic_ give back, restore. 2 repeat; express, render, reproduce; cite, quote: **g- in extenso** repeat in full (verbatim); **g- galt** misquote.

***gjeng'i**[2] _pp of_ **gange**[3]

+**gjen'/givelse** _-n_ (=**-ing**) rendering, reproduction; version (**av** of).

gjen'/gjelḍ _N_ return; reprisal, retribution: **gjøre g-** reciprocate; retaliate; **til g- (for)** in return (for); in retaliation (for); **men til g-** (also) but on the other hand.

gjen'/gjelḍe _V -te_ repay, return; retaliate: **g- ondt med godt** return good for evil.

+**gjen'/gjelḍelse** _-n_ reprisal, retribution (**for** for).

***gjeng'le** _-a_ 1 (little) wheel. 2 stilt. 3 (screw) thread.

+**gjen'/glemt** _A_ - forgotten, left behind.

+**gjen'/grodd** _A_ - (of wounds) healed; (of garden) overgrown, weed-choked: **På g-e stier** On Overgrown Paths (book by Hamsun).

gjeng's _A_ - current, prevailing: **overfall og mord hørte til de g-e begivenheter** assault and murder were everyday occurrences (Sverdrup).

+**gjen'/kalle** _V -kalte_ recall: **g- i erindringen** call to mind; **g- seg** recollect.

+**gjenkal'leliġ** _A_ - revocable.

+**gjen'/kjenne** _V -kjente_ recognize; identify: **nikke g-ende** nod in recognition.

+**gjen'kjøps/rett** _-en jur._ right of redemption.

+**gjen'/klang** _-en_ 1 echo (**av** of). 2: **finne (vekke, vinne) g-** find (awaken, win) response, sympathy.

+**gjen'/komst** _-en_ reappearance, return (**til** to): **Kristi g-** the Second Coming.

+**gjen'/levenḍe** _A_ - surviving: **de g-** the survivors.

+**gjen'/lyd** _-en_ echo.

+**gjen'/lyde** _V -de/-lød, -d/-t_ echo, resound, reverberate (**av** with).

+**gjen'/løse** _V -te bibl._ redeem (Psalms 107, 2).

+**gjen'/løser** _-en bibl._ Redeemer (Job 19, 25).

+**gjen'/mæle** [/mele] _N_: **ta til g- mot** reply, retort to; defend oneself (e.g. against an accusation).

+**gjen'nem** _P_ cf **gjennom**

gjen'nom _P_ 1 through: **g- hele livet** throughout life; **g- ørkenen** across the desert; **g- årene** over the years; **komme seg g-** get through; **slå seg g-** fight one's way to success, struggle through. 2 _(adv.)_ completely, thoroughly: **en g- hederlig mann** an honest man through and through.

+**gjen'nom/arbei'de** _V -et_ work over; overhaul, prepare thoroughly (e.g. soil, a piece of writing, a plan).

gjen'nom/bløyte _V -te/+-bløtte_ drench, soak.

gjen'nom/bore _V -a/+-et_ penetrate, perforate, pierce.

gjen'nom/brott _-et_ (+**/brudd**) 1 breach; _mil._ breakthrough. 2 _fig._ breakthrough, success: **Det nasjonale g-** the National Renaissance (term designating esp. period 1840-70 in Norway); **Det moderne g-** The Period of Realism (term for literary period in Scand. from 1870-90, from a book by Georg Brandes).

+**gjen'nom/brudd** _-et_ cf **/brott**

gjen'nom/fart _-en_ passage.

gjen'nom/føre _V -te_ 1 accomplish; carry out, through, go through with. 2: **g-t** consistent, sustained.

gjen'nom/føring _-a/+-en_ accomplishment, execution (**av** of).

gjen'nom/førliġ _A_ - feasible, practicable.

gjen'nom/gang _-en_ 1 passage; gateway, thoroughfare; transition: **g- forbudt** no through traffic. 2 _astron._ transit. 3 _mus._ passing note.

gjen'nomgangs/figu'r _-en_ character, figure which reappears in various scenes, e.g. of a pageant or play, and unifies them.

+**gjen'nom/gikk** _pt of_ **-gå**

+**gjen'nom/gripenḍe** _A_ - drastic, radical, sweeping.

+**gjen'nom/gå** _V -gikk, -gått_ 1 experience, go through, suffer. 2 examine thoroughly, scrutinize; go through (step by step), study.

gjen'nom/gåenḍe _A_ - 1 through (e.g. train). 2 common, general. 3 _(adv.)_ in most cases, on the whole.

+**gjen'nom/hegle** _V -et_ criticize savagely, tear to pieces.

+**gjen'nom/hullet** _A_ - perforated, punched: **g- med kuler** riddled, shot full of holes.

gjen'nom/kjørsel _-elen, pl -ler_ driving through; passage, thoroughfare: **g- forbudt** no through traffic.

gjen'nom/leve _V -de_ experience, live through, undergo.

gjen'nom/lyse _V -te_ 1 shine light through: **g-t** translucent; luminous. 2 candle (eggs). 3 _med._ fluoroscope, transilluminate.

gjen'nom/pløye *V -pløgde/+-de* 1 investigate thoroughly, reconnoiter (e.g. a country). 2 *fig.* plow, wade through, work one's way through (e.g. a book).
gjen'nom/prøve *V -de* test thoroughly.
gjen'nom/reise *-a/+-en*: **på g- (til)** on the way through, passing through (to).
+gjen'nom/se *V -så, -sett* (=***/sjå**) examine, inspect, look over; look through.
+gjen'nom/siktig *A* - transparent; *fig.* lucid.
+gjen'nom/skinne *V -te* illuminate, shine through: **g-t** radiant, transparent.
+gjen'nom/skinnelig *A* - (=***/skinleg**) translucent.
+gjen'nom/skjære *V -skar, -skåret* (=***/skjere**) 1 intersect, traverse. 2 *math.* (e.g. of chords in a circle) intersect.
gjen'nom/skjæring *-a* cut (e.g. for a railroad).
+gjen'nom/skue *V -et* see through (disguise, intentions, etc.).
gjen'nom/slag *-et* 1 breakthrough. 2 carbon copy.
gjen'nomslags/kraft *-a/+-en mil.* (of a projectile) penetration; *fig.* force.
gjen'nom/snitt *-et* average, mean: **i g-** on the average.
gjen'nom/snittlig *A* - average, mean; on the average.
gjen'nom/syn *-et/*-a* examination, inspection (**av** of).
***gjen'nomsynleg** *A* - transparent.
gjen'nom/syre *V -a/+-et/-te* leaven (dough); *fig.* permeate, pervade.
+gjen'nom/så *pt of* **-se**
+gjen'nom/tenke *V -te* think out, weigh carefully.
gjen'nom/trekk *-en* draft: **sitte i g-** sit in the d-.
+gjen'nom/trenge *V -te* (=***-je**) imbue, permeate.
+gjen'nom/trengende *A* - penetrating, pervasive, piercing.
gjen'nom/våt *A* drenched, soaking wet.
***gje'nom** *P* cf **gjennom**
+gjen'/oppbygge *V -bygde* rebuild, reconstruct.
+gjen'/oppfriske *V -a/-et*: **g- i erindringen** call to mind, revive in the mind (e.g. a scene).
+gjen'/oppleve *V -de* relive.
+gjen'/opplive *V -et* resuscitate, revive.
+gjen'/opprette *V -a/-et* 1 reestablish, restore; repair. 2 retrieve (e.g. a loss).
+gjen'/oppstå *V -stod, -stått* be resurrected, rise again.
+gjen'/oppta *V -tok, -tatt* reopen, resume, take up again.
+gjen'/opptagelse *-n* resumption (**av** of).
+gjen'/part *-en* copy, transcript (**av** of).
+gjen'/reise *V -te* rebuild, reconstruct; raise again, restore.
gjen'/sidig [also si'-] *A*- mutual, reciprocal: **etter g- overenskomst** by mutual consent; *merc.* **g- forsikring** mutual insurance.
+gjen'/sitter *-en, pl -e educ.* repeater.
+gjen'/skape *V -te* recreate; restore.
+gjen'/skinn *-et* reflection (**av** of).
+gjen'/speile *V -te* reflect.
gjen'/stand *-en* 1 object, thing. 2 object, subject (**for** of): **gjøre til g- for** make the subject of; **være g- for** be the object, subject of; **g- for diskusjon** topic of discussion
+gjen'/stod *pt of* **-stå**
+gjen'/stridig *A* - rebellious, unmanageable; obstinate, stubborn.
+gjen'/stå *V -stod, -stått* be left, remain (e.g. matters on the agenda).
+gjen'/svar *-et* rejoinder, response (**til** to).
+gjen'/syn *-et* meeting (again): **på g-** see you later, so long.
+gjen'syns/glede *-n* joy of meeting again, reunion.
+gjen'/ta *V -tok, -tatt* reiterate, repeat: **g- seg** recur; **g- til kjedsommelighet** repeat ad nauseam.
+gjen'/tagen *A -ent, pl -ne* repeated: **g-ne ganger** repeatedly, over and over again.
+gjen'/takelse [also /ta'gelse] *-n* reiteration, repetition; recurrence (**av** of).
+gjen'takelses/tilfelle *-t*: *jur.* **i g-** in the case of a repetition of an offence.
***gjen'te** *-a* cf **jente**
***gjen'te/lag** *-et* cf **jente/**
+gjen'/tok *pt of* **-ta**
+gjen'/valg *-et* reelection: **stille seg til g-** run again (for an office).
+gjen'/valgte *pt of* **-velge**
+gjen'/vant *pt of* **-vinne**
+gjen'/veg *-en* (=**+/vei**) *obs.* short cut: **skyte g-** take a short cut.
+gjen'/velge *V -valgte* reelect.
+gjen'/vinne *V -vant, -vunnet* recover, regain, retrieve: **g- balansen** recover oneself.
+gjenvor'dig/het *-en*: **g-er** hardships, tribulations, troubles.
+gjen'/vunnet *pp of* **-vinne**
+gje'p *-en* cf **geip**
+gje'pe *V -te* cf **geipe**
***gje'r** *V pr of* **gjere**
***gjerande** [jæ'rande] *A* - feasible, practicable; advisable.
***gjerands/laus** [jæ'rans/] *A* futile, idle.
***gjerast** [jæ'rast] *V gjerst, gjordest, gjorst* 1 be in the making; ferment. 2 develop, mature, ripen. 3: **g- på** defy, do on purpose.
gjerd [jæ'r] *-a* 1 manner, way: **ei anna g-** a different w-; **ikkje noka g- på det** no sense to it; **det er berre etter armmanns g-** it's just in the poor man's manner (Vesaas). 2 action, conduct. 3 development, ripening. 4 effect, force. 5 sorcery, witchcraft.
gjerde[1] [jæ're] *N* (=**+gjære**[1]): **være i g-** be afoot, brewing, in the wind.
gjerde[2] [jæ're] *-t* 1 fence; *fig.* barrier. 2 *dial.* cattle pen. 3 *dial.* field.
gjerde[3] [jæ're] *V -a/+-et/*-e* fence (**inn** in).
gjerde/fang *-et* fence materials.
gjerde/smett *-en* (=**+/smutt**) *zool.* wren (Troglodytes troglodytes).
***gjerd/laus** [jæ'r/] *A* confused, disordered.
Gjer'drum *Pln* twp, Akershus.
***gjer'dsle** *-a* enclosure, fence.
***gjere** [jæ're] *V gjer, gjorde, gjort* cf **gjøre**
***gjere/mål** *-et* cf **gjøre/**
***gjer'ne**[1] *-t* (fish) entrails.
gjer'ne[2] [usu. jæ'rne] *Av* 1 gladly, readily, willingly; just as well; possibly: **De kastet g- steiner etter meg, om De våget det** you would gladly throw stones at me, if you dared (Ibsen); **det kan du g- gjøre** you can (just as well) do that if you like; **du kan like g- la være** you may just as well stop, you needn't bother; **det tror jeg g-** I believe that all right, I have no doubt of it; **g- for meg** I have no objection, I'm quite agreeable; OK by me; **ja, gjerne det** yes (OK), why not. 2: **vil(le) g-** should, would like (to); **hvor g- jeg enn ville (om jeg aldri så g- ville), så kan jeg ikke** however (no matter how) much I would like to, I can't; **jeg vil(le) g- ha en kopp kaffe** I would like a cup of coffee. 3 possibly: **det kan g- være** that's quite possible, that may well be; **ungen kunne g- slå den over ende** the child might knock it down. 4 as a rule, generally, usually: **han kom g- om aftenen** he came as a rule in the evening (he would come in the evening).
gjer'ning [usu. jæ'rning] *-a/+-en* 1 work; mission, task: **der har du en g- å gjøre** there you have a mission to fulfill (Falkberget). 2 act, deed: **Apostlenes G-er** *bib.* Acts; **en god g-** a good deed; **falle på sine g-er** get what's coming to one; **i ord og g-** in word and deed; **ta viljen i g-ens sted** give sby credit for trying.
gjer'nings/mann *-en, pl -menn *-menner jur.* criminal, culprit.
gjer'nings/o'rd *-et gram.* verb.
+gjer'nings/sted *-et jur.* scene of the crime.
Gjer'pen *Pln* twp, Telemark.
gjer'rig *A* - (=***gjerug**) miserly, stingy, *(pop.)* tight.
+gjer'rig/het *-en* stinginess.
gjer'rig/knark *-en pop.* tightwad.
***gjer'rig/skap** *-en* stinginess.
***gjer'sle** *-a* deed, doing, esp. in cpds. (**av/, til/**).
Gjer'stad *Pln* twp, Aust-Agder.
Gjer'trud *Prn(f)* Gertrude.
gjer'truds/fugl *-en zool.* black woodpecker (Dendrocopus martius).
***gje'rug** *A* - cf **gjerrig**
gjes'p *-en/+-et* (=***geisp**) yawn.
gjes'pe *V -a/+-et* (=***geispe**) yawn.
+gjess' *pl of* **gås**
gjes't *-en* 1 guest (**hos** at): **en daglig g-** a daily g-. 2 intruder, visitor: **ubudne g-er** unwelcome visitors. 3 customer, patron; (hotel, resort) resident. 4 guest star (at theater).
Gjes'tal *Pln* twp, Rogaland.
gjes'te *V -a/+-et* 1 visit; frequent; afflict. 2 guest star (at theater).
+gjes'te/bud *-et* (=***/bod**) banquet, feast, party.
***gjes'te/heim** *-en* hostel; guest house.
gjes'ter *-en* yeast.
gjestere're *V -te fam.* go visiting; travel the banquet circuit.
gjes'te/rolle *-a/+-en* guest role: **gi g-r** guest star.
+gjes'te/spill *-et* (=***/spel**) guest performance.
gjes'te/vennskap *-en/+-et lit.* hospitality (esp. to strangers).
gjes't/fri *A -tt* hospitable.
+gjes't/fri/het *-en* hospitality: **nyte g-** enjoy h-.
+gjes't/giver *-en* (=***-ar, */gjevar**) innkeeper, landlord.
+gjes't/giveri' *-et* inn.
+gje't *-en* cf **geit**
***gje'tande** *A* - noteworthy.
***gje'te**[1] *V gat, gjete/-i* 1 conjecture, guess. 2 mention, note: **høyre gjete** hear mentioned, spoken of.
gje'te[2] *V -te* 1 herd, tend (goats, sheep, etc.): **g- bort** lose part of the herd. 2 guard, watch: **g- på** keep an eye on.
***gje'ten** *A -e/-i, pl -ne* observant, watchful.
+gje'ter *-en, pl -e* (=***-ar**) herder, shepherd.
+gje'ter/gutt *-en* (=***gjetar/gut**) shepherd boy.
***gje'ti** *pp of* **gjete**[1], *nt of* **gjeten**
+gjet'ning *-a/-en* cf **gjetting**
gje't/o'rd *-et* report, rumor.
***gjets'le** *-a* 1 herding, tending. 2 pasture.
+gjet'te *V -a/-et* (=***gjete**[1]) guess; conjecture, divine: **g- på noe** guess at, make a guess at sth; **g- riktig** hit it right on the nose; **g- seg fram** proceed by conjecture, guess; **g- seg til noe** arrive at sth by guesswork.
+gjet'te/konkurranse [/-ang'se] *-n* guessing contest.
+gjet'ting *-a/-en* (=**+gjetning**) conjecture, guess, *(pop.)* shot in the dark.
+gjett'/verk *-et* guesswork.
+gje'v[1] *A* cf **gjæv**
***gje'v**[2] *C* cf **gid**[1]
***gje'vande** *A* - cf **givende**
***gje'var** *-en* cf **giver**
***gje've** *V gav, gjeve/-i* cf **gi**
***gje'ving** *-a* cf **givning**

+ Bokmål; * Nynorsk; ° Dialect.
After letter: ' stress (Acc. 1); ` tone, stress (Acc. 2); · length.
Below letter: . not pronounced.

***gje'v/mild** *A* cf **gav/**

***gjo'r** *A* cf **gjord**[2]

gjo'rd[1] *-a* **1** cinch. **2** hoop (e.g. on a barrel).

gjo'rd**[2] *A* (=gjor**) ripe.

gjo'rde[1] *V -a/+-et* (=+**gjure, *gjurde**) **1** bind (up), tie (around). **2** *poet.* gird (on a sword).

gjo'rde[2] *pl of* **gjøre, gjere**

+**gjor's** *pt of* **gjørs**[2]

gjor't *pp of* **gjøre, gjere**

***gjo'se** *V gys, gaus, gose/-i* gush, rush forth (water, stream of air).

***gjo'te** *V gyt, gaut, gjote/-i* cf **gyte**

***gju'rde** *V -a* cf **gjorde**[1]

+**gju're** *V -te* cf **gjorde**[1]

+**gju're/tau** *-et* rope (to secure a load of hay).

gju'v *-et* cf **juv**

gjæ'r *-en* yeast.

+**gjæ're**[1] *N* cf **gjerde**[1]

gjæ're[2] *V -a/+-et/+-te* ferment; *fig.* ferment, work: **g-ende krefter** ferment, unrest.

gjæ're[3] *V -a/+-te carp.* bevel, miter.

gjæ'ring *-a/+-en* **1** fermentation; *fig.* ferment, unrest. **2** miter joint.

gjæ'r/kasse *-a/-en carp.* miter box.

gjæ'r/lås *-en/-et chem.* trap (allowing escape of gases).

gjæ'r/sopp *-en bot.* yeast plant (genus Saccharomyces).

gjæ'ser *pl of* **gås**

gjæ'te *V -te* cf **gjete**[2]

***gjætsle** [jes'le] *-a* cf **gjetsle**

gjæv [je'v] *A* fine, splendid; distinguished, eminent; noble; able, capable (**til å** in).

gjæving [je'ving] *-en* distinguished person; outstanding individual.

***gjæv/leik** [je'v/] *-en* **1** eminence, prestige. **2** generosity.

+**gjø'**[1] *-et dial.* barking.

+**gjø'**[2] *V -dde* (=***gøy**[2]) bark (**på** at).

gjø'[3] *V -dde* (=***gjøde**) fatten up.

+**gjø'd** *pt of* **gyde**

***gjø'de** *V -de* cf **gjø**[3]

gjø'dning *-en* fertilizer.

gjøds'el *-la* fertilizer, manure.

+**gjøds'el/kjeller** *-en, pl -e* (=***-ar**) cellar under a cattle barn for storage of manure.

gjøds'le *V -a/+-et* fertilize, manure.

+**gjøg'l** *-et* (=***jugl**) **1** deception, delusion; phantasm. **2** clowning, tomfoolery.

+**gjøg'le** *V -a/-et* (=***jugle**) **1** deceive, delude. **2** clown, play tricks.

+**gjøg'le/bilde** *-t* phantasm.

+**gjøg'ler** *-en, pl -e* clown, juggler; charlatan, quack.

gjø'/gris *-en* fatted hog, pig.

+**gjø'k** *-en* cf **gauk**[1]

gjø'/kalv *-en* fatted calf.

gjø'l *-et* fawning, flattery.

gjø'le *V -te* fawn on, flatter.

***gjøl'me** *V -a* partition (off).

gjø'l/o'rd *pl* flattery.

+**gjøm'me** *V gjømte* cf **gjemme**[1]

+**gjøm'sel** *-elet/-let, pl -ler* cf **gjemsel**

+**gjøm'sle** *-a* cf **gjemsel**

gjø'n *-et* fun, sport: **drive g- med en** make fun of sby, pull sby's leg.

gjø'ne *V -te* jest, joke (**med** with); make fun (**av** of).

+**gjø're** *V gjorde, gjort* (=***gjere**) **1** do; make, cause, render: **g- det godt** be successful, make money; **g- godt** do good; **g- narr (av)** make fun (of); **gjort er gjort** what's done is done. **2** make a difference, matter: **det gjør ingenting** that's all right, that doesn't matter; **g- verken fra eller til** make no difference; **hva gjør det?** what difference does that make? what's the harm in that? **3** (as substitute verb): **skal jeg åpne vinduet? Ja, gjør det** shall I open the window? Yes, do (that); (emphasizing main verb) **snø gjorde det hele natta** it snowed the whole night (Sverdrup); **tror du det? Ja, det gjør jeg** do you believe that? Yes, I do. **4** (with *prep.* and *adv.*): **hvor har han gjort av seg?** where has he gone? what's become of him?; **g- det av med** finish; **g- noe, noen etter** copy, imitate sth, sby; **jeg kan ikke g- for det** I can't do anything about that, I can't help that; **g- noe fra seg, unna** get sth done, out of the way; finish sth; **g- godt igjen** make amends for, set to rights; **g- i stand** put in order, tidy up; **g- om (igjen)** do over, redo, repeat; change, make (**til** into); **g- opp** settle (up); prepare (**g- opp fisk** gut fish; **g- opp tømmer** trim branches and bark from a felled tree; **g- opp varme** light a fire); **g- en til noe** make sby sth; make sth of sby (**g- en til narr** make a fool of sby); **om å g-** important (**det er om å g- å komme tidlig** it's i- to come early). **5** *(refl.)*: **g- seg** look well, have a good effect, make a good show; **g- seg bedre enn man er** pretend to be better than one is; **g- seg håp om** have hopes of; **g- seg opp en mening** make up one's mind; **g- seg til** boast, put on airs; **g- seg til noe** set oneself up as sth (**g- seg til narr** make a fool of oneself); **g- seg umak** take pains, take (the) trouble.

+**gjø're/mål** *-et* (=***gjere/**) (only *pl*) business, duties, tasks.

+**gjø'ren** *en*: **g- og laten** doings.

+**gjø'rlig** *A* - possible; feasible, practicable.

gjør'me *-a* mire, mud; dregs.

gjør'met(e) *A* - muddy, turbid.

+**gjø'rning** *-en archaic*: **i g-en** afoot, brewing, in the wind.

gjø'rs[1] *-en zool.* pike perch, zander (Lucioperca sandra).

+**gjør's**[2] *V gjors, gjors* (=***gjerst**): **g- på noe** do sth in defiance, on purpose; make a point of doing sth.

gjør'tler *-en, pl +-e* brazier (brass moulder).

gjø's[1] *-en naut.* jack (a flag).

+**gjø's**[2] *pt of* **gyse**

+**gjø'/sti** *-en* sty in which pigs are fattened (for slaughter).

+**gjø't** *pt of* **gyte**

+**gjø'v** *pt of* **gyve**

Gjø'v/dal *Pln* twp, Aust-Agder.

+**gjø'vet** *pp of* **gyve**

Gjø'/vik *Pln* town on Mjøsa, Oppland.

gl.=**gammal/+gammel/*gamal**

gla' *V -dde* (=***glade**) **1** set (moon, sun). **2** (of the sun) cast a red glow as it sets.

+**glacé/hanske** *-n* (=***glase/**) kid glove.

gla'd *A* - **1** glad, happy; delighted, pleased (**for** about, because of). **2** animated, lively, merry; skylarking, (slightly) drunk: **de tok seg en g- dag sammen** they made a day of it together. **3** (with *prep.* and *adv.*): **g- i** fond of; in love with; **g- over å høre** delighted to hear; **g- til** grateful for; only too pleased to; **være like g-** not care one way or the other; be indifferent; **"Jeg er like g-," sa gutten, han satt og gråt** "I don't care," said the boy; he was crying (proverb).

***gla'de** *V -de* cf **gla**

gla'delig *Av* **1** cheerfully, gladly. **2** easily: **man kunne g- fiske 1000 kg laks pr. sommer** one could e- fish 1,000 kg salmon a summer (Romsdalsposten).

gladia'tor *-en, pl -to'rer* gladiator.

gla'd-lyndt *A* - (=**/lynt**) cheerful, light-hearted, merry.

***gla'd/vær** *A* cheerful, light-hearted.

***glaf's**[1] *-en* loose-tongued person, (*pop.*) blabbermouth.

***glaf's**[2] *-et* indiscretion.

***glaf'se** *V -a* be loose-tongued.

glam' *+-met/*-et* baying (of a dog).

+**glam'me** *V -a/-et* (=***glame**) bark, bay.

***gla'n** *-et* **1** gaping. **2** gap, opening in the clouds.

gla'ne *V -a/-te* gape, stare (**på** at); gaze (intently).

glan's *-en* **1** brilliance, glitter, radiance; gloss, luster, sheen; *tech.* glaze, polish: **en g- har solen og en annen månen** *bibl.* there is one glory of the sun, and another glory of the moon (I Cor. 15, 41); **sette g- på** give a gloss, polish to. **2** glamor, glory, splendor; *fig.* luster: **g-en var gått av ham** the luster had rubbed off of him; **han klarte prøven med g-** he passed the examination with flying colors; **kaste g- over** add luster to.

+**glan's/bilde** *-t* (=+**/billede, */bilete**) **1** glossy (colored) print, picture. **2** idealized (romanticized) description, picture.

glan'se *V -a/+-et* glisten; cause to glisten.

glan's/full *A* resplendent; brilliant, illustrious.

glan's/laus *A* (=+**/løs**) dead, dull, lackluster.

glan's/nummer [/nommer] *-et, pl -/ +-numre* outstanding act; main attraction, feature (e.g. in a variety show); high point.

glan's/papi'r *-et* glazed, glossy paper.

glan's/perio'de *-n* golden age, heyday.

glan's/rolle *-a/+-en* best part, star role (films, theater).

glan's/tid *-a/+-en* golden days, heyday.

***glan't** *-et* jest, joke.

***glan'te** *V -a* jest, joke.

gla'p *-et* crack, fissure, opening; streak.

gla'pe *V -te* be open, gape.

glapp' *pt of* **gleppe**

gla's *-et* (=+**glass**) **1** glass (substance; container); crystal: **ta seg et g-** have a drink. **2** *naut.* bell (half hour): **slå 8 g-** strike 8 bells. **3** *dial.* window.

***gla's/augo** *pl* (=**/auge**) (eye)glasses.

***gla's/blåsar** *-en* cf **glass/blåser**

gla's/brott *-et* (=***/brot**) (pieces of) broken glass.

***gla'se** *V -a* glaze.

***glasé/hanske** *-n* cf **glace/**

gla's/eple *-t, pl +-r/*-* (=+**glass/**) kind of apple which on ripening has a glassy appearance.

glase're *V -te* (=+**glassere**) **1** glaze. **2** frost, ice (cakes); candy (fruit).

gla's/hus *-et* (=+**glass/**) glass house.

glasia'l *A geol.* glacial.

gla's/karm *-en dial.* window frame.

***gla's/meister** *-eren, pl -rar* cf **glass/-mester**

***gla's/målarstyk'ke** *-t* cf **glass/maleri**

+**glas'ne** *pl of* **glassen**

gla's/plate *-a/+-en* glass plate.

gla's/rute *-a/+-en* window pane.

+**glass'** *-et* cf **glas**

+**glass'/aktig** *A* - **1** glassy, glazed. **2** *chem.* vitreous.

+**glass'/blåser** *-en, pl -e* glass blower.

+**glas'sen** *A -ent, pl glasne* glassy, glazed.

+**glass'/eple** *-t* cf **glas/**

+**glasse're** *V -te* cf ***glasere**

+**glass'/hus** *-et* cf **glas/**

+**glass'/legeme** *-t anat.* vitreous humor (in the eye).

+**glass'/maleri'** *-et* stained glass painting; stained glass (picture).

+**glass'/mester** *-eren, pl -ere/-rer* glazier.

+**glass'/rute** *-a/-en* cf **glas/**

+**glass'/tøy** *-et* **1** glassware. **2** glass fibre.

+**glass'/verk** *-et* glassworks.

+**glass'/øye** *-t* **1** glass eye. **2** *vet.* walleye.

gla's/ull *-a* (=+**glass/**) glass wool.

glasu'r *-en* **1** glaze. **2** frosting, icing.

gla's/vatt *-et/+-en* (=+**glass/**) glass wool.

glatt'[1] *A* - **1** plain, sleek, smooth: **en g- ring** a plain ring; **en g- stil** a smooth (but undistinguished) style. **2** slippery; *fig.* oily, smooth-tongued: **g- føre** slippery going; **en g- tunge** a glib tongue. **3**: **gå g-** be easy; **det gikk ikke så g-** it was not all plain (smooth) sailing. **4**: **gi ham det g-e lag** give him a broadside, *fig.* let him have it.

***glatt'**[2] *pt of* **glette**
glat'te *V -a/+-et* smooth; iron; polish: **g- ut** smooth away, out, straighten out; *fig.* gloss over, iron out (difficulties); *tech.* **g- papir** glaze paper.
glatt`/håra *A* - **(=+-et)** sleek-, smooth-haired.
glatt`/is *-en* icy surface: **komme på g-en** *fig.* be on thin ice.
+glatt`/slepen *A -ent/-et, pl -slepne* ground, polished.
+glatt`/slikket *A* - sleek, smooth.
***glau'p** *pt of* **glupe**
gla`vin *-et poet.* brand, sword.
gle' *V -dde* **(=glede**[2]**)** 1 delight, gratify, please: **det g-r meg å høre det** I'm glad to hear it; **g- en med å gjøre noe** give sby pleasure by doing sth; **g- ens hjerte** do one's heart good. 2 *(refl.)* be glad, happy, pleased: **g- seg for tidlig** count one's chickens before they're hatched; **g- seg over (ved) noe** be delighted with, take great pleasure in; **g- seg til noe** look forward to sth; **jeg g-r meg til det er forbi** I'll be glad when it's over.
+gle'ḍ *pt of* **gli(de)**
gle`de**[1] [\*gle`e] *-a/+-en* 1 gladness, happiness; delight, joy, pleasure: **det er meg en g- å gjøre det it gives me great pleasure to do it, I'm very happy to do it; **hans eneste g-** his only pleasure, his sole delight; **nyte bordets g-r** enjoy good food; **jeg forkynner dere en stor g-** *bibl.* I bring you good tidings of great joy (Luke 2, 10-11). 2 (with *prep.*): **gråte av g-** weep for joy; **ha g- av noe** find comfort, pleasure, satisfaction in sth; **han har ingen g- av det** it won't do him any good, it's not to his interest; **ute av seg av g-** beside oneself with joy; **finne g- i** delight in, take pleasure in; **med g-** gladly; **være til g- for en** be to sby's great delight.
gle`de**[2] [\*gle`e] *V -de/+-et* cf **gle
gle`de/laus *A* **(=+/løs)** cheerless, joyless.
gle`delig *A* - glad, happy; gratifying, pleasant: **g- jul** merry Christmas.
+gle`des/budskap *-et* glad tidings, good news.
+gle`des/dreper *-en, pl -e* **(=*-ar)** killjoy; *(pop.)* wet blanket.
+gle`des/rus *-en/-et* **(=*glede/)** rapture, transport (of joy).
+gle`des/skrik *-et* **(=*glede/)** shout of joy.
gle`de/strålenḍe *A* - beaming, radiant (with joy).
gle`de/stunḍ *-a/+-en* hour, moment of happiness.
***gle`ḍ/sam'** *A* gratifying, pleasant, merry.
glef's *-en/-et* 1 (of a dog) snap. 2 (of food) gulp, snatch, swallow.
glef`se[1] *-a* wild-animal trap, esp. a fox trap.
glef`se[2] *V -a/+-et/-te* 1 (of a dog) snap (**etter** at): *fig.* **g- etter en** bark, snap at sby. 2 bolt, wolf (food).
glei' *pt of* **gli**
***glei'ḍ**[1] *pt of* **gli**
***glei'ḍ**[2] *A* distended, extended, spread (e.g. fingers).
***glei'm** *-en* furtive glance.
***glei`me** *V -a/+-te* 1 steal a furtive glance at; look askance at. 2 look crafty, underhanded.
***glei`ne** *V -a* look askance at, look at sth with a jaundiced eye.
***glei`vre** *V -a* use blasphemous language.
glek`se *-a* cf **glefse**[1]
+glem`me[1] *N* **(=*gløyme**[1]**): gå i g-** be forgotten, sink into oblivion.
+glem`me[2] *V glemte* **(=+glømme, *gløyme**[2]**)** forget, leave (out), omit: **det skal aldri bli g-t Dem** I won't forget this; **g- bort noe** forget sth completely, *(pop.)* clean forget sth; **g- igjen** leave behind; **g- like fort som en lærer** have a memory like a sieve; **g- seg** forget oneself; **g- seg selv** not think about oneself; **ha g-t sine gamle kunster** be out of practice, lose one's touch.
+glem`me/boka *df* **(=+glømme/, *gløyme/): gå i g-** be forgotten, sink into oblivion.
Glem`men *Pln* twp, Østfold.
+glem`sel *-en* **(=+glømsel, *gløymsle)** forgetfulness, oblivion: **dra fram av g-en** rescue from oblivion.
+glem'sk *A* - **(=+glømsk, *gløymsk)** absentminded, forgetful.
+glem`/som· *A -t, pl -me* **(=*gløym/sam)** absentminded, forgetful.
+glem`som/het *-en* absentmindedness, forgetfulness.
glen`ne *-a* clearing, opening (in a forest); stretch of grassland (in a forest or between mountains).
glen`te *-n zool.* kite (Milvus milvus).
***glepp'** *-en* 1 miss, slip. 2 glimpse.
glep`pe *V glapp, +-et/*gloppe/*-i* 1 loosen, work loose. 2 slip, slip away, out of one's grasp. 3 fail: **det glapp for ham ved eksamen** he failed the examination.
°gles`ne *V -a/-et* cf **glisne**
glet'sjer *-en, pl +-e* glacier.
glet`te[1] *-n* break, opening in the clouds: **østa g- gir våt hette** clearing in the east means more rain.
glet`te[2] *-n chem.* lead monoxide, litharge.
***glet`te**[3] *V glatt, glotte/-i* glide, slip: **det glatt ut av henne** she let it slip, let the cat out of the bag.
***glet`te**[4] *V -a/-e* 1 peep, peek. 2 whisper about; hint at. 3 taunt.
***glet`ten** *A -e/-i, pl gletne* slippery.
gli' *V glei, glidd* **(=glide)** 1 glide, slide; drift, flow, slip by: **g-ende skala** sliding scale; **g- bort fra en** drift away from sby; **g- inn i noe** pass, slip into sth; **g- med strømmen** drift with the current; **g- ned** go down, slide down (into one's stomach); *fig.* be acceptable, palatable; **g- opp** slide open; **g- over i** merge, pass into; **g- tilbake i** lapse into; **g- ut** slide (e.g. snow); **g- vekk** give way; vanish. 2 skid, slip (**i, på** on): **g- ut** skid; *fig.* depart from norm, deviate; grow dissolute. 3 move (easily), progress: **det vil ikke g- for meg** I can't get going; **nå begynner det å g-** now things are starting to move.
gli'ḍ *-en/-et* glide, slide; gliding, sliding: **på g-** going; **få en på g-** help sby get started (e.g. in telling a story).
gli`de** [\*gli`e] *V +gled/*gleid, +-d/*-e/*-i* cf **gli
gli`de/flukt *-a* glide; gliding.
gli`de/fly *-et* glider.
gli`de/lås *-en* zipper.
gli`der *-en, pl -e* **(=*-ar)** glider.
gli`de/skala *-en* sliding scale.
***gli`me**[1] *-a* dazzling light, glare.
gli`me[2] *V +-te/*-a/*-de* glow, shine.
***gli`men** *A -e/-i, pl -ne* dazzling.
***gli`me/stein** *-en* jewel, precious stone.
glim`mer *-en* 1 glitter, tinsel. 2 *chem.* mica.
glim`re *V -a/+-et* 1 glitter, glisten: **det er ikke gull alt som g-er** not all is gold that glitters. 2 *fig.* scintillate, shine, sparkle (e.g. by virtue of one's intellect).
+glim`renḍe *A* - brilliant: **han tok seg g- ut** he looked just marvellous.
glim't *-en/-et* 1 flash, glimmer, twinkle. 2 glimpse: **få se et g- av noe** catch a g- of sth.
glim`te *V -a/+-et* flash, glitter, twinkle: **g- fram** gleam.
glim`t/vis *Av* by, in glimpses; momentarily.
glin`se *V -a/+-et* glisten, glitter, shine.
gli'p *-en/+-et* dip net.
gli`pe[1] *-a* crack, small opening.
gli`pe[2] *V -te* come apart (at the seams), come undone; gape: **g- med øynene** peer.
+glipp'[1] *-et* blink.
+glipp'[2] *Av*: **gå g- av** miss, miss out on.
+glip`pe[1] *V glapp, -et* cf **gleppe**
+glip`pe[2] *V -et/-te* blink: **g- med øynene** (the same).
gli'r *-en* squint.
gli`re *V -te* narrow one's eyes, squint.
***gli`ren** *A -e/-i, pl -ne* leaky.
***gli`r/øygd** *A -/-øygt* **(=+/øyd)** squinting.
gli's *-en/+-et* (derisive) grin, sneer.
gli`se *V -te* 1 shine through chinks, cracks. 2 grin (derisively), sneer.
gli`sen *A +-ent, pl -ne* cf **glissen**
glis`ne *V -a/+-et* become sparse, widely scattered.
glis`sen *A +-ent, pl glisne* sparse, thin, widely scattered; cracked, shrunk.
glit`re *V -a/+-et* glitter, sparkle.
Glit`re/tinḍ *Pln* **(=+Glitter/)** mountain in Jotunheimen.
+glit`te *V -a/-et* glaze (e.g. paper), polish.
glit'ter *-eret/glitret* 1 glitter, glittering. 2 tinsel.
glo'[1] *-a, pl glør* 1 ember, live coal: **stå på glør** be on pins and needles. 2 fire, light: **g-en på en sigarett** the l- of a cigarette.
glo'[2] *V -dde* gape, gaze, stare (**etter, på** at).
globa'l *A* global.
globoid [-bo-i'd] *-en* aspirin.
glo'bus *-en* globe.
glo`enḍe *A* - 1 glowing, red-hot: **sanke g- kull på ens hode** heap coals of fire on sby's head. 2 gaudy: **g- farger** g- colors. 3 *fam.*: **på g-flekken** immediately, right away.
glo`/hane *-n dial.* meat roasting on a spit.
glo`/heit *A -t/+-hett* red-hot, scorching hot.
+glo`/het *A* cf **/heit**
Glom'/fjord *Pln* village, Meløy twp, Nordland.
Glom'ma *Pln* Norway's longest river.
***glop** [glå'p] *-et* abyss, canyon.
***glope** [glå`pe] *pp of* **glupe (—*glopi)**
glop`pe[1] *-a* gorge, ravine; opening.
***glop`pe**[2] *pp of* **gleppe**
Glop`pen *Pln* twp in Nordfjord, Sogn og Fjordane.
***glop`pi** *pp of* **gleppe**
glo'r *-et* glitter, tinsel.
+glo`/rake *-n* poker.
***glo`/rauḍ** *A* cf **/rød**
glo`re *V +-et/+-te/*-a* glitter, shine.
glo`ret(e) *A* - gaudy; glaring.
glo'rie *-n/*-a* halo, nimbus.
***glo`r/verdig** *A* - *hum.* glorious.
+glo`/røḍ *A* **(=*/raud)** fiery red.
glo`se[1] *-a/+-en* 1 expression, term, word (e.g. of abuse, or in a foreign language). 2 gloss (in a manuscript text); marginal translation (e.g. in a schoolbook).
glo`se[2] *V +-te/*-a dial.* glow.
glo`se/bok *-a, pl -bøker* notebook containing glosses.
glo`se/forrå'd *-et* vocabulary.
glossa'r *-et, pl -/+-er* glossary.
+glo`/tang *-a, pl -tenger* **(=*/tong)** fireplace tong(s).
***glott'** *-en* cf **gløtt**
***glot`te** *pp of* **glette (=*glotti)**
glo`ve *-a* ravine.
gluf's *-en dial.* breeze, gust of wind.
gluf`se *V -a/+-et dial.* bolt, gulp down, snatch at (food).
glugg'[1] *-en* **(=glugge)** 1 opening, slot, vent; peephole, (small) window; *fam.* eye, *(pop.)* peeper. 2: **skyte for g-** reject (e.g. a suitor).
+glugg'[2] *Av* completely: **le seg g- i hjel** laugh oneself sick, laugh until one's sides ache.
glug`ge *-n* cf **glugg**[1]
***glum`de** *pt of* **glymje**
***glu`me** *V -a* glare, glower.

+ Bokmål; * Nynorsk; ° Dialect.
After letter: ' stress (Acc. 1); ` tone, stress (Acc. 2); · length.
Below letter: . not pronounced.

*glu'meleg A - forbidding, sinister, threatening.
glun't -en dial. boy.
*glu'p[1] -en 1 hollow, ravine. 2 mouthful.
glu'p[2] A excellent, fine, first-rate.
glu'pe V +-r/*glyp, +-te/*glaup, +-t/*glope/*-i dial. bolt, wolf, snatch at (food).
glu'pende A - ravenous, voracious (appetite, hunger, etc.).
glup'sk A - bloodthirsty; greedy; ravenous (etter for): g-e kreditorer hungry creditors.
gly'e -a 1 gelatinous mass, jelly; (of fish, snails, etc.) slime. *2 thin layer of clouds.
gly'et(e) A - gelatinous; slimy.
*glyf's -et aperture, opening.
*glyg'gje V glygde open before one (e.g. a vista).
glyko'se -n chem. glucose.
*glym'je V glumde, glumt boom, roar, thunder.
*gly'p pr of glupe
glyptote'k -et museum for sculpture: G-et museum in Copenhagen.
*gly're V -te stare intently.
glyseri'n -en/+-et chem. glycerin, glycerol.
glytt' -en/+-et cf gløtt
glyt'te V -a/+-et/*-e cf gløtte
*glyv're -a ravine.
*glæ' A -tt 1 pale yellow. 2 flat, insipid.
glø' V -dde (=gløde) 1 glow, shine; cast a glow. 2 fig. be on fire, burn (av with e.g. enthusiasm, indignation, zeal). 3 cause to glow, make red-hot.
+glø'd -en 1 glow. 2 fig. ardor, fervor, glow.
glø'de [*glø'e] V -de/+-et cf glø
glø'de/lampe -a/-en incandescent lamp.
glø'dende A - 1 glowing, incandescent, red-hot. 2 fig. ardent, fiery: en g- tro an ardent faith.
glø'de/tråd -en filament.
gløgg' A gløgt resourceful, quick-witted, smart; apt.
*gløgg'/skap -en acuteness, intelligence, sharp-wittedness.
gløgg'/sy'nt A - acute, penetrating, sharp-witted.
gløgg'/tenkt A - resourceful, quick-witted.
+gløm'me V glømte cf glemme[2]
+gløm'me/boka df cf glemme/
+gløm'sel -elen cf glemsel
+gløm'sk A - cf glemsk
+gløm'/som' A -t, pl -me cf glem/
gløm'te pt of glømme
glø'r pl of glo[1]
glø'se V -te glow, shine (with a reddish lustre).
gløtt' -en/+-et 1 break, rift (in the clouds); chink, crack: på g- ajar. 2 (fleeting) glimpse: få en g- av en catch a g- of sby.
gløt'te V -a/+-et/*-e 1: g- på open slightly (e.g. open the door a crack). 2 peek, steal a furtive glance (på at).
*gløy'me[1] -a cf glemme[1]
*gløy'me[2] V -de cf glemme[2]
*gløy'me/boka df cf glemme/
*gløy'm/sam A cf glem/som
*gløy'msk A - cf glemsk
*gløy'mske -a absentmindedness, forgetfulness.
*gløy'msken A -e/-i, pl -ne absentminded, forgetful.
*gløy'msle -a cf glemsel
gløy'pe V -te swallow; bolt, wolf (food).
*Glå'ma Pln cf Glomma
glå'me V +-te/*-de gape, stare (på at).
Glåm'/fjo'rd Pln fjord, Meløy twp, Nordland.
Glå'm/os Pln twp, Sør-Trøndelag.
*glå'm/øygd A -/-øygt (pop.) bug-eyed.
*glå'p -en blockhead, dunce.
glå'pe V -te gape, stare (på at).
GMT. = Greenwich middeltid
*gnad're V -a grumble, mutter.
gna'g -et 1 gnawing (av of). 2 harping, nagging. 3 birch twigs (used for fodder).
gna'ge[1] V +-er/*gneg, gnog, +-d/*gnege/*-i (=gnage[2]) 1 gnaw, nibble. 2 corrode, wear; chafe, rub: g- seg gjennom, inn i gnaw (wear) through. 3 fig. gnaw at, torment. 4 fret, harp, nag (på on, at): han bad og gnog så lenge at han fikk lov til sist he begged and entreated until at last he was permitted (Asbjørnsen and Moe).
gna'ge[2] V +-de/*-a cf gnage[1]
+gna'ger -en, pl -e (=*-ar) zool. rodent (order Rodentia).
*gna'g/sam' A annoying, tiresome.
*gnag'se V -a toil constantly, (pop.) keep one's nose to the grindstone.
gna'g/sår -et blister, gall, raw place.
*gnal'dre V -a scream, shriek.
gnall' pt of gnelle
gnall'/frost -en (crackling) severe frost.
+gnas'ke V -a/-et crunch, munch.
*gnas'se -n hardy, rugged person.
*gnas't pt of gneste
*gnatt' pt of gnette
*gnau'r -en miser, skinflint, (pop.) tightwad.
*gnau're V -a skimp.
gna'v -et/-en (children's) card game.
+gna'ven A -ent, pl -ne cross, fretful, peevish.
*gnav'le V -a chew slowly, munch.
+gne'd pt of gni
*gne'g pr of gnage[1]
*gne'ge pp of gnage[1] (=*gnegi)
gnei' pt of gni
*gnei'd pt of gnide
gnei's -en gneiss (mineral).
°gnei'st -en cf gnist
*gnei'ste[1] -n cf gnist
*gnei'ste[2] V -a cf gnistre
*gnei'strande Av cf gnistrende
gnel'der -et barking, yelping; shrill, squeal.
gnel'dre V -a/+-et bark, yelp; shrill, squeal.
gnel'dre/bikkje -a derog. yelping dog.
gnell'[1] -et shriek, squeal.
gnell'[2] A gnelt piercing, shrill.
gnel'le V gnall/+gnelte, +gnelt/*gnolle/*-i shrill, squeal.
*gnell'/mæ'lt A - piercing, shrill.
*gnes'te V gnast, gnoste/-i crackle, rustle.
gnett' -a nit.
*gnet'te V gnatt, gnotte/-i crackle, rustle.
gni' V -r, -dde/gnei/+gned, -dd (=*gnide) rub: g- inn rub, work in (e.g. ointment, salve); g- på fiolin saw, scrape away at a violin; g- på skillingen be miserly, stingy, (pop.) squeeze a dollar so hard the eagle screams; g- seg i hendene rub one's hands; fig. congratulate oneself.
gnid'der -eret/gnidret (=*gnitter) 1 cramped writing. 2 delicate whirring sound.
*gni'de V -de/gneid, -d/-e/-i cf gni
+gni'dning -en phys. friction; fig. friction, strife (mellom among).
gnid're V -a/+-et (=*gnitre) write a cramped hand.
gnid'ret(e) A - (=*gnitrut) crabbed, cramped (writing).
gnids'el -en cf gnissel
+gni'er -en, pl -e (=*-ar) miser, skinflint, (pop.) tightwad.
+gni'er/aktig A miserly, stingy.
*gni'kar -en cf gnier
gni'ke V -a/+-et (=+gnikke) 1 rub (intensely, repeatedly). 2 squeal (as a result of friction in a piece of machinery). 3 toil steadily, (pop.) keep one's nose to the grindstone. 4: g- på skillingen be miserly, stingy.
*gni'ken A -e/-i, pl -ne miserly, stingy.
+gnik'ke V -a/-et cf gnike
gnik's -et squeak, squeal; crunch.
gnik'se V -a/+-et squeak, squeal; crunch: gresshoppene g-et the grasshoppers chirped (Evensmo).
gnir'k +-et/*-en dial. squeak.
gnir'ke V -a/+-et dial. squeak.
gnis'le V -a/+-et 1 squeak, squeal; grate. 2: g- med tennene gnash one's teeth.
gniss' -et rubbing; squeaking, squealing.
gnis'se V -a/+-et 1 rub; creak, squeak. 2 work steadily.
+gnis'sel -en rubbing; squeaking, squealing: under gråt og tenners g- bibl. with weeping and gnashing of teeth.
+gnis't -en (=*gneiste[1], *gnister) 1 spark: slå g-er av strike s-s from; være så sint at en spruter g-er be so angry that one gives off sparks; red-hot, spluttering. 2 fig. creative spark, spark of genius, inspiration. 3 iota, trace: han bryr seg ikke en g- om det he doesn't care two hoots about it.
gnis'te V -a/+-et cf gnistre
*gnis'ter -en creak, creaking.
+gnis't/fanger -en, pl -e spark arrester (esp. on steam locomotive).
gnis't/gap -et elec. spark gap.
gnis'tre V -a/+-et (=*gneiste) 1 flash, sparkle; emit sparks: fig. banne så det g-er swear so that the air turns blue, g- av sinne flash fire (in anger). 2 crackle, rustle; squeak, squeal.
gnis'trende Av flashing, sparkling: g- sint furious.
gni'ten A +-ent, pl -ne miserly, stingy; petty.
*gnit're V -a cf gnidre
*gnit'rut A - cf gnidret(e)
*gnit'ter -et cf gnidder
gno'g pt of gnage[1]
*gnol'le pp of gnelle (=*gnolli)
gno'm -en gnome.
*gnos'te pp of gneste (=*gnosti)
+gnos'tiker -en, pl -e (=*-ar) Gnostic.
gnos'tisk A - gnostic.
*gnot'te pp of gnette (=*gnotti)
gnu' V -dde 1 rub: g- på skillingen be miserly, stingy. 2: g- og arbeide toil, work steadily.
gnug'ge V -a/+-et rub, scrape: g- sammen penger scrape together money.
gnuk'ke V -a/+-et dial. rub.
gnu'r -en rubbing; grating.
gnu're V -a/+-te chafe, rub; grate, grind: g-ende disharmonier jarring discords.
gnur'k -en scraping; grating.
gnur'ke V -a/+-et scrape; grate, grind.
gny'[1] -et/*-en clamor, din; fig. (violent) controversy, debate: det stod g- om ham he was a controversial figure.
*gny'[2] -et nagging, pestering.
*gny'[3] V -dde bother, pester.
*gnæ' V -dde (=gnæde) blow cold.
*gnæ'se V -te blow cold.
g-nøkkel [ge'-] -elen, pl -nøkler mus. treble clef.
*gnå' V -dde beg, entreat, implore.
gnå'l -et fussing, nagging; whining.
gnå'le V +-te/*-a fret, fuss, nag; whine: g- på det samme harp constantly on the same thing.
goal [gåll'] -en goal (soccer).
goal/keeper [gåll'/kiper] -en, pl +-e goalkeeper (soccer).
gobelin [gåbeleng'] -et, pl +-er/*- Gobelin tapestry.
go'd A cp bedre, sp best 1 good (for for, med to): jeg gir en g- dag i det I don't give a hang for that; g- dag hello; g- jul merry Christmas; g-t nyttår happy New Year; den er g- that's a good one (e.g. a joke); gå (si seg) g- for en guarantee for sby; du g-este good grief, good heavens, goodness; hva sier du til g-t what do you have to say, what's new; det g-e the good; det g-e ved ham the good thing about him; med det g-e amicably, by friendly means; willingly; for mye av det g-e too much of a good thing; (ikke) få noe for g-e ord og betaling (not) to be had for love or money; i g- tro trusting(ly); det er ikke g-t å si it's

hard to say; **på g-t og ondt** for good or bad; **vil De være så g- å** will you please; **vær så g-** here you are; (if you) please; you're welcome. **2** good=skilled (**til å at**): **g- til å danse** a good dancer. **3** healed, well: **bli g- igjen** recover; **han er like g-** he is as well as ever; **være g- for (til) å** be able to do sth. **4** enough, plenty; considerable: **g- plass** lots of room; **g- tid** plenty of time; **komme i g- tid** arrive early; **legge g-t i** put in plenty (e.g. of wood on fire); **et g-t stykke** a good ways, some distance; **ha g-t med (om)** have plenty of. **5** *(adv.)* **godt** good, well: **det vet du g-t** you know that very well; **gjøre g-t** do good; **gjøre g-t igjen** atone for; **det gjør g-t å høre** it is good to hear; **det gjør ham g-t** it will do him good; **ha det g-t** be comfortable, well off; **nå kan du ha det så g-t** serves you right; **ha g-t av** do one good; **så g-t som** almost, virtually. **6** *(comp.)* **bedre** better (**enn** than): **bli b-** improve; **b- folk** upper-class, well-to-do people; **en b-middag** a first-class dinner; **b- tid** more time; **b- vant** used to better things. **7** *(sup.)* **best** best, first-rate: **etter b-e skjønn** to the best of (my) judgment; **i b-e fall** at the very best; **ditt eget b-e** your own good; **gjøre sitt b-e** do one's best; **det b-e ved ham** the best thing about him; **på b-e måte** in the best possible way; *(adv.)* **b- som** just as, right when; **b- (som) han satt og bad, fikk han se skimtet av noe sort** just as he sat praying, he caught sight of sth black (Asbjørnsen).

+**godaf'ten** *I* cf **aften**

go'ḍ/arta *A* - (=+-**et**) *med.* benign (e.g. tumor); mild (e.g. epidemic).

go'ḍ/bit *-en* tidbit.

goḍda'g *I* cf **dag**

gode[1] [gå'de] *-n hist.* chieftain and priest (Iceland).

go'de[2] *-t, pl* +*-r*/**-* benefit, blessing, boon: **det høyeste g-** the supreme good; **livets g-r** the good things of life.

go'de[3] *N*: **gjøre seg til g-** indulge oneself; **ha til g-** have on one's account; have sth coming; have sth to look forward to; **komme en til g-** benefit one, stand one in good stead; **legge seg til g-** accumulate, lay up.

+**go'deste** *A sp of* **god**

***go'ḍ/far** *-en, pl -fedrar* grandfather.

go'ḍ/fjott *-en* foolishly good-natured person, simpleton.

go'ḍ/fjottet(c) *A* - foolishly good-natured, simpleminded.

+**go'ḍ/gjøre** *V -gjorde,-gjort* (=*/**gjere**): **g- seg** (of food) ripen, season; become full-flavored; (of people) enjoy oneself, feel happy (**med, ved** about, with).

+**go'ḍ/gjørenḍe** *A* - (=*/**gjerande**) beneficent, charitable.

+**go'ḍgjøren/het** *-en* charity.

+**go'ḍ/het** *-en* goodness, kindness; (of quality) excellence: **føle g- for** be fond of; **vær av den g-** be so kind as to.

+**go'ḍhets/fullt** *Av* kindly: **vil De g-sende meg** would you k- send me.

+**go'ḍ/hjertet** [/jærtet] *A* - (=+-**a**, */**hjarta**) kindhearted.

go'ḍ/hug *-en* benevolence, good will, kindness; love, sympathy (**for** for).

***go'dig** *A* - good-natured.

go'ḍ/kjenne *V* +*-kjente*/**-kjende* approve, pass; confirm, O.K., sanction: **ikke g- et krav** disallow a claim.

go'ḍ/kjenning *-a*/+*-en* (=+**-else**) approval; sanction.

go'ḍ/lag *-et* good humor, high spirits.

+**go'ḍ/lienḍe** *A* - (=+/**liendes**, */**lidande**) good-natured, likeable, pleasant.

go'ḍ/lukt [/lokt] *-a*/+*-en* fragrance, good smell; perfume.

go'ḍ/lune *-t*: **i g-** in good humor (mood).

go'ḍ/lynt *A* - (=*/**lyndt**) friendly, good-natured, likeable.

go'ḍ/læte *-t*/**-a* commendation, praise.

go'ḍ/låt *-en* compliments, praise.

***go'ḍ/menne** *-t* good-natured person, *(pop.)* good scout.

godmo'dig *A* - good-natured, kindly.

***go'ḍ/mor** *-a, pl -mødrer* grandmother.

***go'ḍ/mæten** *A -e*/*-i, pl -ne* proud, self-satisfied.

***go'ḍ/møle** *-t* good humor, high spirits.

goḍnatt' *I* cf **natt**

go'dne *V -a*/+*-et*: **g- seg** (of food) ripen, season; become full-flavored.

go'ḍ/o'rḍ[1] *-et* compliment, praise.

god/o'rḍ[2] [gå'd/] *-et hist.* office of chieftain and priest (Iceland).

god's *-et, pl -*/+*-er* **1** (personal) goods, property: **fast g-** *jur.* real property; **jordisk g-** worldly goods. **2** baggage; freight. **3** estate, manor. **4** *tech.* castings. **5** *naut.* rigging.

+**god's/eier** *-en, pl -e* (=*/**eigar**) landed proprietor, squire.

god's/ekspedisjo'n *-en* baggage, freight office.

***go'ḍ/skap** *-en* goodness, kindness; (of quality) excellence.

go'ḍ/skrive *V -skreiv*/+*-skrev*, +*-skrevet*/**-e*/**-i merc.* credit: **g- en** credit sby's account.

goḍ'slig *A* - good-natured, kindly.

go'ḍ/smak *-en* fine, good flavor.

go'ḍ/snakke *V -a*/+*-et* cajole, coax, placate: **g- for, med en** calm sby down; coax, wheedle sby.

god's/stasjo'n *-en* freight station.

god's/tog [/tåg] *-et* freight train.

god's/vogn [/vångn] *-a* boxcar, freight car.

go'ḍ/ta *V -tar*/**-tek, -tok,* +*-tatt*/**-teke*/**-i* accept, acknowledge; approve, pass.

+**goḍt'e** *V -et* cf **gotte**

***go'ḍ/tekke** *-t* kindness.

goḍtem'plar *-en* Good Templar (member of a temperance society).

+**goḍt'er** *pl* of **gotter**

goḍt'/folk *-et* folks; good people; *derog.* Tom, Dick and Harry.

***goḍt'/gjersle** *-a* cf **/gjørelse**

+**goḍt'/gjøre** *V -gjorde,-gjort* (=*/**gjere**) **1** compensate, indemnify for, make good (e.g. a loss). **2** establish, prove.

+**goḍt'/gjørelse** *-n* (=+/**gjøring**, ***gjersle**) **1** compensation, reimbursement. **2** gratuity, tip.

goḍt'/kjøp *-et* bargain: **varer til g-** merchandise at bargain prices.

goḍt'/kjøps *A* - cheap.

goḍt'kjøps/vare *-a*/+*-en* cheap article, piece of merchandise.

go'ḍ/tok *pt of* **-ta**

***go'ḍ/tokke** *-n* kindness.

***go'ḍ/tolug** [/tå·lug] *A* - patient.

+**go'ḍ/troenḍe** *A* - (=*/**truande**, */**truen**) credulous, gullible.

+**go'ḍtroen/het** *-en* credulity, gullibility.

***go'ḍ/truande** *A* - cf **/troende**

***go'ḍ/truen** *A -e*/*-i, pl -ne* cf **/troende**

***go'ḍtruen/skap** *-en* credulity, gullibility.

go'ḍ/tykke *-t* discretion, pleasure: **gjøre noe etter eget g-** do sth arbitrarily.

***go'ḍ/tykken** *A -e*/*-i, pl -tykne* finicky, touchy.

go'ḍ/venner *pl* (=*/**vener**): **bli, være g- med** be good friends with, be close to.

go'ḍ/vilje *-n* good will: **legge g-n til** do the best one knows how.

go'ḍ/villig *A* - (=*/**viljug**) voluntary; unresisting.

***go'ḍ/visleg** *A* - kind: **vil De vere så g- å svare snart?** will you kindly answer soon?

+**go'ḍ/vær** *-et* (=*/**ver**) fair weather.

***gogn** [gång'n] *-a* instrument, tool; apparatus (e.g. loom).

go'l *pt of* **gale**

Go'l *Pln* twp, Buskerud.

+**gol'd** *A* **1** barren, sterile; arid. **2** (of milk cows) dry.

gol'de** *pp of* **gjelde**[1] (=goldi**)

***gol'f**[1] *-en* gulf: **Golfen** the Gulf (of Mexico): **g-en ved Neapel** (now **Napoli**) the Bay of Naples.

gol'f[2] *-en* golf.

gol'f/jakke *-a* light sweater (usu. front-buttoned).

gol'f/kølle *-a*/+*-en* golf club.

+**Gol'f/strømmen** *Pln* (=*/**straumen**) the Gulf Stream.

Gol'gata *Pln* Calvary, Golgotha.

gol'le** *pp of* **gjelle**[2] (=golli**)

gol'v *-et* **1** floor: **gå i g-et** (in boxing) go down, *(pop.)* hit the deck; **slå i g-et** knock out; **han gikk opp og ned på g-et** he paced the floor; **stå på g-et** *dial.* be confirmed; **fare i g-et** *dial., archaic* bear a child. **2** (of a theater) main floor (behind the orchestra); *Brit.* pit.

gol'v/bo'rḍ *-et* floorboard.

gol've *V -a* **1** put in a floor. **2** beat up, thrash soundly.

gol'v/klut *-en* cloth for washing floors.

gol'v/teppe *-t, pl* +*-r*/**-* carpet, rug.

gom [gom'] *-men* cf **gomme**

+**gomle** [gom'le] *V -a*/*-et* chew (slowly), munch; **g- på noe** *fig.* consider, deliberate about sth.

gomme [gom'me] *-n anat.* **1** (in *pl*) gums. **2** *archaic, dial.* palate. **3** fingertip.

gondo'l *-en* gondola.

gondolier [gåndålie'] *-en* gondolier.

***gong'**[1] *-en, pl -er* cf **gang**[1]

***gong'**[2] *-en, pl -er* cf **gang**[2]

***gong'e**[1] *-a* cf **gange**[1]

***gong'e**[2] *V -a* cf **gange**[2]

***gong'e/før** *A* able to walk.

gongong' *-en* gong.

gonoré *-en med.* gonorrhea.

goodtem'plar [god-] *-en* cf **godtemplar**

good/will [gud'/vill] *-en merc.* good will.

gop'le *-a* **1** *bot.* giant bellflower (Campanula latifolia). **2** *zool.* jellyfish, medusa.

***gor'** *-et* cf **gørr**[1]

gor'disk *A* - Gordian: **hugge over den g-e knute** cut the G- knot.

gorgonso'la *-en* Gorgonzola (cheese).

goril'la *-en zool.* gorilla (Gorilla gorilla).

go'ro *-a*/+*-en* (a kind of) wafer (baked on a patterned, rectangular iron).

go'ro/jern [/jæ·rn] *-et* iron for baking **goro**.

+**gorr'** *-et* cf **gørr**[1]

+**gor'r(enḍe)** *Av* cf **gørr**[2], **gørrende**

+**gorr'/kyte** *-a* (=***gor/**) *zool.* minnow (Phoxinus phoxinus).

+**gorr'/myr** *-a* (=***gor/**) sinking slough; morass, swamp.

***gor'/vom'** *-ma anat.* rumen.

***gos** [gå's] *-et* **1** bubbling, gushing, spurt. **2** air current.

***gose**[1] [gå'se] *V -a* evaporate; steam.

gose**[2] [gå'se] *pp of* **gjose** (=gosi**)

***gos'se** *-n* stocky, well-built boy, young man.

***got** [gå't] *-et* (of fish) spawning.

***got/bore** *-a anat.* (of fish) anus.

***gote**[1] [gå'te] *-a* cf **gutu**

***go'te**[2] *-n* cf **goter**

***gote**[3] [gå'te] *pp of* **gyte**

+**go'ter** *-en, pl -*/*-e* (=***gote**[2]) Goth

***goti** [gå'ti] *pp of* **gyte**

gotikk' *-en* Gothic (style).

go'tisk *A* - Gothic.

Got'/lanḍ *Pln* Gotland, Sweden.

got'te *V -a*/+*-et*: **g- seg** gloat, smack one's lips over, triumph (**over** over).

got'ter *pl* candy, goodies.

gouache [guasj'] *-n* gouache.

gouda/ost [gau'da/ost] *-en* cf **gauda/**

gourmand [gurmang'] *-en* gourmand

gourmet [gurme'] *-en* gourmet.

+ Bokmål; * Nynorsk; ° Dialect.
After letter: ' stress (Acc. 1); ` tone, stress (Acc. 2); · length.
Below letter: . not pronounced.

+goutere [gute're] *V -te* cf **gutere**
gov [gå'v] *-et* shower, spray, spume (av of): **om morgenen våknet de i et g- av snø** in the morning they woke in a whirling world of snow (Undset).
***gove[1]** [gå've] *-a* mist, steam.
gove[2] [gå've] *V -a/+-et dial.* steam.
***gove[3]** [gå've] *pp of* **gyve (=*govi)**
gr.=grad(er)
Gr.=Greenwich
gra' *A* 1 (of male animals) procreative, uncastrated. 2 lascivious, lustful.
grabb' *-en tech.* claw.
gra'/bukk [/bokk] *-en* uncastrated goat; *derog.* horny old goat.
gra'd *-en/*-a* 1 degree (of latitude, longitude, temperature, etc.; also *educ., gram., math.*); extent: **i den g-** to such a degree; **i høy g-** to a high degree; **minus ti g-er** ten degrees below (Centigrade, which equals 14° above in Fahrenheit); **til de** [di'] **grader** *fam.* extremely, highly; **til en viss g-** to a certain degree, extent; **tredje g-s forhør** third degree. 2 esp. *mil.* grade, rank: **stige i g-ene** get up in the world.
gra'd/boge [/båge] *-n* **(=*/bue)** *math.* graduated arc.
gra'd/bøye *V -de gram.* compare.
grade're *V -te* 1 grade, graduate (e.g. the scale of a thermometer): **g-straffen** make the punishment fit the crime. 2 *chem.* graduate (salt); alloy (metal).
gra'de/stokk *-en* **(=*grad/)** thermometer.
+gra'ds/forskjell· *-en* difference in degree.
***gra'd/stokk** *-en* cf **grade/**
gra'dteig(s)/kart *-et* topographic map (usu. comprising one degree of longitude, 1/3 degree of latitude).
gra'd/vis *Av* by degrees, gradually.
-graf *-en* -graph, as in **seismog-, teleg-.**
-grafi *-en/-et* -graphy, as in **bibliog-, geog-.**
+gra'fiker *-en, pl -e* **(=*-ar)** graphic artist (e.g. lithographer).
grafikk' *-en* graphic art(s).
gra'fisk *A* - graphic.
grafitt' *-en* graphite (lead).
grafolog [-olå'g] *-en* graphologist.
grafologi' *-en* graphology.
graf'se *V -a/+-et* fumble, paw (at), scramble: **g- til seg** grab.
gra'ham/brød *-et* graham bread.
gra'/hest *-en* stallion; *derog.* horny person.
grak'se *-n* dregs, waste (from processing of whale oil).
gra'l *-en* grail: **den hellige g-** the Holy G-.
gram'[1] *-met* gram (=.035 oz.).
gram'[2] *A -t, pl -me* esp. **g- i hu** angry, wroth.
***gram'de** *pt of* **gremje**
grammatika'lsk *A* - grammatical.
+gramma'tiker *-en, pl -e* **(=*-ar)** grammarian.
grammatikk' *-en* grammar.
gramma'tisk *A* - grammatical.
grammofo'n *-en* phonograph.
grammofo'n/plate *-a/+-en* phonograph record.
+gram'se *V -a/-et* (of animals) snatch at; *fig.*: **g- etter noe** grab, scramble for sth; **g- til seg** be out for everything one can get.
***gram't** *pp of* **gremje**
gra'n *-a bot.* spruce (genus Picea).
Gra'n *Pln* twp, Oppland.
grana't *-en* 1 *bot.* pomegranate (Punica granatum). 2 *chem.* garnet. 3 *mil.* (hand, rifle) grenade; shell.
grana't/eple *-t, pl +-r/*-* pomegranate.
gra'n/bar *-et* spruce needles and twigs.
grand[1] [grang'] *-en* (bridge) no-trump: **gjøre storeslem i g-** score a grand slam in no-trump.
***gran'd[2]** *-en* poor health.
gran'd[3] *-et* cf **grann[1]**
grand[4] [grang'] *A*: **g- galla** full dress affair.
gran'de[1] *-n* grandee.
***gran'de[2]** *-n* sand bar.
grandezza [-es'sa] *-en* grandeur, grandiosity.
+grandgi'velig *A* - cf **grann-**
grandio's *A* grandiose.
grand/melding [grang'/] *-a/+-en* no-trump bid.
gran'd/onkel [/ongkel] *-elen, pl -ler* great-uncle.
grandseigneur [grangsenjø'r] *-en* grand seigneur.
gran'd/tante *-a/+-en* great-aunt.
+grangi'velig *A* - cf **grann-**
granito'l *-en* imitation leather bookbinding.
granitt' *-en* granite.
grann'[1] *-et* bit, particle; trifle: **et (lite) g-** a little; **hvert et g-** every last bit; **ikke det, et g-** not an iota, not the slightest bit; **ikke det skapende g-** absolutely nothing.
grann'[2] *A grant* 1 slender, thin; high-pitched. 2 *archaic (adv.)* plainly, vividly.
gran'ne *-n poet.* neighbor.
gran'ne/lag *-et* neighborhood, vicinity.
+grann/gi'velig *A* - (only *adv.*) exactly, precisely.
***grann'/gjo'rd** *A -/-gjort* artfully made, artistic.
***grann'/leik** *-en* slenderness; beauty, delicacy.
grann'/mælt [+/me'lt] *A* - high-pitched, piping, thin (voice).
***grann'/sam** *A* accurate, precise.
***grann'/semd** *-a* accuracy, exactness.
***grann'/var** *A* careful, prudent; modest, reticent (esp. in helping oneself to food).
+grann'/voksen *A -ent, pl -ne* **(=*/vaksen)** (of) slender (build), thin.
Gra'ns/herad *Pln* twp, Telemark.
gran'ske *V -a/+-et* examine, investigate, study thoroughly; do research: **g- nøye** scrutinize; **et g-ende blikk** a searching look.
+gran'sker *-en, pl -e* **(=*-ar)** investigator, student; researcher, scholar, scientist.
gran'skings/nemnd [/nemd] *-a* investigating committee.
gra'n/skjegg *-et* spruce lichen.
gran't *Av archaic* distinctly, plainly.
Gra'n/vin *Pln* twp, Hordaland.
grape/frukt [grep'/, grei'p/] *-a/+-en* grapefruit.
***grap's** *-et* 1 grab, grabbing. 2 mess: **i grugg (grus) og g-** to smithereens.
gra's *-et* **(=+gress)** grass; (on potato plant) leaves: **bite i g-et** bite the dust; **gå på g-** go to pasture, graze, *fig.* and *pop.* live off the fat of the land (of people); **ha penger som g-** be rolling in money; **slå g-** cut, mow grass, the lawn.
***gra'se** *V -a* weed.
***gra's/enkje** *-a* cf **gress/enke**
***gra's/enkjemann·** *-en, pl -menn(er)* cf **gress/enke-**
gra's/grodd *A -/-grott* grass-grown; overgrown.
gra's/hoppe *-a* 1 grasshopper; *bibl.* locust. 2 jumping firecracker.
grasiø's *A* graceful.
***gra's/kar** *-et* cf **gress/**
+gra's/klipper *-en* **(=*-ar)** lawn mower.
+gra's/løk *-en* **(=*/lauk)** *bot.* chives (Allium schoenoprasum).
gra's/mark *-a* grass field.
gra's/naut *-et* 1 grass-fed cattle (kept for a fee). 2 blockhead, dolt.
gra's/plen *-en* lawn: **det er forbudt å gå på g-en** keep off the grass.
gra's/rot *-a* grass root.
grassa't *A*: **gå, løpe g-** run amuck, run riot.
grasse're *V -te* be rife, prevail; go on a rampage, rage, run rampant.
gra's/strå *-et* blade of grass.
gra's/svor *-en* piece of sod, turf.
gra's/torv *-a* piece of sod, turf.
gra's/tufs *-en* tuft of grass.
gra's/voll *-en* meadow; sod, turf.
Gra'tangen *Pln* 1 twp, Troms. 2 fjord, Gratangen twp.
grateng' *-en* (fish, meat, vegetable) soufflé.
gratiale [gratsia'le] *-t, pl +-r/*-* bonus.
gratie [gra'tsie] *-n* grace; *myth.* one of the three Graces.
gratin [grateng'] *-en* cf **grateng**
gratine're *V -te*: **g-t** au gratin, soufflé.
gra'tis *A* - free, free of charge: **gjøre noe g-** do sth for nothing; **g- adgang** admission free.
gra'tis/passasje'r *-en* deadhead, non-paying passenger.
gratulan't *-en* congratulator, well-wisher.
gratulasjo'n *-en* congratulation.
gratule're *V -te* congratulate (**med** on).
grau't *-en* **(=+grøt)** 1 mush, porridge; **(=havre/)** oatmeal; stewed fruit: **gå som katten om den varme g-en** fight shy of sth. 2 mash, mush (e.g. of snow).
***grau'ten** *A -e/-i, pl -ne* husky (voice); stifled by sobs.
grau'tet(e) *A* - 1 mushy, porridge-like, pulpy. 2 thick, unclear (voice). 3 *fam.*: **g- i hodet** stupid, *(pop.)* soft in the head.
grau't/mælt [+/me'lt] *A* - thick, unclear (voice).
gra'v[1] *-a/+-en* 1 grave, (final) resting place: **kalket g-** *bibl.* whited sepulchre (St. Matthew 23, 27); **legge en i g-en** be the death of sby; **stå på g-ens rand** have one foot in the grave; **vende seg i sin g-** turn over in one's grave. 2 ditch, trench; hole, pit: **den som graver en g- for andre, faller selv i den** he who sets a trap for others, falls into it himself.
***gra'v[2]** *-et* nagging, pestering; worrying: **gnag og grav, ja, det var han vel vant med** he was well accustomed to nagging and pestering (Skram).
gra'v/alvor [/all·vår] *-et* dead seriousness; solemnity, (undue) gravity.
gra'v/alvorlig [/-vå·r-] *A* - portentous, solemn; dead serious.
gra've *V +-er/*grev, grov/+-de, +-d/ *-e/*-i* 1 dig (**etter** for, **opp** up, **ut** out); burrow; poke around, scratch around (**i in**): **g- fram** dig up; *fig.* bring up, rake up (e.g. an old scandal); **g- ned** bury; **spørre og g-** (or **g- og spørre**) ask repeatedly and inquisitively; be inquisitive; **g- ut** dig out, excavate. 2 rankle, trouble: **det grov i ham** he felt troubled; it rankled him. 3 *(refl.)*: **g- seg hjemover** work one's way home (esp. through snow, etc.); **g- seg inn i noe** dig one's way into sth.
gra've/maski'n *-en* steam shovel.
gra'ven/stein *-en* **(=+/sten)** Gravenstein (apple).
+gra'ver *-en, pl -e* **(=*-ar)** gravedigger, sexton.
grave're *V -te* engrave.
grave'rende *A* - 1 grave, serious. 2 *jur.*: **g- omstendigheter** aggravating circumstances.
gra'v/ferd [*/fær] *-a/+-en* funeral, interment.
gra'v/funn *-et archeol.* find (in grave).
gra'v/haug *-en archeol.* barrow, burial mound (tumulus).
gravi'd *A* - pregnant.
gravidite't *-en* pregnancy.
gravitasjo'n *-en* gravitation.
gravite're *V -te* gravitate.
gravite'tisk *A* - pompous, solemn.
gra'v/la *pt of* **-legge, -leggje**
gra'v/laks *-en* corned salmon (lightly salted and allowed to ferment).
+gra'v/legge *V -la, -lagt* **(=*-je)** bury, inter.
gra'v/lund *-en* cemetery, graveyard.
gra'v/mæle [/me'le] *-t* monument, tomb.

gra'v/plass -en burial ground (site); grave.

gra'v/rust -a/+-en deep-seated rust, pitting.

gra'v/røst -a/+-en (=*/røyst) sepulchral voice.

gra'v/skrift -a/+-en epitaph.

+gra'v/sted -et (=*/stad) cemetery plot.

gra'v/støtte -a/+-en tombstone; headstone; archeol. stela.

gra'v/tale -n funeral sermon.

Gra'v/vik Pln twp, Nord-Trøndelag.

gravy'r -en engraving.

gra'v/øl· -et funeral; wake: drikke g- attend a funeral feast, wake.

gravø'r -en engraver.

+gre' V -dde cf greie[3]

*greb'be -a shrew, vixen; spitfire.

*gref't -a 1 grave. 2 ditch, trench; hole, pit.

gregoria'nsk A - Gregorian.

gre'gors/mess(e) en St. Gregory's Mass (March 12th).

grei' A *-tt 1 clear, obvious; open, plain, straightforward: en g- kar a s- fellow; kort og g-t short and snappy, Rett, g-t norsk correct, plain Norwegian (title of book by R. Iversen). 2 easy: det er g- skuring it's plain sailing; it's easy to tell; det er ikke g-t it's not an easy matter, things aren't easy; han er ikke g- å ha med å gjøre he's not easy to deal with.

grei'e[1] -a 1 affair, business, matter; thing, thingumabob; (pl.) gear, paraphernalia, tackle; affairs, things: fam. den derre g-a that thingumajig; dette er fine (gode) g-r a fine business (mess) this is; fam. hele g-a the whole business, the whole kit and caboodle; ikke rare g-r nothing to brag about. 2 knowledge: få g- på find out about (jeg kan ikke få noe g- på ham I can't figure him out); ha g- på have knowledge of, know about. 3 arrangement, order: det er ikke g- på noen ting things are in a mess; som det er noe g- på which is worthwhile (important, useful).

grei'e[2] -t harness.

grei'e[3] V +-de/*-dde (=+gre) comb: g- seg comb one's hair.

grei'e[4] V +-de/*-dde 1 clear, disentangle, straighten (ut out); make right, put straight: g- med arrange; g- opp put to rights, straighten up. 2 be able, manage (å to); (be able to) make (a hill, jump, payment, etc.); get along with, manage, stand. 3 (refl.): g- seg get along, make it, manage; det g-er seg that's enough; det g-er seg nok it'll be all right.

grei'e/kam· -men currycomb.

*grei'leg A - distinct, plain, simple.

grei'n[1] -a/+-en 1 branch; division, section. 2 (of a fork) tine. 3 (of ore) vein. 4 bough, branch: komme på den grønne g- prosper, (pop.) come into the chips.

*grei'n[2] -a arrangement, order: få g- på get into order; learn about; gjere g- på arrange; explain.

grei'n[3] pt of grine

*grei'nad -en arrangement, ordering.

grei'ne[1] V -a/+-te: g- seg branch (ut out), fork.

*grei'ne[2] V -a become more distinct, plainer.

*grei'ne/laus A disorderly, disorganized.

grei'net(e) A - branched, forked.

grei'p[1] -a/-en/-et 1 (manure) fork, pitchfork; forkful. 2 hold (=grep).

grei'p[2] pt of gripe

Grei'p/stad Pln twp, Vest-Agder.

grei'p/vott -en mitten.

grei'/sam· A good at settling things; helpful.

*grei'sle -a arrangement, ordering; settling.

grei'/tenkt A - clear-thinking.

*grei've -n cf greve

*grei'/voren A -e/-i, pl -ne open, plain, straightforward (person).

+gre'/kam· -men cf greie/

Gre'ken/land Pln Greece.

+gre'ker -en, pl -e (=*-ar) Greek.

+grell' A grelt garish, glaring, loud: stikke g-t av mot contrast strongly with.

*grem'je V grem, gramde, gramt cf gremme[2]

*grem'me[1] -t remorse, repentance.

+grem'me[2] V -a/-et 1 grieve, hurt. 2 (refl.): g- seg be annoyed, fret; grieve (over about), rue; g- seg til døde eat one's heart out.

*grem'meleg A - bitter (e.g. cold).

+grem'melse -n grief, sorrow.

+gre'n[1] -en cf grein[1]

*gre'n[2] -et cave, lair.

grenade'r -en grenadier.

gren'd -a neighborhood; group of farms (usu. bearing the same name).

gren'de/lag -et neighborhood; group of farms.

gren'd/skap -en neighborliness.

-grend't A - built-up, developed: tettg- densely built-up.

+gre'ne V -et/-te cf greine[1]

+gre'net(e) A - cf greinet(e)

*gren'je V -a laugh derisively, sneer.

gren'se[1] -a/+-en 1 border, boundary, frontier: g-a mellom Norge og Sverige the f- between Norway and Sweden. 2 borderline, dividing line, limit: dette går over alle g-r this goes beyond all reason. 3 math. (of a function) limit.

gren'se[2] V -a/+-et: g- opp til adjoin, border on; g- til fig. border, verge on; approach.

gren'se/gate -a boundary (demarcation) line.

+gren'se/løs A (=*/laus) boundless, endless, unlimited; extreme(ly): g-t ulykkelig extremely unhappy.

gren'se/pel -en boundary marker.

+gren'se/skjell -et (=*/skil) boundary marker; fig. dividing line, line of demarcation.

+gren'se/tilfelle -t, pl -/+-r borderline case.

gren'se/vakt -a/+-en border guard.

gren'se/verdi· -en 1 math. (of a function) limit. 2 merc. marginal value.

gre'p[1] -et 1 grab, grasp, snatch; grip, hold; handful. 2 move, step: et lykkelig g- a fortunate move; et taktisk g- a tactical move. 3 knack: ha det rette g- på have a k- for. 4 (manure) fork.

+gre'p[2] pt of gripe

gre'pa A - excellent, first-class.

gre'pe -n handful.

+gre'pet[1] pp of gripe

+gre'pet[2] A - (deeply) moved, overwhelmed (av by); with emotion.

*grep'je V -a: g- ein vott put a new grip on (a mitten).

grepp'/lyng -en/-et bot. alpine, trailing azalea (Azalea procumbens).

gre'sk A - Greek.

°gres'ne pl of gressen

+gress' -et cf gras

+gres'se V -a/-et graze.

+gres'selig A - awful, horrible, terrible: (adv.) g- trist awfully sad.

°gres'sen A -ent/-e/-i, pl -ne cf grissen

+gress'/enke -n (=*gras/enkje) grass widow.

+gress'/enkemann· -en, pl -menn grass widower.

+gress'/hoppe -n cf gras/

+gress'/kar· -et bot. gourd, pumpkin, squash, etc. (genus Cucurbita); hum. grass widower.

gre't pt of gråte

+gre'te V gret, grett cf gråte

Gre'te Prn (f)

*grett'[1] -en crossness, peevishness.

+grett'[2] pp of grete

*gret'te V -a/-te be cross, peevish; sulk.

gret'ten A +-ent, pl gretne cross, irritable, peevish.

gre'v[1] -et 1 hoe. 2 (on a horseshoe) calk.

gre'v[2] N cf greve

*gre'v[3] pr of grave

gre've -n (as title: grev) count: komme i g-ns tid come in the nick of time; rike som g-r rich as lords.

grevin'ne -a/+-en countess.

grev'ling -en zool. badger (Meles meles).

grev'ling/hund -en dachshund.

gre'v/skap -et 1 hist. domain of a count. 2 archaic county.

gribb' -en zool. vulture (family Vulturidae).

*grib'be[1] -a shrew, vixen; spitfire.

*grib'be[2] V -a: g- seg frown, scowl.

*grib'ben A -e/-i, pl gribne ugly.

gri'd -et hist., jur. protection, safe-conduct; mercy, pardon, quarter (for criminals, outlaws).

*gri'dug A - up early; diligent, industrious.

griff' -en griffin.

grif'fel -elen, pl grifler 1 slate pencil. 2 bot. style.

grilje're V -te bread meat (and brown it in a frying pan).

grill' -en grill (used in cooking); grill, restaurant.

gril'le[1] -a/+-en caprice, fancy, whim; sette g-r i hodet på en put a bee in sby's bonnet, put ideas in sby's head.

*gril'le[2] V -a 1: det g-er i han he vaguely remembers. 2: g- ein opp put a bee in sby's bonnet.

gril'let(e) A - capricious, whimsical.

grill'/rom [/romm] -met grill, restaurant.

grim'[1] -en folk. (fiddle-playing) supernatural being believed to dwell beneath waterfalls.

gri'm[2] A -t, pl -me hideous, ugly.

Grim' Prn (m)

grima'se -n grimace: gjøre, skjære g-r grimace, make faces.

+grimase're V -te grimace.

gri'me[1] -a 1 halter (horses); muzzle (dogs). 2 grimy streak. 3 dial. patch (shoe).

*gri'me[2] V -a 1 halter (a horse). 2 patch (a shoe).

gri'met(e) A - grimy, streaky.

Grim'stad Pln town, Aust-Agder.

gri'n -et/*-en 1 grimace; sneer. 2 (constant) complaining; fretting, nagging, whining. 3 petty criticism: det danske g- the Danish sneer (of superiority).

+grinak'tig A - amusing, funny.

*gri'nal A cross, peevish.

*gri'na/tagg -en cross, peevish person, (pop.) crosspatch, sourpuss.

grina'tus -en cross, peevish person, (pop.) crosspatch, sourpuss.

grin'd -a 1 gate, wicket: kryss med jernbane i plan med g- guarded railroad crossing. 2 (any) enclosure, pen, e.g. corral, sheepfold; playpen. 3 frame, framework.

grin'de V -a/+-et enclose, fence.

grin'd/gang -en putting cattle in a movable corral (for intensive fertilization).

Grin'd/heim Pln twp, Vest-Agder.

grin'd/kval -en (=+/hval) zool. blackfish, pilot whale (Globiocephala melaena).

grin'd/led -et gate, gateway.

grin'd/sag -a bucksaw, frame saw, whipsaw.

grin'd/stolpe -n gatepost.

gri'ne V grein/+-te, +-t/*-e/*-i 1 grimace, make a face. 2 fret, nag; blubber, whine: g- av scoff, sneer at; g- på nesen av look down one's nose at. 3 be conspicuous, leap at one, stand out: armoden g-te fram poverty shouted at one.

+gri'ne/biter -en, pl -e (=*-ar) old crab; crosspatch, sourpuss.

+ Bokmål; * Nynorsk; ° Dialect.
After letter: ´ stress (Acc. 1); ` tone, stress (Acc. 2); · length.
Below letter: . not pronounced.

gri'net(e) *A* - cross, peevish, sulky.
Grip' *Pln* twp, Møre og Romsdal.
gripe' *V greip/+grep, +grepet/*gripe/ *-i* 1 catch, grab, grasp (**etter** for); apprehend, seize, take hold (of): **g- tak i** (the same). 2 affect, move, seize, stir (cf **g-ende**). 3 (with *prep.* and *adv.*): **g- an** approach, go about, tackle; **g- feil** choose wrongly, miss; **g- (noen) i (noe)** catch (sby) at (sth); **g- inn** intervene, step in; **g- inn i** bear on, have repercussions on, react on (**g- inn i hverandre** interlock); **g- om seg** gain ground, spread; **g- til (noe)** fall back on, have recourse to (sth); grab at, make use of (sth). 4 *(refl.)*: **g- seg i (noe)** catch oneself at (sth).
gri'pe/brett *-et mus.* fingerboard.
gri'pe/klo *-a, pl -klør* (prehensile) claw (e.g. of a lobster).
gri'pende *A* - moving, stirring.
***gri'pi** *pp of* **gripe**
gri's¹ *-en* 1 pig: **det er bare til å gi g-ene** it's worthless, *(pop.)* it's for the birds: **det ligner ikke g-en** you just can't do a thing like that. 2 filthy person; beast, swine; (very) fat person, *(pop.)* lardbucket. 3: **en heldig g-** *hum.* a lucky dog; (in billiards) fluke, lucky shot.
gri's² *-en* groats.
gri's³ *-en* grease.
gri'se *V -a/+-et/+-te* 1 litter. 2: **g- til** dirty, soil; mess up.
gri'se/binge *-n* pigsty.
gri'se/hus *-et* pigsty.
gri'se/mat *-en* slop, swill.
***gris'en** *A -e/-i, pl -ne* cf **grissen**
gri'se/prat *-et/+-en* smutty talk.
gri'seri *-et* dirt, filth; smut.
gri'se/skap *-en* dirt, filth; smut.
gri'se/sylte *-a* pickled pork.
gri'set(e) *A* - dirty, filthy; obscene, smutty.
gri'se/tro *-a* (pig) trough.
griset'te *-a/+-en* grisette; artist's, student's mistress.
gris'/grendt *A* - sparsely populated.
gris'k *A* - grasping, greedy.
+gris'k/het *-en* greed.
gris'le *V -a/+-et* (in baking) give a glossy surface to loaves of bread.
gris'le/brød *-et* bread with an even, firm crust.
gris'ne¹ *V -a/+-et* be sparse, widely scattered.
gris'ne² *pl of* **grissen**
gri's/otte *-a* (very) early morning.
gris'sel *grisla/+-elen, pl grisler* baker's paddle on which **grislebrød** is placed in oven.
gris'sen *A +-ent, pl grisne* (=***grisen**) far apart, scattered; sparse, thin.
***griss'/grendt** *A* - cf **gris/**
gri's/unge [/onge] *-n* baby pig, piglet.
***grjo'n** *-et* fodder (grain).
***grjo'n/vare** *-a* fodder (grain).
***grjo't** *-et* 1 rock, stone. 2 stuff: **det er godt g- i den guten** there is good stuff in that boy.
***grjo't/berg** *-et* stone which can be quarried.
gro'¹ *-a, pl *grør* 1 toad. 2 growth; plankton; potato sprouts (=**groe**).
gro'² *V -dde* grow, sprout: **g- fast** take root; **g- igjen, over** overgrow; **g- opp** crop up; **g- opp som paddehatter** spring up like mushrooms; **g- sammen** heal.
Gro' *Prn (f)*
gro'bian *-en* boor, lout.
gro'blad/kjempe *-a/+-en bot.* plantain (Plantago major).
gro'/botn *-en* (=+/**bunn**) fertile soil.
gro'e *-n* 1 new spring grass. 2 potato sprout. 3 plankton.
grogg' *-en* grog.
gro'/hold *-et dial.* flesh that heals readily.
gro'/kjøtt *-et* flesh that heals readily: **ha dårlig g-** be slow in healing.
grom' *A -t, pl -me* magnificent, splendid; excellent, *(pop.)* grand, swell.
+grom'/gutt *-en* (=*/**gut**) apple of the parents' eye, pet (boy).
grom'/jente *-a* apple of the parents' eye, pet (girl).
Grong' *Pln* twp, Nord-Trøndelag.
gro'p¹ *-a* depression, hollow; pothole (in road).
***grop²** [grå'p] *-et* 1 coarse grain (used for fodder). 2 excavation, hollowing out.
***grope** [grå'pe] *V -a* 1 grind coarsely (grain). 2 excavate, hollow out.
gro'pet(e) *A* - full of hollows.
gro'r *-en* growing, sprouting; growth, vegetation.
***gro'r/botn** *-en* cf **gro/**
***gro'r/sam'** *A* fertile, fruitful.
***gro'r/ver** *-et* cf **gro/vær**
gros [gro'] cf **en gros**
gross' *-et* gross (=12 dozen).
+grosse'rer *-en, pl -e* (=***-ar**) *merc.* wholesale dealer, wholesaler; (big) merchant (often used as title).
grossis't *-en merc.* wholesale dealer, wholesaler.
grotes'k *A* - grotesque.
gro'/tid *-a/+-en* period of (marked) development, growth.
grot'te *-a/+-en* cave, grotto.
***gro'v¹** *-a, pl grøver* brook.
***grov²** [grå'v] *-a* 1 depression, hollow. 2 grave.
gro'v³ *pt of* **grave**
grov⁴ [grå'v] *A cp *-are/*grøvre, sp *-ast/*grøvst* 1 coarse (bread, features, joke, etc.). 2 gruff, rough (person, voice, etc.); rude (**mot** to). 3 big, gross (blunder, injustice, lie, etc.): **g-t med penger** lots of money; **g-t til tørst** terrific thirst; **være g- til å ta seg betalt** demand an exorbitant price.
grov/arbeid [grå'v/arbei'] *-et* 1 unskilled labor. 2 spadework.
grov/brød *-et* coarse, dark rye bread.
grov/bygd *A -/*-bygt* (of person) large-boned; (of building) roughly built.
gro'velig *A* - grievous, gross.
+grov/het [grå'v/] *-en* coarseness, grossness; abusive, rude remark.
+grov/ko'rnet [grå'v/] *A* - 1 coarse-grained. 2 coarse, crude.
***grov/lagd** *A /-lagt* coarsely built, rough.
***grov/leik** *-en* coarseness, grossness, thickness.
grov/lemma *A* - (=+**-et**) coarse-limbed.
grov/maska *A* - (=+**-et**) coarse-meshed.
grov/mælt [+/me'lt] *A* - husky-voiced.
***gro'vne** *V -a* coarsen.
grov/sikta [grå'v/] *A* - (=+**-et**) coarsely sifted.
+grov/skåren *A -ent, pl -ne* (=*/**skoren**) 1 rough cut (e.g. tobacco). 2 coarse, crude.
grov/smed *-en* blacksmith.
+grov/telling *-a/-en* (=*/**teljing**) preliminary (vote) count.
+gro'/vær *-et* (=*/**ver**, ***gror/**) (good) growing weather.
gru' *-a/+-en* horror, terror: **det er en g- å se** it's a horrible, shocking sight; **det slo ham med g-** it made him shudder; **så det var en g-** something awful.
Gru'a *Pln* village, Oppland.
***gru'al** *A* inclined to worry; reluctant, timid, worried.
+gru'be *-n* cf **gruve¹**
+grub'le *V -a/-et* (=***gruvle**) brood, mull over, muse: **g- over noe** meditate, ponder deeply over sth; **g-ende** thoughtfully.
+grub'ler *-en, pl -e* (=***gruvlar**) brooder.
+grubleri' *-et* brooding, meditation, speculation.
grublise're *V -te fam.* brood, mull over, rack one's brains.
gru'e¹ *-a* fireplace, (open) hearth.
gru'e² *V -dde/*-a*: **g- seg** be nervous (about sth approaching); **g- seg for (til)** dread, worry about; hesitate; **jeg g-er meg til eksamen** I'm nervous about the examination.
+gru'e³ *Av* cf **gruve²**
Gru'e *Pln* twp, Hedmark.
gru'elig *A* - awful, horrible, terrible; *(adv.)*: **g- redd** terribly afraid.
***gruf'sen** *A -e/-i, pl -ne* 1 coarse, rough, uneven. 2 muddy, turbid.
gru'/full *A* ghastly, horrible.
grugg' *-et/*-en* dregs, grounds.
***grug'ge** *V -a* become cloudy, turbid.
***grug'gen** *A -e/-i, pl grugne* cf **grugget(e)**
grug'get(e) *A* - full of dregs, grounds; cloudy, turbid.
grum'¹ *A -t, pl -me; archaic* cruel, ferocious; sinister.
***grum'²** *A -t, pl -me* cf **grom**
***grum'de** *pt of* **grymje**
+grum'/het *-en archaic* cruelty, ferocity.
grums [grom's] *-et* dregs, grounds, sediment.
grumse [grom'se] *V -a/+-et*: **g- til** make turbid, muddy.
grumset(e) [grom'set(e)] *A* - 1 cloudy, muddy, turbid. 2 (of a sound) hoarse, husky. 3 (morally) impure, unclean.
***grum't** *pp of* **grymje**
grun'de *V -a/+-et* cf **grunne³**
grunde're *V -te* ground, prime.
grun'dig *A* - exhaustive, thorough; meticulous, painstaking.
+grun'dig/het *-en* thoroughness; meticulosity.
+grundtvigia'ner *-en, pl -e* (=***-ar**) adherent of Grundtvig.
***gru'ne** *V -a* cf **grunne³**
***grun'k** *-en* cf **grunker**
+grun'ker *pl* (=***-ar**) loads of money, *(pop.)* dough, jack.
grunn'¹ *-en* 1 basis, ground(s), reason (**til** for); cause (**til** of): **av hvilken g-** for what reason; **i g-en** after all, all things considered, in reality; **i g-en ikke** not really; **på g- av** on account of, owing to. 2 foundation, ground, groundwork; base, ground, priming; *bot.* base: **fra g-en av** from the ground up; radically; **gå til g-e** be destroyed, ruined; go to rack and ruin. 3 ground, soil; lot, plot, property: **gard og g-** house and grounds; **gå fra gard og g-** go bankrupt, lose one's farm; **gå (kjøre, seile) på g-** run aground; **på norsk g-** on Norwegian soil.
grunn'² *A grunt* shallow; *fig.* shallow, superficial: **grunt vann** shallow water.
grunn- *Pf* basic, fundamental; radical(ly), utter(ly).
grunn'/akkor'd *-en mus.* fundamental harmony.
grunn'/aksje *-n merc.* share of common stock.
grunn'/area'l *-et* area.
grunn'/avgif't *-a/+-en* property tax.
+grunn'/begre'p *-et* fundamental concept.
grunn'/bok *-a, pl -bøker* 1 *admin.* register (of all transactions relating to real estate). 2 *merc.* minutes of business transactions. 3 *educ.* basic book, outline.
grunn'/brott *-et* (=*/**brot**) *naut.* ground breaker, sea breaking over shoal.
grunn'/drag *-et* basic trait, main feature: **i g-** in outline.
grun'ne¹ *-a/-en* 1 shallow(s), shoal. 2: **gå til g-** cf **grunn¹**.
grun'ne² *V -a/+-et* establish, found: **g- på** base, found on; **g- seg på** be based on, rest on (cf **grunnet**).
grun'ne³ *V -a/+-et* (=+**grunde**) mull over, muse, ponder (**på** on): **g- over noe** meditate on sth, ponder sth; **g- ut noe** puzzle out sth.
grun'ne⁴ *V -a/+-et*: **g- opp** shoal.
+grunn'/eier *-en, pl -e* (=*/**eigar**) landowner, property owner.
+grun'net¹ *A* well-founded (e.g. suspicion): **g- frykt for** reason to believe.
grun'net² *P* on account of, owing to:

g- omstendighetene owing to circumstances.
grunn`/fag -et basic courses (required of majors and minors in a university subject).
grunn`fa·gs/stude·renḍe en student taking grunnfag in a subject.
grunn`/farge -n 1 primary color. 2 prime coat (e.g. of paint or varnish).
grunn`/feste[1] -a/+-et anchor.
grunn`/feste[2] V -a/+-et/*-e establish (firmly); confirm, consolidate: en g-et posisjon an established position.
grunn`/fjell -et geol. bedrock.
grunn`/flate -a/+-en base.
grunn`/fonḍ -et merc. capital stock.
grunn`/forskjell· -en basic difference.
grunn`/gi V infl as gi give grounds for, justify.
grunn`/giing -en (=+/giv(n)ing, +/givelse) excuse, justification, reason (for for).
*grunn`/gje(ve) V -gav, -gjeve/-i cf /gi
*grunn`/hått -en essential character.
grun`ning[1] -a/+-en priming; prime coat.
grun`ning[2] -en shoal.
grunn`/la pt of -legge
grunn`/lag -et basis, foundation; grounding: danne g- for form the basis of; legge g-et til lay the foundation of; på g- av on the basis of.
grunn`/laus A (=+/løs) baseless, groundless.
+grunn`/legge V -la, lagt (=*-je) establish, found; lay the basis, foundation of.
+grunn`/leggenḍe A - (=*/leggjande) basic, fundamental, underlying.
+grunn`/legger -en, pl -e (=*-jar) founder.
grunn`/legging -a/+-en (=+-else) establishment, foundation (av of).
+grunn`/linje -a/-en (=*/line) 1 main feature. 2 math. base (line). 3 (tennis) base line.
grunn`/lov [/låv] -en/*-a 1 constitution: Norges g- the C- of Norway. 2 basic, fundamental law.
+grunnlov/givenḍe A - (=*/gjevande): den g- forsamling the constituent assembly.
grunnlovs/brott -et (=+/brudd, */brot) violation of the Constitution.
grunnlovs/dag -en Constitution Day.
grunnlovs/stridig A - unconstitutional.
grunn`/lønn -a/+-en (=*/løn) basic salary, wage.
+grunn`/løs A cf /laus
grunn`/mur -en foundation wall; plinth.
grunn`/not -a, pl -nøter heavily weighted seine.
grunn`/pila·r -en pillar, prop; main support.
grunn`/plan -en ground plan.
grunn`/preg -et basic (essential) character.
grunn`/regel -elen, pl -ler axiom, basic principle, rule.
grunn`/rik A affluent, wealthy.
grunn`/riss -et 1 ground plan. 2 outline (av of).
+grunn`/satte pt of -sette
grunn`/setning *-a/+-en maxim, principle, tenet; math., philos. axiom.
+grunn`/sette V -satte, -satt run aground.
grunn`/sjø -en ground swell.
grunn`/skatt -en property tax.
grunn`/skott -et (=+/skudd, */skot) naut. hit below the water line; fig. death blow.
grunn`/skrift -a/+-en basic text, original.
+grunn`/skudd -et cf /skott
grunn`/stamme +-n/*-a 1 (parent) stock. 2 nucleus.
grunn`/stein -en cornerstone.
grunn`/stilling -a/+-en 1 mil. attention. 2 mus. root position.
grunn`/stoff -et chem. element.
grunn`/stokk -en 1 (parent) stock. 2 nucleus.
+grunn`/støte V -te run aground.
grunn`/syn -et/*-a basic viewpoint.
grunn`/tal -et (=+/tall) cardinal number.
grunn`/tanke -n basic, fundamental idea.
*grunn`/tenkt A - cursory, shallow, superficial.
*grunn`/to -et chem. element.
grunn`/tone -n 1 mus. keynote, tonic; base note of chord. 2 (painting) dominant color; (radio) fundamental tone. 3 fig. keynote.
+grunn`/trekk -et characteristic, essential feature; (pl) outline: i g- in o-.
grunn`/vatn -et (=+/vann) groundwater, subsoil water.
grunn`/verdi· -en land value.
grunn`/vev -et/*-en bot. parenchyma.
grunn`/voll -en basis, foundation, groundwork: legge g-en til noe lay the basis, foundation of sth; rystet i sin sjels g-er shaken to the depths of one's being.
grunn`/æ·rlig A - thoroughly honest, the soul of honesty.
grun't nt of grunn[2]
grun't/gåenḍe A - naut. shallow draft (vessel).
+gru'/oppvek·kenḍe [also gru`/] A - ghastly, horrible, shocking.
grup`pe -a/+-en 1 group (av of); cluster: i g-r på to og tre by twos and threes. 2 mil. (battle) group; section. 3 elec. bank (e.g. of lamps).
+grup`pe/fører -en, pl -e (=*-ar) mil. section leader.
grup`pe/møte -t, pl +-r/*- pol. caucus.
gruppe're V -te group: g- seg form groups, group themselves.
gru's[1] -en/-et 1 gravel. 2 rubble, ruins: legge i g- reduce to rubble; ligge i g- be in ruins; synke i g- crumble, fall in ruins. 3 med. gravel.
gru's[2] A 1 first-rate, magnificent, splendid; grand, swell. 2: ha g-t med have an abundance of, (pop.) be loaded with.
gru`se[1] V -a/+-et gravel: g- opp wash up gravel.
gru`se[2] V -te: g- med squander, waste.
*gru`seleg A - awful, dreadful, frightful.
gru`set(e) A - gravelly.
grus'k A dial. 1 gruff, harsh, stern. 2 (pop.) grand, swell.
+gru`s/lagt A - (=*/lagd) gravelled.
+gru`/som· A -t, pl -me 1 cruel. 2 awful, horrible, terrible: g-t sterk awfully strong; g-t vrøvl terrible nonsense. 3 (in women's speech) awful, hideous, (dress, hat, etc.).
+gru`som/het -en 1 cruelty. 2 atrocity.
+gru`s/strødd A - (=*/strøydd) gravelled, gravel-strewn.
gru`s/tak -et gravel pit.
*grus`te pt of grysje
gru't -en/-et 1 (coffee) grounds. *2 dregs, sediment.
*gru`ten A -e/-i, pl -ne cloudy, turbid.
*gru`v A bent over, stooped.
°gru`val A cf grual
gru`ve[1] -a 1 mine, pit. 2 excavation, hollow. 3 (garage, service station) grease pit.
gru`ve[2] Av (=+grue[3]): dial. falle g- fall flat on one's face; ligge g- lie prone.
+gru`ve/arbei·der -en, pl -e (=*-ar) miner.
+gru`/verdig A - horrible, terrible.
gru`ve/tømmer -et beam (used in shoring up a mine).
*gruv`le V -a cf gruble
*gru`v/sam· A 1 reluctant, worried. 2 disagreeable, unpleasant (work).
gry'[1] -et dawn, daybreak.
gry'[2] V -dde dawn: g- av dag poet. dawn.
gry'l -et growl, grunt.
gry'le V -te growl, grunt.
*grym`je V grym, grumde, grumt grunt; fig. grumble.
gry'n -et 1 (hulled) grain; pearled barley (etc.); (pl) grits, groats: ikke et g- not the slightest, not a trace. 2 tiny tot, tyke. 3 pop. dough, jack.
*gry`nast V -ast become grainy, gritty.
gry`net(e) A - grainy, gritty.
gry`n/graut -en grits porridge.
gry`n/mjøl -et pollard (finely sifted bran).
*gryn`nast V -est, gryntest, grynst shoal (become shallow).
*gryn`ne[1] -a shoal.
*gryn`ne[2] V grynte 1 touch bottom. 2 struggle, wade (e.g. through mud, snow).
gry`n/sodd -et meat broth (with hulled grain).
gryn't -et grunt.
gryn`te V -a/+-et grunt.
*gryn`test pt of grynnast
gry`n/velling -a/-en (grit) gruel.
*gryp`je V gryp, grypte cf grøppe
*grysj`e V grys, gruste cf grøsse
*grysj`eleg A awful, horrible.
gry`te[1] -a 1 kettle, pot: små g-r har også ører little pitchers have big ears. 2 depression, hollow: Oslo ligger i en g- Oslo is located in a (large) depression.
*gry`te[2] V grytte throw, toss.
*gry`te/hodde -a pot handle.
gry`te/klut -en pot holder.
gry`te/krok -en 1 pothook. 2 stove (lid) lifter.
gry`te/lokk -et pot lid.
gry`/tiḍlig A - at the crack of dawn.
Gryt`ten Pln twp, Møre og Romsdal.
+græ`le[1] -a 1 slack wind. 2 overcast, with rain. 3 pale, sickly person.
græ`le[2] V -a/+-et dial. growl, grumble, whine.
*græ`le[3] V -a blow slackly, sluggishly.
græ`len A +-ent, pl -ne dial. 1 chilly, overcast, windy. 2 dun (horse); pale, sickly.
*græ`se V -te blow (cold, sharp wind).
*græ't pr of gråte
grø' V -dde (=grøde[3]) 1 dial. grow, sprout. 2 archaic cure; heal; recover.
*grø`ḍast V grødest, grøddest, grødst get well, recover.
grø`de[1] [*grø`e] -a/+-en bibl., poet. crop, produce, yield: Markens g- Growth of the Soil (novel by Hamsun).
*grø`ḍe[2] -t green spot; crop; offspring.
grø`de[3] [*grø`e] V -de cf grø
grø`de/rik A fertile, fruitful.
*grøḍs't pp of grødast
grøf't -a ditch, trench: kjøre i g-a run (e.g. a car) into the ditch; fig. come to grief.
grøf`te V -a/+-et dig ditches; drain (land) by means of ditches: g- ut (the same).
+grøf`te/graver -en (=*-ar) ditch-digger.
grøf`te/kjøre V -te run a car into the ditch; fig. come to grief.
°grø'n[1] -et cf grjon
grø'n[2] A (=+grønn) 1 green; fresh, verdant: g- av misunnelse green with envy; g- stær med. glaucoma; i det g-e in the fresh air, out of doors; komme på den g-e gren do well for oneself, prosper, (pop.) come into the chips; lengte seg g- etter noe long intensely for sth; love en gull og g-e skoger promise sby the moon. 2 inexperienced, raw: i hans g-e ungdom in his salad days; være g- be a greenhorn, be half-baked. 3 archaic favorable (in a few idioms): gjøre sine hoser g-e hos en go out of one's way to please sby; court sby; sette seg ved ens g-e side sit at one's left side; sove på sitt g-e øre be fast asleep; sleep the sleep of the just.
*grø`ne V -a appear, look green.

+ Bokmål; * Nynorsk; ° Dialect.
After letter: ' stress (Acc. 1); ` tone, stress (Acc. 2); · length.
Below letter: . not pronounced.

grø'n/for [also grø'n/] *-et* (=**+grønn/**) (green) forage, pasturage.
***grø'nka(st)** *V -a(st)* turn green; burst into leaf.
Grøn'/land *Pln* Greenland.
grøn'/landsk *A* - Greenlandic.
+grøn'/lender *-en, pl -e* 1 Greenlander (Eskimo). 2 *hist.* Norse settler in Greenland.
grøn'/lending *-en* 1 Greenlander (Eskimo). 2 *hist.* Norse settler in Greenland.
grø'nlig *A* - (=**+grønnlig**) greenish.
+grønn' *A grønt* cf **grøn[2]**
+grønn'/aktig *A* - greenish.
+grøn'nes *V grøntes* turn green; burst into leaf.
+grønn'/for *-et* cf **grøn/**
+grønn'lig *A* - cf **grønlig**
+grønn'/saker *pl* cf **grøn/**
+grønn'/skolling *-en* cf **grøn/**
+grønn'/svær *-et* greensward, turf.
+grønn'/såpe *-a* cf **grøn/**
grø'n/saker *pl* vegetables.
grøn'ske *V -a/+-et* (appear; make; turn) green.
grø'n/skolling *-en* (=**+grønn/**) greenhorn.
***grø'n/skurd** *-en* unripened grain (mowed for fodder).
grø'n/såpe *-a* (=**+grønn/**) green soap, soft soap.
grøn't *et* 1 (color) green: **kledd i g-** dressed in g-. 2 greens, vegetables; greenery, verdure.
+grøn'tes *pt of* **grønnes**
+grøn't/handler *-en, pl -e* (=***-ar**) fruit and vegetable retailer; *(Brit.)* greengrocer.
grø'n/år *-et* bad year (for crops).
grøpp' *-et* 1 coarsely ground grain, grits (used for fodder). 2 mass of ice (icy ground) ready to thaw.
grøp'pe *V grøpte* 1 grind grain coarsely. 2: **g- seg** form a gritty mass (of sth).
***grø'r** *pl of* **gro[1]**
grøss' *-et* shiver, shudder.
grøs'se *V grøste/+-et/*-a* shiver, shudder: **det g-te i ham** he shuddered; **g- bare ved tanken på** shudder (just) to think of it.
grøs'sen *A +-ent, pl grøsne* shivering, shuddering: **ikke være g- av seg** be aggressive, forward.
+grøs'ser *-en, pl -e* (=***-ar**) thriller (book, film).
+grø't *-en* cf **graut**
***grø'te** *V -te* make (sby) cry: **her er så vent det kan meg g-** it is so lovely here that it could make me weep (Vinje).
***grø'teleg** *A* - melancholy, sad; sentimental; *(adv.)*: **g- vent** so pretty it makes you feel like crying.
+grø'tet(e) *A* - cf **grautet(e)**
grø't/stein *-en* potstone, soapstone.
***grøv'd** *-a* 1 coarseness, roughness. 2 bore, caliber.
grø'ver *pl of* **grov[1]**
***grøv're** *cp of* **grov[4]**
***grøv'st** *sp of* **grov[4]**
***grøy'pe[1]** *-a* channel, groove.
***grøy'pe[2]** *V -te* 1 cut channels, grooves. 2 grind grain.
grå' *A -tt, pl -/-e* 1 gray; grizzled, hoary; overcast (weather); sallow (complexion): **g- eminense** (cf **eminense**); **det setter ham g- hår i hodet** it's enough to give him gray hair; **få sin avskjed på g-tt papir** be summarily dismissed; *mil.* receive a dishonorable discharge; **i mørke er alle katter g-** in the dark everything looks alike. 2 *fig.* drab, dreary, monotonous: **male g-tt i g-tt** paint a gloomy picture. 3 (as a noun, chiefly *poet.*) grayness; gloom: **sommerkveldens g-** the gray of summer eve (Kinck).
+grå'/aktig *A* - grayish, grizzly.
grå'/bein *-en* wolf.
grå'bein/sild *-a* large winter herring.
grå'/bror *-en, pl +-brødre/*-brør* Franciscan, Gray Friar.

grå'dig *A* - greedy, voracious (**etter** for.)
+grå'dig/het *-en* greed, voracity (**etter** for).
grå'e *-n dial.* 1 gray speck, spot 2 wind which ripples water.
grå'/erle *-a zool.* gray wagtail (Motacilla cinerea).
grå'/gås *-a, pl -gjæser/+-gjess zool.* greylag, wild goose (Anser anser).
***grå'/hæ'rd** *A -hært* cf **/håra**
grå'/håra *A* - (=**+-et**) gray-haired, -headed.
grå'/kald *A* - gray and overcast.
***grå'/leitt** *A* grayish, grizzly.
grå'lig *A* - grayish, grizzly.
grå'/lysing *-a/+-en* (=**/lysning**) daybreak, earliest dawn, gray morning light.
grå'/mele'rt *A* - salt-and-pepper (material).
grå'ne *V -a/+-et* 1 turn gray; become overcast, cloud over; *fig.* be getting along in years. 2 dawn.
grå'/pære *-a* small, gray pear.
+grå'/sprengt *A* - (=***/sprengd**) grizzled.
+grå'/spurv *-en* (=***/sporv**) *zool.* (common) sparrow (Passer domesticus).
grå'/stein *-en* granite boulder, stone.
grå't[1] *-en* crying, weeping; tears: **ha g-en i halsen** have a lump in one's throat; **på g-en** on the verge of tears; **svelgje g-en** hold back the tears; **tørr så g-en pent av øyet** now wipe your tears away nicely (Ibsen).
+grå't[2] *pt of* **gråte**
***grå'tar-** *Pf* cf **gråte-**
grå'/tass *-en* wolf.
grå'te *V +-er/*græt, gret/+gråt, +-t/ *-e/*-i* cry, weep (**over** over); blubber, sob: **g- av glede** weep for joy; **g- sine modige tårer** cry one's heart out, weep bitterly; **g- ut** have a good cry; **osten g-er** drops are forming on the cheese.
grå'te/ferdig *A* - half crying, on the verge of tears.
grå'te/kone *-a/+-en* professional mourner.
grå'te/kor *-et* chorus of professional wailers.
grå'te/tone *-n* sobbing tone (voice, instrument).
***grå'/tidleg** *A* - at the crack of dawn.
***grå't/kjøvd** *A -kjøvt* stifled by sobs, tearful.
+grå't/kva'lt *A* - stifled by sobs, tearful.
grå't/mild *A* lachrymose, tearful; whimpering.
***grå't/sam'** *A* lachrymose, tearful; whimpering.
grått'[1] *et* gray (color, clothing, material).
grått'[2] *nt of* **grå**, *pp of* **gråte**
grå'/verk *-et* gray squirrel (fur); miniver.
+grå'/vær *-et* (=***/ver**) 1 cloudy, overcast weather. 2 *fig.* depression, gloom.
GT=**Det gamle testamentet**
gt.=**gate[1]**
gu' *I* cf **gud**
gua'no *-en* guano (fertilizer).
gubb' *-en* whole milk cheese.
gub'be *-n* graybeard, old man: **g-n** *hum.* the old man; *naut.* the skipper.
***gub'beleg** *A* - mighty, powerful; dignified, worthy.
gubb'/ost [/ost] *-en* whole milk cheese.
gu'd *-en* 1 god, God: **dyrke fremmede g-er** *bibl.* worship strange gods; **g- bevar's** (mild oath); **g-ene må vite** heaven knows; **det skal g- vite** that's certainly true; **G- Fader** G- the Father; **g- nåde deg** heaven help you; **g- og hvermann** every Tom, Dick and Harry; **om G- vil** G- willing. 2 (as exclam. or mild oath) good heavens, goodness: **g- for en simpel person** Lord, what a vulgar person. 3 (oath) **gu: (ja)gu var hun det** indeed she was, you bet she was; **(nei)gu om jeg gjør** (I'm) damned if I do; (mild oath) **så gud (sågu, s'gu, sgu, sku)** by heaven, certainly.

gu'd/ba'rn *-et, pl -/*-born* godchild.
+gudbe'dre *I* cf **bedre[1]**
+gu'd/benå'det [also gu'd/] *A* - divine, (heaven-)inspired, highly-gifted.
Gud'/brand *Prn(m)*
Gud'brands/dal(en) *Pln* extended valley running from Lesjaskogsvatn southeastwards to Mjøsa.
gud'brands/døl *-en* inhabitant of Gudbrandsdal.
+gu'd/datter *-a/-en, pl -døtre* (=***/dotter**) goddaughter.
gud'/dom' *-men/*-en* deity, god: **g-men** divinity; the Godhead.
guddom'melig *A* - (=***-domeleg**) 1 divine. 2 *(adv.)*: **vi moret oss g-** we had a perfectly grand time.
***gu'd/dotter** *-a, pl -døtrer* cf **/datter**
+gu'de/bilde *-t* (=***/bilete**) idol.
gu'de/drikk *-en* 1 *myth.* nectar. 2 drink fit for the gods (e.g. a superb wine).
+gu'de/gave *-a/-en* divine gift (esp. the gift of poetry, song).
gu'delig *A* - 1 devout, godly, religious; devotional, pious. 2 *derog.* sanctimonious.
Gudfa'der *N* cf **gud**
gu'd/far *-en, pl +-fedre/*-fedrar* godfather, sponsor.
gudfryk'tig *A* - devout, godfearing, pious.
+gudfryk'tig/het *-en* piety.
+gu'd/hengi'ven *A -ent, pl -ne* devout, godfearing, pious.
***gu'd/hæding** *-a* blasphemy, sacrilege.
gudin'ne *-a/+-en* goddess (**for** of).
gu'd/laus *A* (=**+/løs**) godless, ungodly; atheistic.
***gu'dleg** *A* - cf **gudelig**
gu'd/lik *A* godlike.
+gu'd/løs *A* cf **/laus**
+gu'dløs/het *-en* godlessness, ungodliness; atheism.
***gu'd/løyse** *-a* cf **-løs/het**
gu'd/mor *-a/-en, pl +-mødre/*-mødrer* godmother.
Gud'/mund *Prn(m)*
gudnåds'lig *A* - pitiable, wretched.
Gud'run *Prn(f)*
+gud's/bespot'telse *-n* blasphemy, sacrilege.
gud's/dom' *-men hist.* trial by ordeal (battle, fire, water, etc.).
+gud's/dyrkelse *-n* (=***-ing**) cult, (formal) worship.
gud'sens *A -: fam.* **det er g- sannhet** that's absolutely true; **ikke et g- ord** not a single word.
+gud's/forgå'en *A -ent, pl -ene* abandoned, depraved.
+gud's/forlatt' *A* - godforsaken.
+gud's/fornek'ter *-en, pl -e* atheist.
gud's/frykt **-a/+-en* fear of God, piety.
gud's/hus *-et* (usu.) Christian church; house of God, place of worship.
gudsjam'merlig *A* - pitiable, wretched; *(adv.)*: **han er g- feig** he's a miserable coward.
gu'd/skapt *A -:* **hver eneste g-e dag** every blessed day.
+gudskjelov [gusj'e lå'v] *I* (=**gud skje lov**) fortunately, thank goodness, thank God.
***gu'd/son** [/sån] *-en, pl -søner* cf **/sønn**
gud's/o'rd *-et* 1 (passage of) Scripture; word of God: **denne kveldsbønnen var det eneste g-et han kunne utenad** this evening prayer was the only word of God he knew by heart (Fønhus). 2: **et g- fra landet** a little innocent.
+gud's/tjeneste *-n* (=***/teneste**) (divine) service(s): **etter g-en** after church.
gud's/tru *-a* (=**+/tro**) belief in God.
+gu'd/sønn *-en* (=***/son**) godson.
guf'fen *A -ent, pl gufne* 1 disagreeable, nasty, unpleasant. 2 low, mean, shabby; *(adv.)*: **det var g-t gjort** that was a dirty trick.
guf's *-en/+-et/*-a* (of wind) gust, puff; sudden rush of air, odor; shiver, shudder.

guf`se *V -a/+-et* blow in gusts, gust.
***gug`ge** *V -a* fumble, stammer.
guide [gai'd] *-n* guide; guidebook.
guillotine [giljoti'ne] *-n* cf **giljotin**
gu`l[1] *-a* (**=gule**[2]) steady breeze, wind.
gu`l[2] *A* yellow; sallow: **den g-e fare** the yellow peril; **den g-e flekk** *med.* macula lutea; **det g-e (i egget)** the yolk (of the egg); **g- presse** yellow journalism, the yellow press; **ergre seg g- og grønn** be annoyed to the point of distraction; **g- (og grønn) av misunnelse** afflicted by the green-eyed monster; **slå en g- og blå** beat sby black and blue.
gulasj' *-en* goulash.
Gu`la/ting *Pln hist.* legal assembly held annually at Gulen (Sogn) for western Norway (in Old Norse times).
gu`l/blakk *A -blakt, pl -e* fallow, pale yellow.
gu`le[1] *-n* yellow of the egg.
gu`le[2] *-a* cf **gul**[1]
***gu`le**[3] *-a* yellow (color, shade).
gu`le[4] *V -a/+-et* (of wind) blow gently and steadily.
Gu`len *Pln* twp, Sogn og Fjordane.
+**gu`le/rot** *-a, pl -røtter* cf **gul/**
gu`l/feber *-en* yellow fever.
***gul`ke** *V -a* belch; regurgitate, vomit.
gull' *-et* gold; money, wealth: **det er g- verdt** it's worth its weight in gold; **det er ikke g- alt som glimrer** all that glitters is not gold; **ikke for all verdens g-** not at any price, not for love or money; **love en g- og grønne skoger** promise sby the moon.
gull`/alder *-eren, pl -rer* golden age.
***gul`lan/bragd** *-a* golden glow.
gull`/boksta·v *-en* gilt letter, gold letter.
***gull`/boste** *-n bot.* dandelion (Taraxacum officinale).
gull`/brand *-en* ring finger.
+**gull`/bryllup** *-et* (**=*/bryllaup**) golden wedding.
gul`lende *Av*: **g- ren** spotlessly clean.
gull`/feber *-en* gold fever.
gull`/fisk *-en zool.* goldfish (Carassius auratus).
gull`/flyndre *-a zool.* plaice (Pleuronectes platessa).
gull`/fot *-en* gold standard.
gull`/fugl *-en* gilt, gold bird; *fig.* Croesus; rich heiress.
gull`/førende *A* - auriferous, gold-bearing.
gull`/gruve *-a* gold mine.
gull`/gul *A* golden yellow.
+**gull`/gutt** *-en* (**=*/gut**) apple of the parents' eye, mother's darling, pet (boy).
gull`/høne *-a* **1** *folk.* golden hen (laying golden eggs). **2** *zool.* ladybug (family Coccinellidae).
gu`llig *A* - yellowish; sallow.
gull`/kalv *-en* **1** *bibl.* golden calf (Exodus 32, 4). **2: danse om g-en** be concerned solely with the acquisition of material goods.
gull`/kanta *A* - (**=+-et**) gilt-edged (e.g. securities).
gull`/klausul *-en merc.* gold clause.
gull`/medal·je *-n* gold medal: **drikke til den store g-** drink like a fish.
gull`/merke *-t, pl +-r/*-* gold medal (in sports competition).
gull`/myntfo·t *-en* gold standard.
gull`/papi·r *-et* gilt paper.
gull`/regn [+/rein] *-en bot.* laburnum (Laburnum anagyroides).
***gull`/slegen** *A -e/-i, pl -ne* gold mounted.
gull`/smed *-en* **1** goldsmith; jeweler. **2** *zool.* dragonfly (order Odonata). **3** *zool.* ladybug (family Coccinellidae).
gull`smed/merke *-t* (goldsmith's, jeweler's) hallmark.
gull`/snitt *-et* gilt edge: **en bok i g-** a book with gilt edges.
gull`/stjerne *-a/+-en bot.* gagea, yellow star-of-Bethlehem (Gagea lutea).
gull`/stol *-en* golden chair: **bære på g-** carry in triumph.
+**gull`/strøm·** *-men merc.* flow of gold (into, out of a country).
+**gull`/stukken** [/stokken] *A -et, pl -stukne* gold embroidered.
gull`/vekt *-a/+-en* **1** gold weight; weight in gold. **2** gold scales: **veie sine ord på g-** weigh every word carefully.
gu`lne *V -a/+-et* (turn) yellow.
gul'p *-en/-et* belch; regurgitation; gurgle.
gul`pe *V -a/+-et* belch; regurgitate, vomit; gurgle: **g- opp** throw up.
gu`l/rot *-a, pl +-røtter/*-røter bot.* carrot (Daucus carota).
gu`l/sott *-a/+-en med.* jaundice.
+**gu`l/spurv** *-en* (**=*/sporv**) *zool.* yellowhammer (Emberiza citrinella).
gu`lt *et* yellow (color).
+**gul`v** *-et* cf **golv**
+**gumle** [gom`le] *V -et* cf **gomle**
gumme [gom`me] *-n* "sweet cheese" (brown cheese, boiled from whole cow's milk).
gumme're *V -te* cf **gummiere**
gum`mi *-en* **1** rubber. **2** (chewing) gum.
gum`mi/ball *-en* rubber ball.
gummie're *V -te* gum.
gum`mi/ring *-en* **1** tire. **2** rubber ring (used in canning).
gum`mi/sko *-en, pl -r/+-* tennis shoe.
gum`mi/slange *-n* rubber hose, rubber tube.
gum`mi/strikk *-en* rubber band.
+**gum`mi/såle** *-n* rubber sole.
gump [gom'p] *-en* rump.
+**gung`re** *V -a/-et* boom, rumble.
Gunn' *Prn (f)*
Gun`nar *Prn (m)*
Gunn`/hild *Prn (f)*
gun'st *-en* favor: **stå høyt i ens g-** stand high in sby's favor; **til g- for** in favor of.
+**gun'st/bevi·sning** *-en* favor, kindness.
gun`stig *A* - favorable; propitious: **g- stemt overfor noe** favorably disposed towards sth, in favor of sth.
Gun`/vor· *Prn (f)*
gu'r *-en geol.* diatomite, kieselguhr.
gur`gle *V -a/+-et* **1** gargle: **g- halsen** g- one's throat. **2** gurgle: **våren g-er i hver en bekk** spring is g-ing in every stream (Olaf Bull).
gur`gle/vatn *-et* (**=+/vann**) gargle.
***gur'm** *-et* dregs, grounds.
gur'p *-en dial.* belch.
gur`pe *V -a dial.* belch.
+**gur`se/grøn(n)**¦ *A -grønt* dirty greenish-yellow.
gus't *-en* (of wind) gust.
Gus`tav *Prn (m)*
gus`te *V -a/+-et* blow in gusts, gust.
gus`ten *A +-ent, pl -ne* pale, pallid, wan; feeble, sickly.
***gu't** *-en* cf **gutt**
***gu`te/fjes** *-et* cf **gutte/**
***gu`te/kor** *-et* cf **gutte/**
gute're *V -te* enjoy, relish.
***gu`te/sprengje** *-a* bewitching woman.
+**gutt'** *-en* (**=*gut**) **1** boy; young man. **2** fellow, guy: **g-ene** the boys, the gang; **det var g-en sin** what a boy; attaboy!
+**gutt`/aktig** *A* - cf **gutte/**
guttaper'ka *-en* gutta-percha (a kind of rubber).
+**gut`te/aktig** *A* - boyish.
+**gut`te/fjes** *-et* baby face.
+**gut`te/gal** *A* boy crazy.
+**gut`te/gjeng** *-en* gang of boys.
+**gut`te/kor** *-et* boys' choir.
+**gutt`/unge** [/onge] *-n* boy, *(pop.)* kid, lad; whippersnapper.
guttura'l *A gram.* guttural, velar.
gu`tu *-a* passage for cows; cowpath, trail.
***gu't/unge** [/onge] *-n* cf **gutt/**
guvernan`te *-a/+-en* governess.
guvernø'r *-en* governor.
Gvar'v *Pln* village, Sauherad twp, Telemark.
Gy'da [also jy'-, gy'-] *Prn (f)*
+**gy`de** *V gjød, gydt* cf **gyte**
gyd`je *-a hist.* priestess (in Norse paganism).
***gyf't** *-a* dust.
***gyf`te** *V -a/-e* **1** be dusty. **2** dust (off).
gy`ger *-ra, pl -rer folk.* giantess, (woman)troll.
Gy`/land *Pln* twp, Vest-Agder.
gyl`den[1] *-en* gulden (monetary unit of Holland, worth about $0.26).
+**gyl`den**[2] *A -ent, pl -ne* cf **gyllen**
Gyl`den/dal *Prn* name of Oslo publishing house (=G- Norsk Forlag).
+**gyl`den/lakk** *-en* cf **gyllen/**
gyl`dig *A* - valid; (of money) legal tender: **g- grunn** valid excuse, good reason.
+**gyl`dig/het** *-en* validity: **ha g-** be valid.
gyl'f *-en* fly (e.g. on trousers).
gyl`le *V gylte* **1** cast a golden glow over; gild. ***2** *fig.* boast, brag: **slik åtferd er ikkje noko å g- av** such behavior isn't anything to brag about.
gyl`len *A -ent, pl gylne* **1** gilded: **g-ne lenker** *fig.* g- cage. **2** golden: **g-t hår** g- hair; **den g-ne frihet** glorious freedom; **den g-ne middelvei** the golden mean; **g-ne løfter** glittering promises; **den g-ne regel** the Golden Rule (Matthew 7, 12); **g-ne tider** prosperous times.
gyl'len/lakk *-en bot.* gillyflower, wallflower (Cheiranthus cheiri): **Til min G-** (title of poem by Wergeland).
+**gyl'len/lær** *-et* (**=*/ler**) gilt leather (with relief décor in gilt, silver, colors, used in furniture, wallpaper, etc.).
+**gyl'lenlærs/stol** *-en* (**=*-lers/**) gilt leather chair.
gyl`ne *pl of* **gyllen**
gyl't[1] *-en dial.* pig.
gyl't[2] *A* - gilded.
gyl`te[1] *-a dial.* **1** sow. **2** sled.
gyl`te[2] *pt of* **gylle**
gymkha'na [gym-] *-en, pl -er* gymkhana (sports meet; obstacle race).
gymna's [gym-] *-et, pl -/+-er* (**=*gymnasium**) (junior) college (following *realskole* and preparatory for university entrance; students ab. 16-19 years old).
gymnasias't [gym-] *-en* (junior) college student.
+**gymna'sie/samfunn** [gym-] *-et* cf **gymnas/**
+**gymna'sium** [gym-] *-iet, pl -ier* cf **gymnas**
gymna's/samfunn [gym-] *-et* student organization (of all students at a *gymnas*).
gymnas't [gym-] *-en* gymnast.
***gymnas'tikar** [gym-] *-en* gymnast.
gymnastikk' [gym-] *-en* gymnastics.
gymnastikk'/sal *-en* gymnasium.
gymnastise're [gym-] *V -te* do, perform gymnastics.
gymnas'tisk [gym-] *A* - gymnastic.
***gy`ne** *V -te* glance; stare.
gynekolog [gynekolå'g] *-en* gynecologist.
gynekologi' [gyn-] *-en* gynecology.
gyng`e[1] *-a* swing.
gyng`e[2] *V -a/+-et* rock; swing: **g- seg** swing; **føle seg på g-ende grunn** *fig.* feel oneself on shaky ground, skate on thin ice.
gyng`e/hest *-en* rocking horse.
gyng`e/stol *-en* rocking chair.
***gy`rde** *V -a/-e* bind, fasten with hooks.
***gy`rding** *-a* binding, fastening with hooks.
***gyr`je** *-a* mire, mud.
***gyr`me** *-a* cf **gjørme**
gyro/kompas(s)· [gy'ro/] *-en/-et* gyrocompass.

+ Bokmål; * Nynorsk; ° Dialect.
After letter: ' stress (Acc. 1); ` tone, stress (Acc. 2); · length.
Below letter: . not pronounced.

gyrosko'p [gyro-] -et, pl -/+-er gyroscope.
gy's[1] -et shiver, shudder.
*gy's[2] pr of gjose
gy'se [usu. gy'-] V -te/+gjøs shiver, shudder: det g-er i ham he shivers, shudders; a shiver runs down his back; g- tilbake for noe shrink from doing sth.
+gy'selig [usu. gy'-] A - 1 appalling, dreadful; atrocious, ugly. 2 (adv.) awfully, terribly: han hadde det så g- travelt he was terribly busy.
+gy'sen [also gy'-] en shiver, shudder.
+gy'ser -en, pl -e thriller (book, film).
*gysj'e[1] -a rumor.
*gysj'e[2] V -a gossip; fib.
+gy'sning -en shiver, shudder.
gy'te V -te/+gjøt/*gaut, -t/*gote/*-i 1 pour: g- olje i (på) ilden add fuel to the fire. 2 spawn.
gy'te/fisk -en spawner.
gy'te/plass -en spawning ground.
gyt'je -a/+-en mud.
gyt'je/bad -et mud bath.
gyt'te pt of gyte
gy'v -en/+-et flying (dust, sand, snow): en g- av støv a cloud of dust.
gy've V gauv/+gjøv, +-d/+gjøvet/*gove/*-i fly (e.g. sand; sparks); rage, sweep (e.g. a storm): g- løs på en fly in sby's face, pounce on sby; *sola gyv mot stoveveggen the sun strikes the wall of the house (Vesaas).
gyvel [gy'vel] -en bot. (common) broom, Scotch broom (Cytisus scoparius).
°gæ'ern A -t, pl gærne cf galen
°gæ'len A -ent/-e/-i, pl -ne cf galen
gæ'lisk A - Gaelic.
°gærn [gæ'ærn] A cf galen
gør'je -a mire, mud; muck.
gørr'[1] -et (=+gorr, *gor) 1 mire, mud; muck. 2 half-digested food. 3 junk, trash.
gørr'[2] Av (=+gorr, *gor): kjede seg g- i hjel be bored to tears; være g- lei av noe be completely fed up with sth.
gørr'ende Av cf gørr[2]
gørr'/lei A *-tt completely fed up with.
Gøteborg [jøtebår'g] Pln Gothenburg, Sweden.
gøy'[1] -et/+-en fun, sport: holde (drive, gjøre) g- med make fun of; på g- for fun.
*gøy[2] [jøy'] V -dde cf gjø[2]
gøy'al A amusing, funny.
*gøyme[1] [jøy'me] -t cf gjemme[1]
*gøyme[2] [jøy'me] V -de cf gjømme[2]
*gøymsle [jøy'msle] -a cf gjemsel
*gøys [jøy's] -en 1 bubbling, gushing stream. 2 exaggeration, overstatement.
*gøysar [jøy'sar] -en boaster, braggart.
*gøyse [jøy'se] V -te 1 bubble, gush forth. 2 exaggerate, overstate.
*gøyv [jøy'v] -en flying sand, snow, etc.
*gøyve[1] [jøy've] -a shower, spray; cloud of dust.
*gøyve[2] [jøy've] V -de beat (so dust flies); drift, fly, spray.
*gøyven [jøy'ven] A -e/-i, pl -ne which boils easily.
gå'[1] V +gikk/*gjekk, gått 1 go; go on foot, walk; leave; (of a river, waterfall, etc.) run; (of part of the body) heave, move up and down; (of drawers, furniture, etc.) move, slide; (of machinery) go, run, work: det gikk ham kaldt nedover ryggen a shiver went down his back; gå en tur go for a walk; gå fra et løfte go back on a promise; gå på (en telefonstolpe) knock against, walk into (a telephone pole); gå på ski ski; gå på skøyter ice-skate; hun går alltid med en hvit hatt she always wears a white hat (goes around with a white hat on); ja, så går (gikk) vi da well, let's go; la gå let it go, let it pass; lyset går the light disappears; toget går kl. 20 the train leaves at 8 P.M.; fjæra gikk the spring broke. 2 attend: gå for presten attend confirmation class, read for confirmation; gå i kirken attend, go to church; gå på skole attend, go to school. 3 (of clouds, a storm, etc.) go by, pass over; (of time) go, lapse, pass by: det gikk mot midnatt midnight was approaching. 4 (of a film, play, etc.) play, run. 5 (of a natural phenomenon, e.g. a flood, slide, etc.) come, start; (of light, sound, etc.) come (into sight, into hearing); (of a musical instrument, music, etc.) resound, sound: *Flaumen går, i Noreg er vår the freshets are running, it's spring in Norway (Mortensson). 6 be: gå fint kledd be smartly dressed; gå i første klasse be in the first grade; gå i sitt 20de år be in one's 20th year. 7: det går it is possible, it works out; det går bra (dårlig) things are fine (bad); hvordan går det? how are things going? how are you?; det går ikke it won't work. 8 move (on the market): våre sko går our shoes move (slogan from ad). 9 (with prep. and adv.): gå an be possible, do, pass (det går ikke an that won't do, that's no use); gå av dismount, get off; retire; go off; come off, take place (hva går det av ham? what's the matter with him?); gå (noe) etter overhaul (sth); check (sth); gå for (noe, noen) pass as, for (sth, sby); gå for 100 kroner måneden work for 100 k- a month; gå for seg be doing, go on; happen, take place; gå for å være have the reputation of being; gå (en) forbi escape (the notice of) (sby); gå i close, shut (døra vil ikke gå i the door won't close); gå i luften explode; gå i lås lock; (of a deal) be arranged, concluded; gå i stykker break, go to pieces; gå i stå come to a standstill; det er gått mark i kjøttet the meat has become wormy; det gikk i ham he gave a start; det går i døra sby, sth is at the door; gå igjen recur (hos, i in); (of a ghost, spirit) haunt; gå inn (e.g. of a newspaper) be discontinued; gå fjorden inn (of a ship) put into the fjord; gå hardt inn på (en) be hard on, for (sby); gå innom drop in, visit; gå løs break out, start; gå løs på attack, start in on; gå med come along, go along; be consumed, spent, used up; go (all vinen gikk med til selskapet all the wine was used up for the party); gå med på agree to, fall in with; gå ned go down; decline, decrease, fall off; gå en nær affect, cut one deeply; gå om igjen be repeated; (of a bargain) be annulled: gå opp (in division) come out even; (of ice) break up; gå opp for (en) dawn on (sby); gå opp i result in; (in division) go into (3 går opp i 9 tre ganger 3 goes into 9 three times); be absorbed in, be wrapped up in; gå opp i opp balance, make it even; gå over pass, wear off; gå over i melt, merge, pass into; go down in (e.g. history); gå over til come around to; take up; change over to, turn to; gå på advance, press on, push on; go on, fit; believe, swallow (den går jeg ikke på I don't buy that); make (det går 20 femører på en krone 20 five-øre pieces make a k-); gå til come about, happen; gå under come to an end; fall, go down; go underground; gå unna stand clear; be sold; gå ut fra assume, presume; conclude, take (it); gå ut over affect, hit, cause to suffer (det er alltid kvinnen det går ut over it's always the woman who suffers); gå ut på aim at, be (to the effect) that; gå ved admit. 10 (refl.): gå seg become, get (gå seg vill get lost).
gå'[2] V -dde dial. notice, pay heed to; be aware of (also with til).
gåbort/stas [gå'bort/] -en Sunday-go-to-meeting clothes.
+gå'en[1] A -ent, pl -(e)ne gone; finished (with).
*gå'en[2] A -e/-i, pl -ne attentive, observant.
*gå'/laus A inattentive.
*gå'/løyse -a 1 inattention. 2 oversight.
*gå'ning -en attention: han fekk g- på det he noticed it.
gå'-på'-hug -en drive, enterprise, go.
gå'r N: i g- yesterday; i g- aftes last night, yesterday evening; i g- morges yesterday morning.
+gåraf'tes N cf går
*gå'rast V -ast become, turn streaked, striped.
gå'rd -en cf gard
*gå'r/dag -en cf gårs/
+gå'rd/bruker -en, pl -e cf gard/
+gå'rde N cf garde[3]
+gå'rd/eier -en, pl -e owner of a farm.
+gå'rd/imel'lom Av cf gard/
+gå'rd/lapp -en small farm.
+gå'rd/mann -en, pl -menn cf gard/
+gå'rds/bruk -et cf gards/
+gå'rds/drift -a cf gards/
+gå'rds/gutt -en cf gards/
+gå'rds/hund -en cf gards/
+gå'rds/plass -en courtyard, yard.
gå'rds/rom [/romm] -met courtyard.
*gå're[1] -n (of a tree) annual ring.
gå're[2] -a/-en grain (e.g. in wood).
gå're[3] V -a/+-et grain.
gå'ret(e) A - grained (e.g. leather, wood).
gå'r/kveld N (=går kveld): i g- last night, yesterday evening.
gå'rs/dag -en: g-en yesterday.
gå's -a, pl gjæser/+gjess 1 zool. goose (family Anatidae): det er (som) å skvette vann på g-a it runs off like water from a duck's back. 2 silly woman, simpleton.
*gå'se/auga -t, pl -augo cf /øyne
gå'se/blom [+/blåmm] -en bot. common camomile (Anthemis nobilis).
gå'se/fot -en bot. madwort (Asperugo procumbens).
gå'se/gang -en Indian file, single file.
gå'se/hud -a/+-en goose flesh.
gå'selever/postei' -en pâté de foie gras.
gå'se/marsj -en Indian file, single file.
gå'se/stegg -en gander.
gå'set(e) A - foolish, silly.
+gå'se/øyne pl (=*/augo) quotation marks.
gå'/stol -en walker.
gå's/unge [/onge] -n 1 gosling. 2 bot. catkin (of willow), pussy willow.
gå'te -a/+-en puzzle, riddle; enigma, mystery: det er en g- for meg I can't make head nor tail of it; tale i g-r speak in riddles, incomprehensibly.
gå'te/full A enigmatic, puzzling; mysterious.
gått'[1] -a rabbet (groove in door frame or threshold).
gått'[2] pp of gå[1]
*gå'va A - gifted, talented.
*gå've -a cf gave
*gå've/brev -et cf gave/
*gå've/rik A highly gifted, talented.
*gå've/sending -a gift.

h [hå'] *-en* 1 H, h (letter): **utelate h-ene** drop one's h's. 2 *mus.* (the tone) B.
H=+**Høyre**[2]/***Høgre**
ha'[1] *V hadde, hatt* (=***have**) 1 have: **De må ha meg unnskyldt** you must please excuse me, I beg to be excused; **den som bare hadde en ny bil** if only one had a new car, oh for a new car; **der har vi det** there we have it, that's it; *fam.* **ha det** 'bye, s' long; **ha det bra** be fine, be getting along nicely; (as wish at departure) take care of yourself; **ha det godt** be well off (**nå kan du ha det så godt** there you are, serves you right, you've brought it on yourself); (for use with other adverbs, e.g. **ha det knapt**: see these); **ha det med å lyve** be given to, have a tendency to lie; **han har det mest i kjeften** he is mostly full of hot air, his bark is worse than his bite; **ha for seg** have to do, have in front of one; **ha lite å fare med** lack foundation for one's charges; be not too intelligent, have little gray matter; **ha meget for seg** carry weight, have a lot to recommend it(self), have merit; **ha meget å si** be important, be of significance; **ha noe på seg** have any significance, mean anything; **her har du meg** here I am. 2 get, receive: **ha deg vekk** get away; **ha etter** get, have, inherit from; **ha godt av** be good for, do one good; **ha igjen** get back, get in return (**det skal du ha igjen for** you're going to get it [for doing that]); **hva skal De ha for dette?** what do you want (what are you charging) for this?; **takk skal De ha** thank you; **vi skal ha fisk til middag** we are having (will have) fish for dinner; **vil ha** want. 3 (as auxiliary verb) have: **har du gjort leksene dine? Ja, det har jeg** have you done your lessons? Yes, I have; **hadde** (in place of "would have"): **det hadde jeg aldri drømt om** I would never have dreamed of that (Ibsen); (**ha** often omitted after **kunne, skulle, ville**) **du kunne iallfall prøvd** you could have tried anyway. 4 (with *prep.* and *adv.*): **ha i** (esp. in recipes) add, put in (**ha i litt mel** add a little flour); **ha det i seg** feel; **ha med (noe, noen) å gjøre** deal with (sth, sby); concern, have to do with (sth, sby) (**du har ikke noe med å forsvare ham** it's not your business to defend him); *fam.* **ha opp** open (e.g. the door); **ha på** have on, wear (**hun har en ny hatt på** she has on a new hat); *fam.* **ha litt på** be a little high, tipsy; **han er ikke så syk som man vil ha det til** he isn't as sick as people say. 5 *(refl.)*: **ha seg** be; **hvordan har det seg at du skal reise nå?** how is it that (how come) you are leaving now?; **hvorledes har det seg med stemningen hos folket her ute?** how is the mood of the people out here? (Ibsen).
ha'[2] *I* aha, ha: **si ja og ha** (or **ha og ja**) agree to avoid argument.
ha[3]=**hektar**
Haag [ha'g] *Pln* The Hague.
ha'ben/gut *-et* goods and chattels, personal property: **de solgte hele sitt h- og drog av sted** they sold everything, lock, stock, and barrel, and departed.
habi'l *A* competent; qualified.
habilite're *V -te*: **h- seg** qualify to lecture at universities.
habilite't *-en* qualification.
habitt' *-en* outfit, suit.
ha'bitus *-en*: **åndelig h-** intellectual make-up, moral character.
Ha'de/land *Pln* southern part of Oppland, incl. twps of Brandbu, Gran, Jevnaker, Lunner.
ha'de/lending *-en* person from Hadeland.
+**ha'ende(s)** *A* - cf **havende(s)**
+**ha'/felle** *-a* cf **hag/**[1]
Haf'rs/fjo'rd *Pln* small fjord near Stavanger; scene of final battle in unification of Norway by Harald Hårfagre (traditionally dated A.D. 872).
Haf'slo *Pln* twp, Sogn og Fjordane.
***ha'g**[1] *-en* order; convenience: **til h-s** to one's taste.
***ha'g**[2] *-et* fence, hedge.
ha'g[3] *A* deft, dexterous, handy.
°**ha'ga** *-en* cf **hage**[1]
ha'ge[1] *-n* 1 garden, orchard. 2 (enclosed) pasture.
***ha'ge**[2] *V -a* 1 enclose, fence (in). 2 arrange, manage.
ha'ge/arkitek't *-en* landscape gardener.
ha'ge/benk *-en* garden seat.
ha'ge/bruk *-et* gardening, horticulture.
ha'ge/by *-en* garden city (municipal plots for gardening, with space for small cottages); also as name of certain suburbs, e.g. **Ullevål H-**.
ha'ge/gang *-en* garden path.
+**ha'ge/saks** *-a* hedge shears.
+**ha'ge/sanger** *-en, pl -e* (=***/songar**) *zool.* garden warbler (Sylvia simplex).
ha'ge/sprøyte *-a* sprinkling can, watering can.
ha'g/felle[1] *-a* fence (usu. of felled trees).
***ha'g/felle**[2] *V -a* put up a fence.
***ha'g/hendt** *A* - deft, dexterous, handy.
hag'l *-et* 1 hail, hailstone. 2 buckshot, shot.
hag'l/bye *-a* (=**/bøye**, +**/byge**) hailstorm, shower of hail.
hag'l/børse *-a* fowling piece, shotgun.
hag'le[1] *-a dial.* shotgun.
hag'le[2] *V -a/+-et* hail; pour down, rain down: **slagene h-et ned over ham** the blows rained down on him; **det h-et med skjellsord** terms of abuse poured down.
***ha'gleg** *A* - 1 well-executed. 2 convenient, fit, proper.
***ha'g/leik** *-en* dexterity, skill.
ha'g/lette *-a dial.* sweet and sour milk cheese.
hag'l/ko'rn *-et* 1 hailstone. 2 *med.* sty.
hag'l/skur *-a* hailstorm; shower of hail.
+**hag'l/vær** *-et* (=***/ver**) hailstorm; shower of hail.
ha'g/to'rn *-en bot.* hawthorn (genus Crataegus).
haha' *I* cf **ha**[2]
hai' *-en* 1 *zool.* shark (Squalida). 2 *fig.* sharper, swindler.
+**hai'/aktig** *A* - sharklike.
hai'k *-en* hitchhike, lift.
hai'ke *V -a/+-et* hitchhike.
***ha'k** *-et* cf **hakk**[1]
Ha'ka/dal *Pln* parish, Nittedal twp, Akershus.
ha'ke[1] *-a/+-en* chin.
ha'ke[2] *-n* 1 hook. 2: **en h- ved noe** a catch, drawback to sth.
ha'ke[3] *V -a/+-et* hook: **h- seg fast i (til)** clutch, hang on to; *fig.* buttonhole (sby); carp at, find fault with.
ha'ke/fisk *-en* salmon (trout) with gib (projection on lower jaw during mating season).
+**ha'ke/kors** *-et* (=***/kross**) swastika.
ha'kel *-elen, pl -ler* chasuble.
ha'ke/parente's *-en* (square) brackets.
ha'ke/skjegg *-et* goatee.
ha'ke/spiss *-en* point of the chin.
ha'ke/stift *-en* wall hook.
hakk'[1] *-et* 1 stammer, stutter. 2 indentation, notch. 3: **ikke det (et) h-** not the least bit, not the slightest.
hakk'[2] *N*: **h- i hæl** close on each other's heels, one right after the other.
hak'ke[1] *-a* hoe; pick, pickaxe.
hak'ke[2] *V -a/+-et* 1 chop, hack (**på** in), hoe; chop (up), mince: **h- noe i stykker** chop sth to pieces. 2 (of bird) peck: **h- på en** *fig.* carp at sby, henpeck sby. 3 jerk; stutter: **en h-ende latter** a jerky laugh; **h- og stamme** stutter and stammer; **h- tenner** have one's teeth chattering; **motoren h-er** the motor is jerking.
hak'ke/biff *-en* ground beef, hamburger.
hak'ke/brett *-et* 1 chopping board. 2 *mus.* dulcimer; *hum.* broken-down piano. 3 *naut.* taffrail.
hak'kels(e) *-en* chopped straw (used as fodder).
hak'ke/mat *-en* hash, mincemeat: **gjøre h- av en** make m- of sby.
hak'kende *A* - : *(adv.)* **h- sint** furious, in a towering rage.
hak'ke/spett *-en/*-a* (=+**/spette**) *zool.* woodpecker (family Picidae).
hak'ket(e) *A* - chipped, jagged; (of a knife) dulled.
ha'l[1] *-et* 1 haul, pull: **gjøre et godt h-** make a good haul (catch). 2 *naut.* heeling over, lurch: **le h-** heel to leeward.
ha'l[2] [also: hall'] *N naut.*: **gå en h-** go and haul; **stop en h-** stop and haul; wait a minute.
***hal'd** *-et* cf **hold**[2]
***hal'dar** *-en* cf **holder**
***hal'de** *V held, heldt, halde/-i* cf **holde**[2]
***hal'den** *A -e/-i, pl -ne* 1 held, kept. 2 satisfied (**med** with). 3: **heil og h-** safe and sound.
Hal'den *Pln* town, Østfold.
+**halden'ser** *-en, pl -e* (=***-ar**) person from Halden.
***hal'de/punkt** *-et* cf **holde/**
***hal'di** *pp of* **halde**
Hal'dis *Prn (f)*
Hal'dor *Prn (m)*
***hal'd/sam·** *A* enduring; persevering.
ha'le[1] *-n* 1 tail; (of a fox) brush: **stikke h-n mellom beina** slink away (in shame). 2 (of an airplane, comet, kite) tail; fag end, tail end. 3 *hum.* behind, rear end: **falle på h-n** sit down suddenly; **sette seg på h-n** sit down (and refuse to budge). 4 editorial comment (added to a contributor's article).
ha'le[2] *V -a/-te* 1 haul, pull; drag, tug: **h- ordene ut av en** drag the words out of sby; **h- i** pull, strain at; **h- innpå (inn på) en** catch up with, overtake sby; gain on sby; **h- opp buksene** hitch up one's trousers; **h- (seieren) i land** secure (the victory); come out on top; **h- tiden ut** play for time, procrastinate. 2 *naut.*: **h- an** haul home; **h- i, på land** haul a boat up on the beach; **h- seg** shift (of wind); **h- vekk** haul away.
ha'le/bein *-et* tailbone, *anat.* coccyx.
ha'le/finne *-n* 1 tail fin, *zool.* caudal fin. 2 stabilizer, tail fin (airplane).
ha'le/rot *-a* root of the tail (on horse).
ha'le/tipp *-en* tip of the tail.

+ Bokmål; * Nynorsk; ° Dialect.
After letter: ' stress (Acc. 1); ' tone, stress (Acc. 2); · length.
Below letter: . not pronounced.

half [haff'] *-en* half (in soccer and European handball).

half/back [haff'/bækk, haff'/bekk] *-en* halfback (in soccer).

Hal'fdan *Prn (m)*

hall'[1] *-en archaic, dial.* stone (in names like Haldis, Hallvard).

hall[2] [hå'l] *-en* entrance hall, hallway, vestibule.

hall'[3] *-a/+-en* (large) hall.

hall'[4] *-et dial.* slant, slope: **på h-** aslant.

hal'le *V -a/+-et dial.* incline, slant.

halle'luja' [also: lu'-] *et* hallelujah.

Hall'/gjerd *Prn (f)*

hal'lik *-en* pimp, procurer.

hal'ling[1] *-en* 1 person from Hallingdal. 2 dance (tune) characteristic of Hallingdal.

***hal'ling**[2] *-a* slant, slope.

Hal'ling/dal *Pln* extended valley running through the northern and eastern part of Buskerud county, between Ustevatn and Krøderen.

hal'ling/døl *-en* person from Hallingdal.

hal'ling/kast *-et* wheeling leap characteristic of a Halling dance.

Hal'ling/skarvet *Pln* mountain ridge between Hardanger and Hallingdal.

***hall'/lendt** *A* - slanting, sloping.

hallo' *I* 1 hello (esp. as telephone greeting). 2 hey, hey there; halloo: **h- h-** your attention please.

hallo'/dame *-a/+-en* (woman) radio announcer.

halloi'[1] *-en* (=**haloi**[1]) hullabaloo, uproar.

halloi'[2] *I* (=**haloi**[2]) halloo.

hallo'/mann *-en, pl -menn/*-menner* (man) radio announcer.

hallusinasjo'n *-en* hallucination.

Hall'/vard *Prn (m)*

hall'vards/ok' *-en hist.* St. Hallvard's Day (May 15th; the patron saint of Oslo).

***hall'/år** *-et* bad year for crops.

hal'm *-en* straw.

***hal'me** *V -a* winnow.

hal'm/stakk *-en* strawstack.

hal'm/strå *-et* straw: **gripe etter et h-** clutch at straws.

haloi'[1] *-en* cf **halloi**[1]

haloi'[2] *I* cf **halloi**[2]

hal's *-en* 1 throat; neck (of an animal, a bottle, an article of clothing, a person, violin, etc.): **brøle av full h-** roar at the top of one's voice; **falle en om h-en, falle om h-en på en** throw oneself at sby, throw one's arms around sby; **få, ha noe på h-en** become, be burdened with sth, get, have sth on one's hands; **ha vondt i h-en** have a sore throat; **jeg har det helt opp i h-en** I'm completely fed up with it; **le av full h-** roar with laughter; **med tungen ut av h-en** with one's tongue hanging out; **over h- og hode** at breakneck speed, headlong, head over heels; **på sin h-** body and soul (e.g. **idrettsmann på sin h-** sports enthusiast); **vri, dreie h-en om på en** wring sby's neck. 2 *naut.* (on a sail) tack: **ligge for styrbords h-er** be on the starboard t-. 3 *dial.* forepart of open sailboat. 4 *dial.* neck of land or water. 5: **en hard h-** a hard-bitten, obstinate fellow. 6 (on a musical note) stem.

Hal'sa *Pln* twp, Møre og Romsdal.

hal's/band *-et* necklace; (dog) collar.

hal's/bind *-et* cravat, necktie; stock.

hal's/brann *-en* heartburn.

+**hal's/brekkende** *A* - breakneck, dangerous.

hal's/brune *-n dial.* heartburn.

+**hal's/bånd** *-et* cf **/band**

hal'se *V -a/+-et* 1 bay, give tongue. 2 *naut.* wear (turn sharply).

Hal'se og Har'k/mark *Pln* twp, Vest-Agder.

hal'se/sjuke *-n* (=+**/syke**, ***/sykje**) sore throat, tonsillitis.

hal's/grop *-a* hollow of the throat, neck.

hal's/hogge *V +-er/*-høgg, -hogg/-hogde, -hogd/*-e/*-i* behead, decapitate.

hal's/katarr' *-en* bronchial catarrh, pharyngitis.

hal's/kjede *+-en/+-et/*-a* necklace, strand (e.g. of pearls).

hal's/laus *A* (=+**/løs**): **h- gjerning (dåd)** reckless act, risky undertaking.

+**hal's- og hån'ds/rett** *-en* (=***hand/rett**) *jur.* power of life and death.

hal's/pastill' *-en* throat lozenge.

+**hal's/starrig** [also -star'-] *A* - obstinate, stiff-necked, stubborn.

+**halsstar'rig/het** [also hal's-] *-en* obstinacy, pig-headedness, stubbornness.

***hal's/tole** [/tåle] *-a* vertebra of the neck.

hal's/tørkle *-kleet, pl +-klær/*-kle* neckerchief, scarf.

hal's/virvel *-elen, pl -ler* vertebra of the neck.

hal't *A* - lame, limping.

hal'te *V -a/+-et* 1 hobble, limp. 2: **h-ende** lame (comparison, excuse).

halun'k *-en* boor, lout; scamp, scoundrel.

halv [+hall'] *A* 1 half: **h-e byen** h- the city, town; (as *noun*) **det h-e** h-; **en h- gang til** h- as many again; *fam.* **en h- øl** a h- bottle of beer; **et h-t år** a h- year, h- a year; **klokken h- ni (kl. ½9)** eight-thirty, h-past eight (8:30); **ti over h-** twenty minutes of (the next hour). 2 *(adv.)* **h-t** half, halfway; by halves: **gå h-t om noe** go halves, 50-50 on sth; **h-t om h-t** nearly, well nigh.

***halvan'nan** *Num -anna, halvtanna* cf **-annen**

+**halvannen** [halla'en] *Num -annet* one and a half (1 ½).

hal'vards/ok' *-en* cf **hallvards/**

halv/blind [+hall'/blinn] *A* - half blind.

hal'v/blods [/blot's] *A* - half-blooded, halfbreed.

hal'v/blunde *V -a/+-et* doze.

hal'v/bror *-en, +-brødre/*-brør* half brother.

hal'vdags/post *-en* half (part) time job.

Hal'vdan *Prn (m)*

hal'v/del *-en* half.

***hal'v/dregen** *A -e/-i, pl -ne* half-drawn: **ein h- ande** the slightest hint.

hal'v/død *A* half dead.

hal'v/døs *-en*: **i h-** half asleep.

***hal've**[1] *-a* half.

hal've[2] *V -a/+-et* cf **halvere**

hal'v/edelstei'n *-en* semiprecious stone.

halve're *V -te* (=**halve**[2]) divide in half, in two.

hal'v/fabrika't *-et, pl -/-a/+-er* semi-finished product.

hal'v/feit *A* 1 made of skimmed and unskimmed milk (cheese). 2 *typog.* boldface.

halvfem'te *Num* four and a half (4 ½).

halv'/ferdig *A* - half-finished.

halvfjerde [-fjæ're] *Num* three and a half (3 ½).

hal'v/flaske *-a* half bottle (=3/8 liter) e.g. of beer.

hal'v/gammal *A -t, pl -gamle* (=+**/gammel**) middle-aged; getting along.

+**hal'v/gjort** [/jort] *A* - (=***/gjord**) half-done, half-finished.

hal'v/glad *A* - half-hearted.

hal'v/god *A* medium, moderately good.

hal'v/gras *-et bot.* sedge plant (family Cyperaceae).

hal'v/gud *-en* demigod.

°**hal'v/gåen** *A* - 1: **klokka er h- fire** it is half past three. 2 half way (in pregnancy).

halvhun'dre *Num* (=**halvt-**) fifty (50).

hal'v/høg *A* (=+**/høy**) sotto voce: **h-t** in a low voice.

ha'lv/kule *-a* hemisphere.

+**hal'v/kva'lt** *A* - half-smothered, stifled.

+**hal'v/kvedet** *A* -: **han forstår en h-vise** he can take a hint.

***hal'v/liden** *A -e/-i, pl -ne* (of time) half-gone.

+**hal'v/lodd** *-et* (=***/lott**) half share (in a lottery; in a fishing expedition).

hal'v/lys[1] *-et* (=***/ljos**) half-light, shimmer, twilight.

hal'v/lys[2] *A* (=***/ljos**) shimmering.

hal'v/mett *A* - half full, partly filled-up, still hungry.

hal'v/mørk *A* semi-dark, twilight.

hal'v/mørke *-t* (=***/mørker**) semi-darkness.

hal'v/måne *-n* half-moon; crescent moon.

***hal'vning** *-en* half.

Hal'vor *Prn (m)*

hal'v/part *-en* half.

+**hal'v/påkledd'** *A* - half-dressed.

hal'v/redd *A* - half afraid.

hal'v/rund *A* semicircular.

hal'v/sid *A* (of a dress) half-length, not full length.

hal'v/sirkel *-elen, pl -ler* semicircle.

***hal'v/sole**[1] *-n* cf **/såle**[1]

***hal'v/sole**[2] *V -a* cf **/såle**[2]

hal'v/sove [/så've] *V infl as* **sove** be half asleep, doze, drowse.

hal'v/stikk *-et naut.* half hitch: **dobbelt h-** clove hitch.

hal'v/stor *A* medium sized.

hal'v/strømpe *-a/-en* sock.

hal'v/stude'rt *A* -: **en h- røver** a smatterer, a would-be polyhistor, a Jack of all trades, master of none (Holberg's *Peder Paars)*.

hal'v/søsken *pl* (=***/sysken**) half brothers and half sisters.

+**hal'v/søvn** *-en*: **i h-e** half asleep.

+**hal'v/såle**[1] *-n* half sole.

+**hal'v/såle**[2] *V -te* half-sole.

+**halvt** [hal'(f)t] *-en* half: **h- så vakker som** half as handsome as; **til h-en** halfway; **vi er h- om henne** she belongs to both of us (Ibsen).

halvthun'dre *Num* cf **halv-**

hal'v/time *-n* half hour.

halvtred'je *Num* two and a half (2 ½).

hal'v/veges *Av* (=+**/vegs, /veis**) halfway, midway; almost, in some degree; moderately, so-so: **ha h-lyst til å** have half a mind to.

+**hal'v/vei** *-en*: **på h-en** halfway; **møte en på h-en** meet sby halfway.

+**hal'v/veis** *Av* cf **/veges**

+**hal'v/voksen** *A -ent, pl -ne* (=***/vaksen**) adolescent, teenage.

***hal'v/voren** [/våren] *A -e/-i, pl -ne* average, middling, so-so.

hal'v/øy *-a* peninsula.

+**hal'v/åpen** *A -ent, pl -ne* (=***/open**) half-open.

hal'v/år *-et* half a year.

hal'v/årig *A* - half a year (old).

hal'v/å'rlig *A* - biennial, semiannual.

ham'[1] *+-men/*-en* 1 (outer) skin, slough: **skifte, skyte h-** cast off, shed the (outer) skin. 2 *folk.* form which one assumes as the result of a spell. *3 appearance, form, shape: **den vene h-en hennar** her pretty form (Vesaas).

+**ham'**[2] *Pn ob of* **han**[1]

***ha'mar** *-en, pl hamrar* cf **hammar**

Ha'mar *Pln* city, Hedmark.

Ha'mar/øy *Pln* twp, Nordland.

***ha'me** *V -a*: **h- seg til** doll up, dres up.

ha'mingje *-a folk.* (female) guardian spirit.

hamitt' *-en* Hamite.

hamit'tisk *A* - Hamitic.

ham'le[1] *-a hist.* grommet, oar thong.

ham'le[2] *V -a/+-et*: **h- opp med en** equal, keep up with sby.

ham'le[3] *V -a/+-et* row backwards.

ham'le/band *-et* oar thong.

***ham'leg** *A* - attractive, engaging.

ham'/lett *-en* (=***/let**) *dial.* complexion.

ham'mar *-en, pl hamrer* (=**+hammer, *hamar**) 1 hammer; gavel, mallet; back side of an axe: **komme under h-en** come under the hammer (=be sold at auction). 2 *anat.* malleus. 3 *mus.* hammer (piano). 4 *myth.* Thor's hammer (symbol of Norse paganism): **korset mot h-en** the Cross vs. the hammer. 5 (steep) crag.

ham'mar/slag *-et* (=**+hammer/**) hammer blow: **h- på h- inntil livets siste dag** h- on h- until life's last day (Ibsen).

+**ham'mer** *-eren, pl -ere/hamrer* cf **hammar**

Ham'mer/fest *Pln* seaport, Finnmark (northernmost town in Europe).

ham'n[1] *-a* grazing land, pasture.

ham'n[2] *-a* (=**+havn**[2]) harbor, port; docks: **komme i h-** arrive in port; **ligge i h-** be in port; **nå h-** make port; **søke h-** make for a port; **bringe i h-** *fig.* complete a project successfully.

ham'ne[1] *V -a/+-et* browse, graze; lead to pasture.

ham'ne[2] *V -a/+-et* (=**+havne**[2]) end up, land (**i** in, **på** on): **h- i papirkurven** end up in the wastepaper basket; be discarded, thrown away; **h- på hodet** land on one's head.

ham'ne/by *-en* port, seaport.

***hamne/fut** *-en* cf **havne/fog(e)d**

ham'ne/gang *-en* grazing land, pasture.

ham'ne/hage *-n* (enclosed) pasture.

ham'p *-en bot.* hemp (Cannabis sativa); hemp (bast): **bort i h-en** *fam.* a crazy idea, sth ridiculous, stupid.

ham'pe/reip *-et* hemp rope.

ham're *V -a/+-et* 1 hammer: **h- løs** h- (pound) away. 2 beat (black and blue), thrash: **h- noe inn i en** din sth into sby. 3 pound, thunder; throb.

Ham're *Pln* twp, Hordaland.

ham'ret(e) *A* - mountainous, rough.

ham's *-en* (of a hazelnut) hull, husk; (of clover) dried pod; *fig.* mask, shell.

ham'se[1] *V -a/+-et* shell nuts; remove pods (e.g. from clover) by threshing.

ham'se[2] *V -a/+-et dial., naut.* stand a round of drinks on one's first voyage.

ham'/skifte *-t* shedding of skin; *fig.* changing colors (allegiance).

ham'ster *-eren, pl -rer zool.* hamster (Cricetus cricetus).

ham'stre *V -a/+-et* hoard (food).

han'[1] *-nen* cf **hann**

han'[2] *Pn ob han/+ham/*honom, po hans* 1 he: *dial., fam.* (In front of man's name, not translated, or translated as "that", "that there") **h- far** father (formerly of pastors also); **h- Gunnar** G-; **h- har gått, h- sjømannen, mor** he's gone, that sailor, mother (Bjørnson); *fam.* **h- kan sine ting h-** he knows his stuff, he does. *2 (masculine gender) it; (in expressions about the weather, etc.) it, ("she"): **h- er kald** it's (she's) cold; **h- regner** it's raining. 3 *obs.* you (in addressing man of lower standing).

hanḍ *-a* (=**+hånd**) 1 hand: **døde h-** *jur.* dead h-, mortmain; **for, ved egen h-** by one's own h-; **falle for ens h-** die, fall at the h-s of sby; **for, ved h-en/*h-a** at h-, near; handy, on h-; **få fra h-en/*h-a** get done; **ha frie hender** have a free h-; **gi en noe i h-a (i hende, i hendene)** put sth in sby's h-(s); **legge h- på** use force against; lay a h- on; **sy med h-** sew by h-; **på egen h-** on one's own; **på første h-** (at) first h-; **ha gode kort på h-en** have a good h- (of cards); have a good argument, good chances, etc.; **være stø på h-a** have a steady h-; **slå h-a av en** let sby down; withdraw one's support from sby; **gå en til h-e** assist sby, lend sby a h-; **under h-** confidentially, privately. 2 hand, handwriting.

***han'dar** *N* cf **hånde**

han'ḍ/arbei'ḍ *-et* 1 handwork. 2 needlework.

han'ḍ/bak *-en* back of the hand: **vri h-** try to twist an opponent's arm (cf Indian wrestling).

han'ḍ/ball *-en* 1 *anat.* ball of the thumb. 2 (European) handball.

han'ḍ/bibliote'k *-et, pl -/+-er* reference library (collection).

han'ḍ/bok *-a, pl -bøker* manual; reference book.

***han'de/hov** *-et* moderation.

***han'de/krafs** *-et* grabbing, snatching; free-for-all, rough-and-tumble.

han'del *-elen, pl -ler* 1 business, commerce, trade: **bringe i h-** offer for sale, put on the market; **drive h-** carry on trade, trade; **være i h-en** be on the market, for sale. 2 deal, transaction: **avslutte en h-** close a deal; **gjøre en god h-** pick up a good bargain; **h- og vandel** dealings, method of doing business.

han'dels/avta'le *-n/*-a* trade agreement.

han'dels/balanse [-ang'se] *-n* balance of trade.

han'dels/betjen't *-en* clerk, salesman (in a shop).

+**han'delsborger/skap** *-et* business license.

han'dels/brev *-et* 1 business letter. 2 business license.

han'dels/bu *-a* country store.

Han'dels/departementet [-mang'e] *df* Ministry of Commerce (=U.S. Department of Commerce).

han'dels/fag *-et* 1 commercial course, subject. 2 business, trade (as a profession).

han'dels/flagg *-et* merchant flag.

han'dels/flåte *-n* merchant fleet.

+**han'dels/gartner** *-en, pl -e* (=***-ar**) truck farmer.

han'dels/gymna's *-et* commercial high school (junior college; cf **gymnas**).

han'dels/hus *-et* business house, firm.

han'dels/høgsko'le *-n* (=**+/høyskole**) school of commerce (business administration).

han'dels/kalen'der *-en* business directory.

han'dels/kandida't *-en* Bachelor of Commerce.

han'dels/lag *-et* (local) cooperative society.

han'dels/lære *-a/+-en* Commerce (as a subject of study).

han'dels/mann *-en, pl -menn/*-menner* businessman, merchant.

han'dels/minis'ter *-eren, pl -rer/+ere* Minister of Commerce (=U.S. Secretary of Commerce).

han'dels/polit'isk *A* - politico-commercial, referring to commercial policy.

+**han'dels/regning** [/reining] *-a/-en* (=**/rekning**) commercial arithmetic.

han'dels/reisenḍe *en* traveling salesman.

han'dels/rett *-en* 1 commercial law. 2 civil court.

han'dels/råd *-en* commercial counselor.

han'dels/skip *-et* merchant ship.

han'dels/skole *-n* business school.

han'dels/stanḍ *-en/*-et* business class, profession; commercial world.

+**han'dels/sted** *-et* commercial (trading) center; store.

han'dels/vare *-a/+-en* commodity; merchandise.

+**han'dels/virksomhe't** *-en* commercial activity; business, trade.

han'dels/vitskap *-en* (=**+/vitenskap**) commercial science.

***han'de/makt** *-a* manual strength: **med h-** by hand.

***han'de/verk** *-en*: **ha h-** have a pain in one's hand.

han'ḍ/fallen *A +-ent, pl -falne* at a loss, puzzled, irresolute; dismayed.

han'ḍ/fang *-et* grip, handle.

han'ḍ/fare *V -for, +-t/*-e/*-i* examine, feel, touch (with the hands); handle, lay hands on.

han'ḍ/fast *A* - 1 hefty, robust. 2 tangible. 3 *fig.* heavy-handed, ponderous: **h- humor** robust humor.

***han'ḍ/festing** *-a* cf **hånd/festning**

han'ḍ/flate *-a/+-en* palm (of the hand).

han'ḍ/fritt *A* - dexterously, neatly done.

han'ḍ/gjerning *-a/+-en* needlework, sewing (in school).

han'ḍ/grep *-et* 1 grip (with the hands), hold: **lære h-ene kan du** you can learn the tricks (Bojer). 2 (of an implement, a tool) grip, handle; door handle.

***han'ḍ/ha(ve)** *V -dde, -tt/-vd* handle roughly.

han'ḍ/helse *V -te/*-a* shake hands.

***han'ḍ/høveleg** *A* - easy to handle, handy.

handikap [hæ'ndikæpp] *-et* handicap.

handikappe [hæ'ndikæppe] *V -a/+-et* handicap.

han'ḍ/jern [/jæ'rn] *-et* handcuffs: **legge h- på en** handcuff sby.

han'ḍ/kjerre *-a* handcart.

han'ḍ/kle [also: hang'/] *-et, pl +-klær/*-* (=***/klede**) towel.

han'ḍ/koffert [/koffert] *-en* suitcase, valise.

han'ḍ/kraft *-a/+-en* manual strength: **med h-** by hand.

han'ḍ/lag *-et* knack, manual dexterity; (inborn) skill.

+**han'ḍ/langer** [usu. hån't/] *-en, pl -e* (=***-ar**) 1 apprentice, laborer; (bricklayer's) assistant. 2 *derog.* henchman, minion.

han'dle *V -a/+-et* 1 act: **h- deretter** a- accordingly; **h- etter ens råd** take sby's advice; **h- etter innskytelse** a- on impulse; **h- etter sitt eget hode** follow one's own inclinations; **h- i strid med** a- contrary to, do sth that is at variance with; **h- mot ens ønsker** a- contrary to sby's wishes; **h- resolutt** a- resolutely, take the bull by the horns. 2 deal, do business with, trade; shop: **h- hos Olsen** s- at O-'s; **h- med en** do business with sby; **h- med en vare** deal in a commodity, stock a commodity. 3: **h- om** be about, concern; deal with, treat of.

han'ḍ/leḍ *-en* (=**+/ledd**) *anat.* wrist.

han'dle/dyktig *A* - active, energetic, vigorous.

han'dle/evne *-a/+-en* energy, vigor; ability to act (esp. in a crisis).

+**han'dle/frihet** *-en* (=***/fridom**) freedom of action.

***hand'leg** *A* - convenient, handy.

han'dle/kraft *-a/+-en* energy, vigor.

han'dle/kraftig *A* - energetic, vigorous.

han'dle/måte *-n* conduct; course of action.

+**han'dlenḍe** *en* businessman, merchant.

+**han'dler** *-en, pl -e* (=***-ar**) dealer, merchant.

+**han'dle/sett** *-et* act, (mode of) action.

han'dling *-a/+-en* 1 act, action: **i h-** in practice; **gå fra ord til h-** translate words into deeds; **skride til h-** take action; **straffbar h-** *jur.* offence punishable by law. 2 action, plot (of a play): **h-en foregår** the action takes place, the scene of the story is laid. 3 (usu. religious) ceremony, function.

+**han'dlings/mettet** *A* - action-filled.

han'ḍ/linning *-a/-en* cuff.

han'ḍ/love *-n* palm (of the hand).

han'ḍ/makt *-a/+-en* manual strength: **med h-** by hand, forcibly.

+ Bokmål; * Nynorsk; ° Dialect.
After letter: ' stress (Acc. 1); ` tone, stress (Acc. 2); · length.
Below letter: . not pronounced.

han'ḍ/pant *-en jur.* pledge; lien, mortgage.
***han'ḍ/pengar** *pl* cf **hånd/penger**
han'ḍ/rev *-et* (=**/red, /trev**) balustrade, railing.
hands [hæ'nds] *-en* hands; (in soccer) touching the ball with the hands.
han'ḍ/same *V -a* handle: ***ho h-ar og køyrer kven det er av Førnes-hestane** she h-s and drives any of the F- horses (Vesaas).
***han'ḍsameleg** *A* - easy to handle.
handse [hæ'ndse] *V -a/+-et* (in soccer) touch the ball with the hands.
+**han'ḍ/setter** *-en, pl -e* (=***/setjar**) compositor, typesetter.
***han'ḍs/hjelp** *-a* helping hand.
han'ḍ/skreiv *pt of* **-skrive**
han'ḍ/skrift[1] *-a/+-en* handwriting.
han'ḍ/skrift[2] *-et* manuscript.
han'ḍ/skrive *V infl as* **skrive** write in longhand.
+**han'ḍ/slag** cf **hånd/**
+**han'ḍ/spunnet** *A* - (=***/spunne, *-i**) homespun.
han'ḍ/tak *-et* grip, handle; hilt (on sword); grip (on bicycle); crank, lever.
+**han'ḍ/takes** *V -tok(e)s -takes* (=***/takast**) shake hands.
***han'ḍ/tame** *-en* deftness, dexterity.
han'ḍ/tein *-en* spindle.
hanḍte're *V -te* handle, manage.
hanḍte'ring *-a/-en* 1 handling. 2 business profession, trade.
hanḍte'rlig *A* - (=+**hånd-**) easy to handle.
+**han'ḍ/tok(e)s** *pt of* **-takes**
han'ḍ/tralle *-a* handcar.
han'ḍ/trev *-et* cf **/rev**
han'ḍ/vask *-en* hand washing; clothes to be washed by hand (not machine).
han'ḍ/venḍing *-a/+-en*: **i en h-** in the twinkling of an eye.
***han'ḍ/verje** *-a* hand weapon.
han'ḍ/verk *-et* 1 handicraft. 2 craft, trade.
+**han'ḍ/verker** *-en, pl -e* (=***-ar**) artisan, craftsman.
han'ḍverks/mann *-en, pl -menn/ *-menner* artisan, craftsman; laborer, worker.
han'ḍverks/næring *-a/+-en* craft, trade.
+**han'ḍverks/svenn** *-en* (=***/svein**) journeyman.
han'ḍ/veske *-a* handbag.
***han'ḍ/vol** *-en* handle (of a flail).
han'ḍ/våpen *-et* hand weapon; *mil.* small arm(s).
han'/dyr *-et* cf **hann/**
***han'ḍ/yvle** *-t* hand weapon, e.g. a stick.
°**han'ḍ/øvle** *-t* cf **/yvle**
han'ḍ/åre *-a* oar maneuvered by one hand.
ha'ne *-n* 1 cock; rooster: **den røde h-galer over huset** the house is on fire; **være eneste h- i kurven** be the cock of the walk, the only man in sight; rule the roost. 2 weather vane. 3 (of a barrel) spigot, tap; faucet. 4 (of a gun) hammer: **spenne h-n** cock the gun.
ha'ne/bjelke *-n carp.* tie beam.
+**ha'ne/fjed** *-et* handsbreadth.
ha'ne/gal *-et* cockcrow: **stå opp ved h-** get up at c- (dawn).
+**ha'ne/kylling** *-en* young rooster; *hum.* hothead.
ha'ne/marsj *-en* goose step.
hang'[1] *-en/+-et* bent, inclination, penchant: **ha h- til spirituosa** be addicted to drink.
hang'[2] *pt of* **henge**[2]
hangar [hangga'r] *-en* hangar.
hangar/skip *-et* aircraft carrier.
***hang'e** *V heng, hang/hekk, hange/-i* cf **henge**[2]
hang'le *V -a/+-et* 1: **h- igjennom** get through by the skin of one's teeth, (barely) scrape through. 2 be ailing.
***hang'let(e)** *A* - ailing, sickly.
han'k[1] *-a/+-en, pl *henker* (=***honk**) handle.
han'k**[2] *-en* (=hanke**[1]) loop, noose, strap; bunch (e.g. of keys), string (e.g. of fish).
***han'ke**[1] *-n* cf **hank**[2]
+**han'ke**[2] *N*: **ta hånd i h- med** give a helping hand with, take hold of (a problem); exert one's influence on.
***han'ke**[3] *V -a*: **h- i hop fisk** string fish.
han'ke/kopp *-en* cup with a handle.
han'/kjønn *-et* 1 male sex. 2 *gram.* masculine gender.
han'lig *A* - (=+**hannlig**) male.
hann' *-en* he, male.
Han'na, Han'ne *Prn (f)*
hann'/dyr *-et* male animal.
hann'/hunḍ *-en* male dog.
hann'/katt *-en* tomcat; *hum.* old goat.
+**hann'/kjønn** *-et* cf **han/**
+**hann'lig** *A* cf **hanlig**
han'/rei *-en* cuckold: **gjøre en til h-** cuckold sby.
***han's**[1] *-en* round of drinks (which a sailor stands on his first voyage).
han's[2] *Pn po of* **han**[2] 1 his: **hatten h- h-** hat. *2 (sign of possessive): **garden h- Olav er større enn h- Svein** Olav's farm is larger than Svein's.
Han's *Prn (m)*: **H- og Grete** Hansel and Gretel.
han'sa *+-en/*-a hist.* Hanseatic League.
han'sa/tid *-a/+-en* period during which the Hanseatic League flourished.
***han'se** *V -a* stand a round of drinks (on a sailor's maiden voyage).
hansea't *-en* member of the Hanseatic League.
hansea'tisk *A* - Hanseatic.
+**han'se/forbunḍ** *-et* Hanseatic League (esp. the North German member cities).
***han'ses** *Pn po of* **han**[2]
han'se/stad *pl +-steder* Hanseatic city.
***han'skast** *V -ast* cf **hanskes**
han'ske *-n* glove: **kaste h-n til en** challenge sby, throw down the gauntlet to sby; **oppta h-n** accept a challenge, pick up the gauntlet; **passe som hånd i h-** fit perfectly, hand and glove.
+**han'ske/maker** *-en, pl -e* (=***-ar**) glover.
han'ske/rom [/romm] *-met* glove compartment.
+**han'skes** *V -edes, -es* (=***-ast**): **h- med** come to grips with.
han'ske/skinn *-et* glove leather.
happ' *N*: **hipp som h-** six of one and half a dozen of the other.
***hap'pe** *V -a* chastise, discipline.
haraki'ri *-en* hara-kiri.
Har'alḍ *Prn (m)*
Ha'ram *Pln* twp, Møre og Romsdal.
harang' *-en* harangue.
ha'rḍ *A* 1 hard (bed, battle, heart, metal, stone, times, words, etc.); harsh, severe (loss, person, smile, terms, treatment, voice, weather, etc.): **en h- hand** an iron hand; **dommen var i h-este laget** the verdict was quite severe; *lit.* **i hine h-e dager** in those violent (rugged) days (J. Moe); **sette h-t mot h-t** repel force with force; give measure for measure. 2 hard=stiff, strenuous, tough (climb, contest, exam, walk, work, etc.). 3 *(adv.)*: **han har det h-t** he has a hard time of it; he's very much in love; **sitte h-t i det** be hard up; be in a tough spot; **gå h-t inn på en** be hard on, for sby; press sby; **gå h-t på** press strongly for; **hvor det går h-est for seg** right in the thick of it; **trenge h-t til noe** need sth very badly.
***ha'rḍ/ang** *-en* frozen ground.
Hardang'er *Pln* collective name for the twps around Hardanger Fjord, Hordaland.
hardang'er/fele *-a mus.* Hardanger fiddle (decorated eight-stringed fiddle, four strings of which are actually played, the others sounding sympathetically).
Hardang'er/jøkulen *Pln* the Hardanger Glacier.
+**hardang'er/søm'** *-men* (=***/saum**) type of embroidery characteristic of Hardanger.
ha'rḍ/balen *A +-ent, pl -ne* hardy, tough.
***ha'rḍ/beitt** *A* - hard to cut (grass).
+**ha'rḍ/brent** *A* - (=***/brend**) hard (baked) (esp. bricks).
***ha'rḍe** *-n*: **på h-n** just barely, with difficulty; hard, vigorously.
***ha'rḍ/el** *-et* thunderstorm.
***ha'rḍ/fengd** *A -/-fengt* 1 difficult, troublesome. 2 harsh, heavy-handed.
+**ha'rḍ/frossen** *A -ent, pl -frosne* (=***frosen**) frozen hard.
ha'rḍ/før *A* hardy, robust, tough.
***ha'rḍ/gnuen** *A -e/-i, pl -ne* violent.
ha'rḍ/haus *-en* hard-bitten, sturdy, tough fellow, *(pop.)* hard-nosed character.
ha'rḍ/henḍt *A* - 1 clumsy, heavy-handed; brutal (person). 2 careless, rough, ruthless (actions).
+**har'ḍ/het** *-en* 1 hardness 2 harshness, severity. 3 brutality, hard-heartedness. 4 (of style) awkwardness, stiffness.
ha'rḍ/hjerta *A* - (=+**-et**) hard-hearted, unfeeling.
ha'rḍ/huda [*/hua] *A* - (=+**-et**) thick-skinned; *fig.* callous, thick-skinned, *(pop.)* hard-boiled.
ha'rḍ/huga *A* - callous, unfeeling; *fig.* hard-boiled, rough, tough; dauntless, intrepid.
ha'rḍing[1] *-en* tough person.
ha'rḍing[2] *-en* person from Hardanger.
ha'rḍing/fele *-a mus.* Hardanger fiddle (cf **hardangerfele).**
ha'rḍ/kokt *A* - hard-boiled; *fig.* hard-boiled, rough, tough.
***ha'rḍla** *Av* quite, very.
***ha'rḍleg** *A* - rather, somewhat hard.
***ha'rḍ/leik** *-en* 1 hardness. 2 harshness, severity. 3 brutality, hard-heartedness. 4 (of style) awkwardness, stiffness.
ha'rḍ/lynt *A* - (=***/lyndt**) hard-boiled, rough, tough.
ha'rḍ/nakka *A* - 1 headstrong, obstinate, stiffnecked (person). 2 stubborn, tenacious, unyielding; persistent (e.g. cough, fever): **gjøre h- motstand** resist doggedly.
ha'rḍne *V -a/+-et* harden.
Ha'rḍ/råde *Prn*: **Harald H-** Harald the Ruthless (half-brother of Saint Olaf, and king of Norway 1045-1066).
***ha'rḍ/sett** *A* - 1 headstrong, obstinate, stiffnecked (person). 2 stubborn, tenacious, unyielding; persistent (e.g. cough, fever).
***ha'rḍsleg** *A* - harsh, severe.
***ha'rḍ/sø'kt** *A* - exposed, unsheltered.
ha'rḍ/tukta *A* - undisciplined, unruly, wild.
ha'rḍ/veḍ *-en* hardwood.
***ha'rḍ/voren** [/våren] *A -e/-i, pl -ne* hard.
ha're *-n zool.* hare, jackrabbit (family Leporidae): **ingen vet hvor h-n hopper** no one knows what's going to happen, no one can predict the future; **mange hunder er h-ns død** (=***mange hundar er h-en sin daude**) the mob can destroy the individual.
+**ha're/hjerte** [/jær'te] *-t* (=***/hjarta**): **ha et h-** be chicken-hearted, *(pop.)* be a 'fraidycat.
ha're/hunḍ *-en* beagle.
Ha'r/eid *Pln* twp, Møre og Romsdal.
ha're/labb *-en* 1 hare's (rabbit's) foot: **fare over noe med en h-** give sth a lick and a promise, slur over sth. 2 *bot.* cottonweed (genus Gnaphalium).
ha'rem *-et, pl -/+-er* harem.
ha're/munn *-en* harelip.
ha're/mynt *A* - harelipped.
ha're/pus *-en* bunny (rabbit).
ha're/rug *-en bot.* Alpine bistort (Polygonum viviparum).

+**ha're/skår** -et harelip.

har'k[1] -en clearing of the throat; phlegm, spit.

***har'k**[2] -et junk, rubbish; poor condition.

***har‘kal** A ailing, sickly.

har‘ke V -a/+-et 1 clear one's throat, hawk. *2 be ailing, sickly.

***har‘keleg** A - frail, weak; poor.

***har‘ken** A -e/-i, pl -ne ailing, sickly; rough.

ha'rlekin -en Harlequin.

har'm[1] -en poet., dial. 1 grief, sorrow. 2 anger, indignation.

har'm[2] A angry, indignant (**på** at).

har'm/dirrende A - trembling with indignation, rage.

har'me[1] -n anger, indignation, resentment: **med h-** indignantly; **vekke h-** arouse, cause resentment.

har'me[2] V -a/+-et exasperate, vex: **det h-er meg** it angers me; **h- seg over** feel indignant at, resent.

har'melig A - annoying, exasperating.

har'm/full A angry, indignant.

har'm/fylt A - angry, indignant.

+**har'm/løs** A harmless, inoffensive; innocuous.

harmone're V -te be harmonious; be in harmony, be in keeping (**med** with).

harmoni' -en 1 accord, harmony, unison: **bringe i h- med** harmonize, reconcile with. 2 mus. accord, harmony.

harmo'nika -en, pl +-er mus. accordion (=**trekk/**), concertina; harmonica (=**munn/**).

harmonise're V -te mus. harmonize.

harmo'nisk A - 1 harmonious. 2 mus. harmonic, melodious.

harmo'nium -iet, pl +-ier/*- mus. harmonium, reed organ.

harnis'k -et, pl -/+-er 1 hist. armor. 2: **bringe, sette en i h-** enrage, infuriate sby, make sby see red.

har‘pe[1] -a/+-en 1 harp: **spille på h-** play the h-. 2 (in gardening) screen.

har‘pe[2] V -a/+-et screen.

har‘pe/streng -en harp string.

har‘piks -en resin.

+**har‘piks/holdig** A - (=*/**haldig**) resinous.

harpis't -en harpist.

harpu'n -en harpoon.

harpune'r -en harpooner.

harpune're V -te harpoon.

harr' -en (=***horr**[1]) zool. grayling (Thymallus thymallus).

Har‘ran Pln twp, Nord-Trøndelag.

***har‘re** -n aversion, dislike, hate.

***har‘ren** A -e/-i, pl harne hard; harsh, severe.

harsela's -en fun, teasing: **drive h- med en** tease sby.

harsele're V -te make fun of, tease: **h-ende** sarcastic(ally).

har'sk A - 1 rancid; acrid, bitter. 2 fam. grim, gruff.

har‘ske V -a/+-et: **h- seg** act, be angry, fierce (**over** at).

har‘skne V -a/+-et (=***herskne**) turn rancid.

Har‘stad Pln town on Hinnøya, Troms.

+**har't/ad** Av archaic almost, well-nigh.

+**har't/ko·rn** -et: **slå i h- med noe(n)** lump together with sth (sby).

har'v -a drag, harrow.

har've[1] V -a/+-et drag, harrow (a field).

har've[2] V -a/+-et fish (with a large hook concealed in a bunch of angleworms).

+**ha's** N: **få h- på** get the better of; dispose of; do away with.

hasard [hasa'r] -en 1 gambling, game of chance: **spille h-** gamble. 2 hazard, risk.

hasardiø's A hazardous, risky.

+**hasard/spill** [hasa'r/] -et (=*/**spel**) gambling, game of chance.

ha'se[1] -n 1 back of the knee. 2 hamstring: **smøre h-r** take to one's heels. 3 hock (animals).

***ha'se**[2] V -a hobble (e.g. a horse).

has‘le V -a/+-et hist.: **h- en voll** mark off a combat area (by setting up poles of hazelwood).

+**has‘pe**[1] -n (=+**hasp**) catch, hasp.

has‘pe[2] V -a/+-et 1: **h- på** fasten with a hasp, hasp. 2 reel: **h- av seg** reel off (e.g. a long speech).

+**has‘pel** -elen, pl -ler (of yarn) bobbin.

has‘sel -elen, pl hasler bot. hazel (genus Corylus).

has‘sel/nøtt [also has‘-] -a hazelnut.

has't +-en/*-a haste, hurry: **det har ingen h-** what's the rush? there's no hurry; **ha h-** be busy; **han har ikke noen h- med å** he's in no hurry to; **i all h-** in great haste; **i en h-** headlong; **i h-** hurriedly.

has‘te V -a/+-et 1 hurry. 2 be urgent: **det h-er (med noe)** the matter can't wait, there's no time to lose.

+**has‘telig** Av dial. hastily, hurriedly.

+**ha'/stemt** A - (=*/**stemd**) grandiloquent, high-flown.

has‘tig A - 1 hasty, hurried. 2 abrupt, impetuous, impulsive.

+**has‘tig/het** -en speed, velocity: **med en h- på** at a speed of.

+**has‘tighets/måler** -en, pl -e speedometer.

has't/verk -et 1 hurried work, rush job: **h- er lastverk** haste makes waste. 2 haste, hurry: **ha h-** be in a hurry, rush.

has'tverks/arbeid -et work carelessly and superficially performed.

Has‘/vik Pln village, Hasvik twp, Finnmark.

ha't -et animosity, hate, hatred: **bære, nære h- til en** hate sby, have a hatred of sby; **legge en for h-** make sby the object of one's hate.

***ha‘tal** A malicious, spiteful.

ha‘te V -a/+-et hate; abhor, detest: **h- som pesten** hate like sin; **h- å måtte** hate having to.

ha‘te/full A malicious, spiteful.

+**ha‘ter**[1] -en, pl -e (=*-**ar**) enemy, hater: **være en h- av** hate; abhor, detest.

***ha'ter**[2] -et 1 stinging insect (esp. flies, mosquitoes). 2 bite, itch.

***ha‘tig** A - malicious, spiteful.

***hat‘re** V -a itch, sting.

+**hat'sk** A - malicious, rancorous, spiteful; angry, indignant.

hatt'[1] -en 1 hat; bonnet, cap: **bløt h-** fedora; **stiv h-** bowler, derby; **du skal ikke løfte på h-en før du ser mannen** don't cross your bridges until you get to them; **gi en noe å henge h-en på** give sby cause for complaint; **la h-en gå rundt** pass the hat around (for a collection); **sannelig min h-** (exclam. of surprise) of all things; **ta h-en av for en** take off one's hat to sby; admire sby; **trykke h-en ned over ørene på en** jam sby's hat down over his ears; **være høg i h-en** be cocksure, self-confident, (pop.) be too big for one's britches; **være kar for sin h-** be able to hold one's own, be able to take care of oneself; **være på h- med en** have a nodding acquaintance with sby. 2 (of beer) foam. 3 bot. (of a mushroom) cap. 4: **h-er** hist. members of a political party in eighteenth-century Sweden.

hatt'[2] pp of **ha**[1]

hat‘te/band -et (=+/**bånd**) hatband.

+**hat‘te/brem·** -men hat brim.

hat‘te/forret·ning -a/+-en haberdasher's, milliner's shop.

+**hat‘te/maker** -en, pl -e (=*-**ar**) hatter: **det er forskjell på kong Salomon og Jørgen h-** there's a difference between a king and a cat.

Hatt‘fjell/dal Pln twp, Nordland.

°**hau'**[1] -en cf **hug**

hau'[2] I hey! oh!

hau‘bits -en mil. howitzer.

°**hau'/bitt** -et cf **hug/**

hau'd -en/-et 1 (short for **haud illaudabilis** "not without praise") grade in a university examination (ab.=C). 2 person receiving such a grade.

hau‘g -en 1 hill, knoll, mound; barrow, (grave) mound, tumulus: **gammel som alle h-er** old as the hills. 2 heap, pile: **legge noe i h-** accumulate, heap up sth; **han hadde tjent en h- med penger** he had amassed a great deal of money; **slenge i en h-** throw in a heap.

hau‘ge V -a/+-et 1 pile: **h- seg opp** accumulate, pile up. 2: **h- seg** naut. swell.

hau‘ge/bonde -n (=+**haug/**) folk. "cairn dweller", "undead man" (dead man who continues to live on in a barrow).

Hau‘ge/sund Pln city, Rogaland.

hau‘get(e) A - hilly, undulating.

hau‘ge/vis Av: **i h-** by, in heaps; lots of: **h- av penger** (pop.) oodles of money.

hau‘g/folk -et hill trolls; fairies, gnomes.

+**haugia'ner** -en, pl -e (=*-**ar**) theol. member of religious lay movement founded ca. 1800 by Hans Nielsen Hauge.

hau‘g/kall -en folk. kobold, ogre inhabiting underground places (=/**bonde**).

hau‘g/legge V -la, -lagt hist. bury in a barrow, tumulus.

hau‘g/sky -a meteor. cumulus cloud.

***hau‘g/stall** -en 1 bachelor. 2 widower.

hau‘g/tusse -a folk. kobold, woman of the underground people; also= **huldre**.

hau'k[1] -en zool. hawk (family Falconidae).

hau'k[2] -et halloo, shout.

Hau'k Prn (m)

hau‘ke V -a/+-et call cattle, yodel; hoot, shout.

°**hau‘/kråke** N: **stupe h-** turn somersaults.

hau'ld -en hist. franklin, freeholder, yeoman.

hau's -en 1 head, skull, (pop.) noodle: **spøke og husere i h-en** (of thoughts) run pell-mell through one's head. 2 crag; sunken rock.

Hau's Pln twp, Hordaland.

hau‘se -n cf **haus**

hausse[1] [hå's] -n merc. boom, bull market.

hausse[2] [hå‘se] V -a/+-et merc. operate, speculate (on the assumption of a bullish trend in the market).

hausse/spekulan't -en merc. bull.

***hau'st** -en cf **høst**

***hau'st/bær** A cf **bøst/**

***hau'st/bære** -a cow which calves late in the year.

hau'ste[1] V -a/+-et halloo, shout; hoot.

***hau'ste**[2] V -a cf **høste**

***hau'st/folk** pl cf **høst/**

***hau'st/jamdøgn** -et (=*/**jamdøger**) cf **høst/jevndøgn**

***hau'stleg** A - cf **høstlig**

***hau'st/part** -en cf **høst/**

***hau'st/vinne** -a harvesting.

haut/relieff [å'relieff] -et, pl -/+-er high relief.

ha'v[1] -et 1 sea: **h-ets frihet** freedom of the s-s; **over h-et** above s- level; **på det åpne h-** on the high s-s; **på h-ets** (poet. **h-sens**) **bunn** on the bottom of the s-; **til h-s** out to (at) s-; **ute på h-et** out at s-. 2 ocean: **Det indiske h-** the Indian O-; **vi har lagt et h- mellom oss** we are o-s apart. 3 heavy sea, swell.

***ha'v**[2] -et 1 upturned end of a ski. 2 handle; door handle.

***ha‘vande** A - cf **havende(s)**

***ha‘vands/laus** A 1 empty-handed. 2 idle.

+ Bokmål; * Nynorsk; ° Dialect.
After letter: ' stress (Acc. 1); ‘ tone, stress (Acc. 2); · length.
Below letter: . not pronounced.

+havane'ser -en, pl -e (=***-ar**) 1 person from Havana. 2 Havana cigar.
***ha'vang** -en value, worth; benefit, use.
***-ha'var** -en cf **-haver**
havare're V -te be disabled, wrecked (auto, ship): **h-t** fig. down and out.
havari' -et, pl +-er/*- 1 shipwreck; damage, loss; breakdown (auto, ship). 2 naut. average: **alminnelig h-, felles h-** general a-; **totalt h-** loss of ship, shipwreck. 3 fig. down-and-out condition.
havaris't -en naut. disabled vessel; shipwrecked seaman; fig. down-and-outer.
+ha'v/blikk -et (=***/blik**) dead calm.
ha'v/botn -en (=**+/bunn**) bottom of the sea, sea bed, sea floor.
ha'v/bukt [/bokt] -a bay; arm of the sea.
ha'v/djup -et (=**+/dyp**) deep.
ha'v/dyr -et marine animal.
ha've[1] -n cf **hav**[2]
+ha've[2] -n cf **hage**[1]
***ha've**[3] V hadde, hatt cf **ha**[1]
+ha've/benk -en cf **hage/**
+ha've/bruk -et cf **hage/**
+ha've/by -en cf **hage/**
***ha've/kjær** A - avaricious, grasping, greedy.
***ha'v/elle** -a zool. long-tailed duck (Clangula hyemalis).
+ha'vende(s) A - (=***havande**) valuable, worth having.
+-haver -en (=***-havar**) one who has: **fordringsh-** creditor; **makth-**.
+ha've/saks -a/-en cf **hage/**
+ha've/sanger -en, pl -e cf **hage/**
ha've/sjuk A (=**+/syk**) avaricious, grasping, greedy.
ha've/sjuke -n (=**+/syke**) avarice, covetousness, greed.
+ha've/sprøyte -a/-en cf **hage/**
+ha've/syk A cf **/sjuk**
+ha've/syke -n cf **/sjuke**
ha'v/flate -a/+-en surface of the sea: **over h-n** above sea level.
+ha'v/forskning -en oceanography.
ha'v/fru(e) -a/+-en mermaid.
ha'v/gap -et mouth of a fjord.
ha'v/ga'rd -en (in Arctic regions) outermost edge of drifting ice.
ha'v/gasse -n zool. goosander (Mergus merganser); hum. shrew, xantippe.
ha'v/gul -a (=**/gule**) sea breeze.
ha'v/gående A - seafaring, seagoing.
ha'v/hest -en 1 zool. sea horse (genus Hippocampus). 2 zool. Arctic petrel, fulmar (Fulmarus glacialis).
ha'v/katt -en zool. catfish (Anarrhichas lupus).
ha'v/mann -en, pl -menn/*-menner merman.
+hav'n[1] -a cf **hamn**[1]
+hav'n[2] -a cf **hamn**[2]
+hav'ne[1] V -a/-et cf **hamne**[1]
+hav'ne[2] V -a/-et cf **hamne**[2]
+hav'ne/arbei'der -en, pl -e (=***-ar**) longshoreman, stevedore.
+hav'ne/by -en cf **hamne/**
+hav'ne/fog(e)d -en harbor master.
ha'v/rand -a/+-en edge of the sea, horizon.
hav're -n bot. oats (Avena saliva).
hav're/graut -en oatmeal porridge.
hav're/gryn -et rolled oats (oatmeal).
hav're/lefse -a oatmeal *lefse*: **striskjorte og h-** daily, everyday fare; fig. humdrum existence.
hav're/pose -n bag, sack of oats.
ha'vs/auga** -t (=/auge**) sound (opening out to the sea).
havsens [haf'sens] po df of **hav**[1]
Havs/fjord [haf's/fjor] Pln cf **Hafrs/**
+ha'v/skilpad'de -a/-en (=***/skjelpadde**) zool. sea turtle (order Chelonia).
havs/nød [haf's/] -a/+-en (=***/naud**): **i h-** in danger of shipwreck, in distress.
ha'v/strekning -en/*-a stretch of open sea.
ha'v/stykke -t stretch of open sea.
ha'v/sule -a zool. gannet (Sula bassana).
ha'v/ø'rn -a/-en zool. gray sea eagle (Haliaetus albicilla).
+hawai'er -en, pl -e (=***-ar**) Hawaiian.
hawai'isk A - Hawaiian.
he' I 1 hah (scornful). 2: **he-he** ha ha (dry chuckle).
heade [hed'de] V -a/+-et head (in soccer, play the ball off one's head).
heat [hi't] -et heat (in sports).
hebra'isk A - Hebraic, Hebrew.
+hebre'er -en, pl -e (=***-ar**) Hebrew.
+Hebri'dene Pln (=***Hebridane**) the Hebrides.
Hed'/dal Pln twp, Telemark.
hed'/døl -en person from Heddal.
+he'de -n heath, moor.
+he'den Av: **gå, vandre h-** depart this life.
+he'den/dom' -men heathendom.
+he'den/old N heathen times.
+he'densk A - (=***heidensk**) heathen, pagan.
+he'den/skap -en/-et heathenism, paganism.
+he'der -eren (=***heider**) glory, honor: **komme til h- og verdighet** come into one's own; **vise en h-** honor sby.
+he'der/full A glorious, honorable.
+he'der/kronet A - honored, illustrious.
+he'derlig A - (=***heiderleg**) 1 decent, honest, respectable. 2 honorable: **h- omtale** h- mention.
+he'derlig/het -en honesty, integrity.
+he'ders/bevi'sning -en mark of distinction; token of respect.
+he'ders/dag -en great day, red-letter day (in one's life).
+he'ders/gjest -en guest of honor.
+he'ders/mann -en, pl -menn decent, honest man; gentleman.
+he'ders/pasja -en hum. splendid old man.
Hedm.=Hedmark
Hed'/mark Pln county, Norway.
hed'/marking -en (=***/merking**) person from Hedmark.
***hed'ne** -a hair of the head.
+he'dning -en (=***heidning**) 1 heathen, pagan. 2 godless person. 3 bibl. gentile.
+he'dninge/kristen en, pl -kristne hist. gentile convert to Christianity.
+he'dninge/land -et heathendom, heathen land(s).
+he'dre V -a/-et (=***heidre**) bestow an honor on; honor: **h- din far og din mor** bibl. h- thy father and thy mother (Exodus 20, 12); **h-ende** honorable, respectful; **h-et** honored.
Hed'rum Pln twp, Vestfold.
Hed'vig Prn (f)
hef'te[1] -t, pl +-r/*- 1 delay, hindrance (for to), red tape. 2 jur. (light) imprisonment. 3 merc. lien, mortage. 4 (sword) hilt.
hef'te[2] -t 1 (of a book) number, part; fascicle; issue (**av** of). 2 booklet, brochure, pamphlet. 3 exercise book, notebook; (coupon) book, etc.
hef'te[3] V -a/+-et 1 delay, detain; hold up: **h- en bort** waste sby's time. 2 dial. remain, stay, stop: **vi h-er lite grann ennå** we'll stay a little while yet (Bojer).
hef'te[4] V -a/+-et 1 attach, fasten; paste, stick; sew, staple, stitch: **der h-er stor gjeld på eiendommen** the estate is heavily encumbered; **h- blikket på (ved)** fasten one's eyes on; **h- sammen** bind (staple) into a book; **h- ved** fig. be incident to, involve; **h- seg ved** notice, take notice of; **h- seg ved småting** quibble about trifles, split hairs. 2: **h- for** jur. be legally liable, responsible for.
+hef'telse -n (=***-ing**) merc. encumbrance, lien, mortgage.
hef'te/maski'n -en stapler, stapling machine; tech. bookbinding machine.
***hef'te/sam'** A delaying, time-wasting.
hef'te/vis Av (of a book) in fascicles, in parts.
+hef'tig A - 1 intense, severe, violent: **en h- glede** an intense joy. 2 angry, excited, impetuous; fervent, vehement: **han ble h-** he lost his temper.
+hef'tig/het -en 1 intensity, violence. 2 anger, impetuosity.
hef't/plaster -et adhesive tape.
***he'ga** Av here, hither.
heg'd -a 1 naut. ring in the end of a hawser; staying of a mast. *2 cleverness, skill. *3 economy, moderation.
heg'de V -a/+-et dial. 1 economize. 2: **h- seg** be moderate, know where to stop; control oneself.
+hegelia'ner -en, pl -e (=***-ar**) Hegelian.
hegelianis'me -n Hegelianism.
he'gelsk A - Hegelian.
hegemoni' -et, pl -/+-er hegemony.
hegg' -en bot. European bird cherry (Prunus padus); chokecherry.
heg'ge/bær -et bird cherry.
+heg'le V -a/-et 1 bawl out, rake over the coals. *2 drip; cry.
hegn [heng'n, +hei'n] +-et/*-a fence, hedge; fig. defence, protection.
hegne [heng'ne, +hei'ne] V +-et/*-a fence in; fig. defend, protect.
Heg'ra Pln twp, Nord-Trøndelag.
heg're[1] -n zool. gray heron (Ardea cinerea).
heg're[2] V -a/+-et appear larger (than the actual size, e.g. islands, mountains in the distance); appear as an illusion, mirage.
***heg're**[3] V -a guffaw, roar with laughter.
***heg're/le** V -lo, -ledd guffaw, roar with laughter.
hehe' I cf **he**
hei'[1] -a heath, moor: **h-ene** the hills, the uplands.
hei'[2] I 1 hey, hey there: **h- på deg** hi. 2 hooray, whee (with rapid or sudden movement): **h- hvor det går!** whee, are we ever moving!; **med h- og hopp** and away we go (e.g. in a dance).
hei'a[1] df of **hei**[1], **heie**[1]
hei'a[2] pt of **heie**[2]
hei'a[3] I huzza, let's go; rah rah.
hei'a/gjeng -en cheering section.
hei'a/rop -et cheer; rah rah.
Hei'/dal Pln twp, Oppland.
***hei'den** A -e/-i, pl -ne heathen, pagan.
***hei'densk** A - cf **hedensk**
***hei'den/skap** -en cf **heden/**
***hei'der** -en cf **heder**
***hei'derleg** A - cf **hederlig**
***hei'ders/dag** -en cf **heders/**
***hei'ders/mann** -en, pl -menn (er) cf **heders/**
***hei'ders/skrift** -et testimonial volume (in honor of sby).
***hei'dning** -en cf **hedning**
***hei'dre** V -a cf **hedre**
hei'/døl -en person from Heidal.
hei'e[1] -a coquette, flirt.
hei'e[2] V -a/+-et cheer: **h- på** cheer (a team).
hei'e/ga'rd -en (=**hei/**) farm lying on a heath or upland.
hei'l[1] A (=**+hel**[1]) 1 whole; complete, entire, full, all: **bussen går fem minutter over h-** fam. the bus leaves five minutes past the hour; **det h-e** all of it, the whole business, the whole thing; the whole (e.g. assemblage, society, etc.); **h-e dagen** all day; **h-e gjerdet ramlet ned** the whole fence fell down; **i det h-e** in all; on the whole; **i det h-e tatt** everything considered, on the whole; (not) at all (**jeg vil ikke ha noe med ham å gjøre i det h-e tatt** I don't want anything at all to do with him); **med h-e mitt hjerte** with all my heart, with my whole heart; **over det h-e** all over; **over h-e Europa** all over Europe, over all of Europe. 2 quite a, real: **vinden var nå vokset til en h- storm** the wind had now grown into a regular storm (Sverdrup). 3 (adv.) cf **heilt.**
hei'l[2] I hail: **h- og sæl** good luck greeting (Old Norse, used in mod-

ern times by Norwegian nazis as counterpart to the German Heil Hitler).

*__hei'lag__ *A* cf **hellig**

*__hei'lag/brot__ *-et* cf **hellig/brøde**

*__hei'lag/dag__ *-en* cf **hellig/**

*__hei'lag/dom__ *-(m)en* cf **hellig/**

*__hei'lage__ *V -a* cf **hellige**

*__hei'lag/menne__ *-t* saint.

*__hei'lag/skap__ *-en* holiness, sanctity.

*__heilagtrekong'ars/dag__ *-en* cf **hellig-trekongers/**

*__hei'l/brigd__ *-a* health.

*__hei'l/brigde__ *V -a* cure, restore to health.

hei'ldags/post *-en* full-time job.

hei'le[1] *-n* brain (cf **hjerne**).

hei'le[2] *et* cf **hele**[2]

*__hei'le__[3] *V -a* cf **hele**[3]

*__hei'le/skål__ *-a* cranium, skull.

hei'l/feit *A* (of cheese made from unseparated milk) fat.

hei'l/flaske *-a* ¾ liter bottle for liquor (corresponding approx. to American fifth).

*__hei'l/garde're__ *V -te* cf **hel/**

hei'l/gryn *-et* whole grain.

hei'l/huga *A -* 1 decided, determined; enthusiastic, wholehearted. 2 bold, unafraid.

hei'lko'rn/brød *-et* (loaf of) wheat bread (with some whole kernels).

hei'l/norsk *A -* wholly (and peculiarly) Norwegian (customs, language, objects, etc.).

hei'/lo *-a zool.* golden plover (Charadrius pluvialis).

hei'l/silke *-n* pure silk.

*__hei'l/skap__ *-en* entirety, whole, totality.

hei'l/skinna *A -* (=+**hel/skinnet**) safe and sound: **slippe h-** escape without a scratch.

*__hei'lsleg__ *A -* complete, entire.

hei'l/spenn *N*: **stå i h-** (of a gun) be fully cocked; **være i h-** *fig.* be all tense, keyed up.

hei'l/stat *-en hist., pol.* union of states (not federated); (specif. in Danish history) the United Monarchy.

hei'l/steike *V -te* roast whole: **h-t** barbecued.

*__hei'l/sysken__ *pl* cf **hel/søsken**

hei'lt *Av* 1 completely, entirely, fully; quite, wholly; right; all the way: **h- fra først av** right from the first, from the very first; **h- og holdent** altogether, entirely, wholly; **h- igjennom** right through, to the core; through and through; **h- siden** ever since; **noe h- annet** sth quite different; **skrive det h- ut** write it out completely, in full. 2 quite (=to quite a degree).

hei'l/ull *-a* all wool, pure wool (100% wool).

hei'm[1] *-en* (=+**hjem**[1] **-met**) 1 home: **de måtte gå fra hus og h-** they were thrown out on the street (i.e., dispossessed); **det ble som en annen h-** (+**et annet hjem**) **for ham** it was like a second h- for him; **i h-en** (+**i h-met**) at h-; **stifte h-** marry and settle down. 2 native country; habitat. 3 charitable institution, home. 4: +**det himmelske hjem** *theol.* heaven. *5 world: **i denne h-en** in this w-.

hei'm[2] *Av* (=+**hjem**[2]) 1 home, homeward; back: **bære seieren h-** win the day; **gå nedenom og h-** go to the dogs; **ta h- et stikk** take a trick (cards); **ta noe med seg h-** carry away sth (e.g. from a speech); **vi må h-** we have to be going, we must be getting back. 2: **ta h- en vare** *merc.* import an article. 3: **ta h-slakken** *naut.* haul in a hawser. 4 *theol.* heavenward.

Hei'm *Pln* twp, Sør-Trøndelag.

*__hei'man__ *Av* from home.

*__hei'ma(n)/frå__ *P* from home.

*__hei'ma(n)/følgje__ *-a* dowry.

hei'm/by *-en* home town.

hei'm/bygd *-a* native district (valley, rural community).

hei'me *Av* (=+**hjemme**) at home; back: **føle seg h-** feel at home; **føle seg h- i noe** be conversant with, be up on a subject; **ha h-** live (in a certain place); be indigenous, belong to; **holde seg h-** stay home, indoors; **høre h-** belong; be, hail from (**det hører ingensteds h-** that's neither here nor there); **øst, vest, h- best** there's no place like home.

+__hei'me/brenner__ *-en, pl -e* (=*__-ar__) illicit distiller, *(pop.)* moonshiner.

hei'me/brent *-et* home brew, *pop.* moonshine.

hei'me/dåp *-en* private baptism (at home).

hei'me/fiske *-t* coastal fishing.

+__hei'me/fra__ *P* (away) from home.

hei'me/front *-en* home front; (during World War II) underground resistance movement.

+__hei'me/følge__ *-t* cf **heima(n)/følgje**

+__hei'me/gjort__ [/jort] *A -* (=*__/gjord__) homemade.

hei'me/hage *-n* enclosed pasture (near the farmhouse).

+__hei'me/kjent__ *A -* (=*__/kjend__) acquainted with the locality.

hei'me/koselig *A -* cozy, homey.

hei'me/ku *-a, pl -kyr/+-er* "home cow" (i.e. cow kept on the farm during the summer, instead of being pastured in the mountains).

hei'mel *-elen, pl -ler* (=+**hjemmel**) authority, title (**på** to).

hei'me/laga *A -* homemade.

*__hei'meleg__ *A -* (staying) at home.

hei'mels/mann *-en, pl -menn/*-menner* authority, informant, source.

*__hei'me/marknad__ *-en* cf **hjemme/-marked**

+__hei'me/sitter__ *-en, pl -e* (=*__/sitjar__) stay-at-home; esp. non-voter.

hei'me/styrke *-n* home guard.

+__hei'me/vant__ *A -* (=*__/van__, *__/vand__) at ease, at home.

hei'me/vern [/væ'rn] *-et* home guard.

+__hei'me/værende__ *A -* (staying) at home.

hei'm/fall *-et jur.* reversion; escheat.

hei'm/falle *V (infl as falle)* 1: **h-n** fallen in the clutches (**til** of); doomed. 2 *jur.* revert (**til** to).

hei'm/fast *A -* resident, settled.

hei'm/feste *V -a/+-et/*-e* localize; locate.

hei'm/fus *A* homesick, nostalgic.

hei'm/føding *-en* stay-at-home, *(pop.)* hick, innocent.

hei'm/føre *V -te* 1 bring, carry home: **h- en som sin brud** bring home sby as one's bride. 2 *merc.* import.

*__hei'm/hug__ *-en* homesickness, nostalgia.

*__hei'm/kom(m)e__ *-a* homecoming (e.g. for a new bride).

hei'm/kunnskap *-en* homemaking (as a subject in the schools).

hei'm/land *-et* homeland, native country.

hei'm/laus *A* homeless, outcast.

hei'mle *V -a/+-et* (=**hjemle**) 1 bear out, justify, warrant. 2 *jur.* convey, give title to, vest; prove one's title to.

*__hei'm/lengt__ *-en* homesickness.

hei'mlig *A -* (=+**hjemlig**) 1 domestic, home. 2 cozy, homelike, snug.

hei'm/lov *et/+-en* 1 furlough, leave (to go home). 2: **forunnes h-** *theol.* die.

hei'm/lån *-et* 1 borrowing books (for use outside the library): **lånekort for h-** borrower's card. 2 *merc.* home approval, trial (merchandise).

hei'm/om' *Av* by home: **svippe h-** run home for a moment.

hei'm/over [/åver] *P* 1 homeward; back. 2 *theol.* heavenward, toward the hereafter.

hei'm/rast *-a* the part of a farm's hill pasture lying closest to the house.

*__hei'ms/bolk__ *-en* continent.

hei'm/seter *-setra, pl +setrer/*setrar* summer farm at a relatively low altitude to permit early grazing in the spring and late grazing in the fall.

*__hei'm/sjuk__ *A* homesick, nostalgic.

Hei'ms/kringla *Prn* (Icelandic historical work compiled by Snorri Sturluson, historian and poet, 1179-1241, dealing chiefly with the kings of Norway down to 1177).

*__hei'msleg__ *A -* cf **heimlig**

*__hei'ms/skaut__ *-et* northern sky.

*__hei'ms/soge__ *-a* history of the world.

hei'm/stad *-en* 1 domicile; point of origin. 2 *merc.* home office. 3 *naut.* home port.

hei'mstad/lære *-a* study (in school) of local history and lore.

*__hei'mstad/rett__ *-en admin.* right to public support in one's own district.

hei'm/støing *-en* stay-at-home.

hei'm/støl *-en* mountain pasture near a farm.

+__hei'm/søke__ *V -te* (=*__-je__) 1 afflict, ravage, strike: **de h-te** the victims (of a disaster). 2 haunt, inflict oneself upon. 3 *bibl.* visit upon; punish: **fedrenes synder h-s på barna** the sins of the fathers are visited upon the children.

*__hei'm/til'__ *Av* homeward.

hei'm/veg *-en*: **på h-** on the way (journey, trip) home.

*__hei'm/vist__ *-a* domicile, residence.

hei'n *-en* hone, whetstone.

hei'ne *V *-a/+-te* hone.

+__hei're__ *-n* cf **hegre**[1]

hei's *-en* 1 elevator, hoist: **gå i h-en** be lost, go by the board; go to the dogs; **komme i h-en** get into hot water. 2 *naut.* (of a sail) hoist.

hei'se *V -te/*-a* hoist (up), raise: **h- flagget** put up, run up the flag; **h- hvitt flagg** run up the white flag (surrender); **h- opp buksene** hitch up one's trousers; **h- på skuldrene** shrug one's shoulders; **h- en rå** *naut.* hoist a yard; **h- seil** set sail; **h- seg opp** raise oneself.

+__hei'se/fører__ *-en, pl -e* (=*__-ar__) elevator operator.

hei'se/kran *-a* crane.

hei'se/tå'rn *-et* hoist.

hei't *A -t/+hett* 1 hot: **den h-e sone** the torrid zone; **bli h- om ørene** *fig.* color up, get flustered; **gjøre en helvete h-t** lead sby a dog's life, *(pop.)* make it hotter than hell for sby; **i h-este** (strong oath). 2 ardent, erotic, passionate; intense, violent: **det er h-t mellom dem** they are thicker than thieves. 3: **h-e viner** heady (fortified) wines (having an alcohol content of 16-21 %, e.g. port, sherry).

*__-heit__ *-a* cf **-het**

*__hei'te__[1] *-t* 1 name, term. 2 *hist.* descriptive poetical name (Old Norse poetry).

*__hei'te__[2] *V -a* cf **hete**[4]

*__hei'te__[3] *V heitte/het, heitt* cf **hete**[4]

*__hei'tne__ *V -a* cf **hetne**

*__hei't/vin__ *-en* cf **het/**

hei'v *pt of* **hive**

hekatom'be *-n* hecatomb.

*__he'ke__ *V -a* be doubtful, uncertain.

hekk'[1] *-en* 1 hedge. 2 hurdle (in race).

hekk'[2] *-en* 1 crib, hayrack. 2 *naut.* stern. 3 luggage rack (in R. R. car).

*__hekk'__[3] *pt of* **hange**

hekk'/båt *-en naut.* 1 stern boat. 2 cutter.

*__hek'ke__[1] *-a* frame on the side of sled to hold in a load.

hek'ke[2] *V -a/+-et* (of fowl) nest (brood, hatch).

+__hek'ke/løp__ *-et* (=*__/laup__) hurdles (race).

hek'ke/plass *-en* nesting place.

hekk'/motor *-en* rear engine.

+ Bokmål; * Nynorsk; ° Dialect.
After letter: ' stress (Acc. 1); ` tone, stress (Acc. 2); · length.
Below letter: . not pronounced.

hek'le[1] -*a* 1 flax comb, hackle. 2 hackle (fishing).

hek'le[2] *V* -*a*/+-*et* 1 crochet. 2 comb (flax, hemp), hackle.

+**hek'le/tøy** -*et* crochet work, crocheting.

hek'lung [-ong] -*en* *hist.* nickname of Magnus Erlingsson's supporters.

hek's -*a* 1 sorceress, witch; old hag. 2 *naut.* shackle.

heksame'ter -*eret*/+-*ret*, *pl* -*er*/+-*re* hexameter.

hek'se[1] *V* -*a*/+-*et* practice sorcery, witchcraft; bewitch: **han kan ikke h-** *fig.* he can't do the impossible, can't work miracles; **h- en til seg** draw sby by witchcraft.

***hek'se**[2] *V* -*te* 1 eat voraciously, wolf (food). 2 speak sharply: **h- etter ein** *(pop.)* take sby's head off.

hek'se/dans -*en* 1 wild disorder; running about helter-skelter. 2 *folk.* witches' dance (during the witches' sabbath).

hek'se/gryte -*a* witches' cauldron.

hek'se/kost [/kost] -*en* witches'-broom (also *bot.*).

hek'se/kunst -*en* sorcery, witchcraft: **det er ikke noen h-** that's an easy thing to do.

hek'seri -*et* black magic, sorcery, witchcraft.

hek'se/ring -*en* *bot.* fairy ring.

hek'se/sabbat -*en* witches' sabbath.

hek'se/skott -*et* (=+/**skudd**) crick in the back, touch of lumbago.

***hek'ste** *V* -*a* hold on by the skin of one's teeth.

hek't *N*: **på h-a til å** on the point, verge of; **vi greide det! om det var på h-a noen ganger** we made it! even though it was nip and tuck sometimes (Evensmo).

hek'tar -*et*/-*en*, *pl* - hectare (2.47 acres).

hek'te[1] -*a* hook: **h- og malje** h- and eye; **komme til h-ene** *fig.* come to one's senses.

hek'te[2] *V* -*a*/+-*et* 1 fasten, hook: **h- opp** unhook; **kjolen h-es i ryggen** the dress hooks up the back; **h- seg på en** *fig.* buttonhole sby. 2 arrest, take into custody, *(pop.)* run in.

hek'tisk *A* - 1 hectic. 2 *med.* feverish: **h- feber** hectic fever; **h- rødme** hectic flush.

hek'to -*et*/+-*en*, *pl* - hectogram (3.53 oz.).

hektogra'f -*en* hectograph.

hektografe're *V* -*te* hectograph.

hek'to/gram' -*met* (=**hg**) hectogram (3.53 oz.).

hek'to/liter -*en*, *pl* - (**hl**) hectoliter (2.75 bushels=22 gallons).

he'l[1] *N* (=+**hjel**): **i h-** dead, to death; **arbeide seg i h-** work oneself to death; **slå en i h-** kill sby; **slå tida i h-** kill time; **sulte i h-** die of starvation; **tie noe i h-** suppress (information).

+**he'l**[2] *A* cf **heil**[1]

+**he'l/aften** -*enen*, *pl* -*ener*/-*ner* (which lasts) a whole evening (e.g. film, play).

+**he'l/automa'tisk** *A* - fully automatic.

+**he'l/befa'ren** *A* -*ent*, *pl* -*ne* *naut.* able-bodied (seaman).

+**hel'bred** -*en* health: **ha en god h-** be in good h-.

+**helbre'de** *V* -*et* cure, heal, restore to health: **h- en for en sykdom** cure sby of an illness.

+**helbre'delse** -*n* cure; recovery.

***hel'd** *pr of* **halde**

+**he'ldags/post** [also he'l-] -*en* cf **heildags/**

hel'de[1] -*a* wooden eye, ring at the end of a rope.

hel'de[2] -*a* hobble (esp. for horses).

hel'de[3] *V* -*a*/+-*et* hobble.

hel'dig *A* - 1 fortunate, lucky: **en h- gris** a l- dog; **være h- med noe** be fortunate in sth; *(adv.)* **det traff seg så h- at vi hadde** luckily, we had; *(adv.)* **slippe h- fra noe** escape from sth unhurt, *fig.* get away with sth. 2 advantageous, favorable opportune; beneficial, desirable: **et h- innfall** a happy thought; **et h- øyeblikk** an opportune moment; **den h-ste måte** the best way. 3 successful (**med in**): *(adv.)* **eksperimentet falt h- ut** the experiment turned out well.

hel'dig/vis *Av* fortunately, luckily; as good luck would have it.

***hel'dt** *pt of* **halde**

***he'le**[1] -*a* hoarfrost.

+**he'le**[2] *et* (=**heile**[2]) entity, totality, whole: **i det h- tatt** cf **heil**[1].

+**he'le**[3] *V* -*a*/-*et*/-*te* (=***heile**[3]) heal (up): **h-es** be healed, heal (up).

he'le[4] *V* *-*a*/+-*te* *jur.* receive stolen goods, *(pop.)* fence.

***he'le**[5] *V* -*a* freeze (so that hoarfrost appears).

***he'le/fri** *A* -*tt* frost-free.

+**he'ler** -*en*, *pl* -*e* (=*-**ar**) *jur.* receiver of stolen goods, *(pop.)* fence: **h-en er ikke bedre enn stjeleren** the receiver is no better than the thief.

+**he'leri** -*et*, *pl* -/+-*er* (=***heling**) *jur.* receiving stolen property, *(pop.)* fencing stolen property.

+**he'l/fabrika'ta** *pl* finished goods.

+**he'l/figu'r** -*en* full length (e.g. portrait).

+**he'l/flaske** -*a* cf **heil/**

hel'g -*a*/+-*en* 1 holiday, Sunday (usu. incl. preceding evening); weekend: **ringe h-en inn** ring in the holiday (e.g. on Christmas eve). 2 sacred feeling, sanctity, solemnity: **med h- i sinnet** with a feeling of sanctity in one's heart.

Hel'ga *Prn (f)*

+**he'l/garde're** *V* -*te*: **h- seg** protect one's retreat (usu. *fig.*).

***hel'gd** -*a* holiness, sacredness, sanctity.

***hel'ge** *V* -*a* hallow; render inviolate, sacred.

Hel'ge *Prn (m)*

hel'ge/dag -*en* holiday, holy day.

+**hel'ge/klær** *pl* (=*/**klede**) Sunday (-go-to-meeting) clothes.

Hel'ge/land *Pln* southern part of Nordland county.

hel'ge/lending -*en* person from Helgeland.

hel'ge/mess(e) *en* All Saints' Day (November 1st).

hel'gen -*enen*, *pl* -*(e)ner* 1 *theol.* saint: **gjøre til h-** canonize. 2 person of great moral rectitude, piety: **han er ingen h-** he's no saint.

+**hel'gen/bilde** -*t* saint's image.

hel'gen/dyrking -*a* (=+-**else**) hagiolatry.

helgenin'ne -*a*/+-*en* (female) saint.

***hel'ge/torsdag** -*en* *eccl.* Ascension Day, Holy Thursday.

+**he'l/gryn** -*et* cf **heil/**

Hel'g/øy *Pln* twp, Troms.

Hel'g/øya *Pln* large island in Mjøsa, Nes twp, Hedmark.

he'l/heim -*en* *myth.* the Norse realm of the dead, ruled over by Hel, Loki's daughter.

he'l/hest -*en* *myth.* the steed ridden by Hel in seeking "the companions of Hel", i.e. those who had led evil lives on earth, or, according to another tradition, simply those dying of sickness and old age.

+**he'l/het** -*en* entirety, totality, whole: **i sin h-** as a whole; in full (e.g. a speech).

+**he'lhets/bilde** -*t* overall picture.

+**he'lhets/inntrykk** -*et* general impression.

+**he'lhets/virkning** -*en* general effect, total effect.

helikop'ter -*eret*/-*ret*, *pl* -*er*/+-*re* helicopter.

***he'ling** -*a* cf **heleri**

heliosko'p -*et* helioscope.

heliotro'p -*en* 1 heliotrope (surveyor's instrument). 2 *bot.* heliotrope (Heliotropium peruvianum). 3 *geol.* bloodstone.

he'lium -*et* *chem.* helium.

+**he'lko'rn/brød** -*et* cf **heil-**

hell'[1] -*et* 1 inclination: **på h-** on the slant; waning, on the wane. 2 declivity, incline, slope.

+**hell'**[2] -*et* 1 prosperity, success: **bli, være til h- for** be a benefit to; **ha h- med seg** be successful, succeed; **med h-** successfully. 2 fortune, good luck; piece of good luck: **h- i uhellet** a blessing in disguise; **h-et ville at** as luck would have it; **til alt h-** fortunately, luckily.

°**hell'**[3] *C* cf **eller**

Hell' *Pln* village, Lånke twp, Nord-Trøndelag.

Hel'las *Pln* Greece.

+**hell'/bringende** *A* - beneficial; fortunate, lucky.

hel'le[1] -*a* flag, flagstone; slab of rock.

hel'le[2] *V* *helte* 1 lean: **h- med (på) hodet** hang one's head; **h- seg fram** lean forward; stoop; **h- seg inn til** lean against; **h- seg litt bortpå sengen** lie down and rest awhile. 2 pour: **h- en på dør** throw sby out on his ear; **h- olje på opprørt hav** pour oil on troubled waters; **h- ut** empty. 3 incline, slant, slope (**mot** to, toward); tip: **h- til (en oppfatning)** *fig.* incline, lean towards (a certain view). 4 *poet.* come to an end (e.g. a day); go down, set (e.g. the sun).

hellebar'd -*en* halberd.

hel'le/ba'rn -*et* *zool.* young halibut (Hippoglossus vulgaris).

hel'le/brott -*et* (=*/**brot**, +/**brudd**) quarry (which produces flagstones).

+**helledus'sen** *I* dear me, goodness.

hel'le/fisk -*en* *zool.* halibut (Hippoglossus vulgaris).

hel'le/flyndre -*a* *zool.* halibut (Hippoglossus vulgaris).

+**hel'le/legge** *V* -*la*, -*lagt* (=*-**je**): **h-lagt** paved with flagstone.

helle'n -*en* (=+**hellener**) Greek, Hellene.

+**helle'ner** -*en*, *pl* -*e* cf **hellen**

hellenis'tisk *A* - Hellenistic.

helle'nsk *A* - Greek, Hellenic.

hel'ler[1] -*en*, *pl* +-*e* mountain cave, overhanging rock.

hel'ler[2] *Av* 1 (*comp. of* **gjerne**) rather; just as soon: **h- enn gjerne** most willingly, with the greatest of pleasure; **håret var h- mørkt enn lyst** the hair was dark rather than light; **jo før jo h-** the sooner the better; **han ville jo intet h-** he asked for nothing better (Hoel). 2 either: **h- ikke (ikke h-)** not e-, nor; **ikke jeg, ikke du h-** not I, not you e-. 3 *archaic* (as a question): **hva h-** or perhaps.

hel'le/ristning *-*a*/+-*en*, *pl* *-*ar* *archeol.* Stone and Bronze Age rock carving (esp. in Norway and Sweden).

hel'le/stein -*en* 1 flag, flagstone. 2 slate (or other stone that splits or laminates).

hel'le/tak -*et* slate roof.

+**hel'lig** *A* - (=***heilag**) hallowed, holy, sacred; *derog.* pious, sanctimonious: **de h-e** the saints; **de h-e tre konger** the Magi, the Three Wise Men; **de siste dages h-e** the Latter-day Saints; **det h-e** sacred things; **det aller h-ste** the Holy of Holies; **en h- plikt** a sacred duty; **H- Olav** St. O-; **o h-e enfoldighet** oh sacred simplicity; **holde hviledagen h-** keep the sabbath.

+**hel'lig/brøde** -*n* sacrilege.

+**hel'lig/dag** -*en* holiday: **søn- og h-er** Sundays and h-s.

+**hel'lig/dom'** -*men* 1 (sacred) relic. 2 sanctuary, shrine, temple: **h-mens forheng** *bibl.* the veil of the sanctuary (Leviticus 4, 6).

hel'lige *V* -*et* (=***heilage**) 1 consecrate, dedicate: **h- seg til noe** dedicate, devote oneself to sth. 2 *bibl.* consecrate, hallow, sanctify: **h-et vorde dit navn** hallowed be thy name (Matthew 6, 9); **jeg er Herren som h-er Israel** I the Lord do sanctify I- (Ezekiel 37, 28).

+**hel`lig/gjøre** *V -gjorde, -gjort* consecrate, hallow, sanctify.
+**hel`lig/het** *-en* holiness, sacredness, sanctity: **Hans H-** His Holiness.
+**hel`lig/holde** *V -holdt, -holdt* keep holy, observe (e.g. the sabbath).
+**helligtrekong`ers/dag** *-en* Epiphany, Twelfth Night.
+**helligån'd** *-en*: **den H-** *theol.* the Holy Ghost.
hel`ling *-a/+-en* **1** leaning, stooping, tilting. **2** declivity, incline, slope: **passende h-** just the right s-; **det er på h-en med hans krefter** *fig.* his strength is ebbing away.
+**he`l/lodd** *-et* full share (in a lottery).
+**he`l/melk** [also he'l/] *-a/-en* whole milk.
Hel`mer *Prn (m)*
hel`ming *-en* one half.
+**hel`ning** *-en* **1** declivity, slope. **2** *fig.* inclination, leaning, tendency (**mot** toward).
+**he`l/omven·ding** *-a/-en* about-face (in gymnastics).
***he`l/orar** *pl* bewilderment, confusion.
hel`se[1] *-a* health, vigor: **få igjen full h-** recover one's health completely; **ha god h-** be in good health.
hel`se[2] *V -te* (=+**hilse**) **1** greet, nod to (in greeting): **jeg skal h- fra mor og si takk for lånet** mother says (hello and) thank you (for the loan of sth); **jeg skal h- og si han så morsk ut** *fam.* I'll tell you, he looked fierce (Wiers-Jenssen); **sangeren ble h-t med sterkt bifall** the singer was greeted with (by) heavy applause; **vær h-et** *bibl., obs.* hail. **2** *mil.* salute; **h- med flagget** *naut.* dip the flag (the colors). **3** (with *prep.* and *adv.*): **hels heime** (+**hils hjemme**) greet everyone at home; **h- igjen** return a greeting; **h- på en** greet sby; call on, go and see sby.
hel`se/bot *-a* cure, remedy: **det er h- i skogluften** there is medicine in the forest air.
+**hel`se/bringende** *A -* curative, healthful.
hel`se/direktora·t *-et* Bureau of Health.
hel`se/fa·rlig *A -* injurious to health.
hel`se/heim *-en* sanitarium.
hel`se/laus *A* broken in health, invalid.
hel`se/lære *-a/+-en* hygiene.
hel`se/nemnd [/nemd] *-a* board of health.
hel`se/pass *-et* bill of health.
hel`se/råd *-et* board of health.
***hel`se/sam·** *A* healthy, sound, vigorous.
hel`se/slå *V infl as* **slå**[2] cripple, maim.
hel`se/stasjo'n *-en* clinic, first aid station.
hel`se/stell *-et* public health service.
hel'se/sterk *A* healthy, sound, vigorous; invigorating.
+**hel`se/søster** *-eren/-era, pl -re(r)* public health nurse.
hel`se/tilsyn *-et* hygiene.
+**he`l/side** *-a/-en* full page: **en h-s annonse** a full-page advertisement.
hel`sig *A -* healthy, sound; invigorating.
hel`sike *N* hell: **h-s rart** queer as hell (Evensmo).
+**he`l/silke** *-n* cf **heil/**
hel`sing *-a* (=+**hilsen**) greeting, salutation; regards: **bud og h-** greetings, welcome; **sende en sin h-** give sby one's regards. **2** salute: **besvare en h-** return a s-.
Helsingfor's *Pln* Helsingfors, Finland (Swedish name).
Hel`sinki [usu. but wrongly -sing'ki] *Pln* Helsinki, Finland (Finnish name).
+**he`l/skinnet** *A -* cf **heil/skinna**
+**he`l/skjegg** *-et* beard.
he`l/sott *-a/+-en* *poet.* fatal disease, mortal illness; **ligge i h-** lie at death's door.
+**he`l/spenn** *N* cf **heil/**
hel`st *Av* **1** preferably, rather: **De bør h- gå** you had better go; **h- uten** preferably without; **jeg ville h-** I would prefer to; **jeg vil h- ikke gjøre det** I would rather not do so. **2: hva som h-** anything (whatever); **hvem som h-** anyone; **noe som h-** anything; **når som h-** any moment, any time.
+**he`l/stat** *-en* cf **heil/**
+**he`l/steke** *V -te* cf **heil/steike**
+**he`l/støpt** *A -* (=***heil/støypt**) cast in one piece; harmonious, well-integrated; genuine, unalloyed: **en h- figur** a clearly-drawn figure; **en h- personlighet** a sterling personality.
+**he`l/søsken** *pl* full brothers and sisters.
hel`t *-en* hero (champion; famous person; principal person of a novel, play): **ta det som en h-** take it like a man.
hel`te/dikt *-et* epic.
hel`te/dyrking *-a/+-en* hero worship.
hel`te/dåd *-en* bold exploit, heroic deed.
hel`te/modig *A -* brave, heroic.
hel`te/mot *-et* heroic valor, heroism.
hel`te/motig *A -* cf **/modig**
hel`te/rolle *-a/+-en* part, role of the hero (theater).
+**hel`te/sagn** [/sang'n] *-et* heroic legend.
hel`te/teno·r *-en* *mus.* dramatic tenor (suited to heroic, e.g. Wagnerian, roles).
heltin`ne *-a/+-en* heroine.
+**he`l/ull** *-a* cf **heil/**
***he`l/uv** *-en* inconsiderate, thoughtless person.
***he`luvsleg** *A -* inconsiderate, thoughtless.
+**hel`vede** *-t* cf **helvete**
hel`vete *-t* **1** hell: **gjøre en h- hett** make it hot for one; **gå til h-** go to h-, go to rack and ruin. **2** *(adj.)*: **h-s** damned, hell of a; hellish, infernal; **en (aller) h-s kar** a hell of a fellow; **h-s larm** damnable noise, racket; infernal din.
hel`vetes/eld *-en* (=+**/ild**) *med.* shingles (Herpes zoster).
hel`vetes/maski·n *-en* time bomb.
hel`vetes/stein *-en* *chem.* nitrate of silver.
***helvt** [hel'ft] *-a* half.
hemisfæ're *-n* hemisphere *(geog., anat.)*.
***hem`je** *V -a* cf **hemme**
hem`me *V -a/+-et* (=***hemje**) hamper, hinder, inhibit; check, restrain; arrest, retard: **h-et i veksten** retarded in growth.
+**hem`melig** *A -* **1** secret; concealed, confidential; clandestine: **holde det h-** keep it dark, keep it a secret (**for** from); **h- avstemning** secret ballot. **2** occult; inscrutable: **h-e vitenskaper** the black arts, black magic.
+**hem`melig/het** *-en* **1** secrecy: **i h-** secretly. **2** secret: **betro en en h-** let sby in on a s-; **en offentlig h-** an open s-; **tie med en h-** keep a s-. **3: h-en** the explanation, the (secret) method (**i** of). **4** mystery: **h-er** *bibl.* mysteries; **dere er det gitt å få vite himlenes rikes h-er** it is given unto you to know the mysteries of the kingdom of heaven (Matthew 13,11).
+**hem`melighets/full** *A* **1** secretive. **2** mysterious.
+**hem`melighetsfull/het** *-en* **1** secretiveness. **2** mysteriousness.
+**hemmelighets/kremmeri·** *-et* (undue, unwarranted) secretiveness.
+**hem`melig/holde** *V -holdt, -holdt* keep dark, keep secret.
Hem`(m)ing *Prn (m)*
***hem'n** *-en* cf **hevn**
***hem'nar** *-en* cf **hevner**
***hem`nd** *-a* cf **hevn**
***hem`ne** *V -a/-de* cf **hevne**
Hem`ne *Pln* twp, Sør-Trøndelag.
Hem`/nes· *Pln* twp, Nordland.
***hem`n/fus** *A* evengeful, vindictive.
hem`ning **-a/+-en* **1** hindrance, restriction. **2** *psych.* inhibition: **damene var i ferd med å vrenge av seg sine h-er** the ladies were busy getting rid of their i-s (Hoel).
+**hem`nings/løs** *A* (=***/laus**) uninhibited, unrestrained.
hemoglobi'n *-et* hemoglobin.
hemorroide [hemåro-i'de] *-n* hemorrhoid.
hem`pe[1] *-a* loop (esp. on clothing).
***hem`pe**[2] *V -a* **1** detach, tear off. **2: h- seg opp** improve, thrive.
hem`pe/laus *A* (=+**/løs**) loopless, without loops.
+**hem`se**[1] *-n* (=**hems, hemse/dal**) small loft opening on the living room (in a cabin), a kind of balcony bedroom.
***hem`se**[2] *V -a* **1** grab, snatch; grope for words. **2: h- seg** collect one's thoughts, wits.
Hem`se/dal *Pln* twp, Buskerud.
hem`/sko *-en, pl -r/+-* drag, wheel lock (on a wagon); *fig.* drag, hindrance: **være en h- på noe** hamper, hinder sth.
***hem`te** *V -a* collect, gather, pick.
+**hen'** *Av* away, off, over: **de siste rop døde h- i natten** the last shouts died away in the night (Bjørnson); **falle h- i en døs** fall off in a doze, doze off; **gå h-** (of time) go by, go past, pass by; **hvor bærer det h-?** where is (she, he, it) going?; **hvor skal du h-?** where are you going? where are you off to?; **han gikk h- og døde** he up and died; **se, stirre h- for seg** look, stare vacantly in front of oneself; **si h- for seg** say dreamily, vacantly to oneself. (For other verb phrases see under the verbs; see also **henad, henimot, henover,** etc.)
+**hen'/ad** (of time) towards.
+**hen`/blikk** *-et*: **med h- på** with an eye, a view to.
**hen`de**[1] [+hen`ne] *-t* event, incident; coincidence.
hen`de[2] *N*: **i h-** in hand, in one's hands.
hen`de**[3] [+hen`ne] *V +-te/*-e* **1 happen, occur, take place: **det h-er** it (sometimes) happens (**det h-te han spurte meg** he would sometimes ask me); **det kan h- at jeg må** I may have to (**det kunne h-** I might); **kan h-** maybe; **det h-er seg** it may occur; **det kunne vel h- at Herreper ville ha henne til dronning** you may be sure H- wanted her as his queen (Asbjørnsen). **2** befall, happen to: **det har hendt henne en ulykke** she has met with an accident; **slikt kan h- den beste** these things will happen.
***hen`de**[4] *A -* : **ein h- gong** rarely.
hen`delig *A -* accidental, chance: **et h- uhell** one of those things (=that could happen to anybody).
+**hen`delse** *-n* cf **hending**
+**hen`delses/rik** *A* eventful.
hen'der *pl of* **hand,** +**hånd**
+**hen'der/vridende** *A -* wringing one's hands.
***hen`des/løyse** *-a* trifle; absurdity.
hen`dig *A -* **1** deft, dexterous. **2** convenient, handy, practical.
hen`ding *-a* (=+**hendelse**) **1** event, happening, incident. **2** accident, chance: **ved en (ren) h-** by (pure) c-.
hen`dt *A -* **1** deft, dextrous, handy: **være h- som det høver** be able to handle any problem that comes up, be a jack of all trades. **2: like h-** indifferent.
-hen`dt *A -* -handed, e.g. in **skjelvh-, tomh-**.
+**hen'/falle** *V -falt, -falt*: **h- i grublerier** fall into a reverie; **være h-n til** abandon oneself to, be addicted to.
+**hen'/føre** *V -te* **1** classify, group: **h- til** refer to. **2** entrance, transport.

+ Bokmål; * Nynorsk; ° Dialect.
After letter: ' stress (Acc. 1); ` tone, stress (Acc. 2); · length.
Below letter: . not pronounced.

+hen'/fø·rt *A* - entranced, transported.

***heng'[1]** *-en*: **det er på h-en eller sprengen** one extreme or the other.

heng'[2] *-et dial., poet.* 1 curtain. 2 foliage. 3 declivity, slope: **få h- på skiene** come out (in ski jump) with skis too far down in back. 4 breeze, light gust of wind.

***heng'[3]** *pr of* **hange**

+hen'/gav *pt of* **-gi**

***heng'e[1]** *-t* hanger; something hanging.

+heng'e[2] *V hang, hengt* (=***hange**) 1 be hanging, hang; droop, sag: **h-ende mustasje** drooping moustache; **h- i en tråd (et hår)** hang by a thread (a hair); **h- over bøkene** pore over one's books; **treet h-er fullt av frukt** the tree is loaded with fruit. 2 hang about; idle, loaf, loiter: **han h-er i klubben bestandig** he's always hanging around the club; **stå og h-** lounge about, stand around idle. 3 cling, stick: **h- (fast) i noe** get caught, stuck in sth; **h- i skjørtene på noen** be tied to sby's apron strings; tag after (e.g. one's mother); 4 (with *prep.* and *adv.*): **h- i** keep at it, keep it up, work away; **h- igjen** be retarded, delayed, held back; **h- sammen (i hop)** hang, hold, stick together; be connected, tied up (**med** with) (**det h-er ikke riktig sammen** there's sth wrong here; **hvordan h-er dette sammen?** what is the truth of this matter?); **h- på** hang on, stick to (**h- på som kleggen** hang on like a leech; **vil du være med, så heng på** if you want to come along, hang on (Asbjørnsen)); **h- (med) ved** hold to, stick to.

+heng'e[3] *V -te* (=***hengje[2]**) 1 hang (clothes, a decoration, person, picture, etc., **opp** up). 2: **h- med hodet (vingene)** hang one's head (wings); **h- med nebbet (ørene)** be down in the mouth, mope. 3 (*refl.*): **h- seg** hang oneself; hang, hold on, stick (**i** to); **h- seg fast** cling; **h- seg i den minste ubetydelighet** seize upon the least trifle; **h- seg på** hang on to; *fig.* cling to, stick to.

+heng'e/aks *-et* (=***hengje/**) *bot.* melic grass (Melica nutans).

+heng'e/bjørk *-a* (=***hengje/**) *bot.* weeping birch (Betula verrucosa pendula).

+heng'e/bratt *A* - (=***hengje/**) abrupt, precipitous.

+heng'e/bru *-a* (=***hengje/**) suspension bridge.

+heng'e/hode *-t* (=***hengje/hovud**) killjoy, wet blanket; puritanical person.

+heng'e/køye *-a* (=***hengje/**) hammock.

+heng'e/lås *-en/-et* (=***hengje/**) padlock.

+heng'e/myr *-a* (=***hengje/**) quagmire.

+heng'er *-en, pl -e* (=***hangar**) 1 (clothes) hanger. 2 trailer (e.g. streetcar pulled by a lead car).

+hen'/gi *V -gav, -gitt* 1: **h- seg i** abandon oneself to, indulge in. 2: **h- seg til** dedicate oneself, devote oneself to; *derog.* become addicted to, give oneself up to (e.g. drink).

+hengi'velse *-n* 1 devotion (**til** to), loyalty, selflessness. 2 abandonment; giving oneself (to another).

+hen'/given *A -ent, pl -ne* attached, devoted: **være en h-** be devoted to sby; **Deres h-ne** sincerely yours.

+hengi'ven/het *-en* attachment, devotion: **nære h- for en** be fond of sby.

***heng'je[1]** *-a* 1 fastening, hinge. 2 appendage.

***heng'je[2]** *V -de* cf **henge[3]**

***heng'/sam·** *A* clinging.

heng'sel *-la/-elet/-let, pl +-ler/*-el* (=**hengsle**) hinge: **løfte en dør av h-lene** take a door off its h-s.

heng'sle[1] *-a/-et* cf **hengsel**

heng'sle[2] *V -a/+-et* attach by hinges, hinge.

heng'slet(e) *A* - ungainly.

+hen'/gå *V -gikk, -gått* elapse, pass.

+hen'/hold *N*: **i h- til** *jur.* in accordance, conformity with; pursuant, with reference to.

+hen'/holde *V -holdt, -holdt*: **h- seg til** *jur.* refer to, rely upon.

+hen'holds/vis *Av* respectively.

+hen'/høre *V -te*: **h- til** come under, pertain, relate to.

+hen'/imo·t *P* 1 towards (time). 2 about, approximately (number).

+hen'/kaste *V -et* let fall (a remark), (casually) throw out (a hint): **h-et ytring** casual remark.

***hen'ker** *pl of* **honk**

+hen'/la *pt of* **-legge**

+hen'/lede *V -et*: **h- ens oppmerksomhet på noe** call, draw sby's attention to sth.

+hen'/legge *V -la, -lagt* 1 lay, place; move: **scenen er henlagt til en by** the scene is laid in a city. 2 postpone, shelve, sidetrack: **h- en sak** *jur.* dismiss a case.

***hen'nar** *Pn* cf **hennes**

+hen'ne[1] *Av* away, off (usu. with adv. of place): **der h-** over there; **hvor har du vært h-?** where have you been?; **jeg vet ikke hvor han er h-** I have no idea where he is; **hans tanker var annetsteds h-** his thoughts were elsewhere.

hen'ne[2] *Pn ob of* **hun[6], ho[2]**

hen'nes *Pn po of* **hun[6], ho[2]**

Hen'ning *Prn(m)*

Hen'nings/vær *Pln* fishing village, Vågan twp, Nordland.

+hen'/over [/åver] *P* across, over to.

+hen'/regne [/reine] *V -et*: **h- til** class among, include.

+hen'/rette *V -a/-et* execute, put to death.

+hen'/rettelse *-n* execution.

Hen'rik *Prn(m)*

+hen'/rivende *A* - charming, enchanting, lovely.

+hen'/rykkelse *-n* delight, ecstasy, rapture: **falle i h- over noe** go into raptures over sth.

+hen'/rykt *A* - delighted, enchanted, enraptured (**over** at).

+hen'/sank *pt of* **-synke**

+hen'/satte *pt of* **-sette**

+hense'ende *-n/-t* regard, respect: **i den h-** in this (that) respect; **i h- til** with regard to; **i så h-** in that regard.

+hen'/sette *V -satte, -satt* 1 move, place, transport: **hensatt i hypnose** (usu. *fig.*) put in a trance. 2: **h- seg til** imagine oneself in, transport oneself in imagination to.

+hen'/sikt *-en* intention, purpose; end, object: **ha til h-** have as a purpose, intend (**å** to); **h-en helliger midlet** the end justifies the means; **med h-** intentionally, purposely; **svare til h-en** answer the purpose.

+hen'sikts/løs *A* futile, pointless, purposeless.

+hen'sikts/messig *A* - appropriate, expedient, suitable.

+hen'sikts/svarende *A* - appropriate, expedient, suitable.

+hen'/skyte *V -skjøt, -skutt*: **h- en sak til domstolens avgjørelse** *jur.* refer a matter to the court's decision; **h- seg under** plead.

+hen'/slengt *A* - 1 discarded, thrown away. 2: **en h- ytring** a casual remark; **ligge, sitte h-** lounge, sprawl.

+hen'/slepe *V -te* live (a dreary existence): **h- et helt liv i fattigdom** drag out one's whole life in poverty.

+hen'/sovet [/såvet] *A* - passed away: **h- i Herren** died in the Lord; **de h-de** the dead.

+hen'/stand *-en* 1 *jur.* continuance; reprieve. 2: **på h-** *merc.* on credit, on time.

+hen'/stille *V -stilte, -stilt* refer, submit: **h- til en** request sby (to take a matter under consideration).

+hen'/stilling *-en* appeal, request.

+hen'/stå *V -stod, -stått* be left, remain unsettled (a question).

+hen'/syn *-et* consideration, regard, respect: **av h- til** out of respect for; on account of; **med h- til** with regard to; **ta h- til** consider, take account of; have consideration for, respect; **under h- til** in consideration of.

+hen'/synke *V -sank, -sunket* be absorbed in, lose oneself in.

+hen'syns/betegnelse [/betei·-] *-n* indirect object.

+hen'syns/full *A* considerate, kind, thoughtful.

+hen'syns/fullhet *-en* consideration, regard, thoughtfulness.

+hen'syns/løs *A* 1 inconsiderate, thoughtless. 2 ruthless. 3 reckless, wanton.

+hen'syns/løshet *-en* 1 lack of consideration, thoughtlessness. 2 ruthlessness. 3 recklessness.

+hen'syn/tagen *en* consideration, regard.

hen'te *V -a/+-et* 1 fetch; go after, go and get; bring (a book, chair, doctor, drink, policeman, etc.). 2 come for, come to get; come and take: **vi h-er og bringer** we pick up and deliver; (oath) **fanden h- meg** devil take me, I'll be damned; **vi ble h-et på stasjonen** we were picked up at the station. 3 derive, draw; get: **stoffet er h-et fra middelalderen** the material is drawn (taken) from the Middle Ages.

+hen'/tyde *V -et*: **h- til** allude, refer to, hint at (esp. sth unpleasant).

+hen'/ty·dning *-en* allusion, hint; insinuation.

+hen'/ved *P* close to, nearly.

+hen'/vende *V -te* 1 address, direct; turn: **h- oppmerksomheten på** call, draw attention to. 2: **h- seg til** apply to, approach, turn to.

+hen'/vendelse *-n* application, communication, inquiry (**til** of).

+hen'/vise *V -te* 1 refer (i.e. direct for information), submit: **h- saken til retten** *jur.* let the court decide the matter. 2 allude, refer (**til** to). 3: **være h-t til** be thrown upon (e.g. one's own initiative, resources); compelled, limited (**til** to).

+hen'/vi·sning *-en* reference (**til** to): **under h- til** with r- to.

hen'/ånde *V -et poet.* breathe (lightly), whisper: **et fint henåndende pust av den første kulde** a gentle breath of the first frost (Hamsun).

***hep'ne[1]** *-a* cf **heppe[1]**

***hep'ne[2]** *pl of* **heppen**

***hepp'** *-en* cf **heppe[1]**

***hep'pe[1]** *-a* fortune, (good) luck.

***hep'pe[2]** *V -a* happen (accidentally).

***hep'peleg** *A* - fortunate, lucky.

***hep'pen** *A -e/-i, pl hepne* fortunate, lucky.

***her[1]** [hæ'r] *-en* cf **hær**

her[2] [hæ'r] *Av* here (of place): **alt dette h-** all this (business, stuff), all these (things); **denne, dette, disse h-** this one, these right h-; **det er h- vi skal av** h- is where we get off; **h- er fredelig** it's peaceful h-; **h- har vi ham** (look) h- he is; **h- i landet** in this country (as opposed to other countries); **h- inn, h- inne** in h-; **h- ned, h- nede** down h-; **h- omkring** around h-; hereabouts; **h- opp, h- oppe** up h-; **h- ut, h- ute** out h-; **pu, h- blir for varmt** phew, it's too warm h-; (in hum. dialogue:) **Vær nå forsiktig! Forsiktig meg h- og forsiktig meg der!** (*pop.*) Be careful! Careful shmareful!

***herad** [hæ'rad] *-et* cf **herred**

Herad [hæ'rad] *Pln* twp, Vest-Agder.

***herads/styre** *-t* cf **herreds/**

+heral'diker *-en, pl -e* (=***-ar**) expert in heraldry.

heraldikk' *-en* heraldry.

heral'disk *A* - heraldic.

+**her'/av** *Av* of this: **h- følger at** it follows from this that.
herba'rium *-iet, pl +-ier/*-ium* herbarium.
+**her'/berge¹** *-t* 1 lodging, shelter. 2 *hist.* inn.
+**her'/berge²** *V -et* give shelter to, lodge.
***her'/byrge** *-t* cf **/berge¹**
her'd *-a* 1 *archaic, dial.* shoulder. 2 *poet.* hearth.
her'de *V -a/+-et/*-e* 1 harden: **h- stål** temper steel. 2 harden, inure; *fig.* harden, steel (one's heart). 3: **h- seg** make oneself hardy; nerve, steel oneself (for a blow).
***her'de/blad** *-et* shoulder blade.
her'de/brei *A +-t/*-tt* broad-shouldered.
***her/deild** [hæ'r/] *-a* cf **hær/**
her'dig *A - dial.* hardy, robust; resolute, staunch.
her'ding *-a* hardening, induration; test: ***når det ber i h-a** when it comes to the test.
Her'dla *Pln* twp, Hordaland.
+**her'dne** *V -et lit.* harden, indurate.
***her'd/sam·** *A* enduring, persevering.
her'dsle *-a* (of steel) temper(ing).
He're/foss *Pln* twp, Aust-Agder.
her'/etter *Av* after this; henceforth, hereafter, in the future.
her'etter/dags *Av* from now on, in the future.
***her/fang** [hæ'r/] *-et* cf **hær/**
***her/ferd** [hæ'r/fær] *-a* cf **hær/**
+**her'/fra** *Av* (=*/**frå**) from here; from this: **h- går $ 10** from this must be deducted $10; **vi må se å komme oss h-** we had better get out of here.
+**her'/iblan't** *Av* among them, including.
+**herinn'** *Av* cf **her²**
+**herin'ne** *Av* cf **her²**
her'je *V -a/+-et* 1 devastate, lay waste, ravage (with fire and sword); harry, plunder. 2 *fig.* play havoc with, ravage; leave its mark: **et h-et ansikt** a r-d face.
her'k *-et* 1 junk, rubbish, scrap; nonsense, *(pop.)* balderdash, tommyrot. 2 mob, rabble, riffraff.
***her'ke** *-t* 1 mob, rabble, riffraff. 2 hindrance, obstacle.
***her'ke/muge** *-n* mob, rabble, riffraff.
***her'ker** *pl of* **hork²**
***her'kje** *V -te* 1 lash, secure sth sloppily. 2 resist, retard.
+**her'/komst** *-en* ancestry, descent, parentage.
her'kules/arbeid *-et* Herculean task.
herku'lisk *A -* Herculean.
***her'leg/dom** *-(m)en* glory, magnificence, splendor.
her'lig *A -* 1 glorious, grand, magnificent; *ironic* fine, lovely (e.g. mess): **et h- menneske** a grand person; **et h- måltid** a delightful meal. 2 complete, thoroughgoing: **han fikk h- juling** he got a sound drubbing; **i den h-ste uorden** in the wildest disorder; **han var h- og full** he was gloriously drunk (Hamsun).
+**her'lig/het** *-en* 1 glory, magnificence, splendor: **leve i h- og glede** live in style, live happily; **Salomo i all sin h-** Solomon in all his glory; **hele h-en** *ironic* the whole lot, the whole kit and caboodle. 2 *jur.* manorial right; natural resource; possession, treasure.
***her'm** *-et* 1 mimicry. 2 quotation.
hermafroditt' *-en* hermaphrodite.
her'me¹ *-a* 1 anecdote, tale. 2 herma (pillar with head, orig. of Hermes).
her'me² *V -a/+-et/+-te/*-de* *1 quote. 2: **h- etter** ape, copy, mimic.
her'/med *Av* 1 herewith, with this; *merc.* enclosed. 2 so, thus, with that.
her'me/kråke *-a derog.* imitator, mimic.
her'melin *-en* 1 *zool.* ermine (Mustela erminia). 2 ermine (fur).
+**her'mer** *-en, pl -e* (=*-**ar**) mimic, storyteller.
***her'me/teikn** *-et* quotation marks.
hermetikk' *-en* canned food, canned goods.
hermetikk'/boks *-en* (tin) can.
+**hermetikk'/å'pner** *-en, pl -e* (=*/**opnar**) can opener.
hermetise're *V -te* can, preserve.
herme'tisk *A -* hermetic: **h- lukket** airtight, hermetically sealed.
Her'mod *Prn(m) myth.* name of Odin's messenger.
***hernad** [hæ'rna] *-en* cf **hær-**
+**herne'd** *Av* cf **her²**
+**herne'de** *Av* cf **her²**
he'ro *-en* demigod, hero.
hero'isk *A -* heroic.
heroisme [-o-is'me] *-n* heroism.
herol'd *-en* 1 harbinger, herald. 2 *hist.* herald.
+**heropp'** *Av* cf **her²**
+**herop'pe** *Av* cf **her²**
+**he'ros** *df heroen, pl heroer* cf **hero**
herostra'tisk *A -* notorious: **h- berømmelse** unenviable notoriety.
herr' *N* Mr. (also abbrev. **hr.**; may be used with titles, when it must be omitted in English: *Hr. doktor, hr. professor*, etc.).
her're¹ *-n* 1 lord, master: **h-n til Østråt** the lord of Ø-; **være h- over** be master of, have control over. 2 gentleman; sir; (when addressing a king) sire: **en h- på byen** a man about town (title of book by P. L. Eidem); **mine damer og h-r** ladies and gentlemen; **min h-** sir (now usu. *hum.* or *ironic*). 3 *eccl.* Lord: **Gud H-n** the L- God; **et h-ns vær** devilish weather; **i h-ns navn** for heaven's sake; **i mange h-ns år** for many a long year.
her're² *Av pop.* (this, these) here: **alt dette h-** all this sort of thing; **denne h- kameraten min** *(pop)* this here buddy of mine.
+**her'red** *-et, pl -/-er* (=***herad**) 1 *admin.* township. 2 *hist.*—hundred.
her're/dag *-en hist.* council of nobles (Denmark, Norway).
***her're/dom** *-(m)en* dominion, mastery.
+**her'reds/kasse** *-a/-en* treasury of a township.
+**her'reds/kasse'rer** *-en, pl -e* township treasurer.
+**her'reds/rett** *-en jur.* lower (local) court (=justice of the peace).
+**her'reds/styre** *-t* township board.
her're/dømme *-t* dominion, mastery: **ha h- over** have command, control of.
her're/ekvipe'ring *-a/+-en* men's furnishings; men's (ready-made) clothing store.
her're/folk *-et* 1 aristocracy, nobility. 2 master race.
her're/frisø'r *-en* barber.
her're/gu'd *I* good God; good grief, ye gods.
+**her're/gå'rd** *-en* estate, manor.
her're/konfeksjo'n *-en* men's (ready-made) clothing.
her're/laus *A* (=+/**løs**) ownerless: **h- hund** stray dog.
her're/mann *-en, pl -menn/*-menner* 1 *archaic* aristocrat, nobleman; lord of a manor, squire: **leve som en h-** live a life of ease and luxury, *(pop.)* live the life of Riley. 2 a would-be aristocrat, one with the manners and tastes of a nobleman.
her're/måltid *-et* sumptuous meal.
Her'ren *Prn* The Lord.
her're/sete *-t, pl +-r/*-* castle, country estate, manor.
+**her're/værelse** *-t* 1 library, smoking room. 2 men's room.
+**herrnhu'ter** *-en, pl -e* (=*-**ar**, ***herrnhut**) *eccl.* Moravian Brethren.
herrnhu'tisk *A - eccl.* Moravian.
her'se¹ *-n hist.* local chieftain (esp. West Norway).
her'se² *V -a/+-et* bully, order around.
her'sens *A -* (mild oath) **denne h- menneskenatur** this confounded human nature (Ibsen).
***her/setje** [hæ'r/] *V -sette* cf **hær/**
***her'sk** *A* cf **harsk**
her'/skap *-et, pl -/+-er* 1 master and mistress of a household. 2 gentry, persons of rank: **mine h-er** ladies and gentlemen.
herska'pelig *A -* (=***her'skapleg**) elegant, luxurious; fit for a king.
her'skaps/hus *-et* 1 residence (in the grand style). 2 first family, socially prominent family (in a town).
***her/skare** [hæ'r/] *-n* cf **hær/**
her'ske *V -a/+-et* 1 reign, rule (**over** over): **synden skal ikke h- over dere** for sin shall not have dominion over you (Romans 6, 14); **de h-ende** the rulers, ruling class. 2 predominate, prevail: **h-ende** customary, prevailing; **den h-ende religion** the established religion.
+**her'sker** *-en, pl -e* (=*-**ar**) master, ruler, sovereign: **natten er livet og kvinnen dets h-** the night is life and woman its sovereign (Hamsun).
+**herskerin'ne** *-a/-en* (=***herskarinne**) queen, (female) sovereign.
+**her'sker/mine** *-a/-en* (=*-**ar**/) commanding, dictatorial air.
her'ske/sjuk *A* (=+/**syk**) ambitious, domineering, power mad.
***her'skne** *V -a* cf **harskne**
***her/steds** [hæ'r/] *Av* here, locally.
***her/stell** [hæ'r/] *-et* cf **hær/**
+**her'/til·** *Av* 1 (to) here. 2: **h- kommer** in addition to this, to this must be added; **h- kommer omkostningene** *merc.* to this we must add the charges (e.g. for handling).
+**her'/tillan'ds** *Av* here, in this country.
her'tug *-en* duke.
her'tug/dømme *-t, pl +-r/*-* duchy.
hertugin'ne *-a/+-en* duchess.
+**heru't** *Av* cf **her²**
+**heru'te** *Av* cf **her²**
+**her'/ved** *Av* 1 by this, hereby, herewith. 2 *admin.* concerning this, on this subject. 3 *jur.* by these presents.
+**her/værende** [hæ'r/] *A -* local, of this locality, town: **en h- avis** a newspaper in this town.
Her/øy [hæ'r/] *Pln* 1 twp, Nordland. 2 twp, Møre og Romsdal.
Her/øya [hæ'r/] *Pln* town, Eidanger twp, Telemark (containing plant of Norsk Hydro, near Porsgrunn).
***he's¹** *A* cf **hås**
***hes'²** *-a, pl hesjar* cf **hesje¹**
+**he'se/blesende** *A -* breathless, out of breath; headlong.
+**he's/het** *-en* cf **hås/**
hesj'e¹ *-a* haydrying rack.
hesj'e² *V -a/+-et* dry hay on a rack.
hesj'e/staur *-en* pole, stick (of a haydrying rack).
hesj'e/tråd *-en* wire (of a haydrying rack).
***hes'k** *A* eager; greedy, voracious (**etter** for).
***hes'keleg** *A -* appalling, dreadful, frightful.
Hes'ke/stad *Pln* twp, Rogaland.
+**hes'lig** *A -* hideous, loathsome, ugly.
+**hes'lig/het** *-en* hideousness, ugliness.
hes'pe¹ *-a* hasp.
hes'pe² *-a* skein (of thread, yarn; tangle.
hes'pe³ *V -a/+-et* wind thread, yarn into skein: **h- sammen** tangle.
hes'pel *-elen, pl -ler* skein (of thread, yarn): **greie h-en** *fig.* straighten out difficulties.
hes'pe/tre *-et, pl -/+-trær* 1 yarn bobbin, spool. 2 *pop.* crosspatch, sorehead (esp. a woman); Xantippe.
hes'ple *V -a/+-et* wind thread, yarn into skeins.
hes't *-en* 1 horse; nag, pony; mount: **bruke apostlenes h-er** use shank's

+ Bokmål; * Nynorsk; ° Dialect.
After letter: ' stress (Acc. 1); ' tone, stress (Acc. 2); · length.
Below letter: . not pronounced.

mare, walk; **legge i seg som en h-** eat like a horse; **sette seg på den høge h-en** *fig.* get on one's high horse; **sitte, være til h-** be mounted; **slite som en h-** work like a dog; **stige til h-** mount a horse; **den vingede h-** *myth.* Pegasus. 2 vaulting horse (gymnastics). 3 *naut.* stirrup.
hes'te/blomst *-en bot.* dandelion.
hes'te/dekken *-et, pl -/+-er* horse blanket.
hes'te/drosje *-a/-en* horse-drawn cab, hansom.
hes'te/dum [/domm] *A* **-t**, *pl* **-me** boneheaded.
hes'te/hage *-n* corral, horse pasture.
hes'te/handel *-en* horse trading; horse trade (also *fig.*).
+**hes'te/hode** *-t* (=***/hovud**) horse's head: **være et h- foran** be a little ahead of sby, have the jump on sby.
hes'te/hov *-en* 1 horse's hoof. 2 cloven hoof: **stikke h-en fram** reveal one's true colors, one's real nature. 3 *bot.* coltsfoot (Tussilago farfara).
hes'te/kastan'je *-n bot.* horse chestnut (Aesculus hippocastanum).
hes'te/klede [*/kle'e] *-t* horse blanket.
hes'te/kraft *-a/+-en, pl -krefter/*-er* horsepower.
hes'te/kur *-en* drastic remedy.
hes'te/lass *-et* load (drawn by horses).
hes'te/lengd *-a* (=+**/lengde**) horse's length: **seire med en h-** win by a length (racing).
hes'te/lort [/lor't] *-en* horse manure.
hes'te/pære *-a (pop.)* horse apple.
hes'te/rygg *-en*: **på h-en** mounted, on horseback.
hes'te/sko *-en, pl -r/+-* horseshoe.
+**hes'te/vandring** *-en* horse walk (e.g., while turning a threshing machine).
hes't/folk *-et* cavalry.
Hes'tmann/øy *Pln* island, Lurøy and Rødøy twps, Nordland.
he't'[1] *pt of* **hete**[3], **heite**[3]
+**he't'**[2] *A* cf **heit**
+**-het** *-en* common suffix for abstract nouns, like English -ity, -ment, -ness: **dumhet, frihet, svakhet.**
he'te[1] *-n* 1 heat, warmth: **bære dagens byrde og h-** bear the burden and heat of the day, *(pop.)* do the dirty work. 2 fever. 3 *fig.* ardor, passion, zeal: **i kampens h-** in the heat of the struggle.
***he'te**[2] *-a* 1 heating (up). 2 struggle: **ei hard h-** a tough s-.
+**he'te**[3] *V het/-te, hett* (=***heite**[3]) 1 be called, be named, have the name of: **det er noe som h-er plikt** there is such a thing as duty, there is sth called duty; **han h-er Olav** his name is O-; **hva h-er "dog" på norsk?** what is "dog" (called) in Norwegian? what is the Norwegian for "dog"? 2: **det h-er** it is said; **det h-er ikke slik** that's not correct (language); **nei, det h-er ikke det** no, that's not it, that's not how it is; **som det h-er i visa** as it says in the song, as the song goes. 3 *(refl.)*: **det h-er seg** it's said, rumor has it, they say.
he'te[4] *V -a/+-et* heat: **h- opp h-** up; **det h-et av alle lysene** the candles gave off heat (Undset).
he'te/bølgje *-a/+-en* (=+**/bølge**) heat wave.
***he'te/flage** *-a* heat prostration, sunstroke.
***he'te/moe** *-n* haze, shimmering heat.
heteroge'n *A* heterogeneous.
heterozygo'tisk *A - bot., zool.* heterozygous.
he'te/slag *-et* heatstroke.
hetitt' *-en* Hittite.
hetit'tisk *A* - Hittite.
Het'/land *Pln* twp, Rogaland.
he'tne *V -a/+-et* become, get warm.
het's *-en* agitation, excitement, frenzy.
het'te[1] *-a* hood; cap, cowl; cap (on pen); cowl (of a chimney); *mil.* percussion cap.
+**het'te**[2] *pt of* **hete**[3]
het'te/munk [/mongk] *-en* Capuchin friar.
+**he't/vin** *-en* heady wine (one with a high alcoholic content, ca. 17-21 %; often fortified).
hetæ're *-a/+-en* hetaera.
he'v[1] *-et dial.* grip, handle.
+**he'v**[2] *pt of* **hive**
***he'v**[3] *pr of* **hevje**[1]
he'v/arm *-en* 1 lever. 2 *tech.* cam.
hev'd[1] *-a* *1 fertilizer, manure. *2 farming, tilling. 3: **holde i h-** keep up, keep in good condition, maintain; **være i (god) h-** be in good condition, tillable.
hev'd[2] *-a/+-en* 1 common usage, established custom, tradition. 2 *jur.* prescriptive right, title: **få (ha, *vinne) h- på noe** acquire a title to sth.
hev'de *V -a/+-et* 1 assert, claim, defend (one's opinions, rights); *jur.* acquire prescriptive right, title to: **h- seg** assert oneself, hold one's ground. 2 maintain, preserve, uphold: **h- sin plass, stilling** stand one's ground; **h- sin ære** vindicate one's honor. *3 manure; farm.
***hev'de/fôr** *-et* choice, select hay.
hev'ds/rett *-en jur.* prescriptive right, title.
hev'd/vunnen *A +-et/*-e/*-i, pl -e* sanctioned by usage, time-honored; *jur.* prescriptive.
he've *V -a/+-et/-de* (=***hevje**[1], ***hevje**[2]) 1 lift, raise (an arm, a glass, sunken ship, one's voice, etc.); exalt, praise: **h- til skyene** p- to the skies; **være h-et over mistanke** be above, beyond suspicion. 2 draw, receive (money, wages, etc.); cash (a check, money order). 3 adjourn, dissolve (e.g. a meeting); break off (e.g. an engagement); *jur.* annul (e.g. a contract); dismiss (e.g. a case); raise (e.g. an embargo). 4 *(refl.)*: **h- seg** rise; swell; **det h-et seg røster for** voices were raised in favor of; **h- seg over noe** be, rise above sth; tower above sth.
he'vel *-elen, pl -ler dial.* grip, handle.
+**he'velse** *-n* 1 (of dough) rising. 2 *med.* swelling.
he'vert *-en* pipette, siphon.
***hev'je**[1] *V hev, hov, hove/-i* cf **heve**
***hev'je**[2] *V -a* cf **heve**
hev'le *V -a/+-et dial.* slacken one's pace; catch in time: **h- seg** keep from stumbling.
+**hev'n** *-en* (=***hemn**) revenge, vengeance: **få h- på** be revenged on; **ta h- over** wreak vengeance on; **meg hører h-en til, jeg vil gjengjelde, sier Herren** *bibl.* vengeance is mine, I will repay, saith the Lord (Romans 12, 19).
+**hev'n/akt** *-en* act of revenge.
+**hev'ne** *V -a/-et* (=***hemne**) avenge, take vengeance for, revenge: **det h-er seg** it's certain to bring its own punishment; **h- noe** avenge sth; **h- seg** revenge oneself; **h- seg på en** get even with sby.
+**hev'ner** *-en, pl -e* (=***hemnar**) avenger.
+**hev'n/gjerrig** *A* - (=***hemn/**, ***hemn/gjerug**) vengeful, vindictive.
+**hev'n/lyst** *-a/-en* (=***hemn/**) vengefulness, vindictiveness.
+**hev'n/tørst** *-en* (=***hemn/**, ***hemn/tyrst**) desire, thirst for revenge.
hft. = **hefte**[2], **heftet**
hg = **hektogram**
hi'[1] *-et* winter lair: **gå, ligge i hi** hibernate; *fig.* (also) remain in seclusion.
hi'[2] *I*: **hi-hi** tee-hee.
+**hi'**[3] *Pn f of* **hin**
hia'tus *-en, pl hiater* hiatus.
hickory [hik'kori] *-en bot.* hickory (genus Carya).
Hid'ra *Pln* twp, Vest-Agder.
hi'e *V -a*: **h- seg** hibernate.
hierarki' *-et, pl +-er/*-* hierarchy.
hierar'kisk *A* - hierarchical.
hieroglyf' *-en* hieroglyph.
+**hi'ge** *V -a/-et* (=***hike**) yearn: **h- etter, mot** aspire to, have a craving intense desire for, yearn for, *derog* hanker for.
+**hi'gen** *en* aspiration, craving, yearning; *derog.* hankering.
***hig're** *V -a* shake, tremble (from cold).
***hi'k** *-en* corner; border, fringe.
***hi'ke** *V -a* cf **hige**
hikk' *-en/-et* hiccough, hiccup.
+**hik'ke**[1] *-n* hiccough, hiccup.
hik'ke[2] *V -a/+-et* hiccough, hiccup.
***hik're** *V -a* laugh uproariously.
hik'st *-en/-et* sob; gasp: **med en h- i halsen** with a sob in one's throat.
hik'ste[1] *-n dial.* hiccough, hiccup.
hik'ste[2] *V -a/+-et* 1 sob; catch one's breath, gasp. 2 *dial.* hiccough, hiccup.
Hil'd *Prn (f)* battle goddess in Norse mythology; often as suffix, e.g. **Borgh-, Gunnh-.**
Hil'da, Hil'de *Prn (f)*
hil'der *+-eret/+-ret/*-eren* cf **hildring**
+**hil'det** *A* - : **være h- i** be blinded, misled by; be ensnared in.
hil'dre *V -a/+-et* 1 appear larger (than the actual size, e.g. islands, mountains in the distance). 2 appear as an illusion, fata morgana, mirage: **h- seg inn** be wrapped up (in one's imagination).
hil'dring *-a/+-en* hallucination, illusion; fata morgana, mirage.
+**hill'** *I archaic* hail.
+**hil'le/menn** *I archaic* bless me.
Hil'les/øy *Pln* twp, Troms.
+**hil'se** *V -te* cf **helse**[2]
+**hil'se/fot** *-en*: **være på h- med en** have a nodding acquaintance with sby.
+**hil'sen** *-en* cf **helsing**
+**hil'se/plikt** *-a/-en mil.* compulsory saluting.
+**hil'sning** *-en* 1 salute. 2 greeting, salutation; regards.
***hi'm**[1] *-et* film; membrane.
°**hi'm**[2] *Av* cf **heim**[2]
***hi'me**[1] *-a* haziness.
***hi'me**[2] *V -a* darken, dim, obscure.
°**hi'me**[3] *Av* cf **heime**
him'le *V -a/+-et* 1 die, pass away. 2: **h- med øynene** roll one's eyes, turn one's eyes heavenward (in entreaty, supplication, astonishment). 3: **nordlendingen med den h-ende måltonen** the Nordlending with his high-pitched speech melody (Bojer).
him'lende *Av*: **h- høyt** sky-high.
him'ling *-en* vaulted, paneled ceiling.
him'mel *-elen, pl himler* 1 sky; heavens: **alt mellom h- og jord** everything under the sun; **som lyn fra klar h-** like a bolt from the blue; **på h-en** in the sky; **under åpen h-** in the open air, out in the open. 2 *theol.* heaven: **hva i h-ens navn** what in the name of God; **fare til h-s** ascend to h-; **i den sjuende h-** in the seventh h-; **komme i h-en** go to (get into) h-; **ingen trær kan vokse inn i h-en** no one can attain paradise on earth. 3 canopy (e.g. over a bed).
him'mel/blå *A -tt* azure, sky blue.
***him'mel/bolk** *-en* latitude, zone.
him'mel/fallen *A +-ent, pl -falne*: **bli, være h-** be thunderstruck; **han var h-** you could have knocked him over with a feather.
+**him'mel/fart** *-en theol.* ascension: **Kristi h-** A- of Christ; **Marias h-** Assumption of the Blessed Virgin.
+**him'melfarts/dag** *-en*: **Kristi h-** Ascension Day, Holy Thursday.
***him'mel/ferd** [/fær] *-a* cf **/fart**
+**him'mel/henrykt** *A* - beside oneself with joy, overjoyed.
him'mel/hjørne [/jø'rne] *-t, pl +-r/*-* cardinal point, quarter.
+**him'mel/hvelv** *-et* cf **/kvelv**
him'mel/høg *A* (=+**/høy**) 1 sky-high: **stå h-t over noe** be miles above

sth (in quality). 2 deafening, very loud: **han lo h-t** he laughed immoderately; **hun skrek h-t** she screamed at the top of her lungs.
***him'mel/kropp** *-en* celestial, heavenly body.
him'mel/kvelv *-en/+-et* (=**/kvelving, +/hvelv**) firmament, vault of heaven.
+**him'mel/legeme** *-t* celestial, heavenly body.
him'mel/leite *-t dial.* horizon, skyline.
him'mel/rand *-a/+-en* horizon,skyline.
him'mel/rom [/romm] *-met* heavens; (outer) space.
him'mel/ropende *A* - atrocious, crying to high heaven, glaring.
***him'mels/bragd** *-a* appearance of the sky.
him'mel/seng *-a* canopy bed.
him'melsk *A* - celestial, divine, heavenly: **vår h-e fader** Our H-Father; **en h- saus** a divine sauce.
him'mel/sprett *-en* leap into the air: **leike h- (med en)** toss (sby) in a blanket; flip stones in the air by jumping on the opposite end of a teeter-totter.
him'mel/stormende *A* - heaven-defying, Titanic.
him'mel/strøk *-et* (=***/strok**) latitude, zone: **under fjerne h-** under distant skies; **under våre h-** in our part of the world.
him'mel/syn *-et/*-a dial.* horizon, skyline.
+**him'mel/vendt** *A* - (—*/**vend**) turned heavenward, upward.
him'mel/vid *A* enormous: **de er h-t forskjellige** they are poles apart.
+**him'me/rik** *-et* cf **/rike**
him'me/rike *-t* heaven, paradise.
***him'te** *V -a* 1 behold, perceive. 2 loom.
hi'n *Pn f hi/+hin, nt +hint/*hitt, pl hine* 1 *lit.* that, yonder, yon: **denne (dette, disse)** the latter . . . **h- (h-t, h-e)** the former; **dette og h-t** this and that. *2 the other: **hi veka** last week; **hin dagen** the other day; **hin mannen** (=**hinmannen**) the Devil; **hitt folket** the "other" people underground, usu. = goblins, trolls, etc.); **på hi sida** on the other side, opposite. 3 *obs.* the: **Sigurd h- sterke** S- the strong; **h- rike mann og Lasarus** *bibl.* the rich man and L-.
+**hinan'nen** *Pn* (=***einannen**) *lit.* each other, one another: **ta (bryte, rive) fra h-** take (break, tear) apart.
hin'd *-a/+-en zool.* hind (female of the red deer).
hin'der *-eret/+-ret, pl -er/+-re* 1 fence, obstacle: **være til h- for** be, form an obstacle to. 2 jump (riding): **hoppe h-** clear a jump.
hin'derlig *A* - embarrassing, obstructive.
+**hin'der/løp** *-et* (=***/laup**) steeplechase.
hin'dosta'nsk *A* - Hindustani.
hin'dre *V -a/+-et* 1 hinder, interfere with, obstruct. 2 preclude, prevent: **h- en i å gjøre noe** prevent sby from doing sth.
hin'dring *-a/+-en* obstacle, obstruction (for to): **legge h-er i veien for** put obstacles in the way of; **møte h-er** meet with obstacles.
hin'du *-en* Hindu.
hin'duisk *A* - Hindu.
hing'st *-en* stallion.
hin'k *-et* hop (in hop, step, and jump).
hin'ke *V -a/+-et* 1 hobble, limp: **h- med** hobble along, *fig.* keep up as best one can. 2 hop (on one leg).
Hi'n/mannen *Prn* the devil, *(pop.)* Old Harry, Old Nick, Old Scratch.
hin'ne *-a* membrane; film.
Hinn'/øya *Pln* large island at the border between Nordland and Troms counties.
+**hi'n/sides** *Av* beyond, on the other side of: **h- (graven)** *theol.* in the hereafter, in the next world.
+**hi'n/sidig** *A* - : **det h-e** *theol.* the hereafter, the life to come.
hin't *-et* hint.
hin'te *V -a/+-et* hint (til at).
***hi'pe** *V +-te/*-a* wait expectantly, yearningly.
***hi'pen** *A -e/-i, pl -ne* expectant, longing.
hipp'[1] *-et* cutting remark, *(pop.)* dig.
hipp'[2] *I* hip, hip (hurrah).
hipp'[3] *N*: **bli h- som happ** be six of one and half a dozen of the other.
hip'pen *A +-ent, pl hipne*: **h- etter, på** eager for, keen on.
hippodro'm *-en* hippodrome.
hi'r *-en* apathy, languor (following an excitement).
hir'd *-a/+-en hist.* king's or earl's bodyguard; followers, retainers (a usage revived temporarily by Norwegian nazis for the storm troopers of Quisling).
hir'd/mann *-en, pl -menn/*-menner hist.* member of a king's or earl's bodyguard, retainer.
hir'd/skrå *+-en/*-a hist.* document listing rules of behavior, conduct for the *hird.*
hi're *V -te* be apathetic, languid; not feel well.
hi'ren *A +-ent, pl -ne* drowsy, languid.
hir'se *-n bot.* millet (genus Panicum).
hiss' *-en mus.* B sharp (=C).
his'se *V -a/+-et* agitate, excite, work up; goad, stimulate: **h- opp** egg on, stir, work up; **h- hunden på en** sic a dog on sby; **h- dem på hverandre** set them at each other's throats; **h- seg opp** get excited, work oneself up.
+**his'set** *Av theol.* hereafter, in the next world; up yonder; **både her og h-** both in this world and the next.
his'sig *A* - 1 ardent, eager, keen: **h- etter, på** keen on; hot on the trail of; **ikke så h-** take it easy. 2 angry, irascible, quick-tempered: **bli h-** lose one's temper, *(pop.)* fly off the handle. 3 intense, violent (e.g. discussion, battle). 4 inflamed, irritated (e.g. boil).
+**his'sig/het** *-en* 1 ardor, passion. 2 hastiness, temper. 3 violence. 4 inflammation.
his'sig/propp *-en fam.* hothead.
+**his't** *Av*: **h- og her** here and there, occasionally.
hist. = **historie, historisk**
histo'rie *-a/+-en* 1 history; *fam.* history book: **gå over i h-en** go down in h-; become a part of h-; **professor i h-** professor of (in) h-; h-professor. 2 story, tale: **fortelle h-r** tell stories (anecdotes, jokes). 3 *fam.* (usu. unpleasant) affair, business: **en farlig h-** a dangerous affair; **hele h-en** the whole business.
+**histo'riker** *-en, pl -e* (=***-ar**) historian.
historikk' *-en* historical account, history of sth.
historiogra'f *-en* historiographer.
histo'risk *A* - historical; historic: **det er h-** it's a matter of history, it's on record; **på h- grunn** on historic ground.
Hi's/øy *Pln* 1 island, twp, Aust-Agder. 2 island, Gulen twp, Sogn og Fjordane.
hi't[1] *-a* sheepskin bag.
hi't[2] [also hit'] *Av* here, hither (adv. of motion): **h- inn** in here; **h- og dit** hither and thither; here and there; back and forth; **h- med boka** give me the book, hand over the book; **"Jeg kan bevise det." - "Bevis meg h- og bevis meg dit - jeg gir en god dag i dine beviser."** "I can prove it." "Prove schmove - I don't give a hang about your proofs." (NROrdbok).
hi'ta/for' *P* on this side of.
***hi'tan** *Av* on this side.
***hi'tan/for'** *P* cf **hita/**
***hi'tan/om'** *P* on this side of.
***hi'tare** *A* - cf **hitre**
***hi'tast** *sp of* **hit(a)re** cf **hitterst**
***hi'te** *V -a* cf **hete**[4]
+**hi'ten/for'** *P* cf **hita/**
hi't/over [/åver] *Av* over there, yonder.
Hit'ra *Pln* island, twp, Sør-Trøndelag.
hit're *A* - *cp, sp +hitterst/*hitast* (=***hitare**) nearer: **på den h- side** on this side.
+**hi't/røre** *V -te*: **h- fra** arise out of, be due to, originate in.
***hitt'**[1] *-en* fluke, stroke of luck: **på ein h-** haphazardly, at random.
***hitt'**[2] *nt of* **hin**
***hit'tar** *-en* finder.
hit'te *V -a/+-et* 1 find: **h-s** meet. 2 hit on: **h- på noe** think of sth; **h- ut av** find out, make out (**det er ikke til å h- ut av** it's a complete mystery, *(pop.)* it beats me).
+**hit'te/ba'rn** *-et* foundling.
hit'te/gods [/gots] *-et* (lost and) **found** (property).
hit'ten *A -e/-i, pl hitne* clever, inventive.
+**hit'terst** *sp of* **hitre** (=***hitast**)
+**hi't/tidig** *A* - up to now.
***hit'tig** *A* - clever, inventive.
hi't/til' *Av* 1 so far, up to now. 2 hitherto, till then.
hi'ttil/dags *Av* so far, up to now.
hi'v *+-en/-et* 1 heave, lift; load (e.g. of a scoop shovel). 2 *naut.* heave; heeling, listing.
hi've *V -de/heiv/+hev, -d/*-e/*-i* 1 heave, throw, toss; throw away: **h- av seg** strip off one's clothes; **h- ham på porten** throw him out on his ear; **h- opp** puke, vomit; **h- på seg** slip into (e.g. a coat, dress); **h- seg** throw oneself (e.g. over the railing); **h- seg over ende** flop down (on the ground). 2 lift oneself up, rise suddenly: **h- seg på sprang** start running; **komme h-ende** come suddenly. 3 gasp, wheeze: **h- etter pusten** gasp for breath. 4 *naut.* heave, hoist, throw; heel, list; rise and fall (of the sea): **h- anker, h- opp** hoist anchor; **h- inn på sleperen** shorten the towline; **h- noe over bord** throw sth overboard.
hi'vert *-en* 1 swig, *(pop.)* snort. 2 *naut.* heeling, listing.
***hja'l** *-et* call, cry.
***hja'le** *V -a* call, cry out; sound.
Hjal'mar *Prn(m)*
+**hjal'p** *pt of* **hjelpe**[1]
hjal't *-et* hilt (of a sword).
Hjal't/land *Pln hist.* Norse name for the Shetland Islands.
hjal't/lending *-en hist.* person from the Shetland Islands.
***hjar'ta**[1] *-t, pl hjarto* cf **hjerte**
***hjar'ta**[2] *A* - brave, courageous.
***hjar'tans** *Av* cf **hjertens**
Hjar't/dal *Pln* twp, Telemark.
***hjar'te**[1] *-t* cf **hjerte**
***hjar'te**[2] *-t* cf **hjerter**
***hjar'te/bank** *N* cf **hjerte/**
***hjar'te/ba'rn** *-et* cf **hjerte/**
***hjar'te/blad** *-et* cf **hjerte/**
***hjar'te/blod** *-et* cf **hjerte/**
***hjar'te/dør** *-a* cf **hjerte/**
***hjar'te/feil** *-en* cf **hjerte/**
***hjar'te/glad** *A* - cf **hjerte/**
***hjar'te/infar'kt** *-et* cf **hjerte/**
***hjar'te/lag** *-et* cf **hjerte/**
***hjar'te/laus** *A* cf **hjerte/løs**
***hjar'teleg** *A* - cf **hjertelig**
***hjar'te/mein** *-et* heart disease.
***hjar'te/rom** [/romm] *-met* cf **hjerte/**
***hjar'te/rot** *-a, pl -røter* cf **hjerte/**
***hjar'te/rå** *A -tt* cf **hjerte/**
***hjar'te/sak** *-a* cf **hjerte/**
***hjar'te/slag** *-et* cf **hjerte/**
***hjar'te/sorg** *-a* cf **hjerte/**
***hjar'te/sukk** *-en/-et* cf **hjerte/**

+ Bokmål; * Nynorsk; ° Dialect.
After letter: ' stress (Acc. 1); ' tone, stress (Acc. 2); · length.
Below letter: . not pronounced.

***hjar'te/sår** -*et* cf **hjerte/**

***hjar'te/varm** *A* cf **hjerte/**

***hjar'te/ven(n)** -*en* cf **hjerte/**

***hjar'tig** *A* - 1 kind-hearted. 2 brave, courageous.

***hjas'se** -*n* crown of the head.

+**hje'l** *N* cf **hel**[1]

hjell' -*en* 1 drying rack (for fish). 2 loft of loose boards (in a barn). 3 mountain ledge.

hjell'/bruk -*et* equipment, material for a drying rack (for fish).

hjell'/fisk -*en* fish dried on a rack.

hjel'm -*en* 1 helmet. 2 *dial.* covered stack (of hay or grain).

hjel'm/busk -*en* crest, plume of a helmet.

+**hjel'me** *V* -*a*/-*et* (=***hjelmast**): **h- seg** begin to ripen (grain).

Hjel'me *Pln* twp, Hordaland.

Hjel'me/land *Pln* twp, Rogaland.

***hjel'm/kald** *A* bitter cold.

hjel'p -*a*/+-*en* 1 help; aid, assistance, support: **h-!** help!; **hurtig h- er dobbelt h-** he gives twice who gives quickly; **komme en til h-** come to sby's assistance, rescue; **når nøden er størst er h-en nærmest** it's always darkest before dawn; **ved egen h-** unaided; **være til h- for** be of help to. 2 expedient, means, way out: **ta noe til h-** have recourse to sth, make use of sth; **ved h- av** by means of. 3 help; benefit, use: **det er ingen h- i det** it's of no avail, use.

hjel'pe[1] *V* +*hjalp*/*-*te*, +*hjulpet*/*-*t* 1 aid, assist, help; avail, be of use; be good (**mot** for): **det h-er ikke** it's no use; that's no help, that doesn't do any good. 2 (passive): **h-es at** assist, help one another. 3 (with *prep.* and *adv.*): **h- en av med noe** take sth off sby's hands; **jeg kan ikke h- for det (at)** I can't help it (that); **h- på økonomien** aid, improve one's financial condition; **h- til** lend a hand; **h- en til noe** help sby to get, reach sth. 4 (*refl.*): **h- seg (selv)** get along, manage (by oneself); do everything oneself; **h- seg igjennom** tide oneself over.

***hjel'pe**[2] *V* -*te* cf **hjelpe**[1]

+**hjel'pe/dyktig** *A* - able to help; *mil.* auxiliary (troops).

hjel'pe/fengsel -*et* auxiliary jail.

***hjel'pe/før** *A* able to help.

hjel'pe/kjelde -*a* (=+**/kilde**) 1 aid, help. 2 source (for scholarly work). 3 (*pl*) resources.

hjel'pe/laus *A* 1 helpless. 2 at a loss, at one's wits' end. 3 awkward, clumsy.

***hjel'peleg** *A* - serviceable, useful.

+**hjel'pe/lærer** -*en*, *pl* -*e* (=*-**ar**) assistant teacher; teaching assistant.

+**hjel'pe/løs** *A* cf **/laus**

hjel'pe/løyse -*a* helplessness.

hjel'pe/mannskap -*et* helpers, volunteers.

hjel'pe/middel -*elet*/-*midlet*, *pl* +-*midler*/*-*el* aid, help: **h-er** facilities, resources.

hjel'pe/motor -*en* auxiliary engine.

***hjel'pen** *A* -*e*/-*i*, *pl* -*ne* cf **hjulpen**

hjel'pe/prest -*en* *eccl.* assistant pastor; (*Brit.*) curate.

+**hjel'per** -*en*, *pl* -*e* (=*-**ar**) assistant, helper; ally.

+**hjel'perske** -*n* woman assistant, helper.

hjel'pe/råd -*a*/+-*en*/-*et* aid, expedient, help.

hjel'pes/mann -*en*, *pl* -*menn*/*-*menner* assistant, helper; ally.

hjel'pe/styrke -*n* reinforcement.

+**hjel'pe/tropper** *pl* (=*-**ar**) *mil.* auxiliary troops, auxiliaries.

hjel'pe/verb -*et*, *pl* -/+-*er* auxiliary verb.

***hjel'p/sam'** *A* cf **/som**

***hjel'p/semd** -*a* helpfulness, willingness to help.

+**hjel'p/som'** *A* -*t*, *pl* -*me* helpful, willing to help.

+**hjel'psom/het** -*a*/-*en* helpfulness, willingness to help.

+**hjem'**[1] -*met* cf **heim**[1]

+**hjem'**[2] *Av* cf **heim**[2]

+**hjem'/ad** *Av* homewards.

+**hjem'/by** -*en* cf **heim/**

+**hjem'/bygd** -*a* cf **heim/**

+**hjem'/falle** *V* -*falt*, -*falt* cf **heim/**

+**hjem'/føre** *V* -*te* cf **heim/**

+**hjem'/gående** *A* - homeward bound: **for h-** *naut.* (the same).

+**hjem'/kalle** *V* -*kalte*, -*kalt* recall, summon home.

+**hjem'/komst** -*en* homecoming, return.

+**hjem'/land** -*et* cf **heim/**

+**hjem'le** *V* -*et* cf **heimle**

+**hjem'/lengsel** -*elen*, *pl* -*ler* homesickness, nostalgia.

+**hjem'lig** *A* - cf **heimlig**

+**hjem'/lov** [/låv] *et* cf **heim/**

+**hjem'/løs** *A* cf **heim/laus**

+**hjem'/lån** -*et* cf **heim/**

+**hjem'me** *Av* cf **heime**

+**hjem'me/bane** -*n* home field, grounds (sports): **på h-** *fig.* in familiar territory; **spille på h-** play a home game.

+**hjem'me/brent** -*et* cf **heime/**

+**hjem'me/dåp** -*en* cf **heime/**

+**hjem'me/front** -*en* cf **heime/**

+**hjem'me/gjort** *A* - cf **heime/**

+**hjem'me/hørende** *A* - indigenous, native; having one's home (**i** in).

+**hjem'me/industri'** -*en* 1 domestic industry. 2 home crafts.

+**hjem'me/koselig** *A* - cozy, homey.

+**hjem'mel** -*elen*, *pl* *hjemler* cf **heimel**

+**hjem'me/laget** *A* - cf **heime/laga**

+**hjem'mels/mann** -*en*, *pl* -*menn* cf **heimels/**

+**hjem'me/marked** -*et* domestic market.

+**hjem'me/sitter** -*en*, *pl* -*e* cf **heime/**

+**hjem'me/styrke** -*n* cf **heime/**

+**hjem'me/vant** *A* - cf **heime/**

+**hjem'me/vern** [/væ'rn] -*et* cf **heime/**

+**hjem'me/værende** *A* - (living, staying) at home.

+**hjem'/om'** *Av* cf **heim/**

+**hjem'/over** [/åver] *Av* cf **heim/**

+**hjem'/reise** -*a*/-*en* homeward journey; return journey: **på h-** on the way home.

+**hjem'/sendelse** -*n* sending home; *mil.* demobilization; repatriation.

+**hjem'/sendt** *A* - sent home; *mil.* demobilized; repatriated.

+**hjem'/stavn** -*en*: 1 home, residence. 2 home town, district one hails from.

+**hjem'stavns/beret'tiget** *A* -: **være h- i** have the right to public support in (a certain district).

+**hjem'stavns/rett** -*en* right to public support in one's own district: **ha h- i Oslo** be a legal resident in O-.

+**hjem'/sted** -*et* 1 home town, (native) district, permanent address; domicile. 2 origin, source; scene (**for** of). 3 *merc.* home office. 4 *naut.* home port, port of registry.

+**hjem'/søke** *V* -*te* cf **heim/**

+**hjem'/søkelse** -*n* affliction, misfortune; *bibl.* punishment, visitation.

+**hjem'/ve** -*en* homesickness, nostalgia: **lide av h-** feel homesick.

+**hjem'/vendt** *A* - returned.

Hjer'kinn *Pln* RR station, Dovre twp, Oppland.

hjerne [jæ'rne] -*n* 1 brain, brains: **den lille h-** cerebellum; **den store h-** cerebrum; **få noe på h-n** get sth on the brain, get a fixed idea; **legge sin h- i bløt** rack one's brains; **sykdommen har slått seg på h-n** the illness has affected the brain; **være klar i h-en** be clear-headed. 2 mind: **landets skarpeste h-r** the country's finest minds. 3 nerve center (e.g. of communications, operations).

+**hjerne/blø'dning** -*en* (=*/**bløding**) cerebral hemorrhage.

hjerne/gymnastikk' -*en* mental gymnastics.

hjerne/kiste -*a* skull.

hjerne/masse -*n* gray matter.

+**hjerne/rystelse** -*n* (=*/**risting**) concussion of the brain.

***hjerne/skaking** -*a* concussion of the brain.

hjerne/skalle -*n* (=+**/skall**, */**skal**) cranium, skull.

hjerne/slag -*et* stroke.

hjerne/spinn -*et* figment of the imagination.

hjerne/vinding -*a*/+-*en*, *pl* *-*ar* convolution of the brain.

+**hjer'ta** *A* - (=***hjarta**[2], +**hjerten**) 1 courageous, resolute. 2 desirous: **være h- på** be desirous of; have the courage to.

+**hjer'te** -*t* (=***hjarta**[1]) heart (also *fig.*); core: **av h-t** from the heart; **det gikk ham til h-t** he felt very deeply about it, it stirred his heart; **ha noe på h-** have sth to say (that concerns one deeply); **h-t synker i livet på en** one's heart is in one's boots; **kunne bringe (bære) det over sitt h- (å)** have the heart (to); **legge seg på h-(t)** imprint deeply in one's heart; **det ligger ham på h-(t)** he has it at heart, it concerns him deeply.

+**hjer'te/bank** -*en* palpitation (of the heart).

+**hjer'te/ba'rn** -*et* apple of one's eye, darling.

+**hjer'te/beten'nelse** -*n* (=***hjarte/**) carditis.

+**hjer'te/blad** -*et* *bot.* central leaf, heart.

+**hjer'te/blod** -*et* life-blood, life's blood: **gi sitt h-** give, sacrifice one's life; **skrive med sitt h-** write from the heart.

+**hjer'te/dør** -*a* *poet.* door to one's heart.

+**hjer'te/feil** -*en* (organic) heart disease.

+**hjer'te/glad** *A* - joyful, jubilant.

+**hjer'te/infar'kt** -*et* *med.* infarct of the heart, thrombosis.

+**hjer'te/kammer** -*eret*, *pl* -/-*kamre* *anat.* ventricle.

+**hjer'te/klapp** -*en* 1 palpitation (of the heart). 2 cardiac valve.

+**hjer'te/klemt** *A* - heavy-hearted, oppressed.

+**hjer'te/knuser** -*en*, *pl* -*e* *pop.* charmer, lady-killer.

+**hjer'te/kule** -*a*/-*en* *anat.* solar plexus: **et trykk nede ved h-n** a pain in the s- p-.

+**hjer'te/kval** -*en* agony, anguish.

+**hjer'te/lag** -*et* (kind) heart, kindheartedness: **han har et godt h-** he has a kind heart.

+**hjer'te/lammelse** -*n* heart failure.

+**hjer'telig** *A* - (=***hjarteleg**) 1 cordial, hearty; heartfelt, sincere. 2 (in polite formulas): **h- hilsen (til)** my kindest regards (to); **h- takk** thank you ever so much; **h- til lykke** many congratulations. 3 (*adv.*) deeply, sincerely; extremely: **være h- enig med en** be heartily in accord with sby; **h- dum** really stupid.

+**hjer'telig/het** -*en* cordiality, heartiness, sincerity.

+**hjer'te/løs** *A* callous, heartless.

+**hjer'te/menneske** -*t* person of feeling: **han er et h-** he's all heart.

+**hjer'ten** *A* -*ent*, *pl* -*ne* cf **hjerta**

+**hjer'tens** *Av* (=***hjartans**) deeply, sincerely, extremely: **h- god latter** good, hearty laughter; **h- gjerne** most willingly, with all one's heart; by all means; **h- snill** extremely kind; **h- takknemlig** deeply grateful.

+**hjer'tens/glad** *A* - overjoyed.

+**hjer'tens/god** *A* kindhearted, tenderhearted.

+**hjer'tens/kjær** -*en* dearest, dearly beloved, sweetheart.

+**hjer'ter** -*en*, *pl* - (=***hjarte**[2]) hearts: **h- ni** nine of h-.

+**hjer'ter/ess** -*et* ace of hearts.

+**hjer'te/rom** [/romm] -*met* hospitality: **hvor det er h-, blir det alltid husrom** where there is room in the heart, there is room in the house; where there's a will, there's a way.

+**hjer'te/rot** *-a, pl -røtter* 1 *anat.* muscular bundle of the heart; *fig.* cockles of the heart, innermost heart: **det varmet meg til h-ene** it warmed the very cockles of my heart. 2 *bot.* taproot.

+**hjer'te/rå** *A -tt* cruel, (utterly) ruthless.

+**hjer'te/sak** *-a/-en* cause (to which one is dedicated), matter close to one's heart: **det er en h- for ham** it is a matter of life and death to him.

+**hjer'te/skjærende** *A* - heart-rending: **gråte h-** cry as though one's heart were breaking.

+**hjer'te/slag** *-et* 1 heartbeat. 2 heart attack.

+**hjer'te/sorg** *-a* heartache: **ha h-** be hopelessly (unhappily) in love, be love-sick; **dø av h-** die of a broken heart.

+**hjer'te/styrkning** *-en* drink, pick-me-up, refreshment: **ta en h-** have a quick one.

+**hjer'te/sukk** *-en/-et* 1 long-drawn sigh. 2 expression (of one's inmost feelings).

+**hjer'te/sår** *-et* heartbreak; broken heart: **det var som hun dengang hadde fått h- og de ville aldri gro igjen** it was as if she had once been wounded to the heart and the wounds refused to heal (Undset).

+**hjer'te/tyv** *-en* charmer, lady-killer.

+**hjer'te/varm** *A* warm-hearted.

+**hjer'te/venn** *-en* bosom friend.

hjo'n *-et archaic, dial.* 1 domestic, servant. 2 spouse; *(pl)* married couple.

hjo'n/skap *+-et/*-en archaic* marriage, matrimony.

***hjo'nsleg** *A* - compatible, suited to each other.

hjor'd *-en obs.* 1 drove, flock, herd: **hyrdene var ute på marken og holdt nattevakt over sin h-** *bibl.* shepherds abiding in the field, keeping watch over their flock by night (Luke 2, 8). 2 *bibl.* congregation, flock: **Herrens h-** the Lord's f-, i.e. the Israelites (Jeremiah 13, 17).

hjor't *-en* 1 *zool.* deer (family Cervidae); hart, stag. 2 cardboard target of a deer (in a shooting gallery).

hjor'te/kolle *-a zool.* hind.

+**hjor'te/takk** *-en* (=*/**tagg**) 1 stag's antler. 2 *chem.* (salt of) hartshorn (=ammonium carbonate). 3 cruller (with crossed ends).

+**hjor'tetakk/salt** *-et* (=*-**tagg/**) *chem.* salt of hartshorn (=ammonium carbonate).

Hjuk'se/bø *Pln* RR station, Sauherad twp, Telemark.

hju'l *-et* wheel; hoop (child's toy): **slå h-** turn a cartwheel; (of e.g. a peacock) spread the tail.

hju'l/beint *A* - bowlegged.

hju'l/bår *-a* wheelbarrow.

hju'l/båt *-en* paddle wheel steamer (side-wheeler, stern-wheeler).

+**hju'l/damper** *-en, pl -e* (=*-**ar**) see **/båt.**

***hju'le** *V -a* carry, wheel (in a wheelbarrow).

***hju'l/far** *-et* wheel rut, track.

hju'l/kapsel *-elen, pl -ler* hub cap.

+**hju'l/maker** *-en, pl -e* (=*-**ar**) wheelwright.

+**hjul'pen** *A -ent, pl -ne* (=***hjelpen**) in good shape, well-fixed, well off; helped out (of some difficulty), tided over; relieved, satisfied.

+**hjul'pet** *pp of* **hjelpe**[1]

hju'l/spor *-et* wheel rut, track.

hju'l/visp *-en* (rotary) beater.

***hju'pe** *-a bot.* (rose) hip.

hju'ring *-en* herdsman, shepherd.

hju'ring/jente *-a* shepherd girl.

***hjøl't** *-et vet.* windgall.

Hjør'dis *Prn (f)*

hjø'rne *-t, pl +-r/*-* (=***hyrne**[1]) 1 corner: **bo her like om h-t** live right around the c-; **dreie om h-t** turn the c-; **på h-t av** at the c- of (such and such streets). 2 quarter, region: **jordens fire h-r** the four corners of the earth. 3 humor, mood: **når han var i det h-** when he was in that humor.

hjø'rne/hylle *-a* corner shelf.

hjø'rne/spark *-et* corner (soccer).

hjø'rne/stein *-en* cornerstone (also *fig.*).

hjø'rne/tann *-a, pl -tenner* eyetooth.

Hjørund/fjord [jø'rong/fjor] *Pln* twp, Møre og Romsdal.

Hjø'runga/våg *Pln* bay in Hareid twp, Møre og Romsdal (scene of battle with the Jomsvikings in 986 A.D.).

***hjå'** *P* at, by, with: **h- bror min** at my brother's house.

***hjå'm** *-et* (thin) coating, film (e.g. of dust).

***hjå'/sete** *-t* sitting next to sby.

***hjå'/svæve** *-t* sleeping with sby.

hk = **hestekrefter**

+**H.K.H.** = **Hans (Hennes) Kongelige Høyhet**

hl = **hektoliter**

hm *I* ahem, hm, hum (expression to attract attention, of embarrassment, hesitation, dissatisfaction).

H.M. = **Hans (Hennes) Majestet**

***ho'**[1] *-a* cf **hunn**

***ho'**[2] *Pn ob henne/ho, po hennar/hennes* cf **hun**[6]

hobby [håb'bi] *-en* hobby.

Hobøl [hob'bøl] *Pln* twp, Østfold.

hockey [håk'ki] *-en* hockey.

hockey/kølle *-a/+-en* hockey stick.

***hod'de** *-a* grip, handle.

+**ho'de** *-t* (=***hovud**) 1 head (of a bed, group, nail, person, lettuce, etc.); brains, intelligence: **etter sitt eget h-** according to one's own wishes, in one's own way; **følge sitt eget h-** go one's own way, refuse to listen to advice; **holde h-t kaldt** keep cool, keep a cool head; **kort for h-t** curt, short, snappish; *fam.* slow-witted; **på h-t** head foremost; **nå står det på h-t alt sammen** now everything is upside down, in a mess. 2 *typog.* banner; headline. 3 *anat., bot.* capitulum. 4 bowl (of a pipe).

+**ho'de/brudd** *-et* (=***hovud/brot**) cf **/bry**

+**ho'de/bry** *-et* puzzling, racking one's brains; trouble, worry.

+**ho'de/bunn** *-en* scalp.

+**ho'de/galen** [usu. hug'/gæ'rn] *A -ent, pl -ne fam.* crazy, mad; dizzy.

+**ho'de/gjerde** [/jære] *-t* head (of a bed), headboard.

+**ho'de/kulls** *Av* headlong; precipitate(ly), sudden(ly).

+**ho'de/kål** *-en bot.* (common) cabbage (Brassica oleracea).

+**ho'de/lag** *-et* headgear (for a horse).

+**ho'de/lin** *-et archaic* linen head scarf, headdress.

+**ho'de/løs** *A* headless; *fig.* at a complete loss, silly, stupid.

+**ho'de/pine** *-a/-en* headache.

+**ho'de/pute** *-a* pillow.

+**ho'de/regning** [/reining] *-en* mental calculation, computation.

+**ho'de/rystende** *A* - shaking one's head.

ho'de/sala't *-en* head lettuce.

+**ho'de/skalle** *-n anat.* cranium, skull.

+**ho'de/stup(e)s** *Av* headlong; precipitate(ly), sudden(ly).

+**ho'de/tørkle** *-et* kerchief.

ho'de/verk *-en* headache.

***ho'/dyr** *-et* cf **hunn/**

***ho'e**[1] *-a* cf **hunn**

ho'e[2] *V -a/+-et* halloo, shout.

Hof' *Pln* 1 twp, Hedmark. 2 twp, Vestfold.

hoff' *-et, pl -/+-er* court, royal household.

hoff'/dame *-n* lady-in-waiting.

+**hoffer'de** *-et*: **h- seg** act, be arrogant, overbearing; **h- seg over noe** be stuck-up about sth.

hoffer'dig *A* - arrogant, haughty, proud; presumptuous.

hoff'/folk *pl* courtiers.

hoff'/frøken *-na/+-enen, pl -ner* maid of honor (in a royal court).

hoff'/leverandø'r *-en* purveyor to the royal court.

hoff'/narr *-en* court fool, jester.

hoff'/sjef *-en* lord chamberlain.

hoff'/sorg *-a/+-en* court mourning: **anlegge h-** go into mourning.

hof't *-a* 1 fetter, hobble. 2 obstruction.

hof'te *-a/+-en* 1 *anat.* hip: **vagge i h-ne** swing the hips. 2 *zool.* coxa.

+**hof'te/holder** *-en, pl -e* (=*/**haldar**) girdle (roll-on).

hof'te/skål *-a anat.* hip socket.

hog'de *pt of* **hogge**

hogg'[1] *-et* 1 blow, cut, slash; thud, thump (resulting from a blow). 2 beating, thrashing. 3 cut, incision; *tech.* file cut.

hogg'[2] *pt of* **hogge**

***hogg'/bit** *-en* (steel) chisel.

***hogg'/bratt** *A* - almost perpendicular, vertical.

hog'ge *V -er/*hogg, hogde/hogg, hogd/*-e/*-i* 1 chop, cut; carve, hew; fell. 2 strike (**etter** at, with e.g. an ax, sword, fangs, beak, etc.): **han hogg øksa i stabben** he planted (sank) his ax in the chopping block; **h- tennene i noe** dig, sink one's teeth into sth. 3 grab, snatch: **h- tak i** seize hold of. 4 *naut.* pitch; strike ground (bottom). 5 (with *prep.* and *adv.*): ***h- i** break in (e.g. on a conversation); **h- inn på fienden** charge the enemy (with saber, sword, etc.); **h- opp et skip** break up a ship (for scrap); **h- til** (with an ax, a sword, etc.) chop, strike hard; **h- ut** thin out (a forest). 6 (*refl.*): **h- seg** cut oneself; chop, cut one's way (**igjennom** through); **h- seg fast** grab hold of.

hog'gende *Av*: **h- bratt** perpendicular; **h- stille** stock-still; deathly silent.

+**hog'ger** *-en, pl -e* (=*-**ar**) cutter, hewer.

hog'ge/stabbe *-n* chopping block.

hogg'/jern [/jæ'rn] *-et* (=*/**jarn**) (wood) chisel.

hogg'/orm *-en zool.* adder, viper (Vipera berus).

***hogg'/snøgg** *A -snøgt* quick as a flash.

hogg'/spon *-en* chip.

hogg'/tann *-a, pl -tenner* fang, tusk.

hogg'/våpen *-enet/*-net, pl -en mil.* slashing weapon; battle ax.

Hog'ne *Prn (m)*

hog'old *-a* wooden eye, ring at the end of a rope.

hog'st *-en* cutting, felling; clearing (**av** of).

***hog'ster** *-en* cf **hogst**

h.o.h. = +**høyde**/***høgd over havet**

+**ho'henstaufer** *-en, pl -e* (=*-**ar**) *hist.* Hohenstaufen.

+**ho'henzoller** *-en, pl -e* (=*-**ar**) *hist.* Hohenzollern.

hoi' *I* hey; *naut.* ahoy.

hoi'e *V -a/+-et* halloo, holler.

***ho'/kjønn** *-et* cf **hun/**

°**hok'ken** *Pn f* **hokka,** *nt* **hokke** cf **kven**[3]

***hok're** *V -a* hobble, limp.

hokus/pokus [hok'kus/] *et* hocus-pocus.

***ho'l**[1] *-en* low elevation, rise.

hol[2] [hå'l] *-et* (=+**hull**[1]) 1 hole; (belt) notch, perforation; (tooth) cavity; gap, lacuna: **få h- på en** *fam.* get sby to break his silence, say sth; **ta h- på noe** open and begin to use sth. 2 *fam.* dump, hole (of a room, town, etc.). 3 *fam.* clink, jail.

+ Bokmål; * Nynorsk; ° Dialect.
After letter: ' stress (Acc. 1); ` tone, stress (Acc. 2); ˙ length.
Below letter: . not pronounced.

ho'l[3] *A* (=+hul) 1 empty, hollow; concave: **den h-e hånd** the hollow of the hand; **h- mur** *arch.* cavity wall; **h- sjø** *naut.* hollow sea. 2 *fig.* hollow; empty, false, insincere, *(pop.)* phony: **h-e fraser** empty words.

Ho'l *Pln* 1 twp, Buskerud. 2 twp, Nordland. 3 post office, Tjeldsund twp, Nordland.

***ho'last** *V -ast* become hollow; be hollowed out.

ho'l/brysta *A* - hollow-chested.

hol'd[1] *-et* flesh: **ved godt h-** looking well.

+**hol'd**[2] *-et* (=*hald) 1 grasp, grip, hold. 2 firmness, solidity, substance; backbone, *pop.* guts: **det er ikke h- i ham** he has no guts. 3 pain, stitch in the side. 4 distance, range: **på hundre meters h-** at 100 meters' r-; **på kloss h-** at close r-; **på nært h-** at close quarters. 5 quarter, source: **fra annet h-** from other quarters; **fra høyeste h-** on the highest authority; **fra pålitelig h-** from a reliable source; **på enkelte h-** in some quarters. 6 gang, party (e.g. of workmen).

***hol'dast** *V -ast* fill out.

+**hol'd/bar** *A* 1 durable, hard-wearing; nonperishable. 2 tenable, valid.

+**hol'dbar/het** *-en* 1 durability. 2 tenability, validity.

+**hol'de**[1] *V holdt, holdt* (=*halde) 1 tolerate, withstand; hold (up), last: **det h-er** that's good, that'll go; **h- ut** bear up, endure, stand it; hold up (out); **h- ut med en** bear with sby. 2 (esp. of a carriage, taxi, train, etc.) pull up, stop: **h- inne** break off, cease, stop; **h- opp** hold up, stop. 3: **h- sammen (i hop)** stick together.

+**hol'de**[2] *V holdt, holdt* (=*halde) 1 hold (one's breath, a fort, meeting, an object, a sale, etc.); keep (one's balance, house, the law, livestock, order, a promise, servants, etc.); maintain: **h- kjeft** keep one's mouth shut; **h- senga** keep to one's bed. 2 deliver, give (a sermon, speech, etc.). 3 subscribe to, take (a magazine, newspaper, etc.). 4 (with *prep.* and *adv.*): **h- an** hold it, hold on (stop); rein up; **h- av** be fond of, love, *naut.* bear away; **h- (fast) i noe** hold on (tightly) to sth; clutch, grasp sth (tightly); **h- en i hånden** hold sby's hand; **h- igjen** hold back, restrain; keep shut; **h- for** consider to be, take as being, take for; **h- fra livet** keep at arm's length, at bay; hold off; **h- en med noe** keep sby furnished with sth, keep sby in sth; **h- med** agree, side with; **h- opp (med)** cease, stop; **h- opp** hold up (by robber); **h- på (gal hest)** back (the wrong horse); **h- på med** be busy with; **h- på (med) å gjøre** be doing; keep on doing; be on the verge of doing, be about to do; **h- (fast) på** hold on (tightly) to; maintain, stick to (**h- på sitt** stick to one's own opinion, theory, view, etc.); **h- til** have lodgings, live, stay; **h- ut fra hverandre** distinguish, keep apart; **h- (fast) ved** maintain, stick to. 5 *(refl.)*: **h- seg** hold up, keep, last; endure, wear; restrain oneself; **h- seg for god** consider oneself too good; **h- seg for munnen** hold, keep one's hands over one's mouth; **h- seg for øye** keep in view; **h- seg godt** bear one's years well, keep well-preserved; **h- seg inne** stay in(doors); **h- seg inne med noen** keep in good standing with sby, stay in sby's good graces; **h- seg med** keep company with; **h- seg til** keep to, stick to, turn to; go by, follow.

***hol'de**[3] *V -a*: **h- seg** fill out.

+**hol'den** *A -ent, pl -ne* (=*halden) 1 prosperous, well-to-do. 2: **helt og h-ent** entirely, wholly.

+**hol'de/plass** *-en* 1 bus, streetcar stop. 2 taxi stand.

+**hol'de/punkt** [/pong't] *-et* fixed point; *fig.* basis, ground(s): **politiet hadde intet h-** the police had no clue.

+**hol'der** *-en, pl -e* (=*haldar) 1 holder, stand. 2 *elec.* socket. 3 (on projector) sprocket clamp.

***hol'dig** *A* - full, plump.

+**-hol'dig** *A* - (=*-haldig) bearing, containing: **alkoholh-, malmh-.**

hol'dning *-a/+-en 1 carriage, posture: **ha en dårlig h-** stoop. 2 air, attitude, bearing; backbone, *(pop.)* guts: **innta en fast h-** take a strong stand; **nasjonal h-** patriotic stand.

hol'dnings/laus *A* spineless, wishy-washy.

+**hol'dt**[1] *et*: **gjøre h-** *mil.* come to a halt.

+**hol'dt**[2] *pt of* **holde**[1,2]

+**hol'dt**[3] *I mil.* halt.

ho'le[1] *-n dial.* elevation, ridge.

hole[2] [hå'le] *-a* (=+hule[1]) 1 cave, cavern; den, lair: **våge seg inn i løvens h-** venture into the lion's den. 2 *anat.* cavity.

+**ho'le**[3] *V -te* catch; get hold of, secure; steal, *(pop.)* snitch.

hole[4] [hå'le] *V -a/-te* (=+hule[2]): **h- ut** hollow out.

Ho'le *Pln* twp, Buskerud.

***hole/buar** [hå'le/] *-en* cf **hule/boer**

holet(e) [hå'let(e)] *A* - (=+hullet(e)) 1 bumpy (e.g. a road); full of holes. 2 leaky; *fig.* faulty (e.g. a memory).

hol/fald [hå'l/fall] *-en* (=+hull/) hemstitch.

hol/jern [hå'l/jæ'rn] *-et* gouge.

hol'k[1] *-en naut.* hulk, scow, tub.

hol'k[2] *-en* 1 ferrule (e.g. on a cane). 2 (wooden) tub.

hol'ke *V -a/+-et* (put a) ferrule (on).

ho'l/kinna *A* - (=+hul/kinnet) hollow-cheeked.

***ho'l/kjaka** *A* - hollow-cheeked.

hol/kort [hå'l/] *-et* cf **hull/**

***holl'** *A* bulky, heavy, plump.

Hol'la *Pln* twp, Telemark.

Hol'land *Pln* Holland.

hol'landsk *A* - Dutch.

***hol'leg** *A* - careful, solicitous.

+**hollen'der** *-en, pl -e* (=*hollending) Dutchman (Netherlander): **den flyvende h-** the flying Dutchman.

***hol'lending** *-en* Dutchman.

+**holloi'** *-en* cf **halloi**[1]

***holl'/skap** *-en* cf **hull/**

hol'me *-n* (=*holm) small island, islet; *Brit.* holm.

Hol'men/kollen *Pln* height above Oslo: **Holmenkolldagen** Holmenkoll day (early in March), national ski meet.

Hol'me/strand *Pln* town, Vestfold.

hol'm/gang *-en hist.* "holm-going" (duel fought on a holm, in accordance with certain rules).

Hol'm/ga'rd *Pln hist.* Old Norse name for Novgorod, Russia.

Hol'ms/bu *Pln* town, Hurum twp, Buskerud.

ho'l/mål *-et* (=+hul/) measure of capacity.

***ho'lne** *V -a/+-et* be hollowed out, become hollow.

°**ho'lo** *-a* cf **hole**[2]

***hol/saum** [hå'l/] *-en* cf **hull/søm**

hol/sleiv *-a* (=+hull/) skimmer.

***ho'l/spegel** *-elen, pl -lar* cf **hul/speil**

hol't *-et* grove, wood.

Hol't *Pln* twp, Aust-Agder.

ho'l/tann *-a, pl -tenner* (=+hul/) hollow tooth.

***hol/tong** [hå'l/] *-a* cf **hull/tang**

Hol't/ålen *Pln* twp, Sør-Trøndelag.

Ho'lum *Pln* twp, Vest-Agder.

ho'l/veg *-en* cf **hul/vei**

***ho'l/øygd** *A -/-øygt* cf **hul/øyd**

***hom** [homm'] *-en* little valley.

hom/bot [hom'/] *-a, pl -bøter dial., anat.* hamstring.

home'risk *A* - Homeric.

homi'lie *-n eccl.* homily.

homi'lie/bok *-a/+-en eccl.* book o homilies.

°**homle** [hom'le] *-a* cf **humle**[1]

homme [hom'me] *V -a/+-et dial.* back a horse (by forcing it to move the hindquarters sideways): **h- seg** back (the movement of the horse).

***hom'n** *-a* embryo, fetus.

homofi'l *A* homosexual.

homoge'n *A* homogeneous.

homogenite't *-en* homogeneity.

homony'm *-et* homonym.

ho'mo/seksualite't *-en* homosexuality.

ho'mo/seksuell' *A -elt* homosexual.

homozygo'tisk *A* - homozygous.

homøopa't *-en* homeopathist.

°**ho'n** *-en* cf **hun**[1]

***ho'nk** *-a, pl henker* cf **hank**[1]

honnett' *A* - *archaic* honorable, respectable; cultured, elegant: **h- ambisjon** social ambition.

hon'ning *-en* honey.

hon'ning/kake *-a* a cake containing honey (as one of its ingredients).

Hon'nings/våg *Pln* seaport, Nordkapp twp, Finnmark.

honnø'r *-en* 1 *lit.* honor: **med (full) h-** honorably. 2 *mil.* honor(s), salute: **gjøre h-** salute. 3 honor (bridge).

honnø'r/billett' *-en* reduced-rate ticket (for elderly persons).

honnø'r/kort *-et* honor-card (bridge).

honnø'r/stikk *-et* honor trick (bridge).

***honom** [hå'nåmm] *ob of* **han**[2]

honora'r *-et, pl -/+-er* fee, royalty.

honoratiores [honoratsio'res] *pl* dignitaries, *(pop.)* bigwigs, VIP's.

honore're *V -te merc.* 1 pay (royalties, wages) for, to: **dårlig h-t arbeid** badly paid work. 2 honor (e.g. a check).

honoræ'r *A* honorary (e.g. consul).

hook [huk'] *-en* (in boxing) hook: **en venstre h- til kjeven** a left h- to the jaw.

ho'p *-en* 1 heap, pile. 2 crowd multitude: **alle i h-** all of them; **alt i h-** everything; **en hel h-** a great deal (many); **h-en** the mob, rabble, riffraff; **i h-** together.

+**ho'pe**[1] *N archaic*: **til h-** together; **alt (alle) til h-** everything (everybody).

ho'pe[2] *V -a/+-et*: **h- opp, sammen** accumulate, heap up; **h- seg opp, sammen** accumulate, mount up.

ho'pe[3] *V -a/+-et* back (a horse).

ho'pe/hav *-et* dealings (**med** with), matters, relations (between individuals).

Ho'pen *Pln* twp, Møre og Romsdal.

ho'pe/tal *N* (=+/tall): **i h-** in great numbers.

hopp'[1] *-et* 1 hop, jump, leap: **gjøre et h-** hop, jump, leap, *fig.* omit, skip. 2 jumping; take-off (skiing).

hopp'[2] *I* (expression of delight, usu. accompanied by skipping movements): **hei h-, heisan h-,** etc.

hopp'/bakke *-n* (ski) jumping hill.

hop'pe[1] *-a* mare.

hop'pe[2] *V -a/+-et* hop, jump, leap: **det er likeså godt å h- i det som å krype i det** one might as well be hanged for a sheep as for a goat, *(pop.)* go for broke; **hjertet h-et i livet** (my) heart thumped wildly; **h- bukk** play leapfrog; **h- over noe** miss, omit, skip sth; **h- paradis** play hopscotch; **h- på ski** ski jump.

hop'pende *Av*: **h- glad** beside oneself with joy, overjoyed.

+**hop'per** *-en, pl -e* (=*-ar) jumper (gymnastics); ski jumper.

hop'pe/tau *-et* jump rope.

hopp'la *I* whee, whoops.

hopp'/renn *-et* ski jumping (competition).

hopp'/ski *-a, pl -/-er* jumping ski (used in competition).

hop'sa *-en* old-fashioned hop waltz, lively dance.

hop'sasa *I* tralala (to accompany joyful leaps or skipping).

ho'r *-et* 1 *bibl.* adultery: **du skal ikke bedrive h-** thou shalt not commit a- (Exodus 20, 14). 2 *theol.* fornication.

***hor'd** *-en* person from Hordaland.

Hord. = **Hordaland**
Hor'da/bø *Pln* twp, Hordaland.
Hor'da/land *Pln* county in Western Norway (around Bergen).
hor'de *-n* horde: **den gylne h-** the Golden H-.
ho're[1] *-a* prostitute, whore.
ho're[2] *V -a/+-et/+-te* fornicate, whore.
ho're/hus *-et* brothel, whorehouse.
hor'g[1] *-a* 1 *archeol.* heathen sanctuary (consisting largely of a stone altar, used for private sacrifice). 2 *dial.* flat-topped knoll (with steep sides).
***hor'g**[2] *-a* crowd, multitude.
Hor'g *Pln* twp, Sør-Trøndelag.
horison't *-en* 1 horizon: **dukke opp i h-en** loom up on the h-; **ha fri, vid h-** have a clear view. 2: **sann h-** *astron., naut.* celestial horizon. 3 *geol.* horizon. 4 *fig.* intellectual range, scope: **ha en snever h-** be narrow-minded; **ligge utenfor ens h-** be outside one's experience, interests.
horisonta'l *A* horizontal.
hor'k[1] *-a zool.* ruff (Acerina cernua).
hor'k[2] *-a, pl -er/*herker dial.* 1 (willow) loop on a gate; on a sled runner (as a brake). 2 ski binding.
hormo'n *-et, pl -/+-er* hormone.
hormo'n/prepara't *-et, pl -/+-er* hormone preparation.
ho'rn *-et* 1 horn (true horn; article of horn or shaped like a horn, e.g., a drinking horn; horny substance): **ha et h- i siden til en** bear a grudge against sby; **løpe h-ene av seg** sow one's wild oats; **sette h- på en** cuckold sby; **ta tyren ved h-ene** take the bull by the horns; **trekke h-ene til seg** pull in one's horns. 2 *astron.* cusp of the crescent moon. 3 *mus.* horn; automobile horn: **støte i h-et** blow, sound the horn. 4 (bakery goods) croissant (crescent-shaped roll).
+**ho'rn/aktig** *A* - 1 horny. 2 dead, lifeless (e.g. glance).
ho'rn/blende *+-n/*-a min.* hornblende.
ho'rn/brille *-a/+-en* (*usu. pl.*) horn-rimmed glasses.
ho'rnet(e) *A* - horned.
ho'rn/gjel *-a/-en zool.* needlefish (Belone acus).
ho'rn/hinne *-a anat.* cornea (in eye).
Ho'rnin/dal *Pln* twp, Sogn og Fjordane.
+**ho'rn/kveg** *-et* horned cattle.
ho'rn/mine *-a naut.* sea mine (of the contact type).
ho'rn/musikk' *-en* brass music.
Ho'rn/nes' *Pln* twp, Aust-Agder.
ho'rn/sil *-en zool.* stickleback (family Gasterosteidae).
horosko'p *-et, pl -/+-er* horoscope: **stille ens h-** cast sby's h-.
***horr'**[1] *-en* cf **harr**
***horr'**[2] *-en bot.* flax (genus Linum).
horri'bel *A -elt, pl -le* awful, horrible.
***hor's** *-et* loose woman, slut.
hors d'oeuvre [årdø'ver] *-n* hors d'oeuvre.
***hor'se** *-a* mare.
***hor'se/gauk** *-en zool.* common snipe (Capella gallinago).
Hor'ten *Pln* city, Vestfold.
horten'sia *-en bot.* hydrangea (genus Hydrangea).
ho'r/unge [/onge] *-n derog.* bastard, whoreson.
hor'v[1] *-a* cf **harv**
***hor'v**[2] *-et* fitness, order: **det er ikkje h- med det** there's no sense to it.
***hor've**[1] *V -a* cf **harve**[1]
***hor've**[2] *V -de* happen, turn out: **det h-de seg så til at vi møttest** we met by accident, chance.
***hor'v/elde** *-t* crosspiece on a cow's collar (to close it).
***hor'veleg** *A* - convenient, suitable.
hos [hoss'] *P* at, at sby's (home, house, place, store, etc.), by; in; with; among; from: **den boka ligger inne h- meg** that book is in my room; **det er en svakhet h- ham** that's a weakness in (with) him (of his); **et vers hun hadde lest h- Ibsen** a verse she had read in I-; **han bodde h- lappene i mange år** he lived among the Lapps for many years; **handle h- Olsen** shop, trade at O-'s; **h- oss er kjærligheten snart en vitenskap** with (among) us love will soon be a science (Ibsen); **spise middag h- en** eat dinner at sby's place; **står alt bra til h- Dem?** is everything fine at your place?; **søke råd h- en** seek advice from sby; **utgitt h- X** published by X (at X's); **være i unåde h- en** be in disfavor with sby.
Ho's/anger *Pln* twp, Hordaland.
ho'se *-a* 1 sock, stocking: **gjøre sine h-r grønne hos en** curry favor with sby, go out of one's way to please sby; **lett som fot i h-** as easy as falling off a log. 2 *hist.* hose (for men).
ho'se/band *-et* (=+/**bånd**) (round) garter.
+**ho'sebånds/orden** *-en* (=***hose-bands/**) Order of the Garter.
+**ho'se/lest** *-en* (=*/**leist**) stocking foot.
***hosen** [hå'sen] *A -e/-i, pl -ne* porous, spongy.
hosian'na *I* hosanna.
***ho'/slag** *-et* female.
+**hos/liggende** [hoss'/] *A* - (=*/**liggjande**) *math.* adjacent.
hospita'l *-et, pl -/+-er* hospital: **bringe på h-et** take to the h-; **ligge på h-** be in a h-; **sende en på h-** send sby to a h-.
hospitan't *-en educ.* auditor.
hospite're *V -te educ.* attend class as an auditor.
hospit's *-et, pl -/+-er* hospice; family hotel.
°**hoss'(en)** *Av* cf **korleis**
hos/stående [hoss'/] *A* - adjacent, nearby: **h- bilde** the accompanying picture.
host [hos't] *-en/-el* (single) cough.
hoste[1] [hos'te] *-n* cough, coughing.
hoste[2] [hos'te] *V -a/+-et* cough (**opp** up).
***hos'te**[3] *Av* rather.
hoste/mikstu'r [hos'te/] *-en* cough medicine.
hoste/ri *-a dial.* fit of coughing.
hoste/saft *-a* cough medicine.
hos'tie [also -ti'] *-n eccl.* Host.
***ho't** *-et* menace, threat.
ho'te *V -a/+-et* menace, threaten.
hotell' *-et, pl -/+-er* hotel: **bo på et h-** stay at a h-; **drive et h-** run a h-; **ta inn på et h-** put up at a h-.
hotell'/drift *-a/+-en* hotel management.
hotell'fag/skole *-n* school for hotel management.
hotell'/plass *-en* hotel accommodation.
hotell'/vert *-en* hotel proprietor (manager).
***hott'** *-en* hair (of the head).
hottentott' *-en* Hottentot.
***hot'tut** *A* - rough, uneven (terrain).
ho'v[1] *-en, pl -er/+høver* hoof.
hov[2] [hå'v] *-et archeol.* pagan temple, place of worship (in ancient Scand.).
***ho'v**[3] *-et* adaptation; moderation: **det er ikkje h- med det** it's way out of line.
***ho'v**[4] *pt of* **hevje**[1]
***hov'da** *A* -: **fagert h-** having a fine head.
***hov'de** *-n* 1 head of a bed. 2 rounded peak.
***hov'ding** *-en* cf **høvding**
ho'v/dyr *-et zool.* hoofed animal, ungulate.
***ho've**[1] *V -a* 1 adapt, make suitable. 2 conjecture, surmise.
***ho've**[2] *pp of* **hevje**[1]
+**ho'ved-** *Pf* (=***hovud-**) chief, main, principal.
+**ho'ved/bestan'dde'l** *-en* main ingredient.
+**ho'ved/bok** *-a, pl -bøker merc.* ledger: **avslutte h-en** balance the ledger.
+**ho'ved/bokhol'der** *-en, pl -e* head bookkeeper.
+**ho'ved/bryter** *-en, pl -e elec.* main switch.
+**ho'ved/bygning** *-en* main building.
+**ho'ved/drag** *-et* basic trait, essential feature.
+**ho'ved/dør** *-a* entrance door, main entrance.
+**ho'ved/fag** *-et educ.* major (subject).
+**ho'ved/feil** *-en, pl* - cardinal fault, chief defect.
+**ho'ved/formål** *-et* chief aim, main objective.
+**ho'ved/gate** *-a* main street.
+**ho'ved/gå'rd** *-en* chief residence; main farm.
+**ho'ved/inngang** *-en* main entrance.
+**ho'ved/innhold** *-et* main contents; summary.
+**ho'ved/karakte'r** *-en educ.* average grade, final standing.
+**ho'ved/kasse'rer** *-en* head cashier.
+**ho'ved/kilde** *-n* principal source.
ho'ved/konto'r *-et* main office.
+**ho'ved/kvarte'r** *-et mil.* general headquarters, GHQ.
+**ho'ved/le'dning** *-en* main (gas, water, etc.).
+**ho'ved/linje** *-a/-en* 1 main, principal line (of development). 2 main line (of a RR).
+**ho'ved/mangel** *-elen, pl -ler* chief defect.
+**ho'ved/mann** *-en* chief, leader; ringleader.
+**ho'ved/masse** *-n* bulk, main part.
+**ho'ved/nøkkel** *-elen, pl -nøkler* master key.
+**ho'ved/oppga've** *-a/-en* 1 chief purpose, main task. 2 *educ.* thesis in major subject.
+**ho'ved/perso'n** *-en* 1 leading character, protagonist (theater). 2 head of a household.
+**ho'ved/regel** *-en* axiom, basic principle, rule.
+**ho'ved/reparasjo'n** *-en* complete overhaul.
+**ho'ved/rolle** *-n* leading role.
+**ho'ved/sak** *-en*: **h-en** the chief concern, the main thing.
+**hovedsa'kelig** *A* - (=***hovud/sakleg**) chiefly, mainly, primarily.
+**ho'ved/setning** *-en gram.* main clause.
+**ho'ved/sikring** *-a/-en elec.* main fuse.
+**ho'ved/sogn** [/sångn] *-et* (=+/**sokn**) home parish.
+**ho'ved/stad** *-en, pl -steder* capital (city).
+**ho'ved/stil** *-en educ.* principal essay (in language of student's choice - **bokmål** or **nynorsk**, at examination for University entrance).
+**ho'ved/strømning** *-en* main current: **H-er i det nittende århundredes litteratur** Main Currents in 19th Century Literature (book by Georg Brandes).
+**ho'ved/styrke** *-n* 1 forte, strong point. 2 *mil.* main body (of an army).
+**ho'ved/sum'** *-men* (sum) total.
+**ho'ved/tegning** [/teining] *-en* (=*/**teikning**) *arch.* general plan.
+**ho'ved/trekk** *-et* essential, fundamental feature.
+**ho'ved/vei** *-en* 1 main road. 2 main entrance (to a building).
+**ho'ved/vekt** *-a/-en* 1 chief emphasis: **legge h-en på** emphasize. 2 *gram.* main stress.
Ho'ved/øya *Pln* island, Oslo harbor.
hoven [hå'ven] *A +-ent, pl -ne* 1 distended, swollen. 2 *fig.* conceited, condescending, stuck-up.
hove're *V -te* crow, exult, gloat (**over** at).
hoveri' *-et hist.* villeinage (tenant's obligation to lord, esp. in Denmark).

+ Bokmål; * Nynorsk; ° Dialect.
After letter: ' stress (Acc. 1); ` tone, stress (Acc. 2); · length.
Below letter: . not pronounced.

+**hoveri'/tjeneste** -*n* (=***/teneste**) *hist.* villeinage.
Hovin [hå'vin] *Pln* twp, Telemark.
***ho'vleg** *A* - cf **høvelig**
+**hov'ler** *pl of* **hovold**
hov/mann [hå'v/] -*en*, *pl* -*menn*/ *-*menner* 1 *hist.* courtier, gentleman in waiting. 2 *dial.* clerk of court.
+**hov/mester** [hå'v/] -*eren*, *pl* -*ere*/-*rer* (=***/meister**) 1 headwaiter (maître d' hôtel). 2 *hist.* private tutor; butler.
+**hov'/mod** -*et* arrogance, haughtiness, self-importance: **h- står for fall** pride goeth before a fall.
+**hov'/mode** -*et*: **h- seg (av noe)** boast (about sth).
+**hov'/modig** [also -mo'-] *A* - arrogant, overbearing, stuck-up.
hov'ne *V* -*a*/+-*et* swell: **h- opp** s- up.
***hovold** [hå'vål] -*a* heddle (in weaving).
***ho'v/sam'** *A* lenient, mild, moderate.
ho'v/skjegg -*et* fetlock.
ho'v/slag -*et* 1 hoofbeat. 2 hoofprint.
+**ho'v/slager** -*en*, *pl* -*e* (=***-ar**) blacksmith.
+**ho'v/tang** -*a*, *pl* -*tenger* (=***/tong**) blacksmith's tongs.
***hovud** [hå'vu] -*et* cf **hode**
***hovud-** *Pf* cf **hoved-, hode-**
***hovud/galen** *A* -*e*/-*i*, *pl* -*ne* cf **hode/**
***hovud/gjerd** [/jær] -*a* cf **hode/gjerde**
***hovud/lag** -*et* cf **hode/**
***hovud/sak** -*a* cf **hoved/**
***hovud/sakleg** *Av* cf **hoved/sakelig**
***hovud/skalle** -*n* cf **hode/**
***hovuds/mann** -*en*, *pl* -*menn*(*er*) cf **høveds/**
***hovud/stad** -*en*, *pl* -*er* cf **hoved/**
***hovud/stup** *Av* headlong, precipitate(ly); sudden(ly).
***hovud/tørkle** -*et* cf **hode/**
***hovud/veg** -*en* cf **hoved/**
***hovud/verk** -*et* cf **hode/**
HP = **Høyres Pressekontor**
hr. = **herr**
h.r.adv. = **høgsterettsadvokat**
hs(s). = **handskrift(er)**
+**hu'**[1] -*en* 1 mind: **komme i h-** call to m-, remember. 2 *archaic* craving, desire (**til** for).
+**hu'**[2] *I* 1 oh, ugh (expressing fear, contempt, anger). 2: **huhu** boohoo. 3 whoo (cry of the owl, soughing of the wind). 4: **hu hei** whee.
°**hu'**[3] *Pn* cf **hun**[5]
hu'bro -*en* *zool.* (great) horned owl (Bubo bubo).
hu'd [*hu'] -*a*/+-*en* 1 skin: **ha tykk h-** *fig.* be callous, indifferent; **ha tynn h-** *fig.* be thin-skinned, overly sensitive; **skjelle en h-en full** rake sby over the coals; **sluke med h- og hår** swallow whole; *fig.* **med h- og hår** hook, line, and sinker. 2 hide: **ha en rem av h-en** be cut from the same piece of cloth, share a weakness; **selge h-en før bjørnen er skutt** count one's chickens before they are hatched; **skjære brede remmer av ens h-** make sby pay through the nose. 3 cover, protection (of any kind). 4 *naut.* sheathing.
hu'd/farge -*n* complexion.
hu'd/flette *V* -*a*/+-*et*/*-*e* 1 flay, flog. 2 *fig.* castigate, flay.
hu'd/laus *A* (=+**/løs**) 1 excoriated, raw. 2 *fig.* overly sensitive.
hu'd/orm -*en* blackhead.
hu'd/skifte -*t* shedding (of the skin).
hu'd/sko -*en*, *pl* -*r*/+- *hist.* rawhide shoe.
hu'd/stryke *V* *infl as* **stryke** *bibl.* scourge: **Jesus lot han h- og overgav ham til å korsfestes** he had Jesus scourged and delivered to be crucified (Matthew 27, 26).
hu'd/vev -*et*/+-*en* *bot.* epidermis.
hu'e[1] -*a* (=**huve**) 1 cap; bonnet. 2 *hist.* coif.
°**hu'e**[2] -*t* cf **hode**
hu'e[3] *V* +-*dde*/*-*a* *dial.* holler, shout.
+**hu'e**[4] *V* -*et* *lit.* please: **det h-er meg ikke** I don't like it; I am not pleased with it.
huff' *I* humph, ugh (expressing annoyance, dissatisfaction).
huf's -*et* jerk, tug, wrench: **gjøre et h- på seg** give oneself a shake, shake oneself.
huf'se *V* -*a*/+-*et* 1: **h- (på) seg** give oneself a shake, shake oneself; **h- seg opp** work one's way up. 2 move jerkily, spasmodically; shiver: **h- på seg klærne** jump into one's clothes. 3 botch, bungle.
***huf'sen** *A* -*e*/-*i*, *pl* -*ne* rough, rugged (e.g. terrain).
huf'sopp/seng -*a* wall bunk bed.
hu'g [also *ho'g] -*en* 1 mind; heart, soul: **komme i h-** think; call to mind, remember. 2 craving, desire: **få h- til** have a mind to, want to; **ha h- på noe** be bent on doing sth; **ha h- til** be in a mood to.
hu'ga *A* -: **være h- på noe** be desirous of, feel like doing sth.
***hu'gal** *A* amusing, delightful, pleasant.
***hu'gast** *V* -*ast*: **h- på noko** feel like doing sth.
huga'v -*en* (gruff) old soldier.
***hu'g/bere** [/bære] *V* -*bar*, -*bore*/-*i* be in love with.
+**hu'g/bitt** -*et* (=***/bit**) *dial.* heartburn; nausea.
***hu'g/bod** [/bå] -*et* expectation, presentiment, suspicion.
***hu'g/brann** -*en* interest, passion.
+**hug'de** *pt of* **hugge**[2]
***hu'g/drag** -*et* desire, inclination, interest.
***hu'ge** *V* -*a* 1 recall, remember. 2 desire.
+**hu'gen** *A* -*ent*, *pl* -*ne* cf **huga**
hugenott' -*en* Huguenot.
***hu'g/fallen** *A* -*e*/-*i*, *pl* -*falne* dejected, depressed.
***hu'g/feste** *V* -*e* fix in one's mind.
+**hugg'**[1] -*et* cf **hogg**[1]
+**hugg'**[2] *pt of* **hugge**[1]
***hug'ge**[1] -*n* comfort, consolation.
+**hug'ge**[2] *V* *hugg*/*hugde*, *hugd* cf **hogge**
***hug'ge**[3] *V* -*a* 1 calm down, pacify. 2 cheer, gladden.
+**hug'ger** -*en*, *pl* -*e* cf **hogger**
+**hug'gert** -*en* *naut.* cutlass.
+**hugg'/orm** -*en* cf **hogg/**
+**hugg'/tann** -*en*, *pl* -*tenner* cf **hogg/**
hu'g/heil *A* calm, confident, untroubled.
***hu'g/ill** *A* -*ilt* anxious, concerned.
hu'g/la *pt of* **-legge**
hu'g/lag -*et* disposition, mood, temperament.
***hu'g/laus** *A* dejected, depressed; indifferent.
***hu'gleg** *A* - amusing, delightful, pleasant.
+**hu'g/legge** *V* -*la*, -*lagt* (=***/leggje**) *dial.*, *archaic* fall in love with.
***hu'g/leik** -*en* fancy, imagination, playfulness.
hu'g/lynne -*t* (=***/lynde**) disposition, mood, temperament.
***hu'g/mål** -*et* interest; ideal.
hu'gnad -*en* delight, pleasure: **ha h- av** enjoy; **ingen til h-** to no one's delight.
***hu'gnadleg** *A* - amusing, delightful, pleasant.
hugs [huk's] -*et* *dial.* 1 composure, sense, thoughtfulness. 2 memory.
***hu'g/sam'** *A* agreeable, pleasant: **emnet er ikkje h-t** it is a disagreeable topic (Vesaas).
hugse [huk'se, *hok'se] *V* -*a*/+-*et* (=+**huske**) recall, recollect, remember; bear in mind: **h- feil** be mistaken, remember incorrectly; **husk på at han kommer kl. 11** bear in mind that he is arriving at 11 o'clock; **husk på å skrive** remember to write; **jeg h-er godt den natten** I well remember that night.
hugse/lapp -*en* (=+**huske/**) memo.
***hugsen** [huk'sen] *A* -*e*/-*i*, *pl* -*ne* with a good memory.
hu'g/skott -*et* (=***/skot**) *dial.* fancy, (bright) idea; impulse, inspiration.
***hu'g/snikje** -*a* coquette, flirt.
hu'g/sott -*a*/+-*en* *dial.* melancholy, unhappiness; worry (**for** about).
+**hug'st** -*en* cf **hogst**
***hu'g/stele** *V* -*stal*, -*stole*/-*i* discourage, dishearten.
***hu'g/stemne** -*a* mentality, outlook.
***hu'g/stole** [/ståle] *pp of* **-stele** discouraged, disheartened.
hu'g/stor *A* - broad-minded, high-minded, liberal.
***hu'g/svale** *V* -*a* cf **hu/**
***hu'g/sviv** -*et* fancy, (bright) idea.
***hu'g/syn** -*et*/-*a* idea, thought; fancy, whim.
hu'g/ta *V* *infl as* **ta** (=***/take**) charm, fascinate: ***eit h-ande gutelag** a charming boyishness.
***hu'g/teken** *A* -*e*/-*i*, *pl* -*ne* enamored, fascinated, infatuated.
+**hu'g/tok** *pt of* **-ta**
°**hug'u** -*et* cf **hode**
***hu'g/vill** *A* -*vilt* doubtful, irresolute.
°**hug'ærn** *A* cf **hode/galen**
huhei' *I* ho, whee.
hui'[1] -*en*/-*et*: **i h- og hast** hurriedly, posthaste.
hui'[2] *I* ho, oh boy, whee (expressing pleasure at speed): **h-, hvor det går!** boy, how we're moving!
hui'e *V* -*a*/+*et*/+-*de* (=***huje**) holler, hoot, shout; howl (e.g. the wind).
***hu'je** *V* -*a* cf **huie**
hu'k *N*: **på h-** on one's haunches; **sitte på h-** crouch, squat.
hu'ke[1] *V* -*a*/+-*et*: **h- seg** crouch, squat (**ned, sammen** down); cower.
hu'ke[2] *V* -*te* 1 hook: **h- av** unhook; **h- på** hook on. 2 draw, pull in with a hook. 3: **h- seg fast, h- tak (i)** catch hold (of); get a good grip (on); *fig.* buttonhole (sby). 4 *fam.* grab, snatch, snitch. 5: **h- en talje** *naut.* hook a tackle; **h- ut** unhook, unship.
***hu'ken** *A* -*e*/-*i*, *pl* -*ne* bent, curved.
+**hukom'melse** -*n* memory: **sitere etter h-n** quote from m-; **feste noe i h-n** fix, imprint sth in one's m-; **feste seg i h-n** stick in one's mind.
+**hukom'melses/tap** -*et* loss of memory; *med.* amnesia.
huk'r -*en* *dial.* 1 shiver, shudder. 2 call, crow (of a grouse, partridge).
huk're *V* -*a*/+-*et* *dial.* 1 shiver, shudder. 2 (of a grouse, partridge) call, crow.
+**hu'l** *A* cf **hol**[3]
+**hu'/lag** -*et* cf **hode/**
+**hu'l/brystet** *A* - cf **hol/brysta**
+**hul'd** *A* - cf **hull**[2]
Hul'da *Prn* (*f*)
hul'der -*ra*, *pl* -*rer* 1 *folk.* wicked, alluring siren inhabiting hills and mountains (beautiful in appearance but with a long, cowlike tail). 2 *poet.* any beautiful, alluring woman, femme fatale.
hul'dre/eventyr [also hul'-] -*et* legend about *huldrer* and other subterranean beings.
hul'dre/heim [also hul'-] -*en* hill, mountain inhabited by a *hulder.*
hul'dre/lokk [also hul'-] -*en* enticing melody of a *hulder*; melody learned from a *hulder.*
hul'dren *A* +-*ent*, *pl* -*ene* crazy, half-witted (after having seen a *hulder*).
hul'dre/tjern [/kjæ'rn, also hul'-] -*et* small mountain lake in which the fish belong to a *hulder* and can't be caught.
+**hu'le**[1] -*n* cf **hole**[3]
+**hu'le**[2] *V* -*te* cf **hole**[4]
+**hu'le/boer** -*en*, *pl* -*e* cave dweller, caveman.
+**hu'l/het** -*en* *fig.* hollowness; deception, falsity, humbug.
+**hu'l/jern** [/jæ'rn] -*et* cf **hol/**
+**hul'k** -*en*/-*et* sobbing; sob.
+**hul'ke** *V* -*a*/-*et* sob.
+**hu'l/kinnet** *A* - cf **hol/kinna**
+**hull'**[1] -*et* cf **hol**[2]
+**hull'**[2] *A* *archaic* 1 kind: **være en h-** be fond of sby. 2 faithful, loyal: **være en h- og tro** be faithful to sby. 3 graceful, lovely: **denne mørke,**

hulde hud this dark, lovely skin (Hamsun).
+**hul'le**[1] *V -et* drill holes in.
hul'le[2] *V -a*/+*-et* croon, hum.
+**hul'let(e)** *A* - cf **holet(e)**
+**hull'/falḍ** *-en* cf **hol/**
+**hull'/kort** *-et* punch card (IBM card).
+**hullsa'lig** *A* - *archaic* blissful; gracious.
+**hull'/skap** *-en*: **vise en h- og troskap** be faithful, loyal to sby.
+**hull'/sleiv** *-a* cf **hol/**
+**hull'/søm·** *-men* hemstitch.
+**hull'/tang** *-a* punch (e.g. for leather).
+**hu'l/mål** *-et* cf **hol/**
+**hu'lne** *V -a*/*-et* cf **holne**
+**hu'lning** *-en* depression, hollow.
+**hu'l/rom** [/romm] *-met* cavity, hollow space.
+**hu'l/slipe** *V -te* hollow grind.
+**hu'l/speil** *-et* concave mirror.
+**hu'l/tann** *-en, pl -tenner* cf **hol/**
***hul'ter**[1] *-et* trot.
hul'ter[2] *Av*: **h- til (i) bulter** helter-skelter, pell-mell: **golvet et eneste h- til bulter** the floor one grand confusion (Bojer).
***hul'tre** *V -a* take short steps, trot.
+**hu'l/vei** *-en* sunken road (road with high banks on both sides).
+**hu'l/øyd** *A* - (=+**hol/**, ***hol/øygd**) hollow-eyed.
***hum'** *-et* darkness, gloom (caused by gathering clouds).
huma'n *A* humane; humanistic.
huma'n/etikk' *-en* humanistic ethics.
huma'n/etisk *A* - humanistically ethical.
humanio'ra *pl* the humanities.
humanis'me *-n* humanism.
humanis't *-en* humanist.
humanis'tisk *A* - humanistic.
humanite't *-en* humanity; humaneness.
humanitæ'r *A* humanitarian.
hum'bug *-en* humbug, sham, swindle, *(pop.)* balderdash, bluff.
+**hum'bug/maker** *-en, pl -e* (=***-ar**) charlatan, quack, swindler.
humle[1] [hom'le] *-n bot.* hop (Humulus lupulus).
humle[2] [hom'le] *-a zool.* bumblebee (family Bombidae): **la h-a suse** make merry, put aside one's cares.
humle[3] [hom'le] *V -a*/+*-et* flavor with hops (brewing).
humle/blom +*-men*/**-en bot.* (drooping) avens (genus Geum).
humle/bol *-et* bumblebee's nest.
hum'mel *-en* +**1** see **humul**. **2** *dial.* grain (esp. barley, or mixed barley and rye).
+**hummer** [hom'mer] *-en* (=***-ar**) **1** *zool.* lobster (Homarus vulgaris). **2** *naut.* hole in the masthead through which the halyard goes.
+**hummer/klo** *-a, pl -klør* (=***-ar/**) lobster's claw.
+**hummer/rød** *A* (=***hummar/raud**) red as a lobster, scarlet.
+**hummer/teine** *-a* (=***-ar/**) lobster pot.
hu'mor *-en* humor: **ha, mangle sans for h-** have, lack a sense of h-.
humores'ke *-n mus.* humoresque.
humoris't *-en* humorist.
humoris'tisk *A* - humorous: **ha sans for det h-e** have a sense of humor.
hump[1] [hom'p] *-en* **1** bump, hump (e.g. in a road). **2** lump, thickening. ***3** crag; knoll.
hump[2] [hom'p] *-et* **1** hobbling, limping. **2** bump (of a passenger on a bumpy road).
humpe [hom'pe] *V -a*/+*-et* **1** hobble, limp. **2** bump along (on a rough road): **vogna h-et og ristet** the wagon bumped and shook.
humpet(e) [hom'pet(e)] *A* - bumpy, full of chuckholes (e.g. a road).
humre [hom're] *V -a*/+*-et* **1** neigh, whinny. **2** chuckle.
humre/gauk *-en zool.* common snipe (Capella gallinago).
humse [hom'se] *V -a*/+*-et* **1** hobble, *limp.* **2** chuckle.
hum'ul *-en* singletree, whiffletree.
hu'mus *-en* humus.
hu'mus/jo·rḍ *-a* humus soil.
humø'r *-et* **1** mood, temper; disposition, temperament: **det tar på h-et** it's exasperating; **ha et lyst (tungt) h-** have a cheerful (melancholy) disposition; **når han er i det h-et** when the mood strikes him; **være i h- til** be in the mood to. **2** good humor, high spirits: **sette en i h-** cheer sby up, put sby in a good humor; **miste h-et** be depressed; **ta noe med h-** grin and bear it, put up with sth cheerfully. **3** sense of humor: **en mann med h-, ekte Oslo-h-** a man with a s- of h-, true Oslo humor (Dagbladet).
humø'r/frisk *A* cheerful, in good spirits.
humø'r/fylt *A* - humorous.
humø'r/sjuk *A* depressed, in bad spirits.
hu'n[1] *-en* outer plank from a log.
***hun'**[2] *-en* cf **huner**
***hu'n**[3] *-en* (bear) cub.
+**hun'**[4] *-nen* cf **hunn**
+**hun'**[5] *Pn ob henne*[1], *po hennes* (=***ho**[1]) **1** she: *fam., dial.* (in front of woman's name usu. not translated) **h- Eli E-**; **h- mor** mother; **skal tro, h- Ingrid sitter ensom hjemme** I wonder if I- is sitting home alone (Ibsen). ***2** (feminine gender) it. **3** *obs.* you (in addressing woman of lower standing).
hun'ḍ *-en* **1** dog; hound: **der ligger h-en begravet** there's the rub; **døde h-er biter ikke** dead men do no harm; **gå i h-ene** go to the dogs; **leve (være) som h- og katt** fight constantly; **man skal ikke skue h-en på hårene** appearances are deceptive, you can't judge a book by its cover; **mange h-er er harens død** (see **hare**); **skamme seg som en h-** be thoroughly ashamed of oneself. **2** dog (=person; fellow in general; despicable swine): **en vittig h-** a wit; **være en h- etter noe** be inordinately fond of sth, *(pop.)* be crazy about sth. **3: h-en** *fam.* the devil (in oaths). **4: løpende h-** *arch.* Vitruvian scroll. **5: den store h-** *astron.* Canis Major. **6: røde h-er** *med.* German measles.
+**hun'ḍe/dager** *pl* (=***-ar**) dog days.
hun'ḍe/galskap *-en* hydrophobia.
hun'ḍe/glam· +*-met*/**-et* barking, baying of dogs.
hun'ḍe/hus *-et* **1** doghouse, kennel. **2** *fig.* racket, uproar.
hun'ḍe/kalḍ *A* terribly cold, *(pop.)* cold as hell.
hun'ḍe/kjeks *-en* **1** dog biscuit. **2** *bot.* wild chervil, cow parsley (Anthriscus silvestris).
hun'ḍe/kunst *-en*: **h-er** dog's tricks; *fig.* hanky-panky, monkeyshines.
hun'ḍe/leven *-et* usu. *fig.* pandemonium.
hun'ḍe/liv *-et* dog's life.
hun'ḍe/spann *-et* dog team.
hun'ḍe/tunge [/tonge] *-a* **1** dog's tongue. **2** *bot.* hound's tongue (Cynoglossum officinale). **3** *zool* a kind of flounder (Glyptocephalus cynoglossus).
hun'ḍe/vakt *-a*/+*-en naut.* middle watch, midwatch (12-4 A.M.).
+**hun'ḍe/vær** *-et* (=***/ver**) foul, nasty weather.
***hun'ḍ/fare** *V -for, -fare/-i* browbeat, intimidate, push around.
hun'ḍ/gammal *A -t, pl -gamle* (=+**/gammel**) old as the hills.
+**hun'ḍ/hedensk** *A* - (=***/heidensk**) *archaic* pagan to the core.
Hun'dorp *Pln* village, Sør-Fron twp, Oppland.
***hun'draḍ** *Num* cf **hundre**[2]
hun'dre[1] *-t, pl -*/+*-r* hundred.
hun'dre[2] *Num* (a, one) hundred: **så var h- og ett ute** that did it, that finished it (me).
hun'drede *Num* hundreth.
hun'dre/del *-en* one hundredth.
hun'dre/kroning *-en* hundred *kroner* note.
hun'dretusen/vis *Av* hundreds of thousands (**av** of): **i h-** in h- of t-.
hun'dre/vis *Av* hundreds (**av** of): **i h-** by the hundreds.
hun'dre/år *-et* century.
hun'dreårs/dag *-en* centennial, centenary (**for** of).
hun'dreårs/jubile'um *-eet* centennial, centenary; centennial celebration.
***hun'ḍ/sam** *A* ugly, unpleasant.
hun'ḍse *V -a*/+*-et* browbeat, bully, push around; treat like a dog.
+**hun'ḍsk** *A* - **1** cringing, servile. **2** bullying, contemptuous. **3** debasing, degrading.
hun'ḍs/vott *-en* **1** rear seat on a sled. **2** *naut.* becket, small grommet. **3** *archaic* dirty swine, *(pop.)* SOB.
+**hun'er** *-en, pl* - (=***hun(ar)**) *hist.* Hun.
hunger [hong'er] *-en* hunger (**etter** for): **h- er den beste kokk** h- is the best sauce.
hungers/nød [hong'ers/] *-a*/+*-en* (=***/naud**) famine.
hungre [hong're] *V -a*/+*-et* be hungry, starving: **h- etter** hunger, long for.
hungrig [hong'ri] *A* - hungry, starving (**etter** for).
+**hun'/kjønn** *-et* **1** female sex. **2** *gram.* feminine (gender).
+**hun'lig** *A* - *biol.* female.
+**hunn'** *-en* (=***ho**[1], ***hoe**[1]) female, she.
+**hunn'/djevel** *-elen, pl -ler* she-devil.
+**hunn'/dyr** *-et* (=***ho/**) female animal; *derog.* bitch.
+**hun'ner** *-en, pl-e* cf **huner**
+**hunn'/kjønn** *-et* cf **hun/**
+**hunn'lig** *A* - cf **hunlig**
***hun'tre** *V -a* dawdle, waste time.
hur'd *-a archaic, dial.* door.
Hu'r/dal *Pln* twp, Akershus.
hu'ri **-a*/+*-en, pl -er* houri.
***hur'kel** *-et* rattle (in the throat); snore.
***hur'kle** *V -a* rattle (in the throat); snore.
hur'lumhei *-en* hubbub, hurly-burly, uproar.
hur'pe[1] *-a* biddy, hag, slattern: **den gamle h-a** the old biddy.
hur'pe[2] *V -a*/+*-et* **1: h- på seg** fling, throw on (e.g. one's clothes). **2: h- noe sammen** baste, tack hurriedly (and carelessly).
hur'pet(e) *A* - (of woman) sour, unpleasant.
***hurr'** *-en* dull, humming sound.
hur'ra[1] [also: hurra'] *-et, pl -*/+*-er* cheer, hurrah: **et tre ganger tre h- for** nine cheers for.
hurra'[2] *I* hurrah (**for** for): **det er ikke noe å rope h- for** it's nothing to write home about.
+**hur'ra/gutt** *-en* gay blade; boisterous, noisy fellow.
***hur're** *V -a* **1** eddy, whirl. **2** roll, thunder.
hur'ten *N*: **i h- og sturten** headlong, head over heels.
+**hur'tig** *A* - fast, quick; rapid, speedy: **h- levert** quick work; **h- som lynet** quick as lightning; **h- til bens** fast on one's feet.
+**hur'tig/gåenḍe** *A* - fast, high speed; express.
+**hur'tig/het** *-en* **1** rapidity, speed. **2** dispatch, quickness.
+**hur'tig/koker** *-en, pl -e* pressure cooker.
+**hur'tig/løp** *-et* speed skating.
+**hur'tig/løper** *-en, pl -e* speed skater.
+**hur'tig/rute** *-a*/*-en*: **h-n** steamships trafficking Norwegian coast with fast boats and few calls.
+**hur'tig/tog** [/tåg] *-et* express train.

+ Bokmål; * Nynorsk; ° Dialect.
After letter: ' stress (Acc. 1); ` tone, stress (Acc. 2); · length.
Below letter: . not pronounced.

+hur'tigtogs/fart *-en* express train speed.

+hur'tig/tørrendu *A* - quick drying.

Hu'rum *Pln* twp, Buskerud.

hur'v *-en fam.* flock, herd: **hele h-en** the whole lot, *(pop.)* the whole kit and caboodle.

***hur've** *V -a* do carelessly, slovenly: **la det h-** let things slide.

hu's *-et* 1 (any) building: **h-ene på garden** the b-s on the farm; **et tietasjes h-** a ten-story b-; **Guds h-** the house of God; **det grønne h-** the public toilet; **et offentlig h-** a brothel. 2 house (=home; household): **føre stort h-** live in grand style; **holde h- for** keep h- for; **holde et forferdelig h-** kick up a (terrible) row; rage, storm; **sette h-et på ende** turn the h- upside down; **sønnen i h-et** the son of the h-; **(gå) være i h-et** do housework, help in the house. 3 house (=firm; family; audience; legislature): **et gammelt h-** an old firm; **h-et Windsor** the h- of W-; **en venn av h-et** a friend of the family; **de fikk fullt h-** they got a full h-, a capacity crowd; **for fullt h-** to a capacity audience; **Representantenes H-** the H- of Representatives. 4 lodging, shelter; (machinery) housing; *naut.* deck housing; (snail) shell: **få (berge) i h-** get (e.g. hay) into the barn, under cover; **låne h- hos en** get lodging (for the night) from sby. 5 (other idioms): **(det gikk) h- forbi** it went over sby's head, e.g. of a joke or a taunting remark (=he missed it completely); **de gikk mann av h-e** every man turned out; **(ha, være) til h-e** *archaic* be housed, live.

hu's/apote'k *-et* (family) medicine chest.

husa'r *-en mil.* hussar.

hu's/arbeid *-et* housework.

hu's/arres't *-en* house arrest.

hu's/bank *-en*: **H-en** (short for *Norske stats husbank)* state loan fund for the support of private building (about=FHA).

hu'sbank/lån *-et* building loan (from *Husbanken*).

+hu's/beho'v *-et*: **til h-** for household use; *hum.* barely enough **(han kan ikke mere engelsk enn til h-** his English is barely adequate).

+hu's/bestyrerin'ne *-a/-en* housekeeper.

hu's/bond [/bonn] *-en* 1 *hist.* master of a household. 2 *archaic* husband.

husbonds/folk *-et hist.* master and mistress in a rural household.

husbonds/kar *-en hist.* head servant of a farming household.

hu's/bruk *-et*: **til h-** for household use; *fig.* barely sufficient, nothing to spare.

***hu's/bunad** *-en* furniture.

+hu's/dikter *-en, pl -e* **(=*-ar)** house poet (attached to a newspaper or theater).

hu's/dyr *-et* 1 domestic animal, house pet. 2 livestock.

hu'se[1] *V -a/+-et/+-te* 1 give shelter to, house, put up; contain, hold. 2 harbor (e.g. evil thoughts); *jur.* harbor (a criminal).

°hu'se[2] *V -te* cf **hugse**

***hu'se/mellom** *Av* cf **hus/imellom**

huse're *V -te* 1 do damage, play havoc with, ravage. 2 carry on, rage, storm, *(pop.)* raise hell: **h-med** play (carelessly) with; **spøke og h- i hausen** have thoughts run pell-mell through one's head (Vesaas).

hu's/far *-en, pl +-fedre/*-fedrar* 1 head of the household, man of the house, pater familias. 2 housefather, supervisor of a student dormitory.

hu's/fast *A - hist.* property-owning.

hu's/flid *-en* **(=*/flit)** home crafts, home industry; folk arts: **H-en** store where craft products are sold.

hu's/folk *pl* 1 *hist.* servants. 2 *archaic* servants of a household.

hu's/fred *-en* domestic peace, tranquility.

hu's/frue *-a/+-en archaic* housewife, mistress (of a large household).

+hu's/gerå'd *-et* kitchen utensils.

hu's/gud *-en myth.* household god: **h-er** lares and penates.

***hu's/hald** *-et* cf **/holdning**

***hu's/haldar** *-en* cf **/holder**

***hu's/halderske** *-a* cf **/holderske**

hu's/herre *-n* master of the house.

hu's/hjelp *-a/+-en* domestic help, maid.

+hu's/holder *-en, pl -e bibl.* steward: **den tro og kloke h-, som hans husbond vil sette over sine tjenestefolk** that faithful and wise s-, whom his lord shall make ruler over his household (Luke 12, 42).

+hushol'derske *-a/-en* housekeeper.

+hushol'dning *-en* 1 housekeeping; household: **lede en h-** run a household; **lære h-** learn housekeeping. 2 economy, management: **landh-** farming.

+hushol'dnings/skole *-n* school of home economics.

hu's/imel'lom *Av* from house to house.

husitt' *-en eccl.* Hussite.

+hus'k[1] *-en fam.* memory.

hus'k[2] *-et* rocking, swinging; jarring: **med veldige h-** with big bumps (Evensmo).

hu's/kald *A*: **det er h-t** it's colder in the house (than outside).

hu's/kar *-en hist.* housecarl, retainer.

hus'ke[1] *-a* swing.

+hus'ke[2] *V -a/-et* cf **hugse**

hus'ke[3] *V -a/+-et* rock, swing; seesaw; *naut.* pitch: **han h-et barnet på fanget** he was rocking the child on his lap; **så det husk etter** lickety-split.

+hus'ke/lapp *-en* cf **hugse/**

hus'ke/stue *-a* **(=*/stove)** hullabaloo, row, uproar.

+hu's/klynge *-a/-en* **(=*/klyngje)** clump (cluster) of houses.

+hus'kom/hei *-en* hubbub, hullabaloo, uproar.

+hu's/kors *-et* (member of one's household who is) a cross, a trial; ball and chain.

***hu's/kot'** *-et* small cabin, hut.

hu's/laus *A* **(=+/løs)** homeless, without a roof over one's head.

hu's/lege *-n* family doctor.

+hu's/leie *-a/-en* **(=*/leige)** rent.

hu'slig *A* - domestic; relating to home life; housewifely.

***hu's/lyd** *-en* family, household.

+hu's/lærer *-en, pl -e* **(=*-ar)** tutor.

hu's/mann *-en, pl -menn/*-menner hist.* cotter, crofter (=tenant farmer with life tenure).

hu'smanns/plass *-en* cotter's farm.

hu'smanns/stue *-a* **(=*/stove)** cotter's cottage.

hu's/moderlig *A* - housewifely.

hu's/mor *-a/+-en, pl +-mødre/*-mødrer* housewife, mistress of the house.

hu'smor/skole *-n* school of home economics.

hu'smor/vika'r *-en* household helper (supplied by municipal authorities to families during incapacity of housewife).

hu's/mose [*/måse] *-n* moss used to chink walls.

hus/nov [/nåv] *-a* house corner.

hu's/orden *-en* domestic discipline.

hu's/post *-en* maid's job: **ha h-** do housework, work as a maid.

hu's/postill' *-en* collection of sermons (for home use).

hu's/rom [/romm] *-met* housing, lodging (see **hjerterom**).

hu's/råd *-et* household remedy.

hussitt' *-en* cf **husitt**

hu's/stand *-en/*-et* household.

hu's/stell *-et* housework; home economics, housekeeping.

Hu'stad *Pln* twp, Møre og Romsdal.

hu's/telefo'n *-en* house telephone; inter-office telephone, interphone.

hu's/tomt *-a/+-en* (building) lot, site.

hus'tre *V -a/+-et dial.* shake, tremble from the cold.

hus'tren *A +-ent, pl -ene dial.* 1 sensitive to the cold. 2 chilly (weather).

hus'tru *-a/+-en lit.* wife (nowadays usu. **kone**, esp. in reference to one's own, **frue** to others').

hu's/tyrann' *-en* domestic tyrant, martinet.

+hu's/undersø'kelse *-n* **(=*-ing)** police raid of a home: **foreta en h- hos en** raid, search sby's house.

+hu'/svale *V -te* **(=*hug/svale)** comfort; solace, soothe; refresh.

+hu'/svalelse *-n* **(=*hug/svaling)** balm, comfort, solace.

+hu's/vant *A* - **(=*/vand)** familiar with the house, feeling at home.

hu's/varm *A* feeling, acting as if one is at home (in sby else's home); familiar: **den husholdersken din - er hun ikke blitt temmelig h-, du?** hasn't that housekeeper of yours begun to feel rather much at home? (Undset).

hu's/varme *-n* feeling of intimacy due to residence in the same house.

hu's/venn *-en* **(=*/ven)** friend of the family.

hu's/vert *-en* landlord.

hu's/vill *A -vill* homeless, without a roof over one's head.

hu's/være *-t* **(=/vær)** lodging, shelter.

hu't *I* scat, shoo: **med h- og hei** with a hue and cry (Undset).

hu'te *V -a/+-et* 1 bawl, shout. 2 order (sby) off a place, threaten (sby).

hut'le *V -a/+-et*: **h- bort** fritter away, squander; **h- seg igjennom** just keep body and soul together.

hut're *V -a/+-et* 1 shiver, tremble (from the cold). 2 **(=hukre**[2]**)**.

hut'temegtu' *I* (stronger form of **huttetu**).

hut'tetu' *I* brr (expression of shivering from cold); ow-oo (shuddering at the thought of sth eerie or unpleasant).

***hu'v** *-en* 1 ridge of a roof. 2 bump, knob.

hu've *-a* cf **hue**[1]

***hu've/slag** *-et* edging, trimming of a cap.

HV=Heimevern(et)

***h. v.=har vori** ex-, former.

+hva' *Pn* **(=*kva)** 1 what (interrog. and rel.): **h- behager?** I beg your pardon?; **h- bryr jeg meg om det?** w- do I care about that?; **h- for et hus er det?** w- house is that?; **h- for noe w-?** w-'s that?; **h- gir du meg** (ironic) I like that, how do you like that; **h- kommer det av?** why is that? how do you account for that?; **(og) h- med henne?** (and) w- about her?; **h- om** suppose, w-if; w- about, why not; **h- så** w-then; so w-; **vet du h-** look here, oh but really; do you know w-. 2 what *(adj.)*: **h- slags** what kind of; **h- tid** what time, when (not in reference to hours by the clock). 3 whatever: **h- det (nå) var** w- it was; **han hadde tenkt seg om for lenge, eller h- det var** he had thought it over too long, or w- it was (Hoel); **h- som enn skjer** come what may, w- may happen; **h- som helst** anything at all, anything w-. 4: *(conj.)* **h- enten han vil eller ei** *lit.* whether he will (wants to) or not.

+hva'd *Pn* cf **hva**

+hva'l *-en* cf **kval**[2]

+hva'l/barde *-n* cf **kval/**

Hva'ler *Pln* twp, Østfold.

+hva'l/fanger *-en, pl -e* cf **kval/**

+hva'l/fangst *-en* cf **kval/**

+hva'l/kokeri' *-et* cf **kval/**

+hval'p *-en* cf **valp**

+hval'pe *V -a/-et* cf **valpe**

+hval'pet(e) *A* - cf **valpet(e)**

+hva'l/ross *-en* cf **kval/**

+hva'/somhelst Pn cf hva
+hvass' A hvast cf kvass
+hvel'v -et cf kvelv
+hvel've V -a/-et cf kvelve[1]
+hvel'ving -en cf kvelving[2]
+hvem' Pn (=*kven[1]) 1 who; whom: h- annen, andre, ellers who else; h- der who goes there. 2 whoever: h- De enn (nå, så) vil w- you want; h- som helst anybody (at all).
+hvem'/somhel'st Pn cf hvem
+hve'n pt of hvine
+hvep's -en cf veps
+hvep'se/bol -et cf vepse/
+hver [vær] Pn (=*kvar[2]) each, every: de gikk h- sin vei each went his own way; de hadde h- sitt telt each had his own tent; etter h-t little by little, gradually; as time went on; etter h-t som as; gi h- sitt give every man his due; han kan komme h-t øyeblikk he can come at any moment; h- for seg individually, separately; h- især one and all, each one (of you); h- sin smak (lyst) each man to his own taste (desire), to each his own; litt av h-t a little of everything; noe av h-t many things; det kunne ha blitt til noe av h-t mellom oss to things might have gone much further between the two of us (Ibsen).
+hveran'dre Pn (=*kvarandre) each other: om h- all mixed up; ta maskinene fra h- take the machines apart; tett på h- in rapid succession.
+hver'dag -en weekday, working day.
+hver'dags/bruk N: til h- for everyday use.
+hver'dags/grå A -tt dull, prosaic.
+hver'dags/histo'rie -a/-en story of everyday life.
+hver'dags/klær pl everyday clothes, everyday suit.
+hver'dags/lag -et: i h-et ordinarily, usually.
+hver'dagslig A - (=*kvardagsleg) everyday, ordinary; humdrum, monotonous.
+hver'dags/menneske -t commonplace, ordinary person.
+hver'ken C cf verken[2]
+hver'/mann Pn everybody, everyone; anyone; everyman: Gud og h- (pop.) everybody and his brother.
+hver'v -et cf verv[1]
+hver've V -et cf verve[2]
+hve'se V -te cf kvese
+hves'se V -et/hveste cf kvesse
+hve'te -n cf kveite[1]
+hve'te/bolle -n bun.
+hve'te/brød -et cf kveite/
+hve'tebrøds/dager pl honeymoon.
+hve'te/grøpp -et bruised grain.
+hve'te/kake -n sweet white bread.
+hvi' Av archaic wherefore.
+hvid(d)' -en (=*kvitt[1]) archaic: ikke en h- not a red cent; til siste h- to the last dime.
+hvi'l -en cf kvil
+hvi'le[1] -a/-en cf kvile[1]
+hvi'le[2] V -te cf kvile[2]
+hvi'le/dag -en cf kvile/
+hvi'le/hjem [/jem'] -met cf kvile/heim
+hvi'le/løs A cf kvile/laus
+hvi'le/sted -et resting place: hans siste h- his final r- p-.
+hvi'le/stilling -en cf kvile/
+hvi'le/stund -a/-en cf kvile/
+hvil'ken -et, pl -e 1 what, which; what a: h- deilig dag lit. what a lovely day; h-e foreldre ville gjøre det? what parents would do that?; h- vei which road, way. 2 whatever, whichever: h- De enn (nå, så) vil ha whatever (one) you want; h- som helst any (kind of), whichever. 3 which one(s): "Gi meg så papirene." "Hvilke, herre?" "Now give me the papers." "Which ones, sire?" (Ibsen).
+hvi'n -et cf kvin
+hvi'ne V -te/hven, -t cf kvine
+hvir'vel -en cf virvel[2]
+hvir'vel/dyr -et cf virvel/
+hvir'vel/søyle -a/-en cf virvel/
+hvir'vel/vind -en cf virvel/
+hvir'vle V -et cf virvle
+hvis'[1] C (=*viss[1]) if, in case: h- bare if only; h- det er så if so, if that is the case, supposing that to be the case; h- en skal tro ham to believe him; h- ikke det hadde vært for ham but for him, were it not for him; h- ikke unless, if not.
+hvis'[2] Pn whose; of which, of whom.
+hvis'k -et poet. whisper, whispering; whispered word.
+hvis'ke V -a/-et cf kviskre
+hvis'le V -et cf visle
+hvis'le/lyd -en cf visle/
+hvi't A cf kvit
+hvi'te -n cf kvite[1]
+Hvi'te/havet Pln cf Kvite/
+hvi'te/russer -en cf kvite/
+hvi'te/varer pl cf kvite/
+hvi't/glødende A - white-hot.
+hvi't/kløver -en, pl -e cf kvit/
+hvi't/lett A - cf kvit/
+hvi't/løk [also vi't/] -en bot. garlic (Allium sativum).
+hvi'tne V -a/-et cf kvitne
Hvit'/sten Pln town, Vestby twp, Akershus.
+hvi't/symre -a cf kvit/
+hvitt' -et cf kvitt[1]
+hvit'te V -a/-et cf kvite[3]
+hvit'ting -en cf kviting
Hvit'ting/foss Pln town, Ytre Sandsvær twp, Buskerud.
+hvi't/veis -en cf kvit/
+hvi't/vin -en white wine.
+hvo' Pn archaic who: h- som he who, whoever.
+hvor[1] [vorr'] Av (=*kvar[1]) 1 where: h- ble det av ham? w- did he go? what's become of him?; h- har du gjort av skjorten min? w- have you put my shirt? 2 wherever: h-... enn (nå, så) w-; h- som helst any place, w-.
+hvor[2] [vorr'] Av (=*kor[2]) 1 how: er De gal, h- tør De lit. are you mad, h- dare you (Heiberg); h- er hun ikke tålmodig h- patient she is; h- gammel er du? h- old are you?; h- stor du er h- big you are. 2 however: h-... enn (nå, så) h-.
+hvor/av [vor'/] Av lit. of (from) what, which, whom; how: h- de fleste most of whom; h- kommer det? how does it happen?
+hvordan [vor'dann] Av 1 how: h- det h- so; h- i all verden h- in the world; h- står det til h- are you (etc.); si meg h- han er tell me what he is like. 2 however, no matter how (with enn, så): h- De enn gjør det however you do it; h- været så er no matter how the weather is.
+hvor/etter [vor'/] Av after which, whereupon.
+hvor/for' Av why; wherefore: h- det? why so?; h- i all verden why on earth.
+hvor/fra Av from where; from what: alle vandrer vi uten å vite hvorfra, hvorhen we all wander, not knowing from where or whither (Øverland).
+hvor/hen' [also vorhenn'] Av where; to which; whither.
+hvor/i Av in what, in which; where.
+hvor/iblan't Av among whom, including.
+hvor/imo't Av against which, in return for which; whereas, while.
+hvor/ledes Av how (in what manner); (now usu. hvordan).
+hvor/om' Av about what, about which: h- allting er however that may be.
+hvor/pass Av how far, to what extent.
+hvor/på Av on what, on which; after which, when, whereupon.
+hvor/under Av below, under which; during which.
+hvor/ved Av by what means; at, near which; by means of which.
+hvorvidt [vorrvitt'] C how far, to what extent; whether.
+hvæ'se [ve'se] V -te cf kvese
hy' -et dial. 1 downy beard; sparse grass. 2 complexion. 3 beating, thrashing.
hyasin't -en bot. hyacinth (Hyacinthus candicans).
hy'bel -elen, pl -ler rented room or small apartment (usu. for single person).
+hy'bel/boer -en, pl -e (=*/buar) single person living in a hybel.
+hy'bel/leilighe't -en bachelor's apartment (usu. one-room, with kitchenette and bath).
hybri'd[1] -en hybrid.
hybri'd[2] A - hybrid.
***hy'de** V hydde cf hye[1]
hydran't -en (fire) hydrant.
hydra't -et, pl -/+-er chem. hydrate.
hydrau'lisk A - hydraulic.
hydrofoil/båt [-fåi'l/] -en hydrofoil boat (supported above water by air pressure).
hydroge'n -et chem. hydrogen.
hydrogra'f -en hydrographer.
hydropla'n -et, pl -/+-er naut. hydroplane.
+hy'e[1] V -dde (=*hyde) dial. 1 beat, whip; give sby a hiding. *2: h-ast form skin, heal.
***hy'e[2]** V -a: h- seg become hairy, shaggy; grow moldy.
hye'ne -n zool. hyena (family (Hyaenidae); fig. person who callously profits from another's misfortune.
hy'fe *-a/+-en bot. hypha.
hyf'se V -te/+-a/+-et 1 shake, toss. 2: h- på seg primp, spruce up. 3: h- på en rake sby over the coals.
+hyg'ge[1] -a/-en (=*-je[1]) cheer, comfort; coziness, friendly atmosphere: ha h- av en enjoy sby's company; være til nytte og h- be both useful and pleasant.
***hyg'ge[2]** -t 1 meditation, reflection. 2 comfort, contentment, satisfaction.
+hyg'ge[3] V -a/-et/-de (=*-je[2]) 1: h- for (om) en make sby comfortable. 2: h-seg feel comfortable, make oneself at home; h- seg med enjoy the company of.
hyg'gelig A - 1 cheerful, comfortable, cozy; pleasant, nice: det var da h- å høre I'm pleased to hear that; en h- kveld an enjoyable evening; gjøre det h- for en make sby comfortable; ha det h- enjoy oneself, have a good time. 2 friendly, likeable (person).
***hyg'gen** A -e/-i, pl hygne attentive, observant.
***hyg'gje[1]** -a cf hygge[1]
***hyg'gje[2]** V hygde cf hygge[3]
hygie'ne -n hygiene, public health, sanitation.
hygie'nisk [also -e'-] A - hygienic, sanitary.
***hy'ken** A -e/-i, pl -ne relaxed, slack; stooped.
***hy'kje** V -te bend: h- seg ned bend, crouch down.
+hyk'kelsk A - hypocritical; dissembling, false.
hyk'le V -a/+-et dissemble, play the hypocrite; affect, feign, simulate: h- seg til noe reach one's objective by dissembling.
+hyk'ler -en, pl -e (=*-ar) hypocrite.
+hyk'leri -et (=*hykling) hypocrisy, sham.
+hyk'lersk A - hypocritical.
***hyk'ling** -a cf hykleri
***hy'l[1]** -en cf høl[1]
hy'l[2] -et howl, screech, yell; scream, wail; shriek, squeal, whine.
***hy'l[3]** pr of hylje
+hyl'de[1] V -et cf hylle[4]
***hyl'de[2]** pt of hylje

+ Bokmål; * Nynorsk; ° Dialect. After letter: ' stress (Acc. 1); ' tone, stress (Acc. 2); · length. Below letter: . not pronounced.

+hyl'dest -en cf **hyllest**
hy'le V -te howl, screech, yell; scream, wail; squeal, whine: **h- av latter** scream with laughter; **vinden h-er** the wind is howling.
hy'le/kor -et howling chorus; chorus of howls (e.g. from dissatisfied persons).
+**hy'ler** -en, pl -e (=*-ar) 1 crybaby, whiner. 2 elec. screecher (radio).
Hy'le/stad Pln twp, Aust-Agder.
***hyl'je** V hyl, hylde, hylt cf **hylle**[3]
***hyl'k** -en cf **hølk**
***hyl'ke** -t cf **hølke**
hyll' -en bot. elder (Sambucus niger).
hyl'le[1] -a 1 rack, shelf: **komme på sin rette h-** find one's proper niche in life; **legge på h-a** fig. pigeonhole, shelve; **sette en bok i h-a** put a book on the shelf. 2 bookcase: **åpne h-r** (in library) open stacks. 3 fam. balcony, gallery (theater). 4 shelf (of rock).
hyl'le[2] -t case, covering.
+**hyl'le**[3] V -a/-et/-te (=***hylje**) cover, envelop, wrap.
hyl'le[4] V -a/+-et 1 acclaim, applaud, cheer; hail, pay homage, tribute to. 2 believe in, cherish, uphold (e.g. an opinion, a principle). 3 hist. do homage to, swear allegiance to.
hyl'le/busk -en bot. elderberry bush (Sambucus niger).
hyl'le/bær -et bot. elderberry.
hyl'lest *-a/+-en cheers, ovation; homage, tribute.
Hyl'le/stad Pln twp, Sogn og Fjordane.
hyl'se -a (cartridge) case.
hyl'ster -eret/-ret, pl -er/+-re (=***hylstre**) 1 case, cover. 2 fig. outer covering, shell (e.g. of the human personality).
***hy'me** V -de grow dark, gloomy.
hy'men N anat. hymen.
hym'ne *-a/+-en hymn, ode: **en h- til friheten** an ode to freedom.
hymnologi' -en hymnology.
+**hyn'de** -n/-t cf **hynne**[1]
+**hyn'ne**[1] -n/-t cushion.
°**hyn'ne**[2] -a cf **hedne**
hy'per- Pf hyper-, super-, ultra-.
hyper'bel -elen, pl -ler 1 math. hyperbola. 2 gram. hyperbole.
hy'per/kritisk A - hypercritical.
hy'per/moder'ne A - ultramodern.
hy'per/nervø's A hypersensitive.
hy'per/norvagis'me -n hyper-Norwegian usage (occasioned by a faulty conception of what is Norwegian; e.g. "bjerkebeiner" for "birkebeiner").
hy'per/oksy'd -et chem. superoxide.
***hyp'je** V -a 1 wrap carelessly, heedlessly. 2 hop (off).
hypno'se -n hypnosis.
hypnotise're V -te hypnotize, mesmerize.
hypno'tisk A - hypnotic.
hypnotis'me -n hypnotism.
hypnotisø'r -en hypnotist.
hypofy'se -n pituitary body (gland).
+**hypokon'der**[1] -en, pl -e (=*-ar) hypochondriac.
hypokon'der[2] A hypochondriac.
hypokondri' -en hypochondria.
hypokon'drisk A - hypochondriac.
hypote'k -et jur., merc. mortgage.
hypote'k/bank -en merc. bank (which makes mortgage loans).
hypotenu's -en math. hypotenuse.
hypote'se -n hypothesis: **oppstille en h-** advance, put forward an h-.
hypote'tisk A - hypothetical.
hypp' I giddap.
hyp'pe[1] V -a/+-et drive a horse faster: **h- på en** fig. drive, urge sby on.
hyp'pe[2] V -a/+-et hill, ridge potatoes.
hyp'pe/plog -en ridge plow.
+**hyp'pig** A - frequent: **en h- gjest** a f- visitor.
+**hyp'pig/het** -en frequency.
hy'r[1] -en dial. glimpse, trace: **jeg så ikke h-en av henne** I didn't see hide nor hair of her.
***hy'r**[2] -en ardor, desire, passion: **eg er redd at h-en gjeng av** I'm afraid the desire will weaken (Aasen).
***hy'r**[3] -et clothing (esp. for seamen).
+**hyr'de** -n 1 herdsman, shepherd: **den gode h-** bibl. the good Shepherd (John 10, 11). 2 eccl. pastor.
+**hyr'de/brev** -et (=***hyrding/**) eccl. pastoral letter.
+**hyr'de/diktning** -en (=***hyrding/dikting**) pastoral poetry.
+**hyr'de/taske** -a bot. shepherd's-purse (Capsella bursa pastoris).
+**hyr'de/time** -n lovers' hour.
+**hyr'de/tone** -n 1 sound from a shepherd's flute. 2: **h-r** fig. dulcet notes, tones.
***hyr'ding** -en herdsman, shepherd.
hyrdin'ne -a/+-en shepherdess, shepherd girl.
hy're[1] -a/+-en naut. berth: **få h-** get a b-; **ta h-** ship on board a vessel.
hy're[2] -a 1 naut. wages. 2: **ha sin fulle h- med noe** have all one can do, have one's hands full with sth.
hy're[3] -t/+-n rainwear; naut. oilskins, foul weather gear.
hy're[4] V -te/*-a engage, hire; **h- seg med** naut. ship with.
hy're[5] V -te/*-a: **h- seg** outfit oneself with rainwear; **h- seg til** wrap oneself up.
hy're/konto'r -et naut. hiring hall.
***hyr'g** -et nonsense, rubbish.
***hyr'ne**[1] -t cf **hjørne**
***hyr'ne**[2] V -te growl, grumble.
***hyr'ning** -en horned animal.
***hyr'nt** A - horned.
***hyr'pe** V -te: **h- i hop** contract, draw together; sew up (carelessly).
hy'se[1] -a zool. haddock (Melanogrammus aeglefinus).
hy'se[2] V -te dial. 1 give shelter to, house, put up. *2 fig. entertain (within oneself): **alt han h-er for henne** all that he feels for her.
hysj' I 1 hush. 2 shoo.
hysj'e[1] V -a/+-et 1 hush: **h- på en** h- sby up. 2 shoo (poultry, etc.).
***hysj'e**[2] V hys, huste, hust 1 crumble, sprinkle. 2 hiss, whistle.
***hys'ke** -t 1 family; followers, retinue. 2 ugly person.
hyss' I cf **hysj**
hys'se V -a/+-et cf **hysje**[1]
hys'sing -en 1 string, twine: **det går så lenge h-en holder** it will work for a while, but (it can't go on forever); **gå og bre over deg en h-** go jump in the lake. 2 naut. houseline.
hysteri' -et hysteria.
+**hyste'riker** -en, pl -e (=*-ar) hysteric, hysterical person.
hyste'risk A - hysterical.
hytt' N: **i h- og vær** at random, senselessly.
hyt'te[1] -a 1 cabin, cottage, hut; hovel, shack; summer home: **ha h- på fjellet** have a (summer) cabin in the mountains. 2 naut. poop. 3 tech. smelting works.
hyt'te[2] V -a/+-et look after, take care of: **h- sitt skinn** look out for oneself; **h- seg** look after oneself, protect oneself (**for** against).
hyt'te[3] V -a/+-et make angry gestures, shake one's fist (**til** at).
hyt'te/by -en group of mountain cabins.
hyt'te/tur -en (weekend) trip to a cabin.
hy'v -en: **ta h-en (fatt)** take off, take to one's heels.
°**hæ'** I eh, what; how's that?
hæ'de V +-et/*-de mock, scoff at.
***hæ'deleg** A - derisive, scornful.
***hæ'd/o'rd** -et gibe, taunt.
Hæ'gebo/stad Pln twp, Vest-Agder.
Hæ'ge/land Pln twp, Vest-Agder.
+**hæ'ken** A -e, pl -ne desirous of, greedy, voracious.
***hæ'kje** V -te: **h- seg til** risk, venture.
***hæ'kne**[1] -a desire, greed.
***hæ'kne**[2] pl of **hæken**
hæl [he'l] -en heel (on foot, shoe): **følge, gå, komme (like) i h-ene på en** follow hard on sby's h-s, dog sby's footsteps; **henge i h-ene på en** follow sby slavishly; **skjære av h- og kutte av tå** force sth to fit; **slå h-ene sammen** click one's h-s; **på h-en** naut. (down) by the stern.
hæ'l/jern [he'l/jæ'rn] -et (=*/**jarn**) heel plate (of iron).
hæ'l/kappe -a (heel) counter.
hæl/sene -a anat. Achilles tendon.
hæ'r -en 1 army: **Frelsens H-** the Salvation A-; **tjene i h-en** serve in the a-. 2 host, legion, multitude (**av** of).
***hæ'rd** A hært haired, hairy.
***hæ'r/deild** -a mil. detachment.
hæ're V -te 1 clean butter of hair. 2 winnow grain.
+**hæ'r/fang** -et booty, spoils of war.
hæ'r/ferd [*/fær] -a/+-en military campaign, warlike expedition; raid.
+**hæ'r/fører** -en, pl -e (=*-ar) general, leader of an army.
hæ'r/mann -en, pl -menn/*-menner archaic soldier, warrior.
***hæ'rnad** -en company, flock, troop.
hæ'r/pil -a/+-en hist. "war arrow" (sent around the country districts in Norway as a token of war): **skjære opp h-** summon the tribal districts to war.
***hæ'r/setje** V -sette mil. occupy.
hæ'r/skare -n host, legion, multitude (**av** of): **h-nes Gud** theol. the Lord of Hosts.
+**hæ'r/skjold** -et hist. war shield: **bære, føre h-** harry, ravage a country.
***hæ'r/stell** -et armed forces.
hæ'r/ta V infl as **ta**[1] conquer, occupy: **en h-tt kvinne** an abducted woman.
hæ'r/verk -et 1 hist. plundering, ravaging. 2 jur. wanton destruction of property.
+**hæs** [he's] A cf **hes**[1]
***hæ'se** V -te 1 pant; groan, moan. 2 blow gently (wind). 3 be dried up, parched (by the wind).
***hæ'sen** A -e/-i, pl -ne chapped, parched (skin).
***hætt'**[1] -en danger, risk: **det var h- um det** there was danger of that.
***hætt'**[2] A - dangerous, hazardous, risky.
hæ'v A dial. excellent, splendid.
hø'[1] -a (cupola-shaped) mountain.
hø'[2] I humph.
+**hø'**[3] -et obs. cf **høy**[1]
høf'lig A - courteous, polite (**mot** to).
+**høf'lig/het** -en courtesy, politeness: **h-er** civilities, polite remarks.
+**høf'lighets/fraser** pl civilities, polite remarks.
hø'g A cp -re/+-ere/*-are, sp -st/+-est/*-ast (=+**høy**) 1 high (building, mountain, degree, note, official, polish, price, voice, etc.); tall (person, tree, etc.); exalted; august; lofty: **det er h- dag** it's the middle of the day, it's well on in the day; **det er på h-(e) tid** it's high time; **det var h-t under taket i alle værelsene** all the rooms were high-ceilinged; **h- sjø** heavy sea; **i det h-e** on high; in heaven; **leve h-t på noe** get a lot out of sth; make good use of sth; **ligge h-t** be located on high ground (on an elevation); **det h-e c** high C; **sette h-t** prize, value highly; **spille h-t spill** play for high stakes; **stå h-t** be far advanced; **være h- på pæra** pop. be high-hat, stuck-up. 2 loud (cry, sound, voice, etc.); aloud: **le h-t** laugh out loud; **lese h-t** read aloud; read loudly; **rose i h-e toner** praise to the skies; **snakke h-t om noe** speak openly about sth; **sverge h-t og dyrt** swear solemnly; **tenke h-t** think out loud. 3 great, intense (anger, enthusiasm, joy, wonder, etc.); extreme: **det h-e nord** the extreme north, the far north; **h- alder** advanced, great (old) age. 4 (adv.): **h-t** highly; **h-t elsket** dearly beloved, deeply loved; **h-t regnet** at the most; **h-t utviklet** highly advanced. 5 (comp.): **høgre/+høy-**

ere higher, louder, taller, etc.: **h-re betalt** better paid; **de h-re klasser** the upper classes; **en h-re offiser** a high-ranking officer; **de h-re skoler** the secondary schools (*gymnas*= junior colleges); **et h-re vesen** a superior being. 6 *(sup.)*: **h-st/+h-est** highest, loudest, tallest, etc.; supreme, topmost: **det h-ste** the supreme good; **i det h-ste** at the most; **ære være Gud i det h-ste** glory to God in the highest; **i h-ste grad** extremely, to an extreme degree; **mitt h-ste ønske** my greatest wish, the dream of my life; **på sitt h-ste** at its height.

hø'g/aktuell· *A -elt, pl -e* (=**+høy/**) of great current interest.

***hø'g/altar** *-et* cf **høy/alter**

***hø'g/boren** [/båren] *A -e/-i, pl -ne* cf **høy/båren**

hø'g/borg *-a/+-en* 1 citadel, stronghold. 2 *hist.* acropolis, high place.

høg'd *-a* (=**+høyde**) 1 height; altitude (also *astron.*, *math.*); level; tallness: **flyet er i en h- av 1000 m** the plane is at an altitude of 1,000 m.; **i høyden** on high; *(adv.)* at the most; **stå på h- med** be abreast of, on a level with, equal to; **være på h-en av** be at the culmination of, at the height of. 2 elevation, height, hill, rise: **sol i h-a** sun in the hills (sign in Oslo during skiing season). 3 *mus.* pitch. 4: **på h-a av, på h- med** *naut.* at a latitude of; off (e.g. Cape Horn).

høg'de/drag *-et* range of hills, ridge.

høg'de/hopp *-et* high jump.

hø'g/dele *V -te math.* divide by the golden section.

høg'de/punkt[/pong·t] *-et* height, summit, zenith; *fig.* apex, culmination: **være på sitt h-** be at its height, peak.

høg'de/ror *-et* elevator (on an airplane).

høg'de/rygg *-en* (mountain) ridge.

høg'de/sprang *-et* high jump.

hø'g/ferd [*/fær] *-a* luxurious living: **det er betre velferd enn h-** better to do well than to live well (Aasen, proverb).

hø'g/fjell *-et*: **h-et** the high mountain plateau, above the tree level.

hø'gfjells/sol *-a* 1 mountain sun. 2 *med.* ultraviolet ray treatment.

***hø'g/fløygd** *A -/-fløygt* bombastic, grandiloquent, high-flown.

hø'g/frekven·s *-en* high frequency.

***høgg'** *pr of* **hogge**

***hø'g/hjarta** *A -* bold, brave, courageous.

hø'g/hæla *A -* (=**+høy/hælt**) high-heeled.

***hø'gje** *V -de* elevate, raise.

hø'g/kant *N*: **på h-** edgeways, on (its) edge.

hø'g/konjunktu·r *-en merc.* prosperity, bull market.

***høg'/kyrkjeleg** *A -* cf **høy/kirkelig**

hø'g/land *-et* highland, plateau.

***hø'gleg** *A -* comfortable, easy: **du kjem h- fram til kvelds** you will make it easily by evening (Aasen).

***hø'g/leik** *-en* 1 elevation, highness. 2 loftiness, sublimity.

hø'g/lende *-t* highland, plateau.

***hø'g/lending** *-en* cf **høy/lender**

***hø'g/lydt** *A -* cf **høy/lytt**

+hø'g/lytt *A -* cf **høy/**

***hø'g/mellomal·der** *-en* cf **høy/middelalder**

hø'g/messe *-a/+-en* 1 morning service (Protestant). 2 High Mass (Catholic).

hø'g/mælt [/me·lt] *A -* boisterous, loudmouthed, vociferous.

hø'g/norsk *A -* New Norwegian (in its most conservative and dignified form).

høg're[1] *A -* (=**+høyre[2]**) 1 right, right-handed: **hverken se til h- eller venstre** proceed straight ahead, unswervingly (to a goal or an objective); **ikke kjenne forskjell på h- og venstre** be completely simple, stupid; **kjøre på h- side av veien** keep to the right (of the road); **på h- hand** on one's right; **til h- (for)** to the right (of); **være ens h- hand** be sby's right-hand man. 2 *mil.*: **gjøre h- om** make a right face; **se til h-** eyes right. 3 *pol.* conservative: **Høyre** (name of Conservative Party in Norway).

høg're[2] *cp of* **høg**

hø'g/reist *A -* 1 stately, tall; majestic (e.g. church). 2 *fig.* towering.

høg're/mann *-en, pl -menn/*-menner* member of the Conservative Party (usu. **høyre/**).

hø'g/røsta *A -* (=***/røysta**) loud; boisterous, noisy, vociferous.

hø'g/sesong· *-en* height of a season; busiest (in-season) period.

hø'g/sete *-t* high seat, seat of honor; throne: **sette i h-** enthrone; **sitte i h-** have the place of honor; have the final say-so.

***hø'g/sett** *A -* highly-placed, high-ranking.

høg'/sinn *-et* high-mindedness, nobility.

hø'g/sinna *A -* (=**+høy/sinnet**) high-minded, noble.

hø'g/skole *-n* (=***/skule**) *educ.* technical school of university rank, e.g. College of Engineering, Agriculture, Commerce, etc.

hø'g/slette *-a* highland, plateau.

***hø'g/song** *-en* cf **høy/sang**

hø'g/spenning *-a/+-en elec.* high tension, high voltage.

hø'g/spent *A - elec.* high-tension; *fig.* high-strung; intense.

høgst [hØk'st] *sp of* **høg**

høgst/dags [høk'st/] *Av* at noon, in the middle of the day.

høgstdags/leite *-t* midday, noontime: **ved h-** at noon.

hø'g/stemt *A -* grandiloquent, high-flown.

høgste/rett [høk'ste/] *-en* (=**+høyeste/**) *jur.* Supreme Court.

høg'steretts/advoka't *-en* (=**+høyeste-**) attorney entitled to practice before the Supreme Court.

høgst/nattes [høk'st/] *Av* at midnight, in the dead of night, in the middle of the night.

+hø'g/taler *-en* (=***-ar**, **+høyt/**) loudspeaker.

hø'g/tid *-a/+-en* 1 church holiday: **de tre store h-er** the three great holidays (Christmas, Easter, Pentecost). 2 celebration, festivity (e.g. wedding). 3 (feeling of) awe, solemnity.

***hø'g/tide** *V -a* celebrate.

***høgti'd(e)leg** *A -* cf **høytidelig**

***hø'gtid/sam·** *A* formal, solemn.

hø'gtids/dag *-en* 1 festival, holiday. 2 red-letter day.

hø'g/trykk *-et* 1 high pressure: **arbeide under h-** *fig.* work under great pressure. 2 *typog.* relief printing.

***hø'g/velboren** [/-bå·ren] *A -e/-i, pl -ne* cf **høy/velbåren**

hø'g/verdig *A -* 1 high-grade. 2 *archaic* most reverend, right reverend.

***hø'g/vyrd** *A* highly regarded, respected; honored.

hø'g/ætta *A -* highborn, noble.

+hø'k *-en* hawk: **h- over h** he has met his match; cf **hauk[1]**

***hø'kel** *-elen, pl -lar* hamstring (of an animal).

hø'ker *-eren, pl +-ere/*-rar* small grocer; huckster.

hø'ker/handel *-elen, pl -ler* small grocery store.

hø'kre *V -a/+-et* usu. *derog.* huckster: **h- med** hawk, peddle (out).

hø'l[1] *-en* (underwater) hole, pool (in a river or stream).

°hø'l[2] *-et* cf **hol[2]**

Hø'/land *Pln* twp, Akershus.

Hø'/landet *Pln* twp, Sør-Trøndelag.

***hø'le** *V -te* flatter.

Hø'le *Pln* twp, Rogaland.

***hø'len** *A -e/-i, pl -ne* flattering.

Hø'len *Pln* village, Vestby twp, Akershus.

høl'je *V -a/+-et* pour (**ned** down), rain cats and dogs, pitchforks.

høl'j/regne [+/reine] *V -a/+-et/*-de* pour, rain cats and dogs, pitchforks.

+høl'k *-en* (=***hylk**) *dial.*, *archaic* children's cap; nightcap.

+høl'ke *-t* (=***hylke**) *dial.* (wooden) washtub.

Høl'onda *Pln* twp, Sør-Trøndelag.

***hø'l/o'rd** *-et* adulation, flattery.

***hø'l/sam·** *A* addicted, inclined to flattery.

hø'ne *-a* 1 hen; chicken, fowl, pullet: **blind h- finner også et korn** even a stupid person can come up with a bright idea; **det går den veien h-a sparker** things are going to the dogs; **egget vil lære h-a å verpe** young upstart wants to teach an experienced person; **ha en h- å plukke med en** have a bone to pick with sby. 2 *pop.* fraidy-cat; (esp. of woman) featherbrain.

hø'ne/blund *-en* catnap, forty winks.

Hø'ne/foss *Pln* town, Buskerud.

hø'ne/mor *-a/+-en, pl -er* mother hen.

høn's *pl* 1 chickens, fowl, poultry: **en fjær kan bli til fem h-** one little fact can be distorted by rumor into a great scandal; **gå til sengs med h-ene** go to bed early, with the chickens. 2 *derog.* foolish women.

høn'se/egg *-et* chicken egg.

høn'se/fugl *-en zool.* gallinaceous bird.

høn'se/gar·d *-en* (=***/gård**) poultry yard.

høn'se/hauk *-en zool.* chicken hawk (Astur palumbarius).

høn'se/hjerne [/jæ·rne] *-n derog.* bird brain.

+høn'se/hode *-t* (=***/hovud**) *derog.* bird brain.

høn'se/hus *-et* hen house.

høn'se/netting *-en* chicken wire.

hønseri' *-et, pl +-er/*-* poultry farm.

høn'se/ring *-en* marking ring (used on hens to indicate the layers).

høn'se/stige *-n* chicken runway (ladder-like board to entrance of chicken coop).

+hø'r[1] *-en bot.* flax (genus Linum)

***hø'r[2]** *N*: **bort i h- og heim** beyond reason, utterly fantastic.

+hø'r/bar *A* audible.

hø're *V -te* (=***høyre[1]**) 1 hear; listen (to): **der kan du bare h-** just listen, there you are; see didn't I tell you; **h- en i noe** *educ.* examine sby (orally) in sth, hear sby's lesson; **hør** listen, say (**hør, kan du være med i dag?** say, can you come along today?); **hør her** listen here, look here, now listen; **la seg h-** let oneself be heard (**det lar seg h-** that's more like it, now you're talking); **nå har jeg h-t det også** now I've really heard everything; **som seg hør og bør** as is fitting and proper. 2: **høres** be heard; sound (amazing, false, plausible, true, etc.); **det h-s mye** that sounds like a lot; **det h-s forferdelig ut** that sounds terrible. 3 belong (only in combination with *prep.* and *adv.*): **h- hjemme** belong (to a place, among certain people, etc.); **h- ingensteds hjemme** be neither here nor there, make no sense; **h- inn under** belong under, come under; **h- med til (i)** go with, have to do with, pertain to; be a part of; **h- til** be of, be one of, belong to; have one's home, live; **han h-te til på en liten fjellgard** his home was on a little mountain farm (Bojer); **jeg har h-t en annen til** I have belonged to another

+ Bokmål; * Nynorsk; ° Dialect.
After letter: ' stress (Acc. 1); ` tone, stress (Acc. 2); · length.
Below letter: . not pronounced.

(Ibsen). 4 (with *prep.* and *adv.*): **h- etter** give heed to, listen to; follow, pay attention; (go and) ask, see; **hør etter om han er syk** go see if he is sick; **h- i radioen** hear on the radio; **h- innom** drop in, pay a short visit; **h- opp** cease; **h- på** listen, listen to; hear, tell by; **de kom bare for å h- på** they came just to listen; **det er lett å h- på aksenten at De er amerikaner** it is easy to hear by your accent that you are an American; **h- på radioen** listen to the radio; **h- noe til en** hear sth of (from) sby.

hø're/briller *pl* glasses with built-in hearing aid.

+hø'rer *-en, pl -e* (=***høyrar**) 1 *archaic* hearer, listener: **være ordets gjørere, og ikke bare dets h-e** but be ye doers of the word, and not hearers only (James 1, 22). 2 *hist.* grammar school teacher (to 1806; replaced by **adjunkt**).

hø're/rør *-et/*-a* 1 ear trumpet. 2 stethoscope. 3 telephone receiver.

+hø're/spill *-et* (=***/spel**) radio drama, play.

+hø're/vidde *-a/-en*: **innenfor, utenfor h-** within, out of earshot.

+hø'r/gul *A* flaxen (colored).

hø'rlig *A* - (=***høyrleg**) audible, perceptible.

hør'sel *-la/+-elen* (=***høyrsel**) hearing, sense of hearing.

***hø'se** *V -te* clear the throat, hawk.

+høs't *-en* (=***haust**) 1 crop, harvest: **årets h-** the year's crop (also *fig.*, e.g. of the books published in a given year). 2 autumn, fall; *poet.* declining years, old age: **i fjor h-** last fall (or a year ago this fall); **i h-** this fall; **i livets h-** *poet.* in the sunset of life; **om h-en** in (the) fall; **til h-en** in the fall, this fall.

+høs't/arbeid *-et* harvesting, reaping.

+høs't/bær *A* (of cows) calving in the fall.

+høs'te *V -a/-et* (=***hauste**[1]) 1 approach, draw near (autumn, fall). 2 harvest, reap: **den som sår vind, h-er storm** he who sows the wind shall reap the whirlwind; **h- inn** gather, reap; **se til himmelens fugler: de sår ikke, de h-er ikke** *bibl.* behold the fowls of the air: for they sow not, neither do they reap (Matthew 6, 26); **slik, som du sår, du engang h-er** *bibl.* for whatsoever a man soweth, that shall he also reap (Galatians 6, 7). 3 *fig.* gain, reap, win: **h- erfaring** gain experience, learn by experience; **h- fordel av** benefit by, derive (an) advantage from; **h- fruktene av** reap the fruits of, reap the benefit of; **h- laurbær** win laurels; **h- medynk** gain, win sympathy; **h- stormende bifall** bring down the house.

+høs't/folk *pl* harvesters, reapers.

+høs't/jevndøgn [/-døy·n] *-et* autumnal equinox (September 21st).

+høs'tlig *A* - (=***haustleg**) autumnal.

+høs't/part *-en*: **det var på h-en** it was in the fall.

+høs't/semes'ter *-eret/-ret* fall semester.

høv'ding *-en* chief, chieftain; leader: **åndslivets h-er** the l-s of cultural life.

hø've[1] *-t, pl* - chance, occasion, opportunity: **nytte h-t** take advantage of the opportunity; **ved det h-t** on that occasion.

hø've[2] *V -de* 1 be appropriate, suitable, suit; belong, fit: **h- bra i hop sammen** go, work well together. 2: **h- seg** be convenient; be decent, proper.

hø'veds/mann *-en, pl -menn/*-menner* 1 captain of a fishing boat (Northern Norway); next in command. 2 *hist.* captain, centurion, officer; castellan.

høv'el *-elen, pl -ler carp.* plane.

høv'el/benk *-en* carpenter's bench.

hø'velig *A* - 1 appropriate, fitting, suitable. 2 decent, proper.

høv'el/spon *-en* shaving.

+hø'ver *pl* of **hov**[1]

***hø'ves/vers** *-et* occasional poem, verse for a particular occasion.

***hø've/tal** *-et math.* proportional.

hø'visk *A* - decent, proper; *archaic* courtly, courteous, polite.

høv'le *V -a/+-et* plane: **h- en av** *fig.* rake sby over the coals.

høvleri' *-et, pl +-er/*-* planing mill.

høv're *-t* hame, harness saddle.

høv'ring *-en dial., zool.* lithodes (family Lithodidae).

Høv'ringen *Pln* mountain resort area, Sel twp, Oppland.

Hø'/våg *Pln* twp, Aust-Agder.

høy'[1] *-et* hay.

+høy'[2] *A* cf **høg**

+høy'/akte *V -et* hold in high esteem, honor, venerate.

+høy'/aktelse *-n* deep respect, high esteem.

+høy'/aktuell' *A -elt* cf **høg/**

+høy'/alter *-(e)ret, pl -(e)re* high altar.

+høy'/bane *-n* elevated railway: **h-n** the elevated.

+høy'/bebyg'gelse *-n* high rise apartment(s), building(s); skyskrapers.

høy'/berging *-a/+-en* harvesting of hay.

+høy'/borg *-en* cf **høg/**

+høy'/bygg *-et* high rise apartment, building.

+høy'/båren *A -ent, pl -ne* high-born.

+høy'de *-n* cf **høgd**

+høy'de/drag *-et* cf **høgde/**

+høy'de/hopp *-et* cf **høgde/**

+høy'/dele *V -te* cf **høg/**

+høy'de/punkt [/pong·t] *-et* cf **høgde/**

+høy'de/ror *-et* cf **høgde/**

+høy'de/rygg *-en* cf **høgde/**

+høy'de/sprang *-et* cf **høgde/**

høy'/dott *-en* wisp of hay.

høy'e *V -a/+-et* bring in the hay, do the haying.

+høy'/edel *A -elt, pl -le* high-born, most noble.

***høy'ende** *-t* cushion, pillow.

+høy'en/loft *-et* 1 *hist.* loft, upper story (of a medieval house). 2 *hist.* ceremonial hall (of a castle).

+høy'ere *A - cp of* **høy**[2], cf **høg**

+høy'ere/stående *A* - higher, superior.

+høy'est *A - sp of* **høy**[2], cf **høg**

+høy'este/rett *-en* cf **høgste/**

høy'/feber *-eren, pl -rer* hay fever.

+høy'/fjell *-et* cf **høg/**

+høy'fjells/hotell' *-et* mountain hotel, mountain health resort.

+høy'fjells/sol *-a* cf **høgfjells/**

+høy'/forræderi' [-re·d-] *-et* high treason.

høy'/gaffel *-elen, pl -gafler* hayfork.

+høy'/halset *A* - high-necked: **h- genser** turtleneck sweater.

+høy'/hellig *A* - most holy, sacred.

+høy'/het *-en* 1 elevation, highness. 2 loftiness, sublimity; *bibl.* divine power, divinity: **vil ikke hans h- skrekke eder?** shall not His excellency make you afraid? (Job 13, 11). 3 highness (title): **hans h-** his h-.

+høy'/hælt [/he·lt] *A* - cf **høg/hæla**

+høy'/kant *N* cf **høg/**

høy'/kasse *-a/-en* heavy wooden box filled with hay in which food is placed (to finish cooking after being partially cooked over a fireplace).

+høy'/kirkelig *A* - *eccl.* high church.

+høy'/konjunktu'r *-en* cf **høg/**

+høy'/land *-et* cf **høg/**

Høy'/land *Pln* twp, Rogaland.

Høy'/landet *Pln* twp, Nord-Trøndelag.

høy'/lass *-et* load of hay.

+høy'/lender *-en, pl -e* Highlander.

+høy'lig *Av* extremely, greatly, highly: **bli h- forundret** be greatly surprised.

+høy'/lys *A*: **ved h- dag** in broad daylight.

+høy'/lytt *A* - (=**+høg/**, ***høg/lydt**) loud.

høy'/løe *-a* hay barn.

høy'/meis *-a/-en* frame for loading hay on one's back.

+høy'/messe *-a/-en* cf **høg/**

+høy'/middelal'der *-en* High Middle Ages.

høy'/mo *-et* (of hay) gleanings; hayseed.

+høy'/moder'ne *A* - ultramodern.

+høy'/modig [also /mo'-] *A* - high-minded, noble.

høy'/mole *-a bot.* dock (Rumex domesticus); yellow dock (Rumex crispus).

+høy'/mælt [/me·lt] *A* - cf **høg/**

+høy'ne *V -et* 1 elevate, raise: **h- seg** rise. 2 improve, raise the level of, refine: **h- moralen** improve (public) morals.

+høy'ning *-en* 1 elevation. 2 improvement, refinement (**av** of).

høy'/onn *-a* haying, haymaking season.

***høy'rar** *-en* cf **hører**

***høy're**[1] *V -de* cf **høre**

+høy're[2] *A* - cf **høgre**[1]

+høy'/reist *A* - cf **høg/**

+høy're/mann *-en, pl -menn/*-menner* cf **høgre/**

***høy're/røyr** *-a* cf **høre/rør**

***høy're/spel** *-et* cf **høre/spill**

***høy'rleg** *A* - cf **hørlig**

***høy'rsel** *-la* cf **hørsel**

***høy'rsle** *-a* cf **hørsel**

+høy'/rød *A* bright red, crimson.

+høy'/røstet *A* - cf **høg/røsta**

+høysa'lig *A* - *archaic* of blessed memory, late lamented.

+høy'/sang *-en* 1 hymn, song of praise. 2: **H-en** *bibl.* Song of Solomon, Song of Songs.

+høy'/sesong' *-en* cf **høg/**

+høy'/sete *-t* cf **høg/**

+høy'/sinn *-et* cf **høg/**

+høy'/sinnet *A* - cf **høg/sinna**

+høy'/skole *-n* cf **høg/**

+høy'/slette *-a* cf **høg/**

+høy'/sommer *-eren, pl -ere/-somrer* midsummer.

+høy'/spenning *-en* cf **høg/**

+høy'/spent *A* - cf **høg/**

+høy'st *Av* 1 exceedingly, extremely, highly; most, very: **det er h- sannsynlig** it is more than likely. 2 at the most, at the outside: **h- femti** not more than 50 at the most.

høy'/stakk *-en* haystack.

+høy'st/bydende *A* -: **(den) h-** the highest bidder.

***høy'ste** *V -a* call to sby far off (as a warning).

+høy'/stemt *A* - cf **høg/**

+høy'st/ærede *A* - esteemed, highly honored: **h- herr N.N.** dear Mr. N.N.

høy'/stål *-et* 1 haymow. 2 hayloft.

høy'/såte *-a* haycock; *hum.* (of certain styles of girls' hairdressing) haystack.

+høy't/flyvende *A* - ambitious, high-flying, soaring.

+høy'/tid *-a/-en* cf **høg/**

+høyti'delig *A* - (=***høgtid(e)leg**) 1 festive, solemn; ceremonious, formal: **et h- løfte** a solemn promise; **ved en h- anledning** on a solemn (festive) occasion. 2 serious; pompous, selfimportant: **det var nå ikke så h- ment** it wasn't meant so seriously; **ta en h-** take sby seriously.

+høyti'delig/het *-en* festivity, solemnity; ceremony, formality.

+høyti'delig/holde *V -holdt, -holdt* celebrate, keep, observe; solemnize.

+høy'tids/full *A* festive, solemn.

+høy'tids/stund *-en* festival of commemoration; solemn occasion.

+høy't/lesning *-en* reading aloud.

+høy't/liggende *A* - 1 on high ground. 2 *fig.* elevated, noble.

+høy'/travende *A* - cf **høyt/**

høy'/trev *-et* hayloft.

+høy'/trykk *-et* cf **høg/**

+høy't/stående *A* - high-ranking (e.g. officer); superior (e.g. culture).

+høy't/taler *-en* cf **høg/**

+høy't/travende *A* - bombastic, grandiloquent, (*pop.*) hifalutin.

høy'/tørk *-en* drying, tedding (of hay)

+høyˋ/vandel -elen, pl -ler (small) bundle, truss of hay (for fodder).
+høyˋ/vann(e) -(e)t naut. high tide.
+høyˋ/velbå·ren A -ent, pl -ne high and noble, right honorable; hum. high and mighty.
+høyˋ/verdig A - cf **høg/**
+høyˋ/viktig A - highly important, very important.
***høyˋ/vinne** -a haying, haymaking season.
høyˋ/visk -en (small) bundle, truss of hay (for fodder).
høyˋ/vogn [/vångn] -a hay wagon.
***høyˋ/vondul** -en, pl -vondlar cf /vandel
+høyˋ/ættet A - cf **høg/ætta**
hå'[1] -en zool. piked, spiny dogfish (Ancathias vulgaris).
hå'[2] -a/+-en 1 aftermath (second crop of hay). 2 second mowing (season).
***hå'**[3] V -dde be conscious of, notice, realize: **h- seg** become conscious, remember.
hå'[4] I (often repeated) ho ho; oh ho, ah ha.
°hå'[5] Pn cf **hva**
***hå.=hundreår**
håˋ/ball -en: **h-en** midsummer (between spring work and haymaking).
hå'/brann -en zool. porbeagle shark (Lamna cornubica).
***hå'ḍ** -et derision, mockery, ridicule.
***håˋḍleg** A - 1 disgraceful, outrageous, shameful. 2 contemptuous, scathing: **det er enno søtt på tunga å få vera h-** it is still sweet to the tongue to be scathing (Vesaas).
håˋ/gjel -a/-en zool. nursehound, spotted dogfish (Scylliorhinus stellaris).
***håˋke** -n (=**håk**) 1 fool. 2 tall, skinny person.
hå'/kjerring -a, pl *-ar zool. Greenland shark (Somniosus microcephalus).
Håˋkon Prn(m): **H- Adalsteinsfostre** (king of Norway 934-936); **H- VII** (king of Norway 1905-1957).
håˋl A dial. slippery, smooth.
Håˋlanḍs/dal Pln twp, Hordaland.
***håˋ/laus** A careless, negligent; forgetful, oblivious.
***håˋleg** A - cf **hådleg**
håˋl/is -en dial. slippery ice.
+hålˋk -en cf **holk**[1]
***hålˋkast** V -ast become icy, slippery.
hålˋke -a/-en icy, slippery surface (field, road, etc.).
hålˋke/føre -t icy ground; icy conditions.
hålˋket(e) A - covered with ice, icy.
Håˋloga/lanḍ Pln old name of northern Norway; now an administrative district and bishopric, since 1952 divided into Sør-H- (Nordland) and Nord-H- (Finnmark, Troms).
håˋløyg -en person from Hålogaland.
***håˋ/løyse** -a carelessness, negligence; forgetfulness.
hå'n -en disdain, scorn; insult (**mot** to).
+hån'ḍ -a/-en, pl hender cf **hand**
+hånˋḍ/arbei·ḍ -et cf **hand/**
+hånˋḍ/bak -en cf **hand/**
+hånˋḍ/ball -en cf **hand/**
+hånˋḍ/beve·gelse -n gesture, motion (of the hand).
+hånˋḍ/bibliote·k -et cf **hand/**
+hånˋḍ/bok -a, pl -bøker cf **hand/**
+hånˋde N (=***handar**): **gå en til h-** lend sby a hand; hist. be sby's liegeman.
°hånˋde/lag -et cf **hand/**
+hånˋḍ/fallen A -ent, pl -falne cf **hand/**
+hånˋḍ/fang -et cf **hand/**
+hånˋḍ/fare V -for, -fart cf **hand/**
+hånˋḍ/fast A - cf **hand/**
+hånˋḍ/fest(n)ing -en hist. coronation charter (document executed by an elected king prior to his coronation, in which he agreed to respect the rights and privileges of his subjects, particularly the nobility).
+hånˋḍ/flate -a cf **hand/**
+hånˋḍ/for pt of **-fare**
+hånˋḍ/fritt A - cf **hand/**
+hånˋḍ/full A -en handful: **en h- folk** a h- of people.
+hånˋḍ/gangen A -ent, pl -ne: **h-ne mann** henchman; hist. liegeman.
+hånˋḍ/gemeng· -et 1 brawl, free-for-all, rough-and-tumble. 2 mil. hand-to-hand combat.
+hånˋḍ/gjerning -en cf **hand/**
+hånˋḍ/grep -et cf **hand/**
+hånḍgri'pelig A - concrete, real, tangible; palpable.
+hånḍgri'pelig/het -en 1 concreteness, reality, tangibility. 2: **gå til h-er** come to blows, get violent.
+hånˋḍ/heve V -et/-de enforce, maintain, uphold.
+hånˋḍ/hilse V -te cf **hand/helse**
+hånˋḍ/jern [/jæ'rn] -et cf **hand/**
+hånˋḍ/kjerre -a cf **hand/**
+hånˋḍ/kle [also: hångˋ/] -et, pl -klær cf **hand/**
+hånˋḍ/koffert [/koffert] -en cf **hand/**
+hånˋḍ/kraft -a/-en cf **hand/**
+hånˋḍ/lag -et cf **hand/**
+hånˋḍ/langer [also hånˋt/] -en, pl -e cf **hand/**
+hånˋḍ/ledd -et cf **hand/led**
+hånˋḍ/linning -a/-en cf **hand/**
+hånˋḍ/makt -a/-en cf **hand/**
+hånˋḍ/pant -et cf **hand/**
+hånˋḍ/penger pl 1 merc. deposit (to confirm a deal). 2 mil. enlistment allowance. 3 dial. pocket money.
+hån'ḍs/bredd en handshreadth (width).
+hånˋḍ/skre(i)v pt of **-skrive**
+hånˋḍ/skrift[1] -a/-en cf **hand/**[1]
+hånˋḍ/skrift[2] -et cf **hand/**[2]
+hånˋḍ/skrive V -skre(i)v, -skrevet cf **hand/**
+hånˋḍ/slag -et handshake: **gi hverandre h- på handelen** shake hands on the deal.
+hånˋḍ/spunnet A - cf **hand/**
+hån'ḍs/opprek·ning -en show of hands: **stemme ved h-** vote by a show of hands.
+hån'ḍs/påleg·gelse -n eccl. laying on of hands (in blessing, consecration, rite of confirmation); touch (to effect a cure).
+hån'ḍs/rekning -en assistance, helping hand, (pop.) boost.
+hånˋḍ/tak -et cf **hand/**
+hånˋḍ/takes V -tokes cf **hand/**
+hånˋḍ/ten -en cf **hand/tein**
+hånḍte're V -te cf **hand-**
+hånḍte'ring -a/-en cf **hand-**
+hånḍte'rlig A - cf **hand-**
+hånˋḍ/trykk -et handshake.
+hånˋḍ/vask -en cf **hand/**
+hånˋḍ/vending -a/-en cf **hand/**
+hånˋḍ/verk [also hånˋt/] -et cf **hand/**
+hånˋḍ/verker -en, pl -e cf **hand/**
+hånˋḍverks/mann -en, pl -menn cf **handverks/**
+hånˋḍverks/messig A - 1 handicraft (e.g. organization). 2 craftsmanlike, professional. 3 mechanical, uninspired.
+hånˋḍverks/næring -en cf **handverks/**
+hånˋḍverks/svenn -en cf **handverks/**
+hånˋḍ/veske -a handbag.
+hånˋḍ/våpen -et cf **hand/**
håˋne V *-a/-te deride, mock, ridicule.
hå'n/flir -en/-et derisive, taunting smile, sneer.
+hå'n/latter -en (=***/lått**) derisive, scornful laughter; (pop.) horselaugh.
hå'n/le V -lo, -ledd/*-tt laugh scornfully: **h- av en** laugh sby to scorn.
håˋnlig A - contemptuous, derisive, scornful.
hå'nsk A - contemptuous, derisive.
hå'ns/o·rḍ -et jibe, taunt.
hå'n/staur -en dial. big oaf, clumsy ox.
hå'nt Av: **late h- om** disregard, make light of, pooh-pooh.
hå'p -et hope; anticipation, expectation: **gi godt h- for fremtiden** promise well for the future; **gi lite h-** hold out little hope; **gjøre seg h- om** have hopes of (e.g. success); **h-et er lysegrønt** hope springs eternal (in the human breast); **nære et sikkert h- om at** have every hope that; **sette sitt h- til fremtiden** put one's faith in the future; **være ved godt h-** be of good cheer.
håˋpe V +-te/+-et/*-a hope (**på** for); expect, trust: **det er å h- at** one can only hope that; **h- det beste** hope for the best; **h- i det lengste** hope against hope; **jeg h-er det** I hope so; **jeg h-er ikke han merket noe** I hope he didn't notice anything.
håˋpe/full A 1 hopeful. 2 promising: **en h- yngling** ironic a young hopeful.
håˋp/laus A (=**+/løs**) despairing, hopeless: (adv.) **h-t forelsket** hopelessly in love.
+håˋpløs/het -en despair, hopelessness.
hå'r -et hair; head of hair; bot., zool. seta: **fare (fly, ryke) i h-et på hverandre** fly at one another, come to blows; **h-ene reiste seg på mitt hode** my hair stood on end; **h- i suppa** fly in the ointment; **ikke et h- bedre** not a bit better; **på et h-** by a hair; **stryke en mot h-ene** rub sby the wrong way; **være i h-ene på hverandre** be at logger heads.
håˋr/botn -en (=**+/bunn**) scalp.
+hå'rḍ A cf **hard**
+håˋrḍ/før A cf **hard/**
+håˋrḍ/henḍt A - cf **hard/**
+håˋrḍ/hjertet A - cf **hard/hjarta**
+håˋrḍ/hudet A - cf **hard/huda**
+håˋrḍ/nakket A - cf **hard/nakka**
***håˋr/dregen** A -e/-i, pl -ne 1 dragged by the hair. 2 far-fetched.
Hå'rek Prn(m): **H- av Tjøtta** Norw. chieftain (ab. 965-1036).
hå'ret(e) A - hairy.
håˋr/fager A -ert, pl -re fair-haired: **Harald h-re** Harald Fairhair, first king of Norway (ab. 874-932).
håˋr/fasong· -en hairdo.
håˋr/feste -t hairline.
håˋr/fin A hairline (e.g. crack); fig. minute, subtle; hairsplitting, quibbling.
håˋr/ga·rḍ -en hairline.
håˋr/klipp -en haircut.
+håˋr/kløver -en, pl -e (=***/kløyvar**) hairsplitter, quibbler.
+håˋr/kløveri -et (=***/kløyving**) hair splitting, quibbling, sophistry.
håˋr/nål -a hairpin.
håˋrnål/sving -en hairpin curve.
håˋr/reisenḍe A - hair-raising; appalling, horrible: **det er h-** it's enough to curl your hair (make your hair stand on end).
håˋr/rot -a, pl +-røtter/*-røter root of the hair.
håˋr/rør -et/*-a phys. capillary tube.
+håˋrs/bredd -en (=***/breidd**) hairsbreadth: **ikke vike en h-** not budge an inch.
håˋrs/monn -en (=***/mon**) bit, iota: **ikke en h- bedre** not one bit better.
håˋr/strå -et single hair.
***håˋr/støe** -t growth of the hair; hair (itself).
håˋr/sår A sensitive, tender (to the touch); fig. easily offended.
+håˋr/trukken [/trokken] A -ent, pl -trukne far-fetched.
håˋr/vatn -et (=**+/vann**) hair tonic.
håˋr/vekst -en (growth of) hair.
hå's A (=**+hes**[1]) dial. hoarse, husky: **skrike seg h-** yell oneself hoarse.
+hå's/het -en dial. hoarseness.
hå'/slått -en aftermath (second crop of grass).
hå'/størje -a zool. tunny (Thunnus thynnus).
***hått'** -en 1 perception, sense; memory: **det er ikkje nokon h- i**

+ Bokmål; * Nynorsk; ° Dialect.
After letter: ' stress (Acc. 1); ˋ tone, stress (Acc. 2); · length.
Below letter: . not pronounced.

honom he's indifferent (to the feelings of others). 2 disposition, temper; nature, personality: **ein god h-** affable, friendly personality; **ein vond h-** forbidding personality. 3 property, quality; manner: **ein annan h- i veret** a change in the weather; **på mange h-ar** in many ways.

*__håt'te__ *V -a* 1 notice, perceive. 2: **h- på** call to mind, remember. 3: **h- seg** behave, conduct oneself.

*__håt'tig__ *A -* attentive, perceptive; retentive.

hått'/laus *A* absent-minded, forgetful; negligent.

hå'v *-en* bag net, landing net, scoop net.

Hå'va/mål *Prn* Sayings of the High One, i.e. Odin (poem in the Poetic Edda consisting of proverbs and good advice).

*__hå'var__ *A* backward, bashful.

Hå'/vard *Prn (m)*

hå've *V -a/+-et* catch, land with a scoop net.

°**hå'/voll** *-en* cf **/ball**

I

i'[1] *-en* letter I, i: **sette prikken over i'en** give sth the crowning touch, top sth off.

i'[2] *P* 1 in (the army, a box, bronze, this chapter, evening dress, Norway, the rain, etc.; also before names of communities, districts, and most cities); at, on: **han hev boka i veggen** he flung the book at the wall; **i andre enden av værelset** at the other end of the room; **i annen etasje** on the second floor; **i en avstand** at a distance (**av** of); **i en pris av 10 kroner** (selling) at 10 k-; **i og for seg** in itself, per se; **i Oslo, i Gudbrandsdal** in O-, in G-; **professor i fransk** professor in (of) French; **snuble i en stein** stumble on a stone; **vi var i selskap hos Hansen** we were at a party at H-'s; **i sjøen** *naut.* at sea. 2 (with expressions of time) for; at, during, in; at the present time, this: **først i juni** during the first part of June; **i dag** today; **i julen** at, during Christmas; this Christmas; **i mai** during, in May; this May; **i sommer** this summer; **vi har bodd her i 6 år** we have lived here for 6 years; (with other words expressing time: see these). 3 in, on; into, to (a condition of): **briste i gråt** burst into tears; **falle i søvn** fall asleep; **i brann** afire, on fire; **i stykker** to pieces; **komme i kok** come to a boil; **sette i å le** burst out laughing. 4 *math.* ... to the ... power: **fire i fjerde** four to the fourth power. 5 *(adv.)* in; *fam.* shut: **døra er i** *fam.* the door is shut; **en kurv med poteter i** a basket with potatoes (in it), a basket containing potatoes; **falle i** fall in; **med hull i** with a hole (in it); (with other verbs: see these). 6 (other idioms): **dra i krigen** go to war; **få tak i noe** get hold of sth; **kloss i land** right near land; **slag i slag** in rapid succession.

I' *Pn ob eder/jer, po eders/jer(e)s* 1 *archaic* ye, you *(pl)*: **I skal være der hvor jeg er** *bibl.* where I am, there ye may be also (John 14, 3). 2 *archaic* ye, you (*sg*; used in formal address to person of high rank).

+**iaf'ten** *Av* cf **aften**

+**iaf'tes** *Av* cf **aftes**

+**iak't/ta** *V -tok, -tatt* 1 observe, watch; notice. 2 observe, maintain (laws, rules, etc.); show: **i- forsiktighet** observe caution, proceed cautiously.

+**iak't/tagelse** *-n* cf **/takelse**

+**iak't/tager** *-en, pl -e* cf **/taker**

+**iak't/takelse** *-n* 1 observation; *psych.* perception. 2 observance (**av** of).

+**iak't/taker** *-en, pl -e* observer.

+**iak't/tok** *pt of* **-ta**

iall'/fall *Av* anyway, at any rate, at least, in any case.

ial't *Av* cf **all**

ib. = **ibidem**

ibei't *Av* cf **beit**[2]

i'ben/holt *-en/-et bot.* ebony (genus Diospyros).

+**i'/beregne** [/berei·ne] *V -et* include: **alt i-et** everything included; all things considered.

ibe'risk *A -* Iberian.

I'be/stad *Pln* twp, Troms.

ibi'dem [also: i'bi-] *Av* ibidem (abbr. ibid.).

i'bis *-en zool.* ibis (family Threskiornithidae).

i'/blanda *A -* (= +-**et**) mixed with.

iblan't *Av* 1 at times, occasionally: **en gang i-** once in a while. 2 among (them), intermixed: **med ville blomster i-** with wild flowers among them (Ibsen); (cf also **blant**).

+**iblin'de** *Av* cf **blinde**[1]

*__i'/blå__ *A -tt, pl -/-e* bluish.

+**i'/boende** *A -* inherent, innate.

ib'sensk *A -* Ibsenian.

*__i'/buar__ *-en* inhabitant.

i'd *-a/+-en archaic* activity, effort.

I'da *Prn (f)*

+**ida'g** *Av* cf **dag**

*__i'dast__ *V idest, iddest, idst* feel like, have a mind to (usu. neg.): **han idest knapt (å) røre seg** he barely feels like moving.

Idd' *Pln* twp, Østfold.

*__id'dest__ *pt of* **idast**

idé *-en* 1 idea; concept, notion: **en god i-** a good idea, a happy thought; **gjøre seg en i- om** form an idea of, imagine. 2 ideal: **holde i-ens fane høyt** raise the banner of the i- (Ibsen).

i'de[1] *-a dial.* eddy, whirlpool.

i'de[2] *V -a dial.* eddy.

idea'l[1] *-et, pl -/+-er* ideal: **bruk ikke det utenlandske ord: i-er. Vi har jo det gode norske ord: løgne** don't use the foreign word, "i-s." We have the good Norwegian word, "lies." (Ibsen).

idea'l[2] *A* ideal.

+**idea'l/bilde** *-t* (= *__/bilete__) ideal.

idealise're *V -te* idealize.

idealis'me *-n* idealism.

idealis't *-en* idealist.

idealis'tisk *A -* idealistic.

idealite't *-en* ideality.

idé/assosiasjo'n *-en* association of ideas.

ideell' *A -elt, pl -elle* 1 ideal, perfect: **en i- stilling** an i- position. 2 idealistic, unselfish: **være i-t anlagt** have an idealistic temperament. 3 *jur., merc.* intangible (asset): **i- verdi** good will.

idé/histo'rie *-a/+-en* history of ideas.

+**i'del** *A -* mere; nothing but, sheer.

i'delig *A -* continual, incessant, perpetual.

identifikasjo'n *-en* identification.

identifise're *V -te* identify.

iden'tisk *A -* identical (**med** with): **i- ligning** *math.* i- equation.

identite't *-en* identity.

identite'ts/kort *-et* identity card, ID card.

ideolog [-olå'g] *-en* ideologist, ideologue.

ideologi' *-en* ideology.

ideologisk [-olå'g-] *A -* ideological.

*__i'dest__ *pr of* **idast**

+**ide't** *C* 1 as, just as, when: **i- han kom inn, så han...** on entering, he saw... 2 because, inasmuch as, since.

+**idethe'letatt** *Av* cf **heil**[1]

+**idetmin'ste** *Av* cf **minst**[2]

+**idetsam'me** *Av* cf **samme**

i'dig *A - dial.* diligent, industrious.

idio'm *-et, pl -/+-er* 1 idiom, idiomatic expression. 2 dialect, language.

idioma'tisk *A -* idiomatic.

idiosynkrasi' *-en* allergy, aversion (**for** to).

idio't *-en* 1 idiot, imbecile, (complete) fool, *(pop.)* blockhead, jackass: **gid den gamle i-en ville holde sin munn** how I wish the old fool would shut up (Heiberg). 2 *med.* idiot.

idioti' *-en* 1 idiocy, sheer folly. 2 *med.* idiocy.

idio'tisk *A -* 1 idiotic, (completely) foolish. 2 *med.* idiotic.

*__idk'e__ *V -a*: **i- på** work diligently, industriously.

i'/drett *-en* athletics, sports: **drive i-** engage in athletic activities, sports.

i'dretts/lag *-et* athletic club.

i'dretts/mann *-en, pl -menn/*-menner* athlete, sportsman.

i'dretts/plass *-en* athletic ground, stadium.

i'dretts/stemne *-a/+-et, pl -r/*-* (= +**/stevne**) athletic meet.

*__i'/drott__ *-en* cf **i/drett**

*__ids't__ *pp of* **idast**

I'dun(n) *Prn (f) myth.* Ithunn (goddess, wife of Bragi, who guarded the golden apples eaten by the gods to preserve their youth).

i'duns/eple *-t, pl +-r/*- myth.* one of the golden apples guarded by Ithunn in Asgard.

idyll' *-en* idyl: **deres forhold hadde ikke vært bare i-** their relationship had not been purely idyllic (Elster).

idyl'lisk *A -* idyllic.

+**i'/dømme** *V -dømte*: **i- en noe** *jur.* sentence sby to sth.

°**i'e** *df ia* cf **ide**[1]

+**ifall'** *C* cf **fall**[1]

*__i'/felling__ *-a* inlay; inset, insert.

+**ifer'd** *Av* cf **ferd**

+**ifjo'r** *Av* cf **fjor**

+**ifleng'** *Av* cf **fleng**

+**iflg.** = **ifølge**

+**ifor'/gårs** *Av* cf **for/gårs**

+**ifor'/veien** *Av* cf **for/vegen**

ifrå' *P* (= +**ifra**) cf **frå**

i'/fylling *-a/+-en* filling; fill.

+**iføl'ge** *P* according to, in accordance with.

+**i'/føre** *V -te* 1: **i-t** dressed in. 2: **i- seg** *bibl.* array, attire, clothe oneself in; put on.

-ig *A -* (= *__-ug__) -y (suffix indicating that the word is an *adj.* or *adv.*, e.g. **adskillig** considerable; **fattig** poor; **ferdig** ready).

+**igang'** *Av* cf **gang**[1]

+**igang'/setning** *-a* (= +**/setting**, ***/setjing**) starting (**av** of).

+**igang'/værende** *A -* (= ***/verande**) in progress, ongoing.

ig'de *-a zool.* wagtail (family Motacillidae).

igjen' *Av* 1 again: **ikke mine ord i-** don't repeat this, mum's the word; **komme i-** come a-. 2 back; in re-

turn: **få penger i-** get change (in money); **hilse i-** greet in r-; **komme i-** come back; **holde i-** hold back, restrain (sby); **ta i-** take back; strike back. 3 shut: **(lukke) slå i- vinduet** slam the window s-; **stoppet i-** stopped up. 4 left: **bli i-** be l-, remain (behind); **det er bare to stykker smørbrød i-** there are only two sandwiches l-; **det er langt i-** it's a long way yet; **sitte i-** stay after school.
+**igjen'nem** *P* cf **igjennom**
igjen'nom *P* through: **hele dagen i-** all day long; **hele hans liv i-** throughout the entire course of his life; **hele året i-** all year round; **helt i-** thoroughly; (cf also **gjennom**).
+**igjerde** [ijæ're] *Av* cf **gjerde**[1]
ig'le *-a/-en zool.* leech (class Hirudinea).
ig'le/kone *-a archaic* (female) bloodletter, leech.
ignoran't *-en* ignoramus.
ignore're *V -te* disregard, ignore; cut.
+**igrun'nen** *Av* cf **grunn**[1]
***i`/grøn** *A* greenish.
***i`/grå** *A -tt, pl -/-e* grayish.
igå'r *Av* cf **går**
igå'r/kvelḍ *Av* cf **går/kveld**
+**i'ẖ** *I archaic* oh (startled).
***i'/halden** *A -e/-i, pl -ne*: **med i- penn** with someone else guiding one's pen.
+**ihen'de** *Av* cf **hende**[2]
+**ihen'de/haver** *-en, pl -e* (=***-ar**) *merc.* bearer, holder: **lyde på i-en** be made payable to the bearer.
+**ihen'dehaver/papi·r** *-et* (=***-ar/**) *merc.* any document issued to the bearer, e.g. registered bond.
+**iher'dig** [also i`/] *A* - energetic, persevering, persistent.
+**iher'dig/het** *-en* persistence, tenacity.
+**iẖje'l** *Av* cf **hel**[1]
***i/holen** [i`/hålen] *A -e/-i, pl -ne* concave.
+**iho'p** *Av* cf **hop**
***iho'p/blanḍa** *A* - mixed (up).
***iho'p/draging** *-a* abstract, summary (av of).
***iho'p/leten** *A -e/-i, pl -ne* closed, shut.
***iho'p/sett** *A* - complex, compound.
+**ihu'** *Av* cf **hug**
***i`/hug**[1] *-en* cf **/huge**
+**ihu'g**[2] *Av* cf **hug**
***i`/huga** *A* - ardent, energetic, zealous.
***i`/huge** *-n* 1 ardor, zeal. 2 care, reflection.
+**ihu'/komme** *V -kom, -kommet archaic* 1 be mindful of, bear in mind. 2 *bibl.* remember: **Gud i-kom Noah** God r-ed N- (Genesis 8, 1).
+**ihu'/kommelse** *n archaic* 1: **salig i-** of blessed memory. 2 *bibl.* remembrance: **gjør dette til min i-** this do in r- of me (Luke 22, 19).
+**iẖver'tfall** *Av* cf **fall**[1]
+**iẖvorvel'** *C archaic* although, notwithstanding the fact that.
ikapp' *Av* cf **kapp**[2]
***i'/kjøting** *-a* incarnation.
+**ik'ke** *Av* 1 not; no: **det var i- dårlig** that's not bad, that's pretty good; **han er rik, i- sant?** he is rich, isn't he?; **hun elsker ham i-** she does not love him; **i- det jeg vet** not as far as I know; **i- for det** for that matter, that is to say; **i- noe, noen** not any (**det er i- noen hus i nærheten** there are not any houses nearby). 2 (with affirmative meaning, in rhetorical questions and exclamations): **hvilke muntre bordtaler kunne han i-holde** what gay dinner speeches he used to give (Kielland).
+**ik'keangreps/pakt** *-en* nonaggression pact.
+**ik'ke/røyker** *-en, pl -e* nonsmoker; *(pl)* nonsmoking compartment.
***ikkj'e** *Av* cf **ikke**
***ikkj'e/røykjar** *-en* cf **ikke/røyker**
+**ik'kun** *Av archaic* only.
+**i'/kle** *V -dde* 1 array, attire (in); invest with. 2 clothe, couch, express.
+**i'/kledning** *-en* expression, form, shape; array, embodiment.
+**ikoll'** *Av* cf **koll**[2]
iko'n *-et* icon.
i'ko·rn *-et/+-en* cf **ekorn**
***ikr.** =**ikring**
+**ikraf't/treden** *-en* coming into effect, taking effect.
ikring' *P* about, around.
***ik't** *-a* rheumatism.
ik'te *-n zool.* fluke (class Trematoda).
+**ikvel'ḍ** *Av* cf **kveld**
+**i'l**[1] *-en* 1 *archaic* haste, hurry. 2 *fam.* short for **ilsamtale.**
i'l[2] *-a, pl *iljar dial.* sole (of the foot).
i'l[3] *-a* moldboard (of a plow).
+**i'/la** *pt of* **-legge**
***i'/lag**[1] *-et* insert.
ila'g[2] *Av* cf **lag**[2]
+**i'/lagt** *pp of* **-legge**
+**ilan'ḍ** *Av* cf **land**[1]
+**ilanḍ'/bringe** *V -brakte, brakt archaic* carry on land (from a ship), land.
i'l/brev *-et* special delivery letter.
+**i'l/bud** *-et* special delivery; special delivery messenger.
+**il'ḍ** *-en* cf **eld**
+**il`ḍ/dåp** *-en* cf **eld/**
+**il`ḍe** *V -a/-et* cf **elde**[4]
+**il`ḍe/brann** *-en* conflagration; outbreak of fire.
+**il`ḍenḍe** *Av* cf **eldende**
il'der *-eren, pl -rer zool.* European polecat, fitch (Mustela putorius).
+**il`ḍ/fast** *A* - cf **eld/**
+**il`ḍ/full** *A* cf **eld/**
+**il`ḍ/givning** *-en mil.* firing, shooting.
+**Il`ḍ/landeṭ** *Pln* Tierra del Fuego.
+**il`ḍ/lenḍing** *-en* Tierra del Fuegan.
+**il`ḍ/linje** *-a/-en mil.* firing line; front line.
+**il`ḍ/mørje** *-a* cf **eld/**
+**il`ḍne** *V -a/-et* animate, fire, inspire (**til** to).
+**il`ḍnenḍe** *A* - fiery, inspiring.
+**il`ḍ/prøve** *-n* cf **eld/**
+**il`ḍ/raker** *-en, pl -e* cf **eld/rake**
+**il`ḍ/røḍ** *A* cf **eld/raud**
+**il'ḍs/farlig** *A* - cf **elds/**
+**il`ḍ/sikker** *A -t, pl -sikre* cf **eld/**
+**il`ḍ/sjel** *-a/-en* cf **eld/**
+**il`ḍ/skrift** *-a/-en* letters of fire.
+**il`ḍ/skuffe** *-a* small shovel (for removing ashes from a fireplace).
+**il`ḍ/sprutenḍe** *A* - cf **eld/**
+**il'ḍs/påset·telse** *-n* arson.
+**il`ḍ/sted** [also /ste·] *-et* fireplace, hearth.
+**il`ḍ/tang** *-en, pl -tenger* fire tongs: **jeg ville ikke ta i ham med en i-** I would not touch him with a ten-foot pole.
+**il`ḍ/vann** *-et* firewater.
i'le[1] *-n* 1 (stone) sinker (fishing). 2 *naut.* grapnel (anchor with three or more flukes).
i'le[2] *-a* spring, well.
+**i'le**[3] *V -te* hasten, hurry; run: **i- til hjelp** hurry to one's aid, rescue; **tiden i-er** time flies.
i'/legg *-et* 1 firebox (in stove). 2 insert.
+**i'/legge** *V -la, -lagt*: **i- mulkt** *jur.* fine.
***i'/lengte** *V -a* long, yearn for constantly.
+**i'l/ferdig** *A* - *archaic* hurried, precipitate.
i'l/gods [/gots] *-et* express.
+**ili'ke/må'te** *I* cf **måte**[1]
i'/likne *V -a/+-et* (=+**/ligne**) assess.
+**i'ling** *-en* cf also **eling** shudder, trembling; cold chill.
+**ili've** *Av* cf **live**[2]
***il'k** *-en* 1 *anat.* ball, sole (of foot). 2 callus (on bottom of foot or toe).
***il'ke** *-n anat.* arch (of foot).
***il'ket(e)** *A* - callused.
ill' *A ilt, cp verre, sp verst dial.* 1 painful: **det satte seg noe i-t for bringa** a pain settled in his chest (Falkberget). 2 bad, evil, wicked. 3 nasty, unpleasant: **slite i-t** suffer. 4 angry, cross. (For **verre, verst** see **verre**).
ill. =**illustrasjon, illustrert**
***ill'/beitt** *A* - blunt, dull.
il'le *A -, cp verre, sp verst* 1 bad: **ikke i-** not b-, pretty good; **Mary er nå slett ikke så i- som du tror** M- isn't nearly as b- as you think (Undset). 2 *(adv.)* badly, ill: **i-berørt** hurt, offended; **bli i- ved** feel hurt, depressed; **få høre i- for noe** have sth thrown up to one; **gå i- (med)** turn out badly (with); **hun likte det i-** she did not like it at all (Undset); **se i- ut** look bad; **det står i- til** things are going badly; **ta noe i- opp** take sth amiss; **det var ikke i- ment** it was well meant. 3 *(adv.) fam.* very: **i- sjuk** very sick. (For **verre, verst** see **verre**).
+**il`le/befin·nenḍe** *-t* indisposition, nausea: **lide av et lett i-** be slightly indisposed.
il'/lega·l *A* illegal: **den i-e presse** the underground (resistance) press (in occupied Norway during World War II).
il'/legalite·t *-en* illegality.
il'/legiti·m *A* illegitimate.
il`le/luktende [/loktene] *A* - bad smelling, stinking.
***il`le/læte** *-t* (=**ill/**) expression of disapproval, displeasure.
il`le/varslenḍe *A* - ominous, threatening.
ill`/gjerning [/jæ·rning] *-a/+-en* crime, misdeed.
ill`gjernings/mann *-en, pl -menn/ *-menner* criminal, evildoer, miscreant.
***ill`/gjeten** *A -e/-i, pl -ne* notorious.
***ill`/herveleg** *A* - awful, frightful, terrible: **beit so i- vondt** bit so fearfully hard (Vesaas).
***ill`/hug** *-en* anxiety, care, concern.
ill`/huie *V -a/+-et/+-de* (=***/huje**) scream, yell at the top of one's voice.
***ill`/kynḍt** *A* - cross, ill-natured.
***ill`/menne** *-t* cruel, malicious person.
il'/loja·l *A* 1 disloyal (**mot** to). 2 underhanded, unfair (e.g. competition).
il'/lojalite·t *-en* 1 disloyalty. 2 unfairness.
***ill`/o·rḍ** *-et* blame, censure.
***ill`/råḍig** *A* - treacherous, wicked.
ill`/sinne *-t* towering rage.
ill`/sint *A* - beside oneself with rage, furious, raving.
***ill'/skap** *-en* rage, temper.
ill`/skrike *V infl as* **skrike**[1] scream, yell at the top of one's voice.
+**ill`/svien** *A -ent, pl -ene* (=***/sviden**) 1 agonizing, painful. 2 troubled, worried.
+**ill`/trives** *V -des, -(e)s* (=***-ast**) be unhappy, not enjoy oneself.
***ill`/tru** *V -dde* distrust.
illude're *V -te* be convincing, give a convincing performance (**som** as).
illuminasjo'n *-en* illumination.
illumine're *V -te* illuminate.
illusjo'n *-en* illusion: **gjøre seg ingen i-er om** have no i-s about.
illusjonis't *-en* 1 conjurer, sleight of hand artist. 2 dreamer, visionary.
illuso'risk *A* - illusory.
illustrasjo'n *-en* illustration (**til** of).
illustratø'r *-en* illustrator (**av** of).
illustre're *V -te* illustrate.
***ill`/ver** [/vær] *-et* bad weather, storm.
***ill`/vilje** *-n* hatred, ill will.
+**i'l/marsj** *-en mil.* forced march.
+**i'l/samtale** *-n* priority long distance call (for which a higher rate is paid).
il'sk *A* - angry, ill-tempered, irascible.
***il'skast** *V -ast* be ill-tempered, irascible.
il'ske[1] *-a* 1 anger, rage; hatred, malice. 2 *dial.* nausea; sickness.
il'ske[2] *V -a/+-et*: **i- seg** get angry, excited, work oneself up.

+ Bokmål; * Nynorsk; ° Dialect.
After letter: ' stress (Acc. 1); ` tone, stress (Acc. 2); · length.
Below letter: . not pronounced.

il'sken *A* +*-ent, pl -ne* angry, malevolent.
***il'sleg** *A* - angry, malicious; unpleasant.
+i'l/som· *A* hurried, precipitate.
il't *nt of* **ill**
+i'l/telegram· *-met* (express) telegram.
+il'ter *A -ert, pl -re* 1 angry, hotheaded, irascible. 2 cutting, piercing, sharp (sound). 3 blinding, dazzling (light).
+i'l/tog [/tåg] *-et* express train.
°i'l/tom· *-men* 1 sinker line (fishing). 2 *naut.* anchor cable.
***i'/låt** *-et* bag, sack.
***i'm** *-en* scent, smell.
imaginæ'r *A* 1 imaginary. 2: **i-t tall** *math.* imaginary number. 3: **i- gevinst** *merc.* paper profit.
ima'go *-en zool.* imago (adult insect).
+ima'k *Av* cf **mak**
imbesilite't *-en* imbecility.
imbesill' *A imbesilt* imbecile.
***im'bre** *-n* cf **immer**
+im'bre/dager *pl* (=***-ar**) *eccl.* Ember days.
***i'me**[1] *-a* thin cloud cover.
***i'me**[2] *V -a* smoke, steam; reek.
***ime'dan** *Av* cf **imens**
imel'lom *P* (=**+imellem**) 1 between: **er det noe i- dem?** is there sth b- them?; **i- oss** (also **oss i-**) just b- you, me and the gatepost; **værelser med dør i-** connecting rooms. 2 among: **i- venner** a- friends. 3 *(adv.)* between; occasionally: **legge seg i-** intervene; **engang i-** once in a while; **midt i-** right in between. (See also **mellom**).
+imen's *Av* (=***imedan**) in the meantime, meanwhile.
+imid'ler/tid *Av* at the same time, however, still.
***i'ming** *-en* fine snowfall.
imitasjo'n *-en* imitation (**av** of).
imite're *V -te* imitate: **i-t skinn** imitation leather.
im'/materiell· *A -elt* immaterial, incorporeal, nonmaterial.
immatrikule're *V -te* enroll in a university, matriculate.
immatu'rus *-en* failing grade (on a university examination).
+im'mer *-en* (=***imbre**) *zool.* great northern diver (a loon) (Colymbus immer).
immigran't *-en* immigrant.
immigrasjo'n *-en* immigration.
immigre're *V -te* immigrate.
+immobi'lier *pl* real estate; *jur.* real property.
immu'n *A* immune (**mot** against, from, to).
immunite't *-en* 1 immunity (exemption, special privilege): **diplomatisk i-** diplomatic i-. 2 *med.* immunity (**mot** against, from, to).
+imorgen [imå'ren] *Av* cf **morgen**
+imor'ges *Av* cf **morges**
imo't *P* 1 towards: **se i- kirken** look t- the church; **ta i-** accept, receive. 2 against: **det er meg (henne) i-** I am (she is) opposed to it; **by en i-** be repulsive to one; **få (ha) i- en** develop (have) an aversion to, for sby; **gjøre noen i-** go against sby's will; **middel i-** remedy against, for; **rygg i- rygg** back to back. 3 *(adv.)* against (one); opposite: **like i-** straight across; **si i-** contradict; **tvert i-** on the contrary. (See also **mot**[2]).
imper'ativ[1] *-en gram.* imperative.
imper'ativ[2] *-et*: **kategorisk i-** *philos.* categorical imperative.
imper'ativisk [also -i'v-] *A* - imperative.
im'perfektum *-et gram.* imperfect, preterite.
imperialis'me *-n* imperialism.
imperialis't *-en* imperialist.
imperialis'tisk *A* - imperialistic.
impe'rium *-iet, pl* +*-ier*/**-ium* empire (esp. Roman or British).
impertinen's *-en* impertinence.
impertinen't *A* - impertinent.

implise're *V -te* implicate.
implisitt' *A* - implicit; *(adv.)* by implication.
impone're *V -te* impress: **i-ende** impressive, striking.
impor't *-en* import, importation.
impor't/artik·kel *-elen, pl -artikler* imported article.
importe're *V -te* import.
importø'r *-en* importer.
impoten's *-en* impotence.
impoten't *A* - impotent; sterile.
impregne're *V -te* impregnate; waterproof.
impresa'rio *-en, pl impresarier* impresario.
impresjonis'me *-n* impressionism.
impresjonis't *-en* impressionist.
impresjonis'tisk *A* - impressionistic.
improm'ptu *-et mus.* impromptu.
improvisasjo'n *-en* improvisation.
improvisa'tor *-en* improviser.
improvise're *V -te* improvise.
impul's *-en* 1 impulse; impetus, incentive. 2 *elec.* impulse.
im'pulsiv *A* impulsive.
impulsivite't *-en* impulsiveness.
impul's/kjøp *-et* spur of the moment purchase; impulsive buying.
Im's/land *Pln* twp, Rogaland.
+imø'te *Av* cf **møte**[1]
+imø'te/gå *V -gikk, -gått* answer, counter, meet (arguments); disprove, refute.
+imø'te/gåelse *-n* answer (**av** to), refutation.
+imø'te/komme *V -kom, -kommet* comply with, meet, oblige.
imø'te/kommende *A* - accommodating, obliging; favorable, sympathetic (**mot** to).
+imø'tekommen/het *-en* compliance, considerateness, courtesy.
+imø'te/se *V -så, -sett* anticipate, look forward to; await.
inappella'bel *A -elt, pl -le jur.* final, irrevocable (decree, judgment).
+inatt' *Av* cf **natt**
in blan'ko left blank, not filled in.
incitamen't *-et, pl -*/+*-er* incentive, stimulus; stimulant (**til** to).
incite're *V -te* incite, stimulate.
+incl. =**inklusive**
in corpore [in kår'pore] in toto.
in'deks *-en* 1 index. 2 *eccl.* Index Librorum Prohibitorum: **sette en bok på i-** put a book on the Index. 3 *merc.* price index.
in'deks/fami·lie *-n merc.* wage-earning family approximating average standard of living as determined by price index.
in'deks/regule·ring *-a*/+*-en merc.* adjustment, regulation of the price index.
in'deks/tal *-et* (=**+/tall**) *merc.* price index; index figure.
+in'der *-en, pl -e* (=***-ar**) Indian (person from India).
in'derlig *A* - 1 heartfelt, sincere; fervent; intense: **ha i- lyst** feel strongly inclined; **takke i-** give heartfelt thanks. 2 close, intimate: **et i- forhold** a close relationship. 3 *(adv.)* greatly, heartily, very: **i- glad** very happy; **i- gode venner** very good friends; **i- trøtt** extremely tired; **banne i-** swear heartily.
+in'derlig/het *-en* 1 heartiness, sincerity; intensity. 2 closeness, intimacy.
In'der/øy *Pln* twp, Nord-Trøndelag.
In'dia *Pln* India.
+india'ner *-en, pl -e* (=***-ar**) (American) Indian: **leke i- og hvit** play cowboys and Indians.
india'nsk *A* - (American) Indian.
indifferen's *-en* indifference.
indifferen't *A* - 1 indifferent. 2 *chem.* neutral.
indignasjo'n *-en* indignation.
indigne'rt *A* - indignant.
in'digo *-en* indigo.
in'digo/blå *A -tt, pl -*/**-e* indigo blue.
indikasjo'n *-en* 1 indication. 2 *med.* indication.

indik'ativ *-en gram.* indicative.
indika'tor *-en* 1 indicator (**på** of). 2 *chem.* indicator. 3 *phys.* pressure gauge.
indike're *V -te* indicate.
in'/direk'te *A* - indirect: **i- lys** i- lighting; **i- tale** *gram.* i- discourse.
indise're *V -te* indicate.
+indi'sie/bevi's *-et jur.* (piece of) circumstantial evidence.
indi'sium *-iet, pl* +*-ier*/**-ium jur.* circumstantial evidence.
in'disk *A* - Indian (from India).
indiskresjo'n *-en* indiscretion, tactlessness; act of indiscretion.
indiskre't [also in'-] *A* - indiscreet, tactless.
in'/dispone'rt *A* - indisposed.
indivi'd *-et, pl -*/+*-er* 1 individual, person. 2 *derog.* character.
individualise're *V -te* individualize.
individualis'me *-n* individualism.
individualis't *-en* individualist.
individualis'tisk *A* - individualistic.
individualite't *-en* individuality.
individuell' *A -elt* individual.
In'do/china [/kjina] *Pln* Indo-China.
in'do/europe·isk *A* - Indo-European.
indolen's *-en* indolence.
indolen't *A* - indolent.
in'dre[1] *et* 1 interior: **jordens i-** the i- of the earth. 2 heart, mind: **hans i-** (also) his inner being.
in'dre[2] *A* - inner, inside, interior; internal: **det i- av** the interior of; **det i- menneske** the inner man; **det i- øye** the mind's eye; **i- sammenheng** secret connection.
in'dre/medisi·n *-en med.* internal medicine.
in'dre/medisi·nsk *A* - concerned with internal medicine.
in'dre/misjo·n *-en eccl.* home mission; evangelical work: **I-en** organization of home missions; evangelism.
in'dre/poli·tisk *A* - domestic, internal (policy).
in'dre/sekreto·risk *A* - *anat.* endocrine (gland).
induksjo'n *-en* induction.
in'duktiv *A* inductive.
in dup'lo in duplicate.
induse're *V -te* induce.
industri' *-en* 1 industry. 2: **i-er** *merc.* industrials.
industrialise're *V -te* industrialize.
industrialis'me *-n* industrialism.
industri'/by *-en* industrial, manufacturing town.
industriell' *A -elt* industrial.
industri'/herre *-n* industrialist.
Industri'- og [å] **hån'dverks/departementet** [-mang'e] *df* The Ministry of Industry and Handicrafts.
in'/effektiv *A* ineffective.
in exten'so in full.
infa'm *A* infamous, vile: **situasjonen var i-** it was a dreadful situation (Boo); **en i- bemerkning** a nasty remark.
infanteri' *-et mil.* infantry.
infanteris't *-en mil.* infantryman.
infanti'l *A* infantile.
infantilis'me *-n* infantilism.
infar'kt +*-et*/**-en med.* infarct, infarction (of the heart).
infeksjo'n *-en* infection.
infeksjo'ns/sjukdom *-men*/**-en* (=**+/sykdom**) infectious disease.
inferiø'r *A med., psych.* inferior; moronic.
inferna'lsk *A* - 1 infernal, outrageous. 2 diabolical, fiendish.
infer'no *-et* inferno.
infiltrasjo'n *-en med.* infiltration.
infiltre're *V -te med.* infiltrate.
infinitesima'l/rekning *-a*/+*-en* (=**+/regning**) *math.* infinitesimal calculus.
infin'itiv *-en gram.* infinitive.
infin'itivs/merke *-t gram.* sign of the infinitive (*å* in Norwegian, *to* in English, etc.).
infise're *V -te* infect; *fig.* taint (**med** by, with).

in flagran'te in the very act, red-handed.
inflammasjo'n *-en med.* inflammation.
inflasjo'n *-en* inflation.
inflate're *V -te* inflate.
inflato'risk *A -* inflationary.
influen'sa *-en med.* influenza (flu).
influe're *V -te* influence (**på en** sby).
informasjo'n *-en* **1** information. **2: gi i-er** *archaic* give lessons, private instruction.
informe're *V -te* advise, inform (**om** about).
+**in'fra/rød** *A* (=*/**raud**) infrared.
in'fra/struktu'r *-en* infrastructure, substructure.
infusjo'n *-en* infusion.
infusjo'ns/dyr *-et zool.* paramecium (slipper animalcule).
+**infuso'rie** *-t zool.* paramecium (slipper animalcule).
-ing[1] *-a/-en* suffix like English *-ing* in verbal nouns, e.g. **drikking** drinking; **flytting** moving; **juling** beating (but not like English *-ing* in pres. part. or progressive present).
-ing[2] *-en* designation of person from a particular place, e.g. **vossing** person from Voss.
ing. = **ingeniør**
ing'a *Pn f of* **ingen**
Inga [ing'ga] *Prn (f)*
*__ing'a/leis__ *Av* by no means, in no way.
Inge [ing'ge] *Prn (m)*
Ing'e/borg *Prn (f)*
Ing'e/brikt *Prn (m)*
ing'e/fær *-en/*-a bot.* ginger (Zingiber officinale).
ing'efær/øl *-et* ginger ale.
ing'en *Pn f inga/ingen, nt +intet/*inkje, pl ingen* **1** none; neither (of two); nobody, no one: **i- annen** no one else; **i- av dem** none of them; neither of them; **intet** *obs.* nothing (see **ingenting, ikke noe**); **jeg kjenner i- her** I know no one here; **slett i-** none at all. **2** (as *adj.*) no, not any: **jeg har i- del i dette** I have no part in this (Ibsen); **vi fant i- penger** we didn't find any money.
ingeniør [insjenjø'r] *-en* engineer.
ingeniør/arbeid *-et* engineering; piece of engineering.
+**ing'en/lunde** *Av* by no means, **not at all**; certainly not.
ing'enmanns/land *-et mil.* no-man's-land.
*__ing'en/stad__ *Av* (=***ing'en sta'd**) cf **/steds**
+**ing'en/steds** *Av* (=*/**stad**) nowhere: **overalt og i-** anyplace at all, wherever one happens to be.
ing'en/ting *Pn* (=**ing'en ting'**) nothing, not anything: **det er i-** there's nothing to it; **det gjør i-** it doesn't matter, never mind; **det ligner i-** it makes no sense whatever; it's shameful; **i- biter på ham** nothing bothers him; **i- er som...** nothing can beat...; **i- å snakke om** don't mention it, it's a pleasure; **kunne gjøre noe som i-** be able to do sth as easily as falling off a log; **late som i-** act as if nothing were the matter.
Ing'er *Prn (f)*
*__ing'i__ *Pn f, pl of* **ingen**
ingredien's *-en* ingredient.
Ing'ri(d) *Prn (f)*
Ing'unn [ing'gunn] *Prn (f)*
Ing'vald [also ing'-] *Prn (m)*
Ing'vild *Prn (f)*
in'/habi'l *A* **1** incompetent, unqualified. **2** *jur.* disqualified.
inhabilite't *-en jur.* disqualification.
inhale're *V -te* inhale.
initial [initsia'l] *-en* initial.
initiativ [initsiati'v] *-et* enterprise, initiative: **gripe, ta i-et** seize, take the i-.
initiativ/rik *A* enterprising.
+**initiativ/taker** *-en, pl -e* (=*__-ar__) initiator, originator (**til** of).
injeksjo'n *-en* injection.
injise're *V -te med.* inject.
injurian't *-en jur.* libeler, slanderer.
inju'rie *-n jur.* defamation, libel, slander.
injurie're *V -te jur.* defame, libel, slander.
in'ka *-en* Inca.
inkarnasjo'n *-en* embodiment, incarnation (**av** of).
inkarne're *V -te* embody, incarnate.
inkassa'tor *-en merc.* (debt) collector.
inkas'so *-en merc.* collection of delinquent accounts.
*__in'kje__[1] *Av* cf **ikke**
*__in'kje__[2] *Pn nt of* **ingen**
*__in'kje/kjønn__ *-et* cf **intet/**
*__in'kje/vetta__ *Pn* nothing: **han er eit i-** he's a complete nonentity.
inkl. = **inklusive**
inklinasjo'n *-en* **1** inclination. **2** *archaic* attachment.
inklinasjo'ns/parti' *-et, pl +-er/*- archaic* love match.
inkline're *V -te* **1** incline. **2** *archaic* be in love (**for** with).
inklude're *V -te* include.
in'klusiv *A* inclusive.
in'klusiv(e) *P merc.* inclusive of: **i- emballasje** packing included.
inkog'nito[1] *-et* incognito: **bevare sitt i-** preserve one's i-; **i dypeste i-** strictly i-.
inkog'nito[2] *A -* incognito.
inkommensura'bel *A -elt, pl -le* incommensurable; incompatible.
inkompetanse [inkompetang'se, also in'-] *-n* incompetence.
inkompeten't [also in'/] *A -* incompetent.
in'/kongruen't *A - math.* incongruent, incongruous.
in'/konsekven's *-en* inconsistency.
in'/konsekven't *A -* inconsistent.
inkorpore're *V -te* incorporate.
inkubasjo'n *-en med.* incubation.
inkubasjo'ns/tid *-a/+-en med.* incubation period.
inku'rie *-n* inadvertence, oversight: **ved en i-** through an o-.
inkvisisjo'n *-en eccl.* Inquisition, Holy Office.
inkvisi'tor *-en, pl -to'rer eccl., jur.* inquisitor.
inkvisito'risk *A -* inquisitorial.
in men'te: ha noe i- keep sth in mind.
inn' *Av* in: **i- att** back in; **(gå) i- for retten** (go) before the court; **i- i** into; **ha vinden i- om styrbord, ha vinden styrbord i-** *naut.* have the wind on the starboard side; **i- over** over, upon; **i- på** on (to) (**han kom i- på stien igjen** he got on the path again); **i- til** up against; facing (**han hadde værelse i- til gården** he had a room facing the (court) yard); (with verbs: see these).
in'na *C, Av* cf **innen**
in'na- *pf* (=+**innen-**, ***innan-**) prefix denoting inclusion, location within limits.
in'na/bo'rds *A -* **1** internal (on a ship). **2** *(adv.)* aboard, on board. **3** *hum.* inside (a person): **han hadde fått for mye i-** he was three sheets to the wind, had had too much (to drink).
in'na/bygds *A -* **1** local, within the (country) community. **2** *(adv.)* locally.
in'na/bys *A -* **1** local, within the city (town). **2** *(adv.)* locally.
+**inn'/ad** *P* in, inwards: **i-, i-! Det er ordet! Dit går veien** inward (to man's soul)! That's the word! There goes the path (Ibsen).
+**inn'ad/vendt** *A -* introspective, introverted.
in'na/dø'rs *A -* **1** indoor, inside. **2** *(adv.)* indoors, in the house.
in'na/for' *P* (=***innan/**) inside; within; back of, beyond: **han fikk midtværelset og vi fikk værelset i-** he got the middle room and we got the room beyond (that); **i- våre egne fire vegger** within our own four walls; **kom i- gjerdet** come inside the fence.
in'na/frå *P* (=***innan/**, +**/fra**) from within, from the inside.
in'na/lands *Av* (=***innan/**) internally, within the country.
in'na/landsk *A -* (=***innan/**) domestic, internal.
*__in'nan__ *C, Av* cf **innen**
*__in'nan-__ *pf* cf **inna-**
inn'/anke *V -et jur.* appeal: **i- en dom for høyesterett** carry a case to the Supreme Court.
*__in'nan/om'__ *P* inside, within.
*__in'nar__ *A -, sp innarst* farther in (esp. in a house).
+**inn'/arbei'de** *V -et* **1** incorporate, work in. **2** work up a market for (a product): **i- seg** establish oneself, one's practice. **3** *tech.* appliqué.
in'na/riks *Av* within the country.
in'nariks/fart *-en* domestic shipping.
in'na/riksk *A -* domestic, home, internal.
*__in'narleg__ *A -* (quite) far in, far inward.
*__in'narst__ *A -* cf **innerst**[2]
*__in'narste__ *eit* cf **innerste**
+**in'na/skjæ'rs** *Av* (=*/**skjers**, ***innan/skjers**) in coastal waters (inside the outer reefs).
*__inn'/att__ *Av* cf **inn**
in natu'ra *merc.* in kind.
inn'/avl *-en* (=*/**al**) inbreeding.
innb. = +**innbyggere**/***innbyggjarar**; +**innbundet**/***innbunde(n)**
inn'/barka *A -* (=+**-et**) callous, hardened.
*__inn'/beding__ *-a* invitation.
+**inn'/befat'te** *V -et* embrace, include: **i-et i prisen** i-d in the price.
+**inn'/begre'p** *-et* sum, total; epitome, essence (**av** of).
+**inn'/beret'ning** *-en* report: **avgi i- om** submit a r- on.
+**inn'/beret'te** *V -et* report.
+**inn'/beta'le** *V -te* pay (in): **fullt i-te aksjer** *merc.* fully paid corporate shares; **i-ing** payment.
inn'betalings/kort *-et* money order which deposits money in payee's postal check account.
inn'/bille *V -bilte* lead (sby) to believe, make (sby) believe: **i- seg (at)** imagine (that); labor under a delusion (that).
+**inn'/bilning** *-en* (=*/**billing**) fancy, imagination; delusion, hallucination.
inn'/bilsk *A -* conceited, stuck-up.
+**inn'bilsk/het** *-en* conceit.
inn'/bilt *A -* fancied, imagined; imaginary.
inn'/bilte *pt of* **-bille**
inn'/binding *-a/+-en* (book) binding (**av** of): **en smakfull i-** a tasteful b-.
+**inn'/bitt** *A -* repressed, stifled (anger).
+**inn'/blandet** *A -* (=***-a**) implicated, mixed up in: **bli i- i en sak** get mixed up in a matter.
inn'/blanding *-a/+-en* interference, meddling (**i** in).
+**inn'/blikk** *-et* insight: **få (ha) i- i noe** gain (have) an i- into sth.
+**inn'/bo** *-et* cf **/bu**
+**inn'/bringe** *V -brakte, -brakt* **1** bring in, produce, yield. **2: i-brakt** brought in (as a prisoner).
+**inn'/bringende** *A -* lucrative, profitable.
inn'/brott *-et* (=*/**brot**, +**/brudd**) *jur.* burglary, housebreaking.
inn'brotts/tjuv [/kjuv] *-en* (=+**/tyv**) *jur.* burglar, housebreaker.
+**inn'/brudd** *-et* cf **/brott**
+**inn'brudds/tyv** *-en* cf **innbrots/tjuv**
inn'/bu *-et* (=+**/bo**) furniture, household goods.
+**inn'/bundet** *A -, pl -ne* bound (book).
+**inn'/by** *V -bød, -budt* invite (**til** to): **i- til kritikk** invite criticism.

+ Bokmål; * Nynorsk; ° Dialect.
After letter: ' stress (Acc. 1); ' tone, stress (Acc. 2); · length.
Below letter: . not pronounced.

+innby'delse *-n* invitation (**til** to): **avslå en i-** refuse an i-.
+inn'/bydende *A* - inviting, tempting.
+inn'/byder *-en, pl -e* 1 host. 2 convener; *merc.* promoter.
***inn/byding** *-a* cf **/bydelse**
inn'/bygd[1] *-a* inland district: **i-a** inner part of a district.
inn'/bygd[2] *A -/*-bygt* 1 built-in: **i-elektrisk ledning** concealed electric conduit. 2 surrounded by buildings.
inn'/bygding *-en* person from an **innbygd.**
+inn'/bygger *-en, pl -e* (=***-jar**) dweller, inhabitant.
inn'/byrdes *A* - 1 mutual, reciprocal. 2 *(adv.)* among themselves, with each other; mutually, reciprocally.
+inn'/bytter *-en, pl -e* substitute (in sports).
+inn'/bytting *-a/-en* handing in; swapping.
+inn'/bød *pt of* **-by**
inn'/dele *V -te* 1 classify (**etter** according to); divide (**i** into). 2 graduate (a scale).
inn'/deling *-a/+-en* 1 classification, division (**i** into). 2 graduation (e.g. of a thermometer).
+inn'/dra *V -drog, -dradd* 1 confiscate, seize. 2 call in, retire, withdraw (e.g. money from circulation). 3 abolish (e.g. a department); discontinue, suspend.
+inn'/dragelse *-n* cf **inn/draging**
inn'/draging *-a/+-en* (=**+/dragning**) 1 confiscation, seizure (**av** of). 2 calling in, withdrawal. 3 abolition; discontinuance, suspension.
+inn'/drive *V -dre(i)v, -drevet* collect (e.g. debts, taxes); *jur.* enforce payment through legal measures.
inn'/driving *-a* (=**+/drivning, +/drivelse**) collection (**av** of).
+inn'/drog *pt of* **-dra**
in'ne *Av* 1 indoors, inside; in, within: **i- fra** from inside; **i- hos meg** in my room; **i- i** (emphatic) in, inside; **i- i landet** inland; **i- i meg** inside me, in my heart; **her i-** in here; **jeg er ikke i- i situasjonen** I'm not up on the situation (Ibsen); **midt i- i fjellene** in the heart of the mountains; **i- mot land** near the shore; **i- på scenen** on the stage; **være i- på noe** be on, touch on sth; give consideration to sth (e.g. an idea, subject, etc.). 2 arrived, at hand: **tiden er i-** the time has come. (With verbs: see these.)
-in'ne *-a/+-en* feminine suffix, cf e.g. **venninne** girl friend; **vertinne** hostess.
in'ne/arbeid *-et* work indoors.
in'ne/bar *pt of* **-bære, -bere**
***in'ne/bere** [/bære] *V -bar, bore/-i* cf **/bære**
***in'ne/burd** *-en* implication.
in'ne/bygd *A -/*-bygt* built-in, secluded, surrounded; *naut.* protected (e.g. the captain's bridge).
+in'ne/bære *V -bar, -båret* (=***/bere**) imply.
+in'ne/fra *P* from within.
+in'ne/frosset *A -et/-ent, pl -frosne* (=***/frosen**) icebound: **i-ne kreditter** *merc.* frozen assets.
+in'ne/ha *V -dde, -tt* 1 have in one's possession, own, possess. 2 hold (a position), occupy.
***in'ne/halde** *V -held, -heldt, -halde/-i* cf **/holde**
+in'ne/haver *-en, pl -e* (=***-ar**) owner, proprietor; holder (**av** of).
+in'ne/holde *V -holdt, -holdt* contain, hold.
+in'ne/klemt *A* - 1 jammed in: **i- luft** oppressive, stale air. 2 *fig.* pent-up, suppressed.
inn'/eksersere *V -te mil.* drill (**i** in).
in'ne/liv *-et* indoor life, life indoors.
+in'nen *C, P* (=***inna, *innan**) 1 *(prep.), lit.* inside, within (a circle of friends, an hour, limits, a week, etc.). 2 *(conj.), lit.* before, prior to: **i- du reiser** before you leave.
+in'nen- *Pf* cf **inna-**
+in'nen/at *Av*: **kunne lese i-** be able to read (aloud).
+in'nen/for' *P* cf **inna/**
+in'nen/fra *P* cf **inna/frå**
+in'nen/lands *Av* cf **inna/**
+in'nen/landsk *A* - cf **inna/**
+in'nen/riks *Av* cf **inna/**
+in'nen/riksk *A* - cf **inna/**
+in'nen/skjæ'rs *Av* cf **inna/**
in'ner/dør *-a* inner door.
in'ner/kant *-en* inside edge.
in'ner/lomme *-a* inside pocket.
in'ner/side *-a* inside: **på i-a** on the inside.
+in'nerst[1] *-en hist.* farm laborer (tenant of small landowner who maintains his own household).
+in'nerst[2] *A* - cf **inst**
+in'nerste *et* center, core, heart: **i mitt i-** in my h-.
in'ner/sving *-en* inside curve: **ta i-en på en** cut ahead of sby.
+in'ne/sluttet *A* - 1 reticent, reserved, taciturn. 2 *archaic* enclosed, shut in.
+in'nesluttet/het *-en* reticence, reserve, taciturnity.
+in'ne/sperre *V -et* confine, lock up, shut up: **holde en i-et** keep sby imprisoned.
+in'ne/stengt *A* - (=***/stengd**) confined, locked up, restricted; pent-up (feelings): **i- luft** stuffy air.
+in'ne/stå *V -stod, -stått*: **i- for** guarantee, vouch for.
in'ne/stående *A* - *merc.* (cash) on deposit, (cash) on hand: **ha i-** have invested.
+inn'/ett [also -ett'] *A* - with long suppressed anger; bitter(ly), malicious(ly), savage(ly): **han svor i-** he swore angrily.
inn'/etter *P* 1 in (along, through): **i- fjorden** in through the fjord. 2 *(adv.)* inward, toward the interior.
+in'ne/værende *A* - (=***/verande**) current, present: **i- måned** this month.
inn'/fall *-et* 1 inroad, invasion (**i** into). 2 (sudden) idea, thought; fancy, notion, whim.
inn'/fallen *A +-ent, pl -falne* emaciated, haggard; hollow, sunken.
inn'falls/port [/port] *-en* gateway (**til** to).
inn'falls/vinkel *-elen, pl -ler phys.* angle of incidence.
+inn'/fange *V -et* capture, catch.
+inn'/fant *pt of* **-finne**
+inn'/fart *-en* approach, entrance (**til** to).
+inn'farts/vei *-en* main approach, of road leading to a city.
+inn'/fatning *-a/-en* frame, mounting, setting; border, edging.
+inn'/fatte *V -et* frame, mount, set (**i** in).
inn'/feit *A -t/+-fett* corpulent, obese.
+inn'/felle *V -felte, -felt* inlay, insert.
***inn'/ferd** [/fær] *-a* entrance, entry (**i** into).
+inn'/filtret *A* - entangled, enmeshed, mixed up (**i** in); matted, tangled (also *fig.*).
+inn'/finne *V -fant, -funnet*: **i- seg** appear, show up, turn up; arrive, attend.
inn'/fjo'rding *-en* person from the inner part of a fjord.
+inn'/flette *V -et* interweave; *fig.* insert, put in (e.g. comments, remarks).
+inn'/flydelse [also -fly'-] *-n* cf **/flytelse**
+inn'/flytelse *-n* influence: **gjøre sin i- gjeldende (på)** bring one's i- to bear (on); **stå under i- av** be under the i- of.
+innfly'telses/rik *A* influential.
+inn'/flytter *-en, pl -e* (=***-ar**) 1 new occupant. 2 immigrant; recent comer (to a community).
inn'/fløkt *A* - complex, complicated, tangled.
+inn'/forli've *V -et* 1 incorporate. 2: **i- seg i** familiarize oneself with; **i-et med** conversant, familiar with.
+inn'/forli'velse *-n* 1 incorporation (**i** in). 2 familiarization (**med** with).
+inn'/forstått' *A* -: **erklære seg, (være) i- med noe** accept, agree to sth, be satisfied with sth.
+inn'/fri *V -dde* 1 fulfill, redeem (pledge, promise). 2 *merc.* discharge, pay (obligation), *(pop.)* square (an account).
+inn'/frielse *-n* 1 redemption (**av** of). 2 *merc.* payment.
inn'/ful *A -fult* cunning, sly.
+inn'/funnet *pp of* **-finne**
***inn'/føding** *-en* native.
+inn'føds/rett *-en* (=***innfødings/**) (right of) citizenship: **gi en i-** naturalize sby.
+inn'/født *A* - (=***/fødd**) 1 indigenous, native, native-born: **en i-** a native; **i-e** aborigines. 2 *jur.* having rights of citizenship.
+inn'/føling *-en* empathy, sympathetic understanding.
inn'/føre *V -te* 1 introduce, make known (**i** to); bring in. 2 import (**i** into). 3 enter, register (e.g. birth, marriage) (**i** in). 4 impose, introduce (law, regulation): **i- forbud mot** prohibit.
inn'/føring *-a/+-en* introduction (**i** to).
inn'/førsel *-elen, pl -ler* 1 import, importation (**av** of). 2 entering, registration.
***inn'/førsle** *-a* cf **/førsel**
inn'/gang *-en* 1 entrance, entry (e.g. to a house). 2 *fig.* entrance, entry: **vinne i- hos** gain, win entry into (a group). 3 beginning, threshold (**til** of): **vi står ved i-en til en ny tid** we are at the t- of a new era. 4 *merc.* receipt of payment.
+inn'gangs/bønn *-a,-en* (=***/bøn**) introductory prayer, introit.
inn'gangs/dør *-a* entrance (door).
inn'gangs/kone *-a hist.* woman who is churched following childbirth (purificatory rite).
+inn'gangs/penger *pl* (=***-ar**) entrance fee, price of admission.
+inn'/gi *V -gav, -gitt* 1 send in, submit (application); lodge (complaint). 2 inspire, prompt, suggest. 3 *med.* administer (drugs, poison, etc.).
inn'/gifta *A* - (=**+/giftet, */gift**) intermarried; **i- i** married into (a family).
inn'/gifte *-t* intermarriage; *anthro.* endogamy.
+inn'/gikk *pt of* **-gå**
***inn'/givnad** *-en* impulse, inspiration.
inn'/gjerding [/jæring] *-a/+-en* fencing (in); enclosure, fence.
+inn'/gjøt *pt of* **-gyte**
+inn'/grave're *V -te* engrave, incise.
inn'/grep *-et* 1 interference (**i** in, with), intervention; encroachment, infringement (**i** on). 2 *med.* (surgical) incision, intervention, operation.
+inn'/gripende *A* - far-reaching, vital: **i- forandringer** radical changes.
inn'/grodd *A -/*-grott* 1 deep-rooted, ingrained; confirmed, inveterate. 2 *med.* ingrown (e.g. toenail).
+inn'/gyte *V -gjøt, -gytt* infuse, inspire, instill: **i- redsel** strike terror.
+inn'/gå *V -gikk, -gått* 1 contract, enter into (e.g. an agreement): **i- ekteskap med** marry; **i- et forlik med** come to terms with; **i- et veddemål** make a bet. 2: **i- i** be included in, form a part of.
inn'/gående *A* - 1 incoming; *naut.* inward bound: **for i- entering; i-vindu** window opening inwards. 2 detailed, exhaustive, thorough.
***inn'/hald** *-et* cf **/hold**
***inn'halds/laus** *A* cf **innholds/løs**
***inn'halds/liste** *-a* cf **innholds/**
***inn'halds/rik** *A* cf **innholds/**
inn'/hegning [+/heining] *-a/+-en* fencing (in); enclosure, fence.
+inn'/hente *V -a/-et* 1 obtain, secure: **i- opplysninger om** make inquiries about, obtain information about;

i- tillatelse obtain permission. **2** catch up with, overtake: **i- det forsømte** make up for lost time.

Inn'/herad *Pln* districts around inner Trondheim Fjord.

inn'/hogg *-et*: **gjøre i-** make inroads (**i** on); *mil.* charge.

inn'/hol *A* (=+/**hul**) concave; hollow.

+inn'/hold *-et* **1** contents; content; capacity (**av** of). **2** content, subject matter: **uten i-** empty.

+inn'holds/fortegnelse [/fårtei·nelse] *-n* table of contents.

+inn'holds/liste *-a/-en* table of contents.

+inn'holds/løs *A* empty, inane, without content.

+inn'holds/rik *A* **1** substantial, weighty. **2** eventful: **et i-t liv** a full life.

+inn'/hugg *-et* cf **/hogg**

+inn'/hul *A* cf **/hol**

+inn'/hylle *V -et/-te* envelop, shroud, wrap (**i** in).

***inn'/hyses** *Av* inside (the house).

+inn'/høsting *-a/-en* harvesting, reaping (**av** of); *fig.* acquiring, gathering (experience).

in'ni *P* **1** inside, within. **2** *(adv.)* on the inside, within.

inn'/iblan't *P* **1** among; between. **2** *(adv.)* occasionally, once in a while.

inn'/imel·lom *P* **1** in between. **2** *(adv.)* occasionally, once in a while; now and then.

+inn'/jage *V -et/-de*: **i- skrekk** strike terror (into sby).

+inn'/kalle *V -kalte* **1** call in (a person; a book); summon. **2** call, convene: **i- til møte** call, convene a meeting; **i- til militærtjeneste** *mil.* call to arms, mobilize; call up, draft, induct.

inn'/kalling *-a/+-en* (=+**-else**) summoning; *mil.* mobilization; drafting, induction.

inn'/kapsle *V -et med.* encapsulate, encyst; *tech.* enclose: **i-et i sine meninger** *fig.* rigid in his opinions.

inn'/kasse·re *V -te* **1** accept, receive (applause, praise). **2** *merc.* collect, recover (through legal action).

inn'/kast *-et* **1** firebox door (feed door). **2** (in soccer) throw-in. **3** contribution, remark (in a discussion).

inn'/kjøp *-et* purchase (**av** of): **gjøre i-** go shopping.

+inn'/kjøpe *V -te* buy, purchase (esp. in quantity lots).

inn'kjøps/pris *-en* cost price; purchase price.

+inn'/kjøre *V -te* **1** (of RR) bring in (money), earn, make (by operation). **2** make up time (by driving). **3: i-ende** incoming. **4: i-ing** entering. (cf **/kjørt**).

inn'/kjørsel *-elen, pl -ler* **1** approach, entrance (**til** to). **2** entering: **i- forbudt** do not enter.

inn'/kjø·rt *A* - (=***/køyrd**) **1** broken (to harness); broken in (automobile, horse, road). **2** brought in, stored (of hay).

inn'/klare·re *V -te* clear (goods, merchandise) through customs.

inn'/kokt [/kokt] *A* - boiled down.

inn'/kommande·re *V -te mil.* order out for drill.

***inn'/kom(m)e** *-a* cf **/komst**

inn'/kommende *A* - **1** incoming: **i- skip** arrivals. **2: i- beløp** proceeds (of the sale).

inn'/komst *-en merc.* income, revenue.

+inn'/kreve *V -de merc.* call in, demand payment of; collect, recover.

inn'/kreving *-a/+-en* calling in; collection, recovery (**av** of).

inn'/kvarte·re *V -te* lodge; *mil.* billet, quarter.

+inn'/la *pt of* **-legge**

+inn'/lagt *A* - (=***/lagd**) **1** enclosed (**i** in). **2** inlaid (**med** with). **3: i- på hospital** hospitalized.

inn'/land *-et* **1** home country: **fra i- og utland** from at home and abroad. **2: i-et** the inland, the interior.

inn'lands/is *-en* icecap, inland ice.

inn'lands/klima *-et, pl +-er/*-* (usu. dry) inland climate (opp. of coastal climate).

+inn'/late *V -lot, -latt* **1: i- seg i, på** attempt, embark upon; let oneself in for; **i- seg i samtale med** enter into a conversation with. **2: i- seg med** get mixed up with, have dealings, sth to do with. **3** *jur.* submit (a case to judgment).

+inn'/latende *A* - communicative, friendly, inviting.

***inn'/laup** *-et* cf **/løp**

+inn'/lede *V -et* cf **/leie**

+inn'/ledende *A* - introductory, opening, preliminary.

+inn'/leder *-en, pl -e* chairman.

+inn'/ledning *-en* cf **/leiing**

inn'/legg *-et* **1** installation (of electricity, gas). **2** enclosure; insert. **3** act (in a revue). **4** contribution, plea, speech: **et i- i diskusjonen** a contribution to the discussion; **komme med i-** speak up. **5** *jur.* deposition, statement. **6** *hist.* pauper.

+inn'/legge *V -la, -lagt* **1** admit (to the hospital). **2** install (gas, electricity). **3: i- seg store fortjenester** perform meritorious services, merit gratitude for one's achievements.

+inn'leggs/såle *-n* (=***/sole**) arch support; insole.

***inn'/leiar** *-en* cf **/leder**

inn'/leie *V +-de/*-dde* (=+**/lede**) begin, open (discussion, meeting); introduce: **i- bekjentskap med** strike up an acquaintance with; **i- forhandlinger** enter into negotiations.

inn'/leiing *-a* (=+**/ledning**) **1** beginning, opening. **2** introduction; preface (**til** of). **3** introductory text, work.

inn'/lemme *V -a/+-et* (=***/leme**) annex, incorporate (**i** in), make a part (**i** of): **i- en i familien** make sby a member of the family.

inn'/lemming *-a/+-en* (=+**-else**) incorporation (**av** of).

***inn'/lengst** *A* - inmost, innermost.

+inn'/levelse *-n* cf **/leving**

inn'/leve·re *V -te* hand in, send in; put in (an application); deposit, leave, mail, deliver.

inn'leverings/tid *-a/+-en* (of telegram) time received; (of letter) time posted.

inn'/leving *-a/+-en* (=+**/levelse**) insight (**i** into), intimate understanding.

inn'/losje·re *V -te* lodge, put up, quarter: **i- seg hos** room, take rooms with.

+inn'/lot *pt of* **-late**

inn'/lyd *-en*: **i i-** *gram.* medially.

inn'/lysende *A* - evident, obvious.

+inn'/løp *-et* entrance, inlet (**i** in).

+inn'/løpe *V -løp, -løp(e)t* **1** arrive (letter, report). **2** happen, occur: **det er i-et feil** errors have crept in.

+inn'/løse *V -te* (=***/løyse**) **1** *merc.* redeem. **2** *merc.* cash: **i- pengesedler med gull** convert banknotes into gold.

+inn'/lø·sning *-en* (=***/løysing**) redemption (payment); conversion (**av** of).

inn'/lån *-et merc.* deposit (in bank).

inn'/mari *A* - **1** cunning, sly. **2** thoroughgoing: **en i- kjeltring** a real scoundrel; *(adv.)* thoroughly: **i- ful** sly through and through.

inn'/marisk *A* - cf **/mari**

inn'/mark *-a* fenced, cultivated plot of land near the farmhouse (opp. of **ut/**).

inn'/mat *-en* **1** (edible) entrails, insides; chitterlings, giblets, stuffing. **2** *hum.* insides (of a person); stuffing (of furniture); matter (between covers of a book).

inn'/med *P* alongside, close to, next to.

+inn'/melde *V -te* register (**på** in) (e.g. a school).

inn'/melding *-a/+-en* (=+**/meldelse**) registration.

inn'/om· *P* **1** inside, in; at (esp. of a short visit): **jeg var nettopp i- biblioteket** I just dropped in at the library. **2** inside, within: **i- mitt distrikt** within my district. **3** *(adv.)* in; inside: **stikke i-** drop by, drop in.

+inn'/ordne *-et* **1** arrange, classify. **2: i- seg under** conform, submit to.

inn'/over [/å·ver] *P* **1** across, along; in toward; to the interior of. **2** *(adv.)* inwards, to the inner part, the interior; towards the center.

inn'/pakka *A* - (=+**/pakket**) packed, wrapped (up); bundled up.

+inn'/pakning *-en* (=***/pakking**) packing, wrapping.

+inn'paknings/papi·r *-et* (=***innpakkings/**) wrapping paper.

inn'/pass *-et* entry: **få, skaffe seg i-** gain a foothold, gain entry.

+inn'/passe *V -et* fit, work in (**i** into, with).

+inn'/piske *V -et* **1** beat, drum (sth) into (sby). **2** *pol.* whip (=hold together for united action).

+inn'/pode *V -et* **1** indoctrinate. **2** *bot.* graft. **3** *med.* inoculate.

inn'/prente *V -a/+-et* bring home to, impress upon.

inn'/på *P* **1** close to, close up to: **klokka var nær i- åtte** it was very close to eight o'clock; **i- to hundre gjester** nearly 200 guests. **2** *(adv.)* close, near; close to the farm: **like i-** right next to (one); **det var nær i-** that was a close call. (With verbs: see these).

***inn'på/komen** [/kåmen] *A -e/-i, pl -ne* **1** almost out of. **2** imminent.

***inn'på/leiking** *-a* hint, suggestion.

inn'på/sliten *A +-ent, pl -ne* **1** aggressive, pushing, self-assertive. **2** enfeebled, weakened; worn down; hard up.

+inn'/ramme *V -a/-et* frame; surround.

+inn'/rede *V -et/-te* cf **/reie**[2]

+inn'/re·dning *-en* cf **/reiing**

inn'/registre·re *V -te* register (e.g. an automobile).

***inn'/reie**[1] *-n* **1** arrangement, layout. **2** provision, supply.

inn'/reie[2] *V +-de/*-dde* (=+**/rede**) decorate, furnish (e.g. a house, a room); build, lay out (e.g. an office, a store).

inn'/reiing *-a* (=+**/redning**) furnishings; building, laying out (**av** of): **med ny i-** newly furnished.

inn'/reise *-a/+-en* entry: **i- i Norge** e- into Norway.

+inn'reise/tilla·telse *-n* entry permit, visa.

inn'/retning *+-en/*-a* **1** arrangement, layout, organization. **2** adaptation, conversion (**av** of). **3** appliance, contrivance, device; *(pop.)* doodad, thingumajig.

inn'/rette *V -a/+-et* **1** equip, fit out, furnish. **2** arrange, install, organize. **3: i- seg** adjust; get organized, make oneself comfortable; **i- seg etter** adapt oneself to; **i- seg på å** be prepared to. **4: i-et** constituted; **de er slik i-et disse ungene mine** these youngsters of mine are made like that (Undset).

***inn'/rikes** *A* - within the country.

inn'/rim *-et* assonance, "internal" rhyme (as in skaldic poetry).

+inn'/risse *V -a/-et* carve, engrave.

inn'/rulle·re *V -te mil.* enlist (**i** in).

inn'/rykk *-et* influx, invasion (**av** of, **i** into).

+inn'/rykke *V -et* **1** insert, run (e.g. an advertisement in a newspaper). **2** *typog.* indent. **3: i-ende tropper** entering troops, troops moving in.

+ Bokmål; * Nynorsk; ° Dialect.
After letter: ' stress (Acc. 1); ' tone, stress (Acc. 2); · length.
Below letter: . not pronounced.

+**inn'/rømme** *V* *-et/-rømte* 1 allow, give, grant (e.g. credit, reduction). 2 admit, concede, grant. 3: **i-ende konjunksjon** *gram.* concessive conjunction (e.g. **skjønt** though).

+**inn'/rømmelse** *-n* 1 allowance (e.g. of a rebate). 2 admission, concession: **gjøre en i-** make a c-.

inn'/samling *-a/+-en* collection (**til** for).

inn'/sats *-en* 1 stake (in gambling). 2 contribution, effort: **gjøre en stor i- for** make a great effort for, contribution to.

+**inn'/satt** *en* (=*/**sett**) inmate (of a prison), prisoner.

+**inn'/satte** *pt of* **-sette**

+**inn'/se** *V* *-så, -sett* realize, see, understand.

inn'/segl [+/seil] *-et* *hist.* seal, signet; *fig.* stamp.

+**inn'/seiling** *-en* 1 (seaward) approach (**til** to). 2 earning by sailing.

+**inn'/sende** *V* *-te* contribute, submit (**til** to).

+**inn'/sender** *-en, pl -e* (=***-ar**) contributor (to a newspaper).

inn'/sendt *et* (unsolicited) contribution (to a newspaper).

+**inn'/sette** *V* *-satte, -satt* 1 fit, put in; insert: **innsatt med stener** set with (precious) stones. 2 establish, install; institute; *eccl.* ordain (as a priest): **i- i embete** install in office; **i- en til sin arving** *jur.* make sby one's heir. 3 arrest, take into custody. 4 put up (for sale). 5 deposit (in bank). 6 creosote; faceharden (e.g. skis).

inn'/side *-a/+-en* inside (**av** of): **på i-n** on the i-.

inn'/sig *-et* 1 oozing, seeping in. 2 drifting, (gradual) approach, infiltration: **sildens i-** the coming of the herring. 3 dent, hollow.

+**inn'/sigelse** [also -si'-] *-n* 1 objection, protest: **gjøre i- mot** challenge, protest against. 2: **nedlegge i- mot** enter a demurrer.

inn'/sikt *+-en/*-a* insight (**i** into), understanding (**i** of).

inn'sikts/full *A* insightful, showing insight.

+**inn'/sirkle** *V* *-et* encircle, ring.

inn'/sjø *-en* lake.

inn'/skipe *V* *-a/+-et* 1 put on board, ship. 2: **i- seg** embark, go on board.

inn'/skjerpe *V* *+-a/+-et/-te* enjoin, impress on.

+**inn'/skjøt** *pt of* **-skyte**

inn'/skott *-et* (=*/**skot**, +/**skudd**) 1 insertion, interpolation (e.g. in text); epenthesis (of sound in a word); parenthesis. 2 *merc.* contribution; premium; share (in cooperative apartment house); deposit (in bank); stake (in gambling).

+**inn'/skrenke** *V* *-a/-et* curtail, reduce; limit: **i- seg til** confine, restrict oneself to; be limited to.

+**inn'/skrenket** *A* - 1 limited, restricted: **i- skjenkerett** restricted liquor license (i.e., one permitting the sale of beer and wine only). 2 dense, slow-witted; narrow-minded.

inn'/skrenking *-a/+-en* (=+**-ning**) curtailment, reduction.

+**inn'/skriden** *en* interference, intervention.

inn'/skrift *-a/+-en* inscription; legend.

+**inn'/skrive** *V* *infl as* **skrive** 1 *math.* inscribe. 2: **innskrevet** inscribed; registered (baggage).

inn'/skriving *-a/+-en* (=**-ning**) 1 enrollment, registration. 2 *mil.* enlistment.

+**inn'/skrumpet** [/skrompet] *A* - (=**-a**) shriveled, shrunken.

+**inn'/skudd** *-et* cf **/skott**

+**inn'/skutt** *pp of* **-skyte**

+**inn'/skydelse** [also -sjy'-] *-n* cf **/skytelse**

+**inn'/skyte** *V* *-skjøt, -skutt* 1 insert, interpolate: **i- en bemerkning** interpose a remark. 2 *merc.* deposit; invest (in a business). 3 *mil.* get the range of a target, straddle a target. 4 *tech.* testfire (a gun).

+**inn'/skytelse** [also -sjy'-] *-n* impulse; inspiration.

+**inn'/skyter** *-en, pl -e* (=***-ar**) *merc.* depositor; investor.

inn'/slag *-et* 1 element, leaven, strain: **det mongolske i- i den russiske befolkning** the Mongol s- in the Russian population. 2 weft, woof. 3 flap (of a book).

inn'/smett *-et* shelter.

+**inn'/smigre** *V* *-et* 1: **i- seg** curry favor, ingratiate oneself (**hos** with). 2: **i-ende** ingratiating; charming, winning; coaxing(ly).

+**inn'/snevre** *V* *-et* contract, narrow down.

+**inn'/snike** *V* *-snek, -sneket*: **i- seg** creep, slip in (e.g. an error).

inn'/snitt *-et* cut, incision, notch; dart (in a garment).

***inn'/sokken** *A* *-e/-i, pl -sokne* cf **/sunken**

+**inn'/spare** *-te* *lit.* save.

+**inn'/spilling** *-en* (=*/**speling**) 1 bringing in (money) by playing (of a theater). 2 production; rehearsal (of a film or play). 3 *mus.* recording.

+**inn'/sprøytning** *-en* (=*/**sprøyting**) injection, *(pop.)* shot (**av** of).

+**inn'/spunnet** *A* -, *pl -ne* enmeshed, entangled.

inn'/spurt *-en* finish, last lap (of a race; also *fig.*).

***inn'/steg** *-et* entrance, visit.

innsten'dig *A* - earnest; pressing, urgent: **råde en i- til** earnestly advise sby to, urge sby to.

+**inn'/stevne** *V* *-a/+-et/-te* *jur.* summon: **i-ede** (the) defendant.

+**inn'/stifte** *V* *-et* establish, found, institute.

+**inn'/stiftelse** *-n* establishment, founding (**av** of).

inn'stignings/tjuv [/kjuv] *-en* (=+/**tyv**) cat burglar, second-story man.

+**inn'still/bar** *A* adjustable.

inn'/stille *V* *-stilte* 1 adjust, focus; tune (a radio). 2 adapt, prepare (oneself): **i- seg på** make up one's mind to, prepare to; **i-t** disposed, inclined (**på å** to), minded; **sosialt i-t** socially minded, oriented; **sympatisk i-t** sympathetically disposed. 3 nominate, propose, recommend: **i- til forfremmelse** recommend for promotion. 4 cease, discontinue, suspend (e.g. operations, work); cancel (a performance); *merc.* fail, go into bankruptcy; stop payment (on a check).

inn'/stilling *-a/+-en* 1 adjustment, focus, tuning, (etc.). 2 attitude, outlook. 3 nomination, proposal, recommendation: **få i-** *educ.* get summa cum laude at final university examination. 4 cancellation (of a performance).

inn'/stude're *V* *-te* memorize, study (a role); rehearse.

+**inn'/sunken** [/songken] *A* *-ent, pl -ne* hollow, sunken.

+**inn'/svinget** *A* - (=+/**svunget**) 1 pivoted, swung. 2 concave.

inn'/syn *-et/*-a* view (into).

inn'/søkk *-et* depression, hollow.

+**inn'/så** *pt of* **-se**

+**inn'/ta** *V* *-tok, -tatt* 1 consume, partake of, take: **i- et måltid** eat. 2 capture, storm (a fortress, town). 3 occupy, take (one's place): **i- plassene** on your marks. 4 *fig.* assume, strike, take (an attitude, a position): **i- en avvisende holdning** adopt an unsympathetic attitude; **i- en fast holdning** take a strong stand; **i- et nytt standpunkt** adopt a different position, change one's opinion (see **inntagende, inntatt**).

+**inn'/tagende** *A* - captivating, charming, engaging.

inn'/tak *-et* intake.

+**inn'/takelse** *-n* 1 ingestion (**av** of). 2 capture (**av** of).

+**inn'/tale** *V* *-te* record (speak).

+**inn'/tatt** *A* -: **i- i** charmed by, in love with, *(pop.)* stuck on.

***inn'/teken** *A* *-e/-i, pl -ne* cf **/tatt**

inn'/tekt *-a/+-en* 1 income; profit, receipts, revenue: **ha en i- på** have an income of; **til i- for** for the benefit of. 2: **ta noe til i-** cite sth in support (**for** of), turn sth to (one's) account.

inn'/til' *P* 1 as far as, to; against: **krype i- en** crawl close to sby; **lenet i- veggen** leaning against the wall. 2 until, up to: **i- nå** so far, thus far; **i- videre** until further notice; **i- året 1200** down to the year 1200. 3 not exceeding, up to: **en mulkt av i-** a fine not exceeding. 4 *(adv.)* over to, up to: **sette seg i- bordet** sit up to the table. 5 *(conj.)* until.

inn'/tilbei'ns *A* - pigeon-toed.

inn'/tog [/tåg] *-et* entry: **gjøre, holde sitt i-** make one's e-.

+**inn'/tok** *pt of* **-ta**

+**inn'/traff** *pt of* **-treffe**

+**inn'/tre** *V* *-trådte* commence, set in; happen, occur, take effect: **det har i-trådt en krise** a crisis has arisen.

+**inn'/tredelse** *-n* entrance, entry (**i** into).

+**inn'/treffe** *V* *-traff, -truffet* happen, occur: **det i-traff en ulykke** there was an accident.

+**inn'/trengen** *en* encroachment, intrusion; *mil.* penetration (of a projectile).

+**inn'/trengende** *A* - (=*/**trengjande**) 1 penetrating (e.g. glance). 2 painstaking, thorough (examination). 3 earnest, heartfelt, urgent.

+**inn'/truffet** [/troffet] *pp of* **-treffe**

inn'/trykk *-et* impression (**av** of): **gi i- av å være** give (one) the i- of being, strike (one) as being; **gjøre et fordelaktig i-** create a favorable i-; **ha i- av at** have the i- that.

inn'/trønder *-en, pl +-e/*-ar* person from the north part of Trøndelag (known as **Inn-Trøndelag**).

inn'/tun *-et* *hist.* inner courtyard (around dwelling house of farm).

inn'/tørka *A* - (=+**-et**) dried up, shriveled; dry-as-dust.

inn'/under *P* 1 below, under: **i- jul** just before Christmas. 2 *(adv.)* underneath.

+**inn'/valgte** *pt of* **-velge**

+**inn'/vandre** *V* *-a/-et* immigrate (**i** into).

+**inn'/vandrer** *-en, pl -e* (=***-ar**) immigrant.

inn'/vandring *-a/+-en* immigration.

+**inn'/vant** *pt of* **-vinne**

+**inn'/varsle** *V* *-et* foreshadow, herald, prefigure.

inn'/ved *P* 1 against, close by, to. 2 *(adv.)* close, next to: **sette seg i-** sit up to the table.

+**inn'/velge** *V* *-valgte, -valgt* elect (**i** to).

inn'/vende *V* *-te* object, take exception (**mot** to): **ha å i- mot** object to.

***inn'/vendes** *A* - cf **/vendig**

inn'/vendig *A* - inside, interior; internal, inward: **ha vondt i-** hurt inside; **le i-** laugh inside, inwardly.

inn'/vending *-a/+-en* objection: **gjøre i-er mot** object, take exception to.

***inn'/verke** *V* *-a* cf **/virke**

***inn'/verknad** *-en* cf **/virkning**

***inn'/vertes** *A* - cf **/vortes**

inn'/vie *V* *+-et/-vigde* 1 consecrate, dedicate. 2 *eccl.* ordain (a minister). 3 take into one's confidence; initiate: **i- en i en hemmelighet** let sby in on a secret; **være i-et** *(pop.)* be in the know.

+**inn'/vielse** *-n* (=*/**viing**) 1 consecration. 2 *eccl.* ordination (of a minister). 3 initiation.

Inn'/vik *Pln* twp, Sogn og Fjordane.

+**inn'/vikle** *V* *-et* entangle, implicate, involve: **i- seg i selvmotsigelser** contradict oneself; **i-es i en prosess** get involved in a lawsuit.

+**inn'/viklet** *A* - (=**-a**) complex, complicated, intricate.

+inn'/vilge *V -et*: **i- i** acquiesce in, consent to.

+inn'/vinne *V -vant, -vunnet* 1 acquire, gain (experience, knowledge). 2 recover, retrieve: **i- det tapte** make up one's losses; **i- plass** save space.

+inn'/virke *V -et*: **i- på** affect, act on, influence.

+inn'/virkning *-a/-en* effect, influence (**på** on).

+inn'/voller *pl* (=***/voler**) bowels, entrails, intestines; guts, viscera.

+inn'volls/orm *-en* (=***innvols/**) *zool.* tapeworm (class Cestoda).

inn'/vortes *A* - 1 internal, inward: **det i- menneske** the inner man; **til i- bruk** for internal use. 2 *(adv.)* internally, on the inside.

+inn'/vunnet *pp of* **-vinne**

+inn'/våner *-en, pl -e lit.* inhabitant.

+inn'/ynde *V -et*: **i- seg hos en** curry favor, ingratiate oneself with sby.

+inn'/øve *V -de* drill, train; practice, rehearse (lesson, role).

+inn'/ånde *V -et* breathe in, inhale.

***inn`/åt** *P* close, up to: **sette seg i-** sit up to the table.

in sal'vo 1 safe and sound. 2 free from responsibility.

in`sekt *-et, pl -/+-er* insect.

in`sekt/drepende *A* - insecticidal.

inseminasjo'n *-en* insemination.

insemina'tor *-en* inseminator (esp. of cattle).

insemine're *V -te* inseminate.

insera't *-et, pl -/+-er* (contributed) article, notice (in newspaper).

insig'ne *-t, pl +-ier/*-* (**=insignium**) insignia.

insig'nium *-iet, pl +-ia/+-ier/*-* cf **insigne**

insinuasjo'n *-en* innuendo, insinuation.

insinue're *V -te* 1 insinuate. 2: **i- seg hos en** ingratiate oneself with sby.

insiste're *V -te* insist (**på** on, upon).

inskripsjo'n *-en* inscription.

insolven's *-en* insolvency.

insolven't *A* - insolvent.

insp. =**inspektør**

in spe' future, to be.

inspeksjo'n *-en* 1 inspection, survey. 2 inspectors.

inspektri'se *-a/+-en* (woman) inspector, supervisor.

inspektø'r *-en* 1 inspector, manager, supervisor. 2 *educ.* superintendent of schools.

inspirasjo'n *-en* inspiration.

inspirasjo'ns/kjelde *-a* (=**+/kilde**) source of inspiration.

inspire're *V -te* inspire.

inspise're *V -te* examine, inspect.

in'st *A* - (=**+innerst[2]**) 1 inmost; innermost: **i mitt i-e hjerte** deep down, in my heart of hearts. 2 *(adv.)* at the farthest end, farthest in: **i-inne** at the farthest end of; in one's inmost.

inst. =**institutt**

installasjo'n *-en* 1 installation. 2: **elektriske i-er** *elec.* electric wiring.

installatø'r *-en* electrician.

installe're *V -te* 1 install. 2 *elec.* wire (e.g. a house).

instan's *-en* authority; *jur.* court, legal authority: **føre saken gjennom alle i-er** carry the case through all the courts; **i siste (øverste) i-** in the court of last resort; *fig.* in the final analysis.

***in'ste** *eit* cf **innerste**

instin'kt *-et, pl -/+-er* instinct.

in'stinktiv *A* instinctive.

+instin'kt/messig *A* - instinctive.

institue're *V -te* establish, institute.

institusjo'n *-en* institution.

institutt' *-et, pl -/+-er* institute, institution.

instrue're *V -te* direct (film, play; music).

instruk's *-en* directive, regulation.

instruksjo'n *-en* direction (of a film, play).

in'struktiv *A* instructive.

instruktø'r *-en* 1 coach. 2 director (of a theater).

instrumen't *-et, pl -/+-er* instrument.

instrumenta'l *A* instrumental.

instrumenta'l/musikk· *-en* instrumental music.

instrumentasjo'n *-en mus.* instrumentation, orchestration.

instrumente're *V -te mus.* orchestrate.

+instrumen't/maker *-en, pl -e* (=***-ar**) instrument maker.

instrumen't/tavle *-a/+-en* instrument panel, switchboard.

insubordinasjo'n *-en mil.* insubordination.

insuli'n *-et med.* insulin.

intak't *A* - intact.

°in'te *Av* cf **ikke**

integra'l *-et math.* integral.

integra'l/rekning *-a* (=**+/regning**) *math.* integral calculus.

integrasjo'n *-en math.* integration.

integre're *V -te math.* integrate.

integre'rende *A* - integral.

integrite't *-en* integrity.

intellek't *-et* intellect.

intellektualis'me *-n* intellectualism.

intellektuell' *A -elt* intellectual: **de i-e** the i-s; the intelligentsia; *(pop.)* eggheads, highbrows.

intelligen's *-en* 1 intelligence. 2 intellectuals; intelligentsia.

intelligen's/alder *-eren, pl -rer* mental age.

intelligen's/kvotient [/kvo(t)sien·t] *-en* intelligence quotient (IQ).

intelligen's/måling *-a/+-en* (=***/mæling**) intelligence testing.

intelligen's/prøve *-a/+-en* intelligence test.

intelligen't *A* - intelligent.

intelligen'tsia *-en* intelligentsia.

intendan't *-en* 1 steward. 2 *mil.* quartermaster: **generali-** q- general.

intendantu'r *-en mil.* quartermaster corps.

inten's *A* intense.

intensite't *-en* intensity.

in'tensiv *A* intensive: **i-t jordbruk** i- farming.

intensive're *V -te* intensify.

intensjo'n *-en* intent, intention.

interdik't *-et eccl.* interdict: **belegge et land med i-** lay a country under an i-.

interessant [-ang'] *A* - interesting, of interest: **gjøre seg i-** show off.

interes'se *+-n/*-a* interest (**for** for); (financial) interest (**i** in): **nyhetens i-** the charm of novelty; **se sin i- i noe** find sth to one's advantage; **åndelige i-r** intellectual i-s.

interes'se/konto'r *-et, pl -/+-er merc.* personnel welfare office (to help employees with financial problems).

interes'se/laus *A* (=**+/løs**) uninteresting (subject); indifferent, uninterested (person).

interessen't *-en merc.* partner, stockholder.

interessen't/skap *-et merc.* partnership.

interesse're *V -te* interest: **i- seg for** be interested in, take an interest in.

interesse'rt *A* - 1 interested (person). 2: **i- i** concerned with, interested in. 3 *merc.* involved (in) (to the tune of large amounts): **den i-e kapital** the invested capital.

interferen's *-en phys.* interference.

interfere're *V -te phys.* interfere.

interfolie're *V -te* interleave.

in'terim *-et* interim.

+in'terims/bevi·s *-et* (=***/prov**) *merc.* scrip (certificate).

in'terims/styre *-t* caretaker, provisional government.

interiø'r *-et, pl -/+-er* interior (of a house; a painting).

interiø'r/arkitek·t *-en* interior architect, designer.

interjeksjo'n *-en gram.* interjection.

in'ter/kommuna·l *A* intercommunity; (of schools) consolidated.

in'ter/kontinenta·l *A* intercontinental.

intermes'so *-et, pl -/+-er* intermezzo.

inter'n [also -tæ'rn] *A* internal: **i-medisin** i- medicine; **en i- sak** a domestic affair.

in'ter/nasjona·l *A* international.

in'ter/nasjona·le *-n* International (organization) (song).

interna't *-et, pl -/+-er* boarding school.

interna't/skole *-n* (=***/skule**) boarding school.

interne're *V -te* intern: **i-ing** i-ment.

in'ter/parlamenta·risk *A* - interparliamentary.

interpellan't *-en pol.* parliamentary questioner (of government policy).

interpellasjo'n *-en pol.* parliamentary question (concerning government policy).

interpelle're *V -te pol.* put a question (to the government).

in'ter/planeta·risk *A* - interplanetary.

interpolasjo'n *-en* interpolation.

interpole're *V -te* interpolate.

interpretasjo'n *-en* interpretation.

interprete're *V -te* interpret.

interpunksjo'n *-en gram.* punctuation.

interpunkte're *V -te gram.* punctuate.

interreg'num *+-et/*-umet, pl +-er/*-um* interregnum.

intervall' *-et, pl -/+-er* 1 interval. 2 *mus.* (harmonic, melodic) interval.

intervene're *V -te* 1 intervene (in a nation's affairs). 2 *merc.* pay (commercial paper) for honor.

intervensjo'n *-en* 1 intervention. 2 *merc.* payment (of commercial paper) for honor.

intervju' *-et, pl -/+-er* interview (**med** with).

intervju'e *V -a/+-et* interview.

intervju'/objek·t *-et, pl -/+-er* interviewee (subject of an interview).

+in`tet[1] *et* nothing, nothingness: **den forferdelige tvil foran det store i-** the fearful doubt before the great nothingness (Kinck).

+in`tet[2] *nt of* **ingen**

+in`tet/anende *A* - innocent, unsuspecting.

+in`tet/kjønn *-et gram.* neuter gender.

+in`tet/sigende *A* - insignificant, meaningless: **tomme og i- mennesker** inane and commonplace persons (Egge).

+in`tet/steds *Av* nowhere.

inti'm *A* intimate: **i i- berøring med** in close contact with; **i-t teater** intimate theater (Strindberg).

intimide're *V -te* intimidate.

intimite't *-en* intimacy.

in'/toleranse [/tålerang·se] *-n* intolerance.

in'/toleran·t *A* intolerant.

intonasjo'n *-en gram., mus.* intonation.

intone're *V -te* 1 *gram.* intonate. 2 *mus.* intone.

intr. =**intransitiv**

in'/transitiv *A gram.* intransitive.

intrigan't[1] *-en* intriguer, schemer.

intrigan't[2] *A* - intriguing, scheming.

intri'ge *-n* 1 intrigue. 2 plot (of a story).

+intri'ge/maker *-en, pl -e* (=***-ar**) intriguer, schemer.

intrige're *V -te* intrigue, scheme: **i- seg til noe** gain sth by pulling wires, scheming.

intrika't *A* - complicated, intricate; difficult, ticklish.

introduksjo'n *-en* introduction; letter of introduction.

introduse're *V -te* introduce.

introspekti'v [also in'-] *A* introspective.

intuisjo'n *-en* intuition.

intu'itiv *A* intuitive.

invade're *V -te* invade.

+ Bokmål; * Nynorsk; ° Dialect.
After letter: ' stress (Acc. 1); ` tone, stress (Acc. 2); · length.
Below letter: . not pronounced.

invali'd[1] *-en* invalid.
invali'd[2] *A* - invalid: **bli helt i-** be totally disabled.
invali'de/pensjon [/pangsjo'n] *-en* disability pension.
invalidite't *-en* disablement, invalidism.
invasjo'n *-en* invasion (**av** of).
inventa'r *-et* equipment, fixtures: **et i-** *hum.* a fixture, piece of furniture.
inversjo'n *-en chem., gram., meteor.* inversion.
inverte're *V -te chem., gram.* invert.
investe're *V -te merc.* invest (**i** in).
investe'ring *-a/+-en merc.* investment (**av** of; **i** in).
invitasjo'n *-en* invitation (**til** to).
invite're *V -te* 1 ask, invite: **i- henne ut** offer to take her out; **i- på kaffe** invite for coffee. 2 lead: **i- på (fra) kongen** l- from the king (cards).
invitt' *-en* invitation; lead (cards).
involve're *V -te* involve.
ion [jo'n] *-en/-et phys.* ion.
ionisere [jonise're] *V -te phys.* ionize.
+**ior'den** *Av* cf **orden**
+**iover/morgen** [i-å'ver/måren] *Av* cf **over/morgen**
***i'r** *-en* anxiety, eagerness.
Ira'k *Pln* Iraq.
ira'ksk *A* - Iraqi.
Ira'n *Pln* Iran.
ira'nsk *A* - Iranian, Persian.
i're[1] *-n* (=+**irer**) Irishman.
***i're**[2] *V -a* regret: **i- på** be dissatisfied with; **i-ast, i- seg** be anxious.
+**i'rer** *-en, pl -e* cf **ire**[1]
+**iret'te** *Av* cf **rette**[2]
+**iret'te/sette** *V -satte* rebuke, reprimand, reprove.
+**iret'te/settelse** *-n* 1 reprimand, reproof. 2: **streng i-** *mil.* formal reprimand (before the assembled company).
i'ris *-en* 1 *anat.* iris. 2 *bot.* iris (family Iridaceae).
irise're *V -te* be iridescent: **i-t glass** i- glass.
I'r/land [also ir'-] *Pln* Eire, Ireland.
+**i'r/lender** [also ir'-] *-en, pl -e* Irishman.
i'r/lending [also ir'-] *-en* Irishman.
+**iroke'ser** *-en, pl -e* (=***-ar,** ***irokes**) Iroquois.
ironi' *-en* irony: **blodig i-** deadly i-; **skjebnens i-** the i- of fate.
ironise're *V -te* express oneself ironically (**over** about).
iro'nisk *A* - ironic.
+**irr'** *-et* cf **eir**
ir'/rasjona'l *A math.* irrational (number).
ir'/rasjonell' *A -elt* irrational.
+**ir're**[1] *V -a/-et* cf **eire**
+**ir're**[2] *V -a/-et archaic* lose one's way: **i- om** wander aimlessly.
+**ir're**[3] *V -a/et*: **i- opp** anger, stir up.
ir'/reell' *A -elt* unreal.
ir'/regulæ'r *A* irregular: **i-e tropper** *mil.* irregulars.
ir'/relevan's *-en* irrelevancy.
ir'/relevan't *A* - irrelevant.
ir'/religiø's *A* irreligious.
ir'/religiøsite't *-en* irreligion.
+**ir'ret(e)** *A* - cf **eiret(e)**
+**irr'/gang** *-en* labyrinth, maze.
+**irr'/grønn** *A -grønt* cf **eir/grøn**
irrigasjo'n *-en* irrigation.
irrige're *V -te* irrigate.
irrita'bel *A -elt, pl -le* irritable (also *med.*).
irritabilite't *-en* irritability (also *med.*).
irritamen't *-et, pl -/+-er* irritant.
irritasjo'n *-en* irritation (also *med.*).
irrite're *V -te* annoy, irritate (also *med.*): **i- en til de grader** drive sby crazy; **i- seg over** be annoyed, irritated at, by.
irrite'rt *A* - annoyed, irritated (**over** at).
i'rsk [also ir'sk] *A* - Irish.
i's *-en* 1 ice: **bryte i-en** *fig.* break the i-; **fryse til is** freeze; congeal; **hans blod ble til is** his blood ran cold; **i-en gikk opp** the i- broke up; **i-en legger seg** i- forms (on body of water); **legge, sette på i-** *fig.* put on the shelf, shelve (person, project), *(pop.)* put in cold storage; **skyte is** be ice-covered (by condensation); **våge seg ut på tynn is** *fig.* venture out on thin i-, take a big risk. 2 ice, sherbet; ice cream: **is Melba** peach sundae.
+**isam'men** *Av* cf **sammen**
i's/bein *-et anat.* pubis (of a butchered animal).
i's/berg *-et* iceberg.
i's/bjø'rn *-en zool.* polar bear (Thalarctos maritimus).
i's/brann *-en* scorching of grass (from the sun burning through a thin ice cover).
i's/bre *-en* (=***/brede**) glacier.
+**i's/bryter** *-en, pl -e* (=***-ar**) *naut.* icebreaker (ship).
+**isce'ne/settelse** *-n* (=***/setjing**) (theater) producing, staging; (film) direction.
+**isce'ne/setter** *-en, pl -e* (=***/setjar**) (theater) producer; (film) director.
+**ischias** [isj'iass] *-en* cf **isjias**
i'se[1] *-a zool.* porpoise (Phocaena communis).
i'se[2] *V -a/+-et/+-te* 1 cover (be covered) with ice; turn to ice: **det i-er** ice is forming; **skipet var helt i-et ned** the ship was completely icebound. 2 freeze, put in cold storage. 3 get cold chills: **i- i tennene** set one's teeth on edge.
***i'se**[3] *V -a* cf **isne**
i's/eddik *-en chem.* glacial acetic acid.
i'sende *Av*: **i- kald** icy-cold.
+**iseng'** *Av* cf **seng**
+**isen'k** *Av* cf **senk**
i'sen/kram' *en/et* hardware.
i'senkram/handel *-elen, pl -ler* hardware store.
***ise'r** *Av* cf **især**
i'set(e) *A* - ice-covered, icy.
i's/fast *A* - frozen over (lake, river); icebound (ship).
i's/fjell *-et* iceberg.
i's/flak *-et* ice floe.
i's/fri *A -tt* ice-free, open (e.g. a port).
i's/fugl *-en zool.* kingfisher (Alcedo ispida).
i's/gang *-en* debacle, drifting ice: **det var i- i elva** ice was breaking up and drifting down the river.
i's/hav *-et* arctic, polar sea: **Nordi-et** the Arctic Ocean; **Søri-et** the Antarctic Ocean.
I's/havet *Pln* Arctic Ocean.
+**i'shavs/farer** *-en, pl -e* (=***-ar**) one who sails the Arctic (Antarctic).
i'shavs/skute *-a* arctic, polar vessel.
i's/hockey [/håkki] *-en* ice hockey.
i's/hud *-a/+-en naut.* sheathing (protection against ice floes, etc.).
+**isik'te** *Av* cf **sikte**[1]
i'sing[1] *-en zool.* dab (Limanda limanda).
i'sing[2] *-a/+-en* 1 icing; thin sheet of ice. 2 cold shiver: **i- i tennene** setting one's teeth on edge.
+**isin'ne** *Av* cf **sinne**[1]
isj' *I* phooey, ugh (usu. *fem.*, expressing distaste).
isj'e *V -a/+-et* say *isj.*
isj'ias *-en med.* sciatica.
-isk *A* - -ic, -ical: **filosof-** philosophic; **sto-** stoic; **teoret-** theoretical.
i's/kald *A* ice-cold, icy.
i's/koss *-et/+-en* heap, mass of ice floes frozen solid.
i's/krav *-et* beginning of ice formation on the surface of a lake, river; thin sheet of ice.
i's/krem *-en* ice cream: **en i-** an ice-cream cone.
isl. =**islandsk**
i'/slag[1] *-et* 1 weft, woof. 2 *fig.* sprinkling, strain.
i's/lag[2] *-et* sheet of ice; glaze.
+**i's/lagt** *A* - (=***/lagd**) covered with ice, frozen, icy.
is'lam [also: isla'm] *-en* Islam.
islamit'tisk *A* - Islamic.
I's/land *Pln* Iceland.
i's/landsk *A* - Iceland, Icelandic.
i'slands/mose *-n bot.* Iceland moss (Cetraria islandica).
i's/legg *-en hist.* (crude) skate (fashioned from a sheep's fibula).
+**i's/lender** *-en, pl -e* (=***-ar**) Icelandic sweater.
i's/lending *-en* 1 Icelander. 2 Icelandic pony. 3 Icelandic sweater.
i'/slett *-et* 1 weft, woof. 2 *fig.* sprinkling, strain.
+**i's/løs(n)ing** *-a/-en* (=***/løysing**) breaking up (of ice), thawing.
is'me *-n* ism.
+**i'sne** *V -a/-et* (=***ise**[3]) 1 turn to ice. 2 shiver: **det i-et i henne** her blood ran cold (with terror). 3: **i-ende** freezing, icy; *(adv.)* **i-ende kald** ice-cold.
isoba'r *-en* isobar.
isofo'n *-en gram.* isophone.
isogloss' *-en gram.* isogloss.
isolasjo'n *-en* 1 isolation (segregation; loneliness). 2 insulation (**av** of); insulating material.
isola't *-et, pl -/+-er med.* isolation ward.
isola'tor *-en* insulator.
isole're *V -te* 1 isolate; segregate: **et i-t tilfelle** an isolated case, instance; **han i-er seg** he keeps to himself. 2 insulate: **i-t ledning** *elec.* insulated conductor.
isole'ring *-a/+-en* 1 isolation; segregation. 2 insulation.
i'sop *-en bot.* hyssop (Hyssopus officinalis): **i-en som vokser ut på veggen** *bibl.* the h- that springeth out of the wall (I Kings 4, 33).
isoter'm *-en meteor.* isotherm.
isoto'p *+-et/*-en, pl -er/+- chem.* isotope.
i's/pinne *-n* ice-cream bar on stick.
i's/pose *-n* ice bag.
+**i'/sprenge** *V -te*: **i-t** shot through, sprinkled (with); interspersed (with).
I'srael *Pln* Israel.
+**israe'ler** *-en, pl -e* (=***-ar**) Israeli.
israelitt' *-en* Israelite.
israelit'tisk *A* - Israelitic.
israe'lsk *A* - Israeli.
+**i's/ranun'kel** [-ong-] *-elen, pl -ler bot.* glacier crowfoot (Ranunculus glacialis).
i's/rose *-a/+-en* ice crystal, ice flower (on windowpane); ice pattern.
is'se *-n* crown, top of the head: **fra fot til i-** from head to toe; **skallet i-** bald head.
is'se/bein *-et anat.* parietal bone.
+**i's/skap** *-et* (=***/skåp**) icebox, refrigerator.
i's/svull *-en* thick, rough sheet of ice; patch of ice.
is't *V* cf **idast**
-ist *-en* -er, -ist: **bil-** driver; **fiolin-** violinist; **sosial-** socialist.
°**ista'(d)** *Av* cf **stad**[2]
+**istan'd** *Av* cf **stand**[1]
+**istan'd/settelse** *-n* (=***/setjing**) repair, restoration; overhauling; mending, patching (**av** of).
i's/tapp *-en* icicle.
+**iste'den** *Av* (=+**i stedet,** ***i staden**) instead: **hun giftet seg med broren hans i-** she married his brother i-.
+**iste'den/for'** *P* (=+**i stedet for,** ***i staden for**) instead of, in lieu of: **han gikk i- meg** he went instead of me.
+**iste'det/for'** *P* cf **isteden/for**
***i'/steg** *-et* stirrup.
+**i'/stemme** *V -stemte, -stemt* start singing; chime, join in.
is'ter *-eret/-ret anat.* (leaf) fat: **lyrisk i- og retorisk smult** lyrical bombast and rhetorical ostentation (Ibsen).
is'ter/sild *-a* matie (herring).
is'ter/vom' *-ma* pot belly.
i. st. f. =**i** +**stedet/*****staden for**
+**istfr.** =**istedenfor**
i's/tid *-a/+-en geol.* glacial epoch, ice age.
***is'tre** *-a anat.* layer of leaf fat.
***is'tre/boke** [/båke] *-a anat.* layer of leaf fat.

+istyk'ker *Av* cf **stykke**[1]

+istyk'ker/revet *A* -, *pl -ne* torn (to pieces, shreds); scrap (paper).

+istyk'ker/slått *A* - broken, smashed (to pieces).

+istå' *Av* cf **stå**[1]

+isun'd *Av* cf **sund**[2]

i's/vatn *-et* (=+/**vann**) ice water.

+isvi'me *Av* cf **svime**[1]

isæ'r *Av* 1 especially, particularly. 2: **hver i-** each (by himself), separately.

+iså'/fall *Av* cf **fall**[1]

+it.=**item**

***i'/tak** *-et* grasp, grip.

Ita'lia *Pln* Italy.

+italie'ner *-en, pl -e* (=***-ar**) Italian.

+italienerin'ne *-a/-en* (=***-ar-**) Italian girl, woman.

italie'nsk *A* - Italian.

ita'lisk *A* - Italic.

+it'em *Av archaic* likewise; further.

-ite't *-en* -ity: **human-** humaneness, humanity; **immun-** immunity.

+iti'de *Av* cf **tide**

°it'j *Av* cf **ikke**[1]

+it'le *-n* cf **eitel**

+itrekk' *Av* cf **trekk**[3]

°it'te *Av* cf **ikke**

+itu' *Av* cf **tu**[1]

+itu'/slått *A* - broken, smashed.

i. t. v. = **inntil videre**

I'var *Prn (m)*

+iva're *Av* cf **vare**[2]

+iva're/ta *V -tok, -tatt* attend to, look after, take care of.

+iva're/takelse *-n* (=+/**tagelse**, +/**taking**) attention, care (**av** of).

+iva're/tok *pt of* **-ta**

+ive'g *Av* cf **veg**

+ivei' *Av* cf **veg**

I've/land *Pln* twp, Vest-Agder.

i'ver *-en* ardor, zeal; eagerness, zest; impatience (**etter** for): **med i-** eagerly.

I'ver *Prn (m)*

+iver'k/satte *pt of* **-sette**

***iver'k/setjande** *A* -: **den i- makt** the implementing force.

+iver'k/sette *V -satte, -satt* carry into effect, implement; initiate, start.

+iver'k/settelse *-n* (=*/**setjing**) execution, implementation, realization (**av** of).

i'vre *V -a/+-et* show eagerness, enthusiasm (esp. in speech): **i- for en sak** be an ardent supporter of a cause.

i'vrig *A* - ardent, zealous; eager, enthusiastic, keen: **i- i tjenesten** overzealous, zealous; **være i- etter** be anxious to, *(pop.)* be dying to; **være i- for en sak** be an ardent supporter of a cause.

+iø're/fallende *A* - easy to hear, striking; catchy, tuneful.

+iøy'ne/fallende *A* - conspicuous, glaring, *(pop.)* sticking out like a sore thumb: **lite i-** inconspicuous.

+iå'r *Av* cf **år**[2]

J

j [jådd', je'] *-en* (letter) J, j.

ja'[1] *-et* 1 consent: **han fikk hennes j-** he won her c- (usu. ref. to marriage). 2 aye, yes, affirmative vote: **det var fem ja og ett nei** there were five ayes and one no.

ja'[2] *I* 1 yes: **ja men** (yes) but - -. 2 well (as expression of doubt or uncertainty): **jaja** well.

jabb'[1] *-en* jabberer.

jabb'[2] *-et* jabber.

jab'be[1] *V -a/+-et* trudge, plod: **hun j-et på strømpelesten** she padded in her stockingfeet (Boo).

jab'be[2] *V -a/+-et* jabber; talk indistinctly.

jad'den *I dial* certainly, you bet.

jade [sja'd] *-n* jade.

jaf's *-en/+-et* gob, gulp, mouthful: **i en j-** in one m-.

jaf'se *V -a/+-et*: **j- i seg** chomp, gulp, wolf down (food).

ja'g *-et* 1 chase, hunt. 2 mad rush. 3 prodding, urging: **under stadig j- fra tyskerne** with continual prodding by the Germans.

ja'ge *V -a/+-et/+-de* 1 *lit.* go hunting; chase, hunt (animals): **j- opp** flush; hunt down (criminals). 2 drive (**bort** away, **ut** out): **j- en på dør** turn sby out. 3 fly (**av sted** off), rush, chase (**etter** after): **like over meg j-et skyene** the clouds chased over my head. 4 harass, urge: **de j-et seg opp** they were working themselves up into a rage; **j- på** hurry (sby), urge on; **j-et** harassed, haunted.

+ja'ger *-en, pl -e* (=***-ar**) 1 destroyer (ship). 2 fighter plane. 3 *naut.* flying jib.

+ja'ger/fly *-et* (=***-ar/**) fighter plane.

jag'gu *I* (oath) by God, you may be sure.

jagua'r *-en zool.* jaguar (Felis onca).

jaha' *I* 1 uhuh; yessiree. 2 well - -.

jaja' *I* cf **ja**[2]

+jakett [sjakett'] *-en* cf **sjakett**

jak'ke *-a* (suit)coat; jacket; cardigan (sweater).

***jak'sle** *-n* cf **jeksel**

jak't[1] *-a naut.* (large) sloop.

jak't[2] *-a/+-en* hunt, hunting: **gå på j-** go hunting; **gjøre j- på (en)** chase (sby).

***jak'tar** *-en* hunter.

jak'te *V -a/+-et* go hunting, hunt; chase down: **j- på** hunt for.

jak't/gevæ'r *-et* hunting rifle.

jak't/hund *-en* hunting dog.

jak't/kort *-et* hunting license.

jak't/leopar'd *-en zool.* cheetah (Acinonyx jubatus).

jak't/mark *-a* hunting area: **de evige j-er** the happy hunting grounds (after death).

jak't/rett *-en* 1 hunting rights. 2 hunting law.

jak't/terreng' *-et* hunting ground.

jak't/tid *-a/+-en* hunting season.

***ja'/kvæde** *-t* agreement, consent: **han gav j-t sitt** he gave his c-.

***jal'm** *-en* clang, loud noise.

***jal'me** *V -a* resound.

jam'- *pf* (=+**jevn-**) equally, evenly.

jam'/aldring *-en* (=+**jevn/**) contemporary.

jam'be *-n* iamb.

jam'bisk *A* - iambic.

jamboree [sjambori'] *-n* (in scouting) jamboree (=large camping assembly).

jam'/byrdig *A* - (of) equal (rank, descent): **folk som er deres j-e** people who are their equals (Snorre).

jam'/døger *-eret/-ret* cf **/døgn**

jam'/døgn [+/døyn] *-et* equinox (Mar. 21 and Sept. 23).

jam'en[1] *Av* cf **jammen**

jam'en[2] *C* cf **ja**[2]

jam'/føre *V -te* compare (**med** with) (abbrev. **jf., jfr.**).

jam'/føring *-a/+-en* comparison.

jam'/føttes *Av* with feet together.

jam'/gammal *A -t, pl -gamle* of the same age (**med** as): **de er j-e** they are of the same age.

jam'/god *A* just as good: **j-t med ingenting** as good as nothing.

ja'/minne *-t* consent.

***jam'leg** *A* - cf **jevnlig**

jam'/like *-n* equal, peer.

jam'men *Av* certainly, indeed, to be sure: **j- gjør jeg så** I certainly do; **det skal j- bli artig** that will surely be fun.

jam'mer *-en* 1 lamentation, wailing; complaint. 2 misery.

jam'mer/dal *-en* vale of tears (=the earth, *bibl.*).

jam'mer/full *A* miserable, piteous; plaintive.

jam'merlig *A* - 1 miserable, pitiful. 2 (as *adv.*): **j- feig** terribly cowardly; **frua var j- grå og tynn** the lady was miserably gray and thin (Falkberget).

jam'mer/skrik *-et* cry of distress.

jam'n *A jamt* (=+**jevn**) 1 even; (of surfaces) level, plane, smooth; (of heat) moderate, uniform; (of substances) smooth, uniform; (of movement) constant, regular, steady; (of a slope) gentle, gradual; (of character) balanced, even-tempered, level-headed; *(of numbers) even; (in comparison) equal: ***dei er j-e på storleiken** they are of equal size; **j- gang** steady pace; **j-t og trutt** steadily; **med j-e mellomrom** at regular intervals; **på j- kjøl** on an even keel. 2 ordinary; (of circumstances) average, moderate; (of people) common, mediocre, simple; (of food or manners) homely, natural, simple; unpretentious: **holde seg på det j-e** keep one's feet on the ground; **i j-e kår** in modest circumstances; **den j-e mann** the common man, the man in the street; **et j-t vesen** a natural manner; **et j-t år** an average year.

***jam'nad** *-en* cf **jamne**[2]

***jam'nan** *Av* generally, regularly; constantly.

***jam'nast** *Av* usually: **det gjeng no j- så** that's the way it u- goes.

jam'ne[1] *-n* 1 *bot.* club moss (Lycopodium complanatum). 2 lycopodium powder (a yellow dye made from the plant).

***jam'ne**[2] *-n* (=**jamnad**) 1 constancy, steadiness: **j-n dreg** persistence pays. 2 average: **på j-n** on the a-.

jam'ne[3] *V -a/+-et* (=+**jevne**) 1 flatten, level, smooth (out): +**j- med jorden** destroy, level; **j- vegen** prepare the way; ***det j-er seg** things straighten out. 2 thicken (soup etc., by adding flour).

jam'ning[1] *-en* (=+**jevning**[1]) equal, peer.

jam'ning[2] *-a/+-en* (=+**jevning**[2]) thickening (added to soups and sauces).

jam're *V -a/+-et* complain, fret, wail (**over** about); bemoan, lament: **j- seg** (the same).

jam'/sides *Av* abreast, side by side; alongside, beside, even with; simultaneous: **de stod j-** they stood side by side; **j- med** abreast with, alongside, side by side with.

jam'/stelle *V -stelte, -stelt* place on

+ Bokmål; * Nynorsk; ° Dialect.
After letter: ' stress (Acc. 1); ' tone, stress (Acc. 2); ˙ length.
Below letter: . not pronounced.

an equal footing (**med** with): **j-lte former** alternate forms (of equal status, ref. to linguistic forms in official Norwegian).

jam'/stelling *-a* equality.

jam'/stor *A* equally large, of the same size.

jam't[1] *nt of* **jamn** (=+**jevnt**)

jam't[2] *Av* 1 evenly: **avta j-t** decrease gradually; **dra j-** (of horses) pull equally; **dele j-** divide fairly; **j- og samt** constantly, forever; **j- med** as high as; **j- over** generally. +2 moderately: **j- god** average. (See also **jamn**).

jam'te[1] *-n* cf **jemte**[1]

jam'te[2] *V -a/+-et* meow.

Jam't/land *Pln* cf **Jemt/**

***jam't/over** [/åver] *Av* cf **jamt**[2]

***jam'/vaksen** *A -e/-i, pl -ne* harmoniously developed.

jam'/vekt *-a* balance, equilibrium.

***jam'/vel** *Av* even: **j- om** e- if.

***jam'/vår** *-en* spring equinox.

Ja'n *Prn (m)*

jan. =**januar**

janitsja'r *-en hist.* janissary (soldier of elite corps of Turkish troops).

janitsja'r/musikk' *-en* janissary music (produced by brass and percussion instruments).

Jan Mayen [janmai'en] *Pln* Norwegian island in Arctic Ocean between Greenland and Norway.

janua'r *en* January.

ja'/o'rd *-et* assent, consent: **gi ens j- til noe** give one's c- to sth.

Ja'pan *Pln* Japan.

+**japa'ner** *-en, pl -e* (=***-ar**) Japanese.

japanerin'ne *-a/+-en* Japanese woman.

***japane'sar** *-en* cf **japaner**

***japane'sisk** *A* - cf **japansk**

ja'pansk [also: japa'nsk] *A* - Japanese.

***ja'r** *-en* cf **jare**[1]

jardiniere [sjardiniæ'r] *-n* 1 jardiniere. 2 flower stand.

ja're[1] *-n* (=***jar**) 1 edge. 2 selvage.

***ja're**[2] *V -a* clip, hew along the edge.

+**jargong** [sjargång'] *-en* cf **sjargong**

jar'k *-en* 1 ball (of foot or thumb). 2 corresponding part of shoe.

ja'rl *-en* earl.

Ja'rl(e) *Prn (m)*

ja'rle/dømme *-t, pl +-r/*-* earldom.

***ja'rn** *-et* cf **jern**

***ja'rn/veg** *-en* railroad.

***jar'pe** *-a/-en* cf **jerpe**

***ja'r/slakk** *A -slakt* (of woven piece) loose, slack along the edges.

***ja'r/tegn** [/tengn] *-a* cf **jær/**

***jar'v** *-en* cf **jerv**

***ja'se** *-n* hare.

jas'k *-et* 1 careless, hastily done work. *2 sloppy speech.

jas'ke *V -a/+-et* 1 rush through (a job) carelessly: **j- av, fra seg** dash off, do sloppily. *2 speak carelessly, in slurred fashion.

jas'keri *-et* careless, hasty work.

jas'ket(e) *A* - careless, sloppy, slurred.

jasmin [sjasmi'n] *-en bot.* 1 jasmine (Jasminum). 2 mock orange (Philadelphus coronarius).

jas'å *I* well, well; is that so.

jatt' *-en* yes-man.

jat'te *V -a/+-et* echo the speaker, make continual sounds of agreement: **j- etter en** agree with, imitate sby; **j- med en** express agreement with sby (in an obsequious way).

jat'tet(e) *A* - (of conversation, person) overly agreeable, compliant.

***jau'** *I* cf **jo**[4]

+**javel'** *Av* cf **vel**[4]

+**javiss't** *Av* cf **visst**[3]

jav'l *-et* chattering, gibberish, jabber.

jav'le *V -a* chatter, gabble, jabber.

jazz [jass'] *-en* 1 jazz. 2: **danse j-** dance to jazz music.

jazz/band [jass'/bann, /bæn] *-et* jazz orchestra.

jazze [jas'se] *V -a/+-et* 1 play jazz music. 2 dance to jazz music.

°**je'** *Pn* cf **jeg**[2]

jeep [ji'p] *-en* jeep.

+**jeg**[1] [jei'] *-et* (=***eg**[1]) ego, self: **mitt annet j-** my alter ego; **ens bedre j-** one's better self.

+**jeg**[2] [jei'] *pn ob meg, po min* (=***eg**[2]) I; me; mine: **jeg selv** I myself: **j- er meg selv** I am myself; **det er +meg/+jeg/*eg** it is I (me).

je'ger *-en, pl +-e* 1 hunter: **bjørnej-** bear h-; **kvinnej-** woman chaser. 2 chasseur (infantryman or cavalryman trained for rapid maneuvering).

je'ger/hest *-en* chasseur's horse.

je'ger/korps *-et* (corps of) chasseurs.

+**jeg/form** [jei'/] *-en* first person: **j-roman** novel written in the first person.

°**jei'p** *-en/-et* cf **geip**

jekk' *-en* jack (for lifting heavy objects).

jek'ke *V -a/+-et* jack: **j- opp** jack up; **j- seg opp** act big, swagger; **jekk deg ned!** *fam.* pipe down.

jek'sel *-elen, pl -ler* molar.

jek't *-a* small cargo boat with half deck and sails.

jek'te/bruk *-et* 1 operation of a *jekt.* 2 *jekt* and all its equipment.

***jel'k** *-en* gelding.

Jel'sa *Pln* twp, Rogaland.

Je'l/øy *Pln* island, Østfold.

je'mini *I*: **herre j-** by jiminy.

jem'te[1] *-n* (=**jamte**[1]) person from *Jemtland.*

°**jem'te**[2] *Av* equally, evenly, in the same degree.

Jem't/land *Pln* Jämtland (province in Sweden).

jem't/lending *-en* person from *Jemtland.*

jen'ke *V -a/+-et* even out, smooth over: **j- seg** correct itself, straighten out; conform.

+**jen's** *en*: **pikenes j-** ladies' man.

Jen's *Prn (m)* (form of Johannes).

jen'te *-a* 1 girl. 2 hired girl, housemaid. 3 spinster: **to gamle j-r** two old maids.

jen'te/fut *-en* man who chases after girls.

jen'te/lag *-et* circle, group of girls: **han var sjenert i j-** he was embarrassed in the company of girls.

jen't/unge [/onge] *-n* little girl.

+**jer**[1] [jæ'r] *Pn ob of* **I**

+**jer**[2] [jæ'r] *Pn obs.* your *(pl).*

jeremia'de *-n* jeremiad, lamentation.

+**jeres** [jæ'res] *Pn po of* **I**

jern [jæ'rn] *-et* (=***jarn**) 1 iron: **gammelt j-** scrap i-; **smi mens j-et er varmt** strike while the i- is hot. 2 article made of iron, piece of iron: **flere j- i ilden** several irons in the fire; **slå ham i j-** clap him in irons. 3 iron used in baking (see **krumkake/; vaffel/**). 4 determined person, hard worker.

jern/alder [jæ'rn/] *-en* Iron Age.

jern/bane *-n* 1 railroad, railway: **underjordisk j-** subway; **reise med j-** travel by railway. 2 train: **reise på j-** take the t-. 3 railroad depot, station.

jernbane/mann *-en, pl -menn/*-menner* railroad employee, official.

jernbane/nett *-et* railroad network.

jernbane/stasjo'n *-en* railroad station, train station.

jernbane/vogn [/vångn] *-a* railroad car.

jern/besla'g *-et* iron fittings.

jern/betong' *-en* ferroconcrete, reinforced concrete.

jern/blekk *-et* (=+**/blikk**) sheet iron: **galvanisert j-** galvanized sheet iron.

+**jern/bryllup** *-et* (=***/bryllaup**) seventieth wedding anniversary.

jern/byrd **-a/+-en* ordeal by carrying hot iron.

jern/grep *-et* iron grip.

jern/hand *-a, pl -hender* iron fist, iron hand: **styre med j-** rule with an iron hand.

jern/ha'rd *A* hard as iron, rigid: **j- vilje** iron will; **j- disiplin** rigid discipline.

+**jern/helbred** *-en* iron constitution.

jern/helse *-a* iron constitution.

+**jern/holdig** *A* - (=***/haldig**) ferruginous, having iron content.

+**jern/hånd** *-a/-en* cf **/hand**

+**jern/hå'rd** *A* cf **/hard**

jern/malm *-en* iron ore.

jern/natt *-a/+-en, pl -netter* night in late August when there is a frost.

jern/skodd [/skodd] *A* - ironclad, ironshod: **træd ham ikke med j-hæl** crush him not with an iron heel (Bjørnson).

jern/staur *-en* crowbar, iron bar.

+**jern/støperi'** *-et* (=***/støyperi**) iron foundry.

jern/teppe *-t* 1 iron curtain; safety (fireproof) curtain (formerly used in theaters): **Når j-t faller** When the Iron Curtain Falls (novel, J. Lie, 1903). 2 *fig.*: **bak j-t** behind the Iron Curtain; **ha j-** have a mental block.

jernteppe/land *-et* Iron Curtain country.

jern/tid *-a/+-en* difficult time, time of stress.

jern/tråd *-en* iron wire.

jern/vare *-a/+-en* (usu. *pl*) hardware, ironware.

jernvare/handel *-elen, pl -ler* 1 hardware business. 2 hardware store.

+**jernvare/handler** *-en, pl -e* (=***-ar**) hardware merchant.

jern/verk *-et* ironworks.

jern/vilje *-n* iron will.

jer'pe *-a/-en* hazel hen (grouse), European woodland grouse (Tetrastes bonasia).

+**jers** [jæ'rs] *po of* **I**

jersey/kjole [jø'rsi/] *-n* jersey dress.

jersey/trøye *-a* jersey jacket.

jer'v *-en* wolverine (Gulo luscus).

jes't(er) *-en* yeast.

jesuitt' *-en* Jesuit; Jesuitical person.

jesuit'tisk *A* - Jesuit; Jesuitical.

Je'sus Kris'tus *Prn, po* **Jesu Kristi** Jesus Christ.

jet' *-en* jet.

jeté [sjete'] *-en* jetty.

jet'/fly *-et* jet airplane.

+**jet'/jager** *-en, pl -e* (=***-ar**) jet fighter.

jet'/motor *-en* jet engine.

jetong [sjetång'] *-en* counter, poker chip.

+**jet'te** *-n* giant.

+**jet'te/aktig** *A* - gigantic, giantlike.

+**jet'te/gryte** *-a geol.* pothole.

+**jet'te/stor** *A* gigantic.

+**jet'te/stue** *-a archeol.* megalithic burial chamber from the Stone Age.

+**jev'n** *A* cf **jamn**

+**jev'n-** *Pf* cf **jam-**

Jev'n/aker *Pln* twp, Oppland.

+**jev'n/aldrende** *A* - contemporary, of the same age.

+**jev'n/byrdig** *A* - cf **jam/**

+**jev'n/døgn** [/døyn] *-et* cf **jam/**

+**jev'ne** *V -a/-et* cf **jamne**[3]

+**jev'n/føre** *V -te* cf **jam/**

+**jev'n/føring** *-a/-en* cf **jam/**

+**jev'n/gammel** *A -elt, pl -gamle* cf **jam/**

+**jev'n/god** *A* cf **jam/**

+**jev'n/het** *-en* evenness, smoothness; regularity; plainness.

+**jev'ning**[1] *-en* cf **jamning**[1]

+**jev'ning**[2] *-a/-en* cf **jamning**[2]

+**jev'nlig** *Av* (=***jamleg**) constantly, regularly.

+**jev'n/like** *-n* cf **jam/**

+**jev'n/sides** *P* cf **jam/**

+**jev'n/stor** *A* cf **jam/**

jf. =**jamfør/+jevnfør**

jfr.[1] =**jamfør/+jevnfør**

+**jfr.**[2] =**jomfru**

jibb' *-en* 1 *naut.* act of jibbing. 2 jib, projecting arm (of a crane); boom (of a derrick).

jib'be *V -a/+-et* 1 *naut.* jib. 2: **j- ut** *tech.* swing out (the crane arm).

jnr. =**journalnummer**

jo'[1] *-en* arctic bird of prey, any one

of several skuas and jaegers (Stercorariidae).

jo'[2] *Av* (unstressed, either following verb or finally) after all, of course, you know; (expressing assurance, as of sth on which all would agree; in English also expressed by emphasis on verb): **men det er det jo** but it *is*; **han er jo din sønn** he *is* your son; **det vet du jo** but you *know* that; **jeg hører jo** I *am* listening, I *do* hear you.

jo'[3] *C* the (with comparatives, the second being also preceded by **dess, desto,** or **jo**): **jo fler jo bedre** the more the merrier; **veien blir smalere jo lenger vi går** the road gets narrower the farther we go.

+**jo'**[4] *I* (=***jau**) **1** (in answer to a negative question) yes; certainly: **jo jo** yes indeed, I suppose; **jo visst** of course. **2** (hesitatingly) well - -, ye-es.

jobb' *-en* job, piece of work; work.

job'be *V -a/+-et* **1** *derog.* speculate in stocks. **2** work.

+**job'ber** *-en, pl -e* (=***-ar**) *derog.* speculator.

job'be/tid *-a/+-en* boom period, characterized by much stock market activity (in Norway esp. at end of World War I, 1917-18).

job's/post *-en* piece of bad news.

jockey [jåk'ki] *-en* jockey.

jod [jo'd, jodd'] *-en/*-et* iodine.

jodd' *-en* cf **j**

jod'le *V -a/+-et* yodel.

jo'd/tinktu·r *-en* tincture of iodine.

+**jo'g** *pt of* **jage**

jog'ge *V -a/+-et* jog.

joggu [jog'gu] *I* yes indeed (oath).

Johan' *Prn(m)* (from Johannes).

+**johanit'ter** *-en, pl -e* (=***-ar**) member of the Order of Malta (Order of St. John of Jerusalem).

+**johanit'ter/orden** *-enen* (=***-ar/**) Order of Malta (Order of St. John of Jerusalem).

Johan'ne *Prn(f)*

Johan'nes *Prn(m)*: **J- døperen** John the Baptist.

joho' *I* (emphatic) yes.

joi'k *-en* monotone chant sung by the Lapps (tells story of person or past event).

joi'ke *V -a/+-et* chant in monotone with strong rhythm.

jo'/jo *-en* yo-yo.

jo'ker *-en, pl +-e* joker (playing card).

°**joks** [jok's] *-et* cf **juks**

jo'l[1] *-en bot.* angelica (Archangelica officinalis).

***jo'l**[2] *-a* cf **jul**

jol'le *-a/-en naut.* dinghy, dory, jolly boat.

+**jomen** [jom'men] *Av* (=+**jommen**) really; certainly, surely: **j- sa jeg smør!** don't you believe it!

jom'/fru *-a/+-en* **1** maiden, virgin; *archaic* miss, young lady: **gammel j-** old maid; **J- Maria** the Virgin Mary. **2** *obs.* (except in cpds.) barmaid, housekeeper, shop girl, waitress (cf **kold/, varm/**). **3** *tech.* beetle, ramming machine: **mekanisk j-** pneumatic hammer. **4** *astron.* (def.) Virgo. **5** *bot.*: **j-en i det grønne** fennelflower, love-in-a-mist (Nigella damascena); **naken j-** autumn saffron, naked ladies (Colchicum autumnale).

jom'fru/bur *-et* **1** *hist.* maiden's bower (room where unmarried women slept on medieval farm). **2** *hum.* young girl's room.

jom'fru/dom· *-men* maidenhood, virginity.

jomfru'elig *A* - **1** maidenly; oldmaidish. **2** virgin, virginal: **j- land** virgin land.

Jom'fru'/lanḍ *Pln* island, Telemark.

jomfruna'lsk *A* - **1** affectedly shy, bashful; coy, prissy. **2** spinsterish. **3** effeminate.

+**jommen** [jom'men] *Av* cf **jomen**

joms/viking [jom's/] *-en* member of Danish Viking band which had its stronghold in Jomsborg at the mouth of the Oder.

jo'n *en/-et* cf **ion**

Jo'n *Prn(m)*: **J- blund** the Sandman.

Jon/dal [jon'/] *Pln* valley, Hordaland.

+**jo'ner** *-en, pl -e* (=***-ar**) Ionian.

+**jonglere** [sjångle're] *V -te* cf **sjonglere**

+**jonglør** [sjånglø'r] *-en* cf **sjonglør**

jo'nisk *A* - Ionian, Ionic.

jonsok [jon'såkk] *en* Midsummer Day, St. John's Day (June 24).

jonsok/blom *-en bot.* campion (Lychnis).

jonsok/bål *-et* bonfire celebrating Midsummer Night.

jonsok/koll *-en bot.* bugle (Ajuga pyramidalis).

jonsok/kvelḍ *-en* Midsummer Eve (June 23).

jonsok/natt *-a/+-en* Midsummer Night.

jo'rḍ *-a/+-en* **1** ground: **den bare j-** the bare g-; **innviet j-** consecrated g-; **følge en til j-en** follow sby to the grave (= take part in sby's funeral procession). **2** dirt, earth, soil: **en klump j-** a lump of dirt. **3** land: **leve av j-a** farm for a living. **4** earth, world: **himmel og j-** heaven and earth; **på j-en** on (the) earth; **sette himmel og j- i bevegelse** move heaven and earth.

jo'rḍ/aksen *df* axis of the earth.

+**jo'rḍ/bo** *-en* (=***/bu**) earth-dweller.

***jo'rḍ/bolk** *-en* **1** continent. **2** piece of ground.

jo'rḍ/botn *-en* **1** soil: **på norsk j-** on Norwegian s-. **2** basis: **sunn moralsk j-** sound moral b-.

jo'rḍ/bruk *-et* agriculture, farming: **j-ets krav** the demands of agriculture.

+**jo'rḍ/bruker** *-en, pl -e* (=***-ar**) farmer.

jo'rḍbruks/kandida·t *-en* graduate of college of agriculture.

jo'rḍbruks/lære *-a/+-en* science, study of agriculture.

jo'rḍbruks/skole *-n* agricultural school.

jo'rḍ/bunḍen *A +-ent, pl -ne* earthbound, prosaic, stolid: **hennes j-ne og selvrådige sjel** her earthbound and self-willed soul (Undset).

+**jo'rḍ/bunn** *-en* cf **/botn**

jor'ḍ/bær *-et* strawberry.

jo'rḍ/drott *-en* owner of an estate which is worked by tenants.

+**jo'rḍ/dyrker** *-en, pl -e* (=***-ar**) farmer, one who works the land.

jo'rde[1] *-t, pl +-r/*-* field (cultivated, usu. near houses).

jo'rde[2] *V -a/+-et* **1** bury: **han ble j-et ved kirken** he was buried near the church. **2** ground (an electric wire).

jo'rde/bok *-a, pl -bøker* cadaster (=medieval book setting forth the lands and rights belonging to a manorial estate).

+**jo'rde/ferd** *-a/-en* cf **jord/**

jo'rde/gods [/gots] *-et* landed property, lands.

+**jo'rde/liv** *-et* cf **jord/**

jo'rḍ/eple *-t dial.* potato.

jorde/rik(e) [jor'de/] *-(e)t poet.* earth.

jo'rdet(e) *A* - dirty, muddy.

jo'rḍ/fall *-et* cave-in; landslide.

jo'rḍ/fast *A* - **1** held by the ground, immovable. **2**: **j- eiendom** real estate.

jo'rḍ/ferd [*/fær] *-a/+-en* burial, funeral.

jo'rḍ/feste *V -a/+-et/*-feste* bury, inter.

+**jo'rḍ/festelse** *-n* cf **/festing**

jo'rḍ/festing *-a/+-en* burial, interment.

jo'rḍ/flekk *-en* plot of ground.

+**jo'rḍ/freser** *-en, pl -e* (=***-ar**) cultivator (motorized).

jo'rḍ/frukt *-a/+-en* fruit that grows close to ground (as opposed to tree fruit).

jo'rḍ/funn *-et* archeological find.

jordisk [jor'disk] *A* - earthly, worldly: **j-e levninger** mortal remains.

+**jo'rḍ/klode** *-n* (=***/klote**) world: **j-n** the globe.

jo'rḍ/lapp *-en* patch of ground.

jo'rḍ/ledning *-en* ground wire.

jo'rḍ/liv *-et* existence, life on earth.

jo'rḍ/loppe *-a zool.* flea beetle (Haltica).

jo'rḍ/lov [/lå·v] ***-a/+-en** law relating to land problems.

jo'rḍ/magnetis·me *-n* geomagnetism.

jo'rḍ/mor *-a/+-en, pl -mødrer/+-mødre* midwife.

jo'rḍ/nær *A* close to the soil, earthbound.

jo'rḍ/nøtt groundnut, peanut (Arachis hypogaea).

jo'rḍ/olje *-a/-en* crude oil.

jo'rḍ/omsei·ling *-a/+-en* circumnavigation of the world.

+**jo'rḍ/påkas·telse** *-n* part of committal service when earth is sprinkled on the coffin: **forrette j-** perform graveside ceremony.

jo'rḍ/rotte *-a zool.* European vole, water rat (Arvicola amphibius).

jo'rḍ/røyk *-en* **1** gust of wind bearing dirt, etc. **2** *bot.* fumitory (Fumaria officinalis).

jo'rḍ/skifte *-t* settlement of an estate; change in land ownership; dividing up lands formerly held in common and assigning them to individuals on an equitable basis.

+**jo'rḍskifte/dommer** *-en, pl -e* (=***-ar**) official who directs *jordskifte* with help of two appraisers.

jo'rḍ/skjelv *-en/-et* earthquake.

jo'rḍ/skorpe *-a* earth's crust.

jo'rḍ/slag *-et* **1** type of soil. **2** mildew. **3** affliction such as rash or palsy believed to have come from evil forces in the ground.

jo'rḍ/slå *V infl as* **slå**[2] temporarily cover the roots of a plant with dirt until it can be planted.

jo'rḍ/slått *A* - mildewed, musty.

jo'rḍs/monn *-et* ground, soil (considered in relation to agriculture).

jo'rḍ/styre *-t, pl +-r/*-* locally elected council whose job is to handle questions of land use, including forests.

jo'rḍ/træl *-en* grubber.

jo'rḍ/veg *-en* (=+**/vei**) (cultivated) farmland.

+**jo'rḍ/venḍt** *A* - (=***/vend**) concerned with earthly things, earthbound.

jo'rsal/far *-en* (=+**/farer,** ***/farar**) crusader, one who had made a pilgrimage to Jerusalem (Old Norse Jorsal), esp. of King Sigurd of Norway (1103-30).

jorte [jor'te] *V -a/+-et* chew (its) cud.

***jorte/dyr** *-et* ruminant.

+**jorter** [jor'ter] *-en, pl -e* (=***-ar**) cud-chewer, ruminant.

Jo'rulf *Prn(m)*

Jo'run(n) *Prn(f)*

Jos'te/dal *Pln* twp, Sogn og Fjordane.

jo'tun *jotnen, pl jotner myth.* giant thought to live inside a mountain, at war with gods and men.

Jo'tun/heimen *Pln* **1** mountain range in central part of south Norway. **2** *myth.* home of the giants.

jour/havenḍe [sju'r/] *A* - on duty, on watch.

journal [sjorna'l, sjur-] *-en* journal, logbook, record.

journal/føre *V -te* enter (sth) in a journal (logbook, etc.).

journalisere [sjurnalise're] *V -te* enter (sth) in a journal (logbook, etc.).

journalist [sjurnalis't] *-en* journalist.

journalistikk [sjurnalistikk'] *-en* journalism.

+ Bokmål; * Nynorsk; ° Dialect.
After letter: ' stress (Acc. 1); ` tone, stress (Acc. 2); · length.
Below letter: . not pronounced.

journalistisk [sjurnalis'tisk] *A* - journalistic.
journal/nummer [sjurna'l/nommer] *-et* serial number given to incoming and outgoing letters in a government office (when entered in a journal).
jovia'l *A* jolly, jovial.
jovialite't *-en* joviality.
+**joviss't** *I* cf **visst**[3]
jr. = **junior**
ju'balon *-en* celebration, jubilee.
ju'bel *-en* 1 exultation, shout or song of joy: **latter og j-** laughter and joy. 2 jubilation, transports of joy; hilarity: **under stor j-** amid great acclaim (applause).
+**ju'bel/olding** *-en* 1 person celebrating an anniversary (esp. the 50th). 2 very old man.
ju'bel/år *-et* anniversary, jubilee year: **en gang hvert j-** once in a blue moon.
jubilan't *-en* person or institution celebrating (his, its) anniversary.
***jubile'** *-et, pl* - cf **jubileum**
jubile're *V -te* 1 celebrate an anniversary, a jubilee. 2 exult, rejoice.
jubile'um *-eet, pl* +*-eer*/**-eum* anniversary: **femtiårs j-** 50th a-.
jubile'ums/fest *-en* anniversary celebration, jubilee celebration.
ju'ble *V -a*/+*-et* exult, rejoice, shout with joy.
ju'das *-en* (a) Judas; (a) traitor.
ju'das/kyss *-et*/**-en* Judas kiss, kiss of betrayal.
+**ju'das/penger** *pl* (=***-ar**) Judas money, traitor's wages.
judisiell' *A -elt jur.* judicial.
judi'sium *-et* judgment: **mangle j-** lack j-.
°**ju'ge** *V jaug, jugi* cf **lyge**
jug'l *-et* 1 gaudy finery. 2 empty display, sham. 2 nonsense, rubbish.
jug'le *V -a*/+*-et* 1: **j- (til, ut)** bedizen, deck out. 2 tell a tall story; talk nonsense.
jug'let(e) *A* - bedizened.
jugosla'v *-en* Yugoslav(ian).
***jugosla'var** *-en* cf **jugoslav**
Jugosla'via *Pln* Yugoslavia.
jugosla'visk *A* - Yugoslav(ian).
juks [jok's] *-et* 1 cheating, fudging: **det ble vel noe j- med julegavene i år også** there would probably be some f- on the Christmas gifts this year too (Hoel). 2 junk, trash.
juk's/agn [/angn] *-a* cf **djups/**
juk'se[1] *-a* cf **djups/agn**
jukse[2] [jok'se] *V -a*/+*-et* cheat, fudge.
juk'se/bluse +*-a*/*-en* dickey.
juk'se/fiske *-t* deep-fishing with a handline (cf **djups/**).
+**jukse/maker** [jok'se/] *-en* (=***-ar**) rascal: **j- pipelort, tar igjen og gir bort** (children's saying) Indian giver.
+**jukser** [jok'ser] *-en, pl -e* (=***-ar**) cheater, trickster.
jukseri [jok'seri] *-et* cheating, deceiving, fooling.
ju'l *-a*/+*-en* Christmas (day, season): **feire j-** celebrate C-; **få noe til j-** get sth as a C- present; **gledelig j-, god j-** Merry C-; **holde j-** keep C-; **i j-a** at, during C-.
+**ju'l/aften** *-enen, pl -(e)ner* (=**/aftan**) Christmas Eve: **lille j-** December 23.
ju'le *V -te*/**-a*: **j- opp** beat, thrash, whip; give a licking to sby.
ju'le/bakst *-en* Christmas baking.
ju'le/band *-et* sheaf of grain on pole, or roof peak for birds at Christmas.
ju'le/blot *-et* Old Norse sacrificial feast at Christmastime (about Jan. 12 in the pagan calendar).
ju'le/bo'rd *-et* table spread with Christmas food, esp. in restaurants and at office parties, before Christmas.
ju'le/brennevin *-et* liquor bought (or made) for Christmas.
ju'le/bukk [/bokk] *-en* 1 mummer; masked and costumed person (usu. child) who goes from door to door and is treated with goodies (similar to Am. Hallowe'en trick-or-treaters). 2 fool; affected person.
ju'le/båt *-en* ship which carries Christmas visitors and gifts to and from America.
ju'le/dag *-en* 1 Christmas Day. 2 any day during Christmas season: **annen j-** day after Christmas (Dec. 26).
ju'le/evange'lium *df -iet, pl* +*-ier*/**-ium* Christmas gospel.
ju'le/ferie *-n* Christmas holidays, vacation.
ju'le/gate *-a* street, esp. in business district, decorated for Christmas.
+**ju'le/gave** *-n* (=**/gåve**) Christmas gift, present.
ju'le/geit [/jeit] *-a* 1 = **julebukk.** 2 Christmas bread shaped like goats' horns.
ju'le/glede *-a*/+*-en* 1 Christmas cheer, gaiety, joy. 2 begonia with pink blossoms, sold esp. at Christmas.
ju'le/graut *-en* pudding (usu. rich) eaten on Christmas Eve.
ju'le/gris *-en* pig fattened for Christmas holidays.
ju'le/hefte *-t, pl* +*-r*/**-* Christmas magazine.
ju'le/helg *-a*/+*-en* Christmas season.
+**ju'le/hilsen** *-en* Christmas greeting(s).
ju'le/kake *-a* 1 bread (of a special form) containing raisins, citron, cardamom, etc. 2 *(pl)* Christmas cookies.
ju'le/klapp *-en* Christmas gift.
ju'le/kort *-et* Christmas card.
ju'le/kost *-en* food appropriate to Christmas.
+**ju'le/kurv** *-en* heart-shaped basket of paper (for Christmas tree).
ju'le/kut *-en* racing around wildly on Christmas visits.
ju'le/kvad *-et* Christmas hymn, song.
ju'le/kveld *-en* Christmas Eve.
ju'le/lys *-et* Christmas candle.
ju'le/merke *-t, pl* +*-r*/**-* 1 Christmas seal. 2 prediction, sign: **hvis ikke alle j-r slår feil** if the signs are not altogether wrong.
ju'le/natt *-a*/+*-en, pl -netter* the night before Christmas.
ju'le/nek *-et* sheaf of grain on pole or roof peak for birds at Christmas.
ju'le/nisse *-n* Christmas elf (similar to Santa Claus).
ju'le/presang' *-en* Christmas present.
+**ju'le/sang** *-en* (=**/song**) Christmas song.
ju'le/stemning **-a*/+*-en* Christmas cheer, spirit.
+**ju'le/stri** *-a* (=**/strid**) preparation, rush, work before Christmas.
ju'le/tid *-a*/+*-en* Christmastime.
+**ju'le/travelhet** *-en* Christmas preparation, rush.
ju'le/tre *-et* Christmas tree: **høste j-et** pick off goodies from the C- tree.
ju'letre/fest *-en* after-Christmas party when tree is relighted and candies, etc. are taken from tree and eaten.
ju'letre/fot *-en, pl* +*-føtter*/**-føter* Christmas tree stand.
ju'letre/lys *-et* Christmas tree candle (light).
ju'letre/pynt *-en* Christmas tree decorations.
+**ju'le/uke** *-a*/*-en* cf **/veke**
ju'le/ved *-en* wood chopped for Christmas.
ju'le/veke *-a* Christmas week (Dec. 24-31).
ju'le/øl *-et* Christmas ale.
ju'li *en* July: **fjerde j-** Fourth of J-.
julia'nsk *A* - Julian (calendar).
ju'ling *-a*/+*-en* beating, thrashing.
jum'bo *-en* person who comes in last in a race or sports contest.
jump [jom'p] *-et* hop, jump, leap.
jumpe [jom'pe] *V -a*/+*-et* jump, leap; plop, plump.
jum'per [jømper/jomper] *-en, pl* +*-e* slipover sweater.
jun. = **junior**
junge [jong'e] *-n* 1 boy, young man: **kahytt/** cabin boy. 2 table knife.
jung'el *-en* jungle.
jung/mann [jong'/] *-en, pl -menn*/**-menner* (naval rank) seaman.
ju'ni *en* June: **sjuende j-** J- 7th (commemorating separation from Sweden in 1905).
ju'nior *-en* 1 junior (the younger). 2 sport contestant between 14-16 years old.
jun'ker *-en, pl* +*-e* 1 young nobleman. 2 German Junker.
juno'nisk *A* - Junoesque, stately.
jun'ta *-en* junta.
ju'r *-et* udder.
jur. = **juridisk**
ju'ra *pl of* **jus**
ju'ra/tid *-a*/+*-en geol.* Jurassic period.
juri'dikum *-en* 1 law examination *(examen juridicum)*: **oppe til j-** taking one's l- e-. 2 law degree: **han har tatt j-** he has taken a l- d-.
juri'disk *A* - juridical, legal: **j- kandidat** law graduate; **j- person** juristic person; **j- student** law student; **i j-e spørsmål** in legal matters.
jurisdiksjo'n *-en* jurisdiction.
juris't *-en* jurist; law student; lawyer: **j-ene** the lawyers, the legal profession.
juristeri' *-et* legalistic hairsplitting, quibbling.
jury [ju'ri] *-en* jury (=lay judges); panel of judges (e.g. in a beauty contest).
jury/mann *-en, pl -menn,* **-menner* juror, juryman.
jury/medlem +*-met*/**-(m)en, pl -mer*/**-er* juror; judge (e.g. on a panel of art judges).
jus' *-en, pl jura* jurisprudence, study of law: **lese j-** study law.
°**jus'som** *Av* cf **just/som**
jus't *Av* exactly, just; right now: **han er kommet j- nå** he has just come; **jeg skriver j- til ham** I am writing to him right now; **j- når han kom** just when he came.
juste're *V -te* 1 adapt, adjust (e.g. apparatus). 2 regulate measuring devices to conform with international standards. 3 regulate: **j- lønninger** r- wages.
+**juste'rer** *-en, pl -e* (=***-ar**) official in a district office of weights and measures.
justi's *-en* 1 administration of justice. 2 discipline: **holde (streng) j-** keep (strict) d-.
Justi's/departementet [/-mang'e] *df* Ministry of Justice and Police.
justi's/minis'ter *-eren, pl -rer*/+*-ere* Minister of Justice (=Attorney General).
justi's/mord [/mord] *-et* miscarriage of justice.
justi's/nemnd [/nemd] *-a* parliamentary committee in charge of affairs relating to the Ministry of Justice.
justitiarius [justisia'rius] +*-ien*/**-iusen* Chief Justice.
***jus't/som'** *Av pop.* as if; just like; as it were, sort of.
ju'te[1] +*-n*/**-a* jute.
ju'te[2] *-n* cf **jyde**
ju'te/hamp *-en* jute fiber.
ju'te/lerret *-et, pl* -/+*-er* burlap, gunny.
ju'tul *-en, pl* +*-er*/**jutlar* (=***jøtul**) *folk.* giant thought to live inside a mountain, at war with gods and men.
ju'v *-et* canyon, gorge.
juve'l *-en* jewel; treasure, valuable(s).
+**juve'l/besatt'** *A* - bejeweled, set with jewels.
juvele'r *-en* jeweler.
+**jvf.** = **jevnfør** cf **jfr.**[1]
jy'de *-n* Jutlander.
Jyl'land *Pln* Jutland.
jyl'landsk *A* - Jutlandish, pertaining to Jutland.
jyp'ling *-en* cocky young fellow, young whippersnapper.
jys'k *A* - Jutlandish, pertaining to Jutland.
jy'te *-n* cf **jyde**

°**jæ'kel** *-elen, pl -ler pop.* devil: **det var som bare j-en** (oath).

jæ'r/bu *-en* person from Jæren.

Jæ'ren *Pln* coastal district in southwestern Norway.

jæ'rsk *A* - pertaining to Jæren.

+**jæ'r/tegn** [/tein] *-et* (=***jar/**) 1 omen, sign. 2 miracle.

°**jæ'vel** *-elen, pl -ler* cf **djevel**

jæ'vli(g) *A* - 1 devilish, hellish: **det var da j-** that's a hell of a note. 2 damn, very: **det var j- fint (vanskelig, osv.)** it was damn fine (difficult, etc.).

jø' *I*: **å jø** ah me, oh my.

jø'de *-n* Jew.

+**jø'de/forføl·gelse** *-n* (=***-ing**) persecution of Jews, Jew baiting, pogrom.

Jø'de/land *Pln bibl.* Palestine.

jødin'ne *-a/+-en* Jewess.

jø'disk *A* - Jewish.

+**jøj'e** *I* cf **jøye**

+**jø'kel** *-elen, pl -ler* (=***jøkul**) glacier; arm of a glacier.

***jø'kul** *-en, pl jøklar* cf **jøkel**

Jøl'ster *Pln* twp, Sogn og Fjordane.

Jør'gen *Prn (m)*

Jø'rn *Prn (m)* (abbrev. of Jørgen).

Jø'rund *Prn (m)*

jøss' *I* (very mild oath) gee, my, you bet: **j- bevars** oh sure; **j- for en lyd** my, what a sound; **nei j-** dear me, oh my.

jøs'se/nam' *I* cf **jøss**

jøs'ses *I* cf **jøss**

jøs'sing *-en* 1 Norwegian patriot during World War II (opp. of quisling). 2 person from Jøssingfjord (in Rogaland).

Jøs'sund *Pln* twp, Sør-Trøndelag.

***jø'tul** *-en, pl jøtlar* cf **jutul**

***jø'tul/gryte** *-a* cf **jette/**

jøy'e *I*: **å j-, å j- meg** me oh my, woe is me.

jøy'k *-en* cf **joik**

jøy'ke *V -a/+-et* cf **joike**

jå'/blom *-en bot.* grass-of-parnassus, white liverwort (Parnassia palustris).

jå'l *-et* foolishness, nonsense; showing off.

jå'le[1] *-a* show-off, silly woman.

jå'le[2] *V a/-te* 1 act silly, pretend, put on airs, show off. 2 ridicule: **j- med** make fun of.

jå'le/bukk *-en* fool, show-off.

jå'leri *-et* 1 affectation, showing off. 2 silliness: **noe fordømt j-** infernal idiocy.

***jå'le/skap** *-en* idiotic act or behavior, nonsense, silliness.

jå'let(e) *A* - affected, foolish, silly.

jå'ling *-en* silly, stupid person; simpleton.

K

k [kå'] *-en* (letter) K, k.

K, k=**kommunistpartiet**

°**ka'** *Pn* cf **hva**

kaba'l *-en* 1 solitaire: **legge k-** play s-; **k-en gikk opp for ham** he won the game of solitaire. 2 *fig.* **legge k- om noe** let the cards decide sth.

kaba'le *-n lit.* cabal, intrigue, plot.

kabare't *-en* 1 cabaret: **gå på k-** go to a c-; **opptre på k-** appear, entertain at a c-. 2 sectioned hors d'oeuvre dish. 3 dish consisting of cold meat or fish in gelatin.

kabare't/fat *-et*=**kabaret 2.**

kabb' *-en* chunk of wood, section of a log.

kabbalis'tisk *A* - cabalistic, mystical, secret.

kab'be[1] *-n* 1 chunk of wood, section of a log. 2 *naut.* block (of wood through which rope is run to hold sail in to mast).

kab'be[2] *V -a/+-et dial.* chop, cut, saw across or through: **k- tre** top a tree; **beinet ble k-et av** the leg was cut off; **k-et og huggen ved** firewood.

ka'bel *-elen, pl -ler* cable (rope; wire; electric).

+**ka'bel/lengde** *-n* (=***/lengd**) *naut.* cable length (measure of distance) =1/10 of a nautical mile or usu. 100 fathoms.

Ka'bel/våg *Pln* village, Vågan twp, Nordland.

kabi'n *-en* (=**cabin**) *(aero) naut.* cabin.

kabinett' *-et, pl -/+-er* 1 cabinet (=small room); booth (in beauty salon); salon. 2 royal reception room. 3 *hist.* royal cabinet, council, ministry. 4 (radio, etc.) cabinet.

kabinett's/spørsmål *-et*: **stille k-** demand a vote of confidence (on parliamentary bill).

ka'ble *V -a/+-et* cable, wire.

kabriole't *-en* 1 cabriolet. 2 convertible.

kabyss' *-a/+-en naut.* galley.

kada'ver *-eret, pl -er/+-re* 1 corpse, cadaver, carcass. 2 *pop.* washed-out, worn-out person.

kada'ver/disipli'n *-en* blind, slavish discipline.

ka'der *-eren, pl -rer* cadre (core group, nucleus).

kadett' *-en* cadet (at military or naval school).

kafé *-en* cafe, restaurant.

kafete'ria *-en* cafeteria.

+**kaf'fe** *-n* (=***kaffi**) coffee: **brenne k-** roast c-; **koke k-** make c-; **k-n holder seg varm** the c- is staying warm.

+**kaf'fe/bo'rd** *-et* coffee table.

+**kaf'fe/bønne** *-a* coffee bean.

+**kaf'fe/dokter** *-en* coffee royal (coffee and brandy drink).

+**kaf'fe/erstat'ning** *-en* coffee substitute.

+**kaf'fe/grugg** *-en/-et* cf **/grut**

+**kaf'fe/grut** *-en/-et* coffee grounds.

kaffein [kaffe-i'n] *-en/-et* cf **koffein**

+**kaf'fe/kanne** *-a* coffeepot, coffee server.

+**kaf'fe/kjel(e)** *-(e)n* coffeepot (in which coffee is made).

***kaf'fe/kvern** [/kvæ'rn] *-a* coffee mill.

+**kaf'fe/la'rs** *-en hum.* coffeepot.

kaf'fer *-en, pl +-e* Kaffir.

+**kaf'fe/servi'se** *-t* coffee service, coffee set.

+**kaf'fe/slabbera's** *-et* coffee party, coffee klatch.

+**kaf'fe/tørst** *A* - thirsty for coffee.

+**kaf'fe/tår** *-en* drop, small cup of coffee.

***kaf'fi** *-en* cf **kaffe**

***kaf'fi/stove** [/ståve] *-a* restaurant (in city, featuring rural food).

***kaf'se** *V -a* grab, snatch.

kaf'tan [also: kafta'n] *-en* caftan.

***ka'ge** *V -a* stare: **k- etter** turn and gape at.

kagg' *-en* cf **kagge**[1]

kag'ge[1] *-a/-en* (=**kagg**) 1 keg. 2 barrel float (to float fishing net or seine). 3 stack (esp. of hay).

***kag'ge**[2] *V -a* store, pack in a keg.

+**ka'g/stryke** *V -strøk, -strøket* cf **kak/**

kahytt' *-a naut.* cabin, stateroom.

+**kahytt's/gutt** *-en* (=***/gut**) cabin boy.

kai' *-a/-en* pier, quay, wharf: **legge til (ved) k-en** come alongside the dock.

kai'e *-a zool.* jackdaw (Corvus monedula).

kai'/lengd [also: kai'/] *-a* (=+**/lengde**) (lineal) wharf capacity.

kai'/plass [also: kai'/] *-en naut.* berth.

kaj'akk [also -akk'] *-en* kayak.

+**kajen'ne/pepper** *-en* (=***/pepar**) cayenne pepper.

+**ka'k** *-en* whipping post.

kakadu' *+-en/*-a* (=**/du'e**) cockatoo.

kaka'o *-en* cocoa.

kaka'o/bønne *-a* cocoa bean.

ka'ke[1] *-a* 1 cake, cooky: **bløt/k-** layer cake (usu. filled); **vin og k-r** wine and cakes; **mele sin egen k-** grind one's own axe. 2 *dial.* bread baked in oven (not on top of stove). 3 lump, patty: **klappe k-** patty-cake.

ka'ke[2] *V -a/+-et*: **k- seg** cake; flatten out (like a dough).

ka'ke/boks *-en* cooky tin, cooky jar.

ka'ke/botn *-en* (=+**/bunn**) bottom, base of a layer cake.

ka'ke/bu *-a mil.*: **få ti dagers k-** get ten days in the guardhouse.

ka'ke/fat *-et* cake dish, cake plate.

ka'ke/form *-a* cake tin, cake pan.

ka'ke/linne *-a* period of mild weather early in December, when Christmas baking is being done.

ka'ke/mons *-en* person who is inordinately fond of cake.

kakerlakk' *-en* cockroach.

ka'ke/spade *-n* cake server.

ka'ke/vase *-n* cake stand.

ka'ki *-en* khaki cloth.

ka'ki/farge *-n* khaki color.

ka'ki/skjorte *-a* khaki shirt.

kakk'[1] *+-et/*-en* knock, rap, thump.

kakk'[2] *-en* piggin, small wooden container of stave construction (for milk, etc.).

kak'ke *V -a/+-et* 1 knock, rap: **du trenger ikke k- på** you don't need to k-; **han k-et ut av pipa si** he k-ed his pipe out. 2 (of birds) peck (**på** at). 3 (of clocks) tick.

kak'kel *-elen, pl kakler* glazed tile.

kak'kel/omn *-en* (=+**/ovn**) (iron or tiled) heating stove.

kak'kelomns/krok *-en* (=+**-ovns/**) 1 corner of a room containing a stove. 2 warm, cozy place: **sitte i k-en** sit in the chimney corner.

kak'l *-et* cackle, cackling.

kak'le *V -a/+-et* cackle.

kakler *pl of* **kak'kel**, *pr of* **kak'le**

kakofoni' *-en* cacophony.

kak'se *-n* rural big shot, bigwig; (big) landowner, proprietor.

ka'k/stryke *V infl as* **stryke** whip at the whipping post.

kak'tus *-en* cactus.

kakumina'l *A gram.* cacuminal, retroflex.

ka'l *-en dial.* rope, line used on ships.

kal.=**kalori(er)**

ka'la *-en bot.* 1 calla. 2 water arum.

kalabalikk' *-en* violent battle.

kalamite't *-en* calamity.

kala's *-et, pl -/+-er* big (often a bit unrestrained) party, celebration.

kal'cium *-et* cf **kalsium**

kal'd *A* 1 (of temperature) cold; frigid: **k-t og surt** bitter c-; **k-t/bord** buffet (lunch), *smørgåsbord*; **den k-e**

+ Bokmål; * Nynorsk; ° Dialect.
After letter: ' stress (Acc. 1); ` tone, stress (Acc. 2); · length.
Below letter: . not pronounced.

sone the f- zone; **det ble k-ere i været** the weather grew c-er; **jeg er k- på hendene** my hands are c-. 2 (of person) cold, cool, reserved: **med k-t blod** in cold blood; **holde hodet k-t** keep a cool head; **slå k-t vatn i blodet** cool off (emotions); **k-t vesen** cold manner.

kal'ḍ/bit *-en* cold chisel.

kal'ḍ/blodig [also -blo'-] *A* - cool, composed; (of animals) coldblooded.

+kal'ḍblodig/het [also -blo'-] *-en* coolness, composure.

***kal'de** *-n* cf **kulde**

+kalde'er *-en, pl -e* (=***-ar**) Chaldean.

kalde'isk *A* - Chaldean.

kal'ḍ/flir *-en/+-et* derisive laugh, sneer.

kal'ḍ/flire *V -te* laugh or smile derisively, scornfully.

kal'ḍ/front *-en meteor.* cold front.

kal'ḍ/graut *-en* cold porridge.

***kal'ḍ/hjelm** *-en* cold shiver, feeling of fright.

kal'ḍ/klok *A* coldly calculating.

kal'ḍlig *A* - frightening, unpleasant.

***kal'ḍne** *V -a* cf **kolne**

+kal'ḍ/røyke *V -te* (=***-je**) draw on an unlighted pipe.

kal'ḍslig *A* - 1 cool. 2 creepy, unpleasant.

kal'ḍ/start *-en* cold start (of car).

+kal'ḍ/svette[1] *-n* (=***/sveitte**) clamminess, cold sweat.

+kal'ḍ/svette[2] *V -a/-et* (=***/sveitte**) be in a cold sweat.

***kal'ḍ/tokka** *A* - creepy, unpleasant.

***kal'ḍ/tokke** *-n* shudder, feeling of loathing or fear.

kal'ḍ/voren [*/våren] *A +-ent/*-e/*-i, pl -ne* chilly, cool.

kaleidosko'p *-et, pl -/+-er* kaleidoscope.

kaleidosko'pisk *A* - kaleidoscopic.

***ka'len** *A -e/-i, pl -ne* 1 chilled, numb with cold. 2 frozen, touched by frost.

kalen'der *-eren, pl -rer/+-er* almanac, calendar.

+kalen'der/måned *-en* (=***/månad**) calendar month.

kalen'der/år *-et* calendar year.

kalesj'e *+-n/*-a* 1 calash (a buggy). 2 (folding) top (of baby carriage, buggy, convertible, etc.); *(Brit.)* hood.

kalesj'e/vogn [/vångn] *-a* calash, calèche (light carriage with a folding top).

kalfa'tre *V -a/+-et naut.* caulk.

ka'li *-en/-et* potash.

kali'ber *-en/-et* caliber.

kalibre're *V -te* calibrate.

kalif' *-en* caliph.

kalifa't *-et* caliphate.

+kalifor'nier *-en, pl -e* (=***-ar**) Californian.

kalifor'nisk *A* - Californian.

ka'lium *-et* potassium.

ka'lium/karbona't *-et* potassium carbonate.

kal'k[1] *-en* 1 chalice, cup: *bibl.* **la denne k- gå meg forbi** let this cup pass from me (Math. 26,39). 2 *bot.* calyx.

kal'k[2] *-en* 1 lime, calcium carbonate. 2 mortar, plaster, whitewash: **hvit som k-** white as chalk.

kal'k/brott *-et* (=**+/brudd**) limestone quarry.

+kal'ke[1] *-n* 1 tracing. 2 fresco painting.

kal'ke[2] *V -a/+-et* 1 whitewash: **k-et grav** whited sepulchre; **hvit som en k-et vegg** chalk-white. 2 lime (a field etc.). 3 treat a hide with lime to remove hair.

kalke're *V -te* trace; calque, copy: **k- over levende modell** base (characters) on living models.

kalke'ring *-a/+-en* tracing; (slavish) copy (av of).

kalke'r/papi'r *-et* tracing paper.

kal'k/grav *-a* limestone quarry.

+kal'k/holdig *A* - (=***/haldig**) containing lime.

+kal'k/maleri' *-et* dry fresco, secco.

kal'k/omn *-en* (=**+/ovn**) limekiln.

kal'k/stein *-en* limestone.

kalkulasjo'n *-en* calculation, estimate: *merc.* **k-s/bok** seller's (own) price list; **k-s/pris** cost price.

kalkule're *V -te* calculate, estimate, figure.

kalku'n *-en* turkey.

kalku'nsk *A* - turkey: **stram som en k- hane** stuck-up as a t- cock.

kalky'le *-n* calculation, computation; estimate.

kall'[1] *-en* 1 (old) fellow, (old) man; husband. 2 *dial.* old tree (often with broken or cut-off top).

kall'[2] *-en* vertical axle on old-style mill wheel.

kall'[3] *-et* 1 call; calling, mission; challenge: **følg k-et** follow the call (Wergeland); **mitt k- er ei å svare** it is not my call to answer (Ibsen). 2 vocation: **sjømannens k-** the sailor's v-. 3 parish: **søke et k-** apply for a living.

+kal'la *-en* cf **kala**

kal'le *V +kalte/*-a* 1 call=cry, shout (usu. with **på**): **jeg k-te på ham** I called (to) him. 2 call=summon: **la ham k-** have him c-ed; **k- bort** s- (to one's death); **k- fram** c- forth (to a stage); **k- heim** s- home; **k- inn** c- in, s-; **k- sammen (et møte)** c- (a meeting); **k- til** appoint, name (e.g. as minister, professor); **være kalt til** be c-ed as (by fate or divine will); **k- en til regnskap** c- sby to account; **k- en til live** bring back to life; **jeg k-er Gud til vitne** as God is my witness; **k- til våpen** c- to arms; **k- tilbake** retract. 3 call=name: **Gud k-te lyset dag** God c-ed the light day; **k- hunden for Passopp** c- the dog P-; **den k-es Nordstjernen** it is c-ed "the North Star"; **k- opp en etter hans bestefar** n- sby after his grandfather; ***berre ein småby å k-** just a village so to speak, as it were; *pop.* **k- en c-** sby a name.

+kal'lelse *-n* calling, vocation; call, summons; appointment (to a position).

kal'le/signal [/singna'l] *-et, pl -/+-er* (radio) call signal.

kalligrafe're *V -te* write in elegant style of penmanship.

kalligrafi' *-en* calligraphy.

kalligra'fisk *A* - calligraphic: **skrive k-** write with beautiful flourishes.

kall's/brev *-et* letter of appointment to a pastorate.

kall's/felle *-n* colleague.

kall's/kapella'n *-en* resident curate.

kall's/rett *-en* right to fill certain ecclesiastical positions.

kal'mus *-en* calamus, sweet flag.

kal'mus/rot *-a, pl +-røtter/*-røter* calamus root.

***ka'lne** *V -a* begin to decay, mold or rot.

kalori' *-en* calorie.

+kalori'/beho'v *-et* calorie requirement.

+kalori'/innhol'ḍ *-et* (=***/innhald**) calorie content.

kalosj'e *-n (pl)* galoshes, rubbers.

kalott' *-en* 1 calotte, skullcap. 2 pate, crown. 3 segment of a sphere; *arch.* interior of a dome or cupola.

+kal'sium *-et* calcium.

+kal'sium/fosfa't *-et* calcium phosphate.

+kal'te *pt of* **kalle**

kalu'n *-et* tripe.

kal'v *-en* 1 calf. 2 small island, glacier, or lake beside larger one. 3 wooden wedge used to fasten sod to roof. 4 entrance to salmon trap or the like.

kal'v/beint *A* - knock-kneed.

kal'v/bot *-a, pl -bøter* back of the knee.

kal've[1] *-n* calf (of leg, upper arm).

kal've[2] *V -a/+-et* 1 calve. 2: **k- seg** act frisky. 3 tip, capsize, topple over. 4 (of glacier) calve.

kal've/dans *-en* 1 caper. 2 veal jelly. 3 cold dish, like custard, of heat-thickened colostrum eaten with cinnamon and sugar.

kal've/file't *-en* veal steak.

kal've/kasting *-a/+-en* abortion: **smittsom k-** Bang's disease, brucellosis.

kal've/kjøtt *-et* (=***/kjøt**) veal.

kal've/kryss *-et* 1 lace kerchief worn by men in Louis XIV period. 2 jabot (frilled shirt front).

kal've/steik *-en* veal roast.

kal've/suss *-en* veal jelly.

kal'vet(e) *A* - awkward, calf-like.

kalvinis'me *-n* Calvinism.

kalvinis't *-en* Calvinist.

kalvinis'tisk *A* - Calvinistic.

kalvi'nsk *A* - Calvinistic.

kal'v/tung [/tong] *A* heavy with calf.

kam' *-men, pl -mer* 1 comb. 2 carding tool. 3 (on animal) comb, crest, ridge. 4 *tech.* row of teeth on gear wheel etc. 5 (of mountain, ocean wave) crest, ridge.

kam'/aksel *-en* camshaft.

***ka'mar** *-en* toilet.

kamaril'ja *-en* cabal, clique, group of private advisors.

***kam'b** *-en* cf **kam**

kam'bium *-iet, pl -ium* cambium.

kam'brisk *A* - *geol.* Cambrian.

kam'brium *-et geol.* Cambrian formation.

kamé *-en* cameo.

kame'l *-en* camel; dromedary.

kameleo'n *-en* chameleon.

+kameleo'n/aktig *A* - chameleonic; inconstant.

kame'lia *-en* camellia.

ka'mera *-et, pl +-er/*-* camera.

kameraderi' *-et* camaraderie.

ka'mera/mann *-en, pl -menn/*-menner* cameraman.

kamera't *-en* 1 companion, comrade, friend. 2 member of Communist party.

kamera't/skap *+-et/*-en* comradeship, friendship.

kamera'tslig *A* - friendly; informal.

kam'fer *+-en/*-et* camphor.

kam'fer/drops *-en/-et* camphor lozenges.

kam'fer/dråper *pl* camphorated spirits (cough medicine).

kam'fer/kiste *-a* storage chest made of camphor wood for protection against moths.

kam'fer/kule *-a* mothball.

kam'fre *V -a/+-et* camphorate.

kam'/ga'rn *-et* worsted (yarn).

kamil'le *-n* camomiles.

kamil'le/te *-en* camomile tea.

kami'n *-en* fireplace.

kami'n/hylle *-a* mantelpiece.

kami'n/skjerm *-en* fire screen.

kami'n/teppe *-t, pl +-r/*-* hearth rug.

kam'me *V -a/+-et* comb.

kam'mer *-eret, pl -er/+kamre* 1 chamber, small room (usu. bedroom). 2 *anat.* chamber (e.g. **hjerte/**). 3 public or government office (e.g. **toll/, politi/**). 4 division of a parliament (e.g. in France, Italy, etc.).

kam'mer/herre *-n* chamberlain (court official).

kam'mer/musikk' *-en* chamber music.

+kam'mer/pike *-a/-en* chambermaid.

kam'mers *-et, pl -/+-er* small side room (e.g. large closet, small bedroom, pantry, etc.): **ha oppgjør på k-et** have a scene (between man and wife) in private; **du skal få på k-et** you're going to catch it when we get home.

kam'mer/tone *-n mus.* concert pitch.

kam'p[1] *-en* 1 boulder. 2 round hilltop.

kam'p[2] *-en* 1 battle, fight; struggle: **k-en for tilværelsen** the s- for existence; **indre k-** inner s-; **blåse til k-** call to b-. 2 (sports) contest, match; game.

kampan'je *-n* campaign.

+kam'p/bered't *A* - ready for battle.

+kam'p/dyktig *A* - in fighting trim.

kampe're *V -te* camp, encamp; *fam.* live (temporarily).

kam'pe/stein *-en* boulder, huge rock.
kam'p/felle *-n* buddy, comrade-in-arms.
kam'p/glad *A -* eager to fight; ready to accept a challenge.
kam'p/gny *-et* clamor of battle, din.
kam'p/hane *-n* gamecock.
kam'p/lyst *+-en/*-a* fighting spirit, joy of battle, love of fighting.
kam'p/lysten *A +-ent, p l-ne* eager for battle, eager to fight.
kam'p/mora'l *-en* morale (of troops in battle).
kam'p/resulta't *-et* outcome (of sports event).
kam'p/rop *-et* battle cry.
+**kam're** *pl of* **kammer**
kamufla'sje *-n* camouflage.
kamufle're *V -te* camouflage.
ka'n[1] *-en* khan.
kan'[2] *pr of* **kunne**
Ka'naan *Pln* Canaan: **K-s Land** the Land of C-.
kanaanitt' *-en* Canaanite.
+**kana'dier** *-en, pl -e* (=***-ar**) Canadian.
kana'disk *A -* Canadian.
kana'l *-en* 1 canal, channel; (in house) duct; (underground) sewer. 2 *fig.* channel: **gjennom offentlige k-er** through official c-s.
Kana'len *df* The (English) Channel.
kanalise're *V -te* 1 *tech.* canalize. 2 *fig.* channel.
kanal'je *-n* rascal, rogue, scamp.
kanapé *-en* 1 settee: **k-bord** table used in front of s-. 2 canapé.
kana'ri/fugl *-en* canary.
kana'risk *A -* pertaining to the Canary Islands.
+**Kana'ri/øyene** *Pln* (=***/øyane**) the Canary Islands.
kand. =**kandidat**
kandela'ber *-eren, pl -rer/+-ere* candelabrum.
kandida't *-en* 1 (political etc.) candidate (**til** for). 2 graduate (of higher institution of learning), abbr. **cand.**: **filologisk k-** graduate in letters; **medisinsk k-** graduate in medicine, etc.
kandidatu'r *-en/-et* candidacy.
kan'dis *-en* 1 brown sugar lump, sugar candy. 2 *fam.* noggin.
kandise're *V -te* candy.
kan'dis/sukker [/sokker] *-et* sugar candy.
ka'ne *+-en/*-a* 1 sleigh. *2 bowl with handles on both sides.
ka'ne/fart *-en* sleigh ride (party).
kane'l *-en* cinnamon.
kanevas [kan'neva] *-en/-et* (=+**kanvas**) (embroidery) canvas.
kan'evas/nål *-a* canvas (tapestry) needle.
kang'/kang [also kangkang'] *-en* cancan.
+**kanhen'de** *Av* cf **hende**[3]
kani'n *-en* rabbit.
***kan'nast** *V -ast*: **k- ved (med)** own to, acknowledge as one's own.
kan'ne[1] *-a* 1 can; pot; tankard. 2 *hist.* unit of measure=2 liters.
***kan'ne**[2] *V -a* 1 acknowledge, claim, own to. 2 check, count.
kannele're *V -te* channel, flute, groove.
kannely're *-n* channeling, fluting, groove(s) (as on fluted pillar).
+**kan'ne/støper** *-en, pl -e* (=***/støypar**) 1 pewterer. 2 *fig.*: **politisk k-** armchair politician (from Holberg's play **Den politiske k-**).
+**kan'ne/støperi'** *-et* 1 pewterer's shop. 2 armchair politics.
kanniba'l *-en* cannibal.
kannibalis'me *-n* cannibalism.
kanniba'lsk *A -* cannibal.
kan'nik *-en eccl.* canon (person).
***kan'ning** *-a* 1: **ha k- på** have knowledge of. 2 estimate.
ka'no *-en* canoe.
kano'n[1] *-en mil.* cannon, (big) gun.
ka'non[2] *-en* 1 *eccl.* canon (law, rule, etc.). 2 *mus.* canon, round.
kano'n[3] *Av*: **k- full** dead-drunk.
kanona'de *-n* cannonade.
kano'n/båt *-en* gunboat.
kanone'r *-en, pl -er* gunnery officer (of ensign rank).
kano'n/fotogra'f *-en* "instant" photographer.
kano'n/føde [*/føe] *-a/+-en* cannon fodder.
kanonise're *V -te eccl., fig.* canonize.
kano'nisk *A -* canonical.
kano'n/kule *-a* cannonball.
kano'n/port [/port] *-en* gunport.
kano'n/skott *-et* (=+**/skudd**) cannon shot.
+**kano'n/torden** [/torden] *-en* thunder of cannons.
kanos'sa/gang *-en* humiliating ordeal, self-abasement, eating humble pie.
***kan's** *-en archaic* chance, opportunity.
kanselli' *-et, pl +-er/*-* *hist.* chancery (government administrative office).
kanselli'/språk *-et* official jargon; officialese.
kanselli'/stil *-en* official or formal style; officialese.
kan'skje *Av* perhaps, maybe: **er De tørst k-?** p- you are thirsty?; **k- blir vi ferdige med denne ordboka en gang** m- we'll finish this dictionary sometime.
+**kan'sler** *-en, pl -e* (=***-ar**) chancellor.
kan't *-en* 1 edge; border, edging, rim: **på k-en av stupet** on the r- of the precipice; **ti meter på hver k-** ten meters square; **en krave med k- av kaninskinn** a collar with an edging of rabbit fur. 2 corner (=projecting edge); *fig.* (of character) sharp corner, offensive quality: **runde av k-ene** round off the corners; **fin i k-en** of good quality. 3 (narrow) edge, side: **plankene var lagt k- i k-** the planks were laid s- by s-; **hatten er på k-** the hat is askew (cocked on one s-); **stå på k-** stand on its s-; *fig.* **han er på k- med sin bror** he has fallen out with his brother; **han er på en k-** he is tipsy. 4 direction, quarter; district, parts, region: **fra en annen k-** from another direction; **fra alle k-er** from all directions; **på alle k-er** on all sides, everywhere; **en annen k- av bygda** another part of the valley; **på disse k-er** in this district, in these parts; **hver på sin k-** each in his place, each for his part.
kantarell' *-en bot.* chanterelle (mushroom).
kanta'te *-n/*-a mus.* cantata.
kan'te[1] *V -a/+-et* edge, trim.
kan'te[2] *V -a/+-et* roll over, tumble; tip up on end.
kan'te/band *-et* (=+**/bånd**) edging, piping; tape.
kan'te/stein *-en* stone used in edging; curbstone.
kan'tet(e) *A -* 1 edged, sided. 2 angular, bony, sharp. 3 *fig.* rough, tactless, unpolished.
kanti'ne *-a/-en* 1 *mil.* partitioned chest for field kitchen. 2 canteen.
kanto'n *-en* canton.
kan'tor[1] *-en* cantor; precentor.
°**kanto'r**[2] *-et* cf **kontor**
kan'tre *V -a/+-et* capsize, roll over, tip; (of tide) turn.
+**kan't/sette** *V -satte, -satt* (=***/setje**) edge with stone.
kanutt' *-en* rogue, scoundrel.
kan'vas *-en/-et* cf **kanevas**
ka'os *-et* chaos.
kao'tisk *A -* chaotic.
kap. =**kapittel**
kapa'bel *A -elt, pl -le* capable (**til** of): **en k- arbeider** a c- worker.
kapasite't *-en* 1 capacity. 2 expert. 3 *tech.* capacitance.
kapell' *-et, pl -/+-er* 1 chapel. 2 orchestra (usu. connected with a theater or restaurant).
kapella'n *-en* curate, chaplain.
kapellani' *-et, pl +-er/*-* curacy, chaplaincy.
+**kapell'/mester** *-en, pl -e* (=***/meister**) orchestra conductor.
ka'per *-en, pl +-e hist.* privateer.
ka'pers *-en* capers.
ka'per/skip *-et hist.* privateer.
kapilla'r *-et, pl -/+-er* capillary.
kapilla'r/kraft *-a/+-en* capillary force.
kapilla'r/rør *-et/*-a* (=***/røyr**) capillary tube.
kapillæ'r *A* capillary.
kapita'l[1] *-en* 1 *merc., typog.* capital. 2 *merc.* principal (sum): **k- og renter** p- and interest.
kapita'l[2] *A* cardinal, chief, major: **en k- feil** a colossal error.
kapita'l/flukt *-a/+-en* flight of capital from a country.
kapitalise're *V -te merc.* capitalize (convert a periodic payment into an equivalent capital sum).
kapitalis'me *-n* capitalism.
kapitalis't *-en* capitalist.
kapitalis'tisk *A -* capitalistic.
kapita'l/sterk *A* having a large amount of capital.
kapitél[1] *-et, pl -/+-er* 1 *arch.* capital. 2 capital letter of same height as small letters (antique type).
+**kapit'el**[2] *-elet, pl -ler* cf **kapittel**
kapit'tel *-elet/kapitlet, pl -el/+kapitler* 1 chapter. 2 subject: **det er et k- for seg** that's a separate s-, a case in itself, another story; **han ville ikke inn på det k-** he didn't want to discuss that matter. 3 *eccl.* chapter; chapter house.
kapitulasjo'n *-en* capitulation, surrender.
kapitule're *V -te* capitulate, surrender.
kap'lak' *-en naut.* primage.
kapp'[1] *-en* (of a plank) short piece, stub end.
kapp'[2] *-et* cape, headland, promontory.
kapp'[3] *N*: **om k- (med)** (also **i k-**) in competition (with); **løpe (ro, seile) om k-** run (row, sail) a race.
***kap'past** *V -ast* cf **kappes**
***kap'pe**[1] *-n* fighter, hero.
kap'pe[2] *-a* 1 (woman's) cap (for dusting, sleeping, etc.). 2 cape, cloak; (academic) gown: **ta på sin egen k-** shoulder alone (Evensmo); **bære k-n på begge skuldrer** stay on good terms with both sides. 3 valance. 4 (on shoe) counter. 5 *mil.* jacket (on gun). 6 *naut.* companion, hood. 7 *zool.* mantle.
kap'pe[3] *V -a/+-et* cut (**av** off), cut loose.
kap'pe[4] *V -a/+-et* compete, race.
kap'pe/lyst *-a/+-en* competitive spirit.
+**kap'pes** *V kaptes, har kappes* (=***kappast**) compete, contend, vie (**med** with).
kap'pe/strid *-en* competition, contest, rivalry.
kapp'/ete *V infl as* **ete** compete in eating (see who can eat the fastest or most).
***kapp'/fus** *A* competitive.
kapp'/gang *-en* walking race.
***kapp'/gangar** *-en* cf **/gjenger**
+**kapp'/gikk** *pt of* **-gå**
***kapp'/gjekk** *pt of* **-gå**
+**kapp'/gjenger** *-en, pl -e* (=***/gangar**) walker (participant in a walking race).
kapp'/gå *V infl as* **gå**[1] compete in a walking race.
***kapp'/hug** *-en* competitive spirit.
Kapp'/landet *Pln* Cape Colony.
***kapp'/laup** *-et* cf **/løp**
kapp'/leik *-en* contest.
+**kapp'/løp** *-et* (foot)race.
kapp'/roing *-a/+-en* (=+**roning**) rowing regatta.

+ Bokmål; * Nynorsk; ° Dialect.
After letter: ' stress (Acc. 1); ` tone, stress (Acc. 2); · length.
Below letter: . not pronounced.

kapp'/ruste *V* *-a/+-et* compete in armaments.

kapp'/rustning *-a/+-en* arms race.

kapp'/sag *-a* crosscut saw.

+**kapp'/seila's** *-en* regatta, sailing race.

+**kapp'/seise** *V* *-te* cf **kap/**

kapp'/springe *V* *infl as* **springe** run a race.

Kapp'/staden *Pln* Cape Town.

kapp'/åt *pt of* **/ete**

ka'pre *V* *-a/+-et* capture, grab, seize; get hold of: **det lyktes ham å k- en drosje** he succeeded in getting hold of a taxi.

+**kaprifo'lium** *-ien, pl -ier* (=**kaprifol**) *bot.* honeysuckle, woodbine (Lonicera periclymenum).

kapri'se *-n* 1 caprice, whim; capriciousness. 2 *mus.* capriccio.

kaprisiø's *A* capricious.

kap'/seise *V* *-te* capsize; tip over.

kap'sel *-elen, pl -ler* 1 *pharm., anat.* capsule. 2 watch case; cover. 3 locket. 4 bottle cap, seal. 5 *tech.* metal guard on machine. 6 *bot.* bur, capsule, husk.

kap'sle *V* *-a/+-et* 1 cap (bottle, flask, etc.). 2 encapsulate. 3 administer medicine (in capsule form) to animals.

kapt. =**kaptein**

kaptei'n *-en* 1 captain (of ship team). 2 (rank) captain (=U.S. army captain, air force lieutenant).

kaptei'n/løytnant *-en* naval rank between **løytnant** and **orlogskaptein** (=U.S. lieutenant commander).

+**kap'tes** *pt of* **kappes**

kapu'n *-en* capon.

+**kapusi'ner** *-en, pl -e* (=***-ar, *kapusin**) 1 Capuchin (friar). 2 capuchin monkey.

+**kapusi'ner/munk** [/mongk] *-en* (=***-ar/**) Capuchin friar.

kaputt' *A* - kaput, worn out.

ka'r[1] *-en* 1 man: **full k-** grown m-; **k- om å** m- enough to. 2 fellow, guy: **jeg kjenner k-en** I know the f-. 3 he-man, real man; big shot: **bli k- igjen** feel like a new man; **være k- for noe** be just the man to do sth; **han er k- for sin hatt** he can hold his own; **det koster å være k-** it's expensive to be a big shot. 4 hired hand, servant.

kar'[2] *-et* 1 container, vessel; tub, vat. 2 (salmon) trap. 3 pier (of bridge).

karabi'n *-en* carbine.

karaf'fel *-elen, pl karafler* carafe, decanter.

karakte'r *-en, pl -er* character, nature; characteristic: **landskap uten k-** landscape without distinctive features. 2 person with steadfast, mature character. 3 grade, mark: **gode k-er** good m-s.

karakte'r/ansikt *-et* distinctive face, face full of character.

karakte'r/bok *-a, pl -bøker* report card (in book form).

karakte'r/dannende *A* - (=***/danande**) character forming.

karakte'r/danning *-a/+-en* (=**+/dannelse, */daning**) character formation.

+**karakte'r/egenskap** *-en* characteristic, quality, trait.

karakte'r/fast *A* - having strong character, principled.

karakterise're *V* *-te* characterize.

karakteristikk' *-en* 1 characterization. 2 *math.* characteristic.

karakteris'tikon *-et, pl -ka* characteristic.

karakteris'tisk *A* - 1 characteristic, distinctive: **det k-e ved** the d- feature of. 2 typical (for of).

karakte'r/laus *A* (=**+/løs**) irresponsible, lacking in character, weak.

***karakte'r/lyte** *-t* flaw in (one's) character.

+**karakte'r/løs** *A* cf **/laus**

+**karakte'rløs/het** *-en* lack of character, weakness.

karakte'r/løyse *-a* lack of character, weakness.

karakte'r/rolle *-a/+-en* character part.

+**karakte'r/skuespil'ler** *-en, pl -e* (=***/skodespelar**) character actor.

karakte'r/studie *-n* character study.

karakte'r/styrke *-n* strength of character.

karakte'r/svak *A* weak (in character).

+**karakte'r/trekk** *-et* feature, trait (of character).

karaku'l/sau *-en* karakul sheep.

karambola'sj(e) *-en* 1 carom. 2 clash: **komme i k- med en** have a disagreement, fall out with sby.

karambole're *V* *-te* 1 carom. 2 clash.

karamell' *-en* 1 caramel. 2 caramelized sugar.

karamell'/pudding *-en* caramel pudding.

karante'ne *-n* quarantine; isolation.

karante'ne/flagg *-et* quarantine flag.

Ka'rasjok' *Pln* town, Finnmark.

kara't *-en, pl* - 1 carat. 2 *fig.* glitter of gold.

karava'ne *-n* caravan.

karavell' *-en* cf **kravell**

kar'/bad *-et* tub bath.

karbi'd *-en/-et* carbide.

karbo'l *-en* carbolic acid.

karbo'l/syre *-a* carbolic acid.

karbona'de *-n* 1 meat patty. 2 ground meat for meat patty.

karbona'de/kake *-a* hamburger, meat patty.

karbona't *-et* carbonate.

karbon/papi'r [karbång'/] *-et* carbon paper.

karborun'dum [also -run'-] *-en/-et* carborundum.

karbura'tor *-en* carburetor.

kardang' *-en* universal joint.

kardang'/aksel *-elen, pl -ler* drive shaft (with universal joint).

kardan'sk *A* - *tech.* cardanic (of suspension in gimbals).

ka'rde[1] *-a/-en* card, carding comb.

ka'rde[2] *V* *-a/+-et* card (wool, cotton, etc.).

***ka'rde/borre** *-a* cf **kare/**

kardemom'me *-n* cardamom.

+**kardes'k** *-en* (=***kardeske**) grapeshot.

kardialgi' *-en* cardialgia, heartburn.

kardina'l *-en* 1 *eccl.* cardinal. 2 cardinal (bird).

kardina'l/dyd *-en* cardinal virtue; chief virtue.

kardina'l/punkt [/pongt] *-et* crucial point, crux.

kardiogram' *-met, pl -/+-mer* cardiogram.

kardu's *-a/-en* 1 cartridge, cartouche. 2 tobacco. 3 *pop.* noggin.

kardu's/papi'r *-et* 1 cartridge paper. 2 grey packing paper.

ka're *V* *-a/+-et* 1 dig, poke; rake, scrape: **k- ut av pipa** clean out one's pipe; **k- sammen aska** rake the ashes together. 2: **k- seg** move slowly, with difficulty; **k- seg heim** mosey on home; **k- seg ut av senga** drag oneself out of bed.

+**ka're/borre** *-n* (=***karde/**) *bot.* teasel (Dipsacus).

+**kare'ler** *-en, pl -e* (=***-ar**) Karelian.

kare'lsk *A* - Karelian.

Ka'ren *Prn (f)*

kare't *-en* 1 coach. 2 *fig.*: **hele k-en** the whole shebang.

ka'r/folk *-et* menfolk, men.

karfun'kel *-elen, pl -ler* *archaic* red gem such as ruby or garnet.

***kar'g/hendt** *A* - stingy.

Ka'ri *Prn (f)*

kari'bisk *A* - Cariban, Caribbean.

ka'ries *-en* *med.* decay, as of bone or teeth.

karikatu'r *-en* caricature.

+**karikatu'r/tegner** [/teiner] *-en, pl -e* (=***/teiknar**) caricaturist, cartoonist.

karike're *V* *-te* caricature.

ka'ri/mess(e) *en* St. Catherine's day (November 25).

karjo'l *-en* cariole.

karjo'l/skyss *-en* cart ride.

Ka'rl *Prn (m)*

Ka'rls/vogna [/vångna] *Prn* *astron.* the Big Dipper.

Ka'rls/øy *Pln* twp, Troms.

kar'm *-en* 1 (window, door) frame; sill. 2 (wagon) box, sides. 3 back rest (on sleigh, chair, saddle). 4 *archaic* wagon.

ka'r/mann *-en, pl -menn/*-menner* man.

+**karmelit'ter/munk** *-en* (=***karmelitt/**) Carmelite friar.

karmi'n *-en* carmine.

+**karmi'n/rød** *A* (=***/raud**) carmine red.

karmosi'n/farge *-n* crimson color.

+**karmosi'n/rød** *A* (=***/raud**) crimson red.

kar'm/slede [*/sle'e] *-n* 1 wagon sleigh. 2 one-horse sleigh (with back rest).

kar'm/stol *-en* armchair with high back.

Kar'm/øy *Pln* large island near Haugesund (Rogaland).

karnapp' *-et, pl -/+-er* bay window.

ka'rneval *-et, pl -/+-er* 1 masquerade ball. 2 carnival.

karnøf'fel *-elen, pl karnøfler* 1 knave, scoundrel. 2 beating, dressing down; slap.

karnøf'le *V* *-a/+-et* beat, pummel; dress down: **k-es (med)** fight (with).

karoli'n *-en* 1 early Swedish or German coin. 2 soldier in Charles XII's army (Sweden).

+**karoling'er** *-en, pl -e* (=***-ar**) Carolingian.

karoling'isk *A* - Carolingian.

karoli'nsk *A* - Caroline, Carolinian.

karosseri' *-et, pl +-er/*-* body (of a motor vehicle).

kar'pe *+-n/*-a* carp.

karré *-en* square (formation of e.g. buildings or soldiers).

+**kar're**[1] *V* *-a/-et* cf **kare**

kar're[2] *V* *-a/+-et* *dial.* coo; trill (an r).

kar'ri *-en* curry (powder, sauce); curry.

karriere [kariæ're] *-n* 1 run: **i full k-** at a r-, at a gallop. 2 career (life work).

+**kar'rig** *A* - (=***karg**) 1 miserly, stingy. 2 meager, scanty.

+**kar'rig/het** *-en* unproductiveness (of soil).

kar'ri/saus *-en* curry sauce.

kar'se *-n* cress.

kar'sk[1] *-en* coffee royal (coffee and brandy drink).

kar'sk[2] *A* *-t/*-* healthy, well; bold: **k- og sunn** hale and hearty.

ka'rslig *A* - mannish, like a man.

kar'spore/plante *+-a/-en* pteridophyte.

ka'rs/stykke *-t, pl +-r/*-* feat, stunt; manly deed.

Kar'sten *Prn (m)*

kar't[1] *-en* unripe berry or fruit: **eple/** green apple; *fig.* **ikke si det til en k-** don't tell a soul.

kar't[2] *-et, pl -/+-er* 1 map. 2 chart. 3 agenda; list: **spise/k-** menu; **vin/k-** wine l-.

kar't[3] *-et* gnarl, knot, protuberance.

+**karta'ger** *-en, pl -e* (=***-ar**) Carthaginian.

karta'gisk *A* - Carthaginian.

Karta'go *Pln* Carthage.

kar'te *V* *-a/+-et* start forming fruit.

kartell' *-et, pl -/+-er* cartel.

karte're *V* *-te* check, register (mail, baggage, freight).

+**kar't/legge** *V* *-la, -lagt* (=***-je**) chart, map.

kar't/lesing *-a/+-en* map reading.

+**kar't/negl** [/neil] *-en* (=***/nagl**) malformed fingernail or toenail.

+**kartof'fel** *-elen, pl kartofler* *lit., archaic* potato.

kartogra'f *-en* cartographer.

kartone're *V* *-te* bind (book) in paper boards.

kartong' *-en* 1 thin cardboard, pasteboard. 2 carton. 3 paper board (cardboard book cover). 4 sketch (for mural etc.).

kartote'k *-et, pl -/+-er* card file (index): **føre k- over** keep a file of.
kartote'k/kort *-et* file (index) card.
kartote'k/skap *-et* filing cabinet.
kar't/verk *-et* 1 series of maps or charts of a given area. 2 mapmaking agency.
karusell' *-en* merry-go-round.
karuss' *-en zool.* crucian carp (Cyprinus carossius).
kar've[1] *-n* 1 caraway. 2 *hist.* merchant ship.
kar've[2] *V -a/+-et* 1 carve. 2 cut, shred: **k-a blad** s-ded tobacco.
kar've/akevitt· *-en* caraway-flavored aquavit.
kar've/kål *-en* young caraway sprouts, used in a soup.
kar've/stokk *-en hist.* tally (stick).
ka's *-a* (=**kase**[1]) 1 heap, pile; shock (of grain). 2 burned-over land, used for field.
ka'se[1] *-n* cf **kas**
ka'se[2] *V -a/+-et/+-te* 1 pile up, place in a heap. 2 bury under a pile of stones.
kasein [kase-i'n] *-et/+-en* casein.
kasematt' *-en mil.* casemate.
ka'sen *A +-ent, pl -ne* 1 tainted, not fresh (e.g. fish). 2 faint, weak, worn-out.
***ka'ser** *pl of* **kos**[2]
kaserne [kasæ'rne] *-n* 1 barracks. 2 tenement house.
kasi'no *-et, pl +-er/*-* casino.
kasjmi'r *+-en/*-et* cashmere (cloth).
kasjmi'r/ull *-a* cashmere wool.
kasjott' *-en* (prison) cell.
°**kas'k** *-en* cf **karsk**[1]
kaska'de *-n* cascade.
kaskelott' *-en* sperm whale.
kaskjett' *-en* (visored) cap.
kas'ko *-en* 1 insured vehicle (e.g. ship, plane, car). 2 (short for **k-forsikring**).
+**kas'ko/forsik·ring** *-en* car, plane, ship insurance against damage (does not cover cargo); hull insurance (on waterborne or airborne craft).
***kas'ko/trygding** *-a* =**kaskoforsikring.**
Kas'pi/havet *Pln* the Caspian Sea.
kas'pisk *A -* Caspian: **Det k-e hav** The C- (Sea).
kass' *-en* pack basket (carried on the back).
kas'sa- *pl* cf **kasse-**
kas'sa/appara·t *-et* cash register.
+**kas'sa/behol·dning** *-en* cf **kasse/**
kassa'bel *A -elt, pl -le* ready for the scrap heap, worn-out.
kas'sa/bok *-a, pl -bøker* cf **kasse/**
kas'sa/konto *-en* cash account.
kas'sa/kreditt· *-en* cf **kasse/**
kassasjo'n *-en* 1 dismissal, rejection. 2 cancellation; *jur.* reversal, setting aside. 3 *mil.* demotion; dishonorable discharge.
kassasjo'ns/rett *-en* court of appeal.
kas'se *-a/-en* 1 box: **en k- bøker** a b- of books. 2 case, casing: **en k- øl** a case of beer; **ur/** watchcase. 3 crate (also *derog.* of ship, car, building, etc.). 4 cashbox, till: **være pr. k-** have money in the t-; **hun er i k-n** she is in the cashier's window (in the box office); **fylle k-n** (of plays) draw a good box office; **gjøre opp k-n** balance the cash. 5 fund; treasury: **fattigk-a** poor relief; **sykek-a** sick funds; **det går i statens k-** it goes to the state t-.
kas'se/appara·t[1] *-et* box camera.
kas'se/appara·t[2] *-et* cf **kassa/**
+**kas'se/bedrø·ver** *-en, pl -e* embezzler.
+**kas'se/behol·dning** *-en* cash on hand, cash balance.
kas'se/bok *-a, pl -bøker* cashbook.
kas'se/kreditt· *-en* line of credit.
kas'se/manko *-en* deficit, shortage.
kasse're[1] *V -te* cash: **k- inn penger** receive money.
kasse're[2] *V -te* 1 destroy, discard, scrap; reject (a proposal). 2 cancel; *jur.* reverse, set aside. 3 *mil.* cashier, reduce (in rank).
+**kasse'rer** *-en, pl -e* (=***-ar**) cashier, paymaster, treasurer.
+**kasse'rerske** *-a/-en* (female) cashier.
kasserol'l(e) *-(e)n* saucepan.
***kas'se/styrar** *-en* cashier.
kassett' *-en* 1 *arch.* coffer. 2 *photog.* film or plate holder. 3 small treasure chest.
kas't *-et* 1 cast, fling, throw (of ball, dice, stones, fishing gear, etc.); (in sports) throwing (e.g. the discus); (in knitting) loop: **gjøre et godt k-** make a success of sth (a big haul). 2 jerk, toss: **et k- med hodet** a t- of the head; **et k- i dansen** a leap in the dance. 3 (of wind) gust, squall. 4 fight, struggle: **gi seg i k- med** grapple with, tackle (usu. *fig.*), take hold of. 5 (of garment) throw. *6 wall cupboard (usu. with hole in door, used for toilet articles).
kastan'je *-n* chestnut, horse chestnut: **rake k-ene ut av ilden for en** be sby's cat's-paw.
kastan'je/brun *A* chestnut brown.
kastanjett' *-en* castanet.
kas'te[1] *-n* caste, class.
kas'te[2] *V -a/+-et* 1 throw (**på** at, on); pitch, play (ball); bowl (in cricket); toss: **k- på stikka** throw coins at small stick or line on ground (children's game). 2 throw away: **vi k-a alt vi kunne** we threw away everything we could; **k- et kort** discard; **k- jakka** take off one's jacket. 3 cast (anchor, a glance, fishing gear, lots, pearls before swine, shadow, etc.): **k- etter laks** c- for salmon. 4 lose (leaves, hair), shed; **k- vannet** urinate; **k- hvalper** whelp; **k- kalven** (of a cow) lose the calf. 5 gust: **vinden k-er** the wind g-s. 6 defeat for reelection: **han ble k-et som ordfører** he was d-ed for mayor. 7: **k- seg** toss (e.g. in bed); (of wood) warp; throw oneself; **k- seg bort** throw oneself away (on sby); **k- seg om halsen på en** fall on sby's neck; **k- seg over en** attack, fall upon sby; **k- seg over noe** plunge into sth, throw oneself into sth; **k- seg på kne** fall on one's knees; **k- seg ut** jump out, let oneself fall. 8 (other idioms): **k- av seg** yield a profit; **k- av seg klærne** tear off (toss) one's clothes; **k- bort** throw away, waste (time); **k- glans over noe** lend glory to sth; **k- i fengsel** throw into prison; **k- igjen (en grav)** close (a grave); **k- loss** cast off; **k- med** (snowballs, stones, balls, etc.) throw; **k- om** change direction or manner, turn around suddenly; **k- opp** vomit; **k- opp (en haug)** spade up (a pile of dirt); **k- over** baste, overcast (sewing); **k- (bilen) over** swing (the car) suddenly; **k- (noen) på dør** throw (sby) out; **k- på nakken** toss one's head; **k- på seg** toss, (of horses) pitch; **k- på seg klærne** jump into one's clothes; **k- (skylden) på noen** lay (the blame) on sby; **k- sammen** baste, tack; **k- tilbake (et angrep)** repulse (an attack); **k- ut (en bemerkning)** toss off (a remark); **k- vekk** throw away; **k- vrak på** reject.
kas'te/ball *-en* ball (to play with); *fig.* object of sby's whims.
kas'te/bye *-a* (=+**/byge**) sudden gust, squall.
+**kas'te/bytte** *V -a/-et* (=***/byte**) make an even trade sight unseen.
kas'te/kjepp *-en* 1 throwing stick; *fig.* worthless, insignificant thing. 2 spineless, vacillating person.
kas'te/laus *A* pariah, untouchable.
kastell' *-et, pl -/+-er* 1 citadel, fortified castle. 2 *naut.* poop; forecastle on medieval warship.
+**-kas'telse** *-n* (throwing, casting): **under/** submission, subjection; **ut/** expulsion.
+**kas'te/løs** *A* cf **/laus**
kas'te/not *-a, pl -nøter* casting net.
kas'te/plagg *-et* (a garment) throw.
+**kas'ter** *-en, pl -e* (=***-ar**) caster, thrower.
kas'te/skyts *-et* high trajectory artillery, missile.
kas'te/sluk *-en* casting plug.
kas'te/sting *-et* whip stitch.
kas'tet(e) *A -* gusty, squally; changeable.
kas'te/tørkle *-et* throw.
kas'te/vind *-en* sudden gust.
+**kastilja'ner** *-en, pl -e* (=***-ar**) Castilian.
kastiljan'sk *A -* Castilian.
kastrasjo'n *-en* castration.
kastra't *-en* 1 eunuch; gelding. 2 castrato.
kastre're *V -te* castrate.
kasuis't *-en* casuist.
kasuistikk' *-en* casuistry.
kasuis'tisk *A -* casuistic.
ka'sus *-en, pl -* 1 *gram.* case. 2 case, incident (e.g. of a disease).
kat. =**katolsk**
katafal'k *-en* catafalque.
katakom'be *-n* catacomb.
+**katala'ner** *-en, pl -e* (=***katalan**) Catalonian.
katala'nsk *A -* Catalonian.
katalog [-lå'g] *-en* catalog.
katalogisere [katalågise're] *V -te* catalog.
katalog/pris [-lå'g/] *-en* list price.
katalysa'tor *-en* catalyst.
kataly'se *-n* catalysis.
katalyt'isk *A -* catalytic.
katapul't *-en* catapult.
katarak't *-en* cataract, falls.
katarr' *-en* catarrh.
katarra'lsk *A -* catarrhal.
katastrofa'l *A* catastrophic, disastrous.
katastro'fe *-n* catastrophe, disaster; climax, turning point.
katedra'l *-en* cathedral.
katedra'l/skole *-n* cathedral school; now used of certain public *gymnasia* in cities having a bishop's seat, going back to earlier c- s-s.
kategori' *-en* category, class, type.
katego'risk *A -* categorical.
kateke'se *-n* catechesis.
kateke't *-en* catechist.
katekisasjo'n *-en* catechization.
katekise're *V -te* catechize.
katekis'me *-a/+-en* catechism.
kate't *-en* leg of a right triangle.
kate'ter *-eret/-ret, pl -er/+-re* 1 lectern; teacher's desk. 2 *med.* catheter.
kato'de *-n* cathode.
kato'de/stråle *-n* cathode ray.
katolikk' *-en* (Roman) Catholic.
katolisis'me *-n* catholicism.
kato'lsk *A -* 1 Catholic. 2 catholic, universal. 3 *hum.*: **k- i hodet** crazy.
katri'ne/plomme [/plomme] *-a* French prune.
katt' *-en* 1 cat (Felis): **gå som k-en om den varme grøten** talk all around a subject (without coming to grips with it), avoid an embarrassing subject; **ikke en k-** not a soul; **han er ikke for k-en** he's not to be sneezed at; **ikke mere begrep om det enn k-en** no idea whatever (about sth); **kjøpe k-en i sekken** buy a pig in a poke; **i mørke er alle k-er grå** in the dark everything looks alike; **når k-en er borte, danser musene på bordet** when the cat's away, the mice will play; **som hund og k-** like cats and dogs. 2: **gi k-en i noe** not give a damn about sth. 3: **få k-en** *fam.* be dismissed, get the sack. 4 *naut.* cat (o'-nine-tails).
katt'/auga** *-et, pl -augo* (=/auge**) cf **/øye**
kat'te[1] *-a* cat, esp. female.

+ Bokmål; * Nynorsk; ° Dialect.
After letter: ' stress (Acc. 1); ` tone, stress (Acc. 2); · length.
Below letter: . not pronounced.

kat'te[2] *V -a/+-et* 1 whip with a cat-o'-nine-tails. 2 *naut.* hoist the anchor to the cathead. 3 expel, dismiss.
+**kat'te/aktig** *A* - catlike.
kat'te/blid *A* ingratiating.
+**kat'te/fjed** *-et lit.* cat's footfall: **på k-** stealthily.
kat'te/fot *-en, pl +-føtter/*-føter*: **gå på k-** pussyfoot.
Kat'te/gat' *Pln* Kattegat.
kat'te/hale *-n* 1 cat's tail. 2 *bot.* purple loosestrife (Lythrum salicaria).
kat'te/klo *-a, pl -klør* 1 cat's claw. 2 *dial. bot.* cat's-paw.
kat'te/mat *-en* cat food.
kat'te/musikk' *-en* calling of cats, caterwauling; cacophony, strident music.
+**kat'te/negl** [/neil] *-en* (=***/nagl**) malformed fingernail or toenail.
kat'te/pine *-a/+-en* dilemma, pinch, scrape: **være i k-** be in a pickle, in misery.
kat'te/pus *-en* pussycat.
kat'te/rygg *-en*: **skyte k-** arch one's back, hunch over.
kat'te/vask *-en* a lick and a promise, a quick wash.
katt'/ost [/ost] *-en bot.* mal ow (of malvaceae family).
katt'/ugle *-a zool.* tawny owl (Strix aluco).
kattu'n *-et* calico.
katt'/unge [/onge] *-n* kitten.
+**katt'/øye** *-t* 1 cat's eye. 2 reflector. 3 (gem) cat's-eye.
katzen/jammer [kat'sen/] *-en* 1 hangover. 2 caterwauling.
kau'der/velsk *-et* gibberish.
kau'e *V -a/+-et* call, cooey (to animals).
kauka'sisk *A* - Caucasian.
Kau'kasus *Pln* Caucasus.
kau'ke *V -a/+-et* call, cooey (to animals).
***kau'n** *-en* cf **kong**[1]
***kau'p** *-et* cf **kjøp**
kau'pang *-en hist.* market town.
***kau'pe** *V -te* cf **kjøpe**
kau'r *-en* ripple (on water).
kau're[1] *-n* 1 featherstick (stick whittled into curls along the edge, used for kindling). 2 curled lock (of hair).
kau're[2] *V -a/+-et* 1 curl. 2 whittle into curls. 3: **k- seg** grow and thrive.
kau'ret(e) *A* - curled, spiraled.
***kau's** *pt of* **kjose**
kausa'l *A* causal.
kausalite't *-en* causality.
***kau'se** *-n* 1 log. 2 big shot.
kausjo'n *-en jur.* bond, surety.
kausjone're *V -te jur.*: **k- for** endorse, guarantee, go surety for.
kausjonis't *-en jur.* endorser, guarantor, surety.
kau'stisk *A* - caustic.
kau't *A +-/*-t pop.* arrogant, haughty; proud.
kaute'l *-en/-et jur.* hold harmless clause; precaution, safeguard.
Kautokei'no [also kau'-] *Pln* twp, Finnmark.
kau'tsjuk *-en* caoutchouc, pure rubber.
ka'v[1] *-et* hustle and bustle; turmoil.
ka'v[2] *-et* 1 dense snowfall; heavy spray (from the sea). 2 *archaic* depths of the sea.
ka'v[3] *Av* completely: **k- drukken** dead drunk; **k- norsk** purely Norwegian.
kavai' *-en* greatcoat (old fashioned overcoat).
kavale'r *-en* 1 admirer, escort, partner (at table, at a dance). 2 *hist.* cavalier, gentleman; gentleman-in-waiting.
kavaleri' *-et* cavalry.
kavaleri'/sjokk *-et* cavalry charge.
kavaleris't *-en* cavalryman.
+**kavale'r/messig** *A* - gallant, gentlemanly.
kavalka'de *-n* cavalcade.
***ka'v/båt** *-en* submarine.
ka've[1] *-n* snowstorm.
ka've[2] *V -a/+-et/+-de* 1 flail, strike (the air, water); snatch (**etter** at). 2 paw, scrape. 3 struggle, toil. 4 flounder, swarm.
ka'vende *Av* completely: **k- råtten** rotten through and through.
kave're *V -te* guarantee, take responsibility for.
kave'rings/mann *-en, pl -menn/*-menner* 1 guarantor, sponsor. 2 best man (at wedding).
kaverne [kavæ'rne] *-n med.* cavern (in diseased tissue).
kavia'r *-en* caviar.
kav'l *-en* wooden float (on fishing net).
kav'le[1] *-n* 1 round stick of wood, wooden roller. 2 log used as bridge. 3 (of sea) roller: **fjordens blå k-r** the fjord's blue rollers (Bojer).
kav'le[2] *V -a/+-et*: **k- seg** (of sea) crest; form breakers, white caps.
kav'le[3] *V -a/+-et* attach wooden floats to fishing net.
kav'le/bru *-a* corduroy bridge (logs laid transversely).
kav'le/sjø *-en* choppy sea.
kav'let(e) *A* - choppy, whitecapped.
kav'ring *-en* rusk.
Kbh.=**København**
kedi'v *-en* khedive.
keeper [ki'per] *-en, pl +-e* goalkeeper, goalie.
ke'fir *-en* kefir (a kind of yoghurt).
ke'fir/mjølk *-a* (=+**/melk**) kefir milk.
ke'gel *-elen, pl -ler* (of printer's type) body size, point.
kei [kjei'] *A *-tt* (=+**kjed**) *pop.* fed up (**av** with): **lei og k- av** sick and tired of.
***keie** [kjei'e] *V -a* cf **kjede**[2]
keik[1] [kjei'k] *-en* curve; curvature of the spine.
***keik**[2] [kjei'k] *pt of* **kike**[3]
keik[3] [kjei'k] *A* bent backwards; rigid (in posture), strutting.
keike [kjei'ke] *V -a/+-te* 1 bend backwards. 2 wrangle. 3 *naut.* tack.
***keim** [kjei'm] *-en* disagreeable flavor.
keip [kjei'p] *-en* (=**keipe**) oarlock.
keipe [kjei'pe] *-a* cf **keip**
kei/sam [kjei'/] *A* boring, tiresome.
+**kei'ser** *-en, pl -e* (=***-ar**) emperor, kaiser: **gi k-en hva k-ens er** render unto Caesar the things that are Caesar's.
+**kei'ser/dømme** *-t* (=***-ar/**) empire.
+**keiserin'ne** *-a/-en* (=***-ar/**) empress.
+**kei'serlig** *A* - (=***keisarleg**) imperial.
+**kei'ser/snitt** *-et* (=***-ar/**) Caesarean (operation).
kei'tet(e) *A* - awkward, clumsy; shy.
+**kei'tet/het** *-en* aw wardness, clumsiness; gaucherie.
***keiv** [kjei'v] *A* askew, crooked, wrong.
keive[1] [kjei've] *-a* left hand.
keive[2] [kjei've] *V -a* 1: **k- skoen** wear a shoe down on the side. 2 make a crooked throw.
***keiveleg** [kjei'veleg] *A* - awkward, clumsy; gauche.
keivet(e) [kjei'vet(e)] *A* - *dial.* awkward.
keiv/hendt [kjei'v/] *A* - left-handed; awkward.
kel'ner *-en, pl +-e* waiter.
+**kel'ter** *-en, pl -e* (=***-ar,** ***kelt**) Celt.
kel'tisk *A* - Celtic.
°**kem'** *Pn* cf **hvem**
kem'ner *-en, pl +-e* city treasurer.
kenguru [keng'guru] *-en* kangaroo.
ken'nel *-en* kennel.
ken'nel/klubb *-en* kennel club.
kentau'r *-en* 1 centaur. 2 *astron.* Centaurus.
ke'p *-en* cape.
+**keramiker** [kjera'-] *-en, pl -e* (=***-ar**) ceramist, potter.
keramikk [kjeramikk'] *-en* ceramics; earthenware, pottery.
keramisk [kjera'-] *A* - ceramic.
KF=**Kristelig Folkeparti**
KFUK=**Kristelig forening for unge kvinner** Y.W.C.A.
KFUM=**Kristelig forening for unge menn** Y.M.C.A.
kg=**kilogram**
kgl.=**kongelig**
kgl. res.=**kongelig resolusjon**
kgm.=**kilogrammeter**
kib'be *V -a/+-et pop.* shove (**ut** out; **vekk** away, off); push (aside), throw (out); fire: **alkoholen var en gjøkunge som k-et alt annet av reiret** alcohol was a cuckoo which pushed everything else out of the nest (Sandemose).
+**kid** [kidd'] *-et* cf **kje**[1]
***kidling** [kjil'ling] *-en* cf **killing**
kid/nappe [kidd'/] *V -a/+-et* kidnap.
+**kid/napper** *-en, pl -e* (=***-ar**) kidnapper.
ki'k *-en/+-et* (=+**kikk**) 1 glimpse, peek: **få k- på** catch sight of, get a g- of; **være på k- etter** be on the lookout for. 2 whoop (cough). 3 sprain, twist, wrench.
***ki'kar** *-en* cf **kikkert**
+**ki'ke**[1] *V -te* (=***kikje**) whoop (cough).
ki'ke[2] *V -a/+-et* cf **kikke**
***ki'ke**[3] *V keik, kike/-i* cf **kikke**
***ki'kert** *-en* cf **kikkert**
ki'k/hol [/hål] *-et* peephole.
ki'k/hoste [/hoste] *-n* whooping cough.
***ki'kje** *V -te* cf **kike**[1]
+**kikk'** *-en/-et* cf **kik**
kik'ke *V -a/+-et* (=**kike**[2, 3]) peek, peep, peer: **k- etter** peek at, look for; **k- gjennom** look through (e.g. a manuscript); **k- innom** look in on, drop in.
kik'kert *-en* (=***kikar,** ***kikert**) spyglass, telescope; binoculars; field (opera) glasses.
kik'kert/sikte *-t* telescope sight.
+**kikk'/hull** *-et* cf **kik/hol**
ki'kne[1] *V -a/+-et* lose one's breath (from laughter, coughing, etc.).
ki'kne[2] *V -a/+-et* get a kink from bending or turning suddenly.
kik's *-en* (billiards) miscue.
kik'se *V -a/+-et* 1 (billiards) make a miscue. 2 play marbles.
kik'se/kule *-a* marble.
ki'l *-en* (=**kile**[1]) narrow bay.
+**kil'de** *-n* cf **kjelde**
+**kil'den** *A -ent, pl -ne* delicate, ticklish, touchy (subject, question, etc.).
+**kil'de/skrift** *-et* cf **kjelde/**
+**kil'de/vann** *-et* cf **kjelde/vatn**
+**kil'dre** *V -a/-et lit.* tickle.
ki'le[1] *-n* cf **kil**
ki'le[2] *-n* 1 wedge. 2 (in garment) gore, gusset. 3 cuneiform (writing). 4 (bowling) pin (=**kjegle**[1]).
ki'le[3] *V +-te/*-a* 1 wedge, drive (a) wedge: **k- seg fram** push, elbow one's way ahead. 2: **k- seg ut** taper off. 3 *pop.* dash, rush: **k- fram** d- ahead; **k- i veg** r- off; **k- på** r- on, hurry up; **k- på med arbeidet** plug away at the work.
ki'le[4] *V -te/*-a* tickle: **det k-er i halsen** my throat t-s.
ki'le/bane *-n* (=**kjegle/**) bowling alley.
ki'len *A +-ent, pl -ne* 1 ticklish. 2 *naut.* tippy, unstable.
ki'le/not *-a, pl -nøter* wedge-shaped weir.
ki'le/skrift *-a/+-en* cuneiform writing.
+**ki'le/spill** *-et* (=**kjegle/**) bowling, ninepins.
kilevin'k *-en* blow, slap on jaw or face.
kil'le *I* goat call.
kil'le/bukk [/bokk] *-en* kid, young billy goat.
kil'ling *-en* kid (baby goat).
ki'lo *-et/+-en* kilogram.
ki'lo/gram' *-met* kilogram (=ab. 2.2 lbs).
kilogramme'ter *-en, pl* - kilogrammeter (=ab. 7.2 foot-pounds).
ki'lo/meter *-en* kilometer (=0.62 mile).
ki'lo/watt *-en* kilowatt.
ki'lowatt/time *-n* kilowatt-hour.

kilt [kil't] *-en* kilt.
kil'tre *V -a/+-et* tuck (**opp** up) one's skirt.
ki'm *-en* (=**kime**[1]) 1 embryo, germ. 2 *lit.* seed.
ki'm/blad *-et* 1 cotyledon, embryonic leaf. 2 germ layer: **indre k-** endoderm.
+**kimbrer** [kim'brer] *-en, pl -e* (=***-ar**) Cimbrian.
kimbrisk [kim'brisk] *A* - Cimbrian.
ki'm/celle *-a/-en* germ cell.
ki'me[1] *-n* cf **kim**
ki'me[2] *V -a/+-et/+-te* ring repeatedly; chime, peal: **k- på dørklokken** ring insistently; **det k-er** the church bells are ringing.
ki'ming *-en* 1 horizon. 2 *naut.* projecting part of stern. 3 *naut.* roach (curve in edge of sail).
kimono [ki'mono] *-en* kimono.
kim'se *V -a/+-et*: **det er ikke å k- ad** it's not to be scorned, it's pretty good.
kimæ're *-n* chimera (also *bot., zool.*); fantasy, illusion.
Ki'na *Pln* cf **China**
ki'na/misjo'n *-en* the China mission.
kinematogra'f *-en* 1 *obs.* movie theater. 2 movie projector.
+**kine'ser** *-en, pl -e* (=***-ar**) Chinese.
+**kineserin'ne** *-a/-en* (=***-ar-**) Chinese woman.
kine'sisk *A* - Chinese.
kinestetisk [kineste'tisk] *A* - kinesthetic.
kine'tisk [ki-] *A* - kinetic.
king'el *-elen, pl -ler* 1 spider. 2 spider web.
king'el/vev *-en* spider web.
kini'n *-en* quinine.
kini'n/pille *-a/+-en* quinine pill.
kin'k *-en/+-et* kink, twist; jerk (of head).
kin'kig *A* - delicate, touchy: **spørsmålet er ytterst k-** it's an extremely t- question.
kin'ks *-en* flip, jerk, toss (of head).
kin'kse *V -a/+-*et jerk, toss (esp. the head).
kinn' *-et, pl -/+-er* 1 cheek. 2 *dial.* each of two vertical sides of sth, such as on doorjamb (**dør/**).
Kinn' *Pln* twp, Sogn og Fjordane.
kin'ne[1] *-a* (=+**kjerne**[2]) churn.
kin'ne[2] *V -a* (=+**kjerne**[3]) churn.
kinn'/hest *-en* slap (on the cheek); box (on the ear).
kinn'/skjegg *-et* mutton chop whiskers; sideburns.
kinn'/tann *-a, pl -tenner* molar.
***kin'nung** *-en* doorpost.
ki'no *-en* 1 movie (theater). 2 kino (reddish brown juice of certain tropical trees used for tanning etc.).
ki'no/billett' *-en* movie ticket.
+**ki'no/gjenger** *-en, pl -e* moviegoer.
ki'no/rekla'me *-n* movie ad.
Kin'sar/vik *Pln* twp, Hordaland.
kiosk [kjås'k] *-en* 1 kiosk, newsstand. 2 outdoor telephone booth. 3 garden pavilion.
ki'pe *-a* willow basket.
ki'pen *A +-ent, pl -ne* 1 boisterously happy, frisky, gay. 2: **k- på** crazy about, happy about.
ki'per *-eren, pl +-ere/*-rar* 1 twill (cloth). 2 *archaic* cooper.
***ki'pnast** *V -ast* be gay.
***ki'pne** *-a* cheerfulness, gaiety.
kipp' *-en/+-et* 1 flip; jerk. 2 flopping, slipping (of shoe). 3 blinking (of eye); snapping (of fish). 4 short-haul transportation.
kip'pe[1] *-t, pl +-r/*- dial.* 1 bundle of twigs. 2 piece of branch to string fish on.
kip'pe[2] *V kipte* 1 flip up; jerk. 2 dip (flag). 3 (of shoe) flop, slip up and down. 4 blink or snap repeatedly.
kippers [kip'pers] *-en* kippered herring.
kipp'/skodd [/skodd] *A -/*-skott* with shoes but no socks or stockings.
kip'te *pl of* **kippe**[2]

+**kir'ke** *-a/-en* (=+**kjerke**, ***kyrkje**[1]) church: **gå i k-en** go to c-.
+**kir'ke/bakke** *-n* hill leading up to a church; churchyard, esp. in front of the gate (where official notices were read); church green.
+**kir'ke/bok** *-a, pl -bøker* church register.
+**kir'ke/bryllup** *-et* church wedding.
+**kir'ke/bønn** *-a/-en* common (congregational) prayer.
+**kir'ke/bøsse** *-a* alms box, poor box.
+**kir'ke/departement** [/-mang'] *-et* Ministry of Ecclesiastical Affairs.
+**kir'ke/fader** *-en, pl -fedre* (usu. *pl*) fathers of the Christian church (early ecclesiastical writers).
+**kir'ke/fyrste** *-n* prince of the church, prelate.
+**kir'ke/gang** *-en* attendance at church, churchgoing: **det var hans første k-** it was his first time at church.
+**kir'ke/gjenger** *-en, pl -e* churchgoer.
+**kir'ke/gulv** *-et* church floor: **stå på k-et** be confirmed; **komme nedover k-et** walk down the aisle.
+**kir'ke/gå'rd** *-en* 1 churchyard; graveyard. 2 record of deceased persons.
+**kir'ke/kledd** *A* - dressed for church.
+**kir'ke/klokke** *-a* church bell.
+**kir'kelig** *A* - (=***kyrkjeleg**) church(ly), ecclesiastical; (of person) religious.
+**kir'ke/lys** *-et* altar candle.
+**kir'ke/møte** *-t* church conference, synod.
Kir'ke/nes *Pln* town in Finnmark.
+**Kir'ke- og [å] under'visnings/departementet** [/-mang'e] *df* (=***Kyrkje-**) Ministry of Church and Education
+**kir'ke/rist** *-a* 1 entrance to church yard (with iron gate). 2 area in front of such an entrance.
+**kir'ke/rotte** *-a*: **fattig som en k-** poor as a church mouse (lit. rat).
+**kir'ke/sanger** *-en, pl -e* precentor, minister's assistant.
+**kir'ke/sogn** [/sångn] *-et* parish having a church.
+**kir'ke/spir** *-et* church spire.
+**kir'ke/stol** *-en* pew.
+**kir'ke/sø'kning** *-en* church attendance.
+**kir'ke/tjener** *-en, pl -e* sexton, verger.
+**kir'ke/toneart** *-en mus.* church mode.
+**kir'ke/tukt** *-en* church discipline.
+**kir'ke/tå'rn** *-et* church steeple, tower.
+**kir'ke/ur** *-et* church clock.
+**kir'ke/år** *-et* church year (reckoned from first Sunday in Advent).
+**kiroprak'tiker** *-en, pl -e* (=***-ar**) chiropractor.
kiroprak'tor *-en* chiropractor.
+**kirsch/stang** [kisj'/] *-a, pl -stenger* (=***/stong**) (adjustable) curtain rod.
kir'se/bær *-et* cherry.
Kir'sten *Prn (f)*: **K- giftekniv** a matchmaker (Holberg).
Kir'sti *Prn (f)*
kirur'g *-en* surgeon.
kirurgi' *-en* surgery.
kirur'gisk *A* - surgical.
ki's[1] *-en* pyrites.
kis[2] [ki's] *-en fam.* fellow, guy.
ki'se *V -te/-a* blink, wink; twinkle.
ki'sel *-en chem.* 1 silica. 2 silicon. 3 silicic acid.
+**ki'sel/aktig** *A* - siliceous.
ki'sel/gur *-en* kieselguhr.
ki'sel/stein *-en* siliceous rock, esp. quartz.
+**kis'le** *V -a/-et* (=***kjetle**) have kittens, litter.
kiss [kiss'] *I* call used to attract cats, calves, cows.
kis'te *-a* 1 box, chest, trunk. 2 coffin; *arch.* cist, sarcophagus. 3 fish trap (box type).
kis'te/botn *-en* (=+**/bunn**) bottom of a chest: **ha noe på k-en** have something put away for a rainy day.
kis'te/glad *A* - gleeful, jubilant.
+**kis'te/klær** *pl* (=***/klede**) Sunday best.
kis'te/lokk *-et* lid of chest, coffin lid
Ki'/strand *Pln* twp, Finnmark.

+**ki's/øyd** *A* - (=***/øygd**) having small, blinking eyes.
***ki'tal** *A* cf **kilen**
***ki'te** *V -a* tickle.
***ki'tig** *A* - cf **kilen**
kit'le *V -a/+-et* tickle.
+**kit'ler** *pl of* **kittel**
***kit'lug** *A* - cf **kilen**
kitt' *-et* calking compound, putty.
kit'te *V -a/+-et* calk, putty.
kit'tel [also ki-] *-elen, pl kitler* laboratory coat, smock; maternity dress.
ki'v *-et* quarrel(ing), wrangling.
+**kivak'tig** *A* - quarrelsome.
+**ki'ves** *V kivdes* (=***-ast**) quarrel, wrangle.
***ki'v/sam'** *A* quarrelsome.
***ki'vs/mål** *-et* point of contention, of dispute.
***kja'ge** *V -a* be persistent, keep at sth; nag.
kja'ke[1] *-n pop.* 1 jaw. 2 jowl.
***kja'ke**[2] *V -a* squabble, wrangle.
kja'ke/bein *-et* jawbone.
kjak's *-et* (uneven) cutting, hacking (with scissors).
kjak'se *V -a/+-et* cut unevenly, hack (with scissors etc.).
kjang'el *-et* squabble, wrangle.
kjang'le *V -a/+-et* 1 chomp. 2 chop, hack (with a blunt instrument). 3 squabble.
kjang's *-en pop.* 1 chance, opportunity. 2: **få k-** pick up a girl; **være på k-** be on the make.
kjapp' *A kjapt* fast, quick: **et k-t svar** a pert answer.
kjap'pe *V -a/+-et*: **k- seg** hurry; row with short, quick strokes.
Kjar'tan *Prn (m)*
kja's *-et* 1 fuss; struggle. 2 nagging, pestering.
kja'se *V +-te/*-a* 1 fuss, struggle, tussle (**med** with). 2 nag, pester: **hun k-er hele dagen** she n-s the whole day.
kja'v *-et* bother, fuss, struggle.
kja've *V -a/+-et* struggle, toil.
kje'[1] *-et* kid (goat).
***kje**[2] *Av* cf **ikkje**
+**kje'd** *A* cf **kei**
kje'de[1] [*kje'e] *+-n/+-t/*-a* 1 chain; cordon. 2 track, tread (on caterpillar tractor etc.). 3 necklace. 4 drive (on bicycle).
+**kje'de**[2] *V -a/-et* (=***keie**) bore: **k- seg i hjel** be b-d to death; **komme til å k- seg** get b-d.
kje'de[3] [*kje'e] *V -a/+-et* chain together, link: **k- seg sammen** form a chain.
kje'de/brev *-et* chain letter.
+**kje'delig** *A* - 1 boring, dull, tiresome: **å skrive en ordbok er et k- arbeid** writing a dictionary is drudgery. 2 annoying; embarrassing, unpleasant: **en k- situasjon** an awkward situation; **det var k-** that's too bad.
+**kje'delig/het** *-en* 1 boredom, monotony. 2 *(pl)*: **komme opp i k-er** get into an embarrassing (unpleasant) position.
kje'de/reaksjo'n *-en* chain reaction.
+**kje'de/røyker** *-en, pl -e* (=***-jar**) chain smoker.
kje'de/trekk *-et* chain drive.
+**kje'dsom/het** *-en* boredom: **forgå av k-** be bored to death.
+**kjedsom'melig** *A* - 1 (very) boring, tedious. 2 unpleasant.
+**kjedsom'melig/het** *-en* 1 monotony, tedium, wearisomeness. 2 unpleasantness.
kje'e *V -a/+-et* (of goats) kid.
kjef't *-en* 1 jaw, mouth: **hold k-** shut up, hold your tongue; **ikke en k-** not a soul; **stoppe k-en på en** shut sby up. 2 abuse, scolding: **bruke k- på** abuse; **få k-** get a s-; **grov k-**

+ Bokmål; * Nynorsk; ° Dialect.
After letter: ' stress (Acc. 1); ` tone, stress (Acc. 2); · length.
Below letter: . not pronounced.

abuse, coarse language. 3 *fig.* gap, jaw (e.g. of a fjord, an implement, etc.).

kjeftamen't *-et pop.* 1 jaw structure. 2 gift of gab.

*kjef'tast *V -ast* quarrel, squabble, wrangle.

kjef't/ause *-a* chatterbox, gossip, shrew.

kjef't/bruk *-en/-et* gossiping, jabbering, scolding.

kjef'te *V -a/+-et* jaw, scold.

kjef'te/smelle *-a* chatterbox, gossip, shrew.

+kjeg'l *-et* cf kjekl

kjeg'le[1] [also: kjei'le] *-a/-en* 1 *math.* cone. 2 (bowling) pin (=kile[2] 4).

*kjeg'le[2] *-a* ropemaker's wheel.

+kjeg'le[3] *V -a/-et* cf kjekle

kjegle/bane [kjei'le/] *-n* cf kile/

kjeg'le/snitt *-et math.* conic section.

kjei' *-et fam.* girl, *(pop.)* skirt.

+kje'k *pt of* kike[2]

kjekk' *A kjekt* 1 bold, brave, courageous; daring: holde seg k- put up a brave (or bold) front. 2 buoyant, cheerful, hearty: frisk og k- hale and h . 3 *pop.* fine: en k- pike a f- (great, swell) girl.

kjek'kas *-en* show-off.

kjek'ke *V -a/+-et:* k- seg show off.

kjek'l *-et* argument, quarreling, verbal battle.

kjek'le *V -a/+-et* quarrel.

kjek's[1] *-en, pl -* cracker, dry cooky.

kjek's[2] *-en* gaff (hook).

+kjek's[3] *-en* four-oared, two-man boat used in Nordland.

*kjek'se[1] *-a* obstinate woman.

kjek'se[2] *V -a/+-et* 1 gaff (a fish). 2 *dial.:* k- i take a (verbal) jab at. 3 *dial.* mutter.

kjek't *nt of* kjekk

kje'l *-en* (=kjele[1]) 1 kettle, pot. 2 (steam) boiler. 3 kettle hole.

kjel'de *-a* (=+kilde) 1 fountain, spring. 2 *fig.* source (til of): jeg har det fra en god k- I have it on good authority; en k- til uenighet a s- of discord.

kjel'de/skrift *-et* original document; primary source.

kjel'de/vatn *-et* spring water (usu. mineral water).

kje'le[1] *-n* cf kjel

+kje'le[2] *V -te* cf kjæle[2]

kje'le/dress *-en* coveralls; snowsuit.

+kje'le/flikker *-en, pl -e* (=*-ar) kettle mender, tinker.

kje'le/sjau *-en* cleaning of steam boiler to remove boiler scale and grease.

kjel'ke *-n* sled, toboggan: *fig.* en k- i vegen an obstacle.

kjel'ke/bakke *-n* sliding hill, toboggan slide (or slope).

kjel'ke/føre *-t* (snow conditions for) sledding.

Kjell' *Prn(m)*

Kjel'laug *Prn(f)*

*kjel'le *-a* woman.

+kjel'ler *-en, pl -e* (=*-ar) 1 basement, cellar; vault. 2 dungeon. 3 feuilleton (article or story run at foot of page).

+kjel'ler/eta'sje *-n* (=*-ar/) basement (not a cellar): de bor i k-n they have a b- apartment.

+kjel'ler/hals *-en* (=*-ar/) cellar entrance (outside stairway to basement); bulkhead.

+kjel'ler/lem' *-men* (=*-ar/) trapdoor covering cellar entrance, bulkhead door.

+kjel'ler/mann *-en, pl -menn* (=*-ar/) tapster (at country wedding etc.).

+kjel'ler/nedgang *-en* (=*-ar/) cellar entrance.

kje'l/ost [/ost] *-en* cold dish, like custard, of heat-thickened colostrum eaten with cinnamon and sugar.

kjel'tring *-en* 1 crook, rogue, scoundrel. 2 *pop.* small rusk.

kjel'tring/strek *-en* scoundrelly trick, swindle, villainy.

Kje'l/vik *Pln* village in Finnmark.

*kje'm *pr of* kome[2]

kjem. = kjemisk

*kjem'be[1] *-a* cf kjemme[1]

*kjem'be[2] *V -de* cf kjemme[2]

*kjem'de *pt of* kjemme[2], kjembe[2]

kjemi' *-en* chemistry.

+kjemika'lie *-t, pl -r* (=*kjemikal) chemical.

+kje'miker *-en, pl -e* (=*-ar) chemist, chemistry student, chemical engineer.

kje'misk *A -* chemical; k- fri for entirely without, totally lacking in.

kjem'me[1] *-a* bundle of hay, raked together in orderly fashion for ease in hanging over *hesjer.*

kjem'me[2] *V +kjemte/*kjemde* 1 comb (hair, cotton, etc.). 2 rake hay into orderly bundles.

+kjem'pe[1] *-a/-en* 1 champion; fighter, one mighty in battle; hero. 2 *myth.* giant. 3 (mental, physical, spiritual) giant.

kjem'pe[2] *-a bot.* plantago, plantain.

kjem'pe[3] *-a* forepart of a boat.

kjem'pe[4] *V -a/+-et* 1 contend, do battle, fight *(for* for; om over): de k-ende the combatants, contestants; k- den siste kamp f- one's last battle; k- om prisen contend for the prize; k- til det siste f- to the bitter end. 2 struggle (med with; mot against), work hard; fight: k- fram en sak lead a cause to victory; k- med trange kår contend with poverty; k- med gråten struggle to hold back one's tears; k- med seg selv struggle to keep control of oneself; k- ned suppress; k- seg fram f- one's way, get ahead.

kjem'pe/arbeid *-et* Herculean task.

+kjem'pe/foreta'gende *-t* gigantic undertaking.

kjem'pe/krefter *pl* great strength.

+kjem'pe/messig *A -* gigantic, like a giant, powerful.

+kjem'pe/oppga've *-a/-en* (=*/oppgåve) huge problem or task.

kjem'pe/skritt *-et* giant stride.

kjem'pe/sterk *A* strong as a giant.

kjem'pe/stor *A* giant-sized, huge.

kjem'pe/vekst *-en med.* gigantism.

kjem'pe/vise *-a* heroic ballad.

+kjem'pe/øgle *-a/-en* (=*/ødle) dinosaur.

+kjem'te *pt of* kjemme[2]

*kjen'd *A -* cf kjent

*kjen'de *pt of* kjenne[3]

kjeng' *-en dial.* eye, staple (part of door fastening).

kjeng'e *-a* drinking bowl of wood, with two carved handles.

kjenn' *N:* ha på k- at have a feeling (intuition, suspicion) that.

*kjen'nande *A -* appreciable; perceptible.

+kjenn'/bar *A* noticeable, perceptible.

+kjen'ne[1] *en* little bit, mite, smidgeon.

kjen'ne[2] *N:* gi noe til k- let sth be known, make sth clear; gi seg til k- reveal oneself.

kjen'ne[3] *V +kjente/*kjende* 1 know (a person), recognize; know (e.g. music): kjenn deg selv k- thyself; lære en å k- get to k- sby; være (bli) kjent med be (get) acquainted with; som kjent as is well-known; k- en av utseende k- sby by sight; k- en fra distinguish; jeg kan ikke k- dem fra hverandre I can't tell them apart; k- igjen recognize; k- seg igjen k- a place one has been before; jeg k-er meg ikke igjen I don't recognize the place; k- en på (gangen) know sby by his (walk); k- til know about; k- ut og inn know like the palm of one's hand; k-es ved acknowledge, admit. 2 feel, perceive: k- en lukt notice a smell; k- seg (frisk, ung osv.) f- (healthy, young, etc.); k- etter f-, touch; k- på f- of, touch; (of food) taste; det k-es som it f-s like. 3 pass sentence: k- en skyldig find sby guilty; ti k-es for rett the court finds.

kjen'nelig *A -* 1 appreciable, considerable. 2 discernible, perceptible, recognizable (på by): k- beruset noticeably drunk.

+kjen'nelse *-n jur.* court order, decision, finding, ruling, verdict.

kjen'ne/merke *-t, pl +-r/*-* distinguishing characteristic, mark.

+kjen'ner *-en, pl -e* (=*-ar) connoisseur, expert, judge (of what is good).

+kjen'ner/mine *-a/-en* (=*-ar/) air of a connoisseur, of an expert.

*kjen'ne/spak *A* good at recognizing people.

+kjen'ne/tegn [/tein] *-et* mark, sign (på of).

+kjen'ne/tegne [/teine] *V -et* characterize, distinguish, mark.

kjen'ning[1] *-en* acquaintance.

kjen'ning[2] *-en lit.* kenning (Old Germanic type of poetic metaphor).

kjen'ning[3] *-a/+-en* glimpse, sight, touch; earshot: få k- av land catch s- of land; holde k- med keep contact with.

kjen'nings/signal [/singna'l] *-et* signal letters.

kjenn'/skap *-en/+-et* acquaintance, familiarity (til with); knowledge (til of).

kjen's *A -* familiar, well-known.

kjen'sel *+-elen/*-la* 1 recognition: dra k- på recognize. 2 landfall. 3 feel, touch; feeling.

kjen's/folk *pl pop.* acquaintances, friends.

kjen's/gjerning [/jæ'rning] *+-en/*-a* fact.

kjen'sle *-a* feeling, sense (av of).

kjen'sle/full *A* full of feeling.

*kjen'sleg *A -* 1 companionable. 2 characteristic.

kjen'sle/laus *A* unfeeling, without feeling.

*kjen'sle/sam *A* sensitive, tender.

kjen'sle/var *A* sensitive, tender.

+kjen't *A -* (=*kjend) 1 acquainted, familiar: han er godt k- i byen he knows the town well; felles k-e mutual acquaintances. 2 famous, well-known: en k- personlighet a well-known personality.

+kjen'te *pt of* kjenne[3]

kjen't/folk *pl* acquaintances, friends.

kjen't/mann *-en, pl -menn/*-menner* one who knows the locality; local guide or pilot.

kjepp' *-en* 1 stick (for walking, for herding animals); cudgel. 2 spoke (in wheel).

*kjep'past *V -est, -test, kjepst* 1 compete. 2 push on, work hard at sth.

*kjep'pen *A -e/-i, pl kjepne* competitive.

kjepp'/hest *-en* 1 hobbyhorse. 2 *fig.* consuming interest, obsession.

kjepp'/høg *A* arrogant, cocky, overbearing.

kjepp'/jage *V -a/+-et/+-de* chase off with a stick.

*kjep'test *pt of* kjeppast

*kje'r *-et* 1 container, vessel; tub, utensil, vat. 2 bridge pier. 3 (salmon) trap.

kje'rald *-et, pl -* cf kjørel

+kjer'ke *-a* cf kirke

kjer'ne[1] [also kjæ'rne] *-n* 1 kernel (in a nut), seed (in fruits); pith, heartwood. 2 *bot., chem., phys.* core, nucleus; *mus.* timbre, tonal quality. 3 *fig.* core, essence, heart.

+kjer'ne[2] *-a* cf kinne[1]

+kjer'ne[3] *V -a/-et* cf kinne[2]

+kjer'ne/fysiker *-en, pl -e* =*-ar) nuclear physicist.

+kjer'ne/fysikk' *-en* nuclear physics.

kjer'ne/hus *-et* core.

kjer'ne/kar *-en* real specimen of a man, splendid fellow.

kjerne/mjølk [kjæ'rne/] *-a* (=+/melk) buttermilk.

kjer'ne/punkt [/pongt] *-et* core, crux of the matter; essential point.

kjer'ne/stav *-en* dasher (of a churn).

kjer'ne/sunn *A -sunt* healthy (to the core).

kjer'ne/tropp *-en mil. (pl)* picket troops.

kjer'ne/ved *-en bot.* duramen, heartwood, pith.
kjerr' *-et* (=***kjørr**) 1 brushwood, scrub, thicket. 2 *dial.* bog.
kjer'rat *-en* 1 conveyor (used esp. to drag logs up from the water). 2 waterwheel for driving a hoist.
***kjer're**[1] *-t* grove.
kjer're[2] *-a* 1 (small, two-wheeled) cart. 2 *fam.* jalopy; old car.
kjer're/hjul *-et* cart wheel.
kjer'ring *-a, pl *-ar* 1 old woman, esp. married. 2 *pop.* wife, woman. 3 fall (on skies): *pop.* **reise k-a** get revenge for previous defeat (in sports).
+**kjer'ring/knute** *-n* (=***/knut**) granny knot.
kjer'ring/ris *-et* dwarf birch.
kjer'ring/rokk *-en bot.* horsetail (Equisetum).
kjer'ring/råd *-et* home remedy.
kjer'ring/snakk *-et* old woman's twaddle.
Kjer'ring/øy *Pln* twp, Nordland.
kjer'ris *-en* pulka (one-man Lapp sledge).
kjer'te *-n* candle, taper; torch.
kjer'tel *-elen, pl -ler* 1 lymph gland or node: **lukket k-** ductless gland. 2 musk or scent gland. 3 *geol.* nodule.
kjer'tel/sjuk *A* (=+**/syk**) afflicted with scrofula.
kjer'te/lys *-et* candlelight; torchlight.
kjer'te/svein *-en hist.* candlebearer (at court).
kjer'tler *pl of* **kjertel**
kjeru'b *-en* 1 cherub. 2 *hum.* doorkeeper.
kjeru'bisk *A -* cherubic.
kjer'v *-et* (=**kjerve**[1]) bundle, sheaf (esp. of leafy twigs for fodder).
kjer've[1] *-t* cf **kjerv**
kjer've[2] *V -a/+-et* 1 bundle (leaves etc.). 2 cut leafy twigs for fodder. 3 *dial.* bundle, wrap (a baby).
kje'se[1] *-n* 1 rennet. 2 *zool.* abomasum (fourth stomach of ruminant).
kje'se[2] *V -te* make cheese with help of rennet.
***kjes'ke** *V -a* crave, be hungry (**på** for).
kje's/ost [/ost] *-en* cheese made with rennin (e.g. cheddar).
+**kje'te** *-a* cf **kjæte**[1]
Kje'til *Prn (m)*
***kjet'le** *V -a* have kittens, litter.
***kjet'ling** *-en* kitten.
kjet'te *-a* female cat: **Den store k-a på Dovre** The Big Cat at D- (title of folktale).
+**kjet'ter** *-en, pl -e* (=***-ar**) heretic.
kjetteri' *-et* heresy.
+**kjet'tersk** *A -* (=***-arsk**) heretical.
kjet'ting *-en* chain (e.g. on auto tires, anchor).
+**kje've**[1] *-n* 1 jaw; mandible. 2 mouth (e.g. of tongs).
+**kje've**[2] *-n* cf **keive**[1]
+**kje've/bein** *-et* jawbone.
+**kje've/operasjo'n** *-en* operation on the jaw.
+**kje've/parti'** *-et* jaw (with surrounding area).
+**kje'v/hendt** *A -* cf **keiv/**
+**kjev'l** *-et* argument, squabble.
kjev'le[1] *-t/+-n* rolling pin.
kjev'le[2] *V -a/+-et* roll out (baking).
+**kjev'le**[3] *V -a/-et* argue, squabble.
kjev'le/gras *-et* timothy.
kjo'le *-n* 1 dress, frock, gown. 2 (men's) evening dress, tails: **k- og hvitt** white tie and tails. 3 uniform coat.
kjo'le/liv *-et* bodice (of dress).
***kjo'le/saum** *-en* cf **/søm**
kjo'le/stoff *-et, pl -/+-er* dress material.
+**kjo'le/søm'** *-men* (=***/saum**) dressmaking.
+**kjo'le/tøy** *-et* (=***/ty**) dress material.
kjo'ne[1] *-a* drying house (for grain).
***kjo'ne**[2] *V -a* clean up, put (house) in order.
kjortel [kjor'tel] *-elen, pl -ler* kirtle, tunic; *bibl.* coat.

kjo's *-en* 1 small inlet. *2 grove.
***kjo'se** *V kys, kaus, kose/-i* choose: **k- på** favor, suggest.
kju'ke *-a* 1 growth, lump; fungus of polyporus family; cone. 2 small cheese; milk curd.
kjuk'ling *-en* (=+**kylling**) chick.
+**kjy'le** *V -te* cf **kyle**
°**kjy'r** *-a/-en, pl -* cf **ku**
+**kjy'te** *V -te* cf **kyte**
***kjæ'le**[1] *-a* affectionateness, cuddliness, kittenishness.
kjæ'le[2] [+kje'le] *V -te* 1 caress, fondle, pet. 2 cuddle, nestle (**med** with). 3 coddle, pamper (with *prep.* **for**): **gå ikke omkring og kluss og kjæl for meg!** don't go around coddling me! (Collett Vogt).
kjæ'le/ba'rn *-et* darling, pet (child).
+**kjæ'le/degge** *-n* pet (coddled child or animal).
kjæ'le/gris *-en* cuddly child; pampered person.
kjæ'len *A +-ent, pl -ne* 1 affectionate, cuddly, loving. 2 sensitive, soft, weak: **være k-** be a weakling.
+**kjæ'le/navn** *-et* pet name.
+**kjæ'leri** *-et derog.* 1 cuddling, loving. 2 coddling, sentimentality.
***kjæ'le/synd** *-a* besetting sin, pet (bad) habit.
kjæ'r *A* 1 beloved, dear: **ha noen k-** love sby: **mine k-e** my beloved ones; **k- i** in love with. 2 precious, valued: **intet var henne k-ere** she loved nothing better. 3 (in address, often with weakened meaning): **k-e (deg)** please; **k-e vene** (pretty) please; **her hjelper ingen k-e mor** begging won't help, you're in for it now. 4 (exclam. of surprise): **k-e (meg)** goodness (me), after all.
***kjæ'rast(e)** *-(e)n* cf **kjæreste**
kjæ're *V -te* 1: **k- seg for** complain to. 2: **k- (seg) om** care about.
kjæ're/mål *-et jur.* appeal.
+**kjæ'remåls/utvalg** *-et* (=***/utval**) court of appeals.
+**kjæ'reste** *-n* (=***-ast(e)**) beloved, (boy, girl) friend, lover, sweetheart.
+**kjæ'reste/folk** *-et* (=***kjærast(e)/**) sweethearts.
+**kjæ'resteri** *-et derog.* courting, loving.
kjæ'r/kommen *A -ent, pl -komne* (=***/komen**) welcome: +**en k- anledning** a w- opportunity.
***kjæ'r/leik** *-en* affection, love.
kjæ'rlig [also kjær'-] *A -* affectionate (**mot** towards), fond, loving.
+**kjæ'rlig/het** *-en* 1 affection (**til** for love, passion; *bibl.* charity. 2: **k- på pinne** (candy) sucker.
+**kjæ'rlighets/histo'rie** *-a/-en* love story; love affair.
+**kjæ'rlighets/roma'n** *-en* romantic novel.
+**kjæ'rlighets/sorg** *-a/-en* unhappy love affair.
+**kjæ'r/tegn** [/tein] *-et* caress.
+**kjæ'r/tegne** [/teine] *V -et* caress.
kjæ'te[1] *-a* wantonness, wildness; gaiety, merrymaking.
kjæ'te[2] *V -te*: **k- seg** be gay, cut loose, have fun.
***kjæ'te/full** *A* exuberant, gay.
Kjøbenhav'n *Pln* cf **København**
+**kjøb'/mann** *-en, pl -menn* cf **kjøp/**
+**kjø'd** *-et* cf **kjøtt** 1 *bibl.* flesh: **de to skal være ett k-** they two shall be one f-; **gå all k-ets gang** go the way of all f-. 2 meat (now usu. **kjøtt**).
+**kjø'delig** *A -* carnal, earthly, of flesh. 2 related through blood: **hans k-e bror** his blood brother.
+**kjø'ds/lyst** *-en* (=***kjøt(t)s/**) carnal desire.
kjø'e *-a* small trout.
+**kjø'ge/mester** *-en, pl -e* cf **kjøke/**
+**kjø'ke/mester** *-en, pl -e* (=***/meister**) master of ceremonies at a country wedding etc.
***kjø'ken** *-et* cf **kjøkken**
kjøk'ken *-et, pl -/+-er* (=***kjøken**) 1 kitchen. 2 cuisine: **fransk k-** French c-.

kjøk'ken/benk *-en* kitchen counter.
kjøk'ken/departement [/-mang'] *-et, pl +-er/*-* culinary department, kitchen staff.
kjøk'ken/forkle *-et* kitchen apron.
kjøk'ken/hage *-n* kitchen garden, vegetable garden.
kjøk'ken/kniv *-en* kitchen knife.
kjøk'ken/roma'n *-en* cheap novel.
kjøk'ken/sjef *-en* chef.
+**kjøk'ken/skriver** *-en, pl -e* (=***-ar**) man who meddles and snoops in the kitchen.
kjøk'ken/stell *-et* kitchen work; running a kitchen.
+**kjøk'ken/tøy** *-et* kitchen utensils.
kjøk'ken/veg *-en* (=+**/vei**) kitchen entrance: **gå k-en** use rear entrance.
kjø'l[1] *-en* 1 keel; centerboard (=**senkekjøl**): **vende k-en i været** keel over; **på rett (jevn) k-** on an even k-, upright. 2 *fig.* ship: **på norsk k-** on a Norwegian s-. 3 *bot., zool.* carina. 4 long, low mountain ridge. 5 point of plow.
kjø'l[2] *-en* 1 coolness; cold period. 2 fright, shudder.
***kjøl'd** *-a* 1 cold; coldness. 2 coolness; cold (unpleasant) feeling.
kjøl'e[1] *-a* cf **kjøl**[2]
kjøl'e[2] *V -te* chill, cool: **k- seg** c- off.
kjø'le/disk *-en* refrigerated counter.
kjø'le/lager *-eret, pl -er/+-re* cold storage.
***kjø'leleg** *A -* chilling, horrible; *(adv.)* terribly.
***kjø'len** *A -e/-i, pl -ne* chilly, cool.
Kjø'len *Pln* mountain range between Norway and Sweden (= "the Keel").
+**kjø'ler** *-en, pl -e* (=***-ar**) 1 cooler. 2 *chem.* cooling tube.
kjø'le/rom [/romm] *-met* cooling room, refrigerated storage.
+**kjø'le/skap** *-et* (=***/skåp**) refrigerator.
kjø'le/vatn *-et* (=+**/vann**) coolant, cooling water.
kjø'le/vogn [/vångn] *-a* refrigerator car (railroad).
kjø'l/far *-et* wake; track of keel.
kjø'l/hale *V -te/*-a* 1 lay a boat over on its side for repairs. 2 keelhaul; rebuke with great severity.
kjø'lig *A -* 1 chilly, cool: **en k- mottakelse** a cool reception; **k- mot en** cool to sby. *2 terrible, terrific: **k- til kar** quite a fellow.
kjø'l/makk *-en* (=**/mark**) *zool.* wireworm (Agriotes obscura).
+**kjøl'ne** *V -et* (=***kolne**) cool, cool off.
***kjø'lsleg** *A -* uncomfortable, unpleasant.
***kjø'l/slegen** *A -e/-i, pl -ne* having the chill taken off.
kjø'l/spor *-et* wake; track of keel.
kjø'l/svin *-et* keelson.
kjø'l/vatn *-et* (=+**/vann**) wake (of boat): **i k-et på** in the w- of.
*-**kjøm** *A* accessible: **vegen er framk-** the road is open.
***kjøm'd** *-a*: **vere i k-a** be approaching.
***kjø'n** *A* quick, wise; bold, keen.
kjønn' *-et* 1 sex: **det svake k-** the weaker s-. 2 *gram.* gender.
kjønn's/akt *-a/+-en* copulation, intercourse, mating.
+**kjønn's/bestem'melse** *-n* 1 sex determinant, sex determination. 2 determination of gender.
kjønn's/celle *-a/+-en* sex cell.
kjønn's/del *-en* (external) sex organ, genital.
kjønn's/drift *-a/+-en* sex urge.
+**kjønn's/forskjell'** *-en* sex difference.
kjønn's/laus *A* asexual, sexless; neuter.
kjønn'slig *A -* erotic, sexual.
kjønn's/liv *-et* sex life.

+ Bokmål; * Nynorsk; ° Dialect.
After letter: ' stress (Acc. 1); ' tone, stress (Acc. 2); · length.
Below letter: . not pronounced.

kjønn's/moden *A* *+-ent, pl -ne* sexually mature.
kjønn's/mora'l *-en* sexual morality.
kjønn's/orga'n *-et* sex organ, *(pl)* genitals.
kjønn's/sjukdom *-men* (=+**/syk-**) venereal disease.
+**kjøn'/røk** *-en* (=***/røyk**) lampblack.
kjø'p *-et* 1 buying, purchase (**av** of): **k- og salg** b- and selling; **til k-s** for sale. 2 bargain, deal: **godt k-** b-; **på k-et, attpå k-et** into the b-.
kjø'pe *V -te* buy, purchase (**av** from): **jeg k-te den til min venn for 100 kroner** I bought it for my friend for 100 *kroner*; **alt som kan k-es for penger** anything that can be bought for money; **k- inn** make purchases, shop; **k- opp** b- up; **k- seg noe** b- sth (for oneself); **k- seg løs (fri)** ransom oneself.
kjø'pe/dyktig *A* - able to buy: **k- publikum** buying public.
kjø'pe/evne *-a/+-en* ability to buy.
kjø'pe/kontrak't *-en* sales contract.
kjø'pe/kraft *-a/+-en* purchasing power.
kjø'pe/lysten *A +-ent, pl -ne* eager to buy.
+**kjø'per** *-en, pl -e* (=***-ar**) buyer, purchaser.
kjø'pe/sum' *-men* purchase price.
kjø'pe/tvang *-en* obligation to buy.
kjø'p/mann *-en, pl -menn/*-menner* merchant, storekeeper.
kjø'pmann/skap *-et* commerce, trade.
kjø'p/skål *-a* drink to seal a bargain.
kjø'p/slå *V infl as* **slå** bargain, haggle (**om** for).
kjø'p/stad *-en, pl +-steder/*-er* (selfgoverning) city, town.
+**kjø'p/stevne** *-t* (=**/stemne**) fair, market.
kjø'r *-et/*-en* (=***køyr**) rush: **i ett k-** at a stretch, without a break; on end, running; continually.
+**kjø'r/bar** *A* passable, safe for driving.
kjø're *V -te* (=***køyre**) 1 *(intrans.)* drive, ride; go (in vehicle), go riding: **k- med bil** ride in a car; **k- forbi** overtake, pass; **k- i veg** go ahead; **k- inn i** run into; **k- langsomt** drive slowly; **k- opp** drive up, pull up; **k- opp med** bring up (arguments, cannon); **k- over en** run over sby; **k- på** drive on, go ahead, hurry up; **k- på en** run into sby; **k- en tur** go for a ride; **k- ut** (of horses) run away. 2 *(trans.)* drive, run: **k- bil** drive a car; **k- en film** run a film; **k- kull** haul coal; **k- landevegen** drive the highway; **k- inn** break in (car, horse); **k- noen (seg) i hjel** kill sby (oneself) by driving; **k- en ned** run sby down; **k- noen ut** kick sby out. 3 *(trans.)* drive (**i** into), force, plunge (e.g. a knife): **k- i seg (mat)** gobble up (food); **k- noe fast** get sth stuck.
kjø're/bane *-n* (paved) roadbed; traffic lane.
kjø're/doning *-a/-en* horse-drawn vehicle, rig.
kjø're/fil *-en* lane, line of traffic.
kjø're/kar *-en* driver; teamster.
kjø're/kort *-et* driver's license.
kjør'el *-et, pl -/+-er* (=**kjerald**) container, vessel, esp. of wood.
kjø're/prøve *-n* driver's test.
+**kjø'rer** *-en, pl -e* (=***-ar**, ***køyrar**) driver (of car or team); teamster.
kjø're/retning *-a/+-en* direction of travel.
kjø're/rett *-en* right-of-way.
kjø're/tid *-a/+-en* driving time, travel time.
kjø're/tur *-en* drive, ride.
+**kjø're/tøy** *-et* vehicle.
kjø're/veg *-en* (=+**/vei**) road.
kjø'ring *-a/+-en* 1 driving, riding. 2 hauling, trucking 3 *dial.* thrashing floor.
***kjørr'** *-a* cf **kjerr**
kjør'sel *-elen/-la* drive, driving, ride.
kjør'vel *-en bot.* chervil (Anthriscus cerefolium).

***kjø't** *-et* cf **kjøtt**
***kjø'ta** *Av* cf **kjøtta**
***kjø'te** *V -te* cf **kjøtte**
kjø'ter *-en, pl +-e* cur, mongrel.
***kjø't/meis(e)** *-a* cf **kjøtt/**
***kjø'ts/lyst** *-a* cf **kjøds/**
kjøtt' *-et* (=***kjøt**) 1 meat. 2 pulp (of fruits). 3 flesh (usu. **kjød**, q.v.).
kjøt'ta *Av* (=***kjøta**) *pop.* (for emphasis) absolutely, completely: **k- dum** c- stupid.
kjøtt'/bein *-et* bone (with some meat on).
kjøtt'/berg *-et* mountain of flesh, fat person.
kjøtt'/bolle *-n* meatball (small, finely ground).
kjøtt'/deig *-en* ground meat.
kjøt'te** *V -e* (=kjøte**): **k- seg** flesh up.
kjøtt'/etende *A* - carnivorous.
kjøtt'/farga *A* - (=+**-et**) flesh-colored.
kjøtt'/full *A* fleshy; fat; succulent.
kjøtt'/gryte *-a* 1 meat kettle. 2 *fig.* fleshpot: **lenges tilbake til Egyptens k-r** long for the fleshpots of Egypt.
+**kjøtt'/hue** *-t derog.* meathead (=stupid person).
kjøtt'/kake *-a* meatball.
kjøtt'/klubbe *-a* steak hammer.
kjøtt'/kontroll' *-en* meat inspection.
kjøtt'/kvern [/kvæ'rn] *-a* meat grinder.
***kjøtt'leg** *A* - cf **kjødelig**
kjøtt'/mat *-en* meat dish; meat.
kjøtt'/meis *-a zool.* (great) titmouse (Parus major).
kjøtt'- og [å] **fles'ke/sentra'l** *-en* cooperative sales agency for meat.
kjøtt'/sag *-a* butcher's saw, meat saw.
kjøtt'/suppe *-a* vegetable soup (with meat).
kjøtt'/sår *-et* flesh wound.
kjøtt'/øks *-a* meat-axe.
***kjø'v** *-et* choking up, esp. of ice; damming up.
kjø've *V -de* 1 choke. 2 quench (fire). 3 muffle (sound). 4 dam (because of ice).
kl.=**klasse, klokke**[1]
klabb' *-en pop.* clump; sticky lump: **det ble bare k- og babb** there was a grand confusion, a big mess.
klab'be *V -a/+-et* 1 pat, press together. 2 stick: **det k-er under skiene** snow s-s to the skis; **k- seg** cling, stick. 3 clobber, hit: **k- til en** c- sby.
klab'be/føre *-t* sticky skiing conditions.
klab'bet(e) *A* - sticky; soggy.
klada's *-en* blob, splotch.
kladas'k *en* swat; *(interj.)* plop.
kladd' *-en* 1 rough draft. 2 *dial.* bunch, clump, wad.
klad'de *V -a/+-et* 1 stick: **det k-er** it's sticky (under foot). 2 draft; write a rough draft.
klad'de/blokk *-en* scratch pad.
klad'de/bok *-a, pl -bøker* notebook.
klad'de/smed *-en* bungler, sloppy worker.
klaff'[1] *-en* 1 flap, leaf, lid. 2 *mus.* key (on wind instrument). 3 valve (in heart; machine). 4 plate (on plane, for regulating thickness of cut). 5 (movable) panel.
klaff'[2] *-en* bull's-eye, hit; success.
klaf'fe *V -a/+-et* fit, jibe; work out; be in order.
klaf'fe/bor'd *-et* drop-leaf table.
kla'ge[1] *-a/+-en* 1 complaint, grievance; kick. 2 *lit.* lament, moan, wail.
kla'ge[2] *V -a/+-et/+-de* 1 complain (**over** of; **over at** that; **på** about): **jeg skal k- på deg for far** I'll tell father on you. 2: **k- seg** groan, wail, whimper. 3 confide: **k- sin nød for en** pour out one's trouble to sby.
kla'ge/mål *-et* complaint, grievance, protest; *jur.* claim, demand.
kla'ge/punkt [/pongt] *-et* charge, count, grievance.
+**kla'ger** *-en, pl -e* (=***-ar**) *jur.* complainant, plaintiff.

+**kla'ge/sang** *-en* (=***/song**) dirge, elegy, lament.
kla'ke[1] *-n* 1 crust of ice. 2 *dial.* lump of ice.
kla'ke[2] *V -a/+-et* crust over with ice, begin to freeze.
kla'ket(e) *A* - 1 frosty, icy. 2 frozen.
klakk'[1] *-en* 1 blot, blotch. 2 lump 3 *dial.* underwater fishing bank.
klakk'[2] *-en* claque.
klakk'[3] *pt of* **klekke**[2]
klak'ke *V -a/+-et* 1 crush, hit, pound; clatter. 2 *pop.* dabble, make a mess, smear.
klakø'r *-en* claqueur (member of a claque).
klam' *A -t, pl klamme* clammy; cold and oppressive.
+**klam'me** *-n* 1 bracket(s): **sette i k-r** enclose in b-s; **runde k-r** parentheses; **skarpe k-r** (square) brackets. 2 brace (to enclose several lines).
klam'mer *+-eren/*klamra, pl +-ere/*klamrer* 1 clamp; paper fastener. 2 *dial.* mountain cleft, pass.
+**klammeri'** *-et, pl -er* brawl, loud quarrel, row: **komme i k-** get into a b-.
klam'p *-en* 1 block (of wood or metal). 2 *naut.* chock, clamp, cleat. 3 hobble (drag on a horse): **en k- om foten** a hindrance. 4 hulk (of a man). 5 clamp (on plane).
klam'pe *V -a/+-et* 1 clamp; chock, cleat. 2 clop, clump; stamp.
klam'pet(e) *A* - clumping, noisy.
klam're *V -a/+-et* clutch, grip (sth): **k- seg fast til** clamp onto, cling to, grasp.
kla'n *-en* clan.
klan'der *-et/+-en* blame, censure; rebuke, reprimand.
klan'der/verdig *A* - censurable, deserving a rebuke or reprimand.
klan'dre *V -a/+-et* criticize, find fault with (**for** for).
klang'[1] *-en* 1 ring, sound (esp. of musical instruments or the human voice); clang, peal (of bells): **k-en av stemmer** the s- of voices; **en stemme med lys k-** a clear, high-pitched voice; **klokkenes k-** the p- of bells; **glassenes k-** the clinking of glasses; **med sang og k-** with gay music. 2 *fig.* ring, sound: **et navn med en god k-** a name with a good r-, a good name.
klang'[2] *pt of* **klinge**[2]
klang'/botn *-en* (=+**/bunn**) 1 sounding board. 2 harmony, resonance.
klang'/farge *-n* 1 *mus.* timbre, tone color. 2 tonal effect.
klang'/full *A* resounding, sonorous.
+**klang'/fylde** *-n* (=***/fylle**) sonority, sonorousness.
klang'/preg *-et* tonal quality.
+**klang'/virkning** *-en* (=***/verknad**) tonal effect.
klapp' *-en/+-et* 1 (of sound) clap. 2 pounding (of heart). 3 slap; clapping (of hands); patting: **kyss og k-** kisses and caresses.
klapp'/bo'rd *-et* collapsible table.
klap'pe *V -a/+-et* 1 pat: **k- jorda til** p- the ground; **k- kake** patty-cake; **k- en på kinnet** p- sby's cheek; **k- en på skulderen** p- sby on the back; **kysse og k-** pet. 2 hit, strike: **k- sammen** fold up, snap together, close with a bang; **k- til en** slap, smack sby. 3 (of hands) clap: **k- i hendene** c-, applaud. 4 (of heart) beat. 5 (of ship): **k- til kaia** dock. 6: **k-et og klart** finished, all set to go, open-and-shut.
+**klap'per** *-en, pl -e* (=***-ar**) 1 *eccl.* clapper. 2 slate.
+**klap'per/slange** *-n* (=***/orm**) rattlesnake.
klapp'/jakt *-a/+-en* 1 battue, drive (in hunting). 2 hounding, round up (**på** of), witch hunt: **politiet drev k- på smuglere** the police were rounding up smugglers.
klapp'/myss *-en zool.* hooded seal (Cystophora cristata).

klapp'/salve *-a/-en* round of applause, salvo.
+**klapp'/sete** *-t* folding, tip-up seat (as in auditorium); jump seat (in a car).
klapp'/stol *-en* folding chair.
klap're *V -a/+-et* 1 clatter. 2 rattle (e.g. of snakes). 3 chatter (of teeth).
klap's *-en/+-et* cuff, slap.
klap'se *V -a/+-et* 1 flap. 2 slap: **k- en på baken** spank sby.
kla'r *A* (=***klår**) 1 clear (sky, coast, voice, etc.); transparent (liquid, glass); sheer (cloth). 2 bright (fire, moonlight, sun, etc.; *fig.* eyes). 3 clear=lucid (style); bright, level-headed: **bli k- over noe** realize sth; **k- i hodet** keen, sharp, clearheaded; **ikke riktig k- i toppen** befogged, confused. 4 clear=obvious, plain: **han fikk k-e ord for pengene** he got an earful; **k- beskjed (om)** definite orders, a plain answer; **et k-t blikk (for)** a keen eye (for); **saken er k-** the matter is clear; **det er k-t at** it's obvious that; **det er k-t som dagen** it's clear as daylight. 5 clear =free of, unhindered: **k- veg** clear path; **gå k- av** clear, miss. 6 ready: **k- til start** r- to start; **k-t skip** general quarters; **gjøre k-t** make r-, clear up; **stå k- (til)** be prepared (for). 7 tired, worn-out: **gå k-** tire.
+**kla're**[1] *-a/-en* (=***klåre**[1]) opening, open space (in sky, air, water, woods).
kla're[2] *V -te/*-a* (=***klåre**[2]) 1 clarify, clear (fluids); candle (eggs): **k- kaffe** clear coffee; **k- vin** decant wine. 2 clear (a voice): **k- opp** (of weather) clear. 3 clarify, clear up, elucidate (a problem): **k- begrepene** clarify the concepts. 4 (of a task or person) manage, negotiate: **jeg k-er ikke mer** I can't m- any more; **han k-te biffen** he did the job; **k- sin gjeld** clear one's debt. 5: **k- seg** get along, manage, succeed; **jeg k-te meg til eksamen** I passed the exam; **det får k- seg** that will have to do; **k- seg sjøl** get along by oneself, be on one's own.
klare're *V -te* 1 clear (through customs). 2 *obs.* pay off; pay up.
kla're/skinn *-et* fish skin used to clear coffee.
+**kla'r/gjøre** *V -gjorde, -gjort* 1 clarify, elucidate, explain. 2 make ready.
+**kla'r/het** *-en* 1 brightness, clearness, transparency: **vannets k-** the c- of the water. 2 clarity, insight: **bringe k- i** clear up; **få k- over, komme til k- over** get i- into, arrive at an understanding of.
klarinett' *-en* clarinet.
klarinettis't *-en* clarinetist.
kla'ring *-a/+-en* 1 clearing (of weather, coffee, etc.). 2 *tech.* clearance.
+**kla'r/legge** *V -la, -lagt* (=***klår/leggje**) clarify, explain.
+**kla'rlig** *Av* clearly, obviously.
kla'rne *V -a/+-et* (=***klårne**) clear (of weather, liquids, ideas, etc.), turn clear; clarify: **det k-er opp** it's clearing.
kla'r/signal [/singna'l] *-et naut.* clearance signal; all clear.
kla'r/syn *-et/*-a* vision; intuitive understanding (**for** of).
+**kla'r/sy'nt** *A* - clear-sighted, foresighted.
+**kla'rsynt/het** *-en* clear-sightedness; vision.
kla'r/tenkt *A* - clear thinking.
+**kla'rt/seende** *A* - (=***/sjåande**) clear-sighted, perspicacious.
+**kla'r/vær** *-et* (=***/ver**) clear weather.
+**kla'r/øyd** *A* - (=***/øygd**) 1 *lit.* bright-eyed. 2 clear-sighted, perspicacious.
kla'se[1] *-n* bunch, cluster; *bot.* panicle, raceme.
kla'se[2] *V -a/+-et/-te*: **k- seg** cluster, form clusters.
kla'set(e) *A* - clustered, in clusters.
klas'k *-en/-et* 1 swat; slap. 2 *(interj.)* plop, splash.
klas'ke *V -a/+-et* 1 splash; squish, squash. 2 clatter, clop, crash. 3 clink (glasses). 4 slap: **k- hendene sammen** clap one's hands; **k- seg på låret** s- one's thigh.
klass' *pt of* **klesse**[1]
klas'se *-a/-en* 1 class (of pupils, society, etc.): **en stor k-** a big c-; **de lavere k-r** the lower c-es; **en fiolinist av første k-** a top-ranking violinist; **reise på annen k-** travel second c-. 2 grade (in school): **første k-** first g-. 3 classroom: **han gikk inn i k-n** he went into the c-. 4 classification: **i hvilken k-?** in which c-?
+**klas'se/beviss't** *A* - class-conscious.
klas'se/deling *-a/+-en* class distinction.
klas'se/de'lt *A* - divided into classes.
+**klas'se/forstan'der** *-en* (= ***-ar**) (ab.=) homeroom teacher.
+**klas'se/fradrag** *-et* (=***/frådrag**) deduction (on tax returns).
klas'se/kamp *-en* class struggle.
klas'se/laus *A* (=+**/løs**) classless.
klas'se/rom [/romm] *-met* classroom.
klas'se/skille *-t, pl +-r/*-* class distinction.
+**klas'se/værelse** *-t* classroom.
klassifikasjo'n *-en* classification.
klassifise're *V -te* class, classify, grade.
+**klas'siker** *-en, pl -e* (=***-ar**) 1 classic (writer, work). 2 classicist. 3 student of the classics.
klassisis'me *-n* classicism.
klas'sisk *A* - classic, classical; first-rate.
klat're[1] *V -a/+-et* clamber, climb.
klat're[2] *V -a/+-et dial.* 1 tap; putter. 2 fritter (**bort** away).
+**klat'rer** *-en, pl -e* (=***-ar**) climber.
***klat're/sam'** *A* bungling, puttering.
***klat're/smeđ** *-en* bungler, poor workman.
klatt'[1] *-en* 1 clump (of mud), dab (of butter). 2 blot, splotch. 3 amount, bit: **en k- penger** a small sum of money.
klatt'[2] *-et pop.* difficulty, trouble.
klat'te *V -a/+-et* 1 splotch. 2: **k- bort** fritter away, dribble away; waste.
klat'te/gjelđ *-a/+-en* accumulation of small debts.
+**klat'te/maler** *-en, pl -e* (=***/målar**) slapdash, sloppy painter.
Klau's *Prn (m)*
klau'sul *-en jur.* proviso, restriction, stipulation.
klau'v[1] *-a* hoof.
***klau'v**[2] *pt of* **klyve**
klau'v/dyr *-et* cloven-hoofed animal.
kla've[1] *-n* 1 (animal) collar, neck yoke: **har en k- får en alltid ku** if you have the accessories, you'll always manage to get the thing itself. 2 large compasses for measuring land or trees. 3 wall support (in shape of a compass). 4 calipers (for measuring timber).
kla've[2] *V -a/+-et/+-de* 1 shore up a wall with a **klave**[1] **3**. 2 measure diameter of trees.
klave'r *-et, pl -/+-er* piano: **spille på k-** play the p-.
klaviatu'r *-en/-et* keyboard, keys.
+**klav're** *V -a/-et* clamber, climb, crawl.
kle' *V -dde* (=**klede**[2]) 1 clothe, dress: **k- av en** undress sby; **k- av seg** strip, undress; **k- på en** d- sby; **k- på seg** d-; **k- seg** d-; **k- seg naken** strip; **k- seg om** change (clothes); **k- seg ut (som indianer)** d- up (like an Indian), put on (Indian) costume. 2 cover (as a wall), plate; deck, panel, line: **k- fjellet** c- the mountainside (with trees) (Bjørnson). 3 become, suit: **kjolen k-r henne** the dress b-s her; **Sorgen kler Elektra** Mourning b-s Electra (O'Neill).
+**-kle** *-kleet, pl -klær* cf **klede**[1]
+**kle'be** *V -et/-te* glue, paste; stick; be sticky.
+**kle'be/bånđ** *-et* adhesive tape.
kle'ber *-en* soapstone.
kle'ber/stein *-en* soapstone.
+**kle'brig** *A* - sticky: **k- stoff** s- material; **en k- hjerne** a retentive mind.
kle'de[1] [*kle'e] *-t* 1 cloth. 2 piece of cloth, e.g. throw, kerchief: **en salmebok svøpt i et k-** a hymnbook wrapped in a kerchief (Ibsen).
kle'de[2] [*kle'e] *V -de* cf **kle**
+**kle'de/bon'** *-et archaic* garment(s), raiment.
***kle'de/bunađ** *-en* costume, local dress.
+**kle'de/handler** *-en, pl -e* (=***-ar**) ready-to-wear merchant, clothes dealer.
kle'delig *A* - attractive, becoming, suitable; fitting, proper.
+**kle'delig/het** *-en* suitability; propriety.
***kle'đnađ** *-en, pl -er* attire, clothes, dress.
kled'ning *-en* 1 covering, sheath. 2 clothes, dress, outfit.
klegg' *-en, pl +*-er* 1 horsefly (Tabanidae). 2 *derog.* leech (person who clings to one).
klei'e *V -a/+-de/*-dde dial.* 1 scratch. 2 itch.
***klei'me** *V -de* paste; stick.
***klei'men** *A -e/-i, pl -ne* sticky.
klei'n *A* 1 poorly, sickly; thin and pale. 2 miserable, poor, scanty: **k- til å fiske** a p- fisherman.
+**klei'n/kunst** *-en* small, artistic handicraft; small-scale art.
+**klei'n/smeđ** *-en* locksmith.
***klei'p** *pt of* **klipe**
klei's *A* (of speech, person) lisping, mispronouncing r or s.
klei'se *V -a/+-te* lisp, mispronounce r or s.
klei'set(e) *A* - goocy, soft and sticky.
klei'v[1] *-a* steep rocky ascent.
klei'v[2] *pt of* **klive**
klekk' *A klekt* cf **kløkk**[3]
klek'ke[1] *V klakk, +-et/*klokke/*-i* shake, tremble from fear or excitement.
+**klek'ke**[2] *V -et/klekte* (=***-je**) hatch, incubate: **k- ut** (the same); also *fig.* (of ideas).
+**klek'kelig** *A* - sizable (sum of money), whopping.
klek't *nt of* **klekk,** *pp of* **klekke**[1]
klek'te *pt of* **klekke**[2], **klekkje**
klem' *-men* 1 crush, pinch; emphasis, force: **så det har k-** forcibly, so it hurts; **med fynd og k-** forcibly. 2 hug, squeeze. 3: **på k-** ajar.
klema'tis *-en* clematis.
***klem'de** *pt of* **klemme**[2]
klem'me[1] *-a/+-en* 1 clamp, vise. 2 pinch, squeeze: **få en finger i k-** get one's finger caught. 3 difficulty, scrape, tight spot.
klem'me[2] *V +klemte/*klemde* 1 press, squeeze: **k- til** s- hard; **bilen ble k-t mot veggen** the car was s-d against the wall; **k- seg sammen** cuddle, s- together. 2 hug: **kysse og k-** hand kiss. 3 pinch: **k- fingeren** p- one's finger; **skoen k-er** my shoe p-es. 4 depress, weigh down: **k-t om hjertet** sad of heart. 5: **k- på (til)** fire away, go ahead, keep at it; keep it up. 6 *pop.*: **k- til en** smack sby hard.
klem'/skrue *-n* (=***/skruve**) binding screw, terminal screw.
klem't[1] *-et* toll (of a bell); clang, peal.
+**klem't**[2] *pp of* **klemme**[2]
klem'te[1] *V -a/+-et* ring, toll; clang, peal.
+**klem'te**[2] *pt of* **klemme**[2]
kle'n *A* cf **klein**
kleng'e[1] *-a* (=***-je**[1]) bur.
+**kleng'e**[2] *V -te* (=***-je**[2]) cling, hang, stick (**på** to): **k- seg inn på noen**

+ Bokmål; * Nynorsk; ° Dialect.
After letter: ' stress (Acc. 1); ' tone, stress (Acc. 2); · length.
Below letter: . not pronounced.

force one's company upon sby; **k- seg til** c- to.
+kleng'e[3] *V -te* (=***-je[3]**) extract seeds from pine cones by drying.
+kleng'e/navn *-et* nickname.
+kleng'et(e) *A* - (=***klengjet(e)**) clinging, sticky; importunate.
***kleng'je[1]** *-a* cf **klenge[1]**
***kleng'je[2]** *V -de* cf **klenge[2]**
***kleng'je[3]** *V -de* cf **klenge[3]**
***kleng'je/namn** *-et* cf **klenge/navn**
***kleng'jet(e)** *A* - cf **klenget(e)**
kleng'/stue *-a* (=*/**stove**) building for extracting seeds by drying cones.
kleno'die *-t, pl +-r/*-* (=**+klenodium**) gem, jewel, treasure.
klepp'[1] *-en* 1 lump (in food); ball of flour. 2 knoll, rocky prominence. 3 clog (to restrain a horse).
klepp'[2] *-en* gaff hook.
Klepp' *Pln* twp, Rogaland.
klep'pe[1] *V -a/+-et* 1 make lumpy: **k- seg** lump. 2 gaff (fish).
klep'pe[2] *V -a/+-et* split (fish).
klep'pet(e) *A* - lumpy.
klepp'/fisk *-en* dried cod (split, salted, and dried).
kleptoma'n[1] *-en* kleptomaniac.
kleptoma'n[2] *A* kleptomaniac.
kleptomani' *-en* kleptomania.
kleresi' *-et* clergy.
klerika'l *A* church, clerical.
klerikalis'me *-n* clericalism.
kler'k *-en* *hist.* cleric, clerk; clergyman.
kle's/børste *-n* clothes brush.
kle's/drakt *-a/+-en* attire, costume, dress.
+kle's/henger *-en, pl -e* (=***-(j)ar**) clothes hanger, coat hanger.
kle's/klype *-a* clothespin.
kle's/korg *-a* clothes basket.
kle's/kott *-et* clothes closet.
kle's/plagg *-et* garment, piece of clothing.
***kless'[1]** *-en* slap, smack.
***kless'[2]** *-et* clinging caress.
kles'se[1] *V klass/+kleste, +klest/*klosse/*-i* plop, smack, splash.
kles'se[2] *V kleste* 1: **k- til en "paste"**, slap sby. 2 stammer, stutter; stumble over (one's) words.
+kle's/skap *-et* (=*/**skåp**) closet, wardrobe.
kle's/snor *-a* clothesline.
kle's/tørk *-en* 1 clothes drying: **god k-** good drying weather. 2 drying clothes: **fargerik som k-** colorful as clothes on the line.
kle's/vask *-en* (of clothes) wash, washing.
klett' *-en* (round) bluff, hill.
kle've *-n* 1 (rural) small bedroom off main room; closet. 2 carrel, cubicle (in library).
kli'[1] *-et* bran.
***kli'[2]** *V -dde* feel nauseated, retch.
kli'/brød [also kli'/] *-et* bran bread.
klien't *-en* client.
kliente'l *-et* clientele.
klikk'[1] *-en* clique, set.
klikk'[2] *-en/-et* click: **slå k-** misfire, *fig.* fail; dud.
klikk'[3] *I* click.
klik'ke *V -a/+-et* 1 click; rap, tap, tick. 2 fail, misfire (*lit.* of a gun, also *fig.*): **stemmen k-et** (her, his) voice failed.
+klik'ke/vesen *-et* cliquishness.
kli'ma *-et* climate.
kli'maks *-en* climax.
klimakte'rium *-iet, pl +-ier/*-ium* climacteric, menopause.
+klima't *-et* *archaic* climate.
klima't/feber *-en* endemic fever, tropical fever.
klima'tisk *A* - climatic.
klim'per *-et* plink, plinking (of stringed instrument), strumming.
klim'pre *V -a/+-et* *mus.* plink, pluck, strum; *derog.* plunk.
kli'n *-et* 1 slop, smear. 2 hair oil, pomade. 3 *derog.* caressing, petting.
kli'ne *V -te* 1 coat, daub, spread (paint etc.); smear. 2 paste: **k- opp plakater** put up posters. 3 cling, press close; *derog.* make love, pet.
+kli'neri *-et* 1 slop, smear. 2 *derog.* caressing, petting.
kli'net(e) *A* - 1 gooey, smeary, sticky. 2 importunate, offensive; forward, sticky. 3 clinging, cuddly.
kling' *-en* cf **klining**
Kling'a *Pln* twp, Nord-Trøndelag.
+kling'e[1] *-n* blade (of saber, sword): **gå en hårdt på k-n** press sby (for an explanation); **krysse k-r** cross swords.
kling'e[2] *V klang, +-et/+-t/*klunge/*-i* 1 (of musical tones) ring, sound: **k- ut** die away. 2 (of bells, glass, etc.) clink, jingle, tinkle: *bibl.* **en k-ende bjelle** a t-ing cymbal. 3 echo, resound: **k-ende frost** glittering frost; **k-ende mynt** hard cash; **en k-ende tale** a resounding (ringing) speech. 4 sound: **det k-er som russisk** it s-s like Russian.
klingeling' *I* ting-a-ling.
kling'er *A -ert, pl -re* bell-like; (of voice) high and clear (sometimes piercing, shrill).
kling'/klang *-en/-et* 1 dingdong; 2 empty, meaningless sounds; worthless music.
klinikk' *-en* 1 clinical instruction: **holde k-** have bedside instruction. 2 clinic; small hospital. 3 maternity home, ward.
kli'ning *-en* 1 coating, pasting, spreading. 2 pressing close; caressing. 3 thickly spread flatbread or *lefse*. 4 *naut.* calking.
kli'nisk *A* - clinical.
klin'k *-en/-et* 1 clinking of glasses, *skåling*. 2 marble game.
klink'/bygd *A* - *naut.* clinker-built, lap-jointed.
klin'ke[1] *-a* 1 (old-fashioned) door latch, handle. 2 doorknob.
klin'ke[2] *V -a/+-et* 1 beat, strike. 2 hammer, rivet. 3 repair (also **k- i hop, k- sammen**), esp. earthenware. 4 clink; clink glasses: **jeg vil k- med deg** I want to c- glasses with you. 5 play marbles.
klin'ke[3] *A* - pure: **k- klare tøv** p- nonsense.
klin'ke/kule *-a* marble.
klin'kende *Av* very, extremely: **k- klar** clear as glass.
klin'k/nagle *-n* rivet.
+klin'k/søm' *-met* riveted seam.
+klin't *-en* seaside cliff.
klin'te *-n* 1 *bot.* corn cockle. 2 *bibl.* tares: **skille k-n fra hveten** distinguish the good from the bad.
kli'pe *V kleip, klipe/-i* cf **klype[2]**
klipp' *-et* 1 clip, clipping, snip. 2 *lit.* blink (of eye, light).
+klip'pe[1] *-n* 1 *lit.* cliff. 2 *bibl., lit.* rock: **bygge sitt hus på en k-** build one's house on a r-.
klip'pe[2] *V klipte* 1 cut (with scissors or shears): **k-, k-** (saying used of stubborn persons, from folktale of the Contrary Woman); **k- av** c- off; **k- opp** c- open, slit; **k- over** c- in two; **k- til** trim, shape; **k- ut** c- out. 2 clip (ear, wings); edit (a film); pare (nails); punch (a ticket); shear (sheep); trim (dog, hedge). 3 *lit.* blink: **k- med øynene** b (one's eyes).
+klip'pe/blokk *-en* block of stone, boulder.
+klip'pe/fast *A* - firm as a rock; steadfast, unshakable.
+klip'pe/grunn *-en* rocky ground, rocky land; *bibl.* firm foundation.
klip'pe/kort *-et* commuter's ticket, season ticket (at reduced fares, punched for each use).
klip'pe/maskin [/masji'n] *-en* clippers.
+klip'per *-en, pl -e* (=***-ar**) clipper, cutter (usu. in compounds): **hår/** haircutter; **gress/** lawn mower.
+klip'pe/vegg *en* rocky face of a mountain, mountain wall.
klipp'/fisk *-en* cf **klepp/**
klip's *-en/-et* (decorative) clip.
klirr' *-et* clatter, clinking, jingling.
klir're *V -a/+-et* (noise as of glass or metal) clank, clink, clatter; jingle, rattle.
klisjé *-en* 1 *typog.* block, cut; plate. 2 cliché, stereotype.
+klisjé/aktig *A* - clichéd, stereotyped.
klisjé/anstal't *-en* engraving establishment.
klis'ne *pl of* **klissen**
kliss'[1] *-et* 1 sticky mass, substance, or coating. 2 candy, sucker. 3 sentimental, sugary talk or behavior; overdone lovemaking.
kliss'[2] *I* squish.
klis'se *V -a/+-et* 1 cling, stick: **k- seg sammen** get stuck together. 2 smear. 3 *(impers.)* **det k-er** it makes a squashy sound. 4 lisp; talk babytalk. 5 act in an overly sweet, sentimental way; pet.
klis'sen *A +-ent, pl klisne* 1 gooey, smeary, sticky. 2 overly sweet, sentimental.
klis'set(e) *A* - 1 gooey, smeary, sticky. 2 overly sweet, sentimental.
kliss'/klass[1] *-et* goo, goop.
kliss'-klass'[2] *I* splish-splash, slurpslurp.
klis'ter *-eret/-ret* 1 paste. 2 klister (a soft ski wax).
klis'ter/føre *-t* skiing conditions requiring klister; corn snow, wet snow.
klis'tre *V -a/+-et* paste: **k- seg fast** stick.
klitt' *-en* cliff.
***kli'var** *-en* climber.
kli've *V kleiv, +-d/*-e/*-i* clamber, climb.
***kljå'** *-en* = **klåstein.**
***kljå'/stein** *-en* cf **klå/**
klo' *-a, pl klør* 1 claw (e.g. of animal, lobster; anchor, hook). 2 *hum.* hand: **slå k-a i en** pounce upon sby, get one's hands on sby; **falle i ens klør** fall into sby's clutches; **vise klørne** show one's claws; **med nebb og klør** tooth and nail. 3 hand = handwriting, mark: **det viste mesterens k-** it showed the master's hand. 4 *naut.* clew; reef: **med tre klør i seglet** with three r-s in the sail.
kloakk' [also klo'-] *-en* 1 sewer. 2 *zool.* cloaca.
kloakk'/dyr *-et* *zool.* monotreme.
+kloakk'/ledning *-en* sewer pipe.
kloakk'/rotte *-a* sewer rat.
kloakk'/rør *-et/*-a* sewer pipe.
kloakk'/vatn *-et* (=+/**vann**) sewer water, sewage.
***klo'ast** *V -ast* scratch and claw (each other).
***klo'/berr** *A -bert* clear, distinct, plain; evident, obvious.
+klo'de *-n* (=***klote**) 1 planet. 2 earth, world.
+klod'rian *-en* clod, clumsy fool, oaf.
klo'/dyr *-et* *dial.* beast of prey, predator.
klo'/hammar *-en* claw hammer.
klo'k *A* wise; intelligent, judicious, sensible: **det gjør du k-t i** that is w- of you; **jeg blir ikke k- på (henne)** I can't make (her) out; I can't get w- to (her); **svaret gjorde oss ikke k-ere** the answer made us none the w-r, left us still in the dark. 2 prudent; shrewd; clever: **en k- hund** a smart dog. 3 sane: **er du ikke k-?** are you crazy?; **han er ikke riktig k-** he's not all there, he's off his rocker. 4 knowing the occult: **en k- kone** a wise woman, a quack.
+klo'kelig *Av* (=***klokeleg**) sensibly, wisely.
klo'king *-en* wise person.
***klokk'** *pt of* **kløkke[1]**
klok'ke[1] *-a* 1 bell: **kimer i k-r** ring out ye b-s (hymn). 2 clock, watch: **k-a (+k-n) ett** one o'clock; **k-a er tre** it is three o'clock; **hva er k-a, hvor mange er k-a** what time is it. 3 (bell-shaped) cover (for cheese

etc.). 4 *bot.* bellflower (Campanula).
klok'ke[2] *V -a/+-et* clock: **k- inn** punch in; **bli k-et inn på** be c-ed at.
***klok'ke**[3] *pp of* **klekke**[1]
+klok'ke/blomst *-en* (=***/blome**) bellflower (Campanula).
+klok'ke/bytte *-t* (=***/byte**) watch trading.
lok'ke/forma *A* - (=**+-et**) bellshaped.
klok'ke/jøde *-n* watch peddler (often Jewish).
klok'ke/klang *-en* chime, ringing (of church bells).
klok'ke/klar *A* clear as a bell.
klok'ke/lyng *-en/-et bot.* bell heather (Erica).
klok'kende *Av*: **k- klar** clear as a bell.
+klok'ker *-en, pl -e* (=***-ar**) 1 sexton; precentor (led singing in church; was also often the local schoolmaster). 2 stupid person.
klok'ke/ringing *-a/+-en* bell ringing.
+klok'ker/kjærlighet *-en*: **ha k- for** have a soft spot in one's heart for.
klok'ke/skjørt *-et* bell-shaped skirt.
klok'ke/slett *-et* hour, time (of day): **på k-et (tre)** at the stroke (of three); on the dot.
+klok'ke/spill *-et* (=***/spel**) 1 bells (instrument); carillon, glockenspiel. 2 ringing of bells.
klok'ke/streng *-en* bell rope.
klok'ke/time *-n* (full) hour: **en hel k-** an hour by the clock.
klok'ke/tå'rn *-et* belfry, bell tower, steeple.
klok'ke/ås *-en* beam from which bell swings.
***klok'ki** *pp of* **klekke**[1]
***klo'kleg** *Av* cf **klokelig**
***klo'kne** *V -a* become wiser.
klo'k/skap *-en* 1 understanding, wisdom. 2 judgment, prudence. 3 insight: **etterpå/** hindsight.
***klom'ber** *-ra, pl -rer* mountain cleft, crevice.
***klom'bret(e)** *A* - cut by crevice(s).
klopp' *-a* bridge (of logs), footbridge.
klo'r[1] *-en/-et* chlorine.
klo'r[2] *-et* scratch.
klora'l *-et* chloral.
klo're[1] *V -te/*-a* scratch; claw: **katten k- meg** may the devil take me; **k- ned et par ord** scrawl a few words; **k- seg forbi** c- one's way past; **k- til seg** scrape together; **k-es** fight, s- each other.
klo're[2] *V -te/*-a* chlorinate; bleach; disinfect.
klo'r/kalk *-en* chloride of lime (bleaching powder, disinfectant).
klorofor'm *-en* chloroform.
kloroforme're *V -te* chloroform.
klorofyll' *-et* chlorophyll.
klo'r/syre *-a* chloric acid.
klosett' *-et, pl -/+-er* lavatory, toilet; privy.
klosett'/papi'r *-et* toilet paper.
klosett'/skål *-a* toilet bowl.
kloss'[1] *-en* 1 (usu. wood) block, cleat, clog; wedge. 2 clod, clumsy person.
kloss'[2] *A* - 1 close: **på k- hold** at c-range. 2 right: **k- i veien** r- in the way.
klos'set(e) *A* - awkward, clumsy.
+klos'set/het *-en* clumsiness.
kloss'/hale *V -te* haul tight.
kloss'/majo'r *-en* big oaf, big clod, clumsy ox.
kloss'/reve *V -a/+-et/+-de* close-reef.
klos'ter *-eret/-ret, pl -er/+-re* cloister; convent, monastery; nunnery: **gå i k-** become a monk (or a nun), enter the cloister or m-.
klos'ter/bror *-en, pl +-brødre/*-brør* friar, monk.
klo'ster/lati'n *-en* poor Latin, as used in medieval monasteries.
+klos'ter/løfte *-t* (=***/lovnad**) conventual or monastic vow.
klos'ter/regel *-elen, pl -ler* convent (or monastery) rule.
klos'ter/vesen *-et* monasticism.
klo't *-en* lump.
***klo'te** *-n* cf **klode**

+klo'v[1] *-en* cf **klauv**[1]
***klov**[2] [klå'v] *-et* cleft, crack, split.
+klo'v/dyr [also klå'v/] *-et* cf **klauv/**
***klove**[1] [klå've] *-n* cleft, canyon. 2 forked stick; clamp.
klo've[2] *-a* cleft, hollow in the side of a hill (*Scot.* corrie).
***klove**[3] [klå've] *pp of* **klyve**
***kloven** [klå'ven] *a -e/-i, pl -ne* cloven; cleaved, split.
***klovi** [klå'vi] *pp of* **klyve**
klov'n *-en* clown.
klov'ne *V -a/+-et* (=**+kløvne**) split.
+klov'neri *-et* clownishness, ridiculousness; clowning, tomfoolery.
***klovning** [klå'vning] *-en* one of the two pieces into which log is split.
***klov/sopp** [klå'v/] *-en* bacterium.
+klo'v/syke [also klå'v/] *-n* hoof-and-mouth disease.
klubb'[1] *-en* 1 *dial.* lump. 2 black pudding; dumpling.
klubb'[2] *-en* club, society; (sewing) circle.
klub'be[1] *-a* bat, club, mallet. 2 gavel.
+klub'be[2] *V -a/-et* 1 bat, club, hit. 2 bang, gavel; call to order: **k- ned en taler** take away the floor from a speaker.
klubb'/formann *-en, pl -menn/*-menner* club chairman.
klubb'/genser *-en* club sweater (worn by member of a sports club).
klubb'/loka'le *-t, pl +-r/*-* clubroom.
+klud'der *-eret/kludret* 1 bungling, fumbling (**med** with), sloppy work. 2 scrawling. 3 difficulty, unpleasantness.
+klud're *V -a/-et* 1 bungle, fumble, do a sloppy job of sth: **k- med b**, mess with. 2 scrawl.
***kluf't** *-a* cf **kløft**
***kluf'te** *V -a* cf **kløfte**
kluf't(e)/gran *-a* spruce with two crowns.
***kluf'tet(e)** *A* - cf **kløftet**
klukk[1] [klokk'] *-en/+-et* cluck; (of water) gurgle.
klukk[2] [klokk'] *A* - (of hen) broody.
klukk[3] [klokk'] *I* cluck.
klukke [klok'ke] *V -a/+-et* 1 cackle, cluck, gobble. 2 chortle, chuckle. 3 gurgle.
klukk/høne [klokk'/] *-a* broody hen, setting hen.
+klukk/latter [klokk'/] *-en* (=***/lått**) chortle, chuckle.
klukk/le [klokk'/] *V -lo, -ledd/*-lett* chortle, chuckle.
klump [klom'p] *-en* 1 clod, clump: **en k- jord** a lump of dirt. 2 ball. 3 clog (shoe). 4 bunch, clump.
klumpe [klom'pe] *V -a/+-et* 1 make lumpy: **k- seg** lump, become lumpy. 2 bunch up, wad up: **k- seg sammen** bunch together.
klumpedei(s)e [klompedei'(s)e] *-a* clumsy woman.
klumpet(e) [klom'pet(e)] *A* - lumpy; dumpy, fat.
klump/fot [klom'p/] *-en* clubfoot.
+klump/nese [klom'p/] *-n* (=***/nase**) bulbous, lumpy nose.
klump/rot [klom'p/] *-a* club roo (disease of turnips, radishes, etc., caused by Plasmodiophora brassicae).
klums [klom's] *A* - bewildered, confused, spellbound.
klumse [klom'se] *V -a/+-et*: **k-et** bewildered, confused, spellbound.
klumset(e) [klom'set(e)] *A* - bulging, clumsy, dumpy.
klun'der *-et* 1 botchy, sloppy work. 2 difficulties, problems, unpleasantnesses.
***klun'dre**[1] *-a* gnarl, knot.
klun'dre[2] *V -a/+-et* 1 toil clumsily, ineffectually. 2 struggle: **k- seg fram** s- along.
***klung'e** *pp of* **klinge**[2]
klunger [klong'er] *-eren, pl -rer* bramble, dog brier, wild brier.
klunger/bjørk [klong'er/] *-a* low birch with rough, knotty branches.

klunger/kjerr *-et* bramblebush, brier patch.
klunger/rose *-a/+-en* dog-rose (type of brier).
***klung'i** *pp of* **klinge**[2]
***klungret(e)** [klong'ret(e)] *A* - knotty, thorny.
klunk [klong'k] *-en* 1 (of liquid) gurgle; clunk. 2 drink, swig (esp. from bottle). 3 plink, plunk, strumming (on mus. instrument). 4 (mating) call of capercailzie (**tiur**).
klunke [klong'ke] *V -a/+-et* 1 (of liquid) gurgle; clunk. 2 plink, plunk, strum (**på** on). 3 (of capercailzie) call (with a deep, gurgling sound).
klunke/flaske *-a* pinchbottle (brandy bottle deeply indented on the sides so as to make a clunking sound in pouring).
kluns [klon's] *-en* 1 lump, outgrowth. 2 *dial.* broadbeaked auk. 3 fat, clumsy person; dumpy person.
klun'tet(e) *A* - 1 bulging, lumpy; dumpy. 2 awkward, clumsy.
***klu'se** *V -a* mend, patch.
kluss' *-et* 1 blot, splatter, splotch. 2 mess (**med** with), messing around: **nytt k- med språket** more messing with the language; **bare noe k- et eller annet sted** just some bungling somewhere (Evensmo). 3 fondling, spoiling.
klus'se *V -a/+-et* 1 blot, splatter, splotch. 2 mess (**med** with), mess around; bungle, flounder. 3 fondle, spoil (sby).
klu't *-en* 1 piece of cloth, rag. 2 cloth (e.g. washcloth). 3 sail: **alle k-er vi kunne få på henne** all the canvas we could get on her; **sette alle k-er til** hoist all sails; *fig.* do one's utmost, risk everything.
klu'te/papi'r *-et* rag paper.
+klu'te/samler *-en, pl -e* (=***-ar**) ragpicker.
***klut're** *V -a* fuss, putter.
***klyf'tig** *A* - clever, shrewd.
+klyng'e[1] *-a/-en* (=***klyngje**) cluster, crowd, group (**av** of); knot (of people).
+klyng'e[2] *V -et/-te* 1: **k- seg (til)** cling (to), entwine; **hun k-er seg tett til ham** she clings to him. 2: **k- opp (noen)** hang, string up (sby).
***klyng'je** *-a* cf **klynge**[1]
klyn'k *-et* whimper(ing), whine, whining.
klyn'ke *V -a/+-et* complain, whimper, whine.
kly'pe[1] *-a* 1 clip; clamp; (clothes)pin; tong. 2 *pop.* fist, hand. 3 pinch (of salt etc.). 4 cleft, ravine.
kly'pe[2] *V -te/+kløp, -t/+kløpet* 1 pinch. 2 clamp (with tongs, vise, etc.), squeeze.
klypp' *-et* cf **klipp**
***klyp'par** *-en* cf **kløpper**
klyp'pe *V klypte* cf **klippe**[2]
kly'se *-a* blob, clot, splotch.
klyss' *-et, pl - naut.* hawsehole.
klystér *-et, pl - med.* clyster, enema: **sette et k-** give an e-.
klystér/sprøyte *-a* enema syringe.
+kly've[1] *V kløv/-de, kløvet/-d* climb.
***kly've**[2] *V klyv, klauv, klove/-i* cleave, split.
kly've/led *-et* stile.
kly'ver[1] *-en naut.* jib.
kly'ver[2] *-en, pl -e* (=***-ar**) climber.
kly'ver/bom [/bom'] *-men naut.* jibboom.
klæ [kle'] *V -dde* cf **kle**
Klæ'/bu *Pln* twp, Sør-Trøndelag.
klæde[1] [+kle'de, *kle'e] *-t* cf **klede**[1]
+klæde[2] [kle'de] *V -te* cf **kle**
klæde- [+kle'de-, *kle'e-] *Pf* cf **klede-, kles-**
+klæ'r *pl (df -ne)* (=***klede**) clothes,

+ Bokmål; * Nynorsk; ° Dialect.
After letter: ' stress (Acc. 1); ` tone, stress (Acc. 2); · length.
Below letter: . not pronounced.

clothing: **k- skaper folk** clothes make the man; **i kongens k-** in uniform.

klø' *V -dde* 1 scratch: **k- seg i hodet** s- one's head. 2 itch: **k- (i fingrene) etter noe** i- for sth.

+**klø'e** *-n* 1 scratching: **etter den søte k- kommer den sure svie** after self-indulgence comes the punishment. 2 itch, itching.

kløf't *-a* 1 cleft (e.g. in chin). 2 chasm, crevice. 3 fork (on branch): **gå med k-** divine, dowse (for water). 4 *fig.* breach, cleavage, rift.

kløf'te *V -a/+-et* split: **k- seg** divide, separate.

kløf'tet(e) *A* - 1 cleft; forked. 2 having chasms, crevices, etc.

+**kløkk'**[1] *-en/-et dial.* 1 fright, shock, start. 2 clink, ding.

kløkk'[2] *A kløkt dial.* (=**klekk**) 1 immature, undeveloped. 2 brittle, thin, weak; delicate, tender.

***kløk'ke**[1] *V klokk, klokke/-i* jump, start (from fright, muscle spasm, etc.).

+**kløk'ke**[2] *V kløkte* (=***-je**) *dial.* move (sby emotionally), stir.

***kløk'ken** *A -e/-i, pl kløkne* sensitive, easily moved.

***kløkkj'ast** *V kløktest, kløkst* be moved, touched; be stirred, feel sympathetic.

***kløkkj'e** *V kløkte* cf **kløkke**[2]

kløk't[1] *+-en/*-a* cleverness, cunning, sagacity.

***kløk't**[2] *A* - moved, stirred (**av** by).

kløk't[3] *nt of* **kløkk**[2]

***kløk'te** *pt of* **kløkkje**

***kløk'test** *pt of* **kløkkjast**

kløk'tig *A* - clever, crafty, shrewd.

+**kløk'tig/het** *-en* 1 cleverness, cunning, shrewdness. 2 *archaic* wisdom; insight.

klø'ne[1] *-a* bumbler, clumsy person.

klø'ne[2] *V -te* 1 scrabble, scratch. 2 bumble, fumble (**med** with).

klø'net(e) *A* - awkward, bumbling, clumsy.

+**klø'p** *pt of* **klype**[2]

klø'/pinne *-n* backscratcher.

+**kløp'per** *-en, pl -e* (=***-ar**) crackerjack, expert, whiz: **en k- til å arbeide** a great hand for working.

klø'r *pl of* **klo**

+**klø'v**[1] *-en* (=***kløyv**) 1 *tech.* cleavage. 2 line of cleavage. 3 *pop.* crack, split; cleft; part (in hair).

klø'v[2] *-a* 1 packsaddle. 2 pack (on animal).

+**klø'v**[3] *pt of* **klyve**[1]

+**klø've**[1] *V -de* cf **kløyve**

+**klø've**[2] *V -et* cf **kløvje**

kløv'er *-en, pl-* 1 clover. 2 club (in cards): **melde fire k-** bid four c-s.

kløv'er/eng *-a* clover field.

kløv'er/ess [also /ess'] *+-et/*-en* ace of clubs.

klø'v/hest *-en* packhorse.

kløv'je *V -a/+-et* 1 make up a peck. 2 fasten a pack to a horse. 3 pack (transport by pack animal).

klø'v/meis *-a/-en* pack basket, pannier.

+**kløv'ne** *V -a/-et* cf **klovne**

klø'v/sal *-en* packsaddle.

+**klø'v/sti** *-en* (=***/stig**) pack trail.

kløy'en *A +-ent, pl -ne* soft; effeminate, weak.

***kløy'v** *-en* cf **kløv**[1]

kløy've *V -de* 1 cleave, split: **k- ved** chop wood. 2 divide, separate: **k- seg** d-, split up.

***kløy'vning** *-en* cf **klovning**

klå' *V -dde* 1 scratch; itch. 2 lick, whip. 3 fleece, skin. 4 finger, touch (improperly).

klå'e *-n* 1 itch, itching. 2 mange.

klå'/fingra *A* - (=+**-et**) itchy-fingered, having compulsion to touch things.

***klå'r** *A* cf **klar**

***klå're**[1] *-a* cf **klare**[1]

***klå're**[2] *V -a* cf **klare**[2]

***klå'r/leggje** *V -la(gde), -lagd/-lagt* cf **klar/legge**

***klå'r/leik** *-en* clarity, clearness.

***klå'rne** *V -a* cf **klarne**

***klå'r/syn** *-et/-a* cf **klar/**

***klå'r/ver** *-et* cf **klar/vær**

***klå'r/øygd** *A -/-øygt* cf **klar/øyd**

+**klå'/stein** *-en* (=***kljå/**) warping stone (stone to weight warp threads on upright loom).

***klåt're** *-a* burl, gnarl (on a tree).

km=**kilo/meter**

kna' *V -dde* 1 knead: **godt k-dd** well k-ed; **en k-dd liten fyr** a solid little fellow. 2 roll, rub (sby e.g. in snow).

KNA=**Kongelig Norsk Automobilklubb**

knabb' *-en* 1 knoll, knot (on a mountain). 2 end, piece, stub. 3 chubby person or animal.

knab'be *V -a/+-et* 1 grab, nab, snatch; snitch, swipe. 2: **k-es** fight, tussle.

+**kna'ber** *A -ert, pl -re dial.* neat, nice, well-proportioned.

knagg' *-en* (=***knagge**) 1 peg; hook (for hanging clothes). 2 handle (of scythe); *naut.* (projecting) spoke (on ship's wheel). 3 cog.

kna'k *-et* crack, creak.

kna'ke *V -a/+-et/+-te* crack, creak: **k- og brake** creak and groan; **det k-er i trappa** the stairs creak; **det k-er og går** things are going all right.

kna'kende *A* 1 cracking, creaking. 2 awfully, terrifically: **k- morsomt** great fun.

knakk'[1] *-en* stool.

knakk'[2] *pt of* **knekke**[1]

+**knak'ke** *V -a/-et* knock: **k- på døra** k- on the door.

knakk'/pølse *-a* knackwurst, short sausage.

knall' *-et* 1 bang, explosion, report. 2 crack, pop. 3 catastrophe: **det endte med k-** it ended in c-; **k- og fall** a thunderous downfall.

knall'/blå *A -tt* intensely blue.

knall'/bonbon [/bångbång'] *-en* (frilly) party favor (opens with a bang, contains paper hat etc.).

knal'le *V -a/+-et* 1 bang, explode: **skuddet k-et** the shot rang out. 2 crack, pop; click; smash. 3: **k-ende** bright, dazzling, intense (color).

knall'/effek't *-en* sensation, startling effect.

knal'lert *-en* 1 (percussion) cap. 2 popgun. 3 lightweight motorbike.

knall'/gass *-en* oxyhydrogen.

knall'/hette *-a* (percussion) cap.

knall'/perle *-a* (percussion) cap.

knall'/suksess [/sykse'] *-en* rousing success.

kna'/ost [/ost] *-en* cottage cheese.

kna'pe *-n* 1 *hist.* (knight's) squire. *2 rich, powerful man.

knapp'[1] *-en* 1 button (on bell, clothing, switch): **telle på k-ene** be undecided, try to make up one's mind. 2 knob; head.

knapp'[2] *A knapt* 1 scanty (provisions); narrow (space); scarce: **det er k-t om plassen** space is scarce; **det er k-t med smør** there isn't much butter. 2 hard (times); poor (circumstances): **ha det k-t** be in straitened circumstances. 3 brief, concise, terse (e.g. answer); short (time). 4 bare: **k-e 45 år** a b- (barely) 45; **et k-t minutt** barely a minute. 5 *naut.* poor (wind); slack.

***knap'past** *Av* hardly, scarcely.

knap'pe[1] *V -a/+-et* button: **k- kåpen** button (one's) coat; **k- opp** (e.g. coat) unbutton; **k- ned** (e.g. trousers) unbutton; **k- til** button up.

knap'pe[2] *V -a/+-et*: **k- av** cut down, reduce; **k- av på rasjonene** cut down on the rations.

knap'pe/nål *-a* (straight) pin: **en kunne høre en k- falle** you could hear a p- drop.

knap'penåls/brev *-et* book of pins.

+**knap'pe/støper** *-en, pl -e* (=***/støypar**) button molder, button maker.

+**knap'pet** *A* - buttoned; knobbed, topped with a (gold, silver) knob.

+**knapp'/het** *-en* 1 scarcity, shortage (**på** of). 2 brevity, concision, terseness.

knapp'/hol *-et* buttonhole.

+**knapp'/hull** *-et* cf **/hol**

+**knapp'hulls/blomst** *-en* boutonnière, flower for buttonhole.

***knapp'/nål** *-a* cf **knappe/**

knap't[1] *nt of* **knapp**[2]

knap't[2] *Av* barely, hardly, scarcely: **k- atten år** b- eighteen.

knar'k *-en* crabby old man, curmudgeon, fogey.

knarr'[1] *-en* 1 *hist.* merchantman (ship). 2 type of sailboat.

knarr'[2] *-en* 1 crab, grumbler. 2 (=**kveld/**) night raven.

knarr'[3] *-et* creaking, grating.

knar't[1] *-en* 1 gnarl, knot. 2 crag.

***knar't**[2] *pt of* **knerte**[1]

knar'te *V -a/+-et* chop, hack, rain blows upon.

***knar'te/stav** *-en* knobby cane.

kna's[1] *-et* 1 crackle, crunch, grating. 2 bits, pieces, splinters: **speilet gikk i k-** the mirror broke into a thousand p-s. 3 crunchy candy. 4 fun: **Gud så k-** heavens, such fun.

kna's[2] *Av* crackling: **k- tørr** dry as bone, tinder dry; **en k- tørr tale** a dry-as-dust speech.

kna'se *V -a/-te* crackle, crunch, grate.

kna'sende *Av*: (emphatic) **k- tørr** dry as tinder, explosively dry.

knas'k *-et* crunchy candy; hard candy.

knas'ke *V -a/+-et* chew, crunch.

knas't *-en* 1 gnarl, knot. 2 knob, projection.

kna's/tørr *A -tørt* dry as bone, tinder dry; dry-as-dust.

knatt'[1] *-en* small round hill, hummock, mound, tor.

knatt'[2] *pt of* **knette**

knat'te *V -a/+-et* knock (repeatedly), rap; beat.

knau's *-en* 1 knoll; peak, rock. 2 submerged rock.

knau'set(e) *A* - hilly, rocky.

knav're[1] *-n* nose ring.

knav're[2] *V -a/+-et* put a ring in a hog's snout.

kne' *-et, pl -/+knær* 1 knee: **ligge på k-** kneel; **ligge på knærne for noen** fawn on sby, worship sby; **synke i k-** go down on one's k-s; **på knærne** down-and-out; **til k-s** up to the k-s. 2: (on trousers) **knær i buksene** baggy k-s. 3 (in pipe) elbow, joint. 4 *naut.* bracket.

kne'bel *-elen, pl -ler* 1 gag (in mouth). 2 clapper (of a bell). 3 moustache. 4 tourniquet. 5 *naut.* toggle.

kne'bels/bart *-en* moustache.

+**kne'/beskyt'ter** *-en, pl -e* knee protector.

kne'ble [also **kneb'le**] *V -a/+-et* gag: **k- pressen** g- the press.

kne'bler *pl of* **kne'bel**

kne'/bukser [/bokser] *pl* knee pants.

+**kne'/bøyning** *-en* (=***/bøy(gn)ing**) knee bend; curtsy.

+**kne'/dyp** *A* (=***/djup**) knee-deep.

***kne'e** *V -a* 1 bring to his knees. 2 kneel.

kne'/fall *-et* 1 kneeling bench; communion rail. 2 group of communicants. 3 genuflection, kneeling.

+**kneg'de** *pt of* **knegge**

kne'ge *V -a/+-et* 1 crush, rub. 2 slave, toil; grind away at sth. 3 *pop.* hoard, be stingy.

kne'gen *A +-ent, pl -ne* miserly, stingy.

knegg' *-et* 1 neigh, whinny. 2 call o a grouse, cackle. 3 chuckle.

+**kneg'ge** *V -a/-et/knegde* (=***-je**) 1 (of horse) neigh, whinny. 2 (of grouse) call, cackle. 3 (of person) chuckle.

kne'/gå *V +-gikk/*-gjekk, -gått* 1 walk on (one's) knees. 2 give (sby) the knee, maul (with one's knees). 3 *dial.* hound, press sby for sth.

kne'/høg *A* (=+/**høy**) knee-high.
kne'/høne *-a* chicken, coward, yes-man.
knei'k *-a/-en* 1 bend. 2 short, steep hill: **vi er over k-en** we're over the hump.
knei'ket(e) *A* - hilly, up-and-down.
knei'p *pt of* **knipe**[2]
knei'pe *-a/+-en* pub, saloon, tavern.
kneipp'/brød *-et* whole wheat bread.
+**knei'se** *V -te* 1 lift (one's head), stand up straight. 2 rise proudly, tower up. 3 *fig.* face boldly, brazenly: **k- med hodet** toss one's head.
°**kne'ken** *A -ent, pl -ne* cf **knegen**
knekk'[1] *-en* brittle (type of candy).
knekk'[2] *-en/-et* 1 (slight) bend, bow: **et k- i knærne** a bend of the knees; **k-en i ryggen** the (servile) bow of the back; **k- på kurven** a break in the curve; **k-/stil** a skijumping stance with a sharp bend at the hips. 2 crack: **et k- i glasset** a c- in the glass. 3 crackling, creak, snap: **det gav et k- i trærne** a crackling was heard among the trees. 4 blow, damage, injury: **få en k- for livet** never be the same again, suffer irreparable d-. 5: **ta k-en på** put an end to, overcome; **denne ordboka kommer til å ta k-en på oss** this dictionary will be the end of us.
knek'ke[1] *V knakk, +knekt/*knokke/*-i* 1 crack, snap: **grenen knakk** the branch s-ped; **stemmen knakk** (sby's) voice c-ed. 2 (of noise) crack, creak, snap: **det knakk i isen** the ice creaked. 3 bend, bow: **k- i knærne** bend the knees, double up. 4: **k- sammen** break down, collapse.
+**knek'ke**[2] *V -et/knekte* (=***-je**) 1 crack, snap: **k- nakken på en** break sby's neck. 2 crack (open) (e.g. nuts): **en hard nøtt å k-** a tough problem; **k- en flaske** open a bottle. 3 break, break down, ruin: **k- motet på en** break sby's spirit. 4: **k-et** bent, broken (line; person).
knek'ke/brød *-et* (similar to) rye krisp.
knek'kende *Av* (emphatic) absolutely, terribly: **k- likegyldig** completely indifferent.
+**knek'ker** *-en, pl -e* (=***knekkjar**) cracker: **nøtte/** nutcracker.
***knekkj'e** *V knokto* cf **knekke**[2]
knekk'/parasoll' *-en* parasol with folding handle.
kne'/kort *A* - knee-length.
knek't[1] *-en* 1 fellow, young man. 2 rascal, scamp. 3 jack (in cards). 4 (shelf) bracket.
knek't[2] *pp of* **knekke**[1], **knekke**[2]
knek'te[1] *V -a/-et* discipline, subdue.
+**knek'te**[2] *pt of* **knekke**[2], **knekkje**
kne'le *V -te* kneel: **k- for k-** before.
kne'/ledd *-et* (=*/**led**) knee joint.
+**kne'ler** *-en, pl -e* (=***-ar**) *zool.* (praying) mantis (Mantis religiosa).
kne'p[1] *-et* trick: **bruke k-** resort to t-s.
+**kne'p**[2] *pt of* **knipe**[2]
+**kne'pen** *A -ent, pl -ne* 1 meagre, scanty, small: **k-ent mål** scant measure. 2 closefisted, stingy. 3 narrow: **en k- seier** a n- victory; **et k-ent flertall** a bare majority.
+**kne'pet** *pp of* **knipe**[2]
knepp' *-en/-et* click, ticking: **han kløp låsen igjen; "knepp!" sa den** he closed the lock; "click," it said.
knep'pe[1] *V knepte* 1 button (a garment). 2 clasp, fold: **k- i hop hendene** f- one's hands.
knep'pe[2] *V -a/+-et* 1 click, crack, snap. 2 pluck, plunk (stringed instruments).
knepp'/kake *-a* cookie made with sirup (or honey).
+**knep're** *V -a/-et* clack, put-put; rattle, sputter.
***kner'k** *-en* cf **knirk**
***kner'ke** *V -a* cf **knirke**
kner't[1] *-en* blow, chop.
kner't[2] *-en* 1 little fellow, peanut, shaver. 2 (small) drink, swig.
***kner'te**[1] *V knart, knorte/-i* crackle, glint.
kner'te[2] *V -a/+-et* 1 beat, chop, hack. 2 crack, pop; shoot.
+**kne'/sette** *V -satte, -satt* (=*/**setje**) adopt; acknowledge, recognize.
+**kne'/skjell** *-a/-et* (=*/**skjel**) kneecap.
kne'/skjelv *-en* knocking of the knees (from fright).
kne'/skål *-a* kneecap.
***knes't** *-en* pop, small explosion, sudden sound.
***knes'te** *V knast, knoste/-i -a* pop, make a sudden sound: **det knast ikkje i han** there wasn't a sound out of him.
kne'/strømpe *-a* knee-length sock or stocking.
kne'/stående *A* - on one knee, kneeling (sports).
knett' *-en* pop, small explosion, sudden sound.
knet'te *V knatt, +-et/*knotte/*-i* pop, make a sudden sound: **det knatt ikke i ham** there wasn't a sound out of him.
knickers [nik'kers] *-en* cf **nikkers**
knik's *-et* 1 curtsy. 2 squeak, squeaking.
knik'se *V -a/+-et* 1 curtsy. 2 squeak.
***knik't** *-en* cf **knekt**[1]
***kni'p**[1] *-en* dilemma, pinch: **vere i k- for noko** be short of sth.
kni'p[2] *-et* 1 pinch. 2 stomach cramp (as in colic).
***kni'pal** *A* miserly, stingy
***kni'par** *-en* miser.
kni'pe[1] *-a/+-en* dilemma, fix, pinch: **i k- for noe** in need of sth.
kni'pe[2] *V kneip/+knep, +knepet/ *knipe/*-i* 1 pinch, tweak; press, squeeze: **k- seg i armen** pinch one's own arm; **k- til (med en tang)** clamp (with a pair of pliers); **k- munnen sammen** press one's lips tightly together. 2 grab, snatch; scrounge, snitch, steal. 3 arrest; catch (a criminal). 4 pinch, save (money), be economical: **han k-er på skillingen, men lar daleren gå** he's penny-wise and pound foolish. 5 (impers.): **det k-er (for en)** it is difficult (for sby): **det k-er med penger** money is scarce; **da det knep** when it came to a test, at a pinch, **hvis det k-er** if worst comes to worst. 6 *pop.*: **k- ut** escape, get out. 7 (in cards) finesse: **k- med knekten** f- the jack.
kni'pen *A +-ent, pl -ne* miserly, stingy.
+**kni'peri** *-et* miserliness, stinginess.
kni'pe/tak *-et* difficulty, pinch, scrape: **i et k-** in a p-.
+**kni'pe/tang** *-a, pl -tenger* (=*/**tong**) nippers, (pair of) pliers, tongs.
knip'le *V -a/+-et* make lace.
knip'ling *-en* lace; lacework.
knip'lings/lommetør'kle *-et, pl +-klær/ *-* lace-edged handkerchief.
knip'lings/verk *-et* lacework.
knip'pe[1] *-a vet.* spavin.
knip'pe[2] *-t* bunch, bundle; brace (of birds).
knip'pe[3] *V -a/+-et* bundle: **k- seg** bunch, cluster.
knip's *+-et/*-en* snap (of the fingers); rap.
knip'se *V -a/+-et* 1 snap (the fingers) =**k- med fingrene**. 2 fillip, flick: **k- bort et støvgrann** flick away a grain of dust. 3 shoot, snap (a picture).
knip'sk *A* - prudish.
knir'k *-et/-en* 1 creak, squeak. 2: **uten k-** without a hitch.
knir'ke *V -a/+-et* 1 creak, grate, squeak. 2 have a few bugs, a few squeaks, work with difficulty: **samarbeidet k-et en smule** there were a few hitches in the cooperation.
knir'ke/fri *A -tt* without a jar, with out a hitch.
kni's *-et/-en* snicker.
kni'se *V -te* snicker.
knis'l *-et* 1 crackle, creak. 2 neigh.
knis'le *V -a/+-et* 1 crackle, creak. 2 neigh.
knis'tre[1] *V -a/+-et* 1 whine. 2 crunch.
+**knis'tre**[2] *V -a/-et* cf **gnistre**
+**knit're** *V -a/-et* 1 crackle, rustle: **k-ende kaldt** c-ing cold. 2 glitter, sparkle.
kni'v *-en* knife: **komme under k-en** have an operation; **krig på k-en** fight without mercy, fight to the death; **sette ham k-en på strupen** *fig.* hold a k- at his throat; **han er k-en** he is really sharp, he is in fine form.
kni'v/blad *-et* knife blade.
kni've *V -a/+-et* 1 knife: **k- ned** k-down. 2 compete sharply (**om over**).
kni'vende *Av* extremely, very: **k-skarp kritikk** devastating criticism.
kni'v/rygg *-en* back edge of knife.
kniv's/blad *-et* cf **kniv/**
kniv's/egg *+-en/*-a* knife-edge.
kni'v/skaft *-et* knife handle.
kni'v/skarp *A*: **k- konkurranse** keen competition.
+**kni'v/skjede** *-n* (=*/**skei**) *archaic* knife sheath.
+**kni'v/skjell** *-et zool.* knife-handle, razor clam (Solenidae).
+**Kni'vskjell/odden** *Pln* (=***Knivskjel/**) northernmost point of Norway, on Magerøy.
kni'v/slir *-a* (=/**slire**) knife sheath.
kni'v/smed *-en* cutler.
kniv's/odd *-en* knife tip: **en k- salt** as much salt as will stay on the tip of a (table) knife, a pinch.
kni'v/spiss *-en* knife point.
kni'v/stell *-et* set of table knives.
kni'v/stikk *-et* knife wound, stab; gash.
+**kni'v/stikker** *-en, pl -e* (=***-ar**) stabber.
***knjosk** [kn(j)os'k] *-en* cf **knusk**
KNM=**Den kongelige norske Marine**
knocke [nåk'ke] *V -a/+-et*: **k- ut** knock out.
knock-out [nåkk'aut] *-en* 1 knock-out. 2: **være k-** be knocked out, unconscious; done, out of the running, washed-out.
***knode**[1] [knå'e] *-a* kneaded dough.
***knode**[2] [knå'e] *V -de/-a* cf **kna**
+**knod/ost** [knå'/ost] *-en* cottage cheese.
kno'g *-et* hard work, toil.
kno'ge *V -a/+-et* toil, work hard.
kno'k *-en* 1 knuckle. 2 (soup)bone.
kno'ke[1] *-n* 1 knuckle. 2 (soup)bone.
***kno'ke**[2] *V -a* press, squeeze.
kno'ket(e) *A* - bony, gnarled.
***knok'ke** *pp of* **knekke**[1]
knok'kel *-en, pl knokler* bone knucklebone.
knok'kel/mann *-en* death, personified in a human skeleton.
***knok'ki** *pp of* **knekke**[1]
knok'let(e) *A* - angular, bony.
knoll' *-en* 1 knoll. 2 tuber. 3 *pop.* bean, noggin.
knoll'/forma *A* - (=+**-et**) bulbous.
kno'p *-en, pl* - 1 *naut.* knot (rope); knot (unit of speed). 2 *dial.* clubroot (disease of turnips, radishes, etc.).
kno'pe *V -a/+-et naut.* knot, tie.
knopp' *-en* (=**knupp**) 1 bud: **stå i k-** be in b-. 2 button, knob, lump. 3 *pop.* peach.
knop'pe *V -a/+-et* (=***knuppe**): **k-es** or **k- seg** bud, shoot; **k-ende liv** sprouting life.
knopp'/skyting *-a/+-en bot.* budding, germination.
+**knor't** *-en* gnarl, knot.
***knor'te** *pp of* **knerte**[1]
+**knor'te/kjepp** *-en* cudgel, knobby club.
knor'tet(e) *A* - gnarled, knotty.
***knor'ti** *pp of* **knerte**[1]
kno't *-et* affected, unnatural language.

+ Bokmål; * Nynorsk; ° Dialect.
After letter: ' stress (Acc. 1); ` tone, stress (Acc. 2); · length.
Below letter: . not pronounced.

kno'te *V -a/+-et* use affected, unnatural language (esp. bookish or urban forms instead of native rural forms).
kno'tet(e) *A -* (of language) affected, unnatural.
knott'[1] *-en* 1 button, knob. 2 (building, paving) block; wood block (for burning). 3 cleat (under boot). 4 boy, fellow: **jeg var ikke stor k-en** I was just a little tyke.
knott'[2] *-en zool.* blackfly, sandfly, others of Simuliidae family.
knot'te** *pp of* **knette** (=knotti**)
knubb' *-et/*-en* 1 block of wood, piece of log. 2 push, shove.
knub'be *V -a/+-et* 1 push, shove. 2: **k-es** hassle, wrangle.
knub'be/sild *-a* plump, medium-sized herring.
knubb'/o'rd *-et* harsh or sharp words.
+**knubs** [knup's] *-et* cf **knups**
+**knud'ret(e)** *A -* 1 knotted, knotty. 2 bumpy; jarring, unpleasant. 3 rough, rugged (e.g. hands).
knu'e[1] *-n* cf **knoke**[1]
***knu'e**[2] *V -a* cf **knuge**
+**knu'ge** *V -a/-et* (=***knue**[2]) 1 press, squeeze: **k- hendene sammen** clench one's fists; **k- seg sammen om** grasp, knot oneself around. 2 clasp, embrace, hug: **k- en til sitt bryst** c-sby in one's arms; **hun k-et seg inn til ham** she cuddled up to him. 3 oppress, weigh upon; depress: **en k-ende byrde (sorg)** a crushing weight (sorrow); **føle seg k-et av angst** be weighed down by anxiety.
knul'tre *-a* 1 bumpiness, unevenness (esp. on ice). *2 gnarl, knot.
knul'tret(e) *A -* covered with bumps, ridges.
knupp' *-en* cf **knopp**
***knup'pe** *V -a* cf **knoppe**
+**knup'pet(e)** *A -* pimply: **jeg ble k- over det hele** I got gooseflesh all over (Boo).
+**knup's** *-et* 1 jolt, push, shove. 2 blast, scolding.
+**knup'se** *V -et* 1 jolt, push, shove. 2 bawl out, blast, scold.
***knur'ke** *V -a* growl, grunt.
knur'pe *V -a/+-et* chew noisily, munch.
knurr'[1] *-en* gurnard (any fish of Triglidae family).
knurr'[2] *-et* growl, snarl.
knur're *V -a/+-et* 1 growl, snarl. 2 complain, grumble.
knurr'/hår *-et zool.* whisker.
knur'v *-en dial.* gnarled, stunted creature or tree.
+**knu's/bedå'rende** *A -* absolutely beguiling, bewitching.
knu'se *V -te* 1 crush, smash; break: **k- en kopp** break a cup; **k- stein** c- stone; **et k-ende slag** a c-ing blow; **han k-te hennes hjerte** he broke her heart; **jeg er k-t** I am c-ed. 2 crumble (bread).
knu's/elske *V -a/+-et* 1 be crazy about. 2 hug tightly.
knu'sende *A -* 1 crushing; withering. 2 *(adv.)* totally: **k- sikker** dead sure; **k- likegyldig** t- indifferent, not giving a damn.
knu'se/verk *-et tech.* crushing mill.
knus'k *-en* punk, tinder: **tørr som k-** dry-as-dust.
knus'k/tørr *A -tørt* tinder dry; dry-as-dust.
knus'le *V -a/+-et* be stingy (**med** with).
knus'let(e) *A -* stingy (**med** with).
knus'pe *V -a/+-et* chomp; crunch.
knus'pre *V -a/+-et* chomp; crunch.
knus'sel *-elet/knuslet* stinginess: *dial.* **itte no k-** let's not be stingy (B. Ring).
knus'tre *V -a/+-et* 1 crush. 2 crunch.
***knu't** *-en* cf **knute**
Knu't *Prn (m)*
knu'te *-n* (=***knut**) 1 knot: **knytte en k-** tie a k-; **knytte opp k-n** untie the k-; **slå k- på tråden** knot the thread. 2 *fig.* problem: **løse en k-** solve a p-; **en k- på tråden** a disagreement. 3 bump, lump, nodule. 4 *astron., math.* node.
knu'te/punkt [/pongt] *-et* 1 turning point. 2 crux. 3 junction (of roads, railways, etc.).
+**knu'te/rosen** *N* (=*/**ros**) *med.* erythema nodosum.
knu'tet(e) *A -* knotty.
knutt' *-en* knout.
knuv'l *-en* 1 clod, knot, lump. 2 stocky person.
knuv'le *V -a/+-et* 1 force, push down; press. 2: **k-es** quarrel.
knuv'let(e) *A -* knotty, lumpy.
kny'[1] *-et* sound (of protest): **han gav ikke et k- fra seg** he did not utter the slightest sound.
kny'[2] *V -dde* make a sound of protest, murmur: **k-r du?** are you objecting?
***knysj'e** *V knys, knuste, knust* cf **knuse**
knys't *-en/+-et* murmur, sound of complaint (=**kny**).
***knys'te** *V -a* make a sound (of protest).
***kny'te**[1] *-t* cf **knytte**[1]
kny'te[2] *V -te* (=+**knytte**[2]) 1 knot, tie: **k- garn** make a net; **k- igjen skoen** tie shoelace; **k- opp** untie; **k- tråden igjen** resume a connection; pick up a topic; **k- vennskap med** make friends with. 2 bind, link, unite: **k- to land sammen** l- two countries. 3 add, attach: **k- noen bemerkninger til** add some remarks to; **de er sterkt k-et til hverandre** they are strongly attached to one another. 4 clench, press, squeeze: **k- handa (neven)** c- one's fist. 5 *(refl.)*: **k- seg** form fruit; **det k-er seg for en** one grows tense, tightens up; **k- seg til en** become attached to sby; **det k-er seg en interessant historie til dette** an interesting story is associated with this. 6 *(pp.)*: **k-et til** attached to (e.g. a court), employed by (an institution, organization).
***kny'te/slips** *-et* cf **knytte/**
***kny'ting** *-en* immature berry or fruit.
+**knyt'te**[1] *-t* (=***knyte**[1]) bundle.
+**knyt'te**[2] *V -a/-et* cf **knyte**[2]
+**knyt'te/slips** *-et* necktie (which must be tied each time it is worn).
knytt'/neve *-n* clenched fist; *fig.* brute force, threat.
+**knæ'r** *pl of* **kne**
+**knø'** *V -dde* knead: **k-dd** firm, heavy-set.
knø'l *-en* 1 chunk of wood. 2 lumpish person.
+**knø'len** *A -ent, pl -ne pop.* mean, stingy.
knø'l/kval *-en* (=+/**hval**) *zool.* humpback whale (Megaptera boops).
knø's *-en dial.* brash, arrogant young man; big shot; obstinate fellow.
+**knø't** *pt of* **knytte**[2]
knø'ten *A +-ent, pl -ne* 1 agreeable, nice, pleasant. 2 clever, quick.
knøtt' *-et* chit, mite, peanut.
knøt'ten *A +-ent, pl knøtne* tiny.
knøt'tende *Av* (=**knøtrende**) (emphatic): **k- liten** tiny; **k- stille** absolutely quiet.
+**ko'** *-en, pl kjør* cf **ku**
koafy'r *-en* coiffure, hairdo.
koagule're *V -te* coagulate.
koalisjo'n *-en* coalition.
koalisjo'ns/regje'ring *-a/+-en* coalition government.
kob'be *-n zool.* seal (Phocinae family).
kob'be/fangst *-en* sealing.
+**kob'bel** *-elet/koblet* cf **koppel**
+**kob'ber** *-et* (=+**kopper**[1], ***kopar**) 1 copper. 2 copperplate engraving, print.
+**kob'ber/dank** *-en* copper (coin).
+**kob'ber/hud** *-a/-en* copperplate (on a ship).
+**kob'ber/kis** *-en* copper ore.
+**kob'ber/stikk** *-et* copperplate engraving, print: **k- med kald nål** drypoint engraving.
kob'ber/verk *-et* copper mine.
kob'bung *-en zool. dial.* whelk (Buccinum undatum).
kobb'/unge [/onge] *-n* young seal.
+**kob'le** *V -a/-et* cf **kople**
+**kob'lerske** *-a/-en* procuress.
+**kob'let** *df of* **kobbel**
ko'bolt *-en* cobalt.
ko'bra *-en, pl *-er* cobra.
kodd' *-en* testicle.
kod'de *-n* pillow.
ko'de *-n* 1 code. 2 (on horse) pastern.
ko'deks *-en* 1 (legal) code. 2 codex (=manuscript).
ko'de/skrift *-a/+-en* writing in code.
kodifise're *V -te jur.* codify.
kodil'je *-n*: **hele k-n** the whole bunch, the whole shebang.
kodisill' *-en jur.* codicil.
koeffisien't *-en* coefficient.
+**ko'/fanger** *-en, pl -e* cf **ku/**
koff' *-en* shallow-draft, two-masted merchant vessel; two-master (Dutch type).
koffardi' *-en hist.* merchant marine.
koffardi'/skip *-et hist.* merchant ship.
koffein [kåfe-i'n] *-en/+-et* (=**kaffein**) caffein.
koffer/nagle [kof'fer/] *-n naut.* belaying pin.
koffert [kof'fert] *-en* bag, suitcase, trunk.
+**koffert/løper** *-en* "suitcase skier", who stays at a ski resort and does no skiing.
koffert/mord [/mord] *-et* trunk murder.
+**kof'te** [kof-] *-a* cf **kufte**
kogg' *-en* 1 *dial.* broad rowboat, tender. 2 *hist.* Hanseatic merchant and war vessel.
kog'ger *-et* quiver.
+**kog'le** *V -et* practice magic; bewitch, charm, hex; conjure.
+**kogleri'** *-et* enchantment, magic, spellbinding.
kohesjo'n *-en phys.* cohesion.
koie [kåi'e] *-a* hut, shelter.
***ko'k**[1] *-en* 1 heap, pile. 2 lump (of dirt etc.).
ko'k[2] *-et* 1 cooking. 2 boiling: **bringe i k-** bring to a boil; **sjøen står i k-** the sea is seething (boiling). 3 mess, enough for a meal (esp. of fish). 4 decoction, extract.
kokain [koka-i'n] *-en/+-et* cocaine.
kokar'de *-n* cockade.
ko'ke[1] *-a*: **ei k- fisk** a mess of fish (enough for a meal).
ko'ke[2] *V -te* 1 boil (lit. and *fig.*): **k- bort** b- off; **k- bort i kålen** come to nothing, go up in air; **k- inn** evaporate by b-ing; **k- opp** reach the b-ing point, heat to a boil; **k- over** b- over; *fig.* lose one's temper; **k-ende hett** b-ing hot; **et k-ende mylder** a swarming multitude. 2 cook, make: **k- kaffe** m- coffee; **k- mat** prepare food; **k- olje** refine oil.
ko'ke/bok *-a, pl -bøker* cookbook
ko'ke/fisk *-en* fish suitable for boiling.
ko'ke/kar' *-et* pan, pot to cook in (boil in).
ko'ke/kone *-a* cook (hired for large parties).
ko'ke/kunst *-en* art of cooking, culinary art.
ko'ke/mat *-en* boiled food, hot food.
***ko'ken** *A -e/-i, pl -ne* 1 choked, choky. 2 puckery (as from chokecherries).
ko'ke/plate *-a* electric plate, hotplate; (electric) burner.
ko'ke/punkt [/pongt] *-et* boiling point.
+**ko'ker** *-en, pl -e* (=***-ar**) cooker (apparatus, person).
kokeri' *-et* 1 cooking. 2 cannery, factory where product is prepared by cooking: **flytende k-** whale factory ship.
kokett' *A -* coquettish, flirtatious.
koket'te *-a/+-en* coquette, flirt.
kokette're *V -te* 1 act coquettish, flirt (**med** with): **han k-te med radikalisme** he f-ed with radicalism. 2 show off (**for** for).
koketteri' *-et* coquetry, flirtation (**med** with).
ko'k/heit *A -t/+-hett* boiling hot.
kokk'[1] *-en* cook: **jo flere k-er, dess**

verre søl too many c-s spoil the broth.
kokk'[2] *-en med.* coccus.
kok'ke[1] *-a* (female) cook.
kok'ke[2] *V -a/+-et* cook, prepare food.
kok'ke/kone *-a* woman hired to cook for wedding, party, etc.
+**kok'ke/pike** *-a/-en* (fem.) cook.
***kok'le** *V -a* cf **kakle**
ko'kning *-en* 1 cooking. 2 mess, enough for a meal.
kokong' *-en* cocoon.
+**ko'/kopper** *pl* cf **ku/**
kokos [kok'os] *-en* coconut palm.
kokos/nøtt *-a* coconut.
kokot'te *-a/+-en* cocotte, prostitute.
***kok're** *V -a* whinny; nuzzle.
kok's[1] *+-en/*-a* crock, cup, dipper.
kok's[2] *-en* coke.
ko'k/salt *-et* table salt.
***kok'se** *-a* cf **koks**[1]
kok's/omn *-en* (=+**/ovn**) 1 coke oven. 2 stove using coke.
kol [kå'l] *-et* (=+**kull**[1]) 1 coal: **de hvite k-** "white coals" (i.e. water power). 2 (burning) piece of coal: **sanke glødende k- på ens hode** heap coals of fire on one's head (Rom. 12,20). 3 charcoal: **brenne k-** burn c-.
kol'be *-n* 1 (gun) butt, stock. 2 (corn)cob. 3 *chem.* flask.
Kol'/bein *Prn (m)*
+**kol'be/støt** *-et* (=***/støyt**) blow with butt of rifle.
Kol'/bjø'rn *Prn (m)*
Kol'/botn *Pln* suburb of Oslo, Oppegård twp, Akershus.
***kol/brenne** [kå'l/] *-t* hydrocarbon.
+**kol/brenner** [kå'l/] *-en, pl -e* (=***-ar**) charcoal burner.
Kol'/bu *Pln* twp, Oppland.
+**kol'd** *A* cf **kald**
+**kol'd/brann** *-en* 1 *med.* gangrene. 2 *bot.* dry rot.
+**kol'd/feber** *-en* malaria.
+**kol'd/jomfru** *-a/-en* (in restaurant) woman supervising the preparation of cold dishes.
+**kol'd/krem** *-en* cold cream.
+**kol'd/sindig** [also -sin'-] *A* - 1 cold, cool (of temperament). 2 cool-headed.
+**kol'dt/bo'rd** *-et* "cold table," smørgåsbord.
kole[1] [kå'le] *-a* oil lamp.
***kole**[2] [kå'le] *V -a* blacken (with coal).
kolende [kå'lene] *Av*: **k- svart** pitch-black.
ko'lera *-en* cholera.
+**kole'riker** *-en, pl -e* (=***-ar**) choleric, excitable (person).
koleri'ne *+-n/*-a med.* cholera nostras, sporadic cholera.
+**koleri'ne/dråper** *pl* (=***-ar**) medicine for sporadic cholera.
kole'risk *A* - choleric, easily angered
kol/hydra't [kå'l/] *-et* carbohydrate.
ko'libri [also -li'-] *-en zool.* hummingbird (Trochilidae).
kolikk' *-en* colic.
kol'je *-a zool.* haddock.
***kol'ke** *V -a* bungle, fumble.
kol'kos *-et* collective farm (in Russia).
koll'[1] *-en* (=**kolle**[1]) 1 *dial.* head; crown (of head or hat). 2 hill, peak; rounded mountain top. 3 *bot.* cone-like head (on hops, flowers).
koll'[2] *N*: **slå en i k-** knock sby down; **k- i k-** head over heels.
kollaboratø'r *-en* collaborationist.
kolla's *-en eccl.* collation.
kollasjone're *V -te* 1 collate. 2 confirm (a telegram).
+**koll'/bøtte** *-a*: **gjøre k-** fall on one's head; **slå k-er** turn somersaults.
kol'le[1] *-n* cf **koll**[1]
kol'le[2] *-a* muley cow; female animal (such as moose) without horns.
kol'le[3] *-a* 1 low wooden bowl without handles. 2 wooden container of stave construction, with extended stave as handles; piggin.
***kol'le**[4] *V -a* 1 top (a tree). 2 trim both ends of a log.
kolle'ga *-aen, pl +-er/*-aer* colleague.
kollegia'l *A* collegial.
kollegialite't *-en* collegiality.
kolle'gium *-iet, pl +-ier/*-ium* collegium: **Det akademiske k-** Executive Committee of the University (president and deans); **i samlet k-** at a regular (plenipotentiary) meeting.
kol/leie [kå'l/] *-t, pl +-r/*-* coalfield.
kolleksjo'n *-en* 1 assortment, (salesman's) samples. 2 collection (=fashion display).
kollek't *-en* 1 collection. 2 collect.
kol'lektiv[1] *-et, pl -/+-er* 1 *gram.* collective noun. 2 collective farm.
kol'lektiv[2] *A* collective.
kol'lektiv/bruk *-et* collective farm.
kollektivise're *V -te* collectivize.
kol'le/ku *-a, pl -kyr, +-kuer* hornless cow, muley cow, pollard.
+**kol/lemper** [kå'l/] *-en, pl -e* (=***-ar**) *naut.* coal passer; coal heaver.
kol'let(e) *A* - 1 roundtopped. 2 knolly, rolling. 3 hornless, muley, polled.
kol'li *-et, pl -/+-er* piece of baggage.
kollide're *V -te* collide.
kollisjo'n *-en* collision.
***koll'/kaste** *V -a* cf **kull/**
kolloid [kållo-i'd] *-et* colloid.
kolloidal [kållo-ida'l] *A* colloidal.
kollok'vium *-iet, pl +-ier/*-ium* colloquium, seminar.
koll'/segle *V -a/+-et/+-de* (=+**kull/-seile**) capsize.
kol/mile [kå'l/] *-a* charcoal kiln.
kol/mule [kå'l/] *-n zool.* a kind of cod (Gadus poutassou).
kol/mørk [kå'l/] *A* pitch-dark.
***kolne** [kå'lne] *V -a* cf **kjølne**
kol/oksyd [kå'l/åksy'd] *-et* carbon monoxide.
kolokvin'ter *-en, pl +-e* 1 colocynth; bitterapple. 2 *hum.* drink, pick-me-up.
ko'lon *-et* colon.
koloni' *-en* colony.
kolonia'l *-en* 1 groceries. 2 grocery store.
kolonia'l/butikk' *-en* grocery store.
kolonia'l/handel *-en* grocery store.
kolonia'l/vare *-a/+-en (pl)* groceries.
koloni'/hage *-n* communal garden plots.
kolonisasjo'n *-en* colonization.
kolonisa'tor *-en* colonizer.
kolonise're *V -te* colonize.
kolonis't *-en* colonist, settler.
kolonna'de *-n* colonnade.
kolon'ne *-n arch., mil.* column: **femte k-** fifth c-.
kolora'do/bille *+-n/*-a* Colorado potato beetle.
koloratu'r *-en mus.* coloratura.
+**koloratu'r/sang** *-en* (=***/song**) coloratura singing.
+**koloratu'r/sangerin'ne** *-a* coloratura (soprano).
kolore're *V -te* 1 color. 2 *mus.* embellish.
koloris'tisk *A* - coloristic.
koloritt' *-en* color, coloring, tone.
kol/os [kå'l/] *-en* carbon monoxide.
koloss' *-en* colossus.
kolossa'l *A* colossal, huge; staggering (sum of money).
kolporta'sje *-n* door-to-door selling (esp. of books in rural areas).
kolporte're *V -te* sell door-to-door (esp. books in rural areas).
kolportø'r *-en* salesman, peddler (esp. of books).
kol/stift [kå'l/] *-en* charcoal stick.
kol/stoff [kå'l/] *-et* carbon.
kol/støv [kå'l/] *-et* coaldust.
kol/sur [kå'l/] *A* carbonate.
kol/svart [kå'l/] *A* - coal black.
kol/syre [kå'l/] *-a* carbon dioxide, carbonic acid.
+**kol/tegning** [kå'l/teining] *-en* (=***/teikning**) charcoal drawing.
kolum'ne *-n* column (of figures, of a page).
kol'v *-en* 1 club. 2 clapper (of bell).
+**kol/vannstoff** [kå'l vann'/stoff] *-et* cf **kull/**
Kol'ver/eid *Pln* twp, Nord-Trøndelag.
kom' *pt of* **komme**[2], **kome**[2]
ko'ma *-en* coma.
+**koma'g** *-en* cf **kommag**
kombattan't *-en* combatant.
kombinasjo'n *-en* combination (**av** of); coincidence.
kombinasjo'ns/evne *-a/+-en* ability to combine, insight.
kombine're *V -te* 1 combine. 2 relate (facts); put two and two together.
***kome**[1] [kå'me] *-a* cf **komme**[1]
***kome**[2] [kå'me] *V kjem, kom, kom(m)e/-i* cf **komme**[2]
komedian't *-en derog.* comedian.
kome'die *-n* comedy.
+**kome'die/spill** *-et* (=***/spel**) hypocrisy, playacting.
kome't *-en* comet.
komfort [kåmfå'r] *-en* comfort.
komfortabel [kåmfårta'bel] *A -elt, pl -le* comfortable (not used about a person).
komfy'r *-en* range, stove.
+**ko'miker** *-en, pl -e* (=***-ar**) comedian; comic.
komikk' *-en* comedy, comicality: **et skjær av k-** a touch of comedy.
Kominfor'm *N* Cominform.
Kominter'n *N* Comintern.
ko'misk *A* - comic, comical.
komité *-en* committee.
komm. = **kommune**
kom'ma *-et, pl -/+-er* comma (used also for decimal point, for colon in time figures, and as musical breathing mark).
komma'g *-en* soft foot covering (boot) made of reindeer hide and worn by the Lapps.
kommandan't *-en* commandant, commander, commanding officer.
kommandan't/skap *-et* 1 position of commandant. 2 headquarters, office.
kommande're *V -te* 1 command, order (**til å** to). 2 be in command of, command.
kommande'r/sersjan't *-en* first sergeant (Norwegian army, pre-1930).
kommanditt'/selskap *-et merc.* limited partnership.
komman'do *-en* 1 command (**over** of): **føre k-** be in charge, in c-; **lystre k-** obey orders; **på k-** on c-; **under k-** under c-, under orders. 2 commander (troops).
komman'do/bru *-a* (=+**/bro**) *naut.* bridge (of ship).
komman'do/føring *-a/+-en* leading a command.
kommandø'r *-en* 1 commander (e.g. of the Order of St. Olav). 2 *mil.* commodore (navy).
kommandø'r/kaptei'n *-en mil.* captain (navy).
kom'me[1] *+-t/*-a* (=***kome**[1]) arrival, coming: **vårens k-** the c- of spring.
+**kom'me**[2] *V kom, kommet* (=***kome**[2]) 1 come: **k- gående** c- walking, on foot; **k- hit** c- here; **kom ikke der** *fig.* don't try that; **da kom det** then it came; **k- ditt rike** *bibl.* thy kingdom c-; **k-ende slekter** c-ing generations; *(interj.)* **kom la oss være venner** c- (now) let's be friends. 2 get, go (to a place or into a situation): **k- i hus** get indoors; **k- i vanskeligheter** get into trouble; **jeg k-er ingen veg** I don't get anywhere; **k- langt** go far; **hvor langt var jeg k-et** how far had I gone, where was I; **det k-er en lengst med** that's the best policy; **k- nær(mere)** approach, get close(r); **k- til Oslo** be in Oslo, get (go) to Oslo. 3 arrive, get (somewhere): **gjestene er k-et** the guests have a-d; **vi k-er sent** we're late; **k-er straks** will be right back; **han k-er ofte til oss** he often comes to visit us. 4 happen, occur: **det kom uven-**

\+ Bokmål; * Nynorsk; ° Dialect.
After letter: ' stress (Acc. 1); ` tone, stress (Acc. 2); · length.
Below letter: . not pronounced.

tet it h-ed unexpectedly; **la k- hva k- vil** come what may. 5 *obs.* add, pour, put (in recipes): **k- vann i vinen** mix water into the wine; **kom ett egg i** a- one egg. 6 (with *adv.* and *prep.*): **kom an!** come on!; **k- an' på** be up (to), depend (on); **k-' av** come, stem from; **det k-er av at** it is because of, due to, the result of; **k- a'v med** get rid of; **k- av ste'd** get started, leave; **k- bort** disappear, get lost; get away; **k- bort fra** abandon, get away from, get off (e.g. the subject); **k- borti (en, noe)** get into (sth), get mixed up with (sby, sth); **k- bort til** come over to; **k- et'ter** follow, succeed; catch on, learn; come to fetch (get)! **k- for' en** occur, seem to sby; **k- for en da'g** come out, come to light; **k- forbi** get past, overtake, pass; *(neg.)* **en kan ikke k- forbi at** you can't overlook (ignore) the fact that; **k- (dårlig, godt) fra' noe** acquit oneself (badly, well), (not) get away with sth; **k- fra det** escape, get off; **k- fra hverandre** be separated, drift apart; **k- fram** come forth, come out, emerge; get ahead, make one's way; (of news) become known; arrive, get there, reach a goal; **k- godt med** come in handy; **k- hos noen** be a frequent guest at sby's home; **k- i forbindelse med** get in touch with; **k- i gang (med)** get started (on); **k- (en) i hende** fall into (sby's) hands, reach sby; **k- i hu(g)** remember; **k- i stand** get in order, get started; be realized, take place; **k- i tanker om** realize, think; **k- i veg** get started (e.g. in one's own business); **k- igjen** come back; come again; **k- igjennom** get through, pull through; **k- inn (i)** come, enter (into), get in; **k- inn på** go into, touch upon (a topic); be admitted to, enter (e.g. the university); **k- inn til en** enter sby's room; **k- inn under** belong to, fall within, (a category); **k- løs** get loose; **k- me'd** be included, join; fall in line, join (forces); **det vil k- godt med** that'll be a great help, good to have; **k-' med** bring along, take; bring up, come out with, say, tell; **k- ned** come, get down; **k- ned på beina** land on one's feet; **k- opp** come, get on one's feet, get up (**k- opp i gresk** be examined in Greek); be revealed, come to light; be performed, played; **k- opp i** attain, reach; **byen er k-et opp i tjue tusen** the city has reached a population of twenty thousand; **k- opp i noe** get involved in sth; **k- opp mot** come up against, touch; compare with, equal; **k- over noe** come across, find sth; get over (e.g. a blow), pull through; **k- over en** take sby by surprise; come over one (as an idea); **k- overens** agree (**om** about); **k- på'** come up, happen: **hva som enn k-er på'** no matter what happens; **natta kom på'** night fell; occur to one, remember, think of: **jeg kan ikke k- på' hva han heter** I can't recall his name; **k-' på** amount to (a sum); **k- på det rene med** learn, realize; **k- på tale** be mentioned, be taken into consideration; **k- sammen** get together, meet, mix; **k- til'** get at, secure; get a chance (**la ham k- til** give him a chance, let him try); be born, come into being; **k- (en) til gode** benefit (sby); **k- til seg selv** come to, come to one's senses; **k- til skade** be injured; **k- til stede** arrive (on the scene); **når det k-er til stykket** in a showdown, when all is said and done; **k- til syne** appear, emerge; **k- til verden** be born; **k- til å** happen to (do sth); get to, grow to; be going to, will: **han k-er til å angre dette** he'll regret this; **k- tilbake (til)** come back, return (to); dwell on, recur, repeat; **k- ut** come, get out; be known, revealed, come up; appear, be published (of books etc.); **k- ut av** come out, result (**hva er det k-et ut av det?** what has been the result of it?); get mixed up, lose the thread; **k- ut av det (med en)** get along (with sby); **k- ut for** be exposed to; go through, meet up with; **k- ut på ett** be all the same, come to the same thing, make no difference; **k- utenom noe** deny sth, get around sth; **k- ved** concern; **det k-er ikke ham ved** it's no concern of his; **det k-er ikke saken ved** that's beside the point; **k- videre** get ahead, along; get out, get spread: **la ikke dette k- videre** don't pass this on. 7 *(refl.)*: **k- seg** get better, pull through, recover; happen, result (**hvordan k-er det seg at** how does it happen that); get, go (with *adv.*): **k- seg av gårde (sted)** get started, leave; **k- seg bort (inn, opp, ut osv.)** get away (in, up, out, etc.); **k- seg fram** get ahead, rise (in the world); **(ikke) k- seg til å** (not) get around to; **k- seg unna** get away.

kommensura'bel *A -elt, pl -le* commensurable, commensurate.

kommenta'r *-en* 1 commentary; annotations. 2 comment.

kommenta'tor *-en* commentator.

kommente're *V -te* give, write a commentary on; annotate, comment on.

kommer's *-en* 1 hubbub; carousing, spree. 2 fun, skylarking: **drive k- med** make f- of. 3 struggle, trouble. 4 *archaic* commerce.

kommer'se/lest *-en* old term for load capacity of a ship=2.08 register tons.

kommersialise're *V -te* commercialize.

kommersiell' *A -elt* commercial.

kommi's [kåmmi'] *-en* store clerk, salesperson.

kommisjo'n *-en* 1 commission: **få i k-** be made responsible for doing sth. 2 agency, distributor: **i k- hos** on consignment at (a store). 3 commission, percentage on sales. 4 commission, committee.

kommisjonæ'r *-en* agent, broker, distributor.

kommissaria't *-et, pl -/+-er* commissariat.

kommissæ'r *-en* commissary, commissioner.

kommitten't *-en* consignor.

kommode [komo'de] *-n* bureau, chest of drawers.

kommuna'l *A* civic, local, municipal, town.

Kommuna'l- og [å] **ar'beids/departementet** [/-mang'e] *df* Ministry of Municipal Affairs and Labor.

kommunal'/politikk' *-en* local politics.

kommu'ne *-n* municipality (city, town, or village).

+**kommu'ne/arbei'der** *-en, pl -e* (=* **-ar**) civic employee.

kommu'ne/skatt *-en* municipal (or town) taxes.

kommu'ne/styre *-t* city council, county board, town board, etc.

+**kommu'ne/valg** *-et* (=*/**val**) local election.

kommunikasjo'n *-en* 1 communication. 2 *(pl)* means of communication; connections.

kommunikasjo'ns/middel *-elet/-midlet, pl +-midler/*-el* means of communication.

kommuniké *-et, pl +-er/*-* communiqué, official communication.

kommunio'n *-en eccl.* communion.

kommunise're *V -te* communicate (**til** to; **med** with); connect.

kommunis'me *-n* Communism.

kommunis't *-en* Communist.

kommunis'tisk *A -* communistic.

komp.=**kompani, komparativ**[1,2]

kompagnon [kompanjång'] *-en* cf **kompanjong**

kompak't *A -* compact: **den k-e majoritet** the c- majority (Ibsen).

kompa'n *-en* crony; *derog.* fellow.

kompani' *-et, pl +-er/*-* 1 company: **et lystig k-** a merry c-. 2 partnership; company; corporation: **i k- med djevelen** in p- with the devil. 3 *mil.* company (about 200 men).

kompani'/skap *+-et/*-en merc.* partnership.

kompanjong' *-en merc.* partner.

komparasjo'n *-en* comparison (of *adj.* or *adv.*).

kompar'ativ[1] *-en* comparative (*adj.* or *adv.*).

kompar'ativ[2] *A* comparative.

kompare're *V -te* compare (*adj.* or *adv.*).

kompas(s)' *-en/-et* compass.

kompas(s)'/hus *-et naut.* binnacle; compass case.

kompas(s)'/rose *-a/+-en* compass card.

kompen'dium *-iet, pl +-ier/*-ium* compendium.

kompensasjo'n *-en* compensation.

kompense're *V -te* compensate; indemnify (**for** for).

kompetanse [kompetang'se] *-n* 1 authority, jurisdiction, province. 2 competence.

kompeten't *A* 1 authorized, entitled. 2 competent, qualified.

kompilasjo'n *-en* compilation.

kompila'tor *-en* compiler.

kompile're *V -te* compile.

kompis [kom'piss] *-en pop.* pal, sidekick.

komplek's[1] *-et, pl -/+-er* 1 complex (also *psych.*). 2 block, group (of buildings).

komplek's[2] *A* complex, complicated.

komplemen't *-et, pl -/+-er* 1 *gram.* complement, prepositional phrase. 2 *math.* complement.

komplementæ'r *A* complementary.

komplementæ'r/farge *-n* complementary color.

komple't *A -*: **kaffe k-** continental breakfast; **te k-** tea with sandwiches and cakes.

komplett' *A -* complete; absolute, utter: **en ordbok kan aldri bli k-** a dictionary can never be c-.

komplette're *V -te* complete, fill out (in).

komplikasjo'n *-en* complication.

kompliment [komplimang'] *-en* 1 compliment. 2 *archaic* bow or curtsy.

komplimente're *V -te* compliment (**med** with).

komplise're *V -te* complicate.

komplise'rt *A -* complex, complicated, intricate.

komplott' *-et, pl -/+-er* intrigue, plot (**mot** against).

komponen't *-en* component.

kompone're *V -te* compose; design, plan.

komponis't *-en* composer.

komposisjo'n *-en* composition.

kompos't *-en* compost.

kompos't/haug *-en* compost heap.

kompott' *-en* compote.

kompresjo'n *-en* compression.

kompress' *-en* 1 compress. 2 *typog.*: **k- sats** close (solid) matter.

kompres'sor *-en* 1 compressor. 2 air pump.

komprime're *V -te* compress.

kompromiss' *-et, pl -/+-er* compromise.

kompromitte're *V -te* compromise: **k- seg** (also) ruin one's own reputation.

komse [kom'se] *-a* "komse" (Lapp cradle).

komtes'se *-a* countess.

kondemne're *V -te* condemn (e.g. a house, a ship).

konden's *-en* condensate.

kondensa'tor *-en* 1 *tech.* condenser. 2 *elec.* capacitor, condenser.
kondense're *V -te* condense.
konden's/vatn *-et* (=+/**vann**) condensate.
kondisjo'n *-en* 1 condition, term. 2 condition; state of being: **i god k-** fit, in good (physical) shape. 3 *archaic* (upper) class. 4 *archaic* position (in a house, an office).
kondisjona'lis *-en gram.* conditional: **første k-** present c- tense; **annen k-** past c- tense.
kondisjone'rt *A - archaic* (belonging to the) upper classes: **de k-e** the cultured people.
kondisjo'ns/trening *-a/+-en* physical training (to keep in good condition, shape).
kondit'or *-en* confectioner; fancy baker.
konditori' *-et, pl +-er/*-* 1 confectioner's, pastry shop. 2 tearoom in connection with a bakery.
kondit'or/varer *pl* pastries.
kondolanse [kåndolang'se] *-n* condolence.
kondole're *V -te* express condolences to (sby).
kondo'r *-en zool.* condor.
konduite [kåndu-it'e] *-n* judgment, poise, savoir faire: **vise k-** show tactful understanding.
konduktø'r *-en* conductor (on train etc.); ticket taker.
ko'ne [*kåne] *-a* 1 woman: **en gift k-** a married w-; **en gammel k-** an old w-. 2 wife: **k- og barn** w- and children; **min k-** my w-.
ko'ne/båt *-en* umiak, Eskimo woman's boat.
+**ko'ne/plager** *-en, pl -e* (=***-ar**) wife beater.
ko'net(e) *A - fam.* staid, stodgy, wifish.
konfederasjo'n *-en* cf **konføderasjon**
konfeksjo'n *-en* ready-to-wear clothing.
konfeksjo'ns/forret'ning *-a/+-en* ready-to-wear business.
konfeksjo'ns/sydd *A -* factory made, ready-to-wear.
+**konfeksjon's/søm'** *-men* (=*/**saum**) ready-to-wear manufacturing.
konfek't *-en* 1 candies, chocolates. 2 *fam.* rough treatment: **han sparte ikke på k-en** he didn't pull his punches.
konfek't/eske *-a/+-en* box of candy, chocolates.
konferanse [kånferang'se] *-n* conference (**med** with; **om** about).
konferansier [kånferangsie'] *-en* master of ceremonies, m. c.
konfere're *V -te* 1 confer (**med** with; **om** about). 2 check, compare.
konfesjo'n *-en* confession.
konfesjo'ns/fri *A -tt* secular: **k- stat** country in which there is separation of church and state.
konfesjo'ns/laus *A* (=+/**løs**) 1 secular. 2 nondenominational.
konfet'ti *-en* confetti.
konfidensiell' *A -elt* confidential.
konfirman't *-en* candidate for confirmation, confirmand.
konfirmasjo'n *-en eccl., jur.* confirmation.
konfirmasjo'ns/alder *-en* confirmation age.
konfirmasjo'ns/dress-*en* confirmation suit.
konfirmasjo'ns/kjole *-n* confirmation dress.
konfirme're *V -te eccl., jur.* confirm.
konfiskasjo'n *-en* confiscation, seizure.
konfiske're *V -te* confiscate, seize.
konfiske'ring *-a* confiscation, seizure.
konfity'r *-en* preserves.
konflik't *-en* conflict: **i k- med** in c- with.
konflik't/stoff *-et* cause, source of conflict.
konfor'm *A* conformable (**med** with), in conformity.
konformite't *-en* conformity.
konfrontasjo'n *-en* confrontation.
konfronte're *V -te* confront (**med** with).
konfunde're *V -te* confound, confuse.
konfu's *A* confused.
konfusjo'n *-en* confusion (also *jur.*).
konføderasjo'n *-en* confederacy, confederation.
konfø'derativ *A* confederate(d).
kong'[1] *-en* (=***kaun**) boil (on the neck), carbuncle.
kong'[2] *-en zool.* whelk (Buccinum undatum), an edible snail.
kong'[3] *n* cf **konge**
kong'e *-n* 1 king; (before name) **kong: Helligtrekonger** Twelfth-Day (Jan. 6). 2 kingpin; kingpost. 3: **K-n** the Crown.
kong'e/bok *-a, pl -bøker bibl.* Book of Kings (I and II).
kong'e/brev *-et* special license.
+**kong'e/bryllup** *-et* (=*/**bryllaup**) royal wedding.
+**kong'e/datter** *-a/-en, pl -døtre* (=*/**dotter**) princess.
kong'e/dømme *-t, pl +-r/*-* (=*/**døme**) 1 monarchy. 2 kingdom: **k-et Norge** the k- of Norway. 3 *archaic*: **få k-t** gain the throne.
kong'e/fami'lie *-n* royal family.
kong'e/flagg *-et* royal standard.
kong'e/flyndre *-a zool* plaice (Pleuronectes platessa).
kong'e/hus *-et* dynasty, royal house (or family).
kong'e/krone *-a/+-en* 1 royal crown. 2 *bot.* guinea-hen flower (Fritillaria meleagris).
***kong'el** *-elen, pl -lar* cf **kongle**
kong'elig *A* 1 royal; regal; kingly: **de k-e** the r- family; **Hans k-e høyhet** His R- Highness. 2 as befits royalty: **leve k-** live like a king; **more seg k-** enjoy oneself hugely.
kong'e/lo'sje *-n* royal box.
kongenia'l *A* congenial (**med** with).
kong'e/pjolter *-eren, pl -rer/+-ere* drink of brandy and champagne.
+**kong'e/rekke** *-a/-en* (=***-je**) line of kings; (list of) kings: **den norske k-** the kings of Norway.
kong'e/rike *-t* kingdom: **k-t Norge** the k- of Norway.
+**kong'e/røkelse** *-n* (=*/**røykjelse**) incense.
kong'e/saga *+-en/*ei* saga of the (Norwegian) kings.
+**kong'e/sang** *-en* anthem in honor of the king (**Gud sign vår konge god**).
+**Kong'e/speilet** *Prn* "The King's Mirror", 13th century Norwegian book on manners, travel, etc.
kongestio'n *-en med.* congestion.
+**kong'e/sønn** *-en* (=*/**son**) prince.
kong'e/tiger *-eren, pl -rer/+-ere* Bengal tiger.
kong'e/vatn *-et* (=+/**vann**) *chem.* aqua regia.
kong'e/vennlig *A -* (=*/**venleg**) monarchical, royalist.
kong'e/ø'rn *-a/-en zool.* golden eagl (Aquila chrysaetos).
kong'le *-a/-+en* cone (of pine, spruce, etc.).
konglomera't *-et, pl -/+-er* 1 conglomeration (**av** of). 2 *geol.* conglomerate.
+**kongole'ser** *-en, pl -e* (=***-ar**) Congolese.
kongole'sisk *A -* Congolese.
kongress' *-en* conference, congress, convention.
kong'ro *-a dial.* spider.
kong'ro/vev *-en dial.* spider web.
kongruen's *-en* 1 *math.* congruence. 2 *gram.* agreement (in gender, number, case).
kongruen't *A -* congruent (**med** with).
Kong's/berg *Pln* town, Buskerud.
+**kong's/datter** *-a* (=*/**dotter**) princess.
kong's/emne *-t* heir apparent; pretender to the throne.
kong's/ga'rd *-en* 1 *hist.* royal palace; mansion. 2 king's estate.
***kong's/lyd** *-en* royal family.
kong's/lys *-et bot.* mullein (Verbascum).
+**kong's/sønn** *-en* (=*/**son**) prince.
kong's/tanke *-n* bold thought, great idea.
Kong's/vinger *Pln* town, Hedmark.
ko'nisk *A -* conical.
konjakk' *-en* 1 brandy, cognac. 2 bottle or glass of brandy.
+**konjak'ker** *-en, pl -e* (=***-ar**) *pop.* glass of brandy.
konjakk'/glass *-et* brandy glass, snifter.
konjektu'r *-en* conjecture.
konjugasjo'n *-en biol., gram.* conjugation.
konjuge're *V -te gram.* conjugate.
konjunksjo'n *-en astron., gram.* conjunction.
kon'junktiv *-en gram.* conjunctive, subjunctive.
konjunktu'r *-en (pl)* business conditions, economic conditions: **gode k-er** good times.
konjunktu'r/politikk' *-en* politics based on conditions of the times, economic conditions.
+**konjunktu'r/svingning** *-en* market fluctuations.
konk [kong'k] *A - fam.* bankrupt (short for **konkurs**[2])
konka'v *A* concave.
konke [kong'ke] *V -a/+-et pop.* bankrupt.
konkla've *-t* conclave.
konklude're *V -te* conclude.
konklusjo'n *-en* conclusion.
konkordan's *-en* concordance.
konkorda't *-et, pl +-er/*-* concordat.
konkre't[1] *-et gram.* concrete noun.
konkre't[2] *A -* concrete.
konkretise're *V -te* make concrete.
konkubina't *-et* concubinage.
konkubi'ne *-a/+-en* concubine.
konkurranse [kångkurrang'se] *-n* competition, contest.
konkurranse/dyktig *A -* able to compete, competitive.
konkurren't *-en* 1 competitor, rival. 2 candidate (for a competitive post).
konkurre're *V -te* compete (**med** with; **om** for).
konku'rs[1] *-en* bankruptcy.
konku'rs[2] *A -* bankrupt: **gå k-** go b-.
konku'rs/bu *-et* (=+/**bo**) estate in bankruptcy.
konky'lie *-n* conch shell, (large) snail shell.
+**kon'ning** *-en archaic* king.
konossemen't *-et, pl -/+-er merc., naut.* bill of lading.
konsekven's *-en* 1 consistency: **mangel på k-** inconsistency. 2 consequence: **ta k-ene** take the c-s. 3 conclusion: **dra k-en** draw the c-.
konsekven't *A -* consistent, logical.
konsen's *-en* approval, concurrence, consent.
konsentrasjo'n *-en* concentration.
konsentrasjo'ns/evne *-a/+-en* ability to concentrate.
konsentrasjo'ns/leir *-en* concentration camp.
konsentra't *-et, pl +-er/*-* 1 *chem.* concentrate. 2 *lit.* condensation (**av** of).
konsentre're *V -te* 1 concentrate; center. 2: **k- seg** express oneself succinctly; **k- seg (om)** concentrate (on).
konsen'trisk *A -* concentric.
konsep't *-et* 1 (rough) draft (of a speech, book, etc.). 2 *(pl)* senses: **gå fra k-ene** lose one's head; **bringe fra k-ene** catch off one's guard, disconcert.

+ Bokmål; * Nynorsk; ° Dialect.
After letter: ' stress (Acc. 1); ' tone, stress (Acc. 2); · length.
Below letter: . not pronounced.

konsep't/papi'r *-et* scratch paper, second sheet(s).
konser'n [also -sæ'rn]*-et, pl -/+-er* concern, trust; cartel.
konser't *-en* 1 concert: **gi, holde k-** give a c-. 2 concerto: **A-moll-k-en** (Grieg's) A-minor c-.
konser't/byrå' *-et, pl +-er/*- concert bureau.
konserte're *V -te* give a concert, a recital.
konser't/sal *-en* concert hall.
konservatis'me *-n* conservatism.
konser'vativ *A* conservative.
konserva'tor *-en* curator (e.g. of a museum).
konservato'rium *-iet, pl +-ier/*-ium* conservatory.
konser'ver *pl* canned goods.
konserve're *V -te* 1 keep, preserve. 2 can, preserve (food). 3 protect (against rust etc.).
konserve'rings/middel *-elet/-midlet, pl +-midler/*-el* preservative.
konser'ves/fabrikk' *-en* canning factory.
konsesjo'n *-en* concession, license, rights (**på** to).
+**konsesjo'ns/haver** *-en, pl -e* (=***-ar**) concessionaire, licensee.
konsesjo'ns/lov [/låv] *+-en/*-a* law regulating right to use natural resources (e.g. lakes, waterfalls, etc.).
konsignan't *-en* consignor.
konsignasjo'n *-en* (i on) consignment.
konsignata'r *-en* consignee.
konsigne're *V -te* consign.
konsi'l *-et, pl -/+-er eccl.* council.
konsipe're *V -te* draft (poem. letter); conceive.
konsipis't *-en* draftsman (of a document).
konsi's *A* concise.
konsisten's *-en* consistency.
+**konsisten's/fett** *-et* (=***/feitt**) (cup) grease (in solid form).
Kon's/mo *Pln* twp, Vest-Agder.
konsolide're *V -te* 1 consolidate (debts, funds). 2 strengthen (position). 3: **k- seg** become solid, strong.
konsoll' *-en* 1 shelf. 2 console table. 3 *arch.* corbel.
+**konsoll'/speil** *-et* (=***/spegel**) mirror with shelf beneath.
konsonan't *-en* consonant.
konsonan'tisk *A* - consonantal.
konsonantis'me *-n* consonantism.
+**konsor'ter** *pl* (=***-ar**) *derog.* ilk: **N. N. og k-** N. N. and his i-.
konsortium [kånsår'tsium] *-iet, pl +-ier/*-ium merc.* syndicate.
konspirasjo'n *-en* conspiracy, plot.
konspira'tor *-en* conspirator, plotter.
konspire're *V -te* conspire, plot.
+**kon'st** *-a/-en* cf **kunst**
konst. = **konstituert**
konsta'bel *-elen, pl -ler* policeman.
konstan't[1] *-en* constant.
konstan't[2] *A* - 1 constant, stable. 2 *(adv.)* constantly, invariably.
konstate're *V -te* 1 ascertain, establish, find. 2 declare, demonstrate; show.
konstellasjo'n *-en* 1 *astron.* constellation. 2 combination, relationship: **de politiske k-er** the political situation.
+**kon'stig** *A* - 1 funny, queer, strange. 2 artful, complicated.
konstitue're *V -te* 1 appoint temporarily (as an interim appointment): **k-t statsråd** acting minister. 2 constitute. 3: **k-ende** constitutional, organizing (meeting). 4: **k- seg som** set oneself up as (e.g. a government).
konstitusjo'n *-en* 1 constitution. 2 interim appointment.
konstitusjonell' *A -elt* constitutional.
konstrue're *V -te* construct (building, triangle, etc.), design: **en k-t verden** a hypothetical world.
konstruksjo'n *-en* 1 construction, structure. 2 design; plan. 3 hypothesis, reconstruction.
+**konstruksjo'ns/tegning** [/teining] *-en* (=***/teikning**) construction (constructional) drawing; *naut.* sheer plan (draft).
kon'struktiv *A* 1 structural. 2 constructive.
konstruktø'r *-en* designer.
kon'sul *-en* consul.
konsula't *-et, pl -/+-er* consulate.
+**konsula't/vesen** *-et, pl -/+-er* consular service.
konsulen't *-en* adviser, consultant, counsellor.
konsule're *V -te archaic* consult.
konsultasjo'n *-en* consultation.
konsul'tativ *A* advisory, consultative.
konsulte're *V -te* consult (doctor, lawyer, etc.).
konsulæ'r *A* consular.
konsu'm *-et* consumption (**av** of).
konsumen't *-en* consumer.
konsume're *V -te* consume.
konsumpsjo'n *-en* consumption.
kont [kon't] *-en* creel, knapsack of woven birch strips or willow, with wood end section.
kontak't *-en* 1 contact; touch: **komme i k- med** get in t- with. 2 (electric) connection, plug.
kontak'te *V -a/+-et* contact.
kontaminasjo'n *-en gram.* blend, contamination.
kontan't *A* - 1 cash: **k- betaling** c-payment. 2 forthright, ready; bossy, imperious: **et k- svar** a sharp (quick-witted) answer.
+**kontan't/behol'dning** *-en* cash balance, cash on hand.
+**kontan'ter** *pl* (=***-ar**) cash.
kontan't/rabatt' *-en* cash discount.
kontek'st *-en* context.
kontemplasjo'n *-en* contemplation.
kontem'plativ *A* contemplative.
konten'tum *-et* sound effects.
konte're *V -te merc.* enter.
kon'ti *pl of* **konto**
kontinen't *-et, pl -/+-er* continent.
kontinenta'l *A* continental.
kontingen't *-en* 1 contingent. 2 dues; fee, subscription.
kontingente're *V -te* restrict imports, set a quota.
kontinuasjo'n *-en* repetition of an examination (cf next word).
kontinue're *V -te* repeat an examination (due to absence or failure).
kontinue'rlig *A* - continuous: **k- drift** night and day operation.
kontinuite't *-en* continuity.
kon'to *-en, pl -er/konti merc.* account.
kon'to/kuran't *-en merc.* statement of current account.
konto'r *-et, pl -/+-er* office.
konto'r/betje'nt *-en* clerk, office assistant.
+**konto'r/bud** *-et* office boy.
konto'r/dame *-a/+-en* office girl, secretary.
konto'r/forkle *-et, pl +-forklær/*-* smock.
kontoris't *-en* office clerk.
konto'r/krakk *-en* office stool: **slite k-en** *(derog.)* do office work.
konto'r/loka'le *-t, pl +-r/*-* office, office space.
konto'r/mann *-en, pl -menn/*-menner* clerk; office worker.
konto'r/maski'n *-en* office machine.
konto'r/persona'le *-t* office personnel.
konto'r/post *-en* office job.
konto'r/rekvisi'ta *pl* office supplies.
konto'r/sjef *-en* office manager; department head.
konto'r/søster *-ra/+-eren, pl -rer* (doctor's) office girl, nurse.
konto'r/tid *-a/+-en* business hours, office hours.
kon'tra *P* versus.
kon'tra/bande *-n* contraband.
kon'tra/bass *-en mus.* double bass (string instrument).
kon'tra/bok *-a, pl -bøker* 1 account book. 2 bankbook, passbook.
kon'tra/fei *-et, pl -/+-er hum.* image, likeness, picture.
kontrahen't *-en* contracting party.
kontrahe're *V -te* contract (for).
kontraksjo'n *-en* contraction.
kontrak't *-en* contract.
kontrak't/brott *-et* (=+**/brudd**, ***/brot**) breaking of a contract.
+**kontrak't/messig** *A* - according to contract, contractual.
kontrak't/stridig *A* - contrary to the contract.
kon'tra/ordre *-n* countermand, counterorder.
kon'tra/part *-en* 1 *jur.* opponent. 2 adversary.
kon'tra/punkt [/pongt] *-et mus.* counterpoint.
kontra'ri *A* - contrary; unfavorable (wind etc.).
kon'tra/signatu'r *-en* countersignature.
kon'tra/signe're *V -te* countersign.
kon'tra/spiona'sje *-n* counterespionage.
kontras't *-en* contrast (**til** to).
kontraste're *V -te* contrast (**med** with).
kontras't/farge *-n* contrasting color.
+**kontras't/virkning** *-en* (=***/verknad**) contrasting effect.
kon'tra/vote'ring *-a/+-en* counter ballot (check on the correctness of vote count for a measure by calling for votes from the opposing side).
kon'tre/admira'l *-en* rear admiral.
kontribue're *V -te* contribute.
kontribusjo'n *-en* contribution.
kontroll' *-en* 1 check, checking, inspection (**av** of). 2 control, mastery (**over** over). 3 (in orientation) checkpoint.
kontrolle're *V -te* 1 check, inspect, verify. 2 control, dominate (over).
kontrollø'r *-en* checker, inspector; gatekeeper, ticket taker.
kontrover's *-en* controversy.
kontræ'r *A* 1 contrary. 2 contradictory.
kontuberna'l *-en archaic* roommate.
kontu'r *-en* contour, outline.
ko'nus *-en* cone.
konvall' *-en bot.* lily of the valley (Convallaria majalis).
konvek's *A* convex.
konveksite't *-en* convexity.
konvenien's *-en lit.* convention, conventionality.
konvensjo'n *-en* convention; treaty.
konvensjonell' *A -elt* conventional.
konven't *-et* 1 *eccl.* convent, monastery. 2 *hist.* convention.
konventik'kel *-elen, pl konventikler* conventicle, religious assembly.
konventik'kel/plaka't *-en* ordinance governing religious assembly (in Norway from 1741-1842).
konvergen's *-en* convergence.
konverge're *V -te* converge.
konversa'bel *A -elt, pl -le* talkative.
konversasjo'n *-en* conversation.
konversasjo'ns/leksikon *-et, pl -leksika* encyclopedia.
konverse're *V -te* chatter, converse (**med** with), talk; keep sby entertained: **k- sin borddame** entertain one's dinner companion.
konverte're *V -te merc.* convert.
konverte'rings/lån *-et merc.* conversion loan.
konverti'bel *A -elt, pl -le merc.* convertible.
konvertibilite't *-en merc.* convertibility.
konvertitt' *-en* convert.
konvoi [kånvåi'] *-en* convoy.
konvoiere [kånvåie're] *V -te* convoy.
konvolutt' *-en* envelope.
konvolutte're *V -te* put into an envelope.
konvulsi'visk *A* - convulsive.
konvulsjo'n *-en* convulsion.
kooperasjo'n *-en* cooperation (among members of cooperative): **K-en** the cooperative movement.
ko'/operativ[1] *-en* cooperative (store).
ko'/operativ[2] *A* cooperative.
kooperatø'r *-en* member of cooperative, esp. an official in the movement.

koordinasjo'n *-en* coordination.

koordina't *-en* coordinate.

koordina't/syste·m *-et, pl -/+-er math.* system of coordinates.

koordine're *V -te* coordinate.

ko'p *-en* gaping fool: **i en hop er det alltid en k-** there's always one (fool, idiot) in a crowd.

***kopar** [kå'par] *-en* cf **kobber**

ko'pe *V -te* gape, stare (**på** at).

kopek [kåpe'k] *-en* kopeck, Russian coin=1/100 ruble.

Ko'per/vik *Pln* port town, Rogaland.

kopi' *-en* **1** copy (**av** of), replica. **2** print (of photo).

kopi'/blekk *-et* copying ink.

kopi'/blyant *-en* indelible pencil.

kopi'/bok *-a, pl -bøker* letter book.

kopie're *V -te* **1** copy, duplicate, make carbon copies; mimeograph. **2** print (a photo).

kopie'r/maskin [/masji·n] *-en* copying machine; *tech.* copying lathe.

kopis't *-en obs.* junior clerk; copyist, one who copies art masterpieces.

kop‘le *V -a/+-et* (=+**koble**) **1** tie up (e.g. dogs). **2** couple (R.R. cars). **3** link: **k- inn, k- sammen, k- til** hook up (e.g. electric circuits), connect (by a clutch). **4: k- av** unhook; *fig.* relax.

koplet *df of* **kop'pel**, *pt of* **kop‘le**

kop‘ling *-a/+-en* **1** coupler, coupling (R.R. cars). **2** clutch (in car).

kopp' *-en* **1** cup; *med.* cupping glass; *naut.* drumhead; *arch.* header; *tech.* porcelain insulator: **en k- kaffe** a cup of coffee. **2** vessel; bowl, dish; *(pl)* dishes: **k-er og kar** (all kinds of) dishes.

+**kop‘par**[1] *-et/-en* cf **kobber**

***kop‘par**[2] *pl* cf **kopper**[2]

+**kopp‘/arret** *A -* pockmarked (from smallpox).

kop‘pe *V -a/+-et* **1** *med.* bleed. **2** feed young animal from a cup: **k- opp et lam** bring up a lamb by hand.

kop‘pe/epidemi· *-en* smallpox epidemic.

kop'pel *-elet/koplet* (=+**kobbel**) **1** *mus.* coupler (in an organ). **2** coupling; leash. **3** brace (of dogs), pack. **4** part of harness.

+**kop'per**[1] *-et* cf **kobber**

+**kop‘per**[2] *pl* (=***-ar**) pox; smallpox.

+**kop‘per/dank** *-en* cf **kobber/**

+**kop‘per/hud** *-a/-en* cf **kobber/**

+**kop‘per/kis** *-en* cf **kobber/**

+**kop‘per/stikk** *-et* cf **kobber/**

kop‘pe/sett *-et* cup and saucer.

kopp‘/lam· *-met* lamb fed milk from a cup.

kopp‘/skatt *-en* poll tax.

***kop‘pul** *-en* (=**kuppul**) pebble.

***kopp‘/ærut** *A -* cf **/arret**

ko'pra *-en* copra.

kopulasjo'n *-en* **1** copulation. **2** *hort.* splice grafting.

kopule're *V -te* **1** copulate. **2** splice-graft.

ko'r[1] *-et* **1** choir, chorus (in all English meanings): **i k-** in chorus, simultaneously. **2** church *arch.* chancel, choir.

***kor**[2] [korr'] *Av* cf **hvor**[2]

kora'l *-en mus.* chorale.

kora'l/bok *-a, pl -bøker* hymnal (containing the melodies).

korall' *-en* **1** coral. **2** spike (on spiked collar).

korall'/øy *-a* coral island.

kora'l/musikk· *-en* choral music.

Kora'nen *df* The Koran.

kor‘de *+-n/*-a math.* chord.

korde'l *-en naut.* strand (of a rope).

korderoy [kår'deråi] *-en* corduroy.

kor‘d/fløyel *-elen* corduroy.

kordia'l *A lit.* cordial.

kordialite't *-en* cordiality.

kordong' *-en* **1** cordon. **2** condom.

kordu'an *-en* cordovan (leather), cordwain.

koreogra'f *-en* choreographer; ballet master.

koreografi' *-en* choreography.

kor/for [korr'/fårr] *Av* cf **hvor/**

kor‘g *-a* (=+**kurv**[1]) basket.

kor‘g/ball *-en* basketball.

***kor‘ge/kjerring** *-a* "basket woman", woman who peddles cakes, fruits in baskets.

Kor‘gen *Pln* twp, Nordland.

kor‘g/flaske *-a* wicker bottle; demijohn.

***kor‘g/fletting** *-a* cf **kurv/fletning**

***kor‘gje** *Pn korkje*: **ikkje k-** neither one.

+**kor‘g/møbler** *pl* (=***-ar**) wicker furniture.

kor‘g/stol *-en* wicker chair.

+**ko'r/gutt** *-en* (=***/gut**) *eccl.* acolyte.

***korhel'st** *Av* cf **kvarhelst**

korin't *-en* currant (raisin).

korin'tisk *A -* Corinthian.

kor'k *-en* **1** cork. **2** *bot.* cork cambium, phellogen. **3** cap (on bottle). **4** (traffic) jam, tie-up.

kor‘ka *A -*: **k- dum** absolutely stupid.

kor‘k/belte *-t, pl +-r/*-* lifesaver (of cork).

kor‘ke *V -a/+-et* **1** cork, plug; stopper (a bottle). **2** block (an exit, traffic).

kor‘ke/skrue** *-n* (=/skruve**) corkscrew.

+**kor‘ke/trekker** *-en, pl -e* (=***/trekkjar**) corkscrew.

+**kor‘ketrekker/krølle** *-n* corkscrew curl.

kor‘k/hjelm *-en* pith helmet.

***kor‘kje**[1] *C* cf **verken**[2]

***kor‘kje**[2] *Pn nt of* **korgje**

ko'r/kåpe *-a eccl.* cope.

***ko'r/leis** *Av* how.

ko'rn[1] *-et* **1** grain; cereal(s); in some dial. esp. of barley. **2** kernel, seed; grain, granule.

ko'rn[2] *-et* sight (on a gun): **ta på k-et** hit, take sby off=imitate perfectly.

ko‘rn/aks *-et* ear, head, spike (of grain).

***ko‘rnast** *V -ast* form ears, head.

ko‘rn/band *-et* sheaf (of grain).

+**ko‘rn/blomst** *-en bot.* cornflower (Centaurea cyanus).

ko‘rn/blå *A -tt* cornflower blue.

+**ko‘rn/bånd** *-et* cf **/band**

ko‘rn/dyrking *-a/+-en* grain cultivation, raising of grain.

ko‘rne[1] *V -a/+-et* form granules, granulate.

***ko‘rne**[2] *V -a* get harvested grain into the barn.

ko‘rnet(e) *A -* grainy, granular.

kornett' *-en* cornet.

ko‘rn/kammer *-eret, pl -er/+-kamre* granary.

ko‘rn/mo *-en* (flash of) heat lightning.

ko‘rn/nek *-et* sheaf of grain.

ko‘rn/rauk *-en* grain shock.

ko‘rn/silo *-en* grain elevator.

ko‘rn/sort *-en* cereal, grain.

Ko‘rn/stad *Pln* twp, Møre og Romsdal.

ko‘rn/staur *-en* pole to which grain sheaves are fastened to dry.

kor‘p *-en* raven.

korpora'l *-en* corporal.

korporasjo'n *-en* corporation.

kor‘porativ [also -por'-] *A* corporate.

korpo'rlig *A -* bodily, corporal (e.g. punishment).

kor‘ps *-et* **1** corps. **2** band.

kor‘ps/lege *-n archaic* regimental doctor.

kor‘ps/ånd *+-en/*-a* esprit de corps.

korpulen'se *-n* corpulence.

korpulen't *A -* corpulent, stout.

kor‘pus[1] *-en* **1** (type face) long primer (ab. 10 point). **2** material (e.g. silver) used to make hollow ware.

kor‘pus[2] *-et* **1** body, physique. **2** corpus.

korrek's *-en* correction, reprimand.

korreksjo'n *-en astron.* correction.

korrek't *A -* **1** accurate, correct, exact. **2** conventional, correct, punctilious.

korrekti'v *-et, pl -/+-er* corrective (**til** to).

korrektu'r *-en typog.* proof: **lese k-** read p-.

+**korrektu'r/le·sning** *-en* (=***/lesing**) proofreading.

+**korrektu'r/tegn** [/tein] *-et* (=***/teikn**) proofreader's mark.

korrelasjo'n *-en* correlation.

korrela't *-et* correlate.

korrel'ativ *A* correlative.

korrespondanse [-ang'se] *-n* **1** correspondence; communication. **2** direct connection (between trains, train and boat, etc.).

korrespondanse/ku·rs *-et* correspondence course.

korrespondanse/skole *-n* correspondence school.

korresponden't *-en* **1** correspondent. **2** *merc.* person in charge of correspondence.

korresponde're *V -te* **1** correspond (**med** with; **til** to). **2** connect (**med** with): **toget og båten k-er på Åndalsnes** the train c-s with a boat at Å-.

korresponde'rende *A -* **1** corresponding. **2** connecting.

korrido'r *-en* corridor.

+**korrido'r/poli·tiker** *-en, pl -e* (=***-ar**) lobbyist.

korrige're *V -te* correct; proofread.

korrosjo'n *-en* corrosion.

korrumpe're *V -te* corrupt.

korrupsjo'n *-en* **1** corruption, graft. **2** giving or accepting bribe, special favors. **3** marring (of a text by additions, errors, etc.).

korrup't *A -* (of person, text, etc.) corrupt.

+**kor's** *-et* (=***kross**) **1** cross (also *fig.*): **bære sitt k-** bear one's c-; **gjøre k-ets tegn** make the sign of the c-; **ha det k- på seg** be so cursed, have such a c- to bear; **i k-** crossed; **krype til k-et** humble oneself, repent; **legge armene over (i) k-** cross one's arms, *fig.* be idle, stand idly by; **sitte med bena i k-** sit cross-legged. **2: ikke legge to pinner (strå) i k- for en** do nothing to help, not lift a finger, stand idly by. **3** (mild) oath: **k-, k- og k-** heavens.

ko'r/sang *-en* choir singing, choral singing; song by (Greek) chorus.

+**ko'r/sanger** *-en, pl -e* (=***/songar**) chorister.

korsa'r *-en* corsair.

+**kor's/blomstret** *A - bot.* cruciate, cruciform; brassicaceous.

+**ko'rs/broder** *-en, pl -brødre* canon, member of a chapter in a cathedral or collegiate church.

+**kor's/bånd** *-et* (=***kross/band**) **1** crossed laces (on girl's shoe). **2** class of mail including printed matter, samples, and business papers. **3** *zool.* cruciate ligament.

+**kor‘se** *V -a/-et* (=***krosse**) **1** cross (one's arms); crisscross, tack. **2** mark with a cross; make the sign of the cross: **k- seg** cross oneself; **k- seg over** be shocked at.

korsett' *-et, pl -/+-er* corset.

+**kor's/farer** *-en, pl -e* crusader.

+**korsfes'te** *V -et* crucify.

+**kor's/gang** *-en* **1** via dolorosa. **2** penitential journey. **3** cloister (walk).

+**korsika'ner** *-en, pl -e* (=***-ar**, ***korsikan**) Corsican.

+**kor's/kirke** *-n* cruciform church.

+**kor's/legge** *V -la, -lagt* cross (one's skis etc.), fold (one's arms): **korslagte bein** crossbones.

+**kor's/mess(e)** *en* **1** May 3rd, Holy Rood Day. **2** Sep. 14 (also known as Holy Cross Day).

+**kor's/nebb** *-en zool.* crossbill (Loxia).

***kor/so** [korr'/so] *Av* anyway, in any case: **eg kjem att, k-** I'll be back just the same.

+**kor's/rev** *-en* cross fox, variation of

+ Bokmål; * Nynorsk; ° Dialect.
After letter: ' stress (Acc. 1); ‘ tone, stress (Acc. 2); · length.
Below letter: . not pronounced.

red fox with a black cross on its back.
*kor's/rygg -en anat. lumbar region, small of the back.
+kor's/sting -et cross-stitch.
+kor's/tog [/tåg] -et crusade.
ko'r/stol -en choir stall (one of several chairs placed along the side walls of the chancel).
+kor's/troll zool. starfish (Asterias rubens).
+kor's/vei -en (=+/veg) 1 crossing, crossroad(s): ved neste k- vi møtes we'll meet at the next crossroads (Ibsen). 2 Way of the Cross.
kor't[1] -et card (e.g. Christmas/, playing/, post/, punch/, visiting/, ID/, IBM/): gi k- deal; kikke en i k-ene kibitz, peek behind the scenes; legge k-ene på bordet come clean, lay one's c-s on the table; sitte med alle k-ene have everything working for you, hold all the c-s; sitte med gode (dårlige) k- have a good (bad) hand.
kor't[2] A - brief, concise, short; curt: k- sagt in s-, in summary; innen k- tid before long; gjøre et hode k-ere kill (lit. decapitate); komme til k- be inadequate, fail, lose; (si noe) k- og godt (say sth) clearly, plainly; k- og godt in s-; trekke det k-este strå be on the losing end; være k- for hodet be gruff, short-tempered.
kor't/bo'rd -et card table.
kor't/brev -et double postcard.
kor't/bølgje -a (=+/bølge) shortwave.
kor'te V -a/+-et shorten: k- av en kjole s- a dress; k- av på lønnen skimp one's salary; k- inn på s-, take in; k- tida pass the time (by entertainment).
+kor'telig A - briefly.
*korter ['korte'r] -et quarter hour.
korte'sje -n cortege, procession.
kor'tevare/handel -elen, pl -ler variety store (incl. hardware, porcelain, glass, etc.).
kor'te/varer pl hardware, notions.
+kor't/fattet A - brief, concise, succinct: han er k- i sin tale he is a man of few words.
kor't/film -en short, short subject.
kor't/form -a/+-en shortened form (of a word).
+kor't/fristet A - merc. short-term.
+kor't/het -en brevity, briefness, shortness: i k- briefly.
kor't/hus -et house of cards: slå k-et over ende spoil sby's dreams.
kor't/klipt A - closely clipped, cropped.
kor't/kunst -en card trick.
kor't/leik -en deck of cards.
kor't/liva A - (=+-et) 1 short-lived. 2 archaic short-waisted.
kor't/pusta A - (=+-et) short-winded.
kor't/siktig A - merc. short-dated (loan).
ko'rt/skalle -n anthro. 1 brachycephalic (=broad) skull. 2 brachycephalic person.
kor't/slutning -en 1 elec. short, short-circuit. 2 hum. incorrect conclusion.
kor't/slutte V -a/+-et elec. short-circuit.
+kor't/spill -et (=*/spel) 1 card playing. 2 card game. 3 deck of cards.
kort'/stokk -en deck of cards.
kor't/sy'nt A - shortsighted.
kor't/tenkt A - shortsighted, concerned with immediate advantage only.
kor't/varig A - of short duration, short.
kor't/vegg -en end wall, short wall.
korvett' -en naut. corvette.
koryfé -en leader, top man: en av k-ene one of the brass.
ko's[1] -en course: dra (gå) sin k- go away, leave, skip out.
ko's[2] -en fam. coziness, cozy pleasure: ha k- sammen cuddle up.
*kos[3] [kå's] -a, pl kaser (=*koss[2]). 1 heap, pile, esp. of trees for burning. 2 (burned-over) clearing.
kos[4] A fam. =koselig
kosakk' -en Cossack.
ko'se[1] V -a/-te make things cozy, pleasant (for for): k- seg enjoy oneself, feel delight, have it cozy.
*kose[2] [kå'se] pp of kjose
ko'selig A - comfortable, cozy, snug; delightful, nice, pleasant; friendly.
*kosi [kå'si] pp of kjose
kosme'tika pl cosmetics.
kosmetikk' -en 1 beauty care. 2 cosmetics.
kosme'tisk A - cosmetic.
kos'misk A - cosmic.
kosmonau't -en cosmonaut.
kosmopoli'tisk A - cosmopolitan.
kosmopolitt' -en cosmopolitan, cosmopolite.
kos'mos et cosmos.
koss'[1] -et/+-en heap, pile, esp. of ice chunks frozen into tower formation (in arctic).
*koss'[2] -a cf kos[3]
*koss'[3] Av cf korleis
kost[1] [kos't] -en brush; broom.
kos't[2] -en 1 food; fare: smal k- meagre fare. 2 board: k- og losji b- and room; ha en i k-en have sby as a boarder.
kos't[3] -en jur. costs: dømme en i k- og tæring require the payment of court c-.
kost[4] [kos't] N: k- og mask "costume and mask"=dress rehearsal.
kost[5] [kos't] V: så det k- (etter) at a great speed, furiously.
*kos'tal A costly, expensive.
kos't/bar A 1 costly, expensive. 2 precious. 3: gjøre seg k- be hard to get an answer out of, require a lot of urging.
+kos'tbar/het -en 1 costliness, expensiveness. 2 precious object; treasure, valuable. 3 preciousness.
kos'te[1] V -a/+-et 1 cost: hvor mye k-er det? how much does it c-?; k- hva det k- vil, hva enn det skal k- at all costs, whatever the cost; det har k-et meg mange bitre timer it has c- me many bitter hours; det k-er på it demands great effort, is strenuous. 2 bear the cost of, pay for; spend: k- en fram (til studenteksamen) pay sby's way (to college); k- på (noe, en) spend on (sth, sby); k- seg noe, k- på seg noe allow oneself the luxury of sth, buy sth for oneself; jeg k-er reisen I'll pay for the trip.
kos'te[2] [kos'te] V -a/+-et brush, sweep.
koste/binderi' [kos'te/] -et: hele k-et the whole caboodle (lot, shebang).
*kos'te/laus A free.
kos'telig A - 1 bibl. costly, expensive: en k- perle a pearl of great price. 2 excellent, superb: k-e retter e- dishes. 3 funny, priceless: et k- syn a p- sight.
+kos'tende -t cost, expenditure: til k- at cost.
+kos'ter pl (stolen) goods.
*kos'te/sam' A costly, expensive.
koste/skaft [kos'te/] -et broomstick.
+kos't/forak'ter -en, pl -e finicky eater, fussy person.
*kos't/gjæv A generous (as a host).
+kos't/godtgjørelse -n (=+-ing) per diem.
+kos't/hold -et (=*/hald) fare, meals.
kos'tnad -en cost, expense.
+kos't/penger pl (=*-ar) living expenses; per diem.
kos't/pris -en merc. cost price.
kos't/skole -n boarding school.
kos't/verde [/være] V -a/+-et dial. pay, stand cost (for sth): du skal ikke k- don't go to any expense (Hamsun).
kosty'me -t costume.
kosty'me/ball -et costume ball.
kostyme're V -te costume, dress up.
ko't[1] -en fingerling(s), small fish, fry.
*kot[2] [kå't] -et cf kott
kote[1] [kå'te] -n contour line (on a contour map).
kote[2] [kå'te] -a cottage, hut.
kotelett [kåtelett'] -en 1 chop, cutlet. 2 muttonchop whiskers.
koteri [kåteri'] -et coterie.
kotiljong [kåtiljång'] -en cotillion.
+kot/karl [kå't/] -en hist. cottager, cotter.
kott' -et 1 hut, shed. 2 small room; cubbyhole, fam. hole in the wall. 3 (clothes) closet.
kotur'ne -n buskin, cothurnus: gå på k-r speak in tragic tones; act the prima donna.
ko'v -et dial. 1 heavy shower; fine, thickly falling snow. 2 damming up of a brook by a buildup of ice. 3 (a) cold (=kove).
kove [kå've] -n small room, used as bedroom or storeroom (usu. closed-off section of entryway in log house).
*ko'ven A -e/-i, pl -ne 1 (of air) heavy, oppressive. 2 suffocating; choked up.
ko'vne V -a/+-et suffocate, be suffocating.
+ko'/øye -t, pl -r cf ku/
kr=krone(r)[2]
kra' I caw.
Kra.=Kristiania
kraal [kra'l] -en cf kral
krabas'k -en scourge, whip: få k- get a caning, a whipping.
kraba't -en fellow, rascal: en ordentlig k- a real scamp.
krab'bas/tømmer -et unstamped log in a log run.
krab'be[1] -a/-en 1 zool. crab. 2 naut. wooden drag or grapnel. 3 prongs to hold gem. 4 naut. (pl) gripes. 5 tech. hand hoist.
krab'be[2] V -a/+-et 1 grub, scrabble. 2 crawl, creep: k- til køys scramble into bed. 3 drag, stumble along.
+krab'be/kjent A - (=*/kjend) naut. intimately familiar (with a course).
krab'le V -a/+-et 1 (of animals) crawl, creep, swarm (usu. in krible og k-). 2 finger, fumble with: k- opp scramble to one's feet.
kraf's -et scrape, scratch.
kraf'se V -a/+-et 1 claw, scratch. 2 grub, rake: k- i jorda dig (scratch) in the soil. 3: k- seg fram scratch along, struggle ahead. 4: k- til seg grab, snatch.
kraf't -a/+-en, pl krefter/*krafter 1 force, power, strength (both physical and spiritual): k-ens moment phys. moment of force; av alle krefter with all one's might; rope av alle krefter shout at the top of one's voice; bærende k- mainstay, prime mover; for full k- full steam ahead, at full blast; arbeide for full k- work at top capacity; hemmelige (skjulte) krefter mysterious (hidden) forces; i k- av by virtue of, on the basis of; komme til krefter (igjen) regain one's strength, recuperate; prøve krefter med pit one's strength against; samle krefter gather strength, recuperate; sette i k- put in force; spare på kreftene spare oneself; det tar på kreftene it's exhausting; tre i k- become effective, go into effect. 2 energy, vigor, vitality: han står i sin fulle k- he's at his prime. 3 (pl) effort(s): det er krefter i bevegelse for å e-s are being made to; sette alle krefter inn på å make every e- to; ved forente krefter by joint, combined e-s. 4 dynamic person: være en k- be a dynamo, powerhouse. 5 (dramatic) talent: teatrets beste krefter the theater's leading actors. 6 (soup) stock: koke k- på (et bein) make soup from (a bone).
+kraf't/anstreng'else -n (great) effort, exertion.
kraf't/bein -et soupbone.
kraf't/felt -et electrical field, field of force.

kraf't/for *-et* feed concentrate.

kraf't/idio·t *-en* absolute idiot, prize fool.

kraf'tig *A -* powerful, strong; energetic, vigorous; (of food) heavy, nourishing: **k- bygget** muscular; **et k-slag** a stunning blow; **et k- spark** a good swift kick; **en mann i sin k-ste alder** a man in his prime; **gi en en k- omgang** give sby a real going-over; (emphatic *adv.*) **prisene gikk k- opp** prices skyrocketed; **(protestere) på det k-ste** (protest) vehemently.

+**kraf'tig/bygget** *A -* powerfully built.

kraf't/kar *-en* powerful fellow, strong man.

kraf't/laus *A* (=+**/løs**) 1 powerless, weak. 2 without power.

+**kraf't/ledning** *-en* high-tension line, power line.

kraf't/line *-a* (=**/linje**) line of force.

+**kraf't/løs** *A* cf **/laus**

kraf't/overfø·ring *-a/+-en* transmission of power: **k- på alle fire hjul** 4-wheel drive.

kraf't/papi·r *-et* kraft(paper), brown wrapping paper.

kraf't/papp *-et* building paper.

kraf't/patrio·t *-en* chauvinist, superpatriot.

kraf't/prestasjo·n *-en* display of strength, feat.

kraf't/prøve *-a/+-en* test of endurance, strength.

kraf't/sats *-en* bold assertion or doctrine.

kraf't/spille *-t* waste of energy, strength.

kraf't/stasjo·n *-en* power station.

kraf't/tak *-et* powerful grip, hold; valiant effort: **ta et riktig k-** give it all you've got.

+**kraf't/utfol·delse** *-n* display of energy.

kraf't/uttrykk *-et* oath, swear word.

kraf't/verk *-et* power plant.

kra`ge[1] *-n* collar.

+**kra`ge**[2] *-n* cf **kråke**

kra`ge/bein *-et* clavicle, collar bone.

***kra`ge/blom** *-en* one of several chrysanthemum types.

kra`ge/bryst *-et* dress shirt front.

Kra`ger/ø *Pln* coastal town, Telemark.

+**kra`ge/tær** *pl* cf **kråke/**

kragg' *-en* crooked, dwarfed tree.

kra'k *pt of* **kreke**

kra`ke[1] *-n* 1 crooked, dwarfed person or tree. 2 post with pegs to hang things on. 3 anchor, grapnel, wooden drag. 4 sea monster.

kra`ke[2] *V -a/+-et* 1 drag, slide. 2: **k- seg (fram, opp)** crawl. 3 *dial.* croak, cry.

krakele're *V -te* give a crackle finish to porcelain.

kra`ket(e) *A -* bent, crooked.

+**kra`ke/tær** *pl* cf **kråke/**

+**kraki'ler** *-en, pl -e* (=***-ar**) hothead.

kraki'lsk *A -* bellicose, hotheaded, quick-tempered.

krakk'[1] *-en* stool; (short) bench.

krakk'[2] *-en* poor wretch.

krakk'[3] *-et* crash, economic catastrophe; bankruptcy.

krakk'/mandel *-elen, pl -ler* thin-shelled almond.

kra'l *-en* (=**kraal**) kraal.

kram'[1] *-met* 1 *archaic* wares: **det passet inn i hans k-** it was grist to his mill, it suited his purposes. 2 junk, trash; trifles: **disse moderne skjortene er noe k-** these modern shirts are no good.

kram'[2] *A -t, pl -me* sticky, wet (snow).

kram`/bu *-a* country store, general store.

+**kram`bu/svenn** *-en* clerk in a country store.

kram`/kar *-en* peddler.

***kram`mast** *V -ast* (of snow) pack together.

+**kram`me**[1] *V -a/-et* 1 crumple (**sammen** up), crush. 2 press, squeeze.

kram`me[2] *pl of* **kram**[1]

+**kram`p/aktig** *A -* convulsive; forced, strained, tense: **et k- smil** a f- smile; **holde k-** hang on for dear life (**i** to).

kram`pe[1] *-n* cramp, spasm; tic, twitching; convulsion.

kram`pe[2] *-n* 1 (metal) cramp. 2 staple.

kram`pe/gråt *-en* convulsive sobbing.

+**kram`pe/latter** *-en* (=***/lått**) hysterical laughter.

+**kram`pe/trekning** *-en* convulsion, spasm: **ligge i de siste k-er** be in the throes of death.

kram`se *V -a/+-et* finger, fumble at; clutch.

kram`s/fugl *-en* thrush, waxwing trapped and used as gamebirds.

kra'n *-a* (=+**krane**) 1 (industrial) crane. 2 cock, faucet, tap. 3 long, flexible nozzle from which train tender is supplied with water.

kra`ne *-n* cf **kran**

kra'n/fører *-en, pl -e* (=***-ar**) crane operator.

krang`el *-elet/-let/+-elen* 1 quarrel, squabble, wrangling. 2 contentiousness: **juridisk k-** legal hairsplitting.

krang`le *V -a/+-et* 1 bicker, squabble, wrangle (**med** with; **om** about). 2 pick a quarrel, start trouble.

krang`le/fant *-en* quarreler, troublemaker.

krang`le/pave *-n* quarreler, troublemaker.

krang`let(e) *A -* 1 rough, rugged. 2 quarrelsome.

krang`le/voren *A +-ent, pl -ne* quarrelsome.

kra'nie/brott *-et* (=+**/brudd**) skull fracture.

kra'nium *-iet, pl +-ier/*-ium* cranium, skull.

kran'k[1] *-en* 1 (on a bicycle) (pedal) crank, crank axle bracket. 2 *tech.* crank.

kran'k[2] *A* 1 bad, poor: **uta blank og inna k-** a whited sepulchre. 2 *archaic* sick.

kran's *-en* 1 wreath (of flowers); garland. 2 necklace (of beads, pearls). 3 circle, ring: **i k- om** encircling.

kran`se *V -a/+-et* 1 crown, wreathe. 2 circle, encircle.

+**kran`se/binder** *-en, pl -e* (=***-ar**) wreathmaker.

kran`se/kake *-a* cone-shaped cake of almond macaroon rings with a figure on the top.

kran`se/lag *-et* celebration arranged for workers by building owner when the ridgepole is raised.

kran`se/påleg·ging *-a/+-en* (=+**-else**) part of burial ceremony when wreath is laid on the coffin and eulogy is given.

+**kra'n/spill** *-et tech.* winch.

***krapp'**[1] *pt of* **kreppe**[2]

krapp'[2] *A krapt* 1 narrow, restricted. 2 sharp, short, sudden: **en k- sving** a sudden turn. 3 (of sea) choppy.

krapp'/sjø *-en* choppy sea.

krapy'l *-et* dregs of society, rabble, trash.

kra's *N* cf **knas**[1]

kra`se *V -a/+-te* 1 crackle, crunch. 2 crack, crunch, crush (sth).

krasj [kræsj'] *-en/-et* crash.

krasje [kræsj`e] *V -a/+-et* crash.

kras'l *-et* rustle, scurrying.

kras`le *V -a/+-et* rustle, scurry.

krass' *A krast* crass; coarse, gross: **den k-este uvitenhet** the g-est ignorance; **k- ord** coarse words.

+**kras`se** *V -a/-et* 1 scrape, scratch: **k- på døra** scratch on the door. 2 scribble.

kras't *nt of* **krass**

***kra't** *-et* trash.

kra'ter *-eret/-ret, pl -er/+-re* crater.

kratt' *-et* scrub, underbrush; bushes, thicket.

kratt'/skog *-en* scrub, thicket, underbrush.

krau`me *V -a/+-et dial.* 1 crawl; swarm: **k- seg (opp)** struggle (up). 2 drudge, toil.

***krau`ne** *V -a* 1 dread, shudder (at). 2 complain, whine.

krau'p *pt of* **krype**

kra'v[1] *-et* 1 demand (**på** for; **til** on). 2 claim (**på** on): **ha k- på** have a right to; **moralsk k-** moral c-.

kra'v[2] *-et* ice film; needles, particles of ice.

+**kravat(t)'** *-en* (18th century) cravat.

***krav`de** *pt of* **krevje**

+**kra`ve**[1] *-n* cf **krage**[1]

kra`ve[2] *V -a/+-et*: **k- seg** form ice particles, freeze over.

kravell' *-en naut.* 1 carling (fore-and-aft beam). 2: **på k-**=**k-/bygd.** 3 *hist.* caravel, carvel.

kravell'/bygd *A -/*-bygt naut.* carvel-built (with deck planks flush).

kra'v/full *A* demanding, exacting.

krav'l *-et* 1 climbing (with help of hands), crawling, creeping. 2 struggle, toil. 3 swarm.

kra'v/laus *A* (=+**/løs**) 1 undemanding, unexacting. 2 free from claims, *merc.* unencumbered.

krav`le *V -a/+-et*: **det k-er og kryr** (insects, people, etc.) are swarming everywhere.

kra`v/melding *-a/+-en* demand bid (in bridge).

***kra`v/sam·** *A* demanding.

***kra'vs/mann** *-en, pl -menn(er)* creditor.

***kra'vs/mål** *-et* demand.

kra`v/stor *A* demanding, exacting.

***kravt** [kraf't] *pp of* **krevje**

+**kre'**[1] *-et* 1 poor thing. 2 *lit.* creature, esp. fowl.

kre'[2] *V -dde* string (fish) on a twig.

kreasjo'n *-en* creation (by a dress designer).

+**kreatu'r** *-et, pl -/+-er* cf **krøtter**

kreden'se *V -te archaic* taste before serving; partake of.

kre'dit *-en* 1 credit column: **oppføre til ens k-** enter in the c-. 2 credits: **hans debet er større enn hans k-** his debits exceed his c-.

kreditе're *V -te merc.* credit (to sby's account): **k- en kr 1000 c-** sby with 1000 *kroner.*

krediti'v *-et, pl -/+-er* 1 credentials, letter of accreditation. 2 *merc.* letter of credit.

kre'dit/nota *-en merc.* statement of credit balance.

kre'ditor *-en, pl -o'rer* creditor.

kre'dit/post *-en merc.* credit entry.

kreditt' *-en* credit: **ta på k-** buy on c-.

kreditt'/bank *-en* commercial bank.

kreditt'/opplag *-et* 1 storage in bond (with duty deferred until goods are sold). 2 bonded warehouse.

kreditt'/opply·sning **-a/+-en* credit report: **få k- på noen** get a credit rating on sby.

kree're *V -te* 1 create: **k- en rolle** c- a part (in a new play). 2: **k- noen til æresdoktor** confer an honorary doctor's degree on sby.

kref't *-en* 1 *med.* cancer, cancerous growth, carcinoma. 2 *bot.* canker.

+**kref't/byll** *-en med.* cancerous tumor, carcinoma.

kref'ter *pl of* **kraft**

kref't/skade *-n* cancer.

***kref't/svull** *-en med.* cancerous tumor, carcinoma.

kreg`da *df* the measles.

krei`ste *V -a/+-et* crush, squeeze.

kre'k *-et* miserable creature, poor thing.

kre`ke *V krak/+-te, +-t/*-e/*-i* 1 crawl, creep: **k- seg** drag (oneself). 2 swarm.

kre`ke/bær *-et bot.* crowberry (Empetrum nigrum).

+ Bokmål; * Nynorsk; ° Dialect.
After letter: ' stress (Acc. 1); ` tone, stress (Acc. 2); · length.
Below letter: . not pronounced.

krek'le *-a* cf **krøkle**

krek'ling *-en bot.* crowberry, crowberry shrub (Empetrum nigrum).

*__krek'se__ *-a* 1 crooked branch or twig. 2 crosspatch; ornery, perverse person.

*__krek'seleg__ *A* - contrary, obstinate.

*__krek'sen__ *A -e/-i, pl -ne* contrary, obstinate.

*__kre'l__ *-en* craw, crop, stomach.

kre'm *-en* 1 whipped cream. 2 custard (filling). 3 face cream; cream polish. 4 *fig.* cream, the best (**av** of).

kremasjo'n *-en* cremation.

kremato'rium *-iet, pl +-ier/*-ium* crematorium.

kreme're *V -te* cremate.

kre'm/fløyte *-n* (=+/**fløte**) whipping cream.

Krem'l *Pln* Kremlin.

krem'le *-a* mushroom of russula genus.

+**krem'mer** *-en, pl -e* (=***-ar**) 1 huckster (mercenary person). 2 *dial.* huckster, peddler.

+**krem'mer/aktig** *A* - huckstering, mercenary.

+**krem'mer/hus** *-et* (=***-ar/**) 1 cornet, paper cornucopia (cone-shaped container for candy etc.). 2 *bot.* ochrea.

+**krem'mer/nasjo'n** *-en* (=***-ar/**) nation of shopkeepers (used by Napoleon about the English).

+**krem'mer/sjel** *-a/-en* (=***-ar**) huckster; mercenary soul.

krem't *+-et/*-en* clearing of the throat, hawk(ing).

krem'te *V -a/+-et* clear the throat, hawk.

+**kreng'e** *V -a/-et/-te* (=***-je**) 1 turn suddenly, twist; (of airplane) bank. 2 turn inside out: **k- klærne av kroppen** undress by turning clothes inside out. 3 *naut.* heel, list; overturn: **k- over** overturn.

+**kren'ke** *V -a/-et/-te* (=***-je**) 1 violate (laws, rights, person). 2 hurt, insult, offend.

+**kren'kelse** *-n* (=***-ing**) 1 violation. 2 hurt, insult, offense.

*__kren'kje__ *V -te* cf **krenke**

kreo'l *-en* cf **kreoler**

+**kreo'ler** *-en, pl -e* (=***-ar**) Creole.

+**kreolerin'ne** *-a* (=***kreolarinne**) Creole woman.

kreoso't *-en* creosote.

krepe're *V -te* die (of animals): *hum.* (of people) croak, kick the bucket.

*__krepp'__[1] *-en* 1 narrow passage. 2 decline (in health, esp. of animals).

krepp'[2] *-et* crepe.

krep'pe[1] *-a* narrow passage, strait.

*__krep'pe__[2] *V krapp, kroppe/-i*: **k- i hop** shrink, shrivel.

krep'pe[3] *V krepte/+-a/+-et* 1 make sth narrower, pinch. 2 crepe, crimp, crinkle, curl.

krep'pet(e) *A* - crimped, crinkled, curled.

krepp'/nylon *-et* nylon crepe.

krepp'/papi'r *-et* crepe paper.

krep's *-en, pl -er/+-* crawfish, crayfish: *astron.* **K-en** Cancer, the Crab; **K-ens vendekrets** Tropic of Cancer.

krep's/dyr *-et* crustacean.

krep'se *V -a/+-et* 1 back out of something, crawfish. 2 catch crayfish.

krep'se/gang *-en*: **gå k-** crawfish, retreat.

*__kre'se__ *V -te* be choosy, particular (about food): **k- seg med noko** relish sth, treat oneself to sth.

kre'sen *A +-ent, pl -ne* discriminating, finicky, sophisticated; exclusive; choosy, picky: **en k- publikasjon** an e- magazine, for the d- person, the connoisseur.

*__kre'sne__ *-a* choosiness, discrimination.

Kre'ta *Pln* Crete.

kre'ti *N*: **k- og pleti** all kinds of people; every Tom, Dick, and Harry.

+**kreti'ner** *-en, pl -e* (=***-ar**) cretin.

kretinis'me *-n* cretinism.

kretong' *-en* cretonne.

+**kret's** *-en* (=***krins**) 1 circle, ring: **i k-** in a c-; **slå k- om** rally round; **jordens k-** the terrestrial orb. 2 district (as school, election d-), ward. 3 circle=clique, set: **ledende k-er** leading circles. 4 province, sphere (of activity). 5 cycle, group (of stories).

+**kret'se** *V -a/-et* (=***krinse**) circle (**om, omkring** around): **k- inn** encircle.

+**kret's/fengsel** *-elet, pl -ler* county jail.

+**kret's/formann** *-en, pl -menn* chairman, head of a (e.g. school, election) district.

+**kret's/gang** *-en* circulation; going around (in circles).

+**kret's/løp** *-et* 1 circling (around), gyration: **jordens k-** the earth's course. 2 *med.* circulation: **det store k-** systemic c-; **det lille k-** pulmonary c-.

+**kret's/møte** *-t* district meeting.

+**kre've** *V -de* (=***-je**) 1 ask, claim, demand: **k- betaling av en** d- payment from sby; **k- en for noe** d- sth (returned) from sby; **k- inn skatt** collect taxes; **k- sin rett** d- one's right(s). 2 call for, require: **brevet k-er svar** the letter r-s an answer, must be answered; **k- en til ansvar (regnskap)** call sby to account; **k- livet** cost sby his life; **et arbeid som k-er sin mann** an exacting job, a full-time job.

+**kre'vende** *A* - demanding, exacting.

*__krev'jar__ *-en* collector: **skatte/** tax c-.

*__krev'je__ *V krev, kravde, kravt* cf **kreve**

Kr. F.=**Kristelig Folkeparti**

*__kri'__ *V -dde* 1 want badly, be eager (**etter** for). 2 pelt, pepper.

krib'le *V -a/+-et* 1 crawl, creep. 2 prickle, shiver; itch (to do sth), tickle, tingle: **det k-er i kroppen** (he) feels a tingling in the body.

kri'g *-en* war, warfare: **i k- og kjærlighet er alt tillatt** all's fair in love and war; **åpen k-** open warfare; **å leve er — k- med troll i hjertets og hjernens hvelv** to live is — war with trolls in the vault of the heart and mind (Ibsen); **erklære k-** declare war; **føre k-** wage war; **føre sin k- igjennom** be victorious, get one's way; **være (ligge) i k- med** be at war with.

kri'ge *V -a/+-et* battle, do battle (**med** with), make war (**mot** on).

+**kri'ger** *-en, pl -e* (=***-ar**) warrior: **håpløs er en ensom k-** a lone w- is lost (Ibsen).

kri'gersk *A* - belligerent; martial, warlike; military.

+**kri'ger/ånd** *-en* (=***-ar/**) martial spirit.

kri'g/førende *A* - warring.

kri'g/føring *-a/+-en* warfare.

+**krig's/bytte** *-t* (=***/byte**) booty, spoils of war.

krig's/dans *-en* war dance.

+**krig's/erklæ'ring** *-en* declaration of war.

krig's/fange *-n* prisoner of war.

krig's/fly *-et* warplane.

krig's/fot *-en*: **på k-** in a state of war; **sette på k-** mobilize.

krig's/førsel *-en* warfare.

krig's/herja *A* - (=+**-et**) war-torn; devastated by war.

+**krig's/hisser** *-en, pl -e* (=***-ar**) warmonger.

krig's/humø'r *-et* warring mood: **være i k-** be on the warpath.

krig's/hyl *-et* 1 war whoop. 2 piercing shriek.

krig's/korresponden't *-en* war correspondent.

krig's/kunst *-en* art, science of war.

krig's/list *-a/+-en* stratagem.

+**krig's/lysing** *-a* declaration of war.

krig's/lysten *A +-ent, pl -ne* war-happy, war-loving; bellicose.

krig's/makt *-a/+-en* 1 military power. 2 army; forces, soldiers.

+**krig's/maling** *-a/-en* (=***/måling**) war paint.

krig's/mann *-en, pl -menn/*-menner* 1 *archaic, hum.* soldier, warrior. 2 *jur.* person (either military or civilian) under military command.

krig's/materiell' *-et* war materiel.

krig's/rett *-en* 1 military law. 2 military court, tribunal; court martial.

krig's/rop *-et* battle cry.

krig's/råd *-et* 1 council of war. 2 war council.

krig's/skade *-n* war damage.

+**krig'sskades/erstat'ning** *-en* war indemnity; reparations.

krig's/skip *-et* battleship, warship.

krig's/skole *-n* military academy.

+**krig's/skueplass** *-en* (=***/skodeplass**) 1 theater of operations, theater of war. 2 front, scene of battle.

+**krig's/spill** *-et* (=***/spel**) war game(s).

+**krig's/sti** *-en* (=***/stig**): **på k-en** on the warpath.

krig's/tid *-a/+-en* wartime.

+**krig's/tilstand** *-en* state of war.

+**krig's/tjeneste** *-n* (=***/teneste**) active duty: **gjøre k-** be on a-; **gå i k-** enlist.

+**krig's/tummel** *-en* tumult of war.

+**krig's/vant** *A* - (=***/van(d)**) accustomed to war, seasoned.

krig's/viktig *A* - of military importance.

krig's/øks *-a* battle-axe.

kri'k *-en* 1 bow, corner: **i hver k- og krok** in every nook and cranny. 2 crook, curve, hollow (of arm).

kri'ke *-n* cf **krik**

krikk'/and *-a, pl -ender zool.* teal (Anas crecca).

krill' *-en* curlicue, flourish, scroll (wood carving).

kril'le[1] *-a* (usu. **-a**) measles.

+**kril'le**[2] *V -a/+-et* prickle, tickle.

+**kril'le/hoste** *-n* tickling cough.

kri'm *-et* catarrh, mucus, phlegm; head cold.

Kri'm *Pln* Crimea.

kri'm/full *A* having a cold, stuffed up; plagued with colds.

kri'm/hoste *-n* coughing up phlegm.

krimina'l *A* criminal (only in cpds.).

krimina'l/betje'nt *-en* detective.

kriminalis't *-en* criminologist.

kriminalistikk' *-en* criminology.

kriminalite't *-en* criminality, crime.

krimina'l/lov *-en/*-a archaic* criminal law.

krimina'l/politi' *-et* detective force.

krimina'l/roma'n *-en* crime story; whodunit.

krimina'l/sak *-a/+-en* criminal case.

kriminell' *A -elt* criminal: **k-elt dårlig** shamefully bad.

kriminologi' *-en* criminology.

*__krim's__ *-et* garnish, trim.

*__krim'se__ *V -a* garnish, trim.

kri'm/sjuk *A*: **han er k-** he has a cold.

krim's/krams *-et* fancy ornamentation, folderol, gewgaws, gingerbread, knickknacks.

*__kri'ne__ *V -a* scrawl; decorate with scrolls.

*__kring'__[1] *-en* circle, group: **i k-** around.

*__kring'__[2] *A* 1 agile, nimble. 2 convenient.

*__kring'__[3] *P* around.

*__kring'el__ *-elen, pl -lar* circle, ring.

*__kring'/føtt__ *A* - nimble, quick-footed.

*__kring'/gang__ *-en* bypass, circumvention.

*__kring'/gå__ *V -gjekk, -gått* bypass, circumvent.

kring'/kaste *V -a/+-et* broadcast.

kring'/kasting *-a/+-en* 1 broadcasting. 2 broadcasting system.

kring'kastings/hus *-et* broadcasting station, radio station.

kring'kastings/program' *-met* radio program.

*__kring'/lagd__ *A -/-lagt* circumscribed (circle).

kring'le[1] *-a* 1 disc, round slice, ring (on ski pole etc.). 2 figure 8, pretzel. 3 (large) pastry (in figure 8 shape).

kring'le[2] *V -a/+-et* form bends, figure eights, rings; roll up.

kring'let(e) *A* - scrolled, twisted.

kring'/mæ'lt *A* -fluent, quick-talking.

***kring'/om'** *P* around.
+kring'/sette *V -satte* (=***/setje**) 1 encircle, form a ring around. 2 besiege, surround.
kring'/sjå *-et* 1 panorama, view. 2 guided tour.
krin'k *-en*: **i k- og krok** in every nook and cranny.
+krin'kel *-elen, pl -ler* loop: **gjennom ledens k-ler og krumninger** through the channel's l-s and bends.
+krin'kel/krok *-en* out-of-the-way corner, secret nook.
krinoli'ne *-n* crinoline.
krin's *-en* cf **krets**
krin'se *V -a/+-te* cf **kretse**
***krin'sel** *-elen, pl -lar* circle, circumference.
kri'se *-a/-en* crisis.
kri'se/herja *A* - (=**+-et**) depressed, emergency, hard-hit.
kri'se/lov *-en/*-a* emergency act.
kri'se/løyving *-a* emergency grant.
kri'se/tid *-a/+-en* period, time of crisis; depression.
kri'se/tilstand *-en/*-et* state of crisis, crucial condition.
kri'sis *-en med.* crisis, turning point.
kris'le *V -a/+-et* (=***kritle**) tickle, tingle; prickle, shiver.
kris'telig *A* - 1 Christian, religious: **K- Forening for Unge Menn (Kvinner)** Y.M.(W.)C.A. 2 decent, proper: **på k- vis** in a p- way.
+kris'telig/sinnet *A* - Christian, religious.
kris'ten[1] *en, pl -ne* Christian.
kris'ten[2] *A +-ent, pl -ne* Christian: **den k-ne kirke** the C- church; **i k- jord** in consecrated soil.
Kris'ten *Prn (m)*
kris'ten/dom' *-men* Christianity.
kris'tendoms/kunnskap *-en* knowledge of Christianity (as a school subject), religious knowledge.
kris'ten/folket *df* Christians (=the converted).
+kris'ten/het *-en* Christendom.
kris'ten/mann *-en* (in folktales) Christian person: **Tvi! tvi! Her lukter k-s blod** Fee, fi, fo, fum I smell the blood of an Englishman.
kris'ten/plikt *-a/+-en* Christian duty.
kris'ten/rett *-en hist.* church law.
Kris'ti *po of* **Kristus**
Kris'tian *Prn (m)*: **K- kvart** Christian IV (king 1588-1648).
Kristia'nia *Pln* former name of Oslo, used 1624-1924.
Kristiansan'd (S) *Pln* city, Vest-Agder.
Kristiansun'd (N) *Pln* city, Møre og Romsdal.
Kristi'n(e) *Prn (f)*
kris'tne *V -a/+-et* 1 Christianize, convert. 2 baptize, christen. 3 hallow, sanctify: **i k-et jord** in h-ed ground.
Kristof'fer *Prn (m)*
kris't/to'rn *-en bot.* holly (Ilex aquifolium).
Kris'tus *Prn, po* **Kristi** Christ: **K-i blodsdråper** *bot.* fuchsia; **K-i Himmelfartsdag** Ascension Day; **e.Kr. (etter K-i fødsel, etter K-)** A.D.; **f.Kr. (før K-i fødsel, før K-)** B.C.
kris'tus/skjegg *-et* beard such as Christ wears in religious art.
kri't[1] *-a*: **på k-a** on credit.
***kri't**[2] *-et* cf **kritt**
***kri'te**[1] *V -a* cf **kritte**
***kri'te**[2] *V -a* decorate with scrollwork; scribble.
krite'rium *-iet, pl +-ier/*-ium* criterion.
***kri't/hus** *-et* cf **kritt/**
+kri'tiker *-en, pl -e* (=***-ar**) critic.
kritikk' *-en* 1 criticism (av of): **under all k-** beneath contempt; **være gjenstand for k-** be the target of c-. 2 critique, review (of e.g. book, play). 3: **k-en** the critics, critical opinion. 4 critical ability: **mangle k-** lack self-criticism.
kritikk'/sjuk *A* (=**+/syk**) overly inclined to criticize.
kritise're *V -te* 1 criticize, evaluate. 2 be critical of, censure, find fault with.
krit'isk *A* - critical (in all meanings).
***kri't/kvit** *A* cf **kritt/**
***krit'le** *V -a* cf **krisle**
***kri't/pipe** *-a* cf **kritt/**
+kritt' *-et* (=***krit**[2]) 1 chalk: **et stykke k-** a piece of c-; white. 2 *archaic*: **ta på k-** chalk up (a debt).
+krit'te *V -a/-et* (=***krite**[1]) 1 chalk: **k- en tennisbane** c- a tennis court; **k- opp (et paradis)** c- (for hopscotch). 2 whiten (e.g. shoes, a wall). 3 *archaic* chalk up (a debt).
+kritt'/hus *-et*: **i k-et (hos)** in the graces (of), on the good side (of).
+kritt'/hvit *A* cf **/kvit**
***kritt'/tid** *-a* cf **kritt/**
+kritt'/kvit *A* (=**+/hvit**) chalk white.
+kritt'/pipe *-a* clay pipe.
+kritt'/tegning [/teining] *-en* crayon drawing.
+kritt'/tid *-a/-en geol.* Cretaceous Period.
***krju'pe** *V kryp, kraup, krope/i* cf **krype**
kro'[1] *-a/+-en* inn, public house.
+kro'[2] *-en* craw.
+kro'[3] *V -dde*: **k- seg** be puffed up, strut; boast (av of).
+kroa'ter *-en, pl -e* (=***-ar, kroat**) Croatian.
kroa'tisk *A* - Croatian.
kro'k *-en* 1 hook (on the wall, on a door, fishhook, etc.): **bite på k-en** take, swallow the bait (e.g. be fooled); **få (en fisk; noen) på k-en** hook (a fish; sby); **dra k-** pull fingers (as a test of strength); **spenne k- for en** try to trip sby; *dial.* **vandre k-** spin a top. 2 bend (in river, path, road, etc.): **i k- (og krik)** zigzag; **gjøre en k-** make a detour (side trip). 3 evasive tactic or movement: **han brukte mange k-er** he was extremely evasive, used all the tricks in the bag. 4 (inside) corner, nook, recess; out-of-the-way place: **hjertets lønnlige k-er** the secret r-es of the heart; **drive en opp i en k-** corner, trap sby; **hviske i k-ene** make secret plans, put heads together; **velg imellom lyse vidder og den skumle sorgens k-** choose between shining heights and that dismal sorry hole (Ibsen). 5 poor old person: **"Stå ikke der og glisp", sa kjerringa, "men kom og hjelp en gammel k-."** "Don't just stand there gaping," said the old woman, "but come and help a poor old body." (Asbjørnsen).
kroka'n *-en* almond brittle.
kroka'n/is *-en* ice cream with krokan (butter brickle ice cream).
kro'ke *V -a/+-et* bend, crook: **k- seg sammen** hunch up; **vi k-et oss fram** we wound our way along.
***kro'ken** *A -e/-i, pl -ne* bent, drawn up.
kroke're *V -te* 1 *mil.* sketch a map. 2 croquet (opponent's ball).
kro'ket(e) *A* - 1 bent, crooked, hooked, tortuous; doubled over; (of road or river) winding. 2 complicated, twisted. 3 sly, tricky: **du er så k- i ord du** you're such a tricky talker (Asbjørnsen).
kroki' *-et/+-en* 1 *mil.* sketch, rough map. 2 croquet (of opponent's ball).
krok'ket *-en* croquet.
Kro'k/kleiva *Pln* steep slope in Bærum, with narrow cleft through which old Oslo-Ringerike road passes.
kro'k/lisse *-a* rickrack.
***kro'kne** *V -a* become bent, crooked.
+kro'k/nese *-a/-en* (=***/nase**) hooknose.
krokodil'le *+-a/-en* crocodile.
krokodil'le/tårer *pl* crocodile tears.
***kro'k/o'rdig** *A* - ambiguous, double-talking, evasive.
kro'k/rygg *-en* hunchback: **Inge k-** Norw. king d. 1161.
+kro'k/rygget *A* - (=***/ryggja**) hunchbacked.
kro'k/stav *-en* crook, crosier.
krok'us *-en bot.* crocus.
kro'k/veg *-en* (=**+/vei**) 1 crooked road; roundabout way. 2 devious course, trick: **gå k-er** use indirect or underhand means.
krom [krom'] *-men/-met* chrome.
kroma'tisk *A* - *mus.* chromatic.
kromoso'm *-en/-et* chromosome.
kro'n/blad *-et* petal.
kro'n/dyr *-et zool.* red deer (Cervus elaphus).
kro'ne[1] *-a/+-en* 1 (royal) crown; coronet, tiara; *astron.* corona: **gjøre krav på k-n** claim the throne. 2 (the) Crown (as an institution): **k-ens gods** an estate of the C-. 3 crown=summit (of head, tree, flower, tooth, etc.): **sette k-n på verket** supply the finishing touch. 4 winder (on watch).
kro'ne[2] *-a* 1 krone (Scand. unit of currency; Norw. k-=ab. 14 cents). 2 heads (on coin): **slå mynt og k-** flip a coin, heads or tails. 3 crown (various coins by this name.)
kro'ne[3] *V -a/+-et/+-te* crown: **k- med hell** c- with success.
kro'ne/brud *-a* (=***/brur**) bride with bridal crown.
kro'ne/rulling *-a/+-en* collection for a charitable purpose usu. carried on through the auspices of a newspaper.
kro'ne/stykke *-t, pl +-r/*-* coin *(krone)*.
+krong'le *V -a/-et* cf **krungle**
+krong'le/furu *-a* cf **krungle/**
+krong'let(e) *A* - cf **krunglet(e)**
kro'n/gods *-et* crown land(s).
kro'n/hjort *-en* (red deer) stag with a large rack; royal stag.
kro'n/idio't *-en* absolute idiot, prize fool.
kronikk' *-en* 1 feature article (usu. printed at foot of editorial page). 2 news analysis, report (e.g. on the radio).
kronikø'r *-en* writer of **kronikk.**
kro'ning *-a/+-en* coronation.
kro'nisk *A* - chronic.
kro'n/juve'l *-en* crown jewel.
kronologi' *-en* chronology.
kronologisk [-olå'g-] *A* - chronological.
kronome'ter *-eret/-ret, pl -er/+-re* chronometer.
kro'n/pretenden't *-en* claimant, pretender to the throne.
kro'n/prins *-en* crown prince.
kronprinses'se *-a/+-en* crown princess.
kro'nprins/regen't *-en* prince regent.
kro'n/rake *V -a/+-te* shave the crown of the head.
+kro'n/rega'lier *pl* (=***/regalia**) regalia (1 royal prerogatives. 2 royal emblem).
kro'n/år *-et* bumper year.
krope** [krå'pe] *pp of* **krype** (=kropi**)
***krop'ne** *V -a* become bent; be shrunk.
kropp' *-en* 1 body; fuselage; trunk. 2 *fam., hum.* fellow, guy, man: **en gudsforgåen k-** a wild scamp.
kropp'/due *-a zool.* pouter pigeon (Columba gullurosa).
***krop'pe** *pp of* **kreppe**[2]
***krop'pen** *A -e/-i, pl -ne* shrunk.
***krop'pi** *pp of* **kreppe**[2]
kropp's/arbeid *-et* physical labor.
***kropp's/burd** *-en* bearing.
kropp'slig *A* - bodily, physical.
kropp's/visite're *V -te* frisk, search (a person).
kropp's/øving *-a/+-en* physical culture; physical education.
***kross'** *-en* cf **kors**
***kross/band** *-et* cf **korsbånd**
***kross'/blome** *-n bot.* plant of Cruciferae family.

+ Bokmål; * Nynorsk; ° Dialect.
After letter: ' stress (Acc. 1); ` tone, stress (Acc. 2); · length.
Below letter: . not pronounced.

*kros'se V -a cf korse

*kross'/farar -en cf kors/farer

*kross'/feste V -a/-e cf kors/

*kross'/kyrkje -a cf kors/kirke

*kross'/mess(e) en cf kors/

*kross'/rev -en cf kors/

*kross'/troll -et cf kors/

kross'/ved -en bot. cranberry bush or snowball (Viburnum opulus).

*kross'/veg -en cf kors/vei

kro't -et 1 decorative carving, painting; embroidery; scrollwork. 2 scrawl, scribbling.

kro'te V -a/+-et 1 decorate by carving, painting, or embroidery. 2 scrawl, scribble.

kro't/saum -en (=+/søm) decorative embroidery (not geometric).

*krub'be -a cf krybbe[1]

*krub'be/bitar -en cf krybbe/biter

krugg' -en dial. humpback; hunchback.

*kru'k -en bent, crooked person.

kru'ke V *-a/-te bend the knees; squat.

*kru'ken A -e/-i, pl -ne 1 bent, bowed. 2 despondent, timid.

krukke [krok'ke] -a crock, jar, jug, pitcher, pot: k-n går så lenge til vanns at den kommer hankeløs hjem he's done it once too often.

*kruk'se V -a walk bent over.

krull' -en 1 circle, curl, ring; ball, roll. 2 flourish, scroll. 3 cluster, group.

krul'le V -a/+-et 1 curl, roll: k- på halen r- up its tail; k- seg sammen c- up.

krul'let(e) A - cf krøllet(e)

+krum [krom'] A -t, pl -me arched, bowed, curved; bent, crooked: gå på med k- hals fam. make an all-out effort, put one's heart into it.

+krum/bøyd [krom'/] A bent, bowed down.

krum/kake [krom'/] -a thin, delicate wafer rolled into cone or cylinder, often filled with whipped cream.

+krumme[1] [krom'me] -n 1 bread minus the crust. 2 crumb; bit, morsel.

+krumme[2] [krom'me] V -a/-et 1 bend, curl. 2: k- seg bend, bow; (of hands) clench. 3: ikke k- et hår på ens hode not hurt a hair of sby's head.

+krummelu'r -en (usu. pl) formalities, fuss; tremolos.

+krumning [krom'ning] -en 1 turn, twist; bend, curl, curve. 2 math. curvature.

*krum'p -en raven.

*krum'pe V -a crunch; crush.

+krum/rygget [krom'/] A - bowed, hunchbacked; hunched.

krum/sabel [krom'/] -elen, pl -ler scimitar.

+krum/spring [krom'/] -et caper, gambol: gjøre k- make excuses.

+krum/stav [krom'/] -en crook, crosier.

krum/tapp [krom'/] -en 1 crankpin. 2 fig. kingpin.

krumtapp/aksel -en crankshaft.

*kru'ne -a cf krone[1]

krungle [krong'le] V -a/+-et 1 struggle, toil. 2: k- seg wind; work one's way.

krungle/furu [krong'le/] -a crooked pine tree.

krunglet(e) [krong'let(e)] A - 1 crooked, gnarled, twisted. 2 tortuous; rugged, uneven. 3 difficult, intricate.

krupp' -en croup.

kru's[1] -et/*-a mug, stein, tankard.

kru's[2] -et/+-en 1 curl, fuzz; frizzly hair; ruffle. 2 compliments: gjøre k- for en make a fuss over sby.

kru'se V -a/-te 1 cause ripples: k- seg ripple. 2 (of hair) curl: *k- seg til primp. 3 compliment, flatter.

krusedull' -en 1 flourish, scrollwork. 2 affected movement. 3 (pl) beating around the bush, circumlocutions.

kru'se/mynte -a bot. curled mint (Mentha crispa).

kru'set(e) A - 1 curled, curly, rippling. 2 creased, wrinkled. 3: gjøre hodet k- på en turn sby's head.

krusifik's -et, pl -/+-er crucifix.

*krus'k -en crooked, gnarled tree.

*krus'ken A -e/-i, pl -ne feeble, frail.

krus'le V -a/+-et prickle, shiver, tingle.

krus'let(e) A - scrawny, weak.

*krus'ling -en ailing person.

+kru'sning -en 1 curling, rippling. 2 ripple.

kru's/persil'le -a (curled) parsley.

krusta'de -n croustade, patty shell.

+kru's/tøy -et (=*/ty) earthenware; crock.

+krutt' -et (=*krut) (gun)powder: (være) full av k- (be) a live wire; (skyte med) løst k- (fire) blanks; holde k-et tørt keep one's powder dry, be prepared to fight; han har luktet k- he's seen action; han har ikke oppfunnet k-et he's no shining light, he'll never set the world on fire; han er ikke et skudd k- verd he's not worth the powder to blow him to hell; (ikke) spare på k-et be unsparing (in one's criticism), let go with both barrels.

+krutt'/ho'rn -et (=*krut/) powder horn.

+krutt'/kjerring -a (=*krut/) 1 firecracker. 2 fig. spitfire; flash in the pan.

+krutt'/lapp[also krutt'/]-en (=*krut/) cap for toy pistol.

+krutt'/røyk -en (=*krut/) gunsmoke.

+krutt'/tønne -a (=*krut/, *krut/-tynne) powder keg.

kry'[1] V -dde 1 swarm; be full of: det k-r av ideer (he) is running over with ideas. 2 dial. crawl, creep, drag or pull (oneself).

kry'[2] A +-/*-tt 1 cocky, proud (av of), stuck-up: k- på det hard to please. *2 perky, well.

*kry'ast V -ast get well.

+kryb'be[1] -a (=*krubbe) 1 crib, manger: når k-en er tom, bites hestene poverty makes even the best of friends fall out. 2 day nursery.

+kryb'be[2] -n type of sled.

+kryb'be/biter -en, pl -e (of horses) cribber, crib-biter.

*krydd' -et cf krydder

*kryd'de[1] -a cf krydder

*kryd'de[2] V -a cf krydre

kryd'der -eret/-ret (=*krydd, *krydde[1], +krydderi) seasoning, spice.

+krydderi' -et cf krydder

+kryd'der/nellik -en (=*krydd/) clove.

+kryd'der/sild -a (=*krydd/) pickled herring.

kryd're V -a/+-et spice: k- et foredrag med anekdoter lace a speech with stories.

kry'e V -a/+-et dial. 1 (also k- til) get well, recover. 2: k- seg act cocky, stuck-up.

+kryk'ke -a (=*-je[1]) crutch: gå med k-r use c-es.

*krykkj'e[1] -a cf krykke

krykkj'e[2] -a zool. kittiwake (Rissa tridactyla).

kry'l -en hump (on the back); arch (of the back): treet hadde en k- på seg the tree had a hump.

+kry'l/rygga A - (=+-et, *-ja) humpbacked; arched.

krym'pe V -a/+-et 1 shrink; contract; (of water) ripple. 2: k- seg flinch, shrink, wince. 3 tech. shrink on. 4 fam. celebrate (an occasion) by drinking.

krym'pe/fri A -tt shrink-proof.

*kry'ne V -te discipline, punish.

kry'p +-et/*-en 1 crawling insect, snake, worm; vermin. 2 (+-en) poor creature: stakkars k- (you) poor thing. 3 repulsive person, wretch (also +-en).

kry'p/dyr -et reptile.

kry'pe V kraup/+krøp, +krøpet/ *krope/*-i 1 (of people, animals, plants, etc.) crawl, creep: k- sammen cuddle up, snuggle; alt som kan k- og gå every living being; en må (lære å) k- før en kan gå you have to walk before you run (lit. crawl before you walk); det er like godt å (en kan like gjerne) hoppe (i det) som k- i det you might as well get it over with quick; det k-er i meg it gives me the creeps, makes my flesh crawl. 2 fawn, grovel: k- for en lick sby's boots. 3 (of material) shrink. 4 (in cards) underplay a card; play a lower card (than has been previously played).

+kry'peri -et fawning, groveling.

kry'p/inn -et hole-in-the-wall, hovel; retreat.

*kryp'ling -en cf krøpling

+kry'p/skytter [also -y'-] -en, pl -e (=*-ar) poacher.

kry'p/syl -en dial. miserable creature, poor thing.

kryp't -en crypt.

kryptogram' -met, pl -/+-mer cryptogram.

krysan'temum -en, pl -te'mer/+-temumer (=*krysantem) chrysanthemum.

+krys'ning -en (=*kryssing) 1 cross, hybrid. 2 crossing (av of). 3 naut. cruising, tacking.

kryss' -et 1 cross (mark): i (på) k- across, crosswise; på k- og tvers crisscross, in all directions; gjennomstreife et land på k- og tvers travel the length and breadth of a country; sette k- (i margen av en bok) place a cross mark (in the margin of a book). 2 mus. sharp. 3 (of humans) loin; (of animals) croup, hindquarters. 4 crossing, crossroads: midt i k-et in the middle of the intersection. 5 naut. crown, throat (of an anchor).

krys'se V -a/+-et 1 cross: k- Atlanteren c- the Atlantic; k- av (ut) c- off (out); k- ens vei c- sby's path; k- (over) gata c- the street; brevene våre k-et (hverandre) our letters c-ed; k-et sjekk Brit. c-ed check. 2 cross= intersect: k- hverandre i-; k-ende linjer i-ing lines; lyntogene k-er på Geilo the (west- and eastbound) express trains meet at Geilo. 3 cross=crossbreed. 4 cross= frustrate, thwart: k- ens planer t- sby's plans. 5 naut. tack. 6 naut., mil. cruise, patrol (an area of water). 7 cf krøsse.

+krys'ser -en, pl -e (=*-ar) cruiser.

kryss'/finér -en plywood.

+kryss'/forhør -et (=*/forhøyr) cross-examination.

+kryss'/henvisning -en cross-reference.

+kryss'/ild -en cross fire.

*krys'sing -a cf krysning

kryss'/o'rd -et: gjette (løse) k- work on (solve) a crossword puzzle.

+kryss'ord/oppgave -a (=*/oppgåve) crossword puzzle.

krystall' -en/-et crystal.

krystall'/appara't -et, pl -/+-er crystal set (radio).

krystalli'nsk A - crystalline.

krystallise're V -te crystallize.

*krystall'isk A - cf krystallinsk

krystall'/klar A (=*/klår) crystal clear.

krystall'/kule -a crystal ball.

krys'te V -a/+-et 1 crush, press, squeeze: k- druer c- grapes; k- til sitt bryst p- to one's bosom. 2 (of sorrow or pain) crush, oppress.

+krys'ter -en, pl -e coward.

*kræ'kje/bær -et cf kreke/

*kræ'mar -en cf kremmer

kræ'r pl of krå

*kræ'se V -te cf krese

kræ'sen A +-ent, pl -ne cf kresen

*kræ'v A capable, diligent.

*krø'bel A -elt, pl -le miserable, wretched.

Krø'deren Pln lake in Krødsherad.

Krøds'/herad [/hæra] Pln twp, Buskerud.

***krø'ke**[1] *-t* fish line with two hooks.

+krø'ke[2] *V -te* (=***-je**[2]) 1 bend: **den må tidlig k-es som krok skal bli** training must begin early (lit. to make a hook you must start bending the wood early). 2 hook (elbows, fingers). 3 catch (e.g. fish). 4: **k- seg** bend, bow (down); (of road) turn, twist; **k- seg sammen** curl up, hunch up.

***krø'kje**[1] *-a* woman bent with age.

***krø'kje**[2] *V -te* cf **krøke**[2]

krøk'le *-a* 1 crooked tree. 2 *zool.* smelt (Osmerus eperlanus).

krøll' *-en* 1 curl, curlicue; fold: **ha k- i håret** have curly hair; **det var i én k- alt sammen** it was all crumpled up; **sette k- under navnet** sign one's name with a flourish; **slå k- på nesen** wrinkle up one's nose; **slå k- på seg** curl up, *fig.* cause difficulty, throw a monkey wrench in the works. 2 *zool.* (in male fish) milt.

krøl'le[1] *+-n/*-a* curl: **slå k- på halen** curl one's tail.

krøl'le[2] *V -a/+-et* curl, wrinkle: **k- sammen** crumple up; **k- seg** curl up, wrinkle.

krøl'let(e) *A* - 1 curled, curly. 2 creased, crumpled, wrinkled.

krøll'/fri *A -tt* wrinkle-resistant.

krøll'/hår *-et* hair (as stuffing for furniture).

+krøll'/tang *-a, pl -tenger* (=***/tong**) curling iron.

krøll'/topp *-en* curlyhead, curlylocks, curly top.

krø'nike *-a/+-en* (=***krønik**) 1 chronicle; medieval romance: **K-nes bok** Book of C-s. 2 cock-and-bull story, fairy tale.

krøn'sk *A* - strutting, stuck-up.

+krø'p *pt of* **krype**

+krøp'le *V -et* cripple; dwarf, stunt.

krøp'ling *-en* cripple.

krø's *-et anat.* mesentery.

+krøs'se *V -a/-et fam.* curry favor with, fawn on, flatter; *(pop.)* bootlick.

krø'sus *-en, pl -er* Croesus.

***krø'ter** *-et* cf **krøtter**

krøt'ter *-et, pl* - (=**+kreatur, *krøter**) cattle.

krøt'ter/tråkk *-et* cow trail.

***krøy'pe** *V -te* shrink (of flowers) close: **k- seg i hop** curl up.

krå' *-a, pl krær* corner.

krå'ke *-a* 1 crow. 2: **stupe k-** turn somersaults.

krå'ke/bolle *-n zool.* sea porcupine, sea urchin (Echinoidea).

krå'ke/bær *-et bot.* crowberry (Empetrum nigrum).

krå'ke/fot *-en, pl +-føtter/*-føter* 1 *bot.* club moss (Lycopodium). 2: **spenne k- for en** trip sby.

***krå'ke/føter** *pl* poor writing, chicken tracks.

krå'ke/mål *-et* 1 gibberish, unintelligible talk. 2 pig-Latin. 3 gobbledygook, high-flown language.

krå'ke/reir *-et* crow's nest.

Krå'ker/øy *Pln* twp, Østfold.

krå'ke/smelle *-a* 1 rattle to scare crows away. 2 ratchet brace.

krå'ke/sølv *-et* mica.

krå'ke/ting *-et* crow caucus, gathering of people who handle unimportant matters with a lot of talking.

+krå'ke/tær *pl* scrawls, scribblings, *(pop.)* chicken scratches.

Kråk'/stad *Pln* twp, Akershus.

***krå'ne** *V -a* get well.

krå's[1] *-en* 1 *anat.* gizzard. 2 giblets.

***krå's**[2] *-en* delicacy, tidbit.

+krå'/skap *-et* (=***/skåp**) corner cupboard.

k-solda't [kå'-] *-en* female soldier, WAC.

kst.=**konstituert**

ku' *-a, pl kyr/+kuer* cow; female of other ruminants; clumsy person; stupid female.

Ku'ba *Pln* cf **Cuba**

ku'/band *-et* cow halter (to keep cow in stall).

+kuba'ner *-en, pl -e* (=***-ar**) Cuban.

kuba'nsk *A* - Cuban.

kubb' *-en* 1 chunk (of log). 2 bolts, short lengths (of timber).

kub'be *-n* 1 chunk, log. 2 stump.

kub'be/lys *-et* short, thick candle.

kub'be/stol *-en* chair carved from large section of log.

ku'be *-n* 1 (bee) hive. 2 *geom.* cube.

ku'/bein *-et* crowbar, pinchbar.

+kubikk'/innhold *-et* (=**+/innhald**) cubic volume.

kubikk'/meter *-en, pl* - cubic meter (1.31 cu. yards).

kubikk'/rot *-a, pl +-røtter/*-røter* cube root.

kubikk'/tal *-et* (=**+/tall**) cube (of a number).

ku'bisk *A* - 1 cubic; cube-shaped. 2: **k- ligning** third-degree equation.

kubis'me *-n* cubism.

kubis't *-en* cubist.

kubis'tisk *A* - cubistic.

ku'/bjølle *-a* (=**+/bjelle**) 1 cowbell. 2 *bot.* pasque flower (Pulsatilla).

ku'/brems *-en* botfly (on cows).

ku'bus *-en math.* cube.

ku'e *V -a/+-et* 1 cow, subdue. 2: **k- i veksten** stunt.

+ku'/fanger *-en, pl -e* cowcatcher.

+kuf'fert *-en* cf **koffert**

ku'/for *-et* winter fodder for a cow.

kuf'te *-a* 1 (homespun) jacket (formerly worn by farmers). 2 (knit) sweater (in colorful patterns).

ku'/hud *-a/+-en* cowhide.

kujo'n *-en* coward.

kujone're *V -te* (=***kujonisere**) browbeat, bully.

ku'/kake *-a* cow cake, cow pie, cow's droppings.

kukelu're [also ko-, -lu'-] *V -te*: **sitte og k-** sit brooding, pondering, mope.

+ku'/kopper *pl* (=***-ar**) cowpox.

ku'l *-en* 1 bump, swelling; tumor. 2 knoll (e.g. in ski hill).

kulak(k)' *-en* kulak.

kulan't *A* - *merc.* generous (conditions); obliging (person).

kul'de *-a/-en* 1 cold, coldness (e.g. of the air, weather): **10 graders k-** 10° below (zero, Centigrade). 2 *fig.* chill, coldness, indifference: **hun mottok meg med k-** she received me coldly; **hun viste meg k-** she gave me the cold shoulder; **ensomhetens k-** the coldness of solitude (Vogt); **dødens k-** the chill of death.

kul'de/blanding *-a/+-en tech.* freezing mixture.

kul'de/grad *-en* degree below the freezing point: **det var tre k-er** it was three below zero.

+kul'de/gy'sning *-en* cold shiver, the shivers.

+kul'd/skjær *A* 1 sensitive to cold. 2 *fig.* delicate, tender.

+kul'd/slått *A* - (of liquid) with the chill taken off.

ku'le[1] *-a/-en* cavity, hollow, pit: **hjerte/** heart cavity.

ku'le[2] *-a* 1 (billiard, golf, croquet) ball; globe, pellet, sphere; shot put; marble. 2 (cannon)ball, bullet: **det skal k- til en trønder** strong measures are necessary to get the better of a Trønder (Wessel). 3 *fam.*: **hele kula** the whole gang (bunch). 4 deal (in cards), round or turn in a series. 5 *fam.* (business) coup.

+ku'le[3] *V -a/-te* blow.

ku'le/forma *A* - (=**+-et**) globular; spherical: **k- bakterie** coccus.

ku'le/lager *-eret, pl -er/+-re* ball bearing.

ku'le/ledd *-et anat., tech.* ball-and-socket joint.

ku'le/lyn *-et* ball lightning.

ku'le/mage *-n* potbelly.

ku'le/penn *-en* ball-point pen.

ku'le/ramme *-a* abacus.

ku'le/regn [+/rein] *-et* shower of bullets.

ku'le/rund *A* ball-shaped, round, spherical; beady (eyes).

ku'le/sprøyte *-a obs.* machine gun.

+ku'le/støt *-et* (=***/støyt**) (the) shot put.

+ku'le/støter *-en, pl -e* (=***/støytar**) shot-putter.

ku'let(e) *A* - bumpy.

ku'li[1] *-en, pl -er* coolie.

+ku'li[2] *Av fam.* coolly: **ta det k-** take it easy.

kulina'risk *A* - culinary.

ku'ling *-en* strong wind: **liten k-** strong breeze, **stiv k-** moderate gale, **sterk k-** fresh gale (Beaufort scale).

ku'ling/varsel *-elet/-let, pl +-ler/*-el* gale warning.

kulis'se *-n* flat, sidewing (of stage set): **bak k-ne** behind the scenes; **i k-n** in the wings.

kul'ke *V -a/+-et* 1 guzzle, swill. 2 fiddle, putter (**med** with).

+kull'[1] *-et* cf **kol**

kull'[2] *-et* 1 brood, hatch, litter (e.g. of animals, chickens, children), clutch (of eggs). 2 *jur.*: **lyse i k- og kjønn** legitimate. 3 (school) class; generation.

+kull'[3] *N*: **falle om k-** fall over.

+kull'- *Pf* cf **koll-**

+kull'/brenner *-en, pl -e* cf **kol/**

+kul'lende *Av* cf **kolende**

+kull'/hydra't *-et* cf **kol/**

+kull'/kaste *V -a/-et* (=***koll/**) frustrate, overturn, upset (plans etc.).

+kull'/leie *-t* cf **kol/**

+kull'/lemper *-en, pl -e* cf **kol/**

+kull'/mile *-a* cf **kol/**

+kull'/oksy'd *-et* cf **kol/**

+kull'/os *-en* cf **kol/**

+kull'/seile *V -te* cf **koll/segle**

+kull'/sort [/sort] *A* - coal black.

+kull'/stappende *Av* cf **kol/**

+kull'/stift *-en* cf **kol/**

+kull'/stoff *-et* cf **kol/**

+kull'/støv *-et* cf **kol/**

+kull'/sur *A* cf **kol/**

+kull'/svart *A* - cf **kol/**

+kull'svier/tro *-en* blind faith (**på** in).

+kull'/syre *-a* cf **kol/**

+kull'/tegning [/teining] *-en* cf **kol/**

+kull/vannstoff [kull' vann'/stoff] *-et* carbohydrate.

kulminasjo'n *-en* culmination.

kulmine're *V -te* culminate.

kul'p *-en* deep pool (in brook, river).

***kul's** *-en* cold shiver, the shivers.

kul'se *V -a/+-et* shiver, shudder (e.g. with cold, terror).

***kul'seleg** *A* - cheerless, dismal.

kul'sen *A +-ent, pl -ne* sensitive to cold; shuddering: **k-ende gru** shuddering horror.

kul'ske *V -a/+-et* shiver, shudder (e.g. with cold, terror).

kul't[1] *-en* 1 small block, log, stump; short, thick pole. 2 stout animal or person: **en k- av en gutt** a chunky boy. *3 knoll. 4 *fam.* roughly broken stone (used as fill).

kul't[2] *-en* cult.

kul'te *V -a/+-et* cover or fill with rough stone.

kul'ten *A +-ent, pl -ne* 1 plump, stout. 2 *fam.* poor; annoying, disgusting, wretched: **en k- ferie** a w- vacation; **det var k-t gjort** that was a dirty trick. *3 rotten, spoiled.

kul'tisk *A* - cultic.

kultiva'tor *-en agr.* cultivator.

kultive're *V -te* cultivate.

kultive'rt *A* - cultivated: **k- jord** c- land; **en k- mann** a cultured man.

kultu'r *-en* 1 civilization, culture; cultivation: **uten k-** uncultivated, lacking culture. 2 cultivation (of land, plant, or animal life); culture (e.g. of bacteria): **bringe (legge) under k-** bring under cultivation, cultivate; **være under k-** be under cultivation.

kultu'r/arv *-en* cultural heritage.

+ Bokmål; * Nynorsk; ° Dialect.
After letter: ' stress (Acc. 1); ` tone, stress (Acc. 2); · length.
Below letter: . not pronounced.

kultu'r/beite -*t*, *pl* ⁺-*r*/*- *agr.* cultivated pasture, enclosed pasture.
⁺kultu'r/bærer -*en*, *pl* -*e* (=*/**berar**) culture bearer.
kulturell' *A* -*elt* cultural.
kultu'r/film -*en* documentary film.
kultu'r/folk -*et* (a) civilized people, nation.
kultu'r/histo'rie -*a*/⁺-*en* history of civilization.
⁺kultu'r/krets -*en* (=*/**krins**) civilization, culture area: **Vestens k-** Western civilization.
kultu'r/land -*et* 1 cultured country. 2 *agr.* cultivated land.
kultu'r/liv -*et* cultural life.
kultu'r/mjølk -*a* (=⁺/**melk**) cultured milk.
kultu'r/pause -*n* (temporary) suspension of cultural work; restriction of grants for cultural purposes.
kultu'r/plante -*a*/-*en* cultivated plant.
kultu'r/språk -*et* language of culture.
kultu'r/trinn -*et* cultural stage (of development).
kultu'r/utvikling -*a*/⁺-*en* cultural development.
kul'tus -*en* cult.
kulø'r -*en* 1 color (esp. gay, healthy). 2: **han er ikke i k-** he is not in a good mood. 3 coloring matter.
kulø'rt *A* - colored: **den k-e presse** *derog.* the cheap, sensational weeklies.
kum [kom'] -*men* (wash) basin; (drinking) bowl; (septic) tank; cistern, well.
***ku'mar** -*en*, *pl kumrar* cf **kummar**
kumle[1] [kom'le] -*a* 1 potato dumpling. 2 *dial.* lump.
***kum'le**[2] *V* -*a* knead.
***kum'mar** -*en*, *p kumrar* 1 (flower, tree) bud. 2 *bot.* ament, catkin.
kumme [kom'me] -*n* cf **kum**
⁺kum'mer -*en* affliction, anguish; sorrow.
⁺kum'merlig *A* - miserable, pitifully poor, wretched.
kumpa'n -*en* cf **kompan**
***kum'pe** -*a* 1 potato dumpling. 2 *dial.* lump.
***kum'rar** *pl of* **kummar**
kumulasjo'n -*en* cumulation.
ku'mulativ *A* cumulative.
kumule're *V* -*te* 1 cumulate. 2 *pol.* (in proportional voting) repeat (a candidate's name) one or more times on the ballot.
⁺kun' *Av* just, merely, only: **hun var en gjest k-** she was o- a guest (Ibsen).
kun'de[1] -*n* customer; *(pl)* clientele: **faste k-r** steady customers; **han er k- hos Hansen** he patronizes H-'s shop.
kun'de[2] (old) *pt of* **kunne**
⁺kun'de/krets -*en* (=*/**kr ns**) clientele.
kung' -*en* wild marjoram.
***kun'nande** *A* - experienced, practiced, skilled.
kun'ne *V kan, kunne,* ⁺-*et*/*-*a* 1 **(kan)** can, be able to; **(kunne)** could, was able to: **kan det være sant?** can it be true?; **han kan ikke komme** he can't, isn't able to come; **gjør hva du kan** do what you can; **jeg kunne ikke forstå ham** I couldn't understand him; **hvordan kunne du?** how could you?; **for hjelp ei gavner denne mann som ikke vil hva ei han kan** for help is wasted on a man who does not want to do that which he is not able to do (Ibsen). 2 may, might: **kan være, kan hende** may be; **kan jeg få (se det)?** may I (see it)?; **du kan gå nå** you may go now; **det kan du ha rett i** you may be right about that; **du kan være sikker på at** you may be sure that, rest assured that; **det kan godt være** it may very well be; **han kunne ha vært rik hvis** he might have been rich if; **jeg synes godt du kunne vært litt hyggeligere** I really think you might have been a little more pleasant. 3 know (e.g. a language, lesson, poem, song, etc.); know how to (e.g. perform a skill, play a game, etc.): **kan du norsk?** do you know Norwegian?; **kan du spille sjakk?** do you (know how to) play chess?; **nei, den kan vi** oh, don't give us that, we've heard that before; **jeg ville gjerne danse, hvis jeg bare kunne** I'd like very much to dance, if I only knew how. 4 (other idioms): (following statements) **kan du vite, skjønne** you know, you see; **kan jeg tro** I imagine; **(han) kan ikke for det** (he) can't help it; **det kan greie seg, det kan være nok** that'll do; **det kan vel koste en 5-6 kroner** I guess it costs 5 or 6 *kroner*; **der kan du se** see, I told you so; **det kan være det samme** it's all the same, it makes no difference; **han kan være her når som helst** he'll be here any moment; **eller hva det nå kan være** or whatever it is; **slik kan (kunne) han sitte i timevis** he'll (he'd) sit like that for hours; **jeg kunne ha lyst til å** (I think) I'd like to; **det kunne likne deg** that would be just like you.
***kunn'/gjering** -*a* cf /**gjøring**
⁺kunn'/gjøre *V* -*gjorde*, -*gjort* announce; notify; proclaim.
⁺kunn'/gjørelse -*n* cf /**gjøring**
⁺kunn'/gjøring -*a*/-*en* (=*/**gjering**) (official) announcement; notification; proclamation.
kun'nig *A* - 1 qualified, well informed (**på** in). *2: **det er k- for alle** it is known to everyone.
kunn'/skap -*en* knowledge (**om, til** about): **k-ens tre** the tree of k-; **gode k-er i språk** a good k- of languages.
kunn'skaps/rik *A* learned, well-informed.
⁺kun's *Av archaic* just, merely, only: **det er en mulighet k-** it is o- a possibility (Ibsen).
kun'st -*en* 1 art; artifice: **k-en å** the art of; **de skjønne k-er** the fine arts; **etter alle k-ens regler** according to all the rules of the game; **det å leve er en k-** living is an art (Ibsen). 2 knack, trick: **gjøre k-er** perform t-s; **det er ingen k-** that's easy, there's nothing (no trick) to that; **være ens minste k-** be easy for sby to do.
kun'st/art -*a*/-*en* art form.
⁺kunstfer'dig *A* - 1 expert, skilful (person). 2 elaborate, ingenious (object).
⁺kun'st/gjenstand -*en* art object.
kun'st/gjødsel -*la* (commercial or chemical) fertilizer.
kun'st/grep -*et* artifice, trick.
⁺kun'st/handler -*en*, *pl* -*e* (=*-**ar**) art dealer.
kun'st/handverk -*et* (=⁺/**håndverk**) handicraft.
kun'st/histo'rie -*a*/⁺-*en* history of (the fine) art(s).
kun'stig *A* - 1 artificial, imitation; affected. 2 *dial.* odd, peculiar.
kun'st/industri' -*en* applied art; industrial art.
***kun'st/laup** -*et* cf /**løp**
kun'st/laus *A* artless, simple, unaffected (beauty, manner, style).
⁺kun'stlet *A* - affected, artificial.
⁺kun'st/løp -*et* figure skating.
⁺kun'st/løs *A* cf /**laus**
⁺kun'st/maler -*en*, *pl* -*e* (=*/**målar**) artist (painter).
***kun'stnarleg** *A* - artistic.
⁺kun'stner -*en*, *pl* -*e* (=*-**ar**) artist.
⁺kunstnerin'ne -*a*/-*en* (=***kunstnarin'ne**) artist (woman).
⁺kun'stnerisk *A* - artistic.
⁺kun'stner/lønn -*a*/-*en* (=*-**ar**/) yearly state grant to artists.
⁺kun'stner/temperament [-mang'] -*et* (=*-**ar**/) artistic temperament.
kun'st/pause -*n* deliberate or rhetorical pause.
kun'st/retning -*a*/⁺-*en* school or style of art; art trend.
kun'st/silke -*n* rayon.
kun'st/stoff -*et*, *pl* -/⁺-*er* synthetic organic material (e.g. plastic, synthetic fiber).
kun'st/stopping -*a*/⁺-*en* skilful, invisible mending.
kun'st/stykke -*t*, *pl* ⁺-*r*/*- feat, trick.
kun'st/utstil'ling -*a*/⁺-*en* art exhibit.
kun'st/verk -*et* work of art.
kup' -*et* cf **kupp**
kupé -*en* 1 (train) compartment. 2 coupe.
ku'pe -*a* kind of fishnet, weel.
kupe're *V* -*te* cut off, dock (a tail, e.g. of a horse).
kupe'rt *A* - 1 docked (tail). 2 hilly, undulating: **k- terreng** hilly terrain, rolling country.
⁺kup'ler *pl of* **kuppel**
kuplett' -*en poet.* couplet.
***ku'/poke** -*a* cowpox.
kupong' -*en* coupon: **klippe k-er** clip c-s (=live on dividends).
kupp' -*et* 1 coup. 2: **gjøre et godt kupp** make a good haul. 3 *journ.* scoop.
kup'pel -*elen*, *pl kupler* 1 cupola, dome: **himmelens k-** the vault of heaven. 2 (lamp) bowl, globe. 3 *(pop.)* head, noggin.
°kup'pel/hue -*t* (=⁺/**hode**) *pop.*: **ha k-** have a hangover.
***kup'pul** -*en* cf **koppul**
ku'r[1] -*en* cure, treatment (also *fig.*).
ku'r[2] -*en* 1 court, formal reception: **kongen gir k-** the king is holding court. 2: **gjøre k- til** (pay) court (to), flirt (with), *(pop.)* make up (to).
ku'r/anstalt -*en* sanitarium.
kuran't[1] -*en merc.* price list: **sette k-en** fix prices.
kuran't[2] *A* - 1 current (of money, words). 2 marketable, saleable. 3: **en k- sak** a mere formality.
kura'sje -*n archaic* courage.
kura'tor -*en* 1 guardian, trustee. 2 superintendent; curator.
ku'r/bad -*et* (medicinal) baths, spa.
⁺kur'der -*en*, *pl* -*e* (=*-**ar**) Kurd.
ku're[1] *V* -*a*/-*te* 1 crouch, lie, sit quietly. 2 brood, mope, pine.
ku're[2] *V* -*a*/⁺-*et* 1 take a cure, treatment. 2 *archaic* court, flirt (**til** with).
***ku'ren** *A* -*e*/-*i*, *pl* -*ne* 1 ill. 2 dejected, downcast.
ku'rende *Av* cf **kurrende**
kurér -*en* (diplomatic) courier.
kure're *V* -*te* 1 cure, heal (also *fig.*): **han ble k-t for sin godtroenhet** he was cured of his credulity. 2 doctor, treat: **de k-te på ham med salver** they doctored him with salves (Tryggve Andersen).
ku'r/fyrste -*n hist.* electoral prince.
ku'r/fyrstelig *A* - *hist.* electoral.
ku'rie -*n* curia.
kuriosite't -*en* curio; curiosity: **for k-ens skyld** for the sake of curiosity.
kurio'sum -*umet*, *pl* -*a* curiosity (thing); curio.
kuriø's *A* odd, singular; quaint.
***kur'le**[1] -*a* curl, lock (of hair).
***kur'le**[2] *V* -*a* 1 curl, spiral. 2 coo (also *fig.*); burr, pronounce uvularly.
⁺ku'r/makeri' -*et* flirting, philandering.
kurr'[1] -*et* cooing.
kurr'[2] *A kurt* quiet: **en k- nattetime** a quiet hour of the night (Hamsun).
⁺kur're[1] -*n* 1 knot, tangle (of thread). 2: **det er kommet en k- på tråden mellom dem** they have had a tiff.
kur're[2] *V* -*a*/⁺-*et* coo (also *fig.*).
kur'rende *Av* quietly: **k- stille** quiet as a mouse.
ku'rs[1] -*en* 1 course, direction: **sette k- for** head for. 2 currency; quotation (on the stock exchange); rate of exchange: **ha k-** be current (of money), *fig.* be popular; **stå i høy k-, være i k-** be fashionable, popular.
ku'rs[2] -*et*, *pl* -/⁺-*er* (=**kursus**) course, curriculum.
ku'rs/endring -*a*/⁺-*en* change of course.

kursi'v *-en* italics: **med k-** in italics.
kursive're *V -te* italicize.
+**ku'rs/note'ringer** *pl* (=***-ar**) *merc.* market quotations.
kurso'risk *A* - cursory: **k- pensum** material assigned for reading only.
ku'rs/tap *-et merc.* exchange loss; market loss.
+**ku'r/sted** *-et* (=***/stad**) health resort; sanitarium.
kur'sus *-et, pl* +*kurser*/**kursus* cf **kurs**[2]
ku'rs/verdi· *-en merc.* market or quoted value.
kurta'sje *-n merc.* brokerage.
kur'teis *A archaic* courteous, polite; courtly.
kurtisa'ne *-a*/+*-en* courtesan.
kurti'se *-n* flirtation.
kurtise're *V -te* flirt with.
kurtisø'r *-en* flirt (man).
kurtoasi' *-en lit.* courtesy; courtliness
ku'/ruke *-a* cow cake, cow pie.
ku'/rumpe [/rompe] *-a fam.* cow tail.
+**kur'v**[1] *-en* cf **korg**
kur'v[2] *-en dial.* sausage.
+**kur'v/ball** *-en* cf **korg/**
+**kur'v/blomstret** *A* - *bot.* composite (Compositae).
kur've +*-n*/**-a* 1 *math.* curve: **beskrive en k-** describe a curve; **tegne en k-** draw a graph. 2: **k- i veien** curve in the road.
+**kur'v/flaske** *-a* cf **korg/**
+**kur'v/fletning** *-en* wickerwork.
+**kur'v/møbler** *pl* cf **korg/**
+**kur'v/stol** *-en* cf **korg/**
kusi'ne *-a*/+*-en* cousin (female).
kus'k *-en* 1 coachman, driver. 2 *astron.*: **K-en** Auriga, the Wagoner.
kus'ke[1] *V -a*/+*-et* browbeat, push around.
kus'ke[2] *V -a*/+*-et* drive.
kus'ke/sete *-t* driver's seat (on a coach).
kus'ma *-en* (=***kus'me**) mumps.
ku'/sopp *-en bot.* type of mushroom (Boletus bovinus); other mushrooms of genus Boletus.
kus'te *V -a*/+*-et* keep in discipline, in order.
kus'tus *-en* discipline, order.
ku'/symre *-a bot.* cowslip, primrose (Primula).
ku't *-en dial.* run: **ta k-en** make tracks.
ku'te *V -a*/+*-te dial.* cut (out) and run.
kuti'kula *-en, pl* **-er bot.* epidermis.
ku'/torg *-et fam.* livestock market.
ku'/tråkk *-et* cow path.
kutt' *-et* cut.
kut'te[1] *-a*/+*-en* cowl, monk's habit.
kut'te[2] *V -a*/+*-et* cut (**av** off).
kut'ter *-en, pl* +*-e naut.* cutter.
kuty'me *-n* custom, practice, usage.
ku'v *-en* 1 hump, roundish top. 2 *dial.* haystack.
***ku've**[1] *-a* scaffold(ing).
***ku've**[2] *V -a* 1 round (off). 2 heap (up).
***ku'ven** *A -e/-i, pl -ne* roundish.
ku'/vende *V* +*-te*/**-e naut.* veer, wear.
ku'/vending *-a*/+*-en* 1 *naut.* veering, wearing. 2 about-face.
kuvert [kuvæ'r] *-en* cover, place setting.
ku'vet(e) *A* - arched, rounded.
ku'/vogn [/vångn] *-a* stock car.
ku'vung *-en zool.* 1 sea snail (Buccinum undatum). *2 sea snail shell.
kuvø'se *-n med.* incubator.
+**ku'/øye** *-t, pl -r* (=***/auga**) *naut.* porthole.
***kva'** *Pn* cf **hva**
kvabb' *-en* ooze (esp. *geol.*).
kva'd[1] *-et lit.* lay, poem; song.
kva'd[2] *pt of* **kvede**[2]
kva'der *-eren, pl -rer* 1 *arch.* ashlar. 2 square field.
kva'der/stein *-en arch.* ashlar.
kvadran't *-en astron., math., naut.* quadrant.
kvadra't *-et, pl -/*+*-er* 1 *math.* square: **2 meter i k-** 2 meters s-. 2 *typog.* quadrat (quad). 3 *mus.* natural sign.
kvadra'tisk *A* - 1 square. 2 *math.* quadratic (equation).
kvadra't/meter *-en, pl* - square meter (1.196 sq. yds.).
kvadra't/rot *-a, pl* +*-røtter*/**-røter math.* square root.
kvadre're *V -te* 1 divide into squares. 2 *math.* square.
kvadril'je *-n* quadrille.
kvadrillio'n *-en* quadrillion.
kva'e +*-n*/**-a* (=***kvåe**) resin.
kvakk' *pt of* **kvekke**[1]
kvak'l *-et fam.* bother, trouble; confusion.
kvak'le *V -a*/+*-et archaic* bungle; tamper (**med** with).
+**kvak'/salver** *-en, pl -e* (=***-ar**) quack (doctor); charlatan.
+**kvak'/salveri** *-et* quackery.
kva'l[1] *-en* agony, pain, torment (also *fig.*): **ingen k- stor som geniets** no agony like that of the genius (Collett Vogt).
kva'l[2] *-en* (=+**hval**) whale.
kva'l/barde *-n* baleen, whalebone.
+**kva'l/fanger** *-en, pl -e* (=***-ar**) (person and ship) whaler.
kva'l/fangst +*-en*/**-a* whaling.
kva'l/full *A* agonizing, painful (also *fig.*).
kvalifikasjo'n *-en* qualification.
kvalifise're *V -te* qualify (**som** as): **k- seg til** q- (oneself) for; **k-t flertall** prescribed majority; **k-t forbrytelse** aggravated crime (e.g. assault, larceny).
kval'itativ *A* qualitative; *chem.*: **k- analyse** q- analysis.
kvalite't *-en* quality, nature (of sth): **utsøkt k-** choice, first-class.
kvalite'ts/arbeid *-et* high quality workmanship.
+**kvalite'ts/forring'else** *-n* reduction in quality.
kvalite'ts/vare *-a*/+*-en* high quality goods.
kva'l/kokeri *-et, pl* +*-er*/**-* whale factory ship.
***kvall'** *pt of* **kvelle**
+**kval'm**[1] *-en* fuss, racket, row: **gjøre, lage k-** make a fuss; **k- i gata** street brawl, tumult.
kval'm[2] *A* 1 close, stuffy. 2 ill, nauseated (also *fig.*): **tanken på ham gjør meg k-** the thought of him makes me sick; disgusting, nauseous (also *fig.*).
kval'me[1] *-n* nausea, sickness (also *fig.*).
+**kval'me**[2] *V -a/-et* nauseate, sicken (also *fig.*).
kva'l/rav *-et* spermaceti.
kva'l/ross *-en* walrus.
Kva'l/sund *Pln* twp, Finnmark.
+**kva'lte** *pt of* **kvele**
***kval'v** *pt of* **kvelve**[1]
***kvam'** *-en* hemmed-in valley or inlet.
Kvam' *Pln* 1 parish, village, Oppland. 2 twp, Hordaland. 3 twp, Nord-Trøndelag.
kvam'ne *V -a*/+*-et* be smothered, suffocate.
kvann' *-a* (=**kvanne**) *bot.* angelica (Archangelica officinalis); angelica root or stalks.
kvan'ne *-a*/+*-en* cf **kvann**
kvann'/jol *-en* angelica.
kvann'/rot *-a, pl* +*-røtter*/**-røter bot.* angelica root.
kvan'ta *pl of* **kvantum**
kvan'te/teori· *-en phys.* quantum theory.
kvan'titativ *A* quantitative; *chem.*: **k- analyse** q- analysis.
kvantite't *-en* quantity (e.g. of sound, water).
kvan'tum *-et, pl kvanta* 1 quantity: **et stort k- brennevin** a large q- of brandy. 2 *phys.* quantum.
***kva'p** *-et* soft, humid mass; swelling.
***kva'pe** *V -a* 1 be soft and humid; secrete fluid. 2 swell.
kvapp' *pt of* **kveppe**
kvap'set(e) *A* - fat, obese, swollen.
***kva'p/sott** *-a* dropsy.
***kva'r**[1] *A dial.* quiet, still.
***kva'r**[2] *Av* cf **hvor**[1]
***kva'r**[3] *Pn* cf **hver**
***kvaran'dre** *Pn* cf **hverandre**
***kva'r/dag** *-en* cf **hver/**
***kva'rdags/grå** *A -tt* cf **hverdags/**
***kva'rdags/klede** *pl* cf **hverdags/klær**
***kva'rdags/lag** *-et* cf **hverdags/**
***kva'rdagsleg** *A* - cf **hverdagslig**
***kva'rdags/menneske** *-t* cf **hverdags/**
***kva'rde**[1] *-n* edge, rim; edging (of clothes).
***kva'rde**[2] *V -a* edge, trim (clothes).
kva're *V -a*/+*-te dial.* bring to rest: **k- seg** go to bed; get settled for the night, go to roost (esp. of fowl), rest.
***kvarhel'st** *Av* where.
***kvar'm** *-en* edge, rim; frame; eyelid.
***kva'r/mann** *Pn* cf **hver/mann**
kvar't[1] *-en* 1 quarter (e.g. of an apple, hour): **k- på ti** q- of ten. 2 *mus.* fourth (interval); crotchet. 3 quarte (in fencing). 4 quart (in cards). 5 *naut.* quarter. 6 (of book) quarto.
kvar't[2] *A* - quarter (of): **en k- ost** a quarter (of) cheese; **en k- grad** one fourth degree.
kvarta'l *-et, pl -/*+*-er* 1 quarter (of a year. 2 (city) block.
+**kvarta'ls/avregning** [/-reining] *-a/-en* quarterly statement.
kvar'te *V -a*/+*-et fam.* hook, nab, pilfer.
kvar'tel *-elet, pl -el/*+*-ler* firkin.
kvarte'r *-et, pl -/*+*-er* 1 (of an area) quarter, section; district. 2 *mil.* quarters: **gå i k-, ta sitt k-** take up q-; **ligge i k- hos** be billeted, quartered with. 3 (units of measure) quarter of a barrel; quarter of an **alen** (=6 in.). 4 (of time) quarter of an hour; quarter of the moon: **et k- på (over)** quarter to (past); **et k-s tid** about a quarter of an hour; **akademisk k-** the custom of beginning university lectures a quarter of an hour after the announced time. 5 *mil., naut.* watch.
+**kvarte'r/mester** *-en, pl -e* (=***/meister**) *mil., naut.* quartermaster; coxswain.
kvartett' *-en mus.* quartet.
kvar't/format *-et, pl -/*+*-er typog.* quarto.
kvar'tler *pl of* **kvartel**
kvar't/mil *-a, pl* - nautical mile.
kvar't/rull *-en* quarter plug of tobacco.
kvar'ts *-en* quartz.
kvar'ts/lampe *-a/-en* ultraviolet lamp.
kvartæ'r/formasjo'n *-en geol.* Quaternary formation.
kvartæ'r/tida *df* (=+**/tiden**) *geol.* quaternary period.
kvar't/årig *A* - quarterly.
kvar'v[1] *-et* 1 *dial.* course, round, row (e.g. of logs, timber; in knitting). 2 circle, ring.
kvar'v[2] *pt of* **kverve**[3]
kva's *-et* brushwood, faggots.
kva'se *-n* 1 fish tank, well. 2 (of boat) smack.
kva'si/lærd *A* - quasi-learned.
+**kva'si/vit(en)ska'pelig** *A* - (=***/vitskapleg**) quasi-scientific.
kvass' *A kvast* (=+**hvass**) keen, sharp (also *fig.*): **hun sendte ham et k-t blikk** she gave him a dirty look.
***kvas'se** *-a zool.* turbot (Psetta maxima).
***kvass'/eggja** *A* - sharp-edged.
***kvass'/mæ·lt** *A* - sharp-voiced.
***kvass'/tennt** *A* - sharp-toothed.
kvas't[1] *-en* 1 (powder) puff. 2 bunch (e.g. of flowers), bundle. 3 tassel, tuft. 4 *bot.* cyme.
kvas't[2] *nt of* **kvass**
kvas'te *V -a*/+*-et* 1 brush; paint. *2: **k- på** hurry.
kvas'tet(e) *A* - tasseled.

+ Bokmål; * Nynorsk; ° Dialect.
After letter: ' stress (Acc. 1); ` tone, stress (Acc. 2); · length.
Below letter: . not pronounced.

***kva't** *A* fresh, healthy; high-spirited, fiery; clever, quick.
***kva't/leik** *-en* freshness; buoyancy, vigor.
***kva't/stein** *-en* whetstone.
***kvat'te** *pt of* **kvetje**
***kva'v** *-et* tightness in the chest, throat; wheeziness.
***kvav'ne** *V -a* choke; suffocate.
***kva'vt** *A nt* 1 close, stuffy. 2 nauseated.
kve' *-a* (livestock) fold, pen.
***kve'ḍar** *-en poet.* singer.
kve'de[1] [*kve'e] *-t, pl* +*-r*/**- poet.* lay, song; poem.
kve'de[2] [*kve'e] *V kvad,* +*-et*/*-e/*-i poet.* chant, sing.
Kve'/fjo'rḍ *Pln* cf **Kvæ/fjord**
***kvef's** *-en* cf **veps**
***kvef'se/bol** *-et* cf **vepse/**
+**kve'g** *-et* 1 cattle. 2 blockhead, simpleton.
+**kve'ge** *V -et* 1 refresh (e.g. of air, drink, sleep). 2 allay, soothe: **har du ei et ord som k-er** have you not a word that soothes (Ibsen).
+**kve'g/pest** *-en vet.* rinderpest.
kvei'k[1] *-en* 1 *dial.* refreshment (usu. of food, drink, tobacco): **få en k-** get a pick-me-up. *2 encouragement, enlivenment, stimulation; refreshment.
***kvei'k**[2] *-a* yeast.
***kvei'ke**[1] *-t* kindling.
+**kvei'ke**[2] *V -te* (=*-je) 1: **k- seg** refresh, revive oneself. 2 kindle (fire). *3 encourage, foster, nurse.
***kvei'king** *-a* 1 refreshment. 2 kindling.
***kvei'kje** *V -te* cf **kveike**[2]
***kvei'kne** *V -a* rally, recover, revive.
***kvei'ksle** *-a* 1 origin, rise. 2 kindling.
kvei'l *-en naut.* coil (of rope), fake (single coil).
***kvei'le**[1] *-a* cf **kveil**
kvei'le[2] *V* *-a/+-te *naut.* coil (down, up), fake (down).
kvei'n[1] *-a bot.* bent grass (agrostis).
kvei'n[2] *pt of* **kvine**
***kvei's** *-a* 1 hangover. 2 intestinal worm in fish.
kvei'se *-a* cf **kvise**[1]
***kvei'set(e)** *A* - full of blotches, pockmarked.
***kvei's/sott** *-a* smallpox.
kvei'te[1] *-a* halibut.
kvei'te[2] *-n* (=+**hvete**) wheat.
kvei'te/bolle *-n* small wheat bun.
kvei'te/brøḍ *-et* wheat bread.
kvei'te/mjøl *-et* wheat flour.
kve'ke *-a bot.* couch, quack grass (Agropyron repens).
+**kve'ker** *-en, pl -e* (=***-ar**) quaker.
kvekk'[1] *-en/-et* sudden fright, scare, start.
kvekk'[2] *-et* croak (e.g. of a frog); short, toneless sound: **hun formådde knapt å si et levende k-** she was scarcely able to say a single word (Wiers-Jenssen); **ikke et k-** nothing at all.
kvekk'[3] *Av* completely, quite, utterly: **han lo seg k- i hjel** he laughed himself absolutely to death.
kvek'ke[1] *V kvakk,* +*-et*/*kvokke/*-i* be startled, (give a) start: **k- i** start.
kvek'ke[2] *V -a/+-et* 1 croak (also *fig.*). 2 emit a weak sound, murmur.
***kvek'ken** *A -e/-i, pl kvekne* frightened.
***kvekkj'e** *V -te* frighten, startle.
kvel'ḍ *-en* 1 eve, evening: **god k-** good evening; **i k-** this e-, tonight; **om k-en** during, in the evening. 2 supper: **hva skal vi ha til k-s?** what shall we have for supper?
kvel'ḍe *V -a/+-et* 1 grow towards evening. 2 knock off work in the evening. 3 eat supper. 4 go to bed, rest: **k- seg** (the same).
kvel'ḍing *-a/+-en* dusk, twilight: **i k-en** at dusk.
kvel'ḍ/knarr *-en zool.* nighthawk, nightjar (Caprimulgus europaeus).
kvel'ḍ/sete *-a archaic* period from nightfall to bedtime.
kvel'ḍ/side [*/sie] *-a/+-en*: **utpå k-a** later in the evening.
kvel'ḍ/skingle *-a dial.* bat.
kvel'ḍs/leite *-t*: **ved k-** about, around evening (time).
kvel'ḍs/mat *-en* supper.
kvel'ḍs/mål *-et dial.* 1 supper; evening feeding of livestock. 2 milk which is milked in the evening.
kvel'ḍ/stell *-et* evening (farm, household) chores.
kvel'ḍ/stunḍ *-a/+-en* evening (time).
kvel'ḍs/verd [/vær] *-en archaic* supper.
***kvel'ḍ/svæv** *A* given to becoming sleepy early.
***kvel'ḍ/svæve** *-a bot.* dandelion.
kvel'ḍs/økt *-a* spell of work between dinner and supper.
***kvel'ḍ/verd** [/vær] *-en* cf **kvelds/**
kve'le *V -te/+kvalte* 1 (intrans.) choke, suffocate. 2 (trans.) choke, smother, strangle; *fig.* repress, suppress (e.g. a yawn, laughter, etc.): **k- i spiren** nip in the bud; **k-ende varmt** stifling.
+**kve'ler/slange** *-n zool.* boa, boa constrictor (Boidae).
+**kve'ler/tak** *-et* stranglehold.
kvell' *A kvelt dial.* shrieking, shrill.
***kvel'le** *V kvall, kvolle/-i* speak piercingly, shrilly.
+**kve'lning** *-en* choking: **k-s/anfall** choking fit; asphyxiation; smothering; strangulation; suffocation.
***kvel'p** *-en* cf **valp**
***kvel'pe** *V -a* cf **valpe**
***kvel'pe/sjuke** *-n* cf **valpe/**
+**kve'l/stoff** *-et chem.* nitrogen.
kvel't *nt of* **kvell,** *pp of* **kvele**
kvel'v *-en/-et* (=+**hvelv**) 1 arch, vault. 2 *naut.* overturned boat bottom.
kvel've[1] *V -de/+-a* (=+**hvelve**) 1 arch, vault. 2 overturn (e.g. a boat).
***kvel've**[2] *V kvalv, kvolve/-i* 1 arch, be in arched, vaulted position: **himlene k-r seg** the heavens arch. 2 overturn: **båten kvalv seg** the boat overturned.
***kvel'ving**[1] *-a* overturning.
***kvel'ving**[2] *-en* arch, vault.
***kve'me** *V -a* bustle, flutter, fuss around.
kve'n[1] *-en, pl* *-er* person of Finnish stock (in North Norway).
+**kve'n**[2] *pt of* **kvine**
***kven'**[3] *Pn* cf **hvem**
***kven'de** *-t* woman.
***kven'ḍsk** *A* - very fond of women.
kve'nsk *A* - of Finnish stock (esp. in North Norway).
Kve'n/vær *Pln* twp, Sør-Trøndelag.
kvep'ne *pl of* **kveppen**
kvepp' *-en dial.* fright, scare, start.
kvep'pe *V kvapp,* +*-et*/*kvoppe/*-i dial.* be suddenly frightened, startled; start.
kvep'pen *A* +*-ent, pl kvepne dial.* easily frightened, timorous.
kver'k *-en* 1 throat, gullet: **ta k-en på** exterminate, kill. 2 *naut.* throat (on sail).
kver'ke *V -a/+-et fam.* choke, throttle; quell, smother, stifle (also *fig.*).
***kver'k/svull** *-en* cf **kver/sill**
kvern [kvæ'rn] *-a* (grain) mill; (coffee, meat, nut, pepper) grinder, mill.
kvern/bruk [kvæ'rn/] *-et* gristmill.
kverne [kvæ'rne] *V -a/+-et* 1 turn, whirl (e.g. as a millstone); churn around. 2 buzz, hum.
Kvernes [kvæ'rnes] *Pln* twp, Møre og Romsdal.
kvern/hus [kvæ'rn/] *-et* (rural) grinding mill.
kvern/kall *-en* (mill) waterwheel.
kvern/renne *-a* millrace.
kvern/slåk *-et dial.* narrow millrace.
kvern/stein *-en* millstone.
kvern/vatn *-et* mill head.
***kverr'/setje** *V -sette* arrest; impound, seize.
kver/sill [kvæ'r/] *-a vet.* (horse) strangles.
kverulan't *-en* complainant, grumbler.
kverule're *V -te* complain, grumble; *pop.* grouse.
***kver'v**[1] *-en* circle, ring; whirl.
kver'v[2] *-et* 1 course, round of planks in a boat; row of mesh in a net. 2 short, sudden glimpse.
***kver'v'** *A* 1 lively, quick; clever, intelligent (for one's age). 2 awry, crooked, oblique. 3 transitory.
***kver've**[1] *-a* 1 *dial.* (willow) gate latch. 2 (natural) direction or tack of a boat.
***kver've**[2] *-t* rural neighborhood.
kver've[3] *V kvarv,* +*-et*/*kvorve/*-i* 1 swirl, whirl. 2 disappear.
***kver've**[4] *V -de* 1 circle, swing (around); encircle. 2 distort, twist (e.g. one's view).
***kver'vel** *-elen, pl -lar* cf **virvel**[1]
***kver'vel/vinḍ** *-en* cf **virvel/**
***kver'ven** *A -e/-i, pl -ne* 1 passing, transitory. 2 quick.
***kver'vle** *V -a* cf **virvle**
kve'se *V -te* (=+**hvese**) hiss; wheeze.
kves'se *V -te* sharpen, whet: ***k- på øyro** prick up one's ears.
+**kves'te** *V -et* hurt, injure (usu. in accident).
+**kves'telse** *-n* (bodily) injury.
kves'tor *-en, pl -torer* 1 *hist.* quaestor. 2 (university) bursar, treasurer.
kvestu'r *-et* 1 *hist.* quaestorship. 2 bursarship. 3 bursar's office.
***kvet'je** *V kvet, kvatte, kvatt* cf **kvesse**
+**kve've** *V -de* (=***kvæve**[2]) *dial.* choke; smother; stifle, suppress.
kvi'[1] *V -dde* (=+**kvie,** ***kvide**[2]) 1 whimper, whine; moan. 2: **k- seg** squirm, writhe; **k- seg ved** shrink from; **k- seg for** dread.
***kvi'**[2] *Av* why.
+**kvid'der** *-et* cf **kvitter**
kvi'de[1] [*kvi'e] +*-n*/*-a lit., poet.* agony, pain; sorrow.
***kvi'ḍe**[2] *V -de* cf **kvi**[1]
kvi'de/full *A lit., poet.* distressful; painful.
***kvi'ḍing** *-en* despondent person.
+**kvid're** *V -et* cf **kvitre**
+**kvi'e** *V -dde* cf **kvi**[1]
***kvi'ende** *-t* young cattle.
***kvi'/for'** *Av* cf **kor/**
kvi'ge *-a* heifer.
***kvi'k** *A* 1 alive. 2 lively.
***kvi'ke**[1] *-n* sensitive, tender flesh (e.g. fingernails bitten down to the quick).
***kvi'ke**[2] *V -a* refresh, revive; enliven.
***kvi'kende** *-t* living being.
kvikk' *A kvikt* 1 alert, bright, clever (e.g. answer, person, speech): **han er et k-t hode** he is a live wire; **et k-t svar** a c- reply. 2 fast, quick, rapid. 3 refreshed, strengthened. 4 mobile: **k-/sand** quicksand. 5 *archaic* alive, living.
kvik'ke *V -a/+-et* 1 cheer (**opp** up), enliven. 2 *fam.* **k- seg** hurry.
kvikk'/leire *-a* clayey mud, ooze.
kvikk'/sanḍ *-en* quicksand.
kvikk'/sølv *-et* mercury, quicksilver.
kvik'ne *V -a/+-et* 1 rally, recover, revive; liven (**til** up). 2 accelerate, quicken: **gleden hadde k-et hennes hjerteslag** happiness had made her heart beat faster.
Kvik'ne *Pln* twp, Hedmark.
***kvi'k/sølv** *-et* cf **kvikk/**
kvik't *nt of* **kvikk**
kvi'l[1] *-en/+-a* (=+**hvil**) breathing spell; short rest: **ta seg en k-** take a breather; take a nap.
***kvi'l**[2] *A* rested.
***kvi'ld**[1] *-a* breathing spell, short rest.
***kvi'ld**[2] *A kvilt* rested.
kvi'le[1] *-a* (=+**hvile**[1]) 1 repose, rest: **gå inn til den evige h-** die; **gå (legge seg) til h-/k-** go to bed (i.e. rest); **legge, stede til h-** bury, lay at rest; **være i h-** *phys.* be at rest. *2 bed.
kvi'le[2] *V* +*-te*/*-de* (=+**hvile**[2]) 1 rest (**fra** from, **i** in, **på** on); take a rest;

repose: **h-/k- middag** take an afternoon nap; **h-/k- seg** rest, take a rest; **h-/k- øynene** rest one's eyes; **h-/k- ut** get a good rest, rest up; **på stedet hvil/kvil** *mil.* at ease. 2 (of an operation, work etc.) be suspended, stop. 3 (of cultivated soil) lie fallow. 4 *fig.* rest, weigh upon: **h-/k- i seg selv** be independent, self-contained; **h-/k- over** rest upon; (as a fate) follow, pursue; (of an atmosphere) pervade; **h-/k- på** (of a responsibility) weigh on.

kvi'le/dag *-en* day of rest.

kvi'le/heim *-en* rest home.

kvi'le/laus *A* restless.

***kvi'le/stad** *-en* cf **hvile/sted**

kvi'le/stilling *-a/+-en* 1 resting position. 2 *phys.* state of rest.

kvi'le/stund *-a/+-en* resting period.

***kvi'me** *V -a* bustle, flutter about.

***kvim'sen** *A -e/-i, pl -ne* restless, unsettled.

kvi'n *-et/*-en* (=+**hvin**) shriek.

+**kvin'delig** *A* - cf **kvinnelig**

kvi'ne *V kvein/+-te, +-t/*-e/*-i* (=+**hvine**) shriek (e.g. of an instrument, a person, wind); squeak (e.g. of hinges, an insect, a mouse); (of bullets) whistle.

Kvi'nes/dal *Pln* twp, Vest-Agder.

kvin'k *+-et/*-en* 1 short whining sound; piping. 2 strumming, twanging (e.g. of a stringed instrument).

kvin'ke *V -a/+-et* 1 whimper, whine; pipe; chirp. 2 strum, twang.

kvin'ne *-a/+-en* woman.

+**kvin'ne/aktig** *A* - effeminate.

+**kvin'ne/bedå'rer** *-en, pl -e* ladies' man, lady-killer.

kvin'ne/fore'ning *-a/+-en* women's association, club.

kvin'ne/gunst *-en* woman's favor.

+**kvin'ne/hater** *-en, pl -e* (=***-ar**) misogynist, woman hater.

kvin'ne/jeger *-en, pl +-e* wolf, woman chaser; *(pop.)* skirt chaser.

kvin'ne/kjær *A* fond of women.

kvin'ne/kjønn *-et* female sex, womankind.

kvin'ne/klinikk' *-en* women's clinic.

kvin'ne/ledd *-et* female line in a genealogy.

kvin'ne/lege *-n* gynecologist.

kvin'nelig *A* - 1 feminine, womanly: **det evig k-e** the eternal feminine. 2 female, woman (e.g. doctor, lawyer, novelist, worker).

+**kvin'nelig/het** *-en* femininity, womanliness.

kvin'ne/list *-a/+-en* female cunning, wiles.

kvin'ne/logikk' *-en* feminine logic.

+**kvin'ne/menneske** *-t derog.* woman.

kvin'ne/regimen'te *-t* gynarchy, rule by women.

kvin'ne/sak *-a/+-en* feminism.

kvin'nesaks/kvinne *-a/+-en* feminist.

+**kvin'ne/skikkelse** *-n* 1 female figure. 2 woman (character) (in a literary work): **Ibsens k-r** I-'s women.

+**kvin'ne/sykdom** *-men* women's disease.

kvinn'/folk *-et fam.* woman; womenfolk (also *derog.*).

kvinn'folk/arbeid *-et fam.* woman's work.

Kvinn'/herad *Pln* twp, Hordaland.

+**kvinn's** *pl pop.* women, womenfolk.

kvin't *-en* 1 *mus.* fifth (interval); (violin) treble string; quint (organ stop). 2 quinte (in fencing). 3 quint (in card playing).

kvintessen's *-en* quintessence.

kvintett' *-en mus.* quintet.

kvinti'n *-et* 1 *lit., obs.* bit, particle.

kvi'se[1] *-a* (=**kveise**) pimple.

***kvi'se**[2] *V -a* flare up (also *fig.*).

kvi'set(e) *A* - pimply.

***kvisj'e** *V -a* rattle, rustle faintly.

kvis'kre *V -a/+-et* (=+**hviske**) whisper.

kvis'la *df of* **kvissel**

***kvis'le** *V -a* 1 murmur, ripple, trickle. 2 branch off, ramify. 3 manage, pull through.

kvis'sel *kvisla, pl kvisler* 1 arm, branch (of a river). 2 small wooden fork to wind fishline onto.

kvis't[1] *-en, pl -er* 1 sprig, twig. 2 knot (in lumber). 3 *philol.* side stroke of runic letter.

kvis't[2] *-en* attic, garret; dormer: **på k-en** in the g-.

kvis'te *V -a/+-et* 1 lop (**av** off), trim branches, twigs (from a tree). 2: **k- seg** send out branches, shoots. 3 mark (e.g. a path) with twigs.

kvis'tet(e) *A* - 1 full of twigs, twiggy. 2 knotty (lumber). 3: *naut.* **k-e farvann** turbid waters.

kvis't/fri *A -tt* knotless.

kvis't/kammer *-eret, pl -er/+-kamre* attic (room).

kvis't/ved *-en* 1 branches, twigs (esp. for fuel). 2 knotty wood.

kvi't *A* (=+**hvit**) white: **skyte en h-pinne etter noe** give up hope of getting sth; **de h-e/k-e kull/kol** white coals (=hydroelectric power); **h-/k-saus** white sauce.

kvi't/bjø'rn *-en zool.* polar bear.

kvi'te[1] *-n* (=+**hvite**) white (of an egg, eye).

kvi'te[2] *V -a/+-et* (=+**hvitte**) whiten, whitewash.

***kvi'te/emne** *-t* albumen.

Kvi'te/havet *Pln* White Sea.

***kvi'tel** *-elen, pl -lar* cf **kvittel**

+**kvi'te/russer** *-en, pl -e* (=***-ar**) White Russian.

Kvi'tes/eid *Pln* twp, Telemark.

kvi'te/varer *pl* (cotton, linen) white goods.

kvi'ting *-en* (=+**hvitting**) *zool.* whiting (Gadus merlangus).

Kvi'tings/øy *Pln* twp, Rogaland.

kvi't/kløver *-eren, pl +-e/*-ar bot.* white clover (Trefolium repens).

***kvi't/lauk** *-en bot.* garlic.

+**kvit'ler** *pl of* **kvittel**

+**kvi't/lett** *A* - (=***/leitt**) fair complexioned.

kvi't/mose [*/måse] *-n bot.* sphagnum (moss).

kvi'tne *V -a/+-et* (=+**hvitne**) whiten, (make, become) pale; be (appear) white.

kvi't/nos *-a zool.* white-nosed dolphin (Delphinus albirostris).

kvit're *V -a/+-et* chirp, twitter (also *fig.*).

kvitret *df of* **kvit'ter,** *pl of* **kvit're**

kvi't/rev *-en zool.* white fox.

Kvi't/sjøen *Pln* White Sea.

***kvit'/sunn** *-en eccl.* Pentecost, Whitsuntide.

kvit'sunn/dag *-en eccl.* Day of Pentecost, Whitsunday.

kvit'sunn/helg *-a/+-en eccl.* Pentecost, Whitsuntide.

kvi't/symre *-a bot.* white anemone.

***kvitt'**[1] *-en* cf **hvid(d)**

kvitt'[2] *-et* short peep (of a bird).

kvitt'[3] *et* (=+**hvitt**) white: **kjole og h-/k-** white tie and tails, full dress.

kvitt'[4] *Av* 1: **bli, være k-** get, be rid of (sby, sth). 2: **k- og fritt** debt free. 3: **vi to er k-** we are quits (through with each other). 4 *dial.* beat, tired.

kvitt'[5] *I* peep.

kvit'te *V -a/+-et* 1 balance accounts, settle up. 2: **k- av** deduct, draw, subtract (**i** from, **for** for). 3: *dial.* **det k-r** it doesn't matter, it makes no difference. 4 *dial.* be equal, equivalent (**for** to). 5: **k- seg (av) med** dispose of, part from.

+**kvit'tel** *-elen, pl kvitler* (=***kvitel**) woolen blanket.

kvit'ter *-et/kvitret* chirping, twittering.

kvitte're *V -te* 1 acknowledge, give, write a receipt (**for** for). 2 repay (e.g. a compliment). 3 *fam.* discharge, get rid of (e.g. disagreeable food).

kvitte'ring *-a/+-en* receipt.

kvi't/veis *-en bot.* white anemone.

kvi't/vin *-en* white wine.

kvok'ke** *pp of* **kvekke**[1] (=kvokki**)

kvol'le** *pp of* **kvelle** (=kvolli**)

kvol've** *pp of* **kvelve**[2] (=kvolvi**)

kvop'pe** *pp of* **kveppe** (=kvoppi**)

***kvor've**[1] *-a* hangout, haunt; place of refuge.

kvor've**[2] *pp of* **kverve**[3] (=kvorvi**)

kvo'te *-n* quota.

kvotient [kvosien't] *-en* quotient.

***kvæ'de** *-t* cf **kvede**[1]

Kvæ'/fjo'rd *Pln* twp, Troms.

***kvæ'm** *A* handy.

***kvæ'n** *-en* cf **kven**[1]

Kvæ'nangen *Pln* twp, Troms.

***kvæ'nsk** *A* - cf **kvensk**

***kvæ'se** *V -te* cf **kvese**

***kvæ'v** *-et* 1 heavy breathing. 2 (head) cold; catarrh.

***kvæ've**[1] *-t chem.* nitrogen.

***kvæ've**[2] *V -de* cf **kveve**

***kvæ'ven** *A -e/-i, pl -ne* closed, shut.

***kvå'de** *-a* cf **kvae**

***kvå'e** *-a* cf **kvae**

kvå'l *-en dial.* isolated, roundish elevation.

Kvå's *Pln* twp, Vest-Agder.

kW=**kilo/watt**

kykeliky'[1] [ky-] *-et* crow (of a rooster).

kykeliky'[2] [ky-] *I* cock-a-doodle-doo.

kyklo'p [ky-] *-en* cyclops.

kyklo'pisk [ky-] *A* - cyclopean.

***ky'l** *pr of* **kylje**[1]

***kyl'de** *pt of* **kylje**[1]

+**ky'le** *V -te* fling, hurl, toss.

***kyl'je**[1] *V kyl, kylde* cf **kjøle**[2]

***kyl'je**[2] *V -a* burn coal.

kyl'le *V +-te/*kylte* chop off branches.

kyl'ling *-en* (=**kjukling**) 1 chick. 2 chicken (meat): **k- til middag** c- for dinner. 3 *fig.* greenhorn, whippersnapper.

kyl'ling/bur *-et* chicken coop.

kyl'ling/hane *-n* young rooster.

kyl'ling/høne *-a* mother hen.

***kyl'ne** *-a* (drying) kiln (for grain).

***kyl'p** *-en* (bucket)handle.

***kylte** *pt of* ***kylle**, +**kyle**

***kym'ra(st)** *V -a(st)* curdle (milk).

+**kymrer** [kym'rer] *-en, pl -e* (=***-ar**) Welshman.

kymrisk [kym'risk] *A* - Cymric, Welsh.

***ky'n** *-et* cf **kjønn**

***kyn'd** *-a* kind, nature, sort.

***kyn'de** *-t* natural quality; character, nature, temper.

***kyn'del** *-elen, pl -lar* torch.

kyn'dels/mess(e) *-en eccl.* Candlemas (Feb. 2).

kyn'dig *A* - experienced (**i** in), knowledgeable, skilled, well-informed.

+**kyn'dig/het** *-en* experience, know-how, knowledge, skill (**i** in).

***-kyn'dt** *A* - e.g. **frik-** broad-minded, **godk-** good-natured.

***kyng'je** *V -de* 1 be heard at intervals; vibrate. 2 stretch the neck in order to swallow; have difficulty in swallowing.

+**ky'niker** *-en, pl -e* (=***-ar**) cynic; Cynic.

ky'nisk *A* - cynical.

kynis'me *-n* cynicism; Cynicism.

***kyn'ne** *-t* knowledge; character; temper.

kypriot [kyprio't] *-en* Cypriote.

kypriotisk [kyprio'tisk] *A* - Cyprian.

Kypros [kyp'ros] *Pln* Cyprus.

°**ky'r**[1] *-a/-en, pl* - cf **ku**

ky'r[2] *pl of* **ku**

kyrass [kyrass'] *-et* breastplate, cuirass.

kyrasser [kyrase'r] *-en* cuirassier.

Kyrie eleison [ky'rie elei'sån] *Prn eccl.* Kyrie eleison.

***kyr'kje**[1] *-a* cf **kirke**

***kyr'kje**[2] *V -te* 1 pinch (about the throat); squeeze. 2 swallow with difficulty.

Kyr'kje/bø *Pln* twp, Sogn og Fjordane.

***kyr'kjeleg** *A* - cf **kirkelig**

+ Bokmål; * Nynorsk; ° Dialect.
After letter: ' stress (Acc. 1); ` tone, stress (Acc. 2); · length.
Below letter: . not pronounced.

***kyr'kje/lyd** *-en* congregation, parishioners.
***kyr'kje/songar** *-en* cf **kirke/sanger**
***kyr'kje/stol** *-en* cf **kirke/**
***kyr'kne** *V -a* become stopped up in the throat, have difficulty in swallowing.
ky'r/lag *-et* 1 head, cow as statistical unit. 2 *obs.* cow as unit of value.
***kyrr'** *A kyrt* quiet, still: **Olav K-e** (king) Olav the Quiet (1067-93).
***kyr'tel** *-elen, pl -lar* cf **kjortel**
***ky's** *pr of* **kjose**
ky'se[1] *-a* bonnet, (woman's) hood.
+**ky'se**[2] *V -te archaic* frighten, scare (bort away, off).
ky'se/hatt *-en* poke bonnet.
+**kys'k** *A* chaste, virtuous.
+**kys'k/het** *-en* chastity, virtuousness.
kyss' *-et/*-en* kiss.
kys'se *V -a/+-et/+-te/*kyste* kiss: **k- på fingeren til en** blow, throw sby a kiss; *pop.* **kyss meg bak (imorgen)** go to hell.
kys't *-en* coast, shore.
kys't/båt *-en* coastal steamer.
***kys'te** *pt of* **kysse**
kys't/fart *-en* coastal navigation, traffic.
kys't/linje *-a/+-en* coastline, shoreline.
kys't/vakt *-a/+-en* coast guard.
ky't *-et fam.* boasting, bragging.
***ky'tar** *-en* boaster, braggart.
ky'te *V -te* 1 boast, brag. *2 complain: **dei vil alltid klage og k-** they are always complaining (Aasen).
***ky't/o'rd** *pl* 1 boasting, bragging. 2 chiding, scolding.
***ky've** *V -de* bend down, hang.
kø' *-en* 1 line, queue: **stille seg i k-** form a line, queue up; **stå i k-** stand in line. 2 (billiard) cue. 3 bustle (on dress).
København [kjøbenhav'n] *Pln* Copenhagen.
+**københavner** [kjøbenhav'ner] *-en, pl -e* (=*-**ar**) Copenhagener.
+**kø'/dannelse** *-n* forming a line, queuing up.
kø'e *V -a/+-et* form a line, queue up.
°**kø'l** *-et* cf **kol**
køl'le *-a/+-en* 1 club, mace; (golf) club; (croquet) mallet; (hockey) stick; (police) nightstick. 2 *naut.* (caulking) mallet. 3 *bot., zool.* carina.
Køl'n *Pln* Cologne.
køpenickia'de *-n* bamboozling, swindle (ref. to farcical seizure of power by unauthorized personnel, as in 1906 by a German tailor in Køpenick).
°**kør'j** *-a* cf **korg**
køy' *-a* (=**køye**[1]) berth, bunk: **holde k-a** lie, stay in bed; **gå til k-s** go to bed.
køy'e[1] *-a* cf **køy**
køy'e[2] *V -a/+-et* (also: **k- seg**) go to bed, turn in.
køy'(e)/plass *-en* berth.
***køyne** [kjøy'ne] *-a* boil; pimple.
***køyr** [kjøy'r] *-en/-et* cf **kjør**
***køyrar** [kjøy'rar] *-en* cf **kjører**
***køyre** [kjøy're] *V -de* cf **kjøre**
***køyre/doning** *-a/-en* cf **kjøre/**
***køyre/kar** *-en* cf **kjøre/**
***køyre/veg** *-en* cf **kjøre/**
***køyrsle** [kjøy'rsle] *-a* cf **kjørsel**
køyte [kjøy'te] *-a* 1 hut, (fishing, hunting) shelter. 2 puddle; pond. 3 *pop.* woman tramp.
***kå'** *V -dde* spread, turn (hay).
Kå'/fjo'rd *Pln* 1 village, Finnmark. 2 twp, Troms.
kå'k *-en fam.* house, living quarters: **ha k-** have the house to oneself.
kå'l *-en* 1 cabbage. 2: **gjøre k- på** destroy, do away with; **koke bort i k-en** come to nothing (e.g. of plans, preparations).
kå'l/blad *-et* cabbage leaf.
kå'l/hage *-n* cabbage patch.
+**kå'l/hode** *-et* (=***/hovud**) 1 head of cabbage. 2 *fig.* blockhead.
kå'l/mark *-en* (=**/makk**) *zool.* caterpillar.
kå'l/orm *-en zool.* caterpillar.
kål/ra'bi *-en bot.* kohlrabi (Brassica oleracea); rutabaga (Brassica Napobrassica).
kå'l/rot *-a, pl +-røtter/*-røter bot.* rutabaga.
+**kå'l/sommerfugl** *-en zool.* cabbage butterfly (Pieris brassicae).
kå'pe *-a* 1 (woman's) coat; cloak. 2: *fig.* **dekke med kjærlighetens k-** cover with the cloak of charity.
kå'r *-et* 1 circumstance, condition, environment: **han sitter i gode k-** he is well-off, **trange k-** hardship, poverty. 2 pension (in form of subsistence) paid by new owner of estate, farm to former owner (esp. by son to father). 3 term: **gode k-** good terms. 4 *archaic* choice.
kå'r/brev *-et jur.* contract for sustenance of old people.
kår'de *-n* rapier, sword; (fencing) foil.
kå're[1] *-n* breath of wind; ripple (on water).
kå're[2] *V -a/+-et* choose, select; elect: *poet.* **k- (seg) som brud** choose as one's bride.
+**kå're**[3] *V -a/-et* blow softly, ripple.
Kå're *Prn(m)*
kå'r/folk *-et* pensioners (on own estate, farm).
***kå'rings/sjå** *-et* cf **/skue**
+**kå'rings/skue** *-t* livestock show (for selection of breeding stock).
kå'r/kone *-a* (woman) pensioner (on own estate, farm).
kå'r/mann *-en, pl -menn/*-menner* (male) pensioner (on own estate, farm).
+**kå'rne** *pl*: **folkets k-** "the people's choice" (members of the Storting).
kå'r/stue *-a* pensioner's cottage, room.
+**kå's** *-en* 1 deep channel. 2 course, direction.
kåse're *V -te* lecture (informally, entertainingly).
kåseri' *-et, pl +-er/*-* causerie, informal lecture.
kåsø'r *-en* causeur, (informal) lecturer.
kå't *A* boisterous, frisky, gay; wild; (*pop.*) horny, sexually active.
kå'te[1] *-a* knot, protuberance (on a tree).
***kå'te**[2] *V -a*: **k- seg** be gay.
+**kå't/het** *-en* 1 boisterousness, friskness, wildness; gaiety. 2 practical joke, prank.
***kå't/leik** *-en* gaiety, merriment.
kå't/munna *A -* (=+**-et**) flippant.
***kå'tne** *V -a* be gay, merry; be boisterous.
***kå't/ri** *-a* fit of merriment.
***kå've** *V -a* paw over, stir about (i in); shake.

L

l[1] [el'] *-en* (letter) L, l.
l[2] =**liter**
l. =**lengde**
+**la'**[1] *-et* cf **lad**
la'[2] *N mus.* la.
la'[3] *V +-r/*let, +lot/*let, +-tt/*-te/*-ti* (=**late**[1]) 1 allow, let: **la en få noe** give sby sth (**la meg få et glass vin, takk** please give me a glass of wine); **la en få (gjøre noe)** let sby (do sth); **la gå** at granting that (**la gå!** all right!); **la meg se** let me see; **la oss spise nå** let's eat now. 2 leave (in a given condition): **la bli igjen** leave behind; **la bli (være) å** refrain from, not do (sth), stop; **la det bli (være) med det** leave it at that; **la en (være) i fred** leave sby alone (**la meg være** leave me alone); **la (døra) stå åpen** leave (the door) open; **det lar ingenting tilbake å ønske** it leaves nothing to be desired. 3 cause to be, have (done): **la bygge et hus** have a house built; **la en kalle** have sby called; **la vente på seg** delay, keep sby waiting. 4 **late**: appear, seem; make believe, pretend: **late som (som om)** pretend, simulate; **late som ingenting** pretend to be ignorant of a situation; **late til (å)** appear, seem (to). 5 other idioms: ***late att (opp)** close (open); **late livet** die, lose one's life; **late vannet** urinate. 6: *refl.* **la seg (narre, påvirke, overtale, osv.)** let oneself (be fooled, influenced, persuaded, etc.); **det lar seg ikke gjøre (nekte)** it can't be done (denied); **la seg høre** make oneself heard; **la seg nøye med** be satisfied with; **la seg oppstille som kandidat** run for office.
la'[4] *V -dde* (=**lade**[3]) load (a gun, ship).
la'[5] *pt of* **legge, leggje**
la'[6] *I* la (e.g. tra la la).
la'ban *-en* (young) rascal, scamp; lout.
laban'k *-en* batten, crossbar (e.g. on a door).
labb' *-en* 1 paw, *fam.* hand: **han måtte suge på l-en** he had to take a notch in on his belt (he was hard up); **betale kontant på l-en** pay cash on the line; **gi l-** (to a dog) shake hands. 2 *agr.* end of a harrow tooth. 3 *dial.* outside wool sock.
lab'be *V -a/+-et* 1 pad; trudge. 2: *fam.* **l- til en** smack sby.
+**lab'be/lensk** [also -len'sk] *A -* (=***/lendsk**) *fam.* incomprehensible, meaningless (of a language); rigmarole.
la'ber *A -ert, pl -re meteor., naut.*: **l- bris** moderate breeze.
labi'l *A* labile, unstable; *phys.*: **l-likevekt** unstable equilibrium.
labilite't *-en* instability.
laboran't *-en* 1 laboratory assistant. 2 *pharm.* pharmacist's assistant.
laborato'rie/utstyr *-et* laboratory equipment.
laborato'rium *-iet, pl +-ier/*-ium* laboratory.
labore're *V -te* 1 do laboratory work. 2 *lit.* work (e.g. with a problem).
lab'rador *-en geol.* labradorite.
labyrin't *-en* 1 labyrinth, maze. 2 *anat.* (ethmoidal, membranous, osseous) labyrinth.
labyrin'tisk *A -* labyrinthine.
la'd *-et* 1 low stone wall, layer of stone. 2 pile (e.g. of wood). *3 load, charge (of ammunition). 4 *archaic* head ornament.
ladd'[1] *-en* short, coarse oversock; mukluk.
ladd'[2] *pp of* **la**[4]
***lad'de** *V -a* pad about (in mukluks).
lad'de/vin *-en* cheap, strong wine.
+**la'de**[1] *-n* 1 work frame (e.g. for book-

binding). 2 *archaic* box, case, chest. 3 *archaic* shop. 4 *vet.* toothless section of horse's lower jaw.

+**la'de**[2] *-n/-t* cf **låve**

la'de[3] *V -de* cf **la**[4]

la'de[4] *V -de/+-et* 1 charge (e.g. a battery); *fig.*: **luften er l-t med forventning** the air is charged with expectancy. 2 *archaic* load (a ship): **mitt skip er l-et med** my ship is l-ed with (children's game).

la'de/jarl *-en hist.* earl of Lade.

+**-la'delig** *A* - cf **-latelig**

+**-la'delse** *-n* cf **-latelse**

+**la'den** *en* cf **laten**

+**-la'den** *A -ent, pl -ne* cf **-laten**

+**la'der** *pl* gestures, mannerisms: **i ord og l-** in words and manner.

***la'de/stad** *-en* cf **/sted**

la'de/stasjo'n *-en* battery charging station.

+**la'de/sted** *-et* coastal town (without full urban status).

la'de/stokk *-en* cf **la/**

la'dning *-en* 1 charging (e.g. of a battery); loading (e.g. of a gun, ship). 2 charge (of ammunition, electricity). 3 [lad'-] cargo, load: **en l- salt** a load of salt (also with preps. **av, med**).

lady [lei'di] *+-en/*-a* lady.

laf't *-et/*-a, pl -/+-er* log construction, specif. the corner where timbers are joined together by notching.

laf'te *V -a/+-et* 1 build with logs. 2 join, notch (logs for log house).

laf'te/hus *-et* house, log building.

laf't/stein *-en* cornerstone (foundation stone) under a log building.

la'g[1] *-en hist.* district, territory (having same law).

la'g[2] *-et* 1 layer, stratum; coat (e.g. of paint). 2 class, social stratum: **de høyere l-** the upper c-. 3 company, group; party: **godt l- gjør kortere dag** good company shortens the day; **eie noe i l-** own sth jointly; **i l- med** in the company of; **gi sitt ord med i l-et** put in one's two cents worth; **ha et ord med i l-et** have a say in a decision; ***signe l-et** (greeting to a group); **skille l-** separate; **slå (seg i) l- med** join; **forlovet mann er tapt for venners l-** an engaged man is lost to his circle of friends (Ibsen). 4 (athletic) team; crew; *mil.* squad. 5 (normal) condition; (of people) mood: **gjøre en til l-s** satisfy sby; **holde ved l-** maintain unchanged; **stå ved l-** remain in force, stand (e.g. a regulation, rule); (cf also **lage**[2]). 6 manner, way of behaving: **ha (godt) l- med** have a way with. 7 *naut.* broadside: *fig.* **gi en det glatte l-** give sby a piece of one's mind, tell sby off. 8 (other idioms): **i seneste l-et** pretty (rather) late; **i tidligste l-et** pretty (rather) early; **om (på, ved) l-** almost, approximately (**eller så ved l-** or thereabouts); **gi seg i l- med** tackle, go at sth (e.g. a task).

la'ga *A* -: **det er så l-** it is meant to be, is fated.

***la'g/alder** *-en* cf **lav/**

***la'ga/sild** *-a* cf **lage/**

***la'gast** *V -ast* adjust itself, turn out (well).

***lag'de** *pt of* **leggje**

la'g/deling *-a/+-en* (esp. *bot., geol.*) stratification.

la'g/delt *A* - (esp. *bot., geol.*) laminated, stratified.

***lag'dest** *pt of* **leggjast**

+**la'g/dommer** *-en, pl -e* (=***-ar**) *jur.* presiding judge.

***la'ge**[1] *-n/-t* assigned task.

la'ge[2] *N*: **i l-** in order; **bringe, få i l-** put to rights; **komme ut av l-** get out of order; **ute av l-** (be) out of order; (of people) in a bad mood; **verden er ute av l-** the world is out of joint.

la'ge[3] *V -a/+-et/+-de* 1 make, prepare (**til for**): **l- bråk** make a racket; **l- mat** cook, prepare food; (in sports) **l- mål** score a goal; **l- røre** cause a stir; **l- (en) scene** kick up a fuss, make a scene; **l- til** prepare; **l-et** artificial, fake. 2 arrange, order. 3 *refl.*: **l- seg** (of weather) improve, be good; (of events) turn out well; **l- seg til** prepare, ready oneself for.

***la'ge**[4] *A* - appointed, destined: **han var ikkje liv l-** he wasn't d- to live.

la'ger *-eret, pl -er/+-re* 1 storeroom; warehouse; stock, store: **ha på l-** have on hand, stock; **ha et stort l-** carry a large stock, store. 2 *tech.* bearing.

+**la'ger/behol'dning** *-en* stock, store.

la'ger/frakk *-en* laboratory coat, smock.

la'ger/hus *-et* warehouse.

la'ger/plass *-en* storehouse, storeroom; receiving room.

la'ger/sjef *-en* warehouse manager; shipping clerk.

la'ger/øl *-et* lager beer.

+**la'ge/sild** *-a* (=***laga/**) *zool.* herring-like freshwater fish of salmon family (Coregonus albula).

***la'g/før** *A* cooperative (in teamwork).

+**la'g/fører** *-en, pl -e* (=***-ar**) *mil.* squad leader.

lagg' *-en* croze (groove in barrel stave).

***lag'gar** *-en* cooper.

lag'ge *V -a/+-et* croze (cf **lagg**).

°**la'gje** *-n/-t* cf **lage**[1]

la'g/kake *-a* layer cake.

+**la'g/leder** *-en, pl -e* (=***/leiar**) coach.

la'glig *A* - fitting, proper, suitable; comfortable, easy: **han stod l- til for hogg** he was standing just right for getting his head chopped off (Saga of the Fosterbrothers).

la'g/mann *-en, pl -menn/*-menner* 1 *jur.* presiding judge. 2 *hist.* law speaker (at assemblies).

la'gmanns/rett *-en jur.* circuit court, court of appeals.

la'gnad *-en, pl +*-er* destiny, fate.

la'gnads/tung [/tong] *A* fatal, fateful.

la'gom *Av* (=***lugom**) fitting, proper, suitable.

la'gre *V -a/+-et* store; mature, season (e.g. cheese, wine).

la'g/rett *-en* 1 *jur.* jury. 2 *hist.* court of appeals.

la'g/rette *+-n/*-a* cf **/rett**

la'grette/mann *-en, pl -menn/*-menner* juror.

lag's *N*: **gjøre en til l-** please, satisfy sby.

***la'gs/lem** *-en* member.

la'gs/mann *-en, pl -menn/*-menner* member.

***lag'st** *pp of* **leggjast**

lag't *pp of* **legge, leggje**

la'g/ting *-et* 1 upper section of *Storting*. 2 Faroese parliament.

lagu'ne *+-n/*-a* lagoon.

***la'g/ved** *-en* cord wood.

la'g/vis *Av* 1 in layers, stratified. 2 (in sports) by teams; team against team.

***la'k** *pt of* **leke**[2]

-lak *Prn(m)* e.g. Aslak.

***la'kan** *-et* cf **laken**

la'ke[1] *-n* brine.

la'ke[2] *-n zool.* burbot (Lota lota).

la'ke[3] *-n* 1 patch, rag. 2 poor creature, wretch. 3 *zool.* omasum.

la'ke[4] *V -a/+-et* pickle, put into brine.

lakei' *-en* footman; *derog.* flunky, lackey.

la'ken *-et, pl -/+-er* (bed)sheet.

la'ken/lerret *-et* (linen) sheeting.

la'ken/staut *-en/*-et* (muslin) sheeting.

lakk'[1] *-en/-et* 1 laquer. 2 sealing wax.

+**lakk'**[2] *pt of* **lekke**

lak'ke[1] *V -a/+-et* 1 hop, hobble; amble: **l- i veg** start off (slowly). 2: **det l-r til kvelds** evening is drawing near.

lak'ke[2] *V -a/+-et* seal (with sealing wax).

lakke're *V -te* 1 japan, laquer. 2 paint (a car).

lakk'/segl [+/seil] *-et* (sealing wax) seal.

lakk'/sko *-en, pl -r/+-* patent leather shoe, pump.

+**lakk'/stang** *-a, pl -stenger* (=***/stong**) stick of sealing wax.

lak'mus *-en chem.* litmus.

lak'mus/farge *-n chem.* litmus (dye).

lak'mus/papi'r *-et chem.* litmus paper.

lako'nisk *A* - 1 laconic. 2 *hist.* Laconian.

lak'ris [also -i's] *-en* licorice.

lak'ris/båt *-en* licorice (candy) boat.

+**lak'ris/stang** *-a, pl -stenger* (=***/stong**) licorice stick.

lak's *-en zool.* salmon.

lak'se/elv *-a* salmon river.

lak'se/fiske *-t* salmon fishing.

+**lak'se/flue** *-a* (=***/fluge**) salmon fly (lure).

lakse'r/olje *-a/-en* castor oil.

lak'se/trapp *-a* salmon ladder.

Lak'se/våg *Pln* twp, Hordaland.

laku'ne *+-en/*-a* lacuna (e.g. in a manuscript).

la'-la' *Av* so-so.

lal'le *V -a/+-et* babble (usu. of children); blather, maunder.

lam'[1] *-met* lamb (also *bibl., fig.*): **Guds lam** Lamb of God.

lam'[2] *A -t, pl -me* paralyzed (also *fig.*).

la'ma[1] *-en zool.* 1 llama. 2 llama (wool).

la'ma[2] *-en* (Tibetan) lama.

***lam'b** *-et* cf **lam**[1]

***lam'de** *pt of* **lemje**

lamé *-en* lamé.

lamell' *-en* 1 thin disc, plate (esp. *elec.*). 2 detached building in a group or block of buildings.

+**lamell'/bebyg'gelse** *-n* group of detached apartment buildings.

***la'men** *A -e/-i, pl -ne* cf **lam**[2]

lamente're *V -te* lament, wail.

lam'me[1] *V -a/+-et* cf **lemme**[1]

lam'me[2] *V -a/+-et/+lamte* paralyze: **l-ende redsel** paralyzing fear.

lam'me/kjøtt *-et* (=+**/kjøt**) lamb (meat).

+**lam'melse** *-n* paralysis.

lam'me/steik *-a* lamb roast.

lam'pe *-a/-en* 1 (electric, kerosene, oil) lamp. 2 radio tube.

lam'pe/feber *-en* stage fright.

lam'pe/glas *-et* (=+**/glass**) (lamp) chimney.

lam'pe/kuppel *-elen, pl -kupler* lamp bowl, globe.

lam'pe/lys *-et* lamplight.

lam'pe/skjerm *-en* lampshade.

+**lam'pe/skjær** *-et* lamplight.

lampett' *-en* bracket lamp, sconce.

lam'pe/veike *-n* (=+**/veke**) lamp wick.

lam'/sau *-en* sheep (ewe) which has a lamb.

lam'/slå *V -slo, -slått* paralyze (also *fig.*); stun, stupefy.

***lam't** *pp of* **lemje**

lam'/unge [/onge] *-n* (small) lamb.

lan'd[1] *-et* 1 land (=not sea); shore: **gå (sette) i l-** go (put) ashore; **inne (oppe) i l-et** inland; **på l-** on land; **til l-s** by land; **under l-** close to shore. 2 land, soil, territory: **nytt l-** new territory (also *fig.*); **rydde l-** clear land. 3 country, land (of a nation): **her i l-et** in this c-; **Norges l-** the c- of Norway; **Ja, vi elsker dette landet** Yes, we love this land (Bjørnson); **over hele l-et** all over the country. 4 country, countryside, rural area: **l- og by** country and city; **på l-et** in the country; **den må du lenger ut på landet med** don't try to give me that.

lan'd[2] *-et* (animal) urine (esp. of horses and cows).

Lan'd *Pln* joint name for Fluberg, Nordre Land, Søndre Land, Torpa twps, Oppland.

+ Bokmål; * Nynorsk; ° Dialect.
After letter: ' stress (Acc. 1); ' tone, stress (Acc. 2); ˙ length.
Below letter: . not pronounced.

lan'dauer *-en, pl* ⁺*-e* landau.
lan'ḍ/bruk *-et* agriculture, farming.
Lan'ḍbruks/departementet [-mang·e] *df* Ministry of Agriculture.
lan'ḍbruks/minis·ter *-eren, pl -rer/* ⁺*-ere* Minister of Agriculture.
lan'ḍbruks/produk·t *-et, pl -/*⁺*-er* agricultural product, farm produce.
lan'ḍbruks/skole *-n* agricultural school.
***lan'ḍ/bu** *-en* **(=⁺/boer)** *obs.* country dweller, farmer.
***lan'ḍ/bær** *A* offshore (wind).
lan'ḍ/distrik·t *-et* rural district.
lan'ḍe *V -a/*⁺*-et* land (of an airplane, bird, person, ship).
lan'ḍe/grense *-a/*⁺*-en* border, frontier.
⁺**lan'ḍ/eiendom** *-men* **(=*/eigedom)** estate, landed property.
***lan'ḍe/mellom** *Av* cf **land/imellom**
lan'ḍe/merke *-t, pl* ⁺*-r/*- landmark.
lan'ḍe/plage *-a/*⁺*-en* general plague, scourge; nuisance, pest.
⁺**lan'ḍe/sorg** *-en* public national) mourning.
lan'ḍe/veg *-en* highway; *lit.*: **den slagne l-** the beaten path; **ta l-en fatt** set out on foot.
⁺**lan'ḍeveis/ridder** *-en, pl -e* knight of the road, tramp, vagabond.
⁺**lan'ḍeveis/røver** *-en, pl -e* highwayman.
lan'ḍ/fast *A* - joined, linked (by land): **Norge er l- med Sverige** Norway and Sweden are geographically joined; **øya er blitt l-** the island has been connected to the mainland.
lan'ḍ/feste *-t* abutment (of bridge).
lan'ḍ/flyktig [also -flyk'-] *A* - banished, exiled, in exile.
⁺**lan'ḍflyktig/het** [also -flyk'-] *-en* banishment, exile.
lan'ḍ/gang *-en* **1** disembarkation, landing. **2** *mil.* descent, raid. **3** gangplank, gangway. **4** long (open-faced) sandwich (with a variety of spreads).
lan'ḍgangs/bru *-a* gangplank.
lan'ḍ/handel *-elen, pl -ler* **1** general (country) store. **2** rural trade. **3** overland trade.
⁺**lan'ḍ/handler** *-en, pl -e* **(=*-ar)** country tradesman, storekeeper.
lan'ḍ/handleri· [also -ri'] *-et, pl* ⁺*-er/*- general (country) store.
lan'ḍ/imel·lom *Av* **(=*lande/mellom)** between countries.
lan'ḍings/plass *-en* (airplane, ship) landing place.
⁺**lan'ḍings/sted** *-et* **(=*/stad)** (airplane, ship) landing place.
lan'ḍ/jo·rḍ *-a*: **på l-a** on dry land.
lan'ḍ/kart *-et* (land) map.
lan'ḍ/kjenning *-a/*⁺*-en* landfall, landsighting.
lan'ḍ/kommu·ne *-n* rural district.
lan'ḍ/krabbe *-a/-en* **1** *zool.* land crab. **2** *fig.* landlubber.
***lan'ḍ/kunne** *-a* geography.
***lan'ḍ/laupar** *-en* tramp, vagabond.
***lan'ḍ/lege** *-a* cf **/ligge**
lan'ḍlig *A* - rural, rustic.
⁺**lan'ḍ/ligge** *-t* **(=*/lege)** (usu. fisherman's) time ashore because of bad weather.
lan'ḍ/liv *-et* country, rural life.
lan'ḍ/lov [/låv] *-et/*⁺*-en naut.* liberty; shore leave.
lan'ḍ/lyse *V -te* banish, exile.
lan'ḍ/mann *-en, pl -menn/*-*menner* farmer.
⁺**lan'ḍ/måler** *-en, pl -e* **(=*-ar)** surveyor.
lan'ḍ/not *-a, pl -nøter* shore seine.
***lan'ḍ/nø·rḍing** *-en* northeast wind.
lan'ḍ/nåm *-et hist.* colonization, settling (esp. of Iceland).
lan'ḍnåms/mann *-en, pl -menn/* *-*menner hist.* early settler in Iceland.
***lan'ḍ/røn** *A* offshore (wind).
-lanḍs *Av* e.g. **innen/l-** at home, within the country; **uten/l-** abroad.
⁺**lan'ḍ/satte** *pt of* **-sette**
***lan'ḍs/bate** *-n* benefit to the country.
lan'ḍs/by *-en* village.
lan'ḍs/bygd *-a* rural community: **på l-a** in the country.
lan'ḍs/del *-en* part of the country, section.
lan'ḍs/ende *-n* end of the country: **fra l- til l-** from one end of the country to the other.
lan'ḍsens *A* - **1**: **all l- ulykke** all kinds of misfortune. **2** of the country; provincial, rural.
⁺**lan'ḍ/sette** *V infl as* **sette[1] (=*/setje)** disembark, land (e.g. passengers, troops); beach (a boat).
lan'ḍs/faderlig *A* - paternalistic (of a ruler).
⁺**lan'ḍs/forbunḍ** *-et* league, national federation.
⁺**lan'ḍs/forræ·der** *-en, pl -e* traitor.
⁺**lan'ḍs/forræderi·** *-et* treason.
⁺**lan'ḍs/forvi·se** *V -te* banish, exile.
⁺**lan'ḍs/forvi·sning** *-en* banishment, exile.
⁺**lan'ḍs/gutt** *-en* **(=*/gut)** country boy.
lan'ḍs/gymna·s *-et, pl -/*⁺*-er* rural secondary school (of gymnas).
lan'ḍs/høvding *-en* **(=*/hovding)** (county) governor (in Sweden).
-lanḍsk *A* - **(=*-lendsk)** e.g. **uten/l-** foreign; **vest/l-** of western Norway.
lan'ḍs/kamp *-en* international match (in sports).
lan'ḍ/skap *-et, pl -/*⁺*-er* **1** landscape, scenery. **2** *hist.* province.
lan'ḍskaps/lov [/låv] *-en/*-*a hist.* provincial law.
⁺**lan'ḍs/kjent** *A* - **(=*/kjend)** nationally known, of nation-wide fame.
lan'ḍ/skylḍ *-a/*⁺*-en* land rent; *hist.* property taxes.
lan'ḍs/lag *-et* **1** national team (in international match). **2** nation-wide organization.
⁺**lan'ḍslags/spiller** *-en, pl -e* player on national team.
lan'ḍs/lott *-en, pl *-er* fishing fee (for use of land where net is fastened).
***lan'ḍs/lut** *-en, pl -er* part of the country.
lan'ḍs/mann *-en, pl -menn/*-*menner* compatriot, countryman.
lanḍsmannin'ne *-a/*⁺*-en* compatriot, countrywoman.
lan'ḍs/mål *-et* New Norwegian (language); official name until 1929.
⁺**lan'ḍs/omfattenḍe** *A* - nation-wide.
lan'ḍs/organisasjo·n *-en* national organization: **L-en i Norge** Norwegian Federation of Labor.
lan'ḍs/renn *-et* national (ski) competition, race.
lan'ḍs/skadelig *A* - injurious to the country.
lan'ḍs/styre *-t* government.
lan'ḍs/svik *-et* treason.
⁺**lan'ḍs/sviker** *-en, pl -e* **(=*-ar)** traitor.
⁺**lan'ḍ/sted** *-et* country house; summer cottage.
⁺**lan'ḍ/sti·gning** *-en* landing, disembarkation.
lan'ḍ/storm *-en* **1** *mil.* militia, territorial levy. **2** land storm.
lan'ḍ/stridskrefter *pl mil.* land forces, troops.
⁺**lan'ḍ/stryker** *-en, pl -e* **(=*-ar)** hobo, tramp, vagabond.
***lan'ḍs/veg** *-en* cf **lande/**
lan'ḍ/syn *-et/*-*a naut.* land sighting.
***lan'ḍ/synning** *-en* southeasterly wind.
lan'ḍs/øl *-et* near beer.
lan'ḍ/tange *-n* isthmus.
lan'ḍ/tunge [/tonge] *-a* strip, tongue of land; promontory.
lan'ḍ/tur *-en* trip to the country; picnic.
***lan'ḍ/veges** *Av* by land, overland.
lan'ḍ/vern [/væ·rn] *-et mil.* levy, militia; national guard.
⁺**lan'ḍ/verts** *Av* by land, overland.
Lan'ḍ/vik *Pln* twp, Aust-Agder.
lan'ḍ/vinḍ *-en* land wind.
lan'ḍ vinning *-a/*⁺*-en* **1** acquisition, conquest (also *fig.*). **2** land reclamation.
lang'[1] *-en* **1** addition (to a building); shed. **2** gallery, porch. ***3** long side (e.g. of a building).
lang'[2] *A -t, cp lengre, sp lengst[1]* **1** lengthy, long; (of a person) tall: **l- i ansiktet** crestfallen, glum; **dagen l-** all day long; **i sju l-e og sju brede** forever and ever; **tiden faller meg l-** time hangs heavy on my hands. **2** (as *adv.*): **l-t** far, a long ways; (with comparatives and superlatives) by far, much: **l-t borte** far away; **l-t (i)fra** not at all, far from (it); **(så) l-t fra å være lett, er det...** instead of being easy, it is on the contrary... **l-t om lenge** at long last; **l-t oppe i årene** advanced in years; **l-t på vei til** well on the way to; **(ikke) på l-t nær** not by a long shot, not nearly; **l-t (ut) på natta** late in the night; **det er l-t bedre** it is much better; **det er l-t den beste** it is by far the best; **lenger enn l-t** a long, long way. **3** *(sup.)* **for lengst** long ago; **i det lengste** as long as possible.
⁺**lang'/aktig** *A* - elongated, longish.
lang'/beint *A* - long legged.
lang'/benk *-en* bench (by wall or long side of table).
lang'/bo·rḍ *-et* long table.
lang'/bølgje *-a* **(=⁺/bølge)** low frequency (radio) wave (above 100 m).
lang'/drag *-et*: **trekke i l-** be protracted, drag on, take a long time.
***lang'/dregen** *A -e/-i, pl -ne* drawn-out, lengthy, prolix; boring.
lang'/dryg *A* long lasting, (seemingly) endless; dilatory, slow, tardy.
lang'e[1] *-a zool.* ling (Molva molva).
lang'e[2] *V -a/*⁺*-et* **1** reach **(etter** for). **2** hand, pass **(inn** in, **rundt** around, **ut** out), pass (from hand to hand); sling, heave: **l- i seg** devour; **l- til en** give sby a blow, punch; **l- til seg** grab, help oneself to. **4** run (with long steps), stride: **l- i veg, l- ut** stride off.
lang'e/leik *-en mus.* Norwegian zither (played on one string, with several accompanying strings).
⁺**lang'elig** *A* - **1** gently bending, undulating, winding (e.g. hill, river, valley). **2** imploring, wistful; longing; lingering (e.g. look, note, sound).
lang'e/mann *-en* middle finger.
Lang'e/nes *Pln* twp, Nordland.
Lang'e/sunḍ *Pln* coastal town, Telemark.
lang'/farenḍe *A* - from far away, traveling a long distance.
lang'/fart *-en* long voyage: **i l-** (sailing) in distant waters.
lang'/faste *-a/*⁺*-en eccl., hist.* Lent.
lang'/ferd [*/fæ·r] *-a/*⁺*-en* long journey.
lang'/finger *-eren, pl -rer* middle finger.
lang'/fingra *A* - **(=⁺-et)** long-fingered; *fig.* light-fingered.
Lang'/fjella *Pln* joint name for mountain district from Setesdalsheiene to Dovrefjell.
lang'/flat *A* prostrate: **ligge l-** hurry, rush.
lang'/fredag [also -fre'-] *-en eccl.* Good Friday.
⁺**lang'/fremmed** *A* - **(=*/framand)** guest from far away.
⁺**lang'/fristet** *A* - long-term (e.g. loan).
***lang'/godfar** *-en, pl -godfedrar* great-grandfather.
lang'/grunn *A -grunt* having a long shallow: **det er l-t her** the bottom slopes very gradually here.
lang'/grunne *-a/-en* wide bank, shoal.
***lang'/helde** *-a* hobble (between front and back leg).
***lang'/henta** *A* - far-fetched.
lang'/hus *-et* **1** long house. **2** (church) nave.
lang'/håra *A* - **(=⁺-et)** long-haired.
lang'/kikkert *-en* telescope.
lang'/kost [/kost] *-en* long-handled broom or scrubbing brush.
***lang'/leitt** *A* - long-faced.

***lang'/liva** *A* - (=+**-et**) 1 long-lived. 2 long-waisted.

lang'/minnug *A* - having a good memory.

langmo'dig *A* - 1 forbearing, long suffering. 2 *fam.* drawn-out, tedious.

+**langmo'dig/het** *-en* forbearance, long-suffering.

lang'/orv *-et* long-handled scythe.

lang'/pipe *-a* long-stemmed pipe.

lang'/renn *-et* 1 cross-country race. 2 cross-country skiing.

lang's *P* along: **l- med** along, beside; *naut.* **l- siden av** alongside.

***lang'samleg** *A* - long-lasting, protracted.

***lang'/semd** *-a* boredom, tedium.

lang's/etter *P* along.

lang'/side [*/sie] *-a*/+*-en* long side (of sth).

lang'/siktig [also -sik'-] *A* - 1 *merc.* long-term (e.g. bond), long-dated (e.g. bill). 2 long-range (e.g. plans).

lang'/sint *A* - bearing a grudge for a long time, implacable.

lang'/skalle *-n anthro.* dolichocephalic skull; dolichocephalic person.

lang'/skanket(e) *A* - *fam.* long-legged.

lang'/skip *-et* 1 *hist.* longship (viking war ship). 2 (church) nave.

lang'/skips *A* - *naut.* alongside a ship (from fore to aft).

lang's/med *P* along, alongside.

+**lang'/som'** *A -t, pl -me* (=***/sam**) 1 slow (e.g. boat, horse, man, movement, tempo, work). 2 protracted; boring, dreary; lonesome: **det blir l-t etter deg** it will be l- after you (Hamsun).

+**lang'som/het** *-en* slowness.

+**langsom'melig** *A* - 1 slow. 2 protracted; boring, tiringly long.

lang'/strakt *A* - long (and narrow), extended.

lang'/støvel *-elen, pl -ler* knee boot.

lang'/sy'nt *A* - far-sighted (also *fig.*); hypermetropic.

lang't *Av cp lenger, sp lengst*[1] cf **lang**[2]

langtek'kelig *A* - boringly long, protracted.

+**lang't/fra** *Av* (=***langtfrå**) far from: **han er l- noen helt** he is far from being any hero.

lang'tids/program' *-met, pl -*/+*-mer* long-range program.

lang'tids/varsel *-elet*/+*-let* long-range weather forecast.

+**lang't/ifra'** *Av* (=+**langt ifra**, ***langt ifrå**) far from it, not at all.

+**lang't/rekkende** *A* - *mil.* long-range (artillery); far-reaching.

+**lang'/trukken** [/trokken] *A -ent, pl trukne* drawn-out, protracted (e.g. howl, tone); boring, tedious (e.g. novel, play).

lang'/tur *-en* long hike, trip.

lang'/varig *A* - long(-lasting), prolonged.

lang'/vegg *-en* longitudinal wall.

+**lang'/veis** *Av* (=***/veg(e)s**) far away, (over a) long distance: **hva er det som l- kimer** what is it that chimes far away (Ibsen).

+**lang'veis/fra** *Av* from far away: **duft av blomster l-** (the) scent of flowers from afar (Vogt).

+**lang'/viser** *-en, pl -e* (=***-ar**) minute hand.

lan'ke *-n* hand (in baby talk).

lanoli'n *-en* lanolin.

lan'se *-a*/*-en* 1 lance: **bryte en l- for en (noe)** defend, stand up for sby (sth). 2 *med.* lancet.

lan'se/knekt *-en hist.* lansquenet.

lanse're [langsere] *V -te* launch: **l- en ny plan** launch a new plan, scheme.

lansett' *-en med.* lancet.

lanterne [lantæ'rne] *-a*/+*-en* lantern, light (esp. *naut.*).

La'os *Pln* Laos.

lao'tisk *A* - Laotian.

***la'pe** *V -a* hang flaccidly, loosely.

lapida'risk *A* - lapidary.

la'pis *-en* 1 *chem., med.* silver nitrate. 2 lapis.

lapp'[1] *-en* Laplander, Lapp (now officially called *Same*).

lapp'[2] *-en* 1 patch (of cloth, earth); scrap, slip (of cloth, paper); *fam.* money bill. 2 small thick pancake. 3 loose fold of skin: **kjøtt/l-** dewlap; **øre/l-** ear lobe; *bot.* lobe.

lap'pe[1] *V -a*/+*-et* mend, patch (e.g. clothes, shoes); repair (temporarily); **l- over** overlap.

+**lap'pe**[2] *V -a*/*-et fam.*: **l- til en** smack sby.

+**lap'pe/fog(e)d** *-en* (=***/fut**) superintendent of reindeer husbandry.

+**lap'peri** *-et* 1 botch, patchwork. 2 bagatelle, trifle.

lap'pe/saker *pl* mending, patching materials; repair outfit (for bicycle).

+**lap'pe/skoma'ker** *-en, pl -e* shoe repairman.

lap'pet(e) *A* - 1 patched. 2 *bot.* lobed.

lap'pe/teppe *-t, pl* +*-r*/**-* 1 patchwork quilt. 2 *fam.* hodgepodge.

lap'pisk *A* - Lapp, Lappish.

Lapp'/land *Pln* Lapland (in Sweden).

lapp'/verk *-et* botch, patchwork.

lap's *-en* dandy, dude, fop.

+**lap'salve** *V -a*/*-et naut.* pay (a line with tar). 2 *fam.* drub, thrash.

lap'set(e) *A* - dandyish, dudish, foppish.

lap's/kaus *-en* 1 hash; lobscouse; stew. 2 *fam.* hodgepodge.

lap'sus *-en* slip (of the tongue, pen); lapse (of memory).

La'r/dal *Pln* twp, Vestfold.

***lar'kast** *V -ast* mat; lump.

***lar'ke** *V -a* cuff, slap: **l- til** (the same).

lar'm *-en* 1 noise, racket, tumult: **borte fra byens l-** away from the din of the city. 2 commotion, hullaballoo, uproar: **lite å gjøre l- for** nothing to make a commotion about. 3 *archaic* alarm.

lar'me *V -a*/+*-et* make a din, noise; blare, rumble: **toget l-t av sted** the train clattered off.

La'rs *Prn (m)*

la'rsok *en* August 10th (St. Lawrence's Day).

lar'v *-en* poor creature, fellow; *derog.* scoundrel, wretch.

lar've[1] *-a*/*-en zool.* larva; grub, maggot; caterpillar.

***lar've**[2] *V -a* 1 bungle (e.g. one's work). 2 idle, loaf.

***lar'vet(e)** *A* - ragged, tattered.

Lar'/vik *Pln* town, Vestfold.

***la's** *pt of* **lese**

lasarett' *-et, pl -*/+*-er mil.* field hospital.

lasaro'n *-en* bum, tramp.

+**la'se** *-n* rag.

***la'sen** *A -e*/*-i, pl -ne* 1 cf **laset(e)**. 2 ailing, weak.

+**la'set(e)** *A* - ragged, tattered.

las'k *-en* 1 *naut., tech.* fishplate. 2 *naut., tech.* fish joint. 3 invisible or decorative seam (on leather). 4 *dial.* (cloth) gusset. 5 *dial.* wooden piece to protect against wear.

las'ke[1] *-n* 1 *naut., tech.* fishplate. 2 *dial.* (cloth) gusset. 3 *dial.* wooden piece to protect against wear.

las'ke[2] *V -a*/+*-et* 1 *naut., tech.* fish (a mast, joint); scarf (two beams, planks). 2 *naut.* lash together. 3 sew a decorative seam (in leather).

+**las'ket(e)** *A* - flabby; obese.

***las'ne** *V -a* become loose in the joints.

lass' *-et, pl* - load: **et l- høy** a l- of hay.

las'se/vis *Av*: **selle ved l-** sell wood by the load; **han har penger i l-** he has loads of money.

las'sis *-en* bum, tramp.

las'so *-en* lariat, lasso.

las't[1] *-a*/*-en* 1 burden: **være til l- for noen** be a burden to sby. 2 blame: **legge en noe til l-** blame one for sth. 3 cargo, load: **ta inn l-** take on cargo. 4 *naut.* hold.

las't[2] +*-a*/*-en* 1 damage, harm, injury: **stå l- og brast** stand by (one) through thick and thin; **l- og skam** misfortune and shame. 2 vice: **være slave av en l-** be (a) slave to a vice.

las't/dyr *-et* beast of burden, pack animal.

las'te[1] *V -a*/+*-et* 1 load, take on cargo. 2 carry, hold: **skipet l-r 900 tonn** the ship carries 900 tons.

las'te[2] *V -a*/+*-et* blame, censure.

las'te/bil *-en* (motor) truck.

las'te/båt *-en* cargo boat, ship; freighter.

+**las'te/damper** *-en, pl -e* (=***-ar**) freighter; cargo steamer.

las'te/full *A* dissolute, vicious.

***las'teleg** *A* - deprecatory, disparaging.

+**las'te/linje** *-a*/*-en* (=***/line**) *naut.* load (water) line, Plimsoll line.

las'te/merke *-t, pl* +*-r*/**-* *naut.* load line, Plimsoll mark.

+**las'te/penger** *pl* (=***-ar**) *naut.* cargo duties, tonnage.

las'te/plan *-et* floor, truck bed.

las'te/pram' *-men* barge, lighter.

las'te/rom [/romm] *-met naut.* hold.

las'te/skip *-et* freighter.

las'ting *-en* (cloth) lasting.

la'/stokk *-en* ramrod.

las't/o'rd *pl dial.* reproach, upbraiding.

las't/verdig [also -vær'-] *A* - reprehensible.

las't/verk *-et*: **hastverk er (gjør) l-** haste makes waste.

lasu'r *-en* 1 *chem.* lazurite. 2 glaze, glazing (in ceramics, painting).

lasu'r/blått *et* azure.

la't *A* - indolent, lazy, shiftless.

lat.=**latin(sk)**

la'te[1] *V* +*-er*/**let*, +*lot*/**let*, +*-t*/**-e*/**-i* cf **la**[3] (4,5)

la'te[2] *V -a*/+*-et*: **l- seg** idle, loaf.

-la'telig *A* - e.g. in **till-, uavl-.**

+**-la'telse** *-n* e.g. in **forl-, till-.**

+**la'ten** *en archaic*: **gjøren og l-** affairs, business, doings.

-la'ten *A* +*-ent, pl -ne* e.g. in **etterl-, søtl-.**

laten't *A* - latent.

la't/hans *-en fam.* lazybones, sluggard.

la't/hund *-en fam.* lazybones, sluggard.

lati'n *-en* Latin, *fig.*: **god l-** the accepted view.

+**lati'ner** *-en, pl -e* (=***-ar**) 1 Latin, Roman. 2 Latinist; Latin student.

la'ting *-en fam.* lazybones, sluggard.

***-la'ting** *-a* e.g. in **innl-, oppl-.**

latinise're *V -te* latinize.

lati'nsk *A* - Latin, Roman: **l-e bokstaver** Roman letters, **den l-e kirke** the Roman (Catholic) church; Romance: **de l-e språk** the Romance languages.

lati'n/skole *-n obs.* Latin school, classical *gymnasium.*

la'tmanns/liv *-et* idle life, life of Riley.

latri'ne *-a*/*-en* latrine.

la't/skap *-en* indolence, laziness.

la't/staur *-en fam.* lazybones, sluggard.

la't/stokk *-en fam.* lazybones, sluggard.

+**lat'ter** *-en* laugh, laughter: **bli, være til l-** be a laughingstock; **briste i l-** burst out laughing; **få seg en god l-** have a good laugh; **gjøre seg til l-** make a fool of oneself; **vekke l-** invite ridicule, derision; **holde på å dø av l-** nearly die laughing.

+**lat'ter/dør** [also lat'-] *-a*: **få, slå l-a opp** (begin to) roar with laughter.

+**lat'ter/krampe** [also lat'-] *-n* 1 convulsive, hysterical laughter. 2 *med.* cramp in the risible muscle.

+**lat'terlig** *A* - laughable, ludicrous, ridiculous: **det l-e i** the ridiculousness of; **gjøre en l- figur** cut a ridiculous figure.

+**lat'terlig/gjøre** *V -gjorde, -gjort* hold up to ridicule, make ridiculous.

+ Bokmål; * Nynorsk; ° Dialect.
After letter: ' stress (Acc. 1); ' tone, stress (Acc. 2); · length.
Below letter: . not pronounced.

+lat'ter/milḍ [also lat'-] *A* - given to laughter, mirthful.
+lat'ter/muskel [also lat'-] *-elen, pl -ler* risible muscle.
+lat'ter/salve [also lat'-] *-a/-en* burst of laughter.
+lat'ter/vekkenḍe [also lat'-] *A* - laughable, ludicrous.
Lat'via *Pln* Latvia.
+**lat'vier** *-en* (=***-ar**) Latvian.
lat'visk *A* - Latvian.
lau'd *-en/-et* 1 (short for) **laudabilis.** 2 *fam.* person who has received the mark "laud".
lauda'bel *A -elt, pl -le* deserving of the mark "laud".
lauda'bilis *N* highest mark in final examination for university degree.
Lau'/dal *Pln* twp, Vest-Agder.
lau'g[1] *-et* bath.
lau'g[2] *-et* 1 craft, guild. 2 clique, fraternity (e.g. of artists, writers).
lau'g[3] *pt of* **lyge**
-laug *Prn (f)* e.g. in **Asl-, Gisl-, Oddl-.**
lau'ge *V -a/+-et* bathe: **l- seg** take a bath.
***lau'k** *-en* (=+**løk**[1]) onion; bulb; *fig.*: **han er l-en i laget** he is the top dog.
lau'p[1] *-en* 1 (round) wooden box (with handles). 2 *hist.* unit of measurement (ab. 33 lbs.).
***lau'p**[2] *-et* cf **løp**
***lau'par** *-en* cf **løper**
***lau'par/fant** *-en* tramp, vagabond.
lau'par/rigg *-en* rigging (on a fishing boat).
lau'par/sko *-en, pl -r/+-* skirunner's shoe; kind of moccasin.
***lau'pe** *V -te* cf **løpe**[2]
***lau'pe/tiḍ** *-a* cf **løpe/**
***lau'p/år** *-et* leap year.
lau'r/bær *-et* 1 bayberry. 2 bay, laurel (plant, tree). 3: *fig.* **hvile på sine l-** rest on one's laurels.
lau'rbær/blaḍ *-et* bay leaf.
lau'rbær/krans *-en* laurel wreath; laurels (of victory).
***lau'r/dag** *-en* cf **lør/**
***lau'rdags/friing** *-a* cf **lørdags/frieri**
lau's *A* (=+**løs**) 1 loose=free, unattached: **l- og ledig** free and easy, unfettered; **l-t gods** chattels; **l-e hunder** dogs without leash; **l- krave** detachable collar; **ha en skrue l-** have a screw loose, be nutty; *naut.* **kaste l-** cast off; **rive, slite seg l-** break away, free oneself; **sitte l-t** not be firmly attached; **slå, slippe seg l-** let oneself go; **nå er fanden l-** now there's the devil to pay. 2 loose=lax, slack: **et l-t grep** a loose grip; **l-t vevet** loosely woven. 3 (other idioms): **l-t krutt** blank ammunition (**skyte med l-t** fire blanks); **l- snakk** gossip, idle chatter; **et l-t forhold** an (erotic) affair; **i (ut av) l-e lufta** in (out of) thin air; **(gjøre noe) på livet l-(t)** (do sth) desperately, for dear life (**det går på livet l-** it's a matter of life and death); **gå l- på** attack, go after; go ahead, start (sth); **(snakke sammen om) l-t og fast** (talk about) this and that; **selge i l- vekt** sell by weight (i.e. not packaged); **det bar l-** it started, broke out; (they) started (off); **bære l- på** attack; **uværet brøt l-** the storm broke.
-laus *A* (=+**-løs**) -less (e.g. **heiml-, hvilel-**).
+**lau's/arbeider** *-en, pl -e* (=***-ar**) day laborer.
lau's/bikkje *-a* stray dog.
lau's/blaḍ *-et* loose leaf.
lau's/eld *-en* (accidental) fire.
***lau's/gangar** *-en* cf **løs/gjenger**
lau's/gjelḍ *-a* floating debt.
lau's/hest *-en* reserve, spare horse (led behind the rest).
lau's/kar *-en* 1 day worker. 2 bachelor.
lau's/kjefta *A* - glib, loose-tongued.
***lau'sleg** *A* - cf **løselig**[1]
***lau's/leik** *-en* looseness, slackness (of character, clothing, rules, etc.).
***lau's/livnaḍ** *-en* immorality, loose living.
***lau's/lynt** *A* - changeable, unstable, wavering (person); frivolous (person).
lau's/munna *A* - 1 easy to turn (of a horse). 2 glib, loose-tongued.
***lau's/mynt** *A* - cf **/munna**
***lau'sne** *V -a* cf **løsne**
lau's/rive *V infl as* **rive**[3]: **l- seg** break away, detach oneself, secede; tear oneself away (**fra** from).
lau's/skjegg *-et* false beard.
lau's/snø *-en* loose snow.
lau's/tann *-a, pl -tenner* false tooth.
lau's/unge [/onge] *-n* 1 illegitimate child. 2 *naut.* loose reef point.
+**lau's/øre** *-t* (=+**løs/, */øyre**) chattels, movables; goods, personal property.
***lau't** *pt of* **ljote**
lau'v *-et* (=+**løv**) foliage, leafage; leaf.
***lau'vast** *V -ast* become green (of trees).
lau'v/blaḍ *-et bot.* leaf.
lau've *V -a/+-et* gather leaves (for fodder).
lau'venḍe *Av*: **l- tynn** thin as a leaf.
lau'v/fall *-et* 1 defoliation; fall (of leaves). 2 fallen (dead) leaves.
lau'v/grøn *A* (=+**/grønn**) leaf-green.
lau'v/heng *-et* foliage.
lau'v/hytte *-a* arbor, bower.
lau'v/kjerv(e) *-(e)t* bundle of leafy branches.
lau'v/kniv *-en* knife (to cut leaves for fodder).
lau'v/krone *-a* crown (of a tree).
lau'v/rik *A* - leafy.
lau'v/sag *-a* coping saw, jigsaw.
lau'v/skog *-en* deciduous forest, leafy trees.
lau'v/sprett *-en/-et* foliation, leafing; spring.
lau'v/tak *-et* 1 leafy canopy. 2 gathering of leaves (for fodder). 3 place where one gathers leaves (for fodder).
lau'v/tre *-et, pl -/+-trær* deciduous tree.
lau'v/tynn *A -tynt* leaf-thin.
lau'v/veḍ *-en* hardwood.
lau'v/verk *-et* (=+**løv/**) 1 (ornamental) leafwork. 2 *lit.* foliage.
la'v[1] *-et bot.* lichen.
la'v[2] *A* cf **låg**[4]
la'va *-en* lava.
+**la'v/adel** *-en* cf **låg/**
+**la'v/alder** *-en* (=***lag/**) *jur.* minimum age: **den kriminelle l-** the age of consent.
La'vangen *Pln* twp, Troms.
+**la'v/beint** *A* - cf **låg/**
la've[1] *V -a/-de* 1 dangle, hang down (in clusters). 2 sift down (densely, heavily). 3: **det lyste og l-t av ham** his clothes glittered.
+**la've**[2] *V -et* cf **lage**[3]
laven'del *-elen, pl -ler* lavender (perfume, plant).
lave're *V -te* 1 *naut.* beat, tack. 2 *archaic, fam.* loiter about. 3 shade, wash (a drawing).
+**la'vere/ståenḍe** *A* - inferior (in position, quality); lower (animals).
lavett' *-en mil.* gun carriage.
+**la'v/frekven's** *-en* cf **låg/**
+**la'v/gir** *-et* cf **låg/**
+**la'v/het** *-en* lowness; *fig.* baseness, meanness.
+**la'v/hælt** [/he'lt] *A* - cf **låg/hæla**
La'/vik *Pln* twp, Sogn og Fjordane.
lavi'ne *-n* avalanche (also *fig.*) (**av** of).
+**la'v/komisk** *A* - low-comedy, slapstick.
+**la'v/konjunktu'r** *-en merc.* depression, slump.
+**la'v/lanḍ** *-et* cf **låg/**
+**la'v/loftet** *A* - cf **låg/lofta**
+**la'v/mælt** [/me'lt] *A* - cf **låg/**
+**la'v/mål** *-et* cf **låg/**
+**la'v/pannet** *A* - low-browed; *fig.* base, course, low-minded.
+**la'v/sinnet** *A* - base, low-minded.
+**la'v/sko** *-en, pl -r/-* low shoe, oxford.
la'v/skrike *-a zool.* Siberian jay (Cractes infaustus).
+**la'v/slette** *-a* cf **låg/**
+**la'v/spenning** *-en* cf **låg/**
+**la'v/spent** *A* - cf **låg/**
+**la'v/trykk** *-et* cf **låg/**
+**la'vt/ståenḍe** *A* - inferior, low.
+**la'v/vann(e)** *-(e)t* cf **låg/**
+**la'v/vokst** *A* - cf **låg/**
+**la'v/ættet** *A* - cf **låg/ætta**
***la'v/øyrd** *A -øyrt* flap-eared; *fig.* crestfallen, dejected.
le'[1] *-et* 1 cover, shelter. 2 *naut.* lee, leeward: **i le av** to the lee of.
°**le'**[2] *-et* cf **led**[4]
le'[3] *V -r, lo, ledd/*lett* laugh (**av** at): **le bort** laugh off; **le en like (rett) opp i ansiktet** laugh right in sby's face; **le en ut** laugh sby down; **le over hele ansiktet** grin from ear to ear; **le seg fordervet (fillete)** laugh oneself sick; **den som ler sist ler best** he who laughs last laughs best.
le'a/laus *A* 1 (of a person) loose-jointed; (of a chair) rickety. 2 active, spry.
+**le'be** *-n* cf **leppe**
Le'bes/by *Pln* twp, Finnmark.
***le'ḍ**[1] *-a* side: **til l-s** to the side.
+**le'ḍ**[2] *-en* cf **lei**[1]
le'ḍ[3] *-en, pl *-er* (=+**ledd**[1]) 1 (body) joint: **ute av l-** dislocated. 2 link (*lit.* and *fig.*): **et l- i** a link in. 3 generation: **i tredje og fjerde l-** unto the third and fourth generation. 4 section (of a law).
le'ḍ[4] *-et* barway, gate.
+**le'ḍ**[5] *pt of* **li(de)**[1, 2]
+**le'ḍ**[6] *A* 1 detestable, disgusting, odious; repulsively ugly; evil, wicked (esp. of the devil, supernatural beings). 2 disgusted, tired: **jeg er l- og kjed av det hele** I am sick and tired of the whole business (Lie).
***le'ḍa/laus** *A* cf **lea/**
***le'ḍa/mot** *-et* cf **lede/**
ledd'[1] *-et* cf **led**[3]
ledd'[2] *pp of* **le**[3]
ledd'/dyr *-et zool.* arthropod, articulate animals.
+**led'de/løs** *A* - cf **lea/laus**
+**led'det** *A* - articulated, jointed.
ledd'/gikt *-a* arthritis.
led'dik *-en* till, tray (in a chest, drawer, trunk).
ledd'/knute *-n* 1 *anat.* condyle. 2 rheumatic swelling.
ledd'/orm *-en zool.* annelid.
ledd'/vatn *-et* (=+**/vann**) *anat.* synovial fluid.
ledd'/veḍ *-en bot.* fly honeysuckle (Lonicera xylosterun).
+**le'de**[1] *-n* disgust (**ved** with), distaste (**ved** for), loathing (**ved** of).
+**le'de**[2] *V -et* 1 guide, lead: **l- en på sporet** put sby on the track, give sby a clue; **l- samtalen hen på** lead up to, steer the conversation toward; **l- tanken hen på** call to mind, suggest; **l- til** lead to, result in. 2 be in charge of, conduct (e.g. an orchestra), manage (e.g. a business): **l- et møte** preside at a meeting; **l- trafikken** direct traffic. 3 *tech.* conduct (electricity, heat), pipe (a liquid).
***le'de**[3] *V -a* cf **lee**
+**le'de/bånḍ** *N obs.* leash: **være i ens l-** be dependent on one, be under one's influence.
+**le'de/evne** *-a/-en phys.* conductivity.
+**le'delse** *-n* conduct, direction (of affairs), guidance; management (of a company); leadership: **ta l-n** take command, take the lead.
+**le'de/løs** *A* cf **lea/laus**
+**le'de/mot** *-et* limb.
+**le'de/moti'v** *-et, pl -/-er* leitmotif.
+**le'denḍe** *A* - 1 guiding, leading (idea, principle; personality, politician; position). 2 *phys.* conducting, conductive.
+**le'der** *-en* (=***leiar**) 1 guide, leader. 2 *phys.* conductor. 3 *journ.* editorial.
+**le'der/plass** *-en* 1 place, position of leadership. 2 *journ.* editorial column.

+le'der/skap *-et* leadership.
+le'der/type *-n* leader type.
+-le'des *Av* cf **-leis**
+le'de/stjerne *-a/-en* guiding star, lodestar (usu. *fig.*).
+le'de/tråd *-en* clue; guide.
le'dig *A* - 1 free, idle, unoccupied: **løs og l-** unencumbered, unmarried; **gå l-** be idle, unemployed. 2 untaken, vacant (room, seat, table, etc.): **stå l-** (of a room, apartment) be vacant. 3 (of movements) lithe, supple; easy, free: **lett og l-** at ease. 4 (of clothing) comfortable, loose.
le'dig/gang *-en* idleness: **l- er fandens hodepute** ("idleness is the devil's pillow") idle hands are the devil's helpers.
+le'dig/gjenger *-en, pl -e* idler, loafer.
+le'dig/het *-en* 1 agility, freeness, limberness; ease, poise: **føre seg med l-** act with ease, show poise. 2 idleness, unemployment.
+le'ding *-en* cf **leidang**
***le'd/laus** *A* cf **lea/**
***le'd/mor** *-a* side post(s) on a barway.
+le'dning *-en* (=***leidning**) cable, conduit; line; pipe; wire: **vann/l-** water main.
+le'dnings/evne *-a/-en phys.* conductivity.
+le'dnings/nett *-et* (=***leidnings/**) overhead wires.
+le'd/sage *V -et* accompany (also *mus.*), escort: **l-t av** a-ed by.
+le'd/sagelse *-n* accompaniment (also *mus.*), attendance, escort.
+le'd/sager *-en, pl -e* 1 attendant, escort; companion. 2 *mus.* accompanist. 3 *astron.* satellite.
+le'dsager/grep *-et* come-along (hold used by police on unwilling suspects).
+le'd/sagerske *-a/-en* 1 (woman) attendant, escort; companion. 2 *mus.* (woman) accompanist.
+le'd/tog [/tåg] *-et*: **være i l- med** be an accomplice of, be in league with.
***le'dug** *A* - cf **leug**
***le'd/vatn** *-et* cf **ledd/**
***le'd/verk** *-en* rheumatism.
le'e *V -a/+-et* (=***lede**[3]) move, wiggle (slightly): **l- på** (the same), **l- (på) seg** (the same).
+lef'le *V -a/-et* 1 *lit.* dally, flirt (**med** with). 2: **l- for, med** coax, curry favor, wheedle; pander.
lef'se *-a* "lefse" (thin pancake from rolled dough served buttered and folded).
lef'se/kli(ni)ng *-en* buttered (and sugared) "lefse".
+le'g *A* cf **lek**[4]
***-leg** *A* - cf **-lig**
lega'l *A* legal.
legalise're *V -te* legalize; authenticate.
legasjo'n *-en* legation.
legasjo'ns/råd *-en* counselor of legation.
lega't[1] *-en eccl., hist.* legate.
lega't[2] *-et, pl -/+-er jur.* bequest, endowment, legacy.
legata'r *-en jur.* legatee.
+lega't/stifter *-en, pl -e* (=***-ar**) *jur.* legator; donor of a legacy.
leg'd[1] *-a* 1 (until 1900) system of poor relief, by which a given district supported one pauper: **være på l-** be on relief (usu. living in sby's home). 2 *hist., mil.* number of farms or district which maintained a soldier.
leg'd[2] *-a* (=**legde**[1]) lying position (esp. of grain in a field).
leg'de[1] *-a* cf **legd**[2]
***leg'de**[2] *-t* brood, hatch, litter.
leg'de/folk *pl* community-supported paupers (before 1900).
leg'ds/lem' *+-met/*-(m)en* community-supported pauper.
***le'ge**[1] *-a* 1 (bed) confinement: **ei lang l-** a long confinement. 2 bed, sleeping place. 3 anchorage.
le'ge[2] *-n* doctor, physician.
+le'ge[3] *V -et/-te* cure, heal (also *fig.*).
***le'ge**[4] *pp of* **liggje**
le'ge/attes't *-en* medical (or doctor's) certificate.
+le'ge/behan'dling *-en* medical treatment.
le'ge/bok *-a, pl -bøker* medical guide, manual.
le'ge/dom [+/dåmm] *-men/*-en* 1 healing power. 2 cure, healing. 3 medicament, medicine.
+le'ge/erklæ'ring *-en* medical (or doctor's) certificate.
le'ge/hjelp *-a/+-en* medical aid, advice; medical treatment: **søke l-** consult a doctor.
+le'geme *-t* (=***lekam**) body (animal, human, material, etc.); *(bibl., fig.)*: **Herrens l-** sacramental bread; *lit.* form, shape.
+le'ge/middel *-elet/-midlet, pl -midler* medicament, medicine, remedy.
+le'gemlig *A* - (=***lekamleg**) bodily, corporal; corporeal, physical.
+le'gemlig/gjøre *V -gjorde, -gjort* embody, incarnate.
+le'gems/beska'digelse *-n jur.* assault and battery.
+le'gems/bygning *-en* build, physique.
+le'gems/del *-en* part of the body.
+le'gems/feil *-en* bodily defect.
+le'gems/fornær'me *V -et jur.* assault.
+le'gems/fornær'melse *-n* assault.
+le'gems/høyde *-n* physical stature.
+le'gems/stor *A* life-size.
+le'gems/temperatu'r *-en* body temperature.
legenda'risk *A* - legendary.
legen'de *+-n/*-a* legend (also **l-** on a coin); myth.
+legen'de/dannelse *-n* 1 *hist.* formation of legend. 2 legendary account.
°le'gen/heit *-a* chance, occasion, opportunity.
lege're *V -te* 1 *jur.* bequeath. 2 alloy.
lege'ring *-a/+-en* 1 alloying. 2 alloy.
le'ger/vall *-et* 1 *naut., obs.* leeward shore. 2 *fam., obs.* dilemma, pinch.
+lege/råd *-et med.* remedy.
***le'ge/stad** *-en* resting place; grave.
le'ge/stand *-en/-et* medical profession.
+le'ge/undersøke *V -te* examine (medically).
+le'ge/undersøkelse *-n* medical examination.
le'ge/vakt *-a/+-en* 1 emergency, first aid doctor(s). 2 first aid station; emergency ward.
+le'ge/vitenskap *-en* (=**/vitskap**) medical science, medicine.
+le'ge/vitenskapelig *A* - (=***/vitskapleg**) relating to medical science.
legg[1] *-en, pl +*-er* 1 *anat.* calf, lower leg. 2 (stocking, trouser) leg. 3 (tree) trunk. 4 shank (of an anchor, instrument, tool, etc.).
legg'[2] *-et* 1 crease, fold, pleat; tuck. 2 fold, lift (of paper).
+leg'ge *V la, lagt* (=***-je**) 1 lay, place, put: **l- (sin) elsk på** take a fancy to; **l- hånd på** lay hands on, mistreat; **l- merke til** notice; **l- mye arbeid i** put a lot of work into; **l- ord i munnen på en** put words in sby's mouth; **l- vekt på** emphasize, stress; **l- vinn på** apply oneself to, take special care to; **l- øde** lay waste, destroy; **l- håret** have one's hair done; **l- maske** (of actor) apply make-up. 2 (with *prep.* and *adv.*): **l- an** organize, plan; **l- an på** aim for, intend to, make a point to; **l- an på en** be out to hook (a man), make a pass at (a woman); **l- av** discard, take off, (of a bad habit) break, drop; **l- av(garde) sted** leave, start off; **l- bak seg** leave behind; **l- bort** put aside, away; **l- (en) for hat** begin hating (sby); **l- fra land** shove off; **l- fra seg** put down; **l- fram** advance, present, submit (e.g. evidence, a theory); **l- i** place, put in (**l- i ovnen** light the fire; **l- en annen betydning i** construe differently; **l- hele sin sjel i** throw oneself into; **l- i mørke** darken, black out); **l- i seg** put away (large amounts of food); **l- i vei** set out, start off; **l- igjen** leave behind, leave (**l- igjen beskjed** leave a message); **l- inn** insert, put in, take in (a dress); **l- ned** lay down (arms, etc.); bring down (game); can, preserve (food); mow (a field of hay); invest (money); lengthen (dress); discontinue, stop (a factory, working); **l- om** change, rearrange, reorganize; **l- opp** lay up (reserves), save (money); plan (e.g. a route), prepare (**til** for); cease (an activity, operations); lay down (cards); shorten, take up (a dress); **l- opp (masker)** cast on, lay on (stitches); **l- over** place over; turn (car), bank (plane) sharply; **l- ansvaret over på** shift the responsibility to; **l- på** apply, put on; add to, increase (e.g. prices); **l- på plass** put in place, replace; **l- på røret** hang up (the telephone); **l- en noe på sinne** impress sby with sth, urge sth on sby; **l- på seg** put on weight; **l- på sprang (svøm)** take to one's heels (start swimming); **l- sammen** put together; add up, lump together; fold up; **l- til** add; *naut.* come alongside, dock; **l- til grunn for** use as a base, a starting point; **l- sitt navn til** lend one's name to; **l- til rette** arrange, put in order; **l- til side** lay aside; **l- under seg** conquer, gain control of; **l- ut** lay out, spend (money); let out (a dress); hold forth (on a topic); increase (knitting); **l- ut på** start out on (e.g. a trip); **l- ved** attach, enclose. 3 *(refl.)*: **l- seg** go to bed, lie down; (of the sea, emotions) abate, calm down; (of dust, snow) collect, settle; (of water) freeze; **l- seg bort i** interfere with; **l- seg etter** go in for, go after; **l- seg godt til rette** get settled comfortably; **l- seg imellom** intervene; **l- seg i trening** go into training; **l- seg opp** save up, set aside (e.g. money, supplies); **l- seg opp i** meddle in; **l- seg over på siden** (of a boat) list; **l- seg på alle fire** go down on all fours; **l- seg på sinne** bear in mind; **l- seg til** get into (bad habits); put on, affect (airs); acquire; take up dwelling, settle down; **l- seg til å sove** settle down to sleep; **l- seg ut** put on weight; **l- seg ut med** fall out with.
+leg'ge/tid *-a/-en* (=***-je/**) 1 laying season. 2 *fam.* bedtime.
***leggj'ast** *V legst, lagdest, lagst*: **det legst alltid noe til** there is always something more.
***leggj'e** *V legg, la/lagde, lagt* cf **legge**
legg'/muskel *-elen, pl -ler* calf muscle (*anat.* peroneus).
legg'/støvel *-elen, pl -ler* knee boot.
***le'gi** *pp of* **liggje**
le'gio *en lit.* legion, multitude.
legio'n *-en* 1 legion. 2: **l- er mitt navn; for vi er mange** *(bibl.)* my name is Legion: for we are many (Mark 5,9).
legionæ'r *-en* legionary.
legiti'm *A* lawful, legitimate.
legitimasjo'n *-en* 1 legitimation. 2 identification (document, paper, etc.).
legitimasjo'ns/kort *-et* identification card.
legitime're *V -te* legitimate; justify: **l- seg** establish, prove one's identity.
legitimite't *-en* legitimacy.
+le'g/mann *-en, pl -menn* cf **lek/**
+leg'ning *-en* 1 laying, placing, putting. 2 intellectual bent, turn.
***leg'st** *pr of* **leggjast**
lei'[1] *-a* 1 highway, road: **langt av l-** far away. 2 direction, side: **fra alle**

+ Bokmål; * Nynorsk; ° Dialect.
After letter: ' stress (Acc. 1); ` tone, stress (Acc. 2); · length.
Below letter: . not pronounced.

l-er from all sides. 3 distance: **på lang l-** far and wide, from far off. 4 shipping lane; channel, course.

lei'[2] *pt of* **li**[2]

lei'[3] *pt of* **li**[3]

lei'[4] *A* *-*tt* 1 mean, nasty, unpleasant; (of a situation) embarrassing, unfortunate: **det var l-t** that's too bad; **være l- mot** be nasty to; **være l- til å** be given to, have a way of (bragging, lying, etc.). 2 bored, tired (**av** with, of; also without prep.): **han ble lei hele arbeidet** he got tired of the whole job (Asbjørnsen); **se seg l- på** get sick of looking at; **spise seg l- på noe** get tired of eating sth. 3 sorry: **være l- seg** feel sorry, regret.

***lei'ar** *-en* cf **leder**

***lei'ar/plass** *-en* cf **leder/**

***lei'ar/skap** *-en* cf **leder/**

***lei'ast** *V -ddest, -st* 1 go hand in hand. 2 become bored and disgusted.

***lei'd**[1] *pt of* **li(de)**

***lei'd**[2] *A* cf **lei**[4]

lei'dang *-en* (=+**leding**) 1 *archaic* (sea) warfare. 2 *hist.* conscription for naval defenses. 3 *hist.* fleet of conscripted warships.

lei'de[1] *-t* safe conduct.

***lei'de**[2] *V -de* cf **leie**[5]

lei'de/brev *-et* letter of safe conduct.

lei'der *-en, pl +-e* 1 *naut.* ladder. 2 *naut.* stay.

lei'dner/flaske *-a* Leyden jar.

***lei'dning** *-en* cf **ledning**

***lei'dsle** *-a* cf **leisle**

***lei'e**[1] *-a* 1 boredom. 2 annoying, tiring, unpleasant person or thing.

+**lei'e**[2] *-a/-en* (=***leige**[1]) rent: **til l-** for rent.

lei'e[3] *-t, pl +-r/*-* (=***lægje**[1]) 1 bed (also of a river), couch; (of animals) lair. 2 *geol.* layer, stratum. 3 (correct) position: **ut av l-** dislocated, out of joint (e.g. an arm). 4 *mus.* range (of a voice). 5 *tech.* housing, undercarriage.

***lei'e**[4] *-t* 1 harm, injury. 2 annoyance, vexation.

lei'e[5] *V +-de/*-dde* guide, lead: **l- ved hånden l-** by the hand.

+**lei'e**[6] *V -de* (=***leige**[2]) 1 let, rent (**bort, ut** out): **l- seg inn hos** get lodgings with. 2 hire (for a certain job, period).

+**lei'e/avgift** *-a/-en* rent.

+**lei'e/boer** *-en, pl -e* lodger; tenant.

+**lei'e/folk** *-et* hired help, workers.

+**lei'e/gå·rḍ** *-en* apartment house; tenement building.

+**lei'e/hær** *-en* army of mercenaries.

+**lei'e/kontrak·t** *-en* lease, rent contract.

***lei'ende** *-t* annoying, tiring, unpleasant person or thing.

+**lei'er** *-en, pl -e* (=***leigar**) renter, tenant; lodger.

+**lei'er/mål** *-et jur., archaic* fornication.

*-**lei'es** *Av* e.g. in **bein/l-** by the shortest way; **fram/l-** furthermore, still, yet.

+**lei'e/solda·t** *-en* mercenary.

***lei'e/stanḍ** *-en* cf **lei/**

***lei'e/stjerne** *-a* cf **lede/**

+**lei'e/svenn** *-en* hireling (usu. *derog.*).

+**lei'e/tjener** *-en, pl -e* hired waiter.

+**lei'e/tropper** *pl* mercenaries.

Lei'f *Prn(m)*

lei'/fisk *-en fam.* annoying, tiring, unpleasant person.

***lei'gar** *-en* cf **leier**

***lei'ge**[1] *-a* cf **leie**[2]

***lei'ge**[2] *V -de* cf **leie**[6]

***lei'ge-** *pf* cf **leie-**

***lei'g/lending** *-en* cf **lei/**

lei'ing *-en fam.* annoying, tiring, unpleasant person.

lei'k *-en* (=+**lek**[1]) 1 play, playing: **drive l- med** play, toy with (e.g. one's feelings); **det gikk som en l-** there was nothing to it (e.g. a task). 2 contest, game: **de olympiske l-er** The Olympic Games; **ute av l-en** out of the running, inactive; **slutte mens l-en er god** quit before some-one gets hurt. 3 *archaic* (folk) dancing (now esp. in compounds, e.g. **l-ar/ring**). 4 (of animals esp. birds) mating ritual; (of people) flirtation.

*-**leik** *-en* e.g. in **kjær/l-** love; **ven/l-** beauty.

Lei'kanger *Pln* twp, Sogn og Fjordane.

***lei'kar** *-en* fiddler.

lei'kar/ring *-en* group of folk dancers.

lei'kar/voll *-en* (=***leik/**) (outdoor) field for folk dancing.

lei'ke[1] *-a* plaything, toy.

lei'ke[2] *V -a/-te* (=+**leke**[3]) 1 play: **l- med døden** flirt with death; **l- med en idé** toy with an idea; **l- med ord** play on words. 2 play at, pretend to be. 3 (of animals, esp. birds) mate; (of people) flirt. 4 **l-ende** (as *adv.*): **l-ende lett** easy as pie.

lei'ke/grinḍ *-a/-en* playpen.

lei'ke/kamera·t *-en* playmate.

lei'ken *A +-ent, pl -ne* (=+**leken**) frolicsome, playful.

lei'ke/plass *-en* playground.

lei'ke/stue *-a* playroom; playhouse.

+**lei'ke/søster** *-era/-eren, pl -re(r)* playmate (girl).

+**lei'ke/tøy** *-et* (=***/ty**) plaything, toy (also *fig.*).

lei'ke/værelse *-t* nursery, playroom.

***lei'k/voll** *-en* cf **leikar/**

+**lei'/lenḍing** *-en* tenant farmer.

+**lei'lig/het** *-en* 1 chance, opportunity: **få, ha l- til** get, have the opportunity to; **gripe l-en** seize the opportunity; **(gjøre noe) ved l-** (do sth) at one's convenience, when one has the opportunity. 2 occasion: **ved flere l-er** on several occasions. 3: **etter fattig (ringe) l-** to the best of one's modest abilities, in a small way. 4 apartment, flat: **en fireværelses l-** a four-room a-.

+**lei'lighets/arbeid** *-et* (artistic) work produced for special occasion.

+**lei'lighets/dikter** *-en, pl -e* occasional poet.

+**lei'lighets/tilbud** *-et* chance or special offer.

+**lei'lighets/vis** *Av* occasionally, on occasion.

***lei'n**[1] *-a* 1 slant, slope. 2 side piece (e.g. in loom).

***lei'n**[2] *A* slanting, sloping.

***lei'ne** *V -te* slant, slope.

Lei'n/stranḍ *Pln* twp, Sør-Trøndelag.

lei'r[1] *-en* camp (military, political, prison, recreational, etc.): **ligge i l-** camp; **slå l-** pitch camp; *fig.* go to battle; **liv i l-en** tumult, uproar (in a crowd or group); merriment, merrymaking.

lei'r[2] *-et* (=**leire**[1]) clay, (also *fig.*) mortal clay.

Lei'ranger *Pln* twp, Nordland.

lei'r/bakke *-n* hill of clayey soil.

lei'r/bløyte *-a* clayey mud.

lei'r/botn *-en* (=+**/bunn**) clayey soil; clayey bottom (under water).

lei'r/bål [also **lei'r/**] *-et* campfire.

lei'r/due *-a* clay pigeon.

lei're[1] *-a* cf **leir**[2]

lei're[2] *V -a/+-et* (=***lægre**[1]) 1: **l- seg** camp, pitch camp. 2 *geol.* **l- seg** be deposited.

lei're/mark** *-en* (=/makk**) *zool.* lugworm (Arenicola marina).

lei'ret(e) *A -* clayey.

lei'r/fall *-et* clay slide; hill, slope of moving clayey soil.

lei'r/fat *-et* earthenware dish.

lei'r/fivel *-elen, pl -ler bot.* coltsfoot (Tussilago farfara).

Lei'r/fjo·rḍ *Pln* twp, Nordland.

lei'r/gauk *-en* ocarina.

lei'r/golv *-et* dirt floor.

lei'r/grunn *-en* clayey soil; clayey bottom (under water).

lei'r/jo·rḍ *-a* 1 clayey soil. 2 *chem.* alumina.

lei'r/kar *-et* earthen vessel, pottery.

lei'r/liv [also **lei'r/**] *-et* camping; camp life.

lei'r/plass [also **lei'r/**] *-en* campground, camping place, camp site.

lei'r/ras *-et* clay slide.

lei'r/skreppe *-a* coltsfoot leaf.

+**lei'r/sla·gning** [also **lei'r/**] *-en* setting up camp.

+**lei'r/tøy** *-et* earthenware, pottery.

lei'r/varer *pl* earthenware, pottery.

-leis *Av* (=+**-ledes**) e.g. **ann/l-** differently, otherwise; **så/l-** in this manner, thus.

***lei'/sam** *A* annoying, troublesome.

***lei'/skap** *-en* annoyance; unpleasantness.

***lei'sle** *-a* annoyance, vexation; unhappiness.

lei'st *-en* cf **lest**[1]

lei'/stanḍ *-en*: **i l-** arm in arm; hand in hand.

***lei'ste** *V -a* 1 walk slowly, drag one's feet. 2 last (a shoe).

***lei't**[1] *-en* looking, searching, seeking: **på l- etter** in search of.

lei't[2] *pt of* **lite**

***lei'tar** *-en* looker, searcher, seeker.

lei'te[1] *-t* 1 (approximate) time: **ved dette l-** about this time. *2 elevation, height (giving a good view); horizon.

lei'te[2] *V -a/+-te/+lette* (=+**lete**[4]) hunt (**etter** for), look for, seek: **den som l-er, han finner** he that seeketh findeth (Matt. 7,6); **det skal en l- lenge etter** you'll look a long time for that (i.e. you won't find it); **l- etter ordene** fumble for words; **l- fram** find by searching; **l- opp** hunt up, look up; **l- seg fram** find one's way (by hunting).

lei'te[3] *V -a/+-et/+-te* strain, tax, tire: **l- på** be nerve-racking, taxing.

***leitt'** *nt of* **lei**[4]

*-**leitt** *A* cf **-lett**

lei'v[1] *-a dial.* leaving(s), remain(s), remnant.

lei'v[2] *-en* 1 piece of *flatbrød* or *lefse*. 2 large, thick slice of bread.

Lei'v *Prn(m)*

-leiv *Prn(m)* e.g. **Gunnleiv, Torleiv.**

***lei'vd** *-a* cf **leiv**[1]

***lei've**[1] *-a* cf **leiv**[1]

***lei've**[2] *V -de* cf **levne**[2]

***lei'vning** *-en* cf **levning**

+**le'k**[1] *-en* cf **leik**

***le'k**[2] *-en* cf **lekk**[1]

***le'k**[3] *A* cf **lekk**[3]

le'k[4] *A* (usu. +**leg**) lay (e.g. person, preacher); unlearned.

Le'ka *Pln* twp, Nord-Trøndelag.

***le'kam** *-en* cf **legeme**

***le'kamleg** *A -* cf **legemlig**

le'k/bror *-en, pl +-brødre/*-brør eccl.* lay brother.

+**le'k/dommer** *-en, pl -e* (=***-ar**) juror.

+**le'ke**[1] *-n* cf **leike**[1]

***le'ke**[2] *V lak, leke/-i* cf **lekke**

+**le'ke**[3] *V -te* cf **leike**[2]

+**le'ke/grinḍ** *-a* cf **leike/**

+**le'ke/kamera·t** *-en* cf **leike/**

+**le'ken** *A -ent, pl -ne* cf **leiken**

+**le'ke/plass** *-en* cf **leike/**

+**le'ke/stue** *-a* cf **leike/**

+**le'ke/tøy** *-et* cf **leike/**

lekk'[1] *-en* (=***lek**[2]) 1 leak. 2 leakage (act of leaking).

lekk'[2] *-en dial.* link.

lekk'[3] *A lekt* (=***lek**[3]) leaky.

lekka'sje *-n* leakage (of air, gas, news, water, etc.); leak.

+**lek'ke** *V -et/lekte/lakk, lekt* (=***leke**[2]) leak (air, gas, news, water, etc.).

lek'ker *A -ert, pl lekre* 1 (of food) delicious, luscious. 2 (of clothing) elegant, tasteful; (of a person) appealing, nice, sweet; (of a place) appealing, inviting.

+**lek'ker/bisken** *-en* delicacy, tidbit (also *fig.*); tasty morsel, dish.

+**lekkeri'** *-et archaic* delicacy, tidbit.

lek'ker/munn *-en* epicure, gourmand.

***lekkj'e**[1] *-a* cf **lenke**[1]

***lekkj'e**[2] *V lekte* cf **lenke**[2]

le'k/mann *-en, pl -menn/*-menner* layman.

le'k/predikan't *-en* (=***/preikar**) lay preacher.

lek're *pl and df of* **lekker**

lek'se[1] *-a/+-en* 1 lesson (also *eccl.*); homework. 2 same thing over and over, old story.

lek'se[2] *V -a/+-et* 1: **l- opp** rattle on and on. 2: **l- opp for en** chastise, teach one a lesson.

lek'se/fri *N* without lessons: **det er l- første dag etter ferien** there are no lessons the first day after vacation.

lek'se/pugg *-et* cramming.

lek'sika *pl of* **leksikon**

leksika'lsk *A* - lexical.

lek'sikon *-et, pl leksika/+-er/*-* 1 dictionary. 2 encyclopedia. 3 *fam.* anagrams (=**l-/spill**, a card game).

leksjo'n *-en* 1 lesson (esp. as numbered in a book: **første l-**). 2 *fam.* scolding.

Lek's/vik *Pln* twp, Nord-Trøndelag.

lek't[1] *-a* (=**lekte[1]**) lath.

lek't[2] *nt of* **lekk[3]**

lek'te[1] *-a* cf **lekt[1]**

+lekte[2] *pt of* **lekke, leke[3]**

lek'ter *-en, pl +-e* barge, lighter.

lektie [lek'tsie] *-n* 1 lesson (esp. *eccl.*). 2 something over and over, old story.

lek'tor *-en, pl -to'rer educ.* title for highest rank of secondary school teachers and for certain university teachers.

lektora't *-et, pl +-er/*- educ.* position as *lektor*.

lek'tor/eksa'men *-en educ.* humanities or mathematics degree final (at university), entitling successful candidate to degree of *cand. filol.* and qualifying for position as *lektor*.

lekty're *-n* reading (material).

lell' *Av pop.* after all, all the same, nevertheless.

lem'[1] *-men* 1 trapdoor; shutter. 2 attic; loft. 3 flap.

lem'[2] *+-met/*-(m)en, pl -mer/*-er* 1 limb, member, organ (of the body). 2 member (of a church, family, etc.); inmate.

***le'm[3]** *pr of* **lemje**

***le'me** *V -a* cf **lemme[2]**

lem'en *-et, pl -/+-er zool.* lemming.

lem'en/vandring *-a/+-en* lemming migration.

+lemfel'dig *A* - gentle, lenient, mild.

+lemfel'dig/het *-en* gentleness, leniency, mildness.

***lem'je** *V lem, lamde, lamt* 1 paralyze. 2 beat, drub soundly. 3 roar, thunder.

+lem'/leste *V -a/-et* 1 maim, mutilate. 2 dismember (also *fig.*).

lem'me[1] *V -a/+-et* (=**lamme[1]**) lamb, bring forth lambs.

lem'me[2] *V -a/+-et* (=***leme**): **l- opp** dismember.

lem'pe[1] *+-n/*-a* caution, gentleness: **med l-** cautiously, gently: **med list og l-** by hook or crook.

lem'pe[2] *V -a/+-et* adjust, arrange: **l- på** ease, modify; **l- seg** accommodate, adapt oneself (**etter** to).

lem'pe[3] *V -a/+-et* 1 ease, move carefully, slowly; maneuver (a person). 2 *naut.* stevedore; stow, trim (cargo). 3 throw out; *naut.* heave over board.

lem'pelig *A* - 1 fitting, suitable. 2 gentle, lenient, mild.

+lem'pelse *-n* easement, modification; concession, favor.

lem'ster *A -ert, pl -re* stiff (after strong exertion).

***lem'stre** *V -a* 1 exhaust, fatigue. 2 crush.

le'/mus *-a* small muscle spasm, twitch.

le'n *-et* 1 *hist.* fief. 2 county (in Sweden).

len'd *-a* 1 loin (usu. *bibl., poet.*): **binde opp om sine l-er** gird up one's loins. 2 flank (of an animal); (horse's) shank.

len'de[1] *-t* terrain.

***len'de[2]** *V -e* cf **lande**

len'de/klede [*/klee] *-t* loincloth.

+len'der/mann *-en, pl -menn* cf **lend/**

***len'ding** *-a* 1 landing. 2 landing place.

-len'ding *-en* suffix denoting person's geographic origin e.g. **is/l-** Icelander; **nord/l-** person from Nordland; **sør/l-** person from southern Norway.

len'd/mann *-en, pl -menn/*-menner hist.* feudal lord, nobleman, (royal) vassal.

***-len'dsk** *A* - cf **-landsk**

-len'dt *A* - e.g. **bratt/l-** cliffy, craggy; **myr/l-** marshy.

le'ne[1] *-t, pl +-r/*-* rest (on furniture).

le'ne[2] *V +-te/*-a* lean: **l- seg** lean (**mot, til** against, **på** on).

le'ne/stol *-en* armchair, easy chair.

leng'd *-a* (=**+lengde**) 1 (of distance) length; longitude: **etter hele sin l-e** at full length; **i l-en** in length, long; **på 50° l-e** at longitude 50°. 2 (of time) duration, length: **i l-en** in the long run.

+leng'de *-n* cf **lengd**

leng'de/grad *-en* degree of longitude.

leng'de/hopp *-et* broad jump.

+leng'de/løp *-et* race (on ice skates).

+leng'de/løps/skøyter *pl* (ice) racing skates, speed skates.

***leng'de/mælar** *-en* cf **/mål**

leng'de/mål *-et* linear measure.

leng'de/retning *-a/+-en* longitudinal direction.

leng'de/sprang *-et* broad jump.

***leng'dest** *pt of* **lengjast**

leng'e *Av, cp lenger, sp lengst* 1 for a long time, long: **for l- siden** a long time ago; **ikke på l-** not for a long time; **(ikke) på aldri så l-** (not) for a very long time, for ever so long; **innen l-** before not too long, soon; **langt om l-** at long last, finally; **(gjøre noe) så l-** (do sth) in the meantime; for a time, for the present; **være l- om** take a long time at; **farvel så l-** so long. 2 (*sup.*) **lengst** for a long time; **for lengst** long since, long ago (**jeg var for lengst ferdig** I was finished long ago).

leng'er *cp of* **langt, lenge**

+leng'es *V lengtes, lenges* cf **lengte**

***-leng'es** *Av* cf **-lengs**

***leng'ing** *-a* lengthening, prolongation (**av** of).

***leng'jast** *V -gjest, -dest, lengst* cf **lengte**

***leng'je** *V -de* lengthen, prolong.

leng're *cp of* **lang[2]**

-leng's *Av* (=***-lenges**) e.g. **bak/l-** backward(s); **fram/l-** forward(s).

leng'sel *-elen, pl -ler* (=***lengsle**) longing, yearning (**etter, mot** for).

+leng'sels/full *A* longing(ly), yearning(ly).

***leng'sle** *-a* cf **lengsel**

leng'st[1] *sp of* **lang(t)[2], lenge**

***leng'st[2]** *pp of* **lengjast**

leng't *-en* longing, yearning.

leng'te *V -a/+-et* (=**+lenges**) long, yearn (**etter** for, **etter å** to): **l- hje** be homesick.

+len'k *-en* link.

+len'ke[1] *-a/-en* (=***lekkje[1]**, ***lenkje**) 1 chain, fetter: **legge i l-r** put in chains. 2 lengths of fishnet (fastened together). 3 link (in machinery).

+len'ke[2] *V -a/-et* (=***lekkje[2]**) 1 chain, fetter. 2 hook up, link (**sammen** together).

+len'ke/hund *-en* chained watchdog.

***len'kje** *-a* cf **lenke[1]**

len's *A* - 1 clear, empty, free (from water): **øse l-** bail; *pop.*, esp. *naut.* **slå l-** take a leak (urinate). 2 bare, devoid (**for** of): **l- for penger** broke. 3 *naut.* running downwind.

le'ns/adel *-en hist.* feudal nobility.

len'se[1] *-a* timber boom.

len'se[2] *V -a/+-et/+-te* bail, empty (a boat, well, etc.): **l- seg for** get rid of.

len'se[3] *V -a/+-et/+-te naut.* run before the wind, scud.

len'se/pumpe *-a naut.* bilge pump.

le'ns/herre *-n hist.* feudal lord.

len's/mann *-en, pl -menn/*-menner* 1 administrative official in the country, similar to a sheriff or bailiff. 2 *hist.* vassal.

len'smanns/betjen't *-en* **lensmann's** clerk.

***le'ns/skipnad** *-en hist.* feudalism.

+le'ns/vesen *-et hist.* feudalism.

Len's/vik *Pln* twp, Sør-Trøndelag.

***len'te/krok** *-en* humorist.

***len'ter** *pl* fun; jokes, tricks.

***len'tug** *A* - 1 jesting, jocular. 2 clever, cunning.

Len'/vik *Pln* post office, Nordland.

leopar'd *-en zool.* leopard.

le'pe[1] *-n* cf **leppe**

+le'pe[2] *V -te* hang down unevenly (e.g. of a skirt hem).

le'pet(e) *A* - hanging down unevenly.

lep'je *V -a/+-et* lap, slurp.

lepp' *-en* patch, scrap; strip.

lep'pe *-a/+-en* (=**lepe[1]**, ***lippe**) lip: **ordet ligger meg på l-n** it is on the tip of my tongue; (*anat.*, *bot.*) labium.

lep'pe/lyd *-en* labial (in phonetics).

lep'pe/stift *-en* lipstick.

le'pra *-en* leprosy.

le'pra/basill' *-en* leprosy bacillus.

***le'r[1]** *-et* cf **lær**

+le'r[2] *-et* cf **leir[2]**

+le're *-n* cf **leire[1]**

***ler'eft** *-et* cf **lerret**

+le'r/gjøk *-en* cf **leir/gauk**

***ler'k[1]** *-en* till, tray (in a chest, drawer, trunk).

ler'k[2] *-en bot.* larch.

ler'ke[1] *-a* 1 *zool.* lark. 2 *fam.* lively, merry woman.

ler'ke[2] *-a* hip (pocket) flask.

ler'ke/blid *A* gentle, mild (as a lark).

ler'ke/tre *-et, pl -/+-trær bot.* larch tree.

ler'ret *-et, pl -/+-er* 1 linen (cloth); duck; canvas: **et langt l- å bleke** an endless task. 2 painter's canvas: **det hvite l-** the (movie) screen.

ler'rets/vev *-en* linen weave.

le'se *V +-te/*las, +-t/*-e/*-i* 1 read: **l- opp** read out loud; **l- noe som fanden leser Bibelen** intentionally misinterpret sth; **l- seg til** acquire (knowledge, ideas, etc.) through reading. 2 study: **l- engelsk** study English (as one's major subject); **l- lekser** study one's lessons; do one's homework; **l- med en** study with, be tutored by sby; tutor sby; **l- på spreng** cram; **gå og l- (for presten)** read for the minister (in preparation for confirmation). 3 recite (prayers and other formulas): **l- over en** pray for sby, utter charms for sby; **l- til (fra) bords, for maten** say grace.

le'se/bok *-a, pl -bøker* reader.

le'se/briller *pl* reading glasses.

+le'se/ferdighet *-en* reading ability, proficiency.

***le'se/før** *A* proficient in reading.

le'/segl *-et* (=**+/seil**) *naut.* studdingsail.

le'se/hest *-en* bookworm; diligent reader.

+le'se/hode *-t* one who has a bent for reading, studying.

+le'se/krets *-en* (circle of) readers (of an author, newspaper, etc.).

le'selig *A* - 1 legible. 2 readable, worth reading.

le'se/lyst *-a/+-en* love of reading.

le'se/plan *-en* curriculum, syllabus.

le'se/prøve *-a/+-en* (theater) reading, rehearsal.

+le'ser *-en, pl -e* (=***-ar**) 1 reader. 2 pietist; Haugean (cf **haugianer**).

+le'ser/folk *pl* (=***-ar/**) Haugeans or other pietistic people.

+ Bokmål; * Nynorsk; ° Dialect.
After letter: ' stress (Acc. 1); ' tone, stress (Acc. 2); · length.
Below letter: . not pronounced.

le'se/sal *-en* reading room.
le'se/selskap *-et, pl -/+-er* reading society.
le'se/sirkel *-elen, pl -ler* reading circle; club.
le'se/stoff *-et* reading material, matter.
le'se/stykke *-t, pl +-r/*-* reading selection.
le'se/tone *-n* monotone.
le'se/verdig *A* - readable, worth reading.
+**le'se/værelse** *-t* reading room.
le'/side [*/sie] *-a/+-en* 1 side turned away from the wind. 2 *naut.* lee side.
Lesj'a *Pln* twp, Oppland.
lesjo'n *-en* injury, lesion.
les'ke *V -a/+-et* 1 slake (lime). 2 quench, slake (thirst); refresh.
les'ke/drikk *-en* refreshing drink, thirst-quencher; soft drink.
le'/skur *-et* shed, shelter.
*__le'snad__ *-en* cf **lesning**
+**le'sning** *-en* (=*-**nad, -ing**) 1 reading; studying: **ved nærmere l- av** on closer perusal, study of. 2 reading material.
les'p *A* lisping.
les'pe *V -a/+-et* lisp.
+**less'**[1] *-et* cf **lass**
+**less'**[2] *V* - (=+**lest**[5]) *dial.* act, pretend as if: **mannen l- ikke høre** the man acts as if he doesn't hear (see ***låst**).
les'se *V +-te/*leste* 1 load: **l- på** load, **l- av** unload; **l- noe på en** burden one with sth.
+**les't**[1] *-en* (=***leist**) 1 stocking foot. 2 (cobbler's) last; shoetree; *fig.*: **slå over samme l-** cut, form from the same pattern; **skjære, slå alle over én l-** handle, treat everyone alike; **bli ved sin l-** stick, tend to one's own knitting.
les't[2] *-en, pl *-er obs.* 1 *naut.* last (ab. 4000 lbs.). 2 (dry measure) twelve barrels.
les't[3] *-en dial.* dense grass, grain.
***les't**[4] *N*: **på l-** as a pretense.
+**les't**[5] *V* cf **less**[2]
***les't**[6] *pt of* **låst**
les'te *V -a/+-et dial.*: **l- seg** grow densely.
***les'ter** *-en* cf **lesning**
***le't**[1] *-en, pl -er* cf **lett**[1]
***le't**[2] *pr, pt of* **la**[3], **late**[1]
+**le't**[3] *pt of* **lite**[1]
***le't**[4] *pt of* **låte**
***le'ta** *A* - colored, dyed.
***le'te**[1] *-a* laziness, sloth.
***le'te**[2] *V -a* color, dye.
***le'te**[3] *V -a*: **l- seg** idle, loaf.
+**le'te**[4] *V -te* cf **leite**[2]
***le'ting**[1] *-en* lazybones, sluggard.
+**le'ting**[2] *N* search: **dra på l-** go searching (**etter** for).
let'ne *V -a/+-et* 1 become lighter, ease up, lighten. 2 clear away, up (of fog, weather, etc.).
lett'[1] *-en* (=***let**[1]) color(ing), complexion, hue.
***lett'**[2] *pp of* **le**[2]
lett'[3] *A* - 1 light (in weight, color, construction, intensity, etc.); (of movements) graceful, lithe; mild (in effect, taste, etc.); gentle (e.g. a breeze): **et l- sinn** a cheerful disposition; **sove l-** sleep lightly, uneasily; **ta noe l-** not worry about sth; **være l- på det (tråden)** have loose morals; **være l- på hånden** have a light touch, be careful in handling (sth); **være l- til bens (fots)** be nimble. 2 easy: **bli l- sint** become angry quickly, be hot-tempered; **falle en l-** be easy for sby; **ha l- for noe** have a talent for sth; **slippe l- (fra)** get off easy. 3 slight, superficial: **l- såret** slightly wounded.
+**-lett** *A* - (=***-leitt**) e.g. **lang/l-** long-faced; **rød/l-** ruddy-faced.
+**lett'/anten'nelig** *A* - combustible, inflammable.
+**lett'/beder'velig** *A* - perishable (usu. of food).
lett'/beint *A* - 1 light-footed. 2 irresponsible; shallow.
+**lett'/beve'gelig** *A* - 1 mobile. 2 impressionable, impulsive.
***lett'/budd** *A* - lightly equipped.
***lett'/bær** *A* light, easy to carry.
lett'/båt [also lett'/] *-en* small, light rowboat.
+**lett'/dreven** *A -ent/-et, pl -ne* easy to manage, run (of a farm).
let'te[1] *-n* 1 relief. 2 clearing up (e.g. in the weather).
let'te[2] *V -a/+-et* 1 ease, lighten, relieve; (of work, etc.) make easier; *pop.* steal: **l- for** free of, empty of; *hum.* **l- en for penger** relieve sby of his money; **l- sitt hjerte** get sth off one's chest; *naut.* **l- på roret** ease the helm; **føle seg l-et** feel relieved; **puste l-et** heave a sigh of relief; **det l-er (å)** it's relieving, it helps (to); **været l-er** the weather is improving, it's clearing up. 2 lift: *naut.* **l- anker** weigh anchor; **l- opp** lift (up); **l- på** lift slightly, tip (a hat); **l- på seg** get up, get moving; **l- seg opp** rise. 3 (of airplanes, birds) rise, take off.
+**let'te**[3] *pt of* **leite**[2], **lete**[4]
let'te/ko'rn [*/kånn] *-et* cf **lett/**
let'telig *A* - *1 easy, favorable. 2 *(adv.)* easily, comfortably.
+**let'telse** *-n* cf **lette**[1]
+**let'ter**[1] *-en, pl -e* (=*-**ar**) one who steals from smugglers; hijacker.
+**let'ter**[2] *-en, pl -e* (=*-**ar**) Latvian.
+**let'tet** *A* - lightened; eased, relieved.
+**lett'/fattelig** *A* - easily intelligible.
+**lett'/fengelig** *A* - inflammable.
***lett'/fengen** *A -e/-i, pl -ne* inflammable.
+**lett'/fengt** *A* - (=*/**fengd**) *dial.* 1 accessible, easily obtainable. 2 commodious, convenient. 3 dexterous, handy.
+**lettfer'dig** *A* - 1 frivolous, irresponsible. 2 improper, wanton (in morals).
+**lettfer'dig/het** *-en* 1 frivolity, irresponsibility. 2 impropriety, wantonness.
lett'/flytende *A* - 1 of low viscosity. 2 fluent (in expression).
+**lett'/fordøy'elig** *A* - easily digestible.
***lett'/før** *A* 1 quick (in movement). 2 easy to handle, manage. 3 accessible, easily passable (of a road, etc.).
***lett'/gjengd** *A -/-gjengt* 1 nimble, spry. 2 accessible, easily passable (of a road, etc.).
lett'/hendt *A* - 1 dexterous, handy. 2 gentle, indulgent, lenient.
+**lett'/het** *-en* 1 lightness (of weight). 2 ease, facility (of behavior, manner): **med l-** easily.
+**lett'/håndte'rlig** *A* - easy to handle, manage.
***let'tings/slede** *-n* one-horse sleigh.
let'tisk *A* - Latvian.
lett'/kjennelig *A* - easily recognizable.
lett'/kjøpt *A* - 1 easily come by. 2 cheap, ordinary: **en l- vits** a cheap witticism.
lett'/ko'rn [*/kånn] *-et* grain with little or no kernel.
***lett'/køyrd** [/kj-] *A -køyrt* easy to drive.
Lett'/land *Pln* Latvia.
***lett'leg** *A* - 1 pleasant, comfortable. 2 courteous, polite.
lett'/lending *-en* Latvian.
+**lett'/le'st** *A* - 1 legible. 2 clear, intelligible.
lett'/liva *A* - (=+**-et**) 1 gay, lighthearted. 2 frivolous, irresponsible; superficial.
lett'/lynt *A* - (=*/**lyndt**) 1 gay, lighthearted. 2 frivolous, irresponsible.
lett'/matro's *-en naut.* ordinary seaman.
lett'/metall' *-et, pl -/+-er* light metal.
lett'/rodd *A -/*-rott* easily rowed.
lett'/rø'rt *A* - 1 impulsive, easily set off (e.g. fantasy, laughter, etc.). 2 easily moved, emotional.
+**lettsin'dig** *A* - heedless, rash; frivolous, irresponsible.
+**lettsin'dig/het** *-en* 1 dissoluteness, wantonness. 2 heedlessness, rashness; irresponsibility.
lett'/sinn *-et* heedlessness, rashness; irresponsibility.
lett'/skya *A* - (=+**-et**) lightly overcast.
+**lett'/troende** *A* - cf **/truen**
lett'/truen *A +-ent, pl -ne* credulous, gullible.
+**lett'/vekter** *-en, pl -e* (=*-**ar**) 1 lightweight (boxer, wrestler). 2 light motorcycle. 3 *fig.* person without moral (artistic, intellectual) weight; bluffer.
lett'/vektig *A* - light (also *fig.*), lightweight.
lett'/vint *A* - (=*/**vinn**) 1 easy, facile (work, etc.); handy, ready (method, tool, etc.). 2 heedless, irresponsible (action, person, etc.); superficial. 3 agile, nimble (person).
+**lett'vint/het** *-en* 1 ease, facility, simplicity; handiness, readiness. 2 heedlessness, irresponsibility, superficiality. 3 agility, nimbleness.
+**lett'værs/båt** *-en naut.* fair weather boat.
+**le'ug** *A* - (=***ledug**) agile, limber, lithe.
leukemi' *-en med.* leukemia.
Levang'er *Pln* town (and twp), Nord-Trøndelag.
Levan'ten *Pln* the Levant.
le've[1] *et*: **utbringe et l- for en** call for three cheers for sby.
le've[2] *V -de* be alive, live; exist: **l- kongen** long live the king!; **l- av** live by, on; **l- for** live for (a person, a cause); live on (a certain amount per month); **l- for seg selv** live by oneself, alone; **l- i den tro at** labor under the illusion that; **l- i ufred med** be on bad terms with; **l- i uvitenhet om** be ignorant of; **l- opp igjen** revive (memories), relive (the past); **l- på** live off of, on; **så sant jeg l-er** upon my life.
le've/alder *-en* 1 age, duration of life. 2 *lit.* generation.
le've/brød *-et* livelihood, living, work; bread-and-butter.
+**le'vebrøds/poli'tiker** *-en, pl -e* (=*-**ar**) *derog.* professional politician.
le've/dag *-en* day of one's life: **aldri i mine l-er** never in (all) my born days.
le've/dyktig *A* - viable; capable of living, surviving (also *fig.*).
le've/kostnad *-en* cost of living.
le'vekostnads/indeks *-en* cost of living index.
le'velig *A* - 1 endurable, worth living. 2 habitable, livable.
le've/lysten *A +-ent, pl -ne* full of vitality, zest for life.
le've/mann *-en, pl -menn/*-menner* man about town; fast liver.
le've/måte *-n* 1 mode of living. 2 breeding, manners. 3 *fam.* fare, provisions.
le'ven *-et* 1 commotion, noise, uproar; horseplay, mischief. 2 fun, merriment: **for, på l-** for fun, for the fun of it; **holde l-** make a row; have fun; **holde l- med** ridicule, tease.
***le'vende**[1] *-t* living being, creature.
le'vende[2] *A* - alive, living; lively, vital (e.g. an interest), vivid (e.g. a description, an impression): **l- lys** candles; **l- kraft** kinetic energy; **bli l-** come alive; **(male, tegne) etter l- modell** (paint, draw) from life; **ikke en l- sjel** not a soul; (as *adv.*) **l- grepet** deeply moved; **fortelle noe l-** tell sth vividly; **gjøre noe l-** animate, make sth come alive; **se noe l- for seg** see sth vividly; large as life.
+**le'vende/født** *A* - live-born.
+**le'vende/gjøre** *V -gjorde, -gjort* 1 animate, vivify; *(bibl.)*: **bokstaven slår ihjel, men ånden l-gjør** the letter killeth, but the spirit giveth life

(II Cor. 3,6). 2 evoke; personify; elucidate.
+le've/omkostninger *pl* cost of living.
lev'er *levra, pl *levrar* 1 *anat.* liver. 2: **snakke fra l-en** *fig.* speak one's mind, speak straight from the shoulder; **frisk på l-en** dauntless; vigorous.
leverandø'r *-en merc.* purveyor, supplier.
leveranse [leverang'se] *-n merc.* contract, order; delivery: **på l-** on delivery.
+leveranse/dyktig *A - merc.* able to deliver.
leve're *V -te* 1 furnish, supply, provide (milk, electricity, etc.); bring forward, produce, submit (e.g. proof). 2 deliver, hand in (over), present; give up (ticket).
le've/regel *-elen, pl -ler* maxim, rule (of conduct).
leve'ring *-a/+-en merc.* delivery: **på l-** for, on forward delivery; delivery (wares), order.
+leve'rings/dyktig *A - merc.* able to deliver.
lev'er/mølje *-a* dish consisting of "flatbread" and liver fat.
le've/rop *-et* cheer, hurrah.
lev'er/postei' *-en* liver paste.
lev'er/pølse *-a* liver sausage.
lev'er/tran *-a/-en* cod-liver oil.
le've/sett *-et* mode of living.
le've/standard *-en* standard of living.
le've/tid *-a/+-en* 1 lifetime (of an animal, person; government, etc.). 2 days, time: **i Homers l-** in the days of Homer.
le've/veg *-en* (=+/**vei**) business, career, vocation.
le've/vilkår *-et* living condition.
le've/vis *-a/-en/-et* mode of living.
le've/år *-et* year (of one's life).
levitt' *-en (bibl.)* Levite.
levkøy' *-en bot.* stock (Matthiola annua).
+lev'ne[1] *V -a/-et* cf **livne**
+lev'ne[2] *V -a/-et* (=***leive**[2]) leave: **ikke l- en ære for to øre** not have one good word to say for sby.
+lev'net *-et* (=***livnad**) *lit.* life: **han førte et syndens l-** he led a life of sin.
+lev'nets/løp *-et* career, course of life.
+lev'nets/middel *-elet/-midlet, pl -midler* fare, food, provision.
+lev'nets/skildring *-en* biography, life.
+lev'ning *-en* (=***leivning**) leaving, remain, remnant; (food) scrap: **jordiske l-er** mortal remains; relic (from the past).
lev're *V -a/+-et* (of blood) clot, coagulate.
levvel [le'v vel'] *et* farewell.
lex' *N* (the) law: **Lex Thagaard** a price control law of 1945 assoc. w. W. Thagaard.
l'hombre [lå'mber] *-n* omber (card game).
li'[1] *-a* wooded or grassy hillside, mountainside.
li'[2] *V lei, -dd* (=**lide**[1]) 1 advance, pass, wear on (of time): **når det l-r om litt** after a while; **det lei utpå dagen** the day wore on; **det lei og det skrei** it was getting later and later.
li'[3] *V lei, -dd* (=**lide**[2]) 1 suffer (anguish, hardship, hunger, loss, pain) (av from), be plagued (**av** by). 2 *archaic* like; tolerate.
libel'le *-n* 1 *zool.* dragonfly. 2 (small) spirit level.
libera'l *A* liberal (conditions, law, opinion, person, politics, theology, etc.).
+libera'ler *-en, pl -e* (=***-ar**) liberal (politician; theologian).
liberalis'me *-n* liberalism (usu. political).
liberalite't *-en* 1 generosity. 2 liberality, broad-mindedness.
liberi' *-et, pl +-er/*-* livery.
+liberti'ner *-en, pl -e* (=***-ar**) libertine.
+li'b/haber *-en, pl -e* cf **lieb/**
libret'to *-en mus.* libretto.
lic.=**licentiat**
licentiat [lisensia't] *-en educ.* licentiate (Swedish academic degree, lower than doctorate; reintroduced in Norway for some subjects in 1957).
***li'd**[1] *-et* company, retinue, train.
***lid'**[2] *pr of* **li**[2], **lide**[1]
lid'delig *Av pop.* awfully, extremely, terribly (hungry, sleepy, etc.).
+lid'derlig *A -* cf **liderlig**
li'de[1] *V +led/*leid, +-t/*-e/*-i* cf **li**[2]
li'de[2] *V +led/*leid, +-t/*-e/*-i* cf **li**[3]
***li'delig** *A -* endurable, tolerable.
+li'delse *-n* (=***-ing**) 1 agony, suffering (of body, soul, etc.); hardship, torture: **Kristi l- og død** Christ's Passion and Death. 2 *med., psych.* disease.
+li'delses/felle *-n* fellow sufferer.
+li'delses/histo'rie *-a/-en* tale of suffering: **Kristi l-** the story of Christ's Passion.
li'dende *A -* suffering (**av** from).
li'den/skap *-en* 1 passion, strong feeling (**for** for). 2 object of passion.
+lidenska'pelig *A -* (=***lidenskapleg**) impassioned, passionate; ardent, enthusiastic; fiery, vehement.
li'denskaps/laus *A* (=+/**løs**) dispassionate; apathetic, phlegmatic.
+li'derlig *A -* (=+**lidderlig**) 1 depraved; lewd, licentious; coarse, vulgar. 2 *(adv.), pop.* extremely (=**liddelig**).
+lidt' *pp of* **li**[2,3], **lide**[1,2]
lieb/haber [li'b/] *-en, pl +-e* 1 collector, fancier (e.g. of art objects). 2 *merc.* prospective buyer.
Li'er *Pln* twp, Buskerud.
+lif'lig *A -* 1 blessed, blissful, lovely. 2 *(bibl.)* delightful, precious.
-lig *A -* (=***-leg**) -ly, adjectival ending: **daglig, hyggelig, årlig.**
li'ga *-en, pl *-er* league (of persons, parties, states, etc.); soccer league.
li'ga/kamp *-en* soccer league tournament.
+li'ger/vis *Av*: **l- som** *obs.* just as, in the same way as.
***ligg'** *pr of* **liggje**
+lig'ge *V lå, ligget* (=***-je**) 1 lie; be inactive; rest: **som en reder, så l-er en** you've made your bed, now lie in it; **la noe (f. eks. en sak, arbeid, osv.) l-** put sth (e.g. a matter, work, etc.) temporarily aside; **håret l-er ikke** the hair won't stay put. 2 be sick in bed, be laid up: **l- i meslinger** be down with the measles; **l- syk** be sick in bed; **han har l-et i fire uker** he's been laid up for four weeks. 3 stay (overnight or on a vacation): **hvor skal vi l- i natt** where'll we stay tonight?; **l- på landet** stay (on a vacation) in the country. 4 sit (e.g. of a hen on eggs, of a ship on the water): **båten l-er høyt (lavt) på vannet** the boat sits (rides) high (low) in the water. 5 be located, (of buildings) stand (**ved** by): **det l-er et land mot den evige sne** a country is located near the eternal snows (Bjørnson). 6 (expressing continuing activity): **han l-er og sover** he's sleeping; **jeg lå nettopp og tenkte** I was just thinking (while lying down). 7 (with *adv.* and *prep.*): **l- an** be so situated (**det l-er slik an at** the situation is such that); **det l-er godt, dårlig an for** the conditions are good, bad for; **slik forholdene l-er an** as things stand); **l- bak (ved)** be behind, be at the bottom of; *naut.* **l- bi** lie to; **l- etter** be behind (e.g. in a race, in developments); **l- etter en** be after, pursuing sby; *naut.* **l- for anker** lie at anchor; **l- for en** suit sby (**det l-er for ham** it comes natural to him, he has a gift for it); **l- foran** be ahead (e.g. in a race); **l- framme** be displayed, be in sight; **l- frampå** be greedy; **l- hos en** sleep at sby's house; **l- i** imply, involve (**hva l-er det i det** what does it imply?; **det l-er mere i det enn du tror** there's more to it than you think); **l- i at** be due to, consist of (**feilen l-er i at** the mistake is that; **det l-er i at** it is due to the fact that; **det l-er i sakens natur at** it is in the nature of things that); **l- i blodet** be in one's blood; **l- i det med en** be having an affair with sby; **l- i folder** hang down (e.g. of stockings); **l- i strid med** be at variance with, be enemies of; **l- i trening** be in training; **l- med** sleep, have intercourse with; **det l-er nær å tro (skjønne) at** it is easy to believe (understand) that; **l- omkring** be approximately; **l- over** be above, be higher than, superior to; stay overnight, stay another day; **l- på fiske (jakt)** be fishing (hunting); **l- en på hjerte (sinne)** be of importance to one, weigh on one's mind; **l- godt (dårlig) til** be well (poorly) located, situated; **l- som nr. 1** head the field; **l- til en** be a characteristic of, natural for sby; **l- til grunn for** be at the bottom of, be the basis for; **l- til sengs** be sick in bed; **det l-er langt tilbake i tiden** it's a long time ago; **l- under** be under (the control of); be inferior, lose, succumb (**for** to); be behind, at the bottom of; **l- under for (en last)** be addicted to (a vice); **l- unna** keep away from, lay off of; **l- ved et universitet** study at a university; *naut.* **l- ved vinden** sail close to the wind.
+lig'ge/dag *-en naut.* lay day.
+lig'gende/fe *-et archaic* possessions, property.
lig'ge/stol *-en* lounge or reclining chair; deck chair.
+lig'ge/sår *-et* bedsore.
***liggj'e** *V ligg, låg, lege/-i* cf **ligge**
***liggj'e/dag** *-en* cf **ligge/**
***liggj'e/sår** *-et* cf **ligge/**
lighter [lai'ter] *-en, pl +-e* (cigarette) lighter.
+lign.=**lignende**
+lignamen't [lingn-] *-et* cf **liknament**
+ligne [ling'ne] *V -a/-et* cf **likne**
+lignelse [ling'nelse] *-n* cf **liknelse**
+lignende [ling'nene] *A -* cf **liknende**
+ligning [ling'ning] *-a/-en* cf **likning**
+lignings/nemnd *-a* cf **liknings/nemnd**
+lignings/sjef *-en* cf **liknings/**
+lignings/vesen *-et* cf **liknings/**
ligus'ter *-en bot.* privet (Ligustrum vulgare).
li'k[1] *-et* (dead) body, corpse (also *fig.*): **blek som et l-** pale as death; **ligge l-** lie dead, lie in state; **pynte et l-** lay out a corpse; **et l- i lasten** a corpse on board ship (signifying bad luck), *fig.* sth which hinders, impedes (Ibsen).
li'k[2] *-et naut.* boltrope, leech.
li'k[3] *A* 1 like, similar to: **l-t og ulikt** a little bit of everything; **være seg selv l-** behave as expected, run true to form (usu. *derog.*, ab.=as I expected); **var ikke det l-t seg** isn't that just what you would expect; **han er l- sin far** he resembles (looks like) his father. 2 alike; (of quantities) equal to, identical with: **bytte l-t** trade evenly. 3 *dial.* likely: **det er l-t til (at)** it is probable (that), it looks as if; **var det l-t (seg)** of course not, don't be silly.) 4 *dial.* (esp. in comp. and sup.) good, proper, suitable: **ikke stort l-ere** not much better; **det var l-est at** it would be best if; **mens han var så lik at han kunne** while he was still able to.

+ Bokmål; * Nynorsk; ° Dialect.
After letter: ' stress (Acc. 1); ' tone, stress (Acc. 2); · length.
Below letter: . not pronounced.

+li'k/begjeng'else -n *archaic* funeral.
li'k/bleik *A* pale, white as a corpse.
li'k/brenning -a/+-en cremation.
+li'k/bærer -en, *pl* -e (=*/berar) pallbearer.
li'k/bål -et (funeral) pyre.
li'k/båre -a/+-en bier.
li'ke[1] *en* 1 like, match: **uten l-** unique, unparalleled, unrivaled. 2 equal, peer. 3: **gjøre l- for føden** earn one's keep.
li'ke[2] *N*: **holde ved l-** maintain, preserve.
li'ke[3] *V* +-te/*-a like: **l- seg** be, feel comfortable, happy; enjoy (oneself), like it; **jeg l-er meg godt i Norge** I'm enjoying myself in Norway; **jeg l-er meg ikke riktig i dag** I don't feel quite well today.
li'ke[4] *A* - 1 equal (battle, footing, height, value, etc.): **l- for l-** tit for tat; **stå på l- fot med** be on a par with. 2 *math.* even (number): **la fem være l-** *fig.* be carefree, don't be so cautious. 3 straight (line, road, etc.): **i l- linje** in direct line (of descent).
li'ke[5] *Av* 1 directly, right, straight: **l- opp (ned)** straight up (down); **l- opp i ansiktet på en** right to sby's face; **l- overfor** facing; in relation to; **l- til** all the way to; **l- ut** straight out; **l- ved** close by, close to (**være l- ved å** be right on the point of); **ha l- for hånden** have right at hand. 2 equally, exactly, just (as): **l- +ens/*eins** just the same, likewise; **l- fullt, l- godt** all the same, nevertheless; **l- så godt** just as well; **jeg er l- glad** it's all the same to me; **atter og fram, det er l- langt** back and forth are equally far (Ibsen).
li'ke/arma *A* - (=+-et) having equal arms (esp. *phys.*).
li'ke/arta *A* - (=+-et) homogeneous.
li'ke/beint *A* - (=*/beina) *math.* isosceles.
+li'ke/beret'tiget *A* - having equal rights.
+li'ke/dan' *A* 1 like, (just) the same; similar (**som** to). 2 *(adv.)* in the same way, similarly.
+li'ke/dannet *A* - uniform; *math.* similar.
+li'ke/ens *Av* cf **like[5]**
li'ke/finna *A* - (=+-et) *bot.* abruptly pinnate.
li'ke/forma *A* - (=+-et) uniform; *math.* similar.
li'ke/fram *A* -t, *pl* -me 1 direct, simple, straightforward (action, meaning, person, question, etc.). 2 absolute, downright (duty, nonsense, scandal, etc.).
li'ke/fullt *Av* cf **like[5]**
li'ke/glad *A* - indifferent: **jeg er l- med hva du gjør** I don't care what you do.
li'ke/godt' *Av* cf **like[5]**
+li'ke/gyldig *A* - 1 immaterial, unimportant. 2 indifferent (**for** to); careless (**med** about), heedless.
+li'kegyldig/het -en indifference (**for** to); carelessness (**med** about).
*li'k/eins *Av* (=***like eins**) cf **like[5]**
+li'ke/ledes *Av* likewise; also, besides.
li'kelig *A* - proportionate; equitable, fair.
+li'ke/lydende *A* - 1 homophonic. 2 identically worded.
+li'ke/løpende *A* - 1 straight. 2 parallel.
li'ke/mann -en, *pl* -menn/*-menner match; equal, peer.
*li'kende -t indication, mark, sign (**til** of).
+li'kendes *A* - (=*-andes) likeable.
+li'ke/overfor [/åverfårr] *P* cf **like[5]**
+li'kere *cp of* **lik[3]** (=*-are)
+li'ke/rette *V* -a/-et *elec.* rectify.
+li'ke/retter -en, *pl* -e (=*-ar) *elec.* rectifier.
+li'ke/rettet *A* - *elec.* rectified: **l- strøm** direct current.
li'ke/sida *A* - (=+-et) *math.* equilateral.
+li'ke/sinnet *A* - like-minded, similarly disposed.
li'ke/som' *Av, C* cf **lik/som**
+li'kest *sp of* **lik[3]** (=*-ast)
+li'ke/stille *V* -stilte 1 place on equal footing: **l- kvinner med menn** give women equal rights with men. 2 compare, identify (**med** with).
+li'ke/stilling -en equality (**med** with).
+li'ke/strøm' -men (=*/straum) *elec.* direct current.
li'ke/sæl *A* indifferent.
*li'ke/sæle -a indifference.
+li'ke/så *Av* cf **lik/**
li'ke/til' *A* - 1 direct, straightforward. 2 easy, simple.
+li'ke/vekt -a/+-en *phys.* balance, equilibrium (also *fig.*); composure, equanimity, poise.
+li'ke/vektig *A* - *phys.* balanced, in equilibrium (also *fig.*); composed, equanimous, poised.
+li'kevekts/politikk' -en balance of power policy.
li'ke/vel' *Av* (=***like vel**) all the same, nevertheless; still, yet.
li'k/ferd [*/fæ'r] -a/+-en funeral.
li'k/funn -et discovery of a corpse.
li'k/følgje -t (=+/**følge**) funeral procession.
li'k/halm -en straw upon which a corpse has lain.
+li'k/het -en 1 likeness, resemblance, similarity (**med** to); analogy (**med** with): **i l- med** after the fashion of, like; in conformity with. 2 equality: **l- for loven** equality before the law.
+li'khets/punkt -et point of resemblance, similarity.
+li'khets/tegn [/tein] -et equals sign: **sette l- mellom** consider (two things) equal.
li'k/hus -et mortuary; morgue.
*li'kjast *V* *likjest, liktest, likst* look like, resemble.
li'k/kiste -a casket, coffin.
+li'k/klær *pl* (=*/**klede**) cerements, graveclothes, shroud.
*li'kleg *A* - reasonable; agreeable, pleasant.
*lik'n -a indication, prospect, sign: **l- til godver** prospect for, sign of good weather.
likn. =**liknende**
liknamen't -et (=+**lignament**) 1 *fam.* likeness, anything like: **det fantes ikke l- til møbler** there was not a trace of furniture. 2 reasonableness, sense.
lik'ne *V* -a/+-et (=+**ligne**) 1 look like, resemble; be similar to: **l- på** resemble; **det l-er ham!** that's just like him, that's him all over!; **dette l-er ingenting** this is impossible, unheard of. 2 compare (**med** to). 3 assess (a tax): **l- ut** assess, tax.
+lik'nelse -n (=+**lignelse**) 1 likeness: **i l- av** in the l- of. 2 parable; simile.
lik'nende *A* - (=+**lignende**) comparable, like, similar: **noe l-** sth like that; **eller l-, og l-** etcetera, or the like.
lik'ning -a/+-en (=+**ligning**) 1 (tax) assessment. 2 *math.* equation.
lik'nings/nemnd [/nemd] -a tax commission.
lik'nings/sjef -en tax commissioner.
+lik'nings/vesen -et tax authority.
+li'k/plett -en death spot (on a corpse).
li'k/skap -en likeness, resemblance, similarity (**med** to).
li'k/skjorte -a shroud.
+li'k/skue -t autopsy.
*lik'so *Av* cf **lik/så**
lik'/som' *Av, C* (=**like/som**) 1 *(adv.)* somehow, sort of: **det er l- så mye hyggeligere her nå** it's somehow so much more pleasant here now; **det var l- jeg hørte noe** I seemed to hear sth; **på l-** (in) make-believe. 2 *(conj.)* as, as if; like: **det bor troll i Dem også — l- i meg** there are trolls within you—as in me (Ibsen); **han stanset, l- han ville si noe** he stopped, as if he were going to say sth; **l-...så...** as (like)...so....
*li'kst *pp of* **likjast**
li'k/strå -et: **ligge på l-** lie dead, be laid out.
+li'k/svøp -et shroud, winding sheet.
li'k/syn -et autopsy.
lik'/så *Av* (=**like/**) 1 likewise, the same: **gå bort og gjør du l-** go, and do thou likewise (Luke 10,37). 2 equally, just as: **l- godt** just as well; **l- rik som** just as rich as.
*lik't *A nt of* **lik[3]**
li'k/tale -n funeral oration.
*lik'test *pt of* **likjast**
li'k/tog [/tåg] -et funeral procession.
li'k/to'rn -en corn (on the foot).
li'ktorn/plaster -eret/-ret, *pl* -er/+-re corn plaster.
li'k/tå -a, *pl* -tær *fam.* corn (on a toe).
likvi'd *A* - liquid (assets, funds), having liquid funds (of a firm, person, etc.); liquid (in phonetics).
likvidasjo'n -en *merc.* liquidation.
likvi'der *pl merc.* liquid assets.
likvide're *V* -te 1 *merc.* liquidate (account, claim, debt, etc.). 2 dissolve, do away with, liquidate.
likvidite't -en *merc.* liquidity.
li'k/vogn [/vångn] -a hearse.
likø'r -en liqueur.
lil'je -a/+-en lily.
+lil'je/hvit *A* cf **/kvit**
lil'je/konvall' -en lily of the valley.
lil'je/kvit *A* lily-white.
lil'la *A* - lilac, mauve, pale violet.
+lil'le *df of* **liten**
Lil'le/asia *Pln* Asia Minor.
+lil'le/bror -en little brother, younger brother (pet name).
+lil'le/finger -eren, *pl* -rer little finger: **snu en om sin l-** twist one around one's little finger; **gir en fanden l-en, tar han hele hånden** if one gives the devil an inch, he will take a mile.
+lil'le/gutt -en little boy (pet name).
Lil'le/hammer *Pln* town, Oppland.
+lil'le/hjerne [/jæ'rne] -n cerebellum.
+lil'le/julaf'ten -enen, *pl* -er/-ner night before Christmas Eve.
+lil'le/momp -en little slam (in cards).
+lil'le/putt *en* Lilliput.
Lil'le/sand *Pln* town, Aust-Agder.
+lil'le/slem' -en little slam (in cards).
Lil'le/strøm' *Pln* town, Akershus.
+lil'le/søster -a/-en little sister, younger sister (pet name).
+lil'le/tromme -a *mus.* snare drum.
+lil'le/tå -a, *pl* -tær little toe.
+lil'le/viser -en, *pl* -e hour hand (on clock, watch).
li'm -et 1 glue, mucilage. 2 *dial.* lime.
li'm/band -et gummed or adhesive tape.
li'me[1] -n broom.
li'me[2] *V* -a/+-te 1 glue; size. 2 coat (a tree) with insect lime.
li'm/farge -n color wash, distemper.
li'ming -a/+-en glueing: **gå opp i l-en** come unglued; fall to pieces.
lim'it -en limit (esp. *merc.*).
limite're *V* -te limit (esp. *merc.*).
limona'de -n fruit drink (usu. lemonade).
li'm/pinne -n lime-twig: **gå på l-n** be fooled, taken in.
li'n[1] -et 1 flax. 2 linen; *hist.* linen headdress.
*lin'[2] *A* soft; loose, supple.
li'nd -a *bot.* lime, linden (Tilia).
lin'de[1] -n swaddling band, cloth.
lin'de[2] *V* -a/+-et swaddle, swathe.
Lindesne's [also lin'des/] *Pln* cape, Vest-Agder (Norway's southernmost point).
lin'dre *V* -a/+-et alleviate, relieve, soothe (pain, sorrow, etc.).
lin'dring -a/+-en alleviation, relief.
li'n/duk -en linen (table) cloth.
Lin'd/ås *Pln* twp, Hordaland.
li'ne[1] -a 1 line, (thin) rope; tightrope: **danse på l-** walk on a tightrope. 2 rein: **løpe l-n ut** go the whole hog. 3 longline (in fishing).
*li'ne[2] *V* -a loosen, slacken.
*li'ne[3] *V* -a cf **linjere**
li'ne/bruk -et 1 long-lining (in fishing). 2 longline.

+**li'ne/danser** *-en, pl -e* (=***-ar**) tightrope walker.
li'ne/fiske *-t* long-lining.
lin'/erle [/æ'rle; also -æ'rle] *-a zool.* wagtail (Motacillidae).
lineæ'r *A* linear (also *math.*).
li'n/frø *-et* flaxseed.
lingeri [læŋsjeri'] *-et* lingerie.
lingvafo'n/ku·rs *-et, pl -/+-er* linguaphone course.
lingvis't *-en* linguist.
lingvistikk' *-en* linguistics.
lingvis'tisk *A* - linguistic.
***li'ning** *-a/-en* cf **linning**
linja'l *-en* rule, ruler; scale.
lin'je *-a/+-en* 1 line: **i første l-** first and foremost, primarily; **i like l-** directly; **over hele l-en** all around, all along the line; **på l- med** on a level with. 2 *educ.* course of study, curriculum (in the *gymnasium*), ab.=major.
lin'je/akevitt· *-en* aged aquavit (improved by a long sea voyage, esp. one that has crossed the equator).
lin'je/brott *-et* (=+**/brudd**) line break (e.g. telegraph, telephone).
lin'je/båt *-en* (regularly scheduled) liner, ship.
lin'je/deling *-a/+-en* 1 lineation. 2 *educ.* division into distinct courses of study.
lin'je/fart *-en* regularly scheduled sailing (of a steamship line).
lin'je/mann *-en, pl -menn/*-menner* 1 line soldier. 2 linesman (in soccer).
linje're *V -te* rule (a line, lines).
lin'je/skip *-et* 1 (regularly scheduled) liner, ship. 2 *mil.* ship of the line.
lin'k *-en* chain of radio stations.
***lin'ke** *V -a* 1 dilute, thin. 2 alleviate, relieve, soothe. 3: **l- seg** accommodate oneself (**etter** to), comply (**etter** with). 4: **l- seg** idle, loaf. 5 limp; jerk, toss (oneself).
lin'ks *A tech.* (of screw thread) left-handed.
li'n/kvit *A* flaxen (colored).
linn' *A lint* gentle, mild, soft (movement, touch, weather, etc.); careful, cautious.
lin'ne[1] *-a* mild weather; thaw.
***lin'ne[2]** *V -a* become gentle, mild; mollify, soften.
linne'a *-en bot.* twinflower (Linnaea borealis).
+**lin'net** *-et, pl -/-er* linen (also table linen, underwear, etc.): **vaske sitt skitne l- for alles syne** *fig.* wash one's dirty linen in public.
+**lin'net/skap** *-et* linen closet, cupboard.
lin'ning *-a/-en* (neck, waist) band.
linn'/orm *-en* (man-eating) dragon, serpent.
linn'/salte *V -a/+-et* salt lightly.
linn'/steikt *A* - gently or lightly fried, roasted; baked.
+**linn'/vær** *-et* (=***/ver**) mild weather; thaw.
lino'leum *-en* linoleum.
li'n/olje *-a/-en* linseed oil.
lin'se *-a/+-en* 1 *bot.* lentil (plant, seed): **selge sin førstefødselsrett for en rett linser** sell one's birthright for a mess of pottage (Gen. 25,34). 2 *anat., geol., phys.* lens. 3 a custard tart.
li'n/stoff *-et* linen material.
+**li'n/søm·** *-men* plain needlework, sewing.
lin't *nt of* **linn**
+**li'n/torskemunn** *-en bot.* toadflax (Linaria vulgaris).
li'n/tråd *-en* linen thread.
+**li'n/tøy** *-et* (=***/ty**) linen(s).
***lip'pe** *-a/-en* cf **leppe**
li're[1] *-n, pl* - lira (coin).
li're[2] *-a/+-en* 1 *zool.* shearwater (Puffinus). 2 *mus.* barrel organ, hurdy-gurdy.
li're[3] *V -a/-te*: **l- av** rattle, reel off (song, speech, story, etc.).
li're/kasse *-a/-en* barrel (grind, hand) organ, hurdy-gurdy; *derog.* broken-down musical instrument.
li'rekasse/mann *-en, pl -menn/*-menner* organ grinder.
lir'ke *V -a/+-et* 1 coax, jiggle: **l- med, ved låsen** fumble with, try the lock; **l- døren opp** work the door open. 2 cajole, wangle: **l- seg inn i, ut av** worm one's way into, out of.
***lir'le** *V -a* warble.
li'rum/larum *-et* clang, jangle (of music, words, etc.).
Lis'bet *Prn (f)*
Lis'boa *Pln* Lisbon.
li'se *-a/+-en* alleviation, relief, solace.
Li'se *Prn (f)*
lisen's *-en* 1 license (esp. *admin., merc.*). 2 (radio, TV) listener's permit.
lisen's/avgift *-a/+-en* license fee.
lisensia't *-en* cf **lic-**
lisensie're *V -te* license.
lisitasjo'n *-en admin., merc.* contracting, call for bids.
lisite're *V -te admin., merc.* offer on contract.
***lis'kre** *V -a* coax, wheedle.
***lis'le** *df of* **liten**
lis'/pund *-et obs.* unit of weight (about 18 lbs.).
lis'se *-a* cord, (shoe) lace, string.
+**lis'som** *Av, C cf* **lik/som**
lis't[1] *-a* 1 moulding. 2 selvage. 3 (sports) cross-bar.
lis't[2] *-a/+-en* cunning, slyness: **med l- og lempe** by hook or crook.
Lis'ta *Pln* twp, Vest-Agder.
lis'te[1] *-a* list (of names, words, etc.), inventory.
lis'te[2] *V -a/+-et* slip, sneak, steal: **l- noe fra en** worm something from one; **l- seg** creep, sneak, steal; **l- seg inn på en** creep up on one; **l- seg til å se på** steal a glance at; **l- seg til noe** acquire sth by cunning, stealth.
+**lis'te/bærer** *-en, pl -e* (=***/berar**) person who hands out ballot for a political party outside election precincts.
+**lis'te/forbund** *-et* electoral pact (by which two or more parties can combine their votes).
+**lis'te/fører** *-en, pl -e* (=***-ar**) poll clerk.
+**lis'telig** *Av* cunningly; stealthily.
lis'ter/båt *-en* type of boat used in Lista.
***lis'te/samband** *-et* electoral pact (cf **l-/forbund**).
lis'tig *A* - crafty; cunning, sly, wily.
lis'tring *-en* 1 person from Lista. 2 type of boat used in Lista.
lis't/verk *-et* moulding.
li't[1] *-a/+-en* confidence, trust: **sette sin l- til** put one's trust in.
li't[2] *N*: **i lengste l-en** as long as possible; **i siste l-en** at the last moment, in the nick of time.
li'ta *f of* **liten**
***li'tande** *A* - dependable, reliable, trustworthy.
litani' *-et, pl +-er/*-* litany.
Lit'auen *Pln* Lithuania.
lit'auer *-en* Lithuanian.
lit'auisk *A* - Lithuanian.
***li'ta/voren** [/våren] *f of* **liten/**
li'te[1] *V leit/+let, +-t/*-e/*-i* 1: **l- på** depend, rely on, trust in. 2 *dial.* follow, heed (advice, etc.). 3 *dial.*: **l- seg med** be content, satisfied with. *4 look (**på** at).
li'te[2] *nt of* **liten**
li'te/grann *Av* (=**lite grann**) a little bit, (just) a little.
li'ten *A f lita/+-en, nt lite (df, sg +lille/*litle/vesle), pl små (df små/*smáe), cp mindre, sp minst* 1 little, small: **ikke så lite** quite a bit; *mus.* **et lite intervall** a minor interval; **fra l- av** from childhood on, since I was a child; **som l-** as a child; **både stor og l- (store og små)** both grown-ups and children; **stakkars l-** poor little thing (fellow); **gjøre seg l-** humble oneself; **få en l-** have a baby. 2 *(neut., sg.)* **lite** little; few (cf **litt**): **det er lite folk her** there aren't many people here; **det er lite med (mat)** there's not much (food); **det har lite å si** it is of little importance; **lite eller ingenting** little or nothing; **lite sannsynlig** not very probable. 3 *(comp.)* **mindre** less, smaller; (relatively) small: **et m- bord** a (rather) small table; **m- diktere** minor poets; **ikke (intet) m- enn** no less than, nothing but; **mer eller m-** more or less; **m- heldig** unfortunate; **med m-** unless. 4 *(sup.)* **minst** least, smallest; *(adv.)* at least: **m- mulig** as little as possible; **aller m-** least of all; **den (de) m-e** the youngest child(ren); **det m-e** the least; **ikke det m-e** not the least, nothing at all; **i det m-e** at least; **sist, men ikke m-** last but not least.
***li'ten/voren** [/våren] *A f lita/voren, nt lite/vore, pl små/vorne* fairly small, smallish.
li'ter *-en, pl* - liter (=1.057 U.S. qts.).
li'ter/mål *-et* liter measure.
***li'te/vetta** *Av* little bit.
***li'te/vori** *nt of* **liten/voren**
***lit'le** *df of* **liten**
litogra'f *-en* lithographer.
litografe're *V -te* lithograph.
litografi' *-en* lithography.
litogra'fisk *A* - lithographic(al).
lit'ra *+-en* (designating) letter (for a series, etc.).
litt'[1] *Av* a bit, a little: **l- etter l-** little by little; **l- senere** a little later; **om l-** in a little while; **vent l-** wait a minute; **det er l- lite** it's a bit (too) little.
+**litt'[2]** *Pn* a little: **l- av hvert** odds and ends, a little bit of everything; **l- mat** a little food; **l- å spise** a bit, a little to eat; **han er l- av en** he's sth of a.
+**litt'[3]** *pp of* **lite[1]**
litt.=**litteratur, litterær**
littera't *-en* literary man, man of letters; litterateur, pl. literati.
litteratu'r *-en* literature; belles-lettres.
+**litteratu'r/anmelder** *-en, pl -e* literary reviewer.
litteræ'r *A* literary.
litur'g *-en eccl.* liturgist (during liturgical service).
liturgi' *-en eccl.* liturgy.
litur'gisk *A* - *eccl.* liturgic(al).
li'v *-et* 1 life; liveliness: **aldri i l-et** absolutely never; **med l- og lyst** with a will; **på harde l-et** for dear life; **på l-et løs** for dear life, with might and main (**gå på l-et løs** be a matter of life and death); **på død og l- (l- og død)** absolutely, definitely (**han vil på død og l- gjøre det** he insists on doing it); **blåse l- i** revive, give life to, *fig.* give impetus to; **sette l- i** rouse, stir up; **sette l-et til** die, lose one's life, perish; **stå om l-et** be a case of life or death; **ta l-et av** kill; **true en på l-et** threaten to kill sby; **ville en til l-s** want to get the better of sby, have it in for sby. 2 waist; bodice; body: **fra mors l- av** from birth on; **med l- og sjel** wholeheartedly; **gå en (inn) på l-et** crowd sby, *fig.* put pressure on sby; **ha folk like inn på l-et av seg** have other people (uncomfortably) close to one; **holde seg (en, noe) fra l-et** keep (sby, sth) at a distance; **komme (en, noe) inn på l-et** become closely acquainted with, get to know (sby, sth) very well; **få noe, sette til l-s** dispatch (food), put away.
Li'v *Prn (f)*
li'v/aktig [also -ak'-] *A* - lifelike; vivid.

+ Bokmål; * Nynorsk; ° Dialect.
After letter: ' stress (Acc. 1); ` tone, stress (Acc. 2); · length.
Below letter: . not pronounced.

li'vat A fam. gay, lively.
*li'v/aure -en cf /øre
li'v/belte -t, pl +-r/*- life belt.
li'v/berge V -a/+-et: l- seg (manage to) keep alive, subsist; keep body and soul together.
li'v/berging [also li'v/] -a 1 subsistence (also food, work, etc.). 2 lifesaving.
li'v/bøye -n life buoy.
li'v/båt -en lifeboat.
liv'd -a cover, shelter (for from).
li'v/dyr -et breeding animal, breeder.
*li've[1] -t cover, protection, shelter.
li've[2] N: i l- alive.
li've[3] V -de 1 cover, shelter. 2 save, spare.
li've[4] V -a/+-et: l- opp cheer, perk up; lit. refresh; revivify.
+li'v/egen A -ent, pl -ne (=*/eigen) adscript (of a serf), attached to the soil.
li'venḍe Av: l- redd scared to death.
li'v/full A animated, lively (action, expression, person, etc.); eager.
li'v/garde -n bodyguard.
+li'v/givenḍe A - life-giving.
li'v/gjo'rḍ -a belt, cincture, girdle.
*li'v/hætt A - (mortally) dangerous, perilous.
*liv'je V -a: l- seg subsist.
li'v/kjole -n dress coat, tails.
li'v/ku -a, pl -kyr/+-er breeding cow.
li'v/lanḍsk A - Livonian.
li'v/laus A (=+/løs) dead, inanimate, lifeless.
li'v/lege -n private (or court) physician.
*li'v/lei A -tt world-weary, tired of life.
li'v/lenḍing -en Livonian.
liv'lig A - animated, lively, spirited (animal, conversation, discussion; brisk business, correspondence, etc.); bustling (street, town, etc.).
li'v/line -a life line.
+li'v/løs A cf /laus
li'v/mor -a/+-en anat. uterus, womb.
li'v/mål -et waist measurement.
*liv'naḍ -en cf levnet
liv'ne V -a/+-et liven (opp, til up), revive.
li'v/nære V -te keep alive; l- seg subsist; make a living (av from), support oneself.
li'v/orga'n -et, pl -/+-er mouthpiece (publication).
livré -et, pl +-er/*- livery.
li'v/redd A - deathly frightened; frightened for one's life, f- to death.
+li'v/redning -en lifesaving; rescue.
li'v/reim -a: spenne inn l-a tighten one's belt (also fig.).
+li'v/rem' -ma/-men, pl -mer cf /reim
li'v/rente -a/+-en annuity.
li'v/rett -en favorite dish.
+livs/aften [lif's/] -en old age, evening of life (esp. poet.).
+livsa'lig A - blessed, blissful; delightful, pleasant.
+livs/ansku'else [lif's/] -n life philosophy, view.
livs/arving -en jur. heir, issue.
livs/bane -n career, life.
+livs/beting'else -n vital necessity.
livs/eliksi'r -en elixir of life.
livsens [lif'sens] df po of liv
+livs/erfa'ring [lif's/] -en experience (in life).
livs/fare -n mortal danger, peril.
livs/farlig A - mortally dangerous, perilous.
livs/fjern [/fjæ'rn] A detached, remote (from life).
+livs/fornø'denhet -en necessity (of life).
+livs/forsik're V -a/-et insure one's life.
+livs/forsik'ring -en life insurance.
livs/frisk A healthy, live, vigorous.
+livs/førsel -en conduct, way of living.
livs/gjerning [/jæ'rning] -a/+-en calling, lifework, occupation.
livs/glaḍ A - cheerful, gay, happy.
livs/glede -a/+-en joy of life, joie de vivre.
livs/klok A experienced, wise (in the ways of life).
livs/kraft -a/+-en 1 vital force. 2 vigor, vitality.
livs/kraftig A - vigorous.
livs/kunst -en art of living.
+livs/kunstner -en, pl -e (=*-ar) connoisseur of the art of living.
livs/kvelḍ -en old age, evening of life (esp. poet.).
+livs/ledsager -en, pl -e life partner (man).
+livs/ledsagerske -n life partner (woman).
livs/lyst -a/+-en zest for life.
livs/løgn [+/løyn] -a/+-en life lie, self-delusion (cf Ibsen's The Wild Duck).
+livs/løp -et career, course of life.
*livs/mein -et lifelong damage, hurt, injury.
livs/minne -t, pl +-r/*- memoir(s).
livs/nær A at the heart of, close to life; realistic.
+livs/nødven'dighet -en vital necessity.
+livs/oppholḍ -et livelihood, subsistence.
livs/poli'se -n life insurance policy.
*livs/røynsle -a experience (in life).
livs/sak -a/+-en cause of vital importance, life and death, matter (to which one's life is dedicated).
livs/straff -a/+-en jur. capital punishment; death penalty.
livs/syn -et/*-a life philosophy, view of life.
+livs/tegn [/tein] -et sign of life: gi l- fra seg fig. be heard from (by letter, etc.).
livs/tid -a/+-en lifetime: på l- for life.
+livs/trett A - world-weary, tired of life.
livs/trygd -a life insurance.
li'v/stykke -t, pl +-r/*- bodice.
+livs/udu'gelig [lif's/] A - unsuited to life.
livs/varig A - lifelong: l- fengsel life imprisonment.
livs/verk -et lifework.
livs/viktig A - essential, vital.
livs/vilkår -et living condition.
livs/visdom [/-dåmm] -men/*-en wisdom of life.
livs/ånḍ +-en/*-a vital spirit.
li'v/tak -et waist lock (in wrestling).
li'v/vakt -a/+-en bodyguard.
li'v/vidde -a (=/vidd) waist expansion, measurement.
+li'v/øre -n (=*/øyre) pension paid by new owner of estate, farm to former owner (esp.by son to father).
li'v/åre -a artery.
Ljan [ja'n] Pln section of Oslo.
*ljo'ḍ -en/-et cf lyd[1]
*ljo'ḍ/brigde -t cf lyd/
*ljo'de V -a cf lyde[1]
*ljo'ḍleg A - cf lydlig
*ljo'ḍ/mur -en cf lyd/
*ljo'ḍ/sprang -et cf lyd/
ljo'm -en resounding, echo.
ljo'me V -a/+-et resound, ring; echo.
ljo're [also: jå're] -n smoke vent (in middle of ceiling).
ljore/hol [/hål] -et (=+/hull) smoke vent.
+ljore/stang -a, pl -stenger (=*/stong) pole to open and close smoke vent.
ljore/stue -a (=*/stove) cabin with open hearth and smoke vent.
*ljo's[1] -et cf lys[1]
*ljo's[2] A cf lys[2]
*ljo'se/stake -n cf lyse/
*ljos'ke[1] -n 1 brightening, clearing (e.g. of the weather). 2 gleam, twinkle of light.
*ljos'ke[2] V -a grow light, lighten (e.g. of the weather).
*ljo'sleg A - light (in color).
*ljo's/leik -en lightness (in color).
*ljo's/leitt A - cf lys/lett
*ljo's/mor -a midwife.
*ljo'sne V -a cf lysne
*ljoster [ljos'ter] ljostra cf lyster
*ljo't A hideous, ugly; disagreeable, unpleasant.
*ljo'te V lyt, laut, lote/-i (=lyte[2]) have to; had better: det lyt så vere what must be, must be; du lyt gjere det you'd better do it; "du lyt tåle det," sa mannen, han kasta katten i omnen "you'll have to stand it," said the man, he threw the cat in the oven.
*ljo'ting -en disagreeable person.
*ljo't/leik -en ugliness.
lju'g -et falsehood, lie.
*lju'gar -en cf løgner
lju'ge V +-er/*lyg, laug/+løy, +løyet/*loge/*-i cf lyge
*lju'v A dear (beloved).
*lju'vleg A - agreeable, nice, pleasant; charming.
°ljøs'ke -n cf ljoske[1]
ljå' [also jå'] -en, pl +-er/*-r scythe (with a long handle): mannen med l-en the Grim Reaper.
ljå'/orv -et scythe handle.
ljå'/slått -en mowing, reaping (with a scythe).
ljå'/stubb -en stubble (after mowing).
*L/L =lottlag, lutlag
l. nr. =løpenummer
lo'[1] -a: zool. hei/lo, åker/lo golden plover (Charadrius pluvialis).
lo'[2] -a nap, pile (on cloth, etc.); fluff, fuzz, lint.
lo'[3] -a 1 unthreshed grain. 2 unwinnowed grain.
lo'[4] -a meadow (usu. in place names).
*lo'[5] -a bullet, shot.
lo'[6] -en 1 naut. weatherboard. 2 naut. waters to windward.
*lo'[7] -et dung, manure.
lo'[8] pt of le[2]
LO =Landsorganisasjonen i Norge
lobb' -en lob (in tennis).
lob'be V -a/+-et lob (in tennis).
lob'by -en lobby, vestibule (also British: Parliament Lobby).
lockout [låkk'/aut] -en (labor) lockout.
lockoute [låkk'aute] V -a/+-et lockout (labor).
loco [lo'ko] Av merc. (on the) spot.
loco/vare -a/+-en merc. spot goods.
+lodd'[1] -en fate, lot: falle i ens l- be one's fate, fall to one's lot. 2 portion, share (=lott).
lodd'[2] -et, pl -/+-er 1 lot; lottery ticket; lottery prize: kaste, trekke l- om cast, draw lots for; kjøpe l- buy a lottery ticket; det store l- the big prize. 2 metal weight (on a balance); clock weight; naut. sounding lead; plumb bob, plummet; pile hammer (on pile driver). 3 solder.
*lodd'/bein A perpendicular, vertical.
lod'de[1] -a zool. capelin (Mallotus villosus).
*lod'de[2] -n short, coarse oversock, mukluk.
lod'de[3] V -a/+-et 1 naut., fig. sound; fig. fathom, plumb (e.g. the depths of one's soul). 2 plumb (e.g. a wall). 3 solder.
lod'de[4] V -a/+-et: l- ut raffle off.
lod'de/bolt -en soldering iron.
lod'de/fiske -t cod fishing when the cod follow the capelin to the coastal banks of Finnmark.
lod'de/lampe -a/-en soldering lamp.
lod'de/metall' -et solder.
+lod'den A -ent, pl lodne (=*loden) 1 hairy, hirsute; shaggy; woolly: fam. vende den lodne siden ut show the disagreeable side (of one's nature), be unpleasant. 2 fam. brutish, coarse, low. 3 insidious, sly.
+lodd'/kast(n)ing -en casting of lots.
lodd'/line -a naut. lead line, sounding line.
lodd'/rett A - 1 perpendicular, vertical; down (in crossword puzzles). 2 fam. absolute, bold-faced: l- løgn out-and-out lie.
+lodd'/seddel -elen, pl -sedler lottery ticket.
+lodd'/skott -et (=*/skot, +/skudd) naut. sounding, cast of the lead.
lodd'/snor -a plumb line.
+lodd'/trekning -en drawing lots.
*loden [lå'en] A -e/-i, pl -ne cf lodden
lod'ne pl of +lodden, *loden

lod'ne/gras -et bot. velvet grass (Holcus lanatus).

*__lod'ne/leḍ__ -a: **snu l-a til** turn a deaf ear to.

*__lod'ne/siḍe__ -a: **snu l-a til** turn a deaf ear to.

lo'e V -a 1 fuzz (of woven material): **l- av** shed (e.g. of a carpet). 2: **l- seg sammen** become felted. 3: **l- opp** raise a nap.

Lo'en Pln post office, Stryn twp, Sogn og Fjordane.

lo'et(e) A - fam. nappy, shaggy.

loff[1] [loff'] -en white bread.

loff[2] [loff'] -en fam.: **gå på l-en** bum, loaf around (and beg).

loffe[1] [lof'fe] V -a/+-et 1 naut. luff. 2 force another boat (in sport sailing) to luff.

loffe[2] [lof'fe] V -a/+-et fam. bum, loaf around (and beg).

+**loffer** [lof'fer] -en, pl -e (=*-ar) fam. bum, loafer.

Lo'/foten Pln island group, Nordland.

lo'fot/fiske -t cod fishing in Lofoten (from February to April).

lof't -et 1 ceiling. 2 attic, garret. 3 dial. loft, top story; story. 4 (log) storehouse (in two stories, orig. used as festival quarters).

lof't/bu -a attic storeroom.

lof't/eta'sje -n top (attic) story.

lof'ts/høgd -a top (attic) story.

lof'ts/kammer -eret, pl -er/-kamre 1 attic room. 2 second-story room.

lof'ts/trapp -a attic stairs.

log [lå'g] -en cf **låg**[2]

logarit'me -n math. logarithm.

logarit'misk [also -it'-] A - math. logarithmic.

loge[1] [lå'ge] -n (=+**lue**[1]) blaze, flame (also fig.).

loge[2] [lå'ge] V -a/+-et (=+**lue**[3]) blaze, flame (also fig.).

*__loge__[3] [lå'ge] pp of **lyge** (=*__logi__)

*__logg'__[1] -a cf **lagg**

logg'[2] -en naut. log (for determining distance and speed).

logg'/bok -a, pl -bøker (aero)naut. logbook.

log'ge V -a/+-et 1 naut. heave (drag, pull) the log; log (a ship's speed). 2 naut., fam. put (a seaman) on report, write a seaman up (in a logbook) and impose punishment.

loggia [lådd'sja] -en, pl *-er loggia.

logg'/line -a naut. log line.

+**lo'giker** -en, pl -e (=*-ar) logician.

logikk' -en logic.

lo'gisk A - logical.

*__logn__[1] [lång'n] -a 1 calm, stillness. 2 calm (mirror-like) water.

logn[2] [lång'n] A 1 calm, still. 2 sheltered; cozy, snug.

*__lognast__ [lång'nast] V -ast become calmer, stiller.

*__logne__ [lång'ne] V -a calm, still: **l- seg** grow calm.

log're V -a/+-et 1 wag the tail. 2 fawn (**for** on, over).

loja'l A loyal (citizen, conduct, friend, etc.) (**mot, overfor** to); faithful (to an oath, a vow, etc.).

lojalite't -en loyalty.

lok[1] [lokk'] -et fam. (short for) locomotive.

*__lok__[2] [lå'k] -et cf **lokk**[3]

lo'k[3] -en dial. 1 pond. 2 bot. type of fern (Cystopteris).

loka'l A local.

loka'l/bedø've V -de/+-et anesthetize locally.

loka'l/båt -en boat for local traffic.

loka'le -t, pl +-r/*- (public) hall, room; office: **firmaets nye l-r** the firm's new offices; premises.

loka'l/histo'rie -a/+-en local history.

lokalise're V -te localize (epidemic, story, war, etc.); confine; locate (e.g. a disease); give a local stamp to.

lokalite't -en locality.

loka'l/kjennskap -en knowledge of local condition, things, etc.

+**loka'l/kjent** A - (=*/**kjend**) locally acquainted.

loka'l/patriotis'me -n local patriotism, regionalism.

loka'l/tog [/tåg] -et local train; suburban train.

loka'l/trafikk' -en local (regional) traffic.

*__loke__[1] [lå'ke] -a (window) shutter; (door) bar.

*__lo'ke__[2] -n fist, paw.

*__loke__[3] [lå'ke] V -a cf **lukke**[3]

*__lo'ke__[4] V -a cuff, punch.

Loke [lå'ke] Prn Norse god and mischiefmaker.

lokk'[1] -en lock (of hair): **l-er** tresses.

lokk'[2] -en musical call (to animals); call (e.g. of a bird).

lokk'[3] -et (=*__lok__[2]) 1 cover, lid: **lette på l-et** fig. disclose a little of a secret. 2 pop. whore.

lok'ke[1] V -a/+-et 1 allure, entice, tempt; lure; seduce; **l- fram, ut** coax, wheedle out (e.g. information), elicit. 2 attract, fascinate: **l-ende muligheter** attractive possibilities. 3 call (esp. to an animal); give a mating call.

lok'ke[2] V -a/+-et 1 punch (metal). 2: **l- seg** curl (of hair).

lok'ke/due -a decoy.

+**lok'ke/fat** -et cf **lokk/**

lok'ke/fugl -en decoy.

lok'ke/mat -en bait.

lok'ket(e) A - wavy (of hair).

lok'ke/toner pl 1 bird calls. 2 alluring, siren calls.

lokk'/fat -et (=+**lokke/**) covered dish, bowl.

lokomoti'v -et, pl -/+-er locomotive.

+**lokomoti'v/fører** -en, pl -e (=*-ar) (locomotive) engineer.

lokomoti'v/stall -en roundhouse.

lo'kum -et, pl +-er/*- fam. privy.

lom [lom'] -men/*-en 1 zool. grebe, loon (Colymbus). 2 oar loom.

Lom' Pln twp, Oppland.

*__lom/hunḍ__ [lom'/] -en zool. lemming.

lomme [lom'me] -a 1 pocket (in clothing, in a trunk, etc.): **ha i sin l-** fig. have in one's pocket (palm of one's hand). 2 cavity, hollow (in the earth, etc.).

lomme/bok -a, pl -bøker 1 billfold; wallet. 2 pocket notebook.

lomme/duk -en handkerchief.

lomme/for -et pocket lining.

lomme/kniv -en pocketknife.

lomme/lerke -a hip (pocket) flask.

lomme/lykt -a flashlight.

+**lomme/penger** pl (=*-ar) pocket money, spending money.

lomme/rusk -et pocket fluff, lint.

lomme/tjuv [/kjuv] -en (=+/**tyv**) pickpocket.

lomme/tørkle -et, pl +-klær/*- handkerchief.

lomme/ur -et pocket watch.

+**lomme/utgave** -a/-en (=*/**utgåve**) pocket edition.

+**lompe** [lom'pe] -a cf **lumpe**

lomre [lom're] -a zool. type of flatfish (Pleuronectes microcephalus).

lomvi [lom'vi] -en zool. common guillemot (Uria aalge).

lom'/vær(ing) -en person from Lom.

lo'n -a 1 calm, deep pool (in a river, stream). 2 dial. grassy marsh along such a pool; low meadow by water.

*__lo'net(e)__ A - swampy; puddly.

*__long'e__[1] -a cf **lange**[1]

*__long'e__[2] Av (=*__longo__) long ago, long since.

longør [långgø'r] -en boring, dull part (of a book, play, etc.).

lons [lon's] -en 1 portion, ration (of food). 2 fam. large, thick slice (of bread, meat, etc.).

loope [lu'pe] V -a/+-et loop (an airplane).

*__lopen__ [lå'pen] A -e/-i, pl -ne 1 stiffened (from cold). 2 decomposed; moldered.

lopp' -en dial., zool. frog.

Lop'pa Pln twp, Finnmark.

lop'pe[1] -a 1 zool. flea. 2 small speedboat.

lop'pe[2] V -a/+-et 1 deflea: **l- seg** deflea oneself. 2 fleece, swindle.

lop'pe/kasse -a/-en fam. bed, "fleabag".

+**lop'pe/marked** -et (=*/**marknad**) 1 rummage sale, white elephant sale. 2 Flea Market (in Paris).

lop'pen A -ent, pl loppne frozen; numb.

lop'pe/sirkus -et 1 flea circus. 2 derog. pottering, trifling work.

lop'pe/stikk -et fleabite.

lor'd -en 1 English lord (title); English high official; **l-enes hus** the English House of Lords. 2 fam. English tourist.

lorgnett' -en 1 pince-nez. 2 lorgnette.

lor'je -a flat-bottomed barge.

lort [lor't] -en 1 fam. excrement; turd. 2 dirt, filth.

lorte [lor'te] V -a/+-et dirty, soil, sully.

lortet(e) [lor'tet(e)] A - dirty, filthy; foul.

*__lort/vell__ [lor't/] A -velt dirty, filthy; slovenly.

lo's[1] -en baying (of hunting dogs).

lo's[2] -en naut. (harbor, coastal) pilot.

*__los__[3] [lå's] -et: **kome på l-** start, get going.

lo's/båt -en naut. pilot boat.

lo'se[1] V -a/+-et/-te 1 naut. pilot (a ship); fam., fig. accompany, escort, steer. 2 fam.: **l- etter noe** go about eavesdropping, lurk about and listen for sth.

*__lose__[2] [lå'se] V -a/-te set in motion, start going.

lo's/fisk -en zool. pilot fish (Naucrates ductor).

lo's/flagg -et naut. pilot flag.

lo'sje -n 1 (press, theater) box, loge. 2 fraternal lodge (usu. Freemason). 3 lodge building.

losjemen't -et pop. lodging.

lo'sje/rad -a/+-en (theater) balcony: **første l-** dress circle; **annen l-** upper circle.

losje're V -te lodge, room (**hos** at).

losje'renḍe -en lodger, roomer.

losji' -et, pl -/+-er lodging(s); lodging house.

+**lo'/slitt** A - (=*/**sliten**) threadbare (clothes, person, etc.), shabby, worn (fur).

*__los'ne__ V -a 1 loosen. 2 start going.

lo's/oldermann -en, pl -menn/*-menner naut. pilot master.

+**lo's/penger** pl (=*-ar) naut. pilotage (fee).

loss' A - naut. loose: **gjøre, kaste l-** cast off.

los'se V -a/+-et 1 naut. loose (a hawser, sail, etc.). 2 discharge (cargo); unload (a ship).

+**los'se/arbei'der** -en (=*-ar) naut. hold worker (during unloading).

los'se/bom [/bomm] -men naut. (ship's) derrick.

los'se/gjeng -en naut. unloading team, workers.

°**los'sement** -et cf **losjement**

los'se/plass -en 1 naut. discharging berth. 2 naut. place, port of discharge.

*__los'te__ V -a bark (a tree).

*__lot__[1] [lå't] -en/-et humor, mood, spirits.

+**lo't**[2] pt of **la**[3]**(te)**

*__lota__ [lå'ta] A - disposed, inclined: **eg er ikkje så l-** I am not in the mood.

*__lo'te__ pp of **ljote**

*__loten__ [lå'ten] A -e/-i, pl -ne in (good) humor, mood, spirits.

*__lo'ti__ pp of **ljote**

lott' -en, pl *-er portion, share.

lot'te -a/+-en member of **Norges lotteforening (NLF)**, ab.=WAC.

+**lot'te/fore'ning** -a/-en (=*/**foreining**)

+ Bokmål; * Nynorsk; ° Dialect.
After letter: ' stress (Acc. 1); ' tone, stress (Acc. 2); · length.
Below letter: . not pronounced.

women's defense league (in Norway), ab.=WAC.
lotteri' *-et, pl* +*-er*/*- lottery.
+**lotteri'/gevin·st** *-en* lottery prize.
lott'/fiske *-t* fishing wherein fishermen share in the catch.
lott'/lag *-et* cf **lut/**
lott'/mann *-en, pl -menn*/*-*menner* one who works for share in proceeds.
lo'tus *-en bot.* lotus; lotus tree.
+**lo'tus/blomst** *-en* (=*/**blome**) lotus flower.
*__lo'/ty__ *-et* ammunition.
lo'/tørk *-en* grain drying (process, weather).
lov[1] [lå'v] *-en*/*-*a* law (specific, general and natural), regulation (of a group, society), statute: **etter norsk l-** according to Norwegian law; **(likhet) for l-en** (equality) before the law.
lov[2] [lå'v] *-et*/+*-en* ɪ leave, permission: **få l- til å** be allowed to, get permission to; **gi (en) l- til å** allow (sby) to, give (sby) permission to; **ha l- til å** be allowed, permitted to; **jeg skal få l- til å si** allow me to say, I beg to say. **2** holiday, day off (e.g. from school).
lov[3] [lå'v] *-et*/+*-en* ɪ commendation, praise: **Gud skje l-, l- og takk** the Lord be praised, thank Heaven. **2** character, reputation.
lo'/vart *N* (=+**lu/**): *naut.* **til l-** to windward.
+**lov/bestem·melse** [lå'v/] *-n jur.* statutory enactment, provision.
+**lov/bestem·t** *A* - ɪ *jur.* fixed by law, statutory. **2** constant, regular.
*__lov/bod__ [/bå] *-et* cf **/bud**
lov/bok *-a, pl -bøker* ɪ *jur.* code of laws, statute book. **2** lawbook.
*__lov/brigde__ *-t jur.* change (of a law).
lov/brott *-et* (=+**/brudd**) *jur.* breach, infringement, violation of the law.
+**lov/bryter** *-en, pl -e* (=*-**ar**) lawbreaker.
+**lov/bud** *-et jur.* statutory enactment, provision.
lo've[1] *-n dial.* palm (of the hand, glove, mitten).
+**love**[2] [lå've] *N*: **på tro og l-** on good faith, on one's honor.
love[3] [lå've] *V -a*/+*-et*/*-de*/+*-te* ɪ promise: **å l- er ærlig, å holde besværlig** to promise is one thing, to hold (to) it another; **det l-ede land** the Promised Land. **2** *fam.* assure, guarantee, warrant: **det skal jeg l- for** I will guarantee that, you can be sure of that.
love[4] [lå've] *V* +*-et*/*-*a* *(bibl.), lit.* commend, praise.
lovende [lå'vene] *A* - promising; auspicious.
lov/endring [lå'v/] *-a*/+*-en jur.* change (in the law).
love're *V -te* ɪ *archaic, naut.* beat, tack. **2** *fam.* loiter about.
lov/fast [lå'v/] *A* - ɪ constant, regular. **2** *lit.* fixed by law, statutory.
lov/feste *V -a*/+*-et*/*-*e* establish, fix by law.
+**lovformelig** [låvfår'meli] *A* - lawful, legal: **et l- ekteskap** a lawful marriage.
+**lov/forsla·g** [lå'v/] *-et* bill (in congress, parliament).
+**lov/givende** *A* - (=*/**gjevande**) legislative.
+**lov/giver** *-en, pl -e* (=*/**gjevar**) lawgiver, legislator.
+**lov/gi·vning** *-en* (=*/**gjeving**) legislation.
lov/heimel *-en* (=+**/hjemmel**) *jur.* legal authority, title.
lov/knep *-et* legal trick.
lov/kyndig *A* - (=*/**kunnig**) legally trained: **l- bistand** legal aid.
+**lov/kyndighet** *-en* (=*/**kunne**) ɪ knowledge of law. **2** jurisprudence (usu. *archaic*).
lov/laus *A* - (=+**/løs**) lawless.
lovlig[1] [lå'vli] *A* - lawful, legal, legitimate; valid.
lovlig[2] [lå'vli] *Av* a bit, rather.
lov/lydig [lå'v/] *A* - law-abiding.
+**lov/løs** *A* cf **/laus**
lov/løyse *-a* (=+**/løshet**) lawlessness.
+**lov/medhol·dig** *A* - *jur.* lawful, legal.
+**lov/messig** *A* - ɪ lawful, legal. **2** constant, regular.
*__lovnad__ [lå'vna] *-en, pl -er* promise, vow.
lov/ord [lå'v/o·r] *pl* encomium, words of praise.
lo'/vott *-en* mitten: **jeg hørte lusa hoste i l-en** "I heard the louse coughing in the mitten" (=listen to him talk!).
+**lov/overtre·der** [lå'v/] *-en, pl -e* offender (against the law); criminal.
lov/prise *V* +*-te*/*-*a* extol, laud, praise.
+**lov/sang**[1] *-en* (=*/**song**) hymn, song of praise; paean.
+**lov/sang**[2] *pt of* **-synge**
*__lovseiings/mann__ *-en, pl -menn(er)* cf **lovsige/**
+**lovsige/mann** *-en, pl -menn hist.* law speaker (at the Old Norse *thing*).
lov/stridig *A* - *jur.* illegal.
+**lov/synge** *V -sang, -sunget* sing the praises of; extol.
lov/tale *-n* encomium, eulogy, panegyric.
Lov/tidende *Prn* legal journal.
+**lov/trekkeri·** *-et* (legal) chicanery, pettifoggery.
lov/verk *-et jur.* law code, legislation, system of laws.
Lt.=**Lagtinget**
+**lu'** *-en* cf **lo**[6]
*__lubb'__ *-en* chubby, round figure.
*__lub'be__ *-a* chubby, round figure (girl, fish etc.).
lub'ben *A* +*-ent, pl lubne* chubby, plump.
lucern(e) [lu-, ly-, -sær'n, -sær'ne] *-(e)n* cf **luserne**
Luci'a/fest *-en* Lucia celebration (Dec. 13; cf **Lussinatt**).
lud'der *-et vulg.* tart, whore.
lu'do *-en* ludo (board game similar to parcheesi).
Lud'vig *Prn (m)*
lu'e[1] *-a* (=**luve**) cap.
+**lu'e**[2] *-n* cf **loge**[1]
+**lu'e**[3] *V -et* cf **loge**[2]
*__lu'e__[4] *V -a* sound: **brevet l-ar såleis** the letter reads as follows; **det l-ar så** it sounds like it.
+**lu'ende** *A* - blazing, flaming.
luf'fe[1] *-n* flipper, pectoral (on a seal, whale, etc.).
+**luf'fe**[2] *V -a*/*-et* cf **loffe**[1,2]
*__luf's__ *-en* animal, person with long, straggly hair.
*__luf'se__ *V -a* straggle (of hair).
luf't *-a* air, atmosphere: **i fri l-, i l-a** in the open air; **l- i luka** activity, life, stir; **få l-** get a breath; **få l- under vingene** get a chance (to show what one can do); **gi (sine følelser) l-** give vent to (one's feelings); **gripe ut av l-a** pull out of thin air; **gå i l-a** explode; **ligge i l-a** be in the air, be imminent; **et slag i l-a** a futile effort; **sprenge i l-a** blow up; **svare ut i løse l-a** answer absent-mindedly; (of aircraft) **ta l-a** take off; **trekke l-** breathe, draw a breath; **være l- for en** be nothing to sby, be overlooked by sby.
+**luf't/angrep** *-et* air attack, air raid.
+**luf't/båren** *A -ent*/*-et, pl -ne* (=*/**boren**) airborne.
luf't/drag *-et* breeze, puff of wind; draft.
luf'te *V -a*/+*-et* ɪ air (bedding, dog, room, etc.; also *fig.*), ventilate: **l- seg** get some air; **l- ut** *fig.* clear the air, ventilate; clear out, trim away (esp. between plants, trees, etc.). **2** (of wind) blow lightly. ***3** give off an odor, smell.
+**luf'te/gå·rd** *-en* (=*/**gard**) airing court, yard (in a prison or asylum).
luf'te/luke *-a* air vent.
luf'te/plass *-en* airing court, yard (for an apartment building).
luf'te/tur *-en* airing, short walk outdoors.
luf't/fart *-en* aviation, flying; air traffic, transport.
luf'tfarts/direktora·tet *df* (corresponds closely to) Civil Aeronautics Administration.
+**luf't/fartøy** *-et* (=*/**farty**) aircraft.
*__luf't/ferdsle__ *-a* flight (trip).
luf't/foran·dring *-a*/+*-en* change of climate, air.
luf't/fotografe·ring *-a*/+*-en* aerial photography.
luf't/gevæ·r *-et* air gun, air rifle.
+**luf't/havn** *-a* (=**/hamn**) airport.
luf't/hol [/hål] *-et* (=+**/hull**) ɪ air hole, vent. **2** air pocket.
luf'tig *A* - airy, light (cloth, food, room, etc.); breezy, empty (argument, talk); fleeting, transient (image, thought); (as *adv.*) **l-påkledt** scantily dressed.
luf'ting *-a*/+*-en* ɪ airing; ventilation. **2** (light) breeze. **3** breeziness.
luf't/kastell· *-et, pl -*/+*-er fig.* castle in the air.
luf't/kondisjone·ring *-a*/+*-en* air conditioning.
luf't/kondisjone·rt *A* - air-conditioned.
luf't/lag *-et* atmospheric layer.
+**luf't/le·dning** *-en* ɪ overhead (electric) wire, line. **2** ventilation pipe.
luf't/linje *-a*/+*-en* (=*/**line**) air line, beeline, direct line: **i l-** as the crow flies.
+**luf't/maske** *-a*/*-en* (=*/**moske**) chain stitch (in crocheting).
luf't/motstan·d *-en*/*-*et* air drag; air resistance.
+**luf'tning** *-en* ɪ airing, ventilation. **2** (light) breeze; breeziness; whiff.
luf't/perspekti·v *-et, pl -*/+*-er* aerial perspective.
luf't/post *-en* air mail.
luf't/pumpe [/pompe] *-a* air pump; vacuum pump.
luf't/rør *-et*/*-*a* (=*/**røyr**) ɪ air duct, ventiduct. **2** *anat.* trachea, windpipe.
luf'trørs/katarr· *-en med.* bronchitis.
luf't/sjuk *A* (=+**/syk**) airsick.
luf't/sjuke *-n* (=+**/syke**) airsickness.
luf't/skip *-et* airship.
luf't/slott *-et* castle in the air.
+**luf't/speiling** *-en* (=*/**spegling**) mirage.
luf't/stridskref·ter *pl mil.* air power, strength.
*__luf't/sykje__ *-a* cf **/sjuke**
luf't/tett *A* - airtight, hermetic.
luf't/tom· *A -t, pl -me* void of air, vacuum; *fig.* vacuous.
luf't/trykk *-et* ɪ atmospheric pressure. **2** blast (from an explosion).
luf't/vern [/væ·rn] *-et mil.* antiaircraft defense.
luga'r *-en naut.* berth, cabin.
+**luga'r/pike** *-a*/*-en* (passenger ship) stewardess.
lugg'[1] *-en* ɪ forelock, tuft of hair. **2** *fam.* mop of hair: **fare, komme i l-en på hverandre** fly at, light into each other.
lugg'[2] *-en* ɪ coarse oversock. ***2** large, thick body (usu. of an animal).
lugg'[3] *-et* pull by the hair, hair pulling.
lug'ge *V -a*/+*-et* ɪ pull (by the) hair: **l-s** fight. **2** weed. **3** *typog.* (of colored ink) be too stiff, thick.
lug'ger *-en, pl* +*-e naut.* lugger.
+**lugn** [lung'n] *A* cf **logn**[2]
lu'gom *A* cf **lagom**
lugu'ber *A -ert, pl -re* lugubrious.
lu'ke[1] *-a* ɪ (ceiling, floor, wall) opening, wicket; (bank) window; *naut.* hatch, scuttle: **luft i l-a** activity, life, stir. **2** hatch cover, shutter, trap door cover; skylight. **3** empty space, opening (in a line, row, etc.); loophole (in the law).
lu'ke[2] *V -a*/+*-et*/*-te* weed (also *fig.*).
lu'ke/karm *-en* frame (around an opening); *naut.* coaming.
lu'ke/kolon·ne *-n mil.* open order formation.

***luk'kast** *V -ast* cf **lykkes**
***luk'ke¹** *-a* cf **lykke**
+lukke² [lok'ke] *-t* 1 closure, fastening (cf **lås**). 2 (in phonetics) closure, stop. 3 *archaic* cabinet, closet: **et hemmelig l-** a secret hiding place.
lukke³ [lok'ke] *V -a/+-et* 1 close, shut: **l- munnen på en** silence sby; **l- øynene for** refuse to see, shut one's eyes to. 2 (with *prep., adv.*): **l- for** close to; **l- igjen** close, shut; **l- inn, ut** let in, out (of the door); **l- inne** lock, shut up; **l- opp** open, unlock; **l- til** close, shut; **l- ut** exclude, lock out. 3 *(refl.)*: **l- seg** close (e.g. flowers); **l- seg inne** isolate oneself, lock oneself in one's room. 4: **l-et** closed, shut; closed-in; *fig.* immobile, impassive (e.g. face).
***luk'keleg** *A* - cf **lykkelig**
+lukker [lok'ker] *-en, pl -e* shutter (on camera).
+lukket/het [lok'ket/] *-en lit.* closure; impassivity.
***lukk'/ynsking** *-a* cf **lykk/ønskning**
+lukk/øye [lokk'/] *N*: **Ole l-** the sandman.
+luknings/tid [lok'nings/] *-a/-en* closing time.
luk'rativ *A* lucrative.
+luk's *Av* cf **lukt²**
luksuriø's *A* luxurious.
luk'sus *-en* luxury.
luk'sus/hotell' *-et, pl -/+-er* luxury hotel.
luk'sus/kvinne *-a/+-en* pampered woman living in luxury.
luk'sus/skatt *-en* luxury tax.
lukt¹ [lok't] *-a/+-en* 1 odor, smell; scent, track (of an animal, etc.). 2 sense of smell.
luk't² *Av* clear, directly, straight: **like l-** right straight.
lukte [lok'te] *V -a/+-et* 1 emit an odor; smell (also *fig.*): **det l-er svidd her** it s-s burned (=something's wrong) (Hoel). 2 perceive by odor; smell (also *fig.*): **l- på noe** s-, sniff (at) sth; *fam.* **lukt på den** "smell that" (said when one threatens with one's fist); **l- seg til noe** arrive at by guesswork, smell out.
luktende(s) [lok'tene(s)] *et pop.* perfume.
lukte/sans [lok'te/] *-en* olfactory sense, sense of smell.
lukt/fri [lok't/] *A -tt* odorless.
lukul'lisk *A* - Lucullan, sumptuous.
lul'le *V -a/+-et* lull (to sleep): **l- seg inn i** be lulled by (hope, illusion, etc.); *hum.
***lum'** *A* cf **lummer**
lumba'go *-en med.* lumbago.
lu'men *-et mat., phys.* lumen.
***lum'me** *-a* cf **lomme**
lummer [lom'mer] *A -t, pl lumre* 1 (of air) close, stifling, sultry. 2 oppressive; dead, dull. 3 lewd, suggestive.
lump [lom'p] *-en* thick log, block of wood.
lumpe [lom'pe] *-a* small, somewhat thick potato cake.
lumpen [lom'pen] *A +-ent, pl -ne* 1 low, mean, shabby: *(adv.)* **det var l-t gjort** that was a dirty trick. 2 miserable; paltry, piddling. *3 obtuse, roundish.
+lumpen/het *-en* 1 meanness, shabbiness. 2 dirty, mean trick.
***lum're¹** [lom're] *-a* calm, hazy, warm air.
lumre² [lom're] *pl of* **lummer**
lum'sk [also -o-] *A* 1 deceitful, insidious; treacherous; underhanded. 2 crafty, foxy, sly: **en l- mistanke** a sneaking suspicion.
+lum'skelig *Av* - insidiously, slily.
+lum'sk/het *-en* cunning, deceitfulness; treachery.
lu'n *A* - 1 cozy, snug; sheltered (house, room, valley, etc.); comfortable, genial, warm (person, room, weather). 2 good-natured, pleasant, quiet (person); (quietly) humorous; droll.
lun'd¹ *-en* grove; *poet.* greenwood.
***lun'd²** *-en* melody; (singing) voice.
lun'de *-n zool.* puffin (Fratercula arctica).
Lun'de *Pln* twp, Telemark.
+-lun'de *Av* manner, way, e.g. **ingen/l-, noen/l-.**
lu'ne¹ *-t/*-a* 1 mood, humor: **Jeg i slett l-, Morgenblad?** I in bad humor, M-? (Wergeland). 2 caprice, whim. 3 wit, humor.
lu'ne² *V -a/+-et* shelter; warm; make cozy: **åsenes lave karm som l-er og lukker** the low frame of ridges, which shelters and encloses (Undset).
lu'ne/full *A* capricious, whimsical; changeable, fickle, unpredictable.
lu'net(e) *A* - capricious, whimsical; unpredictable.
lunge [long'e] *-a/+-en* lung: **av sine l-ers fulle kraft, med fulle l-r** at the top of one's lungs.
lunge/beten'nelse *-n* pneumonia.
lunge/brann *-en* pneumonia.
lunge/mos *-en* dish of finely chopped lung (or intestines) cooked in stock.
lunge/sekk *-en anat.* pleura.
lunge/spiss *-en anat.* apex of the lung.
lunge/urt *-a/+-en bot.* lungwort (Pulmonaria).
+lu'n/het *-a/-en* comfort, coziness, warmth; geniality, humor.
lunk¹ [long'k] *-en* 1 warmth. 2: *fam.* **gi kaffekjelen en l-** warm up the coffee pot.
lunk² [long'k] *-en* jog trot.
lunke¹ [long'ke] *V -a/+-et* warm up (a little); take the chill off: **l- på** (the same).
lunke² [long'ke] *V -a/+-et* 1 *fam.* walk slowly, saunter along; move carefully. 2 jog along (usu. of a horse).
lunken [long'ken] *A +-ent, pl -ne* lukewarm, tepid (also *fig.*, cf Revelations 3,16).
lunn' *-en* 1 roller (for ease in moving). 2 skid (for support or elevation). 3 (floor) joist. 4 lever (for lifting lumber). 5 *(pl.)* rights and privileges (attached to landed property): **med lut(er) og l-er** with all portions and privileges.
lun'ne¹ *-a/-en* 1 pile, stack of timber. 2 stack of hay or fodder. 3 skid. 4 joist.
lun'ne² *V -a/+-et* 1 lay rollers. 2 lay skids. 3 lift or move by a lever.
lun'ne³ *V -a/+-et* haul out (of the woods) and pile up (timber).
***lun'nende** *-t* cf **lunn**
Lun'ner *Pln* twp, Oppland.
lunsj [løn'sj] *-en* luncheon, (noon) dinner.
lunsje [løn'sje] *V -a/+-et* lunch.
lun'/stikke *-a* linchpin.
lun't *-et* jog trot.
lun'te¹ *-a* (explosive) fuse; slow match: **lukte l-a** *fig.* smell a rat.
lun'te² *V -a/+-et* jog along (of an animal), saunter (shuffle) along.
+lun'te/trav *-et* (=*/**tråv**) jog trot.
lup'e *-a/+-en* magnifying glass.
lupi'n *-en bot.* lupine (Lupinus).
lu'r¹ *-en* 1 trumpetlike wooden shepherd's horn (similar to an alpenhorn). 2 *hist.* lur (bronze wind instrument). 3 *dial.* roll of bark.
lu'r² *-en* nap, snooze.
lu'r³ *N*: **(ligge) på l- etter** (lie) in ambush, in wait for; **stå på l- etter** be on the watch for.
lu'r⁴ *A* 1 cunning, sly, wily (person). 2 clever, ingenious (e.g. idea), smart.
lu're¹ *V +-te/*-a* 1 eavesdrop; spy, watch. 2 lie in wait (**på** for), lurk. 3 speculate, wonder (**på** about): **l- på noe** (also) scheme. 4 sneak, steal: **l- seg inn på en** sneak up on one; **l- seg fra en, noe** dodge, evade sby, sth. 5 baffle, fool, trick.
lu're² *V -te/*-a* doze, nap.
+lu'ren/dreier *-en, pl -e* foxy, tricky person; rogue, scamp.
+lu'reri *-et* cunning, wile; trickery.
lu're/teppe *-t, pl +-r/*-* coverlet, robe (as a covering).
lu'rifas *-en fam.* sly rogue, scamp.
lu'ring *-en fam.* crafty, cunning person.
lur'k *-en* 1 thick stick. 2 large, heavy animal, object, person.
***lur'ke** *V -a* beat, flog (with a stick).
lu'r/lokk [also lu'r/] *-en* call (to livestock) on a shepherd's horn.
lu'r/passe *V -a/+-et* (in cards) pass (in spite of a high hand) in order to deceive one's opponent.
lur'v *-en* 1 shock (of hair); wisp. 2 ragged, miserable wretch.
lur've¹ *-a* 1 *dial.* rag, tatter. 2 *dial.* sloven (woman).
lur've² *V -a/+-et* make shabby, slovenly, unkempt.
lur've/leven *-et* hubbub, uproar.
***lur'ven** *A -e/-i, pl -ne* ill, unwell.
lur'vet(e) *A* - 1 shabby, slovenly, unkempt; ragged, tattered. 2 coarse, common, low; evil, mean.
Lu'r/øy *Pln* twp, Nordland.
lu's *-a, pl -/*lyser* 1 *zool.* louse (several species including animal, human, plant): **bevege seg som en l- på en tjærekost** move at a snail's pace; **jeg syntes jeg hørte en l- hoste** "I thought I heard a louse cough" (intended to put one in his place). 2 pitiable wretch; greedy, petty person. 3 hairy seed of a rose hip. 4 small stick (forming a design) on a *lusekofte*. 5 *carp.* filler, plug. 6 *naut.* mark on coastal chart indicating a rock awash.
lu'se *V +-te/*-a* 1 delouse. 2 *dial.* beat, drub; box one's ears. 3 (in carpentry) plug a hole, opening. 4 be miserly, niggardly: **l- i hoppet** (in ski jumping) jump too cautiously.
lu'se/fart *-en* miserably slow speed.
+lu'se/knekker *-en, pl -e* (=***-jar**) skinflint.
lu'se/kufte [-kofte] *-a* Norwegian cardigan (in colorful patterns).
lu'se/lønn *-a/+-en* (=*/**løn**) miserable pay, wages.
lu'sen *A +-ent, pl -ne* miserly, niggardly.
luserne [lusæ'rne] *-n bot.* alfalfa (Medicago sativa).
lu'set(e) *A* - 1 infested with lice, lousy. 2 miserable, pitiable, wretched.
lu's/hatt *-en bot.* aconite.
lu'sing *-en* box on the ear; beating, drubbing.
lus'k *-en* tuft of hair; forelock (on a horse).
lus'ke¹ *V -a/+-et* 1 slink, sneak: **l- av** sneak off; **l- seg inn på en** sneak up on sby. 2 get out of, shirk (duty, work, etc.).
°lus'ke² *V -a/+-et* cf **lyske²**
lus'ke/rev *-en* sly, sneaky person.
lus'si/natt *-a/+-en* St. Lucia's Eve (December 12th).
Lus'ter *Pln* twp, Sogn og Fjordane.
lu't¹ *-a/+-en* lye: **gå for l- og kaldt vann** be neglected, left to take care of oneself; **der skal skarp l- til skurvete hoder** desperate diseases need desperate remedies.
***lu't²** *-en* cf **lott**
lu't³ *A* bent (over), stooped.
lu't⁴ *Av* (=**luta, lutende**) extremely, very: **l- lei** sick and tired, thoroughly bored.
***lu't/brev** *-et merc.* stock certificate.
lu't/doven [/dåven] *A +-ent, pl -ne* very lazy, lazy to the core.
lu'te¹ *V -a/+-et* 1 soak, treat in lye. 2: **l- ut noe** wash the lye from sth; *chem.* extract (by dissolving).
lu'te² *V +-a/+-et/-te* bend, lean, stoop; bow, hang down: **l- mot graven be**

+ Bokmål; * Nynorsk; ° Dialect.
After letter: ' stress (Acc. 1); ' tone, stress (Acc. 2); · length.
Below letter: . not pronounced.

near death; **l- seg fram** lean forward.
***lu'te**[3] *V -a* apportion, divide.
lu'te/fisk *-en lutefisk* (cod treated in a lye solution and served boiled).
***lu't/eigar** *-en* shareholder, stockholder.
lu'tende *Av* cf **lut**[4]
lu'tet(e) *A* - treated with lye (solution); (of a favorite type of Norwegian furniture) with lye finish.
lu't/fattig *A* - destitute, penniless.
lu't/fisk *-en* cf **lute/**
+luthera'ner *-en, pl -e* (=***-ar, *lutheran**) Lutheran.
lut'her/dom' *-men/*-en* Lutheranism.
lut'hersk *A* - Lutheran.
***lu't/lag** *-et* (=**lott/**) 1 corporation. 2 cooperative.
lu't/lei *A +-t/*-tt* cf **lut**[4]
+lut're *V -a/-et* purify, refine (feelings, metal, thoughts, etc.); chasten; ennoble.
lu't/rygga *A* - (=**+-et, *-ja**) stoop-shouldered.
***lu't/spel** *-et* lottery.
lutt' *-en mus.* lute.
+lut'ter *A* - all, pure, sheer; nothing but, only: **jeg er l- øre** I am all ears.
lu'v *-en* forelock; fine, thin hair (on an animal).
lu'/vart *N* cf **lo/**
lu've *-a* cf **lue**[1]
+lu'v/slitt *A* - cf **lo/**
lux' *-en phys.* lux.
Luxembourg [lyksambo'r] *Pln*
ly'[1] *-et* cover, shelter, protection: **i ly** protected, sheltered (**av** by, **for** from).
ly'[2] *A -tt* resonant, sound-carrying (house, room, etc.).
ly'[3] *A -tt* mild, soft, somewhat warm (of air, water).
lyb'sk *A* - (of) Lübeck.
lycé(um) *-céet, pl +-céer/*-cé/*-céum educ.* lycée (esp. in France).
ly'd[1] *-en* (=***ljod**) 1 sound: **l-ens hastighet** the speed of sound; **det ble en annen l-** that was a different tune. 2 quiet, silence: **slå til l-** call for order, silence; **slå til l- for noe** advocate sth.
***ly'd**[2] *-en* (group of) people; family.
***ly'd**[3] *A lydt* cf **ly**[3]
***ly'dar** *-en* cf **lytter**
***ly'dar/avgift** *-a* cf **lytter/**
***ly'dast** *V lydest, lyddest, lydst* 1 seem, sound (as if). 2: **l- inn, om** call (on), visit.
ly'd/band *-et* recording tape; taped recording.
ly'dband/opptak *-et* tape recording.
+ly'dband/opptaker *-en, pl -e* (=***-ar**) tape recorder.
ly'd/bok *-a, pl -bøker* talking book (esp. for the blind).
***ly'd/brigde** *-t* vowel mutation, umlaut.
ly'd/bøye *-n* whistling buoy.
+ly'd/bånd *-et* cf **/band**
+ly'd/demper *-en, pl -e* (=***-ar**) (sound) muffler, silencer.
***lyd'dest** *pt of* **lydast**
ly'd/dåse *-n* sound box.
ly'de[1] [*ly'e] *V -de/+lød, -d/+-t* (=***ljode**) 1 sound; be heard; run: **brevet l-er slik, som følger** the letter reads as follows. 2 be made out, registered (**på** in, to); be (**på** for, to the effect that): **sjekken lød på kr 50,00** the check was for 50 *kroner.*
***ly'de**[2] *V -de* cf **lye**[1]
+ly'delig *A* - audible, clear; loud.
ly'd/film *-en* sound film.
ly'dfilm/avi's *-a/+-en* newsreel.
+ly'd/giver *-en, pl -e phys.* body which emits sound waves.
ly'd/himmel *-elen, pl -himler* sounding board (over an orchestra, a speaker, etc.).
+ly'd/hull *-et* (=**/hol**) *mus.* sound hole.
+ly'd/hør *A* 1 keen, sharp (of hearing). 2 attentive, heedful (**overfor** to); sympathetic (**for, overfor** to).
ly'dig *A* - dutiful, obedient (**mot** to).
+ly'dig/het *-en* dutifulness, obedience (**mot** to).
ly'd/laus *A* (=**+/løs**) noiseless, silent, soundless.
ly'dlig *A* - (=***ljodleg**) phonetic.
ly'd/lov [/låv] *-en/*-a gram.* sound law.
ly'd/lære *-a/+-en* 1 *phys.* acoustics. 2 phonetics. 3 phonology.
+ly'd/løs *A* cf **/laus**
+ly'd/malende *A* onomatopoetic.
ly'd/mur *-en* sound barrier.
***ly'dnad** *-en* dutifulness, obedience.
ly'd/o'rd *-et* onomatopoetic word.
ly'd/potte *-a* 1 *mus.* (sound) damper (e.g. in a piano). 2 (motor) muffler.
ly'd/rett *A* - 1 phonetic (according to pronunciation). 2 literal. 3 regular (in agreement with sound laws).
ly'd/rike *-t, pl +-r/*-* dependency.
ly'd/skrift *-a/+-en* 1 phonetic spelling, writing; transcription. 2 alphabetic writing system.
***ly'd/sprang** *-et* ablaut, vowel gradation.
***lyd'st** *pp of* **lydast**
ly'd/tett *A* - soundproof.
+ly'e[1] *V -dde* (=***lyde**[2]) 1 listen (to): **l- etter** inquire about, listen to; **l- innom** drop in. 2 sound.
***ly'e**[2] *V -a* heat, warm (up).
***lyf't** *-et* cf **løft**
***lyf'te** *V -a/-e* cf **løfte**[2]
***lyf'ting** *-en* cf **løfting**
***ly'gar** *-en* cf **løgner**
ly'ge *V laug/+løy, +løyet/*loge/*-i* (=**ljuge**) lie, tell a falsehood: **l- for en l-** to sby; **l- på en** slander sby; **l- sammen** make up; **hvis ikke ryktet l-er** if the rumor is true.
***lygn** [lyng'n] *-a* cf **løgn**
***lygnar** [lyng'nar] *-en* cf **løgner**
***lygne** [lyng'ne] *V -de* abate, subside (of the wind, weather).
***lykel** [ly'kjel] *-elen, pl -lar* cf **nøkkel**
***lyk'kast** *V -ast* cf **lykkes**
lyk'ke *-a/+-en* (=***lukke**[1]) 1 (good) fortune, (good) luck; success: **l- på reisen (turen)** bon voyage; **l- til!** good luck!; **gjøre l-** be a success, a hit; **ha l-n med seg** be lucky; **prøve l-n** try one's luck; **på l- og fromme** at random, in a haphazard way; **til l- med dagen** many happy returns of the day; **til all l-** fortunately; **ønske til l-** congratulate. 2 happiness, joy: **bli til l-** bring happiness, be a source of joy; **tar De livsløgnen fra et gjennomsnittsmenneske, så tar De l-n fra ham med det samme** if you deprive the average person of his illusions, you deprive him of his happiness as well (Ibsen).
lyk'ke/fugl *-en* 1 bird, person who brings luck. 2 fortunate, lucky person.
lyk'ke/hjul *-et* gambling wheel; *lit.* wheel of fortune.
lyk'ke/jeger *-en, pl +-e* fortune hunter.
lyk'kelig *A* - (=***lukkeleg**) 1 lucky; fortunate. 2 happy (**over** about).
+lyk'ke/ridder *-en, pl -e* (=***-ar**) adventurer, soldier of fortune.
lyk'kes *V lyktes, lykkes* (=***lukkast**) prove a success, succeed: **det lyktes ham å gjøre det** he succeeded in doing it.
lyk'ke/skilling *-en* lucky coin.
+lyk'ke/spill *-et* game of chance.
lyk'ke/stjerne *-a/+-en* lucky star.
lyk'ke/tal *-et* (=**+/tall**) lucky number.
lyk'ke/treff *+-et/*-en* stroke of luck.
***lykkj'e**[1] *-a* cf **løkke**[1]
***lykkj'e**[2] *-a* cf **løkke**[2]
+lykksa'lig *A* - (deeply, intensely) blissful, happy; *(bibl.)* blessed.
+lykksa'lig/gjøre *V -gjorde, -gjort* make blissful, happy.
+lykksa'lig/het *-en* (deep, intense) bliss, happiness.
***lykk'/ynsking** *-a* cf **/ønskning**
+lykk'/ønske *V -a/-et/-te* congratulate (**med** on).
+lykk'/ønskning *-en* (=***/ønsking, */ynsking, *lukk/ynsking**) congratulation (**med** on).
lyk't *-a* lantern; (car, street) lamp, light: **lete med lys og l-e** search high and low; **rød l-** red light (at theater or concert hall entrance meaning full house, sold out).
***lyk'te** *V -a* come to an end, finish.
lyk'te/mann *-en, pl -menn/*-menner* ignis fatuus, marshfire; *fig.* will-o'-the-wisp.
+lyk'tes *pt of* **lykkes**
lyk'te/stolpe *-n* lamppost.
+lyk'te/tenner *-en, pl -e* (=***-ar**) lamplighter: **henge i som en l-** work like a dog.
lym'fe *+-n/*-a physiol.* lymph.
lym'fe/kjertel *-elen, pl -ler physiol.* lymph gland.
ly'n *-et* 1 lightning (also *fig.*): **olja l-** greased lightning. 2 flash: **som et l-** like a flash.
+ly'n/avle'der *-en, pl -e* lightning rod; *fig.* one who diverts, turns away anger, wrath.
***lyn'de** *-t* cf **lynne**
***-lyn'dt** *A* - cf **-lynt**
ly'ne[1] *V -te* 1 send out lightning. 2 flash; gleam, glisten (strongly).
***ly'ne**[2] *V -a* become milder, warmer (esp. of the air).
ly'n/eld *-en* lightning.
ly'nende *A* -: **l- fort** (with) lightning speed; **l- flink** brilliantly clever, intelligent; **l- sint** furious, in a rage.
ly'n/fort [/fort] *A* - quick as lightning.
lyng' *-en/-et bot.* heather (Calluna); (blueberry etc.) plant.
+lyng'/blomst *-en* (=***/blome**) heather flower.
Lyng'/dal *Pln* twp, Vest-Agder.
Lyng'en *Pln* twp, Troms.
ly'n/glimt *-en/-et* flash of lightning; *fig.* flash.
Lyng'/ør *Pln* harbor town, Aust-Agder.
+ly'n/ild *-en* cf **/eld**
ly'n/krig *-en* blitzkrieg, "lightning war."
lyn'ne *-t* (=***lynde**) disposition, temperament.
ly'n/nedsla'g *-et* lightning (bolt).
ly'n/rapp *A -rapt* quick as lightning.
lyn'sje *V -a/+-et* lynch.
lyn'sj/justi's *-en* lynch law.
***lyn'sk** *A* - crafty, cunning, sly.
ly'n/skarp *A* sharp (as the zigzag of lightning).
ly'n/snar *A* quick as a flash.
ly'n/stråle *-n* flash of lightning.
-lyn't *A* - (=***-lyndt**) -minded e.g. **fri/l-, god/l-.**
ly'n/tog [/tåg] *-et* (esp. fast) express train.
ly'n/visitt' *-en* quick, short visit.
ly'r *-en zool.* pollack (Gadus pollachius).
ly're *-a/+-en* 1 *mus.* lyre. 2 *mus.* glockenspiel (in a military band). 3 **L-en** *astron.* Lyra, the Lyre.
+ly'riker-*en, pl -e* (=***-ar**) lyric poet.
lyrikk' *-en* lyric poetry; lyric emotion, feeling, mood.
ly'risk *A* - lyric, lyrical (poem, poet; emotion, feeling, mood).
ly's[1] *-et* (=***ljos**[1]) 1 light; lighting: **det gikk et l- opp for meg** it dawned on me; **føre bak l-et** deceive, take in; **få l- i saken** shed light on the matter; **kaste l- på** throw light on; **komme for l-et** be discovered; **stille i et (godt, dårlig, osv.) l-** place in a (good, bad, etc.) light; **stå i l-et for** shade. 2 candle: **levende l-** candle; *tech.* **lampe på 75 lys** a bulb of 75 candles; **rett som et l-** straight as a stick. 3 (intellectual) light; genius, luminary: **han er ikke noe l-** he's no genius.
lys[2] *A* (=***ljos**[2]) light, pale; bright (future, idea); high-pitched (sound, voice); cheerful (mood, temperament); fair (complexion, hair); happy (memories): **midt på l-e dagen** in broad daylight; **til den l-e morgen** till daybreak; **ved (høy)l-**

dag in the (full) light of day; **se l-t på noe** look at sth optimistically; **det er l-t i været** it's clear weather; **han er et l-t hode** he's bright.

+**ly's**[2] *Av*: **l- levende** large as life; **l- våken** wide awake.

ly's/alv *-en* friendly elf.

+**ly's/bilde** *-t* (=***/bilete**) (lantern) slide.

+**ly'sbilde/appara't** *-et* (=***-bilet/**) projector.

ly's/blink *-et* flash(ing) of light(s).

ly's/bryting *-a*/+*-en* (=+**/brytning**) refraction.

***ly's/dæmd** *A -dæmt* fair, light (complexioned).

ly'se[1] *-a* **1** illumination, light; gleam (of light). **2** small torch. **3** *dial.* cod-liver oil.

***ly'se**[2] *-t* (day)light; clearing weather; reflection: **nå fram i l-** get there in daylight.

ly'se[3] *V -te* **1** give (out) light, shine; illuminate, lighten; grow light, dawn; lead (with a light): **banne så det l-er** swear a blue streak; **l- opp** brighten, illuminate, light up. **2** (esp. *admin., jur.*) announce, proclaim: **l- til ekteskap** publish marriage banns. **3**: **l- noe over en** call down sth (blessing, damnation, peace, etc.) upon sby; invoke.

+**ly'se**[4] *Av* light (used before an adjective of color): **l- rødt** pink (usu. written as cpds.: **lyserødt**).

ly'se/krone *-a*/+*-en* chandelier.

ly's/ekte *A* - colorfast (to sunlight).

***lys'er** *pl of* **lus**

ly'se/saks *-a* (pair of) candle snuffers.

+**ly'se/slokker** [/slokker] *-en* (=***/sløkkjar**) **1** candle snuffer. **2** killjoy, spoilsport.

ly'se/stake *-n* candlestick; candelabra.

ly'se/stump [/stomp] *-en* candle end, stub.

+**ly's/fø·lsom** *A* sensitive to light.

ly's/gate *-a* cleared strip in forest for power lines.

ly's/glimt *-et*/**-en* gleam (of light).

ly's/hav *-et fig.* flood, sea of light.

ly's/håra *A* - (=+**-et**) blonde, fair-haired.

ly'sing *-a*/+*-en* **1** announcement: **l- til ekteskap** a- of marriage; banns. ***2** advertisement. **3** dawn; light. **4** (*-en*) *zool.* hake (Merluccius).

ly'sings/blad *-et* gazette (containing public notices, lists of promotions and honors, names of bankrupts, etc.).

ly's/kasse *-a*/*-en* (cellar) window well.

+**ly's/kaster** *-en, pl -e* (=***-ar**) floodlight, searchlight, spotlight.

lys'ke[1] +*-n*/**-a anat.* groin, inguen.

lys'ke[2] *V -a*/+*-et* delouse, pick off lice from.

ly's/kjegle [/kjeile] *-a*/+*-en* (cone-shaped) beam of light.

ly's/kledd *A* -/**-kledt* dressed in light colors.

ly's/kopi· *-en* blueprint (also white or other color), photocopy.

+**ly's/le·dning** *-en* electric (lighting) wire.

+**ly's/lett** *A* - (=***/leitt**) blond, fair (of hair and skin).

+**lys/levende** [ly's le'vene] *A* - cf **lys**[2]

ly's/lokka *A* - (=+**-et**) blond, fair-haired.

lys/løype *-a* lighted ski trail.

+**ly's/måler** *-en, pl -e* (=***-ar**, ***/mælar**) photometer; exposure meter (on a camera).

lys'ne *V -a*/+*-et* (=***ljosne**) (of forest, sky; conditions, eyes, face, etc.) become lighter, brighter; cheer up; brighten, light up; (of day) break, dawn; (of weather) clear up: **l- av dag** dawn.

ly's/nett *-et* (electrical) power network (or grid).

ly'sning *-en* **1** light, shine: **månens l-** the l- of the moon. **2** clearing, let-up (e.g. of the weather); dawn; improvement: **en l- i situasjonen** a turn for the better. **3** clearing, opening (e.g. in the woods). **4** aperture, (door, window) opening; internal caliber, diameter (of a pipe). **5** announcement (esp. of marriage), banns. **6** *archaic* dawn (cf **grå/l-**).

ly's/punkt [/pongt] *-et* **1** point, spot of light. **2** bright spot (in a situation, etc.).

ly's/pære *-a* light bulb.

ly's/redd *A* - **1** afraid of the light of day, of reality. **2** hole-and-corner, shady, underhanded.

ly's/rekla'me *-n* illuminated advertisement, neon sign.

ly's/side *-a*/+*-en* **1** luminous side (e.g. of the earth, moon). **2** bright, favorable side (of a situation, etc.).

ly's/sjakt *-a*/+*-en* light shaft, well.

ly's/skjær *-et* gleam of light.

ly's/sky *A* - **1** photophobic, sensitive to light; avoiding light. **2** hole-and-corner, shady, underhanded.

ly's/stolpe *-n* light pole, post.

ly's/stråle *-n* light ray.

ly's/styrke *-n tech.* candle power.

lys't *-a*/+*-en* **1** desire (=inclination, wish): **l-en driver verket** nothing seems hard to a willing mind; **med l-** willingly, with a will; **ha (få) l- på** feel like, want; **ha (få) l- til å (gjøre)** feel like (doing), want to (do); **hver sin l-** everyone to his liking; **hvis du har l-** if you'd like, if you want to. **2** desire (=lust, passion): **djevelens verk er det som begynner i søt l-** sweet passion is the beginning of the devil's work (Undset). **3** delight, joy, pleasure: **av hjertens l-** most heartily, with a will; **ei blott til l-** not for pleasure alone (motto of Royal Theater in Copenhagen); **så (at) det er en l- (å se)** so (that) it's really a joy (to watch).

+**lys't/beto'nt** *A* - *psych.* pleasurable.

lys'te *V -a*/+*-et*/**-e* desire, want, wish for: **hver mann kan få det han l-er** every man can get what he (really) wants (Nansen).

lys'telig *A* - **1** desirable, inviting; pleasing. **2** gay, lively.

lys'ten *A* +*-ent, pl -ne* covetous, desirous (**etter, på** of); lascivious, lustful.

lys'ter *-ra, pl -rer* fishing spear (with a number of barbed prongs), leister.

+**lys't/følelse** *-n psych.* pleasurable sensation.

lys't/gass *-en* laughing gas.

lys't/hus *-et* garden pavilion, summerhouse; arbor, bower.

lys'tig *A* - gay, lively, merry; mirthful.

+**lys'tig/het** *-en* gaiety, liveliness; fun, merriment.

lys't/kutter *-en, pl* +*-e* (pleasure) yacht.

+**lys't/løgner** [/løyner] *-en, pl -e* (=***-ar**, **/lygnar**) pathological liar.

lys't/mord [/mord] *-et* sex murder.

lys'tre[1] *V -a*/+*-et* catch, spear fish with a leister.

lys'tre[2] *V -a*/+*-et* obey: **l- ens minste vink** be at one's beck and call; respond to, *naut.* answer the helm.

+**lys't/seila's** *-en* yachting; pleasure cruising.

+**lys't/spill** *-et* (=***/spel**) comedy.

lys't/tur *-en* excursion, pleasure trip.

lys't/yacht [/jått] *-en* (pleasure) yacht.

ly's/ved *-en* (rotten) phosphorescent wood.

ly's/verk *-et* (electric) power plant (station, works): **Oslo L-er** Oslo Electric Company.

+**ly's/våken** *A -ent, pl -ne* cf **lys**[2]

ly's/år *-et astron.* light-year.

***ly't** *pr of* **ljote**

ly'te[1] *-t* blemish, defect, fault.

***ly'te**[2] *V lyt, laut, lote/-i* cf **ljote**

***ly'te**[3] *V -a* **1** deform, disfigure, maim. **2** accuse, blame, charge.

ly'te/fri *A -tt* faultless, flawless, unblemished.

ly'te/full *A* blemished, defective, faulty.

ly'te/laus *A* faultless, flawless, unblemished.

lytt' *A nt of* **ly**[2],[3]

+**lyt'te** *V -a/-et* listen (**etter** for; **på, til** to): **l- til** (also) heed (advice, etc.); *med.* auscultate: **l- seg til noe,** know, learn sth by listening.

lyt'te/appara't *-et, pl* +*-er*/**-* detection device.

+**lyt'ter** *-en, pl -e* (=***lydar**) (radio) listener; eavesdropper.

+**lyt'ter/avgift** *-a*/*-en* (radio) listener's fee (for a license to use a radio receiver).

+**lyt'ter/fore'ning** *-en* (radio) listeners' association (advocating more extensive use of *Riksmål* in broadcasting).

+**lyt'ter/lisen's** *-en* (radio) listener's license (for use of a radio receiver).

***ly'v** *-et* alleviation, relief; (medical) remedy.

+**ly've** *V løy, løyet* cf **lyge**

+**læ'**[1] *-et* cf **le**[1]

***læ'**[2] *V lo, lætt* cf **le**[3]

***læ'**[3] *A -tt* (of weather) gentle, mild.

+**læg** [le'g] *A* cf **lek**[4]

***lægd** [leg'd] *-a* **1** lowness, low position. **2** depression, low place (in the terrain).

***læge**[1] [le'ge] *-n* cf **lege**[3]

***læge**[2] [læ'je] *-t* cf **leie**[3]

***læge**[3] [le'ge] *V -et* cf **lege**[2]

læger[1] [le'ger] *-eret/-ret, pl -er*/+*-rer* **1** bed; sleeping place; sleeping shelter (in the mountains). **2** lair.

***læger**[2] [le'ger] *pl of* **låg**[1]

***læ'gje**[1] *-t* cf **leie**[3]

***læ'gje**[2] *V -de* depress, lower, sink.

lægre[1] [le'gre] *V -a*/+*-et* cf **leire**[2]

***lægre**[2] [leg're] *cp of* **låg**[4]

***lægst** [leg'st] *sp of* **låg**[4]

***lækjar** [le'kjar] *-en* cf **lege**[2]

***lækje** [le'kje] *V -te* cure, heal, restore to health.

***lækje/dom** *-(m)en* cf **lege/**

***lækje/råd** *-a* cf **lege/**

'**læ'r** *-et* (=***ler**[1]) leather.

'**læ'r/aktig** *A* - leathery.

lær'd *A* - erudite, learned, scholarly: **de l-e strides** the learned disagree; **den l-e skole** *hist.* the Latin school.

Læ'r/dal *Pln* twp. Sogn og Fjordane.

Læ'rdals/øyri *Pln* village in Lærdal twp.

læ'r/dom' *-men*/**-en* **1** erudition, learning, scholarship: **din megen l- gjør deg rasende** much learning doth make thee mad (Acts 26,24). **2** doctrine, dogma; teaching.

læ're[1] *-a*/+*-en* **1** instruction, teaching: **i l-** in apprenticeship; **liv og l-** life and teaching. **2** branch of knowledge, science, study (**om** of). **3** doctrine, dogma, tenet. **4** lesson, moral (**av** of). **5** gauge, standard of measure.

læ're[2] *V -te* **1** learn (**av** from): **l- å kjenne** get to know, become acquainted with; **l- å sette pris på** come to appreciate; **en l-er så lenge en lever** you live and l-; **det beste en har l-t** the best one can, knows how. **2** teach: **l- en av med** break sby of, teach sby not to; **l- en hvor David kjøpte ølet** give sby a real lesson; **l- fra seg** teach; **l- opp til,** train; **l- seg å bli** learn to be.

+**læ're/anstalt** *-en* educational institution.

læ're/bok *-a, pl -bøker* textbook.

+**læ're/gutt** *-en* apprentice.

læ're/lyst *-a*/+*-en* desire to learn.

læ're/lysten *A* +*-ent, pl -ne* eager to learn.

+**læ're/mester** *-eren, pl -ere/-rer* (=***/meister**) (apprentice's) master;

+ Bokmål; * Nynorsk; ° Dialect.
After letter: ' stress (Acc. 1); ' tone, stress (Acc. 2); · length.
Below letter: . not pronounced.

teacher: erfaring er den beste l- experience is the best t-.
læ're/middel -elet/-midlet, pl +-midler/ *-el teaching aid.
+læ're/nem' A -t, pl -me (=*/næm) apt, quick to learn; easy to teach.
læ're/penge -n: få en l- learn a lesson, det var en dyr l- that was a costly (hard) lesson.
+læ'rer -en, pl -e (=*-ar) (man) teacher; instructor, tutor; (bibl.) master.
læ're/rik A informative, instructive.
+lærerin'ne -a/-en (=*lærarinne) (woman) teacher; instructor, tutor.
+læ'rer/persona'le -t (=*-ar/) teaching staff.
+læ'rer/prøve -a/-en (=*-ar/) degree examination for (grade school) teachers.
+læ'rer/skole -n (=*-ar/) teachers' (training) college, for grade school teachers.
+læ'rer/stand -en (=*-ar/) teaching profession.
+læ'rer/værelse -t teachers' common room, lounge.
læ're/setning *-a/+-en doctrine, dogma, tenet; math. proposition, theorem.
læ're/stol -en 1 chair, professorship. 2 archaic (teacher's) lectern: flokke seg om hans l- become his disciples.
læ're/svein -en archaic. apprentice, disciple.
læ're/tid -a/+-en apprenticeship; training period.
læ're/vogn [/vångn] -a driver-training car.
læ're/år -et (years of) apprenticeship.
læ'rling -en 1 apprentice; disciple, pupil. 2 first degree Mason.
læ'rling/kontrak't -en apprentice's indenture, apprenticeship contract.
+læ'r/reim -a (=+/rem) leather strap, thong.
+læ'r/smøring -a/-en leather dressing; dubbin.
læ'r/villig A - (=*/viljug) docile, easy to teach, teachable.
læse[1] [le'se] V -te cf låse
+læ'se[2] V -te cf lese
*læst [les't] pr of låst
+læstadianer [lestadia'ner] -en, pl -e (=*-ar) adherent of religious movement (esp. spread over Lapland) begun in the 1840's by the Swedish minister Lars L. Læstadius.
*læ't pr of låte
læ'te -t 1 cry, sound (e.g. of an animal, a bird); howl, screech. 2 manner, way. *3 speech; pretense: det var berre l-t hans it was just an act.
*læ'/ver -et mild, thawing weather.
lø' V -dde (=+løe[2], *løde) pile, stack.
+lø'd[1] -en 1 color, hue. 2 characteristic, feature, stamp.
+lø'd[2] pt of lyde[1]
*lø'de V løder, lødde cf lø
lø'dig A - (of precious metal) fine, pure; fig. of worth, sterling, substantial.
+lø'dig/het -en (of metal) fineness, pureness; fig. merit, value, worth.
Lø'dingen Pln twp, Nordland.
lø'e[1] -a hay barn.
+lø'e[2] V -dde cf lø
°lø'en A -ent, pl -ne cf lodden.
+løf't -et (=*lyft) 1 lift; (heavy) weight (to lift); big effort. 2 naut. boom lift.
+løf'te[1] -t promise; pledge, vow.
+løf'te[2] V -a/-et (=*lyfte) 1 lift, raise; l- i flokk combine efforts, join forces. 2 elevate, uplift: i l-et stemning in festive mood, high spirits.
+løf'te/brudd -et breach of promise.
+løf'telse -n 1 exaltation; uplift. 2 enthusiasm; exhilaration.
+løf'te/rik A promising.
+løf'te/stang -a lever (also fig.).
+løf'tet A - 1 elevated, uplifted. 2 enthusiastic, exhilarated.
+løf'ting -en (=*lyfting) naut. poop (deck); poop cabin.
*lø'gleg A - comical, funny, ludicrous; curious, odd.
løgn [+løyn, *løngn] -a/+-en (=*lygn) falsehood, lie; lying: si en l- tell a l-.
+løgn/aktig [løy'n/] A - lying, mendacious; false, untrue.
+løgnaktig/het -en mendacity.
*lø'gnare, -ast cp, sp of løyen
*lø'gne pl of løyen
+løgner [løy'ner] -en, pl -e (=*-ar, *ljugar, *lygar, *lygnar) liar, prevaricator.
+løgnerske [løy'nerske] -n (woman) liar.
løgn/hals [+løy'n/, *løng'n/] -en (terrible) fibber, liar.
løg'ste V -a/+-et accuse of lying: Askeladden som fikk prinsessen til å l- seg The Ashlad who Made the Princess Call him a Liar (Asbjørnsen and Moe).
+lø'k[1] -en (=*lauk) 1 onion. 2 (flower) bulb.
lø'k[2] -en 1 deep, slow-running brook. 2 widening in a brook, stream. *3 puddle, small pool (in a swamp).
løk'ke[1] -a (=*lykkje[1]) loop, noose (of ribbon, rope, thread, etc.).
+løk'ke[2] -a (=*lykkje[2]) 1 enclosure (in a field, meadow), paddock. 2 vacant lot.
+løk't -a cf lykt
+løm'mel -elen, pl lømler lout, scamp.
+løm'mel/alder -en adolescence, awkward age.
*lø'n[1] -a cf lønn[1]
*lø'n[2] -a/-en cf lønn[2]
*lø'ne V -te cf lønne
lønn'[1] -a/+-en (=*løn[1]) 1 payment, return, reward; compensation, remuneration: få l- som forskyldt get what one deserves, served him right. 2 pay, salary, wages.
lønn'[2] -a/-en (=*løn[2]) bot. maple (Acer).
+lønn'[3] N (=*løynd): i l- in secret, secretly.
+lønn'/dom' -men (=*løyn/) secret; mystery.
løn'ne V lønte 1 remunerate, repay, reward: l-ende profitable; l- seg give profit, pay; det l-er seg ikke it isn't worth it (the trouble), it isn't worthwhile. 2 pay (salary, wages).
løn'ne/tre -et, pl -/+-trær maple tree.
+lønn'/gang -en secret passage.
løn'ning -a/+-en 1 pay, salary, wages. 2 naut. gunwale; rail.
løn'nings/dag -en payday.
løn'nings/liste -a pay roll (list).
løn'nings/pose [*/påse] -n pay envelope.
+lønn'/kammer -et bibl., lit. private chamber, closet.
+løn'nlig A - (=*løynleg) clandestine, secret; concealed, hidden.
lønn's/ansiennite't -en seniority (with regard to wages).
*lønn's/auke -n wage increase.
*lønn's/forhøy'else -n wage increase.
+lønn's/forlang'ende et wage demand.
lønn's/klasse -a/-en pay grade.
lønn's/krav -et wage demand.
+lønn's/mottaker -en, pl -e (=*-ar) wage earner.
+lønn's/nedsettelse -n wage cut, reduction.
Lønn's- og [å] pri's/departementet [-mang'e] df Ministry of Salaries and Prices.
+lønn'/som' A -t, pl -me (=*/sam) paying, profitable, remunerative.
lønn's/pålegg -et wage increase.
lønn's/regulati'v -et wage scale.
lønn's/sak -a/+-en matter concerning wages.
lønn's/sats -en wage rate.
lønn's/skala -en salary (wage) scale.
lønn's/slave -n wage slave.
lønn's/stopp -en wage freeze.
+lønn's/taker -en, pl -e (=*-ar) employee, wage earner.
lønn's/tariff' -en wage scale agreement.
lønn's/tillegg -et wage bonus.
lønn's/trekk -et wage deduction.
*lø'n/sam A cf lønn/som
*lø'ns/auke -n cf lønns/
løn'sk A (=*løynsk) crafty, cunning, sly.
løn'te pt of lønne
+lø'p -et (=*laup[2]) 1 race, run, running, heat: hundre meters l- 100-meter race; i l- at a run; dødt l- dead heat. 2 course (of events, of a river, road, etc.), run: i l-et av in the course of; i det lange l- in the long run; i tidens (årets) l- in the course of time (of the year); gi fritt l- give free reins to, let go; månens l- the moon's course. 3 barrel, bore (of gun); pipe (of faucet); naut. channel, fairway. 4 flight of stairs. 5 zool. leg, shank (of wild animals and birds). 6: gå i l-et be ruined, go down the drain.
+lø'pe[1] -n cf løype[2]
+lø'pe[2] V løp, løp(e)t (=*laupe) 1 run; (of ships) sail (at a given speed); (of liquids) flow: ha noe å l- på have enough to spare; la l- let go, not pursue; la munnen l- jabber away; det løp kaldt nedover ryggen på meg chills ran up and down my spine; tennene l-er i vann one's mouth waters; tiden løp fra meg I ran out of time. 2: l- på ski ski. 3 (of contracts) run=be in force, be valid. 4 (of animals) be in heat. 5 with (adv.), (prep.): l- fra run (away) from; l- heldig av turn out well, be successful; l- ned dørene hos en continually pester sby; l- om kapp run a race; l- opp i (of sums) amount to, come to; l- på run into; l- sammen (of milk) curdle; (of lines) converge; (of colors) run; l- sin vei run away; l- ut i join with, mix with.
+lø'pe[3] V -te cf løype[3]
+lø'pe/bane -n career.
+lø'pe/dag -en merc. day of grace.
+lø'pe/grav -a mil. trench.
+lø'pe/gutt -en errand boy.
+lø'pe/ild -en ground fire; bre seg, gå, fare som l- spread, go like wildfire.
+lø'pe/kran -en (overhead) traveling crane.
+lø'pende A - running (feet, meters, etc.); current (business, expenses, rate, year, etc.); open (account, question).
+lø'pe/nummer [/nommer] -eret, pl -er/-numre serial number.
+lø'pe/pass -et e.g. få l- get one's walking papers.
+lø'per -en, pl -e (=*laupar) 1 runner; racer; (express) messenger. 2 (stair, table) runner: den røde l- the red carpet. 3 (domestic) animal in heat. 4 (in soccer) forward. 5 (in chess) bishop. 6 (pigment) muller, pestler. 7 rotating millstone, runner. 8 (brick, stone) stretcher. 9 naut. fall.
+lø'pe/streng -en cf løype/
+-lø'pet A - 1 (of firearms) -barreled. 2 (of rope, yarn) -ply.
+lø'pe/tid -a/-en (=*laupe/) 1 (female animal's) period of heat. 2 merc. term, period of currency.
+lø'ps/dag -en day of (horse) trot.
+løp'sk A - (esp. of a horse) bolting, unmanageable, wild; (of imagination, thoughts) unbridled, wild: løpe l- bolt; run riot (also fig.).
+lørd.=lørdag
+lø'r/dag -en (=*laur/) Saturday.
+lø'rdags/frieri -et bundling.
+lør'dags/vask -en Saturday washing.
Lø'ren/skog Pln twp, Akershus.
+lø's A cf laus
+-løs A cf -laus
+lø's/aktig [also -ak'-] A - 1 irresponsible, unreliable. 2 immoral, loose, wanton.
+lø'saktig/het [also -ak'-] -en 1 irresponsibility, unreliability. 2 immorality, loose living.
+lø's/arbeider -en, pl -e cf laus/
+lø'se V -te cf løyse[2]
+lø'selig[1] A - (=*lausleg) 1 cursory,

hasty; fleeting, transitory; casual, superficial; approximate, rough. 2 (as *adv.*) carelessly, casually, heedlessly; slightly.
+lø'selig[2] *A* - 1 solvable. 2 *lit.* soluble.
+lø'sen *-et* 1 *obs.* countersign, password: battle cry. 2 catchword, slogan; watchword.
+lø'se/penger *pl* (=***løyse/pengar**) ransom.
+lø's/gi *V -gav, -gitt* release, set free.
+lø's/gjeld *-a/-en* cf **laus/**
+lø's/gjenger *-en, pl -e* 1 tramp, vagabond. 2 *pol.* freelancer, independent, mugwump.
+lø's/gjengeri *-et* vagabondage, vagrancy.
+lø's/gjøre *V -gjorde, -gjort* detach, disengage, loosen.
+-lø's/het *-en* cf **-løyse**
+lø's/ild *-en* cf **laus/eld**
løsj'er *-en* blotter holder.
°løs'ke *V -a/-et* cf **luske**[2], **lyske**[2]
+lø's/kjøpe *V -te* ransom, redeem.
+lø's/late *V -lot, -latt* release, set free.
+lø's/munnet *A* - cf **laus/munna**
+løs'ne *V -a/-et* 1 become loose; loosen, work loose; (of ice) break up. 2 discharge, fire (a shot). 3 relax, slacken (e.g. one's grip, hold).
+lø'sning *-en* cf **løysing**[1]
+lø's/rev *pt of* **-rive**
+lø's/reven *A -ent/-et, pl -ne* detached, disconnected, severed; isolated (from context).
+lø's/rive *V -reiv/-rev, -revet* cf **laus/**
+lø's/salg *-et* sale by the piece, by single copies (esp. of newpapers).
+lø's/sloppen [/sloppen] *A -ent, pl -slopne* 1 abandoned, unbridled; riotous, uproarious. 2 *archaic* released, set free.
+lø's/sne *-en* cf **laus/snø**
+lø'st/sittende *A* - loose-fitting.
+lø's/øre *-t* cf **laus/**
Lø'ten *Pln* twp, Hedmark.
+lø'v *-et* cf **lauv**
lø've *-a/+-en* lion (also *fig.*): **fare opp som en l- (og dette ned som en skinnfell)** boast like a lion (but collapse under fire); **i l-ns hule** in the lion's den.
lø've/brøl *-et* roar of a lion.
lø've/manke *-n* lion's mane.
lø've/mot *-et* leonine courage, lionheartedness.
lø've/munn *-en bot.* snapdragon (Antirrhinum).
lø've/tann *-a bot.* dandelion (Taraxacum officinale).
+lø've/temmer *-en, pl -e* (=***/temjar**) lion tamer.
+lø'v/fall *-et* cf **lauv/**
+lø'v/grønn *A -grønt* cf **lauv/grøn**
+lø'v/hytte *-a* cf **lauv/**
løvin'ne *-a/+-en* lioness.
+lø'v/krone *-n* cf **lauv/**
+lø'v/rik *A* cf **lauv/**
+lø'vsals/fest *-en eccl.* Feast of Tabernacles, Sukkoth.
+lø'v/skog *-en* cf **lauv/**
+lø'v/tre *-et, pl -/-trær* cf **lauv/**
+lø'v/verk *-et* foliage.
+løy'[1] *pt of* **lyge**
løy'[2] *A +-t/*- 1 (of wind) light, slack (esp. *naut.*). 2 indolent, lax; slothful.
løy'/benk *-en archaic* couch.
***løy'e**[1] *-t* cf **løyer**
løy'e[2] *V -a/+-et/+-de* (of wind) drop, moderate, slacken (esp. *naut.*): **l- av** calm, moderate.
løy'en *A +-ent, pl +-ne/*løgne, cp *løgnare, sp *løgnast* comical, droll, funny; odd, queer.
+løy'er *pl* (=***løye**) fun, joke.
+løy'erlig *A* - droll, funny; odd, queer.
løy'ert *-en* 1 swaddling cloth, wrap. 2 *naut.* cringle.
+løy'et *pp of* **lyge, lyve**
***løy'nande** *A* - concealable, hidable.
***løy'nd** *-a* cf **lønn**[3]
***løy'nde/råd** *-a* secret plan, plot, scheme.
***løy'n/dom** *-(m)en* secret; mystery.
løy'ne *V +-te/*-de* conceal, hide.
***løy'ne/stad** *-en* hiding place.
***løy'nleg** *A* - cf **lønnlig**
***løy'nsk** *A* - cf **lønsk**
løy'pe[1] *-a* 1 log slide. 2 ski track; marked course (for skiing, cross-country racing).
løy'pe[2] *-n* 1 rennet. 2 abomasum, rennet stomach. 3 fish offal used as animal food.
løy'pe[3] *V -te* 1 set in motion. 2 glide, slide (on ice, snow). 3 peel (bark). 4 curdle (milk). 5 simmer.
***løy'pe/bakke** *-n* skiing hill, slope.
***løy'pe/gut** *-en* cf **løpe/gutt**
løy'pe/streng *-en, pl *-er* aerial cable for transporting loads of hay, wood, etc.
***løy'sande** *A* - 1 able to be unloosened, untied; releasable. 2 soluble, solvable.
***løy'sar** *-en* 1 one who redeems sth from pawn. 2 trigger; release trip.
***løy'se**[1] *-a* 1 loosened mass. 2 active, restless person or animal.
løy'se[2] *V -te* (=+**løse**) 1 let loose; loosen, release, untie (**av, fra** from); come loose. 2 buy, get, take out; ransom, redeem: **l- billett** purchase one's ticket (esp. on a train, bus, etc.); **l- kongebrev** *hist.* get civil marriage license. 3 solve (a problem, riddle, etc.); resolve (a dissonance, a doubt, etc.); accomplish (a task). 4 (with *prep., adv.*) **l- (en) av** relieve, take over from (sby, e.g. a watch); **l- fra** free of, release from (e.g. an obligation, debt, etc.); **l- inn** redeem (e.g. a promise, sth pawned); **l- opp (i)** dissolve (in); **l- opp for** undo, untie (e.g. a sack), *fig.* release, open the way for; **l- ut** buy out, up (e.g. an inheritance, a share); **l- ut av** let loose, release from. 5 (*refl.*): **l- seg fra** free oneself of, renounce; **l- seg opp** dissolve, fade away, melt.
-løy'se *-a* (=**-løs/het**) -lessness e.g. **mot/l-, skam/l-.**
***løy'se/pengar** *pl* cf **løse/penger**
løy'sing[1] *-a* (=+**løsning**) answer, solution (of a problem).
løy'sing[2] *-en* freed serf, slave.
***løy'snad** *-en* 1 payment; redemption (from pawn). 2 solubility.
***løy'sning** *-a* 1 payment; redemption (of a note; of sth from pawn). 2 disintegration, dissolution; dissolving.
løy'tnant *-en* lieutenant.
+løy'tnants/hjerte *-t bot.* bleeding heart (Dicentra spectabilis).
løy've[1] *-t* permission, permit (**på, til** to).
løy've[2] *V -de* allow, permit; grant; appropriate.
***løy've/brev** *-et* (business) license.
løy'ving *-a/+-en* appropriation, grant (e.g. of money).
+lå' *pt of* **ligge**
lå'g[1] *-a, pl læger* fallen log, windfall (tree).
+lå'g[2] *-en* (=***log**) 1 (vegetable) brew, decoction, extract; hay extract (as drink for livestock). 2 (in brewing) water poured over malt.
***lå'g**[3] *pt of* **liggje**
lå'g[4] *A cp -ere/*lægre, sp -est/*lægst* (=+**lav**[2]) low (ceiling, comedy, culture, level of development, morals, number, quality, salary, voice, window, etc.); (in *comp.*) more elementary (e.g. instruction, mathematics).
lå'g/adel *-en* gentry, lesser nobility.
lå'g/alder *-en jur.* minimum age: **kriminell l-** age of consent.
lå'g/beint *A* - short-legged.
Lå'gen *Pln* (water course) e.g. **Gudbrandsdals/l-, Numedals/l-, Suldals/l-.**
lå'g/frekven's *-en elec., phys.* low frequency.
lå'g/gir [/gir] *-et* low gear.
lå'g/halt *A* - lame, limping (because of a short leg); halting.
lå'g/hæla *A* - low-heeled.
lå'g/land *-et* lowland(s) (as opposed to highland(s)).
lå'g/lende *-t* low-lying ground, land.
lå'g/lofta *A* - low-ceilinged.
lå'g/mæ'lt *A* - low-voiced; in a low voice.
lå'g/mål *-et* low level, minimum.
***lå'gne** *V -a* become lower.
***lå'g/skap** *-en* lowness (of action, character).
***lå'g/sku'rd** *-en* bas-relief.
lå'g/slette *-a* lowland plain.
lå'g/spenning *-a/+-en elec.* low voltage; low tension.
lå'g/spent *A* - low-tension.
lå'g/trykk *-et* (in a machine) low pressure; *meteor.* depression, low; low pressure area.
+lå'g/vann(e) *-(e)t* low water; low tide.
+lå'g/vokst *A* - (of animals, people, plants) squat, short.
lå'g/ætta *A* - lowborn.
lå'k *A* 1 (esp. of health) ill, poorly, unwell. 2 (of birth, etc.) low, poor; contemptible, sorry, wretched.
***lå'kne** *V -a* deteriorate, become worse.
***lå'k/skap** *-en* badness; wickedness.
lå'm *-a* track (from sth dragged or from skis).
lå'n[1] *-a* 1 pile (esp. of lumber). 2 long building (esp. a barn); main building (dwelling house). 3 complex of buildings.
lå'n[2] *-et* loan: **oppta et l-** raise a l-; **til l-s** on l-.
lå'ne *V -te* 1 borrow (**av** from; **på** on): **l- seg frem** borrow one's way. 2 lend, loan: **l- bort, ut l-** out.
+lå'ne/bevi's *-et* IOU, promissory note.
lå'ne/fond *-et* loan fund.
+lå'ne/innretning *-en* loan office.
lå'ne/kasse *-a/-en* loan office; loan fund.
+lå'ner *-en, pl -e* (=***-ar**) 1 borrower. 2 lender, loaner.
+lå'ne/seddel *-elen, pl -sedler* pawn ticket.
+lå'n/giver *-en* (=***-ar, */gjevar**) lender (institution, person).
lå'n/o'rd *-et* loanword.
lå'n/ta *V +-r/*-tek, -tok, +-tt/*-teke/*-i* (=***/take**) borrow without owner's consent.
+lå'n/tager *-en* cf **/taker**
+lå'n/taker *-en, pl -e* (=***-ar**) borrower (institution, person).
lå'r *-et* thigh; leg (of a slaughtered animal).
lå'r/bein *-et anat.* femur, thigh bone.
Lå'r/dal *Pln* twp, Telemark.
lå're *V -a/+-et/+-te naut.* lower.
lå'r/hals *-en anat.* neck of the femur.
lå'rhals/brott *-et* (=+**/brudd**) fracture of the femur.
lå'ring *-a/+-en naut.* buttock, quarter (side).
lå's *-en/-et* 1 lock: **under l- og lukke** under lock and key; **gå i l-** lock, spring shut; *fig.* come off, turn out satisfactorily. 2 catch, locket, snap. 3 (in firearms) breech bolt. 4 *carp.* scarf joint. 5 *zool.* bivalve hinge. 6 netfull (of fish). 7 *naut.* shackle.
lå's/boge [/båge] *-n* (=+**/bue**) crossbow.
lå'se *V -te* (=***læse**[1]) 1 lock; padlock: **l- av, ned** lock up; **shut off** (e.g. a room); **l- opp** unlock; **l- ut** let out. 2 (in carpentry) scarf.
+lå'se/besla'g *-et* lock hardware.
lå'se/gjenge *-t/+-n* ward (inside a lock).
+lå'se/smed *-en* locksmith.
***lå's/nål** *-a* safety pin.
***lås't** *V læst, lest, låst* pretend (as if).
***lå's/verk** *-et* (in firearms) breech bolt.
lå't *-en dial.* 1 sound. 2 ring, tone;

+ Bokmål; * Nynorsk; ° Dialect.
After letter: ' stress (Acc. 1); ' tone, stress (Acc. 2); · length.
Below letter: . not pronounced.

tune. 3 whimpering, whining. 4 (noisy) fun, gaiety.
***lå'tar** -*en* complaining person, whiner.
lå'te *V* +-*er*/**læt*, +*låt*/**let*, +-*t*/*-*e*/*-*i* 1 ring, sound (esp. of an instrument, song, tune): **det låt ikke i ham** there was not a sound from him. 2 whimper, whine. 3 *dial.* play (a tune). 4: **l- vel** express pleasure, satisfaction.
-lå'ten *A* +-*ent*, *pl* -*ne* -sounding, e.g. **små/l-, stor/l-.**
lått' -*en* laugh, laughter.
***låt'teleg** *A* - laughable.
***låt'te/løye** -*t* sth laughable.
***lått'/mild** *A* given to laughter, mirthful.
lå've -*n* 1 (grain, hay) barn, loft. 2 threshing floor.
lå've/bru -*a* barn bridge (from ground level to hayloft door).
lå've/dør -*a* barn door.
lå've/svale -*a* *zool.* barn swallow (Hirundo rustica).

M

m[1] [em'] -*en* (letter) M, m.
m[2] =**meter**
M=**meget tilfredsstillende**
°**ma** *Av*: da ma you know.
***m. a.**=**mellom anna**
machiavellisme [makiavellis'me] -*n* Machiavellianism.
***ma'd** -*et* young fish (esp. herring).
+**madagas'ser** -*en*, *pl* +-*e* (=*-**ar**) Madagascan, Malagasy.
madagas'sisk *A* - Madagascan, Malagasy.
madam' +-*men*/*-*ma* 1 obs. Madame, Mrs. (title for middle-class married woman): **m-men** *fam.* the missus, the wife; (heavy) matronly woman. 2 *pop.* midwife.
mada'me +-*n*/*-*a* madame.
mad'dik -*en* *zool.* maggot; *fig.* worm, wretch.
madeira [madei'ra/made'ra] -*en* madeira (wine).
madjar [madsja'r] -*en* Magyar.
madjar(i)sk *A* - Magyar.
Mad'la *Pln* twp, Rogaland.
madon'na -*en* (*ei), *pl* *-*er* (the) Madonna (also picture of the M-).
+**madon'na/aktig** *A* - madonna-like.
madrass' -*en* mattress.
Mad's *Prn (m)*
maf'(f)ia -*en* Mafia.
mag.=**magister**
magasi'n -*et*, *pl* -/+-*er* 1 (ammunition, camera, gun) magazine; storehouse, warehouse. 2 department store. 3 magazine (periodical).
magasine're *V* -*te* store (in attic, warehouse, etc.).
magasi'n/komfy'r -*en* electric stove with thick, insulated lid over one of the heating units for holding in the heat.
magasi'n/omn -*en* (=+/**ovn**) base burner.
ma'ge[1] -*n* 1 bowels, stomach: **ha vondt i m-n** have a stomachache; **ha treg m-** have sluggish bowel movement. 2 abdomen, belly: **gå med en statsråd i m-n** aspire to, have an eye on a cabinet position; **ha (stor) m-** have a (big) paunch; **ligge på m-n for en** grovel for sby, lick sby's boots. 3 bulge, protrusion (on bottle, coffee pot, etc.).
ma'ge[2] *V* -*a*/+-*et* 1 eviscerate, gut (e.g. fish). 2: **m- seg** act important, puff up. *3: **m- seg** eat one's fill, fill up.
ma'ge/belte -*t*, *pl* +-*r*/*- 1 abdominal belt. 2 cigar band.
ma'ge/knip -*et* gripes, stomachache.
ma'ge/mål -*et*: **passe m-** (at meals) eat moderately.
ma'ger *A* -*ert*, *pl* -*re* 1 lean (animal, meat, person, year, etc.); *pop.* skinny, thin: **et m-t kinn** a hollow cheek. 2 meager; poor (pasturage, soil, etc.); scanty (fare, income, resources, etc.). 3 *typog.* lightfaced.
ma'ge/saft -*a* gastric juice.
ma'ge/sekk -*en* stomach.
ma'ge/sjau -*en* *fam.* diarrhea.
ma'ge/sjuke -*n* *fam.* diarrhea.
ma'ge/syre -*a* stomach acid.
ma'ge/sår -*et* gastric ulcer.
***mag'ge**[1] -*a* (of a woman) fat old cow, sow.
***mag'ge**[2] *V* -*a*: **m- seg** enjoy oneself, stuff oneself (with food).
magi' -*en* (occult) magic.
+**ma'giker** -*en*, *pl* -*e* (=*-**ar**) magician.
ma'gisk *A* - magic, magical.
magis'ter -*eren*, *pl* -*rer*/+-*ere* 1 academic title: **m- artium** M.A.; **m scientiarum** M.S. (cf **m-/grad**). 2: **m- bibendi** toastmaster. 3: **sverge til m-ens ord** rely blindly on authority.
magis'ter/grad -*en* university degree granted on passing examinations in one major and two minor subjects and completion of thesis (approximates Ph.D. in U.S.).
magistra't -*en* (until 1922) municipal corporation administrating local government and serving as local representative for federal government.
magna't [also: mangna't] -*en* (industrial, railroad) magnate.
***magne** [mang'ne] *V* -*a*: **m- seg** eat one's fill; gather up courage.
Magne [mang'ne] *Prn (m)*
magnesia [mangne'sia] -*en* *chem.* magnesia.
magnesium [mangne'sium] -*en*/-*et* *chem.* magnesium.
magnet [mangne't] -*en* 1 magnet (also *fig.*). 2 *pop.* magneto (in gasoline engine).
magnet/felt -*et* magnetic field.
magnetisere [mangnetise're] *V* -*te* magnetize.
magnetisk [mangne'tisk] *A* - 1 magnetic (also *fig.*). 2 hypnotizing, mesmerizing.
magnetisme [mangnetis'me] -*n* (esp. *tech.*) magnetism; **dyrisk m-** animal m-.
magnet/jernstein [mangne't/] -*en* magnetite.
magnet/nål -*a* magnetic needle.
magnetofon [mangnetofo'n] -*en* tape recorder.
magnet/stav [mangne't/] -*en* bar magnet.
Magn/hild [mang'n/] *Prn (f)*
Magnor [mang'nor] *Pln* post office, Hedmark.
Magnus [mang'nus] *Prn (m)*
***ma'grast** *V* -*ast* cf **magre**
ma'gre *V* -*a*/+-*et* make thin; become thin; **m-s, m- seg** become thin; **m- inn** shrivel up, waste away.
mahara'ja [also: -rad'sja] -*en* maharaja(h).
mahogni [mahång'ni] -*en* mahogany.
mahogni/pjolter -*eren*, *pl* -*rer*/+-*ere* strong (brandy) highball.
ma'i *en* May.
Mai'a *Prn (f)*
+**ma'i/blomst** -*en* (=*/**blom**) 1 *bot.* plant of the lily family, related to lily of the valley (Maianthemum bifolium). 2 small, artificial flower (for the lapel) sold in May by the Tuberculosis Association.
+**mai'e** *V* -*a*/-*et*: **m- seg ut** bedizen oneself, deck oneself out (gaudily).
ma'i/gull -*en* *bot.* golden saxifrage (Chrysoplenium).
Ma'i/haugen *Pln* folk museum at Lillehammer.
ma'i/nepe -*a* *bot.* early garden turnip (Brassica rapa).
ma'is -*en* (Indian) corn, maize.
ma'is/brennevin -*et* corn whiskey.
maisen'na -*en* cornstarch.
ma'is/gryn -*et* cornmeal.
ma'is/grøpp -*et* cornmeal mush.
ma'is/kolbe -*n* ear of corn.
ma'is/mjøl -*et* cornstarch.
+**ma'i/stang** -*a*, *pl* -*stenger* (=*/**stong**) maypole.
majeste't -*en* majesty (quality, title).
majeste'tisk *A* - majestic.
+**majeste'ts/forbry'telse** -*n* *jur.* lese majesty; high treason.
majo'lika -*en* majolica.
majone's -*en* mayonnaise.
majo'r -*en* (Air Force, Army) major.
majorite't -*en* majority (**på** of): **den forbannede kompakte m-** the damned compact m- (Ibsen); **i m-** in the m-.
majus'kel -*elen*, *pl* -*ler* capital (letter), majuscule.
ma'k *N*: **i m-** leisurely, slowly; **i ro og m-** (the same).
maka'ber *A* -*ert*, *pl* -*re* macabre.
makadamise're *V* -*te* macadamize.
makaro'ni -*en* macaroni.
ma'ke[1] -*n* 1 (animal, shoe, etc.) mate; (marriage) spouse. 2 equal, match; peer: **m-n til (kar)** what a (man); **(hørt) sett på m-n** (*pop.* **makan**) have you ever (heard) seen the like; *pop.* **makan!** isn't that something!
ma'ke[2] *V* -*a*/+-*et*/+-*te* 1 get ready, prepare; arrange, manage: **m- seg** be arranged, work out. 2: **m- seg** take it easy.
+**makedo'ner** -*en*, *pl* -*e* (=*-**ar**, *-**iar**) Macedonian.
makedo'n(i)sk *A* - Macedonian.
ma'ke/laus *A* (=+/**løs**) exceptional, unique; matchless, unequaled; incomparable, incredible.
ma'kelig *A* - 1 easy, soft (e.g. work): **ta det m-** take it e-. 2 comfortable, leisurely, without straining. 3 (of person) ease-loving, indolent.
+**ma'ke/løs** *A* cf /**laus**
+-**maker** -*en*, *pl* -*e* (=*-**makar**) -maker, e.g. **sko/m-, ur/m-.**
ma'ke/skifte[1] -*t*, *pl* +-*r*/*- *jur.* exchange, trade (of real estate).
ma'ke/skifte[2] *V* -*a*/+-*et*/*-*te* *jur.* exchange, trade (real estate).
makk' -*en* cf **mark**[4]
+**makkabe'er** -*en*, *pl* -*e* (=*-**ar**) Maccabee.
mak'ke *V* -*a*/+-*et* *obs.* **m- sammen** join, throw together.
mak'ker -*en*, *pl* +-*e* partner (esp. in cards); fellow worker.
mak'ker/skap +-*et*/*-*en* partnership (esp. in cards); association, dealings (**med** with).
***makk'/eten** *A* -*e*/-*i*, *pl* -*ne* worm-eaten.
mak'ko -*en* (Egyptian) cotton; men's underwear (of Egyptian cotton).
mak'ko/trøye -*a* men's undershirt (of Egyptian cotton).
makk'/verk -*et* botch, mess, poor job; trash.

***ma'kleg** *A* - cf **makelig**
makrell' *-en zool.* mackerel (Scomber scombrus).
makrell'/sky *-a* cirro-cumulus clouds, mackerel sky.
makrell'/størje *-a zool.* tunny (Thynnus thynnus).
mak'ro/kosmos *et* macrocosm.
makro'n *-en* macaroon.
mak'sel *-elen, pl -ler* cut, shape; model, pattern.
maksima'l *A* maximum.
+maksima'l/belas'tning *-en* maximum load.
maksima'l/pris *-en* ceiling price.
maksi'me *-n* maxim.
maksime're *V -te* fix, set the limits (of insurance); maximize.
mak'simum *-umet, pl +-a/*-um* maximum.
mak'sis *N*: **hoppe m-** (of dog, cat) jump through a hoop formed by a person's arm.
mak'sle *V -a/+-et* fashion, form, shape (from pattern).
+ma'ks/vær *-et* (=***/ver**) quiet weather.
mak't *-a/+-en* **1** force, might, strength; authority, power: **av all (sin) m-** with all one's might; **med m-** forcibly; **eksemplets m-** the power of example; **vanens m-** the force of habit; **ha ordet i sin m-** be eloquent, *pop.* have the gift of gab; **holde ved m-** keep in force; **komme til m-en** get the upper hand, gain control; **det står ikke i min m-** I haven't the authority, power (to); **stå ved m-** be (remain) in force. **2** *(pl)* forces (e.g. good, evil forces, forces of nature); powers (=states). **3** (armed) forces.
+mak't/anvendelse *-n* resort to, use of force.
+mak't/begjæ'r *-et* lust for power.
+mak't/bud *-et* dictate, fiat.
mak'te *V -a/+-et* be able (to), manage; be equal to; cope with.
+mak'tes/løs *A* impotent, powerless.
mak't/faktor *-en* factor of power.
mak't/forde'ling *-a/+-en pol.* division (separation) of powers.
+mak't/fullkom'menhet *-en* absolute power: **av egen m-** by (on) one's own authority.
mak't/glad *A* - eager for power, power mad; authoritarian.
+mak't/haver *-en, pl -e* (=***-ar**) ruler; (often *derog.*) potentate, tyrant.
***mak't/laus** *A* (=**+/løs**) impotent, powerless.
+mak't/middel *-elet/-midlet, pl +midler/*-el* forcible means, resource (e.g. to oppose sth); instrument of power.
+mak't/påliggende *A* - important, pressing, urgent.
mak't/sjuk *A* (=**+/syk**) greedy for power, power-seeking.
+mak't/språk *-et* dictatorial command, language.
mak't/stilling *-a/+-en* dominating position, position of power.
+mak't/stjele [also mak't/] *V -stjal, -stjålen/-stjålet* render impotent, powerless; bewitch, conquer, overcome.
makulatu'r *-en* wastepaper, sheets (for use other than printing, reading).
makule're *V -te* **1** *typog.* mark as wastepaper. **2** mark, soil (esp. book, printed matter). **3** paper a (brick) wall with wastepaper before wallpapering.
ma'l *-en* templet (as a pattern; in shipbuilding).
malai' *-en* cf **malay**
malai'isk *A* - cf **malayisk**
Ma'langen *Pln* twp, Troms.
malapropos [-po'] *A* - malapropos.
mala'ria *-en* malaria.
mala'ria/mygg *-en zool.* anopheles (mosquito).
malay [malai'] *-en* Malay.
malayisk [malai'isk] *A* - Malay, Malayan.
ma'le¹ *V +-er/*mel, mol/+-te, +-t/*-e/*-i* **1** grind (coffee, grain, meat); (of water) churn, whirl: **m- på** *fig.* grind away (at), repeat over and over. **2** (of cat) purr.
+ma'le² *V -te* (=***måle²**) **1** paint (a chair, floor, landscape, portrait, etc.): **la seg m-** have one's portrait painted; **m- fanden på veggen** look on the gloomy side. **2** *fig.* depict, portray in words.
maleba'risk *A* - Malabar; (of a language) incomprehensible, meaningless, outlandish.
+ma'le/bok *-a, pl -bøker* (children's) water-coloring book.
+ma'lende *A* - expressive, graphic, vivid.
ma'ler *-en, pl -e* (=***målar**) (house, portrait) painter; artist.
+ma'ler/farge *-n* artist's paint, pigment.
+maleri' *-et* painting, picture; art of painting.
+malerin'ne *-a/-en* (woman) artist, painter.
+ma'lerisk *A* - picturesque; artistic.
+ma'ler/kasse *-a/-en* paint box.
+ma'ler/kost [/kost] *-en* paintbrush.
+ma'ler/kunst *-en* art of painting.
+ma'ler/mester *-en, pl -e* master (house) painter.
+ma'ler/pøs *-en* paintpot.
+ma'ler/svenn *-en* journeyman painter.
°malesjøs'k *A* - malicious, spiteful.
Ma'li *Prn (f)*
+ma'ling *-a/-en* paint.
+ma'lings/slitt *A* - having worn paint, in need of paint.
mali'se *-n* malice, spite.
malisiø's *A* malicious, spiteful.
mal'je *-a/+-en* (=**melle**) eye, eyelet (on shoe): **hekte og m-** hook and eye.
malkonduite [malkånduit'te] *-n* ineptness, maladroitness, mismanagement.
mal'm *-en* **1** ore. **2** copper-base alloy; *(bibl.)* **lydende m-** sounding brass. **3** cast iron. **4** (duramen) heartwood (esp. in coniferous trees). **5** fiber, metal (of person).
Mal'm *Pln* twp, Nord-Trøndelag.
mal'm/båt *-en* ore boat, ship.
mal'men *A +-ent, pl -ne* having good heartwood; *dial.* pithy.
mal'm/full *A* **1** rich (in ore, heartwood, (moral) fiber, metal). **2** sonorous.
mal'm/furu *-a* pine (wood) rich in heartwood.
mal'm/førende *A* - metalliferous, orebearing.
mal'm/gryte *-a* cast-iron kettle, pot.
mal'm/røst *-a/+-en* (=***/røyst**) ringing, sonorous voice: **klokkenes m-** the resounding clang of the bells (Falkberget).
mal'm/tung [/tong] *A* very heavy, ponderous; (of sound, esp. from bells) deep, solemn, somber.
mal'm/ved *-en* heartwood.
mal'm/åre *-a* metalliferous lode, vein.
malplasse'rt *A* - ill-timed, ill-placed, untimely.
+ma'l/strøm' *-men* (=***/straum**) maelstrom (whirlpool); dangerous current(s).
mal't *-et* malt (grain).
mal't/bygg *-et* malting barley.
mal'te *V -a/+-et* malt (convert grain to malt).
mal't/ekstrak't *-en* malt extract.
+malte'ser *-en, pl -e* (=***-ar**) Maltese.
+malte'ser/kors *-et* (=***maltesar/kross**) Maltese cross.
maltrakte're *V -te* maltreat, mishandle.
ma'l/urt *-a/+-en bot.* wormwood (Artemisia absinthium); **dryppe m- i ens beger** *fig.* embitter one's joy.
ma'lurt/beger *-et* cup of bitterness.
Ma'l/vik *Pln* twp, Sør-Trøndelag.
malø'r *-en* ill luck, mishap.
°mam' *N obs.* madam, ma'm.
mamelukk' *-en* **1** *hist.* (Egyptian) Mameluke. **2** *(pl)* pantalets.
mam'ma *-en (*ei), pl *-er* mamma.
mam'ma/dalt *-en* mamma's boy, girl (child who tags after his mother); sissy.
+mam'ma/gutt *-en* (=***/gut**) mamma's boy, sissy.
mam'ma/kjole *-n* maternity dress.
mammon [mam'mån] *-en* mammon.
+mammons/dyrker *-en, pl -e* (=***-ar**) mammon worshipper.
mam'mut *-en zool.* mammoth (Mammuthus).
mam'mut/bygg *-et* huge building; colossus.
+mamsell' *-en obs.* mademoiselle, miss.
ma'n¹ *-a* mane.
+man'² *Pn* one, people, they, you (=**en³ 1**): **m- sier** it is said, people say; **ser m- det!** really! **slikt gjør m- ikke** it just isn't done; (in older cookbooks) **m- tar** take.
-ma'n *A* - maniac, e.g. **biblio/m-; klepto/m-; mono/m-.**
+mand. = **mandag**
+man'/dag *-en* cf **mån/**
Man'/dal *Pln* city, Vest-Agder.
mandalitt' *-en* person from Mandal.
mandan't *-en jur.* mandator, principal (authorizing another to represent him).
mandari'n *-en* **1** mandarin (Chinese official). **2** mandarin orange.
manda't *-et, pl -/+-er jur., merc.* authority, authorization, commission, mandate (**til** to); seat in *Storting.*
mandata'r *-en jur., merc.* agent, authorized person, mandatary.
man'del *-elen, pl -ler* **1** almond. **2** tonsil.
man'del/deig *-en* almond paste.
+man'del/dråper *pl* (=***-ar, /dropar**) almond extract.
man'del/forma *A* - (=**+-et**) almond-shaped.
man'del/olje *-a/-en* almond oil.
man'dig *A* - manly; manfully brave, honorable.
+man'dig/het *-en* manliness.
mandoli'n *-en mus.* mandolin.
man'dsju *-en* Manchu.
mandsju'isk *A* - Manchu.
Mandsju'ria *Pln* Manchuria.
ma'ne *V -a/+-te* **1** admonish, urge (**til** to): **et m-ende opprop** an urgent appeal. **2** charm, conjure: **m- bort** charm away, exorcise; **m- fram** call forth; conjure up (devil, ghost, images, memories); entice, lure. **3** *naut.* pass (an end, rope, etc.).
manér *-en* **1** fashion, manner, way: **gode m-er** good manners. **2** mannerism; (mere) technique.
+manérlig *A* - mannerly, proper.
mane'sje *-n* (circus) ring.
mane't *-a/+-en zool.* jellyfish.
mang' *A mangt, pl mange, cp flere, sp flest* many: **m- en, m- ei, m-t et m- a;** (used substantively) **m-t og meget** much, a lot; **m-e takk** thank you very much; **hvor m-e er klokken?** what time is it?
***mang'-** *pf* cf **mange-**
mangan [mangga'n] *-et/+-en chem.* manganese.
***mang'/bø'lt** *A* - (of farm) divided among several households.
***mang'/dobbel** *A* cf **mange/dobbelt**
***mang'/doble** *V -a* cf **mange/**
mang'e *pl of* **mang**
+mang'e- *pf* (=***mang-**) many-, multi-.
+mang'e/artet *A* - having many kinds, multifarious, varied.
+mang'e/dobbelt *A* - manifold, multiple.
+mang'e/doble *V -a/-et* multiply.
mang'e/farga *A* - (=**+-et**) multicolored, polychromatic.
+mang'e/gifte *-t* cf **mang/**
+mang'e/hånde *A* - multifarious.

+ Bokmål; * Nynorsk; ° Dialect.
After letter: ' stress (Acc. 1); ' tone, stress (Acc. 2); · length.
Below letter: . not pronounced.

+mang'e/kant *-en* polygon.
mang'el *-elen, pl -ler* 1 lack, shortage, want (på of): **av m- på** for w- of; **i m- av** for w- of, in the absence of; **lide m-** suffer deprivation, w-. 2 defect, flaw; drawback (**ved** of).
***mang'e/leis** *Av* in many ways.
mang'el/full *A* deficient, insufficient; defective, faulty.
mang'el/sjukdom [/-dåmm] *-men/*-en* deficiency disease.
+mang'e/lunde *A pl* many kinds of, multifarious; *(adv.)* in many ways.
mang'el/vare *-a/+-en* sth of which there is a lack, shortage: **smør er m-** butter is in short supply.
mang'e/millionæ'r *-en* multimillionaire.
+mang'en *A* cf **mang**
Mang'er *Pln* twp, Hordaland.
+mang'e/sidig *A* - (of aspects, interests, etc.) many-sided, versatile.
+mang'e/sifret *A* - of many figures, running into many figures.
+mang'e/slags *A* - cf **mange**
+mang'e/steds *Av* (=***mang/stad**) in many places.
+mang'e/stemmig *A* - of many voices; *mus.* polyphonic.
+mang'e/tydig *A* - ambiguous, equivocal, open to various interpretations.
+mang'e/årig *A* - (of) long standing, many years'.
***mang'/falde** *V -a* multiply; duplicate, mimeograph.
***mang'/faldig** *A* - cf **-foldig**
***mang'/felde** *-t* multiplicity, variety; plurality.
***mang'/felt** *A* - having many parts, multifarious.
+mangfol'dig *A* - (=***/faldig**) 1 a great many, manifold, many times, numerous: **i m-e år** for many, many years. 2 complex, many-sided, multifarious; versatile: *derog.* **en m- herre** a devious person.
+mangfol'dig/gjøre *V -gjorde, -gjort* multiply; duplicate, mimeograph.
+mangfol'dig/het *-en* multiplicity, variety; plurality.
***mang'/før** *A* versatile.
mang'/gifte *-t* polygamy.
***mang'/kant** *-en* cf **mange/**
mang'le[1] *V -a/+-et* 1 lack; be short of; have no: **m- på** lack of; **det m-er ikke på** there is no lack of, there's plenty of; **det skulle bare m-** I should say not, not on your life; it's out of the question; **jeg m-er ord** I'm at a loss for words; **jeg m-er bestandig penger** I'm always short of money. 2 be missing: **det m-er to sider i boka** two pages in the book are missing. 3 (in expressions of time): **klokken m-er fem minutter på (i) tre** it's five minutes to three. 4 be wrong with: **hva m-er det ham?** what's w- w- him?
mang'le[2] *V -a/+-et* mangle (household linen, etc.).
***mang'/leta** *A* - multicolored, polychromatic.
mang'le/tre *-et* mangle (flat board with a handle, usu. elaborately carved, used to smooth and press clean linen).
***mang'/lynt** *A* - having many moods, temperaments.
***mang'/mannen** *df* the common man.
mang'/ment *A* - in large force, strong in number.
mango [mang'go] *-en* mango (fruit).
mangold [mang'gålt] *-en bot.* spinach beet (Beta vulgaris cicla).
mangrove [manggro've] *-n* mangrove swamp.
***mang'/sidig** *A* - cf **mange/**
mang'/slungen [/slongen] *A +-ent, pl -ne* 1 complex, intricate; difficult. 2 (of people) clever, shrewd; complex, devious.
***mang'/stad** *Av* cf **mange/steds**
***mang'/stemmig** *A* - cf **mange/**
mang't *nt of* **mang**
***mang'/tydig** *A* - cf **mange/**
***mang'/årig** *A* - cf **mange/**
mani' *-en psych.* mania, (also *fig.*) passion: **du har en m- for å gjøre livet vanskelig** you have a mania for making life difficult (Elster d.y.).
manie'rt *A* - (=**manierert**) affected, mannered.
manifes't *-et, pl -/+-er* 1 manifesto, proclamation. 2 (ship's) manifest.
manifestasjo'n *-en* manifestation.
manifeste're *V -te* manifest.
maniky'r(e) *-(e)n* manicure.
manikyre're *V -te* manicure.
manil'a *-en* Manila (cigar, hemp, etc.).
manil'a/hamp *-en* Manila hemp.
manipulasjo'n *-en* manipulation.
manipule're *V -te* manipulate.
ma'nisk *A* - maniacal, manic.
ma'nisk-dep'ressiv *A* manic-depressive.
man'ke *-n* 1 mane (on horse, lion). 2 withers (on horse).
manke're *V -te pop.* be wanting; lack; be wrong: *dial.* **ke som m-er** what's wrong; **hu m-er ingenting** nothing's wrong with her.
man'ko *-en merc.* deficiency, deficit; shortage (**på** of).
mann' *-en, pl menn/*menner* 1 man (=not child, not woman): **alle som en m-** to a m-, unanimously; **et arbeid som krever sin m-** a demanding job. 2 husband: **få, ta til m-** marry; **leve som m- og kone** live as h- and wife. 3 man (=human being): **skipet gikk ned med m- og mus** the ship went down with all on board. 4 *(pl* **mann**) *naut.* hand: **alle mann** all h-s; *mil.* men, troops: **tusen mann** a thousand men.
man'na *-en* 1 *(bibl.)* manna. 2 exudate of flowering (manna) ash.
***man'nast** *V -ast* become a man.
***mann'/dauden** *df* the Black Death.
mann'/dom' *-men/*-en* 1 manhood. 2 manliness; (manly) courage.
mann'/drap *-et archaic* homicide; manslaughter.
+mann'/draper *-en, pl -e* (=***-ar**) homicide, murderer.
man'ne *V -a/+-et* 1: **m- seg opp** buck up, take courage (**til** to); pull oneself together. 2 *naut.* man.
man'ne/bein *-et* 1 *dial.* human bone. 2 *fam.* man.
man'ne/bot *-a, pl -bøter* blood money, wergild (paid to kin of a slain man).
man'ne/fall *-et* (great) loss of life, slaughter (also *fig.*).
***man'neleg** *A* - cf **mandig**
***man'ne/lekam** *-en* human body.
***man'ne/mink** *-en* loss of esteem, respect.
***man'ne/mon(n)** *-en* one's general standing, reputation: **gjere m-** be partial.
man'ne/mål *-et* sound of human voice(s).
mannequin [mannekeng'] *-en* mannequin; model.
***man'ne/tanke** *-n* human thought.
***man'nete** *-a* cf **manet**
***man'ne/verk** *-et* work of man.
man'ne/vett *-et* human sagacity; common sense.
man'ne/vilje *-n* human will.
man'ne/ætt *-a/+-en* human race.
mann'/folk *-et* male, man; he-man, real man; *(pl)* men, menfolk(s).
mann'folk/tekke *-t* a way with men.
mann'folk/vis *-a/-en/-et*: **på m-** in typical male fashion.
mann'/ga'rd *-en* 1 *hist.* gauntlet, line of men: **en m- av fjell** a solid wall of mountains (Bojer). 2 ring of people: **gå m-** comb the terrain; **gjøre m- om en** surround and move in on sby. 3 (on farm) circle of dwelling houses and yard area (as opposed to farmyard).
+mannhaf'tig *A* - 1 (of women) mannish. 2 *archaic* manly.
mann'/jamning *-a* (esp. *hist.*) comparison of two men's achievements, exploits, qualities, etc.
mann'/jamt *A nt* in a body, in full number, plenary.
+mann'/jevning *-a/-en* cf **/jamning**
+mann'/jevnt *A nt* cf **/jamt**
***mann'/kjømd** *A -kjømt* passable (for people); accessible.
mann'/kjønn *-et archaic* male sex.
mann'lig *A* - male; **m- rim** masculine rhyme.
mann's/alder *-eren, pl -rer* 1 generation. 2 *archaic* manhood.
mann's/emne *-t, pl +-r/*-* lad, youth: **et godt m-** a promising lad.
mann's/høg *A* (=**+/høy**) as tall as a man.
mann's/høgd *-a* (=**+/høyde**) height of a man.
mann'/skap[1] *-et, pl -/+-er* crew (also *naut.*), men, *mil.* troops.
***mann'/skap**[2] *-en* manliness, manly courage, daring.
***mann's/kjensle** *-a* feeling of manhood.
mann's/kor *-et* male choir, men's chorus.
***mann'sleg** *A* - cf **mandig**
+mann'sling *-en* dwarf, manikin, pygmy.
+mann's/minne *N* cf **mann**
mann's/mot *-et* (manly) courage, pluck.
mann's/perso'n *-en* male, man (whose name is not known; often *derog.*).
mann's/side [/*sie] *-a/+-en* 1 (in church) men's side. 2 (in family) male line.
mann'/sterk *A* accompanied by many men, well-attended; in large force, strong in number.
mann's/tukt *-a/+-en* stern discipline.
mann's/verk *-et* 1 man's job, men's work. 2 feat; work one man can do (in given period). 3 *hist.* measure of land.
mann'/tal *-et* (=**+/tall**) census; roll call; roster: **føre, oppta m- over** make a list of; **all verden skulle innskrives i m-** *bibl.* all the world should be taxed (Luke 2,1).
mann'tals/liste *-a* (=**+-talls/**) census rolls; register, roster.
+mann'/voksen *A -ent, pl -ne* adult, grown up.
mann'/vond [/vonn] *A* dangerous, vicious; angry, fierce.
manome'ter *-eret/-ret, pl -er/+-re* manometer.
mansa'rd *-en* attic story (under mansard roof).
mansa'rd/tak *-et* mansard roof.
mansjett' *-en* 1 shirt cuff: **støte en på m-ene** hurt one's feelings. 2 *tech.* sleeve (on piston). 3 bobeche.
mansjett'/knapp *-en* cuff link.
mansjett'/skjorte [/sjorte] *-a* dress shirt with French cuffs.
ma'nsk *A* - Manx.
man'tel *-elen, pl -ler* 1 *tech.* jacket (outer covering, casing). 2 *tech.* blast furnace mantle. 3 fireplace mantel(piece). 4 *naut.* runner. 5 *archaic* cloak, mantle.
mantil'je *-n* mantilla.
mantis'se *-n math.* mantissa.
manua'l *-en* 1 *mus.* organ keyboard manual. 2 dumbbell.
manuduksjo'n *-en* private tutoring.
manuduktø'r *-en* private tutor.
manuduse're *V -te* tutor privately.
manuell' *A -elt* manual (labor, etc.).
manufaktu'r *-en merc.* dry goods, textiles.
manuskrip't *-et, pl -/+-er* manuscript.
+manuskrip't/holder *-en, pl -e* (=***/haldar**) copy holder.
manø'ver *-eren, pl -rer* maneuver.
manø'vre *-n* cf **manøver**
manø'vre/dyktig *A* - maneuverable (esp. of ship).
manøvre're *V -te* maneuver (car, oneself, ship, etc.).
m. a. o.=**med andre ord**
map'pe *-a* folder; portfolio.
marabu' *-en* 1 *zool.* marabou (Leptoptilus). 2 marabou feather(s).

+ma'raton/løp *-et* (=*/laup) marathon (race).
ma'r/bakke *-n* (=mol/) drop-off, (under water) shelf.
ma're *-a* 1 incubus: ***m-a rid meg** I have nightmares. 2 (in wrestling): **flyvende m-** flying mare.
ma're/halm *-en bot.* marram grass, matweed (Ammophila arenaria).
ma're/katt *-en zool.* guenon (Cercopithecus).
Ma'ren *Prn (f)*
mareng's *-en* meringue kiss.
***ma're/riden** *A -e/-i, pl -ne* beset, harassed, plagued (as in a nightmare).
ma're/ritt *-et* nightmare.
ma'r/flo *-a zool.* amphipod (Arthrostraca).
mar'g¹ *-en* margin.
+mar'g² *-en* cf **merg**
margari'n *-en* margarine.
+mar'g/bein *-et* cf **merg/**
margeritt' *-en bot.* marguerite, Paris daisy (Chrysanthemum frutescens).
+mar'g/ert *-a* variety of pea.
+mar'g/full *A* marrowy; pithy (also *fig.*).
margi'n *-en merc.* margin.
***margina'l/merknad** *-en* marginal note.
margina'l/note *-n* marginal note.
margina'l/skatt *-en* tax differential (in higher bracket of progressive income tax).
mar'g/laus *A* (=+/løs) marrowless, pithless (also *fig.*); weak.
Margre'te *Prn (f)*
+mar'g/stjålen *A -ent, pl -ne* enervated, powerless.
***ma'r/halm** *-en* cf **mare/**
Ma'ri *Prn (f)*
Mari'e *Prn (f)*
+ma'ri/hand *-a bot.* orchis (Orchis).
ma'ri/høne *-a* 1 *zool.* ladybird, ladybug (Coccinellidae). 2 *dial.* butterfly.
ma'ri/kåpe *-a bot.* lady's-mantle (Alchemilla).
ma'ri/mess(e) *en eccl.* Annunciation Day (25 March).
ma'ri/mjelle *-a bot.* cow wheat (Melampyrum).
mari'n *A* marine.
mari'ne *-n* 1 navy. 2 marine painting, seascape.
+mari'ne/bilde *-t* marine painting, seascape.
mari'ne/blå *A -tt* navy blue.
mari'ne/gast *-en* sailor, seaman.
+mari'ne/maler *-en, pl -e* (=*/målar) marine painter.
marine're *V -te* 1 marinate (e.g. herring). 2 *merc.* damage (goods) with seawater.
ma'ri/nøkkel *-elen, pl -nøkler bot.* moonwort (Botrychium lunaria).
marinøk'le/band *-et bot.* cowslip (Primula veris).
marionett' *-en* marionette, puppet.
marionett'/regje'ring *-a/+-en* puppet government.
+marionett'/spill *-et* (=*/spel) puppet show.
Ma'rit *Prn (f)*
mariti'm [also ma'r-] *A* maritime.
mar'k¹ *-a* 1 ground, land, soil; (cultivated, uncultivated) field. 2 field (of battle, discussion, work, etc.): **arbeide i m-a** do fieldwork; **føre i m-en** advance (an argument); **vike m-en** give ground. 3 *hist.* mark (boundary land).
mar'k² *-a, pl mer'ker¹* unit of weight (now 1/4 kg).
mar'k³ *-a, pl mark* 1 (Finnish, German) mark; earlier Norwegian coin (=1/5 **daler**). 2 unit of land.
mar'k⁴ *-en* (=makk) maggot, worm.
***mar'k⁵** *-et* mark, sign (**på** of).
markan't *A* - marked, pronounced.
***ma'r/katt** *-en* cf **mare/**
+mar'k/blomst *-en* meadow flower, wild flower.
***mar'ke** *V -a* 1 mark, notice. 2 gather fodder (from the forest).
+mar'ked *-et, pl -er* cf **marknad**

+mar'keds/analy'se *-n merc.* market analysis.
+mar'keds/føre *V -te* send, take to market.
+mar'keds/plass *-en* fairground; marketplace.
+mar'ken *-en* cf **marknad**
+mar'kens/gang *-en*: *obs.* **gå m-** go to the fair.
marke're *V -te* 1 indicate, mark; emphasize, stress: **m-t standpunkt** well-defined position. 2 (of hunting dog) point. 3 *math.*: **a m-t** "a" prime (a'). 4 *mil.* represent, simulate (e.g. the enemy in maneuvers).
marketen'ter *-en, pl +-e* 1 *hist.* sutler. 2 *obs.* innkeeper.
marketenteri' *-et, pl +-er/*- hist.* sutlery (=canteen, Post Exchange).
marketen'terske *-a/+-en hist.* woman sutler.
mar'k/ett *A* - worm-eaten.
mar'k/fio'l *-en bot.* dog violet (Viola canina).
mar'k/greve *-n hist.* margrave.
marki' *-en* marquess, marquis.
marki'se *-a/+-en* 1 marchioness, marquise. 2 awning.
mar'k/jo'rdbær *-et* wild strawberry.
+mar'k/kryper *-en, pl -e* (=*-ar) (in sports, of a ball) grounder.
mar'k/mus *-a, pl -/*-myser zool.* field mouse (Microtus agrestis).
mar'knad *-en* (=+marked, +marken) 1 fair, market. 2 (business) market: **flaut m-** slack m-; **overfylle m-en** flood the m-; **varen er på (i) m-et** the item is on the m-. 3 small carnival (with games of chance, etc.).
mar'k/skjeider *-en, pl +-e* mine surveyor.
+mar'k/skriker *-en, pl -e* (=*-ar) one who ballyhoos.
+mar'k/skrikersk *A* -: **m- reklame** advertising ballyhoo.
+mar'k/spist *A* worm-eaten, wormy.
mar'k/stukken [/stokken] *A +-ent, pl -stukne* worm-eaten, wormy.
markø'r *-en* (esp. in billiards) marker, scorekeeper; *agr.* marker.
ma'r/lake *-n dial., zool.* manyplies, omasum.
mar'm *-en dial.* roar of the sea.
mar'me *V -a dial.* (esp. of sea) roar.
marmela'de *-n* marmalade.
mar'mor *-et* marble.
marmore're *V -te* marbleize, marble.
mar'mor/flis *-a/+-en* marble tile.
maro'der *A* - exhausted, played out; (now *usu.*) disabled.
marode're *V -te mil.* maraud, straggle.
marodø'r *-en mil.* marauder; straggler.
maroki'n *-en/-et* (**marokeng**) morocco (leather).
+marokka'ner *-en, pl -e* (=*-ar, *marokkan) Moroccan.
marokka'nsk *A* - Moroccan.
Marok'ko *Pln* Morocco.
mar's *en* March.
Ma'rs *Pln, Prn* Mars.
+ma'rs/boer *-en, pl -e* (=*/buar) Martian.
marsipa'n *-en* marzipan (confection of almond paste).
marsipa'n/brød *-et* marzipan bar.
marsipa'n/gris *-en* marzipan pig.
marsj' *-en* 1 march: **gjøre på stedet m-** mark time (also *fig.*). 2 march (music): **blåse en en lang m-** disregard one completely, not give a hang.
marsjall' *-en* marshal.
marsjall'/stav *-en* 1 field marshal's baton. 2 (at state funeral) flower-entwined staff.
marsjandi'ser *-en, pl +-e obs.* second-hand dealer.
marsjandi'ser/handel *-en obs.* second-hand store.
marsje're *V -te* march.
marsj'/fart *-en naut.* cruising speed.
marsj'/kolon'ne *-n* column of march.

marsj'/konkurranse [/-ang'se] *-n* march contest (with pack, etc.).
marsj'/merke *-t, pl +-r/*-* badge awarded in march contest.
marsj'/takt *-a/-en* march time, tempo.
mar'sk *-en* tideland, salt marsh.
marskal'k [also mar'-] *-en* (ceremony, royal household) marshal; (at funeral) one who carries a flower-entwined staff before the coffin.
ma'r/svin *-et zool.* guinea pig (Cavia porcellus).
Mar'te *Prn (f)*
mar'ter/kammer *-et, pl -/+-kamre* torture chamber.
martialsk [martsia'lsk] *A* - martial.
°mar'tna *-en* cf **marknad**
mar'tre *V -a/+-et* torture (esp. *fig.*).
mar'tyr *-en* martyr.
marty'rium *-iet* martyrdom.
mar'tyr/mine *-a/+-en* air of suffering, martyrized air.
ma'r/ulk *-en* (=+/ulke) *zool.* angler (Lophius piscatorius).
+mar'v *-en* cf **merg, marg**
+mar'v/postei' *-en* a pastry (small round cakes filled with almond paste).
marxis'me *-n* Marxism.
marxis't *-en* Marxist.
marxis'tisk *A* - Marxian.
ma's *-et* bother, difficulty, pother; fuss; fretting; importunity.
***ma'se¹** *-a* fuss-budget; fusser.
ma'se² *V -a/+-te* 1 slave away (**med** at), struggle, toil. 2 fret, fuss; nag; harp.
+ma'se³ *V -te* crush, mash, pound (to pieces).
ma'se/kopp *-en* bothersome, persistent person; fusser; fuss-budget.
ma'se/kråke *-a* fusser; fuss-budget.
ma'set(e) *A* - 1 fussing, fussy (e.g. child); harping, nagging (e.g. woman). 2 taxing, toilsome: **vi har det m-e nå like før jul** we are having a wearing time of it now just before Christmas.
Ma's/fjo'rd *Pln*
mas'k¹ *-en/+-et* (in brewing) mash.
mas'k² *-et* (esp. wood) refuse, scrap, waste.
mas'ke¹ *-a/-en* 1 mask (also *fig.*): **kaste m-n** show one's true colors. 2 (actor's) make-up; disguise. 3 *lit.* masked person.
mas'ke² *-a/-en* (=*moske²) 1 (in crocheting, knitting, etc.) stitch; **legge opp m-r** cast on; **miste m-er** drop a stitch. 2 (in netting) mesh.
mas'ke³ *V -a/+-et* (=*moske³) mesh (a net); **m- opp** reknit, repair (stocking, sweater, etc.).
mas'ke/ball *-et* masquerade ball.
+mas'ke/blomst *-en* (=*/blom, */blomster) *bot.* flower of the Scrophulariaceae family.
mas'ke/kome'die *-n* commedia dell'arte, masque.
maskepi' *-et* collusion, (secret) dealings; hocus-pocus.
maskera'de *-n* masquerade (ball, party).
maske're *V -te* mask; (of actor) make up; camouflage, disguise.
maske'ring *-a/+-en* make-up, mask; disguise.
maskin [masji'n] *-en* engine; machine; *naut.* engine room.
maskin/arbeid *-et* machine work.
maskin/del *-en* machine, machinery part.
maskinell [masjinell'] *A -elt* mechanical.
maskineri [masjineri'] *-et, pl +-er/*-* machinery.
maskin/gevæ'r [masji'n/] *-et* machine gun.

+ Bokmål; * Nynorsk; ° Dialect.
After letter: ' stress (Acc. 1); ` tone, stress (Acc. 2); · length.
Below letter: . not pronounced.

maskin/hall +-*en*/*-*a* machine room (at factory, plant).
maskin/ingeniør [masji'n/insjeniø·r] mechanical engineer.
maskinist [masjinis't] -*en* machinist (esp. *naut.*).
+**maskin/messig** [masji'n/] *A* - machinelike, mechanical.
maskin/pisto·l -*en* submachine gun.
+**maskin/sette** *V* -*satte typog.* compose, set, typeset (on machine).
maskin/skade -*n* (esp. *naut.*) breakdown, engine trouble.
maskin/skrive *V infl as* **skrive** type, typewrite.
maskin/skrue -*n* machine screw.
maskin/telegraf· -*en naut.* engine-room telegraph.
maskot [mas'kått] -*en* (=***maskott**) mascot.
maskuli'n *A* masculine.
mas'kulinum -*umet, pl* -*a*/+-*er gram.* masculine gender; masculine word.
ma's/omn -*en* (=+**/ovn**) blast furnace.
massa'kre -*n* massacre.
massakre're *V* -*te* massacre.
massa'sje -*n* massage.
mas'se -*n* 1 mass (also *phys.*), substance. 2 quantity; multitude; lots: **m-n** the masses; **han har m- penger** he has heaps of money.
+**mas'se/avskjedigelse** -*n* mass dismissal, firing.
mas'se/grav -*a*/+-*en* mass grave.
mas'se/mentalite·t -*en* mentality of the masses.
+**mas'se/morder** -*en, pl* -*e* (=*-**ar**) mass murderer.
mas'se/møte -*t,pl* +-*r*/*- mass meeting.
mas'se/produksjo·n -*en* mass production.
masse're *V* -*te* massage.
mas'se/vis *Av*: **i m-** in great quantities, in masses.
***mas'sing** -*en* cf **messing**
massi'v[1] -*et geol.* massif.
massi'v[2] *A* massive; solid.
massø'r -*en* masseur.
massø'se -*a*/+-*en* masseuse.
mas't -*a* 1 *naut.* mast. 2 (power) pylon; (radio) tower.
mas'te/fisk -*en naut.* mast partner.
mas'te/knapp -*en naut.* truck.
***mas'ter** -*ra* cf **mast**
mas'te/skog -*en* 1 forest of trees suitable for masts. 2 "forest" of masts (on ships lying in harbor).
mas'te/topp -*en naut.* masthead.
mas'te/tre -*et, pl* -/+-*trær* tree suitable for a mast.
mas'tiks -*en* mastic.
mastodon't -*en zool.* mastodon.
masur'ka -*en* mazurka.
ma's/verk -*et arch.* tracery.
ma't[1] -*en* 1 fare, food: **det er m- for Mons** that's just his dish (cup of tea), a real delicacy; **et stykke m-** a slice of bread and butter; (open-faced) sandwich. 2 nourishment: **lite m- i disse kakene** not much n- in these cookies (cakes); **m- i kornet** food value in grain, ripening. 3 meal: **lese for m-en** say grace; **takk for m-en** thanks for the meal (required formula at end of meal, not used in English).
***ma't**[2] *pt of* **mete**
mat.=**matematikk, matematisk**
matado'r -*en* 1 (in bullfighting, cards) matador. 2 magnate, tycoon.
***ma'tast** *V* -*ast* (of grain) ripen.
ma't/auke -*n* home gardening (esp. during WW II).
ma't/bit -*en* bit, morsel of food.
ma't/bo·rd -*et archaic* (set) table.
ma't/bu -*a* larder, pantry.
ma't/bur -*et* storehouse (for food).
match [mæt'sj] -*en* (sports) match.
ma't/dåse -*n* (tin) sandwich box.
ma'te *V* -*a*/+-*et* 1 feed. 2 bait (a fishhook). 3: **m- seg** (of grain) ripen.
+**matema'tiker** -*en, pl* -*e* (=*-**ar**) mathematician.
matematikk' -*en* 1 mathematics. 2 mathematics textbook.
matema'tisk *A* - mathematical.
ma't/eple -*t* cooking apple.
materia'le -*t, pl* +-*r*/*- (=**material**) (building, human, scientific, etc.) material.
+**materia'l/forval·ter** -*en, pl* -*e* stock clerk.
materialise're *V* -*te* materialize.
materialis'me -*n* materialism (also *philos.*).
materialis't -*en* materialist (also *philos.*).
materialis'tisk *A* - materialistic (also *philos.*).
mate'rie -*n* 1 *philos., phys.* matter, substance. 2 subject, topic. 3: **en bok i m-** book in quires, in sheets; unbound. 4 pus: **sette m-** suppurate.
materiell'[1] -*et* matériel; (rolling) stock; materials.
materiell'[2] *A* -*elt* 1 material (comforts, goods, interests, losses, world, etc.). 2 materialistic.
ma't/fat -*et* dish (for, of food): **ta dyktig for seg i m-et** be a big eater; *fig.* be sure to get one's share.
+**ma't/fett** -*et* (=***/feitt**) lard, shortening; cooking fat, drippings.
ma't/fisk -*en* edible fish.
ma't/flo -*a zool.* freshwater crustacean (Gammarus pulex).
+**ma't/frier** -*en, pl* -*e* (=*-**ar**) parasite, sponger (for meals).
***ma't/gjerd** [/jær] -*a* 1 cooking, food preparation. 2 boiled food.
ma't/hug -*en dial.* appetite.
ma't/hus -*et* home where there is good food, where a good table is set.
Mati'as *Prn (m)*
matiné -*en* matinée (concert, lecture, play).
mat'jes/sild -*a* matie (herring).
ma't/jo·rd -*a* humus, topsoil.
ma't/klokke -*a* (esp. on farm) dinner bell.
ma't/krok -*en fam.* hearty eater, one fond of food.
ma't/laging -*a*/+-*en* cookery, cooking: **hun er flink i m-** she is a good cook.
matlasse' *en* quilting.
ma't/lei *A* *-*tt* 1 blasé; lethargic, listless. 2 without appetite.
ma't/lukt [/lokt] -*a*/+-*en* cooking odor.
ma't/lyst -*a*/+-*en* appetite.
ma't/mons -*en fam.* hearty eater, one fond of food; gourmand.
ma't/mor -*a*/+-*en, pl* +*mødre*/*-*mødrer* mistress of the house.
ma't/nyttig *A* - usable as food.
ma't/olje -*a*/-*en* cooking oil.
ma't/pakke -*a*/-*en* (pack) lunch.
ma't/papi·r -*et* wax paper.
ma't/pote·t -*a*/+-*en* eating potato (as opposed to seed potato).
ma't/rest -*en* food particles (e.g. between the teeth); leavings, leftovers.
matriarka'lsk *A* - matriarchal.
matriarka't -*et, pl* -/+-*er* matriarchy.
matrik'kel -*elen, pl matrikler admin.* land register, tax rolls.
matrik'kel/nummer [/nommer] -*et, pl* -/+-*numre admin.* number of property on tax rolls.
matrikule're *V* -*te admin.* enter in the land register, tax rolls.
matri'se -*n tech., typog.* matrix; cut, mat.
ma't/ro -*a*/+-*en* peace and quiet during a meal.
matro'ne -*a*/+-*en derog.* large, sedate (married) woman.
matro's -*en* sailor, (able-bodied) seaman.
matro's/dress -*en* sailor suit.
matro's/krage -*n* sailor collar.
matro's/lu(v)e -*a* sailor's hat.
ma't/smule -*n* bit, morsel of food.
ma't/stasjo·n -*en* station, stopping place (esp. in ski race, bicycle race, etc.) where food is given to contestants.
ma't/stell -*et* cooking, food preparation.
***ma't/stove** -*a* cook shanty.
ma't/strev -*et* 1 toil for one's daily bread; material concerns. 2 *fam.* work involved in cooking a meal.
ma't/strever -*en, pl* -*e* (=*-**ar**) materialist; toiler.
***ma't/så** -*a* bit, morsel of food.
matt'[1] -*en fam.* checkmate.
matt'[2] *A* - 1 faint, feeble, weak (applause, request, smile, voice, etc.). 2 dull, mat, non-gloss (color, glass, metal, etc.); dead, lackluster. 3 (in chess) mate: **gjøre m-** checkmate.
mat'te[1] -*a* mat: **holde seg på m-a** restrain oneself (one's natural inclinations).
mat'te[2] *V* -*a*/+-*et* 1 *obs.* enfeeble, tire, weaken. 2 frost, make non-glossy, mat.
matte're *V* -*te* (esp. of glass, metal) frost.
+**matt'/het** -*en* 1 faintness, fatigue; feebleness, weakness. 2 dullness, flatness; vapidness.
Matti'as *Prn (m)*
+**matt'/slepen** *A* -*ent, pl* -*ne* (of glass) frosted, ground.
***ma't/vand** *A* fastidious, finicky, particular (about food).
ma't/vare -*a*/+-*en (pl)* food, provisions, victuals.
ma't/vatn -*et* (=+**/vann**) household (cooking) water.
ma't/veg -*en* (=+**/vei**): **i m-en** in the food line, in the way of food.
ma't/vett -*en fam.* enterprise, head for (eye to) a good opportunity: **ha godt m-** know how to bring home the bacon.
***mau'k** -*et* liquid (to mix with food); batter, mixture.
mau'le *V* -*a*/+-*et* eat sth by itself, dry (without accompanying liquid); chew, munch.
mau'r -*en* 1 *zool.* ant (Formicidae): **m- i beina** tingling of legs (when they are asleep). 2 *fam.*: **en modig m-** a plucky fellow.
mau're[1] -*n bot.* bedstraw (Galium).
mau're[2] *V* -*a*/+-*et* 1 work diligently. 2 swarm: **det m-er av mennesker** there are swarms of people. 3 (of arm, leg) itch, tingle. 4 *naut.* plug, stop (a leak).
+**mau'rer** -*en, pl* -*e* (=*-**ar**) Moor.
mau'risk *A* - Moorish.
mau'r/tue -*a* (=***/tuve**) ant hill.
mau'ser/gevæ·r -*et* Mauser rifle.
mausole'um -*eet, pl* +-*eer*/*-*eum* (=***mausolé**) mausoleum.
+**ma've** -*n* cf **mage**[1]
mb.=**millibar**
md.=**måned**
mdl.=**medlem**
°**me'**[1] -*et* cf **med**[1]
***me'**[2] *Pn* cf **vi**
°**me'a** *C* cf **mens**
+**me'd**[1] -*et* (=***méd**) 1 bearing(s); landmark. 2 fishing banks; fishing ground. 3 goal: **uten mål og m-** aimlessly.
me'd[2] *C* cf **mens**
me'd[3] *P* 1 with: **ut m- det!** out with it!; **arbeide (leke, snakke, spise, osv.) m- en** work (play, talk, eat, etc.) with sby; **ha vinden m- seg** have the wind with you; **jeg vil ikke ha noe m- det å gjøre** I don't want to have anything to do with it. 2 including (as *adv.*, also, as well, too): **fra og m-** from and including (a given date); **til og med** to and including, even; **jeg traff ham, og henne m-** I met him, and her as well; **det synes jeg m-** I think so too; **vi var fire m- Georg** there were four of us including George; **m- flere** and others, et alia; **m- (meget) mer** et cetera; **m- videre** et cetera. 3 by: **reise m- tog (bil, buss)** travel by train (car, bus); **ta m- makt** take by force; **han begynte m- å si** he began by saying; **hva mener du m- det** what do you mean by that? 4 to: **gift m-** married to; **vise likhet m-** show similarity to; **være snill m- en** be nice to sby; **være vant m-**

be used to. 5 *(adv.)* along (with): **bli, være m-** come along, accompany, join; **være m- i** be a member of; **være m- på** participate, take part in; **gå m- på noe** go along with sth; **jeg tar det m- (meg)** I'll take it along (with me); **de som er m-** the participants, (in theatrical performance) the cast. 6 in: **m- høy (usikker) stemme** in a loud (wavering) voice; **m- kaldt blod** in cold blood; **m- ett ord** in a word, in brief; **m- tiden** in (due) time. 7 about, concerning: **det haster ikke m- det** there's no rush about it; **hva med (egg)?** what about (eggs)?; **hva var dette m- Georg** what was this business about George? **å tenke på dette m- tykkelsen** to think about this business of weight (Hoel). 8 on: **m- vilje** on purpose; **seile m- (et skip)** sail on (a ship). 9 at: **m- fare for** at the risk of; **m- stor fart** at high speed; **m- visse (jevne) mellomrom** at certain (regular) intervals. 10 of: **full m-** full of. 11 (other idioms): **ha lykken m- seg** be lucky; **henge m- hodet** hang one's head; **ti stille m- deg!** be quiet!; **å, du m- din sparing** oh, you and your saving (which you're always harping on). (For expressions with other adjectives, adverbs, nouns and verbs, see these).

med. = **medisin(sk)**

medal'je *-n* medal.

medaljong' *-en* 1 medallion. 2 locket.

medaljø'r *-en* medal engraver, medalist.

***me'ḍan** *C* cf **mens**

+me'd/ansva'rlig *A* - co-responsible, sharing the responsibility.

+me'd/arbeider *-en, pl -e* (=***-ar**) 1 co-, fellow worker; collaborator (e.g. on project); staff member. 2 (of magazine, newspaper) on the staff; contributing editor; contributor, writer: **vår m- i Paris** our (special) correspondent in P-.

me'ḍ/bakke *-n* descent, going downhill (opp. of **mot/**).

+me'd/beiler *-en, pl -e* rival.

+me'd/bestem'mende *A* - concurrent; having a share in determining.

+me'd/borger *-en, pl -e* (=***-ar**) compatriot; fellow citizen, townsman.

+me'd/borgerlig *A* - (=***/borgarleg**) civic: **m- aktelse** respect of one's fellow citizens, reputation.

+me'd/bringe *V -brakte, -brakt* bring along, with: **medbrakt** *hum.* (alcoholic) drinks (brought by participants to party); lunch package (brought along to eating place).

+me'd/broder *-en, pl -brødre eccl.* brother, confrère, fellow believer; colleague.

+me'd/broderlig *A* - fraternal.

me'ḍ/bør *-en* fair wind; *fig.* favor, success.

+me'd/dele *V -te* 1 announce, report, state; inform, notify, tell. 2 communicate, impart (e.g. knowledge) to: **m- seg** be communicated, spread (e.g. doubt). 3 give, grant (discharge, permission, etc.); *eccl.* administer (absolution, the sacraments).

+me'd/delelse *-n* 1 announcement, information, notification (**om** of; **til** to). 2 communication, report (**om** on). 3 grant (**av** of).

+me'ddelelses/trang *-en* desire to communicate, need for expression.

+me'd/deler *-en, pl -e* informant.

+medde'l/som' *A -t, pl -me* communicative; expansive.

+me'd/dommer *-en, pl -e* (=***-ar**) *jur.* judge (in court having several presiding judges).

me'ḍdoms/mann *-en, pl -menn/*-menner jur.* (until 1927) lay judge (now called **doms/**).

me'ḍdoms/rett *-en jur.* (until 1927) designation for criminal court consisting of regular judge and two lay judges.

me'ḍ/drag *-et tech.* 1 line formed with a (carpenter's) marking gauge. 2 groove (in a piece of lumber). 3 (carpenter's) marking gauge.

***me'ḍe** *V -a* 1 aim (**på** at); use as landmark. 2 muse, ponder (**på** on, over).

+me'd/eier *-en, pl -e* (=***/eigar**) co-owner, joint owner.

***me'dels** *A* - cf **middels**

***me'del/tal** *-et* cf **middel/**

***me'del/tiḍ** *N* cf **middel/**

me'ḍ/faren *A +-ent, pl -ne* handled, treated.

+me'ḍ/fart *-en* handling, treatment.

me'ḍ/ferd [*/fær] *-a/+-en* handling, treatment.

me'd/født *A +-/*-født* (=**+/født**) congenital, innate, natural (e.g. ability).

+me'd/følelse *-n* sympathy (**med** for, with).

+me'd/følende *A* - sympathetic.

+me'd/følge *V -fulgte* accompany.

+me'd/før *et*: **i m-** by virtue of, pursuant to; **i embets m-** officially, on official business, professionally.

+me'd/føre *V -te* 1 bring (along) with, carry. 2 entail, involve. 3 bring about, cause, result in.

me'd/gang *-en* good fortune, prosperity, success.

me'd/gi *V -gav, -gitt* admit, grant.

me'd/gift *-a/+-en* dowry.

***me'ḍ/gjeving** *-a* acknowledgement, admission.

+med/gjø'rlig *A* - amenable, manageable, tractable.

***me'ḍ/hald** *-et* cf **/hold**

me'd/hjelp *-a/+-en* assistance, help.

+me'd/hjelper *-en, pl -e* (=***-ar**) assistant, helper; (in the Norwegian Church) pastor's assistant.

+me'd/hold *-et* (=***/hald**) approval, support (**i** of); acceptance (of opinion, view, etc.): **gi en m-** agree with, support sby.

***me'ḍ/hug** *-en* compassion, pity, sympathy.

+me'd/hustru *-a/-en* (esp. *bibl.*) second wife; concubine.

media'n *-en math.* median (line).

medikamen't *-et, pl -/+-er* medicament, medicine.

me'dikus *-en obs.* physician.

me'dio *Av* (esp. *merc.*) in the middle of: **m- januar** mid-January.

medisi'n *-en* medicine.

medisina'l *A* medical.

medisina'l/styre *-t* (central) board of public health.

+medisina'l/vesen *-et* public health administration.

+medisi'ner *-en, pl -e* (=***-ar**) 1 physician. 2 medical student.

medisi'n/mann *-en, pl -menn/*-menner* medicine man.

medisi'nsk *A* - medical (studies, treatment, etc.); medicinal (bath, plant, etc.).

+medisi'n/skap *-et* (=***/skåp**) medicine chest (cupboard).

medisi'n/tran *-a/-en* cod-liver oil (for medicinal use).

medis'ter/deig *-en* mixture of minced fat and lean of pork (with seasonings).

medis'ter/kake *-a* pork sausage (in patty form).

medis'ter/pølse *-a* pork sausage.

meditasjo'n *-en* meditation.

medite're *V -te* meditate.

me'dium *-iet, pl +-ier/*-ium* 1 *math.* mean. 2 (spiritualistic) medium (also *biol., phys.*). 3 *gram.* middle voice. 4 woven cotton fabric.

me'ḍ/kjensle *-a* sympathy.

medl. = **medlem**

me'd/lem' *+-met/*-(m)en, pl -mer/*-er* member; fellow (of a learned society).

me'dlems/bok *-a, pl -bøker* small book (belonging to member of an organization) in which paid dues, etc. are marked: **ha m-a i orden** be a card-carrying member (of a political party).

me'dlems/kort *-et* membership card.

me'dlem/skap *+-et/*-en* membership.

medli'dende *A* - compassionate, pitying, sympathetic (**med** to).

+medli'den/het *-en* compassion, pity, sympathy (**for** for).

me'd/lyd *-en* (=***/ljod**) consonant.

me'd/menneske *-t, pl +-r/*-* fellow (human) being.

meḍmin'dre *C* cf **mindre**

me'd/passasje'r *-en* fellow passenger.

+me'd/regnet [/reinet] *A* - (=***/rekna**) included, taken into account.

+meḍret'te *Av* cf **rett**[3]

+me'd/sammensvo'ren *A -ent, pl -ne* fellow conspirator: **politiet har også arrestert hans m-ne** the police have also arrested his accomplices.

me'd/skapning *-en* fellow creature

me'd/skyldig *A* - (esp. *jur.*) accessory: **være ens m-e** be one's accomplice.

+me'd/spiller *-en, pl -e* (=***/spelar**) (in theater) fellow player; (in cards, sports) partner.

+me'd/søster *-era/-eren, pl -re(r)* fellow woman, sister: **norske kvinner og deres amerikanske m-re** Norwegian women and their American (fellow) sisters.

+me'd/ta *V infl as* **ta**[1] *lit.* 1 bring, take along; include. 2 require: **arbeidet ville m- et par år** the work would r- a couple of years.

+me'ḍ/tatt *A* - (esp. of person) exhausted, weak, worn down; battered, damaged; shabby, worse for wear, worn (e.g. clothing, reputation, wallpaper).

+me'd/tevler *-en, pl -e* (=***-ar**) competitor, opponent, rival.

+medu'sa/hode *-t* (representation of) Medusa's (Gorgon's) head.

***me'ḍ/vetande** *A* - cf **/vitende**

***me'ḍ/veten** *A -e/-i, pl -ne* cf **/viten**

***me'ḍ/vett** *-et* consciousness.

me'ḍ/vind *-en* downwind, tail wind; favoring wind.

+me'd/virke *V -a/ et* contribute (**til** to, towards), cooperate (**til** in).

+me'd/virkende *A* - contributory: **de m-** the performers, those taking part.

+me'd/virkning *-en* (=***/verking, */verknad**) assistance, cooperation; participation: **yte sin m- til** give one's support to.

***me'ḍ/vit** *-et* cf **/vett**

***me'ḍ/viten** *A -e/-i, pl -ne* conscious.

me'd/vitende *A* -: **være m- om** know of (with others), be privy to.

+me'd/viter *-en* (=***-ar**) one who is in on sth (e.g. a secret), one privy to sth.

me'd/ynk *-en* commiseration, pity, sympathy.

me'g[1] [+mei'] *ob of* **jeg**[2], **eg**[2]

+me'g[2] *pt of* **mige**

megafo'n *-en* megaphone.

me'ga/tonn *-et* megaton.

+me'gen *A meget* cf **mye**

+me'get[1] *Pn nt of* **megen**

+me'get/sigende *A* - expressive, meaning, meaningful.

meg'ge *-a dial.* large woman (esp. one who thinks she is sby).

+meg'le *V -a/-et* cf **mekle**

+meg'ler *-en* cf **mekler**

me'/he *-et fam.* spineless person; yes-man.

mei' *-en* (sleigh) runner.

***meidd'** *-a* sleigh track.

mei'e *V -a/+-et/+-de/*-dde* cut, mow, reap: **m- ned** m- down.

mei'e/appara't *-et, pl -/+-er* reaping machine.

meieri' *-et, pl +-er/*-* dairy.

meieri'/smør *-et* (dairy-made) butter.

+ Bokmål; * Nynorsk; ° Dialect.
After letter: ' stress (Acc. 1); ` tone, stress (Acc. 2); · length.
Below letter: . not pronounced.

meieri'/spann *-et* milk can.
meieris't *-en* dairyman.
mei'erske *-a/+-en* dairymaid.
***mei'g** *pt of* **mige**
mei'n *-et* 1 damage, harm, injury; bodily defect. 2 hindrance, impediment.
***mei'n/bægje** *-t* hindrance, impediment.
mei'ne *V -te* (=+**mene**) 1 mean (=have in mind, intend): **hva m-er du?** what do you mean?; **jeg m-te det godt** I meant well; **det var ikke vondt m-t** I (he, she, etc.) didn't mean any harm; **jeg m-te å si ham det** I meant (intended) to tell him. 2 be of (have) the opinion, believe; consider, think: **det er mange som m-er vi er gale** many people think we're crazy; **hva m-er du om det** what's your opinion of that; **det skulle jeg m-e** I should say so (expression of strong agreement). 3 express the opinion, say: **"Det var merkelig," m-te han.** "That's funny," he said.
mei'n/eiḍ *-en* (=+**men/ed**) perjury.
***mei'n/hogg** *-et* damaging, injurious blow.
***mei'n/høve** *-t, pl +-r/*-* bad circumstance, situation.
***mei'nig** *A* - cf **menig**
***mei'nig/mann** *Pn* cf **menig/**
mei'ning *-a/+-en* (=+**mening**) 1 meaning, sense: **finne (få) m- i** make sense of; **gi m-** make sense; **ingen mening** no sense; **i ordets sanne m-** in the true sense of the word. 2 idea, intention: **(gjøre noe) i den beste m-** (do sth) with the best intentions; **det var (ikke) m-en** that was(n't) the idea; **hva er m-en med dette?** what's the meaning of this? 3 conviction, opinion (**om** about): **etter min m-** in my opinion; **danne seg, gjøre seg opp en m- om** form an opinion, make up one's mind about; **ha sine m-ers mot** have the courage of one's convictions; **si sin m-** express one's opinion, speak one's mind; **være av den m- at** be of the opinion, think that.
+**mei'nings/felle** *-n* person of the same opinion.
***mei'nings/før** *A* entitled to give an opinion.
mei'nings/laus *A* meaningless, senseless; absurd.
mei'nings/ytring *-a* expression of opinion.
***mei'nke** *V -a* hinder, impede; prevent.
mei'n/krok *-en* 1 bend in the wrong place (esp. wood). 2 intrigue. 3 contrary, recalcitrant person.
mei'n/laus *A* (=+**men/løs**) 1 without fault, defect; unspoiled. 2 harmless, innocent.
mei'n/rå̤d *-a* intrigue.
***mei'nsleg** *A* - inconvenient, inopportune.
***mei'n/sverjar** *-en* perjurer.
mei'n/svoren *A +-ent, pl -ne* perjured.
mei'nt *A* - (=+**ment**): ***eg er m- på det** I am planning (determined) to do it.
***mei'r** *cp of* **my(kj)e**
***mei'r/smak** *-en* cf **mer/**
mei's¹ *-a/-en* 1 willow basket; willow or rope net. 2 rucksack frame. 3 (in *cpds.*): e.g. **lat/m-** lazybones, sluggard.
mei's² *-a* (=**meise**) *zool.* titmouse (Paridae).
mei'sel *-elen, pl -ler* chisel.
***mei'sk** *-en* mixture; mash.
***mei'ske** *V -a* cf **meske**
mei'sle *V -a/+-et* chisel.
***mei'ster** *-eren, pl -rar* cf **mester**
***mei'sterleg** *A* cf **mesterlig**
***mei'ster/skap** *-en* cf **mester/**
***mei'ster/songar** *-en* cf **mester/sanger**
***mei'ster/stykke** *-t* cf **mester/**
***mei'stre** *V -a* cf **mestre**
mei'te *-a/+-et* fish (with pole).
***mei'tel** *-elen, pl -lar* chisel.
mei'te/mark *-en* (=**/makk**) earthworm.
mek.=**mekanisk**
+**meka'niker** *-en, pl -e* (=***-ar**) machinist; mechanic.
mekanikk' *-en* 1 (science of) mechanics. 2 mechanism.
mekanise're *V -te* mechanize.
meka'nisk *A* - mechanical: **m- jomfru** pneumatic hammer; **m- verksted** machine shop.
mekanis'me *-n* mechanism; contrivance.
***me'ke/dag** *-en* Wednesday.
mek'le *V -a/+-et* arbitrate, mediate (**mellom** between).
+**mek'ler** *-en, pl -e* (=***-ar**) 1 arbitrator, mediator; negotiator. 2 *merc.* broker; agent.
mek'ling *a/+-en* arbitration, mediation.
+**mek'lings/forslag** *-et* compromise proposal (esp. in labor disputes).
mek're *V -a/+-et* baa, bleat (esp. of goats).
mek're/gauk *-en zool.* snipe (Lymnocryptes).
+**meksika'ner** *-en, pl -e* (=***-ar, *meksikan**) Mexican.
meksika'nsk *A* - Mexican.
mek'tig *A* - 1 powerful (e.g. family, government, ruler). 2 (of food) filling, rich. 3 huge, mighty, vast. 4: **være noe m-** be master of sth, have command of sth. 5 *geol.* broad, thick.
me'l¹ *-en* (=+**mele¹**) (high) sand bluff (esp. along river or lake; formed by erosion).
+**me'l²** *-et* cf **mjøl**
***me'l³** *pr of* **male¹**
mel.=**melodi, melodisk**
melankoli' *-en* 1 melancholy. 2 *psych.* melancholia.
+**melanko'liker** *-en, pl -e* (=***-ar**) *psych.* melancholiac, melancholic; manic-depressive.
melanko'lsk *A* - 1 melancholy. 2 *psych.* melancholic.
melas'se *-n* molasses.
+**me'l/bær** *-et* cf **mjøl/**
mel'd *-en* cf **melder¹**
Me'l/dal *Pln* twp, Sør-Trøndelag.
***mel'ḍar** *-en* 1 (book, theater) reviewer. 2 informer.
+**mel'ḍ/bar** *A* (of cards) biddable.
mel'ḍe¹ *+-n/*-a bot.* goosefoot (Chenopodium).
+**mel'ḍe²** *V +-te/*-e* 1 announce, report: **m- av, fra** report; **m- en for (en forbrytelse)** report sby for (having committed a crime). 2 (esp.*) review (book, film etc.). 3 (in cards) bid. 4: **m- seg** (of events) arise, come, e.g. **vinteren m-te seg tidlig i år** winter came early this year; **det m-er seg mange problemer i forbindelse med** many problems arise in connection with; **m- seg hos (for, til) en** appear, report to sby; **m- seg til noe** report, sign up for sth; **m- seg inn i (ut av)** join (resign from); **la seg m-** send one's card in, ask to be announced.
mel'ḍe/plikt *-a/+-en* obligation to report (sth): **løslatt mot m-** released on parole.
mel'der¹ *-en* (=**meld**) grist.
+**mel'ḍer²** *-en, pl -e* (=***-ar**) 1 (in cards) bidder. 2 device for announcing, warning; alarm. 3 (esp.*) reviewer.
mel'ḍe/stokk *-en bot.* lamb's-quarters (Chenopodium album).
mel'ḍing *-a/+-en* 1 announcement, report: **avgi m- om at** report that. 2 (esp.*) review (**av of**). 3 (in cards) bid, bidding.
+**me'l/drøye** *-a* cf **mjøl/**
+**me'l/dugg** *-en* cf **mjøl/dogg**
+**me'le¹** *-n* cf **mel¹**
+**me'le²** *V -te* cf **mjøle**
+**me'len** *A -ent, pl -ne* cf **mjølen**
mele're *V -te* (usu. of fabrics, textiles) blend, mix (colors, shades): **m-stoff** varicolored material.
+**me'let(e)** *A* - cf **mjølet(e)**
Me'l/hus *Pln* twp, Sør-Trøndelag.
me'lis *-en* confectioners' sugar, powdered sugar.
+**mel'k** *-a/-en* cf **mjølk**
+**mel'ke¹** *-n* cf **mjølke¹**
+**mel'ke²** *V -a/-et* cf **mjølke³**
+**mel'ke-** *pf* cf **mjølke-**
+**mel'ke/vei** *-en astron.* Milky Way.
mel'le *-a* cf **malje**
+**mel'lem** *P* cf **mellom**
+**mel'lem/rum** [/romm] *-met* cf **mellom/rom**
mel'lemst *A* - cf **mellomst**
mel'lom *P* 1 between: **m- barken og veden** b- the devil and the deep blue sea; **m- oss sagt** just between you and me; **M- slagene** B- the Battles (Bjørnson); **er det noe m- dem?** is there anything between them? 2 among: ***m- anna** a- other things, inter alia; **m- venner** a- friends.
mel'lom/akt *-a/+-en* (theater) intermission.
mel'lom/alder *-en* *1 (def.) Middle Ages. 2 intermediate age.
Mel'lom-Ame'rika *Pln* Central America.
mel'lom/amerikan'sk *A* - Central American.
***mel'lom/be'ls** *A* interim, provisional, temporary; for the time being.
mel'lom/brun *A* medium brown.
mel'lom/bølgje *-a* (=+**/bølge**) medium frequency radio wave.
mel'lom/dekk *-et naut.* between decks.
mel'lom/distanse [-ang'se] *-n* middle distance (esp. in footracing).
Mel'lom-Europa [-auro'pa] *Pln* Central Europe.
mel'lom/folkelig *A* - international.
mel'lom/fornøgd *A -/*-nøgt* (=+**/fornøyd**) displeased, (a little) unhappy; *pop.* miffed.
mel'lom/golv *-et anat.* diaphragm.
+**mel'lom/handler** *-en, pl -e* (=***-ar**) intermediary, middleman.
***Mel'lom/haveṭ** *Pln* cf **Middel/**
mel'lom/klasse *-a/-en* middle class.
mel'lom/komst *-en* intercession, intervention; mediation.
mel'lom/lag *-et* 1 intermediate (middle) layer. 2 boot, sth given into the bargain.
mel'lom/lande *V -a/+-et* (of plane) make an intermediate landing, stop.
mel'lom/landing *-a/+-en* intermediate landing, stop.
mel'lom/ledd *-et* 1 connecting, intermediate link; medium. 2 *math.* mean. 3 *anat.* middle phalanx. 4 *logic* middle (term).
+**mel'lom/liggende** *A* - interjacent, intermediate (area, field, hill, etc.); intervening (days, hours, time, etc.).
mel'lom/mann *-en, pl -menn/*-menner* go-between, intermediary, middleman.
mel'lom/mat *-en lit.* (between-meal) snack.
+**mel'lom/regning** [/reining] *-en* (=**/rekning**) *merc.* current (open, running) account.
+**mel'lom/regnskap** [/reinskap] *-et* (=**/rekneskap**) *merc.* current account (record).
mel'lomriks/handel *-en* international trade (esp. between Norway and Sweden during their union).
mel'lomriks/veg [+/vei] *-en* road joining Norway and Sweden.
mel'lom/rom [/romm] *-met* interval, space (between): **med m-** at i-s.
mel'lom/skole *-n* (=***/skule**) *obs.* middle school (following grammar school and preceding *gymnasium*).
+**mel'lom/spill** *-et* (=***/spel**) 1 *mus.* interlude. 2 intermezzo (between acts of a drama).
mel'lomst *A* - middle, midmost (in age, position, size).
mel'lom/stemme *+-n/*-a mus.* (in men's chorus) second tenor and baritone; (in mixed quartet) alto

and tenor; (in string quartet) second violin and viola.
mel'lom/stilling *-a/+-en* intermediate position.
mel'lom/stor *A* medium-sized.
+mel'lom/størrelse *-n* medium size.
mel'lom/tid *-a/+-en* (time) interval: **i m-a** meanwhile.
mel'lom/tilstand *-en/*-et* intermediate state; *theol.* interval, state between death and judgment.
mel'lom/ting *-en* sth between, cross: **en m- av kanin og hare** a cross between rabbit and hare.
mel'lom/veg *-en* (=+/**vei**) (usu. *fig.*) middle course, road.
mel'lom/vekt *-a/+-en* middleweight.
mel'lom/verk *-et* (embroidery, lace) insertion.
+mel'lom/værende *-t* (=*/**være**) 1 *merc.* (outstanding) account: **gjøre opp et m-** settle an account. 2 *fig.*: **ordne vårt m-** settle our differences.
+mel'lom/øre *-t* (=*/**øyra**, */**øyre**) *anat.* middle ear.
melodi' *-en* 1 melody (of music, speech, etc.); tune. 2 *fig.*: **den samme m-en** the same old tune.
melo'disk *A* - melodic.
melodiø's *A* melodious.
melodon't *-en fam.* melody.
melodra'ma *-et* melodrama.
melodrama'tisk *A* - melodramatic.
melo'n *-en bot.* cantaloupe (Cucumis melo).
me'l/rakke *-n zool.* arctic fox (Alopex lagopus).
+me'l/sekk *-en* cf **mjøl/**
mel'te *V -a/+-et/*-e* 1 malt (grain). 2 *digest.
***mel'ting** *-a* digestion.
Me'l/øy *Pln* twp, Nordland.
membra'n *-en* 1 membrane. 2 *phys.*, *tech.* diaphragm.
memen'to *-et* memento.
+memoa'rer *pl* (=***-ar**) memoirs.
memoran'dum *-umet, pl -a/*-um* memo, memorandum.
memore're *V -te* memorize.
memoria'l *-en merc.* daybook, journal.
+me'n[1] *-et* cf **mein**
men'[2] *-(n)et, pl -/+-ner*: **det er et m- ved det** *archaic* there is a but to the question; **ikke noe m-** no but(s).
men'[3] *C* but: **m- i all verden** (expressing surprise) what in the world; **nei men, mor** (expressing impatience) good heavens, Mother.
menasjeri' *-et, pl +-er/*-* menagerie.
+me'ne *V -te* cf **meine**
+me'n/ed *-en* cf **mein/eid**
+me'n/eder *-en, pl -e* perjurer.
meng'd *-a* (=+**mengde**) 1 amount, quantity: **i små (store) m-er** in small (large) amounts. 2 great number, multitude; (a) lot(s) of, (a) great many: **en m-e penger** l-s of money; **m-er av, med** large numbers of, lots of; **i (svære) m-er** in abundance. 3 crowd (of people): **m-en** the masses.
+meng'de *-n* cf **mengd**
meng'de/vis *Av*: **i m-** in large quantities; **m- av (med)** lots of.
+meng'e *V -et/-te* (=***-je**) mingle, mix: **m- seg opp i** mix oneself up with (in).
***meng'ing** *-a* mixture.
***meng'je** *V -de* cf **menge**
+me'nig *A* - (=***meinig**) common, rank and file: *mil.* **m- soldat** private; enlisted man.
+me'nig/het *-en* 1 church, religious communion; congregation. 2 adherents, flock, followers.
+me'nighets/blad *-et* parish magazine.
+me'nighets/råd *-et* parish council.
+me'nighets/søster *-eren/-ra, pl -rer* parish nurse.
+me'nig/mann *N* common man, man in the street.
+me'ning *-a/-en* cf **meining**
meningitt [-gitt'] *-en med.* meningitis.
meningit'tisk *A - med.* meningitic.
+me'nings/beret'tiget *A* - entitled to give an opinion.
+me'nings/felle *-n* cf **meinings/**
+me'nings/forskjell *-en* difference of opinion.
+me'nings/løs *A* cf **meinings/laus**
+me'nings/utvek'sling *-en* exchange of views.
+me'nings/ytring *-en* cf **meinings/**
menis'k *-en anat., phys.* meniscus.
+me'n/krok *-en* cf **mein/**
+me'n/løs *A* cf **mein/laus**
menn'[1] *pl of* **mann**
menn'[2] *N*: **så m-** indeed, really, sure enough.
***men'ne** *-t* human being, person.
men'neske *-t* 1 human being, person: **han er et godt m-** he's a fine person; **jeg er bare et m-** I'm only human; **jeg så ikke et m-** I saw nobody, not a soul. 2 man, mankind: **det gamle m-** the Old Adam; **m-ts sønn** Son of Man; **Strindberg som m-** the man S-. 3 *(pl)* men, people: **for Gud og m-r** before God and man; **komme ut blant m-r** get around, meet people; **unge m-r** young people.
men'neske/alder *-eren, pl -rer* generation.
men'neske/ape *-n zool.* anthropoid ape (Pongidae).
men'neske/ba'rn *-et, pl -/*-born* human being, mortal; human child.
+men'neske/eter *-en, pl -e* (=***-ar**) cannibal; man-eater.
men'neske/forstan'd *-en/*-et* human intelligence.
men'neske/føde [*/føe] *-a/+-en* food fit for human consumption.
+men'neske/het *-en* humankind, mankind: **den ganske m-** all m-.
+men'neske/kjenner *-en, pl -e* (=***-ar**) judge of character, one who knows human nature.
men'neske/kjærlig *A* - humane; humanitarian, philanthropic.
men'neske/kropp *-en* human body.
men'neske/kunnskap *-en* knowledge of human nature.
men'neskelig *A* - (=***menneskjeleg**) 1 human. 2 humane.
+men'neskelig/het *-en* humaneness, humanity.
men'neske/liv *-et* human life.
men'neske/materiell' *-et* human material.
+men'neske/rettighet *-en* (=/**rett**) human right, right of man: **Erklæringen om m-ene** Declaration of Human Rights.
men'neske/skildring *-a/+-en* (in literature) delineation of character; (in art) delineation of the human form.
+men'neske/skjebne *-n* (human) destiny, fate.
men'neske/sky *A* - shy (of people).
+Men'neske/sønnen *Prn* (=*/**sonen**) *bibl.* The Son of Man.
men'neske/tap *-et* loss of human life.
men'neske/venn *-en* philanthropist; friend of man.
men'neske/vennlig *A* - philanthropic.
men'neske/verd [*/vær] *-et* human worth.
men'neske/verdig *A* - decent, fit for (worthy of) human beings.
men'neske/vrak *-et* (human) wreck.
men'neske/ånd *+-en/*-a* human spirit; human intellect.
***men'neskja** *df* mankind.
***men'neskjeleg** *A* - cf **menneskelig**
-men'ning *-en* cousin, e.g. **fir/m-**, **tre/m-**.
+me'n/råd *-en* cf **mein/**
+men's *C* (=**med**[1], ***medan**) while.
men'ses *pl* cf **menstruasjon**
menstruasjo'n *-en* menses, menstruation.
menstrue're *V -te* menstruate.
+me'n/svoren *A -ent, pl -ne* cf **mein/**
+me'nt *A* - cf **meint**
-men't *A* - number, e.g. **få/m-**, **mang/m-**.
menta'l *A* mental.
menta'l/hygie'ne *-n* mental hygiene.
menta'l/hygie'nisk *A* - of mental hygiene.
mentalite't *-en* mentality.
+menta'l/undersø'ke *V -te* (=***-je**) *jur., psych.* examine one's mental condition.
+menta'l/undersø'kelse *-n* (=***-ing**) *jur., psych.* mental examination.
men'te *N*: **ha i m-** bear (have) in mind; (in addition) **to i m-** carry two.
men'te/tal *-et* (=+/**tall**) (in addition) number carried.
mento'l *-en chem., pharm.* menthol.
menuett' *-en* minuet.
meny' *-en* menu.
+me'r *A cp of* **mye**
mer'd *-en* 1 fish trap. 2 dip net.
+me're *A cp of* **mye**
+me'r/forbruk [/fårr-] *-et* additional consumption.
mer'g *-en* (=+**marg**[2]) marrow (also *fig.*), medulla, pith (also *fig.*): **den forlengede m-** *anat.* medulla oblongata; **gå gjennom m- og bein** pierce to the marrow (the quick).
***mer'ga** *A* - marrowy, pithy; strong, vigorous.
***mer'gast** *V -ast* acquire strength, vigor.
mer'g/bein *-et* marrowbone.
mer'gel *-en agr., geol.* marl.
***mer'gle** *V -a agr.* marl (=fertilize with marl).
meria'n *-en bot.* marjoram (Origanum).
meridia'n *-en* meridian.
+me'r/inntekt *-a/-en* excess profits.
meri'no *-en/-et* merino (cloth).
meri'no/sau *-en zool.* merino (sheep).
meritt' *-en* (usu. *pl*) meritorious achievements; *fam.* escapades.
meritte're *V -te* merit: **m-t** well deserving of merit.
+mer'jelig *Av* intensely, powerfully.
merkanti'l *A* commercial, mercantile.
merkantilis'me *-n* mercantilism (system).
merkantilis'tisk *A* - mercantilistic.
+mer'k/bar *A* discernible, noticeable, perceptible.
mer'ke[1] *-t* 1 mark (in or on sth, e.g. a blaze, brand, check, label, notch, stamp, tag, etc.): **bære m- av** bear the stamp, show the effects of; **sette (sitt) m- på (i)** mark, leave a (one's) mark on; **sette m-(r) etter seg** leave one's mark, stamp; **sette m- ved** check off. 2 badge, emblem; banner: **under kongens m-** under the royal standard. 3 *naut.* beacon, buoy. 4 *merc.* brand. 5 initials, signature: **han skriver under m-t X** he writes under the signature of X. 6 notice: **bite m- i** notice, take note of; **legge m- til** notice, pay attention to, take notice of.
+mer'ke[2] *V -a/-et/-te* (=***-je**) 1 mark (by blazing, branding, checking, labeling, notching, painting, stamping, tagging, etc.): **m- av** check, mark off; **m- opp** blaze (e.g. a trail), mark; **m- seg ut** stand out; **m- ut** stake out (e.g. lots); **m-et** marked (**m-et av** marked by; **en m-et mann** a marked man). 2 note, pay attention to: **merk!** NB, note; **m- seg** note, make a mental note of; **vel å m-** nota bene, mind you, of course. 3 notice=become aware of, perceive: **jeg m-et ikke noe til det** I didn't notice it; **jeg lot meg ikke m- med noe** I didn't let on (say what I thought, express my feelings, etc.).
mer'ke/dag *-en* memorable day, red-letter day.
mer'ke/lapp *-en* label, tag (esp. on a package).

+ Bokmål; * Nynorsk; ° Dialect.
After letter: ' stress (Acc. 1): ` tone, stress (Acc. 2); · length.
Below letter: . not pronounced.

mer'kelig *A* - **1** notable, remarkable; interesting. **2** odd, peculiar, strange.
+**mer'ke/pæl** *-en* boundary marker; *fig.* landmark, turning point.
mer'ker[1] *pl of* **mark**[2]
+**mer'ker**[2] *-en, pl -e* (=***-jar**) marker (esp. one who marks timber).
mer'ke/sak *-a/+-en* leading issue; plank (in party platform).
mer'kes/mann *-en, pl -menn/*-menner fig., hist.* standard bearer.
+**mer'ke/stang** *-a, pl -stenger* banner, standard (pole).
mer'ke/stein *-en* boundary stone, marker; *fig.* landmark.
***mer'ke/stong** *-a, pl -stenger* cf **/stang**
mer'ke/varer *pl* proprietary (trademarked) goods.
+**mer'ke/øks** *-a* timber marking hammer, pole stamp axe.
mer'ke/år *-et* memorable year.
mer'king *-a* **1** (esp. timber) marking. **2** (road, way) marker.
***mer'kjar** *-en* cf **merker**[2]
***mer'kje** *V -te* cf **merke**[2]
***mer'kje/øks** *-a* cf **merke/**
mer'knad *-en, pl -er* comment, observation, remark; footnote, note.
mer'k/sam *A -t, pl +-me* **1** attentive, observant. **2** aware (**på** of): **ver m- på at** notice that.
Merku'r *Prn (m)* Mercury.
merkver'dig *A* - **1** remarkable, amazing, extraordinary. **2** curious, odd, strange.
+**merkver'dig/het** *-en* **1** remarkableness, singularity. **2** curiosity, oddity; sight, thing worth seeing.
+**mer'le/spiker** *-en, pl -e* (=***-ar**) *naut.* marlinespike.
mer'ling *-en* **1** *naut.* marling. **2** *naut.* marline.
+**mer'l/spiker** *-en, pl -e* cf **merle/**
merr' *-a* mare; hack, jade; *(derog.* of a woman) bitch.
+**mer'ra/bytter** *-en, pl -e* (=***/bytar**) *derog., fam.* horsetrader.
+**mer'ra/flåer** *-en, pl -e* (=***-ar**) *fam.* horse beater; rascal, scoundrel.
mer's *-et naut.* top (sail, mast).
mer'skum *-men/-met* meerschaum.
mer'skums/pipe *-a* meerschaum pipe.
+**me'r/smak** *-en* taste for more: **det gir m-** it whets my appetite for more of the same.
mer's/segl *-et* (=+**/seil**) *naut.* topsail.
+**me'r/utgift** *-a/-en* additional expenditure.
Me'r/åker *Pln* twp, Nord-Trøndelag.
mesallianse [messaliang'se] *-n* misalliance.
mesa'n *-en naut.* spanker.
mesa'n/bom [/bomm] *-men* spanker gaff.
mesani'n *-en* mezzanine.
mesani'n/eta'sje *-n* mezzanine floor.
mesa'n/mast *-a naut.* mizzenmast.
mese'n *-en* Maecenas, patron.
mesena't *-en* cf **mesen**
+**mes'ke** *V -a/-et* (=***meiske**) **1** (in brewing) mash. **2** fatten: **m- seg** gorge, stuff oneself.
+**mes'linger** *pl* (=***-ar**) measles.
meso'n *-en/-et phys.* meson.
mesopota'misk *A* - Mesopotamian.
mes'se[1] *-a/+-en* **1** *eccl.* mass (also *mus.*); protestant church service; protestant liturgy. **2** (trade) fair; exposition. **3** *mil.* mess.
mes'se[2] *V -a/+-et eccl.* chant, intone; say mass.
-mes's(e) *en* -mas, e.g. **kyndelsm-, mikkelsm-.**
mes'se/bok *-a* missal.
mes'se/fall *-et eccl.* no service.
+**mes'se/gutt** *-en* (=***/gut**) (esp. *naut.*) messboy.
mes'se/hakel *-elen, pl -ler eccl.* chasuble.
mes'se/serk *-en eccl.* alb.
mes'se/unifor'm *-a/+-en* mess jacket.
messia'nsk *A* - Messianic.
Messi'as *Prn* (the) Messiah.
+**-mes'sig** *A* - -like, e.g. **bym-, regelm-.**
+**mes'sing** *-en* (=***massing**) **1** brass; orchestral brass. **2: på bare m-en** on one's bare (naked) bottom.
mes'sing/knappa *A* - (=+**-et**) brass-buttoned; (of a cow's horns) brass-tipped.
mes'sing/stake *-n* brass candlestick.
°**mes'som** *Av* almost.
mes't[1] *sp of* **mye**
mes't[2] *Av* almost: **han skremte m-livet av sin mor** he almost frightened his mother to death (Bjørnson); **han var m- på gråten** he was almost crying (Bojer).
***mes'ta** *Av* almost.
+**mes'tbegun'stigelses/klausul** *-en* most-favored-nation clause.
mes'te/delen *df* the greatest part.
+**mes'ten/dels** *Av* for the most part, mostly.
mes'te/parten *df* the greatest part.
+**mes'ter** *-eren, pl -ere/-rer* (=***meister**) **1** master: **være m- for** be responsible for, be behind (e.g. a plan, project); be the perpetrator of (e.g. a practical joke); **være m- i** be an expert in; be adept, proficient at; **det skal jeg være m- for** just leave that to me; **øvelse gjør m-** practice makes perfect. **2** (in sports) champion: **m- i svømming** c- swimmer, **m- på ski** c- skier.
+**mes'terlig** *A* - (=***meisterleg**) masterly.
+**mes'ter/mann** *-en, pl -menn* executioner, hangman.
+**mes'ter/sanger** *-en, pl -e hist.* Meistersinger.
+**mes'ter/skap** *-et* **1** (sports) championship (**i, på** in). **2** masterliness, mastery.
+**mes'ter/skytter** *-en, pl -e* champion marksman; crack shot.
+**mes'ter/stykke** *-t* masterpiece; piece of work by apprentice done for admission to rank of master.
+**mes'ter/verk** *-et* masterpiece.
mesti's *-en* (in Spanish America) mestizo.
+**mes'tre** *V -a/-et* (=***meistre**) master.
°**me't** *A* cf **mæt**
metafo'r *-en* metaphor.
+**metafy'siker** *-en, pl -e* (=***-ar**) metaphysician.
metafysikk' *-en* metaphysics.
metafy'sisk *A* - metaphysical.
metall' *-et, pl -/+-er* metal.
metal'lisk *A* - metallic.
metallurgi' *-en* metallurgy.
metallur'gisk *A* - metallurgic, metallurgical.
metamorfo'se *-n* metamorphosis.
metano'l *-en chem.* methanol.
metate'se *-n* (in linguistics) metathesis.
***me'te** *V mat, mete/-i* cf **mæte**
+**me'te/mark** *-en* cf **meite/**
meteo'r *-en* meteor.
meteor. = **meteorologisk**
meteoritt' *-en* meteorite.
meteorolog [orolå'g] *-en* meteorologist; weatherman.
meteorologi' *-en* meteorology.
meteorologisk [orolå'gisk] *A* - meteorological: **m-e** (short for **M- Institutt**) the weather bureau.
me'ter *-en, pl* - meter (39.37 in.).
me'ter/bølgje *-a* (=+**/bølge**) radio wave length between 1 and 10 meters, used in FM broadcasting.
me'ter/mål *-et* meter-measuring device (e.g. tape measure); yard stick.
me'ter/syste'm *-et* metric system.
me'ter/vare *-a/+-en merc.* piece goods.
me'ter/vis *Av* by the meter: **hun kjøpte kniplinger i m-** she bought yards and yards of lace.
metier [metie'] *-et/+-en* profession, trade; specialty.
+**met'ning**[1] *-a/-en* cf **metting**
***me'tning**[2] *-a* esteem, respect.
meto'de *-n* method.
+**meto'diker** *-en, pl -e* (=***-ar**) methodical person.
metodikk' *-en* methodology.
meto'disk [also -o'-] *A* - methodical.
metodis'me *-n eccl.* Methodism.
metodis't *-en eccl.* Methodist.
metodis't/prest *-en eccl.* Methodist minister.
meto'pe *-n arch.* metope.
metres'se *-a/+-en* mistress (lover).
metrikk' *-en* **1** metrics, prosody. **2** textbook of prosody.
me'trisk *A* - metrical (measurement; poetry).
metrono'm *-en mus.* metronome.
metropo'l *-en* **1** *hist.* (in Greece) metropolis, mother city. **2** capital city, metropolis.
metropolitt' *-en eccl.* metropolitan.
me'trum *+-ret/*-rumet, pl +-ra/*-rum* meter (in poetry).
mett' *A* - **1** full (of food), satisfied: **spise seg m-** eat one's fill. **2** sated: **han kunne ikke se seg m- på** he never got tired of looking at; **gammel og m- av dage** *bibl.* old and full of days (Genesis 35,29).
met'te[1] *-a/-en* fill, satisfaction: **det er ingen m- i denne maten** this food isn't filling; **ha m-n** feel full; **få m-n sin** get one's fill; *fig.* have enough.
met'te[2] *V -a/+-et* **1** feed, fill, satisfy (with food; also *fig.*); satiate. **2** saturate: **en m-et farge** a deep (vivid) color; **markedet er m-et** the market is saturated.
Met'te *Prn (f)*
+**met'tet** *A* - *chem.* saturated (also *fig.*). (cf **mette**[2]).
metting *-a/+-en* saturation.
met'tings/grad *-en* degree of saturation.
***mett'/leik** *-en* fullness; satiety, saturation.
metu'salem *en* Methuselah.
metyll' *-en chem.* methyl.
mezzo/sopra'n [mes'so/, met'so/] *-en* mezzo-soprano.
+**m.fl.** = **med flere**
mg = **milligram**
Mgbl. = **Morgenbladet**
+**m. h. t.** = **med hensyn til**
mi' *Pn f of* **min**
mid'- *Pf* (=+**midt-**) mid-, median.
***mid'/alder** *-en* cf **middel/**
***mid'/alders** *A* - middle-aged.
***mid'/aldrug** *A* - middle-aged.
+**midd'** *-en* cf **mit**
mid'/dag *-en* **1** noon: **kl. 12 m-** twelve o'clock noon. **2** dinner, main meal of the day (often eaten late in the afternoon): **hvile (sove) m-** take an afternoon nap (usu. after dinner). **3** dinner party: **gi (holde) m- for** give a dinner for.
middags/avis *-a/+-en* afternoon paper.
mid'dags/høgd *-a* (=+**/høyde**) meridian altitude (of the sun); *fig.* zenith.
mid'dags/kvil *-en/+-a* afternoon (after-dinner) nap.
mid'dags/leite *-t dial.* dinnertime (late afternoon); (in the country) noontime.
mid'dags/lur *-en* afternoon (after-dinner) nap, siesta.
mid'dags/mat *-en* dinner; food for dinner.
mid'dags/selskap *-et, pl -/+-er* dinner party.
mid'dags/tiḍ *-a/+-en* **1** noon. **2** dinnertime (late afternoon); (in the country) noontime.
mid'dags/økt *-a* (in the country) work period from (second) breakfast to noon.
mid'del[1] *-elet/midlet, pl +midler/*-el* **1** instrument, means (**til** for); expedient, resource: **hensikten helliger m-let** the end justifies the means. **2** drug, preparation, remedy (**mot** against). **3: m-ler** capital, funds; means, wealth.
+**mid'del**[2] short for **middelskole: gå i tredje m-** be in the third class of the **m-**.
+**mid'del/alder** *-en* (=***mid/**) **1** *hist.* Middle Ages. **2** *geol.* Mesozoic period. **3** average age.

+mid'del/alderlig *A* - *hist.* medieval (also *derog., fig.*).
+mid'del/aldersk *A* - medieval; *derog.* benighted, primitive.
+mid'del/aldrende *A* - middle-aged.
+Mid'del/havet *Pln* (=***Mellom/, *Mid/**) the Mediterranean.
+mid'delhavs/farer *-en, pl -e* **1** Mediterranean sailor or ship. **2** *hum.* person of mediocre talents.
+mid'del/klasse *-a/-en* middle class.
+mid'del/mådig *A* - cf **/måtig**
+mid'del/måtig *A* - average, mediocre: **en m- eksamen** an indifferent grade.
+mid'del/punkt [/pongt] *-et* center.
mid'dels *A* - (=***medels**) average, medium, middling.
+mid'del/skole *-n hist.* middle school (following grammar school and preceding *gymnasium*; now called **realskole**).
+mid'del/stand *-en* **1** middle class. **2** *phys., tech.* mean level.
+mid'del/tall *-et* (esp. *math.*) average, mean.
mid'del/tid *N astron.* mean (solar) time.
+mid'del/vei *-en* middle course (way): **den gylne m-** the golden mean.
***mid'el** *-elen, pl -lar* cf **middel[1]**
mid'/faste *-a/+-en eccl.* Mid-Lent (fourth Sunday).
Mid'/ga'rd *Pln myth.* Midgard (abode of humanity).
Mid'gards/ormen *Prn myth.* The Midgard Serpent (coiled around the earth).
***Mid'/havet** *Pln* cf **Middel/**
Mid'/hordland *Pln* judicial district around Bergen (includes several twps).
mid'je *-a/+-en* waist: **smal om m-n** narrow-waisted, slim.
mid'je/smal *A* narrow-waisted, slender.
mid'le *V +-et/*-a archaic* mediate.
+mid'ler[1] *-en, pl -e* (=***-ar**) mediator.
+mid'ler[2] *pl of* **middel[1]**
+mid'lere *A* - mean, middle.
+mid'ler/tidig *A* - interim, provisional, temporary.
mid'let *nt of* **middel,** *pp of* **midle**
***mid'/lies** *Av* midway up the mountainside.
mid'/natt *-a/+-en, pl -netter* midnight.
mid'/nattes *Av pop.* around midnight.
mid'natts/sol *-a* midnight sun.
mid'natts/time *-n* midnight hour.
***mid'/nette** *-t* midnight.
***mid'/punkt** [/pongt] *-et* cf **midt/**
***mid'/sommar** *-en* cf **midt/sommer**
+mid'/sommer *-eren, pl -somrer* cf **midt/**
+mid'sommer/natt *-a/-en* Midsummer Night (Eve).
+mid'/sommers *Av* cf **midt/**
midt' *Av* in the middle: **m- etter** along the middle of; **m- for(an)** right in front of; **m- i** in the middle of; **m- i ansiktet** (also *fig.*) right to one's face; **m- inne i byen** right in the middle of town; **m- (i)mellom** halfway between; **(komme) m- opp i** (come) right in the middle (of); **m- over** right above; **m- på** in the middle of, right on (**m- på dagen, natta** in the middle of the day, night; **m- på gata** right on the street); **m- under** directly below; during, in the middle, midst of.
+midt'- *Pf* cf **mid-**
midt'e *-n* middle, midst: **i vår m-** among us, in our midst.
midt'en *df* the middle: **m- av** the m- of; **på m-** in the m-; **gå av på m-** break in the m-.
midt'erst *sp of* **midtre**
midt'/etter *P* along the middle of.
midt'/fjo'rds *Av* in the middle of the fjord, mid-fjord.
+midt'/linje *-n* (=***/line**) center line, halfway line (sports).
midt/mål *-et* tree's diameter halfway up.
midt'/parti· *-et* central part.
midt'/punkt [/pongt] *-et* center, central point (**for** of); middle (of a line); fess point (on an escutcheon): **Sverdrup var m-et for norsk politisk liv** S- was the focal point (the central figure) of Norwegian political life.
midt're *A -, sp midterst* middle (of three or more uneven numbers).
midt'/skips *Av naut.* midships.
+midt'/sommer *-eren, pl -rer* (=***-ar**) midsummer (esp. of June 24).
+midt'/sommers *Av* in the middle of summer, at the height of summer.
+midt'/veis *Av* (=***/veges, *mid/veges**) midway.
midt'/vinter *-eren, pl -rer* midwinter: **på m-en** in the middle of the winter.
midt'/vinters *Av* in the middle (dead) of winter.
***mid'/veges** *Av* cf **midt/veis**
mid'/vinter *-eren, pl -rer* cf **midt/**
mid'/vinters *Av* cf **midt/**
mi'g[1] *-et dial.* urine.
+mig[2] [mei'] *ob of* **jeg[2]** cf **meg[1]**
mi'ge *V meig/+meg, +meget/*mige/*-i dial.* urinate.
mi'ge/maur *-en dial.* pismire.
mignon/pære [minjå'ng/] *-a* small light bulb (e.g. for use in a chandelier).
migre'ne *-n* migraine.
mika'do *-en* mikado.
***mikj'els/mess(e)** *ei* cf **mikkels/**
mik'kel *-en, pl mikler* Reynard (the fox): **en lur m-** a sly fox.
Mik'kel *Prn (m)*
+mik'kels/mess(e) *en* (=***mikjels/**) *eccl.* Michaelmas (29 Sept.).
Mik'le/gard *Pln* medieval Scandinavian name for Constantinople (now Istanbul).
mikro'be *-n* microbe.
mikrofo'n *-en* **1** microphone. **2** (telephone) transmitter.
mik'ro/kosmos *et* microcosm.
mik'ro/organis'me *-n* microorganism.
mikrosko'p *-et, pl -/+-er* microscope.
mikroskope're *V -te* examine under a microscope.
mikrosko'pisk *A* - microscopic.
mik'se *V -a/+-et* mix; (often *derog.*): **m- sammen** jumble up, muddle.
mik'se/bo'rd *-et* control desk (for sound or video mixer).
+mik'ser *-en, pl -e* (=***-ar**) cocktail mixer.
mik'stum *-et* mixture; mishmash.
mikstu'r *-en* (medicine, smoking) mixture; (*mus.*, on an organ) mixture stop.
mikæli [mike'li] *en* cf **mikkels/mess(e)**
mi'l *-a, pl* - (Norwegian) mile (now 10 km.=6.2 mi.; formerly 11.3 km. =7 mi.); (geographic, nautical, statute) mile.
mil.=**militær**
Mila'no *Pln* Milan
mil'd *A* **1** mild (climate, criticism, person, tobacco etc.); indulgent, lenient (e.g. judge); gentle, soft: **m-est talt** to put it mildly, to say the least; **du m-e himmel** good heavens. **2** *dial.* generous, liberal.
***mil'de** *-a* mildness; gentleness; indulgence, leniency.
+mil'd/het *-en* mildness; gentleness; indulgence, leniency.
mil'dne *V -a/+-et* **1** alleviate, relieve, soothe; soften, subdue. **2** grow gentle, lenient (also **m-es**).
Mil'drid *Prn (f)*
***mil'd/skap** *-en* mildness; gentleness; indulgence, leniency.
***mil'd(s)leg** *A* - fairly mild.
+mil'd/vær *-et* (=***/ver**) mild weather.
mi'le *-a* **1** charcoal kiln. **2** (bridle) bit.
mi'le/lang *A* miles long; very long: **m-e brev** endless letters.
+mi'le/pæl [/pel] *-en* milepost; *fig.* milestone.
mi'le/stolpe *-n* milepost.
mi'le/vid *A* **1** miles wide: **i m- omkrets** for miles around. **2** (adv.) far and wide, for many miles: **m-t omkring** for miles around.
mi'le/vis *Av* miles and miles, many miles.
+milis(s)' *-en* cf **milits**
milit.=**militær**
militaris'me *-n* militarism.
militaris't *-en* militarist.
militaris'tisk *A* - militaristic.
milit's *-en* militia.
militæ'r[1] *-en* military man, soldier.
militæ'r[2] *-et* (the) military.
militæ'r[3] *A* military.
militæ'r/musikk· *-en* **1** military music. **2** military (e.g. regimental) band.
+militæ'r/nekter *-en, pl -e* (=***-ar**) conscientious objector.
militæ'r/perso'n *-en* military man, soldier.
+militæ'r/tjeneste *-n* (=***/tenest(e)**) military service.
miljø' *-et, pl -/+-er* environment, milieu; background, surroundings; social set.
miljø'/bestem't *A* - determined by environment; environmental.
miljø'/skildring *-a/+-en* description of social background.
mill.=**million**
mil'le *-n merc.* thousand: **pro m-** per thousand.
milliar'd *-en* billion.
milliar'd/del *-en* (a) billionth.
milliar'de *Num* billionth.
milliardæ'r *-en* billionaire.
mil'li/bar *-en meteor.* millibar.
mil'li/gram· *-met, pl* - milligram (.015 grains).
mil'li/meter *-en, pl* - millimeter (.04 in.).
millio'n *-en* million.
+millio'n/beløp *-et* (amount of a) million.
millio'n/brann *-en* (over a) million *kroner* (dollar, etc.) fire.
millio'n/by *-en* city of (over) a million inhabitants.
millio'n/del *-en* (a) millionth.
millio'n/tap *-et* loss of (over) a million *kroner* (dollars etc.).
millio'nte *Num* millionth.
millionæ'r *-en* millionaire.
milliono'se *-a/+-en* millionairess.
***mil'lom** *P* cf **mellom**
milorg [mil'årg] *N* = **Militærorganisasjonen,** heart of the armed (military) resistance movement in Norway during World War II.
milorg/mann *-en, pl -menn/*-menner* member of **Milorg.**
mil't *-en/*-et* (=***milte**) *anat.* spleen.
mil't/brann *-en med.* anthrax.
***mil'te** *-n/-t* cf **milt**
+mi'miker *-en, pl -e* (=***-ar**) actor (with special reference to expression and gestures); mimic.
mimikk' *-en* expression (esp. facial), gestures.
mi'misk *A* - expressive, mimic: **m-talent** acting talent.
mimo'se *-a/+-en bot.* mimosa (Mimosa).
+mimo'se/aktig *A* - delicate, (over)-sensitive.
mim're *V -a/+-et* quiver, twitch one's lips (without sound); mumble, quaver.
mi'n *Pn f mi, nt mitt, pl mine* **1** mine, my: **boka mi** my book; **boka er mi** it's my book. **2** (in exclamations) **du store min** (mild oath, *approx.* my heavens). **3** (self-abuse) **jeg min idiot (mitt fe)** what a dope I am.
min.=**minister, ministerium; minutt**
minare't *-en* minaret.
+min'delig *A* - *cf* **minnelig**

+ Bokmål; * Nynorsk; ° Dialect.
After letter: ' stress (Acc. 1); ` tone, stress (Acc. 2); · length.
Below letter: . not pronounced.

***min'der** C 1 unless: **han vil ikkje ha det m- det er nytt** he won't have it unless it's new. 2 (*adv.*) otherwise: **m- hadde eg ikkje sagt det o-** I wouldn't have said it.

°**min'ders** C cf **minder**

min'dre A *cp of* **liten, lite**[2]

min'dremanns/kjensle -*a* feeling of inferiority.

min'dre/tal -*et* (=+/**tall**) minority.

min'dre/verd [*/vær] -*et* inferiority.

min'dre/verdig A - inferior.

+**min'dre/verdighet** -*en* inferiority.

+**min'dreverdighets/komplek's** -*et* cf **mindreverds/**

+**min'dreverds/følelse** -*n* (=+**mindreverdighets/**) feeling of inferiority.

min'dreverds/kjensle -*a* feeling of inferiority.

min'dreverds/komplek's -*et* inferiority complex.

min'dre/årig A - minor, under age.

mi'ne[1] -*a* (coal, silver, etc.; explosive) mine.

mi'ne[2] -*a*/+-*en* air, expression, mien: **gjøre gode m-er til slett spill** grin and bear it, put on a good face; **gjøre m-er til en** make signs to one (by facial expression), make faces, motion; **ikke fortrekke (forandre) en m-** not bat an eye, not move a muscle; **ingen sure m-r** chins up, grin and bear it.

mi'ne[3] V -*a*/-*te* *fam.* blast, blow up: **nisser og dverge bygge i berge, men vi skal m- dem alle herut** brownies and dwarfs dwell in the mountains, but we shall blast them all out (Wergeland).

mi'ne/bor +-*et*/*-*en* drill for making a blasthole (in stone, etc.)

mi'ne/felt -*et* mine field.

mi'ne/melding -*a*/+-*en* radio announcement giving position of World War II mines (or objects which appear to be mines) sighted in Norwegian waters.

miner. =**mineralogisk**

minera'l -*et* mineral.

+**minera'l/holdig** A - containing minerals.

mineralog [-lå'g] -*en* mineralogist.

mineralogi' -*en* mineralogy.

mineralogisk [-lå'gisk] A mineralogical.

minera'l/rik A rich in minerals.

minera'l/rike -*t* mineral kingdom.

minera'lsk A - mineral.

minera'l/vatn -*et* (=+/**vann**) mineral water; usu. carbonated beverage.

mine're V -*te* blast, mine.

mi'ne/skott -*et* (=+/**skudd**) blast, blasting shot.

+**mi'ne/spill** -*et* (=*/**spel**) play of (one's) features.

+**mi'ne/sprenge** V -*te* blast, explode (by mines).

mi'ne/språk -*et* (facial) pantomime.

+**mi'ne/sveiper** -*en*, *pl* -*e* (=*-**ar**) *naut.* mine sweeper.

miniaty'r -*en* miniature: **en Napoleon i m-** a m- Napoleon.

miniaty'r/gevæ'r -*et* small-bore rifle (for sports shooting).

+**miniaty'r/skytter** -*en*, *pl* -*e* (=*-**ar**) small-bore rifle shooter.

minima'l A minimal, minimum.

mi'nimum -*mumet*, *pl* +-*ma*/*-*mum* minimum (**av** of): **m- ett år** at least one year.

mi'nimums/termome'ter -*eret*/-*ret*, *pl* -*er*/+-*re* minimum (temperature) thermometer.

minis'ter -*eren*, *pl* -*rer*/+-*ere* (cabinet, diplomatic) minister.

ministeria'l/bok -*a*, *pl* -*bøker* church register.

ministeriell' A -*ell* ministerial.

ministe'rium -*iet*, *pl* +-*ier*/*-*ium* 1 *admin.* department, ministry. 2: **m-iet** the cabinet.

minis'ter/krise -*a*/-*en* cabinet crisis.

min'k[1] -*en* *zool.* mink (Mustela vison).

min'k[2] -*en* decrease, dwindling, reduction.

min'ke V -*a*/+-*et* 1 decrease, dwindle, shrink. 2: **m- på** reduce; **m- på farten** slow down.

min'ke/mon(n)** -*en* (=minkings/**) degree of loss, reduction, shrinkage.

***min'nast** V *minnest, mintest, minst* cf **minnes**

min'ne[1] -*t* 1 memory, recollection, reminiscence: **m-r fra** memories of (e.g. childhood); **gå (en) av m-** be forgotten (by sby); **ha i friskt m-** remember clearly; **i manns m-** in living memory, in the memory of man; **komme (renne) en i m-** come to one's mind; **legge seg noe på m-** keep sth in mind, pay special attention to sth; **til m- om** in memory of; **ære være hans m-** all honor to his memory. 2 keepsake, souvenir (**fra** from); memorial, monument (**over to**): **til m-** as a keepsake: **reise et m- over** erect a memorial to. 3 *archaic* consent, leave, permission.

min'ne[2] V *minte* 1 remind: **m- en om noe** remind sby of sth; **m- en på** remind sby to (e.g. do sth). 2: **m-s** commemorate; remember; *archaic* be remembered.

***min'ne/blom** -*en* *bot.* forget-me-not (Myosotis).

min'ne/bok -*a*, *pl* -*bøker* 1 (among school children) memory book. 2 memorial volume.

min'ne/dag -*en* 1 commemoration, memorial day. 2 memorable day.

min'ne/fest -*en* commemoration, commemorative festival.

+**min'ne/gave** -*a*/-*en* (=*/**gåve**) 1 memorial (gift); testimonial (gift). 2 keepsake, remembrance, souvenir.

min'nelig A - amicable (compromise, settlement, etc.).

+**min'nelig/het** -*en*: **i all m-** amicably, in a friendly way.

+**min'nelse** -*n* reminder; recollection, remembrance (**om** of) (esp. of sth unpleasant); trace (of illness).

min'ne/o'rd -*et* commemorative words (**om** about).

min'ne/rik A rich in memories; memorable.

+**min'nes** V *mintes* (=***minnast**) 1 remember; commemorate. 2 *archaic* be remembered (**av** by).

+**min'ne/sanger** -*en*, *pl* -*e* (=*/**songar**) minnesinger.

min'nes/merke -*t*, *pl* +-*r*/*- 1 memorial, monument (**for, over to**). 2 relic (**fra, om** of).

min'ne/staup -*et* memorial toast.

min'ne/stein -*en* memorial stone, monument.

min'ne/støtte -*a*/+-*en* memorial column, monument.

min'ne/tale -*n*/*-*a* commemorative, memorial speech.

min'ne/verdig A - memorable.

***min'nig** A - having good memory, able to remember well.

min'ning -*a*/+-*en* admonition, warning; reminder.

minorite't -*en* minority.

minorite'ts/styre -*t* minority rule.

minoritt' -*en* *eccl.* Minorite.

+**minsan't(en)** I cf **sant**

min'ske V -*a*/+-*et* diminish, lessen, reduce.

***min'st**[1] *pp of* **minnast**

min'st[2] A *sp of* **liten, lite**[2]

min'ste/ba'rn -*et* youngest child in the family, the "baby".

min'ste/lønn -*a*/+-*en* (=*/**løn**) minimum wage.

min'ste/sats -*en* minimum (wage) scale.

min'ste/sum' -*men* minimum amount (sum).

***min'test** *pt of* **minnast**

minuen'd -*en* *math.* minuend.

mi'nus[1] -*et*, *pl* -/+-*er* *math.* minus sign (either ÷ or —).

mi'nus[2] A, P *math.* minus; *educ.* (in grading) minus, e.g. M÷, ab. = A—.

mi'nus/flyktning -*en* refugee hampered in choice of employment because of some disability, illness, etc.

minus'kel -*elen*, *pl* -*ler* lower case letter; minuscule.

mi'nus/menneske -*t* (physically, psycholog.) handicapped person.

minutiøs [minutsiø's] A minute (description, difference, observation, etc.).

minutt' -*et*, *pl* -/+-*er* minute: **på m-et** on the dot; **han kommer på m-et** he is coming at once; **han kommer hvert m-** he'll be here at any moment.

+**minutt'/viser** -*en*, *pl* -*e* (=*-**ar**) minute hand.

minø'r -*en* *mil.* miner.

mira'kel -*elet*/-*let*, *pl* -*el*/+-*ler* miracle.

mirakulø's A miraculous.

mis'- Pf mis- (de-, dis-).

+**mis'/akte** V -*et* disdain, scorn.

misantro'p -*en* misanthrope.

misantropi' -*en* misanthropy.

misantro'pisk A - misanthropic(al).

+**mis'/billige** V -*et* disapprove of, frown on.

+**mis'/billigelse** -*n* disapproval (**av** of).

mis'/bruk -*en*/-*et* misuse; abuse (**av** of).

mis'/bruke V -*te*/*-*a* misuse; abuse.

+**mis'/dannelse** -*n* deformity, malformation (**av** of).

+**mis'/dannet** A - deformed, malformed, misshapen.

+**mis'/deder** -*en*, *pl* -*e* *archaic* malefactor, misdoer.

misera'bel A -*elt*, *pl* -*le* miserable, wretched.

misere [misæ're] -*n* failure; unfortunate affair, wretched situation: **etterkrigstidens økonomiske m-** the miserable economic situation of the postwar period.

***mis'/fare** V -*fer*, *for*, *fare*/-*i* 1 go astray, lose the way. 2: **m- seg** do wrong, make a mistake. 3: **m-ast** be destroyed, ruined (e. g. of crops).

+**mis'/forhold** -*et* disparity; disproportion (**mellom** between): **stå i m- til** be out of proportion to; **et skrikende m-** a crying disparity.

+**mis'/fornøyd** A displeased, dissatisfied (**med** with).

+**mis'/fornøyelse** -*n* displeasure, dissatisfaction (**med** with).

mis'/forstå V -*stod*, -*stått* misunderstand; misconceive, misconstrue: **m-tt iver** mistaken (misapplied) zeal.

+**mis'/forståelse** -*n* misunderstanding; misconception, misconstruction (**av** of).

mis'/foster [/foster] -*eret*/*-*ret*, *pl* -*er*/+-*re* deformed fetus; *fig.* monstrosity: **et m- av en roman** a monstrous novel.

***mis'/gjere** V -*gjer*, -*gjorde*, -*gjort*: **m- seg** do wrong.

mis'/gjerning -*a*/+-*en* ill deed, misdeed, offence; *bibl.* iniquity.

***mis'/gjo'rde** *pt of* **-gjere**

mis'/grep -*et* blunder, error, mistake.

+**mis'/hag** -*et* disapproval, displeasure.

+**mis'/hage** V -*et* displease.

+**mis'hags/ytring** -*a*/-*en* expression of displeasure.

***mis'/halde** V -*held*, -*heldt*, -*halde*/-*i* break, fail to fulfill; neglect, put aside: **m-en** neglected, sidetracked.

mis'/handle V -*a*/+-*et* maim, maltreat, mistreat.

mis'/handling -*a*/+-*en* cruelty, maltreatment.

***mis'/hugse** V -*a*: **m- seg** misremember.

mis'/høre V -*te* (=*/**høyre**) mishear.

mis'/høve -*t* disparity; disproportion.

***mis'/jamn** A -*jamt* rough, uneven; unequal.

misjo'n -*en* (diplomatic, religious, life) mission: **ofring til m-en** offering for missions; **hans livs m-** his m- in life.

misjone're V -*te* *eccl.* missionize, proselytize.

+**misjo'ns/fore'ning** -*a*/-*en* *eccl.* mission society.

misjo'ns/mark -*a* *eccl.* mission field.

misjo'ns/selskap *-et eccl.* mission society.
misjo'ns/skole *-n eccl.* **1** mission school. **2** missionary school.
misjo'ns/stasjo'n *-en eccl.* mission (post, station).
misjonæ'r *-en* (usu. *eccl.*) missionary.
mis`/kjenne *V +-kjente/*-kjende* fail to appreciate, misjudge: **et m-t geni** an undiscovered genius.
mis`/kjenning *-a/+-en* (=**+-else**) failure to appreciate, misjudgment (**av** of).
mis`/klang *-en* discord, dissonance, jar.
mis`/kle *V -dde* be unbecoming, not fit or suit: **den hatten m-r henne** that hat is not becoming to her.
mis'k/mask *-et fam.* mishmash; confusion.
mis`/kreditt· *-en* discredit: **komme i m-** be discredited.
mis`/kunn *+en/*ei bibl.* forgiveness, mercy.
mis`/kunne *V +-kunte/*-a: bibl.* **m-seg over** have mercy upon, take pity on.
miskun'nelig *A - bibl.* merciful.
+mis`kunn/het *-en bibl.* mercy.
***mis`kunn/sam·** *A* merciful.
mis`lig *A* - dubious, questionable; shady.
+mis`lig/het *-en* fraud, irregularity; malpractice, misconduct.
+mis`lig/holde *V -holdt, -holdt* (esp. *jur.*) break, default on, fail to fulfill (e.g. a contract).
+mis`lig/holdelse *-n* (esp. *jur.*) breach of contract, default (**av** on).
mis`/like *V -te/*-a* dislike.
mis`/lyd *-en* (=***/ljod**) discord, dissonance.
mis`/lykka *A -* (=**+/lyk(ke)t, */lukka**) abortive, unsuccessful: **frukthøsten var m-** the fruit harvest was a failure.
+mis`/lykkes *V -lyktes, -lykkes* (=***lykkast, */lukkast**) be unsuccessful, fail; fall through, turn out badly.
***mis`/lynt** *A -* **1** capricious, whimsical; unpredictable. **2** naughty, perverse.
+mis`/minnes *V -mintes* (=***-ast**) misremember, remember incorrectly.
mis`/modig *A -* dejected, despondent, dispirited; miserable
***mis`/mon(n)** *-en* unfavorable difference: **gjere m-** be partial.
mis`/mot *-et* dejection, despondency, dispiritedness.
***mis`/mæte** *V -te* disdain, look down upon.
mis`/nøgd *A -/-nøgt* (=**+/nøyd**) displeased, dissatisfied (**med** with).
mis`/nøye *+-n/*-t* displeasure, dissatisfaction.
misogy'n *-en* misogynist.
+mis`/oppfatning *-en* misconception, misunderstanding.
mis'pel *-elen, pl -ler bot.* cotoneaster (Cotoneaster).
***mis`/prenting** *-a* misprint.
mis`/rekne *V -a/+-et* (=**+/regne**): **m-seg** miscalculate.
miss'[1] *-en* **1** *dial.* pussycat. **2** (English) miss.
***miss'**[2] *N* (=**mist**): *dial.* **kaste (skyte) i m-** throw (shoot) and miss (the target); **gå m- av** miss; **ta i mist** be mistaken.
mis'se[1] *V -a/+-et archaic* squint.
***mis'se**[2] *V miste* cf **miste**
mis'se/roma'n *-en* saccharine, sentimental novel for young ladies.
***mis`/steg** *-et* false step, slip.
mis`/stemning *-a/+-en* **1** bad feeling, ill will (**mot** toward). **2** despondency, gloom; bad humor.
mis't *N* cf **miss**[2]
mis`/ta *V -tok, -tatt:* **m- seg** be mistaken, err.
mis`/tak *-et* error, mistake.
***mis`/tale** *V -a/-te:* **m- seg** make a slip of the tongue; blurt out, say too much.
mis`/tanke *-n* suspicion: **ha m- til en** be suspicious of sby; **ha m- om noe** suspect sth.
mis't/benk *-en* hotbed (for plants).
mis'te *V -a/+-et/*-e* (=***misse**[2]) **1** lose (balance, consciousness, contact, control, courage, grip, life, prestige, etc.): **m- både munn og mæle** be dumbfounded, lose one's tongue; **m- fatningen, hodet** lose one's head; **m- trikken** *fam.* miss the trolley. **2** *dial.* (want to) give up, relinquish.
***mis`/teken** *A -e/-i, pl -ne* misconstrued, misinterpreted.
mis'tel/tein *-en bot.* mistletoe (Viscum album).
+mis`/tenke *V -te* (=***-je**) suspect (**for** of): **gjøre en m-t** render one suspect, open to suspicion; **ha noen m-t for** suspect sby of.
+misten'kelig *A -* (=***-tenkjeleg**) suspicious (=open to suspicion): **en m- utseende person** a s- looking character.
+misten'kelig/gjøre *V -gjorde, -gjort* render suspect, throw suspicion on.
***mis`tenkjeleg** *A -* cf **mistenkelig**
+misten'k/som· *A -t, pl -me* (=***/sam**) distrustful, suspicious (nature, person): **m- av seg** having a s- temperament.
+misten'ksom/het *-en* distrustfulness, suspicious nature.
mis`/tillit *+-en/*-a* distrust, lack of confidence (**til** in).
+mis`tillits/forslag *-et pol.* motion for vote of no confidence.
mis`tillits/votum *-et, pl -vota* (esp. *pol.*) vote of no confidence.
mis`/tok *pt of* **-ta**
mis`/tolke *V -a/+-et* misinterpret.
+mis`/tro *-en* cf **/tru**
+mis`/troisk *A -* cf **/truisk**
mis`/tru *-a* distrust, mistrust.
***mis`/truen** *A -e/-i, pl -ne* distrustful, suspicious (nature, person).
+mis`/truisk *A -* mistrustful, suspicious (**mot** of).
+mis`/trøstig [also -øs'-] *A -* **1** disconsolate, discouraged; pessimistic, sad. **2** discouraging: **m-e utsikter** d- prospects.
mis`/tvile *V -te* doubt, have misgivings about.
mis`/tyde *V -de/+-et* misconstrue, misinterpret.
***mis`/tyding** *-a* misunderstanding; misconception, misconstruction.
misun'ne [also mis`/] *V -unte* envy; begrudge (one's food, one's success).
misun'nelig *A -* envious (**på** of).
+misun'nelse *-n* (=***-ing**) envy.
+misun'nelses/verdig *A -* enviable: **lite m-** unenviable.
+misun'ner [also mis`/] *-en, pl -e* (=***-ar**) one who envies.
***mis`/unning** *-a* cf **misunnelse**
mis`/vekst *-en* crop failure.
mis`/visende *A -* **1** deceptive, misleading. **2** *naut., tech.* deviating (from true north because of magnetic influence).
+mis`/visning *-en* (=***/vising**) *naut., tech.* (magnetic) deviation (from true north), error.
***mis`/vokster** *-en* cf **/vekst**
mi't *-en* (=**+midd**) *zool.* mite (Acarina), "worm".
mi'tra *-en eccl.* (bishop's) miter.
mitraljø'se *-a/+-en* (heavy) machine gun.
mitt' *Pn nt of* **min**
mjau'[1] *-et* meow.
mjau'[2] *I* meow.
mjau'e *V -a/+-et* meow.
mjell' *-a* cf **mjøll**
mjell`/snø *-en* dry, loose, powdery (new) snow.
Mjoll'ne *Prn myth.* Mjolner (Thor's hammer).
mju'k *A* (=**+myk**[3]) **1** limber, pliable, supple; springy; soft. **2** compliant, meek, submissive: **gjøre en m-** bring one to heel; **m- som et lam** submissive as a lamb; **m- i knærne** weak-kneed.
mju'ke *V -a* (=**+myke, *mykje**) **1** limber, make pliable; soften: **m-opp** s- up. ***2** beat (up), drub.
***mju'k/hendt** *A -* having soft, fine hands; gentle, having gentle hands.
***mju'k/leik** *-en* pliancy, suppleness; humility, softness.
mju'k/lynt *A -* gentle, soft-hearted, tender.
mju'kne *V -a/+-et* (=**+mykne**) become, make pliable, supple; limber up; soften.
mjø'd *-en* mead (fermented drink including honey): **mjøden farver fortidens skygge blek** mead brightens the pale shadow of the past (Wergeland); **Suttungs m-** *myth.* poetry.
***mjød'm** *-a, pl -ar* hip.
mjø'd/urt *-a/+-en bot.* meadowsweet (Filipendula ulmaria).
mjø'l *-et* (=**+mel**) **1** flour; meal: **+ha rent m- i posen** have a clear conscience. ***2** *bot.* pollen.
mjø`l/bær *-et bot.* bearberry (Arctostaphylos uva-ursi).
mjø`l/dogg *-a/+-en* mildew (also *fig.*).
mjø`l/drikke *-t* mixture of water and meal as drink for livestock.
mjø`l/drøye *-a bot.* ergot (Claviceps purpurea).
mjø`le *V -a/+-te* (=**+mele**) flour, sprinkle with flour: **m- sin egen kake** look out for one's own interests.
mjø`len *A +-ent, pl -ne* mealy (apple, potato).
mjø`let(e) *A -* flour-covered, floury (arm, face, etc.).
***mjø`ling** *-a* pollination.
mjøl'k *-a* (=**+melk**) milk.
mjøl`ke[1] *-n* (=**+melke**[1]) milt (secretion).
mjøl`ke[2] *-n bot.* willow herb (Epilobium).
mjøl`ke[3] *V -a/+-et* (=**+melke**[2]) milk.
mjøl`ke- *Pf* (=**+melke-**) milk.
mjøl`ke/bil *-en* milk truck.
mjøl`ke/bunke [/bongke] *-n* dish of slightly curdled (clabbered) whole milk eaten with sugar and crumbs.
mjøl`ke/butikk· *-en* dairy (for selling milk products and usually some other items such as bread, cold cuts, etc.).
mjøl`ke/feber *-en med.* milk fever.
+mjøl`ke/fett *-et* (=***/feitt**) butterfat.
mjøl`ke/kjerre *-a* milk wagon.
mjøl`ke/krakk *-en* milking stool.
mjøl`ke/ku *-a, pl -kyr/+-er* milch (milk) cow.
mjøl`ke/mann *-en, pl -menn/*-menner* milkman.
mjøl`ke/maski'n *-en* milking machine.
mjøl`ke/mat *-en* food product made from milk.
mjøl`ke/papp *-en* milk cooked and thickened with flour.
mjøl`ke/ringe *-a* dish of slightly curdled (clabbered) whole milk eaten with sugar and crumbs.
mjøl`ke/saft *-a bot.* latex.
mjøl`ke/spann *-et* milk can.
+mjøl`ke/sprengt *A -* (=***/sprengd**) (of breast, udder) charged, heavy with milk.
mjøl`ke/sukker *-et chem.* lactose.
mjøl`ke/syre *-a chem.* lactic acid.
mjøl`ke/tann *-a, pl -tenner* milk tooth.
mjøl`ke/veg *-en astron.* Milky Way.
mjøl`ke/velling *-a/-en* gruel made with milk.
mjøll' *-a* (=***mjell**) dry, loose, powdery (new) snow.
mjø`l/mat *-en* farinaceous food, food made with flour or meal.
+Mjøl'ner *Prn* cf **Mjollne**
mjø`l/sekk *-en* flour, meal sack.

+ Bokmål; * Nynorsk; ° Dialect.
After letter: ' stress (Acc. 1); ` tone, stress (Acc. 2); · length.
Below letter: . not pronounced.

+mjø'l/tråver -en, pl -e (=*-ar) *archaic* tramp, vagrant.
Mjø'sa *Pln* Norway's largest lake, Oppland and Hedmark counties.
mjø's/båt -en boat trafficking Lake Mjøsa.
Mjø's/traktene *df pl* districts around Lake Mjøsa.
mjå' *A* -tt slender, slim; (of the waist) narrow.
***mjå'/herda** *A* - narrow-shouldered.
***mjå'/hund** -en greyhound.
***mjå'/rygg** -en small of the back.
***mjå'/vaksen** *A* -e/-i, pl -ne slender, slim.
M/K=**motorkutter**
ml=**milliliter**
ml.=**mellom**
mm=**millimeter**
+m. (m.) m. med (meget) mer
mnd(r).=**+måned(er)/*månad(er)**
mne'mo/teknikk' -en mnemonics.
mo'1 -en 1 heath, moor, pine barren. 2 *mil* drill grounds; encampment.
mo'2 -et dust, small chaff (e.g. **høy/, sag/**).
***mo'3** *A* -tt close, sultry.
+mo'4 *A* - cf **mod2**
mo'5 *Av*: **m- alene** *fam.* all by oneself.
Mo' *Pln* twp, Telemark; **M- i Rana** twp, Nordland; **M- i Ryfylke** post office, Rogaland.
moaré -en moiré (fabric).
mobb' -en mob.
mobi'l *A* mobile.
mobilise're *V* -te mobilize.
***mo'd1** -et cf **mot1**
mo'd2 *A* - (=**+mo'4**) 1 tired, weary; faint. 2 *archaic* dejected, sad.
-mod1 -et mind (e.g. **tål/, ve/**).
-mod2 *Prn(m)* e.g. **Her/, Tor/.**
***mo'da** *A* - 1 bold, brave, courageous. 2 desirous, eager (**på** for).
moda'l *A gram.* modal.
Mo'/dalen *Pln* twp, Hordaland.
+mo'de1 -n cf **mote1**
mo'de2 *N* cf **mote2**
modell' -en model (**av** of) as e.g. artist's m-; a pattern, representation, standard: **stå m-** pose as a m-; **tegne etter m-** draw from a m-.
modelle're *V* -te model (from clay, wax, etc.).
modelle'r/voks -et modeling wax, plasticine.
modell'/fly -et model airplane.
+modell'/snekker -en, pl -e (=***/snikkar**) patternmaker (in wood, for use in casting, founding).
modell'/studie -n study (drawing, painting) from life (live model).
modellø'r -en modeler.
mo'den *A* +-ent, pl -ne ripe (apple, cheese, grain, etc.); mature (age, person, etc.): **m- for (til)** ready, ripe for; **tidlig m-** early (e.g. apples), precocious.
+mo'den/het -en ripeness; maturity.
+mo'denhets/alder -en (age of) maturity.
+mo'denhets/prøve -a/-en test of maturity.
mo'der -en cf **mor1**
moderasjo'n -en 1 moderation. 2 esp. *merc.* discount, price reduction (**på** on).
modera't *A* - moderate (demand, price, view, etc.): **de m-e** *hist.* conservative liberals (Norw. political group in the 1880's); **m-e former** (of the spelling reforms of 1938 and later) language forms deviating least from those of the preceding (1917) spelling (opposed to **radikale former**).
moderatø'r/lampe -a/-en moderator lamp (from ca. 1840).
modere're *V* -te moderate: **m- seg** control oneself.
+mo'der/jo'rd -en home (mother) soil, native soil.
+mo'der/kirke -n (=***/kyrkje**) mother (parent) church.
+mo'der/land -et homeland, mother country, motherland.
mo'derlig *A* - motherly.

moder'ne *A* - modern; fashionable, up-to-date.
modernise're *V* -te modernize; renovate.
modernis'me -n (in art, literature, theology) modernism.
modernis'tisk *A* - modernistic.
+mo'der/næring -en chief source of livelihood, sustenance.
mo'der/selskap -et *merc.* parent company.
mo'der/skap +-et/*-en maternity, motherhood.
+mo'der/skip -et mother ship.
mo'di *pl of* **modus**
modifikasjo'n -en modification.
modifise're *V* -te modify.
mo'dig *A* - 1 bold, brave, courageous. 2: **gråte sine m-e tårer** cry bitterly, cry one's heart out. 3 *dial.* (as *adv.*) exceedingly, remarkably.
modis't -en milliner, modiste.
***mo'dnad** -en ripeness; maturity.
***mo'dnast** *V* -ast ripen; mature.
mo'dne *V* -a/+-et (also **m-es**) ripen; mature.
mo'dnings/prosess' -en ripening process (e.g. of cheese).
modulasjo'n -en esp. *mus., phys.* modulation.
module're *V* -te esp. *mus., phys.* modulate.
Mo'dum *Pln* twp, Buskerud.
mo'dus -en, pl *modi* 1 *gram.* mood. 2: **m- vivendi** modus vivendi (lat.).
***mo'e** -n 1 heat haze. 2 distant, obscure rain or snow clouds.
***mo'en** *A* -e/-i, pl -ne hazy (air).
***mogeleg** [må'geleg] *A* - cf **mulig**
***mo'gen** *A* -e/-i, pl -ne cf **moden**
***mogleg** [må'gleg] *A* - cf **mulig**
***mo'gnad** -en ripeness; maturity.
***mo'gna(st)** *V* -a(st) cf **modne**
mo'/gopp -en (=***/gop**) *bot.* pasque flower (Anemone).
M. og R.=**Møre og Romsdal**
mogu'l -en Mogul (ruler).
m. o. h.=**meter over havet**
+mohika'ner -en, pl. -e (=***mohikan**) Mohican.
mokasi'n -en moccasin.
***moke1** [må'ke] -a cf **måke2**
***moke2** [må'ke] *V* -a cf **måke3**
mok'ka -en *fam.* mocha coffee.
+mok'ka/kaffe -n (=***/kaffi**) mocha coffee.
mok'ka/kopp -en demitasse cup.
mok'ka/skje -en (=***/skei**) demitasse spoon.
***mol1** [må'l] -a small scattered clouds.
***mol2** [må'l] -en bank, layer of pebbles along a beach.
***mol3** [må'l] -en cf **møll**
mo'l4 *pl of* **male1**
mol'/bakke -n cf **mar/**
+mol'/bo -en (=***/bu**) stupid hick (from Danish stories about inhabitants of Mols in Jutland).
+mol'bo/aktig *A* - dense, stupid; narrow, provincial.
***mol'/bu** -en cf **/bo**
mol'd -a 1 earth, soil, topsoil; humus, mold. 2 *bibl. poet.* (usu. **muld**) dust, earth: **oven m-e** above the sod, above ground (=still alive).
***molde** *V* -a cover with earth; earth, hill (e.g. potatoes); loosen (soil): **m- seg** (of chickens) take a dirt bath.
Mol'de *Pln* city, Møre og Romsdal.
molden *A* +-ent, pl -ne containing humus, mold; moldy.
mol'd/jord -a soil rich in humus, mold.
mol'd/okse -n *dial.* larva of the dungbeetle.
***mol'drast** *V* -ast: **m- opp** crumble away.
mol'd/træl -en grubber, tiller of the soil.
mol'd/varp -en *zool.* mole (Talpa).
***mo'le1** -n bit, particle, piece.
***mole2** [må'le] *V* -a crush, smash.
+molefonken [-fong'ken] *A* -ent, pl -ne *fam.* dejected, downcast, sad; crestfallen.

moleky'l -en/ -et, pl -/+-er *chem., phys.* molecule.
moleky'l/kraft -a/+-en *chem., phys.* molecular force.
moleky'l/vekt -a/+-en *chem., phys.* molecular weight.
molekylæ'r *A* - *chem., phys.* molecular.
moles't -en molestation; damage, injury.
moleste're *V* -te molest; damage, injure.
***mol/eten** [må'l/] *A* -e/-i, pl -ne cf **møll/ett**
moll' -en *mus.* minor.
+moll'/stemt *A* - *lit., poet.* in a minor key; melancholy, sad, somber.
moll'/tone -n *lit., poet.* minor note; melancholy, sad, somber tone.
mollus'k -en *zool.* mollusk (Molusca).
mo'lo -en breakwater, mole.
mo'lok -en *bibl., poet.* Moloch.
mol'te -a *bot.* cloudberry (Rubus chamaemorus).
mol'te/kart -en unripe cloudberry.
mol'te/myr -a cloudberry bog.
***mol'ten** *A* -e/-i, pl -ne tender; crumbling, moldering.
mol'te/sanking -a/+-en cloudberry picking.
molybde'n -en/-et *chem.* molybdenum.
molybde'n/glans -en *chem.* molybdenite.
momen't -et, pl -/+-er 1 aspect, element, factor; feature, point (i of): **et nytt m- i forhandlingene** a new factor in the negotiations. 2 instant, moment. 3 *phys.* moment.
momenta'n *A* momentary; (adv.) instantly: **han døde m-t** he died i-.
momp [mom'p] -en (in cards) slam.
mompe [mom'pe] *V* -a/+-et 1 (in cards) bid a slam. 2 *dial.* chew with a full mouth, stuff oneself.
***mo'n1** -en, pl -er cf **monn**
+mon2 [månn'] *pr of* **monne2**
+mon3 [månn'] *C* I wonder (if): **m- det ikke er noen arvelig galskap i familien** I wonder if there isn't some inherited madness in the family (Ibsen); **hadde han sagt det, mon?** had he really said it? (Hoel).
***mo'naleg** *A* - considerable, goodly; (adv.) completely, effectually, with a vengeance.
monar'k -en monarch.
monarki' -et, pl +-er/*- monarchy.
monar'kisk *A* - monarchic(al).
monarkis't -en monarchist.
monarkis'tisk *A* - monarchist(ic).
monden [månde'n] *A* elegant, fashionable, sophisticated.
***mo'ne** *V* -a cf **monne1**
+monegas'ser -en, pl -e (=***-ar**) Monacan, Monegasque.
+mone'ter *pl fam., obs.* change, dough.
monetæ'r *A* monetary.
mongol [monggo'l] -en 1 Mongol, Mongolian (inhabitant of Mongolia, one who speaks a Mongolian language). 2 *anthro.* Mongoloid.
mongolisme [monggolis'me] -n *med.* mongolism.
mongoloid [monggolo-i'd] *A* - *med.* mongoloid.
mongolsk [monggo'lsk] *A* - 1 Mongolian. 2 *anthro.* Mongoloid.
monn' [also monn'] -en, pl *-er (=***mon1**) 1 advantage, benefit, help. 2 addition, augmentation, increase: **alle m-er drar** every little bit helps. 3 bit, degree: **i noen m-** somewhat, to some degree; **ta sin m- igjen** even things up.
+mon'ne1 [also mon'ne] *V* -a/-et (=***mone**) avail, be of benefit, (to advantage), do good, help: **det m-er ikke stort** it doesn't do much good, it doesn't help much; **det m-er med innsamlingen** the fund-raising is going well.
+mon'ne2 *V* mon, monne (no pp) (=***mune1**) *archaic, poet.* will: **nu mon hun synke** now she will sink (Poetic Edda, tr. Gjessing). 2 may, might: **hva man m- begjære**

whatever one might desire; **monne da** maybe then (Undset). 3 (aux.) do: **svakt m- sol mellom skyer smile** faintly did sun through cloud-banks smile (Bjørnson); ***nyst munde det regna** just now it was raining (Folk song).
monoga'm *A* monogamous.
monogami' *-et* monogamy.
monografi' *-en* monograph.
monogram' *-met, pl -/+-mer* monogram.
monok'kel *-ellen, pl monokler* monocle.
monolitt' *-en* monolith (column, obelisk, etc.): **M-en** (central feature of sculptural decorations in Frogner Park, Oslo, by Gustav Vigeland).
monolog [monolå'g] *-en* monologue.
mono'm *-et, pl -/+-er math.* monomial.
monoma'n *A* monomaniac.
monopo'l *-et, pl -/+-er* monopoly.
monopolise're *V -te* monopolize.
monoteisme [-te-is'me] *-n* monotheism.
monoto'n *A* monotonous.
monotoni' *-en* monotony.
mon's *Av* e.g. **m- alene** completely alone.
Mon's *Prn (m)* also used as typical cat name (=Pussy): **det var mat for M-** that was sth for him, a real treat.
monstran's *-en eccl.* monstrance.
+**monstro'** *C archaic* I wonder (if): **m- det er sant** I wonder if it's true?
mon'strum *-rumet/-ret, pl +-rer/*-rum* monster.
monstrø's *A* monstrous.
monsu'n *-en* monsoon.
monta'sje *-n* 1 *tech.* erection, installation, mounting. 2 esp. *photog.* montage (composite picture; film editing).
+**montenegri'ner** *-en, pl -e* (=**montenegrin**) Montenegrin.
Montene'gro *Pln* Montenegro.
monte're *V -te tech.* erect, install, set up; mount.
montre [mång'ter] *-n* showcase.
+**montro'** *C* cf **tro**[6]
montø'r *-en* fitter; installer.
monumen't *-et, pl -/+-er* monument (over to).
monumenta'l *A* monumental.
mope'd *-en* light motorcycle (motorbike).
mopedis't *-en* one who drives a **moped**.
mopp' *-en* (floor) mop.
mop'pe *V -a/+-et* mop.
mop's *-en* 1 pug (dog). 2 *fam.* person with a pug-like face; *pop.* sour-puss.
mop'se/fjes *-et fam.* pug-like face; *pop.* sour-puss.
mop'set(e) *A* - 1 having a pug face. 2 cross, peevish.
mo'r[1] *-a/+-en, pl mødrer/+mødre* 1 mother (til of): **be for sin syke m-** ask for oneself under pretence of asking for sby else; **han er ikke av m-s beste barn** he is a suspicious character; **her hjelper ingen kjære m-** no use begging or crying here; **ikke en m-s sjel** not a soul; **mor til tusen barn** *bot.* Aaron's beard, mother-of-thousands (Saxifraga sarmentosa). 2 (in exclam. address): **nei mor** [morr'] certainly not (to a girl or woman).
mo'r[2] *-en* Moor; blackamoor.
***mor**[3] [mår'] *-en* chopped meat, sausage.
mo'ra *-en* 1 *jur.* default. 2 *gram.* mora.
mora'l *-en* 1 ethics, morality, moral philosophy. 2 moral conduct, morals. 3 morale (e.g. of troops). 4 moral (of a story): **m-en er, ta din kone med, når du skal gå ut etter øl** the moral is, take your wife along, when you go out for a beer (student song).

+**mora'l/begre'p** *-et* moral concept.
+**mora'l/forkyn'ner** *-en, pl -e* (=***-ar**) moralist, preacher of morality.
moralise're *V -te* moralize.
moralis't *-en* moralist, moralizer.
moralite't *-en* 1 morality. 2 morality play.
mora'l/predikan't *-en* (overzealous, censorious) moralist, moralizer.
+**mora'l/preken** *-en* moralizing lecture, sermon.
mora'lsk *A* - moral (conduct, courage, duty, principle, support, victory, etc.).
mo'ra/rente *-a/+-en merc.* interest on overdue payments.
morass' *-et* morass.
morato'rium *-iet, pl +-ier/*-ium* moratorium.
mo'r/bror [also: mor'/] *-en, pl +-brødre/*-brør* (maternal) uncle, mother's brother: **ha bispen til m-** have good connections.
mo'r/bær *-et bot.* mulberry (Morus).
mord [mor'd] *-et* murder.
***mor'darleg** *A* cf **morderlig**
mord/brann [mor'd/] *-en* arson (with intent to kill).
+**mord/brenner** *-en, pl -e* (=***-ar**) arsonist (who has set fire with intent to kill).
+**morder** [mor'der] *-en, pl -e* (=***-ar**) murderer.
+**morderisk** [mor'derisk] *A* - murderous.
+**morderlig** [mor'derli] *A* - (=***mordarleg**) *fam.* terrific, mighty; *(adv.)* awfully, immensely, terribly: **m- redd** deathly afraid.
+**morderske** [mor'derske] *-a/-en* murderess.
mord/sak [mor'd/] *-a/+-en* murder case.
mord/våpen *-et* murder weapon; murderous weapon.
mo're *V -a/+-et* (=***moroe**) amuse, divert, entertain: **m- seg** amuse, enjoy oneself; **m- seg over** be amused at, enjoy.
mo'r/eld *-en* phosphorescence.
morell' *-en bot.* (morello) cherry (Prunus avium).
more'ne *-n geol.* moraine.
more'ne/jo'rd *-a geol.* soil deposited by a moraine.
mor'/far *-en* (maternal) grandfather, mother's father.
Mor'fevs *Prn* Morpheus.
morfi'n *-en* morphine.
morfinis't *-en* morphine addict.
morfologi' *-en biol., geol., gram.* morphology.
morfologisk [-lå'gisk] *A* - *biol., geol., gram.* morphological.
morgana'tisk *A* - morganatic.
+**morgen** [må'ren, må'ern] *-enen, pl -ner* (=***morgon**) morning: **god m-** good morning; **i m-** tomorrow; **i m- tidlig** tomorrow morning; **i m- aften** tomorrow evening; **i m- åtte dager** a week from tomorrow; **om m-en** in the morning; **tidlig på m-en** early in the morning; **til den lyse m-** till daybreak; **i m- den dag** (even, as soon as) tomorrow.
+**morgen/avi's** *-a/-en* morning newspaper: **M-en** name of Bergen's only morning paper.
morgen/blad *-et* morning newspaper: **M-et** daily newspaper in Oslo.
+**morgen/dag:** **m-en** the next day, tomorrow; *poet.* the morrow, the future.
+**morgen/demring** *-en* (early) dawn, daybreak.
+**morgen/fugl** *-en* early bird.
+**morgen/gave** *-a/-en* morning gift (from husband to wife on morning after wedding night).
+**morgen/gretten** *A -ent, pl -gretne* grumpy in the morning.
+**morgen/gry** *-et* dawn, daybreak.
+**morgen/gymnastikk'** *-en* morning exercises (calisthenics).
+**morgen/kjole** *-n* house coat, robe, wrapper.

+**morgen/kvist** *-en*: **på m-en** early in the morning.
+**morgen/mat** *-en* breakfast (usu. Danish).
Morgen/posten *Prn* daily newspaper in Oslo.
+**morgen/røde** *-n* red light of dawn, sunrise.
+**morgen/side** *-a/-en* **(ut)på m-en** towards morning.
+**morgen/sol** *-a* morning sun(shine); rising sun.
+**morgen/stell** *-et* morning chores (activities, routine).
+**morgen/stemning** *-en* morning atmosphere, mood.
+**morgen/stjerne** *-a/-en* 1 morning star. 2 *hist.* spiked mace (weapon).
+**morgen/stund** *-a/-en* morning (time): **m- har gull i munn** "there is gold in the mouth of the morning" (=the early bird catches the worm).
+**morges** [mår'res] *N*: **i m-, i dag m-** this morning (when referring back to it on the same day); **i går m-** yesterday morning.
mor'gne *V -a/+-et fam.* **m- seg** get the sleep out of one's eyes, awaken fully.
+**morgning** [må'rning] *-en* cf **morgen**
***mor'gon** *-en, pl morg(o)nar* cf **morgen**
***mor'gon/svævd** *A* - sleepy in the morning.
moria'n *-en* Moor; blackamoor.
+**mo'r/ild** *-en* cf **/eld**
***mor'k** *-a, pl merker* cf **mark**[2]
mo'r/kake *-a anat.* placenta.
mor'kel *-elen, pl -ler bot.* morel (Morchella) (a mushroom).
mor'ken *A +-ent, pl -ne* decayed, decaying, rotting (leather, tooth, wood, etc.); brittle (ice).
mor'kne *V -a/+-et* decay, rot; (of ice) become brittle.
mo'r/laus *A* (=+**/løs**) motherless.
mormo'n *-en* Mormon.
mormo'nsk *A* - Mormon.
mor/mor [mor'/] *a/+en* maternal grandmother, mother's mother.
mor'n *I* hello, hi: **m- da** good-bye; **m- igjen** good-bye, so long; **m- m-** (in passing) hello, hi; (when leaving) good-bye; **m- så lenge** so long.
moro [mor'ro] *-a* amusement, enjoyment, fun; entertainment: **for m-(s) skyld** for the fun of it; **ha m- av** make fun of; enjoy; **holde moro** cut up, have fun.
***mo'roe** *V -a* cf **more**
mo'ro/sam' *A -t, pl -me* (=+**morsom**) 1 amusing, enjoyable; entertaining, interesting. 2 funny, humorous, witty. 3 nice, pleasant: **det var m-t å treffe Dem** nice to meet you.
°**mor'ra** *-en cf* **morgen**
mo'rs/arv *-en* maternal inheritance.
mo'rs/dag *-en* Mother's Day (in Norway 2nd Sunday in February).
mor'se *V -a/+-et* telegraph, wire.
mor'se/alfabe't *-et* Morse code.
mor'se/skrift *-a/+-en* Morse code writing.
+**mor'se/tegn** [/tein] *-et* (=***/teikn**) Morse code sign.
mo'rs/folk *-et* mother's people (family, relatives, side of the family).
mo'rs/instin'kt *-et* maternal instinct.
morsk [mor'sk] *A* 1 gruff, severe; fierce, tough. 2 *fam.* strongly disposed, given, inclined **(etter å, til å** to).
mo'r/skap[1] *-en* 1 amusement, enjoyment, entertainment. 2 fun, gaiety, liveliness.
mo'r/skap[2] *+-et/*-en* maternity, motherhood.

+ Bokmål; * Nynorsk; ° Dialect.
After letter: ' stress (Acc. 1); ` tone, stress (Acc. 2); · length.
Below letter: . not pronounced.

mo'rskaps/lekty're *-n* entertaining, light reading (material).
morske [mor'ske] *V -a/⁺-et*: **m- seg** be fierce, gruff, severe.
mo'rs/liv *-et* womb.
mo'rs/merke *-t* birthmark.
mo'rs/mjølk *-a* (=⁺**/melk**) mother's milk: **få noe inn med m-en** be imbued with sth from infancy.
mo'rs/mål *-et* mother tongue.
⁺**mor/som** [mor'/såmm] *A -t, pl -me* cf **moro/sam**
⁺**morsom/het** *-en* 1 amusement, enjoyment; fun. 2 joke, witticism; *pop.* wise crack.
mo'rs/side [*/sie] *-a/⁺-en* maternal side (of one's family).
mo'rs/trygd *-a* mother's pension.
***mo'r/syster** *-a, pl -systrer* (maternal) aunt, mother's sister.
mort [mor't] *-en zool.* roach (Rutilus).
mortalite't *-en* mortality.
Mor'ten *Prn (m)*
mor'tens/gås *-a* roast goose (to be eaten on Martinmas).
mor'tens/mess(e) *en eccl.* Martinmas (11 Nov.)
morter[1] [mor'ter] *-en, pl ⁺-e* mortar (for pulverizing).
mortér[2] *-en mil.* mortar.
mortifikasjo'n *-en jur.* annulment, declaration that sth is null and void (**av** of).
mortifise're *V -te jur.* declare null and void.
mo's[1] *-en* mash, pulp, sauce (of food) e.g. **eple/m-, lunge/m-.**
⁺**mo's**[2] *-et* cf **mose**[1]
mosaikk [mosa-ikk'] *-en* mosaic.
mosa'isk *A - eccl.* Mosaic.
mo'se[1] [*må'se] *-n* 1 *bot.* moss. 2 *dial.* bog, marsh: **ugler i m-n** mischief afoot, trouble brewing. 3 lichen, e.g. **rein/m-, islands/m-.**
***mose**[2] [må'se] *V -a* gather moss (esp. for fodder).
mo'se/bok *en, pl -bøker bibl.* one of the books of the Pentateuch.
mo'se/dott *-en* handful (tuft, wad) of moss.
mo'se/fly *-a* moss- or lichen-covered mountain plateau.
mo'se/funn *-et archeol.* (esp. in Denmark) bog find.
mo'se/grodd *A -/*-grott* moss-covered (also *fig.*), overgrown with moss.
mo'set(e) *A -* mossy.
mosjo'n *-en* 1 (bodily) exercise. 2: **vekke m- om** (in parlimentary procedure) make a motion about.
mosjone're *V -te* (take) exercise.
mosjo'ns/gymnastikk' *-en* bodily exercises, gymnastics.
⁺**mosjø'** *-en hist. fam.* monsieur.
Mo'/sjøen *Pln* town, Nordland.
moské[1] *-en* mosque.
***mos'ke**[2] *-n* cf **maske**[2]
***mos'ke**[3] *V -a* cf **maske**[3]
Mos'ke/nes *Pln* twp, Nordland.
Mos'kenes/straumen *Pln* the Maelstrom.
moskito [moski'to] *-en zool.* mosquito (Culicidae).
moskovitt' *-en* Muscovite.
moskus [mos'kuss] *-en* musk.
moskus/okse *-n zool.* musk ox (Ovibus moschatus).
Mos'kva *Pln* Moscow.
mo'/sott *-a dial.* anemia.
Moss' *Pln* town, Østfold.
°**mosse** [mos'se] *-a* cf **musse**
most [mos't] *⁺-en/*-a* 1 *bibl.* grape juice, must. 2 fermented fruit juice, e.g. hard cider and (Brit.) perry.
moster [mos'ter] *-ra/⁺-eren, pl -rer/⁺-re* (maternal) aunt, mother's sister.
Moster [mos'ter] *Pln* twp, Hordaland.
Moster/øy *Pln* twp, Rogaland.
Mos/vik [mos'/] *Pln* twp, Nord-Trøndelag.
mo't[1] *-et* (=***mod**[1]) 1 courage, pluck, spirit: **friskt m-!** cheer up!; **ha sine meningers m-** have the courage of one's convictions; **holde m-et oppe** keep up one's spirits, keep a stiff upper lip; **samle m-** screw up one's courage; **sette m- i** cheer up, encourage; **ta m-et fra** discourage, dishearten; **være ved godt m-** be of good cheer. 2: **ha m- (på)** want (to do sth).
mo't[2] *-et* 1 meeting: **godt m-** hello (said to sby one meets on a road); ***til m-s** facing, vis à vis. *2 joint, meeting point (e.g. of walls, roads, etc.). *3: **i same m-et** at the same (point in) time. *4 attack (of an illness), cramp.
mo't[3] *P* 1 against, contrary to: **m- all forventning** contrary to all expectations; **m- bedre vitende** against (contrary to) one's better judgment; **(stå) m- himmelen** (be silhouetted) against the sky; **m- loven** against (contrary to) the law; **m- naturens orden** contrary to nature; **Kjerringa m- strømmen** 'The Contrary Woman' (folktale by Asbjørnsen); **jeg har ingenting m- det** I have no objections to it. 2 to, towards: **m- dag** towards day(break) (**M-Dag** a radical political and social movement during the 1920's; also the organ published by the movement); **m- vest** westwards; **midt m-** opposite, facing; **ut m-** out by; **sette kurs m-** make for; **vende m-** face; **være snill (vennlig, uhøflig, osv.) m-** be nice (friendly, rude, etc.) to. 3 (compared) to, versus: **fem m- to** five to two (e.g. of a score, vote, etc.); **det er ingenting m- det jeg hørte** that's nothing compared to what I heard; **i dag er temperaturen 15 grader m- normalt 18** the temperature today is 59 degrees compared to the normal (average) of 65. 4 (in return) for, on (=incident to): **m- betaling, m- å betale** on payment, receipt (of); **ringen leveres tilbake m- annonsens kostende** the ring will be returned on receipt of the cost of the ad; (for use with verbs see these; see also verbs with **imot**).
***m. o. t.** =**med omsyn til**
⁺**mo't/angrep** *-et* counterattack.
mo't/arbeide *V -de/⁺-et* counteract; oppose, work against.
mo't/argumen't *-et, pl -/⁺-er* counterargument.
mo't/bakke *-n* acclivity, ascent: **det gikk smått i m-ene** it was slow going uphill; **i m-** uphill.
⁺**mo't/bevi's** *-et* counter evidence, counterproof, disproof.
⁺**mo't/bevi'se** *V -te* disprove, refute.
***mo't/burd** *-en* cf **/bør**
⁺**motby'delig** *A -* abominable, disgusting, loathsome.
⁺**motby'delig/het** *-en* abomination, disgust, loathing; abominableness, loathsomeness.
***mo't/bærleg** *A -* abominable, disgusting, loathsome.
mo't/bør *-en* 1 contrary wind. 2 *fig.* adversity, opposition, resistance.
mo'te[1] *-n* fashion, vogue: **etter siste m-** in the latest fashion; **gå av m-** go out of fashion; **på m-(n)** in fashion.
⁺**mo'te**[2] *N* (=***mode**[2]): **kjenne seg (godt, underlig, osv.) til m-** feel (good, strange, etc.); **være vel (ille) til m-** feel at ease (uneasy), comfortable (uncomfortable).
⁺**mo'te/dikter** *-en, pl -e* (=***-ar**) fashionable poet.
m'ote/dokke *-a* (woman) clotheshorse.
mo'te/hus *-et* fashion house.
mo'te/journal [/sjurna'l] *-en* fashion magazine.
mo'te/lege *-n* fashionable doctor.
motell' *-et, pl -/⁺-er* motel.
mo'te/o'rd *-et* catchword, fashionable word.
mo'te/prest *-en* fashionable minister (currently in fashion).
mo'te/sak *-a/⁺-en* matter of fashion; fashion, vogue.
mo'te/sjuk *A* fashion crazy.
mo'te/slave *-n* slave of fashion.
motett' *-en mus.* motet.
mo't/fallen *A ⁺-ent, pl -falne* dejected, dispirited, downcast.
⁺**mo't/foranstaltning** [/fårr-] *-en* countermeasure (**mot** against).
⁺**mo't/forestilling** [/fåre-] *-en* expostulation, remonstrance.
⁺**mo't/forslag** [/fårslag] *-et* countermotion, counterproposal.
mo't/gang *-en* adversity, hardship, misfortune.
mo't/gift *-a/⁺-en* antidote.
***mo't/gjerd** [/jær] *-a* 1 countermeasure (**mot** against). 2 affront, insult; injury.
mo't/hake *-n* barb (in an arrow, hook, etc.).
mo't/hug *-en dial.* animosity, aversion, dislike (**for** of).
mo'tig *A -* cf **modig**
moti'v *-et, pl -/⁺-er* 1 motive (**for** of). 2 subject (for a novel, painting, etc.); motif, theme (e.g. in art, music).
motive're *V -te* 1 give grounds for, justify, warrant: **m-t** reasoned, with reasons stated. 2 give adequate motivation for, motivate (e.g. characters in a play).
motive'ring *-a/⁺-en* explanatory statement, grounds, justification.
mo't/kandida't *-en* rival cadidate.
mo't/laus *A* (=⁺**/løs**) despondent, discouraged, disheartened.
mo't/legg *-et* objection, refutation.
⁺**mo't/løs** *A* cf **/laus**
mo't/mann *-en, pl -menn/*-menner* opponent.
mo't/mæle *-t* reply, retort.
mo'tor *-en, pl moto'rer* engine, motor.
mo'tor/båt *-en* motor boat.
⁺**mo'tor/drevet** *A -* engine-, motor-driven.
motorise're *V -te* motorize.
moto'risk *A -* motor (esp. *anat., psych.*).
mo'tor/kasse *-a/-en* engine casing.
⁺**mo'tor/kjøretøy** *-et, pl -/⁺-er* motor vehicle.
mo'tor/kutter *-en, pl ⁺-e* motor-powered fishing cutter.
mo'tor/mann *-en, pl -menn/*-menner* engine mechanic.
mo'tor/sag *-a* power-driven saw (e.g. chain saw).
mo'tor/skade *-n* engine trouble.
mo'tor/skip *-et* motor ship.
mo'tor/stopp *-en/-et* engine failure.
mo'tor/sykkel *-elen, pl -sykler* motorcycle.
mo'tor/syklist *-en* motorcyclist.
mo'tor/veg *-en*(=⁺**/vei**) divided highway, freeway, turnpike.
mo'tor/vogn [/vångn] *-a* 1 motor vehicle. 2 motor car (e.g. surburban electric trolley).
mo't/part *-en* 1 adversary, opponent, opposition. 2 counterpart, opposite number.
mo't/parti' *-et polit.* opposition party.
mo't/pol *-en* 1 opposite. 2 *phys.* opposite pole.
***mo't/prov** *-et* counter evidence, counterproof, disproof.
mots. =⁺**motsatt,** ***motsett, motsetning**
⁺**mo't/sa** *pt of* **-si**
⁺**mo't/satt** *A -* 1 contrary, opposite: **det (stikk) m-e (av)** the (direct) opposite (of); **i m- fall** otherwise, if on the other hand; **uttale seg i m- retning** express oneself to the contrary. 2 (prep.) versus: **by m- land** city versus country.
***mo't/seiing** *-a* cf **/sigelse**
***mo't/setnad** *-en* cf **/setning**
mo't/setning **-a/⁺-en* 1 contrast, opposition: **i m- til** as opposed to, contrary to, in contrast to; clash, disparity. 2 opposite: **de er rene m-er** they are complete opposites.
⁺**mo'tsetnings/forhold** *-et* antagonism, clash of interests (**mellom** between).

***mo't/sett** *A* - cf **/satt**
+mo't/sette *V -satte, -satt*: **m- seg** oppose, resist, set oneself against.
+mo't/si *V -sa, -sagt* contradict: **m- seg selv** c- oneself; **m-gende** conflicting, contradictory.
+mo't/sigelse *-n* contradiction; discrepancy: **m-n mellom evne og higen** the d- between ability and desire (Ibsen).
***mo't/skapt** *A* - annoying, unpleasant.
+mo't/spiller *-en, pl -e* (=***/spelar**) 1 opponent (in cards, chess, tennis, etc.). 2 (in theater) one who plays opposite another actor (ab.= co-star).
mo't/stand *-en/*-et* opposition, resistance (**mot** to, towards) (also *phys., tech.*).
+mo't/stander *-en, pl -e* (=***-ar**) adversary, opponent (**av** of).
+mo'tstands/beve'gelse *-n* resistance movement.
+mo'tstands/dyktig *A* - resistant (**overfor** to): **lite m-** non-resistant, susceptible.
mo'tstands/kraft *-a/+-en* (power of) resistance.
mo'tstands/kraftig *A* - resistant.
+mo't/strebende *A* - (=***/strevande**) grudging, reluctant.
mo't/strid *N* inconsistency, opposition: **stå i m- med (til)** be contrary to, be inconsistent with, run counter to.
mo't/stridende *A* - conflicting (claims, interests, thoughts, etc.), contradictory (accounts, statements, etc.), opposing.
+mo't/strømning *-en* 1 countercurrent. 2 counter movement, reaction.
mo't/stykke *-t, pl +-r/*-* 1 counterpart (**til** of). 2 correlate. 3 contrast, opposite.
mo't/stå *V -stod, -stått* 1 resist, withstand. 2 **m-ende** (esp. *math.*) opposite (e.g. angle, side).
mo't/svare *V -a/-te* be equivalent to, correspond to.
+mo'tsvarig/het *-en* counterpart, match (**til** to).
mott' *-en dial.* moth; mite or other small insect.
+mo't/ta *V -tok, -tatt* 1 receive; welcome (a person): **m- besøk** r- visitors; **bli godt m-tt** r- a hearty welcome; **vi har m-tt Deres brev av** we are in receipt of yours of the. 2 accept (an offer), take (e.g. bribes, orders).
+motta'gelig *A* - cf **mottakelig**
+mo't/tagelse *-n* cf **/takelse**
+mo't/tager *-en, pl -e* cf **/taker**
mo't/tak *-et* *1 counterattack, counterthrust. 2 acceptance; reception. *3 acclivity, ascent.
motta'kelig *A* - amenable, predisposed, susceptible (**for** to).
+motta'kelig/het *-en* amenability, receptivity, susceptibility (**for** to).
+mo't/takelse *-n* 1 reception (of guests, radio signals, etc.); receipt (of a letter, money, etc.) (**av** of). 2 acceptance: **nekte m-** refuse delivery, refuse to accept.
+mo'ttakelses/komité *-en* reception committee.
+mo't/taker *-en, pl -e* (=***-ar**) recipient (e.g. addressee, consignee, payee); receiver (person, radio); (in tennis) striker-out.
+mo'ttaker/appara't *-et* radio receiving set.
mo't/taking *-a/+-en* 1 reception; receipt. 2 acceptance.
***mo't/teken** *A -e/-i, pl -ne* received.
***mot'ting** *-en* cf **mødding**
mot'to *-et, pl +-er/*-* epigraph, motto.
mo't/trekk *-et* countermove (also *fig.*).
mo't/ved *-en* cross-grained (difficult to work with) wood.
mo't/vekt *-a/+-en* counterbalance, counterweight (**mot, til** to).
+mo't/verge *-t* cf **/verje**
mo't/verje *-a* resistance: **sette seg til m-** defend oneself, resist.
mo't/vilje *-n* aversion, dislike, repugnance (**mot** for, of, to).
mo't/villig *A* - (=***/viljug**) grudging, reluctant, unwilling.
mo't/vind *-en* contrary wind, head wind: **i m-** against the w-.
+mo't/virke *V -a/-et* counteract; thwart; neutralize.
+mo't/ytelse *-n* compensation, quid pro quo.
move're *V -te*: **m- seg** move, be in movement; exercise.
m. p. p.=**med +påholden/*påhalden penn**
M/S=**motorsjekte, motorskip**
ms.=**manuscriptum, manuskript**
M/T=**motortankskip**
MTB=**motortorpedobåt**
Mtf. = **+meget/*mykje tilfredsstillende**
mudd' *-en* (=**mut**) fur coat.
mud'der *-eret/mudret* 1 mire, mud. 2 mix-up, muddle: **gjøre m-** kick up a row, make a fuss.
mud'der/botn *-en* (=**+/bunn**) muddy bottom.
mud'der/maskin [/masji'n] *-en* dredger.
mud'der/pram' *-men* (in dredging) mud boat.
mud're *V -a/+-et* 1: **m- opp** dredge; disturb, stir up. 2 *dial.* mumble, mutter.
mu'e *-a* (=***muge**[1]) 1 *dial.* heap, pile. 2 crowd, flock.
muf'fe *-a/+-en* 1 muff. 2 *tech.* muff (in plumbing); sleeve.
muf'fe/kopling *-a/+-en tech.* box (sleeve) coupling.
mu'g *-en* (=***muge**[2]) *dial.* crowd, flock.
***mu'ge**[1] *-a* cf **mue**
***mu'ge**[2] *-n* cf **mug**
mu'ge[3] *V -a/+-et dial.* heap, pile.
mugg'[1] *-en* 1 twill. 2 *vet.* grease heel.
mugg'[2] *-en/-et* 1 mildew, mold: **penicillinet hadde gitt Jan mugg i knærne** *hum.* the penicillin had given Jan shaky knees (Sandemose). 2 sawdust (=**sag/m-**). *3 drizzle. *4: **i m-** secretly. *5 mosquito.
mug'ge[1] *-a* pitcher.
***mug'ge**[2] *-n* 1 moldiness, mustiness. 2 moodiness, sulkiness.
mug'ge[3] *V -a/+-et fam.* fret, grumble (**over** about).
mug'ge[4] *V -a/+-et fam.* work diligently, steadily: **m- sammen penger** scrape together money; **sitte og m- over bøkene** pore over books.
mug'gen *A +-ent, pl mugne* 1 moldy, musty; *fam.* suspicious: **noe m-t ved saken** sth fishy about the case. 2 moody, sulky.
mugg'/smak *-en* moldy taste.
mugg'/sopp *-en* mold fungus.
mug'ne[1] *V -a/+-et* become moldy, mold.
mug'ne[2] *A pl of* **muggen**
m. u. h.=**meter under havflata**
muham.=**muhammedansk**
+muham(m)eda'ner *-en, pl -e* (= ***-ar, *muham(m)edan**) Mohammedan, Moslem.
muham(m)edanis'me *-n* Islam, Mohammedanism.
muham(m)eda'nsk *A* - Mohammedan, Moslem.
mukk[1] [mokk] *-et/*-en* sound, syllable, word: **jeg forstår ikke et m-** I'm completely in the dark, I don't understand a word.
+mukk[2] [mokk] *Av*: **tie m- (m-ende) stille** be completely silent.
***muk'ke**[1] *-a* large heap, mass, multitude.
mukke[2] [mok'ke] *V -a/+-et* grouse, grumble (**mot** at); mutter.
mukkel [mok'kel] *-et/muklet/+-en fam.* fussy, tiresome work.
+mukkende [mok'kene] *Av* cf **mukk**[2]
mukker [mok'ker] *-et/+-en dial.* wood chips.
mulatt' *-en* mulatto.
mulatt'/kvinne *-a/+-en* mulatto woman.
+mul'd *-en* cf **mold**
+mul'de[1] *N geol.* depression, hollow.
+mul'de[2] *V -et* cf **molde**
***mul'de**[3] *pt of* **mylje**
+mul'd/jord *-a* cf **mold/**
+mul'd/varp *-en* cf **mold/**
mul'/dyr *-et zool.* mule (offspring of donkey and mare).
mu'le *-n* 1 (horse's, rifle) muzzle; mouth (of a bag, sack). 2 *dial.* snout.
mu'le/band *-et* (=**+/bånd**) 1 muzzle. 2 drawstring (on a bag, sack).
mu'le/binde *V infl as* **binde** muzzle.
mu'le- og [å] **klau'v/sjuke** *-n* (=***/sykje**) *vet.* hoof-and-mouth disease.
mu'le/pose [*/påse] *-n* nose bag.
mul'/esel *-elet/-let, pl -ler zool.* mule (offspring of stallion and she-donkey).
+mu'lig *A* - (=***mog(e)leg**) possible: **alle m-e mennesker** everybody and his brother, every Tom, Dick, and Harry; **alt m-** everything under the sun, everything imaginable; **(på) alle m-e måter** (in) all p- ways, every p- way; **mest (minst) m-** as much (little) as p-; **om m-** if p-; **så vidt m-** as far as p-; **er det møyen verdt å ville det m-e?** is it worth the trouble to will the possible? (Ibsen).
+mu'ligens *Av* perhaps, possibly.
+mu'lig/gjøre *V -gjorde, -gjort* make possible, permit.
+mu'lig/het *-en* possibility (**for** of).
+mu'lig/vis *Av* perhaps, possibly.
mulje'ring *-a/+-en* (in phonetics) palatalization.
mulje'rt *A* - (in phonetics) palatalized.
mul'kt *-a/+-en* fine, mulct.
mulkte're *V -te* (=**mulkte**) fine, mulct.
+mul'kt/forelegg [/fåre-] *-et jur.* (choice of) fine (in lieu of imprisonment); notice of fine.
mul'le *V -a/+-et* 1 mumble, mutter. 2 hum, murmur.
+mul'm *-et* dense darkness: **i nattens m- og mørke** in the dead of night.
***mul't** *pp of* **mylje**
+mul'te *-n* cf **molte**
multiplikan'd *-en math.* multiplicand.
multiplikasjo'n *-en* (esp. *math.*) multiplication.
multiplikasjo'ns/tabell' *-en math.* multiplication table.
multiplika'tor *-en* 1 *math.* multiplier. 2 multiplication table (with multiplications already done, esp. for use in business).
multiplise're *V -te* (esp. *math.*) multiply.
mul'tiplum *-et, pl multipla math.* multiple (**av** of).
multip'pel *A -t, pl multiple tech.* multiple, multiplex.
mu'mie *-n* mummy.
mumle [mom'le] *V -a/+-et* mumble, mutter.
mummel [mom'mel] *-et* mumbling, muttering.
+mump [mom'p] *-en* cf **momp**
mumpe [mom'pe] *V -a/+-et* cf **mompe**
***mum're** *V -a* snuffle.
***mu'n**[1] *-en, pl -er* cf **monn**
***mu'n**[2] *pr of* **mune**[1]
***mun'd** *-et* time e.g. **kvelds/m-.**
-mund *Prn(m)* e.g. **Her/m-, Sig/m-, Ve/m-.**
***mun'de** *pt of* **mune**[1]
munde'ring *-a/+-en archaic* uniform; *fam.* trappings.
mundu'r *-en archaic* uniform; *fam.* trappings.

+ Bokmål; * Nynorsk; ° Dialect.
After letter: ' stress (Acc. 1); ` tone, stress (Acc. 2); · length.
Below letter: . not pronounced.

***mu'ne**[1] *V pr mun, pl munde* cf **monne**[2]
***mu'ne**[2] *V -a* cf **monne**[1]
mun'/gåt' *-et archaic* home-brewed beer; *dial.* mild, light beer.
munk [mong'k] *-en* 1 monk. 2 *zool.* blackcap (Sylvia atricapilla). 3 *fam.* benedictine liqueur. 4 a children's game: **slå m-** skip stones; play a game in which the participants try to knock down an object placed at a certain distance.
munke [mong'ke] *-a* raised, round, roll-like cake fried in specially formed pan.
munke/kloster [mong'ke/] *-ret, pl -/+-re* monastery.
munke/orden *-en* monastic order.
munke/panne *-a* pan with small, round wells in which to fry *munker.*
munn' *-en* 1 mouth: **m-en står ikke på ham** he talks incessantly; **bruke m-** scold, use abusive language; **hold m-** hold your tongue, shut up; **snakke (tale) en etter m-en** echo, humor, play up to sby; be sby's yes-man; **snakke (rope) i m-en på hverandre** talk (shout) all at the same time. 2 opening (e.g. of bottle, sack).
+munn'/bitt *-et* (=***/bit**) bit (on a bridle).
munn'/bruk *-en/-et fam.* abusiveness, gabbiness, *(pop.)* jaw.
munn'/diaré *-en fam.* incessant babbling, running off at the mouth.
mun'ne *V -a/+-et*: **m- ut i** (of a river) debouch, empty into; (of a street) join, run into; end in.
munn'/full *-en* mouthful.
munn'/harpe *-a/+-en* jew's-harp.
+munn'/hell *-et* adage, saw, saying; byword.
munn'/hole [/håle] *-a anat.* oral cavity.
+munn'/huggeri *-et* bickering, quarreling, wrangling.
+munn'/hugges *V -es/-hugdes, -hugdes* bicker, quarrel, wrangle.
+munn'/hule *-n* cf **/hole**
mun'ning *-en* 1 estuary, mouth, outlet. 2 muzzle (of gun).
mun'nings/hette *-a* muzzle cover, tampion.
munn'/korg *-a* (=**+/kurv**) (animal) muzzle (also *fig.*): **sette m- på en** muzzle sby.
+munn'/kurv *-en* cf **/korg**
+munn'/lader *-en, pl -e* (=***-ar**) muzzle-loading firearm.
***munn'leg** *A* - cf **muntlig**
+munn'/lær *-et fam.* **ha et godt m-** have the gift of the gab.
+munn'- og [å] **klo'v/syke** *-n* cf **mule- og klauv/sjuke**
munn'/rapp *A -rapt* glib, voluble; sassy.
+munn'/skjenk *-en* (=***/skjenkjar**) *bibl.* butler (in charge of wines); cupbearer.
munn'/skåld *-en med.* thrush.
munn'/smak *-en* little taste (of sth).
+munn'/spill *-et* (=***/spel**) harmonica, mouth organ.
munn'/stykke *-t, pl -r/*-* 1 (musical instrument) mouthpiece; (pipe) stem; (cigar, cigarette) holder. 2 (hose, vacuum cleaner) nozzle. 3 filter container (on a gas mask).
+munn's/vær *-et* empty, idle talk, mere words.
***munn'/tame** *-n* fluency (in speaking).
+munn'/tøy *-et* (=***/ty**) gabbiness, jaw.
munn'/vatn *-et* (=**+/vann**) mouthwash.
munn'/vik *-a* corner of the mouth; *anat.* commissure of the lips.
***mun'se** *V -a*: **m- på** sip.
mun'ter *A -ert, pl -re* gay, jovial, merry; cheerful: **i m- stemning** in high spirits.
+mun'ter/het *-en* gaiety, joviality, merriment; cheer(fulness).
+mun'tlig *A* - (=***munnleg**) 1 oral, verbal: **være oppe i m-** take an oral exam. 2 oral, spoken; informal (language, style).
+mun'tlig/het *-en* 1 *jur.* oral proceedings (e.g. in court). 2 *lit.* informality, spontaneity.
muntrasjo'n *-en* gaiety, merriment; amusement, entertainment.
muntrasjo'ns/råd *-en* provider of amusement, fun; life of the party.
mun'tre *V -a/+-et* cheer, enliven: **m- seg** amuse oneself, cheer oneself up.
mu'r *-en* 1 (brick, stone) wall; brickwork, masonry; *dial.* chimney, hearth: **tie som en mur** be silent as death, keep a secret. 2 *fig.* wall (e.g. of misunderstanding).
+mu'r/brekker *-en hist.* battering ram.
+mu'r/brokker *pl* rubble.
+mu'r/bygning *-en* brick building.
***mur'de** *pt of* **myrje**[2]
mu're[1] *-a bot.* blood root, tormentil (Potentilla).
mu're[2] *V -a/+-te* build (of brick, stone); do masonry work: **m- inne** immure, wall in (up); **m- til** brick up, wall up.
mu'rende *Av*: **m- stille** quiet as a mouse, dead quiet; stock still.
mure'ne *-n zool.* moray (Muraenidae).
+mu'rer *-en, pl -e* (=***-ar**) bricklayer, mason.
+mu'rer/mester *-eren, pl -ere/-rer* cf **mur/**
+mu'rer/svenn *-en* (=***murar/svein**) journeyman bricklayer (mason).
mu'r/fast *A* - fixed, immovable: **mur- og naglefaste innretninger** *jur.* immovable fixtures, immovables.
mu'r/hus *-et* brick building, house.
mu'r/kalk *-en* mortar.
mur'mel/dyr *-et zool.* groundhog, woodchuck; marmot (Marmota): **sove som et m-** sleep like a log.
+mu'r/mester *-eren, pl -ere/-rer* (=***/meister**) master bricklayer (mason).
mu'r/puss *-en* plastering; stucco.
murr' *-et* grumble, murmur, mutter.
mur're *V -a/+-et* 1 grumble, murmur, mutter. 2 throb dully (with pain).
mu'r/skei *-a* (=**+/skje**) trowel.
mu'r/stein *-en* brick.
mu'rsteins/farga *A* - (=**+-et**) brick-red.
***mur't** *pp of* **myrje**[2]
°mu'ru *-a/-en* cf **mare**[1]
mu'r/verk *-et* 1 brickwork, masonry. 2 concrete wall.
mu's *-a, pl -/*myser* mouse: **skipet gikk under med mann og m-** the ship was lost with all hands; **ha det travelt som en m- i barselseng** be as busy as a mouse littering (bustle busily about).
mus. =**musikalsk**
mu'se *+-n/*-a* Muse.
***musé** *-et, pl museum* cf **museum**
mu'se/bol *-et* mouse's nest.
mu'se/felle *-a* mousetrap.
mu'se/flette *-a* pigtail, short braid.
mu'se/hale *-n* 1 mouse's tail. 2 *bot.* mousetail (Myosurus minimus). 3 (of hair) pigtail (also of hair gathered and tied with ribbons).
mu'se/hol [/hål] *-et* (=**+/hull**) mousehole.
mu'sel/man *-en, pl -er* 1 Mussulman (Mohammedan). 2 emaciated victim of concentration camps.
mu'sende *Av*: **m- stille** as quiet as a mouse.
mu's/ert *-a* (=***/erter**) *bot.* vetch (Vicia).
+mu'se/stille *Av* (=***/still**) quiet as a mouse.
mu'set(e) *A* - mouse-colored, mousegrey.
muse'um *-eet, pl +-eer/*-eum* (=***musé**) museum.
+muse'ums/gjenstand *-en* museum piece, specimen.
mu's/grå *A -tt* mouse-colored, mousegrey.
musika'lsk *A* - musical.
musikan't *-en* musician, player.
+mu'siker *-en, pl -e* (=***-ar**) musician (e.g. composer).
musikk' *-en* 1 music: **med (under) full m-** in style, with bands playing. 2: **m-en** the musicians, the orchestra.
musikk'/forlag [/fårr-] *-et* music publishing house.
musikk'/handel *-elen, pl -ler* music store.
musikk'/instrumen't *-et, pl -/+-er* musical instrument.
musikk'/konservato'rium *df -iet, pl +-ier/*-ium* conservatory (school) of music.
musikk'/korps *-et* (brass) band.
musikk'/stykke *-t, pl +-r/*-* piece of music, (short) composition.
musikk'/teori' *-en* music theory.
mu'sikus *-en, pl -er/musici archaic* musician.
musise're *V -te* make music, play.
mus'k *-et* 1 dust in the air; drizzle, mist. 2 fiber, stuff, substance (in a person): **det er ikke noe m- i ham** *pop.* there's no push in him.
muskat' *-en* nutmeg.
muskatblom'me [also -kat'/] *-n* mace.
muskatell' *-en* muscatel (wine).
muskat'/nøtt *-a* nutmeg (kernel).
mus'ke *V -a/+-et dial.* drizzle, mist.
muskedun'der *-en* (=**-dundre, +-donner**) blunderbuss.
mus'kel *-elen, pl -ler* muscle.
+mus'kel/brist *-en* muscle rupture, sprain.
mus'kel/bunt *-en* bundle of muscles.
mus'kel/kraft *-a/+-en, pl -krefter/*-krafter* muscular strength.
mus'kel/svinn *-et med.* muscular atrophy.
+mus'kel/trekning *-en* muscular twitch.
muskete'r *-en* musketeer.
muskett' *-en* musket.
mus'k/regn [+/rein] *-et* drizzle, mist.
mus'k/regne [+/reine] *V -a/+-et/+-te/*-de* drizzle, mist.
muskulatu'r *-en* musculature.
muskulø's *A* muscular.
***mus'le** *V -a* niggle, putter.
mus'ling *-en* 1 *zool.* bivalve (Lamellibranchiata); clam, mussel. 2 *anat.* (nasal) concha.
mus'ling/skal *-et* (=**+/skall**) (sea) shell; cockle shell, scallop.
mus'se *-a dial.* young herring.
musseli'n *-et/+-en* muslin.
musse're *V -te* (of seltzer water, wine, etc.) bubble, effervesce, fizz: **m-ende vin** sparkling wine; champagne.
musseron [musserång'] *-en bot.* blewits (Tricholoma).
mus't *-en* 1 *dial.* fog, steam, vapor. 2 fiber, stuff, substance (in a person); enterprise, push.
mustang' *-en* mustang.
musta'sje *-n* moustache.
mu's/våk *-en zool.* common buzzard (Buteo buteo).
mu't *-en* cf **mudd**
mutasjo'n *-en* 1 change of voice. 2 *biol.* mutation.
mu'te[1] *V -a/+-et dial.* 1 bribe; conceal; hide. 2 (of birds) moult.
mu'te[2] *V -a/+-et* apply for a permit (ownership rights) to work a mining claim.
mu'tings/brev *-et* document giving ownership rights to mining claimant.
mutt' *A* - moody, sulky, sullen.
mut'ter[1] *-eren, pl mutrer/+-ere fam.* (the) missus; (the) old lady; ma.
+mut'ter[2] *-en* nut (for a bolt).
+mut'ters *Av*: **m- alene** completely alone.
m. v. =**med videre**
***my'** *-et* cf **mygg**
°my' *A* - cf **mye**
myalgi' *-en med.* myalgia.
my'e *A -, cp +mer/*meir, sp mest* (=**+megen, *mykjen**) 1 much; a great deal, a large amount (of): **ganske (nokså) m-** quite a bit; **ikke så m- som** not even; **uten så m-**

som å without even; **han er m- til kar** he's quite a fellow; **så m- du vet det!** just so you know! 2 *(adv.)* +**meget** very. 3 *(comp.)* **mer, mere** more: **m- enn gjerne** very (more than) gladly; **aldri m-** never again; **han var ikke m-e gal enn at han visste det** he wasn't so crazy that he didn't know that (Hoel); **med (meget) m-** et cetera; **mye vil ha m-** give him an inch and he'll take a mile; **så mye m- som** especially since. 4 *(sup.)* **mest** most: **det m-e** most, the greatest part (**av** of); as much as; **han løp det m-e han kunne** he ran as fast as he could; **for det m-e** generally, mostly; **ha m- å si** be decisive, of greatest importance.

mygg' *-en, pl -'zool.* mosquito (Nematocera); gnat, midge.

myg'ge/stikk *-et* gnat, mosquito bite.

myg'ge/sverm *-en* swarm of mosquitos (or gnats).

mygg'/olje *-a/-en* gnat, mosquito repellent.

myg'l *-et* cf **mugg[2]**

myg'le *V -a/+-et* cf **mugne**

***myg'le/smak** *-en* moldy taste.

myg'let(e) *A* - cf **muggen**

my'/hank *-en zool.* crane fly (Tipulidae); (long-legged) mosquito.

***my'k[1]** *-a* cf **møkk**

***my'k[2]** *-en* 1 limbering, softening. 2 drubbing, thrashing.

+**my'k[3]** *A* cf **mjuk**

+**my'ke** *V -te* cf **mjuke**

+**my'k/het** *-en* 1 pliancy, softness. 2 suppleness.

***my'kje** *V -te* cf **mjuke**

***my'kjen** *A mykje/mye, cp meir, sp mest* cf **mye**

Myk'/land *Pln* twp, Aust-Agder.

***myk'last** *V -ast* 1 be moved (emotionally). 2 be alarmed, frightened. 3 be ashamed, hesitate (**med** to).

***myk'le/sam·** *A* tender-hearted; bashful.

+**my'kne** *V -a/-et* cf **mjukne**

mykolog [-olå'g] *-en* mycologist.

mykologi' *-en* mycology.

***my'l** *pr of* **mylje**

myl'de *V +-te/*-a/*-e* cf **molde**

myl'der *-eret/-ret* multitude, swarm, throng (**av** of).

myl'dre *V -a/+-et* mill, swarm, teem: **det m-et (av folk)** there were swarms (of people).

***myl'je** *V myl, mulde, mult* crumble, crush.

***myl'nar** *-en* cf **møller**

***myl'ne** *-a* cf **mølle**

myl'se** *-a* (=mylske[1]**) 1 crowd, mass, multitude. 2 "sweet cheese" (brown cheese made from cow's milk).

***myl'ske[1]** *-a* cf **mylse**

***myl'ske[2]** *V-a* 1 mix together. 2 lavish; squander.

myn'd** *-a* (=mynde[2]**) 1 character, manner, nature. 2 authority: **makt og m-** power and a-.

myn'de[1] *-n* greyhoud.

***myn'de[2]** *-t* cf **mynd**

myn'dig *A* - 1 authoritative, commanding, masterful (**overfor** towards): **tale m-** speak with authority. 2 of age.

+**myn'dig/het** *-en* authoritativeness; authority: **lokale m-er** local a-ies.

+**myn'dighets/alder** *-en jur.* full legal age, majority: **under m-en** (a) minor.

+**myn'dighets/område** [/åmm-] *-t* sphere of authority.

myn'dling *-en jur.* ward.

***myn'je** *-a* 1 nature, property, quality. 2 fate, lot.

***myn'ne[1]** *-t* estuary; mouth, opening.

°**myn'ne[2]** *V mynte* cf **munne**

myn't *-en* 1 coin. 2 tails (side of a coin where its value is stamped): **slå m- og kron(e)** flip a coin, heads or tails. 3 cash, money; currency: **klingende m-** ready cash. 4 mint (where money is coined).

-myn't *A* - *pop.* -mouthed, e.g. **hare/m-.**

myn'ta *A* - (=+**-et**): **være m- på** be aimed at, be meant for.

myn'te[1] *-a bot.* mint (Mentha).

myn'te[2] *V -a/+-et* coin, mint.

+**myn't/enhet** [also myn't/] *-en* 1 monetary unit. 2 monetary union.

myn't/fot *-en, pl -er* monetary standard (e.g. gold or silver).

myn't/kabinett· *-et* place for display of medals and coins.

+**myn't/mester** *-eren, pl -ere/-rer* (=***/meister**) director of the mint.

myn't/sort *-en* species of coin.

myn't/syste'm *-et* monetary system.

my'r[1] *-a* bog, marsh, swamp.

***my'r[2]** *pr of* **myrje[2]**

***my'r/bær** *-et* cloudberry.

myr'de *V -a/-+-et* murder.

+**myrderi'** *-et* butchery, carnage, massacre.

my'r/drag *-et* marshy tract.

my'r/dun *-a/-et bot.* bog cotton, cotton grass (Eriophorum).

+**my're** *-n* cf **maur**

my'r/fivel *-elen, pl -ler bot.* bog cotton, cotton grass (Eriophorum).

my'r/funn *-et archeol.* bog find.

my'r/hatt *-en bot.* marsh cinquefoil (Comarum palustre).

myria'de *-n* myriad (**av** of).

***myr'je[1]** *-a* cf **mørje**

***myr'je[2]** *V myr, murde, murt* 1 strive, toil. 2 rub.

my'r/jern [/jæ·rn] *-et* bog iron.

***myr'k** *A* cf **mørk**

***myr'ker** *-ret* cf **mørke**

my'r/klegg *-en bot.* lousewort (Pedicularis).

my'r/kongle *-a/+-en bot.* water arum (Calla palustris).

my'r/lende *-t* boggy land, soil.

my'r/lendt *A* - boggy, marshy, swampy.

my'r/malm *-en* bog iron.

my'r/mann *-en, pl -menn/*-menner hist.* (19th century) person who bought or leased worthless land (often marshland) in order to obtain voting rights.

myr'ra *-en* myrrh.

my'r/snelle *-a bot.* marsh horsetail (Equicetum palustre).

my'r/snipe *-a zool.* sandpiper (Calidris alpina).

my'r/soleie *-a bot.* marsh marigold (Caltha palustris).

myr't(e) *-(e)n bot.* myrtle (Myrtus communis).

myr'te/krans *-en* myrtle wreath (esp. used as a bridal wreath).

my'r/ull *-a bot.* bog cotton, cotton grass (Eriophorum).

my'se[1] *-a* whey.

my'se[2] *V -te* peer, squint (**på** at): **m-ende øyne** narrowed eyes.

myse'l *-et, pl -/+-er bot.* mycelium.

My'sen *Pln* twp, Østfold.

my'se/ost [/ost] *-en* cf **mys/**

***my'ser** *pl of* **mus**

my'se/smør· *-et* cf **mys/**

mys'ke[1] *-a bot.* woodruff (Asperula odorata).

***mys'ke[2]** *-n* odor, smell; reek, stench.

°**mys'mer** *-et* cf **mys/smør**

°**mys'mør** *-et* cf **mys/smør**

my's/ost [/ost] *-en primost* (brown cheese made from the whey of cow's milk).

+**mys'/smør** *-et* (=°**mysmer,** °**mysmør,** ***myse/**) 1 cream cheese made from sweet whey. 2 spread for bread made from scalded sour milk mixed with flour and sweetened with syrup.

myste'rium *-iet, pl +-ier/*-ium* 1 mystery. 2 *hist.* mystery play.

mystifikasjo'n *-en* 1 mystification. 2 hoax.

mystifise're *V -te* 1 mystify. 2 hoax, mislead.

+**mys'tiker** *-en, pl -e* (=***-ar**) mystic.

mystikk' *-en* 1 mysticism. 2 mysteriousness, mystery.

mystisis'me *-n* mysticism.

mys'tisk *A* - 1 mystical. 2 mysterious, mystifying.

°**my'su** *-a* cf **myse[1]**

myt. =**mytologi(sk)**

my'te[1] *-n* myth.

my'te[2] *V -te* (of birds) moult.

+**my'te/dannelse** *-n* (=***-ing**) formation of a myth, mythogenesis.

my'te/dannende *A* - myth-forming, mythopoeic.

my'tisk *A* - mythical.

mytologi' *-en* mythology.

mytologisk [-olå'gisk] *A* - mythological.

mytteri' *-et, pl +-er/*-* mutiny.

+**mæ/hæ** [me'/he·] *et* cf **me/he**

***mæ'lar** *-en* cf **måler[1]**

mæ'le[1] *-n archaic* grain measure (15-17 liters).

mæ'le[2] *-t* (power of) speech, voice: **miste mål og m-** become speechless.

mæ'le[3] *V -te* say, speak, utter.

***mæ'le[4]** *V -te* cf **måle[1]**

***mæ'le[5]** *V -te* kick.

***mæ'le/stav** *-en* cf **måle/**

***mæ'ling[1]** *-a* surveying.

mæ'ling[2] *-en* 1 land measurement (now 1,000 m^2). 2 area of a field which one is able to mow in a day.

-mæ'lt *A* - -spoken: **høg/m-, låg/m-.**

mæ't *A dial.* excellent, good, worthy.

mæ'te** *V -te* (=mete**) esteem, regard, value; concern oneself with.

+**mø'[1]** *-en* cf **møy**

mø'[2] *I* moo.

mø'bel *-elet/-let, pl +-ler/*-el/*-lar* 1 piece of furniture: **m-bler** furniture. 2 *archaic* chamber pot.

mø'bel/arkitek't *-en* furniture designer.

mø'bel/lager *-eret, pl -er/+-re* furniture warehouse.

mø'bel/plate *-a/+-en* laminated wood, plywood.

+**mø'bel/snekker** *-en, pl -e* (=***/snikkar**) furniture maker.

+**mø'bel/tapetse'rer** *-en, pl -e* (=***-ar**) (furniture) upholsterer.

mø'bel/trekk *-et* upholstery.

møblement [møblemang'] *-et, pl -/+-er* (set, suite of) furniture.

+**mø'bler** *pl of møbel* (=***-lar**)

møble're *V -te* furnish (a house, room, etc.).

***mø'dast** *V mødest, moddest, mødst* be burdened, plagued (**med** with); grow weary, tire.

***mødd'** *A* - exhausted, tired, weary: **ingen er so m- som eg no, av tvil** no one is as wearied as I am now, of my doubts (Vesaas).

***mød'dest** *pt of* **mødast**

+**mød'ding** *-en archaic* manure pile; rubbish heap; *archeol.* midden.

mø'de[1] [*mø'e] *-a* (=+**møye**) difficulty, inconvenience; pains, toil.

***mø'de[2]** *V -de* burden, plague; tire, weary (sby).

mø'de/full *A* burdensome, laborious, toilsome.

***mø'de/sam·** *A* burdensome, laborious, toilsome.

+**mø'dig** *A* - exhausted, tired, weary.

+**mø'dre** *pl of* **mor[1]**

mø'drehygie'ne/konto'r *-et, pl -/+-er* organization which provides information on child care, contraception, pregnancy, and sex hygiene.

+**mø'dre/kupé** *-en* compartment on trains reserved for mothers with infant children.

+**mø'drene** *A - archaic* maternal: **på m-side** on the mother's side.

+**mø'drene/arv** *-en* maternal inheritance.

mø'drer *pl of* **mor[1]** (=+**mødre**)

***mød'st** *pp of* **mødast**

***møk'** *-a* cf **møkk**

***mø'kje** *V -a* fertilize, manure.

+ Bokmål; * Nynorsk; ° Dialect.
After letter: ' stress (Acc. 1);
` tone, stress (Acc. 2); · length.
Below letter: . not pronounced.

møkk' *-a* (=***møk**) 1 *fam.* dung, manure. 2 *pop.* dirt, filth; rubbish, trash, tripe.
+**møk'ka/vær** *-et pop.* lousy weather.
+**møkk'/dynge** *-a* (=*/**dyngje**) dung heap, manure pile.
møk'ket(e) *A* - dirty, filthy: **m- var hun og fillet** she was dirty and ragged (Undset).
møkk'/greip *-a/-en/-et* manure pitchfork.
***mø'le** *-t* humor, mood, spirits.
møl'je *-a* 1 crumbled *flatbrød* in fat. 2 *fam.* jumble, mishmash; jumbled knot of people.
møll' *-en/+-et, pl* - (=***mol**[3]) *zool.* moth.
møl'le *-a* (=***mylne**) 1 mill (for grinding, crushing): **den som først kommer til m-a får først malt** first come, first served; **få vann på m-a** get grist for one's mill. 2: **lage m-** (in cards) crossruff.
møl'le/bruk *-et* (grinding) mill.
møl'le/dam' *-men* 1 millpond. 2 milldam.
+**møl'ler** *-en, pl -e* (=*-**ar**, ***mylnar**) 1 miller. 2 *zool.* whitethroat (Sylvia).
møl'le/stein *-en* millstone.
+**møll'/ett** *A* - (=*/**eten**) moth-eaten.
møl'le/vatn *-et* (=+/**vann**) mill head.
+**møl'le/ving(e)** *-en* windmill arm, wing.
møll'/middel *-elet/-midlet, pl+-midler/ *-el* moth repellent.
møll'/pose [*/påse] *-n* mothproof clothes bag.
+**møll'/spi'st** *A* - moth-eaten.
***mø'ne**[1] *-a* spinal cord.
mø'ne[2] *-t, pl +-r/*-* ridge of a roof; apex of a gable; circumflex accent (^).
møn'je *-a* minium, red lead.
møn'ster *-eret/-ret, pl -er/+-re* pattern; example, model; design (**for** for, **på** of).
+**møn'ster/beskyt'te** *V -a/-et jur., merc.* protect a design by patent.
+**møn'ster/beskyt'telse** *-n jur., merc.* design patent.
møn'ster/bok *-a, pl -bøker* 1 pattern book (esp. for embroidery, sewing, etc.). 2 sample book (esp. of cloth designs).
møn'ster/bruk *-et* model farm.
møn'ster/gyldig *A* - exemplary, ideal, model.
møn'ster/verdig *A* - exemplary, ideal, model.
møn'ster/verk *-et* classical (or standard) work, ideal, model.
møn'ster/vern [/vær'n] *-et jur., merc.* protection of design.
møn'stre *V -a/+-et* 1 inspect, review (esp. *mil.*); examine, scrutinize, take stock of. 2 assemble, muster (esp. *mil., naut.*). 3 *naut.* (of seamen) ship, sign on (**på**) or sign off, pay off (**av**).
møn'stret(e) *A* - figured, patterned.
møn'string *-a/+-en* 1 *mil.* inspection, review. 2 *naut.* (of seamen) signing on or signing off (a ship).
møn'strings/konto'r *-et naut.* merchant marine shipping (employment) office.
møn's/ås *-en* ridgepole.
møn'sås/skål *-a* house-raising party (with toasts) after the ridgepole is in place; money paid to construction workers after the ridgepole is in place.
mø'r *A* (=***møyr**) 1 (of food, meat) tender. 2 aching, stiff; done in. 3 softened, submissive, weakened.
mø'r/banke *V -a/+-et* (of meat) tenderize (by beating); *fam.* beat black and blue, beat up, drub soundly.
+**mø'r/brad** *-en* (beef, pork) tenderloin.
***mø're** *V -a* muddy, stir up; dredge.
Mø're *Pln* districts of **Nord/m-** and **Sunn/m-** in **M- og Romsdal** county.
mø'ring *-en* inhabitant of Møre.
mør'je *-a* 1 soft mass. 2 (glowing) embers.
mør'k *A* 1 dark (of color, hair, absence of light, etc.). 2 gloomy, somber: **det ser m-t ut** things look dark, the weather is g-; **han ser m-t på** he takes a g- view of.
mør'ke [df mør'ke] *-t* (=**mørker**) dark(ness): **i m-t er alle katter grå** in the dark all cats are grey (everything looks alike).
mør'ke/blå *A -tt* (=**mørk/**) dark blue.
mør'ke/loft *-et* attic (without windows), loft.
mør'ke/mann *-en, pl -menn/*-menner* obscurant; joykiller.
mør'ker *-eret/-ret* cf **mørke**
mør'ke/redd *A* - cf **mørk/**
mør'ke/rom [/romm] *-met* darkroom.
mør'ke/tid *-a/+-en* polar night; *fig.* dark ages.
mør'k/håra *A* - (=+-**et**) dark haired.
***mør'king** *-a* darkening, eclipse.
***mør'kje** *V -te* become, make dark; darken.
+**mør'k/la** *pt of* **-legge**
+**mør'k/laten** *A -ent, pl -ne* darkish, dusky; swarthy.
+**mør'k/legge** *V -la, -lagt* black out (e.g. a city).
***mør'k/leik** *-en* darkness.
+**mør'k/lett** *A* - (=*/**leitt**) dark (of skin), swarthy.
mør'kne *V -a/+-et* become, make dark; darken.
mør'kning *-a/+-en* twilight; darkening.
mør'k/redd *A* - afraid of the dark.
mø'rne *V -a/+-et* become tender.
mør'ser *-en, pl +-e mil.* mortar.
mør'tel *-en* (brick, masonry) mortar.
Mø's/vatn *Pln* large lake, Rauland twp, Telemark.
***mø'tast** *V møtest, møttest, møtst* cf **møte**[2]
mø'te[1] *-t, pl +-r/*-* 1 encounter, meeting (**av** of; **med** with): **m-t er hevet** the meeting is adjourned; **m-t er satt** the meeting is called to order. 2 date, appointment: **avtale m-** arrange to meet (sby), make an appointment. 3 assembly, gathering, meeting; conference, congress. 4 *jur.* session, sitting. 5 *archaic* scene (in play). 6 **i m-** towards; **gå en i m-** walk towards sby; **vi går bedre tider i m-** better times are coming; **stormen slo oss i m-** the storm hit us.
mø'te[2] *V -te* 1 meet; come upon, encounter, run across: **vel møtt** greetings, hello; (when departing) so long (until our next meeting). 2 collect, gather, meet. 3 appear: **m- fram, opp** appear, show up; **m- i retten** appear in court. 4 receive: **hun ble møtt med ovasjoner** she was r-d with ovations. 5: +**m-es**, ***m-ast** meet.
+**mø'te/deltaker** *-en, pl -e* participant (in meeting).
***mø'te/lyd** *-en* group assembled for a meeting.
+**mø'te/plager** *-en, pl -e* (=*-**ar**) heckler (at a meeting).
mø'te/plikt *-a/+-en* obligation to appear; compulsory attendance.
mø'te/protokoll' *-en* minutes (of a meeting).
+**mø'te/sted** *-et* (=*/**stad**) meeting place.
+**møt'rik** *-en* nut (for a bolt).
***møt'st** *pp of* **møtast**
***møt'test** *pt of* **møtast**
møy' *-a* usu. *archaic* maid, maiden; handmaiden; virgin.
møy'/dom [+/dåmm] *-men/*-en* maidenhood; virginity.
+**møy'e** *-a/-en* difficulty: **ha den største m- med å** have great d- in; **det kostet henne stor m-** it was a great effort for her.
+**møy'e/full** *A* burdensome, laborious, toilsome.
***møy'kje** *V -te* 1 dilute, thin. 2 soften.
møy'/kjerring *-a dial.* old maid.
***møy'r** *A* cf **mør**
+**møysom'melig** *A-* burdensome, laborious, toilsome; *(adv.)* laboriously, with difficulty.
***må'**[1] *V -dde* rub, scrape, wear away: **m- av, ut** erase, remove.
må'[2] *pr of* **måtte**
må'[3] *V pr -r archaic* get along, manage: **hun mår bra ellers** otherwise she's fine (Undset); **må i von** get along without, spare.
må'/få *N*: **på m-** aimlessly, at random, haphazard.
må'g *-en archaic* kinsman by marriage, usu. son-in-law or brother-in-law.
må'g/skap *-en archaic* affinity, kinship by marriage.
må'ke[1] *-a/-en* (=**måse**) *zool.* (sea) gull (Laridae).
+**må'ke**[2] *-a* scoop, shovel (for manure, snow).
+**må'ke**[3] *V -a/-et/-te* (=***moke**[2]) clear away, shovel (esp. manure, snow).
må'l[1] *-et* 1 voice: **miste m- og mæle** become dumb, be struck speechless. 2 dialect, language; speech: **ditt m- røper deg** thy s- betrayeth thee (Matth. 26,73). 3: **m-et** New Norwegian (=*landsmål*); **skrive på m-et** write in New Norwegian. *4 errand, matter: **bere opp m-et sitt** state one's errand.
må'l[2] *-et* 1 dimension, measurement; measure: **i fullt m-** in full measure, to the full; **ens dagers m-** the measure of one's days; **holde m-** measure up (**med** to); **nabostrøk som ikke holdt m-** neighborhoods which couldn't keep up (Hoel); **ta m- av** measure, *fig.* size up. 2 unit of areal measure (now) = 1000 square meters (0.247 acres). 3 volumetric unit (now) = 1 deciliter (6.1 cu. in., 0.21 pints). 4 extent, limitation: **med m- og måte** in moderation. 5 (instrument of) measure; standard (of measure).
må'l[3] *-et* aim, end, purpose; goal (also in sports), target; destination, objective (**for** of): **med det m- å** for the purpose of; **m-et helliger midlet** the end justifies the means; **uten m- og med** aimlessly, without purpose; **sette seg m-** set a goal for oneself, have an end in view; **skyte over m-et** (also *fig.*) overshoot the target; **skyte til m-s** shoot at a target; **stå ved m-et** be near one's goal, be on the brink of success.
mål[4] *-et* meal: **et m- mat** a meal.
***må'lar** *-en* cf **maler**
***må'lar/kunst** *-en* cf **maler/**
***må'lar/stykke** *-t* painting, picture.
***må'lar/svein** *-en* cf **maler/svenn**
+**må'l/bandt** *pt of* **-binde**
må'l/bar *pt of* **-bere, -bære**
***må'l/bere** [/bære] *V -bar, -bore/-i* cf **/bære**
+**må'l/beviss't** *A* - determined, purposeful, single-minded; conscious, deliberate.
+**må'lbevisst/het** *-en* purposefulness, single-mindedness.
må'l/binde *V infl as* **binde** nonplus, silence: **Prinsessen som ingen kunne m-** The Princess who Couldn't be Silenced (folktale in Asbjørnsen and Moe).
***må'l/bore** [/båre] *pp of* **-bere** (=*/**bori**)
***må'l/brigde** *-t* change in language.
må'l/bruk *-en/-et* language usage.
+**må'l/bære** *V -bar, -båret* (=*/**bere**) *dial.* 1 state (one's errand). 2 support (a cause by speaking in its behalf).
+**må'l/dommer** *-en, pl -e* (=*-**ar**) finish (goal) referee.
må'le[1] *V -te* (=***mæle**[4]) gauge, measure; evaluate, judge: **kunne m- seg med** come up to, compare with, match; **han m-er to meter** he is two meters tall.
***må'le**[2] *V -a* cf **male**[2]
må'le/band *-et* tape measure.
må'le/brev *-et* 1 surveyor's certificate

of area measure (of a lot, piece of land). 2 naut. certificate of (registered) tonnage.

+må'le/enhet -en unit of measurement.

må'le/glas -et (=+/glass) measuring glass; jigger.

må'l/emne -t dial. business, errand, purpose.

+må'ler[1] -en (=*-ar, *mælar) 1 measurer, surveyor; timber cruiser. 2 gauge, measuring device, meter (e.g. for electricity).

+må'ler[2] -en, pl -e (=*-ar) zool. geometrid moth (Geometridae).

må'le/stav -en (=*mæle/) surveyor's leveling rod.

må'le/stokk -en (=*mål/) 1 measuring rod, ruler. 2 criterion, standard (for for). 3 (on a diagram, map) scale; fig. i stor m- on a large scale.

må'l/fest -en (in sports) scoring spree.

må'l/folk -et adherents of New Norwegian.

må'l/form -a/+-en 1 language form (often used of the two Norwegian written languages). 2 declension, inflection, form.

Må'l/frid Prn(f)

må'l/føre -t, pl -/+-r 1 dialect. 2 one of the two Norwegian written languages (by some considered an erroneous usage).

må'l/føring -a/+-en diction; style.

***må'l/granskar** -en linguist, philologist.

***må'l/gransking** -a linguistics, philology.

***må'ling** -a cf maling

***må'lings/sliten** A -e/-i, pl -ne cf malings/slitt

må'l/kjensle -a feeling for language and good language usage.

må'l/laus A (=+/løs) 1 dumbfounded, speechless. 2 aimless, purposeless, without goal.

må'l/linje -a/+-en 1 scale line (on a diagram, chart, etc.). finish line, goal line.

må'l/lære -a grammar.

+må'l/løs A cf /laus

må'l/mann[1] -en, pl -menn/*-menner adherent of New Norwegian: Far ville våknet i kaldsvette hvis han hadde drømt om at jeg skulle gifte meg med en m- Father would have waked in a cold sweat if he had dreamt I would marry an a- (Sandemose).

må'l/mann[2] -en, pl -menn/*-menner goalkeeper.

***må'l/medviten** A -e/-i, pl -ne (=*/medveten) determined, purposeful, single-minded.

***må'lnad** -en painting, picture.

må'l/reising -a/+-en language movement; (in Norway) movement to make New Norwegian the predominant literary and official language.

+må'l/renser -en, pl -e language purist.

***må'l/rett** A - linguistically correct.

må'l/sak -a/+-en cause, movement for New Norwegian.

Må'ls/elv Pln twp, Troms.

+må'l/setting -a (=*/setjing) goal, objective.

må'ls/mann -en, pl -menn/*-menner spokesman.

må'l/snor -a finish line tape.

***må'l/soge** -a history of a language; language history.

må'l/stang -a, pl -stenger 1 measuring rod. 2 goal post.

***må'l/stokk** -en cf måle/

må'l/strek -en finish line, goal line.

må'l/strev -et work on behalf of national language reform (esp. in Norway).

+må'l/strever -en, pl. -e =*-ar) advocate of national language reform, esp. on behalf of landsmål (New Norwegian).

må'l/tid -et, pl +-er/*- meal: mellom m-ene between m-s.

må'l/trost -en zool. song thrush (Turdus ericetorum).

må'l/vakt -a goalkeeper.

må'l/vennlig A - friendly to New Norwegian.

+må'l/vokter -en, pl -e goalkeeper.

Må'l/øy Pln harbor town, Sogn og Fjordane.

***må'n** -a cf man[1]

***må'nad** -en, pl -er cf måned

***må'nads/lov** et cf måneds/

***må'nads/vis** Av cf måneds/

mån'/dag -en (=+man/) Monday.

må'ne -n 1 moon: avtagende m- waning m-; tiltagende, voksende m- waxing m-. 2 bald patch, spot (on the head).

+må'ned -en (=*månad) month: først (sist) i m-en at the beginning (end) of the month; i denne m- (during) this month; om en m- in a month (from now).

+må'nedlig A - monthly.

+må'neds/gammel A -elt, pl -gamle one month old.

+må'neds/lov [/låv] -en/-et educ. holiday (usu. a Monday) given each month.

+må'neds/skifte -t turn of the month.

+må'neds/skrift -et monthly magazine, periodical.

+må'neds/vis Av for months on end: i m- (the same).

må'ne/fase -n lunar phase.

må'ne/fjes -et fam. moon face (pie face).

+må'ne/formør'kelse -n lunar eclipse.

må'ne/lys[1] -et (=*/ljos) moonlight.

må'ne/lys[2] A (=*/ljos) moonlight, moonlit: fam. bli m-t become lively, be a hubbub.

+må'ne/mørke -t interlunar period.

***må'ne/mørking** -a lunar eclipse.

må'ne/natt -a, pl -netter 1 astron. lunar night. 2 moonlit night.

må'ne/sigd -en crescent moon.

+må'ne/skinn -et (=*/skin) moonlight.

+må'neskinns/lampe -a/-en small lamp giving a subdued, colored light.

må'ne/stråle -n moonbeam.

må'pe V +-te/*-a gape, stare openmouthed.

må'r -en zool. marten (Mustela); marten fur (used as apparel).

°mår'ra N cf morgen

må'r/skinn -et marten fur.

°må'sa N cf mose[1]

må'se -n cf måke[1]

+måskje' Av archaic maybe, perhaps, possibly.

Må's/øy Pln twp, Finnmark.

***må't** -et 1 degree, manner, way: det er vandt å råke m-et it's difficult to do sth just right. 2 moderation: med m- moderately; det er ikkje m- på there is no limit to. 3 goal, mark.

Måt.=måtelig

***må'ta[1]** Av (=*måte[3]) conveniently, suitably: m- stor about the right size.

°må'ta[2] Av cf °måtta

må'te[1] -n 1 manner, way; respect: i like m- same to you; i så m- in this respect; (i) på alle m-r in all respects, in every way; på den (denne) m- in that (this) way (det var på den m-n at that's the way that); på en eller annen m- somehow or other, by some means or other; på ingen m-, ikke på noen m- by no means, absolutely not; så snart jeg på noen m- kan as soon as I possibly can; *til m-s good enough (for you). 2 moderation: holde m- (*halde m-n) observe m-, keep within reasonable limits; med m- in m-; over all m- excessively, inordinately; det får være m- på! there's a (that's the) limit!; det var ikke m- på (det) there was no end to it; it was beyond all measure. 3 gram. archaic mood.

må'te[2] V -a/+-et 1 adapt, fit, put (together): *raudt og blått m-ar godt saman red and blue match well. 2 be suitable: *det m-ar ikkje for meg i dag it isn't convenient for me today.

***må'te[3]** Av cf måta[1]

+må'te/hold -et (=*/hald) moderation, temperance.

+må'te/holden A -ent, pl -ne (=*/halden) moderate, temperate.

+må'teholds/mann -en, pl -menn (=*-halds/) member of temperance society, temperance man.

må'telig A - 1 indifferent, mediocre, second-rate. 2 educ. barely passing mark (in written exam); flunking mark (in oral exam).

måtl.=måtelig

+måtro' C (=*må tru) cf tru[2]

***må't/sam·** A appropriate, convenient, suitable.

***mått'** -en power, strength.

°måt'ta Av (=°måta[2]) don't you know, of course, you know.

måt'te V må, måtte, +-et/*-(a) 1 (må) have to, must; (måtte) had to, must: jeg må gå nå I have to go now; jeg måtte le I had to laugh; (with omitted infinitive) jeg må hjem (bort, til butikken, ut, osv.) I have to go home (away, to the store, out, etc.); du må skynde deg you must hurry, hurry up now; du må ikke snakke sånn you mustn't talk like that; De må unnskylde meg you'll have to excuse me, please excuse me; det må så være it has to be, there's no helping it; jeg må (jamen) si det er flott I (really) must say it's nice; det må jeg si well, I never; det må til it is essential; han må være gal he must be crazy; da måtte jeg være gal then I'd have to be crazy (e.g. to do such a thing); han må (måtte) ha glemt det he must have forgotten it; å ville er å måtte ville to want (to do sth) is to have to want to do it (Ibsen). 2 may, might: må jeg få (gå nå) may I (go now)?; må jeg spørre if I might ask, may I ask?; om jeg så må si if I may (be allowed to) say so; hvem det enn måtte være no matter who it might be, who it is; hva han enn måtte si no matter what he might say, what he says; det er adgang for alle som måtte ønske å delta it is open to all who might wish (all wishing) to participate. 3 (in wishes): må (måtte) du bli lykkelig I wish you happiness; måtte det skje if it only would happen; når det bare måtte vare if it only would (could) last. 4 (other idioms): (preceding statements) du må tro, (following statements) må tro, må tru, må (du) vite you know (cf. also måta, måtro, måvite); det må du si, *du må so seie you can say that; (jeg, du, osv.) måtte kunne (I, you, etc.) should, ought to be able to.

***mått'/laus** A impotent, powerless.

+måvi'te Av cf vite

+ Bokmål; * Nynorsk; ° Dialect. After letter: ' stress (Acc. 1); ` tone, stress (Acc. 2); · length. Below letter: . not pronounced.

N

n[1] [enn'] -*en* (the letter) N, n.

°**n**[2]=**han** (only as a clitic): **har du sett'n?** have you seen him?; **n'Gunvald og jeg** Gunvald and I.

N=**nord;** +**Norge**/***Noreg**

N A=**nordaust**

nab'b(e) -(*e*)*n* 1 peg. 2 knoll.

+**na'bo** -*en* neighbor.

na'bob -*en* nabob.

+**na'bo/bygd** -*a* neighboring (rural) community.

+**na'bo/ga·rd** -*en* neighboring farm.

+**na'bo/lag** -*et* neighborhood, vicinity.

+**na'bo/skap** -*et* 1 neighborhood. 2 neighborliness. 3 neighbor: **fabrikken er et ubehagelig n-** the factory is an unpleasant n-.

+**na'bo/vinkel** -*elen, pl* -*ler* adjacent angle.

nach/spiel [nakk'/spil] -*et* informal party following another.

-nad -*en, pl* *-*er* substantivizing suffix (e.g. in **lovnad, røknad**).

nadd' -*en* point, wedge.

+**nad'/verd** -*en* cf **natt/**

NAF=**Norges Automobil-Forbund; Norsk Arbeidsgiverforening**

naf's -*en*/-*et* munch: **kua tok noen n- av graset** the cow munched a few mouthfuls of grass.

naf'se *V* -*a*/+-*et* munch, nibble (e.g. grass).

naf'ta -*en* naphtha.

naftali'n -*en* naphthalene.

+**na'g** -*et* grudge, resentment: **bære n- til en** bear a grudge against sby.

+**na'ge** *V* -*de*/-*et* gnaw (at), rankle: **skuffelsen n-et ham** his disappointment gnawed at him.

+**nag'el/fast** *A* - cf **nagle/**

+**na'gende** *A* - gnawing, rankling.

nagg' -*et* grudge, resentment.

***nag'l** -*en, pl* *negler* cf **negl**

nag'le[1] -*n* 1 rivet. 2 nail; peg.

nag'le[2] *V* -*a*/+-*et* 1 rivet. 2 nail.

***nag'le/bit** -*et* cf **negle/**

nag'le/fare *V* *in/l as fare* inspect minutely.

nag'le/fast *A* - 1: **mur- og n-e innretninger** fixtures. 2 *fig.* confirmed, established (e.g. fact).

nag'le/gap -*et* *bibl.* print of nails, stigma (John 20, 25).

***nag'le/sprett** -*en* cf **negle/**

naiv [na-i'v] *A* naive; unsophisticated.

naivis'me [na-i-] -*n* style in art (esp. painting) emphasizing artlessness; primitivism.

naivis't [na-i-] -*en* adherent of **naivisme.**

naivis'tisk [na-i-] *A* referring to **naivisme, naivist.**

naivite't [na-i-] -*en* naiveté.

naja'de -*a*/+-*en* naiad.

na'ken *A* +-*ent, pl* -*ne* naked, nude; bare, stripped, uncovered: **kle en n-** undress sby; **nakne armer** bare arms; **en n- holme** a naked reef; **den nakne sannhet** the naked truth.

na'ken/dans -*en* dancing in the nude, striptease dancing.

+**na'ken/danserin'ne** -*a*/-*en* (=*/**dansarinne**) nude dancer, striptease dancer.

na'ken/frøa *A* - (=+-**et**) *bot.* gymnospermous.

***na'ken/frøing** -*en* *bot.* gymnosperm.

+**na'ken/het** -*en* nakedness, nudity.

na'ken/koloni· -*en* nudist colony.

na'ken/kultu·r -*en* nudism.

***na'ken/skap** -*en* nakedness, nudity.

nak'ke -*n* 1 neck (=back of the head, nape of the neck): **sette foten på n-n til en** bring sby under the yoke; **slå med n-n** toss one's head; **ta seg selv i n-n** pull oneself together; **ta bena på n-n** run pell-mell; **ha øyne i n-n** have eyes in the back of one's head. 2 upper part of the shoulders: **bære en sekk på n-n** carry a sack on one's shoulders. 3 hummock, knoll.

nak'ke/drag -*et* blow, clout (on the neck).

nak'ke/grop -*a* hollow of the neck (e.g. of a cow).

nak'ke/hår -*et* hair at the nape of the neck.

nak'ke/kast -*et* toss of the head.

nak'ke/skott -*et* (=+/**skudd**) 1 shot through the head from behind. 2 *pop.* drink with violent effect.

+**nak'ke/speil** -*et* (=*/**spegel -en**) hand mirror.

NAL=**Den norske Amerikalinje A/S**

na'm[1] -*et* *jur.* attachment.

***na'm**[2] *pt of* **neme**

nam'[3] *I* cf **nam-nam**

Nam'dals/eid *Pln* twp, Nord-Trøndelag.

***nam'n** -*et* cf **navn**

nam'-nam' *I* yum-yum.

***nam'ne**[1] -*n* cf **navne**[1]

***nam'ne**[2] *V* -*a* cf **navne**[2]

***nam'ne/skifte** -*t* change of name.

***nam'n/fræg** *A* famous; noteworthy.

nam'n/gjeten *A* +-*ent, pl* -*ne* famous, renowned.

na'ms/mann -*en, pl* -*menn*/*-*menner* *jur.* court official who attaches property.

Nam's/os *Pln* coastal town, Nord-Trøndelag.

na'ms/rett -*en* *jur.* court issuing an attachment.

Nam's/skogan *Pln* twp, Nord-Trøndelag.

Nan'na *Prn (f) myth.* wife of Balder.

Nan'ne/stad *Pln* twp, Akershus.

nan'sen/pass -*et* Nansen passport (issued through the agency of the League of Nations to a stateless person).

napo'leons/kake -*a* Napoleon (pastry).

Na'poli *Pln* Naples.

napp'[1] -*en* nap (short stretch of sleep).

napp'[2] -*et* nibble, tug: **få n-** get a nibble (on the line).

napp'[3] -*et* nap (of wool).

***nap'past** *V* -*ast* cf **nappe**

nap'pe *V* -*a*/+-*et* 1 jerk, tug: **fisken n-er i snøret** the fish is nibbling at the line. 2 pluck, pull, snatch. 3 nab (e.g. a thief). 4: **n-s** fight, quarrel.

nap'pe/tak -*et* set-to, tussle.

***na're** *V* -*a* blow (esp. of cold wind).

+**nar'/hval** -*en* cf **/kval**

narkoma'n[1] -*en* dope addict, narcotic.

narkoma'n[2] *A* addicted to narcotics.

narkomani' -*en* addiction to narcotics.

narko'se -*n* anesthesia.

+**narko'tiker** -*en, pl* -*e* (=*-**ar**) dope addict, narcotic.

narko'tikum -*umet, pl* -*a* narcotic (drug).

narkotise're *V* -*te* anesthetize.

narko'tisk *A* - narcotic.

nar'/kval -*en* *zool.* narwhal (Monodon monoceros).

narr' -*en*/*-*et* 1 jester. 2 fool: **gjøre n- av en** make fun of sby; **holde en for n-** make a f- of sby; **gjøre seg til n-** make a f- of oneself.

+**narr'/aktig** *A* - 1 foolish, ridiculous. 2 conceited, vain.

+**narr'aktig/het** -*en* 1 foolishness. 2 conceit, vanity.

nar're *V* -*a*/+-*et* deceive, delude, fool: **n- penger fra** dupe (cheat) out of money; **n- en opp i stry** make a complete fool of sby; **n- en april** play an April fool's joke on sby.

***nar'releg** *A* - 1 foolish, ridiculous. 2 conceited, vain.

nar're/lue -*a* fool's cap.

nar'reri -*et* 1 deception: **gjøre noe på n-** do sth in order to deceive (sby). 2 fooling, foolishness.

***nar're/skap** -*en* tomfoolery.

nar're/smokk [/smokk] -*en* pacifier.

nar're/strek -*en*/*-*et* foolish prank, tomfoolery.

***nar're/voren** [/våren] *A* -*e*/-*i, pl* -*ne* 1 foolish, ridiculous. 2 conceited, vain.

°**narri** *N* cf **narreri**

+**nar'rifas** -*en* conceited, vain person.

narsis'me -*n* narcissism.

narsiss' -*en* *bot.* narcissus.

nar'v -*en* 1 grain side (of leather). 2 grain (stamped pattern).

nar've *V* -*a*/+-*et* grain (e.g. leather).

Na'r/vik *Pln* city, Nordland.

nasa'l[1] -*en* nasal (sound).

nasa'l[2] *A* nasal.

nasale're *V* -*te* nasalize.

nasalite't -*en* nasality.

nasa'l/lyd -*en* (=*/**ljod**) nasal (sound).

+**nasare'er** -*en, pl* -*e* (=*-**ar**) Nazarene.

***na'se**[1] -*n* cf **nese**

***na'se**[2] *V* -*a* 1 sniff. 2 nose into, pry.

***na'se/bore** -*a* cf **nese/bor**

***na's/ho·rn** -*et* cf **nes/**

***na's/hyrning** -*en* cf **nes/horn**

nasjo'n -*en* nation: **De forente n-er** the United N-s.

nasjona'l *A* national; patriotic: **n-holdning** p- conduct (esp. during WW II); **det n-e** the essence of a people; national characteristics; **N-Samling** "National Unification" (political party founded in 1933 which supported the Nazi movement).

nasjona'l/budsjett· -*et* national budget.

nasjona'l/dag -*en* Independence Day.

nasjona'l/dans -*en* native dance.

nasjona'l/drakt -*a*/+-*en* native (national) costume.

nasjona'l/farge -*n* (in *pl*) national colors.

nasjona'l/forsam·ling -*a*/+-*en* national assembly; parliament.

+**nasjona'l/følelse** -*n* love of country, national awareness, patriotism.

nasjona'l/galleri· -*et* national gallery.

nasjona'l/inntekt -*a*/+-*en* national income.

nasjonalise're *V* -*te* nationalize.

nasjonalis'me -*n* nationalism.

nasjonalis't -*en* nationalist.

nasjonalis'tisk *A* - nationalistic.

nasjonalite't -*en* nationality.

nasjonalite'ts/merke -*t, pl* +-*r*/*- mark of nationality, nationality sign (esp. on vehicles to indicate country of origin).

nasjona'l/kjensle -*a* love of country, national awareness, patriotism.

nasjona'l/råd -*et* national council: **Norske Kvinners N-** N- of Norwegian Women.

nasjona'l/sak -*a*/+-*en* matter of nationwide import(ance).

+**nasjona'l/sang** -*en* national anthem.

nasjona'l/sosialis·me -*n* national socialism.

nasjona'l/sosialis·t -*en* national socialist.

nasjona'l/stat -*en* nation-state.

nasjona'l/tea·ter -*eret*/-*ret, pl* -/+-*tre* national theater.

nasjona'l/økonomi· -*en* national economy.

nasjona'l/økono·misk *A* - pertaining to the economy of a nation.

nasjona'l/ånd -*a* national spirit or soul; patriotic feeling.

nas'k *A* 1 avaricious, greedy. 2 biting, sharp (e.g. of wind).

nas'ke *V* -*a*/+-*et* filch, steal, *(pop.)* snitch.

+**nas'keri** *-et* petty larceny, small thefts, *(pop.)* snitching.
na't *-en* seam (space between adjacent planks).
natalite't *-en* birth rate.
na'te *V -a/+-et* wet down (deck during intense heat).
***na'te-** *Pf* cf **nøtte-**
Nationen [nasjo'nen] *Prn* daily newspaper in Oslo.
na'trium *-et* sodium.
na'tron *-et* soda.
na'tron/salpe'ter *-en* saltpeter.
natt' *-a/+-en, pl netter* 1 night: **god n-** good n-; **hele n-en** all n-; **i n-** last n-; tonight; **midt på n-en** in the middle of the n-; **om n-en** at n-; **til n-en** tonight, this (coming) n-; **n-ens tid(e)** at nighttime; **i n-ens mulm og mørke** in the dark of n-; **det var svarte n-a** it was pitch-dark; **han tenkte på det dag og n-** he thought about it n- and day. 2 *fig.*: **borti n-a** senseless; **dødens n-** death.
natt'/arbeid *-et* night work.
natt'/blind *A* - night-blind.
natt'/bo'rd *-et* night table.
natt'/drakt *-a/+-en* nightclothes.
nat'te *V -a/+-et* 1: spend the night: **n- seg** settle down for the night. 2: **det n-s** night is falling.
nat'te/frost *-en* ground frost, night frost.
+**nat'te/leie** *-t* bed (for a night), bunk.
nat'te/losji' *-et, pl -/+-er* night's lodging.
nat'te/ramn *-en* 1 *zool.* goatsucker (Caprimulgus europaeus). 2 *fig.* nightowl.
nat'te/rangel *-elen, pl -ler* carousing, revel.
nat'ter/gal *-en zool.* nightingale.
nat'te/ro *-a/+-en* rest at night.
nat'te/søvn *-en* sleep at night.
nat'te/vaking *-a* staying awake at night.
nat'te/vakt *-a/+-en* 1 night watch. 2 night watchman.
natt'/fiol *-en bot.* dame's violet, dame's rocket (Hesperis).
natt'/fly *-en zool.* noctuid (night-flying moth).
natt'/hus *-et naut.* binnacle.
nattiné *-en* (late) late show (usually after 11 P.M.).
natt'/kafé *-en* all-night café.
natt'/kjole *-n* nightgown.
natt'/klubb *-en* nightclub.
***natt'/lege** *-a* (=+**natte/leie**) place where one stays the night; night's lodging.
natt'lig *A* - nocturnal.
natt'/lue *-a* nightcap.
natt'/lys *-et bot.* evening primrose (Oenothera).
natt'/mann *-en, pl -menn/*-menner* 1 nightman (man whose duty it was to assist the public executioner and perform unpleasant tasks involving cleaning up at night, e.g. bury carrion). 2 emptier of latrines.
natt'/mat *-en* midnight snack (esp. during a party).
natt'/møbel *-elet/-let, pl +-ler/*-el* chamber pot.
natt'-og-da'g *en bot.* pansy (Vida tricolor).
natt'/portie'r *-en* night clerk.
natt'/potte *-a* chamber pot.
natt'/serk *-en* nightgown.
natt'/skift *-et* night shift.
natt'/skjorte [/sjorte] *-a* nightshirt.
***natt'/staden** *A -e/-i, pl -ne* quartered for the night.
+**natt'/svermer** *-en, pl -e* (=*-**ar**) *zool.* night-flying moth (Heterocera).
natt'/tog [/tåg] *-et* night train.
natt'/vak *A* fatigued (after a sleepless night).
+**natt'/vakt** *-a/-en* cf **natte/**
natt'/verd [*/vær] *-en* *1 supper. 2 communion, the Lord's Supper.
***natt'/voke** [*/våke] *-a* cf **natte/vaking**
natu'r *-en* nature (=temperament, disposition; scenery; primitive or aboriginal condition): **hun er en vanskelig n-** she has a difficult temperament; **den vakre n-en** the beautiful scenery; **menneskene skulle vende tilbake til n-en** man should return to nature; **n-ens orden** the natural order of things.
+**natura'l/hushol'd/ning** *-en* (=*/**hushald**) barter economy.
+**natura'lier** *pl* (=*-**ia**) 1 natural curiosities, specimens (of flowers, plants, etc.). 2 products of the soil: **betale med n-** pay in kind.
naturalise're *V -te* naturalize.
naturalis'me *-n* naturalism.
naturalis't *-en* naturalist (=adherent of naturalism).
naturalis'tisk *A* - naturalistic.
natu'r/ba'rn *-et* child of nature (simple, unsophisticated person).
+**natu'r/bega'velse** *-n* 1 innate ability, natural endowment. 2 person having natural ability.
natu'r/fag *-et* science subject.
natu'r/farga *A* - (=+-**et**) having (only) its natural color(s).
natu'r/fenome'n *-et, pl -/+-er* natural phenomenon: natural genius.
natu'r/folk *-et* primitive group or race.
+**natu'r/forsker** *-en, pl -e* naturalist, natural scientist.
+**natu'r/gransker** *-en, pl -e* (=*-**ar**) naturalist, natural scientist.
+**natu'r/herlighet** *-en* natural resource(s); beauty spot.
natu'r/histo'rie *-a/+-en* natural history (e.g. zoology, botany).
natu'r/histo'risk *A* - pertaining to natural history.
natu'r/katastro'fe *-n* natural catastrophe; act of God.
natu'r/kjensle *-a* feeling for nature, love of nature.
natu'r/kraft *-a/+-en, pl -krefter/*-krafter* natural force; elemental force.
natu'r/lege *-n* nature healer.
natur'lig *A* - 1 natural: **stedet var en n- festning** the place was a n- fortress. 2 inborn, innate, native: **ha n- begavelse for tegning** have an innate talent for drawing. 3 life-sized, normal: **en statue i n- størrelse** a life-sized statue. 4 genuine, unaffected: **hun var så grei og n-** she was so straightforward and u-.
natu'rlig/vis *Av* naturally, obviously, of course.
natu'r/lov [/låv] *-en/*-a* natural law.
natu'r/meto'de *-n* nature method.
natu'r/nødven'dig *A* - inescapable, inevitable.
+**natu'r/nødven'dighet** *-en* physical necessity.
natu'r/park *-en* natural park.
natu'r/produk't *-et, pl -/+-er* natural product.
natu'r/sans *-en* feeling for nature.
natu'r/silke *-n* pure silk, real silk.
+**natu'r/skjønn** *A -skjønt* picturesque, remarkable for the beauty of its scenery.
natu'r/stridig *A* - contrary to nature, unnatural.
+**natu'r/trang** *-en* (=*/**trong**) natural impulse, involuntary inclination.
+**natu'r/tro** *A* - natural, realistic, true to nature.
natu'r/vern [/væ'rn] *-et* conservation of nature, natural resources.
+**natu'r/vitenska'p** *-en* (=/**vitskap**) natural science.
natyrell' *-et* inclination, natural disposition.
+**nau'-** *Pf* (=***naud-**) intensifying prefix (e.g. **naukald** extremely cold).
+**nau'/be** *V -bad, -bedt* (=***naud/**) beg, beseech, entreat, implore.
***nau'd**[1] *-a* cf **nød**
***nau'd**[2] *pt of* **njode**
***nau'd-** *Pf* cf **nau-**
nau'dande** *Av* (=naudende**) intensifying adverb: **n- vakker** extremely pretty; **sitte n- stille** sit perfectly still.
***nau'dar/dom** *-(m)en* 1 misery, privation, wretchedness. 2 narrow-mindedness, niggardliness, pettiness.
***nau'd/be(de)** *V -bad, -bede/-i* cf **nau/**
***nau'dende** *Av* cf **naudande**
***nau'd/fin** *A* cf **nau/**
***nau'd/høve** *-t* crisis, emergency, exigency, necessity.
***nau'dig** *A* cf **nødig**
***nau'dleg** *A* - involuntary, unwilling.
***nau'd/stadd** *A* - cf **nød/stedt**
***nau'd/syn** *-a/-et* necessity, need.
***nau'd/synleg** *A* - essential, necessary.
***nau'd/synt** *A* - essential, necessary.
***nau'd/turft** *-a* cf **nød/tørft**
***nau'd/turveleg** *A* - essential, necessary.
***nau'd/verje** *-a* cf **nød/verge**
+**nau'e** *V -a/-de* 1: **det n-er ikke it** doesn't matter, it's of no consequence. 2: **n- seg** lament, mourn one's lot; **han var slik stelt nå, at han n-a seg** he was reduced to such circumstances now that he mourned his lot.
°**nau'ende** *Av* cf **naudande**
+**nau'/fin** *A* (=***naud/**) extremely fine.
nau's *pt of* **nyse**
nau'st *-et* boathouse.
Nau'st/dal *Pln* twp, Sogn og Fjordane.
nau't[1] *-et* 1 cattle (i.e., common domestic bovine, Bos taurus). 2 blockhead, fool, simpleton.
naut[2] *pt of* **nyte**
+**nau'/tagg** *pt of* **-tigge**
+**nau'te/hår** *-et* cowhair (used particularly in overstuffed furniture).
+**nau'te/kjøtt** *-et* beef.
nau'ten *A* +*-ent, pl -ne* foolish, stupid.
***nau'te/skap** *-en* foolishness, stupidity.
nau't/fall *-et* carcass of cattle (cow, steer).
nau't/ga'rd *-en* 1 pen or enclosure for cattle during the summer. 2 yard adjacent to the outbuildings of a farm.
+**nau'/tigge** *V -et/-tidge/-tagg, -et/ -tigd* (=***naud/**) beg, beseech, implore.
nau'tisk *A* - nautical.
***nau'v**[1] *A* 1 meagre, scanty, scarce. 2 miserly, niggardly, stingy.
***nau'v**[2] *pt of* **nuve**
+**nau'/vakker** *A -ert, pl -vakre* (=***naud/**) extremely pretty.
***nau've** *V -a* bother, damage: **det n-ar ikkje** it doesn't matter.
na'v *-et* hub (of a wheel).
na'var *-en, pl navrer* auger.
***na'vars/hol** [/hål] *-et* auger hole.
***na've** *V -a* fit logs together in a cornerjoint.
+**na'ver** *-en, pl -e* cf **navar**
na'v/hjul *-et* hub sprocket.
navigasjo'n *-en* navigation (act and science).
navigatø'r *-en* navigator.
navige're *V -te* navigate.
nav'le[1] *-n* navel.
nav'le[2] *V -a/+-et* sever and bind up the umbilical cord.
+**nav'le/besku'er** *-en, pl -e* self-centered person; omphalopsychite (member of an ancient Greek sect who practiced gazing at the navel as a means of inducing hypnotic reverie).
nav'le/streng *-en* umbilical cord.
+**nav'n** *-et* (=***namn**) 1 name (**på** of): **dagens n-** n-s in the news; **hva gjør n-et?** what's in a n-?; **i lovens n-** in the n- of the law; **kjært barn har mange n-** a pet child gets many n-s (=call it what you will); **nevne ved n-** mention by n-. 2 reputation, repute: **hans gode n- og**

+ Bokmål; * Nynorsk; ° Dialect.
After letter: ' stress (Acc. 1); ` tone, stress (Acc. 2); · length.
Below letter: . not pronounced.

rykte his good reputation; **vinne seg et n-** build up a reputation.
+nav'ne¹ *-n* (=***namne¹**) namesake.
+nav'ne² *V -a/-et* (=***namne²**) monogram (clothing).
+nav'ne/blekk *-et* marking ink.
+nav'ne/brett *-et* ship's nameplate (on side or stern).
+nav'ne/bror *-en* namesake.
+nav'ne/likhet *-en* similarity of names.
+nav'ne/opprop *-et* roll call.
+nav'ne/plate *-a/-en* nameplate.
+nav'ne/seddel *-elen, pl -sedler* slip of paper bearing one's name (referring esp. to such slips enclosed in sealed envelopes by entrants in contests, contractors submitting sealed bids, etc.).
+nav'ne/skikk *-en* naming, naming customs.
+nav'ne/skilt *-et* nameplate (e.g. of a resident, professional man, manufacturer).
+nav'ne/trekk *-et* **1** autograph, signature. **2** monogram (on clothing).
+nav'n/gitt *A* - designated, named.
+nav'n/gjeten *A -ent, pl -ne* cf **namn/**
+navnkun'dig *A* - renowned, well-known.
+nav'nlig *Av* especially, notably, particularly.
+nav'n/løs *A* **1** anonymous, nameless; obscure. **2** indescribable, unspeakable (e.g. suffering, horror).
+nav'n/o'rd *-et* noun, substantive.
+nav'n/spurt *A* - famous, renowned, well-known.
nazifise're [nasi-] *V -te* nazify.
nazis'me [nas-] *-n* nazism.
nazis't [nas-] *-en* nazi.
nazis'tisk [nas-] *A* - nazi.
NB=**nota bene²**
n. br.=**nordlig bredde**
ndf.=**nedafor, +neden-, *nedan-**
ne' *-et* waning (of the moon): **i ny og ne** off and on, once in a while.
+nean'der/taler *-en, pl -e* Neanderthal man (Homo neandertaliensis).
Nea'pel *Pln* cf **Napoli**
neapolita'nsk *A* - Neapolitan.
***ne'ar** *pl* cf **ne**
nebb' *-en/-et* **1** beak, bill. **2** mouth, nose (human beings): **være bleik om n-et** be pale, green around the gills; **henge med n-et** be crestfallen, down in the mouth. **3** spout (on can, mug). **4** *hum.* impertinent, saucy girl, woman: **hun er et ordentlig n-** she's a real shrew.
***neb'bast** *V -ast* cf **nebbe**
nebb'/dyr *-et zool.* (duck-billed) platypus (Ornithorhynchus anatinus).
neb'be *V -a/+-et*: **n-s** (of birds) peck at each other; *hum.* bill and coo; bicker, wrangle.
***neb'b**e**leg** *A* - neat; finely decorated.
nebbeno'se *-a* pert, saucy girl.
neb'bet(e) *A* - impertinent, pert, saucy: **svare nebbete** give a sharp answer.
+nebb'/tang *-a, pl -tenger* (=**+nebbe/, */tong**) pair of pliers.
necessæ'r *-en* cosmetics case, toilet case.
ne'd [also ne'] *Av* down: **n- med roret** ease d- the helm; **han gikk opp og n- på gulvet** he walked the floor; **han var kommet dypt n-** he had come d- far (in the world); **prisene er gått n-** prices have come d-, have been reduced.
ne'da- *Pf* (=**+neden-, *nedan-**) below.
+ne'd/ad *Av* downhill, downwards: **det går hurtig n- med ham** *fig.* he's going downhill fast.
+ne'dad/gående *A* - declining, sinking: **n- priser** falling prices.
+ne'dad/vendt *A* - downcast (eyes), facing downwards.
ne'da/for' *P* (down) below.
***ne'da/frå** *Av* cf **nedefra**
***ne'da/føre** *P* cf **/for**
***ne'dan** *P* below; from below.
***ne'dan-** *Pf* cf **neda-, neden-**
***ne'dan/for'** *P* cf **neda/**
***ne'dan/om'** *P* cf **neden/**
ne'd/arva *A* - (=**+-et**) inherited; traditional.
+ne'd/arves *V -edes, -et* be handed down, transmitted.
ne'da/til' *Av* (=***nedan/**) below; at the bottom, on the underside.
ne'd/att *Av* cf **ned**
+ne'd/be *V -ba, -bedt* invoke, pray for: **n- Herrens velsignelse** invoke the Lord's blessing.
ne'd/brent** *A* - (=/brend**) burnt down, burnt to the ground.
+ne'd/brutt *A* - broken: **han er n- på sjel og legeme** he is b- in body and spirit.
+ne'd/bryte *V -braut/-brøt, -brutt* break down, destroy, ruin: **drikk og utsvevelser n-er hans helbred** drink and debauchery are ruining his health.
+ne'd/brytende *A* - destructive, detrimental, ruinous: **virke n- på** have a detrimental effect on.
+ne'd/brøt *pt of* **-bryte**
ne'd/bør *-en* precipitation (e.g. rain, snowfall, hail).
ne'dbør/fattig *A* - dry (region, season).
ne'dbør/mengd *-a* (=**+/mengde**) amount of precipitation.
+ne'd/bøyet *A* - **1** bowed down. **2** afflicted, weighed down (with grief).
+ne'd/dykket *A* - submerged.
+ne'd/dysse *V -et* hush up (e.g. scandal), put an end to, quiet (e.g. rumor).
ne'de *Av* **1** below, down: **der n-** d-there; **n- i sydhavsøyene** d- in the South Sea Islands. **2** down-and-out, run-down **gården lå så n-** the farm was so run-down.
+ne'de/fra *Av* (=**+neden/, neda/frå**) from down below.
+ne'den- *Pf* cf **neda-**
+ne'den/for' *P* cf **neda/**
+ne'den/fra *Av* cf **nede/**
+nedenn.=**nedennevnte**
+ne'den/nevnte *A* - mentioned, referred to below.
+ne'den/om' *P* (=***nedan/**) down below: **vi gikk n- ura** we walked d-below the rocky slope; *(adv.)* **gå n- og hjem** go to the bottom (=drown; also *fig.*).
+ne'den/stående *A* - mentioned, referred to below.
+ne'den/til *Av* cf **neda/**
+ne'den/under *P* below, beneath, underneath; downstairs.
+ne'der/del *-en* lower part: **n-en av en kjole** the skirt of a dress.
+ne'der/drektig *A* - base, scoundrelly, villainous.
+ne'derdrektig/het *-en* baseness, meanness, vileness.
ne'der/lag *-et* defeat; reverse, setback: **lide n-** be defeated, suffer defeat.
Ne'der/land *Pln* the Netherlands.
ne'der/landsk *A* - Dutch.
+ne'der/lender *-en, pl -e* (=**/lending**) Netherlander, Dutchman.
+ne'derst *sp of* **nedre** cf **nedst**
+ne'der/tysk *A* - Low German.
***ne'd/ervd** *A -/-ervt* cf **/arva**
***ne'd/erving** *-a* inheritance, transmission (of characteristics).
ne'd/etter *P* down: **n- bakken** d-the hill.
ne'd/fall *-et* collapse, downfall; defeat.
ne'dfalls/frukt *-a/+-en* windfall (of fruit).
ne'dfalls/sott *-a/+-en* epilepsy.
ne'd/fart *-en* descent (**til** to).
ne'd/for' *P* **1** down; below. **2** dejected, despondent.
ne'dfor/kommen *A +-ent, pl -komne* (=***-komen**) low, run-down (health, spirits).
ne'd/gang *-en* **1** descent, passage down (to a place); entrance: **alle n-er var sperret** all e-s were blocked. **2** decline, fall; decrease: **romerrikets n-** decline of the Roman Empire; **prisenes n-** drop in prices.
ne'dgangs/tid *-a/+-en* depression, slump (economic); period of decadence, deterioration.
ne'd/grodd *A -/*-grott* overgrown, overrun (garden); ingrown (toenail).
ne'd/gående *A* - declining, descending; falling.
+ne'd/hengende *A* - **1** hanging down, pendulous. **2** *bot.* cernuous, drooping (flowers, trees).
ne'di *P* cf **ned**
ne'd/igjen'nom *P* down through.
ne'd/isa *A* - (=**+-et**) **1** icebound, ice-covered, icy. **2** frozen.
+ne'd/kalle *V -kalte, -kalt* call down, invoke, summon: **n- forbannelser over en** call down curses (maledictions) on sby.
ne'd/kast *-et* drop; airdrop (delivery of supplies, troops, etc. by parachute).
+ne'd/kjempe *V -a/-et* **1** overcome, vanquish (enemy). **2** choke down, fight back (anger, tears).
+ne'd/komme *V -kom, -kommet* be delivered of, give birth to: **hun n-kom i går** she gave birth (her child was born) yesterday.
+ne'd/komst *-en* **1** delivery: **kvinne som venter sin n-** expectant mother. **2** descent.
+ne'd/la *pt of* **-legge**
+ne'd/lagt *A* - (=***/lagd**) **1** laid down, deposited. **2** discontinued, disused, dismantled (fortifications). **3** embodied, implanted (instincts). **4** relinquished, resigned (office, position). **5** canned, preserved.
+ne'd/lastet *A* - (=***-a**) loaded down, overloaded: **skipet var n- dypere enn tillatt** the ship was loaded beyound the legal limit.
+ne'd/late *V -lot, -latt* condescend, deign, stoop (**til** to).
+ne'd/latende *A* - condescending, patronizing.
+ne'dlaten/het *-en* condescension, patronizing air.
+ne'd/legge *V -la, -lagt* (cf also **legge ned**) **1** lay down, place. **2** abdicate; discontinue, give up, relinquish, resign: **n- kronen** abdicate; **n- en forretning** discontinue, close down a business; **n- arbeidet** cease work, strike; **n- våpnene** lay down one's arms, cease fighting. **3** demolish, dismantle: **n- befestninger** dismantle fortifications. **4** deposit, invest: **n- store kapitaler i et foretagende** i-capital in a business venture. **5** bag, bring down: **han nedla villsvinet med et velrettet skudd** he brought down the boar with a wellaimed shot. **6** stop thinking about: **jeg kan ikke n- det** I can't get it out of my mind. **7** *jur.* prepare, file: **n- påstand om (døds)straff** demand the (death) penalty. **8** can, pickle, preserve (fish, fruit, etc.).
+ne'd/lot *pt of* **-late**
ne'd/med *P* by, down along.
ne'd/om' *P* by, down to: **hun gikk n- steinrøysa** she walked down past the heap of stones.
ne'd/over [/åver; also nedd'/] *P* down, downwards: **gå n- trappa** go, walk downstairs.
ned'over/bakke *-n* downhill.
ne'd/på *P* down (on): **legge seg n-** take a nap.
ne'd/rakking *-a/+-en* abuse, vilification.
ne'dre *A* -, *sp nedst/+nederst* lower: **n- Donau** the lower Danube.
Ne'dre Ei'ker *Pln* twp, Buskerud.
+ne'drig *A* - base, contemptible, mean.
+ne'drig/het *-en* baseness, meanness, villainy.
+ne'd/ringet *A* - décolleté, low-necked; (of gowns) low-backed.
+ne'd/ringning *-en* neck opening (of an evening gown).
+ne'd/ri'vning *-en* demolition, tearing down.

+ne'd/ruste *V -a/-et* disarm, reduce armaments.
+ne'd/rustning *-a/-en* (=***/rusting**) disarmament, reduction of armaments.
+ne'd/sable *V -a/-et* **1** cut down, massacre, slaughter. **2** criticize caustically, scathingly: **boka ble n-et av kritikken** the book was savagely attacked by critics.
+ne'd/satt *A* - diminished, reduced: **til n-e priser** at r- prices; **n- takst** r- rate (railway fares); **hans arbeidskraft var sterkt n- etter sykdommen** his capacity for work was considerably diminished after his illness.
+ned/satte *pt of* **-sette**
***ne'd/setjande** *A* - cf **/settende**
+ne'd/sette *V -satte, -satt* **1** abate, lower, reduce; depreciate, discredit, disparage: **n- prisene** cut, lower prices; **n- en straff** *jur.* mitigate, reduce, remit part of a sentence; **det har n-satt ham i mitt omdømme** it has lowered him in my regard. **2** appoint: **n- en kommisjon** a- a commission.
+ne'd/settelse *-n* **1** decrease, reduction; detraction, disparagement. **2** appointment. **3** establishment, settlement.
+ne'd/settende *A* - (=***/setjande**) belittling, depreciatory, disparaging.
+ne'd/sittet *A* - worn down (by being sat on): **sofaen var godt n-** the sofa was well-worn (Hoel).
+ne'd/skjæring *-a/-en* **1** cutback, reduction (expenditures, prices, wages, etc.). **2** pruning, truncating (trees). **3** cut (erosion). **4** neck opening (dress): **V-formet n-** V-neck. **5** rebuff, snub.
+ne'd/skrive *V -skreiv/-skrev, -skrevet* **1** commit, reduce to writing, record. **2** *merc.* reduce (outstanding amount, debt); reduce the book value of assets, bonds, stocks: **n- aktivers nominelle verdi** reduce the book value of assets.
+ne'd/skriver *-en, pl -e* chronicler, recorder: **n-en** the writer.
+ne'dskrivnings/bidrag *-et* subsidy to private individuals for construction of housing.
ne'd/slag *-et* **1** fall, reduction (i of e.g. prices). **2** hit, impact (e.g. of projectiles); landing (in jumping). **3** condensation; *chem.* precipitation. **4** *mus.* downbeat, thesis (downbeat stroke). **5** downdraft (chimney).
ne'dslags/distrik't *-et, pl -/+-er* catchment, fluvial basin (area from which a river draws its water).
ne'dslags/felt *-et* field of fire (artillery).
ne'dslags/område *-t, pl +-r/*-* field of fire (artillery).
ne'd/slaktning *-a/+-en* butchery, killing, slaughter (av of).
+ne'd/slitt *A* - worn-down; exhausted, fatigued.
ne'd/slående *A* - depressing, discouraging, disheartening.
ne'd/slått *A* - dejected, depressed, downcast.
+ne'dslått/het *-en* dejection, depression, despondency.
ne'd/snødd *A* - snow-covered, snowed over.
neds't *sp of* **nedre** (=**+nederst**)
+ne'd/stamme *V -a/-et* be descended, descend (**fra** from); be derived, derive from (word).
+ne'd/stemme *V -stemte* **1** chill, dampen, discourage: **n-ende nyheter** discouraging news. **2** moderate, tone down: **han måtte n- sine fordringer** he had to tone down his demands. **3** defeat, vote down: **regjeringen ble n-t** the government was defeated. **4** *mus.* lower the tone, pitch of; modulate.
+ne'd/stemt *A* - **1** dejected, downcast; subdued. **2** modulated: **med n-kvint** mus. with m- treble string (violin).
ne'd/stigende *A* - descending: **stamme i rett n- linje** be lineally descended (**fra** from).
+ne'd/sti'gning *-en* (=***/stiging**) descent (act of descending; declivity).
Ne'd/strand *Pln* twp, Rogaland.
ne'd/sylta *A* - (=**+-et**) pickled, preserved: **n- i forkjølelse** in the midst of a bad cold.
+ne'd/tegne [/teine] *V -a/-et* commit to paper, writing, note down.
ne'd/trykt *A* - dejected, depressed, discouraged: **han var aldeles n-** he was utterly discouraged.
+ne'dtrykt/het *-en* depression, melancholia.
ne'd/tur *-en* trip down: **på n-** on the way down.
ne'd/verdige *V -et* debase, degrade: **n- seg til noe** stoop to sth.
ne'd/verdigende *A* - debasing, degrading.
ne'd/vote're *V -te* defeat, vote down: **forslaget ble n-t med stort flertall** the measure was defeated by a large majority.
ne'd/vurde're *V -te* depreciate, devalue, downgrade.
***ne'd/væ'pning** *-a* disarmament.
***ne'd/åt** *P* down (to).
negasjo'n *-en* negation.
ne'gativ¹ *-et* negative (image, plate, pole).
ne'gativ² *A* negative.
negativite't *-en* negativeness.
ne'ger *-eren, pl -rer/+-ere* negro.
ne'ger/arbeid *-et* drudgery: **gjøre alt n-et** do all the dirty work.
nege're *V -te gram.* negate.
ne'ger/kvarte'r *-et, pl -/+-er* negro quarter.
ne'ger/kyss *-et* chocolate-covered cooky.
ne'ger/vennlig *A* - negrophile.
+negl [nei'l] *-en* (=***nagl**) **1** nail (fingernail, toenail): **han er en hard n-** he's a tough customer; **bite n-er** bite one's nails (habitually). **2** *bot.* claw, unguis (claw-like base of certain petals).
+negle/band [nei'le/] *-et* cuticle, nailfold.
+negle/bit *-en* frostbite of fingernail, fingertip.
+negle/børste *-n* nail brush.
+negle/fil *-a* nail file.
negle/lakk *-en* nail polish.
negle/rot *-a* root of the nail.
+negle/saks *-a* nail scissors.
+negle/sprett *-en* frostbite of fingernail, fingertip.
neglisjé *-en* negligée.
neglisje're *V -te* ignore, neglect.
negotiere [negåsie're] *V -te* negotiate.
negres'se *-a/+-en* negress.
negroid [negro-i'd] *A* - negroid.
nei'¹ *-et* no: **gi en sitt n-** refuse, reject sby (e.g. a suitor); **hun vil ikke høre (noe) n-** she won't take no for an answer; **si n- til en innbydelse** refuse an invitation.
nei'² *I* **1** no: **n-, slett ikke** no, by no means; **n- da** no indeed. **2** indeed, really, well, etc.: **n-, bare se** just look, do look; **n-, nå har jeg aldri hørt maken** well, I never heard the like of it; **han er aldri blitt til noe stort, n-** indeed, he's never amounted to anything much. **3: n- men** (also **neimen**) exclamation of surprise): **n- men mor da!** but mother - -!; **n- men visste du ikke dette?** what, didn't you know this?
+nei'/da *I* cf **nei²**
nei'e¹ *V +-de/*-a* curtsy, make (drop) a curtsy.
***nei'e²** *V -a* say no.
nei'e³** *V -dde* (=njode**) clinch (bend a nail over); rivet (bolts); butt (two plates together).
neigu' [also: neig'gu] *Av* (oath) indeed not: **n- om jeg gjør** I'll be damned if I will; **n- om han det har** I'll be damned if he has.
nei'men¹ *Av* indeed not: **n- om jeg gjør som han sier** I'll be blessed if I'll do as he says.
nei'men² *I* cf **nei²**
***nei'se** *V -te* provoke (with offensive allusions), slur (**med** with).
***neit'te** *V -a* cf **nekte**
***neit'ting** *-a* cf **nekting**
+ne'k *-et* sheaf (of grain).
nekrolog [-olå'g] *-en* obituary (biographical article).
nek'tar *-en* nectar.
nek'te *V -a/+-et* (=***neitte**) deny; decline, refuse: **jeg kan ikke n- (for) at** I must admit (I can't dispute) that; **n- å vedkjenne seg sitt løfte** go back on one's promise; **n- seg hjemme** refuse to see ayone; **han n-er seg ingenting** he does anything he pleases.
+nek'telse *-n* cf **nekting**
+nek'ter *-en, pl -e* (=***-ar**) conscientious objector (to military service).
nek'ting *-a/+-en* (=**+-else, *neitting**) denial; negation; *gram.* negative: **to n-er opphever hverandre** two negatives make an affirmative.
+nel'de *-n obs.* nettle (cf **nesle**).
nel'lik *-en* **1** *bot.* pink (Dianthus plumarius); carnation (Dianthus caryophyllus). **2** cloves (spice).
+nel'lik/spiker *-eren, pl -rer/+-er* (=***-ar**) tack.
+nem' *A -t, pl -me* (=***næm**) *obs.* easy, simple; convenient, handy; easy to get along with: **det er ikke så n-t** it's no easy matter.
+-nem' *A -t, pl -me* (=***-næm**) suffix denoting quickness of apprehension, handiness, etc.: **fingernem** adroit, dexterous, handy; **lærenem** quick at learning.
***ne'me** *V nam, nome/-i* notice, perceive.
ne'mesis *en* nemesis: **det går en n- igjennom livet** a n- runs through our lives (Ibsen).
nem'lig *Av* namely, that is, you see: **det kan n- tenkes at . . .** you see, it is possible that . . .
+nem'me *-t* (=***næme**) (quickness of) apprehension, aptitude, turn (**for, til** for): **han har lett n- for kjemi** he has an aptitude for chemistry.
***nem'nande** *A* - mentionable, worth mentioning.
***nem'nar** *-en* cf **nevner**
nemnd [nem'd] *-a* **1** committee. **2** jury (in Old Norse times the group selected at the assembly to render decisions in legal matters).
***nem'ne¹** *-t* name, term.
***nem'ne²** *V -de* cf **nevne**
***nem'ning** *-a* **1** designation, name. **2** *gram.* defining, limiting word (article, demonstrative, etc.).
***nen'nast** *V nennest, nentest, nenst* cf **nenne**
nen'ne *V nente/+-et* bear to, bring oneself to, have the heart to: **jeg n-er ikke å gjøre det** I don't have the heart to do it; **n-er du virkelig å si det?** can you bear to say it?
+nenn'/som' *A -t, pl -me* considerate, gentle: **med n- hånd** with a gentle touch.
+nenn'som/het *-en* care, consideration, gentleness.
***nen'st** *pp of* **nennast**
***nen'test** *pt of* **nennast**
neolit'tisk *A* - neolithic.
ne'on *-en* neon.
ne'on/lys *-et* neon light.
ne'on/rør *-et/*-a* neon tube.
ne'pe *-a* **1** *bot.* turnip (Brassica rapa). **2** *hum.* large or thick pocket watch.
***ne'pen** *A -e/-i, pl -ne* **1** brisk, quick. **2** delicate, sensitive: **med n- og nærtakande hug** with a delicate and sensitive mind (Skogstad).

+ Bokmål; * Nynorsk; ° Dialect.
After letter: ' stress (Acc. 1); ' tone, stress (Acc. 2); · length.
Below letter: . not pronounced.

nepotis'me *-n* nepotism.
***nep'pe**[1] *-t* bunch, bundle (e.g. of wool).
***nep'pe**[2] *V nepte* squeeze together: **n- hendene** fold one's hands.
+nep'pe[3] *Av* hardly, scarcely: **han slapp med nød og n-** he had a narrow escape; **det var med nød og n- at jeg bar ham** I had all I could do to carry him; **n- .... førenn** no sooner .... than.
Nep'tun *Prn (m)* Neptune.
°ne'r *Av* cf **ned**
°ne're *Av* cf **nede**
***ner'k** *-en* vital force, vitality.
ner'ts *-en* mink.
ner'ts/kåpe *-a* mink coat (for women).
ner've *-n* **1** *anat.* nerve: **ha sterke n-er** have strong n-s; **hun går meg på n-ene** she gets on my n-s. **2** *bot.* vein. **3** *fig.* feeling, spirit, temperament; **en fin n- for poesi** a feeling for poetry; **det er n- i hennes spill** there is temperament (style) in her playing. **4** line of communication; main thread.
ner've/feber *-en* typhoid.
ner've/krig *-en* war of nerves.
ner've/lege *-n* neurologist.
ner've/pirrende *A* - hair-raising, nerve-racking.
+ner've/sammenbrudd *-et* nervous breakdown.
ner've/sjokk *-et* nervous shock.
ner've/sjukdom *-men* neurosis.
ner've/sliten *A +-ent, pl -ne* neurotic.
ner've/slitende *A* - nerve-racking.
+ner've/svak *A* neurasthenic, neurotic.
ner've/syste'm *-et, pl -/+-er* nervous system.
nervø's *A* nervous: **ha et n-t temperament** have a n- temperament.
nervøsite't *-en* nervousness.
ne's *-et* headland, promontory.
Ne's *Pln* twp, Buskerud; twp, Sør-Trøndelag; twp, Hedmark.
ne's/bygding [also ne's/] *-en* inhabitant of Nes.
+ne'se *-a/-en* (=***nase**[1], ***nos**[1]) **1** nose: **få en lang n-** be disappointed; **ha bein i n-n** have backbone, courage; **peke n- av** thumb one's n- at; **sette n-n høyt (i været)** put on airs; **ta en ved n-n** hoodwink sby, pull the wool over sby's eyes. **2** sense of smell; *fig.* flair for: **ha en fin n- for** have a flair for, a nose for. **3** projecting part of sth (e.g. a mountain, ship, plane, etc.).
ne'se/bein *-et* nasal bone.
+ne'se/blod *-et* nosebleed: **han blør n-** his nose is bleeding.
+ne'se/bor *-et* nostril.
+ne'se/drypp *-et* nasal drip.
+ne'se/grev *-et* prominent nose (e.g. Roman nose); person with such a nose; nosey person.
+ne'se/grus *Av* prone, prostrate: **falle n-** fall flat on one's face; **kaste seg n- for** grovel before, kowtow to.
+ne'se/hule *-n* nasal cavity.
+ne'se/klemme *-a* **1** (pl) pince-nez. **2** barnacle (=instrument with two hinged branches for pinching the nose of an unruly horse).
+ne'se/lyd *-en* nasal (sound).
+ne'se/perle *-a/-en* nosedrip; *fig.* impertinent, impudent person.
+ne'se/ring *-en* nose ring.
+ne'se/rot *-a, pl -røtter* root of the nose.
+ne'se/rygg *-en* bridge of the nose.
+ne'se/styver *-en, pl -e* poke, punch in the nose: **få en n-** *fig.* be severely reprimanded; get a setback.
+ne'se/tipp *-en* tip of the nose; **han kan ikke se ut over sin egen n-** he can't see beyond his nose.
+ne'se/vinge *-n anat.* ala, wing of the nose (nostril).
+ne'se/vis *A* fresh, impertinent, impudent (**mot** towards).
+ne's/ho'rn *-et* (=***nas/**) *zool.* rhinoceros (family Rhinocerotidae).
ne's/konge *-n hist.* petty king (ruled over a limited amount of territory —often only a headland—along Norway's coast during the Viking period; generally a term of contempt).
nes'le *-a bot.* nettle (genus Urtica).
nes'le/feber *-en* nettle rash (Urticaria).
+nes'le/sommerfugl *-en zool.* (small) tortoiseshell butterfly (Vanessa urticae).
Nes'na *Pln* twp, Nordland.
Ne's/odden *Pln* twp, Akershus.
Nes'se/by *Pln* twp, Finnmark.
Nes'set *Pln* twp, Møre og Romsdal.
nes't[1] *+-et/*-en, pl +-/+-er* tack (=temporary stitch).
nes't[2] *A* - next; **n- best** second best; **n- eldst** n- oldest; **n- etter** immediately following; **n- nederste** second from the bottom; **n- sist** n- to the last; **den n-e igjen** the one after that; **på n-e side** on the following page; **(det) n-e år, (den) n-e dag, n-e morgen** the n- (following) year, day, the morning after; **den tredje i n-e måned** on the third of n- month.
nest[3] *P obs.* next after, next to.
nes'te[1] *-n bibl.* neighbor: **elsk din n-** love thy n-.
nes'te[2] *V -a/+-et/*-e* baste, tack (=secure by temporary stitching).
nes'te/kjærlig *A* - charitable, kindly.
+nes'te/kjærlighet *-en* benevolence, charity.
nes'te/mann *en* next in line; next man.
nes'ten *Av* almost, nearly: **n- aldri** hardly ever; **n- alltid** nearly always; **n- ikke** hardly; **n- ingen** hardly any, anybody; **få det n- gratis** get it for practically nothing.
nes't/formann *-en, pl -menn/*-menner* deputy chairman, vice-president.
+nes't/følgende *A* - following, next.
nes't/kommande'rende *en* second in command: **n- på vakten** *naut.* second officer of the deck.
nes'tor *-en* dean, senior member (from Nestor, oldest and wisest of the Greeks in the Trojan War).
***ne't** *A* cf **nett**[2]
***ne'ter** *pl of* **not**[2]
***net'je**[1] *-a* fatty membrane.
***net'je**[2] *V -a*: **n- seg** (of fish) be caught in a net or seine.
***net'le** *-a* cf **nesle**
nett'[1] *-et* net (netting; grid, network, system; *med.* amnion, caul): **gå i n-et** fall into a trap; **sette n-et opp** put up the net (tennis): **geodetisk n-** geodetic grid.
nett'[2] *A* - **1** nice, pretty; neat, tidy: **en n- liten formue** a t- little fortune; **det er en n- historie** *ironic* that's a pretty kettle of fish; **du er en n- en** *ironic* you're a fine fellow, you are. ***2** just: just now: **n- som du vil** just as you wish.
net'te[1] *V -a/+-et* net (e.g. a tennis ball).
net'te[2] *V -a/+-et*: **n- seg** make oneself neat, pretty up.
net'ter *pl of* **natt**
nett'/hendt *A* - deft, dexterous.
nett'/hinne *-a* retina.
net'ting [also net'-] *-en* (steel, wire) netting, screen.
nett'/mage *-n zool.* reticulum (of ruminating animals).
net'to[1] *-en* net: **n-beløp** n- amount; **n-fortjeneste** n- profit.
net'to[2] *Av* **1** net; **alle priser er n-** all prices are n-, no discount; **det innbrakte meg kr 100 n-** I cleared 100 *kroner*. **2** *pop.* naked; **barnet spaserte på stranden ganske n-** the child was walking around on the beach stark n-.
nett'/opp *Av* exactly, just, precisely; **n- nå** this very moment; **jeg så ham n- i dag** I just saw him today; **n- det jeg ventet** the very thing I expected; **det er n- saken** that is just the point; **n- som** just as; **jeg skulle n-...** I was just going to...
net'to/vekt *-a/+-en* net weight.
nett'/verk *-et* network.
neur- *Pf* (=**nevr-**) neuro-.
neuralgi' *-en* neuralgia.
neural'gisk *A* - neuralgic.
neurasteni' *-en* neurasthenia.
+neuraste'niker *-en, pl -e* (=***-ar**) neurasthenic.
neuraste'nisk *A* - neurasthenic.
neuritt'[1] *-en* neuritis.
neuritt'[2] *-en anat.* dendrite (of a nerve cell).
neurolog [-olå'g] *-en* neurologist.
neuro'se *-n* neurosis.
+neuro'tiker *-en, pl -e* (=***-ar**) neurotic.
neuro'tisk *A* - neurotic.
neu'tron *-en/-et* cf **nøytron**
***ne'vast** *V -ast* cf **neves**
ne've[1] *-n* fist, handful: **knytte n-ene** clench one's fists; **true en med n-n** shake one's fist at sby; **det sitter et par gode n-r på ham** he knows how to use his fists; **en n- jord** a handful of earth; **fra han var en n- stor** since he was a tiny boy (cf **nevestor**).
***ne've**[2] *V -a* grasp, seize.
ne've/helse *V -te/*-a*: **n-s** shake hands (**med** with).
ne've/nyttig *A* - adept, handy.
ne'ver *nevra, pl *-rar* birch bark.
ne've/rett *-en* jungle law, law of force.
ne'ver/kont [/kont] *-en* birch(bark) bag, basket: **gå med n-en** roam around without possessions or fixed purpose, be a rolling stone.
ne'ver/lur *-en* (shepherd's) horn (covered with birchbark).
ne'ver/skrukke [/skrokke] *-a* birchbark basket, pail (for fish, berries, etc.).
ne'ver/tak *-et* birchbark roof.
+ne'ves *V -edes, -es* (=***nevast**) shake hands (**med** with).
ne've/slag *-et* **1** blow of one's fist. **2** handclasp: **et siste n-** a final h-.
ne've/stor *A* big as a fist, fist-sized (=knee-high to a grasshopper).
+ne've/takes *V -tok(e)s* (=***/takast**) shake hands (**med** with).
ne'v/gilde *-t hist.* head tax, poll tax (capitation).
nev'nd *-en* cf **nemnd**
+nev'ne *V -te* (=***nemne**[2]) mention, name: **for ikke å n-** not to mention; **n- ved navn** mention by name; **n- en ting ved dens rette navn** call a spade a spade; **som allerede n-t** as mentioned before; **særlig kan n-s** special mention may be made of.
+nev'nelse *-n*: **med navns n-** by name.
+nev'ner *-en, pl -e* (=***nemnar**) denominator.
+nev'ne/verdig *A* - worth mentioning: **ikke i n- grad** not to any appreciable extent.
nevr- *Pf* cf **neur-**
nev'ra *df of* **never**
nevø' *-en* nephew.
n. f. =**nord for**
N. F. D. S. =**Nordenfjeldske Dampskibsselskab**
NGO =**Norges Geografiske Oppmåling**
Ng. tf. =**noenlunde tilfredsstillende**
NHH =**Norges handelshøgskole**
Nhl. =**Nordhordland**
ni' *Num* nine: **alle n-** all n-; **i n- av ti tilfeller** n- times out of ten.
+ni'- *Pf* cf **nid-**
***ni'/auge** *-a* cf **/øye**
***nib'be** *-a* sharp point or corner, esp. on stones or mountains.
ni'd *-et* **1** insult, libel. **2** envy, malice.
ni'd- *Pf* (=**+ni-**) intensively.
Ni'daros *Pln* **1** diocese, incl. Nord- og Sør-Trøndelag, Nordmøre, Romsdal. **2** *hist.* old name of city of Trondheim.
ni'/del *-en* ninth (part).
ni'd/glane *V -a/-te* stare intently (**på** at).
ni'd/glo *V -dde* stare intently (**på at**).
ni'd/hauke *V -a/+-et* call, shout loudly.
nid'ing *-en* coward, dastard.
nid'ings/verk *-et* dastardly deed, piece of villainy.

+ni'd/kjær *A* 1 zealous. 2 *bibl.* (of God) jealous (Exodus 34, 14).
+ni'dkjær/het *-en* 1 fervor, zeal. 2 *bibl.* jealousy (Deut. 32, 16).
+ni'/dobbelt *A* - (=*/dobbel) ninefold.
nids'k *A* - 1 envious, spiteful. 2 niggardly.
ni'd/skrift *-et* lampoon, libel.
+ni'd/stang *-a, pl -stenger* (=*/stong) *hist.* in Old Norse times a pole surmounted by some insulting figure, placed so as to face the dwelling or country of one's enemy for the purpose of both scorning him and injuring him through sympathetic magic.
+ni'd/stirre *V -a/-et* (=*-stire) stare hard (**på** at).
ni'd/vers *-et* (verse) lampoon.
ni'd/vise *-a/+-en* libellous ditty, song.
ni'ende *Num* ninth: **det n- og tiende bud** the tenth commandment (in American Protestant catechismus).
ni'ende/del *-en* cf **ni/**
+ni'er *-en, pl -e* (=*-ar) number nine; ninespot (in cards).
nie'se *-a/+-en* niece.
nif's *A* creepy, dreadful, frightening.
***ni'gje** *V -de* cf **neie**[1]
+ni'/glane *V -a/-te* cf **nid/**
+ni'/glo *V -dde* cf **nid/**
+ni'/halet *A* -; **n- katt** *naut.* cat-o'-nine-tails.
+ni'/hauke *V -a/-et* cf **nid/**
nihilis'me *-n* nihilism.
nihilis't *-en* nihilist.
nihilis'tisk *A* - nihilistic.
nikk'[1] *-en/-et* nod; **være på n- med** have a nodding acquaintance with.
+nikk'[2] *-et* trick.
nik'ke *V -a/+-et* 1 nod (**til** to): **n- bifallende** n- approval; **n- god morgen** n- good morning. 2 head (a ball, e.g. in soccer).
nik'ke/dokke *-a* 1 mechanical doll. 2 *fig.* yes-man.
nik'kel *-en* nickel.
nik'kers *-en* knickers.
Nikola'i *Prn(m)* Nicholas.
nikoti'n *-en* nicotine.
+nikoti'n/forgif'tning *-en* (=*/forgifting) nicotine poisoning, nicotinism.
nikoti'n/fri *A -tt* denicotinized.
nikoti'n/slave *-n* nicotine addict; heavy smoker.
nik's *N*: **null og n-** not a thing; **på null komma n- tid** in no time at all.
ni'/lese *+-te/*-las* read assiduously.
Nil's *Prn(m)*
nil's/mess(e) *en* St. Nicholas's Day (Dec. 6th).
nim'bus *-en* halo, nimbus.
nim'rod *-en* Nimrod; great hunter.
ni'p *-en* cf **nipe**
ni'pe *-a* (=+nip) mountaintop with extremely steep flanks.
nipp'[1] *-en/-et*: **være på n-et** be on the point, verge (of): **han var på n-et til å drukne** he was very close to drowning.
+nipp'[2] *-et* sip.
nip'pe *V -a/+-et* sip, taste (**til** of): **n- til vinen** sip the wine.
nip'pel *-elen, pl nipler tech.* nipple.
+nipp'/flo *-a* (=*/flod) neap tide.
nip's *+-en/*-et* knickknack, trinket.
nip's/figu'r *-en* knickknack, piece of bric-a-brac.
+nip's/gjenstand *-en* knickknack, ornament, piece of bric-a-brac.
nip's/saker *pl* knickknacks, trinkets.
nirva'na *-en/-et* nirvana.
ni'se *-a zool.* porpoise (Phocaena communis).
nisj'e *-n* niche, recess.
***nis'k** *A* cf **nidsk**
nis'se *-n* pixie, puck (usu. thought of as short, gray-clad, with red stocking cap): **en gammel n-** an old fogey.
Nis'se/dal *Pln* twp, Telemark.
nis'se/lu(v)e *-a* red stocking cap (trad. assoc. with the *nisse*).
nis'te[1] *-a* lunch (basket, box), provisions (for the road).
nis'te[2] *V -a/+-et*: **n- ut** provision, supply with food.
+ni'te *-n* blank (in a lottery).
niti'd *A* - (of a piece of work) dainty, elegant, neat.
nitra't *-et, pl -/+-er* nitrate.
nitre're *V -te* treat with nitric acid.
nitroge'n *-et* nitrogen.
nitroglyseri'n *-en/+-et* nitroglycerin.
nit'te *V -a/+-et* rivet (bolts); clinch (nails); butt (two plates together).
Nit'te/dal *Pln* twp, Akershus.
nit'ten *Num* nineteen.
nit'tende *Num* nineteenth.
nit'tende/del *-en* cf **nitten/**
nit'ten/del *-en* nineteenth (part).
nit'ti *Num* ninety.
nit'ti/del *-en* ninetieth (part).
nit'tiende *Num* ninetieth.
nitt'/nagle *-n* rivet.
nivelle're *V -te* level (e.g. in surveying); level out (a road, class distinctions, etc.).
+nivelle'r/kikkert *-en* surveyor's level.
nivå' *-et, pl -/+-er* level, plane, standard: **ned til havets n-** down to sea level; **et høyt moralsk n-** a high moral plane; **senke n-et** lower the standard.
+ni'/øye *-n zool.* lamprey (Petromyzon marinus).
nja' *I*: **n-, jeg skulle hjem i grunnen** well, you know I should really go home.
***njo'de** *V nyd, naud, node/-i* cf **neie**[2]
Njor'd *Prn myth.* god of prosperity, father of Frey and Freya.
***njo's** *-a* (=*njosn): **få n- av** get wind of.
***njo'sne** *V -a* be on the lookout for, reconnoitre, scout.
***njo'sning** *-a* reconnaissance.
NKL=**Norges Kooperative Landsforening**
NKN=**Norske Kvinners Nasjonalråd**
NKP=**Norges Kommunistiske Parti**
n. l.=**nordlig lengde; norske lov**
NLH=**Norges landbrukshøgskole**
NM=**norgesmesterskap(et)**
N. N.=**nomen nescio: hr. N. N.** John Doe.
NN fange [enn'enn'-] *-n* prisoner in windowless cell (of a concentration camp), from German Nacht und Nebel.
+NNO=**nordnordost**
+no'[1] *Av* cf **nå**[2]
°no[2] *nt of* **noen**
+NO=**nordost**
no.=**nummer**
no'a/o'rd *-et anthro.* noa word (word substituted for a taboo word).
no'bel [also nå'-] *A -elt, pl -le* noble (=highminded, generous; distinguished-looking).
nobel'/pris *-en* Nobel prize.
nobilite't *-en* nobility, esp. *hist.* old Roman nobility.
noblesse [nåbles'se] *+-n/*-a* nobility; upper classes, upper crust.
***no'de**[1] *-t* ball (of thread, yarn, etc.).
***no'de**[2] *pp of* **njode** (=*nodi)
+no'en *noe, pl noen* (=*nokon) 1 some; somebody, someone; something: **atten hundre og noe** 1800 and something; **det kommer noen** somebody (someone) is coming; **han har kjøpt noen bøker** he has bought some books; **ja, du sier noe** there's something in that, you said it; **noe av det verste** about the worst, some of the worst, the worst of it; **noe av en kunstner** something of an artist; **noe bedre** something better; **det er noe i det** there's something to it (that); **noe slikt** something like that; **vil du ha noe erter?** do you want some (of these) peas? 2 (in comp., neg., and interrog. sentences) any; anybody, anyone; anything: **er det noen der?** is there anyone there?; **han er høyere enn noen jeg kjenner** he is taller than anyone I know; **har noe hendt?** has anything happened?; **ikke noen** not any (one); **han er ikke noen taler** he isn't any speaker; **ikke noe** no, not any (thing); **det er ikke noe hus i nærheten** there is no house nearby; **det gjør ikke noe** it doesn't make any difference; **jeg har aldri sett noe slikt** I've never seen anything like that. 3 *(adv.)* somewhat; *(neg.)* any: **ikke noe bedre** not any better; **noe bedre** somewhat better. 4 (other idioms and phrases): **for noen mennesker!** what (awful) people!; **for noe tull!** what nonsense!; **hva for noe, noen** what, which; **noen gang** any time, ever; **har du noen gang sett henne?** have you ever seen her?; **noen hver** one and all; **noen (noe) og (av) hver (hvert)** both the one and the other, one thing and another; a little of everything; **på noen måte** in any way, possibly; **noe nær** almost, nearly; **noe så nær** approximately, just about; **noe, noen som helst** any whatever; anyone, anything whatever; **han tok ikke med seg noe som helst** he didn't take along anything whatever (at all); **det var noe til kar** he's quite a guy, he's some fellow, what a (fine) fellow he is.
+no'en/gang *Av* cf **noen**
+no'en/lunde *Av* passably, tolerably; approximately, more or less: **etter at n- ro var falt over forsamlingen** after the gathering had more or less quieted down; **ha det n-** not feel too bad; **n- presentabel** fairly presentable; **n- tilfredsstillende** fair (grade in *gymnasium*).
+no'en/sinne *Av* at any time, ever.
+no'en/slags *A noe-, pl noen-* some kind of: **han hadde vært n- reisende** he had been some kind of traveling salesman (Sandel).
+no'ensomhel'st *Pn* cf **noen**
+no'en/steds *Av* anywhere; somewhere.
+no'e/nær *Av* cf **noen**
+no'gen [also: nå'gen] *pn noget, pl nogen* cf **noen**
***nogg'** *pt of* **nyggje**
***nog'ge** *pp of* **nyggje** (=*noggi)
***no'g/grann** *A -grant* accurate, exact, punctual.
nok' *Av* 1 enough (**av** of; **til** for): **bare det beste er godt n-** only the best is good e-; **det er n- av dem som** there are e- of those who; **det er n- til meg** it's e- for me; **har du fått n-?** have you had e-?; **n- av (om) det** e- (said) of that; **ikke n- med det** not only that, that isn't all; **n- sagt** e- of that; e- said; **stor n-** large e-. 2 (unstressed, immediately following the verb) all right, probably, to be sure: **det blir n- regn** it will most probably rain; **det kan n- være** that may be so; **han kommer n- i morgen** he'll come tomorrow all right.
***no'ka** *Pn f of* **nokon**
nok'ke *-n* (=+nokk) 1 *naut.* yardarm: **babords n-** port yardarm. 2 peak.
***no'ko** *Pn nt of* **nokon**
***no'ko/leis** *Av* somehow.
***no'ko/lunde** *Av* cf **noen/**
***no'kon** *Pn f noka, nt noko, pl -/-re* cf **noen**
***no'kon/gong** *Av* cf **noen**
***no'kon/stad** *Av* cf **noen/steds**
***no'ko/sinne** *Av* cf **noen/**
***nokre** [nok're] *Pn pl of* **nokon**
nok'/sagt *-en* 1 enough said: **n-, de reiste** to make a long story short, they left. 2 *pop.* blankety-blank: **han er en n-** he's a so-and-so, a you-know-what.
+nok'/som' *Av* enough, sufficiently: **n- bekjent** famous, well-known; **jeg kan ikke n- takke Dem** I can't thank you enough.

+ Bokmål; * Nynorsk; ° Dialect.
After letter: ' stress (Acc. 1); ` tone, stress (Acc. 2); · length.
Below letter: . not pronounced.

nok'/så *Av* fairly, rather, tolerably: **hun er n- søt** she is rather charming, nice.
noktur'ne *-n mus.* nocturne.
no'lo *-en* nullo (in whist, etc.).
no'lo/kort *pl* nullo cards.
noma'de *-n* nomad.
nomadise'rende *A* - nomadic.
noma'disk *A* - nomadic.
***no'me** *pp of* **neme**
***no'men** *A -e/-i, pl -ne* cf **nommen**
nomenklatu'r *-en/-et* nomenclature.
***no'men/skap** *-en* lameness, palsy.
***no'mi** *pp of* **neme**
nominasjo'n *-en* nomination.
nominativ [nom'-] *-en* nominative: **i n-** in the nominative case.
nominell' *A -ell* nominal; **kursene er n-e** the rates are n-.
nomine're *V -te* nominate.
nommen [nom'men] *A -ent, pl nomne* (=***nomen**) numb; paralyzed.
nomne [nom'ne] *pl of* **nom(m)en**
no'n[1] *-et* hour of the afternoon meal (in some rural areas), around three o'clock.
non'[2] *-en/-et* (abbrev. of Latin non contemnendus) poor (=lowest grade with which one can pass a university examination).
nonchalanse [nångsjalang'se] *-n* nonchalance.
nonchalant [nångsjalang't] *A* - nonchalant.
nonfigurativ [nånn/fig'urativ] *A* abstract, non-figurative: **n- kunst** abstract art.
non'ne *-a/+-en* **1** nun: **bli n-** take the veil. **2** *zool.* nun moth (Lymantria monacha).
non'ne/kloster *-ret, pl -er/+-re* convent, nunnery.
non'sens *-et* nonsense.
no'ns/leite *-t* time around three in the afternoon.
no'ns/tid *-a/+-en* time around three in the afternoon.
no'r *-et* **1** cove. **2** mite (infant, small child).
no'rd *Av* (also N) north, northerly: **n- for** n- of; **det høye n-** the far north; **rett n-** due north; **dra n- og ned** go to hell; **i n-** in the north; **mot n-** to the n- (cf **Norden**).
nord. =**nordisk**
***no'rda** *Av* from the north, northerly.
no'rda/drag *-et* northerly breeze, wind.
no'rda/fjells *Av* Norway north of Dovre: **jeg er en nykomling her n-** I am a newcomer here north of Dovre.
no'rda/fjelsk *A* - characteristic of the land and people north of Dovre.
no'rda/for' *P* northward, to the north of: **n- fjellene** north of the mountains.
No'rd-Ame'rika *Pln* North America.
+**no'rd/amerika'ner** *-en, pl -e* (=*-**ar**) North American.
no'rd/amerika'nsk *A* - North American.
***no'rdan/etter** *P* from the north.
***no'rdan/om'** *P* cf **norden/**
***no'rdan/til'** *Av* cf **norda/**
no'rda/sno *-en* biting wind from the north.
no'rda/til'** *Av* (=nordan/**) from (in) the north: **vinden har vendt seg n-** the wind has veered round to the north.
no'rd/atlan'tisk *A* - North Atlantic.
No'rd-Aurdal *Pln* twp, Oppland.
nordau'st *Av* (=+**nordøst**) northeast.
no'rda/vind *-en* north wind, northerly wind.
+**no'rda/vær** *-et* (=*/**ver**) norther.
no'rd/bu *-en* (=+/**bo**, */**bue**) Scandinavian.
No'rd/dal *Pln* twp, Møre og Romsdal.
Norden [nor'den] *Pln* Scandinavia (incl. Denmark, Finland, Iceland, Norway, Sweden); (also) Norden, the North, the Nordic countries.
+**no'rden-** *Pf* cf **norda-**
+**no'rden/for'** *P* cf **norda/**
+**no'rden/fra** *P* cf **nord/frå**
+**no'rden/om'** *P* (=*-**an/**) northward of, round the north of: **n- Skottland** round the north of Scotland.
+**no'rden/vind** *-en* cf **norda/**
Norder/hov [nor'der/håv] *Pln* twp, Buskerud.
***norder/landsk** [nor'der/] *A* - (=*/**lendsk**) Nordic, Northern, Scandinavian.
no'rd/etter *Av* in a northerly direction.
no'rd/fjo'rding *-en* **1** native of Nordfjord. **2** horse of the Nordfjord breed.
No'rd/fold *Pln* twp, Nordland.
+**no'rd/fra** *P* from the north: **vinden er n-** the wind is northerly.
No'rd-Fron *Pln* twp, Oppland.
No'rd-Frøya *Pln* twp, Sør-Trøndelag.
no'rd/frå *P* (=+/**fra**) from the north.
no'rd/gående *A* - northbound (e.g. express, ship); northerly (e.g. current).
no'rd/hav *-et* northern sea.
no'rd/himmel *-en* northern sky.
No'rd/hordland *Pln* northern section of Hordaland county (north of Bergen).
no'rd/i *P* in the north, northward: **n- dalen** in the northern part of the valley.
no'rd/igjen'nom *P* northward through: **de reiste n- skogen** they traveled northward through the forest.
No'rdis/havet *Pln* the Arctic Ocean.
nordisk [nor'disk] *A* - Scandinavian (usu. including Denmark, Finland, Iceland, Norway, Sweden); (more loosely) Nordic, Norse, Northern: **de n-e riker** the Northern kingdoms; **de n-e språk** the Scandinavian languages; **den n-e type** the Nordic type; **n- mytologi** Norse mythology.
No'rd/kapp *Pln* North Cape.
No'rd/kyn *Pln* twp, Finnmark (=Kinnarodden, the northernmost point on the mainland of Norway).
no'rd/kyst *-en* northern coast.
nordl. =**nordlig**
Nordl. =**Nordland**
No'rd/land *Pln* county, north of Trøndelag; (also, loosely) North Norway in general.
no'rdlands/jekt *-a* sloop designed primarily to sail in coastal waters; type of boat used in Nordland.
no'rd/landsk *A* - characteristic of Nordland.
no'rd/lending *-en* native of Nordland.
No'rd/li *Pln* twp, Nord-Trøndelag.
no'rdlig *A* - northerly, northern: **på n-e breddegrader** in northern latitudes; **vinden er n-** the wind is northerly.
no'rd/lys *-et* (=*/**ljos**, */**lyse**) northern lights (aurora borealis).
no'rd/mann [also norr'/] *-en, pl -menn/*-menner* Norwegian.
No'rd/marka *Pln* the wooded hill district of Oslo (north of the populated section), used as a recreational area.
+**No'rd-Norge** *Pln* (=*-**Noreg**) Norway north of Trøndelag.
No'rd-Odal *Pln* twp, Hedmark.
no'rd/om' *P* northward of, to the north of.
+**nordo'st** *-en* northeast.
+**nordo'st/kuling** *-en* northeasterly gale.
no'rd/over [/åver] *P* north, northward.
no'rd/pol *-en* north pole.
No'rd/polen *Pln* the North Pole.
+**no'rdpols/farer** *-en, pl -e* (=*-**ar**) arctic explorer.
no'rd/på *P* (=**nord på**) to the north, up north.
No'rd-Rana *Pln* twp, Nordland.
nordre [nor'dre] *A* - (=***nørdre**) northern.
No'rd/reisa *Pln* twp, Troms.
Nordre Lan'd [nor'dre] *Pln* twp, Oppland.
+**no'rd/rinnende** *A* - (of water) flowing, running northward.
***no'rd/røn** *A* (of wind) northerly.
No'rd/sjøen *Pln* the North Sea.
no'rd/stjerne *-a/+-en* North Star (Polaris).
No'rd/strand *Pln* southernmost administrative unit in Oslo.
No'rd-Trøndela'g *Pln* county encompassing townships on both sides of central and upper Trondheim Fjord.
No'rd-Varang'er *Pln* twp, Finnmark.
+**no'rd/vendt** *A* - (=*/**vend**) facing north, with a northerly view.
nordves't *Av* northwest: **n- til nord** northwest by north; **n- for** northwest of.
nordves'tlig *A* - northwesterly.
No'rd/vik *Pln* twp, Nordland.
No'rd-Vågsøy *Pln* twp, Sogn og Fjordane.
+**nordøs't** *Av* cf **-aust**
No're *Pln* twp, Buskerud.
***Noreg** [nå'reg] *Pln* cf **Norge**
+**Nor'ge** *Pln* (=***Noreg**) Norway.
+**nor'ges/mesterska'p** *-et* national championship (of Norway).
+**nor'ges/salpe'ter** *-en* Norwegian saltpeter.
No'rheim/sund *Pln* twp, Hordaland.
nor'm *+-en/*-a* norm, standard.
norma'l[1] *-en* norm, standard: **over n-en** above normal; **under n-en** subnormal (person), substandard (quality).
norma'l[2] *-en math.* perpendicular line or plane, esp. one perpendicular to a tangent line of a curve at the point of contact.
norma'l[3] *A* normal (regular; average, mean; sane): **vi får ikke n-e forhold igjen** normal conditions will never return again; **over det n-e** above average.
normalise're *V -te* normalize; standardize (e.g. text of a manuscript); correct the spelling (according to the latest norm).
norma'l/plan[1] *-et math.* perpendicular plane, esp. one perpendicular to a tangent line of a curve at the point of contact.
norma'l/plan[2] *-en educ.* curriculum plan (in grade schools).
norma'l/spor *-et* standard gauge (railroad track).
norma'l/tid *-a* standard time.
Normandie [normandi'] *Pln* Normandy.
+**norman'ner** *-en, pl -e* (=***normann**) Norman.
norman'nisk *A* - Norman.
nor'mativ *A* normative.
norme're *V -te* establish, prescribe, regulate.
nor'n *en* Norn (West Norwegian dialect formerly spoken in the Hebrides, Shetland, and Orkneys).
nor'ne *-a/+-en* **1** *myth.* Norn (one of the goddesses of fate, usu. represented as three in number). **2** *bot.* lady's slipper (Calypso bulbosa).
norrøn [nor'røn] *A hist.* Norwegian (including Icelandic, Faroese, the Norse settlements in Ireland, etc.) during the Viking period.
+**norrøna/folk** [nor'røna/] *-et poet.* Norwegians (esp. in the Old Norse period).
No'r/sjø *Pln* twp, Telemark.
nor'sk *A* - Norwegian: **jeg sa ham min mening på godt n-** I told him what I thought in good N- (i.e., in no uncertain terms).
+**nor'sk/amerika'ner** *-en, pl -e* (=*-**ar**) Norwegian-American.
nor'sk/dansk[1] *-en* Norwego-Danish (language).
nor'sk/dansk[2] *A* - Norwego-Danish.
nor'sk/dom' *-men/*-en* Norwegianness: **den kommunistiske ungdommen i Norge mangler n-** the communist youth in Norway lacks patriotic feeling (Tidens Tegn 1922);

n-men i Amerika Norway in America.

Nor'ske/havet *Pln* the Norwegian Sea (the North Atlantic between Norway and Greenland).

nor'ske/kysten *df* the Norwegian coast.

+**nor'sk/født** *A* - (=*/**fødd**) Norwegian born.

+**nor'sk/het** *-en* 1 Norwegianness: **han arbeidet for n- i skrift og tale** he worked for the promotion of Norwegian characteristics in writing and speech. 2 Norwegianism: **n-er i språket hos Holberg** Norwegianisms in Holberg's language.

nor'sk/norsk *A* - ultra-Norwegian.

norvagise'rende *A* - Norwegianizing.

norvagis'me *-n* Norwegianism.

***nos**[1] [nå's] *-a, pl naser* cf **nese**

no's[2] *-a* precipitous mountain peak.

nose** [nå'se] *pp of* **nyse** (=nosi**)

noss' *-et* mite, very small child.

no't[1] *-a, pl nøter* seine, trawl net.

***not**[2] [nå't] *-a, pl neter* cf **nøtt**

no't[3] *-a* groove made in the edge of a plank.

no'ta *-en, pl* *-er note; bill, invoice; memorandum: **ta seg ad notam** note, take note of.

nota'bel *A -elt, pl -le* distinguished, notable, noteworthy.

notabe'ne[1] *-t, pl +-r/*-* nota bene, NB

+**notabe'ne**[2] *Av* mark you, (please) note.

notabilite't *-en* notability; notable person, VIP.

nota'r *-en* notary.

nota'rius pub'licus *en* notary public: **få et dokument attestert hos n-** have a document notarized.

nota't *-et, pl -/+-er* note: **gjøre n-er** take n-s.

no't/bas *-en* foreman of a seine gang, master seiner.

no't/bruk *-et* 1 seines. 2 seine gang.

no't/båt *-en* seine boat or barge.

no'te[1] *-n* note (annotation; diplomatic; bank; musical): **forsyne med n-r** annotate; **100 pund i gull og n-r** 100 pounds in gold and notes; **n-r som skal besvares** (diplomatic) notes that must be answered; **n- under teksten** footnote; **spille etter n-r** play by note; **være med på n-ene** go along, play along.

***note**[2] [nå'te] *pp of* **nyte**

***no'te/bas** *-en* cf **not/**

no'te/blad *-et* sheet of music.

no'te/papi'r *-et mus.* music paper.

note're *V -te* 1 note, take (**ned** down); enter, record: **n- seg noe** make a note of sth; **bli n-t** be reported, given a citation by a policeman. 2 *merc.* quote (prices): **n- kursen på** quote the rate of exchange for. 3 *merc.* debit, put down: **De kan n- meg for ti kroner** you can put me down for 10 *kroner*. 4 mention, point out.

note'ring *-a/+-en* 1 noting, recording, (policeman's) report. 2 *merc.* (market) quotation: **særlig billig n-** special price.

no'te/stati'v *-et, pl -/+-er* music rack, music stand.

no'te/stol *-en* (folding) music stand.

no't/fiske *-t* seining.

no't/hund *-en* hired member of a seine gang.

no't/høvel *-elen, pl -ler* beading plane.

***noti** [nå'ti] *pp of* **nyte**

***no'/tid** *-a* cf **nå/**

***no'/tidig** *A* - cf **nå/**

notifikasjo'n *-en dipl., jur.* notification.

notifise're *V -te dipl., jur.* notify.

noti's *-en* 1 note, notice: **ikke ta n- av** pay no attention to. 2 short article, story (in newspaper).

noti's/blokk *-en* scratch pad.

noti's/bok *-a, pl -bøker* notebook.

no't/kast *-et* cast of a seine, trawlnet.

no't/lag *-et* fishing group, seine gang.

No't/odden *Pln* town, Telemark.

noto'risk *A* - notorious.

no't/steng *-et* enclosure of fish in a seine, trawlnet; fish so caught.

nov [nå'v] *-a* 1 notched (and dovetailed) corner of a log house. 2 exterior corner of a house.

nov. =**november**

novasjo'n *-en* 1 *jur.* novation. 2 innovation (e.g. in language).

***nove** [nå've] *pp of* **nuve**

novelet'te *-a/+-en* cf **novellette**

novel'le *-a/+-en* short story, tale.

novellet'te *-a/+-en* short story (shorter than a **novelle**).

novellis't *-en* short story writer.

novellis'tisk *A* - having characteristics of a short story (esp. lively, exciting): **n- teknikk** short story technique.

novem'ber *en* November.

novem'ber/storm *-en* November storm.

***no'/verande** *A* - cf **nå/værende**

***novi** [nå'vi] *pp of* **nuve**

novi'se *-a/+-en* neophyte, novice.

nr. =**nummer**

NRK=**Norsk rikskringkasting**

NS=**Nasjonal Samling**

NSB=**Norges statsbaner**

NT=**Det nye testamentet**

NTB=**Norsk telegrambyrå**

ntf.=**Noenlunde tilfredsstillende**

NTH=**Norges tekniske høgskole**

nto=**netto**[1,2]

nty.=**nedertysk**

nu'[1] *-en* trough.

+**nu'**[2] *-et* present moment: **i ett n-** in a jiffy, trice; **i samme n-** at that very instant, just then; **leve i n-et** live for the moment.

+**nu'**[3] *Av* cf **nå**[2]

nubb' *-en* brad, tack.

+**nub'be**[1] *-n* shot (of liquor).

nub'be[2] *V -a/+-et* tack.

nub'be[3] *V -a/+-et* down liquor by the shot glass.

+**nu'bier** *-en, pl -e* (=***-ar**) Nubian.

nu'bisk *A* - Nubian.

nudd' *-en* brad, tack (shoemaking).

nud'de *V -a/+-et* peg (shoes).

nu'del *-elen, pl -ler* noodle.

nudis'me *-n* nudism.

nudis't *-en* nudist.

nudis'tisk *A* - nudist.

nuf'se *V -a/+-et* nudge, poke.

nugg'[1] *-en* cold gust, draft.

nugg'[2] *-et* friction, rubbing; chafe mark.

nug'ge *V -a/+-et/+nugde* 1 rub, scrape. 2 nudge, shove.

null'[1] *-en/-et* 1 cipher, zero; zero point (on a scale): **termometret står på n-** the thermometer reads zero. 2 *fig.* nonentity.

null'[2] *Num* 1 zero: **n- grader** z- degrees (on thermometer). 2 nothing (=**ingenting**): **n- og niks** not a thing.

nullan't *-en* taxpayer who pays no income tax (due to deductions exceeding gross earnings).

nullite't *-en* invalidity, nullity; nobody (ref. to a person).

null'/meridia'n *-en* prime meridian.

null'/punkt [/pongt] *-et* zero (e.g. on a thermometer); *tech.* datum point: **hans mot stod nær n-et** his courage was just about gone.

+**null'/skattyter** *-en, pl -e* (=***-ar**) taxpayer who pays no income tax (due to deductions exceeding gross earnings).

num.=**numerus, numerisk**

Nu'me/dal *Pln* large valley of Eastern Norway.

nu'me/døl *-en* native of Numedal.

nume'risk *A* - numerical: **de var motstanderne n- underlegne** they were outnumbered by their opponents.

nu'merus *-en math.* number.

+**num'men** *A -ent, pl numne* cf **nommen**

nummer [nom'mer] *-eret, pl -er/+numre* 1 number; item: **bli n- én** come in first (in a competition). 2 size: **jeg bruker n- 43 i sko** I wear a size ten shoe. 3 issue (of a magazine, newspaper). 4: **gjøre (et) stort n- av** *fig.* make much of.

nummerere [nommere're] *V -te* number: **n- fortløpende** number consecutively; **n-te plasser** reserved seats.

nummer/orden [nom'mer/] *-en* numerical order.

nummer/skilt *-et* 1 key tag. 2 license plate. 3 number (on horse, etc.).

***numre** [nom're] *V -a* cf **nummerere**

nu'natak [-takk] *-en geog.* nunatak (in arctic regions, a mountain completely surrounded by glacial ice).

nuntius [nun'tsius] *-en* nuncio.

nuperel'ler *pl* tatting.

nupp'[1] *-en* 1 nob (tiny skin protuberance). 2 nubbin (e.g. of a gooseberry).

nupp'[2] *-et* jerk, pull, tug.

nup'pe *V -a/+-et* pluck, pull, snatch.

nup'pet(e) *A* - nubbly, rough.

nur'k *-en/+-et* 1 manikin (=small, stunted person); small child. 2 deficiency, lack: **treet er i n-en** the tree is stunted; **være i n-en for penger** *fam.* be in financial straits.

nur'ket(e) *A* - stunted.

°**nur'v** *-en* manikin.

nus'le *V -a/+-et* 1 (e.g. of cattle) rummage around looking for fodder. 2 putter around.

***nuss'**[1] *-en* scent.

+**nuss'**[2] *-et* baby, small child (used as term of endearment).

nus'se *V -a/+-et* 1 scent, sniff. 2 putter around.

nus'set(e) *A* - childish, infantile.

nu't *-en* mountain peak: ***dei gode gamle n-ane** the good old m- p-s (Aasen).

+**nu'/tid** *-en* cf **nå/**

+**nu'/tidig** *A* - cf **nå/**

+**nu'/tildags** *Av* cf **nå/**

nu'tria *-en* nutria (fur of the coypu).

nu'v[1] *-en* round hill.

***nu'v**[2] *A* blunt; (of persons) dull, surly.

***nu've** *V nyv, nauv, nove/-i* round off.

***nu'veleg** *A* - blunt; (of persons) dull, surly.

+**nu'/værende** *A* - cf **nå/**

NV=**nordvest**

ny'[1] *-et* new moon; waxing moon: **i ny og ne** off and on, once in a while.

ny'[2] *A -tt* 1 new, novel; modern, recent: **av ny dato** recent; **i den nyere tid** in recent times; **intet nytt under solen** nothing new under the sun; **nye poteter** early potatoes; **nytt av året** new this year; **på ny, nytt** anew; **spørre nytt (om)** get news (of). 2 other, second: **han er en ny Ibsen** he's a s- I-; **ta fram en ny flaske** get out another bottle.

-ny *Prn(f)* e.g. Dagny, Signy.

+**ny'/ankommen** *A -et, pl -komne* newly, recently arrived; newcomer.

nyanse [nyang'se] *-n* nuance, shade.

nyansere [nyangse're] *V -te* shade (off), vary; make delicate distinctions.

nyansert [nyangse'rt] *A* - nuanced, shaded.

+**ny'/anskaffelse** *-n* recent acquisition.

ny'/bakt *A* - (=*/**baka**) freshly baked; *fig.* newfangled (e.g. ideas), (of persons) newly fledged: **n- kandidat** young man just out of college.

ny'/barbe'rt *A* - freshly shaved.

+**ny'/begyn'ner** *-en, pl -e* beginner, novice; *derog.* greenhorn.

Ny'berg/sund *Pln* post office, Hedmark.

+**ny'/brent** *A* - (=*/**brend**) recently burnt: **n- kaffe** freshly roasted coffee.

+ Bokmål; * Nynorsk; ° Dialect. After letter: ' stress (Acc. 1); ' tone, stress (Acc. 2); · length. Below letter: . not pronounced.

ny'/brott -*et* (=**/brot**) newly cleared ground; new farm; *fig.* pathfinding, pioneering.

ny'brotts/mann -*en, pl -menn/*-menner* backwoodsman (one who clears ground for cultivation); *fig.* pathfinder, pioneer.

ny'brotts/verk -*et* act of clearing ground; *fig.* act of extending frontiers (in the realm of ideas), pioneering.

ny'/bygd[1] -*a* colony, settlement.

ny'/bygd[2] *A* -/*-*bygt* recently built.

ny'/bygg -*et* house, etc. in the process of construction or recently completed.

+ny'/bygger -*en, pl -e* colonist, pioneer, settler.

+ny'/bygning -*en* new construction; reconstruction.

ny'/bær *A*: **n- ku** cow that has recently calved.

***ny'd** *pr of* **njode**

ny'/danne *V* -*a*/+-*et* create, coin (a word); reconstruct.

+ny'/dannelse -*n* new formation, neologism; regeneration: **språklige n-r** linguistic innovations.

+ny'delig *A* - (very) attractive, delightful; (of person, esp. women) charming; (of food) delicious; (of objects) beautiful; **en n- pike** a very pretty girl; **en n- utsikt** an exquisite view; **du er en n- en** *ironic* you're a fine one, you are; **en n- historie** a real mess, a pretty kettle of fish.

+ny'delse -*n* cf **nytelse**

ny'/dyrke *V* -*a*/+-*et* bring under cultivation.

***ny'e** *V* -*a*: **n- oppatt** renew, renovate.

ny'/emisjo'n -*en merc.* new issue (e.g. of stock).

+ny'/erver'velse -*n* recent acquisition.

ny'/fallen *A* +-*ent, pl -falne* newly fallen: **hvit som n- snø** white as the n- f- (driven) snow.

ny'/fiken *A* +-*ent, pl -ne* curious, inquisitive.

+ny'fiken/het -*a*/-*en* curiosity, inquisitiveness.

***ny'/fikne** -*a* curiosity, inquisitiveness.

ny'/forlova [/fårlå·va] *A* - (=***-et**) recently engaged (to be married).

+ny'/fundlen'der -*en, pl -e* (=***-ar**) Newfoundlander (person, dog).

ny'/fødd *A* -/*-*født* (=+**/født**) newborn.

ny'/føding -*en* newly born child; *derog.* greenhorn.

+ny'/født *A* - cf **/fødd**

***nyg'gje** *V nygg, nogg, nogge/-i* 1 bump (**mot** against), rub; damage by bumping and rubbing: **båten ligg og nygg seg mot berget** the boat is pounding against the rock. 2 *fig.* bother, nag: **dei nygg på meg etter det** they keep after me about it.

ny'/gift *A* - newly married.

nyg'le -*a* (boat) plug.

ny'/gresk *A* - Modern Greek.

ny'/hende** -*t* (=/hending**) novelty, recent event.

ny'/hending -*a* cf **/hende**

+ny'/het -*en* newness, novelty; (piece of) news: **ingen n-er er gode n-er** no news is good news.

+ny'hets/sending -*a*/-*en* news broadcast.

+ny'hets/stoff -*et* news, newsworthy material.

+ny'hets/tjeneste -*n* news service.

***ny'ing**[1] -*a* renewal.

ny'ing[2] -*en* bonfire, fire (built in the open).

***ny'kel** -*elen, pl -lar* cf **nøkkel**

ny'/kjerna *A* - (=+**-et**) freshly churned.

***nykk'**[1] -*en* cf **nøkk**

nykk'[2] -*en*/+-*et* jerk, tug.

nyk'ke[1] +-*n*/+-*t*/*-*a* whim: **jeg skal nok pille de n-ene ut av ham** I'll cure him of those ideas all right.

+nyk'ke[2] *V nykte* jerk, pull.

***nyk'ke/blom** -*en bot.* water lily (Nymphaeaceae).

nyk'ket(e) *A* - capricious, whimsical.

***nykkj'e** *V nykte* cf **nykke**[2]

***nyk'le/blom** -*en* cf **nøkle/**

***ny'/klede** *pl* cf **/klær**

ny'/klekt *A* - recently hatched.

+ny'/klær *pl* (brand) new clothes.

+ny'/kommer -*en, pl -e* newcomer.

ny'/laga *A* - (=+**-et**) freshly made (e.g. tea).

***ny'/lagd** *A* -/-*lagt* cf **/lagt**

ny'/lage *V* -*a*/+-*et*/+-*de*: **nylaget ord** neologism.

+ny'/lagt *A* - freshly laid, newlaid (e.g. eggs).

ny'/lende -*t* newly cleared land.

ny'lig *A* - recent; lately, recently: **n- utkommen** recently published; **nå n-** just now; **til for n-** until recently.

ny'lon [also=nai'lånn] -*et* nylon.

nylon/snøre -*t* nylon cord.

nylon/strømper *pl* nylon hose.

+ny'/ma'lt *A* - freshly painted.

nym'fe -*a*/+-*en* nymph.

nymfoma'n *A* nymphomaniac.

ny'/motens [also: ny'/] *A* - *derog.* newfangled.

ny'/måne -*n* new moon.

nynn' -*et* humming.

nyn'ne *V* -*a*/+-*et* hum.

ny'/norsk[1] -*en* 1 Modern Norwegian (after 1500). 2 New Norwegian (one of Norway's two official written languages).

ny'/norsk[2] *A* - 1 Modern Norwegian. 2 New Norwegian.

ny'/oppdaga *A* - (=+**-et**) recently discovered.

ny'/ordning -*a*/+-*en* rearrangement, reorganization: **den europeiske n-en** the New Order in Europe.

ny'p -*et* nip, pinch.

ny'pe[1] -*a* hip (=ripe fruit of wild rose).

ny'pe[2] -*a* pinch: **en n- salt** a p- of salt.

ny'pe[3] *V* -*te* nip, pinch.

ny'pe/lus -*a* seed of the (rose) hip.

ny'pe/puré -*en* purée of (rose) hip.

ny'pe/rose -*a*/+-*en bot.* dog rose (Rosa canina).

ny'pe/to'rn -*en bot.* sweetbriar, wild briar (Rosa eglanteria).

ny'/pote't -*a*/+-*en* new potato; early potato(es).

ny're -*a*/+-*en*/-*et* 1 *anat.* kidney. 2 *tech.* (flint) nodule. 3: **granske hjerter og n-er** *fig.* search (our, men's) hearts.

ny're/beten'nelse -*n* nephritis.

ny're/grus -*en*/-*et* kidney stone, renal calculus.

ny're/sjukdom -*men* kidney disease.

ny're/stein -*en* kidney stone.

ny's -*en* sneeze.

ny'se *V naus*/+-*te*/+*nøs*, +-*t*/**nose*/*-*i* sneeze.

ny'se/rot -*a bot.* Christmas rose, hellebore (Helleborus niger).

nysgjerrig [nysjær'ri] *A* - curious, inquisitive (**etter** about); *derog.* nosey: **gjøre en n-** rouse sby's curiosity.

+nysgjerrig/het -*en* curiosity, inquisitiveness.

nysgjerrig/per -*en* nosey person.

ny'/si'lt *A* - (=***/sila**) fresh from the cow.

ny'/slakta *A* - freshly slaughtered.

ny'/slått *A* - (=***/slegen**) 1 (of hay) new-mown. 2 (of coins) freshly minted: **fin som en n- toskilling** smart-looking.

***nys'n** -*a* cf **nyss**[1]

***nys'ne** *V* -*a* peek, spy.

ny'/snø -*en* new fallen snow.

nyss'[1] *en* (=***nysn**) hint, information, news: **få n- om** learn about.

nyss'[2] *Av* (=***nyst**) lately, recently; just now.

nys'selig *A* - cute, sweet.

***nys't** *Av* cf **nyss**[2]

ny'/starta *A* - (=+**-et**) newly begun.

***nys'te**[1] -*t* cf **nøste**[1]

***nys'te**[2] *V* -*a* cf **nøste**[2]

+ny'/stemt *A* - (=***/stemd**) (of music instrument) recently tuned.

ny'/sølv -*et* German silver, nickel silver.

ny'te *V naut*/+*nøt*, +-*t*/**note*/*-*i* 1 enjoy: **n- godt av** benefit from; **n- livet** enjoy life; **han n-er alminnelig aktelse** he is widely respected. 2 partake of (food, drink); imbibe: **jeg har ikke nytt noe i dag** I haven't eaten today.

+ny'telse -*n* (=***-ing**) enjoyment, pleasure, zest: **det var en stor n-** it was delightful; **finne n- ved** enjoy; **forhøye n-n av** give an added zest to; **han levde et liv i n-** his life was one round of pleasure.

+ny'telses/middel -*elet*/-*midlet, pl -midler* stimulant (e.g. alcohol, tobacco; opp. to **nærings/m-**).

+ny'telses/syk *A* pleasure loving, self-indulgent.

ny'/testamen'te -*t, pl* +-*r*/*- New Testament.

ny'/testamen'tlig *A* - New Testament.

ny'/tid -*a*/+-*en* 1 contemporary period. 2 *geol.* Tertiary and Quaternary periods.

***ny'ting** -*a* cf **nytelse**

***ny'tings/middel** -*elet*/-*midlet, pl* +-*midler*/*-*el* cf **nytelses/**

***ny'tings/sjuk** *A* cf **nytelses/syk**

+ny'/trukket [/trokket] *A* -: **n- fisk** fresh fish.

nytt'[1] *nt of* **ny**[2]

+nytt'[2] *pp of* **nyte**

nyt'te[1] -*a*/+-*en* use; advantage, benefit: **dra, få, ha n- av** benefit from, have use for; **gjøre n- for seg** make oneself useful; **det gjør samme n-n** it serves the same purpose, *fam.* it's all the same; **til n-** of use; **til ingen n-** to no avail, useless.

nyt'te[2] *V* -*a*/+-*et* 1 use, utilize; take advantage of: **n- høvet (leiligheten)** seize, take advantage of the opportunity; **n- på, n- seg av** take advantage of; **n- tida** use the time to best advantage. 2 avail, be of use: **det n-er ikke** it's no use; **det n-er deg ikke** it won't do you any good; **hva kan det n- (å gjøre noe)** what's the use (of doing sth).

+nyt'te/gjenstand -*en* 1 useful object. 2 *archeol.* utensil.

+nyt'te/hensyn -*et* practical, utilitarian consideration.

nyt'te/laus *A* useless.

***nyt'teleg** *A* - serviceable, useful.

+nyt'te/løs *A* cf **/laus**

nyt'te/mora'l -*en* utilitarianism.

***nyt'ten** *A* -*e*/-*i, pl nytne* economical, frugal.

***nyt'te/sam** *A* economical, frugal.

nyt'te/vekst -*en* useful plant.

nyt'tig *A* - useful (**for** for a person; **til** for a purpose); advantageous, serviceable: **det er n- å vite** it's worth knowing; **gjøre seg n- i huset** make oneself useful around the house.

+nyt'tig/gjøre *V* -*gjorde, -gjort* (usu. with **seg**) turn to account, utilize.

nytt'/år -*et* (=**ny/**) New Year; **godt n-** Happy New Year.

+nytt'års/aften -*enen, pl -(e)ner* New Year's Eve.

nytt'års/dag -*en* (=**nyårs/**) New Year's Day; **annen n-** January 2.

nytt'års/helsing -*a* (=+**/hilsen**) New Year's greeting(s).

***ny'v** *pr of* **nuve**

ny've[1] -*a* furrow (of the brow), wrinkle.

ny've[2] *V* -*de* bend (end of a nail, etc.).

ny'/år -*et* cf **nytt/**

ny'/års/dag -*en* cf **nyttårs/**

***næ'kje** *V* -*te* denude.

***næ'le** *V* -*te* baste, tack.

***næ'm** *A* 1 receptive, susceptible. 2 handy, practical.

***-næm** *A* cf **-nem**
***næ'me** *-t* apprehension, grasp.
***næ'men** *A -e/-i, pl -ne* quick to learn.
***næ'ming** *-en* greenhorn, novice; pupil.
***næ'pen** *A -e/-i, pl -ne* 1 deft, quick. 2 exact.
nær[1] *A cp +-mere/*-(m)are, sp +-mest/*-(m)ast* 1 close, near(ly); almost: **det ligger n- å tro** it's very likely, the chances are; **det gikk n- innpå ham** it hit him hard; **gå, komme en for n-** take excessive liberties with sby; **ikke n- så** not nearly as; **ikke på langt n-** not by a long shot, not nearly; **n- sagt alle** nearly all: **jeg hadde n- sagt** I almost said, was close to saying; **(det var) på n-e nippet** (that was) a close shave: **stå en n-** be intimate with, close to sby; **ta seg n- av (noe)** take (sth) to heart, be hurt (by sth); **vi er stadig like n-** we're getting nowhere; **være n- på (ved) å** be close to, on the point of (doing sth). 2 except (for): **på én n-** with the exception of one; **så n- som** except for. 3 *(comp.)* **nærmere** closer, nearer; more explicit(ly): **en n- forklaring** a more detailed explanation; **han kom ikke n- inn på saken** he didn't go into details: **jeg må få (vite) n- beskjed** I'll have to have more detailed information; **la oss snakke n- om det senere** let's talk more about it later; **se n- på** take a closer look at; **ved n- ettertanke** on second thought. 4 *(sup.)* **nærmest** closest, nearest; most essential(ly), really; almost, practically: **de n-e dagene** the next few days; **en kunne n- tro at** you'd almost believe that; **det var n- en verdslig tanke** it was really a worldly thought; **enhver er seg selv n-** charity begins at home; **ens n-e** those closest to one; **på det n-e** almost.
nær[2] *P* close, near to; **han er undergangen n-** he is on the verge of ruin; **være døden n-** be at death's door; **n- sagt** almost, just about.
+nær'r/beslek'tet *A* - closely related.
+nær'r/bilde *-t photog.* close-up.
Nær'r/bø *Pln* twp, Rogaland.
nær're[1] *V -te* 1 feed, nourish, sustain; **n- seg av** live on; **n- en slange ved sin barm** nourish a viper in one's bosom. 2 *fig.* entertain (hopes, thoughts), harbor (doubt, suspicion); **n- interesse for** take an interest in; **n- kjærlighet til** love; **jeg n-r ingen tvil om at** I have no doubt that.
nær're[2] *Av*: **n- på, ved (=+nær på, ved)** nearly; **det var n- på, jeg skulle sagt De til deg** I almost said "De" to you (Undset).
nær'renḍe *A* - nourishing, nutritious.
+nær'r/forestående *A* - imminent, impending.
nær'r/gåenḍe *A* - aggressive **(mot** towards), bold, forward; tactless, personal: **hun kommer med n- bemerkninger** she indulges in personalities.
+nær'rgåen/het *-en* forwardness, indiscretion.
+nær'r/het *-en* nearness, vicinity: **her i n-en** in the vicinity, nearby; **jeg bor i umiddelbar n- av stasjonen** I live within easy reach (walking distance) of the station.
nær'rig *A* - miserly, stingy.
nær'ring[1] *-a/+-en* 1 food, sustenance: **gi ilden ny n-** add fuel to the flames; **ta n- til seg** take nourishment. 2 business, livelihood: **sette tæring etter n-** live within one's income.
***nær'ring**[2] *-en* large headland.
nær'rings/drivenḍe *A* - in business, trade: **de n-** the business community.
+nær'rings/frihet *-en* (=*/**fridom)** free enterprise, free choice of occupation.
nær'rings/grein *-a* branch of industry.
nær'rings/kjelde *-a* means of subsistence, resource.
nær'rings/liv *-et* industry, trade.
nær'rings/middel *-elet/-midlet, pl +-midler/*-el* foodstuff.
nær'rings/politikk' *-en* economic policy.
nær'rings/rik *A* nutritious.
nær'rings/sorg *-a/+-en* financial difficulty.
nær'rings/veg *-en* (=+/**vei)** industry; occupation, source of income.
+nær'rings/verdi' *-en* (=*/**verd(e))** food value.
nær'rings/vett *-et* economic knowhow, good business head.
nær'r/kamp *-en* hand to hand combat; (in aviation) dogfight; (in boxing) infighting.
***nær'r/komen** [/kåmen] *A -e/-i, pl -ne* (practically) finished; empty; hopeless.
nær'r/kone [*/kåne] *-a archaic* midwife.
***nær'r/leik** *-en* nearness, vicinity **(av** of).
+nær'r/liggenḍe *A* - 1 nearby, neighboring. 2 natural, obvious: **av n- grunner** for o- reasons; **en n- tanke** an idea which immediately suggests itself.
nær'r/lys *-et* low beam (on headlight of car).
nær'me[1] *V -a/+-et* bring, draw near; *(refl.)* approach, draw near: **natten n-er seg** night is falling; **n- seg land** approach land; **timen n-er seg** the hour is at hand.
°nær'me[2] *Av* almost, nearly.
+nær'mere *cp of* **nær**[1] (=***-are)**
+nær'mest *sp of* **nær**[1] (=***-ast)**
+nær'mest/følgenḍe *A* - following, next.
***nær'rom** *Av* about; almost.
+nær'r/på *Av* nearly.
+nær'r/sagt *Av* cf **nær**[2]
nær'r/skyld *A* - (=+/**skyldt)** closely related.
***nær'r/skylding** *-en* close relative.
nær'r/ståenḍe *A* - close, intimate: **en n- venn** an i- friend.
nær'r/synt *A* - myopic, nearsighted.
***nær'r/søken** *A -e/-i, pl -ne* aggressive, forward.
+nær'r/tagenḍe *A* - (=*/**takande)** sensitive, touchy.
+nær'rtagen/het *-en* sensitivity, touchiness.
***nær'r/takande** *A* - cf **/tagende**
nær'r/trafikk' *-en* local traffic; local calls (telephone).
+nær'r/vær *-et* (=*/**vere,** */**være)** presence: **i fremmedes n-** before company.
+nær'r/værenḍe *A* - (=*/**verande)** existing, present; attentive: **de n-** those present; **for n-** at present; **n- forfatter** the present writer; **ikke riktig n-** engrossed, preoccupied.
Nær'r/øy *Pln* twp, Nord-Trøndelag.
+næst [nes't] *Av* cf **nest**[2]
+næste [nes'te] *-n* cf **neste**[1]
+næsten [nes'ten] *Av* cf **nesten**
+nø' *V -dde* (=+**nøde)** 1 compel, force, oblige: **n- en til (å gjøre noe)** force sby (to do sth); **+nødt/*nøydd** compelled **(til å** to), forced. 2 urge; **han lot seg ikke lenge n-** he didn't need much urging.
NØ =**nordøst**
nø'd *-a/+-en* (=***naud**[1]) 1 necessity, need; destitution: **n- lærer naken kvinne å spinne** necessity is the mother of invention: **i n-en skal en kjenne sine venner** a friend in need is a friend indeed; **i n-ens stund** in the hour of need; **lide n-** suffer privation; **være i n- for** lack, want. 2 danger, distress; difficulty: **det har ingen n-** no danger of that; **det har ingen n- med ham** don't worry about him; **i største n-** in extreme danger; **med n- og neppe** (cf **neppe**[2]); **til n-** at most, barely, with difficulty; in a pinch. 3 =**barnsnød.**
nø'd/anker [also nø'd/] *-eret, pl -er/-(e)re* sheet anchor.
nø'd/bremse *-a/-en* (=+/**brems)** emergency brake.
nø'd/dåp *-en* emergency baptism (e.g. when an infant's life is in danger).
+nø'de *V -de* cf **nø**[1]
nø'd/forbin'ḍing *-a/+-en* first-aid dressing.
+nø'd/havn *-a* (=/**hamn)** port of refuge: **søke n-** put into a port of refuge.
nø'd/hjelp *-a/+-en* makeshift.
nø'dig *A* - (=***naudig)** 1 *archaic* or *dial.* essential, necessary: **har du vennskapen min n- nå da?** do you need my friendship now? (Undset). 2 (with **vil**) reluctantly, unwillingly: **jeg vil n- såre ham** I would rather not hurt his feelings.
nø'd/lanḍe *V -a/+-et* make a forced landing.
+nø'd/lidenḍe *A* - 1 destitute, distressed, needy: **de fattige og n-** the poor and needy. 2: **en n- veksel** *merc.* a defaulted, dishonored note (=note which maker refuses to pay upon legal presentation).
nø'd/løgn [/løyn] *-a/+-en* white lie.
nø'd/rakett' *-en* distress rocket.
nø'd/rett *-en jur.* jus necessitatis (=case involving legal act of necessity); **ytterste n-** justifiable homicide.
nø'd/rop *-et* cry of distress.
+nø'd/saget *A* - compelled, forced, obliged **(til å** to).
nø'ds/arbeid *-et* relief work.
nø'ds/fall *-et*: **i n-** in an emergency, pinch.
+nø'ds/foranstaltning *-en* emergency measure.
nø'd/signal [/singna'l] *-et, pl -/+-er* distress signal.
+nø'd/steḍt *A* - distressed (e.g. areas), in distress (e.g. ships), indigent.
+nø'ds/tilfelle *-t* emergency: **i n-** in case of need, in an e-.
nø'ds/tilstanḍ *-en/*-et* distress.
nø'd/stilt *A* - distressed.
nø'ds/år *-et* year of the locust (=drought, hardship).
+nøḍ't *A* - cf **nø**[1]
+nø'd/tvungen [/tvongen] *A -ent, pl -ne* compelled (by necessity).
+nø'd/tørft *-en*: **forrette sin n-** relieve oneself.
+nø'd/tørftig̣ *A* - 1 (strictly) necessary: **det n-e** the necessities of life. 2 meagre, scanty.
+nø'dtørftig/het *-en* meagerness, scantiness.
nø'd/utgang *-en* emergency exit.
+nø'd/utvei *-en* emergency measure, last resort.
nødven'dig *A* - necessary **(for** for, to); essential: **en n- slutning** an inescapable conclusion.
+nødven'dig/gjøre *V -gjorde, -gjort* compel, necessitate.
+nødven'dig/het *-en* necessity **(av** of): **gjøre en dyd av n-** make a virtue of n-, do sth because one has to.
+nødven'dighets/artik'kel *-elen, pl -artikler* necessity of life.
+nødven'dig̣/vis *Av* necessarily, perforce.
+nø'd/verge *-t* (=/**verje)** *jur.* self-defense: **gripe til n-** act in s-.
nøff' *-et* grunt, oink (of a pig).
nøf'fe *V -a/+-et* (of a pig) grunt, oink.
nøg'd[1] *-a* sufficiency.
nøg'd[2] *A -/*nøgt* (=+**nøyd)** contented, pleased, satisfied **(med** with).
***nø'gnare** *cp of* **nøyen**
***nø'gne** *pl of* **nøyen**
+nøkk' *-en* (=***nykk**[1]) water sprite (in shape of man, horse, etc.).

+ Bokmål; * Nynorsk; ° Dialect.
After letter: ' stress (Acc. 1); ` tone, stress (Acc. 2); · length.
Below letter: . not pronounced.

nøk'kel -*en*, *pl nøkler* 1 (door) key (til to). 2 clue, key (e.g. to a code). 3 *mus.* clef. 4 (telegraph) sender. 5 wrench.
nøk'kel/ba'rn -*et* "key child" (both of whose parents work and who is given a house key and left to fend for itself after school).
nøk'kel/hank -*a*/+-*en*, *pl* +-*er*/*-*henker* (=*/**honk**) bunch of keys; key ring.
nøk'kel/hol [/hål] -*et* (=+/**hull**) keyhole.
nøk'kel/knippe -*t* bunch of keys.
nøk'kel/o'rd -*et* 1 key word; catchword. 2 (in crossword puzzle) clue(s).
nøk'kel/ost [/ost] -*en* clove cheese.
nøk'kel/perso'n -*en* key man.
nøk'kel/pipe -*a* shank (of a key).
nøk'kel/pung [/pong] -*en* cf **nøkle/**
nøk'kel/roma'n -*en* roman à clef (=novel in which actual persons and events are disguised as fiction).
nøk'kel/skjegg -*et* bit, web (of a key).
nøk'kel/stilling -*a*/+-*en* key position.
nøk'ke/rose -*a*/+-*en bot.* (white) water lily (Nymphaea alba).
nøk'le/bein -*et* clavicle, collarbone.
nøk'le/blom[+/blåmm]-*en*(=***nykle/**) *bot.* cowslip (Primula veris).
nøk'le/pung [/pong] -*en* key case.
nøk'ler *pl of* **nøkkel**
nøk'le/ring -*en* 1 key ring. 2 bow (of a key).
nøk'tern *A* 1 sober (=not intoxicated, temperate): **han har vært n- i lang tid nå** he's been on the wagon for a long time now. 2 serious, sober; matter-of-fact, prosaic; levelheaded, realistic; (e.g. of furnishings) plain, simple.
+**nøk'tern/het** -*en* 1 sobriety. 2 sobermindedness; practicality; plainness.
nø'le[1] -*a* large trough.
+**nø'le**[2] *V* -*te* hang back, hesitate: **han nølte ikke med å komme oss til hjelp** he was not slow in coming to our assistance; **n-ende** halting(ly), hesitant(ly).
+**nø'len** *en* hesitation; stalling.
+**nø'le/politikk'** -*en* delaying tactics, policy of delay.
***nø'rding** -*en* norther, northerly wind.
***nør'dre** *A* -, *sp nørdst* cf **nordre**
***nø're**[1] -*t* 1 restorative; tinder. 2 oxygen.
nø're[2] *V* -*te* 1 *dial.* nourish; restore, revive: **n- opp** fatten up. 2 kindle (a fire): **n- opp** light a fire; **n- på (varmen)** feed the fire.
+**nø's** *pt of* **nyse**
+**nøs'te**[1] -*t* (=***nyste**[1]) 1 ball (of yarn, string, thread). 2 *pop.* butterball (animal, person).
+**nøs'te**[2] *V* -*a*/-*et* (=***nyste**[2]) 1 wind up (thread) into balls. 2: **n- seg** bunch, cluster together (e.g. clouds).
nøs'te/kopp -*en* box (for balls of yarn, thread).
+**nø't** *pt of* **nyte**
nø'ter *pl of* **not**[1]
nøtt' -*a* 1 nut; *pop.* head: **ei hard n- å knekke** a difficult problem, a puzzler, a tough nut to crack; **hun er ikke riktig i n-a** *pop.* she's off her nut. 2 lump: **en liten n- under huden** a little swelling under the skin.
nøt'te/brun *A* nut-brown.
nøt'te/frukt -*a*/+-*en* nuciform (=nutshaped) fruit.
nøt'te/hams -*en* husk of a nut.
nøt'te/kjerne -*n* kernel of a nut.
+**nøt'te/knekker** -*en*, *pl* -*e* (=*/**knekkjar**) 1 nutcracker. 2 *hum.* person adept at solving knotty problems.
Nøt'ter/øy *Pln* twp, Vestfold.
nøt'te/skrike -*a zool.* (common) jay (Garrulus glandarius).
nøt'te/tre -*et* walnut (wood): **et n-s bord** a w- table.
nøyak'tig *A* - accurate, exact, precise; *(adv.)* exactly, just: **klokka er n- 2** it's 2 o'clock sharp.
+**nøyak'tig/het** -*en* accuracy, precision, preciseness.

+**nøy'd** *A* - cf **nøgd**[2]
***nøy'dd** *A* - cf **nø**[1]
***nøy'de** *V* -*de* cf **nø**[1]
***nøy'e**[1] -*t* satisfaction: **få sitt n-** get enough.
nøy'e[2] *V* +-*de*/*nøgde*: **n- seg** or **nøyes:** be content, satisfied (**med** with); **det kan jeg ikke n-s med** that's not good enough for me; **n-s med å se til** be content to watch.
+**nøy'e**[3] *A* - 1 close, exact; intimate: **det kan jeg ikke si så n-** I can't say exactly; **det vet jeg ikke så n-** I don't know exactly; **ha n- kjennskap til** have an intimate knowledge of; **kjenne en n-** know sby intimately; **passe n- på** keep a sharp watch out; **være n- inne i (en sak)** know (a matter) through and through. 2 meticulous, particular, strict: **han ser ikke så n- på pengene** he's not so particular (careful) with his money; **holde n- på** be particular, strict about; **ikke ta (regne) det så n- med** not be so particular, strict about; **være n- på det** be demanding, strict.
***nøy'en** *A nøye*, *pl nøgne* accurate, exact, precise.
+**nøy'e/regnende** [/reinene] *A* - particular (**med** about), scrupulous; closefisted (e.g. with money): **han er ikke så n- i bruken av sine midler** he is rather unscrupulous about his means.
+**nøy'e/seende** *A* - attentive, vigilant.
+**nøy'/som'** *A* -*t*, *pl* -*me* (=*/**sam**) easily satisfied; modest, unassuming.
+**nøy'som/het** -*en* (=*/**semd**) contentment, moderation.
***nøy'te**[1] *V* -*a* 1 use. 2 enjoy, partake of (food).
nøy'te[2] *V* -*te*: **n- seg** hurry.
***nøy'ten** *A* -*e*/-*i*, *pl* -*ne* industrious, persevering; quick.
nøytra'l *A* neutral (power, zone; *chem.* reaction; *elec.* field): **de n-e** the neutral powers; **holde seg n-** observe neutrality.
nøytralise're *V* -*te* neutralize (make neutral; counteract).
nøytralise'ring -*a*/+-*en* neutralization.
nøytralite't -*en* neutrality.
nøytralite'ts/brott -*et* (=+/**brudd**) breach of neutrality.
+**nøytralite'ts/krenkelse** -*n* (=*-**ing**) violation of neutrality.
nøytralite'ts/vakt -*a*/+-*en* vigilance (incl. defense) against breach of neutrality.
nøy'tron -*en*/-*et* (=**neutron**) neutron.
nøy'trum -*umet*, *pl* -*a*/+-*er*/*-*um gram.* neuter.
nå'[1] *V* -*dde* arrive at, reach; accomplish, attain: **nå (ikke nå) bussen, toget** catch (miss) the bus, train; **nå et mål** attain a goal; **nå fram** reach one's destination, goal; **nå i** get hold of; **nå en i telefonen** get hold of sby by telephone; **nå igjen (inn på)** catch up with, overtake; **nå langt i verden** go far in the world; **nå opp til** attain; **jeg nådde så vidt å bli ferdig** I just barely finished; **så langt øyet når** as far as the eye can see; **vi nådde ikke så mye i dag** we didn't get much done today.
+**nå'**[2] *Av* (=***no**[1]) 1 (accented) now; at this moment: **nå for tida** nowadays; **nå og da** now and then; **nå til dags** nowadays; **fra nå av** from now on; **hva nå** what next. 2 (unaccented) after all, really: **det er nå ikke en gang sant** after all, it's not even true; **skal nå det være kunst?** is that really supposed to be art?.
nå'[3] *I* (surprise) really; (questioning) well; (calming) there, there; (in reply) I see; (hesitation) o-o-h: **nå ja** oh well; **å nå** oho.
nå'/bleik *A* deathly pale, ghastly.

+**nåd'a** *I* now what, what next.
nå'de[1] -*n* grace, favor; leniency, mercy: **av Guds n-** by the grace of God; **be om n-** beg for mercy; **Deres N-** Your Grace; **finne n- for ens øyne** find favor in sby's eyes; **la n- gå for rett** temper justice with mercy; **leve på andres n-** live on charity; **overgi seg på n- og unåde** surrender unconditionally; **ta til n-** restore to favor; **uten n- og barmhjertighet** mercilessly, ruthlessly.
nå'de[2] *V* +-*et*/*-*a*: **gud n- deg** may God have mercy on you; **(gud) n- deg, hvis** - God help you, if -.
nå'de/full *A* compassionate, merciful.
+**nå'de/gave** -*n* (=*/**gåve**) 1 *eccl.* charisma, gift of grace. 2 *fig.* gift, talent: **frekkhetens n-** a talent for brass.
nå'de/laus *A* (=+/**løs**) merciless, ruthless, unmerciful.
nå'de/middel -*elet*/-*midlet*, *pl* +-*midler*/*-*el eccl.* (in *pl*) means, vehicles of divine grace (esp. the sacraments).
nå'de/skott -*et* (=+/**skudd**) coup de grace, shot putting an animal out of its misery.
+**nå'de/støt** -*et* (=*/**støyt**) coup de grace, death blow.
nå'dig *A* - 1 *bibl.* merciful: **Gud være oss n-** may God have mercy on us; **vår n-e frelser** our merciful Savior. 2 gracious (**mot** to): **han er god og n-** he is kind and g-; **vår n-ste konge** our most gracious king.
+**nå'dsens/brød** -*et* (bread of) charity: **spise n- hos en** live on sby's charity.
nå'e -*n dial.*, *poet.* corpse.
***nå'eleg** *A* - sickly; stunted (in growth).
+**nå'/gjeldende** *A* - current, present (=currently in force).
nå'l -*a* needle (compass, knitting, phonograph, pine, sewing, etc.); pin; brooch: **han var så fattig, at han ikke eide n-a i veggen** he was as poor as a church mouse; **hun stod (satt) som på n-er** she was on pins and needles; **som å lete etter ei n- i en høystakk** like looking for a n- in a haystack; **træ i ei n-** thread a n-.
***nå'l/auge** -*t* cf **/øye**
nå'le/brev -*et* paper of needles, pins.
+**nå'le/penger** *pl* (=*-**ar**) pin money.
nå'le/pute -*a* pin cushion.
nå'le/stikk -*et* pinprick.
nå'le/tre -*et*, *pl* -/+-*trær bot.* conifer (Coniferae).
nå'/levende *A* - contemporary, living: **de n-** our contemporaries.
nå'/lys -*et* (=*/**ljos**) corpse candle (light resembling a candle's flame sometimes seen in churchyards and believed to presage sby's death).
+**nå'l/øye** -*t* eye of a needle.
nå'm -*et hist.* taking, only in **landnåm** land taking (in 9th century Iceland).
***nå'me** *Av*: **ikkje (på) n- nær** nowhere near; **han kjende seg ikkje på nåmenær slik som dei andre ville ha det til** he didn't feel at all the way the others said he should (Vesaas).
når'[1] *Av* when (=at what time): **n- blir vi ferdig med denne ordboka?** when will we be through with this dictionary?; **n- som helst** (at) any time (at all); **n- på dagen** what time of the day.
når'[2] *C* 1 (of events in the present or future, or repeated events) when, whenever: **n- vi kom fram, pleide han å stå i døra** when(ever) we arrived, he was standing in the door. 2 if: **n- vi bare kunne leve av solskinn** if we could only live on sunshine.

nå'risle/gras *-et bot.* twinflower (Linnaea borealis) (used esp. in folk medicine for treatment of skin diseases, e.g. shingles).
når'somhelst *Av* cf **når**[1]
***nå's/fall** *-et* death.
+nå'/tid *-a/-en* 1 present, present time: **i n-a** in our time; **n-ens mennesker** the present generation. 2 *gram.* present tense: **i n-** in the p- t-.
+nå'/tidig *A* - contemporary, current, modern.
+nå'tids/menneske *-t* modern (person): **vi n-r** we moderns.
+nå'/tildag's *Av* (=**+nå til dags**) nowadays.
nåt'le *V -a/+-et* stitch (shoes).
nåt'lerske *-a* woman who stitches shoes.
+nåvel' *I* well (then).
+nå'/værende *A* - current, present, prevailing.

O

o'[1] *-en* (letter) O, o.
°o'[2] *A* - cf **od**
+o'[3] *I lit.* oh.
+O=**ost**[2]
+o.=**omkring**
'o- *Pf* cf **u-**
o. a.=**og +annet/*anna, og andre** et al.
oa'se *-n* oasis.
o. a. st.=**og andre +steder/*stader**
obduksjo'n *-en* autopsy.
obduse're *V -te* perform an autopsy on.
obelis'k *-en* obelisk.
o'berst *-en* colonel.
oberstin'ne *-a/+-en* colonel's wife (used as title).
oberstløy'tnant *-en* lieutenant colonel.
objek't *-et, pl -/+-er gram., philos.* object: **gjøre en til o- for vitser** make sby the target of witticisms.
objekti'v[1] *-et, pl -/+-er photog.* objective (lens).
ob'jektiv[2] *A* objective.
objektivite't *-en* objectivity.
obla't *-en* 1 *eccl.* altar bread, wafer. 2 seal.
obligasjo'n *-en merc.* bond: **en o- på tusen kroner** a 1000-*kroner* bond.
obliga't *A* - 1 inevitable, obligatory. 2 *mus.* obligato (=indespensable, necessary, in ref. to a voice composition).
obligato'risk *A* - obligatory: **o-e kurser** required courses.
oblikk' *A oblikt* oblique (*gram.*= other cases than the nominative).
obo *-en* oboe.
obois't *-en* oboe player, oboist.
OBOS=**Oslo bolig- og sparelag**
ob's *A - pop.* aware (**på** of) (short for **observant**).
obs.=**observer**
obscøn [åpskø'n] *A* obscene.
obscønitet [åpskønite't] *-en* obscenity.
observant [åpsærvang'] *A* - observant.
observasjo'n *-en* observation: **legge inn til o-** send to hospital for o-.
observa'tor *-en* (scientific) observer.
observato'rium *-iet, pl +-ier/*-ium* observatory.
observatø'r *-en* (diplomatic) observer.
observe're *V -te* observe (esp. *astron., med., naut.*); **observer** observe, notice; NB (usu. abbrev. as **obs.**).
obsku'r *A* obscure.
obskuran't *-en* obscurant (=know-nothing, anti-intellectual, opponent of clear thinking).
obskurite't *-en* obscurity.
°obstana'sig *A* - cf **obsternasig**
+obsterna'sig *A pop.* obstinate, stubborn; willful.
obstrue're *V -te* obstruct.
obstruksjo'n *-en* obstruction.
***o'd** *A* - excited, wild; in heat.
odalis'k *-en* odalisque (woman in harem).
odd' *-en* (knife, sword) point: **verge med o- og egg** defend with sword and spear (=all one's might).
Odd' *Prn(m)*
Od'da *Pln* twp, Hordaland.
Odd'/bjørg *Prn(f)*
Odd'/bjø'rn *Prn(m)*
od'de[1] *-n* headland, point (of cape or peninsula); spit of land.
od'de[2] *-n* odd man (in game, group).
od'de[3] *A* - odd (numbered): **par og o-** odd and even.
***od'de/mann** *-en, pl -menn(er)* arbitrator, umpire.
Od'der/nes *Pln* twp, Vest-Agder.
od'de/tal *-et* (=**+/tall**) odd number.
Odd'/laug *Prn(f)*
odd's *pl* odds (horse racing).
o'de *-n* ode.
o'del *-en* property owned under an alodial system (freehold, udal; cf **odelsrett**); the right to hold such property: **ta garden på o-** take the farm by alodial right; **få noe til o- og eie** get sth for one's very own.
o'dels/bonde *-n, pl -bønder* freeholder (farmer owning property under *odelsrett*).
+o'dels/båren *-et, pl -ne* (=***/boren -e/-i**) born to the heritage, entitled by birth.
o'dels/ga'rd *-en* ancestral farm, freehold (farm owned under *odelsrett*).
+o'dels/gutt *-en* (=***/gut**) oldest son and heir (to an *odelsgard*).
o'dels/jente *-a* heiress (to an *odelsgard*).
o'dels/jo'rd *-a* freehold (land held under *odelsrett*).
o'dels/lov [/låv] *-en/*-a* law about *odel*, alodial law.
o'dels/mann *-en, pl -menn/*-menner* freeholder (=**odelsbonde**).
o'dels/rett *-en* alodial (udal) rights (form of property ownership acquired by a family to a farm held for at least 20 years, whereby members of family have right to redeem it within five years of sale).
o'dels/ting *-et* lower house of Norwegian legislature (elected at same election as upper house, self-constituted as 3/4 of whole legislature).
o'delstings/proposisjo'n *-en* bill originating in the *Odelsting*.
O'din [also o'-] *Prn(m) myth.* chief of gods (cf Woden, Wotan), from whose name we have Wednesday.
odiø's *A* 1 odious. 2 malicious: **en o- kritikk** m- criticism.
***o. dl.**=**og dilikt**
o'dle *V -a/+-et* 1 gain alodial right (*odelsrett*) to. 2 cultivate (land, plants).
odontolog [odåntolå'g] *-en* odontologist.
odontologi' *-en* odontology.
odyssé *-en* odyssey (also of the poem), travel tale.
odø'r *-en* odor (usu. unpleasant).
off.=**offentlig**
offensiv[1] [åf'fangsiv] *-en* offensive: **ta o-en** take the o-.
offensiv[2] *A* offensive (only *mil.*).
of'fentlig *A* - public: **det o-e** the government; **en o- bygning** a public building; **et o- hus** a house of ill fame; **en o- hemmelighet** an open secret; **det o-e liv** public life; **o- rett** public law; **gjøre noe o-** make sth public; announce publicly; **opptre o-** appear in public.
+of'fentlig/gjøre *V -gjorde, -gjort* announce, publish; make public.
+of'fentlig/gjørelse *-n* announcement, publication (**av** of).
+of'fentlig/het *-en* (def.) the public: **komme til o-ens kunnskap** become generally known; **ligge o-en til byrde** be a public charge.
of'fer *-eret, pl -er/+ofre* 1 (gift) offering, offertory, sacrifice (**til** to). 2 sacrifice, self-sacrifice: **kreve et o-** demand a sacrifice; **et tungt o-** a heavy sacrifice. 3 victim (**for** of); casualty, martyr.
of'fer/dag *-en* day of offering (in church).
offere're *V -te merc.* offer (for sale).
of'fer/lam' *-met* sacrificial lamb; *fig.* innocent victim.
offer'te *-n merc.* offer.
of'fer/vilje *-n* generosity, willingness to sacrifice.
of'fer/villig *A* - (=***/viljug**) generous, willing to sacrifice.
+of'fervillig/het *-en* generosity, willingness to sacrifice.
offise'r *-en* officer (**i** in).
offisiell' *A -elt* official.
offisi'n *-et, pl -/+-er* 1 dispensary, pharmacy. 2 print shop.
offisiø's *A* semi-official, unofficial; **o-e forhandlinger** informal talks.
off/set [åff'/sett] *-en* offset (printing).
off/side [åff'/said] *Av* offside (sports).
o. fl.=**og +flere/*fleire** et al.
O'/foten *Pln* district, Nordland.
°of're[1] *pl of* **offer**
of're[2] *V -a/+-et* 1 give an offering (**til** to); make a sacrifice. 2 sacrifice (**for** for): **o- livet** s- one's life. 3 devote (one's life, time) (**på** to): **han hadde ikke o-et saken en tanke** he had not given the matter a thought; **hun o-et seg for saken** she devoted herself to the cause.
°o'/frysk(j)e *-t* cf **u/friske**
of'se[1] *-n* 1 recklessness, violence; ***take til med ein o-** start recklessly. 2 abundance, superfluity (**med** of): **ingen o- med penger** no excess of money (Hamsun). 3 bad storm; flood.
***of'se**[2] *V -a* boast, exaggerate: **o- seg** show pride.
***of'seleg** *A* - enormous, tremendous.
***of'sen** *A -e/-i, pl -ne* reckless, violent.
of'te *Av* 1 often: **hvor o-** how many times; **så o- jeg kan** as often as I can; **titt og o-** time and again. 2 (in *comp.*) several times; (with *neg.*); **ikke oftere** never again. 3 (in *sup.*): **som oftest** as a rule.
og[1] [å] *C* and: **og så videre (osv.)** and so forth (etc.); **bøker og bøker, fru Blom** there are books and books, Mrs. B-; **han gikk og gikk** he walked and walked; **kom og spis** come and eat; (in various phrases where it is omitted in English) **jeg lå og leste** I lay reading; **hun er ute og går** she

+ Bokmål; * Nynorsk; ° Dialect.
After letter: ' stress (Acc. 1); ` tone, stress (Acc. 2); · length.
Below letter: . not pronounced.

is out walking; **vi skal ut og skyte** we're going out shooting; **hold opp og skrik** (more correctly: **å skrike**) stop crying; (sometimes confused with **å**) **det er lett og** (should be **å**) **gjøre** it's easy to do.

og[2] [+å', *å'g] *Av* (=***au**) also, too (=**også**, now usu. in final position): **det er underlig og** it's a strange thing, too.

Ogna [og'na] *Pln* twp, Rogaland.

Ogn/dal [og'n/] *Pln* twp, Nord-Trøndelag.

også [+ås'så, *åg'så] *Av* 1 also, too: **han o-, o- han** he too; **her o-, o- her** here too; **o- du, min sønn Brutus** you too, (my son) B-. 2 (as introd. particle) even: **o- uten det** even without that; **om o-** even if; **jeg gav ham alt, o- min kjærlighet** I gave him everything, even my love. 3 (as mild intensive) indeed, in fact, of course, really, you see: **er det nå o- sant?** is it really true?: **det gjør jeg o-** indeed I do; **han var da o- den første** after all, he was the first. 4 (expressing annoyance or surprise): **det var o- et spørsmål** what a question; **Den hellige Antonius — også en bok å lese nettopp nå** St. Anthony—what a book to be reading just now (Hoel); **så skulle da o-** well, I'll be—; **du får gjøre det, eller o- skal jeg...** you'd better do it or (else) I'll...; **pokker o-** damn it anyway. 5 (*dial.*, confused with **å**); **det er vanskelig o- få gjort det** it's hard to do it.

o. h.=**over havet**

o'hm *en elec.* ohm.

ohoi [ohåi'] *I* ahoy.

oi [åi'] *I* oh (cry of pain or surprise): **oi oi** cry of dismay.

oie [åi'e] *V* -*a*/+-*et* cry out, scream: **de oia og bar seg** they shouted and carried on; **o- seg** moan, wail; **o- seg over noe** cry out in amazement about sth.

***ok**[1] [å'k] -*et* cf **åk**

***o'k**[2] *pt of* **ake**[1]

o k [o' kå', o' ke', åkei'] *Av* all right, O.K.

oka'pi -*en zool.* okapi.

okari'na -*en mus.* ocarina.

***oke** [å'ke] -*n* 1 cleat, crossbar. 2 yoke.

o'ker[1] -*en* ocher (ochre).

***oker**[2] [å'ker] -*et* cf **åger**

o'ker/gul *A* ocher yellow.

okkul't *A* - occult.

okkulte'rende *A* - *naut.* occulting light (=navigational light whose beam is interrupted at regular intervals by a brief period of darkness).

okkultis'me -*n* occultism.

okkupan't -*en mil.* occupier, occupying forces.

okkupasjo'n -*en mil.* occupation (of a territory or country).

okkupe're *V* -*te* 1 *mil.* occupy (a territory or country). 2 *jur.* take possession of (unowned goods, land).

***ok'le** -*a*/-*et* cf **ankel**

***okre** [å'kre] *V* -*a* cf **ågre**

oksa'l/syre -*a chem.* oxalic acid.

okse [ok'se] -*n* ox; bull: **sterk som en o-** strong as an ox; **den kommer også fram som kjører med o-r** better late than never.

okse/bryst [ok'se/] -*et* brisket of beef.

+okse/hode -*t* (=***/hovud**) 1 head of an ox. 2 hogshead (unit of liquid measure=51 gallons).

okse/kalv -*en* bull-calf.

okse/kjøtt -*et* (=***/kjøt**) beef.

okse/spann -*et* team of oxen.

okse/steik -*a* roast beef.

oks/høvel [ok's/] -*elen, pl* -*ler* timber plane.

oksidenta'l *A* occidental.

+oksidenta'ler -*en, pl* -*e* (=***-ar**) occidental.

Oksiden'ten *Pln* the Occident.

***ok'sl** -*a* cf **aksel**[1]

oksy'd -*et chem.* oxide.

oksydasjo'n -*en chem.* oxidation.

oksyde're *V* -*te chem.* oxidize.

oksyge'n -*et chem.* oxygen.

okt.=**oktober**

oktae'der -*eret, pl* +-*(e)re*/*-*er* octahedron.

oktan't -*en astron.* octant.

okta'v -*en* 1 octave. 2 octavo; book in octavo format.

okta'v/forma't -*et* octavo format.

oktett' -*en mus.* octette.

okto'ber *en* October.

oktroa' -*en hist.* octroi (=1 concession granted by a legal authority. 2 duty levied by a city).

oktroaje're *V* -*te hist.* octroy (=grant a privilege, concession): **o-t** chartered.

okula'r -*et, pl* -/+-*er* eyepiece, ocular (lens).

okulasjo'n -*en hort.* budding (=grafting of a single bud into a stock).

okule're *V* -*te hort.* bud (=graft a single bud into a stock).

o'l[1] -*a* (=**ole**) leather strap.

***o'l**[2] *pt of* **ale**

o. l.=**og** +**lignende**/***liknande**

O'la *Prn(m)*

o'la/bukse -*a* blue jeans.

O'laf *Prn(m)* cf **Olav**

O'laug *Prn(f)*

O'lav *Prn(m)*

Ola'va *Prn(f)*

o'lavs/dagen *df* St. Olaf's Day (July 29, supposedly the day of the death of king Olaf Haraldsson in 1030).

+o'lavs/kors -*et* cross of the Order of St. Olaf (honorary Norwegian royal order).

o'lavs/orden *en* (short for): **Sankt O-** Order of St. Olaf.

+o'lavs/ridder -*en, pl* -*e* (=***-ar**) knight of the Order of St. Olaf (honorary Norwegian royal order).

***ol'/boge**[1] [/båge] -*n* cf **al/bue**[1]

***ol'/boge**[2] [/båge] *V* -*a* cf **al/bue**[2]

ol'de/ba'rn -*et, pl* -/*-*born* great-grandchild.

ol'de/far -*en, pl* +-*fedre*/*-*fedrar* great-grandfather.

ol'de/mor -*a, pl* -*mødrer*/+-*mødre* great-grandmother: **fanden og hans o-** the devil and his dam (also=a lot of nonsense, all that rot).

Ol'den *Pln* post office, Sogn og Fjordane.

+ol'den/borger -*en, pl* -*e* (=***-ar**) *hist.* member of the royal House of Oldenborg.

ol'den/borre -*a*/-*en zool.* cockchafer (Melolontha melolontha); June beetle.

ol'der -*eren*/-*ra, pl* -*rer*/*-*rar bot.* alder (tree or shrub of the genus Alnus).

ol'der/mann -*en, pl* -*menn*/*-*menner hist.* 1 master of a guild. 2 either of the two foremen of the council of the German Wharf in Bergen.

ol'd/frue -*a*/+-*en* housekeeper (in an institution, hotel, hospital).

ol'd/funn -*et* archeological find.

+ol'd/gransker -*en, pl* -*e* (=***-ar**) archeologist.

ol'ding -*en* 1 (very) old, elderly man; graybeard. 2 infirm old man.

+ol'ding/aktig *A* - senile.

+ol'd/kirke -*a*/-*en* usu. def. (the) early (Christian) church.

oldn.=**oldnorsk**

ol'd/nordisk *A* - Old Scandinavian.

ol'd/norsk *A* - Old Norwegian; Old Norse.

ol'd/saker *pl* objects of antiquity.

ol'd/tid -*a*/+-*en* antiquity; prehistory.

o'le -*a* cf **ol**[1]

O'le *Prn(m)*

olean'der -*en, pl* +-*e bot.* oleander (Nerium oleander).

+Ole lukkøye [lokk'øye] *Prn* the Sandman.

-olf *Prn(m)* cf **-olv**

oligarki' -*et, pl* -/+-*er* oligarchy.

oligar'kisk *A* - oligarchic(al).

+o. lign.=**og lignende**

o. likn.=**og liknende**

Oli'ne *Prn(f)*

oli'ven -*en* olive.

oli'ven/olje -*a*/-*en* olive oil.

ol'je[1] -*a*/-*en* oil: **amerikansk o-** castor o-; **helle (gyte) o- på (i) ilden** *fig.* add fuel to the fire; **helle o- på sjøen (bølgene), dempe sjøen (bølgene) med o-** pour oil on troubled waters; **den siste o-** *eccl.* Extreme Unction, *fam.* the finishing touches, the final polish.

ol'je[2] *V* -*a*/+-*et* 1 oil: **som et olja lyn** like greased lightning. 2 (of a liquid) form into drops like oil.

Ol'je/berget *Pln* the Mount of Olives.

+ol'je/brenner -*en, pl* -*e* (=***-ar**) oil burner.

ol'je/farge -*n* oil color.

ol'je/fyring -*a*/+-*en* oil burning; oil heating.

+ol'je/holdig *A* - (=***/haldig**) containing oil, oily.

ol'je/hyre -*t*/+-*n* oilskins (clothing used by fishermen, etc.).

ol'je/kake -*a* oil cake; *bibl.* cake of oiled bread (Ex. 29, 23).

+ol'je/klær *pl* (=***/klede**) oilskin clothing.

+ol'je/le'dning -*en* (=***/leiding**) oil pipe.

ol'je/lerret -*et* oilskin.

+ol'je/maleri' -*et* oil painting.

ol'jet(e) *A* - oily.

ol'je/trøye -*a* oilskin jacket.

+ol'je/tøy -*et* oilskin clothing.

oll' -*en* noise, racket: shouting.

ol'le[1] -*a* spring.

***ol'le**[2] *V* -*a* 1 make noise, shout. 2 gush forth.

***ol'lo** *Av* quite; completely: **for o-** in all.

ol'm *A* (of animals, *hum.* of people) angry; vicious: **et o-t blikk** a glowering look.

ol'me *V* -*a*/+-*et*: **o- seg** work oneself into a rage; **o- på noe** look angrily at sth.

***ol/mose** [ål'/måse] -*a* cf **al/misse**

olsok [ol'/såkk] -*en* St. Olaf's Day (July 29, supposedly the day of the death of king Olaf Haraldsson in 1030).

olsok/dag -*en* cf **olsok**

***ol'ster** -*en* noise, racket; shouting.

***ol'stre** *V* -*a* 1 make noise, shout. 2 gush forth.

O'luf *Prn(m)*

-olv *Prn(m)* e.g. in **Torolv (Torolf)**.

olympia'de -*n* Olympiad, Olympic Games.

olym'pisk *A* - Olympic.

+O'-løp=**orienteringsløp**

o'm[1] -*en* distant, dull sound.

om'[2] *C* 1 if, in case: **hva skal dette bety, om jeg tør spørre?** what does this mean, if I might ask?; **om jeg ikke ser deg igjen** in case I don't see you again; **om... bare if...** only; **om... enn, om... så, selv om** although, even if; **om så var** even so, if that were the case; **som om** as if. 2 if, whether: **jeg vet ikke om han er her** I don't know if (whether) he is here; **tro om det er sant** wonder if it's true. 3 used to introduce emphatic answers (="how can you ask..."): **om jeg vil (kan, gjør, etc.)** and how, you bet; **nei (nei så menn) om jeg vil** not on your life.

om'[3] *P* 1 around: **om hjørnet piler en pike** a girl whisks around the corner (Olaf Bull); *(adv.)* **høyre (venstre) om** right (left) face; *(adv.)* **se seg om** look around. 2 about, concerning: **en bok om elefanter** a book about elephants; **vi snakket ikke om deg** we weren't talking about you. 3 during, in (=time within which): **om dagen (natta)** during the day (night); **om morgenen** in the morning; **her om dagen** the other day; **nå om dagen** nowadays. 4 (of future time) in: **om en uke** in a week; **om litt** in a little while. 5 per: **to ganger om dagen** two times a day. 6 *(adv.)* again, repeatedly: ***om att, om igjen** again; **om og om igjen** again and again; **skrive noe om** rewrite sth. 7 (other idioms): **om å gjøre** important, necessary; **hva er det om å gjøre?** what's the matter? what's troubling you?; **ham (meg) om det** let him (me) worry about (take care of) that; **han er om seg** he's sharp, he's a go-getter; **jeg var alene om det** I did it myself, I am solely responsible; **år om annet** year after year; (for uses with other verbs: see these).

o. m.=**og** +**mer**/***meir**

o. m. a.=**og mye** +**annet**/***anna, og mange andre**

+**om'/adresse're** *V -te* readdress; forward (mail).

omarb.=**omarbeidd**

om'/arbei'de *V -de/+-et* revise, rewrite (a book); adapt (a play).

om'/att *Av* cf **om**[3]

***om'/bere** *V -bar, bore/-i* dispense with, do without.

+**om'/bestem'me** *V -bestemte*: **o- seg** change one's mind.

***om'/boḍ** *-et* cf **/bud**

***om'bods/manṇ** *-en, pl -menn(er)* cf **ombuds/**

ombo'rḍ *Av* cf **bord**[1]

+**ombo'rḍ/værendẹ** *A* -: **de o-** those on board.

om'/bore** [/båre] *pp of* **-bere** (=-i**)

om'/bot *-a/+-en, pl -bøter* improvement, reform.

+**om'/brakk** *pt of* **-brekke**

+**om'/brakte** *pt of* **-bringe**

+**om'/brekke** *V -brakk, -brukket* make up (=arrange type matter into columns or pages); overrun (=rearrange lines or columns of type).

om'/brekning *+-en/*-a* making up, overrunning (of type matter).

om'breknings/feil *-en, pl* - mistake committed during **ombrekning** (usu. resulting in a misplaced line of type).

+**om'/bringe** *V -brakte, -brakt* 1 deliver (e.g. mail), distribute. 2 *obs.* destroy, kill.

+**om'/bringelse** *-n* delivery, distribution.

+**om'/brukket** [/brokket] *pp of* **-brekke**

***om'/bryting** *-a* cf **/brekning**

***om'/brøyte** *-t* alteration, change.

+**om'/bud** *-et* civil position, office.

om'buds/mann *-en, pl -menn/*-menner* 1 civil official to whom one can appeal administrative decisions; a grievance officer. 2 *hist.* bailiff.

om'/bygging *-a/+-en* alteration, rebuilding.

+**om'/bytning** *-en* exchanging, replacement, substitution.

+**om'/bytte** *-t* (=***/byte**) change, exchange; change of clothes: **til o-** for a change.

+**om'/bæring** *-en* delivery, distribution.

om'/bøter *pl of* **-bot**

om'/danne *V -a/+-et* convert, remodel, transform (**til** into).

om'/debatte'rt *A* - under discussion: **et meget o- spørsmål** a much debated question.

om'/deling *-a/+-en* distribution.

om'/dispute'rt *A* - disputed: **en o- sak** a d- case.

+**om'/dreining** *-en* turning; revolution, rotation: **200 o-er i minuttet** 200 rpm.

om'/dømme *-t* (=***/døme**) judgment, opinion; powers of judgment: **folks o-** public opinion.

+**om'/døpe** *V -te* rebaptize; rename.

+**om'/egn** [/ein] *-en* environs, surrounding area.

om'/ekspede're *V -te* forward (mail), reship (goods).

omelett' *-en* omelette.

o'men *-et, pl -/+omina* omen.

+**omenskjøn't** *C* although.

om'/fang *-et* 1 dimensions, extent, size: **av stort o-** extensive, sizable; **i det o- omstendighetene tillater** as far as circumstances permit; **saken begynte å anta større o-** the case began to assume larger proportions; **planens o-** the scope of the plan. 2 circumference: **trestammen er to meter i o-** the tree trunk is two meters in c-. 3 *mus.* range.

om'fangs/rik *A* bulky; extensive; voluminous.

om'/far *-et, pl* - round (of stitches, boards, logs, etc.).

***om'/farast** *V -forst, -farest* (of two people approaching each other from opposite directions) pass by without seeing each other.

+**om'/fatte** *V -a/-et* (=***/fate**) cover, encompass, include.

+**om'/fattendẹ** *A* - (=***/fatande**) comprehensive, extensive: **en alt o- interesse** an interest in all things.

+**om'/favne** *V -et* embrace.

+**om'/favnelse** *-n* embrace.

+**om'/flakkendẹ** *A* - roaming, rootless, vagrant.

+**om'/flytt** *A* - surrounded (**av** by) (a body of water).

om'/flødd *A -/*-flødt* covered, inundated (**av** by).

+**omforla'telse** *I* cf **forlatelse**

+**om'/forme** *V -a/-et* reform, remodel.

+**om'/former** [also åm'/] *-en, pl -e* (=***-ar**) reformer.

***om'/fo'rst** *pt of* **-farast**

om'/fram' *P* (=+**/framt**) 1 ahead of, before; except for; in addition to. 2 *(adv.)* extra, in addition; exceptionally, unusually: ***ei o- ven jente** an exceptionally beautiful girl.

om'fram/arbeid *-et* extra work.

om'førsels/handel *-en* itinerant selling, peddling.

om'/gang *-en* 1 round (of drinks, of a boxing match, of knitting stitches, etc.); period, section (of a competition or game): **i første o-** to begin with; **i siste o-** last of all. 2 rotation, turn: **gå på o-** be used in turn; rotate; **holde på o-** subscribe (to a paper) jointly. 3 treatment (esp. of rough or violent nature): **de fikk en hard o-** they were treated roughly. 4 association, company, intercourse (also sexual): **ha o- med** be associated with; **han er ingen o- for deg** he's not fit for you; **uforsiktig o- med** carelessness with. 5 (in soccer) half time.

om'gangs/form *-a/+-en* social convention(s); *(pl)* social amenities.

+**om'gangs/krets** *-en* circle of acquaintances.

om'gangs/sjuke *-n* communicable disease; epidemic (usu. of stomach flu).

om'gangs/skole *-n* ambulatory school (formerly common in sparsely settled rural areas of Norway).

***om'gangs/sykje** *-a* cf **/sjuke**

om'gangs/tone *-n* social atmosphere, (conversational) tone (of a circle).

om'gangs/venn *-en, pl *-er* (=***/ven**) close friend, frequent associate.

+**om'/gi** *V -gav, -gitt* encircle, encompass, surround: **o- seg med** surround oneself with (e.g. friends).

+**om'/giing** *-a/-en* redeal (at cards).

+**om'/gikk** *pt of* **-gå**

+**om'/gikkes** *pt of* **-gå(e)s**

+**omgi'velser** *pl* surroundings; environment.

***om'/gjekst** *pt of* **-gåast**

***om'/gjenge** *-t* association, company, intercourse (also sexual) (cf **omgang**[4]).

omgjeng'elig *A* - sociable; easy to get along with.

+**omgjeng'elig/het** *-en* sociability.

+**om'/gjerde** *V -et* enclose, fence in.

***om'/gjevnaḍer** *pl* cf **/givelser**

+**om'/gjo'rde** *V -et* gird (**med** with): **o- sin lend** *bibl.* g- one's loins.

***om'/grep** *-et* concept(ion), idea.

om'/gå *V -gikk, -gått* 1 evade: **o- loven** get around the law. 2 *mil.* outflank, turn the flank of.

***om'/gåast** *V -gåst, -gjekst, -gåst* cf **/gåes**

+**om'/gåelse** *-n* 1 evasion. 2 *mil.* outflanking.

+**om'/gåendẹ** *A* - 1 immediate, prompt: **pr. o-, med o- post** by return mail; **vente o- svar** expect an answer by return mail. 2 *mil.* flanking (movement).

+**om'/gåes** *V -gikkes, gå(tte)s* (=+**/gås**, ***/gåast**) 1 associate with, have intercourse with: **si meg hvem du o-, og jeg skal si deg hvem du er** a man is known by the company he keeps; **vanskelig (lett) å o-** hard (easy) to get along with. 2 deal with, handle, treat: **o- med varsomhet** handle with care; **o- med tanker om** be thinking about, have in mind. 3 (of two people approaching each other from opposite directions) pass by without seeing each other.

***om'/gå'st** *pr, pp of* **-gåast**

om'/handle *V -a/+-et* deal with, discuss (e.g. a case, question): **den o-de sak** the matter in question.

om'/heng *-et, pl* - (enclosing) curtain.

om'hengs/seng *-a* four-poster bed (with curtains).

om'/hug *-en* (=+**/hu**) care, concern: **vise o- for** be solicitous about.

***om'hug/sam** *A* careful (**for** about), painstaking.

omhyg'gelig *A* - care (**for, om** about), painstaking, studied; *(adv.)* with great care.

+**om'/hylle** *V -et/-hylte* envelop, wrap (**med** in).

+**om'/igjen** [/ijenn] *Av* cf **om**[3]

om'/innreie *V* +*-de*/**-dde* (=+**-rede**) refurbish.

ominø's *A* ominous.

om'/kalfa'tre *V -a/+-et* 1 *naut.* recaulk. 2 *fam.* radically, totally change; completely redo.

om'/kamp *-en* rematch.

+**omkapp'** *Av* cf **kapp**[3]

om'/kjøring *-a/+-en* 1 detour. 2 rerun.

+**om'/klamre** *V -a/+-et* clasp, cling to.

om'/kledd *A -/*-kledt* having changed one's clothes.

***om'/komen** [/kåmen] *A -e/-i, pl -ne* at a loss; excessively selfconscious, shy.

+**om'/komme** *V -kom, -kommet* be lost, perish.

om'/kontrahe'rt *A* - contracted for.

om'/kopling *-a/+-en* reconnection, recoupling.

omkos'tning [also åmm'/] +*-en*/**-a* charge, cost, expense: **betale o-ene** defray the expenses; **bli dømt til å betale sakens o-er** be sentenced to pay court costs.

omkr.=**omkring**

om'/kranse *V -a/+-et* encircle, wreathe.

+**om'/krets** *-en* circumference: **10 meter i o-** ten meters in c-; **i fem mils o-** within a radius of five miles; **i miles o-** for miles around.

omkring' *P* around; about: **gå o-** walk around; **her (der) o-** here (there) abouts; **o- klokka 11** around 11 o'clock; **gjøre o-** *archaic* turn around; **ta o-** embrace.

omkring'/ståendẹ *A* - : **de o-** the bystanders.

***om'/krins** *-en* cf **/krets**

+**omkull'** *Av* cf **kull**[3]

***om'/kvarv** *-et* round (of logs in a log house or planks in a boat).

+**om'/kved** *-et, pl* - (=***/kvede**) refrain; *fig.* saying, statement repeated ad nauseam.

***om'/kverve** *-t* area, district.

***oml.**=**omlag**

***om'/lag** *-et* surrounding layer; covering.

+ Bokmål; * Nynorsk; ° Dialect.
After letter: ' stress (Acc. 1); ' tone, stress (Acc. 2); · length.
Below letter: . not pronounced.

om'/laging *-a* change, transformation.
om'/land *-et* surrounding country, district.
om'/lasting *-a/+-en* reloading; transshipment (**av** of).
+**om'/legge** *V -la, -lagt* alter, change over (e.g. a factory).
om'/legging *-a/+-en* alteration (**av** of), change, rearrangement; replacement.
+**om'/liggende** *A* - (=*/**liggjande**) surrounding.
om'/lyd *-en* (=*/**ljod**) *gram.* vowel mutation (umlaut).
+**om'/lydt** *A* - (=*/**lydd**) *gram.* (of vowels) mutated, umlauted.
*__om'/lægre__ *V -a* besiege.
+**om'/løp** *-et* (=*/**laup**) 1 revolution, rotation: **månens o- om jorda** the moon's revolution about the earth. 2 circulation: **blodets o- i legemet** the c- of blood in the body; **ha o- i hodet** be alert, quick-minded; **sette i o-** put into c- (e.g. money, rumors).
+**om'løps/tid** *-a/-en* period of revolution (e.g. of a heavenly body); circulation period (e.g. of money); period of rotation (e.g. of crops); period of maturation (e.g. of a forest).
om'me *Av* at an end, over, past: **tida er o-** the time is up; **før (innen) året er o-** before the year is over.
om'n *-en* (=+**ovn**) 1 oven, stove; furnace: **legge i o-en** light the fire. 2 *astron.* Fornax.
om'nibus *-en* bus, omnibus.
om'ns/brød *-et* bakery bread.
om'ns/krok *-en* chimney corner, inglenook.
om'ns/rør *-et/*-a* (=*/**røyr**) stovepipe.
om'ns/varme *-n* stove heat.
om'n/sverte *-a* stove black (stove polish).
om'/organise're *V -te* reorganize.
+**om'/plante** *V -a/-et* replant, transplant.
omr. =**område**[1]
+**om'/regne** [/reine] *V -a/-et* recalculate; convert (**i** to): **o- dollar i kroner** convert dollars to *kroner*.
+**omregnings/kurs** [åm'reinings/] *-en* rate of exchange.
+**om'/reisende** *A* - itinerant, touring, traveling.
+**om'/ringe** *V -a/-et* surround.
om'/riss *-et, pl* - contour, outline: **Norges historie i o-** an outline of Norwegian history.
*__om'/rit__ *-et* cf **/riss**
*__om'/røding__ *-a* (=*/**røde**) discussion, mention.
*__om'/romme__ *V -a*: **o- seg** find a way out (of a predicament), gain time (to make a decision).
om'/rå *V -dde*: **o- seg** reflect, take extra time to make a decision.
*__om'/råd__ *-a* deliberation, reflection; time for reflection.
om'/råde[1] *-t, pl +-r/*-* area, territory; *fig.* domain, field: **være sakkyndig på et o-** be an expert in a field, line (of study, work, etc.).
*__om'/råde__[2] *V -de* cf **/rå**
om'råde/plan *-en* plan for the building or development of a given area (section of a city, etc.).
om'råde/sjef *-en* area commander (in the Norwegian National Guard).
*__oms.__ =**omsetjing, omsett**
+**om'/satte** *pt of* **-sette**
om'seg/gripende [+-sei/] *A* - expanding, spreading.
*__om'/segn__ *-a* declaration; report.
*__om'/setjing__ *-a* cf **/setting**
*__om'/setnad__ *-en* cf **/setning**
om'/setning *+-en/*-a* 1 business, sale(s); turnover: **en o- på fem millioner** a t- of five million. 2 conversion (of money). 3 *typog.* resetting.
om'setnings/avgift *-a/+-en* sales tax.
om'setnings/skatt *-en* sales tax.

+**om'/sette** *V -satte, -satt* (=*/**setje**) 1 realize (in monetary terms), sell. 2 convert (money). 3 *typog.* reset. *4 translate.
+**omset'telig** *A* - (of securities, etc.) negotiable, (of goods) salable.
+**om'/setting** *-en* (=*/**setjing**) *1 translation. 2 *typog.* resetting.
omsi'der *Av* at last, at length, finally; eventually.
+**om'/sikt** *-en* circumspection; discretion, foresight.
+**om'sikts/full** *A* circumspect, prudent; discreet.
om'/skape *V -a/-te* transform (**til** to): **man glemmer at Norge ved dampen og telegrafen er omskapt til et annet og moderne land** one forgets that Norway has been transformed by steam and the telegraph to a new and modern country (J. Lie, ab. 1900).
+**om'/skar** *pt of* **-skjære**
om'/skifte *-t, pl +-r/*-* 1 alteration, change. 2 change, substitute (i.e., one item which is used in place of another, e.g. a set of clothes, team of horses).
omskif'telig *A* - changeable, inconstant, variable.
+**om'/skiftelse** *-n* (=**-ing**) change, fluctuation, vicissitude: **skjebnens o-r** the v-s of fate.
+**om'/skipe** *V -et* reload (from one ship to another), transship.
*__om'/skipnad__ *-en* rearrangement, reorganization.
+**om'/skjære** *V -skar, -skåret* circumcise.
+**om'/skreven** *A -ent/-et, pl -ne* (=*/**skriven**) 1 discussed, mentioned (in writing). 2 *math.* circumscribed. 3 rephrased, rewritten.
om'/skrift *-a/+-en* 1 copying (**av** of), rewriting. 2 transcription.
+**om'/skri'vning** *-en* 1 rewriting. 2 circumlocution, euphemism, paraphrasing.
+**om'/skåret** *pp of* **-skjære**
om'/slag *-et* 1 (sudden) change, turnabout: **o- i været** change in the weather. 2 cover, wrapper; dust jacket (of a book). 3 *med.* compress, poultice.
+**om'slags/tegning** [/teining] *-en* (=*/**teikning** *-a*) cover design.
+**om'/slutte** *V -a/-et* enclose, envelop, surround; embrace, hug.
+**om'/slynget** *A* - entwined: **tett o-e** locked in an embrace.
+**om'/snakket** *A* - discussed; gossiped about.
om'/snudd *A -/*-snutt* reversed, turned about; (of persons) totally changed.
*__om'/snunad__ *-en, pl -er* alteration, change.
+**omson'st** *Av archaic.* in vain.
om'/sorg *-a/+-en* care, concern: **dra o- for** take care of, look after.
+**om'sorgs/full** *A* careful, considerate, thoughtful.
+**om'/spenne** *V -spente* enclose, envelop; span: **o-ende** comprehensive, far-reaching.
+**om'/spring** *-et* (=*/**sprang**) re-servicing (of a female animal that has not conceived as a result of the original servicing).
*__om'/spurd__ *A -spurt* in demand.
*__om'/stende__ *-t* circumstance, condition, situation.
omsten'delig *A* - detailed, elaborate; lengthy; (of persons) long-winded: **forklare o-** explain at great length.
+**omsten'delig/het** *-en* elaborateness, long-windedness; fussiness, particularity.
+**omsten'dig/het** *-en* circumstance: **etter o-ene** considering the c-s, taking the c-s into consideration; **formildende o-er** extenuating c-s; **under alle o-er** at any rate, in any case; **under ingen o-er** by no means, on no account; **gjøre o-er** stand on ceremony; **det kommer an på o-er** that all depends; **sitte i gode o-er** be well-off (financially); **være (komme) i o-er** be (get) pregnant.
+**omsten'dighets/kjole** *-n* maternity dress.
+**om'/stille** *V -stilte* readjust, rearrange, reset; switch over; invert, transpose: **o- seg til nye forhold** adapt oneself to new circumstances; **o- produksjonen fra krigs- til fredsbasis** (re)convert, switch over from wartime to peacetime production.
om'/stilling *-a/+-en* readjustment, rearrangement; switching over; inversion; transposition.
om'stillings/vanske *-n* difficulty of readjustment.
+**om'/streifende** *A* - stray; *(noun)* tramp, vagabond.
+**om'/streifer** *-en, pl -e* (=*__-ar__) tramp, vagrant.
om'/stridd *A -/*-stridt* (=+/**stridt**) disputed: **et o-t spørsmål** a controversial issue, matter.
+**om'/styrte** *V -a/-et* overthrow.
+**om'/støte** *V -te* annul, invalidate (a decision), refute (an argument).
+**om'/stående** *A* - 1 on the reverse side: **se o- (side)** see the next page, overleaf. 2: **de o-** the bystanders.
*__om'/sut__ *-a* care, concern: **ha o- for** take care of, look after, worry about.
+**om'/sverme** *V -a/-et* 1 swarm about, around. 2 surround (admiringly): **en o-t dame** an attractive, much-courted lady.
*__om'/sviv__ *-et* roving, wandering; evasion, flight; rotation.
+**om'/svøp** *-et* circumlocution, evasion; red tape: **gjøre o-** beat around the bush; **etter (med) mange o-** after (with) much beating around the bush; **uten o-** straight to the point.
+**om'svøps/fri** *A -tt* candid, frank, straight to the point.
+**om'svøps/full** *A* evasive, quibbling.
om'/sydd *A -/*-sytt* altered (by sewing), resewn.
om'/syn *-et* consideration, regard: **med o- til** concerning, as regards.
om'syns/laus *A* inconsiderate, thoughtless.
om'syns/ledd *-et* indirect object.
om'/tale[1] *-n/*-a* discussion, mention, report: **en o- i avisen** a notice in the newspaper; **kjenne av o-** know by repute; **være gjenstand for o-** be discussed, be the subject for comment.
+**om'/tale**[2] *V -te* discuss, mention, refer to: **den o-te** the beforementioned, the one in question.
om'/tanke *-n* reflection, thought; consideration: **handle uten o-** act thoughtlessly; **vise o-** show consideration, thoughtfulness.
+**omten'k/som'** *A -t, pl -me* (=*/**sam**) thoughtful.
om'/tenkt *A* - thoughtful.
omtr. =**omtrent**
omtren't *Av* 1 about, approximately: **de er o- like store** they are of about the same size; **det er o- en kilometer dit** it's about a kilometer away; **så o-** just about. 2 almost, nearly: **det er o- det samme** it's almost the same thing; **det er o- ferdig** it's nearly finished.
omtren'tlig *A* - approximate; inexact, vague; *(adv.)* about.
+**om'/tumlet** *A* - tossed about: **en o- tilværelse** a stormy, unsettled life.
+**omtvis'telig** *A* - debatable, disputable.
+**om'/tvistet** *A* - disputed: **et o- spørsmål** a point in question, a controversial issue.
om'/tykt *A* - liked, regarded: **godt o-** highly regarded.
om'/tåka *A* - (=+/**tåket**) dim, hazy, unclear; befogged, befuddled, groggy (from drinking or concussion).
+**om'/valg** *-et* (=*/**val**) reelection.
om'/vandrende *A* - itinerant, traveling.

om'/vankende *A* - itinerant, traveling.
om'/veg *-en* (=+/vei) 1 detour, roundabout way: **gjøre (gå) en o-** take a detour. 2: **på (ad) o-er** *fig.* indirectly, by devious means.
***om'/veg(e)s** *Av* indirectly.
+om'/veltning *-en* (=*/velting) revolution, upheaval.
om'/vende *V* +-te/*-e convert (**til** to): **bli o-t, o- seg** be converted, get religion.
+om'/vendelse *-n* conversion (**til** to).
om'/vending *-a/+-en* 1 reversal. *2=**omvendelse.**
+om'/vendt[1] *A* - (=*/vend) 1 inverted, reversed, the other way around; opposite: **det o-e av** the opposite of; **stå i o- forhold til** be inversely proportional to. 2 cf **omvende; omvendt**[2].
om'/vendt[2] *Av* conversely, inversely; on the other hand: **og o-** and vice versa.
+om'/verden *-en* (=*/verd) surroundings, outside world: **avsondret fra o-en** cut off from the outside world.
+om'/viklet *A* - wound (**med** with), wrapped (in).
+om'/viser *-en, pl -e* (=*-ar) guide.
+om'/vi·sning *-en* guided tour.
om'/vurde·re *V -te* reevaluate.
onane're *V -te* masturbate.
onani' *-en* masturbation.
+ond [onn'] *A* (=vond) bad, evil; hateful, malicious: **den o-e** the evil one (i.e. the devil); **det o-e** evil; **de o-e** the wicked; **et o-t smil** a malicious smile, smirk; **med o-t skal o-t fordrives** one must fight fire with fire; **o-e ånder** evil spirits; **fri oss fra det o-e** deliver us from evil; **gi o-t fra seg** scold; **gjøre o-t** do harm; **på godt og o-t** for better or for worse, whatever this may mean; **dele o-t og godt** share happiness and sorrow, for better or for worse; **se o-t til (på)** look hatefully at; **slite o-t** suffer; **være av det o-e** be a bad thing; (see also **vond** for other idioms containing **ond**).
+ond/artet [onn'/] *A* - 1 *med.* malignant, pernicious. 2 *fam.* (of persons) ill-tempered, malicious.
+onde [on'de] *-t, pl -r* 1 evil: **et nødvendig o-** a necessary e-; **det minste av to o-r** the lesser of two e-s. 2 disease, malady: **legemets o-r** the diseases of the body.
***on'der** *-dra, pl -drar* cf **ånder**
+ond/sinnet [onn'/] *A* - ill-tempered, malicious, vicious: **o- sladder** malicious gossip.
+ond/skap [onn'/] *-en* 1 malice, spite, wickedness: **hun var bare sladder og o-** she was nothing but gossip and malice. 2 malicious, spiteful act.
+ondskaps/full [onn'-] *A* malicious, spiteful, vicious.
ondulasjo'n *-en* (hair) waving.
ondule're *V -te* wave (hair).
***ong'lar** *pl of* **ongul**
***ong'le** *V -a* cf **angle**
***ong'ul** *-en, pl onglar* fishhook.
onkel [ong'kel] *-elen, pl -ler* uncle; *fam.* pawnbroker.
onn' *-a* work season on a farm (e.g. haying season, plowing season); *haste; hard work.
on'ne[1] *V -a* work on a farm during an *onn*.
***on'ne**[2] *V -a*: **o- på, o- seg** hurry, make haste.
on'ne/graut *-en* porridge served to the workers at the end of an *onn*.
on'ne/kar *-en* farm worker (hired for the duration of an *onn*).
on'ne/mellom *Av* (=***onn/imellom**) between working seasons on a farm (usu. between plowing and haying seasons).
on'nig** *A* - (=annig**) bustling, industrious.
***onn'/imellom** *Av* cf **onne/mellom**
***on'nor** *f of* **annan**
***on'nor/kvar** *f of* **annan/**
***on'nor/leis** *A* - cf **ann/**
onomatopoetisk [-po-e'tisk] *A* - onomatopoetic.
onsd.=**onsdag**
ons/dag [on's/] *-en* Wednesday.
Ons/øy [on's/] *Pln* twp, Østfold.
ontologi' *-en* ontology.
ontologisk [-lå'gisk] *A* - ontological: **det o-e gudsbevis** the o- argument.
onyk's *-en* onyx.
***o'p**[1] *-et* empty space, hole, opening.
+op'[2] *Av* cf **opp**
opa'l *-en* opal.
+op'/efter *P* cf **opp/etter**
***o'pen** *A -e/-i, pl -ne* cf **åpen**
***o'pen/berr** *A -bert* cf **åpen/bar**
***o'pen/berre** *V -a* cf **åpen/bare**
***o'pen/berring** *-a* cf **åpen/baring**
***o'pen/dage** *V -a* cf **opp/**
o'pera *-en* opera, opera house: **gå til o-en** become an opera singer; **komisk o-** opéra comique.
+o'pera/sanger *-en* (=*/songar) opera singer.
+o'pera/sangerin'ne *-a/-en* opera singer (female).
operasjo'n *-en* operation (financial, military, surgical): **foreta en o- på en** operate on sby.
operasjo'ns/basis *-en mil.* base of operations.
operasjo'ns/bo'rd *-et med.* operating table.
op'erativ *A med.* operative (e.g. treatment); *mil.* operational.
operatø'r *-en med.* operator.
opere're *V -te* operate.
operet'te *-n* comic opera, musical comedy, operetta.
operet'te/helt *-en* comic opera hero.
opia't *-et* opiate.
opinio'n *-en* (public) opinion.
opinio'ns/dannende *A* - influencing public opinion.
opinio'ns/måling +*-en*/**-a* public opinion poll.
+opinio'ns/ytring *-a/-en* expression of public opinion.
o'pium *-en* opium.
o'pium/valmue *-n bot.* opium poppy (Papaver somniferum).
***o'pnar** *-en* cf **åpner**
***o'pne** *V -a* cf **åpne**
***o'pning** *-a/-en* cf **åpning**
opos'sum *-en zool.* (Virginian) opossum (Didelphis virginiana).
opp' *P* 1 up, upwards (motion; cf **oppe**): **o- av** (up) out of (e.g. bed, a pocket, the water); **o- gjennom tiden (årene)** through the ages (years); **o- i landet** inland; **(gå) o- i o-** come out even; **o- i under** amazed, astonished; **o- i årene** on in years; **o- imot** up against, close to, approaching; **han har o- imot 1000 kroner** he has close to 1000 *kroner*; **o- med deg!** get up!; **o- med hendene!** stick 'em up!; **o- med humøret** chin(s) up; **o- og ned** up and down, back and forth; **(stå) rett o- og ned** (stand) erect, at attention; **(vende) o- ned** (turn) topsy-turvy, upside down; **o- til** up against, up to, as much as; **det kan bli o- til 10 graders frost** it can get as much as 10 below; **helt o- til våre dager** right up to the present; **det er o- til deg** it's up to you; **(være, ligge) like o- til** (be located) right next to; **alle mann o-** *naut.* all hands on deck; **vite verken o- eller ned** be at a loss, be totally confused. 2 open: **o- med døra** open the door; **knappe o-** unbutton; **lukke o-** open; **pakke o-** unpack. 3 again: **(gjøre noe) o- att** (do sth) again; **det er det samme o- og o- igjen** it's the same old story; **friske o-** refresh; **male o-** repaint; **ta noe o- igjen** repeat sth; **ta o- igjen** reassume. 4 (with other verbs, see these, e.g.): **gjøre o-** settle (accounts); **gjøre o- varme** light a fire; **lese o-** read aloud, recite; **rope o-** call (a list of names).
+opp'/ad *P* up, upwards.
+opp'ad/gående *A* - advancing (e.g. prices), rising (e.g. temperature), upward: **o- bevegelse** u- motion.
+opp'ad/strebende *A* - ambitious, aspiring; *hum.* upturned (e.g. nose).
+opp'ad/vendt *A* - upturned, upward.
opp'/agite'rt *A* - worked up, wrought up.
***opp'/al** *-et* breeding, raising (of livestock).
***opp'/alen** *A -e/-i, pl -ne* brought up, fostered, reared.
+opp'/arbeide *V -dde/-et* 1 build up, develop, work up: **o- en forretning** build up a business; **det o-dde seg en fiendtlig stemning mot ham** a hostile mood was forming against him. 2 make, manufacture: **o- store reserver** create large reserves (e.g. in a corporation). 3 work off: **o- ferier** make up vacation time.
opp'/att *Av* cf **opp**
+opp'/beva're *V -te* keep, preserve, save.
+opp'/beva·ring *-a/-en* 1 preservation, safekeeping (**av** of). 2 *merc.* safe-deposit box. 3 checkroom; storage.
+opp'/blande *V -a/-et* admix, dilute (e.g. liquids).
+opp'/blomstring *-a/-en* flourishing (**av** of), growth, prosperity.
+opp'/bløtt *A* - soaked, sodden, soggy (e.g. roads).
***opp'/blåsen** *A -e/-i, pl -ne* cf **/blåst**
opp'/blå·st *A* - inflated; swollen; arrogant, conceited, pompous.
+opp'/brakt *A* - exasperated, indignant: **være o- på en** be i- at sby.
+opp'/brakte *pt of* **-bringe**
opp'/brett *en* cuff (on trouser leg); turned-up sleeves.
opp'/bretta *A* - (=+-et) rolled up (sleeves); turned up (brim, cuffs).
+opp'/bringe *V -brakte, -brakt* 1 anger, provoke. 2 capture, seize (a ship).
+opp'/brudd *-et* breaking up, departure, striking camp: **det var alminnelig o-** everybody was leaving (e.g. from a party), there was a general exodus.
opp'/brukt *A* - consumed, exhausted, expended (e.g. money, resources, supplies).
+opp'/bud *-et* (=*/bod) 1 call-up, mobilization (of military forces), muster (of police). 2 summoning: **med o- av sine siste krefter** with a mustering of one's ebbing strength.
+opp'/by(de) *V -bød, -budt* 1 call up, mobilize (military forces). 2 exert, make use of, summon: **o- all sin kraft, evne** summon all one's strength, ability.
+oppby'delse *-n* exertion; summoning: **med o- av alle våre krefter** with a s- of all our strength.
+opp'/bygge *V -bygde* 1 build, build up, reconstruct. 2 edify, uplift (also *ironic*): **jeg skal o- dem med et lite panorama** I'll edify them with a little panorama (Jonas Lie).
oppbyg'gelig *A* - (=**oppbyggjeleg**) edifying, uplifting: **det var o- å høre på** *ironic* that was edifying to listen to.
+oppbyg'gelse *-n* (=*/bygging) 1 edification. 2 *eccl.* prayer meeting.
***oppbyg'gjeleg** *A* - cf **oppbyggelig**
+opp'/bød *pt of* **-by**
opp'/dage *V -a/+-et* discover; detect, find, find out.
+oppda'gelse [also opp'/] *-n* (=*-ing) detection, discovery (**av** of).
+oppda'gelses/reise *-a/-en* expedition, voyage of discovery.
+oppda'gelses/reisende *-n* explorer.
+opp'/dager [also /da'ger] *-en, pl -e* (=*-ar) 1 discoverer (e.g. of land,

+ Bokmål; * Nynorsk; ° Dialect.
After letter: ' stress (Acc. 1); ` tone, stress (Acc. 2); · length.
Below letter: . not pronounced.

chemical elements): **Amerikas o-** the d- of America. 2 detective.
*__opp'/daging__ *-a* cf **/dagelse**
Opp'/dal *Pln* twp, Sør-Trøndelag.
opp'/daling *-en* person from Oppdal.
+__opp'/dekning__ *-en* (=*/**dekking**) setting (a table); meal set out, spread.
opp'/dikta *A* - (=+**-et**) fictitious, imaginary, made up.
opp'/disking *-a*/+*-en* (=+**-ning**) sumptuous meal, spread.
+__opp'/dra__ *V -drog, -dradd/-dratt* 1 bring up, educate, rear; improve (sby's) manners: **o- på en** take sby in hand. 2 train (domestic animals).
opp'/drag *-et* assignment, mission, task: **få i o- å** be assigned to.
+__oppdra'gelse__ *-n* 1 education, upbringing; breeding, manners: **mangle o-** have no manners. 2 *hum.* corkscrew.
+__opp'/dragende__ *A* - educational.
+__oppdra'ger__ *-en, pl -e* educator, instructor.
+__opp'drags/giver__ *-en, pl -e* one who assigns a task (on the administrative level).
+__opp'/dratt__ *pp of* **-dra**
+__opp'/dre(i)v__ *pt of* **-drive**
+__opp'/drett__ *-et* breeding, raising (of domestic animals); young stock.
+__opp'/drette__ *V -a/-et* breed, raise (domestic animals, livestock); *derog.* raise children haphazardly, irresponsibly.
+__opp'/drevet__ *pp of* **-drive**
opp'/drift *-a*/+*-en* 1 buoyancy (of objects). 2 ambition, drive: **ha o- i seg** be ambitious.
+__opp'/drive__ *V -dre(i)v, -drevet* 1 force up, raise: **høyt oppdrevne priser** excessive prices. 2 cultivate, develop: **en godt oppdrevet gård** a well-cultivated farm. 3 obtain, procure: **ikke til å o-** not obtainable, not to be had.
+__opp'/drog__ *pt of* **-dra**
op'pe[1] *V -a*/+*-et*: **o- seg** exert oneself; show off.
op'pe[2] *Av* 1 up (location; cf **opp**); upstairs; out of bed; (of a recuperating patient) up and about; under consideration (e.g. a case): **der (her) o-** up there (here); **o- fra** from above; **o- fra landet** from the inland districts; **være (seint) o-** stay up (late); **sitte o-** sit up (waiting for sby); **være o- i (engelsk, fransk osv.)** be taking an examination in (English, French, etc.); **være o- i det** be occupied with sth; **være o- i tiden** be of current interest; **være o- i årene** be getting along in years; **være høyt o- og langt nede** be alternately exuberant and despondent; **stykket var sist o- i 1939** the last time the play was performed was in 1939. 2 open (e.g. window, door): **banken var o- ennå** the bank was still open.
+__op'pe/bar__ *pt of* **-bære**
+__op'pe/bie__ *V -et* wait for.
+__op'pe/bære__ *V -bar, -båret merc.* collect, earn, receive (interest, revenue, etc.).
+__op'pe/børsel__ *-elen, pl -ler merc.* collection, receipt (of revenue).
+__op'pe/båret__ *pp of* **-bære**
op'pe/gående *A* - (of patient) ambulatory, not confined to bed, up and around.
Op'pe/gård *Pln* twp, Akershus.
+__opp'/elske__ *V -et* cherish, foster, nurture: **stiklinger hun selv hadde o-et** cuttings she herself had nurtured.
op'pesen *A -, pl -*: **være o-** be in high spirits, feel great.
opp'/etter *P* up (along); upward.
+__opp'/fange__ *V -a/-et* 1 catch (e.g. a ball, glance, word): **det korte øyekast som jeg o-et** the brief glance which I caught. 2 intercept, pick up: **o- et nødsignal** pick up an SOS.
+__opp'/fant__ *pt of* **-finne**
+__opp'/farende__ *A* - fiery, hotheaded, irascible.
+__opp'/farenhet__ *-en* irascibility, vehemence.
opp'/fatning +*-en*/*__-a__ 1 apprehension, understanding: **være sein i o-en** be slow on the uptake. 2 conception: **etter min o-** in my opinion; **subjektive o-er** subjective judgments; **hans o- av rollen** (also:) his reading of the part.
opp'fatnings/evne *-a*/+*-en* (power of) apprehension, perception.
opp'/fatte *V -a*/+*-et* 1 comprehend, understand: **o- et vink** take a hint. 2 construe, interpret.
+__opp'/fattelse__ *-n* cf **/fatning**
+__opp'/finne__ *V -fant, -funnet* devise, invent; fabricate: **han har ikke oppfunnet kruttet** he's not too bright.
+__oppfin'nelse__ *-n* (=*__-ing__) invention (av of).
+__opp'/finner__ *-en, pl -e* (=*__-ar__) inventor.
*__opp'/finning__ *-a* cf **/finnelse**
+__oppfinn'/som'__ *A -t, pl -me* (=*/**sam**) ingenious, inventive, resourceful.
+__oppfinn'som/het__ *-en* ingenuity, inventiveness, resourcefulness.
opp'/fiska *A* - (=+**-et**) depleted of fish, fished out.
+__opp'/flamme__ *V -a/-et* arouse, fire with zeal, inflame.
+__opp'/flaske__ *V -a/-et* bring up, raise, spoon-feed (**på** on).
+__opp'/flytning__ *-en* advance, promotion (in school).
opp'/for' *P* 1 up, upward: **o- bakke** uphill. 2 above: **det ligger o- byen** it is located a- the town.
+__opp'/fordre__ *V -a/-et* 1 exhort, urge: **o- en til å holde en tale** call on sby for a speech. 2 demand, require: **dette o-er til omhyggelig overveielse** this demands, requires careful consideration; **føle seg o-et til å gjøre noe** feel called upon to do sth.
+__opp'/fordring__ *-en* appeal, request, summons: **ha o- til** feel called upon to.
+__opp'/fostre__ [/fostre] *V -a/-et* bring up, rear; cherish, foster.
opp'/fostring [/fostring] *-a*/+*-en* rearing, upbringing; fostering.
+__opp'/friske__ *V -a/-et* 1 renew, renovate, touch up; revive: **o- gamle minner** reminisce, revive old memories. 2 refresh: **han følte seg o-et** he felt refreshed.
+__opp'/funnet__ *pp of* **-finne**
opp'/fylle *V -fylte, -fylt* 1 fill, fill up: **hele værelset er o-t av bøker** the whole room is filled with books; **være o-t av noe** be engrossed with sth. 2 comply with, fulfill, gratify: **o- sine plikter** discharge one's duties; **o- et ønske** fulfill, gratify a wish.
oppfyl'lelig *A* - capable of being fulfilled, gratified, realized.
+__oppfyl'lelse__ *-n* (=*__-ing__) fulfillment: **gå i o-** be fulfilled, come true.
opp'/fyring *-a* lighting a fire.
+__opp'/føre__ *V -te* 1 build, erect (e.g. a house). 2 perform, present, put on (a play, opera, etc.): **o- scener** make a scene. 3 make an entry (in a ledger, list, etc.). 4: **o- seg (godt, dårlig)** behave, conduct oneself (well, poorly).
+__opp'/førelse__ *-n* 1 construction (**av** of), erection (e.g. of a house). 2 performance, presentation (of a play, opera, etc.).
+__opp'/førsel__ [also -før'-] *-en* behavior, conduct: **vise god o-** be well-mannered, conduct oneself properly.
opp'/gang *-en* 1 ascent, rise: **prisene er i o-** prices are climbing. 2 ascendancy, rising: **landet er i o-** the country is on its way up; **solens o-** sunrise. 3 entrance, stairway (e.g. in an apartment building), stairwell: **det er seks leiligheter i denne o-en** six apartments (not on the same floor) are served by this entrance; **vi bor i samme o-** we live in apartments sharing the same entrance. 4 breaking up (of ice).
opp'gangs/sag *-a* gate saw, sash saw.
opp'gangs/tid *-a*/+*-en* boom period, period of prosperity.
+__opp'/gav__ *pt of* **-gi**
+__opp'/gave__ *-a/-en* 1 duty, job, task: **det er en vanskelig o-** it's a tough job; **ha til o-** have as one's job; **han har fått til o- å** he's been assigned, instructed to; **jeg ser det som min o- å** I consider it my duty to; **være o-n voksen** be equal to the task. 2 problem (e.g. in mathematics, chess, etc.): **løse (regne) en o-** solve a p-. 3 (in school) assignment; composition: **rette o-r** grade papers; **skrive en o-** write a composition. 4 statement: **spesifisert o- over** itemized s- of.
+__opp'/gi__ *V -gav, -gitt* 1 abandon (e.g. a plan), give up (e.g. a struggle), resign from (e.g. a position): **o- en** give sby up as lost (i.e., incorrigible); **o- kampen** give up the struggle, throw in the sponge; **o- håpet om** give up hope of; **o- ånden** give up the ghost. 2 relinquish, waive (one's interests, rights): **o- sitt bo** turn over one's estate (e.g. to disposition by a court). 3 declare, state: **o- detaljer** give details; **o- sine inntekter** state one's income (e.g. for income tax purposes); **o- navn og adresse** give one's name and address; **o- nøye** specify. 4 assign (e.g. a subject for discussion or study): **o- pensum (til eksamen)** assign a reading list (curriculum) (in preparation for an examination); **forelese over oppgitt emne** lecture on an assigned topic (as part of the Norwegian doctoral examinations); (cf also **gi opp, oppgitt**).
opp'/gift *A* - remarried.
opp'/gitt *A* - 1 dejected, in despair, resigned. 2 assigned (cf **oppgi** 4).
+__opp'/givelse__ *-n* 1 abandonment (**av** of), giving up (e.g. of a project); relinquishment, waiver (e.g. of one's interests, rights). 2 declaration, statement (e.g. of income).
+__opp'/givende__ *-t* declaration, statement.
*__opp'/gjer__ [/jær] *-et* cf **/gjør**
*__opp'/gjerd__ [/jær] *-a* cf **/gjør**
+__opp'/gjort__ [/jort] *A* - (=*/**gjord**) decided, settled.
+__opp'/gjør__ *-et* (=*__-gjer__) 1 adjustment (**av** of), settlement (e.g. of an account, dispute). 2 clash, reckoning, scene: **holde o- med en** have a showdown, have it out with sby; **o-ets dag** the day of reckoning.
opp'/glødd *A* -/*__-glødt__ 1 red-hot. 2 *fig.* enthusiastic (**over** about); ecstatic, on fire.
opp'/gulp *-et* regurgitation; (bird) pellet.
opp'/gående *A* - ascending, rising (e.g. sun, terrain, prices), improving: **for o-** upward bound; **det er o- tider** business is on the upgrade.
opp'/gått *A* - trampled, trodden: **en o- sti** a beaten path.
*__opp'/gåve__ *-a* cf **/gave**
opph. =**opphavlig**
opp'/hakka *A* - (=+**-et**) chopped, hacked up: **en o-et stil** a choppy style.
*__opp'/hald__ *-et* cf **/hold**
*__opp'halds/ver__ *-et* cf **oppholds/vær**
opp'/hav *-et* 1 beginning, origin, source. 2 *hum.* father or mother.
opp'/havlig *A* - original.
opp'havs/mann *-en, pl -menn*/*__-menner__ author, instigator (**til** of).
opp'havs/rett *-en* author's, inventor's rights.
+__opp'/hengt__ *A* - hung up, suspended.
+__opp'/hete__ *V -a/-et* heat up.
opp'/heve *V -a*/+*-et*/+*-de* 1 annul, cancel, nullify, rescind (e.g. a contract, decree, decision, policy). 2: **o- hverandre** neutralize each other; **sakens**

omkostninger ble o-et *jur.* the costs of the law suit were assumed by both defendant and plaintiff.

+**opp'/hevelse** *-n* 1 annulment, cancellation, discontinuation (**av** of). 2 *(pl)* objections, protestations: **gjøre mange o-er over** make a big fuss about, grumble about; **uten o-er** without further ceremony.

+**opp'/hisse** *V -a/-et* 1 incite, provoke: **o- en til å gjøre noe** egg sby on to do sth. 2 excite, inflame, infuriate.

+**opp'/hisselse** *-n* agitation, excitement.

opp'/hjelp *-a/+-en* aid, encouragement (**av** of), promotion (e.g. of government subsidized industries).

opp'/hogging *-a/+-en* breaking up, scrapping (e.g. a ship); cutting up (e.g. wood).

+**opp'/hold** *-et* (=***/hald**) 1 cessation, pause, stop: **det regnet uten o-** it rained incessantly; **etter et øyeblikks o-** after a moment's pause; **jeg vil uten o- skrive til Bergen** I am going to write to B- without delay; **i dag er det o-** today it isn't raining. 2 sojourn, stopover: **et o- på Capri** a sojourn in C-. 3 livelihood, support: **tjene til livets o-** earn one's living.

+**opp'/holde** *V -holdt, -holdt* 1 delay, detain: **jeg o-er Dem** I'm keeping you. 2 support, sustain: **o- livet** keep body and soul together. 3: **o- seg** stay, reside. 4: **o- seg over noe** criticize, take exception to sth.

+**opp'holds/rom** [/romm] *-met* living room; lounge.

+**opp'holds/sted** *-et* 1 residence. 2 place to stay.

+**opp'holds/tilla'telse** *-n* residence permit (for foreigners).

+**opp'holds/vær** *-et* weather without rain.

+**opp'/hope** *V -et* accumulate, amass, pile up.

+**opp'/ho'pning** *-en* (=***/hoping**) accumulation, pile.

opp'/hovna *A* - (=+**-et**) swollen.

***opp'/høgje** *V -de* cf **/høye**

+**opp'/hør** *-et* 1 cessation, stop: **uten o-** continually, unceasingly. 2 conclusion, end, termination.

+**opp'/høre** *V -te* cease, come to an end, stop: **o- med** discontinue (e.g. the work), suspend (e.g. hostilities); **ilden opphører!** cease fire!

+**opp'hørs/salg** *-et* closing-out sale.

+**opp'/høye** *V -de/-et* (=***/høgje**) 1 elevate, raise: **o- et tall i annen (tredje, fjerde) potens** square (cube, raise to the fourth power) a number. 2 exalt, glorify, praise: **o- seg** *bibl.* exalt oneself; **den seg selv o-er, skal fornedres** whosoever shall exalt himself shall be abased (Matt. 23, 12). 3: **o-et** (as *adj.*) elevated, lofty (e.g. style, thoughts); noble, sublime: **o-et ro** sublime calm, serenity; **med o-et forakt** with lofty scorn.

+**opp'høyet/het** *-en* elevation, grandeur, sublimity (of style, thought, etc.).

opp'/i *P* (=**opp i**) up in, into: **legge seg o- noe** interfere in sth; **midt o-** right in the midst of.

opp'/igjen'nom *P* up through: **alle årene o-** through all the years (Undset).

+**opp'/ildne** *V -et* incite, inflame, rouse to action.

opp'/imot *P* (=**opp imot**) against, towards; approaching, close to: **det kostet o- 1000 kroner** it cost close to 1000 *kroner*.

+**opp'/irre** *V -a/-et* exasperate, irritate, provoke: **o- en til raseri** goad sby into a fury.

opp'/jaga *A* - (=+**-et**) (of wild game) flushed; (of people) jittery, jumpy.

+**opp'jaget/het** *-en* jumpiness.

+**opp'/kalle** *V -kalte*: **o- en etter** name sby after (e.g. a child after its father).

opp'/kalling *-a/+-en* 1 (telephone) call. 2 naming (after sby).

opp'/kast *-et* vomit.

+**opp'/kaste** *V -a/-et* 1 throw up (e.g. a dike, wall); dig (e.g. a grave); vomit. 2 turn up: **en o-et nese** a turned-up nose. 3 *fig.* raise (e.g. a doubt, question): **o- seg** assume (e.g. a position); **o- seg til dommer** set oneself up as judge.

opp'/kava *A* - (=+**/kavd**, +**/kavet**) 1 agitated, disturbed. 2 busy; overcome, overwhelmed (e.g. by conflict, strife, work).

opp'/kjeftig *A* - audacious, impudent, shameless.

opp'/kjøp *-et* (large-scale) buying (up), purchase (**av** of); cornering.

+**opp'/kjøper** *-en, pl -e* (=***-ar**) buyer (**av** of); speculator.

opp'/kjørsel *-elen, pl -ler* 1 driving up. 2 approach, driveway.

+**opp'/klare** *V -te* 1: **o-ende vær** clearing weather. 2 explain, throw light on, unravel (e.g. question, obscure point, mystery): **mysteriet ble o-t** the mystery was cleared up, solved; **o- et omtvistet punkt** elucidate a disputed point.

opp'/klaring *-a/+-en* 1 clearing up (of weather). 2 elucidation, explanation.

opp'/kledd *A -/*-kledt* clothed; equipped, furnished.

opp'/kok *-et* 1 bringing (sth) to a boil; parboiling; reboiling. 2 *fig.* rehash (e.g. of old stories).

***opp'/kome** [/kåme] *-a* cf **/komme**

opp'/komling *-en* parvenu, social climber, upstart.

opp'/komme *-a/+-et* 1 underground spring, vein; *fig.* source (e.g. of inspiration, strength). 2 wealth of ideas: **det er ikke noe o- i ham** he offers little in the way of original ideas.

opp'/komst *-en* 1 beginning, rise (e.g. of capitalism): **i o-** rising. 2 development, progress.

+**opp'/konstrue're** *V -te* invent, manufacture (e.g. difficulties).

opp'/krav *-et*: **mot o-** C.O.D. (cash on delivery).

opp'/krever *-en, pl -e* (=***-jar**) collector; tax collector.

***opp'/kveik** *-en* encouragement.

+**opp'/kvikke** *V -a/-et* enliven, excite, stimulate.

+**opp'/kvikkelse** *-n* excitement, stimulation.

+**opp'/kvikker** *-en, pl -e* (=***-ar**) 1 stimulant, tonic. 2 (alcoholic) drink, pick-me-up.

oppl.=**opplag; oppløsning**

Oppl.=**Oppland**

opp'/lag *-et* 1 stock, store(s), supplies (on hand): **varer på o-** stored goods, stockpile. 2 edition, issue (of books, newspapers): **boka utkom i et o- på 1000 eksemplarer** a thousand copies of the book were printed; **nytt o-** reissue, reprint. 3: **i o-** (of ships) laid up.

opp'lags/næring *-a/+-en* food reserve (e.g. in a plant).

opp'lags/tal *-et* (=+**/tall**) number of copies in a printing (of a book, magazine, newspaper, etc.).

opp'lags/tomt *-a* depot, storehouse.

+**opp'/lagt** *A* - (=***/lagd**) 1 in a good mood, in fine fettle: **o- på, til** inclined to (sth); in the mood for. 2 certain, obvious, open and shut: **det er (ganske) o-** there's no question about it; **et o- flertall** a clear majority; **en o- vinner** a sure bet (e.g. in horse racing); **spille o-e kort** lay down a (winning) hand. 3 laid up (e.g. ships), stored: **o-e penger** savings.

opp'/land *-et* hinterland, trading area; surrounding area (e.g. of a city): **Oslo har et stort o-** Oslo serves a large area.

Opp'/land *Pln* county, eastern Norway.

opp'/landsk *A* - of or pertaining to Oppland county.

+**opp'/late** *V -lot, -latt* 1 open (one's ears, eyes, mouth, etc.). 2: **o- sin røst** open one's mouth, speak.

+**opp'/latt** *A* - (=***/laten**) open, receptive (**for** to).

***opp'/laup** *-et* cf **/løp**

opp'/legg *-et* 1 laying-up (e.g. of ships), storing: **o- av fonds** reserve of funds. 2 (in knitting) casting-on (of stitches). 3 (in soccer) setting-up (of scoring opportunities). 4 initial conception, introduction, presentation: **planen var dårlig i o-et** the plan was poorly worked out. 5 subject (for discussion); underlying idea, plot (of a play).

opp'/lending *-en* native of Oppland.

+**opp'/leser** *-en, pl -e* (=***-ar**) reciter.

opp'/lesing *-a/+-en* (=+**/lesning**) reading (aloud), recitation.

opp'/lett *A* - not raining.

***opp'/lette** *-a* (=+**/lett**) pause; temporary cessation (esp. of rain).

opp'/leve *V -de* 1 experience, live through (adventures, crises, events, etc.): **han har o-d mye** he has had many interesting experiences. 2 live (long enough) to see: **han o-de ikke frigjøringen** he didn't live to see the liberation.

°**opple'velse** *-n* (=***-ing**) adventure, experience: **hvert nummer var en o-** every number was a thrill (a treat); **vi ble en o- rikere** this (experience) gave us a memory for life.

opp'/liva *A* - (=+**-et**) refreshed; animated, gay.

opp'/livende *A* - enlivening, exhilarating.

+**opp'/li'vning** *-en* (=***/living**) resuscitation, revival.

+**opp'livnings/forsøk** *-et* (=***opplivings/**) attempt to resuscitate (sby, sth).

+**opp'/lot** *pt of* **-late**

opp'/lyse *V -te* 1 illuminate, light up: **en sterkt o-t sal** a brightly lit hall. 2 elucidate, make clear. 3 inform, state: **o- en om noe** inform sby about sth; **han o-te at banken var stengt** he said the bank was closed. 4 enlighten: **vi lever i en o-t tid** we live in an enlightened age.

opp'/lysende *A* - enlightening, informative, instructive.

opply'sning [also opp'/] *+-en/*-a* (=***/lysing**) 1 illumination, lighting (e.g. of a room, street). 2 clarification, enlightenment; education: **arbeide for folkets o-** work for popular education. 3 information: **en o-** a piece of information; **o-er** information; **nærmere o-er** particulars.

opply'snings/arbeid *-et* educational work.

+**opply'snings/forbund** *-et*: **Arbeidernes O-** League for Workers' Education.

opp'lysnings/tid *-a/+-en* (age of) Enlightenment.

opp'/ly'st *A* - 1 illuminated, lighted. 2 educated, informed; enlightened.

opp'/læring *-a* training.

opp'/læ'rt *A* - trained.

+**opp'/løftende** *A* - edifying, elevating, inspiring: **et o- syn** *ironic* an edifying spectacle.

+**opp'/løp** *-et* 1 gathering of crowds; commotion, disturbance, riot. 2 finishing spurt (in a race). 3 *naut.* run (of a torpedo boat).

+**opp'/løpen** *A -ent, pl -ne* (of adolescents) lanky, overgrown.

+**opp'/løse** *V -te* 1 break up, disperse (e.g. a crowd), dissolve (e.g. a marriage, a partnership, a substance in a liquid): **o- seg i** dissolve into, turn into; **et ansikt o-t i gråt (latter)** a face dissolved in tears (laughter).

+ Bokmål; * Nynorsk; ° Dialect.
After letter: ' stress (Acc. 1); ` tone, stress (Acc. 2); · length.
Below letter: . not pronounced.

2 decompose (e.g. an organism), disintegrate. 3 destroy, disorganize: **en o-ende tidsånd** a disrupting spirit of the age. 4: **o-t hår** loosened (i.e., not bound up) hair. 5 *mus.* resolve (a dissonance).
+**opplø'selig** *A* - soluble.
+**opp'/lø'sning** *-en* cf **/løysing**
+**opp'lø'snings/middel** *-elet/-midlet, pl -midler* solvent.
+**opp'lø'snings/prosess'** *-en* process of disintegration.
opp'/løysing *-a* (=+**/løsning**, ***/løysning**) 1 decay, decomposition, disintegration: **jeg vet så omtrent hva tid o-en begynner** I know just about when decomposition sets in (Ibsen); **være i o-** (e.g. of authority, power) be crumbling. 2 dissolution (e.g. of a marriage, partnership). 3 *mus.* resolution of a discord.
***opp'/løysning** *-a/-en* cf **/løysing**
+**opp'/magasine're** *V -te* store, warehouse (e.g. furniture).
opp'/mann *-en, pl -menn/*-menner* arbitrator; umpire.
opp'/marsj *-en* (troop) deployment; marching (e.g. of demonstrators): **være i o-** be approaching, impending.
opp'/med *P* (up) along, (up) by: **gutten hadde kløvet o- masten** the boy had climbed up (along) the mast; **o- elva lå det garder** there were farms along the river.
opp'/merking *-a/+-en* marking (**av** of); marker (e.g. a blaze).
+**oppmer'k/som'** *A -t, pl -me* 1 attentive, observant: **bli, være o- på** notice, become aware of; **gjøre o- på noe** call, draw attention to sth; **høre meget o-t etter** listen very attentively. 2 considerate, thoughtful (**mot** of).
+**oppmer'ksom/het** *-en* 1 attention, attentiveness: **følge med o-** follow closely, pay close attention to; **vekke o-** attract attention. 2 consideration, courtesy; compliment, gift: **vise en kvinne stor o-** be very attentive to a woman, ply a woman with gifts and compliments; **hjertelig takk for o-en i anledning av** many thanks for (your) thoughtfulness at the time of (the death of a member of the family, etc.).
***opp'/mode** *V -a* encourage, request.
***opp'/moding** *-a* encouragement, request: **på o-** on r-.
+**opp'/muntre** *V -a/-et* 1 cheer (up). 2 encourage, urge: **o- en til noe** encourage sby to (do) sth.
+**opp'/muntrende** *A* - cheering, encouraging: **lite o-** discouraging.
+**opp'/muntring** *-en* encouragement (**til** to), incentive.
+**opp'muntrings/premie** *-n* consolation prize.
+**opp'/my'kning** *-en* limbering up (e.g. before athletic events).
opp'/måling *-a/+-en* (=***/mæling**) 1 measuring, surveying; survey. 2 society responsible for topographical and hydrographic surveys: **Norges Geografiske O-** Norwegian Geodetic Survey.
+**opp'/navn** *-et* (=***/namn**) nickname.
+**opp'/nevne** *V -te* appoint, designate, nominate.
opp'/norske *-a/+-et* (esp. of language) make more Norwegian, Norwegianize.
opp'/nå *V -dde* attain, gain, reach; obtain, secure: **o- å** manage to; **o- en alder av** reach the age of; **o- enighet** arrive at agreement; **o- en fordel** gain an advantage; **o- sin hensikt** attain one's goal, purpose; **det samme kunne o-es ved** the same purpose could be served by; **hva har du tenkt å o- på den måten?** what do you think that (way of going about it) will get you?.
oppnå'elig *A* - attainable, obtainable.
opp'/ofre *V -a/-et* sacrifice: **o- sitt liv for sitt land** lay down one's life for one's country; **o- seg (for)** dedicate, devote oneself (to).
+**opp'/ofrelse** *-n* sacrifice, self-sacrifice: **med o- av** at the price of.
+**opp'- og** [å] **a'v/gjort** [/jort] *A* - settled and done.
opp'/om' *P* up around, up to: **han var o- i dag og spurte etter deg** he dropped in today and asked about you.
opponen't *-en* opponent (at doctoral disputation at university).
oppone're *V -te* oppose: **o- mot en** o- sby.
opportu'n *A* opportune, timely.
opportunis'me *-n* opportunism.
opportunis't *-en* opportunist.
opposisjo'n *-en* opposition (in all English senses): **være i o- til** be opposed to.
opposisjonell' *A -elt* oppositional; given to argumentativeness.
+**opposisjo'ns/lysten** *A -ent, pl -ne* argumentative, disputatious.
opposisjo'ns/parti' *-et, pl +-er/*-* opposition party.
+**opposisjo'ns/trang** *-en* compulsion to oppose.
opp'/over [/åver] *P* up, uphill: **o- trappene** up the stairs.
opp'/pakning *+-en/*-a* burden, load; *mil.* pack: **en soldat med full o-** a soldier with full field pack.
+**opp'/passer** *-en, pl -e* (=***-ar**) *archaic* servant; *mil.* orderly.
+**opp'/plantet** *A* -: **med o-ede bajonetter** with fixed bayonets.
opp'/pussing *-a/+-en* (=+**/pusning**) reconditioning, renovation, touching up.
oppr. =**opprinnelig**
opp'/ramsing *-a/+-en* rattling off, reeling off: **o- av alt det jeg hadde på meg** reeling off of everything I had on (Heiberg).
+**opp'/rant** *pt of* **-rinne**
+**opp'/redd** *A* - (=***/reidd**): **sengen står o-** the bed is made.
+**opp'/regning** [/reining] *-en* enumeration (**av** of).
+**opp'/reise** *V -te* 1 erect, raise (e.g. a monument, statue): **o-t** erect, upright. 2 reestablish, restore: **o- ens ære** restore one's honor. 3 *bibl.* raise (up), resurrect: **o- fra de døde** raise from the dead.
+**opp'/reisning** *-en* 1 amends, compensation, reparation. 2 restoration (e.g. of one's honor, reputation); satisfaction. 3 *jur.* remedy at law; restitution of civil rights.
***opp'/reist** *-en* cf **/rør**
+**opp'/reklame're** *V -te* ballyhoo, make exaggerated claims for.
opp'/rensking *-a/+-en* cleaning out.
opp'/rett [also åpp'-] *A* - (esp. of posture) erect, straight, upright.
+**opp'/rette** *V -a/-et* 1 establish, found (e.g. an agency, business, institution). 2 conclude, enter into (e.g. an agreement, contract): **o- et testamente** make a will. 3 compensate for, make good (e.g. damage, loss).
+**opp'/retter** *-en, pl -e* (=***-ar**) founder.
+**opp'rett/holde** *V -holdt, -holdt* 1 maintain, uphold (e.g. discipline, order). 2 sustain: **nok til å o- livet** enough to s- life.
+**opp'/revet** *A -, pl -ne* 1 cut, torn up. 2 agitated, shaken, shattered (e.g. nerves).
+**opprik'tig** *A* - genuine, sincere; candid, frank: **o- talt** frankly speaking, to tell the truth.
+**opprik'tig/het** *-en* candor, frankness, sincerity.
+**opp'/rinne** *V -rant, -runnet poet.* come, dawn (e.g. daylight): **den dag o-er aldri** that day will never come.
+**opprin'nelig** *A* - 1 original; *(adv.)* originally. 2 natural, unsophisticated: **en o- natur** an u- personality; **ekte og o-e følelser** genuine and u- feelings.
+**opprin'nelig/het** *-en* 1 originality. 2 primitivity.
+**opprin'nelse** *-n* origin, source.
+**opp'/rivende** *A* - agonizing, harrowing.
opp'/rop *-et* 1 roll call. 2 offer (e.g. at an auction, sale).
+**opp'/rulle** *V -a/-et* 1 roll up (e.g. shades). 2 *mil.* roll up (the flank of an army). 3 display, unfold (e.g. a panorama, spectacle).
+**opp'/runnet** *pp of* **-rinne**
opp'/rusting *-a/+-en* rearmament: **Moralsk O-** Moral R-.
opp'/rydding *-a/+-en* (=+**/rydning**) cleaning up, tidying (**av** of).
opp'/rykk *-et* advancement, promotion.
+**opp'/rykning** *-en* promotion: **o- i gradene** p- in grade (e.g. in civil service).
+**opp'/rømt** *A* - elated, in high spirits, spirited.
opp'/rør *-et* 1 commotion, excitement: **i (sterkt, vilt) o-** (greatly) agitated; **sette byen i o-** set the town on end; **være i o-** be in an uproar. 2 insurrection, rebellion, revolt: **gjøre o-** rebel, revolt (**mot** against).
opp'/rørende *A* - revolting, shocking: **det er o-** it's an outrage, it's s-.
+**opp'/rører** *-en, pl -e* (=***-ar**) insurgent, rebel.
+**opp'rørs/akt** *-en*: **lese o-en** read the riot act.
opp'/rø'rsk *A* - 1 defiant, mutinous, rebellious. 2 (of stomach) upset.
opp'/rø'rt *A* - 1 agitated, rough (e.g. sea). 2 indignant, shaken, stirred up (**over** about).
opp'/rådd *A* - 1 at a loss (**for** for), lacking. 2 helpless, perplexed, puzzled.
+**opp'/sa** *pt of* **/si**
+**opp'/sagt** *pp of* **/si**
opp'/samling *-a/+-en* accumulation, collection, gathering.
+**opp'/sang** *-en* 1 chanty, work song. 2 fighting song: **O- for frihetsfolket i Norden** Battle Hymn for the Freedom Lovers of Scandinavia (Bjørnson).
opp'/sats *-en* 1 article, essay, paper. 2 centerpiece, epergne. 3 caster, cruet stand. 4 *mil.* sighting gear (on a cannon).
+**opp'/satt** *A* - 1 bent upon, determined to, set (up)on: **o- på å gjøre noe** intent upon (anxious to be) doing sth. 2 (e.g. of a woman's hair, type for a book, a prize, troops) arranged, set up.
+**opp'/satte** *pt of* **-sette**
***opp'/sede** *V -a* bring up, educate.
***opp'/seding** *-a* education, upbringing.
***oppsei'eleg** *A* - cf **oppsigelig**
***opp'/seiing** *-a* cf **/sigelse**
+**opp'/seiling** *-en*: **være under o-** 1 (of a ship) approach, draw near. 2 be in the air, in the offing; **et uvær er under o-** a storm is brewing.
+**oppset'sig** *A* - stubborn.
+**oppset'sig/het** *-en* stubbornness.
opp'/sett[1] *-et* article, essay, paper.
***opp'/sett**[2] *A* - cf **/satt**
+**opp'/sette** *V -satte, -satt* 1 postpone, put off: **oppsett ikke til i morgen hva du kan gjøre i dag** don't put off til tomorrow what you can do today; **o- på ubestemt tid** postpone indefinitely. 2 *archaic* draw up (a contract, will, etc.). (cf also **sette opp.**)
+**opp'/settelse** *-n* delay, postponement, putting off: **saken tåler ingen o-** the matter is urgent.
+**opp'/si** *V -sa, -sagt* 1 fire, give notice: **o- en leilighet** give notice of moving (from an apartment); **jeg er blitt oppsagt** I've been fired. 2 call in (a loan), terminate (a contract). (cf also **si opp.**)
+**oppsi'gelig** *A* - (e.g. of an annuity, a contract) terminable; redeemable (e.g. bonds).
+**opp'/sigelse** *-n* dismissal, notice: **en måneds o-** a month's n- (of termina-

tion on a job); **uten o-** without previous notice; **på o-** terminable (e.g. a contract).

+**opp'sigelses/konto** *-en merc.* savings account subject to prior notice to the bank of large withdrawals.

opp'/sikt *-a/+-en* 1 superintendence, supervision: **ha o- med** be in charge of, watch over; **holde under o-** supervise. 2 attention, sensation: **gjøre, vekke o-** create a stir.

+**opp'sikts/vekkende** *A* - (=+**oppsikt/**) sensational.

+**opp'/sitter** *-en, pl -e* (=***/sitjar**) 1 leaseholder, tenant farmer (Eastern Norway). 2 *jur.* freeholder.

opp'/skaka *A* - (=+**-et**) flustered, perturbed, startled (**av** by).

opp'/skakende *A* - disquieting, perturbing, upsetting.

+**opp'/skjær** *-et* cold cuts.

opp'/skjørta *A* - (=+**-et**) bustling, excited, flustered.

+**opp'/skremt** *A* - (=***/skremd**) alarmed, frightened, startled.

opp'/skrift *-a/+-en* 1 recipe (**på** for). 2 formula: **romanen er laget etter den gamle o-en** the novel is written according to the familiar f-.

+**opp'/skrive** *V -skrev, -skrevet* 1 make a note of, write down. 2 use up (paper in writing). 3 *merc.* increase the face value of stock.

opp'/skrubba *A* - (=+**-et**) abraded, scraped (up).

opp'/skrudd *A* - (=***/skruva**) 1: **et o- tempo** an increased tempo. 2 exorbitant (e.g. prices). 3 bombastic, high-sounding (e.g. style).

opp'/skrytt *A* - (=***/skrøytt**) ballyhooed, blatantly advertised.

+**opp'/skyte** *V -skjøt, -skutt* 1 postpone. 2: **oppskutt** coiled, raised; *mil.* (of ammunition) expended.

+**opp'/skåret** *A* - cut, sliced; slashed.

opp'/slag *-et* 1 placard, poster; posting (of a placard): **bekjentgjøre ved o-** post (a notice); **o- om portotakster** notice concerning postal rates. 2 *mus.* upbeat. 3 opening (of a book). 4 breaking of an engagement. 5 beginnings (**til** to), material, theme (for a play, novel, etc.). 6 cuff; lapel.

opp'slags/bok *-a, pl -bøker* reference book.

opp'slags/brev *-et* letter breaking an engagement.

opp'slags/tavle *-a* bulletin board.

opp'slags/verk *-et* reference work.

opp'/slitende *A* - backbreaking, fatiguing; enervating.

+**opp'/sluke** *V -te* 1 devour, swallow up; absorb: **en alt o-ende interesse** an all-absorbing interest. 2 *bibl.* annihilate, destroy; swallow up: **Herren skal o- dem i sin vrede** the Lord shall swallow them up in his wrath (Psalms 21, 9).

+**opp'/slutning** *-en* 1 *mil.* closing up (of ranks). 2 support (**om** for); rallying round.

+**opp'/snappe** *V -a/-et* snatch up; intercept (e.g. a letter).

opp'/sop *-et* sweepings.

opp'/spa'rt *A* - (=***/spara**) accumulated (e.g. capital, interest, savings), saved (up); pent-up (e.g. rage).

opp'/spedd *A* -/*-*spett* diluted, thinned.

opp'/spi'lt *A* - (=***/spila**) 1 distended: **med o-e øyne** wide-eyed. 2 *fig.* excited.

+**opp'spilt/het** *-en* 1 distension. 2 *fig.* excitement.

opp'/spinn *-et* fabrication, falsehood: **det er bare o-** it's a pack of lies.

+**opp'/spore** *V -a/-et/-te* run to earth, track down (e.g. an animal, a criminal); ferret out (e.g. the truth).

opp'/spytt *-et* expectoration, spittle.

opp'/stabla *A* - (=+**-et**) piled, stacked (up).

opp'stad/gogn [/gångn] *-a* small vertical loom used to weave rugs.

opp'/staka *A* - (=+**-et**) marked with stakes, staked out.

opp'/stand *-en* rebellion, revolt, uprising: **gjøre o-** revolt.

+**oppstan'delse** *-n* 1 *bibl.* resurrection. 2 excitement, fuss, stir: **det var stor o-** there was a great to-do.

+**opp'/stander** *-en, pl -e* (=***-ar**) standard, upright (post).

opp'/stasa *A* - (=+**-(e)t**) decked out, dressed up.

+**opp'/stemt** *A* - (=***/stemd**) excited, in high spirits.

opp'/stigende *A* - ascending, rising: **i o- linje** in lineal ascent (genealogy); **o- saft** *bot.* rising sap.

+**opp'/sti'gning** *-a/-en* (=***/stiging**) 1 ascent, rising (e.g. of a balloon). 2 climbing (e.g. of a mountain, steep terrain). 3 (upward) incline, slope.

+**opp'/stille** *V -stilte* 1 arrange, place; post, set up: **o- et eksempel** give an example; **virke o-t** give the effect of being contrived, artificial. 2 advance (a theory), set forth (e.g. a proposal), lay down (a rule). 3: **o- seg** present oneself (for consideration, etc.) (cf also **stille opp**).

opp'/stilling *-a/+-en* arrangement, order, position: (as mil. command) **o-!** fall in!; **ta o-** take up a position (e.g. to watch a parade), fall into line. (Cf also **oppstille.**)

+**opp'/stod** *pt of* **-stå**

***opp'/stode** [/ståe] *-a* cf **/standelse**

+**opp'/stopper** *-en, pl -e* (=***-ar**) snub nose, turned-up nose.

opp'/strammer *-en, pl -e* (=***-ar**) 1 pick-me-up, tonic. 2 reprimand, talking-to.

+**opp'/stukket** [/stokket] *A* -, *pl -ne* 1 (e.g. of one's face) stung, swollen. 2 (of road) staked out, surveyed. 3 (of itinerary) planned: **de o-ne veier** the beaten paths. 4 *naut.* (of line) slack.

opp'/stuss *-et* hullabaloo, uproar: **gjøre, vekke o-** raise hell.

opp'/stykking *-a/+-en* division, splitting up (**av** of).

+**opp'/styltet** *A* - (=***/styltra**) pompous, stilted (e.g. speech).

opp'/styr *-et* excitement, hullabaloo, uproar.

+**opp'/støt** *-et* belch, burp; regurgitation: **få moralske o-** have an attack of moral platitudes.

+**opp'/stå** *V -stod, -stått* 1 *bibl.* rise from the dead. 2 arise, come into existence: **det oppstod et rykte** a rumor sprang up; **det var o-tt en tvist** a dispute had arisen. 3: **o-ende** projecting (e.g. cliff), vertical. 4: **o-tt** (of persons) out of bed, up.

+**opp'/suge** *V -de* absorb; sponge up.

+**opp'/summe're** *V -te* 1 sum up (e.g. evidence). 2 total up (e.g. a bill).

opp'/sving +*-et*/**-en* 1 flight, soaring (e.g. of birds). 2 advance, progress; boom (e.g. economic, industrial): **ta o-** make strides, progress.

opp'/sydd *A* -/*-*sytt archaic* sewn up: **o-e klær** readymade clothes.

opp'/syn *-et*/**-a* 1 aspect, face, look: **jeg liker ikke o-et på ham** I don't like his looks. 2 charge, supervision: **føre, ha o- med noe** have charge of, look after, supervise sth. 3 inspection, surveillance: **være under o- (av)** be under s- (of). 4 inspector; inspector's office.

opp'syns/mann *-en, pl -menn/*-menner* inspector; attendant, warden.

+**opp'/søke** *V -te* 1 hunt up, look for, seek out. 2 go to see, pay a visit to.

+**opp'/ta** *V -tok, -tatt* 1 accept, admit, take (up, in): **o- en i familien** take sby into the family, accept sby as one of the family; **o- hansken** accept a challenge, take up the gauntlet; **artikkelen ble opptatt i avisen** the article was accepted by, printed in the paper. 2 occupy, take up (one's time, thoughts, interest, etc.): **en sak som o-r sinnene** a case of general interest, which attracts wide attention. 3 (other idioms): **o- bestillinger** take orders (for merchandise, etc.); **o- forhør over** hold an inquiry about; **o- en fortegnelse over** make a list of; **o- kart over** make a map of; **o- et lån** arrange, make a loan; **o- en sak til doms** submit a case to judgment. (cf also **ta opp.**)

+**opp'/tagelse** *-n* cf **/taking**

opp'/tak *-et* 1 recording (of sound) (**av** of), taking (of films, photographs); (film) shot; record, transcription. 2 initiative; starting point: **gjøre o-et til** take the initiative for. 3 placing of land under cultivation. 4 digging, pulling up (of root crops, e.g. potatoes); pickings (e.g. residue of hay rakings). 5 *educ.* admission (of pupils).

+**opp'/takelse** *-n* cf **/taking**

+**opp'takelses/prøve** *-a/-en* cf **opptaks/**

+**opp'/taker** *-en, pl -e* (=***-ar**) 1 recorder. 2 (potato) digger. 3 (bottle) opener.

opp'/taking *-a/+-en* 1 acceptance, admission (to a school, group, organization, etc.). 2 making, taking (of orders, a loan, etc., cf **oppta** 3).

opp'taks/prøve *-a/+-en* entrance examination.

opp'/takt **-a/+-en* 1 *mus.* upbeat. 2 anacrusis (metrics). 3 preliminaries, prelude (**til** to).

***opp'/tamd** *A -tamt* practiced, trained.

+**opp'/tatt** *A* - busy, engaged, occupied (**av, med** with); absorbed (**av** by, **med** in): **denne plassen er o-** this seat is taken; **jeg er svært o- i øyeblikket** I'm very busy at the moment; **han er meget o- av arbeidet sitt** he's all wrapped up in his work.

+**opp'/tegnelse** [/teinelse] *-n* memorandum, note; *(pl)* memoirs.

***opp'/teken** *A -e/-i, pl -ne* cf **/tatt**

+**opp'/telling** *-a/-en* (=***-teljing**) counting), enumeration (**av** of).

+**oppten'kelig** *A* - (=***-tenkjeleg**) conceivable, possible.

opp'tennings/ved *-en* kindling (wood).

opp'/til' *P* 1 up against. 2 (=**opp' til**) as much as, up to and including: **en torsk kan bli o- 20 år gammel** a cod can live up to 20 years.

+**opp'/tjene** *V -te* acquire, earn: **o- seg en formue** build a fortune.

opp'/tog [/tåg] *-et* parade, procession.

+**opp'/tok** *pt of* **-ta**

+**opp'/tre(de)** *V -trådte, -trådt* 1 appear (in court), perform (on the stage): **o- under falsk navn** go under an alias. 2 act, behave: **o- bestemt overfor en** be firm with sby; **o- på egen hånd** act on one's own; **o- som** act as, in the capacity of. 3 (of natural events and diseases) occur.

+**opp'/treden** *-en* 1 appearance, performance (e.g. on the stage). 2 behavior, conduct. 3 action.

+**opp'/tredende** *A* -: **de o-** the actors, performers.

+**opp'/trekkeri** *-et* extortion, swindling: **slike priser er det rene o-** such prices are highway robbery.

+**opp'/trinn** *-et* 1 episode, incident; scene (e.g. in a play). 2 riser (of stairs).

+**opp'/trukket** [/trokket] *A* -, *pl -ne* drawn up.

+**opp'/trykk** *-et* reissue, reprint.

+**opp'/trådte** *pt of* **-tre(de)**

+**opptuk'telse** *-n* (=***/tukting**) discipline: **naturen gikk over o-n** the temptation became too strong.

+**opp'/tøyer** *pl* disorders, riots: **gjøre o-** start a riot.

opp'/under *P* (=**opp under**) 1 up

+ Bokmål; * Nynorsk; ° Dialect.
After letter: ' stress (Acc. 1); ' tone, stress (Acc. 2); · length.
Below letter: . not pronounced.

under: **støtte o-** support. 2 under, underneath: **o- fjellet** high up on the mountainside; **o- land** near land.
opp'/vakt *A* - bright, intelligent.
+opp'/vakte *pt of* **-vekke**
+opp'/varme *V* *-a/-et* heat, warm, warm up: **o-et mat** warmed-over food.
opp'/varming *-a/+-en* heating, warming.
+opp'/varte *V* *-a/-et* serve, wait on: **o- en med** regale sby with (stories); **o- ved bordet** wait on table.
+opp'/varter *-en, pl -e* (=***-ar**) waiter.
+oppvar'tning *-en* (=***/varting**) attention, service.
opp'/vask *-en* 1 dishwashing; (washed) dishes, utensils: **pikene gjorde o-en ferdig i en fart** the girls washed the dishes in a jiffy. 2 (violent) squaring of accounts; settlement of one's social obligations.
opp'vask/klut *-en* dishcloth, dishrag.
opp'vask/kum [/kom'] *-men* sink.
opp'vask/maski'n *-en* dishwasher.
opp'vask/vatn *-et* (=**+/vann**) dishwater.
opp'/ved *P* (up) by, next to.
+opp'/veie *V* *-de* balance, compensate (for), make good, offset (e.g. deficiencies, losses).
+opp'/vekke *V* *-vakte, -vakt* 1 rouse, stir (e.g. anger, sympathy). 2 *bibl.* restore to life: **o- fra de døde** raise from the dead.
opp'/vekst *-en* adolescence, youth: **i o-en** while growing up.
+opp'/vigle *V* *-a/-et* agitate, stir up (e.g. the masses).
+opp'/vigler *-en, pl -e* agitator, demagogue.
+opp'/vigleri' *-et* agitation; subversive activity.
+opp'/vise *V* *-te* exhibit, show: **en vil ikke kunne o- maken til dette** you won't find its equal.
+opp'/vi'sning *-en* demonstration, exhibition.
+opp'/voksende *A* -: **den o- slekt** the coming generation.
***opp'/vokster** *-eren, pl -rar* cf **/vekst**
opp'/ø'st *A* - excited, wrought up.
+opp'/øve *V* *-de* develop, train (e.g. one's faculties); practice.
op'på *P* on, upon; on top (of).
***opp'/åt** *P* up to.
+oprin'delig *A* - cf **opprinnelig**
opsjo'n *-en* option: **ta o- på noe** take an o- on sth (e.g. on film rights from an author).
opte're *V* *-te* choose, opt.
+op'tiker *-en, pl -e* (=***-ar**) optician.
optikk' *-en* optics.
optima'l *A* optimum (e.g. conditions).
optimis'me *-n* optimism.
optimis't *-en* optimist.
optimis'tisk *A* - optimistic.
op'timum *-et* optimum.
op'tisk *A* - optical.
o'pus *-et* opus.
***o'r**[1] *+-a/-en* *bot.* alder (genus Alnus).
***o'r**[2] *P* from, out of (also **ut or**): **Viv vaknar or tankane sine** V- awakens from her thoughts (Vesaas).
ora'kel *-elet/-let, pl -el/+-ler* oracle: **oraklet i Delfi** the Delphic o-.
orangutang' *-en* *zool.* orangutang (Rango pygmaeus).
oransje[1] [orang'sje] *-n* *bot.* orange (fruit, tree).
oransje[2] [orang'sje] *A* - orange (colored).
oransje/gul *A* orange yellow (colored).
***o'rar** *pl* delirium, ravings.
ora'tor *-en* orator.
orato'risk *A* - oratorical.
orato'rium *-iet, pl +-ier/*-ium* *mus.* oratorio.
o'rd *-et* 1 word: **o- for o-, o- til annet** w- for w-, letter perfect; **det ene o- tok det annet** one w- led to another; **et o- i rette tid** a w- in season, at the right time. 2 proverb, saying: **det er et gammelt o- som sier** there's an old saying that goes; **du kjenner vel det gamle o-et** you surely know the old saying. 3 Word of God: **i begynnelsen var o-et** in the beginning was the Word (John 1, 1). 4 ability, opportunity to speak; contribution to a debate: **o-et er fritt** the meeting is open for discussion; **få o-et** be given, get the floor; **føre o-et** be the speaker, play the main role; **føre det store o-** talk big, shoot one's mouth off; **ha (gripe, ta) o-et** have (seize, take) the floor; **ha o-et i sin makt** be a gifted speaker; **ta o-et for en** speak in sby's behalf; **ta o-et fra en** interrupt sby; **ta til o-e** begin speaking. 5 reputation, talk (about sth): **gå o- av (om)** be famous, much talked about; **ha o- (på seg) for å** be reputed to, have a reputation for; **ha et godt (dårlig) o- på seg** have a good (bad) reputation. 6 promise, word of honor: **et o- er et o-** a promise is a promise; **gi en sitt o- på noe** promise sby sth; **gå fra sitt o-** break a promise; **holde (stå ved) sitt o-** keep one's word; **tro (ta) en på o-et** take sby at his word; **være mann for sitt o-** be capable of keeping a promise. 7 (idioms with adj.): **med andre o-** in other words; **med ett o-** in short, in a word; **(ikke) for gode o- og betaling** (not) for love or money; **godt o- igjen** no offence meant; **for et (godt) o-** for little cause, over nothing; **på første o-et** at the first asking, immediately; **med rene o-** straightforward, in so many words; **det var rene o- for pengene** that's putting it plainly, that's laying it on the line; **det er et sant o-** that's certainly true, you said it; **store o- og fleskefett sitter ikke fast i halsen** big words come easy. 8 (idioms with verbs): **han fikk ikke o- for seg** he couldn't (find words to) express himself; **gi en et o- med på veien** give sby a bit of parting advice; **ha et o- med (i laget)** get one's two cents worth in; **ha sine o- i behold** turn out to be right; **la et o- falle** mention, drop a hint; **før jeg visste o-(et) av det** before I realized it, before I could say Jack Robinson.
ord.=**orden**
***o'rdast** *V* *-ast* converse, talk.
+o'rd/bilde *-t* word image.
o'rd/blind *A* word-blind.
+o'rdblind/het *-en* *psych.* dyslexia, word blindness.
o'rd/bok *-a, pl -bøker* dictionary, lexicon.
o'rd/danning *-a/+-en* (=**+-else**) word formation.
o'rde[1] *N*: **komme til o-** make oneself heard; **ta til o-** begin to speak.
o'rde[2] *V* *-a/+-et* discuss, mention: **jeg skal o- det til ham** I'll m- it to him; **o- innpå** bring up, mention.
o'rde/lag *-et* expression, words.
or'den *-enen, pl +-ener/*-nar* 1 order (=arrangement, organization, system): **det hører til dagens o-** that's an everyday occurrence; **for o-s skyld** as a matter of form, to keep the record straight, to make sure; **ha god o- på** have in good order, well-organized; **holde o-** maintain discipline, keep order; **alt er i o-** it's all fixed, set; everything's in order; **bringe i o-** put in order, organize; **det er i o-** that's all right, OK, forget it; **det er i sin o-** that's as it should be; **det går nok i o-** it will work out all right; **være i o-** (of a machine, etc.) be in working condition; be correct, as it should be; **ha nervene i o-** have good nerves; **i alfabetisk o-** (also) alphabetically arranged; **i den skjønneste o-** in the very best shape; **i tur og o-** one after the other, in turn; **naturens o-** the order of nature; **sluttet o-** *mil.* closed order; **en ny tingenes o-** a new state of affairs. 2 order (=decoration, title). 3 order (=classification, e.g. in biology, zoology). 4 order (=group, e.g. a religious order). 5 orderliness (=good behavior).
or'dens/band *-et* (=**+/bånd**) 1 ribbon of a royal order. 2 *zool.* catocala, underwing.
or'dens/karakte'r *-en* (school) grade for behavior.
or'dens/mann *-en, pl -menn/*-menner* 1 person of orderly, regular habits. 2 monitor (in a classroom).
or'dens/menneske *-t, pl +-r/*-* person of orderly, regular habits.
or'dens/politi' *-et* patrolmen, policemen on the beat; riot squad.
or'dens/promosjo'n *-en* presentation ceremony (of royal orders).
or'dens/regn [+/rein] *-et* granting of royal orders in wholesale lots.
or'dens/sans *-en* sense of order.
or'dens/tal *-et* (=**+/tall**) ordinal numeral.
or'dens/vern [/væ'rn] *-et* auxiliary, special police.
or'dentlig [also: år'ntli] *A* - 1 orderly: **alt var pent og o- i huset** the house was attractive and o- in all respects. 2 correct, proper, respectable: **en o- pike** a decent girl; **han fører et svært o- liv** he lives a very orderly life; (*adv.*) **o- gift** properly married; **det brenner ikke o-** it doesn't burn properly; **du får kle på deg o-** be sure and dress properly (i.e. warmly enough). 3 proper, real, regular: **det var et o- måltid** that was a real meal; **er det ikke moro å bo på et o- turisthotell da?** isn't it fun to live in a regular tourist hotel? (Bang-Hansen); **det 96de o-e Storting** the 96th regular (session of) Parliament; **vi har ikke hatt en o- ferie på tre år** we haven't had a real vacation in three years; (*adv.*) **det var o- snilt av deg** that was really extremely nice of you; **nå fikk du o-!** now you really caught it!
***o'rd/fang** *-et* vocabulary.
o'rd/fattig *A* - (of a language) having a limited vocabulary; (of a person, also) of few words, taciturn.
+o'rd/flom' *-men* (=***/flaum**) sea, torrent of words.
o'rd/forråd *-et* vocabulary.
+o'rd/fører *-en, pl -e* (=***-ar**) 1 spokesman: **være o- for** act as, be s- for. 2 mayor: **o- i Oslo** m- of Oslo.
+o'rd/gyter *-en, pl -e* windbag.
+o'rd/gyteri *-et* verbiage, verbosity.
o'rd/hag *A* eloquent; quick-witted.
***o'rd/hegd** *-a* eloquence, rhetoric.
o'rd/hitten *A* *+-ent, pl -hitne* quick at repartee, quick-witted.
+o'rd/holden *A* *-ent, pl -ne* (=***/halden**) as good as one's word, reliable.
ordinan's *-en* *eccl.* ordinance.
ordinasjo'n *-en* 1 *eccl.* ordination. 2 prescription (of drugs).
ordina't *-en* *math.* ordinate.
ordine're *V* *-te* 1 *eccl.* ordain: **han skal o-s** he is going to be o-ed. 2 prescribe (drugs).
ordinæ'r *A* 1 ordinary, regular, usual. 2 common, vulgar.
o'rd/kast *-et* altercation, dispute: **de var oppe i et o-** they had words.
o'rd/klasse *-a/-en* part of speech.
+o'rd/kløveri *-et* (=***/kløyving**) hairsplitting.
o'rd/knapp *A* *-knapt* succinct; reticent, taciturn: **en o- mann** a man of few words.
+o'rd/kunstner *-en, pl -e* (=***-ar**) artist, virtuoso with words.
o'rd/la *pt of* **-legge, -leggje**
***o'rd/lag** *-et* cf **orde/**
+o'rd/legge *V* *-la, -lagt* (=***/leggje**): **o- seg** express oneself.
***o'rd/leie** *V* *-dde*: **o- seg** express oneself.
o'rd/liste *-a* word list.
o'rd/lyd *-en* wording (e.g. of a document, letter, text): **etter o-en** lit-

erally; **følge o-en av en kontrakt** observe the terms of a contract.
or'dne *V -a/⁺-et* 1 organize, put in order: **o- opp i** put in order; **o-ede forhold** law and order; **et vel o-t samfunn** a well-organized society. 2 arrange, fix, take care of: **jeg skal o- det** I'll take care of it, fix it; **o- med** arrange, take care of; **det o-er seg** everything will be, will turn out all right. 3 pay, settle (e.g. an account): **o- seg med** make financial arrangements, come to an (usu. financial) agreement with.
or'dning *-a/⁺-en* 1 arrangement, organization, system. 2 (usu. financial) settlement: **treffe en o-** reach a s-.
ordonnan's *-en* (=⁺**ordonans**) *mil.* orderly.
***o'r/drag** *-et* extract; abstract, summary.
or'dre *-n* command, order(s): **etter o-** to order; **etter høyeste o-** on highest authority; **i o-** on order; **(en veksel) til o- av** (a check) to the order of.
⁺**or'dre/seddel** *-elen, pl -sedler* (=*/**setel**) order blank.
o'rd/rett *A* - literal, verbatim: **sitere o-** quote v-, word for word.
o'rd/rik *A* copious; verbose, wordy.
***o'rd/sending** *-a* greeting, message.
o'rd/skifte *-t* 1 argument, exchange of words. 2 debate, discussion.
⁺**o'rd/skiller** *-en, pl -e* (=*/**skilar**) space bar (on typewriter).
o'rd/skvalder *-eret/-ret* blather, verbiage.
⁺**o'rd/snill** *A* - adept at selection of the correct word or phrase.
⁺**o'rd/spill** *-et* (=*/**spel**) play on words, pun.
⁺**o'rd/språk** *-et* adage, proverb, saying.
o'rd/stilling *-a/⁺-en* word order.
o'rd/strid *-en* altercation, argument, dispute.
⁺**o'rd/strøm'** *-men* torrent of words.
⁺**o'rd/styrer** *-en, pl -e* (=*-**ar**) moderator (of a discussion); chairman (of meeting).
ord. t. =**ordenstall**
o'rd/tak *-et* (=/**tøke**) adage, saying; *hist.* battle cry.
⁺**o'rd/valg** *-et* choice of words, phraseology.
o'rd/viss *A dial.* 1 quick at repartee, quick-witted. 2 as good as one's word, trustworthy.
o're *-a* cockeye, lug (on harness).
***o'r/eigne** *V -a* dispossess, expropriate.
o're/kjerr *-et* alder brake, thicket.
o're/kratt *-et* alder thicket.
org. =**organisasjon; organisk**
orga'n *-et, pl -/⁺-er* 1 organ (of body, institution, newspaper). 2 voice (quality): **et godt o-** a fine voice. 3 agency (of the UN).
organ'di *N* mull, organdy.
organisasjo'n *-en* organization.
⁺**organisasjo'ns/frihet** *-en* (=*/**fridom**) freedom to organize (e.g. a union).
organisasjo'ns/tvang *-en* coercion to join a union; union shop.
organisa'tor *-en* organizer.
organisato'risk *A* - organizing.
organise're *V -te* organize: **o-t arbeidskraft** organized, union labor.
orga'nisk *A* - organic: **o- kjemi** o- chemistry.
organis'me *-n* organism.
organis't *-en* organist.
or'ge *V -a/⁺-et fam.* forage, rustle, steal.
or'gel *-elet/⁺-let, pl ⁺-ler/*-el* organ: **spille på o-** play the o-; **han spiller alltid for fullt o-** *mus.* he always plays on full organ (with the organ on full); *fig.* he always gives it his all.
or'gel/brus *-et* organ peal.
or'gel/pipe *-a* organ pipe.
or'gie *-n* orgy.
⁺**orienta'ler** *-en, pl -e* (=*-**ar**) Oriental.
orientalis't *-en* orientalist.
orienta'lsk *A* - Eastern, Oriental.
Orien'ten *Pln* the Orient.
oriente're *V -te* orient: **være o-t** be oriented, be conversant, familiar (with a problem, situation, etc.); **o- seg** find one's bearings; **han kunne ikke o- seg** he had lost his bearings.
oriente'ring *-a/⁺-en* orientation.
⁺**oriente'rings/løp** *-et* orientation race (=cross-country race in which the runners must plot their own course).
⁺**oriente'rings/løper** *-en, pl -e* runner in an orientation race.
oriente'rings/sans *-en* sense of direction.
origina'l¹ *-en* 1 original (e.g. of a document). 2 character, eccentric.
origina'l² *A* 1 original. 2 (of persons) eccentric, odd, queer.
originalite't *-en* 1 originality. 2 eccentricity.
origina'l/vare *-a/⁺-en* liquor bottled in bond (e.g. Scotch whiskey).
ori'go *-en math.* origin of coordinates.
or'k *-et* effort, strain.
ork. =**orkester**
orka'n *-en* hurricane.
⁺**orka'n/aktig** *A* - hurricane-like.
Or'k/anger *Pln* twp, Sør-Trøndelag.
Or'k/dal *Pln* twp, Sør-Trøndelag.
or'ke¹ *-a/⁺-et* effort, strain.
or'ke² *V -a/⁺-et* 1 be able (to), manage: **alt han o-et** all he could manage; **jeg o-er ikke å gjøre det** I haven't the strength to do it. 2 bear, stand; bring oneself to: **han o-et ikke å straffe gutten** he couldn't bring himself to punish the boy; **jeg o-er ikke den fyren** I can't stand that fellow.
orkes'ter *-eret/⁺-ret, pl -er/⁺-re* orchestra (may also include bands): **for fullt o-** with pomp and circumstance; in full view.
orkes'ter/grav *-a/⁺-en* orchestra pit.
orkes'ter/plass *-en* orchestra seat.
orkestre're *V -te* orchestrate.
orkidé *-en bot.* orchid (family Orchidaceae).
Or'k/land *Pln* twp, Sør-Trøndelag.
⁺**Or'kn/øyene** *Pln* (=*/**øyane**) the Orkney islands, the Orkneys.
or'kn/øying *-en* Orcadian, Orkneyan (inhabitant of the Orkneys).
or'kn/øysk *A* - Orcadian, Orkneyan.
orlog [å'rlåg] *-en*: **til o-s** in the navy.
orlogs/flagg *-et* naval ensign (flag, standard).
orlogs/flåte *-n* (=*/**flote**) fleet of warships, navy.
orlogs/gast *-en* sailor, seaman (in navy).
orlogs/kaptei'n *-en* (navy) commander.
or'lon *-et* orlon.
orlov [å'rlåv] *-en mil.* furlough, leave (of absence).
or'm *-en* 1 serpent, snake: **Ormen lange** "The Long Serpent" (King Olav Tryggvason's warship). 2 *archaic* maggot, worm (cf **mark** for modern term). 3 *med.* (intestinal) worm: **ha o-** have w-s. 4 *lit.* gnawing, pangs (of conscience, anxiety, etc.): **sorgens tærende o-** the consuming p-s of sorrow (Ibsen). 5 mania, passion: **hans o- var teatret** the theater was his p-.
Or'm *Prn(m)*
or'me *V -a/⁺-et*: **o- seg** move sinuously; wriggle (along like a snake, worm).
⁺**or'me/aktig** *A* - vermiform, wormlike.
or'me/bol *-et* (=/**bøle**) vipers' nest.
or'me/ga'rd *-en hist.* snake pit (=method of execution).
or'me/gras *-et* bracken, fern.
⁺**or'me/gå'rd** *-en* cf /**gard**
or'me/ham' *⁺-men/*-en* cast-off, shed snake's skin.
***o'r/mekta(st)** *V -a(st)* grow faint, languish.
or'me/telg *-en bot.* male fern (Dryopteris filix-mas).
***o'r/minnast** *V infl as* **minnast** be on the verge of falling asleep.
or'm/slo *-a zool.* blindworm, slowworm (Anguis fragilis).
or'm/stukken [/stokken] *A ⁺-ent, pl -stukne* worm-eaten; decayed.
ornamen't *-et, pl -/⁺-er* ornament.
ornamenta'l *A* decorative, ornamental.
ornamente're *V -te* ornament.
ornamentikk' *-en* ornamentation, ornamenting art.
orna't *-et eccl.* canonicals, vestments: **i fullt o-** wearing one's v-.
ornitolog [-lå'g] *-en* ornithologist.
ornitologi' *-en* ornithology.
⁺**or'ntlig** *A* - cf **ordentlig**
or're *-n zool.* black grouse (Lyrurus tetrix).
orr'/fugl *-en zool.* black grouse.
orr'/hane *-n zool.* blackcock, male black grouse.
orr'/høne *-a zool.* female black grouse, heath hen.
***o'r/sake** *V -a* excuse.
o.r.sakf. =⁺**overrettssakfører/*-ar**
***o'r/saking** *-a* apology, excuse.
***o'r/sku'rd** *-en* judgment, verdict.
ort¹ [or't] *-a hist.* coin (=80 **øre**), 1/5 **spesiedaler**.
ort² [or't] *-en* drift (horizontal mine shaft).
ortodok's *A* - orthodox.
ortodoksi' *-en* orthodoxy.
ortofo'n *A* orthophonic.
ortografi' *-en* orthography.
ortogra'fisk *A* - orthographical.
ortope'd *-en* orthopedist.
ortopedi' *-en* orthopedics.
ortope'disk *A* - orthopedic.
or'v *-et* 1 handle of a scythe. 2 willow ring (used to hold a gate in place).
o's¹ *-en* 1 (strong) odor. 2 smoke (e.g. from a lamp).
o's² *-en/-et* mouth (of a river), outlet.
***o's³** *pt of* **ase**
O's *Pln* twp, Hedmark, Hordaland.
***osb.** =**og så bortetter**
oscillasjo'n *-en* oscillation.
oscilla'tor *-en* oscillator.
oscille're *V -te* oscillate.
o'se *V -te* 1 reek (also *fig.*): **o- av brennevin** r- of liquor; **o- av hykleri** r- of hypocrisy. 2 (of a lamp, oven) smoke; steam: **o- i vei** (of a car) roar away.
osea'n *-et, pl -/⁺-er* ocean.
⁺**osea'n/damper** *-en, pl -e* (=*-**ar**) ocean liner.
oseanogra'f *-en* oceanographer.
oseanografi' *-en* oceanography.
oseanogra'fisk *A* - oceanographical.
O'sen *Pln* twp, Sør-Trøndelag.
osfr. =**og så frametter** etc.
os'ke *-a* (=⁺**aske**) ash(es): **komme fra o-a i elden** go from (out of) the frying pan into the fire.
os'ko/rei *-a* (=⁺**åsgårds/**) company of dead spirits (on horseback) who ride through the air (esp. at Christmastime) sweeping human beings along with them.
Oslo [os'lo] *Pln* Oslo.
Oslo/fjo'rden *Pln* Oslo Fjord.
⁺**oslo/frokost** *-en* (=*/**frukost**) "Oslo breakfast" (breakfast or late morning meal provided for school children in Oslo and some other communities, instituted in 1931).
oslo/jente *-a* girl from Oslo.
oslo/mann *-en, pl -menn/*-menner* inhabitant, native of Oslo.
osma'n *-en* Ottoman.
osman(ni)sk [-ma'nsk, -man'nisk] *A* - Ottoman.
osmo'se *-n* osmosis.
osmo'tisk *A* - osmotic.
oso'n *-en/-et* ozone.
⁺**oso'n/holdig** *A* - ozonic.

⁺ Bokmål; * Nynorsk; ° Dialect.
After letter: ' stress (Acc. 1); ` tone, stress (Acc. 2); ' length.
Below letter: . not pronounced.

os'p -*a bot.* aspen (Populus tremula).
os'pe/tømmer -*et* aspen (timber).
os'pe/ved -*en* aspen (wood).
oss' *ob of* **vi** (also, *dial.*=**vi**).
ost[1] [os't] -*en* 1 cheese: **kjøpe en halv o-** buy half a cheese. 2=**ostestoff.**
+**o'st**[2] *Av* from, toward the east.
+**oste** [os'te] *V* -*a*/-*et*: **o- seg** curdle.
oste/høvel [os'te/] -*elen, pl* -*ler* cheese slicer (of Norwegian construction, functioning like a plane).
oste/klokke -*a* cheese dish with cover.
oste/løype -*n* rennet.
oste/mark -*en* (=**/makk**) larva of the cheese fly (Piophila casei).
osten'tativ *A* ostentatious.
oste/skorpe [os'te/] -*a* cheese paring, cheese rind.
oste/stoff -*et* curd.
+**Ostindia** [ostin'dia] *Pln* the East Indies.
+**ostindisk** [ostin'disk] *A* - East Indian.
***ostre** [os'tre] -*a* cf **østers**
osv.=**og så videre** etc.
Ot.=**Odelstinget**
***o'te** -*a* fight; competition, rivalry: **midt i ota** in the midst of his struggle (Vesaas).
o'ter -*eren, pl* -*rer* 1 *zool.* otter (Lutra vulgaris). 2 (fishing) otter.
o'ter/fjøl -*a* (fishing) otter board.
otium [o'tsium] -*et* leisure (time); retirement.
Ot. prp.=**Odelstingsproposisjon**
o'tre *V* -*a*/+-*et* 1 fish with an otter board. 2 *dial.* back, crawfish: **o- seg** move, worm one's way.
Otta [ot'ta] *Pln* twp, Oppland.
Ot'tar *Prn (m)*
***ottast** [ot'tast] *V* -*ast* cf **ottes**
otte[1] [ot'te] -*a* early morning: **stå opp i o-a** get up at the crack of dawn.
otte[2] [ot'te] -*n* anxiety, apprehensiveness, fear.
otte/full *A* anxious, apprehensive, uneasy.
otte/laus *A* free from anxiety, unconcerned.
Otter/øy [ot'ter/] *Pln* twp, Nord-Trøndelag.
+**ottes** [ot'tes] *V* -*es*, -*es* (=***ottast**) be anxious, apprehensive, uneasy.
otte/sam' [ot'te/] *A* 1 apprehensive, fearful. *2 dangerous, risky.
+**otte/sang** [ot'te/] -*en* (=***/song**) matins, matin song.
ottoma'n -*en* Ottoman; ottoman.
outrere [utre're] *V* -*te* exaggerate, overdo: **hun kler seg o-t** she overdresses.
out/rigger [au'trigger] -*en, pl* +-*e* outrigger.
out/sider [au'tsaider] -*en, pl* +-*e* outsider (esp. *pol.* or sports).
ouverture [uverty're] -*n* 1 *mus.* overture. 2 beginning, opening (**til** to); advance, overture.
***ov-** [å'v-] *Pf* extraordinarily.
***ova-** [å'va-] *Pf* (=+**oven-**) from above.
***ova/bu'rd** [å'va/] -*en* precipitation.
***ova/dotten** *A* -*e*/-*i, pl* -*dotne* thunderstruck.
ova/for' *P* above, higher up (than).
ova/frå *P* down, from above: **alt godt kommer ovenfra** all good things come from heaven; **behandle en ovenfra og nedad** treat sby with condescension.
ova'l[1] -*en* oval.
ova'l[2] *A* oval.
ova/lys** [å'va/] -*et* (=/ljos**) light from above.
***ovan** [å'van] *Av* above, from above; in the bargain.
***ovan-** [å'van-] *Pf* cf **ova-**
***ovan/bu'rd** -*en* cf **ova/**
ovande** [å'vande] *Av* (=ovende**) exceedingly, extremely.
***ova/nemnd** [å'va/] *A* -*nemnt* cf **oven/-nevnt**
***ovan/etter** [å'van/] *P* from above.
***ovan/for'** *P* cf **ova/**
***ovan/lys** -*et* cf **ova/**
***ovan/nemnd** *A* - cf **oven/nevnt**
***ovan/om'** *P* cf **oven/**
***ovan/over** [å'van/åver] *P* cf **oven/**
***ovan/på** *P* cf **ova/**
***ovan/renn** -*et* cf **ova/**
***ovan/til'** *Av* cf **ova/**
ova/på [å'va/] *P* 1 on, upon; on top of: **komme o-** come out on top, pull through (e.g. difficulties); **være o-** be sitting pretty, on top of the world. 2 upstairs. 3 (time) after, following.
ova/renn -*et* inrun (upper slope of a ski jump, above the jumping point; cf **unnarenn**).
ova'rium -*iet, pl* +-*ier*/*-*ium* ovary.
ovasjo'n -*en* ovation.
+**ovasjo'ns/messig** *A* - *lit.* enthusiastic, overwhelming: **o- bifall** deafening applause.
ova/til [å'va/till] *Av* above, at the top; from above.
***ov/bunad** [å'v/] -*en* extravagance, luxury.
***ov/dyr** [å'v/] *A* extremely expensive, high-priced.
O've *Prn (m)*
+**oven** [å'ven] *Av* above, from the top: **fra o-** from on high; **o- i kjøpet** in addition, into the bargain; (as *prep.*) **o- vanne** afloat.
***ovende** [å'vende] *Av* cf **ovande**
+**oven/for** [å'ven/fårr] *P* cf **ova/**
+**oven/fra** [å'ven/] *P* cf **ova/frå**
+**ovenn.**=**ovennevnte**
+**oven/nevnt** [å'ven/] *A* - above-mentioned.
+**oven/om'** *P* above, higher than.
+**oven/over** [å'ven/åver] *P* above.
+**oven/på** *P* cf **ova/**
+**oven/stående** *A* - the above, the foregoing.
+**oven/til'** *P* cf **ova/**
over [å'ver] *P* 1 over: **o- det hele** all over, everywhere; **bli natta o-** stay overnight; **det verste er o-** the worst is o-; **hoppe o-** jump o-, skip. 2 above: **o- enhver mistanke** a- suspicion; **meter o- havet (m.o.h.)** meters a- sea level. 3 across: **gå o- gata** walk a- the street, cross the street. 4 about: **det er noe rart o- ham** there's sth strange a- him; **en bok (en tale) o- et emne** a book (a speech) a- a subject. 5 via: **reise til Bergen o- Oslo** travel to Bergen v- Oslo. 6 beyond: **O- Evne** B- Human Power (play by Bjørnson); **det går o- min forstand** it's b- my comprehension. 7 in excess of, more than: **det var o- hundre mennesker der** there were more than 100 people present. 8 past (in time): **kl. er ti over to** it's ten p- two, 2:10. 9 at, of, on account of: **henrykt o-** delighted at (e.g. a prospect); **stolt o-** proud of; **være herre o-** be master of. 10 (other idioms): **et kart o- byen** a map of the city; **brekke (klippe) o-** break (cut) in two; **snakke o- seg** be out of one's head; **ønske ondt o- en** invoke (wish) evil on sby. (With other nouns and verbs, see these.)
over/administre'rt [å'ver/] *A* - bureaucratized: **vi er et o- land** we are a country enmeshed in bureaucratic red tape.
over/all [å'verål, also å'-] -*en* (=+**/alls**) overalls.
overalt [åveral't] *Av* 1 everywhere: **o- i verden** e- in, in all parts of the world. 2 *naut.* overall: **lengde o-** overall length (of a ship).
+**over/anstrenge** [å'ver/] *V* -*te* overwork, work too hard: **o- seg** overtax one's strength.
+**over/anstrengelse** -*n* overexertion, overwork.
+**over/antvorde** *V* -*et archaic* entrust, hand over.
over/arbeide *V* -*de*/+-*et* 1 polish, rework (e.g. an article, monograph). 2: **o- seg** overexert, overwork oneself.
over/arm -*en* upper (part of the) arm.
over/balanse [å'ver/balang'se] -*n* lack of balance: **ta o-** lose one's balance.
+**over/bebyr'de** -*et* overburden, overload.
+**over/befol'ket** *A* - overpopulated.
+**over/bega'vet** *A* - overly gifted, talented: **hun er ikke o-** she's not what you would call brilliant.
+**over/belas'te** *V* -*a*/-*et* overload.
***over/berande** *A* - cf **/bærende**
+**over/bevi'se** *V* -*te* 1 convince (**en om** sby of): **la seg o-** allow oneself to be persuaded; **o-ende** convincing (e.g. argument); **o-t** convinced (**om** of); **o- seg om** convince oneself of (e.g. the truth). 2 *archaic, jur.* convict (**om** of).
+**over/bevi'sning** -*en* conviction, firm belief, persuasion: **handle etter sin o-** have the courage of one's convictions.
+**over/bitt** -*et* (=***/bit**) overbite, receding jaw; *odont., vet.* overshot.
over/blikk -*et* 1 panorama, view. 2 general, overall idea; breadth of outlook: **han mangler o-** he lacks a broad view of things; **skaffe seg o- over en sak** gain a comprehensive view of a matter.
overbord [åverbo'r] *Av* cf **bord**[1]
+**over/brakte** [å'ver/] *pt of* **-bringe**
+**over/bredsel** -*elet*/-*let, pl* -*ler* (=***/breisle**) blanket, quilt.
+**over/bringe** *V* -*brakte*, -*brakt* bring, convey, deliver (e.g. a letter, message, thanks).
+**over/bringer** -*en, pl* -*e* bearer (e.g. of news).
+**over/brode'rt** *A* - 1 embroidered (all over). 2 overelaborated.
+**over/bud** -*et* higher bid (at an auction).
+**over/by** *V infl as* **by**[2] 1 outbid: **o- en på en auksjon** o- sby at an auction. 2 outdo, surpass.
over/bygd *A* -/*-*bygt* covered, roofed over.
over/bygg -*et* superstructure.
over/bygning -*en* superstructure.
+**over/bærende** *A* - 1 indulgent, lenient (**mot** to). 2 condescending, patronizing (e.g. smile).
+**overbæren/het** -*en* indulgence, lenience: **vise o- mot en** bear with sby.
+**over/dekke** *V* -*dekte*, -*dekt* 1 cover: **en o-t veranda** a covered veranda. 2 *lit., fig.* conceal, cover up.
over/del -*en* top, upper part (**av** of).
+**over/denge** *V* -*te* cover, load with: **o- en med skjellsord** heap abuse on sby.
over/dimensjone'rt *A* - oversized.
+**over/dra** *V* -*drog*, -*dradd*/-*dratt* 1 overlay (e.g. copper with gold). 2 assign, delegate; surrender: **o- en et verv** delegate a task to sby; **o- sine rettigheter til en annen** relinquish one's rights to another.
+**over/dragelse** -*n* (=***/draging**) assignment, conveyance, delegation: **o- av fast eiendom** conveyance of real property.
+**over/dre(i)v** *pt of* **-drive**
+**over/dreven** *A* -*ent, pl* -*ne* exaggerated, excessive.
+**over/drive** *V* -*dre(i)v*, -*drevet* 1 overdo: **hun o-er sin sparsommelighet** she carries her thriftiness too far; **sport må ikke o-s** sports must not be overdone. 2 exaggerate, overstate: **o- betydningen av noe** overemphasize the significance of sth.
+**over/drivelse** -*n* (=*-**ing**) 1 excess, immoderation: **forsiktig inntil o-** cautious to a fault. 2 exaggeration, overstatement.
***over/driven** *A* -*e*/-*i, pl* -*ne* cf **/dreven**
***over/dryving** -*a* cf **/drivelse**
+**over/dynge** *V* -*a*/-*et* 1 pour over. 2 *fig.* heap upon, overwhelm (e.g. with abuse).
+**over/døve** *V* -*de*/-*et* drown out, suppress: **orkestret o-et koret** the orchestra drowned out the chorus; **o- den indre stemme** stifle the voice of conscience.
+**overdådig** [åverdå'di] *A* - excessive,

lavish, sumptuous; (of vegetation) luxuriant.

+**overdådig/het** *-en* luxuriousness, sumptuousness; profusion: **leve i o-** live like a king.

***overeins** [åverei'ns] *Av* cf **overens**

over/ekspone're [å'ver/] *V -te* overexpose (film).

overende [åveren'ne] *Av* cf **ende**[3]

+**overens** [åvere'ns] *Av* (=***-eins**): **komme o- om noe** agree, come to an agreement about sth; **komme godt o- (med)** get along well (with); **stemme o-** agree, correspond, harmonize.

+**overens/komst** *-en* 1 agreement, arrangement, settlement: **inngå, treffe en o-** enter into a contract. 2 contract (document itself).

+**overens/stemmelse** *-n* accordance, agreement, harmony: **i o- med** in accordance with.

+**overens/stemmende** *A* -: **o- med** consistent with, in agreement with.

over/eta'sje [å'ver/] *-n* upper story.

overf. =**overført**

over/fall *-et* (sudden) assault, attack.

+**over/falle** *V -falt, -falt* assault, attack.

overfalls/mann *-en, pl -menn/*-menner* assailant.

overfalls/vatn *-et* (=+**/vann**) sluice water powering an overshot waterwheel.

+**over/fart** *-en* crossing, passage.

+**over/fladisk** *A* - cf **/flatisk**

over/flate *-a/+-en* surface.

+**overflate/behan'dling** *-en* treatment of a surface (e.g. wood).

overflate/hinne *-a* surface tension.

over/flatisk *A* - cursory, shallow, superficial.

over/flod *+-en/*-a* abundance, profusion; superfluity: **det er o- på markedet** there is a glut in the market; **til o-** abundantly, more than needed.

over/flyging *-a/+-en* overflight.

+**over/flytte** *V -a/-et* move, transfer.

+**overflø'dig** [also å'ver-] *A* - superfluous: **De er o- her** you're not needed here; **enhver forklaring vil være o-** any explanation will be s-; **gjøre o-** render s-.

+**overflø'dig/het** *-en* abundance, surplus; superfluity.

+**overflø'dighets/ho'rn** *-et* cornucopia, horn of plenty.

+**over/fløye** [å'ver/] *V -et* 1 excel, outstrip, surpass. 2 *mil.* outflank.

over/for' *P* 1 confronted, face to face with, opposite: **stillet o- et valg** faced with a choice. 2 towards: **hans følelser o- henne** his feelings for her; **like o-** faced with, in comparison with, in front of.

over/fore *V -a/+-et/+-te* overfeed (animals).

over/frakk *-en* overcoat.

over/fuse *V -te* bawl out, jump all over (sby).

over/fylt *A* - crammed, glutted (e. g. market), (over)crowded, packed.

over/følsom [/-såmm] *A -t, pl -me* oversensitive.

over/føre *V -te* 1 convey, move, transport (**til** to). 2 carry forward (e.g. a sum in a ledger), transfer (**på** to): **o-t** transferred; **i o-t betydning** in a figurative sense, figuratively. 3 transmit (e.g. a disease, electric power, radio broadcast). 4 *med.* transfuse (blood); graft, transplant (skin).

over/føring *-a/+-en* 1 transferring, transporting (**av** of e.g. funds, goods, property). 2 transmission (e.g. of a disease, electricity, broadcast). 3 *med.* transfusion (of blood); grafting, transplanting (of skin). 4 *psych.* transference (of affections, emotions). (Cf also **føre over.**)

over/førsel *-elen, pl -ler merc.* balance brought forward.

over/gang *-en* 1 crossing, passage (e.g. of a river, mountains): **o-en over Det røde hav** the crossing of the Red Sea. 2 crossing (e.g. of a road and railroad line); pass (e.g. over mountains); gangway, overpass: **o- for fotgjengere** pedestrian crossing, crosswalk. 3 change, transition; period of change: **o- til katolisismen** conversion to Catholicism; **det er bare en o-, sa reven, han ble flådd** it's just a passing phase, said the fox, he was being skinned; **hans stemme er i o-** his voice is changing; **stå på o-en til** be on the point of transition to. 4 *mil.* desertion (to the enemy). 5 =**overgangsbillett.** 6 area directly below the critical point of a ski-jumping hill: **han slo ned i o-en** he landed below the critical point.

overgangs/alder *-en* 1 puberty. 2 change of life.

overgangs/billett' *-en* (bus, streetcar) transfer.

overgangs/tid *-a/+-en* period, time of transition.

+**over/gi** *V -gav, -gitt* 1 deliver, hand over, turn over. 2 commit, entrust: **Fader! I dine hender o-r jeg min ånd!** Father, into thy hands I commend my spirit (Luke 23, 46). 3 give up, surrender: **o- seg til sin skjebne** resign oneself to one's fate. (Cf also **gi over**).

+**over/gikk** *pt of* **-gå**

over/gitt *A* - (=***/gjeven**) 1 (completely) exhausted; despairing, despondent. 2 astonished, startled.

+**over/givelse** *-n* capitulation, surrender.

+**over/given** *A -ent, pl -ne* abandoned, unrestrained: **o- lystighet** u- merriment.

over/gjekk *pt of* **-gå**

***over/gjeven** *A -e/-i, pl -ne* cf **/gitt**

over/grep *-et* 1 *gymn.* upper grip (=overhand). 2 act of tyranny: **begå o- mot en** infringe on sby's rights.

over/grodd *A -/*-grott* overgrown.

over/gå *V infl as* **gå** 1 exceed, outdo, surpass (e.g. expectations): **o- i antall** outnumber; **o- seg selv** outdo oneself; **Kristi kjærlighet o-r all kunnskap** the love of Christ passeth knowledge (Eph. 3, 19). 2 excel, be superior to: **vi tilgir ikke vår likemann at han o-r oss** we cannot forgive one of our equals for excelling us (Hamsun). 3 (esp. of misfortunes, catastrophes, etc.) befall, happen to: **den skam som overgikk ham** the shame that befell him. (Cf also **gå over.**)

over/hale *V -te/*-a* overhaul (e.g. a motor, ship); *naut.* overhaul, slacken (a rope).

over/haling *-a/+-en* 1 overhaul (e.g. of a motor, ship). 2 heeling over, lurch(ing) (of a boat). 3 *fam.* intoxication. 4 dressing down: **gi ham en o-** rake him over the coals.

Over/halla *Pln* twp, Nord-Trøndelag.

***over/hand** *N* cf **/hånd**

***over/hangande** *A* - cf **/hengende**

+**over/helle** *V -te* douse, soak (**med** with).

over/hendig *A* - 1 great, huge, powerful: **o- med, til** great amounts of; **det er o- med sild i år** there's lots of herring this year; **en o- arv** a huge inheritance; **et o- vær** a violent storm. 2 (as *adv.*) exceedingly, extremely: **ikke snakk så o- fort** don't talk so tremendously fast.

+**over/heng** *-et* 1 overhang. 2 bothering, pestering.

+**over/hengende** *A* - 1 overhanging. 2 imminent, impending (danger).

over/herredømme *-t* hegemony, supremacy.

+**over/hode** *-t* chief, head.

+**overhodet** [åverho'de] *Av* 1 at all: **han har o- ikke vært her** he hasn't been here at all; **kommer han o-?** *is* he coming? 2 altogether; in general; on the whole: **det var o- ikke hans sterke side** in general it was not his forte.

+**over/holde** [å'ver/hålle] *V -holdt, -holdt* comply with, keep, observe.

over/hus [å'ver/] *-et* upper house (of a legislature, esp. def. the British House of Lords).

over/høre *V -te* (=***/høyre**) 1 examine (orally); catechize (**i** on). 2 overhear. 3 ignore, pretend not to hear.

over/høvle *V -a/+-et* 1 plane (over). 2 dress down: **gi en overhøvling** call sby on the carpet.

+**over/høyhet** *-en* hegemony, supremacy.

+**over/hånd** *N*: **få o- over** get the better of, get the upper hand, prevail over; **ta o-** make headway; **sykdommen tok o-** the illness got out of hand.

+**overhånd/tagende** *A* - growing, rampant, spreading.

+**over/ile** *V -te*: **o- seg** act precipitately, rashly.

+**over/ilelse** *-n* indiscretion, rashness.

+**over/i'lt** *A* - hasty, precipitate, rash.

over/jordisk [å'ver/jordisk] *A* - 1 above ground. 2 *fig.* supernatural; celestial, ethereal.

over/kant [å'ver/] *-en* 1 rim, top, upper edge. 2: **i o- (av)** at the utmost limit (of); a little too much (of).

over/kikado'r *-en hum.* (self-appointed) inspector, supervisor.

+**over/kjøre** *V -te*: **bli o-t** get run over.

over/klasse *-a/-en* upper class(es).

over/komman'do *-en mil.* high command, GHQ; supreme command.

+**over/komme** *V -kom, -kommet* 1 come across, lay hands on. 2 be able (to manage), be equal to: **han har så mye arbeid som han kan o-** he has all the work he can handle. (Cf also **komme over.**)

+**over/kom'melig** *A* - 1 feasible, practicable. 2 moderate, reasonable (prices).

over/kompense're *V -te* overcompensate.

+**overkors** [åverkår's] *Av* cf **kors**

over/kropp [å'ver/] *-en* upper part of body (down to waist).

over/køy *-a* (=**/køye**) upper bunk; upper berth.

+**over/la** *pt of* **-legge**

over/lag[1] *-et* upper layer.

over/lag[2] *Av* exceedingly, extremely, very: **o- snill** extremely kind; **o- med bær** lots of berries; **o- til kar** an unusual fellow.

over/lagt *A* - premeditated: **o- mord** p- murder.

over/lang *Av* cf **lang**[2]

over/langsynt *A* - (extremely) farsighted.

over/lappe *V -a/+-et* overlap.

+**over/last** *-en* 1 damage, injury, molestation: **lide o-** suffer d-, i-. 2 injustice, maltreatment: **kjempe mot o-** fight against injustice.

over/late *V +-lot, +-latt/*-late/*-i* entrust with, leave, turn over to: **De kan trygt o- saken til meg** you can safely leave the matter in my hands.

***over/laups** *Av* excessive, surplus.

+**over/ledning** *-en elec.* current leakage.

over/lege *-n* medical director (of hospital, asylum, or section of a hospital).

over/legen *A +-ent, pl -ne* 1 superior: **han er enhver situasjon o-** he's the master of any situation; **være en o-** be superior to sby. 2 masterly: **en o- fiolinist** a consummate violinist; **rollen var o-t spilt** the part was brilliantly played; **vinne o-t** win

+ Bokmål; * Nynorsk; ° Dialect.
After letter: ' stress (Acc. 1); ' tone, stress (Acc. 2); · length.
Below letter: . not pronounced.

with ease. 3 aloof, haughty, supercilious: **opptre o-t** behave arrogantly.

+overlegen/het *-en* 1 superiority. 2 haughtiness.

over/legg *-et* 1 deliberation, reflection: **etter modent o-** after due deliberation. 2 premeditation: **med o-** deliberately, on purpose.

+over/legge *V -la, -lagt* consider, deliberate (about), reflect (upon).

+over/legning *-en* deliberation, discussion.

over/leppe *-a* upper lip.

***over/ler** *-et* cf **/lær**

over/lesse *V +-te/*-leste* 1 load down, overload. 2: **en o-t stil** *fig.* a ponderous style.

+over/leve *V -de* live through, outlive, survive: **det o-er jeg aldri** it will be the death of me; **o- seg selv** outlive one's day; **Vi o-er alt** we will live through all (Nordahl Grieg).

+over/leve're *V -te* 1 deliver, hand over. 2 hand down, transmit (e.g. a custom). 3 *mil.* pass on (an order).

over/leve'ring *-a/+-en* 1 delivery, handing over. 2 transmission. 3 tradition: **muntlig o-** oral t-.

+overligge/dag *-en naut.* day of demurrage, lay day.

+over/ligger *-en, pl -e* lintel.

+over/liste *V -a/-et* dupe, outwit, take in.

+over/lot *pt of* **-late**

over/lykkelig *A -* overjoyed.

over/lys *-et* ceiling light.

+over/lær *-et* upper (part of a shoe), vamp.

over/lærer *-en, pl -e* (=***-ar**) 1 principal (of grammar school). 2 instructor (esp. in commercial and technical secondary schools).

+over/løper *-en, pl -e* 1 defector, deserter. 2 *agr.* barren, farrow cow, mare, etc.

over/makt *-a/+-en* predominance, superiority; superior force: **kjempe mot o-en** fight against odds.

over/mann *-en, pl -menn/*-menner* superior (in ability, etc.): **være fandens o-** go the devil one better.

over/manne *V -a/+-et* overpower, overwhelm.

over/mektig *A -* superior; overpowering.

over/menneske *-t, pl +-r/*-* superman.

over/menneskelig *A -* superhuman.

over/mett *A -* surfeited.

***over/mod** *-et* cf **/mot**

over/moden *A +-ent, pl -ne* overripe; overmature (e.g. stand of timber).

over/modig *A -* arrogant, insolent, overbearing.

***over/mon(n)** *-en* superiority.

+over/morgen [å'ver/mårn] *N*: **i o-** the day after tomorrow.

over/mot [å'ver/] *-et* arrogance, insolence.

over/mål *et* excess, plethora, superabundance: **til o-** to excess, to a fault.

+overmåte [åvermå'te] *Av* exceedingly, extremely.

+over/natte [å'ver/] *V -a/-et* spend the night, stay overnight.

over/naturlig *A -* 1 supernatural. 2 abnormal: **i o- størrelse** larger than life.

over/oppsyn *-et* superintendence, supervision; superintendent, supervisor.

+overordentlig [åverår'ntli] *A -* extraordinary.

+over/ordnet [å'ver/] *A -* (=***/ordna**) 1 superior: **min o-de** my chief. 2 responsible: **en o- stilling** a r- position. 3: **en o- setning** *gram.* an independent clause.

over/plagg *-et* outer garment.

over/pris *-en* 1 overcharge. 2 extra charge.

over/produksjo'n *-en* overproduction.

over/rakte *pt of* **-rekke**

over/raske *V -a/+-et* 1 surprise, take by surprise: **bli o-t over noe** be surprised at sth; **han ble o-t av regn** he was caught in the rain; **o- en med noe** s- sby with sth. 2 amaze, astonish.

+over/raskelse *-n* (=***-ing**) 1 surprise: **en ubehagelig o-** an unpleasant s-. 2 amazement: **til min store o-** to my utter a-.

over/reise *-a/+-en* (=**/reis**) crossing, passage.

+over/rekke *V -rakte, -rakt* present (formally): **jeg o-er Dem dette album** I p- you with this album (Ibsen).

+over/rekkelse *-n* (formal) presentation (av of).

+over/renne *V -rente, -rent* 1 overrun. 2 pester, plague: **være o-t av** be annoyed, pestered by. 3: **o-t** extremely busy, occupied.

over/representert *A -* overrepresented (in a legislature).

over/rett *-en hist.* appellate court (in Bergen, Oslo, Trondheim; abolished in 1936).

+overretts/sakfører *-en, pl -e* (=***-ar**) *hist.* attorney admitted to practice before the appellate court (abolished in 1936; title survives).

over/risle *V -a/+-et* sprinkle; irrigate.

+over/rumple *V -a/-et* catch off guard, take by surprise.

overs [å'vers] *Av*: **til overs** in addition, remaining; superfluous, unneeded: **ha noe til o-** have sth left over; **ha til o- for en** like, be fond of sby.

+overs. =**oversettelse, oversatt**

+overs. anm. =**oversetterens anmerkning**

over/sanselig [å'ver/] *A -* extrasensory; metaphysical, transcendental.

+over/satte *pt of* **-sette**

+over/se *V -så, -sett* (=***/sjå**) 1 overlook (=forgive; not see): **jeg skal o- det denne gangen** I'll overlook (forget, ignore) it this time; **det oversså jeg** I overlooked that, that escaped my attention. 2 neglect, slight, underestimate (sby). 3 *lit.* see in its totality, survey (e.g. a problem, situation); assess, estimate (consequences). (Cf also **se over.**)

+over/sende *V -te* dispatch, transmit.

+over/sette *V -satte, -satt* translate (**til** into): **fritt oversatt** freely translated.

+over/settelse *-n* translation, version (**av** of).

+over/setter *-en, pl -e* translator.

over/side [*/sie] *-a/+-en* top side, upper side.

over/sikt **-a/+-en* 1 general view, perspective, survey (e.g. of terrain, a problem). 2 outline, summary, synopsis (**av** of).

over/siktlig *A -* 1 surveyable, viewable, visible. 2 easy to grasp, lucid, well arranged.

oversikts/kart *-et* small-scale map.

+over/sitte *V -satt, -sittet* 1 *jur.* disregard (e.g. a court order). 2: **o-ende** *bot.* epigynous.

over/sjøisk [/sjø'isk] *A -* (=***/sjøsk**) overseas: **skip i o- fart** oceangoing vessel, vessel engaged in overseas commerce.

***over/sjå** *V infl as* **sjå**[2] cf **/se**

+over/skar *pt of* **-skjære**

over/skjegg *-et* mustache.

+over/skjære *V -skar, -skåret* 1 cut (in two), sever; cut short; cut through. 2 (of textiles) crop, shear.

over/skjønn *-et* (=***/skjøn**) reappraisal, revaluation.

over/skott *-et* (=***/skot, +/skudd**) 1 excess, surplus (e.g. of strength, vitality): **et o- på** an excess of; **være i o-** be in excess. 2 balance, profit: **forretningen gikk med o-** the business was operated at a profit; **gi et o-** yield a profit.

overskotts/menneske *-t* buoyant, sanguine individual.

+over/skred *pt of* **-skride**

+overskrevs [åverskref's] *Av* cf **skrevs**

+over/skride [å'ver/] *V -skred, -skredet* 1 cross (e.g. a border), overstep, transgress. 2 *fig.* exceed, overstep, transgress.

+over/skridelse *-n* 1 excess, overexpenditure. 2 transgression (**av** of).

over/skrift *-a/+-en* 1 heading (**på** of). 2 caption, headline. 3 salutation (of letter).

+over/skudd *-et* cf **/skott**

+over/skue *A -et* survey: **o- ulykkens omfang** s- the extent of the disaster.

+overskuelig [åversku'eli] *A -* easy to grasp, lucid, well arranged: **i en o- framtid** in the foreseeable future.

over/skya [å'ver/] *A -* (=**+-et**) cloudy, overcast.

+over/skygge *V -et* overshadow, put into the shade; eclipse (also *fig.*): **alt o-ende** paramount.

+over/skytende *A -* additional, excess, surplus: **det o- beløp** the excess, the surplus; **for hver o- dag** for each additional day.

+over/skåret *pp of* **-skjære**

over/slag *-et* 1 (rough) calculation, (rough) estimate: **gjøre et o- over** make a (rough) estimate of. 2 *elec.* flashover.

***oversleg** [å'versle(g)] *Av* exceedingly, extremely.

over/spent [å'ver/] *A -* excitable, highstrung, hysterical; overwrought, quixotic: **o-e forventninger** exaggerated expectations.

+overspent/het *-en* overwrought state; quixotism.

+over/sprøyte *V -a/-et* squirt over; splash, splatter (**med** with).

+over/stadig *A -* 1 effervescent, hilarious; intoxicated, tipsy. 2 *(adv.)* excessively: **i o- godt humør** bubbling over with good spirits; **o- beruset** roaring drunk.

over/stemme *+-n/*-a mus.* upper register (of a voice).

+over/stemple *V -a/-et* cancel, surcharge (e.g. stamps).

+over/stenke *V -et* splash, splatter.

+over/stige *V -steg, -steget* exceed, go beyond, surpass: **inntekten o-er utgiften med kr 1000** income exceeds expenditures by 1000 *kroner*; **o- en hindring** surmount an obstacle; **o-ens krefter** exceed one's strength.

over/stikk *-et* overtrick (cards).

+over/stod *pt of* **-stå**

+over/stry'kning *-en* crossing-out, deletion (**av** of).

+over/strømmende *A -* effusive, gushing, profuse.

+over/stråle *V -te* eclipse, outshine, overshadow.

overstyr [åversty'r] *Av* cf **styr**[2]

over/styre [å'ver/] *-t* directorate, top management.

over/styrmann *-en, pl -menn/*-menner naut.* officer of the deck.

+over/stå *V -stod, -stått* get (sth) over with; get through (sth): **det verste er o-tt** the worst is over; **han overstod sykdommen** he recovered from the illness; **o-tt** over, through; **vel o-tt** "well gotten through" (greeting heard after a holiday, e.g. Christmas; ab. equal to "glad you're back").

+over/svømme *V -svømte, -svømt* flood, inundate; overrun: **vi blir o-t av dårlige bøker** we are deluged with trashy books.

+over/svømmelse *-n* deluge, flood, inundation.

over/syn *-et* survey, view.

+over/søster *-era/-eren, pl -re(r)* head nurse.

over/så[1] *V -dde* sow, strew: **o-dd med** strewn, studded with; **himmelen var o-dd med stjerner** the heavens were star-spangled, studded with stars.

+over/så[2] *pt of* **-se**

+over/ta *V -tok, -tatt* take over (a position); undertake (a task).

+over/tagelse *-n* cf **/taking**

over/tak *-et* 1 arm grip (wrestling).

2: få, ha o-et over en gain, have the upper hand over sby.

+over/takelse -n cf /taking

over/taking -a/+-en taking possession (av of); acceptance (e.g. of a position).

*over/talde pt of -telje

over/tale V -a/-te persuade, prevail upon: han lot seg o- til å komme he let himself be talked into coming.

+over/talelse -n persuasion (av of).

+overtalelses/kunst -en art, gift of persuasion.

+over/talende A - persuasive.

+over/tall -et majority, surplus: være i o- be in the majority.

+over/tallig A - additional, extra, in excess: en o- a supernumerary.

over/ta'lt pp of -telje, -tale

over/tann -a, pl -tenner upper tooth.

+over/tegne [å'ver/teine] V -a/-et oversubscribe (e.g. a loan).

*over/telje [å'ver/] V -tel, -talde, -talt persuade, prevail upon.

over/tid -a/+-en overtime.

overtids/arbeid -et overtime work.

overtids/beta'ling -a/+-en overtime pay.

+over/tok pt of -ta

over/tone -n harmonic, overtone.

over/tramp -et failure (in sports).

+over/tre(de) V -trådte, -trådt break, violate (e.g. a commandment, law).

+over/tredelse -n breach, transgression, violation (av of).

+over/treffe V -traff, -truffet exceed, surpass: o- forventninger s- expectations; o- seg selv outdo oneself.

over/trekk -et 1 slipcover (for furniture). 2 film, layer: et o- av maling a coat of paint. 3 overdraft (bank account).

over/trekke V infl as trekke 1 coat; (slip)cover. 2 overdraw (an account).

over/trene V -a/+-et/+-te overtrain.

+over/tro -en superstition; superstitious faith (på in).

+over/troisk [å'ver/tro-isk] A - superstitious.

+over/trukket [å'ver/trokket] A - 1 overcast (sky). 2 pp of overtrekke.

+over/trumfe [å'ver/tromfe] V -et cap, go one better, outdo.

over/trøtt [å'ver/] A - dog-tired, exhausted.

+over/trådte pt of -tre

overtvert [åvertvær't] Av cf tvert

over/tyde [å'ver/tyde, */tye] V -de/+-et convince (om of).

+over/tøy -et overcoat: uten o- without a coat on.

+over/vann -et cf /vatn

+over/vant pt of -vinne

+over/var pt of -være

over/vatn -et (=+/vann) 1 surface water (e.g. on top of ice), flood water (in a mine). 2: ta o- naut. ship water.

+over/veie V -de consider, think over: o- på ny reconsider; vel o-d well-advised; vi har o-d alle sider ved denne sak we have considered this matter from all sides.

+over/veielse -n consideration, deliberation: etter moden o- after careful consideration; etter nærmere o- on second thought; ta under o- consider; vi har saken under o- the matter is under review.

+over/veiende Av 1 predominant, prevailing: den langt o- del av by far the major part of; det o- antall the great majority. 2 (adv.) chiefly, mainly: det er o- sannsynlig it is highly probable.

over/vekt -a/+-en 1 excess weight: betale o- pay for excess baggage. 2 majority: med to stemmers o- by a m- of two. 3 predominance, superiority; decisive influence.

over/vektig A - overweight (e.g. baggage, letter, person).

over/velde V -a/+-et overcome, overwhelm: det o-er meg I am overwhelmed; it takes my breath away; være o-t med gjøremål be snowed under with work.

over/veldende A - overwhelming, staggering: et o- nederlag a crushing defeat.

over/vettes A - excessive, inordinate.

+over/vinne V -vant, -vunnet conquer, defeat; master (one's feelings, emotions): o- en vanskelighet surmount a difficulty; o- ham get the better of him; hvis du bare kunne o- deg til å si du til henne if you could only get yourself to say "du" to her (=call her by her first name) (Ibsen).

+over/vinnelse -n self-conquest, mastery (av of): det koster o- it goes against the grain, you have to force yourself.

over/vintre V -a/+-et 1 spend the winter, winter. 2 hibernate.

+over/vokst A - overgrown (e.g. with weeds).

+over/vunnet pp of -vinne

over/vurde're V -te overestimate, overrate: en o-t forfatter an overrated author.

+over/vær -et presence: i vitners o- in the p- of witnesses.

+over/være V -værer, -var, -vært attend, be present at, watch.

+over/våke V -te look after, watch over.

+over/ømfin'tlig A - oversensitive; med. allergic.

+over/øse V -te 1 pour over, upon. 2 fig. heap upon, shower upon: o- en med skjellsord heap abuse on sby, shower sby with abuse.

over/årig A overaged, superannuated.

over/åring -en superannuated person (esp. an official).

ovf. =ovafor

ov/god [å'v/] A unusually good.

*ov/hug -en overwhelming desire, passion (på for).

*ovig [å'vig] A - cf avig

ov/kar [å'v/] -en exceptional fellow.

ov/kast -et exploit (e.g. exceptional catch of fish); exceptional throw (in sports).

*ovleg [å'vleg] A - excessive, extreme.

*ov/læte [å'v/] -t 1 hullabaloo. 2 arrogance, insolence.

*ov/mektig A - extremelypowerful; dominating: ho stend yverfor eitkvart o- she faces something overpowering (Vesaas).

*ov/menne -t superman.

ov/mod -et (=/mot) arrogance, insolence.

*ov/modig A - cf over/

*ov/mot -et cf /mod

+ov'n -en cf omn

+ov'ns/brød -et cf omns/

+ov'ns/krok -en cf omns/

+ov'ns/rør -et cf omns/

+ov'ns/varme -n cf omns/

+ov'n/sverte -a cf omn/

*ov/nøgd [å'v/] -a abundance, profusion.

*ovre [åv're] V -a: o- seg show oneself; express oneself; alt som o-ar seg i tida every issue of our times.

*ov/rike [å'v/] -t violence; tyranny.

*ov/rikje V -te overcome, overwhelm: det o-er meg it's too much for me.

*ovring [åv'ring] -a 1 ascent, rising (esp. of the sun). 2 fig. appearance; occurrence; phenomenon.

ov/stor [å'v/] A extremely large.

*ov/tru -a cf over/tro

*ov/truen A -e/-i, pl -ne cf over/troisk

*ovund [å'vunn] -a cf avund

*ovunde [å'vunde] V -a cf avunde

*ov/undre [å'v/] V -a admire.

+oxford/beve'gelsen [åk'sfård/] df (=*/rørsla) the Oxford movement (later called MRA).

ozelot [åselo't] -en zool. ocelot (Felis pardalis).

P

p [pe'] -en 1 (letter) P, p. 2 (adj.) mus. piano. 3 (abbr. for) post, pro.

pa. =prima

p. a. =pro anno

pace[1] [pe's] -n 1 pace, speed. 2: gi p- set the p-.

pace[2] [pe'se] V -a/+-et 1 set pace. 2 lit. drive (sby) to take initiative; hurry (sby) on.

pad'de -a zool. toad (Bufo vulgaris).

*pad'de/dyr -et zool. Amphibia.

pad'de/hatt -en toadstool: skyte opp som p-er spring up like mushrooms.

pad'del -elen, pl padler paddle.

pad'le V -a/+-et paddle.

pad'le/åre -a paddle.

paff' A - dumbfounded, speechless, taken aback.

pag. =pagina

pa'gina -en page; page number.

pagine're V -te paginate.

pago'de -n 1 pagoda. 2 lit., fam. gingerbread architecture.

pai' -en pie.

pakett' -en packet (boat); coastal steamer.

Pakista'n Pln Pakistan.

pakista'nsk A - Pakistani.

pakk' -et 1 rabble, riffraff. 2 fam. baggage: pikk og p- bag and b-.

pakk'/bu -a storeroom, warehouse; baggage room.

pak'ke[1] -a/-en package; pack (of sth); bundle (of letters).

pak'ke[2] V -a/+-et 1 pack; wrap. 2 tech. pile (lengths of iron). 3 (with prep. and adv.): p- inn wrap up, make a package of; p- ned pack (away), stow (away); p- om repack; p- opp (ut) unpack; unwrap; p- sammen make up (e.g. a parcel); close up shop, pack up (and leave). 4 (refl.) p- seg get out, get packing, take off; pakk deg ut get out, scram; p- seg inn wrap oneself (up); p- seg sammen become packed close together, crowd together.

pak'kende Av: p- full chock-full.

pakkenel'lik -en: p-er little packages; odds and ends (of luggage).

pak'ke/post -en parcel post.

+pak'ker -en, pl -e (=*-ar) 1 packer, wrapper (person). 2 agr. packer (on self-binder).

pakk'/esel -elet/-let, pl +-ler/*-el 1 donkey, mule (used for carrying). 2 hum. beast of burden (person).

pakk'/full A crowded, packed solid; chock-full.

pakk'/hus -et storehouse, warehouse.

pakk'/is *-en* pack ice.
pakk'-kasse *-a/-en* box, crate.
pak'ning **-a/+-en* 1 boxing, packing. 2 washer (in faucet); *elec.* gasket. 3 *med.* (hot, cold) pack. 4 pack (on sby's back). 5 (road) fill. 6 pack (of cigarettes).
pak't *-a/+-en* 1 *pol.* agreement, pact. 2 *bibl.* covenant. 3: **i p- med** in keeping with; **i p- med tiden** in tune with the times.
***pak'tar** *-en* leaseholder, tenant farmer.
pak'te *V -a/+-et dial.* lease, rent out.
pa'l[1] *-en naut.* pawl: **hive p-** pawl; ratchet.
pa'l[2] *Av fam.* (sit) tight, (stand) stock-still: **ligge p-** lie flat on one's back.
palass' *-et, pl -/+-er* palace.
palass'/revolusjo'n *-en hist.* palace revolution; *fig.* coup.
palata'l[1] *-en gram.* palatal (sound).
palata'l[2] *A gram.* palatal.
palatalise're *V -te gram.* palatalize.
+palat's *-et* cf **palass**
pala'ver *-en, pl +-e* palaver.
pa'le *-n zool.* young coalfish (Pollachius virens).
palé *-et, pl +-er/*-* mansion, small palace.
paleogra'f *-en* paleographer.
paleografi' *-en* paleography.
paleolit'tisk *A* - paleolithic.
paleontolog [-lå'g] *-en* paleontologist.
paleontologi' *-en* paleontology.
Palesti'na *Pln* Palestine.
palett' *-en* (painter's) palette.
pa'l/hjul *-et* ratchet wheel.
palisa'de *-n* palisade, stockade.
paljett' *-en* sequin, spangle.
pall' *-en* 1 *hist.* raised section of floor; bench. 2 shelf (in house; mining).
pal'lium *-iet, pl +-ier/*-ium eccl.* pallium (woolen vestment).
pall'/tosk *-en zool.* stone crab (Lithodes maia).
pal'me[1] *-n bot.* palm (Palmaceae): **stå med p-er i hendene** *fig.* be vindicated, triumph.
+pal'me[2] *V -et* (=***pelme**) 1 *naut.* haul in (rope, sail). 2 *dial.* strike (sby with the hand), throw (sth at sby).
pal'me/hage *-n* palm garden; winter garden (e.g. in hotel).
pal'me/søndag *en* (=***/sundag**) Palm Sunday.
pamfi'lius *-en lit.* favorite: **lykkens p-** lucky dog.
pamflett' *-en pol.* lampoon.
pam'p *-en pop.* person who has gained leading, lucrative position in an organization (esp. in labor union); boss.
pam'pa *-en, pl -s* pampa(s).
pan'ama/hatt *-en* panama (hat).
pan'/amerika'nsk *A* - Pan-American.
pandemo'nium *-iet* 1 pandemonium. 2 *lit.* hell; dwelling place of pagan gods.
pando'ra/eske *-a/+-en* Pandora's box.
panegyrikk' *-en* panegyric; excessive praise.
panegy'risk *A* - panegyrical.
pane'l *-et, pl -/+-er* paneling; dado, wainscoting.
pane'le *V -te* panel: **p- av** wall off by paneling.
pane'ling *-a/+-en* paneling.
pane'l/omn *-en* (=**+/ovn**) electric radiator (panel-shaped and fastened to wall).
pang'[1] *-et* bang, sharp noise.
pang'[2] *I* bang; ping.
pan'/germa'nsk *A* - Pan-German(ic).
panikk' *-en* panic.
+panikk'/artet *A* - panicky.
pa'nisk *A* - panicky: **p- redsel** sudden, inexplicable fear.
pan'k *-en* bundle (of clothes).
pan'ne[1] *-a* 1 pan: **være pott og p-** be the boss. 2 *hist.* firepan (on gun).
pan'ne[2] *-a/+-en* forehead: **renne p-n mot veggen** butt one's head against a stone wall.
+pan'ne/brask *-en hum., archaic* skull.
pan'ne/hole [/håle] *-a* (=**+/hule**) frontal sinus.
pan'ne/hår *-et* bangs; forelock.
pan'ne/kake *-a* pancake (like crêpe suzette).
pan'ne/lin *-et* linen headscarf.
pan'ne/lugg *-en* hair or curl falling over the forehead; bangs, forelock.
panop'tikon *-et* panopticon (orig. prison where all prisoners are visible to guard; later a curiosity show, waxworks exhibit).
panora'ma *-et, pl +-er/*-* panorama.
pan'ser *-et, pl -/+-e* 1 armor, coat of mail; armor plate. 2 hood (of car). 3 *zool.* carapace, (protective) shell.
pan'ser/bil *-en* armored car, bulletproof car.
+pan'ser/hvelv *-et* (walk-in) safe.
pan'ser/skip *-et* armor-plated ship, ironclad.
pan'ser/vern [/vær'n] *-et* antitank defences.
pan'ser/vogn [/vångn] *-a* armored car; tank.
pan'/slavisk *A* - Pan-Slavic.
pan'sre *V -a/+-et* 1 armor, armor plate. 2: **p- seg** *fig.* cover oneself, protect oneself.
pan't *-et* 1 *jur.* deposit, security. 2 *jur.* mortgage. 3 forfeit (in game). 4 symbol (e.g. of love).
pan'te *V -a/+-et* 1 pawn. 2 *jur.* levy distress upon (sby): **p- en for skatt** seize sby's property in payment of taxes.
pan'te/brev *-et jur.* deed, mortgage.
pan'te/gjeld *-a/+-en jur.* mortgage debt.
pan'te/gods *-et jur.* mortgaged properties other than houses or land.
panteisme [pante-is'me] *-n* pantheism.
panteist [pante-is't] *-en* pantheist.
panteistisk [pante-is'tisk] *A* - pantheistic.
pan'te/leik *-en* (game of) forfeits.
+pan'te/låner *-en, pl -e* (=***-ar**) pawnbroker.
pan'te/mann *-en hist.* distrainer, levier; tax assessor.
pan'ter *-eren, pl -ere/-rer zool.* leopard, panther (Felis pardus).
pan'te/regis'ter *-eret/-ret, pl -er/+-re* register of mortgages.
pan'te/rett *-en jur.* 1 mortgage. 2 mortgage law.
***pan'te/skuld** *-a jur.* debt on a mortgage.
+pan't/haver *-en, pl -e* (=***-ar**) *jur.* mortgagee, mortgage bondholder.
pan't/obligasjo'n *-en jur.* mortgage deed.
pantomi'me *-n* pantomime.
+pan't/sette *V -satte, -satt* (=***/setje**) 1 pawn. 2 *jur.* give mortgage or security.
***pap'a** *-en* cf **pappa**
papegøy'e *-n zool.* parrot (Psittacus).
papiljott' *-en* 1 curler (for hair). 2 parchment paper (to broil food in). 3 papillote (for decorating roast or chop bone ends).
papill' *-en* papilla.
papi'r *-et, pl -/+-er* 1 paper. 2 document; *(pl)* securities: **kikke en i p-ene** *fam.* check up on sby, look into sby's affairs. 3 person (judged by character, morals, etc.): **han er et dårlig p-** he's a shady customer.
+papi'r/bestem'melse *-n* paper regulation, on paper only.
papi'r/handel *-elen, pl -ler* paper trade; stationery shop.
papi'r/innsamling *-a/+-en* paper collection.
papi'r/kniv *-en* letter opener, paper knife.
papi'r/korg *-a* (=**+/kurv**) wastepaper basket.
papi'r/kule *-a* spitball.
papi'r/lapp *-en* piece, scrap of paper.
papi'r/mølle *-a* 1 paper mill. 2 *fig.* red tape.
+papi'r/penger *pl* (=***-ar**) bills, paper money.
papi'r/tutt *-en* paper cone; roll of paper.
papis't *-en* papist.
papisteri' *-et* papism.
papis'tisk *A* - papistic.
papp' *-en* 1 cardboard. 2 pap (in cpd. **melke/p-**).
pap'pa *-en* (=***papa**) papa.
pap'pa/båt *-en fam.* commuter ferry ("daddy boat"), esp. morning or late afternoon run.
pap'pa/dalt *-en fam.* daddy's pet (child always trailing its father).
+pap'pa/gutt *-en derog.* young man living off wealthy father; young man being advanced in a business because of influential father.
pap'penheimer *-en, pl +-e*: **kjenne sine p-e** *hum.* know what to expect of (certain) people.
papp'/eske *-a* cardboard box; carton.
papp'/kartong *-en* carton.
papp'/masjé *-en* papier-maché.
pap'rika *-en* paprika.
pap's *-en fam.* pop (pet name for **pappa**).
papy'rus *-en/-et* papyrus.
pa'r [also: par'] *-et* 1 couple, pair (of): **et p- sko** a p- of shoes; **et p- briller** a p- of glasses; **siste p- ut** last couple out; **et elskende p-** a loving couple; **et p- ord** a couple of (a few) words; **et p- og tredve** thirty-odd. 2 even (number): **p- og odde** even and odd.
para'bel *-elen, pl -lèr* 1 parable. 2 *math.* parabola.
para'de *-n* 1 inspection, parade: **ligge på p-** lie in state; **sitte på p-** sit on exhibition. 2 *mil.* parade. 3 *mil., educ.* punishment (e.g. reporting early on holidays). 4 (in fencing) parry. 5 (in riding) checking, pulling up (horse).
para'de/marsj *-en mil.* special step used for parade purposes; parade march.
parade're *V -te* 1 *mil.* parade. 2 show off. 3 be punished (in mil. school).
para'de/seng *-a* bed of state.
paradig'ma *-et, pl +-er/ gram.* paradigm.
paradi's *-et, pl -/+-er* 1 *bibl.* Garden of Eden. 2 paradise. 3: **hoppe p-** play hopscotch. 4 *fam.* top gallery of a theater.
paradi's/fugl *-en zool.* bird of paradise (Paradisaeidae).
paradi'sisk *A* - heavenly: **i p- drakt** naked.
paradok's *-et, pl -/+-er* paradox.
paradoksa'l *A* paradoxical.
+paradok's/maker *-en, pl -e* (=***-ar**) paradoxer.
parafe're *V -te jur.* countersign.
parafi'n *-en* 1 kerosine. 2 paraffin. 3 petroleum.
parafi'n/olje *-a/-en* 1 kerosine. 2 mineral oil, paraffin oil.
parafi'n/omn *-en* (=**+/ovn**) kerosine stove.
parafi'n/voks *-en* paraffin wax.
parafra'se *-n* paraphrase (also *mus.*).
par'agon *-en merc.* sales slip, sales book.
paragra'f *-en* 1 *jur.* article, clause, paragraph; section (of the law). 2 section (of a book).
+paragra'f/rytter *-en, pl -e* (=***-ar**) pedant; one who sticks to the letter of the law.
+paragra'f/tegn [/tein] *-et* (=***/teikn**) section mark (§).
parallell'[1] *-en* 1 *math.* parallel line. 2 *mil.* parallel trench. 3 *fig.* parallel: **trekke en p- mellom** draw a p- between.
parallell'[2] *A -ell* parallel (**med** with).
+parallell'/forsky've *V infl as* **forskyve** *math.* displace parallel to sth.
parallellis'me *-n* 1 parallelism (**med** with). 2 *lit.* stanza of poetry repeating idea of previous stanza thus intensifying it.
parallellite't *-en* parallelism.
parallell'/klasse *-a/-en educ.* parallel class (at same level).

parallell'/kople *V* *-a/+-et elec.* hook up in parallel, shunt.
parallellogram' *-met, pl -/+-mer* parallelogram.
paraly'se *-n med.* (complete) paralysis; general paresis (third stage of syphilis).
paralyse're *V -te* paralyze; *elec.* neutralize.
+paralyt'iker *-en, pl -e* (=***-ar**) paralytic.
paralyt'isk *A* - paralytic.
pa'ra/nøtt *-a bot.* brazil nut (Bertholletia excelsa).
paraply' *-en* umbrella.
pa'ra/psykisk *A* - extrasensory.
parasitt' *-en* parasite.
parasitte'rende *A* - parasitical.
parasit'tisk *A* - parasitic.
parasoll' *-en* parasol, sunshade.
para't *A* - prepared, ready (**til** to).
pa'ra/tyfus *-en med.* paratyphoid.
+par'der *-en, pl -e bibl.* leopard.
pardong' *-en* 1 *mil.* pardon, quarter. 2 (expletive) sorry.
par'e *V -a/+-et* 1 couple; match (e.g. socks); pair off (e.g. guests at table). 2 (of domestic animals) couple, mate: **p- seg** (of wild animals) mate.
parente's [also: parangte's] *-en* 1 parenthesis; square bracket. 2 sth enclosed within parentheses: **i p- bemerket** parenthetically speaking.
parente'tisk *A* - parenthetic.
pare're¹ *V -te* 1 draw rein, pull up. 2 parry; *fig.* ward off (e.g. a blow, question); (in chess) counter.
pare're² *V -te*: **p- ordre** *mil.* obey.
pare'r/plate *-a/+-en mil.* (hilt) guard.
parfor'se/jakt *-a/+-en*: **gå på p-** ride to the hounds.
parfy'me *-n* perfume.
parfy'me/flaske *-a* perfume bottle.
parfyme're *V -te* perfume, scent.
parfymeri' *-et, pl +-er/*-* perfumery.
parga's *-et dial., fam.* baggage.
par'/hest *-en* either of two horses in a span; *fam. pl* inseparable friends.
pa'ri *A* - *merc.* par: **i p-** at p-.
pa'ria *-en* pariah; social outcast.
pa'ria/kaste *-n* pariah caste.
pa'ri/kurs *-en merc.* par rate of exchange.
par'ings/akt *-a/+-en* copulation, mating act.
+pari'ser *-en, pl -e* (=***-ar**) Parisian.
pari'ser/gul *A* chrome yellow.
+pariserin'ne *-a/-en* (=***parisarinne**) Parisian woman, Parisienne.
pari'ser/loff [/loff] *-en* French bread.
+pari'ser/modell' *-en* (=***-ar/**) (of clothing) Paris model.
pari'sisk *A* - Paris, Parisian.
parite't *-en* parity; par.
par'k *-en* 1 park. 2 (artificial) fishpond. 3 *mil.* park; materiel.
par'k/anlegg *-et* grounds; park.
parke're *V -te* park (e.g. a car).
parke'rings/lys *-et* parking light.
parke'rings/plass *-en* parking lot, parking space.
parkett' *-et* 1 (in theater) orchestra (section for audience). 2 parquet floor.
parkett'/golv *-et* parquet (inlaid) floor.
parkett'/stav *-en* parquet block, parquetry.
parkome'ter *-eret/+-ret, pl -er/+-re* parking meter.
par'k/tante *-a/+-en* woman playground-supervisor for small children.
+par'k/vesen *-et admin.* department of grounds and parks.
parlamen't *-et, pl -/+-er* 1 Parliament. 2: **gatens p-** crowd, mob.
+parlamenta'riker *-en, pl -e* (=***-ar**) 1 parliamentarian. 2 member of Parliament.
parlamenta'risk *A* - parliamentary (e.g. expression, government): **p- immunitet** legislative immunity.
parlamentaris'me *-n* parliamentary government (with a cabinet responsible to the parliament).
parlamente're *V -te* 1 *mil.* negotiate. 2 palaver; haggle.
parlamentæ'r *-en mil.* negotiant; bearer of a flag of truce.
parlamentæ'r/flagg *-et* flag of truce.
+par'/løp *-et* pair skating.
parlø'r *-en* phrase book.
parmesa'n/ost [/ost] *-en* parmesan (cheese).
parnass' *-et* Parnassus (lofty world of poets): **det norske p-** Norwegian classic writers.
parodi' *-en* 1 parody (**på** of). 2 *fam.* caricature.
parodie're *V -te* mimic; parody.
paro'disk *A* - ludicrous.
paro'le *-n* 1 slogan, watchword. 2 *mil.* order, password: **lystre p-** obey orders; **møte på p-n** appear at morning meeting (of police); **møte ved p-n** (mil. officers') meeting to receive orders of the day. 3: **på p-** on word of honor.
+par're *V -et* cf **pare**
parsell' *-en* lot, parcel, plot (of land).
parselle're *V -te admin.* divide, parcel out (land into lots).
par't *-en* 1 part (also *naut.*); portion, share: **for min p-** I for my part, I for one. 2 *jur.* party.
parte're *V -te* (of carcass) carve, cut up; dismember, quarter.
parterr(e) [partær'] *-(e)t* 1 ground floor; section for audience in back of orchestra, usu. under balcony. 2 *hort.* flower bed. 3: **p-/brytning** ground wrestling.
+par't/haver *-en, pl -e* (=***-ar**) *merc.* joint owner, partner.
parti' *-et, pl +-er/*-* 1 part (of a book, piece of music, wall, etc.); view (in photo, drawing, etc.); role. 2 (hunting, political) party; side, team; table (of bridge, whist, etc.): **ta p-** take sides. 3 game (of cards, billiards, etc.): **et p- sjakk** a g- of chess. 4 *merc.* consignment, lot: **et p- barnevogner** a consignment of baby buggies. 5 (marriage) match: **et godt p-** a good m-, a catch.
parti'/avi's *-a/+-en pol.* party organ, party paper.
partiell [partsiell'] *A -elt* partial (=not whole).
parti'/felle *-n pol.* fellow member (of a party).
+parti'/gjenger *-en, pl -e pol.* party man.
parti'/gruppe *-a/+-en pol.* 1 party wing. 2 members of a political party in a parliament.
+parti'/hensyn *-et pol.* party considerations: **ta p-** play politics.
partik'kel *-elen, pl partikler* particle (also *gram.*).
partikulæ'r *A jur.* particular, special.
parti'/linje *-a/+-en pol.* party line.
parti'/mann *-en, pl -menn/*-menner* *pol.* party man.
+parti'/poli'tiker *-en, pl -e* (=***-ar**) (loyal) party politician.
parti'/politikk' *-en* party politics.
partisa'n *-en* 1 *mil.* partisan (a weapon). 2 guerrilla, partisan (fighter).
partisa'n/krig *-en* guerrilla warfare.
partisipp' *-et, pl -/+-er gram.* participle.
par'tisk [also: partis'k] *A* - biased (e.g. judge, decision).
+partisk/het *-en* bias, partiality.
+parti'/taing [/ta-ing] *-a/-en* (=***/taking**) taking sides.
+parti'/traver *-en, pl -e* (=***/tråvar**) party hack.
partitu'r *-en/-et, pl -/-er mus.* score.
pa'rtner *-en, pl +-e* 1 partner (e.g. in cards, dance). 2 *merc.* joint owner, partner.
partout [partu'] *Av*: **ville p-** insist on.
partout/kort *-et* (permanent) pass (e.g. at theater).
+par't/reder *-en, pl -e* (=***/reiar**) joint owner of a ship.
+par'ts/forhan'dling *-en* negotiations in a dispute, esp. labor dispute.
par'ts/innlegg *-et* 1 *jur.* plea, pleading (in lawsuit). 2 biased, one-sided presentation.
***par'ts/lag** *-et* cooperative society.
***par'ts/tinging** *-a jur.* negotiations in a dispute, esp. labor dispute.
par'/tåa *A* - (=+-et) *zool.* two-toed.
parveny' *-en* parvenu, upstart.
par'/vis *A* - by couples, in pairs.
parykk' *-en* toupee, wig: **gå med p-** wear a w-.
+parykk'/maker *-en, pl -e* (=***-ar**) wigmaker.
parykk'/tid *-a/+-en* "the Age of Wigs" (Baroque and Rococo periods).
pasien't *-en* patient.
pasifise're *V -te* pacify.
pasifis'me *-n* pacifism.
pasifis't *-en* pacifist.
pasifis'tisk *A* - pacifist(ic).
pa'sja *-en* pasha; *fam.* man accustomed to being waited on.
pa'sje *-n hist.* page (boy).
pa'sje/hår *-et* pageboy haircut.
pasjo'n *-en* 1 *bibl.* Passion. 2 *archaic* love, passion. 3 hobby, intense interest.
pasjone'rt *A* - ardent, keen, passionately fond of.
+pasjo'ns/blomst *-en* (=***/blome**) *bot.* passionflower (Passiflora).
+pasjo'ns/skuespill *-et* passion play.
+pasjo'ns/spill *-et* (=***/spel**) passion play.
+pasjo'ns/uke *-a/-en* Holy Week.
pas'ning *-a/+-en* 1 care, tending. 2 fit (of clothes, machinery). 3 pass (in soccer).
pass'¹ *-en* pass (in card game): **melde p-** pass; *fig.* give up.
pass'² *-et* passport.
pass'³ *-et* 1 mountain pass. 2 pace (gait).
pass'⁴ *-et* care, tending (**av** of).
pass'⁵ *N*: **til p-** suitable; **det er til p- til ham** that serves him right; **gjøre det til p- for** do sth satisfactorily for; **gjøre noen til p-** satisfy sby; **ikke riktig til p-** not feeling well.
passa'bel *A -elt, pl -le* not too bad, passable.
passa'sje *-n* 1 passage; traffic, transit (of people); gait (of horses); *astron.* transit (across meridian): **fri p- til** free access to. 2 channel, narrows, straits; arcade, passageway. 3 *lit., mus.* passage (e.g. in a book, a mus. composition).
passasje'r *-en* passenger.
passasje'r/tog [/tåg] *-et* passenger train.
passasje'r/vogn [/vångn] *-a* passenger coach.
passa't *-en* trade wind; area of trade winds.
passa't/vind *-en* trade wind.
pass'/bilde *-t* passport photo.
pass'/båt *-en* flat-bottomed boat with outboard motor (for 4–8 people).
pas'se¹ *V -a/+-et* (in card game) bid pass, pass.
pas'se² *V -a/+-et* (in ball game) pass.
pas'se³ *V -a/+-et* 1 fit; be appropriate, suit; apply: **det p-er** that's fine, suitable; that's convenient; **p- dårlig** be unsuitable, not fit; **kjolen p-er godt** the dress fits well; **rødt p-er meg ikke** red doesn't suit me, isn't becoming to me. 2 (with *prep.* and *adv.*): **p- med** fit in with; agree with; **p- på** apply to, fit; **p- sammen** go together, suit each other; fit together; **p- til** go with, match. 3 (*refl.*): **p- seg** be proper, suitable, do. (See also **passende.**)
pas'se⁴ *V -a/+-et* 1 mind, watch; look after, take care of, tend: **p- leiligheten** watch one's chance, opportunity; **p- sitt (eget)** mind one's (own) business; **p- telefonen** answer

+ Bokmål; * Nynorsk; ° Dialect.
After letter: ' stress (Acc. 1); ' tone, stress (Acc. 2); · length.
Below letter: . not pronounced.

the telephone; **p- tiden** watch the time, be punctual. 2 (with *prep.* and *adv.*): **p- opp** be on the lookout for, waylay; **p- på** mind, take care of, watch; be careful, look out, watch out; **p- på barna** take care of, watch the children. 3 *(refl.)*: **p- seg** look out, watch out (**for** for); watch oneself; **p- seg selv** take care of oneself; **pass deg selv** mind your own business.

pas'se[5] *A* - fair, moderate, suitable: **p- stor** about the right size; **så p-** medium, so-so.

passé *A* - passé, unfashionable.

pas'selig *A* - 1 fitting, suitable: **så p-** (just) passable, tolerable; **føle seg så p-** feel just so-so. 2 *(adv.)* conveniently; fittingly.

pas'sende *A* - 1 according to custom; correct. 2 fitting, suitable; just right: **noen p- ord** some appropriate words.

+**pas'ser** *-en, pl -e* (=***-ar**) pair of compasses, dividers.

passe're *V -te* 1 go past, pass by, through; cross (the equator, a line, etc.): **p- revy** pass in review. 2 happen, occur. 3 pass (be permissible): **du kan til nød p-** at a pinch you will do; **p- for** pass as.

+**passe'r/seddel** *-elen, pl -sedler* (=***/setel**) pass, permit; carnet (for car).

pass'/fotografi' *-et, pl +-er/*-* passport photo.

pass'/gang *-en* 1 (of animals) pace, pacing (lateral gait); amble. 2 (of humans) slow pace, walk.

+**pass'/gjenger** *-en, pl -e* (=***/gangar**) pacer.

passia'r *-en* chat, talk.

passia're *V -te* chat, talk (**med** with).

pas'siv[1] *-en gram.* passive: **i p-** in the p-.

pas'siv[2] *A* passive (e.g. person, resistance; *chem.* metal).

pas'siva *pl* liabilities.

passivite't *-en* passivity.

pass'/kontroll' *-en* 1 passport examination. 2 passport officials.

pass'/kort *-et* passing hand (in card game).

pass'/melding *-a/+-en* bid of pass (in card game).

pas'sus *-en* sentence; (short) passage (of writing).

pass'/vise'ring *-a/+-en* supplying a passport with a consular visa.

pass'/visitasjo'n *-en* examination of passports (usu. in transit).

pas'ta *-en* dough; (dry or wet) paste.

pastell' *-en* pastel (=pastel coloring matter, crayon, painting process, picture).

pastell'/farge *-n* pastel color.

pasteurisere [pastørise're] *V -te* pasteurize.

+**pastiche** [pastisj'] *-n* cf **pastisj**

pastill' *-en* lozenge, pastille.

pastinakk' *-en bot.* parsnip (Pastinaca sativa).

pastisj' *-en* pastiche.

pas'tor *-en* pastor (form of address).

pastora'l *A* pastoral.

pastora'le *-n* 1 pastoral play. 2 *mus.* pastorale.

pastora't *-et, pl -/+-er admin.* pastorate (the office, calling); benefice.

pastø's *A* impasto, pastose (thickly applied paint).

paten't[1] *-et, pl -/+-er* patent (on invention; of nobility, etc.); certificate, commission (**som** as): **ha p- på sannheten** have a monopoly on the truth.

paten't[2] *A* - dependable, first-class: **en p- venstremann** a solid supporter of *Venstre.*

+**paten't/beskyt'tet** *A* - protected by patent.

patente're *V -te* patent, take out a patent on.

+**paten't/haver** *-en, pl -e* (=***-ar**) patentee.

paten't/krav *-et* application for a patent.

paten't/medisi'n *-en* patent medicine; *ironic* nostrum.

paten't/middel *-elet/-midlet, pl +-midler/*-el* nostrum.

paten't/smørbrød *-et* usu. a fried egg on bread.

pa'ter *-en, pl -rer/+-e eccl.* Father.

paterfami'lias *en hum.* pater, paterfamilias.

paternite't *-en* paternity.

paternos'ter *-et* 1 Lord's Prayer. 2 each of the large beads of a rosary; rosary.

paternos'ter/verk *-et* endless chain conveyor.

pate'tisk *A* - showing pathos, feeling; high-flown (speech, style).

+**patient** [pasien't] *-en* cf **pasient**

pa'tina *-en* patina.

patine're *V -te* become covered with patina; treat chemically to produce patina.

patolog [-olå'g] *-en* pathologist.

patologi' *-en* pathology.

patologisk [-olå'gisk] *A* - pathological; diseased, morbid.

patos [pa'tås] *-en* passion, pathos.

patriar'k *-en* patriarch.

patriarka'lsk *A* - patriarchal.

patrio't *-en* patriot.

patrio'tisk *A* - patriotic.

patriotis'me *-n* patriotism.

+**patri'sier** *-en, pl -e* (=***-ar**) patrician.

patri'sisk *A* - patrician.

patro'n[1] **-a/+-en* 1 *mil.* cartridge. 2 *tech.* model, pattern; chuck (on machine or workbench).

patro'n[2] *-en* patron, protector; *hum.* fellow; queer fish.

patro'n/belte *-t* cartridge belt.

patro'n/hylse *-a* cartridge (case), shell.

patronise're *V -te* patronize (protect condescendingly).

patro'n/taske *-a mil.* cartridge pouch.

patrul'je *-n* patrol (military, police, boy scouts, etc.).

patrulje're *V -te* patrol.

patrul'je/vogn [/vångn] *-a* patrol car.

patt' *A* - (of chess) stalemated.

pat'te[1] *-en/*-a* nipple, teat (of animal); nipple (of human); *pop.* woman's breast: **gi p-** give breast to, suckle.

pat'te[2] *V -a/+-et* 1 (of child) nurse, suck, suckle. 2 drag at (e.g. a pipe).

pat'te/ba'rn *-et, pl -/*-born* baby, bottle baby, suckling.

+**pat'te/dyr** *-et zool.* mammal.

pat'te/gris *-en* suckling pig.

pau'ke *-n mus.* kettledrum.

pauli'nsk *A* - Pauline (of or pertaining to the apostle Paul).

paulu'n *-et, pl -/+-er archaic* pavilion, tent; *hum.* abode, dwelling: **slå sine p-er opp** *bibl.* raise one's tents.

Pau'lus *Prn* Paul (usu. the apostle).

***pau're** *V -a* work diligently but slowly.

pau'se *-n* pause, stop; break, respite; intermission; *mus.* rest.

pause're *V -te lit.* pause; *mus.* rest.

pau'se/signal [/singna'l] *-et* radio signal repeated during a pause (in Norway a short melody composed for the purpose).

pa've *-n* 1 *eccl.* pope: **strid om p-ns skjegg** hairsplitting, quarrel about nothing. 2 *derog.* domineering, self-important person; boss.

pa've/dømme *-t* papacy.

+**pa've/kirke** *-n*: **p-n** the Roman Catholic Church.

pa'velig *A* - papal.

pa'vet(e) *A* - *derog.* arrogant, domineering, self-important.

paviljong' *-en* pavilion.

paviljong'/syste'm *-et, pl +-er/*-* cottage system (of institutions).

pd.=**pund**

pea/nøtt [pi'/] *-a* peanut.

peau-de-pêche-jakke [pådøpe'sj-] *-a* velveteen jacket.

pedago'g *-en* 1 pedagogue, teacher. 2 professor, teacher of pedagogy (education).

pedagogikk' *-en* pedagogy (usu. called Education in U.S.).

pedago'gisk *A* - pedagogical.

pedagur'k *-en pop.* dry, dull teacher; sourpuss.

peda'l *-en* pedal (e.g. on bicycle, car, musical instrument); treadle.

pedan't *-en* pedant.

pedanteri' *-et* pedantry.

pedan'tisk *A* - pedantic.

pedell' *-en* janitor.

Pe'der *Prn(m)*

pediky'r *-en* chiropody, pedicure.

pe'gasus *-en* 1 *myth., astron.* Pegasus. 2 *zool.* small Chinese fish (Pegasidae).

+**pe'gl** *-en* cf **pel**[1]

***pei'k**[1] *-et* cf **pek**[1]

***pei'k**[2] *-et* cf **pek**[2]

***pei'ke** *V -a/-te* cf **peke**

***pei'ke/finger** *-eren, pl -rar* cf **peke/**

pei'le *V -a/+-et/+-te* 1 *naut.* take a bearing; sound (e.g. the pumps, the tanks). 2 (of radio) locate: **p- inn** (the same).

pei'le/stokk *-en naut.* gauge.

pei'ling *-a/+-en* 1 *naut.* bearings, soundings: **ta p-** take (one's) bearings, s-. 2 *fam.*: **få p- på** catch sight of; learn about; **ha p- på** know about; **ha ikke p- (på det)** have no idea (about it); **ta p- på** aim at, head for.

pei'p *pt of* **pipe**[2]

pei's[1] *-en* fireplace, hearth (in Norway usu. in a corner).

pei's[2] *-en* 1 penis (of animal). 2 whip: **få p-** get a beating.

pei'se *V -a/-te* 1 whip; beat, strike. 2: **p- på** go ahead, work hard; go very fast, speed.

pei'se/stue *-a* (special) room with a fireplace.

pei's/helle *-a* flat stone or piece of iron forming the floor of a fireplace.

pei's/hylle *-a* mantelpiece, mantelshelf.

pei's/krakk *-en* fireplace stool.

pei's/krok *-en* fireplace corner, inglenook.

pei's/pipe *-a* fireplace chimney.

+**pei's/puster** *-en, pl -e* (=***-ar**) bellows.

pe'k[1] *-et*: **gjøre en et p-** play a joke on sby; trick sby.

+**pe'k**[2] *-et* (=***peik**[2]) hint, pointer.

+**pe'ke** *V -te* (=***peike**) point: **p- fingre av** make derisive gestures, p- derisively at; **p- mot** *fig.* p- to, towards; **p- på** call attention to, refer to; indicate; **p- ut** p- out, select.

+**pe'ke/finger** *-eren, pl -rer* forefinger, index finger.

+**pe'ke/pinn(e)** *-(e)n* 1 pointer. 2 directions, guidance, hint.

+**pe'ke/stokk** *-en* pointer.

+**pekinge'ser** *-en, pl -e* (=***-ar**) Pekingese (dog).

pekuniæ'r *A* financial, pecuniary.

pe'l[1] *-en hist.* measure, 1/4 **pott** (for liquids, ab.=1/2 pint).

+**pe'l**[2] *-en* cf **påle**[1]

pela'gisk *A* - pelagic.

pelargo'nium *-iumen, pl -ier bot.* geranium (Pelargonium).

***pe'le** *V -a* cf **pelle**

°**pelemen't** *-et* 1 strife; quarreling, wrangling. 2 joke, trick; acting up.

pelika'n *-en zool.* pelican (Pelecanus).

pell' *-et archaic* fine cloth (esp. silk and satin).

+**pel'le** *V -a/pelte* (=***pele**) 1 pick (berries) (cf also **pille**[3]). 2: **p- en ned** *fam.* pick sby off (by shooting).

pel'me *V -a/+-et* cf **palme**[2]

pelotong' *-en* platoon (in infantry).

pel's *-en* 1 (animal) fur, hide. 2 fur (or fur-lined) coat. 3 *hum.* skin: **få på p-en** get a beating, hiding; **redde p-en** save one's skin.

pel's/dyr *-et* fur-bearing animal.

pel'sdyr/farm *-en* fur farm.

pel'se *V -a/+-et* 1 kill and skin (fur-bearing animal). 2 grow fur. 3 raise (e.g. foxes) for fur.

pel's/fora *A* - (=+**-et**) fur-lined.

+**pel's/handler** *-en, pl -e* (=***-ar**) furrier.

pel's/jeger *-eren, pl +-ere/*-rar* trapper.

pel's/kåpe *-a* fur coat.

pel's/lue *-a* (=**/luve**) fur cap.

pel's/vare *-a/+-en* usu. *(pl) merc.* hides or skins (with hair or feathers on).

pel's/verk *-et* furs.

pem'mikan [also -ka'n] *-en* pemmican.

pe'n *A* 1 nice (dress, face, funeral, girl, house, manners, weather, etc.); (of clothing, appearance, etc.) neat, trim; honest, respectable, upstanding (e.g. citizen): **den p-e handa** the right hand. 2 good-looking, handsome (object, person, etc.); nice, pretty (handwriting, painting, poem, singing, etc.). 3 (quite) good (job, position, etc.); fine, (very) good (achievement, exam, performance, etc.); goodly, handsome, nice, very favorable (profit, sum, wage, etc.). 4 *(adv.)* nicely, etc.; merely, simply, without further ado: **nå får du p-t finne deg i det** now you'll simply have to accept it; **sitte p-t til bords** sit nicely at table.

pena't *-en*: **p-er** (Roman) *myth.* penates (household gods).

pendant [pangdang'] *-en* counterpart.

pen'del *-elen, pl -ler* 1 *phys.* pendulum. 2 *elec.* pendant lamp.

+**pen'del/beve'gelse** *-n phys.* pendulum movement.

pen'del/kjøring *-a/+-en* (=***/køyring**) (esp. of buses) running a through route.

pen'del/ur *-et* pendulum clock.

pen'dle *V -a/+-et* oscillate (also *fig.*): **p- mellom Norge og Amerika** shuttle between Norway and America; **p- over** swing over.

***peng'** *-en* cf **penge**

peng'e *-n* (=***peng**) (usu. *pl*) money: **alle p-ne mine** all my m-; **for en billig p-** for a small sum; **ha p-r** be rich; **mange p-r** lots of m-; **norske p-r** Norwegian m-; **p-ne på bordet** cash on the line, *(pop.)* fork out your money.

+**peng'e/anbring'else** *-n merc.* investment (i in).

+**peng'e/anvi'sning** *-en merc.* check.

peng'e/aristokrati' *-et* plutocracy.

+**peng'e/avpresning** *-en* (=***/avpressing**) *jur.* blackmail.

peng'e/brev *-et* registered letter containing money (indicated on envelope); postal money order.

+**peng'e/flom'** *-men* flood of money (in good times).

peng'e/folk *pl* financiers; the wealthy.

+**peng'e/forle'genhet** *-en* pecuniary embarrassment.

peng'e/fyrste *-n* money baron, tycoon.

peng'e/gras *-et bot.* rattle, yellow rattle (Rhinanthus crista-galli).

peng'e/grisk *A* - avaricious.

+**peng'e/hensyn** *-et* pecuniary consideration.

peng'e/hjelp *-a/-en* pecuniary aid.

+**peng'e/hushol'dning** *-en* money economy.

peng'e/kjær *A* fond of money.

peng'e/lens *A* penniless.

peng'e/lotteri' *-et* lottery in which money is the prize.

peng'e/mann *-en, pl -menn/*-menner* capitalist.

+**peng'e/midler** *pl* capital, means.

peng'e/pressing *-a/+-en* extortion.

+**peng'e/puger** *-en, pl -e* (=***-ar**) miser.

peng'e/pung [/pong] *-en* purse.

+**peng'er** *pl of* **penge**

peng'e/saker *pl* financial affairs, money matters.

+**peng'e/seddel** *-elen, pl -sedler* (=***/setel**) bill (piece of paper money).

+**peng'e/skap** *-et* (=***/skåp**) safe.

peng'e/sorg *-a/+-en* (usu. *pl*) financial, money worries.

peng'e/sterk *A* financially strong, wealthy.

peng'e/stykke *-t, pl +-r/*-* coin.

peng'e/urt *-a/+-en bot.* pennycress (Thlaspi arvense).

+**peng'e/utpresning** *-en* extortion.

+**peng'e/utpresser** *-en, pl -e* extortionist.

+**peng'e/vanskeligheter** *pl* financial difficulties.

peng'e/velde *-t* plutocracy.

peng'e/verdi' *-en* (=***/verd(e)**) cash value, monetary value.

+**peng'e/vesen** *-et* finance.

peni'bel *A -elt, pl -le* embarrassing, painful, unpleasant.

penicilli'n *-et* penicillin.

***pe'ning** *-en* cf **penning**

pe'nis *-en anat.* penis.

penn'[1] *-en* 1 pen: **bringe, føre i p-en** pen, write down; **la p-en løpe** write down ideas as they occur to one; **med bred p-** with broad strokes of the p-; **uttrykket falt meg i p-en** the expression slipped in (as I was writing). 2 author, pen, writer: **en av landets skarpeste p-er** one of the keenest writers in the country.

penn'[2] *-en* peen (back of hammer).

penna'l *-et, pl -/+-er* pencil box.

pen'ne/drag *-et* stroke of the pen; jotting, notation.

+**pen'ne/feide** *-n* literary controversy, feud.

pen'ne/før *A* able to write (well).

pen'ne/knekt *-en derog.* journalist, scribbler.

pen'ne/kniv *-en* penknife, pocketknife.

pen'ne/prøve *-a/+-en* curlicue, doodle; *lit.* first work of a writer, literary exercise.

pen'ne/skaft *-et* penholder.

+**pen'ne/skjær** *-et* nib, pen point.

pen'ne/splitt *-en* pen point.

pen'ne/strøk *-et* stroke of the pen.

+**pen'ne/tegning** [/teining] *-en* (=***/teikning**) 1 pen-and-ink drawing, sketch. 2 *lit.* sketch.

+**pen'ning** *-en* (=***pening**) 1 *hist.* penny. 2 *dial.* money.

pen's *-en* switch (on railroad).

pens. =**pensjonist**

pen'se *V -a/+-et* 1 switch (e.g. a train). 2 *fig.* direct, lead: **pens utviklingen inn i det riktige løp** direct the development into the right course (Dagbladet).

pen'se/jern [/jæ'rn] *-et* (=***/jarn**) switch key.

pen'sel *-elen, pl -ler* (paint) brush; *med.* swab.

pen'sel/strøk *-et* brushstroke.

pen'se/mann *-en, pl -menn/*-menner* switchman.

pensjon [pangsjo'n] *-en* 1 pension: **livsvarig p-** life p-. 2 board and room: **full p-** b- and r-; **ha en i p-** have sby as a boarder. 3 (rarely) boarding house, pension.

pensjonat [pangsjona't] *-et, pl -/+-er* boarding house, pension.

pensjonat/skole *-n* boarding school.

pensjonere [pangsjone're] *V -te* pension, pension off.

pensjonist [pangsjonis't] *-en* pensioner.

pensjons/alder [pangsjo'ns/] *-en* retirement age with right of pension (pensionable age).

+**pensjons/beret'tiget** *A* - entitled to pension.

pensjons/innskott *-et* (=+**/innskudd**) contribution to pension fund.

pensjons/kasse *-a/-en* pension fund.

pensjons/ordning *-a/+-en* pension system.

pensjonær [pangsjonæ'r] *-en* boarder, guest.

pen'sle *V -a/+-et* 1 paint (with brushstrokes), retouch (with small brush). 2 *med.* swab.

pen'sum *-et, pl pensa* curriculum; required course of study; required reading.

penteri' *-et* (=**pentri**) *naut.* pantry.

peo'n *-en* (=**pion**) *bot.* peony (Paeonia).

+**peo'n/rød** *A* (=***/raud**) red as a peony.

+**pe'p** *pt of* **pipe**[1]

pe'par *-en* cf **pepper**

peparmyn'te *-a* cf **pepper/**

pe'par/møy *-a* cf **pepper/**

pe'par/rot *-a, pl -røter* cf **pepper/**

pe'par/svein *-en* cf **pepper/svenn**

+**pe'pet** *pp of* **pipe**[1]

+**pep'per** *-en* (=***pepar**) pepper.

+**pep'per/bøsse** *-a* pepper shaker.

+**pep'per/kake** *-a* spiced cooky (rolled flat).

+**pep'per/ko'rn** *-et* peppercorn.

+**pep'per/kvern** [/kvæ'rn] *-a* pepper mill.

+**peppermyn'te** *-a* 1 peppermint (candy). 2 *bot.* peppermint (Mentha piperita).

+**pep'per/møy** *-a* (=+**/mø**) old maid.

+**pep'per/nøtt** *-a* peppernut (small ball-shaped cooky).

+**pep'per/rot** *-a bot.* horseradish (Armoracia rusticana).

+**pep'per/svenn** *-en* bachelor.

pep're *V -a/+-et* season with pepper; *fig.* spice (a story).

pepsi'n *+-en/*-et chem.* pepsin.

per' *P* esp. *merc.* 1 per: **pr. mann** p- person; **pr. måned** p- month; monthly; **pr. stykke** apiece. 2 near, over: **pr. Oslo** near, over O-. 3 by: **pr. bil** by car; **pr. kontant** cash. 4 on (date): **pr. 1ste januar** on Jan. 1. 5 (in bookkeeping) by.

Pe'r *Prn(m)*: **P- og Pål** Tom, Dick, and Harry (from folktale by Asbjørnsen and Moe).

perfeksjone're *V -te* perfect.

perfeksjonis'me *-n* perfectionism.

perfeksjonis't *-en* perfectionist.

perfeksjonis'tisk *A* - perfectionist.

perfek't *A* - perfect: **han kan sine ting p-** he knows his stuff to perfection.

perfekti'bel *A -elt, pl -le* perfectible.

per'fektum [also -fek'-] *-umet, pl +-er/+-a/*-um gram.* perfect.

perfi'd *A* - faithless; perfidious.

perfidite't *-en* perfidy.

perfore're *V -te* perforate.

pergamen't *-et, pl -/+-er* 1 parchment. 2 *lit.* document, manuscript.

pergamen't/papi'r *-et* parchment paper.

per'gola *+-en/* ei* 1 *arch.* pergola. 2 arbor, bower.

peria'l *-en* 1 *hum., archaic* intoxication. 2 *arch.* tower above apse in stave church.

perife'r *A* peripheral, subordinate.

periferi' *-en* periphery (**av** of); outskirts (of a city).

perife'risk *A* - peripheral, subordinate.

pe'rikum *-en bot.* St.-John's-wort (Hypericum).

perio'de *-n* 1 period (of time; cycle, phase; epoch, era, etc.). 2 *gram.* (compound) sentence, period; periodic sentence. 3 *fam., med.* menses. 4 *elec.* cycle (of alternating current). 5 (in telephones) pay period (e.g. 3 minutes).

+**perio'de/dranker** *-en, pl -e* alcoholic, dipsomaniac.

perio'de/vis *Av* periodically.

periodisite't *-en* periodicity.

perio'disk [also -o'-] *A* - periodic.

perisko'p *-et, pl -/+-er* periscope.

perkola'tor *-en* percolator.

perkole're *V -te* percolate.

perkusjo'n *-en med., mil.* percussion.

per'le[1] *-a/+-en* 1 pearl; *fig.* gem, jewel.

2 bead. 3 drop (of liquid); bead (of sweat).
per'le[2] *V* -*a*/+-*et* 1 bead, form beads; (e.g. of sweat, dew) drip, roll; pearl. 2 (of drink) effervesce, sparkle. 3 *fig.*: **p-ende latter** rippling laughter; **spille p-ende rent** play with clear, rippling tones.
per'le/band -*et* (=**+/bånd**) string of pearls or beads.
+per'le/blomst -*en* (=***/blom**) *bot.* grape hyacinth (Muscari).
+per'le/fisker -*en*, *pl* -*e* (=***-ar**) pearl diver, pearl fisher.
per'le/ga'rn -*et* pearl cotton (or wool; a mercerized yarn).
per'le/halsband -*et* (=**+/halsbånd**) pearl necklace.
per'le/humø'r -*et* extra good humor, high spirits.
per'le/høne -*a* *zool.* guinea hen (Numididae).
per'le/kjede +-*en*/+-*et*/*-*a* pearl necklace; string of beads.
per'le/mor -*et*/+-*en* mother-of-pearl.
per'lemor/sky -*a* mother-of-pearl (nacreous) cloud (in stratosphere).
per'le/musling -*en* 1 *zool.* pearl oyster (Pinctada margaritifera). 2 pearl mussel (in European rivers).
per'lende *A* - excellent (=**perle/**).
per'le/port [/port] -*en*: **p-en** *bibl.* the Pearly Gates.
per'le/rad [*/ra] -*a*/+-*en* row of pearls.
per'le/venn -*en* (=***/ven**) best friend.
per'lon -*et* perlon (synthetic fiber much like nylon).
per'm[1] -*en* binding, cover (of a book): **lese fra p- til p-** read from c- to c-.
per'm[2] -*en* *mil., pop.* leave (short for **permisjon**).
permanen't[1] -*en* permanent (wave).
permanen't[2] *A* - permanent, perpetual.
permanen'te *V* -*a*/+-*et* give a permanent (wave).
permisjo'n -*en* 1 *mil.* leave. 2 leave of absence (from any position). 3 *hum., archaic* (*pl*) unmentionables (underdrawers).
permitte're *V* -*te* grant leave; send home (for a short period).
per'm/tida *df* *geol.* the Permian (period).
Pernil'le *Prn(f)* (servant girl in several plays by Holberg).
perpendik'kel -*elen*, *pl* *perpendikler* pendulum.
perpendikulæ'r[1] -*en* *math.* perpendicular line.
perpendikulæ'r[2] *A* perpendicular (**på** to).
perpe'tuum mo'bile *et* perpetual motion machine.
perplek's *A* bewildered, perplexed.
perrong' -*en* platform (at station).
per's[1] -*en* ironing, pressing; fold, press (of material): **ligge i p-** be under a weight, lying in a press.
per's[2] *N*: **skal (må) til p-** is forced to yield, gets one's comeuppance; is in for sth.
pers. =**personlig**
per'se[1] -*a* press (for meat); (wine)-press.
per'se[2] *V* -*a*/+-*et* 1 press, squeeze. 2 force (sth) in, out, upon (sby); drive (sby) hard. 3 iron, press (esp. men's clothing).
per'se/jern [/jæ'rn] -*et* (=***/jarn**) tailor's pressing iron.
persepsjo'n -*en* *psych.* perception.
+per'ser -*en*, *pl* -*e* (=***-ar**) Persian.
per'se/sylte -*a* pressed (collared) headcheese.
Per'sia *Pln* Persia (now Iran).
+persia'ner -*en*, *pl* -*e* (=***-ar**) Persian lamb.
+persia'ner/kåpe -*a* (=***-ar/**) woman's coat of Persian lamb.
persien'ne -*n* Venetian blind.
persifla'sje -*n* (=**+persiflasj**) good-humored ridicule.
persifle're *V* -*te* ridicule good-humoredly.
persil'le +-*a*/-*en* *bot.* parsley (Petroselinum).
persil'le/blad -*et* 1 leaf of parsley. 2 *fig.* delicate, fragile person.
persil'le/rot -*a*, *pl* +-*røtter*/*-*røter* parsley root.
persil'le/smør' -*et* parsley butter.
per'sisk *A* - Persian.
pe'rsok *en* *dial.* St. Peter's Day (June 29).
perso'n -*en* 1 person (also *gram., jur.*); personage, personality: **for min p-** (as) for me personally; **i egen (høye) p-** in person; **vennligheten i egen p-** friendliness personified; **uten p-s anseelse** without respect of persons. 2 character (in book, play), (*pl*) cast, characters, dramatis personae. 3 *derog.* creature.
persona'le -*t* personnel, staff.
persona'l/histo'rie -*a*/+-*en* biography.
persona'lia *pl* biographical data.
persona'l/sjef -*en* chief of staff (in institution); personnel manager (in business).
persona'l/unio'n -*en* *hist.* union of countries under a common ruler (as Norway and Sweden 1814—1905).
persona'sje -*n* *derog.* character, person.
perso'n/bil -*en* passenger car, private car.
personell' -*et* *mil.* personnel.
personell'/kapella'n -*en* *hist.* assistant pastor (paid by pastor himself).
perso'n/galleri' -*et* *lit.* (cast of) characters (in a literary work).
personifikasjo'n -*en* personification (**av** of).
personifise're *V* -*te* personify.
***perso'nleg/dom** -(*m*)*en* cf **/het**
perso'nlig *A* - 1 personal; private: **p- frihet** individual liberty; **p- konto** private account; **p- samtale** person-to-person call. 2 (*adv.*) personally; in person.
+perso'nlig/het -*en* personality (=character, figure); individuality; (*pl*) personalities (=insults).
+perso'nlighets/spaltning -*en* *psych.* schizophrenia, split personality.
+perso'nlighets/type -*n* *psych.* personality type.
perso'n/takst -*en* fare.
perso'n/tog [/tåg] -*et* passenger train.
perso'n/vogn [/vångn] -*a* passenger car.
perspekti'v -*et*, *pl* -/+-*er* perspective: **det å ha elsket mange, det gir p- i livet** to have loved many gives p- in life (Kinck).
+perspekti'v/tegning [/teining] -*en* (=***/teikning**) perspective drawing.
perspire're *V* -*te* *med.* perspire.
per't -*en* *naut.* footrope.
per'ten *A* +-*ent*, *pl* -*ne* *dial.* fastidious, fussy, particular.
perten'tlig *A* - correct, meticulous; punctilious; (*pop.*) persnickety.
Peru' *Pln* Peru.
+perua'ner -*eren*, *pl* -*e* (=***-ar**) Peruvian.
perua'nsk *A* - Peruvian.
perver's *A* 1 contrary, perverse. 2 *med.* (sexually) perverted, unnatural.
perversite't -*en* *med.* perversion; abnormality.
perversjo'n -*en* *med.* perversion.
pe'se *V* +-*te*/*-*a* 1 breathe heavily, pant, puff; blow out (e.g. smoke): **p- i vei** puff away. 2 (of sports) pace.
pese'ta -*en*, *pl* -*s* peseta (monetary unit of Spain).
pes'k -*en* reindeer jacket (chiefly used by Lapps).
pe'so -*en*, *pl* -*s*/+-*er* peso (monetary unit of Mexico, etc.).
pessimis'me -*n* pessimism.
pessimis't -*en* pessimist.
pessimis'tisk *A* - pessimistic.
pes't -*en* pest, plague (also *hum.*, of person): **hate en som p-en** hate sby like poison.
pes't/byll -*en* 1 *med.* bubo. 2 *fig.* open sore; disgrace.
***pes't/fengd** *A* -/-*fengt* pestiferous, plague-stricken.
pestilen's -*en* pestilence.
pes't/lik -*et* corpse of one dead of plague.
Pe'ter *Prn(m)*
pe'ters/penge -*n* *hist., eccl.* Peter's pence.
pe'tet(e) *A* - prim.
petime'ter -*eren*, *pl* -*re* pedantic, petty bureaucrat.
petisjo'n -*en* *admin.* petition.
petit [pøti'] -*en* 1 *typog.* 8 point. 2 *journ.* =**petitartikkel.**
petit/artik'kel -*elen*, *pl* -*artikler* *journ.* short, usu. humorous or chatty commentary by regular columnist, printed in small print (**petit**).
petit/journalist [pøti'/sjurnalis't] -*en* one who writes *petit* articles; ab.= columnist.
petit/noti's -*en* news item printed in small print.
Pe'tra *Prn(f)*
+Pe'tri *po of* **Peter** (only *bibl., eccl.*)
petro'leum -*en* 1 petroleum. 2 gasoline, kerosine.
petro'leums/lampe -*a*/-*en* kerosine lamp.
petro'leums/omn -*en* (=**+/ovn**) kerosine stove.
Pet'ter *Prn(m)*: **lille P- spillemann** the little finger (from children's verse).
pe'tum -*en* stem tobacco for pipe smoking.
pfal'z/greve -*n* *hist.* (title) Count Palatine.
p. g. a.=**på grunn av**
pi' *en*, *pl* - *math.* pi.
pianis't -*en* pianist.
+pianistin'ne -*a*/-*en* (woman) pianist.
pia'no -*et*, *pl* -*er* piano; (*adj., adv.*) piano: **ta det p-** *pop.* take it easy.
pianofor'te -*t*, *pl* +-*r*/*- piano, pianoforte.
pia'no/kasse -*a*/-*en* piano box.
pia'no/krakk -*en* piano bench.
piano'la -*et* pianola, player piano.
piassa'va/kost [/kost] -*en* piassava broom (chiefly for decks and streets).
pickles [pik'kels] -*en* pickles.
pickup [pikk'øp] -*en* pickup (on phonograph).
pidestall' -*en* pedestal.
piece [pje's] -*n* piece, short play; article, story (in newspaper); booklet, leaflet, pamphlet.
piete't -*en* respect, reverence, veneration (**for, mot, overfor** to, for).
piete'ts/full *A* reverent.
+piete'ts/følelse -*n* cf **/kjensle**
+piete'ts/hensyn -*et* respect, reverence.
piete'ts/kjensle -*a* (feeling of) respect, reverence, veneration.
+piete'ts/løs *A* irreverent.
pietis'me -*n* Pietism; *derog.* bigotry.
pietis't -*en* Pietist; *derog.* "holy" person, bigot.
pietis'tisk *A* - pietistic.
pigg'[1] -*en* 1 spike (e.g. on fence, tool, ski pole); barb (on wire). 2 quill, spine (on animal); prickle, thorn (on plant): **vende p-ene ut** *fig.* bristle. 3 mountain peak (e.g. **Galdhøpiggen**). 4 *naut.* forepeak, afterpeak, gaff (of sail).
pigg'[2] *A* - 1 feeling well, in fine shape: **være p- på noe** be eager about sth. 2 *dial.* full, stuffed (with food); drunk.
pig'ge *V* -*a*/+-*et* 1 (using a stick with a spike, e.g. a ski pole): **p- i mål** (push ahead to) reach (one's) goal; **p- i vei, p- på, p- seg (nedover** down) hurry, increase speed, push on (skiing or sledding). 2 *fam.* plod, walk: **p- av, p- av gårde** hurry off, run off; (*pop.*) push off, scram; **vi må p- oss hjem** we must get along home; **p- seg fram** plod along. **3: p- opp** excite; *fig.* prod, stimulate. **4: p- seilet** *naut.* raise the sail apeak.
pig'get(e) *A* - 1 barbed, prickly; quilled, spiky. 2 *fig.* prickly, unfriendly (person).

pigg`/hakke -a (railroad) pick, pickax.
pigg`/hå -en *zool.* spiny dogfish (Squalus acanthias).
pigg`/sko -en, *pl* -r/+- spiked shoe, track shoe.
pigg`/sopp -en *bot.* hydnum (Hydnaceae).
pigg`/stav -en pikestaff, pole (with metal point); ski pole.
pigg`/svin -et cf **pinn/**
pigg`/trạ̊d -en barbed wire.
pigg`trạ̊d/gjerde [/jæ're] -t, *pl* +-r/*- barbed wire fence.
pigg`trạ̊d/sperring -a/+-en barbed wire barricade.
pigg`/var -en *zool.* turbot (Bothus or Rhombus maximus).
pigmen't -et, *pl* -/+-er pigment.
***pi'k[1]** -en fine point (usu. of iron).
+**pi'k[2]** -et grudge: **jeg tror at Gud har et p- til meg** I think God has a g- against me (N. Grieg).
pi'kajor *I* by Jove.
pikan't *A* - piquant; highly-flavored; spicy, suggestive.
pikanteri' -et piquancy.
+**pi`ke** -a/-en **1** girl (child), young girl; *poet.* maid, maiden: **gammel p-** old maid; **p-nes Jens** ladies' man. **2** maid, servant: **fast p-** full-time maid; **holde p-** have a maid.
piké -en piqué (cloth).
+**pi`ke/ba'rn** -et girl (child); young girl (usu. teenager).
+**pi`ke/histo'rie** -a/-en (erotic) affair.
+**pi`ke/jeger** -en, *pl* -e girl chaser, skirt chaser.
+**pi`kelig** *A* - girlish.
+**pi`ke/lill** -en *poet.* lass.
+**pi`ke/navn** -et **1** girl's name. **2** maiden name.
pike're *V* -te **1** quilt (cloth). **2** hurt, insult, pique.
pikett' -en *mil.* picket (detachment); sentinel; stand-by.
+**pi`ke/værelse** -t maid's room.
pikk'[1] +-et/*-en knock, tap; peck; tick (of watch).
pikk'[2] -en *pop.* penis.
pikk'[3] *et*: **p- og pakk** bag and baggage.
pik`ke[1] -a small hoe, pick.
pik`ke[2] *V* -a/+-et **1** (e.g. of a bird) peck. **2** knock, tap. **3** tick. **4: p- opp** collect, pick up.
pikk`/lue -a pointed man's cap (Setesdal).
pik'kolo -en **1** *mus.* piccolo. **2** bellboy, bellhop.
pik'kolo/fløyte -a/+-en *mus.* piccolo.
pik'nik -en picnic.
+**pik`ter** -en, *pl* -e (=*-ar) Pict.
pik'tisk *A* - Pictish.
pi'l[1] -a/-en **1** arrow: **fare av sted som en p-** be off like a shot. **2** clock (on a stocking). **3** (in game) dart. **4** *fig.* bolt, dart, shaft.
pi'l[2] -a/-en *bot.* willow (Salix).
pila'r -en **1** column, pillar; *fig.* foundation. **2** pier in river.
pilas'ter -eren, *pl* -rer pilaster.
***pi`le[1]** -n cf **pille[3]**
pi`le[2] *V* +-te/*-a hurry, run, scurry (**av sted** off).
pil`e/grim· -en pilgrim.
pil`egrims/ferd -a/+-en pilgrimage.
pil`egrims/vandring -a/+-en pilgrimage.
pi`le/regn [+/rein] -et shower of arrows.
pi`le/skott -et (=+/**skudd**) **1** arrow shot. **2** shoot (of willow).
pi`le/spiss -en arrowhead.
pi`le/tre -et, *pl* -/+-trær *bot.* willow (Salix).
pil`/grim· -en cf **pile/**
pil'k -en jig, spoon hook (for fishing).
pil`ke *V* -a/+-et **1** fish with jig, spoon. **2** pick, pluck; pick up.
pil`le[1] -a/+-en *pharm.* pill: **en bitter p- å svelge** *fig.* a bitter p- to swallow.
+**pil`le[2]** -n **1** *arch.* column, pillar; pier. **2** *fig.* foundation.
+**pil`le[3]** *V* -a/-et/*pilte* **1** pick, pluck: **fuglen p-er seg** the bird is preening itself; **p- erter (reker)** shell peas (shrimp); **p- fjærene av en fugl** pluck (feathers from) a bird; **p- i maten** pick at the food; **p- med (på, ved)** finger, touch; **p- seg i nesen** pick one's nose; **p- ut av en** cure, rid sby of (e.g. bad manners). **2: p- av (bort, vekk)** beat it, scram; **p- seg (hjem)** get going, start for (home).
+**pil`len** *A* -ent, *pl* *pilne* **1** finicky, meticulous. **2** brittle, fragile.
pill'/erter *pl* *bot.* (garden) peas (Pisum sativum).
+**pil`le/triller** -en, *pl* -e (=*-ar) **1** *hum.* (of pharmacist) pill roller. **2** *zool.* scarab (Scarabaeus sacer).
+**pill`/råtten** *A* -ent, *pl* -råtne rotten to the core.
pilo't [also pai'låt] -en **1** pilot. **2** *pop.* queer duck, odd fellow.
pil's -en (=**pilsner**) (light) beer: **en p- takk** one beer, please.
pil'sener/øl -et Pilsner beer; light beer.
pi`l/snar *A* swift as an arrow.
pil'sner -en, *pl* +-e cf **pils**
pil't -en **1** small boy. **2** small, weak man, weakling.
pil`te *V* -a/+-et go, run, scurry: **p- av** hurry off.
pim'pe *V* -a/+-et booze, tipple.
pimpenll`le/rose -a/+-en *bot.* burnet (Scotch) rose (Rosa spinosissima).
pim'p/stein -en *geol.* pumice.
°**pi`nade** *I* cf **pine/død**
+**pi`n/aktig** *A* - distressing, painful; difficult, unpleasant: **p-e tider** lean times; **p- økonomi** scrupulous economy.
+**pi`naktig/het** -en distress, pain (esp. due to poverty); penuriousness.
***pi`nast** *V* *pinest, pintest, pinst* **1** be tortured, suffer prolonged pain. **2** be tormented with longing (**etter** for).
pi`ne[1] -a/+-en **1** pain, torment, torture: **den evige p-** eternal damnation; **død og p-** (*hum.* oath) hell's bells. **2** anguish, suffering: **gjør p-n kort** get it over with quickly; don't keep me in suspense.
pi`ne[2] *V* -te **1** torture: **p- livet av** torture to death (also *fig.*); **p-s** be racked (with pain), be tortured (by e.g. rheumatism), suffer. **2** cause anguish, pain, worry; pain, torment. **3** force, stuff: **p- inn i, gjennom** squeeze in, into, through; **p- ut** force out; extort (e.g. money, a secret); **p- seg opp til veggen** squeeze up against the wall (Bojer). **4** (with *adv.*): **p- på (penger)** **1** be parsimonious, stretch one's funds; **p- sammen (penger)** scrape together (money); **p- ut** exploit (e.g. the soil).
pi`ne/benk -en rack: **legge en på p-en** put sby on the r-; *fig.* keep sby on tenterhooks.
+**pi`ne/død** *I* (oath) by God, damn it.
pi`ne/full *A* painful.
pi`nende *Av*: **p- gjerrig** extremely, painfully stingy.
***pi`ne/sam** *A* cf **pin/**
***pi`nest** *pr of* **pinast**
pi`net(e) *A* - stingy.
ping'/pong -en ping-pong.
pingvi'n -en *zool.* penguin (Spheniscidae).
pin`je +-n/*-a *bot.* stone pine (Pinus pinea).
pin'k -en *dial.* weak brandy; milk punch.
pi`nlig *A* - **1** painful (subject); embarrassing, unpleasant (moment, situation). **2** meticulous (care), scrupulous (attention to detail, cleanliness). **3: p- forhør** torture, (the) third degree.
+**pi`nlig/het** -en awkwardness, embarrassment; painfulness.
pin`ne[1] -n **1** stick (e.g. kindling, twig, croquet); chopstick; knitting needle; row of knitting; peg (to close door); perch, roost (for bird); pin (in piston); stake (for plants); tiller (on boat). **2** *zool.* small, thin fish; **vandrende p-** walking stick (insect Phasmidae). **3** (idioms): **falle av p-n** fall off one's perch, topple from high position; **ikke legge to p-er i kors** not lift a finger (for sby or sth); **kaste, skyte en hvit pinn etter noe** give sth up for lost, regard sth (e.g. a friendship) as over and done with; **rive, vippe en av p-n** get sby fired; **sette en p- for** put a stopper to; **stiv som en p-** stiff as a board, reserved; **stå på p- for en** be at sby's beck and call, serve, wait on sby hand and foot.
pin`ne[2] *V* -a/+-et **1: p- opp (ved)** chop (kindling wood). **2** hammer (pegs into footwear).
pin`ne/kjøtt -et (=*/**kjøt**) steamed or roasted mutton (usu. on sticks over open fire or in kettle, West Norwegian delicacy).
pin`nende *Av* absolutely: **stå p- fast** be a- stuck.
+**pinn`e/spill** -et (=*/**spel**) **1** jackstraws ("pickup sticks"). **2** tipcat.
pin`ne/stol -en chair with spindled back.
pin`ne/ved -en kindling wood: **bli til p-** (of wooden structure) be shattered to bits.
+**pinn`/svin** -et *zool.* hedgehog (Erinaceus europaeus); porcupine (Hystrix cristata).
***pin's** -a/-en cf **pinse**
pi`n/sam** *A* (=pine/**) **1** stingy. **2** embarrassing, painful.
pin'se -a/-en (=***pins**) Pentecost, Whitsuntide (7th Sunday after Easter).
pin'se/aften -en evening before Pentecost, Whitsunday.
pin'se/dag -en Pentecost, Whitsunday: **annen p-** day after Pentecost.
pin'se/kveld -en evening before Pentecost, Whitsunday.
+**pi'nsel** -elen, *pl* -ler (=***pinsle**) torment, torture.
pin'se/lilje -a/+-en *bot.* (white or paper) narcissus (Narcissus poeticus).
pin'se/tid -a/+-en: **ved p-** around Pentecost, Whitsuntide.
pinsett' -en pincers, tweezers.
pin'se/venn -en (=*/**ven**) Pentecostalist.
+**pin'se/vær** -et **1** (good) weather during Pentecost. **2** religious revival.
pin'sjer -en, *pl* +-e *zool.* pinscher (Doberman and Miniature).
***pi'nsle** -a cf **pinsel**
+**pi`n/som·** *A* -t, *pl* -me embarrassing, painful.
***pi'nst** *pp of* **pinast**
***pi'ntest** *pt of* **pinast**
pio'n -en cf **peon**
pione'r -en pioneer (also *mil.* and *fig.*).
pione'r/arbeid -et pioneer work; *fig.* breaking new ground.
pi'p -et whistle; cheep, chirp; whine.
pi'pe[1] -a **1** pipe (in organ); fife, steam whistle (usu. on ship); whistle: **danse etter ens p-** dance to sby's tune, follow orders; **da fikk p-n en annen lyd** then he changed his tune; **stikke p-n i sekk** give up. **2** pipe (for tobacco): **en p- tobakk** a pipe(ful) of tobacco (ready for smoking); **ikke en p- tobakk verd** valueless. **3** chimney (e.g. on building, lamp); smokestack (e.g. on train, heating plant); vent (e.g. for air, steam). **4** barrel (of gun); iron pipe (in glass blowing). **5** pipe (barrel for liquids; measure for wine). **6** fluting, piping (in clothing).
pi'pe[2] *V* *peip*/+*pep*, +*pepet*/*-*e*/*-*i* **1** (e.g. of bird) cheep; (e.g. of door, old person's voice) creak, squeak; (of animal) whimper, whine; (of human) snivel, whimper; (e.g. of

+ Bokmål; * Nynorsk; ° Dialect.
After letter: ' stress (Acc. 1); ` tone, stress (Acc. 2); · length.
Below letter: . not pronounced.

bullets, storm) whine, whistle; (e.g. of breathing) wheeze, whistle; (of person, through his fingers) whistle: **p- en ut** boo, hiss, whistle sby off the stage; **p-ende instrument** squeaking instrument. 2 *naut.* pipe: **p- fall-rep** p- the side; **p- fast** p- belay; **p- til** p- dinner. 3 flute (a collar).
pi'pe/bo'rd *-et* pipe rack.
pi'pe/brann *-en* chimney fire.
+pi'pe/hode *-et* (=*/**hovud**) pipe bowl.
pi'pe/konser't *-en* hissing, jeering (at theater).
pi'pe/krage *-n* ruff.
pi'pe/lort [/lort] *-en* (tobacco) heel.
+pi'pe/renser *-en, pl -e* (=*/**reinskar**) pipe cleaner.
pi'pe/rør *-et/*-a* pipestem.
pi'pe/stilk *-en*: **p-er til bein** scrawny, sticklike legs; legs like pipestems.
pi'pet(e) *A* - 1 porous (cheese, bread). 2 (of cloth) fluted.
pi'pe/tobakk' *-en* pipe tobacco.
pipet'te *-n* (**pipett**) (eye)dropper, pipette.
pip'l *-et* trickle.
pip'le *V -a/+-et* 1 trickle: **svetten p-et fram** beads of sweat appeared, broke out. 2: **p- fram (ut)** (e.g. of light, smoke) filter, pour out; come out gradually; (e.g. of emotion) break out slowly; **en p-ende uro** a prickly restlessness.
pi'p/lerke *-a zool.* pipit (Anthus).
pipp' *-et* 1 cheep, chirp, peep. 2 courage, strength: **det tok nesten p-et fra oss** it almost knocked us out.
pip'pe *V -a/+-et* 1 cheep, chirp. 2: **p- fram (opp, ut)** peep up, sprout.
pi'r[1] *-en* pier (usu. of stone).
pi'r[2] *-en zool.* small mackerel (Scomber scombrus).
pira't *-en* 1 pirate. 2 *fig.* piratical publisher.
***pi'ren** *A -e/-i, pl -ne* 1 scrawny, slight, thin: **han er ikkje p-** he's not to be trifled with. 2 stingy.
***pir'k[1]** *-en* finicky person.
pir'k[2] *-et* 1 tiresome, detailed work. 2 petty criticism.
pir'ke *V -a/+-et* 1 pick, poke (**i** in; **med** with); fiddle, finger (**på, ved** at): **p- fram, ut av en** get (e.g. a confession, information) out of sby; **p- i mat** pick at food; **p- i sand** dig, poke in sand; **p- negler** clean (one's) nails; **p- på et sår** pick at a sore; **p- seg i tennene** pick one's teeth. 2 *fig.* criticize, pick at: **p- på, ved en** carp at, pick on sby; **p- ved** meddle with. 3: **p- seg** *fam.* move slowly; **p- seg fram** crawl ahead.
pir'ke/arbeid *-et* tiresome, detailed work.
+pir'keri *-et* petty criticism.
pir'ket(e) *A* - 1 pedantic. 2 niggling, picky.
pirquet/prøve [pirke'/] *-a/+-en* Pirquet test (for tuberculosis), tuberculin test.
pir're *V -a/+-et* 1 excite, stimulate, titillate (e.g. appetite, feeling, smell, taste); provoke (e.g. curiosity). 2: **det p-et i dem** they had a prickly sensation.
pir'relig *A* - excitable, irritable, touchy.
piruett' *-en* pirouette.
piruette're *V -te* pirouette.
pi'rum *A - fam., archaic* drunk.
pi'r/ål *-en zool.* hagfish (Myxine glutinosa).
pis'k *-en* 1 crop, whip: **få p-** get a whipping; **ha p-en over seg** be under sby's heel; **holde en under p-en** make sby toe the mark. 2 pigtail. 3: **på en p-** *fam.* tipsy, *(pop.)* high.
piskadau'sen *I archaic, dial.* (mild oath).
piskantull' *I archaic, dial.* (mild oath).
pis'ke *V -a/+-et* 1 beat, lash, whip: **p- livet av** beat, flog to death; **p- løs på** flog, whip; **p- på** whip; **p- på en** *fig.* urge sby (to do sth); *(pop.)* build a fire under sby; **p- seg til å gjøre noe** drive oneself to do sth. 2 (e.g. of rain, sleet, snow, waves) beat: **kvistene p-er i vinden** the branches lash back and forth in the wind; **regnet p-er ned** the rain pelts down; **seilet p-er i vinden** the sails beat, flap sharply in the wind; **snøen p-er ham i ansiktet** the snow whips his face. 3 beat (e.g. eggs), whip (e.g. cream).
pis'ke/snert *-en* 1 whiplash. 2 flick.
piss' *-et pop.* piss, urine.
pis'se *V -a/+-et pop.* 1 piss, urinate. 2 (e.g. of ants) excrete poison.
+pis'se/trengt *A* - (=*/**trengd**) *pop.* needing to urinate.
pissoa'r *-et, pl -/+-er* urinal.
pis't[1] *-en* 1 cheep, peep (e.g. of bird). 2 weakling. 3 strand: **noen p-er av hår** thin, stringy hair. 4 ring fence (in circus).
pis't[2] *I* pst; hey, hi.
pis'te *V -a/+-et* 1 cheep, squeak, whimper. 2 make sound of pst (to get sby's attention).
pisto'l *-en* pistol.
pistong' *-en* 1 *mil.* nipple (on percussion lock of gun). 2 *mus.* piston, valve (on wind instrument).
pis'tre *V -a/+-et* (e.g. of bullets, storm) whine, whistle; (e.g. of dog) whine (softly); speak with a squeaky voice.
pis'tre/flette *-a* thin, stringy braid (of hair).
pis'tret(e) *A* - 1 stringy, thin (e.g. bush, hair). 2 squeaky, whining.
pit'le *V -a/+-et* 1 pick (e.g. berries), pluck (sth) apart. 2 trip, walk with a short step: **p- seg** hurry. 3 *(adv.)*: **p-ende liten** very small, tiny.
pit'/props *pl* pitprops (round timbers of various lengths used in mines to support roof).
pit're *V -a/+-et* 1 *dial.* spurt out (in thin stream). 2 prick, stick; tingle: **det p-et i henne av innestengt jubel** she tingled with repressed ecstasy (Bang-Hansen).
pittores'k *A* - picturesque.
+pjal't *-en* 1 rag, *(pl)* tatters: **slå sine p-er sammen** *fig., hum.* join forces; marry. 2 coward, weakling.
+pjal'tet(e) *A* - 1 in rags, tattered. 2 cowardly, mean, spineless.
pjan'k *-et* 1 *derog.* bundle, parcel (e.g. of baggage). 2 paltriness, worthlessness; foolishness, nonsense, twaddle.
pjatt'[1] *-en* nitwit.
pjatt'[2] *-et* empty chatter, nonsense, twaddle.
pjat'te *V -a/+-et* blather, chatter idly.
pjat'tet(e) *A* - chattering (e.g. person), twaddling (talk).
pjek'kert *-en naut.* pea coat (jacket).
pjokk' *-en* little fellow, shaver; lad, youngster.
pjol'ter *-eren, pl +-ere/+-rer/*-rar* highball, whiskey and soda.
pjol'ter/glas *-et* (=+/**glass**) highball glass.
pjol'tre *V -a/+-et fam.* drink highballs.
pjus'k[1] *-en* 1 *pop.* (term of endearment for child or animal) poor dear, darling. *2 coward, weakling. 3 *dial.* strand, tuft (of hair).
pjus'k[2] *A* - 1 shabby; tousled, unkempt. 2 looking unwell.
pjus'ke *V -a/+-et* blow; make messy.
pjus'ket(e) *A* - messy, rumpled, unkempt; dishevelled, straggly, windblown.
pjut're *V -a/+-et* 1 bubble, seethe, simmer; dance. 2 mumble, prattle; twitter.
pk. =**pakke[1]**
pkt. =**punkt**
pl. =**plansje; plass**
***pla'** *V plar, pla* have as a habit, usually do (sth): **han p-r vere her** he's usually here.
pladas'k *Av* flop, plop, plump: **falle p-** fall smack (e.g. on one's seat).
plaff' *-et* bang.
plaf'fe *V -a/+-et* 1 bang, shoot: **p- løs på** blaze away at, take a pot shot at; **p- ned** pick off. 2 blow, breathe (e.g. smoke): **p- ut med** blurt out.
***pla'gar** *-en* bore, pest, tormentor.
pla'ge[1] *-a/+-en* 1 *bibl.* plague: **Egyptens p-r** the p-s of Egypt. 2 affliction, illness, pain: **hver dag har nok med sin egen plage** sufficient unto the day is the evil thereof (Matt. 6, 34). 3 bother, worry; nuisance, pest.
pla'ge[2] *V -a/+-et/+-de* afflict; bother, pester, plague; torment, trouble: **p- livet av en** pester sby to death; **p-et av tannpine** suffering from a toothache.
pla'ge/ånd *+-en/*-a* 1 *folk.* tormenting spirit. 2 nuisance, pest; tormentor; importunate person.
plagg' *-et* article, piece of clothing; garment.
plagia't *-et, pl +-er/*-* (piece of) plagiarism.
plagie're *V -te* plagiarize; copy, imitate (slavishly).
+pla'g/som' *A -t, pl -me* (=*/**sam**) burdensome (e.g. relationship); annoying, irksome (e.g. task); tiresome, troublesome (e.g. person).
plaka't[1] *-en* 1 bill, placard, poster; public notice, sign. 2 (theater) playbill: **stykket ble tatt av p-en** the play was taken off the program.
plaka't[2] *A* - 1 *pop.* dead drunk, plastered. 2 *(adv.)* absolutely: **p- umulig** a- impossible.
plaka't/søyle *-a/+-en* advertisement display pillar.
plaka't/tavle *-a* billboard.
plakett' *-en* plaque.
pla'n[1] *-en* 1 plan; project; design, scheme: **legge p-er om å** make plans to. 2 blueprint, drawing, map (**over** of). 3 timetable.
pla'n[2] *-et* level, plane (e.g. of intelligence); *math.* plane: **ligge, være i p-** be (on a) level (**med** with).
pla'n[3] *A* flat, level, plane.
plane're *V -te* 1 flatten, level; plane, smooth. 2 *fam., hum.* plan.
plane't *-en* 1 planet. 2 *fam.* forehead, skull: **få en i p-en** get one on the bean, noggin, smacker.
planeta'risk *A* - planetary.
plane't/bane *-n* orbit of a planet.
plane't/syste'm *-et, pl -/+-er* planetary system.
pla'n/fri *A -tt*: **p-tt kryss** crossing with overpass (grade separation).
pla'n/geometri' *-en* plane geometry.
plan'k *-en* planking.
plan'ke *-n* board, plank.
plan'ke/adel *-en hum.* timber barons.
plan'ke/bu *-a* shack, shed (of boards).
+plan'ke/bærer *-en, pl -e* (=*/**berar**) sawmill worker who carries planks.
plan'ke/ende *-n* deal end, plank end.
plan'ke/gjerde [/jære] *-t, pl +-r/*-* board fence.
plan'ke/kapp *-en* deal ends, plank cuttings.
plan'ke/kledning *-en* planking.
plan'kton *-et* plankton.
pla'n/la *pt of* **-legge, -leggje**
pla'n/laus *A* (=+/**løs**) aimless, desultory, random.
+pla'n/legge *V -la, lagt* (=*-**je**) make plans for; plan, project; contemplate.
+pla'n/løs *A* cf /**laus**
+pla'n/messig *A* - methodical, planned, systematic; according to plan.
pla'n/overgang *-en* grade crossing.
plansje [plang'sje] *-n* 1 plate (in book). 2 wall chart. 3 *typog.* plate.
plansjett [plangsjett'] *-en* planchette (used with ouija board).
plansje/verk [plang'sje/] *-et, pl -/+-er* book containing plates.
pla'n/slipe *V -te/*-a* make plane (by grinding).
planta'sje *-n* 1 plantation. 2 newly planted forest; nursery.
+planta'sje/eier *-en, pl -e* (=*/**eigar**) planter; fruit grower.

plan'te[1] +-*a*/-*en* **1** plant; seedling. **2** *fam., derog.* character: **han er en fin p-** he's a nice specimen.

plan'te[2] *V -a*/+-*et* **1** plant: **p- inn** transplant (from woods to garden or house); **p- om (ut)** replant, transplant. **2** *fig.* plant (e.g. flag, fist, kiss); implant (e.g. desire, doubt, idea): **p- seg** seat oneself, *(pop.)* plunk oneself down.

plan'te/etende *A* - herbivorous.

plan'te/farge *-n* vegetable dye.

+**plan'te/fett** *-et* (=*/**feitt**) vegetable fat.

plan'te/papi·r *-et* porous paper used to press plants.

plan'te/rike *-t* vegetable kingdom.

plan'te/saft *-a* juice of plant, sap.

plan'te/skole *-n* nursery.

plan'te/vekst *-en* vegetation.

plan'te/vev *-et* plant tissue.

plan'tning *-en* **1** planting. **2** afforestation.

pla'n/økonomi· *-en* planned economy.

plap're *V -a*/+-*et* **1** chatter away, gab; rattle off (sth); patter (a foreign language). **2: p- ut med noe** blabber, blurt out sth, let the cat out of the bag.

***plap're/mynt** *A* - blabber-mouthed: **so er han rusen og p- bliven** then he became drunk and b- (Vesaas).

plase're *V -te* cf **plassere**

plas'k *-et* splash.

plas'ke *V -a*/+-*et* **1** splash; plop. **2** (of raindrops) patter.

plas'kende *Av*: **p- full** dead drunk; **p- våt** sopping wet.

plas'k/regn [+/rein] *-et* drenching rain, pelting rain; downpour, heavy shower.

plas'k/regne [+/reine] *V -a*/+-*et*/+-*te*/*-*de*: **det p-er** it's pouring, coming down in buckets.

plas'k/våt *A* drenched, soaked; dripping wet.

plas'ma *-et* plasma.

plass' *-en* **1** (geographical) place, spot; ship's position. **2** place, position, rank (in series); place (in race). **3** (proper) place: **på p-** in its place; (as *interj.*) take your places; **det er på sin p- å** it is appropriate, fitting to; **sette en på (sin) p-** put sby in his place; **sette noe på (sin) p-** put sth back in its place. **4** (assigned) seat (at table, in theater, etc.); berth: **bestille p-** make reservations; **en ledig p-** a vacant berth (seat); **en tom p- ved bordet** an empty seat at table; **ta p-** be seated; all aboard. **5** room, space; accommodations (**til** for): **få p- til** get room for; **gi p- for** give way to; **godt om p-** plenty of room; **gjøre p- for** make room, space for; **mangel på p-** lack of space. **6** (on RR or ship) class. **7** job, position (as employe): **få p-** get a post, situation. **8** (city) square; marketplace; circle: **Rådhus/p-en** City Hall Square. **9** (camp, play, etc.) ground(s). **10** (cotter's) farm: **en liten p- under hovedgården** a small holding under the main farm.

plass'/angst *-en* (=*/**angest**) *psych.* agoraphobia.

+**plass'/anviser** *-en, pl -e* usher.

+**plass'/bespa·rende** *A* - space-saving.

plass'/billett· *-en* reserved seat ticket.

plas'se- *Pf* cf **plass-**

plasse're *V -te* **1** place (e.g. object in a particular spot, players in a game, winners in contest): **p- seg** take up a position; place (in a contest); **p- seg midt i sofaen** place (seat) oneself in the middle of the sofa. **2** *merc.*: **p- penger** invest, place money; **p- en kontrakt** place a contract. **3** *mus.* place (the voice).

plass'/folk *-et* cotters, sharecroppers.

+**plass'/gutt** *-en* cotter's boy, son of sharecropper.

+**plass'/hensyn** *-et* considerations of space.

plass'/mangel *-en* lack (shortage) of space.

+**plass'/oppsi·gelse** *-n* **1** discharge. **2** walkout.

plas't *-en* plastic(s).

plas'ter *-eret*/*-ret, pl -er*/+-*re* **1** adhesive bandage (tape). **2** plaster, salve: **som p- på såret** *fig.* as a sop to one's pride; by way of consolation.

plastic [plas'tikk] *-en* cf **plast**

plastikk' *-en* **1** plastic art. **2** plastic gymnastics or dancing.

plastili'n *-et* Plasticine.

plas'tisk *A* - plastic (arts, clay, features, personality, proportions, sculpture, species, style, surgery, etc.).

plas'tre *V -a*/+-*et* plaster (a wound).

plata'n *-en bot.* plane tree, sycamore (Platanus).

pla'te *-a*/+-*en* **1** plate, sheet, slab (of glass, metal, wood, etc.); (chocolate) bar; (table) top; (table) leaf; (on armor) breastplate; *naut.* shell plating, esp. *biol.* lamina; (phonograph) record. **2: slå en p-** *fam.* lie, tell a fib.

+**pla'te/arbeider** *-en, pl -e* (=*-**ar**) sheet metal worker.

pla'te/saks *-a* sheet metal shears.

+**pla'te/skifter** *-en, pl -e* (=*-**ar**) automatic record changer.

pla'tina *-et* platinum.

pla'tina/blond *A* platinum blond.

pla'tina/rev *-en zool.* platinum fox (Vulpes argentata).

plato'nisk *A* - Platonic (e.g. ideas, love).

platt' *A* - **1** coarse, vulgar; dull, flat. **2** *(adv.)*: **falle, kaste, legge seg p-** fall, throw oneself, lie prone, flat (on one's face); **sette seg p- ned** sit right down. **3** *(adv.)*: **seile p-** *naut.* run dead before the wind. **4** *(adv.)* absolutely, quite: **p- umulig** a- impossible.

plat'te *V -a*/+-*et* flatten, roll (metal).

+**plat'ten/slager** *-en, pl -e* (=*-**ar**) swindler; *(pop.)* con man.

plat'terdings *Av hum.* completely, quite.

platt'/form *-a*/+-*en* platform (e.g. on streetcar, in RR station; also *fig.*).

platt'form/billett· *-en* platform ticket.

platt'/fot *-en, pl* +-*føtter*/*-*føter med.* flatfoot.

+**platt'/het** *-en* coarseness, vulgarity; coarse, vulgar expression.

plat'ting *-en* **1** *naut.* sennit (=braided cord). **2** flagstones; flagstone paving.

+**platt'/søm·** *-men* **1** satin stitch. **2** clout nail.

platt'/tysk *A* - Low German.

platå' *-et, pl* +-*er*/*- plateau, tableland.

plausi'bel *A -elt, pl -le* plausible.

+**plebei'er** *-en, pl -e* (=***plebei**) plebeian; uncultivated person.

plebei'isk *A* - plebeian; common, vulgar.

plebisitt' *-en*/*-et* plebiscite.

pleb's *-en* **1** *hist.* plebs. **2** (the) common people; *derog.* vulgar, uncultivated person(s).

pledd' *-et* **1** lap robe, lap rug. **2** (Scotch) plaid.

pledd'/reim *-a* carrying strap with handle (esp. for lap robe).

plede're *V -te jur.* plead (a case; *fig.* a cause).

plei'e[1] *-a*/+-*en* **1** care, nursing (of people, animals). **2** care (of hair, skin); care, tending (of people, animals, plants): **sette en i p-** place sby in a nursing or foster home. **3** cultivation (of higher interests).

+**plei'e**[2] *V -de* **1** care for, nurse, tend (one's nails, a person, plant, etc.); cultivate (friendship, interests, talents, etc.). **2** be in the habit of, be used (**å** to), usually (do): **han p-de å komme hver dag** he used to come every day; **jeg p-er ikke å gjøre det** I don't usually do it (that).

plei'e/ba·rn *-et* foster child; *admin.* child under 14 years old placed in foster home.

plei'e/forel·dre *pl* foster parents.

plei'e/heim *-en* (=+/**hjem**) nursing home, rest home; orphanage; foster home.

plei'e/mor *-a*/+-*en, pl -mødrer*/+-*mødre* foster mother.

+**plei'er** *-en, pl -e* (=*-**ar**) male nurse.

plei'erske *-a*/+-*en* (female) nurse.

plek'si/glas *-et* (=+/**glass**) *tech.* plexiglass (trademark).

plek'ter *-eret*/*-ret, pl -er*/+-*re mus.* plectrum.

ple'n *-en* lawn.

plena'r- *Pf* cf **plenums-**

ple'n/frø *-et* grass seed (suitable for lawn).

+**ple'n/klipper** *-en, pl -e* (=*-**ar**) lawn mower.

plen't *Av* **1** *fam.* quite, right, surely: **sette seg p- ned** sit right down; **du slår deg p- i hjel** you'll surely kill yourself. **2** absolutely, finally: **hun skal p- snakke om alt** she just has to talk about everything; **svare p- nei** give a flat refusal.

***plen'te** *V -a*: **p- seg** be reticent, shy.

plenty [plen'ti] *Av* plenty: (as noun) **p- med penger** p- of money.

ple'num *-et admin.* plenary: **møte i p-** hold a plenary session (in Norway esp. of Storting and Supreme Court).

+**ple'nums/behan·dle** *V -a*/*-et admin.* discuss in plenary session.

+**ple'nums/beslut·ning** *-en admin.* plenary decision.

ple'nums/møte *-t, pl* +-*r*/*- plenary session.

pleonas'me *-n* pleonasm.

pleonas'tisk *A* - pleonastic.

ples'ken *-en* (small, thin) cooky (containing no fat).

ple'ti *N*: **kreti og p-** Tom, Dick and Harry; anybody.

+**plett'**[1] *-en* mark, spot; speck; blot, blotch, stain (also *fig.*): **først på p-en** first (one) on the spot; **vite på en p-** know to a hair, to the letter; **sette p- på sitt rykte** stain, sully one's reputation.

plett'[2] *-en* **1** plate (esp. silver plate): **ekte p-** Sheffield plate. **2** plated (metallic) ware. **3** *naut.* soup plate.

+**plet'te** *V -et* defile, stain, sully.

plette're *V -te* **1** plate (e.g. metal, esp. with silver). **2** electroplate, galvanize. **3** plate (textiles, thread).

+**plet'tet(e)** *A* - **1** dirty, stained; *fig.*: **p- fortid** doubtful past; **p- rykte** tarnished reputation; **et liv p- av laster** a life sullied by vice. **2** spotted (e.g. animal, insect); mottled, spotted (e.g. bird, plant); speckled (e.g. fish).

+**plett'/fri** *A -tt* **1** immaculate, spotless (esp. clothing). **2** blameless, spotless (e.g. reputation).

pleuritt' *-en* (=**plevritt**) *med.* pleurisy.

pli' *-en* poise, polish.

plik't *-a*/+-*en* duty, obligation (**mot, overfor** to, towards): **en kjær p-** a pleasant duty; **p- til å betale** o- to pay.

plik't/arbeid *-et* duty, work required (of owner or occupant of land by state or community); *hist.* work required of a cotter; drudgery (work done from sense of duty only).

plik't/dans *-en* obligatory dance.

plik'te *V -a*/+-*et* be obligated (**å** to).

+**plik't/forsøm·melse** *-n* neglect of duty.

+**plik't/følelse** *-n* cf /**kjensle**

+**plik't/hensyn** *-et* obligation: **av p-** from a sense of duty.

plik'tig *A* - (duty) bound, obliged (**til å** to): **kjennes p- til å betale** be held liable to pay; **p- til å avlegge regnskap for** accountable for.

+ Bokmål; * Nynorsk; ° Dialect.
After letter: ' stress (Acc. 1); ` tone, stress (Acc. 2); · length.
Below letter: . not pronounced.

plik't/kjensle *-a* sense of duty, obligation.

plik't/menneske *-t, pl* +*-r*/**-* person with a strong sense of duty.

+**plik't/messig** *A* - dutiful, obligatory; *(adv.)* from a sense of duty.

+**plik't/oppfyl·lende** *A* - conscientious, dutiful.

+**plik't/oppfyl·lenhet** *-en* conscientiousness, devotion to duty.

+**plik't/skyldig** [also -sjyl'-] *A* -: **p-st** *(adv.)* as in duty bound, dutifully.

plik't/tru *A -tt* (=+**/tro**) conscientious, faithful.

plik't/truskap *-en* (=+**/troskap**) conscientiousness, faithfulness.

plik't/visitt· *-en* duty call, visit.

+**plik't/øvelse** *-n* (in sports) prescribed figure or exercise required of all contestants (esp. in figure skating).

plim'/soller *-en, pl* +*-e naut.* old, unseaworthy ship, often heavily insured; coffin ship.

pli'r *-et* narrowed eyes, squint; blink, twinkle.

pli're *V -te* look with narrowed eyes, squint (**mot** at); blink; twinkle, wink.

+**pli'r/øyd** *A* - having blinking, narrowed eyes; having twinkling (or winking) eyes.

plissé *-en* pleating.

plisse're *V -te* pleat.

plissé/skjørt *-et* pleated skirt.

+**plis'tre** *V -et* cf **plystre**

plitt' *-en naut.* 1 enclosed space aft or forward in a boat. 2 footboard aft or forward.

plo'g *-en* plow; plow, wedge (flight formation of some migratory birds): **sette p-** make a snowplow (position of skis in breaking speed).

+**plo'g/får** *-a* (=***/for**, +**/fure**) (plow) furrow.

plo'g/hest *-en* plow horse.

plo'g/jern [/jæ·rn] *-et* (=***/jarn**) plowshare.

plo'g/land *-et* arable land; land being plowed; land already under cultivation.

***plo'gnad** *-en* plowing; plowed land.

+**plo'g/skjær** *-et* (=***/skjer**) plowshare.

plo'g/velte *-a* sod turned up by plow; furrow.

plom'be *-n* 1 seal (of lead, esp. on baggage, electric meters). 2 *odont.* filling; *hort.* filling (in tree).

plombe're *V -te* 1 seal (by affixing lead seal). 2 fill (tooth; cavity in tree).

plom'me[1] *-a bot.* plum (Prunus).

plomme[2] [plom'me] *-a*/+*-en* yolk: **ha det som p-n i egget** live the life of Riley.

plot'te *V -a*/+*-et* plot (on chart).

plot'te/bo'rd *-et* plotting board.

+**plud'der** *-eret*/*-ret* gabble, jabbering; cozy chat, small talk; prattle (of baby).

+**plud'der/hose** *-n hist.* trunk hose.

+**plud're** *V -a*/*-et* chat, jabber; prattle.

plugg' *-en* 1 nail, peg, plug; (metal, wood) tack. 2 stocky, sturdy boy or fellow.

plug'ge *V -a*/+*-et* 1 fasten (sth) with peg (e.g. sole to shoe), drive peg (into sth). 2 plug, stop up: **p- mat i en** *fam.* get some food into sby. 3 *fig.* hammer (e.g. lessons into sby's head).

plukk[1] [plokk'] *-en* 1 a card game. 2: **hver p- og pille** every smitch and smidgen.

plukk[2] [plokk'] *-et* 1 picking (**av** of). 2 bit, piece, scrap. 3: **ikke det p-** not the least bit.

plukke [plok'ke] *V -a*/+*-et* 1 gather, pick (e.g. berries, flowers): **p- i stykker** pick, tear to pieces; *fig.* criticize, tear apart (e.g. an article); **p- sammen** collect (e.g. clothing, tools); **p- jordbær under snøen** game of forfeits (kiss under cover of a sheet). 2 clean, pluck (e.g. feathers); fleece: **ha en høne å p- med noen** have a bone to pick with sby; **p- en for penger** clean sby out of his money; **p- en i spill** win over sby in a game; **p- ut** choose, pick out; **p- noe ut av en** extort (e.g. information, confession) from sby; cure, rid sby of sth (e.g. bad manners). 3 finger, pick, touch: **p- på et sår** pick at a scab; **p- seg i nesen** pick one's nose. 4 *geol.* remove the finer metals from ore.

+**plukker** [plok'ker] *-en, pl -e* (=***-ar**) picker (person; device for picking berries, fruit, etc.).

plukk/fisk [plokk'/] *-en* 1 dried fish (usu. cod, haddock) prepared in white sauce. 2 *fig.* hash: **bli til p-** fall apart; **gjøre p- av** beat to a pulp; make hash, mincemeat of; **boka er bare p-** the book is mere hackwork.

+**plukk/råtten** [plokk'/] *A -ent, pl -råtne* rotten to the core.

+**plump**[1] [plom'p] *-et* flop, plop, splash (also *interj.*).

+**plum'p**[2] [also: plom'p] *A* 1 large and awkward (e.g. animal); rough (hand); clumsy, crude (piece of work). 2 coarse, crude, tasteless (manner, person, remark); boorish, rude.

+**plumpe** [plom'pe] *V -a*/*-et* flop, plop, plump (**i** in, into): **p- opp i** accidentally find oneself in (e.g. a particular situation); **p- til å si, gjøre noe** accidentally say, do sth; **p- ut med** blurt out with.

plum/pudding [plom'/] *-en* plum pudding.

+**plum're** [also: plom're] *V -a*/*-et archaic* confuse, muddle, muddy.

plun'der *-eret*/*-ret fam.* bother, tiresome work, trouble: **det er sånt p- med fletter** braids are such a bother (Bang-Hansen).

***plun'der/sam** *A* troublesome.

plun'dre *V -a*/+*-et* have no end of trouble, struggle, toil (**med** with).

plun'dret(e) *A* - complicated, inconvenient, troublesome.

plura'lis *-en gram.* plural.

pluralite't *-en* majority, plurality.

plus'/kvamperfek·tum *-et gram.* pluperfect.

pluss'[1] *-et, pl -*/+*-er* 1 *math., phys.* plus; positive (e.g. terminal), plus quantity. 2: **t**+ *educ.* B plus. 3 advantage, asset.

pluss'[2] *P* plus.

plus'se *V -a*/+*-et*: **p- på** add (to); **jeg skulle ha bare fem kroner, men han p-et på én til** I was supposed to get only five *kroner*, but he added one more.

°**plus'sen** *A -ent, pl plusne* cf **pløsen**

plutokra't *-en* plutocrat.

plutokrati' *-et* plutocracy.

+**plut'selig** *A* - sudden; *(adv.)* suddenly.

plyn'dre *V -a*/+*-et* loot, plunder, rob: **p- byen** sack the town.

plyn'drings/tog [/tåg] *-et* raid (by robbers, or by soldiers in enemy territory).

plysj' *-en* plush.

plysj'/møblement [/-mang·] *-et* furniture upholstered with plush.

plys'tre *V -a*/+*-et* (=**plistre**) 1 whistle; (e.g. of wind) whine, whistle; (e.g. of bird) sing: **p- middag** skip dinner.

pløg'de *pt of* **pløye**

pløg'sel *-la* (=**pløgsle**) 1 plowing. 2 arable land, plowed field.

plø'se[1] *-a* 1 tongue (in shoe). 2 loose fold (of skin).

plø'se[2] *V -te*: **p- seg** (e.g. of dough) rise; (of skin) form loose folds.

plø'sen *A* +*-ent, pl -ne* 1 bloated, swollen. *2 porous.

plø'set(e) *A* - bloated, swollen; (of skin) baggy: **p- under øynene** having bags under one's eyes.

pløy'/bo'rd *-et* matchboard (board with tongue and groove).

pløy'e *V pløgde*/+*pløyde* 1 plow: **p- hav, sjø** sail the seas; **p- ned** p- under; **p- opp** turn up; **p- opp veiene** p- the roads (to remove snow); **p- seg igjennom** cut through (e.g. barricade, mountain); make one's way through (e.g. crowds); plow, wade through (reading matter). 2 *carp.* tongue and groove, match.

pløy'er *-en, pl -e* (=***-ar**) plowman.

***plå'ge**[1] *-a* cf **plage**[1]

***plå'ge**[2] *V -a* cf **plage**[2]

PM=**promemoria**

pneuma'tisk *A* - (=**pnevmatisk**) pneumatic.

***p. o.**=**postopneri**

pocket/bok [påk'kit/] *-a, pl -bøker* paperback (book).

po'dagra *-en med.* gout.

po'de[1] *-n hum.* hopeful, offspring, scion: **håpefull p-** (*ironic*, of young man) young hopeful.

po'de[2] *V -a*/+*-et* (=**pote**[2]) 1 *agr.* graft. 2 *med.* inoculate. 3: **p- inn** *fig.* imprint, teach.

po'de/kniv *-en* grafting knife.

po'deks *-en fam.* rear, seat (of body).

po'de/kvist *-en agr.* graft, scion.

po'de/voks *-et agr.* grafting wax.

po'dium *-iet, pl* +*-ier*/**-ium* platform, podium, stage.

poe'm *-et, pl -*/+*-er* usu. *hum.* epic or long lyric poem.

poeng' *-et, pl -*/+*-er* 1 point (in games, sports): **få, gjøre p-** score a point; **vinne på p-** (esp. in boxing) win on points. 2 *educ.* mark, grade point. 3 *fig.* point: **gode p-er** good p-s (e.g. in article); **p-et i** the p- of (e.g. a story, speech); **hva er p-et med dette?** what is the p- of this?

+**poeng'/beregning** [/berei·ning] *-en* computing of score (or grades).

+**poeng'/stilling** *-a*/*-en* placing.

poengte're *V -te* 1 emphasize, underscore; point up. 2 *agr.* give points to animals on exhibit, place.

poesi' *-en* poetry.

poesi'/album *-et, pl -*/+*-er* (handwritten) poetry album.

poesi'/fattig *A* - dry, unpoetic.

poesi'/fylt *A* - poetic, romantic.

poesi'/laus *A* (=+**/løs**) prosaic.

poe't *-en* usu. *ironic* poet.

poet.=**poetisk**

poe'tisk *A* - poetic.

pogro'm *-en* pogrom.

+**point** [poeng'] *-et* cf **poeng**

pointer [påi'nter] *-en, pl* +*-e* pointer (dog).

+**pointere** [poengte're] *V -te* cf **poengtere**

poka'l *-en* 1 cup (i.e. prize). 2: **tømme en p- for** *lit.* drink a toast to. 3 decorative goblet.

poka'l/renn *-et* cup race.

***po'ke** *-a* smallpox.

po'ker *-en* 1 poker (cards). 2 *naut.* poker (iron).

po'ker/ansikt *-et, pl -*/+*-er* poker face.

po'ker/fjes *-et* poker face, *(pop.)* poker puss.

+**po'ker/spill** *-et* (=***/spel**) game of poker.

+**pokka** [pok'ka] *Av* cf **pukka**

pok'ker *I* the deuce, devil (used in variety of oaths; milder, more humorous than *fanden*): **det var som p-** well, I'll be damned; **for p-** confound it, damn it, hang it; **gi p-en i noe** not give a damn, a hoot about sth; **hva p-** what in the devil, hell, thunder; **jeg bryr meg p- om det** I don't give a damn, hoot about it; **p- ta ham** blast, curse him, devil take him; **p- til kar** heck, hell of a fellow; **som bare p-en** like the devil (himself).

pok'kers *A* - confounded, damned, infernal: **et p- arbeide** a devil of a job.

pok'kers/dom· *-men*/**-en* deviltry.

pokule're *V -te* carouse.

po'l[1] *-en* 1 pole (north, south; magnetic, etc.); *elec.* terminal (positive, negative). 2 *fig.* pole (either as a fixed point or as one of two ex-

tremities): **den faste p- i hans arbeid** the central core of his work.
po'l[2] *-en* cf **pole**
po'l[3] *-et fam.* (state-owned) liquor store (short for **Vinmonopolet**).
pol.=**politisk**
polakk' *-en* Pole.
pola'r *A* polar: **p-e motsetninger** p-opposites.
pola'r/ekspedisjo·n *-en* polar expedition.
pola'r/ferd [*/fær] *-a/*+*-en* cf **pol/**
*****pola'r/forsker** *-en, pl -e* (=***-ar**) polar explorer.
polarise're *V -te* **1** polarize. **2** *fig.* concentrate, fix.
polarite't *-en* polarity.
pola'r/luft *-a* polar air.
pola'r/natt *-a/*+*-en* polar night.
pola'r/sirkel *-elen, pl -ler* polar circle.
pola'r/stjerne *-a/*+*-en* Stella Polaris, North Star.
pola'r/strøk *-et* polar area.
po'le *-n* (=**pol**[2]) (in ball playing) fly (=high ball): **slå en p-** hit a f-.
+**pole'miker** *-en, pl -e* (=***-ar**) controversialist, disputant, polemist.
polemikk' *-en* controversy, dispute, polemics (usu. in the press).
polemise're *V -te* carry on a controversy (**mot** against), polemize.
pole'misk *A* - controversial, polemic.
Po'len *Pln* Poland.
polen'ta *-en* polenta (Italian dish of cornmeal mush).
polen'ta/graut *-en* (=+**/grøt**) polenta pudding (Norwegian dish served with red fruit sauce).
polen'ta/gryn *-et* fine cornmeal (for porridge or pudding).
pole're *V -te* **1** buff, polish. **2**: **føre et p-t språk** *fig.* use cultivated (polished) language.
+**po'l/farer** *-en, pl -e* (=***-ar**) polar explorer.
po'l/ferd [*/fær] *-a/*+*-en* polar expedition.
+**po'l/flukt** *-a/-en* polar flight.
po'li/klinikk· *-en* policlinic.
po'lio *-en med.* polio.
po'lio/epidemi· *-en med.* polio epidemic.
poliomyelitt' *-en med.* poliomyelitis.
poli's *-en fam.* cop, policeman.
poll'se *-n* (insurance) policy.
polis'k *A* - arch, roguish, sly.
politi' *-et* **1** police: **p-et** the Police. **2** *pop.* (**p-en**) policeman.
politi'/attes·t *-en* police certificate; (after 1945) paper certifying patriotic behavior during Nazi occupation; written permission from police (for special privileges).
politi'/betjen·t *-en* (police) officer, policeman.
politi'/bil *-en* patrol car, police car.
politi'/forhør *-et* (=***/forhøyr**) police interrogation.
politi'/fullmek·tig *-en* assistant chief of police, desk sergeant.
politi'/hund *-en* police dog.
politi'/kammer *-et* **1** police station. **2** police authorities.
+**poli'tiker** *-en, pl -e* (=***-ar**) politician (also *derog.*).
politikk' *-en* **1** politics (also *derog.*): **det gikk p- i saken** it became a matter of p-, politics got mixed up into it. **2** policy (of party, government, person): **det er dårlig p- å spare på skillingen og la daleren gå** it's a poor p- to be penny wise and pound foolish.
politi'/konsta·bel *-elen, pl -ler* policeman.
polit'ikus *-en hum., derog.* politician.
politi'/mann *-en, pl -menn/*-menner* police officer, member of the police force.
+**politi'/mester** *-eren, pl -ere/-rer* (=***/meister**) chief of police.
politise're *V -te derog.* talk politics; scheme, speculate.
polit'isk *A* - political.
politi'/stasjo·n *-en* police station.
politu'r *-en* **1** polish. **2** *fig.* breeding, polish.
pol'ka *-en* polka (dance).
po'l/kalott· *-en* polar ice cap.
poll' *-en* **1** round fjord with narrow inlet. **2** *dial.* small lake. **3** *dial.* round valley bottom.
pol'len *-et bot.* pollen.
+**pol'len/undersøkelse** *-n* (=***-ing**) pollen analysis.
pollusjo'n *-en med.* pollution.
Polmak [pol'makk] *Pln* twp, Finnmark.
po'lo *-en* polo.
polone'se *-n* polonaise (dance): **gå p-** dance the p-.
po'lsk *A* - Polish: **p- riksdag** pandemonium, uproar.
polsk/dans [på'ls/] *-en* couple dance in 3/4 time.
pol'stre *V -a/*+*-et* pad, stuff, upholster: **p-et celle** padded cell.
polyfo'n *A* polyphone, polyphonic.
polyga'm *A* polygamous.
polygami' *-et* polygamy.
polygo'n *-en/-et math.* polygon.
polyhis'tor *-en hist.* person with encyclopedic knowledge.
polykro'm *A* polychrome.
+**polyne'sier** *-en, pl -e* (=***-ar**) Polynesian.
polyne'sisk *A* - Polynesian.
polyno'm *-et, pl -/*+*-er math.* polynomial.
polypp' *-en* **1** *zool.* polyp. **2** *med.* (*pl*) adenoids.
polyteisme [-te-is'me] *-n* polytheism.
polyteist [-te-is't] *-en* polytheist.
polytek'nisk *A* - technological.
poma'de *-n* pomade (hair oil).
pomadise're *V -te* pomade.
pomeran's *-en bot.* bitter orange (Citrus aurantium).
pomolog [-lå'g] *-en* pomologist.
pomologi' *-en* pomology (=fruit science).
pomo'r/handel *-en hist.* Pomor trade (White Sea Russian trading with Norway; ended in 1914).
pomp[1] [pom'p] *-en* pomp: **p- og prakt** p- and circumstance.
+**pomp**[2] [pom'p] *-en* **1** behind, seat (child's language). ***2** small, fat person (male). ***3** *fam.* dull, slow person.
pompadu'r *-en* lady's (small) bag; sewing or work bag.
pompeia'nsk *A* - Pompeian.
+**pompet(e)** [pom'pet(e)] *A* - **1** *dial.* chunky. **2** *fam.* dull, slow.
pompong' *-en* pompon.
pompø's *A* dignified, stately; pompous.
pon'dus *-en* authority, gravity, weight: **prestelig p-** clerical gravity.
pongtong' *-en* **1** pontoon. **2** *arch.* (weighted iron box used as) bridge pier.
pongtong'/bru *-a* pontoon bridge.
pon'ni *-en* pony.
°**pons** [pon's] *-en* cf **punsj**
+**pontifika'lier** *pl* (=***-ar**) **1** canonicals. **2** *hum.* official costume; elegant robes.
pool [pu'l] *-en merc.* pool.
pop.=**populær**
pop'lin *-et* poplin (textile).
pop'pel *-elen, pl popler bot.* poplar (Populus).
popularise're *V -te* popularize.
popularite't *-en* popularity.
popularite'ts/jakt *-a/*+*-en* popularity seeking.
popula's *-en* mass, populace.
populæ'r *A* popular.
populæ'r/konser·t *-en* pop concert.
+**populæ'r/vitenskapelig** *A* -: **p- tidsskrift** popular science magazine.
po're[1] *-a/*+*-en* (skin) pore; minute opening (e.g. in earth).
***pore**[2] [på're] *V -a* poke, prick.
porfy'r *-en* porphyry.
pornografi' *-en* pornography
pornogra'fisk *A* - pornographic.
por's *-en bot.* (sweet) gale (Myrica gale).
Porsang'er/fjo·rd *Pln* fjord in Finnmark.
porsele'n *-et* china, porcelain.
porsele'ns/dokke *-a* china doll; child's doll with only head and hands of china; *fig.* pretty but empty-headed young woman.
porsele'ns/fat *-et* porcelain dish.
Por's/grunn *Pln* city, Telemark.
porsjo'n *-en* **1** lot, measure, quantity: **en p- juling** a good beating; **i små p-er** in small doses. **2** helping, portion, serving (of food); ration: **en p- graut** a helping of porridge.
porsjone're *V -te* parcel, portion (**ut** out).
port [por't] *-en* **1** gate, gateway; doorway; entrance: **få (hive, jage, kaste, sette) en på p-en** fire sby, send sby packing; **bolig i p-en** apartment next to entrance (and with direct access to it). **2** (sports) gate (in slalom skiing). **3** *naut.* port(hole): **åpne p-ene** open the p-s. **4** gate (in canal or dock). **5** *anat.* pylorus. **6** gateway, pass (in mountain border).
portal [porta'l] *-en arch.* gateway, portal.
portechaise [pårt(e)sje's] *-n* sedan chair.
porteføl'je *-n* **1** briefcase, portfolio. **2** *merc.* portfolio (of securities). **3** portfolio (=office of cabinet minister): **minister uten p-** minister without p-.
portefø'l'je/vare *-a/*+*-en merc.* leather goods (esp. briefcases, etc.).
portemoné *-en* billfold, purse: **åpne for p-en** be generous.
+**port/forbud** [por't/] *-et* (=***/forbod**) *mil.* confinement to barracks; *fig.* limited access.
+**port/handler** *-en, pl -e* (=***-ar**) person selling from (usu.) a booth in a gateway.
port/hus *-et archaic* brothel.
portier [portie'] *-en* doorman (in hotel), hall porter.
portiere [portiæ're] *-n* drape, portiere (in door opening).
+**portner** [por'tner] *-en, pl -e* (=***-ar**) **1** doorman (in office building, apartment house). **2** *med.* pylorus.
+**portnerske** [por'tnerske] *-n* woman doorkeeper (usu. in apartment house).
port/nøkkel [por't/] *-elen, pl -nøkler* key to main entrance door.
porto [por'to] *-en* postage.
porto/fri *A -tt* **1** postpaid. **2** exempt from payment of postage (e.g. official mail, by franking privilege).
porto/takst *-en* postal rates.
porto/tillegg *-et* (postal) surcharge.
portrett' *-et, pl -/*+*-er* **1** picture, portrait (**av** of). **2** (literary) portrayal.
portrett'/byste *-a/-en* portrait bust.
portrette're *V -te* **1**: **la seg p-** *lit.* have one's portrait painted. **2** *hum.* photograph. **3** *lit.* portray.
portrett'/galleri· *-et, pl* +*-er/*- portrait gallery.
+**portrett'/likhet** *-en* likeness (of a picture).
portrettø'r *-en* portrait painter.
port/rom [por't/romm] *-met* **1** gateway; entranceway (to courtyard). **2** room (usu. for gatekeeper) next to driveway, entrance.
port/stolpe *-n* gatepost.
Portugal [por'tugal] *Pln* Portugal.
+**portugiser** [portugi'ser] *-en, pl -e* (=***-ar, *portugis**) **1** Portuguese. **2** *naut.* Portuguese ship.
portugisisk [portugi'sisk] *A* - Portuguese.
portulakk' *-en bot.* **1** (edible) purslane (Portulaca oleracea). **2** (deco-

+ Bokmål; * Nynorsk; ° Dialect.
After letter: ' stress (Acc. 1); ˋ tone, stress (Acc. 2); · length.
Below letter: . not pronounced.

rative) purslane (Portulaca grandiflora).

port/vakt [por't/] *-a/+-en* 1 gatekeeper. 2 *mil.* guard.

port/vin [por't/] *-en* port wine.

portø'r *-en* 1 orderly (in a hospital); stretcher-bearer; *archaic* chairman (of sedan chair). 2 redcap, skycap.

porø's *A* porous.

po'se[1] [*på'se] *-n* bag, pouch, sack: **en p- konfekt** a bag of candy; **få både i p- og sekk** have one's cake and eat it too; **ha p-r i benklærne** have bags in one's (trouser) knees; **p-r under øynene** bags under one's eyes; **ha rent mel i p-n** have a good conscience, be completely honest; **tale rent ut av p-n** speak frankly.

po'se[2] [*på'se] *V -a/+-et/+-te* 1: **p- seg (ut)** (e.g. of clothing) bag; (e.g. of skin) bag, swell; (e.g. of sails) balloon, swell out. 2: **p- ut** (e.g. of a skirt) balloon; stuff (e.g. animal skin in drying).

po'se/not *-a, pl -nøter* purse net (for fishing).

pose're *V -te* pose (**som** as); put on airs, strike poses.

po'set(e) [*på'set(e)] *A* - baggy; puffy, swollen.

po'se/tur *-en* hike, ski trip with sleeping bag.

posisjo'n *-en* 1 position, *fig.* standing, status: **han har litt av en p- her** he has something of a reputation here. 2 *naut.*: **bestemme sin p-** take one's bearings; **gi sin p-** give one's position. 3 *mil.* disposition, position. 4 position, posture (e.g. in fencing). 5 *mus.* position (e.g. on violin).

+posisjo'ns/angivelse *-n* giving of position (e.g. in air, at sea).

po'sitiv[1] *-en gram.* positive (degree).

po'sitiv[2] *-en/-et photog.* positive.

positi'v[3] *-et* barrel organ, grind organ.

po'sitiv[4] *A* 1 positive (advantage, answer, electricity, film, numbers, etc.). 2 affirmative, favorable: **p-handelsbalanse** favorable balance of trade; **p- kritikk** constructive criticism; **et p-t livssyn** an optimistic philosophy; **p-t innstillet** favorably inclined, sympathetic; **reagere p-t** react favorably. 3 empirical, real: **de p-e vitenskaper** the empirical sciences; **et p-t bidrag** a real contribution.

positivis'me *-n* positivism.

positivis't *-en* positivist.

positro'n *-en/-et* phys. positron.

positu'r *-en* affected attitude, pose: **stille seg i p-** pose (for effect), posture.

possemen't *-et, pl -/+-er* passementerie, (fancy, lace) trimmings.

pos'sessiv *A gram.* possessive.

pos't[1] *-en* 1 (window) post; stud (in building); ledge, windowsill. 2 pump.

pos't[2] *-en* 1 *mil.* post; checkpoint, position, station: **fremskutt p-** picket, outpost; **stå på p-** stand guard; **ta p-** take up a vantage point; **være på p-** *fig.* be on (one's) guard. 2 job: **få p-** get a j-, a position; **ha p-** have a j- (e.g. as maid, office worker).

pos't[3] *-en* 1 item (in a series). 2 *merc.* entry (in bookkeeping); block, holding (e.g. of securities); lot.

pos't[4] *-en* 1 mail (**til** for): **sende i p-en** mail; **med p-en** by mail. 2 (rarely) post office; postman.

pos't/adres'se *-a/+-en* mailing address.

posta'l *A* postal.

postamen't *-et, pl +-er/*-* pedestal.

+pos't/anvi'sning *-en* money order: **p-til utlandet** foreign m-.

pos't/boks *-en* post-office box.

+pos't/bud *-et* mailman, postman.

pos't/båt *-en* mail boat, packet boat.

pos't/date're *V -te* postdate.

pos'te *V -a/+-et* mail, post.

postei' *-en* 1 pasty; patty (creamed food in a patty shell); (meat) pie; tart. 2 (liver) paste, spread.

pos't/ekspedisjo'n *-en* 1 branch post office, postal station. 2 handling of mail.

pos't/ekspeditø'r *-en* mail clerk.

poste're[1] *V -te* post, station (men).

poste're[2] *V -te* enter, post (e.g. item, sum, usu. in bookkeeping).

poste restante [pås't restang't] general delivery.

poste'ring *-a/+-en* 1 *mil.* posting (of men). 2 *merc.* entry, item (in bookkeeping).

poste'rings/feil *-en* mistake in entry (bookkeeping).

pos't/flagg *-et* 1 mail, postal flag (in Norway swallow-tailed flag with emblem, painted on mailboxes and carried by mail boats). 2 checkpoint marker (e.g. in a race).

+pos't/forbin'delse *-n* postal communication.

pos't/gang *-en* mail delivery.

pos't/giro [/sjiro] *-en merc.* postal bank account system by which money can be deposited and transferred.

pos'tgiro/blankett' [-sjiro/] *-en* postal giro blank (used somewhat like a check).

pos'tgiro/nummer [-sjiro/nommer] *-et* postal giro account number.

pos't/ho'rn *-et* postman's signal horn (used on stamps, postal flags and mailboxes).

posthu'm *A* posthumous.

pos't/hus *-et* post office.

pos't/hylle *-a* letter rack.

postill' *-en* book of sermons (arranged according to the church year).

pos't/kasse *-a/-en* mailbox.

pos't/konto'r *-et* post office.

+pos't/legge *V -la, -lagt* mail.

pos't/mann *-en, pl -menn/*-menner* post office employee, clerk; mailman.

+pos't/mester *-en, pl -e* (=*/**meister**) postmaster.

pos't/nett *-et* postal network.

+pos't/ombæ'ring *-en* mail delivery.

***pos't/opnar** *-en* cf **/åpner**

***pos't/opneri** *-et* cf **/åpneri**

pos't/oppkrav *-et* collect on delivery: **sende mot p-** send C.O.D.

pos'tordre/forret'ning *-en* mail-order house.

pos't/sekk *-en* mailbag.

pos't/sending *-a/+-en* postal shipment.

pos't/skip *-et* mail boat, packet boat.

postskrip'tum *-et, pl +-er/+-skripta/*-* postscript.

pos't/sparebank *-en* postal savings bank.

+pos't/sted *-et* postal station, post office.

pos't/stempel *+-(e)let/*-elen, pl -ler* postmark.

+pos't/søster *-en med.* head nurse (female).

***pos't/tilvising** *-a* cf **/anvisning**

postula't *-et, pl -/+-er* postulate.

postule're *V -te* postulate.

pos't/verk *-et* postal service.

pos't/veske *-a* mailbag.

pos't/vogn [/vångn] *-a* mail car (on train).

posty'r *-et archaic* fuss, noise, row.

+pos't/åpner *-en, pl -e* (=*/**opnar**) (rural) postmaster.

+pos't/åpneri' *-et* (rural) postal station.

posø'r *-en* poseur, show-off, stuffed shirt.

+po'te[1] *-n* paw (hum. for hand).

po'te[2] *V -a/+-et* cf **pode**[2]

po'te/kniv *-en* cf **pode/**

po'te/kvist *-en* cf **pode/**

poten's *-en* 1 potency, power (esp. sexual). 2 *math.* power: **i annen p-** to the second p-, squared; **i høyeste p-** *fig.* to the highest degree.

potense're *V -te* 1 intensify. 2 *math.* raise to a higher power.

potensia'l[1] *-et phys.* potential.

potensia'l[2] *A gram.* potential (mood).

potensiell' *A -elt* potential (energy, plant, etc.).

poten't *A - med.* (sexually) potent.

potenta't *-en* potentate.

pote't *-a/+-en* potato.

pote't/binge *-n* potato bin (in cellar).

+pote't/blomst *-en* (=*/**blome**) potato blossom.

pote't/brennevin *-et* distilled liquor produced from potatoes.

pote't/ferie *-n* potato vacation (given by schools for potato harvest).

pote't/gras *-et*: **p-et er frosset** the potato plants are frozen.

pote't/grev *-et* potato hoe.

pote't/kake *-a* 1 potato cake (layer cake using grated, raw potatoes in dough). 2 =**p-/lumpe.** 3 potato pudding (hot dish made something like macaroni with cheese, meat, or eggs).

+pote't/kjeller *-en, pl -e* (=*-**ar**) potato cellar.

pote't/kreft *-en* potato blight.

pote't/lumpe [/lompe] *-a* round, thick pancake of potatoes and flour.

pote't/mjøl *-et* potato starch.

pote't/onn *-a* potato planting, harvesting.

+pote't/oppta'ker *-en, pl -e* (=*-**ar**) potato digger.

pote't/prest *-en hist.* 18th-century minister who preached cultivation of the potato (at expense of spiritual values).

pote't/puré *-en* potato purée.

pote't/sala't *-en* potato salad.

+pote't/setting *-a/-en* potato planting.

pote't/skrell *-et* potato peel.

+pote't/skreller *-en, pl -e* (=*-**ar**) potato peeler.

pote't/sprit *-en* potato spirits.

pote't/stappe *-a* mashed potatoes.

pote't/åker *-eren, pl -rer* potato field.

po'te/voks *-et* cf **pode/**

potpurri' *-en/-et, pl -er/*- mus., fig.* potpourri (**av** of).

pott' *-en* 1 *hist.* measure equal to about one quart. 2: **være p- og panne** be the boss, the one who makes all the decisions.

+pott'/aske *-a* cf **/oske**

pot'te[1] *-a* 1 (small, round) kettle, pot: **tett som ei p-** absolutely watertight. 2 flowerpot. 3 chamber pot; pottie. 4 *tech.* melting pot. 5 (in cards) pot (of money).

pot'te[2] *V -a/+-et* pot, (re)plant (in pots).

+pot'te/blomst *-en* potted flower.

pot'te/blått *et* homemade blue color (from urine and vitriol).

pot'te/leire *-a* potter's clay.

+pot'te/maker *-en, pl -e* (=*-**ar**) potter.

+pot'temaker/arbeid *-et* (=*-**ar/**) earthenware, pottery.

+pot'temaker/hjul *-et* (=*-**ar/**) potter's wheel.

pot'te/plante *+-a/-en* potted plant.

+pot'te/skår *-et* potsherd.

pott'/oske *-a* (=+/**aske**) potash.

pott'/øl *-et archaic* small beer (sold by the **pott**).

p. r. =**poste restante**

pr.[1] =**per**

pr.[2] =**presis**

pragma'tisk *A* - pragmatic.

Pra'ha *Pln* Prague.

prai'e *V -a/+-et/+-de* 1 *naut.* call, hail: **p- et skip** ask a ship for identification; **utkikken p-er** the watch calls out. 2: **p- en bil** hail a taxi.

+prai'e/hold *-et* (=*/**hald**) hailing distance: **på p-** within h- d-.

prakk' *-et* 1 inconvenience, trouble. 2 troublesome detail work.

prak'ke *V -a/+-et* 1: **p- på** palm off on, saddle with, wish on. 2 putter: **p-es med** be bothered with (esp. dull, tiresome work). *3 scrape together, squeeze out. *4 annoy, bother.

+prak'ker *-en, pl -e* (=*-**ar**) sharper; miser.

prak'sis *-en* practice (as opp. to theory); practice (e.g. of a doctor); custom, practice: **i p-** in p-.

prak't *-a/+-en* magnificence, splendor;

pomp and circumstance: **i sin fulle p-** in all his (her, its) glory.

prak't/eksempla·r *-et, pl -/+-er* magnificent copy (e.g. of a book); beauty, jewel, treasure: **p- (av et dyr)** fine specimen (of an animal).

prak't/elskende *A* - fond of display.

prak't/full *A* elegant, gorgeous (e.g. costume, display), magnificent (e.g. building); marvellous (e.g. poem, view), splendid (e.g. performer).

prak't/glad *A* - showy.

praktikan't *-en* (=***praktikand**) 1 trainee. 2 *med.* intern.

+**praktikan't/tjeneste** *-n med.* internship.

+**prak'tiker** *-en, pl -e* (=***-ar**) practical man; practitioner.

prak'tikum *-et* 1 *educ.* university examination testing students' ability to apply theoretical knowledge: **gå opp til p-** take the *praktikum* examination. 2 *eccl.* studies of a practical nature for theologians (after other exams).

praktise're *V -te* 1 make use of, put into practice. 2 practice (e.g. as a doctor, lawyer). 3 *hum., archaic* maneuver (sby into a place or posture).

prak'tisk *A* - practical (person, tool, activity, etc.); handy, useful: **i det p-e liv** in practical life; **p- sans** practical turn of mind; **p- talt** practically, virtually.

prak't/kar *-en* 1 sturdy, powerfully built man. 2 brick, first-rate fellow.

prak't/lyst *-a/+-en* love of display.

prak't/stjerne *-a bot.* campion (Melandrium).

prak't/stykke *-t, pl +-r/*-* museum piece, showpiece.

+**prak't/utfoldelse** *-n* display; *derog.* ostentation.

prak't/verk *-et, pl -/+-er* elegant, deluxe edition (of book).

+**pra'l** *-et* boasting, bragging, swaggering.

+**pra'le** *V -te* boast, brag (**av** about): **p- med** flaunt, show off.

+**pra'l/hans** *-en* braggart.

pram' *-men* 1 (flat-bottomed) rowboat. 2 barge: **en født bærer, en p- gjennom skogene** a born carrier, a b- through the woods (Hamsun).

+**pram'/penger** *pl* (=***-ar**) barge fee, lighterage.

prang'e *V -a/+-et* 1 be resplendent. 2 be pretentious. 3: **p- (med) seil** *naut.* crowd, press sails. 4 *dial.* trade; bargain.

pra't *-en/-et* 1 chat, talk: **komme i p- med** get to chatting with. 2 *fam.* idle chatter, nonsense.

pra'te *V -a/+-et* 1 chat, converse, talk: **p- det bort** talk as if it (e.g. a problem) didn't exist; **p- over seg** not know what one is saying, be in delirium; **p- en rundt** talk sby into sth. 2 prate, prattle, talk nonsense: **å du p-er!** what nonsense!

+**pra't/maker** *-en, pl -e* (=***-ar**) loquacious person; windbag.

+**pra't/som·** *A -t, pl -me* (=***/sam**) talkative.

pre' *-et* 1 *educ., archaic* high honors, summa cum laude. 2 advantage.

preben'de *+-n/*-t eccl.* prebend; prebendary.

predestine're *V -te* predestine.

predikan't *-en eccl.* preacher.

predika't *-et, pl -/+-er* 1 *gram., philos.* predicate. 2 designation, name, title.

pre'dikativ *A gram.* predicative.

predika'ts/o'rd *-et gram.* predicate word.

+**predi'ke** *V -et* cf **preke**[2]

+**predi'ke/bro(de)r** *-en, pl -brødre eccl.* Dominican.

prefek't *-en* prefect.

preferanse [preferang'se] *-n* 1 *lit.* advantage; precedence. 2 (tariff) preference; *merc.* preference (as in stocks).

preferanse/aksje *-n* preferred stock.

prefere're *V -te* 1 *econ.* prefer, give priority to. 2: **p- (i) spar** make a preference bid of spades (bridge).

prefige're *V -te gram.* prefix.

prefik's *-et, pl -/+-er* prefix.

pre'g *-et* 1 character, feature, stamp: **bære p- av sannhet** give the impression of truth; **sette p- på** leave its mark on, stamp. 2 stamp (e.g. on coin, silverware); *typog.* relief.

pre'ge *V -a/+-et* 1 engrave, impress, stamp (usu. on metals; also *fig.*). 2 characterize, color, influence; mark. 3 *typog.* make (a cut); engrave, emboss (paper). 4 strike (medals). 5 coin (money).

pre'g/laus *A* (=+**/løs**) featureless, uninteresting.

pregnan's *-en* pithiness, pregnancy; significance (usu. in art).

pregnan't *A* - pithy, pregnant; significant, weighty.

***prei'k** *-et* cf **prek**

***prei'kar** *-en* preacher.

***prei'ke**[1] *-a* cf **preken**

***prei'ke**[2] *V -a* cf **preke**[2]

prejudika't *-et, pl -/+-er jur.* precedent.

prejudise're *V -te* prejudge, prejudicate, prejudice: **p-t veksel** *jur.* invalid note (because owner failed to follow laws).

+**pre'k** *-et* (=***preik**) 1 harangue, sermonizing. 2 nonsense, twaddle. 3 chat.

prekave're *V -te* 1: **p- seg** be on one's guard. 2 *dial.* take care of.

+**pre'ke**[1] *-a* cf **preken**

+**pre'ke**[2] *V -te* (=***preike**[2]) 1 *eccl.* deliver a sermon, preach (gospel). 2 lecture; agitate for (sth), preach: **p- en ørene fulle av noe** din, drum sth into sby's ears. 3 converse, talk; talk nonsense.

+**pre'ken** *-en* (=***preike**[1]) 1 sermon: **holde en p-** deliver a s- (**om** on). 2 lecture, preaching: **holde en p- for en** lecture sby, give sby a lecture.

+**pre'ken/samling** *-en* book (collection) of sermons.

+**pre'ke/stol** *-en* pulpit: **på p-en** in the p-.

+**pre'ke/søndag** *-en* Sunday for which sermon is scheduled.

+**pre'ke/tone** *-n* often *derog.* sermonizing, unctuous tone.

prekeve're *V -te* cf **prekavere**

pre'/klusiv *A jur.* preclusive: **p-t proklama** notice to creditors, barring claims not lodged before a certain date.

prek'tig *A* - beautiful, fine, gorgeous; excellent, noble; magnificent, splendid.

prekæ'r *A* precarious: **i en p- stilling** in an embarrassing position.

prela't *-en eccl.* prelate.

preliminæ'r *A* preliminary.

prel'le *V -a/+-et*: **p- av (mot)** glance off (from); **p- av på** glance off; *fig.* (of advice, reproaches) be lost, make no impression on (sby).

prelude're *V -te mus.* play a prelude; play a voluntary.

prelu'dium *-iet, pl +-ier/*-ium* 1 *mus.* prelude; voluntary. 2 *lit.* long (often tiresome) introduction.

pre'mie *-n* (=***premi**) 1 prize, reward; cup, trophy. 2 bounty (paid for wild animal). 3 prize (for prize bond, lottery bond). 4 *merc.* (insurance) premium; option (in forward buying). 5 *naut.* premium (on bottomry loan).

+**pre'mie/belønne** *V -et/-belønte* reward with a prize.

pre'mie/idio't *-en* prize idiot.

pre'mie/konkurranse [-ang·se] *-n* prize competition.

pre'mie/ku *-a* prize cow (also *derog.*, of woman).

pre'mie/obligasjo'n *-en* (state) lottery bond (in Norway), prize bond.

première [premiæ're] *-n* first night, opening (night) (of play or film), première (**på** of).

premie're *V -te* give a prize; reward with a prize.

pre'mie/renn *-et* cup race.

première/stemning [premiæ're/] *-a/+-en* festive and expectant mood of a first-night audience.

premie'r/løytnant *-en* 1 *hist.* first lieutenant. 2 lieutenant.

premie'r/minis'ter *-eren, pl -rer/+-e* premier, prime minister.

pre'mie/sats *-en* premium rate.

+**pre'mie/vinner** *-en, pl -e* (=***-ar**) prize winner.

premiss' *-en/+-et* 1 condition, term: **etter veddemålets p-er** by the terms of the bet; **på mine p-er** on my terms. 2 *philos.* premise. 3 *jur.* (*pl*) grounds.

+**pre'n** *-en* bodkin (awl-like instrument for making holes in leather).

pren't *-et* 1: **på p-** in print. *2 print, printed matter.

***pren'tar** *-en* printer.

pren'te *V -a/+-et* 1 imprint (**inn i** into; also *fig.*): **sorgen står p-et i hans ansikt** sorrow is i-ed on his face. *2 print.

pren'te/svarten *df hum.* "printshop gremlin" (imaginary cause of printers' errors).

***pren'te/verk** *-et* printing shop.

***pren'te/ville** *-a* misprint.

prenumeran't *-en* subscriber.

prenumere're *V -te* subscribe.

prep. =**preposisjon**

preparan't *-en* preparateur, preparator (in laboratory, museum, pharmacy); lab assistant.

prepara't *-et, pl -/+-er chem.* preparation, product.

prepare're *V -te* 1 mount, prepare (e.g. skins, insects); impregnate (e.g. materials); conserve, preserve (e.g. foodstuffs, usu. chemically). 2 *lit.* brief (e.g. person, group); prepare (e.g. speech, students): **p- seg til eksamen** prepare (oneself), study for an examination.

preposisjo'n *-en gram.* preposition.

prerogati'v *-et, pl -/+-er* prerogative.

pres. =**presens**

presang' *-en* gift, present: **gi en noe i p-** give sby a gift.

presang'/kort *-et* gift card.

presbyte'r *-en, pl +-e eccl.* 1 *hist.* presbyter. 2 elder.

presbyteria'ner *-en, pl -e* (=***-ar**) Presbyterian.

presbyteria'nsk *A* - Presbyterian.

preseden's *-en* precedent.

presen'ning *-en* tarpaulin.

pre'sens *et gram.* present (tense).

+**present**[1] [presang'] *-en* cf **presang**

presen't[2] *A* - in one's memory: **jeg har det ikke p-** I don't have it clearly in mind, it has slipped my memory.

presentabel [presangta'bel] *A -elt, pl -le* 1 presentable, fit to be seen. 2 acceptable (e.g. idea), suitable (e.g. clothes).

presentasjon [presangtasjo'n] *-en* 1 *merc.* presentation (of bill). 2 introduction, presentation (**av** of).

presenter/brett [presangte'r/] serving tray.

presentere [presangte're] 1 introduce, present (e.g. person): **får jeg p-** may I p-. 2 present (e.g. bill, concert, interpretation of a character, play, surprise); show (e.g. a dress): **korguttene p-te seg for første gang** the choir boys appeared for the first time. 3: **p- gevær** *mil.* present arms.

presep'tor *-en hist.* tutor.

preser've *-n* (usu. *pl*) shield (to protect clothing from perspiration).

preserve're *V -te* preserve (e.g. eggs).

+ Bokmål; * Nynorsk; ° Dialect.
After letter: ' stress (Acc. 1); ` tone, stress (Acc. 2); · length.
Below letter: . not pronounced.

pre'ses *-en* chairman, president (esp. of academic organization).
prese'teris *N* (=**prae ceteris**) *educ.* highest mark (=summa cum laude).
preseteris't *-en* one who has passed examinations for a degree with the mark of **preseteris.**
presiden't *-en* chairman, president (in Norway only of presiding officers of the *Storting*).
presiden't/skap *-et* **1** (collectively) the *presidents* of the *Storting*. **2** board of directors, directorate, executive committee.
preside're *V -te* preside (over a meeting); sit at head of table (as host).
presi'dium *-iet, pl* +*-ier*/**-ium* **1** chairmanship: **stå under ens p-** be under sby's c-. **2** directorate.
presi's *A* **1** precise (e.g. definition, statement); accurate (e.g. person, machine): **være p-** be on time. **2** *(adv.)* exactly, just so, precisely: **omtrent p-** just about; **det er ikke p- det samme** that's not quite the same; **kl. 9 p-** 9 o'clock sharp.
presise're *V -te* **1** emphasize, point out. **2** define (one's position); amplify, formulate, specify.
presisjo'n *-en* **1** accuracy, exactness; punctuality. **2** precision (e.g. in a gun, machine).
presisjo'ns/arbeid *-et* precision work.
presiø's *A* affected, precious.
preskribe're *V -te jur.* invalidate: **p-t gjeld** prescribed debt (invalid through lapse of time).
preskripsjo'n *-en jur.* limitation.
press' **1** pressure, weight; *fig.* burden (e.g. illness); strong influence, moral pressure; press (in clothing): **legge et tungt p- på sine omgivelser** *fig.* put a damper on one's surroundings; **legge i p-** press (e.g. flowers, meat); **legge p- på en** bring pressure to bear on sby; **levere bukser til p-** take trousers to be pressed; **øve p- på** exert pressure on. **2** force, forcing (e.g. of motor): **for fullt p-** at full force; **sette p- på** hurry up (e.g. the work), improve efficiency; **under p- av seil** crowding all sails. **3** *mus.* forcing (usu. of voice).
pres'se[1] *-a* **1** press (e.g. baler for hay, juicer for fruit, vegetables). **2** *typog.* (printing) press: **gå i p-n** go to p-; **nytt opplag er under p-n** a new edition is in p-.
pres'se[2] *-a*/*-en* press; journalists, reporters: **få god p-** get good coverage (e.g. of event), reviews (e.g. of book, play).
pres'se[3] *V -a*/+*-et* imprint; press (e.g. clothes, hay, steel); squeeze out (e.g. juice); condense (e.g. a speech): **p- noen** force, press sby (e.g. to do sth); **p- penger av en** blackmail sby; **p- på** crowd; **p- seg** force one's way (**fram** forward); **p- seg i hop** be compressed.
pres'se/byrå· *-et* news agency.
+**pres'se/feide** *-n* controversy, lively debate in the press.
pres'se/fotogra·f *-en* press photographer.
+**pres'se/frihet** *-en* freedom of the press.
+**pres'se/jern** [/jæ·rn] *-et* iron, pressing iron.
+**pres'se/klede** *-t* press cloth.
pres'se/konto·r *-et* information office, public relations bureau.
pres'se/lo·sje *-n* press box.
pres'se/mann *-en, pl -menn*/* *-menner* journalist, reporter, representative of the press.
+**pres'se/meddelelse** *-n* press release.
presse'rende *A* - pressing, urgent.
pres'se/sekretæ·r *-en* press secretary, public relations man.
press'/gjeng *-en hist.* press gang.
press'/gjær *-en* compressed yeast.
press'/luft *-a* compressed air.
pres't *-en eccl.* clergyman, minister, pastor; (Catholic) priest: **gå for p-en** attend confirmation class, read for confirmation.
prestasjo'n *-en* achievement, performance, piece of work: **en fremragende p-** an outstanding p- of w-; **en enestående p-** a unique achievement.
pres'te/frue *-a*/+*-en* minister's wife.
pres'te/ga·rd *-en* (=+**/gård**) parsonage, rectory.
pres'te/gjeld *-et* parish (served by one minister).
pres'te/kall *-et* call, parish.
pres'te/kjole *-n* cassock, vestment.
pres'te/kone *-a* minister's wife.
pres'te/krage *-n* **1** clergyman's ruff. **2** *bot.* (oxeye) daisy (Chrysanthemum leucanthemum). **3** *zool.* ringed plover (Charadrius hiaticula).
pres'telig *A* - clerical, priestly.
pres'te/lære *-a*/+*-en*: **i p-** studying for the ministry.
pres'te/læ·rt *A* - trained for the ministry.
pres'te/mann *-en, pl -menn*/**-menner* *fam.* parson: **på tomannshånd kan du s'gu trygt legge hele p-en til side** in private you can safely put aside the whole parson (Kielland).
pres'te/offer *-et eccl.* offering to the minister by the congregation.
preste're *V -te* achieve (e.g. good grades); perform, produce, supply (e.g. ideas, money).
pres'te/sjuke *-n* (=+**/syke,** ***/sykje)** *med.* clergyman's sore throat.
pres'te/skap *-et* clergy.
pres'te/stand *-en*/**-et* clerical profession.
+**pres'te/vielse** *-n* ordination.
prestin'ne *-a*/+*-en* priestess.
presti'sje *-n* prestige.
+**presti'sje/hensyn** *-et* considerations of prestige, matter of prestige.
presti'sje/tap *-et* loss of face, prestige.
pre'sumptiv *A* presumptive; supposed: **den p-t dyktigste** the supposedly most capable.
pretenden't *-en* pretender (to a throne); claimant.
pretende're [also: pretangde're] *V -te* lay claim, pretend.
pretensiøs [pretangsiø's] *A* pretentious; demanding.
pretensjon [pretangsjo'n] *-en* claim, pretension.
prete'ritum *-umet, pl -um*/+*-a gram.* preterite (tense).
pretiosa [presio'sa] *pl* valuables.
pre'tor *-en, pl -torer hist.* praetor.
pret'te *-a* trick.
+**pret'te/maker** *-en, pl -e* (=***-ar)** teaser, trickster.
Preussen [prøy'sen] *Pln* Prussia.
prevensjo'n [-vang-] *-en* birth control, contraception.
pre'ventiv[1] [-vang-] *-et, pl -*/+*-er med.* contraceptive.
pre'ventiv[2] [-vang-] *A* preventive, prophylactic: **p-e midler** contraceptives.
pr.gj. =**prestegjeld**
pri'ar *-en, pl* +*-e* (=+**-er)** *naut.* clew line (on Nordland boat); brail (on Sunnmøre boat): **stikke i p-en** reef the sail.
prikk'[1] *-en* **1** dot, point: **ligne på en p-** be identical; **på en p-, på p-en** to a T, exactly; ***versa i visa er på ein p-** like the verses of the song are exactly alike (Vesaas). **2** spot (e.g. on skin, fur): **sorte p-er i huden** blackheads. **3** (in sports) bull's-eye; black mark, check. **4: den vesle p-en** *fam.* that little shaver.
prikk'[2] *-et* prick, puncture.
prik'ke *V -a*/+*-et* **1** prick, puncture. **2** dot: **p- opp et mønster** mark out a pattern with a dotted line. **3** prickle, tingle: ***det p-a i han** he was on pins and needles (Vesaas); **det p-et i huden** the skin tingled. **4** tap, touch; *fig.* tease: **p- på en** pick at sby.
prik'ket(e) *A* - dotted (line, material); spotted (e.g. mirror).
prikk'/fri *A -tt* **1** (in sports) without black marks, perfect. **2** *fam.* excellent, faultless.
prikk'/hogge *V infl as* **hogge** (using special hammer) chip (e.g. dangerously smooth steps); hew, shape (flagstone).
prik'le *V -a*/+*-et* **1** prickle, tingle: **p- i en av spenning** be on pins and needles. **2** dibble (in transplanting). **3** *dial.* putter (with clumsy or numb fingers).
prik'le/pinne *-n agr.* dibble.
pril'lar/ho·rn *-et mus.* buck horn (with tongue and finger holes; a wind instrument).
***pril'le** *V -a* finger (e.g. mus. instrument).
pri'm[1] *-en* **1** *mus.* key note, tonic; prime (unison). **2** (in fencing) prime; vertical cut usu. directed at head. **3** *eccl.* prime (early service).
pri'm[2] *-en*/*-et* soft cheese, spread (made of whey).
pri'm[3] *-et* nonsense.
pri'ma *A* - *merc.* first (class), prime (quality); *fam.* choice, first-class, very fine.
primadon'na +*-en*/**ei* leading lady (in theater); prima donna (in opera); also *hum., derog.*
primadon'na/nykke +*-n*/+*-t*/**-a* prima donna airs.
pri'mas *-en* **1** *eccl.* primate (e.g. in Anglican and Orthodox churches; unofficially, the bishop of Oslo in Norway). **2** *mus.* leader of (and soloist in) gypsy orchestra.
+**prima'ter** *pl* (=***-ar)** *zool.* primates.
pri'ma/veksel *-elen, pl -ler merc.* first of exchange, prime bill of exchange.
pri'me *V -a*/+*-et*/+*-te* **1** talk nonsense. **2** fib, lie: **p- i noen** tell sby a fib; **p- sammen en grunn** make up a reason.
pri'mitiv *A* primitive.
primitivite't *-en* crudeness, primitiveness.
pri'mo *Av* **1** in the early part of: **p- august** *merc.* August 1-10. **2** in the first place.
pri'm/signe [/singne] *-a*/+*-et eccl.* mark with the sign of the cross before baptism.
pri'm/stav *-en hist.* calendar stick, wooden computus.
pri'm/tal *-et* (=+**/tall)** *math.* prime number.
pri'mula *-en, pl* **-er* **1** *bot.* primrose (Primula). **2** trademark name of a Norw. process cheese.
pri'mus *-en* primus (portable kerosene stove).
pri'mus mo'tor *en lit.* founder, promoter (**i** of).
primæ'r *A* **1** earliest, original (e.g. rock). **2** chief, primary: **p-t ansvar** *jur.* primary claim.
primæ'r/spole *-n elec.* primary coil.
prin's *-en* prince.
prin'selig *A* - princely: **mitt p-e jeg står i pant** my p- self is pawned (Ibsen).
prinses'se *-a*/+*-en* princess.
prin's/gema·l *-en* prince consort.
prinsipa'l[1] *-en* **1** *merc.* employer, head (e.g. of a business). **2** *mus.* principal.
prinsipa'l[2] *A jur.* chief, primary (e.g. proposal): **stemme p-t for et forslag** vote in the affirmative on the first ballot.
prinsipa't *-et hist.* principate.
prinsipiell' *A -elt* in principle: **p-enighet** agreement in p-; **p- motstander** opponent in p-.
prinsipp' *-et, pl -*/+*-er* principle: **av p-** on p-; **etter dette p-** on, according to this p-; **livsløgnen er det stimulerende p-** the life-lie is the stimulating p- (Ibsen).
+**prinsipp'/avgjørelse** *-n* decision on principle (with details of application left for later discussion).
prinsipp'/fast *A* - firm (e.g. policy), of principle (e.g. a man of p-); high-principled.

+prinsipp'/rytter *-en, pl -e* (=***-ar**) doctrinaire.
prinsipp'/spørsmål *-et* matter, question of principle.
prin's/regen't *-en* prince regent.
pri'or *-en eccl.* prior.
priorin'ne *-a/+-en eccl.* prioress.
priorite're *V -te jur.* give priority to: **p-t pant** first mortgage, preferential claim; **skattekrav er p-t** tax claims have priority (e.g. in an estate).
priorite't *-en* 1 priority. 2 *jur.* mortgage.
+priorite'ts/haver *-en, pl -e* (=***-ar**) mortgagee.
priorite'ts/lån *-et* mortgage loan.
priorite'ts/rett *-en* 1 priority (e.g. idea, rank). 2 *jur.* preferred claim, right of priority.
prip'pen *A -ent, pl pripne* testy, touchy: **moralsk p-** morally priggish.
pri's[1] *-en* fame; praise: **(han) synger ekteskapets p-** (he) sings the praise of marriage (Garborg); **takk og p-** thank the Lord.
pri's[2] *-en* prize, reward (e.g. in competition); reward (e.g. for catching criminal): **bære p-en, vinne p-en** have the advantage, win, get first place. 2 (pirate's) prize: **gi til p-** abandon, desert.
pri's[3] *-en* price (**på** of): **for enhver p-** at all costs, at any p-; **i en viss p-** at a certain p-; **ikke for noen p-** under no circumstances; **komme i p-** go up in p-, increase in value; **sette p- på** appreciate, set store by, value; **til billig p-** at a low p-, cheap(ly).
pri's[4] *-en* pinch of snuff: **ta seg en p-** take a p- of s-.
pri's/avhandling *-a/+-en* prize essay, dissertation.
pri's/avslag *-et* discount, rebate, reduction.
pri's/avtale *-n* price agreement.
+pri's/belønne *V -et/-belønte* award a prize to (a person), for (an accomplishment).
pri's/billig *A -* inexpensive, lowpriced.
pri'se[1] *-a/+-en naut.* prize (confiscated boat, ship).
pri'se[2] *V -a/+-et* 1 extol, glorify, praise; commend, laud: **pris ingen lykkelig før han er i sin grav** proclaim no one happy until he is in his grave; **p- en i høye toner** praise sby to the skies; **p- sin lykke** be happy about one's (unexpected) luck. 2 enjoy, make use of: **p- maten** eat with good appetite; **p- sommeren** dress in a summerly way.
pri'se[3] *V +-te/*-a* price, set a price on.
pri'se/domstol *-en naut., jur.* prize court.
pri'selig *A -* laudable, praiseworthy.
pri'se/mannskap *-et naut.* prize crew (i.e. of a seized ship).
pri'se/rett *-en naut., jur.* prize court.
pri's/fall *-et* fall in prices.
+pri's/gi *V -gav, -gitt* abandon, give up (**til** to, to the mercy of); throw to the wolves.
pri's/indeks *-en merc.* price index.
pri's/kamp *-en merc.* price war.
pri's/konkurranse [-ang'se] *-n* prize competition.
pri's/kontroll' *-en admin.* 1 price control. 2 price control office.
pri's/krig *-en* price war.
pri's/kuran't *-en merc.* price list.
pri's/lapp *-en* price label, price tag.
prisma'tisk *A -* prismatic.
pris'me *-t* prism.
pris'me/kikkert *-en* (=***/kikert**) field glasses.
pris'me/krone *-a* crystal chandelier.
+pri's/nedsettelse *-n* price cut, reduction in (of) price: **offisiell p-** rollback.
pri's/nedslag *-et merc.* price cut, reduction of prices.
pri's/nivå' *-et, pl -/+-er* price level.
pri's/note'ring *-a/+-en merc.* quotation (of market values).
priso'n *-en hist.* prison, esp. of prison ship during Napoleonic wars: **han satt i "p-en" i lange år** he was confined to a British prison ship for many years (Ibsen).
+pri's/oppgave *-a/-en educ.* question for the solution of which a prize is awarded.
pri's/regule'ring *-a/+-en* price regulation.
pri's/stigning *-en* (=***/stiging**) rise in prices.
pri's/stopp *-en/-et* price stabilization, price ceiling: **innføre p-** freeze prices.
pri's/verdig *A -* praiseworthy.
+pri's/vinner *-en, pl -e* (=***-ar**) prize winner.
priv. =**privat**
priva't *A -* private (e.g. expenses, interest, property, school); personal, private (e.g. car, life, opinion); confidential.
priva't/bil *-en* private (passenger) car.
+priva't/bolig *-en* (private) residence; home.
priva't/bruk *N*: **til p-** for personal use.
priva't/detekti'v *-en* private detective, private eye.
priva't/forbruk *-et* private consumption.
priva'tim *Av* in private, privately; secretly.
privatis't *-en* student who has prepared for examinations at an unauthorized school or privately.
privatis't/eksa'men *-en* an examination esp. prepared for a *privatist.*
pri'vativ *A gram.* privative.
priva't/liv *-et* privacy, private life: **p-ets fred må være hellig** one's private life must be sacred (Heiberg).
priva't/mann *-en, pl -menn/*-menner* private person: **som p-** as an individual; as a private citizen; in private life.
priva't/perso'n *-en* individual, private person.
priva't/presep'tor *-en hist.* student advisor at a university (chosen by student from professors; system abandoned 1948).
priva't/rett *-en jur.* civil law.
priva't/sak *-a/+-en* personal or private matter.
priva't/sekretæ'r *-en* private secretary.
priva't/skole *-n* private school.
priva't/time *-n* private lesson.
priva't/undervise *V -te* give private lessons.
priva't/undervi'sning *-a/+-en* private lessons.
prive't *-et, pl -/+-er* privy.
privil. =**privilegert**
privilege're *V -te* grant privilege to; charter, license: **p-t behandling** privileged treatment; **p-t krav** preferred claim.
privile'gium *-iet, pl -ier/*-ium* (=***privileg**) privilege (e.g. of the nobility): **den eldstes p-** the right of seniority; **kvinnens p-** woman's prerogative.
pro'[1] *I* whoa (actual sound is a voiceless bilabial trill).
pro'[2] *P* 1 pro: **p- og kontra** p- and con; **p- tempore** at the present time, at this writing. 2 per: **p- anno** p- year; **p- persona** p- person.
pro'- *Pf* pro-.
proba't *A -* effective, infallible, tested (e.g. remedy).
probe're *V -te* 1 *merc.* test, try (e.g. product). 2 assay (e.g. gold in ore).
proble'm *-et, pl -/+-er* problem: **løse et p-** solve a p-; **sette p-er under debatt** take up p-s for discussion (Brandes).
problema'tisk *A -* doubtful, problematic.
proble'm/ba'rn *-et, pl -/*-born* problem child.
proble'm/stilling *-a/+-en* approach to a problem, way of posing a problem: **falsk p-** (also) asking the wrong questions.
produksjo'n *-en* 1 manufacture, production (**av** of). 2 output, production.
produksjo'ns/auke *-n* increase in production.
produksjo'ns/evne *-a/+-en* potential, productive capacity.
+produksjo'ns/midler *pl* (=***/middel**) means of production.
+produksjo'ns/omkostninger *pl* costs of production, prime costs.
produksjo'ns/pris *-en* cost of production, cost price.
+produksjo'ns/ø'kning *-en* cf **/auke**
produk't *-et, pl -/+-er* 1 product (**av** of). 2 manufacture, production: **eget p-** of one's own make; homemade.
prod'uktiv *A* productive.
produktivite't *-en* productivity.
produsen't *-en* producer.
produse're *V -te* manufacture, produce; raise (e.g. wheat); *derog.* turn out (e.g. literary works): **p- seg** *hum.* display one's talent (e.g. in music, wit).
pro'e *V -dde* say whoa (to horse).
prof. =**professor**
profa'n *A lit.* profane (=secular; uninitiated; irreverent).
profanasjo'n *-en* profanation (**av** of).
profane're *V -te lit.* debase, profane: **hvorfor skulle jeg også p- mine egne idealer?** why should I debase my own ideals? (Ibsen).
profesjo'n *-en* occupation, trade, work (usu. a craft).
profesjonell' *A -elt* professional (e.g. house painter, skill, tennis player).
profesjonis'me *-n* (in sports) professionalism.
profesjonis't *-en* professional (sportsman).
profes'sor *-en, pl -so'rer* professor (**i** of; **ved** at).
professora't *-et, pl -/+-er* chair, professorship.
profe't *-en* prophet.
profete're *V -te* prophesy.
profeti' *-en* prophecy: **p-ens gave** the gift of p-.
profe'tisk *A -* prophetic.
+profe't/skikkelse *-n* (personality resembling the) figure of a prophet.
profe't/skjegg *-et* long beard like that of a prophet.
proff[1] [proff'] *-en* 1 (student language) prof (short for professor). 2 (in sports) pro (short for professional).
proff[2] [proff'] *A -* (of sports) professional.
profi'l *-en* 1 contour, profile, silhouette (**av** of). 2 *arch.* cross-section drawing; moulding; sectional iron, steel. 3 *tech.* vertical cross section (e.g. of planned road); clearance, border of right-of-way (of railroad). 4 *geol.* earth's layers; drawing of earth's layers. 5 profile, sketch (e.g. of person).
profile're *V -te* 1 draw profile or cross section (of sth). 2 shape (e.g. moulding, frieze). 3 *eng.* draw, plan (by giving details in cross section).
profita'bel *A -elt, pl -le archaic* profitable.
profite're *V -te* cf **profittere**
profitt' *-en merc.* profit: **med p-** at a p-.
+profitt'/begjæ'r *-et* lust for gain.
profitte're *V -te* gain, profit (**av** by).
profitt'/jeger *-en, pl +-e derog.* profit seeker.
profitø'r *-en* profiteer.

+ Bokmål; * Nynorsk; ° Dialect.
After letter: ' stress (Acc. 1); ' tone, stress (Acc. 2); · length.
Below letter: . not pronounced.

profor'ma *A* - 1 *jur.* pro forma. 2 (purely) formal: **det er rent p-** it is just a matter of form.

profor'ma/faktu'ra *-en* pro forma invoice.

profor'ma/selskap *-et* paper corporation.

profylak'se *-n* prophylaxis (prevention of disease).

profylak'tisk *A* - prophylactic.

progno'se *-n* prediction, prognosis: **stille en p-** make a p-.

prognostise're *V -te* foretell, prognosticate.

prognos'tisk *A* - prognostic.

program' *-met, pl -/⁺-mer* 1 program (=booklet, plan, prospectus, etc.): **hva har du på p-met i kveld?** what's on the agenda for tonight?; **det gikk etter p-met** things went off according to schedule. 2 *educ.* publication on an academic occasion, often containing scientific articles or annual reports. 3 manifesto, programmatic statement; *pol.* platform. 4 catchword, slogan; goal.

program'/blad *-et* (radio, TV) guide.

⁺**program'/erklæ'ring** *-en pol.* manifesto (of a party), platform.

⁺**program'/forplik'tet** *A* - committed to the party platform.

programma'tisk *A* - *mus.* programmatic.

⁺**program'/messig** *A* - according to schedule.

program'/post *-en* item on a program.

program'/tale *-n/*-a* manifesto, programmatic speech.

progresjo'n *-en math.* progression.

progressiv [prog'ressiv] *A* progressive: **p- skatt** graduated system of taxation.

prohib'itiv *A* prohibitive.

projeksjo'n *-en geog., math., phys.* projection.

⁺**projeksjo'ns/tegning** [/teining] *-en* (=*/**teikning**) *math.* projection.

⁺**projekt** [prosjek't] *-et* cf **prosjekt**

projektør [prosjektø'r] *-en* cf **prosjektør**

projise're *V -te* project (**på** on) (also *math., psych., tech.*).

prokla'ma *-et jur.* notice: **preklusivt p-** cf **preklusiv.**

proklamasjo'n *-en admin.* proclamation (**av** of).

proklame're *V -te* proclaim.

proklit'isk *A* - *gram.* proclitic.

prokrus'tes/seng *-a* Procrustean bed.

proku'ra *-en/⁺-et* power of attorney.

prokura'tor *-en* 1 attorney (usu. *derog.*). 2 quibbler, sophist.

prokura'tor/knep *-et* pettifogging, sharp practice.

prokuris't *-en* confidential secretary; person having power of attorney, right to sign (for a firm).

proleta'r *-en* proletarian.

⁺**proleta'r/beve'gelse** *-n* proletarian movement.

⁺**proleta'r/dikter** *-en, pl -e* (=***-ar**) poet of the proletariat.

proletaria't *-et, pl -/⁺-er* proletariat: **det akademiske p-** the white-collar p-.

proletarise're *V -te* pauperize, proletarianize; degrade.

prolog [-lå'g] *-en* prologue.

prolongasjo'n *-en merc.* (also theater) prolongation (e.g. of contract, loan).

prolonge're *V -te merc.* extend (e.g. contract): **p- en veksel** renew a note; **p- et gjestespill** extend a contract of a guest performance.

promemo'ria *-et/⁺-en, pl ⁺-er/*-* memo, memorandum (abbrev. PM); chronological survey (of a problem).

promena'de *-n* promenade (movement in dance; elegant path, street, walk; stroll).

promena'de/dekk *-et* promenade deck.

promena'de/konser't *-en* outdoor concert.

promene're *V -te* promenade, stroll.

promil'le *-n* thousandth: **fem p-** one half of one percent (.005).

⁺**promil'le/kjører** *-en, pl -e* (=***-ar,** */**køyrar**) driver (operating a motor vehicle) whose alcohol content in the blood is above the legal minimum, which in Norway is .05 percent (**en halv promille**).

promil'le/prøve *-a/⁺-en* test for determining alcohol content of blood.

prominen't *A* - prominent.

promosjo'n *-en* conferring of degree (in Norway used about the doctor's degree only).

promove're *V -te* confer a (doctor's) degree upon.

prompe [prom'pe] *V -a/⁺-et pop.* break wind, fart.

promp'te *A* - 1 prepared, ready: **p-e varer** merchandise ready for delivery immediately. 2 prompt, punctual: **betale p-** pay p-ly.

promulgasjo'n *-en* promulgation (**av** of).

promulge're *V -te* promulgate.

prono'men *-et, pl -/⁺-er gram.* pronoun.

pronomina'l *A gram.* pronominal.

propagan'da *-en* propaganda; publicity: **gjøre p- for** make p- for, publicize.

propagan'da/appara't *-et* propaganda machine.

propagande're *V -te* carry on, make propaganda (**for** for); propagandize.

propagandis't *-en* propagandist.

propage're *V -te* 1 propagate. 2 make propaganda for.

propedeutikk' *-en* (=**propedevtikk**) propaedeutic (introductory course, school; introductory textbook).

propedeu'tisk *A* - (=**propedevtisk**) propaedeutic: **p-e kurser** preparatory courses (often introductory courses at a university).

propell' *-en* propeller.

propell'/aksel *-elen, pl -ler* propeller shaft.

propel'ler *-en, pl ⁺-e* cf **propell**

⁺**propell'/ving** *-en* (=*/**veng**) propeller wing.

pro'per *A -ert, pl -re* 1 careful, thorough (e.g. piece of work). 2 clean, neat, tidy (person).

propone're *V -te*: **p- en skål** *archaic* propose a toast.

proporsjo'n *-en* proportion: **statuen mangler p-** the statue is out of p-; **geometrisk p-** *math.* geometrical p-.

proporsjona'l *A* proportional, proportionate (**med** to): **omvendt p-** inversely proportional.

proporsjonalite't *-en math.* proportionality.

proporsjone'rt *A* - proportioned.

proposisjo'n *-en pol.* bill: **kongelig p-** government b-.

propp' *-en* 1 plug; stopper; cork, top (of bottle). 2 *fam.* short, fat, stocky person, esp. boy.

prop'pe *V -a/⁺-et* 1 cork (bottle); plug (e.g. hole, opening). 2 cram, stuff (e.g. ideas, knowledge into sby's head); stuff (esp. food): **p- kaker i et barn** stuff a child with cookies; **p- seg med mat** stuff oneself with food.

prop'pende *Av*: **p- full** chock-full, packed.

propp'/full *A* brimfull, chock-full; packed (e.g. theater).

propp'/mett *A* - *pop.* (of person) gorged, stuffed, stuffed full (with food).

proprietæ'r *-en hist.* wealthy farmer, landowner.

prop's *-en* pitprops (used in mining).

pro ra'ta pro rata; proportionate(ly).

prorek'tor *-en* vice-president (of a university).

pro'sa *-en* prose: **livets p-** the trivialities of life.

pro'sa/dikt *-et* prose poem.

⁺**prosa'iker** *-en, pl -e* (=***-ar**) 1 prose writer. 2 *derog.* prosy person.

prosa'isk *A* - 1 prose (writing). 2 prosaic, unimaginative (e.g. person); banal, ordinary, trivial.

prosais't *-en* prose writer.

pro'sa/litteratu'r *-en* prose literature.

pro'sa/stil *-en* prose style.

prosede're *V -te*: **p- en sak for retten** *jur.* conduct, plead a case before the court.

prosedy're *-n jur.* plea, pleading; proceedings; hearing, trial.

prosek'tor *-en med.* prosector (one who dissects).

proselytt' *-en* convert, proselyte.

prosen't *-en* percent; percentage (**av** of); ratio: **5 p- renter** 5 % interest; **få p-er på** get a percentage (discount) on.

prosen't/del *-en* percentage.

prosen't/sats *-en merc.* percentage.

prosen't/sølv *-et* alloy with low silver content (usu. 10—40 % used for tableware, loving cups, etc.

prosen't/tal *-et* (=⁺/**tall**) percentage, ratio.

prosen't/vis *A* - in percentages, percent.

prosesjo'n *-en* parade, procession: **gå i p-** parade.

prosess' *-en* 1 procedure; process: **kunstig p-** technical p-. 2 *jur.* (civil) action, case, (law)suit; rules of legal procedure: **føre p- med** be involved in a lawsuit with; **gjøre kort p-** settle (sth) summarily; **kriminell p-** criminal case, trial. 3 *biol.* process (protruding part of an organism esp. on a knuckle).

prosess'/fullmek'tig *-en* trial lawyer.

⁺**prosess'/maker** *-en, pl -e* (=***-ar**) litigious person.

prosessuell' *A -elt* procedural.

pro'sit *I* (God) bless you (said to one who sneezes).

prositt' *I* cf **prosit**

prosjek't *-et, pl -/⁺-er* plan; project (**for** for).

prosjekte're *V -te* plan, project.

prosjekti'l *-et, pl -/⁺-er* missile, projectile; bullet.

⁺**prosjek't/maker** *-en, pl -e* (=***-ar**) crank, eccentric; crackpot inventor.

prosjektø'r *-en* (=**projektør**) floodlight; spotlight; projector.

proskribe're *V -te hist.* proscribe (exile, outlaw).

prospek't *-et, pl -/⁺-er* 1 scene, view, vista; picture (in perspective). 2 *mus.* facade, front (of organ). 3 *merc.* brochure, prospectus. 4: **ha noe i p-** have expectation, p-s of sth.

prospek't/kort *-et* picture postcard.

⁺**prospek'tus** *-en merc.* prospectus.

pros'se *V -a/⁺-et mil.* couple.

prost [pros't, pro'st] *-en eccl.* dean (of a cathedral); pastor in charge of area including several parishes.

pros'tata *-en* 1 *anat.* prostate (gland). 2 *fam.* prostatitis.

prosti [prosti'] *-et, pl ⁺-er/*- eccl.* deanery (office of dean); area in charge of a *prost.*

prostinne [prostin'ne] *-a/⁺-en eccl.* wife of a *prost.*

prostitue're *V -te* 1: **p- seg** disgrace oneself; make oneself ridiculous. 2 *(adj.)*: **p-t kvinne** prostitute; **mannlig p-t** male prostitute.

prostitusjo'n *-en* 1 disgrace, humiliation. 2 prostitution: **offentlig p-** legalized p-.

prot. =**protestantisk**

protegé [protesje'] *-en* protégé.

protegere [protesje're] *V -te* patronize, protect.

protein [prote-i'n] *-et* protein.

proteksjo'n *-en* patronage, protection: **stå under ens p-** be under sby's p-.

proteksjonis'me *-n pol.* protectionism.

proteksjonis't *-en pol.* protectionist.

proteksjonis'tisk *A* - *pol.* protectionist.

protektora't *-et, pl -/⁺-er pol.* pro-

tectorate: **stille et land under p-** set up a p- over a country.
prote'se *-n med.* prosthesis (e.g. artificial limb, false teeth).
protes't *-en* protest, protestation.
protestan't *-en eccl.* Protestant.
protestan'tisk *A* - Protestant.
protestantis'me *-n* Protestantism.
proteste're *V -te* protest; remonstrate; lodge a protest (**mot** against).
protokoll' *-en* **1** *pol.* protocol. **2** *jur.* records (e.g. court proceedings): **føre p-en** keep the r-. **3** *merc.* books, ledger. **4** minute book, minutes; teacher's grade book.
protokolle're *V -te* enter, record; register; take down; take legal cognizance of.
protokoll'/føre *V -te* keep minutes, keep records; register.
protokoll'/komité *-en admin.* committee (of 10 chosen from and by members of the *Odelsting*) whose duty it is to check the books and records of the administration and the work of the state auditor.
pro'ton *-en/-et, pl -er/*- phys.* proton.
protoplas'ma *-et, pl +-er/*- biol.* protoplasm.
prototy'p *-en* prototype.
protte [prot'te] *V -a/+-et* **1** say whoa *(pro)*: **p- på hesten** say whoa to the horse. **2** *dial.* putter.
pro'v *-et* **1** *jur.* deposition, evidence. **2** proof. ***3** sample.
prov. =**provins; provisjon**
prov. bas. = **provisjonsbasis**
pro've *V -a/+-et jur.* depone, testify.
+provençaler [provangsa'ler] *-en, pl -e* (=***-ar**) Provençal.
provençalsk [provangsa'lsk] *A* - Provençal.
provenien's *-en* origin, source; provenance.
proven't *-et, pl +-er/*- eccl., hist.* maintenance for life at cloister in return for property or money given to the church.
***pro'v/føring** *-a* argumentation, demonstration, proof.
provian't *-en* provisions, supplies.
proviante're *V -te* provision, take in supplies.
+provian't/forval'ter *-en, pl -e* (=***-ar**) manager and bookkeeper of public supplies; paymaster (in navy); steward.
+provian't/skriver *-en, pl -e* (=***-ar**) assistant to paymaster (in navy); keeper of stores.
provin's *-en* **1** *hist.* province. **2** *admin.* district, province, region. **3**: **p-en** the provinces (as opposed to the capital).
+provin's/boer *-en, pl -e* provincial.
***provin's/dansk** *A - derog.* provincial Danish (in ref. to Dano-Norwegian).
provinsialis'me *-n* provincialism.
provinsiell' *A -elt* provincial.
provisjo'n *-en* **1** *archaic* provisions. **2** *merc.* commission, percentage: **fast p-** flat commission.
provisjo'ns/basis *-en* commission basis.
provi'sor *-en, pl -so'rer* head dispenser, pharmacist who works in a pharmacy.
proviso'risk *A* - provisional, temporary: **p- benskinne** emergency splint.
provokasjo'n *-en* **1** provocation; incitation, instigation. **2** challenge, demand (for an answer, explanation).
provokato'risk *A* - inflammatory, provocative; challenging.
provokatø'r *-en* agent provocateur.
provose're *V -te* **1** incite, instigate, provoke. **2** *pol.* incite, stimulate (sby) to crime.
***pro'vs/kraft** *-a* cogency, evidential force.
pru'd *A* - *archaic* glorious, noble; proud.
prun'k *-en* display, ostentation, pomp.
+prun'k/løs *A* simple, unostentatious.
prupp' *-en pop.* fart.
prup'pe *V -a/+-et pop.* fart.
+prus't *-et* snort.
+prus'te *V -a/-et* puff, snort.
pru'te *V -a/+-et* bargain, dicker, haggle: **p- av (ned) på** get price down by haggling.
pru'tings/monn *-en* (=**+prutnings/, */mon**) margin (between asking and selling price).
pry'd *-en* adornment, decoration, ornament (**for** of, to): **han er en p- for sin stand** he is an o- to his profession.
pry'd/busk *-en* ornamental shrub.
***pry'de[1]** *-a* cf **prydelse**
pry'de[2] *V -a/+-et* adorn, decorate; grace.
pry'delig *A - archaic* attractive, decorative.
+pry'delse *-n* (=***pryde[1], *prydnad**) decoration, ornamentation.
***pry'dnad** *-en* cf **prydelse**
+pry'd/søm' *-men* (=***/saum**) embroidery.
pry'l *-et* beating, thrashing, whipping: **en drakt p-** a beating, *(pop.)* a good licking; **få p-** *fig.* get a tongue-lashing, sharp criticism.
pry'le *V -te* beat, thrash, whip; *(pop.)* lick: **p- en fordervet** beat sby senseless; **p- en opp** beat sby up; **p- løs på en** beat up on sby.
pry'lert *-en* strapping fellow.
præ'rie *-n* prairie.
præ'rie/brann *-en* prairie fire.
præ'rie/ulv *-en zool.* coyote (Canis latrans).
prø've[1] *-a/+-en* **1** test, trial (**av** of); ordeal: **på p-** on trial, probation; on approval; **sette på p-** put to the test, try; **stå sin p-** stand the test. **2** examination; rehearsal; audition; fitting: **gå opp til skriftlig p-** take the written examination. **3** sample, specimen (**av, på** of). **4** *math.* check, proof.
prø've[2] *V -de* **1** test, try (**å** to); try out: **p- fisken** try the fishing, see if the fish are biting; **p- krefter med en** match, measure, pit strength against sby; **p-ende** scrutinizing, searching; **p- på (å)** try, endeavor (to); **p-et** proved, tried. **2** examine; rehearse; audition: **p- på** try (clothes) on. **3** sample. **4** experience, try, undergo: **han fikk p- litt av hvert** he went through a great deal. **5** *(refl.)*: **p- seg** prove oneself (itself), have a go (**på at**), try (sth); **p- seg fram** proceed tentatively, throw out a feeler; **p- seg med en** try one's tricks with sby.
prø've/ark *-et typog.* proof sheet; sample sheet.
prø've/ballong· *-en* **1** *meteor.* pilot balloon. **2** *fig.* feeler, trial balloon.
prø've/bok *-a* **1** *merc.* sample book. **2** *typog.* book with samples of print.
prø've/drift *-a/+-en* experimental operation (of factory, mine, etc.)
prø've/eksempla'r *-et* sample, sample copy.
prø've/fly *V infl as* **fly** test, test-fly.
prø've/hopp *-et* trial jump.
prø've/kjøre *V -te* (=***/køyre**) make test run (e.g. car, train); test (by running; machinery etc.); rehearse, run through (e.g. ceremony).
prø've/klut *-en* **1** sampler. **2** *fam.* guinea pig.
prø've/kolleksjo'n *-en merc.* sample assortment.
+prø'velse *-n* (=***-ing**) **1** critical examination, scrutiny, test: **fornyet p-** reexamination; **til p- i Høyesterett** *jur.* to scrutiny by the supreme court; **underkaste noe en p-** subject sth to scrutiny. **2** affliction, ordeal; trial, tribulation; *fig.* (of person) annoyance, burden, trial: **gjennomgå hårde p-r** be sorely tried; **han er en p-** he is a cross; **p-ns tid** time of trial.
prø've/pakke *-a/-en merc.* sample, sample package.
prø've/rom [/romm] *-met* fitting room.
prø've/rør *-et/*-a* (=***/røyr**) test tube.
prø've/sal *-en* rehearsal room.
prø've/skott *-et* (=**+/skudd**) trial shot.
prø've/stein *-en* criterion, (acid) test; touchstone (**på** of).
+prø'vet *A* - experienced, seasoned; tested, tried: **p- gull** hallmarked, sterling gold.
prø've/tid *-a/+-en* **1** apprenticeship; probationary period. **2** *bibl.* ordeal, time of trial. **3** *merc.* period of approval.
prø've/trykk *-et* **1** trial print (of graphics). **2** steam pressure used in testing (e.g. boiler, tank).
prø've/tur *-en* trial run, trial try.
***prø'ving** *-a* cf **prøvelse**
+prøy'sser *-en, pl -e* (=***-ar**) Prussian.
+prøysser/disipli'n *-en* (=***-ar/**) Prussian discipline (=severe d-).
+prøysser/ånd *-en* (=***-ar/**) Prussianism, (militaristic) spirit of the Prussians.
prøy'ssisk *A* - Prussian.
***prå'm** *-en* cf **pram**
prå's *-en* **1** *archaic* cheap candle; poor, weak light. **2**: **det går en p- opp for en** *hum.* a light dawns on one.
psal'ter *-en/-et* psalter.
pseud. =**pseudonym[1,2]**
pseudony'm[1] *-et* (=**psevdonym**) pseudonym.
pseudony'm[2] *A* pseudonymous.
ps't *I* hey, pst (getting attention).
pst. =**prosent**
psyk. =**psykologisk**
psy'ke *-n* mentality, mind, psyche: **den primitive p-** primitive mentality.
psykia'ter *-eren, pl +-ere/*-rar* psychiatrist.
psykiatri' *-en* psychiatry.
+psykia'triker *-en, pl -e* cf **psykiater**
psykia'trisk *A* - psychiatric.
psy'kisk *A* - mental, psychic.
psy'ko/analy'se *-n* psychoanalysis.
psy'ko/analyse're *V -te* psychoanalyze.
+psy'ko/analyt'iker *-en, pl -e* (=***-ar**) psychoanalyst.
psy'ko/analyt'isk *A* - psychoanalytic(al).
psykolog [-lå'g] *-en* psychologist.
psykologi' *-en* psychology.
psykologise're *V -te* psychologize.
psykologisk [-lå'gisk] *A* - psychological.
psykopa't *-en* psychopath.
psykopa'tisk *A* - psychopathic.
psyko'se *-n* psychosis.
psy'ko/soma'tisk *A* - psychosomatic.
psy'ko/teknisk *A* - psychotechnical.
p. t. =**pro tempore**
ptoleme'isk *A* - Ptolemaic.
ptro' *I* cf **pro[1]**
puberte't *-en* puberty.
puberte'ts/alder *-eren, pl -rer/+-ere* (age of) puberty.
publikasjo'n *-en* publication (**av** of).
pub'likum *-et* **1** the public: **det store p-** the general p-. **2** audience, spectators; readers, subscribers; clientele, customers: **han har et stort p-** he has a large following, he is popular.
+pub'likum(m)er *-en, pl -e* (=***-ar**) *hum.* spectator; man in the street.
pub'likums/interes'se *+-n/*-a* public interest; audience interest.
pub'likums/suksess [/sykse·] *-en* hit (e.g. play, performance).
publise're *V -te* **1** make public. **2** print, publish.
publisite't *-en* publicity.
pud'del *-elen, pl pudler* **1** poodle:

+ Bokmål; * Nynorsk; ° Dialect.
After letter: ' stress (Acc. 1); ' tone, stress (Acc. 2); · length.
Below letter: . not pronounced.

p-ens kjerne the crux of the matter. 2 (in bowling) ball thrown into wrong lane.
pud'der *-eret/pudret* (cosmetic) powder.
pud'der/dåse *-n* compact.
pud'der/kvast *-en* powder puff.
pud'der/sukker *-et* 1 (granulated) sugar. 2 *fig.* dirty granular snow.
pud'ding *-en* pudding (as dessert or main dish).
pud're *V -a/+-et* powder (e.g. one's face); dust (e.g. plant); drench, sprinkle (e.g. hair with gray).
pudrett' *-en agr.* night soil, sludge.
pueri'l *A* puerile.
puff'¹ *-en* 1 hassock; ottoman. 2 puff (on sleeve etc.).
puff'² *-en/-et* 1 push, shove; nudge, poke, prod (also *fig.*). 2 puff (on cigar; of locomotive).
puf'fe *V -a/+-et* 1 elbow, push, shove; nudge, poke: **p- til** poke (etc.). 2 puff (e.g. on a cigar; of a locomotive): **p- av sted** chuff, chug, puff away, off; travel (by train); **ein gong um dagen kjem ein båt p-ande** once a day a boat comes puffing along (Vesaas).
+puff'/erme *-t* (=*/**erm)** puff sleeve.
+pu'ge *V -a/-et derog.* hoard, scrape together (money).
+pu'ger *-en, pl -e derog.* hoarder, miser.
pugg' *-et* cramming, rote learning.
pug'ge *V -a/+-et* cram, grind (in studying for exams); learn by rote.
pugg'/hest [also pugg'/] *-en fam.* grind (person).
pu'h *I* phew, whew (indicating weariness, heat, dismay).
pu'ke *-n archaic* devil.
pukk [pokk'] -en crushed stone, gravel (in Norway often of granite).
pukka [pok'ka] *Av* absolutely: **p- nødt til** forced to (do sth).
pukke [pok'ke] *V -a/+-et* 1 crush (ore). 2 crush, grind, hammer (stones to make gravel). 3 cover, gravel (road). 4: **p- en til å gjøre noe** *fam.* force sby to do sth, intimidate sby into doing sth; **p- på** assert, insist on; **p- på sin rett** stand on one's right. 5 complain; grumble, mutter.
pukkel [pok'kel] *-elen, pl pukler* 1 hump (e.g. on camel). 2 hunched back. 3: **få, gi på p-en** get, give a scolding; be criticized, criticize; *(pop.)* catch hell, get it in the neck.
pukkel/rygga *A* - **(=+-et)** hunchbacked.
pukk/hammar [pokk'/] *-en, pl -hamrer* (=**+/hammer)** spalling or stone hammer.
pukk/maski'n *-en* stone-crushing machine.
pukk/stein *-en* crushed stone.
pukk/verk *-et* battery, stamp(ing) mill.
pul'der *-en dial.* spray.
pul'dre *V -a/+-et dial.* spurt; trickle; roll out, well up.
pul'je *-n* 1 (in sports) heat (=group of contenders pitted directly against each other): **i samme p-** in the same h-; pitted against each other; **i p-r på tre og tre** by groups of three. 2 (in cards) kitty, pool.
pul'je/vis *Av* (in sports) by groups (contending in same heats).
pul'k *-en* reindeer sleigh (boat-shaped, partly enclosed, without runners).
pull' *-en* crown (of hat).
pul'ler(t) *-en naut.* bitt, bollard.
pull'/over *-en, pl +-e* (sleeveless) pullover sweater.
pul's *-en* pulse: **i takt med tidens egen p-** in step with the tempo of the times (Hoel).
pulse're *V -te* 1 beat, pulsate, throb: **p-ende liv** throbbing life. 2 *elec.* (of direct current) pulsate: **p-ing** pulsation.
puls'/slag *-et* pulse beat; rhythmic beat of a machine: **tidens p-** the rhythm of the times.
puls'/vante *-n* wrist warmer (knitted, almost fingerless, long glove).
+puls'/varmer *-en, pl -e* (=***-ar)** pulsewarmer, wristlet.
puls'/åre *-a* (=***/år)** artery (also *fig.*)
pul't *-en* desk (e.g. in a school).
pulte'r/kammer *-et, pl -/+-kamre* storeroom.
pul't/lokk *-et* desk cover.
pul't/ost [/ost] *-en* soft, sharp cheese of sour, skimmed milk, used as spread (similar to but not identical with cottage cheese).
pul'ver *-et, pl -/+-e* powder (e.g. baking, medical).
pul'ver/form *-a/+-en*: **i p-** in powdered form.
pul'ver/heks *-a archaic* hag, hex, old witch.
pulverise're *V -te* pulverize; smash.
pu'ma *-en, pl *-er zool.* cougar, panther, puma (Felis concolor).
pumpe¹ [pom'pe] *-a* pump.
pumpe² [pom'pe] *V -a/+-et* 1 pump (e.g. air, liquid); (of heart) beat; (of blood) spurt: **hårdt p-et** (of tires) pumped up hard; **p- en kanon** clean a cannon; **p- en sykkel** inflate, pump up the tires on a bicycle; **p-lens** empty, dry out (e.g. ship); **p-magen** pump out the stomach. 2 *fig.* pump (for information): **p- en tilståelse ut av en** p- a confession out of sby.
pumpe/mann [pom'pe/] *-en, pl -menn/ *-menner naut.* petty officer in charge of pumps (esp. on tankers).
+pumpe/spiker [pom'pe/] *-eren, pl -er/ -rer* (=***-ar)** tack.
punche [pøn'sje] *V -a/+-et* punch.
punche/dame *-a/+-en* punch girl (at IBM machine).
punching/ball [pøn'sjing/] *-en* punching bag.
pun'd *-et, pl -* 1 pound (weight). 2 pound (English money). 3 *bibl.* pound (=ability, talent): **grave sitt p- ned i jorden** bury one's talents (cf Luke 19, 20; Matt. 25, 25).
***pun'dar** *-en* steelyard.
+pu'ner *-en, pl -e* (=***-ar)** *hist.* Phoenician; esp. Carthaginian.
+pu'ner/krig *-en* (=***-ar/)** Punic War.
pung [pong'] *-en* 1 purse: **det sved i p-en** it really hurt the pocketbook; **løse på p-en** loosen the pursestrings. 2 bag, pouch (usu. for shot, tobacco). 3 *zool.* pouch (e.g. of kangaroo). 4 *anat.* scrotal sac, scrotum.
pung/dyr [pong'/] *-et* marsupial, pouched mammal.
punge [pong'e] *V -a/+-et*: **p- ut** *fam.* come across, cough up, pay; **p- ut med** fork out.
pung/rotte [pong'] *-a zool.* opossum (Didelphis virginiana).
pu'nisk *A* - Punic.
pun'kt [also: pong't] *-et, pl -/+-er* 1 dot (over letter i; in Braille; in *mus.*); spot (e.g. on bird egg): **et lyst p-** *fig.* a bright spot; **klag ikke under stjernerne over mangel på lyse p-er i ditt liv** complain not under the stars of a lack of bright spots in your life (Wergeland); **til p- og prikke** exactly, in every detail, to the letter. 2 point (e.g. in time, development); period, stage (e.g. in negotiations); *astron., math., phys.* point (e.g. of freezing; on a line). 3 place, point (of land), spot: **fra dette p-** from this spot. 4 *fig.* point (e.g. in a discussion): **p- for p-** p-by p-; **på det p-** on that p-; **det springende p-** the salient p-; the heart of the matter. 5 *typog.* point (type size).
punkte're *V -te* 1 (of tire) puncture; get, have a flat (tire), a puncture; (of etching) point, stipple; (of pattern making) perforate, puncture; (of sculpture) point. 2 dot (e.g. letters), mark with accent mark; *mus.* dot (a note); dot (a drawing, line, painting): **p-t rune** dotted rune.
pun'ktlig [also: pong'tli] *A* - precise, punctual: **love p- levering** promise immediate delivery.
+punktlig/het *-en* promptness, punctuality.
pun'ktum *-et, pl -/+-er gram.* period (the sign); paragraph (e.g. of a speech); stop (in telegraphy): **sette p- for noe** end, put a stop to sth; **og dermed p-!** and that's that! that's all I have to say!
pun'kt/vis [also: pong't/] *A* - point by point.
pun'sj *-en* punch (hot drink): **svensk p-** Swedish p- (an arrack liqueur).
pun'sj/bolle *-n* 1 punch bowl. 2 (pastry) roll filled with custard flavored with Swedish punch.
+pun't/lær *-et* (=***/ler)** tough, high-grade leather (used for soles and boots).
+pun'tlærs/mage *-n hum.* cast-iron stomach.
pupill' *-en anat.* pupil.
pup'pe *-a/+-en zool.* chrysalis, cocoon
+pu'r *A* 1 pure, real, unadulterated (e.g. gold); absolute (necessity); dire (need); mere (youth); pure (fabrication, speculation), sheer (nonsense): **av p- ondskap** out of sheer spite, pure malice; **Guds ord forkyntes p-t og rent** *bibl.* God's word was preached without adulteration. 2 *archaic* clean; (morally) pure. 3 *(adv.)*: **p- ung** extremely young, in the first flush of youth.
puré *-en* purée.
+pu'rende *Av*: **p- ung** extremely young (cf **pur**).
puris'me *-n gram.* purism (esp. avoidance of foreign words).
puris't *-en gram.* purist.
puris'tisk *A* - puristic.
+purita'ner *-en, pl -e* (=***-ar, *puritan)** 1 *hist.* Puritan. 2 puritan.
purita'nsk *A* - 1 *hist.* Puritan(ic). 2 puritan(ic).
pur'k *-en* 1 *fam.* little fellow, shaver, tyke. 2 *pop.* cop, policeman.
pur'ke *-a* sow (also *derog.* of woman).
pur'ke/ful *A* crafty, foxy, sly.
pur'ket(e) *A* - *dial., fam.* ornery.
pur'k/otte *-a*: **i p-a** at the crack of dawn.
pur'l *-et* murmur, purl.
pur'le *V -a/+-et* murmur, purl.
pur'pur *-et* purple (color, dye; note that it may include also crimson and scarlet); purple-colored cloth; purple robe (indicating high office): **ta ikke p-et, Julian** *fig.* do not let yourself be crowned, J- (Ibsen).
+pur'pur/rød *A* (=***/raud)** crimson, scarlet.
purr' *-et* 1 frizz, very curly hair: **brenningens svulmen under det hvite p- av skum** *fig.* the breakers' swell under the white, frizzly foam (Kjær). 2 *dial.* brush, scrub (esp. of oak).
pur're¹ *-n bot.* leek (Allium porrum).
pur're² *V -a/+-et* 1 *naut.* rouse, waken: **p- ut** rout out; **p- vakten** call the watch. 2 remind, send reminder to, warn: **p- på en** remind sby. 3 *lit.* rumple (hair); draw, stroke (fingers through hair): **p- seg i håret** scratch one's head (in perplexity).
+pur're/løk *-en* (=***/lauk)** cf **purre**
pur're/skriv *-et* written reminder.
purser [pø'rser] *-en, pl +-e* purser.
+pu'r/ung [/ong] *A* very young (cf **pur**).
pu's *-en fam.* 1 kitty, pussy (esp. used for one's own housecat). 2 bunny (rabbit). 3 (term of endearment for woman) baby, darling.
pu'se/katt *-en* pussy, pussycat.
+puselan'ke *-n fam.* paddy, tootsywootsy (esp. of child's hand, foot; or animal paw).
pus'ke *V -a/+-et dial.* 1 finger, play with, rumple. 2 fix (e.g. one's hair): **p- seg til** clean up, get (oneself) ready. 3 putter about.

pus'ket(e) *A* - *dial.* poorly, run-down; rumpled, seedy.
pus'l *-et* (=**putl**) **1** puttering (**med** with). **2** rustling (faint noise).
pus'le *V* *-a*/+*-et* (=**putle**) **1** busy oneself, fiddle, finger, putter (**med** with). **2** make a faint noise; move softly: **p- omkring** shuffle about (e.g. in slippers), walk slowly and softly; **det begynte å p- i gatene** traffic was starting up in the streets (Evensmo).
pus'le/arbeid *-et* petty, puttering work; trifles.
+**pus'leri** *-et* **1** puttering. **2** rustling.
+**pus'le/spill** *-et* (=*/**spel**) jigsaw puzzle.
pus'let(e) *A* - poky, sluggish; sickly.
pus'ling *-en* **1** small, weak person or animal; slowpoke. **2** *folk.* dwarf.
puss'[1] *-en* *med.* matter, pus.
puss'[2] *-en* **1** best (clothes): **i full p-** all dressed up; **i sin beste p-** in one's Sunday best, in one's best bib and tucker; **trekke i p-en** *fam.* dress in formal clothes. **2** polish (of silver); finish (of woodwork); dressing (of carcass). **3** plaster; stucco =**mur/p-**).
puss'[3] *-et* practical joke, trick: **gjøre, spille en et p-** play a t- on sby; **det skulle være et p- til ham** it would be a t- on him.
puss'[4] *I* sic: **p- ta'n** sic 'im.
pus'sa *A* - *pop.* drunk, plastered, swacked.
pus'se[1] *V* *-a*/+*-et* **1** polish, shine (glass, metal, shoes, a stove, etc.); clean (e.g. a rifle); brush (teeth): **p- nesen** blow one's nose; **p- opp** do over, redecorate, renovate; **p- på** brush up, polish (e.g. one's style), tidy up. **2** trim (meat, vegetables, a wick, etc.); dress (e.g. stone); sand, smooth (a floor, table top, etc.). **3** plaster. **4** (*refl.*) **p- seg** clean up, spruce up.
pus'se[2] *V* *-a*/+*-et* sic: **p- en hund på noen** s- a dog on sby.
pus'se/fille *-a* polishing cloth.
pus'se/ga'rn *-et* cotton waste.
pus'se/middel *-elet*/*-midlet*, *pl* +*-midler*/**-el* polish (for furniture, metal, etc.).
pus'se/skinn *-et* chamois skin (for polishing, washing, etc.).
pus'sig *A* - curious, funny, odd; amusing, droll: **p- nok** curiously enough, a funny thing; **det p-e er** the queer thing is.
pus't *-en*/*-et* **1** breath: **kort i p-en** short of b-; **ta p-en fra en** take one's b- away; **trekke p-en** breathe. **2** breather, pause: **en p- i bakken** a breather. **3** puff (of steam, wind, etc.), whiff; gust: **et p- av liv** a lively air.
pus'te *V* *-a*/+*-et* **1** breathe; huff, pant: **p- tungt** breathe hard. **2** blow, puff (**på at**): **p- glass** blow glass; **p- opp ilden** fan the embers, blow on the coals; **p- til hatet** fan hatred. **3: p- på** take a breather, a rest; **p- ut** catch one's breath; draw a sigh of relief. **4** (*refl.*): **p- seg opp** inflate oneself, swell up.
pus'te/rom [/romm] *-met* break, breather, respite.
pus'te/rør *-et*/**-a* blowgun (such as a peashooter).
+**pus'te/øvelse** *-n* breathing exercise.
pu's/unge [/onge] *-n* kitty-cat; (as pet name for child) kitten.
pu'te *-a* **1** pillow; pad; cushion: **sy p-r under armene på en** make things too easy for sby, pamper sby. **2** esp. *carp.*, *naut.* bolster. **3: p-r** *naut.* bilge ways. **4** *arch.* torus.
pu'te/krig *-en* pillow fight.
pu'te/var *-et* pillowcase, pillowslip.
put'l *-et* cf **pusl**
put'le *V* *-a*/+*-et* cf **pusle**
put're *V* *-a*/+*-et* **1** bubble, simmer, sputter; (esp. of water) seethe; (of motor) chuff, putt. **2** fret, whimper. **3** *dial.* chatter, gabble, prattle.

putt' *-en* cf **pytt**[1]
put'te *V* *-a*/+*-et* place, put (**i** in): **p- en i hullet** *fam.* put sby in the clink; **p- i lommen** pocket; **p- i seng** put to bed.
put'tis *pl* puttees.
pygmé *-en* pygmy.
pygméisk *A* - pygmy.
pyjamas [pysja'mas] *-en* pajamas.
pyjamas/bukse [/bokse] *-a* pajamas bottoms, trousers.
pyjamas/jakke *-a* pajama jacket, top.
+**pyk'niker** *-en*, *pl* *-e* (=***-ar**) pyknic (short, powerful person).
pyk'nisk *A* - pyknic.
pyl'se *-a* cf **pølse**
pyn't[1] *-en* **1** point (of land). **2** brink, edge (of cliff, hill).
pyn't[2] *-en* **1** decoration, trimming. **2** dress, finery: **i full p-** all dressed up, in all its, one's finery.
pyn'te *V* *-a*/+*-et* **1** adorn, decorate, dress up; garnish, trim; beautify: **p- opp** decorate, smarten up; **p- på** smarten up, touch up; gloss, varnish over; **p- på et regnskap** doctor an account; **p- på en rekord** (in sports) better, improve a record. **2** straighten up, tidy up: **p- på** (the same). **3** look well; be decorative, brighten (the prospect): **hun p-er (opp) i landskapet** she pretties up the landscape. **4** (*refl.*): **p- seg** dress up; adorn, deck oneself out (**med** with).
pyn'te/band *-et* (=+/**bånd**) decorative ribbon.
pyn'te/dokke *-a* *derog.* (of woman) doll.
pyn'te/duk *-en* embroidered, decorative tablecloth (or mat).
pyn'te/forkle *-et*, *pl* +*-forklær*/**-* fancy apron, party apron.
'**pyn'te/gjenstand** *-en* knickknack, piece of bric-à-brac.
pyn'te/handkle *-et*, *pl* +*-handklær*/**-* (=+/**håndkle**) guest towel, ornamental towel (hung over towels in use).
pyn'telig *A* - neat, proper, tidy: **en p- stue** a tidy room; **p- språk** proper language.
pyn'te/lommetørkle *-et*, *pl* +*-lommetørklær*/**-* ornamental handkerchief (e.g. for suit breast pocket).
pyn'te/sjuk *A* (=+/**syk**) inordinately fond of finery, fancy clothes, jewelry.
pyn'te/varer *pl* fancy goods, notions.
pyoré *-en* *odont.* pyorrhea.
pyramida'l *A* pyramidal.
pyrami'de *-n* pyramid.
+**Pyrene'ene** *Prn* (=***Pyreneane**) the Pyrenees.
pyroma'n *-en* pyromaniac.
pyromani' *-en* pyromania.
+**pyrr'hus/seier** *-eren*, *pl* *-rer* (=*/**siger**) Pyrrhic victory.
py'se[1] +*-n*/**-a* *fam.* poor devil, wretch; sissy, weakling.
+**py'se**[2] *V* *-te*: **p- for (med)** *fam.* coddle, pet, spoil.
py'sen *A* +*-ent*, *pl* *-ne* (=**pyset(e)**) delicate, sensitive, sissified.
pytagore'er *-en*, *pl* *-e* (=***-ar**) Pythagorean.
pytagore'isk *A* - Pythagorean.
pytt'[1] *-en* puddle.
pytt'[2] *I* pooh, tut: **p- sann** it doesn't matter, makes no difference, that's all right.
pytt'[3] *N*: **p- i panne** meat and potato hash.
pyt'te *V* *-a*/+*-et* pooh-pooh.
+**pæ'l** *-en* cf **påle**[1]
+**pæ'le**[1] *-n* cf **påle**[1]
+**pæ'le**[2] *V* *-a*/*-te* cf **påle**[2]
pæ'le[3] *V* *-a*/+*-te* *dial.* exert oneself, work hard: **p- og dra** pull and pull (Jølsen).
°**pæl'me** *V* *-a* cf **pelme**
pæ're[1] *-a* **1** pear. **2** (light) bulb. **3** *pop.* head: **bløt på p-a** balmy, imbecile, soft-headed.
+**pæ're**[2] *Av* *fam.* utterly, very: **p- dansk** out-and-out Danish; **p- full** dead drunk.

pø' *N*: **pø om pø** gradually, little by little.
pø'bel *-elen*, *pl* *-ler* **1** mob, rabble; riffraff. **2** boor, cad: **en utsøkt p- a** complete b- (Elster d. y.).
+**pø'bel/aktig** *A* - boorish, plebeian, vulgar.
pø'bel/herredømme *-t* mob rule.
pø'bel/språk *-et* coarse, common, vulgar language.
pø'h *I* poof, pooh, tut.
+**pø'l** *-en* (=***pøyle**) **1** mud puddle; pool, puddle (of sth spilled, e.g. blood). **2** mess, mire, morass. **3** *bibl.* lake of fire and brimstone.
+**pøl'le** *-n* cylindrical bolster, pillow
pøl'se *-a* sausage; frankfurter, wiener: **det er ingen sak med den p-a som er for lang** better to have too much than too little; **en p- i slaktetiden** a drop in the bucket; **rosinen i p-a** (see **rosin**); **varm p-** hot dog.
+**pøl'se/bod** *-en* cf /**bu**
pøl'se/bu *-a* hot dog stand.
+**pøl'se/gutt** *-en* (=*/**gut**) hot dog seller, vendor.
+**pøl'se/maker** *-en*, *pl* *-e* (=***-ar**) sausage maker.
pøl'se/pinn(e) *-(e)n* sausage peg (to tie up ends of casing): **koke suppe på en p-** make much of an unimportant matter.
pøl'se/skinn *-et* sausage casing, skin.
pøl'se/snabb *-en* end piece of smoked or summer sausage.
pøl'se/snakk *-et* *fam.* nonsense, rubbish.
pøl'se/tarm *-en* intestine used for sausage casing.
pøl'se/vev *-et* *fam.* nonsense, rubbish.
pøl'se/vogn [/vångn] *-a* hot dog wagon.
pønite're *V* *-te* *eccl.* do penance; repent.
+**pøn'se** *V* *-et* cf **pønske**
pøn'ske *V* *-a*/+*-et* (=+**pønse**) meditate, muse, ponder; speculate (**på** about, on): **p- på** dream of, think of; **p- på hevn** plan revenge; **p- ut** arrive at by thinking, think out; devise, think up.
pø's *-en* **1** esp. *naut.* bucket; dipper, grab, scoop (on excavating machine). **2** *fam.*, *hum.* old, unsightly hat.
pø'se *V* *-te* pour: **det p-er ned** the rain is p-ing down; **p- på** keep pouring (e.g. drink).
pø's/regne [+/reine] *V* *-a*/+*-et*/+*-te*/**-de* pour down (rain), rain in torrents.
pøy'k *-en* *dial.* lad, young boy.
***pøy'le** *-a* cf **pøl**
på' *P* **1** on, upon (a beach, bicycle, Broadway, ceiling, chair, the coast, one's head, an island, Karl Johan, Monday, a page, the way, etc.); at (a certain time, the corner, school, the top, etc.); in (the attic, the bottle, a cafe, the country, the heavens, Hønefoss, Lillehammer, Nordland, Norwegian, a picture, etc.): **gang på gang** time after (upon) time; **kapteinen på skipet** the captain of the ship; **langt på natt** late at night; far into the night; **midt på dagen** in the middle of the day; **på avstand fra hverandre** at a distance from each other; **på besøk** on a visit, visiting; **(bevertes) på det beste** (be treated) in the best possible way; **på seg** on, on one(self); **har du en sigarett på deg?** do you have a cigarette on you?; **på vidt gap** wide open; **tidlig på året** early in the year; **være på'n** *fam.* have one on, be high; be at it, be working. **2** at (=towards); onto; to: **dra, reise**

+ Bokmål; * Nynorsk; ° Dialect.
After letter: ' stress (Acc. 1); ` tone, stress (Acc. 2); · length.
Below letter: . not pronounced.

på fjellet, på landet go to the mountains, the country; (of time) **fem på to** five to two; **jeg skal på postkontoret** I'm going to the post office; **kaste stein på noen** throw stones at sby; **komme inn på scenen** come on the stage. 3 (with expressions of distance, time) for; in: **den rikeste mannen på mange mil** the richest man for many miles (around); **han gjorde det på tre minutter** he did it in three minutes; **har ikke vært her på en stund** hasn't been here for a while. 4 by, by means of; with: **kjenne noe på lukten** recognize sth by its odor. 5 of: **enden på visen** the end of the song; **gjeld på 10 kroner** debt of 10 kr. 6 *(adv.)* on: **det er sist på med ham** *fam.* he's on his last legs; **et bord med lampe på** a table with a lamp on it; **lyset står på** the light is on; **med krone på** wearing a crown, with a crown on. (For use with verbs, e.g. **drive, gå, samle på:** see these).

p. å. = **poståpneri**

på'/akta *A* - (=⁺**-et**) noticed, paid attention to.

***på'/ankande** *A* - *jur.* which can be appealed.

⁺**på'/anke** *V -a/-et* 1 *jur.* appeal. 2 complain about.

⁺**på'/begyn'ne** *V -begynte* begin, commence, start (on); *jur.* institute.

⁺**på'/bero'pe** *V -te*: **p- seg** cite, invoke, plead (in support of one's position).

på'/binding *-a* 1 binding, tying on; knitting on. 2 binding (e.g. on skis).

⁺**på'/bud** *-et* (=***/bod**) bid, command, order (**om å** to).

⁺**på'/by** *V -bød, -budt* command, order, require: **påbudt** prescribed.

på'bygg *-et* addition, extension (e.g. to a house).

⁺**på'/dikte** *V -a/-et* ascribe, attribute, impute: **p- en noe** ascribe sth to sby.

⁺**på'/dra** *V -drog, -dradd/-dratt* 1 bring on, entail, incur (e.g. expenses). 2 *(refl.)*: **p- seg** incur (e.g. responsibility); catch, contract (a cold, disease, etc.).

⁺**på'/dutte** *V -a/-et*: **p- en noe** impute sth to sby.

⁺**på'/dømme** *V -dømte jur.* adjudicate, adjudge, decide.

på'/emning *-a* 1 intention, plan. *2 beginning, start.

på'/fallende *A* - conspicuous, marked, striking; peculiar, strange: **p- lik** strikingly similar.

på'/fugl *-en* 1 *zool.* peafowl; peacock (Pavo). 2 *fig.* vain, showy person.

på'fugl/hane *-n zool.* peacock (Pavo cristatus).

⁺**på'fugl/øye** *-t* (=***/auga, */auge**) *zool.* peacock butterfly (Vanessa); emperor moth (Saturnia).

på'/funn *-et* idea, notion; device, invention; fabrication.

på'/fyll *-et* 1 fill (e.g. gravel, sand). 2 fill-up; second helping.

på'/fylling *-a/⁺-en* 1 bottling, filling (up). 2 fill, filling.

***på'/fynster** *-eret, pl -rar* cf **/funn**

⁺**på'/følgende** *A* - ensuing, following, subsequent.

⁺**på'/føre** *V -te* 1 *merc.* enter, insert. 2 cause, inflict: **p- en utgifter** put sby to expense.

på'/gang *-en* 1 going at, setting to work, tackling (anew); pressing ahead. 2 influx, inrush; pressing; press, throng: **p- av turister** influx of tourists.

på'gangs/mot *-et* go-ahead, push; courage to press forward.

⁺**på'/gikk** *pt of* **-gå**

⁺**på'/gjeldende** *A* - concerned, in question, referred to: **p- år** the year in question; (as noun) **den p-** the party (person) concerned, in question.

⁺**på'/gripe** *V -gre(i)p, -grepet* apprehend, arrest, take into custody.

⁺**på'/gå** *V -gikk, -gått* be in progress, go on.

på'/gående *A* - aggressive, driving, pushing; insistent, persistent.

⁺**på'gåen/het** *-et* aggressiveness, drive, push; determination, persistence.

***på'/halden** *A -e/-i, pl -ne* cf **/holden**

på'/heng *-et* 1 clinging, hanging around. 2 hangers-on, heelers.

⁺**på/heng'elig** *A* - clinging, importunate.

på'hengs/motor *-en* outboard motor.

på'/hitt *-et* 1 impulse, inspiration; idea, thought. 2 fabrication, sth made up.

***på'/hitten** *A -e/-i, pl -hitne* ingenious, inventive, resourceful.

⁺**på'/holden** *A -ent, pl -ne* (=***/halden**) 1: **med p- penn** with sby else holding the pen (for one who cannot sign his own name). 2 [på'/h-] = **påholdende.**

⁺**på'/holdende** *A* - close-fisted, tight; frugal, sparing.

⁺**på'/hvile** *V -te* be incumbent on, lie with, rest with: **ansvaret p-er ham** the responsibility lies with him.

⁺**på'/hør** *-et* hearing, presence: **i hans p-** in front of him, in his p-.

på'k *-en* switch; (short) rod, stick.

⁺**på'/kalle** *V -kalte* 1 call upon, invoke. 2 beseech, entreat, implore. 3 claim, demand: **p- ens oppmerksomhet** attract, get sby's attention.

⁺**på'/kjenne** *V -kjente* 1 *jur.* decide. 2 *tech.* strain, stress.

på'/kjenning *-a/⁺-en* (strong) action, effect, influence; (physical, psychic) strain, stress (**på** on).

⁺**på'/kjære** *V -te jur.* appeal (e.g. a judgment).

⁺**på'/kjøre** *V -te* 1 collide with, hit, run into. 2 cart (earth, sand, etc.) onto (a lot, road, etc.).

⁺**på'/kjørsel** *-elen/-la* being run into (av by).

på'/kledd *A -/*-kledt* (fully) clothed, dressed.

⁺**på'/klederske** *-n* (actresses') dresser.

⁺**på'/kledning** *-en* 1 attire, clothes, dress. 2 dressing.

⁺**på'/kommende** *A* - 1: **i p- tilfelle** in case of need, should the occasion arise. 2 *naut.*: **p- bredde** latitude in (or arrived at); **p- plass** point of destination.

***på'/kostande** *A* - worth spending money on.

⁺**på'/krevd** *A* - (=***/kravd**) called for, requisite, necessary.

På'l *Prn(m)* Paul.

på'/la *pt of* **-legge**

på'lands/vind *-en* onshore wind, sea breeze.

på'le¹ *-n* (=⁺**pæl(e)¹**) pale, pole, stake.

***på'le²** *V -a* (=⁺**pæle²**) drive pales, stakes, etc.; enclose, mark off with pales, poles, stakes.

på'/legg *-et* 1 cheese, meat, spread (for sandwiches). 2 increase, raise, rise (**på in**) (prices, rent, wages, etc.). 3 duty, excise, impost. 4 injunction, order (**om å** to). 5 strengthening piece (e.g. cheek or fish on mast. 6 laying (e.g. of linoleum).

⁺**på'/legge** *V -la, -lagt* (=***-je**) 1 lay on, put on. 2 impose (e.g. taxes) on. 3 enjoin, order; charge. 4 increase, raise (usu. **legge på**).

***på'/leit** *-en* (strong) action, effect, influence; strain, stress.

påli'telig *A* - (=***pålitande**) dependable, trustworthy (friend, worker, etc.); reliable (information, person, watch, etc.).

på'ls/mess(e) *en eccl.* feast of Conversion of St. Paul (25 January).

på'/lydende¹ *-et merc.* face value.

på'/lydende² *A* - specified, stated (sum, value, etc.)

⁺**på'/løpe** *V -løp, -(e)t* esp. *merc.* accrue, accumulate.

på'/melding *-a/⁺-en* signing up (for membership, tickets, etc.).

på'/minne *V -minte* esp. *bibl.* admonish, exhort; remind (**om** about, of).

på'/minning *-a/⁺-en* (=⁺**-else**) admonition, warning.

på'/mønstre *V -a/⁺-et naut.* ship, sign on.

⁺**på'/nøde** *V -de* force on, obtrude, press on: **p- en sine tjenester** force one's services on sby.

⁺**på'/pakning** *-en* 1 *fam.* dressing-down, severe reprimand. 2 packing on.

påpas'selig *A* - (=***-passig**) 1 attentive, careful, watchful (esp. in one's work). 2 careful, thrifty.

⁺**på'/peke** *V -te* 1 call attention to, indicate, point out. 2: **p-ende** *gram.* demonstrative.

⁺**på'/regne** [/reine] *V -et* count on, expect, reckon on.

⁺**på'/rørende** *A* - (as noun) relation, relative: **de p-** the bereaved family, next of kin.

***på'/røyning** *-a* strain, stress.

°**på'sa** *-n* 1 bag. 2: **p-n** (term of endearment) lad, shaver.

⁺**på'/satt** *A* - (=***/sett**) 1 attached, put on: **med p- bajonett** with fixed bayonet. 2 (of fire) incendiary, intentional.

⁺**på'/se** *V -så, -sett* ensure, see to it (at that).

⁺**på'/seilet** *A* - (=***/segla**) 1 *hum.* (very) drunk. 2 *naut.* run afoul of, run into.

på'ske *-a/-en eccl.* 1 Easter. 2 Passover.

⁺**på'ske/aften** *-en* Easter eve.

på'ske/brun *A* brown, tanned from Easter vacation (in the mountains).

på'ske/dag *-en* Easter Sunday: **annen p-** Easter Monday; **første p-** Easter Sunday.

på'ske/egg *-et* Easter egg.

på'ske/ferie *-n* Easter vacation.

på'ske/helg *-a/⁺-en* Easter holiday(s).

på'ske/lam' *-met eccl., hist.* paschal lamb; (of Christ) Paschal Lamb.

***på'ske/laurdag** *-en* cf **/lørdag**

på'ske/lilje *-a/⁺-en bot.* daffodil (Narcissus pseudo-narcissus).

⁺**på'ske/lørdag** *-en* Easter eve.

⁺**på'ske/morgen** [/måren] *-en* (=***/morgon**) Easter morning.

på'ske/trafikk' *-en* Easter traffic (by vacationers).

på'ske/tur *-en* Easter vacation trip (esp. to the mountains to ski).

på'ske/veke *-a* (=⁺**/uke**) Easter week, Holy Week.

***på'/skjøning** *-a* cf **/skjønnelse**

⁺**på'/skjønne** *V -skjønte* acknowledge, appreciate; reward: **p- en med 100 kroner** r- sby with 100 *kroner.*

⁺**på'/skjønnelse** *-n* acknowledgement, appreciation; bonus, reward.

på'/skott *-et* (=***/skot**) excuse, pretence, pretext: **under p- av** on the pretext of.

⁺**på'/skrevet** *A* - labeled, signed: **få sitt pass p-** get a piece of sby's mind, get it good and proper.

på'/skrift *-a/⁺-en* inscription, legend, superscription; address (e.g. on letter).

⁺**på'/skudd** *-et* cf **/skott**

⁺**på'/skynde** *V -te* accelerate, hasten, quicken.

på'/stand *-en/*-et* assertion, contention, theory; claim: **gjøre, nedlegge p- på** *jur.* claim, lay claim to; **p- står mot p-** it's your word against his.

på'/stigende *A* - (as noun) entering passengers, passengers getting on (a bus, train, etc.).

på'/stå *V -stod, -stått* claim, contend, maintain; assert, insist.

påstå'elig *A* - mulish, obstinate, stubborn: **p- på** insistent on (e.g. one's rights).

på'/sydd *A* - sewed on: **p- lomme** patch pocket.

på'/syn *-et/*-a* sight: **i alles p-** in front of everybody, publicly.

⁺**på'/så** *pt of* **-se**

⁺**på'/ta** *V -tok, -tatt* 1 *(refl.)*: **p- seg**

assume (the blame, responsibility, etc.); take upon oneself. 2 *(refl.)*: **p- seg** take on, undertake (a job, task, etc.); **p- seg å** undertake to (see **påtatt**).
+**påta'gelig** *A* - cf **påtakelig**
påta'kelig *A* - palpable, tangible.
på'/tale[1] *-a/-en 1 censure, reprimand, reproof. 2 esp. *jur.* accusation, indictment.
på'/tale[2] *V -a/-te* 1 protest against; criticize. 2 esp. *jur.* bring to court; prosecute.
+**på'tale/myndighet** *-en* (=*/**makt**) prosecuting authority; state's attorneys.
+**på'tale/unnlatelse** *-n jur.* dropping of charges.
+**på'/tatt** *A* - assumed, false, put on (air, name, piety, etc.).
+**på'/tegning** [/teining] *-en* 1 *admin.* endorsement, signature. 2 marking (e.g. with pattern).
på'/tenkt *A* - contemplated, intended, planned.
+**på'/treffe** *V -traff, -truffet* meet (accidentally), run into.
+**på'/trengende** *A* - (=*/**trengjande**) 1 insistent, importunate, obtrusive. 2 pressing, urgent: **p- nødvendig** urgently needed.
+**på'trengen/het** *-en* importunity, intrusiveness, obtrusiveness.
på'/trykk *-et* influence, pressure (**fra** by).
+**på'/tvang** *pt of* **-tvinge**
+**på'/tvinge** *V -tvang, -tvunget* 1 force upon. 2 *(refl.)*: **p- seg** force itself upon.
på'/tår *-en fam.* extra drop, sip (of coffee, tea, etc.).
+**på'/vente** *N*: **i p- av** in expectation (anticipation) of.
*__på'/verke__ *V -a* cf **/virke**
*__på'/verknad__ *-en, pl -er* cf **/virkning**
+**på'/virke** *V -a/-et* (=*/**verke**) act on, affect, influence: **p-et** (slightly) intoxicated, under the influence (of liquor).
+**påvir'kelig** *A* - easy to influence, susceptible.
+**på'/virkning** *-en* (=*/**verking**, */**verknad**) influence: **under p- av** under the i- of.
på'/vise *V -te* 1 *archaic* point out, show. 2 demonstrate, establish, prove. 3 detect (the presence of).
påvi'selig *A* - demonstrable, provable: **uten p- grunn** for no apparent reason.

Q

q [ku'] *-en* (the letter) Q, q (not used in native words).

R

r [ærr'] *-en* (letter) R, r.
R=**reaumur, regina, rex, riktig**
ra' *-et* moraine, ridge.
ra'bagast *-en* devil-may-care fellow, rascal, rogue.
rabal'der *-eret/-ret* crash, noise; hullaballoo, racket, uproar.
rabal'der/møte *-et*, pl *+-r/*-* disorderly meeting; meeting with heated discussion.
+**rabal'sk** *A* - rebellious, refractory.
rabar'bra *-en* rhubarb.
rabar'bra/graut *-en* rhubarb pudding.
rabar'bra/stilk *-en* rhubarb stalk.
rabatt'[1] *-en* border (in a garden); shoulder (of road).
rabatt'[2] *-en* discount (**på** of).
rabb' *-en* (=**rabbe**) stony ridge (usually treeless).
rab'bel *-elet/rablet* scribbling.
rab'bet(e) *A* - (of landscape) ridged.
+**rabbi'ner** *-en, pl -e* (=***rabbi(n), -ar**) rabbi.
rabia't *A* - fanatic, rabid, raving.
rab'le *V -a/+-et* 1 scribble: **r- ned** jot down. 2: **det r-er for ham** he is losing his mind; he is becoming confused.
rabulis't *-en* agitator, demagogue.
rabulis'tisk *A* - agitatorial, demagogic.
race [re's] *-t* (in sports) race.
racer [re'ser] *-en, pl +-e* racer (person, horse, boat, car, etc.).
racer/bil *-en* racing car.
racer/sykkel *-elen, pl -sykler* racing bicycle.
racket [ræk'ket] *-en* (tennis) racket; (pingpong) paddle.
ra'd[1] [*ra'] *-a/+-en* 1 row (**med** of) (e.g. potatoes, trees, seats): **fem dager på r-** five days in a r-; **i rekke og r (i r- og rekke)** lined up in rows; one after the other; ***stande i r-** stand in a r-. 2 string (of beads).
*__ra'd__[2] *A* 1 quick. 2 straight: **r-e vegen** straight ahead.
ra'dar *-en* radar.
+**ra'd/brekke** *V -et* 1 break on the wheel; maim. 2 mangle (a name), murder (a language).
radd' *-en* fellow, rascal.
*__rad'de__ *V -a* chatter, talk foolishly.
*__ra'de__[1] *V -a* chatter.
ra'de[2] *V -a/+-et* arrange in rows, line up.
rade're *V -te* 1 erase. 2 etch.
rade'r/gummi *-en* ink eraser.
rade'ring *-a/+-en* etching.
rade'r/nål *-a* etching needle.
*__ra'd/hendt__ *A* - quick of hand.
radia'l *A* (=**radiell**) radial.
radia'tor *-en, pl -to'rer* radiator.
radiell' *A -elt* cf **radial**
ra'dig *A* - 1 (of road) easy, straight. 2 quick: **det går r- med slåtten** the haying is coming along fine.
radika'l *A* radical; thoroughgoing.
+**radika'ler** *-en, pl -e* (=***-ar**) radical.
radikalise're *V -te* make more radical.
radikalis'me *-n* radicalism.
radikan'd *-en math.* radical.
ra'dio *-en* radio: **jeg hørte det i r-en** I heard it on the r-; **kjøpe r-** buy a r-; **sette på (slå av) r-en** turn on (turn off) the r-; **tale i r-** speak on the r-.
ra'dio/aktiv *A* radioactive.
ra'dio/aktivite't *-en* radioactivity.
ra'dio/anten'ne *-a/+-en* radio antenna.
ra'dio/appara't *-et, pl -/+-er* radio, receiving set.
ra'dio/bil *-en* 1 mobile recording and broadcasting car or truck. 2 bump car, dodgem car (in amusement park).
ra'dio/bo'rd *-et* table for radio.
ra'dio/grammofo'n *-en* radio-phonograph combination.
ra'dio/link *-en* relay (station).
radiolog [-lå'g] *-en* radiologist.
radiologi' *-en* radiology.
ra'dio/mast *-a* radio tower.
+**ra'dio/mottaker** *-en, pl -e* (=***-ar**) radio receiver.
ra'dio/orkes'ter *-eret/-ret, pl -er/+-re* orchestra regularly employed by a radio station.
ra'dio/rør *-et/*-a* (=*/**røyr**) radio tube.
+**ra'dio/sender** *-en, pl -e* (=***-ar**) radio transmitter.
+**ra'dio/taushet** *-en* radio silence.
ra'dio/tea'ter *-eret/-ret, pl -er/+-re* radio theater.
ra'dio/telegrafe're *V -te* send a message by radio.
ra'dio/telegrafis't *-en* radio operator.
ra'dio/telegram' *-met* radiogram.
ra'dium *-et/+-en* radium.
ra'dium/behan'dling *-a/+-en* radium therapy, treatment.
ra'dius *-ien, pl -ier* radius.
*__rad'l__ *-et* chatter, talk.
*__rad'le__ *V -a* chatter, talk.
*__ra'dleg__ *A* - fast, quickly.
+**ra'd/mager** *A -ert, pl -re* emaciated, skin and bones.
*__ra'd/mælt__ *A* - speaking rapidly.
*__radt'__ *Av* cf **ratt**[2]
raff' *A raft pop.* elegant, modish, smart (short for **raffinert**).
raffina'de *-n* loaf (lump) sugar.
raffinement [-mang'] *-et, pl +-er/*-* sophistication, subtlety.
raffine're *V -te* refine (oil, sugar, style).
raffineri' *-et, pl +-er/*-* refinery.
raffine'rt *A* - elegant, refined; sophisticated, subtle.
raf's *-et* careless work.
raf'se *V -a/+-et* 1: **r- til seg** grab. 2: **r- noe fra seg** do sth hastily.
raf't *-a/-en* 1 lath, pole. 2 eave rafter (esp. lower rafter of roof).
raf'te *V -a/+-et* lay rafters.
raf'te/stokk *-en* top log of long side of building.
+**ra'ge** *V -a/-et* jut, project; rise, tower: **r- fram** protrude; **r- i været, r- opp** stand out, tower; **r- opp over**

+ Bokmål; * Nynorsk; ° Dialect.
After letter: ' stress (Acc. 1); ` tone, stress (Acc. 2); · length.
Below letter: . not pronounced.

dominate, overlook; *fig.* excel, surpass.
ra'ge[2] *V -a/+-et* stagger, weave.
ragg' *-et* 1 thick, shaggy hair (e.g. on goat). 2 coarse, bushy hair (e.g. on man).
rag'ge/sokk *-en* cf **ragg/**
rag'get(e) *A* - (of dog, horse, man etc.) having bushy hair, shaggy.
ragg'/sokk *-en* (=**ragge/**) heavy socks made from goat hair or coarse wool.
+**rag'lan/erme** *-t* (=*/**erm**) raglan sleeve.
rag'lan/frakk *-en* raglan coat.
Ragna [rang'na] *Prn(f)*
Ragnar [rang'nar] *Prn(m)*
+**ragna/rokk** [rang'na/] *et* (=***ragnarok**) 1 *myth.* end of the world. 2 catastrophe, Armageddon.
Ragn/hild [rang'n/hill] *Prn(f)*
Ragn/vald [rang'n/vall] *Prn(m)*
ragu' *-en* (=***ragout**) ragout (stew).
raid [rei'd] *-et* raid.
rai'de *-n* string of reindeer and sleds tied together.
rai'/gras *-et bot.* rye grass (Lolium).
ra'jah [also: ra'dsja] *-en* rajah.
ra'je *-a* 1 long stick. 2 tall, thin man.
ra'k[1] *-et* 1 jetsam, junk. 2: **på r-** wandering. 3 (candle) wick.
ra'k[2] *pt of* **reke**[4]
ra'k[3] *A* 1 erect, straight (posture). 2 direct, straight (course, road): **r-t fram** straight ahead.
ra'k[4] *A* (of fish) partially fermented.
ra'ka[1] *N* cf **rake**[2]
ra'ka[2] *A* - : **r- fant** dead broke.
ra'k/aure *-n* Norw. delicacy, consisting of trout which has been partially fermented.
ra'ke[1] *-a* 1 poker (fire). 2 (grass) rake.
ra'ke[2] *N*: **rubb og r-** every scrap.
ra'ke[3] *V -a/-+te* 1 rake: **r- i asken** poke, stir the ashes; **r- til seg** r- in (the money). 2 shave (sby): **r- seg** shave (oneself).
+**ra'ke**[4] *V -et/-te* 1 concern: **det r-er ikke ham** it's none of his business. 2: **r- uklar med** get into a quarrel with.
+**ra'ke**[5] *V -et* cf **rage**[1]
ra'ke/fisk *-en*=**rak/aure**
ra'ke/kniv *-en* razor.
ra'kende *A* - : **r- revnende likegyldig** totally indifferent.
rakett' *-en* rocket.
rakett'/fly *-et* jet, rocket-propelled plane.
+**rakit'is** *-en* cf **rakitt**
rakit'isk *A* - rachitic.
rakitt' *-en* rachitis, rickets.
rakk'[1] *-et* riff-raff, scum: **mannfolk er noe r-** men are no good.
rakk'[2] *pt of* **rekke**[3]
rak'ke[1] *-n* 1 dog; male fox. 2 dog (term of abuse).
rak'ke[2] *-n naut.* truss.
rak'ke[3] *V -a/+-et*: **r- ned på** make derogatory remarks about, run down; **r- til** dirty, soil.
rak'kel *-elet/raklet* 1 poor work. 2 tall, thin person.
+**rak'ker** *-en, pl -e* (=*-**ar**) 1 rascal, scoundrel, villain: **din r-** you rascal. 2: **r-en** the devil; **fy til r-en** what the devil. 3 a card game. 4 *hist.* executioner's assistant; scavenger.
+**rak'ker/fant** *-en* (=*-**ar/**) rascal.
+**rak'ker/knekt** *-en* (=*-**ar/**) rascal, villain, wretch. 2 *hist.* executioner or his assistant.
+**rak'ker/unge** [/onge] *-n* (=*-**ar/**) brat, scamp.
Rak'ke/stad *Pln* twp, Østfold.
rak'l *-et* cf **rakkel**
rak'le[1] *-n bot.* ament, catkin.
rak'le[2] *V -a/+-et* 1 ramble, roam, wander. 2 stroll; walk slowly, unsteadily. 3 bungle, putter.
rak'le/føre *-t* (of roads) heavy going.
rak'le/hane *-n* cock (hybrid of capercaillie and black cock).
rak'let *df of* **rakkel**
rak'le/tre *-et, pl -/+-trær* tree (brush) bearing catkins.
rak'ne *V -a/+-et* 1: **r-, r- opp** (e.g. cloth) unravel; (of boat) break up, come apart. 2 *fig.* fall apart, unravel.
rak'ne/fri *A -tt* run-proof.
ra'k/rygga *A* - (=+**-et**) 1 erect, upright. 2 *fig.* courageous, upright.
rak'st[1] *-en* (=**rakster**) 1 raking. 2 grass, hay, straw.
***ra'kst**[2] *pt of* **rekast**
rak'ste/kulle *-a* woman who rakes hay.
rak'ster *-en* cf **rakst**[1]
+**rak'te** *pt of* **rekke**[4]
+**ra'k/ørret** *-en* cf **/aure**
***ra'l** *-et* talk, gossip.
***ra'le** *V -a* chatter, talk.
ralje're *V -te*: **r- over** jeer at, make fun of, scoff at.
***rall'** *-et* rambling, roving.
ral'lar *-en* migrant worker (esp. on RR construction); tramp; *(pop.)* gandy dancer.
ral'lar/vise *-a/+-en* ballad (composed or sung) by **rallar.**
ral'le *V -a/+-et* 1 (death) rattle. 2 roam, tramp. 3 chatter, talk.
ral'le/lyd *-en* rale, (bronchial) rattle.
ram'[1] *-en* paw (of bear).
ram'[2] *-en* 1 gable. 2 attic room, loft.
ram'[3] *N* blow, hit, stroke: **få r- på** hit home, get in a blow at.
ram'[4] *A -t, pl -me* 1 acrid, pungent, strong (taste, smell). 2 firm, sincere: **det er r-me alvor** it is in dead earnest; **for r-me alvor** for keeps, in earnest. 3 rough, strong.
ra'ma/skrik *-et* outcry (of indignation), protest: **det ble et r-** there was a hue and cry.
ram/bukk [ram'/bokk] *-en* 1 pile driver. 2 battering ram.
ram'le *V -a/+-et* 1 clatter, rattle, rumble. 2 collapse, fall (with a crash), tumble: **r- over ende** fall; **r- sammen** cave in, crash.
ram'let *df of* **rammel**
ram'me[1] *-a/+-en* 1 border, frame (of door, picture, structure); rim (of glasses); setting (of play, story); box (in newspaper). 2 framework, scope: **innenfor r-n av denne organisasjon** within the f- of this organization.
ram'me[2] *V -a/+-et/+ramte*: **r- inn** frame (a picture).
ram'me[3] *V -a/+-et/+ramte* ram (down), drive (in) (e.g. a pile).
+**ram'me**[4] *V -a/+-et/+ramte* 1 hit, strike (object, target); hit off (likeness): **r- kraftig** strike home. 2 (of a calamity) befall, overtake: **r-et av sykdom** struck down by illness. (see also **r-ende**).
ram'mel *-elen/-elet/ramlet* clatter, crash, noise.
ram'me/list *-a* 1 molding. 2 frame (in beehive).
+**ram'mende** *A* - 1 incisive, pointed, telling (criticism, remark); pertinent, to the point. 2: **r- svart** absolutely black.
ram'me/sag *-a* gang mill (saw frame with several blades).
ram'n *-en zool.* raven (Corrux corax).
ram'ne/krok *-en* hole, one-horse town, Podunk.
ram'ne/mor *-a/+-en, pl +-mødre/*-mødrer* negligent (unnatural) mother.
Ram'/nes *Pln* twp, Vestfold.
ram'n/svart *A* - black as a raven, coal black.
ram'/ost [/ost] *-en dial.* sharp cheese (=**gammelost**).
ram'p *-en* 1 rabble, riff-raff, scum. 2 boor; common, vulgar person.
ram'pe *+-n/*-a* 1 ramp, platform. 2 front edge of stage floor (footlights).
ram'pe/feber *-en* stagefright.
+**ram'pe/gutt** *-en* rude, uncouth boy; brat.
ram'pe/lys *-et* footlights: **i r-et** in the limelight.
ram'pe/strek *-en* (act of) vandalism.
ram'pet(e) *A* - ill-bred, rude, uncouth.
rampone're *V -te* damage.
ram's[1] *-en bot.* ramson (Allium ursinum).
ram's[2] *N*: **på r-** by heart.
ram'/salt *A* - 1 heavily salted. 2 *fig.* caustic (remark), salty (joke, story).
ram'/salte *V -a/+-et* salt heavily.
ram'se[1] *-a/+-en* jingle, rigmarole.
ram'se[2] *V -a/+-et*: **r- opp** rattle off, reel off.
ram'/skrike *V infl* as **skrike**[2]
ram'/sterk *A* (of coffee) exceptionally strong; (of food) hot, pungent.
ram'/svart *A* - coal-black.
ra'n *-et* 1 robbery (**på** of); *fig.* rape (e.g. of Europe). 2 booty, loot.
Ra'na *Pln* twp, Nordland.
ran'd *-a/+-en, pl render* 1 boundary, edge (of cliff, horizon), outline; rim: **i den første r- av skumringen** at the beginning of twilight. 2 *fig.* brink: **på vanviddets r-** on the b- of madness. 3 stripe (in material, of pattern); brim (of bottle, pail); groove (of ski); welt (of shoe).
Ran'da/berg *Pln* twp, Rogaland.
+**ran'd/bemer'kning** *-en* marginal note.
***ran'de**[1] *-n* narrow ridge (esp. on mountain side).
ran'de[2] *V -a/+-et* 1 edge, rim (e.g. coin, shoe): **det r-s** it is dawn. 2 stripe.
Ran'de/sund *Pln* twp, Vest-Agder.
ran'det(e) *A* - 1 edged, rimmed. 2 striped.
Ran'di *Prn(f)*
Ran'ds/fjo'rd *Pln* lake, southern Norway.
ran'd/stat *-en* border state (esp. the Baltic countries after WW I).
ran'd/sydd [also rann'/] *A -/*-sytt* welted.
***ra'ne**[1] *-n* 1 point (of land), protruding cliff. 2 pole, tall and narrow tree. 3 tall, thin man.
ra'ne[2] *V -a/-te* 1 rob (person, institution). 2 steal: **r- til seg makten** usurp the power.
rang'[1] *-en* 1 *mil.* rank: **ha r- som** have the r- of. 2 rank, station, status (in social order): **av annen r-** second class; **fiolinist av r-** eminent violinist; **gjøre en r-en stridig** contend for precedence, be a close competitor.
***rang'**[2] *A* cf **vrang**
***rang'e**[1] *-a* cf **vrange**
+**rang'e**[2] *V -a/-et* 1: **hesten r-r det hvite i øynene** the horse shows the whites of his eyes. 2: **r- av (seg) klærne** pull clothing off inside out.
rang'el[1] *-elen, pl -ler* bender, binge, carouse: **gå på r-** go on a spree, paint the town red.
rang'el[2] *-elet/-let, pl +-ler/*-* lanky person.
rangere [rangsje're] *V -te* 1 arrange, range (in place). 2 rank: **musikken r-er over teksten** the music outranks the text. 3 shunt, switch (train).
ranger/stasjo'n [rangsje'r/] *-en* switchyard.
+**ran'g/følge** *-n* order of precedence, ranking.
rang'le[1] *-a* 1 rattle (toy). 2 *archeol.* device of large and small rings fastened together used as sleigh bells.
rang'le[2] *V -a/+-et* 1 carouse, celebrate, go on a spree (a bender). 2 stagger, walk unsteadily. 3 roam, stroll, wander.
rang'le[3] *V -a/+-et* jingle (bells, keys); rattle (bones).
rang'le/fant *-en* drunkard, tippler.
***rang'leg** *A* - incorrect, wrong.
rang'le/pave *-n* drunkard, tippler.
***rang'/læte** *-a* obstinacy, waywardness.
rang'/orden *-en* hierarchy, order of rank.
+**rang's/forskjell'** *-en* (=*/**skilnad**)

difference in rank (of social station in life).
rang'/snudd *A* -/*-*snutt* 1 backwards, turned inside out, twisted. 2 intractable, perverse.
rang's/perso'n *-en* person of rank.
rang'/stige *-n* hierarchy; social ladder.
***rang'/strupe** *-n* cf **vrang/**
***rang'/svæv** *A* sleepy at the wrong time; insomniac.
rang'/søles *Av* counterclockwise.
ran'k *A* 1 erect, straight, upright (carriage of body, stem, tree, tower). 2 *fig.* proud, self-assured: **en r- personlighet** an independent personality, one who holds his head high. 3. *naut.* crank, crank-sided, tender (of ship inclined to heel over).
ran'ke[1] +-*n*/*-*a* 1 *bot.* bine, vine; tendril; runner. 2 vine-like ornamentation.
ran'ke[2] *N*: **ride, ride r-** ride a cock-horse to Banbury cross (nursery rhyme spoken while dandling child on one's knee).
+**ran'ke**[3] *V* -*a*/-*et* straighten: **r- seg (opp)** straighten up.
ran'ke[4] *V* -*a*/+-*et*: **r- seg** grow (like a vine), twine, wreath.
ranking/liste [ræ'nking/] -*a* list of winners (in order of rank).
+**ran'k/vokst** *A* - erect, straight.
***rann'** *pt of* **renne**[1]
ran'/sake *V* -*a*/+-*et*/+-*te* 1 ransack, search (house, ship, woods, one's heart, etc.). 2 look through, study (place, problem, situation).
ran'sel -*elen, pl* -*ler* knapsack, schoolbag (worn on back).
ra'ns/mann -*en, pl* -*menn*/*-*menner* bandit, robber.
+**ran't** *pt of* **renne**[1], **rinne**
***ran'te** -*n* knoll, ridge.
ranun'kel -*elen, pl* -*ler* *bot.* buttercup, crowfoot (Ranunculus).
ra'n/væring -*en* person from Rana.
ra'p[1] -*en* wild grass (Poa pratensis).
ra'p[2] -*en*/-*et* belch.
ra'p[3] -*et* 1: **stjerne/r-** falling star. 2 earthquake, landslide.
***ra'pe**[1] -*n* esp. dwarf birch found in mountain regions (Betula noma).
ra'pe[2] *V* -*a*/-*te* belch.
ra'pe[3] *V* -*a*/-*te* 1 (of stars) fall, (of earth, rock) slide, shift (under one's foot), (of foothold) slip. 2: **r- for vettet** lose one's mind. *3 rush: **r- av stad på villska r-** off wildly (Vesaas).
***ra'p/gras** -*et* meadow grass (Poa), spear grass (Poa rigida).
rapp'[1] -*en*/-*et* blow (of stick); cut, flick (of whip); rap (of ruler).
rapp'[2] -*en*/-*et*: **på røde r-n** at once, instantly, this minute.
rapp'[3] -*en* *obs.* (slang) rucksack.
rapp'[4] *A* *rapt* fast, fleet, quick: **r- på tungen** glib, quick of tongue; *(pop.)* quick on the trigger.
rapp'[5] *I* quack (of duck).
rap'pe[1] *V* -*a*/+-*et*: **r- til** cut, lash (with whip); rap, strike (with stick).
rap'pe[2] *V* -*a*/+-*et*: **r- seg** be quick about it, hurry, hustle.
rap'pe[3] *V* -*a*/+-*et*: **r- til seg** grab, snatch, steal.
rap'pe[4] *V* -*a*/+-*et* *tech.* roughcast.
rap'pe[5] *V* -*a*/+-*et* quack.
+**rap'pen/skralle** -*n* fishwife, scold, shrew.
rapp'/føtt *A* - (=/**fota**, +/**fotet**) fleet, light-footed, swift of foot.
rapp'/høne -*a, pl* -*høns* *zool.* grouse, partridge (Perdix perdix).
rapp'/kjefta *A* - fast talking, glib, smooth (of speech).
rappor't -*en* 1 report: **avlegge (gi) r-** give a r-. 2 contact, rapport: **være i r- med** be in r- with. 3 (of textiles) repeat.
rapporte're *V* -*te* 1 report. 2 (of hunting dog) report game.
rapportø'r -*en* 1 rapporteur, reporter. 2 hunting dog.

rapp'/tunga [/tonga] *A* - (=+-**et**) glib of tongue.
rap's -*en* *bot.* rape (Brassica napus).
rap'se *V* -*a*/+-*et* filch, pilfer.
+**rap'seri** -*et* petty larceny, pilfering.
rapsodi' -*en* rhapsody.
rapso'disk *A* - rhapsodic.
rap't *nt of* **rapp**[4]
rap'tus -*en* 1 *med.* fit, seizure, spell. 2 *fig.* sudden desire to do sth; craze; fancy, notion, passing mood.
ra'r *A* 1 odd, quaint, queer; strange: **r- av seg** strange in manner. 2 (usu. with negatives) good, remarkable: **det er ikke r-e greiene** it's not much good; **det står ikke så r-t til med dem** they do not feel very well, they are not well off; **få noe rart** (children's language) get a treat.
ra'ring -*en* odd, quaint, queer person; character, eccentric; *(pop.)* nut, oddball.
rarite't -*en* curio; curiosity, rarity.
ra's -*et* 1 avalanche, landslide (**av** of), snowslide. 2 sudden and violent gust of air.
ra'se[1] -*n* 1 *anthro.* race. 2 *zool.* blood, breed, stock; breeding. 3 *fig.* breed, kind of person: **en underlig r-** a strange breed.
ra'se[2] *V* -*a*/+-*te* 1 be furious, fume, rage; rave (see also **r-ende**). 2 *fig.* (of fever, plague, war) rage. 3 (of river) rush, sweep over; tear along, (of storm) wreak havoc: **han r-te avsted** he rushed madly off; **r- ut** subside, spend itself; **ungdommen r-er** youth must have its fling. 4 fall, roll, slide (e.g. in avalanche): **det r-er av taket** snow is sliding off the roof; **r- sammen** cave in, collapse; **jernbanen r-er ut** an earthslide is undermining the RR; **r- utfor** rumble down.
ra'se/ansikt -*et, pl* +-*er*/*- aristocratic (distinguished, thoroughbred) face; handsome, striking face (often with an exotic cast).
ra'se/blanding -*a*/+-*en* racial mixture.
ra'se/dyr -*et* pedigreed, purebred animal; thoroughbred.
ra'se/fordom [/fårrdåmm] -*men*/*-*en* race prejudice.
ra'se/hat -*et* race hatred.
ra'se/merke -*t, pl* +-*r*/*- distinctive feature, trait of a breed or race.
ra'sende *A* - 1 angry, furious, mad: **se r- på** look daggers at. 2 *(adv.)* awfully, terribly: **r- forelsket** madly in love.
rase're *V* -*te* clear (an area), level (with the ground), raze.
raseri' -*et* fury, rage.
+**raseri'/anfall** -*et* fit, paroxysm of rage.
ra's/galen *A* +-*ent, pl* -*ne* insane, raving mad.
rasjo'n -*en* ration.
rasjona'l *A* rational: **r- størrelse** *math.* r- quantity.
rasjonalise're *V* -*te* *psych.* rationalize. 2 *merc.* make more efficient (by application of scientific principles).
rasjonalise'rings/eksper't -*en* efficiency expert.
rasjonalis'me -*n* rationalism.
rasjonalis't -*en* rationalist.
rasjonalis'tisk *A* - rationalistic.
rasjonell' *A* -*elt* 1 rational. 2 efficient.
rasjone're *V* -*te* ration.
rasjone'rings/kort -*et* ration card.
ras'k[1] -*et* trash: **rusk og r-** odds and ends.
ras'k[2] *A* 1 fast, quick, rapid: **i r-t trav** at a brisk pace; **r- på foten** light of foot, agile; **r- på hånden** deft.
ras'ke[1] *V* -*a*/+-*et* *1 dig, mess, rake (in refuse). 2: **r- sammen** scrape together, collect hastily. 3: **r- til seg** snatch, steal.
ras'ke[2] *V* -*a*/+-*et* hurry: **r- på** hurry up; **r- noe unna** get sth done hurriedly.
ras'ke/skog -*en* scrub forest.

ras'ke/slått -*en* second haying, poor hay harvest.
+**ras'k/het** -*en* alacrity, promptness.
ras'le *V* -*a*/+-*et* (=**ratle**) 1 (of chain, snake, wheels) rattle. 2 (of knitting needles) click; clink, jangle; (of metals) ring. 3 (of leaves, paper, rain, wind, water) rustle, swish; (of jewelry, Christmas tree ornaments) tinkle.
Ras'mus *Prn (m)*
ras'p[1] -*a* 1 coarse file, rasp. 2 grater. 3 *hum.* fig wine. 4 *vet.* malanders.
ras'p[2] -*et* 1 rasping. 2 *(pl)* bread crumbs. 3 *zool.* (fish) scales.
ras'pe *V* -*a*/+-*et* 1 grate, rasp (potatoes, hooves). 2 make a rasping sound. 3 strip, tear: **r- løv** strip leaves; **r- med seg** snatch, strip off; **r- på seg klærne** tear into, throw on one's clothes.
ras'pe/ball -*en* potato dumplings.
ras'pe/tunge [/tonge] -*a* scold, sharp-tongued person.
***ras't**[1] -*a* 1 field, meadow, piece of land (esp. **heim/r-, ut/r-**). 2 row (e.g. of plants).
ras't[2] -*en* 1 break, halt, rest: **hun hadde ikke r- eller ro** she could get no peace; **holde r-** call a halt, take a breather, a rest. 2 (in steelmill) bosh.
***ras't**[3] -*et* stretch (of road one can walk without rest). 2 difficult piece of road.
ras'te *V* -*a*/+-*et* rest, stop.
ras'ter -*eret*/+-*eren, pl* -/+-*rer* screen (in photoengraving).
ras't/laus *A* (=+/**løs**) fidgety, restless.
+**ras't/løs/het** -*en* (=***rastløyse**) restlessness.
ra't -*et* trash, waste.
rat'ata -*en* *hum.* behind, duff, fanny.
ra'te[1] -*n* 1 installment: **kjøpe på r-** buy on i-. 2 price, rate (for freight).
ra'te[2] *V* -*a*/+-*et* discard, reject.
ra'te/beta'ling -*a*/+-*en* installment plan.
+**ra'te/salg** -*et* (=*/**sal**) selling on the installment plan.
ra'te/vis *A* - on the installment plan.
ratifikasjo'n -*en* ratification.
ratifise're *V* -*te* ratify.
rat'le *V* -*a*/+-*et* cf **rasle**
***rat'le/orm** -*en* *zool.* rattlesnake (Crotalus and Sistrurus).
rat'sj *I* rip (sound of cloth tearing).
ratt'[1] -*et* (steering) wheel.
+**ratt'**[2] *Av* (=***radt**) 1 easily, lightly, quickly: **like r-** anyway, just as well. 2 direct, straight: **r- fram** straight ahead. 3 absolutely, quite: **det er r- forbi** it's all over.
ratt'/kjelke -*n* sled equipped with steering wheel.
ratt'/lås -*en*/-*et* steering wheel lock.
°**rau'** *A* -*tt* cf **rød**
***rau'd**[1] *pt of* **ry**[3]
rau'd[2] *A* cf **rød**
***rau'd/bete** -*a*/-*en* cf **rød/**
***rau'de**[1] -*n* 1 blush. 2 yolk.
***rau'de**[2] *V* -*a* appear red: **det r-er på marka** the field is red (with berries).
***Rau'de/havet** *Pln* cf **røde/**
rau'd/eik -*a* *bot.* red oak (Quercus rubra).
***Rau'de/krossen** *Prn* cf **Røde Kors**
rau'd/fisk -*en* *zool.* rosefish (Sebastes marinus).
rau'd/furu -*a* *bot.* red pine, Norway pine (Pinus resinosa).
+**rau'd/hals** -*en* *zool.* red-breasted wagtail (Sylvia rubecula).
***rau'd/håra** *A* - cf **rød/håret**
rau'd/knapp -*en* *bot.* red scabious (Knautia arvensis).
rau'd/kolle -*a* red breed of cows (common in Eastern Norway).

+ Bokmål; * Nynorsk; ° Dialect.
After letter: ' stress (Acc. 1); ' tone, stress (Acc. 2); · length.
Below letter: . not pronounced.

*rau'dleg A - cf rødlig
*rau'd/leitt A - cf rød/lett
*rau'd/leta A - cf rød/lett
rau'd/mose [/måse] -n bot. reddish-colored marsh moss (Sphagnum).
*rau'd/nakke -n zool. pochard (Aythya ferina).
*rau'dne V -a cf rødme[2]
rau'd/rev -en zool. red fox (Canus vulpes).
*rau'd/russ -en cf rød/
rau'd/spette -a zool. flounder (Pluronectes platersa).
*rau'd/strupe -n cf rød/
rau'd/syre -a bot. red sorrel (Rumex).
rau'd/åt(e) -a zool. red copepod (Calanus finmarchensis).
rau'k[1] -en/-et shock (of grain); stack (of leaves, peat).
rau'k[2] pt of ryke
rau'ke V -a/+-et shock, stack.
Rau'/land Pln twp, Telemark.
Rau'ma Pln river in Romsdal.
*rau'n -a/-en cf rogn[1]
rau's A (=*raust[2]) 1 generous, munificent (med with). *2: r- til å good at.
rau'se V -a/+-te 1 plunge, pour, tip: r- ut slide, slip. 2 dash, run. 3 work carelessly. 4: r- med penger throw one's money around.
*rau'st[1] -et cf røst[2]
*rau'st[2] A - cf raus
*rau'ste V -a raise a roof.
*rau'st/leik -en 1 generosity. 2 skill.
rau't[1] -et/+-en mooing sound (of cow, walrus); bellow, roar (of bull, herd).
rau't[2] pt of ryte
rau'te V -a/+-et (of cow) low, moo; (of ox, also) bellow, roar.
rau'v -a pop. behind, rear, seat: arse: hver gang noe er riktig moro, blir en slått i r-a every time anything is really fun, one gets a kick in the butt (Sandemose).
ra'v[1] -en/+-et dried fat, flesh from around fins of halibut.
ra'v[2] -et amber.
ra'v[3] Av (intensive): r- ruskende gal stark raving mad.
*ra'vande Av cf ravende
*ra've[1] -n 1 rag, torn clothing. 2 strip.
+ra've[2] V -a/-et lurch, reel, stagger.
ra'vende Av (=*ravande): r- gal completely mad; r- mørkt pitch-dark.
+ra'v/gal A (=*/galen) 1 absurd, crazy. 2 absolutely wrong (e.g. answer).
ra'v/gul A amber yellow.
rav'l -et trash.
rav'le V -a/+-et 1 chatter. *2 reel, stagger.
+rav'n -en cf ramn
+rav'ne/krok -en cf ramne/
+rav'ne/mor -a/-en cf ramne/
rayon [rai'ån] -et rayon.
razzia [ras'sia] -en raid.
rdl=+riksdaler/*-ar
+re' V -dde cf reie[2]
reagen's -en chem. reagent.
reagen's/glas -et (=+/glass) chem. test tube.
reagen's/rør -et/*-a (=*/røyr) chem. test tube.
reage're V -te 1 chem., psych. react (med with, på to). 2 react, respond (overfor, på to); take action (mot against).
reaksjo'n -en 1 chem., psych. reaction. 2 reaction (mot against); pol. reactionary movement, party, trend.
reaksjonæ'r A reactionary.
reak'tor -en tech. reactor.
rea'l A 1 actual, real: r-e verdier jur. concrete values; r-e fag educ. scientific subjects. 2 [re'al] honest, worthy (of act or person); real, regular: en r- dram a whale of a drink; et r-t mannfolk a regular he-man.
rea'l/artium [/artsium] -en artium degree with specialization in scientific subjects (realfag).
rea'l/fag -et scientific subjects (incl. mathematics).
rea'l/gymna's -et gymnasium emphasizing scientific subjects.
rea'lia pl realia (objects used as illustrations in teaching).
realisa'bel A -elt, pl -le 1 practicable. 2 merc. realizable e.g. assets.
realisasjo'n -en 1 carrying out, realization (of plans). 2 merc. sale, selling (av of).
+realisasjo'ns/salg -et (=*/sal) clearance sale.
realise're V -te 1 carry out, realize (hopes, plans). 2 merc. sell (for cash): r- alle sine eiendeler sell all one's properties (often at reduced price); r- sin handel liquidate one's business.
realis'me -n realism.
realis't -en 1 realist. 2 educ. one studying or holding a degree in science.
realis'tisk A - realistic.
realite't -en 1 reality: i r-en in r-; r-er facts. 2 essence, kernel: sakens r- the facts of the case, the heart of the matter.
+realite'ts/avgjørelse -n (=*/avgjerd, */avgjersle) 1 adm., jur. decision on a point of substance. 2 final decision.
realite'ts/behan'dle V -a/+-et jur. consider the substance of a case.
rea'l/kommenta'r -en commentary, notes (on content of a text).
rea'l/linje -a/+-en (=*/line) educ. natural science curriculum (in gymnasium).
rea'l/lønn -a/+-en (=*/løn) econ. real wages (calculated acc. to price level).
rea'l/opply'sning *-a/+-en, pl *-ar information on a point of fact.
+rea'l/poli'tiker -en, pl -e (=*-ar) practical politician; power politician.
rea'l/skole -n school following grammar school and preceding gymnasium; now incorporated in latter as its first two years, plus a third year (ages ab. 14—16).
rea'l/verdi' -en (=*/verd(e)) true value (e.g. of property); (pl) physical assets.
re'/assuranse [-ang'se] -n reinsurance.
re'/assure're V -te reinsure.
reaumur [reåmy'r] N Réaumur (thermometer with freezing point at 0° and boiling point at 80°): 10 grader r- ten degrees R- (ab. 60° F).
rebell' -en rebel.
rebel'sk A - rebellious.
re'bus -en rebus.
+re'bus/løp -et race in which the laps (stages) are indicated by a rebus (usu. published in newspapers).
recensen't -en critic, reviewer.
recense're V -te 1 review (a book). 2 censure.
recensjo'n -en review (av of).
recess' -en hist. recess, statute, treaty.
recessiv [res'sesiv] A biol. recessive.
rechts [rekj'ts, rek's] A - 1 tech. (of screw thread) right-handed. 2 (adv.) (on the) right.
recipien't -en 1 chem. receiver (of distilled product). 2 phys. receiver (of air pump).
rec'tum en rectum.
re'd[1] -en harbor, roads.
*re'd[2] -et crest of hill.
+re'd[3] pt of ri
red.=redaktør(en); redaksjon(en)
redaksjo'n -en 1 editing, editorship: under r- av edited by. 2 draft, version: en ny r- a new draft (redaction). 3 editorial staff, editors. 4 editorial office(s).
redaksjonell' A -elt editorial.
redaksjo'ns/artik'kel -elen, pl -artikler editorial.
redaksjo'ns/sekretæ'r -en assistant editor.
redaktø'r -en editor.
redd' A - 1 afraid, frightened, scared: er du r- meg? are you afraid of me?; r- av seg timorous. 2: r- for concerned about; han er r- for sakene sine he is careful with his things; jeg er r- for at det går galt I'm afraid things will go badly.
*red'dast V -ast cf reddes
red'de V -a/-et rescue, salvage, save (fra from): r- livet save one's (own) life; r- seg escape, save oneself.
+red'des V -edes, -es (=*reddast) be frightened (for of).
redd'/hare -n cowardly, timorous person: din r- (you) fraidycat, scaredy-cat.
redd'/hug -en cowardice, fear, respect.
red'dik -en bot. radish (Raphanus).
+redd'/som' A -t, pl -me awful, frightful, ghastly.
+re'de[1] en 1: gjøre r- for explain, give an account of, review; account for (e.g. money). 2: få (skaffe seg) r- på discover, find out, get wind of; ha god r- på know all about; ha r- på know about; holde r- på keep track of.
+re'de[2] -t cf reir
+re'de[3] V -et 1 lit. comb (e.g. one's hair), make (e.g. bed); make ready, prepare: som man r-er, så ligger man you've made your bed, so you can lie in it. 2: r- ut (en sak) clarify, explain (an affair).
+re'de[4] A - prepared, ready, willing (til to): ha et svar på r- hånd have a ready answer, not be at a loss; holde seg r- be in readiness; r- penger ready cash, money.
+re'de/bon' A archaic ready, willing (til to).
+re'de/gjøre V -gjorde, -gjort: r- for clarify, explain.
+re'de/gjørelse -n account, explanation, statement (for of).
+re'delig A - fair, honest, straightforward: ærlig og r- fair and square; (adv.) really and truly.
+re'delig/het -en honesty, integrity.
+re'der -en, pl -e (=*reiar) shipowner.
+rederi' -et, pl -er 1 shipping company, firm of shipowners. 2 shipping business.
+re'dig A - 1 easy, simple: r- mann easy man to deal with. 2 clear (air).
redige're V -te 1 edit. 2 draft, formulate.
redingot [red'inggått] -en frock coat.
+red'ning -en 1 escape, rescue (from danger, death). 2 hope, resource; deliverance, salvation: den eneste r- the only way out.
+red'nings/aksjo'n -en rescue (expedition).
+red'nings/anker -eret/-ret last hope, resort.
+red'nings/belte -t, pl +-r/*- life belt, preserver.
+red'nings/bluss -et flare.
+red'nings/bøye -n life buoy.
+red'nings/båt -en lifeboat; rescue boat (for lifesaving, patrolling coast).
+red'nings/dåd -en heroic rescue, lifesaving exploit.
+red'nings/flåte -n 1 life raft. 2 fleet of ships especially constructed for and engaged in rescue operations.
+red'nings/line -a lifeline.
+red'nings/løs A lost, without hope: r-t fortapt irretrievably lost.
+red'nings/mann -en, pl -menn deliverer, lifesaver, rescuer.
+red'nings/medal'je -n lifesaving medal.
+red'nings/planke -n 1 plank used by drowning person to save self. 2 fig. last hope, resort.
+red'nings/selskap -et organization engaged in rescue operations.
+red'nings/skøyte -a rescue ship.
+red'nings/vest -en life jacket, life vest.
re'/doble V -a/+-et redouble (in bridge).
red'sel -elen, pl -ler (=*redsle) 1

fear, horror, terror (**for** of): **krigens r-ler** the horrors of war. 2 fright, monstrosity, nightmare.

+red'sels/full *A* awful, frightful, terrible; dreadful, frightening: **en r-seng** a vile bed; **en r- håndskrift** an abominable hand.

+red'sels/gjerning *-en* frightful, horrible deed.

+red'sels/herredømme *-t* reign of terror.

+red'sels/kabinett· *-et* chamber of horrors.

+red'sel/slagen *A -ent, pl -ne* horror-, terror-, panic-stricken, terrified.

+re'd/skap *-en/-et, pl -er* (=***rei/**) 1 equipment, implement, tool (**til** for); (surgical) instrument; (hunting) gear; (fishing) tackle; (kitchen) appliance, utensil; *physiol.* organ. 2 *fig.* (of person) instrument, tool: **bruke en som r-** use sby as a cat's paw.

+re'dskaps/bu *-a* tool shed.

+re'dskaps/kasse *-a/-en* toolbox.

+re'dskaps/skur *-et* tool shed.

***red'sle** *-a* cf **redsel**

reduksjo'n *-en* reduction (**av** of); conversion (from one set of values to another).

reduksjo'ns/tabell· *-en adm., merc.* conversion table.

redupliseʹre *V -te gram.* reduplicate.

reduse're *V -te* reduce (**til** to): **r-t** down-at-the-heel, shabby.

reell' *A -elt* 1 real: **det r-e** material values. 2 honest, sincere: **ha r-e hensikter** have honorable intentions.

refekto'rium *-iet, pl -ium/+-ier eccl.* refectory.

referanse [referang'se] *-n* reference: **ha gode r-r** have good r-s.

refera't *-et, pl -/+-er* account (**av** of), report; summary (of book): **r- av et møte** minutes of a meeting.

referen'dum *-et* referendum.

referen't *-en* reporter (e.g. of a meeting); stenographer (e.g. in legislature).

refere're *V -te* 1 cover (news), report (a meeting). 2 refer (**til** to): **dette r-r seg til** this refers to. 3: **r-ende** objective, merely reporting.

reflek's *-en* 1 reflection (of light). 2 *physiol.* reflex.

+reflek's/beve'gelse *-n* reflex action.

ref'leksiv *A gram.* reflexive.

refleksjo'n *-en* reflection.

reflektan't *-en* applicant; prospective buyer.

reflekte're *V -te* 1 *phys.* reflect. 2 reflect (**over** upon), think (about). 3 *merc.* consider: **r- på tilbudet** consider the offer.

reflekte'rt *A* - reflective; philosophical.

reflek'tor *-en* reflector; *astron.* reflecting telescope.

refor'm *-a/+-en* reform (**av, i** of).

reformasjo'n *-en* 1 change, reformation. 2 **R-en** *hist.* the Reformation.

reformasjo'ns/tid *-a/+-en* period of reformation.

reforma'tor *-en* 1 reformer. 2 *hist.* leader in the Reformation.

reforme're *V -te* reform.

reforme'rt *A* - 1 reformed. 2 *hist.* Reformed.

refor'm/iver *-en* reforming zeal.

refor'm/vennlig *A* - reformist.

refraksjo'n *-en* refraction.

refreng' *-et, pl -/+-er* refrain.

+refreng'/sanger *-en, pl -e* (=***/songar**) popular singer (usu. also member of orchestra).

ref'se *V -a/+-et/-te* castigate, chastise, punish; admonish, reprimand, scold.

+ref'selse *-n* (=***-ing**) reprimand; *mil.* disciplinary action, punishment.

+ref'ser *-en, pl -e* (=***-ar**) castigator, chastiser.

***ref'sing** *-A* cf **refselse**

refu'ge *-n* traffic island.

refunde're *V -te* refund; reimburse.

refuse're *V -te* refuse (to receive), reject (book, painting).

refusjo'n *-en merc.* refund, reimbursement.

refyse're *V -te* cf **refusere**

reg.=**register, registrert**

regale're *V -te* 1 regale: **r- seg (over)** enjoy. 2 treat (**med** with).

+rega'lier pl (=***regalia**) regalia.

regat'ta *-en, pl *-er* regatta.

re'gel *-elen, pl -ler* rule (**for** for): **gjøre seg til r-** make a r- of; **et unntak fra r-en** an exception to the r-; **i r-en, som r-** as a rule.

re'gel/bunden *A +-et, pl -ne* 1 regular. 2: **r- geistlig** r- clergy.

re'gel/fast *A* - regular.

re'gel/laus *A* (=**+/løs**) irregular, unruly.

+re'gel/messig *A* - regular (e.g. features, habits): **r- puls** normal pulse; **r- tilbakevendende** returning at regular intervals.

+re'gelmessig/het *-en* regularity.

re'gel/rett *A* - regular; orderly.

regenere're *V -te* regenerate.

regen't *-en* ruler, sovereign; regent.

regen't/skap *-et* regency.

regi [resji'] *-en* direction, production, staging (of film, stage production): **i Max Reinhardts r-** under M- R-'s direction.

regime [resji'me] 1 government, regime, rule. 2 *med.* regimen (regulations related to diet).

regimen't *-et, pl -/+-er mil.* regiment.

regimen'te *-t* government rule.

regio'n *-en* region, *fig.* **de høyere r-er** a high intellectual plane; **de nedre r-** the lower floors (of a building), basement.

regiona'l *A* regional.

regiona'l/plan *-en* regional plan.

regissere [resjisse're] *V -te* direct (esp. a film).

regissør [resjissø'r] *-en* director (of film, play).

regis'ter *-eret/-ret, pl -er/+-re* 1 (alphabetical) index, table of contents (in book); record book, register (e.g. of laws); census (of births and deaths), directory (of voters). 2 *mus.* range, register (of instrument, voice); **et stort r-** a wide register (also *fig.*). 3 *mus.* stop (of organ). 4 *typog.* register (line esp. of pages back to back). 5 gamut (of expression, feeling).

regis'ter/bind *-et* index volume (of set, series of books).

regis'ter/tonn *-et naut.* register ton (measure of internal capacity of ships = 100 cu. ft.).

registre're *V -te* 1 register; take inventory; keep census records. 2 notice, take note of: **r- med interesse** note with interest.

registre'rings/appara't *-et phys.* recorder, registering apparatus.

registre'rings/pliktig *A - naut.* obliged to register.

regje're *V -te* 1 govern, reign, rule, (**over** over): **la seg r-** allow oneself to be dominated; **det er kona som r-r** it's the wife who wears the pants. 2 bluster, brawl, row; (of children, animals) frolic, romp: **r- med** browbeat, bully.

regje'ring *-a/+-en* 1 government, rule: **dårlig r-** misrule. 2 cabinet, government, ministry (in parliamentary government): **danne r-** form a government; **møte i r-en** cabinet meeting. 3 reign, rule (=period): **under kong Haakons r-** during King Haakon's reign.

regje'rings/advoka't *-en* attorney general.

regje'rings/avi's *-a/+-en* official organ of the government.

regje'rings/bygning *-en* government office building.

regje'rings/dyktig *A* - : **r- flertall** working majority.

+regje'rings/flertall *-et* (=***/fleirtal**) parliamentary majority (in support of cabinet).

regje'rings/form *-a/+-en* form of government.

regje'rings/konto'r *-et* (governmental) bureau, office.

+regje'rings/kretser *pl* government circles.

regje'rings/krise *-a/-en* cabinet crisis.

regje'rings/orga'n *-et, pl -/+-er* official organ of the government; party press (of ruling party).

regje'rings/parti· *-et, pl +-er/*-* government party, party in power.

regje'rings/sjef *-en* prime minister.

regje'rings/tid *-a/+-en* reign.

reg'le[1] *-a* 1 jingle, nonsense verse, rigmarole. 2 story (with set sentences that are frequently repeated); anecdote: **hun var fylt av sladder og regler om bygdefolk** she was full of gossip and stories about the people of the community (Kinck).

***reg'le**[2] *V -a* rattle off, tell.

reglement [-mang'] *-et, pl -/-er* regulations.

reglemente'rt *A* - regular, prescribed, statutory.

+reglements/stridig [-mang's/] *A* - irregular, out of order.

reg'le/smed *-en* storyteller, teller of tall tales: **O, din fandens r-** You damned liar (Ibsen).

regn [+rei'n, *reng'n] *-et* rain; *fig.* shower (e.g. of arrows, honors, abuse), hail (of bullets): **se ut til r-, trekke opp til r-** look like rain; **etter r- kommer solskinn** after tears comes joy.

***reg'nal** *A* rainy.

regn/bløyte [+rei'n/, *reng'n/] *-a* soaking rain.

regn/boge [/båge] *-n* rainbow.

regn/bolk *-en* prolonged rain.

+regn/bue *-n* cf **/boge**

+regnbue/hinne *-a* (=***-boge/**) *anat.* iris.

regn/bye *-a* (=**+/byge, /bøye**) shower, squall.

regn/dråpe *-n* (=***/drope**) raindrop.

regne[1] [+rei'ne, *reng'ne] *V -a/+-et/ +-te/*-de* rain; *fig.* hail, pour, shower: **når det r-er på presten, så drypper det på klokkeren** when the chief is honored, some of it rubs off on his subordinates.

+regne[2] [+rei'ne, *reng'ne] *V -a/-et* cf **rekne**

+regne/bok [+rei'ne/, *reng'ne/] *-a, pl -bøker* cf **rekne/**

+regne/brett *-et* cf **rekne/**

+regne/feil *-en* cf **rekne/**

+regne/ferdighet *-en* skill in using figures.

+regne/maski'n *-en* cf **rekne/**

+regne/mester *-en, pl -e* arithmetician: **jeg er ikke noen r-** I have a poor head for figures.

+regne/stav *-en* cf **rekne/**

+regne/stykke *-t* cf **rekne/**

regn/frakk [+rei'n/, *reng'n/] *-en* raincoat.

regn/full· *A* rainy.

regn/hatt *-en* 1 hood, waterproof hat. 2 umbrella.

regn/hyre *-t/+-n* oilskins.

+regning [rei'ning] *-a/-en* cf **rekning**

+regnings/art *-a/-en* cf **reknings/**

+regnings/blankett· *-en* blank bill.

+regnings/bud *-et* bill collector.

+regnings/svarende *A* - profitable.

regn/kappe [+rei'n, *reng'n/] *-a* raincoat, slicker.

regn/kåpe *-a* raincoat.

regn/luft *-a/+-en* rain-bearing air.

+regn/måler *-en, pl -e* (=***-ar, */mælar**) rain gauge, udometer.

regn/orm *-en* angleworm, earthworm.

regn/plagg *-et* garment used in rain.

+ Bokmål; * Nynorsk; ° Dialect.
After letter: ' stress (Acc. 1); ' tone, stress (Acc. 2); · length.
Below letter: . not pronounced.

+regn/skap [rei'n/] -*et* cf **rekne/**
+regnskaps/bok -*a*, *pl* -*bøker* account book.
+regnskaps/fører -*en*, *pl* -*e* bookkeeper, treasurer; scorer (in games); paymaster (armed forces); purser (passenger ship); bursar (college).
+regnskaps/førsel -*en* keeping of accounts.
+regnskaps/kyndig *A* - skilled in accounts.
+regnskaps/messig *A* - pertaining to accounts.
+regnskaps/plikt -*a*/-*en* duty to keep accounts.
+regnskaps/post -*en* item (in accounts).
+regnskaps/år -*et* fiscal year.
regn/skur [+rei'n/, *reng'n/] -*en* shower.
regn/sky -*a* rain cloud.
+regn/skyll -*et* downpour; cloudburst.
regn/slag -*et* rain cape.
regn/tid -*a*/+-*en* rainy season, esp. of monsoons.
regn/tung [/tong] *A* heavy with rain.
+regn/tykk *A* -*tykt* dark with clouds (about air, sky), foggy.
+regn/tykning -*en* drizzle.
+regn/tøy -*et* (=*/**ty**) waterproof clothing.
regnvass/tønne -*a* (=*/**tynne**) rain barrel.
regn/vatn -*et* (=+/**vann**) rainwater.
+regn/vær -*et* (=*/**ver**) rainy weather: **det blir r-** it is going to rain.
+regnværs/dag -*en* rainy day.
regn/våt *A* wet with rain.
regresjo'n -*en* regression.
regress' -*en* *jur.* legal remedy, recourse: **ha r- til** have (right of) recourse against; **søke r- hos** have (right of) recourse against (sby).
reg'ressiv *A* *gram.* regressive.
reguladetri' -*en* 1 *math.* rule of three. 2 *hum.* complicated calculation.
regularise're *V* -*te* regularize.
regulati'v -*et*, *pl* -/+-*er* (regulation concerning) wage scale.
regula'tor -*en* *tech.* governor, regulator, throttle.
+regule'r/bar *A* adjustable.
regule're *V* -*te* 1 regulate (prices, a river, traffic, wages, watch). 2 grade (a road); straighten (teeth). 3 lay out, plan (an area, streets, town); develop.
regule'rings/plan -*en* area development plan.
regulæ'r *A* 1 regular; normal, ordinary. 2 *fig.* proper, real: **et r-t slagsmål** a r- fight.
reg. vm. =**registrert varemerke**
rehabilite're *V* -*te* rehabilitate.
rei'[1] -*a* 1 company of riders on horseback; crowd: **en r- av friere** a throng of suitors. 2=**oskorei.**
rei'[2] *pt of* **ri**[2]
***rei'ar** -*en* cf **reder**
***rei'ar/lag** -*et* company of shipowners.
***rei'd** *pt of* **ri**[2]
Rei'dar *Prn (m)*
Rei'dun *Prn (f)*
***rei'e**[1] -*n* accessories, equipment, fittings: **ein vevstol med all sin r-** a loom with all its fixtures.
rei'e[2] *V* +-*de*/*-*dde* (=**re**) 1 convey (on horseback), ride: **r- høyet heim** drive home the hay. 2 make (a bed); make ready, prepare (sth): **r- ned (håret)** smoothe down (one's hair); **r- opp** make (a bed). *3 pay: **r- skatten** pay the taxes. *4: **r- ut** equip. *5 dress (hides).
***rei'e**[3] *A* - cf **rede**[4]
***rei'e/bo'rd** -*et* serving table.
***rei'eleg** *A* - 1 honest, straightforward. 2 regular, proper.
***rei'ing** -*a* preparation; equipment.
rei'k -*a* 1 stripe. 2 furrow, groove. 3 part (in hair).
***rei'kar** -*en* drifter; stroller.
rei'ke *V* -*a*/+-*et* roam, stroll.
rei'm -*a* (=+**rem**) 1 strap; thong; leash: **kjøre alt hva r-er og tøy kan holde** drive at top speed. 2 belt: **spenne r-a inn** *fig.* tighten one's belt. 3 strip, stripe (of skin): **ha en r- av huden** suffer from the same weakness.
rei'm/skive -*a* pulley.
rei'n[1] -*a* 1 grass-grown strip at edge of field. 2 ridge, river bank.
rei'n[2] -*en* reindeer (Rangifer tarandus).
***rei'n**[3] *pt of* **rine**
rei'n[4] *A* (=+**ren**) 1 (physically) clean: **hennes føtter de er ikke ganske r-e** her feet - - they're not quite clean (Ibsen); **r- og pen** nice and clean; **få r-t på** change underwear, (of children) get clean diapers; **gjøre r-t** clean (e.g. house); **gjøre r-t bord** clear the decks; **en r- profil** a clean-cut profile. 2 (morally) pure, chaste: **de r-e av hjertet** the pure of heart; **r- for synd** free from sin; **r- samvittighet** clear conscience. 3 (physically) pure, unadulterated: **av det r-este vann** of the purest water; **det r-e flagg** (the Norwegian flag without the Swedish mark of union); *mus.* pure (pitch); perfect (interval). 4 *fig.* (nothing but, the pure) sheer; complete; perfect: **r- fortjeneste** clear profit; **en r- galskap** a regular passion; **r-e barnet** a mere child; **r-e krigen** a regular war. 5 clear, plain, simple: **få r- beskjed** get sth straight from the shoulder; **r-e ord for pengene** plain words; **r-t ut sagt** frankly speaking; **snakke r-t** speak clearly (of a child); **snakke r-t ut** speak one's mind. 6: **på det r-e** certain, clear; **bringe på det r-e** ascertain; **være på det r-e med** be clearly aware of.
***rei'nad** -*en* equipment, furnishings.
rei'n/beite -*t*, *pl* +-*r*/*- grazing land for reindeer.
rei'n/blom [+/blåmm] +-*men*/*-*en* *bot.* 1 (white) crowfoot (Dryas octopetala). 2 glacier crowfoot (Ranunculus glacialis).
rei'n/dyrke *V* -*a*/+-*et* 1 cultivate; *fig.*: **r- sine egenheter** cultivate one's eccentricities; **r-t hedning** heathen through and through; **r-t sosialisme** pure socialism. 2 isolate (bacteria).
***rei'ne** -*a* cf **rein**[1]
reineclaude [reneklå'd] -*n* *bot.* greengage (plum).
rei'n/fann -*en* *bot.* tansy (Tanacetum vulgare).
rei'n/ferdig *A* - cleanly.
+rei'n/gjøre [also rei'n/] *V* -*gjorde*, -*gjort* clean: **r-ing** (house) cleaning.
***rei'n/hald** -*et* cf **/hold**
rei'n/hekla *A* - honest, straightforward.
+rei'n/hold -*et* (=*/**hald**) 1 cleaning (av of). 2 keeping of reindeer.
rei'n/ho'rn -*et* reindeer horn.
rei'n/hårig *A* - 1 dependable. 2 real, unmitigated (of **rallare**).
rei'n/lav -*et* *bot.* reindeer lichen (Cladonia).
***rei'n/leik** -*en* cleanliness, purity.
+rei'n/lender -*en*, *pl* -*e* (=*-**ar**) dance with a polka step (similar to schottische).
+rei'n/levnet *et* monastic life.
***rei'n/livd** *A* -/-*livt* 1 celibate. 2 decent, ethical, moral.
rei'n/mose [*/måse] -*n* *bot.* reindeer moss (Cladonia).
***rei'n/sam** *A* clean.
rei'ns/bukk [/bokk] -*en* reindeer buck.
rei'ns/dyr -*et* reindeer.
***rei'nse** *V* -*a* cf **rense**
***rei'n/semd** -*a* cleanliness.
***reinseri'** -*et* cf **renseri**
***rei'nse/verk** -*et* cf **rense/**
***rei'nsing** -*a* cf **renselse**
***rei'nske** *V* -*a* cf **renske**
***rei'nske/verk** -*et* cf **rense/**
rei'n/skrift -*a* clean copy.
rei'n/skrive *V* *infl as* **skrive** make a clean copy of, transcribe.
rei'n/skure *V* +-*te*/*-*a* scour, scrub.
+rei'n/skåren *A* -*ent*/-*et*, *pl* -*ne* (=*/**skoren**) clean-cut (features); planed (planks); boned and cleaned (meat).
rei'nslig *A* - cleanly.
+rei'nslig/het -*en* cleanliness.
rei'n/spikka *A* - pure, real, true.
+rei'n/strøk -*et* area frequented by reindeer.
rei'nt *Av* (=+**rent**) completely, entirely, quite: **r- ut** frankly (speaking); **r- vitenskapelig** purely scientific.
rei'n/vaske *V* -*a*/+-*et* 1 clean, wash clean. 2 clear (sby's name).
rei'n/vatn -*et* clean water.
rei'p -*et* rope.
***rei'par/bane** -*n* cf **reper/**
***rei'pe** *V* -*a* tie with rope.
rei'p/helde -*a* bight, loop (of rope).
+rei'p/slager -*en*, *pl* -*e* (=*-**ar**) ropemaker.
rei'r -*et* (=+**rede**[2]) nest.
***rei're** *V* -*a*: **r- seg** nest.
rei's[1] -*a*/+-*en* cf **reise**[1]
rei's[2] -*et* 1 rise, rising. 2 V-shaped log pile.
***rei's**[3] *pt of* **rise**[3]
rei'se[1] -*a*/+-*en* journey, trip, voyage; (*pl*) travel(s): **gjøre en r-** take a trip; **ligge, være på r-** be on a trip, be traveling; **lykke på r-en** have a good trip.
rei'se[2] *V* -*te* 1 go (away), leave- **r- bortom** run over to (e.g. for a couple of days); **r- fra** leave; **så reis med Gud** then go with God (Ibsen); **r- med noe** run off with sth, take sth along; **reis og ryk** *fam.* go to hell, get out; **(hushjelpen) r-te på dagen** (the maid) quit the same day (without notice); **r- på landet** go to the country; **r- sin vei** leave, move; quit; **r- ut i verden** go out into the world. 2 journey, travel (**med** by): **vi r-ste 500 km i dag** we covered 500 kilometers today; **r- i** travel=be a traveling salesman in (sth, e.g. tobacco); **r- om (omkring)** travel around; **r- på turné** (e.g. theater group) be on tour; **r- sjøvegen** go by sea; **r- til fots** travel on foot; **være ute og r-** be traveling. 3 be lost, disappear, vanish; leave hurriedly: **de var redde for at broen skulle r-** they were afraid the bridge would wash out (Undset); **nå r-er siste resten av hans vett** now the last of his senses are taking leave of him (Ibsen); **båthuset r-te på sjøen** the boathouse was taken by the waves; **trollet var r-t opp igjennom pipa** the troll had vanished up the chimney (Asbjørnsen). (See also **reisende**).
rei'se[3] *V* -*te* 1 raise=lift (up), set up: **r- bust** bristle; **r- (tønnen) på ende** set (the barrel) up. 2 raise= build, erect: **r- forsvaret** rebuild one's defences. 3 raise=stir up: **r- sak** bring suit; **r- støv** r- the dust; **r- tvil** give rise to doubts; **r- vilt**, flush, start game. 4 raise=procure (e.g. an army, money). 5 (*refl.*): **r- seg** arise, rise; get up, recover; revolt: **fjellet r-te seg foran dem** the mountain towered before them; **folket r-te seg** the people rose in revolt; **havet r-te seg** the sea heaved (swelled); **r- seg opp** get on one's feet; **r- seg over ende** sit up.
rei'se/akkrediti'v -*et* letter of credit.
+rei'se/beskri'velse -*n* account of journey, book of travels, travelogue.
rei'se/brev -*et* travel account (e.g. in newspaper), travelogue.
rei'se/byrå' -*et*, *pl* +-*er*/*- travel agency.
rei'se/feber -*en* excitement before a trip.
rei'se/felle -*n* traveling companion.
rei'se/ferdig *A* - ready to leave (for trip).
rei'se/fot -*en*: **leve (være) på r-** always be going somewhere, on the move; **stå på r-** be about to leave (for a trip).
+rei'se/følge -*t* (=*/**følgje**) 1 fellow

traveler(s): **få r-** get traveling companions. 2 (organized) party of tourists, travelers.

+rei'se/fører *-en, pl -e* (=***-ar**) travel guide (book, person).

rei'se/gods *-et* baggage.

+rei'se/godtgjørelse *-n* travel allowance.

rei'se/grammofo'n *-en* portable phonograph.

rei'se/handbok *-a, pl -handbøker* (=**+/håndbok**) guidebook.

rei'se/kledd *A -/*-kledt* dressed for travel.

rei'se/koffert [/koff-] *-en* suitcase, traveling bag.

rei'se/kone *-a* woman traveling with a married man as his wife (but not married to him).

+rei'se/leder *-en, pl ˙-e* (=***/leiar**) guide, tour director, tour leader.

rei'se/liv *-et* 1 travel. 2 tourist traffic.

rei'se/lyst *-a/+-en* desire to travel, *poet.* wanderlust.

rei'sende *en* 1 traveler, passenger. 2 commercial traveler, traveling salesman (i of). 3 tramp.

rei'se/pass *-et* 1 *archaic* passport. 2 *fam.* sudden, unfriendly dismissal, discharge.

+rei'se/penger *pl* (=***-ar**) money for travel; passage money.

rei'se/plan *-en* 1 itinerary. 2: **ha r-er** be thinking of a trip.

rei'se/radio *-en* portable radio.

rei'se/selskap *-et, pl -/+-er* 1 traveling companion(s); companion(s) on a conducted tour. 2 party of tourists.

rei'se/sjekk *-en* traveler's check.

rei'se/skildring *-a/+-en* description of trip; book of travels, travelogue.

rei'se/stipen'd *-et* travel grant.

+rei'se/vant *A -* (=***/van(d)**) experienced (as traveler), used to traveling.

***rei'sing** *-a* 1 erection, raising; bearing, carriage. 2 movement, rise, stirring (of people); revolt, uprising (cf **mål/r-**). 3 framework (of house). 4 bottom layer of grain sheaves in granary.

***rei'/skap** *-en* cf **red/**

***rei'sle** *-a* 1 preparation. 2 transportation.

rei'sning **-a/+-en* 1 erection, raising (e.g. of building); pitching (of tent); bearing, carriage, erectness (of body). 2 ascent, slope; pitch (of roof). 3 grandeur, nobility: **et drama med r-** a drama in the grand manner. 4 rebellion, revolt, uprising. 5 *naut.* rigging.

***rei'st[1]** *-en* brake (on sled, sleigh).

***rei'st[2]** *-et* fish scales.

***rei'ste** *V -a* 1 scale (fish). 2 punish.

rei's/ved *-en* wood piled in a **reis** (for later transport).

rei's/verk *-et* (wooden) framework of building.

***rei't[1]** *-a* 1 groove, row (for planting). 2 line, mark, stripe.

rei't[2] *-en* small cultivated field (for kitchen garden).

rei't/bruk *-et hist.* farming of very small cultivated pieces of land.

***rei'te** *V -a* 1 dig furrows; hill up (plants). 2: **kornet r-er seg** the grain is lying flat in lines and strips. 3 anger, annoy, tease.

***rei'ten** *A -e/-i, pl -ne* annoying, provoking, teasing.

***rei'ug** *A -* ready.

***rei'ug/skap** *-en* readiness.

rei'v[1] *-a/-en* fishing line (used in fresh water).

rei'v[2] *-en* swaddling clothes.

rei'v[3] *pt of* **rive[3]**

rei've *V +-de/-a/+-et* swaddle; *bind, wind around; *bandage.

***rei'vst** *pt of* **rivast**

rei'v/unge [/onge] *-n* infant.

rejeksjo'n *-en* failure (in examinations).

rejek't *A - :* **gå r-** flunk out.

rejise're *V -te* fail, flunk (sby in exam).

re'k *-et* 1 drifting, loitering, roaming: **r- av turister** running around of tourists; **komme på r-** be adrift, drift around. 2 jetsam; drift; trash, waste. *3 gentle wind.

rek.=**rekommandert**

rekam'bio/veksel *-elen, pl -ler merc.* redraft.

***re'kar/fant** *-en* cf **reke/**

***re'kast** *V rekst, rakst, -est/-ist* tramp about; drift.

re'ke[1] *-a zool.* shrimp (Macrura natantia).

re'ke[2] *-a dial.* snow shovel.

***re'ke[3]** *-t* 1 path. 2 tracks.

re'ke[4] *V rak/+-te, +-t/*-e/*-i* 1 drift, loiter, roam. 2 *dial.* drive (sby) away. 3 hunt.

re'ke/fant *-en* bum, floater, tramp.

re'kel *-elen/+-elet/+-let, pl -ler* tall, lanky person; *(pop.)* tall drink of water.

+re'ker *-en, pl -e* (=***-ar**) tramp, vagabond.

re'ke/saus *-en* shrimp sauce.

re'ke/smørbrød *-et* open-face shrimp sandwich.

re'ke/trål *-en* shrimp trawler.

+rek'ke[1] *-a* (=***rekkje[1]**) 1 ship's rail: **over r-a** overboard; **forsvinne over r-a** *fam.* jump ship. 2 rack (e.g. for plates).

+rek'ke[2] *-a/-en* (=***rekkje[2]**) 1 row (**av** of) (persons, things); line (e.g. of ancestors): **i første r-** above all, primarily; **stå i r- og rad** be lined up. 2 file, rank (of soldiers): **en mann ut av r-ene** a man gone from the ranks (Hamsun). 3 chain, range (e.g. of mountains); series. 4 number: **en r- (av) år, tilfeller** a number of years, cases, 5 *math.* column, progression, row; series. 6 *zool.* phylum.

rek'ke[3] *V rakk, +rukket/*rokke/*-i* 1 extend, reach **knapt en ser så langt, som staven r-er** one can hardly see as far as the stick can r- (Ibsen); **så vidt mine evner r-er** as far as it lies within my (ability) power; **øyet rakk ei utom egen tram** his vision did not extend beyond his own doorstep (Kinck). 2 catch, reach (e.g. train); have time to do (sth): **r- fram** arrive, get (**til** to) (e.g. goal, place). 3 be adequate, sufficient: **r- til** suffice. 4 continue, last: **r- mot kveld** get on towards evening; **veien varte og rakk** the road went on and on (Sverdrup).

+rek'ke[4] *V rakte, rakt* (=***rekkje[3]**) 1 extend, give, hold out (e.g. hand); stretch (**fram** out, **i været** up, **mot** toward, **opp** up, **ut** out); reach (e.g. a shelf): **r- tunge av** stick out tongue at. 2 give, hand (sth to sby): **Hedvig, å rekk meg den knipetangen** H-, please hand me that pair of pliers (Ibsen).

+rek'ke[5] *V* **rekte** (=***rekkje[4]**) loosen: **r- opp** unravel.

+rek'ke/følge *-n* (=***rekkje/følgd**) order: **i alfabetisk r-** in alphabetical o-.

+rek'ke/hus *-et* row housing; row house.

+rek'ke/vidde *-a* (=***/vidd**) 1 range (e.g. of sound, guns), reach (e.g. of arm, fire): **utenfor min r-** beyond my reach. 2 range, scope (of abilities, intellect). 3 effect, scope (e.g. of plan); extent (e.g. of damage).

***rekkj'e[1]** *-a* cf **rekke[1]**

***rekkj'e[2]** *-a* cf **rekke[2]**

***rekkj'e[3]** *V rekte* cf **rekke[4]**

***rekkj'e[4]** *V rekte* cf **rekke[5]**

***rekkj'e/tal** *-et* ordinal number.

rekk'/verk *-et* banister, guardrail, handrail; parapet, railing.

reklamasjo'n *-en* claim, complaint (about goods received): **gjøre r-** demand refund, make complaint.

rekla'me *-n* 1 advertisement, publicity: **det er ingen r- for stedet** that's no recommendation for the place. 2 advertising: **falsk r-** misleading a-; **r-ens makt er stor** it pays to advertise.

rekla'me/byrå˙ *-et, pl +-er/*-* advertising agency.

rekla'me/felttog [/-tåg] *-et* advertising campaign.

rekla'me/mann *-en, pl -menn/*-menner* advertising man.

rekla'me/plaka't *-en* advertising poster, sign.

reklame're *V -te* 1 advertise: **r- for noe** a-, publicize sth. 2 complain, demand refund.

rekla'me/søyle *-a/+-en* pillar, post displaying advertising.

+rekla'me/tegner [/teiner] *-en, pl -e* (=***/teiknar**) commercial artist.

***rekla'me/øyemed** *-et*: **i r-** for publicity purposes.

rek'ling *-en* wind-dried fat or flesh around fins, usu. of halibut (=**rav**).

***rek'nande** *A -* worth considering.

rek'ne *V -a/+-et* (=**+regne[2]**) 1 calculate, compute, do arithmetic; figure, reckon. 2 consider, deem, regard (**for, som** as); count, include (**blant** among, **til** in): **r- en noe til gode** count sth in one's favor, credit one with sth. 3 (with *prep.* and *adv.*): **r- etter** check over, go over; go by, judge by; **r- med** allow for, reckon with, take into account; count on; **r- om** recalculate; convert (**r- dollars om til kroner** convert d- to k-); **r- opp** enumerate, read off (one by one); **r- over noe** make an estimate of sth; **r- på noe, noen** count on, rely on sth, sby; **r- ut** estimate, figure out.

rek'ne/bok *-a* 1 arithmetic book. 2 notebook for arithmetic problems.

rek'ne/brett *-et* abacus.

rek'ne/feil *-en* error in arithmetic, miscalculation.

rek'ne/maski'n *-en* calculating machine, computer.

***rek'ne/meister** *-eren, pl -rar* cf **regne/mester**

rek'ne/skap *-en* (=**+regn/**) 1 account(s); balance sheet; (in games, sports) scoring: **føre, holde r-** keep the accounts. 2 *fig.* account; difference, quarrel, score: **avlegge r- (for)** give an a-ing (for) (e.g. actions); **kalle en til r-** hold sby responsible; **jeg har et gammelt r- å avgjøre med ham** I have an old score to settle with him (Krag).

rek'ne/stav *-en* slide rule.

rek'ne/stykke *-t, pl +-r/*-* arithmetic problem.

rek'ning *-a* 1 bill; account. 2 arithmetic.

rek'nings/art *-a/-en* one of the four basic arithmetical operations (e.g. addition).

rekognose're *V -te* explore, reconnoitre.

rekommandasjo'n *-en* registration (of letter).

rekommande're *V -te* register (letter).

rekonstrue're *V -te* 1 reconstruct (sth destroyed; a series of events). 2 reorganize (business, group); reshuffle (cabinet).

rekonstruksjo'n *-en* reconstruction (**av** of).

rekonvalesen's *-en* convalescence.

rekonvalesen't *-en* convalescent.

rekonvalesen't/heim *-en* (=**+/hjem**) convalescence home, rest home.

rekor'd *-en* record (e.g. in sports): **r- i stupiditet** a r- in stupidity; **slå alle r-er** break all r-s.

rekor'd/arta *A -* (=**+-et**) record, record-breaking.

+rekor'd/innehaver *-en, pl -e* (=***-ar**) holder of a record.

rekor'd/jag *-et* craze for record-breaking.

+ Bokmål; * Nynorsk; ° Dialect.
After letter: ' stress (Acc. 1); ' tone, stress (Acc. 2); ˙ length.
Below letter: . not pronounced.

+rekor'd/messig *A* - record-breaking: **r-e lave priser** r- low prices.
rekor'd/tid -*a*/+-*en*: **på r-** in record time.
rekreasjo'n -*en* recreation, relaxation.
+rekreasjo'ns/opphold -*et* (=*/opphald) holiday, rest cure.
rekree're *V* -*te*: **r- seg** recuperate, take a rest or vacation.
rekrutt' -*en* 1 recruit: **utskrive r-er** call in r-s. 2 beginner (in field of work).
rekrutte're *V* -*te* recruit.
rekrutt'/skole -*n* training school for recruits.
rek'ster -*en* 1 *fam.* roaming, tramping. 2 *dial.* cow path; pasture. 3 driftwood, flotsam.
***rek'ster/veg** -*en* cow path.
re'k/stokk -*en* driftwood, log.
rek'ta/klausul -*en* *merc.* restrictive endorsement.
rektang'el -*elet*/-*let*, *pl* +-*ler*/*-*el* rectangle.
rektang'el/kart -*et* topographic map (in rectangular form).
rektangulær [rektanggulæ'r] *A* rectangular.
rek'ta/veksel -*elen*, *pl* -*ler* *merc.* nonnegotiable bill.
***rek'te** *pt of* **rekkje**[3,4]
rektifise're *V* -*te* *chem.* rectify.
rek'tor -*en*, *pl* -*to'rer* 1 president (of college, university). 2 principal (of gymnasium, secondary school).
rektora't -*et* 1 presidency (of university). 2 position of principal (of gymnasium).
re'k/ved -*en* driftwood.
re'kviem -*et* requiem.
rekviren't -*en* *jur.* claimant.
rekvire're *V* -*te* 1 *mil.* requisition (rooms, food). 2 *jur.* claim, order. 3 *merc.* order, send for.
rekvisisjo'n -*en* 1 requisition; document of requisition. 2 *mil.* forced requisition.
rekvisit'a *pl* 1 accessories, equipment. 2 props, stage properties.
rekvisitt' -*et*, *pl* +-*er*/*- cf **rekvisita**
reky'l -*en* kick, recoil (of gun).
reky'l/kano'n -*en* recoil gun.
rel. =**relativ**[1]
relasjo'n -*en* relation (**til** to), connection: **stå i (ha) r- til** have a bearing upon, be connected with.
rel'ativ[1] -*et* *gram.* relative (e.g. pronoun).
rel'ativ[2] *A* 1 relative: **alt er r-t i denne verden** there is nothing absolute in this world. 2 *(adv.)* comparatively, relatively: **økonomisk står vi r-t dårligere** economically we are comparatively worse off.
relativis'me -*n* relativism.
relativis't -*en* relativist.
relativis'tisk *A* - relativistic.
relativite't -*en* relativity.
relativite'ts/teori' -*en* theory of relativity.
relé -*et*, *pl* +-*er*/*- *elec.*, *mil.* relay.
relegasjo'n -*en* dismissal (from university).
relege're *V* -*te* dismiss, expel.
relé/stasjo'n -*en* relay station.
relevan's -*en* relevance.
relevan't *A* - relevant.
relieff' -*et*, *pl* -/+-*er* 1 relief (of landscape, sculpture). 2 *fig.*: **stå i klar r-** stand out clearly; **stille i r-** delineate clearly, set off.
religio'n -*en* religion: **r- i skolen** religious instruction in school.
+religio'ns/forføl'gelse -*n* (=*-**ing**) religious persecution.
+religio'ns/frihet -*en* (=*/**fridom**) freedom of religion.
religio'ns/krig -*en* religious war.
religio'ns/samfunn -*et* religious society; church, sect.
+religio'ns/stifter -*en*, *pl* -*e* (=*-**ar**) founder of a religion.
religio'ns/undervi'sning -*a*/+-*en* religious education.
religiø's *A* religious (art, home, person, etc.); sacred (music); devotional (books); devout, pious (attitude, manner): **han kom snart i strid med de r-e i bygda** he soon fell out with the brethren in the district.
religiøsite't -*en* religiosity; piety.
relik'vie -*n* (sacred) relic.
relik'vie/skrin -*et* reliquary.
re'ling -*a*/+-*en* *naut.* gunwale, rail.
+rem' -*ma*/-*men* cf **reim**
***rem'be** *V* -*de*: **r- seg** stretch (one's limbs).
remburs [rangbu'rs] -*en* banker's credit, letter of credit: **åpne r-** open a credit (available to seller).
rembursere [rangburse're] *V* -*te* reimburse.
reme'die -*t*, *pl* +-*r*/*- cf **remedium**
reme'dium -*iet*, *pl* +-*ier*/*-*ium* 1 *archaic* remedy. 2 *(pl)* paraphernalia. 3 *fam.* *(pl)* fuss: **det er så mange r-ier med ham** there's so much f- with him.
reminisen's -*en* reminiscence.
remis [remi'] *A* - (esp. in chess) drawn, tied; a draw, a tie.
remis'se -*n* remittance.
remitten't -*en* payee.
remitte're *V* -*te* 1 *merc.* remit. 2 *med.*: **r-ende feber** remittent fever.
rem'je *V* -*a*/+-*et* 1 *fam.* bawl, howl; roar, wail. 2 (of goats) bleat.
remonte're *V* -*te* 1 *mil.* supply with fresh horses. 2 *bot.* flower a second time: **r-ende rose** remontant rose.
remplassere [ramplase're] *V* -*te* replace.
rem'pling -*en* small beeves (30—80 kg.).
rem'se[1] -*a* 1 strip (cloth, land, paper). 2 jingle, long string of words, rigmarole.
rem'se[2] *V* -*a*/+-*et* 1 cut into strips. 2 *dial.*: **r- opp** rattle off.
remula'de -*n* mayonnaise sauce flavored with condiments.
+re'n *A* cf **rein**[4]
***ren'de**[1] *V* -*a* make (weave) stripes in (cloth).
***ren'de**[2] *pt of* **renne**[3]
***ren'det(e)** *A* - striped.
rendezvous [rangdevu'] -*et* date, rendezvous.
+re'n/dyrke *V* -*et* cf **rein/**
***re'ne** *V* -*a* 1 lose flavor, taste flat; (of drink) turn sour. 2 (of food) cool. 3 (of alcohol) lose effect.
renega't -*en* 1 *hist.* Christian who joins the Mohammedan faith. 2 renegade.
renessanse [renessang'se] -*n* renaissance, renascence; revival: **r-n** the Renaissance.
renessanse/menneske -*t*, *pl* +-*r*/*- a Renaissance personality (usu. of creative, robust, wide-ranging person).
reng'er pl of **rong**
***reng'je** *V* -*de* cf **vrenge**
***reng'je/bilete** -*t* cf **vrenge/bilde**
+re'n/gjøre [also re'n/] *V* -*gjorde*, -*gjort* cf **rein/**
+re'n/het -*en* 1 cleanness. 2 chastity: **r- før ekteskapet** pre-marital c-. 3 purity: **sjelelig r-** p- of soul; **stemmens r-** clarity, p- of voice.
+re'n/hold -*et* cf **rein/**
+re'n/hårig *A* - cf **rein/**
+ren'ke -*n* *(pl)* plots, tricks, underhanded means; secret intrigues, wiles.
+ren'ke/full *A* crafty, underhand, wily.
+ren'ke/smed -*en* plotter, schemer.
+ren'ke/spinn -*et* net, web of intrigue.
renn' -*et* 1 run, running: **i ett r-** in one swoop, without stop; **legge på r-** start running; **r- fra taket** running (of water) from the roof; **felen gjorde noen kåte r-** the violin made some gay runs (Bjørnson). 2 meet, race esp. on skates, skis). 3 *fig.* **det var et r- av tiggere** they were overrun (pestered) by beggars; **r- med gutter** running around with boys; **r- på dørene** constant run of people at the door.
***ren'nar** -*en* (fast) runner.
ren'ne[1] -*a* 1 gutter, (small) trench. 2 downsput, gutter, rainpipe. 3 chute (e.g. for grain). 4 crack, fissure, lead (in subsoil, rock). 5 *naut.* (narrow) channel, lane: **Den norske r-** the Norwegian Channel. 6 groove (e.g. in wood, metal).
ren'ne[2] *V* +*rant*/**rann*, +*rent*/**runne*/ *-*i* 1 (of people) run, run around; fly: **r- etter** run after; **r- på** run down, run into; **r- på kjelke** go sledding; **r- på ski** go skiing; **r- på skøyter** go skating; **r- sin vei** run away; **r- ut** (of horses) run away; **r- ut og inn** run in and out. 2 (of liquids) pour, run: **de spilte så svetten rann** they played till the sweat rolled off them (Bojer); **r- full** fill up; **r- over** run over; **r- tom** run dry; **r-ende øyne** runny eyes. 3: **r- på en** (of a feeling, drunkenness, etc.) grow stronger, take the upper hand. 4 rise; spring: **r- opp** (of plants) shoot up (see **rinne**).
ren'ne[3] *V* +*rente*/**rende* 1 run, stick, thrust: **e- kniven i en** stick a knife in sby; **r- hodet mot veggen** run one's head against a stone wall; **r- et skip i senk** ram, sink a ship. 2 wind (up): **r- garn** w- yarn (on boom, spindle). 3 *dial.* pour: **r- melk** skim milk. 4 *(refl.)* **r- seg fast** get stuck.
ren'ne/bom [/bomm] -*men* 1 warp beam. 2 yarn reel (=**/stol**).
Ren'ne/bu *Pln* twp, Sør-Trøndelag.
***ren'ne/drev** -*et* driving snow; snow flurry.
ren'ne/ga'rn -*et* warp.
ren'ne/knute -*n* (=*/**knut**) running knot.
ren'ne/løkke -*a* slip knot.
ren'ne/snare -*a* slip noose.
ren'ne/stein -*en* gutter.
ren'nesteins/språk -*et* gutter speech, vulgar language.
ren'ne/stol -*en* (large) yarn reel (for warping).
Ren'nes/øy *Pln* twp, Rogaland.
ren'ning[1] -*a* 1 running. 2 sunrise (=**sol/**). 3 warp.
ren'ning[2] -*en* sapling, shoot.
renommé -*et* reputation, repute; fame.
renons [renång's] *A* - (of card suit) void: **gjøre seg r-** void one's hand (e.g. in spades); **r- på noe** devoid of, lacking sth; (in cards) void of.
renonsere [renångse're] *V* -*te*: **r- på** give up, renounce.
renovasjo'n -*en* street cleaning; collection and disposal of refuse; sanitation; sewage disposal.
+renovasjo'ns/vesen -*et* department of sanitation.
renove're *V* -*te* *archaic* clean streets, collect garbage, etc.
+re'ns/dyr -*et* cf **reins/**
+ren'se *V* -*a*/-*et* (=***reinse**) 1 clean (e.g. fingernails, fish, seed); dry-clean (clothes); cleanse, rinse. 2 filter, purify; winnow (grain); disinfect. 3 clear, rid (**for** of); weed (a field): **r- opp** clean out, dredge. 4 *fig.* cleanse, purge, purify; clear (of charge): **r- luften** clear the air. 5 *(refl.)* **r- seg for** clear oneself of (e.g. suspicion), purge oneself.
***ren'sel** -*et* 1 path (of fish). 2 rheumatic pains.
+ren'selse -*n* (=***reinsing**) 1 cleansing. 2 *eccl.* purgation, purification.
+ren'se/middel -*elet*/-*midlet*, *pl* -*midler* cleaning compound.
+ren'se/prosess' -*en* cleaning process.
+renseri' -*et* (=***reinseri**) dry-cleaning establishment.
+ren'se/verk -*et* (=***reinse/**, ***reinske/**) fanning mill, winnower.
+ren'ske *V* -*a*/-*et* (=***reinske**) 1 clean. 2 clear (e.g. throat, name); clean out (woods): **r- opp i** clean up (e.g. affair, social conditions); **isen r-es opp** the ice is breaking up.
+re'n/skrev *pt of* **/skrive**

+**re'n/skrift** *-a/-en* cf **rein/**
+**re'n/skrive** *V infl as* **skrive** cf **rein/**
+**re'n/skure** *V -te* cf **rein/**
+**re'n/skåren** *A -ent/-et, pl -ne* cf **rein/**
***ren'sle** *-a* 1 running (e.g. of fish); streaming (of water). 2 course, run (e.g. for logs).
+**re'nslig** *A* - cf **reinslig**
+**re'nslig/het** *-en* cf **reinslig/**
+**ren't** *pp of* **renne**[2], **renne**[3]
renta'bel *A -elt, pl -le* profitable.
rentabilite't *-en* profitableness: **foretagendets r- er tvilsom** it is doubtful whether the undertaking will pay.
ren'te[1] *-a/+-en* 1 *(usu. pl)* interest (**av** on); dividend(s): **gi igjen med r-r** pay back (e.g. an insult) with i-; **r-s r-r** compound i-; **ta 6 % i r-** charge 6 % interest. 2 *hist.* rent, esp. ground rent. 3 annuity, income, pension: **leve av sine r-r** live on one's i-, have independent means.
***ren'te**[2] *V -a*: **r- seg** accrue interest.
+**ren'te**[3] *pt of* **renne**[3]
+**ren'te/bærende** *A* - interest-bearing.
ren'te/dag *-en* 1 date interest is due. 2 (in banking) each day interest accrues.
ren'te/fot *-en* rate of interest.
ren'te/fri *A -tt* free of interest: **r-konto** non-interest-bearing account.
ren'te/kammer *-et hist.* exchequer.
rentenis't *-en* rentier (one who lives on income from investments).
+**ren'tes/rente** *-a/-en* (=***rente/**) compound interest.
ren'te/tap *-et* loss of interest.
rentie'r [-e'] *-en* rentier (see **rentenist**).
+**re'n/trykk** *-et* clean proof.
+**re'nt/ut** *Av* cf **reint**
+**re'n/vaske** *V -et* 1 wash clean. 2: **r- ens navn** clear one's name (esp. of suspicion, charges).
reo'l *-en* 1 bookcase, book shelves. 2 (nest of) pigeon holes; rack (for tools).
reorganise're *V -te* reorganize.
+**re'p** *-et* cf **reip**
reparasjo'n *-en* 1 mending (e.g. of clothing); restoration (of art work); repair(s) (**av** of): **omfattende r-er** thorough overhauling, reconditioning. 2 *lit.* improvement, reform. 3 *hist.* (payment of) reparations.
+**reparasjo'ns/verksted** *-et, pl -er* (=***/verkstad**) repair shop; garage.
reparatø'r *-en* mechanic, repairman.
repare're *V -te* 1 fix, mend, repair. 2 make amends (e.g. for hastily spoken word). 3 *hum.* drink (to get over a hangover).
repatrie're *V -te* repatriate.
+**re'per/bane** [also re'per/] *-n* (=***reipar/**) rope walk, ropework (=rope factory).
repertoa'r *-et, pl +-er/*-* repertoire, repertory (**av** of): **ukens r-** performances this week.
repete're *V -te educ.* repeat, review.
repetisjo'n *-en* 1 *educ.* review (**av** of). 2 (theater) rehearsal. 3 *mus.* repeat. 4 *mil.* refresher course.
+**repetisjo'ns/øvelse** *-n* (=**-ing**) *educ., mil.* review (exercise).
repetitø'r *-en* (at theater) coach, rehearser; chorus master.
replikk' *-en* 1 remark, reply (in conversation, public discussion). 2 lines, speech (in play). 3 repartee: **kvikk i r-en** quick at reply.
replikk'/skifte *-t* dialogue, exchange (of words).
+**replikk'/veksel** *-en* (=+**/veksling**) dialogue, exchange (of words).
replise're *V -te* reply, retort.
reporta'sje *-n* 1 news service, reporting. 2 commentary, coverage (**fra** from, of).
reporter [repå'rter] *-en, pl +-e* reporter.
repos [repå'] *+-en/*-et* 1 landing (on stairway). 2 platform.
***repp'** *-en* cluster of farms, hamlet, neighborhood.
repr.=**representant; representert**

+**represa'lier** *pl* (=***-ar**) reprisals: **ta r- mot** make r- against.
representan't *-en* 1 representative (**for** of). 2 agent; deputy. 3 delegate; member of legislature (etc.): **R-enes hus** House of Representatives.
representan't/skap *-et* board, council; stockholders' committee.
representasjo'n *-en* 1 *pol.* delegation, representation. 2 *merc.* agency. 3 *admin.* (official) entertainment; allowance for entertainment.
representasjo'ns/konto *-en* expense account (for entertainment).
representasjo'ns/utgifter *pl* entertainment expenses.
represen'tativ *A* 1 representative, typical (**for** of): **et r-t utvalg** a r- selection (e.g. of goods, poems). 2 *pol.* representative (government). 3 highly qualified, select: **en r- forsamling** a select audience; **en r- skikkelse** a distinguished(-looking) figure. 4 ceremonial, social: **r-e plikter** social obligations.
represente're *V -te* 1 represent (=exemplify, signify; correspond to; be member of assembly, agent of firm, etc.). 2 entertain, perform official social functions.
repriman'de *-n* reprimand.
repri'se *-n* 1 resumption (of interrupted work): **i r-r** in installments. 2 rerun, revival (of film, play). 3 *mus.* repeat.
repri'se/kino *-en* second-run movie house.
reproduksjo'n *-en* reproduction (**av** of).
reproduse're *V -te* reproduce.
+**re'p/slager** *-en, pl -e* cf **reip/**
repti'l *-et, pl +-er/*-* reptile.
+**republika'ner** *-en, pl -e* (=***-ar**) 1 republican. 2 Republican. 3 *zool.* sociable weaverbird (Philetaerus socius).
republika'nsk *A* - 1 republican. 2 Republican.
republikk' *-en* 1 republic. 2 *lit.*: **den litterære r-** the republic (=world) of letters.
reputasjo'n *-en archaic* reputation.
***re's** *-et* 1 crest, ridge. 2 rise. 3 size, volume.
res.=**resolusjon**
rese'da [also re'] *-en bot.* mignonette, reseda (Reseda odorata).
+**resensen't** *-en* cf **recensent**
resepsjo'n *-en* 1 reception. 2 reception desk; lobby. 3 *jur.* acceptance, recognition (of foreign law).
resep't *-en* 1 precription: **ekspedere en r-** make up a prescription; **fåes kun på r-** obtained only on doctor's p-; **gi r- på** write a p- for. 2 conception, idea: **følge sin egen r-** follow his own rules.
resepta'r *-en* dispenser.
res'eptiv *A* receptive.
reseptivite't *-en* receptivity.
reseptu'r *-en* dispensary.
reservasjo'n *-en* 1 doubts, reservation. 2 (Indian) reservation (usu. **reservat**).
reserva't *-et, pl -/+-er* 1 (Indian) reservation. 2 (wild life) preserve.
reser've *-n* 1 reserve (financial, military, etc.) (**av** of): **bruke av r-n** tap the reserve; **ha store r-r av proviant** have a large stock of provisions; **i r-** in r-. 2 (in sports) substitute(s); (on auto) spare.
reser've/del *-en* spare part.
reser've/hjul *-et* spare wheel.
reser've/lege *-n* resident physician (assistant to head physician at hospital, clinic).
reser've/offise'r *-en* reserve officer.
reserve're *V -te* reserve (e.g. rooms, tickets); earmark: **r- seg** reserve (the right to sth); **r- seg imot** guard oneself against, provide against.
reserve'rt *A* - aloof, guarded, reserved; cool (**overfor** towards).
+**reser've/tropper** *pl* (=***-ar**) *mil.* reserves.

reser've/utgang *-en* emergency exit.
reservoa'r *-et, pl -/+-er* reservoir.
residen's *-en* 1 (noble, royal) residence. 2 *hum.* (private) residence.
reside're *V -te* 1 *lit.* (of nobility, royalty, high official) live, reside. 2 *eccl.*: **r-ende kapellan** assistant pastor. 3 *hum.* live: **han r-er oppe på kvisten** he makes his residence in a room under the eaves.
resignasjo'n *-en* (feeling of) resignation: **med r-** resignedly.
resigne're *V -te* forego, give up (e.g. goal, wish); capitulate (e.g. in face of opposition); resign oneself (to one's fate).
resigne'rt *A* - resigned, uncomplaining.
res'iprok *A* 1 *jur.* reciprocal (e.g. agreement, will). 2 *gram.* reciprocal (pronoun, verb).
resisten's *-en med.* resistance to infection.
resisten't *A* - *med.* resistant.
resitasjo'n *-en* declamation, recitation.
resitati'v *-et, pl -/+-er* recitative.
resite're *V -te* declaim, recite.
res. kap.=**residerende kapellan**
reskon'tro *-en* 1 *merc.* current account. 2 current account book.
reskrip't *-et hist., jur.* ordinance, rescript.
resolusjo'n *-en admin.* resolution; decree: **stille en r-** propose a resolution; **vedta en r-** adopt a resolution: **kongelig r-** royal decree (decision made by king's cabinet).
+**resolusjo'ns/forslag** *-et* motion, proposal for a resolution.
resolutt' *A* - resolute; quick, unhesitating.
+**resolutt'/het** *-en* resoluteness; promptness, quickness.
resolve're *V -te* resolve; decree.
resonans [resonang's] *-en* 1 *phys.* resonance. 2 echo; resonance, response.
resonans/botn *-en* (=+**/bunn**) sounding board.
resong' *-en* 1 reason, sound sense: **bringe en til r-** bring sby to his senses. 2 coherence.
resonnement [resonnemang'] *-et, pl -/+-er* 1 argumentation, reasoning. 2 mode of reasoning.
resonne're *V -te* 1 argue; reason; think (**over** through): **r-ende stil** expository style. 2 *dial.* criticize, scold.
resonnø'r *-en* 1 argumentative person. 1 raisonneur; author's mouthpiece, spokesman.
resorbe're *V -te physiol.* absorb (e.g. foodstuffs), assimilate, resorb.
resorpsjo'n *-en physiol.* resorption.
resp.=**respektive**
respek't *-en* respect (**for** for): **det står r- av ham** he inspires r-; **gjøre noe av r-** do sth out of r-; **ha r- for** stand in awe of; **med r- å melde** with all due deference; **sette seg i r-** make oneself r-ed.
respekta'bel *A -elt, pl -le* respectable (=honorable; quite good; considerable).
respekte're *V -te* 1 respect. 2 *fig.* honor (e.g. agreement).
+**respek't/inngytende** *A* - awe-inspiring, impressive; commanding respect.
res'pektiv *A* respective.
res'pektive *Av* respectively.
respek't/laus *A* (=+**/løs**) disrespectful (**imot, overfor** to, towards).
+**respek't/stridig** *A* - disrespectful (**imot, overfor** to, towards), insubordinate.
respirasjo'n *-en* respiration.

+ Bokmål; * Nynorsk; ° Dialect.
After letter: ' stress (Acc. 1); ` tone, stress (Acc. 2); · length.
Below letter: . not pronounced.

respitt' *-en* 1 period of grace, respite. 2 (in sports) handicap.
respon'sum *-umet, pl* *+-a/*-um* (=***respons**) *jur.* (expert) opinion: **avgi r-** give an o-; **sakførers r-** counsel's o-.
ressur's *-en (pl)* means, (natural) resources.
res't *-en* rest; remainder (also *math.*), remnant: **bli, stå, være til r-** remain; be still due; be in arrears (**med** with); **r-er** remnants; leftovers; **for r-en** see **forresten.**
restanse [restang'se] *-n (pl)* arrears: **være i r-** be in arrears.
restan't *-en* person in arrears with payment.
restaurant [restaurang'] *-en* restaurant (incl. coffee-shop, dining room, lunch room): **gå på r-** eat at a r-.
restaurasjo'n *-en* 1 restoration (**av** of) (e.g. picture, building). 2 *hist.* Restoration. 3 restaurant.
restauratri'se *-a/+-en* woman manager of restaurant, esp. ship's restaurant.
restauratø'r *-en* 1 restorer (of art). 2 owner, manager of restaurant.
restaure're *V -te* renovate, restore (work of art).
restaure'rings/arbeid *-et* reconstruction, restoring (e.g. of fossil, painting).
+res't/behol'dning *-en merc.* 1 balance. 2 surplus stock.
+res't/belø'p *-et merc.* balance.
***res'te** *V -a* cf **restere**
res'te/middag *-en fam.* dinner of leftovers.
+reste're *V -te* (=***reste**) 1 *merc.* remain to be paid. 2 *fam.* be in arrears (see **r-ende**).
+reste'rende *A* - remaining (sum): **r- beløp** balance; **r- skatter** tax arrears.
+res'te/salg *-et* clearance sale.
res't/gjeld *-a/+-en* outstanding debt.
restitue're *V -te* 1 *jur.* restore (money); rehabilitate, restore (to one's rights, former rank). 2 cure, store (to health). 3 reconstruct, restore (text).
restitusjo'n *-en* 1 *jur.* compensation, damages. 2 restoration (of text to original spelling). 3 *jur.* rehabilitation.
res't/opplag *-et* unsold stock; remainders.
res't/parti' *-et, pl +-er/*-* remainder, surplus (of unsold goods).
res't/produk't *-et* by-product, waste product.
restriksjo'n *-en* restriction.
res'triktiv *A* restrictive.
resultan't *-en phys.* resultant.
resulta't *-et, pl -/+-er* result (**av** of): **hvor utgangspunktet er galest, blir tidt r-et originalest** when the point of departure is maddest, the results are often the most original (Ibsen).
resulta't/laus *A* (=**+/løs**) fruitless, vain (effort); ineffective (treatment).
resulte're *V -te* result: **r- i** result in; lead to.
resymé *-et, pl +-er/*-* résumé, summary (**av** of).
resyme're *V -te* summarize: **for å r-** to sum up.
retardasjo'n *-en* retardation; *naut.* seconds a chronometer slows up pr. 24 hrs.
retarde're *V -te* delay, retard; (of chronometer) slow up.
retensjo'n *-en jur., med.* retention.
retiré *A* - guarded, reserved.
retire're *V -te* 1 *mil.* retreat; *fam.* withdraw. 2: **r- seg** *fam.* recover (from illness).
ret'ne *V -a/+-et dial.* straighten.
ret'ning *-a/+-en* 1 direction; course: **i r- av** in the d- of; **i r- nord-sør** in a north-south d-. 2 *fig.* course, direction: **i alle r-er** in all respects; **i samme r-** along the same lines; **i r- av** with respect to; **noe i den r-** sth of that kind. 3 tendency, trend; (intellectual, political, religious, etc.) movement: **en radikal r-innen bevegelsen** a radical wing of the movement. 4 *mil.* adjusting (e.g. sights on cannon); *educ.* correcting, grading; *gymn., mil.* dressing up (of line).
ret'nings/linje *-a/+-en* (=***/line**) 1 line of direction (of a movement), outline, plan. 2 *pol. (pl)* directives, lines of guidance, platform.
ret'nings/lys *-et* (=***/ljos**) direction light (on car).
+ret'nings/viser *-en, pl -e* (=***-ar**) 1 sign (e.g. in road, street). 2 signal arrow, light (on vehicle); direction indicator.
+reto'riker *-en, pl -e* (=***-ar**) rhetorician; orator.
retorikk' *-en* rhetoric.
reto'risk *A* - rhetorical.
retor'te *-n* 1 *chem.* retort. 2 gas retort.
retrett' *-en mil.* retreat: **gjøre r-** retreat.
+retrett'/stilling *-en · mil.* (prepared) position (to fall back on); *hum.* retirement post.
re'trospektiv *A* retrospective.
retroversjo'n *-en* reverse translation (into the original).
rett'[1] *-en* 1 course (of meal). 2 dish, portion (of food): **dagens r-** special.
rett'[2] *-en* 1 jurisprudence, justice, law: **la nåde gå for r-** temper justice with mercy. 2 court (of law), tribunal: **for r-en** before the c-, in c-; **gå r-ens vei** go to c-, take legal action; **møte for r-en** appear in c-; **sette r-** convene c-; **ti kjennes for r-** the judgment of the c- (introductory phrase when passing sentence).
rett'[3] *-en* 1 right (**til** to): **i sin r-** within one's r-(s); **komme til sin r-** come into one's own; show to (one's) advantage. 2 right (as opposed to wrong); rightness, straightness: **få r-** prove right, turn out to be right; **gi en r-** admit sby is right; agree with sby; **gjøre r- for noe** give compensation for sth, reimburse; **få r- og skjel** get one's rights; **gjøre r- (og skjel) for seg** acquit oneself well; do the right thing; **ha r-** be right; **r- skal være r-** give the devil his due, in all fairness. (See also **rette[1], rettes.**)
rett'[4] *A* 1 straight (back, line, etc.); direct: **r- fram** straight ahead; blunt(ly), straight out; *(adv.)* **r- fram for seg** straight in front of one; **r- på** bluntly; **r- som et lys** stiff as a ramrod, straight as a stick; **r- så** *naut.* steady (as you go); **stå r-** stand at attention. 2 correct, right (amount, angle, method, place, road, etc.); lawful, rightful; *dial.* right (in the head): **r-ere sagt** (to put it) more correctly; **r- nå** at this very moment, right now; **r- og slett** *(adv.)* mere; pure and simple; quite simply; **r- som vi gikk** just as we were going; **r- som det er (var)** all at once, suddenly; at intervals, every once in a while. 3 *(adv.)*, *archaic* just; really.
***ret'tar** *-en* executioner.
***ret'tar/bot** *-a* cf **retter/**
***ret'tar/gang** *-en* cf **retter/**
***ret'tar/stad** *-en* cf **retter/sted**
ret'te[1] *-a/+-en* right side (e.g. of cloth).
ret'te[2] *N* 1: **til r-** in order, straight, to rights; **finne seg til r-** adapt oneself (**i** to), make the best of it; **komme til r-** be found, turn up; **snakke, tale en til r-** make sby listen to reason. 2: **med r-** lawfully, rightfully. 3: **gå i r- med en** call sby to account, upbraid sby; **stå til r-** be called to account.
ret'te[3] *V -a/+-et/*-e* 1 right, straighten; correct, rectify: *mil.* **r- inn et geledd** dress up a rank; **r- på** straighten; correct; remedy. 2 direct (**mot** against); aim, point (**mot at**): **r- en takk til en** extend a word of thanks to sby; **r- et spørsmål til en** direct a question to sby. 3 execute; punish: **r- baker for smed (smed for baker)** make the innocent suffer for the guilty. 4 *(refl.)* **r- seg etter** be regulated according to; go by; comply with; conform to; **r- seg opp (i været)** draw oneself up, straighten up.
ret'te/ba'rn *-et fam.* (one's) real child (not step-, adopted child).
ret'telig *A* - 1 proper, real, regular: **en r- kar** a real man. 2 *(adv.)* by rights, really, rightly: **som vi r- skulle hatt** which by rights we should have had. *3 *(adv.)* quite, very: **r- snill** very kind.
+ret'telse *-n* correcting; correction (**av** of).
+ret'ter/bot *-a/-en, pl -bøter hist.* amendment (to law code).
+ret'ter/gang *-en jur.* legal action, procedure.
+ret'tergangs/ordning *-a/-en* rules of legal procedure.
+ret'ter/sted *-et* (=***rettar/stad**) place of execution.
***ret'tes** *N*: **til r-** aright; **hjelpe ein til r-** help sby out, straighten sby out; **koma til r- med ein** get along with sby; **leggja noko til r- for ein** prepare sth for sby. (See also **rette[2]**.)
ret'te/snor *-a* guide, rule (of conduct); example.
***rett'/fengen** *A -e/-i, pl -ne* legally acquired.
rett'/ferd [*/fær] *-a/+-en* (=**+/ferdighet**) justice.
rettfer'dig *A* - 1 fair, just. 2 *bibl.* righteous.
+rettfer'dig/gjøre *V -gjorde, -gjort* justify.
+rettfer'dig/het *-en* cf **rett/ferd**
+rettfer'dighets/sans *-en* sense of justice.
rettferds/kjensle *-a* sense of justice.
***rett'/følgd** *-a* consistency.
+rett'/haveri *-et* insistence, obstinacy, pigheadedness.
+rett'/haversk *A* - argumentative, insistent, obstinate.
***ret'tig** *A* - just, proper, right.
+ret'tig/het *-en jur.* privilege, right: **borgerlige r-er** civil rights.
ret'ting *-a/+-en* correction (**av** of).
rett'/kjenne *V +-kjente/*-kjende admin.* confirm, verify.
rett'/kommen *A +-ent, pl -komne* (=***/komen**) entitled (**til** to); honestly acquired.
rett'/kval *-en* (=**+/hval**) *zool.* right whale (Balaena).
rett'/laus *A* 1 outlawed, without legal rights. 2 anarchical, lawless (e.g. conditions).
+rett'/lede *V -et* cf **/leie**
+rett'/ledning *-en* cf **/leiing**
rett'/leie *V -de* direct, guide; give (sby) directions.
***rett'/leies** *Av* straight ahead.
rett'/leiing *-a* directions; guidance.
+rett'/linjet *A* - (=***/lina**) 1 *math.* rectilinear. 2 *fig.* honest, straightforward.
+rett'/løs *A* cf **/laus**
+rett'/messig *A* - lawful, legal, legitimate; proper, rightful.
rett'/nå *Av* cf **rett[4]**
+rett's/avgjø'relse *-n* judicial decision.
+rett's/begre'p *-et* conception of justice.
+rett's/belæ'ring *-en* charge (to the jury), summing up.
+rett's/beskyt'telse *-n* legal protection.
+rett's/betjen't *-en* officer of the court.
+rett's/beviss'thet *-en* conception of, sense of justice.
rett's/ferie *-n* court vacation (July 1—Aug. 15, Dec. 24—Jan. 1).
+rett's/forføl'gelse *-n* legal proceedings.
+rett's/følelse *-n* sense of justice.
rett's/grunnlag *-et* legal basis.
rett's/gyldig *A* - legal, valid.
rett's/handling *-a/+-en* act of the court, judicial act.

rett's/heimel *-en* legal basis, proof, title; validity: **skaffe seg r-** prove one's title (to sth).
rett's/histo'rie *-a/+-en* legal history.
rett's/hjelp *-a/+-en* legal aid.
+**rett's/hjemmel** *-en* cf **/heimel**
rett'/side [*/sie] *-a/+-en* face (of material), right side.
+**rett'/sindig** *A* - honorable, upright.
rett'/sinn *-et* honesty, uprightness.
+**rett'/skaffen** *A -ent, pl -skafne* honorable, upright; righteous.
+**rett'skaffen/het** *-en* honesty, uprightness; integrity, righteousness.
rett's/kjemi' *-en* forensic chemistry, chemical jurisprudence.
+**rett's/kjennelse** *-n* decision of, finding by the court.
rett's/kjensle *-a* sense of justice.
rett's/kraftig *A* - legally binding.
rett's/krav *-et* legal claim.
+**rett's/krenkelse** *-n* (=*-**ing**) violation of the law.
+**rett'/skri'vning** *-a/-en* (=*/**skriving**) orthography, spelling: **engelsk r-** English s-; **r-en av 1917** the orthography of 1917.
+**rett's/kyndig** *A* - learned in the law, legally trained: **r- bistand** legal advice.
rett'slig *A* - judicial, legal: **et r- forhør** a court hearing; **skride inn r-** prosecute sby; **reise r- tiltale mot en** make a charge against sby.
rett's/lærd *en* lawyer, man of law.
+**rett's/løs** *A* cf **rett/laus**
rett's/maskineri' *-et* machinery of justice.
rett's/medisi'n *-en* forensic medicine, medical jurisprudence.
rett's/medisi'nsk *A* - medico-legal.
rett's/møte *-t, pl +-r/*-* session, sitting (of a court).
+**rett's/område** *-t* jurisdiction.
+**rett's/oppgjør** *-et* (=*/**oppgjer**) legal settlement.
rett's/orden *-enen, pl -ner* legal system.
+**rett's/pleie** *-n* administration of justice.
rett's/prinsipp' *-et, pl -/+ er* (basic) legal principle.
rett's/sak *-a/+-en* case; (court) trial; lawsuit.
rett's/sal *-en* courtroom.
+**rett's/sikkerhet** *-en* law and order, rule of law.
*****rett's/skipnad** *-en* legal system.
+**rett's/skriver** *-en, pl -e* (=*-**ar**) clerk of court.
rett's/stat *-en* state governed by law (opp. of police state).
*****rett's/stell** *-et* administration of justice, judicial system.
rett's/stridig *A* - illegal, unlawful.
rett's/subjek't *-et, pl -/+-er* legal person.
rett's/vern [/væ'rn] *-et* legal protection.
+**rett's/vesen** *-et* administration of justice, judicial system.
+**rett's/villfarelse** *-n* judicial error.
+**rett's/vitenskap** *-en* (=/**vitskap**) jurisprudence, law.
rett's/vitne *-t, pl +-r/*-* court witness.
*****rett'/svæv** *A* sleepy at the right time (opp. of **rangsvæv**).
*****rett'/synt** *A* - clear-sighted, perceptive.
rett'/søles *Av* with the sun.
+**rett'/tenkende** *A* (=*/**tenkjande**) right-minded.
rett'/tenkt *A* - right-minded.
rett'/tidig *A* - **1** at time due, in time, punctual. **2: r- behandling** early treatment.
+**rett'/troende** *A* - (=*/**truande**) **1** *eccl.* believing, having the right faith; orthodox. **2** *fig.* orthodox.
+**rett'/troenhe't** *-en* orthodoxy.
*****rett'/viljug** *A* - honorable, upright.
rett'/vinkla *A* - (=+-**et**) *math.* rectangular, right-angled.
rett'/vis *A* **1** fair, just (**mot** to). **2** honorable.
*****rett'/vise** *-a* honor; justice.
rett'/visende *A* - *naut.* true (course).
retu'r *-en* **1** return trip, trip home: **tur r-** round trip. **2** *merc.*: **varer sendt i r-** goods returned. **3: på r-** in decline (of abilities, economic position, health), on the wane; past one's prime.
retu'r/billett' *-en* return ticket.
retu'r/mjølk *-a* (=+/**melk**) milk returned by dairy to (original) owner at reduced price.
returne're *V -te* return (e.g. goods, letter).
retu'r/veksel *-elen, pl -ler merc.* redraft.
retusj' *-en* added touch (to painting), retouching.
retusje're *V -te* retouch (painting, photograph); give finishing touches to (literary product).
+**reuma'tiker** *-en, pl -e* (=*-**ar**, **revmatiker**) rheumatic.
reuma'tisk *A* - (=**revmatisk**) rheumatic.
reumatis'me *-n* (=**revmatisme**) rheumatism.
°**rev**[1] [ræv'] *-a* cf **rauv**
re'v[2] *-en* **1** *zool.* fox (Vulpes vulpes): **Mikkel r-** Reynard the f-; **ha en r- bak øret** have tongue in cheek, be up to some trick; **det stikker en r- under** there is some trick (deceit). **2** fox scarf, fur piece.
re'v[3] *-et naut.* reef (part of rail).
re'v[4] *-et* bank (in sea), reef.
+**re'v**[5] *pt of* **rive**[3]
revanche [revang'sj] *-n* cf **revansj(e)**
revansj(e) [revang'sj] *-(e)n* compensation, reparation, revenge (for deed, in games): **få, ta r-** retaliate.
revansj(e)/parti' *-et, pl +-er/*-* **1** *pol.* Revenge Party (1870 in France). **2** (of games) extra round, return game.
*****re've**[1] *-a* vixen (female fox).
re've[2] *V -a/+-et/+-de naut.* reef (a sail).
+**re've**[3] *V -et* cf **reive**
re've/bjølle *-a* (=+/**bjelle**) *bot.* foxglove (Digitalis purpurea).
re've/fôr *-et* food for foxes.
re've/ful *A* sly as a fox.
re've/hi *-et* fox burrow.
+**re've/hold** *-et* (=*/**hald**) fox farming.
revel'je *-n* reveille.
re've/mat *-en* fox food.
re've/pels *-en* fox fur; *fig.* fox, fly fellow.
reveren's *-en* **1** respect, veneration. **2** (show of) veneration, e.g. bow, curtsy.
reveren'ter *Av*: **r- talt** saving your reverence, to speak bluntly.
rever's *-en* **1** reverse side (of coin). **2** facing, lapel (of clothing). **3** *fig.* the other side of the picture. **4** reverse: **sette motoren i r-** put the motor in r-.
reversi'bel *A -elt, pl -le* reversible.
re've/saks *-a* fox trap.
re've/strek *-en* sharp trick; hanky-panky.
+**re'vet** *pp of* **rive**[3]
revide're *V -te* **1** revise (sth written): **den r-te oversettelse** the r-d translation. **2** *merc.* audit (accounts). **3** adjust (wage scale); alter, revise (decree, opinion).
revi(e)r [reviæ'r/revi'r] *-et, pl +-er/*-* **1** *naut.* navigable mouth of river. **2** hunting grounds. **3** *fig.* field (of study, specialty).
revisjo'n *-en* **1** revision; adjustment, alteration (**av** of). **2** *merc.* auditing, taking of inventory. **4** auditor(s): **r-en kommer i dag** the a-(s) will be here today.
revi'sor *-en, pl -so'rer* accountant, auditor: **statsautorisert r-** certified public accountant.
*****rev'je** *V -a* bubble: **det r-ar på sjøen** the sea is bubbling (of the bubbles caused by presence of fish).
rev'le[1] *-n* piece of weaving, strip of cloth.
+**rev'le**[2] *-n* sandbank (usu. parallel to shore).
+**revma'tiker** *-en, pl -e* (=*-**ar**) cf **reumatiker**
revma'tisk *A* - cf **reumatisk**
revmatis'me *-n* cf **reumatisme**
+**rev'ne**[1] *-a* cf **rivne**[1]
+**rev'ne**[2] *V -a/-et* cf **rivne**[2]
+**rev'ne/ferdig** *A* - bursting (**av** with) (curiosity, food).
revol'te *-n* (=+**revol't**) revolt.
revolte're *V -te* rebel, revolt, rise up (**mot** against).
revolusjo'n *-en* revolution (**mot** against).
revolusjone're *V -te* revolutionize.
revolusjonæ'r *A* revolutionary.
revol'ver *-en, pl +-e* **1** revolver. **2** revolving part of a machine.
revol'ver/mann *-en, pl -menn/*-menner* gunman.
re'v/tik *-a* vixen (female fox).
re'v/tispe *-a* vixen (female fox).
revy' *-en* **1** review (esp. *mil.*): **holde r-** inspect the troops; **passere r-** file past. **2** (theater) revue (entertaining medley of skits, songs, dances).
revy'/tea'ter *-eret/-ret, pl -er/+-re* revue theater (often with cabaret).
revy'/vise *-a/+-en* song from a revue; popular song.
Rhi'nen *Pln* Rhine river, Germany.
Rhi'n/land *Pln* Rhineland, Germany.
+**rhin'sk/vin** *-en* cf **rinsk/**
rhododen'dron *-en* rhododendron.
ri'[1] *-a* **1** (violent) attack, fit (e.g. of illness); birth pangs; (sudden) onset (e.g. of bad weather); paroxysm (e.g. of laughter); epidemic: **ei ri med meslinger** a spell of measles. **2** period of bad weather; spell (e.g. of desire to work): **arbeide i rier** work in fits and starts. **3** a few minutes; moment: **der skal han stande ei lita ri** there he shall stand a little while (Ballad).
ri'[2] *V rei, ridd* (=**ride**) **1** ride (**på** on) (broom, horse, etc.); ride horseback; sit astride: **han rir ikke den dag han saler** he is a slow starter, he takes his time. **2** (with *prep., adv.*): **ri stormen av** ride out the storm; **ri for ankeret** *naut.* ride at anchor; **ri inn** break in (horse); **ri på** be mounted on, ride (horse, motorcycle, etc.); **ri på staven** ride one's ski pole to brake one's speed. **3** (*refl.*) **ri seg en tur** *lit.* go for a horseback ride.
+**ribb'/bein** [also ribb'/] *-et anat.* rib: **så mager en kan telle r-ene** so skinny you can count the ribs.
+**ribb'/ben** *-et* cf **/bein**
rib'be[1] *-a/+-en* **1** spareribs. **2** *gymn.* (stall) bar.
rib'be[2] *V -a/+-et* **1** pick, pluck (e.g. feathers); gather, strip, (e.g. berries, often using tool): (of wild goose) **r- sin egen barm** pluck its own breast. **2** fleece, pluck; rob, skin (sby of his money); denude, strip (e.g. house of furniture): **r-et for alle illusjoner** completely disillusioned; **r-et for min siste drøm** divested of my last dream (Garborg).
+**rib'be/fett** *-et* fat around ribs of pork.
+**rib'ben** *-et* cf **ribb/bein**
rib'be/steik *-a* roasted spareribs.
rib'be/vegg *-en gymn.* stall bars.
*****ri'd** *pr of* **ri**[2]
-rid *Prn(f)* e.g. in **Gud/r-, Ing/r-.**
*****ri'dar** *-en* rider (on horseback).
ridd' *pp of* **ri**[2]
*****rid'darleg** *A* - cf **ridderlig**
+**rid'der** *-en, pl -e* (=*-**ar**) **1** knight: **r- av St. Olav** k- of (the Order of) St. Olav; **r- av den bedrøvelige skikkelse** Knight of the Rueful Countenance; **slå seg til r- på** make oneself important by; **damenes r-**

+ Bokmål; * Nynorsk; ° Dialect.
After letter: ' stress (Acc. 1); ` tone, stress (Acc. 2); · length.
Below letter: . not pronounced.

champion of the ladies; *hum.* **lande-veiens r-** vagabond (lit. knight of the road). **2: arme r-e** french toast.

+rid'der/borg *-a/-en* (=***-ar/**) knight's castle.

+rid'der/diktning *-en* chivalric poetry.

+rid'der/kors *-et* knight's cross.

+rid'derlig *A* - (=***riddarleg**) chivalrous.

+rid'derlig/het *-en* chivalrousness.

+rid'der/orden *-en* (=***-ar/**) order of knighthood.

+rid'der/skap *-et* (=***-ar/**) knighthood.

+rid'ders/mann *-en, pl -menn* (=***-ars/**) *archaic* knight; gentleman.

+rid'der/spore *-n* (=***-ar/**) 1 knight's spur. 2 *bot.* larkspur (Delphinium).

+rid'der/tid *-a/-en* (=***-ar/**) age of chivalry.

+rid'der/vesen *-et* knighthood.

ri'de [*ri'e] *V +red/*reid, +-d/*-e/*-i* cf **ri**[2]

ri'de/bukse *-a* riding breeches.

ri'de/dyr *-et* mount.

+ri'de/foged *-en hist.* bailiff.

ri'de/hest *-en* mount, saddle horse.

ri'de/knekt *-en* groom.

ri'dende *A* - mounted, riding.

ri'de/pisk *-en* crop, riding whip.

ri'de/sal *-en* riding saddle.

ri'de/stell *-et* riding gear, trappings.

+ri'de/sti *-en* (=***/stig**) bridle path.

ri'de/støvel *-elen, pl -ler* riding boot.

ri'de/tur *-en* (horseback) ride.

+ri'de/tøy *-et* riding gear, trappings.

ri'de/veg *-en* (=**+/vei**) bridle path (esp. prepared with sand).

+ri'dning *-en* (=***riding**) riding.

rif'le[1] *-a* 1 rifle. 2 rut (in road); rifling (in gun); furrow (of skin); fluting (on edge of coin).

rif'le[2] *V -a/+-et* 1 flute, groove, rifle (an object). 2 ripple (e.g. water), ruffle.

rif'let(e) *A* - fluted (object); ridged (nails); rippled (water); (of guns) rifled.

rif't *-a* 1 scratch (on skin, in paint); break (in clouds); tear (in cloth). **2: r- om noe** great demand for sth. 3 *med.* stitch (in back).

rigabal'sam *-en* home remedy of oil, alcohol, and tincture of saffron.

***ri'ge** *V -a* rock, sway.

rigg' *-en* 1 *naut.* rigging. 2 *fam.* gear, outfit, rig.

rig'ge *V -a/+-et* 1 equip, rig (a ship): **r- i stand et måltid** get up a meal; **r- opp** rig up; **r- til** fix, prepare. 2 *fam.* dress up, equip with clothes; *hum.* **r- av seg klærne** remove one's clothes.

***rig'le** *V -a* 1 rock, stand unsteadily, sway. 2 gurgle, rattle.

rigorø's *A* rigorous, severe, strict.

ri'k *A* 1 opulent, rich, wealthy: **den r-e mann** the rich man (Dives); **de r-e** the rich. 2 abounding, rich (**på** in); copious; fruitful: **en r- høst** a bumper crop; **r-e evner** great gifts; **et r-t liv** a full life; **et r-t utvalg** a wide choice.

-rik *A* full of, rich in, e.g. **begivenhets/r-** eventful.

ri'k/dom' *-men/*-en* 1 opulence, riches, wealth. 2 abundance, copiousness, wealth (**på** of).

ri'ke *-t* kingdom; empire, realm, state: **hva i all verdens r-** what on earth, what in the world; **Norges r-** the kingdom of Norway; **Det britiske r-** the British Empire.

ri'kelig *A* - abundant, ample, generous: **vi har r- tid** we have plenty of time; **r- med mat** an abundance of food.

+ri'k/holdig *A* - rich (of metallic vein); abundant, copious, rich (e.g. collection).

ri'king *-en fam.* rich person, *(pop.)* plutocrat.

***ri'kje** *V -te* rule.

***rik'ke**[1] *-a* streak, wavy vein (in wood).

rik'ke[2] *V -a/+-et* (usu. *neg.*) move, stir: **han r-et seg ikke av flekken** he did not budge from the spot.

***rik'le** *V -a* cf **vrikle**

ri'k/mann *-en, pl -menn/*-menner* man of wealth, capitalist.

***ri'kne** *V -a* grow richer.

rikosjett' *-en/-et* ricochet (rebounding projectile).

rikosjette're *V -te* ricochet.

rik's[1] *+-en/*-et* 1 chirp, chirr (of grasshoppers). 2 creak, squeak: **r- av årene** squeak of the oars. 3 prick, smart, tingle (of blow, cold).

rik's[2] *-en* (short for **r-/telefon**) long distance call: **ta en r-** make a long distance call.

rik's- *Pf* of the state; national, official.

rik's/advoka't *-en* Attorney General, State Attorney.

rik's/arki'v *-et, pl -/+-er* National Archives.

rik's/bank *-en* national bank, state bank.

rik's/dag *-en* national assembly, parliament (Denmark, Sweden).

+rik's/daler *-en, pl -e* (=***-ar**) *hist.* silver coin (=four *kroner*), used in Norway until 1875.

rik'se *V -a/+-et* 1 chirp, chirr (of grasshoppers). 2 creak, squeak: **han kom r-nde med en trillebør** he came creaking along with a wheelbarrow. 3 *fam.* (short for **rikstelefonere**) make a long distance telephone call.

***rik'sens** *po*: **r- stell** affairs of state.

rik's/eple *-t* gold orb with cross (emblem of sovereignty).

rik's/forsam'ling *-a/+-en hist.* assembly of king's advisors and vassals; esp. of the constitutional assembly of Norway in 1814.

+rik's/forstan'der *-en, pl -e* regent.

rik's/grense *-a/+-en* border, frontier: **r-n** Norway's border with Sweden, Finland, Russia.

+rik's/kansler *-en, pl -e* (=***-ar**) chancellor.

rik's/kringkas'ting *-a/+-en* state broadcasting system: **Norsk r-** the Norwegian Broadcasting System.

rik's/meklingsmann *-en, pl -menn/*-menner* national labor arbitrator.

rik's/mål *-et* 1 (opp. of **dialekt**) official language (of a country). 2 (opp. of **landsmål, nynorsk**) Dano-Norwegian, one of the two official languages of Norway (name used esp. by its supporters). 3 (opp. of **bokmål**) traditional Dano-Norwegian (esp. as advocated by **Foreldreaksjonen**).

+rik'småls/fore'ning *-a/-en* society for advancement, preservation of **riksmål** (in sense 2).

rik'småls/mann *-en, pl -menn/*-menner* supporter of **riksmål** (in sense 2 or 3).

rik's/nett *-et* national broadcasting network.

rik's/program' *-met* nationwide radio program (opp. of local).

rik's/rett *-en* court of impeachment (in Norway 14 members of the **Lagting** and 7 Supreme Court justices).

rik's/revisjo'nen *df* government board of auditors.

rik's/råd[1] *-en hist.* member of State Council.

rik's/råd[2] *-et hist.* State Council.

rik's/segl [+/seil] *-et* state seal.

rik's/språk *-et* official (standard) language.

rik's/styre *-t, pl +-r/*-* national government.

rik's/tea'ter *-eret/-ret, pl -er/+-re* state traveling theater (estab. in Norway 1949).

rik's/telefo'n *-en* 1 state telephone system. 2 long distance: **ta en r-** make a long distance call.

rik'stelefon/samtale *-n/*-a* long distance telephone call.

rik's/trygdeverk *-et admin.* national social insurance system.

rik's/veg *-en* state highway: **R-50** H- 50.

rik's/våpen *-et* national coat of arms.

***rik't** *-en* creak, squeak.

rik'te *V -a dial.* creak, squeak: **det r-er i døra** the door creaks (Fønhus).

rik'tig *A* - 1 correct, right; proper: **det går ikke r- for seg** sth is not right, there's sth wrong. 2 downright, regular, thoroughgoing. 3 (usu. *neg.*) sane: **han er ikke r-** he isn't right in his head, he's crazy. 4 *(adv.)* exactly, for certain: **jeg vet ikke r-** I don't exactly know. 5 *(adv.)* really, very; quite: **r- livlig** quite lively.

+rik'tig/het *-en* accuracy, correctness; rightness, truth; propriety: **det har sin r-** it is quite correct, it is a fact.

+rik'tig/nok' *Av* 1 (intensive) certainly, indeed. 2 (concessive) to be sure; true enough.

ri'l *-en* reel (folk dance, usu. with three couples).

+ril'le[1] *-n* groove.

+ril'le[2] *V -a/-et* groove.

***ri'm**[1] *-ma* board; crossbar, rung; pole.

ri'm[2] *-et/+-en* frost, hoarfrost, rime.

ri'm[3] *-et* 1 (end) rhyme. 2 rhyme, verse (poem with end rhyme).

ri'me[1] *V -a/+-et/+-te* frost: **det r-er på vinduet** the window is f-ing over.

ri'me[2] *V -a/+-et* 1 rhyme (**med, på** with). 2 rhyme; write verse, doggerel. 3 agree, make sense: **det r-r ikke** this doesn't check, m- s-; **jeg får ikke dette til å r-** I can't see that this makes sense.

ri'melig *A* - reasonable (amount, demand, excuse, price, etc.); fair, just; amenable: **som r- er (kunne være)** as is (was) to be expected: **til r- pris** at a reasonable price.

+ri'melig/het *-en* 1 reasonableness, sense: **innenfor r-ens grenser** within reason. 2 likelihood, probability: **det er all r- for (at)** it seems likely (that).

ri'melig/vis *Av* most likely, probably.

+ri'meri' *-et derog.* 1 doggerel. 2 rhyming.

ri'met(e) *A* - 1 covered with frost. 2 *dial.* (of eye) edged with pus.

ri'm/fri *A -tt* unrhymed.

ri'm/frost *-en* hoarfrost, (white) frost.

ri'm/o'rd *-et* rhyme (word).

ri'm/smed *-en* poetaster, rhymester.

***ri'nald** *-en zool.* gurnard (Triglidae).

Rin'/dal *Pln* twp, Møre og Romsdal.

***rin'de** *-n* bank, ridge; high hill.

***ri'ne** *V rein, rine/-i* 1 affect, impress: **det rin ikkje på han** it doesn't affect him. 2 pain, sting: **det rin upp i nasen** it stings in the nose. 3 scream, squeal, whinny.

ring'[1] *-en* 1 (prize, Saturn's smoke, wedding, etc.) ring; hoop: **kaste r-** play quoits; **ta (d)en r- og la den vandre** (children's game) ab.= Button, button, who's got the button. 2 circle: **gå (kjøre) i r-** go in c-s; **kjøre i r- med en** lead sby a dance; **r-er under øynene** circles under one's eyes; **slå på r-en** (children's game) ab.=Run, goose, run; **slå r- om** form a c- around. 3 link (in chain). 4 tire; (tire) rim.

ring'[2] *A dial.* 1 small (number, size); low (price). 2 poor (quality).

+ring'/blomst *-en* (=***/blom**) *bot.* marigold (Calendula).

ring'/brynje *-a* coat, shirt of mail; byrnie, hauberk.

+ring'e[1] *-a* (=***ringje**[1]) (usu. round) wooden container for milk.

+ring'e[2] *V -te* (=***ringje**[2]) 1 ring; peal, toll: **det r-er** (the) bells are ringing. 2 call, ring, telephone. 3 (with *prep., adv.*) **det r-er for ørene (mine)** my ears are ringing; **det r-er i telefonen** the phone is ringing; **r- opp** call up, give a ring, phone; **r- over en ring,** toll for one's funeral; **r- på ring** the doorbell; **det r-er på døra** the doorbell is ringing.

ring'e[3] *V -a/+-et* 1 encircle, ring; circle (around): **r- inn** encircle, surround; hem in. 2 provide with a ring, ring (e.g. bull, tree). 3 *(refl.)*: **r- seg** form a ring; form ringlets; coil.

+ring'e[4] *A* 1 humble, lowly (e.g. birth): **etter min r- evne** to the best of my h- ability; **ingen r-ere enn** no less a person than, none other than. 2 feeble, inferior, poor (ability, quality, work, etc.). 3 insignificant, trifling (e.g. gift). 4 *archaic.* little, slight, small: **ikke den (aller) r-este interesse** not the slightest interest.

+ring'e/akt *-en* contempt, disdain, scorn (**for** for).

+ring'e/akte *V -a/-et* despise, disdain, scorn; slight (sby).

+ring'e/appara't *-et* (=***ringje/**) (electric) bell.

Ring'e/bu *Pln* twp, Oppland.

+ring'e/klokke *-a* signal bell (to call field workers); alarm clock; doorbell, electric bell; bicycle bell.

+ring'e/ledning *-en* bell wire.

Ring'e/rike *Pln* twp, Oppland.

ring'e/riking *-en* person from Ringerike.

ring'/finger *-eren, pl -rer* ring finger (in Norway usu. fourth finger on right hand).

ring'/fjell *-et astron.* crater of the moon.

ring'/forlova *A* - (=**+-et**) *fam.* formally engaged (with exchange of rings).

***ring'je**[1] *-a* cf **ringe**[1]

***ring'je**[2] *V -de* cf **ringe**[2]

***ring'/laup** *-et* circuit, circulation (of blood), cycle: **naturens r-** the cycle of Nature; **et r- av plikter** a round of duties.

ring'le[1] *-a* 1 curl, spiral. 2 (child's) rattle, small bell.

ring'le[2] *V -a/+-et* 1 curl up. 2 *(refl.)*: **r- seg** twist, wind itself.

ring'le[3] *V -a/+-et* jingle (coins, bells), tinkle (Christmas-tree ornaments, sleigh bells).

ring'/mur *-en hist.* circular wall, surrounding wall (of fort, town).

ring'/orm *-en* ringworm.

ring'/perm *-en* loose-leaf binder.

ring'/rev[1] *-en pol.* (sly) fox.

ring'/rev[2] *-et* atoll.

Ring's/aker *Pln* twp, Hedmark.

+ring'/spill *-et* (game of) quoits.

+rin'ne *V rant, runnet lit.* 1 rise; spring (**opp** up): **r- en i hu, i minne, i sinne** come to one's mind; **runnet av bondeslekt** (come) of peasant stock; **solen r-er** the sun is r-ing; **dagen rant** dawn broke. 2 (of time) elapse, pass, slip by. 3 (of currents of thought, impressions, etc.) run, stream (**sammen** together). 4 *obs.* (of fluid) flow, run (see **renne**).

rin'sk/vin *-en* (=**+rhinsk/**) Rhine wine.

***ri'om/til'** *Av* now and then.

ri'p[1] *-a, pl *-ar* (=**+ripe**[1]) edge; *naut.* gunwale, railing.

***ri'p**[2] *-et* 1 scratch. 2 scratching sound (usu. of throat).

+ri'pe[1] *-a* cf **rip**[1]

ri'pe[2] *-a* 1 rift, scratch. 2 cleft, pass.

ri'pe[3] *V -a/+-te* 1 score; scratch. 2: **r- av (i)** strike (a match).

ri'pe[4] *V -a/+-te* rip, tear (**av** off).

ri'p/måt *-et dial., carp.* (marking) gauge.

ripos't *-en* 1 (fencing) riposte. 2 repartee.

riposte're *V -te* 1 riposte, counter. 2 retort.

***ripp'** *-en* haste, hurry.

rip'pe[1] *V -a/+-et* 1: **r- opp, r- opp i** drag up, rake up (the past, painful memories). 2 *dial.* scale fish.

***rip'pe**[2] *V -a* 1 hurry. 2 clear out, run away.

rip's[1] *-en bot.* red, white currants (Ribes sativum).

rip's[2] *-en* rep (a textile).

rip's/busk *-en* currant bush.

***ri'r** *-en* veined, knotted wood.

ri's[1] *-en bot.* rice (Oryza sativa): **japansk r-** puffed r- (used as desert in Norway); **r- i karri** r- curry.

ri's[2] *-et* 1 twigs (on bush, tree, etc.); bush, greenery, top of plant (e.g. potato). 2 brush, brushwood. 3 (birch) rod, whip; esp. *(bibl.)* rod (of punishment): **binde r- til egen bak** raise trouble for oneself. 4 spanking, whipping; *fig.* criticism: **få r-** get a s-; **r- og ros** a mixed reception.

ri's[3] *-et* ream (of paper).

***ri's/bit** *-en* year-old (billy goat, pig, ram).

ri'se[1] *-n* (Norse) *myth.* giant.

ri'se[2] *V +-te/*-a* 1 birch, flog, thrash. 2 stake (e.g. tomatoes).

***ri'se**[3] *V reis, -e/-i* 1 arise, rise (**opp** up). 2 (of horse) rear up. 3 get over (a blow, disease). 4 tower.

***ri'seleg** *A* - gigantic, Herculean.

+ri'sen/gryn *-et* cf **ris/**

ri's/gjerde [/jære] *-t* 1 fence (of small trees and twigs placed between logs). 2 low fence of small branches with openings for placing grouse snares.

ri's/graut *-en* (=**+/grøt**) rice pudding.

ri's/gryn *-et* (grain of) rice.

risika'bel *A -elt, pl -le* hazardous, risky, uncertain.

risike're *V -te* risk, run (take) a risk, take a chance on.

ris'iko *-en* 1 risk: **løpe en r-** run a r-; **med r- for** at the r- of; **på egen r-** at one's own r-. 2 *merc.* object of insurance: **bære en r-** cover a r- (with possible loss); **en god r-** a good r-; **forsikring på første r-** first r-.

ris'iko/momen't *-et* element of risk.

ris'k *-en* chance, risk: **ta r-en** take a c-, run a r-.

ris'ke[1] *-a bot.* milk fungus (Lactarius).

***ris'ke**[2] *-a vet.* disease of horses (causing them to roll over and scratch backs).

riskon'tro *-en* cf **reskontro**

ri's/kost [/kos't] *-en* 1 broom (of imported straw and rushes). 2 seamark of such a broom on a stake used in sheltered waters. 3 *dial.* brush pile.

ris'le[1] *-a dial.* 1 bush, treetop. 2 large broom. 3 head of grain.

ris'le[2] *V -a/+-et* 1 murmur, ripple, trickle: **solens gule lys r-et ned** *fig.* the yellow light of the sun filtered down. 2 run: **det r-et kaldt nedover ryggen på ham** cold shivers ran down his spine. 3 sprinkle (flour). 4 strip (berries off bushes).

ri's/mjøl *-et* rice flour.

ris'p *-et* 1 slash, slit. 2 scratch (on skin, surface). 3 scales removed from fish.

ri's/papi'r *-et* 1 rice paper (made from Tetrapanax papyriferum). 2 cigarette paper.

ris'pe[1] *-a* anecdote, jolly story.

ris'pe[2] *V -a/+-et* 1 rip, slash, tear (esp. body, also clothing). 2 rip, tear off (e.g. leaves from bush, tree): **r- fisk** clean fish. 3 carve, score, scratch (e.g. in bark): **nu r-et en rakett over himmelen** now a rocket streaked across the sky (Hamsun).

ris'pende *Av* intensive: **hun var rivende, r- gal** she was completely and hopelessly mad.

riss' *-et* 1 mark, scratch; fine crack (in ice); (of eyes) slit; (of leather) groove. 2 contour, outline: **i skarpe r-** in sharp contours. 3 diagram, drawing; ground plans; sketch: contour tracing (of patterns on cloth). 4 *fig.* thumbnail sketch (e.g. of sby's character).

Ris'sa *Pln* twp, Sør-Trøndelag.

ris'se *V -a/+-et* 1 draw up (ground plans); outline, sketch. 2 carve, cut (with sharp instrument on e.g. stone, metal); blaze (tree); cut, cut up (e.g. meat); score (e.g. ham); scratch: **r- inn i historiens tavler** inscribe on the tablets of history (Krag).

+ris'se/fjær *-a* 1 drawing pen, ruling pen. 2 ink compasses.

ris't[1] *-a* (=**+vrist**) instep (of foot, shoe).

ris't[2] *-a* 1 grate (in fireplace for cooking on), grating (over drain), grill (in oven); *hist.* grill (instrument of torture). 2 scraper (for shoes). 3 bars, grille (on gate, window).

ris't[3] *-a dial.* 1 ridge (of mountain). 2 hill, slope.

ris't[4] *-en/+-et* shake, shaking.

°ris't[5] *-et* cf **reist**[2]

+ris't[6] *N* rest (usu. with **ro**): **han har verken r- eller ro** he cannot rest; **uten r- og ro** without rest.

ris'te[1] *V -a/+-et* toast (bread); broil, grill (fish, meat); roast (chestnuts, coffee beans).

ris'te[2] *V -a/+-et/*-e* (=**+ryste**) 1 shake (sby, sth): **r- (en) av seg** discourage, shake (sby); **r- (noe) av seg** shake sth off; dismiss (e.g. worries); **r- i (på) noe(n)** shake sth, sby; **r- ned** shake down (e.g. apples); **r- på hodet** shake one's head; **r- på seg** shake oneself. 2 shake, tremble (see also **ryste**).

ris'te[3] *V -a/+-et/*-e* carve, esp. runic letters: **r- inn** imprint.

ris'tel *-elen, pl -ler* colter (on plow).

***ris't/høg** *A* with high instep; *fig.* defiant, proud.

ristorne're *V -te merc.* return; cancel.

ristor'no *-en merc.* return of premium.

Ri's/ør *Pln* town, Aust-Agder.

***ri't** *-et* drawing, sketch.

ri'te *V -a/+-et dial.* draw; write.

+ri'ter *pl of* **ritus**

rit'sj-rat'sj *I* 1 rip (sound made by tearing cloth). 2 opening words of a children's song and game: **r- fillebom-bom-bom.**

ritt' *-et* (horseback) ride: **en halv times r-** a half hour's r-.

+ritt'/mester *-eren, pl -ere/-rer* (=***/meister**) *mil.* captain (of horse).

ritua'l *-et, pl -/+-er eccl.* ritual; (order of) service (e.g. marriage); *fig.* ritual, tradition.

ritua'l/mord *-et* ritual murder.

rituell' *A -elt* 1 *eccl.* ritual. 2 conventional.

rit'us *-en, pl +riter eccl.* rite. 2 *hum.* habitual manner of excessive ceremoniousness.

***ri'v**[1] *-en* beam, roller (in loom).

***ri'v**[2] *-et* 1 toil: **r- og slit** t- and labor. 2 pain, stitch. 3 rift.

***ri'v**[3] *-et anat.* rib.

+ri'v[4] *Av*: **r- ruskende gal** stark raving mad, insane (of person); dead wrong (of idea).

riva'l *-en* competitor, rival.

rivalin'ne *-a/+-en* (female) rival.

rivalise're *V -te* compete, vie (**med** with): **r-ing** rivalry.

rivalite't *-en* competitiveness, rivalry.

***ri'var** *-en* hustler; careless worker.

***ri'vast** *V reivst, rivist* fight, wrestle.

ri've[1] *-a* rake.

***ri've**[2] *-a* crack, crevice, fissure.

ri've[3] *V reiv/+rev, +revet/*rive/*-i* 1 tear; raze, tear down. 2 gash, scratch (e.g. one's finger). 3 grate, shred (nuts, vegetables, etc.). 4 grind (colors); rub, work (**inn** in). 5 bite, burn, rasp: **akevitten r-er godt i halsen** the aquavit burns all the way down one's throat; **r- i nesen** tickle the nose. 6 pluck, pull, snatch; carry, take. 7: **r-es** fight, scuffle, wrestle. 8 (with *prep., adv.*): **r- av** pull, tear off; **r- av seg klærne**

+ Bokmål; * Nynorsk; ° Dialect.
After letter: ' stress (Acc. 1); ' tone, stress (Acc. 2); · length.
Below letter: . not pronounced.

pull, strip off one's clothes; **r- av seg vitser** crack, reel off jokes; **r- en noe i nesen** rub sth in, throw sth up to one; **r- i** (stand) treat; **r- med seg** carry away, sweep along (**r- en med seg i fallet** pull sby down with one); **r- opp** break open, tear open; reopen (e.g. wound); **r- til seg** grab, snatch (**r- handa til seg** pull, snatch one's hand away); **r- tvers over** tear in two (straight across). 9 (refl.) **r- seg i håret** tear one's hair; **r- seg løs** tear oneself away (**fra** from).

ri'vende A - 1 rapid, torrential, violent (rain, storm, stream, etc.); terrific: **r- fart** breakneck (furious, t-) speed. 2 (adv.) extremely, terribly: **r- gal** stark raving mad.

ri've/skaft -et rake handle.

ri've/tind -en tooth (on rake).

*****ri'v/hest** -en hustler; careless worker.

rivie'ra -en Riviera.

ri'v/jern [/jæ'rn] -et (=*/**jarn**) 1 grater. 2 fig. sharp-tongued person; hustler: **hun er et r- til å arbeide** she is a real h-.

riv'ne[1] -a (=+**revne**[1]) 1 rip, tear (in cloth). 2 crack (in stone), crevice, fissure: **r- i skyene** break in the clouds; **isen slår r-r** the ice breaks up.

riv'ne[2] V -a/-et (=+**revne**[2]) 1 crack (e.g. ice); rip (e.g. cloth); split (of head in headache). 2 (adv.): **det er meg r-nde likegyldig** it is utterly immaterial to me; I couldn't care less.

ri'vning -en conflict, discord, friction.

*****riv'nut** A - full of cracks, cracked.

*****rjo'me** -n cf **rømme**[1]

Rju'kan Pln town, Telemark.

ro'[1] -a, rør/+-er dial. 1 corner. 2 rivet head.

ro'[2] -a tech. burr, wire edge (left after sharpening).

ro'[3] -a/+-en rest; calm, stillness; peace, quiet; composure, equanimity: **bringe (stille) til ro** bring to rest; calm down, quiet; **falle, komme til ro** calm down; **gå til ro** go to bed; **ha ro på seg** be calm, not restless; **i ro** at rest, in peace, still; undisturbed; **ro og mak** leisure and comfort (**i ro og mak** leisurely); **slå seg til ro** settle down; compose oneself (**slå seg til ro med noe** be, rest content with sth); **ta det med ro** take it easy.

ro'[4] V -dde 1 row (boat): **r- fiske** engage in fishing by rowboat for a living. 2: **r- seg for langt ut** fig. get out beyond one's depth; stick one's neck out; **r- seg i land** crawfish, try to back out of an awkward situation; **nå ror han** fam. now he's trying to back out (Hoel; in reference to Nazi fellow travelers during occupation of Norway).

Ro'a Pln village, Hadeland.

Ro'ald Prn (m)

Ro'an Pln twp, Sør-Trøndelag.

*****ro'ande** A - (time, place) possible to row in: **det er så grunt det er ikkje r-** it is so shallow one can't row there; **det er ikkje r- i dag** the weather is so bad one can't row today.

Ro'ar Prn (m)

roast/biff [rås't/] -en broiled steak; underdone roast beef.

+**rob'be** V -a/-et plunder, rob.

rob'ber -en, pl +-e rubber (in card game).

+**robe** [rå'be] -n 1 gown, robe. 2 evening gown.

robinsona'de -n Robinsonade (novel reminiscent of Defoe's Robinson Crusoe).

robot [ro'båt] -en robot.

+**robot/aktig** A - like a robot; mechanical.

robus't A - 1 robust, rugged, sturdy: **r- samvittighet** tough conscience (Ibsen). 2 derog. coarse, rough.

ro'/båt -en rowboat.

*****rod** [rå'] -et fish skin.

+**ro'de[1]** -n cf **rote**[1]

*****rode[2]** [rå'e] -n cf **røde**[2]

*****rode[3]** [rå'e] V -a cf **rodne**

*****rode[4]** [rå'e] pp of **ry**[2] (=*rodi)

+**ro'de/kors** -et hist. Holy Rood; cross, crucifix.

*****rodne** [rå'dne] V -a 1 redden, turn red. 2 brush liquid on flatbrød to color.

+**ro'e[1]** -n 1 beet; sugar beet. 2 rutabaga. 3 turnip.

ro'e[2] V -a/+-et: **r- seg** become quiet, settle down.

+**ro'er** -en, pl -e (=*-ar) one who rows (a boat); (in sports) oarsman, rower.

ro'e/sukker [/sokker] -et beet sugar.

Rog. =**Rogaland**

Ro'ga/land Pln county, southwestern Norway.

*****rogg'** -et 1 fear, respect. 2 effort, initiative.

*****rog'ge** V -a speed up.

rogn[1] [rång'n] -a bot. rowan tree, European mountain ash (Sorbus aucuparia).

rogn[2] [rång'n] +-a/-en (fish) roe, spawn.

rogne/bær [rång'ne/] -et berries of rowan tree: **Reven og r-ene** the Fox and the Grapes (Aesop's fable as retold in Norway).

rogn/fisk [rång'n/] -en roe-carrying fish (female).

rogn/kjekse [rång'n/] -a zool. lumpfish (Cyclopterus lumpus).

rojalisme [råjalis'me] -n royalism.

rojalist [råjalis't] -en monarchist, royalist.

rojalistisk [råjalis'tisk] A - royalistic.

rok [rå'k] -et cf **rokk**[2]

roka'de -n castling (in chess): **kort r-** king c-; **lang r-** queen c-.

*****roke[1]** [rå'ke] -n cf **råke**[1]

*****roke[2]** [rå'ke] V -a fill to the brim, to overflowing.

*****roke[3]** [rå'ke] pp of **ryke**

roke're V -te castle (in chess).

*****roki** [rå'ki] pp of **ryke**

rokk'[1] -en 1 spinning wheel; hum. bicycle. 2 bot. horsetail (Equisetum).

rokk'[2] -et (=**rok**) sea spray, spindrift; driving rain, snow; storm: **fjorden stod i et eneste r-** the fjord was black with s-; **r- og fokk, r- og vær, storm og r-** rain and blizzard, snow and s-.

+**rok'ke[1]** -a zool. skate (fish) (Rajidai).

+**rok'ke[2]** V -a/+-et budge, move: **r- på seg** rock, constantly moving (in sitting position); **ikke r- på seg** refuse to budge; **r- på hodet** wag one's head. 2 shake (decision, faith, opinion): **han er ikke til å r-** he can't be budged. 3 stomp, walk heavily. 4 hum. bicycle.

*****rok'ke[3]** pp of **rekke**[3]

rok'ke/hjul -et wheel (of spinning wheel).

+**rok'ke/hode** -t (=*/**hovud**) 1 distaff (of spinning wheel). 2 fam. fool.

rok'ke/snor -a cord on spinning wheel.

*****rokk'/ga'rde** -n huge wave, wall of seawater.

*****rok'ki** pp of **rekke**[1]

ro'/klubb -en rowing club.

°**ro'ko** -a cf **reke**[2]

rokok'ko -en rococo (period, style).

*****rok/ver** [rå'k/] -et storm with sea spray.

Rol'f Prn (m)

ro'lig A - 1 calm, peaceful, quiet (conditions, person); steady (flame, market); serene, tranquil (water). 2 quiet, subdued (color, decor, pattern). 3 calm, controlled, quiet (attitude, speech). 4: **ta det r-** take it easy; calm down.

Rol'lag Pln twp, Buskerud.

rol'le -a/+-en part, role: **falle ut av r-n** forget one's part (lines); act out of character; **spille en r-** play a p-, r-; be of importance, matter (**det spiller ingen r-** it doesn't matter, it makes no difference).

+**rol'le/beset'ning** -en cast (of play); casting.

rol'le/bok -a (theater) script.

rol'le/fag -et (special) line (of acting), specialty: **Aabels r- har ligget i den komiske retning** Aabel's specialty has been comic parts (Tidens Tegn).

rol'le/hefte -t, pl +-r/*- (in theater) lines, part, script.

+**rol'ling** -en toddler.

roll'/mops -en rolled herring, rollmops.

*****rol'p** -et nonsense, twaddle.

*****rol'pe** V -a 1 talk nonsense. 2 bundle up, roll up.

*****rol's** -et drivel, nonsense.

*****rol'se** V -a talk nonsense.

Rol'v Prn (m)

Rol'vs/øy Pln twp, Østfold.

rom[1] [rom'] +-men/*-en rum (drink).

rom[2] [rom'] -met 1 space (also math., phys.); place, room (**til** for): **gi r-** make r- (**for** for); astron. **r-met** space; **tid og r-** time and s-. 2 compartment, section (hist. in viking ships, the space between ship's ribs where one rower could sit); room; naut. hold: **på r-met mitt** in my room.

rom[3] [rom'] A -t, pl -me 1 roomy, spacious; plenty of: **i r- tid** in plenty of time; **r-t omkring ham** plenty of room around him. 2 naut. open (sea): **i r- sjø** in the open sea; **holde seg i r- sjø** keep out to sea; **r- vind** fair (leading) wind; **seile r-t** run free, sail large.

Ro'm Pln cf **Roma**

Ro'ma Pln Rome.

roma'n -en novel.

roma'n/figu'r -en character in a novel.

+**roma'n/forfat'ter** -en, pl -e (=*-ar) novelist.

roma'n/helt -en hero in a novel.

romani [rom'ani] N Romany (language spoken by the gypsies).

Roma'nia Pln Romania.

romanis't -en 1 jur. lawyer specializing in Roman law. 2 educ. philologist having Romance languages as specialty.

roma'n/litteratu'r -en novels (as body of literature).

romanse [romang'se, -ang'se] -n 1 lit. ballad, romance. 2 mus. romance.

roma'nsk A - 1 Romance (language): **r-e folkeslag** Latin peoples. 2 arch. Romanesque: **r- stil** R- style.

+**roman'tiker** -en, pl -e (=*-ar) 1 romantic. 2 Romanticist.

romantikk' -en 1 romance. 2 Romanticism.

roman'tisk A - romantic.

*****ro'mar/tal** -et cf **romer/tall**

rom'be -n math. rhombus.

rom'be/porfy'r -en geol. rhombporphyry.

rom'bisk A - rhombic, rhomboid.

*****ro'me** V -a cf **romme**

Ro'me/dal Pln twp, Hedmark.

ro'me/gras -et bot. bog asphodel (Narthecium ossifragum).

+**ro'mer** -en, pl -e (=*-ar) Roman.

+**ro'mer/bad** -et (=*-ar/) Turkish bath; steam bath.

Ro'me/rike Pln twp, part of Akershus.

ro'me/riking -en person from Romerike.

+**romerin'ne** -n (=*romarinne) Roman (woman).

+**ro'mer/kirken** df the Church of Rome, the Roman Catholic Church.

+**ro'mer/rett** -en (=*-ar/) jur. Roman law.

+**ro'mer/riket** df (=*-ar/) hist. the Roman Empire.

ro'mersk A - Roman.

+**ro'mer/tall** -et Roman numeral.

rom/fang [rom'/] -et phys. cubic content, volume.

+**rom/farer** -en, pl -e (=*-ar) astronaut, space traveler.

rom/fart -en space travel.

rom/ferd [*/fær] *-a/+-en* space journey, space trip.
***rom/frek** *A* voluminous.
rom/geometri· *-en* solid geometry.
rom/helg *-a/+-en hist.* Dec. 27—Jan. 5; now most commonly Dec. 27—31 ("half holidays", days which form part of Christmas season).
rom/hendt *A -* generous.
+rom/innhold *-et* (=***/innhald**) capacity, cubic content.
rom/jul *-a/+-en* Dec. 27—31 (see **romhelg**).
rom.-kat.=**romersk-katolsk**
***romleg** [rom'leg] *A -* cf **romslig**
romme [rom'me] *V -a/+-et* 1 accommodate, seat (e.g. hall); hold, take (e.g. bottle): **det r-es ikke flere her** there is no space for more here. 2 *fig.* hold; imply, involve; conceal, contain. 3 *naut.* (of wind) veer so as to become more favorable.
rommelig [rom'meli] *A -* 1 roomy, spacious (house). 2 loose (clothing). 3 ample (time, means): **leve r-** live comfortably; **ta r- tid** take plenty of time. 4 tolerant (person); broad, elastic: **r- samvittighet** accommodating conscience.
rom/mål [rom'/] *-et* cubic measure, measure of capacity.
rom/pudding [rom'/] *-en* rum pudding.
rom/punsj [rom'/] *-en* rum punch.
***rom/sam** [rom'/] *A* roomy, spacious.
rom/skip [rom'/] *-et* spaceship.
romslig [rom'sli] *A -* (=***romleg**) 1 (of clothing) loose fitting, roomy. 2 (of attitude) generous, tolerant. 3 (of salary) substantial: **han har det r-** he has ample means.
+romslig/het [rom'sli/] *-en* generosity, tolerance.
romstere [romste're] *V -te* 1 mess, poke around, rummage; bank, knock about (**med** with).
***rom/stor** [rom'/] *A* voluminous.
+rom/tent *A -* (=***/tennt**) *dial.* having widely spaced teeth.
***romus** [rå'mus] *A -* generous, lavish.
°**ron'd** *-a, pl render* cf **rand**
***rone** [rå'ne] *-n* cf **råne**[1]
rong' *-a, pl renger dial.* stem; stern (of boat).
ro'p *-et* call (**om** for), calling; cry, shout (**til** to): **sette i et r-** utter a cry.
ro'pe *V -te/*-a* 1 call, cry, shout (**etter, om, på** for; **til** to). 2 (with *prep., adv.*) *mil.* **r- an** challenge; **r- etter** shout after, at; call for; *mil.* **r- i gevær** call to arms; **r- om, på** call for, shout for (e.g. help); **r- opp** call out (e.g. names on list); **r- på** (by radio) call (another station).
+ro'per[1] *-en, pl -e* (=***-ar**) *folk.* shrieking ghost (of slain child).
+ro'per[2] *-en, pl -e* cf **ropert**
ro'pert *-en* megaphone.
roquefort [råkefå'r] *-en* Roquefort (cheese; in U.S. often called "blue cheese").
ro'r[1] *-en* 1 rowing: **en times r-** an hour's r-. 2: **være i r- med** go out fishing with (sby). 3 *dial.* space for one rower.
ro'r[2] *-et* 1 *naut.* helm, tiller, wheel; rudder: **stå til r-s** be at the helm (also *fig.*); **ta r-et** take over the helm. 2 *aeronaut.* (the) controls; elevator, rudder.
ro'r/bu *-a* fisherman's shanty.
+ro'r/gjenger *-en, pl -e* helmsman.
ro'r/kult *-en* tiller (esp. on smaller boats or sailing vessel).
ro'r/mann *-en, pl -menn/*-menner* helmsman.
ro'r/pinne *-n* tiller.
ro'rs/folk *pl* oarsmen, rowers.
ro'r/skade [*/skae] *-n* damage to the rudder.
ro'rs/kar *-en* oarsman, rower (often hired in fishing season in Nordland).
+ro'r/stang *-a, pl -stenger* (=***/stong**) tiller.
ro'r/tø'rn *-en* time, trick, turn at the helm.
***ro's**[1] *-a* 1 landslide. 2 furrow; stripe.
***ros**[2] [rå's] *-a* cf **rosen**
ro's[3] *-en* praise, honor: **få, gi r-** get, give p-; **til r- for** in h- of.
ro'sa *A -* pink, rose-colored.
***ro'se**[1] *-a* cf **rosse**
ro'se[2] *-a/+-en bot.* rose (Rosaceae).
ro'se[3] *V -te/*-a* commend, praise: **r- en i høye toner** sing sby's praises, eulogize; **r- seg av** be proud of, boast, brag; **r-ende omtale** laudatory notice.
***rose**[4] [rå'se] *V -a* hurt slightly, scratch, scrub.
***ro'se/busk** *-en* cf **rosen/**
ro'se/knopp** *-en* (=/knupp**) cf **rosen/**
***ro'se/kål** *-en* cf **rosen/**
+ro'se/maling *-a/-en* (=***/måling**) rose painting (decorative floral painting on walls, ceilings, and furniture in rural areas, developed in the 18th Century from baroque and rococo elements).
+ro'sen *en* (=***ros**[2]) *med.* erysipelas.
+ro'sen/busk *-en* rosebush.
ro'sende *A -* commendatory, laudatory.
+ro'sen/knopp *-en* rosebud; *fig.* a young girl.
ro'sen/krans *-en* 1 garland of roses. 2 *eccl.* rosary.
ro'sen/kål *-en bot.* Brussels sprouts (Brassica oleracea gemmifera).
+ro'sen/munn *-en poet.* mouth like a rosebud, rosy lips.
+ro'sen/rød *A* rose-colored (also *fig.*= optimistic); rosy.
+ro'sen/skjær *-et* rosy hue.
ro'set(e) *A -* flower-adorned, flowery (furnishings, paper).
rosett' *-en* 1 bow; rosette (on dress, in hair). 2 *bot.* circular cluster of leaves. 3 *elec.* rosette (round plate covering a connection).
rosett'/bakkels *-en/*-et* rosette (a cooky); timbale.
+ro'se/vindu *-et* (=***/vindauga, */vindauge**) *arch.* rose window.
ro'/signal [/singna'l] *-et, pl -/+-er mil.* taps.
rosi'n *-a/+-en* raisin: **r-en i pølsen** the climax, the prize (usu. of pleasant surprise)
+ro'/skap *-et* (=***/skåp**) corner cabinet, cupboard.
rosmari'n *-en bot.* rosemary (Rosmarinus officinalis).
rosmari'n/lyng *-en/-et bot.* wild rosemary (Andromeda polifolia).
+ros'se *-a* (=***rose**[1]) gust of wind, squall (esp. sudden downdrafts from the mountains).
***ros'se/gauk** *-en zool.* common snipe (Gallinago caelestis).
ross'/mål *-en dial.* walrus.
***ros't** *-a* cf **rast**[3]
ros't/biff *-en* cf **roast/**
ros'te[1] *-n* 1 mash. 2 ores for roasting.
ros'te[2] *V -a/+-et* 1 mash, calcine (malt). 2 *metall.* roast, torrefy (ores).
ro's/verdig [also -vær'-] *A -* commendable, praiseworthy.
ro't[1] *-a, pl +røtter/*røter bot., gram., lit., math.* root: **ha sin r- i** be rooted in, stem from; **korn på r-** standing crop of grain; **rykke opp med r-** pull up by the r-s, uproot; exterminate, wipe out; **slå (sette, skyte) r-** strike r-s, take r-; **uten r- i virkeligheten** without foundation in reality.
ro't[2] *-et* disorder, litter, mess (**av** of); meddling: **slikt r-** such a mess, what a mess.
***rot**[3] [rå't] *-et* cf **råte**
***ro't**[4] *-et* attic, loft.
***rota/hol** [rå'ta/hål] *-et* poor shack (of a house), ramshackle house.
***rotal** [rå'tal] *A* dirty, uncleanly (work).
+rotaria'ner *-en, pl -e* (=***-ar**) Rotarian.
rotasjo'n *-en* rotation.
rotasjo'ns/presse *-a typog.* rotary press.
***rota/skap** [rå'ta/] *-en* cf **råtten/**
ro't/bløyte *-a* a soaking rain, a thorough soaking.
ro'te[1] *+-n/*-a* 1 *gymn., mil.* file: **førstemann i r-n** file leader. 2 *mil.* smallest subdivision of a conscription district. 3 group of farms which keeps up a section of road by work in kind; the section of road itself.
***rote**[2] [rå'te] *-n* cf **råte**
ro'te[3] *V -a/+-et* 1 dig, grub; putter about (in garden); poke, rake (in ashes); (of pigs) root: **r- opp** stir up; **r- opp i noe** rake up sth; **r- opp marka** dig up the grass (soil); **r- ut** cover up, erase (e.g. tracks). 2 *fig.* mess, root, rummage (**i, om, nedi,** in e.g. drawers), search (**etter** for) sth: **r- fram** dig up, uncover; **r- igjennom** search through; mess around in; **r- sammen** mix up; **r- til** make untidy (e.g. livingroom). 3 *(refl.)*: **r- seg bort i, inn i** get oneself involved in, mixed up in. 4 *dial.* struggle with (heavy or unpleasant work); putter, waste (time).
***rote**[4] [rå'te] *pp of* **ryte**
+ro'te/forstan'der *-en, pl -e* (=***-ar**) director of a district draft board (prior to 1953).
+ro'te/hode *-t* (=***/hovud**) *fam.* confused, messy person; blunderhead.
ro'te/kopp *-en fam.* messy, untidy person.
ro't/ekte *A -* 1 *hort.* own-root(ed), ungrafted. 2 absolutely genuine, original; homegrown, native.
+ro'te/mester *-en, pl -e* (=***/meister**) 1 superintendent of road maintenance (in a **rote**). 2=**/forstander.**
***roten** [rå'ten] *A -e/-i, pl -ne* cf **råtten**
ro't/ende *-n* 1 butt, trunk end of tree, stalk, or pole. 2 *naut.* thick end of spar.
***roten/skap** [rå'ten/] *-en* cf **råtten/**
rote're *V -te* rotate: **r-ende** rotary.
ro'tet(e) *A -* 1 disorderly, messy (person, place). 2 confused, disordered (thinking, writing).
ro't/fast *A -* 1 well-rooted (plant, tree). 2 *fig.* acclimatized, anchored, deeply rooted: **jeg var r- i egen jord** I was rooted in my own soil (Evensmo).
ro't/feste *V -a/+-et* 1: **r- seg** root, establish firm roots (of plants). 2 *lit.* (of person) establish roots, feel at home: **en r-et skikk** an established custom; **en r-et fordom** a deeply ingrained prejudice.
ro't/frukt *-a/+-en* (edible) root; *(pl)* root crops.
ro't/fylling *-a/+-en odont.* pulp canal therapy, root filling.
+ro't/hogger *-en, pl -e* (=***-ar**) *fig.* one who saps (undermines) sth (e.g. beliefs, established customs), a radical.
***roti** [rå'ti] *pp of* **ryte**
ro't/knoll *-en* edible root, tuber.
ro't/laus *A* (=**+/løs**) 1 rootless (plant). 2 *fig.* (of people) rootless, without traditions. 3 *geol.* (of earth, rock layer) displaced.
***rot'ne** *V -a* cf **råtne**
ro'tor *-en elec., naut.* rotor.
ro't/o'rd *-et gram.* root word.
+ro't/skudd *-et bot.* sucker.
ro't/stappe *-a dial.* mashed rutabaga.
ro't/staving *-a/+-en* (=**+-else**) *gram.* root syllable.
ro't/stokk *-en bot.* rhizome, root stock.
ro't/stue *-a* (=**/stove**) *dial.* cottage without a loft (raftered ceiling).
rot'te[1] *-a* 1 *zool.* rat (Rattus). 2 *fig., hum.*: **fattig r-** one who is poor

+ Bokmål; * Nynorsk; ° Dialect.
After letter: ' stress (Acc. 1); ` tone, stress (Acc. 2); · length.
Below letter: . not pronounced.

as a church mouse; **en gammel r-** a wily bird.
rot'te[2] *V* -*a*/+-*et*: **r- seg sammen** conspire (**imot** against), gang up (on).
rot'te/felle -*a* rattrap.
rot'te/gift -*a*/+-*en* 1 rat poison. 2 *fam.* strangler (mixture of wine and beer).
rot'te/hale -*n* 1 rat's tail. 2 larva (of fly family Cristalis).
rot'te/hund -*en* dog, esp. rat terrier.
rot'te/katt -*en* cat good at catching rats.
rot'te/krutt -*et* (white) arsenic.
rot'te/rumpe [/rompe] -*a* 1 rat's tail. 2 *bot.* pepper elder (Peperomia). 3 compass or keyhole saw.
rot'te/skjerm -*en* *naut.* rat guard.
*__rot/tev__ [rå't/] -*en* smell of decay.
rott'ing -*en* 1 rattan. 2 flogging.
rotun'de -*n* 1 *arch.* rotunda. 2 round, open space.
ro't/vekst -*en* root crop.
ro't/velsk *A* - thieves' cant; gibberish.
ro't/velte -*a* tree uprooted by wind.
rov [rå'v] -*et* 1 plundering, stealing; kidnapping (**av** of), preying (of animals): **(ute) på r-** on the prowl; in search of prey, booty; **drive (jorda) på r-** exploit (the soil); usu. *hum.* **gå på r-** pilfer. 2 booty, loot; prey (e.g. children, women): **være et r- for** be a prey to, fall prey to (e.g. flames, emotion).
Rov'de *Pln* twp, Møre og Romsdal.
rov/drift [rå'v/] -*a*/+-*en* ruthless exploitation of a natural resource (**på** of).
rov/dyr [rå'v/] -*et* beast of prey.
ro've -*a* *dial.* tail.
*__roven__ [rå'ven] *A* -*e*/-*i*, *pl* -*ne* 1 loose, loosened (e.g. of grass); broken up, dissolved (e.g. fish liver). 2 porous (esp. of ice).
rover[1] [rå'ver] -*en*, *pl* +-*e* rover (scout).
rove'r[2] -*et* *naut.* navigable mouth of (large) river.
*__ro've/troll__ -*et* tadpole.
rov/fisk [rå'v/] -*en* predatory fish.
rov/fiske -*t* overfishing.
rov/fugl -*en* bird of prey, *zool.* raptorial bird (also *fig.*).
rov/grisk *A* predatory, rapacious.
rov/lyst -*a*/+-*en* rapaciousness.
rov/mord -*et* murder with intent to rob.
royalty [råi'elti] -*en* *merc.* royalty.
R.S.O.O. = +**ridder**/***riddar av St. Olavs Orden**
RT = **registertonn**
*__ru'__[1] -*a* (loose) winter wool (of sheep).
+__ru'__[2] *A* -/-*tt*, *pl* - 1 rough (e.g. beard, surface, tongue); *fig.* rough (e.g. behavior, weather). 2 gruff, hoarse, rasping (e.g. sound, throat). 3 *bot.* scabrous.
ru'/bank -*en* *carp.* jointer plane.
+__rubb'__ *N*: **r- og stubb** bag and baggage, every scrap.
rub'be *V* -*a* 1 *dial.* scrub, scale (fish); *naut.* smooth (rope). 2 *dial.* push roughly, shake. 3 gather (material when sewing).
rub'ben *A* +-*ent*, *pl* *rubne* rough, uneven.
ru'bel -*elen*, *pl* -*ler* ruble.
rubi'n -*en* ruby.
rubrikk' -*en* 1 column, section, space (e.g. for name). 2 category, group, head. 3 *typog.* caption, head, headline.
rubrise're *V* -*te* 1 categorize, classify, pigeonhole. 2 line (notebook, register) into sections.
*__ru'd__ -*et* clearing (common ending of place names: **Hassel/r-, Linde/r-.**)
*__rud'de__ *pt of* **rydje**
rudimen't -*et*, *pl* -/+-*er* usu. (*pl*) rudiments (**av** of). 2 *biol.* rudiment (of undeveloped organ). 3 *fig.* survival (e.g. of old custom).
rudimentæ'r *A* 1 rudimentary. 2 surviving.
ru'd/kall -*en* *folk.* first settler of a farm (as a mythical figure).
*__rud'nad__ -*en* clearing (of land).
*__rud'ning__ -*en* cf **rydning**
ru'e -*a* cf **ruve**[1]
+__ru'else__ -*n* contrition; *eccl.*: **anger og r-** repentance and c-.
ruff'[1] -*en*/-*et*: **i en r-** in a jiffy, in no time; *dial.* **i samme r-et** that very minute.
ruff'[2] -*en* deckhouse, forecastle, poop.
+__ruf'fe__ *V* -*a*/-*et* pander, procure.
+__ruf'feri__ -*et* pandering, procuring; keeping a brothel.
+__ruf'ferske__ -*n* procuress.
ru'g -*en* *bot.* rye (Secale); **tall grass** (of Secale family); rye seed.
ru'g/brød -*et* rye bread.
rug'de -*a* *zool.* woodcock (Scolopax rusticola).
rug'de/trekk -*et* flight of woodcocks at mating time.
*__ru'ge__[1] -*a* small dung heap.
ru'ge[2] *V* -*a*/+-*et* 1 brood, sit on (eggs): **r- ut** hatch. 2 *fig.* brood, pore (over).
ru'ge/egg -*et* egg for hatching.
ru'ge/høne -*a* brooding, sitting hen.
ru'ge/kasse -*a*/-*en* brooding box.
ru'ge/maski'n -*en* incubator.
ru'ge/plass -*en* hatching place (for wild birds).
ru'ge/tid -*a* brooding time; brooding season.
rugg' -*en* large, heavy person (animal, object); giant.
*__rug'gal__ *A* tottering, rocking (e.g. of boat).
rug'ge[1] -*a* a big woman.
rug'ge[2] *V* -*a*/+-*et* 1 move; (cause to) budge: **steinen var ikke til å r-** the stone could not be moved. 2 rock (e.g. boat, chair): wag (head); **r- på seg, r- seg fram og tilbake** rock back and forth. 3 lumber, move heavily; **Isak r-et saktelig bortover til dem** I- l-ed slowly over to them (Hamsun).
rug'ge/stol -*en* *dial.* rocker.
ru'g/kake -*a* round loaf of rye bread.
rug'l -*et* 1 shaking, tottering, wobbling. 2 (of throat, voice) roughness. 3 *fam.* sth falling apart, trash. 4 unreliability. 5 *zool.* corallinaceae (which tears fishing nets) (Lithothamnion).
rug'le *V* -*a*/+-*et* lurch, totter; shake, sway; (of boat) lurch, rock; lie insecurely.
rug'let(e) *A* - tottering, wobbly; unsteady.
ru'/håra *A* - (= +-**et**) wire-haired, rough coated (usu. of dogs).
ruin [ru-i'n] -*en* 1 ruin; destruction (e.g. after war): **ligge i r-er** lie in r-s. 2 disaster, downfall; bankruptcy, failure, ruin: **det er den rene r-** it is completely ruinous; **gå sin r- i møte** be on the road to r-; **han er sin r- nær** r- stares him in the face. 3 *fig.* shadow (of person), wreck (of a life).
ruinere [ru-ine're] *V* -*te* 1 destroy, ruin, spoil: **så r-t på sjelen var han blitt allerede dengang** *fig.* his soul was already so demoralized at that time (Ibsen). 2 break, go bankrupt, ruin (economically).
ruin/haug [ru-i'n/] -*en* débris, heap of ruins, rubble.
ru'/jern [/jæ'rn] -*et* (= */**jarn**) pig iron.
ru'ke -*a* 1 heap of hay; peat. 2 cow dung.
ruk'ke[1] -*a* cf **rynke**[1]
ruk'ke[2] *V* -*a*/+-*et* cf **rynke**[2]
+__ruk'kel__ -*elet*/*ruklet* 1 *dial.* rattling sound in throat, hoarseness. 2 junk, trash.
+__rukket__ [rok'ket] *pp of* **rekke**[3]
ruk'ket(e) *A* - cf **rynket(e)**
*__ruk'l__ -*et* 1 rattling sound in throat. 2 trash.
ruk'let(e) *A* - 1 uneven, wrinkled. 2 (of voice) hoarse.
rula'de -*n* 1 *mus.* roulade, run. 2 dish of meat, fish usu. rolled in a dough (or cabbage leaf). 3 = **rulleterte.**
rulett' -*en* 1 roulette (a game). 2 roller (making furrow in top of screw); wheel (baker's, bookbinder's, shoemaker's). 3 stuffed cabbage leaf (= **rulade** 2).
rull' -*en* 1 roller (of wood or metal, esp. in *agr.*); large mangle; grooved rolling pin (for *flatbrød* making); warp beam (on loom); (of fishing) reel fastened to gunwale. 2 roll (e.g. cake, clothing, coins); twist (of tobacco); pressed cold meats (= **rullepølse**); coil (of wire); roll (of silk); *naut.* turn of the boom. 3 *folk.* waltz-like folk dance; *dial.* epilogue; refrain (of song).
rul'le[1] -*a* 1 skid (e.g. for ship). 2 mangle, mangling room. 3 scroll. 4 *mil.*, *naut.* roll, roster: **føre r-en** keep the roster; **stå i r-ene** entered in the rolls. 5 *anat.* trochlea. 6 *photog.* squeegee roller.
rul'le[2] *V* -*a*/+-*et* 1 roll; (esp. of blood) course: **la pengene r-** put money in circulation; squander one's money; **r- opp** disclose, reveal, unfold; discover, unravel (e.g. a crime); **r- opp gardinet** pull up, raise the window shade; **r- på r'en** roll one's r's; **r- seg r-** (e.g. in the grass). 2 mangle (linen); calender, press (paper, etc.).
rul'le/bane -*n* *aeronaut.* runway.
rul'le/blad -*et* *mil.* record sheet (of soldier); *fig.*: **ha rent r-** have a clean record.
+__rul'le/bøtte__ -*a* *derog.* dishpan, tub (of ship with strong tendency to roll).
+__rul'le/fører__ -*en*, *pl* -*e* (= *-**ar**) *mil.* keeper of the rolls, registrar.
rul'le/gardi'n -*a*/+-*en*/-*et* (sun) blind, (window) shade.
rul'le/lager -*et*, *pl* - +-*e* roller bearing.
*__rul'len__ *A* -*e*/-*i*, *pl* *rulne* round.
rul'le/pølse -*a* collared lamb or beef, pressed and sliced into cold cuts.
rul'le/skøyte -*a* roller skate.
rul'le/stein -*en* 1 pebble, rolling stone. 2 *geol.* erratic boulder.
rul'le/stol -*en* wheelchair.
rul'le/terte -*a* jelly roll.
rul'le/tobakk' -*en* sliced plug, twist tobacco.
rul'le/trapp -*a* escalator.
+__rul'le/tøy__ -*et* (= */**ty**) mangling (flat pieces, flatwork).
rul't -*en* *dial.* 1 roly-poly man. *2 walk, trot.
rul'te[1] -*a* *dial.* roly-poly woman, girl.
rul'te[2] *V* -*a*/+-*et* *dial.* waddle; make sth rock, shake.
rul'ten *A* +-*ent*, *pl* -*ne* roly-poly (person); broad, roundish (boat).
+__rum__ [rom'] -*met* cf **rom**[2]
rumba [røm'ba] -*en* rumba.
+__rume'ner__ -*en*, *pl* -*e* (= *-**ar**, ***rumen**) Romanian.
rume'nsk *A* - Romanian.
rumle [rom'le] *V* -*a*/+-*et* rattle, rumble: **r- med** (cause to) r-.
+__rumme__ [rom'me] *V* -*et* cf **romme**
rummel [rom'mel] -*et*/+-*en*/+*rumlet* rumbling; din, rumble, tumult.
rumpe [rom'pe] -*a* 1 (human) behind, rear, seat; buttocks, rump: **få ris på r-a** get a spanking on the behind; **sid i r-a** *fig.* having lead in one's pants, slow-moving. 2 tail (of animal, mythical being). 3 *fig.*: **en r- av røk** a trail of smoke; **alt vondt drar på en lang r-** all evil leaves a long wake (Undset).
rumpe/balle -*n* *anat.* buttock.
rumpe/tange -*n* *anat.* (human) coccyx; tailbone.
rumpe/taske -*a* small (leather, cloth) pouch attached to belt.
rumpe/troll -*et* tadpole.
*__rum'ple__ *V* -*a* move, upset.
rumstere [romste're] *V* -*te* cf **romstere**
run [røn'n] -*et* 1 *merc.* run (on a bank, store). 2 crowd: **et r- av pressefolk**

a c- of newsmen. 3: seile for r- naut. sign on for a single run.

-run Prn(f) suffix in e.g. Gud/r-, Sol/r-.

+run'ḍ[1] -en archaic arch, curve, rounding (e.g. window); circle, ring, sphere (e.g. of earth, fig. eternity); curvature (of earth); dome (of sky).

run'ḍ[2] A 1 round; circular; globular; (of note, voice) full: i r-e tall in r-numbers. 2 (of wine) full-bodied. 3 (of fish) not cleaned, whole; (of timber) whole (not trimmed flat on the sides): legge seg r- go to bed fully clothed. 4 (of person) generous, liberal: med r- hand generously, open-handedly. 5 (=not sharp) affable, good-natured; sociable; bland, inoffensive, smooth: et r-t svar a diplomatic answer; være like r- be unaffected, undisturbed. 6 (adv.) around: det går r-t for meg I'm completely at sea; drikke r-t pass the cup a-; dial., lit. ha det r-t med mat og drikke have an abundance of food and drink; r-t om(kring) a- (about) (r-t omkring i landet a- the country), r-t regnet in round numbers, roughly speaking; sove r-t sleep a- the clock; velte r-t capsize, turn over.

+run'ḍ/aktig A - roundish.

*run'dast V -ast become round, fill out.

run'ḍ/boge [/båge] -n (=+/bue) archaic round arch.

+run'ḍ/brenner -en, pl -e (=*-ar) 1 Argand burner or lamp (with tubular wick). 2 hum. Casanova, philanderer.

run'ḍ/dans -en 1 round dance (couple dancing, in which dancers circle the room). 2 spinning, whirling movement. 3 naut. fife rail.

run'de[1] -n 1 round (of inspection, boxing, watchman); beat (of policeman, postman, soldier); lap (of race). 2: ta seg en r- take a walk, stroll.

run'ḍe[2] V -a/+-et 1 (make) round, round off; perfect (e.g. ideas, language); bend, curve (sth): r- leppene round the lips; r- av round off (sum). 2 round (e.g. cape, corner); circle (e.g. field, market place): r- år turn a round number of years (in Norway 50, 60 etc.; usu. cause for special celebration). 4 (refl.): r- seg (of back) bend, grow round; (of breast, cheek) curve, fill out: r- seg i mel og velmakt wallow in flour and opulence (Kielland).

*run'de[3] pt of rynje

+run'ḍebords/konferanse [/-ang'se] -n (=*-bord/) round table (conference).

run'delig A - abundant, ample; (of person) generous, liberal.

run'ḍ/gang -en 1 circuit, round; turn, tour (of stores, duties, visits): livets trivielle r- life's endless round of trivialities. 2 (round) gallery.

+run'ḍ/hodet A - anthro. brachycephalic, roundheaded.

run'ḍ/holt -en/-et naut. spar.

+run'ḍ/håndet A - (=+-a) generous, liberal.

run'ḍing -en 1 rolling, rounding; rounding, rotundity (e.g. hips, lips). 2 circle, place (e.g. intersection in front of building); ring; curvature (of earth); curve (e.g. of lips, road). 3 (act of) circling, rounding.

run'ḍ/jule V -te/*-a beat up thoroughly, lick, thrash.

run'ḍ/kast -et 1 somersault. 2 net fishing from land in shallow water.

run'ḍ/kinna A - (=+-et) round-cheeked.

run'ḍ/kjøring -a/+-en rotary, traffic circle.

run'ḍ/kysse V infl as kysse 1 kiss repeatedly, thoroughly. 2 kiss every one present in turn.

run'ḍ/pinne -n round (knitting) needle.

run'ḍ/reise -a/+-en round trip.

run'ḍreise/billett· -en round trip ticket.

run'ḍ/rygga A - (=+-et) round-shouldered.

+run'ḍ/sang -en mus. 1 round (festive song sung by all guests at dinner table). 2 rondo, round, roundelay.

run'ḍ/skrift -a/+-en round hand (writing).

run'ḍ/skriv -et admin. circular letter, directive.

+run'ḍ/skue -t panorama.

run'ḍ/skål ei/+en toast drunk by everybody, the whole party.

+run'ḍ/spørring -a/-en poll (av of).

+run'ḍ/stjele V -stjal, -stjålet am. rob (sby) of everything; clean (sby) out.

run'ḍ/stykke -t, pl +-r/*- hard roll.

*run'ḍ/sviv -et 1 circulation (e.g. of planet). 2 revolution (e.g. of wheel).

run'ḍt P around (the corner, one's neck, North Cape, the world, etc.), round: året r- all year r-.

run'ḍ/tur -en round trip, trip: vi tar en kort r- gjennom utstillingsområdet let's take a look around the exhibition grounds (Tidens Tegn).

run'ḍ/tømmer -et untrimmed timber.

ru'ne[1] -a/+-en 1 rune, runic letter; fig. mysterious secret, symbol: kaste r-er etter (over, på) en practice magic on sby. 2 runic-like inscription, line, mark: risse ens r-er set up a memorial to sby; extol, glorify sby.

*ru'ne[2] -n 1 streaming down (e.g. grain into a mill); earth slide, stone slide; moving flock (of animals). 2 sapling; bush; clump of trees.

ru'ne[3] V -a/+-et cast charms and spells, engage in secret arts; bewitch, charm.

ru'ne/bomme [/bomme] -a/+-en folk. magic drum (Lapp).

ru'ne/innskrift -a/+-en runic inscription.

ru'ne/kall -en sorcerer, wizard (using runes).

+ru'ne/mester -eren, pl -ere/-rer (=*/meister) rune carver, runemaster.

ru'ne/skrift -a/+-en runic writing.

ru'ne/stav -en vertical stroke in runic letter.

ru'ne/stein -en rune stone, stone with runic inscription.

+runge [rong'e] V -a/-et boom, resound, ring; peal (out); re-echo: slå i bordet så det r-er bang the table so it echoes.

+rungende [rong'ene] A - resounding, ringing: r- latter (also) peals of laughter.

*runke [rong'ke] V -a move lazily; rock, sway.

runn' -en (=runne[1]) dial. bush, copse, thicket.

run'ne[1] -n cf runn

*run'ne[2] pp of renne[2]

*run'nen A -e/-i, pl runne 1 arisen (pp of renne[2]). 2 (of wood) streaked.

runner [røn'ner] -en, pl +-e naut. runner (agent for seamen's boardinghouse).

+run'net pp of rinne

*run'ni pp of renne[2]

runolog [-lå'g] -en runologist.

runologi' -en runology (the scientific study of runes).

*run't pp of rynje

ru'/pane'l -et carp. rough panel (used under other wall surfacing).

*rup'le V -a move; disturb, mess up.

ru'r -en 1 scab (on sore). 2 zool. acorn barnacle (Balanus balanus).

ru's[1] -en/-et 1 drunkenness, intoxication: være i en lett r- be mildly intoxicated; sove r-en ut sleep it off. 2 fig. ecstasy, transport of joy: en r- av glede (the same).

*ru's[2] -et scale, shell.

ru's/drikk -en, pl *-er intoxicant.

ru'se[1] -a fish trap (funnel-shaped basket); fish pot, weir.

ru'se[2] V -a/-te 1 rush (imot towards): r- ned pour down; en storm r-ste opp a storm suddenly came up. 2 rotate at high speed: r- en motor gun a motor (while in neutral).

ru'se[3] V -a intoxicate.

ru's/gift -a/+-en intoxicating drug.

rush [røsj'] -en/-et rush: det verste r-et the worst r-; en hel r- med penger a flood of money.

rush/tid -a/+-en rush hour.

rush/trafikk· -en rush hour traffic.

*ru'sings/middel -et/-midlet intoxicant.

rus'k[1] -en giant, hulk: en stor og lubben r- av en tenor a large and chubby hulk of a tenor (Aftenposten); en svær r- av en engelskmann a huge hulk of an Englishman.

rus'k[2] -et 1 trash: r- og rask dust and dirt, this and that. 2 mote, particle: få et r- i øyet get a piece of dust in one's eye.

rus'k[3] -et cold, wet, windy weather; drizzle.

rus'k[4] A - fam., hum. out of one's mind, having lost one's wits.

rus'ke[1] -a big woman; slattern.

rus'ke[2] V -a/+-et shake; jerk, tug, twitch (usu. with i): r- i en (also fig.) shake sby; r- en i håret rumple sby's hair; det r-et i skigarden the fence shook (Evensmo); r- opp shake up, stir up (things); pull up; r- en opp (av) rouse, shake sby up (from); r- sammen throw together; r- noe unna (fra seg) do sth slovenly and hurriedly; dial. r- på seg move.

rus'ke[3] V -a/+-et dial. drizzle.

*rus'ken A -e/-i, pl -ne drizzly, unsettled (weather).

rus'kenḍe Av: riv, r- gal stark, raving mad.

rus'ket(e) A - 1 drizzly, unpleasant (weather). 2 (of hair) messy, untidy.

+rus'ke/vær -et (=*/ver) drizzly, unpleasant weather.

ru'/skinn -et suède.

rus'kom/snusk -et 1 dish of leftovers, esp. fried. 2 fig. hodgepodge, mishmash.

+Rus'/lanḍ Pln cf Russ/

rus'le V -a/+-et (=rutle) 1 amble, stroll; plod, shuffle: vi må nok r- well, we have to be moving (toddling) along. 2 move, stir; fumble: r- med putter with (sth).

rus'le/tog [/tåg] -et hum. local, milk train (slow train that makes every stop).

russ'[1] -en cf russer

russ'[2] -en (member of) graduating class of a gymnasium (esp. during last few months of school year, when many special activities are held).

rus'se/avi's -a/+-en newspaper published only on May 17 by the russ of the year.

rus'se/fest -en celebration party held by russ.

rus'se/lue -a (=*/luve) blue or red cap worn by russ.

+rus'ser -en, pl -e (=*-ar) Russian.

russerin'ne -a/+-en Russian woman.

rus'se/tid -a/+-en period when one is russ (esp. last two months before exams).

rus'sisk A - Russian: på r- in R-.

Russ'/lanḍ Pln Russia.

+russ'/lær -et (=*/ler) Russia leather.

rus't[1] -a rust (on iron, plants, etc.; a color): hvor møll og r- fortærer where moth and r- corrupt (Matt. 6, 19).

*rus't[2] -a 1 grove; slope with (esp. deciduous) trees. 2 hill, ridge.

*rus't[3] pp of rysje

+ Bokmål; * Nynorsk; ° Dialect.
After letter: ' stress (Acc. 1); ' tone, stress (Acc. 2); · length.
Below letter: . not pronounced.

***rus'ta** *A* - cf **rusten**

+**rus't/beskyt'tende** *A* - rust-preventing.

rus't/brun *A* rust brown, rust-colored.

rus'te1 *V* -*a*/+-*et* (=+**rustne**) 1 corrode, rust: **skruen er r-et fast** the screw is rusted in tight; **r- opp** corrode, destroy. 2 *fig.* (of person, feeling, ability) grow rusty: **gammelt vennskap r-er ikke** old friendship never dies.

rus'te2 *V* -*a*/+-*et* 1 *mil.* arm (**mot** against): **r- seg** a- oneself. 2 equip, prepare: **r- seg** get ready (**til** for): **r- ut** equip (**med** with); **godt r-et** well endowed, equipped.

***rus'te3** *pt of* **rysje**

rus'ten *A* +-*ent*, *pl* -*ne* (=***rusta**, ***rustet(e)**) 1 (e.g. of metal) rusty; rust-colored. 2 *fig.* hoarse, husky (voice).

rus't/fri *A* -*tt* 1 (of metals) rustproof, stainless (knives etc.). 2 without rust.

rustifise're *V* -*te* countrify, rusticate.

rus't/kammer -*et* (=*/**kammers**) arsenal, reservoir, storehouse (**av** of).

+**rus'tne** *V* -*a*/-*et* cf **ruste1**

rus'tning +-*en*/*-*a* 1 armament; armor; (coat of) mail: **i full r-** in full panoply. 2 equipment (for expedition).

rus'tnings/industri' -*en* armament industry.

+**rus'tnings/kappløp** -*et* armaments race.

+**rus't/rød** *A* (=*/**raud**) rust-colored.

Rut' *Prn(f)* Ruth.

ru'te1 -*a* 1 diamond, square (in cloth, flooring, gameboard, etc.). 2 (window)pane.

***ru'te2** -*a* cf **ruter**

ru'te3 -*a*/+-*en* 1 route. 2 schedule; service; line, run: **fast r-** regular service, run; **gå i (fast) r- (mellom)** ply (between); **i r-** on time; **holde r-n** run on schedule, on time; **på r-n** en route, on the run (e.g. to Oslo); **sette flere vogner inn på r-n** add more cars to the run. 3 *fam.* (short for **rutebil**): **kjøre med r-a** take the bus.

***ru'te4** *V* -*a* 1 carouse. 2 clamor, make a noise. 3 storm.

ru'te/bil -*en* (scheduled) bus.

ru'te/bok -*a* schedule (bus, RR, etc.), timetable.

ru'te/båt -*en* coastal steamer.

ru'te/fart -*en* regular service.

ru'te/fly -*et* (scheduled) plane.

ru'te/kart -*et* 1 road map; schedule (bus, train, etc.). 2 *naut.*, *mil.* chart.

***ru'te/meter** -*en*, *pl* - square meter.

***ru'te/mål** -*et* square measure.

+**rute'ner** -*en*, *pl* -*e* (=*-**ar**) Ruthenian.

rute'nsk *A* - Ruthenian.

ru'te/papi'r -*et* graph paper.

ru'te/plan -*en* timetable.

+**ru'ter** [also: ru'ter] -*en* (=***rute2**) diamond (in cards): **melde r-** bid diamonds.

+**ruter/dame** -*a*/-*en* (=***rute/**) queen of diamonds.

ru'tet(e) *A* - 1 (of textiles) checked; plaid. 2 squared (paper).

ru'te/trafikk' -*en* regular service, traffic.

ruti'ne -*n* 1 routine: **ha r- i** have skill in. 2 *fig.*, *derog.* mechanical skill (e.g. in writing novels). 3 *mil.*, *naut.* schedule, timetable (for work).

ruti'ne/arbeid -*et* routine work.

+**ruti'ne/messig** *A* - routine.

rutine'rt *A* - experienced, skilled, trained (**i** in).

rut'le *V* -*a*/+-*et* cf **rusle**

rut'sje *V* -*a*/+-*et* 1 glide, rush, slide (**ned** down). 2 *hum.*: **komme r-ende** come a-running.

rut'sje/bane -*n* slide (e.g. on playground; into water; for toboggan); roller coaster.

+**rutt'** *nt of* **ru**

rut'te *V* -*a*/+-*et*: **r- med** be free with, have the use of, squander (resources, time).

***ru'v** -*et* bulk, volume.

ru've1 -*a* (=***rue**) heap; lump; stack.

ru've2 *V* -*de*/*-*a* 1 appear large, loom, tower (up); bulk. 2 be imposing, impressive.

ru'velig *A* - 1 big, broad. *2 bushy, shaggy.

ru'ven *A* -*e*/-*i*, *pl* -*ne* 1 bulky; impressive. 2 bushy, shaggy.

***ruv'le** -*a* furrow, unevenness, wrinkle.

***ruv'let(e)** *A* - bumpy, rough, uneven.

***ru'v/sam** *A* bulky; imposing.

ry'1 -*et* fame, renown, reputation (**for** for); report: **det går ry av en, av noe** sby, sth is famous; **høre godt ry om (noen)** hear (sby) spoken well of.

***ry'2** *V* *raud*, *rode*/-*i* cf **ry3**

ry3 *V* -*dde* 1 (of dry particles) pour, sift. 2 crumble, fall apart. 3 swarm.

+**ry'4** *A* -*tt* cf **ru1**

***ry'd** *pr of* **rydje**

ryd'de *V* -*a*/+-*et* (=***rydje**) clear (land, space, a street, the way, etc.); straighten up, tidy: **r- av veien, til side** do away with, get rid of; clear aside, away; **r- opp** clean, straighten, tidy up; **r- sammen** put (things) together; **r- vekk** clear away.

ryd'dig *A* - cleared, made roomy; neat, orderly (also *fig.*, of one's mind).

ryd'ding -*a*/+-*en* (=***rydjing**) act of clearing; (a) clearing (in woods).

***ryd'je** *V* *ryd*, *rudde* cf **rydde**

***ryd'jing** -*a* cf **rydding**

ryd'ning -*en* clearing (in woods).

ryd'nings/mann -*en*, *pl* -*menn*/*-*menner* pioneer.

ry'e1 -*a* rag rug (for floor); tied shag rug (for bed, floor; also used as wall hanging).

***ry'e2** -*n* stony mountain heath.

***ryf't** -*a* cf **ryfte**

ryf'te** -*t* (=ryft**) 1 width of the woven fabric. 2 strip of woods.

***ryg'd** -*a* 1 horror, terror. 2 marvel, miracle.

***ryg'de** *pt of* **ryggje**

ry'ger *pl* people from Rogaland.

rygg' -*en*, *pl* *-*er* 1 back: **bak ens r-** behind one's back; **legge, sette r-en til** put one's back to it; **r- mot r-** back to back; **skyte r-** arch one's back; **vende en r-en, vende r-en til en** turn one's back on sby; **få en til å fryse på r-en** make the chills run down one's spine. 2 esp. *mil.* rear: **falle en i r-en** attack sby from the r-; **ha en i r-en** be backed by sby, have sby on one's side, behind one; **ha r-en fri, dekket** be covered in the r-. 3 (roof, mountain, underwater) ridge; back (of book, chair, coat, one's hand, etc.); spine (of book). 4 saddle (of meat).

rygg'/bein -*et* *anat.* spinal column, backbone.

ryg'ge *V* -*a*/+-*et* 1 back (car, horse), move backward, reverse; retreat, step back. 2: **r- ved** disturb, upset: **det kunne r- ved folks tro** it might u- people's faith.

Ryg'ge *Pln* twp, Østfold.

+**ryg'ges/løs** *A* depraved, dissolute, licentious.

rygg'/finne -*n* *zool.* dorsal fin.

***ryg'gje** *V* *rygde* cf **rygge**

***ryg'gje/laus** *A* cf **rygges/løs**

rygg'/merg -*en* (=+/**marg**) 1 *anat.* spinal marrow (cord). 2 *fig.* backbone, courage.

rygg'/rad [*/ra] -*a*/+-*en* 1 *anat.* spine; spinal column. 2 *fig.* backbone, courage, fortitude.

rygg'/sekk -*en* knapsack, rucksack.

rygg'/skjold -*et* *zool.* carapace.

rygg'/stykke -*t*, *pl* +-*r*/*- 1 back piece (of slaughtered animal, fowl). 2 back (of person), usu. *(pl) hum.*

rygg'/stø -*et* 1 back (of seat), support for the back. 2 *fig.* (moral, financial) backing, support.

+**rygg'/svømming** -*a*/-*en* (of swimming) backstroke.

rygg'/søyle -*a*/+-*en* *anat.* spinal column, vertebral column.

rygg'/tak -*et* wrestling: **ta r-** wrestle.

rygg'/tavle -*a* *dial.* (surface of the) back; vertebra.

***rygg'/tole** [/tåle] -*a* vertebra.

rygg'/virvel -*elen*, *pl* -*ler* vertebra.

ry'ke *V* *rauk*/+*røk*, +*røket*/*roke*/*-*i* 1 smoke, steam: **ovnen r-er** the stove is smoking; **r-ende** steaming; **r-ende varm** piping hot. 2 (of dust, rain, snow, etc.) fly, swirl; (of e.g. person) dart, fly, rush (**avsted** away, off). 3 fall (suddenly), go; break, burst, snap; go wrong, go to pot; *educ.*, *fam.* flunk: **r- i luften** come to nothing; go up in the air; **r- i stykker, i tu** fall, fly apart, go to pieces; **r- og reise** (mild oath) go to the devil; **r- over ende** fall over; (of plan) be wrecked, come to naught; **r- uklar** disagree, fall out (**med** with). 4 (with *prep.*, *adv.*): **r- i, på** fly at, rush at (**r- i tottene på hverandre** fly at one another's throats); **r- opp** (of bad weather, storm, etc.) break loose (**det r-er opp med, til en storm** a storm is brewing); **r- over ende** be upset, fall over; be wrecked, come to grief.

rykk' -*en*/-*et* 1 jerk, tug: **stanse med et r-** stop suddenly. 2 (of involuntary motion) start; twinge (of pain): **det gikk som et rykk gjennom henne** a light twinge passed through her (Undset). 3 spurt, (period of) sudden activity, streak: **arbeide i r-** work by fits and starts; **et r- inntraff der fisken ble borte** a short period occurred during which the fish disappeared (from its regular haunts).

+**ryk'ke** *V* *rykte* (=*-**je**) 1 jerk, pull, tug (**i** at): **r- bort** snatch away (one's life); **r- en i ermet** pull at sby's sleeve; **r- inn** insert (an advertisement, notice, etc.); **r- opp med roten** pull up by the roots; **r- på skulderen** shrug one's shoulders. 2 start (suddenly); shake, twitch: **r- til** give a start, jump (back); **det r-et i ansiktet** his face twitched. 3 move: **r- fram** (esp. of an army, expedition, etc.) advance, march onward, move on; *fig.*, *mil.* **r- i marken** start a campaign (**mot** against); **r- inn** (esp. of an army) move in; **r- nærmere** approach, draw closer; **r- opp** advance, move up, be promoted; **r- seg unna** move away; **r- ut med** come out with, disclose; part with. 4 dun (**for** for).

***ryk'ke/drikkar** -*en* periodic drinker; alcoholic.

+**ryk'ker** -*en*, *pl* -*e* (=*-**jar**) 1 bill collector. 2 dun.

+**ryk'ker/brev** -*et* (=*-**jar/**) dunning letter.

ryk'ke/vis *Av* by fits and starts, jerkily, spasmodically.

***rykkj'e** *V* *rykte* cf **rykke**

***ryk'kut** *A* - jerky.

rykk'/vis *Av* cf **rykke/**

+**ryk'ning** -*en* nervous twinge; jerk, twitch (in muscle), twitching.

ryk'te1 -*t*, *pl* +-*r*/*- 1 report, rumor (**om** about). 2 reputation: **mitt gode navn og r-** my good name and r-.

ryk'te2 *pt of* **rykke, rykkje**

+**ryk'te/maker** -*en*, *pl* -*e* (=*-**ar**) gossip, rumormonger.

+**ryk'tes** *V* -*es*/-*edes*, -*es* be rumored, get about (**at** that).

ryk'te/smed -*en* gossip, rumormonger.

***ry'le** *V* -*te* 1 roar, scream. 2 grunt.

ryl'lik -*en* cf **røllik**

***ryn'je** *V* *ryn*, *runde*, *runt* gush, pour, stream; echo, roar, thunder: **folket ryn utor kyrkja** people pour out of the church; **det ryn i fjella** the mountains echo.

+**ryn'ke1** -*a*/-*en* (=***rukke1**) 1 line, wrinkle; fold, furrow (of skin): **r-r**

ved øynene crow's feet. 2 gather, shirring, tuck (in cloth).

+**ryn'ke**[2] *V -a/-et* 1 knit, wrinkle (one's brow); frown, scowl (in anger): **r- på nesen** turn up one's nose. 2 gather, shirr (material).

+**ryn'ket(e)** *A* - 1 wrinkled (clothing; skin of fruit, person). 2 gathered, shirred.

ry'pe *-a zool.* ptarmigan, white grouse (Lagopus).

ry'pe/bær *-et bot.* bearberry (Arctostaphylos Alpina).

ry'pe/kull *-et* brood of ptarmigan, white grouse.

ry'pe/stegg *-en* cock grouse, male ptarmigan.

ry'r *A dial.* 1 having a grainy, porous substance; (of wood) dry, rotten; (of snow) dry, grainy; (of flour) dry, fluffy. 2 evanescent, impermanent; (of food) quickly used up, uneconomical; (of money) fleeting, insufficient: **det blir r-t folket her** people don't get old here (Aanrud).

***ry'r/leik** *-en* impermanence, inadequacy.

***ry'rne** *V -a* be used up quickly, disappear.

***ry's**[1] *-en* chill, shiver, shudder.

***ry's**[2] *pr of* **rysje**

rysj' *-en* ruche, ruching (on women's garments).

***rysj'e** *V rys, ruste, rust* cf **røsse**

+**rys'ke** *V -a/-et* (=***-je**) *dial.* 1 pluck, pull; tear (**ut** out). 2 pull up (flax by the root).

***ryss'** *-en* boy.

***rys'se** *-a* mare.

+**rys'te** *V -et* shake (esp. *fig.*), shock; tremble.

+**rys'telse** *-n* shaking, shock (**ved** at).

+**rys'tende** *A* - 1 appalling, shocking: **r- tragedie** s- tragedy. 2 quaking, shaking, trembling.

+**rys'tet** *A* - shaken (esp. *fig.*); shocked: **r- til sin sjels innerste s-** to the depths of one's being.

ry'te *V raut/+røt, +-tt/*rote/*-i dial.* 1 growl, grunt, snarl. 2 snore. *3 fall, plunge.

ryt'me *-n* beat, cadence, rhythm.

rytmikk' *-en* rhythmics.

ryt'misk *A* - rhythmic.

+**rytt'**[1] *pp of* **ryte**

+**rytt'**[2] *nt of* **ry**[3]

+**ryt'ter** *-en, pl -e* (=***-ar**) 1 horseman, rider. 2 tab (on index card).

+**ryt'terske** *-n* horsewoman.

+**ryt'ter/statue** *-n* equestrian statue.

+**ryt'ter/veksel** *-elen, pl -ler merc.* accomodation bill.

***ræ'/fugl** *-en* bird of prey.

***ræ'kje** *V rækte* clear the throat, hawk.

***ræ'l** *-en* pole, stick.

***ræ'le** *V -a* 1 clean a pipe. 2 talk nonsense.

Ræ'lingen *Pln* twp, Akershus.

+**ræ'r** *pl of* **rå**[1]

***ræ'se**[1] *-t* drain.

***ræ'se**[2] *V -te* 1 roam, run. 2 flow.

°**ræv'** *-a* cf **rauv**

***rø'**[1] *V -dde* cf **rydde**

***rø'**[2] *V -dde* cf **røde**[2]

+**rø'be** *V -et* cf **røpe**

+**rø'd** *A* (=***raud**[2]) red (e.g. hair, pencil, dress); (of skin) florid, flushed; rosy; red; *pol.* communist, radical, red: **(hun) ble både r- og blek** (her) color came and went; **den r- mann** the Red Man, Indian; **det r- gull** *poet* (red) gold; **i dag r-, i morgen død** here today, gone tomorrow; **ikke eie et r-t øre** be dead broke, not have a red cent; **ivrig og r- i hodet** excited and flushed (Kielland); **r- av skam** blushing with shame; **r- i kammen** flushed with anger; **r-e hunder** German measles; **virke som en r- klut** be highly annoying, irritating.

+**rø'd/aktig** *A* - reddish.

+**rø'd/bete** [also rø'/] *-a/-en bot.* beet (Beta vulgaris rapacea).

+**rø'd/brun** *A* reddish brown.

***rø'de**[1] *-a* conversation, talk.

rø'de[2] *-n* (=***rode**[2]) red (color), redness; blush, flush.

rø'de[3] *V -de* chat, talk.

+**Rø'de/havet** *Pln* (=+**det røde hav**) the Red Sea.

+**Røde Kor's** *Prn* (=***Raudekrossen**) Red Cross.

+**rødekor's/søster** *-a/-en, pl -søstre(r)* Red Cross nurse.

Rø'de/nes *Pln* twp, Østfold.

rø'd/flammet(e) *A* - flushed, streaked with red.

+**rø'd/glødende** *A* - fiery red, glowing red.

+**rø'd/grøt** *-en* red pudding (usu. made of fruit juice).

+**Rø'd/hette** [also rø'd/] *Prn* Red Riding Hood.

+**rø'd/hud** *-en* redskin, North American Indian.

+**rø'd/håret** *A* - red-haired, redheaded.

+**rø'd/kinnet** *A* - red-cheeked.

+**rø'd/knapp** *-en* cf **raud/**

+**rø'd/kolle** *-a* cf **raud/**

+**rø'd/lett** *A* - (=***raud/leitt**, ***raud/leta**) red-cheeked, red-faced, ruddy.

+**rø'dlig** *A* - (=***raudleg**) reddish.

+**rød'me**[1] *-n* blush (of shyness, pleasure); flush (of anger); reddening (e.g. of dawn); redness.

+**rød'me**[2] *V -a/-et* (=***raudne**) blush, flush, redden.

+**rø'd/musset** *A* - red-cheeked, red-faced, ruddy.

+**rø'd/randet(e)** *A* - (of eye) red-rimmed; (of cloud) red-streaked; (of paper, textiles) red-striped.

+**rø'd/rev** *-en* cf **raud/**

+**rø'd/russ** *-en* graduating student at regular, not commercial *gymnasium* (who wears a red cap during last weeks of school year; cf **blåruss, russ**).

+**rø'd/rutet(e)** *A* - red-checked.

+**rø'd/spette** *-a zool.* plaice (Pleuronectes platessa).

+**rø'd/sprengt** *A* - florid, ruddy, weather-beaten; (of eyes) bloodshot.

+**rø'd/strupe** *-n zool.* (European) robin (Erithacus rubecula).

+**rødt'** *et* red (color): **kledt i r-** dressed in r-; **ha r- på leppene** have lipstick on.

+**rø'd/vin** *-en* red wine; burgundy, claret.

Rø'd/øy *Pln* twp, Nordland.

røff' *A røft* rough (=coarse; primitive; not precise): **et r-t overslag** a r- estimate.

røf'fel *-elen, pl -ler* rebuke, reprimand: **få en r-** be called on the carpet.

røf'le *V -a/+-et* rebuke, reprimand.

°**røf'te** *-t* cf **ryfte**

+**rø'k**[1] *-en* cf **røyk**

+**rø'k**[2] *pt of* **ryke**

+**rø'ke** *V -te* cf **røyke**

+**rø'kelse** *-n* (=+**røykelse**, ***røykjelse**) incense.

+**rø'kelses/kar'** *-et* censer.

+**rø'ker** *-en, pl -e* cf **røyker**

+**rø'ket**[1] *pp of* **ryke**

+**rø'ket**[2] *A* - (=**røykt**) smoked.

+**rø'k/farvet** *A* - cf **røyk/farga**

***rø'kje** *V -te* search: **r- etter** inquire about, investigate, search for.

°**røkk'** *-et* cf **rykk**

***rø'knad** *-en, pl -er* inquiry, investigation.

+**rø'kning** *-en* cf **røyking**

+**rø'k/ovn** *-en* cf **røyk/omn**

***rø'k/sam** *A* careful, sedulous; industrious.

røk't *-a/+-en* care, tending (**av** of).

røk'te *V -a/+-et* 1 look after, take care of, tend (animals, plants). 2: **r- et ærend** perform an errand; **r- sin dont** *hum.* do one's duty, tend to one's chickens.

+**rø'k/teppe** *-t* cf **røyk/**

+**røk'ter** *-en, pl -e* (=***-ar**) caretaker, herdsman, keeper; tender of livestock.

rø'l *-et dial.* loud chatter; boasting; nonsense.

Røl'/dal *Pln* twp, Hordaland.

rø'le *V +-te/*-a dial.* chatter loudly; talk incoherently (as in delirium).

røl'lik *-en* (=**ryllik**) *bot.* yarrow (Achillea millefolium).

***røm'd** *-a* 1 roominess, spaciousness. 2 (outer) space.

***rø'me** *V -de* cf **rømme**[2]

røm'ling *-en* (=***røming**) deserter, fugitive, runaway (**fra** from).

røm'me[1] *-n* heavy cream, esp. that formed on top of milk allowed to thicken.

røm'me[2] *V +rømte/*rømde* 1 vacate; leave, quit: **r- byen** leave town. 2 flee, run away (**fra** from); escape; *mil.* desert: **r- hjemmefra** run away from home. *3 have space for, house; make roomier, widen. 4 *(refl.)*: **r- seg** clear one's throat. *5: **r-ast** get roomy, grow roomier: **det r-est på** there is plenty of room.

røm'me/graut *-en* cream porridge (Norwegian delicacy).

røm'me/kolle *-a* dish, consisting of clabbered whole milk strewn with sugar and crumbs.

***røm'meleg** *A* - roomy, spacious.

+**røm'ning** *-en* (=***rømming**) 1 vacating (**av** of). 2 desertion; escape (**fra** from); *naut.* (also) jumping ship. *3 expansion, widening.

Røm'/skog *Pln* twp, Østfold.

Røn'naug *Prn (f)*

+**røn'ne** *-a* hovel, shack, tumble-down house.

røn'tgen/appara't *-et, pl -/+-er* X-ray apparatus.

røn'tgen/behan'dling *-a/+-en* X-ray therapy, treatment.

+**røn'tgen/bilde** *-t* (=***/bilete**) X-ray picture.

røn'tgen/fotografe're *V -te* take an X-ray.

røntgenolog [-lå'g] *-en* radiologist.

røn'tgen/stråle *-n* X-ray.

rø'pe *V -te/+-et* 1 betray; disclose, give away. 2 display, evince, show; tell. 3 *(refl.)*: **r- seg** give oneself away.

***rø'r**[1] *-a* edge (e.g. of table).

rø'r[2] *-et/*-a* (=***røyr**[3]) 1 (drain, gas, heating, stove, water) pipe, piping; (glass, metal, paper, radio) tube (also *anat., bot., zool.*); conduit. 2 (rifle, cannon) barrel; bore. 3 (plant) reed (also *fig., mus.*); cane. 4 (cigarette holder, pipe) stem. 5 (telephone) receiver. 6 drinking straw. 7 *hum.* stovepipe hat.

rø'r[3] *-et* nonsense: **sludder og r-** stuff and n-.

rø'r[4] *pl of* **ro**[1]

Rø'ra *Pln* twp, Nord-Trøndelag.

rø're[1] *-a* 1 batter. 2 chaos, mess: **det var ei einaste r-** it was one big m-.

rø're[2] *-a/+-et* commotion, excitement; disturbance, restlessness: **et voldsomt r-** a huge uproar; **vekke r-** stir up excitement.

rø're[3] *V +-te/*-de* 1 move, stir, touch (also of emotions); *lit.* concern: **det r-er ham personlig** it c-s him personally; **se, men ikke r-** look, but don't touch. 2 mix, stir; agitate: **rørt vann** troubled water. 3 prattle, talk nonsense. 4 (with *prep., adv.*): **r- i grøten** stir the porridge; **r- opp** stir up; **r- opp i** rake up, revive (e.g. old rumors); **r- på seg** move, stir; get a little exercise; get busy, get to work; **r- (mel) ut i vann** mix (flour) with water; **r- ved** touch; touch on; meddle, tamper with; encroach upon. 5 *(refl.)*: **r- seg** move, stir.

+ Bokmål; * Nynorsk; ° Dialect.
After letter: ' stress (Acc. 1); ` tone, stress (Acc. 2); ˙ length.
Below letter: . not pronounced.

rø're/kopp -*en* blockhead, fool.
+**rø'relse** -*n* 1 activity, movement: **liv og r-** busy activity. 2 agitation, emotion, excitement. 3 feeling, sentiment, sentimentality. 4 current, movement.
rø'rende *A* - moving, pathetic, touching.
rø'ret(e) *A* - confused, mixed-up; nonsensical, unclear.
rø'r/gate -*a* passage for conduits carrying water to hydroelectric plant.
rø'r/gras -*et bot.* reed (canary) grass (Phalaris arundinacea).
rø'rig *A* - active, agile, vigorous: **rask og r-** hale and hearty.
+**rø'r/le'dning** -*en* (=*/**leidning**) conduit, pipeline.
+**rø'r/legger** -*en*, *pl* -*e* (=*-**jar**) plumber; pipe fitter, pipelayer.
rø'rlig *A* - moveable: **r- gods** *jur.* household effects, personal property; **r- kapital** free capital.
rø'r/muffe [/moffe] -*a* pipe socket, pipe union.
Rø'r/os *Pln* (mining) town and twp, Sør-Trøndelag.
rø'r/post -*en* pneumatic dispatch, pneumatic post.
rø'rsle -*a* 1 movement (of body). 2 activity (of business). 3 current, movement (of the times).
rø'r/sopp -*en bot.* boletus (family Boletaceae).
rø'r/sukker [/sokker] -*et* cane sugar.
+**rø'r/tang** -*a*, *pl* -*tenger* (=*/**tong**) pipe wrench.
***rø'seleg** *A* - cf **røslig**
+**røs'ke** *V* -*a*/-*et* (=***ryskje**) 1 shake, tug. 2 rip (berries off), pull up (grass, flax).
røs'lig *A* - (=***røseleg**) husky, sturdy; fine-looking, handsome, stately.
+**røs'se** *V* -*te* (=***rysje**) *dial.* 1 sift down (as snow), stream down; topple down; disintegrate, fly apart (e.g. cobweb). 2 tremble with fear: ***det rys i han** it chills his blood, he shivers; **det røst i kropp** it made one shudder (Falkberget).
røss'/lyng -*en*/-*et bot.* heather (Calluna vulgaris).
røs't[1] -*a*/+-*en* (=***røyst**) 1 voice; *fig.* voice (of conscience, heart, truth): **la sin r- høre i avisen** express one's ideas in the paper. 2 *lit.* song (esp. of nightingale), sound (of animal); *fig.*: **bølgens sakte r-** the soft whisper of the waves; **kanonens r-** the sound of the cannon; **stormens veldige r-** the cry of the storm.
røs't[2] -*et* (=***raust**[1]) 1 rafters; arch, gable. 2 *naut.* chains, channels (on sailing ship).
Røs't *Pln* twp, Nordland.
***røs'te**[1] *V* -*a* cf **røyste, rauste**
+**røs'te**[2] *V* -*et* cf **roste**[2]
røs't/stue -*a* raftered cottage (no ceiling).
røs't/tak -*et* raftered roof.
+**rø't** *pt of* **ryte**
***rø'tast** *V røttest* strike root.
***rø'te**[1] -*t* 1 (network of) roots. 2 ferns. 3 *fig.* family background, origins.
***rø'te**[2] *V røtte*: **r- seg** strike root.
***rø'ter** *pl of* **rot**[1]
+**røt'ter** *pl of* **rot**[1]
***røt'test** *pt of* **røtast**
rø've *V* -*a*/+-*et*/+-*de* 1 loot, pillage, rob. 2 kidnap, rape. 3 *fig.* steal (a kiss).
+**rø'ver** -*en*, *pl* -*e* (=*-**ar**) bandit, robber: **falt blant r-e** *bibl.* fell among thieves; **halvstudert r-** ignoramus.
+**rø'ver/histo'rie** -*a*/-*en* 1 story about robbers. 2 *fam.* cock-and-bull story, yarn.
+**rø'veri** -*et* robbery.
+**rø'ver/kjøp** -*et* big bargain.
+**rø'ver/kule** -*n* 1 den of robbers. 2 *fig.* **gjøre sitt hjerte til en r-** keep one's dissent to oneself.
+**rø'ver/stat** -*en hist.* predatory states (particularly Morocco, Algiers, Tunis and Tripoli).
+**rø'ver/unge** [/onge] -*n hum.* rascal, scamp.
røy' -*a*, *pl* *-*ar zool.* female of capercaillie (Tetrao urogallus), wood grouse.
+**røy'e** -*a* cf **røyr**[1]
røy'k -*en* 1 smoke: **det gikk opp i r-** nothing came of it (e.g. plans); **få, ta seg en r-** have a smoke; **gå som en r-** be done in a jiffy, go like a flash; **gutten i r-en** bold, venturesome fellow. 2 fumes; steam (e.g. from kettle, lake).
+**røy'k/dykker** -*en*, *pl* -*e* "smoke diver" (fireman with gas mask).
+**røy'ke** *V* -*te* (=*-**je**) 1 smoke (tobacco): **r- inn en pipe** break in a new pipe; **r- snadde** smoke a pipe; **r- ut en sigar** finish smoking a cigar. 2 cure, smoke (fish, meat); fumigate: **r- ut** smoke out (usu. animal from cave); *fig.* force sby to tell the truth.
røy'ke/fisk -*en* smoked fish; fish for smoking.
+**røy'ke/flesk** -*et* smoke-cured bacon.
+**røy'ke/jakke** -*a* smoking jacket.
+**røy'ke/kupé** -*en* smoking compartment.
+**røy'ke/laks** -*en* smoked salmon.
+**røy'kelse** -*n* cf **røkelse**
Røy'ken *Pln* twp, Buskerud.
røy'ke/pølse -*a* smoked sausage.
+**røy'ker** -*en*, *pl* -*e* (=*-**jar**) (of person) smoker.
+**røykeri'** -*et* smokehouse.
+**røy'ke/saker** *pl* smoking things (tobacco, pipes, etc.).
+**røy'ke/skinke** -*a* smoke-cured ham.
+**røy'ke/tobakk'** -*en* smoking tobacco.
røy'k/farga *A* - smoke-colored.
røy'k/fri *A* -*tt* smokeless.
røy'k/hatt -*en* chimney pot, turncap.
røy'king -*a* smoking.
***røy'kjar** -*en* cf **røyker**
***røy'kje** *V* -*te* cf **røyke**
***røy'kjelse** -*t* cf **røkelse**
***røy'kje/pølse** -*a* cf **røyke/**
røy'k/kana'l -*en* flue, smoke duct.
+**røy'k/legge** *V infl as* **legge** *agr.*, *mil.* cover with a smoke screen.
røy'k/offer -*et*, *pl* -/*-*ofre* offering of incense.
røy'k/omn -*en* 1 *hist.* corner fireplace (without chimney). 2 *mil.* smudge fire (for directions at sea).
røy'k/ring -*en* smoke ring.
røy'k/sky -*a* cloud of smoke.
røy'k/sopp -*en bot.* puffball (Lycoperdon).
røy'k/stue -*a* (=/**stove**) *hist.* simple dwelling, usu. of logs, containing an open fireplace at the center of the room, with a smoke hole directly above.
røy'k/svak *A* smokeless (e.g. powder).
røy'k/teppe -*t* smoke screen.
***røy'nd** -*a* experience; reality: **i r-a** in reality.
***røy'n/dom** -(*m*)*en* 1 attempt, effort. 2 experience, reality.
***røy'ne**[1] -*t* experiment, trial.
røy'ne[2] *V* -*te* *1 test, try; experience, live through; observe: **r- ut** explore; **r- seg** test oneself, try one's wings. **2: det r-er på** it is exhausting, it is hard on one; **når det r-er på** in a pinch, in a showdown, when things get tough.
***røy'nleg** *A* - actual, true.
røy'nsle -*a* experience; fact.
røy'r[1] -*a* (=+**røye**) *zool.* char (Salvelinus alpinus).
***røy'r**[2] -*a*, *pl* -*ar anat.* groin.
***røy'r**[3] -*a*/-*et* cf **rør**[2]
***røy're** *V* -*te* lash, tie up, wind.
***røy'r/gras** -*et* cf **rør/**
***røy'r/leggjar** -*en* cf **rør/legger**
***røy'r/leidning** -*en* cf **rør/ledning**
Røy'r/vik *Pln* twp, Nord-Trøndelag.
røy's -*a* heap of stones, stone pile; heap, pile (**med** of).
***røy'se/katt** -*en* cf **røys/**
røy'sert -*en* high boots; rubber boots.
røy'set(e) *A* - rocky, stony (terrain).
røy's/katt -*en zool.* weasel (Mustela erminea).
***røy'st** -*a* cf **røst**[1]
***røy'star** -*en* voter.
***røy'st/bruk** -*en*/-*et* use of voice.
røy'ste** *V* -*a* (=røste**[1]) vote (**på** for).
***røy'ste/før** *A* eligible to vote.
***røy'ste/rett** -*en* (right to) vote.
***røy'ste/setel** -*elen*, *pl* -*lar* ballot.
***røy'te**[1] -*a* 1 dampness. 2 loss of hair, moulting, shedding. 3 *fig.* dressing-down, talking-to.
røy'te[2] *V* -*te*/+-*a* moult (feathers), shed (hair of animals).
***røy'te/ver** -*et* damp weather.
***røy've**[1] -*t* 1 wool from one sheep. 2 bulk, size, volume.
***røy've**[2] *V* -*de* 1 move: **r- seg** move (oneself). 2 touch: **det hadde ikkje vore r-t** it was untouched.
***røy'ven** *A* -*e*/-*i*, *pl* -*ne* bulky, voluminous.
rå'[1] -*a*, *pl ræer* pole; *naut.* crossbeam (of mast), yard.
rå'[2] -*en*, *pl* -*r* stake set in ground, used to impale sheaves of grain for drying.
rå'[3] *V* -*dde* (=**råde**) 1 advise (**til** to), counsel. 2 be master (**over** over); reign, rule; predominate, prevail. 3 *archaic* interpret, rede (e.g. a dream). 4 (with *prep.*, *adv.*): **råde bot på** remedy; **rå for** be master of, have control of; **rå fra** advise against; **rå med** control, handle, manage; ***rå med seg** collect oneself, come to one's senses; ***rå or** pull through, recover; come to one's senses. 5 *(refl.)*: ***rå seg** buy, get hold of, secure (for oneself); **rå seg selv** act on one's own account, be one's own master.
rå'[4] *A* -*tt* 1 raw (fruit, hides, meat, sugar, etc.); crude, unrefined (oil, ore, etc.): **rå biff** rare beef; **sluke noe rått** devour sth raw; *fig.* swallow sth hook, line and sinker. 2 coarse (expression, laugh, person, voice, etc.); crude, rough (copy, form, stone); raw, vulgar (behavior, joke, etc.); brutal, rude (e.g. treatment): **le rått** guffaw, roar. 3 cold, damp, raw (weather, wind, etc.): **rå ved** green (damp) wood. 4 exorbitant, shameless (demand, price, etc.). 5 *fam.* (intensifying *adj.*, *adv.*): **rått gøy** more fun than a barrel of monkeys.
***rå'ast** *V* -*ast* grow damp, moist (e.g. of drying hay).
rå'/balanse [/balang'se] -*n merc.* trial balance.
rå'/band -*et naut.* roband.
rå'/barka *A* - (=+-**et**) 1 undertanned (leather). 2 *fam.* coarse, rough (person).
rå'/bukk [/bokk] -*en zool.* male roe deer (Capreolus capreolus).
rå'/bygg -*et* framework, structure (of building).
rå'd[1] -*a*/+-*en* 1 expedient; remedy; way (out): **det blir vel ei r- sth** will most likely turn up; **det er det r- for (med)** that can be taken care of, remedied; **ikke vite sin arme r-** be at a loss, be at one's wits' end. 2 chance, possibility: **i dag var det ikke r- for annet** today there was no getting out of it (B. Lie); **så fort r- er** as soon as possible; *fam.* **mulighets r-** at all possible, humanly possible. 3 provision, store, supply; means, wealth: **ha god, dårlig r-** be well, badly off; **ha r- til** be able to afford.
rå'd[2] -*en* councilor (member of a council); cabinet member.
rå'd[3] [*rå'] -*et*/*-*a* 1 advice, counsel: **et godt r-** a good piece of advice; **r- og dåd** work and deed; **spørre en om r- (til r-s), ta en med på r-** ask sby's advice, consult sby. 2 conference, consultation, deliberation; counsel: **holde r-** hold a conference, council (of war); **legge opp r-** de-

liberate, take counsel; **være med på r-** take part in deliberations.
rå'd[4] *-et* council: **Kongens r-** *hist.* the Royal C-; (nowadays) the King's Cabinet; **Det økonomiske og sosiale r-** C- for Economic and Social Affairs (UN).
rå'd/bot *-a, pl -bøter dial.* corrective, remedy (**for** for); improvement, reform.
*__rådd'__ *A* - 1 decided (**på** upon): **eg er ikkje r- på det** I don't intend to do it. 2 advised (**til å** to). 3 provided: **for lite r- på det** not adequately provided with it.
rå'de *V -de* cf **rå**[3]
Rå'de *Pln* twp, Østfold.
*__rå'/dele__ *-t* boundary.
rå'delig *A* - advisable.
*__rå'den'__ *A -e/-i, pl -ne* arranged, placed: **ille r-** badly off.
rå'dende *A* - 1 existing, prevailing. 2: **den r-** the master (mistress).
rå'de/rett *-en* freedom of action, use, disposal (**over** of).
rå'de/rom [/romm] *-met* freedom of action, latitude.
rå'd/føre *V -te*: **r- seg med** consult, take counsel with.
rå'd/givende *A* - (=*__/gjevande__) advisory, consultative.
+**rå'd/giver** *-en, pl -e* (=*__-ar__, *__/gjevar__) advisor, consultant, counselor.
råd/gjerd [rå'/jær] *-a dial.* expedient, remedy (**mot** against) steps. 2 deliberation; decision.
*__rå'd/gjevande__ *A* - cf **/givende**
*__rå'd/gjevar__ *-en* cf **/giver**
rå'd/hitten *A* +*-ent, pl -hitne dial.* resourceful.
rå'd/hus *-et* city hall, town hall.
rå'dig *A* - 1: **være r- over** be master of, have control over. *2 resolute.
+**rå'dig/het** *-en* command, disposal (**over** of): **stille noe til ens r-** put sth at one's d-; **stå til r-** be at one's d-.
+**rå'd/la** *pt of* **-legge**
rå'd/laus *A* 1 bewildered, helpless; perplexed, puzzled; confused, irresolute. 2 *dial.* hopeless, impossible: ***alt dette r-e** the hopelessness of it all (Vesaas).
+**rå'd/legge** *V -la, -lagt* consult, deliberate; make plans.
+**rå'd/legning** *-en* (=**/legging**) consultation, deliberation.
+**rå'd/løs** *A* cf **/laus**
+**rå'dløs/het** *-en* (=*__/løyse__) 1 irresolution, perplexity. *2 hopelessness, impasse.
rå'd/mann *-en, pl -menn/*-menner* town official (ab.=deputy mayor, who directs administration and prepares budget proposals).
+**rå'd/rik** *A* eager to have power; authoritarian.
rå'ds/dreng *-en hist.* chief hired man, farm manager.
rå'ds/forsam'ling *-a/+-en* board, council (meeting).
rå'ds/herre *-n hist.* councilor; senator.
+**rå'd/sla'gning** *-en* conference, consultation, deliberation.
+**rå'd/slå** *V -slo, -slått* consult, deliberate.
rå'd/snar *A* quick-witted, resourceful; resolute.
+**rå'd/snill** *A -snilt archaic* clever, shrewd.
+**rå'd/spørre** *V -spør, -spurte, -spurt* (=*__/spørje__) consult, hear the opinion of.
rå'ds/republikk' *-en* one of the republics of the U.S.S.R.
rå'd/stue *-a archaic* jail: **han sitter på r-a** he is in j-.
*__rå'd/vald__ *-et* command, (right of) disposal; authority, competence.
*__rå'dvalds/midel__ *-elen, pl -lar merc.* free capital.
*__rå'dvalds/rett__ *-en jur.* right of disposal.
*__rå'd/velde__ *-t* control, mastery (**over** of).
rå'd/vill *A -vilt* bewildered, confused; irresolute, perplexed, undecided.
*__rå'd/ville__ *-a* dilemma, embarrassment, quandary.
*__rå'd/vis__ *A* resourceful.
rå'/dyr *-et zool.* roe deer (Capreolus capreolus).
*__rå'e__ *-n* dampness.
rå'/emne *-t, pl* +*-r/*-* raw material.
rå'/flott *A* - *fam.* lavish.
+**rå'/gjenger** *-en, pl -e* (=*__/gangar__) careless pedestrian, jaywalker.
rå'/gummi *-en* crepe rubber.
+**rå'/het** *-en* rawness; crudity; coarseness; brutality; chill, dampness; (a) crude act, remark.
rå'/hogge *V infl as* **hogge** roughhew.
rå'/jern [/jœ'rn] *-et* (=*__/jarn__) pig iron.
rå'k[1] *-a* 1 open channel (in ice). 2 cow path, trail. *3 furrow, stripe.
rå'k[2] *-et* chance (meeting): **på eit r-** at a guess, roughly; at random.
rå'/kald *A* raw (weather, wind).
*__rå'kast__ *V -ast* meet: **kvar skal vi r-** where shall we m-.
+**rå'ke**[1] *-n* (=*__roke__[1]) heaping measure: **for å sette r- på motgangen** to make our hard luck complete (Nansen).
*__rå'ke__[2] *-n* saliva.
*__rå'ke__[3] *V -a* moisten.
rå'ke[4] *V -a/+-te* 1 hit, strike. 2 come upon, meet: **r-es m-**; **r- bort i (opp i, ut for)** run into; **r- opp for** *dial.* run out of; **r- på** come across; **r- sammen** run into each other; **r- til å** happen to.
+**rå'/kjører** *-en, pl -e* (=*__-ar__, *__/køyrar__) reckless driver.
rå'/kjøring *-a/+-en* (=*__/køyring__) reckless driving.
rå'/kost *-en* uncooked fruits and vegetables.
rå'kost/jern [/jærn] *-et* grater.
rå'l *-et dial.* cry, scream; noise.
*__rå'le__ *V -a* feel, fumble; scratch, scrape (together).
rå'/lendt *A* - damp, soggy (terrain); marshy.
*__rå'm__ *-et* accident, chance: **på et r-** by c-; at random.
rå'/malm *-en* crude ore.
rå'/mark *-a* damp, soggy ground.
rå'/materia'le *-t, pl* +*-r/*-* raw material.
*__rå'me__[1] *-a* cf **ramme**[1]
rå'me[2] *-n* dampness, moisture, sogginess.
*__rå'me__[3] *V -a* cf **ramme**[4]
+**rå'/melk** [also rå'/] *-a/-en* cf **/mjølk**
*__rå'men__ *A -e/-i, pl -ne* damp, moist.
rå'/mjølk *-a* colostrum, first milk.
*__rå'm/skott__ *-et* random shot.
rå'ne[1] *-n* boar.
*__rå'ne__[2] *V -a* 1 (of hay) become wet again. 2 get better (after illness).
rå'/nokke *-n* (=+__/nokk__) *naut.* boom end, yardarm.
rå'/olje *-a/-en* crude oil.
+**rå'pert** *-en* cf **ropert**
rå'/rand *-a* 1 incompletely baked strip under crust (usu. in bread). 2 section in center of hide unaffected by tanning process.
rå's *-a* 1 cow path, trail. 2 earth, stone slide. 3 open channel (in ice). 4 (sailing) channel.
rå'/segl *-et* (=+__/seil__) *naut.* square sail.
rå'/silke *-n* raw silk, shantung.
rå'/skap *-en* coarseness; brutality; vulgarity.
*__rå'ske__ *-n* moisture.
*__rå'sken__ *A -e/-i, pl -ne* moist.
rå'/skinn *-et* 1 crude, brutal person. 2 vulgar person.
+**rå'/skjær** *-en* (=*__/skjer__) dried fish (usu. cod, coalfish).
rå'/slag *-et* pieces of newly slaughtered animal; fresh fish; esp. entrails and waste.
rå'/steikt *A* - rare (meat); underdone (bread).
rå'/stoff *-et, pl -/+-er* raw material (**for** for).
rå'/sukker [/sokker] *-et* unrefined sugar.
+**rå't** *-en* cf **råte**
rå'/tamp *-en* hoodlum, rowdy.
rå'/tass *-en* hoodlum, rowdy.
+**rå'te** *-n* (=+__råt__, *__rot__[3], *__rote__[2]) decay, rotting.
+**råt'ne** *V -a/-et* (=*__rotne__) decompose, rot (also *fig.*, e.g. morals): **r- ned** be ruined by rotting.
rått' *nt of* **rå**[4]
+**råt'ten** *A -ent, pl råtne* (=*__roten__) 1 decayed, rotten: **r- snø (is)** melting snow (ice) (and therefore insecure). 2 damp, mouldy. 3 *fig.* unmanly, weak; morally corrupt; filthy.
+**råt'ten/skap** *-en* (=*__rota/__) rottenness; *fig.* corruption.
*__rå'v__ *-et* roof.
rå'/vare *-a/+-en* raw material.
+**rå'/vær** *-et* (=*__/ver__) raw weather (cold, wet).

S

s [ess'] *-en* 1 (letter) S, s. 2 *pop.*= **særdeles tilfredsstillende** (highest grade).
S=**Senterpartiet; sør,** +__syd__
s.=**side; substantiv; søndre**[2]
sa *pt of* *__seie,__ +__si__[1]
*__SA__=**søraust**
sabb' *-en pop.* 1 slow, slovenly person; slob. 2 big man; wealthy man.
sab'bat *-en* sabbath.
sab'bats/år *-et* sabbatical (year).
sab'be[1] *-a pop.* slovenly woman; slattern.
sab'be[2] *V -a/+-et* 1 slog, slosh. 2 splash, squish.
sab'be/føre *-t* slushy walking; bad going.
sab'bet(e) *A* - 1 sloshy. 2 sloppy, slovenly.
sa'bel *-elen, pl -ler* sabre; (officer's) sword: **rasle med s-en** rattle the sabre (=threaten war).
+**sa'bel/hefte** *-t* sabre (sword) hilt.
sa'bel/rasling *-a/+-en* sabre rattling= warlike maneuvers.
+**sa'bla** *A* - (euphemism for Satan) damnable, damned.
sa'ble *V -a/+-et*: **s- ned** cut down, mow down (with sword); *fig.* slaughter, slay (e.g. in a critical review).
sabota'sje *-n* sabotage.

+ Bokmål; * Nynorsk; ° Dialect.
After letter: ' stress (Acc. 1); ' tone, stress (Acc. 2); ˑ length.
Below letter: . not pronounced.

sabote're *V -te* sabotage.

sabotø'r *-en* saboteur.

Sachsen [sak'sen] *Pln* Saxony (Germany).

sa'del *-en* cf **sal**[1]

sadis'me *-n* sadism.

sadis't *-en* sadist.

sadis'tisk *A -* sadistic.

safe [sei'f] *-n* safe (vault).

saffia'n *-et* morocco (leather).

safi'r *-en* sapphire.

safi'r/blå *A -tt* sapphire (blue).

safra'n *-en bot.* saffron (Crocus sativus); a strong yellowish dye.

saf't *-a* 1 sap (of plants and trees). 2 juice (of fruits or meat); syrup (as in cough syrup): **presse s-a av en sitron** squeeze a lemon dry; **druens saft** *poet.* wine (cf **druesaft**). 3 *fig.* strength, vigor, vitality: **s- og kraft** vim and vigor.

saf'te *V -a/+-et* 1 make juice from (berries, fruit); juice (in Eng. only oranges). 2: **s- seg** (of berries) excrete juice.

saf'tig *A -* 1 juicy (fruit); lush (grass). 2 *fig.* juicy, racy (story); broad (humor); pithy, pungent (style).

saf'tig/grøn *A* (=+**/grønn**) lush and green.

saf't/laus *A* (=+**/løs**) sapless; feeble, withered.

+**saf't/ogvann** [/åvann·] *-et* a fruit drink (mixture of water and berry juice).

saf't/rik *A* juicy, succulent.

saf't/spenning *-a/+-en bot.* turgor (sap pressure).

saf't/suppe *-a* fruit soup (made with fruit juices, prunes, raisins and sago).

sa'g *-a* 1 saw. 2 sawmill: **kjøre tømmer til s-a** transport timber to the s-.

sa'ga *+-en/**ei* (=***soge**[1]) 1 saga (Old Norse prose narrative). 2 *lit.* history: **utflytternes s-** the h- (saga) of the emigrants. 3 story (**om** about), esp. biographical: **hans s- er ute** his day is done; **hun er ute av s-en** she is out of the picture (the running); **en s- blott** a thing of the past.

+**sa'ga/skriver** *-en, pl -e* writer of sagas; historian.

sa'ga/stil *-en lit.* style of the Old Norse sagas (=concise, oral, vigorous).

sa'ga/tid *-a/+-en* saga age (about 800—1300 A.D., when events of Old Norse sagas occurred).

sa'g/blad *-et* saw blade.

sa'g/bruk *-et* sawmill.

***sag'de** *pt of* **seie**

***sag'dest** *pt of* **seiast**

sa'ge *V -a/+-et/+-de* saw (**av** off; **over** through): **s- av (over) den gren en selv sitter på** saw off the branch one is sitting on.

Sa'gene *Pln* section of Oslo.

sa'g/flis *-a* sawdust.

sa'g/krakk *-en* sawhorse.

sa'g/mjøl *-et* (fine) sawdust.

sa'g/mo *-et* sawdust.

sa'g/mugg *-en/+-et* (fine) sawdust.

+**sagn** [sang'n] *-et* legend, myth; tradition: **det går et s-** there is a t-; **få syn for s-** see for oneself.

+**sagn/aktig** [sang'n/] *A -* legendary, mythical; fabulous.

sagn/figu'r *-en* legendary (mythical) figure, character.

sagn/helt *-en* legendary (mythical) hero.

sagn/konge *-n* legendary king.

+**sagn/krets** *-en* cycle of legends.

sa'go *-en* sago.

sa'go/gryn *-et* sago (in granular form).

sa'go/palme *-n bot.* sago palm (Metroxylon rumphii).

sa'go/velling *-a/-en* sago gruel.

sagra'da/pille *-a/+-en pharm.* type of laxative pill (made from an extract of the bark of buckthorn (Rhamnus purshiana)).

sa'g/sku'r(ḍ) *-en* 1 sawing. 2 cut made by a saw.

sag't *pp of* **seie, si**[1]

sa'g/tagga *A -* (=+**-et**) saw-toothed (e.g. mountains).

sa'g/takka *A -* (=+**-et**) 1 saw-toothed. 2 *bot.* serrate. 3 *zool.* serratus (muscle).

sa'g/tann *-a, pl -tenner* saw tooth.

+**sa'g/tent** *A -* (=***/tennt**) saw-toothed.

sa'hib *-en* sahib.

sa'k *-a/+-en* 1 (legal) case, lawsuit: **anlegge s- mot** bring (legal) action against; **føre (tale) ens s-** defend, speak for sby; **sikker i sin s-** sure that one is right. 2 matter; affair, business: **s-en er den, ser du, at...** you see, the point is, that...; the situation is that...; **s-ene står godt (dårlig)** the situation is good (bad); **det er en annen s- med deg** you're in a different position; **det er en s- for seg** that's quite another matter (story); **det er en avgjort s-** no question about that; **det er ikke hvermanns s-** it is not the business of just anybody; **det er nettopp s-en** that's just the point; **det er så sin s-** it's not easy, it's a touchy business (also used as an expression of hesitation or indecision); **det er ingen s-** that's no problem, that's an easy matter; **blande seg i andres s-er** meddle in (stick one's nose into) other people's business; **for den s-s skyld** for that matter; **la det bli min s-** let me worry about that; **det gjelder s- og ikke person** it's a question of facts, not personalities; **gjøre felles s-** join forces; **gjøre sine s-er godt** do one's work well; **gå like på s-en** go straight to the point; **holde seg til s-en** stick to the subject at hand, the point; **la oss komme til s-en** let's get down to business; **være inne i s-ene** know all about sth, know the ropes. 3 cause: **en god s-** a worthy c-. 4 thing (usu. *pl*): **s-er og ting** (all kinds of) things, this and that; **det var s-er** that was really sth; **det var ikke store s-ene** there wasn't much to that; **etterglemte s-er** lost and found. 5 food or drink: **kraftige s-er** heavy food (or strong drink); **sterke s-er** hard liquor; **det var sterke s-er!** that was powerful stuff!; **søte s-er** goodies.

***sa'ka** *A -* guilty.

sakari'n *-en* saccharin.

***sa'ke** *V -a* 1 accuse; complain: **s- seg** complain. 2 abandon; discard, slough (at cards).

+**sa'ke/fall** *-et* (=***sak/**) *jur., archaic* proceeds from the collection of fines.

+**sa'kes/løs** *A jur.* blameless, innocent: **overfall på s- mann** attack on an innocent party.

***sa'k/fall** *-et* cf **sake/**

+**sa'k/fører** *-en, pl -e* (=***-ar**) (trial) lawyer.

+**sa'k/førsel** *-elen, pl -ler* (=***/førsle**) pleading of a legal case.

+**sakk'** *pt of* **søkke**[2]

sak'ke *V -a/+-et* 1 slow down, move with diminished speed: **s- akterut (av, bakut)** lag (fall) behind; **s- på farten** decrease speed. 2: **s- av** *dial.* (esp. of rain, wind, etc.) diminish. 3 *naut.* run with reverse engines.

***sa'k/kunne** *-a* cf **/kyndighet**

***sa'k/kunnig** *A -* cf **/kyndig**

sa'k/kunnskap *-en* expert knowledge of a subject.

+**sa'k/kyndig** *A -* expert, competent in a subject.

+**sa'kkyndig/het** *-en* 1 *lit.* expert knowledge of a subject. 2 those possessing expert knowledge of a subject: **hva sier s-en?** what do the experts say?

***sa'k/laus** *A* cf **sakes/løs**

sa'klig *A -* factual, impartial, objective: **s- kritikk** unbiased criticism.

+**sa'klig/het** *-en* impartiality, objectivity.

sa'k/liste *-a* 1 court agenda. 2 subject index (=**sakregister**).

***sa'k/løyse** *-a* guiltlessness, innocence.

sak'n *-et* (=+**savn**) 1 lack, privation, want: **lide s-** suffer privation; **ordboka kommer til å avhjelpe et lenge følt s-** the dictionary will meet a long-felt need. 2 loss; bereavement: **føle s-et av noe** miss sth.

sak'naḍ *-en* 1 lack, want. 2 loss; bereavement: **ein stor s-** a bitter loss.

***sak'naḍ/dauḍe** *-n* widely mourned death.

sak'ne *V -a/+-et* (=+**savne**) 1 be without, lack, want: **s- ord til å uttrykke** be at a loss for words; **han s-er ingenting** he has everything he needs. 2 miss: **de s-ede** the missing (persons); **når s-et du det først?** when did you first notice it was gone?; **vi s-er ham sterkt** we miss him very much.

sakra'l *A* consecrated, holy, sacred.

sakramen't *-et, pl -/+-er* sacrament: **alterens s-** Holy Communion.

sakramenta'l *A* sacramental.

sa'k/regis'ter *-eret/-ret, pl -er/+-re* subject index.

sakristi' *-et, pl +-er/**- sacristy, vestry.

sakrosan'kt *A -* sacrosanct.

sak's[1] *-a* 1 (pair of) scissors, shears. 2 steel-jawed trap: **gå i s-a** fall into the trap (laid for one); **sitte i s-a** be in a jam, a tough spot.

sak's[2] *-en* gap between the ends of skis when seen from the side during a ski jump: **han ble trukket for s-** he was marked down (on points for form) for not holding his skis even.

***sak's**[3] *-et* (large) knife.

+**sa'ks/anlegg** *-et* lawsuit, prosecution.

+**sa'ks/behan'dling** *-a/-en* court proceedings, trial.

sak'se *V -a/+-et* 1 plagiarize (by "clipping out", usu. referring to one newspaper using material taken from another). 2 "scissor" (place two objects, supposed to be parallel, at an angle to each other, usu. referring to the position of skis during a jump): **skiene s-et i nedslaget** his skis were not parallel when he landed.

sak'se/dyr *-et zool.* earwig (Forficula auricularia).

sak'se/klo *-a zool.* pincers.

sak'se/krok *-en naut.* sister hook.

+**sak'ser** *-en, pl -e* (=***-ar**) Saxon.

saksifra'ga *-en bot.* saxifrage (Saxifraga herba).

sak'sisk *A -* Saxon.

saksofo'n *-en* saxophone.

+**sa'ks/omkos'tninger** *pl* court costs.

sak's/sverd *-et* short one-edged sword (used during the Old Norse saga period).

+**sa'k/søke** *V -te* (=***-je**) prosecute, sue, take to court.

+**sa'k/søker** *-en, pl -e* (=***-jar**) plaintiff.

***sa'k/søkje** *V -te* cf **/søke**

sa'k/søkte *df* the defendant.

sak'te[1] *V -a/+-et* cf **sakne**

sak'te[2] *A -* 1 quiet, soft(ly); gentle: **snakke s-** speak quietly, softly; **en s- vind** a gentle wind; **så s-!** easy now! 2 slow(ly): **kjøre s-** drive s-; **slå s-** *naut.* slow the engine.

***sak'te**[3] *Av* cf **saktens**

sak'telig *A - poet.* soft; gentle; quiet.

sak'tens [also: sak'-] *Av* (=**sakte**[3]) surely, to be sure; undoubtedly: **det kan han s- gjøre** he can surely do that, that's no trick for him.

saktmo'dig *A -* gentle, meek, mild.

+**saktmo'dig/het** *-en* gentleness, meekness, mildness.

sak'tne *V -a/+-et* decrease (in intensity, speed, violence): **s- av** decrease (in intensity); **s- (på) farten** slow down; **stormen s-er** the storm is dying down; **uret mitt s-er 10 minutter på et døgn** my watch loses 10 minutes a day.

sa'l[1] *-en* saddle: **sitte fast (løst) i s-en**

fig. be in a secure (insecure) position.
sa'l[2] *-en* large hall; auditorium.
***sa'l**[3] *-et* cf **salg**
+sal. =**salig**
salaman'der *-eren, pl -rer/+-ere* salamander.
sala'mi/pølse *-a* salami.
Sal'angen *Pln* twp, Troms.
sala't *-en* 1 lettuce. 2 salad.
sala't/bestikk· *-et* salad set (fork and spoon).
+sala't/hode *-t* head of lettuce.
sa'l/boge [/båge] *-n* (=+**/bue**) saddlebow.
salde're *V -te econ.* 1 pay (the balance of a debt). 2 balance (an account).
sal'do *-en, pl -er/saldi econ.* balance (of a debt).
sa'le *V +-te/*-a* saddle.
+sal'g *-et* (=***sal**[3]) sale: **til s-s** for sale.
+sal'g/bar *A* salable.
sa'l/gjo'rd *-a* cinch (on a saddle).
+sal'gs- *Pf* (=***sals-**) sales.
+sal'gs/honora'r *-et* commission on sales.
+sal'gs/lag *-et* marketing cooperative.
+sal'gs/nota *-en* bill, invoice.
+sal'gs/pris *-en* sale price, selling price.
+sal'gs/regning [/reining] *-a/-en* account sale(s).
+sal'gs/sentra'l *-en* marketing center.
+sal'gs/sjef *-en* sales manager.
+sal'gs/teknikk· *-en* sales technique.
+sal'gs/vare *-a/-en* article, commodity, product.
+sal'gs/verdi· *-en* sale value.
sa'lig *A -* 1 *bibl.* blessed: **s-e er de fattige i ånden** b- are the poor in spirit; **bli s-** be saved; **enhver blir salig i sin tro** let him believe it if it makes him happy; **gjøre s-** save. 2 *hum.* or *archaic* deceased (abbr. **sal.**): **min s- mor** my dear, departed mother. 3 blissfully happy: **et s- smil** a blissful smile. 4 *fam.* tipsy.
+sa'lig/gjørende *A -* saving: **det eneste s-** the only thing, the most important thing.
+sa'lig/het *-en* 1 blessedness, salvation. 2 bliss, ecstasy. 3: **nei, min s- om jeg gjør** *fam.* damned if I will.
+sa'lighets/sak *-a/-en* 1 matter pertaining to salvation. 2 matter of great import to one.
sa'ling *-a* 1 *naut.* crosstrees, trestletrees. 2 *arch.* profile (wooden frame).
sa'lings/ho'rn *-et naut.* outrigger.
salisy'l *-en/-et* salicyl; salicylic acid.
salisy'l/syre *-a* salicylic acid.
sa'l/knapp *-en* saddle horn, pommel.
+sa'l/maker *-en, pl -e* (=***-ar**) saddler.
sal'me *-n* 1 hymn. 2 psalm.
sal'me/bok *-a, pl -bøker* 1 hymnal, hymnbook. 2 *fam.* deck of cards.
+sal'me/dikter *-en, pl -e* (=***-ar**) hymnist.
sal'me/nummer [/nommer] *-et, pl -/+-numre* hymn number.
sal'me/vers *-et* verse or stanze (of a hymn).
salmiakk' *-en* ammonium chloride, sal ammoniac.
salmiakk'/spiritus *-en* ammonia water.
salmis't *-en* psalmist; the Psalmist (David).
salmo'dikon *-en/-et mus.* monochord.
salomo'nisk *A-* Solomonic.
salong' *-en* 1 drawing room. 2 lounge (on a ship, in a hotel). 3 (literary) salon.
salong'/bo'rd *-et* coffee table.
+salong'/fähig [/fe-ig] *A -* presentable in society; poised; *hum.* housebroken.
salong'/gevæ'r *-et* (small-bore) rifle.
salong'/løve *-a/+-en* drawing room lion, ladies' man.
+salong'/radika'ler *-en, pl -e* (=***-ar**) parlor pink, drawing room radical.
salong'/vogn [/vångn] *-a* club car, parlor car.
salpe'ter *-en* niter, saltpeter.
+salpe'ter/holdig *A -* nitrous, saltpetrous.
salpe'ter/syre *-a* nitric acid (HNO_3).
sa'l/pute *-a* saddle pad.
***sa'l/reie** *-n* saddle gear.
sa'l/rygga *A -* (=+**-et**, ***-ja**) swaybacked.
***sa'ls-** *Pf* cf **salgs-**
sa'ls/dør *-a* entrance door.
***sa'ls/lag** *-et* cf **salgs/**
***sa'ls/pris** *-en* cf **salgs/**
***sa'ls/sentra'l** *-en* cf **salgs/**
sal't[1] *-et, pl +-er/*-* salt.
sal't[2] *A -* salt, salty: **s-e pine, død og s-** (mild oaths).
sa'l/taske *-a* saddlebag.
***sal't/biten** *A -e/-i, pl -ne* lightly salted.
***sal't/brim** *-et* salt crust.
+sal't/bøsse *-a* saltcellar, saltshaker.
Sal't/dal *Pln* twp, Nordland.
sal'te *V -a/+-et* salt; (of meat) cure, pickle.
Sal'ten *Pln* section of Nordland.
+sal'ter *-en, pl -e* (=***-ar**) salter (person who salts fish, meat, etc.).
sal't/fisk *-en* salted fish.
+sal't/holdig *A -* (=***/haldig**) saline, salty.
sal't/kar *-et* saltcellar, saltshaker.
sal't/kjøtt *-et* (=***/kjøt**) salted meat.
sal't/ko'rn *-et* grain of salt.
sal't/lake *-n* brine, pickle.
sal't/mat *-en* salted (preserved) food (esp. meats and fish).
saltomorta'le *-n* somersault: **gjøre, slå en s-** somersault, turn a s-.
sal't/sild *-a* pickled herring.
+sal't/sprengt *A -* (=***/sprengd**) (lightly) salted; (of rocks) salt-covered.
sal't/støtte *-a/+-en bibl.* pillar of salt.
sal't/syre *-a* hydrochloric acid.
+sal'tvanns/fisk *-en* saltwater fish.
sal't/vatn *-et* (=+**/vann**) salt water.
sal't/væring *-en* inhabitant of Salta.
salutt' *-en* salute.
salutte're *V -te* salute.
sal've[1] *-a/-en* 1 ointment, salve. 2 salvo, volley; round of applause: **en grusom s-** a devastating remark.
sal've[2] *V -a/+-et* anoint.
Sal've *Prn (m)*
+sal'velse *-n* 1 anointment. 2 unction: **han talte med s-** he spoke with u-.
+sal'velses/full *A* unctuous(ly); ministerial(ly).
sa'l/veske *-a* saddlebag.
salvi'e *-n bot.* sage (Salvia).
salvi'e/te *-en* sage tea.
salæ'r *-et, pl -/+-er* fee.
sam'- *Pf* co-, pan-.
-sam *A* also cf **-som** -some.
***sa'man** *Av* cf **sammen**
***sa'man/felling** [also: sa'man/] *-a* joining; joint.
***saman/hangande** *A -* cf **sammen/hengende**
***saman/likne** *V -a* cf **sammen/ligne**
***saman/likning** *-a* cf **sammen/ligning**
***saman/setjing** *-a* cf **sammen/setning**
***saman/sett** *A -* cf **sammen/satt**
***saman/skot(t)** *-et* cf **sammen/skudd**
***saman/støyt** *-en* cf **sammen/støt**
***saman/sverjing** *-a* cf **sammen/svergelse**
sam'/arbeid *-et* cooperation.
sam'/arbeide *V -de/+-et* cooperate.
sama'rie *-n* cassock, chasuble (minister's gown).
samarita'n *-en* Samaritan: **den barmhjertige s-** the good S-.
+samaritanerin'ne *-a/-en* (=***samaritanarinne**) Samaritan woman.
samarita'nsk *A -* Samaritan.
samaritt' *-en* practical nurse.
samaritt'/ele'v *-en* practical nursing student.
sam'ba *-en* samba.
sam'band *-et* 1 communication, connection: **i s- med** in connection with. 2 union.
sam'bands/offise'r *-en* liaison officer.
+Sam'bands/statene *Pln* (=***-ane**) the United States (of America).
+sam'bands/tjeneste *-n* (=***/teneste**) *mil.* communication section.
sam'/beite *-t* common pasture.
sam'/binding *-a* unification, union.
sam'/bruk *-et/-en* common or joint tillage.
***sam'/bunden** *A -e/-i, pl -ne* joined, united.
sam'/bygding *-en* person from same rural community (as another person).
***sam'd** *A -* in agreement (**med** with).
***sam'de** *pt of* **semje**[2]
+sam'/drektig *A -* unanimous.
+samdrek'tig/het *-en* unanimity.
sam'/drift *-a* joint operation.
***sam'/drøg** *A* harmonious.
sa'me[1] *-n* Lapp.
***sa'me**[2] *V -a*: **det s-er seg ikkje** it is not fitting, proper.
***sa'me**[3] *Pn* cf **samme**
+sam'/eie *-t* (=***/eige**) joint ownership; sth jointly owned: **ha noe i s-** own sth jointly.
***sam'/eine** *V -a/-te* unite.
sam'/eksisten's *-en* coexistence: **fredelig s-** peaceful c-.
***sa'meleg** *A -* befitting, proper.
***sa'me/leis** *Av* similarly; in the same way.
***sam'/felt** *A -* steady, uninterrupted.
***sam'/fengd** *A -/ fengt* blended, mixed.
sam'/ferdsel [/færsel] *-la/+-elen* (=***/ferdsle**) communication; traffic (between two points).
Samferdsels/departementet [-mang'e] *df* Ministry of Transport and Communications.
sam'ferdsels/middel [-færsels/] *-elet/midlet, pl +-middel/*-el* means of communication.
***sam'/feste** *-t* connection.
***sam'/folkeleg** *A -* international.
sam'/full *A* complete, whole: **i tre s-e dager, år, etc.** for three whole days, years, etc.
sam'/funn *-et* 1 community; society: **den mann må være en borgerfiende, som kan ville ødelegge et helt s-** that man must be an enemy of the people who can wish to destroy an entire community (Ibsen); **de nedbrytende krefter i s-et** the destructive forces in society. 2 communion: **ha (komme i) s- med** be (get into) c- with; **det jødiske s-** the Jewish c-; **de helliges s-** the C- of Saints. 3 association, organization: **Militære S-** the Military Society.
***sam'funns/bate** *-n* commonweal, public good.
+sam'funns/beva'rende *A -* conservative.
+sam'funns/borger *-en, pl -e* (=***-ar**) citizen, member of society.
sam'funns/drama *-et, pl -/+-er* social drama.
sam'funns/farlig *A -* dangerous to society.
sam'funns/fiende *-n* enemy of society, public enemy.
sam'funns/fiendtlig *A -* antisocial, inimical to society.
sam'funns/forhold *-et* social conditions.
sam'funns/gagnlig [/gangnli] *A -* of public utility, socially beneficial.
***sam'funns/huga** *A -* interested in the welfare of society; philanthropic.
sam'funns/hus *-et* community center.
***sam'funns/høveleg** *A -* socially suitable.
sam'funns/klasse *-a/-en* social class.
sam'funns/kunnskap *-en* sociology.
sam'funns/lag *-et* social stratum.
sam'funns/liv *-et* community life, social existence.

+ Bokmål; * Nynorsk; ° Dialect.
After letter: ' stress (Acc. 1); ` tone, stress (Acc. 2); · length.
Below letter: . not pronounced.

sam'funns/lære -a/+-en civics.
sam'funns/maskineri' -et mechanics of social structure.
+sam'funns/messig A - social.
sam'funns/nyttig A - of public utility, socially beneficial.
sam'funns/orden -en social order.
sam'funns/plikt -a/+-en civic duty, social duty.
sam'funns/proble'm -et, pl -/+-er social problem.
sam'funns/reformasjo'n -en social reformation.
sam'funns/reforma'tor -en social reformer.
*sam'funns/skipnad -en social organization.
sam'funns/støtte -a/+-en pillar of society.
+sam'funns/vitenskap -en sociology; social studies.
sam'funns/ånd +-en/*-a public spirit.
+sam'/følelse -n 1 feeling of unity, solidarity. 2 sympathy: **ha s- med en** sympathize with sby.
*sam'/hald -et cf /hold
*sam'/haldig A - cohesive, unanimous.
sam'/handel -en commerce, trade.
*sam'/helde -t cf /hold
+sam'/hold -et (=*/hald) agreement, concord; solidarity, unity.
sam'/hug -en compassion, sympathy.
+sam'/hørig A - closely bound, interdependent; solidary.
+sam'hørig/het -en interdependence, solidarity.
*sam'/høve -t agreement, conformity, harmony: **i s- med** according to.
sa'misk A - Lappish.
sam'/kjensle -a sympathy.
*sam'/kjøm A agreeing: **det vart ikkje s-t** it didn't agree.
*sam'/kjønn -et common gender.
sam'/kjøre V -te (=*/køyre) coordinate (electrical power stations).
sam'/klang -en harmony.
*sam'/kom(m)e -a gathering, meeting; reunion.
*sam'/kroning -en bot. gamopetalous plant (Metachlamydeae).
sam'/kvem' -met (=*/kvæme) 1 contact; intercourse: **ha s- med** have contact, dealings with. 2 company. 3 communication.
saml.=**samling**
sam'la A - (=+-et) collected; joined, united: **s-ede verker** collected works.
sam'/lag -et 1 association; group (**av** of). 2 state liquor store.
*sam'/lage V -a bring in agreement, harmonize.
sam'le V -a/+-et 1 collect, gather (things, money, people, etc.): **s- inn, på, sammen** collect; **s- seg** collect, compose oneself; **s- seg om** unite around (e.g. a cause); **ikke noe å s- på** not worth much, not worth bothering with. 2 merge, unite: **s-riket** unite the kingdom. 3 attract: **s- oppmerksomheten om seg** become the center of attention.
sam'le/band -et conveyor belt; assembly line.
+sam'le/bind -et anthology, collection (of writings).
+sam'le/bånd -et cf /band
sam'le/fabrikk' -en assembly plant (e.g. for automobiles).
+sam'/leie -t (=*/lege) coitus, sexual intercourse.
sam'le/lense -a chain of logs used to gather up floating timber.
sam'le/linse -a/+-en convex lens.
sam'le/mappe -a portfolio.
+sam'ler -en, pl -e (=*-ar) 1 collector (e.g. of coins, stamps). 2 compiler (e.g. of scientific data). 3 *anthro.* food-gatherer.
+sam'let A - cf **samla**
*sam'/leta A - unicolored.
sam'ling -a/+-en 1 assembling, collecting, gathering; collection; unification (of a nation); meeting (of a group of people), session (of a legislature). 2 sense(s): **være ved full s-** be in one's right mind; **være (gå) fra sans og s-** be (go) out of one's mind.
sam'lings/merke -t, pl +-r/*- symbol of unity (e.g. banner, flag); rallying point (e.g. of a political party).
sam'lings/punkt -et, pl -/+-er rallying point: **et s- i den bitre politiske strid** a r- in the bitter political contest.
sam'lings/regje'ring -a/+-en coalition government.
+sam'lings/sted -et (=*/stad) place of meeting, rendezvous.
sam'/liv -et life together: **ekteskapelig s-** married life; **et lykkelig s-** a happy marriage.
sam'/lyd -en (=/ljod) harmony.
+sam'/løp -et skating in pairs.
+sam'/ma'lt A - (=*/malen) (of flour) ground whole.
+sam'me *Pn* (=*same[3]) 1 (the) same: **den s- mannen** the s- man; **s-dag(en), år(et), etc.** the s- day, year, etc.; **i s- retning** in the s-direction. 2 (in phrases expressing lack of distinction, difference): **det er (meg) det s-** it's all the s-, it makes no difference (to me); **det er ett og det s-** it's precisely the s-thing, there's no difference at all; **det får (kan) være det s-** never mind, forget it; **det går for det s-** it's all the s-, it doesn't make any difference; **det kommer ut på det s-** it amounts to the s- thing, it's all the s-. 3 (in expressions of time): **i det s-** just then, at that (the same) instant, moment; **i det s- falt mannen ned gjennom pipa** just then the man fell down the chimney (Asbjørnsen); **jeg møtte ham i det s- han kom ut av huset** I met him just as, at the same moment he came out of the house; **med det s-** right away, immediately, at the same time, while you're at it; **jeg skal gjøre det med det s-** I'll do it right away; **tar De livsløgnen fra et gjennomsnittsmenneske, så tar De lykken fra ham med det s-** if you take the average man's illusions from him, you deprive him of his happiness at the same time (Ibsen); **vær så snill og hent boka mi, og ta med brillene mine med det s-** please get my book, and bring my glasses while you're at it; **med det s- vi snakker om det** while we're on the subject.
+sam'men *Av* (=*saman) together: **s- med** t- with, in company with; **alle s-** all (of them, us, you); **alt s-** all (of it); **til sammen** (all) together; **to og to s-** two by two; **ha noe s-** have sth in common; **ta to s-** decrease (in knitting). (For expressions with verbs, e.g. **kalle s-, sette s-, ta seg s-**: see these).
+sam'men/arbeide V -de/-et combine (into a whole), unify: **s- seg** cooperate, work together; **de s-et seg** they met each other half way.
+sam'men/bitt A - clenched, contracted; dogged, persevering: **det var noe s- hos ham** there was sth determined about him; **med s-e tenner** with clenched teeth.
+sam'men/blanding -a/-en blending, mingling, mixture.
+sam'men/bretta A - (=+-et) folded.
+sam'men/brudd -et collapse, crash, debacle (firm, government, stock market, etc.); *med.* breakdown, crackup: **et nervøst s-** a nervous breakdown.
+sam'men/bundet A - tied together.
+sam'men/dradd A - 1 contracted, shrunken. 2 abridged, summarized (e.g. report).
+sam'men/drag -et resumé, summary (**av** of).
+sam'men/fall -et 1 coalescence, merger (**med** with); *gram.* syncretism. 2 collapse, crash (**av** of).
+sam'men/fallen A -et, pl -falne broken-down, collapsed; shrunken.
+sam'men/fatte V -a/-et 1 join, unite. 2 recapitulate, summarize: **s-ende fremstillinger** summation.
+sam'men/filtre V -a/-et snarl, tangle (e.g. hair, threads).
+sam'men/føyning -en joint, seam: **gi seg, gå opp i s-en** give, come apart at the joints, seams.
+sam'men/heng -en 1 connection, interdependence, relationship: **ha s-med, stå i s- med** be connected with, related to; **i denne s-** in this connection, in reference to this. 2 coherence, cohesion, continuity: **s-en i Norges historie** the continuity in the history of Norway; **se noe i en større s-** see sth as part of a greater whole, in a wider perspective. 3 sense, truth (of an event or situation): **kjenne hele s-en** know the true facts of a case, situation; **så fortalte hun hele s-en** then she told the whole story; **det er ingen s- i dette** this doesn't make any sense. 4 context: **ordet betyr noe annet i denne s-** the word means sth different in this c-; **rive ut av s-en** lift out of c-.
+sam'men/hengende A - connected, related; continuous, unbroken; coherent, consistent: **en s- fremstilling** a coherent account; **et s- hele** a continuous whole.
+sam'men/holde V -holdt, -holdt 1 hold together. 2 collate, compare.
+sam'men/kalle V -kalte call together, convene (assembly, meeting, etc.).
+sam'men/klemt A - compressed, squeezed together.
+sam'men/knepet A -: **med s-ne lepper** tight-lipped; **med s-ne øyne** with narrowed eyes, slit-eyed.
+sam'men/komst -en meeting, social gathering; conference (**av** of).
+sam'men/krøpet A - crouched, huddled over.
+sam'men/lagt A - combined, totaled; put together.
+sam'menlegg/bar A collapsible.
+sam'men/ligne V -a/-et (=/likne) compare (**med** with); liken (**med** to): **de kan ikke s-s** they can't be compared, they're not in the same class; **s-ende** comparative.
+sam'men/ligning -en (=/likning) comparison: **i s- med** compared with, to; **dra, trekke en s-** make a c-; **ikke tåle s- med** not be in the same class with; **uten s-** (with comparatives) by far, far and away; **uten s- for øvrig** otherwise no c-.
+sam'menlignings/grunnlag -et basis for comparison.
+sam'men/satt A - (=*saman/sett) 1 composed, made up (**av** of): **maskinen er s- av mange deler** the machine is composed of many parts. 2 *gram., bot.* compound (leaf, word); *bot., math.* composite (flower, number). 3 complex (e.g. character, nature).
+sam'men/setning -en (=*saman/, *saman/setjing) 1 combining; composition, makeup (e.g. of a committee, of gases). 2 *gram.* compound, compounding: **ordet er dannet ved s-** the word is formed by compounding.
+sam'mensett/bar A *gram.* compoundable, capable of forming compounds.
+sam'men/skudd -et contribution (to a common purpose, e.g. a party).
+sam'menskudds/fest -en party at which each person pays his share; Dutch treat, potluck.
+sam'men/slutning -en 1 amalgamation, merger: **en s- av partiene** a m- of the parties. 2 organization, society, union.
+sam'men/smeltning -en amalgamation, fusion (**av** of).
+sam'men/snø'rt A - constricted.
+sam'men/stilling -en 1 grouping to-

gether; juxtaposition. 2 comparison (**av** of).

+samˋmen/stimling *-en* crowding together; crowd, throng.

+samˋmen/støt *-et* 1 collision: **et s- mellom en bil og en buss** a c- between an auto and a bus. 2 clash, controversy; run-in; *mil.* skirmish: **hans mange s- med politiet** his many altercations with the law. 3 coincidence, concurrence: **s- av tilfeldigheter** coincidence.

+samˋmen/støtende *A* - 1 adjoining, contiguous. 2 coincidental.

+samˋmen/sunken [/songken] *A -ent, pl -ne* collapsed, sunken; *fig.* prostrate.

+sammensu'rium *-iet, -ier* conglomeration: **det blir et s-** that will be a mess, hodgepodge.

+samˋmen/sveiset [also: sam'men/] *A* - welded together (e.g. steel plates, elements of a nation).

+samˋmen/sverge *V -et/-svor*: **s- seg** conspire (**om å** to), plot (**mot** against).

+samˋmen/svergelse *-n* (=***saman/sverjing**) conspiracy, plot.

+samˋmen/svoren *en, pl -svorne* conspirator.

+samˋmen/treff *-et* 1 accidental, chance meeting: **vårt s- i Trondheim** our chance meeting in T-. 2 coincidence: **et merkverdig heldig s- av omstendigheter** a lucky, remarkable c-.

+samˋmen/trekning *-en* contraction.

+samˋmen/trengt *A* - 1 crowded together. 2 condensed: **et s- referat** a concise account.

+samˋmen/trykt *A* - compressed.

+samˋmen/vokst *A* - grown together; coalesced, fused: **hans øyebryn er s-** his eyebrows meet; **han var så s- med oss** he had become a part of our family circle; **s-e tvillinger** Siamese twins.

+samˋme/steds *Av* in the same place; **sst.**=ibid.

***samˋ/namn** *-et* cf **/navn**

Samˋnanger *Pln* twp, Hordaland.

+samˋ/navn *-et gram.* common noun.

***samˋ/nemnar** *-en* common denominator.

***samˋ/nemne** *-t* cf **/navn**

samˋ/nordisk *A* - pan-Scandinavian.

samˋ/norsk[1] *-en* (projected) pan-Norwegian language, to be formed by the interfusion of *Bokmål* and *Nynorsk*.

samˋ/norsk[2] *A* - pan-Norwegian, esp. in referring to the (projected) all-Norwegian language *(samnorsk)*.

samoje'd *-en* Samoyed.

samoje'd/hund *-en* Samoyed (dog).

samoje'disk *A* - Samoyed(ic).

samˋ/ordne *V -a/+-et* coordinate.

samova'r *-en* samovar.

***samˋ/røde** *-a* conversation.

samˋ/røre *V -te* 1 mix together. 2 confound, confuse, merge.

samˋ/røring *-a/+-en* 1 mixture. 2 confusion, merger.

***samˋ/rø(y)stes** *A* - unanimous.

samˋ/rå *V -dde*: **s- seg** consult together, deliberate (**om** about); **s-dd** agreed.

samˋ/råd *+-et/*-a* consultation: **møtes til s-** meet for c-; **i s- med** after c-with, in agreement with.

***samˋ/råde** *V -de* cf **/rå**

sam's *A* - 1 common, joint. 2 of one kind; unsorted. 3 agreed (**om** about; **med** with).

+samˋ/sang *-en* choral or group singing.

samˋ/skatt *-en* taxation of joint income (of husband and wife).

samˋ/skipnad *-en* association, organization: **Student/s-en** the Students' Association.

***samˋ/song** *-en* cf **/sang**

+samˋ/spill *-et* (=***/spel**) 1 *mus.* ensemble (playing), harmony: **det var utmerket s-** they played together excellently. 2 (sports) teamwork: **det var dårlig s- mellom løperne** there was poor t- between the runners. 3 interaction, interplay: **et s- av mange faktorer** an interplay of many factors.

+samˋ/staves *V -des, -es* (=***/stavast, */stave**) agree; harmonize.

***samˋ/stelt** *A* - agreed.

+samˋ/stemme *V -stemte* 1 attune, bring into harmony with: **tekst og musikk var godt s-t** text and music were in accord. 2 agree, concur: **de andre s-te i dette** the others c-ed in this.

+samˋ/stemmig *A* - agreeing, concordant: **s- mening** unanimous opinion.

+samˋstemmig/het *-en* agreement, unanimity.

***samˋ/stendig** *A* - agreeing, unanimous; constant, steady.

***samˋ/stevjast** *V -ast* be in harmony with, harmonize with.

samˋ/stundes *Av* 1 simultaneously. 2 contemporaneously.

samˋ/svar *-et* accord, conformity: **i s- med** in accordance with.

samˋ/svare *V -a/-te* be equivalent to, correspond to: **s-ende** corresponding.

***samˋ/syn** *-et/-a* collective, unified view.

***sam't[1]** *pp of* **semje[1]**

sam't[2] *Av*: **jamt og s-** constantly, continually.

+sam't[3] *P* in addition to, plus, together with: **De har fornærmet meg s- min kone** you have insulted me and my wife as well.

samˋ/tale[1] **-a/-en* 1 conversation, talk: **føre en s-** carry on a conversation (**med** with); **gi s-n en annen retning** change the subject; **en s- under fire øyne** a tête-à-tête. 2 (telephone) call: **bestille en s-** place a c-.

samˋ/tale[2] *V +-te/*-a* converse, talk (**med** to; **om** about): **forstå den kunst å s-** understand the art of conversation; **vi måtte s- med Los Angeles over Denver** our calls to L- A- had to be routed through D-.

samˋtale/avgift *-a/+-en* charge (for telephone call).

samˋtale/emne *-t, pl +-r/*-* subject, topic of conversation.

samˋ/tid *-a/+-en* 1 age, time: **Fredrik den store satte liten pris på s-ens tyske diktning** Frederick the Great had a low opinion of the German literature of his time. 2 contemporaries (collective): **Holberg og hans s-** H- and his c-.

samˋ/tidig [also -ti'd-] *A* - 1 simultaneous: **de to begivenheter skjedde nesten s-** the two events occurred almost at the same time; **de kom s-** they arrived at the same time. 2 contemporary: **Holberg og Voltaire var s-e** H- and V- were contemporaries.

+samˋtlige *pl* all, one and all: **s- gjester** all the guests; **s- bestod eksamen** all passed the exam.

***samˋ/tonande** *A* - in agreement, unanimous.

samˋ/tykke[1] *-t* approval, sanction; consent: **foreldrene gav sitt s- til partiet** the parents gave their blessing to the match; **få, ha ens s- til noe** obtain, have sby's c- to sth; **nekte sitt s- til noe** withhold one's c- to sth.

+samˋ/tykke[2] *V -et* (=***-je**) acquiesce (**i** in), assent, consent.

samurai' *-en* samurai.

samˋ/velde *-t* commonwealth: **Det britiske S-** the British C-.

***samˋ/vere** *-a* cf **/vær**

***samˋ/verknad** *-en* cooperation.

samˋ/vett *-et* cf **samvittig/het**

***samˋvetts/agg** *-et* pangs of conscience, remorse.

***samˋvetts/full** *A* cf **samvittighets/**

***samˋvetts/laus** *A* cf **samvittighets/løs**

***samˋvetts/sak** *-a/-en* cf **samvittighets/**

samˋ/virke *-t* 1 cooperation, joint action. 2 system of cooperatives.

samˋvirke/lag *-et* cooperative society.

+samˋ/virkende *A* - concurrent, cooperative; interacting.

***samˋ/vit** *-et* cf **samvittig/het**

***samˋvits/agg** *-et* cf **samvetts/**

+samvit'tig/het *-en* (=**sam/vett**) conscience: **med god s-** with a clear c-; **på ære og s-** on one's honor; (jokingly) **hva har du på s-en?** what's on your mind? what can I do for you?; **ha sin s- fri** have a clear c-; **ta noe på s-en** take the responsibility for sth.

+samvit'tighets/full *A* conscientious, painstaking, scrupulous.

+samvit'tighets/løs *A* conscienceless, unprincipled, unscrupulous.

+samvit'tighets/nag *-et* pangs of conscience, twinge of remorse.

+samvit'tighets/sak *-a/-en* matter of conscience.

+samvit'tighets/skruppel *-elen, pl -skrupler* qualm, scruple of conscience.

+samvit'tighets/spørsmål *-et* 1 personal question. 2 matter of conscience.

+samˋ/vær *-et* (=***/vere**) being together, company, life together: **Simon kjente seg sky og usikker i s- med henne** S- was shy and unsure of himself in her company (Undset); **vi ble gode venner under vårt s- i Norge** we became good friends during our stay (together) in Norway; **kameratslig s-** friendly gathering; **takk for s-et** thank you for a very pleasant time.

***samˋ/yrke** *-t* cooperation, joint action.

san' *N* cf **sann[1]**

+sanato'rie/opphold *-et* rest, stay in a sanatorium.

sanato'rium *-iet, pl +-ier/*-ium* 1 sanatorium. 2 health resort.

san'd *-en* sand: **løpe ut i s-en** come to nothing, fizzle out; **strø s- på** hush up, smooth over (an affair).

San'd *Pln* twp, Rogaland.

sanda'l *-en* sandal.

San'dar *Pln* twp, Vestfold.

san'd/blåsing *-a/+-en* sandblasting.

san'd/botn *-en* (=**+/bunn**) sandy bottom.

san'd/dyne *+-n/*-a* dune.

san'de *V -a/+-et* 1 sprinkle, strew with sand. 2 sand up (e.g. spring, well).

San'de *Pln* twp, Møre og Romsdal, Vestfold.

San'de/fjo'rd *Pln* town, Vestfold.

San'd/eid *Pln* twp, Rogaland.

san'del *-en* sandalwood.

+san'delig *Av* cf **sannelig**

san'del/tre *-et bot.* sandalwood tree (red: Pterocarpus santalinus; white: Santalum album).

san'det(e) *A* - sandy, sanded.

+san'd/flukt *-a/-en* (=***/flog**) sand drift.

san'd/fokk *-et* (=***/fok**) blowing sand.

san'd/grunn *-en* sandy soil.

san'd/jo'rd *-a* sandy soil.

san'd/kake *-a* 1 cooky (made of butter, flour, and almonds, baked in small metal forms). 2 pound cake.

san'd/kasse *-a/-en* sandbox.

san'd/ko'rn *-et* grain of sand.

san'd/mel *-en* sandbank.

San'd/nes *Pln* seaport, Rogaland.

San'dnes/sjøen *Pln* lake and twp, Nordland.

san'd/papi'r *-et* sandpaper.

san'd/sekk *-en* sandbag.

***san'd/skjel** *-a zool.* soft clam (Mya arenaria).

+ Bokmål; * Nynorsk; ° Dialect.
After letter: ' stress (Acc. 1); ˋ tone, stress (Acc. 2); · length.
Below letter: . not pronounced.

san'ḍ/skure *V* *+-te/*-a* scour with sand.
San'ḍ/staḍ *Pln* twp, Sør-Trøndelag.
san'ḍ/stein *-en* sandstone.
san'ḍ/storm *-en* sandstorm.
san'ḍ/strø *V* *-dde* 1 sand, sprinkle with sand (e.g. a floor; formerly, a document to dry the ink). 2 *fig.* whitewash (sby's actions).
san'ḍ/tak *-et* sandpit.
San'ḍ/torg *Pln* twp, Troms.
sandwich [sæ'n(d)vitsj] *-en* sandwich.
san'ḍ/ørken *-enen, pl -(e)ner* (sandy) desert.
San'd/øy *Pln* twp, Møre og Romsdal.
sane're *V* *-te* 1 clear away; rebuild, reconstruct (e.g. a section of a city). 2 *merc.* reorganize (e.g. a corporation), restore (finances).
sane'ring *-a/+-en* 1 clearance; reconstruction: **s- av usunne bydeler** slum clearance. 2 *merc.* reorganization, restoration.
+sang'[1] *-en* (=***song**[1]) 1 song. 2 singing. 3 canto.
+sang'[2] *pt of* **synge**
+sang'/bar *A* singable; melodious.
+sang'/bok *-a, pl -bøker* songbook.
+sang'/bunn *-en* 1 *mus.* soundboard (of an instrument), sounding board. 2 *fig.* response; feeling, sensitivity: **hans poesi fant ingen s- i samtiden** his poetry found no response in his own time; **hun var uten s- for det lyriske** she had no feeling for the lyrical.
+sang'er *-en, pl -e* (=***songar**) singer; chorister, vocalist; bard, minstrel, troubadour; warbler (bird).
+sang'er/bro(de)r *-en, pl -brødre* member of a choral society, glee club.
+sangerin'ne *-a* (=***songarinne**) (female) singer (esp. opera, concret); songstress.
+sang'/fore'ning *-a/-en* choral society, glee club.
+sang'/fugl *-en* songbird, warbler.
+sang'/kor *-et* choir.
sang're *V* *-a/+-et* whimper, whine; (e.g. of a violin) squeal.
+sang'/stemme *-n* singing voice.
+sangvi'niker *-en, pl -e* (=***-ar**) optimist, sanguine person.
sangvi'nsk *A* - sanguine; hopeful, optimistic.
sanite't *-en* 1 health, hygiene. 2 *mil.* medical corps.
sanite'ts/binḍ *-et* sanitary napkin.
+sanite'ts/fore'ning *-a/-en* (=***/foreining**) 1 the Gray Ladies (=volunteer workers of the Red Cross who provide nonprofessional care and services for the sick and convalescent in hospitals). 2 any society concerned with the problems of hygiene.
sanite'ts/solda't *-en* corpsman, medic.
sanitæ'r *A* hygienic, sanitary.
sanitæ'r/anlegg *-et* plumbing (e.g. in an apartment building).
+san'k *pt of* **synke**
san'ke *V* *-a/+-et* 1 collect, gather, round up (also with **inn, sammen**): **han har s-et erfaringer i livets skole** he has amassed experiences in the school of life. 2 pick: **s- aks** glean; **s- bær** p- berries; **s- opp** p- up.
+san'ker *-en, pl -e* (=***-ar**) 1: **bær/s-** berry picker. 2 *anthro.* food gatherer.
sanksjo'n *-en* 1 sanction; assent, permission. 2: **militære, økonomiske s-er** military, economic sanctions.
sanksjone're *V* *-te* authorize, sanction.
san'kt *N* saint.
sankt-ber'nhards/hunḍ *-en* St. Bernard (dog).
sankthan's [also: sang'kt-] *en* Midsummer Day, St. John's Day (June 24th).
+sankthan's/aften *-en* Midsummer Eve (June 23rd).
sankthan's/bål *-et* Midsummer Eve bonfire.
sankthan's/fest *-en* Midsummer Eve festival.
sankthan's/kvelḍ *-en* Midsummer Eve (June 23rd).
sankthan's/orm *-en* *zool.* glowworm (Lampyris noctiluca).
sanktvei'ts/dans *-en* *med.* St. Vitus' dance, chorea.
sann'[1] *N* 1: **for s-, min s-, s-** (usu. **s-t) for dyden** fairly mild emphatic expressions (by George, sure enough, etc.). 2 used as emphatic particle at end of a statement: **nei, om det var så greitt s-!** oh, if it were only that easy!; ***men far sjølv s-!** but father himself! (Vesaas); **nei takk s-** no thanks; **pytt s-** who cares?
sann'[2] *A* *sant* 1 true; genuine, real: **det er s-t** that's true (also: by the way); **dette er Guds s-e ord** these are the true sayings of God (Rev. 19, 9); **en s- venn** a real friend; **gi et s-t bilde av noe** give a faithful, true picture of sth; **s-t å si** to tell the truth; **ikke s-t?** isn't that so? don't you agree? etc.; **det var et s-t ord** you said a mouthful; **det kan være noe s-t i det** there might be an element of truth in that; **det er så s-t som det er sagt** that's sure as shooting. 2: **så s-t** if ever, if only, whenever; **så s-t jeg lever (står her)** as sure as I'm alive (standing here); **de gikk tur hver dag, så s-t det var godt vær** they took a walk every day, provided it was good weather; **hvis jeg så s-t kunne det** if I only could do it.
+sann'/dru *A* - truthful, veracious; honest, sincere.
+sann'/drømt *A* - (=***/drøymd**) having one's dreams come true: **han var s-** his dreams came true.
san'ne *V* *-a/+-et* 1 confirm, verify; experience the truth of: **du kommer nok til å s- mine ord** you'll learn (to your regret) that what I say is true. 2: **s- seg, s-es** (e.g. of a prophecy) be borne out.
san'nelig *Av* certainly, indeed, to be sure; *bibl.* verily: **det har du s- rett i** you're most certainly right; **han visste s- ikke hva han skulle si** he didn't have the faintest idea what he should say; **s- sier jeg eder** verily I say unto you (Matt. 5, 18); **s- min hatt** of all things, why I never; **s- om (jeg gjør det)** darned if (I'll do it); **så s-** by golly.
sann'/ferdig [also -fær'-] *A* - 1 truthful, veracious. 2 *(adv.)* really.
***sann'/feste** *V* *-a/-e* confirm, verify.
+sann'/het *-en* (=**sanning**) truth, veracity: **av barn og fulle folk skal man høre s-en** out of the mouths of babes and sucklings; **når jeg skal si s-en** to tell the truth, to be perfectly honest; **uten å tre s-en for nær** without overstepping the bounds of truth.
+sann'hets/iver *-en* fervor, zeal for the truth.
+sann'hets/kjærlig *A* - truthful, veracious.
+sann'hets/kjærlighet *-en* truthfulness, veracity; love of truth.
+sann'hets/o'rḍ *-et* word of truth; word of admonition, warning.
San'ni/dal *Pln* twp, Telemark.
san'ning *-a* cf **sann/het**
***san'nings/kjær** *A* truthful, veracious.
***sann'/kjenne** *V* *-kjende* acknowledge, recognize.
***sann'/leik** *-en* truth, veracity.
***sann'/o'rḍig** *A* - truthful, veracious; honest.
***sann'/røynd** *A* *-røynt* confirmed, verified by experience.
+sann'/si(g)er *-en, pl -e* soothsayer.
sann'/spådd *A* *-/*-spått* foretold, prophesied: **bli s-** have one's predictions come true.
sannsy'nlig *A* - likely, probable, reasonable.
+sannsy'nlig/het *-en* likelihood, probability: **det er liten s- for at de kommer** it is not very likely that they will come; **etter all s-** in all probability.
+sannsy'nlighets/beregning [/berei'-ning] *-en* calculation of possibilities; *math.* calculus of probability.
+sannsy'nlighets/bevi's *-et* demonstration, evidence of probability.
+sannsy'nlig/vis *Av* in all likelihood, probably.
san's *-en* sense: **sunn s-** common s-; **ha s- for** appreciate; have a s-, understanding of; **komme til s- og samling** come to one's s-s; **være (gå) fra s- og samling** be (go) out of one's mind (senses); **være ved sine s-ers fulle bruk** be in possession of all of one's faculties.
+san's/bar *A* discernible, perceptible.
san'se *V* *-a/+-et/+-te* 1 perceive; be(come) aware of, notice, realize: **s- på** be aware of, notice; **s- seg** come to one's senses, collect one's wits. 2 remember.
san'se/bedra'g *-et* illusion.
san'se/evne *-a/+-en* sensory faculty.
san'se/inntrykk *-et* sense impression.
san'se/kake *-a* box on the ear.
san'se/kvalite't *-en* quality of sense perception.
san'se/laus *A* 1 senseless, unconscious: **han var halvt s- etter det voldsomme slag** he was knocked half senseless by the violent blow. 2 distracted, frantic: **s- av skrekk** f- with terror. 3 senseless, stupid: **hun måtte høre på hans s-e snakk** she had to listen to his senseless drivel.
san'selig *A* - 1 material, perceptible, physical: **den s-e verden** the material world. 2 sensual, voluptuous: **han er en s- natur** he is a sensualist; **en s- munn** a sensual mouth.
+san'se/løs *A* cf **/laus**
***san'se/løyse** *-a* unconsciousness; distraction, frenzy; witlessness.
san'se/orga'n *-et, pl -/+-er* sense organ.
***san'se/vildring** *-a* illusion.
***san'se/ville** *-a* illusion.
san'skrit *et* Sanskrit.
sanskulott [sangkylått'] *-en* *hist.* sans-culotte.
+san'sning *-en* sensation, sense perception.
+san't[1] *N* (=**+santen**): **min s-, min s-en; s- for dyden** fairly mild emphatic expressions (by George, sure enough, etc.).
san't[2] *nt of* **sann**[2]
santa'l *-en* Santal (=Kolarian people in Bengal).
santa'l/misjo'n *-en* missionary work among the Santals.
+san'ten *N* cf **sant**[1]
sappø'r *-en* *mil.* sapper.
saprofyt' *-en* saprophyte.
saprofyt'isk *A* - saprophytic.
sapø'r *-en* cf **sappør**
saraban'de *-n* *mus.* saraband.
+sarase'ner *-en, pl -e* (=***-ar, *sarasen**) Saracen.
sardell' *-en* *zool.* anchovy (Engraulis encrasicholus).
sardi'n *-en* sardine.
+sardi'nier *-en, pl -e* (=***-ar**) Sardinian.
sar'g *-en* 1 *carp.* frame (holding legs of chair or table together). 2 *mus.* curved side, rib of a stringed instrument.
Sargas'so/haveț *Pln* the Sargasso Sea.
sargas'so/tang *-en/-et* gulfweed, sargasso.
sarkas'me *-n* sarcasm; gibe, sarcastic remark.
sarkas'tisk *A* - sarcastic.
sarkofa'g *-en* sarcophagus.
sar'ping *-en* resident of Sarpsborg.
Sar'ps/borg *Pln* town, Østfold.
sa'rt *A* - delicate, soft, tender; (of color) pale, subdued: **jeg går i de s-este vårlengslers følge** I am accompanied by the tenderest longings of spring (Collett Vogt).

sar'v *-et* refuse, trash; nasty mess.
***sar've** *V -a* do sth in a slapdash manner.
SAS=Scandinavian Airlines System
***sa't** *pt of* sitje
sa'tan *-en* 1 (the) devil: **han er en s- til å arbeide** he's one helluva good worker. 2 (as oath): **det var som s-** well, I'll be damned; **hold opp for s-** stop, damn it all; **kjøre (løpe, etc.) som bare s-** drive (run, etc.) like hell; **gi s- i** not give a damn for. 3: **s-s** damned; **denne s-s båten** this d- boat.
sata'nisk *A* - diabolical, fiendish, satanic.
satellitt' *-en* satellite.
sateng' *-en* sateen.
satine're *V -te* glaze (e.g. paper).
sati're *-n* satire.
+sati'riker *-en, pl -e* (=*-ar) satirist.
satirise're *V -te* satirize.
sati'risk *A* - satirical.
satisfaksjo'n *-en lit.* satisfaction.
satra'p *-en* satrap.
sat's *-en* 1 *typog.* composition, type matter. 2 *mus.* movement; compositional form. 3 explosive or inflammable mixture (e.g. for use in fireworks, match heads, etc.). 4 mash (from which an alcoholic beverage is brewed or distilled). 5 proverbial saying: **jeg har lest på trykk — — og satsen er sann — — "ingen blir profet i sitt eget land"** I have read it in print — — and the saying is true — — "no man is a prophet in his own land" (Ibsen). 6 (in ski jumping) takeoff: **ta s-** take off; *fig.* begin on sth.
sat'se *V -a/+-et* 1 gamble (**på** on); speculate (e.g. in investments, stocks): **s- en femmer** bet a fiver. 2 take off (e.g. in ski jumping).
+satt'[1] *pt of* **sitte**, *pp of* **sette[1]**
+satt'[2] *A* - mature, sedate.
+sat'te *pt of* **sette[1]**
sa'tyr *-en* satyr.
sau' *-en* 1 sheep. 2 *pop.* blockhead, dolt, nincompoop.
***sau'/al** *-et* cf **saue/**
sau'/bikkje *-A* cf **saue/**
sau'/bukk [/bokk] *-en* ram.
saucisse [såsiss'] *-n* cf **såsiss**
***sau'd** *pt of* **sjode, syde**
Sau'da *Pln* twp, Rogaland.
sau'e/al *-et* sheep breeding.
+sau'e/avl *-en* cf **/al**
sau'e/bikkje *-a* sheep dog.
sau'e/fjøs *-et* sheep cote.
sau'e/flokk *-en* flock of sheep.
***sau'e/ga'rde** *-n* enclosure, stall for sheep in a stable.
sau'e/kjøtt *-et* (=*/kjøt) mutton.
sau'e/kve *-a* sheep cote, sheep fold.
sau'e/saks *-a* sheep shears.
sau'e/sanking *-a* collecting the sheep.
***sau'e/skap** *-en* silliness, stupidity.
sau'e/skinn *-et* sheepskin.
sau'g *pt of* **suge**
Sau'/herad *Pln* twp, Telemark.
sau'/kjøtt *-et* cf **saue/**
sau'/lam· *-met* female lamb.
***sau'm** *-en* cf **søm[1], søm[2]**
***sau'me** *V -a* cf **sømme[1]**
sau'm/fare *V infl as* **fare[2]** examine minutely, go over critically.
sau'p[1] *-et* buttermilk.
sau'p[2] *pt of* **supe[2]**
sau'p/graut *-en* buttermilk porridge.
***sau'r** *-en* dirt.
***sau're** *V -a* dirty, make unclean.
***sau'ret(e)** *A* - dirty.
sau's *-en* 1 gravy; sauce. 2 solution (e.g. in moistening tobacco leaves). 3 tobacco juice.
***sau'/saks** *-en* cf **saue/**
sau'se *V -a/+-et* 1 moisten (e.g. tobacco leaves); secrete tobacco juice: **tobakken s-er** the tobacco secretes juice. 2: **s- inn (med)** grease, lubricate, rub in (with).
sau'se/kopp *-en* gravy bowl.
sau'se/nebb *-en* (=/nebbe) gravy boat (pitcher).
sau'se/skei *-a* (=+/skje) gravy spoon.
sau'/skinn *-et* cf **saue/**
***sau's/kopp** *-en* cf **sause/**
sa'v *-et* fish entrails, etc. used as bait (for lobsters).
savan'ne *-n* savanna.
sa've *-n* sap.
sa've/never *-ra, pl -rer* birchbark (from young trees).
sav'l *-et* 1 saliva, slobber. 2 drivel, twaddle.
sav'le *V -a/+-et* 1 slaver, slobber. 2 talk nonsense.
+sav'n *-et* cf **sakn**
+sav'ne *V -et* cf **sakne**
sb.=substantiv
s. br.=sørlig +bredde/*breidd
sce'ne *-n* 1 scene: **s-n er en liten by i Norge** the s- is a small town in Norway; **avisene brakte bilder av s-n for mordet** the newspapers carried pictures of the s- of the murder; **første s-** s-one; **en rørende s-** a touching s-; **kona mi lager aldri s-r** my wife never creates s-s. 2 (theatrical) stage: **for åpen s-** with the curtain up; **utenfor s-n** offstage; **gå over s-n** walk across the stage, *fig.* (of a dramatic work) be played; **gå til s-n** go on the stage (i.e. become an actor); **sette i s-** direct (a play); **skrive for s-n** write for the theater.
+sce'ne/arbei'der *-en, pl -e* (=*-ar) stagehand.
sce'ne/foran'dring *-a/+-en* 1 change of scene (theater). 2 sudden, unexpected change (e.g. in a course, situation, weather).
sce'ne/kunst *-en* acting, dramatic art.
sceneri' *-et, pl +-er/*-* scenery (theater décor, setting; landscape).
sce'ne/tekke *-t* stage presence.
+sce'ne/vant *A* - (=*/van, */vand) confident, experienced, possessing stage presence: **jeg kysset henne s-** I kissed her with aplomb (Gunnar Larsen).
+sce'nevant/het *-en* confidence, experience, stage presence.
sce'nisk *A* - scenic, theatrical.
scherzo [sker'tso] *-en mus.* scherzo.
schizofren [sjitsofre'n, ski-] *A* schizophrenic.
schizofreni [sjitsofreni', ski-] *-en* schizophrenia.
schlager [sjla'ger] *-en, pl -e* cf **slager**
schæfer [sje'fer] *-en, pl +-e* Alsatian (dog), German shepherd dog.
scooter [sku'ter] *-en, pl +-e* (motor) scooter.
score [skå're] *V -a/+-et* score (e.g. a goal in soccer).
sculler [skøl'ler] *-en, pl +-e* scull(er).
s. d.=+samme dag; +se/*sjå dette
Sdm.=Sunnmøre
+se' *V* så, sett (=*sjå[2]) 1 see: **se godt (dårlig)** have good (bad) eyes; **la meg se** let me see; **jeg så ham i går** I saw him yesterday; **har du noen gang sett Villanden?** have you ever seen The Wild Duck?. 2 look (**på** at): **han stod og så ut av vinduet** he was looking out the window; **se her** look here; **se mørkt på** take a gloomy view of. 3 (exclamation): **se for en deilig dag!** oh, what a wonderful day!; **nei se, er det deg** we-e-ll, look who's here; **se så, det er gjort** there, that's done. 4 see=understand: **han er en slusk, det ser jeg nå** he's a bum, I see that now; **han er en rik mann, ser du** you see, he's a rich man; **der ser du** I told you so. 5 (idioms): **jeg ser gjerne at** it would please me if, I'd be very glad if; **jeg ser helst** I would prefer that; **stort sett** for the most part, by and large; **være vel (ille) sett hos en** be in sby's good graces (disfavor). 6 (with *adv.* and *prep.*): **se en an** size sby up; **se sine folk an** be careful about with whom one becomes involved; **se tiden an** bide one's time, sit back and wait; **en ser av dette** this shows, hence; **se bort fra** disregard, ignore; **se etter** follow with the eyes; look, search for; look after, take care of, tend to; check, investigate; **se etter i en bok** consult a book; **se etter at alt er i orden** check that everything is OK; **se noe etter i sømmene** look sth over carefully; **jeg skal se etter om han er hjemme** I'll see if he's home; **se fram til** look forward to; **se igjennom** leaf through (papers, a book, etc.); **se ned på** despise, look down on; **se opp for** watch out for; **se opp til** look up to; **se opp til en** pay sby a visit; **se over** glance, look over; **se på** look at; pay attention to, be particular about; tell by; **han ser nøye på pengene** he's not free with his money; **jeg kunne se på ansiktet hans at** I could tell by the expression on his face that; **se til** look at; be sure to, see to; be in the company of; drop in; **hun er pen å se til** she's nice to look at; **hun er bare et barn å se til** she is apparently only a child; **jeg har sett til Georg** I've been to see George, have looked at George; **se til at det ikke gjentar seg** see that it doesn't happen again; **se til å komme deg ut** get out of here; **se mye til en** see a lot of sby; **se (inn) til en** drop in on, visit sby; **se ut** present an appearance; **se glad ut** look happy; **hvordan ser han ut?** what's he look like?; **hvordan er det du ser ut!** you look a mess!; **se ut som** appear, look like; **se ut til** be in prospect; appear, seem; **det ser ut til regn** it looks like rain; **det ser ut til at jeg har glemt det** it seems, looks like I've forgotten it; **han er 70 år, men det ser han ikke ut til** he's 70 years old, but he doesn't look it; ***sjå åt** look after, see to, take care of. 7 (*refl.*): **se seg for** be careful, watch out; **se seg i stand til** consider oneself able to, see one's way to (doing sth); **se seg nødt til** feel compelled to; **se seg om** look around (**etter** for); **se seg sint på noe (en)** be sick of looking at sth (sby); **se seg tilbake** look back, around; **se seg tvunget til** feel forced to; **se seg ut** pick out for oneself.
°se'a *Av* cf **sia**
seanse [seang'se] *-n* séance.
se'bra *-en* zebra.
se'd [*se] *-en* 1 custom, tradition, usage: **gammel s- og skikk** an old custom. 2: **s-er** morals; culture, refinement.
seda't *A* - sedate, staid.
***sedd'** *pp of* **sjå[2]**
+sed'del *-elen, pl sedler* (=*setel) 1 slip of paper; note. 2 bank note.
+sed'del/bank *-en* bank of issue (e.g. a Federal Reserve bank).
+sed'del/bok *-a, pl -bøker* wallet.
+sed'del/dekning *-en* legal reserve.
+sed'del/masse *-n* circulation, issue of bank notes.
***se'de** *V -a* bring up, educate.
se'delig *A* - ethical, moral; chaste, virtuous.
+se'delig/het *-en* moral conduct; chastity, virtue.
se'de/lære *-a/+-en* ethics, moral philosophy.
se'der *-en, pl +-e* cedar.
se'der/tre *-et, pl -/+-trær bot.* cedar (Cedrus libani).
sedimen't *-et, pl -/+-er* sediment.
sedimentæ'r *A* sedimentary.
***se'ding** *-a* education, upbringing.
***se'd/laus** *A* immoral, licentious.
+sed'ler *pl of* **seddel**
***se'd/løyse** *-a* immorality, licentiousness.

+ Bokmål; * Nynorsk; ° Dialect.
After letter: ' stress (Acc. 1); ` tone, stress (Acc. 2); · length.
Below letter: . not pronounced.

***se'dug** *A* - courteous, well-bred.
***se'dug/skap** *-en* moral conduct; chastity, virtue.
se'd/vane *-n* custom, habit, practice: **etter s-** as is customary, as is my wont; **mot s-** contrary to usual practice; **en gammel s-** a time-honored custom.
se'dvane/rett *-en* prescriptive law; common law (England and the United States).
sedva'nlig *A* - customary, habitual, usual.
+sedva'nlig/vis *Av* habitually, ordinarily, usually.
+se'er *-en, pl -e* (=***sjåar**) prophet, seer.
+se'er/evne *-a/-en* gift of prophecy.
+se'erske *-n* prophetess.
+se'es *V sås/sees, sees* (=**+ses**) meet: **de s- ofte** they m- often; **ja, så s- vi kl.** to well, be seeing you at two o'clock.
sefy'r *-en* zephyr.
seg [+sei] *Pn* (obj. *pron.* referring back to a 3rd-person subject of the clause in which it stands) him(self), her(self), it(self), one(self) them(selves): **seg imellom** among themselves; **han er liten (stor) av seg** he's small (large); **han er for seg** he's aggressive, forward; **det er noe helt for seg** that's quite another matter; **han er noe for seg** he's an odd one; **være i en klasse for seg** be sth quite apart; **hver for seg** separately; **i og for seg** actually, in itself; **med hele seg** with (one's) whole self; **om seg** smart, keeping one's eyes open; **det har noe på seg** there's sth to be said for it; **nei, var det likt seg!** why, of course not! (cf also expressions with verbs listed under these).
***se'ge**[1] *-n* muscle.
***se'ge**[2] *V -a* move slowly.
***seg'el** *-let, pl -el* cf **segl**[2]
+se'get *pp of* **sige**
***segg'** *-en, pl -er* huge man.
***segje** [sei'e] *V segjer, sa, sagt* cf **si**[1]
seg'l[1] [+also: seil] *-et* seal, signet: **et brev med hengende s-** a letter with appended seal; **sette sitt s- under et dokument** affix one's seal to a document; **under vår hånd og rikets s-** under our hand and seal.
seg'l[2] *-et* (=**+seil**) sail: **for fulle s-** with all sails set, at top speed.
***seg'lar** *-en* cf **seiler**
seg'l/area'l *-et* spread of canvas, sail.
seg'l/båt *-en* sailboat; yacht.
seg'l/duk *-en* canvas, sailcloth.
seg'le *V -a/+-et* (=**+seile, *sigle**[2]) sail: **s- forbi en** pass sby; **s- inn (penger)** earn (money) by sailing; **s- over ende** fall over; **s- på (India)** s- (regularly) to (India); **s- på** run into; **la en s- sin egen sjø** leave sby to his fate.
seg'l/føring *-a* spread of canvas, sail.
seg'l/gar'n *-et* twine (used in sewing sails).
seg'l/lakk [+also sei'l/] *-en* sealing wax.
+seg'l/maker *-en, pl +-e* (=***-ar**) sailmaker.
seg'l/ring [+also: sei'l/] *-en* signet ring.
seg'l/skip *-et* sailing ship, vessel.
seg'l/skute *-a* sailing ship, vessel.
segmen't *-et, pl -/+-er* segment.
segmente're *V -te* segment.
***seg'n** *-a* legend, myth, tradition.
+segne [sei'ne] *V -a/-et* drop, sink down; collapse, succumb: **s- under en byrde** collapse under a burden.
+segne/ferdig [sei'ne/] *A* - dog-tired, ready to drop: **s- av tretthet** ready to drop from exhaustion.
segregasjo'n *-en* apartheid, segregation.
segrege're *V -te* segregate.
sei' *-en zool.* coalfish, pollack (Pollachius virens).
***sei'ande** *A* - mentionable.
***sei'ast** *V sa(gde)st* say about oneself: **han seiest vilja reisa** he says he wants to leave; **det seiest it is** said.
sei'/biff *-en* pollack fried or baked with onions.
sei'd *-en hist.* magic, sorcery, witchcraft (esp. as practiced in Old Norse times by a special group of women and involving indecent ceremonies whose object was to bring death and ruin to an enemy).
sei'de *V -a/+-et* practice magic, sorcery, witchcraft.
sei'del *-elen, pl -ler* beer stein, tankard.
sei'd/mann *-en, pl -menn/*-menner* magician, sorcerer.
***sei'e** *V seier, sa(gde), sagt* cf **si**[1]
***sei'e/måte** *-n* mode of expression.
+sei'er *-eren, pl -rer* (=***siger**) victory: **vinne s-** gain a v-; **føre en sak fram til s-** carry a matter through to success; **s-en over egennytten og fordommen** the triumph over self-interest and prejudice.
+sei'er/herre *-n* conqueror, victor, winner.
+sei'er/rik *A* conquering, triumphant, victorious.
+sei'ers/gang *-en* triumphal procession, victorious advance: **gå sin s- verden over** gain entry around the world.
+sei'ers/hette *-a* caul.
+sei'er/sikker *A -ert, pl -sikre* cocksure, supremely confident.
+sei'ers/krans *-en* laurel wreath, victory wreath.
+sei'ers/rus *-en* elation, intoxication of victory.
+sei'ers/tog [/tåg] *-et* triumphal procession.
+sei'ers/vilje *-n* determination to win.
+sei'er/sæl *A* triumphant, victorious.
+sei'er/vant *A* - unconquered, victorious.
sei'g[1] *pt of* **sige**
sei'g[2] *A* 1 (e.g. of meat, leather, etc.) tough; (of liquids) thick, viscous; (of metals) ductile. 2 (of people) persevering, stubborn, tough. 3 slow: **de s-e bønder, som aldri kan få fart i seg** those poky farmers who can never get a move on (Kielland). 4 (of work, bad weather, etc.) long-lasting, never-ending: **dagen hadde vært både s- og slitsom** the day had been both long and tiresome (Falkberget).
***sei'g/leik** *-en* 1 resistance, tenacity, toughness. 2 dilatoriness, slowness.
sei'g/liva *A* - (=**+-et**) stubborn, tenacious of life, hard to kill.
***sei'g/meis** *-a/-en* dilatory, slow person.
***sei'gne** *V -a* toughen.
sei'g/pine *V -te* put on the rack, torment constantly.
sei'/kake *-a* fish ball (made of pollack).
+sei'l *-et* cf **segl**[2]
+sei'l/areal *-et* cf **segl/**
+seila's *-en* navigation, sailing; voyage; regatta.
+sei'l/bar *A* 1 (of bodies of water) navigable. 2 (of ships) seaworthy. 3 (of freight payments) remunerative.
+sei'l/båt *-en* cf **segl/**
+sei'l/duk *-en* cf **segl/**
+sei'lduks/båt *-en* canvas boat.
+sei'le *V -te* cf **segle**
+sei'ler *-en, pl -e* 1 yachtsman. 2 sailing ship, sailer: **en god s-** sailing ship that performs well.
+sei'ler/lue *-a* yachting cap.
+sei'l/fly *-et* glider.
+sei'l/føring *-a/-en* cf **segl/**
+sei'l/ga'rn *-et* cf **segl/**
+sei'l/klar *A* ready to sail.
+sei'l/maker *-en, pl -e* cf **segl/**
+sei'l/meter *-en, pl* - international unit of measurement expressed in meters used to indicate the size of a racing sloop (cf **seksmeter**).
***sei'l/ryggja** *A* - swayback(ed).
+sei'l/skip *-et* cf **segl/**
+sei'l/skute *-a* cf **segl/**
+sei'l/sport *-en* yachting.
+sei'l/tur *-en* cruise, sail: **på s-** out sailing.
***sei'n**[1] *pt of* **sine**[1]
sei'n[2] *A* 1 late: **s-t på kvelden (dagen, etc.)** l- in the evening (day, etc.); **s-t eller tidlig** sooner or later; **s-t og tidlig (tidlig og s-t)** at all times, continually; **bedre s-t enn aldri** better l- than never; **komme s-t** come, be l-; **komme (for) s-t til** miss (a train, etc.); **stå s-t opp** get up l-; **være s-t oppe** stay up l-; **være s-t ute** miss the boat. 2 slow: **være s- av seg** be s- (by nature); **være s- i vendingen** be slow-moving, s- on the uptake; **han var ikke s- til å** he didn't hesitate, wait to, he wasn't s- in; **(noe) som s-t vil glemmes** (sth) which will long be remembered. 3 *(comp.)*: **før eller s-ere** sooner or later; **i den s-ere tid** lately, of late. 4 *(sup.)*: **i den s-este tid** very recently; **jeg må ha det s-est fredag** I need it by Friday at the latest.
***sei'n/drøg** *A* - dilatory, slow, tardy.
+sei'n/høstes *Av* (=***/haustes**) in the late autumn, fall.
sei'nke *V -a/+-et* (=**+sinke**[2]) delay, slow up.
***sei'n/kjøm** *A* late developing.
***sei'nleg** *A* - dilatory, slow, tardy.
***sei'n/leik** *-en* slowness, tardiness.
***sei'n/stundes** *Av* late: **s- i 1870-åra** late in the 1870's.
sei'n/tenkt *A* - slow-thinking, slow-witted: **bare en sjenert, s-, ensom og uerfaren bondestudent** only a shy, s-, lonely and inexperienced country student (Hoel).
***sei'n/voren** [/våren] *A -e/-i, pl -ne* dilatory, slow, tardy.
+sei'r *-en* cf **seier**
+sei're *V -a/-et* (=***sigre**) be triumphant, victorious; conquer, win: **s- eller falle** conquer or die; **s- over en** be victorious over, defeat sby.
+sei'rende *A* - conquering, victorious.
+sei'rer *pl of* **seier**
sei'se *V -a/+-et* 1 capsize, overturn. 2 *naut.* secure with a line, frap, seize.
sei'sing *-en* 1 capsizing, overturning. 2 *naut.* line used to secure sth, seizing.
seismogra'f *-en* seismograph.
***se'k** *-a* luxuriant meadow.
sek.=**sekund**[1]
sekan't *-en* secant.
se'kel *-elet/+-let, pl +-ler/*-el* (=**+sekulum**) century.
se'kel/skifte *-t, pl +-r/*-* turn of the century.
sekk' *-en, pl *-er* bag, sack: **få både i pose og s-** gain a double advantage (ab.=have one's cake and eat it too); **kle seg i s- og aske** dress in sackcloth and ashes.
sek'ke/band *-et* sack cord, string.
+sek'ke/bevil'gning *-en admin.* lump appropriation.
sek'ke/lerret *-et* sackcloth, sacking.
+sek'ke/løp *-et* sack race.
sek'ke/pipe *-a* bagpipe.
sek'ke/strie *-n* sacking.
+se'kler *pl of* **sekel**
sekon'd/løytnant *-en* second lieutenant.
sekresjo'n *-en* secretion.
sekre't[1] *-et, pl -/+-er* secretion.
sekre't[2] *-et, pl -/+-er* privy seal.
sekretaria't *-et, pl -/+-er* secretariat.
sekreto'risk *A* - secretory.
sekretæ'r *-en* 1 secretary (=official; officer of state; desk; less commonly of a stenographer). 2 clerk (e.g. c- of court). 3 *zool.* secretary bird (Sagittarius serpentarius).
sek's *Num* six: **så det sa s-** vigorously.
sek'sa *-en* (small) banquet, dinner, light supper (for members of a club, etc.).
seksage'sima *A* - *eccl.* Sexagesima (eighth Sunday before Easter).

sek's/arma *A* - (=**+-et**) hexapodous; six-armed.

sek's/del *-en* (a) sixth.

+sek's/dobbelt *A* - (=***/dobbel**) sixfold, sextuple.

sek's/doble *V -a/+-et* multiply by six.

+sek'ser *-en, pl -e* (=***-ar**) number six; six-spot (in cards, dice).

seksjo'n *-en* section.

sek's/kant *-en* hexagon.

sek's/kanta *A* - (=**+-et**) hexagonal.

+sek's/løper *-en, pl -e* six-shooter.

sek's/meter *-en, pl +-e* six meter (-class) boat.

sek's/rada *A* - (=**+-et**): **s- bygg:** six-rowed barley.

°sek'sring *-en* cf **seks/æring**

sek's/sifra *A* - (=**+-et**) written with six ciphers (e.g. 100,000).

sek'st *-en mus.* sixth.

sekstan't *-en* sextant.

sek'sten [+sei'sten] *Num* sixteen.

sek'stende [+sei'stene] *Num* sixteenth.

sek'sten/del [+sei'sten/] *-en* **1** (a) sixteenth (part). **2** *mus.* sixteenth note.

sekstett' *-en* sextet.

sek'sti *Num* sixty.

sek's/tida *df* (=**+/tiden**): **ved s-** about six (o'clock).

sek'stiende *Num* sixtieth.

sek'sti/åra *pl df* (=**+/årene**) the sixties.

***sek'string** *-en* cf **seks/æring**

seksua'l/angst *-en* sex phobia; frigidity.

seksua'l/drift *-a/+-en* sexual instinct.

+seksual/forbry'telse *-n* sex crime.

seksualite't *-en* sexuality.

seksua'l/lære *-a/+-en* sex hygiene, instruction.

seksua'l/opplysning *+-en/*-a* sex hygiene, instruction.

seksua'l/undervisning *-a/+-en* sex hygiene, instruction.

seksuell' *A -elt* sexual.

sek's/æring *-en* boat with three pairs of oars.

sek's/åring *-en* six year old (esp. a horse).

+sek't[1] *-a/-en* denomination, sect.

sek't[2] *-en* champagne, sack.

+sekte'rer *-en, pl -e* (=***-ar**) sectarian.

sekte'risk *A* - sectarian.

sek'tor *-en* sector.

+sek't/vesen *-et* sectarianism.

+sekula'r/geistlig *en* secular cleric.

sekularise're *V -te* secularize.

+se'kulum *-et, pl sekler* cf **sekel**

sekulæ'r *A* secular.

sekun'd[1] *-en* (in fencing) parry in seconde; (in printing) second leaf of a quire; *mus.* second.

sekun'd[2] *-et/*-en, pl -/+-er* second: **på s-et** immediately.

sekun'da *A* - *merc.* **1** second. **2** inferior, second-rate.

sekundan't *-en* second (e.g. in a duel, prizefight).

sekun'da/varer *pl* second-rate goods, merchandise.

sekun'da/veksel *-elen, pl -ler merc.* second exchange (=negotiable duplicate of draft).

sekunde're *V -te* **1** back up, second (a person). **2** accompany, join (e.g. in singing).

sekun'd/meter *-en, pl* - meters per second (used esp. in measuring the velocity of wind).

+sekun'd/viser *-en, pl -e* (=***-ar**) second hand (on a watch).

sekundæ'r *A* secondary.

sekundæ'r/spole *-n elec.* secondary coil.

sekven's *-en* sequence.

se'l[1] *-en zool.* seal (suborder Pinnipedia).

se'l[2] *-et* (house on) a mountain summer farm (=*seter*).

+se'l[3] *N* cf **sjel**

***se'l[4]** *pr of* **selje[2]**

Sel' *Pln* twp, Oppland.

-sel *Sf* substantivizing suffix, e.g. in **oppførsel, trivsel.**

Sel'/bu [also sel'/] *Pln* twp, Sør-Trøndelag.

sel'bu/mønster *-et* design, pattern from Selbu.

sel'bu/vott *-en* mitten from Selbu (black pattern on white background).

***sel'de** *pt of* **selje[2]**

se'le[1] *-n* **1** harness; reins (for horses): **legge s- på en hest** harness a horse; **legge seg i s-n** apply oneself, get down to work. **2** suspender: **en overall med s-r** overalls with s-s.

se'le[2] *V -a/+-te* harness (e.g. a horse): **s- av** unharness; **s- på** harness, hitch up.

se'le/bot *-a* cf **sæle/**

seleksjo'n *-en* selection.

sel'ektiv *A* selective.

selektivite't *-en* selectivity.

se'le/pinne *-n* harness pin.

se'le/pute *-a* harness pad (to avert chafing).

+se'le/tøy *-et* (=***/ty**) harness (of draft animals).

+se'l/fanger *-en, pl -e* (=***-ar**) sealer (person or vessel).

se'l/fangst *-en* sealing, seal hunting.

+sel'ge [also sel'le] *V solgte, solgt* (=***selje[2]**) sell: **s- seg** sell out (one's ideals, for reward); **s- sitt liv dyrt** make violent resistance (in a hopeless battle); **s- ut** sell out (at lower prices); **han er solgt** he is lost, is in a hopeless situation.

+sel'ger *-en, pl -e* (=***seljar**) salesman; seller, vendor; commercial traveler.

se'l/hund *-en zool.* seal.

***sel'jar** *-en* cf **selger**

sel'je[1] *-a bot.* (goat) willow (Salix caprea).

***sel'je[2]** *V sel, selde, selt* cf **selge**

Sel'je *Pln* twp, Sogn og Fjordane.

sel'je/fløyte *-a/+-en* willow flute.

sel'jemanna/mess(e) *en hist.* July 8th (holy day dedicated to the memory of the martyrs at Selja near Nordfjord).

Sel'/jo'rd *Pln* twp, Telemark.

sel'le[1] *-n* **1** miner. **2** fellow: **en underlig s-** a strange f-.

+sel'le[2] *V sollte, sollt* cf **selge**

+sel'ler *-en, pl -e* cf **selger**

selleri' *-en* celery (plant, root, stalk).

selleri'/rot *-a* celery root.

selo't *-en* fanatic, zealot.

selo'tisk *A* fanatical.

se'ls/bø *-en* enclosure adjoining a mountain summer farm.

sel'/skap *-et, pl -/+-er* **1** company: **dårlig s-** bad c-; **i s- med** in the c- of; **det er s- i (en bok, flaske, pipe)** (a book, bottle, pipe) is good c-; **for s-s skyld** to keep (one) c-; **gjøre en s-, holde en med s-** keep sby c-. **2** party: **ha (holde) s-** give a p-. **3** association, society: **lærde s-er** learned societies. **4** company (=business venture): **være direktør i et stort s-** be the head of a large c-. **5** society: **det gode s-** good s-.

selska'pelig *A* - (=***selskapleg**) **1** gregarious, sociable: **mennesket er et s- vesen** man is a gregarious animal. **2** convivial, social: **ha s- dannelse** have good manners; **leve s-** move in social circles, society; **være s- anlagt** feel at home in society. **3** (in mining) sympathetic (e.g. minerals).

+selska'pelig/het *-en* sociability; entertaining, social life, society: **delta meget i s-en** move about a great deal in society; **dyrke s-en** entertain a lot, go out a great deal.

***selska'pleg** *A* - cf **selskapelig**

+sel'skaps/antrekk *-et* formal evening clothes.

sel'skaps/bror *-en, pl +-brødre/*-brør* convivial person, good mixer.

sel'skaps/dame *-a/+-en* (woman's) companion; woman adept in the social graces.

sel'skaps/dans *-en* ballroom dancing.

sel'skaps/kjole *-n* party dress.

sel'skaps/kledd *A -/*-kledt* dressed for a party.

+sel'skaps/lek *-en* (=***/leik**) parlor game.

sel'skaps/liv *-et* entertaining, parties, society: **s-ets gleder** the pleasures of society.

sel'skaps/loka'le *-t, pl +-r/*-* banqueting room, reception room.

sel'skaps/løve *-a/+-en* social lion.

sel'skaps/mann *-en, pl -menn/*-menner* convivial person, partygoer.

sel'skaps/reise *-a/+-en* conducted tour.

sel'skaps/rett *-en* corporation law.

se'l/skinn *-et* sealskin.

sel's/nepe *-a bot.* cowbane, water hemlock (Cicuta virosa).

+se'l/som' *A -t, pl -me* mysterious, strange; odd, singular, unusual.

sel'ters *-en* seltzer (water), club soda.

+sel'v[1] *-et* (=***sjølv[1]**) ego, personality, self: **hva er da det gyntske s-?** what is the (essential) Gyntian self? (Ibsen).

+sel'v[2] *Pn* cf **sjølv[2]**

+sel'v[3] *Av* even: **s- min far** e- my father; **s- om** e- if, (al)though.

+sel'v/aktelse *-n* self-respect.

+sel'v/angivelse *-n* income tax form, return.

+selvan'nen *Pn* cf **annen**

+sel'v/antennelse *-n* spontaneous combustion.

+sel'v/assuranse [/-ang'se] *-n merc.* self-insurance.

+sel'v/bebrei'delse *-n* self-reproach.

+sel'v/bedra'g *-et* self-deception, self-delusion.

+sel'v/beha'g *-et* complacency, self-satisfaction, smugness.

+sel'v/beha'gelig *A* - complacent, self-satisfied, smug.

+sel'v/beher'skelse *-n* self-control, self-restraint.

+sel'v/beher'sket *A* - self-controlled, self-possessed.

+sel'v/berget *A* - cf **sjølv/berga**

+sel'vbergings/politikk' *-en* policy of self-sufficiency; (economic, political) independence.

+sel'v/bestal'tet *A* - self-appointed, self-constituted.

+sel'vbestemmelses/rett *-en* right of self-determination.

+sel'v/betje'ning *-en* self-service.

+sel'v/betrak'tning *-en* introspection, self-observation.

+sel'v/beviss't *A* - conscious (of self); conceited, self-important.

+sel'vbevisst/het *-en* consciousness (of self); conceit, self-importance.

+sel'v/binder *-en, pl -e* cf **sjølv/**

+sel'v/biografi' *-en* autobiography.

+sel'v/bygger *-en, pl -e* person who builds his house with his own hands.

+sel'v/død *A* cf **sjølv/daud**

+sel've *Pn* cf **sjølve**

+sel'v/eiende *A* - personal, private: **s- jord** private property.

+sel'v/eier *-en, pl -e* owner, proprietor.

+sel'v/erver'vende *A* - self-supporting.

+sel'veste *Pn* cf **sjølveste**

+sel'v/forak't *-en* self-contempt.

+sel'v/forglem'mende *A* - self-denying, self-sacrificing.

+sel'v/forher'ligelse *-n* self-exaltation, self-glorification.

+sel'v/forne'drelse *-n* self-abasement, self-degradation.

+sel'v/fornek'telse *-n* self-abnegation, self-denial.

+sel'v/forskyl'dt *A* - self-inflicted: **hans elendighet er s-** his misery is his own fault, of his own making.

+sel'v/forsvar *-et* self-defense.

+sel'v/forsy'nende *A* - self-sufficient.

+sel'vforsynings/politikk' *-en* policy of self-sufficiency; (economic, political) independence.

+ Bokmål; * Nynorsk; ° Dialect.
After letter: ' stress (Acc. 1); ' tone, stress (Acc. 2); · length.
Below letter: . not pronounced.

+sel'v/følelse -n pride, self-respect; egotism, conceit.
+sel'v/følge -n matter of course: **ta noe som en s-** take sth for granted.
+selvføl'gelig A - 1 inevitable, natural; evident, obvious. 2 *(adv.)* of course; obviously.
+selvføl'gelig/het -en matter of course; naturalness; banality, truism.
+sel'v/gitt A - 1 axiomatic, self-evident: **en s- forutsetning** a self-evident assumption. 2 (e.g. of laws) given by oneself.
+sel'v/gjort [/jort] A - cf **sjølv/**
+sel'v/glad A - self-satisfied, smug.
+sel'v/god A cf **sjølv/**
+sel'vgod/het -en self-importance, self-righteousness.
+sel'v/hersker -en, pl -e autocrat.
+sel'v/hevdelse -n cf **sjølv/hevding**
+sel'v/hjelp -en cf **sjølv/**
+sel'v/hjulpen A -ent, pl -ne resourceful, self-sufficient.
+sel'v/innlysende A - obvious, self-evident.
+sel'v/ironi' -en self-irony (an irony directed at oneself, ab.=not taking oneself too seriously).
+sel'v/iro'nisk A - self-ironic.
+sel'visk A - selfish.
+sel'v/klok A cf **sjølv/**
+sel'v/kontroll' -en self-control, self-restraint.
+sel'v/kost -et cf **sjølv/**
+sel'v/kostende A - cf **sjølv/kost**
+sel'v/kritikk' -en cf **sjølv/**
+sel'v/krit'isk A - cf **sjølv/**
+sel'v/laget A - cf **sjølv/laga**
+sel'v/lyd -en cf **sjølv/**
+sel'v/lysende A - luminous.
+sel'v/læ'rt A - cf **sjølv/**
+sel'v/mord [/mord] -et cf **sjølv/**
+sel'v/morder [/morder] -en, pl -e suicide (person).
+sel'vmords/forsøk [-mords/] -et attempted suicide.
+sel'v/motsigelse -n self-contradiction: **innvikle seg i s-r** contradict oneself.
+sel'v/motsigende A - self-contradictory.
+sel'v/mål -et unintentional score (esp. in soccer when one kicks the ball past one's own goalkeeper for a score).
+selvom [sel'låmm] C cf **om[2], selv[3]**
+sel'v/oppholdelse -n self-preservation.
+sel'voppholdelses/drift -a/-en instinct of self-preservation.
+sel'v/opplevd A - experienced personally.
+sel'v/oppofrelse A - self-sacrifice.
+sel'v/oppofrende A - self-sacrificing.
+sel'v/opptatt A - self-centered.
+sel'v/overvinnelse -n self-conquest.
+sel'v/pinsel -en self-torture.
+sel'v/portrett' -et self-portrait.
+sel'v/respek't -en self-respect.
+sel'v/ros -en cf **sjølv/**
+sel'v/rådig A - cf **sjølv/**
+sel'vrådig/het -en obstinacy, pig-headedness, wilfulness.
+sel'v/sagt A - 1 matter of course, obvious, self-evident. 2 *(adv.)* of course.
+sel'v/samme A - identical, selfsame.
+sel'v/sikker A -ert, pl -sikre self-assured, self-confident; cocksure, smug.
+sel'vsikker/het -en self-confidence; cocksureness.
+sel'v/skiftende A -: **s- arvinger** *jur.* heirs who distribute an estate on an informal basis, by agreement (without referring the matter to court).
+sel'v/skreven A -ent, pl -ne natural, obvious (choice): **s- til stillingen** the obvious choice for the post.
+sel'v/skryt -et cf **sjølv/**
+sel'v/skudd -et cf **sjølv/skott**
+sel'vskyldner/kausjonis't -en *jur.* surety.
+sel'v/starter -en, pl -e self-starter.
+selvsten'dig A - cf **sjølv-**
+selvsten'dig/het -en autonomy, independence.
+sel'v/studium -iet private study.
+sel'v/styr -et cf **sjølv/**
+sel'v/styre -t home rule, local autonomy.
+sel'v/suggestio'n [-sjo'n] -en autosuggestion.
+sel'v/syn -et cf **sjølv/**
+sel'v/tekt -en cf **sjølv/**
+sel'v/tilfred's A - complacent, self-satisfied, smug.
+sel'v/tillit -en cf **sjølv/**
+sel'v/tukt -en cf **sjølv/**
+sel'v/utløser -en, pl -e self-timer.
+sel'v/valgt A - self-chosen (e.g. subject of a lecture).
+sel'v/voldt A - self-imposed, self-induced, self-inflicted.
***sem'** *pr of* **semje[2]**
Sem' *Pln* twp, Vestfold.
semafo'r -en semaphore.
semafore're V -te semaphore.
semafo'r/flagg -et semaphore flag.
semaforis't -en semaphorist.
***-semd** -a nominal suffix corresponding to adjectives ending in **-sam**, e.g. **spar/s-; tol/s-.**
semen't -en cement.
semente're V -te cement.
semen't/omn -en (=+**/ovn**) cement kiln.
semes'ter -eret/+-ret, pl -er/+-re (school, university) semester; term of six months.
semes'ter/avgift -a/+-en semester's registration fee, tuition.
se'mi/fina'le -n semifinal.
se'mi/kolon -et semicolon.
semina'r -et, pl -/+-er 1 seminary. 2 seminar. 3 teachers' college.
seminaris't -en 1 student at, graduate from a teachers' college. 2 *derog.* half-baked, sophomoric scholar.
seminaris'tisk A - 1 referring to teachers or teachers' colleges: **s-utdannelse** education as a teacher. 2 half-baked, sophomoric, superficial.
semina'rium -iet, pl +-ier/*-ium cf **seminar**
semitt' -en Semite.
semit'tisk A - Semitic.
***sem'jast** V -ast agree; come to terms.
***sem'je[1]** -a 1 agreement; concord, harmony. 2 contract; treaty: **s-a i Verdun** the T- of V-.
***sem'je[2]** V *sem, samde, samt* 1 fit together (pieces, parts). 2 bring into agreement, harmony. 3 =**semjast.**
+sem'mel -elen, pl *semler* small white bun.
sem'ske V -a/+-et suede: **s-t skinn** chamois leather; **s-ede sko** suede shoes.
semu'le/gryn -et (=+**semulje/**) semolina (middlings of wheat, used esp. to make pudding).
***se'n[1]** -a cf **sene**
+se'n[2] A cf **sein[2]**
sen. =**senior**
sena't -et, pl +-er/*- senate.
sena'tor -en, pl -to'rer senator.
sen'de [+sen'ne] V +-te/*-e 1 send; dispatch: **s- en av gårde, på dør** s- sby about his business; **s- bud (etter, på en)** s- word (for sby); **s- en i døden** s- sby to his death; **s- en et par ord** drop sby a line; **s- ut en bok** publish a book; **s- ut på markedet** introduce, release (a new product); **s- videre** forward (e.g. mail). 2 deliver: **varer s-es gratis** free delivery. 3 hand, pass: **vær så snill og send meg sukkeret** please pass me the sugar; **s- rundt** hand, pass around. 4 propel, throw: **s- et egg i hodet på en** hit sby in the head with an egg; **s- en et smil (blikk)** smile (glance) quickly at sby; **s- et skudd etter en** fire a shot at sby (running away); **s- til værs** throw into the air. 5 transmit (e.g. a radio program, telegraph message).
***sen'de/bod** [/bå] -et cf **/bud**
+sen'de/bud -et (=***/bod**) 1 *obs.* message, word (that is sent). 2 messenger; emissary, envoy.
sen'de/ferd [*/fær] -a/+-en *hist.* errand, mission.
sen'de/gods [+sen'ne/gots] -et baggage, freight.
+sen'de/hastighet -en transmission speed.
sen'de/lag [+sen'ne/] -et delegation.
sen'de/mann [+sen'ne/] -en, pl -menn/*-menner ambassador, envoy; delegate; emissary, messenger.
+sen'der -en, pl -e (=*-ar) 1 sender. 2 transmitter; broadcasting station.
+sen'der/anlegg -et (=*-ar/) broadcasting set or station.
sen'de/tid [+sen'ne/] -a/+-en broadcasting time.
sen'ding[1] [+sen'ning] -a/+-en 1 sending; transmitting, transmission. 2 consignment, load. 3 gift. 4 transmitted program.
sen'ding[2] [+sen'ning] -en person who is sent, (esp. in **utsending** delegate, envoy).
sen'dings/korg -a basket containing a gift (e.g. of food).
+se'n/drektig A - slow, tardy.
se'ne -a (=***sen[1]**) sinew; tendon.
se'ne/drått -en cramp (of tendons).
se'ne/hinne -a *anat.* synovial membrane; (in eye) sclera.
se'ne/knute -n *anat.* ganglion.
+se'ne/skjede -n *anat.* synovial sheath, tendon sheath.
+se'neskjede/beten'nelse -n *med.* tenosynovitis (inflammation of tendon sheath).
***se'ne/slir** -a cf **/skjede**
se'ne/sterk A sinewy.
se'ne/strekk -en/-et sprain, strained tendon.
se'net(e) A - sinewy (arm); gaunt (face).
seng' -a bed: **frokost på s-a** breakfast in b-; **gå i s, gå til s-s** go to b-; **holde s-a, ligge til s-s** stay in b- (often ill); **re opp en s-** make a b-; **slå opp en s-** turn down a bed; **ta en på s-a** visit sby before he is up; **være oven s-e** be up, be well again.
seng'- *Pf* cf also **senge-**
seng'e/benk -en wooden bench that can be turned into a bed.
seng'e/botn -en (=+**/bunn**) bottom of a bed; bed boards.
seng'e/fjøl -a side board of a bed.
+seng'e/forlegger -en, pl -e throw rug used beside a bed, bedside carpet.
seng'e/halm -en straw used as mattress.
seng'e/hest -en bed rail(s).
+seng'e/hygge -a/-en bed jacket.
seng'e/kamera't -en bedfellow.
seng'e/kant -en edge of bed.
***seng'e/kone** -a woman in confinement.
+seng'e/liggende A - (=***/liggjande**) confined in bed; bedridden.
***seng'e/mat** -en food given a woman in confinement.
seng'e/plass -en 1 sleeping accommodations. 2 bed.
seng'e/stokk -en edge of a bed.
seng'e/stolpe -n bedpost.
seng'e/teppe -t bedspread.
seng'e/tid -a/+-en bedtime.
+seng'e/tøy -et bedclothes.
seng'e/varme -n bed warmth.
seng'e/væting -a/+-en bed-wetting.
+seng'/klær *pl* (=***/klede**) bedclothes.
***seng'/kone** -a cf **senge/**
+se'n/høstes Av cf **sein/**
seni'l A senile.
senilite't -en senility.
se'nior -en 1 senior. 2 sports contestant over 16 (or 18) years of age.
se'nior/sjef -en managing director of a firm which also has a younger director subordinate to him.
se'nit -et zenith.
Sen'ja *Pln* island, Troms (second largest in Norway).
+sen'k N: **i s-** down, to the bottom of the sea; **renne en båt i s-** sink a boat by ramming into it; **skyte**

et skip i s- sink a ship (by cannon fire).
+sen'k/bar A which can be lowered.
+sen'ke V -a/-et (=+søkke[2], *søkkje[2]) 1 sink (e.g. a ship). 2 let fall, lower: s- hodet l- one's head; han s-et blikket his glance fell; s- i jorden inter; s- prisene l- the prices. 3: s- seg fall, sink (down); natten s-er seg night falls; terrenget s-er seg the terrain becomes lower.
sen'ke/kjøl -en naut. centerboard.
sen'king -a (=+senkning) 1 lowering; reduction; sinking. 2 depression, dip, hollow (in terrain).
sen'knings/reaksjo'n -en sedimentation rate.
senn' N: i s-, om s- at a time, each time; en om s- one at a time; one by one.
sen'na -en senna.
sen'ne/gras -et a sedge (Carex vericaria or Carex aquatilis) which the Lapps dry and put in their shoes for warmth.
sen'nep -en mustard.
sen'neps/gass -en mustard gas.
sen'neps/gul A mustard yellow.
sen'neps/ko'rn -et mustard seed.
sen'neps/krukke [/krokke] -a mustard pot.
sen'neps/plaster -eret/-ret, pl -er/+-re mustard plaster.
sen'neps/saus -en mustard sauce.
sensasjo'n -en sensation (big event, etc.).
sensasjonell' A -elt sensational.
sensasjo'ns/avi·s -a/+-en derog. scandal sheet.
sensasjo'ns/jakt -a/+-en hunt for sensations or sensational news.
sensasjo'ns/lyst -a/+-en wish to create or experience sensations.
sensibel [sangsi'bel] A -elt, pl -le sensitive, susceptible; impressionable; delicate: være s- for noe be s- to sth.
sensibilite't -en sensitiveness; sensitivity.
sen'sitiv A sensitive.
+se'n/sommer -eren, pl -somre late summer: på s-en late in the summer.
sen'sor -en, pl senso'rer 1 censor. 2 educ. person who grades papers and oral examinations.
sensualis'me -n sensualism.
sensuell' A -elt sensual.
sensu'r -en 1 censorship. 2 (list of) examination results: s-en faller i morgen the results will be announced tomorrow.
sensure're V -te 1 censor. 2 grade examination papers (or candidate's answers at an oral examination).
+se'n/tenkt A - cf sein/
senten's -en aphorism, maxim, saying.
sen'ter[1] -en, pl +-e center (player).
sen'ter[2] -eret/-ret, pl +-rer/*-er cf sentrum
sen'ter/forward -en center forward (in soccer).
sen'ter/half [/haf] -en center halfback (in soccer).
Sen'ter/parti·et Prn "the Center Party" (name of a Norwegian political party formerly called Bondepartiet).
sentimenta'l A sentimental.
sentimentalite't -en sentimentality.
sentra'l[1] -en 1 center, central agency, headquarters (for for). 2 nationwide marketing organization. 3 telephone central, exchange.
sentra'l[2] A central.
sentra'l/administrasjo'n -en central (in Norway state, in U.S. Federal) administration.
sentra'l/bo'rd -et switchboard.
sentra'l/fyring -a/+-en central heating.
sentralisasjo'n -en centralization.
sentralise're V -te centralize.
sentra'l/nervesystem -et central nervous system.
sentra'l/skole -n consolidated school.
sentra'l/varme -n central heating.
sen'tre V -a/+-et pass the ball (in ball game, esp. soccer).
sentre're V -te center.
sentrifuga'l A centrifugal.
sentrifuga'l/kraft -a/+-en centrifugal force.
sentrifu'ge -n centrifuge.
sentrifuge're V -te centrifugate, centrifuge.
sentripeta'l A centripetal.
sen'trum -rumet/-ret, pl -ra/+-rer/*-rum (=senter[2]) 1 center: være i begivenhetenes s- be in the c- of events. 2 (main) business district, downtown.
sen'trums/bor· -et center bit.
sen'trums/parti· -et, pl +-er/*- middle-of-the-road political party.
separasjo'n -en jur. separation.
separa't A - separate.
separatis'tisk A - separatist, separatistic.
separa'tor -en, pl -torer separator (for milk).
separe're V -te separate.
+se'pe -n cf såpe[1]
se'pia -en sepia.
se'pia/brun A sepia brown.
sept. = september
septem'ber en September.
sep'ter -eret/-ret, pl -er/+-re scepter.
septett' -en septet.
sep'tik/tank -en septic tank.
septi'm -en mus. seventh; septuplet.
septi'm/akkor'd -en mus. seventh chord.
septuage'sima A - eccl. Septuagesima (3rd Sunday before Lent).
*ser [sæ'r] A cf sær
se'ra pl of serum
sera'f -en seraph.
sera'fisk A - seraphic.
serai' -et 1 caravansary, serai. 2 seraglio.
+ser'ber -en, pl -e (=*-ar) Serb, Serbian.
ser'bisk A - Serbian.
serbokroa'tisk A - Serbo-Croatian.
*sere [sæ're] V -a cf sære
seremoni' -en ceremony.
seremoniell'[1] -et ceremonial.
seremoniell'[2] A -elt 1 ceremonial. 2 ceremonious.
+seremoni'/mester -en, pl -e (=*/meister) master of ceremonies.
serena'de -n serenade.
se'rie -n series.
se'rie/fabrikasjo'n -en mass production.
se'rie/kamp -en match in a series (esp. of soccer).
se'rie/kopla A - (=+-et, +/kobla, +/koblet) (of electrical circuit elements) coupled in series.
seriø's A serious: s- musikk classical music.
ser'k -en, pl *-er shift, slip (woman's undergarment).
*serleg [sæ'rleg] A - cf særlig
serpenti'n -en serpentine, streamer.
*sers [sæ'rs] A - cf særs
sersjan't -en sergeant.
sertifika't -et, pl -/+-er certificate; driver's license; pilot's license.
sertifise're V -te license: s- en bil get a car licensed.
se'rum -et, pl sera/*- serum.
servan't -en washstand.
serve[1] [sø'rv] -n serve (in tennis).
serve[2] [sø'rve] V -a/+-et serve (in tennis).
serve're V -te 1 wait on (at table). 2 serve: s- mat s- food; s- en historie usu. derog. tell a story.
serve'ring -a/+-en serving: dårlig s- poor service; nekte en s- refuse to serve sby.
serve'rings/brett -et serving tray.
serve'rings/dame -a/+-en waitress.
service [sø'rvis] -n service.
service/bil -en tow truck; wrecker.
serviett' -en napkin.
+serviett'/holder -en, pl -e (=*/haldar) napkin holder.
serviett'/mappe -a envelope-shaped napkin holder.
serviett'/ring -en napkin ring.
servi'l A servile.
servilite't -en servility.
servi'se -t, pl +-r/*- service, set (of china, dinnerware, etc.).
servitri'se -a/+-en waitress.
servitutt' +-et/*-en, pl -/+-er jur. easement; servitude.
servitø'r -en waiter.
+se's V sås, ses cf sees
se'sam -et sesame: s- lukk deg opp open s-.
sesjo'n -en 1 session. 2 mil. (meeting of) draft board; medical examination (or examiners): innkalt til s- called up by one's draft board.
sesong' -en season: i s-en in s-; utenfor s-en off s-.
sesong'/arbeid -et seasonal work.
sesong'/billett· -en season ticket.
sesong'/kort -et season ticket.
sess' -en 1 seat. 2 buttocks, rear: være tung i s-en "be heavy in the rear", be slow-moving. 3 dial. terrace.
ses'se V -a/+-et 1 seat. 2: s- seg take a seat.
*se't[1] -et cf sett[2]
*se't[2] pr of setje
*se'te[1] -a 1 period of sitting down. 2 stay. 3 seat.
se'te[2] -t, pl +-r/*- 1 seat: bringe en til s- seat sby; komme til s- get seated. 2 buttocks, rear. 3 abode, residence; headquarters. 4 saddle (on bicycle, etc.).
*se'te[3] pp of sitje
se'te/bad -et sitz bath.
se'te/fødsel -elen, pl -ler breech, breech presentation.
*se'tel -elen, pl -lar cf seddel
se'ter -ra, pl +-rer/*-rar chalet, summer dairy (usu. in mountains).
se'ter/bruk -et mountain summer dairying.
se'ter/bu -a chalet cabin.
se'ter/drift -a/+-en mountain summer dairying.
se'ter/hytte -a chalet cabin.
se'ter/jente -a dairymaid at a summer dairy; chalet girl.
se'ter/stell -et mountain summer dairying.
se'ter/vang -en (fenced-in) meadow near chalet.
se'ter/voll -en (fenced-in) meadow near chalet.
Se'tes/dal Pln valley, Aust-Agder.
se'tes/døl -en person from Setesdal.
*se'ti pp of sitje
*set'jar -en cf setter[1]
*set'je V set, sette cf sette[1]
*set'jing -a cf setting
*set'nad -en equipment, outfit.
*set'ne V -a (of liquid) clear; settle out (residue).
set'ning +-en/*-a 1 gram. clause; sentence. 2 maxim, saying. 3 math. theorem. 4 setting, settling (av of).
set'nings/lære -a/+-en syntax.
se'tre V -a/+-et go to the summer pasture in the mountains with the cattle, or work there as a dairymaid.
Set'/skog Pln twp, Akershus.
*sett'[1] -en stake, wager.
sett'[2] -et 1 setting, putting out (e.g. of fishing nets); sth that is put out, set. 2 collection; nest (of tables); service, set: et s- undertøy a set of underwear. 3 succession (e.g. of impressions, sounds): i ett s- all the time. 4 manner, way: han gjorde det på sitt eget s- he did it in his own w-; på s- og vis in a w-, when you come right down to it. 5 jump, start: med ett s- suddenly, with a bound, a start; det gav et s- i henne she started. 6 (log) jam.

+ Bokmål; * Nynorsk; ° Dialect.
After letter: ' stress (Acc. 1); ` tone, stress (Acc. 2); · length.
Below letter: . not pronounced.

sett'[3] pp of se, sjå[1]

*sett'[4] pp of setje

sett'/bo'rd -et one of a nest of snack tables, nesting table.

+set'te[1] V satte, satt (=*setje) 1 place, put, set (with nouns): s- alt på ett brett put all one's eggs in one basket; s- en annonse i avisen put an ad in the paper; s- barn til verden bring children into the world; s- barn på en pike get a girl with child; der s-er jeg aldri mine bein mer I'll never set my foot there again; s- bo build a home, settle; s- bremsene på put on the brakes; s- farge på add color, zest to; s- grenser for set limits for; s- hunden på en sic the dog on sby; s- høyere prefer; s- knopper bud; s- (sin) lit til trust in, place one's faith in; s- livet inn på stake one's life on; s- livet til lose one's life, be killed; s- merker leave marks, traces; s- ondt blod create bad blood (mellom between); s- sitt navn under sign; s- penger i omløp (banken) put money into circulation (the bank); s- penger inn i invest in; s- sitt preg på leave one's mark, impression on; s- pris på appreciate; s- skrekk (støkken) i en put the fear of God in sby; s- skylden på put the blame on; s- (en) spiss på add zest, relish to; s- spor leave traces, tracks; han har satt spor etter seg he has made a lasting impression, he has achieved lasting results; s- en stevne make an appointment (to meet sby); s- en stopper for put a stop to; s- store øyne open one's eyes wide (in surprise); s- sin vilje igjennom get one's way; s- vilkår fix terms; s- sin ære i noe take pride in (doing) sth. 2 go, move, start (usu. suddenly): s- av sted (gårde) set off, rush away; s- etter start out after (in pursuit); s- fra land put out to sea; s- i å (suddenly) begin to (laugh, cry, shout, etc.); s- i et hyl let out a yell; s- i gang (med) get started (with); s- inn med (of weather) begin; det satte inn med regn a rainy spell began; s- mot land head for land; s- over cross (e.g. a river), jump (e.g. a fence); s- på sprang start running; s- til go all out; s- utfor take off downhill (usu. skiing). 3 assume, suppose: sett at (om) suppose that, what if; sett at vi aldri blir ferdige med denne ordboka! what if we never finish this dictionary! 4 (participial forms): komme s-ende come in a rush, dashing; møtet er satt the meeting is called to order; retten er satt the court is in session. 5 (with adv. and prep.): s- av let off, out (of a vehicle); set aside (for, til for) (e.g. money, time); s- bort lay, put aside; farm out, place (e.g. a child); s- fast catch, jail; stump, trip (on a question); get (e.g. one's foot) stuck; s- for hitch up; s- fra seg put down; s- fram set out (for display, on the table); advance, set forth (theory, proposition, etc.); s- høyt esteem, hold in high regard; s- i gang start (a car); s- i stand fix, put in working order; s- en i stand til å enable sby to; s- i verk start (a project); s- igjennom carry through, put into effect; s- en inn put sby in jail; s- en inn i noe explain sth to sby, familiarize sby with sth; s- inn med coat, impregnate with; s- noe inn risk sth; s- med adorn, set with (e.g. precious stones); s- opp draft, write (document); make ready, put on (a train); put on (a cheerful face); incite, stir up (mot against); raise (e.g. a tent); s- over ferry across; put on (the coffee); s- på put on (e.g. coffee), set (the table); raise (a calf); turn on (the current); s- en på gata evict sby; s- en på noe give sby an idea; s- på prøve put to the test; s- på spill risk, gamble with; s- på spissen exaggerate; s- på sporet put on the right track; s- til lose, squander; add (in cooking); estimate at; assign (sby to do sth); s- til livs consume, eat; s- ut expose (a child); start (a rumor); arrange (a melody); s- ut av drift discontinue; s- ut av kraft declare null and void; s- ut i livet put into effect; s- en utenfor exclude sby. 6 (refl.): s- seg (ned) sit down; s- seg settle, jell, become set, firm; s- seg fast get stuck (i in, på to); get a foothold; s- seg for(e) decide, set one's mind on; s- seg i bevegelse start moving; s- seg i forbindelse med get in touch with; s- seg i hodet get into one's head; s- seg imot oppose, protest against; s- seg inn i familiarize oneself with; s- seg opp sit up; s- seg opp mot rebel against; s- seg opp for natta (of chickens) perch, roost for the night; s- seg opp på mount (e.g. a horse); s- seg på sitt remain adamant; s- seg til (rette) get settled (comfortably) in a chair; s- seg til å gjøre noe set about doing sth; s- seg til motverge defend oneself, fight back; s- seg ut over disregard, overrule; det satte seg verk i såret the wound festered.

*set'te[2] pt of setje

+set'te/dommer -en, pl -e jur. substitute judge.

+set'te/ferdig A - (of plant) ready to be transplanted.

+set'te/fisk -en hatchery-produced fish for stocking.

+set'te/ga'rn -et setnet.

+set'te/kasse -a (typesetter's) case.

+set'te/maski'n -en typesetting machine; linotype.

+set'te/pote't -a/-en seed potato.

+set'ter[1] -en, pl -e (=*setjar) typog. compositor.

set'ter[2] -en, pl +-e setter (bird dog).

setteri' -et, pl +-er/*- composing room.

+set'te/verge -n jur. guardian appointed for one occasion only, in the absence or inability of the guardian otherwise functioning.

+set'ting -a/-en (=*setjing) putting, setting.

settlement [set'telment] -et settlement.

se'v[1] -et (=+siv) bot. rush.

*se'v[2] -et underground well.

+sever'dig A - worth seeing.

+sever'dig/het -en attraction, sight.

Severi'n Prn (m)

sev'je -a sap.

+sev'je/løp -et sap flow.

se'v/matte -a rush mat.

SF=Sosialistisk Folkeparti

s. f.=sør for

sfinks [sving'(k)s] -en sphinx.

+sfinks/aktig A - sphinxlike.

sfære [svæ're] -n sphere.

sfærisk [svæ'risk] A - spheric.

sg.=singularis

Sg.=+særdeles/*særs godt

sgu [sku'] I cf gud

sh.=shilling

shaker [sjei'ker] -en, pl +-e (cocktail) shaker.

shanti [sjan'ti] -en cf sjanti

sharper [sja'rper] -en, pl +-e sharper; sharp person.

shelter/dekk [sjel'ter/] -et naut. shelter deck.

sheriff [sjer'rif] -en sheriff.

sherry [sjer'ri] -en sherry.

Shet/land [sjett'/] Pln Shetland.

shet/landsk A - Shetland(ic).

shetlands/ponni -en Shetland pony.

+Shetlands/øyene pl (=*/øyane) the Shetland Isles.

shet/lending -en Shetlander.

shilling [sjil'ling] -en, pl -s/- shilling.

shipping [sjip'ping] -en shipping business: begynne i, gå inn i s- go into the s- b- as a career.

shirting [sjir'ting] -en cf sjirting

Shl.=Sunnhordland

shoppe [sjåp'pe] V -a/+-et shop.

shopping [sjåp'ping] *-a/+-en shopping.

shopping/bag [sjåp'ping/bægg] -en shopping bag.

shorts [sjå'rts] -en shorts.

show [sjåu', sjåv'] -et show (entertainment).

+si'[1] V sa, sagt (=*seie) 1 say: du sier ikke det! sier du det! you don't say!; en sier at it is said that; ja, du kan så si that's for sure; jeg behøver ikke å si at needless to say; jeg sier ikke mer 'nuff said; nå, det må jeg si well, I never; om jeg selv skal si det if I say so myself; om jeg så må si if I may say so; (det er) å si, det vil si (dvs.) that is (i.e.); så å si so to speak; ha mye å si (hos) have great influence (with); ha noe en skulle ha sagt have sth to say (=have influence); han kan få sagt det he can find the right words; kort sagt in short; mellom oss sagt just between us; rent ut sagt actually, to tell the truth; snart sagt almost, nearly; som sagt as stated; som sagt, så gjort no sooner said than done. 2 tell: kan De si meg veien til stasjonen? can you tell me the way to the station?; (ikke) la seg si (not) take advice; si sannheten tell the truth; var det ikke det jeg sa? didn't I tell you?. 3 mean: det har ingenting (ikke stort) å si that doesn't mean anything (much), is of no (little) consequence; det er ikke sagt at that doesn't mean that, it doesn't follow that, it isn't certain that; hva skal det si? what's that supposed to mean?; hva skal dette si? what's the meaning of this?; vet du hva det vil si (å) do you know what that (it) means (to). 4: sies be said; det sies at I've heard that. 5 (with adv. and prep.): si bort give away (e.g. a secret); si etter repeat; si fra express one's opinion, speak up (about sth); inform, tell; han ville verken si fra eller til he wouldn't commit himself; si fram recite; speak out; si (i)mot contradict, object to; det er mye å si både for og imot there's a lot to say on both sides; hva vil De si med det? what do you mean by that?; si opp give notice; cancel; si noe like opp i øynene på en say sth straight to sby's face; si på criticize, find fault with; det er ikke noe å si på det there's nothing wrong with that; si til say, tell to; speak out; si noe rett (bent) ut say sth straightforwardly; si ved (til) seg selv say to oneself. 6 (with impersonal subject) make a noise: "tripp trapp," sa det i brua "clip clop," said the bridge (Asbjørnsen). 7 (refl.): si seg enig med express one's agreement with; si seg god for guarantee; det sier seg selv it goes without saying, it stands to reason.

si'[2] f of sin

si'[3] A cf sid

si'[4] N: på si on the side, in addition.

si'- Pf continuously.

si'a Av, C cf siden

+siame'ser -en, pl -e (=*-ar) Siamese.

siame'sisk A - Siamese.

Sibi'r Pln Siberia.

sibi'rsk A - Siberian.

*si'/breidd A -/-breitt evenly spread (hay).

sibyl'le -a/+-en sibyl.

sibylli'nsk A - Sibylline.

Sici'lia Pln Sicily.

sicilia'ner -en, pl -e (=*-ar) Sicilian.

sicilia'nsk A - Sicilian.

si'd A 1 long, loose-fitting; hanging down. 2 (of air) heavy, close. 3 of terrain) low and swampy. 4: være

s- til do a lot of; **han er s- til å drikke** he is a heavy drinker.
-si'ḍa *A* - -sided.
***si'ḍan** *C* cf **siden**
sidd' *-a* (=**+sidde**) length (of garment).
si'de [*si'e] *-a/+-en* **1** side (of a person, an object, a question, etc.); aspect (of a personality, a matter, etc.): **s- om s-** s- by s-; **fra begge s-r** mutually; **fra min s-** for my part; **med hendene i s-n** with arms akimbo; **over s-n** *naut.* overboard; **på s-n** on the side, in addition; **på s-n av** alongside; **på den annen s-** on the other s-, *fig.* on the other hand; **på denne s-n (av) jul** before Christmas; **på vår s-** on our s-; **til s-** aside; **sette til s-** put away, set aside; disregard; **til alle s-r** in all directions; **ved s-n av** beside, next (door) to; **han har sine gode s-r** he has his good points; **stå ved ens s-** *fig.* stand by sby; **være (komme) på den riktige s-n av en** be (get) on the right s- of sby. **2** page (in a book, newspaper, etc.).
side/bane *-n* branch line (of railroad).
side/bein *-et* rib: **dette er mat som legger seg på s-a** this is food that sticks to your r-s (=fattens).
side/blikk *-et* side glance.
side/bygning *-en* wing (of a building); annex.
side/dal *-en* branch valley.
side/flesk *-et* side of pork.
side/form *-a/+-en* alternative form (of a word); in Norwegian school practice, a form permitted in pupils' written work but not in textbooks.
side/gate *-a* side street.
+side/hensyn *-et* ulterior motive.
side/kamera't *-en* seatmate.
+side/langs *A* - **1** to the side. **2** sideways.
side/lengs *A* - (=***/lenges**) sideways.
+side/linje *-n* **1** (sports) sideline. **2** (RR) branch line. **3** *zool.* lateral line. **4** branch (of family).
side/lomme [/lomme] *-a* side pocket.
side/mann *-en, pl -menn/*-menner* person next to sby, person on one's left, right.
+si'den *Av, C* (=**sia**, ***sidan**) **1** since: **jeg har ikke sett ham s- kl. 2** I haven't seen him s- 2 o'clock; **jeg har ikke sett ham s- han var gutt** I haven't seen him s- he was a boy; **det er ikke lenge s- han kom** it's not been (a) long (time) s- he arrived; **jeg reiste i fjor og har ikke vært i Norge s-** I left last year and haven't been in Norway s-; **s- det er sommer kan vi bade** s- it's summer we can go swimming; **like s-** ever s-. **2: (for) . . . s-** ago; **det var for lenge (10 år) s-** it was a long time (10 years) ago; **jeg så ham for en uke s-** I saw him a week ago. **3** afterwards, later (on), then: **vi skal spise aftens sammen, og s- skal vi i teatret** we are going to have supper together, and then we're going to the theater; **du skal få resten av pengene s-** you'll get the rest of the money later (on); **s- etter** thereafter.
si'den/svans *-en zool.* waxwing (Bombycilla garrulus).
si'de/ordne [*si'e/] *V -a/+-et* coordinate.
si'der *-en* cider.
si'de/rom [/romm, *si'e/] *-met* side room; side compartment.
si'de/ror [*si'e/] *-et* rudder (controlling horizontal movement).
side/sjø *-en* waves from the side.
side/spark *-et* **1** kick to the side. **2** sideswipe (criticizing remark).
side/spor *-et* **1** siding (track). **2** sidetrack: **komme inn på et s-** get sidetracked.
side/sprang *-et* **1** sideways leap. **2** digression.
+side/stille *V -stilte* **1** place side by side. **2** compare. **3** put on an equal footing.
side/stilling *-a/+-en* **1** juxtaposition. **2** comparison. **3** equality (av of).
side/stilt *A* - **1** compared (**med** with); juxtaposed. **2** (of) equal (rank). **3** *bot.* (of leaf) lateral.
side/stykke *-t, pl +-r/*-* **1** sidepiece. **2** counterpart; match; parallel (**til** to): **som savner s-** unparalleled. **3** side (of handloom).
side/veg *-en* (=**+/vei**) lane, side road; backroad.
side/vogn [/vångn] *-a* sidecar.
si'ḍ/lenḍt *A* - (of terrain) low and swampy.
+si'/drikke *V -drakk, -drukket* drink like a fish.
si'ḍ/rumpa [/rompa] *A* - (=**+-et**) *pop.* big-bottomed, dumpy; *fig.* clod-like, slow-moving; timid.
siḍt' *Av* a lot, heavily, much (cf **sid**).
+si'ende *et* cf **sigende**
sies'ta *-en* siesta.
sif'fer *-et, pl -/+sifre* cipher (code).
sif'fer/skrift *-a/+-en* cipher (secret writing).
sifong' *-en* siphon.
-sif'ra *A* - (=**+-sifret**) -ciphered, -digit.
si'g[1] *-et* **1** sag; sinking, sliding, slipping movement: **gå med s- i knærne** walk with give in the knees; **komme i s-, på s-** begin to move, slide slowly; **være i s-** be moving, drifting, sliding slowly. **2** sth that sags, slides, moves slowly: **et jevnt s- av folk** a steady stream of people. **3** trickle of water in the ground; swampy area.
+sig[2] [sei'] *Pn* cf **seg**
siga'r *-en* cigar.
sigarett' *-en* cigarette.
sigarett'/etui' *-et, pl +-er/*-* cigarette case.
sigarett'/merke *-t, pl +-r/*-* cigarette brand.
sigarett'/munnstykke *-t, pl +-r/*-* cigarette holder.
sigarett'/stump [/stomp] *-en* cigarette butt.
+sigarett'/tenner *-en, pl -e* (=***-ar**) (cigarette) lighter.
sigarillo [-il'jo] *-en, pl -s* cigarillo (small cigar).
siga'r/kasse *-a/-en* cigar box.
Sig'/bjø'rn *Prn (m)*
sig'd *-en* sickle.
Sig'/dal *Pln* twp, Buskerud.
+sig'dal/frokost *-en* Sigdal breakfast, a balanced lunch served in some Norwegian elementary schools, named after the twp Sigdal, where it was first tried.
si'ge *V seig, +seget/*sige/*-t* **1** ooze, seep, trickle: **s- (inn) over, på** (of darkness, emotions, fatigue, etc.) slowly come, steal over. **2** sag, sink, slide: **s- igjen, sammen** (e.g. of eyelids) close slowly; **s- i hop, sammen** collapse; **s- i kne** sink to one's knees; **s- i knærne** walk with give in the knees; **s- over ende** sink to the ground; **s- tilbake** sink back. **3** move slowly; drift: **båten seig fram gjennom tåken** the boat glided slowly through the fog; **isen har seget fra land** the ice has slipped away from the shore; **karene seig inn etter hvert** the men drifted in gradually.
si'gel *-elet, pl +-ler/*-el* sign, symbol (in shorthand).
***si'gen** *A +-ent, pl -ne* **1** shrunken, sunk. **2** exhausted, tired.
+si'gende *et* (=**+siende**): **etter s- . . .** they say that . . .; from what I hear . . .; **etter eget s-** by his (her) own account.
***si'ger** *-eren, pl -rar* cf **seier**
***si'ger/herre** *-n* cf **seier/**
***si'ger/krans** *-en* cf **seiers/**
***si'ger/viss** *A* - confident of success, of victory.
Sig'/frid *Prn (f)*
sight/seeing [sai't/si-ing] *-en* sightseeing.
sight/seer [sai't/sier] *-en, pl +-e* sightseer.
sigill' *-et* seal.
***sig'le[1]** *-t* millrind (crossbar in upper millstone).
***sig'le[2]** *V -a/-de* cf **segle**
Sig'/munḍ *Prn (m)*
sign. =**signatum**
signal [singna'l] *-et, pl -/+-er* signal; call; *mil.* telegram; signal corps (insignia): **gi s-** give a (the) signal; **gi s- til angrep** give the signal for attack; **på et gitt s-** at a prearranged signal; **endre s-er** change signals, *fig.* change one's policy.
signalement [singnalemang'] *-et, pl -/+-er* description (of a person), signalment: **gi et s- av en** give a description of sby; **s-et stemmer** the description fits (him, her, etc.).
signalere [singnale're] *V -te* signal.
signal/flagg [singna'l/] *-et* signal flag.
signal/fløyte *-a* signal whistle.
signal/ho'rn *-et* **1** (auto) horn. **2** *mil.* bugle.
signalisere [singnalise're] *V -te* signal.
signal/klokke [singna'l/] *-a* signal bell.
signal/lykt *-a* signal lantern.
signal/lys *-et* signal light.
signal/mann *-en, pl -menn/*-menner* signalman.
signal/pisto'l *-en* signal pistol.
signal/språk *-et* signal language.
signatar [singnata'r] *-en* signatory.
signatar/makt *-a/+-en* signatory power.
signatur [singnatu'r] *-en* **1** signature (e.g. of name; music; gathering of book, etc.). **2** *pharm.* signature (abbrev. **sig.**=contents or directions for use on label). **3** *typog.* nick (in type). **4** catalogue number (of a book).
signe [sing'ne] *V -a/+-et* **1** *archaic* consecrate (a child, in place of baptizing) by making the sign of the cross. **2** bless: **Gud s- deg** God b- you; (old-fashioned terms of greeting, esp. in the country) **Gud s-** God b-; **s- møtet** b- our meeting; **god dag og s- arbeidet** howdy, and God b- your work. **3** heal by magic signs and formulas.
Signe *Prn (f)*
signe/kall *-en* magic healer.
signe/kjerring *-a, pl *-ar* wise woman, witch.
signere [singne're] *V -te* sign.
signet [singne't] *-et, pl -/+-er* seal, signet.
signet/ring *-en* seal ring, signet ring.
signifikati'v *A* significative; meaningful.
signing [sing'ning] *-a/+-en* blessing.
Sig'ny *Prn (f)*
***si'grar** *-en* victor.
***si'gre** *V -a* cf **seire**
Sig'rid *Prn (f)*
Sig'run' *Prn (f)*
***si'/grøn** *A -nt* **1** evergreen. **2** nonfading green.
Sig'urḍ *Prn (m)*
Sig'/vard *Prn (m)*
+sigøy'ner *-en, pl -e* (=***-ar**) gypsy.
+sigøy'nerske *-n* gypsy woman.
si'k[1] *-a* **1** grassy, lush meadow near farmhouses. **2** small bog, swamp.
si'k[2] *-en zool.* type of whitefish (Coregonus lavaretus).
***si'k[3]** *-et* small well, trickle of water in the ground.
sika'de *-n zool.* cicada (family Cicadidae).
***si'ke[1]** *-t* cf **sik[3]**
si'ke[2] *V -a/+-et* drain, empty (liquid):

+ Bokmål; * Nynorsk; ° Dialect.
After letter: ' stress (Acc. 1); ` tone, stress (Acc. 2); · length.
Below letter: . not pronounced.

s- av e- completely (e.g. liquid and dregs in a container).
***sik'kel** *-et* cf **sikl**
sik'ker *A -ert, pl sikre* 1 safe, secure: **isen er ikke s-** the ice isn't safe; **være s- for en** be safe from sby; **være på den s-re siden** be on the safe side; **han er ikke s- for** he has a tendency to. 2 certain, sure: **ha s- tro på** believe firmly in; **vite (tro) s-t** know (believe) conclusively, for sure; **vær s-** you bet; **være s- på** be sure of; **være s- på hånden** have a steady hand; **er det s-t at han kommer?** is he definitely coming?; **vet du det så s-t?** are you really sure about it?. 3 (of people) confident; firm; reliable: **en s- venn** a true, reliable friend; **s- i sin sak** confident that one is right.
+sik'ker/het *-en* 1 safety, security (**for** from; **mot** against): **for s-s skyld** just in case, for safety's sake. 2 certainty: **vite med s-** know for sure. 3 *merc.* surety (**for** for). 4 confidence, poise. 5 proficiency, skill (**i** in).
+sik'kerhets/foranstaltning *-en* safety measure.
+sik'kerhets/følelse *-n* feeling of safety, security.
***sik'kerhets/hvelv** *-et* safe-deposit vault.
***sik'kerhets/lenke** *-a/-en* safety chain; chain guard; door chain.
+sik'kerhets/nål *-a* safety pin.
+sik'kerhets/rådeț *df* the Security Council (of the UN).
+sik'kerhets/venti'l *-en* safety valve.
sik'kerlig *Av* assuredly.
Sik'kils/dalen *Pln* valley, Nord-Fron twp, Oppland.
sik'l *-et* (=**+sikkel**) 1 trickle. 2 salivation. 3 saliva.
sik'le[1] *-a* small brook.
sik'le[2] *V -a/+-et* 1 trickle; ripple. 2 drivel, drool, salivate. 3: **s- etter noe** want (to get) sth badly.
sik'le/smekke *-a* bib.
siko'ri *-en* chicory.
sik're[1] *V -a/+-et* 1 make safe, secure; protect: **s- mot** guard against, render safe from. 2 assure, guarantee: **s- seg** get hold of, make sure that one has. 3 put under restraint (e.g. a dangerous criminal or maniac). 4: **s-et** *jur.* assured, insured.
sik're[2] *pl of* **sikker**
sik'ring *-a/+-en* 1 securing; protection. 2 *jur.* preventive detention (security measures taken against a criminal, esp. habitual, after jail sentence has expired, as e.g. detention in an institution). 3 safety catch (e.g. on gun). 4 *elec.* fuse.
sik'rings/boks *-en* fuse box.
sik'rings/fonḍ *-et merc.* contingency fund.
sik'rings/kost *-en* minimum diet (giving the necessary vitamins, minerals and proteins).
sik'rings/middel *-elet/-midlet, pl +-midler/*-el jur.* security measure (e.g. as used according to law against habitual lawbreakers).
sik'rings/tavle *-a* fuse panel.
+sik'rings/tjeneste *-n* 1 *mil.* counter intelligence, security. 2 safety measures (e.g. in industry).
sik'/sak' *et* zigzag: **bevege seg i s-** zigzag.
sik'sak/lyn *-et* lightning bolt, chain lightning.
sik'spens/lue *-a* type of cloth cap (flat, low, with a visor).
sik't[1] *-a* sieve, strainer.
sik't[2] *-en* 1 sight: **betalbar ved s-** payable at s-; **på kort s-** at short s-; **planlegge på lang s-** plan with a long-range objective in mind. 2 visibility.
+sik't/bar *A* 1 clear: **været er s-t** the weather is c-; the visibility is good. 2 visible.
+sik'tbar/het *-en* visibility.
sik'te[1] *-t, pl +-r/*-* 1 sight: **få s- av land** catch s- of land; **tape av s-** lose s- of; **i s-** in s-; **få land i s-** sight land; **ha noe i s-** be within s- of sth; have a purpose in mind; **målet er i s-** the goal is in s-. 2 aim: **ta s-** take a-; **ta s- på noe** a- at sth; **planen har videre s- enn...** the plan aims further than (only).. 3 sights (of a gun).
sik'te[2] *V -a/+-et* 1 aim (**på at**): **s- inn målet** sight the target; **s- inn kikkerten** adjust the binoculars, bring the binoculars into focus. 2: **s- til** hint at, refer to (indirectly).
sik'te[3] *V -a/+-et jur.* charge, indict: **s- en for mord** charge sby with murder.
sik'te[4] *V -a/+-et* sift: **s- korn** s- grain; **aspirantene blir s-et grundig før opptaket** the aspirants are carefully screened before admittance; **forfatteren burde ha s-et materialet bedre** the author ought to have sifted his material better.
+sik'tede *df jur.* the accused, the defendant.
sik'te/ko'rn *-et* front sight (of a gun).
sik'te/linje *-a/+-en* (=***/line**) line of sight.
+sik'telse *-n jur.* charge, indictment; accusation: **reise s- mot** prosecute.
sik'te/mjøl *-et* bolted (sifted) flour (esp. rye).
sik'te/punkt *-et, pl -/+-er* sighting point.
-sik'tig *A* - 1 -term (e.g. **kort/s-**). 2 looking (e.g. ahead), -sighted.
sik'ting *-a* 1 aiming. 2 charge, indictment. 3 sifting (of flour).
sik't/veksel *-elen, pl -ler merc.* sight draft.
si'l[1] *-en* strainer.
si'l[2] *-en zool.* sand launce (family Ammodytidae).
sil'ḍ *-a, pl *-ar zool.* herring (Clupea harengus): **daud som ei s-** dead as a dormouse.
+sil'de *Av obs.* late: **årle og s-** early and l-.
sil'ḍebeins/mønster *-eret/-ret* herringbone pattern.
sil'ḍe/bruk *-et* 1 herring fishing outfit (including boat, nets, etc.). 2 very big shoal of herring.
sil'ḍe/fiske *-t* herring fishery.
sil'ḍe/ga'rn *-et* herring net.
sil'ḍe/gryn *-a* thick soup containing pieces of herring, barley, and vegetables.
sil'ḍe/konge *-n zool.* herring king, oarfish (Regalecus glesne).
sil'ḍe/lake *-n* herring brine.
sil'ḍe/mjøl *-et* herring meal.
sil'ḍe/not *-a, pl -nøter* herring sweep net.
sil'der *-eret/-ret* 1 purl, trickle; small brook. 2 purling, trickling sound.
***sil'ḍe/reist** *-et* herring scale.
sil'ḍe/sala't *-en* salad of sliced pickled herring, beets, onion, etc.
***sil'ḍe/salslag** *-et* herring fishermen's cooperative marketing organization.
sil'ḍe/steng *-et* catch of herring made with sweep net.
sil'ḍe/stim *-en* shoal of herring.
sil'ḍe/syner *pl* sights, marks that indicate the location of a shoal of herring (e.g. birds, whales following the shoal).
+sil'dig *A* - late.
sil'ḍ/olje *-a/-en* herring oil.
sil'dre[1] *-a* 1 small brook. 2 *bot.* saxifrage (genus Saxifraga).
sil'dre[2] *V -a/+-et* purl, trickle.
si'le *V -te/*-a* 1 filter, strain (e.g. juice, milk); sift. 2 pour: **regnet s-er ned** the rain is p-ing down.
si'le/klede [*/klee] *-t* strainer cloth.
silentium [silen'(t)sium] *-et* silence.
si'le/sup *-en* cf **sil/**
silhuett [siluett'] *-en* silhouette.
si'l/hår *-et* strainer cloth made of hair.
sili'cium *N chem.* silicon.
silika't *-et, pl -/+-er chem.* silicate.
siliko'se *-n med.* silicosis.
Sil'jan *Pln* twp, Telemark.
sil'ke *-n* silk: **blank s-** satin.
sil'ke/ape *-n zool.* guereza (genus Colobus).
sil'ke/atlask *-en* satin.
+sil'ke/bløt *A* soft as silk.
sil'ke/fin *A* smooth as silk.
sil'ke/føre *-t* excellent skiing conditions with new snow that has a soft but carrying surface.
sil'ke/hanske *-n* 1 silk glove. 2: **ta på (en, noe) med s-r** handle (sby, sth) with kid gloves.
sil'ke/hatt *-en* silk hat.
sil'ke/hår *-et* soft, silky hair.
sil'ke/orm *-en zool.* silkworm (Bombyx mori).
sil'ke/papi'r *-et* tissue paper.
sil'ke/snor *-a* silk cord.
sil'ke/strømpe *-a* silk stocking.
***sil'ke/svans** *-en zool.* waxwing (Bombycilla garrulus).
+si'l/klede *-t* cf **sile/**
***sil'le** *V -a* flow, pour; drip, trickle rapidly.
si'lo *-en* 1 silo. 2 (in mining) bin.
si'lo/for *-et* ensilage.
+sil're *V -et* cf **sildre[2]**
si'l/regn [+/rein] *-et* steady, pouring rain.
si'l/regne [+/reine] *V -a/+-et/+-te/*-de* rain heavily and steadily, pour.
si'l/sup *-en* sip, cupful of milk fresh from the cow.
silu'r/tiḍa *df geol.* the Silurian period.
si'l/våt *A* dripping wet.
si'me *-n* rope (esp. of hair).
Si'men *Prn (m)*
si'mili *N* 1 costume jewelry. 2 *fig.* sth artificial, imitation, sham.
sim'le *-a* 1 female reindeer. 2 hard roll.
simoni' *-en eccl.* simony.
sim'pel *A -elt, pl -le* 1 plain, simple, uncomplicated: **s-t flertall** simple majority; **s- forbrytelse** misdemeanor; **s- tro** innocent faith; **av den s-le grunn** for the simple reason; **ganske s-t (fordi)** quite simply (because). 2 coarse, common, vulgar: **en s- fyr** a common fellow, a heel; **s-t språk** coarse language; **det var s-t gjort** that was a mean trick.
+sim'pelt/hen' *Av* simply: **han tør s- ikke gjøre det** he s- doesn't dare do it.
sim'pleks *-en* simpleton.
simplifise're *V -te* simplify.
simulan't *-en* simulator.
simule're *V -te* simulate.
simulta'n *A* simultaneous (**med** with).
+simulta'n/oversettelse *-n* simultaneous translation.
simulta'n/parti' *-et, pl +-er/*-* simultaneous game (of chess).
si'n *pn f si/+sin, n sitt, pl sine* 1 his, her(s), its, their(s), one's (own) (usu. referring back to subject of clause): **mannen går inn i huset sitt** the man walks into his (own) house; **kall tingen ved sitt rette navn** call a spade a spade; **han gikk s- vei** he went his way; **de gikk hver s- vei** they went their several ways; **prøve s- lykke** try one's luck; **ta s- død av** die from; **være det beste i sitt slag** be the best of its kind. 2 peculiar, special: **det har s- sjarme** there's a special charm about it, it has a charm of its own; **det har s-e fordeler** there are certain advantages in it; **han har s-e grunner** he has good reasons, he knows what he's doing. 3 (used to express exceptional number or size): **grana er s-e 40—50 meter høy** the spruce tree is a good 40 or 50 meters tall; **han tjener s-e hundre tusen i året** he makes a cool hundred thousand a year. 4 *(pl)* dear ones, family: **ernære seg og s-e** support oneself and one's family, dear ones. *5 (used

as a possessive form): **mannen sin hatt** (=⁺**mannens hatt**) the man's hat; **det er sonen min s- gard (sitt hus, si ku, s-e hestar)** it's my son's farm (house, cow, horses); **Kven eig det huset? Det er Ola sitt** Who owns that house? It's Ola's; **sope unna sjøl si dør** sweep in front of his own door (Falkberget). 6 (other idioms): **i s- alminnelighet** in general; **i s- tid** formerly, at one time; **det er på s- plass** it is proper; **på sitt sted** in the proper place; **på sine steder** in places; **til s-e tider** at times, occasionally; **alt til s- tid** everything in due time; **få sitt fram (igjennom)** get one's way; **gi enhver sitt** give everyone his due; **gjøre sitt (til noe)** do one's share, make one's contribution (to sth); **gå hver til sitt** go each to his own (house, work, business, etc.); **ha nok med sitt** have one's hands full with one's own affairs; **ha sitt på det tørre** have nothing to worry about; **holde på (bli ved) sitt** stick to one's guns, not give in; **legge sitt til** make one's contribution to, contribute one's share to; **ligge på sitt siste (ytterste)** be breathing one's last; **passe sitt, stelle med sitt** mind, tend one's own affairs; **tenke sitt (om noe)** have one's own opinion (about sth); **tenke på sitt** be occupied with one's own thoughts; **det var gutten (karen) sin!** what a guy!, attaboy!; **djevelen hjelper sine** the devil helps those who belong to him, his kind; **det tar s- tid** it takes a while, it's not done in a hurry.

sin=**sinus**

sin'der *-eret/-ret* cinder, dross, slag.

sin'ders *-en* cinders (used for fuel).

sin'dig *A* - calm, careful; deliberate, steady; soberminded; thoughtful.

sin'dre *V -a/⁺-et* 1 crumble, crush. 2 (of hot iron) spark.

⁺**sin'drig** *A* - cf **sinn/rik**

***si'ne**[1] *V sein, sine/-i* 1 glide slowly. 2 sink down; cause pressure, feel heavy.

si'ne[2] *V -a/⁺-et* (of cow or woman) dry up.

sineky're *-n* sinecure.

sineky're/stilling *-a/⁺-en* sinecure.

sing.=**singularis**

sing'el[1] *-en* a coarse gravel.

sing'el[2] *-et* (=⁺**singl**) tinkle, tinkling: ***med eit s- i øyro som når ein fin og glasskjøyr ting hev sprunge sund** with a tinkling in the ears like the sound which is heard when a delicate object of glass is broken (Vesaas).

sing'el[3] *A -elt, pl -le* single.

sing'elton *-en* singleton (card).

⁺**sing'l** *-et* cf **singel**[2]

sing'le *V -a/⁺-et* tinkle; make a splintering sound.

sing'le/bjølle *-a* tinkling bell.

single/sculler [sing'el/skøller] *-en, pl ⁺-e* scull, one-man racing boat.

sing'let *-en* singlet (short-sleeved undershirt).

singott' *I obs.* skoal.

Sing's/ås *Pln* twp, Sør-Trøndelag.

singularis [singgula'ris] *en gram.* singular.

singulær [singgulæ'r] *A* singular, unique.

sin'k *-en/-et* zinc.

⁺**sinkadu's** *-en pop.* powerful body blow, wallop.

⁺**sin'ke**[1] *-n* 1 slow person; straggler (usu. of slow learner); retarded pupil. 2 delay.

⁺**sin'ke**[2] *V -a/-et* cf **seinke**

sin'ke[3] *V -a/⁺-et carp.* dovetail.

sin'k/kvitt *et* (=⁺**/hvitt**) zinc oxide, zinc white.

sinn'[1] *-et* 1 mind: **fra s- og sans** out of one's m-; **i (på) s- og skinn** (both) internally and externally, through and through; **i sitt stille s-** inwardly, to oneself, in one's heart; **i sjel og s-** through and through; **sjuk på s-et** mentally ill; **sette s-ene i bevegelse (opprør)** cause a stir; **skifte s-** change one's m-; **være til s-s å** have a m- to, intend to; **være rolig (urolig) til s-s** be easy (uneasy) in one's m-; **ute av øye, ute av s-** out of sight, out of m-. 2 disposition, mood, temperament: **etter ens s-** to one's liking; **ha s- for** have an eye for, be of such a temperament as to be able to appreciate; **ha et vanskelig s-** be moody; **ha et vennlig s-** be of a kindly disposition; **være tung (lett) av s-** be melancholy (lighthearted). (Cf also **sinne**[2]).

***sinn'**[2] *eit* 1 time: **eit s-** once, at one t-; **eitkvart s-** some t-. 2 recent past: **(her) i s-** recently, a short while ago.

sin'na *A* - 1 angry (esp. suddenly but briefly): **han er s- av seg** he is quick-tempered. *2 disposed, minded.

sin'na/tagg *-en* spitfire.

⁺**sinn'/bilde** *-t* (=***/bilete**) allegorical figure; symbol.

⁺**sinn'/billede** *-t* cf **/bilde**

sin'ne[1] *-t* anger, temper: **i fullt s-** furiously.

sin'ne[2] *N*: **falle (renne) en i s-** come to one's mind; **få i s-** get into one's head; **ha i s- å** have in mind to, intend to; **ha ondt i s-** mean no good, have evil intentions; **legge en på s- å** urge sby to; **ligge en på s-** be close to one's heart.

sin'ne/lag *-et* 1 disposition, temper, temperament. 2 sentiment, opinion.

⁺**sin'net** *A* - disposed, minded.

⁺**sinn'/rik** *A* clever, ingenious: **en s- oppfinnelse** an i- invention.

⁺**sinn's/beve'gelse** *-n* agitation, emotion; excitement.

⁺**sinn's/forvir'ret** *A* - insane; out of one's mind.

⁺**sinn's/forvir'ring** *-a/-en* insanity.

⁺**sinn's/lidelse** *-n* mental illness.

⁺**sinn's/likevekt** *-en* mental balance; equanimity.

sinn's/opprør *-et* agitation; frenzy.

sinn's/ro *-a/⁺-en* equanimity.

sinn's/sjuk *A* (=⁺**/syk**) mentally ill, insane, mad.

sinn's/sjukdom *-men/*-en* (=⁺**/sykdom**) mental disease, mental illness, insanity.

sinn's/stemning **-a/⁺-en* mood, spirits, state of mind.

sinn's/styrke *-n* courage; strength of mind; steadfastness.

sinn's/svak *A* 1 insane, mad. 2 absurd, preposterous.

⁺**sinn's/syk** *A* cf **/sjuk**

⁺**sinn's/sykdom** *-men* cf **/sjukdom**

sinn's/tilstand *-en/*-et* state of mind.

sino'ber *-en* cinnabar.

⁺**sino'ber/rød** *A* (=***/raud**) cinnabar red.

***sin's/imel'lom** *Av* among themselves; mutually.

sin't *A* - angry: **s- på en** a- with sby; **s- for noe** a- about sth; **han blir s- for ingenting** he gets a- over nothing.

si'nus *-en* 1 *math.* sine. 2 *anat.* sinus.

sinusitt' *-en med.* sinusitis.

si'nus/kurve *-n math.* sine curve.

sionis'me *-n* Zionism.

sionis't *-en* Zionist.

si'p *-et* (=**sipp**) 1 moaning, whining. 2 drip, drizzle.

si'pe *V -a/-te* 1 moan, whine. 2 drip, drizzle.

si'pet(e) *A* - (=**sippet(e)**) 1 tearful, teary, whining. 2 prudish, squeamish.

°**sip'le** *V -a/-et* 1 drip, trickle. 2 moan, whine.

sipp' *-et* cf **sip**

sip'pe[1] *-a* girl or woman who weeps or complains easily.

sip'pe[2] *V -a/sipte* be on the verge of tears; moan, whine.

sip'pet(e) *A* - cf **sipet(e)**

⁺**sip're** *V -et* trickle.

⁺**si'r** *-en obs.* ornament.

si'ra *-en archaic* Sir (title used to the clergy).

***si'/rann** *pt of* **-renne**

sira't *-et, pl -/⁺-er* ornament.

si'/regn [⁺/rein] *-et* steady, pouring rain.

si'/regne [/reine] *V -a/⁺-e /⁺-te/*-de* rain steadily.

sire'ne *-a/⁺-en* siren.

sire'ne/prøve *-a/⁺-en* siren test (e.g. of air raid siren).

si'/renne *V infl as* **renne**[2] flow evenly and copiously.

siriss' *-en zool.* cricket (family Gryllidae).

⁺**sir'ka** *Av* cf **cirka**

sir'kel *-elen, pl -ler* circle: **løpe i s-** run in c-s; **den onde s-** the vicious c-; **ferdes i de beste, i de høyeste sirkler** move in the best, in the highest c-s.

sir'kel/boge [/båge] *-n* (=⁺**/bue**) *math.* arc of a circle.

sir'kel/rund *A* circular.

sir'kel/sag *-a* circular saw.

sir'kel/sektor *-en math.* sector of a circle.

sir'kle *V -a/⁺-et* circle: **s- inn** encircle.

sirkulasjo'n *-en* circulation.

sirkule're *V -te* circulate.

sirkulæ're *-t, pl ⁺-r/*-* circular.

sir'kus *-et* 1 circus: **gå på s-** go to the c-. 2 big, tumultuous noise, pandemonium.

sir'kus/artis't *-en* circus performer.

sir'kus/klovn *-en* circus clown.

sir'kus/mane'sje *-n* circus ring.

si'rlig *A* - 1 elegant; refined. 2 neat, orderly, tidy.

⁺**si'rlig/het** *-en* 1 elegance. 2 neatness, orderliness, tidiness.

sir's *-en* calico.

⁺**sir'ts** *-en* cf **sirs**

si'/runne** *pp of* **-renne** (=/runni**)

sir'up *-en* syrup.

sir'ups/kake *-a* cooky made with syrup.

sir'ups/snipp *-en* thin diamond-shaped cooky made with syrup.

sisa'l/hamp *-en* sisal hemp.

sisele're *V -te* chase (metal).

siselø'r *-en* chaser (of metal).

si'sik *-en zool.* siskin (genus Carduelis).

⁺**sisilia'ner** *-en, pl -e* (=***-ar**) Sicilian.

sisilia'nsk *A* - Sicilian.

Sis'sel *Prn (f)*

sis'sel/rot *-a bot.* polypody (Polypodium vulgare).

sis't[1] *A* - last, latest; (of two) latter: **s-e gang** the last time; **s-e halvdel av** the latter half of; **de s-e nyhetene** the latest news; **de s-e dagers hellige** the Latter Day Saints; **i s-e øyeblikk** at the last moment; **i det s-e, i den s-e tid** lately, recently; **i de s-e årene** (during) the last few years; **gi den s-e olje** administer extreme unction; **ligge på det s-e** be near death; **synge på s-e vers** be on one's last legs.

sis't[2] *Av* last, (the) last time: **s- jeg så ham** the last time I saw him; **s- i juni** late in June; **s- men ikke minst** last but not least; **takk for s-** thank you for (your hospitality) the last time (we were together); **til s-** at last, finally; **til syvende og s-** at long last, in the last resort; **vente til s-** wait to the last; **være s- på** be near death; **det er lenge siden s-** it's been a long time since the last time (we were together); **det er det jeg s- av alt vil gjøre** that's the last thing I want to do.

sis'te/mann *en* 1 last person to arrive. 2 hindmost. 3 person getting the poorest results in a competition.

⁺ Bokmål; * Nynorsk; ° Dialect.
After letter: ' stress (Acc. 1); ` tone, stress (Acc. 2); · length.
Below letter: . not pronounced.

sis'ten *N* tag: **leke s-** play t-.
+sis't/leden *A -ent, pl -ne* (the) last (used with dates): **s- 17. mai** last May 17th.
+sis't/nevnte *A* - the last mentioned, the latter.
sis't/på *Av* at last, eventually, finally.
***si'/stundes** *Av* late.
si'su *-en* perseverance, stamina (Finnish word).
si'syfos/arbeid *-et* Sisyphean task (=one requiring continual and often ineffective effort).
***si't** *pr of* **sitje**
sitadell' *-et* citadel.
sitan't *-en jur.* plaintiff.
sit'ar *-en* zither.
sita't *-et, pl -/+-er* quotation.
sita't/fusk *-et* misquotation.
***sita't/teikn** *-et* quotation mark.
site're *V -te* quote: **s- Ibsen** q- I-; **s- bibelen** q- from the Bible.
***sit'je** *V sit, sat, sete/-i* cf **sitte**
***sit'je/plass** *-en* cf **sitte/**
+sit're *V -a/-et* quiver, tremble, vibrate.
sitro'n *-en* lemon.
sitro'n/gul *A* lemon yellow.
sitro'n/saft *-a* lemon juice.
+sitro'n/sommerfugl *-en zool.* brimstone butterfly (Gonepteryx rhamni).
sitro'n/syre *-a chem.* citric acid.
si'trus/frukt *-a/+-en* citrus fruit.
sitt' *nt of* **sin**
+sit'te *V satt, sittet* (=***sitje**) **1** sit (**på** on): **s- godt (vondt)** s- comfortably (uncomfortably); **s- i tanker** s- quietly, idly (lost in thoughts); **s- igjen** stay after school; be left (**med** with); **s- inne med** contain, possess; **s- med** have on hand (not be able to get rid of); **s- ned** s- down; **s- oppe** stay up late (e.g. reading); **s- over** s- out (e.g. a dance); **s- på** ride along; **vil du s- på?** want a ride?; **s- på noe** s- on sth (to prevent others from getting it); **så satt vi der** so there we were (in a tough spot). **2** be (located in, on): **s- fint i det** be in a spot; **s- godt (trangt) i det** be well (poorly) off; **s- i gjeld** be in debt; **s- nederst i klassen** be at the bottom of the class; **s- inne** be in jail; **s- i velstand** be well-to-do; **han s-er i Stortinget (regjeringen)** he is in the *Storting* (the cabinet); **det s-er en stygg kjeft på ham** he has a foul mouth; **hatet til ham s-er dypt i meg** I hate him from the bottom of my heart; **nøkkelen s-er i døra** the key is in the door; **sykdommen s-er i lungene** the disease is located in the lungs; **vite hvor esset s-er** (in cards) know where the ace is. **3** stick, be stuck: **s- fast** be stuck; **banke inn en spiker så den s-er** pound in a nail so it holds; **den satt!** that one (i.e. that remark) struck home!; that's telling him!; **båten ble s-ende et godt stykke fra stranden** the boat was grounded quite a ways from the shore; **jeg kan ikke la skammen s- på meg** I must rid myself of the disgrace. **4** (of clothes) fit: **dressen s-er utmerket** the suit fits wonderfully. **5 s- og: jeg s-er og leser** I'm reading; **han har sittet og ventet lenge** he's been waiting a long time.
+sit'te/bad *-et* sitz bath.
+sit'te/plass *-en* seat: **det er tusen s-er** there are a thousand s-s.
situasjo'n *-en* situation: **en spent s-** a state of tension, a tense s-; **s-ens alvor** the gravity of the s-; **redde s-en** save the s-; **sette en inn i s-en** brief sby; **utnytte s-en** make the most of the occasion; **være s-ens herre** be master of the s-.
situe'rt *A* - situated (esp. financially): **godt s-** well off.
+si'v *-et* cf **sev**[1]
***si've**[1] *V seiv, sive/-i* cf **sive**[2]
si've[2] *V +-a/+-et/*-de* (=**sive**[1]) filter, ooze, percolate: **s- inn** seep in, trickle through; **s- ut** (e.g. of a rumor) leak out.
Si'vert *Prn(m)*
sivi'l *A* civilian.
+sivi'l/arbei'der *-en, pl -e* (=***-ar**) "civilian worker" (conscientious objector who is assigned civilian work in place of military service).
sivi'l/forsvar *-et* civil defense.
sivi'l/ingeniør [/insjeniø'r] *-en* (graduate) engineer (Bachelor of Engineering).
sivilisasjo'n *-en* civilization.
sivilise're *V -te* civilize.
sivilise'rt *A* - civilized.
sivilis't *-en* civilian.
sivi'l/kledd *A -/*-kledt* in civilian clothes; (of policeman) plainclothes.
sivi'l/prosess' *-en jur.* civil proceedings.
sivi'l/rett *-en jur.* civil law.
***siv'je** *V -a* **1: s- seg** become related by marriage. **2: sivja** related by marriage.
+si'v/matte *-a* (=***sev/**) rush mat.
si'/våt *A* dripping wet.
sj. = **+sjelden**[1,2]/***sjeldan**, ***sjeld/synt**
***sjab'be** *V -a* plod, shuffle.
sja'ber *A -ert, pl -re* **1** (of state, quality) poor. **2** poorly, sick (often from hangover).
sjablon [sjablång'] *-en* **1** *tech.* template (metal pattern). **2** *fig.* stereotype.
+sjablon/messig *A* - routine, stereotype, unoriginal.
sjagreng' *-en* shagreen.
sja'h *-en* shah.
sjaka'l *-en zool.* jackal (Canis aureus).
sjakett' *-en* **1** cutaway. **2** (men's) morning dress.
sjakk' *-en* **1** chess. **2** check, checkmate: **sette (kongen) s-** c- the king; **si s-** say c-; **holde en i s-** usu. *fig.* keep sby in check.
sjakk'/brett *-et* chessboard.
sjakk'/brikke *-a/+-en* chessman.
sjak'kel *-elen, pl sjakler naut.* shackle (U-shaped metal fitting).
sjakk'/matt *A* - checkmate.
sjakk'/parti' *-et, pl +-er/*-* game of chess.
+sjakk'/spill *-et* (=***/spel**) **1** chess. **2** set of chessboard and chessmen.
sjakk'/trekk *-et* move (in chess): **et klokt s-** *fig.* a clever move.
sjakk'/turne'ring *-a/+-en* chess tournament.
sjak'le *V -a/+-et naut.* shackle.
sjak're *V -a/+-et* **1** *derog.* barter, peddle. **2: s- med noe** offer sth for sale; **s- med seg selv** sell (oneself) to the highest bidder, do anything for a profit.
sjak't *-a/+-en* pit, shaft.
sja'l *-et* shawl.
+sjalott'/løk *-en* (=***/lauk**) *bot.* shallot (Allium ascalonicum).
sjal'te *V -a/+-et* shunt, switch: **s- inn** switch on, turn on; *fig.* include, insert, make use of; **s- over** switch over, change; **s- ut** switch off, turn off; *fig.* eliminate, remove.
sjalu' *A* - jealous (**på** of).
sjalupp' *-en obs.* barge.
sjalusi' *-en* **1** jealousy. **2** *obs.* Venetian blinds. **3** roll top (of desk); roll door (of cabinet).
sjalusi'/drama *-et, pl -/+-er* crime of passion.
sjama'n *-en* shaman.
sjampinjong' *-en bot.* type of mushroom (genus Psalliota).
sjam'po *-en* shampoo.
sjampone're *V -te* shampoo.
sjang'le *V -a/+-et* **1** (of person) stagger. **2** (of object) sway.
sjang'let(e) *A* - **1** staggering; swaying. **2** gaunt, skinny.
sjanse [sjang'se] *-n* chance: **han har gode s-r** his c-s are good; **han har ingen s-r, ikke en s-** he hasn't got a c-; **ikke mange s-r** not much c-; **ta s-en på noe** take a c- on sth, risk doing sth; **ta s-r** take risks.
+sjanse/seila's *-en fig.* gamble.
+sjanse/spill *-et* gamble.
sjan'ti *-en mus.* chantey, shanty.
sjapp' *-a* (=***sjap'pe**) **1** often *derog.* shop, store: **stenge s-a** close up shop. **2** low-grade barroom; dive.
sjargong' *-en* **1** jargon. **2** (teen-age) slang.
sjar'k *-en* type of motorboat used for fishing and transport.
sjar'latan *-en* charlatan.
sjar'm *-en* (=**charme**) charm.
sjarmant [sjarmang't] *A* - (=**charmant**) charming.
sjarme're *V -te* (=**charmere**) charm.
sjar'm/troll *-et* "charm pixie" (endearing term used of young girl).
sjarmø'r *-en* (=**charmør**) lady-killer.
sjas'k *+-et/*-en* **1** mud, sludge, slush. **2** negligence, slovenliness. **3** work that has been done in a slovenly manner.
sjas'ke *V -a/+-et* **1** shuffle, slush (e.g. through mud); give a shuffling, smacking sound. **2: s- noe av, unna, fra seg** do, finish sth quickly and negligently, slovenly.
sjas'ket(e) *A* - **1** creased, rumpled, tousled; bedraggled. **2** negligent, slatternly, slovenly. **3** flabby.
sjasmi'n *-en bot.* jasmine (genus Jasminus).
sjatte're *V -te* shade (a drawing).
sjatte'ring *-a/+-en* shading; shade; nuance.
sjau' *-en* **1** heavy work, toil; stint, task. **2** occasional work, esp. on the docks (loading, unloading). **3** noise, racket, uproar; noisy fun: **de holdt en svare s-** they were very noisy; **være ute på s-** be out having fun.
sjau'e *V -a/+-et* **1** work heavily, toil. **2** work at loading or unloading. **3** make a noise, be noisy; have fun. **4** carry on, fuss (**med** over).
+sjau'er *-en, pl -e* (=***-ar**) stevedore.
sje'f *-en* boss, chief, head; commanding officer: **være s- for noe** be the boss, the head of sth.
sje'f/redaktø'r *-en* editor-in-chief.
sje'fs/ga'rd *-en* (=**+/gård**) farm owned by the State and given as residence to the commanding officer of a company.
sje'fs/kokk *-en* chef.
sjei'de *V -a/+-et* separate ore from rock by crushing it with a hammer.
sjei'der *-en, pl +-e* miner who separates ore from rock by crushing it with a hammer.
sjei'k *-en* sheik.
sjekk' *-en* **1** check (of money). **2** *pop.* check (inspection).
sjekk'/bok *-a, pl -bøker* checkbook.
sjek'ke *V -a/+-et pop.* check, inspect: **s- opp noe** check up on sth.
sjekk'/hefte *-t, pl +-r/*-* checkbook.
sjek'te *-a* type of fishing boat (ab. 20 feet long, pointed at both ends) mainly used on the inner coast.
sje'l *-a/+-en* soul: **menneskets udødelige s-** the immortal s- of man; **av hele sin s-** with all one's heart; **med liv og s-** heart and s-; **min s-, min sel** mild oath expressing sincerity or used for emphasis; **det gjorde du min sel rett** i you did just what you should have; **ikke en mors s-** not a single solitary person; **ikke en s- var å se** not a s- was in sight; **være s-en i** be the heart and s- of (e.g. a project, enterprise).
+sjel'den[1] *A -ent, pl -ne* **1** rare: **en s-gang** rarely, very seldom; **et s-t maleri** a r- painting; **du er en s-mann å se på disse kanter** we don't see you around here often; **han har s-e gaver** he has r- talents. **2** exceptional, unusual: **maten er s-t god** the food is exceptionally good; **et s-t godt stykke** an unusually good play; **i s- grad** exceptionally, unusually; **han er s- flink til å spille fiolin** he's an exceptionally gifted violinist.

+sjel'den[2] *Av* (=***sjeldan**) rarely, seldom: **han er s- her** he is rarely here; **s- eller aldri** hardly ever.

+sjel'den/het *-en* rarity, sth rare (object, occurrence, sight, etc.).

***sjel'd/fengd** *A -/-fengt* rare; rarely obtained.

sjel'd/sy'nt *A* - rare; rarely seen.

+sje'le/dyp *-et* depths of the soul.

sje'le/fred *-en* peace of mind.

sje'le/glad *A* - delighted (**over** at), happy as a lark.

***sje'le/kunne** *-a* (science of) psychology.

sje'le/kval *-en* agony (of soul).

sje'le/lege *-n* mind-healer (often of a minister).

sje'lelig *A* - mental, spiritual; of the soul.

sje'le/liv *-et* mental life; spiritual life; psychology.

sje'le/lære *-a/+-en* (science of) psychology.

sje'le/messe *-a/+-en* mass for the soul (of sby dead), requiem.

sje'le/nød *-en* (spiritual) agony: **i s-** troubled (by religious anxieties).

sje'le/ro *-a/+-en* peace of mind.

sje'le/røkt *-a/+-en* care of the soul (e.g. of minister's work).

sje'le/sorg *-a/+-en* =**/røkt**

+sje'le/sørger *-en, pl -e* (=**/sørgjar**) minister, pastor, priest.

sje'le/vandring *-a/+-en* transmigration of souls.

sje'l/full *A* soulful.

+sje'l/løs *A* (=***/laus**) soulless.

sje'ls/evne *-a/+-en* mental faculty: **varig svekkede s-r** permanently impaired mental faculties.

sje'ls/styrke *-n* strength of mind.

sjenanse [sjenang'se] *-n* bashfulness, diffidence, shyness.

sjene're *V -te* 1 bother, trouble; embarrass; hamper, handicap: **s-er det Dem at jeg røker?** do you mind if I smoke? does my smoking bother you?; **såret s-er ham ennå** the wound is still giving him trouble; **s-ende** embarrassing; **en s-ende hoste** a troublesome cough; **s-ende hårvekst** superfluous hair. 2: **s- seg** be, feel embarrassed, self-conscious, shy; **jeg s-er meg for å be ham om penger** I hesitate to ask him for money; **han s-er seg ikke for å stemme på seg selv** he has the nerve to vote for himself; **sjener deg ikke** (often *ironic*) go right ahead, help yourself.

sjene'rlig *A* - disturbing, troublesome; embarrassing.

sjene'rt *A* - 1 bashful, shy. 2 embarrassed.

+sjene'rt/het *-en* 1 bashfulness, shyness. 2 embarrassment.

sjenerø's *A* generous.

sjenerøsite't *-en* generosity.

sjene'ver *-en, pl +-e* Holland gin, Hollands.

sjene'ver/krukke [/krokke] *-a* Hollands jug (tall and cylindrical with short, narrow neck).

+sjen'kel *-elen, pl -ler* leg (of a horseman).

Sjernar/øy [sjæ'rnar/] *Pln* twp, Rogaland.

sjeselong' *-en* chaise longue (lounge).

sjeté *-en* jetty; breakwater.

+sjet'landsk *A* - cf **shetlandsk**

sjetong' *-en* chip (for playing).

sjet'te *Num* sixth: **en s- sans** a s- sense.

sjet'te/del *-en* cf **seks/**

sjeviot [sjev'jått] *-en* cheviot.

sjeviot/sau *-en* cheviot sheep.

+sjev're *V -a/-et* 1 (of flag, sail) flap. 2 (of person, voice) quiver, shake.

sjevrå' *N* kid leather, kidskin.

sjib'bolet *et* shibboleth.

sjika'ne *-n* slander.

sjikane're *V -te* slander.

sjikanø's *A* slanderous.

sjik't *-et* 1 layer, stratum (e.g. in rock). 2 shift (mining).

sjimpan'se *-n zool.* chimpanzee (Anthropopithecus troglodytes).

sjing'el *-en* shingle (women's hair style).

sjing'le *V -a/+-et* shingle (hair).

sjiraff' *-en zool.* giraffe (Giraffa camelopardalis).

sjiraff'/hals *-en* giraffe's neck.

sjirok'ko *-en* sirocco (hot, dry wind).

sjir'ting *-en* (book) cloth: **en bok i s-** a clothbound book.

sjir'ting/bind *-et* cloth binding.

sjod'di *-en* shoddy (reclaimed wool).

***sjo'de** *V syd, saud, sode/-i* cf **syde**

sjo'fel *A -elt, pl -le* contemptible, low, mean: **en s- beskyldning** a mean accusation; **han gjorde meg en s- strek** he played a dirty trick on me; **det var s-t gjort av ham** that was a mean thing for him to do.

+sjo'fel/het *-en* 1 lowness, meanness. 2 low, mean act, utterance.

***sjo'g** *-en* roar, swish (of water).

sjo'ge *V -a* (of turbulent water, esp. a river) roar, swish.

sjogse [sjok'se] *V -a/+-et* (of black-cock) give a hissing sound during play.

sjokk' *-et* shock: **få (et) s-** get a s-; **gi en et s-** give sby a s-; **nyheten kom som et s- på meg** the news came as a s- to me.

+sjokk'/behan'dling *-en* shock treatment.

+sjok'ke *V -a/-et* 1 (of walking) shuffle. 2 (of sound) swoosh.

sjokke're *V -te* shock: **s-t over** s-ed at.

sjokola'de *-n* chocolate.

sjokola'de/automa't *-en* chocolate automat.

sjokola'de/kake *-a* chocolate cake.

sjokola'de/konfek't *-en* chocolate candy.

sjokola'de/plate *-a/+-en* chocolate bar.

sjokola'de/selskap *-et, pl -/+-er* party (usu. for children) where cake and hot chocolate are served.

sjongle're *V -te* 1 juggle: **s- med baller** j- balls. 2 juggle, play: **taleren s-te med en rekke tall** the speaker juggled a lot of figures; **s- med fakta** (also) juggle the facts around.

sjonglø'r *-en* juggler.

sju'[1] *Num* seven; **De s- søstre** the S- Sisters (mountains, waterfalls); **min munn er lukket med s- segl** I won't betray the secret; **vente i s- lange og s- breie** wait indefinitely.

sju'[2] *I dial.* (you) see.

sju'/arma *A -*: **s- lysestake** seven-branched candelabrum.

sju'/del *-en* seventh part: **en s-** one seventh.

sju'ende *Num* seventh: **den s- himmel** the s- heaven; **s- far i huset** (in a fairytale) the s- ancestor; *fig.* very old person; **til s- og sist** at long last, eventually; in the end; when all is said and done; **Syvende Sans** pocket diary (lit. the seventh sense).

sju'ende/del *-en* cf **sju/**

+sju'er *-en, pl -e* (=***-ar**) seven (e.g. a card, dice throw).

sju'k *A* (=**+syk**) 1 ill, sick: **s- etter** s- with longing for, crazy about, dying (to); **syk til døden** deathly ill; (as title of book by Kierkegaard) Sick unto Death; **et s-t hode (sinn)** a deranged mind; **et s-t smil** a sickly, wan smile; **ligge s- av** be ill, laid up with. 2 decadent, perverted: **Syk kjærlighet** Perverted Love (novel by Hans Jæger); **vi lever i en s- tid** we are living in a period of decadence.

sju'k/dom' *-men/*-en* disease, illness, sickness.

sju'kdoms/forfall *-et* sick leave.

sju'kdoms/tilfelle *-t* case of illness.

sju'kdoms/årsak *-a/+-en* cause of illness.

sju'ke *-n* (=**+syke, *sykje**) disease, illness, sickness.

sju'ke/attes't *-en* certificate of illness.

sju'ke/besø'k *-et* sick call (by doctor, friend, etc.): **gå på s-** call on a sick person.

sju'ke/bil *-en* ambulance (car).

+sju'ke/båre *-a/-en* (=***/bår**) stretcher.

sju'ke/heim *-en* home, sanitarium.

sju'ke/hus *-et* hospital.

sju'ke/kasse *-a/-en* national health insurance: **stå i s-en** be a member of the national health insurance.

+sju'kelig *A* - cf **sjuklig**

sju'ke/luga'r *-en naut.* sick bay, sick berth.

+sju'ke/penger *pl* (=***-ar**) sick pay.

sju'ke/pleie *-a/+-en* cf **syke/**

sju'ke/pleierske *-a* cf **syke/**

sju'ke/seng *-a* sickbed.

sju'ke/stell *-et* care of the sick.

sju'ke/stue *-a* first aid room, nurse's office; infirmary.

+sju'ke/søster *-era/-eren, pl -re(r)* (=***/syster**) nurse.

sju'ke/trygd *-a/+-en* health insurance.

+sju'ke/vokter *-en, pl -e* (=***/vaktar**) *mil.* (hospital) orderly.

***sju'king** *-en* cf **sjukling**

sju'klig *A* - (=**+sjukelig, +sykelig**) 1 sickly, often sick. 2 (of color) sickly, wan. 3 abnormal, exaggerated: **en s- nysgjerrighet** an abnormal curiosity. 4 morbid: **en s- fantasi** a m- imagination.

sju'kling *-en* (=***sjuking**) sick creature, sick person.

sju'k/melding *-a/+-en* doctor's certificate that patient is unfit for work for a certain period.

+sju'k/meldt *A* - (=***/meld**) on sick leave.

sju'kne *V -a/+-et* (=**+sykne**[2]) 1 become sick, sicken. **+2: sykne hen** waste away, decline.

sju'mils/fart *-en*: **med s-** at very high speed (=the speed of seven-league boots).

sju'mils/steg *-et* giant stride.

sju'mils/støvel *-elen, pl -ler*: **ta s-ene på** forge rapidly ahead.

°sju'r[1] *-a* cf **skjor**

°sju'r[2] *A* 1 stiff (from exercise). 2 slow, slow-moving: **det gikk s-t** things moved slowly. 3 (of person) weak and cowardly, wretched.

Sju'r *Prn(m)*

sju'rs/messe) *on dial.* old name for December 23 (or 12).

sjus'k *-et* negligence, slovenliness (in work).

sjus'ke[1] *-a* slattern.

sjus'ke[2] *V -a/+-et* work in a negligent, slovenly manner: **s- arbeidet fra seg** hurry through one's work.

sjus'ke[3] *V -a/+-et dial.* 1 (of water) swish. 2 plop (e.g. when sth is pulled out of a bog). 3 (of black-cock) hiss (during play).

+sjus'keri *-et* negligence, slovenliness.

sjus'ket(e) *A* - negligent, slovenly.

***sju'/skjære** *-a bot.* type of cranesbill (Geranium).

+sju'/sover *-en, pl -e* (=***-ar**) sleepy-head.

sjy' *+-en/*-et* jus (meat juice served with meat in place of gravy).

°sjæ'l *Pn* cf **sjølv**[2]

Sjælland [sjel'lann] *Pln* Zealand (Danish island).

sjællandsk [sjel'lansk] *A* - Zealand(ic).

sjællending [sjel'lenning] *-en* Zealander.

sjø' *-en* 1 ocean, sea: **i åpen (rum) s-** on the open s-, high s-s; **på s-en, til s-s** at s-; **(reise) til s-s** (go) to s-; **ved s-en** by the s- (side); **seile sin egen s-** shift for oneself, be on one's own; **(ikke) tåle s-en** be a good (bad) sailor; **verken på land eller s-** absolutely nowhere. 2 (sea) water;

+ Bokmål; * Nynorsk; ° Dialect.
After letter: ' stress (Acc. 1); ` tone, stress (Acc. 2); · length.
Below letter: . not pronounced.

sea (=surface conditions): **båten tok inn mye s-** the boat shipped a lot of water; **høy (svær, tung) s-** high (heavy) s-; **s-en gikk høyt** the s-s ran high; **springe til s-s** jump overboard. 3 billow, swell, wave: **en stor s- gikk over båten** a large w- swept over the boat; **s-ene rullet inn** the w-s rolled in. 4 lake (=**innsjø**).

sjø'/assurandø'r *-en* marine underwriter.
sjø'/aure *-n* sea trout.
sjø'/bad *-et* 1 swim in the sea; sea bathing. 2 seaside baths, seaside resort.
sjø'/bein *-et* sea legs: **sette s-** walk with legs apart to keep one's balance on swaying deck.
sjø'/botn *-en* (=+/**bunn**) bottom of a lake, fjord, sea.
sjø'/bu *-a* boathouse (on the seacoast).
****sjø'/bu'rd** *-en* 1 rough, breaking sea. 2 din, noise from breaking sea.
sjø'/by *-en* seaside town; seaport.
sjø'/båt *-en* sea boat: **en god s-** a good s-.
sjø'/djevel *-elen, pl -ler zool.* devilfish, devil ray (Dicerobatis).
sjø'/drev *-et* spray from rough sea.
+**sjø'/dyktig** *A* - seaworthy.
+**sjø'dyktighets/attes't** *-en* certificate of seaworthiness.
sjø'e *V -a/+-et*: **det s-er** the waves are getting high(er).
sjø'/elefan't *-en zool.* sea elephant, elephant seal (Cystophora proboscidea).
sjø'/fall *-et* 1 difference between tide and ebb, spring tide. 2 time from tide to ebb, time when tide is falling.
sjø'/farende *A* - seafaring.
+**sjø'/farer** *-en, pl -e* (=***-ar**) seafarer.
sjø'/fart *-en* navigation, shipping.
sjø'farts/bok *-a* discharge book (folder where a sailor's service record is entered).
sjø'/finn *-en* Lapp living on the coast as a fisherman.
sjø'/fly *-et* seaplane.
sjø'/folk *pl* sailors, seamen.
sjø'/forkla'ring *-a/+-en jur.* protest (after an accident at sea).
sjø'/fugl *-en* seabird.
***sjø'/før** *A* seaworthy.
***sjø'før/leik** *-en* seaworthiness.
sjø'/gang *-en* agitated, heavy sea; storm.
sjø'/grense *-a/+-en* territorial limit.
sjø'/grøn *A* (=+/**grønn**) sea-green.
sjø'/gutt *-en* (=*/**gut**) sea boy, ship boy; young sailor.
sjø'/gående *A* - seagoing.
sjø'/helt *-en* naval hero.
sjø'/hus *-et* big boathouse; storehouse, warehouse at a wharf.
sjø'/kadett' *-en* naval cadet.
sjø'/kart *-et* chart.
***sjø'/katt** *-en zool.* blenny, wolf fish (Anarrhichas lupus).
sjø'/klar *A* ready to put to sea.
sjø'/krigsskole *-n* naval academy.
sjø'/ku *-a zool.* sea cow (order Sirenia).
+**sjø'l** *Pn* cf **sjølv**[2]
+**sjø'l-** *Pf* cf **selv-, sjølv-**
sjø'/laks *-en* (ocean) salmon.
sjø'/lei *-a* sea route.
+**sjø'l/eiende(s)** *A* - cf **selv/**
sjø'/leies *Av* (=+/**leis**) by sea.
sjø'/lik *-et* corpse of sby drowned.
sjø'/lilje *-a/+-en zool.* crinoid, sea lily (order Crinoidea).
sjø'/liv *-et* life at sea; a sailor's life.
***sjøl'v**[1] *-et* cf **selv**[1]
sjø'lv[2] *Pn* (=+**selv**[2], +**sjøl**) 1 (her-, him-, it-, my-, one-, your-)self, (our-, them-, your-)selves: **s- takk** (in response to being thanked) same to you; **kongen s- var til stede** the king himself was present; **det må du s- om** that's up to you; **han er ærligheten s-** he is honesty itself; (with personal pronouns) **om (når) jeg s- skal si det** if I say so myself; **du skal elske din neste som deg s-** thou shalt love thy neighbor as thyself (Lev. 19, 18); **det blir verst for deg s-** it will be worst for you yourself; **han (det) er noe for seg s-** he (it) is sth quite apart, extraordinary; **av seg s-** of its (one's) own accord, by itself; **det følger av seg s-** it's a matter of course; **for seg s-** alone, by oneself; **hos seg s-** in one's own house; **i (og for) seg s- (er det en bra idé)** in itself (it's a fine idea); **gå inn til seg s-** go to one's own room (to be alone); **snakke med seg s-** talk to oneself; **være seg s-** be oneself; **du var og ble deg s- til slutt** in the final analysis you were yourself (Ibsen). 2 (with ordinal numbers): **jeg kommer s- annen** I won't be alone, I'll have someone with me; **s-tolvte, osv.** with 11 other people (i.e. with oneself as the twelfth), etc.
***sjø'lv/beden** *A -e/-i, pl -ne* 1 on one's own initiative: **han gjorde det s-** he did it without having been asked. 2 without invitation, self-invited.
sjø'lv/berga *A* - self-sufficient, self-supporting: **være s- med mat** be s- in food, have enough food.
sjø'lv/berging *-a* 1 self-support. 2 self-preservation.
+**sjø'lv/binder** *-en, pl -e* (=***-ar**) *agr.* binder, self-binder.
sjø'lv/byrg *A* conceited, self-important.
sjø'lv/daud *A* (of animal) dead from accident or disease (so that the meat isn't edible).
***sjø'lv/daude** *V -a* (of animal) die without having been slaughtered.
sjøl've *Pn* (=+**selve**) (her-, him-, it-)self; (the) very: **s- den luften hun innånder** the very air she breathes; **en bok av s- N.N.** a book by N.N. himself; **det var som s- (fanden)** I'll be — (damned); **drikke av s- flaska** drink straight from the bottle; **sove på s- jorda** sleep on the bare ground; ***s- seg= seg sjølv.**
sjøl've/folk *-et* the master and his family (used by servants).
***sjø'lv/eigande** *A* - cf **selv/eiende**
***sjø'lv/eigar** *-en* cf **selv/eier**
+**sjøl'veste** *Pn* (=+**selveste**, ***sjølvaste**) (her-, him-)self: **s- kongen** the King himself.
***sjø'lv/gjeven** *A -e/-i, pl -ne* self-evident.
sjø'lv/gjort [/jort] *A* - done, made by oneself: **s- er velgjort** self-done is well done (=if you want it done well you have to do it yourself).
***sjø'lv/gløymande** *A* - cf **selv/forglemmende**
sjø'lv/god *A* self-righteous, self-satisfied, smug.
sjø'lv/hevding *-a* self-assertion.
sjø'lv/hjelp *-a* self-help.
***sjø'lv/hjelpen** *A -e/-i, pl -ne* cf **selv/-hjulpen**
***sjø'lv/hug** *-en* egoism.
***sjø'lv/kalla** *A* - self-appointed.
sjø'lv/kjensle *-a* pride, respect; conceit, egotism.
sjø'lv/kjær *A* egotistic, self-loving.
sjø'lv/klok *A* opinionated; conceited.
sjø'lv/kost *-et* what sth has cost a person who later wants to sell it: **selge til s-** sell at cost, without a profit.
sjø'lv/kritikk' *-en* self-criticism.
sjø'lv/kritisk *A* - self-critical.
sjø'lv/laga *A* - made by oneself.
***sjø'lv/laus** *A* unselfish.
sjø'lv/lyd *-en* vowel.
***sjø'lv/lysande** *A* - cf **selv/lysende**
sjø'lv/læ'rt *A* self-taught.
***sjø'lv/medviten** *A -e/-i, pl -ne* arrogant, conceited, self-important.
sjøl'v/melding *-a* (income) tax return: **sende inn s-** file one's (income) tax return.
***sjøl'v/mint** *A* - without having had to be reminded.
sjøl'v/mord [/mord] *-et* suicide: **begå s-** commit s-.
***sjø'lv/motseiing** *-a* cf **selv/motsigelse**
sjø'lv/nøgd *A -/*-nøgt* complacent, self-satisfied.
sjø'lv/ros *-en* self-praise: **s- stinker** s- is no praise.
sjø'lv/råden *A +-ent, pl -ne* headstrong, self-willed.
sjø'lv/rådig *A* - cf **/råden**
***sjø'lv/rådvald** *-et* self-determination.
***sjø'lv/sagd** *A -/-sagt* cf **selv/sagt**
sjø'lv/sikker *A -ert, pl -sikre* cf **selv/**
sjø'lv/skott *-et* cocked gun (set out for animals, robbers, etc.).
***sjø'lv/skriven** *A -e/-i, pl -ne* cf **selv/-skreven**
sj'ølv/skryt *-et* self-praise.
***sjø'lvsleg** *A* - selfish.
sjø'lv/stende *-t* autonomy, independence.
sjø'lv/stendig *A* - autonomous, independent, self-governing; having a mind of one's own.
sjø'lv/styr *-et*: **på s-** on one's own; being one's own master.
***sjø'lv/styren** *A -e/-i, pl -ne* headstrong, obstinate, self-willed.
sjø'lv/syn *-et/*-a* seeing for oneself: **overbevise seg om noe ved s-** convince oneself of sth by seeing for oneself.
sjø'lv/tekt *-a/+-en jur.* taking the law into one's own hands.
***sjø'lv/te'nt** *A* - (of fortune, property) self-acquired, self-made.
sjø'lv/tillit *-en* assurance, self-confidence.
sjø'lv/tukt *-a* self-discipline.
***sjø'lv/tøyming** *-a* self-command, self-control.
***sjø'lv/valda** *A* - cf **selv/voldt**
***sjø'lv/viljande** *A* - voluntary.
***sjø'lv/vø'rdnad** *-en* self-esteem, self-respect; pride.
sjø'/løve *-a/+-en zool.* sea lion (genus Otaria).
sjø'/makt *-a/+-en* sea power.
sjø'/mann *-en, pl -menn/*-menner* sailor, seaman.
sjø'manns/heim *-en* (=+/**hjem**) 1 hotel for sailors. 2 seamen's home.
sjø'mann/skap *+-et/*-en* seamanship.
+**sjø'manns/kirke** *-a/-en* (=*/**kyrkje**) Norwegian church for sailors in a foreign port (also contains reading room, etc.).
sjø'manns/skole *-n* school educating deck officers for the merchant marine.
sjø'manns/språk *-et* nautical language, sailors' language.
sjø'manns/stand *-en/*-et* sailors as a vocational or social group.
sjø'manns/trøye *-a* pea jacket, reefer.
sjø'manns/vals *-en* lively waltz (often with text that deals with sailors and life at sea).
sjø'manns/vise *-a* song about sailors and life at sea.
sjø'/merke *-t, pl +-r/*-* landmark, seamark; beacon.
sjø'/mil *-a, pl* - geographical mile, nautical mile.
sjø'/mål *-et* 1 ocean level. 2 line between water and land at high tide. 3 coastal dialect.
sjø'/offise'r *-en* naval officer.
sjø'/orm *-en* sea serpent.
+**sjø'/pinnsvin** *-et* (=*/**piggsvin**) *zool.* sea porcupine, sea urchin (class Echinoidea).
sjø'/pølse *-a zool.* holothurian, sea cucumber (order Holothuroidea).
sjø'/reise *-a/+-en* (sea) voyage.
sjø'/rett *-en* maritime law.
sjø'/rokk *-et* spray of sea during storm.
+**sjø'/røver** *-en, pl -e* (=***-ar**) pirate.
+**sjø'/røveri** *-et* piracy.
sjø'/same *-n* Lapp living on the coast as a fisherman.
+**sjø'/sette** *V -satte* (=*/**setje**) launch (boat, ship).

sjø'/sjuk *A* (=+/syk) seasick.
sjø'/sjuke *-n* seasickness.
sjø'/skadd *A -/*-skadt* damaged at sea.
sjø'/slag *-et* 1 naval action, sea battle. 2 *fam.* noisy, hard-drinking party.
+sjø'/speil *-et* (=*/**spegel**) mirror-like surface of calm sea.
sjø'/sprøyt *-en/+-et* spray of sea, sea splash.
sjø'/sterk *A* a good sailor (=not easily seasick).
sjø'/stjerne *-a zool.* sea star, starfish (order Asteroidea).
sjø'strids/krefter *pl* naval forces.
sjø'/støvel *-elen, pl -ler* seaboot; rubber boot.
+sjø'/syk *A* cf **/sjuk**
+sjø'/syke *-n* cf **/sjuke**
sjø'/territo'rium *-iet, pl +-ier/*-ium* territorial waters.
sjø'/tokt *-et* cruise.
sjø'/trygd *-a/+-en* marine insurance.
sjø'/trøye *-a* pea jacket, reefer.
sjø'/tunge [/tonge] *-a zool.* a kind of flounder (Glyptocephalus cynoglossus).
sjø'/ulk *-en* old salt (sailor).
+sjø'/vant *A* - (=*/**van(d)**) used to the sea, at home on a ship.
sjø'/vatn *-et* (=+/**vann**) seawater.
sjø'/veg *-en* (=+/**vei**) sea route: **s-en til India** the s- to I-.
sjø'/veges *Av* by sea, by the sea route.
sjø'/veik *A* easily seasick.
+sjø'/verts *Av* by sea, by the sea route.
sjø'/vær *-et* 1 good weather at sea. 2 *dial.* fishing trip at sea.
+sjø'/ørret *-en* cf **/aure**
***sjå'1** *-et* fair, esp. cattle show.
***sjå'2** *V ser, såg, sett/sedd* cf **se**
***sjå'ande** *A* - 1 worth seeing. 2 which can be seen, visible. 3: **det er s- til det** it looks like it, it appears so.
***sjå'ar** *-en* cf **seer**
sjåfø'r *-en* 1 driver. 2 chauffeur.
+sjåfø'r/lærer *-en, pl -e* (=***-ar**) driving instructor.
sjåfø'r/skole *-n* driving school.
***sjå'leg** *A* - 1 visible. 2 considerable, noticeable; outstanding.
***sjå'/sam** *A* (of place, spot) affording a good view.
sjåssé *-en* cf **chaussé**
sjåvinis'me *-n* chauvinism.
sjåvinis't *-en* chauvinist.
sjåvinis'tisk *A* - chauvinistic.
sk.=**skilling**
s.k.=**+såkalt/*såkalla**
ska'1 *V -dde* (=**skade2**) damage, hurt, injure; be bad for: **s- ens rykte** damage one's reputation; **s- sin sak** damage one's cause; **det kan aldri s-, det s-der aldri, det s-der ikke (å forsøke)** it doesn't hurt, it does no harm (to try); **tørken har s-dd åkeren** the drought has been bad for the field; **s- seg** hurt oneself; **han s-dde seg på en sag** he hurt himself on a saw; **s-dd** (or **+s-det**) casualty, injured person.
°ska'2 *pr of* **skulle**
skabb' *-et* 1 mange, scale, scabies; the itch. 2 *bot.* dandelion (Taraxacum officinale).
skab'bet(e) *A* - 1 mangy, scabby. 2 morally inferior, trashy: **et s- får** a black sheep.
skabb'/hals *-en archaic* blockhead, dunce; rascal.
+-ska'belig *A* - cf **-skapelig**
skabelo'n *-en* 1 pattern, templet; gauge. 2 form, shape.
skaberakk' *-et* monstrosity.
skabil'ken *-et, pl -/+-er* fright, scarecrow.
***ska'ḍ-** *pf* extremely, very, e.g. in **s-/god, s-/sterk.**
ska'de1 [*ska'e] *-n* 1 damage, harm, injury: **av s- blir man klok** experience is the best teacher; **gjøre s- på** damage; ***gå (ut) på s-** lead to injury, go wrong; **komme til s-** be damaged, injured; **ta s- av** be damaged by; **ta s- på forstanden (sjelen)** be damaged mentally (morally); **han har ingen s- av å** it won't do him any harm, it won't hurt him to; (often positive) **du kan uten s- være litt høfligere** it wouldn't hurt you to be a little more polite. 2 detriment, loss: **til (stor) s- for** to the (great) detriment of. 3 misfortune: **(det er) s- at** (it's) too bad that; **det er stor s-** it's a great pity; **jeg kom i s- for å** I had the misfortune, was unfortunate enough to, made the mistake of.
ska'de2 [*ska'e] *V -de* cf **ska1**
ska'de/bot [*ska'e/] *-a* compensation, indemnification; *jur.* damages.
***ska'ḍe/dauḍe** *-n* tragic death (=a death which represents a great loss, esp. to the community).
ska'de/dyr [*ska'e/] *-et* pest, vermin; beast of prey.
+ska'de/forsik'ring *-en* casualty insurance.
ska'de/fri [*ska'e/] *A -tt* 1 uninjured. 2 *merc.* claim free (e.g. insurance policy on which no claims have been submitted).
+ska'de/fro *A* malicious, rejoicing in the misfortune of others.
+ska'defro/het *-en* malice, malicious pleasure.
+ska'de/fryd *-en* malice, malicious pleasure.
***ska'ḍe/gleḍe** *-a* malice, malicious pleasure.
***ska'ḍe/laus** *A* cf **skades/løs**
+ska'de/lidd *A* - injured: **den s-e** the injured party; the claimant, insured.
ska'de/lidende [*ska'e/liande] *A* - injured: **den s-** the injured party; the claimant, insured.
ska'delig *A* - detrimental, harmful, injurious: **en s- innflytelse** a pernicious influence.
+ska'des/erstat'ning *-en* compensation, indemnity; *jur.* damages: **kreve s- av en** sue sby for damages.
+ska'de/skutt *A* - maimed; wounded (without being killed).
+ska'des/løs *A* 1 unharmed, uninjured. 2 indemnified: **holde en s- for et tap** compensate, reimburse sby for a loss.
+ska'det *A* - cf **ska1**
ska'de/verk [*ska'e/] *-et* harm.
skaf'fe1 *V -a/+-et* 1 get (hold of), obtain, procure: **s- en noe** get sth for sby; **s- av veien** get rid of; **s- til veie** arrange for, procure; **s- seg** get (for oneself), gain, win; **s- seg respekt (venner)** win respect (friends); **s- seg av med** get rid of. 2 cause (sorrow, trouble, unpleasantness). 3 *archaic* do (=**bestille2**): **han har ingenting med det å s-** he has nothing to do with it.
skaf'fe2 *V -a/+-et naut.* eat.
+skaf'fe/tøy *-et naut.* tableware.
skafott' *-et, pl +-er/*-* scaffold.
skaf't *-et* 1 handle, shaft, shank; (boot) leg. 2 *bot.* scape. 3 *zool.* rachis.
skaf'te/støvel *-elen, pl -ler* jackboot, top boot.
***ska'g** *-et* exposed spot.
***ska'ge1** *-n* cape, promontory.
***ska'ge2** *V -a* project, protrude.
Ska'gen *Pln* The Skaw.
Ska'gerak' *Pln* Skagerrak.
ska'k *-et* (powerful) jolt, shaking.
***ska'kal** *A* jarring, jolting.
***ska'ke1** *V skjek, skok, skjeke/-i* cf **skake2**
ska'ke2 *V -a/+-et* (=**skake1**) 1 shake; jolt, tremble: **s- av sted** bump along (on a rough road); **s- opp** jar, shake up, unsettle (emotions); **s- på seg** shake oneself (e.g. a dog); **hun gråt så hun s-et** she wept so much she shook, trembled; **vinden s-et huset** the wind shook the house *dial.* **s- sammen** strike together (e.g. the hands). 2 *naut.* overhaul (a tackle). 3 *naut.* (of the wind) come round, shift.
skakk' *A skakt* askew, crooked; sagging, twisted: **et s-t smil** a twisted smile; **ha et s-t syn på tingene** have a warped viewpoint.
skak'ke1 *N*: **på s-** aslant, tilted; **gå på s-** go badly.
skak'ke2 *V -a/+-et* slant, tilt: **s- på hodet** cock one's head.
skakk'/kjø'rt *A* - (=*/**køyrd**) 1 inclining, (e.g. of a horse) pulling to one side. 2 *fig.* perverse, wrongheaded.
skakk'/mynt *A* - wry-mouthed.
skak't *nt of* **skakk**
ska'l1 *-et* (=+**skall**) 1 shell (of eggs, mussels, nuts, etc.): **er perlen vekk, hva gjelder s-et?** if the pearl is gone, of what value is the s-? (Ibsen); **trekke seg inn i sitt s-** *fig.* withdraw into oneself. 2 peel (e.g. of bananas, oranges), rind (of melons, pumpkins, etc.), skin (of apples).
skal'2 *pr of* **skulle, *skule2**
ska'la *-en* scale; dial: **i forminsket, stor s-** on a reduced, large scale.
skal'd *-en hist.* skald (court poet in Old Norse times); (also *lit.*) poet.
skal'de/dikt *-et* skaldic poem.
skal'de/kvad *-et* skaldic lay.
***skal'de/kveḍe** *-t* minstrelsy, skaldic art.
***skal'dre** *V -a* clatter, rattle.
skal'd/skap *-en* minstrelsy, skaldic art.
ska'l/dyr *-et zool.* shellfish.
***ska'le** *V -a* cf **skalle3**
ska'l/frukt *-a bot.* achene.
skal'k1 *-en* 1 heel (of a loaf of bread or cheese). 2 bowler (hat).
skal'k2 *-en* rogue, scoundrel.
+skal'k/aktig *A* - mischievous, roguish.
skal'ke *V -a/+-et*: **s- lukene** batten down the hatches.
***skal'ke/herming** *-a* burlesque, parody.
+skal'ke/skjul *-et* (=*/**skjol**) blind, camouflage: **tjene som (til) s-** serve as c-.
skal'ke/strek *-en/*-et* mischievous prank.
***skal'ket(e)** *A* - mischievous, roguish.
+skall' *-et* cf **skal1**
***skal'la** *A* - cf **skallet(e)**
+skall'/dyr *-et* cf **skal/**
skal'le1 *-n* 1 cranium, forehead, skull; pate. 2 Lapplander's moccasin.
skal'le2 *V -a/+-et* butt, smash one's head (into sby, sth).
+skal'le3 *V -a/-et* (=***skale**) peel, scale (**av** off): **s- av seg** peel off, shed.
+skal'le/panne *-n* baldpate.
+skal'let(e) *A* - (=***skalla**) bald, baldheaded.
+skall'/frukt *-a/-en* cf **skal/**
skalmei'e *-a/-en mus.* shalm, shawm (reed flute).
skal'p *-en* scalp.
skalpe're *V -te* scalp.
skal'p/jeger *-en, pl -e* scalp hunter.
skal'te *V -a/+-et*: **s- og valte med noe** do as one likes with sth.
skal'v *pt of* **skjelve**
skam' *-ma/+-men* 1 disgrace, ignominy, shame: **det er s- å** it's a s- to; **det er s- av deg** you ought to be ashamed; **det er (både) synd og s-** it's really too bad; **fy for s-!** shame!; **føle s- over** be ashamed of; **gjøre s- på en** outdo sby, put sby to shame; **(med) s- å si** to tell the truth, to one's shame. 2 sense of decency: **bite hodet av all s-** disregard the dictates of common decency; **er det ikke s- i ham? har han ikke s- i livet?** has he no sense of decency?; **for s-s skyld** out of

+ Bokmål; * Nynorsk; ° Dialect.
After letter: ' stress (Acc. 1); ' tone, stress (Acc. 2); ˙ length.
Below letter: . not pronounced.

common decency; **han eier ikke s-** he has no sense of decency. 3 (as mild oath): **det blir du s- nødt til** well, you'll just have to; **han har s- rett** I have to admit he's right; **s- ta deg** hang you, anyway. (Cf also **skamme.**)

skam'/bein *-et anat.* pubic bone.

+**skam'/bud** *-et* (=*/**bod**) ridiculous bid, offer.

skam'/djerv *A* shamefully bold.

***skam'/fare** *V -fer, for, fare/-i* cf **skamfere**

skam'/ferd [*/fær] *-a* disaster, failure.

+**skamfe're** *V -te* (=**skam/fare**) disfigure, maim; ruin, spoil.

skam'/file *V -te naut.* abrade, chafe.

skam'/flekk *-en* blot, stain (on one's honor, reputation).

***skam'/for** *pt of* **-fare**

skam'/full *A* ashamed, shamefaced.

+**skam'/følelse** *-n* feeling, sense of shame.

skam'/gød *A* excellent, extremely good.

skam'/hogge *V infl as* **hogge** 1 damage, spoil (e.g. forest, trees) by excessive cutting, felling; ruin, spoil (woodwork) by faulty cutting. 2 cut severely, maim by cutting (e.g. one's hand, foot).

skam'/kjensle *-a* feeling, sense of shame.

skam'/kjøp *-et* steal, tremendous bargain.

skam'/laus *A* (=+/**løs**) brazen, shameless, wanton.

***skam'leg** *A* - cf **skammelig**

+**skam'løs/het** *-a/-en* brazenness, shamelessness, wantonness.

***skam'/løyse** *-a* =**skamløshet**

+**skam'me**[1] *N*: **bli (stå) til s-** be put to shame, be outdone; **gjøre en til s-** put sby to shame, overshadow sby; **gjøre noe til s-** overshadow sth (e.g. sby's accomplishments); give the lie to sth, prove sth to be false, unfounded (e.g. fears, hopes, sby's trust); **(tilstå) med s-** (confess) shamefully, with a feeling of shame.

skam'me[2] *V -a/+-et* 1: **s- seg** be ashamed (of oneself); **skam deg!** shame on you!. 2: **s- en ut** scold sby sharply, take sby to task.

skam'me/krok *-en*: **sette et barn i s-en** put a child in the corner (as punishment), make a child stand in the corner.

skam'mel *-elen, pl skamler* (foot)-stool.

skam'melig *A* - (=***skamleg**) disgraceful, scandalous, shameful: **det er s-** it's an outrage, a shame, it's shameful.

+**skam'/plett** *-en* blot, stain (on one's honor, reputation).

skam'/pris *-en* ridiculously low price.

skam'/rose *V -te/*-a* praise fulsomely.

+**skam'/rødme** *-n* blush (with shame).

skam'/skjelle *V -skjelte* abuse, revile scandalously.

skam'/skyte *V infl as* **skyte** maim, wound (without killing).

skam'/slå *V -slo, -slått/*-slege/*-i* beat severely, thrash.

skam'/vett *-et* feeling, sense of shame.

skand. =**skandinavisk**

skanda'l/avi's *-a/+-en* scandal sheet.

skanda'le *-n* disgrace, scandal; scandalous scene: **der har vi s-n!** just what I expected! that does it!; **gjøre s-** cause a scandal; make a scene.

skandalise're *V -te* 1 disgrace, scandalize. 2 compromise (by involving one in a scandal).

skandalø's *A* disgraceful, scandalous.

+**skan'/dekk** *-et naut.* plank-sheer.

skande're *V -te* scan (poetry).

skandina'v *-en* Scandinavian.

Skandina'via *Pln* Scandinavia.

skandina'visk *A* - Scandinavian.

skandinavis'me *-n* Scandinavianism (movement for closer cooperation among Scandinavians).

skandinavis't *-en* adherent, supporter of Scandinavianism.

+**skan'd/skrift** *-et* lampoon, libel.

skan'k *+-en/*-a, pl *skjenker* leg, shank: **røre s-ene** *pop.* shake a leg.

skann'/tile *+-n/*-t* cf **skarn/**

skan'se[1] *-n* 1 *mil.* earthwork, entrenchment: **være den siste på s-n** be the last one to yield. 2 *naut.* quarterdeck.

skan'se[2] *V -a/+-et mil.* construct earthworks, entrenchments.

skan'se/kledning *+-en/*-a naut.* bulwark.

skan'se/verk *-et mil.* fortification consisting of a series of earthworks.

***skan't** *-en* 1 yardstick. 2 (measured) part, portion.

skan'te *V -a/+-et* 1 measure (out). 2 fit, square, trim (lumber).

skan'/tile *-t* cf **skarn/**

+**ska'p**[1] *-et* (=***skåp**) cabinet, closet, cupboard: **hun bestemmer hvor s-et skal stå** she wears the pants in that (the) family.

ska'p[2] *-et* form, shape.

-skap *-en/-et* substantival suffix, e.g. **bror/s-; mester/s-; viten/s-.**

+**ska'p/aktig** *A* - affected, pretentious.

+**ska'p/drikker** *-en, pl -e* one who drinks on the sly.

ska'pe *V -a/-te* 1 create, form, make; bring about, cause: **s- etter** copy, imitate; **s- om** transform; **s- til** form, make into; **i begynnelsen s-te Gud himmelen og jorden** in the beginning God created the heaven and the earth (Gen. 1, 1). 2: **s- seg** act affectedly, put on an act, show off; **ikke skap deg sånn** stop carrying on, showing off like that. 3: **s-t** created, shaped; **vel s-t** shapely, well-built; **være som s-t for (til å)** be cut out for (to); **det er ikke mening s-t i det** it doesn't make any sense at all; **det var ikke råd s-t å** it was utterly impossible to; **jeg forstår ikke det (guds) s-te ord av det** I don't understand a single word of it.

+**ska'pelig** *A* - cf **skaplig**

+**-ska'pelig** *A* - adjectival suffix, e.g. **sel/s-; viten/s-.**

+**ska'pelse** *-n* 1 *eccl.* creation, formation (e.g. of the world). 2 form, shape.

+**ska'pelses/akt** *-en* act of creation.

+**ska'pelses/histo'rie** *-n bibl.* story of creation.

ska'pende *A* - 1 creative. 2: **ikke det (guds) s- grann** not the least thing.

+**ska'per** *-en, pl -e* (=*-**ar**) creator, maker, originator: **S-en** God, the Creator.

+**ska'per/evne** *-n* (=*-**ar/**) creative ability, creativeness.

+**ska'per/glede** *-n* (=*-**ar/**) enthusiasm for, joy of creating.

+**ska'peri** *-et* affectation, pretentiousness.

+**ska'per/kraft** *-en* (=*-**ar/**) creative ability, power.

ska'per/makt *-a/+-en* (=*-**ar/**) creative ability, power.

+**ska'per/verk** *-et* (=*-**ar/**) work of creation: **Guds s-** the Creation.

***ska'ping** *-a* cf **skapelse**

ska'p/laus *A* - 1 formless, shapeless. 2 deformed, misshapen.

ska'plig *A* - (=+**skapelig**) 1 comfortable, suitable, well-arranged. 2 proper, well-behaved.

***ska'p/løyse** *-a* 1 formlessness. 2 deformity.

***ska'pnad** *-en* 1 appearance, form, shape; figure. 2 condition, order.

ska'pning *-en* 1 creature. 2 creation: **s-ens herre** lord of c- (=man).

+**ska'p/sprenger** *-en, pl -e* safecracker.

ska'r[1] *-et* 1 cleft, cut; gap, pass (in mountains). 2 chip, scratch (in wood, glass, etc.); nick. *3 loss.

ska'r[2] *-et* burnt part of a wick.

ska'r[3] *pt of* ***skjere**[3], +**skjære**[3]

skarabé *-en* 1 *zool.* scarab (Scarabaeus sacer). 2 scarab (=gem cut in the form of a beetle).

***ska'rd** *-et* cf **skar**[1]

***ska'rde** *V -a* 1 decrease, diminish. 2 nick, notch.

ska'rdet(e) *A* - 1 full of clefts, (of a mountain range) jagged. 2 (of wood, glass, etc.) chipped.

ska're[1] *-n* band, flock, multitude (av of).

ska're[2] *-n* (snow) crust.

***ska're**[3] *V -a* 1 pile up, stack. 2 join (timber). 3 rake together (a fire). 4 snuff (wick). 5: **s- seg** (of snow) crust.

ska're/føre *-t* hard (sleighing, walkable) snow.

ska're/snø *-en* crusted snow.

***skar'k** *-en* nag.

***skar'ke** *V -a* 1 walk with tedious slowness. 2 become decrepit, infirm.

***skar'ken** *A -e/-i, pl -ne* decrepit, infirm.

+**skarla'gen** *-et* (=***skarlak**) scarlet.

+**skarla'gen/rød** *A* scarlet.

+**skarla'gens/feber** *-en* scarlet fever.

***ska'r/lak** *-et* cf **skarlagen**

***ska'rlaks/feber** *-en* cf **skarlagens/**

***ska'rlaks/klede** *-t* scarlet cloth.

ska'rn *-et* 1 dirt, excrement, filth: **dra en opp av s-et** raise sby from the gutter. 2 beast, brute (person).

+**ska'rn/aktig** *A* - evil, wicked.

ska'rn/tile *-t* manure trough (space between lines of stalls in a stable).

skar'p *A* 1 sharp (corner, edge, knife, mind, tone of voice, tongue, etc.): **s- ammunisjon** live ammunition; **s- konkurranse** keen competition; **s- ost** strong, s- cheese; **en s- kritikk (dom)** a severe criticism (sentence); **en s- lukt** an acrid smell; **et s-t lys** a clear, blinding light; **en s- stemme (skrik)** a piercing voice (scream); **en s- vind** a biting wind; **skyte med s-t** fire live ammunition; *fig.* let him have it; **trekke en s- grense** make a clear distinction; **være s- av seg** be bright, sharp. 2 acute, keen, sensitive (sensory organs): **ha et s-t blikk for** have a keen eye for; **et s-t hode** a keen mind; **høre s-t etter** listen intently to; **se s-t på** look intently, searchingly at.

skar'p/ladd *A -/*-ladt* loaded (gun with live cartridges).

skar'p/lendt *A* - sandy (soil).

+**skar'p/retter** *-en* (=*-**ar**) executioner; hangman.

+**skar'p/seiler** *-en, pl -e* (=*/**seglar**) fast sailer (ship).

+**skar'p/sindig** *A* - clever, discerning; shrewd, sharp.

+**skarpsin'dig/het** *-en* acumen, cleverness, shrewdness.

skar'p/sinn *-et* acumen, cleverness, shrewdness.

skar'p/skodd *A -/*-skott* 1 roughshod. 2 *fig.* incisive, overwhelming (e.g. argument); extremely competent, proficient (person).

+**skar'p/skytter** *-en, pl -e* (=*-**ar**) sharpshooter.

+**skar'p/skåren** *A -ent, pl -ne* (=*/**skoren**) 1 sharp cut (e.g. planks). 2 clear-cut (e.g. profile): **et s-t ansikt** a rugged face.

skar'p/slipt *A* - sharp-edged.

skar'p/synt *A* - eagle-eyed, sharp-sighted.

***skar're**[1] *-n* nag.

***skar're**[2] *V -a* 1 walk falteringly, unsteadily. 2 be feeble in body and health.

skar're[3] *V -a/+-et* 1 (e.g. of a grouse) make a whirring noise. 2 burr, use a uvular r: **s- på r'en** (the same). 3 *dial.* clear one's throat noisily, hawk.

skar'v[1] *-en zool.* cormorant (Phalacrocorax carbo).

skar'v[2] *-en* rogue, scoundrel.

skar'v[3] *-et* stony mountain terrain.

skar'v[4] *-et dial.* rubbish, trash.

***skar'val** *A* fragile; frail, infirm.

***skar've**[1] *V -a* 1 liquidate, settle (an

account, a claim). 2 be feeble, infirm.

skar've[2] *A* - miserable, worthless, wretched.

skar've- *Pf* worthless, e.g. **s-/gamp; s-/jente.**

***skar've/dom** *-men/-en* meanness, misery, wretchedness.

***skar've/ferd** [/fær] *-a* failure, unsuccessful expedition.

***skar'veleg** *A* miserable, worthless; rascally, scoundrelly.

skar've/pakk *-en* rabble, riffraff.

skar've/strek *-en* rascally, scurvy trick.

skar've/stykke *-t* rascally act, deed.

skar'v/kjeft *-en* abusive, coarse language, invective.

skar'v/øks *-a* adze.

ska't *-et* 1 top, toppings of a tree. 2 (sea) shelf.

ska'te[1] *-a zool.* skate (genus Raja).

***ska'te**[2] *-a zool.* magpie (Pica pica).

ska'te[3] *-n* desiccated tree (without branches).

ska'te[4] *V -a/+-et* prune, top a tree.

***ska'ten** *A -e/-i, pl -ne* narrow (toward the top).

skatoll' *-et, pl -/+-er* escritoire, secretary, writing desk.

skatt' *-en* 1 treasure: **samle eder s-er i himmelen** lay up for yourselves t-s in heaven (Matt. 6, 20). 2: **min s-** my darling. 3 excise, tax(es): **legge s- på** impose, place a tax on; **utskrive s-** levy taxes.

+skatt'/bar *A* assessable, taxable.

skat'te *V -a/+-et* 1 assess, tax. 2 pay taxes (**til** to). 3 appreciate, cherish, prize.

+skat'te/ansettelse *-n* assessment.

+skat'te/borger *-en, pl -e* (=***-ar**) taxpayer.

skat'te/byrde *+-n/*-a* burden of taxation, tax burden.

+skat'te/foged *-en* (=**+/fogd, */fut**) (income) tax collector.

skat'te/fri *A -tt* tax-exempt.

***skat'te/fritak** *-et* tax exemption.

***skat'te/fritaking** *-a* tax exemption.

***skat'te/fut** *-en* cf **/foged**

+skat'te/graver *-en, pl -e* (=***-ar**) treasure hunter.

skat'te/klage *-a/+-en* formal appeal for reduction of an excessive assessment or tax.

skat'te/lette *-n* (=**+/lettelse**) tax reduction, relief.

skat'te/likning *-a/+-en* assessment of taxes.

skat'te/liste *-a* tax roll.

+skat'te/nedsettelse *-n* tax reduction.

+skat'te/nekter *-en, pl -e* (=***-ar**) one who refuses to pay taxes.

+skat'te/oppkrever *-en, pl -e* (=***-jar**) tax collector.

skat'te/pliktig *A* - 1 liable for taxes (person). 2 taxable (income, property). 3 (as noun, *pl* **s-e**) taxpayer.

skat'te/prosen't *-en* tax rate.

skat'te/pålegg *-et* 1 taxation. 2 increase of taxation.

+skat'te/seddel *-elen, pl -sedler* (=***/setel**) tax bill.

+skat'te/snyter *-en, pl -e* (=***-ar**) (income) tax evader, tax dodger.

+skat'te/snyteri *-et* (income) tax evasion, tax dodging.

skat'te/svikt *+-en/+-et/*-a* shortage in tax revenues (=below estimate).

skat'te/takst *-en* 1 valuation of real property (by tax assessors). 2 assessed valuation.

skat'te/trekk *-et* withholding tax.

skat'te/trykk *-et* burden, pressure of taxation.

skat'te/vesen *-et* tax authorities; revenue service.

+skat'te/yter *-en, pl -e* cf **skatt/**

skat'te/år *-et* fiscal (tax) year.

skatt'/kammer *-et* 1 treasury. 2 *fig.* goldmine, storehouse (e.g. of information).

skatt'/land *-et hist.* tributary land, colony.

+skatt'/legge *V -la, -lagt* (=***-je**) assess, tax.

+skatt'/likning *-a/-en* (=**+/ligning**) cf **skatte/**

+skatt'/mester *-en, pl -e* (=***/meister**) treasurer.

+skatt'/seddel *-elen, pl -sedler* (=***/setel**) cf **skatte/**

skatt'/skyldig *A* - liable for payment of taxes.

+skatt'/yter *-en, pl -e* (=***-ar**) taxpayer.

+skatt'/øre *-n* (=***/øyre**) tax rate.

Skat'val *Pln* twp, Nord-Trøndelag.

°skau' *-en* cf **skog**

Skau'gum· *Pln* private estate of King Olav, in Asker.

Skau'n *Pln* twp, Sør-Trøndelag.

skau't[1] *-et* head covering, kerchief (for women and children).

skau't[2] *-et* (=**+skjøt**) *naut.* sheet (rope that regulates angle of a sail).

skau't[3] *pt of* **skyte**

skau'v *pt of* **skuve, skyve**

ska'v *-et* 1 scrapings, shavings. 2 peeled bark used as emergency fodder.

skavan'k *-en* defect, flaw, weakness: **ha sine s-er** have one's shortcomings.

***ska've**[1] *V skov, skove/-t* cf **skave**[2]

ska've[2] *V +-de/+-et/*-a* (=**skave**[1]) cut, scrape, whittle: **s- bark** strip bark.

ska'/vind *-en* damaging wind.

ska'v/kniv *-en* scraper; spokeshave.

skav'l *-en* 1 scraper; spokeshave. 2 snowdrift. 3 breaker, long crested wave.

skav'le *V -a/+-et* 1: **s- seg** (of snow) accumulate in steep drifts. 2 (of waves) break.

skav'let(e) *A* - 1 drifty (snow). 2 crested (waves).

Skeds/mo [sjess'/] *Pln* twp, Akershus.

skei[1] [sjei'] *-a* (=**+skje**[1]) 1 spoon: **gi en noe inn med s-er** spoonfeed sby; **ta s-en i en annen hånd** mend one's ways. 2 casting ladle. 3 weaver's reed. 4 spoon (lure).

skei[2] [sjei'] *-et* cf **skeid**

+skei/binder [sjei'/] *-en, pl -e* (=***-ar**) person who makes the weaver's reed in a loom.

skei/blad [sjei'/] *-et* bowl of a spoon.

skeid [sjeid] *-et* 1 race; course, heat: ***i eitt s-** without stopping. 2 horse race. *3 *educ.* course (**i** in). 4 *hist.* horse fight.

skeie[1] [sjei'e] *V -a/+-et/+-de* 1: **s- ut av veien** take the wrong course, direction. 2: **s- ut** *fig.* kick over the traces, strike out; lead a dissolute life.

skeie[2] [sjei'e] *V -a/+-et/+-de* 1: **s- ut** discharge, dismiss; cashier. 2 *naut.* knock off (work).

skei/full [sjei'/] *en* (table)spoonful.

skei'/leit *-et* (=**+skylight**) skylight.

skei/mat [sjei'/] *-en* food eaten with a spoon.

skein [sjei'n] *pt of* **+skinne**[1], ***skine**

skeine [sjei'ne] *V -te* deviate, swerve, veer.

skeis [sjei's] *A* good-for-nothing, worthless.

***skeise**[1] [sjei'se] *-a* skate.

***skeise**[2] [sjei'se] *V -a* skate.

***skeise/rennar** [sjei'se/] *-en* skater.

skei/sluk [sjei'/] *-en* spoonbait.

skeit [sjei't] *pt of* **skite**

skeiv [sjei'v] *A* crooked, lopsided; oblique, slanting; distorted (thoughts, viewpoint, etc.): **s-e hæler** heels worn down on one side; **en s- stilling** an awkward position; **en s- vinkel** an acute or obtuse angle; **komme i et s-t forhold til en** find oneself in an awkward relationship to sby; **la tingene gå sin s-e gang** let things slide; **se med s-e øyne på, se s-t til** look askance at, with jaundiced eye at; **smile s-t** smile wryly. (Cf also **skeive.**)

***skei/vatn** [sjei'/] *-et* cf **skje/vann**

skeiv/beint [sjei'v/] *A* - bowlegged.

skeive[1] [sjei've] *N*: **på s-** askew, crooked; **gå på s-** turn out badly, go wrong; **legge hodet på s-** cock one's head.

skeive[2] [sjei've] *V -a/+-et* make crooked, set at an angle; stagger: **s- skoene (hælene)** wear heels down on one side; **s- med** place at an angle, cock (e.g. one's head); **s- til** look sideways at, look askance at.

***skeiv/ferd** [sjei'v/fær] *-a* 1 unlucky journey. 2 misfortune.

***skeivle** [sjei'vle] *V -a* bring out of joint, unhinge.

***skeivleg** [sjei'vleg] *A* - unfortunate, unlucky.

***skeivne** [sjei'vne] *V -a* become distorted.

***skeiv/syn** [sjei'v/] *-a/-et* distorted view.

+skeiv/øyd [sjei'v/] *A* - (=***/øygd**) slant-eyed.

skep'sis *-en* scepticism.

+skep'tiker *-en, pl -e* (=***-ar**) sceptic.

skeptisis'me *-n* scepticism.

skep'tisk *A* - sceptical.

sket'sj *-en* 1 sketch. 2 skit.

ski'[1] *-a, pl -/-er* ski: **gå, løpe, stå på s-** ski.

+ski'[2] *-a* cf **skie**

+ski'b *-et* cf **skip**

ski'/bakke *-n* ski hill.

+skib'/brudd *-et* shipwreck: **lide s-** be shipwrecked; *fig.* fail in life, be ruined, go on the rocks.

+skib'/brudden *A -ent, pl -brudne* shipwrecked; castaway; *fig.* on the rocks, ruined.

ski'/binding *-a/+-en* (ski) bindings.

+skid'den *A -ent, pl skidne* cf **skitten**

ski'e *-a* (=**+ski**[2]) 1 sawed and split piece of firewood. 2 wooden fence rail.

Skien [sje'en] *Pln* city, Telemark.

skif'er *-en* schist, shale, slate: **tekke med s-** slate (e.g. a roof).

skif'er/brott *-et* (=**+/brudd**) slate quarry.

skif'er/stein *-en* slate.

skif'er/tak *-et* slate roof.

skif'ret(e) *A* - slaty.

skif'rig *A* - slaty.

skif't *-et* 1 change, changing (e.g. of clothes, seasons). 2 lap (of a journey). 3 (work) shift.

skif't/arbeid *-et* shift work.

skif'te[1] *-t, pl +-r/*-* 1 change, changing (e.g. of clothes, government, routine, etc.). 2 lap (of a journey); *archaic* relay station. 3 (work) shift. 4 settlement of a deceased person's estate; distribution, division of an inheritance: **holde s- (i et bo)** settle an estate. 5 *arch.* course (=layer of bricks in a wall). 6 *agr.* course, shift.

skif'te[2] *V -a/+-et* 1 change (clothes, color, name, trains), exchange (glances, words), shift (gears): **s- fot** shift from one foot to the other; **s- ham** (of snakes) slough the skin; **s- tenner** cut one's second teeth; **s- inn** put in operation (as a replacement); **s- om** alter, change; **s- over i (til)** change to; **s- på** alternate, make a change; change diapers of; **s- noe ut** replace sth; **s-es om, til (å gjøre noe)** take turns (doing sth). 2 *naut.* move (cargo), shift (the helm). 3 assign, divide (among); administer, settle (an estate): **s- ut** partition (**til** among). 4: **s-ende** changeable, changing, varying: **s-ende skydekke** variable cloud cover; **s-ende tider** changing times; **med s-ende hell** with varying success.

+skif'te/behan'dling *-a/-en jur.* administration of an estate.

skif'te/bruk *-et* crop rotation.

+ Bokmål; * Nynorsk; ° Dialect.
After letter: ' stress (Acc. 1); ' tone, stress (Acc. 2); · length.
Below letter: . not pronounced.

skif'te/forret'ning *-a/⁺-en jur.* administration of a decedent estate.
***skif'te/laus** *A* monotonous, uniform.
skif'te/lokomoti'v *-et, pl -/⁺-er* switching locomotive.
skif'te/nøkkel *-elen, pl -nøkler* 1 monkey wrench, pipe wrench. 2 (typewriter) shift key.
skif'te/rett *-en* 1 *jur.* law pertaining to management of decedent estates. 2 *jur.* probate court.
skif'te/samling *-a/⁺-en jur.* meeting of the beneficiaries and heirs of a decedent estate (presided over by the administrator).
skif'te/spor *-et* (railroad) siding.
***skif'te/straum** *-en elec.* alternating current.
skif'te/takst *-en jur.* official valuation of the property of a decedent estate.
skif'te/tast *-en* (typewriter) shift key.
skif'te/vis *Av* alternately, by turns.
⁺**skif'tning** *-en* alteration, change; nuance.
ski'/føre *-t* skiing conditions.
ski'/føring *-a/⁺-en* skiing technique.
ski'/ga'rd *-en* rail fence.
ski'/heis *-en* ski lift.
ski'/hopp *-et* ski jump.
⁺**ski'/hopper** *-en, pl -e* (=***-ar**) ski jumper.
ski'/hæl *-en* ski boot heel (concave to permit fastening of bindings).
ski'/idrett *-en* ski sport.
ski'/kjelke *-n* sled with skis as runners.
skikk' *-en* 1 custom, practice, usage: **s- og bruk** accepted practice, customary; **ha for (til) s-** be in the habit of, be used to; **som s- er** as is customary. 2 (good) condition, order: **få i s-, få s- på** set in order, get in shape; **holde s- på** keep in order, keep under control; **så det har s-** with a vengeance. 3 *dial.* form, shape (=**skikkelse**).
***skik'ka** *A* - cf **skikket**
skik'ke[1] *V -a/⁺-et* 1: **s- seg** behave, conduct oneself; improve (one's conduct); **s- seg i** accept (a situation); **s- seg til** be suitable for. 2: **det s-er seg** it is proper, seemly.
skik'ke[2] *V -a/⁺-et* send: **s- bud etter** send for.
skik'kelig *A* - 1 decent, good, reasonable: **et s- måltid** a decent meal, a square meal; **få s- lønn** receive decent, reasonable wages; **været var noenlunde s-** the weather was halfway decent. 2 proper, (often=) inoffensive: **en s- fyr** a harmless fellow; **en meget s- pike** a very proper girl; **oppføre seg s-** behave properly.
⁺**skik'kelse** *-n* 1 form, shape, stature: **i s- av** in the form of. 2 character, figure (e.g. in literary work).
⁺**skik'ket** *A* - (=***skikka**) cut out, fitted, suited (**for, til** for): **gjøre seg s- til** qualify oneself for; **mindre s- for** hardly suited for.
***ski'l**[1] *-et* cf **skill**
***ski'l**[2] *-et* cf **skjell**[2]
***ski'l**[3] *et* cf **skjel**[2]
***ski'l**[4] *pr of* **skilje**[2]
***skil'de** *pt of* **skilje**[2]
skil'der/hus *-et* sentry box.
⁺**skilderi'** *-et* picture.
skil'dre *V -a/⁺-et* depict, describe, portray.
skil'dring *-a/⁺-en* description, portrayal (**av** of).
***ski'le** *V -a* distinguish, make out.
***skil'je**[1] *-t* cf **skille**[1]
***skil'je**[2] *V skil, skilde, skilt* cf **skille**[2]
***skil'je/mynt** *-en* cf **skille/**
***skil'je/teikn** *-et* cf **skille/tegn**
⁺**skill'** *-en* (=***skil**[1]) part (in the hair)
⁺**skil'le**[1] *-t* (=***skilje**[1]) division, partition; border, dividing line.
⁺**skil'le**[2] *V skilte* (=***skilje**[2]) 1 part, separate: **s- at** part, separate; **s- en av med, s- en ved noe** rid sby of sth, take sth away from sby; **s- bukkene fra fårene, klinten fra hveten** separate the sheep from the goats (the men from the boys), the chaff from the wheat; **s- fra hverandre** separate; **s- ut** pick out, separate; **s- ut fra hverandre** keep separate; **skilt** divorced. 2: **s- seg** be divorced; (of milk) curdle, separate out; **s- seg av med** part with; **s- seg godt fra (med) det** acquit oneself well, give a good account of oneself; **s- seg ut fra** be different from, stand out among; **s-s (at)** part, separate, be divorced; **la seg s-(s) (fra sin mann, kone)** be divorced (from one's husband, wife). 3 distinguish (**fra** from, **mellom** between), make a difference: **de var så like at de ikke kunne s-s fra hverandre** they were so alike that they couldn't be told apart; ***det er ikkje stort som skil** there's not much difference. 4 concern, matter to: **det s-er ikke deg** (also **skjeller**) it's none of your business; ***det skil ikkje meg** it doesn't matter to me.
***skil'leg** *A* - 1 probable, reasonable. 2 distinct, plain.
⁺**skil'le/linje** *-a/-en* dividing line, line of demarcation.
⁺**skil'le/mur** *-en* partition wall.
⁺**skil'le/mynt** *-en* small change; coins.
⁺**skil'le/tegn** [/tein] *-et* punctuation mark.
skil'le/veg *-en* crossroads: **vi står på s-en** we're standing at a c-.
skil'le/vegg *-en* partition.
⁺**skil'le/vei** *-en* cf **/veg**
skil'ling *-en hist.* coin=1/120 of a *daler* (ab.=1 cent): **spare på s-en og la daleren gå** be penny-wise and pound-foolish; **tjene seg en pen s-** clean up, earn a pretty penny.
skil'linge *V -a/⁺-et*: **s- sammen** club together, raise a subscription.
skil'nad *-en* 1 difference (**på** in). 2 separation (**fra** from).
***skil'ning** *-a* discrimination, distinction; judgment.
***ski'l/o'rd** *-et* condition, restriction, term.
⁺**skil'/padde** *-a/-en* (=***skjel/**) 1 tortoise, turtle: **forloren s-** mock turtle. 2 tortoise shell.
⁺**skil'padde/suppe** *-a* turtle soup: **forloren s-** mock turtle soup.
***ski'ls** *N* cf **skjels**
***ski'ls/dom** *-(m)en* divorce decree.
***ski'ls/mann** *-en, pl -menn(er)* arbitrator.
⁺**skil's/misse** *-n* divorce: **få, oppnå s-** obtain a d- (**fra** from).
⁺**skil'smisse/dom'** *-men* divorce decree.
⁺**skil'smisse/grunn** *-en* grounds for divorce.
***ski'ls/mon(n)** *-en* difference, distinction.
***ski'ls/mål** *-et* divorce; separation.
skil't[1] *-et, pl -/⁺-er* 1 badge (e.g. police badge); plate (e.g. keyhole plate, nameplate, license plate); sign (e.g. advertising sign, street sign). 2 *fig.* cover-up (**for** for).
skil't[2] *pp of* ⁺**skille**[2], ***skilje**[2]
skil'te[1] *V -a/⁺-et*: **s- med** display, parade, show off.
⁺**skil'te**[2] *pt of* **skille**[2]
skil't/vakt *-a/⁺-en mil.* sentry: **stå s-** be on sentry duty.
⁺**ski'/løp** *-et* skiing.
⁺**ski'/løper** *-en, pl -e* (=***/laupar, */løypar**) skier.
ski'/løype *-a* ski track, trail.
ski'/låm *-a* ski track, trail.
skim'le[1] *-a* fish-shaped board used to drive herring into the net.
skim'le[2] *V -a/⁺-et* 1 mold (mould). 2 grow dappled. 3 fish with a **skimle**.
skim'let(e) *A* - 1 moldy. 2 (of horses) roan (gray or red with mixture of white).
skim'mel *-elen, pl skimler* 1 mold. 2 dapple-gray horse.
skim'mer *-et* gleam, shimmer.
skim're *V -a/⁺-et* gleam, glimmer, glint.
skim't *-en/⁺-et* 1 flash, gleam. 2 glimpse.
skim'te *V -a/⁺-et* 1 appear dimly, in vague outline: **s- fram** pierce the darkness. 2 glimpse, make out; see dimly, vaguely. 3 *fig.* have an inkling of.
***ski'n** *-et* cf **skinn**[2]
***ski'n/daud** *A* cf **skinn/død**
***ski'ne** *V skein, -e/-i* cf **skinne**[2]
sking'er *A -ert, pl -re* 1 piercing, strident. 2 (of colors) garish, glaring.
sking're *V -a/⁺-et* screech, shriek, shrill: **s-ende falsk** painfully out of tune; **s-ende farver** loud colors; **s-ende skrik** piercing cry.
***ski'ni** *pp of* **skine**
skin'ke *-a* ham.
⁺**skin'ke/erme** *-t* leg-of-mutton sleeve.
skin'ke/steik *-a* roast (leg of) pork.
skinn'[1] *-et* 1 hide, skin; leather; fur, pelt; (drum) head: **det gylne s-** the Golden Fleece; **en skal ikke selge s-et før bjørnen er skutt** don't count your chickens before they're hatched; **gå ut av sitt gode s-** jump out of one's skin; **han er bare s- og bein** he's just a bag of bones, just skin and bones; **hva i (djevelens, fandens, pokkers) s- og bein!** what the hell!; **holde seg i s-et** control oneself; **løpe (renne) som et tørt (pisket) s-** run like mad; **være redd for sitt s-** be afraid for one's life; **våge sitt s-** risk one's life; **våt til s-et** soaked to the skin. 2 old person: **et stakkars s-** a poor old fellow, woman; **han er et ærlig s-** he's an honest old fellow.
⁺**skinn'**[2] *-et* (=***skin**) 1 gleam, light, shining (of the sun, moon, a lamp, etc.). 2 appearance(s), show: **s-et bedrar** appearances are deceiving; **bevare (redde) s-et** keep up appearances (save face); **gi et s- av** give the appearance, a semblance of; **gi seg et s- av (å gjøre noe)** pretend (to do sth); **ha s-et imot seg** have appearances against one; **med et visst s- av** with a semblance of.
skinn'- *pf* imitation, mock, sham; pseudo-.
⁺**skinn'/angrep** *-et mil.* feint, mock attack.
***skin'nar** *-en* flayer.
⁺**skinnba'rlig** *A* - apparent, manifest, real: **den s-e djevel** the devil incarnate.
⁺**skinn'/besatt'** *A* - fur-trimmed.
⁺**skinn'/bevi's** *-et* specious argument, proof.
⁺**skinn'/bind** *-et* leather binding, cover.
skinn'/bløyte *-a* thorough drenching, soaking.
skinn'/bok *-a, pl -bøker* 1 parchment manuscript. 2 *dial.* leather billfold.
skinn'/brev *-et* parchment document.
⁺**skinn'/død** *A* (=***skin/daud**) apparently dead.
⁺**skin'ne**[1] *-a* (=***skjene**[1]) 1 rail, track: **gå på s-r** run on t-s. 2 splint (e.g. for a broken arm, leg, etc.).
⁺**skin'ne**[2] *V skinte/skein, skint* (=***skine**) (e.g. of the sun, moon, a polished surface, radiant face) shine: **s- av** (e.g. of a face) shine with (happiness, etc.); *dial.* **s- av (opp)** dry up; **s- fram** appear, become apparent; **s- igjennom** show through, be apparent; **la det s- igjennom at** hint that; **det s-er over** *dial.* that's going too far; **s-ende** glittering, sparkling; radiant.
⁺**skin'ne/bein** *-et anat.* shinbone, tibia.
⁺**skin'ne/buss** *-en* rail bus.
⁺**skin'ne/gang** *-en* rails, track.
skinn'/egg *-et* egg without a shell.
⁺**skin'ne/legg** *-en* fibula.
⁺**skin'ne/legging** *-a/-en* track laying.
⁺**skin'ne/løs** *A* trackless (e.g. trolley).
⁺**skinn'/fektning** *-en* sham battle.
skinn'/fell *-en* sheepskin blanket: **fare**

opp som en løve og falle ned som en s- speak up confidently and then fall flat.
skinn'/fille -a patch of hide, skin.
skinn'/hanske -n leather glove.
+**skinn'/hellig** A - hypocritical.
+**skinn'hellig/het** -en hypocrisy.
skinn'/hyre -t/+-n oilskins.
skinn'/kåpe -a fur coat.
skinn'/mager A -ert, pl -re skin and bones, skinny.
skinn'/manø'ver -eren, pl -rer feint, mock attack.
skinn'- og [å] **bei'n/fri** A -tt skinned and boned.
skinn'/rygg -en 1 leather chair back. 2 leather back (of book): **i s-** bound in half leather.
+**skinn'/syk** A envious, jealous (**på** of).
+**skinn'/syke** -n envy, jealousy.
skinn'/tryte -a bot. whortleberry (Vaccinium myrtillus).
+**skinn'/tøy** -et furs; leather clothing.
+**skinn'/veng** -a (=+/**vinge**, */**vengje**) zool. bat (order Chiroptera).
+**skin't** pp of **skinne**[2]
***ski'n/år** -et year of drought.
ski'p -et 1 ship, vessel: **om bord på et s-** on board s-; **reise med s- til** go by s- to; **sende varer med s-** send goods by s-; **sende varer i norske s-** ship goods in Norwegian bottoms. 2 arch. nave. 3 typog. galley.
***ski'p/broten** [/bråten] A -e/-i, pl -ne cf **skib/brudden**
***ski'p/brot(t)** -et cf **skib/brudd**
ski'pe[1] V -a/+-et 1 send, transport by ship. 2: **s- inn** embark, take on board; **s- seg inn til Oslo** take ship for O-. 3: **s- ut** disembark, discharge; export overseas.
ski'pe[2] V -a/-et 1 organize, regulate: **s- til** arrange. 2 establish, settle. 3: **s- seg vel** turn out well.
***ski'pelig** A - decent, orderly.
***ski'ping** -a arrangement, establishment, organization.
***ski'pings/møte** -t organizing meeting.
skip'le V -a/+-et confuse, disarrange, disturb; ruin.
ski'pnad -en, pl *-er arrangement, organization; regulation.
skip'per -en, pl +-e skipper.
skip'per/skjønn -et judgment based on experience and practice, rule of thumb.
skip'per/skrøne -a sea yarn, tall tale.
skip'per/tak -et short, intensive all-out effort: **ta et s-** make an all-out effort.
skip'/pund -et weight of 160 kilograms (ab. 350 lbs.).
ski'p/reide -a hist. in the Viking period, a coastal district whose inhabitants were responsible for manning and equipping a warship.
***ski'p/sam** A careful, skilful at arranging one's affairs.
+**skip's/bygger** -en, pl -e (=*-**jar**) shipbuilder, shipwright.
skip's/båt -en 1 ship's boat. 2 zool. nautilus (Nautilus pompilius).
skip's/fart -en navigation, shipping; shipping industry.
+**skip's/fører** -en, pl -e (=*-**ar**) shipmaster.
+**skip'sfører/eksa'men** -en (=*-**ar/**) examination for a shipmaster's certificate.
+**skip's/gutt** -en (=*/**gut**) cabin boy; apprentice seaman.
skip's/handel -elen, pl -ler ship chandler.
skip's/journal [/sjurna'l] -en ship's log.
skip's/kjeks -en hardtack, ship biscuit.
skip's/lei -a shipping lane, ship's channel (inside outer band of islands).
+**skip's/leilighet** -en accommodation, passage: **få s- til** obtain p- to.
skip's/liste -a registry book; shipping list.
skip's/mekler -en, pl -e (=*-**ar**) ship broker.
+**skip's/reder** -en, pl -e (=*/**reiar**) shipowner.
skip's/råd -et council on board ship (at sea).
skip's/side [*/sie] -a/+-en ship's side: **fritt fra s-** free overside, ex ship; **levere fritt ved s-** deliver free alongside ship.
skip's/skrov [*/skråv] -et (=+/**skrog**) ship's hull.
skip's/verft -et (=*/**verv**) shipyard.
Skip/tvet [locally sjæt've] Pln twp, Østfold.
ski'r A cf **skjær**[4]
***ski're** V -a 1 clear (a fluid). 2 baptize.
ski'/renn -et skiing competition, ski meet.
***ski'/rennar** -en skier.
***ski'r/leik** -en clarity, purity.
***ski'rne** V -a (of a fluid) clear, deposit its sediment.
***ski'rsel** -la, pl -ler baptism, christening.
***ski'rs/eld** -en cf **skjærs/**
***ski'rsle** V -a baptize, christen.
skis'ma -et, pl -/+-er schism.
+**ski'/smøring** -en (=/**smurning**) ski wax.
ski'/spor -et ski track.
ski'/sport -en skiing.
skis'se -a/+-en outline, rough drawing, sketch (**av** of).
skis'se/bok -a, pl -bøker sketchbook.
skisse're V -te outline, sketch.
ski'/stav -en ski pole.
***ski't** -en cf **skitt**[1]
ski'te V skeit, +-t/*-e/*-i 1 defecate. 2: **det s-er vi i** we don't give a damn about it.
***ski'ten** A -e/-i, pl -ne cf **skitten**
ski'/terreng' -et ski terrain.
skit'ne[1] V -a/+-et become or make dirty: **s- til (ut)** dirty, soil.
skit'ne[2] pl of **skitten**
***ski't/semd** -a dirtiness, filthiness.
skitt'[1] -en/-et (=***skit**) 1 dirt, filth; rubbish, trash: **bry seg s- om noe** not give a damn about sth; **prate s- og lort** talk nonsense, rubbish; **s- i det!, s- la gå!** oh, the hell with it! 2 good-for-nothing; mean, rotten person.
skitt[2] A miserable, rotten, worthless: **det var s-** that's too bad.
skitt'- Pf disgusting, miserable, worthless, e.g. **s-/bok.**
+**skitt'/bemer'kning** -en dirty crack, remark.
skit'ten A +-ent, pl skitne (=***skiten**) 1 dirty, filthy: **en s- affære** a f- business. 2 obscene, smutty: **ha en s- munn** be foul mouthed.
skit'ten/ferdig A - slovenly.
+**skit'ten/tøy** -et 1 dirty clothes. 2 fig. dirty linen.
skitt'/fyr -en scamp, worthless fellow.
+**skitt'/gutt** -en rascal, scamp.
skitt'/unge [/onge] -n brat.
skitt'/viktig A - self-important, stuck-up.
+**skitt'/vær** -et (=*/**ver**) miserable weather.
ski'/tupp -en tip of a ski.
ski'/tur -en skiing; ski trip: **ta seg en s-** go out skiing.
ski've[1] -a 1 disc: **skyte på s-** shoot at a target; **være s- for** fig. be the butt of, target for. 2 dial (on a telephone). 3 face (on a clock, watch). 4 slice (of bread, cheese, meat, etc.): **skjære i s-er** slice. 5 tabletop. 6 bot. gill (on mushroom). 7 zool. bell, umbrella (on jellyfish).
ski've[2] V -a/+-et slice: **s- seg** flake, come off in flakes.
ski've/plog -en disc plow.
ski've/sopp -en bot. a mushroom (family Agaricaceae).
***skja'ge** V -a reel, stagger.
***skja'l** -et 1 dance, entertainment. 2 visit.
***skja'le** V -a 1 entertain. 2 pay a visit.
+**skje'**[1] -a/-en cf **skei**[1]
skje'[2] V -dde happen, occur, take place: **Og det s-dde i de dage** And it came to pass in those days (Luke 2, 1); **gud s- lov!** thank God!; **skal s-** will do; **s- din vilje** Thy will be done; **ingen skade s-dd** no harm done.
skjeb'be -a zool. perch (genus Perca).
Skje'/berg Pln twp, Østfold.
+**skje'/binder** -en, pl -e cf **skei/**
+**skje'/blad** -et cf **skei/**
+**skje'bne** -n destiny, fate, lot: **dele s- med en** cast one's l- with sby; **finne seg i sin s-** be resigned to one's fate; **friste s-n** tempt fate; **lide samme s-** meet the same fate; **s-n ville det annerledes** fate decreed otherwise.
+**skje'bne/bestem't** A - destined, doomed, fated.
+**skje'bne/gudin'ne** -n goddess of fate: **s-ne** the Fates, Parcae.
+**skje'bne/svanger** A -ert, pl -re fatal, fateful, momentous: **s- for** fatal to.
+**skje'bne/time** -n fateful hour, hour of destiny.
+**skje'bne/tro** -en fatalism.
+**skje'bne/tråd** -en web of fate.
+**skje'bne/tung** [/tong] A momentous.
***skjed'de**[1] V -a (of skins) dry out.
skjed'de[2] pt of **skje**[2]
+**skje'de** -n 1 scabbard, sheath: **stikke sverdet i s-n** sheathe one's sword. 2 anat. vagina. 3 bot. sheath.
+**skje'de/kne** -et bot. knotgrass (Polygonum aviculare).
skjef'te[1] -t, pl +-r/*- 1 small of the stock (on a gun). 2 = **s-/gras.**
skjef'te[2] V -a/+-et/*-e haft; stock (e.g. a rifle).
skjef'te/gras -et bot. scouring rush (Equisetum hiemale).
skjef'ting -en implement having a handle.
+**skje'/full** en cf **skei/**
skjegg' -et beard (on humans, animals, grain heads, etc.); bit, web (on key); naut. cutwater; typog. deckle edge: **le i s-et** laugh up one's sleeve; **mumle i s-et** mumble in one's beard; **sitte (igjen) med s-et i postkassa** be left holding the bag; **ta s-et** shave off one's beard.
+**skjeg'get(e)** A - (=***skjeggja**, ***skjeggjet(e)**) bearded, whiskered; unshaven; shaggy (tree).
skjegg'/laus A (=+/**løs**) beardless.
skjegg'/sopp -en med. sycosis.
skjegg'/stubb -en (beard) stubble.
skjegg'/tråd -en zool. barbel.
skjegg'/vekst -en growth of beard.
skjeg'le V -a squint.
***skjeg'l/øygd** A -/-øygt cf **sjel/øyd**
***skje'k** pr of **skake**[1]
***skje'ke** pp of **skake**[1]
***skje'kel** -elen, pl -lar corner, edge.
°**skje'ker** pl of **skåk**
***skje'ki** pp of **skake**[1]
***skjekkj'e**[1] -a: **på s-** aslant, to one side.
***skjekkj'e**[2] V sjekte 1 bend out of position. 2 distort, twist.
***skje'l**[1] -a/-et cf **skjell**[1]
+**skje'l**[2] et (=***skil**[3]) 1 right, the right thing: **gjøre rett og s- mot enhver** do the right thing by everybody. 2 grounds, reason: **ha s- til** have r- for. 3 understanding: **komme til s-s år og alder** reach the age of discretion, grow up.
***skje'l**[3] -et cf **skjell**[2]
+**skje'le** V -te (=***skjegle**) 1 squint: **s- til** look out of the corner of one's eye at, look askance at. 2 be cross-eyed.
skjelett' -et, pl -/+-er skeleton.
+**skjell'**[1] -a/-et (=***skjel**[1]) 1 shell, mussel. 2 flake, scale; dandruff. 3: **kne/s-** kneecap, patella.
+**skjell'**[2] -et (=***skil**[2], **skjel**[3]) border line (e.g. between estates); distinction, separation.

+ Bokmål; * Nynorsk; ° Dialect.
After letter: ' stress (Acc. 1); ' tone, stress (Acc. 2); · length.
Below letter: . not pronounced.

skjel'lakk -en shellac.
+skjell'/dyr -et (=*skjel/) zool. pangolin, scaly anteater (Manis).
***skjel'le**[1] -a 1 rattle. 2 cold wind.
skjel'le[2] V skjelte scold: s- og smelle fuss and fume, rant and roar, storm and rage; s- på en bawl sby out, scold sby; s- en ut abuse, revile sby.
+skjel'le[3] V skjelte be sby's business, concern: hva s-er det deg? what business is it of yours?.
+skjel'let(e) A - scaly, shelly: s- blekksopp bot. shaggy ink cap (Coprinus comatus).
+skjel'lig A - 1 just, reasonable: s- grunn sufficient cause. 2 (adv.) distinctly, plainly; quite, really.
+skjell'/sand -en (=*skjel/) sand mixed with crushed seashells.
skjell's/o'rd -et insult, word of abuse.
skjel'm[1] -en cf skolm
skjel'm[2] -en 1 rascal, rogue: en kan gjøre en s- urett one must give the devil his due; neste gang er en s- take the chance while you have it, don't depend on doing sth later. 2 joker, wag: ha en s- bak øret have a trick up one's sleeve.
skjel'msk A - roguish, waggish.
skjel'ms/stykke -t, pl +-r/*- practical joke, prank.
+skjel'ne V -a/-et distinguish, make out: jeg kunne ikke s- dem fra hverandre I couldn't tell them apart; s- mellom discriminate between; som lar seg s- distinguishable.
***skje'l/padde** -a cf skil/
+skjel's N (=*skils): komme til s- år og alder reach the age of discretion, grow up.
***skjel'te**[1] -n skull.
***skjel'te**[2] -n shivering, trembling.
skjel'te[3] pt of skjelle[2],[3]
***skjel'tre** V -a spread thinly.
skjel'v[1] -en/-et shaking, trembling; quaver (of the voice); jitters: hun hadde nå fått s-en i seg she was now shaking (trembling) like a leaf.
skjel'v[2] A shaky; quavering (voice): han er s- på hånden his hand is unsteady.
skjel've V skalv, +-et/*skolve/*-i quake, shake, tremble; (of a voice) quaver: blad som s-er i vinden leaves which tremble in the wind; hans stemme skalv his voice quavered; jorden skalv under oss the earth shook, trembled under us; s- av frykt tremble with fear.
skjel'ven A +-ent, pl -ne quivering, shaking, trembling; tremulous (e.g. smile, voice).
skjel've/tone -n mus. tremolo.
skjel'v/hendt A - with trembling hands.
skjel'v/mæ'lt A - quavering, tremulous (voice).
***skjel'v/redd** A - quaking with fear.
+skje'l/øyd A - (=*skjegl/øygd) cross-eyed; squint-eyed.
skje'ma -et, pl -/+-er 1 pattern, scheme, system: etter et s- according to a (fixed) pattern. 2 blank, form, questionnaire: fylle ut et s- fill out a form.
+skje'/mat -en cf skei/
skjematise're V -te schematize.
skjema'tisk A - schematic.
skje'ma/velde -t rule of red tape.
***skjem'd**[1] -a (feeling of) shame.
***skjem'd**[2] A skjemt cf skjemt[2]
***skjem'dar/verk** -et shameful act, deed.
***skjem'mast** V skjemdest, skjemst cf skjemmes
skjem'me V +skjemte/*skjemde 1 disfigure, mar, spoil: s- en kniv dull a knife; s- bort spoil (e.g. a child); s- ut ruin, spoil. *2 talk disparagingly of: s- på scold; s- seg be ashamed. 3 bring shame to: navnet s-er ingen what's in a name; hun hadde s-t ut slekten så stygt she had brought great shame down on the family (Undset); s- seg ut disgrace oneself.
+skjem'mes V skjemmes/skjems, skjemtes, skjems (=*skjemmast) be ashamed (for over, ved of): s- for en be ashamed (of a dishonest act) in sby's presence; du s- ei for din mor you're not ashamed to lie to your mother (Ibsen).
+skjem's pr, pp of skjemmes
***skjem'sle** -a 1 disgrace, shame. 2 rebuke, reprimand.
***skjem'st** pp of skjemmast
skjem't[1] -en/*-et 1 banter, jocularity. 2 jest, joke: på s- in jest.
+skjem't[2] A - (=*skjemd[2]) 1 damaged, ruined, spoiled. 2 blunt, dull (e.g. knife). 3 ashamed: *eg er s- utav det I'm a- about it.
skjem'te[1] V -a/+-et banter, jest, joke (med with).
+skjem'te[2] pt of skjemme
skjem'te/gauk -en joker, wag.
+skjem'tes pt of skjemmes
***skjem'te/teikning** -a caricature.
skjem'te/vise -a comic song.
+skjem't/som' A -t, pl -me (=*/sam) bantering, jocular, merry.
+skje'n pt of skinne[2]
skjen'de V -a/+-et 1 damage, desecrate. 2 rape, ravish.
skjen'dig A - disgraceful, outrageous, scandalous.
+skjen'dig/het -en disgrace, outrage.
***skje'ne**[1] -a cf skinne[1]
skje'ne[2] V -a/+-te 1 (of cattle) stampede; (e.g. of rabbits) run every which way. 2: s- ut swerve.
***skje'ne/bein** -et cf skinne/
***skje'ne/gang** -en cf skinne/
***skje'ne/legg** -en cf skinne/
skjen'k -en 1 drink; drinks (in general). 2 bar, counter, sideboard. 3 gift, present: få til s- get as a gift.
+skjen'ke V -et/-te (=*-je) 1 pour (e.g. coffee, tea, liquor): s- glasset fullt fill the glass; s- for gjestene serve the guests (liquid refreshment); s- i pour into, fill (a glass, cup); s- opp fill (by pouring); s- ut serve (alcoholic) drinks. 2 bestow, give, present (til to): s- noe hele sin oppmerksomhet give sth all one's attention; s- en minnegave present a memorial gift.
***skjen'ker** pl of skank
+skjen'ke/rett -en (on-sale) liquor license.
+skjen'ke/stue -a (=*skjenkje/stove) bar, tavern.
***skjen'kjar** -en archaic host, server of drinks.
***skjen'kjar/svein** -en =skjenkjar.
***skjen'kje** V -te cf skjenke
***skjen'kje/rett** -en cf skjenke/
***skjen'kje/stove** -a cf skjenke/stue
skjenn' -et scolding: få s- get a s-.
***skjen'nast** V skjentest, skjenst cf skjenne
skjen'ne V skjente 1 reprimand, scold: s- på en s- sby. 2: s-s bicker, squabble, wrangle.
+skjen'ne/preken -en (=*/preike) severe scolding, tongue-lashing.
+skjen'neri -et altercation, quarrel, row.
+skjen'sel -elen, pl -ler disgrace, dishonor, ignominy.
+skjen'sels/dåd -en infamous deed, outrage.
+skjen'sels/gjerning [/jæ'rning] -en infamous action, outrage.
skjen'te pt of skjene[2], skjenne
***skjen'test** pt of skjennast
***skjen'st** pp of skjennast
skjep'pe -a archaic dry measure =ab. 1/2 bushel (2 pecks): måle en s-n full let sby have it right in the teeth; sette sitt lys under en s- hide one's light under a bushel (Matt. 5, 15).
***skjer'**[1] [sjæ'r] -et cf skjær[1]
***skjer'**[2] [sjæ'r] -et cf skjær[2]
***skjer'de** V -a/-e deplete, diminish.
skjer'ding -en chimney hook.
***skjere**[1] [sjæ're] -a sickle.
***skjere**[2] [sjæ're] -n colter (on plow).
***skjere**[3] [sjæ're] V skar, skore/-i cf skjære[3]
skjer'f -et muffler, sash, scarf; kerchief.
***skjer/ga'rd** [sjæ'r/] -en cf skjær/gård
skjer'm -en 1 cover, screen, shield. 2 casing, guard; fender (on car). 3 (eye, lamp) shade. 4 shoulder pad (in a dress). 5 bot. umbel.
+skjer'm/bilde -t (=*/bilete) fluoroscope picture.
skjer'm/blomstra A - (=+-et) bot. umbelliferous.
skjer'm/brett -et (folding) screen.
skjer'me V -a/+-et protect, shield (mot against, from); elec. screen.
***skjer'm/hu(v)e** -a visor cap.
skjer'm/plante +-a/-en bot. umbelliferous plant.
skjer'p -et mining excavation, prospect.
skjer'pe[1] V +-a/-te/+-et 1 prospect (for metals, ore). 2 drill for oil.
skjer'pe[2] V +-a/-te/+-et 1 sharpen (e.g. a knife), whet (e.g. the appetite); crispen (e.g. flatbread, crackers); dry (e.g. fish, hay): dial. det s-er, s-es på the frost has come, has hit. 2 intensify (e.g. hostilities), make more rigorous (e.g. regulations), tighten up; aggravate: s- motsetningen intensify the contrast.
+skjer'pelse -n aggravation, increase, intensification.
skjer'pende A - aggravating, intensifying.
skjerr' A skjert skittish.
***skjer're** V -a frighten, startle.
***skjer/slipar** [sjæ'r/] -en cf skjær/sliper
skjer'v[1] -en 1 mite: enkens s- the widow's m- (Mark 12, 41—44); gi sin s- contribute one's share. 2 crushed rock; shards.
***skjer'v**[2] -et bare, denuded mountain range.
Skjer'v/øy Pln twp, Troms.
+skje'/sluk -en cf skei/
***skjes'se**[1] -a appetite.
***skjes'se**[2] V skjeste crave.
***skjes'se/mat** -en delicacy.
***skje'v**[1] pr of skave[1]
+skje'v[2] A cf skeiv
+skje'/vann -et nitric acid.
***skje've**[1] N cf skeive[1]
+skje've[2] V -et cf skeive[2]
***skje'vel** -elen, pl -lar stick (with bark removed).
+skje'v/het -en 1 crookedness, lopsidedness. 2 bias, one-sidedness, slant. 3 med. curvature of the spine.
+skje'v/øyd A - cf skeiv/
***skjo'l** -et cover, shelter; shed.
skjol'd[1] -en 1 spot, stain. 2 patch (of discoloration, or of a different color).
skjol'd[2] -et shield; escutcheon; shell (of tortoise): føre i sitt s- have in mind, intend.
Skjol'd Pln twp, Rogaland.
skjol'd/borg -a/+-en rampart, wall of shields.
skjol'dbrusk/kjertel -elen, pl -ler anat. thyroid gland.
skjol'de V -a/+-et discolor.
skjol'det(e) A - discolored, stained.
skjol'd/knapp -en shield boss.
skjol'd/lue -a archaic cap with a visor.
skjol'd/lus -a zool. scale insect (family Coccidae).
skjol'd/møy -a hist. amazon, female warrior.
skjol'd/rand -a/+-en, pl -render shield rim.
skjo'r -a (=+skjære[1]) 1 zool. magpie (Pica pica). 2 chatterbox.
skjo're/reir -et magpie nest.
skjorte [sjor'te] -a shirt; (with national costume) blouse: han eier ikke s-a på kroppen he doesn't own the s- on his back.
skjorte/bryst [sjor'te/] -et shirtfront.
+skjorte/bytte -t (=*/byte) change of shirts.

+**skjorte/erme** *-t* (=***/erm**) shirtsleeve: **i s-r** in (one's) s-.
skjorte/flak *-et* shirttail.
skjorte/knapp *-en* shirt button.
skjorte/linning *-a/-en* neckband, wristband (of a shirt).
+**skjort/erme** [sjor`t/] *-t* cf **skjorte/**
***skjo't** *A* quick, swift.
***skjo`te** *V skyt, skaut, skote/-i* cf **skyte**
***skjo't/før** *A* fleet, swift.
+**skju'l** *-et* 1 cover, shelter; shed. 2 hiding (place): **legge s- på noe** conceal, make a secret of sth; **ligge i s-** be hidden; **engler daler ned i s-** angels float down (to earth) unseen (Christmas carol)
+**skju`le** *V -te* conceal, hide (**for** from): **s- seg for en** h- from sby; **s-t** concealed, hidden; *fig.* covert, latent; **s-t betydning** hidden meaning; **s-te krefter** latent powers, strength; **en s-t fare** a latent danger; **en s-t hentydning** a covert hint; **i det s-te** in secret, secretly; **holde noe s-t** hide sth; **holde seg s-t** keep out of sight.
+**skju`le/sted** *-et* hiding place.
°**skju'r** *-a* cf **skjor**
skjæ'ker *pl of* **skåk**
+**skjæ'r**[1] *-et* (=***skjer**[1]) reef, skerry: **et blindt s-** a sunken rock.
+**skjæ'r**[2] *-et* (=***skjer**[2]) cutting edge of a tool; (plow)share.
skjæ'r[3] *-et* 1 gleam, reflection (**av** of), sheen. 2 tinge, tint, touch (of color).
skjæ'r[4] *A* (=***skir**) 1 delicate, pure, sheer. 2 plain, pure, simple: **det er det rene s-e bedrageri** it is fraud pure and simple.
skjæ'r[5] *A* (e.g. of wheat) ready for the sickle, ripe.
+**skjæ`re**[1] *-a* cf **skjor**
***skjæ`re**[2] *-a* scissors.
+**skjæ`re**[3] *V skar, skåret* (=***skjere**[3]) 1 cut, slice, trim; (of wind) bite; (of sound) penetrate, pierce; (of light) blind, glare: **s- alle over en kam** judge, treat all alike; **s- ansikt, grimaser** make a face; **s- en i hjertet** wring one's heart; **s- hverandre, sammen** (of lines) intersect; **s- tenner** grind one's teeth; **fanden s- (meg)** strong oath. 2 castrate, geld. 3 (of motion) sheer, swerve; move with great speed: **s- klar, fri (av noe)** avoid, dodge (sth); **s- ut (fra kurs, veien)** swerve off (course, the road). 4 (with *adv.*): **s- av** cut off (a piece of sth); interrupt; **s- bort** cut away, prune; **s- for** carve; **s- i (å gråte, skrike)** burst out (crying, screaming, etc.); **s- i** (of colors) shade into (another color); **s- i øynene** (of light) blind, hurt one's eyes; **s- inn i** intersect; **s- ned** cut down, decrease, reduce (e.g. armaments, expenses); **s- opp** carve up, cut, operate on; **s- over** cut (into two pieces); **s- til** cut out (from a pattern); **s- tilbake** cut back (a tree, bush); **s- under** (e.g. of skis into snow, a boat into a wave) dig down into; **s- ut** carve, cut out. 5 (*refl.*): **s- seg** cut oneself; (of milk) curdle; (of a voice) break, crack; **s- seg i fingeren** cut one's finger; **s- seg ut** stand out.
+**skjæ`rende** *A* - 1 cutting (e.g. edge, tool, remark). 2 biting, bitter, sharp (e.g. cold, wind). 3 piercing, shrill (e.g. sound, voice). 4 dazzling (e.g. light), glaring (e.g. color, constrast, light).
+**skjæ'r/gå'rd** *-en* (=***skjer/gard**) skerries; archipelago.
Skjæ'r/hallen *Pln* twp, Østfold.
+**skjæ`ring** *-a/-en* 1 cutting. 2 intersection. 3 cut, passage (for road or railroad).
+**skjæ`rings/punkt** *-et* (point of) intersection.
+**skjæ'r/myssel** *-elen, pl -ler* skirmish.
skjæ`rne *V -a/+-et* ripen, yellow.
skjæ`rs/eld *-en* (=+**/ild**) 1 *eccl.* purgatory. 2 *fig.* ordeal.
+**skjæ'r/sliper** *-en, pl -e* (=***skjer/slipar**) (knife, scissors) grinder.
+**skjærsom'mer** *-en, pl -e/-somrer poet.* midsummer: **hun er seksten s-e gammel** she is sixteen summers old (Ibsen).
skjær/torsdag [usu. -tå'rs-] *-en* Maundy Thursday: **hvis s- falt på langfredag** if the impossible should happen.
+**skjø'd** *-et* 1 lap: **legge hendene i s-et** remain a passive spectator, sit back; **sitte med hendene i s-et** be idle, twiddle one's thumbs. 2 bosom, womb: **i familiens s-** in the bosom of one's family; **i jordens s-** in the womb of earth.
+**skjø`de/hund** *-en* lap dog.
+**skjø`des/løs** *A* (=***skøyte/laus**) 1 careless, negligent, slovenly: **s- med sitt utseende** careless of one's appearance. 2 devil-may-care, nonchalant, reckless.
+**skjø`desløs/het** *-en* (=***skøyte/løyse**) 1 carelessness, slovenliness: **en s-** an act of negligence. 2 nonchalance.
+**skjø`de/synd** *-a/-en* besetting sin.
+**skjø`ge** *-a/-en* (=***skjøkje**) prostitute, whore.
***skjø`kje** *-a* cf **skjøge**
skjøl'p *-en* 1 gouge. 2 *naut.* score (e.g. in a block).
***skjø'n** *-et* cf **skjønn**[1]
***skjø`nar** *-en* cf **skjønner**
***skjø`ne** *V -a/-te* cf **skjønne**
***skjø`neleg** *A* - intelligible.
***skjø'n/laus** *A* without understanding.
+**skjønn'**[1] *-et* (=***skjøn**) 1 discernment, understanding: **ha s- på** understand. 2 estimate, judgment, opinion: **anslå etter et s-** estimate roughly; **avgi et s- i en sak** give an o- in a case; **etter beste s-** to the best of one's judgment; **etter mitt s-** in my o-; **handle etter s-** use one's own discretion.
+**skjønn'**[2] *A skjønt* 1 beautiful, lovely; (of food) delicious: **den s-e** the fair one; **det s-e** the beautiful; **de s-e** the fair sex; **i den s-este orden** in apple-pie order, shipshape. 2 fine, noble: **de s-e kunster** the fine arts.
+**skjøn`ne** *V skjønte* (=***skjøne**) 1 understand; discern, realize: (at the end of statements) **s-er du, kan du s-** you know, you see; **så vidt jeg s-er (kan s-)** as far as I can make out, apparently; **jeg s-te på ham at** I could tell, I understood by his manner that; **s- seg på** know about, have an understanding of; **ikke s- seg på en** not be able to figure sby out. 2 *dial.* assess, estimate, judge: **s- på noe** make an assessment of sth. 3: **s- på** (=**på-skjønne**) (properly) appreciate, evaluate.
+**skjøn`ner** *-en, pl -e* (=***skjønar**) connoisseur.
+**skjønn'/het** *-en* beauty.
+**skjønn`hets/idea'l** *-et* ideal of beauty.
+**skjønn`hets/konkurranse** [/-ang'se] *-n* beauty contest.
+**skjønn`hets/middel** *-elet/-midlet, pl -midler* beauty preparation, cosmetic.
+**skjønn`hets/pleie** *-n* beauty treatment.
+**skjønn`hets/plett** *-en* beauty spot, mole.
+**skjønn`hets/prepara·t** *-et* beauty preparation.
+**skjønn`hets/salong·** *-en* beauty parlor (salon, shop).
+**skjønn`hets/sans** *-en* sense of beauty.
+**skjønn`hets/verdi·** *-en* esthetic value.
+**skjønn`hets/åpenbaring** *-en* (a) stunning beauty.
+**skjønnjom'fru** *-en poet.* fair maiden.
skjønn'/litteratu·r *-en* belles lettres, (imaginative) literature; fiction.
skjønn'/litteræ·r *A* belletristic, literary.
***skjønn`/sam** *A* cf **/som**
***skjønn`/semd** *-a* cf **skjøn/**
+**skjønn's/forret·ning** *-a/-en* appraisal, valuation.
+**skjønn`/skrift** *-a/-en* calligraphy.
+**skjønn's/mann** *-en, pl -menn* appraiser, assessor.
+**skjønn's/messig** *A* - approximate, estimated: **en s- beregning** a rough estimate.
skjønn's/nemnd [/nemd] *-a* commission of appraisers, experts.
+**skjønn`/som·** *A -t, pl -me* (=***skjøn(n)-/sam**) discerning, discriminating: **et s-t utvalg** a judicious selection.
+**skjønn`som/het** *-en* discernment, discretion, discrimination.
+**skjønn's/sak** *-en* matter of opinion.
+**skjønn'/ånd** *-en* bel esprit, esthete.
skjøn's *N*: **på s-** obliquely.
***skjø'n/sam** *A* cf **skjønn/som**
***skjøn`se** *V -a* place, put in an oblique position.
***skjø'n/semd** *-a* discernment, discretion, discrimination.
***skjø'n/setje** *V -te* appraise, estimate.
+**skjøn`ske** *V -a/-et* cut obliquely, cut on a bias; *naut.* steer an oblique course.
***skjø'ns/mann** *-en, pl -menn(er)* cf **skjønns/**
***skjø'ns/nemnd** *-a* cf **skjønns/**
+**skjøn't**[1] *nt of* **skjønn**[2]
+**skjøn't**[2] *C* although, though.
skjøn`te** *pt of* **skjøne**, **`skjønne
skjø'r[1] *-et* 1 curdled milk, sour milk. 2 *dial.* core, kernel (of grain).
skjø'r[2] *A* (=***skøyr**) 1 brittle, delicate, fragile. 2 cracked, crazy, loony: **s- i hodet** off one's rocker.
skjø'r/buk *-en* scurvy.
***skjø`re** *V -te* clear, sweep away.
+**skjø`r/levner** *-en, pl -e* licentious person, *bibl.* fornicator.
+**skjø`r/levnet** *-et bibl.* debauchery, fornication.
skjø`rne *V -a/+-et* become brittle, crumble; make brittle, friable.
skjø`r/ost [/ost] *-en* cottage cheese.
***skjør`pe** *V -te* (of animals) puff, snort.
skjør't *-et, pl -/+-er* 1 skirt; petticoat. 2 *pop.* dame, skirt, tomato.
skjør`te *V -a/+-et*: **s- opp** tuck up one's skirts.
skjør`te/jeger *-en, pl +-e* skirt chaser.
skjør`te/kant *-en* skirt hem.
+**skjør`te/regimen·te** *-t* petticoat government, rule.
+**skjø't**[1] *-en* (=***skøyt**) connection, joint: **uten s-** in one piece.
+**skjø't**[2] *-et* cf **skaut**[3]
+**skjø't**[3] *-et* coattail.
+**skjø't**[4] *pt of* **skyte**
+**skjø`te**[1] *-t* (=***skøyte**[3]) deed of conveyance.
+**skjø`te**[2] *V -te* (=***skøyte**[4]) convey, deed (**til** to).
+**skjø`te**[3] *V -te* (=***skøyte**[4]) join, lengthen: **s- på** add (a piece of cloth), fill out.
+**skjø`te/le·dning** *-en* extension cord.
+**skjø`tes/løs** *A* cf **skjødes/**
+**skjøt'sel** *-en* care, management.
+**skjø't/stue** *-a hist.* public room on the German Wharf in Bergen.
+**skjøt`te** *V -a/-et* (=***skøyte**[5]) look after, take care of: **s- seg selv** get along on (one's) own; **ikke s- om** not care about.
+**skjø'v** *pt of* **skyve**
skjå'[1] *-en* transparent membrane, (from a cow's stomach).
skjå'[2] *-en* shack, shanty.
Skjå'k *Pln* twp, Oppland.
skjå'k/vær *-en* person from Skjåk.
+**skle'(d)** *pt of* **skli**
sklero'se *-n med.* sclerosis.
skli' *V -dde/sklei, sklidd* (=***sklide**) glide, skid, slip (on icy or slippery surface).
***skli'de** *V -de/skleid, sklidd/sklide/-i* cf **skli**
skli'e *-a* slide.

+ Bokmål; * Nynorsk; ° Dialect.
After letter: ' stress (Acc. 1); ` tone, stress (Acc. 2); · length.
Below letter: . not pronounced.

skli'/sikker *A -ert, pl -sikre* nonskid.
sko'[1] *-en, pl -r/+-* shoe: **over en lav s-** indiscriminate(ly); on a large scale, wholesale; **han vet hvor s-en trykker** he knows where the s- pinches (where the difficulty is); **være oppe før fanden får sko på** get up at an unearthly hour.
sko'[2] *V -dde* 1 shoe (e.g. a horse). 2: **s- seg** enrich oneself (at others' expense).
+**sko'/bespa'rer** *-en, pl -e* (shoe) cleat.
sko'/børste *-n* shoe brush.
***skodar** [skå'ar] *-en* onlooker, spectator.
***skodd'** *-a* cf **skodde**[1]
skod'de[1] *-a* (=***skodd**) fog, mist.
+**skod'de**[2] *-n* (window) shutter.
skod'de/banke *-n* fogbank.
skod'det(e) *A* - foggy.
***skode** [skå'e] *V -a* look at, view: **s- etter** look for.
***skode/spel** *-et* cf **skue/spill**
***skode/spelar** *-en* cf **skue/spiller**
***skodespelarin'ne** *-a* cf **skuespillerinne**
Skod'je *Pln* twp, Møre og Romsdal.
***skodnad** [skå'dna] *-en* inspection, viewing.
sko'/eske *-a/+-en* shoe box.
skof't *-en/-et* absenteeism.
skof'te *V -a/+-et* absent oneself from work, shirk: **en som s-er** an absentee.
sko'g *-en* forest, wood: **han kan ikke se s-en for bare trær** he can't see the forest for the trees; **som en roper i s-en får en svar** you get from others the kind of treatment your conduct entitles you to.
sko'g/botn *-en* forest, woodland floor.
sko'g/brann *-en* forest fire.
sko'g/bruk *-et* forestry, lumbering.
sko'g/bryn *-et* edge of a forest.
+**sko'g/bunn** *-en* cf **/botn**
+**sko'g/eier** *-en, pl -e* (=***/eigar**) owner of forest.
Sko'ger *Pln* twp, Vestfold.
sko'g/fattig *A* - sparsely wooded.
sko'ggangs/mann *-en, pl -menn/*-menner hist.* outlaw.
+**skog'ger/latter** *-en* roar of laughter; horselaugh.
+**skog'ger/le** *V -lo, -ledd* roar with laughter; guffaw.
sko'g/grense *-a/+-en* timberline.
sko'g/holt *-et* grove.
sko'g/kant *-en* edge of a wood.
sko'g/katt *-en* Angora cat.
sko'g/kledd *A -/*-kledt* wooded.
sko'g/laus *A* treeless.
sko'g/leies *Av* through a forest.
sko'g/lendt *A* - wooded.
sko'g/li *-a* wooded slope (of hill or mountain).
+**sko'g/løs** *A* cf **/laus**
***sko'g/løyse** *-a* deforestation; lack of forest.
Skogn [skång'n] *Pln* twp, Nord-Trøndelag.
sko'g/planting *-a/+-en* 1 afforestation. 2 wooded area, section.
+**skog're** *V -et* roar with laughter.
sko'g/rik *A* heavily timbered, wooded.
skogs/arbeid [skok's/] *-et* lumbering.
+**skogs/arbei'der** *-en, pl -e* (=***-ar**) lumberjack, woodman.
skogs/drift *-a/+-en* logging, lumbering.
skogs/folk *-et* lumberjacks, woodmen.
skogs/fugl *-en* woodland bird.
skogs/kar *-en* lumberjack, woodman.
sko'g/skole *-n* (elementary) school of forestry.
sko'g/snar *-et* 1 copse, grove. 2 *dial.* strip of woods.
+**skogs/rå** [skok's/] *-en* forest spirit (esp. one which appears to people lost in a forest).
sko'g/sti *-en* (=***/stig**) forest, woodland path.
sko'g/stjerne *-a bot.* chickweed wintergreen (Trientalis europaea).
skogs/ved [skok's/] *-en* pine, spruce wood.
skogs/veg *-en* (=+**/vei**) forest, woodland road.
sko'g/troll *-et* forest goblin.
+**sko'g/tykning** *-en* (=***/tykke**) thicket.
Sko'gul *Prn(f) myth.* a valkyrie.
+**sko'g/vokter** *-en, pl -e* (=***/vaktar**) forest ranger.
sko'/ho'rn *-et* shoehorn.
sko'/hæl *-en* heel (of a shoe).
***sko'k** *pt of* **skake**[1]
skokk' *-en* 1 crowd, flock, throng. 2 *archaic* threescore.
skok'ke/vis *Av*: **i s-** (in) great numbers (of), lots (of).
skok'le[1] *-a/-en*: **s-r** shafts (e.g. of a plow).
***skok'le**[2] *V -a* hobble, stump.
sko'/krem *-en* shoe polish.
***skol** [skå'l] *-et* 1 heavy shower. 2 splash.
+**skolas'tiker** *-en, pl -e* (=***-ar**) scholastic, schoolman.
skolastikk' *-en* scholasticism.
skolas'tisk *A* - scholastic.
+**skol'de** *V -et* cf **skålde**
sko'le[1] *-n* (=***skule**[1]) 1 school (institution, building, etc.): **s-n** (in contrast to the university, often used to mean) the secondary schools; **danne s-** form a s- (of thought); **gå i s- hos** be instructed by; **gå på (i) s-** go to s-; **holde s-** teach s-; **i livets s-** in the s- of life; **ta en i s-** take sby to task; **være av den gamle s-** belong to the old s- (of thought, behavior, etc.). 2 schooling, training (i in).
***skole**[2] [skå'le] *V -a* 1 rinse, wash. 2 splash.
sko'le[3] *V -a/+-te* (=***skule**[3]) school, train: **en vel s-t stemme** a well-trained voice.
sko'le/ba'rn *-et, pl -/*-born* school child.
sko'le/benk *-en* school bench: **vi har sittet på s-en sammen** we went to school together.
+**sko'le/besty'rer** *-en, pl -e* cf **/styrer**
sko'le/bok *-a, pl -bøker* schoolbook, textbook.
sko'le/bruk *-en/-et*: **til s-** for school use.
sko'le/dag *-en* school day: **han var en dovenlars i s-ene** he was a lazybones in his school days.
sko'le/direktø'r *-en* superintendent of schools (for one of eleven districts into which Norway is divided for school purposes).
sko'le/eksem'pel *-elet/-let* perfect illustration (**på** of).
sko'le/ele'v *-en* pupil.
sko'le/fag *-et* subject (in school).
sko'le/fest *-en* school party.
sko'le/film *-en* educational film.
sko'le/fly *-et* training plane.
sko'le/forkle *-et* (girls') smock (esp. for school use).
sko'le/frakk *-en* coat worn in school (like a lab coat).
sko'le/fri *N*: **ha s-** have a day off from school, a holiday.
+**sko'le/frokost** *-en* (=***/frukost**) breakfast or (late morning) lunch.
sko'le/gang *-en* education, schooling; school attendance.
sko'le/ga'rd *-en* school yard.
+**sko'le/gutt** *-en* (=***/gut**) schoolboy.
+**sko'le/gå'rd** *-en* cf **/gard**
sko'le/hage *-n* school garden.
sko'le/heim *-en* (=+**/hjem**) reform school.
+**sko'le/holder** *-en, pl -e* teacher (esp. in an ambulatory school).
sko'le/hygie'ne *-n* school hygiene.
sko'le/idrett *-en* school athletics, sport.
sko'le/idrettsmerke *-t, pl +-r/*-* medal, pin granted for school athletics.
sko'le/inspektø'r *-en* superintendent of schools.
***sko'/leist** *-en* cf **/lest**
sko'le/kamera't *-en* schoolmate.
sko'le/kjøkken *-et, pl -/+-er* school kitchen (for home economics instruction).
sko'le/klasse *-a/-en* (school) class.
sko'le/konto'r *-et* administrative office in Ministry of Education, having supervision over schools.
+**sko'le/krets** *-en* school district.
sko'le/kringkasting *-a/+-en* radio programs for use in school instruction.
***sko'le/krins** *-en* cf **/krets**
sko'le/lege *-n* school doctor.
sko'le/lys *-et* bookish student, grind.
+**sko'le/lærer** *-en, pl -e* (=***-ar**) schoolteacher.
sko'le/mann *-en, pl -menn/*-menner* educator, pedagogue.
sko'le/mat *-en* lunch carried by schoolchild.
+**sko'le/mester** *-en, pl -e* (=***/meister**) schoolmaster.
+**sko'lemester/tone** *-n* pedagogical, pedantic manner of expression.
sko'le/moden *A +-ent, pl -ne* of school age.
+**sko'le/penger** *pl* (=***-ar**) tuition.
+**sko'le/pike** *-a/-en* schoolgirl.
sko'le/plan *-en* course of instruction, curriculum.
sko'le/plikt *-a/+-en* compulsory school attendance.
sko'le/pliktig *A* - of school age: **i s-alder** of compulsory school age.
sko'le/psykolog [/-lå'g] *-en* school psychologist.
skole're *V -te* school, train.
sko'le/råd *-et* teachers' council.
sko'le/skip *-et* training ship.
+**sko'/lest** *-en* 1 (shoe) last; shoe tree. 2 *zool.* grenadier, rattail (deepwater fish, Coryphaenoides rupestris).
sko'le/stue *-a* schoolroom.
sko'le/styre *-t, pl +-r/*-* board of education.
+**sko'le/styrer** *-en, pl -e* (=***-ar**) principal (esp. of a private school or an adult extension school).
sko'le/tannpleie *-a/+-en* school dental care.
sko'le/tea'ter *-(e)ret, pl -/+-re* "school theater" (arrangement permitting school pupils to attend regular theater performances at reduced prices).
sko'le/tid [*/ti] *-a/+-en* 1 school session. 2 school days.
sko'le/tur *-en* school outing.
+**sko'le/utgave** *-a/-en* (=***/utgåve**) school edition.
sko'le/veg *-en* (=+**/vei**) way to and from school.
+**sko'le/vesen** *-et* educational system.
sko'le/veske *-a* small satchel (for school books).
sko'le/år *-et* school year.
sko'/lisse *-a* shoelace.
***skol'le** *V skolte* appear, seem; look imposing, loom.
skol'm *-a/-en* (=**skjelm**[1]) 1 pod. 2 shell (of shellfish).
skol'me *V -a/+-et* shell (peas).
***skol/orm** [skå'l/] *-en zool.* millipede (class Diplopoda); centipede (class Chilopoda).
skol'p *-en* 1 quiver. 2 *derog.* inhabitant of the Nordland coast.
skol'pe/jern [/jæ'rn] *-et* gouging chisel.
skol't *-en* 1 forehead; skull; top of the head; head. 2 knoll. 3 top of a hill. 4 round reef.
skol'te/finn *-en* Lapp living in Neiden and in Finnish Lappland, belonging to Greek Orthodox Church.
skol'te/lapp *-en* (=**/finn**).
skol've** *pp of* **skjelve** (=skolvi**)
+**skoma'ker** *-en, pl -e* (=***-ar**) shoemaker: **s-, bli ved din lest** s-, stick to your last (=don't try to do what you don't know about).
+**skoma'ker/mester** *-eren, pl -ere/-rer* master shoemaker.
sko'ning[1] *-a/+-en* shoeing.
sko'ning[2] *-en* 1 ferrule; shoe. 2 hem (on skirt).
***skon'k** *-a, pl skjenker* cf **skank**
+**skon'ner** *-en, pl -e* cf **skonnert**
skon'nert *-en* schooner.

skon'rok -en 1 hard roll. 2 hardtack, ship's biscuit.
sko'/puss -en shoeshine, shoe polishing.
+sko'/pusser -en, pl -e (=*-ar) bootblack, shoeshine.
*skor[1] [skå'r] -a footstool, step.
*skor[2] [skå'r] -a cf skår[1]
*skorde[1] [sko're] -a prop, support.
*skorde[2] [sko're] V -a shore up, support.
*skor/dyr [skå'r/] -et insect.
*skore[1] [skå're] -a groove; notch, nick.
*skore[2] [skå're] V -a 1 cut grooves, notches: s- på horna show signs of getting old. 2 cut down, fell.
*skore[3] [skå're] pp of skjere[3]
sko'/reim -a, pl *-ar shoelace.
skor/fast [skå'r/] A 1 (of farm animals) stuck in a place (e.g. ledge, cliff) from which it can't get out. 2 in a fix, in a difficult position, stuck.
skor/feste [skå'r/] -t 1 spot (in cliffs, mountains) from which there is no exit. 2 difficult position, fix, spot.
*skori [skå'ri] pp of skjere[3]
skor'pe -a crust.
+skor'pe/dannelse -n incrustation.
skor'pet(e) A - crusty.
skorpio'n -en scorpion.
skorsone'r/rot -a bot. black salsify (Scorzonera hispanica).
skor'/stein -en 1 open fireplace. 2 chimney, smokestack; funnel.
+skor'steins/feier -en, pl -e (=*-ar) chimney sweep.
skor'steins/pipe -a chimney, smokestack.
skort [skor't] -en lack, shortage (på of).
skorte[1] [skor'te] -a cleft (in cliff, mountain).
skorte[2] [skor'te] V -a/+-et 1 be insufficient, lack. 2: s- på be a shortage of; det s-er ham ikke på mot he isn't lacking in courage.
*skor'tne V -a clot, congeal, harden.
*skor'v -et naked cliff, mountain.
+sko'se[1] -a/-en gibe, sneer, taunt.
+sko'se[2] V -et/-te gibe at, sneer at, taunt.
sko'/slit -et wear of shoes.
sko'/snute -a/-en tip of a shoe.
sko'/spenne -a/+-en/-et shoe buckle.
sko'/spiss -en tip of a shoe.
sko'/svein -en hist. personal servant, valet.
sko'/sverte -a shoe polish; blacking.
+sko'/såle -n (=*/sole) sole of a shoe.
*skot [skå't] -et cf skott[3]
*skote[1] [skå'te] -a cf skåte[1]
*skote[2] [skå'te] V -a cf skåte[2]
*skote[3] [skå'te] pp of skyte (=*skoti)
*skotning [skå'tning] -en prematurely born farm animal.
skot'sk A - Scots, Scotch, Scottish: s- rutet plaid, tartan.
skott'[1] -en (=skut[2]) stem or stern of a boat; stem or stern room, compartment.
skott'[2] -et 1 naut. bulkhead. 2 shed.
skott'[3] -et (=+skudd, *skot) 1 shot (of, with a gun; at a goal in sports); round of ammunition: løst s- blank; skarpt s- round of live ammunition; klar til s- ready to fire; få s- på get a shot at; komme på (i) s- get within range; skyte s- på s- fire shot after (upon) shot; stå for skudd (e.g. of a hunting dog) be steady under fire; be under fire; være i skuddet (of a commercial product) be popular, sell well. 2 bot. shoot, sprout; fig. heir, scion: sette, skyte s- sprout.
skott'/dag -en leap day.
skot'te[1] -n Scot, Scotchman, Scotsman.
skot'te[2] V -a/+-et glance, peek: s- bort på en glance over at sby.
skot'te/histo'rie -a/+-en anecdote about (stingy) Scot(s).
skot'te/toget df the Scottish Campaign of 1612, during the Kalmar war.
skott'/fri A -tt 1 invulnerable. 2: gå s- get off scot-free.
skott'/gamp -en old horse that will soon have to be killed.
*skott'/hald -et cf skudd/hold
skott'/hyll(e) en game in which one tries to hit a wooden pin with an iron or a stone disc.
skott'/kalv -en prematurely born (dead) calf.
Skott'/land Pln Scotland.
*skott'/lending -en Scot, Scotchman.
skott'/mål -et range (of a firearm).
+skott'/penger pl (=*-ar) bounty.
skott'/premie -n bounty: sette opp s- på ørn put a b- on eagles.
skott'/redd A - (esp. of dog, horse) gunshy.
skott'/sikker A -ert, pl -sikre 1 proof against shooting; bulletproof. 2 (of dog, horse) not gunshy.
*skott'/skive -a cf skyte/
*skott's/mål -et cf skuss/
skott'/sår -et (gun)shot wound.
skott'/våpen -et firearm.
skott'/år -et leap year.
sko'/tupp -en tip of a shoe.
+sko'/tvinge -n archaic shoelace.
+sko'/tøy -et (=*/ty) footwear.
*skot/år [skå't/] -et cf skott/
*skov[1] [skå'v] -et 1 move; progress. 2 attack; fight; brief tumult. 3 short time, while; time: to-tre s- two or three times.
*sko'v[2] pt of skave[1]
sko've[1] -a caking, crust (that sticks to sth, e.g. a pan).
sko've[2] V -a/+-et/+-de 1 clean, free (e.g. a pot) of crust. 2: s- seg form a crust.
*skove[3] [skå've] V -a appear in spurts, unevenly.
sko'vet(e) A - crusty.
skov'l -a/+-en 1 bucket, dipper (e.g. on excavator). 2 blade, vane (e.g. of turbine). 3 paddle. 4 shovel.
skov'le V -a/+-et scoop, shovel.
skov'l/hjul -et paddle wheel.
skr.=skriftlig
skrabb' -en 1 dry, stony patch in a field. 2 rattletrap (car), jalopy.
skrak'l -et (=+skrakkel) 1 rattling, shaking. 2 sth ramshackle; rattletrap. 3 tall thin person.
skrak'le V -a/+-et rattle, shake.
skrak'le/føre -t road conditions when lumps of ice or frozen earth make vehicles rattle.
skrak'let(e) A - 1 ramshackle, rickety. 2 (of person) tall and thin.
skra'l A 1 scant, slack; in a poor way: det går s-t things are going badly; s- med a lack of. 2 poorly, in bad health.
+skrall'[1] -et crack, crash, thunder; peal (e.g. of laughter).
skrall'[2] pt of skrelle[2]
+skral'le[1] -a rattle.
+skral'le[2] V -a/-et 1 clatter, crash, rattle. 2 (of sound) blare, peal.
skram'le V -a/+-et clatter, rattle: s- med kasseroller r- pans.
skram'le/orkes'ter -(e)ret, pl -/+-re children's "band" of lids, saucepans, etc.
+skram'me[1] -a/-en (=*skråme[1]) scratch.
+skram'me[2] V -et scratch, scuff.
skram'mel -elet/skramlet 1 clatter, rattle. 2 junk, scrap.
skrang'el -et/+-en clatter, rattle.
skrang'le[1] -a thin, bony person.
skrang'le[2] V -a/+-et clatter, rattle: s- med penger r- money around.
skrang'le/kjerre -a worn, rickety cart; rattletrap.
skrang'let(e) A - 1 loose-jointed and rattling, rickety. 2 (of person) thin and bony.
skrang'le/veg -en road that causes vehicles to rattle.
skrang'le/verk -et rattletrap.
skrang'le/voren [+/vårren, */våren] A +-ent, pl -ne rattling, ready to fall apart.
skran'ke -n 1 bar, barrier. 2 (in gymnastics) parallel bars. 3 (office) counter. 4 jur. bar: ved s-n at the b-.
skran'ke/advoka't -en trial lawyer.
skran'te V -a/+-et 1 be ailing, show signs of poor health. 2 not feel well. 3 be in a decline, a lapse; not be thriving.
skran'ten A +-ent, pl -ne 1 ailing, in poor health, unwell. 2 sensitive, tender.
skra'p -et 1 scraping sound, scratch. 2 rubbish, trash.
skra'pe[1] -a 1 scratch. 2 scraper. 3 currycomb.
skra'pe[2] -a/+-en reprimand.
skra'pe[3] V -a/+-te 1 scrape; pare (vegetables); scale (fish): s- bunnen scrape the bottom of the barrel; s- sammen scrape up (money); s- til seg rake in (money); bukke og s- bow and scrape; være s-t for be cleaned out of, completely lacking in. 2 (of animals) paw the ground, scratch. 3: s- ut med. curette.
+skra'per -en, pl -e (=*-ar) scraper.
+skra'p/handler -en, pl -e (=*-ar) junkman.
skra'p/haug -en junk (scrap) heap: kaste noe på s-en throw sth on the scrap heap.
skra'p/jern [/jæ'rn] -et (=*/jarn) scrap iron.
skra'p/kake -a 1 cake, bread made from the last scrapings of dough. 2 hum. youngest child, born long after the others.
skra'p/kasse -a/-en junk box.
*skrapp'[1] pt of skreppe[2]
+skrapp'[2] A skrapt 1 capable; quick. 2 nimble; handsome, pretty.
skra'p/slått -en uneven, stony area which yields little grass and has to be mowed by hand.
+skrap't nt of skrapp[2]
skra'p/ut N scrape (in oldfashioned greeting, together with a low bow).
*skras'l -et (=*skratl) cf skrassel
skras'le V -a/+-et (=skratle) 1 rattle. 2 guffaw, laugh loudly.
skras'sel -en/-et 1 rattling sound. 2 guffaw, loud laugh.
*skra't -et 1 cackle. 2 power, the upper hand (over sby).
*skra'te V -a 1 cackle. 2 reprimand, scold.
*skrat'l -et cf skrasl
skrat'le V -a/+-et cf skrasle
skratt' -et/-en 1 cackling. 2 guffaw, loud laughter.
skrat'te V -a/+-et 1 grate, give a shrill sound, shriek; crash, rattle. 2 cackle. 3 guffaw, laugh loudly.
skratt'/le V -lo, -ledd/*-lett guffaw.
*skrau'v -a foam (e.g. on beer).
*skrau've V -a 1 take up much space. 2 foam.
*skra've V -a chatter, talk.
skrave're V -te hachure, hatch, shade.
skrav'l[1] -a pop. kisser, mouth: jeg gav ham en på s-a I hit him in the m-, in the face; hold s-a på deg shut up, shut your trap.
skrav'l[2] -en chatterbox.
skrav'l[3] -et chatter, jabbering.
skrav'le[1] -a chatterbox, talkative woman.
skrav'le[2] V -a/+-et chatter, jabber: s- i vei chatter away.
+skrav'le/bøtte -a (=*/bytte) chatterbox.
skrav'le/kopp -en chatterbox.
skrav'let(e) A - talkative.
+skre' V -dde (=*skræ) 1 cut across (e.g. a piece of cloth) at an oblique angle. 2 slant, slope. 3 grind coarsely (to grits). 4 sift, sort out; reject, throw away. 5 spill; spoil.
skre'd[1] [*skre'] -et 1 avalanche;

+ Bokmål; * Nynorsk; ° Dialect.
After letter: ′ stress (Acc. 1); ‘ tone, stress (Acc. 2); · length.
Below letter: . not pronounced.

(land)slide. 2 collapse, slump (e.g. of prices); radical change.

+**skre'd**[2] *pt of* **skride**

+**skred'der** *-en, pl -e* (=*-**ar**) tailor.

+**skredderi'** *-et* 1 tailoring. 2 tailor's workshop.

+**skred'der/kritt** *-et* (=*-**ar/**) tailor's chalk.

+**skred'der/mester** *-eren, pl -ere/-rer* master tailor.

+**skred'der/saks** *-a* (=*-**ar**) tailor's shears.

+**skred'der/sydd** *A* - (=*-**ar/**) tailored, tailor-made; made-to-measure.

***skre'de** *-a* cf **skred**[1]

***skre'de/laup** *-et* marks from a landslide.

skrei'[1] *-a* flock (**av** of), host, swarm (of sth advancing speedily).

skrei'[2] *-en* cod (in spawning period).

skrei'[3] *pt of* **skri**[1]

Skrei'a *Pln* hilly area, town, Østre Toten twp, Oppland.

***skrei'd** *pt of* **skri**[1]

***skrei'de** *V -de* 1 push to the side: **skreid loka ifrå** unbolt the door. 2: **s- seg** run on ice or snow (e.g. skating, skiing).

skrei'/fiske *-t* winter fishing of cod.

skrei'k *pt of* **skrike**[2]

skrei'/torsk *-en* cod (in spawning period).

skrei'v *pt of* **skrive**

+**skre'k** *pt of* **skrike**[2]

skrekk' *-en* 1 alarm, fright, terror: **få seg en s- i livet** get a fright; **være blek av s-** be pale with t-. 2 (strong) aversion: **ha en s- for noe** have an a- to sth; be scared of sth; **snakkesalige folk er min s-** talkative people are my pet a-.

+**skrek'kelig** *A* - awful, frightful, terrible: **han så s- ut** he looked t-; (as *adv.*) **det er s- varmt her** it's terribly hot here.

+**skrekk'/innjagende** *A* - terrifying.

+**skrekk'/regimen'te** *-t* (reign of) terror.

+**skrekk'/slagen** [also skrekk'/] *A -ent, pl -ne* terrified, terror-stricken.

skrekk'/velde *-t* (reign of) terror.

skrell'[1] *-en/+-et* 1 bang (e.g. of thunder), detonation. 2 crack (e.g. in a plate).

skrell'[2] *-et* peel; rind, skin.

***skrel'le**[1] *-a* cf **skralle**[1]

skrel'le[2] *V skrall/+skrelte, +skrelt/*skrolle/*-i* 1 boom, crash, explode; echo, resound. 2 (e.g. of a plate) become cracked.

***skrel'le**[3] *V skrelte* 1 bang, do sth with a bang: **s- en dør igjen** bang a door shut. 2 crack (e.g. a cup).

skrel'le[4] *V skrelte/*-a* peel (**av** off): **de s-er av drømmene** they shed their dreams (Evensmo).

***skrel'le/lått** *-en* booming laughter.

+**skrel'ler** *-en, pl -e* (=*-**ar**) (apple, potato) peeler.

skrel'te *pt of* **skrelle**[2,3]

skrem'me *V +skremte/*skremde* alarm, frighten, terrify; threaten (**med** with): **du skremte meg** you gave me a fright; **banken skremte ham med tvangsauksjon** the bank threatened him with foreclosure; **et skremt uttrykk** a terrified expression; **s-ende nyheter** alarming news; **s- opp** alarm, start, startle (e.g. birds).

+**skrem'me/bilde** *-t* frightening description; bogey, bugbear.

skrem'melig *A* - frightening, terrifying.

+**skrem'me/skudd** *-et* warning shot.

skrem'sel *-elet/-let, pl +-ler/*-el* 1 terror, threat. 2 scarecrow; boogeyman; ugly person.

***skrem'sle** *-a* 1 fright, scare. 2 (in *pl*) ghosts; haunting.

skren'se *V -a/+-et/+-te* swerve: **bilen s-et borti gjerdet** the car s-d into the fence.

skren't *-en* 1 steep slope; cliff; escarpment. 2 edge of a precipice.

skrepp' *-et* 1 quack, quacking sound. 2 praise. 3 bragging.

skrep'pe[1] *-a* bag, sack, wallet.

***skrep'pe**[2] *V skrapp, skroppe/-i* 1 slide noisily. 2 give a rattling, scraping sound. 3 shrink.

skrep'pe[3] *V skrepte* 1 (of bird) quack. 2: **s- av noe, noen** praise sth, sby; brag about sth, sby. 3 (often of sth that later on shrinks or turns out to be smaller or less than it appears) look big, impressive.

skrep'pe/handel *-en* peddling.

+**skrep'pe/handler** *-en, pl -e* (=*-**ar**) peddler.

skrep'pe/kar *-en* peddler.

***skrepp'/sam** *A* given to praising or bragging.

skre'v[1] *-et* 1 (long) step, stride. 2 crotch: **over s-s** astride; **til s-s** up to the c-.

+**skre'v**[2] *-et*: **gå over s-et** go too far, be an outrage.

+**skre'v**[3] *pt of* **skrive**

skre've *V -a/+-et/+-de* 1 straddle, stride, walk with big steps: **s- over noe** step over sth. 2 stand with feet wide apart, astride.

skrev's *Av* astraddle, astride, striding: **over s-, s- over** astride.

skre'v/stor *A* long-legged, able to take long steps.

skri'[1] *V skrei, +skridd/*skride/*-i* (=**skride**) 1 slide, slip. 2 glide, run (on skates or skis). 3 advance, proceed, walk with a slow, solemn gait; stride. 4 advance, proceed; develop, make progress: **s- fram** advance; make progress; **hvi skrider menneskeheten så langsomt frem?** why does humanity make such slow progress? (Wergeland); **begivenhetene s-r fram** events are unfolding, proceeding; **s- inn** take measures, steps; **s- inn mot misbruk** take measures against abuse; **s- til noe** take the step of doing, beginning, starting sth; **s- til verket** go to work. 5 go, pass: **det lir mens det s-r** time is going by.

skri'[2] *V -dde* slide, slip.

skriben't *-en* writer.

+**skriben't/virksomhet** *-en* literary activities.

+**skrib'le** *V -a/-et* 1 scribble. 2 write in a superficial, lighthearted manner.

+**skrib'leri** *-et* scribbling.

skri'de [*skri'e] *V +skred/*skreid, +skredet/*skride/*-i* cf **skri**[1]

+**skri'e** *-a* cf **skred**[1]

skrif't[1] *-a/+-en* 1 alphabet, system of writing; letters; type: **gotisk s-** Gothic letters, script; **hemmelig s-** secret alphabet, cipher. 2 handwriting, writing: **lese s-** be able to read; **s-en på veggen** the handwriting on the wall; **hun har (en) vakker s-** she has (writes) a beautiful hand. 3 literary work, writing(s); scripture: **gå inn for noe i s- og tale** advocate sth in writing as well as in speech; **Den hellige s-** the Holy Writ; **de hellige s-er** the Holy Scriptures.

skrif't[2] *-et, pl -er/*-* document; publication: **et oppbyggelig s-** an edifying (religious) p-; a tract; **samlede s-er** collected writings.

***skrif't**[3] *-et* cf **skrifte**[1]

skrif't/art *-en* 1 (kind of) hand, script. 2 *typog.* fount.

+**skrif't/bilde** *-t* 1 *typog.* typeface. 2 visual picture, impression of sth written (word, line, page).

+**skrif'te**[1] *-t* (=***skrift**[3]) confession, shrift: **gå til s-** go to confession; confess.

skrif'te[2] *V -a/+-et* confess; hear confession, shrive.

skrif'te/ba'rn *-et, pl -/*-born* penitent.

skrif'te/far *-en, pl +-fedre/*-fedrar* (father) confessor.

skrif'te/mål *-et* confession.

skrif'te/stol *-en* confessional.

skrif't/klok *A* 1 *bibl.* (as noun) scribe. 2 versed in the Scriptures. 3 book-learned.

skrif'tlig *A* - in writing, written: **s- svar** written reply; **kan jeg få det s-?** will you give (often: confirm, repeat) it (to me) in writing?

skrif't/lærd *A* - 1 versed in the Scriptures. 2 book-learned.

skrif't/o'rd *-et* Bible passage.

skrif't/språk *-et* literary (=written) language.

+**skrif't/sted** *-et* Bible passage.

***skrif't/styrar** *-en* editor of a periodical.

skrif't/trekk *-et* stroke (of handwriting).

skri'k *-et* 1 scream, yell; call (of animal). 2 screaming, yelling: **s- og skrål** screaming, bawling; noisy confusion; **dette s-et etter høyere lønn** this clamor for higher wages; **mye s- og lite ull** much ado about nothing. 3: **siste s-** the latest fashion.

***skri'kar/unge** [/onge] *-n* cf **skriker/**

+**skri'ke**[1] *-a* (=*-**je**) *zool.* jay (genus Garrulus).

skri'ke[2] *V skreik/+skrek, +skreket/*skrike/*-i* 1 scream, shout, yell; (of animals) bellow, call; (of a crow) caw: **s- etter, på** scream for; **s- i, opp** let out a yell; **s- om** shout about, for. 2 bawl, cry, shriek: **s- fra seg** (e.g. of a baby) cry oneself out. 3 (of hinges, snow, wheels, etc.) creak, squeak. 4: **s- mot himmelen** *fig.* cry to high heaven. (See also **s-ende.**)

***skri'ke**[3] *V -a* move, shake; bring out of position, disturb.

skri'kende *A* - 1 crying (also *fig.*), flagrant, glaring (e.g. injustice): **en s- motsetning** a glaring contrast. 2 (of colors) glaring, loud.

+**skri'ker** *-en, pl -e* (=*-**ar**) 1 loudmouth; demagogue. 2 (howling) baby, brat.

+**skri'ker/unge** [/onge] *-n* (=*-**ar/**) howling brat.

skri'k/hals *-en* 1 animal or person who cries, yells a lot; crybaby. 2 demagogue, loudmouth.

***skri'kje** *-a* cf **skrike**[1]

***skrik'ke** *V -a* (of animal, e.g. calf) caper, jump.

***skrim'sel** *-et* brief appearance, glimpse.

***skrim'sle** *V -a* 1 glimpse; make out (sth). 2 glow, shine faintly.

skri'n *-et* 1 reliquary, shrine. 2 (fairly small) box, chest; casket.

+**skri'n/legge** *V -la, -lagt* (=*-**je**) abandon, shelve (e.g. plans); bury, enshrine.

skrinn' *A skrint* 1 (of person or domestic animal) lean, scraggy, scrawny. 2 (of soil) barren, poor. 3 (e.g. of fare, food) lean, giving little nourishment.

***skrin'ne** *-a* area, field that is barren, yields little.

skrinn'/lendt *A* - (of area) having barren, poor soil.

skrin't *A nt of* **skrinn**

***skri'pe** *V -a* caress, pet.

skri'pen *A +-ent, pl -ne* 1 (esp. of animal) friendly, wanting to be petted. 2 shy.

***skri'p/læte** *-a/-et* ingratiating manner.

+**skritt'** *-et* 1 step, stride; pace: **gå et s-** take a step; **holde s- med** keep in step with; **holde s- med tiden** move with the times; **holde en på tre s-s avstand** keep sby at arm's length; **s- for s-** step by step; **tre s- fra livet!** keep your distance! 2 *fig.* measure, step: **ta det første s-** make the first move; **ta s- til** take the necessary s-s to; **ta s-et** make the decision; **ta s-et fullt ut** go (the) whole hog. 3 pace, walk: **kjøre i s-** drive (a horse) at a walk. 4 crotch, groin: **sparke en i s-et** kick sby in the g-.

+**skrit'te** *V -a/-et* pace, stalk, stride;

walk: **s- av (opp)** pace off; **s- ut** stride briskly.

skritt'/gang -*en* walk, walking pace.

skritt'/teller -*en*, *pl* -*e* pedometer.

skri'v -*et* (=+**skrivelse**) 1 (official) letter; document. 2 *hum.* missive.

***skri'var** -*en* cf **skriver**

***skri'var/brød** -*et* cf **skrive/**

skri've *V* *skreiv*/+*skrev*, +*skrevet*/ **skrive*/*-*i* 1 write (**til** to; **om** about): **s- diktat** take dictation; **s- falsk** commit forgery; **s- noe rent** make a clean copy of sth, w- sth out; **sier og s-er ti** (emphatically) ten (10), ten repeat ten; **hva s-er vi i dag?** what's the date today?; **det s-es i avisen at** it says in the paper that; **det skrevne ord** the written word; **som skrevet står** as is written, as the Bible says; **det står skrevet** it is written, decreed (e.g. by fate); the Bible says; **det står ingen steder skrevet at** there's no law that; **hvor står det skrevet?** who says so? what's your authority? 2 (with *prep.* and *adv.*): **s- av** copy, transcribe; **s- etter** copy; write according to (e.g. a norm); write for (i.e. request); **s- fra seg** renounce in writing; **s- inn** enter (e.g. in a ledger); **s- om** write about; rewrite; **s- opp** write down, make a note of; **det kan du s- opp** you can be sure of that; **s- på en** charge to one's account; **s- på for en** go good for, countersign for sby; **s- på noe** be writing sth (e.g. a book); **s- på maskin** type; **s- sammen** write, slap together; **s- til** add (in writing); **s- under (på noe)** endorse, sign (sth); **s- ut** fill (e.g. a notebook) with writing; write out in full; decree in writing, announce (e.g. new tax laws, general conscription); **s- en ut** discharge sby (e.g. from a hospital); **s- ut stemmene** *mus.* transcribe the parts. 3 (*refl.*): **s- seg** write one's name as; **s- (seg) noe bak øret** make a mental note of sth, keep sth in mind; **s- seg for** put oneself down for, pledge (on a contribution or subscription list, etc.); **s- seg for presten** register for confirmation; **s- seg fra** be derived from, be due to, originate with; date from; **s- seg inn** enter one's name, register; **s- seg opp** work oneself up (while writing); **s- seg tom** (of an author) write oneself out.

skri've/bok -*a*, *pl* -*bøker* copy book, excercise book.

skri've/bo'rd -*et* (office) desk: **sitte ved s-et** be sitting at one's desk.

skri'vebords/lampe -*a*/-*en* desk lamp.

skri'vebords/skuff -*en* desk drawer.

+**skri've/brød** -*et* thin round cake, baked in an iron and then given an extra coating of very thin batter in which a line pattern is "written" with a serrated piece of birch bark.

skri've/feil -*en* writing error, slip of the pen.

skri've/før *A* 1 able to write. 2 able at writing.

skri've/kløe -*n* writer's itch.

skri've/krampe -*n* writer's cramp.

skri've/kunst -*en* 1 art of writing. 2 penmanship.

+**skri'velse** -*n* cf **skriv**

skri've/lyst -*a*/+-*en* itch, urge to write (e.g. articles, books).

skri've/lysten *A* +-*ent*, *pl* -*ne* itching to write.

skri've/mappe -*a* portfolio (of writing materials).

skri've/maski'n -*en* typewriter.

skri'vemaskin/dame -*a*/+-*en* typist.

skri've/papi'r -*et* writing paper.

skri've/penn -*en* recording pen, stylus.

skri've/pensel -*elen*, *pl* -*ler* writing brush.

skri've/pult -*en* writing desk (often tall).

+**skri'ver** -*en*, *pl* -*e* (=***-ar**) 1 (rural) judge. 2 clerk, scribe; *secretary (e.g. of an association).

+**skri'ver/gå'rd** -*en* residence of a **skriver.**

+**skri'veri** -*et*, *pl* -*er* 1 scribbling, writing. 2 poorly written article.

+**skri'ver/kar** -*en* (=***-ar/**) *archaic* clerk.

skri've/saker *pl* writing materials.

skri've/stell -*et* writing set; inkstand.

skri've/stue -*a* 1 *archaic* writing room. 2 (in modern business organization) typing pool.

+**skri'v/feil** -*en* cf **skrive/**

skrofulo'se -*n* *med.* scrofula.

skrofulø's *A* *med.* scrofulous.

+**skrog** [skrå'g] -*et* (=***skrov**[2]) 1 *naut.* hull. 2 carcass: **koke suppe på s-et** boil the bones for soup. 3 frame; central part, chassis. 4 wreck, wretch.

***skrokk'** *pt of* **skrøkke**

skrok'ke** *pp of* **skrøkke** (=skrokki**)

***skrokken** [skrok'ken] *A* -*e*/-*i*, *pl* *skrokne* cf **skrukken**

***skrokne** [skrok'ne] *V* -*a* cf **skrukne**[1]

***skrol'le**[1] *V* -*a* loom, take up much space.

skrol'le**[2] *pp of* **skrelle**[2] (=skrolli**)

***skro'p** -*et* bragging.

***skro'pe** *V* -*a* brag.

skrop'pe** *pp of* **skreppe**[2] (=skroppi**)

***skrop'pen** *A* -*e*/-*i*, *pl* *skropne* shrunk(en).

skro't -*et* 1 scrap metal; junk, trash. 2 a pity, too bad: **det var s- at jeg mistet kniven** it's a pity I lost the knife.

skro't/haug -*en* junk heap, pile.

skrott' -*en* 1 carcass. 2 body: **få noe i s-en** get sth to eat. 3 berry, fruit pulp (after juice has been extracted); core (of apple, pear).

skrov[1] [skrå'v] -*et* 1 porous mass. 2 sth ramshackle, worn.

***skrov**[2] [skrå'v] -*et* cf **skrog**

skroven [skrå'ven] *A* +-*ent*, *pl* -*ne* porous, spongy.

skrov/is [skrå'v/] -*en* loose, porous ice (e.g. on top of other ice).

***skrov'ne** *V* -*a* become porous.

skru' *V* -*dde* (=**skrue**[2], **skruve**[2]) 1 screw, turn: **s- av** screw off, unscrew; turn off (e.g. a faucet, radio); **s- for, til** fasten, screw down; **s- ned** turn down (e.g. a lamp), *fig.* depress (prices); **s- opp** open, turn up, unscrew; *fig.* increase (prices, often artificially); **s- på** turn on; **s- tilbake** turn back (e.g. time, progress, the clock); **s- seg opp** (of a sound, storm, etc.) increase in strength; (of a person) inflate oneself, put on airs; **s-et** *archaic* artificial, put on (e.g. manners); (of people) peculiar, queer. 2 (of ice) pack together, press: **isen s-er seg opp** the ice is packing; **skipet ble s-dd ned av isen** the ship was pressed down (i.e. sunk) by the ice.

skrubb'[1] -*en* 1 wolf. 2 scrubbing brush. *3 severe person.

skrubb'[2] -*et* 1 scrubbing. 2 abrasion (of the skin). 3 reprimand, scolding: **få s-** get a s-. 4 beating, licking, thrashing.

skrub'be[1] -*a* *zool.* type of flounder (Pleuronectes flesus).

skrub'be[2] *V* -*a*/+-*et* 1 scrub; rub. 2 brake, drag: **s- med foten** brake with one's foot when sledding; **s- nedpå** (of a ski) go through the snow, scrape. 3 skin: **s- (seg på) kneet** skin one's knee. 4 dress down, scold. 5: **skrubb av** (slang) clear out, go away; don't give me that.

skrub'bet(e) *A* - 1 coarse, rough, uneven; chopped. 2 (of fungus) scaly.

skrubb'/høvel -*en* *carp.* scrub plane.

+**skrubb'/sulten** *A* -*ent*, *pl* -*ne* (=***/svolten**) ravenous.

skru'/blyant -*en* automatic pencil.

skru'd -*et* vestments.

skru'e[1] -*n* (=**skruve**[1]) 1 screw. 2 *naut.* propeller. 3 peculiar character, person: **han er en underlig s-** he's a queer duck.

skru'e[2] *V* +-*dde*/*-*a* cf **skru**

skru'e/gang -*en* screw thread.

+**skru'e/hode** -*t* screwhead.

+**skru'e/kork** -*en* screw cap on a bottle.

skru'e/lokk -*et* screw cap on a jar.

skru'e/snitt -*et* screw threading tool.

skru'e/stikke -*a* (=+**/stikk**) vise.

+**skru'e/tang** -*a*, *pl* -*tenger* (=***/tong**) adjustable pliers.

skru'e/tvinge -*a* clamp.

skru'/is -*en* pack ice.

skru'/jern [/jæ'rn] -*et* screwdriver.

skrukk[1] [skrokk'] -*en* wrinkle.

***skrukk**[2] [skrokk'] *N*: **i s-** packed together; **siga i s-** collapse.

skrukke[1] [skrok'ke] -*a* 1 wrinkle. 2 small basket of (birch) bark.

skrukke[2] [skrok'ke] *V* -*a*/+-*et* 1 wrinkle. 2: **s- seg** form wrinkles; shrink.

skrukken [skrok'ken] *A* +-*ent*, *pl* *skrukne* shrunken.

skrukket(e) [skrok'ket(e)] *A* - wrinkled.

skrukke/troll [skrok'ke/] -*et* *zool.* wood louse (Oniscus).

skrukne[1] [skrok'ne] *V* -*a*/+-*et* become wrinkled, wrinkle.

skrukne[2] [skrok'ne] *pl of* **skrukken**

+**skru'/kork** -*en* cf **skrue/**

skrull' -*en* 1 screwy idea, notion (also +-*et*). 2 eccentric, odd person, screwball.

skrul'le -*a* 1=**krumkake.** 2 eccentric, odd, screwy woman.

***skrul'len** *A* -*e*/-*i*, *pl* *skrulne* cf **skrullet(e)**

skrul'let(e) *A* - (=***skrullen**) cracked, crazy.

skrul'ling -*en* crazy person.

skru'/lokk -*et* cf **skrue/**

skrumle [skrom'le] *V* -*a*/+-*et* give a hollow, rattling sound.

skru'/mor -*a* nut (on a bolt).

skrumpe [skrom'pe] *V* -*a*/+-*et* shrink: **s- inn (i hop, sammen)** s-, shrivel (up).

skrumpen [skrom'pen] *A* +-*ent*, *pl* -*ne* shriveled, shrunken.

skrump/lever [skrom'p/] -*ra*/+-*eren*, *pl* +-*rer*/*-*rar* *med.* cirrhosis of the liver.

***skrun'de** *pt of* **skrynje**

***skrun't**[1] -*en* cavity.

***skrun't**[2] *pp of* **skrynje**

skru'/nøkkel -*elen*, *pl* -*nøkler* monkey wrench (esp. adjustable-end wrench).

skrup'pel -*elen*, *pl* *skrupler* scruple: **gjøre seg (få) s-er over noe, ved noe** have s-s about sth; **uten s-er** unscrupulous.

+**skrup'pel/løs** *A* (=***/laus**) unscrupulous, without scruples.

skrupulø's *A* scrupulous.

+**skru'/skøyte** -*a* ice skate (which can be screwed on shoes).

+**skru'/trekker** -*en*, *pl* -*e* screwdriver.

skru'v -*en* 1 *archaic* laced brim on a type of woman's cap. 2 top part of a tall cupboard. 3 sounding board above a pulpit. 4 shock (of grain).

***skruv-** *Pf* cf **skru-**

skru've[1] -*n* cf **skrue**[1]

skru've[2] *V* +-*de*/*-*a* cf **skru**

***skry'** -*et* coughed-up mucus.

***skry'e**[1] -*a* mucus cough.

***skry'e**[2] *V* -*dde* cough up mucus.

***skryf'te** *V* -*a* cf **skrøfte**

***skryf'te/rug** -*en* cf **skrøfte/**

***skrykkj'e** *V* *skrykte* wrinkle (by cramming).

***skrym'sle** -*a* ghost.

***skryn'je** *V* *skryn*, *skrunde*, *skrunt* 1 rattle, rumble. 2 brag.

***skry'p** *A* unlasting, unsubstantial.

+ Bokmål; * Nynorsk; ° Dialect.
After letter: ' stress (Acc. 1); ' tone, stress (Acc. 2); · length.
Below letter: . not pronounced.

***skry'pleg** *A* - perishable; transitory.
skry't *-et* (=***skrøyt**) bragging.
***skry'te**[1] *-t* 1 dry tree. 2 skeleton.
skry'te[2] *V -te/+skrøt, -t* (=***skrøyte**) boast, brag (av of).
skry'ten** *A -e/-i, pl -ne* (=skrøyten**) ugly.
skry'te/pave *-n* boaster, braggart.
+**skry'ter** *-en, pl -e* (=***-ar, *skrøytar**) boaster, braggart.
skry't/hals *-en* boaster, braggart.
skry't/laup *-en* boaster, braggart.
***skry've** *V -de* shock (grain).
***skræ'** *V -dde* cf **skre**
***skræ'kte** *V -a* croak, emit a hoarse, raucous scream.
***skræ'len** *A -e/-i, pl -ne* feeble, weak.
skræ'ling *-en* weak, pitiful person, wretch.
***skræ'me**[1] *-a* fright, scare.
***skræ'me**[2] *V -de* cf **skremme**
***skræ'meleg** *A* - cf **skremmelig**
***skræ'msle** *-a* cf **skremsle**
***skræ'ne** *V -a* dry out; harden, shrink.
***skræ'r** *pl of* **skrå**[2]
skrøf'te *V -a/+-et* 1 extract the ripest grain from a sheaf by knocking it against sth. 2 punish, beat up.
skrøf'te/rug *-en* ripest part of rye (extracted from the sheaves by knocking them against sth).
***skrøk'ke** *V skrokk, skrokke/-i* shrink (often by drying up).
skrøm't *-et* 1 ghosts; uncanny things or goings-on. 2 illusion, imagination; bluff, feint: **på s-** feinted, as a bluff or joke; **uten s-** sincere, unfeigned.
skrøm'te *V -a/+-et* (of ghosts) appear, be afoot: **det s-er** the ghosts are about.
***skrøm't/heilag** *A* hypocritical.
***skrøm't/laus** *A* sincere, unfeigned.
skrø'ne[1] *-a* 1 fib, lie; tall story. 2 anecdote, (good) story.
skrø'ne[2] *V -te/*-a* 1 fib, lie. 2 tell (tall) stories, anecdotes: **s- sammen** invent.
+**skrø'ne/maker** *-en, pl -e* (=***-ar**) storyteller; liar.
skrø'ne/pave *-n* fibber, liar; storyteller.
skrø'ne/smeḍ *-en* (=/**pave**).
skrø'pelig *A* - 1 *lit., fig.* fragile, frail; weak: **et s- kar** *bibl.* a frail vessel; **kvinnene, det er en s- slekt** women, they're a sorry lot (Ibsen); **ånden er villig, men kjødet er s-** the spirit is willing, but the flesh is weak (Matt. 26, 41). 2 decrepit, in bad shape, sickly; ramshackle, rundown; bad, (of) poor (quality): **s- med fortjenesten** poor earnings.
+**skrø'pelig/het** *-en* 1 brittleness, fragility; frailness, frailty: **i all s-** in a modest way, in all humility. 2 defect, fault, infirmity; weakness.
+**skrø'pelighets/synḍ** *-en* sin of infirmity.
+**skrø't** *pt of* **skryte**[2]
***skrøy't** *-et* cf **skryt**
***skrøy'tar** *-en* cf **skryter**
***skrøy'te** *V -te* cf **skryte**[2]
***skrøy'ten** *A -e/-i, pl -ne* cf **skryten**
***skrøy't/sam** *A* boastful.
***skrøy'v** *-et* boast; exaggeration.
***skrøy've**[1] *-t* sth that appears big, that looms.
***skrøy've**[2] *V -de* 1 loom. 2: **s- opp** exaggerate, overpraise.
***skrøy'veleg** *A* - bombastic.
skrå'[1] *-a/-et* (plug of) chewing tobacco; chaw, chew.
skrå'[2] *+-en/*-a, pl *skrær hist.* 1 parchment manuscript. 2 codex, collection of statutes.
skrå'[3] *V -dde* 1 cut (across sth) at an oblique angle, diagonally. 2 walk (across sth) at an oblique angle, diagonally: **s- over gaten** cross the street.
skrå'[4] *V -dde* chew tobacco.
skrå'[5] *A -tt, pl -/*-e* oblique, slanting; *(adv.)* at an angle, diagonally: **solskinnet falt s-tt inn av vinduet** the sunshine came in through the window at an angle; **de s- bredder** the stage; **på s-** aslant, at an angle, diagonally.
skrå'l *-et* racket, shout(ing), uproar: **skrik og s-** yelling and screeching; **s- etter, på** clamor, demand (for).
skrå'le *V -te/*-a* bawl, shout, yell; clamor: **s- en sang** bawl out a song; **han s-te (etter) på mer øl** he was yelling for more beer.
skrå'l/hals *-en* loudmouth, vociferous person.
***skrå'me**[1] *-a* cf **skramme**[1]
***skrå'me**[2] *V -a* bruise, scar, scratch.
skrå'met(e) *A* - bruised, scarred, scratched.
skrå'ne *V -a/+-et/+-te* 1 slant, slope, tilt: **s- nedover** slope downwards; **s- oppover** rise, slope up. 2 level, make oblique, give a slant.
skrå'ning *+-en/*-a* 1 declivity, incline, slope: **jevn s-** gentle i-, smooth s-. 2 *tech.* gradient, pitch.
skrå'/plan *-et* 1 *phys.* inclined plane. 2 *fig.* downward path; moral decline: **komme (ut) på s-et** wander from the straight and narrow.
skrås' *Av* at an angle, diagonally: **på s-** (the same).
skrå'/sikker *A* confident, positive.
skrå'/snitt *-et* bevel cut.
skrå'/stilt *A* - placed in a slanting position, at an angle.
skrå'/tak *-et* slanting roof.
skrå'/tobakk *-en* chewing tobacco.
+**skrått'/liggenḍe** *A* slanting, sloping: **et s- jorde** a sloping field.
***skrå've** *V -a* grate, rattle, rustle.
skubb' *-en/-et* 1 push, shove: **gi en et s-** push sby, give sby a s-. 2 push, stimulus: **et s- framover** a forward p-.
skub'be *V -a/+-et* 1 push, shove: **s- fra seg** push away, try to get rid of; **s- fram, i været** boost; **s- på** boost, stimulate; **s- til side, vekk** push aside, away. 2: **s- seg (mot)** rub (against); shift one's weight, fidget; **s- seg fram** push one's way ahead.
+**skudd'** *-et* cf **skott**[3]
+**skudd'/dag** *-en* cf **skott/**
+**skud'der/mudder** *et* chaos, confusion: **gå i s-** dissolve into chaos; go by the board.
+**skudd'/fri** *A -tt* cf **skott/**
+**skudd'/holḍ** *-et* (=***skott/hald**) range (of aim, shot): **komme innenfor s-** come within r-; **utenfor s-** beyond r-.
+**skudd'/linje** *-a/-en* line of fire, trajectory: **komme i s-en** *fig.* be in an exposed position.
+**skudd'/penger** *pl* cf **skott/**
+**skudd'/premie** *-n* cf **skott/**
+**skudd'/sikker** *A -ert, pl -sikre* cf **skott/**
+**skudd'/sår** *-et* cf **skott/**
+**skudd'/veksling** *-en* exchange of fire, shots.
+**skudd'/vidde** *-a/-en* range (of fire).
+**skudd'/våpen** *-et* cf **skott/**
+**skudd'/år** *-et* cf **skott/**
Sku'de/nes *Pln* twp, Rogaland.
Sku'denes/havn *Pln* town, Rogaland.
+**sku'e**[1] *-t* 1 appearance, sight: **komme til s-** appear; **bære, stille til s-** display, show off. 2 survey. 3 sight, spectacle: **et storslått s-** a magnificent s-. 4 (cattle) show.
+**sku'e**[2] *V -et* (=***skode**) behold, see: **s- ut over mengden** survey the populace; **det var herlig å s-** it was a magnificent sight; **en skal ikke s- hunden på hårene** (don't judge the dog from its coat) appearances are deceptive.
+**sku'e/brøḍ** *-et bibl.* shewbread: **det er bare s-** *fig.* it's only window dressing.
+**sku'e/lysten** *A -ent, pl -ne* curious, eager (to see, watch).
+**sku'e/plass** *-en* 1 scene (**for** of). 2 stage, theater.
+**sku'e/spill** *-et* (=***skode/spel**) 1 play. 2 scene; spectacle.
+**sku'e/spiller** *-en, pl -e* (=***skodespelar**) actor.
+**skuespillerin'ne** *-a/-en* (=***skodespelarinne**) actress.
skuff [skoff'] *-en* cf **skuffe**[1]
skuffe[1] [skof'fe] *+-n/*-a* drawer: **stjele, ta av s-n** (of employee) steal money out of the cash register.
+**skuffe**[2] [skof'fe] *-a* shovel.
+**skuffe**[3] [skof'fe] *V -a/-et* 1 shovel: **s- i seg** s- in the food. 2 *dial.* push, shove.
skuf'fe[4] *V -a/-et* 1 disappoint: **han har s-et meg dypt** he has d-ed me deeply; **føle seg s-et** feel d-ed. 2 *archaic* deceive, delude.
skuffel [skof'fel] *skufla, pl skufler* shovel.
+**skuf'felse** *-n* disappointment.
+**skuf'fenḍe** *A* - 1 deceptive; lifelike: **s- likhet** deceptive likeness. 2 disappointing.
skufle [skof'le] *V -a/-et* shovel.
***skuf's** *-en* speed: **setje s- i ein** speed sby up.
***skugg'** *-et* shadow: **i s- og skjol** on the sly, secretly.
***skug'ge**[1] *-n* cf **skygge**[1]
***skug'ge**[2] *V -a* cf **skygge**[3]
***skug'ge/heim** *-en* otherworld, world of shadows.
***skug'ge/redd** *A* - jittery, nervous: **han er ikkje s-** he's got plenty of nerve.
skukk' *-en* hayloft.
***skul'ḍ** *-a* cf **skyld**[1]
***skul'ḍ/auke** *-n* aggravating circumstances.
***skul'ḍ/bunden** *A -e/-i, pl -ne* debt-ridden.
***skul'de** *V -a* cf **skylde**[1]
+**skul'der** *-eren, pl -rer* 1 shoulder: **dra, trekke på s-en** shrug; **slå en på s-en** slap sby's back; **stå s- ved s-** stand s- by s-; **stå på ens s-** build on sby's achievements. 2 upper part of a mountain slope; mountain plateau.
+**skul'der/bein** *-et* shoulder bone.
+**skul'der/blaḍ** *-et* shoulder blade.
+**skul'der/klaff** *-en* shoulder strap (board U.S. Navy, loop U.S. Army).
+**skul'der/stropp** *-en* shoulder strap.
+**skul'der/trekk** *-et* shrug: **han hadde bare et s- til overs for deres lidelser** he merely shrugged at their sufferings.
***skul'ḍ/fri** *A -tt* cf **skyld/**
***skul'ḍ/før** *A* of sound mind, responsible for one's actions.
***skul'ḍ/gjeving** *-a jur.* charge.
skul'dig [+skul'di] *A* - cf **skyldig**
***skul'ding** *-a* accusation.
***skul'ḍ/kjensle** *-a* feeling of guilt.
***skul'ḍ/laus** *A* innocent.
***skul'ḍ/løyse** *-a* innocence.
***skul'ḍ/mann** *-en, pl -menn(er)* debtor.
***skul'ḍ/mink** *-en* extenuating circumstances.
***skul'ḍ/minkande** *A* - extenuating.
***sku'le**[1] *-n* cf **skole**[1]
***sku'le**[2] *V skal, skulle, skula* cf **skulle**
***sku'le**[3] *V -a* cf **skole**[3]
sku'le[4] *V -te* look furtively, squint, steal a sidelong glance (**til** at); look embarrassed, as if having a bad conscience; give an ugly look.
Sku'le *Prn(m)*
sku'le/dunk *-en* slop jar, swill pail.
***sku'le/krins** *-en* cf **skole/krets**
sku'lenḍe *A* - furtive, squinting.
sku'ler *pl* slop, swill.
skul'k *-et/+-en* shirking; malingering.
skul'ke *V -a/-et* 1 shirk: **s- unna** s- one's duty. 2 be absent without good cause; malinger: **s- skolen, arbeidet** play truant from school, work.
skul'ke/sjuke *-n* malingering, truancy.
skul'le *V skal, skulle, +-et/*-a* (=***skule**[2]) 1 (simple future, conditional) shall, will; should, would: **jeg skal gjøre det** I'll do it; **hva skal det være** what'll you have (of food, drink, etc.); **hva (hvor) det**

skal være no matter what (where); **det skal bli** as you wish; **skal — — skal ikke** shall I or shan't I; what to do?; (at end of statement) **skal jeg si deg** let me tell you; **(det) skal (skulle) jeg tro** I would imagine, I guess so; **det skulle ikke forbause meg** it wouldn't surprise me; **du skulle ikke ville?** you wouldn't want to?; **skulle det være mulig?** is that possible? 2 (duty, obligation) must, shall; ought to, should: **du skal ikke** you mustn't, *bibl.* thou shalt not (Ex. 20, 3); **det er ikke som det skal være** that's not as it should be; **jeg vet ikke hva jeg skal tro** I don't know what to think; **sannheten skal fram** the truth must out; **skulle vi ikke gå?** shouldn't we leave? 3 is (was) going to, is (was) supposed to: **skal vi snart spise?** are we going to eat soon?; **hva skal De her?** what are you doing (do you want) here?; **det var ikke det vi skulle snakke om** that's not what we were supposed to talk about; **jeg skulle akkurat til å si** I was just going to say; **hva var det jeg skulle sagt?** what was I going to say? 4 is (was) said to: **han skal være rik** he is said to be rich; **han skal ha lest mye** I've heard he's studied a lot. 5 (with *adv.* of motion) is (was) getting, going: **skulle av** be getting off; **skulle opp** be getting (going) up; **han skulle til byen etter øl** he was going to town for some beer (a song). 6: **s- til** be necessary, needed; **det skulle noe til** it took quite a bit; **jeg hadde ikke den frekkheten som skulle til** I didn't have the necessary brashness. 7: **skal tro (om)** (I) wonder (if).

skul'pe +-*n*/*-*a* *bot.* silique (seed capsule).

skulptu'r -*en* sculpture.

skulpturell' *A* -*elt* sculptural.

skulptø'r -*en* sculptor.

skul's *A* - (=**skult**) (of persons settling sth so that neither owes the other) even, quits.

skul'se *V* -*a*/-*et* (=***skulte**) (of two persons) settle a mutual account.

skul't *A* - cf **skuls**

skul'te *V* -*a*/-*et* cf **skulse**

skum[1] [skom'] -*met* 1 foam, froth, lather; scum; spray. 2 *fam.* champagne.

skum[2] [skom'] *A* (=**skym**) (half) dark, dim.

sku'mast** *V* -*ast* (=skymast**) cf **skumre**

skum/brott [skom'/] -*et* white breaker.

skum/dott -*en* cap of foam.

sku'me** *V* -*a* (=skyme**) cf **skumre**

skum/gummi [skom'/] -*en* foam rubber.

skum/hatt -*en* cap of foam.

+**skum/hvit** *A* cf **/kvit**

***sku'ming** -*a* cf **skumring**

skum/kvit [skom'/] *A* foamy white.

skum'le [also: skom'le] *V* -*a*/-*et* insinuate; pass on rumors (**om** about), whisper: **det s-es om underslag** they say there's been an embezzlement.

+**skum'leri** [also: skom'leri] -*et*, *pl* -*er* (usu. *pl*) insinuation; rumor.

skumma/mjølk [skom'ma/] -*a* skim milk.

skumme [skom'me] *V* -*a*/-*et* 1 foam, froth, lather: **en s-ende elv** a foaming river; **s- av raseri** froth with rage; **såpen s-er ikke** the soap doesn't lather. 2 skim: **s- fløten** *fig.* get the best part of sth; harvest the results.

skum'mel *A* -*elt*, *pl* *skumle* 1 dismal, gloomy; eerie: **en s- gate** a d- street; **et s-t strøk** a bad district, part of town. 2 sinister; ugly: **en s- type** an u- customer; **et s-t blikk** a s- glance; **omgås med skumle planer om noe** harbor s- plans of (doing) sth. 3 fishy, suspicious: **virke s-t** seem s-; **det ser meg litt s-t ut** I think it's a bit fishy.

+**skummer** [skom'mer] *A* -*ert*, *pl* *skumre* half dark, dim.

+**skummet/melk** [skom'met/] -*a*/-*en* cf **skumma/mjølk**

skump [skom'p] -*en*/+-*et* (hard or sudden) push; poke, shove.

skumpe [skom'pe] *V* -*a*/-*et* 1 poke, push: **s- inn i** bump into; **s- til** bump (sby). 2 bump (along), jolt, rattle (e.g. on a bad road).

+**skum'pel/skudd** -*et* outcast.

skumple [skom'ple] *V* -*a*/-*et* bump, jolt.

+**skum're** [also: skom're] *V* -*et* (=***skume, *skyme, *-ast**) grow dark, dusk: **det s-er** it's getting dark.

skum'ring [also: skom'ring] -*a*/-*en* (=***skuming**) dusk, twilight.

skumrings/time -*n* hour of twilight: **holde s-** sit in the dark (=not turn on the light).

+**skum/skjær** [skom'/] -*et* (=***/skjer**) coulter (on plow).

***skum/skott** -*et* dusk, twilight.

+**skum/slokker** [skom'/slokker] -*en*, *pl* -*e* (=***/sløkkjar**) foam extinguisher.

skum/sprut [skom'/] -*en* spray.

skum/sprøyt -*en*/-*et* spray.

+**skum/svett** *A* - (=***/sveitt**) lathering, in a lather.

skum/topp -*en* crest of foam.

***skun'de** *V* -*a* cf **skynde**

***skun'ding** -*a* cf **skynding**

skunk [skong'k] -*en* *zool.* skunk (Mephitis mephitica).

sku'r[1] -*a* shower (of hail, rain, or missiles).

sku'r[2] -*en* cf **skurd**[2]

***sku'r**[3] -*en* *zool.* sparrow (Passer domesticus).

sku'r[4] -*et* shack, shanty, shed.

sku'rd[1] -*en* (wood)carving.

sku'rd[2] -*en* (=**skur**[2]) 1 cutting, mowing of grain. 2 harvest time. 3 ripe grain that is to be cut. 4 cutting of lumber into planks etc. 5 dressed, finished lumber. 6 cut; cut profile. 7 notch.

sku'rd/last -*a*/-*en* dressed, finished lumber.

sku'rd/onn -*a* harvesting, harvest work; (period of) harvest.

***sku'rd/treskjar** -*en* cf **skur/tresker**

sku're *V* +-*te*/*-*a* 1 rub, scour, scrub: **s- gulv** scrub floors; **s- kniver med sand** scour knives with sand (to remove spots). 2 grate, grind, scrape (**mot** against): **det får s-, la det s-** let it ride, don't do anything about it. 4 move quickly, speed: **det går s-ende** it's going at a great rate.

+**sku're/bøtte** -*a* (=***/bytte**) scrub pail.

sku're/fille -*a* wash rag (for floors).

sku're/klut -*en* wash rag (for floors).

sku're/kone -*a* cleaning woman, scrubwoman.

sku're/pulver -*et* cleanser, scouring powder (for floors and sinks).

sku'ring -*a*/-*en* 1 scrubbing. 2 reprimand, scolding, talking to. 3: **det er grei s-** anyone can see that; that's easy to tell.

skur'k -*en* scoundrel, villain.

+**skur'k/aktig** *A* - villainous.

skur'ke/fjes -*et* villain's face.

skur'ke/rolle -*a*/-*en* part (in play, book) of a villain: **spille s-en** play the villain.

skur'ke/strek -*en* (piece of) villainy, vile trick.

sku'r/last -*a*/-*en* cf **skurd/**

***skur'n** -*a* shell (e.g. of egg).

***skur'ne** *V* -*a* peel (e.g. an egg).

sku'r/onn -*a* cf **skurd/**

skur're *V* -*a*/-*et* grate, jar: **s- i ørene** grate on one's ears.

+**sku'r/tresker** -*en*, *pl* -*e* combine (harvester).

skur'v -*en* 1 scab, scabies. 2 *med.* favus; *vet.* ringworm.

skur've -*a* crust, scab (on wound).

skur'vet(e) *A* - scabby, scurfy, scurvy: **det skal skarp lut til s-e hoder** (sharp lye is needed for scurfy heads) it takes harsh measures to reform a hardened sinner.

skus'le *V* -*a*/-*et* (=**skutle**): **s- bort** waste, throw away, spend recklessly.

+**skuss'/mål** -*et* certificate of character; reference, testimonial; reputation.

sku't[1] -*en* 1 overhanging cliff. 2 eaves. 3: **gjøre s-, slå s-** shade the eyes with one's hand. 4 shack, shed. 5 lean-to.

sku't[2] -*en* cf **skott**[1]

sku'te[1] -*a* *naut.* craft, vessel; ship (esp. sailship).

***sku'te**[2] *V* -*te* row backwards.

sku'tel -*elen*, *pl* -*ler* shuttle.

sku'tel/svein -*en* *hist.* 1 servant who waits at table. 2 title of type of courtier in Old Norse times.

skut'le *V* -*a*/-*et* cf **skusle**

sku't/rygga *A* - (=***-ja**, +**-et**) stoop-shouldered.

+**skutt'** *pp of* **skyte**

+**skut'te** *V* -*et* shake: **s- seg** shake oneself, shrug; shiver; **s- på seg** shrug, toss; **s- noe av seg** toss off.

***sku'v**[1] -*en* 1 tassel. 2 heap, pile.

***sku'v**[2] -*et* push.

sku've *V* +-*de*/*-*a* cf **skyve**

+**skvad're** *V* -*et* chatter.

skvadro'n -*en* squadron.

skvadrone're *V* -*te* bluster, boast, brag.

skvadronø'r -*en* blusterer, braggart.

***skva'ke** *V* -*a* chatter.

***skvakk'** -*en* bark, yelp.

***skvak'ke** *V* -*a* bark.

skva'l -*et* 1 dishwater; diluted, thin drink. 2 rippling, splashing sound. *3 shell.

skval'der -*eret*/-*ret* chatter; noisy, stupid talk.

skval'dre *V* -*a*/-*et* chatter, prattle.

+**skval'dre/bøtte** -*a* (=***/bytte**) chatterbox.

skva'le *V* -*a*/+-*te* splash: **s- i seg** drink, gulp down.

skval'ler/kål -*en* *bot.* goutweed (Aegopodium podagraria).

skval'p -*en*/+-*et* lapping, ripple, splash.

skval'pe *V* -*a*/-*et* 1 lap, ripple. 2 splash, make a splash: **s- med bøtta** splash with the bucket (in hauling up water from well).

skval'pe/sjø -*en* choppy sea.

skvam'ple *V* -*a*/-*et* splash.

skvat're *V* -*a*/-*et* (=***skvate**) (e.g. of magpie) chatter.

skvatt' *pt of* **skvette**[1]

skvett'[1] -*en* 1 splash, spray: **s- fra bilene** splash from passing cars. 2 dash, drop: **en s- øl** a drop of beer. 3 small (rain) shower.

skvett'[2] -*en* *zool.* part of certain compound bird names, e.g. **stein/s-**.

skvett'/bo'rd -*et* *naut.* washboard.

skvet'te[1] *V* *skvatt*, +-*et*/**skvotte*/*-*i* 1 spatter, squirt: **han kjørte så søla skvatt** he spattered up mud as he drove along. 2 rain in small showers. 3 jump, start: **han skvatt av lyden** he started at the noise; **s- i, til** give a start; **s- opp** jump up; **s- tilbake for** be startled at, retreat from. 4 hop, skip, run a short distance: **s- over gata** cross the street in two jumps.

skvet'te[2] *V* -*a*/-*et*/*-*e* 1 splash, squirt: **s- vatn** s- water; **det er som å s- vatn på gåsa** it runs like water from a duck's back. 2 (e.g. of a dog) let water, urinate (esp. in squirts).

skvet'ten *A* +-*ent*, *pl* *skvetne* 1 jittery, jumpy. 2 nervous; reticent: **hun er så s- av seg** she is so nervous, shy. 3 scared; cowardly: **han er ikke s-**

he's no sissy; he's got what it takes.
skvett'/lapp -en splash guard (on automobile).
+**skvett'/lær** -et (=*/ler) fender, leather mudguard (on front of wagons).
skvett'/skjerm -en fender (of car, bicycle, wagon).
skvi'p -et sth diluted, "dishwater", thin drink.
skvi's -en squeeze (in bridge).
skvi'se V -a/-et/+-te squeeze (in bridge).
skvot'te** pp of **skvette**[1] (=skvotti**)
+**skvul'p** -et lap, ripple.
+**skvul'pe** V -a/-et lap, ripple; splash.
skvæ'r A -t/*- 1 naut. square. 2 honest, square. 3 (adv.) completely, square, straight: **han kjørte s- i fjellveggen** he drove square into the rock; **bli s- gærn** pop. go crazy.
skvæ're V -a/-et/+-te 1 naut. square (yards of a ship). 2: **s- opp** settle, square up (account, dispute).
skvæ'r/rigga A - (=+-et) naut. square-rigged.
skvæ'r/segl -et (=+/seil) naut. square sail.
sky'[1] -a cloud (av of): **det er ikke en s- på himmelen** there isn't a cloud in the sky (also fig.); **heve, løfte til s-ene** praise to the skies; **sveve oppe i s-ene** have one's head in the c-s; **i s-, mot s-** skywards; **gleden stod høyt i s-** they were happy as larks; **sette nesen i s-** stick one's nose in the air (i.e. appear stuck-up); **(synge, skråle) i vilden s-** (sing, yell) at the top of one's voice.
+**sky'**[2] -en 1 fear: **føle s- for noe** have a f- of sth; shrink from sth. 2 awe, veneration. 3 bashfulness.
sky'[3] V -dde avoid; shrink from; shun: **s- (en, noe) som pesten** avoid (sby, sth) like the plague; **ikke s- noen anstrengelse** not shrink from any effort; **brent barn s-r ilden** (a burnt child avoids the fire) once bitten twice shy.
sky'[4] A -, pl +-/*-e bashful, diffident; shy, timid, wary: **en s- hest** a shy horse (i.e. difficult to catch).
sky'/banke -n bank, mass of clouds.
+**sky'/brudd** -et (=/brott) cloudburst.
sky'/dekke -t cloud cover, cloudiness, overcast: **skiftende s-** variable cloud cover.
sky'/dott -en cloudlet.
sky'/drag -et cloud movement.
***sky'/drått** -en cloud movement.
sky'e V -a/-et (of clouds) form: **s- over (på, til)** cloud over.
sky'et(e) A - cloudy, overcast.
skyf'fel -elen, pl +skyfler hoe, scraper.
skyf'le V -a/-et hoe, scrape; clean (e.g. garden).
sky'/floke -n dense cloud formation.
sky'/fri A -tt unclouded; clear (sky).
sky'/full A cloudy.
***skyg'de** pt of **skyggje**
***skygg'**[1] -et gauze, veil.
skygg'[2] A skygt reticent, shy, wary.
+**skyg'ge**[1] -n (=***skugge**[1]) 1 shadow: **(ikke) en s- av tvil** (not) a s- of a doubt; **gripe (jage) etter en s-** catch at (chase) s-s; **kaste s-** cast a s-; **løpe fra (springe over) sin egen s-** attempt the impossible; **stille en i s-n** fig. overshadow sby; **tre i s-n for** be overshadowed by; **en s- av seg selv** a s- of one's former self. 2 shade (also in meaning of ghost, spirit); shading (e.g. on a drawing): **det var 30 grader i s-n** it was 86 degrees in the shade; **nattens s-er** the shades of night. 3 visor (on cap); brim (on hat).
***skyg'ge**[2] -t shading; shady place.
+**skyg'ge**[3] V -et/skygde (=***skugge**[2], ***skyggje**) 1 shade; cast a shadow; fig. obscure: **s- for** block the light, shade from; **s- for øynene** shade one's eyes; **s- over** cast a shadow over. 2 shade (drawing). 3 shadow, tail (sby).
+**skyg'ge/aktig** A - shadowy; vague.
+**skyg'ge/bilde** -t 1 shadow figure, silhouette (**av** of). 2 phantom; ghost.
+**skyg'ge/bokser** -en, pl -e shadow-boxer.
+**skyg'ge/full** A shady.
+**skyg'ge/legge** V -la, -lagt shade.
+**skyg'ge/lue** -a cap with visor.
+**skyg'ge/regje'ring** -a/-en shadow cabinet (one in name only).
+**skyg'ge/side** -a/-en 1 shady side, shade: **livets s-** the seamy side of life. 2 disadvantage, drawback (**ved** of).
***skyg'ge/stein** -en rock crystal.
+**skyg'ge/tilvæ'relse** -n: **føre en s-** lead (a) shadowy existence.
+**skyg'ge/tre** -et, pl -/-trær shade tree.
***skyg'gje** V skygde cf **skygge**[3]
***skygg'/lapp** -en cf **sky/**
***skyg'ne** V -de look after; look around, spy.
+**sky'/het** -en shyness.
sky'/høg A sky-high.
***sky'l** pr of **skylje**
sky'/lag -et cloud layer (bank), overcast.
+**sky'/lapp** -en blinder(s), blinker(s): **gå med s-er** (also fig.) wear b-s.
sky'/laus A clear, cloudless, unclouded.
skyl'ḍ[1] -a/+-en (=***skuld**) 1 blame, fault, guilt: **gi en s-en for** blame sby for; **ha s-en for** be to blame for, be the cause of; **legge, kaste s-en på** lay, place, throw the blame on; **ta s-en på seg** take the blame; **tilstå sin s-** confess one's guilt; **s- i** to blame for, the cause of; **uten egen s-** through no fault of one's own. 2 crime, sin: **forlat oss vår s-** forgive us our trespasses (debts). 3 sake: **for ens s-** for sby's sake; **for den saks s-** for that matter, as far as that's concerned; **for min (din) s-** for me (you), for my (your) s-; **for min s- kan du gjerne** as far as I'm concerned go right ahead, it's all right by me. 4 archaic tax. 5 debt: **stå i s- til** be in d- to. 6 dial relationship: **være (i) s- med** be related to.
skyl'ḍ[2] A - related (**med, til** to): **de er s-** they are r-.
+**skyl'ḍ/betyng'et** A - guilt-ridden, guilty.
+**skyl'ḍ/beviss't** A - conscience-stricken, guilty.
+**skyl'ḍbevisst/het** -en sense of guilt.
skyl'ḍe[1] V +-te/*-a (=***skulde**) 1 owe: **s- (bort) penger** o- money; **s- en en unnskyldning** o- sby an apology; **jeg s-er meg selv å gjøre det** I o- it to myself to do it. 2 accuse, blame: **de s-te ham for tyv** they accused him of being a thief; **s- fra seg** put the blame on sby else; **s- på en** blame sby; **s- på noe** (also) give sth as the reason. 3 * or archaic have the duty, be obliged (å to).
***skyl'de**[2] pt of **skylje**
+**skyl'ḍes** V -tes, -es be due to; arise from, be caused by, be the work of: **det s- at** it is due to the fact that.
skyl'ḍ/folk -et relatives.
+**skyl'ḍ/fri** A -tt 1 guiltless, innocent. 2 dial. free of debt.
+**skyl'ḍ/følelse** -n feeling of guilt.
skyl'dig A - (=***skuldig**) 1 guilty (**i** of): **s- i mord** g- of murder; **gjøre seg s- i en feil** fall into an error. 2 due: **vise s- respekt** show d- respect. 3 in debt: **bli, være s-** owe; **hva blir jeg s-?** how much do I owe you?; **bli svar s-** be at a loss for an answer; **være en (stor) takk s-** owe sby a debt of gratitude. 4 liable (**til** to); in duty bound, obliged (**til å, å** to): **s- til dødsstraff** liable to capital punishment.
+**skyl'dig/het** -en duty: **gjøre sin s-** do one's d-; fulfil an obligation.
***skyl'ding** -en relative.
skyl'ḍ/mark -a/+-en unit used in assessing value of land, for taxation purposes.
skyl'ḍnaḍ -en duty, obligation.
+**skyl'dner** -en, pl -e debtor.
+**skyl'ḍ/satt** A - (=*/sett) jur. (of land) assessed.
***skyl'ḍ/setje** V -te cf /sette
skyl'ḍ/setning +-en/*-a jur. assessment (of land).
+**skyl'ḍ/sette** V -satte (=*/setje) jur. assess (land).
skyl'ḍ/skap -en/+-et (family) relationship: ***for s- skuld** for kinship's sake.
+**skyl'ḍ/spørsmål** -et question of guilt: **avgjøre s-et** settle question of defendant's guilt or innocence.
***sky'le**[1] -t 1 hiding place. 2 shack, shed.
***sky'le**[2] V -te 1 cover; hide. 2 dial. wash; rinse.
+**sky/light** [skei'/leit] -et cf **skei/leit**
***skyl'je** V skyl, skylde, skylt cf **skylle**[2]
***skyl'/jings/kar** -et dishpan.
+**skyll'** -et 1 rolling, wash (of waves against coast, shore). 2 downpour, heavy precipitation; shower.
+**skyl'le**[1] -n 1 flood, flow (e.g. of water, or abuse). 2 food refuse, slop.
+**skyl'le**[2] V skylte (=***skylje**) 1 pour: **vannet s-te inn (ned)** the water p-ed in (down); **bli s-ende rød** flush violently; **musikken s-te over ham som veldige havbølger** fig. the music engulfed, swept over him like huge waves. 2 wash: **s- i land** w- ashore; **s- noe ned med** w- sth down with; **en mann ble s-t overbord** a man was w-ed overboard. 3 rinse, wash (clothes, dishes, vegetables, one's mouth, etc.): **s- ut** w- out.
+**skyl'le/bolle** -n fingerbowl.
+**skyl'le/bøtte** -a slop pail; fig. flood of abuse, severe reprimand.
+**skyl'le/kopp** -en rinsing bowl.
+**skyl'ler** pl cf **skuler**
+**skyl'le/vann** -et rinse water.
+**skyll'/regne** [/reine] V -a/-et rain in torrents.
***skyl't** pp of **skyle**[2], **skylje, skylle**[2]
***skyl'te** pt of **skyle**[2], **skylle**[2]
sky'm A cf **skum**[2]
***sky'mast** V -dest cf **skumre**
***sky'me** V -de cf **skumre**
+**skym'es** V -tes, -tes cf **skumre**
***sky'ming** -a cf **skumring**
***sky'n** -et cf **skjønn**[1]
+**skyn'ḍe** V -te (=***skunde**) 1 hurry: **s- fram** accelerate, speed up; **s- på** accelerate, speed up (sby, sth); hurry up, push on. 2: **s- seg** hurry (up); **s- seg med noe** hurry up with sth; **skynd deg å komme** please come quickly.
***skyn'del** -elen, pl -lar 1 torch. 2 shuttle.
+**skyn'ḍing** -a/-en (=***skunding**) haste, hurry: **i s-en** in (one's) h-; **i største s-** in the greatest h-, as quickly as possible.
+**skyn'ḍ/som'** A -t, pl -me hasty, hurried: **et s-t tilbaketog** a h- retreat.
***sky'ne** [also: sjø'ne] V -a f **skjønne**
sky'/pumpe [/pompe] -a meteor. waterspout.
***sky'r**[1] -et cf **skjør**[1]
***sky'r**[2] A cf **skjør**[2]
***sky're** V -te (of fish) flee, shy away.
***skyr'ne** V -a cf **skjørne**
°**sky'ru** -a sickle.
sky/segl [skai/, skei/] -et (=+/seil) naut. skysail.
+**sky'/skraper** -en, pl -e (=*-ar) skyscraper.
skyss' -en 1 archaic transport of travelers by horse or boat (esp. according to statute or route, schedule). 2 ride: **få s-** get a r-; **takk for s-en** thanks for the r-. 3 hurry, speed: **han fikk s-** he was thrown out, chased away.
skys'se V -a/+-et 1 drive, give (sby) a ride: **s- en over vannet** ferry sby across the lake. 2 chase, drive (away): **s- en av gårde** chase sby away, off.

skyss'/hest -en archaic horse kept for conveyance of passengers.

skyss'/kar -en archaic coachman, driver.

skyss'/skifte -t archaic inn where travelers changed horses.

sky'te V skaut/+skjøt, +skutt/*skote/*-i 1 fire, shoot (etter, på at) (gun, bullet, arrow, ball, puck, etc.): s- av discharge, fire (gun); s- bort use up (ammunition, usu. wastefully); s- feil (forbi) miss the mark; s- løs på blaze away at; s- mål score a goal; s- ned shoot down, kill on the spot; s- nyttår inn fire a salute to the New Year; s- over shoot too high, overshoot the mark; s- ut launch (e.g. rocket). 2 (of plants; fig. of people, esp. children) grow, (of buds) shoot: s- knopper bud; s- rot strike, take root; s- vekst grow, develop. 3 move rapidly: s- fart put on speed; s- forbi pass quickly, shoot past; s- opp bob up; s- opp i vinden naut. gain the wind, move upwind; s- seg fram move forward quickly. 4 push, shove: s- døra for shut the door; s- fra seg push away; s- fram push forward; project, jut out, protrude; s- brystet fram throw out one's chest; s- ham slough one's skin; s- i været raise up, stick up (one's nose, shoulders, etc.); s- rygg (skuldre) arch, hunch up one's back (shoulders); s- slåen for døra bolt the door (i.e. shoot the bolt); s- til side push aside; fjorden s-er en arm langt inn i landet fig. an arm of the fjord cuts far into the land. 5 blast (rock etc.). 6 (other idioms): s- ansvaret fra seg shirk one's responsibility; s- inn put in; contribute, invest (money); s- inn under submit to (sby's judgment); s- opp (et tau) naut. coil up (a line); skutt sats typog. leaded matter; s- seg i mellom (of events) intervene; s- seg inn under (bak) noe use sth as a pretext, hide behind sth; s- til contribute; s- ut delay, postpone.

sky'te/bane -n rifle range; shooting gallery.

sky'te/bas -en foreman of construction crew using explosives.

sky'te/bomull [/bommull] -a guncotton.

sky'te/felt -et artillery range.

+sky'te/ferdighet -en ability in shooting; marksmanship.

sky'te/matte -a blasting mat (used to cover small blast sites).

sky'te/prøve -a/+-en shooting test (for hunting license).

+sky'ter -en, pl -e (=*-ar) "rod", shooter.

sky'te/skive -a target; (of person) object, target (e.g. for ridicule).

sky'te/skole -n mil. shooting course.

+sky'te/skår -et (=*/skor(e) -a) mil. embrasure (=opening in wall or parapet for shooting).

sky'te/våpen -et firearm(s).

*skyt'je -a arch. extension, lean-to; woodshed.

skyt'nings/stue -a hist. 1 tavern. 2=skjøtstue.

skyt's -et artillery: kjøre opp med s-et bring up the big guns; kjøre opp med tungt s- (also) fig. bring up strong arguments.

+skyt's/engel -elen, pl -ler guardian angel.

+skyt's/helgen -en patron saint.

+skyt's/ånd -en guardian spirit.

skyt'tel -elen, pl skytler shuttle.

+skyt'ter -en, pl -e (=*-ar) rifleman; hunter: en god s- a good shot, marksman.

+skyt'ter/grav -a/-en (=*-ar/) trench.

+skyt'ter/konge -n (=*-ar/) national shooting champion.

+skyt'ter/lag -et (=*-ar/) rifle club.

+skyt'ter/linje -a/-en (=*-ar/) 1 skirmish line. 2 hunters posted to intercept game.

+skyt'ter/medal'je -n (=*-ar/) marksmanship medal.

+skyt'ter/post -en (=*-ar/) hunter's post.

+sky'v/bar A movable, sliding.

sky've V skauv/+skjøv, +skjøvet/*skove/*-i (=skuve) push: s- bort, fra seg dismiss, p- aside, shirk (unpleasant thought, duty, responsibility, etc.); s- en til side p- sby aside; s- på p-, fig. act upon, stimulate.

sky've/dør -a sliding door.

sky've/port [/port] -en gate with doors that slide open or shut.

+sky'ver[1] en, pl -e 1 stop latch (on lock). 2 pusher (for food, used by children).

*sky'ver[2] A -ert, pl -re quickly consumed, short-lived.

skøy' +-en/*-et fun, jokes, teasing: på s- for fun.

skøy'e V -a/+-et/+-de have fun; joke (med with).

+skøy'er -en, pl -e (=*-ar) joker, rascal.

+skøy'er/aktig A - given to pranks, impish, mischievous.

skøy'er/fant -en joker, prankster.

+skøy'er/fjes -et (=*-ar/) impish, mischievous face.

+skøy'er/strek -en prank, (pl) mischief.

*skøyr [sjøy'r] A cf skjør[2]

*skøyt [sjøy't] -en cf skjøt[1]

skøyte[1] [sjøy'te] -a fishing smack.

+skøyte[2] [sjøy'te] -a skate: gå på s-er skate.

*skøyte[3] [sjøy'te] -a/-et cf skjøte[1]

*skøyte[4] [sjøy'te] V -te cf skjøte[2]

+skøyte[5] [sjøy'te] V -te cf skjøtte

*skøyte[6] [sjøy'te] V -te cf skjøte[3]

+skøyte/bane [sjøy'te/] -n skating rink.

+skøyte/is -en skating ice.

*skøyte/laus [sjøy'te/] A cf skjødes/løs

*skøyte/leidning -en cf skjøte/ledning

+skøyte/løp [sjøy'te/] -et 1 skating. 2 skating contest, race.

+skøyte/løper -en, pl -e skater.

+skøyte/løperske -n (female) skater.

*skøyte/løyse [sjøy'te/] -a cf skjødes-løs/het

+skøyte/publikum [sjøy'te/] -met audience at skating contest.

+skøyte/stevne -t (official) skating contest.

*skå' A -tt, pl skå(e) oblique; at an angle, diagonally.

skå'k -a, pl skjæker shaft (of carriage): slå på s-a og mene merra criticize by inference, by attacking sth that is connected with what one really means to criticize.

skå'k/sky A - (of horse) afraid of the shafts.

skå'l[1] -a 1 bowl: en s- (med) melk a b- of milk. 2 saucer: kopp og s- cup and s-. 3 dish, plate (e.g. in frukt/s-). 4 toast: utbringe en s- for en drink a t- to sby; nå tar vi en s- let's all drink.

skå'l[2] I skoal; (to) your health.

*skå'l/blom -en bot. ranunculus.

skål'de V -a/+-et scald.

skål'dende A scalding.

skål'd/heit A scalding hot.

skål'd/varm A scalding hot.

skå'le[1] -n 1 archaic dwelling house; house containing large hall for festive use. 2 shack, shed. 3 corridor in outbuilding.

skå'le[2] V -te/*-a drink a toast: s- for en, noe drink (a toast) to sby, sth; s- med en drink a toast with sby; s- med hverandre (of two persons) drink to one another.

+skå'l/gave -a/-en (=*/gåve) gift of money (put in gift bowl at country wedding).

skå'l/harv -a disc harrow.

skå'l/pund -et obs. unit of weight, slightly larger than a pound (498 grams).

skå'l/tale *-a/-en speech (at table) concluded by a toast.

+skå'l/taler -en, pl -e (=*-ar) speaker who proposes a toast.

skå'l/vekt -a balance, scales.

*skå'n -a hard crust.

skå'ne[1] V -a/+-te 1 spare (e.g. life): s- en for noe s- one (e.g. the trouble of) sth. 2 be careful of: s- sin helbred take care of one's health; s- øynene take care not to strain one's eyes.

*skå'ne[2] V -a slant, slope.

Skå'ne Pln Scania (in Sweden).

skå'ning -en Scanian.

Skå'n/land Pln twp, Troms.

skå'nsel +-elen/*-la leniency, mercy, pity: vise s- show p-; uten s- merciless.

skå'nsel/laus A (=+/løs) merciless, pitiless, ruthless.

skå'nsk A - Scanian.

+skå'n/som' A -t, pl -me (=*/sam) considerate; gentle; lenient: et s-t vaskemiddel a g- detergent; vi må fortelle ham det så s-t som mulig we must tell him as gently as possible.

+skå'nsom/het -en consideration; gentleness.

*skå'p -et cf skap[1]

*skå'p/drikkar -en cf skap/drikker

skå'r[1] -a (=*skor[2]) cleft in mountain; ledge.

skå'r[2] -en (=skåre[2]) swath.

+skå'r[3] -et 1 chip, notch; cut, incision: et s- i gleden a fly in the ointment. 2 (broken) piece, shard.

+skå're[1] -a (=*skore) 1 cut, incision. 2 cleft, ravine.

skå're[2] -n cf skår[2]

skå're[3] -n (test) score.

+skå're[4] V -a/-et/-te score (goal in soccer).

+skå're[5] V -a/-et/-te 1 make a cut, incision into; notch. 2: s- på horna pop. (of horned farm animals, fig. of people) show signs of ageing.

Skå're Pln twp, Rogaland.

+skå'ret pp of skjære[3]

skå'r/ung [/ong] -en (=/unge) 1 yearling seagull. 2 young boy on his first fishery.

+skå'te[1] -a (=*skote[1]) 1 (window) shutter. 2 bar, bolt (for locking door).

+skå'te[2] V -a/-et (=*skote[2]) back the oars (in rowing).

Skå't/øy Pln parish, Telemark.

S/L=+salgslag/*sals-

*sla'[1] -et slope.

*sla'[2] A slatt sloping.

slabb' -en sloppy or seedy-looking man; slob.

slab'be[1] -a sloppy or seedy-looking woman; slattern.

slab'be[2] V -a/+-et slop, splash; spill (food) on one's clothes; eat noisily.

slabbedas'k -en lazy, good-for-nothing fellow.

slabbera's -et coffee party; hen party.

slab'bet(e) A - sloppy.

slad'der -en/*-et gossip: fare med s- spread g-.

+slad'der/aktig A - gossipy.

slad'der/hank -en tattletale.

slad'der/histo'rie -a/+-en piece of gossip; slander.

slad're V -a/+-et 1 gossip (om about). 2 tell (på on), (pop.) blab.

+slad're/bøtte -a (a) gossip.

slad're/kjerring -a, pl *-ar (woman) gossip.

+slad're/speil -et busybody, window mirror.

°sla'e -n cf slede

slaf's -et 1 smack (of lips); slurp. 2 slush.

slaf'se V -a/+-et 1 (esp. of dogs) eat noisily: s- i seg maten gulp down food noisily. 2 (e.g. of rain, snow) splash down.

+ Bokmål; * Nynorsk; ° Dialect.
After letter: ' stress (Acc. 1); ' tone, stress (Acc. 2); · length.
Below letter: . not pronounced.

slaf'se/føre *-t* (= +**slapse/**) slushy road condition(s).
slaf'set(e) *A* - slushy.
sla'g[1] *-et* 1 blow, hit, punch (with fist, hammer, weapon; of fate, life, etc.); knock (on door, the head, in engine, etc.), rap: **falle for det første s-** lose quickly, give up easily; **et s- i luften** an empty gesture; **ha fritt s-** have free hands (to act); **kunne stå for s-** be strong, able to withstand blows; **med ett slag** at one blow, suddenly; **s- i s-** thick and fast, without pause; **slå et s- for** strike a blow for (a cause). 2 beat (in music, of heart), stroke (in tennis, golf; of clock, engine, etc.): **på s-et tolv** on the stroke of twelve; **klokka dro opp til s-** the clock prepared to strike. 3 beating (of heart, waves, rain, wind, etc.), flapping (of sth hanging loose, wings, etc.), striking (of one object against another). 4 battle; game (of cards, chess, etc.): **s-et er tapt (vunnet)** the day is lost (won); **her skal s-et stå** the battle will take place here; **s-et på Stiklestad stod i 1030** the battle of S- took place in 1030. 5 heart attack (stroke); blow, shock (to nervous system): **få s-** have a heart attack; **nyheten kom som et s-** the news came as a shock. 6 singing, warbling of birds: **jeg hørte måltrostens muntre s-** I heard the cheerful warbling of the song thrush (Asbjørnsen). 7 short run, trip; *naut.* tack: **gå et s- over gulvet** take a turn around the room; **slå et s-** take a walk; **ta det i små s-** take it easy. 8 (esp. rain) cape. 9 (animal) tracks: **s- etter bjørn (ulv, osv.)** bear (wolf etc.) tracks. 10 lapel (on dress or jacket).
sla'g[2] *-et* 1 kind, sort: **varer av alle s-** all kinds of merchandise; **er hun av det s-et?** (usu. *derog.*) is she that kind of person?; **all s-** all kinds of; **det eneste i sitt s-** the only one of its kind. 2 race: **grisen er av et godt s-** this pig is of a good r-. 3 *pop.*: **hva s-?** what's that?; ***kva er d- -ta for s-?** what's this? 4: **det er slikt s-** one is as good as the other.
+**sla'g/anfall** [also: sla'g/] *-et* heart attack; stroke.
sla'g/benk *-en, pl* *****-er** bench which opens into a bed.
sla'g/bjø'rn *-en* killer bear.
sla'g/bo'rd *-et archaic* folding table.
***sla'ge** *V -a* 1 *naut.* tack. 2 reel, stagger, totter.
+**sla'gen** *A -ent, pl -ne* beaten; struck: **en s- mann** a defeated man; **s- med blindhet** s- blind; **den slagne landevei** the beaten track.
sla'ger *-en, pl* +*-e* (popular) hit (tune).
sla'ger/melodi' *-en* (popular) hit (tune).
sla'g/ferdig *A* - quick-witted, witty.
+**sla'gferdig/het** *-en* wit.
slagg' *-en/-et* 1 slag; cinder; clinker. 2 *lit. (pl)* impurity; refuse. *3 slavering.
slag'ge *V -a/+-et* 1 form slag. 2 remove slag from: **s- fyren** clean up (slag) the furnace. *2 salivate, slaver, slobber.
slagg'/spett *-et tech.* slice bar.
sla'g/kraft *-a/+-en* 1 striking power. 2 effect, effectiveness.
sla'g/kraftig *A* - (e.g. of army) having great striking power; effective.
sla'g/lodd *-et* 1 hard solder. 2 clock weight (e.g. in grandfather clock).
sla'g/mark *-a* battlefield.
***sla'gne** *V -a* 1 (e.g. of wood) become moist, saturated. 2 (e.g. of board) warp.
sla'g/o'rd *-et* slogan; motto.
sla'g/orden *-en* battle array, battle order.
sla'g/plan *-en* plan of action, of campaign.
sla'g/regn [+/rein] *-et* very hard, lashing rain.
+**slag's** *en/et* (=**slag**[2]) 1 kind of, sort of: **all(e) s-** all kinds of, various; **den s- (ting)** that sort of thing, things like that; **en, et s-** a sort of, some kind of; **han er en s- dikter** he's a sort of poet, a poet of sorts; **hva s-** what kind of, what sort of; **mange s-** many kinds of. 2 kind, sort, type: **av det beste s-** of the best sort, variety; **det er enestående i sitt s-** it's outstanding of its kind.
slag's/bror *-en, pl* +*-brødre/*-brør* brawler, fighter.
sla'g/side [*/sie] *-a/+-en* 1 *naut.* list. 2 lopsidedness.
sla'g/skip *-et* battleship.
slag's/kjempe *-a/+-en* bully, fighter.
+**sla'g/skygge** *-n* (=*/**skugge**) sharply outlined shadow; *fig.* overshadowing personality.
slag's/mål *-et* (fist)fight; controversy: **komme i s- om noe** get into a fight about sth (**med** with).
+**sla'g/sted** *-et* (=*/**stad**) battle site.
sla'g/støvel *-elen, pl -ler* high boot.
sla'g/sverd *-et* broadsword.
sla'g/tilfelle [also sla'g/] *-t, pl -/+-r* apoplexy, heart attack, stroke.
sla'g/ur *-et* striking clock.
sla'g/verk *-et* 1 striking mechanism in clock. 2 percussion (in orchestra).
sla'g/vol *-en* swingle, swiple on flail.
slakk'[1] *-en* slack (in rope): **ta inn s-en** (esp. *naut.*) haul the rope taut, take up the s-.
slakk'[2] *A slakt* (=**slak**) 1 (of rope) slack; (of curve, slope) gentle, slight. 2 (of ice) loose; (of sailing water) partially free from ice; (of current in water) weak.
slak'ke *V -a/+-et* 1 *naut.* slacken (e.g. a line): **s- ned, på farten** cut speed, slow down; **s- opp** ease the helm; **s- på** ease (e.g. the helm), slacken (e.g. a line). 2 (of ice) break up, become less packed.
slak'ne *V -a/+-et* 1 become (more) lax, slack. 2 (of wind) die down.
slak't[1] *-et* 1 slaughtered animal. 2 stock (being raised for market). 3 meat.
slak't[2] *nt of* **slak, slakk**[2]
slak'te *V -a/+-et* butcher, slaughter: **s- ned** butcher; massacre.
slak'te/dyr *-et* stock (being raised for market).
slak'te/fe *-et* stock (being raised for market).
slak'te/hus *-et* abattoir, slaughterhouse.
slak'te/kniv *-en* butcher's knife.
slak'te/maske *-a* slaughtering mask.
+**slak'ter** *-en, pl -e* (=*****-ar**) butcher.
+**slak'ter/benk** *-en* (=*****-ar/**) bench where animal is stretched out for skinning and dismemberment: **som et lam som føres til s-en** *bibl.* or *fig.* like a lamb that is led to the slaughter.
+**slak'ter/butikk'** *-en* (=*****-ar/**) butcher shop.
slakteri' *-et* 1 slaughterhouse; packing house. 2 butchery, carnage, massacre.
+**slak'ter/kniv** *-en* cf **slakte/**
+**slak'ter/øks** *-a* (=*****-ar/**) butcher's axe.
slak'te/tid *-a/+-en* slaughtering season.
slak't/offer *-et, pl -/+-ofre* sacrifice; hecatomb.
sla'/låm *-en* slalom (skiing).
sla'låm/bakke *-n* slalom hill.
sla'låm/renn *-et* slalom race, competition.
sla'låm/ski *-a, pl -/-er* slalom ski.
+**slam'** *-met* mud, ooze; sludge; slime.
slam'mer *-et* banging (e.g. of door, to shut it).
slam'p *-en* 1 idler, loafer, lounger. 2 boor; rascal.
slam'pe *V -a/+-et* walk heavily and noisily; blunder along.
slam'pet(e) *A* - lazy; boorish, impertinent, vulgar.
slam're *V -a/+-et* bang (e.g. door): **s- med dørene** b- doors.
slam's *-en* slovenly, untidy man.
slam'se[1] *-a* slovenly, untidy woman.
slam'se[2] *V -a/+-et* 1 *dial.* dangle. 2 slush, splash. 3: **s- i seg** gulp down (food) noisily.
slam'set(e) *A* - (=***slamsen**) sloppy, untidy.
slang'[1] *-en* stealing, petty theft (usu. in connection with children stealing apples from a tree).
slang'[2] [slæng] +*-en/*-et* slang.
+**slang'**[3] *pt of* **slenge**[1]
slang'e[1] *-n* 1 snake: **s-n** *bibl.* the serpent; **s-n i paradiset** the nigger in the woodpile. 2 serpentine, twisting line: **en s- av røyk** a t- l- of smoke. 3 (garden) hose; inner tube.
+**slang'e**[2] *V -a/-et*: **s- seg** 1 (e.g. of line) snake, twist. 2 stretch out (one's body), relax.
+**slang'e/agur'k** *-en* snake cucumber.
+**slang'e/menneske** *-t, pl* +*-r/*-* contortionist.
+**slang'e/skinn** *-et* snakeskin.
+**slang'e/temmer** *-en, pl -e* snake charmer.
slan'k *A* slender, slim.
slan'ke *V -a/+-et* 1 make thin(ner), have a slimming effect. 2: **s- seg** reduce (e.g. by dieting).
slan'ke/kur *-en* reducing diet.
slant' *-en* 1 bit, coin; small amount of money. 2 drop (**av** of) (e.g. at bottom of glass).
***sla'pe** *V -te* dangle limply.
slap'ne *V -a/+-et* become (more) lax.
slapp'[1] *A slapt* 1 loose, slack (line, reins, etc.); lax (morals); relaxed: **s-e priser** sluggish prices; **en s- smak** a flat, insipid taste; **s-e trekk** flabby features; **omsetningen er s-** business is slow; **henge s-t ned** hang slack, sag. 2 (of person) feeble, weak; *fig.* insipid, spineless.
slapp'[2] *pt of* **sleppe**[1], +**slippe**
+**slap'pe** *V -a/-et* 1 loosen, relax: **s- taket** loosen one's hold, grip. 2 relax, make lax, limp: **virke s-ende** have a relaxing effect; make (one) limp; **s- av** relax; slack off.
+**slap'pelse** *-n* relaxation; falling off, flagging.
slapp'/fisk *-en* lazy, inactive person.
+**slapp'/het** *-en* laxness, limpness.
slap's *-et* slush.
slap'se/føre *-t* cf **slafse/**
slap'set(e) *A* - slushy.
slaraf'fen/land *-et* land of milk and honey; imagined country of superfluity and no work.
slaraf'fen/liv *-et* life in clover, life of leisure.
slar'k[1] *-en* rascal, scamp.
slar'k[2] *-et* too loose fit, play, wobble (e.g. in machinery part, usu. causing rattle).
slar'ke *V -a/+-et* 1 hang loosely; fit too loosely. 2 shuffle (walk); saunter, drift; jerk (its way).
slar'ket(e) *A* - 1 dangling, loose; fitting too loosely. 2 (e.g. of grip) lax, limp, loose.
slar'v[1] *-en* 1 slouch, sloven. 2 untrustworthy person. 3 loudmouth.
slar'v[2] *-et* 1 sloppy, untidy work. 2 slander; loose talk.
slar've *V -a/+-et* 1 work slovenly, untidily. 2 slander; talk loosely.
***slar'veleg** *A* - slatternly, slovenly.
***slar'ven** *A -e/-i, pl -ne* cf **slarvet(e)**
slar'vet(e) *A* - (=***slarven**) 1 slovenly, untidy. 2 (of person) chattering, slandering. 3 (of talk) slanderous.
slas'k[1] *-en* lazybones, slouch.
slas'k[2] *-et* slush.
slas'ke *V -a/+-et* 1 walk in slush; splash along. 2 (of sth wet) flap, slap, smack.
slas'ket(e) *A* - 1 slushy. 2 dangling, loose; flabby.
slat'ten *A* +*-ent, pl slatne* flabby, limp; sagging, wobbly.

slat'ter *-en, pl +-e* athlete's disease characterized by loosening of ligaments, esp. of patellar ligament ("trick knee").

slau'r *-en* scamp.

***sla'v** *-en* cf **slaver**

sla've[1] *-n* slave.

sla've[2] *V -a/+-et* drudge, slave, toil.

sla've/binde *V infl as* **binde** enslave, reduce to slavery.

+sla've/driver *-en, pl -e* (=***-ar**) slave driver.

sla've/handel *-en* slave trade: **hvit s-** white slavery.

+sla've/handler *-en, pl -e* (=***-ar**) slave trader.

+sla'ver *-en, pl -* (=***-ar, *slav**) Slav.

slaveri' *-et* 1 slavery; drudgery, toil. 2 *hist.* penitentiary; imprisonment.

sla've/sinn *-et* servility, slave mentality.

slavin'ne *-a/+-en* (female) slave.

sla'visk[1] *A -* Slavic, Slavonic.

sla'visk[2] *A -* slavish, submissive: **en s- etterligning** a slavish imitation.

slavo'n *-en* Slavonian.

slavo'nsk *A -* Slavonian.

sle'de [*sle'e] *-n* 1 sledge, sleigh: **det kom en mann med en s- i veien** (a plan) was blocked by an obstacle; **kjøre i s-** go sleighing. 2 *mil.* (cross) slide (artillery). 3 *naut.* launching (cradle).

slede/føre *-t* (road conditions for) sleighing.

slede/hund *-en* sled dog.

slede/tur *-en* sleigh ride.

sleg'd *-a* (long) groove, hollow.

***sle'ge** *pp of* **slå[2]**

sle'gel *-elen, pl -ler* cf **sliul**

***sle'gest** *pp of* **slåst**

+sleg'ge *-a* (=***sleggje**) 1 sledgehammer: **bruke (stor)s-a** bring overwhelming, powerful arguments to bear to win one's point. 2 (in sports) hammer.

+sleg'ge/kast *-et* (in sports) hammer throw.

+sleg'ge/kaster *-en, pl -e* (=***sleggje/-kastar**) (in sports) hammer thrower.

***sleg'gje** *-a* cf **slegge**

***sle'gi** *pp of* **slå[2]**

***sle'gist** *pp of* **slåst**

slei'd *-en* slide valve (on steam engine).

slei'k *-en* 1 lick. 2 sweets. 3 lick-spittle (person).

+slei'ke *V -a/-te* cf **slikke**

***slei'ken** *A -e/-i, pl -ne* fawning, wheedling.

***slei'kje** *V -te* cf **slikke**

***slei'kje/pott** *-en* cf **slikke/**

***slei'k/munn** *-en* cf **slikk/**

slei'p *A* 1 slick, slippery (surface); slimy. 2 ingratiating; shifty, sly.

slei'pe *-a* 1 sth slippery. 2 snail.

Slei'pne *Prn myth.* Odin's horse.

slei's *-en naut.* slice bar.

***slei'sk** *A* cf **slesk**

***slei'ske** *V -a* cf **sleske**

slei't *pt of* **slite**

slei'v[1] *-a* (wooden) ladle.

slei'v[2] *-en* 1 impudent fellow, lout. 2 sideways, skidding movement of ski as it touches snow (following a jump).

slei'v[3] *-et* slovenly speech; gossipy, irresponsible talk.

slei've *V -a/+-et/+-de* 1 slouch, trudge (along). 2 stagger, swerve. 3 talk, write carelessly, recklessly; gossip, tattle. 4: **han s-et av seg en tale** he rattled off a speech.

slei'vet(e) *A -* 1 deviating, swerving. 2 loose, relaxed, slouching. 3 careless, slovenly. 4 gossiping, tattling.

slei'v/kjeft *-en* flap-jaw, gossipmonger.

slei'v/kjefta *A -* flap-jawed, gossipmongering.

***slekkj'e** *V slekte* slacken.

slek't *-a/+-en* 1 family, kin, lineage: **være (stå) i s- med** be related to, be akin to. 2 generation (of man); *mankind*: **kommende s-er** coming generations; **fra s- til s-** from generation to generation. 3 race, stock: **kvinnene — det er en skrøpelig s-** women — they're a sorry lot (Ibsen). 4 *bot.* genus.

***slek'tast** *V -ast*: **s- på ein** resemble, take after sby.

slek'te[1] *V -a/+-et*: **s- på en** resemble, take after sby.

***slek'te[2]** *pt of* **slekkje**

slek't/ledd *-et* (=***/led**) generation.

slek'tning *-en* relation, relative.

slek't/regis'ter *eret, pl +-rer/*-er* genealogy.

slek't/skap *+-et/*-en* 1 kinship, relationship: **stå i nær (fjernt) s- med** be closely (distantly) related to. 2 affinity, connection.

slek'ts/kjensle *-a* feeling for family; clannishness, family pride.

slek'ts/ledd *-et* generation.

+slek'ts/navn *-et* (=***/namn**) family name, surname.

+slek'ts/stolthet *-en* family pride.

slem'[1] *-men* slam (bridge).

slem'[2] *A -t, pl -me* bad, (of children) naughty: **være s- etter** have a weakness for; **være s- imot en** treat sby badly; **være s- til å (lyve, skryte, osv.)** be given to, have an inclination to (lie, brag, etc.).

slem'me *V -a/+-et/+slemte* separate, wash (e.g. ore).

+slem'men *df* bad boy.

+slem'ming *-en* bad boy (or girl).

slen'drian *-en* ingrained apathy, routine: **bli i den gamle s-** go along in the same old rut.

sleng'[1] *-en, pl *-er* 1 fling, toss: **s- med kroppen** swing (toss) of the body. 2 peculiarity, turn (e.g. of style of speech or writing); gait: **den s-en var ikke til å ta feil av** you couldn't miss that g- (Bang-Hansen). 3 *dial.* sth occurring sporadically; refrain of a ballad. 4 *fam.*: **i s-en** at the same time; **kjøp to trådsneller i s-en** buy two spools while you're at it.

+sleng'[2] *-et* circle, clique, gang.

+sleng'/bemer'kning *-en* casual, passing remark; gibe.

+sleng'e[1] *V +slang/*slong, +-t/*slunge/*-i* 1 (of objects) dangle, flop, swing (loosely, e.g. in the wind). 2 (of people) saunter, slouch along; stagger: **gå og s-** loaf around; **ligge og s-** lie around (in a disorderly fashion). 3 chance, happen (along): **i blant s-er det en svær rusk** now and then a big one comes along; **s- forbi** drop by; **s- til** happen, turn out.

+sleng'e[2] *V -te* (=***slengje**) fling, sling, throw: **s- en noe i ansiktet** t- sth in sby's face; **s- med armene** wave one's arms; **s- på (seg) klærne** slip into, t- on one's clothes; **s- rundt** swing around; **s- seg ned** t- oneself to the ground.

+sleng'e/navn *-et* nickname.

sleng'et(e) *A -* loose-jointed, slouching.

***sleng'je** *V -de* cf **slenge[2]**

***sleng'je/namn** *-et* cf **slenge/**

***sleng'je/o'rd** *-et* cf **sleng/**

***sleng'je/skott** *-et* cf **sleng/**

sleng'/kappe *-a* opera cloak.

sleng'/kyss *-en/-et* blown kiss.

sleng'/o'rd *-et* gibe, jeer, taunt.

sleng'/skott *-et* (=**+/skudd**) random, stray shot.

slen'tre *V -a/+-et* 1 saunter (along). 2 loaf, lounge.

sle'p *-et* 1 tow, towing: **på s-** in tow. 2 load (of sth being towed); train (on dress or cloak). 3 path or track along which sth is dragged. 4 drudgery, toil.

sle'pe[1] *-a* path.

sle'pe[2] *V -te* 1 drag, haul, tow: **s- med seg, s- på** drag along; **s- sammen (av gårde)** scrape together (money); **s- seg (av gårde)** crawl, drag oneself around, (of time) pass slowly. 2 drag, trail (along behind sth); struggle, toil, work hard: **s-ende** (of motion) shuffling, slouching; (of speech) careless, drawling.

sle'pe/båt *-en* tugboat.

+sle'pen *A -ent, pl -ne* polished; polite, refined.

sle'pe/not *-a, pl -nøter* dragnet, townet.

+sle'per *-en, pl -e* (=***-ar**) 1 tugboat. 2 towline.

sle'pe/rive *-a* buck rake, hay sweep.

sle'pe/tau *-et* 1 towline. 2 dragline, guide rope.

sle'pe/trosse *-a naut.* hawser.

slepp' *-en/-et* (=**+slipp[2]**) 1: **gi s- på** give up, let go, relinquish. 2 dropping of supplies by parachute.

slep'pe[1] *-a geol.* fissure.

slep'pe[2] *V slapp, +sloppet/*sloppe/*-i* (=**+slippe**) 1 let go, release; drop: **s- en av syne** let sby out of one's sight; **s- kuene** let out the cows; **s- løs** let loose, set free; **s- løs på** turn loose on, sic (e.g. a dog) on; **s- noe (i golvet)** drop sth (on the floor); **s- taket** lose one's grip; **s- tråden** leave off (discussion), lose the thread. 2 avoid, be spared from; get out of, not have to: **s- billig (lett)** get off easy; **s- ubehageligheter** avoid, be spared (from) unpleasantness; **du skal s- å vaske opp i dag** you won't have to wash the dishes today. 3 leave off, stop: **hvor var det vi slapp?** where did we leave off? 4 escape, go, slip: **s- bort** escape; **s- fri** go free; **s- løs** get free, free oneself; **s- med (f. eks. skrekken)** escape, get off with (e.g. a scare); **det slapp ut av hånden min** it slipped out of my hand. 5 (with *prep.* and *adv.*): **s- forbi** let (sby) pass; get past, pass; **s- fra** avoid, get away from, get out of; **s- fram** get by, get past; pass (a test); **s- inn** let in; get in, slip in; **s- opp** give out, run short (e.g. of supplies); **s- opp for** run out of; **s- til** get a chance; **s- ut** let out; escape, get out. 6 *(refl.)*: **s- seg løs** let oneself go.

slep'pe[3] *V -te* let go, release, relinquish (cf **sleppe[2]** 1).

***slep'pen** *A -e/-i, pl slepne* 1 butterfingered. 2 *fig.* generous, openhanded.

slepp'/hendt *A -* 1 butterfingered. 2 *fig.* generous, open-handed.

+sles'k *A* (=***sleisk**) fawning, ingratiating, oily.

+sles'ke *V -a/-et* (=***sleiske**) butter up, fawn (**for en** on sby): **s- seg fram** get ahead by fawning.

+sles'k/het *-en* fawning, obsequiousness.

+sle't *pt of* **slite**

slet'ne *V -a/+-et* become more even, smoothed out.

***slett'[1]** *-a* cf **slette[1]**

slett'[2] *-et*: **klokke/s-** hour, time.

slett'[3] *A -* 1 even, level, smooth: **rett og s-** pure and simple. 2 (morally) bad, poor (in quality): **du s-e tid** mild oath.

slett'[4] *Av*: **s- ikke** not at all, absolutely not; **rett og s-** quite simply.

slet'te[1] *-a* 1 plain, plateau; (in ski jump) outrun. 2 opening (in woods).

slet'te[2] *-a* sleet.

slet'te[3] *V -a/+-et* 1 level, smooth. 2: **s- ut** delete, erase; eradicate, wipe out; **s- ut vansker** smooth away difficulties.

***slet'te[4]** *V -a/-e* fling, throw.

slet'te/land *-et* level country.

°slet'tes *Av* cf **slett[4]**

+slett'/het *-en* badness, vileness, wickedness.

slett'/høvel *-elen, pl -ler* carpenter's plane.

+ Bokmål; * Nynorsk; ° Dialect.
After letter: ' stress (Acc. 1); ' tone, stress (Acc. 2); · length.
Below letter: . not pronounced.

slett'/lendt *A* - characterized by level country.
+sle'v *-en* cf **sleiv**[1]
sle've[1] *-a zool.* blindworm, slowworm (Anguis fragilis).
***sle've**[2] *-n/-a* saliva.
sle've[3] *V -a/+-et* drool, slobber.
***sli'**[1] *-et* scum, slime.
***sli'**[2] *A -tt* avaricious, greedy (**etter** for).
***sli'ast** *V -ast* become slimy.
+sli'brig *A* - 1 slippery. 2 dirty, obscene, smutty.
+sli'brig/het *-en* dirtiness, obscenity, salacity: **en s-** a dirty joke.
+slid'der/sladder *-et* fiddle-faddle.
Sli'dre *Pln* district (including Øystre and Vestre Slidre twps), Oppland.
+sli'el *-en* cf **sliul**
sli'k *A* 1 like that, such: **en s- mann** such a man, a man like that; **s- er han** that's the way he is, that's what he's like; **noe s-t** sth like that, such things; **har du hørt s-t!** have you ever heard the likes!; **s- en fin dag!** what a wonderful day! 2 *(adv.)*: **slik** like that (this), in such a way, to such a degree; **s- er det** that's the way it is; **s- at** so that; **s- saken nå står** as matters now stand; **s- som det blåste!** the wind was terrific!; **gjør det s-** do it like this.
***sli'kje** *V -te* 1 glisten, shine. 2 smooth.
slikk'[1] *-en* 1 lick; sweets. 2 little bit, smattering (of sth): **han kjøpte det for en s- (og ingenting)** he bought it for a song. 3 mud mixed with clay to afford an oozy bottom.
+slikk'[2] *-et* lick (act of licking, e.g. by dog).
slik'ke *V -a/+-et* (=**+sleike, *sleikje**) lick; lap: **s- noe i seg** lap up (e.g. milk); **s- seg om munnen** lick one's chops; **s- på noe** lick sth; **s- sol** absorb sunshine.
slik'ke/pott *-en* 1 forefinger. 2 sweet tooth (person). 3 (rubber) scraper.
+slik'keri *-et, pl -er* sweets.
+slikk'/munn [also slikk'/] *-en* sweet tooth.
+slikk'/munnet *A* - having a sweet tooth.
slikk'/voren [+/vårren, */våren] *A* *+-ent, pl -ne* sweet toothed.
sli'm *-et* 1 scum, slime. 2 mucus, phlegm. 3 foulness, vileness.
sli'me *V -a/+-et/*-de* 1: **s- til** cover with slime, dirty. 2 secrete slime.
sli'met(e) *A* - 1 slimy; mucous. 2 foul, vile.
sli'm/hinne *-a* mucous membrane.
sli'm/hud [*/hu] *-a/+-en* 1 mucous membrane. 2 slimy skin.
sli'm/ål *-en zool.* borer, hagfish (Myxine glutinosa).
slin'd *-a* beam, crossbeam.
sling'er *-en* rolling; vacillation, wavering: **ingen s- i valsen** no nonsense.
sling're *V -a/+-et* 1 lurch, reel, stagger; (e.g. of ship) roll, sway. 2 vacillate, waver. 3 *dial.* (e.g. of road) twist, wind.
sling're/brett *-et naut.* fiddle.
sling're/kjøl *-en naut.* bilge keel.
sling'rings/monn *-en* tolerance of movement (e.g. of joint).
sling'se *-a* cf **slintre**
slin'tre *-a* 1 muscular fibre; shred of meat. 2 wisp (of hair).
slin'tret(e) *A* - stringy (meat); bony, skinny (person).
+sli'p *-en* 1 grinding. 2 ground edge (of instrument, tool). 3 log stump (used as raw material for wood pulp), pulpwood.
sli'pe *V -te/*-a* 1 grind, hone, sharpen; cut (e.g. glass); polish (e.g. marble). 2 *fig.* sharpen (e.g. one's wits); improve, polish (e.g. a speech).
sli'pe/middel *-elet/-midlet, pl +-midler/ *-el* abrasive.
sliperi' *-et, pl +-er/*-* 1 grinding shop. 2 lapidary's workshop. 3 pulp mill.
sli'pers *pl* (railroad) ties.
sli'pe/stein *-en* grindstone, whetstone.
sli'pe/stikke *-a* bar (=short piece of stone or wood used to hold knife, scythe, etc. in position against grindstone).
sli'pe/tømmer *-et* pulpwood.
slipp'[1] *-en* 1 *naut.* slip (of propeller). 2 *naut.* slip, slipway (inclined plane sloping to water on which ships are built or repaired). 3 hoist (e.g. in service station, garage).
+slipp'[2] *-en/-et* cf **slepp**
+slip'pe *V slapp, sloppet* cf **sleppe**[2]
slip's *-et* necktie, tie.
slip's/knute *-n* tie knot.
slip's/nål *-a* stickpin, tiepin.
sli'r *-a* (=**slire**) 1 scabbard; sheath. 2 *geol.* schlieren.
sli're *V -te* skid, slip.
sli're/kniv *-en* sheath knife.
sli'ring *-en* (big) sheath knife.
slis'k *-en* 1 *naut.* fender, skid. 2 fish net (hung on side of ship into which catch is thrown).
slis'ke *V -a/+-et* fawn (**for** on), ingratiate oneself.
slis'ket(e) *A* - fawning, obsequious, oily.
+sliss' *-en* 1 slit (e.g. in door); placket, slit (e.g. in skirt). 2 *carp.* mortise.
+slis'se *V -et* 1 slit. 2 *carp.* provide with a mortise, tenon.
sli't *-et* 1 drudgery, grind, toil: **s- og slep** drudgery. 2 friction, strain, wear and tear. 3 *dial.* sprain.
slita'sje *-n* wear and tear.
+sli'tbar/het *-en* durability.
sli'te *V sleit/+slet, +slitt/*slite/*-i* 1 pull, rip, tear: **s- i noe** pull, tug at sth; **s- i stykker** tear up (apart); **s- opp** pull up; **s- over** tear in two; **s- seg** (of horses) break loose; **s- seg løs** free oneself, pull loose, tear away. 2 wear: **s- ut (opp)** wear out; **s- på (nervene)** fray, wear down (one's nerves); **s-t** worn (out). 3 toil, work hard; struggle: **s- seg igjennom noe** s- through sth; **s- seg i hjel** kill oneself working.
sli'te/bane *-n* wearing surface; tread.
sli'ten *A +-ent, pl -ne* exhausted, tired, worn out.
sli'te/sterk *A* durable.
sli'te/styrke *-n* durability, wearing quality.
slit'ne *V -a/+-et* 1 snap. 2 tear loose.
+sli't/som' *A -t, pl -me* (=***/sam**) hard, strenuous, tiring.
+slitt' *pp of* **slite**
+sli'ul *-en* (=***slegel**) flail, swingle.
slo'[1] *-a zool.* blindworm, slowworm (Anguis fragilis).
***slo'**[2] *-a* path, route.
slo'[3] *-et* fish entrails.
slo'[4] *pt of* **slå**[2]
slodd' *-a/-en* (=**slodde**) 1 drag, heavy harrow. 2 handsleigh; toboggan.
slod'de *V -a/+-et* drag, harrow.
slo'e[1] *-n* 1 improvised sled (of tree branches, scrub) used to move hay down steep slope. 2 improvised brake (of heavy branches) to which a load is affixed to slow its descent down steep slope. 3 lazy fellow.
slo'e[2] *V -a/+-et* move a load by an improvised sled.
slok[1] [slå'k] *-en bot.* fern (order Filicales).
***slok**[2] [slå'k] *-et* millrace; large trough.
***slokk'** *pt of* **sløkke**[1]
+slokke[1] [slok'ke] *V slokte* (=**+sløkke**[2], ***sløkkje**) extinguish, put out (fire, light); quench (e.g. thirst): **den sorgen er s-t** that problem is solved.
slok'ke**[2] *pp of* **sløkke**[1] (=slokki**)
slokne [slok'ne] *V -a/+-et* be extinguished, go out; *fig.* die.
slom [slom'] *-en zool.* smelt (Osmerus eperlanus).
***slong'** *pt of* **slenge**[1]
sloppe** [slop'pe] *pp of* **sleppe**[2] (=sloppi**)
+sloppet [slop'pet] *pp of* **sleppe**[2], **slippe**
***slo'se** *-a* amusing story, yarn.
+sloss [sloss'] *pt of* **slåss**
***slost** [slos't] *pt of* **slåst**
slott' *-et* castle, chateau, palace.
slott's/bakke *-n* hill forming an approach to a castle.
slott's/herre *-n* lord of the manor.
slott's/park *-en* castle, palace park.
slott's/plass *-en* palace square.
slott's/vakt *-a/+-en* palace guard; guardhouse.
slova'k *-en* Slovak.
slova'kisk *A* - Slovak, Slovakian.
+slove'ner *-en, pl -e* (=***-ar, *sloven**) Slovene.
slove'nsk *A* - Slovene, Slovenian.
slu' *A* - (=***sløg**) crafty, cunning, sly.
slubb' *-en* slattern, slut.
slub'bert *-en* boor, lout, scoundrel; scamp.
+slub're *V -a/-et* gurgle, slurp: **s- noe i seg** imbibe sth noisily, slurp.
sludd' *-et* (=**+slut**[1]) sleet, slush.
slud'de *V -a/+-et* (=**+slute**[1]) fall as sleet, sleet.
slud'der *-eret/+sludret* nonsense, rubbish; *(pop.)* baloney, tommyrot.
slud're *V -a/+-et* talk nonsense, twaddle; jabber; *(pop.)* jaw.
+slud're/bøtte *-a* windbag.
sluf'fe *-a* two-seated sleigh.
sluf's *-et* sludge, slush.
sluf'se *V -a/+-et* get dirty, soil; splash.
slugg' *-en* slug (metallurgy).
+slu'/het *-en* craftiness, cunning, slyness.
slu'ing *-en* crafty, wily person, slyboots.
slu'k[1] *-en* spoon bait.
slu'k[2] *-et* 1 abyss, chasm. 2 *fam.* machine requiring exorbitant operating expenses; *(pop.)* oil burner (automobile). 3 manhole; opening.
slu'ke *V -te* devour, gobble up, swallow (also *fig.*): **s- maten** bolt one's food; **han tror han har s-t all verdens visdom** he thinks he knows everything.
slu'k/hals *-en* glutton.
+slukke [slok'ke] *V -et* cf **slokke**[1]
+slukk'/øret *A* - crestfallen, drooping.
+slukne [slok'ne] *V -et* cf **slokne**
+sluk't *-en* gorge, ravine, narrow pass.
slu'k/voren [+/vårren, */våren] *A* *+-ent, pl -ne* avaricious, greedy.
+sluk'/øret *A* - cf **slukk/**
slum' *-men* 1 slum. 2 institutions, people engaged in social work in slums.
slum'/kvarte'r *-et, pl -/+-er* slum area.
+slum'mer *-en* slumber; nap, snooze.
slump [slom'p] *-en* 1 chance, hazard: **det var rent ved en s- jeg oppdaget det** it was by mere accident I discovered it; **på (en) s-** at a guess, roughly; at random, in round numbers; **han lar alt gå på s-** he has a happy-go-lucky approach to things. 2 some, a good deal, a chunk: **en god s- penger** a handsome sum of money. 3 remainder: **s-en av pengene** the rest of the money.
slumpe [slom'pe] *V -a/+-et* 1 do (sth) at random: **s- i vei** set out without a definite plan. 2 be fortunate enough, have the good luck to (do sth): **s- til noe** chance upon, stumble across sth.
slumpe/hell [slom'pe/] *-et* stroke of good fortune; windfall.
slumpe/høve *-t* chance, fluke.
slumpe/lykke *-a/+-en* stroke of good luck.
slumpe/skott *-et* random shot.
slumpe/treff *-et* stroke of good luck; chance, fluke.
slumre [slom're] *V -a/+-et* 1 doze, slumber. 2: **s- inn** *poet.* die, pass away. 3 (e.g. of feelings, passions) be quiescent, lie dormant.
slum're/teppe *-t, pl +-r/*-* afghan, blanket.
slumse [slom'se] *V -a/+-et* 1 pour,

splash water carelessly. 2 work carelessly, in a slapdash manner.

slumset(e) [slom'set(e)] *A* - careless, reckless, rough.

+**slum'/søster** *-era/-eren, pl -re(r)* (=*/**syster**) welfare worker.

slunge** [slong'e] *pp of* **slenge**[1] (=slungi**)

slunken [slong'ken] *A +-ent, pl -ne* 1 lank, lean: **en s- pung** a slender purse. 2 flabby, loose, slack.

slun'te *V -a/+-et* (=**sluntre**) 1 saunter (along). 2 idle away (time): **s- unna** evade, shirk work.

slun'tre *V -a/+-et* cf **slunte**

slupp' *-en naut.* sloop; pinnace.

slu're *V -a/+-et/+-te* slide, slip; skid.

+**slur'fe** *V -a/-et* slurp.

slur'k *-en* gulp, mouthful, swallow; pull (at the bottle), swig.

***slur'ke** *V -a* gulp, swallow eagerly: **s- noe i seg** gulp sth down.

slur'p *-en/+-et* noisy swallow, slurp.

slur'pe *V -a/+-et*: **s- i seg** imbibe noisily, slurp.

slur'v[1] *-en* slipshod, slovenly person.

slur'v[2] *-et* carelessness, negligence; slipshod, sloppy work.

slur've[1] *-a* careless, sloppy woman, slattern.

slur've[2] *V -a/+-et* work in a careless, slipshod manner; be slipshod.

slur'vet(e) *A* - careless, negligent; slatternly, slovenly.

slu'se *-a/+-en* 1 floodgate, sluice: **han åpnet sin vredes s-r** *fig.* he allowed his anger to pour forth. 2 (canal) lock. 3 air lock.

slu'se/penger** *pl* (=-ar**) canal toll, lockage.

slu'se/port [/port] *-en* (canal) lock gate.

slus'k *-en* 1 careless, slipshod worker. 2 bum, tramp; hoodlum, ruffian. 3 section hand, *(pop.)* gandy dancer (railroad).

slus'ke *V -a/+-et* work in a careless, slipshod manner (**med** with).

slus'ke/arbeid *-et* careless, slipshod work.

+**slus'keri** *-et* carelessness, negligence (in appearance, work).

slus'ket(e) *A* - slipshod, sloppy (work); unkempt, untidy (appearance).

+**slu't**[1] *-et* cf **sludd**

slu't[2] *A* - stooping.

+**slu'te**[1] *V -a/-et* cf **sludde**

***slu'te**[2] *V -a/-te* stoop; (e.g. of branches) hang down.

slut'ning *+-en/*-a* 1 conclusion, end, ending. 2 conclusion (=decision, deduction): **dra (trekke) en s-** conclude, come to a c-. 3 closing (e.g. of electric circuit, of chain).

slut'nings/akkor'd *-en mus.* final chord.

slut'nings/kjede [*/kjee] *+-en/+-et/*-a* chain of reasoning.

+**slut'nings/rekke** *-n* chain of reasoning.

slu't/rygga *A* - (=+**-et**, ***-ja**) humpbacked, stoop-shouldered.

slutt'[1] *-en* end, ending, finish: **s-en på** the end of (sth); **i s-en av** at the end of (period of time); **til s-** at last, finally; **få (gjøre) s- på** put an end to; **ta s-** end, come to an end.

slutt'[2] *A* - at an end, finished, over: **det er s- med (på) krigen** the war is over.

+**slutt'/bemer'kning** *-en* closing, final remark.

slut'te *V -a/+-et* 1 conclude (=end, finish) (**med** with, by); quit, stop. 2 close (electric circuit, chain or ring), move together: **i s-et tropp** in close formation; **en s-et krets** a closed circle; **Ringen s-et** The Ring is Closed (novel by Hamsun). 3 (e.g. of doors, windows; occasionally of clothes) fit tightly; clasp (sby in one's arms). 4 conclude (=decide, deduce). 5 conclude (=enter into) (e.g. agreement, treaty). 6 (with *prep.*): **s- av** finish; **s- opp om** close ranks around, *fig.* support, stand behind; **s- sammen** join, merge. 7 *(refl.)*: **s- seg om** close around, grip; **s- seg sammen** join together, unite; **s- seg til** associate with, join, side with; conclude, figure out; agree to, concur in.

+**slut'telig** *Av* eventually, finally, ultimately.

+**slut'ter** *-en, pl -e* (=***-ar**) jailer, turnkey.

slutt'/sats *-en mus.* final movement.

+**slutt'/seddel** *-en* (=*/**setel**) *merc.* contract, formal agreement.

slutt'/spurt *-en* final spurt, finish (of race, preparations for exam, etc.).

slutt'/stein *-en* capstone, keystone.

slutt'/strek *-en/*-et* 1 line (at foot of column of figures; or marking end of book or chapter). 2: **sette s-** *fig.* (bring to) conclusion, end, finale.

slutt'/stykke *-t, pl +-r/*-* 1 keeper, strike (on door). 2 breech action (of gun).

slutt'/sum' *-men* total.

slutt'/tid *-a/+-en* finishing time.

sly' *-et* 1 scum, slime. 2 fish entrails.

sly'e *-a* slut, whore.

slyng' *-en/-et* 1 loop, turning, winding. 2 tangle: **s- på linjen** crossed wires.

+**slyng'e**[1] *-a/-en* (=***slyngje**[1]) sling.

+**slyng'e**[2] *V -et/-te* (=***slyngje**[2]) 1 coil, twine, wind: **s- armene om** put one's arms around (sby); **s- seg** (e.g. of road) twist, wind; **s- seg om hverandre** intertwine. 2 fling, hurl, sling: **s- ut forbannelser** hurl abuse (at sby). 3 extract (honey).

+**slyng'e/kaster** *-en, pl -e hist.* slinger.

slyng'el *-elen, pl -ler* scoundrel, villain.

+**slyng'el/aktig** *A* - rascally, villainous; dirty, low-down.

slyng'el/alder *-en* (the) awkward age, (the) teens.

slyng'el/strek *-en* dirty, low down trick.

***slyng'ing** *-a* cf **slyngning**

***slyng'je**[1] *-a* cf **slynge**[1]

***slyng'je**[2] *V -de* cf **slynge**[2]

+**slyng'ning** *-en* 1 twining, winding; intertwining. 2 tracery (ornamentation); flourish (signature). 3 extraction (of honey).

slyng'/plante *+-a/-en bot.* creeper, rambler.

slyng'/rose *-a/+-en bot.* rambling rose.

slyng'/tråd *-en bot.* tendril.

***sly'sen** *A -e/-i, pl -ne* unfortunate, unlucky.

+**slys'ne** *V -a* do sth unfortunate, unlucky.

***slæ'r** *pr of* **slå**[2]

***slæt'te** *-t* 1: **dags/s-** day's work (e.g. haying, mowing). 2 hayfield.

***slø'**[1] *V -dde* drag (behind).

***slø'**[2] *A -tt* cf **sløv**

***slø'g** *A* cf **slu**

***sløg'd** *-a* cunning, slyness.

+**slø'ke** *-a* (=***sløkje**) *bot.* angelica, archangel (Angelica silvestris).

***sløk'ke**[1] *V slokk, slokke/-i* be extinguished, go out.

+**sløk'ke**[2] *V sløkte* cf **slokke**[1]

***sløkkj'e** *V sløkte* cf **slokke**[1]

slø'r[1] *-en* 1 sidewind (in sailing). 2: **på en s-** three sheets to the wind (=drunk).

slø'r[2] *-et* 1 veil: **dra et s- fra noe** disclose, reveal sth; **lette s-et** unveil, *fig.* withdraw the v-; **ta s-et** become a nun, take the v-. 2 haze, mist. 3 netting: **mygge/s-** mosquito n-. 4 *bot., zool.* indusium. 5 *zool.* facial disc (of owl).

slø're *V +-te/*-de* 1 *naut.* run before the wind. 2 blur, dim, fog. 3 deaden, muffle.

slø'ret(e) *A* - 1 blurred, dimmed, veiled. 2 indistinct, muffled (e.g. voice).

slø'se *V -te* 1 waste: **s- bort, vekk** fritter away, squander; **s- med penger, tid** squander money, time. 2 *dial.* gossip (**om** about).

+**slø'ser** *-en, pl -e* (=***-ar**) spendthrift, wastrel.

+**sløseri'** *-et* waste (**med** of).

slø'set(e) *A* - extravagant, wasteful (**med** with).

slø'v *A* (=***slø**[2]) 1 blunt, dull (e.g. edge, knife); dim, weakened. 2 apathetic, lethargic, listless.

+**slø've** *V -a/+-et* 1 blunt, dull (e.g. knife). 2 deaden, dim, dull (the senses); render apathetic: **s-es** grow dull, listless.

+**slø'v/het** *-en* 1 bluntness. 2 apathy, lethargy, stupor.

+**slø'vhets/tilstand** *-en* listlessness, stupor, torpor.

slø'v/sinn *-et* 1 apathy, lethargy, torpor. 2 *psych.* dementia praecox; stupor.

slø'v/skodd *A -/*-skott* (of horse) smooth-shod (=with dulled calks).

slø'v/tenkt *A* - slow-witted.

+**sløy'** *A* 1 (of business) dull, slack. 2 *dial.* artful, crafty (=**slu**).

sløy'd *-en* 1 carpentry, woodwork; sloyd. 2: **metall/s-** metalwork.

sløy'd/benk *-en* carpenter's bench.

sløy'de *V -a/+-et* do woodwork.

sløy'd/sal *-en* carpentry workshop (in school).

sløy'e[1] *V sløgde/+sløyde* clean (fish).

+**sløy'e**[2] *V -de/-et* ease up, slacken: **s- av** (the same).

sløy'fe[1] *-a/+-en* 1 bow, bowknot, bow tie. 2 loop; loop line (railroad).

sløy'fe[2] *V -a/+-et* 1 cut out, omit; discontinue, take (e.g. a train) out of service. 2 *mus.* slur (e.g. two notes). 3: **s- seg** (e.g. of cable) loop.

slå'[1] *-a* bolt (on door): **skyve s-a for, fra** bolt, unbolt the door; **under lås og s-** under lock and key.

slå'[2] *V slo, +slått/*slege/-i* 1 beat (=hit, knock, strike): **s- beina vekk under** knock the bottom out of (e.g. an argument); **klokka s-r fem** the clock strikes five; **s- en for penger** touch sby for money, put the touch on sby; **s- hull i (på)** knock, put a hole in; **s- en i møte** (e.g. of odor) assail, face sby; **s- takten** beat time. 2 beat (=defeat, surpass): **s- den!** b- that if you can!; **s- en (i sjakk)** b- sby (at chess); **det s-r alt** that b-s everything, takes the cake; **s- en rekord** break a record. 3 strike (=occur to, impress): **det slo meg** it struck me; **s-ende** striking (e.g. resemblance, truth). 4 cut, mow (grain, grass, hay). 5 pour (liquids) (usu. with *adv.* **av, i, på, ut**). 6 jerk: **s- med nakken** toss one's head; **s- med armene** wave one's arms. 7 do, perform (with various nouns): **s- alarm** raise the alarm; **s- ball** play ball; **s- bru over** bridge; **s- eld (ild)** strike fire; **s- feil** fail, go wrong, miscarry; **s- følge** go along (**med** with); **s- hjul** turn cartwheels; **s- hånden av** disregard, neglect; **s- knute** tie a knot; **s- krøll** arch, curl; **s- lag** join forces; **s- leir** set up camp; **s- rot** take root; **s- en sirkel** draw a circle (with compass); **s- et slag (nedover gata)** take a walk (down the street); **s- et slag for** strike a blow for (a cause); **s- triller** warble; **s- en vits** crack a joke; (for use with other nouns: see these). 8 (with *prep.* and *adv.*): **s- an** become popular, catch on; (of vaccination) take; strike up a conversation (**med** with); **s- an tonen** strike the keynote; **s- av** turn off (e.g. light, radio); knock (sth) off; **s- av farten** slow down; **s- av en handel** strike a bargain, make a

+ Bokmål; * Nynorsk; ° Dialect.
After letter: ' stress (Acc. 1); ` tone, stress (Acc. 2); · length.
Below letter: . not pronounced.

deal; **s- av en prat** have a chat; **s- av på (prisen)** reduce (the price); **s- bort** push, wave aside (e.g. objections, unpleasant thoughts); **s- bort i latter** laugh off; **s- etter** look up (in book, dictionary); **s- etter en** hit at sby; **s- fast** fasten, nail down; ascertain, determine; agree upon, settle (sth); **s- for** close (blinds); bolt; **s- fra seg** put up a fight, strike back; **s- fra seg tanker** dismiss thoughts; **s- frampå** propose, suggest; **slå hen** disregard, ignore, make light of; **s- hen i spøk (latter)** pass off as a joke (laugh off); **s- i** pound in (nail), slam (door); burst out with (a scream); **s- i bordet** pound the table; **s- i hjel** kill; **s- i stykker** break (apart, to pieces); **s- igjen** strike, fight back; **s- igjennom** penetrate, come through; become a hit, catch on, (of person) make a name for oneself, score a success; **s- inn** smash, stave in; **s- inn på** enter upon, take off on; **s- løs (på)** strike out (at); **s- ned** beat down, suppress (e.g. revolt), dash (e.g. hopes); turn down (e.g. collar), lower (one's eyes), close (umbrella), reduce (prices); (of lightning) strike; (of birds) alight, swoop down; (of smoke) blow down; **s- ned i en** occur to sby, strike sby; **s- ned på** jump, pounce on, (of birds) swoop down on, *fig.* crack down on; **s- ned på maskin** type; **s- om** throw, wrap around (e.g. coat around one's shoulders, string around package); (of weather, mood, opinion, etc.) change, shift; turn around; **s- om seg** hit out in all directions, wave one's arms; *fig.* toss around; **s- om seg med penger** throw one's money around; **s- om seg med ros** be lavish with praise; **s- om seg med sitater** toss off quotations right and left; **s- opp** open (book, door, umbrella); look up (in book, dictionary); post (bill, placard); pitch, raise (e.g. tent); turn up (e.g. collar); (of flames) leap up, (of smoke) rise; (of newspaper story) give much publicity to, blow up out of proportion; cast on (stitches), prepare (bread dough); burst into, burst out with (scream, laugh, etc.); **s- opp med en** break up with sby; **s- over** pull, throw over; (of waves) engulf, sweep over; **s- over i (til)** change, switch over to; **s- på** beat, strike; hint at, suggest; turn on (light, radio, etc.); **s- på flukt** put to flight; **s- på tråden** ring up; **s- stort på** live it up, live in style; **s- sammen** strike together; close (e.g. umbrella), fold up; amalgamate, combine; **s- til** hit, strike at; agree to, accept an offer, take sby up on sth; (of prophecy) come true; succeed, turn out well, live up to expectations; **s- til blods** beat (sby) bloody; **s- under seg** subjugate; **s- ut** knock, pour, spread out; (of disease, rash) break out; **s- ut av tankene** put out of one's mind, forget; **s- ut med armene** gesticulate wildly; **s- vekk** wave aside; make light of. **9** *(refl.)*: **s- seg** hurt oneself; (of wood, metal) warp, buckle; **s- seg gjennom** fight one's way through; **s- seg i hjel** be killed; **s- seg løs** tear oneself loose, free oneself; let oneself go, let one's hair down; **s- seg ned** settle down; sit down; **s- seg opp** get ahead, rise in the world; **s- seg opp på** make capital of; **s- seg på** go in for, take to; **s- seg på forstanden** affect one's mind; **s- seg sammen** join forces; **s- seg selv på munnen** contradict oneself; **s- seg til** settle, stay; **s- seg til ro** settle down, take it easy; **s- seg vrang(t)** balk, cause trouble, go wrong.

slåbrok [slåb'råkk] *-en* (men's) dressing gown, robe.

+**slådd'** *-en* cf **slodd**

slå'ende *A* - **1** striking (e.g. resemblance). **2** conclusive, convincing (e.g. argument).

°**slå'k** *-et* cf **slok[2]**

slå'/maski'n *-en* mowing machine, reaper.

slå'p *-en* daydreamer, idler; lout.

slå'pe *-a bot.* blackthorn, sloethorn (Prunus spinosa).

slå'pe/bær *-et bot.* sloeberry.

slå'pen *A* +*-ent, pl -ne* **1** gaunt, lank, lean; loose-jointed. **2** careless, nonchalant.

slå'pe/to'rn *-en bot.* blackthorn, sloethorn (Prunus spinosa).

***slå'pne** *V -a* become gaunt, lank, lean.

+**slåss'** *V sloss, slåss* (=***slåst**) fight, struggle (**med, mot, over** with, against, about); come to blows, scrap, wrangle: **s- med et problem** grapple with a problem; **s- mot overmakten** fight against heavy odds; **s- som ville dyr** fight tooth and nail.

+**slåss'/bikkje** *-a* dog which is constantly fighting.

+**slåss'/hanske** *-n* brass knuckles, knuckleduster.

+**slåss'/kjempe** *-a/-en* fighter; bully, rowdy.

***slås't** *V slost, slegest/-ist/slåst* cf **slåss**

***slås'tar** *-en* bully, rowdy.

***slås't/kjempe** *-a* cf **slåss/**

***slå'te** *-a* pole, rod.

slått'[1] *-en* haying (cutting, mowing); hayfield.

slått'[2] *-en* (country) air, melody; dance.

slått'[3] *pp of* **slå[2]**

slåt'te *-a* hayfield.

slåt'te/folk *-et* haymakers, mowers.

slåt'te/graut *-en* porridge (served at festivities marking end of haying).

slåt'te/kar *-en* haymaker, mower.

slåt'te/mark *-a* hayfield.

slåt'te/teig *-en* strip of hayfield.

slått'/onn *-a* haying (season).

smad'der *et*: **slå i s-** smash to pieces.

smad're *V -a/+-et* **1** smash to pieces, smash up: **s- fjeset på en** bash sby's face in. **2** annihilate, destroy.

sma'k *-en* taste: **etter s-** to t-; **etter min s-** to my liking, t-; **hver sin s-** t-s differ, there's no accounting for t-s; **falle i ens s-** be to one's liking; **få s- for** develop a t- for.

sma'ke *V -a/+-te* **1** taste: **s- av t-** like; **s- på** sample, t- (sth); **s- til (maten)** season (food) to taste; **s- seg fram** cook, season food by trial and error. **2**: (of food, etc.) **det s-er** it tastes good.

sma'ke/bit *-en* (=**/bete**) sample, taste.

sma'kelig *A* - (=***smakleg**) agreeable, palatable.

sma'k/full *A* **1** in good taste, tasteful. **2** tasty.

smak'ke *V -a/+-et* smack (one's lips).

sma'k/laus *A* **1** improper, in poor taste. **2** insipid, tasteless.

***sma'kleg** *A* - cf **smakelig**

+**sma'k/løs** *A* cf **/laus**

+**sma'kløs/het** *-en* cf **-løyse**

sma'k/løyse *-a* **1** bad, poor taste. **2** insipidity, tastelessness.

sma'ks/evne *-a/+-en* (sense of) taste.

sma'ks/orga'n *-et* organ of taste; taste bud.

sma'ks/prøve *-a/+-en* sample, taste.

sma'ks/retning *-a/+-en* (prevailing) style, taste.

sma'ks/sak +*en/***ei* matter, question of taste.

sma'l *A* **1** narrow; (of people) slender, slim: **den s-e vei** the straight and narrow (path). **2** meager, scanty: **settes på s- kost** be placed on short rations. **3** insignificant, trifling: **det er en s- sak for ham** it's quite easy for him (to do).

sma'le[1] *-n* **1** sheep. **2**: **hele s-n** the whole crowd, shebang.

sma'le[2] *V -a/+-et* crack, pop.

+**sma'le[3]** *V -te* narrow, taper.

sma'le/beist *-et* nanny goat; sheep.

sma'le/fjøs *-et* sheepcote.

sma'l/ende *-n* narrow end.

sma'l/film *-en* 8- or 16-millimeter film.

sma'l/hans *N* poverty, want: **det var s- i huset** they had little to eat.

***sma'lke** *V -a* narrow, taper.

small' *pt of* **smelle[3]**

sma'l/legg *-en, pl* **-er* calf (of leg).

sma'lne *V -a/+-et* **1** become narrower. **2** narrow, taper.

sma'l/rygg *-en* small of the back.

+**sma'l/skuldret** *A* - narrow-shouldered.

sma'l/spora *A* - (=+**-(e)t**) **1** narrow-gauge (track). **2** narrow-minded.

+**smal't** *pt of* **smelle[3]**

smarag'd *-en* emerald.

smarag'd/grøn *A* (=+**/grønn**) emerald green.

sma'rt *A* - smart (=clever, tricky; fashionable).

+**sma'rt/het** *-en* smartness.

smash [smæsj'] *-et* smash (in tennis).

smashe [smæsj'e] *V -a/+-et* smash (esp. tennis).

smas'k *-en* **1** noisy chewing; smack (of the lips); loud, smacking kiss. **2**: **slå i s-** *dial.* smash to pieces.

smas'ke *V -a/+-et* chew one's food noisily; smack one's lips; kiss loudly.

smat're *V -a/+-et* bang, crackle, rattle.

smatt'[1] *-en/-et* smack, smacking sound.

smatt'[2] *pt of* **smette[2]**

smat'te *V -a/+-et* smack one's lips: **s- på hesten** gee to a horse; **s- på pipen** suck one's pipe.

smau' *-et* alley, lane, narrow passage.

smau'g *pt of* **smyge**

smau's *-en* **1** blowout, spree. **2** *pop.* chop, jaw: **hold nu din s-** keep your trap shut (Bojer).

sme'd *-en* smith (e.g. blacksmith, locksmith, etc.): **enhver er sin egen lykkes s-** every man is the architect of his fortune, the master of his destiny; **passe på som en s-** keep a sharp lookout.

+**sme'de[1]** *V -et archaic* **1** forge: **s- mens jernet er varmt** strike while the iron is hot. **2** *fig.* invent, make up (lies, stories).

+**sme'de[2]** *V -et* deride, ridicule.

+**sme'de/dikt** *-et* lampoon.

+**sme'de/skrift** *-et* libel.

+**sme'd/gutt** *-en* (=***/gut**) smith's apprentice.

+**smed'je** *-n* cf **smie[1]**

smei'k *-en* caress, endearment, kiss.

+**smei'ke** *V -te* (=***-je**) caress, fondle.

smei'ken *A* +*-ent, pl -ne* affectionate loving; ingratiating.

***smei'kje** *V -te* cf **smeike**

smei's *-en dial.* **1** mass. **2** lick, whack.

smei'se *V -te/***-a* slap, smack: **s- på (til)** attack vigorously, pitch into.

***smei't** *pt of* **smite**

smekk'[1] *-en/+-et* (=***smikk** **1** click, smack, snap. **2** rap, slap: **slå to fluer med ett s-** kill two birds with one stone. **3** blow, loss (e.g. economic, financial).

smekk'[2] *-en* (trouser) fly.

smekk'/dør *-a* door with (spring) latch.

+**smek'ke[1]** *-a* (=***smikke[1]**) bib (for child; on apron or costume).

smek'ke[2] *V -a/+-et/+smekte* (=***smikke[2]**) **1** click, smack, snap: **s- med tungen** smack one's tongue. **2** rap, slap: **hun s-et til ham over fingrene** she gave him a rap across the fingers. **3** bang, slam: **s- døren i, igjen** s- the door. **4** *dial.* make a sucking sound (as when walking in deep mud).

smek'ker *A -ert, pl smekre* **1** slender, slim. **2** (of boats) elegant, trim.

smekk'/feit *A* very fat.

smekk'/full *A* chuck-full.

smekk'/lås *-en/-et* (spring) latch, snap lock.
smek're *pl of* **smekker**
smek'te *V +-et/*-a* long, pine (**etter** for).
smek'tende *A* - languishing; seductive(ly).
smell' *-en/-et* click, crack; pop, smack; bang, slam; report (of gun): **skjell og s-** scolding and abuse.
smel'le[1] *-a bot.* carpet pink, moss campion (Silene acaulis).
smel'le[2] *-a* cracker (party favor).
smel'le[3] *V small/+smalt, +smelt/ *smolle/*-i (intrans.)* click, crack, pop; snap; slam; (of gun) bang: **frosten smalt i veggene** the frost crackled in the walls; **døra s-er igjen** the door slams; **s- i med** burst out with (e.g. a remark); **s- løs** open fire; (of sound, laughter) break out, explode; **s- opp** snap open; **skjelle og s-** cf **skjelle.**
smel'le[4] *V smelte (trans.)* crack, snap; slam: **s- igjen døra** s- the door; **s- med svepen** crack the whip.
smel'lende *Av*: **s- feit** very fat.
+**smel'ler** *-en, pl -e* (=***-ar**) *zool.* click beetle (Elateridae).
smell'/feit *A* (=+**/fet**) very fat.
smell'/fin *A* exceedingly fine, first-rate.
smell'/kyss *-en/-et* loud, smacking kiss.
smell'/vakker *A -ert, pl -vakre* cracking, (superlatively) fine, handsome.
smel't *pp of* **smelle**[3,4]
+**smel't/bar** *A* fusible.
smel'te[1] *-a zool.* smelt, sparling (Osmerus eperlanus).
smel'te[2] *-a* metal mass: **hele s-a** the whole lot.
smel'te[3] *V -a/+-et/*-e* ɪ *(intrans.)* melt; *(trans.)* melt, smelt: **s- om** melt down, remelt. 2 blend, fuse: **s- i hverandre** blend, mix together; **s- sammen** blend, mix together; (e.g. of metals) fuse; melt away.
+**smel'te**[4] *pt of* **smelle**[4]
smel'te/digel *-elen, pl -ler* crucible, meltingpot: **komme, være i s-en** undergo a complete transformation.
smel'te/hytte *-a* smelter, smelting works.
smel'telig *A* - fusible: **lett s-** highly f.
smel'te/omn *-en* (=+**/ovn**) (smelting) furnace.
smel'te/punkt *-et* melting point; fusing point (of metals).
smel'te/sikring *-a/+-en* (safety) fuse.
***sme're** *V -a* ɪ curry favor with, wheedle. 2 smirk.
***sme'ren** *A -e/-i, pl -ne* cloying, mawkish, nauseating.
smer'gel *-en* emery.
smer'gel/lerret *-et* emery cloth.
smer'gel/skive *-a* emery wheel.
smer'gle *V -a/+-et* grind, polish with emery.
smer'te[1] *+-n/*-a* ɪ ache, pain: **han har store s-r** he is in great pain. 2 grief, sorrow.
smer'te[2] *V -a/+-et* ɪ ache, be painful. 2 grieve: **det s-et meg dypt** it cut me to the quick.
smer'te/fri *A -tt* painless; *(adv.)*: **s-tt** painlessly.
smer'te/full *A* painful.
+**smer'te/fylt** *A* - agonizing, cruel, painful.
smer'telig *A* distressing, painful: **et s- tap** a grievous loss.
+**smer'tens/ba'rn** *-et* enfant terrible, problem child.
+**smer'tens/budskap** *-et* sad news, tidings.
+**smer'tens/leie** *-t poet.* bed of pain, sorrow.
smer'te/ri *-a* severe attack of pain.
smer'te/stillende *A* - analgesic, pain-relieving.
smet'te[1] *-a/-et* narrow aperture, opening.
smet'te[2] *V smatt, +-et/*smotte/*-i* move quickly, slip: **s- gjennom døra** s- through the door; **s- i klærne** s- into one's clothes; **s- unna** s- away.
smet'te[3] *V -a/+-et/*-e* squeeze into, thread: **han s-et seg gjennom hullet i gjerdet** he squeezed himself through the hole in the fence.
smi' *V -dde* (=***smide**) ɪ forge (metal), work: **s- mens jernet er varmt** strike while the iron is hot. 2 whittle (wood). 3 make (e.g. plans). 4 fling, toss (**bort** away).
+**smi'/bar** *A* malleable.
***smi'de** *V -de* cf **smi**
smi'dig *A* - adaptable, lithe, supple (e.g. language, person); flexible, pliant (e.g. law, rod); ductile (metal): **en handelsmann må være ferm, s-** a merchant has to be vigorous and pliant (Bjørnson).
+**smi'dig/het** *-en* adaptability, flexibility, suppleness.
smid'je *-a* cf **smie**[1]
smi'e[1] *-a* blacksmith shop; forge, smithy.
***smi'e**[2] *V -a/-dde* whittle (cf **smi**).
smi'e/avl *-en* forge, hearth.
smi'e/belg *-en* forge bellows.
smi'e/kol [/kål] *-et* smithing coal (low sulphur and ash content).
smi'e/ste *-et* anvil.
+**smi'e/tang** *-a, pl -tenger* (=***/tong**) blacksmith's tongs.
smi'ger *-en* flattery.
smig're *V -a/+-et* flatter: **s- grovt** spread it on thick, lay it on with a trowel; **s- seg inn hos en** ingratiate oneself with sby; **jeg s-er meg med at** I like to think that; **et s-ende tilbud** a f-ing offer.
+**smi'grer** *-en, pl -e* (=***-ar**) flatterer.
+**smig'reri** *et* flattery, obsequiousness.
smi'/jern [/jæ'rn, also smi'/] *-et* wrought iron.
smi'jerns/lampe *-a/-en* wrought iron lamp.
***smikk'** *-en* cf **smekk**[1]
***smik'ke**[1] *-a* cf **smekke**[1]
***smik'ke**[2] *V -a* cf **smekke**[2]
smi'/kol [/kål] *-et* (=+**/kull**) cf **smie/**
smi'l *-en/-et* smile: **være lutter s-** be all s-s.
smi'le *V -te* smile (**av, til** at, on): **det er da ikke noe å smile av** that's nothing to laugh at; **lykken s-te til ham** fortune s-ed on him.
smi'le/band *-et* (=+**/bånd**): **dra, trekke på s-et** smile, break into a smile.
***smi'le/dokk** *-a, pl -dekker* dimple.
+**smi'le/hull** *-et* (=**/hol**) dimple.
smin'ke[1] *+-n/*-a* make-up, rouge; grease paint.
smin'ke[2] *V -a/+-et* make up: **s- seg** make up one's face.
sminkø'r *-en* make-up man (movie, studio, theater).
sminkø'se *-a/+-en* make-up woman (movie, studio, theater).
smis'ke *V -a/+-et* ɪ be ingratiating, fawn on sby: **s- for** try to ingratiate oneself with. 2 gossip: **s- og tiske** whisper (gossip). 3 smile, smirk.
smis'ket(e) *A* - ɪ fawning, ingratiating. 2 smiling, smirking.
***smi'te** *V smeit, smite/-i* ɪ smear, spread. 2 slip, steal away.
***smi'ten** *A -e/-i, pl -ne* fawning, ingratiating.
***smi'ti** *pp of* **smite**
smitt' *-en*: **hver s- og smule** every particle.
smit'te[1] *-n* ɪ contagion, infection: **utsette seg for s-** expose oneself to i-. 2 *typog.* color (transferred by contact). 3 sizing (into which yarn is dipped prior to weaving).
smit'te[2] *V -a/+-et* ɪ (e.g. of disease, high spirits) be catching, contagious: **eksemplet s-er** the example is contagious. 2 infect; influence: **bli s-et av en sykdom** catch a disease; be contaminated; **det var ditt eksempel som s-et ham** it was your example that influenced him. 2: **s- av** (of color) come, rub off. 3 size yarn (before weaving).
+**smit'te/bærende** *A* - infectious.
+**smit'te/bærer** *-en, pl -e* (=***/berar**) carrier (of infection).
smit'te/evne *-a/+-en* infectiousness.
smit'te/fare *-n* danger of infection.
smit'te/fa'rlig *A* - infectious.
smit'te/fri *A -tt* noninfectious.
smit'te/førende *A* - infectious.
smit'te/kjelde *-a* (=+**/kilde**) source of infection.
+**smit'te/spreder** *-en, pl -e* (=***/spreiar**) carrier (of infection).
smit'te/stoff *-et* infectious matter, virus.
+**smitt'/som'** *A -t, pl -me* (=***/sam**) catching, contagious, infectious.
***smju'ge** *V smyg, smaug, smoge/-i* cf **smyge**
sml. =+**sammenlign**/***samanlikn**
***smoge**[1] [små'ge] *-a* narrow passage, refuge.
smoge**[2] [små'ge] *pp of* **smyge** (=smogi**)
***smog'ne** *V -a* dwindle, narrow.
smoking [små'king] *-en* dinner jacket, tuxedo.
smoking/skjorte *-a* tuxedo shirt.
smokk [smokk'] *-en* ɪ guard (for sore finger). 2 nipple.
***smo'le**[1] *-a* cf **smule**[1]
***smo'le**[2] *V -a* ɪ break, crack (sth). 2 be noisy.
***smol'le**[1] *V -a* snicker.
smol'le**[2] *pp of* **smelle**[3] (=smolli**)
***smol't** *-et* cf **smult**
°**smo'rte** *pt of* **smøre**
smot'te[1] *-a* alley, lane; narrow passage.
***smot'te**[2] *pp of* **smette**[2]
***smott'/hol** [/hål] *-et* cf **smutt/hull**
***smot'ti** *pp of* **smette**[2]
smp. =**smeltepunkt**
sms. =**sammensetning**
+**smst.** =**sammesteds**
+**smu'g**[1] *-et* cf **smau**
smu'g[2] *N*: **i s-** on the sly, secretly, surreptitiously.
smu'g/brenning *-a/+-en* moonshining.
smu'g/handel *-en* illicit trade, traffic (e.g. bootlegging).
smug'le *V -a/+-et* smuggle: **s- varer inn (i)** s- goods in(to).
+**smug'ler** *-en, pl -e* (=***-ar**) smuggler.
+**smug'ler/gods** [/gots] *-et* (=***-ar/**) contraband, smuggled goods.
+**smug'ler/sprit** *-en* (=***-ar/**) bootleg, moonshine.
+**smug'ler/trafikk'** *-en* (=***-ar/**) smuggling.
+**smug'ler/vare** *-a/-en* (=***-ar/**) contraband, smuggled goods.
smu'g/trafikk' *-en* illicit trade, traffic.
+**smukk'** *A smukt* comely, handsome, pretty: **det s-e kjønn** the fair sex; **et s-t resultat** a fine outcome; **jeg måtte s-t bli hjemme** I had to stay home (with as good grace as I could summon); **si s-e ting** pay handsome compliments.
+**smuk'kas** *-en fam.* beau brummel, sheik.
smu'l *A* calm, smooth: **i s-t farvann** in calm waters.
smul'der *-et* crumbs, small fragments.
smul'dre *V -a/+-et* ɪ crumble, decompose, disintegrate: **s- bort** crumble away. 2 demolish, pulverize.
smu'le[1] *-n* ɪ crumb: **s-r er også brød** a little is better than nothing. 2 *lit.* tiny bit, trifle: **hver s-** every single bit.
smu'le[2] *V +-te/*-a* break into small fragments, pieces: **s- seg** crumble, fall into small pieces.
smu'lne *V -a/+-et* (of the sea) become calmer, smoother.
smul't *-et* lard.
smul't/bakkels(e) *-(e)n/*-(e)t* deep fried bakery goods (e.g. crullers, doughnuts).

+ Bokmål; * Nynorsk; ° Dialect.
After letter: ' stress (Acc. 1); ` tone, stress (Acc. 2); · length.
Below letter: . not pronounced.

smul't/ring *-en* doughnut.
***smu'rde** *pt of* **smørje**[2]
smu'rning *-en* 1 grease, lubricant; *(pop.)* bribe. 2 drubbing, thrashing.
***smu'rnings/ler** *-et* oiled leather.
+**smu'rte** *pt of* **smøre**
+**smus'ket** *A* - black, dark, dirty (in color).
+**smuss'** *-et* dirt, filth: **kaste s- på en** besmirch, smear sby.
smuss'/blad *-et* muckraking paper, yellow journal.
+**smus'se** *V -et*: **s- til** dirty, soil.
+**smus'sig** *A* - dirty, filthy, grimy; indecent, sordid.
smuss'/konkurranse [/-ang·se] *-n* unfair competition.
smuss'/litteratu·r *-en* pornography.
smuss'/omslag *-et* dust jacket.
smuss'/presse *-a/+-en* muckraking press, yellow press.
smuss'/tittel *-elen, pl -titler typog.* bastard title, half title.
smutt' *N*: **kaste, slå s-** skip stones (across water).
+**smut'te** *V -a/-et* glide, slip: **s- bort** s- away; **s- fra** give the slip to.
+**smutt'/hull** *-et* hiding-place, hideout, refuge.
smy'g *-en* sneak; *(pop.)* creep.
smy'ge *V smaug/+smøg, +smøget/ *smoge/*-i* slip, sneak, steal: **s- av (på) seg** slip off (on) (e.g. clothes); **s- for en** crawl, grovel before sby; **s- seg inn (ut)** sneak in (out); **s- seg inn til** nestle (snuggle) up to; **s- seg om** cling around.
smy'g/stol *-en* cf **smøy/**
smyk'ke[1] *-t, pl +-r/*-* ornament, piece of jewelry; *(pl)* jewelry.
+**smyk'ke**[2] *V -et/smykte* adorn, decorate, embellish: **s- seg** deck oneself out.
smyk'ke/skrin *-et* jewel box, case.
smyk'ke/stein *-en* jewel, precious stone.
smy'le *-t* (=+**smyle/bunke**) *bot.* wood hairgrass (Aira flexuosa).
***smæ'ling** *-en* 1 inconsequential, insignificant person. 2 miser.
***smæ're** *-n bot.* clover, trefoil (genus Trifolium).
***smær're** *cp of* **små**[1]
***smæs't** *sp of* **små**[1]
***smæt'te** *V -a* diminish, make small.
+**smø'g** *pt of* **smyge**
smør'[1] *-et* butter: **legge s- på flesk** gild the lily, overdo sth; **ja(jo)men sa jeg s-** (used as expression of disbelief or ironically after sth has not come up to expectations; from the saying: **jamen sa jeg s-, sa kjerringa, hun fikk smult på brødet** that's some b-, said the old woman, she got lard on her bread).
***smø'r**[2] *pr of* **smørje**[2]
***smør'/auga** *-t* cf **/øye**
smør'/blid *A* overly bland, smirking.
+**smør'/blomst** *-en* (=***/blom(e), */blomster**) *bot.* buttercup (Ranunculus acris).
smør'/brød *-et* sandwich (usu. open-faced).
smør'/bukk *-en* 1 roly-poly boy (from fairy tale by Asbjørnsen and Moe), "Butterball". 2 *bot.* orpine (Sedum telephium).
+**smø're** *V smurte* (=***smørje**[1]) 1 butter (e.g. bread): **s- for tykt på** exaggerate, lay it on too thick; **s- mat** make sandwiches; **s- en om munnen** butter sby up. 2 grease, lubricate, oil (e.g. machine); wax (skis); smear: **s- seg i ansiktet (med olje)** rub one's face (with oil); **s- seg med tålmodighet** be patient; **s- seg til** mess oneself (or one's clothes) up; **det går som smurt** it's going, working without a hitch. 3 bribe (i.e. grease sby's palm). 4 beat, lick, thrash. 5: **s- sammen** daub (painting); scribble (letter, novel, etc.).
+**smø're/kanne** *-a* oilcan.
+**smø're/kopp** *-en* grease cup.
+**smø're/middel** *-elet/-let, pl -midler* lubricant.
+**smø're/olje** *-a/-en* lubricating oil.
+**smø'rer** *-en, pl -e* (=***smørjar**) 1 *naut.* greaser, oiler. 2 *derog.* artistic, literary hack.
+**smø'reri** *-et* 1 daubery. 2 scribbling. 3 piece of artistic, literary trash.
smør'et(e) *A* - greasy; ingratiating (e.g. smile); oily, unctuous (e.g. voice).
smør'/farge *-n* coloring (added to butter).
smør'/form *-a/+-en* butter form.
smør'/graut *-en* porridge (of flour, butter, and water or milk).
smør'/gul *A* butter-colored.
smør'/gås *-a* (Swedish) open-faced sandwiches and hors d'oeuvres.
+**smø'ring** *-a/-en* (=***smørjing**) 1 greasing, lubrication. 2 ski wax. 3 *fam.* bribe, tip, *(pop.)* greasing (sby's palm).
***smør'jar** *-en* cf **smører**
smør'je[1] *-a* 1 grease, lubricant. 2 soft mass: **hele s-a** the whole kit and caboodle.
***smør'je**[2] *V smør, smurde, smurt* cf **smøre**
***smør'jing** *-a* cf **smøring**
smør'/kniv *-en* butter knife.
smør'/krem *-en* filling (made of butter, eggs, and powdered sugar).
smør'/kule *-a* butter ball.
smør'/ogbrød [/åbrø·] *-et* cf **/brød**
smør'/papi·r *-et* greaseproof paper (wax paper).
+**smør're/brød** *-et* cf **smør/**
smør'/side [*/sie] *-a/+-en* (the) buttered side.
smør'/teno·r *-en* affected, tearfully emotional tenor.
smør'/øskje *-a* wooden butter dish.
+**smør'/øye** *-t* melted lump of butter (in center of dish of porridge).
smøy'e *V +-de/*-gde* 1 thread (rope, thread, etc.). 2 slip: **s- av (på)** s- off (on) (e.g. clothes).
***smøy'eleg** *A* - (overly) reticent, shy; shrewd, sly.
***smøy'en** *A -e/-i, pl -ne* agile, pliable, supple.
***smøy'gde** *pt of* **smøye**
smøy'/stol *-en* (=+**smyg/**, ***smøye/**) belt loop.
små'[1] *A -tt, pl -/*-e, cp *smærre, sp *smæst* 1 little, small: **i det s-** on a small scale; **i stort og s-tt** in all things; **med stort og s-tt** including everything; **skrive med s-tt** write with small letters. 2 inconsequential, poor: **s-tt stell** poor conditions; **det er bare s-tt** it's of little consequence; **det er s-tt med** there's little of; **det så s-tt ut** the prospects were poor; **det ble s-tt om mat** food supplies ran short. 3 (used substantively): **småen** the little one; **småene** the children; **ha s-tt** have a baby, children. 4 *(adv.)*: **s-tt** gradually, slightly; slowly; **s-tt om senn** little by little; **så s-tt** a little, little by little; **og så begynte han å filosofere så s-tt** and then he gradually began to philosophize (Hoel).
små'[2] *pl of* **liten, små**[1]
+**små'/aktig** *A* - 1 insignificant. 2 narrow-minded, petty.
små'/banne *V -a/-bante* swear a little.
små'/ba·rn *pl* babies; small fry.
+**små'/belø·p** *pl* paltry, trifling amounts.
små'/blomstra *A* - (=+**-et**) 1 having small flowers. 2 (of fabrics) sprigged.
små'/bonde [/bonne] *-n, pl -bønder* operator of small farm.
små'/bo·rd *pl* small tables (e.g. in café, restaurant).
+**små'/borger** *-en, pl -e* (=***-ar**) 1 member of the lower middle class, petty bourgeois. 2 *derog.* babbit, philistine. 3 *hum.* baby, infant.
+**små'/borgerlig** *A* - (=***/borgarleg**) 1 of the lower middle class, bourgeois. 2 philistine.
små'/bruk *-et* small farm.
+**små'/bruker** *-en, pl -e* (=***-ar**) operator of a small farm.
små'bruks/skole *-n* agricultural school (for small-farm operators).
små'/by *-en* small town.
+**små'by/aktig** *A* - small-town.
små'/båt *-en* rowboat; ship's boat.
små'/deler *pl* particles; small parts.
små'/fallen *A +-ent, pl -falne* moderate; on the small side.
små'/fe *-et* goats and sheep.
små'/feil *en, pl* - minor defect, error; peccadillo.
små'/felt *A* - moderate; on the small side.
***små'/ferdig** [/færig] *A* - 1 slow-working. 2 on the small side, smallish. 3 modest, petty.
små'/fisk *-en* small fry.
små'/flire *V -te* chuckle, grin.
små'/folk *pl* 1 people of humble means; common people, ordinary people. 2 small fry, tots.
+**små'/forlovet** [/fårlå·vet] *A - hum.* going steady; pinned.
små'/fryse *V infl as* **fryse**[1] shiver.
små'/fugl *-en* small bird, songbird.
små'/gate *-a* side street.
små'/gris *-en* piglet.
+**små'/gutt** *-en* (=***/gut**) little boy.
små'/handel *-elen, pl -ler* small-scale trading.
små'/hus *-et* cottage, small house.
små'/høy *-et* short, fine hay (used to feed goats and sheep).
små'/jente *-a* little girl.
små'/kake *-a* (small) cake, cooky; *(pl)* cookies, pastry.
små'/kar *-en* 1 little fellow. 2 insignificant person.
+**små'/kirke** *-a/-en* (=***/kyrkje**) chapel (privately financed as auxiliary to main church).
små'/klasse *-a/-en* class attended by children in a **småskole** (7—10 years of age).
+**små'/knegge** *V -a/-et/-knegde* (=***-je**) whinny (softly); chuckle.
små'/koke *V -te/*-a* simmer.
små'/kol [/kål] *-et* (=+**/kull**) slack coal.
små'/konge *-n* petty king.
små'/koselig *A* - congenial, cozy, pleasant (in a small or simple way).
+**små'/kveg** *-et* goats and sheep.
små'kårs/folk *pl* people of humble, modest means.
små'kårs/mann *-en, pl -menn/ *-menner* person of humble, modest means.
+**Smål.** =**Smålenene**
små'/le *V -lo, -ledd/*-lett* chortle, chuckle.
+**Små'/lenene** *Pln* former name of Østfold.
små'lig *A* - 1 narrow-minded, petty. 2 niggardly, stingy.
+**små'lig/het** *-en* 1 narrow-mindedness, pettiness. 2 meanness, stinginess.
små'/lo *pt of* **-le**
***små'/log** [/låg] *-et* goats and sheep.
***små'/læte** *-t* humility, modesty.
små'/låten *A +-ent, pl -ne* modest, reserved, unassuming.
små'/mann *-en, pl -menn/*-menner* common, humble man.
små'/maska *A* - (=+**-et**) fine-meshed.
***små'/minke** *V -a*: **s- seg til** condescend, stoop to.
+**små'/morsom** [/morsåmm] *A -t, pl -me* amusing, diverting (in a minor way).
små'/mønstra *A* - (=+**-et**) small patterned, (e.g. of material) sprigged.
små'ningom *Av* gradually: **så s-** (the same).
små'/nytt *et* bits, scraps of news, filler (in newspaper).
***små'/nøgd** *A -/-nøgt* modest, undemanding.
små'/o·rd *-et gram.* particle.
små'/pen *A* prettyish, pretty (without character).

+små'/penger pl (=*-ar) (small) change.

+småpi'ke -n little girl.

små'/plukk [/plokk] -et trifles: det var ikke s- it was no small thing.

*små'/poke [/påke] -a smallpox.

små'/prate V -a/+-et chat, make small talk.

små'/pussig A - amusing, droll (in low-keyed way).

små'/regne [+/reine] V -a/+-et/+-te/*-de drizzle, sprinkle.

+små'/rolling -en kid, (tiny) tot.

små'/rutet(e) A - (=/ruta) 1 with small windowpanes. 2 (of cloth) checked, checkered (with small checks).

små'/sei -en zool. small billet, coalfish (Pollachius virens).

små'/sild -a sprats.

små'/skjenne V -skjente chide, grumble (på at sby).

små'/skog -en brushwood (with small trees), copse.

små'/skole -n school for children 7—10 years of age.

*små'/skoren [/skåren] A -e/-i, pl -ne cf /skåren

små'/skrift -et pamphlet.

+små'/skåren A -ent, pl -ne (=*/skoren) 1 cut into small pieces. 2 narrow-minded, petty.

små'/snakke V -a/+-et chatter, chitchat; mumble (to oneself).

+små'/sparer -en, pl -e (=*-ar) small depositor.

+små'/spiker -eren, pl -rer/+-er (=*-ar) small nail (less than 2 inches long).

små'/springe V infl as springe jog, trot along.

+små'/sted -et (=*/stad) crossroads, village; (pop.) whistle-stop.

små'/stein -en pebble.

små'/stunder pl breaks, brief rests; intervals, pauses.

+små'/stykker pl (=*/stykke) 1 bits; short, small pieces. 2 playlets (theater); short musical compositions.

+små'/summer pl (=*-ar) driblets, petty sums.

små'/svein -en archaic little boy.

små'/tenkt A - shortsighted.

små'/ting -en 1 small object, thing. 2 bagatelle, trifle.

små'/torsk -en small cod (generally found in fjords); codling.

små'/troll -et 1 small troll. 2 brat, ill-behaved child (also used hum. and affectionately).

smått' nt of små[1]

småt'teri -et, pl +-er/*- small things; bagatelle, trifle.

små'/tærende A -: han er s- he is a poor eater, he eats like a bird.

*små'/tøk A moderate, temperate.

små'/ved -en kindling.

små'/vilt -et small game.

*små'/voren A -e/-i, pl -ne 1 fairly small. 2 petty; stingy.

*SN=Dei sameinte nasjonane cf FN

snabb' -en bit, end (e.g. of sausage).

sna'bel -elen, pl -ler 1 proboscis; trunk. 2 beak, rostrum (of ancient warship). 3 hum. human nose, (pop.) schnozzle.

sna'bel/sko -en, pl -r/+- peaked, pointed shoe.

+sna'bel/skøyter pl (old-fashioned) skates with runners curled up in front.

snadd' -en 1 dial. muzzle, snout; gift of gab. 2 zool. ringed seal (Phoca hispida).

snad'de -a (short-stemmed) tobacco pipe.

snad'der -eret/+snadret cackling, quacking (of fowl); fig. gabbling, jabbering.

snad're V -a/+-et 1 (of fowl) cackle, quack. 2 fig. gabble, jabber.

+snaf's -et dirt, filth, muck.

*snaf'se V -a gobble (food).

*sna'ge V -a chafe, rub; bump.

sna'k A sneaking; avaricious, greedy.

sna'ke V -a/+-te 1 nab, purloin: s- til seg appropriate (by devious means). 2 prowl, slink, sneak: s- etter nose around for, try to secure.

snakk' -et 1 conversation, talk: gi seg, komme i s- med talk, enter into c- with. 2 gossip: s-et går om at the latest g- is that. 3 chattering, idle talk, twaddle: å, s- oh, nonsense.

snak'ke V -a/+-et speak, talk (med with, to; om about): du s-er! well, I never!; snakk om at luften går ut av ballongen t- about the air going out of the balloon (=being deflated) (Hoel); s- forbi hverandre t- at cross purposes; s- en fra noe t- sby out of (doing sth); s- frampå om hint at; s- over seg be out of one's head, talk irrationally; s- til en t- to sby; give sby a talking to; s- ut speak up, speak one's mind; s- ut med en have a good talk with sby, get things settled; s- seg bort fra t- oneself out of; s- seg opp get oneself worked up (by talking); s-es ved t- things over.

+snak'ker -en, pl -e (=*-ar) blowhard, chatterbox.

+snak'ke/salig A - garrulous, loquacious; long-winded.

+snak'ke/tøy -et: ha et godt s- have the gift of gab.

+snakk'/som· A -t, pl -me (=*/sam) garrulous, talkative.

snapp' A snapt dial. brisk, lively.

snap'pe V -a/+-et grab, snatch: s- opp catch, intercept, pick up; s- etter luft gasp for air.

snapp'/hane -n 1 blunderbuss. 2 hist. Danish guerilla (in war with Sweden over Scania).

snap's -en nip, schnaps; shot (of brandy, aquavit, etc.).

snap'se V -a/+-et tipple.

snap/shot [snæpp/sjått] -et snapshot.

sna'r[1] -et 1 brushwood, copse, thicket. 2 dial. snarl, twist.

sna'r[2] A quick, swift; of short duration: s- som et lyn quick as lightning; s- av seg quick-tempered; s- til å quick to (e.g. comprehend); (adv.) cf snart.

+sna'r/bedt A - (=*/beden) accommodating, willing.

sna're[1] -a/+-en 1 snare. 2 fig. pitfall, trap: bli hengende i sin egen s- be hoist on one's own petard; stille en s- for en set a trap for sby.

sna're[2] V -a/+-et 1 snare, trap. 2 dial. wrap (sth around one); lace, tie; turn, twist.

sna're/fangst -en snaring (av of).

sna're/fugl -en snared bird (esp. grouse).

sna'r/fengd A -/-fengt (=/fengen) easily obtained, secured.

*sna'r/føtt A - nimble-footed.

+sna'r/gjort [/jort] A - (=*/gjord) quickly done, hastily done.

*sna'r/hug -en presence of mind, resourcefulness.

*snar'ke V -a snore; snort.

*sna'r/kjøm A coming quickly.

sna'r/kjøp -et self-service.

sna'rkjøps/butikk· -en self-service store.

sna'rlig A - speedy; (adv.) quickly, shortly, soon.

*snar'p[1] pt of snerpe[3]

snar'p[2] A keen, sharp; fig. perspicacious.

*snar'past V -ast become sharper.

*sna'r/ræde -a cf /rådighet

sna'r/rådig A - quick-witted, resourceful.

+sna'rrådig/het -en presence of mind, resourcefulness.

sna'r/sint A - fiery, quick-tempered.

*snar't[1] -en brand, firebrand.

*snar't[2] pt of snerte[1]

sna'rt[3] Av 1 quickly, soon: vi må s- gå we have to go soon; det er s- gjort that is quickly done, that can easily happen; så s- (som) as soon as; aldri så s- no sooner. 2 almost, nearly; hardly: s- sagt almost, nearly; det er s- ti år siden it's almost ten years ago; jeg er s- ferdig I'm nearly finished; jeg vet s- ikke I hardly know. 3: s- det ene s- det andre now this now that. 4 snarere sooner; if anything, rather: det er s- det motsatte it is, if anything, the opposite; jeg ville s- si at I'd prefer to say that; jeg tror s- at I'm more inclined to believe that. 5 snarest soonest, as soon as possible: som (aller) s- for just a moment.

*snar'te V -a cut, trim (e.g. a wick).

sna'r/tenkt A - quick-witted, resourceful.

*sna'r/truen A -e/-i, pl -ne credulous.

sna'r/tur -en flying trip, visit.

*sna'r/tøk A quick to learn.

sna'r/veg -en (=+/vei) shortcut.

sna'r/vending -a 1 emergency, pinch. 2 flying trip, visit. 3: i en s- in passing.

sna'r/visitt· -en flying visit.

sna'r/ærend -et hurried errand.

*sna'se V -a sniff, snort, snuff.

snas'k -et 1 goodies, sweets. 2 discard, refuse, rubbish.

snas'ke V -a/+-et 1 chew, crunch greedily and noisily. 2 nab, snatch. 3 prowl, slink, sneak.

snau' A *-tt 1 bare (e.g. ground, rock, mountain); bald: klippe s- crop closely. 2 broke, impoverished. 3 bare=scant, scarce; skimpy, stingy: i s-este laget a bit on the skimpy side; det er en s- time igjen there's just barely an hour left; han er ikke s-ere enn at he is generous enough to; prestene pleide ellers å være s-e med skysspenger the ministers used to skimp on payment to the coachmen (Falkberget). 4 (adv.) s-t barely, scarcely; s-t nok barely, scarcely; s-t regnet as a minimum, as a low estimate.

snau'e V -a/+-et/+-de (=snøye[2]) 1 crop close (e.g. a tree, dog's ears, etc.). 2 drain, empty, scrape clean. 3: s- seg run out (of money); han hadde s-et seg for kontanter he had run out of cash.

snau'/fjell -et bare, naked rock.

snau'/flekk -en bare spot.

snau'/gnage V infl as gnage[1] crop (grass, pasture) closely; gnaw clean.

snau'/hogge V infl as hogge clear (land).

snau'/hogst -en clearing (of land).

snau'/klippe V -klipte clip, crop close.

snau'/skalle -n bald head or person.

*snau'/sliten A -e/-i, pl -ne threadbare, worn.

snav'l -a/-en derog. jaw, snout: hold s-a keep your trap shut.

snav'le V -a/+-et grumble crossly, peevishly.

+sne'[1] -en cf snø[1]

+sne'[2] V -dde cf snø[2]

*sne'd[1] -et cut, slash: han fekk ikkje s- på det he didn't get the hang of it; han gjorde meg eit godt s- he really pulled a good one on me; i s- askew, aslant.

+sne'd[2] N cf snei

*snedd' -a hurry.

*sned'de V -a: s- seg hurry.

sned'den A +-ent, pl snedne brisk, lively, quick.

sne'dig A - astute, crafty, wily.

+sne'dig/het -en astuteness, craftiness, cunning.

+snegl [snei'l] -en (=+snile/*snigel) 1 zool. snail (class Gastropoda). 2 mus. scroll (on a violin). 3 (snile) hum. rascal.

+snegle [snei'le] V -a/-et (=*snigle): s- seg av sted crawl, move at a snail's pace.

+snegle/fart [snei'le/] -en 1 snail's pace:

+ Bokmål; * Nynorsk; ° Dialect. After letter: ' stress (Acc. 1); ` tone, stress (Acc. 2); · length. Below letter: . not pronounced.

med s- at a snail's pace. 2 *mus.* slow tempo.
+**snegle/gang** *-en* snail's pace.
+**snegle/hus** *-et* 1 snail shell: **trekke seg inn i sitt s-** retire into one's shell. 2 *anat.* cochlea.
+**sne'/hvit** *A* cf **snø/kvit**
snei' *+-en/*-a* 1 slice. 2: **på s-** aslant, askew; **med hatten på s-** with the hat on one ear. 3 *naut.* **få s- på vinden** get a good wind (to sail by).
***snei'd** *pt of* **snide**
***snei'e**[1] *-a* reproach, upbraiding.
snei'e[2] *V +-de/*-dde* 1 cut, slice on the slant. 2 walk obliquely; cut across. 3: **s- borti** brush (against), graze. 4 gibe, sneer; reproach.
snei'/o'rd *-et* sarcastic remark, taunt.
snei's[1] *-a* 1 nail, peg; knitting needle. 2 drying pole (on which ten sheaves of barley, rye, etc. are placed to dry): **dra kornet opp på s-** put the grain up to dry.
snei's[2] *-a/+-et* (=+**snes**) score.
snei'se *V -a/-te* 1 place sheaves of wheat, rye, etc. on the drying pole. 2 reproach, taunt.
sne'k[1] *-en* pungent, sharp odor.
+**sne'k**[2] *pt of* **snike**[1]
***sne'ke** *V -a* smell, stink.
snek'ke**[1] *-a* (=-je**) 1 snail shell. 2 endless screw, worm.
+**snek'ke**[2] *-n* 1 *hist., poet.* ship, vessel. 2 sailboat (small, open, pointed, may have motor).
+**snek'ker** *-en, pl -e* (=***snikkar**) cabinetmaker, joiner; carpenter.
+**snek'ker/blyant** *-en* carpenter's pencil.
+**snekkere're** *V -te dial.* carpenter, do joiner's work.
+**snekkeri'** *-et* 1 cabinetmaker's, joiner's trade. 2 cabinetmaker's, joiner's workshop.
+**snek'ker/mester** *-eren, pl -ere/-rer* master joiner.
+**snek'ker/svenn** *-en* journeyman joiner.
***snekkj'e** *-a* cf **snekke**[1]
+**snek're** *V -a/-et* (=***snikre**) 1 carpenter, do joiner's work. 2 fix, repair sth: **s- i hop** put, throw sth together.
snel'le[1] *-a* 1 reel; spindle; spool. 2 nail, pin (which fastens the cross piece to the runner on a timber sled). 3 *hum.* short, vivacious young girl or woman.
snel'le[2] *V -a/+-et*: **s- inn** roll, wind up; reel in.
snel'le/tråd *-en* sewing thread (usu. cotton on wooden spools).
+**sne'/lø'sning** *-en* cf **snø/løysing**
+**snep'pe** *-a/-en* cf **snipe**
snep'pert *-en* lancet, scarificator.
sner'k *-en* (=***snerke**) thin coating, crust (of ice); skin (on liquids, esp. on hot milk).
+**sner'ke** *V -a/+-et* (=***-je**): **s- seg** become covered with a thin coating, crust, film; **mjølka s-a seg** skin formed on the (hot) milk.
sner'ket(e) *A* - coated, filmed.
***sner'kje** *V -a* cf **snerke**
sner'p *-et* cf **snerpe**[1]
sner'pe[1] *-a* (=**snerp**) awn (on grain).
sner'pe[2] *-a* 1 prude. *2 bold, sharp person.
***sner'pe**[3] *V snarp, snorpe/-i*: **s- sammen** contract, draw together.
sner'pe[4] *V +-et/*-te* cause to contract, pucker, shrink: **s- munnen sammen** purse the lips (in disapproval); **s-ende** astringent.
sner'peri *-et* prudishness.
sner'pet(e) *A* - prim, prudish, strait-laced.
sner're *V -a/+-et* growl, snarl.
sner't *-en* 1 cracker, snapper, whiplash. 2 crack, flick, lash (of a whip). 3 touch (e.g. of sarcasm); cutting, sarcastic remark. 4 glimpse; hint (av of).
***sner'te**[1] *V snart, snorte/-i* cf **snerte**[2]
sner'te[2] *V -a/+-et/*-e* 1 flick, strike lightly with a whip. 2 graze, rub lightly against: **s- innom** drop in on sby (for a visit). 3 hurry, move quickly. 4 make cutting, nasty remarks at sby.
sner'ten *A +-ent, pl -ne* 1 natty, smart. 2 dexterous, handy. 3 light-footed, quick.
Sner'ting/dal *Pln* twp, Oppland.
+**sne's** *-et* cf **sneis**[2]
+**sne'se/vis** *Av*: **i s-** by the score, in scores.
sne'v *-en* 1 faint odor. 2 hint, inkling, touch; remnant, trace. 3 bit, particle: **ikke s-en** not the least bit.
+**sne'/vann** *-et* cf **snø/vatn**
sne'ver *A -ert, pl -re* confined, narrow, restricted; (of people) narrow-minded: **i en s- vending** in a pinch; **i s-reste forstand** in the narrowest (most restricted) sense.
sne'ver/syn *-et/*-a* narrow-mindedness, narrow outlook.
sne'ver/sy'nt *A* - narrow, narrow-minded.
snev're *V -a/+-et*: **s- seg inn** grow narrower, narrow.
sni'bel *-elen, pl -ler* long-tailed coat, tails.
***sni'de** *V sneid, snide/-i* advance, walk obliquely, on a slant.
sni'del *-elen, pl -ler* sickle (for cutting leaves).
***sni'di** *pp of* **snide**
***sni'gel** *-elen, pl -lar* cf **snegl**
***snig'le** *V -a* cf **snegle**
***snig'le/hus** *-et* cf **snegle/**
***sni'k**[1] *-en* cf **snek**[1]
sni'k[2] *-en* sneak; *(pop.)* creep.
+**sni'ke**[1] *V snek, sneket* (=***snikje**) 1 sneak, skulk about; creep, slink, steal away. 2 be obsequious, fawn: **s- etter** try to obtain by sneaking around, obsequiously; beg for. 3: **s- seg inn** creep in (e.g. an error in a text); slink, steal in; **s- seg til å gjøre noe** do sth on the sly; **s- til seg** contrive to get hold of sth by devious means; sponge. 4: **s-ende** insidious.
***sni'ke**[2] *V -a* cf **sneke**
+**sni'ke**[3] *V -te* (=***snikje**) (of animal) beg (**etter** for).
sni'ken *A +-ent, pl -ne* 1 fawning, obsequious, oily. 2 furtive, hidden, stealthy.
+**sni'ker** *-en, pl -e* (=***-jar**) sneak; freeloader, sponger.
***sni'kjar** *-en* cf **sniker**
***sni'kje** *V -te* cf **snike**[1,3]
***sni'kje/dyr** *-et* parasite.
***sni'kje/gjest** *-en* freeloader, sponger; parasite.
***sni'kje/plante** *-a/-en* parasite.
***snik'kar** *-en* cf **snekker**
+**snikk'/snakk** *-et* fiddle-faddle, nonsense.
***sni'k/meldar** *-en* informer, *(pop.)* stool pigeon.
***sni'k/melde** *V -e* inform against, *(pop.)* stool on.
sni'k/mord [/mord] *-et* assassination.
+**sni'k/morder** [/morder] *-en, pl -e* (=***-ar**) assassin.
sni'k/myrde *V -a/+-et* assassinate.
***snik're** *V -a* cf **snekre**
+**sni'k/skytter** *-en, pl -e* (=***-ar**) sniper.
snil'd *A* cf **snill**
+**sni'le** *-n* cf **snegl**
snill' *A snilt* kind, nice (**med, mot** to); good, well-behaved: **s-e deg** term of address; (to children) **vær s- (gutt, pike) nå** be (a) good (boy, girl) now; (preceding a statement, or as a separate statement) **vær s- (og), vær så s- (å, og)** please; (following a statement) **er du (De) s-** please; **være s- i ansiktet (øynene)** have a kind face (eyes).
snil'le[1] *-t* genius, talent; ingenuity, originality.
***snil'le**[2] *V -a* decorate, dress up: **s- på orda sine** take the sting out of one's words, mince words.
Snill'/fjo'rd *Pln* twp, Sør-Trøndelag.
***snill'sleg** *A* - good-natured, kind.
snil't *nt of* **snill**
sni'pe *-a* 1 *zool.* snipe (genera Capella and Limnocryptes). 2 snipe (type of boat).
snipp'[1] *-en* 1 corner, end (e.g. of handkerchief). 2 collar (on men's shirts). 3 diamond-shaped cooky (usu. made with syrup).
+**snipp'**[2] *I* used to indicate the end of a story: **s- snapp snute, nå er eventyret ute** and that's the end of the story.
snip'pe *V -a/+-et* blubber, whimper.
***snip'pen** *A -e/-i, pl snipne* 1 sudden, unexpected. 2: **s- og snau** chagrined and empty-handed. 3 niggardly, stingy.
snip'pe/proletaria't *-et* white-collar proletariat.
snipp'/kjole *-n* full dress, tails.
snir'kel *-elen, pl -ler* 1 spiral (movement); flourish, frill, scroll; *mus.* tremolo. 2 *hum.* (for **sirkel**) **de finere, høyere snirkler** the hoity-toity.
snir'klet(e) *A* - embellished, ornate (e.g. handwriting, ornamentation); florid (e.g. style); excessively formal (conduct, speech); tortuous (e.g. road).
snitt'[1] *-en* (small) open-faced sandwich (usu. *pl*).
snitt'[2] *-et* 1 cut (in sth, of a garment), incision; section. 2 edge (of a book). 3 knack, trick: **det skal et eget s- til** it takes a special knack. 4: **se (passe) sitt s- til å** see (watch for) one's chance to.
snit'te *V -a/+-et* 1 cut, slice (**av, opp** off, up); carve, whittle. 2: **s- seg til** take advantage of an opportunity.
snit'te/bønne *-a* (=***/baune**) *bot.* kidney bean (Phaseolus vulgaris).
snitt'/flate *-a/+-en* cut, edge.
snitt'/verk *-et* carved work, carving.
+**sni've** *-a/-en vet.* glanders.
***snjo'** *-en* cf **snø**[1]
sno'[1] *-a/+-en* 1 sharp, biting wind. 2 scent (of sth).
sno'[2] *V -dde* (=***snoe**) 1 blow coldly, sharply. 2 get the scent (of sth).
+**sno'**[3] *V -dde* 1 twine, twist. 2: **s- seg** turn, twist; squirm; pick one's way; **vite å s- seg** know how to get ahead.
snobb' *-en* 1 snob; self-important person. 2: **s-en** the circle, group of snobs.
snob'be *V -a/+-et*: **s- seg** be a snob, be snobbish; give oneself airs.
snob'beri *-et* snobbery, snobbishness.
***snob'be/skap** *-en* snobbery, snobbishness.
snob'bet(e) *A* - 1 snobbish. 2 classy, stylish.
+**snob'bet/het** *-en* 1 snobbishness. 2 stylishness.
sno'dig *A* - 1 amusing, droll, funny. 2 cheerful, friendly, pleasant. *3 nice, clever.
***sno'e** *V -a* cf **sno**[2]
+**sno'g** *-en* cf **snok**
sno'k *-en zool.* grass snake (Natrix natrix).
sno'ke *V -a/+-et/+-te* sniff around; spy.
sno'p[1] *-et* goodies, sweets.
°**sno'p**[2] *A* fast, quick, speedy.
sno'pe *V -a/+-et/+-te* 1 chew, munch. 2: **s- (bort)** fritter away, squander (money, time).
°**snopt** [snop't] *Av* cf **snupt**
sno'r[1] *-a* cord, string; leash; line; (on a uniform) braid; (on a robe) girdle; (toilet) chain: **gå etter en s-** walk in a straight line; **som perler på en s-** one after the other, like pearls on a string.
***sno'r**[2] *-et* cf **snørr**
sno'r/bein *A* straight as an arrow: **den s-e vegstubben** the straightaway (Vesaas).
snor'k *-en/-et* snore.
snor'ke *V -a/+-et* 1 snore. 2 catch one's breath, gasp. 3 snort (of animals).
snor'kel *-elen, pl -ler* snorkel.

***snor'ken** *A -e/-i, pl -ne* shrivelled, shrunk together.
snor'k/sove [/såve] *V infl as* **sove** lie snoring, sleep and snore.
snor'pe** *pp of* **snerpe**[3] (=snorpi**)
sno'r/rett *A* - straight as an arrow (lit. as a string).
snor'te** *pp of* **snerte**[1] (=snorti**)
***snor'ten** *A -e/-i, pl -ne* cf **snurt**[2]
+**snot'tet(e)** *A* - snotty, with a running nose.
snu'[1] *-en* turn, turning: **sein (snar) i s-en** slow (quick) on one's feet; **ha en s- på det** find a way out.
snu'[2] *V -dde* turn; turn around, back: **s- mot** turn toward, face; **s- om** turn around; **s- opp ned på** turn upside down; **s- på** turn (over); **s- (på) skillingen** pinch pennies; **s- seg** (of a person) turn around; (of the wind, public opinion, etc.) change, shift; **forstå, vite å s- seg** know how to, be good at accommodating oneself to circumstances.
snub'be *V -a/+-et* clip, cut (**av** off): **s- av** cut one short, snub.
snub'bet(e) *A* - **1** blunted, curtailed. **2** cross, curt (e.g. answer).
***snubb'/o'rd** *-et* affront, snub.
snub'le *V -a/+-et* **1** stumble, trip (over **noe** over sth). **2** err, sin. **3: det ligger s-ende nær** it's so obvious it stares you in the face, hits you in the eye.
snu'e *-n* head cold.
snuf's *-en/+-et* **1** sniff, sniffle; snort. **2** a person who is continually sniffling, sniffing.
snuf'se *V -a/+-et* sniff, sniffle; snort (esp. of animals).
snu'ing *-a* turning: **snar i s-a** quick, alert.
snul'tre *V -a/+-et*: **s- seg** slink (away), sneak (off).
***snu'nad** *-en* alteration, change; activity, bustle.
***snu'ning** *-a* cf **snunad**
snupp' *-en* **1** corner, point, tab. **2: i en s-** in a jiffy.
snup'pe[1] *-a fam.* chubby little thing.
snup'pe[2] *V -a/+-et* **1** grab, snatch. **2** snip: **s- av** cut, clip off; *fig.* cut short, dismiss.
snup'pet(e) *A* - **1** scanty, scarce. **2** snippy.
***snup't** *Av* **1** entirely, quite. **2** abruptly, suddenly.
***snu'r** *-en* knot, tangle; *fig.* quarrel, squabble.
***snu'rast** *V -ast* become complicated, get entangled.
***snu'ren** *A -e/-i, pl -ne* complicated, entangled.
***snur'ke** *V -a* cf **snorke**
***snur'kle** *V -a* rattle (in the throat).
snur'p[1] *-en/-et* **1** gathering (of a sack). **2** loose stitch (used in basting, tacking). **3** pursing of the lips. **4** purse net, seine; a catch of fish contained in such a net.
***snur'p**[2] *A* wrinkled; testy, touchy.
snur'pe[1] *-a* disagreeable, irritable person; prude.
snur'pe[2] *V -a/+-et* **1** sew up (carelessly): **s- sammen** baste, draw together. **2** pucker up, purse (the lips). **3** fish with a purse seine.
snur'pe/band *-et* drawstring.
snur'pe/not *-a, pl -nøter* purse net, seine.
+**snur'per** *-en, pl -e* (=***-ar**) **1** fisherman using a purse seine. **2** purse boat, seiner.
snur'pet(e) *A* - **1** puckered, pursed (lips, mouth). **2** prudish.
snurr' *-en* **1** rotating, whirling motion. **2** snarl, tangle. **3** curl, frill. **4: på s-** aslant, at an angle; **sette hatten på s-** to wear one's hat at a rakish angle, on the side of one's head; **på en s-** mildly intoxicated, high.
snurr'/bart *-en* cf **snurre/**
snur're *V -a/+-et* **1** buzz, hum, whirr. **2** revolve, rotate; spin, twirl, whirl; twist.
snur're/bart *-en* mustache.
snur're/bass *-en* (=***/basse**) (humming) top, whirligig.
***snur'ren** *A -e/-i, pl snurne* offended, put out.
+**snur're/piperi** [also -ri'] *-et, pl -er* **1** *archaic* bric-a-brac, knickknacks. **2** frills, pedantic formalities; oddities.
snur're/vad *-et* Danish seine.
+**snur'rig** *A* - droll, funny, ludicrous; odd, queer: **en s- fyr** an odd duck.
+**snur't**[1] *-en*: **se s-en av** get a glimpse of.
snur't[2] *A* - (=**snurten**) affronted, offended.
snu's *-en/+-et* **1: få s-en i** get wind of sth. **2** snuff, pinch of snuff: **ikke en s-** not a scrap.
snu's/dåse *-n* snuffbox.
snu'se *V -te/*-a* **1** sniff; nose, smell (**opp** out; e.g. a bone, a secret): **s- inn lufta** draw air in through one's nostrils. **2** poke one's nose into other people's business, pry into other people's affairs. **3** take snuff.
snu's/fornuf't *-a/+-en* matter-of-factness, prosiness, shortsighted reasoning.
snu's/fornuf'tig *A* - pedestrian, prosy, self-satisfied.
snu's/hane *-n* inquisitive person, snoop.
snu's/ho'rn *-et* **1** antenna, feeler: **ha sine s- ute** make inquiries on the q.t., put out feelers. **2** snuffbox.
snus'k *-et* meanspiritedness, shabbiness.
snus'ke *V -a/+-et* **1** sniff, snuff. **2** slink, sneak.
+**snus'keri** *-et* **1** dirt, filth, grime. **2** meanspiritedness, shabbiness.
snus'ket(e) *A* - **1** dirty, filthy, slovenly. **2** contemptible, meanspirited.
snu's/tobakk' *-en* snuff.
snu'te *-en/+-a* (=***snut**) **1** muzzle, snout; *(pop.)* chops, snoot: **få på s-n** get a good dressing down, scolding; **gi ham et slag over s-n** sock him in the face; **hold s-en på deg!** shut your trap! **2** person: **pr. s-** pro persona. **3** end, point, tip (of sth).
snu'te/bille *+-n/*-a zool.* snout beetle, weevil (Curculionidae).
***snuv'le** *V -a* cf **snøvle**
***sny'd** *pr of* **snydje**
***snyd'de** *pt of* **snydje**
+**sny'd(en)** *Av* cf **snyte**[3]
***snyd'je** *V snyd, snydde* nose, smell out.
***snyk'te** *V -a* sob.
snyl'te *V -a/+-et* (=***snyltre**) be a parasite (**på** on); *fig.* sponge off sby; *(pop.)* freeload.
snyl'te/dyr *-et* (=***snyltre/**) *bot., zool.* parasite.
snyl'te/gjest *-en* **1** sponger, *(pop.)* freeloader. **2** parasite.
+**snyl'ter** *-en, pl -e* (=***-ar**) *bot., zool.* parasite; sponger, *(pop.)* freeloader.
+**snyl'teri** *-et bot., zool.* parasitism; sponging, *(pop.)* freeloading.
***snyl'tre** *V -a* cf **snylte**
***sny'rel** *-elen, pl -lar* snailshell; spiral.
***snyr'pe** *V -te* cf **snurpe**[2]
***snyr'te** *V -a/-e* adorn, decorate, dress.
***sny't** *-en* crest, top; point, tip.
sny't(a) *Av* cf **snyte**[3]
sny'te[1] *-a* **1** muzzle, snout. **2** point, tip.
sny'te[2] *V -te/+snøt, snytt* **1** cheat, dupe, swindle: **s- noen for noe** bamboozle sby out of sth, *(pop.)* gyp sby out of sth. **2: s- seg** blow one's nose. **3: s- lyset** snuff out a candle. **4: død og s-!** damnation.
sny'te[3] *Av*: **s- full** drunk as a lord.
sny'te/ho'rn *-et hum.* long, pointed nose, *(pop.)* ski snoot; person with such a nose.
+**sny'ten/strup'** *-en hum.* cheat, imposter, swindler.
+**sny'ter** *-en, pl -e* (=***-ar**) cheat, impostor, swindler.
sny'teri *-et* deception, fraud, swindle.
sny'te/skaft *-et hum.* nose, *(pop.)* ski snoot; person with such a nose.
***snæ'ken** *A -e/-i, pl -ne* biting, cutting (wind).
***snæ'kje** *V -te* **1** blow hard and cold. **2** make cutting, sarcastic remarks.
***snæ're**[1] *-a* breeze, gust of wind.
***snæ're**[2] *-t/+-n* brushwood.
snæ're[3] *V -te dial.* **1** roam, wander about. **2** blow gently, ripple (as wind blowing across water). **3** bind, tie. **4** ensnare, seduce.
snø'[1] *-en* snow: **evig s-** perpetual snows; **hvor er s-en fra i fjor?** where are the snows of yesteryear? **vi får s-** it's going to snow; **den hvite s-** cocaine.
snø'[2] *V -dde* (=***snøe**) snow: **s- inne, ned, under** be snowbound, trapped in the snow.
snø'/bad *-et* bath in snow.
snø'/ball *-en* snowball: **kaste s- på hverandre** throw snowballs at each other.
+**snø'/bar** *A* (=***/berr**) devoid of snow, snowless.
snø'/bil *-en* weasel (=a tracked vehicle used in snow); snowmobile.
snø'/blind *A* snowblind.
snø'/bre *-en* **1** firn, névé, snow field. **2** glacier.
snø'/briller *pl* snow goggles.
snø'/brøyting *-a* act of clearing snow, snowplowing.
snø'/dekt *A* - snow-covered.
snø'/drev *-et* driving snow.
snø'/drive *-a* snowdrift.
***snø'e** *V -a* cf **snø**[2]
snø'/fall *-et* snowfall.
snø'/fane *-a* snowdrift.
+**snøf'fel** *-elen, pl snøfler* insolent lout.
snø'/fille *-a* (heavy, wet) snowflake.
***snø'/fjom** *-et* (=+**/fjon**) (light, fluffy) snowflake.
snø'/floke *-n* (large, heavy) snowflake.
+**snø'/fnugg** *-et* particle of snow, (tiny) snowflake.
snø'/fokk *-et* blowing, drifting snow.
snø'/fonn *-a, pl *-fenner* **1** snowdrift. **2** firn, névé, snow field.
+**snø'/freser** *-en, pl -e* (=***-ar**) (rotary) snowplow.
snøf't *-et* **1** sniff, snort. **2** sniffle, snuffle.
snøf'te *V -a/+-et* **1** sniff, snort. **2** sniffle, snuffle; blubber, snivel.
snø'/full *A* filled with snow.
+**snø'/føyke** *-a* (=***-je**) blowing, drifting snow; blizzard.
***snøg'd** *-a* speed, velocity.
snøgg' *A snøgt* brisk, quick, rapid.
***snøg'ge** *V -a* hasten, hurry: **s- seg** hurry up.
snøgg'/tenkt *A* - quick-witted.
snøgg'/tog [/tåg] *-et* express (train).
snøgg'/vending *-a* quick turn: **i en s-** in a pinch.
snøgg'/ærend *-et* quick trip, hasty errand.
snø'/grense *-a/+-en* snow line.
snøg't *nt of* **snøgg**
snø'/hare *-n zool.* alpine, mountain hare (Lepus timidus).
snø'/hatt *-en* cap, covering of snow.
Snø'/hetta *Pln* mountain top in the Dovre.
snø'/hol [/hål] *-et* (=+**/hull**) cavity, hollow in snow.
snø'/hus *-et* snow house; igloo.
snø'/hytte *-a* snow hut; igloo.
snø'/kav *-et* (=***/kave**) (heavy) snowfall, snowstorm.
snø'/kjetting *-en* snow chains.
snø'/klokke *-a bot.* snowdrop (Galanthus nivalis).
snø'/kvit *A* snowy, snow-white; *poet.* innocent, pure (as the driven snow).

+ Bokmål; * Nynorsk; ° Dialect.
After letter: ' stress (Acc. 1); ` tone, stress (Acc. 2); · length.
Below letter: . not pronounced.

snø'/lykt *-a* snow lantern (=cone of packed snow with candle inside).
snø'/løysing *-a* melting of snow; season when this occurs.
snø'/mann *-en, pl -menn/*-menner* snowman.
snø'/mus *-a zool.* snow weasel (Mustela nivalis).
+**snø'/måking** *-a* (=***/moking**) clearing, shovelling away of snow.
snø'/plog *-en* snowplow.
snø're[1] *-t, pl +-r/*-* cord; line, fishline: **ikke få s-t i bånn (bunnen)** fail to achieve one's goal, *(pop.)* not get to first base).
snø're[2] *V -te* bind, lace, tie: **s- opp** unlace, untie; **s- til, sammen** tie up, draw together; **s- seg sammen** draw together, knot; *archaic* **s- seg** wear a corset.
snø're/fiske *-t* fish with hook and line.
+**snø're/hull** *-et* eyelet (on boot or shoe).
snø're/kjøre *V -te* (=***/køyre**) do skijoring (ski or sled with locomotion furnished by a horse, reindeer, etc.).
snø're/liv *-et* 1 corset, laced bodice. 2 *fig.* anything that binds or constricts; straitjacket.
snø're/sko *-en, pl -r/+-* laced shoe.
snø're/støvel *-elen, pl -ler* lace-up boot.
snø'ring *-a* lace, lacing.
snørr' *-a/+-et* (=***snor**[2]) snot.
snør'ret(e) *A* - snot-nosed, snotty.
snørr'/hoven [/håven] *A +-ent, pl -ne* conceited, self-important, stuck-up.
snørr'/unge [/onge] *-n* snotty brat; greenhorn, person not dry behind the ears.
snørr'/viktig *A* - conceited, self-important, stuck-up.
+**snørr'viktig/het** *-en* conceit, self-importance.
snø'se *V -te* 1 scent, smell, get wind of. 2 sniff, snuff. 3 snort (esp. as a sign of contempt and disbelief).
snø'/skavl *-en* (steep) snowdrift.
snø'/skjerm *-en* snow fence.
snø'/sko *-en, pl -r/+-* snowshoe.
snø'/skred *-et* (=***/skrede**) avalanche, snowslide.
+**snø'/skuffe** [/skoffe] *-a* (=***/skuffel**) snow shovel.
snø'/slaps *-et* slush.
snø'/sokk *-en* galosh, overshoe.
snø'/storm *-en* snowstorm.
snø'/sørpe *-a* slush.
+**snø't** *pt of* **snyte**[2]
+**snøtt'** *Av* cf **snau**
snø'/tung [/tong] *A* heavy with snow; snow-bearing (e.g. wind).
+**snø'/tykke** *-t* (=***/tjukke** *-a*) driving snow, snowstorm.
snø'/ugle *-a zool.* snowy owl (Nyctea nyctea).
snø'/vatn *-et* water from melted snow.
***snø'/ver** *-et* cf **/vær**
snø'/vinter *-eren, pl -rer* snowy winter.
snøv'l *-et* snuffle, snuffling.
snøv'le *V -a/+-et* (=***snuvle**) 1 snuffle, talk through one's nose. 2 cry hoarsely (birds).
snøv'let(e) *A* - 1 nasal, snuffling. 2 conceited, self-important.
+**snø'/vær** *-et* snowy weather.
***snøy'e**[1] *-a* 1 damage, destruction. 2 bare spot; desolate region.
snøy'e[2] *V +-de/*-dde* cf **snaue**
***snøy'pe** *V -te* conceal, hide: **s- seg** steal away.
snø'/yr *-et* fine, flying snow.
snå'l *A* 1 droll, odd, queer. 2 greedy, stingy. *3 neat, pretty. *4 quick, light of foot.
snå'le *V +-te/*-a*: **s- seg til noe** obtain sth by stealth.
snå'ling *-en* character, eccentric.
snå'p *A* agile, deft; quick, swift.
***snå'rt** *A nt of* **snål**
Snå'sa *Pln* twp, Nord-Trøndelag.
snå've *V -a/+-et* stumble, trip: **s- i ordene** stammer.
+**so'**[1] *-en archaic* sow.
***so'**[2] [also: så'] *Av, C* cf **så**[3]
+**SO** = **sørøst**
soaré *-en* soirée (evening party).
so'bel *-elen, pl -ler zool.* sable (Mustela zibellina); fur of the sable.
+**so'ber** *A -ert, pl -re* sober, temperate; sedate, sober-minded.
***sod** [så'(d)] *-et* 1 boiling. 2 meat broth.
so'da *-en* 1 *chem.* soda. 2 seltzer, soda water.
so'da/vatn *-et* (=+**/vann**) club soda, mineral water, seltzer, soda water.
sodd' *-et* 1 broth, soup (consisting of cabbage or grain with meat). 2 bree (juice remaining from the boiling of fish or meat). 3 fodder (consisting of grain, bits of chaff, and kitchen slops).
sode** [så'e] *pp of* **sjode, syde** (=sodi**)
***sod'ning** *-en* anything that is boiled; a mess.
sofa [sof'fa] *-en, pl -er* sofa.
sofa/benk *-en* day bed, sofa bed, studio couch.
sofa/bonde [sof'fa/bonne] *-n, pl -bønder* gentleman farmer.
sofa/hjørne *-t, pl +-r/*-* sofa corner.
sofa/krok *-en* sofa corner.
sofa/pute *-a* sofa cushion; pillow.
Sofie [såfi'e] *Prn (f)* Sophia.
sofis'me *-n* sophism.
sofis't *-en* sophist.
sofisteri' *-et* sophistry.
sofis'tisk *A* - sophistical.
***sog** [så'g] *-et* cf **sug**
***sog/ba'rn** [så'g/] *-et* suckling.
***sog/dyr** [så'g/] *-et* mammal.
***soge**[1] [så'ge] *-a* 1 saga, story, tale. 2 history.
***soge**[2] [så'ge] *pp of* **suge**
***soge/mann** [så'ge/] *-en, pl -menn/*-menner* teller of folktales, sagas.
***sogi** [så'gi] *pp of* **suge**
***sog/mor** [så'g/] *-a* wet nurse.
+**sogn** [sång'n] *-et* cf **sokn**
Sogn [sång'n] *Pln* the southern part of Sogn og Fjordane county.
Sogn/dal [sång'n] *Pln* twp, Sogn og Fjordane.
+**sogne** [sång'ne] *V -a/-et* cf **sokne**[1]
+**sogne/ba'rn** [sång'ne/] *-et* cf **sokne/**
+**sogne/bud** *-et eccl., hist.* sick call (=visit by the local clergyman to the sick and dying).
+**sogne/bånd** *-et eccl.* obligation of parishioners to avail themselves exclusively of the services of the local pastor.
+**sogne/kall** *-et* cf **sokne/**
+**sogne/kirke** *-a/-en* (=**sokne/, */kyrkje**) *eccl.* parish church.
+**sogne/prest** *-en* cf **sokne/**
+**sogne/råd** *-et* cf **sokne/**
sogning [sång'ning] *-en* person from Sogn.
+**-sogning** [sång'ning] *-en* cf **-sokning**
soia [såi'a] *-en* cf **soya**
soignere [soenje're, soanje're] *V -te* groom: **s-t** neat, trim, well-groomed.
sokk'[1] *-en* sock (=short stockings; also on horse).
***sokk'**[2] *pt of* **søkke**[2]
sok'ke[1] *V -a/+-et* blaze (=strip a tree of bark as far up as one can reach).
***sok'ke**[2] *pp of* **søkke**[2]
sok'ke/brok *-a, pl -brøker hist.* stocking breeches.
+**sok'ke/holder** *-en, pl -e* garter.
sok'kel *-elen, pl sokler* 1 base, pedestal, plinth. 2 *typog.* bed (in hand press).
+**sok'ke/lest** *-en* (=***/leist**) stocking foot: **på s-en** in one's stocking feet.
sok'ket(e) *A* - stockinged (esp. a horse).
***sok'ki** *pp of* **søkke**[2]
+**sok'ler** *pl of* **sokkel**
sok'n *-a/+-et* (=+**sogn**) *eccl.* parish.
Sok'n/dal *Pln* twp, Rogaland.
sok'ne[1] *V -a/+-et* (=+**sogne**): **s- til** be associated with, belong to, hail from a particular district, parish, organization, etc.
sok'ne[2] *V -a/+-et* drag, sweep (**etter** for): **s- i elva** drag the river.
sok'ne/ba'rn *-et, pl -/*-born eccl.* parishioner; *(pl)* flock.
***sok'ne/bod** [/bå] *-et* cf **sogne/bud**
Sok'ne/dal *Pln* twp, Sør-Trøndelag.
sok'ne/kall *-et eccl.* 1 parish incumbency, living. 2 parish (served by one pastor).
+**sok'ne/kjerke** *-a* cf **sogne/kirke**
***sok'ne/lyd** *-en eccl.* congregation, parishioners.
sok'ne/prest *-en* (=+**sogne/**) *eccl.* minister, parish pastor; rector, vicar.
sok'ne/råd *-et eccl.* parish council.
-sok'ning *-en* (=+**-sogning**) suffix denoting the parish a person is associated with or hails from: **akers/s-, vangs/s-.**
sokra'tisk *A* - Socratic.
so'l *-a* sun, sunlight: **med s-a** clockwise, from east to west; **mot s-a** counterclockwise, from west to east; **når en snakker om s-a, så skinner den** speak of the devil.
So'la *Pln* twp, Rogaland.
sola'r/olje *-a/-en* solar oil; gas oil (from petroleum).
***so'l/auga** *-t* cf **/øye**
so'la/veksel *-elen, pl -ler* (unduplicated) bill of exchange, promissory note.
so'l/bad *-et* sun bath.
so'lbad/olje *-a/-en* suntan oil.
so'l/bake *V -a/-te* sunbathe.
so'l/bakke *-n* sunlit hill, slope.
so'l/blank *A* sunlit, sunny.
+**so'l/blender** *-en, pl -e* (=***-ar**) lens hood.
+**so'l/brent** *A* - (=***/brend**) sunburned, tanned.
+**so'lbrent/het** *-en* sunburn, tan.
so'l/brille *-a/+-en* dark glasses, sun glasses.
so'l/bær *-et bot.* black currant (Ribes nigrum).
so'lbær/saft *-a* black currant juice.
+**sol'd** *-en* 1 *mil.* pay, recompense: **stå, være i ens s-** be in sby's pay. 2 *(bibl.)* reward: **syndens s- er døden** the wages of sin is death (Romans 6, 23).
solda't *-en* soldier: **den ukjente s-** the Unknown Soldier.
solda't/ånd *+-en/*-a* soldierly spirit.
so'l/dirrende *A* - quivering, vibrating (of air, caused by heat of the sun).
so'l/dis *-en* heat haze.
so'l/dogg *-en bot.* sundew (genus Drosera).
so'l/drukken [/drokken] *A +-ent, pl -drukne* sun-intoxicated.
***so'le**[1] *-n* cf **såle**[1]
so'le[2] *V -a/+-te*: **s- seg** sun oneself; sunbathe; *fig.* bask (in the admiration, favor of others).
***so'le**[3] *V -a* cf **såle**[2]
so'le/fall *-et* sunset.
so'le/glad [also /gla] *-et* sunset.
solei'e [also so'l/] *-a bot.* buttercup (Ranunculus acris).
so'le/klar *A* crystal clear, obvious, self-evident.
so'l/fest *-en* festival in honor of the sun.
so'l/flekk *-en* sunspot.
+**so'l/formør'kelse** *-n* solar eclipse.
so'lgangs/bris *-en* breeze shifting with the sun's course or motion.
so'lgangs/vind *-en* wind shifting with the sun's course or motion.
so'l/glimt *-en/-et* glimpse of the sun.
so'l/gløtt *-en/-et* glimpse of the sun.
+**solgte** [sål'te] *pt of* **selge**
so'l/hjul *-et archeol.* sun wheel (e.g. in Scandinavian rock carvings).
***so'l/hov** [/håv] *-et* winter solstice.
+**so'l/hverv** *-et* cf **/verv**
+**so'l/høyde** *-n* sun's meridian.
soli'd *A* - solid, sound, substantial; sturdy (shoe); solidly built (house); reliable, trustworthy; solvent (business): **s-e kunnskaper** thorough knowledge.
solida'risk *A* - solidary: **opptre s-** make common cause with, stand solidly together; **stå s- med** stand

shoulder to shoulder with; *jur.* guarantee jointly and severally; **være s- ansvarlig for** be jointly and severally responsible for.
solidarite't *-en* 1 *jur.* joint liability. 2 solidarity.
solidarite'ts/kjensle *-a* feeling of solidarity.
solidite't *-en* 1 solidity (e.g. of building). 2 strength, stoutness, sturdiness. 3 solvency, soundness (e.g. of firm).
so'lidum *N jur.*: **in s-** jointly.
solis't *-en* soloist.
solitæ'r *-en* solitaire (i.e. a precious stone, esp. a diamond, set by itself).
so'l/konge *-n hist.* sun king, i.e. Louis XIV.
***so'l/kverv** *-en* cf /verv
soll'[1] *-en* 1 flatbread crumbled in milk. 2 mixture of cheese and milk.
***soll'**[2] *-en* 1 racket, uproar (as of many voices). 2: **sanke s- på en gang** up on sby.
so'l/laus *A* sunless; *fig.* bleak, joyless.
***sol'le** *V -a* bawl, roar.
So'l/lia *Pln* twp, Hedmark.
sollisitan't *-en* favor-seeker, petitioner.
+**soll'te** *pt of* **selle**[2]
+**so'l/løs** *A* cf /laus
***so'l/mørke** *-t* (=*/**mørk(n)ing**) solar eclipse.
so'l/nedgang *-en* sundown, sunset.
so'l/nære *-t astron.* perihelion.
so'lo[1] *-en* 1 solo. 2: **S-** name of a soft drink.
so'lo[2] *A* - 1 solo. 2 alone, by oneself.
so'lo/parti' *-et, pl* +*-er*/*- solo part.
so'l/oppgang *-en* sunrise.
+**so'lo/sang** *-en* (=*/**song**) solo singing.
+**so'lo/sanger** *-en, pl -e* (=*/**songar**) solo singer, solo vocalist, soloist.
+**so'l/plett** *-en* sunspot.
so'l/renning *-a*/+*-en* sunrise (when the first rays strike the mountain tops).
so'l/rik *A* sunny.
so'l/røyk *-en* heat haze.
so'l/segl *-et* (=+/**seil**) *naut.* awning.
so'l/side [*/sie] *-a*/+*-en* southern exposure, sunny side (e.g. of house, street, etc.): **et værelse til s-n** a room facing south; **på livets s-** favored by fortune.
+**so'l/sikke** *-n bot.* sunflower (Helianthus annuus).
+**so'l/skinn** *-et* (=*/**skin**) sunshine; *fig.* favor, good fortune; gladness, joy.
+**so'lskinns/ba'rn** *-et* happy child.
+**so'lskinns/buss** *-en* bus with transparent top.
+**so'lskinns/dag** *-en* sunny day.
so'lskinns/tak *-et* sunroof.
so'l/skive *-a* 1 sun disk. 2 sundial.
so'l/skjerm *-en* eyeshade; sunshade, sun visor.
so'l/sky *-a* sunlit cloud.
so'l/sprett *-en*/*-et* sunrise.
so'l/steik *-en* broiling hot sun.
so'l/steikt *A* - sunbaked.
so'l/stikk *-et* sunstroke.
so'l/streif *-et* glimmer of sunlight; sunbeam.
so'l/strime *-a*/+*-en* shaft of sunlight, sunbeam.
so'l/stråle *-n* sunbeam; ray of the sun.
+**so'lstråle/fortel'ling** *-a*/*-en* (=*/**forteljing**) idyll, sunny story.
so'l/syste'm *-et, pl* -/+*-er* solar system.
+**so'l/tilbeder** *-en, pl -e* (=*-**ar**) sun worshipper.
so'l/tørke *V -a*/+*-et* dry in the sun: **s-t klippfisk** sun-dried split cod.
So'lund *Pln* twp, Sogn og Fjordane.
solung [so'long] *-en* person from Solør.
so'l/ur *-et* sundial.
solusjo'n *-en tech.* rubber solution.
***sol'v** *-en* broom.
so'l/varm *A* sunny, sunwarmed.
so'l/varme *-n* solar heat; warmth of the sun.
so'l/vegg *-en* sunny wall: **ligge, sitte i s-en** sun oneself.

So'l/veig *Prn (f)*
so'l/vendel *-elen, pl -ler bot.* sunflower (Helianthus annuus).
so'l/vending *-a*/+*-en* solstice.
+**so'l/vendt** *A* - (=*/**vend**) exposed to the sun; with a southern exposure.
solven's *-en* solvency.
solven't *A* - solvent.
so'l/verv *-et* (=+/**hverv**, */**kverv**) solstice.
So'lør *Pln* district, Glomma valley.
+**so'l/øye** *-t poet.* sun disk (esp. as seen through cloud and mist); beaming, radiant eye.
som'[1] *C* 1 as, like: **det samme som** the same as; **som barn** as a child; **være som en far** be like a father; **som du vil** as you wish; **som om** as if; **som sagt** as mentioned; **som takk for** by way of thanks; **slik som** how, the way; **så . . . som . . .** as. . as. . .; **gjør som jeg gjør** do as (like) I do; **trett som han var** tired as he was; (or) no matter how tired he was; **han hadde som et slags håp** he had sort of a hope (Hoel). 2 (before superlatives): **som oftest** generally, usually; **som snarest** for just a moment, briefly; **som verst** most intensely (**når det regnet som verst** at the height of the storm). 3 how: **jøss, som du snakker!** goodness, how you talk! **tjui! som det gikk mann** how they travelled! (Bojer). 4 as, when: **best som, rett som** just as, when. 5 where: **de steder som han hadde vært** the places where he had been.
som[2] [som'] *Pn -t, pl -me* some: **s-me steder** in some places; **s-me tider** sometimes.
som'[3] *Pn* (relative) that, which, who, whom: **de som** they who, those which; **den som** he who, whoever, that which; **det som** that which, what (**det som han sa** what he said); **hva som** what; **hva som er** no matter what; **hvem som** who; **de som er med** the participants, (in theatrical performances) the cast; **de som var til stede** those present.
+**-som** *A* (=*-**sam**) -some.
soma'tisk *A* - somatic.
somle [som'le] *V -a*/+*-et* 1 dawdle, loiter. 2 fumble, muddle: **s- bort** manage to lose, mislay; fritter away, squander, waste (opportunities, time).
+**somle/bøtte** [som'le/] *-a* dawdler, loiterer, slowpoke.
somle/kopp *-en* dawdler, loiterer, slowpoke.
somle/pave *-n* dawdler, loiterer, slowpoke.
somlet(e) [som'let(e)] *A* - dawdling, loitering; confused, slow.
somle/tog [som'le/tåg] *-et* local, milk train.
***som'mar** *-en, pl somrar* cf **sommer**
***som'mar/mål** *N* cf **sommer/**
***som'mars-** *Pf* cf **sommer-**
***som'mar/so'lkverv** *-en* cf **sommer/-solverv**
***som'mar/veg** *-en* cf **sommer/vei**
somme [som'me] *pl of* **som**[2]
sommel [som'mel] *-elet/somlet* 1 dawdling, fiddling. 2 confusion, snafu.
+**-som'melig** *A* - adjectival suffix, e.g. **frukt/s-** pregnant; **møy/s-** troublesome.
+**som'mer** *-eren, pl -ere/somrer* (=***sommar**) summer: **forrige s-** the summer of last year; **i fjor s-** last summer; **i s-** this summer; **(langt) ut på s-en** late in the summer; **om s-en** in the summer; **s-en 1960** the summer of 1960; **til s-en** next summer.
+**som'mer/bolig** *-en* summer cottage (home, residence).
+**som'mer/bruk** *-en*/*-et*: **til s-** for summer use, wear.
+**som'mer/dag** *-en* 1 summer day. 2 first day of summer (April 14th).
+**som'mer/ferie** *-n* summer vacation.
+**som'mer/fugl** *-en* 1 *bot.* butterfly (order Lepidoptera). 2 *poet.* charming, graceful girl: **Agnes, min deilige s-** A-, my darling skylark (Ibsen).
+**som'mer/føre** *-t* summer roads.
+**som'mer/gjest** *-en* visitor (e.g. at a summer resort).
+**som'mer/halvår** *-et* summer half-year (=the six month period from April 14th to October 14th).
+**som'mer/hus** *-et* summer cottage.
+**som'mer/kjole** *-n* summer frock.
+**som'mer/klær** *pl* summer clothes.
+**som'mer/ku'rs** *-et* summer school.
+**som'merlig** *A* - (=***sommarleg**) summery.
+**som'mer/mål** *-et* April 14th (=the beginning of the summer half-year).
+**som'mer/opphold** *-et* a stay for the summer.
+**som'mer/pensjonat** [/pangsjona·t] *-et* summer resort.
+**som'mer/sko** *-en, pl* -/*-r* summer shoe.
+**som'mer/sol** *-a* summer sun.
+**som'mer/so'lverv** *-et* summer solstice.
+**som'mer/tid** *-a*/*-en* 1 summer. 2 daylight saving time.
+**som'mer/ull** *-a* wool from the second shearing.
+**som'mer/varme** *-n* summer heat.
+**som'mer/vei** *-en* summer road (i.e. one that can only be used during the summer).
+**som'me/steds** *Av* in some places.
som'me/tider *Av* cf **som**[2]
somnambulis'me *-n* sleepwalking, somnambulism.
°**som'ne** *V -a* cf **sovne**
+**som'rer** *pl of* **sommer**
+**som'res** *V -edes, -es* become, pass into summer.
***so'm/stad** *Av* in some places, somewhere.
***so'm/tid** *Av* at times, sometime(s).
son [så'n] *-en, pl* +*sønner*/**søner* (=+**sønn**) son.
So'n *Pln* seaport, Akershus.
sona'te *-n mus.* sonata.
son'de *-n* 1 *geol.* core drill. 2 *med.* probe. 3 *meteor.* radiosonde.
sonde're *V -te* 1 *geol.* explore (e.g. by means of a core drill). 2 *med.* probe. 3 reconnoiter: **s terrenget** see how the land lies. 4 sound out (e.g. an individual about an idea, proposition, etc.).
+**son'dre** *V -a*/*-et* differentiate, distinguish, make a distinction between: **s- noe ut** segregate, set something apart.
so'ne[1] *-a*/+*-en* zone.
so'ne[2] *V -a*/+*-te* 1 atone for, explate (e.g. crime, sin). 2: **s- en straff** serve a sentence.
***sone/dotter** [så'ne/] *-a, pl -døtrer* granddaughter (on male side).
so'ne/inndeling *-a*/+*-en* classification, division into zones.
***sone/kone** [så'ne/kåne] *-a* cf **sønne/**
***sone/son** [så'ne/sån] *-en, pl -søner* grandson (on male side).
sonett' *-en* sonnet.
***song'**[1] *-en* cf **sang**[1]
***song'**[2] *pt of* **syngje**
***song'ar** *-en* cf **sanger**
***song'/fugl** *-en* cf **sang/**
***song'/kor** *-et* cf **sang/**
***song'/lag** *-et* choral society, glee club.
***song'/mål** *-et* singing voice.
so'n/offer *-et, pl* -/+*-ofre* propitiatory sacrifice.
sono'r *A* resonant, sonorous.
sonorite't *-en* resonance, sonority.
so'p *-et* sweep; sweepings.
***so'par** *-en* able, hard-driving person.
so'pe[1] *V* +*-te*/**-a* sweep: **s- av seg** brush (oneself) off; **s- ren for**

+ Bokmål; * Nynorsk; ° Dialect.
After letter: ' stress (Acc. 1); ` tone, stress (Acc. 2); · length.
Below letter: . not pronounced.

noe clear, sweep out something from a room.
***sope²** [så'pe] *pp of* **supe²**
so'pe/lime *-n* (=***sop/**) besom, broom.
so'pen *A* ⁺*-ent, pl -ne dial.* 1 ravenously hungry. 2 quick.
***sopi** [så'pi] *pp of* **supe²**
***so'p/lime** *-n* cf **sope/**
***so'pling** *-en* besom, broom.
so'pne *pl of* **sopen, soppen**
sopp' *-en* 1 *bot.* fungus; mushroom, toadstool (family Agaricaceae). 2 dry rot, mildew.
sop'pe¹ *-a* 1 log jam. 2 raft of ca. 1200 logs.
sop'pe² *V -a/⁺-et* join logs into rafts.
sop'pe³ *V -a/⁺-et* hunt for mushrooms (esp. cows).
sop'pen *A* ⁺*-ent, pl sopne* fungous, spongy.
sopp'/skade [*/skae] *-n* damage caused by dry rot, mildew.
sopra'n *-en* soprano.
so'p/rein *A* completely clean, cleared.
***sor** [så'r] *-et* (thin) crust of ice.
sordi'n *-en mus.* mute, sordino.
sordine're *V -te mus.* mute (an instrument); *fig.* subdue, tone down (noise, etc.).
***sore** [så're] *V -a* to be frozen up, icebound.
⁺**so'ren/skriver** *-en, pl -e* (=***-ar**) *jur.* judge (chief magistrate of a rural district).
⁺**so'renskriver/fullmek'tig** *-en jur.* judge's deputy.
⁺**so'renskriveri** *-et* district presided over by the chief magistrate of a rural district; office of such a magistrate.
sor'g *-a/⁺-en* 1 grief, mourning, sorrow: **bære s-** be in mourning. 2 anxiety, care, worry: **den tid, den s-** I'll worry about that when the time comes.
***sor'gal** *A* grieved, sorrowful.
sor'g/fri *A -tt* carefree.
sor'g/full *A* sad, sorrowful.
sor'g/laus *A* (=⁺**/løs**) 1 carefree. 2 unconcerned.
sor'g/mild *A* melancholy.
***sor'g/mod** *-et* sadness, sorrowfulness.
***sor'g/modig** *A* - cf **sørg/**
sor'g/tung [/tong] *A* grief-stricken.
So'ria Mo'ria *Pln* a fairy-tale castle in story by this name (traced to islands in Red Sea).
⁺**sorl** [sor'l] *et* cf **surl**
⁺**sorle** [sor'le] *V -et* cf **surle**
sor'p *-et* sludge, slush; mire, mud.
sor'pet(e) *A* - sludgy, slushy, sodden.
sor't¹ *-en* 1 kind, sort: **en ny s- epler** a new variety (kind) of apples; **han var av den snille s-en** he was a kind sort. 2 grade, quality: **av første s-** of the finest quality.
⁺**sort²** [sor't] *A* - cf **svart²**
sorte're *V -te* 1 screen, sort: **s-posten** sort the mail; **s-t** handpicked. 2 be under the jurisdiction of, belong (under).
sorti' *-en* exit; retirement (from a position, etc.).
sortiment [sårtimang'] *-et* assortment, range.
sortiments/bokhandel *-elen, pl -ler* (general) bookshop.
⁺**sort/kledd** [sor't/] *A* - cf **svart/**
Sort/land [sor't/lann] *Pln* twp, Nordland.
⁺**sort/smusket** [sor't/] *A* - swarthy.
⁺**so's** *-en* cf **saus**
⁺**so'se** *V -et/-te* dawdle, fool around, waste time.
so'se/kopp *-en* dawdler, disorganized person.
sosia'l *A* social.
sosia'l/demokra't *-en* Social Democrat.
sosia'l/demokrati' *-et* Social Democracy; **s-et** the Social Democratic party.
Sosia'l/departementet [/-mang'e] *df* Ministry of Social Affairs.

sosialise're *V -te* nationalize (e.g. railroads, transport), socialize.
sosialise'rings/politikk' *-en* nationalization (socialization) policy.
sosialis'me *-n* socialism.
sosialis't *-en* socialist.
sosialis'tisk *A* - socialistic: **S- Folkeparti** Socialistic People's Party.
sosia'l/kura'tor *-en* staff consultant at a hospital, asylum, penitentiary (who exercises both advisory and administrative functions).
⁺**sosia'l/lovgi'vning** *-en* social legislation.
sosia'l/minis'ter *-eren, pl -rer/⁺-ere* Minister of Social Affairs.
sosia'l/poli'tisk *A* - socio-political.
sosia'l/trygd *-a/⁺-en* social welfare (inclusive term for social insurance, e.g. disability insurance, workman's compensation, unemployment compensation, social security, child support, etc.).
sosia'l/økono'm *-en* economist.
sosia'l/økonomi' *-en* economics.
sosia'l/økono'misk *A* - economic.
sosiete't *-en* society: **den høyere s-** high society, haut monde; *(pop.)* the upper crust.
sosiete'ts/dame *-a/⁺-en* grande dame, society lady.
sosiolog [-lå'g] *-en* sociologist.
sosiologi' *-en* sociology.
sosiologisk [-lå'gisk] *A* - sociological.
so't *-a/⁺-et/⁺-en* 1 soot. 2 *naut.* pump casing.
so'te *V -a/⁺-et* soot, soot (up): **s- seg ned, til** dirty, foul oneself (with soot).
so'tet(e) *A* - sooty.
so't/farga *A* - (=⁺**-et**) blackish, sooty color.
so't/luke *-a* soot vent (of a chimney and soot box).
sott [sott'] *-a/⁺-en* disease, sickness; pest, pestilence.
sotte/død [sot'te/] *-en hist.*: **dø s-en** die on a sickbed (instead of on field of battle).
sotte/seng *-a* sickbed; deathbed: **dø på s-** die on a sickbed.
***sott/næm** [sott'/] *A* susceptible to infection, communicable diseases.
sous/sjef [su'/] *-en* assistant manager (e.g. in a bank).
sov [så'v] *pt of* **sove**
sove [så've] *V* ⁺*-er/*søv, sov,* ⁺*-et/ *-e/*-i* sleep, be asleep: **s- av seg** sleep off; **s- fra noe** drop off to sleep (and thus miss or avoid sth); **sov godt!** sleep tight! **s- hen** die, pass away; **s- hos** sleep with; **s- inn** go to sleep; die, pass away; **s- middag** take a nap after dinner; **s- over seg** oversleep; **s- ut** get slept out; sleep off; **ta noe å s- på** take sth to make one sleep.
sove/by [så've/] *-en* bedroom town.
⁺**sove/hjerte** *-t* (=***/hjarta, /hjarte**): **ha godt s-** be a sound sleeper.
sove/kupé *-en* sleeping compartment (train).
sove/middel *-elet/-midlet, pl ⁺-midler/ *-el* sleeping pill, soporific.
sove/plass *-en* 1 sleeping accommodation. 2 berth (e.g. on boat, train).
sove/pose [*/påse] *-n* sleeping bag.
sove/pulver *-et, pl -/⁺-e* sleeping powder.
sove/pute *-a* pillow.
⁺**sover** [så'ver] *-en, pl -e* (=***-ar**) *archaic* sleeper, sleepyhead.
sove/rom [så've/romm] *-met* bedroom.
sove/sal *-en* dormitory, (large) sleeping quarters.
sove/sjuke *-n med.* sleeping sickness (Encephalitis lethargica).
sove/sofa [/soffa] *-en* sofa bed, studio couch.
⁺**sove/syke** *-n* cf **/sjuke**
sove/tablett' *-en* sleeping pill.
sove/vogn [/vångn] *-a* sleeper, sleeping car (on train).
⁺**sove/værelse** *-t* bedroom.
Sov'jet *et* Soviet; the Soviet Union.

sovjet'isk *A* - Soviet.
Sovjet'/samvel'det *Pln* the Soviet Union, U.S.S.R.
sovjet'/vennlig *A* friendly, well-disposed towards the Soviet Union.
***sovl** [sov'l] *-en* besom, broom.
sov'ne *V -a/⁺-et* fall asleep: **s- inn** *lit.* pass away.
***so/voren** [så'/våren] *Pn -e/-i, pl -ne* cf **så/**
soya [såi'a] *-en* soy, soya.
soya/bønne *-a* (=***/baune**) soybean.
soya/mjøl *-en* soy meal.
soya/olje *-a/-en* soybean oil.
SP =**Senterpartiet**
sp. =**spalte¹**
spa' *V -dde* (=***spade²**) spade: **s- opp et bed** dig up a plot.
spa'(d) *-et dial.* (thin) broth.
spa'de¹ [*spa'e] *-n* 1 shovel, spade; *mil.* entrenching tool. 2 spadeful: **tre s-r jord** three spadefuls of earth.
***spa'de²** *V -de* cf **spa**
spa'de/stikk *-et* spadeful: **gjøre det første s-** break the first ground (esp. at ground-breaking ceremonies).
spa'de/tak *-et* spadeful.
spaghet'ti *-en* spaghetti.
spa'k¹ *-en* 1 *naut.* handspike. 2 joy stick (airplane).
spa'k² *A* 1 meek, submissive, unresisting. 2 gentle, mild (breeze, sea).
⁺**spakfer'dig** *A* - mild, quiet, subdued.
spa'k/lynt *A* - (=***/lyndt**) gentle, meek, mild.
spa'kne *V -a/⁺-et* 1 become more amenable, pliable, tractable. 2 subside (rain, snow, wind).
⁺**spa'k/vær** *-et* (=***/ver**) calm, quiet weather.
spalie'r *-et* espalier, trellis: **danne s-** form a lane, line the route of a parade, procession.
spal'te¹ ⁺*-n/*-a* 1 column (of printed matter, type). 2 *bot., zool.* opening, slit. 3 *geol.* cleft, crevice, fissure.
⁺**spal'te²** *V -a/-et* cleave, divide, split: **s- seg** divide, split; **en s-t personlighet** a split personality.
spal'te/breidd *-a* (=⁺**/bredde**) *typog.* column width.
⁺**spal'te/fyll** *-et/-a journ.* filler.
spal'te/golv *-et* lath flooring.
spal'te/korrektu'r *-en* galley proof.
spal'te/plass *-en* space (in a newspaper): **avisen gir ham s-** the columns of the newspaper are open to him.
spaltis't *-en* (newspaper) columnist.
spal'tnings/prosess' *-en* process of chemical decomposition.
***spa'n** *-et* stretching, tension.
***spa'nande** *A* - cf **spennende**
spanda'bel *A -elt, pl -le* generous, open-handed; spendthrift.
spande'r/bukser [/bokser] *pl*: **trekke s- på** be more generous, openhanded than usual; treat the crowd.
spande're *V -te* 1 expend, spend; make use of, sacrifice. 2 stand (e.g. a round of drinks), treat: **s- noe på en** treat sby to sth; **s- noe på seg selv** indulge oneself.
***spa'ne** *V -a* cf **spenne³**
⁺**spang'** *-a* cf **spong**
Spang'er/eid *Pln* twp, Vest-Agder.
Spa'nia *Pln* Spain.
⁺**spa'nier** *-en, pl -e* (=***spanjar**) 1 Spaniard. 2 *naut.* dogvane.
⁺**spanierin'ne** *-a/-en* (female) Spaniard Spanish woman.
***spa'ning** *-a* cf **spenning**
spanjo'l *-en* 1 Spaniard. 2 Spanish snuff.
⁺**span'ke** *V -a/-et* strut.
spankule're *V -te* strut.
spann'¹ ⁺*-et/*-a* span (of fingers; period of time): **et s- av år** a s- of years.
spann'² *-et* span, team (of horses, oxen, etc.).
spann'³ *-et* 1 bucket, pail. 2 *hist.* unit

of weight (ab. 20 lbs.); unit of taxation (ab. 3 dollars).

***spann'**[4] *pt of* **spenne**[2]

***spann'**[5] *pt of* **spinne**

spann'/reim *-a* knee strap (used to hold an article over the knee while working on it).

span'sk *A* - 1 Spanish: **s- vegg** folding screen. 2 conceited, stuck-up, supercilious. 3 undependable, untrustworthy.

span'ske *V -a/+-et* give oneself airs, show off, swagger: **s- seg** (the same).

span'ske/sjuke *-n* Spanish influenza, flu.

span'sk/grøn *A* (=+**/grønn**) verdigris.

span'sk/rør *-et/*-a* (=***/røyr**) *bot.* rattan cane (genus Calamus): **få av s-et, få s-** get a caning.

span't[1] *-et naut.* frame; rib, timber: **stå i s-** be in frame.

+**span't**[2] *pt of* **spinne**

span'te *V -a/+-et naut.* frame (a ship).

span'te/verk *-et naut.* framing, framework.

spa'r[1] *-en* spades (cards): **s- er trumf** spades are trump.

***spa'r**[2] *-et* broad tack (used in soling shoes).

spa'r[3] *A* stingy: **være s- på** *dial.* be sparing of.

Spar'/bu *Pln* twp, Nord-Trøndelag.

spa're *V -a/-te* 1 save: **s- penger, tid** s- money, time; **spinke og s-** pinch pennies. 2 spare: **s- en for noe** s- sby for sth; **s- øynene** s- one's eyes. 3 (with *prep., adv.*): **s- inn** save (by economizing); **s- opp, sammen** save up; **s- på** collect; be sparing with, save; **s- på kreftene** conserve, save one's strength. 4 (*refl.*) take it easy; **ikke s- seg** exert oneself to the limit, spare no pains.

spa're/bank *-en* savings bank.

+**spa're/bøsse** *-a* (=***/børse**) savings bank (for small coins); dime bank.

spa're/gris *-en* piggy bank.

spa're/kampan'je *-n* economy drive.

spa're/kasse *-a/-en* savings bank, savings and loan association.

spa're/klubb *-en* savings club.

+**spa're/penger** *pl* (=***-ar**) savings.

spa're/politikk' *-en* policy of economy, retrenchment.

spa're/program' *-met* austerity program, program of retrenchment.

+**spa'rer** *-en, pl -e* (=***-ar**) depositor; saver.

spa're/skilling *-en*: **s-er** modest savings.

spa're/øks *-a* economy axe: **bruke s-a på et budsjett** cut a budget to the bone.

spar'k[1] *-en* "kick sled" (short for **spark/støtting**).

spar'k[2] *-et* 1 kick; *fig.* contemptuous, cutting scorn. 2 **få s-en** be fired; (*pop.*) be canned, thrown out on one's ear.

spar'ke *V -a/+-et* kick: **s- bakut** kick up its heels, lash out (a horse); **s- en på dør, s- en ut** boot, kick sby out; fire sby; **det går dit høna s-er** things are going to pot.

spar'ke/bukse [/bokse] *-a* infant rompers, sleeper.

spar'kel *-elen, pl -ler* putty knife (for spackling).

+**spar'ke/pike** *-a/-en* chorus girl.

spar'ke/sykkel *-elen, pl -sykler* scooter.

spar'kle *V -a/+-et* fill, spackle, stop up (holes in walls, woodwork prior to painting).

+**spar'k/støtting** *-en* (=***/stytting**) "kick sled" (scooter on runners; similar in appearance to a small dogsled but without the dogs).

sparla'ken *-et* (=+**-lagen**) *archaic* (bed) curtain.

***spa'r/semd** *-a* economy, thrift.

+**spa'r/som'** *A -t, pl -me* (=***/sam**) 1 scant, sparse, thin. 2 economical, thrifty (**med** with).

+**spa'rsom/het** *-en* economy, thrift (**med** with).

+**sparsom'melig** *A* - economical, thrifty.

+**sparsom'melig/het** *-en* economy, thrift.

+**sparsom'melighets/hensyn** *-et*: **av s-** for reasons of economy.

+**sparta'ner** *-en, pl -e* (=***spartan**) Spartan.

sparta'nsk *A* - Spartan.

spa's *-en* jest, joke: **for (i) s-** in fun, jokingly.

spa'se *V +-te/*-a* banter, jest, joke: **s- med jenter** tease (flirt with) girls.

spase'r/drakt *-a/+-en* street dress, suit.

spase're *V -te* promenade, stroll, walk.

spase'r/sko *-en, pl -r/+-* walking shoe.

spase'r/stokk *-en* cane, walking stick.

spase'r/tur *-en* stroll, short walk.

+**spa's/maker** *-en, pl -e* (=***-ar**) joker, wag.

spa't *-en geol.* spar: cf **felt/s-, fluss/s-.**

spa'tel *-elen, pl -ler* spatula.

spatium [spa'tsium] *-iet, pl +-ier/*-ium* 1 period, space of time. 2 *typog.* interval, space between letters.

spatiøs [spatsiø's] *A* spacious.

spatt' *-en* spavin.

***spau'ke** *V -a* dig, root, rummage.

spe'[1] *+en/*eit* mockery, ridicule, scorn; **spott og s-** contempt, derision.

spe'[2] *V -dde* dilute, thin, water down: **s- opp i, s- til** add to (for purposes of dilution, thinning); *fig.* contribute.

spe'[3] *A -dt, pl -de* cf **sped**

speaker [spi'ker] *-en, pl +-e* 1 speaker (of the assembly, legislature). 2 radio announcer.

spe'/ba'rn *-et* cf **sped/**

spe'd *A* 1 slender, slight, tiny. 2 delicate, tender (e.g. buds, leaves); immature, young: **deres s-e alder** their tender years. 3 frail, weak; insignificant: **en s- stemme** a feeble voice; **en s- film** a worthless film.

spedal'sk *A* - leprous.

+**spedal'sk/het** *-en* leprosy.

spe'd/ba'rn *-et, pl -/*-born* baby, infant (in arms).

***spe'de** *V -de* cf **spe**[2]

spede're *V -te* dispatch, forward, transship (goods and merchandise).

spe'd/gris *-en* suckling pig.

spedisjo'n *-en* dispatch, forwarding, transshipment (of goods and merchandise); brokerage.

spedisjo'ns/firma *-et, pl +-er/*-* broker, forwarding agents, shipping firm.

speditø'r *-en* broker, forwarding agent, shipper.

spe'd/kalv *-en* sucking calf.

spe'd/lemma *A* - (=+**-et**, ***/lema**) frail, slight; slender-limbed.

***spe'e** *V -a* deride, ridicule, scoff at.

speedometer [spidome'ter] *-eret/-ret* speedometer.

+**spe'ge** *V -et* cf **speke**

***spe'gel** *-elen, pl -lar* cf **speil**

***spe'gle** *V -a* cf **speile**

***spei'ar** *-en* cf **speider**

spei'de [*spei'e] *V -a/+-et* (=***speie**) 1 be on the lookout, on the watch (**etter for**); observe carefully, peer, spy (out). 2 *mil.* reconnoiter, scout, send out patrols.

+**spei'der** *-en, pl -e* (=***spei(d)ar**) 1 *mil.* observer, scout, spy. 2 (boy, girl) scout.

+**spei'der/gutt** *-en* boy scout.

+**spei'der/kniv** *-en* boy scout's knife.

+**spei'der/pike** *-a/-en* girl scout.

***spei'e** *V -a* cf **speide**

+**spei'el** *-en* cf **speil**

+**spei'l** *-et* (=+**speiel**, ***spegel**) glass, looking glass, mirror: **se seg i s-et** look in the mirror. 2 *med.* speculum.

+**spei'l/bilde** *-t* image, reflection (**av** of); (accurate) copy, reproduction.

+**spei'l/blank** *A* glassy, mirrorlike; shiny, smooth.

+**spei'le** *V -te* (=***spegle**) 1 mirror, reflect: **s- seg** be mirrored, reflected; look in the mirror. 2 fry (an egg).

+**spei'l/egg** *-et* fried egg.

+**spei'l/glass** *-et* plate glass.

+**spei'l/glatt** *A* - slippery, smooth as glass.

+**spei'l/skrift** *-a/-en* mirror writing, reversed script.

***spei'si/dalar** *-en* cf **spesi/daler**

spe'k *-en* frozen earth.

+**spe'ke** *V -te* (=***spekje**) 1 *dial.* freeze. 2 cure, smoke (fish, meat, etc.). 3 (*bibl.*) **spege sitt kjød** mortify the flesh (Col. 3,5).

+**spe'ke/fjel** *-en* cf **spikke/fjøl**

spe'ke/flesk *-et* cured (or) smoked bacon, ham.

spe'ke/kjøtt *-et* (=***/kjøt**) cured (dried) meat.

+**spe'kelse** *-n* asceticism, mortification of the flesh.

spe'ke/mat *-en* cured (or) smoked fish, meat.

spe'ken *A +-ent, pl -ne* cured (or) smoked.

spe'ke/pølse *-a* smoked sausage.

spe'ke/sild *-a* 1 salt herring. 2 a skinny person, (*pop.*) beanpole.

spe'ke/skinke *-a* smoked ham.

***spe'kje** *V -te* cf **speke**

spekk' *-et* blubber, fat.

spek'ke *V -a/+-et* 1 lard: **s- dyrekjøtt** lard reindeer meat. 2 stuff (e.g. turkey): **s- en stek med persille** garnish a roast with parsley. 3 cram, fill (up): **en s-et pengebok** a bulging wallet. 4 pare, scrape away blubber, fat.

+**spek'ke/fjel** *-en* cf **spikke/fjøl**

+**spekk'/hogger** *-en, pl -e* (=***-ar**) *zool.* grampus, killer whale (Orcinus orca).

***spe'kne** *V -a* be cured, smoked.

+**spektak'(k)el** *-elet/spektaklet, pl spektakler* cf **spetakkel**

spektra'l/analy'se *-n* spectroscopic analysis.

spektrosko'p *-et* spectroscope.

spek'trum *-ret/*-rumet, pl +-rer/*-ra* spectrum.

spekulan't *-en* speculator; *derog.* gambler.

spekulan't/hus *-et* house built with an eye for a quick profit; jerrybuilt house.

spekulasjo'n *-en* speculation (e.g in stocks): **kjøpe på s-** buy on speculation, speculatively.

spekulasjo'ns/øyemed *-et*: **i s-** on speculation, speculatively.

spek'ulativ *A* speculative.

spekule're *V -te* 1 gamble, speculate (e.g. on the stock exchange). 2: **s- over, på** ponder, rack one's brains over, wonder about; *pop.* mull over.

+**spel**[1] [spæ'l] *-en* cf **spæl**

***spe'l**[2] *-et* cf **spill**[1]

***spe'lar** *-en* cf **spiller**[1]

***spe'le** *V -a/-te* cf **spille**[2]

***spe'leg** *A* - hazardous, risky.

***spe'le/mann** *-en, pl -menn(er)* cf **spille/**

spe'/lemma *A* - cf **sped/**

***spe'l/ferd** [/fær] *-a* concert tour.

***spe'l/jakt** *-a* cf **spill/**

+**spell'** *-et* cf **spill**[1]

+**spel'le** *V spelte* cf **spille**[2]

***spe'l/mann** *-en, pl -menn(er)* cf **spille/**

***spe'l/stykke** *-t* play.

***spe'l/tile** *-t* stage.

°**spendere** [spande're] *V -te* cf **spandere**

+ Bokmål; * Nynorsk; ° Dialect.
After letter: ' stress (Acc. 1); ` tone, stress (Acc. 2); · length.
Below letter: . not pronounced.

***spe'n/dyr** -et mammal.

spe'ne -n 1 teat (on an animal's udder). 2 bot. parasitic fungus (Taphrina pruni) attacking plums; bladder plum (a plum attacked by such fungus).

***spe'nel** -elen, pl -lar mill spindle.

spe'ne/varm A warm (as fresh milk from a cow's udder).

speng'er pl of spong

***speng'ing** -en sled, sleigh studded with iron.

***speng'je** V -de mount, stud (e.g. sleigh).

spen'ler pl of spennel

spenn' -et 1 strain, tension, tightness: sette pistolhanen i s- cock the pistol; stå i s- be tense, under tension. 2 span (of bridge). 3 naut. shroud. 4 kick.

spen'na Av completely, wholly: han er s- gal he is absolutely mad, raving.

spen'ne[1] -a/-et/+-en buckle, clasp; bobbypin, clip; belt, shoe buckle; archeol. fibula.

***spen'ne[2]** V spann, sponne/-i move, stir: det spann ikkje i han he didn't show a spark of life.

spen'ne[3] V spente (=*spane) 1 stretch; tense, tighten; strain: s- bein for (under) trip up; s- buen draw the bow; s- buen for høyt aim too high; s- geværet cock the gun; spent tense (cf spent). 2 (with adv., prep.): s- av (seg) take off, unfasten; s- for hitch up (horses); s- fra unhitch (horses); s- i buckle; s- inn tighten up; s- om embrace, encompass, span; s- opp unbuckle; s- over extend, stretch over; s- på (seg) buckle on, fasten; s- ut let out, unloosen; s- seg ut stretch out, unfold.

spen'ne[4] V spente kick: hesten s-er the horse lashes out in all directions; s- beina mot noe brace oneself against sth; s- i exert oneself, take hold; s- til kick.

spen'ne/bok -a, pl -bøker clasped book.

spen'nel -en, pl spenler little willow loop, ring (used to fasten a gate).

spen'nende A - (=*spanande) exciting, tense, thrilling.

+spen'ner -en, pl -e (=*-ar) 1 tension adjuster. *2 check, stop bolt. *3 bridge support.

spen'ne/tak -et cf spenn/

spen'ning -a/+-en (=*spaning) 1 tension, tightening. 2 excitement, suspense: holde en i s- keep sby in suspense. 3 elec. potential, voltage.

spenn'/kraft -a/+-en elasticity, resilience; tension.

spenn'/tak -et 1 foothold, grip: ta s- brace oneself, plant one's feet solidly. 2 effort, exertion; struggle.

spenn'/trøye -a strait jacket.

spenn'/vidd -a (=/vidde) span (of an arch, a bridge); fig. range, scope.

spen'sel -elet/-let, pl +-ler/*-el strap, strop; half belt (e.g. on the back of a coat, vest).

spen'st -en flexibility, suppleness.

+spen'stig A - resilient, springy, supple.

+spen'stig/het -en resilience, springiness, suppleness.

spen't A - 1 taut; strained, tense: stå, leve på en s- fot med be on strained terms with. 2 eager, expectant; in suspense: s- på eager, excited (jeg er så s- på å høre I just can't wait to hear; jeg er s- på resultatene I'm anxious, eager to learn about the results); med s-e forventninger with high expectations.

spen'te pt of spenne[3,4]

spe'/o'rd -et gibe, taunt.

Sper'illen Pln lake, Ådal twp, Buskerud.

sper'ma -et sperm.

spermasett'/kval -en (=+/hval) zool. sperm whale (Physeter macrocephalus).

spermasett'/olje -a/-en sperm oil.

spermatoso' -en spermatozoon.

***sper'm/kval** -en (=+/hval) zool. sperm whale (Physeter macrocephalus).

sper're[1] -a 1 crossbar, rafter, strut; log. 2 brace of fish (hung up to dry).

sper're[2] V -a/+-et 1 bar, block, close (off); obstruct: s- av block off, close off; s- inne confine, lock up; s- opp open wide (e.g. the eyes); s- ute exclude, keep out; s-et for closed to (e.g. traffic). 2 typog. space type widely (for emphasis).

sper're[3] V -a/+-et 1 set crossbars, rafters in place (by pairs). 2 hang up (fish) to dry (two and two).

sper're/ballong' -en barrage balloon.

sper're/eld -en (=+/ild) barrage (antiaircraft, artillery).

sper're/gods [/gots] -et special handling package.

sper're/hjul -et ratchet wheel.

+sper're/ild -en cf /eld

sper're/tak -et raftered ceiling.

sper're/verk -et 1 framework (of a house). 2 ratchet mechanism (e.g. in a clock).

sper'ring -a/+-en 1 bar, barrier, obstruction. 2 blockade, embargo.

spes. =spesiell, spesifikk

speseri' -et, pl +-er/*- seasoning, spice.

speseri'/hylle -a spice shelf.

spesia'l A special.

spesia'l/arbeid -et specialist work; specialization.

+spesia'l/arbeider -en, pl -e (=*-ar) specialist.

spesia'le -t specialty.

spesialise're V -te specialize: s- seg (also) prepare, train (for for).

spesialis't -en specialist.

spesialite't -en specialty.

+spesia'l/løp -et free skating.

spesia'l/stål -et steel alloy; high quality steel (for a specific purpose).

+spesia'l/utdannet A - specially trained.

+spesia'l/verktøy -et special purpose tools.

+spe'si/daler -en, pl -e (=*-ar) hist. rix-dollar (coin used to 1873, worth ab. one dollar).

spesiell' A -elt special, particular.

spesifikasjo'n -en specification.

spe'sifikk [also spes'-] A -fikt specific.

spesifise're V -te 1 itemize (e.g. an account, a bill). 2 specify (e.g. a claim).

***spe't** -et cf spett[3]

spetak'kel -elet/spetaklet, pl +spetakler 1 fright, scarecrow. 2 noise, racket, uproar; riot, row: holde s- cause a row, make a racket; holde s-med make fun of.

+spetak'kel/maker -en, pl -e (=*-ar) noisy person; brawler, rioter, rowdy.

spett'[1] -en (=spette[1]) zool. woodpecker (family Picidae).

+spett'[2] -en fleck, spot.

spett'[3] -et crowbar, lever (farm implement).

spet'te[1] -a cf spett[1]

spet'te[2] -a 1 fleck, spot. 2 zool. flounder (Platichthys flesus); plaice (Pleuronectes platessa).

spet'te/flyndre -a zool. flounder (Platichthys flesus); plaice (Pleuronectes platessa).

+spet'tet(e) A - mottled, speckled, spotted.

spidd' -et spit: steike på s- roast on a spit.

spid'de V -a/+-et impale, pierce, spike: s- på bajonett run through with a bayonet.

spi'k -a, pl *-ar (pine) splinter.

spi'ka Av: s- gal stark, raving mad; utterly wrong.

spi'ke V -te splinter; smash.

spi'kende Av: s- gal stark, raving mad; utterly wrong.

+spi'ker -eren, pl -er/-rer (=*-ar) nail, spike: det er sikkert som s-(en) i veggen it's absolutely certain; koke suppe på en s- make sth out of nothing (allusion to a folktale); treffe s-en på hodet hit the nail right on the head.

+spi'ker/fast A - absolutely certain.

+spi'ker/hode -t nail head.

+spi'ker/slag -et 1 hammer blow (on nails). 2 stud, studding.

+spi'ker/tønne -a cask full of spikes (the criminal was placed inside and the cask rolled over a precipice).

spikk' -et 1 splinter, whittling. 2 practical joke, prank.

spik'ke[1] -n zool. sparrow (Passer domesticus).

spik'ke[2] V -a/+-et whittle; cut, slice up.

spik'ke/fjøl -a chopping board (for cutting up meat, fish etc.).

spi'kre V -a/+-et nail: s- fast nail down; root to the spot; s- til (igjen) vinduene nail the windows shut.

***spi'l** -a/-en, pl -ar cf spile[1]

***spil'der** Av cf spildrende

spil'dre[1] -a (fence) picket; lath, slat.

***spil'dre[2]** V -a splinter.

spil'drende Av: s- naken stark naked; s- ny brand, spanking new.

spil'dre/verk -et framework (of laths or slats).

spi'le[1] -a/-en (=*spil) 1 lath. 2 stay (e.g. in a corset).

spi'le[2] V -te/*-a 1 distend, spread, stretch. 2 dilate, open wide. 3: s- opp agitate, arouse. 4: s- seilene naut. boom the sails out.

+spil'/fekteri' -et cf spill

spil/kum [spil'/komm] -men small bowl.

+spill'[1] -et (=+spell, *spel[1]) 1 play, playing: et s- med ord playing with words; ut(e) av s-et out of the running; drive s- med en make fun of, tease sby; gi (ha) fritt s- give (have) a free rein. 2 acting; play-dramatic work. 3 gambling; card-playing: høyt s- high stakes; sette på s- risk, stake; spille et høyt s- play for high stakes, a dangerous game; stå på s- be at stake. 4 game (or part of a game, e.g. a hand, a round, etc.); the equipment for a game (e.g. deck of cards, board, men, etc.). 5 (of light, flames, a smile, eyes, etc.) flickering, play, sparkling. 6 mating call (of game birds).

+spill'[2] -et loss, waste.

+spill'[3] -et naut. capstan, winch, windlass.

+spill'[4] Av: s- naken stark naked; s- våken alert, keen, wide-awake.

spil'le[1] -t loss, waste: gå til s- go to waste.

+spil'le[2] V spilte (=+spelle, *spele) slop, spill, waste; lose: det er spilt på ham it's wasted on him; det var spilt umake it was labor lost.

spil'le[3] V spilte 1 play (a game, musical instrument, piece of music, role, trick, etc.); (of a film, play) be playing, showing: s- en film run, show a film; s- en rolle play a part; det s-er ingen (en stor) rolle it makes no (a lot of) difference. 2 act, pretend to be: s- en rolle play a part; s- komedie put on an act. 3 gamble. 4 (of light, flames, smile, eyes, etc.) flicker, play, sparkle: s- i det grønne have a green tint. 5 (of game birds) call (the mating call). 6 (with prep., adv.): s- bort gamble away, lose through gambling; s- hos en take music lessons from sby; s- høyt play for high stakes; s- inn enter in, be a factor; record (a song, etc.); make (a film); s- mot (in sports) play against; (in the theater) play opposite; s- om play for (sth as stakes); s- opp strike up (music); s- ut lead (with a card); (in a game) have the first move; s- den ene ut mot den andre play one off against the other. 7 (refl).

s- seg opp improve, get warmed up; (of a team) rally.
+spil'le/bank *-en* gambling casino; bank of a casino (=funds out of which winnings are paid).
+spil'le/bo'rd *-et* 1 card, gaming table; bridge table. 2 *mus.* console (of an organ).
+spil'le/bule *-n* gambling den; *pop.* gambling joint.
+spil'le/djevel *-en* gambling demon.
+spil'le/dåse [also spil'-] *-n* music box.
+spil'le/film *-en* feature film.
+spil'le/kort *-et* cf **spill/kort**
+spil'le/lykke *-a/-en* luck in gambling.
+spil'le/mann *-en, pl -menn* fiddler, musician.
spil'le/merke *-t* counter, jeton.
+spil'lende *Av*: **s- gal** stark, raving mad; utterly wrong; **s- våken** wide-awake.
+spil'ler[1] *-en, pl -e* (=***spelar**) 1 player (music, sports, theater); actor, performer. 2 gambler, speculator; declarer (in card playing).
+spil'ler[2] *Av*: **s- ny** brand, spanking new.
+spil'le/regel *-elen, pl -ler* rule of the game.
+spil'le/rom [/romm] *-met* clearance, latitude, scope: **ha fritt s-** have a free hand.
+spil'le/time *-n* music lesson.
+spill'/fekteri *-et* dissimulation, humbug.
+spill'/jakt *-a/-en* shooting (grouse, partridges) during mating season.
+spill'/kort *-et* playing cards.
spill'/kraft *-a/+-en* potential, unutilized power.
spill'/olje *-a/-en* waste oil.
+spillop'per *pl* jokes, pranks, tricks.
+spillopp'/maker *-en, pl -e* joker, trickster, wag.
***spill'/sam** *A* extravagant, wasteful.
***spill'/sjuk** *A* leprous.
***spill'/sykje** *-a* leprosy.
spill'/va'ken *A +-ent, pl -ne* wide-awake.
spill'/vatn *-et* (=+**/vann**) wastewater, discharge (e.g. from a turbine); sewage.
+spill'/vå'ken *A -ent, pl -ne* cf **/vaken**
spil'/tau [also: spil'/] *-et* horse stall.
+spil'te *pl of* **spile**[1], **spille**[1,3]
spina'l *A anat.* spinal.
spina't *-en* spinach.
Spin'd *Pln* twp, Vest-Agder.
spin'del *-elen, pl -ler* spindle.
spin'del/vev *-en/+-et* cobweb, spider web.
spinett' *-et, pl +-er/*- mus.* spinet.
spin'ke *V -a/+-et*: **s- og spare** pinch pennies, scrape and save.
+spin'kel *A -elt, pl -le* slender, thin (e.g. figure); delicate, fragile, frail (e.g. build, voice); flimsy (e.g. construction, plot).
***spin'lar** *pl of* **spinnel**
spinn' *-et* 1 yarn. 2 mesh, net, web: **dette s- av løgn og bedrag** this web of lies and deceit (Ibsen). 3 loop, roll, spin (airplane); spin (automobile): **gå i s- for en** get confused.
spin'naker *-en, pl -e naut.* spinnaker.
spin'ne *V +spant/*spann, +spunnet/*spunne/*-i* 1 spin: **s- opp, sammen** make up (lies, tales). 2 (of cats) purr; (of planes) hum. 3: **s- (seg) ut** unwind (e.g. a ball of yarn).
spin'ne/hus *-et hist.* house of correction (esp. for women).
spin'ne/kjerring *-a, pl *-ar* 1 spinner woman. 2 *poet.* spider.
***spin'nel** *-en, pl spinlar* spindle.
+spin'ner *-en, pl -e* (=***-ar**) 1 spinner. 2 kind of silk moth (Bombyx).
spinneri' *-et, pl +-er/*-* textile mill.
spin'ne/rokk *-en* spinning wheel.
+spin'nerske *-n* textile worker (female).
spin'ne/side [*/sie] *-a/+-en* distaff side, female line: **på s-n** by the female line; on the mother's side.
spin'ne/stoff *-et* textile material.
spin'ning *-a* 1 spinning: **vinningen går opp i s-en** expenses absorb the profits. 2 skein (of yarn). 3 purring (e.g. of motor).
***spinn'/kjerring** *-a* cf **spinne/**
spio'n *-en* secret agent, spy.
spiona'sje *-n* espionage.
spione're *V -te* carry on espionage work, spy.
***spi'r**[1] *-en* 1 dash, squirt of sth. 2 small mackerel (=**pir**). 3 forelock. 4 strange sight.
spi'r[2] *-et* 1 spire, steeple. 2 *poet.* scepter. 3 point (on reindeer's horn).
spira'l *-en* coil, spiral, whorl.
spira'l/bor [/bårr] *-et* twist drill; spiral bit; screw auger.
spira'l/fjør *-a* (=+**/fjær**) coil (spiral), spring; hairspring (in a watch).
spira'l/madrass' *-en* (coiled) spring mattress.
spira'l/tråd *-en* cord.
spira'l/tåke *-a astron.* spiral nebula.
spiran't *-en* fricative, spirant.
spiran'tisk *A* - fricative, spirantic.
spi're[1] *-a naut.* boom, spar.
spi're[2] *-a/+-en* 1 beginnings (**til** of); germ, seed, sprout: **kvele noe i s-n** nip sth in the bud. 2 aspiring, embryo poet, scholar, teacher, etc.; *ironic* young hopeful.
spi're[3] *V -te* begin to grow, germinate, sprout: **et s-ende håp** a dawning hope; **s- fram** grow, spring forth.
spire'a *-en bot.* spirea (genus Spiraea).
+spi're/dyktig *A* - capable of germinating; fertile.
spi're/evne *-a/+-en* capacity, power of germination.
spi're/tid *-a/+-en* time of germination, sprouting.
spirill' *-en zool.* spirillum (genus Spirillum).
spiritis'me *-n* spiritism.
spiritis't *-en* spiritist.
spiritis'tisk *A* - spiritualistic.
spiritualis'me *-n* spiritualism.
spiritualite't *-en* brilliancy, wit.
spirituell' *A -elt* 1 bright, clever, witty. 2 (rarely) spiritual.
spirituo'sa *pl* hard liquor: **viner og s-** wines and spirits.
spir'itus *-en* alcohol; alcoholic liquors, spirits.
spirituø's *A* alcoholic.
spirrevipp' *-en* whippersnapper; dude, fop.
spi's *-en dial.* fireplace, hearth.
+spi'se[1] *-n* dish, food: **kostelige s-r** *(bibl.)* precious dishes.
+spi'se[2] *V -te* eat: **spise en av** put off sby (e.g. with promises); **s- frokost** have breakfast; **s- på noe** munch sth; **s- seg mett** *(refl.)* eat one's fill.
+spi'se/bestikk' *-et* flatware: **et s-** knife, fork and spoon.
+spi'se/bo'rd *-et* dining table.
+spi'se/eple *-t* eating apple.
+spi'se/gjest *-en* boarder.
+spi'se/kart *-et* bill of fare, menu.
+spi'se/krok *-en* dining alcove.
+spi'se/kvarte'r *-et, pl -/-er obs.* eating establishment.
+spi'selig *A* - edible.
+spi'se/pinne *-n* chop stick.
+spi'se/rør *-et* esophagus, gullet.
+spi'se/sal *-en* dining hall; canteen, refectory.
spi'se/salong' *-en* dining room (on ship).
+spi'se/seddel *-en, pl -sedler* bill of fare, menu.
+spi'se/sjokola'de *-n* chocolate (for eating).
+spi'se/skje *-a/-en* table spoon.
+spi'se/sted *-et* café, lunchroom, restaurant: **godt s-** a good place to eat.
+spi'se/stell *-et* dinner service.
+spi'se/stue *-a* dining room.
+spi'se/varer *pl* food, provisions.
+spi'se/vogn [/vångn] *-a* diner, dining-car.
spis'k *A* snippy.
+spis'/kammer *-eret, pl -er/-re* pantry.
spiss'[1] *-en* 1 point, tip; *math.* apex, cusp: **i s-en** at the head, leading; **sette på s-en** accentuate, point up, push (sth) to an extreme; **stå i s-en for** be the leader of. 2 *(pl)* bigshots, VIP's; leaders (of society). 3 Pomeranian (=**s-/hund**). 4 *journ.* editorial (= **s-/artikkel**).
spiss'[2] *A* 1 pointed, sharp: **s- halsutringning** V-shaped neck. 2 *fig.* cutting, sarcastic, sharp (answer, remarks).
spiss'/artikkel *-elen, pl -artikler* lead article (in a newspaper).
spiss'/boge [/båge] *-n* cf **/bue**
+spiss'/borger *-en, pl -e* (=***-ar**) babbitt, philistine.
+spiss'/borgerlig *A* - (=***/borgarleg**) bourgeois, philistine.
spiss'/bub *-en* joker, prankster; rogue.
+spiss'/bue *-n* (=**/boge**) pointed (Gothic) arch; ogive.
+spiss'bue/stil *-en* Gothic style.
spiss'/bur *-en* joker, prankster; rogue.
spiss'/båt *-en naut.* sharp-sterned vessel.
spis'se *V -a/+-et* 1 sharpen: **s- munnen** protrude, pucker up the lips: **s- ører** prick up one's ears. 2: **s- seg** taper, taper off. 3 scour (grain).
+spis'ser *-en, pl -e* (=***-ar**) 1 sharpener; cf **blyant/s-** pencil sharpener. 2 *archaic* a quick one, pick-me-up.
+spissfin'dig *A* - hair-splitting, quibbling, sophistic.
+spissfin'dig/het *-en* hair-splitting, quibbling, sophistry.
spiss'/gatta *A* - (=+**-et**) *naut.* sharp-sterned.
+spiss'/gatter *-en, pl -e* (=***-ar**) *naut.* sharp-sterned vessel; double-ender.
spiss'/hakke *-a* pickaxe.
spiss'/kål *-en* early (spring) cabbage, sweet cabbage.
spiss'/mus *-a, pl -/*-myser zool.* shrew (Sorex araneus).
spiss'/rot *N* gantlet: **gå, løpe s-** run the gantlet (e.g. of adverse criticism).
spiss'rot(s)/gang *-en* running the gantlet.
spiss'/skjegg *-et* goatee.
spiss'/slede [also: spiss'/] *-n* cutter (sleigh).
spiss'/vinkla *A* - (=+**-et**) acute-angled.
***spi't**[1] *-en* point, tip.
***spi't**[2] *-et* affront, insult; derision, scoffing.
***spi'te** *V -a* impale, transfix; sharpen.
***spi'tig** *A* - cf **spydig**
spi't/o'rd *-et* sarcastic remark; *pop.* nasty crack.
Spit's/bergen *Pln* Spitzbergen (now called Svalbard).
spjel'd *-et* 1 (stove) damper; throttle valve. 2 corner shelf (e.g. for knickknacks). 3 gore, gusset (in dress). 4 temple (in loom).
spjel'k *-en* 1 splint. 2 temple (in a loom). 3 *pop.* shrimp; twerp.
spjel'ke *V -a/+-et* apply a splint: **s- opp** prop one's eyes open (with matchsticks).
spjer're *V -a* (=+**spjære**) rip, slash, tear; **s- seg** fall to pieces, split.
spjer't *-en* little dandy.
spjer'te *V -a/+-et*: **s- seg** show off, strut around.
spjer'ten *A +-ent, pl -ne* small and cocky.
spju't *-et* cf **spyd**
spjæ'ling *-en pop.* shrimp, twerp.
+spjæ're *V -a/-et/-te* cf **spjerre**
spjå'k *-et* 1 getup; *pop.* dolling up. 2 *pop.* dolled-up person, person tastelessly dressed. 3 mimic; *pop.* copy-cat.
spjå'ke *V -a/+-et/+-te*: **s- seg til (ut)** dress, rig oneself out grotesquely, outlandishly.

+ Bokmål; * Nynorsk; ° Dialect.
After letter: ' stress (Acc. 1); ' tone, stress (Acc. 2); · length.
Below letter: . not pronounced.

spjå'ket(e) *A* - dolled up, dressed tastelessly.
spleen [spli'n] *-en* ill humor, spite, spleen.
splei's *-en* 1 splice. 2 *pop.* hitching (=marrying). 3 Dutch treat; bottle party. 4 *pop.* bungler, jerk.
splei'se *V -a/+-te* 1 splice. 2 *pop.* get hitched, tie the knot (=get married). 3 go Dutch.
splei'se/lag *-et* (party where each guest brings his own contribution) Dutch treat, potluck; bottle party.
spli'd *-en* discord, dissension, division: **vekke s-** cause dissension, make trouble.
+spli'd/aktig [also -ak'ti] *A* - contentious, disharmonious: **s- med seg selv** divided against oneself.
splin't *-en* 1 bit, fragment, splinter. 2 cotter pin. *3 tramp.
+splin'ter *Av*: **s- naken** stark naked; **s- ny** brand new.
+splin'tre *V -a/-et* shatter, shiver (e. g. glass, mirror), splinter: **s-es** be shattered, smashed.
splin't/sikker *A -ert, pl -sikre* shatterproof.
splitt' *-en* 1 rent, slit, split; fly. 2 nib (of pen). 3 cotter pin. 4 swallowtail (cleft end of flag).
split'te *V -a/+-et* 1 slash, split. 2 disperse, scatter. 3 divide, separate. 4: **s- seg** break, split up; divide one's attention. 5: **s-es** be broken, split up.
+split'telse *-n* 1 break-up, distintegration. 2 dispersal, scattering. 3 discord, dissension, disunion (**av** of).
split'tende *Av*: **s- gal** stark, raving mad.
split'ter *Av*: **s- naken** stark naked; **s- ny** brand new; **s- (pine) gal** mad as a hatter.
splitt'/flagg *-et* naval ensign (with swallow-tails), pennant.
splitt'/kein *-en* split cane (plywood used in ski construction).
splitt'kein/ski *-a, pl -/-er* split cane skis.
splitt'/nagle *-n* split rivet.
spm. =**spørsmål**
°spo'l[1] *-en* cf **spord**
***spo'l**[2] *-en* 1 horizontal bar (e.g. in a gate). 2 strip of cloth; band, stripe in dyed material.
spo'le[1] *-n* 1 bobbin; reel; spool. 2 coil (radio).
spo'le[2] *V +-te/*-a* reel, spool, wind.
spo'le/maskin [/masji'n] *-en* bobbin winder.
spole're *V -te* ruin, spoil, wreck.
spo'l/orm *-en zool.* roundworm (Ascaris lumbricoides).
spo'n *-en* 1 chip, filing, shaving. 2 shingle. 3 wooden spoon. 4 *hist.* decorative shield placed on the bow and stern of a ship.
spondé *-en* spondee.
spong' *-a, pl spenger* 1 clasp, mounting (of metal). 2 small footbridge. 3 marking, spot on a cow.
spo'n/korg *-a* chip basket.
spon'ne** *pp of* **spenne**[2] (=sponni**)
spo'n/tak *-et* shingle roof.
sponta'n *A* spontaneous.
spontanite't *-en* spontaneity.
sponta'n/utvik'ling *-a/+-en* spontaneous development.
spo'r *-et* 1 footprint, track (**av, etter** of); (in hunting) scent: **bringe, sette på s-et** put on the (right) track; **følge, komme i ens s-** follow sby's example, in sby's footprints; **føre av s-et** throw off the track; **komme inn i et nytt s-** enter a new phase, proceed in a new direction; **komme, være på s-et** be, get on the track, (of hunting dog) on the scent. 2 trace (**av, etter** of): **ikke (det) s-** not a bit, not at all; **ikke s- av** not a trace of; **bære s- av** show traces, signs of; **sette dype s-** make a lasting impression, have great influence; **utslette s-ene av** wipe out all traces of. 3 track (train) rail; rut (from a car or wagon wheel): **fortsette i det gamle s-** continue in the same old rut; **gå, komme av s-et** be derailed. 4 (screwdriver) slot (in screw).
spora'disk [also -a'-] *A* - isolated, sporadic.
spo'r/avstand *-en/*-et* gauge (of a railroad).
spo'rd *-en* 1 tail (of a fish, reptile); fish. 2 extreme end of a wharf.
spo're[1] *-n* spur; *fig.* incentive, stimulus (**til** to).
spo're[2] *-n bot., zool.* spore.
spo're[3] *V -a/+-et/+-te* 1 scent, track: **s- opp** track down. 2: **s- av** derail; *fig.* be diverted from an objective; **s- ut** jump the tracks; *fig.*, (*pop.*) go off one's nut.
spo're[4] *V -a/+-et/+-te* spur (e.g. one's horse); *fig.* egg, urge on.
spo're/hus *-et bot.* sporangium (spore case).
+spo'ren/streks *Av* forthwith, immediately, without delay.
spo're/plante *-a/-en bot.* cryptogam, spore plant.
spo'r/hund *-en* bloodhound; *fig.* sleuth.
spo'r/laus *A* (=+/**løs**) invisible, trackless: **s-t forsvunnet** vanished without a trace.
spo'r/leik *-en* (=+/**lek**) game of following a trail.
spo'r/lys *-et mil.* tracer (bullet).
+spo'r/løs *A* cf /**laus**
spo'r/sans *-en* dog's ability to track, sense of smell; *fig.* aptitude, flair, perception.
spo'r/skifte *-t archaic* (railroad) switch.
spo'r/snø *-en* fresh snow (in which tracks of game can be followed).
spor't *-en* 1 sport: **drive s-** go in for sports. 2 amusement, pastime: **det ble s- blant gutter å henge bakpå biler** it became a pastime among boys to snag rides on cars.
spor'te *V -a/-et* go in for sports.
spor'tel *-elen, pl -ler* administrative fee.
spor'ts/artik'kel *-elen, pl -artikler* 1 piece of sports equipment. 2 sports article (in a newspaper).
spor'ts/dilla *df* sports craze.
spor'ts/fiske *-t* gamefish.
+spor'ts/fisker *-en, pl -e* (=*-**ar**) angler, fisherman.
spor'ts/forret'ning *-a/-en* sporting goods store.
spor'ts/idio't *-en* sports nut.
spor'ts/journalist [/sjurnalis't] *-en* sportswriter.
spor'ts/kvinne *-a/-en* sportswoman, woman athlete.
spor'tslig *A* - sporting: **s- anlagt** devoted to sports.
spor'ts/mann *-en, pl -menn/*-menner* athlete, sportsman.
+spor'ts/messig *A* - sportsmanlike.
spor'ts/sko *-en, pl -r/+-* hiking shoe, sports shoe.
spor'ts/strømpe *-a/-en* athletic sock; golf stocking; (sports) kneesock (used with knickers).
spor'ts/vogn [/vångn] *-a* 1 push-cart, stroller. 2 sports car.
spor'ts/ånd *+-en/*-a* (spirit of) sportsmanship.
sporty [spå'rti] *A* - active (interested) in sports, athletic; (being) a good sport.
***spor'v** *-en* cf **spurv**
spo'r/veg *-en* (=+/**vei**) streetcar line; trolley line.
spo'r/veksel *-elen, pl -ler* (railroad) switch.
***spor'v/hauk** *-en* cf **spurve/**
spo'r/vidde *-a* gauge (of a railroad).
spo'r/vogn [vångn] *-a* streetcar, trolley car.
spot'sk *A* - derisive, sardonic, sneering; contemptuous, mocking.
spott' *-en* derision, ridicule, scorn: **drive s- med** deride, mock at; **gjøre seg til s- og spe, være hvermanns s-** be, become an object of public ridicule, a laughing-stock; **halvt i s- og halvt i alvor** half mockingly and half seriously; **det er s- og skam** it's a great shame.
spot'te *V -a/-et* 1 deride, mock, ridicule: **s- med, over** make fun of, mock. 2 defy, frustrate: **det s-er enhver beskrivelse** it baffles description. 3 (*bibl.*) blaspheme (Acts 2, 13).
spot'te/fugl *-en* 1 *zool.* mockingbird (Mimus polyglottos). 2 mocker, scoffer (person).
spot'te/gauk *-en* mocker, scoffer.
***spot'teleg** *A* - blasphemous.
+spot'ter *-en, pl -e* (=*-**ar**) derider, mocker, scoffer; blasphemer.
spott'/pris *-en* bargain price, low price: **få det til s-** get it dirt-cheap.
spo've *-n* (=***spue**) *zool.* curlew (Numenius arquatus).
spra'de[1] *-n* dandy, dude, show-off.
spra'de[2] *V -a/-te* show off, strut around, swagger.
spra'de/basse *-n hum.* dandy, dude, show-off.
+sprag'let(e) *A* - (=***spreklet(e)**) motley, multicolored, pied; gaudy, showy (e.g. clothes).
spra'ke[1] *-n bot.* juniper shrub, tree (Juniperus communis).
spra'ke[2] *V -a/+-te* 1 crack, crackle, snap (e.g. fire, machine gun): **s-ende tørr** dry as a bone. 2 sparkle: **s- fram** burst forth.
sprakk' *pt of* **sprekke**[2]
***spra'le** *V -a* flounder; kick, squirm, wriggle.
sprang'[1] *-et* 1 bound; jump, leap, spring: **gjøre et s- i mørket** take a leap in the dark; **i store s-** by leaps and bounds; **med et s-** at a single bound; **stå på s-et til å** be on the point of (doing sth); **ta s-** take a running jump; **ta en på s-** overtake sby; **våge s-et** take the plunge. 2 run: **i s-et** on the r-; **legge (sette) på s-** start running.
sprang'[2] *-et* lace (edge), tatting.
sprang'[3] *pt of* **springe**
sprang'/vis *Av* 1 by jumps, leaps. 2 *mil.* by rushes (across open terrain).
spratt' *pt of* **sprette**[2]
+spre' *V -dde/-dte* cf **spreie**[2]
+spre'de[1] *-t* cf **spreie**[1]
+spre'de[2] *V -te* cf **spreie**[2]
+spre'de/linse *-a/-en* concave lens.
+spre'der *-en, pl -e* cf **spreier**
+spre'dning *-en* cf **spreiing**
sprei'e[1] *-t* (=+**sprede**[1]) spread.
sprei'e[2] *V +-de/*-dde* (=+**spre(de)**[2]) 1 scatter, spread (e.g. hay, wings, light rays, information): **s- for alle vinde** scatter to the four winds. 2 scatter, split (e.g. group, mole, clouds): **s-dt** distracted; split; **bo s-dt** live far apart, scattered; **s-dte eksempler på** sporadic examples of; **s- seg, s-es** scatter, separate; be spread.
+sprei'er *-en, pl -e* (=*-**ar**, +**spreder**) spreader; (lawn) sprinkler.
sprei'ing *-a* (=+**spredning**) 1 diffusion, scattering, spreading; spread. 2 *mil.* dispersal of forces.
spre'k *A* active, spry, vigorous: **han er s- for sin alder** he's pretty spry for his age.
+spre'k/het *-en* spryness, vigor, vitality.
spre'king *-en* active, vigorous individual; (*pop.*) spry old gaffer.
sprekk' *-en* chink, crack, crevice (**i** in): **slå s-er** crack.
+sprekk'/dannelse *-n geol.* fissuration, fissure formation.
+sprek'ke[1] *-n* cf **sprekk**
sprek'ke[2] *V sprakk, +sprukket/*sprokke/*-i* break, burst, crack; split: **s- av latter** split one's sides laughing; **stemmen hennes sprakk på de høye toner** her voice broke on the high notes. 2: **sprukken** raw, rough; **sprukne hender** chapped hands.

sprek'ke/ferdig *A* - nearly bursting, splitting: **s- av latter** ready to burst out laughing.

sprekk'/fri *A -tt* free of cracks, fissures; smooth, unbroken.

*__sprekkj'e__ *V sprekte* (cause sth to) break, burst, crack.

+**sprekk'/mett** *A* - gorged to the point of bursting.

*__spre'k/leik__ *-en* spryness, vigor, vitality.

*__sprek'let(e)__ *A* - cf **spraglet(e)**

*__spre'l__[1] *-et* cf **sprell**[1]

*__spre'l__[2] *Av* cf **sprell**[2]

*__spre'le__ *V -a/-te* cf **sprelle**

*__spre'le/mann__ *-en, pl -menn(er)* cf **sprelle/**

+**sprell'**[1] *-et* (=*__sprel__) 1 kicking, squirming, wriggling; exertion, struggle. 2 disturbance, fuss: **gjøre, lage s-** kick up a row. 3 spree; *(pop.)* cutting loose.

+**sprell'**[2] *Av* (=*__sprel__): **s- levende** full of life and vitality (vim and vigor); *(pop.)* bright-eyed and bushy-tailed, full of beans.

+**sprel'le** *V -a/-et/sprelte* (=*__sprele__) flail, flounder; kick, squirm, wriggle; strive and struggle.

+**sprel'le/mann** *-en, pl -menn* jumping jack.

sprell'/le'vende *A* - cf **sprell**[2]

+**sprel'sk** *A* - audacious, frisky, lively: **s- fantasi** vivid imagination.

spreng' *-en* 1 extreme pressure; pell-mell haste: **(arbeide) på s-** (work) at high pressure, against time; **lese på s-** cram. *2 tympanitis. 3 dentist's plug, wedge. *4 *bot.* bearberry (Arctostaphylos uva-ursi).

spreng'/bombe [/bombe] *-a/+-en* fragmentation, high explosive bomb; anti-personnel bomb.

+**spreng'e** *V -te* (=*__-je__) 1 break (open), burst, shatter: **s- døra** break down the door; **det s-er (i strupen)** (one's throat) feels as if it will burst. 2 disperse, scatter, spread (=break up a crowd). 3 blast, blow up (with explosives); explode; **s- i luften** blow up. 4 exhaust, overexert, wear out: **s- en hest** disable a horse (by overriding); **s- seg** overstrain oneself, work oneself to death. 5 (bookbinding) sprinkle. 6 salt lightly (e.g. fish). 7: **s- av sted (forbi, fram)** ride (a horse) at a gallop, at top speed; hurry, rush. 8: **s-t** (also) flushed.

spreng'/feit *A -feitt/+-fett* overly plump.

spreng'/fly *V infl as* **fly**[4] run for all one is worth.

spreng'/frost *-en* black frost.

spreng'/granat *-en* high explosive shell.

*__spreng'/hug__ *-en* uncontrollable, ungovernable desire.

*__spreng'je__ *V -de* cf **sprenge**

spreng'/kald *A* freezing, frigid, icy cold.

*__spreng'/kjøld__ *-a* cf **/kulde**

spreng'/kjøre *V -te* (=*__/køyre__) drive at breakneck speed.

spreng'/kraft *-a/+-en* explosive force; blast effect.

spreng'/kulde *-a/-en* frigid temperature, icy cold.

spreng'/ladning *-en* explosive, main charge, war head.

spreng'/lese *V infl as* **lese** cram (e.g. for an examination).

spreng'/lærd *A* - erudite, extremely learned.

+**spreng'ning** *-en* 1 (=**sprenging**) bursting, dispersal, explosion etc. **(av of): partiets s-** the party split. 2 arch, instep (of shoe).

+**spreng'/rød** *A* (=*__/raud__) flushed.

spreng'/sats *-en* explosive mixture.

spreng'/stoff *-et* explosive.

*__spreng'/to__ *-et* explosive.

spreng'/verk *-et arch.* strut (roof beams).

sprett'[1] *-en* 1 dandy, dude, show-off; *(pop.)* squirt. 2 bounce, elasticity, spring. 3 (small) explosive charge. 4 spatter, splash, squirt. 5 mosquito larvae. 6: **sol/s-** peep of dawn.

sprett'[2] *-en/-et* 1 jerk, jump, twitch. 2 shoot, sprout: **stå i s-** be breaking into leaf.

sprett'/boge [/båge] *-n* (=+**/bue**) boy's crossbow.

*__spret'te__[1] *-a* pole, slat, stick.

spret'te[2] *V spratt, +-et/*sprotte/*-i* 1 bound, jump, leap; jerk, twitch. 2 drift, fly (e.g. snow, chips); gush, splash, spurt (e.g. blood). 3 break loose (suddenly): **så kaldt at flisen s-er** biting cold. 4 shoot forth, sprout. 5 (of sun) peep.

spret'te[3] *V -a/+-et/*-e* 1 cut, rip, slit open (**opp** up) (e.g. fish; lining, seam of a garment): **s- opp en bok** cut the pages of a book; **s- opp magen på en** slash sby wide open. 2 spray, spurt, squirt. *3 scatter, spread. 4: **s- fra** unhitch.

spret'te/kniv *-en* seamstress' knife (used to rip up linings, seams).

spret'ten *A +-ent, pl spretne* brisk, frisky, lively.

spret'tende *A* frolicsome, lively; (adv.): **s- full** teeming (**av** with).

spret'tert *-en* slingshot.

sprett'/fyr *-en* dandy, dude, show-off.

*__spret'ting__ *-en* dandy, dude, show-off.

sprett-i-vass'fat *-en* dandy, dude, show-off.

spri'[1] *-et naut.* sprit.

spri'[2] *V -dde naut.* set the sail by means of the sprit.

+**spri'ke** *V -te* (=*__-je__) 1 distend, spread; bristle. 2 stand out; gape, show (e.g. a garment): **s- med armer og bein** sprawl; **s-ende** conspicuous, glaring.

*__spri'kjande__ *A* - 1 bursting, swelling. 2 bombastic; conspicuous, glaring.

*__spri'kje__ *V -te* cf **sprike**

*__spri'kje/stakk__ *-en* crinoline.

+**sprik'/vort** *-et archaic* proverb, saying.

spring'[1] *-en* (water) faucet, tap.

+**spring'**[2] *-et* 1 bound, jump, leap; sudden transition (e.g. in thought). 2 *geol.* ledge, projection; fault. 3 *naut.* sheer (=fore-and-aft curvature of a vessel; position of a ship riding at anchor). 4 fountain, spring. 5 elasticity, spring (in shoe).

spring'ar *-en* 1 roundel (=Norwegian folk dance in $^3/_4$ time). *2 *zool.* tunny fish (Thunnus thynnus).

spring'/brett *-et* spring board.

spring'/dans *-en* roundel (Norwegian folk dance in $^3/_4$ time).

spring'e *V sprang, +sprunget/*sprunge/*-i* 1 bound, jump, leap: **s- bukk** leapfrog; **s- i klærne** tear on one's clothes; **s- i været** leap up; **s- opp som en løve (og dette ned som en skinnfell)** roar like a lion (and give in like a lamb). 2 run: **s- etter noe** run over and get sth. 3 blow up, burst, explode; (of corks) pop: **s- i luften** blow up, explode. 4 (of liquids) gush, spout, squirt. 5 (of flowers) bud, open; bloom, blossom (=**s- ut**). 6: **s-ende** disconnected, incoherent; salient: **det s-ende punkt** the main point. 7 (with *prep., adv.*): **s- (ut) av** have its origin in; **s- fram** jut out, project (e.g. cliff, balcony); be obvious (e.g. a contrast); **s- i (igjen)** slam shut (e.g. door); **s- i øynene** be obvious, hit one in the eye; **s- om** (of wind) shift (suddenly); **s- opp** open (e.g. a wound, glued joint); fly open (e.g. a door); **s- over** omit, skip.

+**spring'er** *-en, pl -e* (=*__-ar__) 1 jumper (e.g. horse). 2 knight (chess). 3 *zool.* dolphin (Delphinus delphis); tunny fish (Thunnus thynnus).

+**spring'/flo** *-a* (=*__/flod__) spring tide.

spring'/frø *-et bot.* touch-me-not (Impatiens noli me tangere).

spring'/madrass' *-en* coil spring mattress.

spring'/marsj *-en mil.* forced march.

spring'/vatn *-et* (=+**/vann**) fountain.

+**sprin'kel** *-elen, pl -ler* bar, picket, post (in a fence, gate).

+**sprin'kel/kasse** *-a/-en* crate.

+**sprin'kel/verk** *-et* grating.

sprin'kler *-en, pl +-e* sprinkler (system).

sprin't *-en* sprint.

sprin'te *V -a/+-et* sprint.

sprin'ter *-en, pl -e* sprinter.

spri'/segl *-et naut.* spritsail.

spri't *-en* 1 alcohol, spirits. 2 denatured alcohol; *(pop.)* booze, rotgut.

spri'te *V -a/+-et*: **s- opp** add alcohol to, *(pop.)* spike.

+**sprog** [språ'g] *-et* cf **språk**

+**sproglig** [språ'gli] *A* - cf **språklig**

*__sproke__ [språ'ke] *-a* (little) chink, crack.

*__sprokke__ [sprok'ke] *pp of* **sprekke**[2] (=*__sprokki__)

+**spros'se** *-a/-en* 1 rung (in a ladder). 2 crossbar, crosspiece; *arch.* mullion, transom.

*__sprot__ [språ't] *-et* small bar, pole, stick.

*__sprote__ [språ'te] *-n* 1 lath, stick. 2 clasp, hook. 3 dandy, dude, show-off.

*__sprot'ne__ *V -a* unravel (linings, seams).

*__sprot'te__[1] *-a* placket, slit (of a garment).

*__sprotte__[2] [sprot'te] *pp of* **sprette**[2] (=*__sprotti__)

+**sprud'le** *V -a/-et* bubble, gush, well; effervesce, sparkle, (also *fig.*).

+**sprukket** [sprok'ket] *pp of* **sprekke**[2]

sprunge[1] [sprong'e] *-a* chink, crack, crevice; fissure.

*__sprunge__[2] [sprong'e] *pp of* **springe** (=*__sprungi__)

+**sprunget** [sprong'et] *pp of* **springe**

spru't[1] *-en* 1 gush, spurt, stream; spindrift, spray; burst (of laughter): **stå i s-** splash, spurt. 2 *zool.* squid (Ommastrephes sagittatus).

spru't[2] *Av*: **s- rød** red, scarlet (of a person).

sprut'/bakkels(e) *-(e)n/*-(e)t* cruller.

spru'te *V -a/+-et/*-te* 1 gush, spout, spurt; spatter, splash, squirt; (of sparks) fly. 2 explode (e.g. with anger, laughter).

spru'tende *Av*: **s- rød** red as a turkey cock, scarlet (of a person).

spru't/regne [+/reine] *V -a/+-et/+-te/*-de* (of rain) gush, pour.

+**spru't/rød** *A* (=*__/raud__) red, scarlet (of a person).

*__spry'd__ *-et cf* **spri**[1]

*__spræ'k__ *A* cf **sprek**

*__spræ'l__ *-en* bobtail (esp. on sheep).

*__spræ'n__ *-en* spurt, squirt.

*__spræ'ne__ *V -te* spurt, squirt.

sprø' *A -tt* 1 crackly, crisp, short. 2 brittle, friable; delicate, feeble, frail. 3 *fam.* crazy, foolish, weak-minded.

sprø/steikt *A* - crisp, short.

sprøtt' *nt of* **sprø**

sprøy't[1] *-en/+-et* dash, squirt; spatter, splash; foam, spindrift, spray.

sprøy't[2] *-et* nonsense.

sprøy'te[1] *-a* 1 spray, syringe; watering can; fire engine (extinguisher, pump). 2 hypodermic, shot (**av** of). 3 (a game of cards).

sprøy'te[2] *V -a/+-et/*-te* 1 spray, squirt; infect (e.g. serum); (of whales) blow. 2 gush, spatter, splash; sprinkle.

sprøy'te/flaske *-a chem.* wash bottle.

sprøy'te/full *A* dead drunk.

+**sprøy'te/gal** *A* mad as a hatter, stark, raving mad.

sprøy'te/hopp *-et* concave-shaped ski jump.

+**sprøy'te/maling** *-a/-en* (=*__/måling__) spray painting.

+ Bokmål; * Nynorsk; ° Dialect.
After letter: ' stress (Acc. 1); ` tone, stress (Acc. 2); · length.
Below letter: . not pronounced.

sprøy'te/vogn [/vångn] *-a* water wagon.
sprøy'te/væske *-a/+-en* (garden) spray, insecticide.
språ'k *-et* language, speech: **s-ets opprinnelse** the origin of the language; **fuglenes s-** the language of birds; **disse tall taler sitt tydelige s-** these figures speak volumes; **han ville ikke ut med s-et** he hesitated to speak out; **på vårt s-** in our language.
+språ'k/blomst *-en derog.* gem; howler.
språ'k/bruk *-en/-et* (language) usage.
språ'k/feil *-en* grammatical error, solecism.
+språ'k/ferdighet *-en* command of a language, linguistic proficiency.
+språ'k/forsker *-en, pl -e* (scientific) linguist; philologist.
språ'k/forvir'ring *-a/+-en* Babel, confusion of languages.
+språ'k/følelse *-n* feeling for language, style.
språ'k/føring *-a/+-en* diction.
språ'k/geni [/sjeni'] *-et, pl +-er/*-* linguistic genius (ability and person).
språ'k/grense *-a/+-en* language boundary.
språ'k/histo'rie *-a/+-en* language history.
språ'k/kjensle *-a* feeling for language style.
språ'k/konsulen't *-en* language consultant (e.g. in publishing house or government office).
språ'k/kunst *-en* literary art.
språ'klig *A* - linguistic, of language.
språ'k/lyd *-en* phone, phoneme.
språ'k/lære *-a/+-en* grammar.
+språ'k/lærer *-en, pl -e* (=***-ar**) language teacher.
språ'k/mann *-en, pl -menn/*-menner* linguist, philologist.
språ'k/mektig *A* - skilled, versed in languages.
språ'k/politikk' *-en* linguistic policy; politics of language ("glottopolitics").
+språ'k/renser *-en, pl -e* purist.
språ'k/sak *-a/+-en* (usu. in the definite form) the cause of New Norwegian.
språ'k/sans *-en* feeling, instinct for language; (style).
språ'k/strid [*/stri] *-en* linguistic controversy, dispute (e.g. of Dano-Norwegian and New Norwegian).
språkv. =**språkvitenskapelig**
språ'k/vitska'p *-en* (=**+/vitenskap**) linguistics: **sammenlignende s-** comparative philology.
språ'k/vitska'plig *A* - (=**+/vitenskapelig**) of or pertaining to linguistic science; grammatical, linguistic.
språ'k/øy *-a* linguistic island, pocket.
***spu'e** *-n* cf **spove**
***spu'ne** *-n* spinning; purring.
spun'ne** *pp of* **spinne** (=spunni**)
+spun'net *pp of* **spinne**
+spun'ning *-a naut.* rabbet.
spun's *-et* 1 bung. 2 bunghole. 3 *naut.* graving piece. 4 lozenge, square (in cloth).
spun'se *V -a/+-et* 1 bung (e.g. a cask); plug. 2 *naut.* patch with a graving piece.
spun's/hol [/hål] *-et* (=**+/hull**) bunghole.
***spu'r/dag** *-en* question.
***spu'rde** *pt of* **spørje**
spu'r/lag *-et* intelligence, news: **få s- på** find out about, learn about.
***spu'rnad** *-en, pl -er* inquiry.
***spu'rning** *-a* question, riddle.
spur't *-en* spurt.
spur'te¹ *V -a/+-et* spurt.
+spu'rte² *pt of* **spørre**
+spur'v *-en* (=***sporv**) *zool.* sparrow (Passer domesticus): **en s- i tranedans** completely outclassed, utterly out of one's element; **skyte s-er med kanoner** kill flies with a sledgehammer.
+spur've/hauk *-en zool.* sparrow hawk (Accipiter nisus).
***spu'r/vis** *A* inquiring, inquisitive.
sput'nik *-en* sputnik.
sp. v. =**spesifikk vekt**
spy'¹ *-et* 1 puke, vomit. 2 blowfly larva.
spy'² *V -dde* vomit; belch (**ut** forth), emit; spew: **s- gift** vent one's spleen; **s- ut varer** (of factory) pour out goods.
spy'd *-et* (=**spjut**) spear; dart, javelin.
Spy'de/berg *Pln* twp, Østfold.
spy'dig *A* - (=***spitig**) sarcastic, withering.
+spy'dig/het *-en* derision, sarcasm; gibe, sarcastic remark, taunt; *(pop.)* nasty crack.
spy'd/kast *-et* javelin throw; javelin throwing.
spy'/ferdig *A* - ready to heave, vomit.
+spy'/flue *-a* (=***/fluge**) *zool.* blowfly, bluebottle (fly) (Calliphora vomitoria).
+spy'/gatt *-et* (=***/gat**) *naut.* scupper, hole.
spy'le *V -te* flush (with hose and water); *naut.* swab (the deck).
***spyr'je** *V spyr, spurde, spurt* cf **spørje**
spytt' *-et* saliva; spit, spittle, sputum.
spyt'te *V -a/+-et* spit (**på** on): **s- i bøssa** make a (financial) contribution; *(pop.)* cough up, shell out; **s- i nevene** roll up one's sleeves; **s- opp** cough up (spit) blood; **s- seg selv i ansiktet** degrade, demean oneself (by speaking against one's own conviction).
spyt'te/bakk *-en* (=**+/bakke**) spittoon.
spytt'/kjertel *-clen, pl -ler* salivary gland.
+spytt'/slikker *-en, pl -e* bootlicker, lickspittle.
***spæ'je** *V -a* cf **speide**
spæ'l *-en* (bob)tail (e.g. on sheep).
spæ'l/sau *-en* short-tailed sheep.
spø'k *-en* jest, joke, prank; witticism: **det ble ham en dyr s-** it cost him a pretty penny; **det er ikke (ingen) s-** it's no laughing matter; **drive s-en for vidt** carry the joke too far; **for (i) s-** as a joke, for the fun of it; **han forstår ikke s-** he can't take a joke; **slå noe hen i s-** laugh sth off.
+spø'ke *V -te* (=***-je**) 1 jest, joke (**med** with, about): **det er ikke til å s- med** it is no laughing matter; **han er ikke til å s- med** he is dangerous, not to be trifled with; **en s-ende tone** a joking (lighthearted) tone. 2 return (from the dead), walk again (after death): **det s-er i huset** the house is haunted; **i de kristne skikker s-er meget gammelt hedenskap** a great deal of paganism still lives in the Christian practices; **det s-er i hodet på meg** I am haunted (possessed) by an idea, an idea fills me. 3: **det s-er for (en, noe)** there is danger of (sth); it looks bad for (sby), e.g. **det s-er for garden** there is danger of losing the farm (Bojer).
+spø'ke/fugl *-en* joker, wag.
+spø'ke/full *A* jocose, jocular; facetious, jesting.
+spø'kelig *A* - (=***spøkjeleg**) creepy, dangerous, spooky.
+spø'kelse *-t* (=***spøkjelse**) 1 apparition, ghost, spectre; *(pop.)* spook: **se s-er ved høylys dag** be frightened of one's own shadow. 2 *zool.* stick insect, walking stick (family Phasmatidae).
+spø'kelses/aktig *A* - ghostly, spectral, weird.
+spø'kelses/histo'rie *-a/-en* ghost story.
+spø'keri *-et* ghosts; haunting.
***spø'kje** *V -te* cf **spøke**
***spø'kjeleg** *A* - cf **spøkelig**
***spø'kjelse** *-t* cf **spøkelse**
***spø'kjen** *A -e/-i, pl -ne* cf **spøkelig**
***spø'ne** *V -te* kick, thrust; exert oneself.
spør' *pr of* **spørre, spørje**
+spør'ger *-en, pl -e* (=***spørjar**) interrogator, questioner.
***spør'jast** *V spørst, spurdest, spurst* cf **spørre**
***spør'je** *V spør, spurde, spurt* cf **spørre**
***spør'je/hug** *-en* curiosity, inquisitiveness.
***spør'je/melding** *-a* cf **spørre/**
***spør'je/time** *-n* cf **spørre/**
+spør're *V spør, spurte* (=***spørje**) 1 ask, inquire (**etter** for; **om** about); ask a question (questions), examine: **spør om hun var glad** was she ever happy!; **s- opp** look up (sby); **s- på noe** ask the price of sth; **s- til en** make inquiries about sby; **s- ut** interrogate, pump (e.g. for news, information); **s- seg for, fram** make inquiries, ask for directions; **det spørs/*spørst (om)** I wonder (if), it's a question (of whether), it's questionable (if); **s-ende** doubtful, inquiring, *gram.* interrogative. 2 *archaic* hear (about), learn: **s- til** hear about; **s-es/*s-jast** be heard, be told.
+spør're/lyst *-a/ en* curiosity, inquisitiveness.
+spør're/lysten *A -ent, pl -ne* curious, inquisitive.
+spør're/melding *-a/-en* asking bid (bridge).
+spør're/o'rd *-et gram.* interrogative.
+spør're/setning *-en* interrogative sentence.
+spør're/skjema *-et* questionnaire.
+spør're/syk *A* (over) curious, inquisitive; burning with curiosity.
+spør're/syke *-n* inquisitiveness, nosiness.
+spør're/tegn [/tein] *-et* question mark.
+spør're/time *-n* question period (e.g. in parliament).
+spør's *pr of* **spørres** cf **spørre**
spør's/mål *-et* 1 question; inquiry (**etter** about): **gjøre, stille et s-** ask a question; (*not* **spørre et s-**); **komme med et s-** ask a question. 2 matter, problem: **et aktuelt s-** a current p-; **det er s- om (liv og død)** it's a matter of (life and death); **det er et annet s-** that's another matter; **det er (bare) et s- om** it's just a question of (whether).
+spør'småls/tegn [/tein] *-et* (=***/teikn**) question mark.
+spør'/vis *A* cf **spur/**
spø't *-et* knitting.
***spø'te¹** *-a* knitting needle.
spø'te² *V +-te/*-a* knit.
***spø'te/trøye** *-a* knitted jacket.
spøtt' *et*: **ikke det s-** not in the least, not the slightest.
°spøt'te *V -a* cf **spytte**
spå' *V -dde* 1 foretell, predict, prophesy the future; forecast; tell fortunes: **s- (en) i handa** read one's palm; **s- (en) i kaffegrut** read (sby's) fortunes by coffee grounds. 2 bode, presage, promise: **det s-r ilt for ham** it doesn't look good for him.
spå'/dom' *-men/*-en* prediction, prophecy: **s-men gikk i oppfyllelse** the prophecy came true.
spå'/kjerring *-a, pl *-ar* fortune-teller.
spå'/kone [*/kåne] *-a* fortune-teller.
spå'/kvinne *-a/+-en* fortune-teller; *hist.* prophetess, sibyl.
spå'/mann *-en, pl -menn/*-menner* fortune-teller; *hist.* prophet, soothsayer.
+spå'n *-en* cf **spon**
***spå'/vis** *A* having the gift of prophecy.
+squeeze [skvi's] *en* cf **skvis**
sr. =**senior**
S/S =**steamship**
***s. st.** =**same stad¹**
st. =**stasjon; store**

St. =Santa, Santo, Sankt
sta'[1] *A* -, *pl* -/*-e bullheaded, obstinate, stubborn: **være s- på noe** stick to one's guns.
°**sta'**[2] *Av* cf **stad**[2]
sta'b -en (esp. *mil.*) staff: **han hører til s-en** he's on the staff.
stab'be[1] -n 1 stump. 2 chopping block. 3 rounded reef. 4 chunky boy.
stab'be[2] *V* -a/+-et toddle; trudge.
stab'be/stein -en (roadside) guard stone.
stab'bur -et storehouse (on pillars).
stab'burs/loft -et 1 storehouse (=**stabbur**). 2 loft in **stabbur**.
stab'burs/nøkkel -en, *pl* -nøkler storehouse key.
stab'burs/pølse -a summer sausage.
***sta'/be(de)** *V infl as* **be(de)** beg earnestly, implore.
***sta'/beint** *A* - dead ahead, straight ahead.
sta'/beis [also -bei's] -en an old fogy, stick-in-the-mud.
sta'bel -elen, *pl* -ler 1 pile, stack (e.g. of lumber). 2 hinge pin. 3 *naut.* slip: **gå (løpe) av s-en** be launched (a ship, also *fig.*); **stå på s-en** be on the stocks, under construction.
+**sta'bel/avløpning** -en launching.
stabi'l *A* stable, steady.
stabilisa'tor -en stabilizer.
stabilise're *V* -te stabilize, steady.
stabilite't -en stability.
stab'le *V* -a/+-et 1 pile, stack (e.g. lumber). 2: **s- på beina** raise, get sby on his feet; (also *fig.*) organize, raise.
+**sta'bler** *pl of* **stabel**
sta'bs/sjef -en *mil.* chief of staff.
+**stab'ur** -et cf **stabbur**
sta'd[1] [*sta] -en, *pl* +steder/*stader *1 place: **i s-en for** instead of; **i min s-** in my place, in my shoes; **ingen s-** nowhere; **til s-es** present. +2 *archaic* city: **Oslo stad** the city of Oslo; (esp. in cpds.) **berg/s-, hoved/s-** etc. 3: **i s-** a little while ago, just now; in a little while.
***sta'd**[2] *Av* away: **gå s- og sjå** go and look.
Sta'd [usu. statt'] *Pln* promontory, Sogn og Fjordane.
***stadd'** *A* - cf **stedd**
***sta'de**[1] -n pile, stack.
+**sta'de**[2] -t level, plane, plateau.
***sta'de**[3] *V* -a settle down, stop.
***sta'de**[4] *pp of* **stande**
***sta'den** *A* -e/-i, *pl* -ne having stood: **for lite s-** not yet ripe.
sta'd/feste *V* -a/+-et/*-e affirm, confirm, ratify (e.g. a document, one's rights, etc.).
sta'd/festing -a/+-en (=+-**else**) confirmation, ratification.
***sta'di** *pp of* **stande**
+**sta'dier** *pl of* **stadium**
sta'dig *A* - 1 stable, steady: **s- vær** settled weather. 2 constant, continual, incessant: **stå i s- forbindelse med** be in constant touch with. 3 (*adv.*) constantly: **i s- stigende grad** to an ever increasing extent; **vi foretar s- forbedringer** we are continually making improvements; **s-vekk** invariably, without fail.
+**sta'dig/het** -en 1 stability, steadiness. 2: **til s-** constantly, continually.
sta'dion -et stadium.
sta'dium -iet, *pl* +-ier/*-ium phase, point, stage: **et overvunnet s-** a thing of the past.
***sta'dleg** *A* - cf **stedlig**
***sta'd/namn** -et cf **steds/navn**
sta'ds/arki'v -et, *pl* -/+-er municipal archives.
Sta'ds/bygd *Pln* twp, Sør-Trøndelag.
sta'ds/fysikus -en city health officer, city medical officer.
sta'ds/ingeniør [/insjeniø'r] -en city engineer.
stafett' -en 1 baton. 2 relay race.
+**stafett'/løp** -et (=***/laup**) relay race.
stafett'/pinne -n baton.
staffa'sje -n 1 figures in a landscape. 2 extras (in theater); background, décor.
staffeli' -et, *pl* +-er/*- easel.
staffe're *V* -te 1 adorn, decorate (often in a tasteless manner). 2 fell (a seam); belt, line, stripe.
sta'g -et *naut.* stay: **gå over s-** put about, tack.
sta'ge *V* -a/+-et *naut.* stay (e.g. a mast); put about, tack.
stag'ge *V* -a/+-et 1 check, curb, restrain. 2 hush, pacify, soothe.
stagnasjo'n -en stagnation.
stagne're *V* -te stagnate.
sta'g/vende *V* +-te/*-e *naut.* put about, tack.
***sta'/halde** *V infl as* **halde** clutch, grab hold, hang on.
+**sta'/het** -en bullheadedness, obstinacy, stubbornness.
sta'ke[1] -n 1 pole, stake. 2 candlestick. 3 tall, skinny person; (*pop.*) beanpole. 4 *naut.* spar buoy.
sta'ke[2] *V* -a/+-et/+-te 1 drive, pound stakes (in the ground); mark out with stakes. 2 pole a boat; **s- seg fram** pole a boat. *3 **s- (seg)** stumble, totter.
stakitt' -et paling, picket fence.
+**stakitt'/sprosse** -a/-en picket.
stakk'[1] -en skirt.
stakk'[2] -en rick, stack (e.g. of hay).
stakk'[3] *pt of* **stikke**[2], **stinge**
stak'kar -en, *pl* -er miserable wretch; poor creature; (*pop.*) poor devil.
stak'kars *A* - pitiable, poor, wretched: **s- deg!** you poor thing; **s- krok** poor old soul.
stak'kars/dom' -men/*-en 1 poverty; misery, wretchedness. 2 cowardice, degradation, depravity.
stak'karslig *A* - 1 poor, poverty-stricken; pitiable, miserable, wretched. 2 contemptible, despicable.
stak'kars/ting -en/-et 1 poor soul, wretch. 2 contemptible person.
stakka'to *Av* staccato.
stak'ke *V* -a/+-et stack (e.g. hay).
+**stak'kel** -en, *pl* **stakler** cf **stakkar**
+**stak'ket** *A* - brief, fleeting, short.
+**stakk'/åndet** *A* - breathless, out of breath.
stak're *V* -a/+-et feel sorry for, pity (lit. say "**stakkar**" to sby).
sta'l *pl of* **stele**
Sta'l/heim *Pln* resort, Vossestrand, Hordaland.
stall' -en 1 barn, stable: **sette en hest på s-en** stable a horse. 2 racing stable. 3 *hist.* dais, elevation (for pagan gods).
stal'lare -n *hist.* king's marshal.
stall'/bror -en, *pl* +-brødre/*-brør confederate, crony, partner in crime.
stall'/dreng -en stableboy.
stall'/dør -a stable door.
stal'le *V* -a/+-et 1 stable (a horse). 2 (of locomotive, trolley) go to the barn. 3 (of horses) urinate.
stall'/fore *V* -a/+-et/+-te stall-feed.
stall'/kar -en groom, stableboy.
stall'/trev -et hayloft.
+**stall'/vekke** -a (=***-je**) horse bell.
stam' *A pl* -me stammering: **være s-** stammer.
stam'/aksje -n *merc.* share of common stock.
stam'/bane -n trunk line (railroad).
stam'/bok -a, *pl* -bøker 1 family album, guest book. 2 *vet.* studbook. 3 *archaic* genealogy.
stam'bok/føre *V* -te *vet.* enter in a studbook.
stam'/bo'rd -et regular customer's table (e.g. in a restaurant).
stam'/far -en, *pl* +-fedre/*-fedrar ancestor, progenitor.
stam'/fisk -en parent fish.
stam'/gjest -en regular customer, patron; habitué.
stam'/gods [/gots] -et entailed estate.
stam'/herre -n heir, owner of entailed estate.
stam'/hus -et entailed estate.
stam'/kafé -en haunt (café where one is a regular patron).
stam'me[1] +-n/*-a 1 stem, trunk: **eplet faller ikke langt fra s-n** he's a chip off the old block. 2 blood, stock, strain. 3 nation, race, tribe. 4 *gram.* stem, theme. 5 stem (of key).
+**stam'me**[2] *V* -a/-et: **s- fra** be descended from, descend from; come, hail from; be due to, originate in.
stam'me[3] *V* -a/+-et stammer, stutter.
stam'/mor -a, *pl* -mødrer/+-mødre ancestress.
stam'n -en (=+**stavn**) bow; stem, stern: **fra s- til s-** from stem to stern.
Stam'/nes *Pln* twp, Nordland.
stam'p[1] -en tub.
stam'p[2] -en *pop.* pawnshop: **i s-en** at the pawnbroker's, (*pop.*) in hock.
stam'p[3] -en/-et 1 stamp, stomp. 2 pestle. 3 heaving, pitching sea. 4 sacrifice bid.
stam'pe[1] -a 1 stamper, stamping mill. 2: **stå i s-** be at a standstill, mark time.
stam'pe[2] *V* -a/+-et 1 stamp, tramp, trample: **s- i jorda** stamp the ground; **s- mot brodden** knock one's head against the wall, (*bibl.* kick against the pricks); **s- seg fram** trudge. 2 beat, crush, pound: **s- graut** stir porridge. 3 full, mill (e.g. cloth). 4 *naut.* pitch, plunge, pound: **s- av gårde** (also train) chug away.
stam'pe[3] *V* -a/+-et hock, pawn.
stam'pe/jo'rd -a packed earth.
stam'pe/melding -a/+-en sacrifice bid (bridge).
stam'pe/sjø -en *naut.* head sea.
stam'pe/verk -et stamper, stamp mill.
stam'/tavle -a family tree, genealogical table, pedigree.
stam'/tre -et, *pl* -/+-trær family tree.
stan'd[1] *en* 1 condition, order, state: **i s-** in (working) order, ready; **i god s-** in fine shape; **i s- til å** capable of, in a position to; **ute av s- til å** incapable of, in no position to; **bringe, få i s-** bring about, effect; **gjøre i s-** put in order, repair; **holde i s-** keep in order, in a state of repair; **komme i s-** get in order, repair; come about, be arranged; **se seg i s- til å** find oneself able to, see one's way to; **sette i s-** put in order, repair; **sette i s- til å** enable to, put in a position to. 2 position; (of a barometer) level, reading: **holde s-** hold one's own (**mot** against), not retreat. 3 (of dog) point; (of hunter) station. 4 *archaic*: **på s-** instantly.
stan'd[2] -en/*-et, *pl* +stender/*- 1 (social) class, group; profession; social status; station (in life): **av s-** of quality, noble; **(gifte seg) under sin s-** (marry) beneath oneself. 2 *hist.* estate (of the realm): **den tredje s-** the Third Estate.
stan'd[3] -en (exbihition) stand.
stan'dard -en standard.
stan'dard/forma't -et standard size (e.g. of a book).
standardise're *V* -te standardize.
stan'dard/meto'de -n standard method.
stan'dard/mål -et standard measure.
+**stan'dard/utgave** -a/-en (=***/utgåve**) standard edition.
stan'dard/verk -et standard work.
standa'rt -en banner, standard.
***stan'de** *V* stend, stod, stade/-i cf **stå**[2]
+**stan'der** -en, *pl* -e (=***-ar**) 1 standard, upright post; *naut.* stanchion. 2 bore hole (e.g. for dynamite). 3 *naut.* pennant.
stan'd/fugl -en non-migratory bird.

+ Bokmål; * Nynorsk; ° Dialect.
After letter: ' stress (Acc. 1); ' tone, stress (Acc. 2); · length.
Below letter: . not pronounced.

+standhaf'tig *A* - resolute, steadfast, unflinching; persevering.
+standhaf'tig/het *-en* resolution, steadfastness; perseverance.
stan'd/kvarte'r *-et mil.* base of operations, headquarters.
stan'd/punkt *-et, pl -/-er* 1 point, position; level, standard. 2 attitude, point of view, standpoint: **innta et s-** take (up) a position; **ta s- til** decide on, make up one's mind about.
stan'dpunkt/karakte'r *-en* mark based on classwork (given e.g. in *gymnasium* before *artium* examination).
stan'd/rett *-en* court-martial; military court.
stan'ds/fordom [/fårdåmm]*-men* class prejudice.
+stan'ds/forskjell' *-en* class distinction.
***stan'ds/høveleg** *A* - elegant, high-class.
+stan'ds/messig *A* - elegant, high-class.
stan'ds/perso'n *-en archaic* person of rank; of quality.
sta'ne *V -a/-te dial.* halt, stop.
+stang' *-a, pl stenger* (=***stong**) 1 bar, pole, rod; lever, staff, stick; shaft: **på halv s-** at half mast; **holde en s-en** be a match for sby, hold one's own against sby. 2 (of gold, silver) bar, ingot. 3 *naut.* topmast. 4 bow, side, temple (of glasses).
Stang'a/land *Pln* twp, Rogaland.
stang'e *V -a/+-et* butt, gore, toss: **s- hornene av seg** sow one's wild oats.
Stang'e *Pln* twp, Hedmark.
+stang'/fiske [also stang'/] *-t* fishing rod.
+stang'/fisker *-en, pl -e* angler.
+stang'/jern [/jæ'rn] *-et* bar iron.
+stang'/lorgnett' [/lårnj-] *-en* lorgnette.
+stang'/selleri *-en bot.* celery (Apium graveolens).
+stang'/såpe *-a* bar soap.
Stang'/vik *Pln* twp, Møre og Romsdal.
stang'/vis *A - dial.* (of bulls, goats, etc.) butting, enraged.
stan'k[1] *-en* stench, stink (**av** of).
***stan'k[2]** *-et* groan, moan.
***stan'ke** *V -a* groan, moan.
+stan'kel/bein *-en zool.* crane fly, daddy longlegs, tipula (family Tipulidae).
stannio'l *-et* tin foil.
stan's *-en* break, halt, pause: **uten s-** continuously, steadily.
stan'se[1] *-n* stamper, stamping machine.
stan'se[2] *V -a/+et/+-te* 1 come to a halt, stop: **s- lenge** stay a long time; **s- (helt) opp** come to a (dead) stop; **s- ved** stop at; dwell upon. 2 check, halt, stop: **s- driften** discontinue operations, stop work; **s- blødningen** staunch the flow of blood; **s- i veksten** stunt.
stan'se[3] *V -a/+-et*: **s- ut** punch, stamp.
stan'se/maski'n *-en* punch, punch press.
sta'pel *-elen, pl -ler* 1 (separate) bell tower (near church). 2 foundation under a church spire. *****3 pile, stack. 4 (short for **s-plass**).
sta'pel/plass *-en hist.* emporium, trade center (Middle Ages).
sta'pel/vare *-a/+-en* staple (commodity).
***stap'le** *V -a* 1 pile, stack (up). 2 fumble: **s- på orda** grope for words.
stap'pa *A* - crammed, stuffed.
stap'pe[1] *-a* 1 dish of mashed vegetables (esp. potatoes). 2 crushed ice (in sea).
stap'pe[2] *V -a/+-et* 1 crush, mash. 2 cram, fill, stuff: **s- noe i munnen** pop sth in one's mouth.
stap'pende *Av*: **s- full** crammed full.
stapp'/full *A* chock-full, crammed full.
stapp'/mett *A* - crammed full (of food).
sta'r[1] *-en* (=**+stær[1]**) *zool.* starling (Sturnus vulgaris).
***sta'r[2]** *-en* cf **stær[2]**
***sta'r[3]** *-et* 1 gazing, staring; glance, look. 2 iris (of eye).
sta'r/blind *A* purblind.
sta're[1] *-n* cf **star[1]**
***sta're[2]** *V -a* gaze, stare.
+starr' *-en* cf **storr**
sta'rt *-en* start; take-off.
sta'rt/bane *-n* airstrip, runway (for take-off).
sta'rte *V -a/+-et* start; take off (e.g. an airplane): **s- egen forretning** open a business.
+sta'rter *-en, pl -e* (=***-ar**) 1 starter. 2 self-starter.
sta'rt/grop *-a* starting hole.
sta'rt/kapita'l *-en* initial capital.
sta'rt/klar *A* ready to start.
sta'rt/linje *-a/+-en* (=***/line**) starting line.
sta'rt/motor *-en* starter.
sta'rt/nummer] [/nom-] *-et, pl -/+-numre* start number (in skiing, cross-country races, etc.).
sta'rt/pisto'l *-en* starter's pistol.
sta'rt/skott *-et* (=**+/skudd**) starting shot.
star'v *-et dial.* effort, toil.
star've *V -a/+-et dial.* drudge, toil: **s- av** die, perish.
sta's *-en* 1 finery, Sunday best: **i full s-** all dressed-up; **til s-** for dress. 2 decoration, embellishment: **bare til s-** only for show. 3 frills, gewgaws, trash: **s- for turister** trash for tourists; **hele s-en** the whole business, the whole mess. 4: **(gå, sitte, stå) på s-** be idle, on display, *(pop.)* all dressed up and no place to go. 5 celebration, festive occasion, party: **gjøre s- på** lionize, make a fuss over. 6 fun; festive mood; pleasure: **det er ingen s-** it's no fun (of no special value); **det er ingen s- ved ham** he's nothing to write home about.
sta's/drakt *-a/+-en* dress clothes; *(pop.)* one's best bib and tucker.
sta'se *V -a/+-et/+-te*: **s- opp, til, ut** deck out, dress up, rig out.
sta'selig *A* - fine, handsome, stately; magnificent.
stasjo'n *-en* depot, station: **følge en på s-en** see sby off.
stasjone're *V -te* station.
stasjo'ns/by *-en* village grown up around RR station.
stasjo'ns/bygning *-en* (RR) depot, station.
+stasjo'ns/mester *-en, pl -e* (=***/meister**) station master.
stasjo'ns/sjef *-en* airport manager; station manager (at airport).
stasjo'ns/vogn [/vångn] *-a* 1 boxcar (used within the confines of a station). 2 station wagon.
stasjonæ'r *A* stationary.
sta's/kar *-en* 1 elegantly dressed person, swell. 2 fine man, *(pop.)* swell guy.
sta's/kjole *-n* party dress.
+sta's/klær *pl* (=***/klede**) Sunday best.
sta's/stue *-a* (=**/stove**) parlor.
sta't *-en* state: **s-en** (also) the government; **De forente s-er** the United States; **en s- i s-en** a state within the state; **i s-ens tjeneste** in the government service; **s- og kommune** state and local authorities.
stata'risk *A* -: **s- lesning, pensum** reading assigned for thorough study or memorization.
sta'telig *A* - dignified, imposing, stately.
Stathel'le *Pln* twp, Telemark.
statikk' *-en* statics.
sta'tisk *A* - static: **s- sans** sense of balance.
statis't *-en* (film) extra; (theater) supernumerary, walk-on.
statisteri' *-et* group of supernumeraries, walk-ons (theater).
+statis'tiker *-en, pl -e* (=***-ar**) statistician.
statistikk' *-en* statistics.
statis'tisk *A* - statistical.
statis't/rolle *-a/+-en* walk-on part (films, theater).
stati'v *-et, pl -/+-er* (hat) rack; (flower, umbrella) stand; (camera) tripod; post (in high jumping).
sta'tlig *A* - government(al).
sta'tor *-en elec.* stator.
sta'ts/advoka't *-en* district attorney, prosecuting attorney, public prosecutor.
sta'ts/akt *-a/+-en* official ceremony; *(pl)* state papers.
sta'ts/autorise'rt *A* - certified: **en s-revisor** a c- public accountant.
sta'ts/bane *-n* national railway: **Norges S-r** Norwegian State Railways.
sta'ts/bank *-en* national bank.
sta'ts/bankerott' *-en* bankruptcy of the government.
+sta'ts/bi'drag *-et* government grant, subsidy.
+sta'ts/borger *-en, pl -e* (=***-ar**) citizen, national, subject.
+sta'tsborger/brev *-et* citizenship, naturalization papers.
+sta'ts/borgerlig *A* - civil (e.g. rights).
sta'ts/budsjett' *-et* national budget.
+sta'ts/dannelse *-n* form(ation) of government, polity.
+sta'ts/drevet *A* - state-operated.
sta'ts/drift *-a/+-en* state control, ownership.
+sta'ts/eiendom *-men* government property.
sta'ts/embetsmann *-en, pl -menn/*-menner* government official.
sta'ts/fengsel *-elet/-let, pl +-ler/*-el* national penitentiary, prison.
sta'ts/fiende *-n* enemy of the state.
sta'ts/flagg *-et* national flag.
+sta'ts/forfat'ning *-en* constitution.
sta'ts/funksjonæ'r *-en* civil servant, government worker.
sta'ts/gjeld *-a/+-en* public debt.
sta'ts/handling *-a/+-en* official act.
+sta'ts/hemmelighet *-en* state secret.
sta'ts/institusjo'n *-en* government institution.
sta'ts/kalen'der *-eren, pl -rer/+-ere* government yearbook (listing officials etc.).
sta'ts/kasse *-a/-en* national treasury.
+sta'ts/kirke *-a/-en* established church, state church.
sta'ts/konsulen't *-en* government advisor, consultant.
sta'ts/kontroll' *-en* government control.
sta'ts/kupp *-et* coup d'état.
sta'ts/laus *A* (=**+/løs**) stateless.
sta'ts/lære *-a/+-en* 1 theory of the state. 2 political science.
+sta'ts/løs *A* cf **/laus**
sta'ts/lån *-et* goverment loan.
sta'ts/makt *-a/+-en* 1 government authority. 2 the executive, legislative, judicial divisions of the government: **s-ene** the government; **den fjerde s-** the fourth estate (the press).
sta'ts/mann *-en, pl -menn/*-menner* statesman.
sta'tsmanns/kunst *-en* statecraft; statesmanship.
sta'ts/maskineri' *-et* machinery of government.
+sta'ts/midler *pl* (=***-ar**) government funds.
sta'ts/minis'ter *-eren, pl -rer/+-ere* prime minister.
sta'ts/obligasjo'n *-en* government bond.
sta'ts/ordning *-a/+-en* political system.
sta'ts/papi'r *-et, pl -/+-er* government bond.
sta'ts/pensjonis't [-pang-] *-en* government pensioner.
sta'ts/politi' *-et* government police.
+sta'ts/regnskap [/reinskap] *-et* (=***/rekneskap**) national budget.
sta'ts/religio'n *-en* established religion, state religion.
sta'ts/rett *-en* 1 constitutional law. 2 international law.

sta'ts/rettslig *A* - constitutional.
sta'ts/revisjo'n *-en* general accounting office.
sta'ts/råd[1] *-en* cabinet minister.
sta'ts/råd[2] *-et* cabinet meeting (presided over by King).
sta'ts/sekretæ'r *-en* 1 *hist.* secretary of state. 2 (since 1947 in Norway) undersecretary.
sta'ts/sjef *-en* head of state.
sta'ts/skatt *-en* government tax.
sta'ts/stipen'd *-et, pl* - government scholarship, stipend.
sta'ts/stipendia't *-en* government scholar.
sta'ts/styre *-t* 1 administration of the state. 2 government authority.
+**sta'ts/støtte** *-a/-en* government aid.
sta'ts/tilskott *-et* government aid, grant, subsidy.
+**sta'ts/tjeneste** *-n* government service.
+**sta'ts/tjenestemann** *-en, pl -menn* civil servant, government employee.
statsv. = **statsvit(en)skap(elig)** pertaining to political science.
sta'ts/vitskap *-en* (=+**/vitenskap**) political science.
sta'ts/vitska'pelig *-en* (=+**/vitenskapelig**) of or pertaining to political science.
sta'ts/økono'm *-en* political economist.
sta'ts/økonomi' *-en* political economy.
+**statt'/holder** [also statt'/] *-en, pl -e* (=***/haldar**) governor, viceregent.
sta'tue *-n* statue (**av** of).
statue're *V -te*: **s- et eksempel på en** make an example of sby.
statuett' *-en* statuette.
statu'r *-en* stature.
sta'tus *-en* 1 status. 2 *merc.* annual statement (of net worth), balance sheet.
+**sta'tus/oppgjør** *-et merc.* annual statement (of net worth), balance sheet.
sta'tus/oversikt [/åver-] **-a/*+*-en merc.* balance sheet.
statutt' *-en/*+*-et, pl -er* statute.
stau'de -n *hort.* perennial.
stau'de/bed' *-et hort.* bed, border of perennials.
***stau'k** *-en* elderly, clumsy person.
***stau'ke** *V -a/-et* 1 walk unsteadily (with the aid of a cane). 2 halt, stammer.
stau'p[1] *-et* 1 beaker, goblet. 2 chuck hole.
***stau'p**[2] *pt of* **stupe**
stau'pet(e) *A* - bumpy, full of holes.
stau'r *-en* 1 pole, stake. 2 bungler; bumpkin, lout.
stau're *V -a/*+*-et* 1 place (grain sheaves) on stakes (for drying). 2 *dial.* ram (stake, stick) into (ground); pound with stick. 3 *dial.* stumble, totter.
stau'ret(e) *A* - awkward, clumsy.
stau'r/hyrning *-en* (=**/henning, /hynning**) *zool.* grampus, killer whale (Orcinus orca).
stau'r/lag *-et* 1 pair of pickets in a rail fence connected with a willow band. 2 section of rail fence between two such pickets. 3 unit of four oblique pickets in a rail fence.
stau't[1] *-en/-et* (cotton) sheeting, long-cloth.
stau't[2] *A* +*-/***-t* 1 healthy, hefty, strapping. 2 capital, excellent, first-rate.
sta'v *-en* 1 staff, stick: **bryte s-en over en** condemn, denounce sby; **gå med s-** use a cane; **ta s-en i hånd** take to the road (often = go begging). 2 pole, ski pole; pole-vault. 3 stave (in wooden vessel, runic letters, stave churches): **falle i s-er** fall apart; usu. *fig.* be overcome with amazement, be lost in thought. 4 stripe (in cloth). 5 rod (in eye); bacillus.
Stavang'er *Pln* seaport, Rogaland county.
sta'v/bakte'rie *-n* bacillus.
sta've *V -a/*+*-et* 1 spell: **s- og legge sammen** put two and two together. 2 stumble, totter (=**stavre**). 3: **s- seg** push with one's poles (as in skiing).
sta've/bok *-a, pl -bøker* speller.
+**sta'velse** *-n* cf **staving**
sta've/måte *-n* spelling (**på** of).
Sta'vern [-værn] *Pln* town, Vestfold.
sta'vet(e) *A* - striped (e.g. sail).
sta'v/hopp *-et* pole vault.
sta'ving *-a/*+*-en* 1 syllable (=+**stavelse**). 2 spelling.
+**sta'v/kar** *-en archaic* (=**stakkar**) beggar.
+**sta'v/kirke** *-a/-en* (=***/kyrkje**) stave church.
sta'v/laus *A* without a cane; brisk.
sta'v/lykt *-a* (cylindrical) flashlight.
sta'v/magnet [/mangne't] *-et* bar magnet.
+**stav'n** *-en* cf **stamn**
+**stav'ns/bunden** *A -et, pl -ne hist.* adscript, bound to the soil.
+**stav'ns/bånd** *-et hist.* adscription, serfdom.
+**stav're** *V -a/-et* stump (along), toddle, walk stiffly.
sta'v/rim *-et* alliteration.
sta'v/sprang *-et* pole vault, pole vaulting.
sta'/væring *-en* person from Stadsbygd.
std. = **standard**
ste'[1] *-et* anvil.
ste'[2] *V -dde* (=**stede**[2]) 1 *archaic* bury: **s- i jorden, til hvile** lay to rest. 2 *lit.* **stedes** be placed (e.g. in danger). 3 employ, hire: **s- seg** hire out. 4 straighten, tidy up (e.g. a room).
steari'n *-en* stearin; paraffin wax.
steari'n/lys *-et* (paraffin wax) candle.
ste'/ba'rn *-et, pl -/***-born* stepchild: **samfunnets s-** stepchildren of society; the underprivileged.
+**ste'd** *-et, pl -er* place; spot; locality, location; passage (in book): **alle s-er** everywhere; **et s-** someplace, somewhere (**det er her et s-** it's here somewhere); **ikke noe s-** nowhere; +**i s-** a little while ago; **i ditt s-** in your position, shoes; **i s-et for** instead of; **på s-et** on the spot, immediately; **på s-et hvil** at ease; **på sine s-er** in places, in spots; **dra, komme av s-** leave; **finne s-** occur, take place; **ikke komme av s-et** make no headway, progress; **ta i barns s-** adopt; **være en i fars s-** be like a father to sby.
+**ste'/datter** *-a/-en, pl -døtre(r)* stepdaughter.
stedd' *A* - (=+**stedt**, ***stadd**): **ille s-** in a bad way.
+**ste'de**[1] *N*: **til s-** present; **komme til s-** arrive, show up.
ste'de[2] *V -de* cf **ste**[2]
+**ste'd/egen** *A -ent, pl -ne* indigenous, local.
+**ste'der** *pl of* **stad**[1]
+**ste'd/feste** *V -a/-et* localize, locate.
+**ste'd/finnende** *A* - existing, prevailing, taking place.
+**ste'd/fortre'dende** *A* - deputy.
+**ste'd/fortre'der** *-en, pl -e* deputy, lieutenant, substitute.
+**ste'd/funnen** *A -funnet, pl -funne* having (recently) occurred.
+**ste'dig** *A* - bullheaded, obstinate, stubborn.
+**ste'dig/het** *-en* bullheadedness, obstinacy, stubbornness.
+**ste'd/kjent** *A* - (person) acquainted with (a locality).
+**ste'dlig** *A* - (=***stadleg**) local.
+**ste'd/o'rd** *-et gram.* pronoun.
+**ste'ds/angi'velse** *-n* information as to location; reference (in a book).
+**ste'd/sans** *-en* sense of locality, orientation.
+**stedse** [stet'se] *Av* cf **stetse**
+**ste'ds/navn** *-et* place name.
+**ste'ds/tillegg** *-et* living allowance (e.g. in overseas employment).
+**stedt'** *A* - cf **stedd**
ste'/far *-en* stepfather.
Stef'fen *Prn (m)* Stephen.
ste'g[1] *-et* 1 step, stride; hop. 2 (of a stair) step; (of a ladder) rung.
+**ste'g**[2] *pt of* **stige**[2]
ste'ge *V -a/*+*-et* stride.
+**ste'get** *pp of* **stige**[2]
stegg' *-en, pl* **-er* 1 cock, male bird. *2 repulsion; frightening, repulsive creature.
***stegg'leg** *A* - frightful, hideous, ugly.
***steg'l** *-et* cf **steile**[1]
***steg'le**[1] *-a* fishing line.
steg'le[2] *V -a/*+*-et* 1 *hist.* break on a wheel. *2 rear (=**steile**).
stei'g pt of **stige**[2]
Stei'gen *Pln* twp, Nordland.
stei'k[1] *-a* roast: **en fet s-** a fat prize; **vil du være med på leken, får du også smake steken** you have to take the bitter with the sweet; **rar som s-** queer, unique.
stei'k[2] *-en* heating, roasting.
+**stei'ke** *V -te* (=***-je**) roast: **s- i en panne** fry; **s- i ovn (sol)** bake; **s- på rist** broil, grill; **fanden s-** (oath); **s-ende** (see below).
+**stei'ke/fisk** *-en* fish for panfrying.
stei'kende *Av*: **s- varmt** scorching hot; **s- sint** furious, raving.
+**stei'ke/ovn** *-en* (baking) oven.
+**stei'ke/panne** *-a* frying pan.
+**stei'ke/plate** *-a* baking sheet.
+**stei'ke/spidd** *-et* spit.
stei'k/heit *A* broiling, scorching hot, sweltering.
***stei'kje** *V -te* cf **steike**
***stei'kje/fisk** *-en* cf **steike/**
***stei'kje/omn** *-en* cf **steike/ovn**
***stei'kje/panne** *-a* cf **steike/**
+**stei'l** *A* 1 steep; abrupt, precipitous, sheer. 2 stiff-necked, uncompromising, unyielding.
+**stei'le**[1] *-n* (=***stegl**) *hist.* stake on which wheel was placed for breaking bodies of criminals: **dømt til s- og hjul** sentenced to be broken on the wheel.
+**stei'le**[2] *V -et/-te* rear (e.g. a horse); *fig.* bridle, take umbrage (**over** at).
+**stei'l/skrift** *-a/-en* backhand (writing).
stei'n *-en* rock, stone; boulder; (in fruit) pit, seed, stone; testicle; (precious) stone (=**edel/s-**): **det falt en s- fra mitt hjerte** I was greatly relieved; it was a load off my mind; **legge s- til byrden** add to one's burden; **sove som en s-** sleep like a log; **rund s-** pebble; **gi s-er for brød** give stones for bread (Luke 11,11).
Stei'n *Prn (m)*
+**stei'n/aktig** *A* - stony; *fig.* expressionless, unfeeling.
stei'n/alder *-eren, pl -rer archeol.* Stone Age: **eldre s-** the Paleolithic; **yngre s-** the Neolithic.
Stei'nar *Prn(m)*
stei'n/art *-a/-en geol.* kind, variety of rock.
stei'n/ask *-en bot.* European ash (Fraxinus excelsior).
stei'n/bit *-en zool.* lumpfish, lumpsucker (Cyclopterus lumpus).
stei'n/blind *A* stone-blind, blind as a bat.
stei'n/blokk *-en* block of stone; boulder.
stei'n/botn *-en* (=+**/bunn**) rocky, stony bottom (e.g. of a lake).
stei'n/brott *-et* (=+**/brudd**) stone quarry.
stei'n/bru *-a* stone (masonry) bridge.
+**stei'n/brudd** *-et* cf **/brott**
+**stei'n/bryter** *-en, pl -e* (=***-ar**) 1 quarryman, quarry worker. 2 construction worker (on highways, roads).
stei'n/bu *-a* stone cabin, hut.
stei'n/bukk [/bokk] *-en zool.* Alpine ibex (Capra ibex); **S-en** Capricorn;

+ Bokmål; * Nynorsk; ° Dialect.
After letter: ' stress (Acc. 1); ` tone, stress (Acc. 2); · length.
Below letter: . not pronounced.

S-ens vendekrets Tropic of Capricorn.

+stei'n/bunn *-en* cf **/botn**

stei'n/daud *A* cf **/død**

stei'n/dolp *-en zool.* wheatear (Oenanthe oenanthe).

stei'n/død *A* (=**/daud**) stone-dead; *(pop.)* dead as a doornail.

stei'n/døv *A* stone-deaf.

stei'ne *V -a/+-et* 1 stone (e.g. sby to death): **s- med sitt blikk** look daggers at; **s- ned** cover with stones (in a cache). 2 polish with stone.

stei'n/eik *-a bot.* holly oak, holm oak (Quercus ilex).

stei'nende *Av*: **s- hard** hard as rock.

stei'net(e) *A* - rocky, stony; *fig.* expressionless, unfeeling.

stei'n/flis *-a* flagstone; (stone) tile.

stei'n/fri *A -tt* 1 (of ground) free of stones. 2 (of fruit) seedless, stoneless; pitted, stoned.

stei'n/frukt *-a/+-en bot.* stone fruit; drupe.

stei'n/ga'rd *-en* stone fence, stone wall.

***stei'n/gjengen** *A -e/-i, pl -ne* cf **/gått**

stei'n/gods [/gots] *-et* earthenware, faience.

stei'n/grunn *-en* stony soil; *(bibl.)* stony places (Matthew 13,5).

stei'n/gått *A* - fossilized, petrified.

***stei'n/haldig** *A* - cf **/holdig**

stei'n/ha'rd *A* hard as stone, stony; *fig.* adamant, hard-hearted.

stei'n/helle *-a* 1 flat stone, slab of rock. 2 doorstep; flagstone.

+stei'n/hjerte *-t* (=***/hjarte**) heart of stone.

+stei'n/hogger *-en, pl -e* (=***-ar**) stonecutter, stonemason.

+stei'n/holdig *A* - (=***/haldig**) rocky, stony (ground).

stei'n/kast *-et* throw with a stone; stone's throw.

+stei'n/kaster *-en, pl -e* (=***-ar**) catapult, sling.

stei'n/kiste *-a* sarcophagus.

Stei'n/kjer' *Pln* seaport, Nord-Trøndelag.

stei'n/kledd *A -/*-kledt* stone covered (terrain).

stei'n/kløver *-en bot.* melilot (genus Melilotus).

stei'n/kol [/kål] *-et* (=**+/kull**) anthracite (coal).

stei'nkol/tjære [-kål/kjære] *-a* coal tar.

+stei'n/kull *-et* cf **/kol**

stei'n/la *pt of* **-legge, leggje**

+stei'n/lagt *A* - (=***/lagd**) paved.

stei'n/laus *A* (of ground) free of stones; (of fruit) stoneless, seedless.

+stei'n/legge *V -la, -lagt* (=***-je**) pave.

stei'n/lendt *A* - rocky, stony (terrain).

stei'n/mark *-a* rocky, stony field, terrain.

stei'n/mjøl *-et* stone dust.

+stei'n/pukker [/pokker] *-en, pl -e* (=***-ar**) rock crusher (esp. in road construction).

stei'n/purke *-a zool.* ruff (Acerina cernua).

stei'n/ras *-et* rockslide.

stei'n/rik *A* 1 (of terrain) rocky, stony. 2 affluent; wealthy.

stei'n/røys *-a* cairn; rock-covered slope.

+stei'n/satt *A* - 1 brick, stone lined, paved. 2 weighted (with stones).

+stei'n/setning *-en* 1 (stone) paving. 2 *archeol.* cromlech.

+stei'n/sette *V -satte* (=***/setje**) 1 line with brick, stone; pave. 2 weight (with stones).

stei'n/skred *-et* avalanche, rockslide.

stei'n/skvett *-en zool.* wheatear (Oenanthe oenanthe).

stei'n/sopp *-en bot.* edible mushroom (Boletus edulis); cep(e), flap-mushroom.

stei'n/sprang *-et* loosening, sliding of rock (on a steep hillside).

+stei'n/støtte *-a/-en* stone statue.

stei'n/tavle *-a* stone tablet.

stei'n/trapp *-a* flight of stone steps.

stei'n/trykk *-et* 1 lithograph. 2 lithography.

+stei'n/tøy *-et* (=***/ty**) crockery, earthenware, stoneware.

stei'n/vegg *-en* stone wall; rocky precipice.

stei'n/ørken *-enen, pl -(e)ner* wasteland of stone.

+ste'k[1] *-a/-en* cf **steik[1]**

+ste'k[2] *-en* cf **steik[2]**

+ste'ke *V -te* cf **steike**

***ste'kke[1]** *-t* enclosure in a barn.

+stek'ke[2] *V -et/-te* clip (e.g. bird's wings); *fig.* check, restrain: **s- vingene på en** curb sby.

***stekkj'e[1]** *-a* stack (e.g. of fodder).

***stekkj'e[2]** *V stekte* stack (up).

***ste'lar** *-en* cf **stjeler**

ste'le *V stal, +stålet/*stole/*-i* (=**+stjele**) 1 steal; deprive of. 2: **s- seg** slip, sneak (away); **s- seg til (noe)** do (sth) on the sly; gain (sth) by stealth.

stell' *-et* 1 care(s), chores, work: **husets s-** housework. 2 administration, management: **landets styr(e) og stell** the administration (public affairs) of the country. 3 order, system: **få s- på tingene** get things in order; **jo, det er s-!** *hum.* that's a fine mess! **det er dårlig (smått) s- med (noe, noen)** (sby, sth) is in a bad way; **få et annet s- på tingene** reorganize things, put them back on their feet. 4: **på s-** crazy, out of one's mind. 5 service, set; gear: **hele s-et** the whole business.

stel'le[1] *-t dial.* place, spot.

stel'le[2] *V stelte* 1 care for, look after, take care of (chores, housework); tend: **s- for en** (also=) keep house for sby; **s- med (om)** care for, tend; look after, work with. 2 arrange; fix (meals): **s- (med) på** fix, repair; **s- det slik at** fix it so that; **s- til** arrange, make, fix up; prepare; **s- til bråk** stir up trouble. 3: **s- seg** fix oneself up, get ready; **s- seg i stand til** get ready for; **s- seg (galt, godt** etc.**)** get oneself into a (bad, good) situation (a fix, a mess); **s- seg selv** do one's own housekeeping.

stel'le/bo'rd *-et* table used in washing and dressing a baby; cf bathinette.

stel'le/tid *-a/+-en* baby's bath time; chore time.

stel'ling *-a* 1 care, tending. 2 *hist.* tending of a neighbor's stock in return for goods and services. 3 scaffold(ing).

***stel'p** *-et* hindrance, obstacle: **meir s- enn hjelp** more hindrance than help.

***stel'pe** *V -te* hinder, obstruct.

stem' *-men* 1 dam, embankment. 2 sluice gate. 3 pond, pool, reservoir.

+stem'/jern [/jæ'rn] *-et* chisel.

stem'me[1] *+-n/*-a* 1 voice: **med høy s-** in a loud v-. 2 *mus.* part, voice; (organ) stop. 3 vote: **avgi sin s-** vote, cast one's vote.

+stem'me[2] *V stemte* 1 vote (**for, på** for). 2 tune (a musical instrument). 3 dispose, put in a given mood (cf also **stemt 3**). 4 agree, be correct; tally: **få til å s-** make come out right, tally (e.g. of balancesheet); **det s-er** that's right; *(pop.)* check, that checks: **det s-er med det jeg har hørt** that agrees with what I've heard. 5 (with *prep., adv.*): **s- i** begin to sing, break into song, strike up (instrumental music); chime in, join in singing; **s- opp** break into song (etc.); **s- overens** agree, be in agreement; **s- ned** tone down, moderate.

stem'me[3] *V +stemte/*stemde* 1 block, stem, stop (esp. the flow of a liquid): **s- for** block, dam; **s- strømmen** stem the tide. 2 press, set, thrust: **s- føttene mot** brace one's feet against.

stem'me/band *-et* (=**+/bånd**) *anat.* vocal cord.

+stem'me/beret'tiget *A* - entitled to vote.

stem'me/bruk *-en/-et* use of the voice, voice production.

+stem'me/bånd *-et* cf **/band**

stem'me/føring *-a/+-en mus.* voice production.

stem'me/gaffel *-elen, pl -gafler mus.* tuning fork.

+stem'me/gi'v(n)ing *-en* voting.

+stem'me/høyde *-n mus.* pitch.

+stem'me/krets *-en* voting district.

+stem'me/kveg *-et derog.* ignorant, stupid voters (who vote as they are told).

stem'me/laus *A* (=**+/løs**) 1 mute. 2 (of sounds) voiceless.

stem'me/leie *-t mus.* (vocal) register.

+stem'me/likhet *-en* tie vote.

stem'me/lyd *-en* voiced sound.

+stem'me/midler *pl mus.* singing voice.

***stem'me/nål** *-a* darning needle.

stem'me/prakt *-a/+-en* magnificent voice.

+stem'mer *-en, pl -e* (=***-ar**) tuner.

stem'me/rett *-en* franchise: **alminnelig s-** universal suffrage.

stem'meretts/alder *-en* voting age.

+stem'me/seddel *-en, pl -sedler* ballot.

stem'me/skifte *-t*: **han er i s-t** his voice is changing.

stem'me/tal *-et* (=**+/tall**) number of votes.

+stem'me/teller *-en, pl -e* election board clerk.

stem'me/u'rne *-a/+-en* ballot box.

stem'ne[1] *-a/+-et* (=**+stevne[1]**) 1 convention, meeting, rally: **sette en s-** make an appointment (tryst) with sby. 2 *hist.* council (meeting); fair.

stem'ne[2] *V -a/+-et/+-te/*-de* (=**+stevne[2]**) 1 head, steer (**mot** for): **hold fram som du s-er** keep going as you have started. 2 *jur.* serve sby with a summons, subpoena sby: **s- for retten** have the law on sby. 3 *hist.* call a (council) meeting, summon.

***stem'ne/lei** *-a* course, direction.

stem'ne/møte *-t* cf **+stevne/**

stem'ne/vitne *-t, pl +-r/*- jur.* bailiff.

stem'ning[1] *-a/+-en* (=**+stevning**) 1 *jur.* writ. 2 *jur.* subpoena, petition, summons: **forkynne s- for motparten** serve the defendant with a summons.

stem'ning[2] *-en* 1 tuning (up) (**av** of). 2 atmosphere, feeling; frame of mind; humor, mood, spirit(s); animation, enthusiasm: **i s- til å** in a mood to; **komme, være i (høy) s-** get, be in high spirits. 3 (popular) opinion, sentiment: **vinne s- for seg** gain (popular) support.

+stem'nings/beto'nt *A* - emotional, sentimental.

stem'nings/bølgje *-a* (=**+/bølge**) wave of (public) sentiment.

stem'nings/full *A* moving; lyrical, poetic.

stem'nings/fylt *A* - emotional; lyrical, poetic.

stem'nings/menneske *-t, pl +-r/*-* emotional, impulsive person.

+stem'nings/utbrudd *-et* (=**/utbrott**) outburst of emotion, feeling.

+ste'/moderlig *A* - unfair, unjust: **bli s- behandlet** be treated unfairly.

ste'/mor *-a/+-en, pl -mødrer/+-mødre* stepmother.

+ste'mors/blomst *-en* (=***/blom**) *bot.* pansy (Viola tricolor).

stem'pel *+-(e)let/*-elen, pl -ler* 1 stamp (die, punch, ram, tool). 2 stamp (hallmark, mark, postmark): **geniets s-** the stamp of genius; **få s- på seg for å være** be branded, stigmatized as; **sette sitt s- på noe** leave one's mark on sth. 3 piston, plunger.

stem'pel/avgift *-a/+-en* excise tax, stamp tax.

stem'pel/farge *-n* ink (used for stamp pads).

stem'pel/merke *-t, pl* +*-r*/**-* revenue stamp.

stem'pel/papi'r *-et* paper bearing an official (usu. revenue) stamp.

+**stem'pelpapir/forval'ter** *-en, pl -e* (=***-ar**) (government) revenue service (in charge of excise taxes).

stem'pel/pliktig *A* - taxable, subject to stamp tax.

stem'pel/pute *-a* stamp pad.

+**stem'pel/stang** *-a, pl -stenger* piston rod.

stem'pel/sverte *-a* ink (used for stamp pads).

stem'ple *V -a*/+*-et* 1 stamp; brand; cancel (stamp): **s- en som** brand, stigmatize sby as. 2 shore up (e.g. sides of a ditch).

Stem's/haug *Pln* twp, Møre og Romsdal.

+**stem't** *A* - 1 (of sounds) voiced. 2 *mus.* in tune, tuned. 3 disposed: **(krigersk, vennlig osv.) s-** in a (martial, friendly, etc.) mood; **s- for** inclined to.

+**stem'te** *pl of* **stemme**[1,2]

+**ste'n** *-en* cf **stein**

***sten'd** *pr of* **stande**

+**sten'der**[1] *-en* pillar, post, support.

+**sten'der**[2] *pl of* **stand**[1]

+**sten'der/forsam'ling** *-a*/*-en hist.* legislative assembly (e.g. the French States-General prior to 1789).

sten'dig *A* - constant, steady: **støtt og s-** incessantly.

steng' *-et* seine; catch, seine-full.

***steng'e**[1] *-t* bar, barrier.

+**steng'e**[2] *V -te* (=***-je**) 1 bar, block; bolt, lock; close, shut: **alle utveier er s-t for oss** there's no way out for us; **s- av** shut, turn off; **s- døren for** lock the door to; **s- for** block out; **s- forretningen, sjappa** close, close down (a business); **s- inne** hem, shut in; **s- seg ute fra** cut oneself off from, close one's mind to; **s- ute** lock out. 2 seine (fish). 3 support with stakes (e.g. sweet peas).

steng'el *-elen, pl -ler bot.* stalk, stem.

steng'er *pl of* +**stang**/***stong**

+**steng'e/tid** *-a*/*-en* (of businesses, stores) closing time.

***steng'je** *V -de* cf **stenge**[2]

+**steng'sel** *-elet*/*-let, pl -ler* (=***stengsle**) bar, bolt; barrier (**for, mot** to, against), fence.

+**sten'k** *-et* drop, splash, spray; speck, spot; dash, touch, trace (**av** of): **kaste s- over navnet** give sby a bad name.

+**sten'ke** *V -et* splash, spatter; sprinkle, (**med** with); muddy, spot.

stenogra'f *-en* stenographer (e.g. in parliament).

stenogra'f/dame *-a*/+*-en* secretary, stenographer.

stenografe're *V -te* take down in shorthand.

stenografi' *-en* shorthand, stenography.

stenogra'fisk *A* - shorthand, stenographic.

stenogram' *-met, pl -*/+*-mer* shorthand note, report.

stensi'l *-en* stencil: **skrive en s-** cut a stencil.

stensile're *V -te* stencil; duplicate (by stencil).

sten'tor/røst *-a*/+*-en* (=***/røyst**) stentorian voice.

sten'tor/stemme +*-en*/**-a* stentorian voice.

step'pe[1] +*-n*/**-a* steppe.

step'pe[2] *V -a*/+*-et* tap dance.

+**step'per** *-en, pl -e* (=***-ar**) tap dancer.

stereofo'nisk *A* - stereophonic.

stereometri' *-en* stereometry.

stereome'trisk *A* - stereometric.

stereosko'p *-et* stereoscope.

stereoty'p *A* hackneyed, stereotyped.

stereotype're *V -te* stereotype.

stereotypi' *-en* stereotypy.

steri'l *A* 1 barren, sterile. 2 sterilized.

sterilisasjo'n *-en* sterilization.

sterilise're *V -te* 1 castrate, spay. 2 sterilize.

sterilite't *-en* 1 sterility. 2 sterilization.

ster'k *A* 1 powerful, strong; (of sound) loud: **det er ikke hans s-e side** it's not his strong point, forte; **s-e drikkevarer** strong drinks; **s- kulde, varme** intense cold, heat; **s-e nerver** nerves of steel; *(adv.)* **s-t fristet** sorely tempted; **s-t interessert** deeply interested. 2 durable, solid, sturdy: **den er dobbelt så s-** it has twice the wear in it.

ster'k/bygd *A -*/**-bygt* (of physique) solidly built, well built.

***ster'k/helsa** *A* - robust.

***ster'k/leik** *-en* force, strength.

ster'kne *V -a*/+*-et* grow stronger, strengthen.

+**ster'k/strøm'** *-men elec.* power current (for light, heat, power etc.) cf **svak/s-**.

+**ster'kstrøms/anlegg** *-et* power plant.

ster'kt *et* hard liquor.

+**ster'kt/virkende** *A* - efficacious, potent, powerful.

sterling [stø'rling] *-en* sterling: **pund s-** pound s-.

sterling/blokk *-a*/*-en* sterling area, bloc.

***ster're** *V -a*: **s- imot** resist.

***ster'ren** *A -e*/*-i, pl sterne* bullheaded, stubborn.

ster's *-en naut.* larder, pantry.

ster't *-en* cf **stjert**

***ster'te** *V -a*/*-e* 1 slave, toil: **eg s-a og bar** I struggled along with my load. 2 tighten the reins (on a horse).

+**ste'/sønn** *-en* (=***/son**) stepson.

stetosko'p *-et, pl -*/+*-er* stethoscope.

+**stet'se** *Av* always, constantly: **for s-** eternally, forever.

+**stet'se/varig** *A* - everlasting, perpetual.

***stett'**[1] *-a* doorsteps, stoop.

stett'[2] *-en* stem (of glass); feet (of pot).

stet'te[1] *-a* tub.

stet'te[2] *V -a*/+*-et* 1 help, serve; satisfy. 2 support (e.g. a demand).

stet'te/glas *-et* (=+**glass**) stemmed glass, goblet.

ste'v *-et* 1 *mus.* burden, chorus (of a song). 2 short, improvised (folk) verse, (usu. 4-line rhymed stanzas).

***stev'jar** *-en* singer (of **stev**).

***stev'jast** *V -ast* cf **stevjes**

stev'je *V -a*/+*-et* make **stev**; carry on a (dialogue) contest in the improvisation of **stev.**

+**stev'jes** *V* -as/-es (=***-ast**) (See **stevje**).

ste'v/kamp *-en* contest in making **stev.**

ste'v/leik *-en* contest in making **stev.**

+**stev'n** *-en naut.* bow, prow, stem; stern: **stikk i s-** dead ahead.

+**stev'ne**[1] *-t* cf **stemne**[1]

+**stev'ne**[2] *V -a*/*-et*/*-te* cf **stemne**[2]

+**stev'ne/møte** *-t* assignation, rendezvous; *poet.* tryst.

+**stev'ne/vitne** *-t* cf **stemne/**

+**stev'ning** *-a*/*-en* cf **stemning**[1]

steward [stju'erd] *-en* steward.

stewardess [stjuerdess'] *-a*/+*-en* stewardess.

S. tf. =**Særdeles tilfredsstillende**

Sth =**Stockholm**

+**sti'**[1] *-en* (=***stig**[1]) 1 path; footpath, trail, walk: **holde sin s- ren** keep to the strait and narrow (cf Psalms 119,9). 2 (pig) sty.

+**sti'**[2] *-en*/*-et* (=***stig**[2]) sty (on the eye).

***sti'**[3] *-et* (farm) chores.

***sti'e** *V -a* do the chores (livestock).

+**sti'/finner** *-en, pl -e* pathfinder.

stif't[1] *-en* 1 tack; (phonograph) needle; (wire) nail; tumbler (in lock); pin (in tooth). 2 slate pencil; lead (for pencils; cf **blyant/s-**). 3: **slå s-(en)** do a handspring.

stif't[2] *-et* 1 *hist.* diocese. 2 *hist.* (charitable) foundation, institution, esp. one for unmarried gentlewomen.

stif't/amtmann *-en, pl -menn*/**-menner hist.* prefect (=chief administrative officer having jurisdiction over an area corresponding to a diocese; in effect in Norway 1692—1918).

stif'te[1] *V -a*/+*-et* 1 establish, found: **s- bekjentskap med** become acquainted with; **s- en forening** form a society; **s- et fond** set up a fund; **s- fred** make peace; **s- gjeld** run up debts; **s- hjem** make a home. 2 instigate, stir up: **s- ufred** start a quarrel.

stif'te[2] *V -a*/+*-et* nail, tack; staple.

stif'te/appara't *-et* stapler.

+**stif'telse** *-n* (=***-ing**) 1 establishment, foundation, institution (**av** of). 2 charitable institute, philanthropic organization.

+**stif'ter** *-en, pl -e* (=***-ar**) creator, founder, originator (**av** of).

***stif'ting** *-a* cf **stiftelse**

stif'ts/ga'rd *-en* (=+**/gård**) *hist.* residence of a prefect: **S-en (i Trondheim)** now used as a royal residence.

stif'ts/prost [/prost] *-en hist.* archdeacon (in effect in Norway until 1922).

stif'ts/stad *-en* cathedral city.

stif't/tann *-a, pl -tenner* pivot tooth.

***sti'g**[1] *-en* cf **sti**[1]

***sti'g**[2] *-et* cf **sti**[2]

sti'g/brett *-et, pl -*/+*-er* running board (automobile); footboard, step (railroad car).

+**sti'g/bøyle** *-n* (=***/bøyel**) 1 stirrup. 2 *anat.* stapes (bone in ear).

sti'ge[1] *-n* 1 ladder; *fig.* social ladder. 2 ladder (gymnastics).

sti'ge[2] *V steig*/+*steg,* +*steget*/**stige*/**-i* 1 go, step, stride: **s- over et gjerde** step over a fence. 2 ascend, climb, rise (e.g. of thermometer): **veien s-er** the road is climbing. 3 *fig.* go up, grow, increase; rise: **prisene s-er** prices are rising. 4 (with *prep., adv.*): **s- av** get off (bus, train, etc.), dismount (a horse); **s- fram** emerge, loom out (of darkness, fog, etc.); be known, win renown; **s- ned** descend; **s- opp** ascend; **s- på** get on (bus, train, etc.), mount (a horse); **s- til hest** mount (a horse).

+**sti'ge/le'dning** *-en* riser (main conduit for electricity or water).

+**sti'ger** *-en, pl -e* (=***-ar**) 1 mine captain. 2 riser (=**stigeledning**).

***sti'gi** *pp of* **stige**[2]

***sti'ging** *-a* cf **stigning**

stigmatise're *V -te* stigmatize.

sti'gning +*-en*/**-a* (=***-ing**) ascent, rising; gradient, rise; increase (**i** of): **være i s-** be on the increase, be on the upgrade.

sti'gnings/forhold *-et* gradient.

+**sti'g/trinn** *-et* running board (automobile); footboard, step (railroad car).

***sti'ke** *V -a* stitch.

stikk'[1] *-et* 1 prick, stab; bite, sting (**av** of); pang, twinge. 2: **holde s-** hold good, hold water (e.g. a theory). 3 trick (cards). 4 *naut.* hitch. 5 engraving, print.

stikk'[2] *Av* diametrically, directly: **s- imot** in direct opposition to, in the teeth of; **s- i strid med** at variance with; *naut.* **s- i sta n** dead ahead.

stikk'/bekken *-et, pl -*/+*-er* bedpan.

stikk'/brev *-et* wan ed circular, poster: **sende ut s- etter en** circulate a lawbreaker's descri tion.

stik'ke[1] *-a* 1 peg, pin, stick: **kaste på s-a** toss pennies (at a line or object to see who can come closest). 2 vise (=**skru/s-**).

stik'ke[2] *V stakk,* +*stukket*/**stukke*/**-i* 1 prick, stab, stick; cut, pierce;

+ Bokmål; * Nynorsk; ° Dialect.
After letter: ' stress (Acc. 1); ' tone, stress (Acc. 2); · length.
Below letter: . not pronounced.

thrust (**etter** at): **s- hull på** prick, puncture. 2 put, stick, thrust; hand: **s- fingeren i jorda og lukte hvor en er** take stock of the situation, get the lie of the land; **s- hendene i lomma** put one's hands in one's pockets; **s- hodene sammen** put heads together; **s- ild (varme) på, s- *i* brann** set fire to; **når det stakk ham** when it struck him; ***det stikk gjennom henne** the thought strikes her (Vesaas); bite, sting (e.g. of insects); **det s-er i brystet** I have sharp pains in my chest; **s- i øynene** (of light) hurt one's eyes, blind, dazzle. 3 go (esp. of a sudden or temporary motion), run; come, go (to visit): **s- av, inn, ut** (see below). 4 engrave: **s- i kopper** do copper engraving. 5 embroider, stitch. 6 (in cards) cover, take: **stikk den!** (try to) top that! beat that if you can! 7 *naut.* let out (a line); (of ships) draw (water). 8 (with *prep., adv.*): **s- av (gårde)** run away, beat it; **s- av mot** contrast to, stand out against; **s- bort** hide, put away; **s- dypt** (of ships) draw much water, *fig.* be deep-seated; **det s-er ikke dypt** it's superficial; **s- fram** jut out; **s- i** be concealed in, be found in; **s- i å** (suddenly) start to; **s- innom, oppom** drop in (by, up); **s- en ned** knife, stab sby; **s- opp** project, stick out; **s- på kruset** drink from the mug, hit the bottle; **s- til seg** pocket; **s- til side** put aside; **s- til havs** put out to sea; **s- noe til en** give sth to sby on the sly; **s- under** be concealed (**det s-er noe under her** there's sth behind, at the bottom of this); **s- under stol(en)** conceal, suppress; **s- ut** lay out, plot; *naut.* let out (a line); drink down, empty (a glass), toss off; depart, leave; **s- en ut** defeat, eliminate sby from competition. 9 *(refl.)*: **s- seg** get stung (**på** by), prick oneself (**på** on); **s- seg bort** go away, go off; **s- seg fram** thrust oneself forward, make oneself conspicuous; **s- seg ut** stand out, be conspicuous.

stik'kel *-en, pl stikler* 1 burin, graver. 2 cotter, key. *3 spike. *4 horn tip (e.g. of deer).

stik'kels/bær *-et bot.* gooseberry (Ribes grossularia).

stik'ken *df*: **late i s-** leave in the lurch.

stik'kende *A* - pricking, stabbing, stinging: **s- øyne** ferrety eyes; **komme s- med noe** hand one sth (on the sly).

stikk'/flamme *+-n/*-a* spurt of flame.

stikk'/hevert *-en* dropper, pipette, (small) siphon.

stikk'/kontak't *-en elec.* outlet.

stikk'/lomme *-a* side-pocket, slash pocket.

stikk'/o'rd *-et* 1 (theater) cue. 2 *typog.* headword. 3 catchword, slogan; password.

stikk'/pille *-a/+-en* 1 *med.* suppository. 2 sarcasm: **komme med s-r** be sarcastic.

stikk'/prøve *-a/+-en* random sampling, spot check.

stikk'/renne *-a* (covered) drain.

stikk'/sag *-a* compass saw, keyhole saw.

stikk'/teppe *-t, pl +-r/*-* quilt.

stikk'/våpen *-et* pointed (thrusting) weapon.

stik'le *V -a/+-et* 1 deride, sneer (**på** at). 2 engrave. *3 *hort.* plant slips.

+stikleri' *-et, pl -er* sarcasm, scorn.

Stik'le/stad *Pln* historical site, Verdal twp, Nord Trøndelag; (St. Olaf's last battle, 1030 A.D.).

stik'ling[1] *-en* sapling; cutting, slip.

stik'ling[2] *-en zool.* stickleback (family Gasterosteidae).

+stik'ning *-en* 1 stitching. 2 embroidery. 3 engraving. 4 planting of cuttings, slips.

stik'te *V -a/+-et* 1 walk uncertainly: **s- på foten** limp. 2 stammer. *3 allude (**på** to).

sti'l *-en* 1 style (=manner, touch; elegance, etc.): **bunden og ubunden s-** verse and prose; **i samme s-** along the same line; **i stor s-** on a grand scale; **stå, være i s- med** be in keeping with; **det må være s- over det** it must be in keeping, in good style. 2 (school) exercise, paper, theme: **norsk s-** Norwegian composition.

sti'l/art *-a/-en* style.

sti'l/brott *-et* (=+**/brudd**) inconsistency in style; bad style.

sti'le *V -te/*-a* 1 compose; address (e.g. a letter to sby). 2 aim, head (**mot, på** for); *(pop.)* make a bee line for; *fig.* aim at, aspire to do sth: **s- høyt** aim high, be ambitious; **s- rett på** bear down on.

sti'le/bok *-a, pl -bøker* notebook (in which themes are written and handed in).

stilett' *-en* stiletto.

sti'l/full *A* correct, distinguished; graceful, stylish, tasteful.

+sti'l/følelse *-n* (feeling for) style.

+sti'l/hopper *-en, pl -e* (=***-ar**) ski-jumper with excellent form.

sti'lig *A* - elegant, smart, stylish.

stilise're *V -te* formalize, stylize.

stilis't *-en* stylist.

stilistikk' *-en* stylistics.

stilis'tisk *A* - stylistic.

stil'k *-en, pl *-er* stalk, stem; *bot.* peduncle: **øynene hans stod på s-er** he stared in amazement, his eyes were popping out of his head.

sti'l/karakte'r *-en* points, rating given for form (esp. ski jumping).

stil'ket(e) *A* - stalklike, stalky; *bot.* petiolate.

sti'l/kjensle *-a* (feeling for) style.

sti'l/kunst *-en* stylistic art, style.

+sti'l/kunstner *-en, pl -e* (=***-ar**) stylist.

still' *A stilt* calm, quiet, still; (cf **stille**[5]).

stilla's *-et, pl -/+-er* scaffolding.

sti'l/laus *A* (=+**/løs**) devoid of style, undistinguished.

+still'/bar *A* adjustable.

stil'le[1] *-a* calm, lull: **i storm og s-** in calm and stormy weather; **i s-** becalmed.

***stil'le**[2] *-t* tuning instrument (e.g. tuning fork).

stil'le[3] *V stilte* 1 alleviate, relieve (e.g. need, pain); calm, quiet down (e.g. a person); quench, satisfy, still (e.g. hunger, longing, thirst). 2 *dial.*: **s- seg** sneak; **s- seg inn på** stalk.

stil'le[4] *V stilte* 1 place, set; make, put (in various idioms): **s- en fordring** make a claim, demand; **s- et forslag** make a motion (proposal); **s- krav til** make demands on; **s- en et spørsmål** ask sby a question; **s- et ur** set (adjust) a watch; **være godt (dårlig) s-t** be well (badly) off. 2 furnish, provide (e.g. troops): **s- garanti (kausjon) for** give security, go bail for. 3 appear, report (*mil.*, sports): **s- til militærtjeneste** report for duty. 4 (with *adv., prep.*): **s- for retten** bring to trial; **s- fram** display, present, set out; **s- en fritt** give sby a free hand, leave (sth) to sby's discretion; **s- i skyggen** eclipse, overshadow; **s- opp** place in order, set up; draw up, line up; present, propose (e.g. a theory); **s- opp imot** match with, present opposition to; **s- en overfor noe** confront, face sby with sth; **s- på beina** raise (an army, troops); **s- (tingene) på hodet** turn topsy-turvy, put the cart before the horse; **s- sammen** set side by side, compare; **s- til skue** display, make a show of; **s- ut** display, exhibit; **s- utenfor** exclude. 5 *(refl.)*: **s- seg** stand, take up a position; **s- seg i kø, s- seg opp** take one's place in line, line up; **s- seg vennlig (fiendtlig) overfor** take a friendly (hostile) attitude towards; **s- seg likegyldig (skeptisk, osv.) til** be unconcerned (sceptical, etc.) about; **s- seg til tjeneste** offer one's services; **s- seg til valg** run for public office.

+stil'le[5] *A* - calm, quiet, still: **(ti) s-!** (be) quiet!; **i det s-** on the sly, secretly; **i sitt s- sinn** inwardly, to oneself; **bli s-** fall silent, stop; **stå (ligge) s-** stand (lie) still, be at a standstill, (of business) be slack, (of factory, machines, etc.) be idle; **s- vann har dypest grunn** still waters run deep.

stil'/leben *-et* still life.

Stil'le/havet *Pln* the Pacific Ocean.

stil'lehavs/øy *-a* island in the Pacific; South Sea island.

+stil'le/sittende *A* - sedentary.

+stil'le/skru(v)e *-n* 1 adjusting screw. 2 *mil.* elevating arc (of a cannon).

stil'le/stående *A* - 1 stagnating, static, stationary. 2 stolid (e.g. expression).

+stil'let *A* - situated: **være godt, dårlig s-** be well, badly off, in good, bad circumstances; **være meget uheldig s-** be placed at a great disadvantage; **s- overfor** faced with.

still'/farende *A* - quiet, unobtrusive, unassuming.

still'/ferdig [also -fær'-] *A* - quiet, unobtrusive, unassuming.

+still'/het *-en* silence, stillness; calmness, peace, tranquility: **i all s-** privately, quietly.

stil'ling *-a/+-en* 1 position, posture, standing; pose, stance: **ens s- i samfunnet** one's social standing; **gå i s-** *mil.* take up (defensive) positions; **innta en s-** take a position (post); pose; **sakenes nåværende s-** the present state of affairs. 2 situation: **s-ens herre** master of the s-; **s-en voksen** equal to the s-. 3 employment, job, occupation; position, post. 4 position=attitude, stand: **ta s- til** take a stand on. 5 *naut.* scaffolding (along the side of a ship under repair).

stil'lings/krig *-en mil.* trench warfare; war of position.

stilliss' *-en zool.* goldfinch (Carduelis carduelis).

still'/skrue *-n* cf **stille/**

***still'sleg** *A* - calm, quiet, still.

still'/stand *-en/*-et* stagnation, standstill (**i** in); lull (in conversation, fighting).

***still'/ståande** *A* - cf **stille/**

+still'/tiende *A* - (=***/teiande**) implied, tacit (e.g. agreement): **det var en s- avtale** it was tacitly agreed.

still'/verk *-et* signal control center (railroad); yard signal box.

sti'l/lære *-a/+-en* stylistics.

+sti'l/løs *A* cf **/laus**

sti'l/møbel *-elet, pl -ler* (piece of) period furniture.

stil'ne *V -a/+-et* abate, calm down, subside; die away, quiet down: **s- av** (the same).

+sti'l/oppgave *-a/-en* composition, exercise, paper.

sti'l/prøve *-a/+-en* literary exercise.

sti'l/rein *A* in pure style, pure (e.g. pure Renaissance).

sti'l/retting *-a* correction, grading of compositions, exercises.

sti'l/sans *-en* sense of style.

sti'l/sikker *A -ert, pl -sikre* correct, with a sure feeling for style.

stil't *nt of* **still**

stil'tre *V -a/+-et* 1 stumble, walk stiffly. 2: **s- seg** pussyfoot, sneak, tiptoe.

sti'm[1] *-en* 1 crowd, multitude, throng (av of). 2 school (e.g. of fish), swarm.

sti'm[2] *-en* steam: **få s-en opp** get up the s-.

sti'm[3] *-en/+-et* commotion, disorder, tumult (cf **stim**[1]).

+sti'/mann *-en, pl -menn hist.* highwayman, outlaw.

sti'm/båt *-en* steamboat.

sti'me *V -a/+-et/+-te* 1 crowd, flock, swarm: **s- forbi** swarm past; **s- til havs** set sail for the open sea. 2 (of fish) shoal, swarm.

stim'le *V -a/+-et* crowd, flock, throng: **s- sammen** flock, huddle (together); **de s-er om ham** they flock around him.

stim'mel *-en, pl stimler* crowd, multitude, throng (**av** of).

stimulans [stimulang's] *-en* stimulant; incentive (**til** to).

stimule're *V -te* stimulate; incite (**til** to).

stim'ulus *-en* stimulus (**til** to).

sting' *+-et/*-en, pl +-/*-er* 1 sting (e.g. of a bee). 2 catch, stitch (e.g. in the side). 3 stitch (sewing; surgical).

sting'e *V -a/+-et/stakk, *stunge/-i* 1 sting; butt. 2 pierce, prick, stab (also *fig.*).

***sting'e/sag** *-a* cf **stikk/**

sting'/sild *-a zool.* stickleback (family Gasterosteidae).

stin'k *-en* stench, stink.

stinkado'r *-en* evil-smelling cigar.

+stin'k/bombe [/bombe] *-a/-en* stink bomb.

+stin'k/dyr *-et zool.* skunk (Mephitis mephitis).

+stin'ke *V -a/-et* stink; reek (**av** of): **selvros s-r** self-praise is no recommendation.

+stin'k/potte *-a* 1 *hist., mil.* stinkpot. 2 *pop., derog.* stinkpot.

stinn' *A stint* 1 stiff, unbending. 2 bloated, distended (**av** by); thick. 3 compact, dense, solid: **skodda stod s-** the fog was dense.

stin'te[1] *-a* 1 *zool.* vendace (Coregonus albula). 2 *zool.* goldfinny (Ctenolabrus rupestris).

stin'te[2] *V -a/+-et dial.* exert oneself: ***det skal s-ast om eg orkar** it will be a question if I can make it.

stipen'd *-et, pl -* (=**stipendium**) fellowship, scholarship.

stipendia't *-en* fellow, scholar.

stipen'die/fond *-et* scholarship fund.

***stipen'dium** *-iet, pl +-ier/*-ium* cf **stipend**

+stip'le *V -a/-et* stipple.

+stip'let(e) *A -* stippled.

stipule're *V -te* stipulate.

***sti'r** *-en* gazing, staring: **det gav folk ein s-** that created a sensation, woke people up.

+stir're *V -a/-et* (=***stire**) gaze, stare (**på** at): **s- frekt og vedholdende på en** stare sby out of countenance; **s- med store øyne på** be all eyes; **s- olmt på** glare at sby; **s- stivt framfor seg** stare into space.

***sti'r/øygd** *A -/-øygt* with a fixed stare.

sti'v *A* 1 stiff (=rigid, taut, wooden, etc.): **en s- time** a solid hour; **holde ørene s-e** keep one's ears open, listen attentively; **s- kuling** moderate gale; **se (stirre) s-t** look (stare) steadily. 2 excessive, unreasonable: **s-e priser** steep prices; **et s-t stykke** a bit thick, pretty stiff; **synes De ikke det er litt s-t?** isn't that a bit thick? 3: **s- i (historie)** good at (history).

sti'v/beint *A -* 1 stiff-legged. 2 *fig.* inelastic, inflexible, rigid.

***sti've[1]** *-t* cf **stivelse**

sti've[2] *V -a/+-et* starch: **s- av, opp** prop, shore up; *fig.* bolster up, steady, strengthen.

sti'velse *-n* (=***stive[1]**) starch; *chem.* amyl.

sti've/skjorte [/sjorte] *-a* dress shirt, *(pop.)* boiled shirt.

+sti've/tøy *-et* (=***/ty**) starched linen (esp. dress shirts).

+sti'v/frossen *A -ent, pl -frosne* (=***/frosen**) frozen stiff.

sti'v/fryse *V infl as* **fryse[1]** be frozen stiff; freeze solid.

sti'v/hatt *-en* bowler, derby.

+sti'v/het *-en* 1 stiffness, rigidity; tautness. 2 formality, reserve.

sti'v/krampe *-n med.* tetanus.

***stiv'le** *V -a* hinder, stifle, stop.

sti'v/nakka *A -* (=**+-et**) stiff-necked; *fig.* headstrong, obstinate, stubborn.

sti'v/nakke *-n* obstinate, stubborn person; *(pop.)* bullhead.

stiv'ne *V -a/+-et* 1 stiffen; congeal, harden, set: **s- til** (the same). 2 settle in a rut, stagnate. 3 be paralyzed: **det fikk hans blod til å s- i årene** it made his blood run cold.

sti'v/piska *A -* (=**+-et**) whipped (e.g. cream).

sti'v/sinn *-et* obstinacy, stubbornness; *(pop)* bullheadedness.

sti'v/sinna *A -* (=**+-et, +/sint**) obstinate, stubborn; *(pop.)* bullheaded.

+sti'v/stikker *-en, pl -e* self-willed, stuffy person: **rektor var en gammel s-** the principal was an old sourpuss (Hoel).

+sti'v/øyd *A -* wide-eyed; *(pop.)* bug-eyed.

+stje'le *V stjal, stjålet* cf **stele**

+stje'ler *-en, pl -e* (=***stelar**): **heleren er ikke bedre enn s-en** the fence is as bad as the thief (see **heler**).

stjer'ne *-a/+-en* star; *typog.* asterisk; blaze (e.g. on horse): **ha en høy s- hos en** stand high in sby's favor; **lese i s-ne** read (sby's fortune) in the stars; **full av s-r** star-studded; **en ny s-** a rising s- (e.g. in the films).

stjer'ne/banner *-et*: **S-et** the Star-Spangled Banner.

+stjer'ne/bilde *-t* (=***/bilete**) *astron.* constellation.

+stjer'ne/blomst *-en* (=***/blom**) 1 *bot.* (any) starflower. 2 *bot.* stitchwort (Stellaria holostea).

stjer'ne/himmel *-en* starry sky, firmament; *poet.* starry heavens above: **den nordlige s-** the northern skies.

stjer'ne/hær *-en poet.* host of stars.

stjer'ne/idrett *-en* sports event dominated by a handful of outstanding performers.

+stjer'ne/kikker *-en, pl -e* (=**+/kiker, */kikar**) 1 astronomer, stargazer. 2 *zool.* stargazer (family Uranoscopidae).

stjer'ne/kikkert *-en* (=**+/kikert**) (astronomic) telescope.

+stjer'ne/klar *A* (=***/klår**) starlit, starry: **det er s-t ute** it's a starry night.

stjer'ne/rap *-et* falling star, shooting star.

stjer'ne/skott *-et* (=**+/skudd, */skot**) 1 falling star, shooting star. 2 sparkler.

+stjer'ne/tyder *-en, pl -e* (=***-ar**) astrologer.

stjer'ne/tyding [*/tying] *-a/+-en* astrology.

stjer'ne/tåke *-a astron.* nebula.

stjer'ne/vrimmel *-en, pl -vrimler* host, multitude of stars.

stjer'ne/år *-et astron.* sidereal year.

stjer't *-en* 1 *zool.* (of a bird) tail, uropygium. 2 *naut.* lanyard, tail.

***stjor'n** *-a* 1 administration, conduct, management; rule. 2 chores (of cattle).

***stjor'nar** *-en* administrator, manager.

***stjor'ne** *V -a* 1 administer, manage. 2 care for (cattle), do chores.

Stjø'r/dal *Pln* twp, Nord-Trøndelag.

Stjør'na *Pln* twp, Sør-Trøndelag.

+stjå'len *A -ent, pl -ne* stealthy, stolen.

+stjå'let *pp of* **stjele**

stk.=**stykk(er)**

sto'[1] *-a* milking place, resting place (for cows).

sto'[2] *-et* stud (=herd of mares and stallions).

+sto'[3] *pt of* **stå[1]**

Stock/holm [ståk'/] *Pln* Stockholm (capital of Sweden).

+stock/holmer *-en, pl -e* (=***-ar**) person from Stockholm.

sto'd *pt of* **stande, stå[1]**

Sto'd *Pln* twp, Nord-Trøndelag.

+stod'der *-en, pl -e* (=***stotar**) *archaic* beggar, ragamuffin, tramp.

+stod'der/konge *-n hist.* policeman, sheriff's deputy (who kept beggars and transients under surveillance).

***stode** [stå'e] *-a* position, situation.

stoff' *-et, pl -/+-er* 1 matter, stuff, substance. 2 fabric, material. 3 innate quality, makings (**til** of). 4 subject-matter, theme, topic: **gi s- til ettertanke** give food for thought.

stoff'lig *A -* material, physical.

stoff'/skifte *-t physiol.* metabolism.

+stoff'skifte/sykdom *-men med.* metabolic disorder.

°stoge [stå'ge] *-a* cf **stue[1]**

***stogg'** *-en/-et* breathing spell, pause, stop (**i** in).

***stog'ge** *V -a* pause, stop.

sto'/hest *-en* studhorse.

sto'/hingst *-en* studhorse (stallion).

+sto'iker *-en, pl -e* (=***-ar**) stoic.

stoisisme [sto-isis'me] *-n* stoicism.

sto'isk *A -* stoic.

stokk'[1] *-en* 1 beam, log, (tree)trunk: **over s- og stein** over stock and stone; **sove som en s-** sleep like a log. 2 stick; cane, walking stick; *mus.* baton; stake: **gå med s-** use a cane. 3 stalk, stock (e.g. on cabbage, vines). 4 block; stocks (for punishment). 5 deck (of cards). 6 crew, hands, working force.

stokk'[2] *pt of* **støkke[2]**

stokk'[3] *Av*: **s- blind** stone blind; **s- døv** stone deaf; **s- konservativ** reactionary, ultraconservative.

stokk'/and [also ståkk'/] *-a, pl -ender zool.* mallard (Anas platyrhynchos).

stokk'/døv *A* cf **stokk[3]**

stok'ke[1] *V -a/+-et* 1 shuffle (cards): **s- av** *dial.* remove fish (from nets). 2 *naut.* stock the anchor. 3 *hist.* put (lawbreakers) in the stocks. 4: **s- seg** be paralyzed (e.g. the organs of speech).

stok'ke[2]** *pp of* **støkke[2]** (=stokki**)

Stok'ke *Pln* twp, Vestfold.

stok'ke/bru *-a* log bridge.

stok'ke/far *-et* round of logs (e.g. in a log cabin).

stok'ke/lag *-et* round of logs.

stokk'/eld *-en* (=**+/ild**) bonfire, open fire (of logs or log-ends).

stok'ke/lengd *-a* (=**+/lengde**) length of log (as a unit of measurement).

Stok'ken *Pln* twp, Aust-Agder.

stokk'/ende[1] *-n* (cut) end of log.

stok'kende[2] *Av* completely.

stok'ke/pryl *-et* caning.

stok'ke/slag *-et* blow with a cane, stick.

***stok'ket(e)** *A -* brief, short-lived, transitory.

stokk'/fisk *-en* stockfish (dried in open air without salt).

+stokk'/ild *-en* cf **/eld**

stokk'/rose *-a/+-en bot.* hollyhock, rose mallow (Althaea rosaea).

stokk'/verk *-et* floor, story.

Stok'mark/nes *Pln* seaport, Hadsel twp, Nordland.

Stok'/sund *Pln* twp, Sør-Trøndelag.

sto'l *-en* 1 chair: **falle mellom to s-er** fall between two stools; **sette en s-en for døren** present sby with an ultimatum; **stikke noe under s-** conceal sth, hold sth back. 2 pew; pulpit; throne. 3 loom. 4 *mus.* bridge (e.g. of a violin).

sto'la *-en* stole.

sto'l/arm *-en* chair arm.

sto'le[1] *V +-te/*-a*: **s- på en** depend upon, rely upon, trust sby; **ikke s- på en** distrust sby.

***stole[2]** [stå'le] *pp of* **stele**

+sto'l/gang *-en med.* bowel movement, stool.

+ Bokmål; * Nynorsk; ° Dialect.
After letter: ' stress (Acc. 1); ' tone, stress (Acc. 2); · length.
Below letter: . not pronounced.

***stoli** [stå'li] *pp of* **stele**
sto'l/kant *-en* edge of a chair.
sto'l/kjerre *-a* two-wheeled cart (with seats).
stoll' *-en* (=***stull**) (mining) drift, gallery; adit.
***stol'p** *-a* deep track in the snow.
stol'pe[1] *-n* pole, post; studding (in a building): **snakke oppad s-r og nedad vegger** run off at the mouth.
stol'pe[2] *V -a/+-et* stalk, walk stiffly; (of children) toddle.
stol'pe/bu *-a* building on pillars (e.g. storehouse).
stol'pe/sjø *-en* choppy sea.
+stol'pre *V -a/-et* stalk, walk stiffly; (of children) toddle.
+stol'pret(e) *A* - awkward, stiff (e.g. style).
sto'l/rad *-a/+-en* row (of seats).
sto'l/rygg *-en* chair back.
sto'l/sete *-t, pl +-r/*-* chair seat.
stol't *A* - **1** proud; arrogant, haughty: **være s- av, over** be proud of, take pride in. **2** *poet.* noble, splendid. **3** *bot.* **s- Henriks melde** all-good, good-king-henry (Chenopodium bonus Henricus).
+stol'telig *Av* magnificently, majestically, proudly.
+stol't/het *-en* pride; arrogance: **sette sin s- i** pride oneself on.
stoltse're *V -te* strut around.
stomle [stom'le] *V -a/+-et* grope, lurch, stagger.
***stom'n** *-en* stump; trunk.
+stomp [stom'p] *-en* cf **stump**[1]
***stong'** *-a, pl stenger* cf **stang**
***stong'/ja'rn** *-et* cf **stang/jern**
St. O. O. =**Sankt Olavs Orden**
stope** [stå'pe] *pp of* **stupe** (=stopi**)
stop'le *V -a/+-et* **+1** stipple. ***2** pile, stack. ***3** fumble: **s- på orda** stumble on one's words. ***4** (of sea) billow, roll.
stopp'[1] *-en* **1** stop; halt, standstill: **sette s- for noe** put a stop to sth; **si s-** put a stop (for to); protest; stop (functioning). **2** bus, streetcar stop.
stopp'[2] *-en/-et* stuffing; filling, padding.
°stop'pe[1] *-a* path, track.
stop'pe[2] *V -a/+-et* stop; come to a halt, standstill; bring to a halt, hold up: **s- brått** come to a dead stop; **s- en** take the wind out of sby's sails; **s- munnen på en** shut sby up; **s- opp** come to a standstill; **s- på signal** stop on request (e.g. a bus).
stop'pe[3] *V -a/+-et* **1** cram, fill, stuff: **s- igjen** stop up; **s- møbler** upholster furniture; **s- pipa** fill one's pipe; **s- ut** stuff (e.g. animals); **s-ende full** chuck full. **2** darn (e.g. stockings).
stop'pe/ga'rn *-et* darning (mending) yarn.
stop'pe/klokke *-a* stop watch.
stop'pe/nål *-a* darning needle.
stop'pe/plikt *-a/+-en* obligation to stop (e.g. at traffic signals).
+stop'per *-en, pl -e* (=***-ar**) **1** stop, stopper; (door) stop, thumb latch (on lock): **sette en s- for** put a stop to. **2** *naut.* stopper.
stop'pe/signal [/singna'l] *-et, pl -/+-er* stop light.
stop'pe/sopp *-en* darning egg.
+stopp'e/sted *-et* (=***/stad**) stop (esp. bus, streetcar).
stop'pe/teppe *-t, pl +-r/*-* stitched quilt.
stop'pe/ur *-et* stop watch.
stopp'/signal [/singna'l] *-et, pl -/+-er* cf **stoppe/**
stopp'/skive *-a* washer.
***stopul** [stå'pull] *-en, pl stoplar* cf **støpul**
sto'r *A større, størst* **1** big, large; great (e.g. distance, height, a man, ideas, etc.); high (e.g. sea, a tree, mountain); capital (letters); important (events): **de s-e** grown-ups; bigshots; **Karl den s-e** Charlemagne; Charles the Great; **s-t sett** generally speaking, for the most part; **et s-t intervall** *mus.* a major interval; **du s-e (storeste) verden (gud, min)** mild oath (e.g. my heavens); **i s-t** en gros, wholesale; **i det s-e og hele** in general, on the whole; **en sjekk s- kr 100** *merc.* a check for 100 *kroner*; **føre det s-e ord** lay down the law; **gjøre det s-t** be (economically) successful; **se s-t på (tingene)** take the large view; **seire s-t** win hands down; **slå noe s-t opp** make a lot of sth; **være s- av seg** be proud, think well of oneself; **være s- på det** put on airs, be snooty, stuck-up. **2 (ikke) s-t, større** (not) much: **ikke s-t annet enn** nothing much but, little more than; **det er ikke s- ved det** there's not much to that, that doesn't amount to much; **det er ikke noe større** it's not very much, of little consequence; **det gjør ikke s-t fra eller til** it doesn't make much difference one way or the other; **du er ikke s-t bedre** you're not much better; **han sa ikke s-t (større)** he didn't say much. **3** *(comp.)*: **større** (comparatively) big, important: **en s-aften** a big evening; **et s- parti** a large shipment; **en s- middag** a dinner party; banquet; formal dinner; **ikke noe s- (til)** not (very) much (of a). **4** *(sup.)*: **størst: s-e delen (av)** most (of), the majority (of); **med s-e fornøyelse** with the greatest of pleasure.
+sto'r/aktig *A* - haughty, overbearing, proud.
+sto'raktig/het *-en* haughtiness, pride, superciliousness.
+sto'r/artet *A* - (=**+-a**) grand, magnificent, splendid; capital, excellent, first-rate, *(pop.)* swell, tiptop.
sto'r/bedrif't **-a/+-en* **1** (large-scale) industrial concern. **2** great achievement.
sto'r/blomstra *A* - (=**+-et**) large-flowered (e.g. design of a shirt).
sto'r/bonde [/bonne] *-n, pl -bønder* farmer with large holdings; well-to-do farmer.
Stor'/britan'nia *Pln* Great Britain.
+sto'r/bukk [/bokk] *-en* **1** large, powerful reindeer. **2** *(pop.)* big shot; bigwig.
sto'r/by *-en* big city, metropolis.
sto'r/båt *-en naut.* long boat.
Stor'd *Pln* twp, Hordaland.
Sto'r/dal *Pln* twp, Møre og Romsdal.
***sto'r/dom** *-(m)en* greatness.
sto'r/dåd *-en* deed, exploit; great achievement: **øve s-** perform a great deed (feat of valor, glorious deed).
sto're/bror *-en* big brother: **spille s-** play the heavy-handed father to sby.
Sto'r/egga *Pln* "Big Edge" (declivity of the continental shelf which makes up the western Norwegian coast).
Sto'r-Elvdal *Pln* twp, Hedmark.
sto're/slem' *-men* grand slam (bridge).
+sto'r/eter *-en, pl -e* (=***-ar**) glutton.
+sto're/viser *-en, pl -e* (=***-ar**) minute hand.
sto'r/fe *-et* cattle.
sto'r/felt *A* - imposing, magnificent, sublime; on a grand scale.
sto'r/finans [/finang's] *-en* high finance.
sto'r/fisk *-en* large game fish.
sto'r/fiske *-t* unusually large catch of fish.
Sto'r/fjo'rd *Pln* twp, Troms.
sto'r/flire *V -te* guffaw, laugh loudly.
sto'r/folk *-et* magnates; *(pop.)* big shots, VIP's.
+sto'r/forbry'ter *-en, pl -e* (=***-ar**) arch criminal, public enemy; *(pop.)* big-time criminal.
sto'r/fremmend *N* (=**+/fremmed, */framand**) distinguished guest.
sto'r/fugl *-en zool.* wood grouse (Tetrao urogallus); (collective name for) grouse (family Tetraonidae).
sto'r/fyrste *-n hist.* (Russian) grand duke (i.e. son of the czar).
+sto'rfyrsten/dømme *-t hist.* (Russian) grand duchy.
sto'r/fyrstin'ne *-a/+-en hist.* (Russian) grand duchess.
sto'r/gard *-en* big farm; landed estate.
sto'r/gate *-a* avenue, boulevard; main street.
sto'r/glad *A* - beaming with delight, joy; *(pop.)* pleased as Punch.
sto'r/gråte *V infl as* **gråte** sob.
+sto'r/handler *-en, pl -e* (=***-ar**) large-scale operator (in commerce), wholesaler.
sto'r/hav *-et* ocean.
sto'r/hending *-a archaic* outstanding, significant event.
sto'r/hertug *-en* grand duke.
sto'rhertug/dømme *-t, pl +-r/*-* (=***/døme**) grand duchy.
sto'r/hertugin'ne *-a/+-en* grand duchess.
+sto'r/het *-en* **1** grandeur, greatness. **2** great person.
+sto'rhets/tid *-a/-en* days of glory, golden age.
+sto'rhets/vanvidd *-et psych.* megalomania.
sto'r/hjerne *-n anat.* cerebrum.
+sto'r/hopper *-en, pl -e* (=***-ar**) star skijumper.
***sto'r/huga** *A* - elevated, high-minded.
sto'r/hundre *-t, pl +-r/*- hist.* long hundred (=120).
sto'r/industri' *-en* big (heavy, large-scale) industry.
sto'ring *-en pop.* bigwig, big shot, VIP.
stor'k *-en zool.* stork (Ciconia ciconia).
sto'r/kar *-en pop.* bigwig, big shot, VIP; higher-up.
***sto'rkars/armod** *-a* genteel shabbiness.
stor'ke/nebb *-en* **1** stork's beak. **2** *bot.* crane's-bill, geranium (genus Geranium). **3** (large) tweezers.
sto'r/kjefta *A* - (=**+-et**) **1** broad-jawed. **2** big-mouthed, bragging.
sto'r/klokke *-a* **1** large bell. **2** *bot.* giant bellflower (Campanula latifolia).
+stor'kne *V -a* cf **størkne**
sto'r/kobbe *-n zool.* bearded seal (Phoca barbata).
sto'r/konvall' *-en bot.* David's-harp, Solomon's-seal (Polygonatum multiflorum).
sto'r/kornet(e) *A* - coarse-grained.
+sto'r/kors *-et* grand cross.
+sto'r/kveg *-et* cattle.
sto'rkårs/mann *-en, pl -menn/*-menner* man of means.
***sto'r/lagd** *A -/-lagt* large of frame.
+sto'r/laten *A -ent, pl -ne* grand, grandiose: **det s-ne ved ham** his (true) greatness.
sto'r/le *V infl as* **le** laugh uproriously, roar with laughter.
sto'r/leik *-en* size, stature (**av** of).
+sto'r/lemmet *A* - (=***/lem(m)a**) heavy limbed; with heavy branches.
sto'rlig *Av* exceedingly, greatly.
sto'r/lynt *A* - elevated, high-minded; ambitious, proud.
***sto'r/læte** *-t* pride; arrogance, vanity.
stor'/låten *A +-ent, pl -ne* elevated, high-minded; arrogant, proud.
stor'm *-en* storm, tempest; *meteor.* strong gale; outburst (**av** of); storm (e.g. of applause): **en s- i et vannglass** a tempest in a teacup; **(inn)ta med s-** *mil.* carry by assault, take by storm (e.g. a citadel); *fig.* carry away, sweep; **løpe s- på** *mil.* storm (e.g. a fortress); **så vind og høste s-** sow the wind and reap the whirlwind.
stor/makt *-a/-en* Great Power.
sto'rmakts/politikk' *-en* great-power politics.
+stor'm/angre'p *-et mil.* assault, storm.

sto'r/mann *-en, pl -menn/*-menner* chieftain, great man; magnate; notable; man of distinction, prominent figure.
+sto'rmanns/gal *A* (=***/galen**) megalomaniac.
sto'rmanns/galskap *-en* megalomania: **han har s-** he has a swelled head.
sto'rmanns/vis *-en*: **på s-** in grand style.
sto'r/maska *A* - (=**+-et**) widemeshed.
sto'r/mast *-a naut.* mainmast.
stor'm/dekk *-et naut.* hurricane deck.
+stor'm/dreven *A -ent/-et, pl -ne* stormtossed.
stor'me *V -a/+-et* **1** storm; fly, rush; rage: **det s-er** a gale is blowing; **de s-et sperringene** they rushed the barricades; **s- løs på en** rush at sby, *pop.* go for sby; **s- en festning** *mil.* take a fortress by storm. **2: s-ende** stormy, tempestuous; **det gjorde s- lykke** it was a tremendous success, it brought down the house; *(adv.)* **s-ende glad** overjoyed.
sto'r/mektig *A* - mighty; arrogant, high and mighty.
+sto'r/mester *-eren, pl -ere/-rer* grand master (e.g. of a fraternal organization, lodge).
stor'm/flod [*/flo] *+-en/*-a* deluge, flood (due to storm).
stor'm/fugl *-en* **1** *zool.* fulmar (Fulmarus glacialis). **2** bird flying in a storm.
stor'm/full *A* stormy; tempestuous, tumultuous.
stor'm/kast *-et* gust of wind, squall.
stor'm/klokke *-a* tocsin.
stor'm/krok *-en* window fastener, hook.
+stor'm/løp *-et* (=***/laup**) *mil.* assault, onslaught.
stor'm/melding *-a/+-en* storm warning.
***sto'r/mod** *-et* **1** courage. **2** arrogance, insolence.
sto'r/modig *A* - **1** elevated, highminded; noble; courageous. **2** arrogant, proud.
sto'r/mogu'l *-en*: **s-en** the Great Mogul.
stor'm/reim *-a* chin strap.
***stor'm/sam** *A* stormy, tempestuous, tumultuous.
stor'm/segl *-et* (=**+/seil**) *naut.* storm sail.
stor'm/signal [/singna'l] *-et, pl -/+-er* storm signal.
stor'm/skritt *pl*: **med (i) s-** by leaps and bounds.
stor'm/sky *-a* storm cloud.
stor'm/stige *-n hist., mil.* scaling ladder.
stor'm/svale *-a zool.* stormy petrel (Hydrobates pelagicus).
stor'm/tropp *-en mil.* storm troop; assault party, shock troop.
stor'm/varsel *-elet/-let, pl -el/+-ler* storm warning.
stor'm/vind *-en* gale, squall, storm.
+stor'm/vær *-et* (=***/ver**) stormy weather.
sto'r/mønstra *A* - (=**+-et**) largepatterned.
***sto'r/nasa** *A* - impertinent, saucy; *(pop.)* fresh.
sto'r/nøgd *A -/*-nøgt* (=**+/nøyd**) *dial.* demanding, exacting; greedy.
***sto'rom** *Av* to a considerable degree, extent.
***sto'r/o'rdig** *A* - bombastic, grandiloquent.
sto'r/part *-en* larger share: **s-en** (also) the majority (**av** of).
sto'r/politikk' *-en* international (power) politics.
sto'r/polit'isk *A* - pertaining to international politics.
sto'r/produsen't *-en* large-scale producer.
storr' *-en* (=**+starr**) *bot.* sedge grass (genus Carex).
sto'r/reint *A nt*: **gjøre s-** do housecleaning.
+sto'r/rengjø'ring *-a/-en* (thorough) housecleaning, e.g. spring cleaning.
sto'r/rutet(e) *A* - (pattern) with large checks.
+sto'r/røyker *-en, pl -e* avid smoker.
sto'r/rådig *A* - autocratic, dominating, imperious.
sto'r/sal *-en hist.* large salon (generally on the second floor).
sto'r/segl[1] *-et, pl* - (=**+/seil**) *naut.* mainsail.
sto'r/segl[2] [+/seil] *-et, pl* - great seal.
+stor'segl/beva'rer *-en, pl -e* (=***-ar**) *hist.* keeper of the great seal, Lord Chancellor (England).
sto'r/sei *-en zool.* large billet, coalfish (Pollachius virens).
+sto'r/seil *-et* cf **/segl**
sto'r/sild *-a* large herring (ab. 12 in. in length).
sto'r/sinn *-et* breadth of mind, highmindedness, liberality.
sto'r/sinna *A* - (=**+-et**) large-minded, liberal, magnanimous.
+sto'rsinnet/het *-en* breadth of mind, greatness of spirit, large-mindedness.
sto'r/sint *A* - cf **/sinna**
sto'r/sirkel *-elen, pl -ler* great circle.
sto'r/skog *-en* big forest, deep woods.
sto'r/skole *-n hist.* upper elementary school.
sto'r/skratte *V -a/+-et* laugh uproariously, roar with laughter.
sto'r/skrike *V infl as* **skrike[1]** bawl, scream vociferously, squall.
+sto'r/skryter *-en, pl -e* (=***-ar**) braggart; *(pop.)* blowhard, loudmouth.
+sto'r/slagen *A -ent, pl -ne* grand, impressive, splendid; great, sublime.
sto'r/slegge *-a* sledge-hammer: **bruke s-a** use one's big guns (**på** on).
sto'r/slått *A* - grand, impressive, splendid.
***sto'r/snut** *-en* arrogant, haughty, overbearing person.
sto'r/snuta *A* - (=**+-et**) arrogant, haughty, overbearing.
+sto'rsnutet/het *-en* arrogance, haughtiness, superciliousness.
sto'r/spove *-n zool.* curlew (Numenius arquata).
sto'r/sti'lt *A* - **1** comprehensive, grandiose, large-scale. **2** *typog.* having large type.
sto'r/stue *-a* (=**/stove**) **1** *hist.* fine, imposing residence. **2** *hist.* living room, parlor: **kolbrenneren måtte inn i s-a til dronningen** the charcoal burner had to go into the queen's p. (Asbjørnsen).
sto'r/tak *-et* all-out effort.
sto'r/talende *A* - bombastic, grandiloquent; boasting, bragging.
+sto'rtalen/het *-en* bombast, grandiloquence; boastfulness, bragging.
+sto'r/taler *-en, pl -e* (=***-ar**) orator, spellbinder.
sto'r/tenkt *A* - **1** large-scale. **2** largeminded, liberal, magnanimous.
sto'r/tid [*sto'r/ti] *-a/+-en* days of glory, golden age.
sto'r/ting *-et* Storting (=Norway's parliament).
sto'rtings/kvinne *-a/+-en* woman deputy, member of parliament.
sto'rtings/mann *-en, pl -menn/*-menner* deputy, member of parliament.
sto'rtings/presiden't *-en* president of parliament.
sto'rtings/proposisjo'n *-en* parliamentary bill.
sto'rtings/representan't *-en* deputy, member of parliament.
sto'rtings/sesjo'n *-en* session of parliament.
sto'rtings/tidende *en* record of transactions of the *Storting* (ab.=Congressional Record).
+stor'tings/valg *-et* (=***/val**) election for parliament, general election.
sto'rtings/vedtak *-et* act of parliament.
+sto'r/trives *V -des* (=***-ast**) enjoy oneself (very much), feel at home.
sto'r/troll *-et* huge troll.
sto'r/tromme [/tromme] *-a* bass drum: **slå på s-a** use big (boastful) words; talk big.
sto'r/tute *V -a/+-et* howl, sob.
sto'r/tyrk *-en*: **S-en** *hum.* the Grand Turk, i.e. sultan.
***sto'r/tøk** *A* generous, open-handed; prodigal, wasteful.
sto'r/tå *-a, pl -tær* big toe.
***sto'r/vaksen** *A -e/-i, pl -ne* cf **/voksen**
sto'r/vask *-en* big wash, washing; *fig.* clean-up.
sto'r/veg *-en* (=**+/vei**) highway, main road.
sto'r/veges *Av* (=**+/veies**) exceedingly, extremely; *(adj.)* grand, magnificent.
+sto'r/vei *-en* cf **/veg**
+sto'r/veies *Av* cf **/veges**
sto'r/verk *-et* great achievement, deed; magnum opus, monumental work.
sto'r/vilt *-et* big game.
sto'rvilt/jeger *-en, pl +-e* big game hunter.
sto'r/visi'r *-en* grand vizier.
+sto'r/voksen *A -ent, pl -ne* (=***/vaksen**) big, huge, large (in size).
sto'r/voren [+/vårren, */våren] *A +-ent, pl -ne* bulky, large (e.g. a book).
sto'r/ætta *A* - (=**+-et**) highborn.
+sto'r/øyd *A* - (=***/øygd**) big-eyed, wide-eyed.
***stotar** [stå'tar] *-en* cf **stodder**
***stotar/konge** *-n* cf **stodder/**
***stote** [stå'te] *V -a* cf **stotre**
sto'tre *V -a/+-et* (=***stote, +stotte**) stammer, stutter: **s- fram** burst out (speaking); **s-ende** haltingly.
+stot'ret(e) *A* - quavering, tremulous.
+stot'te *V -a/-et* cf **stotre**
stove [stå've] *-a* cf **stue[1]**
St. prp. =**stortingsproposisjon**
straba's *-en* (usu. *pl*) exertions; hardships.
strabasiø's *A* fatiguing, strenuous.
straff' *-a/+-en* **1** punishment; penalty; chastisement; retribution (**for** for): **til s-** by way of punishment; **til s- for** as punishment for. **2** *jur.* imprisonment; penalty: **hun kom på s-** she went to prison.
straff'/ansvar *-et jur.* penalty of the law; criminal liability: **unnlatelse av . . . medfører s- etter loven** any person failing to . . . will be prosecuted to the full extent of the law.
straff'/arbeid *-et jur.* imprisonment at hard labor.
+straff'/bar *A jur.* punishable: **det er en s- handling å** it is against the law to.
+straff'bar/het *-en jur.* **1** criminal liability. **2** criminal nature (of an act).
straf'fe *V -a/+-et* **1** punish; castigate, chastise; exact retribution for; **s- seg** bring its own punishment; **s- strengt** punish severely. **2** *jur.* sentence: **s- en på livet** sentence sby to death. **3: s-ende** punishing, punitive: **et s-ende blikk** a reproachful, reproving look.
straf'fe/bataljo'n *-en mil.* hard labor battalion.
straf'fe/dom' *-men* **1** *jur.* sentence. **2** *eccl.* judgment.
straf'fe/domstol *-en jur.* criminal court.
straf'fe/eksersi's *-en mil.* punishment tour (with full field pack); fatigue drill.
straf'fe/ekspedisjo'n *-en mil.* punitive expedition.

straf'fe/kast *-et* penalty throw (sports).
straf'fe/klausul *-en jur.* penalty clause (in a contract).
straf'fe/koloni· *-en* convict colony.
straf'fe/likne *V -a/+-et* (=**+/ligne**) assess penalties (e.g. those imposed in late payment of state and federal income taxes).
straf'fe/lov [/låv] *-en/*-a* criminal law; criminal code.
straf'fe/middel *-elet/-midlet, pl +-midler/*-el* punitive measure.
straf'fe/måte *-n* manner, mode of punishment.
straf'fe/poeng· *-et* penalty goal (rugby, soccer).
straf'fe/porto *-en* extra postage (paid for having put on too little).
+straf'fe/preken *-en* reprimand; severe lecture.
straf'fe/rett *-en* 1 right to punish. 2 *jur.* criminal law.
straf'fe/sak *-a/+-en jur.* criminal case.
straf'fe/spark *-et* penalty kick (rugby, soccer).
straf'fe/tale *-n/*-a* reprimand; severe lecture.
+straf'fe/trusel *-elen, pl -ler* threat of punishment.
straf'fe/utmå'ling *-a/+-en jur.* fixing of the sentence.
straff'/fange *-n* convict, prisoner.
straff'/fri *A -tt* exempt from punishment; with impunity.
+straff'fri/het *-en* exemption from punishment, impunity.
***straff'/lagd** *A -/-lagt* punishable.
straff'/skyldig *A -* (=***/skuldig**) culpable, deserving of punishment.
stra'k *A* erect, straight, upright: **på s- arm** at arm's length; on outstretched arm(s).
strakk' *pt of* **strekke**[1]
stra'kne *V -a/+-et* be tightened; become erect, straight.
strak's *Av* 1 (of time) immediately, right away: **s- over jul** right after Christmas; **s- på timen (på stedet)** right away, then and there; **klokka er s- tolv** it's nearly 12 o'clock; **kommer s-** be right there; **det er s- noe annet** that's quite another matter. 2 (of location) close, directly: **s- under** directly beneath; **s- utenfor** right outside. 3 (*conj.*) as soon as: **s- han så henne** as soon as he saw her.
strak'te *pt of* **strekke**[2], **strekkje**[2]
stram' *A -t, pl -me* 1 taut, tight; tight-fitting: **gå på s- line** walk a tightrope; **holde i s-me tøyler** keep a tight control over. 2 erect, stiff, upright. 3 *fig.* forbidding, rigid, unbending; hidebound, strict. 4 acrid, rank, sharp (smell).
+stram'/buks [/boks] *-en obs.* 1 tight-fitting trousers. 2 caning, spanking.
***stra'me** *V -a* cf **stramme**
stramei' *-en* canvas (foundation for embroidery stitches).
+stram'/het *-en* 1 tautness, tightness. 2 stiffness; harshness, severity. 3 strictness. 4 acridity.
stram'me *V -a/+-et* 1 tighten (up); draw tight: **s- tøylene** draw rein. 2 *fig.* increase, intensify, stiffen (e.g. demands): **s- disiplinen** tighten up the discipline; **s- inn (livreima)** cut down expenses, tighten one's belt; **s- en opp** buck sby up; **s- seg opp** pull oneself together, straighten up.
+stram'mer *-en, pl -e* (=***-ar**) tightener (esp. for skis).
+stram'ning *-en* tightening (e.g. a cord, credit, etc.) (**av** of).
+stram't/sittende *A -* tight-fitting.
stran'd *-a, pl strender* beach, shore, seashore: **fare land og s- rundt** roam all around the country.
Stran'd *Pln* twp, Rogaland.
Stran'da *Pln* twp, Møre og Romsdal.
+stran'd/bredd *-en* (=***/breidd**) beach.
stran'de *V -a/+-et* 1 be stranded, run aground; be shipwrecked (**på** on). 2 fail, miscarry: **s- på** break down (come to grief) because of.
Stran'de/barm *Pln* twp, Hordaland.
stran'd/gate *-a* shore street.
stran'd/hogg *-et hist.* foray, raid (esp. by pirates, Vikings, in which they went ashore and ravaged the countryside).
stran'd/linje *-a/+-en* (=***/line**) shoreline.
stran'd/promena'de *-n* esplanade, shore promenade.
stran'd/rek *-et* flotsam.
stran'd/rett *-en* 1 access to the beach, right to use the beach. 2 *hist.* right to claim merchandise washed ashore from shipwrecked vessels.
stran'd/rug *-en bot.* lyme grass (Elymus arenarius).
+stran'd/satte *pt of* **-sette**
+stran'd/setning *-en naut.* beaching, running aground.
+stran'd/sette *V -satte* 1 *naut.* beach, run aground. 2 abandon sby, cast sby away.
+stran'd/sitter *-en, pl -e* (=***/sitjar**) seaside resident (non-landowning).
+stran'd/sted *-et* seaside settlement.
Stran'd/vik *Pln* twp, Hordaland.
***strang'** *A* acrid, bitter, sharp.
strang'e *-n* log (of small tree).
strangulasjo'n *-en* strangulation.
strangule're *V -te* strangle.
stran't *-en* 1 long, thin, shriveled-up plant. 2 tuft of hair. 3 lanky, spindly person; spindlelegs.
stran'te *V -a/+-et* project, shoot up in the air.
stran'ten *A +-ent, pl -ne* (=**stran-tet(e)**) lanky, spindly; shriveled.
+strass' *-en* strass (=brilliant glass of high lead content used in artificial gems): **s-/perle** s- bead.
strate'g *-en* (=**+strategiker**) strategist.
strategi' *-en* strategy.
+strate'giker *-en, pl -e* (=***-ar**) cf **strateg**
strate'gisk *A -* strategic.
+stra'ten/røver *-en* highwayman, highway robber.
stratosfæ're *-n* stratosphere.
stratosfæ'risk [also -æ'-] *A -* stratospheric.
stratt' *-en* 1 (dry, thin) shrivelled-up stalk. 2 feeble, frail old man. 3 bullheaded, obstinate person.
***strat'te** *V -a*: **s- imot** resist.
strau'k *pt of* **stryke**
***strau'm** *-en* cf **strøm**
***strau'm/drag** *-et* cf **strøm/**
***strau'm/kjelde** *-a* cf **strøm/kilde**
***strau'm/kvervel** *-elen, pl -lar* cf **strøm/virvel**
***strau'm/laus** *A* cf **strøm/løs**
***strau'm/line** *-a* cf **strøm/linje**
Strau'ms/nes *Pln* twp, Møre og Romsdal.
***strau'p** *pt of* **strupe**[2]
+stre'be *V -a/-et*: **s- etter** aim at, strive for.
+stre'be/bjelke *-n arch.* strut.
+stre'be/bue *-n arch.* flying buttress.
+stre'ben *en* effort, endeavor.
+stre'be/pila'r *-en arch.* buttress.
+stre'ber *-en, pl -e* climber, status seeker.
+stre'ber/type *-n* pushy type, status-seeking type.
+stre'd *pt of* **stride**
+stre'de *-t* (=***strete**[1]) 1 crooked, narrow street; alley, lane: **på gater og s-er** in highways and byways. 2 strait: **Magellans s-** the S-s of Magellan.
+strei' *pt of* **stri**[2]
strei'f *-et* 1 gleam, ray (**av** of). 2 glimpse, peep. 3 touch.
strei'fe *V -a/+-et* 1 ramble, roam, rove: **s- omkring** roam, wander at large. 2 glance at: **blikket s-et Synnøve** he g-d at S- (Bjørnson). 3 brush, graze, touch: **han ble s-et i halsen** the bullet grazed his throat; **s- inn på et emne** touch lightly on a subject. 4 occur: **tanken har aldrig s-et meg** the idea has never occurred to me.
strei'f/lys *-et* 1 fitful, unsteady light. 2 sidelight; *fig.* incidental information; glimpse.
strei'f/skott *-et* (=**+/skudd**) grazing shot.
strei'f/sår *-et* grazing, slight wound.
strei'f/tog [/tåg] *-et mil.* hit and run foray, raid.
strei'k *-en* strike: **gå til s-** go on s-.
strei'ke *V -a/+-et* 1 go on strike, strike. 2 refuse to function, operate (e.g. brakes).
+strei'ke/bryter *-en, pl -e* (=***-ar**) strikebreaker; *(pop.)* fink, scab.
+strei'ke/frihet *-en* right to strike.
strei'ke/kasse *-a/-en* strike fund.
strei'ke/ordre *-n* order to strike.
strei'ke/rett *-en* right to strike.
strei'ke/vakt *-a/+-en* picket: **gå s-** picket, walk the picket line.
strei'ke/varsel *-elet/-let, pl -el/+-ler* notice of a strike.
***strei't** *-et* exertion, hardship.
***strei'te** *V -a* exert oneself.
stre'k *-en/*-et* 1 line, stroke; dash, streak: **etter (på) en s-** exactly, precisely; **gå over s-en** go too far, exceed the limit; **sette s- under** underline; **slå en s- over** cross out, strike out, *fig.* forget about; **s- i regningen** disappointment, unforeseen obstacle; snag. 2 (compass) point, direction: **en s- mot vest** a point to the west; **vinden holder seg på samme s-en** the wind is still from the same direction. 3 prank, trick: **gale s-er** crazy pranks, shenanigans.
stre'ke *V -a/+-et/+-te* draw lines, rule (e.g. sheet of paper): **s- opp** outline, sketch; **s- over** cross out, run one's pen or pencil through; cancel, delete; **s- under** underline; emphasize.
strekk' *-en/-et* 1 stretch, tension; elasticity: **ligge i s-** be in traction. 2 sprain. 3 run; *naut.* tack. 4 straight line: **i ett s-** at a stretch; **på s-** in a row.
+strekk'/bar *A* elastic; ductile.
+strekk'bar/het *-en* elasticity; ductility.
strekk'/bukse [/bokse] *-a* ski pants; stretch pants.
strek'ke[1] *V strakk, +strukket/*strokke/ /*-i* 1 extend, reach. 2 avail; be sufficient, suffice: **s- til** go round, last; **få inntektene til å s- til** make both ends meet.
+strek'ke[2] *V strekte/strakte* (=***-je**) 1 draw out, stretch; expand (e.g. metals); extend, reach; *naut.* haul taut (a sail): **s- bena** stretch one's legs; **s- ut** extend, reach out; **s- ut armene etter** reach towards; **s- våpen** lay down one's arms, surrender. 2 *(refl.)*: **s- seg** extend, reach, stretch (between); strain a point; **s- seg (i full lengde)** stretch oneself; **s- seg etter** reach for; **s- seg over** cover, embrace; **s- seg så langt som mulig** do the best one can.
+strek'ke/muskel *-elen, pl -ler anat.* extensor muscle.
strekk'/fisk *-en* 1 *arch.* supporting beam. 2 *naut.* rigging screw, turnbuckle.
***strekkj'e**[1] *-a* distance, stretch.
***strekkj'e**[2] *V strekte/strakte* cf **strekke**[2]
strekk'/spenning *-a/+-en* tensile stress.
stre'k/måt *-et carp.* (marking) gauge.
***strek'nad** *-en* elasticity; ductility.
strek'ning *-en/*-a* 1 stretching. 2 area, territory; distance, stretch.
stren'de *V -a/+-et/*-e dial.* 1 roam, wander; *(pop.)* gad, knock about; hurry, hustle. 2 shovel away (mire, mud).
stren'der *pl of* **strand**
stre'ne *V -te* 1 hurry hustle; (of cows) run ahead; roam, wander. 2 scour (an area).

streng'[1] *-en, pl *-er* 1 string (bow, violin); cord, wire; strand: **ha flere s-er på sin bue** have many talents. 2 *fig.* chord; feeling: **alltid slå på den samme s-en** be always harping on the same thing; **spille på de nasjonale s-ene** appeal to national feelings.

streng'[2] *A* 1 severe, stern, strict (**mot** with); hard, harsh, rigorous; *pop.* tough; austere, exacting, stringent: **leve i s-e kår** be in straitened circumstances; **settes på en s- prøve** be put to a severe test. 2 *(adv.)*: **holde s-t på** observe rigorously; **s-t tatt** strictly speaking, in the strict sense of the word.

streng'e/instrumen't *-et mus.* stringed instrument.

streng'e/leik *-en* (=+**/lek, *streng/**) *mus.* stringed instrument (e.g. harp, zither).

+**streng'e/spill** *-et* (=***/spel**) playing upon stringed instruments; music.

+**streng'/het** *-en* severity, strictness (**mot** with); harshness, rigorousness; austerity, exactitude, stringency.

***streng'je** *V -de* 1 tighten: **s- opp fela** tune up the fiddle. 2 treat harshly, severely.

streng'le *V -a/+-et* string (e.g. beans).

***streng'/leik** *-en* harshness, rigorousness, severity.

streptokokk' *-en* streptococcus.

streptomyci'n *-et* streptomycin.

***stre't** *-et* exertion; grind, toil.

***stre'te**[1] *-t* cf **strede**

***stre'te**[2] *V -a* 1 exert oneself, wear oneself out. 2: **s- imot** resist.

stre'v *-et* 1 exertion; effort, endeavor; work. 2 drudgery, grind, toil.

***stre'val** *A* 1 hardworking, industrious. 2 laborious, toilsome.

stre've *V -de/*-a* 1 strive, struggle, work (**etter** for). 2 drudge, slave, toil (**med** at).

+**stre'ver** *-en, pl -e* (=***-ar**) 1 plodder. 2 adherent: cf **bak/s-, mål/s-**. 3 cross-beam, support.

+**stre'v/som'** *A -t, pl -me* (=***/sam**) 1 hardworking, industrious. 2 laborious, toilsome.

+**stri'**[1] *-a* (daily) struggle, toil; everyday cares, drudgery (see also **jule-stri, strid**[1]).

stri'[2] *V -dde/strei, -dd* (=**stride**) battle, fight, struggle (**for** for): **han har så mye å s- med** he has so many things to worry about, so much to do; **s- mot** (also) be contrary to, run counter to; **s- mot fornuften** be incompatible with, be against common sense; **s- mot loven** be illegal; **s-es om pavens skjegg** split hairs; **s-es om** contend, dispute about; **s- den gode strid** fight the good fight (2 Tim. 4,7).

stri'[3] *A -tt* cf **strid**[2]

+**stri'-**[1] *Pf* cf **strid-**

+**stri'-**[2] *Pf* cf **strie-**

stri'd[1] [*stri'] *-en* 1 battle, fight, struggle (**for** for; **imot** against): **den daglige s-** the daily struggle (for existence); **dra i s-** go to war; **åpen s-** open hostility. 2 conflict, controversy, dispute; disagreement, quarrel (**mellom** among, between; **om** about, over): **bilegge en s-** settle a dispute; **det har vært stor s- om dette punkt** this point has been hotly contested; **handle i s- med loven** act in defiance of the law; **stå i (direkte) s- med** be in (direct) conflict with, be at complete variance with; **vekke s-** stir up strife.

stri'd[2] *A* 1 hard, rigorous: **en s- dag** a strenuous day. 2 obstinate, stubborn: **s- på (sin rett)** insistent on (one's rights). 3 bristly, rough, wiry (beard, hair). 4 stiff (wind); rapid, swift (current); torrential (river): **det regner i strie strømmer** it's raining cats and dogs.

+**stri'd/bar** *A* argumentative, bellicose, quarrelsome.

+**stri'd/bar/het** *-en* pugnacity, quarrelsomeness.

stri'd/bukk [/bokk] *-en* hardhead, stubborn person.

stri'de [*stri'e] *V* +*stred/*streid, +-d/*-e/*-i* cf **stri**[2]

stri'dende [*stri'ande] *A* - fighting, struggling; contending, disputing: **s- imot** contrary to; **de s- parter** *jur.* the litigants.

stri'd/gråte *V infl as* **gråte** weep bitterly.

stri'dig *A* - headstrong, refractory, willful: **gjøre en noe s-** dispute sth with sby, contend for sth with sby; **gjøre en rangen s-** contend for precedence, superiority with sby.

+**stri'dig/het** *-en* 1 stubbornness, willfulness. 2 (usu. *pl*) conflict, controversy, dispute.

stri'd/lynt *A* - (=***/lyndt**) combative, disputatious.

stri'd/regne [+/reine] *V -a/+-et/+-te/ *-de* pour down, rain in torrents (cats and dogs).

***stri'd/sam** *A* argumentative, quarrelsome.

strid's/emne *-t, pl +-r/*-* subject of controversy, dispute.

strid's/eple *-t* bone of contention.

strid's/folk *-et poet.* warriors.

***strid's/før** *A* in fighting condition, trim.

strid's/hanske *-n* gauntlet: **kaste s-n til** challenge.

strid's/hest *-en* charger, war horse.

strid's/hingst *-en* charger, war horse (stallion).

strid's/hug *-en* fighting spirit; love of fighting, pugnacity.

strid's/huga *A* - combative, eager to fight, pugnacious.

strid's/hær *-en* army.

stri'd/sinna *A* - (=+**-et**) pugnacious.

strid's/krefter *pl* armed forces, military forces.

strid's/lyst *-a/+-en* fighting spirit; love of fighting, pugnacity.

strid's/lysten *A +-ent, pl -ne* combative, eager to fight, pugnacious.

strid's/makt *-a/+-en* armed forces, military forces.

strid's/mann *-en, pl -menn/*-menner* warrior, champion of a cause.

strid's/punkt *-et* issue in dispute, point at issue.

strid's/skrift *-et* polemic article, pamphlet.

strid's/spørsmål *-et* controversial question, point at issue.

+**strid's/vant** *A* - (=***/van(d)**) battle-hardened, seasoned.

strid's/vogn [/vångn] *-a* 1 *hist.* war chariot. 2 tank.

strid's/øks *-a* battle-ax: **begrave s-en** bury the hatchet.

strid's/årsak *-a/+-en* cause of controversy, dispute.

***stri'd/voren** [/våren] *A -e/-i, pl -ne* 1 headstrong, refractory, willful. 2 severe, strict.

stri'e *-n* burlap, sacking; buckram.

stri'e/sekk *-en, pl *-er* gunny sack.

stri'e/skjorte [/sjorte] *-a* cf **stri/**

+**strig'le**[1] *-n* currycomb.

+**strig'le**[2] *V -a/-et* curry, groom (a horse).

stri'k *-en dial.* little boy; *pop.* kid.

strikk' *-en* 1 elastic cord, string; rubber band. 2 shoddy.

+**strik'ke**[1] *-a/-en* cord, rope; halter: **en skal ikke tale om s- i hengt manns hus** never mention rope in the house of a hanged man.

strik'ke[2] *V -a/+-et* knit: **strikk en rett og to vrange** knit one purl two.

strik'ke/ga'rn *-et* knitting yarn.

strik'ke/maski'n *-en* knitting machine.

strik'ke/pinne *-n* knitting needle.

+**strik'kerske** *-n* woman who knits (or tends a knitting machine).

strik'ke/trøye *-a* knitted jacket, sweater.

+**strik'ke/tøy** *-et* (=***/ty**) knitting.

strikk'/fille *-a* woolen rag.

strik'king *-a/+-en* (=+**strikning**) knitting.

+**strik's** *A* strict; exacting, scrupulous.

+**strik't** *A* - strict.

strik'te *Av lit.* strictly.

stri'l *-en derog.* inhabitant of the coast esp. north and west of Bergen.

stri'le/mål *-et derog.* dialect of the coastal area around Bergen.

stri'me[1] *-a/+-en* 1 stripe, welt. 2 strip (e.g. of land); streak (e.g. of light).

+**stri'me**[2] *V -te/-et* streak, strip, stripe.

***stri'mel** *-elen, pl -lar* cf **strimmel**

stri'met(e) *A* - streaked, striped.

strim'le *V -a/+-et*: **s- opp** shred, cut up into shreds.

strim'mel *-elen, pl strimler* 1 strip (e.g. of paper, land). 2 border, frill.

Strin'da *Pln* twp, Sør-Trøndelag.

stringens [stringgen's] *-en* cogency, stringency (of logic).

stringent [stringgen't] *A* - closely reasoned, cogent.

stri'pe[1] *-a/+-en* stripe; band, shaft, streak; strip: **en s- jord** a strip of land; **en s- av himmelen** a streak of sky; **S-a** *fam., hum.* upper section of Karl Johansgate, the main street of Oslo.

+**stri'pe**[2] *V -a/-et/-te* streak, stripe.

stri'pet(e) *A* - 1 streaked, striped. 2 willing to work during a strike. 3 (in World War II) *derog.* inclined to favor or collaborate with the Nazis.

+**strip's** *-en* flogging, thrashing.

stri'/skjorte [/sjorte] *-a* sackcloth shirt; *fig.* (ab. =hairshirt): **s-a og havrelefsa** everyday activity (after a holiday; cf "back to the salt mines").

***stri't** *-et* cf **stret**

stritt' *nt of* **stri**[3]

+**strit'te** *V -a/-et* 1 bristle. 2: **s- imot** resist, struggle against; **s- imot med hender og føtter** fight tooth and nail.

stro'fe *+-n/*-a* stanza, strophe.

stro'fisk *A* - stanzaic, strophic.

***strok** [strå'k] *-et* 1 (river) current; rapids (=+**stryk**). 2 crowd, multitude. 3 noise, racket. 4 whetstone. 5 stroke (e.g. of pen). 6 district, region (=+**strøk**).

***stroke**[1] [strå'ke] *-a* 1 beating, drubbing. 2 narrow passage. 3 long row, series.

***stroke**[2] [strå'ke] *V -a* 1 be noisy. 2 ramble, rave; swarm.

stroke**[3] [strå'ke] *pp of* **stryke** (=stroki**)

***stroke/fant** [strå'ke/] *-en* tramp, vagrant; *(pop.)* bum.

***strokk'** *-en* (butter) cask, churn.

strok'ke** *pp of* **strekke**[1] (=strokki**)

***strong'ul** *-en, pl stronglar* (fence) rail.

strope** [strå'pe] *pp of* **strupe**[2] (=stropi**)

stropp' *-en* 1 strap, strop; loop, sling. 2 *naut.* strap; grommet.

***strop'pe**[1] *-a* cf **stropp**

+**strop'pe**[2] *V -a/-et* 1 *naut.*: **s- inn (en blokk)** strop (a block). 2 tie (in bundles).

+**strop'pe/holder** *-en, pl -e* (=***/haldar**) garter belt.

+**strukket** [strok'ket] *pp of* **strekke**[1]

struktu'r *-en* structure.

strukturell' *A -ell* structural.

stru'ma *-en med.* goiter, struma.

strun'k[1] *-en* 1 wooden bucket, cask. *2 clumsy fellow, oaf.

strun'k[2] *A* erect, straight, upright: **stiv og s-** as straight as a poker.

strun't *-en* 1 cone (e.g. of paper; ice cream). 2 *dial.* churlish, surly person; hardhead. 3 *fam.* foolishness, nonsense.

+ Bokmål; * Nynorsk; ° Dialect.
After letter: ' stress (Acc. 1); ' tone, stress (Acc. 2); · length.
Below letter: . not pronounced.

strun'ten *A* *+-ent, pl -ne dial.* cantankerous, perverse; cross, sullen.
stru'pe[1] *-n* throat: **fukte s-n** wet one's whistle; **sette en kniven på s-n** give sby an ultimatum; **skjære s-n over på en** cut sby's throat.
***stru'pe**[2] *V stryp, straup, strope/-i* cf **strupe**[3]
stru'pe[3] *V -te* (=***strupe**[2]) **1** choke, strangle; throttle (an engine).
+stru'pe/hode *-t anat.* larynx.
stru'pe/hoste [/hoste] *-n med.* croup: **falsk s-** acute catarrhal laryngitis.
stru'pe/lyd *-en* guttural sound, *gram.* guttural.
stru'pe/tak *-et* strangle hold.
stru'pe/tone *-n mus.* throaty tone.
***struss'** *-en* cf **struts**
stru't *-en* **1** point. **2** nozzle, spout. **3** snout.
strut's *-en zool.* ostrich (Struthio camelus): **gjøre som s-en** bury one's head in the sand.
+strut'se/fjær *-a* ostrich feather.
strut'se/politikk' *-en* ostrich-like policy.
***strut's/fjør** *-a* cf **strutse/fjær**
+strut'te *V -a/-et* be nearly bursting, bulge (**av** with): **s-ende** buxom, healthy; **et s-ende sunt menneske** a person glowing with health.
stry' *-et* **1** hards, hurds, tow. **2**: **narre en opp i s-** fool, pull the wool over sby's eyes.
stry'/dott *-en* handful of tow (used to clean a gun).
stry'k[1] *-et* rapid.
stry'k[2] *-et* beating, drubbing, thrashing.
stry'ke *V strauk/+strøk, +strøket/*strøke/*-i* **1** stroke=brush, pat, smooth: **s- en over håret** stroke sby's hair. **2** iron (clothes). **3** coat, cover (with oil, paint, etc.). **4** *mus.* bow. **5** lower, strike (a flag, sail). **6** cancel, delete, strike out; cut out, discontinue. **7** fail (an examination), flunk: **han strøk til eksamen** he flunked the exams. **8** move quickly, rush, swish: **s- av sted** dash off; **s- sin kos (sin vei)** disappear, go away, *(pop.)* beat it, clear out. **9** (as pres. p.): **s-ende** rapid, lively; **det er s-ende avsetning på varene** the goods sell like hot cakes. **10** (as pp.): **strøken** level (cup, spoon). **11** (with *adv.*, prep.): **s- av** remove, rub off, wipe off; **s- av med run off with**; **s- med** die, go the way of all flesh; be destroyed (in a catastrophe); **s- en mot hårene** rub sby the wrong way; **s- over** cross out; **s- ut** blot, delete; cross out, erase; iron out (wrinkles); hurry out.
stry'ke/bo'rd *-et* table for ironing.
stry'ke/brett *-et* ironing board.
stry'ke/fjøl *-a* ironing board.
stry'ke/flate *-a/+-en* striking surface (e.g. on matchbox).
stry'ke/instrumen't *-et, pl -/+-er* stringed instrument (played with a bow).
stry'ke/jern [/jæ'rn] *-et* iron, flatiron.
stry'ke/kandida't *-en* candidate who fails his examinations or has no chance of passing them.
stry'ke/klede [/klee] *-t, pl +-r/*-* ironing cloth.
stry'ke/kvartett' *-en* string quartet.
stry'kende *Av*: **det går s-** things are moving fast; it's going at a good clip; we're making good time, etc. (See also **stryke.**)
stry'ke/prosen't *-en* percentage of candidates failing their exams.
stry'ker *-en, pl -e* (=***-ar**) **1** *mus.* string (player): **s-ne** the strings. **2** candidate who fails his examinations or has no chance of passing them.
strykeri' *-et* laundry.
+stry'kerske *-n* ironing woman.
+stry'ke/tørr *A -tørt* ready for ironing.
+stry'ke/tøy *-et* ironing.
stry'king *-a/+-en* (=**+-ning**) **1** ironing: **vask og s-** laundry. **2** crossing out, deletion; failure. **3** *geol.* strike.
strykni'n *-en* strychnine.
Stry'n *Pln* twp, Sogn og Fjordane.
***stry'p** *pr of* **strupe**[2]
***stry'pe**[1] *-t* narrow pass.
+stry'pe[2] *V -te* cf **strupe**[3]
***stry'te** *-a* **1** snout. **2** narrow pass.
***stræ'ne** *V -te* cf **strene**
strø'[1] *-et* litter, sawdust, straw (on stable floor).
strø'[2] *V -dde* scatter, sprinkle, strew: **s- om seg med (penger)** scatter, spend (money) lavishly; **s- sand i maskineriet** throw a monkey wrench into the works; **s- sand på** hush up, smooth over; **s-dd (omkring)** scattered, strewn (about).
+strø'/bemer'kning *-en* casual, offhand remark.
strø'/halm *-en* straw bedding.
strø'k[1] *-et* **1** stroke (of bow, brush, hand, pen, etc.). **2** coat (of paint). **3** *geol.* strike, vein. **4** area, district; section (of a city): **s-et** *hum.* (favorite) promenade, main shopping street.
+strø'k[2] *pt of* **stryke**
+strø'ket *pp of* **stryke**
strø'k/vis *Av* here and there, sporadically.
+strøm' *-men* (=***straum**) **1** current (of water; electricity). **2** heavy flow, flood, stream (**av** of) also *fig.* (e.g. of tears, people, thoughts, etc.): **følge med s-en** go along with the crowd; **"Kjerringa mot s-en"** "The Contrary Woman" (folk tale by Asbjørnsen); **tidens (livets) s-** the course of time, events.
+strøm'/brudd *-et elec.* break in the circuit.
+strøm'/bryter *-en, pl -e elec.* circuit breaker; switch.
+strøm'/buss *-en* trackless trolley.
+strø'm'/drag *-et* **1** steady movement (of air, water). **2** rapid.
+strøm'/fall *-et* fall of current (in river, or due to tides).
+strøm'/forbruk *-et* consumption of electricity.
+strøm'/forde'ler *-en, pl -e elec.* (current) distributor.
+strøm'/førende *A - elec.* live (e.g. wire, rail).
+strøm'/gang *-en* course, direction of a current.
+strøm'/kilde *-n elec.* power supply.
+strøm'/krets *-en elec.* circuit.
+strøm'/leder *-en, pl -e elec.* conductor.
+strøm'/linje *-a/-en* streamline: **(de nye bilene) var en ren orgie i s-r** (the new cars) were a regular orgy of streamlining (Morgenbladet).
+strøm'/linjet *A -* streamlined.
+strøm'/løs *A elec.* dead (e.g. wire).
Strømm' *Pln* twp, Vestfold.
+strøm'me *V -et/strømte* (=***strøyme**) **1** flow, gush, run, stream; (of rain) pour: (often impersonal) **det s-er med (blod)** (blood) is streaming; **s- over (av)** overflow (with). **2** *fig.* flock, pour: **s- inn** (also) file in; **s- på** crowd in; **s- sammen** congregate, flock together; **s- til** come flocking.
+strøm'me/vis *Av*: **i s-** in streams, torrents.
+strøm'/måler *-en, pl -e* **1** *elec.* meter. **2** current meter (in a watercourse).
+strøm'ning *-en* **1** flow, stream. **2** current, trend: **litterære s-er** literary t-s.
strøm'pe *-a/-en* sock, stocking: **s-r** hose.
strøm'pe/band *-et* (=**+/bånd**) (round) garter.
+strøm'pe/holder *-en, pl -e* (=***/haldar**) garter; garter strap (on a corset, girdle).
+strøm'pe/lest *-en* (=***/leist**) stocking feet.
strøm'pe/skaft *-et* stocking leg.
strøm'pe/sokk *-en* sock (formed by cutting down a stocking).
strøm'pe/stopping *-a/+-en* darning of stockings.
strøm'pe/strikk *-en* elastic band, garter.
+strøm'/rasjone'ring *-a/-en* rationing of electricity.
+strøm'/retning *-a/-en* **1** *elec.* direction of current. **2** *naut.* (also) set of the current.
+strøm'/skifte *-t* **1** reversing of the current, turn of the tide. **2** reversal, shift in public feeling.
+strøm'/styrke *-n* **1** *elec.* amperage. **2** force, strength of a current (river).
+strøm'/vender *-en, pl -e elec.* commutator, reversing switch.
+strøm'/vending *-a/-en* **1** reversing of the current; turn of the tide. **2** reversal, shift in public feeling.
+strøm'/virvel *-elen, pl -ler* eddy, whirlpool.
strø'/sand *-en hist.* sand (for blotting).
strø'/skei [/sjei] *-a* (=**+/skje**) perforated spoon for sprinkling sugar or cinnamon.
strø'/sukker [/sokker] *-et* granulated sugar.
+strø'/tanker *pl* (=***-ar**) aphorisms.
***strøy'** *-et* cf **strø**[1]
***strøy'e** *V -dde* cf **strø**[2]
***strøy'me** *V -de* cf **strømme**
strøy'pe *V -te* choke, strangle.
***strøy'pe/orm** *-en zool.* boa constrictor (Constrictor constrictor).
strå'[1] *-et* straw; blade of grass: **høyt på s-** high up (in society), up in the world; **ligge på strå** *archaic* be laid out (as a corpse); **trekke s-** draw (lots); **trekke det korteste s-** get the worst of it; **ikke legge to s- i kors** not lift a finger.
***strå'**[2] *V -dde* cf **strø**[2]
strå'/død *-en* (=***/daude**) natural death (in bed).
strå'/farga *A* - (=**+-et**) straw-colored.
strå'/fletning *-en* plaited straw; straw plaiting.
strå'/for *-et* (hay, straw) fodder.
strå'/hatt *-en* straw hat.
°**strå'k** *-et* cf **strok**
strå'/korg *-a* straw basket.
strå'/kost [/kost] *-en* straw besom, broom.
strå'l *-et* (small) shoal of fish, esp. of herring.
strå'le[1] *-n* **1** beam, ray (of light, *fig.* of hope). **2** jet, squirt, (thin) stream (of liquid). **3** radial spoke; ray, spine (of the fin of a fish); frog (of the hoof of a horse); fourchette (of a glove).
strå'le[2] *V -te/*-a* **1** beam, radiate, shine; (also *fig.*) be radiant, sparkle: **s- ut** radiate. **2** spray, squirt (a liquid). (See also **strålende.**)
strå'le/bunt *-en phys.* pencil of rays.
strå'le/forma *A* - (=**+-et**) **1** shaped like a ray; straight. **2** star-shaped.
strå'le/glans *-en* radiance, refulgence.
strå'le/hav *-et poet.* flood, ocean of light.
strå'le/kreft *-en* **1** *vet.* foot canker. **2** *med.* cancer.
strå'lende *A* - **1** beaming, radiant, shining; glittering, sparkling. **2** (of weather) clear, sparkling. **3** *fig.* brilliant, glorious, gorgeous, spectacular; marvellous, wonderful.
strå'le/omn *-en* (=**+/ovn**) electric heater.
strå'le/sopp *-en bot.* actinomycete, ray fungus (belonging to the group Actinomycetes).
strå'le/varme *-n phys.* radiant heat, radiation heat.
strå'le/vell *-et poet.* flood, ocean of light.
+strå'le/virkning *-en* radiation effect.
strå'ling *-a/+-en phys.* radiation, radioactivity.
strå'lings/fare *-n* danger of radioactivity.
strå'/mann *-en, pl -menn/*-menner* straw man; figurehead, *(pop.)* stooge.
strå'/moden *A +-ent, pl -ne* partially ripened (e.g. barley, rye).

strå'/sekk *-en* straw mattress.
strå'/tak *-et* thatched roof.
+**strå'/tekke** *V -tekte* thatch.
strå'/visk *-en* wisp of straw.
St. tid.=**Stortingstidende**
+**stu'** *-en* cf **stuv**
stua'sje *-n naut.* stowage.
stubb' *-en* 1 stub (e.g. of arm, finger, pencil); stubble (grain, beard). 2 (of a song) snatch.
stub'be[1] *-n* 1 (tree) stump. 2 *dial.* (short) sturdy boy.
***stub'be**[2] *V -a* 1 stump, trudge along. 2 cut off.
+**stub'be/bryter** *-en, pl -e* (=***-ar**) stump puller.
stub'be/golv *-et* insulation flooring.
stub'be/loft *-et* insulation space below attic floor.
stub'bet(e) *A* - 1 stubby, stubbly. 2 *dial.* surly.
+**stubb'/loft** *-et* cf **stubbe/**
stubb'/mark *-a* stubble field.
stubb'/rumpa [/rompa] *A* - docked, short-tailed.
stubb'/åker *-en* stubble field.
stud.=**studiosus, student**
***stud'de** *pt of* **stydje**
studen't *-en* (university) student (including graduates; actually, anyone who has taken the **artium** degree): **bli s-** matriculate.
studen't/by *-en* student housing area: **S-en (på Sogn)** student dormitories (at Sogn, Oslo).
studen't/eksa'men *-en* matriculation examination (final examination in *gymnasium*, entrance examination at the university).
+**studen'ter-** *Pf* cf **student-**
Studen'ter/samfundet *Prn* The (Norwegian) Students' Association.
studen't/fabrikk' *-en hist.* "student factory" (school run by private individuals to prepare students for the matriculation examination).
studen't/heim *-en* residence hall for students.
studen't/hus *-et* residence hall for students.
studentiko's *A* student, undergraduate (usu. =jolly, lively).
studen't/lag *-et* student club.
studen't/lue *-a* (=**luve**) student cap (special cap with long tassel, worn on special occasions by all who have matriculated).
studen't/må'llag *-et* association of students advocating usage of New Norwegian.
studen't/samband *-et* students' association, club, corps.
studen't/samfunn *-et* students' association, club, corps.
studen't/samskipnad *-en* student welfare association (operates dormitories, union, etc.).
+**studen't/uke** *-a/-en* orientation week (at the university).
stude're *V -te* 1 study; pore over, scrutinize carefully; ponder, puzzle (**på** over): **s- nøye** make a close study of. 2 go to the university, receive a higher education; study (e.g. law, medicine): **la en s-** send sby to college; **s- ved universitetet** go to the university. 3: **s-ende** (university) student (in contrast to **student**, which includes university graduates).
stude'r/kammer *-et* (=***/kammers**) study.
stude'rt *A* - *archaic* 1 affected, studied. 2 educated, learned.
+**stude'r/værelse** *-t* study.
stu'die *-n* study; sketch (**av** of): **drive s-r** carry on, conduct studies.
+**stu'die/begren'sning** *-en* restricted enrollment (based on available space and scholastic achievement).
+**stu'die/leder** *-en, pl -e* (=***-ar**) leader of a study group.
stu'die/lån *-et* student loan.
+**stu'die/opphold** *-et* (temporary) residence in a foreign country for purposes of study.
stu'die/ordning *-a/+-en* curriculum.
stu'die/plan *-en* curriculum.
stu'die/reise *-a/+-en* study tour.
stu'die/sirkel *-elen, pl -ler* study circle, group.
stu'die/tid *-a/+-en* college days, student days.
+**stu'die/øyemed** *-et*: **i s-** for purposes of study.
studi'ne *-a/+-en hum.* woman (university) student.
stu'dio *-et, pl -/+-er* studio (musical, radio): **Store S-** large auditorium at national broadcasting studios.
studio'sus *-en* (university) student, esp. in titles: **stud. jur.** law student, **stud. philol.** student of philology, etc.
stu'dium *-iet, pl +-ier/*-ium* study (**av** of), esp. scientific or academic; *(pl)* studies (**i** in): **kaste seg over s-iene** throw oneself into one's s-s.
***stud'nad** *-en* cf **stønad**
stu'e[1] *-a* (=**stove**) 1 cottage, hut: **sette s-a på taket** raise the roof, turn the house upside down. 2 room; living room. 3 (in hospital) ward.
stu'e[2] *V -a/+-et* (=**stuve**) 1 pack, stow: **s- sammen** pack, squeeze together (like sardines); **s- ned (vekk)** stow away; **s- seg sammen** crowd together; **s- lasten** *naut.* stow the cargo. 2 blunt, dull. 3 sprain. 4 cream (vegetables): **s-ede erter** c-ed peas.
stu'e/arres't *-en* house arrest.
stu'e/bygning *-en* (farm) house, residence.
+**stu'e/dikter** *-en, pl -e* (=***-ar**) closet poet, ivory tower poet.
stu'e/dør *-a* door to livingroom.
stu'e/gris *-en* homebody, stay-at-home.
stu'e/hus *-et* dwelling house, residence.
stu'e/liv *-et* indoor, sedentary life.
stu'e/luft *-a* close, stuffy air of a room.
stu'e/lærd *A* - academic, bookish, pedantic.
***stu'e/lån** *-a* farm dwelling (usu. two-storied, extended log house).
stu'e/menneske *-t, pl +-r/*-* homebody, stay-at-home.
+**stu'e/pike** *-a/-en* maid, parlormaid.
stu'e/plante *-a/-en* 1 potted plant, room (indoor) plant. 2 homebody, stay-at-home.
+**stu'er** *-en, pl -e* (=***-ar**) stevedore.
stu'ert *-en naut.* steward.
stu'ert/skole *-n naut.* steward's school.
stu'e/temperatu'r *-en* room temperature.
stu'e/ur *-et* (wall) clock, grandfather's clock.
stu'e/varme *-n* room temperature; indoor warmth; coziness.
°**stug'u** *-a* cf **stue**[1]
stu'ing *-a/+-en* 1 *naut.* stowing; storage. 2 creamed dish (e.g. carrots).
stu'ke *V -a/+-et/+-te* 1 *tech.* rivet, swage, upset (e.g. a bolt). 2 bump, jar; sprain.
stukk' *-en* stucco.
stukkatu'r *-en* stuccowork.
stukke** [stok'ke] *pp of* **stikke**[2] (=stukki**)
+**stukket** [stok'ket] *pp of* **stikke**[2]
stukk'/verk *-et* stuccowork.
°**stu'l** *-en* cf **støl**[1]
***stul'd** *-en* theft.
***stul'k** *-en* awkward, clumsy person.
***stull'** *-en* cf **stoll**
stul'le *V -a/+-et* 1 putter around: **s- med** work with. 2 stump, trudge along. 3 care for (cattle).
stum' *A -t, pl -me* 1 dumb, mute, speechless (**av** with): **en s- person** a mute; **s- av skrekk** struck speechless with terror. 2 silent, taciturn; unspoken: **når du er dum, da vær blott s-** if you are stupid, keep silent (and no one will know); **bokstaven h er s- i hjerte** the letter *h* is silent in *hjerte.*
***stu'mende** *A* - cf **stummende**
stum'/film *-en* silent film.
+**stum'/het** *-en* dumbness, muteness; silence: **så en kveld vil s- ruge langs vår lange kyst** then one night will silence fall upon our long, long coast (Hamsun).
stumle [stom'le] *V -a/+-et* cf **stomle**
stum'mende *Av*: **s- mørk** black as pitch.
stum'/mørk *A* pitch-dark.
stump[1] [stom'p] *-en* 1 stub, stump; bit, fragment, piece; butt (of cigar, cigarette); snatch (e.g. of a song): **redde s-ene** save the pieces; **slå i s-er og stykker** smash to pieces. 2 *hum.* buttocks; little scamp, tiny tot. 3 *naut.* lower topsail. 4 *tech.* (of a hat) body.
+**stum'p**[2] [also: stom'p] *A* 1 blunt, dull. 2 *jur.*: **s- vold** injury sustained by a blunt weapon. 3 *math.*: **s-vinkel** obtuse angle.
stumpe [stom'pe] *V -a/+-et* 1 stump, trudge along, stumble. 2 bump, knock, thump. 3 (of a garment) be too short (at some point). 4 crush out (e.g. a burning cigarette). 5 *naut.* reef, shorten a sail.
stumpet(e) [stom'pet(e)] *A* - 1 (too) short, skimpy. 2 coarse, heavy.
stumpe/vis [stom'pe/] *Av* bit by bit.
+**stump/nese** [stom'p/] *-n* snub nose.
+**stump/neset** *A* - snub-nosed.
+**stump/vinklet** *A* - (=+**-a**) obtuse-angled.
stum're *V -a/+-et* stumble, totter; grope.
stum's *Av* (=***stups**) abruptly, suddenly.
+**stum'/tjener** *-en, pl -e* (coat) stand, hallstand.
stun'd *-a/+-en* 1 moment, while: **all den s-** considering, seeing that, since; **en god s-** a good while; **fra første s- (av)** right from the start; **i denne s-** right away; **i samme s-** at the same moment, simultaneously; **om en liten s-** in a little while; **noen s-** ever; **avgjørelsens (prøvelsens) s-** the hour of decision (trial); **til min siste s-** until my dying day. 2 *(pl)* time: **gi seg gode s-er** take one's time; **ha s-er til** have occasion, time for; **nå om s-er** nowadays.
stun'de[1] *V -a/+-et* 1 long, yearn (**etter for**): **s- mot** look forward to. 2 approach: **det s-r mot kvelden (til kvelds)** evening is drawing nigh; **vinteren s-er til** winter is near.
***stun'de**[2] *pt of* **stynje**
***stun'de/mellom** *Av* cf **stund/imellom**
+**stun'des/løs** *A* (=***stund/laus**) restless: **Den s-e** The Busybody (comedy by Holberg).
stun'de/vis *Av* from time to time, occasionally.
stun'd/imel'lom *Av* (=***stunde/-mellom**) at intervals, now and then.
***stun'd/laus** *A* cf **stundes/løs**
stun'dom' *Av* at times, now and then, sometimes.
***stun'd/vis** *Av* cf **stunde/**
stunge** [stong'e] *pp of* **stinge** (=stungi**)
stungen [stong'en] *A +-et, pl -ne*: **s-ne runer** *hist.* pointed runes.
***stun't** *pp of* **stynje**
stu'p *-et* 1 cliff, precipice. 2 header; dive, plunge; (sports) diving; (airplane) dive.
stu'p/bratt *A* - precipitous.
stu'pe *V -te/*stup, *staup, *stope/*-i* 1 dive, plunge; fall (dead; headlong, prone): **s- kråke** turn a somersault; **s- på nesen** fall flat, (of airplane) nose over; **s- uti** plunge in. 2 (of terrain) drop steeply: **s- opp** climb steeply.

+ Bokmål; * Nynorsk; ° Dialect.
After letter: ' stress (Acc. 1); ' tone, stress (Acc. 2); · length.
Below letter: . not pronounced.

stu'pe/brett *-et* diving board, springboard.
stu'pende *Av*: **s- mørk** pitch-dark.
+**stu'per** *-en, pl -e* (=*-**ar**) (sports) diver.
stu'pe/tå'rn *-et* (high) diving platform, tower.
stupi'd *A* - stupid.
stupidite't *-en* stupidity.
stu'p/mørk *A* pitch-dark.
stu'p/mørke *-t* (=*/**mørker**) pitch-darkness.
*****stu'pne** *V -a* droop, sink down.
*****stup'pe** *-a* pitfall.
+**stu'p/rød** *A* blood-red.
*****stu'ps** *Av* cf **stums**
°**stu'pul** *-en* cf **støpul**
stu'r[1] *-en* melancholy, sadness.
stu'r[2] *A* 1 dejected, downcast, moping; *(pop.)* blue. 2 depressing, gloomy: **en s- oktoberkveld** a gloomy October night (Ibsen).
stu're *V -te/*-a* 1 droop, mope; be depressed, melancholy, *(pop.)* blue. 2: **s-ende stilt** oppressively silent.
stu'ren *A* +*-ent, pl -ne* depressed, downhearted, sad; *(pop.)* blue.
*****stur't** *-en* cf **styrt**
stur'te *V -a/+-et* cf **styrte**
+**stur'ten** *N*: **i hurten og s-** in headlong haste, pell-mell.
stus'le *V -a/+-et* putter around.
+**stus'lig** *A* - cf **stusslig**
+**stuss'**[1] *-en* 1 (hair) trim; docking. 2 to-do, uproar. 3 end piece; (pipe) stub; connecting pipe.
stuss'[2] *A stust* 1 brusque, curt, gruff. *2 quiet, taciturn.
stus'se[1] *V -a/+-et* crop, dock, trim.
stus'se[2] *V -a/+-et* be surprised, taken aback; start (**over** at).
stuss'lig *A* - empty, lonesome; dull, monotonous, tedious.
stus't *nt of* **stuss**[2]
stu't *-en* 1 ox, steer. 2 *derog.* boor, oaf.
+**stu't/aktig** *A* - boorish, oafish.
stu'te/fjøs *-et* ox stable.
*****stu'teleg** *A* - boorish, crude, oafish.
stu'tet(e) *A* - boorish, crude, oafish.
stutt' *A* - 1 short. 2 brusque, curt, gruff.
stutt'/beint *A* - short-legged.
stut'te *V -a/+-et* 1 curtail, shorten. 2: **s- opp** creep, ride up (clothing).
stutteri' *-et, pl +-er/*-* stud farm.
stutt'/hose *-a* short hose.
stutt'/hugsen *A* +*-ent, pl -ne dial.* forgetful.
stutt'/høy *-et* short hay.
+**stut'ting** *-en* (=**stytting**[2]) *dial.* short sled for hauling timber.
stutt'/kjerre *-a dial.* (small) two-wheeled cart.
*****stutt'/minnig** *A* - *dial.* forgetful.
stutt'/mæ'lt *A* - brusque, curt.
*****stutt'ne** *V -a* become shorter.
stutt'/orv *-et* short-handled scythe.
stutt'/synt *A* - shortsighted.
stutt'/tenkt *A* - inconsiderate, thoughtless.
stutt'/trøye *-a* short jacket.
*****stutt'/vaksen** *A -e/-i, pl -ne* cf **/voksen**
stutt'/varig *A* - short-lived, transitory; of short duration.
+**stutt'/voksen** *A -ent, pl -ne* (=+/**vokst**) undersized.
stu'v *-en* (=+**stu**) 1 tree stump. 2 remnant (e.g. of cloth). 3 bird's tail.
*****stu'var** *-en* cf **stuer**
stu've *V -a/+-et* cf **stue**[1]
*****styd** [stø'] *-a* cf **stø**[1]
*****styd'je** *V styd, studde, studd* cf **stø**[3]
*****stygg'**[1] *-en* (=***stygge**) antipathy, aversion: **få s- til ein** take a dislike to sby.
stygg'[2] *A stygt* 1 bad (=dangerous, harmful): **en s- ulykke** a b- accident; **det ser s-t ut** it looks bad. 2 bad (=evil, malicious, mean): **det var s-t gjort** that was a dirty trick; **s- mot en** mean to sby; **det var s-t av ham** that was mean of him; **han er s- til å** he has a bad habit of; **en s- gutt** a bad boy. 3 bad (=unfavorable, unpleasant): **s-t vær** foul weather; **en s- lukt** a vile smell. 4 bad (=repulsive, ugly): **en s- håndskrift** an ugly handwriting; **s-e ord** bad words; **en s- kjole** an ugly dress. 5 *(adv.)*: **jeg er s-t redd for at** I'm really afraid that.
*****styg'ge** *-n* cf **stygg**[1]
styg'ge/dom' *-men/*-en* 1 deviltry, malevolence, witchcraft. 2 abomination, horror.
styg'gelig *A* - fearfully, terribly: **ta s- feil** be grievously mistaken.
styg'gelse *-t* monster, ogre.
styg'ge/mannen *df* the devil.
styg'gen *df* 1 *hum.* fright, scarecrow. 2 the devil.
+**styg'ges** *stygdes, -es* (=*-**jast**) be disgusted (**ved** by); feel loathing (for).
+**styg'ge/vær** *-et* cf **stygg/**
+**stygg'/het** *-en* repulsiveness, ugliness; evil, filth; filthiness, wickedness.
styg'ging *-en* nasty, repulsive person; fright, scarecrow.
*****styg'gjast** *V stygdest* cf **stygges**
*****styg'gje** *V stygde* frighten, scare off; repel.
stygg'/kald *A* frightfully cold.
stygg'/mye *A* - a great deal of.
stygg'/sint *A* - frenzied, raving.
+**stygg'/vær** *-et* (=**stygge/**, */**ver**) bad weather, storm.
*****sty'k-** *Pf* cf **ste-**
stykk' *N*: **arbeide på (per) s-** work on a piecework basis.
stykk'/arbeid *-et* piecework.
styk'ke[1] *-t, pl +-r/*-* 1 bit, piece; (of cattle) head: **et s- kake** a p- of cake; **s- for s-** p- by p-; **femti øre s-t** fifty *øre* apiece; **for (per) s-et** apiece; **i s-r** broken, in p-s; **(gå, rive, skjære, slå, osv.) i s-r** (go, rip, cut, knock, etc.) to p-s; **et lekkert støkke** *pop.* (of woman) a tasty morsel. 2 (in business letters and papers) unit (of): **i dag har vi sendt Dem to s-r (stkr.) skrivemaskiner** we have today sent you two typewriters. 3 (as noun substitute): **vi var en 10—12 s-r til stede** there were 10 or 12 of us present. 4 (usu. short) distance, a ways: **et lite s-** a little ways. 5 film, play; musical composition; article, piece: **det går et godt s- på** there's a good film (play) at. 6 piece of bread, sandwich; slice: **jeg skal ha to s-r med geitost og ett s- med skinke** I'll have two goat cheese sandwiches and one ham sandwich. 7: **når det kommer til s-t** when it comes to the point (the chips are down), when it counts; when all is said and done; after all, in the final analysis. 8 problem (in arithmetic).
+**styk'ke**[2] *V -a/-et/stykte* (=*-**je**): **s- opp** cut, split up, divide; **s- ut** parcel out.
styk'ke/vis *Av* piecemeal; by the piece, piece by piece.
stykk'/gods [/gots] *-et* 1 *naut.* general or miscellaneous cargo. 2 parcels (railroad).
*****stykkj'e** *V -a* cf **stykke**[2]
stykk'/junker *-en, pl +-e mil.* master sergeant, artillery corps (until 1930).
stykk'/last *-a/-en naut.* general or miscellaneous cargo.
styk'kom/til' *Av* 1 piece by piece. 2 now and then; part of the way.
stykk'/pris *-en merc.* unit price.
+**stykk'/salg** *-et* (=*/**sal**) retail sale, retail selling.
stykk'/takst *-en merc.* unit rate; going rate.
*****sty'k/mor** *-a, pl -mødrer* cf **ste/**
*****sty'l** *-en* (of straw) stalk, stem.
+**styl'te**[1] *-n* cf **styltre**[1]
+**styl'te**[2] *V -et* walk on stilts: **s- seg opp** put on airs.
*****styl'tre**[1] *-a* (=+**stylte**[1]) stilt: **gå på høye s-r** put on airs; speak in a grandiloquent, high-flown manner.
*****styl'tre**[2] *V -a* walk as though on stilts.
+**stym'per** [also -ym'-] *-en, pl -e* 1 poor devil, wretch. 2 coward, weakling.
+**stym'per/aktig** [also -ym'-] *A* - 1 miserable, wretched. 2 bungling, cowardly.
*****sty'n** *-et* cf **stønn**[2]
*****styng'** *-en* cf **sting**
*****styn'je** *V styn, stunde, stunt* cf **stønne**
*****sty'p** *pr of* **stupe**
sty'r[1] +*-et/*-en* commotion, ruckus, uproar: **holde s-** make c-; **på s-** confused, crazy.
sty'r[2] *-et* control, management: **s- og stell** management, running (e.g. of a house); **gå over s-** fail, go on the rocks, (of an engagement) be broken; **ha s- på** have control of, have under control; **holde s- på** control, keep under control; keep track of, make out; **sette over s-** squander (e.g. money).
+**sty'r/bar** *A*: **s-t luftskip** dirigible.
sty'r/bo'rd *N naut.* starboard.
*****styr'd** *A* cf **støl**[2]
*****styr'dne** *V -a* cf **stølne**
sty're[1]*-t, pl +-r/*-1* handlebar; steering gear; *naut.* helm: **stå for s-t** rule the roost, wear the pants in the family; **ta s-t** assume control. 2 administration, control, management: **s- og stell** conduct, management. 3 board of directors, executive committee: **i s-t** on the board (etc.).
sty're[2] *V -te* 1 guide, pilot, steer (a boat, car, etc.): **s- rett mot (på)** head straight for, bear down on. 2 govern, rule (e.g. a country); direct, be the head of, manage (e.g. a business, a house, etc.): **s- med** manage, take care of; **s- over** rule over. 3 control, keep in check. restrain: **s- seg (sin lyst)** curb, restrain oneself. 4 *gram.* govern (a case).
+**sty're/beslut'ning** *-en* resolution by the board (committee).
sty're/fjør *-a zool.* tail feather, rectrix.
sty're/form *-a/+-en* system of government.
sty're/hus *-et naut.* pilothouse, wheelhouse.
+**sty'relse** *-n* 1 administration, government, management (**av** of). 2 dispensation, (divine) providence. 3 *gram.* object (of a preposition).
sty're/makt *-a/+-en* (the) authorities, (the) government.
sty're/medlem [/-lemm] +*-met/*-(m)en, pl +-mer/*-(m)er* member of the board (exec. comm.).
sty're/møte *-t, pl - +-r/*-* board meeting.
sty're/måte *-n* system of government.
sty'ren *A* +*-ent, pl -ne* 1 rebellious, ungovernable; crazy, mad. 2 flustered, perturbed; frightened, scared.
sty're/protokoll' *-en* minutes of a board meeting.
+**sty'rer** *-en, pl -e* (=*-**ar**) 1 regent, ruler. 2 chairman (e.g. of a meeting); manager (e.g. of a firm); school principal. 3 *naut.* steersman.
sty'res/makt *-a/+-en* cf **styre/**
sty'res/mann *-en, pl -menn/*-menner* 1 regent, ruler. 2 *archaic* helmsman.
+**sty're/stang** *-a, pl -stenger* (=*/**stong**) 1 steering gear; connecting rod. 2 *naut.* guide rod. 3 plough handle.
sty're/vedtak *-et* resolution by the board.
sty're/vol *-en dial.* 1 *naut.* tiller. 2 (of an airplane) joy stick.
sty're/åre *-a* steering oar.
sty'ring *-a/+-en* 1 dominance, lead, rule; administration, government. 2 *naut.* handling of the tiller, steering. 3 *tech.* steering gear, controls (e.g. of an automobile, airplane); reversing gear; valve gear: **miste s-en** lose control.
sty'rings/verk *-et* (the) administration, government.

***styr'je** *V -a* cause a disturbance, riot, uproar.

***styr'k** *-en* fortifying, strengthening.

styr'ke[1] *-n* 1 strength (of person, army, material; liquid, feeling etc.): **det er ikke hans s-** it's not his strength (forte, strong point); **prøve s- med en** measure one's strength against sby. 2 force, power, vigor; intensity (of stress), volume (of sound); potency: **uttale med s-** express forcibly, vigorously. 3 (armed) force(s); command: **overlegne s-r** superior forces.

+**styr'ke[2]** *V -a/-et/-te* (=***-je**) 1 fortify, invigorate, strengthen: **s- seg på** restore oneself with (by means of). 2 *archaic* confirm, verify. *3 encourage, urge (**til** to). 4: **s-ende** fortifying, refreshing, stimulating.

styr'ke/belte *-t* (=***styrkje/**) *hist.* girdle of strength (worn by warriors to insure success in battle).

styr'ke/drikk *-en* (=***styrkje/**) stimulating drink, tonic (e.g. brandy, cordial).

styr'ke/dråpe *-n* (=***styrkje/**) stimulating drink, tonic (e.g. brandy, cordial).

styr'ke/forhold *-et* relative strength (**mellom** of).

styr'ke/grad *-en* degree of intensity, strength.

+**styr'kelse** *-n* fortifying, strengthening (**av** of); invigoration, refreshment.

styr'ke/middel *-elet/-midlet, pl +-midler/*-el* (=***styrkje/**) tonic.

styr'ke/prøve *-a/+-en* test, trial of strength.

***styr'kje** *V -te* cf **styrke[2]**

sty'r/laus *A* (=+**/løs**) unbridled, ungovernable, unruly.

styr'/mann *-en, pl -menn/*-menner* *naut.* mate; coxswain (e.g. of a longboat, racing shell).

styr'manns/skole *-n naut.* mate's school (i.e. one preparing candidates for the mate's examination).

***styr'me** *V -de* rush, storm forth.

***sty'rnad** *-en* administration, management; housekeeping.

styr't *-en* (=***sturt**) 1 shower; shower bath. 2 *lit.* inundation (e.g. of insults) (**av** of).

styr'te *V -a/+-et* (=***sturte**) 1 dash, plunge, rush: **s- av sted** dash off; **s- i seg** gulp, wolf down; **komme s-ende** come running. 2 fall down, topple over: **s- i grus** fall into ruin; **s- om** fall dead; **s- sammen** cave in, collapse, fall down. 3 overthrow, throw down: **s- regjeringen** topple the government. 4 (*refl.*): **s- seg** (of terrain) drop off sharply; (of person) plunge, throw oneself; **s- seg ut i fordervelse(n)** ruin oneself; **s- seg over noe** fall upon sth (a victim); throw oneself into (a task); **s- seg ut** jump out (e.g. of a window).

styr'te/ferdig *A* - ready to drop (e.g. with fatigue).

styr'te/gods [/gots] *-et naut.* bulk cargo (which can be loaded through a chute).

styr'tende *Av* tremendously: **s- rik** rolling in money.

styr'tning *-en* 1 falling, plunging, rushing. 2 precipice.

styr't/regn [+/rein] *-et* torrential rain; downpour.

styr't/regne [+/reine] *V -a/+-et/+-te/*-de* pour down; (*pop.*) come down in buckets, rain cats and dogs.

styr't/rik *A* rich as Croesus, rolling in money.

styr't/sjø *-en* big wave, breaker; heavy sea.

***styr'ven** *A -e/-i, pl -ne* awkward, clumsy, stiff.

+**sty'r/vol** [/vål] *-en* cf **styre/**

styr'/volt *-en* 1 *hist.* a four-handed card game. 2 *hist.* low card not used (in ombre).

***styt'te[1]** *-a* cf **støtte[1]**

***styt'te[2]** *V -a/-e* cf **støtte[2]**

***styt'ting[1]** *-a* abbreviation.

***styt'ting[2]** *-en* cf **stutting**

sty'v *-en* 1 bird's tail. 2 *derog.* buttocks, rump.

***sty'v-** *Pf* cf **ste-**

***sty've** *V -de* top.

***sty'ven** *A -e/-i, pl -ne* silly, simple.

+**sty'ver[1]** *-en, pl -e hist.* stiver (small copper coin); *fig.* piddling amount, sum.

+**sty'ver[2]** *-en, pl -e* jolt; *fig.* reprimand, setback.

***stæ'le** *V -te* 1 pile, stack. 2 stimulate, urge. 3 steel (an axe, oneself).

+**stæ'r[1]** *-en* cf **star(e)[1]**

+**stæ'r[2]** *-en* (=***star[2]**): **grønn s-** *med.* glaucoma; **grå s-** *med.* cataract.

+**stæ'r/blind** *A* (=+**stær blind**) blind as a bat.

+**stæ'r/kasse** *-a/-en* starling's birdhouse.

stø'[1] *-a* 1 boat landing. 2 *dial.* river bank. *3 back, support (of chair).

stø'[2] *V -dde* (=**støe[2]**) steady, support; *fig.* assist, help: **s- seg mot** lean against.

stø'[3] *A -tt* firm, steady; dependable, reliable: **være s- på** be sure of, depend upon; **være s- på hånden** have a s- hand.

***stø'de** *V -de* cf **stø[2]**

stø'dig *A* - firm, steady; dependable, reliable.

+**stø'e[1]** *-a* cf **stø[1]**

+**stø'e[2]** *V -dde* cf **stø[2]**

***stø'e/punkt** *-et* cf **støtte/**

stø'/hendt *A* - sure-handed.

+**stø'/het** *-en* steadiness; reliability.

støkk' *-en* start; shock.

°**støk'ke[1]** *-t* cf **stykke[1]**

støk'ke[2] *V stokk, +-et/+støkt/*stokke/*-i* 1 be startled, give a start, jump: **det stokk (+støkk) i ham** he gave a start. *2 break in two, burst, split. *3 pour, trickle (e.g. blood, sweat).

+**støk'ke[3]** *V støkte* (=***-je**) 1 scare, startle. 2 flush game (hunting). *3 fell (tears).

støk'ken *A +-ent, pl støkne* 1 brittle, fragile. 2 timorous.

***støkkj'e** *V støkte* cf **støkke[3]**

stø'l[1] *-en* 1 open milking-place for cows at a mountain summer farm. 2 mountain summer farm.

stø'l[2] *A* (=**stør[3]**) 1 stiff, sore (in one's muscles): **stiv og s-** (the same). 2 slow, sluggish (e.g. in one's thinking).

stø'le *V -a/+-te* 1 go to a mountain summer pasture with cattle. 2: **s- seg** rest during grazing (cattle).

***stø'leg** *A* - steady; dependable.

***stø'/leik** *-en* steadiness; reliability.

+**stø'l/het** *-en* stiffness.

stø'lne *V -a/+-et* (=**størne**) grow stiff, stiffen.

stø'ls/bu *-a* chalet, herdsman's cabin at a mountain summer farm.

stø'ls/jente *-a* dairymaid at a mountain summer farm.

***stø'n** *-et* cf **stønn[2]**

stø'nad [*støna] *-en* aid, assistance, benefit.

***stø'ne** *V -a* become steadier.

°**støng'** *-en* cf **sting**

°**stønn'[1]** *-a* cf **stund**

stønn'[2] *-et* (=***støn**) groaning, moaning; gasp, groan, moan.

+**støn'ne** *V -et/stønte* (=***stynje**) groan, moan.

+**stø'pe** *V -te* cf **støype**

+**stø'per** *-en, pl -e* cf **støyper**

+**støperi'** *-et, pl -er* cf **støyperi**

+**stø'pe/skje** *-a/-en* cf **støype/skei**

+**stø'pning** *-en* 1 casting, founding; pouring (of concrete). 2 cast, mold; character, type; stature: **han var av en annen s-** he was a man of a different cast (mold).

+**støp'sel** *-elet/-let, pl -ler* (=***støypsel**) *elec.* plug.

+**stø'pul** *-en* (=***stopul**) bell frame, belfry.

+**stø'r[1]** *-en zool.* sturgeon (Acipenser sturio).

°**stø'r[2]** *-en* cf **staur**

stø'r[3] *A* cf **støl[2]**

***stø're** *V -te* stimulate, urge, (**til** to).

Stø'ren *Pln* twp, Sør-Trøndelag.

+**stø'r/het** *-en* cf **støl/**

stø'r/hus *-et dial.* cookshack, washhouse.

stør'je *-a zool.* 1 tunny (Thynnus thynnus). 2 (often used term for) large fish (also in *cpds.*).

+**stør'kne** *V -a/-et* (=***storkne**) 1 harden, set, solidify; coagulate, congeal (blood). 2 *fig.* become hackneyed, stereotyped.

stø'rne *V -a/+-et* cf **stølne**

stør're *cp of* **stor**

+**stør'relse** *-n* 1 size; area, extent, magnitude; height, tallness; bulk, quantity, volume: **av middels s-** medium-sized; **av passende s-** of a suitable size; **i naturlig s-** lifesize; **ordnet etter s-** arranged according to size. 2 personage, personality, star. 3 *math.* quantity.

stør'st *sp of* **stor**

stør'ste/delen *df* the bulk, the greatest part, the majority (**av** of): **for s-** for the most part, generally.

stør'ste/parten *df* the bulk, the greatest part; the majority (**av** of).

+**stø't** *-et* cf **støyt**

+**stø't/demper** *-en, pl -e* shock absorber.

+**stø'te** *V -te* cf **støyte**

+**stø'tende** *A* - objectionable, offensive, shocking.

+**stø'ter** *-en, pl -e* (=***støytar**) pestle.

+**stø't/fanger** *-en, pl -e* (=***støyt/fangar**) (automobile) bumper.

+**stø't/pute** *-a* buffer (e.g. on a railroad car); *fig.* buffer, cushion.

støtt' *Av* always, continually: **s- og stadig** constantly.

+**stø't/tann** *-a, pl -tenner* tusk.

støt'te[1] *-a/+-en* 1 support (e.g. brace, pillar, stanchion; buttress, prop). 2 monument, pillar, statue (**av** of): **en s- av ild** a pillar of fire. 3 *fig.* mainstay, pillar, supporter: **sannhetens og frihetens ånd — det er samfundets s-r** the spirit of truth and freedom — these are the pillars of society (Ibsen). 4 backing, support; grant, subsidy: **gi en sin s-** back sby; **få s- av** be backed by; get a grant from.

+**støt'te[2]** *V -a/-et* (=***stytte[2]**) 1 brace, support: **s- opp** prop, shore up; **s- under** serve as a base for. 2 *fig.* back up, endorse, support; aid, help: **s- forslaget** second the motion; **tre s-ende til** come to sby's aid. 3 (*refl.*): **s- seg til** fall back on, rely on; lean, steady oneself on.

+**støt'te/aksjo'n** *-en* relief action, campaign.

+**støt'te/fag** *-et* minor field of study (for the M.A. degree).

+**støt'te/punkt** *-et* 1 point of support, support. 2 *mil.* base.

+**støt'te/stav** *-en* staff; *fig.* prop, support.

+**støt'te/vev** *-et physiol.* connective tissue.

+**stø't/tone** *-n gram.* glottal catch (in Danish).

+**stø't/vis** *Av* by fits and starts, spasmodically; intermittently.

stø'v *-et* 1 dust; pollen: **tørke s-** dust (furniture). 2 *bibl., lit.* clay, mortal remains: **s- er du, og til s- skal du vende tilbake** dust thou art and unto dust shalt thou return (Gen. 3, 19); **s-ets år** age of man, days of our years (70 years).

+**stø'v/aktig** *A* - dustlike.

stø'v/briller *pl* goggles.

+**stø'v/bærer** *-en, pl -e* (=***/berar**) *bot.* stamen.

+**stø'v/drager** *-en, pl -e bot.* stamen.

+ Bokmål; * Nynorsk; ° Dialect.
After letter: ' stress (Acc. 1); ` tone, stress (Acc. 2); · length.
Below letter: . not pronounced.

stø've *V -a/+-et* 1 be dusty; raise dust: **det s-er fra veien** dust is blowing from the road; **møblene er s-ete** the furniture is covered with dust. 2: **s- opp** nose, smell out, track down game; **s- omkring** rush around. 3: **s-ende(s)** fine, vigorous; **det gikk rent s-ende(s)** it went swimmingly; **komme s-ende(s)** strutting, swaggering along.
stø've/brett *-et* dustpan.
stø've/klut *-en* dustcloth.
stø've/kost *-en* duster.
støv'el *-elen, pl -ler* boot; (ankle-high) shoe; *naut.* sea boot: **være på støvlene** be slightly high.
støv'el/knekt *-en* bootjack.
støv'el/lisse *-a* bootlace.
støv'el/skaft *-et* bootleg.
støv'el/snute *-n* toe of a boot.
støv'el/stropp *-en* bootstrap.
+**støv'el/såle** *-n* (=*/sole) boot sole.
støv'el/tramp *-et* stamping of boots.
stø'vende *A* - first-rate, splendid, *(pop.)* swell.
+**stø'ver** *-en, pl -e* (=***-ar**) 1 hound, hunting dog, (e.g. a beagle); retriever: **en s- etter** *fig.* eager for, on the lookout for. 2 energetic person, hard worker: **en s- til å** good at.
stø'vet(e) *A* - dusty; *fig.* antiquated, old-fashioned.
stø'v/fin *A* dustlike, powdery (e.g. snow).
+**stø'v/fnugg** *-et* dust particle, speck of dust.
stø'v/frakk *-en* duster.
stø'v/grann *-et* dust particle, speck of dust.
stø'v/grå *A -tt* dust colored.
***stø'ving** *-a* pollination.
stø'v/knapp *-en bot.* anther.
stø'v/ko·rn *-et* 1 dust particle, speck of dust. 2 pollen.
stø'v/lag *-et* layer of dust.
+**støv'le**[1] *-n* cf **støvel**
støv'le[2] *V -a/+-et* stomp, trudge.
støvlett' *-en* snowboot.
stø'v/plage *-a/+-en* dust nuisance, problem.
stø'v/regn [+/rein] *-et* drizzle, mist.
+**stø'v/samler** *-en, pl -e* (=***-ar**) dust catcher (e.g. a piece of furniture); dust collector (in iron and steel work).
stø'v/sky *-a* cloud of dust.
stø'v/suge *V infl as* **suge** vacuum, clean with a vacuum cleaner.
+**stø'v/suger** *-en, pl -e* (=***-ar**) vacuum cleaner.
stø'v/tørking *-a* (=+**/tørring**) dusting (e.g. of furniture).
støv/veg *-en* (=+**/vei**)
stø'v/vei *-en bot.* pistil.
støy' *-en* noise; din, racket, uproar: **lage s-** make noise; interference (in radio).
+**støy'e** *V -a/-et/-de* make a noise, racket; **s-nde** boisterous, noisy.
støy'/filter *-eret/-ret, pl -er/+-re elec.* static filter, reducer (radio).
støy'/kontroll· *-en* sound inspection.
støy'pe *V -te* (=+**støpe**) cast, found; pour (concrete): **sitte som s-t** fit like a glove; **s- lys** make candles.
støy'pe/form *-a/+-en* casting mold, mold.
støy'pe/gods [/gots] *-et* castings; foundry products.
støy'pe/jern [/jæ'rn] *-et* cast iron.
støy'pe/lys *-et hist.* (molded) candle.
støy'pe/omn *-en* (=+**/ovn**) foundry furnace.
+**støy'per** *-en, pl -e* (=***-ar**, +**støper**) caster, founder.
støyperi' *-et, pl* +*-er/**- (=+**støperi**) foundry.
støy'pe/skei [/sjei] *-a* casting, foundry ladle: **komme i s-a** (+**støpeskjeen**) (e.g. of an institution) be reshaped, be radically changed; **i s-en med ham som mislykket gods** throw him into the meltingpot as a failure (Ibsen).
støy'pe/stål *-et* cast steel.
støy'/plage *-a/+-en* noise nuisance; din, racket (e.g. from radios, traffic, etc.).
***støy'psel** *-elet/-let* cf **støpsel**
***støy're** *V -te* drive poles into the ground; place sheaves (of grain) on poles (for drying).
støy't *-en* (=+**støt**) 1 push, shove, thrust; jab; stab; shot, stroke; (in shotput) putting: **gi s-et til noe** cause, launch, originate sth; **gi det siste s-** finish off. 2 blow, bump, jolt; shock: **stå for en s-** take a blow, *(pop.)* take it; **ta s-en** bear the brunt, take the blow. 3 gust (of wind). 4 blast, toot (of a horn). 5 gulp, swallow, swig (of liquor). 6 *gram.* glottal (stop).
***støy'tar** *-en* pestle.
støy'te *V -te* (=+**støte**) 1 push, shove, thrust; jab, stab; shoot. 2 bump (**borti, mot** into), jolt, thump; bruise (an apple): **s- seg** bump (oneself). 3 hurt, offend: **s-ende** offensive; **det norske teaterspråk er rått og s-ende** Norwegian theatrical language is coarse and offensive (Ibsen); **bli (være) s-t over** be offended at. 4: **s- i** sound (a horn). 5 grind, pound (with pestle). 6 (with *prep., adv.*) **s- an mot** offend against, outrage; **s- bort** push away, reject; **s- fra seg** push away, reject; alienate; **s- fram (ordene)** press (the words) out; **s- opp til** abut on, adjoin; **s- på** come upon, encounter, run into (across, up against); **s- til** bump, jar, prod; abut, adjoin; (of complications with an illness) arise, set in; **s- sammen** collide; **s- ut** push out, exclude.
***støy'te/stein** *-en* stumbling block.
***støy't/fangar** *-en* cf **støt/fanger**
***støy't/tann** *-a, pl -tenner* cf **støt/**
stå'[1] *N*: **gå i s-** come to a dead stop, standstill; stop short.
stå'[2] *V stod, stått* (=***stande**) 1 stand; be, be located: **s- brud** be a bride; **s- modell for** pose for; **s- i butikk (bak disken)** work in a store; **s- på en liste** be on a list; **s- som** be, serve as (e.g. chairman, leader); **la det s-** let it be, leave it alone; **det s-r og faller med** it's all up to, it all depends on; **maten s-r på bordet** the food is on the table, dinner is served; **som en s-r og går** just as one is; **her stod slaget** the battle was fought here; **skogen (kornet) s-r bra** the woods (the grain) are doing fine; **så stod jeg der** so there I was (in a jam). 2 be written; says: **s-r det noe om ham i brevet?** is there anything about him in the letter?; **det s-r i avisen** it says in the paper; the paper says. 3 (e.g. of a factory, machinery) halt, stop; be idle, be at a standstill: **munnen s-r ikke på ham** he talks incessantly; **uret s-r** the clock has stopped. 4 take place; (of battles) be fought: **når skal bryllupet s-?** when's the wedding? 5 (e.g. of boats, wind) come, go, move: **s- til sjøs** put out to sea; **vinden s-r fra vest** the wind is from the west. 6 last: **festen stod i flere dager** the party l-ed several days; **kulda stod ikke lenge** the cold didn't l- long. 7 remain in place, stick fast: **båten s-r på grunn** the boat is aground; **slå i en spiker så den s-r** drive in a nail so that it sits; **dette kortet s-r** this card is good. 8 (expressing continuing action): **s- og henge** hang around; **han stod og ventet i en halv time** he waited (was waiting) for half an hour; **mor s-r midt oppe i sildesalaten** mother's right in the middle of (making) the herring salad (Ibsen). 9 protrude, stick out, up; (of liquids) splatter, squirt; (of dust) fly, rise; (of odors, warmth, etc.) come from, radiate from: **det stod en kald gufs fra døra** a blast of cold came from the door; **det s-r respekt av ham** he inspires respect, is respected; **støvet stod omkring oss** the dust flew around us. 10 (with *prep., adv.*): **s- av** get off; **s- bak** stand behind, *fig.* sponsor, support; be at the bottom of; **s- en bi** assist sby; **s- en dyrt** cost sby a lot; **dette kommer til å s- ham dyrt** he'll pay dearly for this; **s- dårlig** be in a bad way, a weak position; **s- etter** be after (e.g. sby); **så det s-r etter** with a vengeance; **s- fast** stand firm, hold one's own; **(ikke) s- for** (not) bear, stand (criticism, examination, punishment, etc.); (not) resist (temptation, a person, etc.); **s-' for** be in charge of (arrangements, an organization, work, etc.); (see also **dør, fall, tur**); **s- for' en** be in sby's mind or memory, seem to sby; **det s-r for' meg at** I seem to remember, it seems to me that; **s- foran** stand in front of, *fig.* be on the verge of, on the eve of; **s- fritt** remain neutral, keep an open mind; **s- en fritt** be at sby's option; **det s-r deg fritt å velge** you are free to choose; **s- hen** *archaic* be in abeyance, be deferred; **la det s- hen** let it wait for now; **s- høyt** rank, stand high, be at a premium; **s- i** be in, (danger, debt, one's power, relationship); be on (fire); (of money) be invested in; **djevelen s- i alt som minner, djevelen s- i alle kvinner** devil take everything that reminds one, devil take all women (Ibsen); **s- i med en** have an affair, intimate relations with sby; **s- igjen** be left (behind, remaining); **s- imot** be opposed to, resist, withstand; **s- klart for en** be clear to sby, dawn on sby; **s- midt oppe i noe** be in the midst of sth; **s- mot himmelen** be silhouetted against the sky; **s- om (livet)** be a matter of, involve (life and death); **s- opp** stand up, get up, get out of bed; **s- opp under** reach to; **vannet stod ham opp under armene** the water reached to his armpits; **s- over** be above, superior to; (of an article) be delayed, not yet printed; live through, survive; **s- overfor** be faced with, confronted with (e.g. difficulty, problem); be on the threshold of (advancement, development); **s- på** (of radio, faucet) be (turned) on; (of wind) be coming straight at one; (of sun) beat down; be going on, last (**mens det stod på** while it lasted); be the matter (**hva er det som s-r på?** what's up? what's wrong?; **hva s-r det på?** what's the hitch?); be at (odds, stake, the zenith), in (the balance, the sky), on (end, good terms, a list, sby's side, etc.): **det s-r på henne** it's in her name (or: it depends on her); **s- på sitt** be adamant, insist on one's rights; **s- på ski** ski (esp. downhill); **s- sammen** (also of colors) be matched, suit; **s- svakt** be in a weak position, have no leg to stand on; **s- til** go with, match; **hatten s-r til drakten** the hat matches the suit; **hvordan s-r det til?** how are you?; **det s-r bra til** things are fine; (of an examination) be good enough for, be worth (a given grade); **hvis det s-r til meg** if it's up to me; **la det s- til** let 'er rip, pull out all the stops, take a chance; **det s-r til liv** *hum.* (as answer to an inquiry of one's condition) oh, I'll live; **s- til pumpene** *naut.* man the pumps; **s- til tjeneste** be at (one's) service; **s- til værs** stick straight up; **ikke s- til å** not capable of being (e.g. changed, helped, saved); **s- tilbake** be left, remain, be yet to come; be backward; **s- tilbake for** be behind, inferior to; **han s-r ikke tilbake for noen** he's second to none; **s- under**

be subordinate to, inferior to; be under (authority, command, control of sth); **s- under vann** be submerged, under water; **s- ut** project, stick out, (of gases, liquids) pour out; **s- ut med** stand, tolerate; **s- ute** (of money) be outstanding; **s- ved** be at, near, next to; hold to, keep (a promise, offer, etc.). **II** *(refl.)*: **s- seg (godt)** get along, manage (well); **s- seg for (mot)** resist; **s- seg på** benefit, gain from. (See also **s-ende.**)

stå‘ende *A* - standing=fixed, permanent (e.g. offer, order, price); stock (e.g. argument, character, expression, phrase); *phys.* stationary (waves); upright, vertical: **s- buffet** buffet supper; **bli s-** remain standing, remain in force; **bli s- ved** abide by, stick to (e.g. a decision); **på s- fot** off hand, on the spur of the moment.

+ståhei’ *-en* hullabaloo, racket, uproar.

stå’k *-et* **I** din, noise, racket. **2** struggle, toil: **strev og s-** (the same).

stå‘ke *V* *-a/+-et* **I** make a noise, racket. **2** bustle, struggle, toil (**med** with).

stå’/kort *-et* winning card (cf **stå[3]** 7).

stå’l[1] *-et* **I** steel: **bløtt s-** mild steel; **herdet s-** case hardened steel. **2** (cutting) tool.

stå’l[2] *-et* **I** hayloft. **2** pile of hay, straw. **3** (of fish) shoal.

stå’/lampe *-a/-en* floor lamp.

stå‘l/band *-et* **I** magnetic steel tape (for recording). **2** (steel) tape measure. **3** steel hoop.

stå‘l/blank *A* bright as steel.

stå‘l/blå *A* *-tt* steel(y) blue.

stå‘l/briller *pl* steel-rimmed spectacles.

+stå‘let *pp of* **stele**

stå‘l/fjør *-a* steel spring.

stå‘l/grå *A* *-tt* steel grey.

stå‘l/hjelm *-en* steel helmet.

stå‘l/is *-en* blue ice.

stå‘l/kant *-en* steel edge (e.g. on skis).

stå‘l/mantel *-elen, pl -ler* steel casing, jacket.

stå‘l/omn *-en* furnace, hearth.

stå‘l/orm *-en zool.* blindworm (Anguis fragilis).

stå‘l/panser *-et* armor, armor plate.

stå‘l/penn *-en* steel pen.

stå‘l/plate *-a/+-en* steel plate; ship plate.

stå‘l/rør *-et/*-a* (=***/røyr**) steel tube; steel chair, table leg.

+stå‘l/satt *A* - steel plated; *fig.* firm, resolute: **s- mot** steeled against.

+stå‘l/sette *V* *-satte* (=***/setje**) plate with steel; *fig.* harden, steel (character).

stå‘l/stut *-en hum.* bulldozer.

stå‘l/svamp *-en vet.* capped hock.

stå‘l/tråd *-en* steel wire.

stå‘l/ull *-a* steel wool.

stå‘l/vaier *-en, pl +-e/+-vairer* steel wire; steel cable.

stå‘l/verk *-et* steelworks.

stå’/man *-a* clipped mane; crest (of horse).

stå’/plass *-en* standing room (e.g. in a theater).

***ståss’** *-et* bustle, unrest.

***stås‘se** *V* *-a* work busily.

stått’ *pp of* **stå[2]**

su’[1] *-a* sow.

su’[2] *-a* undertow.

su’[3] *-a* joint between two planks (esp. in boat).

+su’[4] *V* *-dde* cf **suge**

+s. u.=svar utbes

sub’/alpi‘n *A* subalpine.

subb’[1] *-en* down-at-the-heels, seedy individual.

subb’[2] *-et* **I** shuffling, sloshing gait (as e.g. in walking through mire, slush). **2** refuse, slops, waste; *fig.* filthy, scummy existence, work; deadly monotonous work.

sub‘be[1] *-a* seedy, slovenly woman.

sub‘be[2] *V* *-a/+-et* **I** clean, sweep: **s- bort (vekk)** fritter, squander away; **s- inn penger** rake in money hand over fist; **s- sammen** scrape together hastily; **s- til seg** seize money, property ruthlessly, feather one's nest. **2** shuffle, slouch along: **s- seg** drag oneself along. **3** work in filth and muck; drudge, slave, toil (with no appreciable result); **la tingene s-** let things slide.

sub‘be/føre *-t* muddy and wet condition of the road.

sub‘bet(e) *A* - **I** shuffling, slouching (gait). **2** messy, slovenly (person, work); muddy, sloppy, wet.

subj.=subjekt

subjek’t *-et, pl -/+-er* **I** *gram., mus.* subject. **2** *fam.* down-at-the-heels, seedy individual; sot.

sub’jektiv *A* subjective.

subjektivis’me *-n* subjectivism.

subjektivite’t *-en* subjectivity.

+subjek’ts/antyder *-en, pl -e gram.* anticipatory subject.

subli’m *A* sublime.

sublima’t *-et, pl -/+-er chem.* sublimate, esp. corrosive sublimate (mercury chloride).

sublime’re *V* *-te* **I** *chem.* sublime; purify, refine. **2** *psych.* sublimate.

sublimina’l *A* *psych.* subliminal.

submari’n *A* submarine.

subordinasjo’n *-en* subordination.

subret’t(e) *-a/+-en* soubrette.

subsi’die/politikk‘ *-en* policy of subsidization (e.g. farm support prices).

+subsi’dier *pl* (=***-ar**) subsidies.

subsidie’re *V* *-te* subsidize.

subsidiæ’r *A* subsidiary; alternate: **s-t 30 dagers fengsel** alternatively 30 days' imprisonment.

subskriben’t *-en* subscriber (to a work appearing in instalments).

subskribe’re *V* *-te* subscribe (to a work appearing in instalments).

subskripsjo’n *-en* subscription (to a work appearing in instalments).

subst.=substantiv

substan’s *-en* substance.

substansiell’ *A* *-elt* substantial.

sub‘stantiv *-et, pl -/+-er gram.* noun, substantive.

substantive’re *V* *-te gram.* substantivize.

sub‘stantivisk *A* - *gram.* noun, substantive; nominal, substantival.

substitue’re *V* *-te* substitute.

substitusjo’n *-en* substitution.

substitutt’ *-en/-et* substitute.

substra’t *-et, pl -/+-er* substratum.

subti’l *A* subtle.

subtilite’t *-en* subtlety.

subtrahen’d *-en math.* subtrahend.

subtrahe’re *V* *-te math.* subtract.

subtraksjo’n *-en math.* subtraction.

sub’/tropisk *A* - subtropical.

subvene’re *V* *-te* subsidize; subvene.

subvensjo’n *-en* subsidy; subvention.

succes [sykse’] *-en* cf **suksess**

***sud-** *Pf* cf **syd-, sør-**

+Su’der/øyene *Pln* (=***/øyane**) *hist.* the Hebrides.

su’derøying *-en hist.* Hebridean.

***Su‘d/landa** *Pln* the southern countries, lands.

***su‘d/landsk** *A* - cf **syd/**

***su‘dleg** *A* - cf **sørlig**

***su‘d/lending** *-en* cf **syd/**

su’/drag *-et* undertow.

su‘d/røn *A* *archaic, dial.* southerly (esp. of wind).

suffige’re *V* *-te gram.* suffix.

suffik’s *-et, pl -/+-er gram.* suffix.

suffisanse [suffisang’se] *-n* self-assurance, self-confidence.

suffisant [suffisang’t] *A* - **I** solid, substantial. **2** assured, self-assertive, self-confident.

sufflé *-en* soufflé.

suffle’re *V* *-te* prompt (theater).

sufflø’r *-en* prompter (theater).

sufflø’r/kasse *-a/-en* prompter's box (theater), prompt box.

sufflø’se *-a/+-en* woman prompter (theater).

suffragett(e) [sufrasjett’] *-a/+-en* suffragette.

***suf’t** *-a* **I** nutritious juices in food. **2** bit, particle.

+su’g *-et* (=***sog**) **I** draw, suck; sucking, suction. **2** gnawing, hollow feeling, twinge (e.g. of hunger, remorse).

***su‘gar** *-en* cf **suger**

***su‘gar/unge** [/onge] *-n* suckling.

su‘ge *V* *+-er/*syg, saug/+sugde, +sugd/*soge/*-i* **I** suck (often with **på**); absorb; attract, draw: **s- inn, opp, til seg** absorb, suck up; **s- kraften ut av** sap the vitality of; **s- på labben** live on nothing, starve; **s-seg fast** cling to; **s- til seg** draw irresistibly; **s- ut** exploit; **s- (ut) av sitt eget bryst** learn by personal experience. **2** ache; feel hollow: **s-ende** irresistible, unextinguishable, unappeased.

+su‘gen *A* *-ent, pl -ne* hungry: **på s- mave** on an empty stomach.

su‘ge/pumpe [/pompe] *-a* suction pump.

+su‘ger *-en, pl -e* (=***-ar**) **I** *zool.* bloodsucker, leech; *fig.* extortionist. **2** suction apparatus, e.g. a filter for home or office building.

su‘ge/rør *-et/*-a* (=***/røyr**) **I** (drinking) straw. **2** suction pipe.

su‘ge/skål *-a zool.* sucking disk, sucker.

sugg’ *-en* big, strong animal or person, an "ox".

sug‘ge *-a* **I** sow; *fig.* fat, sloppy woman; slob. **2** *zool.* crucian carp (Carassius carassius).

suggere’re *V* *-te psych.* hypnotize; suggest: **s-ende** hypnotic; suggestive.

suggesti’bel *A* *-elt, pl -le psych.* suggestible.

suggestion [-sjo’n] *-en psych.* (hypnotic) suggestion; fixation.

sug’gestiv *A* **I** suggestive. **2**: **s-t spørsmål** *jur.* leading question.

suite [svit‘te] *-n* suite (hotel; musical; retinue).

sujett [sysjett’] *-et, pl -/+-er* subject, theme.

suka’t *-en* citron (preserved rind).

sukk’ *-en/-et* sigh; soughing (e.g. of the wind).

suk‘ke *V* *-a/+-et* sigh; sough (e.g. the wind): **s- etter** long, yearn for.

sukker [sok’ker] *-et* sugar: **s-et mitt** *pop.* sugar, sweetie.

sukker/bit [sok‘ker/] *-en* sugar lump.

sukker/brød *-et* a cake (of eggs, flour and sugar).

sukker/ert *-a bot.* sugar pea (Pisum sativum macrocarpon).

+sukker/holdig *A* - (=***/haldig**) saccheriferous; saccharine, sugary.

sukker/kavring *-en* (sweet) rusk, zwieback.

sukker/klype *-a* sugar tongs.

sukker/kopp *-en* sugar bowl.

sukker/kulø’r *-en* caramel (burnt sugar for coloring).

sukker/lake *-n* **I** sugar water (used in canning). **2** sweetened brine.

sukker/nepe *-a bot.* rutabaga, Swedish turnip (Brassica napobrassica).

+sukker/roe *-n bot.* sugar beet (Beta vulgaris saccharifera).

sukker/rør *-et/*-a bot.* sugar cane (Saccharum officinarum).

sukker/saks *-a* "sugar shears" (formerly used to cut refined sugar into cubes or lumps).

sukker/sjuk *A med.* diabetic.

sukker/sjuke *-n med.* diabetes.

sukker/skei [/sjei] *-a* (=**+/skje**) sugar spoon.

sukker/skål *-a* sugar bowl.

+sukker/syk *A* cf **/sjuk**

+sukker/syke *-n* cf **/sjuke**

sukker/søt *A* saccharine, sugary, sweet as sugar (e.g. a smile, voice, etc.).

+ Bokmål; * Nynorsk; ° Dialect.
After letter: ’ stress (Acc. 1); ‘ tone, stress (Acc. 2); · length.
Below letter: . not pronounced.

+sukker/tang -a, pl -tenger 1 sugar tongs. 2 (-en/-et) bot. honeyware, sweet tangle (Laminaria saccharina).
sukker/topp -en (old-fashioned) sugar loaf (in cone shape).
+sukker/tøy -et candy, sweets.
sukker/unge [/onge] -n little darling.
sukker/vatn -et (=+/vann) sugar water.
*suk'l -et gurgling.
suk'le V -a/+-et gurgle.
sukre [sok're] V -a/+-et 1 sugar, sweeten: s- ned preserve. 2 fig. sugar-coat: s- pillen sugar-coat the pill.
suksesjo'n -en succession.
suksess [sykse'] -en (=succes) lit. success: bli en s- be a hit.
suk'sessiv A successive: s- gradually.
+suk's/omsi'der Av hum. gradually, step by step.
+su'l -et (=suvl) fish, meat foods (in contrast to breadstuffs).
sulamit'ten df hele s- pop. the whole shebang.
Sul'/dal Pln twp, Rogaland.
su'le[1] -a zool. gannet (family Sulidae; common gannet Moris bassana).
su'le[2] -a dial. fork; crotch; reel (for fishline); gore, patch; neckyoke (on pig).
*su'le[3] -a cf søyle
su'le[4] V -a/+-et dial. reel (opp in); yoke (a pig).
sul'fa/prepara't -et, pl -/+-er sulfa drug.
sulfa't -et, pl -/+-er chem. sulfate.
sulfi'd -et/+-en chem. sulfide.
sulfitt' -en chem. sulfite.
sul'ke V -a/+-et 1 dirty, soil: s- noe til get sth dirty, soil sth. 2 gurgle.
*sul'kut A - soiled.
sulky [sul'ki] -en sulky.
sull'[1] -en lullaby; lilt, tune.
sull'[2] -et murmur, ripple.
sul'le V -a/+-et 1 croon, hum; murmur, ripple (e.g. a brook). 2 fritter away time: gå og s- putter around.
sul'lik -en fam. idling, incompetent, lazy person.
+sul't -en (=*svolt) hunger, starvation: lide s- og savn suffer privations.
sul'tan -en sultan.
+sul'te V -a/-et cf svelte[1], svelte[2]
+sul'te/død -en: dø s-en starve to death.
+sul'te/fore V -a/-et/-te cf svelte/
+sul'te/ga'sje -n starvation wage.
+sul'te/grense -a/-en minimum needed for survival.
+sul'te/kunstner -en, pl -e professional faster.
+sul'te/kur -en cf svelte/
+sul'te/lønn -a/-en starvation wage.
+sul'ten A -ent, pl -ne (=*svolten) hungry (etter for): s- som en skrubb hungry as a bear (lit. wolf).
+sul'te/streik -en hunger strike.
sum'[1] -men amount, sum; (sum) total; result (av of): hele s-men the sum total; i s- in toto.
sum'[2] -met buzzing, humming.
*sum'[3] -met cf svøm
*sum'[4] Pn cf som[2]
*su'mar -en cf sommer
*sum'd A sumt able to swim.
*sum'de pt of symje
*sum'/fot -en webbed foot.
*sum'/fugl -en webfooted bird.
*sum'le V -a cf somle
*sum'lut A - cf somlete
summa'risk A - 1 concise, summary. 2 jur. summary (e.g. proceedings).
sum'ma summa'rum 1 the grand total. 2 in short, when all is said and done.
sum'me[1] V -a/+-et buzz, drone, hum.
sum'me[2] V -a/+-et: s- seg collect oneself, gather one's wits about one.
*sum'mel -elet/-let cf sommel
summe're V -te add: s- opp add up, sum up.
sum'me/tone -n dial tone.

sum'p [also: som'p] -en marsh, morass, swamp.
+sum'p/aktig [also: som'p/] A - marshlike, swampy.
sum'pet(e) [also: som'pet(e)] A - marshy, swampy.
sum'p/feber [also: som'p/] -en med. swamp fever; malaria.
sum'pig [also: som'pi] A - marshy, swampy.
sum'p/lendt [also: som'p/] A - marshy, swampy (ground).
sum'p/strekning [also: som'p/] *-a/-en fen, marshland, swamp.
*sum'/stad Av cf som/
*sum't pp of symje
*sum'/tid Av cf som/
sun'd[1] -et channel, inlet, sound; strait(s).
+sun'd[2] A cf sunn
sun'd[3] A 1 asunder, in bits, fragments, pieces. 2 (adv.): bryte (i) s- break, smash asunder, to pieces; rive (i) s- tear to pieces.
Sun'd Pln twp, Hordaland.
*sun'/dag -en cf søn/
*sun'd/broten [/bråten] A -e/-i, pl -ne asunder, broken, smashed.
sun'd/mage -n zool. sound, swimming bladder (of a fish).
sun'd/mann -en, pl -menn/*-menner hist. ferryman.
*sun'dre V -a cf søndre[1]
+sun'd/reven A -ent, pl -ne (=*/riven) torn (to pieces).
+sun'd/slitt A - (=*/sliten) torn to pieces.
sun'd/slått A - broken, smashed; injured.
+sun'd/sprengt A - (=*/sprengd) cracked (to pieces); blown up.
sun'd/toll -en 1 archaic ferry toll. 2 hist. "sound toll" (exacted by Danish authorities until 1857 for passage through the Øresund).
*sunge [song'e] pp of syngje
+sunget [song'et] pp of synge
*sungi [song'i] pp of syngje
+sunket [song'ket] pp of synke
sunn' A sunt fit, healthy, sound; healthful, wholesome: en s- sjel i et s-t legeme mens sana in corpore sano; s- fornuft common sense; s- omdømme sound judgment.
sunn- Pf south.
*sun'nan Av from the south.
Sunn'/dal Pln twp, Møre og Romsdal.
sunn'/daling -en person from Sunndal.
+sun'ne V -a/-et lit. 1: s- seg collect one's thoughts, gather one's wits about one. 2: s- seg på turn sth over in one's mind, weigh.
Sunn'/fjo'rd Pln district in Sogn og Fjordane.
sunn'/fjo'rding -en person from Sunnfjord.
+sunn'/het -en health, vitality; healthiness, wholesomeness; soundness.
+sunn'hets/fa'rlig A - injurious, unhealthy, unwholesome.
+sunn'hets/pleie -n hygiene: offentlig s- public hygiene.
+sunn'hets/skadelig A - injurious, unhealthy, unwholesome.
+sunn'hets/tilstand -en state of one's health; public health.
Sunn'/hordland Pln southwestern district of Hordaland.
Sunn'/møre Pln district in Møre og Romsdal.
sunn'/møring -en person from Sunnmøre.
Sunn'/ylven Pln twp, Møre og Romsdal.
sun't nt of sunn
su'p -en nip, swig; sip; dram, shot.
supé -en (elegant) evening meal.
su'pe V +-er/*syp, saup/+-te, +-t/*sope/*-i 1 draw (up), drink in, suck in (e.g. air). 2 tipple, fam. hit the bottle.
+su'per[1] -en (=*-ar) heavy drinker, (pop.) boozer.
su'per[2] A fam. super; outstanding, wonderful.

super'b A superb.
supe're V -te dine; sup.
su'per/elegan't A - very elegant.
su'per/fin A extra fine, superfine.
su'per/fosfa't -et chem. superphosphate.
superintenden't -en hist. bishop (in Denmark and Norway immediately following the Reformation).
superkar'go -en naut. supercargo.
super'lativ[1] -en gram. superlative (degree).
super'lativ[2] -et, pl -/+-er superlative.
superlati'visk A - superlative.
superso'nisk A - supersonic.
supi'num -et gram. supine.
sup'pe -a broth, soup, stock: hele s-a the whole lot (pop.) the whole kit and caboodle; koke s- på noe (pop.) make a big case out of sth.
sup'pe/ause -a soup ladle.
sup'pe/blokk -en soup concentrate (in bar form).
+suppeda's -en 1 awkward state of affairs, (pop.) kettle of fish: være i en s- (pop.) be in a fine fix, be in the soup. 2: hele s-en the whole lot, (pop.) the whole kit and caboodle.
sup'pe/gryte -a soup kettle, pot.
+sup'pe/hue -t pop. blockhead, lunkhead.
sup'pe/kjøtt -et (=*/kjøt) beef from which to make soup.
sup'pe/lapskaus -en a thin hash.
sup'pe/skei [/sjei] -a (=+/skje) soup spoon.
sup'pe/terri'n -en soup tureen.
+sup'pe/øse -a cf /ause
supplean't -en deputy, substitute.
supplement [supplemang'] -et, pl -/+-er supplement (til to).
+supplements/bind -et supplement, supplemental volume.
supplements/vinkel -elen, pl -ler math. supplement.
supplementæ'r A supplementary.
supple're V -te 1 supplement. 2: s- hinannen complement each other. 3: s- seg selv have power to co-opt (e.g. a committee).
+supple'rings/valg -et (=*/val) bye-election (English Parliament); special election (to fill a vacated seat).
supplikan't -en hist. petitioner, supplicant.
supplikk' -en hist. petition, supplication.
suppone're V -te assume, presuppose, suppose.
supposisjo'n -en supposition; suspicion.
supprime're V -te suppress.
su'pra/denta'l -en gram. alveolar, supradental.
supremati' -et supremacy.
su'r A 1 acid, sour (e.g. ground, milk, etc.); acerbate, sharp (e.g. fruit); chem. acetous: bite i det s-e eple swallow a bitter pill. 2 decayed (e.g. trees); rotten (e.g. fish, meat). 3 dank, foul (e.g. weather). 4 disagreeable, unpleasant; hard, laborious: han gjorde livet s-t for henne he led her a dog's life. 5 crabby, cross, surly: ingen s-e miner no complaints, please. 6 (adv.) hard: s-t ervervede sparepenger hard-earned savings.
su'r/apal -en crab apple.
su'r/brød -et sourdough bread.
su'r/deig -en 1 leaven, sourdough: en s- i europeisk åndsliv a leaven in the intellectual life of Europe. 2: av samme s- derog. birds of a feather, of a kind.
su'r/eple -t crab apple.
+su'r/het -en 1 acidity, sourness. 2 crossness, peevishness, sourliness.
*su'rkast V -ast become moldy, musty.
*su'rke[1] -a layer of mold.
*sur'ke[2] V -a cf surkle
sur'kle V -a/+-et (=*surke[2]) gurgle, murmur, ripple (e.g. a brook); squish.
sur'kle/lyd -en gurgling sound.

su'r/kål *-en* 1 cabbage cooked with vinegar, sugar, and caraway: **svinestek med surkål** pork roast with sour cabbage.

sur'l *-et* 1 murmur, ripple. 2 buzz, drone (e.g. of voices).

sur'le *V -a/+-et* 1 murmur, ripple. 2 buzz, drone, hum (e.g. voices).

su'r/maga *A -* (=**+/mavet**) suffering acid indigestion; *fig.* cross, peevish, surly.

su'r/mjølk *-a* sour milk.

su'rmjølk(s)/graut *-en* sour milk porridge.

su'r/mule *V -a/+-et* pout, sulk.

su'r/myse *-a* sour whey.

Su'rna/dal *Pln* twp, Møre og Romsdal.

su'rne *V -a/+-et* 1 become, turn acid, sour. 2 *fig.* be (turn) bitter; sulk.

su'r/ost [/ost] *-en* cottage cheese; sour milk cheese.

surr'[1] *-et/+-en* 1 buzz, drone, hum (av of); bustle. 2 confusion: **det går i ett s-** for **en** one is thoroughly confused.

surr'[2] *Av*: **gå, løpe s-** be confused; **gå s- i** get things mixed up; **det går i s- for meg** I am getting mixed up.

sur're[1] *V -a/+-et* 1 buzz, drone, whir; simmer, sizzle (e.g. in a frying pan). 2 be confused, muddled; **det s-et i hennes hode** her brain was reeling.

sur're[2] *V -a/+-et naut.* lash, secure.

sur'realisme *-n* surrealism.

sur'realist *-en* surrealist.

sur'realistisk *A -* surrealistic.

sur'ret(e) *A -* 1 confused, jumbled; crazy, silly. 2 (slightly) drunk, intoxicated, *(pop.)* lit.

sur'ring *-a/+-en naut.* fastening, lashing.

surroga't *-et, pl -/+-er* substitute (for for).

su'r/sild *-a* pickled herring.

su'r/smak *-en* acid, sour taste.

su'r/stoff *-et chem.* oxygen.

su'r/søt *A -* sour-sweet.

sur've *V -a/+-et* fret, whine.

+su'r/øyd *A -* (=***/øygd**) bleary-eyed, rheumy-eyed.

su's *-en/-et* 1 sigh, sough, whisper (e.g. of wind); whistling, whizzing (e.g. of bullet); roaring, rushing (e.g. of water); rustling (e.g. of leaves); hum (of voices); sizzle (e.g. of frying pan); buzzing, ringing (in one's ears). 2 *poet.* (giving a sense of elevation, emotional uplift): **historiens s-** the rustle (the song) of history. 3 pursuit of pleasure; gay, mad whirl: **leve i s- og dus** lead a life of riot and revel; *(pop.)* live it up.

su'se *V -te/*-a* 1 sigh, sough, whisper (e.g. wind); simmer, sing (e.g. of kettle); whir, whistle, whiz (e.g. a bullet); roar, rush along; buzz, ring (in one's head); rustle; sizzle: **i s-ende fart** at top speed; **s- av sted** race along; **s- forbi** flash past. 2 (of sound in ears) ring; (of blood) boil, race, roar. 3 live a life of dissipation, *(pop.)* live it up; waste one's substance.

su'se/ladd *-en fam.* 1 fool, silly person, *(pop.)* nut. 2 dissolute drunkard, sot.

su'set(e) *A - fam.* absent-minded, confused; muddled (from drinking).

sus'l *-et* (=**sutl**) 1 splash(ing). *2 slop (water).

sus'le *V -a/+-et* (=**sutle**) 1 splash; gurgle, murmur. 2: **s- vekk** fritter away, squander.

suspek't *A -* suspect, suspicious.

suspendere [suspangde're] *V -te* suspend.

suspensiv [sus'pangsiv] *A* suspensive: **s-t veto** s- veto.

suspensjon [suspangsjo'n] *-en* suspension.

+suss' *-en* kiss (baby talk).

+sus'se *V -et* kiss (baby talk).

su't *-a* 1 whimper, whine. 2 anxiety, care, concern; grief, sorrow.

su'tar(e) *-(e)n archaic* shoemaker.

sutene're *V -te* cf **sutinere**

sutenø'r *-en* pimp.

sutine're *V -te*: **s- seg** *lit.* manage, support oneself (**med** on).

sut'l *-et* 1 splash(ing). *2 slop (water).

su't/laus *A* unconcerned, without worries.

sut'le *V -a/+-et* 1 splash; gurgle, murmer. 2: **s- bort** fritter away, squander.

***su't/løyse** *-a* carelessness; unconcern.

sut're *V -a/+-et* fret, whimper, whine.

sut'ret(e) *A - fam.* fretting, whimpering, whiney.

sutt' *-en fam.* pacifier.

sut'te *V -a/+-et*: **s- på** suck, suck at.

sut'ter *-et* fretting, whimpering.

sutu'r *-en med.* suture.

suveni'r *-en* souvenir.

suvere'n[1] *-en* sovereign.

suvere'n[2] *A* 1 *pol.* sovereign: **s-e rettigheter** s- rights. 2 sovereign, unique: **Giottos kunst er s-** G-'s art is s-. 3 high-handed, independent.

suverenite't *-en* sovereignty.

suv'l *-et* cf **sul**

SV=**sørvest**

sva'[1] *-et* bare, smooth, sloping rock (usu. by water).

sva'**[2] *V -dde* (=svade**[2]) loosen, peel easily (e.g. bark).

***sva'**[3] *A -tt* damp, moist.

svab'be *V -a/+-et* slosh, splash; slop.

sva'ber *-eren, pl -rer/+-ere naut.* swab.

sva'/berg *-et* bare, smooth, sloping rock (usu. by water).

sva'bre *V -a/+-et naut.* swab down (the deck).

sva'da *-en* claptrap, *(pop.)* hot air.

***sva'de**[1] *-n* sap.

***sva'de**[2] *V -de* cf **sva**[3]

sva'g *-et* 1 swaying. 2 *naut.* **ligge på s-** swing at anchor (to wind and tide).

sva'ge *V -a/+-et* cf **svaie**

svai' *A* 1 lissome, pliable, willowy. 2 arched, bowed (usu. concavely), sway.

svai'e *V -a/+-et/+-de* 1 bend, sway (to and fro); toss. 2 *naut.* swing at anchor.

svai'/rygg *-en* sway-back.

svai'/rygga *A -* (=**+-et, *-ja**) sway-backed.

sva'k *A* 1 feeble, weak (of body, mind, strength, etc.); ailing, infirm: **den s-e** the weakling; **det s-e kjønn** the weaker sex; **stå s-t** be in a weak position, have no leg to stand on; **stå s-t (være s-) i** be poor in (a school subject); **være s- for** have a weakness for; **være s- overfor** be unable to resist; be indulgent with. 2 faint (idea, smell, smile, sound, etc.), slight (breeze, impression, hope, etc.); gentle, mild, weak (medicine); low-tension (electric current); weak (market).

+sva'kelig *A -* delicate, infirm, sickly.

+sva'kelig/het *-en* delicate health, infirmity, weakness.

+sva'k/het *-en* weakness; failing, weak point; infirmity; indulgence: **ha en s- for** have a weakness for, be partial to.

+sva'khets/tegn [/tein] *-et* sign of weakness.

+sva'k/strøm' *-men* low-power current (usu. below 1 ampere, for communications and electronic purposes).

+sva'kstrøms/ingeniør [/insjenjø'r] *-en elec.* electronics (communications) engineer.

+sva'k/synt *A -* having bad eyesight.

sva'l[1] *-a* hall, hallway, vestibule.

sva'l[2] *A* cool.

Sva'l/bard *Pln* island group, usu. called Spitzbergen (Norw. possession).

sva'le[1] *-a zool.* swallow (family Hirundinidae): **en s- gjør ingen sommer** one swallow does not make a summer.

+sva'le[2] *-n* coolness.

sva'le[3] *V -a/+-te* cool (sth), cool (sth) off: **s- seg** cool (oneself) off.

sva'le/drikk *-en, pl -er* (=***/drykk**) cooling, refreshing drink.

sva'le/hale *-n* 1 swallow's tail. 2 *zool.* swallowtail (butterfly) (Papilio machaon). 3 *tech.* dovetail (joint etc.).

sva'le/urt *-a/+-en bot.* greater celandine, swallowwort (Chelidonium majus).

sva'l/gang *-en* vestibule; covered balcony.

+sva'l/het *-en* coolness.

***svall'**[1] *-et* chatter, talk.

***svall'**[2] *pt of* **svelle**

***sval'le** *V -a* chatter, talk.

sva'lne *V -a/+-et* become cool.

sval't *pt of* **svelte**

***svam'** *pt of* **svemje, svømme**

***svam'le** *V -a* 1 splash; swim, wade. 2 doze.

svam'p *-en* sponge: **drikke som en s-** drink like a fish.

+svam'p/aktig *A -* porous, spongy.

svam'pet(e) *A -* 1 porous, spongy. 2 bloated, swollen.

***svam're** *V -a* run around, swarm.

sva'ne[1] *-a/+-en zool.* swan (subfamily Cygninae): **Svanen** *astron.* the Swan.

***sva'ne**[2] *V -a* diminish, shrink; get better.

sva'ne/hals *-en* 1 swan's neck, swanlike neck. 2 *tech.* gooseneck.

sva'ne/kvit *A* snowy white: **S-** Swanwhite (folktale figure).

+sva'ne/sang *-en* (=***/song**) swan song.

+svang'[1] *N*: **gå, komme i s-** be rampant, rife.

+svang'[2] *pt of* **svinge**[1]

svang'[3] *A dial.* empty, hungry.

svang'e *-n* (horse's) flank.

svang'er *A -ert, pl -re* pregnant; **være s- med** be teaming with (e.g. ideas).

svang'er/skap *+-et/*-en* pregnancy.

+svang'erskaps/avbrytelse *-n* abortion.

svang'ne *V -a/+-et*: **s- ned** diminish, shrink.

Sva'n/hild *Prn (f)*

svan's *-en* 1 tail. 2 *mil.* (of a gun carriage) trail. 3 one-man cross-cut saw.

svan'se *V -a/+-et* 1 wag, wave (a tail). 2 flounce, mince, scurry around: **svinse og s-** flutter, scurry around.

+svan't *pt of* **svinne**

sva'r *-et* answer, reply (**på** to); response, return: **s- utbes** please reply, RSVP; **som s- på** in reply to; **bli s- skyldig** be at a loss for an answer; ***stå til s-s** be accountable, responsible; ***ta til s-s** answer, reply; ***vere til s-s** be available, present.

sva'r/brev *-et* letter of reply.

sva'r/brevkort *-et* prepaid answer card.

sva're[1] *V -a/-te* 1 answer, reply; respond (**på** to): **s- for** answer for, be responsible for; **s- på et spørsmål** answer a question; **s- til** answer to=correspond to, fit; agree with, be in keeping with; match; **(ikke) s- til forventningene** (not) come up to expectations. 2 pay (a fee, tax etc.): **s- skatt** pay taxes. 3 *(refl.)* pay off, pay one's way (e.g. of a business venture).

sva're[2] *A -* big, tremendous, vast: **en s- makt** huge power; **et s- spetakkel** big uproar; **s- til kar** big fellow (ironic).

***sva'r/hitten** *A -e/-i, pl -hitne* quick-witted, *(pop.)* fast on the draw.

sva'r/laus *A* (=***/løs**) at a loss (for a reply), speechless.

+ Bokmål; * Nynorsk; ° Dialect.
After letter: ' stress (Acc. 1); ` tone, stress (Acc. 2); · length.
Below letter: . not pronounced.

***svar'm** -en confusion, giddiness; tumult; swarm.
sva'r/o'rd -et gram. answer word, e.g. "yes", "no".
sva'r/skriv -et 1 letter of reply. 2 jur. defendant's answer, pleading.
svar't[1] et black: **gjøre s- til hvitt** prove that b- is white; **ha noe s- på hvitt** have sth in writing (in black and white).
svar't[2] A - 1 black: **for s-e** (oath); **s- av folk** black with people; **s- som en feier** as black as the ace of spades. 2 dark; desolate: **midt på s-e natten** in the dead of night; **midt i s-e skogen** in the densest forest. 3 dirty, soiled: **s- på fingrene** having dirty hands. 4 bare, barren (ground); empty, fishless (sea). 5 black, hopeless, pessimistic: **en s- dag** a black day; **se allting s-** look on the dark side.
+svar't/aktig A - blackish.
svar't/alv -en myth. malignant elf.
svar't/bak -en zool. black-backed gull (Larus marinus).
svar'te/bok -a book (containing magic formulas etc.), black book; sorcerer's book.
svar'te/bror -en, pl +-brødre/*-brør Black Friar, Dominican.
svar'te/børs -en black market.
svar'tebørs/hai -en black marketeer.
svar'te/dauđen df hist. the Black Death.
Svar'te/haveț Pln the Black Sea.
svar'te/kunst -en black art, necromancy.
+svar'te/kunstner -en, pl -e (=*-ar) necromancer, sorcerer.
***svar'te/lars** -en fam. coffeepot.
svar'te/liste -a/+-en blacklist.
svar'te/marja +en/*ei Black Maria, paddy wagon.
Svar'ten Prn 1 black horse, Blackie. 2 the devil.
svar'te/per en (in cards) old maid (using jack as odd card).
svar't/farga A - dyed black.
svar't/flekket(e) A - with black spots.
svar't/handel -en black market trading.
svar'ting -en dark-haired, dark-skinned person; black man.
svar't/kledd A -/*-kledt dressed in black.
svar't/kol [/kål] -et bituminous coal.
svar't/krøllet(e) A - curly black.
***svar't/leitt** A - swarthy.
svar'tne V -a/+-et darken, grow dark: **s- for øynene på en** have one's eyes grow dim; black out.
svar't/older -eren/-ra, pl +*-rer/*-rar cf /or
svar't/or -a/+-en (=/older) bot. black alder (Alnus glutinosa).
svar't/sidet(e) A - with black flanks (e.g. a cow).
svar't/sinn -et depression, melancholy.
svar't/sjuk A envious, jealous.
svar't/sjuke -n envy, jealousy.
svar't/skjorte [/sjorte] en hist. Black Shirt, fascist.
+svar't/smuska A - cf **sort/smusket**
svar't/syn -et pessimism.
svar't/sy'nt A - pessimistic.
svar't/trost -en zool. blackbird; common thrush, merl (Turdus merula).
+svar't/øyd A - (=*/øygd) black-eyed.
svar't/år -et bad year (for fish, crops), famine year.
svar'v -en dial. curve, turn; circular movement; semicircle.
svar've V -a/+-et 1 turn. 2 form, turn in a lathe.
svar've/jern [/jæ'rn] -et turning chisel.
+svar'ver -en (=*-ar) lathe operator, turner.
svar've/stol -en (crude) lathe (without flywheel).
svas'se V -a/+-et dial. splash; slosh (through mud and water).
sve' -a burnt-over land.
sve'a/velde -t hist. Swedish empire.
svecis'me -n gram. Swedicism (Swedish expression in another language).
+sve'd[1] -en cf **svette[1]**
+sve'd[2] pt of **svi[1]**
***sve'de[1]** -n cf **svie**
+sve'de[2] V -et cf **svette[2]**
+sve'er pl (=*-ar) hist. Swedes; inhabitants of Svealand.
svei'[1] -en dial. arch, curve, sway.
svei'[2] pt of **svi[1]**
***svei'd** pt of **svide[1]**
***svei'e** V -a (=*sveige) bend, curve: **s- seg** (the same).
svei'g[1] -en twig.
svei'g[2] A 1 bent, curved, sway. 2 damp, wet.
***svei'ge** V -a cf **sveie**
***svei'gne** V -a become damp, moist.
svei'k pt of **svike**
***svei'm** -en hovering about; disturbance, unrest.
***svei'me** V -a hover about.
svei'n[1] -en 1 hist. stripling, youth; swain. 2 (male) virgin.
***svei'n[2]** -en cf **svenn**
Svei'n Prn(m)
***svei'ne/prøve** -a cf **svenne/**
svei'n/kall -en dial. bachelor.
***svei'n/stykke** -t cf **svenne/**
Svei'nung [-ong] Prn(m)
svei'p[1] -et dial. blow (with a whip).
svei'p[2] -et dial. swaddling cloth.
***svei'pe[1]** -a swaddling cloth.
svei'pe[2] V -a/+-et 1 naut. sweep (the sea for mines). 2 dial. whip.
svei'pe[3] V -te 1 swaddle, wrap (e.g. a baby). 2 beam (in weaving).
***svei'pe/duk** -en swaddling cloth.
+svei'per -en, pl -e naut. mine sweeper.
svei's -en 1 gift, knack: **ha en egen s- med noe** have a way with sth. 2 aplomb, style: **få s- på noe** fix sth up, get sth going. 3 well combed hair (usu. of young boys).
svei'se V -te/*-a weld: **s- sammen** join, weld.
svei'sen A +-ent, pl -ne chic, smart, stylish.
+svei'ser[1] -en, pl -e (=*-ar) welder.
svei'ser[2] -en, pl -e (=*-ar) foreman on dairy farm.
svei't -a/+-en 1 mil. wing (air force). 2 hist. band, group of fighting men.
Svei'ts Pln Switzerland.
+svei'tser -en, pl -e (=*-ar) 1 Swiss. 2 hist. member of the Swiss guard.
+sveitserin'ne -a/-en (=*sveitsarinne) Swiss woman.
svei'tser/ost [/ost] -en Swiss cheese.
svei'tsisk A - Swiss.
***sveitt'** A - cf **svett**
***sveit'te[1]** -n cf **svette[1]**
***sveit'te[2]** V -a cf **svette[2]**
svei'v[1] -a 1 crank, handle. *2 antler.
svei'v[2] -en/+-et 1 swing, turn; bend, curve; curl. swirl. 2 flipper (on seal).
svei'v[3] pt of **svive**
svei've V -a/+-et/-de 1 crank, rotate, turn: **s- opp** crank, wind up. 2 flicker, move, roam; sway.
+svei've/spill -et 1 barrel organ, hand organ. 2 naut. capstan, winch.
***sve'k[1]** -et cf **svekk[2]**
+sve'k[2] pt of **svike**
+sve'ket pp of **svike**
+svekk'[1] -en cf **zweck**
svekk'[2] +-en/*-et med. rickets.
+svek'ke V -et/svekte (=*-je) 1 enfeeble, impair, weaken: **s- ens helse, krefter** impair one's health, sap one's strength (cf **sjelsevne**). 2 modify, soften (e.g. one's stand).
+svek'kelse -n impairment, weakening.
***svekkj'e** V -te cf **svekke**
+svek'ling -en weakling.
svel'g[1] -en, pl *-er gulp, swallow; swig.
svel'g[2] -et 1 throat; pharynx. 2 abyss, chasm, gulf: **et bunnløst s-** a bottomless abyss.
svel'gje V -de/+-et 1 swallow: **s- sin stolthet** pocket one's pride. 2 lit. wallow (e.g. in luxury). 3 lit.: **s-ende** gaping, yawning (e.g. abyss).
***svel'g/knut** -en larynx.
***svell'** -et ice sheet (on a field).
***svell'/brend** A -brent damaged by ice (e.g. grass).
***svell'/brune** -n damage from ice (e.g. to grass).
svel'le V +svelte/*svall, +svelt/*svolle/*-i 1 swell: **s- ut** bulge, swell out. 2 ooze.
***svel'lut** A - frozen, slippery (from ice).
svel't -en cf **sult**
svel'te[1] V svalt, +-et/*svolte/*-i (=+sulte) starve: **s- i hjel** starve to death; **s- seg** starve oneself.
svel'te[2] V -a/+-et/*-e (=+sulte) starve; underfeed (e.g. cattle): **s- ut** starve into submission.
svel'te/fore V -a/+-et/+-te underfeed (e.g. cattle).
svel'te/kur -en reducing diet.
svel'te/lønn -a/+-en (=*/løn) starvation wage.
svel't/ihel N (=+/ihjel) 1 death from starvation. 2 bare existence. 3 pauper.
sve'lung [-ong] -en dial. young salmon.
Svel'/vik Pln seaport, Vestfold.
***svem'je** V svem, svam. svome/-i cf **svømme**
Sven' Prn(m)
***sveng'je** V -de make slimmer: **s- seg** pull in one's stomach.
+svenn' -en (=*svein[2]) 1 journeyman. 2 archaic stripling, youth; swain. 3 hist. page, squire. 4 (male) virgin.
+sven'ne/brev -et certificate attesting to the completion of one's apprenticeship.
+sven'ne/prøve -a/-en journeyman's examination (at close of appren ticeship).
+sven'ne/stykke -t journeyman's work (test piece for completing apprenticeship).
sven'sk A - Swedish.
sven'ske -n 1 Swede. 2 zool. greenfinch (Chloris chloris).
sve'pe -a (buggy) whip.
sve'pe/slag -et blow with a (buggy) whip.
sve'pe/snert -en 1 tip of whip. 2 lash of a whip.
+sve'r pr of **sverje**
sver'd -et 1 sword: **det er et tveegget s-** it cuts both ways; **slå på s-et** rattle the saber. 2 naut. leeboard.
sver'd/fisk -en zool. swordfish (Xiphias gladius).
+sver'd/hefte -t (sword) hilt.
sver'd/hjalt -et (sword) hilt.
sver'd/lilje -a/+-en bot. yellow flag, yellow iris (Iris pseudacorus).
sver'd/odd -en sword point.
sver'd/side [*/sie] -a/+-en male line (of descent).
sver'd/slag -et sword blow, cut: **uten s-** without striking a blow (firing a shot).
sver'd/slire -a (sword) scabbard.
+sver'd/sluker -en, pl -e (=*-ar) sword swallower.
+sver'ge V -et/svor, -et/svoret (=*sverje) 1 swear, take an oath: **s- på s-** to (=affirm the truth of); **s- til s-** by (=vow devotion to). 2 curse: **han svor så det lyste om ham** he swore until the air was blue, cussed like a trooper.
+Sverige [svær'je] Pln (=*Sverike) Sweden.
***sver'je** V sver, svor, svore/-i cf **sverge**
sver'kel -elen, pl -ler pivot, rotary joint.
sver'm -en crowd, throng; flock (e.g. of birds), swarm (e.g. of insects).
sver'me V -a/+-et 1 swarm (e.g. insects, people): **s- som bier** swarm like locusts. 2 daydream, lose oneself in revery; romance: **s- for** be crazy about; be passionately fond of; have a crush on, moon over.
+sver'mer -en, pl -e (=*-ar) 1 dreamer, visionary; romantic. 2 fanatic,

zealot. 3 *zool.* hawkmoth (family Sphingidae).
svermeri' *-et* 1 infatuation, passion. 2 fanaticism; enthusiasm; craze, mania. 3 beloved object, person; flame.
sver'merisk *A* - 1 romantic, quixotic, visionary. 2 fanatical; enthusiastic.
sver'me/tid *-a* 1 swarming season (e.g. for bees). 2 *hum.* adolescent love.
Sver're *Prn (m)*
sver'te[1] *-a* 1 blacking, polish. 2 printer's ink.
sver'te[2] *V -a/+-et* 1 blacken; cover with soot: **s- av** color off. 2 *fig.* blacken, malign; *(pop.)* smear. 3 *dial.* curse, swear.
sver'ting *-en tech.* batten, brace.
***sver'vel** *-elen, pl -lar* eddy, whirlpool.
***sver'vle** *V -a* eddy.
+**svett'** *A* (=***sveitt**) perspiring, sweaty.
+**svet'te**[1] *-n* (=***sveitte**[1]) perspiration, sweat: **s-n hagler av en** the sweat is running off sby.
+**svet'te**[2] *V -a/-et* (=***sveitte**[2]) perspire, sweat.
svet'te/drivende *A - med.* diaphoretic, sudorific.
svet'te/duk *-en* 1 *naut.* coarse scarf worn by firemen. 2 *eccl.* veronica.
svett'te/perle *-a/+-en* drop of sweat.
svet'te/reim *-a* sweat band.
svet'te/tokt *-et* attack of sweating (as e.g. before an examination).
sve'v *-et* 1 glide, flight; ride (in skiing). 2 *zool.* plankton.
+**sve've**[1] *-a* (=***svæve**[1]) *bot.* hawkweed (genus Hieracium).
sve've[2] *V -de/+-et/*-a* float, glide, hover; *fig.* fluctuate, vacillate; **s- i den tro at** labor under the delusion that; **s- i fare** be in danger; **s- i frykt, uvisshet** be in the greatest anxiety, uncertainty; **s- i luften** hang suspended in mid-air; **s- mellom liv og død** hover between life and death.
sve've/fly *-et* glider.
sve'vende *A* - floating; *fig.* uncertain, vague; be in suspense, undecided.
***svev'n** *-en* cf **søvn**
***svev'n/laus** *A* cf **søvn/**
***svev'n/løyse** *-a* cf **søvn/**
***svev'n/orar** *pl* drowsy, drugged state (on being awakened from a sound sleep).
***svev'nug** *A* - cf **søvnig**
svi'[1] *V -dde/+sved/svei, -dd/*-de/*-di* (=***svide**[1]) smart, sting: **han får s- for det** he'll pay for it (suffer the consequences).
svi'[2] *V -dde* (=***svide**[2]) burn, scorch, singe; *fig.* hurt, sting: **hun har s-dd grauten** she has burnt the porridge; **s- av** burn off, set fire to; **s- seg** (e.g. of food) burn; burn oneself.
svi'bel *-elen, pl -ler bot.* hyacinth (Hyacinthus orientalis).
***svi'de**[1] *V sveid, svide/-i* cf **svi**[1]
***svi'de**[2] *V -de* cf **svi**[2]
svi'e *-n* sharp stinging pain, smarting: **tort og s-** *jur.* injury, tort; *fig.* disgrace, insult.
+**svi'e/merke** *V -et* cf **svi/**
***svif'tuns/voke** [/våke] *-a* cf **syftesok**
***svi'g** *-et* bark and branches used as fodder.
***svi'ge**[1] *-a/-en* pliant, springy stick.
***svi'ge**[2] *V -a* bend.
+**svi'ger/datter** *-a/-en, pl -døtre(r)* (=***/dotter**) daughter-in-law.
svi'ger/far *-en, pl +-fedre/*-fedrar* father-in-law.
+**svi'ger/foreldre** *pl* parents-in-law.
svigerin'ne *-a/+-en* sister-in-law.
svi'ger/mor *-a/+-en, pl -mødrer/+-mødre* mother-in-law; **s-s tunge** *bot.* narrow-leaved sword aloe (Aloe arborescens).
+**svi'ger/sønn** *-en* (=***/son**) son-in-law.
svi'/jern [/jæ·rn] *-et* branding iron.
svi'k *-et* 1 treachery, treason; betrayal (**mot** of); faithlessness, perfidy; guile. 2 *jur.* deception, fraud; **begå s-** commit fraud.
+**svi'k/aktig** *A* - 1 treacherous; faithless. 2 *jur.* fraudulent; **handle s-** act with intent to defraud.
+**svi'kaktig/het** *-en* 1 treachery; perfidy. 2 *jur.* fraud.
svi'ke *V sveik/+svek, +sveket/*svike/*-i* 1 betray, be disloyal to; shirk (duty, responsibility). 2 deceive, disappoint.
+**svi'ke/full** *A* cf **svik/**
+**svi'ker** *-en, pl -e* (=***-ar**) traitor.
svi'k/ferd [*/fær] *-a/+-en* treachery; perfidy.
svi'k/full *A* treacherous; faithless, perfidious.
svikk' *-en archaic* bung, spigot.
svikk'/bor *-et/*-en* gimlet.
svi'k/laus *A* (=+**/løs**) dependable, reliable, trustworthy.
svi'k/råd [*/rå] *-a/+-et* betrayal, treachery, treason.
***svi'k/sam** *A* faithless, false, perfidious.
svik't *-en/+-et/*-a* 1 failure, giving way, sinking: **isen gav s-** the ice gave way. 2 departure, deviation (e.g. from course). 3 elasticity, flexibility. 4 deficiency, shortage. 5 compromise, weakness.
svik't/brett *-et* springboard.
svik'te *V -a/+-et* 1 fail, give way: **beina s-et** his legs gave way; **bremsene s-et** the brakes failed. 2 disappoint, fail (to come up to expectations). 3 betray, desert; let (sby) down; leave in the lurch: **s- sin plikt** shirk one's duty. 4 give out, run short. 5: **s-ende** failing (e.g. eyesight, health); disappointing, unsteady, weak; **på s-ende grunnlag** on an unsound basis.
svill' *-a/+-en* 1 sill (horizontal timber in foundation of wall); threshold. 2 crosstie (railroad track).
+**svil'le** *-n* cf **svill**
svi'me[1] *N*: **i s-** unconscious; **slå i s-** knock out.
svi'me[2] *V -a/+-et/+-te* 1 faint: **s- av, bort** faint (dead) away. 2 reel: **det s-er for ham** he feels faint. 3 bustle, scurry around.
+**svi'men** *A -ent, pl -ne* 1 unconscious. 2 dizzy.
+**svi'/merke** *V -a/-et/-te* (=***/merkje**) brand.
***svi'me/slegen** *A -e/-i, pl -ne* knocked unconscious.
svi'me/slå *V -slo, -slått* knock unconscious, stun.
+**svi'met(e)** *A* - bewildered, confused, dazed.
svim'le[1] *V -a/+-et* (=**svimre**) be, feel dizzy; reel: **s- overende** collapse, fall senseless; **det s-er for en** sby feels dizzy, is overcome. (Cf **s-ende.**)
svim'le[2] *pl of* **svimmel**
svim'lende *A* - dizzying; enormous, prodigious; fantastic, staggering (e.g. losses).
svim'ling *-en bot.* (bearded) darnel (Lolium temulentum).
svim'mel *A -elt, pl svimle* dizzy, faint; bewildered, confused, dazed.
svim're *V -a/+-et* cf **svimle**[1]
svim'ren *A +-ent, pl -ene* dizzy, faint, giddy.
***svim'rig** *A* - dizzy, faint, giddy.
svi'n *-et* hog, pig, swine; *fig.* brute, pig, swine: **full som et s-** dead drunk; **ha sine s- på skogen** be engaedg in questionable dealings.
+**svi'n/aktig** *A* - 1 beastly, rotten (e.g. weather); annoying. 2 *(adv.)* extremely, very: **jeg synes s- synd på deg** I'm awfully sorry for you (Borgen); **han var s- hyggelig mot oss** he was terribly nice to us.
svin'del *-en* humbug, trickery; swindle: **drive s-** swindle.
+**svin'del/foretagende** *-t* bogus, fraudulent enterprise, swindle.
svin'dle *V -a/+-et* cheat, swindle: **s- seg inn i** delude oneself into thinking sth; **s- seg til noe** obtain sth by fraud.
+**svin'dler** *-en, pl -e* (=***-ar**) swindler.
+**svindleri'** *-et* swindle, swindling.
svi'ne *V -a/+-et/+-te*: **s- til** dirty, make dirty, soil; defile, smear, sling mud at.
svi'ne/al *-et* hog breeding.
svi'ne/arbeid *-et* 1 filthy, nasty work. 2 drudgery.
svi'ne/beist *-et* brutal, ruthless person.
svi'ne/binde *V infl as* **binde** 1 bind hand and foot, hogtie. 2 *naut.* moor head and stern.
svi'ne/blom [+/blåmm] *-en bot.* ragwort (genus Senecio).
svi'ne/bust *-en* pig's bristles.
+**svi'ne/fett** *-et* (=***/feitt**) lard.
svi'ne/fylking *-a/+-en hist.* wedge-shaped battle formation.
svi'ne/heldig *A* - (unusually) lucky, a lucky devil.
svi'ne/hell *-et* fluke, stroke of good luck.
svi'ne/hund *-en* dirty dog, swine; *(pop.)* s.o.b.
svi'ne/kam· *-men* saddle of pork.
svi'ne/kjøtt *-et* (=***/kjøt**) pork.
svi'ne/kotelett· *-en* pork chop.
+**svi'ne/lær** *-et* (=***/ler**) pigskin.
svi'ne/pakk *-et* rabble, riffraff, scum.
svi'ne/pels *-en* dirty dog, swine; *(pop.)* s.o.b.
svi'ne/pest *-en vet.* necrotic enteritis.
svi'neri *-et* 1 filth, filthiness, swinishness. 2 lechery, lewdness, smut; corruption. 3 annoyance, nuisance: **gikt er noe s-** rheumatism is a damn nuisance.
svi'ne/rot *-a, pl +-røtter/*-røter bot.* woundwort (genus Stachys).
svi'ne/steik *-a* roast pork.
+**svi'ne/sti** *-en* pigsty.
sving' *-en, pl -/-er* 1 swing(ing); oscillation, vibration; (with the hand) flourish, sweep; (in writing) flourish; (in boxing) swing; activity, motion: **få s- på** get started; **i s-** active, going, working; **i full s-** in full swing; **komme i s-** get started; **sette i s-** start; **det ble ordentlig s- på det** things really got rolling, were in good shape. 2 bend, curve (in a road, etc.), turn. 3 detour, side trip: **ta en s- bort til bordet** take a trip over to the table. 4 accent, lilt; style, tone (also *et*): **litt svensk s- på ordene** a Swedish turn of phrase (accent).
sving'/bru *-a* swing bridge, swing drawbridge.
sving'/dør *-a* revolving door.
+**sving'e**[1] *V svang, svunget* cf **svinge**[2]
sving'e[2] *V +-et/+-te/*-a* (=**svinge**[1]) 1 swing, wave; brandish (a sword), flourish (e.g. a glass). 2 swing = circle, pivot; turn (e.g. in dancing, driving, skiing, etc.). 3 swing = fluctuate, oscillate. 4 (with *prep., adv.*): **s- med** brandish, flourish; **s- med armene** wave one's arms around; **s- mellom** fluctuate between; **s- om** (of feelings, opinions, etc.) change, shift; **s- om hjørnet** turn the corner; **s- opp foran** (with a car) pull up in front of; **s- opp med** dance with; lead off with, start off with; bring out, produce; **s- til side** sverve, turn aside. 5 *(refl.)*: **s- seg** pivot, turn around; leap, swing (oneself e.g. onto or off a horse); dance, trip the light fantastic; **s- seg opp (i verden)** get ahead, rise, succeed (in the world); (cf **s-ende**).
+**sving'e/krets** *-en elec.* oscillating circuit.
sving'el *-elen, pl -ler bot.* fescue grass (genus Festuca).

+ Bokmål; * Nynorsk; ° Dialect.
After letter: ' stress (Acc. 1); ` tone, stress (Acc. 2); · length.
Below letter: . not pronounced.

sving'ende *A* - 1 swinging; fluctuating, oscillating etc. 2 powerful, strong; *(adv.)* extremely: **for s-** (oath).
sving'e/tal *-et* (=+/tall) *phys.* frequency (of oscillations).
sving'et(e) *A* - winding, full of curves (e.g. a highway).
sving'e/tid *-a/+-en phys.* period (of oscillation).
sving'/hjul *-et* balance wheel, fly wheel.
sving'/kraft *-a/+-en phys.* tangential force.
sving'/kran *-en* (overhead) traveling crane.
+sving'ning *-en* (=***svinging**) 1 swing; oscillation, vibration. 2 fluctuation, variation; turn (e.g. to the left).
+sving'nings/tal(l) *-et* cf **svinge/**
sving'om *-en fam.* dance: **få seg en s-** go dancing.
sving'/sag *-a* pendulum saw.
+sving'/stang *-a, pl -stenger* parallel bar.
sving'/stol *-en* swivel chair.
sving'/tapp *-en* pivot, trunnion.
svinn'[1] *-et* 1 decrease, loss, shrinkage; wastage, waste (**av, i** of). 2 *med.* atrophy.
***svinn'**[2] *A svint* slender, slim; light eater.
+svin'ne *V svant, svunnet* 1 decline, decrease, dwindle: **s- hen** fade away, slip by; **s- inn** dwindle, shrink. 2 disappear, vanish: **svunne tider** bygone days.
svinn'/prosen't *-en* percentage of waste, wastage.
+svinn'/sott *-a/-en med., obs.* consumption.
svin'se *V -a/+-et* 1 wag, wave (a tail); swing (one's hips). 2 bustle, scurry, scuttle about: **s- og svanse** fidget, flutter, scurry about.
svi'nsk *A* - 1 foul, nasty (e.g. weather). 2 dirty, filthy, smutty.
***svi'nsleg** *A* - dirty, filthy, unclean.
svin't[1] *-en* flying trip, visit.
svin't[2] *A* - quick, speedy, swift.
svin'te *V -a/+-et* hurry, rush: **s- innom** pop in (on sby); **s- seg** hurry.
svi'n/toks *-en zool.* badger (Melus melus).
svin't/ærend *-et dial.* rush errand, quick trip.
***svi'p** *-en* 1 appearance; resemblance: **ein s- av morsfolket** a touch of his mother's family. 2 feature, peculiarity, trait: **det er ikkje nokon s- med det** there's no sense to it.
***svi'pe** *V -a* 1 appear: **s- på** resemble (in appearance). 2 shape: **s- til** fix up, get in order.
***svi'p/hag** *A* artful, skillful.
***svi'p/laus** *A* flat, insipid, without character.
***svi'pleg** *A* - impressive, stately; clever.
***svi'p/lik** *A* having some resemblance.
svipp' *-en* flying trip, visit: **ta deg en s- ut til oss** *fam.* drop out to our house.
svip'pe *V -a/+-et*: **s- innom (hos)** make a flying trip (to), pop in, run over (to).
svipp'/tur [also svipp'/] *-en* flying trip, visit.
svi'r *-en* 1 carousing: **drikk og s-** drinking and c-; **på en s-** on a binge. 2 pleasure: **en sann s-** a real joy.
svi're *V +-te/*-a* carouse, *(pop.)* booze: **s- bort (penger)** waste (money) on drink.
svi're/bror *-en, pl +-brødre/*-brør* boon companion.
svi're/lag *-et* drinking bout; *(pop.)* drunken brawl.
+svirr' *-et* buzz, whir, whiz.
svir're *V -a/+-et* buzz, whir, whiz; swing, swirl: **det s-er med rykter** rumor is rife.
***svir't** *-en* flashing movement.
***svir'te** *V -a* move, travel like a flash.
svis'ke *-a* 1 prune: **være vekk som en (kokt) s-** disappear into thin air. 2 *dial.* faint-hearted person.
svis'ke/graut *-en* prune pudding.
svis'ke/kompott· *-en* stewed prunes.
svis'ke/prins *-en obs.* clerk in grocery store.
svis'ke/suppe *-a* fruit soup with prunes.
+svit'sen *en* cf **switzend**
svi'v *-et* 1 swing, turn. 2 floating, gliding. 3 movement: **tankene hans var kommet på s-** his thoughts had wandered (Singdahlsen). 4 (sudden) idea, notion.
svi've *V sveiv, +svivd/*svive/*-i* 1 revolve, rotate, turn: **s- om** revolve, *fig.* be a question of, involve. 2 slide, slip (to one side). 3 float, hover, soar. 4 occur: **det sveiv for henne alt hun hadde hørt om spøkelser** everything she had heard about ghosts passed through her mind (Undset). 5 drift, lounge; saunter, stroll; ramble, rove.
svi've/sott *-a vet.* staggers.
svi'/vø·rde *V +-te/*-e* (=+/**være**) humiliate, insult; scorn.
***svi'/vø·rdeleg** *A* - cf **/vørdslig**
svi'/vørdslig *A* - (=+/**vørslig**) contemptuous, derisive, scornful.
***svode** [svå'e] *-a* 1 scratch, surface wound. 2 bare mountain (slope).
svoger [svå'ger] *-eren, pl -rer/+-ere* brother-in-law.
svoger/skap *+-et/*-en* affinity, relationship by marriage.
Svol'der *Pln hist.* island in Baltic Sea where King Olav Tryggvason was ambushed and killed (A.D. 1000).
***svole** [svå'le] *-a* cf **svale**[1]
svol'k *-en* 1 stick, switch; cudgel; *pop.* branches used to fasten a raft together. 2 beating, thrashing. 3 powerful, well-built man or boy.
svol'ke *V -a/+-et* beat, drub, thrash (with a cudgel).
***svoll'** *-en* cf **svull**
svol'le** *pp of* **svelle** (=svolli**)
***svol't** *-en* cf **sult**
svol'te** *pp of* **svelte**[1] (=svolti**)
***svol'ten** *A -e/-i, pl -ne* cf **sulten**
Svol'/vær *Pln* seaport, Nordland.
svome** [svå'me] *pp of* **svemje** (=svomi**)
svo'r[1] *-en* (pork) rind.
svo'r[2] *pt of* **sverge, sverje**
svo'rd *-en* cf **svor**[1]
***svore** [svå're] *pp of* **sverje**
+svo'ret *pp of* **sverge**
***svori** [svå'ri] *pp of* **sverje**
***svorte**[1] [svor'te] *-a* black color, dye; (black) shoe polish.
***svorte**[2] [svor'te] *V -a* blacken.
svovel [svå'vel] *-en/+-et chem.* brimstone, sulfur.
+svovel/aktig *A* - sulfurous.
+svovel/blomme *-n* (=*/**blome**, +/**blomst**) *chem.* flowers of sulfur.
***svovel/brenne** *-a chem.* hydrogen sulfide.
svovel/farga *A* - (=+-**et**) sulfurous, sulfur-colored.
svovel/gul *A* brimstone, sulfur yellow.
+svovel/holdig *A* - (=*/**haldig**) sulfurous.
svovel/jern [/jæ'rn] *-et* (=*/**jarn**) *chem.* ferrous sulfide.
svovel/kis *-en chem.* pyrites.
svovel/predikan't *-en* fire-and-brimstone preacher.
+svovel/pøl *-en* bottomless pit, everlasting fire (of hell).
svovel/sur *A chem.* sulfate.
svovel/syre *-a chem.* sulfuric acid.
svovel/sy'rling *-en chem.* sulfurous acid.
+svovel/vann'stoff *-et chem.* hydrogen sulfide.
svov'le *V -a/+-et* 1 treat with sulfur; disinfect, fumigate with sulfur. 2 (of a preacher) threaten with the everlasting fire of hell.
svull' *-en* (=***svoll**) 1 rough sheet of ice. 2 abscess, boil.
svul'len *A +-ent, pl svulne* swelled, swollen.
svull'/finger *-eren, pl -rer* festered, swollen finger; *med.* felon.
+svul'me *V -a/-et* 1 distend, swell; *naut.* fill (e.g. sails); roll (e.g. sea): **s- av stolthet** swell with pride; **s- opp** bloat, swell up. 2: **s-ende** full, overflowing, swelling; inflated, luxuriant: **s-ende språk** bombastic language.
+svul'men *en* swelling (e.g. sound).
+svul'ne *V -a/-et* become swollen.
+svul'st *-en* 1 bombast, turgidity. 2 *med.* tumor: **godartede, ondartede s-er** benign, malignant tumors.
+svul'stig *A* - bombastic, high-flown, turgid.
+svul'stig/het *-en* bombast, turgidity.
+svunget [svong'et] *pp of* **svinge**[1]
+svun'nen *A -et, pl -e* cf **svinne**
+svun'net *pp of* **svinne**
+svupp' *-et* 1 pop. 2 quick, sudden movement: **i en s-** in the twinkling of an eye.
+svup'pe *V -a/-et* pop (e.g. corks), squish (e.g. water).
***svæ'le** *-a* 1 smoke, vapor. 2 noisy party.
svæ'r *A* 1 heavy, massive; huge, large, tremendous (in size or extent); (of people) fat, husky, stout: **s-t så mange ord det er i denne ordboka** my, there are lots of words in this dictionary; **(det er) s-t som det regner** it's quite a rain; **det er s-t med** there's a lot, plenty of. 2 difficult, hard: **falle en s-t** be difficult for one; **ha s-t for (ved) å** have trouble, difficulty in, find it difficult to. 3 exceptional, outstanding- **s- til å** extremely good at; **s-t til** great, remarkable.
***svæ're** *V -te* oppress, trouble.
svæ'rende *Av* extremely, very.
+svæ'r/lemmet *A* - heavy-limbed.
svæ'rt *Av* extremely, very: **s- mange** very many, an awful lot; **slite s-** work oneself to the bone; **jeg vil s- gjerne** I'd like to very much; **er det så s- om å gjøre?** is it so terrifically important?
+svæ'r/vekter *-en, pl -e* (=***-ar**) heavyweight (boxer).
***svæ'v** *A* sleeping.
***svæ've**[1] *-a* cf **sveve**[1]
***svæ've**[2] *V -de* put sby to sleep.
***svæ've/drikk** *-en, pl -er* (=*/**drykk**) sedative: sleeping potion.
+svøm' *-men* (=***sum**[3]) swimming: **legge på s-** begin to swim.
+svøm'me *V svømte* (=***symje**) 1 swim (over across): **s- i blod** run with blood, welter in blood; **s- i tårer** be bathed in tears. 2 float: **s-ende last** *naut.* floating cargo; **s-ende øyne** bleary eyes.
+svøm'me/basseng· *-et, pl -/-er* swimming pool.
+svøm'me/belte *-t* life jacket, life preserver.
+svøm'me/blære *-a zool.* (of a fish) sound, swimming bladder.
+svøm'me/dyktig *A* - able to swim.
+svøm'me/finne *-n zool.* fin.
+svøm'me/fot *-en, pl -føtter* web foot.
+svøm'me/fugl *-en zool.* web-footed bird.
+svøm'me/hall *-en* swimming pool (indoor).
+svøm'me/hud *-a/-en* web.
+svøm'mer *-en, pl -e* swimmer.
+svøm'merske *-n* (woman) swimmer.
+svøm'me/tak *-et* swimming stroke.
+svø'p *-et* 1 shroud; swaddling clothes. 2 *bot.* involucre.
+svø'pe[1] *-n* scourge, whip: **Attila var en s- i Guds hånd** Attila was a scourge of God.
+svø'pe[2] *V -te* swaddle, swathe; wrap.
***svø'r** *A* out of (sth): **det er ikkje s-t** it can't be denied.
swagger [svæg'ger] *-en, pl -e* swagger (coat).
swing' *-en* swing (music, dance).
swing'/pjatt *-en pop.* zoot suiter.

swiss'/roll *-en* jelly roll, Swiss roll.

switzend [svit'senn] *N* sweet-scented chewing tobacco.

sy' *V -dde* sew: **sy etter mål** make to order; **sy i en knapp** sew on a button; **sy om** make over, remodel; **sy puter under armene på** bolster up, pamper; **sy sammen** stitch together.

sy'/atelie'r *-et* couturier, (high-class) dressmaker's shop.

sybaritt' *-en* sybarite.

sybarit'tisk *A* - sybaritic.

sy'/bo'rd *-et* sewing cabinet, sewing table (with drawers).

+**sy'd** *Av* (also *N*) cf **sør**

+**syd-** *Pf* cf **sør-**

sy'/dame *-a/+-en* dressmaker, seamstress.

sy'de *V* *+-et/*saud*, *+-et/*sode/*-i* (=***sjode**) boil, seethe.

+**Sy'den** *Pln* the South; the Mediterranean countries.

+**sy'd/frukter** *pl* tropical fruits.

+**sy'd/landsk** *A* - (=***sud/**) southern; tropical.

+**sy'd/lending** *-en* (=***sud/**) southerner, esp. a person from the Mediterranean countries.

+**sy'd/pol** *-en* cf **sør/**

+**Sy'd/polen** *Pln* cf **sør/**

+**sy'dpols/kalot'ten** *df* polar icecap (South Pole).

+**sydves't**[1] *-en* cf **sørvest**[1]

+**sydves't**[2] *Av* cf **sørvest**[2]

+**sydves't/landsk** *A* - cf **sør-**

+**sydves'tlig** *A* - cf **sør-**

+**sydøs't/landsk** *A* - cf **sør/**

+**sydøs'tlig** *A* - cf **sør-**

syenitt' *-en* syenite.

+**sy'erske** *-n* seamstress (dressmaker).

syf'ilis *-en* syphilis.

syfilit'tisk *A* - syphilitic.

+**sy'/forening** [/fåre·ning] *-a/-en* sewing circle.

***syf'te**[1] *-t* cf **søfte**

***syf'te**[2] *V -a/-e* 1 shake, sift, swing. 2 *naut.* pull together (sail).

syf'te/band *-et* cf **søfte/**

syf'tesok *en hist.* Saint Swithun's Day (July 2).

***sy'g** *pr of* **suge**

+**syg'/dom'** *-men* cf **sjuk/**

***sygner** [syng'ner] *pl* people from Sogn.

+**sy'k** *A* cf **sjuk**

+**sy'k/dom'** *-men* cf **sjuk/**

+**sy'kdoms/forfall** *-et* cf **sjukdoms/**

+**sy'kdoms/tegn** [/tein] *-et* symptom.

+**sy'kdoms/tilfelle** *-t* cf **sjukdoms/**

+**sy'kdoms/årsak** *-a/-en* cf **sjukdoms/**

+**sy'ke** *-n* cf **sjuke**

+**sy'ke/attes't** *-en* cf **sjuke/**

+**sy'ke/bil** *-en* cf **sjuke/**

+**sy'ke/forsik'ring** *-a/-en* health insurance.

+**sy'ke/gymnas't** *-en* physiotherapist.

+**sy'ke/hjem** *-met* cf **sjuke/heim**

+**sy'ke/hus** *-et* cf **sjuke/**

+**sy'ke/leie** *-t* 1 illness. 2 sickbed.

+**sy'kelig** *A* - cf **sjuklig**

+**sy'kelig/het** *-en* 1 illness, infirmity. 2 morbidity.

+**sy'ke/passer** *-en, pl -e mil.* hospital, medical orderly.

+**sy'ke/pleie** *-n* nursing.

+**sy'ke/pleier** *-en, pl -e* (male) nurse.

+**sy'ke/pleierske** *-a/-en* (female) nurse.

+**sy'ke/seng** *-a* cf **sjuke/**

+**sy'ke/søster** *-era/-eren, pl -re(r)* (female) nurse.

+**sy'ke/trygd** *-a/-en* cf **sjuke/**

+**sy'ke/værelse** *-t* sickroom.

***sy'kjast** *V syktest, sykst* become ill, sick; be ailing; long (**etter** for).

***sy'kje** *-a* cf **sjuke**

syk'kel *-elen, pl sykler* bicycle, cycle, *(pop.)* bike.

syk'kel/dekk *-et* bicycle tire.

syk'kel/kjede [*/kjee] *+-en/+-et/*-a* bicycle chain.

syk'kel/klokke *-a* bicycle bell.

+**syk'kel/løp** *-et* bicycle race.

syk'kel/nett *-et* (bicycle) mud guard.

syk'kel/pumpe [/pompe] *-a* bicycle pump, hand pump.

syk'kel/ring *-en* bicycle tire.

syk'kel/slange *-n* inner tube (for a bicycle tire).

syk'kel/stall *-en* bicycle shed.

syk'kel/stati'v *-et, pl -/+-er* bicycle stand.

+**syk'kel/sti** *-en* (=***/stig**) bicycle path.

syk'kel/styre *-t* handlebar.

syk'kel/veske *-a* bicycle tool kit.

Sykk'/ylven *Pln* twp, Møre og Romsdal.

syk'le *V -a/+-et* ride a bicycle; *(pop.)* bike.

+**syk'ler** *pl of* **sykkel**

syklis't *-en* cyclist; bicycle rider.

syklo'n *-en* cyclone.

sy'/klubb *-en* sewing circle.

syk'lus *-en* cycle.

***syk'n** *-a* cf **søkn**

***syk'ne**[1] *-a* cf **søkn**

+**sy'kne**[2] *V -a/-et* cf **sjukne**

***syk'ne/dag** *-en* weekday, workday.

sy'/korg *-a* (=**+/kurv**) sewing basket.

***sy'kst** *pp of* **sykjast**

***sy'ktest** *pt of* **sykjast**

sy'l *-en* awl, gimlet.

Syl'fest *Prn (m)*

sylfi'de *-a/+-en* sylph.

+**sylfi'de/aktig** *A* - sylphlike.

***syl'gje** *-a* cf **sølje**

sylin'der *-eren, pl -rer/+-ere* 1 cylinder. 2 *fam.* silk hat, top hat.

sylin'der/blokk *-a/-en* cylinder block.

sylin'der/formа *A* - (=**+-et**) cylindrical.

sylin'drisk *A* - cylindrical.

***syl'je** *-a* cf **sølje**

***syl'le** *V sylte* make **soll.**

syllogis'me *-n* syllogism.

syllogis'tisk *A* - syllogistic.

syll'/stokk *-en* sill (i.e. horizontal timber serving as foundation of a wall).

sy'l/spiss[1] *-en* (of an awl, gimlet) point, tip.

sy'l/spiss[2] *A* extremely sharp, pointed.

syl'te[1] *-a* pickled pork, pressed into loaf shape and sliced.

syl'te[2] *V -a/+-et* can, preserve; pickle: **være s-t ned i arbeid** *fig.* be buried, swamped with work.

syl'te/agur'k *-en* gherkin.

syl'te/eddik *-en* pickling vinegar.

syl'te/flesk *-et* pickled pork.

syl'te/glas *-et* (=**+/glass**) canning jar.

syl'te/labb *-en* pickled pig's foot.

syl'te/sjau *-en* canning.

syl'te/sukker [/sokker] *-et* sugar used in canning, preserving.

+**syl'te/tøy** *-et* (=***/ty**) jam.

syl'te/voks *-et* paraffin wax (used to seal jars of preserved fruit).

***syl'v** *-et* cf **sølv**

***sym'** *pr of* **symje**

sy'/maski'n *-en* sewing machine.

symbio'se *-n* symbiosis.

symbo'l *-et, pl -/+-er* symbol.

symbolikk' *-en* symbolism.

symbolise're *V -te* symbolize.

symbo'lsk *A* - symbolic.

symfoni' *-en* symphony.

+**symfo'niker** *-en, pl -e* (=***-ar**) composer (of symphonies).

symfoni'/konser't *-en* symphony concert.

symfoni'/orkes'ter *-eret/-ret, pl -er/+-re* symphony orchestra.

symfo'nisk *A* - symphonic.

***sym'je** *V sym, sumde, sumt* cf **svømme**

symmetri' *-en* symmetry.

symme'trisk *A* - symmetrical.

sympate'tisk *A* - sympathetic.

sympati' *-en* sympathy: **ha s- for, med** be in sympathy with, feel sympathy for.

sympatise're *V -te* sympathize (**med** with).

sympa'tisk *A* - 1 sympathetic. 2 appealing, engaging, pleasing: **en s- mann** an attractive man.

sympati'/streik *-en* sympathy strike.

sympatisø'r *-en* sympathizer; fellow traveller.

symposion [sympo'siånn] *-iet, pl +-ier/*-ion* (=**symposium**) symposium.

sympto'm *-et, pl -/+-er* symptom (**på** of).

symptoma'tisk *A* - symptomatic (**for** of).

sym're *-a bot.* anemone (genus Anemone).

sy'n *-et/*-a, pl -/+-er/*-ar* 1 sight, vision; eyesight: **et vakkert s-** a beautiful sight; **for s-s skyld** for the sake of appearances; **få s- for sagn** see for oneself; **få s- på** catch sight of; **ha s- for** have an eye for; **miste s-et** lose one's eyesight; ***se seg s- med (til)** eye an opportunity to, see a possibility for; **så langt s-et rekker** as far as the eye reaches. 2 vision (=apparition, mirage): **se s-er** have visions; **se s-er ved høylys dag** see ghosts in broad daylight. 3 outlook, view: **skifte s-** change one's opinion; **det er mitt s- på saken** that's the way I look at the matter. 4 face: **like (midt opp) i s-et på en** right to sby's face. 5 appraisal, survey. (Cf **syne.**)

synago'ge *+-n/*-a* synagogue.

***sy'nast** *V -test, -st* cf **synes**

+**sy'n/bar** *A* (=***/berr**) apparent, evident, obvious; easily perceptible, visible.

syn'd *-a/+-en* 1 sin: **ikke la en dø i s-en** not let sby off too easily; **fedrenes s-er hjemsøkes på barna** the sins of the fathers are visited upon the children (Ibsen, quot. from Exodus 20, 5). 2 too bad: **det er s-** it's a pity, a shame; **det er s- på ham** it's too bad about him, I feel sorry for him; **synes s- på** be sorry for. 3: **det er s- å si at** it would be wrong to say that, one can hardly say that.

syn'de *V -a/+-et* sin, commit a sin: **s- mot** offend against.

syn'de/bukk [/bokk] *-en* scapegoat, whipping boy.

syn'de/byrde *+-en/*-a* burden of guilt, sin.

syn'de/fall *-et eccl.* fall of man (from divine grace).

syn'de/fri *A -tt* free from sin, sinless.

syn'de/full *A* sinful.

+**syn'der** *-en, pl -e* (=***-ar**) sinner: offender (**mot** against).

syn'de/regis'ter *-eret/-ret, pl -er/+-re* catalogue, list of one's sins.

synderin'ne *-a/+-en* (female) sinner.

+**syn'derlig** *A* - *lit.* 1 particular, peculiar, special: **av ingen s- betydning** of no particular importance; **i s- grad** particularly; **ikke i noen s- grad** not to any great extent. 2 *(adv.)* especially, notably, particularly: **det er ikke s- vanskelig** it's not particularly difficult.

syn'de/træl *-en* (=**+/trell**) slave of sin.

syn'd/flod [*/flo] *+-en/*-a* 1 deluge, flood; catastrophe: **etter oss kommer s-en** after us the deluge (Madame Pompadour). 2 *(bibl.)* **s-en** the Flood (Genesis 7).

syn'd/fri *A -tt* cf **synde/**

syn'dig *A* - 1 sinful; guilty. 2 awful, horrible: **i en s- forvirring** in an awful mess; **holde et s- leven** make an awful racket.

syndikalis'me *-n* syndicalism.

syndikalis't *-en* syndicalist.

syndikalis'tisk *A* - syndicalistic.

syndika't *-et, pl -/+-er* combine, syndicate.

***syn'dleg** *A* - deplorable, regrettable, unfortunate.

***syn'd/løyse** *-a* sinlessness.

***syn'dre** *A* - cf **søre**[2]

+**syn'ds/bekjen'nelse** *-n* confession (of sins).

+ Bokmål; * Nynorsk; ° Dialect.
After letter; ' strees (Acc. 1); ' tone, stress (Acc. 2); · length.
Below letter: . not pronounced.

+syn'ds/erkjen'nelse *-n* consciousness, realization of guilt, sin.

+syn'ds/forla'telse *-n* (=***-ing**) absolution, remission of sins.

sy'ne[1] *N*: **i s-** in sight; **ute av s-** out of sight; **komme til s-** come into view, appear; **miste, tape av s-** lose sight of; **slippe av s-** let out of (one's) sight.

sy'ne[2] *V -te* show; indicate, point out: **s- en omkring** show sby around; **s- fram** show; **s- håndbak** hand wrestle, Indian wrestle.

sy'ne[3] *V -te* appraise, value; inspect, look over.

+sy'nes *V syn(e)s, syntes, syn(e)s* (=***-ast**) 1 be visible, come into view: **det s-** it is perceptible, visible; **flekken s- nesten ikke** the stain hardly shows at all. 2 appear, seem: **det s- som om** it looks as if; **det s- så** so it seems; **det s- å være en eller annen feil** there seems to be some mistake; **som det s-** apparently. 3 think; be of an opinion (**om** about): **jeg s- at** it seems to me that, I think; **hva s- De** what do you think; **gjør som De s-** do as you think best, use your own discretion. 4: **s- om** like; **jeg s- godt om det** it suits me, I like it very much; **jeg s- ikke om det** I don't like it. 5: **s- synd på** be sorry for, pity.

***sy'n/fare** *V -fer, -for, -fare/-i* inspect, survey.

***syng'** *pr of* **syngje**

+syng'e *V sang, sunget* (=***-je**) sing; ring (out), warble: **s- etter noter, fra bladet** sing from music; **s- fore** lead (the singing); **s- med** join in (the singing); **s- på siste verset** be on one's, its last legs; **s- ut** sing out, speak up; **så det sang** so it echoed, rang.

+syng'e/måte *-n* technique of singing.

+syng'e/spill *-et* ballad opera, Singspiel.

+syng'e/stykke *-t* ballad opera, Singspiel.

***syng'je** *V syng, song, sunge/-i* cf **synge**

sy'ning[1] *-a* 1 appearance, showing: **være i s-a** emerge; bob up, pop up. *****2 horizon: **dei gamle fjell i s-om** the ancient peaks against the sky (Aasen).

+sy'ning[2] *-en* sewing; needlework: **gå opp i s-en** come unsewed.

+syn'ke *V sank, sunket* cf **søkke**[1]

+syn'ke/ferdig *A* - cf **søkke/**

+syn'ke/not *-a, pl -nøter* cf **søkke/**

synko'pe *-n* 1 *mus.* syncopation. 2 *gram.* contraction, syncope.

synkope're *V -te* 1 *mus.* syncopate. 2 *gram.* syncopate.

synkretis'me *-n* 1 *eccl.* syncretism. 2 *gram.* syncretism.

synkro'n *A* synchronous.

synkroni' *-en* synchronism, synchrony.

synkronise're *V -te* synchronize.

synkro'nisk *A* - synchronic.

sy'n/kverve *V -de/+-a/+-et* bewilder, blind, confuse.

sy'n/kverving *-a* hallucination, (optical) illusion, mirage.

sy'nlig *A* - perceptible, visible; conspicuous, noticeable; apparent; *(adv.)* obviously, visibly: **han var s- skuffet** he was v- disappointed.

Syn'nøve *Prn (f)* name of heroine of Bjørnson's novel *S- Solbakken.*

syno'de *-n* synod.

synony'm[1] *-et, pl -/+-er* synonym.

synony'm[2] *A* synonymous.

synop'sis *-en* synopsis.

+synop'tiker *-en, pl -e* (=***-ar**) synoptist.

synop'tisk *A* - synoptic: *(bibl.)* **de s-e evangelier** the synoptic Gospels.

+syn's *pr, pp of* **synes**

sy'ns/bedra'g *-et* hallucination, (optical) illusion.

sy'ns/evne *-a/+-en* sight; power, sense of sight.

sy'ns/felt *-et* field of vision.

sy'ns/grense *-a/+-en* horizon.

sy'ns/inntrykk *-et* visual sensation.

sy'nsk *A* - 1 clairvoyant, gifted with second sight. 2 visionary: **en s- fantasi** a v- imagination.

+sy'nsk/het *-en* 1 clairvoyance, second sight. 2 visionariness.

+sy'ns/krets *-en* field of vision, horizon; *fig.* intellectual horizon.

sy'ns/leite *-t* horizon.

sy'ns/linje *-a/+-en* line of vision.

sy'ns/måte *-n* outlook, view.

sy'ns/nemnd *-a* [/nemd] inspection, survey commission.

sy'ns/nerve *-n* optic nerve.

sy'ns/orga'n *-et, pl -/+-er* organ of sight, vision.

sy'ns/punkt *-et* point of view, standpoint, viewpoint.

sy'ns/rand *-a/+-en* horizon.

***sy'ns/stad** *-en* point of view, standpoint, viewpoint.

***syn'st**[1] *pp of* **synast**

***syn'st**[2] *A* - southernmost.

sy'ns/vidde *-a/+-en* range of vision, visibility: **utenfor s-** out of sight.

sy'ns/vinkel *-elen, pl -ler* angle of vision; *fig.* point of view.

***sy'nt** *A* - perceptible, visible: **her er s-** there is a good view here.

syntak's *-en* syntax.

syntak'tisk *A* - syntactical.

+syn'tes *pt of* **synes**

synte'se *-n* synthesis.

synte'tisk *A* - synthetic.

sy'/nål *-a* (sewing) needle.

***sy'p** *pr of* **supe**

+sy'/pike *-a/-en* 1 *archaic* seamstress. 2 *zool.* poor cod (Gadus minutus).

sypress' *-en bot.* cypress (genus Cupressus).

sy're[1] *-a* 1 *chem.* acid; *dial.* buttermilk, sour whey. 2 *bot.* common sorrel, sour dock (Rumex acetosa).

sy're[2] *V *-a/+-et/-te* 1 leaven (batter, dough). 2 *dial.* mope, sulk; whine.

sy're/bad *-et* acid bath.

sy're/ballong' *-en* carboy (container for acids).

sy're/fast *A* - acid resistant.

sy're/flaske *-a* carboy (bottle for acids).

sy're/fri *A -tt* non-acid.

sy're/grad *-en* degree of acidity.

+sy'rer *-en, pl -e* (=***-ar**) Syrian.

sy're/vekt *-a/+-en* acid content.

***syr'gje** *V -de* cf **sørge**

***syr'gjeleg** *A* - cf **sørgelig**

Sy'ria *Pln* Syria.

syri'n *-en bot.* lilac (Syringa vulgaris).

syri'n/busk *-en* (=**/buske**) lilac bush.

sy'risk *A* - Syrian.

sy'rlig *A* - 1 sour, sourish; subacid, tart. 2 *fig.* peevish, sour; caustic, satirical.

+sy'rlig/het *-en* 1 sourness, subacidity; tartness. 2 *fig.* peevishness, sourness; causticity.

sy'rling *-en chem.* acid: **svovel/s-** sulfurous acid.

sy'/saker *pl* sewing things.

sy'/silke *-n* sewing silk.

***sysken** [sysj'en] *-a* cf **søsken**

sy'/skole *-n* sewing school.

sy'/skrin *-et* sewing box.

***sys'le**[1] *-a hist.* (administrative) district.

sys'le[2] *V -a/+-et* be busy, be occupied, putter (**med** with).

***sys'le/mann** *-en, pl -menn(er)* cf **syssel/**

sys'sel *-elen/-elet, pl +sysler* (=***sysle**[1]) 1 business, chore, pursuit. 2 *hist.* (administrative) district (in Norway); shire; office as governor of such a district. 3 district (of Svalbard).

sys'sel/mann *-en, pl -menn/*-menner* (=**sysle/**) 1 *hist.* district governor, royal official (in Norway). 2 district governor (of Svalbard; equal in rank to **fylkesmann** elsewhere).

+sys'sel/sette *V -satte* (=***/setje**) 1 employ, give work to, keep busy: **holde sysselsatt** keep employed. 2 occupy; absorb, engross: **s- seg med** busy oneself with.

syste'm *-et, pl -/+-er* system: **sette i s-** reduce to a system, systematize.

+systema'tiker *-en, pl -e* (=***-ar**) systematizer; methodical, systematic person.

systematise're *V -te* systematize.

systema'tisk *A* - methodical, systematic.

+syste'm/maker *-en, pl -e* (=***-ar**) systematizer.

syste'm/skifte *-et, pl +-r/*-* change in (political) system.

syste'm/tvang *-en gram.* force of analogy; systemic pressure.

***sys'ter** *-era, pl -rer* cf **søster**

***sys'ter/dotter** *-a* cf **søster/datter**

***sys'terleg** *A* - cf **søsterlig**

***sys'ter/mann** *-en, pl menn(er)* brother-in-law (sister's husband).

***sys'ter/son** [/sån] *-en* cf **søster/sønn**

sy'/stove [/ståve] *-a* cf **/stue**

***sys'trungar** [-ongar] *pl* (first) cousins.

sy'/stue *-a* (=**/stove**) dressmaker's shop.

sy'/svorte [/svorte] *-a zool.* common thrush (Turdus merula).

sy't *-et* 1 whimpering, whining. 2 care, worry.

sy'te *V -te* 1 whimper, whine: **s- for** dread. 2 care, take care: **s- for** look after.

sy'ten *A +-ent, pl -ne* 1 anxious, apprehensive; solicitous (**for** about). 2 whimpering, whining.

+sy'ter *-en, pl -e* (=***-ar**) whimperer, whiner.

sy'tet(e) *A* - whimpering, whining.

sy'/tråd *-en* (sewing) thread.

***sy't/sam** *A* careful, solicitous.

sytten [søt'ten] *Num* 1 seventeen. 2 (mild oath, euphemistic for Satan): **hva s- kommer det deg ved** how in thunder does it concern you (Undset).

syttende [søt'tene] *Num* seventeenth: **syttende mai** 17th of May (Independence Day; Constitution Day).

sytten/del [søt'ten/] *-en* a seventeenth (1/17).

syttendemai/tale [søttenema'i/] *-en/*-a* Independence Day speech (Norway).

syttendemai/tog [søttenema'i/tåg] *-et* Independence Day parade, procession (Norway).

sytti [søt'ti] *Num* seventy.

sytti/del *-en* a seventieth (1/70).

syttiende *Num* seventieth.

sytti/åring *-en* septuagenarian.

+sy'/tøy *-et* (=***/ty**) needlework.

+sy'v *Num* cf **sju**

+sy'v/armet *A* - cf **sju/arma**

Syv'de *Pln* twp, Møre og Romsdal.

+sy'vende *Num* cf **sjuende**

Sy'ver *Prn (m)*

***syv'je** *V -a* fall asleep; be drowsy.

***syv'jug** *A* - drowsy, sleepy.

+sy'vmils/skritt *-et* cf **sjumils/steg**

+sy'vmils/støvel *-elen, pl -ler* cf **sjumils/**

+sy'v/sover [/såver] *-en, pl -e* cf **sju/**

+syvsover/dag *-en hist., eccl.* Seven Sleepers' Day (July 27th).

***sæ'/bygg** *-en* person from Setesdal.

Sæ'/bø *Pln* 1 twp, Hordaland. 2 post office, Hjørundfjord twp, Møre og Romsdal.

sæd [se'd] *-en* 1 seed; germ, grain. 2 semen, sperm. 3 *(bibl.)* offspring, progeny.

sæd/celle [se'd/] *-a/+-en* sperm cell.

***sæ'de** *-t* seed; germ, grain.

***sæ'de/land** *-et* arable land.

***sæ'ding** *-en zool.* glaucous gull (Larus hyperboreus).

sæ'l *A* 1 fortunate, happy; wonderful: **heil og sæl** (Old Norse) greeting (revived by Norwegian Nazis). 2: **være like s-** be indifferent, don't care; **jeg er like s-, sa gutten, han gråt** "I don't care," said the boy, as he cried. 3 *archaic* blessed: **den s-e mø Maria** the B- Virgin Mary (Undset).

***sæ'last** *V -ast* die.
***sæl'de**[1] *-a* sieve.
sæl'de[2] [+sel'le] *V -a/+-et/*-e* sift (through a sieve).
***sæ'le**[1] *-a* 1 (good) fortune, happiness. 2 bliss, salvation.
***sæ'le**[2] *V -a* make happy; praise.
sæ'le/bot *-a* 1 act of charity, humane deed: **det er ingen s-** it serves no purpose, there's no use. 2 compassion, pity: **for s-s skyld** out of pity.
***sæ'ling** *-en* poor wretch, *(pop.)* poor devil.
***sæ'lke**[1] *-a* contentment, well-being.
***sæ'lke**[2] *V -a* make happy.
sæ'r *A* 1 singular, strange; eccentric, odd, peculiar. 2 cranky, crotchety.
sæ'r- *Pf* extra, special.
sæ'r/avtale *-en/*-a* special agreement.
sæ'r/behan'dling *-a/+-en* special handling (e.g. of a package).
+**sæ'r/beskat'ning** *-en admin.* special assessment, surtax.
særde'les *A* - 1 special: **en s- fornøyelse** a s- pleasure. 2 *(adv.)* especially, particularly; exceedingly, extremely; (short for **s- godt, s- tilfredsstillende**) outstanding (school grade, ab.=A+).
+**særde'les/het** *-en*: **i s-** especially, particularly; in particular.
sæ'r/domstol *-en jur.* special court, tribunal.
***sæ're** *V -a*: **s- seg ut** be different.
+**sæ'r/egen** *A -ent, pl -ne* 1 characteristic, distinctive (for of); special: **en s- smak** a flavor all its own; **s- for** peculiar to. 2 odd, singular, strange.
+**sæ'regen/het** *-en* 1 characteristic, distinctive quality. 2 oddness, peculiarity.
+**sæ'r/eie** *-t* (=*/**eige**) *jur.* separate estate (esp. of a married woman).
+**sæ'r/hensyn** *-et* special consideration.
***sæ'r/høve** *-t* special case, condition.
***sæ'r/hått** *-en* characteristic, peculiarity.
sæ'r/interes'se *+-n/*-a* private, special interest.
sæ'r/kjenne *-t* characteristic, distinguishing (salient) feature; criterion: **et s- for** a hallmark of.
sæ'r/klasse *-a/-en* special class (e.g. for handicapped children): **det står i en s-** it's in a class by itself.
sæ'rlig *A* - 1 special; exceptional: **en sak av s- interesse** a matter of particular interest; **en s- anledning** a special occasion; **i s- grad** particularly; **ikke i noen s- grad** not to any great extent. 2 *(adv.)* especially: **ikke s- stor** not very big.
+**sæ'rling** *-en* crank, eccentric.
***sæ'r/lynt** *A* - (=*/**lyndt**) eccentric, peculiar.
***sæ'r/menne** *-t* crank, eccentric.
sæ'r/merke[1] *-t, pl +-r/*-* characteristic, criterion, distinguishing feature.
+**sæ'r/merke**[2] *V -te* (=***-je**) be characteristic, distinctive of; characterize.
***sæ'r/merkjande** *A* - characteristic, distinctive.
***sæ'r/merkje** *V -te* cf **/merke**[2]
sæ'r/merkt *A* - characteristic, distinctive.
sæ'r/norsk *A* - distinctively Norwegian.
sæ'r/preg *-et* character, distinctive feature, stamp.
sæ'r/prege *V -a/+-et* characterize, stamp; **s-et** characteristic, distinctive.
***sæ'r/prent** *-et* offprint.
sæ'r/rett *-en* (special) privilege.
+**sæ'r/rettighet** *-en* (special) privilege.
sæ'rs *A* - 1 special: **det er noe s- ved henne** there is sth s- about her. 2 *(adv.)* especially, particularly; exceedingly, extremely: **s- god** very good.
+**sæ'r/skilt** *A* - (=*/**skild**) 1 distinct, individual, separate; special. 2 *(adv.)* apart, individually, separately; especially: **sende s-** send under separate cover.
sæ'r/skole *-n* school for retarded children.
sæ'r/stilling *-a/+-en* exceptional position: **innta en s-** hold a unique position.
***sæ'r/stode** [/ståe] *-a* exceptional, unique position.
sæ'r/syn *-et* exception; rare, unusual thing, sth quite exceptional, unique.
sæ'r/sy'nt *A* - rare, unusual; unique.
sæ'r/trykk *-et* offprint.
***sæ'r/voren** [/våren] *A -e/-i, pl -ne* odd, peculiar, strange.
***sæ't** *-et*: **det er ikkje s- på** you can't depend on it.
***sæ'tande** *A* - dependable, reliable, trustworthy.
sæte[1] [se'te] *-t* cf **sete**[2]
sæte[2] [se'te] *V -te dial.* 1 heed, mind, pay attention to. 2 mean, signify; be conclusive, crucial, decisive. 3: **s-endes** dependable, reliable, trustworthy.
***sæ'te**[3] *V -te* cf **såte**[2]
sæter [se'ter] *sætra, pl +-rer/*-rar* cf **seter**
***sætt'** *-en* agreement, settlement.
***sætt'tast** *V -ast* agree, be reconciled.
°**sø'** *-et* cf **sodd**
+**SØ**=**sørøst**
+**sø'delig** *A* - cf **søtelig**
+**sød'me** *-n* sweetness; *fig.* charm, delight, joy: **det første møtes sødme** the s- of the first encounter (Bjørnson).
+**søf'te** *-t* (=***syfte**[1]) *naut.* lanyard; reef.
+**søf'te/band** *-et naut.* hawser below the yard.
***sø'g** *-et* talk; humming (of voices).
***søgg'** *A søgt* damp, soggy.
***søg'gast** *V -ast* become damp, soggy.
***søgne** [søng'ne] *V -a* become damp, soggy.
Søgne [søng'ne] *Pln* twp, Vest-Agder.
***sø'k** *-en* demand, inquiry (**etter** for); hunt, search.
+**sø'ke** *V -te* (=***-je**) 1 hunt, look for; search, seek: **s-ende** inquiring, searching; **s- etter** look, search for; **s- opp** look up (see also **opp/s-**); **s- seg ut** pick, select; **s- sin egen fordel** look out for oneself. 2: **s- å** attempt to, try to. 3 go to, move toward; frequent: **s- havn** put in to harbor; **s- hjelp hos** turn to sby for help; **s- ly** take shelter; **s- omgang med** associate with; **s- sammen** join forces; **krake s-er make** birds of a feather flock together. 4 apply (**om** for) (a job, a license, etc.): **s- avskjed** resign; **s- (seg) bort, vekk** apply for a transfer, try to get away. 5 *archaic* attack, go after. (See also **søkt.**)
+**sø'ke/lys** *-et* searchlight: **komme i s-et** be in the limelight, exposed to (public) scrutiny.
***sø'ken** *A -e/-i, pl -ne* aggressive; inquisitive.
+**sø'ker** *-en, pl -e* (=***-jar**) 1 searcher, seeker (e.g. after truth). 2 applicant, petitioner. 3 *tech.* rangefinder, viewfinder.
***sø'kjar** *-en* cf **søker**
***sø'kje** *V -te* cf **søke**
søkk' *-et* depression, hollow.
søkk'/blaut *A* drenched (to the skin), soaking wet.
søk'ke[1] *-t* 1 *naut.*: **ta s-** ship water. 2 sinker (in fishing).
søk'ke[2] *V +sakk/*sokk, +-et/*sokke/*-i* (=+**synke**) 1 sink (e.g. into liquid, mud, etc.); settle (e.g. dust): **s- i jorda** sink into the ground, disappear without a trace; **sola synker i vest** the sun is sinking in the west. 2 decline, decrease (e.g. in estimation, status, value, etc.); fall: **s- i kne** fall to one's knees; **s- ned til** sink down to; lower oneself to; **s- (død) om** fall dead; **s- sammne** collapse; **barometret (termometret) synker** the barometer (thermometer) is falling. 3 swallow; digest: **synke maten** s- (digest) one's food. 4: **det søkker (sakk) i ham** it gives (gave) him a jolt; his heart sank.
+**søk'ke**[3] *V -te* cf **senke**
søk'ke/ferdig *A* - (=+**synke/**) (of ship) ready to (liable to) sink: **et s- skip** a sinking ship. 2 (of person) ready to drop.
+**søk'ke/myr** *-a* (=***søkkje/**) quagmire.
søk'kende *Av*: **s- borte** disappeared without a trace; **s- full** dead drunk; **s- stille** dead quiet, quiet as a mouse; **s- våt** dripping wet.
søk'ke/not *-a* (=+**synke/**) sink seine.
søk'ke/stein *-en* sinker (fishing).
søkk'/full *A* 1 brimful, chock-full, *(pop.)* jammed to the gunnels (gunwales). 2 drunk as a lord, *(pop.)* plastered.
***søkkj'e**[1] *-a* quagmire.
***søkkj'e**[2] *V -te* cf **senke**
søkk'/lasta *A* - (=+**-et**) fully loaded, loaded to the gills (gunnels) (**med** with).
søkk'/rik *A* rolling in money, *(pop.)* filthy rich.
søkk'/tung [/tong] *A* heavy as lead.
søkk'/våt *A* drenched, soaking wet, wringing wet.
+**søk'n** *-a* (=***sykn(e)**) weekday, workday.
sø'knad [*sø'kna] *-en, pl *-er* application, petition (**om** for).
sø'knads/frist *-en* grace period (for an application to be received).
sø'knads/skjema *-et, pl -/+-er* application form.
+**søk'ne/dag** *-en* weekday, workday.
+**sø'kning** *-en* 1 quest, search. 2 clientele, customers, patronage: **dårlig s-** poor boxoffice.
sø'ks/mål *-et jur.* lawsuit, legal proceedings: **anlegge s- mot en** sue sby.
sø'kt *A* - artificial, far-fetched, strained: **en s- vits** a far-fetched joke.
sø'l *-et* 1 mess, messing around: **jo flere kokker, dess mere s-** too many cooks spoil the broth. 2 dish water; slop. 3 mire, mud, slush.
sø'le[1] *-a* mire, mud, slush; *fig.* filth, mire.
sø'le[2] *V -te* 1 dirty, soil, (also *fig.*): **s- ned** blacken, tarnish (e.g. one's reputation); **s- på bordet** make a mess of the table, slop, spill food; **s- på seg, s- seg til** spill on oneself, make a mess of oneself; **s- til** dirty, soil. 2 mess (around), waste: **s- bort** fritter away, squander (money, time).
sø'le/pytt *-en* (mud) puddle.
sø'le/skvett *-en* splash of muck, mud.
sø'let(e) *A* - dirty, muddy; sloppy, slushy.
sø'le/vatn *-et* (=+/**vann**) dirty, muddy water.
søliba't *-et* celibacy.
søl'je *-a hist.* type of Norwegian silver brooch.
***sø'lt** *A* - sunny.
søl'v *-et* silver: **havets s-** fish; **tale er s-, men taushet er gull** speech is silver but silence is golden.
+**søl'v/aktig** *A* - silvery.
søl'v/alder *-en* silver age.
søl'v/arbei'd *-et* silverwork.
+**søl'v/arbei'der** *-en, pl -e* (=***-ar**) silversmith.
søl'v/barre *-n* silver ingot.
søl'v/besla'g *-et* silver mounting.
søl'v/beslått· *A* - silver mounted.
søl'v/blank *A* silvery.
søl'v/blekk *-et* (=+/**blikk**) sheet silver.

+ Bokmål; * Nynorsk; ° Dialect.
After letter: ' stress (Acc. 1); ' tone, stress (Acc. 2); · length.
Below letter: . not pronounced.

søl'v/brudepar *-et* (=*/**brur(e)par**) husband and wife celebrating their silver wedding anniversary.
+**søl'v/bryllup** *-et* (=*/**bryllaup**) silver wedding anniversary.
søl'v/erts *-en* silver ore.
søl'v/fat *-et* silver dish, vessel.
søl'v/fot *-en merc.* silver standard.
+**søl'v/gehal't** *-en* silver content (e.g. *in ore*).
søl'v/glans *-en* 1 silvery lustre, radiance. 2 *chem.* argentite, silver sulfide.
søl'v/glinsende *A* - silvery.
søl'v/gran *-a bot.* silver fir (Abies alba).
søl'v/grå *A -tt* silver gray; (of a person) silver-haired.
søl'v/klang *-en poet.* silvery sound, tinkle.
søl'v/klar *A* 1 (of air, water) limpid. 2 (of sounds) silvery.
søl'v/kre *-et zool.* silverfish (Lepisma saccharina).
søl'v/kvit *A* white as silver.
søl'v/liknende *A* - silvery.
søl'v/medal'je *-n* silver medal (esp. one awarded in sports competition).
søl'v/myntfot *-en merc.* silver standard.
søl'v/papi'r *-et* aluminum foil, tinfoil.
+**søl'v/penger** *pl* (=*-**ar**) 1 silver coins. 2 *(bibl.)* pieces of silver (Matthew 26, 15).
søl'v/plett *N* silver plate.
søl'v/poka'l *-en* 1 silver cup (awarded in sports competition). 2 *hist.* silver goblet.
søl'v/puss *-en* silver polish.
søl'v/rev *-en* silver fox.
søl'v/saker *pl* silver, silverware.
+**søl'v/skjær** *-et* silvery radiance, shimmer.
søl'v/slå *V infl as* **slå**[2] mount with silver: **s-tt** mounted in silver.
søl'v/smed *-en* silversmith.
+**søl'v/tøy** *-et* (=*/**ty**) silver, silverware.
+**søl'vtøy/skap** *-et* cupboard (for silverware, silver plate).
+**søm'**[1] *-men* (=***saum**) 1 sewing: **drive med s-** do sewing. 2 seam; *archaic* hem: **forloren s-** false hem; **gå noe etter i s-mene** examine sth painstakingly, go over sth with a fine-toothed comb. 3 *anat.* suture.
+**søm'**[2] *-met* (=***saum**) nail, spike; horseshoe nail.
***søm'd** *-a* dignity, decorum, honor.
***sø'me** *V -de* cf **sømme**[2]
***sømeleg** *A* - cf **sømmelig**
+**søm'/fare** *V -for, -faret* cf **saum/**
+**søm'me**[1] *V -a/-et* (=***saume**) *archaic* embroider, sew.
søm'me[2] *V +-et/+sømte/*sømde* (=***søme**) 1 befit, behoove, beseem: ***det sømde honom ikkje it** did not befit him. 2: **s- seg** be becoming (fitting, proper).
søm'melig *A* - (=***sømeleg**) decent, decorous, proper (**for** for); fitting, seemly.
+**søm'melig/het** *-en* decency, decorum, propriety.
+**søm'melighets/følelse** *-n* sense of decency, propriety.
+**søm'melighets/hensyn** *-et*: **av s-** for decency's sake, out of decency.
Søm'na *Pln* twp, Nordland.
søn'/dag *-en* (=***sun/**) Sunday: **om s-en** on Sundays; **på s-** on Sunday; **aldri på en s-** never on Sundays.
søn'dags/arbeid [also: søn'-] *-et* work done on Sunday.
søn'dags/ba'rn [also: søn'-] *-et* Sunday child (=lucky child): **være et s-** be born under a lucky star.
+**søn'dags/betrak'tning** *-en* Sunday devotion(s).
søn'dags/boksta'v *-en* dominical letter.
søn'dags/fred [also: søn'-, */fre] *-en* Sabbath calm, peace.
+**søn'dags/klær** [also: søn'-] *pl* (=*/**klede**) Sunday best, Sunday-go-to-meeting clothes.
søn'dags/skole [also: søn'-] *-n* Sunday school.
Søn'de/led *Pln* twp, Aust-Agder.
+**søn'den/** *Pf* cf **sønna/**
+**søn'der** *Av*: **i s-** to bits, to pieces; **s- og sammen** totally (destroyed), e.g. **slå s- og sammen** rout (thoroughly), smash (to bits).
+**søn'der/flenge** *V -et* rip, slash, tear to pieces; tear asunder.
+**søn'der/jysk** *A* - from North Schleswig (South Jutland from the Danish point of view).
+**søn'der/knuse** *V -te* crush, destroy, ruin completely: **s-ende** crushing, withering (e.g. blow, remark); *(bibl.)* **s-t** broken-hearted, prostrate; contrite.
+**søn'der/lemme** *V -et* dismember; *fig.* cut, slash to pieces (e.g. an article, a book).
+**søn'der/rive** *V -rev, -revet* 1 pull, tear to pieces: **s-reven** torn by grief, prostrate. 2 *(bibl.)* rend (one's clothes as a sign of grief).
+**søn'dre**[1] *V -et* (=***sundre**) *archaic* 1 crush, shatter. 2 part, separate, split.
+**søn'dre**[2] *A* - cf **søre**[2]
+**Søn'dre Hø'land** *Pln* (=***Syndre**, ***Søre**[2]) twp, Akershus.
+**Søn'dre Lan'd** *Pln* (=***Syndre**, ***Søre**[2]) twp, Oppland.
+**sønn'** *-en* cf **son**
søn'na *Av* from the south.
søn'na/drag *-et* southerly breeze.
søn'na/fjells *Av* in the south of Norway, to the south of the Dovre (ab.=Østlandet).
søn'na/fjelsk *A* - southern and eastern (Norway).
søn'na/for' *P* south of.
søn'na/frå *P* (=+/**fra**) from the south.
***søn'naleg** *A* - southerly, southern.
***søn'nan/etter** *P* from the south.
***søn'nan/om'** *P* south of.
søn'na/til' *Av* (=***sønnan/**) in (from) the south.
søn'na/trekk *-et* southerly breeze.
søn'na/vind *-en* south wind, southerly wind.
+**søn'na/vær** *-et* (=*/**ver**) southerly gale; souther.
+**søn'ne/datter** *-a/-en, pl -døtre(r)* granddaughter (son's daughter).
+**søn'ne/kone** *-a archaic* daughter-in-law.
+**søn'nen/** *Pf* cf **sønna/**
+**søn'ne/sønn** *-en* grandson (son's son).
+**søn'nesønns/sønn** *-en* great-grandson.
+**sønn'lig** *A* - filial.
+**søn'- og** [å] **hel'lig/dager** *pl* Sundays and holidays.
°**søn'st** *A* - cf **synst**[2]
***søp'le** *V -a* sweep.
søp'le- *Pf* cf **søppel-**
søp'pel *-elet/søpla/søplet* garbage, trash; *dial.* sweepings.
søp'pel/bil *-en* garbage truck.
søp'pel/brett *-et* dustpan.
+**søp'pel/dynge** *-a* garbage heap.
søp'pel/haug *-en* garbage heap.
søp'pel/kasse *-a/-en* garbage can, trash barrel.
+**søp'pel/kjører** *-en, pl -e* (=*-**ar**, */**køyrar**) garbage collector.
søp'pel/sjakt *-a/+-en* garbage disposal shaft.
sø'r *Av* south: **i s-** in the s-; **mot s-** to the s-; **s- for** s- of (see also **Syden**).
sør- *Pf* (=***sud-**, +**syd-**) south, southern.
Sø'r-A'frika/sambandet *Prn* Union of South Africa.
Sø'r-Ame'rika *Pln* South America.
Sø'r-Audnedal *Pln* twp, Vest-Agder.
Sø'r-Aukra *Pln* twp, Møre og Romsdal.
Sø'r-Aurdal *Pln* twp, Oppland.
sørau'st *Av* southeast, southeasterly.
sørau'stlig *A* - southeastern, southeasterly.
***sø'r/bær** *A* - southward (current).
sø're[1] *V -a/+-et*: **s- seg** (of a current) travel southward; (of wind) blow toward the south.
sø're[2] *A* - (=+**søndre**[2]) southernmost.
sø'ren *I* (mild oath) drat it! I'll be hanged!
Sø'ren *Prn(m)*
+**sø'r/enne** *-a zool.* roach (Rutilus rutilus) (a fish).
sø'r/etter *P* southward.
Sø'r/fjo'rd *Pln* twp, Troms.
Sø'r/fold *Pln* twp, Nordland.
Sø'r-Fron *Pln* twp, Oppland.
Sø'r-Frøya *Pln* twp, Sør-Trøndelag.
+**sør'ge** *V -a/-et/-de* (=*-**je**) 1 grieve, mourn; be in mourning: **s- over** grieve for, mourn. 2: **s- for** attend to, arrange; provide, make provision for; see to, take care of: **sørg endelig for å** be sure to, see to it that; **s- for seg og sine** provide for oneself and family; **s- for seg selv** shift for oneself; **s- spesielt for at** see that.
+**sør'ge/bind** *-et* mourning band (around one's arm).
+**sør'ge/bud** *-et* sad news, tidings; news of a death.
+**sør'ge/budskap** *-et* sad news, tidings; news of a death.
+**sør'ge/dikt** *-et* elegy.
+**sør'ge/drakt** *-a/-en*: **bære s-** be dressed in mourning.
+**sør'ge/flor** *-et* mourning crepe.
+**sør'ge/hus** *-et* house of mourning.
+**sør'ge/høyti'delighet** *-en* commemorative service.
+**sør'ge/kappe** *-a* (=***sørgje/**) *zool.* mourning cloak (Nymphalis antiopa).
+**sør'ge/kledd** *A* - in mourning, wearing mourning.
+**sør'ge/klær** *pl* mourning clothes.
+**sør'gelig** *A* - (=***sørgjeleg**) sad, lamentable, tragic; disastrous, grievous: **det er s- at** it is deplorable that; **det er det s-e** the pity of it is; **jeg ble s- skuffet** I was sadly disappointed.
+**sør'ge/marsj** *-en* funeral march.
+**sør'ge/pil** *-a/-en bot.* weeping willow (Salix babylonica).
+**sør'ge/rand** *-a/-en, pl -render* black edge (e.g. on envelopes, note paper used in death announcements); black border (e.g. around newspaper obituaries of famous people); *fam.* dirty fingernails.
+**sør'ge/sang** *-en* dirge.
+**sør'ge/skare** *-n* funeral procession, mourners.
+**sør'ge/spill** *-et* tragedy.
+**sør'ge/år** *-et* year of mourning.
***sør'gje** *V -de* cf **sørge**
***sør'gjeleg** *A* - cf **sørgelig**
sørgmo'dig *A* - sad, mournful, sorrowful.
+**sørgmo'dig/het** *-en* sadness, melancholy.
+**sø'r/helling** *-a* (=*/**hall**) southern slope.
Sø'r/ishavet *Pln* Antarctic Ocean.
sørl.=**sørlig**
Sø'r/landet *Pln* area along the southern coast and immediate inland districts of Norway (incl. esp. Vest- and Aust-Agder).
sø'rlands/idyll' *-en* an idyllic scene typical of nature in Sørlandet (esp. on the coast).
sø'r/landsk *A* - pertaining to Sørlandet.
sø'r/lending *-en* person from Sørlandet.
Sø'r/li *Pln* twp, Nord-Trøndelag.
sø'rlig *A* - southern, southerly: **s-breidd/**+**bredde** (latitude) south.
+**Sø'r-Norge** *Pln* Southern Norway (south of border between Trøndelag and Nordland).
Sø'r-Odal *Pln* twp, Hedmark.
sø'r/om' *P* to the south of.
+**søro'st** *Av* southeast, southeasterly.
sø'r/over [/åver] *Av* southward(s).
sør'p *-et* cf **sørpe**
sør'pe *-a* 1 sludge, slush. 2 mash (feed).

sør`pe/føre *-t* sludgy, slushy conditions (e.g. of roads).
sør`pet(e) *A* - sludgy, slushy.
sø`r/pol *-en* south pole.
Sø`r/polen *Pln* (=+**Syd/**) the South Pole.
sø`r/på *Av* down south.
Sø`r-Rana *Pln* twp, Nordland.
Sø`r/reisa *Pln* twp, Troms.
sø`r/side [*/sie] *-a* south side (e.g. of a house).
Sø`r-Trøndelag *Pln* South Trøndelag.
Sø`rum *Pln* twp, Akershus.
Sø`rum/sand *Pln* village, Sørum twp, Akershus.
Sø`r-Varang`er *Pln* twp, Finnmark.
sørves't[1] *-en* ɪ southwest; southwester (wind). 2 sou'wester (hat).
sørves't[2] *Av* southwest (**for** of).
sørves't/landsk *A* - pertaining to southwestern Norway.
sørves'tlig *A* - southwest, southwesterly.
Sø`r-Vågsøy *Pln* twp, Sogn og Fjordane.
+**sørøs't** *Av* cf **søraust**
sørøs't/landsk *A* pertaining to southeastern Norway.
+**sørøs'tlig** *A* cf **søraustlig**
Sø`røy/sund *Pln* twp, Finnmark.
+**søs`ken** *pl* (=***sysken**) brother(s) and sister(s), siblings.
+**søs`ken/ba`rn** *-et* (first) cousin.
+**søs`ter** *-a/-en, pl søstre* (=***syster**) sister.
+**søs`ter/datter** *-a/-en, pl -døtre(r)* niece (sister's daughter).
+**søs`ter/lag** *-et hist., eccl.* order of nuns, sisters; sisterhood.
+**søs`terlig** *A* - (=***systerleg**) sisterly.
+**søs`ter/selskap** *-et merc.* associated company.
+**søst`er/skip** *-et* sister ship.
+**søs`ter/sønn** *-en* nephew (=sister's son).
sø't *A* ɪ sweet; sugary; unsoured (e.g. milk). 2 *fig.* delightful, pleasant; good, kind, sweet (**mot** to); cute, nice: **etter den s-e kløe kommer den sure svie** after a pleasant experience come the bitter consequences; **sove s-t** sleep soundly; **vær s- og** please, be an angel and.
+**sø`t/aktig** *A* - sweetish.
sø`t/apal` *-en, pl *-aplar* apple tree (bearing eating apples).
sø`te[1] *-a bot.* gentian (Gentiana).
sø`te[2] *V -a/+-et* sweeten.
+**sø`telig** *A* -: **sove s-** sleep soundly.
sø`te/middel *-elet/-midlet, pl +-midler/ *-el* sweetening.
sø`t/eple *-t, pl +-r/*-* eating apple.
sø`te/rot *-a bot.* gentian (Gentiana).
+**sø`t/laden** *A -ent, pl -ne* cf **/laten**
+**sø`t/laten** *A -ent, pl -ne* (=***/låten**) ɪ cloying, saccharine, sugary. 2 maudlin, mawkish.
+**sø`tlaten/het** *-en* ɪ cloyingness, sugariness. 2 mawkishness.
***sø`t/leik** *-en* sweetness.
sø`tlig *A* - ɪ cloying, saccharine, sugary; sweet(ish). 2 maudlin, mawkish.
***sø`t/læte** *-t* ɪ cloyingness, sugariness. 2 mawkishness.
sø`t/mjølk *-a* (=+**/melk**) fresh milk.
sø`tne *V -a/+-et* become sweeter, ripen (e.g. fruit).
sø`t/ost *-en* unspiced cheese made of (sweet) cow's milk.
sø`t/pote`t *-a/-en bot.* sweet potato (Ipomoea batatas).
sø`t/smak *-en* sweet taste.
sø`t/suppe *-a* ɪ soup made with prunes, raisins, etc. 2 *hum.* high-sounding, well-meaning but empty phrases; *(pop.)* baloney.
°**søt`ten** *Num* cf **sytten**
sø`t/vier *-en, pl +-e bot.* bittersweet, woody nightshade (Solanum dulcamara).
***sø`t/voren** [/våren] *A -e/-i, pl -ne* sweetish.
***sø'v** *pr of* **sove**
Søv`de *Pln* twp, Møre og Romsdal.

***sø`ve** *V -de* lull (to sleep); calm, soothe.
°**søves't** *-en* cf **sørves't**[1]
søv`n *-en* (=***svevn**) sleep; **dysse en i s-** lull sby to s-; **falle i en dyp s-** fall fast asleep, fall into a deep s-; **sove den rettferdiges s-** sleep with a clear conscience, sleep the s- of the just.
søv`n/drukken [/drokken] *A +-ent, pl -drukne* drowsy, sleep drugged.
søv`n/dyssende *A* - soporific.
søv`ne *N*: **i s-** asleep, sleeping; **gå i s-** walk in one's sleep; **snakke i s-** talk in one's sleep.
+**søv`n/gjenger** *-en, pl -e* (=***/gangar**) sleepwalker, somnambulist.
+**søv`ngjenger/aktig** *A* - sleepwalking, somnambulistic.
+**søv`n/gjengeri`** *-et* sleepwalking, somnambulism.
søv`n/gretten *A +-ent, pl -gretne* cranky, cross (from being asleep).
søv`nig *A* - (=***svevnug**) drowsy, sleepy.
+**søv`nig/het** *-en* drowsiness, sleepiness.
søv`n/laus *A* (=+**/løs**) sleepless.
søv`n/liknende *A* - (=+**/lignende**) sleep-like (state).
+**søv`n/løs** *A* cf **/laus**
+**søv`nløs/het** *-en* insomnia, sleeplessness.
***søv`n/løyse** *-a* insomnia, sleeplessness.
søv`n/tung [/tong] *A* drowsy, drugged with sleep.
***søy`de** *V -de* ɪ heat. 2 sigh, whisper (e.g. the wind).
søy`e *-a* ewe.
søy`e/lam` *-met* (female) lamb.
søy`le *-a/+-en* ɪ column, pillar. 2 pile, support. 3 *elec.* **volta/s-** voltaic cell, couple.
søy`le/gang *-en arch.* colonnade.
søy`le/hall *+-en/*-a arch.* peristyle.
søy`le/helgen *-enen, pl -(e)ner eccl., hist.* stylite.
***søy`r** *-en* (of trees) dry rot.
***søy`re** *V -te* allow to decay, rot; spoil.
så'[1] *-a* chaff, husk (of grain): **ikke s-a igjen** not a speck left.
så'[2] *-en* wooden tub (with handles).
så'[3] *V -dde* seed, sow: **så vind og høste storm** sow the wind and reap the whirlwind.
+**så'**[4] *pt of* **se**
så'[5] *Av* ɪ so, such, thus: **så som så** so-so (expressing moderate dissatisfaction); **så vidt** just barely; **så å si** so to speak; **så bra en mann** such a fine man; **om så** even if; **om så skal være** if necessary; **om så var** if it were thus, if such were the case; so what; **(bedre, større, osv.) enn som så** (better, larger, etc.) than that; **ikke mer enn som så** no more than that, nothing at all; only so-so; **hvorfor er det så dyrt?** why is it so expensive?; **når det er så** such being the case; **vær så snill** please. 2 then (=subsequently): **og så skal jeg tilbake til Amerika** and then I'm going back to America; **gi meg boka, så skal jeg lese for deg** give me the book and I'll read to you. 3: **i så fall** in that case; **i så henseende (måte)** in that respect.
så'[6] *C* ɪ so (that): **så at** so that. 2: **så . . (som) . .** as . . as . . (**så godt som** as good as, almost, practically; **så mye jeg kan** as much as I can; **så vidt jeg vet** as far as I know).
så'[7] *I* oh, indeed, really? there now, be calm: **jaså!** oh, really! **se så** there now; **så menn** indeed.
s. å. =**samme år**
***så'd** *-et* germ, seed.
+**så'dan** *A -t, pl -ne* cf **sånn**
***så`d/slag** *-et* kind, type of seed.
så`/erle *-a zool.* yellow wagtail (Motacilla flava thunbergi).
+**så'es** *pt of* **se(e)s**
såfram't *C* (=+**såfremt**) if, provided that.
så`/frø *-et* seed (seed grain).
***så'g** *pt of* **sjå**[3]

+**såga'r** *Av* even, in fact, indeed.
så'/gauk *-en zool.* wryneck (Jynx torquilla).
***så`/gidn** *-a* vibrating air.
sågodt'/som` *Ao* cf **god**
+**så/kalt** *A* - (=***/kalla**) so-called.
såkorn *-et* seed (seed grain).
så'l *-a/-en/-et dial.* ɪ poor wretch, *(pop.)* poor devil. 2 lazy sluggish person. *3 soul (cf **sjel**).
***så`last** *V -ast* die.
sål'd *-et* ɪ riddle (=coarse sieve for winnowing grain). 2 *hist.* quantity of grain equaling approx. 80 kilograms.
***sål`de** *V -a* cf **sælde**[2]
+**så`le**[1] *-n* (=***sole**[1]) ɪ sole. 2 (of a carpenter's plane) bottom. 3 *naut.* false keel.
+**så`le**[2] *V -a/-te* (=***sole**[3]) sole (shoes): **s- og flikke** put soles and heels on shoes.
+**så`le/beskyt`ter** *-en, pl -e* sole protector (e.g. cleat, hobnail).
+**så'/ledes** *Av* (=**/leis**) ɪ in this manner, like this, like that; so, thus. 2 accordingly, therefore.
+**så`le/lær** *-et* sole leather.
+**såleng'e** *Av* cf **lenge**
***så`lut** *A* - ɪ awkward, clumsy. 2 miserable, pitiable, wretched.
+**så'/lydende** *A* - which read as follows.
***så'm** *A* dark, dim; dull.
så`/mann *-en, pl -menn/*-menner* sower.
så'/maski`n *-en* seeder, sowing machine.
***så`men** *A -e/-i, pl -ne* dark, dim; dull.
såmenn' *Av* cf **menn**[3]
***så`ming** *-en* dull, lethargic person.
***så`mleg** *A* - dark, dim; dull.
***så`mut** *A* - apathetic, lethargic, sluggish.
+**så'n** *A* cf **sånn**
***så`nad** *-en* sowing; seed (seed grain).
+**sånn'** *A sånt, pl sånne* (=+**sådan**) ɪ like that, such: **en s- mann** such a man, a man like that; **s- er han** that's the way he is, that's what he's like; **noe s-t** something like that, such things; **har du hørt s-t!** have you ever heard the likes!; **s- en fin dag!** what a wonderful day! 2 (as *adv.*): **sådan, sånn** like that (this), in such a way, to such a degree; **s- er det** that's the way it is; **s- at** so that; **s- som** like; **gjør det s-** do it like this; **s- i blant** every once in a while; **det koster s- en to-tre kroner** it costs about two or three *kroner*.
så'/pass *Av* enough, this much: **jeg ville ønske jeg hadde s- meget** I wish I had even that much; **men s- meget vet vi** but this much we do know; **planen var s- vellykket at** the plan was so successful that.
så`pe[1] *-a* soap.
så`pe[2] *V -a/+-te* soap; lather, wash with soap: **s- inn** lather (one's face), rub soap on (cloth).
+**så`pe/aktig** *A* - soaplike; soapy.
så`pe/boble *-a/-en* soap bubble.
+**så`pe/koker** *-en, pl -e* (=***-ar**) ɪ soapmaker. 2 *fam.* blockhead, lunkhead, nitwit.
så`pe/kopp *-en* soap dish.
så`pe/skum [/skomm] *-met* lather, soapsuds.
så`pe/skål *-a* soap dish.
så`pe/spon *-en* soap flakes.
så`pe/urt *-a/+-en bot.* soapwort (Saponaria officinalis).
så`pe/vaske *V -a/+-et* wash with soap (and water).
så`pe/vatn *-et* (=+**/vann**) soapy water; soapsuds.
så'r[1] *-et* wound; sore, ulcer: **rive opp et gammelt s-** reopen an old wound.

+ Bokmål; * Nynorsk; ° Dialect.
After letter: ' stress (Acc. 1); ` tone, stress (Acc. 2); · length.
Below letter: . not pronounced.

så'r[1] *A* painful, sore; *fig.* sensitive; sad, whimpering: **det s-e punkt** the sore spot, subject; **angre s-t på noe** regret sth bitterly; **gråte s-t** sob.
+**så'r/bar** *A* susceptible, vulnerable: **s-t punkt** weak spot; chink in one's armor.
+**så'rbar/het** *-en* vulnerability.
så'r/beint *A* - footsore.
så're *V -a/+-et* injure, wound; *fig.* hurt, offend, wound: **s- en dypt** cut sby to the quick, hurt sby deeply; **s- ens følelser** hurt sby's feelings; **s- ens stolthet** wound sby's pride.
så'rende *A* - cruel, harsh, painful: **en s- bemerkning** a cutting remark.
så'r/feber *-eren, pl -rer/+-ere* septic fever, septicemia.
så'r/føtt *A* - footsore.
+**så'r/het** *-en* soreness, tenderness; *fig.* sensitiveness.
***så'r/hjarta** *A* - 1 anxious, apprehensive; uneasy. 2 sensitive, touchy.
***så'r/huga** *A* - anxious, concerned, worried.
***så'rke** *-n* eruption, rash (e.g. on one's face).
+**så'r/tent** *A* - (=*/**tennt**) having sensitive teeth, tender gums.
+**så'r/øyd** *A* - bleary-eyed, with bloodshot eyes.
+**så's** *pt of* **se(e)s**
+**såsan't** *C* cf **sann**[2]
såsiss' *-en* (=**saucisse**) small sausage.
+**såsna'rt** *C* cf **snar**[3]
+**så'/som'** *C* 1 for example. for instance. 2 *archaic* inasmuch as.
såså' *I* easy does it, there now.
så'te[1] *-a* (rounded) pile, small stack (e.g. of hay, straw).
så'te[2] *V -a/+-et* (=***sæte**[2]) rick, stack (e.g. hay, straw).
så'te/høy *-et* hay in ricks.
+**såvel'** *Av* cf **vel**[4]
+**såvidt'** *Av* cf **vid**
+**såviss't** *Av* cf **visst**[2]
***så'/voren** [/våren] *A -e/-i, pl -ne* such.

T

t[1] [te'] *-en* 1 (letter) T, t. 2 *educ.* grade, mark for **tilfredsstillende.**
t[2]=**tonn**[2]; **tara**
t.=**til**[1]; **time**[1]
ta'[1] *V +-r/*tek, tok, +tatt/*teke/*-i* (=***take**) 1 take (=get for oneself, e.g. a bride, a fort, a hurdle, a prize, a snapshot; punishment, responsibility, etc.); have (a drink); charge (a price); steal: **ta i arv** inherit; **ta bladet fra munnen** speak out, speak one's mind; **ta del i** take part in; **ta eksamen** take a degree; **ta en med det gode** win one over by kindness; **ta farvel** say goodbye; **ta feil** be mistaken; **ta knekken på en** cook one's goose, finish one off; **ta mot til seg** gather up one's courage; **ta natten til hjelp** burn the midnight oil; **ta ordet** speak up, take the floor; **ta plass!** all aboard, take your seats; **ta en pust i bakken** take a breather; **ta tiden** time. 2 grab, grip; handle: **kåpen tar meg i armene** the coat is tight around my arms; **vinden (sola) tar her** the wind (sun) is strong here; **ta en i hånden** shake hands with sby; **ta fatt** grab hold; **ta beina fatt** get going, leave, pick up one's feet (and go); **ta beina på nakken** quicken one's pace, run for it; **ta fatt på** begin, start in on; **ta i favn** embrace; **ta omkring** embrace; **ta skjeen i en annen hånd** mend one's ways, turn over a new leaf; **ta tak** wrestle. 3 reach (**etter** for), touch; **ta i** take hold of, touch; **ta på** handle, touch; **ta til** reach for, resort to: **ta varsomt, slyngel, på et kongelig barn** handle a royal child carefully, scoundrel (Ibsen); **ta bakken, vannet** hit, land on the ground, on the water; **ta bunnen** (of a boat, a swimmer) hit, touch bottom; **ta hull på** broach a subject; break (money); **ta land** make landfall. 4 catch (a ball, fish, a thief, etc.); reach; **ta varme** catch fire; **ta en** *fig.* catch sby, trip sby up; **ta en på kornet** take aim at; hit off, imitate. 5 take (=react to; endure, stand); endure, last; **han kan ikke ta en operasjon til** he can't take another operation; **hvor lenge vil det ta?** how long will it take? 6 go, start off: **ta til Hamar** go to H-; **vi skulle ta over fjellet** we were going to go over the mountain(s); **ta på sprang** begin running; **ta på vei** carry on (terribly); fly off the handle. 7 (with *prep., adv.*): **ta av** be less, diminish, drop off; take off (weight); cut (a deck of cards); **ta av for noe** protect, shelter from sth; **ta av seg (tøyet)** take off one's wraps; **ta etter** be like, take after; **ta for** take to be; **jeg tok ham for en prest** I took him to be a minister; **ta for god fisk** take as gospel; **ta en for seg** take one to task; **ta for seg av** help oneself to; feel one's way; **ta i** endeavor, put forth effort, undertake; begin, launch into, take hold of; speak out (up); **ta fatt i** grab hold of, grip; **ta sin hånd i** touch; **ta igjen** take back; fight back; answer, talk back; catch up with, overtake; **ta det igjen** get even; **ta imot (mot)** receive; stand for, swallow, tolerate (an insult etc.); **ta inn (hos)** find lodging (at); **ta opp** take up (a question, problem, etc.); dig up (potatoes, etc.); **ta opp igjen** repeat, resume; **ta ille opp** be angry over, take amiss; **ta det opp med** be a match for, cope with; **ta på** tell severely on; attack, set upon; *fam.* begin (**å** to); **det tar på kreftene** it takes it out of one, one is played out; **ta på seg (tøyet)** dress, put on (wraps); **ta til (med)** begin, start (with); **de tok til å lete etter ham** they started looking for him; **ta til orde (gjenmæle)** speak up (in reply); **ta til seg** eat; **ta unna** *dial.* alleviate, ease; **ta unna for en** ease one's burden, work, etc.; **ta ut** pick out, select; **ta ved** begin; accept, take on; **bilisten har tatt ved en bot** the motorist has accepted a fine. 8 (*refl.*): **ta seg** *dial.* change in appearance, quality; lose freshness; (of female animals) conceive; **ta seg av en** look after, take care of one; deal with, handle one; **ta seg for** be busy with, do; **ta seg for pannen** clasp one's hand to one's forehead; **ta seg i akt, i vare** take care, watch out (**for** for); **ta seg i det** check (stop) oneself; **ta seg opp (igjen)** improve, pick up; **ta seg på tak** go out of one's way, take pains; **ta seg sammen** pull oneself together; **ta seg til** busy oneself with, do; **ta seg til (brystet)** move one's hand to (one's breast); **ta seg til rette** help oneself (**av** to); **ta seg ut** appear, look; put oneself out, strain oneself.
°**ta**[2] *P* cf **av**
tab'be[1] *-n fam.* blunder, boner, *(pop.)* boo-boo: **gjøre en t-** make a b-.
+**tab'be**[2] *V -a/-et fam.* blunder, make a boner: **t- seg (ut)** make a fool of oneself, make a big blunder.
+**tab'be/forsik'ring** *-a/-en* liability insurance (for property damage caused by an individual).
tabell' *-en* (conversion, multiplication, time, etc.) table.
tabella'risk *A* - tabular; tabulated.
taberna'kel *-elet/-let, pl +-ler/*-el bibl., eccl.* tabernacle.
tablett' *-en med.* lozenge, tablet.
tablå' *-et, pl +-er/*-* 1 tableau; pageant. 2 (as interj.) surprise!; curtains.
+**tablå/messig** *A* - tableau-like.
ta'bu *-et* taboo.
+**ta'bu/forestilling** [/fåre-] *-en* taboo concept.
tabula'tor *-en* tabulator (on a typewriter).
taburett' *-en* 1 stool, taboret; folding stool (with cloth seat). 2 *pol.* cabinet position.
***ta'd** *-et* manure.
+**ta'fatt** *A* - irresolute, perplexed, puzzled; helpless.
taf'fel *-elet/taflet* 1 *archaic* (festively laid) table. 2 (royal) banquet: **heve t-et** end the meal; **holde åpent t-** have open house for dinner.
taf'fel/musikk' *-en* dinner music.
taf'fel/ur *-et* bracket clock, mantle or table clock (in a casing or glass dome).
taf's *-et/*-en* 1 tuft, wisp (of hair, thread, etc.): **komme i t-** ravel, tangle. 2 *fam.* pitiable fellow, poor wretch.
taf'se *V -a/+-et* fray, ravel, tatter: **t- opp** (the same).
***taf'sen** *A -e/-i, pl -ne* cf **tafset(e)**
taf'set(e) *A* - (=***tafsen**) ragged, tattered, (un)raveled; (of hair) dishevelled.
taf't *-et* taffeta.
ta'gal *A dial.* silent, taciturn.
tag'de *pt of* **tie, teie**[1]
+**-ta'gelig** *A* - cf **-takelig**
+**-ta'gelse** *-n* cf **-takelse**
+**-ta'ger** *-en, pl -e* cf **-taker**
tagg'[1] *-en* (=***tagge**[1]) 1 point, tip; prong, tine (e.g. of antler); barb, spike, spine; sharp mountain peak, top. 2 *dial.* scallop (on cloth). 3 *pop., (pl)* hemorrhoids, piles.
tagg'[2] *pt of* **tigge**[1]
***tag'ge**[1] *-n* cf **tagg**[1]
tag'ge[2] *V -a/+-et* clip, cut; jag, notch.
***tag'ge**[3] *V -a* pacify, quiet, silence.
tag'get(e) *A* - jagged, notched, toothed; barbed, spiked, thorny.
tag'l *-et* 1 hair of a horse's mane or tail. 2 *dial.* flax ready for spinning.
tag'ne *V -a/+-et dial.* fall silent.
taifu'n *-en* typhoon.
-ta'ing *-a/+-en* cf **-takelse, -taking**
ta'k[1] *-et* 1 roof. 2 ceiling: **det er lavt under t-et (hos en)** there is a low ceiling (in sby's house), *fig.* sby's horizon is limited; **bo under t- med** live in the same house, under the same roof with.
ta'k[2] *-et* 1 grasp, grip, hold: **få t- i, på** get hold of, seize; get the hand, knack of, understand; **grasp, make**

out; **miste (sleppe) t-et** lose one's grip. 2 bout, scuffle, tilt: **ta (et) tak med en** wrestle with one. 3 (oar, swimming) pull, stroke, sweep; turn (of a key, shovel, etc.). 4 effort, exertion; ability, energy: **et tungt t-** a big effort; **i harde t-** (with) full force, with all one's might; **ta seg på t-** exert oneself, make an effort. 5 fit, paroxysm, spell (of illness, pain, work, etc.); period, stage: **rykke fram i t-** advance by stages; **t- om t-** alternately. 6 *dial.* instant, moment; while: **stanse et t-** stop a while. 7 (tool) handle. 8 (clay, gravel, sand) pit.

***ta'kande** *A* - 1 enthralling, moving. 2 ready (to take), ripe.

***ta'kast** *V tekst, tokst, tekest/-ist* 1 fight, wrestle (with each other); contend, dispute, quarrel. 2 be burdened, be plagued: **ha mykje å t- med** suffer great hardships.

ta'k/bjelke *-n* roof beam, rafter.

+ta'k/drypp *-et* (=***/drop**) dripping from the roof (eaves).

***ta'ke** *tek, tok, teke/-i* cf **ta**[1]

-ta'kelig *A* - e.g. **an/t-, mot/t-.**

+-ta'kelse *-n* e.g. **del/t-, mot/t-.**

+-ta'ker *-en, pl -e* (=***-ar**) e.g. **av/t-, del/t-.**

***ta'ke/skjerr** *A -skjert* cf **tak/skjær**

ta'k/halm *-en* (roofing) thatch.

-ta'king *-a/+-en* e.g. **del/t-, mot/t-.**

takk'[1] *-a/+-en* 1 thanks; gratitude, reward (**for** for): **det var t-en jeg fikk** that was all the gratitude I got. 2 thank you, thanks; (as polite refusal) no thanks. 3 please: **det blir fem kroner, t-** five *kroner*, please. 4 (idioms): **da skal du ha t-, da skal de fattige ha t-** *fam.* it's no use, one is helpless; **ja (nei) t-** yes (no), thank you; (ironic, scornful rejection) no, thank you! **ja t-** (in answer to an offer) yes please; **mange (tusen) t-** many thanks, thanks so much; **selv (sjøl(v)) t-** same to you, don't mention it; **si t- for seg** bow out, take one's leave; **som t-** by way of thanks, in return (**for** for); **t- for sist** thanks for our last time together (polite greeting to host); **t- skjebne** just my luck; **t- som byr** *fam.* thanks (for offering).

°takk'[2] *-en* branch (of antler); point; sharp peak; cog, notch, tooth.

ta'k/kammer *-et, pl -/+-kamre* attic room.

tak'ke[1] *-a* round iron griddle (esp. for baking *flatbrød*).

tak'ke[2] *N*: **ta til t- (med)** be satisfied (with), take what one gets (without complaint).

tak'ke[3] *V -a/+-et* 1 thank, give thanks (**for** for): **t- for seg** thank one's host for hospitality; **ingenting å t- for** don't mention it, not at all, you're welcome; **(jo) jeg t-er** (ironic) indeed! **t- meg til å få betale for seg** I prefer to pay for myself, thanks (J. Lie); **t- til** be thankful, be satisfied; **t-et være** thanks to, owing to. 2 **t- av** resign, retire (from office, service).

tak'ke/brev *-et* thank-you letter.

+tak'ke/bønn *-a/-en* (=***/bøn**) prayer of thanks(giving).

+tak'ke/gudstje'neste *-n* (=***/gudsteneste**) thanksgiving service.

***tak'ke/helsing** *-a* note, word of thanks.

tak'ke/kort *-et* (usu. printed) thank-you card, note.

tak'kel *-elet/-let, pl +takler/*-el naut.* tackle: **lense, ligge for t- og tau** lie ahull.

takkela'sje *-n naut.* rigging.

+tak'ke/skrivelse *-n* (official) letter of thanks.

tak'ket(e) *A* - jagged, ragged; notched, serrated; pointed; (of antler) branched.

***takk'/laus** *A* thankless, unacknowledged, unappreciated.

+takknem'lig *A* - 1 appreciative, grateful, obliged; thankful (**for** for; **mot** to). 2 promising, rewarding, worthwhile.

+takknem'lig/het *-en* gratefulness, gratitude; thankfulness.

+takknem'lighets/gjeld *-a/-en* debt of gratitude: **stå i t- til en** owe one a debt of gratitude.

***takk'/sam** *A* appreciative, grateful, obliged; thankful.

***takk'/semd** *-a* gratefulness, gratitude; thankfulness.

+takksi'gelse *-n* expression of thanks, thanksgiving.

takkskyl'dig *A* - : **være en t-** be indebted (obliged) to one.

ta'k/lampe *-a/-en* ceiling light.

tak'le *V -a/+-et* 1 *naut.* rig; *fam.* bedizen, rig out, up; **t- av** dismantle, take off, unrig. 2 *naut.* overlay, whip (a line). 3 (in hockey, soccer) tackle; assail, bombard (with questions, etc.); tackle (a problem).

ta'k/list *-a* cornice molding.

+ta'k/løk *-en* (=***/lauk**) *bot.* houseleek (Sempervivum tectorum).

ta'kom/til' *Av dial.* now and then, off and on.

ta'k/papp *-en* roofing paper, tar paper.

ta'k/ras *-et* slide of snow from a roof.

ta'k/renne *-a* 1 eaves trough, gutter. 2 *fam.* downspout.

ta'k/rygg *-en* ridge of a roof.

+ta'k/rytter *-en, pl -e* ridge turret (usu. for decoration or for a clock).

ta'k/rør *-et/*-a bot.* ditch reed (Phragmites communis).

tak's[1] *-en bot.* yew (Taxus).

tak's[2] *-en zool.* dachshund.

taksame'ter *-eret/-ret, pl -er/+-re* fare meter, taximeter.

taksasjo'n *-en* appraisal, assessment, valuation; estimate.

taksasjo'ns/forret'ning *-a/+-en* appraisement, assessment, valuation.

taksa'tor *-en* appraiser, assessor.

takse're *V -te* appraise, assess, value; estimate, size up: **t-t polise** *admin.* valued policy.

takse'rings/mann *-en, pl -menn/*-menner* appraiser, assessor.

ta'k/skjegg *-et* eaves.

+ta'k/skjær *A* (=***take/skjerr**) *dial.* (esp. of horse when it is to be taken in from the field) skittish.

***ta'ks/mål** *-et* fight, struggle; argument, dispute.

ta'k/sperre *-a* rafter.

ta'k/spon *-en* (roofing) shingle.

tak'st *-en* 1 charge, fare, rate. 2 appraisal, assessment, valuation.

ta'k/stein *-en* (roofing) slate, tile.

+tak'st/forhøy'else *-n* increase in charges, fare, rate.

tak'st/mann *-en, pl -menn/*-menner* appraiser, assessor.

ta'k/svale *-a zool.* martin (Delichon urbica).

tak't *-a/-en* 1 (esp. *mus.*) time; rhythm, tempo: **i t-** in step, keeping time; **slå t-en** beat time, keep time. 2 *mus.* bar, measure. 3 stroke (of engine, oar, etc.). 4 discretion, tact.

ta'k/tekking *-a/+-en* 1 roofing. 2 roofing material (also **+/tekning**).

tak't/fast *A* - in time, measured, rhythmic(al).

tak't/full *A* discreet, tactful.

+tak't/full/het *-en* discretion, tact.

+tak'tiker *-en, pl -e* (=***-ar**) tactician.

taktikk' *-en* tactic, (esp. *mil.*) tactics.

tak'tisk *A* - tactic(al).

tak't/laus *A* (=**+/løs**) indiscreet, tactless.

+tak'tløs/het *-en* tactlessness; a tactless act.

tak't/løyse *-a* tactlessness; a tactless act.

+tak't/måler *-en, pl -e* (=***-ar**) metronome.

tak't/stokk *-en* (conductor's) baton.

tak't/strek *-en mus.* bar (line).

+ta'k/vindu *-et* skylight.

ta'k/ås *-en* purlin, roof beam.

ta'l *-et* (=**+tall**[1]) (e.g. *gram., math.*) number; figure, numeral: **t-et på disiplene** the number of disciples; **uten t-** innumerable.

ta'la/trost *-en dial., zool.* song thrush (Turdus ericetorum).

***tal'de** *pt of* **telje**

ta'le[1] *-n/*-a* 1 speech, talk; speaking, talking: **få en i t-** get a chance to speak to (see) one; **ikke t- om** certainly not, not at all, out of the question; **ikke t- om annet** certainly, of course; by all means; **t-ns bruk** the faculty (power) of speech; **være på t-** be mentioned, be discussed; **være t- om** be talk about, be discussed. 2 speech (=address, oration): **holde en t-** give, make a speech.

ta'le[2] *V -a/-te* 1 speak, talk (**for** for, **med** with, **mot** against, **om** about, **til** to): **t- ens sak** make a plea for one, plead one's case; **t- en til rette** remonstrate with one; **t- med en under fire øyne** speak to one in private; **t-ende blikk** meaningful glance; **t-ende vitnesbyrd** eloquent, striking testimony; **t- rent ut av posen** speak bluntly, straight from the shoulder; **t- sitt tydelige språk** tell its own tale; **t- til ens fordel** speak in one's favor, to one's advantage. 2 give a speech, speak; orate. 3 (with *prep., adv.*): **t- for** go to show, indicate, point towards; call for (strong measures, etc.); make for (good relations, etc.); **t- imot, mot** argue, tell, weigh against; be unfavorable to; make unlikely; invalidate; weaken; **t- med** put in a word, add one's bit (to the conversation); **t- over seg** rave, wander (in one's mind); **t-es ved (om)** speak, talk (about) with sby; **t- ut** have one's say, speak up; finish speaking.

***ta'le/dryg** *A* garrulous, loquacious, talkative.

ta'le/evne *-a/+-en* faculty or power of speech.

ta'le/feil *-en* speech defect, speech impediment.

+ta'le/ferdighet *-en* fluency, skill in speaking.

ta'le/figu'r *-en* figure of speech.

ta'le/film *-en* sound film.

+ta'le/flom' *-men* (=***/flaum**) torrent of speech, talk.

+ta'le/frihet *-en* (=***/fridom**) freedom of speech.

ta'le/før *A* able, qualified to speak (in public).

+ta'le/gaver *pl* (=***/gåver**) eloquence, fluency.

***ta'l/eining** *-a* numerical unit.

ta'le/kunst *-en* art of speaking, oratory, rhetoric.

ta'le/mål *-et* spoken (colloquial) language.

ta'le/måte *-n* 1 manner of speaking, mode of expression. 2 locution, phrase; commonplace, platitude: **bare t-r** empty phrases.

talen't[1] *-en hist.* (monetary unit, weight) talent.

talen't[2] *-et* aptitude, gift, talent; talented person.

talen't/full *A* gifted, talented.

talen't/laus *A* (=**+/løs**) inept, ungifted, untalented.

ta'le/orga'n *-et, pl -/+-er anat.* organ of speech.

ta'le/port [/port] *-en hist.* gate (in cloister) where visitors could talk to inmates of cloister.

+ta'ler *-en, pl -e* (=***-ar**) speaker; orator.

+ta'ler/stol *-en* (=***-ar**) rostrum, speaker's platform; lectern.

+ Bokmål; * Nynorsk; ° Dialect.
After letter: ' stress (Acc. 1); ' tone, stress (Acc. 2); · length.
Below letter: . not pronounced.

ta'le/rør *-et/*-a* (=***/røyr**) 1 speaking tube. 2 mouthpiece, spokesman.
ta'le/språk *-et* spoken (colloquial) language.
ta'le/stasjo'n *-en obs.* pay telephone (booth).
ta'le/stemme *+-n/*-a* speaking voice.
+ta'le/strøm· *-men* flow of talk; torrent of speech, talk.
ta'le/tid [*/ti] *-a/+-en* time allotted for speaking (esp. on telephone).
+ta'le/trengt *A* - (=***/trengd**) having desire, urge to speak, express oneself; garrulous, loquacious, talkative.
tal'g *-a/+-en* tallow.
+tal'g/aktig *A* - sebaceous, tallowy.
tal'g/lys *-et* tallow candle.
tal'g/okse [/okse] *-n* (=***/ukse**) *dial., zool.* titmouse (Parus major).
tal'g/tit *-en* (=***/tite**) *dial.* titmouse.
ta'lisman *-en* talisman.
tal'je[1] *-a/-en naut., tech.* (block and) tackle.
tal'je[2] *-n* 1 waist. 2 build, figure, form.
tal'k *-en* talc.
tal'kum *-en* talcum powder.
tall'[1] *-a* (=***toll**[1]) *dial.* pine (tree).
+tall'[2] *-et* cf **tal**
+tall'/angi'velse *-n* statement of a number.
ta'l/laus *A* (=**+tall/løs**) countless, innumerable, numberless.
tal'le *-n* 1 *dial.* dung (esp. of goat and sheep). 2 oily, tallowy dirt from sheep's wool.
+tall'/enhet *-en* numerical unit.
+taller'ken *-en* (=***tallerk**) 1 (dinner, lunch, or soup) plate: **en t- suppe** a plate of soup; **flyvende t-** flying saucer. 2 *tech.* disk (in disk valve).
+taller'ken/demper *-en, pl -e* plate silencer (doily used between serving plate and dinner plate, etc.).
+taller'ken/hylle *-a* dish, plate shelf.
+taller'ken/rekke *-a/-en* plate rack to place plates upright in, usu. in kitchen.
+tall'/forhold *-et* numerical ratio.
+tall'/løs *A* cf **tal/laus**
+tall'/messig *A* - numerical.
+tall'/o'rd *-et* cf **tal/**
+tall'/rekke *-a/-en* series of numbers.
+tall'/rik *A* cf **tal/**
+tall'rik/het *-en* abundance, numerousness.
+tall'/skive *-a* cf **tal/**
+tall'/størrelse *-n* number, numerical quantity or size.
+tall'/syste'm *-et* cf **tal/**
+tall'/tegn [/tein] *-et* 1 figure, numerical sign, symbol. 2 *naut.* numeral (numbered) pennant.
+tall'/verdi· *-en* numerical value.
***tal'mast** *V -ast* waste away (from disease).
***tal'me** *V -a* (esp. of disease) plague, trouble.
Tal'mud *Prn* Talmud.
talong' *-en* 1 (in cards) stock, talon. 2 stub (of check, money order, etc.).
ta'l/o'rd *-et* numeral.
ta'l/rik *A* abundant, numerous.
ta'l/skive *-a* dial.
ta'ls/mann *-en, pl -menn/*-menner* spokesman; *(bibl.)* advocate (of Christ); **t-en** the Comforter (Holy Ghost).
ta'l/syste'm *-et, pl -/+-er* numerical system.
***ta'lt** *pp of* **telje**
***ta'lte** *pt of* **tale**[2]
***ta'l/teikn** *-et* cf **tall/tegn**
***ta'l/verde** *-t* cf **tall/verdi**
***ta'm**[1] *-et* training (esp. of animals): **denne hesten har godt t-** this horse is well trained.
tam'[2] *A -t, pl -me* tame (affair, animal, poem, etc.); domestic; lame (e.g. reply); docile, tractable (person).
tamaris'k *-en bot.* tamarisk (Tamarix).
tam'bak *-en* 1 tombac (guinea gold, red brass). 2 *pop.* watch made of tombac.
tambu'r [also tam'-] *-en* 1 tambour (as drum, drummer, embroidery hoop, wall supporting a dome). 2 *tech.* cylinder, drum, roller.
tamburi'n *-en* 1 tambourine. 2 embroidery hoop, tambour.
tambu'r/majo'r *-en* drum major.
***tam'd** *A tamt* domesticated, tamed; controlled, subdued.
***tam'de** *pt of* **temje**
tam'/dyr *-et* domestic(ated) animal.
ta'me *-n* proficiency, skill; practice, training.
***ta'me/fag** *-et educ.* subject requiring proficiency and skill.
+tam'/het *-en* domesticity, tameness.
tam'p *-en* 1 esp. *naut.* end, rope end: **på t-** pulled, stretched all the way out, up; **t-en brenner** (game) you're getting warm, *fig.* the situation is critical. 2 esp. *naut.* flogging (with a rope end). 3 *fam.*: **på t-en** at the end, finish; on the decline. 4 *dial.* longish lump, piece. 5 *dial.* large, hulking fellow; lout, scamp.
tam'pe *V -a/+-et* esp. *naut.* beat, flog.
tampong' *-en* 1 *med.* plug, tampon, wad; sponge. 2 *typog.* dabber.
tam'/rein *-en* domesticated reindeer.
***tam'se** *V -a* 1 chew or munch slowly. 2 fumble for words. 3 fool around, fuss.
tam'/tam· *-men* tom-tom.
ta'n *-et* 1 *dial.* distension, extension, stretching. 2 run, running. 3 exertion, strain.
Ta'na *Pln* twp, Finnmark.
***ta'nande** *A* -: **i t- jag** at top speed, at a gallop.
+tan'de[1] *-n* cf **tanne**
***tan'de**[2] *pt of* **tenje**
tan'dem· *-en* tandem (as bicycle, in tandem engine, team of horses).
tandem/sykkel *-elen, pl -sykler* tandem bicycle.
tan'der *A -ert, pl -re* delicate, frail (beauty, glance, person, etc.); sensitive, tender (flower, person, skin, etc.); gentle (mood, voice, etc.).
***tan'dre** *V -a* 1 berate, chide, scold; abuse, revile. 2 kindle, light, set fire to.
+ta'ne[1] *-n* cf **tanne**
ta'ne[2] *V -a/+-et dial.* 1 distend, extend, stretch. 2 run; gallop: **t-ende jag** galloping, top speed. 3 plod, trudge.
+tang'[1] *-a, pl tenger* (=***tong**) 1 (pair of) forceps, nippers, pincers, pliers, tongs; curling iron. 2 *dial.* (in stave church) double horizontal beam connecting columns.
tang'[2] *-en/-et bot.* kelp, seaweed (order Fucales).
tang'/art *-en/-a* species of seaweed.
+tang'/aske *-a* kelp ash.
tang'e *-n* 1 spit, tongue of land. 2 tang (on carpenter's plane, file, knife, etc.).
tangens [tang'gens] *+en/*ein math.* tangent (of angle).
tangent [tanggen't] *-en* 1 *mus.* (organ, piano) key. 2 *math.* tangent (line).
tangential [tanggentia'l] *A math.* tangential.
tangere [tangge're] *V -te* esp. *math.* be tangent to; border on, touch (upon).
tang'/fjære *-a* (=***/fjøre**) stretch of beach full of seaweed.
tang'/fødsel *-elen, pl -ler med.* forceps delivery.
tang'/loppe *-a zool.* beach flea, sand flea (Orchestiidae).
tang'/nål *-a zool.* pipefish (Syngnathidae).
tango [tang'go] *-en* tango.
tang'/sprette *-a zool.* butterfish (Pholis gunnellus).
tan'k[1] *-en* 1 tank (for oil, water, etc.). 2 *fam.* tanker, tankship. 3 *naut.* tanker shipping. 4 *merc.* stock in a tanker (ship).
tan'k[2] *-en, pl -s mil.* tank.
***tan'kar** *-en* tankard.
tan'k/bil *-en* tank truck.
tan'k/båt *-en* tanker, tank ship.
tan'ke *-n* 1 thought (på of); idea; intention: **det ble med t-n** it was never realized, it never came off; **falle i t-r** become absorbed in thought, fall into a reverie; **ha t-ne med seg** have one's wits about one; **jeg kom på den t-n (at)** the idea (thought) struck me, occurred to me (that); **komme på andre t-r** change one's mind; **stå i egne t-r** be in a brown study, be lost in a reverie, in one's own thoughts; **ved t-n** at the thought; **jeg gyser bare ved t-n på det** I shudder at the very thought of it. 2 dash, trace, touch: **suppen trenger bare en t- salt** the soup needs just a dash of salt; **få, ha en t-** (of food) be slightly spoiled (due to beginning decay).
tan'ke/arbeid *-et* mental effort; intellectual pursuit.
tan'ke/bygning *-en* philosophical system, structure of ideas, thoughts.
tan'ke/eksperimen't *-et, pl -/+-er* hypothesis, supposition.
tan'ke/flukt *-a/+-en* (=***/flog**) 1 imagination, soaring of thoughts. 2 *psych.* rapid, illogical skipping from one subject to another.
tan'ke/foster *-eret/-ret, pl -er/+-re* brainchild.
tan'ke/full *A* contemplative, pensive, thoughtful.
+tan'kefull/het *-en* contemplation, pensiveness, thoughtfulness.
tan'ke/føring *-a/+-en* thought process, way of thinking; mentality, mind.
tan'ke/gang *-en* thought process, way of thinking; mentality, mind.
tan'ke/gymnastikk· *-en* mental gymnastics.
+tan'ke/innhold *-et* (=***/innhald**) (store of) ideas, thought content.
tan'ke/laus *A* (=**+/løs**) thoughtless, unreasoning; featherbrained, scatterbrained; imprudent.
+tan'ke/lek *-en* (=***/leik**) mental exercise, game.
+tan'ke/leser *-en, pl -e* (=***-ar**) mind reader.
+tan'ke/løs *A* cf **/laus**
+tan'keløs/het *-en* cf **-løyse**
tan'ke/løyse *-a* (=**+/løshet**) imprudence, rashness, thoughtlessness.
tan'ke/operasjo'n *-en* intellectual undertaking, process of mental activity or thought.
tan'ke/overfø'ring *-a/+-en* telepathy.
+tan'ker *-en, pl -e* (=***-ar**) tanker, tankship.
+tan'ke/rekke *-a/-en* (=***/rekkje**) chain, train of thought, sequence of thought(s).
***tan'ke/rett** *A* - logical.
tan'ke/rik *A* rich in thought (ideas).
tan'ke/spinn *-et* fantasy, figment, speculation.
tan'ke/sprang *-et* (sudden) transition of thought.
***tan'ke/spreidd** *A* - absent-minded, preoccupied.
tan'ke/språk *-et* (terse) aphorism, apothegm.
tan'ke/strek *-en* dash (—).
tan'ke/tom· *A -t, pl -me* empty-headed, vacant, vacuous.
tan'ke/tung [/tong] *A* thought-laden.
+tan'ke/vekkende *A* - (=***/vekkjande**) thought-provoking.
+tan'ke/verden *-en* (=***/verd**) world of ideas; ideal world.
+tan'ke/virksomhet *-en* mental activity, thinking.
tan'ke/øving *-a/+-en* (=**+-else**) mental exercise, practice, training.
tan'k/fart *-en* tanker shipping.
tan'k/skip *-et* tanker, tankship.
tan'k/vogn [/vångn] *-a* tank car.
tann' *-a, pl tenner* tooth (*anat.*, also on tool, wheel, etc.); prong, tine (on fork, rake, etc.): **føle en på tennene** sound one out; **få blod på t-** (see **blod**); **holde t- for tunge re-**

strain oneself; keep back a remark; **slå ut en t-** give up an idea, plan; **tennene løper i vann** (one's) mouth is watering; **tidens t-** ravages of time.

tann'/bein *-et anat.* dentin.

tann'/bisse *-n* (in babytalk) tooth.

tann'/byll *-en* gumboil.

tann'/børste *-n* toothbrush.

tann'børste/bart *-en* toothbrush moustache.

+tan'ne *-n* snuff (on a candlewick).

+tan'ne/bisse *-n* cf **tann/**

tan'net(e) *A* - (esp. *bot.*) dentate, toothed.

tann'/felling *-a/+-en* losing of (milk) teeth.

tann'/forma *A* - (=**+-et**) dentiform, tooth-shaped.

tann'/ga'rd *-en* row of teeth; sth that resembles row of teeth.

tann'/glas *-et* (=**+/glass**) glass for one's toothbrush (and mouthwash).

tann'/hals *-en* neck of a tooth.

tann'/hjul *-et* cogwheel, gear, toothed wheel.

tann'/kitt *-et* temporary filling for teeth.

tann'/kjøtt *-et anat.* gingiva, gum.

tann'/krem *-en* toothpaste.

tann'/laus *A* (=**+/løs**) toothless (also *fig.*)

tann'/lege *-n* dentist.

+tann'lege/høyskole *-n* dental college.

tann'lege/stol *-en* dental chair, dentist's chair.

tann'/lyd *-en* dental (sound).

***tann'/lækjar** *-en* cf **/lege**

+tann'/løs *A* cf **/laus**

+tann'løs/het *-en* toothlessness.

tann'/pasta *-en* toothpaste.

tann'/pine *-a/+-en* toothache.

+tann'/pirker *-en, pl -e* (=***-ar**) toothpick.

tann'/pleie *-a/+-en* care of the teeth, dental care.

tann'/pulver *-et* tooth powder.

tann'/rot *-a, pl +-røtter/*-røter* 1 root of a tooth. 2 *bot.* coralwort (Dentaria bulbifera).

tann'/røkt *-a/+-en* care of the teeth, dental care.

+tann'/råte *-n* (=***/rote**) dental caries, tooth decay.

tann'/stein *-en* tartar (on teeth).

+tann'/stikker *-en, pl -e* (=***-ar**) toothpick.

+tann'/tekniker *-en, pl -e* (=***-ar**) dental technician.

tann'/verk *-en* (severe) toothache.

***ta'n/sprang** *-et* flying run.

+tan't[1] *-en/-et* 1 *bibl., lit.* trumpery, vanity; fantasy, nonsense. 2 *dial.* fun, joke.

***tan't**[2] *pp of* **tenje**

tan'talus/kval *-en* torment of Tantalus.

tan'te *-a/+-en* 1 aunt; great-aunt. 2 (more loosely) woman friend of family.

+tan'te/aktig *A* - reminding one of, being typical of an (old) aunt; old-maidish.

tantieme [tangtie'me] *-t merc.* bonus, commission (on profits), percentage.

ta'p *-et* loss (**av** of); (in hunting) loss of scent or track.

+ta'p/bringende *A* - *merc.* carried on at a loss, involving a loss, losing.

ta'pe *V -te/*-a* 1 lose (battle, game, lawsuit, money, troops, etc.): **gi t-t** give in, give up; **gå t-t** be lost; **t- av syne** lose sight of; **t- for noen, noe** be beaten by, lose to sby, sth; **t- hodet** *fig.* lose one's head; **t- interessen** lose interest (**for** in); **t- lysten** lose desire (**til** for); **t- på noe** lose by (doing) sth, worsen one's position. 2 (*refl.*): **t- seg** become poorer in appearance; deteriorate; die away, fade away.

+ta'per *-en, pl -e* (=***-ar**) loser.

tape't *-et, pl -/+-er* 1 wall covering (of cloth); wallpaper. 2: **bringe på t-et** bring up, introduce; **ha på t-et** have scheduled, have on the program; **være på t-et** be under discussion.

tape't/dør *-a* wallpapered jib door.

tape't/prøve *-a/+-en* wallpaper sample.

tapetse're *V -te* paper (=hang wall covering, wallpaper).

+tapetse'rer *-en, pl -e* (=***-ar**) paperhanger.

tapiok'a *-en* tapioca.

tapi'r *-en zool.* tapir (Tapiridae).

+tap'ning *-en* 1 pumping, tapping (**av** of) (body cavity, courage, liquid, etc.); draining (of land, strength). 2 tap (beer, wine). 3 *carp.* dovetailing.

tapp' *-en* 1 projection; *anat.* apophysis, process. 2 spigot, tap; bung, stopper. 3 dowel, pin, pintle; axle journal; pivot (also *fig.*). 4 *carp.* tenon. 5 *tech.* tap (for forming internal screw threads). 6 *dial.* small, heavyset, powerful fellow or animal. 7 *dial.* dot, wisp.

tap'pe *V -a/+-et* 1 draw (off), pump, tap (body cavity, courage, liquid); drain (land, strength, etc.): **t- en for noe** bleed one for sth, drain one of sth; **t- ut** drain. 2 *carp.* dovetail.

tap'pe/kran *-a* faucet, tap.

tap'pen/strek *-en mil.* tattoo; (military) pageant or parade.

+tap'per[1] *-en, pl -e* (=***-ar**) tapper (one who taps, e.g. beer).

tap'per[2] *A -ert, pl tapre* bold, courageous, valiant; energetic, persevering.

+tap'per/het *-en* boldness, courage, valor.

tapp'/hol [/hål] *-et* (=**+/hull**) 1 *carp.* mortise. 2 bunghole; taphole. 3 pivot hole.

ta'ps/konto *-en merc.* loss account.

ta'ps/liste *-a* usu. *mil.* casualty list.

ta'ps- og [å] **vin'nings/konto** *-en merc.* profit and loss account.

tap's/prosen't *-en* percentage of losses.

ta'ra *-en chem., merc.* tare.

tarantell' *-en* 1 *zool.* tarantula (Lycosa tarantula). 2 *mus.* tarantella.

ta're *-n* 1 *bot.* kelp, sea tangle, sea wrack (order Laminariales). 2 *dial.* sea bottom covered with sea wrack.

+ta're/aske *-a* kelp ash.

ta're/brenning *-a* kelp burning (to produce kelp ash).

ta're/bruk *-et dial.* heap of sea wrack (on a beach).

tare're *V -te chem., merc.* tare.

ta're/torsk *-en* cod which keeps to the coastal shoals.

tariff' *-en* scale, table of rates or charges; wage scale; wage agreement.

tariff'/avtale *-n/*-a* wage agreement.

tariff'/krig *-en* rate war (esp. between insurance companies).

+tariff'/messig *A* - concerning tariff; in accordance with tariff.

+tariff'/oppgjør *-et* wage negotiations, settlement.

tariff'/sats *-en* wage scale.

tariff'/stridig *A* - in conflict with, resisting a wage agreement.

tar'm *-en* 1 bowel, gut, intestine; catgut. 2 *fig.* sth which resembles an intestine.

tar'm/gang *-en* intestinal canal.

+tar'm/innhold *-et* (=***/innhald**) intestinal contents.

tar'm/kana'l *-en* intestinal canal.

tar'm/katarr' *-en med.* enteritis.

tar'm/saft *-a* digestive juice (of small intestine).

***tar'm/sig** *-et* (intestinal) hernia, rupture.

tar'm/slyng *-en med.* volvulus.

tar'm/streng *-en, pl *-er* catgut, gut.

tar'm/tott *-en* (intestinal) villus.

tarpei'isk *A* - Tarpeian.

tar't *-en dial.* young, small salmon.

tarta'r *-en* (=**tatar**) Tartar, Tatar.

tarta'r-smørbrød *-et* steak tartare sandwich (raw beef with raw egg).

tar'v[1] *+-en/+-et/*-a* 1 demand(s), need, requirement. 2 good, interest(s): **vareta sitt t-** look after one's own interests.

***tar'v**[2] *pr of* **turve**

***tar'val** *A* destitute, indigent, needy.

tar'velig *A* - 1 humble, modest, simple; frugal, plain. 2 cheap, poor, wretched. 3 lowdown, mean, shabby: **t-e insinuasjoner** contemptible insinuations. *4 necessary, needful.

+tar'velig/het *-en* 1 frugality, modesty, plainness. 2 caddishness, meanness; shabbiness; commonness, vulgarity.

***tar'vende** *-t* tool; necessity, requirement.

tar'v/laus *A* needless, unnecessary.

***ta'se**[1] *-n* 1 rag, tatter. 2 poor (pitiable) fellow.

***ta'se**[2] *V -a* 1 be unraveled. 2 be enfeebled, weakened.

tas'ke *-a* 1 bag, pouch, satchel; briefcase; holster. 2 hussy, wench; slut, tart.

tas'ke/gras *-et bot.* shepherd's purse (Capsella bursa-pastoris).

tas'ke/krabbe *-a/-en zool.* (edible) crab (Cancer pagurus).

+tas'ken/spiller *-en, pl -e* 1 conjurer, illusionist, sleight-of-hand artist. 2 *fam.* charlatan, impostor, swindler.

+tas'kenspiller/kunst *-en* conjuring, legerdemain, sleight of hand.

tas'le *V -a/+-et* (=**tatle**) 1 pad, pat, shuffle; rustle, swish. 2 fool around, putter.

tass' *-en* 1 animal which pads or shuffles about. 2 tiny gnome or troll. 3 tiny, insignificant person (or animal); kid, tot; tiny, insignificant object, thing. 4 paw.

tas'se[1] *-n* cf **tass**

tas'se[2] *V -a/+-et* 1 pad, shuffle; rustle, swish. 2 drag about, slouch around.

tas't *-en* (organ, piano, typewriter) key.

tastatu'r *-en/-et* (organ, piano, typewriter) keyboard.

tata'r *-en* cf **tartar**

ta'ter *-en, pl +-e* 1 gypsy, Romany; tramp. 2 *fam.* hellion, rascal, scamp.

+ta'ter/følge [also ta'-] *-t* (=***/følgje**) band of gypsies.

ta'ter/jente *-a* gypsy girl.

ta'ter/kjerring *-a, pl *-ar* (old) gypsy woman, gypsy crone.

ta'ter/språk *-et* Romany (language).

tat'le *V -a/+-et* cf **tasle**

tatove're *V -te* tattoo.

+tatt/ *pp of* **ta**[1]

tau' *-et* rope: **få, ha strekk på t-et** sail with taut rigging under strong wind, *pop.* be (slightly) tipsy; **hoppe t-** jump rope.

tau'/bane *-n* aerial (suspension) railway; funicular railway; telpher.

tau'/båt *-en* towboat, tugboat.

tau'e *V -a/+-et* tow.

tau'/ende *-n* end of a rope; end (short piece of rope).

***tau'g**[1] *-et cf* **tau**

+tau'g[2] *pt of* **tie**

***tau'g**[3] *A* mild, quiet, subdued.

***tau'g/før** *A* dilatory, slow, tardy.

***tau'gleg** *A* - (somewhat) dilatory, slow, tardy.

***tau'g/lyn(d)t** *A* 1 impassive, phlegmatic, stoical. 2 long-suffering, patient.

***tau'g/mæ'lt** *A* - slow of speech, slow-speaking.

tau'/kveil *-en* coil of rope.

***tau'm** *-en* cf **tom**[1]

***tau'm/laus** *A* free, unhindered, unimpeded.

tau's[1] *-a dial.* 1 maid, servant girl; girl. 2 unmarried mother. 3 chippy, tart.

+tau's[2] *A* mute, silent, taciturn.

+ Bokmål; * Nynorsk; ° Dialect.
After letter: ' stress (Acc. 1); ` tone, stress (Acc. 2); · length.
Below letter: . not pronounced.

+tau's/het *-en* muteness, silence, taciturnity.
+tau'shets/løfte *-t* pledge, promise of silence or secrecy.
+tau'shets/plikt *-a/-en jur.* duty of civil official, member of the professions not to divulge confidential matters: **pålegge en t-** pledge sby to secrecy.
tau's/kjerring *-a, pl *-ar dial.* 1 old maid. 2 (young) unmarried mother.
tau'/stige *-n* rope ladder.
tau'/stump [/stomp] *-en* (short) piece of rope, rope end.
tau't pt of **tyte**[2]
tautologi' *-en* tautology.
tautologisk [-lå'gisk] *A* - tautological.
tau'/trekking *-a/+-en* tug of war (also *fig.*) (**mellom** between).
tau'/verk *-et* cordage, ropes; (ship's) rigging.
***tau'vre** *V -a* bewitch, cast a spell over, hex.
***tau'vre/kall** *-en* sorcerer, wizard.
ta've *-n dial.* 1 rag, tatter. 2 dry stalk, stem.
tav'l *-et hist.* 1 game played on a board. 2 game board.
tav'le *-a* 1 (stone) slab, tablet. 2 (bulletin, hymn) board; blackboard, scoreboard. 3 panel (to draw on, paint on), plaque; (writing) slate. 4 chart, list, table. 5 (bee) comb. 6 *dial.* check (on game board).
+tav'le/kritt *-et* (=***/krit**) (blackboard) chalk.
taxi [tak'si] *-en* taxi (cab).
T. B. =**tuberkelbasiller**
tbc. =**tuberkulose**
***t. d.** =**til dømes**
te'[1] *-en* tea (plant; drink; party): **hun er ofte borte i teer** she is often out to tea.
te'[2] *V -dde dial.* 1 show; disclose, reveal: **te seg** appear, become visible. 2: **te seg** behave, carry on.
teak [ti'k] *-en* teak.
teak/tre *-et* 1 *bot.* teak tree (Tectona grandis). 2 teakwood.
team [ti'm] *-et* team (e.g. of advisers, players).
tea'ter *-eret/-ret, pl -er/+-re* 1 theater: **gå i t-ret** go to the theater; **Holbergs t-** the t- (=drama) of Holberg. 2 stage: **gå til t-ret** go on the stage, become an actor, actress; **spille t-** play a part, put on an act. 3 *derog.* contrived, showy.
tea'ter/effek't *-en* dramatic effect, stage effect.
+tea'ter/forestilling [/fåre-] *-a/-en* theatrical performance.
+tea'ter/gal *A* stage-struck.
+tea'ter/gjenger *-en, pl -e* playgoer, theatergoer.
tea'ter/histo'rie *-a/+-en* history of the theater; stage history.
tea'ter/kikkert *-en* opera glasses.
+tea'ter/kritiker *-en, pl -e* (=***-ar**) drama critic.
+tea'ter/maler *-en, pl -e* (=***/målar**) scene painter, stage decorator.
tea'ter/salong' *-en* (theater) auditorium.
tea'ter/sjef *-en* theater manager.
tea'ter/skole *-n* drama school, school of dramatics.
tea'ter/stykke *-t, pl +-r/*-* (stage) play.
teatra'lsk *A* - theatrical; *derog.* histrionic, stagy.
te'/bo'rd *-et* tea table; tea wagon.
te'/brød *-et* "tea bread" (dry cake made in loaves about an inch thick and cut into diagonal strips).
ted'di/bjø'rn *-en* teddy bear.
tef't *+-en/*-a* 1 scent (of animal or person); **få t- av noe** get wind of sth; **jeg har en t- av** I have a suspicion. 2 sense of smell; flair, nose (**for** for).
***tef'te** *V -a* (esp. of animals) nose out, scent, smell.
te'ge *-a zool.* bug, insect (order Heteroptera).
teg'l [+also: tei'l] *-et* brick; (drain, roof) tile.
teg'l/omn [+also: tei'l/] *-en* (=**+/ovn**) brick, tile kiln.
tegl'/stein *-en* brick; (drain, roof) tile.
teglsteins/farge *-n* brick, tile color (red).
tegl/verk *-et* brick works, tile works.
+tegn [tei'n] *-et* (=***teikn**) 1 sign (**på, til** of): **korsets t-** the s- of the cross. 2 *astron.* sign=constellation: **i Andromedas t-** under the sign of A-; **i samarbeidets t-** *fig.* in the spirit of cooperation; **hele verden stod ennå i krigens t-** the whole world was still under the shadow of war (Falkberget). 3 sign=(alphabetic) character; (punctuation) mark. 4 sign=symbol: **knele som t- på underkastelse** kneel as a sign of submission. 5 sign=gesture: **gi t- til å** make a s- to; **gjøre t- til** make s-s of. 6 sign=indication, mark: **ikke t- til** not a sign of. 7 sign=omen; miracle.
+tegne [tei'ne] *V -a/-et* (=***teikne**) 1 draw, sketch; design (furniture, house, etc.); *fig.* depict, paint: **t- opp** make a sketch of, sketch out; **t-et etter naturen** drawn from life. 2 list, note, write (**ned** down); sign for (a firm); bind (by signature), underwrite; subscribe for; take out (insurance, a policy): **t- en for (beløp)** put sby down for (sum); **t- aksjer** subscribe for shares, take shares (**i** in). 3 give promise of being, promise to be: **t- til å bli** (the same); **dagen t-er varm** the day promises to be warm (Undset). 4 *(refl.)*: **t- seg** be outlined, be silhouetted (**mot** against); appear; enroll, enter one's name; **t- seg for (beløp)** contribute, sign up for (sum).
+tegne/bestikk' [tei'ne/] *-et* case (set) of drawing instruments.
+tegne/blokk *-en* drawing pad.
+tegne/blyant *-en* artist's pencil.
+tegne/bok *-a, pl -bøker* billfold, wallet; coloring book.
+tegne/bo'rd *-et* drawing table.
+tegne/brett *-et* drawing board.
+tegne/film *-en* (animated) cartoon (film).
+tegner [tei'ner] *-en, pl -e* (=***teiknar**) 1 designer; draftsman; illustrator; sketcher. 2 subscriber (e.g. for shares).
+tegne/stift [tei'ne/] *-en* 1 thumbtack. 2 *fam.* traffic button.
+tegn/forkla'ring [tei'n/] *-en* key, legend (explaining symbols used, as on a map, etc.).
+tegning [tei'ning] *-en* (=***teikning -a**) 1 drawing, sketch (**av** of), design, plan (e.g. of a house). 2 drawing, sketching; designing, drafting. 3 subscription (for shares); enrolment, signing up; taking out (of insurance, a policy); underwriting. 4 *lit.* outline, silhouette; line, feature (e.g. of a face). 5 depiction, description (e.g. of character).
+tegnings/innby'delse *-n* prospectus.
+tegnings/liste *-a* subscription list.
+tegn/setning [tei'n/] *-en* punctuation.
+tegn/skrift *-a/-en* picture writing.
+tegn/språk *-et* sign language.
+tegn/syste'm *-et* system of signals or signs.
te'/handel *-en* 1 tea trade. 2 tea shop.
***tei'e**[1] *-a* cf **tægje**
***tei'e**[2] *V teier, tagde, tagt* cf **tie**
tei'e/bær *-et* (=***tåge/**) *bot.* stone bramble (Rubus saxatilis).
tei'g *-en* 1 parcel, strip of field or land; *dial.* certain strip of a field (which yields so much grain, can be mowed within a certain time, etc.); *fam.* separate section of flat surface. *2 (newspaper) column.
tei'g/blanding *-a/+-en hist., agric.* system of rundale, strip farming.
+tei'g/bytte *-t* (=***/byte**) 1 *agric.* exchange of strips of land (e.g. for crop rotation). 2 boundary, division between two strips of farm land.
***tei'ing** *-a* silence.
***tei'ings/lovnad** *-en* pledge, promise of silence or secrecy.
***tei'ings/skyldnad** *-en jur.* duty of civil official, member of the professions not to divulge confidential matters.
***tei'kn** *-et* cf **tegn**
***tei'knar** *-en* cf **tegner**
***tei'kne** *V -a* cf **tegne**
***tei'kne/bestikk'** *-et* cf **tegne/**
***tei'kne/bok** *-a, pl -bøker* cf **tegne/**
***tei'kne/stift** *-en* cf **tegne/**
***tei'kning** *-a* cf **tegning**
***tei'kn/setjing** *-a* cf **tegn/setning**
tei'n *-en* 1 *dial.* root sucker, offshoot from a stump. 2 *dial.* thin rod or stick; (in hand spinning) spindle.
tei'ne *-a* 1 fish trap (of thin wooden slats). 2 *dial.* hopper (on grinding mill). 3 *dial.* (willow) basket, pannier.
tei'nt *-en* (skin) color, complexion.
tei'nung *-en dial.* root sucker, offshoot from a stump.
Tei's *Prn (m)*
tei'ste *-n zool.* black guillemot (Cepphus grylle).
***te'k** *pr of* **ta(ke)**[1]
te'/kanne *-a* teapot.
te'/kasse *-a/-en* tea chest (for shipping tea).
te'ke** *pp of* **ta(ke)**[1] (=teki**)
te'kest** *pp of* **takast** (=tekist**)
te'/kjel(e) *-(e)n* teakettle.
te'/kjøkken *-et, pl -/+-er* small room with hotplate for light housekeeping.
tek'ke[1] *-t dial.* roof; thatch.
tek'ke[2] *-t* 1 a pleasant manner; modesty, unpretentiousness. 2 ability to attract; appeal, charm: **ha loppe/t-** attract fleas; **ha gutte/t-** attract boys.
+tek'ke[3] *V tekte* (=***tekkje**[2]) cover, deck; roof, shingle, thatch.
tek'kelig *A* - decent, nice, proper; respectable, well-behaved; modest, unassuming: **legge ansiktet i t-e folder** assume a proper expression.
+tek'kes *V tektes, tekkes* (=***-jast**) 1 please. 2 be satisfied with, put up with: ***du får t-ast** you'll have to take what we can offer you.
tek'king *-a/+-en* (=**+tekning**) roofing (e.g. shingling, thatching).
***tekkj'ast** *V tektest, tekst* cf **tekkes**
***tekkj'e**[1] *-a* cf **tekke**[1]
***tekkj'e**[2] *V tekte* cf **tekke**[3]
***tekk'/leik** *-en* attractiveness, comeliness, pleasantness; modesty, unpretentiousness.
tekn. =**teknisk**
teknifise're *V -te* mechanize, modernize.
+tek'niker *-en, pl -e* (=***-ar**) technician; expert.
teknikk' *-en* 1 technique; technical skill. 2 technology; technical specialization; engineering.
+tek'ning *-en* cf **tekking**
tek'nisk *A* - 1 technical: **t- prøvetur** *naut.* trial run. 2 technological: **et t- museum** a museum of technology.
teknokrati' *-et* technocracy.
teknokra'tisk *A* - technocratic.
teknolog [-lå'g] *-en* technologist.
teknologi' *-en* technology.
teknologisk [-lå'gisk] *A* - technological.
te'/kopp *-en* teacup.
tek'sle[1] *-a* cooper's adz.
tek'sle[2] *V -a* 1 chisel, hollow out with a cooper's adz. 2 *dial.* (esp. of birds) screech (piercingly, staccato-like).
tek'st[1] *-a/-en* 1 text (from Bible, of a book, document, letter, play, sermon, etc.); (film) subtitle; (music) libretto, words: **holde seg til t-en** stick to the subject; **lese en t-en** give one a lecture, give one

a piece of one's mind. 2 *typog.* paragon.

°**tek'st**[2] *-en, pl -* timber boom.

***tek'st**[3] *pr of* **takast**

***tek'st**[4] *pp of* **tekkjast**

tek'ste *V -a/+-et* subtitle (a film).

+**tek'st/forfat'ter** *-en, pl -e* (=*-ar) librettist, writer of lyrics; script-writer.

teksti'l *-en/-et, pl -er/*-* 1 textile. 2 textile industry.

+**teksti'l/arbeider** *-en, pl -e* (=*-ar) textile worker.

teksti'l/fabrikk· -en textile mill.

teksti'l/varer *pl* textiles.

tek'st/kritikk· *-en* textual criticism (to establish original text).

tek'st/kritisk *A -* of textual criticism.

+**tek'st/rekke** *-a/-en* (=*/**rekkje**) *eccl.* one of the prescribed texts (epistle, gospel, or lesson) for a holy day.

tekstu'r *-en* texture.

+**tek'st/utgave** *-a/-en* (=*/**utgåve**) (critical) edition (e.g. of literary text).

-tekt *-a/+-en* taking, e.g. **inn/t-, ved/t-, vold/t-.**

+**tek'tes** *pt of* **tekkes**

***tek'test** *pt of* **tekkjast**

te'l[1] [also: tæ'l] *-et dial.* 1 (back) ground of woven material. 2 fine wool nearest sheep's skin. 3 floor, ground. 4 base material in (molded) grindstone. 5: **god t- i gutten** good stuff in the boy.

***te'l**[2] *pr of* **telje**

tel.=**telefon**

Tel.=**Telemark**

te'le[1] *-n* (deep) frost, ice (in the soil); layer of frozen earth.

te'le[2] *-n* inhabitant of Telemark.

te'le[3] *V -a/+-et* (of snow, soil, etc.) freeze hard, solid.

te'le/døl *-en* inhabitant of Telemark.

telefo'n *-en* telephone (apparatus); telephone exchange: **være ansatt på, ved t-en** *fam.* work for the phone company; **bestille en t-** place a call; **i t-en** on the t-; **t- til deg** you're wanted on the phone.

telefo'n/abonnen't *-en* telephone subscriber.

telefo'n/anlegg *-et* telephone exchange; telephone system (also in one's house); *fam.* telephone company.

telefo'n/appara't *-et, pl -/+-er* telephone set (apparatus, instrument).

+**telefo'n/beskje'ḍ** *-en* telephone message.

telefo'n/boks *-en* pay station, telephone booth (enclosed or not).

telefo'n/dame *-a/+-en fam.* central, operator.

telefone're *V -te* call, ring (up), telephone: **t- med** carry on a conversation by telephone with; **t- til en** call sby.

+**telefo'n/forbin'delse** *-n* telephone connection.

telefoni' *-en* telephony.

telefo'nisk *A -* telephonic; by telephone, telephoned.

telefonistin'ne *-a/+-en* (woman) telephone operator.

telefo'n/katalog [/-lå'g] *-en* telephone book (directory).

telefo'n/kiosk [/kjåsk] *-en* telephone booth.

+**telefo'n/mottaker** *-en, pl -e* (=*-ar) telephone receiver.

telefo'n/nett *-et* network of telephone lines.

+**telefo'n/oppring'ning** *-en* telephone call.

telefo'n/rør *-et/*-a* (telephone) receiver (handset).

telefo'n/samband *-et* telephone connection.

telefo'n/sentra'l *-en* telephone exchange; central.

telefo'n/tråḍ *-en* telephone wire.

telefo'n/ur *-et* clock which gives time (by human voice) when certain number is dialed.

telefo'n/verkeṭ *df* the (state-owned) telephone company.

te'le/foto *-et* telephoto(graph).

te'le/fri *A -tt* (of soil) free from frost, ice.

telegra'f *-en* telegraph; *fam.* telegraph company.

+**telegra'f/bud** *-et* 1 telegraphic message. 2 telegraph messenger boy.

telegrafe're *V -te* telegraph, wire; send by semaphore; *naut.* order, send via engine room telegraph.

telegrafi' *-en* telegraphy.

telegra'fisk *A -* telegraphic.

telegrafis't *-en* telegrapher, telegraph operator.

telegrafistin'ne *-a/+-en* (woman) telegrapher, telegraph operator.

+**telegra'f/le'dning** *-en* telegraph wire.

telegra'f/melḍing *-a/+-en* telegraphic message.

telegra'f/nøkkel *-en, pl -nøkler* telegraph key.

telegra'f/stolpe *-n* telegraph pole.

+**telegra'f/tegn** [/tein] *-et* (=*/**teikn**) sign for letter or number in telegraphic alphabet.

telegra'f/verkeṭ *df* government institution having administration of telegraph, telephone, radio and broadcasting services.

telegram' *-met, pl -/+-mer* telegram.

telegram'/adres'se *-a/+-en* cable address.

telegram'/blankett· *-en* telegram blank.

telegram'/byrå· *-et, pl +-er/*-* wire service: **Norsk T- (NTB)** Norwegian Wire Service.

telegram'/stil *-en* telegraphic style.

te'le/grop *-a* hole (in a road) caused by spring thaw.

+**te'le/kommunikasjo'ner** *pl* (—*-ar) telecommunications.

te'leks *-en* (short for) teleprinter exchange, a European network of teletype communication.

telekse're *V -te* send by **teleks.**

te'le/løysing *-a* (=+/**løsning**) spring thaw.

Telem.=**Telemark**

Te'le/mark *Pln* county in S. Norway, west of the Oslofjord.

te'le/marking *-en* 1 person from Telemark. 2 (in skiing) telemark turn.

te'lemarks/ku *-a* (breed of cattle) Telemark (similar to Ayrshire).

te'lemarks/sving *-en* telemark turn (in skiing).

teleologi' *-en* teleology.

teleologisk [-lå'gisk] *A -* teleological.

telepati' *-en psych.* telepathy.

telepa'tisk *A -* telepathic.

te'le/printer *-en, pl +-e* teleprinter, teletypewriter.

telesko'p *-et, pl -/+-er* telescope.

televisjo'n *-en* television.

tel'g *-en bot.* fern (Dryopteris).

tel'gje *V -de* 1 hew, shape with an axe. 2 whittle; cut shavings from.

tel'gje/kniv *-en* sheath knife.

tel'gje/øks *-a* broadaxe, timber axe.

***tel'jar** *-en* cf **teller**

***tel'je** *V tel, talde, talt* cf **telle**[2]

***tel'je/appara't** *-et* cf **telle/**

***tel'le**[1] *-a* young conifer.

+**tel'le**[2] *V talte/telte* (=***telje**) 1 count (days, money, people, etc.): **t- en ut** (in boxing) count one out; **t- på knappene** be in a quandary, be on the fence. 2 comprise, encompass, number: **flokken talte elleve dyr** the flock numbered eleven animals. 3 count (=consider, include, number among): **t- en blant sine beste venner** number one among one's best friends. 4 count (=be of consequence, mean sth). 5 (with *prep., adv.*): ***t- av, fra** dissuade from, advise against; **t- etter, over** count over, recount; **t- med** count in, include; be of consequence, count; **t- opp** count out (e.g. so many bills); count up (e.g. votes); ***t- til** persuade, urge.

+**tel'le/appara't** *-et, pl -/+-er* turnstile; counter.

+**tel'le/maski'n** *-en* adding machine; counter.

+**tel'le/måte** *-n* method of counting: **den nye t-n** (in Norway) naming the tens before the digits (**førtien** instead of **en og førti).**

+**tel'ler** *-en, pl -e* (=***teljar**) 1 *math.* numerator. 2 cashier, teller; ballot clerk; census taker. 3 counter.

+**tel'le/verk** *-et tech.* counter, odometer.

tellu'rium *-iet, pl +-ier/*-ium chem.* tellurium.

tel'ne *-a* 1 *dial.* floor plank. 2 *naut.* edge of a sail or net; boltrope, rope edging on sail or net.

tel't *-et* tent: **holde seg ved t-ene** stay close to home; **slå t-** pitch t-.

tel't/duk *-en* tent canvas.

tel'te[1] *V -a/+-et* 1 pitch, set up (a tent). 2 camp, go camping, live in a tent.

+**tel'te**[2] *pt of* **telle**[2]

tel't/leir *-en* camp.

tel't/liv *-et* camping; nomadic life.

tel't/plugg *-en* tent peg.

tel't/slå'ing *-a/+-en* pitching a tent.

+**tel't/stang** *-a, pl -stenger* (=*/**stong**) tent pole.

tel't/tur *-en* camping trip.

tel't/vogn [/vångn] *-a* 1 covered wagon. 2 *mil.* (canvas-covered) transport truck.

***tem'** *pr of* **temje**

te'ma *-et, pl -/+-er lit., mus.* theme.

te'/maski'n *-en* samovar, tea urn.

tema'tisk *A - gram., mus.* thematic.

***tem'je** *V tem, tamde, tamt* cf **temme**

+**tem'me** *V temte* (=***temje**) 1 break, tame (animals). 2 control, subdue, tame (action, emotions): **Troll kan temmes** Taming of the Shrew (Shakespeare).

tem'melig *Av* quite, rather, somewhat: **så t-** *lit.* a good deal, quite a bit.

+**tem'mer** *-en, pl -e* (=***temjar**) tamer.

tem'pel *-elet/-let, pl -el/+-ler* temple.

tem'pel/herre *-n hist.* (Knight) Templar.

+**tem'pel/ridder** *-en, pl -e* (=*-ar) *hist.* (Knight) Templar.

tem'pera *-en* tempera.

tem'pera/farge *-n* tempera.

+**tem'pera/maleri·** *-et* tempera painting.

temperament [-mang'] *-et, pl -/+-er* 1 temperament. 2 temperamental nature.

temperaments/full *A* temperamental.

+**temperaments/svingning** *-en* change of mood.

temperatu'r *-en* temperature: **en t- av 100°** a t- of 100°.

temperatu'r/fall *-et* temperature drop.

temperatu'r/kart *-et* map showing mean temperatures for a given time.

temperatu'r/kurve *+-n/*-a* graphed curve of temperature changes.

temperatu'r/måling *-a/+-en* temperature measurement, reading.

tempere're *V -te* temper: **t-t vin** wine at room temperature; **t-t sone** temperate zone.

tem'po *-et, pl -/tempi* tempo, time.

tem'pora *pl of* **tempus**

temporæ'r *A* temporary.

tem'pus *-et, pl tempora gram.* tense.

Tem'sen *Pln* cf **Themsen**

+**te'n**[1] *-en* cf **tein**

***te'n**[2] *pr of* **tenje**

tena'kel *-elen, pl -ler typog.* copy holder.

+**te'nar**[1] *-en* (=+**tennar**, ***tinar**) *dial.* burl, knot (hard area in fir or spruce wood).

***te'nar**[2] *-en* cf **tjener**

***te'nar/halḍ** *-et* employ, keeping of servants.

+ Bokmål; * Nynorsk; ° Dialect. After letter: ' stress (Acc. 1); ` tone, stress (Acc. 2); · length. Below letter: . not pronounced.

***tenarin'ne** *-a* cf **tjenerinne**
+ten'de *V -te* cf **tenne²**
tenden's *-en* 1 tendency, trend: **ha fallende t-** tend to fall; **t- stø** prices steady. 2 proclivity, propensity. 3 bias, pitch, slant; purpose: **historie-skrivning med t-** slanted historical writing (Winsnes).
tendensiø's *A* biased, slanted.
tenden's/roma'n *-en* tendentious novel; novel with a purpose.
ten'der *-en, pl +-e* tender (for locomotive); *naut.* supply ship.
tende're *V -te* tend: **t- mot** have a tendency toward; lean toward; aim toward.
***ten'dre** *V -a* light.
***te'ne** *V -te* cf **tjene**
***te'nel** *-elen, pl -lar naut.* boltrope, rope edging on sail or net.
***te'nest** *-a* cf **tjeneste**
***te'nest/dreng** *-en* (male) servant; hired man.
***te'neste** *-a* cf **tjeneste**
***te'neste/makt** *-a* authority, power.
***te'neste/mann** *-en, pl -menn(er)* cf **tjeneste/**
***te'nest/jente** *-a* servant girl; hired girl.
***te'nestleg** *A* - cf **tjenstlig**
***te'nest/viljug** *A* - cf **tjenst/villig**
teng'er *pl of* **tang¹, tong**
***ten'je** *V ten, tande, tant* 1 stretch (sth out). 2 run fast, sprint: **han kom t-ande** he came running.
+ten'k/bar *A* conceivable, imaginable.
+ten'ke *V -te* (=***-je**) 1 think (**over** over, **på** about); consider, dwell, reflect (**på** on): **t- så det knaker** rack one's brains. 2 think (=be of the opinion); believe: **t- sitt** draw one's own conclusions, have one's own views; **t-te jeg det ikke** I thought as much. 3 intend, mean (**til** for): **blomstene var t-t til deg** the flowers were meant for you; **i neste uke t-er jeg å bli ferdig** I intend to be finished next week. 4 imagine, suppose: **det kunne t-es** that (it) is conceivable, possible, that could be so; **tenk (bare, det)** just imagine, just think (**tenk at jeg skulle møte deg her** fancy meeting you here); **du har vel glemt det nå, kan jeg t-** you've probably forgotten it now, I suppose; **tenk om** imagine if, think if, what if. 5 (with *prep., adv.*): **t- etter** consider, think of, weigh; **t- for (med) seg selv** think to oneself; **t- godt om** think well of; **t- ut** devise, work out. 6 *(refl.)*: **t- seg** fancy, imagine, picture (**det kunne jeg godt t- meg** I can very well imagine that; **jeg kunne godt t- meg å** I wouldn't mind); plan to go (**jeg har t-t meg til Sverige i morgen** I plan to go to Sweden tomorrow); **t- seg om** consider, think over, weigh; **t- seg til** guess, imagine.
+ten'ke/evne *-a/-en* ability to think, reasoning ability.
+ten'ke/frihet *-en* freedom of thought.
+ten'kelig *A* - (=***tenkjeleg**) conceivable, imaginable, possible: **på alle t-e måter** in every c- way.
+ten'ke/måte *-n* mentality, mode of thought, way of thinking.
+ten'ker *-en, pl -e* (=***tenkjar**) philosopher, thinker.
+ten'ker/panne *-a/-en* high forehead.
+ten'ke/sett *-et* mentality, mode of thought.
***ten'king** *-a* cf **tenkning**
***ten'kjar** *-en* cf **tenker**
***ten'kje** *V -te* cf **tenke**
***ten'kjeleg** *A* - cf **tenkelig**
***ten'kje/måte** *-n* cf **tenke/**
+ten'kning *-en* (=***tenking**) 1 philosophizing, thinking. 2 mode of thought, way of thinking. 3 philosophy: **gresk t-** Greek thought.
+ten'k/som' *A -t, pl -me* (=***/sam**) reflective, thoughtful.
+ten'ksom/het *-en* reflectiveness, thoughtfulness.
***ten'kt** *A* - 1 intended: **eg er t- på** I intend to (do). 2 suspected: **for eitt kjend, til ti t-** convicted of one thing, suspected of everything. 3 reflective, thinking. 4 (also +) hypothetical, imaginary.
-tenkt *A* - -thinking, e.g. **få/t-, snar/t-.**
***ten'leg** *A* - cf **tjenlig**
+ten'nar *-en* cf **tenar¹**
+tenn'/bar *A* combustible, flammable, inflammable.
ten'ne¹ *V +tente/*tende* 1 light; fire, ignite, kindle (also *fig.*); set off (an explosion, a mine), start (an internal combustion engine); switch on, turn on (electric light): **lynet t-te fyr i taket** the lightning set fire to the roof; **t- (et) bål** make, start a bonfire; **t- lyset** turn on the light. 2 (with *prep., adv.*): **t- opp** light, make a fire; **t- på** light, set fire to.
***ten'ne²** *V -te* fit teeth into (sth); file (a saw).
+ten'ner¹ *-en, pl -e* 1 lighter. 2 percussion cap. 3 *naut.* lighter.
ten'ner² *pl of* **tann**
+ten'ner/skjærende *A* - anguished, bitter, teeth-gnashing; teeth-gritting: **t- besluttsomhet** fighting determination (Scott).
tenn'/hette *-a* percussion cap.
ten'ning *-a/+-en* 1 lighting. 2 igniting, setting off. 3 ignition (e.g. in car).
ten'nings/nøkkel *-elen, pl -nøkler* ignition key.
ten'nis *-en* tennis.
ten'nis/ball *-en* tennis ball.
ten'nis/bane *-n* tennis court.
ten'nis/sko *-en, pl -r/+-* tennis shoe.
tenn'/ladning *-en* firing, priming charge; detonator.
tenn'/nål *-a* firing pin.
tenn'/plugg *-en* spark plug.
tenn'/sats *-en* percussion cap; (**fire-**arm) primer.
tenn'/stikke *-a dial.* match.
***-tennt** *A* - cf **-tent**
teno'r *-en* tenor.
***te'nt¹** *pp of* **tene**
ten't² *pp of* **tenne¹**
+-tent *A* - (=***-tennt**) toothed, e.g. **sår/t-.**
tenta'kel *-elen, pl +-ler* tentacle.
tenta'men *-en* (non-final) written exam (in secondary schools, testing student's progress in a subject).
ten'tativ *A* tentative.
ten'/åra *pl df* (=**+/årene**) the teens.
ten'/årig *A* - teenage.
ten'/åring *-en* teenager.
teodolitt' *-en geol.* theodolite.
teokrati' *-et pol.* theocracy.
teokra'tisk *A - pol.* theocratic.
teol. =**teologisk**
teolog [-lå'g] *-en* theologian.
teologi' *-en* theology.
teologisk [-lå'gisk] *A* - theological.
teore'm *-et, pl -/+-er math.* theorem.
+teore'tiker *-en, pl -e* (=***-ar**) theoretician.
teoretise're *V -te* theorize.
teore'tisk *A* - theoretical.
teori' *-en* theory (**om** about): **sosialismens t-** the t- of socialism.
teosen'trisk *A* - theocentric.
teoso'f *-en* theosophist.
teosofi' *-en* theosophy.
teoso'fisk *A* - theosophical.
te'/potte *-a* teapot.
***tep'pe¹** *-a* block, obstruction, stopping up; constipation.
tep'pe² *-t, pl +-r/*-* 1 bedspread, blanket, quilt; coverlet; (heavy) tablecloth. 2 carpet, rug. 3 tapestry, wallhanging. 4 (theater) curtain: **t-t faller** curtain (stage direction). 5 *fig., lit.* cover, covering: **gressets bløte t-** the soft carpet of grass (Ibsen).
***tep'pe³** *-t* damper, shutter.
tep'pe⁴ *V tepte* block, plug, stop (up).
+tep'pe/banker *-en, pl -e* (=***-ar**) rug beater.
tep'pe/gras *-et bot.* brook grass (Catabrosa aquatica).
+tep'pe/lagt *A* - carpeted.
°tep'pen *-et* cf **teppe²**
tep'pe/rot *-a bot.* tormentil (Potentilla tormentilla).
tep'te *pt of* **teppe⁴**
terapeu't *-en* therapeutist, therapist.
terapeu'tisk *A* - therapeutic.
terapi' *-en* therapy.
***ter'gar** *-en* tease.
ter'ge *V -a/+-et* heckle, tease.
ter'm *-en* (scientific) term.
ter'me *-n* 1 *hist.* bath. 2 *geol.* hot spring.
termi'n *-en* 1 period, term; semester (of school year). 2 deadline, due date. 3 installment.
termi'n/handel *-elen, pl -ler merc.* trade in futures; hedging.
terminologi' *-en* terminology.
terminologisk [-lå'gisk] *A* - terminological.
ter'minus *-en, pl termini* term: **en grammatisk t-** a grammatical t-.
termi'n/vis *A* installment, periodic: **betale t-** pay by i-s.
ter'misk *A* - thermal.
termitt' *-en* 1 *zool.* termite. 2 *chem.* thermite.
termome'ter *-eret/-ret, pl -er/+-re* thermometer.
ter'mos/flaske *-a* thermos (bottle).
termosta't *-en* thermostat.
ter'ne¹ [also: tæ'rne] *-a/+-en* 1 *archaic* girl, maid, maiden. 2 handmaiden: **Osloprinsesse og terner** Miss Oslo and princesses (attendants).
ter'ne² *-a zool.* tern (Sterna).
ternet(e) [tæ'rnet(e)] *A* - checked, flecked, plaid.
ter'ning [also: tæ'rning] *-en* 1 die (*pl* dice): **kaste t-(er)** play dice; **t-en er kastet** the die is cast. 2 cube (as of bread, bouillon). 3 check, square (in material).
terning/forma *A* - (=**+-et**) cube-shaped.
terning/kast *-et* throw of the die.
+terning/spill *-et* (=**+/spell, */spel**) 1 dice game, *(pop.)* crap game. 2 set of dice.
te'/rose *-a/+-en bot.* tea rose (Rosa fragrans).
ter'pe *V -a/+-et* cram, plug (**på at**): **t- i seg** *dial.* force (food) down; **t- noe inn i hodene på dem** cram sth into their heads; **t- seg igjennom** struggle through (usu. a textbook).
terpenti'n *-en* turpentine.
terpenti'n/klut *-en* turpentine compress.
terpenti'n/olje *-a/-en* (oil of) turpentine.
terrakot'ta *-en* terra cotta; terra cotta ware.
terra'rium *-iet, pl +-ier/*-ium* terrarium.
terras'se *-n* terrace: **T-n** (short for) Victoria T-, government buildings (used as Gestapo headquarters in WW II).
***ter're¹** *-n* 1 drying. 2 drying weather. 3 sth to dry grain on.
***ter're²** *V -a* dry.
***ter're³** *V -a* heckle, tease.
terreng' *-et* 1 open country; terrain: **kupert t-** hilly country. 2 ground, territory: **tape t-** lose g-.
+terreng'/løp *-et* cross-country race.
+terreng'/løper *-en, pl -e* cross-country runner.
terres'trisk *A* - terrestrial.
ter'rier *-en, pl +- e* terrier.
terri'n *-en* tureen.
territoria'l/farvatn *-et* (=**+/farvann**) territorial waters.
territoria'l/grense *-a/+-en* territorial limits.
territo'rium *-iet, pl +-ier/*-ium* territory; region.
ter'ror *-en* terrorism.
terrorise're *V -te* terrorize.
terroris't *-en* terrorist.
ter's *-en* 1 *mus.* third. 2 (in fencing, cards) tierce. 3 *naut.* toggle; fid.
tersett' *-en* terzet, trio.

+ter'skel [also tær'-] *-elen, pl -ler* threshold: **på t-en til livet** on the t- of life.
ter't *-en* young salmon.
ter'te *-a* tart.
ter'te/fin *A* finicky, prissy; uppity.
tertia [tær't(s)ia] *-en typog.* great primer type (ab. 18 pt.).
ter'/tit· *-en zool.* titmouse (a bird: Parus major).
tertiær [tærtsiæ'r] *A* tertiary.
tertiær/bane *-n* lightly built, narrow gauge train, for local use.
tertiær/tiḍa *df geol.* the Tertiary period.
te'se *-n* hypothesis, tenet, thesis.
te'/servi·se *-t, pl +-r/*-* tea service.
te'/sil *-en* tea strainer.
te'/skei [/sjei] *-a* (=+**/skje**) teaspoon (smaller than American teaspoons).
te'/sort *-en* variety of tea.
tess' *A* - (usu. *neg.)* amount to sth, be worth sth; capable (of work): **hunden var ikke stort t-** the dog wasn't much good; **lite t-** not much good, no good.
***tes'se** *V -a* be of use, suitable, worth sth: **han t-er ikkje stort** he's not much help.
tes't *-en* test (esp. *psych.*).
testamen't *-et, pl +-er/*-* cf **testamente**
testamenta'risk *A - jur.* testamentary.
testamen'te *-t, pl+-er/*-* **1** *jur.* testament, will. **2** *(bibl.)* Testament.
testamente're *V -te jur.* bequeath, will (to).
testa'tor *-en jur.* testator.
tes't/batteri· *-et, pl +-er/*- psych.* battery of tests.
tes'te *V -a/+-et psych.* test.
teste're *V -te jur.* **1** attest, testify. **2** will.
testik'kel *-elen, pl testikler anat.* testicle.
testimo'nium *-iet, pl +-ier/*-ium* (written) testimonial; *adm.* certificate.
tete [te't] *-n* **1** head of the line, lead position: **gå i t-n** take the lead. **2: tête-à-tête** private conversation, twosome.
tet'ne *V -a/+-et* become denser, thicken; condense.
+tet'ning *-en* cf **tetting**
+tet'nings/list *-a* weather stripping.
tetrae'der *-eret, pl +-(e)re/*-er math.* tetrahedron.
tett' *A* - **1** dense (crowd, foliage, population, smoke, thicket, etc.), thick (fog, hair, shrubbery); compact, thickset (person); **t- av, med noe** full of, thick with sth; **t- i t-** cheek by jowl, shoulder to shoulder; closely packed, set thickly, studded; **t- luft** stuffy air. **2** impervious (to light, water, etc.); tight (weave); watertight (barrel, ship); plugged up, stopped (nostril, pipe, etc.), swollen (throat): **holde tett** hold one's tongue, keep a secret, keep silent (**med** about). **3** close, near: **t- i hop** close together; **t- innpå** right behind; **drikke t-** drink heavily; **t- opptil** right close to, right up against; **t- på hverandre** in rapid succession; **t- utenfor** just (right) outside; **t- ved** close by, near by.
+tett'/befol·ket *A* - densely populated.
tett'/bygd *A -/*-bygt* **1** built up, closely built, densely populated. **2** (of person) compactly, solidly built; close-knit, stocky.
tet'te[1] *-n* **1** starter (such as cream or butterwort) put in bottom of milk container to make milk thicken. **2**=**tettemjølk.**
tet'te[2] *V -a/+-et* **1** make tight; calk, fill, etc. **2** thicken milk by putting starter in bottom of container. **3: t- seg** crowd together; compress, shrink.
tet'te/gras *-et bot.* butterwort (Pinguicula vulgaris).
tet'te/gubbe *-n* snail (formerly used as milk starter).
tet'te/mjølk *-a* (=+**/melk**) Norwegian type of yogurt (see **tette**).
tett'/grend *-a* densely populated area.
tett'/grenḍt *A* - densely populated.
+tett'/het *-en* **1** closeness, density; compactness, concentration. **2** stuffiness, tightness.
tet'ting *-a/+-en* (=+**tetning**) **1** making tight; calking, filling, weather stripping, etc. **2** calking, weather stripping (material). **3** thickening (of milk by use of starter).
***tett'/leik** *-en* see **tetthet.**
tett'/maska *A* - (=+**-et**) close-meshed, fine-meshed.
tett'/pakka *A* - (=+**-et**) close, tightly packed; crowded (**med** with).
+tett'/sittenḍe *A* - (=***/sitjande**) close-set (eyes); close fitting, snug, tight (clothing).
+tett'/skrevet *A* - (=***/skriven**) closely written.
tett'/sluttenḍe *A* - snug, tight fitting.
+tett'/vokst *A* - (=***/vaksen**) **1** dense; compact, solid; hard. **2** (of person) squarely built, thick-set.
teuto'n *-en* Teuton.
teuto'nsk *A* - Teutonic.
te'v *-en* **1** *dial.* breath. **2** scent, smell (**av** of).
+te'/varmer *-en, pl -e* (=***-ar**) coffee warmer, tea cozy.
te'/vatn *-et* (=+**/vann**) water for tea; weak tea.
te've[1] *-a* bitch, jade, whore.
te've[2] *V -a/+-et dial.* **1** pant; *breathe. **2** reek, stink. ***3** scent; follow a scent.
***tev'je** *V -a* smell, stink.
tev'le *V -a/+-et* **1** compete, race; fight, struggle (**med** with). **2** *dial.* exert oneself, hurry.
tev'le/før *A* able, ready to compete.
+tev'ler *-en, pl -e* (=***-ar**) *dial.* competitor, contestant.
tev'ling *-a/+-en* competition, race (**med** with; **om** for).
te'/vogn [/vångn] *-a* tea cart, tea wagon.
Tf.=**Tilfredsstillende**
tg=**tangens**
t. h.=**til høgre**
Thẹm'sen *Pln* the Thames.
+Thọ'r *Prn* cf **Tor**
+ti[1] *C archaic* **1** hence, therefore: **ti kjennes for rett** *jur.* therefore the court decrees. **2** because, for, since.
ti'[2] *Num* ten
°ti[3] *P* cf **i[2]**
°ti'a *df of* **tid[1]**
tia'ra *-en* tiara.
Tibe't *Pln* Tibet.
+tibeta'ner *-en, pl -e* (=***-ar**) Tibetan.
tibeta'nsk *A* - Tibetan.
ti'd[1] [*ti'] *-a/+-en* **1** time (=period; age, epoch, times; season; fourth dimension): **all den t-** as long as, since (**all den t- du er i byen kan du godt besøke henne** as long as you're in town you can just as well visit her); **alle t-ers** all-time (**alle t-ers sjanse** chance of a lifetime; **det var alle t-ers** *fam.* that was the best ever, tops, simply great); **avtale en t-** make an appointment; **den tid(a)** at the time, when; **den t- den sorg** worry about that when the t- comes, sufficient unto the day is the evil thereof; **for t-en** at the moment, at the present t- (**nå for t-a** nowadays); **fra t-enes morgen** from time immemorial; **få t- på seg** get, have (some) t-; gain t-; **før i t-a** before, previously; **gi seg (god) t-** take one's (sweet) t-; **ha god t-** have sufficient t-; **ha t-en for seg** have (spare) t-; **hva t- går toget** what t- does the train leave; **i rett t-** at the right t-; on t-; **i sin t-** at one t-; **i t-e** (see **tide**); **kommer t-, kommer råd** when the t- comes the right expedient will present itself; don't cross that bridge until you get to it; **på lang t-** for a long t-; **se t-en an** bide one's t-, wait and see; **t-en er inne (til å)** now's the t- (to); **t-ens tann** the ravages of t-; **til enhver t-** at all t-s; **til rett t-** in due course; **alt til sin t-** all in good t-, everything in its season; **til sine t-er** at certain t-s, from t- to t-. **2** *gram.* tense.
***ti'ḍ[2]** *A* **1** frequent. **2** ice-free, unfrozen.
***ti'ḍ-** *Pf* cf **tids-**
***ti'ḍare** *cp of* **tidt**
***ti'ḍar/morgonen** *df* the beginning of time.
***ti'ḍast** *sp of* **tidt**
ti'ḍ/bolk *-en* period (of time); age.
ti'd/bøye *V infl as* **bøye[3]** *gram.* conjugate (a verb) in its various tenses.
***tidd'** *A* - **1** (of cow) pregnant; fertile. **2** having an appetite.
ti'de [*ti'e] *N*: **i t-** at the right time, in time, on time, **i t- og utide** in season and out (of season); **på t-** about time, high time.
ti'/del *-en* (fraction) tenth.
+ti'denḍe *-n* (=***tidend**) **1** piece of news; *(pl)* news, tidings; information. **2** *archaic* newspaper (exc. in names of papers, e.g. **Drammens T-**).
***tidend/fus** [ti'en/] *A* curious, inquisitive, prying.
Ti'dens Tegn [tei'n] *Prn* (formerly) daily newspaper in Oslo.
+ti'de/vatn *-et* (=+**/vann**) tide.
+ti'de/verv *-et* era, period.
***ti'ḍ/feste[1]** *-t* an established date.
ti'd/feste[2] *V -a/+-et/*-e* **1** date (to a certain time or period). **2: t-et** dated, outdated.
***ti'ḍ/følgje** *-a* cf **tids/**
***ti'ḍ/føtt** *A* - nimble footed.
***ti'ḍ/gjengd** *A -/-gjengt* frequent (visitor).
***ti'ḍ/høveleg** *A* - contemporary, in keeping with the times.
ti'dig *A - dial.* **1** early rising. **2** brisk, chipper, hale and hearty; brave and cheerful. **3** amusing; pleasant.
ti'd/kort *en/+et* amusement, pastime.
tidl.=+**tidligere/*tidlegare**
+ti'd/lang *en lit.* period, time, while.
ti'ḍ/laus *A* (=+**/løs**) **1** timeless. **2** (as noun) autumn crocus (Colchicum autumnale).
ti'dlig *A* - **1** early: **bli t- voksen** mature e-; **det var ikke for t-** it wasn't too e-; it was none too soon; **for t-** premature (birth, death, etc.); **han er t- oppe** he's up e-; he's an e- riser. **2** *(adv.)* soon: **hvor t- kan vi vente å høre fra ham** how soon can we expect to hear from him. **3** *(comp.)*: **t-ere** earlier; former (owner, president, student, etc.), previous (events, years, etc.). **4** *(sup.)*: **t-st** earliest, soonest; **svar kan ventes t-st lørdag** (an) answer can be expected by Saturday at the e-.
ti'dlig/dags *Av* early (in the day).
ti'dlig/pote'ter *pl* early potatoes.
+ti'd/løs *A* cf **/laus**
+ti'dløs/het *-en* timelessness.
***ti'ḍ/nemning** *-a* dating, indication of time.
ti'/dobbelt *A* - (=***/dobbel**) tenfold, ten times; many times (as much).
ti'/doble *V -a/+-et* increase tenfold.
tids' *A - dial.* wrong: **ka e t-** what's the matter?
tid's- *Pf* (=***tid-**) time.
tid's/alder *-eren, pl -rer* age, epoch, era.
+tid's/angi·velse *-n* dating, indication of time.
tid's/avsnitt *-et* period.
+tid's/begren·sning *-en* time limit.

+ Bokmål; * Nynorsk; ° Dialect.
After letter: ' stress (Acc. 1); ` tone, stress (Acc. 2); · length.
Below letter: . not pronounced.

+tid's/bespa'relse *-n* saving of time: **til t-** to save time.
+tid's/bespa'rende *A* - time-saving.
+tid's/bilde *-t* (=***/bilete**) picture of the times.
+tid's/enhet *-en* unit of time.
***ti'd/setje** *V -te* appoint, fix, set (a date).
tid's/faktor *-en* time factor.
+tid's/fordri'v *-et* pastime.
tid's/frist *-en* delay, grace (period), respite.
+tid's/følge *-a* (=***-je**) chronological order, chronology.
tid's/grense *-a/+-en* deadline, time limit.
+tid's/innstilling *-a/-en* time scale.
tid's/innstilt *A* - controlled by a time mechanism: **t- bombe** time bomb.
***ti'd/skifte** *-t* cf **tids/**
***ti'd/skrift** *-a/-et* cf **tids/**
+tid's/messig *A* - contemporary, modern, up-to-date.
+tid'smessig/het *-en* modernity, quality of being up-to-date.
+tid's/måler *-en, pl -e* (=***-ar**) timer (e.g. on time relay apparatus).
tids'/nok' *Av* in time; early, soon enough: **komme t-** be on time; **vi kommer t- fram** we will get there soon enough (Bjørnson).
tid's/nød *-a/+-en* lack of time: **komme i t-** be caught short by l-.
tid's/punkt *-et* time; moment: **på det t- da** at the m- when.
tid's/rekning *-a* (=**+/regning**) reckoning (of time); calendar; chronology: **i vår t-** in the Christian era.
tid's/rom [/romm] *-met* period (**av** of; **fra, til** from, to).
tid's/signal [/singna'l] *-et, pl -/+-er* time signal.
tid's/skifte *-t* change in the times; beginning of an era.
tid's/skrift *-et/*-a* magazine, periodical.
tid's/spille *N* waste of time.
tid's/spørsmål *-et* question of time.
tid's/studium *-iet, pl +-ier/*-ium* time study.
+tid's/svarende *A* - worth spending time on, worth the time spent.
tid's/ånd *+-en/*-a* spirit of the times.
***tidt'** *Av cp tidare, sp tidast* cf **titt²**
+ti'd/taker *-en, pl -e* (=***-ar**) timekeeper.
***ti'd/trøyte** *-t* entertainment; pastime.
***ti'dug** *A* - cf **tidig**
***ti'd/vand** *A -vant* capricious, unpredictable.
***ti'd/vatn** *-et* cf **tide/**
+ti'e *V -dde/tagde, -dd/tagd* (=***teie²**) be silent, keep quiet, (**om** about); become, fall silent, stop talking; stop making a noise: **t- i hjel** kill by silence; give the silent treatment to; suppress (an unpleasant fact); **t- (stille) med noe** keep quiet about sth; **t- til** say nothing, let pass in silence; **ti stille** hold your tongue, shut up, silence.
ti'en *A +-ent, pl -ne/+-ene* frostfree, thawed, unfrozen.
+ti'ende¹ *-n* (=***tiend**) tithe: **gi t- av** pay a t- on.
ti'ende² *Num* tenth.
ti'ende/del *-en* cf **ti/**
ti'ende/plikt *-a/+-en* obligation to tithe.
+ti'er *-en, pl -e* (=***-ar**) **1** (figure) 10. **2** ten-*krone* bill, tenner, ten-spot. **3** contestant, wearing number 10; (streetcar line) number 10.
+ti'ere *cp of* **titt²**
+ti'est *sp of* **titt²**
+ti'/fold *A* - (=***/fald**) tenfold, ten times; many times.
+tig'd *pp of* **tigge²**
ti'ger *-eren, pl -rer/+-ere zool.* tiger (Felis tigris).
+ti'ger/aktig *A* - tigerlike.
tigerin'ne *-a/+-en* tigress.
ti'ger/katt *-en* **1** *zool.* margay (Felis tigrina). **2** *fam.* tiger. **3** *fam.* (of aggressive, temperamental young woman) spitfire, wildcat.
ti'ger/sprang *-et* leap, spring of (or like) a tiger.
ti'ger/stad *-en*: **T-en** *hum.* (of Oslo) tiger city (because of its reputed coldness toward strangers).
tig'ge¹ *V tagg, +-et/*-e/*-i* (=**tigge²**) beg (**om** for), beseech, implore; solicit: **t- penger** s- money.
tig'ge² *V +tigde/+-et/*-a* cf **tigge¹**
+tig'ger *-en, pl -e* (=***-ar**) beggar.
+tig'ger/aktig *A* - beggarly, like a beggar.
+tig'ger/brev *-et* (=***-ar/**) begging letter; letter of solicitation.
+tig'ger/gang *-en* (=***-ar/**) beggary; collecting, soliciting funds.
+tiggeri' [also tig'-] *-et* begging; beseeching, importuning; solicitation (of funds).
+tig'ger/munk *-en, pl -e* (=***-ar/**) mendicant friar.
+tig'ger/pose *-n* (=***-ar/**) beggar's sack.
+tig'ger/stav *-en* (=***-ar/**) beggar's staff: **bringe til t-en** ruin (financially).
+tig'ger/sti *-en* beggar's path: **komme på t-en** become a beggar.
***tig'le** *V -a* economize, save.
ti'k *-a* **1** bitch, vixen. ***2** ewe. **3** *archaic* strumpet, wench.
ti'/kamp *-en* decathlon.
ti'/kant *-en* decagon.
tikk' *-et* tick, ticking (**av** of).
***tik'ke¹** *-a* cf **tik**
tik'ke² *V -a/+-et* **1** tick. **2** *dial.* tag; play tag.
tikk'-takk' *I* tick-tock.
ti'/krone *-a* ten-*krone* note (or coin).
ti'/kroning *-en* ten-*krone* note (or coin).
tik'se¹ *-a* cf **tik**
tik'se² *V -a/+-et dial.* **1** berate, call sby a name. ***2** tear; knock, peck.
til'¹ *P* **1** to; for (direction, destination, recipient): **avreise t- Bergen** departure for B-; **et brev t- deg** a letter for you; **lese t- artium** study for (*artium*) exam; **telle t- ti** count to ten; **t- og med** up to and including; *(adv.)* even, in addition. **2** (of time) till, until; by; at: **t- påske** until Easter, by E-, at E-; **t- jul** until (etc.) Christmas; **mandag t- fredag** Monday through Friday. **3** of (membership, possession, relationship): **sønn t- Jørgen** son of J-, J-'s son; **nøkkelen t- døra** the key to the door; **Fru Inger t- Østråt** Lady I- of Ø-; **kjærlighet t- barn** love of (for) children. **4** *fam.* a . . . of a: **det var fanden t- kropp** that was a hell of a fellow (Ibsen); **det var mye t- pipe, tenkte Espen Askeladd** that's a honey of a whistle, thought E- the Ashlad (Asbjørnsen). **5** as: **t- svar** as an answer; **t- takk** as thanks; **utnevne t- statsråd** appoint (as) minister. **6** accompanying, with: **en dram t- maten** a drink with the meal. **7** at, on, to (with nouns in **-s**): **t- bords** at, to the table; **t- lands** on land. **8** (with **å**): **han t- å hogge** he started to chop (Asbjørnsen); **det er ikke til å tro** it's unbelievable; **komme t- å** be going to; happen to. **9** *(adv.)* more; additional: **en t-** one more; **t- og med** even. **10** (as *adv.* complement with verbs: see these, e.g.): **bli t-** come into being; **få en t- å** get sby to; **må t-** is necessary, unavoidable; **skal t-** is needed (**det skal mange penger t-** lots of money is needed); **slå (dra) t-** hit hard; **strømme t-** pour in; **ta t-** start; **være t-** exist.
til² *C* **1** till, until: **like t- han kommer** clear until he comes. **2** *dial.* the (with *comp*): **t- lenger det led, t- knappere ble det for kona** the longer it was, the more difficult it became for the woman (Asbjørnsen).
+tilak'ters *Av* cf **akters**
til'/bad *pt of* **-be(de)**
tilba'ke *Av* **1** back, backward(s) (in movement, in time): **gå t-** subside (**feberen var gått t-** the fever had s-d); **vise t-** reject, repudiate. **2** behind (of place), backward (in development): **bli t-** remain, stay behind; **stå t- for** be inferior to. **3** left (over): **ha t-** have left (over).
+tilba'ke/beta'le *V -te* pay back, refund; reimburse, repay.
tilba'ke/beta'ling *-en* refund, repayment, return.
tilba'ke/blikk *-et* backward glance, retrospective view: **kaste et t- på** look back upon.
+tilba'ke/blitt *A* - left, remaining.
tilba'ke/fall *-et* **1** *med.* relapse. **2** *jur.* reversion (to original owner). **3** backsliding, falling back; return (**til** to). **4** *jur. psych.* instance of recidivism.
tilba'ke/gang *-en* decline, fall, recession: **være i t-** decline, fall off.
+tilba'ke/holde *V -holdt, -holdt* **1** detain, hold back (e.g. a passenger). **2** curb, stifle, suppress (e.g. expression of feeling).
+tilba'ke/holdelse *-n* **1** detention (**av** of). **2** suppression.
+tilba'ke/holden *A -ent, pl -ne* aloof, reserved (**overfor** toward); modest, retiring.
+tilba'keholden/het *-en* aloofness, reserve; modesty, reticence.
+tilba'ke/holdt *pt, pp of* **-holde**
+tilba'ke/kalle *V -kalte* **1** call back, recall (e.g. an ambassador). **2** retract, revoke, take back; withdraw (a proposal).
+tilba'ke/kallelse *-n* **1** recall (**av** of). **2** retraction, revocation; withdrawal.
tilba'ke/komst *-en* return.
+tilba'ke/legge *V -la, -lagt* **1** leave behind; pass: **et t-lagt stadium** a thing of the past. **2** cover, travel.
+tilba'ke/leve're *V -te* hand back, return.
+tilba'ke/liggende *A* - backward, underdeveloped.
tilba'ke/reise *-a/+-en* return journey (trip, voyage).
°tilba'kers *Av* cf **tilbake**
tilba'ke/skritt *-et* step backward(s); retrogression: **det betegner et t-** it means a step backward(s).
tilba'ke/slag *-et* **1** kick, recoil, repercussion; backfire, backwash. **2** backspace (on typewriter). **3** reaction, swing back (to previous position, situation, etc.). **4** *biol.* atavism, throw-back.
tilba'ke/stående *A* - **1** *archaic* standing back, in the rear: **de t-** the people in the rear. **2** backward: **t- barn** b- children. **3** left behind: **de t-** the rest.
tilba'ke/tog [/tåg] *-et mil.* retreat, withdrawal (also *fig.*): **være på t-** retreat.
+tilba'ke/tredelse *-n* (=**+/treden**) resignation, retirement, withdrawal (**fra** from).
+tilba'ke/trekning *-en* (=***/trekking**) retraction, withdrawal (e.g. of troops).
+tilba'ke/trengt *A* - (=***/trengd**) **1** forced, pushed back. **2** repressed, suppressed.
+tilba'ketrukken/het [-trokken/] *-en* retirement, seclusion.
+tilba'ke/trukket [/trokket] *A -, pl -trukne* **1** drawn back, retracted, withdrawn; set back. **2** retiring, secluded.
tilba'ke/tur *-en* return trip: **på t-en** on the way back.
tilba'ke/veg *-en* (=**+/vei**) way back, home: **på t-en** on the way back.
tilba'ke/vendende *A* - **1** returning. **2** periodical, recurrent, recurring.
+tilba'ke/virkende *A* - (=***/verkande**) **1** retroactive: **t- kraft** r- force. **2** *gram.* reflexive.
+tilba'ke/virkning *-en* effect; reaction, repercussion (**på** on).
+tilba'ke/vise *V -te* reject, repudiate.

+tilba'ke/vi'sning *-en* rejection, repudiation (av of).

+tilba'ke/værende *A* - left behind, remaining: **de t-** the rest.

°tilba'rs *Av* cf **tilbake**

til'/be(de) *V infl as* **be(de)** 1 worship. 2 adore, idolize.

+tilbe'delse [also til'/] *-n* (=***/beding**) 1 worship (av of). 2 adoration, adulation.

+til'/beder *-en, pl -e* (=***-ar**) 1 worshiper. 2 devoted admirer, suitor.

+til'/behø'r *-et* accessories; appurtenances; paraphernalia; equipment, fittings, fixtures: **med alt t-** and all that goes with it.

+til'/bere'de *V -te* fix, make ready, prepare (food, etc.).

+til'/bere'dning *-en* (=**+-else**) fixing, making, preparation (av of; til for).

+tilbli'velse *-n* birth, coming into existence, genesis; establishment, founding; origin (av).

+tilbli'velses/histo'rie *-n* genesis, story of creation.

***til'/bod** [/bå] *-et* cf **/bud**

+til'/brakte *pt of* **-bringe**

***til'/brigde** *V -a* adapt, modify.

+til'/bringe *V -brakte, -brakt* 1 pass, spend (time): **t- tiden med å lese** spend one's time reading. 2 *(pp.)* **tilbrakt** delivered.

+til'/bud *-et* 1 bid, offer (om of; om å to); quotation; proffer: **fordelaktig t-** bargain. 2 *merc.* supply: **t- og etterspørsel** s- and demand.

***til'/budd** *A -/-butt* equipped, supplied; repaired.

+til'budt *pp of* **-by(de)**

***til'/bunad** *-en* 1 equipment; preparation.

+tilbunn's *Av* cf **botn**

***til'/burd** *-en* 1 event, happening, occurrence. 2 behavior, procedure.

+til'/by(de) *V infl as* **by(de)** offer: **t- noen en krone** offer sby a crown; **t- seg å** offer to (do sth).

til'/bygg *-et* addition, annex, extension (til to).

+til'/bytte *V -et*: **t- seg** get in exchange, *(pop.)* by swapping.

+til'/bød *pt of* **-by(de)**

tilbø'rlig *A* - fitting, proper, suitable.

+tilbøy'elig *A* - 1 disposed, inclined (til to): **t- til å tro** i- to believe. 2 susceptible; apt; having a tendency (til to): **t- til å bli forkjølet** susceptible to colds.

+tilbøy'elig/het *-en* 1 disposition, inclination (til to). 2 tendency; predisposition, susceptibility (til to).

+til'/danne *V -a/-et* fashion, shape.

+til'/dekke *V -dekte* cover, veil.

til'/dele *V -te* allot, assign (e.g. a task); award (e.g. a prize).

+tilde'ls *Av* cf **del**

+til'/dikte *V -et* add to (a poem, story, etc.).

+til'/diktning *-en* addition (to poem, story, etc.).

+til'/dra *V -drog, -dradd/-dratt:* **t- seg** attract, draw (attention); happen.

***til'/drag** *-et* attraction.

+til'/drage *V -drog, -dradd/-dratt* cf **/dra**

+til'/dragelse [also -dra'-] *-n* event, happening: **selsomme t-r** strange e-s.

***til'drags/kraft** *-a* power of attraction.

+til'/dratt *pp of* **-dra(ge)**

til'/driv *-et* 1 motivation: ***dei varige sjelelege t-a hos menneska** the enduring psychological motivations of man (Koht). 2 impulse, stimulus (til to). 3 disposition, tendency.

+til'/drog *pt of* **-dra(ge)**

+til'/dømme *V -dømte jur.* award.

***ti'le** *-t* 1 (plank, wood) floor. 2 (theater) stage.

+til'/egne [/eine] *V -a/-et* (=***/eigne**) 1 dedicate (til to). 2: **t- seg** appropriate, take possession of. 3: **t- seg** acquire, master, pick up (e.g. a language, a subject).

+til'/egnelse [/einelse] *-n* (=***/eigning**) 1 dedication (av of; til to). 2 appropriation, usurpation. 3 acquisition, mastery (av of); understanding.

***til'/eigne** *V -a* cf **/egne**

***til'/emning** *-a* beginning, plan: **i t-** in preparation.

+tilen'de *Av* cf **ende**[1]

+tilen'de/bringe *V -brakte, -brakt* complete, conclude, terminate.

+tilen'de/bringelse *-n* completion, conclusion, termination (av of).

***til'/etla** *A* - intended, intentional.

+til'/falle *V -falt, -falt* (of money) come, fall, go to; (of duties) devolve upon: **overskottet skulle t- bykassa** the surplus was to go to the city treasury.

+tilfal's *A* - cf **fals**[2]

til'/fang *-et* material, substance (til for).

tilfel'dig *A* - (=**+tilfellig, *tilfelleleg**) 1 accidental, chance, fortuitous. 2 casual, incidental: **t-e forbipasserende** c- passersby. 3 occasional, random: **en t- jobb** an odd job. 4 *philos.* accidental. 5 *(adv.)* (also) at random, by chance.

+tilfel'dig/het *-en* accident, chance, coincidence: **mer enn en t-** no mere coincidence.

tilfel'dig/vis *Av* accidentally, by (any) chance; as it happens; incidentally: **jeg vet t- om en** I happen to know of someone.

til'/felle *-t, pl -/+-r* 1 case, instance, occurrence (av of): **det er t- at** it is true that; **for alle t-s skyld** just in case; **for det t- at** in case (of); **i ethvert t-** in any case, in any event; **i så t-** in that case, if so; **i t- av** in case of, in the event of. 2 occasion: **ved det t-** on that o-; **t-t gjør tyver** opportunity makes thieves. 3 chance, coincidence: **t-t førte dem sammen** chance brought them together; **ved et t-** accidentally, by chance. 3 *fam.* case; attack, fit (of disease).

***tilfel'leleg** *A* - cf **tilfeldig**

+tilfel'lig *A* - cf **tilfeldig**

+tilfel'lig/het *-en* cf **tilfeldig/**

til'/flukt *-a/+-en* refuge, resort, sanctuary: **finne t- hos** find shelter with; **ta t- til** take refuge in; resort to.

til'flukts/rom [/romm] *-met* (bomb) shelter.

+til'flukts/sted *-et* (=***/stad**) refuge, sanctuary, shelter.

+til'/flyte *V -fløt, -flytt* accrue to, fall to; be granted, supplied with (esp. of information).

+til'/flytte *V -et* move to (a place).

+til'/fløt *pt of* **-flyte**

tilforla'telig *A* - 1 dependable, reliable, trustworthy. 2 *(adv.)* certainly, positively.

+tilfor'n *Av archaic* before, formerly, of yore.

tilfred's *A* - content, satisfied (med with).

+tilfred's/het *-en* content, contentment, satisfaction (med with): **til hans fulle t-** to his complete s-.

+til'freds/stille *V -stilte* satisfy, give satisfaction (med with).

+til'freds/stillelse *-n* satisfaction (med with).

til'freds/stillende *A* 1 satisfactory. 2 *educ.* (used as a grade in the secondary schools) ab.=average (C): **ikke t-** failure; **meget/*mykje t-** very good (B-A); **noenlunde t-** ab.=poor (D); **særdeles t-** excellent (A+).

+til'/frosset *A* - frozen (over).

+tilful'le *Av* cf **fulle**

+til'/føket *A* - buried in drifts, drifted.

til'/føre[1] *-t* occasion, opportunity; **med t- av Dykkar brev** with regard to your letter.

+til'/føre[2] *V -te* bring in, supply (with): **t- nytt blod** b- in new blood.

til'/førsel *-elen, pl -ler* sth brought in, supply: **t-en til våre markeder** the supply to our markets.

til'førsels/linje *-a/+-en* supply line.

***til'/førsle** *-a* cf **/førsel**

+til'/føye *V -de* 1 add; attach. 2 cause, do, inflict (injustice, injury) upon.

+til'/føyelse *-n* 1 addendum, addition (til to). 2 infliction (av of).

til'/gang *-en* 1 access, approach (til to). 2 supply; influx: **t-en på fisk** the supply of fish; **t-en på arbeidskraft** the labor market. *****3 event, occasion; plot, sequence of events.

til'/gi *V -gav, -gitt* 1 forgive. 2 excuse: **t- at jeg går først** excuse me for preceding you.

til'/gift *+-en/*-a*: **(få, gi) i t-** (get, give) as a bonus, sth thrown in.

+til'/gitre *V -et* cover with a lattice, grill, grate.

+tilgi'velig *A* - excusable, forgivable.

+tilgi'velse *-n* (=***-ing**) forgiveness (for for): **syndens t-** *(bibl.)* f- of sins.

***til'/gjenge** *-t* admission, entrance.

tilgjeng'elig *A* - 1 accessible, approachable; available, open (for to). 2 (of a literary work) accessible, comprehensible: **vanskelig t-** difficult.

***til'/gjerd** *-a* affectation, artificiality.

***til'/gje(ve)** *V -gav, -gjeve/-i* cf **/gi**

***til'/gjeving** *-a* cf **/givelse**

+til'/gjort [/jort] *A* - (=***/gjord**) 1 affected, artificial. 2 (of fish) cleaned.

+til'gjort/het *-en* affectation, artificiality.

tilgo'de *Av* cf **gode**[2]

+tilgo'de/gjøre *V -gjorde, -gjort* make use of, utilize: **t- seg** take advantage of.

tilgo'de/havende *et* account outstanding, balance, credit.

+tilgo'de/se *V -så, -sett* attend to, look after, take care of.

+tilgo'de/skrive *V -skrev, -skrevet* credit.

til'/grensende *A* - adjoining, contiguous, neighboring.

til'/grodd *A -/*-grott* 1 overgrown (garden, path). 2 healed over (wound).

***til'/hald** *-et* cf **/hold**

***til'halds/løyve** *-t* residence permit.

***til'halds/stad** *-en* cf **tilholds/sted**

***til'/helde** *-t* cf **/hold**

til'/heng *-et* 1 appendix. 2 *derog.* crowd, following, hangers-on.

+til'/henger *-en, pl -e* (=***-(j)ar**) 1 adherent, follower, supporter; devotee (av of). 2 trailer.

***til'/hjelp** *-a* aid, assistance, help.

+til'/hold *-et* 1 lodging, shelter, stay: **ha sitt t-** be, stay (usu. temporarily). 2 injunction, order; caution, warning.

+til'holds/sted *-et* hangout, haunt; den, nest.

***til'/hug** *-en* inclination, tendency.

***til'/hygge** *-t* refuge, reliance.

+til'/hylle *V -a/-et/-te* cover, shroud; cloak, hide, veil.

+til'/høre *V -te* belong to; **alt slikt t-er middelalderen** all that is part of the Middle Ages; **å t- en annen** to be another's.

til'/hørende *A* - (=***/høyrande**) belonging to, going with; attached: **alt t-** all that goes with (it).

+til'/hører *-en, pl -e* (=***-ar, */høyrar**) listener: **t-e** audience; **ærede t-e** ladies and gentlemen.

+til'hører/krets *-en* audience: **en stor t-** a large audience (following).

til'/høve *-t dial.* 1 circumstance, condition: **under slike t-** under such circumstances. 2 opportunity (til to).

***til'/høyrsle** *-a* accessory, adjunct; belonging(s), fitting(s), paraphernalia.

+tilhån'de *Av* cf **hånde**

+ Bokmål; * Nynorsk; ° Dialect.
After letter: ' stress (Acc. 1); ' tone, stress (Acc. 2); · length.
Below letter: . not pronounced.

*tilin'kjes/gjering -a cf tilintet/gjørelse
+tilin'tet/gjøre V -gjorde, -gjort annihilate, crush, destroy; obliterate: **han følte seg t-gjort** he felt crushed, humilated.
+tilin'tet/gjørelse -n annihilation, destruction, obliteration (av of).
+tilin'tet/gjørende A - crushing, destructive, obliterating: **et t- smil** a withering smile.
til'/jamning -a/+-en 1 leveling, smoothing off. 2 gram. vocalic assimilation.
til'je -a 1 archaic or dial. floorboard; poet. dance floor: **dansen går over t-** the dance is trod in the hall (ballads). 2 (loose) floorboard (in rowboat or sailboat).
+til'/juble V -et acclaim, cheer, hail.
til'/kalle V -kalte/*-a call (in), send for, summon: **t- troppene** call up the troops.
til'/kalling -a/+-en (=+-else) call, calling up, summons (av of).
+til'/kaste V -et throw, toss (to sby).
+til'/kjempe V -et: **t- seg** earn, gain (by struggle), win: **t-et livsvisdom** hard-earned wisdom; **t- seg adgang** fight one's way in; **t-et fatning** hard-won composure.
+til'/kjenne V -kjente accord, award, grant: **bli t-t barnet** get custody of the child.
+tilkjen'ne/gi V -gav, -gitt declare, make known; express, show (e.g. one's displeasure).
+tilkjen'ne/givelse -n declaration, expression, notification (av of).
+til'/knappet A - buttoned (up); fig. aloof, closed, reserved.
+til'knappet/het -en aloofness, reserve.
+til'/knytning -en (=*/knyting) 1 attachment, connection, tie (til with): **i t- til** in c- with, in amplification of, as a supplement to. 2 fig. affinity, association, relevance.
+til'knytnings/punkt -et point of connection, of contact, of departure.
+til'/knyttet A - connected with, tied to; affiliated with.
+til'/koble V -a/-et (=+/kople) attach, connect (to); couple, hook up; put (a motor) in gear: **t-et** hooked up, in gear.
+til'/komme V -kom, -kommet: usu. **det t-er en** one is entitled to, has a right to; **det t-er ikke meg å dømme** it is not for me to judge; ***t-en** mature, of advanced years.
til'/kommende A - (=*/komande) coming, future: **hennes (hans) t-** her (his) fiancé(e).
til'/kopling -a/+-en attachment, connection, coupling.
til'/laga A - (=+-et) 1 made, prepared. 2 fig. affected, artificial.
til'/laging -a preparation (av of).
til'/late V infl as late[1] 1 allow, permit (å to); suffer, tolerate: **parkering t-t** parking permitted. 2: **t- seg** dare, presume, take the liberty to: **herved t-er vi oss å meddele Dem** we have the honor to inform you.
tilla'telig A - allowable, permissible: **på grensen av det t-e** (skating) on thin ice.
+tilla'telse -n permission (til to).
*til'/laten A -e/-i, pl -ne allowed, permitted.
*til'le V -a drip -a drip, flow, trickle.
til'/legg -et 1 adding, addition: **ved t- av** by adding. 2 increase, raise; bonus; surcharge: **t- i lønn** salary raise. 3 addendum, appendix, supplement: **med utfyllende t-** with supplementary remarks. 4 agr. breeding (av of).
+til'/legge V -la, -lagt 1 accord, ascribe to, credit: **t- seg æren** take the c-. 2 add to, attach: **t- saken stor betydning** attach great significance to the matter.
til'leggs/avgift -a/+-en surcharge.
+til'leggs/bemer'kning -en supplementary remark.
+til'leggs/bestem'melse -n additional provision, codicil, rider.
+til'leggs/bevil'gning -en additional concession; supplementary grant.
til'leggs'porto -en additional postage, surcharge.
til'leggs/skatt -en surtax.
til'leggs'spørsmål -et supplementary question.
+tillei'e Av cf **leie**[2]
*til'/leiing -a cause, impulse.
til'/lempe V -a/+-et adapt: **t- seg a-**, adjust (oneself) (**etter, til** to).
+til'/liggende A - (=*/liggjande) 1 belonging to, going with. 2 adjacent, adjoining.
+tilli'ke Av also, as well, besides, too.
+tilli'ke/med P along, together with.
til'/lit -a/+-en confidence, faith, trust (**til** in): **i t- til** in reliance on; **nyte allmenn t-** enjoy public confidence; **bli fradømt allmenn t-** lose one's civil rights.
*til'lit/sam A confident, trusting.
til'lits/brott -et (=+/brudd) breach of confidence, trust.
+til'lits/erklæ'ring -en vote of confidence.
til'lits/forhold -et position, relationship of trust.
til'lits/full A confident, trusting.
+til'litsfull/het -en confidence, trustfulness.
til'lits/mann -en, pl -menn/*-menner representative, spokesman; shop steward.
*til'lits/ombod -et position of honor, of trust.
til'lits/tap -et loss of civil rights.
til'lits/verv -et position of honor, of trust.
til'lits/votum -et, pl -vota vote of confidence.
+til'lit/vekkende A - inspiring confidence.
+tilliv's Av cf **liv**
+til'/lokkelse -n attraction, charm; allurement, temptation (**for** to): **miste sin t-** pall.
+til'/lokkende A - alluring, attractive, charming; seductive (offer; woman).
+til'/lot pt of **-late**
til'læ'rt A - acquired, learned, trained; artificial.
+til'/løp -et (=*/laup) 1 inflow, influx (of people, water). 2 running start (to a high jump or pole vault). 3 fig. beginning, (preliminary) effort; approach, attempt (**til at**). 4 hint, sign, suspicion (**til** of): **t- til værforandring** signs of a change in the weather.
+til'/lyse V -te announce (e.g. a meeting).
til'/med Av besides, moreover, on top of (this); even, to boot.
til'/må'lt A - allotted, apportioned, meted out: **knapt t-** scanty.
*til'/måting -a adaptation, adjustment, fitting.
*til'måts/tal -et proportion.
*til'måts/val -et proportional representation.
+til'/navn -et (=*/namn) cognomen, nickname.
+tilnær'melse -n cf **/nærming**
+tilnær'melses/vis Av approximately: **ikke t- riktig** far from correct, not even close.
+til'/nærmet A - (=*/nærma) approximate: **t- tall** round number.
til'/nærming -a/+-en (=+/nærmelse) 1 approach, rapprochement: **t- av de to målformene** rapprochement of the two language forms (directive given to Norsk språknemnd by the Storting). 2: **gjøre t-er** make advances, overtures, passes. 3 approximation (**til** to).
*til'nærmings/verde [/være] -t approximate value, estimate.
+tilovers [tilå'vers] Av cf **overs**
+tilovers/blitt A - left-over, remaining.
til'/passe V -a/+-et adapt, adjust, fit: **t- seg nye forhold** adjust to new conditions.
til'/passing -a/+-en (=+/pasning) adaptation, adjustment (**av** of; **etter, til** to).
til'passings/evne -a/+-en (=+tilpasnings/) ability to adapt, adjust; adaptability.
+til'/plikte V -et jur. require: **t-et å betale** ordered to pay.
+til'/re V -dde (=+/rede) damage, injure, maul: **ille t-dd** in bad condition, (pop.) roughed up.
+til'/regne [/reine] V -et attribute to, blame on, charge with.
*til'/reiing -a manufacture, preparation (**av** of).
til'/reisende A - visiting: **de t-** the visitors; **en ny t-** a new arrival.
tilrek'nelig A - (=+/regnelig) accountable, responsible, of sound mind, sane: **ikke t-** non compos mentis.
+tilret'te/legge V -la, -lagt arrange, organize, prepare; adapt, adjust (e.g. instruction).
+tilret'te/vise V -te rebuke, reprimand.
+tilret'te/vi'sning -en rebuke, reprimand.
+til'/rive V -rev, -revet: **t- seg** seize, usurp.
til'/rop -et cry, shout (of warning, etc.); heckling, jeering; acclamation, cheering.
til'/råde V -de (=+/rå) advise, counsel, recommend: **t- en å** advise sby to.
tilrå'delig A - advisable.
til'/råding -a/+-en 1 advice, recommendation. 2 admin. proposal, proposition, recommendation.
til'rådings/nemnd -a advisory committee.
tils.=til +sammen/*saman
+til'/sa pt of **-si**
+til'/sagn [/sangn] -et assurance, promise (**om** of).
+tilsal'gs Av cf **salg**
+tilsam'men A cf **sammen**
+til'/satte pt of **-sette**
+til'/se V -så, -sett inspect, keep an eye on, watch.
*til'seg/komen [/kåmen] A -e/-i, pl -ne thoroughly awake; come to.
*til'/segn [/sengn] -a cf **/sagn**
*til'/seiing -a cf **/sigelse**
+til'/sende V -te send (to): **jeg har fått det t-t** it was sent to me.
til'/setning -en 1 addition; additive, admixture (**av** of). 2 seasoning; dash.
+til'/sette V -satte (=*/setje) 1 add (to); mix, season: **t-satt kinin** with quinine added; **t-satt vitaminer** vitamin enriched. 2 appoint (to a position). 3 naut. set, spread (sails).
+til'/setting -a/-en (=*/setjing) appointment (**av** of).
+til'/si V -sa, -sagt 1 order (cab, etc.); archaic call in, summon. 2 leave a call for (sby) (usu. long distance, for a certain time). 3 grant, pledge, promise.
+tilsi'de/sette V -satte, -satt 1 disregard, ignore, neglect; pass over (in promotions). 2 jur. reverse, set aside.
+tilsi'de/settelse -n disregard, neglect, slight(ing): **med t- av** in defiance of.
til'/sig -et gentle inflow, seepage, tributary; fig. nourishment: **få t- (av)** be fed (by).
+til'/sigelse -n (=/siing) 1 calling, order, summons. 2 (long distance) call (for a specified person).
+til'/sikte V -et aim at, have in view, intend: **t-et** deliberate, intended, intentional; **den t-ede virkning** the desired result.
+tilska'de/kommet A -, pl -komne (=*/kom(m)en) injured: **den tilskadekomne** the victim.
+til'/skikkelse -n chance, decree, dispensation; (turn of) fate: **ved skjebnens t-** as fate would have it.
*til'/skipa A - adjusted, arranged.
+til'/skjære V infl as **skjære**[3] cut (cloth); trim (shrubbery).

+til`/skjærer *-en, pl -e* (=***/skjerar**) (shoemaker's, tailor's) cutter.
***til`/skodar** [/skåar] *-en* cf **/skuer**
til`/skott *-et* (=***/skot**) 1 contribution, grant, subsidy (**til** to). 2 *fig.* addition, contribution, supply: **t- til utviklingen** contribution to development.
+til'/skrev *pt of* **-skrive**
til`/skrift *-a/+-en* address; heading.
+til'/skrive *V -skrev, -skrevet* 1 ascribe, attribute to; blame, credit. 2 *archaic* write to; add (in writing).
+til`/skudd *-et* cf **/skott**
+til`/skuer *-en, pl -e* spectator; *(pl)* audience.
+til`skuer/plass *-en* 1 (spectator) seat. 2 auditorium, grandstand, etc.
***til'/skunding** *-a* cf **/skyndelse**
***til`/skuv** *-en* impulse, stimulus; encouragement, stimulation; **gje t- til** prompt, stimulate.
+til'/skynde *V -te* encourage, prompt, stimulate; incite, instigate (**til** to).
+til'/skyndelse *-n* impulse, stimulus; encouragement, stimulation; incitation, instigation (**til** to).
til`/slag *-et* 1 hit, strike (of fish). 2 bang of auctioneer's gavel "knocking down" an item: **få t-et** get one's bid accepted, have sth knocked down to one. 3 *tech.* flux.
til'/slutning *-en* (=***/slutnad**) 1 affiliation; connection: **i t- til** in c- with, in continuation of. 2 acceptance, approval, endorsement (**til** of); response, support, sympathy: **i t- til** in support of. 3 adherents, following; (good, poor) attendance. 4 *gram.*: **med fast t-** checked (vowel); **med løs t-** free.
+til'/sluttet *A* - affiliated, attached, connected: **stå t- en forening** be a member of a society.
til'/sløre *V -te* 1 veil; conceal: **t-te bondepiker** brown Betty with whipped cream.
+til'/smu'rt *A* - (=***/smurd**) smeared.
+til'/smusse *V -et* 1 dirty, soil. 2 *fig.* blacken, defile, sully: **t- fedrelandet** besmirch, smear one's country.
+til'/snakke *V -et* 1 accost, talk to (a stranger, esp. for no good purpose). 2 reprimand.
+til'/snike *V -snek, -sneket* acquire insidiously, by sneaky means: **t- seg tillit** worm one's way into (sby's) confidence.
+til'/snikelse *-n* (=***-ing**) trickery; deliberate misrepresentation, willful suppression of facts.
til`/snitt *-et* appearance, character, stamp.
***til'/snunad** *-en* direction, turn, twist (of fate).
til'/snødd *A -/*-snøtt* snow-covered.
til'/snø'rt *A* - laced up.
+til'/spisse *V -et* point, sharpen, taper: **t-et** pointed, sharpened; exaggerated: **t- seg** become critical, more acute.
til`/sprang *-et* 1 running start. 2 attempt, effort (*til* at, to).
til`/stand *-en/*-et* 1 condition, state: **i dårlig t-** in poor c-; **i bevisstløs t-** (in an) unconscious (s-). 2 situation: **den nåværende t-** the present s-; **det skulle bli t-** that would be a mess.
+til'/stede[1] *V -te lit.* allow, grant, permit (**at** to).
+tilste'de[2] *Av* cf **stede[1]**
+tilste'de/komst *-en* arrival: **ved hans t-** on his a-, when he arrived.
+tilste'delig *A* - admissible, allowable, permissible.
+tilste'de/værelse *-n* 1 presence. 2 existence, occurrence (**av** of).
+tilste'de/værende *A* - in attendance, present: **de t-** those p-.
+til'/stelning *-en* (=***/stelling**) 1 arrangement, preparation (**av** of). 2 entertainment, festivity, party.
***til'/stemne** *-a* direction, tendency, trend; attempt, effort (**til** to).
+til'/stille *V -stilte* forward, remit; send, transmit (to).
til'/stod *pt of* **-stå**
+til'/stoppe *V -et* block, clog, plug; stop up.
+til'/strebe *V -et* strive for, toward; aspire to.
tilstrek'kelig *A* - 1 adequate, enough, sufficient.
+tilstrek'kelig/het *-en* adequacy, sufficiency.
+til'/strømning *-en* (=***/strøyming**) 1 flow, rush: **t- av blod** r- of blood. 2 flocking, influx (of people, capital); crowd (**av** of): **det er stor t- til stykket** people are flocking to the play.
+til'stundende *A* - approaching, coming, forthcoming.
***til'/styrking** *-a* encouragement, impulse, stimulus; recommendation, support.
***til'/støring** *-a* see **/styrking**
+til'/støte *V -te* befall, happen (to): **jeg er redd det har t-t ham noe** I'm afraid he has had an accident.
+til'/støtende *A* - 1 adjacent, adjoining, neighboring. 2 unexpected, unforeseen (circumstances).
til'/stå *V -stod, -stått* 1 admit, confess, own up to; *jur.* plead guilty. 2 *lit.* accord, grant; allow.
+til'/ståelse *-n* (=***-ing**) admission, confession.
tilsv. =**tilsvarende**
til`/svar *-et* 1 reply. 2 *jur.* liability: **på eget ansvar og t-** on one's own responsibility.
+til'/svare *V -te* correspond, (be) equal (to).
til'/svarende *A* - corresponding, equivalent; comparable, proportional.
+til'/sverge *V infl as* **sverge** swear to, vow (sby): **t- en troskap** s- allegiance to sby.
+til'/svindle *V -et*: **t- seg noe** get sth by fraud.
til`/syn *-et/*-a* 1 inspection, supervision: **holde skarpt t-** keep a sharp watch. 2 manager, superintendent, supervision. 3 *pol.* (international) trusteeship.
+tilsy'ne/komst *-en* appearance.
+tilsy'ne/latende *A* - apparent, ostensible, seeming; deceptive, feigned; *(adv.)* apparently, ostensibly.
***til`syns/havar** *-en* inspector, proctor.
+til`syns/havende *-en* inspector, proctor.
til`syns/mann *-en, pl menn/*-menner* 1 director, inspector, supervisor. 2 *(bibl.)* bishop.
til`syns/nemnd *-a* board of supervisors, of control; directorate, steering comittee.
til`syns/rådet *df pol.* the Trusteeship Council (of the UN).
+til'/søle *V -te* soil, sully (**av** by).
+til'/så[1] *V -dde* sow (an area).
+til'/så[2] *pt of* **-se**
+til'/ta *V -tok, -tatt* 1 grow, increase: **t- i vekt** add weight. 2: **t- seg** take over, usurp (authority).
+til'/tagende *A* - growing, increasing, waxing (e.g. moon): **være i t-** be growing.
til`/tak *-et* 1 attempt; enterprise, undertaking, venture: **et nytt t-** a new v-. 2 effort, exertion: **det er et enormt t- å gå og legge seg** it's an enormous effort to go to bed (Boo). 3 initiative; daring: **mangle t-** lack enterprise, i-.
***til`tak/sam** *A* enterprising.
til`taks/laus *A* - (=**+/løs**) unenterprising, without initiative.
til`taks/lyst *-a/+-en* drive, enterprise, initiative.
til`taks/løs *A* cf **/laus**
til`taks/løyse *-a* lack of initiative.
til`taks/råd *-et* (community) planning commission (e.g. to promote industry and tourism).
til`/tale[1] **-a/-en* 1 address: **gi svar på t-** give tit for tat, return the compliment. 2 *jur.* charge, indictment: **reise t- mot en** bring a charge against sby; **være under t-** be under i-.
+til'/tale[2] *V -te* 1 address, speak to. 2 *jur.* charge, indict, prosecute. 3 appeal to, attract, please (see **t-ende**).
til`tale/benk *-en* prisoner's dock: **sitte på t-en** be on trial, stand trial.
+til`tale/beslut'ning *-en jur.* indictment.
til'/talende *A* - attractive; appealing, pleasing; commendable, likeable.
til`tale/o'rd *-et* term of address.
+til'/talte *df* (the) accused, defendant.
***til'/teljing** *-a* appeal, demand, request.
+til'/tenke *V -te* intend for: **den kulen var t-t meg** that bullet was meant for me.
til'/tjukning *-a* clouding up: **t- til regn** *meteor.* increasing cloudiness, turning to rain.
+til'/tok *pt of* **-ta**
+til'/trakk *pt of* **-trekke**
+til'/tre *V -trådte* 1 enter into, upon, take over (a position); step into; embark upon, start (a journey). 2 concur with, subscribe to, sign (an agreement, pact).
+til'/tredelse *-n* 1 accession (**i** to); beginning (of a term of office), entry. 2 agreement, concurrence, endorsement (**til** of).
+til'tredelses/preken *-en* inaugural sermon.
+til'tredelses/tale *-n* inaugural address.
+til'/trekke *V -trakk, -trukket* 1 attract, draw; captivate, fascinate.
+til'/trekkende *A* - alluring, attractive, fascinating.
+til'/trekning *-en* attraction, charm, fascination.
+til'treknings/kraft *-en* 1 *phys.* force of attraction. 2 power of attraction.
+til'/trenge *V -te* need: usu. **t-es** is n-ed; **t-t** n-ed.
+til'/tro[1] *-en* cf **/tru[1]**
+til'/tro[2] *V -dde* cf **/tru[2]**
til'/tru[1] *-a* confidence, faith, trust (**til** in): **vinne t-** gain acceptance.
til'/tru[2] *V -dde* credit with; believe, expect of: **det kunne jeg t- ham** *(pop.)* I wouldn't put it past him.
+til'/trukket [/trokket] *pp of* **-trekke**
+til'/trådte *pt of* **-tre**
+til'/tuske *V -a/-et*: **t- seg** get by barter.
+til'/tvinge *V -et*: **t- seg** gain by force; **t- seg adgang** force one's way in; **t- seg oppmerksomhet** compel attention.
+til'/tykning *-en* cf **/tjukning**
***til'/tøk** *A* enterprising, full of initiative.
***til'/tøke** *-t* enterprise; undertaking.
***til'/tøken** *A -e/-i, pl -ne* cf **/tøk**
+til'/vant *A* - (=***/vand**) 1 accustomed, used (to): **godt t- a-** to comfort. 2 customary, habitual: **det t-e** the usual thing.
+tilvei'e/bringe *V -brakte, -brakt* 1 find, procure, provide (e.g. money, proof). 2 bring (about), produce (a result).
til`/vekst *-en* 1 addition, growth, increase (**i** of). 2 recruitment (**av** of) (e.g. younger talents). 3 *math.* increment
+til'/vende *V -te*: **t- seg** appropriate, embezzle.
+til'/venning *-en* (=***/venjing**) addiction, habituation; adaptation (**til** to).
***til'/verande** *A* - existing.
***til'/vere** *-a* cf **/værelse**
***til'verings/rett** *-en* right to exist.
***til'/verke** *V -a* cf **/virke**
***til'/verknad** *-en* cf **/virkning**
***til'/verk(n)ing** *-a* cf **/virkning**

+ Bokmål; * Nynorsk; ° Dialect.
After letter: ' stress (Acc. 1); ` tone, stress (Acc. 2); · length.
Below letter: . not pronounced.

*til'/vik -et 1 help, helpfulness, service. 2 tendency.

+til'/virke V -a/-et (=*/verke) make, manufacture (e.g. a product); prepare, process (e.g. fish).

+til'/virkning -en manufacture; preparation, processing (av of).

til'/vise V -te 1 merc. OK (a bill) for payment. 2 refer.

til'/vising -a/+-en reference, referral.

+tilvis'se Av cf visse[2]

*til'/vokster -en 1 addition, increase. 2 development, growth.

til'/være -t cf /værelse

+tilvæ'relse -n (=/være, +/vær) being, existence, life: kampen for t-n the struggle for e-; en t- etter døden a l- after death; *han lever i det nye tilværet med heile seg he lives his new l- with his whole being (Vesaas).

tilå'rs/kommen A +-ent, pl -komne (=*/komen) along in years, middle-aged, no longer young.

*ti'm pr of timje

*ti'mast V timdest, timst cf times

*tim'ber -et cf tømmer

*tim'd -a sight; first glimpse (av of).

*tim'de pt of timje

*tim'dest pt of timast

ti'me[1] -n 1 hour: bestille t- hos tannlegen make an appointment at the dentist's; for en t- siden an hour ago; i en t- for an hour; om en t- in an hour (after an hour has passed); på en t- in an hour (throughout an hour's time); på t-n at once, instantly; 60 kilometer i t-n 60 kilometers an (per) hour; 20 kroner t-n 20 kroner an (per) hour. 2 class, lesson (period): ha t- i norsk teach a Norwegian class; jeg har t- nå I'm teaching a class now; ta t-r i norsk take (private) Norwegian lessons.

*ti'me[2] V -de bring (oneself) to, feel like, have the energy to (see times).

*ti'me[3] V -de chime.

Ti'me Pln twp, Rogaland.

ti'me/beta'ling -a/+-en hourly pay, wage: få t- be paid by the hour.

ti'me/beta'lt A - paid by the hour: t- arbeid timework.

time/charter [tai'm/sja'rter] -et/-chartret naut. time charter (=contract for use of cargo ships).

ti'me/glas -et (=+/glass) hourglass.

ti'me/lang A hour-long, lasting for hours; endless.

ti'melig A - earthly, temporal, wordly; secular.

+ti'me/lærer -en, pl -e (=*-ar) educ. (usu. part-time) teacher, paid by the hour.

ti'me/lønn -a/+-en (=*/løn) hourly pay, wage.

ti'me/lønt A - paid by the hour.

ti'me/plan -en educ. (class) schedule, timetable.

+ti'mes V -tes, -es (=*-ast) 1 befall, happen; be granted (å to). 2 dial. (usu. neg.) allow (bring) oneself to, feel like, have the energy to.

+ti'me/skriver -en, pl -e (=*-ar) timekeeper.

ti'me/slag -et striking of the hour.

ti'me/tabell' -en (class) schedule; timetable.

ti'me/tal -et (=+/tall) 1 (number of) hours (worked): i t- for hours. 2 numbers of clock.

ti'me/vis Av: t- or i t- for hours, hour after hour.

+ti'me/viser -en, pl -e (=*-ar) hour hand.

tim'ian -en bot. thyme (Thymus).

*tim'je V tim, timde, timt glimpse, perceive: alt som ein kan t- av låtar all the sounds one can p- (Vesaas).

timotei' -en bot. timothy (Phleum pratense).

*tim'st pp of timast

*tim't pp of timje

+ti'mtes pt of times

*tin' -et cf tinn[1]

*ti'nar -en cf tenar[1]

tin'd -en 1 (mountain) peak, pinnacle, summit, top (also fig.). 2 merlon (on a battlement). 3 tine, tooth (on an implement, a tool).

+tin'de[1] -n cf tind

tin'de[2] V -a/+-et set teeth into sth (as a rake).

+tin'de/besti'ger -en, pl -e mountain climber.

+tin'de/besti'gning -en mountain climbing.

*tin'de/klivar -en mountain climber.

*tin'der[1] -ra, pl -rer anat. diaphragm.

+tin'der[2] -et sparkle, twinkle; sheen, shine; light timbre (of voice).

tin'det(e) A - crenelated; peaked; toothed.

tin'dre V -a/+-et scintillate, sparkle, twinkle; glitter, shine; beam, flash (with anger, joy, etc.); tinkle: det t-er av glede i hennes øyne her eyes sparkle with joy; t-ende sparkling, etc.; (adv.) t-gal hopping mad; t- morsom sparkling; t- våken wide awake.

tin'd/ved -en bot. sea buckthorn (Hippophaë rhamnoides).

ti'ne[1] -a round or oval bentwood box, with handled lid which is pressed between two upright projections.

ti'ne[2] V -a/-te melt (bort away) (av off); thaw (opp out).

*ti'ne[3] V -te 1 winnow (chaff from) grain. 2 pick fish from a net.

ting'[1] -en, pl - thing (either of physical objects, or of non-material "things"=affair, matter; often very vague in its reference): gjøre t-en enda verre make matters still worse; ingen verdens t- absolutely nothing, nothing whatever; kunne sine t- know one's job, one's stuff; passe sine t- attend to one's business; de tjente penger så det var store t- fam. they earned money hand over fist.

ting'[2] -et (usu. small, helpless) being, creature: et riktig forførende lite t- med smilehuller og kruset hår a really enchanting little c- with dimples and curly hair (Scott).

ting'[3] -et 1 hist. thing (legislative and judicial assembly of free men in Scandinavian Middle Ages): holde t- hold a meeting, council. 2 jur. court (session): til t-s to c-. 3 legislature, parliament: komme på t-et be elected to parliament (=the Storting). 4 assembly (of representatives, e.g. of sports clubs).

ting'/bok -a, pl -bøker jur. court register.

ting'/bu -a hist. hut in which tingmann lived while at the Alting (in Iceland).

+ting'e[1] N: på t- poet. at the thing (see ting[3] 1); at court.

ting'e[2] V -a/+-et 1 bargain (om for), dicker, haggle (om over); negotiate. 2 book, contract for, reserve; subscribe (på to): t- på put in a request for, speak for.

ting'el/tangel -(e)let raucous musical entertainment.

+ting'er -en, pl -e (=*-ar) subscriber.

ting'est [also ting'-] -en little thing; (pop.) dingus, doohickey.

ting'/fred -en hist. conditions of peace, armistice (supposed to prevail during thing).

ting'/hus -et courthouse.

*ting'ings/mann -en, pl -menn(er) negotiator.

ting'/lag -et (smallest) judicial district.

ting'le V -a/+-et tinkle.

ting'/lese V -te jur. file, record, register.

+ting'lig A - jur. real: t- rett law (rights) of real property.

ting'/lyse V -te hist., jur. announce legal action at public assembly (the thing), giving it binding force.

ting'lysings/attes't -en registration certificate.

ting'/mann -en, pl -menn/*-menner 1 member of parliament (Storting). 2 hist. delegate at a thing; follower of a particular chief (see gode[1]).

ting'/muge -n crowd of people at a thing.

*ting'/sete -a session of the Storting.

ting's/rett -en jur. law of real property.

ting'/stue -a (=*/stove) hist. courtroom.

ting's/vitne -t, pl +-r/*- archaic taking of evidence, testimony.

ting'/voll -en hist. plain traditionally used for meeting of thing.

Ting'/voll Pln twp, Møre og Romsdal.

*tin'kle V -a tinkle.

tinktu'r -en 1 pharm. tincture (e.g. of iodine). 2 thin solution of bronze-tinted lacquer.

tinn' -et 1 chem. tin (an element). 2 pewter (bowl, button, plate, vase, etc.).

Tinn' Pln twp, Telemark.

tinn'/fat -et pewter dish.

tinn'/folie -n tinfoil.

tin'ning -en anat. temple.

tin'ning/bein -et anat. temporal bone.

tinn'/solda't -en tin soldier.

+tinn'/taller'ken -en (=*/tallerk) pewter plate, platter.

tin't -en dial. small beaker, jar; vial.

tin'te -a zool. bladder worm (Cystercicus); vet., (pl) measles (a tapeworm).

ti'-pakning +-en/*-a pack of ten cigarettes.

tip'le V -a/+-et dial. 1 drip. 2 tipple.

tipp'[1] -en end, extremity, tip (esp. of body part).

tipp'[2] -en 1 dump (in filling). 2 dump body (on truck).

tipp'[3] -et cf tips

tipp- Pf great-great-.

+tip'pe[1] -a dial. 1 biddy, hen. 2 hum. (of girl) chick.

tip'pe[2] V -a/+-et 1 tip (e.g. a waiter). 2 bet (on), predict: t- på guess. 3 bet in a (betting) pool.

tip'pe[3] V -a/+-et tip (over), unbalance.

tip'pe[4] V -a/+-et dial. dribble, drip; press out in drops.

tip'pe/kupong' -en betting slip, post coupon.

+tip'pe/midler pl (=*-ar) surplus receipts from the state-run betting pool (used for support of athletics and science).

tip'pe/premie -n (=*/premi) prize for winning a betting pool.

+tip'per -en, pl -e (=*-ar) 1 bettor (in pool). 2 dump body, dump truck.

tip'pe/selskap -et, pl -/+-er (betting) pool organization.

tipp(e)tipp' I (used to call chickens) chick-chick-chick.

tipp'/oldefar -en, pl +-fedre/*-fedrar great-great-grandfather.

tipp'/oldemor -a/+-en, pl -mødrer/+-mødre great-great-grandmother.

tipp'/vogn [/vångn] -a dump car, tipcart.

tip's -et, pl - 1 dope, inside information, odds, tip. 2 gratuity, tip.

tira'de -n 1 tirade (flood of words). 2 mus. run.

tiraljø'r -en mil. skirmisher.

*ti're V -te 1 stare; peek. 2 gleam, sparkle.

*ti'ren A -e/-i, pl -ne gleaming, sparkling.

ti'ril/tunge [/tonge] -a (=*tiri/) bot. babies' slippers (Lotus corniculatus).

*tir'le V -a blow gently; chirp, twitter.

tir're V -a/+-et tease; provoke.

+ti'rs/dag -en (=*tys/) Tuesday.

+ti'r/øyd A - (=*/øygd) dial. bright-eyed, with sparkling eyes.

°tis'/dag -en cf tirs/

tis'ke *V -a/+-et* whisper; buzz, gossip, tattle.
tis'pe *-a* 1 *zool.* bitch. 2 hussy, whore.
tiss'[1] *-et* pee (children's word).
°**tiss'**[2] *A* - cf **tids**
tis'se *V -a/+-et* pee (children's word).
tis't *-en dial.* strand, tuft, wisp.
tis'tel *-elen, pl -ler bot.* thistle (Cirsium).
tis'tet(e) *A* - wispy.
ti't *-en* (=**tite**[1]) *dial.* 1 small bird (as titmouse); small fish. 2 nubbin.
ti'tal/syste'm *-et* (=+**titall/**) decimal system.
tita'n[1] *-en myth.* titan.
tita'n[2] *-et chem.* titanium.
tita'nisk *A* - titanic.
ti'te[1] *-a* cf **tit**
ti'te[2] *V -a* chirp, twitter.
ti'ting *-en dial.* snow bunting; junco; grey sparrow.
+**tit'ler** *pl of* **tittel**
tit're *V -a/+-et* 1 quiver, tremble; shiver: ***det t-ar i Viv med ho les*** V- shivers as she is reading (Vesaas). 2 twitter.
titre're *V -te chem.* titrate.
titre'r/væske *-a/+-en chem.* titrant.
titt'[1] *-en* 1 glimpse, peek(ing): **stå på t-** peek; **leke t-** play peekaboo (see also **titter 2**). 2 *fam.* brief visit: **takk for t-en** thanks for dropping in.
titt'[2] *Av, cp +tiere/*tiare, sp +tiest/*tiast* (=***tidt**) 1 often: **t- og ofte** again and again; **så t-** *(conj.)* whenever. 2 *(comp.)* again; oftener. 3 *(sup.)* usually; most often: **som t-** as a rule; *dial.* **rett som t-** every once in a while.
tit'te *V -a/+-et* 1 peek, peep; glance: **t- opp** look up. 2: **t- innom** drop in, look in on.
tit'tel *-elen, pl titler* title (**på** of) (book, person, etc.): **legge bort titlene** drop (name) formalities, use the pronoun *du*.
tit'tel/blad *-et* title page.
+**tit'tel/innehaver** *-en, pl -e* (=***-ar**) title holder.
tit'tel/kamp *-en* championship game, match.
tit'tel/rolle *-a/+-en*: **spille t-n** play the lead (in a drama).
+**tit'ter** *-en, pl -e* (=***-ar**) 1 one who peeks; Peeping Tom. 2 "It" in hide-and-seek: **t-n på hjørnet** hide-and-seek.
titulatu'r *-en* form of address, title.
titule're *V -te* address (sby as): **en som selv t-er seg geni** a self-styled genius.
titulæ'r *A* titular.
+**titu'sener** *pl* tens of thousands.
ti'ur *-en zool.* capercaillie, wood grouse (Tetrao urogallus).
ti'ur/høne *-a* capercaillie, wood grouse hen.
ti'ur/leik *-en* capercaillie mating game (also of wooded area where this usually takes place).
tiv'oli *et* amusement park, carnival.
ti'/øre *-n* (=**/øring**) ten *øre* coin.
ti'/år *-et* decade.
ti'/års *A* - ten-year-old; ten-year; tenth.
ti'års/dag *-en* tenth birthday; tenth anniversary (**for** of).
tja' *I* hm, well (doubt; indifference; polite regret).
***tjad're** *V -a* chatter, jabber.
tjaf's *-en* 1 tuft, wisp; tangle. 2 *dial.* bite, snatch.
tjaf'set(e) *A* - shaggy, tangled, unkempt: **boka er t- i kantene** the edges of the book are ragged (Bojer).
***tjasen** [kja'sen] *A -e/-i, pl -ne* exhausted, fatigued.
tjau [kjau'] *-et* (=**tjug**) *dial.* score (20).
tjeld[1] [kjel'] *-en zool.* oyster catcher (Haematopus ostralegus).
tjel'd[2] *-et* 1 *hist.* tapestry. 2 *hist.* canvas shelter, tent. 3 *dial.* shawl.
tjel'de *V -a/+-et hist.* 1 hang with tapestries. 2 roof over with canvas; pitch a tent.
Tjel'd/sund *Pln* twp, Nordland.
+**tje'ne** *V -te* (=***tene**) 1 serve (one's country, a master, a purpose, etc.); be of service; minister (**til** to): **t- som hushjelp hos noen** serve as household help in sby's house; **t- i krigen** serve in the war; **t- til noe** be used as, serve as sth; tend to: **hva t-er det til** what's the good of that; **t- til ens heder, ære** be to one's credit; **t- til ingenting** do no good; **t- sin verneplikt** serve one's time in the military. 2 earn (a living, money, a reward), gain, make (a fortune, a profit, etc.): **t- på noe** make a profit on sth. 3 *(refl.)*: **t- seg opp penger** earn and save up money: **t- seg rik** make a fortune. 4: **t-t** served; **jeg er ikke t-t med det** it is not to my advantage.
+**tje'ner** *-en, pl -e* (=***tenar**[2]) servant; butler, valet.
+**tje'ner/bolig** *-en* servants' quarters (house).
+**tje'ner/fløy** *-a/-en* servant's wing.
+**tjenerin'ne** *-n* (=***tenarinne**) woman servant; chambermaid, maid; *(bibl.)* handmaiden.
+**tje'ner/skap** *-et* domestic staff, servants.
+**tje'ner/stab** *-en* domestic staff, servants.
+**tje'ner/stand** *-en* servant class.
+**tje'nest-** *Pf* cf **tjenst-**
+**tje'neste** *-n* (=***tenest(e)**) *(admin., eccl., mil., etc.)* service; favor, good turn, kindness: **den ene t- er den annen verd** one good turn deserves another; (usu. *dial.*) **etter t-n** after services, after church; **gjøre en en t-** do one a favor; **gjøre t- som** be used as, serve as; **til t-** of service; at (one's) disposal; **være i t- hos en** be employed in one's household.
+**tje'neste-** *Pf* also cf **tjenst-** servant, service, serving: **t-/pike.**
+**tje'neste/anlig'gende** *-t* official business.
+**tje'neste/attes't** *-en* testimonial of service.
+**tje'neste/brev** *-et* official communication.
+**tje'neste/dyktig** *A* - fit for military service.
+**tje'neste/folk** *-et* (=***teneste/**) servants; hired help.
+**tje'neste/fri** *A -tt* off duty, on leave.
+**tje'neste/frihet** *-en* leave.
+**tje'neste/frimerke** *-t* official stamp (postage), service stamp.
+**tje'neste/gutt** *-en* hired man.
+**tje'neste/iver** *-en* eagerness to serve, zeal.
+**tje'neste/kar** *-en* (=***teneste/**) hired man.
+**tje'neste/kvinne** *-a/-en* (=***teneste/**) *hist.* woman servant.
+**tje'neste/mann** *-en, pl -menn* 1 *hist.* man servant. 2 official, public servant.
+**tje'neste/merke** *-t* official stamp (postage), service stamp.
+**tje'neste/pike** *-a/-en archaic* maid, servant girl; hired girl.
+**tje'neste/plikt** *-a/-en* duty to serve, official duty.
+**tje'neste/reise** *-a/-en* official trip.
+**tje'neste/sak** *-a/-en* official business, matter.
+**tje'neste/skriv** *-et* official communication.
+**tje'neste/tid** *-a/-en* 1 period of service. 2 office hours.
+**tje'neste/udyktig** *A* - unfit for military service.
+**tje'nlig** *A* - (=***tenleg**) fit, usable; serviceable, useful: **det er t- å** it pays to.
+**tje'nst-** *Pf* also cf **tjeneste-** service.
+**tje'nst/gjøre** *V -gjorde, -gjort admin., mil.* fulfill one's duty, serve.
+**tjen'st/gjørende** *A* - on active duty.
+**tje'nst/ivrig** *A* - eager, zealous; *(pop.)* an eager beaver.
+**tje'nstlig** *A* - (=***tenestleg**) official: **ad t- vei** through o- channels.
+**tjen'st/villig** *A* - helpful, obliging.
+**tje'nstvillig/het** *-en* helpfulness, obligingness.
***tjere** [kje're] *-a* cf **tjære**[1]
tjern [kjæ'rn] *-et* (=**tjørn**) pond, small lake, tarn.
t-jern [te'-jæ'rn] *-et tech.* T bar.
tjerne/blom [kjæ'rne/, +/blåmm] *-en dial.* water lily.
***tjerv** [kjær'v] *A* flat-tasting, tasteless.
tjo[1] [kjo'] *-et* neck of a scythe or sickle (part that fits into the handle).
tjo[2] [kjo'] *I* whoop of joy, yippee.
***tjod** (kjo'] *-a* nation, people.
***tjodleg** [kjo'dleg] *A* - national.
***tjod/skap** [kjo'd/skap] *-en* nationality.
tjoe [kjo'e] *V -a/+-et* whoop with joy; shout.
tjon [kjo'n] *-et dial.* 1 (of thing) annoyance, irritation; clumsy person, fool. 2 chore(s), toil. *3 harm; destruction.
tjone [kjo'ne] *V +-te/*-a dial.* 1 be busy at, bustle, putter. 2 care for, take care (**for, med** of). *3 harm; destroy, ruin.
***tjonsleg** [kjo'nsleg] *A* - disagreeable, nasty, ugly.
***tjor**[1] [kjo'r] *-en* ox.
tjor[2] [kjo'r] *-et* tether.
tjore [kjo're] *V -a/+-te* stake, tether; *naut.* make fast, moor.
***tjore/fektar** [kjo're/] *-en* cf **tyre/-fekter**
°**tju** [kju'] *-en* cf **tjuv**
+**tjua/gutt** [kju'a/] *-en* (=***/gut**) *hum.* kid, rascal, scamp (orig. used of the street boys of Bergen, now mostly to imply good humor).
tjue[1] [kju'e] *Num* twenty.
°**tjue**[2] [kju'e] *V -a* steal.
tjue/del *-en* (fraction) twentieth.
+**tjueen** [kjue-e'n] *Num* twenty-one.
tjueførste [kjuefør'ste] *Num* (=***-fyrste**) twenty-first.
tjuende [kju'ene] *Num* twentieth.
tjuende/dag *-en* Jan. 13 (in older times, the last day of Christmas).
tjuende/del *-en* cf **tjue/**
tjug [kju'g] *-et* cf **tjau**
tjuge[1] [kju'ge] *-a* (hay) fork, forked pole.
tjuge[2] [kju'ge] *Num* cf **tjue**[1]
tjukk [kjukk'] *A tjukt* (=+**tykk**) 1 thick (lips, plank, soup, etc.); dense (darkness, forest, etc.); muddy, turbid (liquids, etc.): **t-t av folk** a huge crowd; **midt i t-e byen** right in the middle of the city. 2 corpulent, fat, stout; swollen; *fam.* pregnant. 3 *pop.* stupid: **t- i hue** dense. 4 thick (=very improbable, unlikely, etc.): **den var for t-** don't hand me that; **humbugen blir for t-** the humbug is becoming too obvious.
tjukka [kjuk'ka] *df pop.* (of a girl, woman) fatso.
tjukkas [kjuk'kas] *-en* (=+**tykkas**) *pop.* (of a boy, man) fatso.
***tjukke**[1] [kjuk'ke] *-a* 1 fog; dense air; whirling snow. 2 curd.
tjukke[2] [kjuk'ke] *-n* cf **tjukn**
tjukken [kjuk'ken] *df pop.* (of a boy or man) fatso.
tjukk/eng [kjukk'/] *-a* meadow with a heavy stand of grass.
tjukk/fallen *A +-ent, pl -falne* heavy-set, stout.
***tjukk/huding** *-en zool.* pachyderm; *fig.* thick-skinned (insensitive) person.
tjukking [kjuk'king] *-en pop.* fat person, fatso.

+ Bokmål; * Nynorsk; ° Dialect.
After letter: ' stress (Acc. 1); ' tone, stress (Acc. 2); · length.
Below letter: . not pronounced.

tjukk/legg [kjukk'/] *-en* calf (of the leg).
***tjukk/leik** *-en* thickness.
tjukk/maga *A* - (=**+-et**) paunchy, pot-bellied, stout.
tjukk/mjølk *-a* curdled whole milk.
tjukk/mæ·lt *A* - with tearchoked voice.
***tjukk/ver** *-et* fog, foggy weather, mist.
tjukn** [kjuk'n] *-a* (=tjukke**[2]) girth, thickness.
tjukne [kjuk'ne] *V -a/+-et* (=**+tykne**) 1 become denser, fatter, thicker. 2 (of weather) become cloudier, darker, foggier: **t- til** (the same).
tjuv [kju'v] *-en* (=**+tyv**) 1 robber, thief; burglar. 2: **t- i lyset** (candle) snuff.
+tjuv/aktig [kju'v/] *A* - larcenous, thieving.
tjuve/gods [kju've/gots] *-et* stolen goods.
tjuve/pakk [kju've/] *-et* pack of thieves.
tjuveri [kju'(v)eri] *-et, pl +-er/*-* (=**+tyveri**) larceny, stealing, theft (**av** of).
tjuv/fiske [kju'/] *V -a/+-et* fish unlawfully.
***tjuving** [kju'(v)ing] *-a* larceny, stealing, theft.
tjuv/jo [kju'v/] *-en zool.* jaeger (Stercorarius parasiticus).
***tjuv/kjenne** [kju'/] *V infl as* **kjenne**[3] accuse (sby) of, berate (sby) for stealing.
tjuv/lese *V infl as* **lese** 1 read in secret, surreptitiously. 2 read over someone's shoulder.
+tjuv/lytte *V -a/-et* 1 listen to radio program without paying (state fee). 2 listen to forbidden radio program.
***tjuv/sam** *A* larcenous, thieving.
***tjuv/skap** *-en* theft.
tjuv/start *-en* false start, jumping the gun.
tjuv/starte *V -a/+-et* jump the gun, start before the gun goes off.
tjuv/trene *V -a/+-et/+-te* practice, train in secret.
tjære[1] [kjæ're] *-a* (=***tjøre**) tar.
tjære[2] *V -a/+-et* tar (a boat, rope, etc.).
+tjære/aktig *A* - tarry.
tjære/blom [+/blåmm] *+-men/*-en bot.* catchfly (Viscaria vulgaris); alpine campion (Viscaria alpina).
tjære/bre *V -dde* tar.
+tjære/brenner *-en, pl -e* (=***-ar**) tar maker.
tjære/farge *-n* coal tar dye.
+tjære/låg *-en* (=***/log**) liquid distilled in tar making (prob. =creosote oil).
tjære/papp *-en* tarpaper.
+tjære/smu·rt *A* - (=***/smurd**) tarred, tarry.
tjære/såpe *-a* tar soap.
tjæret(e) [kjæ'ret(e)] *A* - tarred, tarry.
tjære/tønne [kjæ're/] *-a* tar barrel.
***tjære/veie** *-a* (see **/låg**).
Tjølling [kjøl'ling] *Pln* twp, Vestfold.
Tjøme [kjø'me] *Pln* twp, Vestfold.
tjømling [kjøm'ling] *-en* person from Tjøme.
***tjøre** [kjø're] *-a* cf **tjære**[1]
tjørn [kjør'n] *-a* cf **tjern**
Tjøtta [kjøt'ta] *Pln* twp, Nordland.
***tjå** [kjå'] *V -dde* 1 hound, plague, torment. 2 rub, wear (against sth).
tjåk [kjå'k] *-et dial.* drudgery, toil, work.
tjåke [kjå'ke] *V -a/+-et dial.* drudge, toil, work.
tjåk/sam [kjå'k/, +samm] *A dial.* burdensome, toilsome, wearisome.
***tjåleg** [kjå'leg] *A* - burdensome, toilsome, wearisome.
tlf. =**telefon**
***to'**[1] *-a, pl tør* patch of grass.
to'[2] *-et/+-en* 1 innate ability, personal quality, stuff: **det er god to i ham** there's good s- in him. 2 tow; carded wool.
to'[3] *Num* two: **begge to** both of you, them, us; *(archaic* or *dial.)* **de var to e(i)ne** there were just the two of them; **gå på to** stand up; be on one's hind legs; **to ganger** twice; **to og to** by (in) twos, two by two; **to-tre** two or three; **være to om** share in (a task, a decision); **det skal vi bli to om** I'll see to it you don't get your way.
toalett' *-et, pl -/+-er* 1 (dress, grooming) toilet. 2 formal gown, dinner dress. 3 lavatory, powder room. 4 stool, toilet.
toalett'/bo·rd *-et* dressing table.
+toalett'/bøtte *-a* (=***/bytte**) slop pail.
toalett'/papi·r *-et* toilet paper.
toalett'/skrin *-et* vanity case.
toalett'/såpe *-a* toilet soap.
to'/arma *A* - (=**+-et**) two-armed.
tobakk' *-en* tobacco.
tobakk's/dåse *-n* tobacco tin.
tobakk's/pipe *-a* tobacco pipe.
tobakk's/pung [/pong] *-en* tobacco pouch.
tobakk's/rull *-en* roll of tobacco.
to'/beint *A* - two-legged: **t- dyr** biped.
tod'di *-en* toddy.
+to'/dekker *-en, pl -e* (=***-ar**) double-decker (plane, ship).
to'/deling *-a/+-en* 1 bisection; dichotomy. 2 bifurcation, forking.
to'/de·lt *A* - 1 besicted, divided into two parts: **t- badedrakt** two-piece bathing suit. 2 *mus.* double time. 3 bifurcated, forked.
+to'/dobbelt *A* - (=***/dobbel**) double(d).
+to'e *V -et archaic* wash: **t- sine hender** wash one's hands (of a problem, in allusion to Pilate).
to'/egga *A* - (=**+-et**): **t- tvillinger** fraternal twins.
***to'/eine** *Av* alone together, two alone.
+to'er *-en, pl -e* (=***-ar**) 1 (number, rating, etc.) two; two-spot; deuce. 2 (in rowing) two-man shell.
to'/eta·sjes *A* - two-story.
to'/fasa *A* - (=**+-et**) *elec.* two-phase.
***tof'le**[1] *-a* cf **tøffel**
***tof'le**[2] *V -a* cf **tøfle**
to'frø/blada *A* - (=**+-et**) *bot.* dicotyledonous.
***to'frø/blading** *-en bot.* dicotyledon.
tof'te *-a* seat (in boat), thwart.
tog [tå'g] *-et* 1 train: **reise med t-et** go by t-. 2 parade, procession: **gå i t-** parade. 3 excursion, expedition: **vikingenes tog** the forays of the vikings.
to'ga [also: tå'ga] *-en* toga.
toge [tå'ge] *V -a/+-et* be in a procession, march, parade.
+tog/forbin·delse [tå'g/] *-n* (train) connection, service: **hvordan er t-n med Bergen?** what trains are there for Bergen?
+tog/forsin·kelse *-n* (train) delay.
+tog/fører *-en, pl -e* (=***-ar**) (train) engineer.
***togg'** *pt of* **tyggje**
tog'ge** *pp of* **tyggje** (=toggi**)
***togn** [tång'n] *-a* silence.
***togne** [tång'ne] *V -a* grow, extend, stretch out; become slack (from being stretched).
tog/rute [tå'g/] *-a/+-en* timetable (for trains).
tog/skifte *-t* change of trains.
tog/tabell· *-en* timetable (for trains).
tog/tid [*/ti] *-a/+-en* train time.
+to'/hendig *A* - *mus.* for two hands.
to'k[1] *-en dial.* clod, fool.
to'k[2] *pt of* **ta**[1]
tokai'er *-en* Tokay (wine).
to'kammer/syste·m *-et pol.* bicameral system.
***toke** [tå'ke] *-a* roof.
***tokk'** *-en* little bit, particle, *(pop.)* smidgen.
tok'ke[1] *-n dial.* 1 feeling, impression. 2 nature (of a person): **han har en god t-** he is congenial.
tok'ke[2] *V -a/+-et dial.* move, shove: **t- seg** make room, move over.
***tok'ke/laus** *A* disagreeable.
***tok'keleg** *A* - agreeable.
***tok'ke/løyse** *-a* disagreeableness.
tok'n *-a* gills.
to'/krone *-a* (=**/kroning**) two-*kroner* coin.
toksi'n *-et med.* toxin; poison.
tok'sisk *A* - *med.* toxic.
***to'kst** *pt of* **takast**
tok't[1] *-a/+-en* attack, siege, spell.
tok't[2] *-et* (ocean) trip; (training) cruise; sea expedition: **på t-** cruising.
***tol** [tå'l] *-et* cf **tål**
+tol'der *-en, pl -e* cf **toller**
***tole** [tå'le] *V -te* cf **tåle**
tole'do/klinge *-n* Toledo (blade).
***tol'e/kniv** *-en* cf **tolle/**
***tolen** [tå'len] *A -e/-i, pl -ne* able to stand a lot; patient; sturdy.
toleranse [tålerang'se] *-n* tolerance (**for, overfor** of).
tolerant [tålerang't] *A* - tolerant (**overfor** of).
tolerere [tålere're] *V -te* tolerate; overlook, permit.
Tol'ga *Pln* twp, Hedmark.
***tolig** [tå'lig] *A* - cf **tålig**
tol'k *-en* interpreter; spokesman: **gjøre seg til t- for** become the spokesman of.
tol'ke *V -a/+-et* 1 interpret (lit. and *fig.*). 2 act as interpreter (for), spokesman of.
+tol'ker *-en, pl -e* (=***-ar**) interpreter (esp. *mus.*).
tol'king *-a/+-en* (=**+tolkning**) interpretation; presentation.
toll'[1] *-a* (=***tall**[1]) (young) pine.
toll/[2] *-en* 1 customs, duty, tariff (**på** on). 2 bureau of customs.
toll'[3] *-en* cf **tolle**[1]
tol'laks/mess(e) *en archaic* December 23.
+toll'/angivelse *-n* customs declaration.
toll'/avgift [/a'vjift] *-a/+-en* duty.
toll'/behan·dling *-a/+-en* clearance through customs.
+toll'/beskyt·telse *-n* protection (by tariff).
toll'/betjen·t *-en* customs officer.
toll'/bu *-a* customs house.
***tol'le**[1] *-n* (=**toll**[3]) *dial.* peg, pin; *naut.* thole(pin).
tol'le[2] *V -a* 1 charge duty. 2 pay duty.
Tol'lef *Prn (m)*
***tolleg** [tå'leg] *A* - cf **tålelig**
tol'le/gang *-en* oarlock.
tol'le/kniv *-en* sheath knife.
tol'le/pinne *-n naut.* thole(pin).
tol'ler** *-en, pl -e* (=-ar**) 1 customs officer. 2 *(bibl.)* publican.
toll'/fri *A -tt* duty free.
+toll'/frihet *-en* (=***/fridom**) duty-free status.
toll'/grense *-a/+-en* 1 border, customs boundary. 2 *fig.* tariff barrier.
toll'/inspektø·r *-en* chief customs officer (within one district).
toll'/kammer *-et* 1 customs office. 2 bureau of customs.
+toll'/kasse·rer *-en, pl -e* (=***-ar**) collector of customs.
toll'/klare·ring *-a/+-en* clearance through customs.
toll'/kniv *-en* cf **tolle/**
toll'/krig *-en* tariff war.
toll'/mur *-en* tariff barrier.
toll'/pliktig *A* - dutiable.
+toll'/sted *-et* customs house; port of entry.
toll'/tariff· *-en* tariff schedule(s).
toll'/vern [/væ'rn] *-et* tariff protection.
toll'/vesen *-et* bureau of customs, customs service.
***toll'/vind** *-en dial.* beam wind.
toll'/visitasjo·n *-en* customs inspection.
***tol/mod** [tå'l/] *-et* cf **tål/**
***tolmodig** [tålmo'di(g)] *A* - cf **tålmodig**
***tolmods/arbeid** [tål'mots/arbei] *-et* work requiring close and patient effort (e.g. dictionary making).

***tols** [tå'ls] *N* cf **tål**

***tol/sam** [tå'l/] *A* cf **tål/som**

tol/semd** *-a* (=tål/**) tolerance.

***tolug** [tå'lug] *A* - cf **tålig**

tol'v *Num* twelve: **ha t- av hvert** have a dozen of each; **på halv t-** halfway, unfinished; sloppy, unorganized; askew.

tol'v/del *-en* (fraction) twelfth.

+tol'ver *-en, pl -e* (=***-ar**) 1 number 12 (of anything); highest rating in a medical school examination. 2 sth that arrives, leaves at 12 o'clock.

tol'vfinger/tarm *-en anat.* duodenum.

tol'v/skilling *-en hist.* twelve-shilling piece (one tenth of a *riksdaler*).

tol'vte *Num* twelfth: **selv t-** *archaic* he (she, I) and eleven others.

tol'vte/del *-en* cf **tolv/**

+tom'[1] *-men* (=***taum**) *dial.* 1 (fish) line, string. 2 rein.

tom'[2] *A -t, pl -me* empty (bottle, chair, house, page, pleasure, threat, words, etc.); bare, deserted, vacant; empty-headed, expressionless, vapid.

t. o. m.=**til og med**

+to'manns/bolig *-en* duplex.

to'manns/bridge [/bridsj] *-n* two-handed bridge.

to'manns/hand *N*: **på t- med noen** alone with sby; **få en på t-** catch sby alone, get sby off by himself.

to'manns/telt *-et* two-man tent.

tom'as/fosfa't *-en/-et chem.* Thomas phosphate (basic slag, used as fertilizer).

tom'as/mess(e) *en hist.* St. Thomas day (Dec. 21).

+to'/master *-en, pl -e* (=***-ar**, ***/masting**) two-master.

toma't *-en* tomato.

toma't/ketsjup [/ketsjøpp] *-en* tomato ketchup.

toma't/puré *-en* tomato purée.

toma't/suppe *-a* tomato soup.

tom'bola *-en* lottery (usu. for charitable purpose).

tom'/flaske *-a* empty bottle.

tom'/gang *-en* idling (of an engine): **gå på t-** idle.

tom'/gods [/gots] *-et* empties, empty containers.

tom'/hendt *A* - (=***/hendes**) 1 empty-handed. 2 *fig.* without resources: **vi reiser t- en dag** one day we will depart empty-handed (Øverland).

+tom'/het *-en* blankness, emptiness; barrenness, desolation; futility, vanity: **hans død har etterlatt t-** his death has left a void.

+tom'hets/følelse *-n* feeling of emptiness, desolation.

+tom'/hjernet *A* - empty-headed, inane.

tom'me *-n* 1 (ab.=) inch. 2 *dial.* thumb.

tom'mel *-elen, pl tomler* thumb.

tom'mel/finger *-eren, pl +-rer/*-rar* (=***tumars/**) thumb.

Tommeli'se *Prn* Thumbelina.

Tommeli'ten *Prn* Tom Thumb.

+tommelomsk [tommelom'sk] cf **tummelumsk**

tom'mel/tott *-en* thumb: **ha to t-er på hver neve** be all t-s.

tom'mel/tå *-a, pl -tær zool.* big toe.

tom'me/skrue *-n* thumbscrew.

tom'me/stokk *-en* folding rule.

tom'/reipa *A* - (=**/reipes**) *dial.* without a load; empty-handed; footloose.

tom'/rom [/romm] *-met* 1 emptiness, space, void: **det ble et stort t- etter ham** he left a great v-; **stirre ut i t-met** stare into space. 2 *phys.* vacuum.

toms [tom's] *-en* empty head, fool.

tomse [tom'se] *V -a/+-et* fool around, talk nonsense: **t- med tankene** woolgather (Evensmo).

tom'/sekk *-en* empty sack.

tomsen [tom'sen] *A +-ent, pl -ne* cf **tomset(e)**

tomset(e) [tom'set(e)] *A* - 1 confused, flustered. 2 daffy, deranged.

tomsing [tom'sing] *-en* 1 fool, idiot. 2 insane person, loony.

tom'skips/linje *-a/+-en naut.* light waterline mark.

tom't *-a* 1 (building) lot, site. 2 yard; open (storage) area. 3: **på gamle t-er** at the (old) homestead, on familiar ground.

tom'te *-n folk.* (ab.=) brownie, gnome, puck.

tom'te/gubbe *-n folk.* brownie, gnome, little (old) man.

tom'te/spekulasjo'n *-en* speculation in (usu.) city lots.

***to'nad** *-en* 1 cloth, thread, yarn (esp. linen, hemp). 2 stuff: **det er t- i den karen** there's something to that fellow.

tona'l *A mus.* tonal.

tonalite't *-en mus.* tonality.

to'ne[1] *-n* 1 *mus.* note; pitch, tone: **en høy t-** a high note; **gi t-n** strike the pitch; *fig.* call the tune. 2 *mus.* air, melody, tune: **t-en på Ja vi elsker** the melody of *Ja vi elsker;* **til t-ne av** to the strains of. 3 sound, tone; music, song: **t-ns makt** the power of music; **lerkens t-** the song of the lark. 4 tone (of voice); intonation, pitch: **i en spørrende t-** in a questioning tone; **rose i høye t-er** praise extravagantly; **nordlandsk t-** North Norwegian speech melody. 5 manners, style: **god t-** good form; **falle ut av t-n** commit a faux pas; **finne t-n** hit the right note. 6 *fig.* note, ring, strain, tone: **en lyrisk t-** a lyrical strain. 7 (of colors) nuance, tint, tone: **i en lys t-** in light colors.

to'ne[2] *V -a/+-et/+-te* 1 sound; echo, resound, sing: **kirkeklokkene t-te i vinden** the church bells sang in the wind (Hoel); **t- ut** be resolved, die away. 2 *photog.* tone.

to'ne[3] *V -a/+-et/+-te* 1 show: **t- (rent) flagg** show one's (true) colors. 2 appear; loom (**fram** forth, up). 3 *poet.* disappear, fade (**bort, hen** away; **ut** out).

***to'ne**[4] [tå'ne] *V -a* stretch.

To'ne *Prn(f)*

+to'ne/angi'vende *A* - setting the tone, style-setting: **de t-** the leaders of fashion.

to'ne/art *-a/-en* 1 tone (of voice). 2 *mus.* key; mode.

to'ne/dikt *-et* composition, tone poem.

+to'ne/dikter *-en, pl -e* (=***-ar**) composer.

to'ne/fall *-et* inflection, intonation, tone; accent.

to'ne/følgje *-t* (=+**/følge**) *mus.* 1 progression, tone sequence. *2 accompaniment.

to'ne/givande** *A* - (=/gjevande**) setting the tone, style-setting: **dei t-** the leaders of fashion.

+to'ne/høyde *-n* pitch.

to'ne/klang *-en mus.* timbre.

to'ne/kunst *-en* (art of) music.

+to'ne/kunstner *-en, pl -e* (=***-ar**) musician, esp. composer.

to'ne/lag *-et* inflection, musical accent: **de to norske t-ene** the two Norwegian pitch accents.

+to'ne/løp *-et mus.* run.

+to'ne/rekke *-a/-en* (=***/rekkje**) sequence, succession of notes.

to'ne/skala *-en mus.* scale.

to'ne/stige *-n mus.* scale.

to'ne/vell *-et poet.* flow (swell) of notes, music; symphony of sound.

to'n/fikse'ring *-a photog.* combined toning and fixing.

***tong'** *-a, pl tenger* cf **tang**[1]

to'nika *-en mus.* 1 keynote, tonic. 2 basic chord, tonic triad.

to'nisk *A* - 1 *mus.* key, tonic. 2 *med.* tonic.

to'n/laus *A* (=+**/løs**) soundless; toneless; flat, expressionless; unaccented.

***tonn'**[1] *-a* cf **tann**

tonn'[2] *-et* ton (in Norway=2204.6 lbs.).

tonna'sje *-n* tonnage.

+-tonner *-en, pl -e* (=***-ar**) -ton: **tre/t-** three-ton.

tonsill' *-en anat.* tonsil.

tonsu'r *-en* tonsure.

topa's *-en* topaz.

topogra'f *-en* topographer; surveyor.

topografi' *-en* topography.

topogra'fisk *A* - topographic(al).

topp'[1] *-en* 1 top (of a mountain, tower, tree, etc.); peak, summit; *fam.* head, noggin: **fra t- til tå** from head to foot; **t- på skjeen** a heaping spoonful; **være klar i t-en** *fam.* be sober; have a clear head. 2 *fig.* acme, pinnacle: **det er t-en** that beats everything; **t-en av urett** the height of injustice; **føle seg, være på t-** *fam.* feel, be tip-top, in the pink of condition. 3 *naut.* mast; masthead: **i t-, til t-s** (of sails) hoisted. 4 crest (of feathers), tuft (of hair); topknot.

topp'[2] *N* **tipp t-** tip-top.

***top'pe**[1] *-a* bung, spigot, tap.

top'pe[2] *-n dial.* rooster.

top'pe[3] *V -a/+-et* 1 (of a plant, tree, etc.) develop, form a top; (of waves) comb, crest; culminate, reach a summit. 2 top (=put a top on); *naut.* top (a boom, a derrick). 3 top (=take a top off, e.g. a plant, a tree). 4 (*refl.*) **t- seg** (of waves) comb, crest; stick (its, their) tops up into the air; reach a high point (i in). 5: **t-et** crested, topped; heaped high; brimfull, good measure.

top'pende *Av* 1 brimfull, full to overflowing. 2 absolutely, plumb: **t- gal** p- crazy.

topp'/fart *-en* top speed.

topp'/figu'r *-en* 1 crowning figure, statue. 2 figurehead.

topp'/hogge *V infl as* **hogge** top (a tree).

topp'/hu(v)e *-a dial.* stocking cap.

topp'/jakt *-a/+-en* hunting of large birds that sit in the treetops.

topp'/klasse *-a/-en* top class (in sports); first class, first-rate.

topp'/lanter'ne *-a/+-en naut.* toplight, masthead light.

topp'/lente *-a naut.* lift (cable from yard to masthead).

topp'/lokk *-et* cap, cover, lid; cylinder head.

topp'/lu(v)e *-a* stocking cap; knit cap; wool toque.

topp'/mage *-n* potbelly.

topp'/møte *-t* summit meeting.

topp'/mål *-et* 1 full, generous measure. 2 height (of sth); extra, more besides, top: **t-et av frekkhet** the height of insolence.

topp'/må'lt *A* - heaped.

topp'/note'ring *-a/+-en* top price (on stock exchange, etc.).

topp'/pris *-en* top price (on goods, etc.).

topp'/punkt *-et* apex, summit; *math.* vertex.

topp'/segl *-et* (=+**/seil**) topsail.

topp'/sjø *-en* breaker, crested wave.

topp'/skott *-et* (=+**/skudd**) *bot.* top shoot (on tree).

topp'/sukker [/sokker] *-et* cone of refined sugar (from which pieces are cut).

topp'/vinkel *-elen, pl -ler math.* vertical angle.

***tor'**[1] [tå'r] *-et* audacity, daring, temerity.

***to'r**[2] *-et* low, slow fire.

°tor[3] *P* out of.

To'r *Prn(m) myth.* Thor, Old Norse god of thunder.

To'ra *Prn(f)*

to'/rada *A* - (=+**-et**) two-rowed; *bot.* distichous.

+ Bokmål; * Nynorsk; ° Dialect.
After letter: ' stress (Acc. 1); ` tone, stress (Acc. 2); · length.
Below letter: . not pronounced.

to'rad/bygg -*en* two-rowed barley.

+**to'/rader** -*en pl -e* (=*-**ar**) accordion with two rows of bass buttons.

To'r/alf *Prn (m)* (=/**alv**)

To'r/bjørg *Prn (f)*

Tor/bjø'rn [tor'/] *Prn (m)*

to'rde *pl of* **tore**[2]

+**torden** [tor'den, tor'-] -*en* cf **tore**[1]

+**torden/brak** [tor'den/] -*et* 1 (thunder) clap, crash of thunder. 2 thunderous noise.

+**torden/bye** -*a* cf **tore/**

+**torden/gud** -*en* god of thunder (=Thor).

+**torden/kile** -*n* 1 thunderbolt. 2 thunderstone.

+**torden/røst** -*a*/-*en* thunderous voice, voice of thunder.

+**torden/skrall** -*et* 1 thunderclap. 2 *fig.* blow, shock.

+**torden/sky** -*a* thundercloud.

+**torden/tale** -*n* fulmination, thundering speech.

+**torden/vær** -*et* cf **tore/**

Tor/dis [tor'/] *Prn (f)*

tordi'vel [also tor'/] -*elen, pl -ler zool.* dung beetle (Geotrupes).

+**tordne** [tor'dne] *V* -*a*/-*et* (=***tore**[3]) 1 thunder; crash, roar. 2 (of person) storm.

to're[1] -*a* (=+**torden**) thunder.

to're[2] *V tør*/*-*er, -de, -t* 1 dare, venture: **han kan ei leve, tør ei dø** he cannot live, dares not die (Ibsen). 2 can, may; will most likely; could: **det tør anses for sikkert** it can be safely assumed; **jeg tør nok si** I can safely say; **tør jeg spørre** may I ask.

***to're**[3] *V* -*a* cf **tordne**

To're *Prn (m. f)*

toreador [tåreadå'r] -*en* toreador.

to're/bye -*a* thunder shower.

to're/dønn -*et* rumble of thunder.

to're/slått -*en* clap, crash, roar of thunder.

+**to're/vær** -*et* (=*/**ver**) thunderstorm.

tor'g -*et* (city) square; market (place): **bringe til t-s** peddle (e.g. gossip); **på åpent t-** publicly; **(stå) ledig på t-et** (be) available, idle.

tor'g/dag -*en* market day.

tor'g/direktø'r -*en* official in charge of city's market square.

Tor/geir [tor'/] *Prn (m)*

tor'g/føre *V infl as* **føre**[1] take to market.

tor'g/handel -*en* marketing, market trade.

tor'g/kone [*/kåne] -*a* market woman.

tor'g/pris -*en* market price.

Tor/grim' [tor'/] *Prn (m)*

To'ril (To'r/hild) *Prn (f)*

torlaks/mess(e) [tor'-] *en* cf **tollaks/**

To'r/leif *Prn (m)* (=/**leiv**)

***tor'men** *A* -*e*/-*i, pl -ne* (of tree) stunted; slow growing.

Tor/mod [tor'/] *Prn (m)*

to'rn -*en* 1 thorn: **en t- i kjødet** *(bibl.)* a t- in the flesh. 2 *zool.* ray, spine. 3 prong (of a buckle).

***torne**[1] [tå'rne] *V* -*a* dry (out, up).

***to'rne**[2] *V* -*a* cf **tordne**

to'rne/busk -*en bot.* wild rose bush (Rosa canina).

to'rne/full *A* painful, thorny.

to'rne/krans -*en* crown of thorns.

tor'ne/krone -*a*/+-*en* crown of thorns.

to'rne/kvist -*en* thorny branch.

Tornerose [to'rnero'se] *Prn* Sleeping Beauty.

tornerose/søvn -*en* 1 long sleep (of Sleeping Beauty), magic sleep. 2 quiet, untroubled existence.

to'rnet(e) *A* - thorny.

tornis'ter -*eret*/-*ret, pl -er*/+-*re* 1 *mil.* nosebag. 2 *hist.* backpack.

***to'r/næm** *A* slow-learning.

To'r/olf *Prn (m)*

tor'p -*et dial., hist.* croft (small farm).

Tor'pa *Pln* twp, Oppland.

torpede're *V* -*te* torpedo.

torpe'do -*en* 1 torpedo. 2 *zool.* electric ray (Torpedinidae).

torpe'do/båt -*en mil.* torpedo boat.

+**torpe'do/jager** -*en, pl -e* (=*-**ar**) *mil.* destroyer.

+**tor'per** -*en, pl -e* (=*-**ar**) *hist.* crofter (small farmer).

°**to'r/prata** *A* - talked out.

tors/dag [to'rs/, tå'rs/] -*en* Thursday.

torsjo'n -*en* 1 *med., phys.* torsion. 2 *med.* torsioning.

tor'sk -*en* 1 *zool.* cod (Gadus callarias). 2 *hum.* fool (usu. **tosk**).

tor'ske/dum [/domm] *A* -*t, pl -me* dumb as a cod, stupid as a goose.

tor'ske/fangst -*en* 1 cod fishing. 2 catch (of cod).

tor'ske/fiske -*t* cod fishing.

tor'skelever/tran -*a*/-*en* cod-liver oil.

tor'ske/munn -*en bot.* butter-and-eggs, toadflax (Linaria vulgaris).

Tor'sken *Pln* twp, Troms.

To'rs/nes *Pln* twp, Østfold.

tor'so -*en* torso.

***tor'stal** *A* frequently thirsty, parched.

***tor'ste** -*n* cf **tørste**[1]

Tor/stein [tor'/] *Prn (m)*

***tor'stug** *A* - frequently thirsty, parched.

tor't[1] +-*en*/*-*a* injury, insult, wrong; disgrace, humiliation; *jur.* tort: **t- og svie** insult and injury.

to'rt[2] *pp of* **tore**[2]

tortu'r -*en* torture.

torture're *V* -*te* torture.

torturis't -*en* torturer.

tortu'r/kammer -*et, pl* -/+-*kamre* torture chamber.

+**tortu'r/redskap** -*et* (=*/**reiskap**) instrument of torture.

***tor'v**[1] -*a* necessity, need, requirement.

tor'v[2] -*a*/-*et* 1 (piece of) sod, turf: **under t-a** beneath the sod (=buried). 2 peat: **brenne t-** burn p-.

+**tor'v**[3] -*et* cf **torg**

Tor/vald [tor'/] *Prn (m)*

Tor'va/stad *Pln* twp, Rogaland.

tor've[1] -*a* (piece of) sod, turf: ***under t-a** beneath the sod (=buried).

***tor've**[2] *V* -*a* gather peat.

tor'v/myr -*a* peat bog.

tor'v/spade [also: /spae] -*n* peat spade.

tor'v/strø -*et* (=*/**strøy**) peat moss (dried, for bedding animals).

tor'v/tak -*et* 1 sod roof. 2 gathering of peat; place where peat is gathered.

tory [tå'ri] -*en* Tory.

***tos** [tå's] -*et* 1 ravelings, threads; poor material. 2 sth insignificant, useless.

***tose** [tå'se] *V* -*a* 1 ravel up. 2 putter at sth useless.

to'/seters *A* - coupe, two-seater (car, plane).

to'/sidig *A* - two-sided; bilateral (e.g. treaty).

to'/sifra *A* - (=+-**et**) two digit (number).

tos'k -*en* 1 *dial.* cod. 2 fool: **for en t- hun hadde vært** what a f- she had been (Skram).

+**tos'ke/hode** -*t* (=*/**hovud**) blockhead, fool, idiot.

+**tos'keri** -*et* foolishness, stupidity.

tos'ke/skap -*en* foolishness, stupidity.

tos'ket(e) *A* - foolish, silly, stupid.

to'/spann -*et* team (of two horses, hitched to wagon).

to'/spent *A* - two-horse (e.g. carriage).

to'stavings/o'rd -*et* two-syllable word.

+**to'/stemmig** *A* - for two voices, two-part: **t- sang** duet.

***tot** [tå't] -*et* buzz, hum (of voices); sighing (of wind), swish (of waves).

+**to'/takter** -*en, pl -e* (=*-**ar**) two-cycle engine.

to'takts/motor [also to'-] -*en* two-cycle engine.

tota'l *A* total: **slå t-t feil** fail completely.

+**tota'l/avhold** -*et* total abstinence.

+**tota'lavholds/mann** -*en, pl -menn* teetotaler.

total'/forli's -*et naut.* total loss.

tota'l/frede *V* -*a*/+-*et* protect against hunting the year round, throughout the country (=no open season).

***tota'l/fråhald** -*et* cf /**avhold**

tota'l/inntekt -*a*/+-*en* total income.

tota'l/inntrykk -*et* general, total impression.

totalisa'tor -*en* parimutuel (machine), totalizator.

totalis't -*en* teetotaler.

totalite't -*en* totality.

totalitæ'r *A* totalitarian.

***tote** [tå'te] *pp of* **tyte**[2]

to'tem -*et* totem.

to'tem/dyr -*et* totem, totemic animal.

To'ten *Pln* twps of Østre and Vestre Toten, Eina and Kolbu (on west side of Lake Mjøsa), Oppland.

***toti** [tå'ti] *pp of* **tyte**[2]

to'tning -*en* person from Toten.

to'/toms *A* - two-inch.

+**tot/schläger** [tå't/sjleger] -*en, pl -e* blackjack.

tott'[1] -*en* 1 tuft: **komme i t-ene på hverandre** fall to quarreling, get into a fight. 2 plug, wad: **t-er i ørene** p-s in one's ears.

tott'[2] -*en* thumb (children's lang., short for **tommeltott**).

tott'[3] *A* - *naut.* taut; tight; (of ice) packed.

tot'te *V* -*a*/+-*et* 1 pull out a tuft. 2 *naut.* tighten.

touche [tusj'] -*n* 1 *mus.* fanfare, flourish: **gi t-** sound a flourish. 2 *mus.* keyboard; fingerboard.

touchere [tusje're] *V* -*te* offend: **føle seg t-t** feel offended.

tout-à-fait [tuttafe'] *Av* completely.

to'v -*et dial.* sth matted; tangle.

Tov/dal [tå'v/] *Pln* twp, Aust-Agder.

to've[1] -*n dial.* 1 jumble, tangle. 2 wisp.

to've[2] *V* -*a*/+-*et dial.* twist together; tangle.

Tove [tå've] *Prn (f)*

to'ven *A* +-*ent, pl -ne dial.* matted; tangled.

to'vne *V* -*a*/+-*et dial.* become matted, tangled.

to'/øre -*n* (=/**øring**) two-øre piece.

to'/årig *A* - biennial.

to'/åring -*en* two-year-old.

to'/å'rs *A* - two-year-old.

tpt. =**transporteres**

trabele're *V* -*te fam., dial.* tramp, trot, trudge (back and forth).

tra'd -*et dial.* enclosure, fenced-in field.

trade [tre(i)'d] -*n* 1 *naut.* commerce, trade; merchant shipping. 2 business; trade, work: **være i t-en** be busy.

tradisjo'n -*en* tradition.

tradisjonell' *A* -*elt* traditional.

tradisjo'ns/bestem't *A* -, *pl -e* set by tradition, traditional.

tradisjo'ns/bunden *A* +-*ent*/+-*et, pl -ne* bound by tradition, traditional.

tradisjo'ns/rik *A* rich in traditions; honorable.

traff' *pt of* **treffe**

+**traf'fes** *pt of* **treffes**

trafika'bel *A* -*elt, pl -le* open to traffic, passable.

trafikan't -*en* 1 driver, motorist, traveler. 2 *merc.* trader, trafficker.

trafikk' -*en* 1 traffic, transportation; communications, service. 2 trade, traffic; carrying on, goings on, practices.

trafikke're *V* -*te* 1 trade, traffic (**i, med in**). 2 traffic (a road); service (a steamship route); ply, provide (regular) service.

trafikk'/fly -*et* commercial plane.

trafikk'/fyr -*et* traffic light.

trafikk'/konsta'bel -*elen, pl -ler* traffic officer.

trafikk'/kultu'r -*en* respect for traffic laws and consideration for other drivers.

trafikk'/minis'ter -*eren, pl -rer*/+-*ere* minister of communications, of transport.

trafikk'/regel -*elen, pl -ler* traffic law, regulation.

trafikk'/retning *-a/+-en* direction of traffic.

trafikk'/signal [/singna'l] *-et, pl -/+-er* traffic light; traffic sign.

trafikk'/skilt *-et, pl +-er* traffic sign.

trafikk'/stans *-en* traffic block, jam, tie-up.

trafikk'/øy *-a* safety island.

trafikk'/åre *-a* traffic artery.

tra'fo =**transformator**

***traf's** *-et* rag, ravelings, threads.

***traf'se** *V -a* become ragged, ravel out.

***traf'set(e)** *A* - ragged, shaggy.

trage'die *-n* tragedy: **den greske t-** Greek t-.

tragedien'ne *-a/+-en* tragedienne.

+tra'giker *-en, pl -e* (=***-ar**) tragedian.

tragikk' *-en* tragedy; tragic aspect, nature (**i** of).

tra'gi/komisk *A* - tragicomic.

tra'gisk *A* - tragic: **det t-e** tragedy; the tragic (side of sth); **det t-e er** the sad part of it is.

trakasse're *V -te* badger, pester, (*pop.*) ride.

trakasseri' *-et, pl +-er/*-* badgering, pestering (*pop.*) riding.

trakeide [trake-i'de] *-n bot.* tracheid.

°trakk'[1] *-et* cf **tråkk[2]**

trakk'[2] *pt of* **trekke**

°trak'ke *V -a* cf **tråkke**

+trak't[1] *-a* cf **trekt**

trak't[2] *-a/+-en* area, region; tract: **på disse t-er** in these parts.

trakta't *-en* 1 (religious) tract. 2 *pol.* treaty.

trakta't/brott *-et* (=**+/brudd**) *pol.* breach of (a) treaty.

+trak'te[1] *V -a/-et* cf **trekte**

trak'te[2] *V -a/+-et* aspire (**etter to**), long, strive (**etter** for); covet, have designs on.

+trak'te/kaffe *-n* percolator coffee.

traktement [-mang'] *-et* 1 treatment. 2 refreshments, (a) treat.

trakte're *V -te* 1 (stand) treat: **t- med (på)** serve. 2 *lit.* handle, play (musical instrument).

trakte'ring *-a/+-en* refreshments, (a) treat.

+trak't/formet *A* - (=**+-a**) funnel-shaped.

trak'tor *-en, pl -to'rer* tractor.

tra'l *-et dial.* 1 rubbish, trash. 2 drudgery.

tralala' *I* tra-la-la.

tra'le *-a/+-en dial.* latticework (e.g. on veranda); latticed veranda.

tra'le/verk *-et* latticework, trellis; picket fence.

trall' *-en* 1 humming, singing; tune, *2: **på den t-en** in that humor, mood, vein.

tral'le[1] *-a* 1 baggage cart, platform truck. 2 (RR) handcar. 3 ore car, tramcar (used in mine). 4 *naut.* launching cradle.

tral'le[2] *V -a/+-et* hum; sing, troll.

tral'le/bane *-n* tram railway, tramroad (in mining).

tral'le/hjul *-et* wheel on a cart, tramcar, trolley, etc.

tral't *-en* (slow) movement, pace; routine: **i den gamle t-en** in the same old rut.

tram' *-men* 1 (front, back) steps; stoop. 2 *dial.* platform, scaffolding, (speaker's) stand. *3 bank, brim.

***tra'me** *V -a* level; fill to the brim.

tram'/gjeng *-en* group of amateur actors who perform on a platform or stage to promote some political idea.

tram'p[1] *-en* 1 bum, tramp. 2 tramp steamer; tramp shipping. 3 vagabondage: **på t-en** bumming around; **ta t-en** tramp on foot to another harbor (looking for a seaman's job).

tram'p[2] *-et* stamp(ing), tramp(ing): **tunge t-** heavy stamping.

tram'p/båt *-en* tramp ship (=unscheduled freighter).

tram'pe *V -a/+-et* stamp, tramp (**på** on); trample: **t- i golvet** stamp one's feet (in anger); **t- ned** trample under foot; **t- takten** beat the rhythm with one's foot.

tram'p/fart *-en* tramp shipping (see **trampbåt**).

trampoli'ne *-n* trampoline.

trampoli'ne/sprang *-et* trampoline leap.

tra'n *-a/-en* 1 cod-liver oil. 2 train oil (from seal or whale blubber), whale oil.

trance [trang'se] *-n* trance.

tranchere [trangsje're] *V -te* carve (meat).

tra'ne *-a zool.* crane (Grus grus).

tra'ne/bær *-et bot.* cranberry (Oxycoccus quadripetalus).

tra'ne/dans *-en* "dance of the cranes": **en spurv i t-** a dwarf among giants.

tra'ne/hals *-en* 1 crane's neck. 2 *bot.* alfilaria, pin grass (Erodium cicutarium).

+trang'[1] *-en* (=***trong[1]**) 1 need, want (**til** for, of): **føle t- til** feel a n- for, feel impelled to; **være i t- om** *dial.* (be in) need (of). 2 desire, urge (**til** for, to); longing (**til for**): **det er min sjel en frydfull t- å gjeste Norges dale** it is a joyous urge of my soul to visit the valleys of Norway (Wergeland).

+trang'[2] *A* (=***trong[2]**) 1 narrow (fjord, path, valley, etc.); cramped, tight (coat, room, shoe, etc.); constricted: **den t-e port** (*bibl.*) the narrow gate; *fam.* **være t-t om saligheten** be a tight squeeze. 2 difficult, hard, straitened (circumstances): **ha det t-t** be hard up; **t-e tider** hard times. 3 narrow-minded; stupid: **være t- i nøtta** *pop.* be a dunce, be slow on the uptake. 4 confined, limited, restricted (conditions, environment, etc.).

+trang'/bodd *A* -: **være t-** live in cramped quarters.

+trang'/brystet *A* - 1 having breathing difficulties; asthmatic, short of breath. 2 narrow-minded, straitlaced.

+trang'brystet/het *-en* narrow-mindedness.

+trang'/pustet *A* - short of breath.

+trang'pustet/het *-en* breathing difficulties (asthma, etc.).

+trang'/syn *-et* narrow-mindedness, narrowness.

+trang'/synt *A* - narrow-minded.

+trang'/vi'ksk *A* - from Podunk; provincial, small-town (ref. to imaginary town Trangvik, created by J. Hilditch in his satirical paper Trangviksposten, 1900—1907).

tra'n/lampe *-a/-en* (train, whale) oil lamp.

transaksjo'n *-en merc.* transaction.

tra'n/salve *-a/-en pharm.* salve with a cod-liver oil base.

transatlan'tisk *A* - transatlantic.

transcendenta'l *A* transcendental.

transforma'tor *-en tech.* transformer.

transforma'tor/vikling *-a/+-en tech.* transformer coil.

transforme're *V -te* covert, transform.

transfusjo'n *-en med.* transfusion.

tran'sitiv *A gram.* transitive.

transitt' *-en* transit (through a country).

transitte're *V -te* convey, pass through (a country).

transitt'/gods [/gots] *-et* goods for, in transit (across, through a country).

transitt'/handel *-en* business of transporting goods through the country.

transkribe're *V* -te transcribe.

transkripsjo'n *-en* transcription.

translasjo'n *-en eccl., phys.* translation.

translatø'r *-en* (authorized, official) translator.

transmisjo'n *-en tech.* transmission.

transmitte're *V -te tech.* send, transmit.

+transp. =**transporteres**

transparent[1] [transparang'] *-et* transparency (=color slide); (also= transparent banner, used in a parade). 2 summer apple.

transparent[2] [transparang'] *A* - transparent.

transpirasjo'n *-en* 1 perspiration. 2 *bot.* transpiration.

transpire're *V -te* 1 perspire. 2 *bot.* transpire.

transplantasjo'n *-en* 1 *med.* grafting, transplantation. 2 *folk.* transference of disease from person to object.

transplante're *V -te med.* graft, transplant.

transpone're *V -te mus.* transpose.

transpor't *-en* 1 conveyance, transport(ation); express. 2 load, shipment; convoy. 3 *merc.* amount carried (brought) forward; transfer, exchange.

transporta'bel *A -elt, pl -le* movable; portable.

transpor't/bańd *-et* (=**+/bånd**) conveyor belt.

transport'/byrå' *-et, pl +-er/*-* express agency, company.

transporte're *V -te* 1 carry, move, transport. 2 *merc.* carry, bring forward.

transpor't/middel *-elet/-midlet, pl +-midler/*-el* means of transportation.

transportø'r *-en* 1 *math.* protractor. 2 conveyor. 3 feed dog (on sewing machine).

tran't *-en* mouth, snout, (*pop.*) trap.

Tra'n/øy *Pln* twp, Troms.

trape's[1] *-en* trapeze.

trape's[2] *-et, pl -/+-er math.* trapezoid.

trapp' *-a* (flight of) stairs, steps; staircase, stairway: **slite t-ene** haunt the authorities; **stå på t-en** stand on one's doorstep; **være på t-ene** be in the making, on the way; **tre t-er opp** up three flights.

trap'pe *V -a/+-et dial.* 1 stamp, tramp. 2: **t-seg** form steps.

trap'pe/avsats *-en* (stair) landing.

trap'pe/gang *-en* 1 stairway. 2 hall leading to (or from) stairs. 3 sidestepping (in skiing).

trap'pe/oppgang *-en* (inside) stairway.

trap'per *-en, pl +-e* trapper.

trap'pe/steg *-et* 1 *dial.* stairstep. 2: **gjøre t-** climb by sidestepping (in skiing).

trap'pe/stein *-en* stone doorstep.

trap'pe/stol *-en* step stool.

+trap'pe/trinn *-et* (stair) step.

trap'pe/vask *-en* washing of stairways; charwoman's work.

***tra'sal** *A* - fragile, frail.

***tra'sast** *V -ast* become raveled, shaggy.

tra'se *-n dial.* 1 rag, shred: **i filler og t-r** in shreds and patches. 2 slattern.

trasé *-en* projected canal, roadway (on drawings, or staked out in terrain).

trase're *V -te* draw up, stake out a canal, roadway.

tras'k *-et* 1 stamp(ing), tramp(ing), trampling. 2 drudgery, tiresome rounds.

tras'ke *V -a/+-et* stamp, tramp; plod, slog, trudge; drudge.

trass'[1] *-en/-et* (=**+tross**) defiance; contumacy, obstinacy: **på t-** in defiance, in spite; **på t- av** despite, in spite of; **+til tross for** despite, in spite of, notwithstanding.

trass'[2] *P* (=**tross[2]**) in spite of: **+tross alt** after all, all the same, in spite of everything; **t- i** in spite of;

+ Bokmål; * Nynorsk; ° Dialect.
After letter: ' stress (Acc. 1); ' tone, stress (Acc. 2); · length.
Below letter: . not pronounced.

+tross det at although, in spite of the fact that.
trass'/alder *-eren, pl -rer/+-e psych.* difficult, obstinate age.
trassa't *-en merc.* drawee.
tras'se *V -a/+-et* 1 bid defiance to, defy; hold one's own against, stand up to: **t- enhver beskrivelse** d- (all) description. 2 brave, face (danger, the elements, gunfire, etc.).
+tras'sel *-et dial.* 1 tangle. 2 rustling.
trassen't *-en merc.* drawer.
trasse're *V -te merc.* draw (**på** on); demand.
tras'sig *A* - defiant; obstinate, stubborn; unyielding.
+tras'sig/het *-en* defiance; obstinacy, stubbornness.
+tras't *-en* cf **trost**
trat'te *-n merc.* draft.
trau' *-et* oblong wooden bowl; trough.
***trau'd** *A* disinclined, unwilling.
***trau'd/beden** *A -e/-i, pl -ne* reluctant.
***trau'de** *Av* reluctantly.
***trau'dig** *A* - contrary, unwilling.
***trau'dsleg** *A* - somewhat unwilling.
trau'g *-et* cf **trau**
+trau'rig *A* - *archaic* melancholy, sad; dismal, tragic.
trau'ske *-a bot.* creeping crowfoot (Ranunculus repens).
trau'st *A* - firm, solid, steady; reliable: **t- som et fjell** f- as a rock.
***trau'stleg** *A* - quite set, solid.
trau'st/leik *-en* firmness, strength.
trau't *pt of* **tryte²**
***trau'tal** *A* strenuous, tiring.
***trau'te¹** *-n* long, strenuous job; difficult problem.
***trau'te²** *V -a* toil hard and long.
***trau'ten** *A -e/-i, pl -ne* difficult.
+tra'v *-et* cf **tråv**
+tra'valig *A* - (=***travleg**) *dial.* difficult, toilsome, troublesome.
tra've¹ *-n dial.* 1 rag. 2 (poor) wretch; poor little thing.
+tra've² *V -a/-et/-de* cf **tråve**
tra'vel *A -elt, pl -le* busy (day, life, man, street, town, etc.): **få, ha det t-t** become, be busy (**med** with).
+tra'vel/het *-en* activity, business; bustle, noise.
+tra'ver *-en, pl -e* cf **tråver¹**
+tra'ver/bane *-n* cf **tråv/**
traverse're *V -te* traverse.
travesti' *-en* travesty.
+tra'v/hest *-en* cf **tråv/**
+tra'v/kjører *-en, pl -e* (=***tråv/køyrar**) sulky driver.
+tra'v/kjøring *-en* cf **tråv/**
tra'vle *pl of* **travel**
***tra'vleg** *A* - cf **travalig**
+tra'v/løp *-et* cf **tråv/**
tre'¹ *-et, pl -/+trær (df pl trea/ +trærne)* 1 tree: **livets t-** the t- of life; **ta midt på t-et** take a middle position (between two opposite viewpoints); be reasonable. 2 wood: **skjære i t-** do woodcarving.
tre'² *V +trådte/*tro(d), trådt/*trådd* (=***trede**) 1 step, tread (**på** on); trample: **t- en menuett** dance a minuet; **t- istedenfor en** replace one, step into one's place. 2 enter: **t- inn** come in; **t- inn i** (also) join (as a member); **t- (inn) i tjeneste** enter (into) service; **t- i kraft** come into effect; **t- i underhandling** enter into negotiations (**med** with). 3 (with *prep., adv.*): *mil.* **t- av** break ranks, fall out; **t- av på naturens vegne** answer nature's call; **t- fram** come, step forward, up; appear, stand forth; **t- sammen** assemble, meet; **t- støttende til** come to the rescue; **t- tilbake** stand, step back; retire; **t- ut** step out; retire, withdraw.
+tre'³ *V -dde* cf **træ**
tre'⁴ *Num* three.
trea'k(el) *-et/+-en dial.* licorice.
+tre'/aktig *A* - 1 tree-like. 2 woody. 3 (of expression, etc.) wooden; expressionless.
tre'/art *-a/-en* kind of tree.
+tre'/bar *A* treeless.
tre'/bein *-et* wooden leg.
tre'/beint *A* - three-legged.
tre'blåse/instrumen't *-et, pl -/+-er* woodwind instrument.
+tre'/blåser *-en, pl -e* (=***-ar**) woodwind player.
+tre'/bonner *pl* clogs, wooden-soled shoes.
tre'/bukk [/bokk] *-en* 1 sawhorse. 2 stiff, unyielding person. 3 *zool.* longicorn beetle (Cerambycidae).
+tre'/bunner *pl* cf **/bonner**
***tre'de** *V trod, trådt* cf **tre²**
tre'/del *-en* (fraction) third.
tre'/dele *V -te* divide into three parts, trisect: **t-t speil** triple mirror; **t-t tau** three-strand rope.
+tre'de/mølle *-a* treadmill.
+tred'evte *Num* cf **trettiende**
tred'je (also tred'de] *Num* third: **det t- rike** the third empire (term launched by Ibsen in his play Emperor and Galilean, 1873; used by German Nazis after 1923 about Nazi Germany).
tred'je/del *-en* cf **tre/**
tred'jegrads/forhør *-et* (=***/forhøyr**) (the) third degree.
tred'je/klasses *A* - third class; third rate.
tred'je/mann *-en* number three, third man; third party.
tred'je/part *-en* third (of sth).
tred'je/stand *-en/*-et* third estate (=middle class).
***tred'jung** *-en* (fraction) third.
tre'/dobbelt *A* - (=***/dobbel**) triple.
tre'/doble *V -a/+-et* triple.
+tred've *Num* cf **tretti**
***tre'/eining** *-a eccl.* trinity.
tre'en *A -ent, pl -ne* 1 stiff, wooden; woody. 2 boring, dry.
+tree'nig *A* - *eccl.* triune.
+tree'nig/het *-en eccl.* trinity.
+tre'er *-en, pl -e* (=***-ar**) (number, rating, etc.) three; trey (in cards).
tre'/eta'sjes *A* - three-story.
tre'et(e) *A* - 1 stiff, wooden; woody; calloused. 2 boring, dry.
tre'/fall *-et dial.* trees blown down by the wind.
tre'/fasa *A* - (=+**-et**) *elec.* three-phase.
treff' *+-et/*-en* 1 chance, coincidence, turn of events; stroke (of luck, etc.); **på t-** *dial.* at random, haphazardly. 2 hit (of a shot): **8 t- på 10 skudd** 8 hits out of ten shots. 3 *fam.* meeting: **skulle ut på t-** had a date.
tref'fe *V +traff/*trefte, +truffet/*treft* 1 hit, strike (an obstacle, one's taste, one's weak point, a target, etc.): **den traff** that hit home (a sore spot); **t- sakens kjerne** strike to the root of the matter. 2 come across, meet; find, happen upon: **t- på noen** bump, run into sby; **t- sin overmann** meet more than one's match; **t-es** be found, seen; be gotten in touch with; meet. 3 make (a choice, a decision, preparations); take (measures, precautions, etc.). 4 (with *prep., adv.*): **t- inn, til** happen, occur (esp. suddenly); **t- til (å, at)** happen (to, that). 5 *(refl.)* **t- seg** happen, so happen; **det traff seg så heldig at** fortunately it so happened that.
tref'fende *A* - striking, telling, witty; appropriate, apt, pertinent (criticism, remark).
+tref'fer *-en, pl -e* 1 good strike, telling blow. 2 hit, success.
+tref'fes *V traffes, treffes* 1 come together, (of two people, objects) meet. 2 come upon, run into (each other, sth). 3 can be reached, found; accepts (callers, patients, etc.).
tref'fe/tid [also /ti] *-a/+-en* office hours, reception hours.
+treff'/sikker *A -ert, pl -sikre* accurate, sharp-shooting; exact, precise; striking, telling *(lit.* and *fig.)*.
+treff'sikker/het *-en* accuracy, marksmanship; wit.
tre'/flis *-a* chip, sliver, splinter (of wood).
+tref'ning *-en* encounter, skirmish; *mil.* action, engagement.
+tre'/fold *A* - *archaic* three-fold, three times.
+tre'/foldig *A* - *archaic* treble, three-fold, triple, triune: **t- hurra** rah, rah, rah.
+trefol'dig/het *-en eccl.* trinity: **t-s fest, søndag** Trinity Sunday.
tre'fore'dlings/industri' *-en* wood (forest) products industry.
tre'/fot¹ *-en, pl +-føtter/*-føter* peg leg, wooden leg.
tre'/fot² *-en* 1 tripod, trivet. 2 kettle with three feet. 3 three-legged stool.
tre'g *A* dull, slow, sluggish; languid, listless, torpid; *phys.* inert (mass), viscous (liquid).
tre'ge¹ *-n dial.* 1 regret, remorse; grief. 2 annoyance, irritation.
tre'ge² *V -a/+-et dial.* 1 regret, repent (**på** of). 2 anger, annoy, irritate: **t- over** be angry, gripe.
tre'ge/full *A dial.* melancholy, sad, sorrowful.
tre'gelig *A* - *dial.* aggravating, annoying, irritating.
***tregg'** *A tregt* 1 solid, strong, tight. 2 slow, sluggish.
+tre'g/het *-en* 1 slowness, sluggishness. 2 *lit., phys.* inertia; viscosity.
tre'/grense *-a/+-en* timberline.
tre'gt/flytende *A* - sluggish.
tre'/hendt *A dial.* awkward, clumsy (with one's hands).
tre'/hest *-en* 1 wooden horse. 2 *fam.* blockhead, woodenhead.
tre'hjuls/sykkel *-elen, pl -sykler* tricycle.
tre'/hode *-t* 1 head carved in wood. 2 *fam.* blockhead, woodenhead.
+tre'/hvit *A* cf **/kvit**
***tre'/høgda** *A* - three-story.
***trei'sk** *A* cf **tresk**
trei'v *pt of* **trive**
***trei'vst** *pt of* **trivast**
***tre'k** *A* thick.
tre'/kant *-en math.* triangle (also *fig.* of marital t-).
tre'/kanta *A* - (=+**-et**) triangular; three-sided; three-cornered.
trekk'¹ *-en* 1 draft; current of air. 2 irritation, catarrh (of the eye).
trekk'² *-et* 1 pull; pulling; stroke (of a brush): **i ett t-** at one go, at one stretch; **i t-** in succession, on end, running. 2 feature (of a face, a landscape, a work, etc.), line; side (of a matter, a situation, etc.); trait (of character): **kraftige t-** strong features. 3 twitch, wince (in one's face); shrug (of one's shoulder). 4 movement; flight, migration (esp. of bees, birds), passage: **gå på t-** *fam.* (of a prostitute) walk the streets to solicit business. 5 (in business, chess, politics, etc.) move; (in cards) trick. 6 (furniture) covering, upholstery; cloth case for a musical instrument). 7 *mus.* crook (on a valve instrument). 8 (+*-en*) deduction; (in sports) point loss (because of bad form, etc.); withholding (tax); *naut.* allotment. 9 scenery cable (for lowering and raising backdrops, etc.).
trekk'/basun *-en* slide trombone.
trekk'/dyr *-et* draft animal; work-horse.
+trek'ke *V trakk, trukket* (=***-je**) 1 drag, lug; draw (a card, a chance, a crowd, a conclusion, a sword, etc.); pull (a lever, a tooth, a wagon, etc.) tow: **t- lodd** draw a chance, a lot (**om** for); **(komme) t-ende med noe** drag in sth; bring up sth; **t- med seg** drag along with oneself; bring about, effect; **t- på** draw on (a fund, a reserve); **t- på årene** begin to get old; **t- te** let tea steep; **t- tøy** stretch (damp) linen prior to mangling; **t- veksler** make demands (**på** on). 2 absorb, soak up. 3 crank, turn (a machine, a wheel, etc.); wind (**opp** up). 4: **t- på** shrug

(one's shoulders), twitch; make a facial gesture; **t- på smilebåndet** smile. 5 deduct; withhold (tax); (in sports) take off points (e.g. for bad form); *naut.* draw an allotment. 6 (esp. of animals, birds) migrate, trek; (esp. of people) go, wander; *fam.* (of prostitute) walk the streets to solicit business. 7 (of clouds, a storm, etc.) move across the sky; (of smoke, fumes, etc.) blow, drift: **det t-er opp til uvær** a storm is brewing, gathering; **t- bort** clear away, up. 8 be drafty, blow: **det t-er her** there is a draft here. 9 (in a board game) move. 10 cover, upholster. 11 draw, mark, outline; (with a compass, dividers) describe. 12 (with *prep., adv,*): **t- an** (of a hunting dog) stalk a bird which has been scented; **t- av** fire, pull the trigger; **t- for** draw, pull shut (e.g. curtains); **t- fra** draw aside; subtract; **t- opp** pull out, up; uncork; wind up; **t- på det** hesitate; **t- til** pull (tightly) shut, **t- (et forslag) tilbake** withdraw (a proposal). 13 *(refl.)*: **t- seg** pull out (of a group), withdraw (from an agreement); **t- seg sammen** contract, shrink; close in, tighten; (of a catastrophe, clouds, etc.) build up to, gather; **t- seg tilbake** retire, withdraw; fall back **(fra** from); **t- seg ut** drop, step out **(av** of); withdraw **(av** from); **t-s med** be burdened, encumbered with.

+**trek'ke/ga'rn** -*et* drawnet.

trekk'/fugl -*en* bird of passage, migratory bird.

trekk'/full *A* drafty.

trekk'/hol [/hål] -*et* (=+**/hull**) airhole, draft, vent.

trekk'/hund -*en* sled dog; dog trained to pull anything.

***trekkj'e** *V* -*te* cf **trekke**

trekk'/kraft -*a*/+-*en* draft, pulling power, tractive force.

trekk'/luke -*a* draft (door), vent.

trekk'opp/bil -*en* wind-up car.

trekk'/papi'r -*et* blotting paper.

trekk'/plaster -*eret*/-*ret*, *pl* -*er*/+-*re* 1 (mustard, onion, etc.) plaster; *med.* vesicant. 2 attraction, drawing card.

+**trekk'/spill** -*et* (=***/spel**, +**/spell**) accordion.

trekk'/venti'l -*en* draft, ventilator.

tre'/klang -*en* *mus.* common chord, triad.

***tre'k/leik** -*en* size, thickness.

tre'/kloss -*en* 1 block of wood. 2 *derog.* blockhead, dope; stick: **han sitter der som en t-** he sits there like a bump on a log.

tre'/kløver -*en*, *pl* +-*e* 1 three-leaf clover. 2 threesome, trio.

***tre'kne** *V* -*a* get fat, thick; thicken.

trek'ning -*en* 1 (at a raffle) draw(ing); pull(ing). 2 movement, spasm, twitch; flicker, shiver, shudder.

trek'ning/liste -*a* list of numbers drawn in a lottery.

tre'/kol [/kål] -*et* (=+**/kull**) charcoal.

tre'/kopp -*en* wooden dish (bowl, cup).

tre'/krone -*a* crown, top of a tree.

trek't -*a* (=+**trakt**) funnel.

trek'te *V* -*a*/+-*et* (=+**trakte**) 1 pour sth through a funnel; filter, strain. 2 percolate; steep.

+**tre'/kull** -*et* cf **/kol**

trekvar't *A* - three-fourths, three-quarters.

tre'/kvit *A* *dial.* like freshly-scrubbed wood.

tre'/last -*a*/-*en* lumber.

tre'/laus *A* treeless.

+**trel'ke** *V* -*a*/-*et* cf **trælke**

+**trell'** -*en* cf **træl**[1]

+**trell'/binde** *V* -*bandt*, -*bundet* cf **træl/**

+**trell'/dom'** -*men* cf **træl/**

+**trel'le** *V* -*a*/-*et* cf **træle**

+**trel'le/arbeid** -*et* cf **træle/**

+**trel'le/kår** -*et* cf **træle/**

+**trell'/kvinne** -*a*/-*en* cf **træl/**

+**tre'/løs** *A* cf **/laus**

tre'/masse -*n* wood pulp.

+**tre'/master** -*en*, *pl* -*e* (=***/masting)** three-master (ship).

+**tre'/mel** -*et* cf **/mjøl**

tre'/menning -*en* second cousin **(av** of).

tre'mils/grense -*a*/+-*en* three-mile limit.

tre'/mjøl -*et* wood flour, wood meal (finely ground sawdust); wood dust (from wood borers).

+**trem'me** -*n* bar, slat, trellis; rung, spindle, wood strip.

+**trem'me/verk** -*et* grillwork, latticework, trellis.

tremulan't -*en* *mus.* tremolo, vibrato.

tremule're *V* -*te* sing, play with vibrato; vibrate.

tre'n[1] -*et* *archaic, mil.* train; baggage train.

+**tre'n**[2] *pt of* **trine**

tre'ne[1] *V* -*a*/+-*et*/+-*te* practice train (esp. in sports).

tre'ne[2] *V* -*a*/+-*et* *dial.* become wooden, woody.

+**tre'ne**[3] pl of **treen**

+**tre'ner** -*en*, *pl* -*e* (=***-ar)** (sports) coach, trainer.

trene're *V* -*te* delay, slow up (sth, to gain time).

***treng'ast** *V* *trengst, trongst, trungest*/-*ist* cf **trenges**

***tren'gd** -*a* narrowness; crowding; need.

treng'e[1] *V* +-*te*/**trong*, +-*t*/**trunge*/*-*i* have need **(til** for), need **(å** to), require (see **t-ende**).

+**treng'e**[2] *V* -*te* (=***-je)** 1 crowd, force, press; advance, push **(fram** forward, onward): **t- igjennom** penetrate, pierce through; prevail; **t- inn** creep (drift, seep) in; **t- inn i** dip deeply into, probe; penetrate, permeate; **t- inn på en** press sby hard; **t- på** crowd, push (forward); **t-es** crowd, press, throng **(om** around); be crowded, be pressed. 2 *(refl.)*: **t- seg inn** force one's way in, intrude, push in; **t- seg på** (of person) be aggressive, pushy; (of idea) be forced in upon one; **t- seg sammen** crowd, press together.

treng'ende *A* - 1 destitute, indigent, needy. 2: **et t- behov** a pressing need.

+**treng'es** *V* *trengs, trengtes, trengs* (=***-ast)** 1 be needed, be necessary. 2 (see **trenge**[1]).

***treng'je** *V* -*de* cf **trenge**[2]

+**treng's** *pr, pp of* **trenges**

treng'sel -*la*/+-*elen*, *pl* -*ler* 1 crowding, pushing and shoving; crowd, crush. 2 bad times; distress, need, trouble.

treng'sels/tid -*a*/+-*en* time of need, of trouble.

***treng'sle** -*a* cf **trengsel**

***treng'st** *pr of* **trengast**

tre'ning -*a*/+-*en* practice, training.

tre'nings/drakt -*a*/+-*en* sweat suit, track suit, training suit.

+**tre'nings/løp** -*et* (=***/laup)** practice run.

tre'nings/overall [/å'verål] -*en* sweat suit (sports).

+**tren'ne** *Num* *archaic* three.

trepane're *V* -*te* *archaic, med.* trepan, trephine.

tre'/pinne -*n* 1 wooden peg, pin. 2 (of person) stick.

tre'/propp -*en* wooden plug.

tre'/rada [*/raa] *A* - (=+**-et)** three-row.

+**tre'/raders** *A* - (of accordion) having three rows of keys.

Tres'/fjo'rd *Pln* twp, Møre og Romsdal.

+**tres'k** *A* (=***treisk)** 1 *lit.* crafty, cunning; *dial.* clever, wise. 2 *dial.* contrary, stubborn. 3 *dial.* laborious; slow.

+**tres'ke** *V* -*a*/-*et*/-*te* (=***-je)** thresh.

tre'/skei [/sjei] -*a* wooden spoon.

tres'kel -*elen*, *pl* -*ler* *dial.* threshold.

+**tres'kelig** *A* - *dial.* 1 crafty, wily. 2 annoying, vexatious; infamous.

+**tres'ker** -*en*, *pl* -*e* (=***-jar)** thresher.

+**tres'ke/verk** -*et* threshing machine.

+**tres'k/het** -*en* *archaic* craftiness, cunning, deceit.

***treskj'ar** -*en* cf **tresker**

+**tre'/skje**[1] -*a*/-*en* cf **/skei**

***treskj'e**[2] *V* -*te* cf **treske**

***tre'/skjefting** -*en* equipment, tool with wooden handle.

***tre'/skjerar** -*en* cf **/skjærer**

***treskj'e/verk** -*et* threshing machine.

+**tre'/skjærer** -*en*, *pl* -*e* (=***/skjerar)** wood-carver.

tre'/sko -*en*, *pl* -*r*/+- wooden shoe.

tre'/sku'rd -*en* (wood) carving.

tre'/slag -*et* type of wood.

tre'/sliperi' -*et*, *pl* +-*er*/*- pulp mill.

tre'/smak -*en* 1 taste of, like wood. 2 numbness, stiffness (from sitting too long on a wooden bench).

tre'/snitt -*et* wood-block; woodcut.

tre'/snuta *A* - (=+**-et)** *dial.*: **t- hatt** three-cornered hat.

tre'/sort -*en* type of wood.

tre'/sprit -*en* wood alcohol.

tress' -*et* 1 (in poker) three of a kind. 2 *archaic* sixty.

+**tres'se** -*a*/-*en* (silver or gold) braid.

tre'/stamme +-*n*/*-*a* (tree) trunk.

tre'/steg -*et* hop, step, and jump.

tre'/stjerners [/stjæ'rners] *A* - three-star.

tre'/stre'ks *A* - *educ.* triply underlined (error = serious error).

+**tre'/strøken** *A* -*ent*/-*et*, *pl* -*ne* *mus.*: **den t-ne oktav** the three-line octave; **t- tone** any of the notes in the three-line octave.

tre'/tal -*et* (=+**/tall)** figure, number three.

+**tret'ne** *V* -*et* cf **trøtne**

tre'/topp -*en* treetop.

+**trett'** *A* - cf **trøtt**

***tret'tande/helga** *df* Epiphany, Twelfth Day (Jan. 6).

tret'te[1] -*a*/+-*en* dispute, quarrel **(mellom** between; **om** about).

+**tret'te**[2] *V* -*a*/-*et* cf **trøtte**

tret'te[3] *V* -*a*/+-*et*/*-*e* quarrel **(med** with; **om** about).

tret'te/kjær *A* quarrelsome.

***tret'te/mål** -*et* matter under dispute, point of contention.

tret'ten *Num* thirteen.

tret'tende *Num* thirteenth.

tret'tende/dag -*en* Epiphany, Twelfth Day (Jan. 6).

tret'ten/del -*en* (fraction) thirteenth.

tret'te/sjuk *A* cantankerous, contentious, quarrelsome.

+**trett'/het** -*en* fatigue, weariness.

+**trett'hets/følelse** -*n* feeling of fatigue, weariness.

tret'ti *Num* thirty.

tret'ti/del -*en* (fraction) thirtieth.

tret'tiende *Num* thirtieth.

tre'/ull -*a* excelsior.

tre'v[1] -*et* *dial.* 1 loft; loft space; floor of a loft. 2 hay barn. 3 balcony in a church.

+**tre'v**[2] *pt of* **trive**

°**tre'valig** *A* - cf **travalig**

tre'vare/fabrikk' -*en* woodworking factory.

tre've -*n* *dial.* grain shock (of 24 sheaves).

+**tre'ven** *A* -*ent*, *pl* -*ne* 1 obstinate, reluctant; monotonous, slow: **det gikk smått og t-t med meg** I worked slowly and ineffectually (Evensmo). 2 *dial.* hearty, quick; active, energetic.

tre'/verdig *A* - *chem.* trivalent.

tre'/verk -*et* woodwork; wood (construction, decorations).

+**tre'vet** *pp of* **trive**

+**tre'/virke** -*t* lumber, timber.

+**trev'l** -*en* (=***trevle)** 1 raveling, thread; rag, shred, tuft: **ikke en t-** not a shred. 2 fiber: **med hver t-**

+ Bokmål; * Nynorsk; ° Dialect.
After letter: ' stress (Acc. 1); ' tone, stress (Acc. 2); · length.
Below letter: . not pronounced.

av sin kropp in every fiber of her body ((Hoel); **til siste t-** to the last ounce (of his strength).

trev'le V -a/+-et 1 ravel, shred. 2 fumble, grope (etter for): **t- seg fram** feel one's way along.

trev'let(e) A - (of edge) raveled out, ragged, shaggy; fibrous; tufted.

***tre'/vyrke** -t cf /virke

tre'/åring -en three-year-old.

Tr.heim = **Trondheim**

***tri'** Num cf **tre**[4]

tria'de -n lit. triad.

triang'el -elet/-let, pl +-ler/*-el esp. math., mus. triangle.

triangulere [-anggule're] V -te 1 math. triangulate. 2 hort. graft by inserting scion cuts into wedge-shaped cut in stem.

triangulær [-anggulær] A math. triangular.

tri'as/tida df the Triassic Period.

tribuna'l -et tribunal.

tribu'ne -n bandstand, platform; reviewing stand, tribune; bleachers, grandstand.

+tribu'ne/sliter -en, pl +-e (=*-ar) sports fan (one who wears down the bleachers).

tributt' -en 1 tribute. 2 contribution, offering. 3 token of appreciation, of respect; acknowledgment.

+trick [trikk'] -et, pl tricks cf **trikk**[2]

***tridje** [tri'e] Num cf **tredje**

***trif'se** -a patch, rag, scrap.

trigonometri' -en trigonometry.

trigonome'trisk A - trigonometric.

triki'n -en (=***trikine**) zool. trichina (Trichinella spiralis).

trikino'se -n med. trichinosis.

trikinø's A med. trichinous.

trikk'[1] -en streetcar, trolley car (or two or three in tandem): **ta t-en** take the s- (trolley).

trikk'[2] -et (=+**trick**) trick.

trik'ke V -a/+-et take the trolley.

trik'ke/billett' -en streetcar ticket.

+trik'ke/skinne -a streetcar track.

trik'ke/stall -en (street)car barn.

trik'ke/stans -en failure of streetcar service.

trikolor [-lå'r] -en tricolor.

trikot [trikå'] -en 1 tricot (a knitted fabric). 2 tights made of t-.

trikota'sje -n 1 knitwear (hosiery, lingerie, etc.). 2 store selling k-.

+trill'[1] -en 1 trill, trilling. 2 dial. small disc; pulley; top.

trill'[2] Av: **t- rund** rolypoly, round as a ball: **det gikk t- rundt for ham** he was completely confused.

tril'le[1] -a (horsedrawn) buggy, phaeton, small carriage.

tril'le[2] -a/+-en 1 mus. trill: **slå t-r** sing t-s. 2 (of birds) warble.

tril'le[3] V -a/+-et 1 roll (a ball, dough, etc.); trundle (a hoop); wheel (a bicycle, a wheelbarrow, etc.); (of rain, tears, etc.) roll, trickle: **han lo så tårene t-et** he laughed until he cried. 2 mus. trill; (esp. of birds) roll, trill, warble.

tril'le/bår -a (=/**bør**) wheelbarrow.

tril'lende Av: **t- rund** rolypoly; round as a ball.

+tril'le/pike -a/-en girl hired to air baby in its buggy.

tril'ling -en 1 triplet. 2 triple-barreled shotgun.

trillio'n -en quintillion.

trill'/rund A cf **trill**[2]

trilobitt' -en zool. trilobite.

trilogi' -en trilogy.

***tril'te** V -a run, toddle, trip (along).

trim' -men 1 trim (of a ship in the water, of an airplane's cargo). 2 trim (=condition, order): **være på (i) t-** (esp. naut.) be in trim; be in condition, shape.

trim'me V -a/+-et 1 naut. trim. 2 trim (a dog, a lawn, a tree, etc.).

+trin' -et cf **trinn**[1]

+tri'ne V -te/tren, -t lit. step, tread, walk.

+trinn'[1] -et 1 step, tread; (on ladder) rung: **t- for t-** step by step; **tunge t-** heavy footsteps. 2 level, stage (of civilization, development, etc.).

+trinn'[2] A trint 1 chubby, plump, round. 2 archaic, (adv.) **t-t** around: **t-t om** round about.

+trinn'/vis A - gradual, stepwise; (adv.) step by step: **stigende t-** built in tiers.

trin'se[1] -a 1 dial. jagging wheel, pastry wheel; rolling pin for making flatbrød. 2 (shoemaker's) roulette, tracing wheel. 3 caster (under furniture). 4 pulley. 5 basket or ring on ski pole.

trin'se[2] V -a/+-et 1 dial. roll, flatten (with a pastry wheel or flatbrød rolling pin). 2 roll, tumble. 3 dial. sling, whirl around.

+trin't nt of **trinn**[2]

***trin'te** V -a roll, roll over, tumble.

tri'o -en mus. trio.

tripp' -en 1 step, tripping. 2 short trip; naut. run.

trip'pe V -a/+-et 1 toddle; trip (around, along, etc.); mince. 2 take small steps; shift from one foot to another (from impatience, etc.). 3 favor a sore foot, limp.

trippel/allianse [trip'pel/alliang'se] -n Triple Alliance.

trippel/entente [trip'pel/angtang'te] -n Triple Entente.

tripp'-trapp'-tre'/sko I 1 one-two-three (as when three children are evenly graduated down the scale). 2 game (ab. =) tick-tack-toe.

tri'se -a waitress on a passenger ship.

tris'se -a 1 lit. pulley. 2 anat. trochlea.

***tris'sel** -elen, pl trislar pulley.

tris'se/verk -et block and tackle.

tris't A - gloomy, melancholy, sad; bleak, dismal, dreary: **det var da t-** that's too bad.

+tris't/het -en gloom, sadness; bleakness, dreariness.

+tritt' -et step: **holde t-** keep step (pace), keep up (**med** with); **komme i t-** fall into step.

trium'f -en 1 triumph, victory. 2 exultation: **med t- i stemmen** in a triumphant voice.

triumfa'tor -en victor.

trium'f/boge [/båge] -n (=+/**bue**) triumphal arch.

triumfe're V -te 1 triumph, win. 2 crow, exult, gloat.

trium'f/tog [/tåg] -et triumphal procession.

triumvira't -et triumvirate.

***tri'vast** V trivst, treivst, trivest/-ist cf **trives**

tri've V treiv, +trevet/+trivd/*-e/*-i dial., fam. (suddenly) grab, seize, snatch (**etter, til** at, for): **t- i, t- tak i** take hold of.

tri'velig A - 1 plump, round, well-fed; buxom, healthy; (of plants) luxuriant. 2 inviting, pleasant; comfortable, cosy.

***tri'ven** A -e/-i, pl -ne active, healthy, thriving.

+tri'ves V -des, -(e)s (=***trivast**) 1 (of a person) feel comfortable, content; get along; be happy, enjoy oneself: **han t- i Norge** he likes it in Norway. 2 (of plants, enterprises, etc.) flourish, prosper, thrive; do well.

***tri'vest** pp of **trivast**

trivialite't -en 1 triviality; commonplace. 2 banality, truism.

triviell' A -elt common(place), ordinary; dull, boring, trivial.

***tri'vist** pp of **trivast**

triv'le V -a/+-et dial. fumble, grope (**etter** for): **t- seg fram** g- one's way.

tri'vnad -en dial. well-being; development, growth, prosperity.

+triv's pp of **trives**

triv'sel -en well-being; development, growth, prosperity: **handelens t-** the growth of trade.

***triv'st** pr of **trivast**

triø'r -en agr. grain-sorting machine.

Tr.lag = **Trøndelag**

tro'[1] -a, pl -er/*trør 1 (feeding, watering) trough. 2 wooden water conduit.

***tro'**[2] -a trampled area.

+tro'[3] -en cf **tru**[1]

***tro'**[4] -et (wooden) poles, staves; roof planking.

+tro'[5] V -dde cf **tru**[2]

tro'[6] pt of **trå**[3], **tre**[2]

+tro'[7] A -, pl - cf **tru**[3]

***tro'd** pt of **trede**

tro'e -a dial. pole, esp. a fishing pole.

+tro'ende[1] N: **stå til t-** be believed, trusted; be accepted (as true).

+tro'ende[2] A - 1 believing, devout: **en t-** a believer; **bli t-** be converted; **lite t-** of little faith. 2 trusted; trustworthy: **t- til litt av hvert of** whom anything might be expected; **lite t- (t-s)** dubious, questionable.

+tro'/fast A - cf **tru/**

+tro'fast/het -en dependability, reliability, trustworthiness.

trofé +-et/*-en, pl -er trophy.

+tro'/hjertig A - cf **tru/hjerta**

Tro'ja Pln Troy.

+troja'ner -en, pl -e (=*-ar) Trojan.

troja'nsk A - Trojan.

troké -en trochee.

trokéisk A - trochaic.

+tro'lig A - cf **trulig**

troll' -et 1 folk. troll, monster, ogre; goblin; (also) any kind of evil, supernatural creature: **det var t-det, 'sa haugkjerringa** that's a hell of a note, said the witch (Asbjørnsen and Moe). 2 (esp. of women) shrew, spitfire, vixen; (of children) brat, imp: **være et t- til å ete** be an absolute glutton. 3 evil power, spirit; capricious, ill-natured tendency, inclination: **å leve er krig med trolle i hjertets og hjernens hvelv** life is an endless war against trolls in one's heart and brain (Ibsen). 4 sorcery, witchcraft: **det går t- i ord** what is said will come true (mentioning, referring to sth dangerous can make it happen). 5: **t- i eske** jack-in-the-box. 6 core of a boil; (painful) swelling.

troll'/binde V infl as **binde** cast a spell over (sby); spellbind.

troll'/bær -et bot. baneberry (Actaea spicata).

troll'/dom' -men/*-en 1 sorcery, witchcraft, wizardry. magic, spell.

+troll'doms/aktig A magic, mystical.

troll'doms/kraft -a/+-en, pl -krefter/*-er magic power.

troll'doms/kunst -en art of magic, witchcraft.

troll'doms/makt -a/+-en magic power.

trol'le V -a/+-et 1 practice witchcraft, work magic. 2 bewitch, cast a spell (on sby), hex: **t- fast** bewitch. 3 conjure (**fram** forth, up, etc.).

Trol'le/botn Prn folk. (in medieval ballads) country (in far north) where trolls are thought to live.

trol'let(e) A - bad, naughty.

trolley/buss [trål'li/buss] -en trackless trolley, trolleybus.

troll'/ga'rn -et trammel net.

troll'/gryte -a geol. kettle hole, pothole.

troll'/ham' -men folk. form, shape into which sby, sth is turned by magic; enchantment.

troll'/hegg -en bot. buckthorn (Rhamnus).

troll'/katt -en folk. supernatural cat; witch's cat which steals milk and food.

troll'/kjerring -a, pl *-ar 1 folk. female troll, esp. an old one. 2 witch 3 firecracker.

troll'kjerring/spytt -et folk. star jelly, witches'-butter (a blue-green algae e.g. Nostoc commune); a yellow slime mold (Fuligo septica); foamy larva case of a spittle insect. All thought to be vomit of a witch's cat.

troll'/krabbe -a/-en zool. lithodes crab (Lithodes maja).

***troll'/kunnig** *A* - cf **/kyndig**

troll'/kunst *-en* art of magic, witchcraft.

troll'/kvinne *-a/+-en* witch.

+troll'/kyndig *A* - versed in the art of magic.

troll'/mann *-en, pl -menn/*-menner* sorcerer, wizard.

troll'/mjøl *-et agr.* calcium cyanamide (a fertilizer, weed killer).

troll'/pakk *-et derog.* 1 (pack of) trolls. 2 sorcerers. 3 naughty children.

troll'/ring *-en* 1 magical ring. 2 magic circle (usu. *fig.*).

troll'/skap *-en/+-et* 1 magic, witchcraft. 2 illness due to witchcraft. 3 troll people. 4 naughtiness.

troll'slig *A* - *dial.* bad, naughty (as if bewitched).

+troll'/speil *-et* magic mirror.

troll'/stilt *A* - *folk., mus.* (of a violin) tuned to play melodies learned from the underground fairies.

troll'/tak *-et dial.* 1 very strong grip. 2 test of strength.

+troll'/tøy *-et derog.* evil spirits, troll folk, witches.

troll'/unge [/onge] *-n* 1 child of a troll. 2 naughty child.

troll'/urt *-a/+-en bot.* enchanter's nightshade (Circaea lutetiana).

+troll'/øye *-t* magic eye (turning indicator on radio).

+tro'/love [/låve] *V -et* cf **tru/**

+tro'/lovelse [/låvelse] *-n* engagement.

trol'sk *A* - trollish, witchlike; bewitching, enchanting, magic: **en t- stemning ligger over byen** bewitching air rests over the city (Arbeiderbladet).

+tro'/løs *A* cf **tru/laus**

+tro'løs/het *-en* faithlessness, treachery; deception (**mot** towards).

+tromle[1] [trom'le] *-a/-en* cf **trommel**

tromle[2] [trom'le] *V -a/+-et* roll (a lawn, etc.).

tromme[1] [trom'me] *-a* drum (instrument, container): **slå på t-** beat the d- (also *fig.*=advertise, advocate sth).

tromme[2] [trom'me] *V -a/+-et* 1 drum, beat the drum; **t- sammen** *hum.* drag out, rope in (e.g. members of a family, polit. party). 2 beat (a rhythm, in a rhythmic way), drum, tap: **t- på bordet** tap the table; **regnet t-er på taket** the rain drums on the roof; **det t-et i ørene** his ears throbbed.

tromme/hinne *-a anat.* ear drum, tympanic membrane.

+tromme/hvirvel *-en* cf **/virvel**

+tromme/ild *-en* 1 barrage, drumfire. 2 *fig.* barrage, running fire (of questions, comments, etc.).

trommel [trom'mel] *-elen, pl tromler* cylinder, metal drum.

trommel/bremse *-a/+-en* (=**+/brems**) friction brake utilizing a drum.

trommelom [trommelom'] *I* rat-a-tat (sound of drumming).

+trommer [trom'mer] *-en, pl -e* (=***-ar**) drummer.

tromme/sjuke [trom'me/] *-n vet.* bloat, tympanitis.

tromme/skinn *-et* drum head.

+tromme/slager *-en, pl -e* (=***-ar**) drummer.

tromme/stikke *-a* drumstick.

+tromme/virvel *-elen, pl -ler* roll of drums.

trompet [trompe't] *-en* 1 trumpet: **blåse i t-** blow the t- (also *fig.*). 2 *naut.* sheepshank (knot).

+trompeter [trompe'ter] *-en, pl -e* (=***-ar**) 1 trumpeter, trumpet player. 2 clumsy oaf. 3 *zool.* bee that fans air into hive.

trompetere [trompete're] *V -te* 1 play a trumpet. 2 trumpet (e.g. of elephant).

trompetist [trompetis't] *-en* trumpeter, trumpet player.

+trompet/støt [trompe't/] *-et* (=***/støyt**) blare, blast (of trumpets).

Troms [trom's] *Pln* county in northern Norway.

Tromsø [trom'sø] *Pln* city, Troms.

Tromsøy/sund [trom'søy/sunn] *Pln* twp, Troms.

Trom/øy [trom'/] *Pln* twp, Aust-Agder.

tro'n/arving *-en* heir to the throne.

+tro'n/besti'gelse *-n* accession to the throne.

Tron'd *Prn (m)*

Tron'de/nes *Pln* twp, Troms.

Tron'd/heim *Pln* city, Sør-Trøndelag.

+tron'dhjems/suppe *-a* soup of milk, rice, raisins, and sugar.

tro'ne[1] *-a/+-en* throne (seat; office; institution): **sitte på t-n** be a monarch, rule; *hum.* sit on the potty; **stå for t-n** *eccl.* come to judgment, stand before God's throne.

tro'ne[2] *V -a/+-et* hold sway, rule; be enthroned; sit on a throne (also *hum.*); dominate (e.g. the landscape).

+tro'n/frasigelse *-n* abdication.

+tro'n/følge *-n* (=***/følgje**) order, right of succession (to the throne).

+tro'n/følger *-en, pl -e* (=***-jar**) successor to the throne.

***trong'[1]** *-en* cf **trang[1]**

***trong'[2]** *pt of* **trenge[1]**

***trong'[3]** *A* cf **trang[2]**

***trong'/budd** *A -/-butt* cf **trang/bodd**

***trong'leg** *A* - quite narrow, tight.

***trong'/rømd** *A -rømt* narrow, tight.

***trong'/røme** *-t* cramped, tight quarters; crush.

***trong's/mål** *-et* compelling necessity.

***trong'st** *pt of* **trengast**

***trong'/syn** *-a/-et* cf **trang/**

***trong'/synt** *A* - cf **trang/**

tro'n/himmel *-elen, pl -himler* canopy (over a throne).

tro'n/pretenden't *-en* pretender to the throne.

+tro'n/røver *-en, pl -e* (=***-ar**) usurper.

tro'n/skifte *-t, pl +-r/*-* accession of a new ruler.

tro'n/stol *-en* throne (seat).

tro'n/tale **-a/-en* speech from the throne (in the *Storting*; now a report on the state of the nation, read by the monarch, corresponding in the U.S. to the president's message on the state of the Union).

tro'ntale/debatt' *-en* (parliamentary) debate following the **trontale**.

tro'pe *-n* trope (rhetorical figure); musical embellishment.

tro'pe/hjelm *-en* sun helmet.

+Tro'pene *Pln* (=***-ane**) the tropics.

tro'pisk *A* - tropical.

***tropp'[1]** *-a* cf **trapp**

tropp'[2] *-en* 1 troop (of actors, scouts, soldiers, etc.); company: **holde t-** keep up (**med** with); **i samlet, sluttet t-** in a body; **slutte t-en** bring up the rear. 2 *archaic* circle, clique.

trop'pe *V -a/+-et*: **t- av** *mil.* break up, disband; **t- inn** enter, march into; **t- opp** march into position, move up; show up; turn out.

***trop'pe/rørsle** *-a* troop movement.

+tropp's/fører *-en, pl -e* (=***-ar**) 1 *mil.* section leader. 2 scoutmaster.

tropp's/sjef *-en mil.* section leader.

***tros** [trå's] *-et* fallen branches, brush (in the forest).

+tro's/artik'kel *-elen, pl -artikler eccl.* article of faith.

+tro's/bekjen'nelse *-n eccl.* 1 belief, faith. 2 creed, declaration of faith.

***trose** [trå'se] *V -a* 1 gather brush; brush out (an area). 2 break, crush. 3 make a snapping noise, crack.

***troseleg** [trå'seleg] *A* - brittle, fragile.

+tro's/felle *-n* fellow believer.

+tro's/fellesskap *-et* community of religion, religious fellowship.

+tro's/frende *-n* fellow believer.

+tro's/frihet *-en* religious freedom.

+tro's/handling *-en* 1 religious action (behavior, declaration). 2 *eccl., hist.* auto-da-fé.

+tro's/iver *-en* religious fervor, zeal.

+tro'/skap *-en* cf **tru/**

+troskyl'dig *A* - cf **tru/**

+troskyl'dig/het *-en* innocence, naiveté; simplicity; trust, unsuspicious nature: **i all t-** in all innocence.

+tro's/lære *-a/-en* 1 study of religion; dogmatics; creed. 2 faith, religious belief.

+tro's/regel *-elen, pl -ler* dogma.

+tro's/retning *-en* creed, denomination, religious persuasion.

+tross'[1] *-en* cf **trass[1]**

+tross'[2] *P* cf **trass[2]**

+tro's/sak *-en* matter of faith.

+tross'/alder *-eren, pl -ere/-re* cf **trass/**

+tro's/samfunn *-et* religious community; church, creed, denomination.

+tro's/sannhet *-en* religious truth, verity.

tros'se[1] *-a naut.* hawser (large rope).

+tros'se[2] *V -et* cf **trasse**

+tro's/setning *-en* religious doctrine, dogma, tenet.

+tros'sig *A* - cf **trassig**

+tro's/skifte *-t* change of religion, of faith (as during the Reformation).

tros't *-en* (=**+trast**) *zool.* thrush (Turdus).

+tro's/vitne *-t* religious martyr; missionary.

***trot** [trå't] *-et* 1 cessation, conclusion, end. 2 absence, lack (e.g. of food).

***trote[1]** [trå'te] *-n* inflammation, swelling.

***trote[2]** [trå'te] *V -a* become tired, give up.

trote[3]** [trå'te] *pp of* **tryte[2]** (=troti**)

***troten** [trå'ten] *A -e/-i, pl -ne* cf **truten**

+tro'/tjener *-en, pl -e* faithful retainer, trusted servant.

***trot'ne** *V -a* swell (up).

***trott'** *-en* diligence; endurance; strength.

***trot'te** *V -a* endure (sth), hold out, stand; have the strength for.

***trot'tig** *A* - 1 diligent, industrious; persevering. 2 hardy, rugged, tough.

trott'/laus *A* changeable, unstable; soon bored, tired.

***trott'/løyse** *-a* lack of perseverance, of diligence.

trottoa'r *-et, pl +-er/*- archaic* sidewalk.

+tro'/verdig [also -vær'-] *A* - cf **tru/**

tru'[1] *-a* (=**+tro[3]**) 1 belief, faith (**på** in); creed: **den kristne t-** the Christian faith (creed); **den rette t-** the accepted creed, orthodoxy; **enhver blir salig i sin tro** each man his own faith (=believe what you will). 2 confidence, faith, trust (**på, til** in): **i den t- at** convinced that; **i god t-** in good faith; ***dei har god t- til han** they have great faith in him. 3 *archaic* assurance, troth; trustworthiness: **min t-** in truth, upon my word; **på tro og love (ære)** on one's honor.

tru'[2] *V -dde* (=**+tro[5]**) 1 believe, have faith (**på** in). 2 be of the opinion, think: **du kan (må) t-** you bet, you can be sure; **jeg t-dde han var død** I thought he was dead; **kan (skal, skulle) jeg t-** I should think, I suppose; **må t-** of course, you know (esp. to express sarcasm, doubt, or scorn); **t- godt om en** think well of one. 3 (as *introd. particle*) wonder: **t- hvor langt en kan komme frem** I wonder how far one can get (Scott); ***skal (må) t- han kjem** wonder if he'll come. 4 trust (**på** in): ***t- ein vel** have faith in sby; **t- en til noe** believe sby capable of sth (usu. *derog.*) e.g. ***det er du t-dd til** this is what one could expect of you (Vesaas). 5 *(refl.)* **t- seg til** dare; confide in.

+ Bokmål; * Nynorsk; ° Dialect.
After letter: ' stress (Acc. 1); ` tone, stress (Acc. 2); · length.
Below letter: . not pronounced.

tru'[3] *A* +-/*-*tt*, *pl* +-/*-*e* (=+**tro**[7]) faithful, loyal (**mot** to); devoted, staunch, true; trusty; accurate, close (copy, imitation, etc.): **lang og t- tjeneste** long and faithful service; **tradisjonen t-** according to tradition; **være, bli en t-** be faithful to one (**han er oss t-** he is f- to us).
***tru'ande** *A* - cf **troende**
trubadu'r *-en* troubadour.
tru'/dom' *-men*/*-*en* faith, religion.
***tru'/doms-** *Pf* cf **tros-**
+**tru'e** *V -a/-et* cf **truge**[2]
***tru'en** *A -e/-i, pl trugne* 1 credulous, gullible, unsuspecting. 2 faithful, trustworthy.
+**tru'ende** *A* - (=***trugande**) threatening; imminent.
tru'/fast *A* - 1 faithful, loyal; dependable. 2 firm, steady, strong (grip, hold).
+**truffet** [trof'fet] *pp of* **treffe**
***tru'g** *-en* snowshoe.
tru'ge[1] *-a/-en* snowshoe.
tru'ge[2] *V -a/+-et* (=+**true**) threaten; intimidate, menace: **t- en med neven** shake one's fist at one; **t- en på livet** threaten one's life; **t- en til noe** intimidate one into (doing) sth; **la seg t-** let oneself be intimidated (bullied).
***tru'gen** *A -e/-i, pl -ne* cf **truen**
***tru'gne** *pl of* **tru(g)en**
***trug'sel** *-elen, pl -lar* cf **trusel**
trug's/mål *-et* threat.
tru'/hjerta *A* - 1 ingenuous, simple, trusting. 2 honest, reliable, trustworthy.
+**trukket** [trok'ket] *pp of* **trekke**
tru'/laus *A* faithless, perfidious, treacherous (**mot** to).
tru'lig *A* - (=+**trolig**) 1 likely, probable; *(adv.)* probably. 2 *(adv.)* faithfully, persistently.
trul'le *V -a/+-et fam.* trundle.
***tru'/lovar** [/låvar] *-en* best man, maid of honor.
tru'/love [/låve] *V -a/-de/+-et/+-te archaic* betroth, engage.
***tru'/loving** [/låving] *-a* betrothal, engagement.
***tru'/løyse** *-a* faithlessness, perfidiousness, treachery.
trumf [trom'f] *-en* trump; trump card: **ha en t- i bakhånd(en)** have sth up one's sleeve.
trumfe [trom'fe] *V -a/+-et* trump; play trump: **t- igjennom** force through; **t- ut med** persist in using.
trumf/ess [trom'f/] +*-et*/*-*en* ace of trumps; *fig.* ace card.
trumf/kort *-et* trump (card).
***trum'me** *V -a* cf **tromme**[2]
trumpet(e) [trom'pet(e)] *A* - sulky, sullen, surly.
***tru'/mål** *-et*: **i t-** in confidence, confidentially.
***tru'nad** *-en* confidence, reliance, trust.
***tru'ne** *-a* cf **trone**[1]
trung'e** *pp of* **trenge**[1] (=trungi**)
trung'est** *pp of* **trengast** (=trungist**)
trupp' *-en* (circus, theater) troop; company, ensemble.
***tru'/røken** *A -e/-i, pl -ne* sincere; conscientious.
***tru'/røkne** *-a* sincerity; conscientiousness.
tru'se *-a/+-en* panty.
+**trus'el** *-elen, pl -ler* (=***trugsel**) menace, threat (**mot** to).
+**trus'els/brev** *-et* threatening letter.
trus'k *-en dial.* (of old ship) tub; (of person) poor wretch, slob.
tru'/skap *-en* (=+**tro/**) allegiance, fidelity: **sverge hinannen evig t-** swear to be true to each other forever; **sverge kongen t-** swear allegiance to the king.
***tru'/skifte** *-t* cf **tros/**
tru'/skyldig *A* - (=+**tro-**) innocent, trusting; simple, unaffected.
trust [trøs't] *-en merc.* trust (=financial combine).
***trus'te** *pt of* **trysje**
trust/kontroll' [trøs't/] *-en* 1 regulation of trusts. 2 agency which regulates trusts.
tru't *-en* 1 *dial.* muzzle, snout. 2 *hum.* lips, mouth, *(pop.)* smacker: **sette t-** pout, purse one's lips.
***tru'ten** *A -e/-i, pl -ne* puffy, swollen.
tru't/munn *-en* pout.
trut'ne *V -a/+-et* (of wood) swell; *fam.* get fat; puff up.
trutt' *Av, nt of* **tru**[3] faithful(ly); long and regular(ly); steadi(ly).
***tru'/vedkjen'ning** *-a* 1 belief, faith. 2 creed, delaration of faith.
tru'/verdig [also -vær'-] *A* - (=+**tro/**) 1 honest, reliable, trustworthy. 2 unsophisticated, unspoiled; appealing.
+**try'bel** *A -elt, pl -le* dismal, dreary: **t- til sinns** depressed, troubled.
tryg'd *-a/+-en* 1 insurance, esp. through government agencies (social security, medicine, etc.). *2 guarantee, protection, security.
tryg'de[1] *V -a/+-et* 1 insure (through govt. agencies). *2 guarantee, secure.
tryg'de[2] *pt of* **trygge**[1], **tryggje**[2]
tryg'de/brev *-et hist.* safe-conduct letter.
tryg'de/kasse *-n* communal organization for medical insurance.
***tryg'de/lag** *-et* insurance company.
tryg'de/premie *-n* (social) insurance premium.
+**tryg'de/taker** *-en, pl -e* (=***-ar**) insurance buyer, insured.
***try'gel** *-elen, pl -lar* small trough.
trygg' *A trygt* 1 safe, secure (**for** from). 2 at ease, confident; assured, reassured, sure (**på** of): **være t- på en, noe** be certain, sure of one, sth; be able to rely on one, sth; **vær t- på det** be sure of that.
***tryg'ge**[1] *-a* cf **tryggje**[1]
+**tryg'ge**[2] *V -a/-et/trygde* (=***tryggje**[2]) insure; make safe, protect, secure (**mot** against); make solid, steady: **t- ens kår (vilkår)** secure sby's economy.
+**trygg'/het** *-en* 1 safety, security. 2 assurance, confidence.
+**trygg'hets/følelse** *-n* confidence, feeling of security, peace of mind.
tryg'ging *-a/+-en* insurance, safety, security.
tryg'gings/fond *-et* insurance fund.
***tryg'gings/rådet** *df* the Security Council (of the UN).
***tryg'gje**[1] *-a* safety, security; protection, reassurance.
***tryg'gje**[2] *V -a/trygde* cf **trygge**[2]
***trygg'leg** *A* - (quite) safe, secure.
***trygg'/leik** *-en* 1 safety, security. 2 assurance, confidence.
Tryg(g)'ve *Prn (m)*
tryg'le *V -a/+-et* beg, beseech, wheedle (**om** for).
tryg't *nt of* **trygg**
trykk'[1] *-en* 1 *fam.* blow; push, shove: **stå for en t-** withstand a blow. 2 print: **boken er i t-en** the book is being printed; **fin t-** fine p-; **på t-** in p-; **sende i t-en** send to press.
trykk'[2] *-et* 1 press, squeeze; heaviness, pressure (also *tech.*). 2 oppression, pressure; stress, weight. 3 *gram.* stress.
trykk'/boksta'v *-en* block letter.
+**tryk'ke** *V trykte* (=***-je**) 1 force, press, push; pinch, squeeze: **t- av** fire, pull, squeeze the trigger; **t- en i hånden** shake one's hand; **t- et kyss** plant a kiss (**på** on); **t- på knappen** press the button. 2 depress, oppress, weigh heavily; force, push down (prices): **føle seg t-et** feel uncomfortable; **t- markedet** *merc.* depress the market. 3 print (a book, a pamphlet, a pattern, etc.): **t- av (noe)** duplicate (sth e.g. by ditto, mimeograph, etc.).
+**tryk'ke/ferdig** *A* - cf **trykk/**
+**tryk'ke/frihet** *-en* freedom of the press.
+**tryk'ke/maski'n** *-en* printing machine (for cloth, etc.).
+**tryk'kende** *A* - heavy, oppressive; depressing.
+**tryk'ker** *-en, pl -e* (=***-jar**) pressman, printer, (printing) press operator.
trykkeri' *-et, pl* +*-er*/*- 1 printer, printing company, print shop. 2 press room. 3 place where cloth is printed.
+**tryk'ke/sted** *-et* (of book, etc.) place of printing, where published.
+**tryk'ket** *A* - 1 (of mood, market) depressed. 2 printed (also **trykt**).
+**tryk'ke/år** *-et* year of printing.
trykk'/feil *-en* misprint, typographical error.
+**trykk'feils/djevel** *-en hum.* "printshop gremlin" (imaginary cause of printer's errors): **t-en har vært ute** there are misprints.
trykk'/ferdig *A* - (of manuscript) ready for the printer; (of corrected proof) ready to print.
***trykkj'ar** *-en* cf **trykker**
***trykkj'e** *V -te* cf **trykke**
trykk'/kabi'n *-en* pressurized cabin (in aircraft).
trykk'/knapp *-en* 1 snap (fastener). 2 push button.
+**trykk'/koker** *-en, pl -e* (=***-ar**) pressure cooker.
trykk'/luft *-a* compressed air.
+**trykk'/måler** *-en, pl -e* (=***-ar**) manometer, pressure gauge.
trykk'/papi'r *-et* book paper, newsprint.
trykk'/pumpe [/pompe] *-a* force pump, pressure pump.
+**trykk'/sak** *-en* 1 (in *pl*) printed matter. 2 publication, volume; published item.
trykkseksten [-sei'sten] *en* hard sock, wallop.
trykk'/side [*/sie] *-a/+-en* printed page.
trykk'/svak *A gram.* unaccented, unstressed; weakly stressed.
+**trykk'svak/het** *-en gram.* lack of accent, of stress.
trykk'/sverte *-a* printer's ink: **det er ikke verd å spandere t- på** it's not worth the ink to print it.
***tryk'nad** *-en* suitability for printing.
tryk'ning +*-en*/*-*a* 1 printing. *2 pinching, squeezing; pressure.
tryl'le *V trylte/+-et* 1 conjure (**bort** away, **fram** forth, up); do, work magic. 2 *archaic* bewitch, cast a spell.
tryl'le/binde *V infl as* **binde** *lit.* bewitch, spellbind.
tryl'le/drikk *-en* magic potion.
tryl'le/fløyte *-a* magic flute.
tryl'le/formula'r *-en/-et, pl -er*/*- incantation, magic words, spell.
+**tryl'le/krets** *-en* magic circle, ring.
tryl'le/kunst *-en* 1 magic; witchcraft. 2 conjuring, magic trick.
+**tryl'le/kunstner** *-en, pl -e* (=***-ar**) conjurer, magician.
tryl'le/o'rd *-et* magic word(s).
+**tryl'leri** *-et* enchantment, magic; spell, witchcraft.
tryl'le/ring *-en* 1 magic ring. 2 magic circle.
tryl'le/slag *-et* magic touch, touch of a wand.
+**tryl'le/speil** *-et* magic mirror.
tryl'le/stav *-en* magic wand.
try'ne *-t* 1 snout: **sette t-** pout. 2 *pop.* mouth, face, puss: **få en i t-et** get one in the kisser.
try'n/tyrk *-en* 1 *folk.* man-eating being with a pig snout. 2 *archaic* Turk.
***try's** *pr of* **trysje**
Try'sil *Pln* twp, Hedmark.
***trysj'e** *V trys, truste, trust* 1 clean up (a field, etc.). 2 break up, crush. 3 crack, snap.
trys'ling *-en* person from Trysil.
***trys'te** *V -a/-e* press, squeeze.
try'te[1] *-a* 1 *zool.* perch (Perca fluviatilis). 2 *bot.* bog bilberry (Vaccinium uliginosum).
try'te[2] *V traut*, +*-t*/**trote*/*-*i* fail, run

dry (out, short), stop: ***det tryt ikkje** there is no lack (of that); **det vil ikke t- på noe** there'll be no end to sth.

Try'vass/høgda *Pln* forested ridge in Oslo.

træ' *V -dde* (=+**tre**[2], ***træde**[2]) thread (a needle, sth through an opening, etc.); string (pearls, etc.).

***træ'de**[1] *-t* 1 fenced-in area. 2 fallow field.

***træ'de**[2] *V -de* cf **træ**

træ'l[1] *-en* (=+**trell**) 1 *hist.* bondman, bondwoman, thrall. 2 slave (**av** of, to e.g. one's emotions, money, work, etc.); (hard) worker. 3 callus.

træ'l[2] *-et dial.* drudgery, toil and trouble.

træ'l/binde *V infl as* **binde** chain, fetter; enslave.

træ'l/bunden *A +-ent/+-et, pl -ne* bound, chained, fettered; enslaved (**av** by).

træ'l/dom· *-men/*-en* bondage, servitude, slavery; *hist.* thralldom.

træ'le *V -a/+-et* (=+**trelle**) slave, struggle, work (hard).

træ'le/arbeid *-et* 1 work for slaves. 2 slaving.

træ'le/kår *-et* slavery; conditions of servitude.

træ'le/merke *-t* mark branded on a slave; *fig.* servility.

træ'lke *V -a/+-et* (=+**trelke**) *dial.* enslave.

træ'l/kvinne *-a/+-en* bondwoman, female slave.

***træ'l/lyn(d)t** *A* - servile.

***træ'l/sam** *A* toilsome; toiling.

***træ'lut** *A* - callused.

Træ'na *Pln* twp, Nordland.

trø'[1] *-a/-et* (=+**trøe**[1], ***trøde**[1]) enclosure, fold; small field.

***trø'**[2] *-et* (noise of) tramping.

trø'[3] *V -dde* cf **trå**[3]

***trø'**[4] *V -dde* put on roof planking.

trøb'bel *N* trouble.

***trø'de**[1] *-a* cf **trøe**[1]

***trø'de**[2] *-t* cf **trø**[1]

+**trø'e**[1] *-a* (=***trøde**[1]) *dial.* 1 footrest, pedal. 2 treadle (on a loom). 3 stepladder.

°**trø'e**[2] *-a* cf **troe**

trøf'fel *-elen, pl +trøfler bot.* truffle (Tuber melanosporum).

Trøg'/stad *Pln* twp, Østfold.

°**trøkk'** *-en* cf **trykk**[1]

***trøm'** *-en* edge, rim.

Trøn'de/lag *Pln* area around the Trondheimsfjord, often used of all of Nord- and Sør-Trøndelag.

trøn'der *-en, pl -e* person from Trøndelag, from Trondheim.

trøn'der/fe *-et* breed of cattle native to Trøndelag: **rødt t-** light, red-horned breed; **sidet t-** hornless, black-flanked breed.

trøn'dsk *A* - (from) Trøndelag.

°**trøng'(s)** *pr of* **trenge(s)**

***trø'r** *pl of* **tro**[1]

***trøs'k** *-en* 1 rounded sidewall in box or pail; same in fiddle. 2 rotted wood (=**fausk**). 3 bag. 4 big fellow.

+**trøs'ke**[1] *-n med.* thrush.

°**trøs'ke**[2] *V -a/-et* cf **treske**

trøs't *-a/+-en* (=***trøyst**) comfort, consolation, solace.

trøs'te *V -a/+-et* (=***trøyste**[1]) 1 comfort, console: **(Gud) t- (og bære) meg** (expressing chagrin) good heavens; heaven help me. 2 esp. *naut.* rely upon, trust (that sth is strong enough, etc.). 3 *(refl.)* **t- seg** be comforted; **t- seg med** take comfort in; **t- seg til** dare, venture; trust oneself to; think oneself able to; *obs.* rely upon; ***jærbuen trur på skillingen og t-ar seg til Gud** the man from Jæren believes in the money and trusts in God (Garborg).

trøs'te/full *A* comforting, consoling.

trøs'te/premie *-en* consolation prize.

+**trøs'ter** *-en, pl -e* (=***-ar**) comforter, consoler.

trøs'te/rik *A* richly comforting, consoling.

+**trøs'tes/løs** *A* (=***/laus**) 1 inconsolable. 2 hopeless. 3 drab, dreary.

+**trøs'te/spiser** *-en, pl -e* compulsive eater.

trøs'tig *A* - calm, confident, undaunted; *(adv.)* confidently, without fear or hesitation.

trøt'ne *V -a/+-et* (+usu. **tretne**) tire.

trøtt' *A* - (+usu. **trett**) 1 fatigued, tired, weary (**av** from, of): **gå t-** get tired, tire (**av** of). 2 *fam.* apathetic, listless. 3 *fam.* boring, tiresome, uninteresting: **en t- vits** a tired joke.

trøt'te *V -a/+-et* (+usu. **trette**) tire (**ut** out): **t-s** become tired.

***trøt'te/sam** *A* cf **trøtt/**

+**trøtt'/het** *-en* (+usu. **trett/**) 1 (of people, metals, etc.) fatigue; weariness. 2 apathy, listlessness. 3 boredom.

***trøtt'/leik** *-en* 1 (of people, metals, etc.) fatigue; weariness. 2 apathy, listlessness. 3 boredom.

***trøtt'/sam** *A* tiring.

trøy'e[1] *-a* jacket (used of a variety of garments, now esp. of men's and woman's undershirts, but formerly also of suitcoats, sweaters, and vests).

trøy'e[2] *V -dde dial.* pass, spend (the time): **t- seg** amuse oneself.

+**trøy'e/erme** *-t* (=***/erm**) coat (jacket, sweater) sleeve.

trøy'e/lomme [/lomme] *-a* coat (or jacket) pocket.

***trøy's** *-a* bowl with a lip.

trøy'/sam *A -t, pl +-me dial.* amusing, fun, funny.

***trøy'/skap** *-en* entertainment, pastime.

+**trøy'som/het** *-en* amusement, fun; joke.

***trøy'st** *-a* cf **trøst**

***trøy'ste**[1] *V -a* cf **trøste**

***trøy'ste**[2] *V -a/-e* 1 make hard, strong, sturdy. 2 dare, have the strength (to); *(refl.)* **t- seg til** (the same).

***trøy'stes/laus** *A* cf **trøstes/løs**

***trøy't** *-en* conclusion, end; bustle (of finishing sth).

***trøy'tande** *A* -: **det er ikkje t- lenger** there is no use staying longer.

trøv'te *V -te dial.* 1 complete, finish (a job); hold out, last (a given period): **t- på** keep it up. 2 work: **t- seg** busy, exert oneself; **t- seg med** get along on.

***trøy'ten** *A -e/-i, pl -ne* diligent, persevering.

***trøyt'ne** *V -a* cf **trøtne**

***trøy't/sam** *A* cf **trøtt/**

***trøytt'** *A* - cf **trøtt**

***trøyt'te** *V -a* cf **trøtte**

trå'[1] *-a/+-en poet., dial.* desire, yearning (**etter** for).

trå'[2] *V -dde poet., dial.* long, yearn (**etter** for).

trå'[3] *V -dde/tro/*trod, -dd* (=**trø**[3]) step, tread (**i** into); stamp, tramp; trample: **t- bremsen inn** step on the brake; **t- feil** take a false step; miss one's footing, slip; **t- vannet** tread water.

trå'[4] *A -tt* 1 persistent, unchanging; *(adv.)* constantly, persistently, regularly. 2 contrary, obstinate; which offers resistance; (of surface) sticky: **det går t-tt** it's slow going. 3 rancid, spoiled (e.g. butter).

trå'/bil *-en* (child's) pedal car.

trå'/bukk *-en dial.* contrary, obstinate person.

trå'd *-en* thread (also *fig.*); line, wire; filament: **falle i t- med** be in line with; **ha en på t-en** (in telephoning) have sby on the line; **løs på t-en** of loose morals; **rød t-** governing idea, leitmotif; **ta opp t-en** pick up the thread (of what one was saying, etc.); **trekke i t-ene** manipulate (behind the scenes), pull wires.

+**trå'd/aktig** *A* - threadlike.

trådd' *pp of* **tre**[2], **trå**[2,3]

trå'd/ende *-n* end of (a) thread; short piece of thread.

trå'd/glas *-et* (=+**/glass**) 1 safety glass, wire glass. 2 filigree glass.

trå'd/laus *A* (=+**/løs**) wireless, radio.

***trå'/dom** *-(m)en* 1 aspiration, desire. 2 endurance, perseverance.

trå'd/snelle *-a* spool; spindle.

trå'd/stift *-en* wire nail, wire tack.

trådt' *pp of* **tre**[2], **trede**

+**trådt'e** *pl of* **tre**[2]

trå'd/vindsel *+-elen/*-elet/*-let, pl +-ler/*-el* spool of thread (cardboard center).

trå'e *-n dial.* endurance, perseverance, stamina.

trå'en *A +-ent, pl -(e)ne dial.* rancid, spoiled.

trå'kig *A* - *lit.* tiresome.

tråkk'[1] *-a* yard (much trampled area, e.g. a farmyard, area in front of a farmhouse).

tråkk'[2] *-et* 1 stamp(ing), tramp(ing); steady running back and forth, traffic: **husmorens t- i huset** the housewife's many steps about the house. 2 pedaling, treadling. 3 track, trail, worn path (esp. of animals).

tråk'ke *V -a/+-et* stamp, tramp, tread; trample (**på** on); pack down; side step (in skiing): **t- dagen lang** be on the move all day; **t- en på tærne** step on sby's toes; **t- ned** trample (e.g. flowers); **t- opp** trample (e.g. a path).

+**tråk'ker** *-en, pl -e* (=***-ar**) person that tramples, esp. one who packs down the snow on a ski hill.

tråk'le *V -a/+-et* 1 baste: **t- en jakke** baste up a coat; **t- noen sting** take some basting stitches. 2 move carefully, laboriously.

tråk'le/sting *-et* basting stitch.

trå'l *-en naut.* 1 trawl net. 2 trawling.

trå'le *V -a/+-et/+-te* 1 trawl (fish). 2 *fig.* drag, search (a building, an area).

***trå'/leik** *-en* slowness, sluggishness.

+**trå'ler** *-en, pl -e* (=***-ar**) *naut.* trawler.

trå'l/fiske *-t* trawling.

***trå'/læte** *-t* reluctance, unwillingness.

***trå'nad** *-en* rancidity, spoilage.

trå'ne *V -a/+-et dial.* 1 become rancid, spoil. 2 long, yearn.

***trå'/skap** *-en* 1 defiance; obstinacy, refractoriness. 2 sulkiness, sullenness, surliness.

trå'/smak *-en* rancid, spoiled taste; taint.

trå'/sykkel *-elen, pl -sykler* bicycle (also of motor bike).

***trå'/søken** *A -e/-i, pl -ne* demanding, importunate, pushy.

trått' *Av cf* **trå**[4]

trå'v *-et* (=+**trav**) trot; trotting: **ride i t-** ride at a trot.

trå'v/bane *-n* racetrack (for harness racing), trotting track.

trå've *V -a/+-et* (=+**trave**[2]) 1 trot. 2 tramp, trudge.

+**trå'ver**[1] *-en, pl -e* (=***-ar**, +**traver**) trotter.

***trå'/ver**[2] *-et* unchanging weather (over a long period).

***trå'vers/bolk** *-en* period of unchanging weather.

trå'v/hest *-en* (=+**trav/**) trotter.

trå'v/kjøring *-a/+-en* (=***/køyring**) harness racing.

***trå'v/køyrar** *-en* cf **trav/kjører**

+**trå'v/løp** *-et* (=***/laup**) harness racing; trotting race.

tsa'r *-en* czar.

+**tset'se/flue** *-a* (=***/fluge**) *zool.* tsetse fly (Glossina).

tsjek'a *-en* cheka (secret Soviet police organization 1917—1922; *fig.* of other secret police).

+ Bokmål; * Nynorsk; ° Dialect.
After letter: ' stress (Acc. 1); ` tone, stress (Acc. 2); · length.
Below letter: . not pronounced.

tsjekk' *-en* cf **tsjekker**
+tsjek'ker *-en, pl -e* (=***-ar, tsjekk)** Czech.
tsjek'kisk *A* - Czech.
tsjekkoslova'k *-en* Czechoslovakian.
Tsjekkoslova'kia *Pln* Czechoslovakia.
tsjekkoslova'kisk *A* - Czechoslovakian.
+tsju' *I* shoo.
T. T. = **Tidens Tegn**
+tu'[1] *N*: **i tu** broken, in pieces; **slå i tu** break.
°tu[2] *P* cf **utor**
tub. =**tuberkulose**
tu'ba *-en, pl* **-er* *mus.* tuba.
+tubb' *-en* 1 tuberculosis. 2 T.B. ward (of a hospital).
tu'be *-n* 1 tube (of paint, toothpaste) 2 *anat.* Fallopian tube; Eustachian tube.
tuber'kel *-elen, pl -ler med.* tubercle.
tuber'kel/basill' *-en med.* tubercle bacillus.
tuberkuli'n/prøve *-a/+-en med.* tuberculin test.
tuberkulo'se *-n med.* tuberculosis: **åpen t-** active t-.
tuberkulø's *A* tuberculous.
+tu'e[1] *-a dial.* wash cloth; scouring cloth (of heavy, coarse material esp. for scrubbing floors).
tu'e[2] *-a* (=**tuve**) hillock, mound; clump, tuft (of grass), patch (of berries, mushrooms, etc.); (large) ant hill: **lita t- velter stort lass** little strokes fell great oaks.
tuff' *-en geol.* tuff.
tuf's[1] *-en* 1 tuft (of hair); cluster. 2 *folk.* supernatural being (often in shape of a fuzzy ball of yarn) that can harm people or animals. 3 small, insignificant person, pipsqueak, shrimp; (old) codger, (young) squirt, twirp, wretch.
tuf's[2] *-et* 1 snarl, tangle; tuft; sth matted together. 2 sth insignificant miserable, shabby: **det ble bare t- med dem** they never got anywhere.
tuf's[3] *A* 1 miserable, poorly, sickly. 2 seedy, shabby, shaggy.
tuf'se[1] *-a dial.* 1 snarl, tangle; sth matted together. 2 slattern.
tuf'se[2] *V -a/+-et* 1 mat, snarl, tangle (usu. refl.: **t- seg**). 2 be tufted. 3 mess (**til up**); mess around, putter; diddle, tog with.
tuf'set(e) *A* - 1 matted, shaggy, snarled; tangled; messy, shabby. 2 confused, dotty; fumbling. 3 puny, sickly, weak; depressed.
tuf'sing *-en dial.* (=**tufs**[1] **3**).
tuf't *-a dial.* (building) lot; site.
***tuf'te**[1] *-n* brownie, goblin (see **tomte**).
tuf'te[2] *V -a/+-et* lay a foundation: **t- på** build on.
tuf'te/kall *-en* brownie, little old man.
tug'ge *-a* 1 *dial.* bite, mouthful. 2 *hist.* pacifier, sugartit (for a baby).
tu'ja *-en bot.* arborvitae (Thuja).
tuk'l *-et* (=+**tukkel**) fumbling; mess; trouble.
tuk'le *V -a/+-et* 1 bumble; fiddle, fumble, mess (**med** with). 2 caress, (*pop.*) paw.
tuk't *-a/+-en* 1 discipline; (of dogs) training; (esp. *bibl.*) admonition, chastisement, correction: **i Herrens tukt** in the a- of the Lord (Eph. 6,4); **tankens t-** the discipline of thought. 2 (esp. *bibl.*) decorum, propriety, seemliness: **i t- og ære** with shamefacedness and sobriety (I Tim. 2,9); **med t- å melde** *hum.* saving your presence.
tuk'te *V -a/+-et* 1 discipline; chastise, reprimand, reprove; (esp. *bibl.*) chasten, punish. 2 beat (up), flog (in order to discipline or subdue); drive, force (sby to do sth). 3 *tech.* hew (stone with a chisel). 4 (*refl.*): **t- seg** discipline oneself.
+tuk'telse *-n* discipline; punishment; reprimand.
+tuk'te/mester *-eren, pl -ere/-rer* (=***/meister)** taskmaster.
tuk't/hus *-et lit.* penitentiary, prison.
tuk'thus/fange *-n* jailbird, prisoner.
tuk'thus/kandida't *-en fam.* criminal, crook.
tuk'tig *A* - *lit.* modest, virtuous.
tuk't/laus *A* (=+**/løs**) *lit.* 1 undisciplined, wild. 2 immoral; unseemly.
tulipa'n *-en bot.* tulip (Tulipa gesneriana).
+tulipa'n/løk *-en* (=***/lauk**) tulip bulb.
tull'[1] *-en* 1 ball, tuft (e.g. of wool); small bundle, roll: **t- i t-** bundled up, rolled together. 2 roly-poly child. 3: **gå i t-** go in circles; become jumbled, tangled; become a confusion, a mess. 4 *fam.* dummy, dunce, nitwit: **en t- og en tosk var han** what a blockhead he was (Falkberget).
tull'[2] *-et* 1 foolishness, nonsense, rubbish: **slikt t- og tøys** such stuff and nonsense. 2 *fam.* trouble: **få t- med politiet** get into trouble with the police.
tull'/ball *-en pop.* idiot, nitwit.
tul'le[1] *-a pop.* stupid woman.
tul'le[2] *-a fam.* little girl; lass; tot (endearing term).
tul'le[3] *V -a/+-et* 1 roll, spin around; twiddle (e.g. one's thumbs), twine, twist. 2 bundle, tuck, wrap (**inn i** in, **om** around, **sammen** together, up). 3 frisk, romp, tumble (**omkring, rundt** around). 4 fool around, meddle, tamper (**med** with). 5 talk foolishness, nonsense; behave like a fool. 6 confuse: **t- noen rundt** confuse sby, turn sby around. 7 (*refl.*): **t- seg** wander (**inn i** into) by mistake; **t- seg bort** get lost, lose one's way; become entangled, get mixed up (**i** in, with).
tul'le[4] *V -a/+-et dial.* croon, hum.
tul'len *A* +*-ent, pl tulne* 1 crazy, wild. 2 beside oneself, dizzy, giddy.
tullerus'k *A* - crazy, wild.
tul'let(e) *A* - crazy, wild.
tul'ling *-en fam.* half-wit, idiot.
tull'/jente *-a* crazy, silly girl.
tull'/prat *-et* foolish talk, nonsense.
***tull'/skap** *-en* nonsense, twaddle.
tull'/snakk *-et* foolish talk, nonsense.
tulupp' *-en archaic* (men's) furlined greatcoat.
***tu'mars/finger** *-eren, pl -rar* cf **tommel/**
***tu'me** *-n* cf **tomme**
tumle [tom'le] *V -a/+-et* 1 topple, tumble (**om** over); lurch, stagger, totter. 2 frisk, gambol, romp; swing, whirl about (esp. in a dance): **t- i vei** rush away. 3 (esp. of sea, waves, etc.) toss about; (of emotions, thoughts, etc.) become confused, jumbled; tumble, whirl; go round and round. 4: **t- med** handle, manage; deal, grapple, struggle with; (of thoughts) turn over in one's mind. 5 (*refl.*): **t- seg** frisk, play about, romp; throw oneself (**inn i** into e.g. excesses, etc.).
tumle/plass *-en* 1 playground. 2 *fig.* arena.
+tumler [tom'ler] *-en, pl -e* (=***-ar)** 1 *zool.* tumbler pigeon. 2 *zool.* (type of) dolphin (Tursiops truncatus).
tumling [tom'ling] *-en* 1 round-bottomed beaker, sometimes weighted at the bottom. 2 roly-poly toy.
tummel [tom'mel] *-en* tumult, uproar; turmoil.
+tummelumsk [tommelom'sk] *A* -: **t- i hodet** confused, giddy, lightheaded.
***tumsen** [tom'sen] *A -e/-i, pl -ne* cf **tomsen**
***tumsing** [tom'sing] *-en* cf **tomsing**
***tumsut** [tom'sut] *A* - cf **tomset(e)**
tumul't *-en lit.* disturbance, tumult, uproar.
tumultua'risk *A* - *lit.* tumultuous.
tu'n *-et* yard (courtyard, farm yard) usu. surrounded by a cluster of farm buildings.
***tun'der** *-eret/-ret* cf **tønder**
tun'dra *-en, pl* **-er* *geol.* tundra.
Tu'ne *Pln* 1 twp, Østfold. 2 large island on which Sarpsborg is located.
+tune'ser *-en, pl -e* (=***-ar)** Tunisian.
tune'sisk *A* - Tunisian.
tu'n/fisk *-en zool.* tuna; tunny (Thunnus thynnus).
tung [tong'] *A cp tyngre, sp tyngst* 1 heavy (book, build, food, load, responsibility, sea, taxes, work, etc.); ponderous (architecture, language, movement, etc.); oppressive (atmosphere, heat, mood, silence, etc.); 2 difficult, hard (road, task, times, etc.): **falle en t-t for brystet** be objectionable, unpleasant for one, stick in one's throat; **ha t-t** have difficulty (**for** in, with); find it difficult (**for** to); **selv i den tyngste motgang** even in the greatest adversity (Evensmo). 3 grievous, painful, sad (fate, loss, news, etc.). 4 brooding, melancholy (disposition, landscape, mood, etc.). 5 dull, slow, sluggish (in comprehension, etc.); stodgy (expression, face, etc.).
***tung/alde** [tong'/] *-a* ocean wave.
tung/arbeid [tong'/] *-et* heavy work.
+tung/bedt *A* - (=***/beden)** *dial.* slow to comply.
***tung/blæ'st** *A* - out of breath; short-winded.
tunge[1] [tong'e] *-a/+-en* 1 tongue (of fire, of land, of a railroad switch, *dial.* of a shoe); index, pointer, tongue (e.g. of a scale); scallop: **holde t-en rett i munnen** watch one's step, one's P's and Q's; **ligge en på t-en** be on the tip of one's tongue; **med t-a ut av halsen** with one's tongue hanging out; **splittflagg med t-** ensign with three swallow tails; **ta på t-en** mention, repeat, say; **være t-en på vektskålen** be the deciding factor. 2 tongue (=language). 3 *zool.* sole (Solea solea).
***tunge**[2] [tong'e] *-n* 1 weight (measure, additional w-). 2 heaviness, sleepiness.
tunge[3] [tong'e] *V -a/+-et* 1: **t- seg** form tongue(s), scallops; (of fire) lick out. 2: **t- ut** scallop; divide.
tunge/bånd *-et* (=+**/bånd**) *anat.* frenum: **løse t-et på en** loosen sby's tongue; **være godt skåret for t-et** have the gift of gab.
tunge/blad *-et* blade of the tongue.
+tunge/bånd *-et* cf **/band**
+tunge/ferdig *A* - fluent, glib.
+tungeferdig/het *-en* fluency, glibness.
tunge/mål *-et* language, tongue.
tunge/rapp *A -rapt* fluent, glib.
tunge/rot *-a, pl +-røtter/*-røter* root of the tongue.
tunge/rygg *-en* back of the tongue.
tunge/spiss *-en* tip of the tongue.
tunget [tong'et] *A* - cf **tungete**
tunge/tale [tong'e/] *-n/*-a eccl.* gift of tongues, speaking in tongues.
+tunge/taler *-en, pl -e* (=***-ar)** *eccl.* one who speaks in tongues, pentecostalite.
tunget(e) [tong'et(e)] *A* - scalloped, tongued.
tung/før [tong'/] *A* heavy of step, slow-moving.
***tung/føtt** *A* - heavy-footed.
tung/hørt *A* - (=***/høyrd)** (partially) deaf, hard of hearing.
+tunghørt/het *-en* deafness, hardness of hearing.
tung/industri' [tong'/] *-en* heavy industry.
+tung/lest *A* - (=***/lesen)** hard to read, heavy going.
***tung/lynde** *-t* gloom, heavy spirit; melancholy.
tung/lynt *A* - (=***/lyndt)** gloomy, melancholy.
+tung/nem' *A -t, pl -me* (=***/næm)** dull, slow learning.
tung/olje *-a/-en* tung oil (China wood oil).
tung/pusten *A* +*-ent, pl -ne* (=**/pusta,** +**/pustet)** asthmatic, short-winded.

tung/rodd *A* -/*-*rott* 1 hard to row. 2 *fig.* difficult to handle.
***tung/sam** *A* burdensome, difficult, sad.
+**tungsindig** [tongsin'di] *A* - gloomy, melancholy, moody; dismal, sad.
+**tungsindig/het** *-en* gloom, melancholy, moodiness; sadness.
+**tung/sinn** [tong'/] *-et* depression, gloom, melancholy.
tung/sint *A* - depressed, gloomy, heavy-hearted.
***tung/svævd** *A* -/-*svævt* (=*/**svæv**): **han er t-** he's a heavy sleeper.
tungt/fordøy·elig [tong't/] *A* - hard to digest, heavy.
tungt/vatn *-et* (=+/**vann**) heavy water.
+**tungt/veiende** *A* - weighty.
***tung/vatn** [tong'/] *-et* cf **tungt/**
tung/vekt *-a*/+*-en* heavyweight.
tung/vint *A* - (=*/**vinn**) 1 hard (work), laborious, tiring. 2 clumsy, unwieldy; inconvenient. 3 (of person) slow-moving; awkward, heavy.
tu'nika *-en, pl* *-*er* tunic.
Tu'nis *Pln* Tunis.
tu'n/kall *-en folk.* friendly spirit belonging to a particular farm; elf.
tunn'[1] *-et dial.* circle, whirl: **ri i t-** ride in circles; **t- i t-** round and round, end over end; **snakke folk i t-** confuse people with talk.
***tunn'**[2] *A tunt* cf **tynn**
***tun'ne**[1] *-a* cf **tynne**[1]
***tun'ne**[2] *V -a* circle around, spin, whirl.
tunnel' [also tun'-] *-en* tunnel.
tunnel'/bane *-n* subway.
***tunn'/hærd** *A -hært* cf **tynn/håra**
***tun'ning** *-a* circular course, orbit, round.
***tunn'/vange** *-n anat.* temple.
***Tu'ns/berg** *Pln* cf **Tøns/**
tu'n/tre *-et, pl* -/+*-trær folk.* tree planted in a farmyard, originally where the owner was buried; formerly honored by sacrifices.
tu'n/vo'rd *-en folk.* friendly spirit belonging to a particular farm; elf.
tupe're *V -te* rat (women's hair, by combing in).
tupp'[1] *-en* 1 bud, tip (e.g. of finger, nose, ski). 2 *dial.* rooster. 3 pet name for child or young animal.
+**tupp'**[2] *I*: **t-, t-, t-** chick-chick-chick (to call hens).
tup'pe[1] *-a* 1 *fam., dial.* biddy, hen. 2 *fam.* young girl, "chick".
tup'pe[2] *V -a*/+*-et* 1 kick (a ball). 2 tamp (a cigarette). 3 *dial.* jerk.
tu'r[1] *-en* 1 trip; stroll, walk; excursion, outing, tour; drive, ride, spin: **gå, kjøre, ri en t-** take a walk, a ride (on horseback), a drive; **ta (seg) en t- til byen** take a trip to town. 2 journey, trip, voyage: **god t-** bon voyage; *dial.* **stå på t-** be ready to go, travel; **t- returbillett** round trip ticket. 3 turn: **etter t-** by turns, in rotation, one after the other; **i t- og orden** in due course, one by one; **stå for t-** be next (in line). 4 (dance) figure. 5 *fam.* spell (of carousing, drinking, insanity, etc.).
°**tu'r**[2] *P* cf **utor**
tur'ban *-en* turban.
tu'r/billett' *-en* one-way ticket.
turbi'n *-en tech.* turbine.
turbi'n/båt *-en* turbine-propelled ship, turbiner.
tu'r/binding *-a*/*-en* loose type of ski binding used for cross-country skiing.
turbi'n/hall +*-en*/**-a* turbine room.
turbi'n/hjul *-et* turbine wheel.
turbi'n/skovl *-a*/+*-en* turbine blade; vane.
tu'r/dans *-en* folk dance consisting of several figures.
+**tur'de** *V tør, turde, -et* cf **tore**[2]
***tu're**[1] *-n* large spigot.
tu're[2] *V -a*/+*-te* 1 roam, rove, wander (**omkring, rundt** around); *fam.* take a trip (on foot, on skis). 2 *pop.* go on a bender, hang one on; carouse, revel: **t- fra seg** have one's fling, sow one's wild oats. 3 *pop.* celebrate: **t- bryllup** hold a wedding celebration. 4: **t- fram** continue (recklessly, wildly) on one's course.
tu're/basse *-n fam.* carouser, drinker, rounder.
tu're/lag *-et* drinking party.
+**tu'rer** *-en, pl -e* (=***-ar**) reveler, rounder.
***tur'ft** *-a* necessity, need.
***tur'ftig** *A* - needful, needy.
+**tu'r/gjenger** *-en, pl -e* hiker, hiking or skiing enthusiast.
tu'r/gåing *-a*/+*-en* cross-country skiing or hiking.
Tu'rid *Prn (f)*
turis'me *-n* touring, tourism; tourist trade.
turis't *-en* tourist.
turis't/byrå· *-et, pl* +*-er*/*- travel agency.
+**turisteri'** *-et derog.* tourism, tourist business.
+**turis't/fore·ning** *-en* organization to promote hiking and tourism: **Den Norske T-** Norwegian Travel Association.
+**turis't/fører** *-en, pl -e* (=***-ar**) guide, tour leader.
turis't/hotell· *-et* tourist hotel.
turis't/hytte *-a* tourist cabin (often in the mountains).
turis't/klasse *-a*/*-en* tourist class.
+**turis't/messig** *A* - for tourists, touristy; tourist.
turis't/sesong· *-en* tourist season.
***tur'k** *-en* cf **tørk**[1]
***tur'ke** *V -a* cf **tørke**[2]
turki's *-en* turquoise.
turki's/blå *A -tt* turquoise blue.
+**tu'r/leder** *-en, pl -e* (=*/**leidar**) tour guide.
tu'rn *-en* gymnastics.
tu'rn/appara't *-et, pl* -/+*-er* gym apparatus.
turné *-en* tour (of road show, etc.): **gå på t-** go on the road.
tu'rne *V -a*/+*-et* do gymnastics.
+**tu'rner** *-en, pl -e* (=***-ar**) gymnast, turner.
turne're *V -te* 1 *mil.* evade, outflank. 2 turn (a compliment, a phrase); parry, retort.
turne'ring *-a*/+*-en* 1 *hist.* joust, tournament, tourney. 2 (sports) tournament. 3 *hist.* joust. 4 *fam.* go on the road; barnstorm.
tu'rnips *-en* turnip.
tu'rn/sko *-en, pl* -*r*/+- gym shoe, sneaker, tennis shoe.
tur'nus *-en lit.* 1 round, round trip. 2 rotation; rotation period.
***turr'** *A turt* cf **tørr**
tur't *-a bot.* blue lettuce (Lactuca alpina).
tu'r/tal *-et* (=+/**tall**) revolutions per minute.
tur'tel/due *-a* turtledove: **t-ns røst** *(bibl.)* the voice of the turtle (Song of Solomon 2, 12).
°**tu'ru** *-a* cf **tvare**
***tur'vande** *A* - needy; needed.
***tur've** *V tarv, -te, -t* need: **han tarv det vel** he needs it badly; **du tarv ikkje tvile** you needn't doubt it; **eg turvte ha gjort det** I ought to have done it.
tu'r/veg *-en* (=+/**vei**) tour route; hiking trail.
tu'r/vis *Av* by turns.
tu'sen[1] *-et, pl* -/+*-er* thousand: **t-er og atter t-er** t-s and t-s; **to t-** two t-; **(mange) t- takk** thank you ever so much; **t- umulig** utterly impossible.
tu'sen[2] *Num* thousand: **T- og en natt** Arabian Nights; **de t- hjem** every home; all of Norway's homes (orig. a quotation from Bjørnson's national anthem.
tu'sen/bein *-et zool.* millipede (class Diplopoda); centipede (class Chilopoda).
tu'sende *Num* thousandth.
tu'sen/del *-en* (fraction) thousandth.
***tu'sende/part** *-en* (fraction) thousandth.
+**tu'sen/fold** *Av* thousandfold, thousand times.
+**tu'sen/foldig** *A* - a thousandfold.
tu'sen/fryd *-en* (=*/**frygd**) *bot.* English daisy (Bellis perennis).
+**tu'sen/kunstner** *-en, pl -e* (=***-ar**) 1 magician, sleight-of-hand artist. 2 jack-of-all-trades.
tu'sen/stemmig *A* - thousandvoice(d).
tu'sen/tal *-et* (=+/**tall**) 1 **på t-et** in the eleventh century. 2 **i t-** by the thousands.
tu'sen/tals *A* - (=+/**talls**) thousands of.
tu'sen/vis *Av*: **i t-** by the thousands; **t- av t-** of.
tu'sen/år *-et* millennium, thousand years.
tu'sen/årig *A* - thousand year(s old); ancient, hoary: **det t-e rike** the millennium.
tu'senårs/rike *-t*: **t-t** the millennium.
tusj' *-en* India ink.
tusj'e *V -a*/+*-et* (use) India ink.
tusj'/penn *-en* drawing pen (used with India ink).
+**tusj'/tegning** [/teining] *-en* (=*/**teikning**) ink drawing, wash drawing.
tus'k *-et dial.* hullabaloo, noise; games, joking; whispering.
tus'ke[1] *V -a*/+*-et dial.* 1 move quietly; tiptoe; putter around. 2 whisper; talk in a low voice; call (sby) quietly. 3 have fun, make noise.
tus'ke[2] *V -a*/+*-et* bargain, barter; make a deal, trade: **t- bort** trade off; **t- seg til** get (one's) hands on; **t- til seg** buy, make a swap for.
tus'k/handel *-en* barter, swap, trade.
***tus'l** *-et* pottering around.
tus'le *V -a*/+*-et* (=+**tutle**) 1 rustle, swish. 2 be (quietly) busy, putter (**med** with). 3 go, pad, walk (around) quietly, slowly; **gå og t-** (the same).
tus'let(e) *A* - feeble, puny; small and weak.
tus'ling *-en* (=**tutling**) weakling.
tus'/mørk *A* dim, dusky, twilight.
tus'/mørke *-t* (=*/**mørker**) dusk, twilight.
***tus'ne** *V -a* become dry, stiff.
tuss' *-en* (=**tusse**[2]) 1 *myth.* giant, troll (living in the mountains and an enemy of gods and men). 2 *folk.* gnome, goblin, pixie; *dial., folk.* spirit in human or animal form which attracts good fortune to a dwelling; spirit in cat form which steals milk and food; spirit in form of shaggy ball of thread, yarn, etc.
tus'se[1] *-a* 1 *folk.* female sprite; pixie woman. 2 *dial.* halfwit girl.
tus'se[2] *V -a*/+*-et* pad, plod.
tus'se/flette *-a folk.* elflock.
tus'se/fløyte *-a folk.* fairy flute.
tus'se/ladd *-en* pale, insignificant-looking person; weakling.
tus'set(e) *A* - 1 puny, unprepossessing. 2 crazy, wild (**etter** for).
tus't[1] *-a dial.* flail.
tus't[2] *-en* 1 clump; cluster; tangle. 2 lock, wisp (of hair); bunch. 3 nitwit. 4 *bot.* sedge grass (Kobresia).
***tus't**[3] *pp of* **tysje**
tus'te[1] *-a dial.* 1 snarl, tangle. 2 messy, slovenly woman.
tus'te[2] *V -a*/+*-et* 1 bumble, putter (at). 2 snarl, tangle; straggle. 3: **t- seg bort** get lost.
***tus'te**[3] *pt of* **tysje**
tus'tet(e) *A* - 1 disheveled, messy; snarled, straggling. 2 feeble.
Tus'tna *Pln* twp, Møre og Romsdal.
tus'tret(e) *A* - *dial* 1 disheveled, tangled. 2 ailing, sickly.
***tu'sul** *-en, pl tuslar* 1 ghost, sprite. 2 nonentity; weakling.

+ Bokmål; * Nynorsk; ° Dialect.
After letter: ' stress (Acc. 1); ` tone, stress (Acc. 2); · length.
Below letter: . not pronounced.

tu't¹ *-en* 1 nozzle, spout; lip, opening. 2 *pop.* mouth, *(pop.)* smacker, snout. 3 *naut., pop.* head, john, toilet.
tu't² *-et* 1 howl. 2 (of horns) blast, toot.
***tu'tar/ho'rn** *-et mus.* horn.
tu'te *V -a/+-et* 1 howl; hoot: **en må t- med de ulver som er ute** one must howl with the wolves one is with (=when in Rome do as the Romans do). 2 blow, honk, toot (horn, instrument, etc.). 3 bawl, cry, weep; bellow, howl: **t- ørene fulle på en** din sth into one's ears.
+tu'te/kanne *-a* (=***tut/**) wooden ale tankard with a spout.
+tut'le *V -a/-et* cf **tusle**
tut'let(e) *A -* 1 poorly, sickly. 2 foolish, halfwitted. 3 awkward.
tut'ling *-en* cf **tusling**
tut're *V -a/+-et dial.* 1 shiver. 2 whimper. 3 chatter.
+tutt' *-en* 1 paper cornucopia (for candy, etc.); paper (cone-shaped) plant shield. 2 roll of coins. 3 *dial.* lock, tuft (of hair); bun, knot (of hair).
tu've *-a* cf **tue²**
***tu'vut** *A -* hummocky, humpy.
t. v.=**til venstre**
tva'g *-et agr.* animal urine.
***tva'ge** *V -a* (of animals) stale, urinate.
tvang'¹ *-en* 1 coercion, compulsion, force; *jur.* duress; constraint, restraint: **med t-** by force, forcibly; **bruke t- på** coerce; **under t-** under duress. 2 tyranny: **nå har dere fått t- og trelldom** now you have gotten tyranny and slavery (Snorre).
+tvang'² *pt of* **tvinge²**
tvang'/fri *A -tt* free, unconstrained; easy, informal.
tvang'/laus *A* (=**+/løs**) free, unconstrained; easy, informal.
tvang's/arbeid *-et* forced labor; hard labor.
tvangs'arbeids/anstalt *-en* house of correction, workhouse.
tvang's/auksjo'n *-en* forced sale, foreclosure.
tvang's/fore *V -a/+-et* force-feed.
+tvang's/forestilling [/fåre-] *-en* obsession; compulsion, compulsive idea.
tvang's/handling *-a/+-en* 1 compulsive action. 2 sth done under compulsion.
+tvang's/innlegge *V -la, -lagt* commit (to a mental hospital).
tvang's/middel *-elet/-midlet, pl +-midler/*-el* coercive measure.
***tvang's/råd** *-a* coercive measure.
tvang's/situasjo'n *-en* situation where there is no choice; emergency.
tvang's/tanke *-n* compulsion; obsession.
tvang's/trøye *-a* straitjacket.
+tva're *-a* (=***tvore**) stirring stick (for porridge).
***tvarr'** *pt of* **tverre²**
+tve'- *Pf* also cf **tvi-**
+tve'/beite *-t* (=***tvi/**) team (of horses).
+tve'/bitt *-et* two fish caught at the same time (on the same line).
+tve'/bo *A - bot.* dioecious.
+tve'/deling *-a/-en* bisection, dichotomy, halving (**av** of).
Tve'de/strand *Pln* city, Aust-Agder.
+tve'/drakt *-a/-en* discord, dissension.
+tve'/egget *A -* (=**+-a**) double-edged, two-edged: **et t- sverd a t-** sword (usu. *fig.*).
+tve'/fold *A -* double, twofold; *(adv.)* doubly.
+tve'/føttes *Av dial.* with both feet.
***tve'ge¹** *V -a* stagger, walk heavily.
tve'ge²** *pp of* **två** (=tvegi**)
+tve'/hake *-a/-n* cf **tvi/**
tvei't¹ *-a dial.* 1 angled cut in a tree trunk (to fell it); split. 2 small furrow; groove; hollow.
***tvei't²** *-en* chip; splint.
Tvei't *Pln* twp, Vest-Agder.
+tve'/kamp *-en* duel, single combat (**med** with).
+tve'/kjønnet *A -* (=**-a**) bisexual, hermaphroditic.
+tve'/kroket(e) *A -* bent double, doubled up: **le seg t-** laugh one's head off.
+tve'/lyd *-en gram.* diphthong.
***tveng'** *-en* 1 strap (with a buckle). 2 wedge in a plane.
+tven'ne *Num* cf **to³**
***tve'rel** *-elen, pl -lar* churn handle.
tver'ke¹ *N*: **på t-** crosswise, in the way; awry; awkward, frustrating; **komme på t- for** hinder, thwart; come at an inconvenient (awkward) time for.
***tver'ke²** *V -a* act perversely.
tverr' *A tvert* 1 cross (beams, streets, etc.), crosswise, lying at right angles to each other. 2 cross, grumpy; sullen, surly. 3 reluctant, stubborn, unwilling. (See also **tvers** and **tvert**).
tverr'/berg *-et* 1 (mountain) spur. 2 mountain across the end of a valley.
tverr'/bjelke *-n* crossbeam, cross member.
tverr'/blei *-en* (=**/bleig**) 1 wedge (for splitting logs). 2 *fig.* cross, contrary person.
tverr'/bratt *A -* precipitous, sheer-sided.
tverr'/bukk [/bokk] *-en* contrary, ornery person.
tverr'/dal *-en* 1 side valley. 2 *geol.* valley that runs counter to the direction of the geological layers.
tverr'/djup *A*: **det er t-t** there is a sudden drop-off.
+tverr'/driver *-en, pl -e* (=***-ar**) crosspatch; sourpuss.
+tverr'/dyp *A* cf **/djup**
tver're¹ *-a* 1 *dial.* edge, end (surface). 2: **på t-** sideways; on unfriendly terms.
***tver're²** *V -a/tvarr, -a/tvorre/-i* diminish: **det tvarr i kokinga** it boiled down (Aasen).
tverr'/gate *-a* cross, side street.
tverr'/gående *A -* cross, transverse.
+tverr'/het *-en* 1 contrariness, orneriness. 2 crabbiness, sulkiness, surliness.
tverr'/kast *-et* sudden movement to the side.
***tverr'/laga** *A -* inconvenient, inopportune.
+tverr'/ligger *-en, pl -e* (=***-jar**) cross member, crosspiece; (between goal posts) crossbar.
tverr'/mål *-et* diameter.
tverr'/pinne *-n* 1 crosspin. 2 sourpuss; ornery person.
+tverr'/plattfot *en* fallen metatarsal (transverse) arch.
tverr'/pomp [/pomp] *-en* crab, sourpuss; ornery coot.
+tverr'/rykke *V -rykte* (=***/rykkje**) jerk suddenly.
tverr'/side [*/sie] *-a/+-en* end (surface).
tverr'/sikker *A -ert, pl -sikre* cocksure, positive (**på** of).
***tverr'/skap** *-en* contrariness, orneriness.
tverr'/skip *-et arch.* transept (of church).
+tverr'/skips *Av naut.* athwart, thwartships, transversely.
***tverr'/sku'rd** *-en* cross section, section.
tverr'/snitt *-et* cross section, section.
tverr'/snu¹ *-en dial.* sudden turn.
tverr'/snu² *V -dde* 1 turn crosswise: **t-dd** contrary. 2 turn sharply, suddenly.
tverr'/sprang *-et* gallop, top speed.
***tverr'/spreng** *-en elec.* short circuit.
***tverr'/stane** *V -a/-te* cf **/stanse**
+tverr'/stang *-a, pl -stenger* (=***/stong**) crossbar.
tverr'/stanse *V -a/+-et* break off, end, stop suddenly.
tverr'/strek *-en* cross stroke; slash.
tverr'/stripe *-a/+-en* cross stripe, transverse stripe; crossbar.
tverr'/sum' *-men* sum of the digits in a number.
tverr'/tre *-et, pl -/+-trær* 1 crosspiece, cross strip. 2 crosspatch, ornery person.
tverr'/ved *-en* wood with twisted grain.
tverr'/vegg *-en, pl *-er* end wall, short wall.
tverr'/vende *V +-te/*-e* turn sharply, suddenly.
tver's *Av* across; *naut.* abreast, abeam, athwart: **på t-** *(dial., fam.* **på tvert)** across, crosswise, transversely; **komme på t-** be amiss, go wrong; **t- gjennom** clean, straight through; **t- over** (right, straight) across; **t- på** across, athwart, at right angles to.
+tver's/over *P* cf **tvers**
tver't¹ *nt of* **tverr**
tver't² *Av* 1 abruptly, sharply; flatly: **bryte over t-** break (**med** with); cut the matter short. 2 right, squarely: **t- imot** (quite) contrary to, on the contrary; **t- om** on the contrary. 3 crossly, curtly.
+tver't/imo't *Av* cf **tvert²**
+tver't/om' *Av* cf **tvert²**
+tve'/sidig *A - lit.* bilateral, two-sided.
+tve'/sprang *-et* cf **tvi/**
+tve'/syn *-et* cf **tvi/**
+tvett' *-en lit.* cleansing (of sins, etc.).
***tvet'te¹** *-t* 1 wash(ing). 2 strong liquid for washing (lye, urine).
tvet'te² *V +-et/*-a (bibl.)* cleanse, wash.
+tve'/tunget [/tonget] *A* - fork-tongued, two-faced.
+tve'/tydig *A -* 1 ambiguous, equivocal; dubious: **i en t- stilling** in an equivocal position. 2 indelicate, risqué, suggestive.
+tve'tydig/het *-en* 1 ambiguity, equivocation; an ambiguous position. 2 double entendre, indelicate remark.
tvi' *I* 1 pfui, phoo (e.g. for spitting or expressing disgust); phooey; phew: **t- deg** *archaic* shame on you; **t- være** *dial.* (the same). 2 *folk.* said (with or without spitting) to assure good fortune: **t- t-** good luck.
tvi'- *Pf* (=**tve-**) 1 two-. 2 intensively: **t-/holde.**
***tvi'/auke** *V -a* double, redouble.
***tvi'/beite** *-t* cf **tve/**
***tvi'/botna** *A -* double-bottomed.
+tvi'/brent *A -* (in hide-and-seek): **t-** plus player's name 1 — 2 — 3 you're out!; **t- meg** free!
***tvi'bu/plante** *-n bot.* dioecious plant.
***tvi'/burar** *pl* twins.
***tvi'/drag** *-et* cf **tve/drakt**
***tvi'/eggja** *A -* cf **tve/egget**
tvi'/felt** *A -* (=/fald**) double.
***tvi'/føtt** *A -* two-legged.
tvi'/hake *-a/+-n* double chin.
+tvi'/holde *V -holdt, -holdt* (=***/halde**) 1 hold tight: **t- krampaktig** hang on for dear life. 2 maintain (a position, opinion, etc.): **han t-t blikket** he forced himself to look steadily (Evensmo); **t- på** insist.
***tvi'/huga** *A -* in doubt, of two minds, irresolute.
***tvi'/høgda** *A -* two-story.
***tvi'ke** *V -a* be doubtful, irresolute; waver.
***tvi'/kjønna** *A -* cf **tve/kjønnet**
tvi'/kroket(e) *A -* cf **tve/**
tvi'/krøkt *A -* bent double.
***tvi'k/sam** *A* doubtful, undecided.
tvi'l *-en, pl -/*-ar* doubt (**om** of); misgiving(s): **dra i t-** call in question, throw doubt on; **ingen t- om det** no doubt about that; **uten t-** undoubtedly.
tvi'le *V -te/*-a* 1 doubt; be doubtful, skeptical: **t- om, på** be in doubt about; *(adj.)* **t-ende** doubting, skeptical; doubtful. 2 *dial.* be afraid, have misgivings (**for** about): **jeg t-te mest for at jeg kom for tidlig** I was most afraid that I came too early (Scott).
+tvi'ler *-en, pl -e* (=***-ar**) doubter, skeptic.
***tvi'/ljod** *-en* cf **tve/lyd**
***tvi'/ljode** *V -a* 1 echo. 2 diphthongize.
tvill' *-en* twill.
tvi'l/laus *A* (=**+/løs**) undoubting,

unquestioning; *(adv.)* **t-t** undoubtedly, without a doubt.
tvil'ling -*en* twin.
tvil'ling/hjul -*et* dual wheel.
tvil'ling/par -*et* pair of twins.
tvi'l/rådig *A* - doubtful, irresolute, undecided (**om** about).
+tvi'lrådig/het -*en* feeling of doubt, indecision, irresolution.
***tvi'l/sam** *A* cf **/som**
tvi'ls/mål -*et* doubt, misgiving; questionable point; uncertainty.
***tvi'ls/måte** -*n*: **i t-** in doubt, in question.
+tvi'l/som· *A* (=***/sam**) doubtful, dubious, questionable; problematic, uncertain.
+tvi'lsom/het -*en* 1 dubiousness. 2 imponderable; uncertainty; question.
tvi'ls/spørsmål -*et* moot point, point in dispute, questionable point.
tvi'ls/tilfelle -*t*, *pl* -/+-*r* 1 doubtful case, case in question, moot case. 2: **i t-** in case of doubt.
***tvi'/lyd** -*en* cf **tve/**
tving'e[1] -*a* vise; clamp, cramp; *archaic* buckle.
tving'e[2] *V* +*tvang*/*-*a*, +*tvunget*/*-*a* 1 coerce, compel, force; constrain, restrain: **t- en til handling** force one's hand; **t- fram** force (out); effect, obtain (an admission, a decision, etc.); **t- noe igjennom** enforce sth; railroad sth through; **t- sin vilje igjennom** work one's will, have one's own way. 2 *(refl.)*: **t- seg** force oneself; constrain, restrain oneself.
tving'ende *A* coercive; compelling: **t- nødvendighet** absolute necessity.
***tvin'le** *V* -*a* 1 turn, twine, twist. 2 reel; topple.
tvin'ne[1] *V* -*a*/+-*et* 1 twine, twist, wind: **t- opp** unravel, untwist, unwind. 2 *(refl.)* **t- seg** get twisted; twist, wind; **t- seg opp** come unraveled, untwisted; **t- seg sammen** get entangled.
***tvin'ne[2]** *Num* cf **to[3]**
***tvinn'/tråd** -*en* (spun) thread.
***tvin'te** *V* -*a* reel, stagger, totter.
tvi'/sprang -*et* *dial.* gallop: **på t-** at top speed.
tvis't[1] -*en* conflict, dispute: **et t-ens eple** an apple of discord.
tvis't[2] -*en* 1 cotton waste. 2 twist (e.g. silk); fine metal strand.
tvis'te/mål -*et* conflict, dispute; *jur.* civil case.
tvis'te/punkt -*et*, *pl* -/+-*er* controversial point, point of conflict.
+tvis'tes *V* -*edes*, -*es* argue, contend (**om** over).
tvi'/syn -*et* 1 ambivalence, duality. 2 ironic, paradoxical view of life (assoc. with name of A. O. Vinje); split personality.
tvi'/synt *A* - ambivalent, dual; ironic, paradoxical.
***tvi'/ta(ke)** *V* -*tek*, -*tok*, -*teke*/-*i* 1 hesitate, stammer, talk stumblingly. 2 repeat.
***tvi'/tunga** [/tonga] *A* - cf **tve/tunget**
***tvi'/tydig** *A* - cf **tve/**
***tvo'[1]** *pt of* **två**
***tvo'[2]** *Num* cf **to[3]**
***tvoge[1]** [två'ge] -*a* washcloth.
***tvoge[2]** [två'ge] *V* -*a* dabble, splash.
***tvore** [två're] -*a* cf **tvare**
tvor're** *pp of* **tverre[1]** (=tvorri**)
tvungen [tvong'en] *A* +-*ent*, *pl* -*ne* 1 compulsory, obligatory, required. 2 forced, obliged; duty-bound. 3 constrained; cramped; restricted: **med en rar, t- stemme** in a queer, strained voice (Undset).
+tvunget [tvong'et] *pp of* **tvinge[2]**
***tvæ'r[1]** *pr of* **två**
***tvæ'r[2]** *A* cf **tverr**
tvæ're *V* -*a*/+-*et*: **t- ut** drag, pad, stretch out.
+tvætte [tvet'te] *V* -*et* cf **tvette[2]**
***två'** *V* *tvær*, *tvo*, *tvege*/-*i* wash.
***tvått'** -*en* wash(ing).
***tvåt'te/vatn** -*et* wash water.
tweed [tvi'd] -*en* tweed (material).
***ty'[1]** -*et* cf **tøy[2]**
ty'[2] *V* -*dde* 1 have recourse, resort, turn (**hen til, til** to); fall back on; seek, take refuge (**til** in). 2: **t- seg** *dial.* attach oneself (**med, til** to), seek the company (of).
°ty'[3] *I* hush, ssh.
Ty' *Prn(m)* *myth.* Tyr (god of war).
***ty'd** *A* 1 friendly, sociable. 2 gentle; soft; easy to handle.
Ty'/dal *Pln* twp, Sør-Trøndelag.
ty'de[1] [*ty'e] *V* -*dde* *archaic, dial.* denote, mean, signify: ***B. sluttar lure på kva ølet t-er** B. stops wondering what the beer signifies (Vesaas).
ty'de[2] [*ty'e] *V* -*dde*/-*et* 1 decipher, interpret, make out: **t- runer** d- runes; **t- drømmer** i- dreams. 2: **t- på** imply, indicate, suggest.
ty'delig *A* - 1 clear, evident, obvious: **sammenhengen var t-** the connection was o-. 2 conspicuous, marked, pronounced: **en t- forbedring** a p- improvement. 3 distinct, sharp (image) plain (writing): **jeg husker t-** I remember distinctly.
+ty'delig/gjøre *V* -*gjorde*, -*gjort* clarify, elucidate, explain; make clear.
+ty'delig/het -*en* clarity, clearness; distinctness; plainness.
ty'delig/vis *Av* clearly, evidently, obviously.
ty'ding [*ty'ing] -*a*/+-*en* (=**+tydning**) 1 explanation, interpretation. *2 meaning, sense.
***ty'dleg** *A* - friendly, pleasant.
+ty'dning -*en* cf **tyding**
***ty'd/skap** -*en* friendliness, pleasantness.
ty'ende -*t* *archaic* servant, serving folk.
tyfoid/feber [tyfo-i'd/] -*en* typhoid fever.
tyfo'n -*en* typhoon.
ty'fus -*en* typhus (fever).
***ty'gel** -*elen*, *pl* -*lar* bridle rein.
***tygg'** *pr of* **tyggje**
+tyg'ge[1] -*a* 1 bite, mouthful; chew, cud. 2 *pop.* jaw: **få en på t-a** get one in the kisser.
+tyg'ge[2] *V* *tygde* (=***-je**) 1 chew, masticate. 2 *fig.* chew, grind away (**på at, on** e.g. the same subject, etc.): **t- på noe** mull over sth, turn sth over in one's mind.
tyg'ge/gummi -*en* chewing gum.
***tyg'gje** *V* *tygg*, *togg*, *togge*/-*i* cf **tygge[2]**
***tyg'gje/gummi** -*en* cf **tygge/**
***tyg'le** *V* -*a* keep in check, rein.
ty'kje -*n* *dial.* devil: **hva i han t-** what the d-.
+tykk' *A* *tykt* cf **tjukk**
+tyk'kas -*en* cf **tjukkas**
tyk'ke[1] -*t* *archaic, dial.* (personal) judgment; opinion: **etter (eget) t-** according to one's (own) wish; at will.
+tyk'ke[2] -*t*/-*n* cf **tjukke[1]**
+tyk'ke[3] *V* *tykte* cf **tykkje**
+tyk'kelse -*n* thickness (depth; layer).
***tyk'ken** *A* -*e*/-*i*, *pl* *tykne* offended; irritable, touchy.
tyk'kes** *V* *tyktes*, -*es* (=tykkjast**) *archaic, dial.* 1 be of the opinion, think; seem: **det t- meg** it seems to me, meseems, methinks; **jeg t-** I think, it seems to me; **t- om** like. *2 consider oneself, regard oneself: **han tyktest vere kar** he considered himself quite a fellow.
+tykk'/fallen *A* -*ent*, *pl* -*falne* cf **tjukk/**
***tykkj'ast** *V* *tyktest*, *tykst* cf **tykkes**
***tykkj'e** *V* *tykte* 1 be of the opinion, think; believe: **t- monn i** think well of; **t- om** like; **t- synd i** feel sorry for. 2: **t- på** feel offended, piqued, vexed (at).
+tykk'/legg -*en* cf **tjukk/**
+tykk'/maget *A* - cf **tjukk/maga**
+tykk'/melk -*en* thick, sour milk; yogurt.
+tykk'/mæ·lt *A* - cf **tjukk/**
+tykk'/sak -*en* (of fat boy, man) fatty, tub.
+tykk'/tarm -*en* colon, large intestine.
+tyk'ne *V* -*a*/-*et* cf **tjukne**
+tyk'ning -*en* 1 depths of the forest; thicket. 2 *fig.* obscureness.
***tyk'st** *pp of* **tykkjast**
tyk'te *pt of* **+tykke[3]**, ***tykkje**
***tyk'test** *pt of* **tykkjast**
+tyk't/flytende *A* - viscous.
***ty'/lapp** -*en* cf **tøy/**
tyl'ft -*a* dozen.
°ty'lig *A* - cf **tydelig**
tyll' +-*en*/*-*et* tulle.
tyl'le *V* -*a*/+-*et*: **t- i seg** guzzle, pour down, swill; *fig.* fill oneself with.
tympa'n -*en* 1 *mus.* timpani. 2 *arch.* tympanum. 3 *anat.* eardrum, tympanum. 4 *typog.* tympan.
ty'ne *V* -*te* 1 plague, torment, torture: **t- livet av en** plague the life out of one. 2 destroy, kill. 3: **t- bort** *dial.* lose; waste. 4 *dial.* chide, scold.
tyng'd -*a* (=**+tyngde**) 1 heaviness, weight; *phys.* gravity. 2 solidity, weightiness (of mind, reasoning, etc.); emphasis. 3 body, mass: **store t-er av storsild utenfor kysten** great masses of herring off the coast (Morgenbladet).
tyng'de/kraft -*a*/+-*en* force of gravity.
tyng'de/lov [/låv] -*en*/*-*a* law of gravity.
tyng'de/punkt -*et* 1 center of gravity. 2 central point (of an argument).
+tyng'e *V* -*de*/-*et* (=***-je**) weigh down; lie heavy, weigh (**på** on); oppress, press; hamper: **t-es av noe** have sth on one's mind, be oppressed by sth.
+tyng'ende *A* - burdensome, heavy, oppressive.
***tyng'je** *V* -*de* cf **tynge**
tyng're *cp of* **tung**
tyng'sel +-*en*/*-*tyngsla*, *pl* *tyngsler* (=***tyngsle**) burden, weight; heaviness: **skatter og tyngsler** taxes and tributes.
tyng'st *sp of* **tung**
tynn' *A* *tynt* thin (air, cloth, log, grass, liquid, person, plot, etc.); slender, slim; *pop.* skinny; meager, sparse; weak (coffee, tea, etc.): **be t-t** beg ingratiatingly; **t-t besatt** (of an audience) small house; **t-t med** little of; **t- som en strek** thin as a rail; **i t-este laget** on the thin side.
tyn'ne[1] -*a* cf **tønne**
tyn'ne[2] *V* -*a*/+-*et*/*-*te* 1 (make) thin: **t- ut** thin out (plants, etc.); dilute. 2: **tynnes** get thin(ner), (of hair, etc.) thin out.
tynn'/håra *A* - (=+-**et**) balding, sparse-haired.
tyn'nings/hogst -*en* thinning (of a forest, by chopping down trees).
tynn'/kledd *A* -/*-*kledt* thinly dressed; lightly dressed.
+tynn'/slitt *A* - (=***/sliten**) (of nerves, clothes) worn thin.
tynn'/tarm -*en* small intestine.
Tyn'/set *Pln* twp, Hedmark.
tyn't *nt of* **tynn**
+tyn't/befol·ket *A* - sparsely populated.
tyn't/flytende *A* - (of fluid) thin.
tyn't/øl -*et* *archaic* old type of weak, home-brewed beer; small beer.
ty'pe -*n* 1 kind, type (**av** of): **t-n på en streber** the typical climber. 2 *typog.* type.
ty'pe/lære -*a*/+-*en* typology.
ty'pe/metall· -*et* type metal.
ty'pisk *A* - typical.
typogra'f -*en* 1 printer, typographer. 2 *zool.* bark beetle (Scolytus typographus).
typografi' -*en* typography.
typogra'fisk *A* - typographical.
***typ'pe** *V* *typte* make cone-shaped, put a point on; top.
ty'r -*en* (=***tjor[1]**) 1 bull: **ta t-en ved**

+ Bokmål; * Nynorsk; ° Dialect.
After letter: ' stress (Acc. 1); ` tone, stress (Acc. 2); · length.
Below letter: . not pronounced.

hornene take the b- by the horns. **2 T-en** *astron.* Taurus.
+**Ty'r** *Prn(m)* cf **Ty**
tyrann' *-en* **1** despot, tyrant. **2** *zool.* tyrant bird (Tyrannidae).
tyranni' *-et* tyranny.
tyrannise're *V -te* tyrannize.
tyran'nisk *A* - tyrannical.
***ty're** *-t* cf **tyri**
+**ty're/fekter** *-en, pl -e* (=***-ar**) bullfighter.
+**ty're/fektning** *-en* bullfighting.
ty're/hals *-en* bull neck.
ty're/nakke *-n* bull neck.
ty'r/hjelm *-en bot.* a type of aconite, resembling monkshood (Aconitum septentrionale).
ty'ri *-en* (=***tyre**) **1** pine pitch. **2** dead, resinous, pine wood (formerly used for lighting).
ty'ri/fakkel *-elen, pl -fakler* pine torch.
ty'ri/flis *-a* chip, splinter of resinous pine wood.
Ty'ri/hans *Prn* (another name for) Ash Lad, a fairy tale character.
ty'ri/rot *-a, pl +-røtter/*-røter* pine root.
ty'ri/spik *-a, pl *-ar* pine splinter.
ty'ri/stikke *-a* pine stick (used formerly as torch).
tyr'k *-en* (=+**-er**, ***-ar**) Turk.
Tyr'kia *Pln* Turkey.
tyr'kisk *A* - Turkish: **t- and** *zool.* Muscovy duck (Cairina moschata).
***tyr'me** *V -de* **1** take it easy, take one's time. **2** be easy on, spare.
+**tyro'ler** *-en, pl -e* (=***-ar**) Tyrolean, Tyrolese.
+**tyrolerin'ne** -a/-en (=***-ar-**) Tyrolean woman.
tyro'lsk *A* - Tyrolean.
***tyrs't** *A* - cf **tørst**[2]
***tyrs'te** *V -a/-e* cf **tørste**[2]
***ty's** *pr of* **tysje**
tys'/bast *-en bot.* mezereon (Daphne mezereum), a flowering shrub.
***ty's/dag** *-en* cf **tirs/**
Tys'/fjo'rd *Pln* twp, Nordland.
***tysj'e** *V tys, tuste, tust* (of footsteps) rustle; walk softly.
tys'k *A* - German.
+**tys'ker** *-en, pl -e* (=***-ar**) German.
tys'k/fiendtlig *A* - anti-German.
+**tys'k/het** *-en* Germanism.
Tys'k/land *Pln* Germany.
tys'k/vennlig *A* - pro-German.
Tys'/nes *Pln* twp, Hordaland.
+**tyss'** *I* hush.
+**tys'se** *V -et* **1** hush (sby). **2** *dial.* (of river) sing, gurgle.
tys't *A* - hushed, quiet, soundless; mute, silent, still: **det er t- om hans navn** his name is never spoken (Vogt); **når han tier, er det tyst** when he falls silent, all is hushed (Hamsun).
+**tys'te** *V -a/-et* **1** silence: **t- ned** hush up. **2** *lit.* inform, spy.
+**tys'ter** *-en, pl -e lit.* informer, stool pigeon.
+**tys't/het** *-en* silence.
+**tys'tne** *V -et* grow silent, quiet down: **t- hen** die away.
Tys'/vær *Pln* twp, Rogaland.
***ty'te**[1] *-a* **1** small bump, lump. **2** nodule of hard stone in softer stone. **3** *bot.* lingonberry.
ty'te[2] *V -te/taut/+tøt, tytt/*tote/*-i* **1** filter, ooze, seep; leak, trickle (**ut** out). **2** *dial.* (of sound) howl, sough; buzz, cackle; whimper; complain.
***ty'te/bær** *-et* cf **tytte/**
ty'ting *-en* cf **tytte/bær**
***tyt'te** *-a* girl, woman.
+**tyt'tebær** *-et* (=***tyte/**) *bot.* lingonberry, mountain cranberry, red whortleberry (Vaccinium vitis idaea).
+**ty'v** *-en* cf **tjuv**
+**ty'v/aktig** *A* - cf **tjuv/**
+**ty've** *Num* cf **tjue**[1]
ty'/ved *-en bot.* mezereon (Daphne mezereum), a flowering shrub.
+**ty've/gods** [/gots] *-et* cf **tjuve/**
+**ty've/koster** *pl* stolen goods.
+**ty'vende** *Num* cf **tjuende**
+**ty'vende/del** *-en* cf **tjue/**
+**ty've/pakk** *-et* cf **tjuve/**
+**tyveri'** *-et, pl -er* cf **tjuveri**
+**tyveri'/alar'm** *-en* burglar alarm.
+**ty'v/lytte** *V -a/-et* cf **tju/**
+**ty'v/starte** *V -et* cf **tjuv/**
***tæ'** *V -dde* untie; unravel.
***tæ'ge/bær** *-et* cf **teie/**
tæ'ger *pl of* **tåg**[1]
tæ'gje** *-a* (=teie**[2]) basket braided of roots or twigs.
°**tæ'l** *-et* cf **tel**[1]
***tæ'pe** *V -te* touch lightly; step lightly (as on a sore foot).
tæ'r *pl of* **tå**[1]
***tæ're**[1] *-t* bit, morsel: **ikkje t-t** not a bit.
tæ're[2] *V -te* **1** consume, corrode: **t- på** drain, eat into; be a strain on, tax; make inroads on; irritate, prey upon (e.g. one's mind); rankle; *(adj.)* **t-ende** consuming (desire, grief, thirst, etc.); corrosive; **t-s bort, vekk** be consumed; waste away. **2** *archaic* devour, eat.
tæ're/skilling *-en* money laid by for a rainy day, savings.
tæ'ring *-a/+-en* **1** *archaic* consumption, use: **sette t- etter næring** live according to one's means. **2** corrosion, pitting (esp. of metal). **3**: **ta seg t- av noe** let sth prey on one's mind; be rankled by sth. **4** wasting away; *med.* consumption, tuberculosis.
tæ'rings/sjuk *A* tubercular.
***tæ'se**[1] *-a* slipper.
***tæ'se**[2] *V -a* **1** wear out (sth). **2** (of weather) melt (the snow). **3** shuffle, trudge.
***tæ'se/ver** *-et* thawing weather.
tæt'ter *pl of* **tått**
+**tø'** *V -dde, -dd* (=***tøye**[2]) thaw (**opp** out, up); also *fig.* loosen up.
tød'del *-elen, pl tødler* jot, tittle; iota: **ikke en t-** not one i-.
***tø'de** *-a* manure.
tøff'[1] *A tøft* tough (fellows; job; literature).
tøff'[2] *I*: **t- t-** chug-chug; put-put.
tøf'fe *V -a/+-et* chug, put-put.
tøf'fel *-elen, pl tøfler* (=***tofle**[1]) slipper: **under t-en** hen-pecked.
+**tøf'fel/blomst** *-en* (=***/blom(e)**) *bot.* slipperwort (Calceolaria).
tøf'fel/dyr *-et zool.* paramecium.
tøf'fel/helt *-en* hen-pecked husband.
tøf'fel/regimen'te *-t* female rule (in household).
tøf'le *V -a/+-et* (=***tofle**[2]) pad, plod, shuffle; trot, trudge.
***tø'k** *A* ready; fit (usu. as suffix).
tø'ler *pl dial.* **1** doodads, goods and chattels, knick-knacks: **han måtte pakke t-ene sine** he had to pack his things. **2** storage chest; *fig.* storehouse: **i hennes minners t-** in the recesses of her memories (Wiers-Jensen).
+**tøl'per** *-en, pl -e lit.* boor, lout, oaf.
+**tøl'per/aktig** *A* - *lit.* boorish, loutish, oafish.
+**tøm'** *-men* cf **tømme**[1]
***tø'me** *V -de* cf **tømme**[2]
+**tøm'me**[1] *-n* (=**tøm**) rein: **holde en i t-** keep sby in check, restrain sby.
tøm'me[2] *V +tømte/*tømde* **1** drain, empty (**for** of); drink up: **stua t-es** the room empties, is emptied. **2** *(refl.)* **t- seg** empty one's bowels, purge oneself.
+**tøm'me/kjøre** *V -te* drive (horse) with reins; *fig.* keep (a person) under one's thumb.
+**tøm'me/løkke** *-a* bight, loop (of reins).
tøm'mer *-et* (standing) timber; (cut) logs; (trimmed) lumber.
+**tøm'mer/fløyter** *-en, pl -e* (=***-ar**, +**/fløter**) log driver, river driver.
tøm'mer/fløyting *-a* (=+**/fløting**) river driving (of logs).
tøm'mer/flåte *-n* log raft.
tøm'mer/hake *-n* peavey, pike pole.
+**tøm'mer/hogger** *-en* (=***-ar**) lumberjack; woodcutter.
tøm'mer/hogst *-en* (=***/hogster**) logging; woodcutting.
+**tøm'mer/hugger** *-en* cf **/hogger**
tøm'mer/hus *-et* log house.
+**tøm'mer/kjører** *-en, pl -e* (=***-ar**, ***/køyrar**) log trucker, one who drives logs to loading place, river, or mill.
tøm'mer/klave *-n* log caliper.
tøm'mer/koie *-a* cabin, shanty at a logging camp.
tøm'mer/lunne *-a/-n* log pile.
tøm'mer/mann *-en, pl -menn/*-menner* **1** carpenter. **2** *hum.* hangover. **3** *zool.* type of wood beetle (Acanthocinus aldilis).
tøm'mermanns/bile *-a* carpenter's broadax.
tøm'mermanns/blyant *-en* carpenter's pencil.
+**tøm'mermanns/passer** *-en, pl -e* (=***-ar**) carpenter's compass.
+**tøm'mer/merker** *-en, pl -e* (=***/merkjar**) timber cruiser.
tøm'mer/merking *-a/+-en* timber cruising (marking trees for cutting).
tøm'mer/mester** *-en, pl -e* (=/meister**) master carpenter.
+**tøm'mer/måler** *-en, pl -e* (=***-ar**) timber cruiser.
tøm'mer/sag *-a* crosscut saw.
tøm'mer/saks *-a* lug hood.
tøm'mer/skog *-en* logging woods.
tøm'mer/stokk *-en* log: **dra, rulle t-er** snore loudly.
tøm'mer/veg *-en* (=+**/vei**) logging road.
tøm'mer/velte *-a* log slide; place where logs are dumped; log conveyor; pile of logs (as at bottom of a log slide).
tøm'mer/øks *-a* timber ax, esp, carpenter's broadax.
***tøm're**[1] *-a* wooden structure of a house.
tøm're[2] *V -a/+-et* **1** carpenter, do carpentry, hammer; build, erect: **t- opp** put up (a house); **t- sammen** slap together. **2** *fig.* build, construct (a plan, etc.): **t- noe sammen** knock sth together.
+**tøm'rer** *-en, pl -e* (=***-ar**) *archaic* carpenter.
+**tøn'der** *-eret/-ret* (=***tunder**) tinder.
tøn'ne *-a* (=**tynne**[1]) **1** barrel, cask, drum; *obs.* volumetric measure ab. 4 bushels (for fish, grain, potatoes, etc.): **tomme t-r ramler mest** empty barrels rattle most (=empty heads make the most noise). **2** *obs.* areal measure, ab. 1 acre. **3** *naut.* mooring buoy. **4** *naut.* crow's nest (esp. on a fishing boat, whaler, etc.) **5.** *zool.* hardened cuticle or integument enclosing fly pupa.
tøn'ne/band *-et* (=+**/bånd**) (barrel) hoop.
tøn'ne/gjo'rd *-a* (barrel) hoop.
+**tøn'ne/hvelv** *-et arch.* barrel arch, barrel vault.
Tøn'nes *Prn(m)*
tøn'ne/stav *-en* barrel stave.
tøn'ne/tapp *-en* bung.
tøn'ne/vis *Av*: **i t-** by the barrel; in large quantities.
Tøn's/berg *Pln* city in Vestfold.
***tø'r**[1] *pl of* **to**[1]
+**tø'r**[2] *pr of* **tø**
+**tør'**[3] *pr of* **tore**[2], **turde**
tør'k[1] *-en* **1** drying: **henge tøy til t-** hang the washing out to dry; **ha tennene på t-** *hum.* have protruding teeth. **2** *dial.* drought, dry period. **3** *fam.* blow, wallop; **en t- i trynet** a w- on the kisser.
+**tør'k**[2] *-en* cf **tyrk**
tør'ke[1] *+-a/-en* **1** drought, dry spell. **2** *agr.* drying house; shed.
tør'ke[2] *V -a/+-et* **1** dry (**inn up, ut** out); become dry. **2** wipe (**av** off, **opp** up, a glass, one's hands, etc.); mop (one's brow): **t- støv** dust; **t- vekk en tåre** wipe away a tear; **faen t- meg** (oath). **3** **t- til en** *(fam.)*: strike sby. **4** *(refl.)*: **t- seg** dry oneself.

tør'ke/anlegg *-et* drying plant.

tør'ke/appara't *-et, pl -/+-er* drying apparatus e.g. electric hairdryer.

tør'ke/hus *-et hist.* drying house for grain (equipped with drying kiln).

tør'ke/klut *-en* dustcloth, rag.

tør'ke/loft *-et* loft where clothes were hung to dry; drying house for grain.

tør'kende *Av*: **t- gal** *fam.* absolutely crazy.

tør'ke/omn *-en* (=**+/ovn**) kiln (for drying hops, wood, etc.)

tør'ke/plass *-en* 1 drying place (where fish are spread out to dry). 2 drying area (with clotheslines).

+**tør'ker** *-en, pl -e* (=***-ar**) 1 person who lays fish out to dry; one who works in drying room of a whale factory. 2 drying apparatus e.g. hair dryer.

tørkeri' *-et* drying house, room; kiln (room).

+**tø'rke/sommer** *-en, pl -e/-somrer* (=***-ar**) dry summer.

tør'ke/stati'v *-et* 1 drying rack, e. g. clothesrack. 2 dish drainer.

+**tør'ke/vær** *-et* (=***/ver**) drying weather, wind.

tør'ke/år *-et* year with long dry period in spring or summer.

tør'kle *-kleet, pl +-klær/*-kle* kerchief.

tør'kle/snipp *-en* point of (the) kerchief.

tø'rn *-en/-et* 1 shift (on watch, of work, etc.); *fam.* spell (of work); turn (in line, at a task, etc.): **spille t-** *naut.* do in shifts, take turns. 2 (demanding) job, task; *fam.* battle, bout, tilt: **en hard t-** a real battle, a tough job. 4 brunt, impact. 5 *naut.* turn (of a line, chain around a cleat, spar, etc.); coil, kink, twist (in a line, chain): **ta t-** belay (a line, rope); *fig.* restrain oneself.

tø'rne *V -a/+-et* 1 turn; *naut., tech.* turn over (an engine, etc., periodically); change, shift, (course, direction, etc.); swing. 2 bump, hit, run (**imot, på** into); *naut.* foul: **t- sammen** collide, take issue (**med** with). 3 (with *prep., adv.*): **t- inn, til, ut** *naut.* turn in, to, out; **t- opp** *naut.* bring to.

tørr' *A tørt* dry (climate, facts, lecture, manner, wine, wit, etc.): **ikke t- bak ørene** not d- behind the ears, immature; **med t-e never** with bare knuckles; **få t-t på kroppen** get dry clothes on; **på det t-e** on dry land; **ha sitt på det t-e** *fig.* be safe, secure; **t-e tårer** dry tears (=no tears at all); **t-t brød** plain bread with nothing on it; **uten vått eller t-t** without drink and food.

tørr'/banne *V -a/-bante* swear softly, under one's breath.

tørr'/batteri' *-et, pl +-er/*-* dry cell.

tørr'/dokk *-a/+-en* 1 *naut.* dry dock. 2: **ligge i t-** *fam.* be on the wagon.

+**tør're** *V -et* cf **tørke**[2]

+**tør're/anlegg** *-et* cf **tørke/**

+**tør're/appara't** *-et* cf **tørke/**

Tør'res *Prn (m)*

tørr'/feie *V -a/+-et* sweep (without sprinkling with water).

tørr'/fisk *-en* 1 (air-)dried fish. 2 *fam.* bore; dry, colorless person.

+**tørr'/flue** *-a* (=***/fluge**) dry fly (used in fishing).

tørr'/for *-et* dry fodder.

tørr'/furu *-a* dead (dry) pine.

tørr'/gran *-a* dead (dry) spruce.

+**tørr'/het** *-en* dryness; lack of imagination, spirit.

tørr'/hoste[1] *-n* dry, hacking cough.

tørr'/hoste[2] *V -a/+-et* 1 cough, hack without producing phlegm). 2 cough to attract attention, warn.

tørr'/høy *-et* dried hay.

tørr'/is *-en* 1 dry ice. 2 brittle ice.

Tør'ris *Prn (m)*

tørr'/kledd *A -/*-kledt* dressed in dry clothes.

+**tørr'/legge** *V -la, -lagt* (=***-je**) 1 drain, dry out (a swamp, etc.). 2 bar the sale of liquor (in an area).

***tørr'/leik** *-en* dryness.

tørr'/lendt *A -* dry (soil etc.).

tørr'/mat *-en dial.* dry food (e.g. bread etc., in contrast with meats or liquids).

tørr'/mjølk *-a* (=**+/melk**) powdered milk.

tørr'/pinne *-n fam.* bore; dry, colorless person; an old stick.

tørr'/prate *V -a/+-et* carry on a polite conversation.

+**tørr'/råte** *-n* (=***/rot(e)**) dry rot (of potatoes, wood, etc. caused by fungus).

tørr'/skinna *A -* (=**+-et**) dry, with dry clothes.

tørr'/skodd [/skodd] *A -/*-skott* dry-shod, with dry feet.

tørr'/snø *-en* dry snow.

+**tørr'/sommer** *-eren, pl -somrer* (=***-ar**) dry summer.

tørr'/sprit *-en* canned heat.

tørr'/stoff *-et* solids (left after liquid is removed).

tørr'/ved *-en* dry wood.

tørr'/vittig *A -* with a dry sense of humor.

+**tørr'/vær** *-et* (=***/ver**) drought, dry weather.

+**tørr'/øyd** *A -* dry-eyed.

°**tør's** *pr of* **tore**[2]

+**tør'st**[1] *-en* cf **tørste**[1]

tør'st[2] *A -* (=***tyrst**) thirsty.

tør'ste[1] *-n* (=**+tørst**[1], ***torste**) thirst (**etter** for): **en tår over t-en** a drop too many, more (drink) than is good for one.

+**tør'ste**[2] *V -a/-et* 1 be thirsty, thirst (**etter** for). 2 *lit.* yearn.

tør'ste/drikk *-en* refreshing drink, thirst quencher.

+**tør'stig** *A - archaic* thirsty.

tør't *nt of* **tørr**

tø's *-a* 1 *archaic* girl. 2 *fam.* tart, wench.

+**tø't** *pp of* **tyte**[2]

tø'v *-et* 1 nonsense; foolishness, monkey business: **det er så mye tull og t- med kvinnfolka** there's so much nonsense and monkey business with women (Haalke). *2 felting, fulling. *3 clumsy, ineffectual work.

tø've[1] *V -de/+-et/*-a* 1 talk nonsense; fool around, joke: **la oss nå bare ikke stå her og t-** let's not just stand here and fool around (Undset). 2 felt, full (cloth). *3 jutter; fiddle, fumble (at sth).

tø've[2] *V -de archaic* 1 tarry. 2 hesitate, wait: **t-ende** hesitantly.

tø've/kopp *-en* buffoon, fool.

tø'vet(e) *A -* foolish; silly; crazy.

tøv're *V -a/+-et dial.* delay, wait; drag out.

+**tø'/vær** *-et* thaw.

+**tøy'**[1] *-en* (=***tøyg**) 1 *dial.* extending, stretching: **gi t-** bend, expand, give; (of a person) give in, yield. 2 *tech.* elasticity.

+**tøy'**[2] *-et, pl -er* (=***ty**[1]) 1 (esp. in cpds.) equipment, implement(s), tool(s), e.g. **kjøkken/t-, skrive/t-**; material, stuff, ware, e.g. **fot/t-, sko/t-, sølv/t-**. 2 cloth, fabric, e.g. **dress/t-, ull/t-**. 3 clothes: **vaske t-** do the laundry, wash clothes. 4 baggage, luggage: **sette inn t-et** check the baggage. 5 *typog.* rejected type (to be recast). 6 *tech.* (paper) pulp.

tøy'e[1] *V +-de/*-gde* 1 extend, pull, stretch (**ut out**): **t- i** haul, pull; **t- på** pull, stretch. 2 *fig.* stretch; make sth last: **t- en bestemmelse** stretch a regulation; **t- tobakken** make the tobacco last (as long as possible). 3 (*refl.*): **t- seg** extend, pull oneself, stretch; *fig.* give, stretch; stretch a point; be compliant; **t- seg langt for en** go out of one's way for one.

***tøy'e**[2] *V -a* cf **tø**

tøy'elig *A -* 1 elastic. 2 *fig.* flexible; compliant.

+**tøy'elig/het** *-en* 1 elasticity. 2 *fig.* flexibility; compliancy.

***tøy'g** *-en* cf **tøy**[1]

***tøy'gje** *V -de* cf **tøye**[1]

+**tøy'/hus** *-et mil., archaic* arsenal.

+**tøy'/lapp** *-en* patch, piece of cloth.

+**tøy'le**[1] *-n* rein (also *fig.*): **gi en frie t-r** give one free r-.

+**tøy'le**[2] *V -a/-et* bridle, check, rein; control, curb, restrain.

+**tøy'les/løs** *A lit.* unbridled, uncurbed, unrestrained; licentious, profligate, riotous; wild.

+**tøy'lesløs/het** *-en lit.* lack of restraint; licentiousness; riotous behavior.

***tøy'me** *V -de* bridle, rein; control, curb, restrain.

***tøy'r** *-en* thaw.

+**tøy'/rull** *-en* bolt of cloth.

tøy's *-et* nonsense.

tøy'se[1] *-a* silly woman.

tøy'se[2] *V -a/+-et/-te* 1 act foolishly, be silly: **neimen som jeg t-er!** what a fool I am! (Evensmo). 2 talk nonsense; fool around, joke: **du vet da godt at jeg bare t-er** you know very well I'm only joking (Undset). *3 prepare drinks for domestic animals. *4 dabble, mess, muddle with.

+**tøy'se/bøtte** *-a* clown, goof, silly fool.

tøy'se/kopp *-en* clown, goof, silly fool.

tøy'set(e) *A -* crazy, foolish, silly.

+**tøy'/sko** *-en* cloth-top shoe.

+**tøy'te**[1] *-a* coquette, hussy, minx.

***tøy'te**[2] *V tøytte* drink greedily, gulp.

***tøy'/ver** *-et* cf **tø/vær**

tå'[1] *-a, pl tær* toe: **gå på tå** tiptoe; **lett på tå** light of foot (esp. in dancing); **på tå hev** *gymn.* on your toes; **stå på tærne** stand on tiptoe.

tå'[2] *-a dial.* patch of ground that is bare of snow.

tå'[3] *V -dde dial.* unravel, untwist: **tå i trevlene** unravel the threads.

°**tå'**[4] *P* cf **av**

***tå'en** *A -e/-i, pl tåne* free of snow, unfrozen.

tå'g[1] *-a, pl tæger* 1 root fiber; slender root. 2 *fig.* fiber, shred.

***tå'g**[2] *-et* cattle pen.

***tå'ge/bær** *-et* cf **teie/**

tå'get(e) *A - dial.* raveled; fibrous.

+**tå'/gjenger** *-en, pl e zool.* digitigrade.

tå'/hette *-a* 1 toe box(ing). 2 toe cap.

tå'ke *-a* 1 fog; haze, mist; mistiness: **kunstig t-** *mil.* smoke screen. 2 *astron.* nebula.

tå'ke/banke *-n* fog bank.

+**tå'ke/bilde** *-t* hazy picture.

tå'ke/flekk *-en med.* nebula (in cornea); nubecula.

tå'ke/full *A* foggy, hazy, misty.

tå'ke/heim *-en lit.* land of fog and mist (also *fig.*): **Nord i T-en** In Northern Mists (book by Fridtjof Nansen).

+**tå'ke/legge** *V -la, -lagt* (=***/leggje**) *mil., fig.* lay a smoke screen; confuse, dim, obscure (e.g. the facts).

tå'ke/lur *-en* fog horn.

tå'ke/signal [/singna'l] *-et, pl -/+-er* fog signal.

tå'ke/slør *-et* veil of fog, mist.

tå'ke/syn *-et/*-a* 1 *med.* foggy vision. 2 hazy vision, nebulous view.

tå'ket(e) *A -* foggy, hazy, misty.

+**tå'ke/verden** *-en lit.* hazy, misty world.

+**tå'ke/vær** *-et* foggy, hazy, misty weather.

tå'l *-et* (=***tol**) patience; calmness, equanimity: **gi t-** be patient; have, show patience; **slå seg til t-s** be content (**med** with), resign oneself (**med** to).

tå'le *V -te* (=***tole**) bear, endure, stand; take, put up with; stand for, tolerate: **han t-er ikke kaffe** coffee disagrees with him; **t- en fornærmelse** pocket (swallow) an insult; **kjærligheten t-er alt** (*bibl.*)

+ Bokmål; * Nynorsk; ° Dialect.
After letter: ' stress (Acc. 1); ' tone, stress (Acc. 2); · length.
Below letter: . not pronounced.

love endureth all things (I Cor. 13,7).
tå'lelig *A* - (=***tolleg**) **1** bearable, tolerable. **2** fair, passable, so-so: **så t-** not too bad.
tå'lig *A* - (=***tolig**) **1** composed, patient, resigned; calm, tame. **2** fair, passable, so-so.
tål'/mod *-et* patience.
tålmo'dig *A* - (=***tolmodig**) patient.
+tålmo'dig/het *-en* patience.
+tålmo'dighets/arbeid *-et* job requiring patience, trying job.
+tålmo'dighets/prøve *-a/-en* test of one's patience.
tå'ls *N* cf **tål**
+tå'l/som' *A -t, pl -me* (=***/sam, *tol/sam**) **1** patient, resigned. **2** forbearing, tolerant.
+tå'lsom/het *-en* **1** composure, patience, resignation. **2** forbearance, tolerance.
***tå'ne** *V -a* become bare of snow..
tå'pe *-n* fool, ninny, simpleton.
tå'pelig *A* - dumb, foolish, idiotic.
+tå'pelig/het *-en* foolishness, idiocy, stupidity.
tå'r *-en* drop (of sth to drink).
***tå'rast** *V -ast* start to cry.
tå're *-a/+-en* tear, teardrop: **få t-er i øynene** get t-s in one's eyes; **ha lett for å ta til t-ene** cry easily.
+tå're/flom' *-men* (=***/flaum**) flood of tears.
tå're/full *A* tearful.
tå're/gass *-en* tear gas.
tå're/kana'l *-en anat.* lacrimal canal, l- duct, tear duct.
+tå're/kva'lt *A* - stifled by sobs, tear-choked.
tå're/mild *A* given to tears, weepy.
tå're/perse *-a* **1** tear-jerker. **2** *fam.* weepy person.
+tå're/strøm' *-men* flood of tears.
tå're/vætt *A* - **1** wet with tears; tear-soaked, tear-stained. **2** sentimental; drippy (with sentimentality).
tå're/våt *A* tear-filled, wet with tears; teary.
***tå'r/mild** *A* cf **tåre/**
tå'rn *-et* **1** tower; (church) steeple; (castle) turret (also *mil., naut.*). **2** (in chess) castle, rook.
tå'rne *V -a/+-et* **1** heap, pile (**opp** up). **2** *(refl.)*: **t- seg** accumulate, gather, pile up; **t- seg opp** rise, tower; pile up.
tå'rn/fløy *-a/+-en* **1** weather vane on a steeple. **2** wing of a building containing a steeple or tower.
tå'rn/glugge *-n* tower window.
tå'rn/høg *A* (=**+/høy**) high as a tower, towering.
tå'rn/spir *-et* spire (on a steeple).
tå'rn/svale *-a zool.* swift (Apus apus).
tå'rn/ugle *-a zool.* barn owl (Tyto alba).
tå'rn/ur *-et* tower clock.
tå'rn/urt *-a/+-en bot.* tower cress (Arabis turrita, Turritis glabra).
***tå'r/øygd** *A -/-øygt* teary-eyed.
tå'/spiss *-en* **1** point of the toe: **på t-ene** on tiptoe. **2** **danse t-** do toe-dancing.
tå'/støyt *-en* toe patch (on sole of shoe).
tå'te *-a* **1** pacifier, sugartit. **2** nipple on a baby bottle. **3** *fam.* mouth: **hold t-a på deg** shut your m-.
tå'te/flaske *-a* baby bottle.
tå'te/smokk [/smokk] *-en* nipple (on a baby bottle).
tått' *-en, pl tætter/*tåttar* **1** *dial.* strand, thread. **2** *hist.* short story; anecdote, episode (in ON literature). ***3** quality, strain, tendency (of character).
***tåt'tut** *A* - striped, veined.

U

°**u'**[1] *-en* (letter) U, u.
u[2] *Pn* cf **du**[2]
u- *Pf* un-; in- (negative).
u.=**under**[2]
***u'/aktande** *A* - invalid; not worthy of attention, valueless.
+u'/aktet *P* **1** *lit.* despite. **2** *(conj.)* although, even though.
+u'/aktsom [/-såmm] *A -t, pl -me* careless, heedless, unthinking; inadvertent: **u-t drap** negligent homicide, manslaughter.
+uakt'som/het *-en* carelessness, negligence: **grov u-** gross n-.
u'/aktuell' *A -elt, pl -e* not of current interest; unfashionable.
+ualmin'nelig *A* - exceptional, uncommon, unusual; extraordinary, remarkable, rare.
+u'/anet *A* - cf **u/ant**
+u'/anfektet *A* - composed, unaffected, undisturbed; unmoved, untouched (**av** by), indifferent, uninterested.
+uangri'pelig *A* - **1** unassailable, unimpeachable; blameless, irreproachable, spotless. **2** impregnable, unconquerable. **3** (of capital) tied up, untouchable.
+u'/anmel'dt *A* - unannounced; (of book) not reviewed.
+uanse'lig *A* - inconspicuous; insignificant (looking); ordinary, plain, undistinguished; unimpressive.
+uanse'lig/het *-en* insignificance (in appearance), plainness, unimpressiveness.
+u'/ansett *P* **1** irrespective of, no matter, regardless of. **2** *(adv.)* in any case, no matter what.
+u'/ansten'dig *A* - **1** immodest, improper, indecent; lewd, obscene. **2** disgraceful, inexcusable, shocking (e.g. wages).
+uansten'dig/het *-en* **1** immodesty, impropriety, indecency. **2** an improper remark.
+u'/anstrengt *A* - effortless, unstrained.
u'/ansva'rlig *A* - **1** *jur.* not (legally) responsible, not accountable (**for** for); lay, unofficial. **2** irresponsible.
+uansva'rlig/het *-en* **1** *jur.* freedom from responsibility. **2** irresponsibility.
u'/a'nt *A* - (=***/ana**) unsuspected; undreamed (of): **u-e muligheter** possibilities undreamed of.
+uanta'gelig *A* - cf **uantakelig**
+uanta'kelig *A* - unacceptable; inadmissible.
+u'/antastet *A* - unassailed; unchallenged, unhindered, unmolested.
+uanven'delig *A* - **1** unusable; useless. **2** inapplicable.
uappetitt'lig *A* - **1** unappetizing, uninviting, unsavory. **2** disgusting, repulsive; nasty.
+uappetitt'lig/het *-en* repulsiveness, unattractiveness, unsavoriness.
uar'tig *A* - *lit.* **1** impolite, rude. **2** naughty; illbred, poorly trained.
+uar'tig/het *-en* **1** discourtesy, rudeness; rude remark. **2** naughtiness; lack of breeding, training.
u'/artikule'rt *A* - inarticulate; unexpressed; primitive.
+uatskil'lelig *A* - inseparable: **u- forbundet** i-ly connected.
+u'/avbrutt' *A* - continual, steady, unbroken; uninterrupted.
u'/avgjort [/avjor't] *A* - undecided, unsettled; pending: **u- kamp** draw, tie.
u'/avgrensa *A* - (=**+-et**) unbounded.
uavhen'delig *A* - inalienable.
u'/avhengig *A* - independent (**av** of); autonomous, sovereign.
+u'avhengig/het *-en* independence; autonomy, sovereignty.
+u'avhengighets/erklæ'ring *-en* declaration of independence.
+u'/avhentet *A* - unclaimed.
+u'/avhjel'pelig *A* - inevitable, unavoidable; which cannot be helped.
u'/avkorta *A* - (=**+-et**) unabridged, uncurtailed; unstinted; *(adv.)* in full.
uavla'telig *A* - **1** eternal, unceasing. **2** constant, continual, incessant.
+uavset'telig *A* - **1** *jur.* irremovable: **u- dommer** judge with a lifetime position. **2** *merc.* unsalable.
uavven'delig *A* - inevitable, unavoidable.
+u'/avvi'dende *A* - cf **/avvitende**
uavvi'selig *A* - inescapable, unavoidable; compelling (duty), urgent (necessity).
u'/avvi'tende *A* - unknowing, unwitting: **meg u-** unbeknownst to me, without my knowledge.
UB=**Universitetsbiblioteket**
U. B.=**uten botn/bunn** (on nautical maps).
u'/barbe'rt *A* - **1** unshaved, unshaven. **2** *fam.* rough, unexpurgated.
+u'/barmhjer'tig *A* - cruel, merciless, pitiless (**mot** toward).
+ubarmhjer'tig/het *-en* cruelty, mercilessness, lack of pity (**mot** toward).
***ub'be** *V -a*: **u- seg** bristle up.
u'/bearbeidd *A* - raw, unworked; rough, undressed; undigested.
+u'/bebodd' *A* - uninhabited.
+ubebo'elig *A* - uninhabitable.
+u'/bebyg'd *A* - not built (on, up), vacant (lot); uninhabited (region).
***u'/beden** *A -e/-i, pl -ne* cf **/bedt, /buden**
+ubedra'gelig *A* - *lit.* sure, unmistakable: **et u- tegn** an u- sign.
+u'/bedt *A* - (=***/bedd, */beden**) **1** (do sth) unasked, unordered. **2** (come) uninvited.
+u'/befer'det *A* - untraveled (e.g. road).
+u'/befes'tet *A* - **1** *mil.* unfortified. **2** inexperienced; impressionable, weak: **ung og u-** young and impressionable.
+u'/beføy'd *A* - unjustified.
+u'/bega'vet *A* - ungifted, unintelligent; dull, stupid.
+u'/begren'set *A* - boundless, limitless; unlimited.
+ubegri'pelig *A* - incomprehensible. **2** *(adv.)* unbelievably, unusually.
+u'/begrun'net *A* - groundless, unfounded.
+u'/beha'g *-et* distaste (**ved** for), feeling of displeasure.
+ubeha'gelig *A* - disagreeable, unpleasant (**mot** towards); distasteful; uncomfortable (**for** for).
+ubeha'gelig/het *-en* disagreeableness, unpleasantness; annoyance, nuisance, trouble: **være utsatt for u-er** be placed in an unpleasant position; **si u-er** say disagreeable (mean, sarcastic) things.
+u'/behen'dig *A* - clumsy, unhandy; awkward.
+ubehen'dig/het *-en* clumsiness, unhandiness; blunder.
+u'/beher'sket *A* - uncontrolled, un-

restrained; uninhibited; lacking in self-control.
***ubehjel'pelig** *A* - 1 helpless. 2 awkward, clumsy.
+u'/behjel·psom [/-såmm] *A* clumsy, maladroit, unskilled.
+u'/behøv·let *A* - boorish, rude.
***u'/beinug** *A* - unhelpful, unwilling to help.
u'/beist *-et* beast, monster.
***u'/bekjen·t** *A* - 1 unknown: **meg u-** u- to me. 2 unacquainted (**med** with).
+u'/bekref·tet *A* - unconfirmed.
+u'/bekvem· *A* - 1 inconvenient; poorly situated. 2 uncomfortable; awkward.
+u'bekvem/het *-en* 1 inconvenience. 2 discomfort.
+u'/bekym·ret *A* - unconcerned, untroubled, unworried (**om** about); carefree.
+u'bekymret/het *-en* unconcern.
+u'/belei·lig [also -lei'-] *A* - 1 inconvenient, inopportune; awkward, unwelcome. 2 (of wind) contrary.
+u'/beman·net *A* - unmanned.
+u'/bemer·ket *A* - unnoticed; unobserved: **føre en u- tilværelse** live in obscurity.
+u'bemerket/het *-en lit.* obscurity.
+u'/bemid·let *A* - of limited means, unmoneyed, without a fortune.
+uben'dig *A* - uncontrollable.
***u'/benev·nt** *A* - nameless: **u- tall** abstract number.
+u'/benyt·tet *A* - unused.
+uberegnelig [uberei'neli] *A* - 1 incalculable. 2 unpredictable; capricious, fickle; erratic.
+u'/beret·tiget *A* - 1 ineligible; unauthorized (**til** to). 2 unwarranted; unjustified.
uber'gelig *A* - *dial.* 1 uninhabitable, unlivable. 2 excessive, monstrous.
+u'/berø·rt *A* - 1 undisturbed; untouched, virgin(al). 2 (emotionally) unaffected, unmoved (**av** by).
+u'/besatt· *A* - unoccupied (seat; country); available, unfilled (position).
+u'/besei·ret *A* - unconquered.
+u'/besin·dig *A* - rash, senseless, thoughtless; hasty.
+ubesin'dig/het *-en* rashness; senseless behavior, thoughtless act.
+u'/beskje·den *A -ent, pl -ne* forward, immodest, pushy.
+u'beskjeden/het *-en* forwardness, immodesty, pushiness.
+u'/beskjef·tiget *A* - unemployed.
+u'/beskre·vet *A* -, *pl -ne* 1 blank, unwritten. 2 undescribed.
+ubeskri'velig *A* - indescribable: **u- lykkelig** deliriously happy.
+u'/beskå·ret *A* -, *pl -ne* uncut; unabridged; in full.
+u'/beslutt·som [/-såmm] *A* indecisive, irresolute, undecided.
+ubeslutt'som/het *-en* indecision, irresolution.
+u'/besmit·tet *A* - immaculate (conception); unsullied (**av** by).
+u'/best *-et* cf **/beist**
+u'/bestan·dig *A* - 1 changeable, inconstant, vacillating. 2 capricious. 3 *chem.* unstable.
+ubestem'melig *A* - indefinite, indeterminate; fuzzy, vague; indefinable, nondescript.
u'/bestem·t *A* - indefinite (also *gram.*); unspecified, vague; indeterminate, undecided, undetermined.
+u'bestemt/het *-en* indefiniteness, vagueness; indecision, indetermination.
+ubestik'kelig *A* - incorruptible, uncompromising.
+u'/bestridd· *A* - (=**+-stridt**) unchallenged; uncontested, undisputed.
+ubestri'delig *A* - incontestable, incontrovertible, indisputable.
+u'/besva·rt *A* - unanswered.
+u'/besvæ·r(e)t *A* - unaffected, unbothered, untroubled; unconstrained; carefree.
+u'/besør·get *A* - not executed, uncompleted: **u-ede brev** dead letters.
+ubeta'lelig *A* - invaluable, priceless; a scream, very funny.
+u'/beten·ksom [/-såmm] *A* inconsiderate, thoughtless, unthinking; careless, heedless, imprudent.
+ubeten'ksom/het *-en* inconsiderateness, thoughtlessness; carelessness, heedlessness, inadvertence.
+ubeti'melig *A* - ill-timed, inopportune, untimely.
+u'/betin·get *A* - absolute, unconditional, unqualified; implicit, wholehearted; *(adv.)* absolutely, unconditionally, without reservation.
+u'/beto·nt *A* - *gram.* unaccented, unstressed.
+ubetving'elig *A* - uncontrollable; invincible, unconquerable, untamable.
+ubety'delig *A* - 1 insignificant, unimportant; inconsiderable, trifling, trivial. 2 mediocre, ordinary: **en u- mann** a nobody.
+ubety'delig/het *-en* 1 insignificance, unimportance; triviality. 2 mediocrity, nobody, nonentity. 3 a suspicion, a trifle.
+ubeve'gelig *A* - 1 immovable, stationary; motionless. 2 impassive, rigid; stiff.
+ubeve'gelig/het *-en* 1 immobility. 2 impassivity, rigidity.
+u'/beviss·t *A* - subconscious, unconscious: **det u-e sjeleliv** the (life of the) unconscious (Hamsun).
+u'bevisst/het *-en* unconsciousness; the subconscious.
+u'/bevok·st *A* - bare, without plant growth.
+u'/bevok·tet *A* - unguarded (e.g. moment, RR crossing).
+u'/bevæ·pnet *A* - 1 unarmed. 2: **det u-e øye** the naked eye.
+u'/billig *A* - unfair, unjust, unreasonable.
***u'/bjåleg** *A* - improper, inappropriate, unsuitable.
u'/blanda *A* - (=**+-et**) pure, unadulterated; unalloyed (e.g. metal; pleasure); unmixed: **u- beundring** unqualified admiration.
u'/blid *A* 1 (of a person) unfavorable, unkind. 2 (of climate, fate) hard, harsh, inclement. 3 (of terrain) rough, rugged.
u'/blodig *A* - bloodless (victory, war).
+u'/blu *A* - shameless, unreasonable (demands); exorbitant, extortionate (prices).
+u'/blufer·dig *A* - bold, immodest, shameless.
***u'/blyg** *A* cf **/blu**
ubo'telig *A* - (=***ubotleg**) irremediable, irreparable; hopeless.
u'/botferdig *A* - impenitent, unrepentant.
***u'/brigda** *A* - unchanged.
***ubrig'deleg** *A* - unchangeable.
***u'/brukande** *A* - cf **ubrukelig**
+u'/brukbar *A* cf **ubrukelig**
ubru'kelig *A* - unsuitable, unusable, useless; unfit: **han er u- som lærer** he is no good (impossible) as a teacher.
u'/brukt *A* - unused, unutilized: **nesten u-** as good as new; **u-e frimerker** mint stamps.
+u'/brutt *A* - 1 intact, unbroken, unopened (e.g. letter). 2 continuous, uninterrupted: **i u- strøm** in an u- stream.
ubry'telig *A* - fast, inviolable, unbreakable (e.g. friendship); unassailable (e.g. agreement), unshakable (e.g. resistance).
***u'/brøytt** *A* - 1 uncleared (road). 2 unchanged.
***u'/budd** *A -/-butt* unprepared.
+u'/buden *A -ent, pl -ne* uninvited.
+u'/bundet *A* - (=***/bunden**) 1 free, unrestricted; unbound, unfettered: **u- stil** prose (style). 2 *gram.* indefinite.
***u'/byde** *-t* damage.
u'/bygd[1] *-a archaic* wilderness.
u'/bygd[2] *A -/*-bygt* 1 not (yet) built. 2 *archaic* uninhabited.
***u'/bøn** *-a* curse.
+u/bønnhø'rlig *A* - 1 inexorable, inflexible, unrelenting. 2 inescapable, inevitable, unavoidable.
+ubønnhø'rlig/het *-en* 1 inexorability, inflexibility. 2 inevitability.
***u'/bøtande** *A* - hopeless, incorrigible, inveterate; irremediable.
ubøy'elig *A* - 1 inflexible, unbending, unyielding; merciless, relentless. 2 *gram.* uninflected.
***u'/bøygd** *A -/-bøygt* 1 unbent, unbowed. 2 *gram.* uninflected.
u'/båt *-en* submarine, U-boat.
u'båt/krig *-en* submarine warfare.
UD=**Utenriksdepartementet**
+udad'lelig *A* - blameless, irreproachable.
u'/danna *A* - (=**+-et**) 1 uncultured, vulgar. 2 uncultivated; unschooled, untrained.
u'/date·rt *A* - undated.
***u'/daude** *-n* violent death.
ude'lelig *A* - indivisible.
u'/de·lt *A* - 1 undistributed; undivided (e.g. attention, estate); unqualified (admiration): **u- skole** ungraded school. 2 *(adv.)* altogether, wholly: **ikke u- sympatisk** not altogether pleasant.
u'/deltakende *A* - cold, detached, indifferent.
u'/diploma·tisk *A* - undiplomatic.
u'/disipline·rt *A* - undisciplined.
+u'd/merket *A* - cf **ut/**
udre'pelig *A* - indestructible: **et enig, stolt folk er u-** a proud, united people is i- (Kinck).
udrik'kelig *A* - not fit to drink, undrinkable.
u'/dryg *A* (=**+/drøy**) which is used up too rapidly; uneconomical, unsubstantial.
+udu'elig *A* - cf **udugelig**
udu'gelig *A* - incapable, incompetent; unfit, unusable (**til** for).
+udu'gelig/het *-en* 1 incapability, incompetence, unfitness. 2 *lit.* incapable, incompetent person.
u'/dyd *-en* (=***/dygd**) 1 blemish, fault, flaw. 2 immorality, vice. *3 incapacity, uselessness.
u'/dyktig [also -dyk'-] *A* - 1 incapable, incompetent, unfit (**til** for). 2 disabled.
+u'dyktig/het [also -dyk'-] *-en* 1 incapability, incompetence, unfitness. 2 incapable, incompetent person.
u'/dyr *-et, pl df -a* 1 beast, (wild) animal. 2 (of a person) beast, monster.
u'/dyrka *A* - (=**+-et**) uncultivated.
+udø'delig *A* - (=***udøyeleg**) deathless, immortal, undying.
+udø'delig/het *-en* immortality: **er det ikke hjertelag, geni og ulykke, Gud giver udødelighetens fagreste kranser?** is it not to mercy, genius, and misfortune God gives the fairest wreaths of i-? (Wergeland).
***udøm'meleg** *A* - extraordinary.
u'/dåd *-en* atrocity, crime, outrage; evil deed, misdeed.
u'/edel *A -elt, pl -le* 1 (of metals) base, unrefined. 2 (of actions) ignoble, low, vulgar.
+u'/effen *A -ent, pl -efne*: **ikke u-** not too bad.
+u'/egennytte *-n* altruism.
+u'/egennyttig *A* - altruistic, unselfish.
+u'/egentlig *A* -: **i u- forstand** in a figurative sense; improperly.
+u'/egnet [/einet] *A* - unfit(ted), unsuited; unsuitable (**til** for).
***u'/einig** *A* - cf **/enig**
***u'/eins** *A* - cf **/ens**

+ Bokmål; * Nynorsk; ° Dialect.
After letter: ' stress (Acc. 1); ` tone, stress (Acc. 2); · length.
Below letter: . not pronounced.

u'/ekte *A* - 1 artificial, false, imitation. 2 not authentic (or genuine), spurious. 3 bogus, counterfeit, sham; affected, feigned, insincere. 4 born out of wedlock; illegitimate. 5: **u- sammensetning** *gram.* separable verb. 6: **u- brøk** *math.* improper fraction.
u'/elskver'dig *A* - grudging, ungracious, unobliging (**mot** towards).
uen'delig *A* - 1 endless, infinite, interminable; eternal, perpetual, unending; boundless, limitless: **i det u-e** indefinitely. 2 *(adv.)* exceedingly, extremely, immensely: **u-liten** infinitely small, infinitesimal.
+**uen'delig/het** *-en* endlessness, infinity (also *math.*); boundlessness: **en u- av** an infinite number of, no end of; **i u-** endlessly.
+**u'/enig** [also -e'-] *A* - in disagreement: **bli, være u-** differ, disagree (**med** with).
+**ue'nig/het** *-en* disagreement, discord (**mel'lom** among).
+**u'/ens** *A* - dissimilar, unlike.
+**u'/ensartet** *A* - of dissimilar, unlike types; heterogeneous; incongruous.
+**u'ensartet/het** *-en* diversity, heterogeneity, incongruity.
+**u'/ens(e)t** *A* - unheeded, unnoticed; obscure.
u'er [also: u'r] *-en, pl* +*-e zool.* rosefish (Sebastes marinus).
+**u'/erfa'ren** *A* *-ent, pl -ne* inexperienced.
+**u'erfaren/het** *-en* inexperience.
+**uerhol'delig** *A* - *merc., jur.* unobtainable; irrecoverable, uncollectable: **u-e fordringer** bad debts.
+**uerstat'telig** *A* - irreparable, irreplaceable, irretrievable.
***u'/etande** *A* - inedible.
+**uetterret'telig** *A* - dishonest, false, unreliable.
+**uetterret'telig/het** *-en* dishonesty, falsity, unreliability.
***u'/fallen** *A* *-e/-i, pl -falne* 1 unqualified, unsuited. 2 not fallen.
+**u'/farbar** *A* impassable.
u'/farga *A* - (=+-et) 1 natural-colored, undyed. 2 objective, uncolored (report).
u'/fa'rlig *A* - 1 not dangerous, safe: **ikke u-** not without danger. 2 harmless; unexciting.
+**u'/farvet** *A* - cf **u/farga**
ufat'telig *A* - 1 incomprehensible, inconceivable. 2 fantastic, unbelievable.
+**u'/feilbar** *A* infallible; unerring (instinct), unfailing (remedy).
+**ufeilba'rlig** *A* - 1 unerring, unfailing. 2 *(adv.)* inevitably, inexorably.
+**ufeilba'rlig/het** *-en* infallibility.
u'/ferd [*/fær] *-a/+-en archaic., dial.* misfortune: **fare ei u-** suffer a m-. 2 brutal, violent behavior.
u'/ferdig *A* - 1 incomplete, unfinished; *dial.* not ready. 2 immature, uncultivated.
uff' *I* oo, oof, ugh; oh dear (often combined with **da, ja, jo, nei**); expresses unpleasant feelings, e.g. alarm, uneasiness; aversion, disgust; irritation; regret: **uff, du gjør meg så redd** oo, you frighten me so (Bjørnson); **uff da, hugg han ikke fingeren av!** ugh, he chopped off his finger! (Ibsen).
uffameg [+uff' a mei'] *I* oh dear me (exclamation of irritation).
uf'fe *V* *-a/+-et*: **u- seg** complain, groan (i.e. say **uff**).
u'/fin *A* 1 coarse, crude, unrefined. 2: **hunden gjorde seg u- på teppet** the dog made a mess on the rug.
+**u'fin/het** *-en* coarseness, crudeness; a crude remark.
u'/fisk *-en* noxious fish, rough fish.
u'/fjelg *A* 1 uncared for, unkempt (e.g. garden, person); unappetizing, unpleasant (place). 2 coarse, low, vulgar. 3 creepy, frightening (events).
u'/flaks +*-en/*-et* bad luck.
u'/flidd *A* - messy, unkempt, untidy.
uforan'derlig *A* - 1 immutable, unalterable, unchangeable. 2 constant, steady, unchanging.
u'/foran'dra *A* - (=+-et) unaltered, unchanged.
+**uforbe'derlig** *A* - confirmed (bachelor, drunkard), incorrigible, inveterate (optimist).
+**u'/forbeholden** *A* *-ent, pl -ne* forthright, frank, open (e.g. admission); unqualified, unreserved, unrestrained (e.g. admiration).
+**u'/forberedt** *A* - unprepared; extemporaneous; unexpected.
+**u'/forbin'dende** *A* - *jur.* non-committal; not binding; informal.
+**u'/forbin'dtlig** *A* - not binding, without obligation.
+**u'/forblom'met** *A* - blunt, unambiguous.
+**u'/fordelaktig** *A* - 1 disparaging (remarks), unfavorable (impression). 2 disadvantageous, unprofitable (dealings). 3 detrimental, harmful (**for** to).
u'/forder'va *A* - (=+-et) uncorrupted, unspoiled.
+**ufordra'gelig** *A* - *lit.* 1 detestable, unbearable. 2 intolerant, truculent.
+**ufordra'gelig/het** *-en lit.* 1 repulsiveness. 2 intolerance, truculence.
+**u'/fordøy'd** *A* - unassimilated, undigested (also *fig.*).
+**ufordøy'elig** *A* - indigestible; heavy.
+**ufore'nlig** *A* - (=+**uforenelig**) incompatible, irreconcilable (**med** with).
+**u'/forfal'sket** *A* - authentic, genuine, unadulterated; pure, real: **den u-ede sannhet** the unvarnished truth.
+**u'/forfer'det** *A* - (=*/**forfælt**, */**forfærd**) fearless, intrepid, undaunted.
+**u'forferdet/het** *-en* dauntlessness, fearlessness, intrepidity.
+**uforgjeng'elig** *A* - everlasting, immortal, undying; imperishable, indestructible: **u- stoff** material that wears forever.
+**uforgjeng'elig/het** *-en* immortality; imperishability, indestructibility.
+**uforglem'melig** *A* - unforgettable.
+**uforgri'pelig** *A* -: **hans u-e mening** his dictum, his pronouncement; his unshakeable conviction.
+**u'/forholdsmessig** *A* - disproportionate, inordinate, out of all proportion; unreasonable.
+**uforkla'rlig** *A* - inexplicable, strange, unaccountable: **på en u- måte** unaccountably.
+**u'/forkla'rt** *A* - unexplained.
+**u'/forknytt'** *A* - unabashed, undismayed.
+**u'/forkor'tet** *A* - (=+-a) complete, unabridged, uncut: **u- brøk** unreduced fraction.
+**uforkren'kelig** *A* - *lit.* immortal, imperishable, indestructible; sacred.
+**uforlig'nelig** *A* - (=+**uforliknelig**) incomparable, matchless; inimitable.
+**uforli'kelig** *A* - (=***uforlikleg**) incompatible, irreconcilable, quarrelsome.
u'/forlik't *A* - at odds, in disagreement (**med** with): **være u-** quarrel; **u-e saker** unfinished business.
u'/forlova [/fårlå'va] *A* - (=+-et) not engaged (to marry).
u'-forma *A* - (=+-et) u-shaped.
+**ufor'melig** *A* - formless, shapeless; amorphous.
u'/formell' *A* *-elt, pl -e* informal.
+**u'/formin'sket** *A* - unabated, undiminished.
+**u'/formu'ende** *A* - 1 poor, without means. 2 *lit.* incapable, without ability; helpless.
u'/fornuf't **-a/+-en* folly, foolishness; absurdity, irrationality.
u'/fornuf'tig *A* - foolish, senseless; absurd, irrational.
+**u'/forret'tet** *A* -: **med u- sak** having failed in one's mission, without success.
+**u'/forsag't** *A* - brave, undaunted, undismayed.
+**u'/forsik'tig** *A* - careless, incautious (**med** with); injudicious, rash.
+**u'forsik'tig/het** *-en* carelessness, lack of caution.
+**u'/forskam'met** *A* - bold, brazen, impertinent; impudent, insolent, shameless: **u-ede priser** exorbitant prices.
+**u'forskam'met/het** *-en* impertinence, impudence, insolence; insult, piece of impudence (etc.).
+**u'/forskyl'dt** *A* - undeserved, unmerited, unprovoked; *(adv.)* through no fault (merit) of (one's) own.
+**u'/forso'nlig** *A* - implacable, intransigent; irreconcilable (contrasts), uncompromising (enemies).
+**uforso'nlig/het** *-en* implacability, intransigence, irreconcilability.
u'/forstan'd *-en/*-et* foolishness, imprudence; lack of judgment.
u'/forstan'dig *A* - foolish, imprudent, unwise.
+**u'/forstil't** *A* - sincere, undisguised, unfeigned.
u'/forstyr'ra *A* - (=+-et) undisturbed; uninterrupted.
uforstyr'relig *A* - imperturbable, serene, unruffled: **hans u-e humør** his unfailing good humor.
+**uforstå'elig** *A* - impossible to understand, incomprehensible, unintelligible.
u'/forstå'ende *A* - uncomprehending; unappreciative, unsympathetic (**overfor** to): **leger og tannleger står ofte u- overfor hverandre** doctors and dentists often fail to understand one another (Dagbladet).
u'/forsva'rlig *A* - 1 indefensible, unexcusable, unpardonable. 2 irresponsible, reckless: **en u- handling** an i- act; **u- kjøring** reckless driving.
+**u'/forsø'kt** *A* - untried: **ikke late noe middel u-** leave no stone unturned.
+**u'/forsør'get** *A* - (=*/**forsyrgd**) unprovided for.
+**u'/forta'lt** *A* - (=*/**fortald**) aside from, not to speak of: **hans andre gode egenskaper u-** to say nothing of his other good qualities.
uforta'pelig *A* - inalienable (rights).
+**u'/fortje'nt** *A* - (=*/**fortent**) undeserved, unmerited.
+**u'/fortol'let** *A* -: **u-ede varer** goods that have not been through customs, on which duty has not been paid.
+**u'/fortrø'den** *A* *-ent, pl -ne* dogged, indefatigable, tireless: **u-t** *(adv.)* steadily.
+**u'fortrø'den/het** *-en* indefatigability, perseverance, tireless effort.
+**u'/fortø'vet** *Av archaic* forthwith, without delay.
+**u'/forutsett** *A* - unforeseen.
u'/forva'rende *A* - (usu. *adv.*) 1 unexpectedly, without warning. 2 accidentally, inadvertently, unintentionally.
+**ufrakom'melig** *A* - inescapable, unavoidable.
uframkom'melig *A* - impassable.
u'/franke'rt *A* - unstamped.
+**u'/fraven'dt** *A* - (usu. *adv.*) (look) fixedly, intently, unswervingly.
+**ufravi'kelig** *A* - absolute, fixed, unalterable: **et u- vilkår** an indispensable condition.
u'/fred *-en* 1 discord, dissension, strife; enmity, war: **leve i u-** feud; be at odds, war (**med** with). 2 uneasiness, unrest; disturbance, trouble.
ufre'delig *A* - strife-torn, unpeaceful: **det var u- i Norge** there was strife in N-. 2 belligerent, quarrelsome, warlike.
***u'freds/bod** [/bå] *-et* tidings of war.
+**u'freds/stifter** *-en, pl -e* (=*-**ar**) mischief-maker, trouble-maker; warmonger.

u'freds/tid [*/ti] *-a/+-en* time of strife, wartime.
***u'/fredt** *A* - strife-torn; unsafe (for wild animals).
***u'/freista** *A* - untried.
+ufremkom'melig *A* - cf **-fram-**
u'/fri *A -tt* 1 enslaved, in bondage, not free; oppressed, without political rights. 2 confined, cramped, restrained. 3 awkward, constrained, inhibited; bound (e.g. by one's prejudices).
***u'fri/dom** *-(m)en* cf **/het**
+u'fri/het *-en* 1 bondage, slavery; oppression: **leve i u-** be oppressed. 2 confinement, restraint. 3 awkwardness, constraint, restriction.
u'/frisk *A* 1 stale; oppressive (air). 2 (of person) decadent, perverted. *3 ill, unwell.
u'/friske [/frisje] *-t dial.* 1 insecurity, uneasiness. 2 sth causing uneasiness, as a ghost, a predatory animal.
u'/frivillig *A* - (=***/friviljug**) involuntary, unintended, unintentional: **u- komisk** unintentionally funny, ludicrous.
+u'/fruktbar *A* barren, sterile; infertile, unproductive; arid, fruitless, unfruitful: **u-e diskusjoner** f- discussions.
***u'/fryskje** *-t* cf **/friske**
***u'/fræv** *A* barren, sterile; infertile, unproductive.
u'/frø *-et dial.* bad seed; weed(s).
***u'/frødd** *A -/-frøtt* non-bearing, unfertilized.
uf's *-a/-en dial.* 1 cliff, precipice. 2 eaves.
uf'se/dråpe *-n* (=***/drope**) *dial.* drip from the eaves.
+u'/fullbåren *A -ent, pl -ne* (=***/fullboren**) embryonic, premature; abortive, imperfect.
+u'/fullendt *A* - (=***/fullenda**) incomplete, unfinished.
u'/fullkommen *A +-ent, pl -fullkomne* (=***/fullkomen**) defective, imperfect.
+u'fullkommen/het *-en* defect, shortcoming; defectiveness, imperfection.
***u'fullkommen/skap** *-en* cf **/het**
***u'/fullnøgd** *A -/-nøgt* dissatisfied, unsatisfied.
u'/fullsten'dig *A* - defective, imperfect, incomplete; fragmentary, uncompleted, unfinished.
u'fylle/fat *-et* 1 huge dish. 2 (of person) bottomless pit; heavy eater or drinker.
u'/fyse *-a dial.* 1 sth nasty, disgusting, uninviting (filth, mud, slop, etc.). 2 ugly beast, repulsive creature.
ufy'selig *A* - 1 unappetizing, uninviting. 2 disgusting, loathsome; filthy, swinish. 3 (of roads, walking conditions) muddy, sloppy; (of weather) raw and cold, wet.
u'/fysen *A +-ent, pl -ne* 1 (=**ufyselig**). 2 *dial.* not eager, unwilling.
+u'/født *A* - (=***/fødd**) unborn.
+ufø'lsom *A* insensitive; callous, unfeeling, unsympathetic (**overfor** to).
+ufø'lsom/het *-en* insensitivity; callousness, lack of feeling, of sympathy.
u'/før *A* - 1 disabled, immobilized, invalided. 2 *dial.* impassable.
***u'/føre**[1] *-a* cf **ufør/het**
u'/føre[2] *-t* 1 bad roads, hard going, unbroken trail. 2 *fig.* impasse; roadblock: **saken er kommet opp i et u-** the affair has reached an impasse.
u'føre/trygd *-a/+-en* disability insurance.
+u'før/het *-en* disability, invalidism.
+u'førhets/trygd *-a/-en* cf **uføre/**
***u'/førleg** *A* - 1 disabled, invalided. 2 difficult to travel, impassable.
***u'før/leik** *-en* cf **/het**
***-ug** *A* - cf **-ig**
u'/gagn [/gangn] *-et* damage, harm, injury; mischief: **gjøre u-** do m-, play tricks.
u'gagns/kråke [-gangns/] *-a* mischief-maker, vandal.
u'/garde'rt *A* - unguarded, unprotected.
ugg'[1] *-en dial.* 1 bristle, quill; fin; hackle, mane: **reise u-** bristle; rise to one's defence. 2 mosquito larva, small water creatures.
ugg'[2] *-en dial.* 1 raw cold. 2 anxiety, fear; respect: **de hadde fått en prest som det stod ugg av** they had gotten a minister who inspired them with respect.
ug'ge *-n dial.* 1 fin. 2 gill(s).
ug'gen *A +-ent, pl ugne dial.* 1 raw cold. 2 shivering.
ug'get(e) *A* - *dial.* 1 finned, finny; bristled, quilled. 2 shivering (=**uggen**).
***ugg'leg** *A* - shivery, unpleasant.
***ugg're** *V -a* (of fish) flutter, quiver its fins (to hold its position against the current).
***ugg're/hår** *-et* bristle, quill.
+ugid'delig *A* - listless; indolent, lazy, sluggish.
+ugid'delig/het *-en* listlessness; indolence, laziness, sluggishness.
u'/gift *A* - single, unmarried.
u'/gild *A* 1 *jur.* disqualified; invalid. 2 *hist.* uncompensated (by wergild).
***u'/gilde** *V -a* disqualify, invalidate; overrule, reverse; disapprove (of), disallow.
***u'gild/skap** *-en* disqualification, invalidity.
+ugjendri'velig *A* - irrefutable.
+ugjenkal'lelig *A* - irredeemable, irrevocable; *(adv.)* irrevocably: **u-tapt** i- lost; **for u- siste gang** for the absolutely last time.
+ugjenkjen'nelig *A* - unrecognizable.
+u'/gjennomførlig [also -fø'r-] *A* - impracticable, unfeasible, unworkable.
+u'/gjennomsiktig *A* - 1 *phys.* opaque. 2 dim; obscure; inscrutable.
+ugjennomsku'elig *A* - impenetrable, inscrutable, obscure.
+ugjennomtreng'elig *A* - impenetrable (darkness, forest, problem), impervious (**for** to, e.g. acids etc.), proof (**for** against); *mil.* impregnable.
***u'/gjerande** [/jærande] *A* - impossible, impracticable.
***u'/gjerd** [/jær] *-a* bad practice, usage; misdeed.
u'/gjerne [/jæ'rne] *Av* not gladly, reluctantly, unwillingly; hate to: **miste deg vil jeg u-** I would be loath to lose you (Undset).
u'/gjerning [/jæ'rning] *-a/+-en* bad deed, misdeed; crime (**mot** against).
u'gjernings/mann [-jæ'rnings/] *-en, pl -menn/*-menner* criminal, evildoer, malefactor.
***u'/gjo'r(d)** *A -gjort* unripe.
u'/gjort [/jort] *A* - undone, unfinished: **ønske noe u-** wish sth undone.
+u'/gjørlig [also -jø'r-] *A* - impossible (to do), unfeasible.
u'/glad *A* - 1 depressed, sad, unhappy. 2 reluctant, unwilling, without pleasure. 3 dispirited, melancholy, morose.
ug'le *-a* 1 *zool.* owl (Strigidae); little owl (Athene noctua): **det er u-r i mosen** things are not what they seem to be; there is mischief (trouble, sth) brewing; **føre u-r til Aten** carry coals to Newcastle. 2 *zool.* owlet moth (Noctuidae).
+ug'le/se *V -så, -sett* look askance at; dislike, ostracize.
***u'/gløymande** *A* - unforgettable.
u'/grammatika'lsk *A* - ungrammatical.
u'/gras *-et* weed(s).
u'gras/harv *-a* weeding harrow.
u'gras/klo *-a* weeding fork.
u'/grei *A *-tt* confused, disordered, tangled; ambiguous, indistinct, obscure; erratic, naughty.
u'/greie[1] *-a* 1 confusion, mess, mixup; tangle. 2 difficulty, hitch, trouble: **i u-** out of order; **u- med, på** trouble with. 3 discord, misunderstanding (**mellom** between).
u'/greie[2] *V +-de/*-dde* 1 tangle; disorder, mess up. 2 *(refl.)* **u- seg** become disordered, tangled.
***u'/grein** *-a* disorder, mess.
+u'/gress *-et* cf **/gras**
+u'grisk *A* - Ugrian, Ugric.
u'/grunna *A* - (=**+-et**) groundless, unfounded, ungrounded.
ugu'delig *A* - 1 godless, ungodly; impious, unholy. 2 depraved, reprobate. 3 enormous, immense: **et u-leven** an ungodly racket; **en u-masse penger** an outrageous amount of money.
+ugu'delig/het *-en* impiety, ungodliness; depravity, sinfulness.
+u'/gunst *-en* disfavor, displeasure: **i u-** in disfavor; **ved skjebnens u-** as ill luck would have it.
u'/gunstig *A* - unfavorable (e.g. attitude, terms) (**for** to); detrimental, harmful; adverse (e.g. balance of trade); unpropitious (time): **u-skjebne** bad luck, ill fortune.
ugyl'dig [also u'/] *A* - invalid, null and void: **gjøre u-** annul, invalidate.
***u'/hag** *A* - awkward, clumsy.
***u'/ha'gleg** *A* - inconvenient, unhandy.
u'/handte'rlig [also -te'r-] *A* - unhandy, unmanageable, unwieldy.
+uhe'derlig [also u'/] *A* - (=***/heiderleg**) dishonorable; degrading; dishonest.
***u'/hegd** *-a* mass (**med** of).
u'/heil *A* (=**+/hel**) 1 defective, fragmentary, incomplete. *2 dilapidated, tumble-down.
+uhelbre'delig *A* - incurable.
uhel'dig *A* - 1 unfortunate, unlucky (**med** with); unsuccessful. 2 inopportune, ill-timed; awkward: **et u-uttrykk** an awkward expression. 3 adverse, disadvantageous; detrimental, injurious: **komme i et u-lys** appear in an adverse light.
uhel'dig/vis [also uhel'di vi's] *Av* unfortunately.
u'/hell *-et* bad luck, misfortune; accident, mishap: **ha u- med noe** fail in sth; **et hell i u-et** a blessing in disguise.
+u'hell/svanger *A -ert, pl -re* dangerous, fatal; ominous, sinister.
u'hell/varslende *A* - foreboding, ominous, sinister.
+u'/hemmet *A* - (=***/hemja**) uninhibited, unrestrained, unrestricted.
u'/hemna** *A* - (=/hemnd**) cf **/hevnet**
***u'/hende** *-t* accident, misfortune.
+u'/hensiktsmessig *A* - unappropriate, inexpedient, irrational.
***u'/heppast** *V -ast* fail, go wrong, not succeed; have an accident.
***u'/heppe** *-a* accident, misfortune.
***u'/heppeleg** *A* - (of situation) unfortunate.
***u'/heppen** *A -e/-i, pl -hepne* (of person) unlucky.
+u'/hevnet *A* - (=***u/hemna**) unavenged.
+u'/hildet *A* - (=***-a**) impartial, objective; unbiased, unprejudiced.
u'/hindra *A* - (=**+-et**) free (access), unhindered, unobstructed.
u'/histo'risk *A* - unhistorical.
uhjel'pelig *A* - beyond (past) help; hopeless, incurable: **u- fortapt** irretrievably lost.
+u'/hjelpsom [/-såmm] *A -t, pl -me* (=***-sam**) unhelpful, unobliging.
+u'/hjemlet *A* - *jur., lit.* baseless, without grounds; unauthorized, unlawful, unwarranted.
+u'/holdbar *A* 1 not durable; perishable. 2 fallacious, untenable (e.g. arguments); impossible to main-

+ Bokmål; * Nynorsk; ° Dialect.
After letter: ' stress (Acc. 1); ' tone, stress (Acc. 2); · length.
Below letter: . not pronounced.

tain: **u-e boligforhold** indefensible housing conditions.
uhor'velig *A* - enormous, tremendous: **det var u- til bør han hadde lagt på** he had put on a monster of a load (Kinck).
***u'/hug** *-en* dislike, distaste; reluctance.
***u'/huga** *A* - with distaste, dislike; reluctantly.
***u'/huggande** *A* - disconsolate, inconsolable.
***u'/hu'gleg** *A* - disagreeable, unpleasant.
***u'/hu'gnaḍ** *-en* displeasure, dissatisfaction.
+u'/humsk *A* - 1 filthy, nauseating, unappetizing. 2 corrupt, repulsive, revolting: **u- agitasjon** unsavory agitation.
+u'humsk/het *-en* 1 filth, nastiness; repulsive thing(s). 2 corruption, evil.
u'/hygge *+-a/+-en/*-et* 1 cheerlessness; desolate, dismal, unpleasant atmosphere. 2 eeriness; eerie, sinister feeling, uneasiness; horror.
u'hygge/kjensle *-a* feeling of desolation, eeriness, uneasiness.
uhyg'gelig *A* - 1 cheerless, dismal, dreary; uncomfortable, unpleasant. 2 ominous, sinister; eerie, uncanny, weird: **i en u- grad** to an alarming degree; **være u- til mote** be disquieted, troubled, uneasy.
***u'/hyggje** *-a* cf **/hygge**
u'/hyre[1] *-t* monster; monstrous beast, ogre (also *derog.* of people).
+uhy're[2] *A* - 1 enormous, huge, immense; colossal, gigantic, tremendous. 2 *(adv.)* exceedingly, extremely, tremendously.
+uhy'rlig *A* - 1 enormous, huge, immense. 2 monstrous, outrageous, shocking: **det u-e** the grotesque.
+uhy'rlig/het *-en* grotesqueness, monstrosity, outrageousness.
***u'/hæv** *A* poor, not very useful.
uhøf'lig *A* - discourteous, impolite.
+uhøf'lig/het *-en* discourtesy, impoliteness.
***u'/høg** *A* inconvenient, uncomfortable, unsuitable.
uhø'rlig *A* - inaudible, soundless.
u'/hø'rt *A* - (=***/høyrd**) 1 not heard; unheard, without a hearing. 2 unheard of, unprecedented; shameless, shocking: **u-e lidelser** unprecedented suffering.
u'/høvelig *A* - 1 inappropriate; inconvenient. 2 improper, unseemly.
u'/høvisk *A* - *lit.* discourteous; improper, indecent, unseemly; lewd, smutty.
+u'/hånḍte'rlig *A* - cf **/handterlig**
+u'/imotsag't *A* - unchallenged, uncontested, undisputed; *(adv.)* incontestably, indisputably.
+uimotsi'(g)elig *A* - incontestable, indisputable, undeniable: **u- sant** undeniably true.
uimotstå'elig *A* - irresistible (e.g. person); overpowering, overwhelming (e.g. desire): **u- komisk** i-ly funny.
+uimotta'gelig *A* - cf **uimottakelig**
+uimotta'kelig *A* - immune, resistant, not susceptible (**for** to); proof: **u- for kritikk** proof against criticism.
+u'/innbundet *A* - (=***/innbunden**) unbound.
+uinndri'velig *A* - irrecoverable: **u-e fordringer** bad debts.
+u'/innfridd *A* - unfulfilled (promises); *merc.* unpaid, unredeemed.
+u'/innløst *A* - uncashed, unredeemed; unpaid.
u'/innpakka *A* - (=**+-et**) not packed, not wrapped.
+u'/innskrenket *A* - absolute (e.g. monarch); unbounded, unlimited, unrestricted.
+uinnta'gelig *A* - cf **uinntakelig**
+uinnta'kelig *A* - impregnable.
+u'/innviet *A* - 1 profane, unconsecrated, unhallowed. 2 uninitiated (**i** in).
u'/interessant [/-ang'] *A* - boring, uninteresting.
u'/interesse'rt *A* - indifferent; disinterested, uninterested.
u'/jamn *A* *-jamt* 1 rough, uneven (road, style, surface, etc.). 2 unequal (portions, etc.); broken, irregular. 3 erratic, variable; inconsistent.
+u'/jevn *A* cf **/jamn**
+u'jevn/het *-en* 1 bumpiness, roughness, unevenness. 2 inequality; difference, disparity. 3 irregularity; inconsistency.
U K=**United Kingdom; utta(k)ingskomiteen**
+u'/kallet *A* - (=***-a, +/kalt**) 1 uncalled, uninvited. 2 gratuitous, uncalled-for.
u'/kamera'tslig *A* - uncomradely, unsporting.
+u'/kampdyktig *A* - disabled, unfit for battle.
uka's *-en* ukase; dictum, ultimatum.
+u'ke *-a/-en* cf **veke**[1]
+u'ke/blaḍ *-et* cf **veke/**
+u'ke/dag *-en* cf **veke/**
+u'ke/gammel *A* *-elt, pl -gamle* cf **veke/gammal**
+u'ke/havenḍe *en* (duty officer, etc.) of the week, person on duty for the week.
+u'ke/kort *-et* week's pass, ticket, etc.
+u'ke/lang *A* cf **veke/**
+u'ke/lønn *-a/-en* cf **veke/**
+u'ke/lønnet *A* - paid by the week.
+u'ke/magasi'n *-et* weekly (magazine).
+u'kentlig *A* - weekly; per week; by the week: **tre ganger u-** three times a week, weekly.
+u'ke/oversikt *-en* week's survey.
+u'ke/penger *pl* cf **veke/**
+u'ke/revy' *-en* weekly newsreel.
+u'ke/vis *Av* cf **veke/**
+u'/kirkelig *A* - anticlerical, nonchurch; secular, worldly.
ukjen'nelig *A* - unrecognizable: **gjøre seg u-** disguise oneself.
+ukjen'nelig/het *-en* unrecognizability: **til u-** beyond all recognition.
u'/kjennskap *-en/+-et* ignorance (**til** of), lack of acquaintance (**til** with).
+u'/kjent *A* - (=***/kjend**) 1 strange, unfamiliar, unknown (**for** to) (country, person, road, etc.); obscure (artist, writer, etc.): **en u- størrelse** an unknown quantity; a dark horse; **det store u-e** the Great Unknown. 2 ignorant (**med** of); unacquainted (**med** with).
u'/kjure *-a dial.* 1 filthiness, lewdness; brutality; coarseness. 2 slattern, unsavory person; fiend, monster; lecher.
u'/kjær *A* unwelcome: **det var ham ikke u-t å** he was not averse to.
u'/kjæ'rlig *A* - uncharitable; unkind; hateful, unloving.
+u'kjærlig/het *-en* lack of charity; unkindness; hate.
u'/kjønna *A* - (=**+-et**) *bot., zool.* asexual.
uklan'derlig *A* - blameless, irreproachable; faultless.
u'/klar *A* 1 dim, hazy; cloudy, muddy; indistinct, obscure, vague. 2 confused, uncertain, unclear; ambiguous, muddled; delirious, light-headed. 3 *naut.* foul: **rake u-** run afoul (**av** of); *fam.* **rake, ryke u-** fall out, have a row (**med** with).
+u'klar/het *-en* 1 dimness, haziness; cloudiness, muddiness, opacity; fuzziness, vagueness; obscureness. 2 confusion, uncertainty; lack of clarity; ambiguity, muddle; delirium.
ukle'delig *A* - unbecoming (clothing, conduct).
u'/klok *A* unwise; ill-considered, imprudent, injudicious.
u'klok/skap *-en* unwisdom; folly, imprudence, injudiciousness.
u'/konfirme'rt *A* - *eccl.* not (yet) confirmed (usu. age 14).
+u'/kontrolle'rbar *A* unverifiable (information).
***u'/kosta** *A* - free, gratis.
Ukrai'na *Pln* the Ukraine.
+ukrai'ner *-en, pl -e* (=***-ar**) Ukrainian.
ukrai'nsk *A* - Ukrainian.
***u'/kravd** *A* *-/-kravt* voluntary.
+ukren'kelig *A* - (=***ukrenkjeleg**) inviolable, sacred, sacrosanct; *jur.* immune.
+ukren'kelig/het *-en* inviolability, sacredness, sacrosanctity; *jur.* immunity.
ukris'telig *A* - unchristian, ungodly: **stå opp u- tidlig** get up at an ungodly hour.
u'/kritisk *A* - uncritical.
+u'/kron(e)t *A* - (=***/krona**) uncrowned.
+u'/krutt *-et* (=***/krut**) weed(s): **u- forgår ikke** you can't get rid of a bad penny.
***uk'se** *-n* cf **okse**
+uku'elig *A* - indomitable, irrepressible, unconquerable: **u- var deres visshet** their confidence was u- (N. Grieg).
ukule'le *-n mus.* ukulele.
u'/kultive'rt *A* - 1 uncultured. 2 *agr.* uncultivated; not purebred.
u'/kultu'r *-en* lack of culture; lack of breeding.
***u'/kunnig** *A* - cf **/kyndig**
+u'/kunstlet *A* - artless, natural, unaffected; simple, unsophisticated.
u'/kuran't *A* - not current, out of fashion; *merc.* unsalable.
+u'kvems/o'rḍ *-et* term of abuse; abusive language: **bruke u- mot en** call sby names.
ukvin'nelig *A* - unfeminine, unwomanly.
u'/kyndig [also -kjyn'-] *A* - ignorant (**i** of), unskilled, untrained (**i** in).
+ukyn'dig/het *-en* ignorance (**i** of), lack of skill or training (**i** in).
+u'/kysk *A* unchaste, wanton; immodest, lewd, sensuous.
u'l[1] *+-et/*-en* 1 howl, howling (of animals, wind, etc.); hoot; *fam.* bawling, yelling. 2 blast, scream, screech (of ship's horn, siren, tires).
u'l[2] *A dial.* rancid, spoiled, tainted.
u'/ladd *A* *-/*-ladt* 1 unloaded (gun). 2 *phys.* uncharged.
u'/lag *+et/*eit* disorder: **i u-(e)** out of order; out of sorts.
***u'/lagast** *V -ast* get out of order.
+u'/lage *N* cf **/lag**
+u'/la'glig *A* - inconvenient, unsuitable.
ula'n *-en mil.* uhlan.
u'-land *-et* cf **utviklingsland**
ulas'telig *A* - blameless, faultless; immaculate, impeccable, irreproachable: **u- fransk** faultless French.
***u'lde** *pl of* **ylje**
u'le *V -te/*-a* 1 howl; bawl; hoot. 2 blast, blow, toot (on a horn or siren).
+ule'gelig *A* - 1 incurable (disease), non-healing. 2 *fig.* irremediable.
+u'/legemlig *A* - bodiless, disembodied; incorporeal, spiritual.
+ulei'lige *V -et* bother, incommode, inconvenience: **u- seg** take the trouble, put oneself out (to do sth).
+ulei'lig/het *-en* inconvenience, trouble: **gjøre seg den u- å** go to the trouble of; **komme til u-** cause i-.
u'/lempe *-a/+-en* difficulty, disadvantage, drawback (**ved** to): **til u- for** to the inconvenience of.
ulem'pelig *A* - inconvenient.
u'/lenḍe *-t* rough, rugged terrain; wilderness.
u'/lenḍt *A* - difficult to traverse, rugged; pathless, trackless.
+ulen'kelig *A* - (=***ulenkjeleg**) ungainly; loose-jointed.
ule'selig *A* - illegible; unreadable.
u'/leska *A* - (=**+-et**) unslaked.
Ul'f *Prn (m)*
***u'/liḍande** *A* - cf **ulidelig**
uli'delig *A* - excruciating; insufferable, intolerable, unbearable.

u'/lik *A* 1 different (from), dissimila,r unlike. 2 unequal (size, value, etc.). 3 *dial.* unfitting, unseemly; bad, unreasonable: **det var ikke så rent u-t, sa kongen** that wasn't at all bad, said the king (Asbjørnsen and Moe).
u'/like *A* - 1 unequal (age, distribution, length, struggle, etc.); uneven. 2 odd (day, number, etc.). 3 *(adv.)* by far, far, much (better), bigger, etc.).
u'like/finna *A* - (=+-et) *bot.* odd-pinnate.
+**u'/likevektig** *A* - out of equilibrium, unbalanced.
+**u'lik/het** *-en* difference, inequality.
***u'/li'kleg** *A* - disagreeable; unreasonable.
***u'/livnad** *-en* dissipation, immorality.
u'livs/sår *-et lit.* fatal wound; irreparable damage.
***u'/ljod** *-en/-et* cf **/lyd**
ul'k *-en* (=**ulke**) 1 *zool.* sea scorpion (Cottus). 2 *naut.* old salt, old tar.
ul'ke *-a* cf **ulk**
***ul'keleg** *A* - repulsive.
ull' *-a* wool: **kjenne u-a** know one's (that) type, kind; **være av samme u-a** be cut from the same cloth, be birds of a feather.
ul'len *A* +*-ent, pl ulne* 1 wool(en). 2 shaggy, woolly (hair, tuft, etc.); heavy, thick (cloud, fog, smoke, etc.). 3 fuzzy, vague, woolly (sound, thinking, voice, etc.).
Ul'lens/aker *Pln* twp, Akershus.
Ul'lens/vang *Pln* twp, Hordaland.
Ul'le/vål *Pln* section of Oslo.
ull'/ga rn *-et* wool yarn.
+**ull'/hode** *-t* (=***/hovud**) 1 curlyhead, woolly head. 2 part of spindle on which yarn is wound.
ull'/hår *-et* 1 underfur, underhair; body hair. 2 curly, woolly hair.
ull'/håra *A* - (=+-et) 1 woolly-haired; furry. 2 *bot.* villous.
Ull's/fjo'rd *Pln* twp, Troms.
ull'/sky *-a* woolly cloud.
ull'/teppe *-t, pl* +*-r/**- (woolen) blanket.
ull'/trøye *-a* 1 wool undershirt. 2 wool sweater.
ull'vare/fabrikk' *-en* woolen goods factory, woolen mill.
ul'me *V -a/*+*-et* 1 smoulder (lit. and *fig.*): **det u-er i asken** the ashes are s-ing; **u-ende misnøye** s-ing dissatisfaction. 2 *dial.* (of the weather) be close, sultry.
u'lne *V -a/*+*-et dial.* become rancid, tainted; spoil.
u'/logisk *A* - illogical.
***u'/lot** [/låt] *-et* bad humor.
+**u'/lovende(s)** [/låv-] *Av dial.* without permission.
ulovlig [-lå'vli] *A* - illegal, illicit, unlawful; against the rules, not permitted.
+**ulovlig/het** [-lå'vli-] *-en* 1 illegality, unlawfulness; lawlessness, transgression; sth illicit.
Ul'rik *Prn(m)*
Ul'riken *Pln* highest of Bergen's seven mountains.
ul's/blakk *A -blakt dial., vet.* light grey, with a dark stripe down the back.
Ul'/stein *Pln* twp, Møre og Romsdal.
ul'ster *-eren, pl -rer* ulster.
***u'lt** *pp of* **ylje**
ult. =**ultimo**
ultima'tum *-et, pl -/*+*-er* ultimatum.
ul'timo *Av merc.* at, by the end of the month, usu. after the 21st of the month: **u- april** end of April.
ul'tra *Av* ultra.
ul'tra/fiolett' *A* - ultraviolet.
ul'tra/lyd *-en* supersonic sound, ultrasound.
ultramari'n *-et* ultramarine (blue).
ul'tra/radika'l *A* extremely radical.
+**ul'tra/rød** *A* (=***/raud**) infrared.
***u'/lugom** *A* inconvenient, unhandy, unsuitable.
***u'/lukke** *-a* cf **/lykke**
***uluk'keleg** *A* - cf **ulykkelig**
u'/lune +*-et/***-a* bad humor.
ul'v *-en* wolf; *fig.* fiend; bear; bad-tempered or vicious person: **u- i fåreklær** wolf in sheep's clothing; **en u- etter pikene** a girl-chaser, a wolf.
Ul'v *Prn(m)*
ul've/binne *-a* she-wolf.
ul've/grav *-a* pit for trapping wolves.
ul've/grå *A -tt* light brownish-gray.
ul've/hund *-en* wolf dog, wolfhound.
ul've/hunger *-en* ravenous hunger, wolfish appetite.
ul've/skinn *-et* wolfskin.
ul've/stue *-a* (=**/stove**) pit for trapping wolves.
Ul'/vik *Pln* twp, Hordaland.
ul'v/unge [/onge] *-n* 1 wolf cub. 2 cub scout.
u'/lyd *-en* raucous, unpleasant sound; discord, dissonance; *fig.* disharmony.
uly'dig *A* - disobedient: **være u- mot** disobey.
+**uly'dig/het** *-en* disobedience (**mot** against).
***u'/lydnad** *-en* disobedience.
u'/lykke *-a/*+*-en* 1 accident; calamity, disaster; harm, injury: **gjøre en u- på en** inflict harm, injury on sby; **gjøre en u- på seg** do away with oneself; **være ute for en u-** have an accident. 2 bad luck, ill fortune, misfortune; unfortunate thing; downfall, ruin, undoing: **komme i u-(a)** *fam.* become pregnant out of wedlock; **stygg som en u-** ugly as the devil; **så ville u-n** as bad luck would have it; **til u-** detrimental (**for** to).
+**u'lykke/bringende** *A* - fatal; disastrous.
+**u'lykke/bringer** *-en, pl -e* sby, sth that brings bad luck; jinx.
ulyk'kelig *A* - 1 unhappy; distressed. 2 disastrous, unfortunate; ill-fated, ill-starred: **u- forelsket** hopelessly in love.
ulyk'kelig/vis *Av* unfortunately; as luck would have it.
+**u'lykkes/budskap** *-et* (=***/bodskap**) bad tiding, tragic news.
+**u'lykkes/forsik'ret** *A* - insured against accidents.
u'lykkes/fugl *-en* 1 bird of ill omen. 2 accident-prone, jinxed person; Jonah.
u'lykkes/profe't *-en* alarmist, prophet of doom; Cassandra.
+**u'lykkes/sted** *-et* (=***/stad**) scene of an accident or disaster.
u'lykkes/tilfelle *-t, pl -/*+*-r* accident.
u'lykkes/trygd *-a/*+*-en* accident insurance.
u'lykke/svanger *A -ert, pl -re* dangerous, ominous.
u'lykke/varslende *A* - ominous.
+**ulykksa'lig** *A* - ill-fated, unfortunate, unlucky; unhappy.
u'/lyst *-a* 1 disinclination, reluctance (**til** to). 2 aversion, dislike; displeasure, distaste: **gjøre noe med u-** do sth reluctantly.
u'/lysten *A* +*-ent, pl -ne* disinclined, reluctant (**på** to).
u'lyst/kjensle *-a* feeling of reluctance; aversion; dislike.
***ulæ'kjeleg** *A* - cf **ulegelig**
u'/lærd *A* - illiterate, unlettered; unlearned; without higher education.
u'/læ'rt *A* - untrained (**i** in).
***u'/læ'st** *A* - cf **/låst**
***u'/læte** *-a* 1 unpleasant sound; shriek. 2 (**-t**) disturbance, misbehavior.
+**u'/lønnsom** [/-såmm] *A* (=***/lønsam**) unprofitable; not worthwhile.
u'/lønt *A* - 1 unprofitable. 2 (usu. **ulønnet**) unpaid (workers); honorary, volunteer.
+**ulø'selig** *A* - (=***uløyseleg**) indissoluble (e.g. bonds), insoluble, unsolvable (e.g. problem).
u'/løyst *A* - (=+**/løst**) unsolved; unresolved.
u'/løyves *Av dial.* without permission.
u'/lå'st *A* - unlocked.
u'/låt *-en* (horrible) noise, racket.
***um'** *P, C* cf **om**[1,2]
***u'/mage** *-n* 1 weakling. 2 child, youth.
u'/mak *-en* bother, inconvenience, trouble: **gjøre seg den u-e** take the pains; **u-en verd** worth the trouble.
u'/make[1] *V -a/*+*-et* 1 bother, inconvenience, trouble. 2 *(refl.)* **u- seg** bother, go out of one's way (to); exert oneself.
+**u'/make**[2] *A* - (=***-a**) mismatched, odd, without a mate (glove, shoe).
***u'mak/laus** *A* easy-going; lazy.
u'mak/redd *A* - *dial.* lazy.
+**u'/ma'lt**[1] *A* - unpainted; natural color.
+**u'/ma'lt**[2] *A* - unground, whole (grain).
u'/mandig *A* - effeminate, unmanly.
+**uman'dig/het** *-en* effeminacy, unmanliness.
+**umane'rlig** *A* - 1 unmannerly, unseemly; awkward. 2 excessive, enormous; *(adv.)* immensely, terribly.
um'bra *-en* umber.
+**um'brer** *-en, pl -/-e* (=***-ar**) Umbrian.
um'brisk *A* - Umbrian.
+**u'/medde'lsom** [/-såmm] *A -t, pl -me* silent, taciturn, uncommunicative.
+**u'/medgjø'rlig** [also -jø'r-] *A* - 1 hard to deal with, ornery, unaccommodating; stubborn, uncooperative. 2 (of object or situation) difficult (to manage, overcome, etc.).
+**umedgjø'rlig/het** *-en* intractability, stubbornness.
+**u'/medli'dende** *A* - lacking compassion, unsympathetic.
***u'/medvi'ten** *A -e/-i, pl -ne* 1 subconscious, unconscious. 2 instinctive, intuitive.
***u'/megd** *-a* 1 weakness. 2 childhood.
u'/melo'disk *A* - harsh, unmelodic.
***u'/meltande** *A* - indigestible; heavy.
***u'/melteleg** *A* - indigestible.
***u'/menne** *-t* 1 weakling. 2 (=**umenneske**).
u'/menneske *-t, pl* +*-r/**- inhuman person; fiend; beast, brute; devil.
umen'neskelig *A* - inhuman; bestial, brutal, cruel; hard-hearted, unsympathetic.
+**umen'neskelig/het** *-en* inhumanity; bestiality, brutality, cruelty; hard-heartedness, lack of sympathy.
***umen'neskjeleg** *A* - cf **umenneskelig**
***u'/merkande** *A* - cf **umerkelig**
umer'kelig *A* - 1 gradual, imperceptible, unnoticeable: **en u- overgang** an i- transition. 2 [u'/mærkeli] ordinary, unremarkable; usual.
u'/metta *A* - (=+-et) 1 unfilled (e.g. demand), unsated (e.g. appetite), unsatisfied. 2 *chem.* unsaturated.
umet'telig *A* - insatiable.
+**u'/middelba'r** *A* - 1 direct (evidence, link, result, etc.); first-hand (e.g. knowledge); immediate (cause, vicinity, etc.). 2 spontaneous, unreserved; emotional, impulsive, lively (person, work of art, action).
+**u'middelbar/het** *-en* 1 directness, immediacy. 2 impulsiveness, spontaneity.
u'/mild *A* - 1 gruff, harsh; stern, strict; unfriendly. 2 inclement, rough, severe; forbidding.
+**umin'delig** *A* - cf **uminnelig**
umin'nelig *A* - immemorial: **siden u-e tider** since time i-.

+ Bokmål; * Nynorsk; ° Dialect.
After letter: ' stress (Acc. 1); ' tone, stress (Acc. 2); · length.
Below letter: . not pronounced.

***u'/minnig** *A* - forgetful, oblivious.

+umiskjen'nelig *A* - clear, evident, unmistakable.

***u'/missande** *A* - cf **umistelig**

umis'telig *A* - 1 inalienable (e.g. rights). 2 indispensable: **gjøre seg u-** make oneself i-. 3 priceless (e.g. values).

+u'/misten'ksom [/-såmm] *A* - trusting, unsuspecting, unsuspicious.

***um'me** *Av* cf **omme**

u'/moden *A* +*-ent, pl -ne* 1 unripe; green. 2 callow, immature.

+u'/modenhet *-en* 1 unripeness; greenness. 2 callowness, immaturity.

u'/moderne [/modæ'rne] *A* - old-fashioned, out-of-date.

***umogeleg** [umå'gleg] *A* - cf **umulig**

***u'/mogen** *A* *-e/-i, pl -ne* cf **/moden**

***umogleg** [umå'gleg] *A* - cf **umulig**

u'/mora'l *-en* immorality.

u'/mora'lsk *A* - immoral.

u'/motive'rt *A* - 1 unmotivated; gratuitous, groundless; startling, surprising; unprovoked, wanton. 2 *(adv.)* for no reason at all; without any obvious reason.

+umu'lig *A* - (=***umog(e)leg**) 1 impossible (=not possible): **det er meg u- å** it's i- for me to. 2 impossible (=unacceptable): **hun er u- i kortspill** she's i- at cards; **gjøre seg u-** (also) make oneself an outcast; spoil one's chances. 3 *(adv.)* not possibly: **det kan du u- gjøre** you can't p- do that.

+umu'lig/gjøre *V -gjorde, -gjort* make, render impossible; preclude, prevent.

+umu'lig/het *-en* 1 impossibility (**av** of). 2 impossible person.

+umu'lius *-en* clumsy, incompetent, impossible person.

u'/myndig [also -myn'-] *A* 1 minor, not (yet) of age, under age. 2 (of adult) legally incompetent.

+umyn'dig/gjøre *V -gjorde, -gjort* (=***/gjere**) 1 *jur.* declare incompetent. 2 *fig.* deprive of freedom of action and independence.

+u'myndig/het *-en* 1 *jur.* minority; wardship. 2 *fig.* immaturity; lack of independence.

u'/mynta *A* - (=+**-et**) unminted: **u- sølv** silver bullion.

u'/mælende *A* dumb, without power of speech.

u'/møble'rt *A* - unfurnished.

u'/mønstra *A* - (=+**-et**) not figured, plain, unpatterned.

umå'lelig *A* - 1 not measurable; imponderable. 2 enormous; immeasurable, vast.

u'/må'lt *A* - unmeasured.

***u'/måte** *-n*: **til u-, u-s** to excess.

+u'/måteholden *A* *-ent, pl -ne* (=***/måtehalden**) excessive, immoderate, intemperate.

umå'telig *A* - enormous, immense (crowd, extent, number, success, etc.); tremendous, vast; intense (cold, hunger, pride, etc.); *(adv.)* enormously, immensely, etc.

u'/nasjona'l *A* 1 foreign, un-Norwegian. 2 unpatriotic: **u- holdning** u- conduct (esp. during World War II).

u'/natu'r *-en* affectation, artificiality, unnaturalness.

u'/natu'rlig *A* - 1 unnatural; abnormal, perverted. 2 affected, artificial, forced.

+u'/navngitt *A* - anonymous, unnamed.

+und- *Pf* cf **unn-**

un'da *P* cf **unna**

***un'dan** *P* cf **unna**

un'das *N* cf **ad undas**

un'der[1] *-et, pl -/+-e* 1 marvel, miracle, wonder: **det var et Guds u-** it was a real miracle, a wonder; **ikke (intet) u- at** no wonder that; **være, bli opp i u-** *dial.* be, become highly astounded, surprised (**over** at). 2 *dial.* (used as adj. or adv.) inconceivable, unbelievable: **et u-s syn** an u- sight.

un'der[2] *P* 1 under (age, control, five dollars, a false name, repair, the table, treatment, the Tudors, water, etc.); below (deck, the equator, the surface, etc.), beneath (one's dignity, a clear sky, the window, etc.), underneath. 2 close to, near, right up to (the coast, land, etc.); at the foot of (a mountain, a ridge, etc.): **like u- jul** just before Christmas. 3 at the time of, during (a meal, the war, etc.); in the process of, while: **u- kjørselen** while driving. 4 amidst, in the midst of, to the accompaniment of (cheers, loud music, silence, etc.). 5 *(adv.)* below, beneath, underneath; down: **gå u-** (of ship, sun) go down, sink; be lost, come to an end. (With other verbs, see these.)

un'der/ansikt *-et* chin, lower part of the face.

un'der/arm *-en* forearm, lower part of the arm.

un'der/art *-a/-en* *biol.* subspecies.

un'der/avde'ling *-a/+-en* subdivision.

un'der/balanse [/balang'se] *-n* *merc.* deficit: **være i u-** show d-; be in the red.

+un'der/bandt *pt of* **-binde**

+un'der/bega'vet *A* - of subnormal intelligence, slow, ungifted.

+un'der/be'nklær *pl*: **lange u-** long underwear; **korte u-** shorts.

un'der/betale *V -te/*-a* underpay.

+un'der/beviss't *A* - subconscious.

+un'derbevisst/het *-en* 1 subconscious: **i u-en** in one's s-. 2 subconscious feeling (**om** of).

+un'der/binde *V -bandt, -bundet* *med.* ligate, tie.

+un'der/bitt *-et* (=***/bit**) protruding jaw; *odont., vet.* undershot jaw.

+un'der/brakte *pt of* **-bringe**

***un'der/breisle** *-a* blanket (used to sleep on).

+un'der/bringe *V -brakte, -brakt* esp. *mil.* billet, quarter.

un'der/bruk *-et* 1 croft, tenant farm, subdivision (of larger farm). 2 appendage, subsidiary; branch, wing (of a larger enterprise).

un'der/bukse [/bokse] *-a* underpants; drawers, trunks.

+un'der/bundet *pp of* **-binde**

***un'der/bu'rd** *-en* litter (e.g. in a stall).

+un'der/by *V* *infl as* **by[2]** underbid, undercut, undersell.

+un'der/bygge *V -bygde, -bygd* 1 found, lay a foundation for (e.g. an enterprise). 2 substantiate, support (e.g. an experiment, a theory).

underda'nig *A* - 1 subservient: **gjøre seg (noe, noen) u-** master (sth), subjugate (sby); **være noen u-** be subservient to sby. 2 humble, obsequious, servile.

+underda'nig/het *-en* 1 subservience. 2 humbleness, humility; obsequiousness, servility.

+un'der/deilig *A* - *archaic* divinely beautiful, gorgeous.

un'der/dønning *-en* ground swell (also *fig.* of hidden emotions).

+un'der/ernæ'ring *-a/-en* malnutrition, undernourishment.

+un'der/ernæ'rt *A* - malnourished, undernourished.

un'der/eta'sje *-n* basement (floor); bottom story, lower floor.

un'der/forstå *V -stod, -stått* 1 imply, understand: **u-tt** implicit, implied, understood. 2: **være u-tt med** accept, consent to.

un'der/full *A* - 1 miraculous; wonder-working. 2 marvellous, wonderful.

+underfun'dig *A* - 1 artful, crafty, shrewd; cunning, wily. 2 clever, subtle; mischievous, roguish, sly: **Hamsuns u-e stil** H-'s roguishly subtle style.

+underfun'dig/het *-en* 1 craftiness, cunning, trickery. 2 cleverness, slyness, subtlety.

un'der/gang *-en* 1 destruction, ruin: **verdens u-** end of the world. 2 railroad underpass.

+un'der/gikk *pt of* **-gå**

un'der/gitt *A* - subject; subordinate: **u- skjebnens tilfeldigheter** subject to the buffetings of fate.

+un'der/givelse *-n* *lit.* subjection, subservience.

+un'der/given *A* *-ent, pl -ne* cf **/gitt**

***un'der/gi'vnad** *-en* cf **/givelse**

un'der/gjerning *-a/+-en* miracle, miraculous deed.

+un'der/gjørende *A* - miraculous, wonder-working.

un'der/grave *V* *infl as* **grave** undermine (also *fig.*, e.g. of one's health); sap, subvert.

+un'dergravings/forsøk *-et* attempt to undermine; attempted subversion.

un'der/grep *-et* *gymn.* undergrip, reverse grip.

un'der/grunn *-en* 1 subway, underground railway. 2 *geol.* subsoil. 3 underworld (of criminals). 4 resistance movement, underground movement (in World War II).

+un'der/gå *V -gikk, -gått* experience, undergo; be subjected to, suffer.

***un'der/hald** *-et* cf **/hold**

***un'der/halde** *V* *infl as* **halde** cf **/holde**

***un'der/haldning** *-a* cf **/holdning**

***underhan'd** *Av* cf **hand**

+un'der/handle *V -a/-et* negotiate (**med** with).

+un'der/handling *-a/-en* negotiation: **være i u-er** negotiate (**med** with).

***underhan'ds/bod** [/bå] *-et* confidential bid, offer.

+un'der/hold *-et* 1 maintenance (**av** of); subsistence, (financial) support. 2 sustenance; necessities of life.

+un'der/holde *V -holdt, -holdt* 1 keep (alive, up); maintain, support. 2 amuse, entertain: **u- gjestene** e- one's guests. 3: **u- seg med** converse, talk with.

+un'der/holdende *A* - amusing, entertaining.

+under/hol'dning *-en* 1 amusement, diversion, entertainment. 2 (=**underhold**).

+underhol'dnings/bi'drag *-et* alimony, support money (for children).

+underhol'dnings/litteratu'r *-en* light reading.

+underhol'dnings/plikt *-a/-en* obligation to support (e.g. one's children).

+underhån'den *Av* confidentially, privately, secretly.

+un'derhånds/akkor'd *-en* private, secret agreement.

+un'derhånds/avtale *-n* private, secret agreement.

+un'derhånds/kjøp *-et* private, secret purchase.

+un'derhånds/opply'sning *-en* confidential, secret information.

+un'derhånds/salg *-et* private, secret sale.

un'der/jordisk [/jor'disk] *A* - 1 subterranean, underground: *mil.* **u- rom** dugout; bombshelter. 2 illegal, underground, underworld. 3 *folk.* netherworld: **de u-e** the n- people; the hillfolk (gnomes, goblins, etc., said to live underground).

un'der/kant *-en* 1 bottom edge, underside. 2 lowest limit, minimum: **ligge i u-** be at or below the acceptable minimum (of wages, a sports performance, etc.).

+un'der/kaste *V -a/-et* 1 conquer; subject, subordinate: **u- seg et land** c- a country. 2 *fig.* subject; expose to, lay open to: **u- noe en revisjon (kritikk)** subject sth to revision (criticism); **det kan ikke være tvil u-et** it cannot be open to question, be doubted. 3 *(refl.)*: **u- seg** acquiesce, submit; **u- seg** (with object), e.g. **u- seg en eksamen** undergo an examination; **u- seg en operasjon** submit to having an operation.

+un'der/kastelse *-n* 1 conquest, sub-

jection, subjugation (av of). 2 acquiescence, compliance, submission (av of; til to).
*un'der/kjake -n cf /kjeve
un'der/kjeft -en pop. lower jaw.
+un'der/kjenne V -kjente, -kjent 1 jur. disallow, not approve, reject; override, reverse. 2 fail, refuse to appreciate or recognize; underestimate; belittle.
+un'der/kjeve -n lower jaw; anat. mandible.
un'der/kjole -n slip.
+un'der/kjøpe V -te lit. bribe, suborn.
un'der/klasse -a/-en: u-en the lower classes.
*un'der/klede pl cf /klær
+un'der/klær pl (=*/klede) underclothes, underwear.
un'der/kropp -en lower part of the body (below the waist).
un'der/kue V -a/+-et subdue, subjugate, suppress; cow, henpeck.
+un'der/kuelse -n (=*-ing) subjugation, suppression (av of).
+un'der/la pt of -legge
un'der/lag -et basis, substratum; base, foundation, undercoating; mat, pad, underlay.
+un'der/lagt pp of -legge
un'der/legen A +-ent, pl -ne inferior.
+un'derlegen/het -en inferiority.
+un'derlegenhets/følelse -n feeling of inferiority.
+un'der/legge V -la, -lagt 1: u- seg conquer, overcome, subjugate. 2: u-lagt subject to; alt som lever er u-lagt kjærlighetens gjenskapermakt all that lives is subject to the creative force of love (Bjørnson).
un'der/leppe -a/+-en 1 lower lip. 2 bot. lower half of crown on a labiate plant.
un'derlig A - 1 queer, singular, strange. 2 archaic, (bibl.) marvelous, wonderful.
+un'der/liggende A - supporting, underlying; sub, subordinate: de u- realiteter the u- realities.
*un'der/lippe -a cf /leppe
+un'der/liv -et 1 anat. abdomen, belly; esp. med. (internal) female organs. 2 bodice, camisole.
+un'derlivs/sykdom -men abdominal disease.
un'der/mann -en, pl -menn/*-menner 1 inferior: bli ens u- come out second best. 2 bottom man (in acrobatics).
*un'der/medvit -et subconscious(ness).
un'der/mine're V -te 1 set a (dynamite) charge: u-t bru a mined bridge. 2 mine (field, harbor, etc.). 3 undermine (attitudes, etc.).
+un'der/måler -en, pl -e (=*-ar) 1 undersized person (animal, thing); runt (e.g. of fish) below legal limit. 2 moron, non-entity, second-rater.
un'der/må'ls A - pygmy, undersize; deficient; below standard.
un'der/offise'r -en non-commissioned officer (N.C.O.), petty officer.
un'der/ordna A - (=+-et) inferior, subordinate (also gram.); minor, secondary: av u-et betydning of minor significance; de u-ede one's subordinates.
un'der/ordne V -a/+-et subordinate: u- seg (under) submit to; u-ende konjunksjoner gram. subordinating conjunctions.
un'der/ordning -a/+-en subordination (av of) (also gram.); subjection, submission.
un'der/plagg -et underclothes.
+un'der/prikke V -a/-et place dots under crossed-out word or letter to restore it (=stet).
un'der/pris -en bargain, cut-rate prices; reduction: selge til u- sell at a sacrifice; få noe til u- get sth at a bargain; han oversatte bøker til u- he translated books at starvation wages (Hoel).
un'der/representе'rt A - underrepresented.
+un'der/retning [also -ret'-] -en information (om about): få u- be informed; til u- for Dem for your i-.
un'der/rett -en jur. lower court.
+un'der/rette V -a/-et advise, inform (om about): godt u-et well i-ed.
*un'der/sam A (easily) astonished, surprised.
un'der/setning *-a/+-en philos. minor premise.
+un'der/setsig A - squat, stocky, thickset.
un'der/side [*/sie] -a/+-en underside (av of).
un'der/sjø -en lit. ground swell.
un'der/sjøisk [/sjø-isk] A - submarine, underwater.
un'der/skjorte [/sjorte] -a undershirt.
un'der/skjønn¹ -et (=*/skjøn) jur. 1 preliminary appraisal. 2 preliminary appraiser.
+un'der/skjønn² A -skjønt divinely beautiful.
un'der/skjørt -et petticoat; underskirt; half-slip.
un'der/skog -en 1 underbrush, undergrowth. 2 fig. used of young students, researchers, etc. who will eventually grow into the higher positions.
un'der/skott -et (=+/skudd, */skot) 1 merc. loss; deficit: gå med u- show a d-. 2 deficiency, shortage (av of).
+un'der/skre(i)v pt of -skrive
+un'der/skre'vne N the undersigned; hum. yours truly.
un'der/skrift -a signature.
+un'der/skrive V -skre(i)v, -skrevet 1 endorse, sign (a document, etc.): han u-er seg he signs himself. 2 endorse, subscribe to, underwrite (an idea, etc.).
+un'der/skriver -en, pl -e (=*-ar) lit. signatory, signer.
*un'der/skri'vne N cf /skrevne
+un'der/skudd -et cf /skott
un'der/slag -et 1 embezzlement: gjøre u- embezzle; u- av hittegods withholding found property. 2 sum embezzled: dekke u-et repay the e-d money.
+un'der/slep -et embezzlement.
un'der/slå V infl as slå¹ 1 embezzle, misappropriate. 2 conceal.
+un'der/spi'st A -: være u- have eaten (or drunk) in advance so that one is prepared (e.g. for work, a party, etc.); be fortified (for sth).
un'derst sp of undre²
un'der/stell -et chassis; landing gear; undercarriage (of plane, train, wagon, etc.).
un'derstells/behan'dling -a/+-en undercoating of automobile chassis.
un'der/stemme +-n/*-a mus. lower part.
un'der/streke V -a/+-et/+-te 1 underline, underscore. 2 emphasize, stress.
*un'der/støe -a base, foundation; substratum; basis.
+un'der/støtte V -a/-et support (financially); subsidize.
+un'der/støttelse -n support; financial assistance; alimony; (unemployment) relief.
+un'der/stå V -stod, -stått: u- seg dare, presume (å to).
+un'der/søke V -te 1 examine, inspect, scrutinize (e.g. a document, an object). 2 check up on, probe, search (e.g. a person, sby's pockets, a story): se u-ende på en look searchingly at one. 3 explore, investigate, study (e.g. a problem, a theory, a crime).
+un'der/søkelse -n 1 examination, inspection, scrutiny (av of). 2 check-up, probe, search (av of). 3 exploration, investigation, study (av of).
+un'dersøkelses/kommisjo'n -en fact-finding, investigating committee (commission).
*un'der/søking -a cf /søkelse
*un'der/sø'kje V -te cf /søke
un'der/sått -en 1 archaic, pol. subject. 2 fam. dogs, underpinning.
+un'der/tallig A - deficient, short.
+un'der/tegne [/teine] V -a/-et 1 endorse, sign: u- seg sign (in a certain way). 2 merc.: u-et undersubscribed.
+un'der/tegnede [/teinede] N the undersigned; hum. yours truly.
+underti'den Av now and then, sometimes.
un'der/tittel -elen, pl -titler subhead, subheading, subtitle.
+un'der/trykke V -trykte, -trykt oppress (e.g. a people); repress (e.g. a sigh); suppress (e.g. one's feelings; a book): de u-te the downtrodden.
+un'der/trykkelse -n oppression, repression, suppression (av of).
+un'der/trykker -en, pl -e oppressor, tyrant.
un'der/trøye -a undershirt.
un'der/tvinge V infl as tvinge¹ lit. subdue, subjugate; repress.
+un'der/tøy -et (=*/ty) underwear.
un'der/utvikla A - (=+-et) underdeveloped.
+un'der/vanns A - submarine, underwater.
+un'dervanns/båt -en (=*-vass/) submarine, U-boat.
un'der/varme -n warmth from below; (in oven) lower burner.
*un'dervass/båt -en cf undervanns/
+undervei's Av 1 en route, in transit, on the (one's) way. 2 naut. under way.
un'der/vektig A - 1 short-weighted, underweight. 2 fig. light, without substance.
+un'der/verden -en (=*/verd) 1 infernal regions, netherworld. 2 underworld.
un'der/verk -et miracle, wonder: kaffen gjør u-er coffee does w-s; verdens sju u-er the seven w-s of the world.
un'der/vise V -te instruct, teach: u- i norsk teach Norwegian.
undervi'sning -a/+-en instruction, teaching (i of); lessons (e.g. in French, swimming).
undervi'snings/råd -et Council of Secondary Education (supervises instruction in all gymnasier).
+un'der/vurde're V -te underestimate, underrate, undervalue.
undi'ne -a/+-en lit., folk. undine; beautiful but heartless woman.
un'dorn -en dial., archaic 1 afternoon meal (ab. 3 PM). 2 afternoon.
*un'dral A cf undren
*un'drande A: det er ikkje u- it's no wonder.
*un'drast V -ast cf undres
un'dre¹ V -a/+-et 1 astonish, surprise: det u-er meg I am surprised. 2 wonder (på about): u-ende øyne wondering eyes. 3 (refl.): u- seg (=u-s) be surprised, marvel, wonder (over at, på about): det skulle ikke u- meg I wouldn't be surprised (om if); u-er meg på hva jeg får å se over de høye fjelle wonder what I will get to see beyond the high mountains (poem, Bjørnson).
+un'dre² A - sp underst lower.
*un'dren A -e/-i, pl -ene (=*undral, *undrig) astonished, surprised.
+un'dres V -edes, -es (=*undrast) wonder: (jeg) u- på, om det er hendt noe galt I w- if sth has gone wrong.
*un'drig A - cf undren
un'dring -a/+-en wonder, wonderment.
undula't -en zool. budgie bird, budgerigar (Melopsittacus undulatus).
*u'ne¹ -n contentment, satisfaction:

+ Bokmål; * Nynorsk; ° Dialect.
After letter: ' stress (Acc. 1); ` tone, stress (Acc. 2); · length.
Below letter: . not pronounced.

han hev så god ein u- he enjoys himself so much (poem, Garborg).
*__u'ne__² *V unte* be content, satisfied; thrive; enjoy oneself, like it.
unek'telig *A* - undeniable, without a doubt.
*__u'neleg__ *A* - comfortable, enjoyable, pleasant.
+__unev'nelig__ *A* - (=*/**nemneleg**) 1 unmentionable: **de u-e** unmentionables (esp. of woman's panties). 2 inexpressible.
+__u'/nevnt__ *A* - (=*/**nemnd**) 1 anonymous, nameless, unnamed: **en som skal være u-** one who shall be n-. 2 unmentioned.
ung [ong'] *A cp yngre, sp yngst* young; juvenile, youthful: **den yngre (d.y.)** junior; **en yngre mann** a fairly young (youngish) man; **i (en) u- alder** at an early age; **i mine u-e dager** in my younger days; **u- og gammel** the y- and the old; **u- pike** (young) girl; **de u-e** young people, youth.
+__ungarer__ [ungga'rer] *-en, pl -e* (=*-**ar**, *__ungar__) Hungarian.
Ungarn [ung'ga·rn] *Pln* Hungary.
ungarsk [ung'ga·rsk] *A* - Hungarian.
ung/dom [ong'/, +/dåmm] *-men/*-en* 1 youth; adolescence: **i u-men** in youth. 2 young people, youth; young person: **"u-men raser", sa kjerringa, hun hoppet over et halmstrå** "Youth will have its fling," said the old woman, as she jumped over a straw.
ungdommelig [ongdåm'meli] *A* - (=*__ungdomleg__) youthful.
+__ungdommelig/het__ *-en* youthfulness.
ungdoms/arbeid [ong'dåms/] *-et* 1 youth work. 2 (artistic, literary) work done in one's youth.
+__ungdoms/erin'dring__ *-en* memory from one's youth.
+__ungdoms/herberge__ *-t* youth hostel.
ungdoms/kriminalite't *-en* juvenile crime, delinquency.
ungdoms/lag *-et* young people's society.
ungdoms/rørsle *-a* youth movement.
ungdoms/skole *-n* continuation school; (since 1959) ab.=junior highschool.
ungdoms/sløvsinn *-et psych.* dementia praecox.
ungdoms/verk *-et* youthful work (of art), work done in an author's (artist's, musician's) youth.
unge [ong'e] *-n* 1 young (of animals). 2 *fam.* baby, child, youngster; *(pop.)* brat, kid: **sette u- på en** *pop.* get sby with child; **våre barn, andre folks u-r** our children, other people's brats (saying).
unge/flokk *-en* brood, flock of young (e.g. birds); bunch of kids.
unge/mas *-et* nagging and fussing of children.
+__unger/svenn__ [ong'er/] *-en archaic, lit.* young swain.
unge/skrik [ong'e/] *-et* 1 baby's cry. 2 shouting of children.
ung/fe [ong'/] *-et* heifer; young bull.
ung/folk *-et*: **u-et** the young (married) couple, the young folks (esp. on a farm).
+__ung/gutt__ *-en* (=*/**gut**) young boy, youth.
ung/hest *-en* one-year-old (horse), young horse.
ung/jente *-a* young girl.
ung/kar [ong'/] *-en* bachelor: **u- og spillemann** young and unattached, *hum.* lighthearted and gay.
*__ung/lyd__ [ong'/ly] *-en* young people, young folks.
*__ung/menne__ [ong'/] *-t* young person.
ung/merr *-a* filly, young mare.
ung/møy *-a poet.* young maiden.
+__ung/pike__ *-a/-en* young girl.
+__ungpike/bok__ *-a, pl -bøker* book for young girls.
ung/skog *-en* 1 young forest. 2 rising generation (of writers, etc.).
unifor'm *-a/+-en* uniform.
uniforme're *V -te* 1 outfit (with a uniform). 2 make uniform, standardize.
uni'k *A* unique.
u'nikum *-et* unique person, specimen; rarity.
unio'n *-en pol.* union: **U-en** usu. of the union between Norway and Sweden 1814—1905 (or of Norway and Denmark 1397—1814).
unionell' *A -elt* (relating to the) Union (of Norway and Sweden).
unio'ns/flagg *-et* flag of the Norway-Sweden union.
unio'ns/merke *-t* device (in upper left-hand quarter of flag) marking the union of Norway and Sweden.
unio'ns/strid [*/stri] *-en* strife due to political union (of countries), esp. Norway-Sweden.
uniso'n *A* unisonous: **synge u-t** sing in unison.
unita'r *-en* (=+__unitarier__) Unitarian.
unita'risk *A* - Unitarian.
univ.=**universal; universitet**
univer's *-et* universe.
universa'l *A* universal.
universa'l/geni [/sjeni'] *-et, pl +-er/*-* universal genius.
universa'l/middel *-elet/-midlet, pl +-midler/*-el* cure-all, panacea.
universell' *A -elt* universal; pertaining to the universe.
universite't *-et, pl -/+-er* university: **U-et i Oslo (Bergen)** the U- of Oslo (Bergen); **gå på u-et** go to the u-.
universite'ts/bibliote'k *-et* university library.
universite'ts/stipendia't *-en* university fellow (ab.=post-doctoral fellow in U.S.A.; has obligation to do research and a small amount of teaching).
Unn' *Prn(f)*
un'na *P* 1 away from; clear of; out from under: **(stå) u- vinden** (sail) before (away from) the wind. 2 *(adv.)* away, off: **langt u-** far away, far off; **vike u-** fall away, turn aside. 3 *(adv.)* done, finished; aside, out of the way: **gjøre noe u-** get done, finished with sth; **gå u-** (of merchandise) be sold, sell; **u- for u-** *fam.* surely and steadily forward, further. 4 *dial.* down from; down, downwards (also *adv.*): **det drypper u- taket** it's dripping (down) from the roof; **helle u-** slope downwards.
un'na/bakke *-n* downhill slope.
+__un'na/gjort__ [/jort] *A* - (=*/**gjord**) accomplished, done, out of the way.
*__un'na/gøymd__ *A -gøymt* hidden away.
un'na/renn *-et* landing slope (on ski-hill).
un'na/tak *-et* cf **unn/**
*__un'na/teken__ *A -e/-i, pl -ne* except(ed); *(prep.)* aside from, with the exception of.
+__unn'/dra__ *V -drog, -dradd/-dratt* 1 deprive of, withhold from: **u- en sin hjelp** w- one's assistance from sby. 2: **u- seg** avoid, elude, evade; escape, get out of, shirk (e.g. responsibility); **u- seg oppmerksomhet** escape attention.
un'ne *V +unte/*unnte* 1 be glad about, not grudge (sby sth good); wish (sby sth bad, with feeling "it serves him right"): **det skal være deg vel unt** you are quite welcome to it; **ikke u-** begrudge, grudge; **vel unt** you're welcome. 2 *archaic* wish (one well, ill, etc.); allow; give, grant: **Gud u- deg glede** God grant you joy (Undset). 3 *(refl.)* **u- seg noe** allow oneself sth, indulge in sth.
+__unn'/fallen__ *A -ent, pl -falne* pliable, weak, yielding (**overfor** to).
+__unn'/fallende__ *A* - cf **/fallen**
+__unn'fallen/het__ *-en* compliancy, pliability, weakness.
+__unn'/fange__ *V -et* conceive (child, idea, poem, etc.).
+__unn'/fangelse__ *-n* conception (**av** of).
+__unn'/fly__ *V -dde* escape, flee, run away from.
+__unn'/gikk__ *pt of* **-gå**
+__unn'/gjelde__ *V -te* pay, suffer for: **han skal u- for dette** he'll pay for this.
unn'/gå *V infl as* **gå**¹ 1 avoid, shun: **det kan ikke u- å** it can't help but; **det kan ikke u-(e)s** it can't be a-ed, can't be helped. 2 escape, evade (danger); avert (catastrophe): **u-ens oppmerksomhet** escape one's attention.
Un'ni *Prn(f)*
+__unn'/komme__ *V -kom, -kommet* escape.
+__unn'/late__ *V -lot, -latt* fail, neglect, omit (**å** to).
+__unn'/latelse__ *-n* failure, neglect (**av å** to.)
+__unn'latelses/synd__ *-en* sin of omission.
+__unn'/lot__ *pt of* **-late**
+__unn'/sa__ *pt of* **-si**
+__unn'/satte__ *pt of* **-sette**
+__unn'/se__ *V -så, -sett*: **u- seg for** be ashamed, embarrassed, reluctant to; **ikke u- seg for** (also) have the gall, nerve to.
*__unn'/sedd__ *pp of* **-sjå**
+__unnse'else__ *-n* bashfulness, modesty: **uten u-** unblushingly.
+__unnse'lig__ *A* - bashful, modest, shy.
+__unnse'lig/het__ *-en* bashfulness, modesty, shyness.
+__unn'/setning__ *-en* aid, assistance, rescue; reinforcements, relief: **komme en til u-** come to one's rescue.
+__unn'setnings/ekspedisjo'n__ *-en* relief expedition, rescue party.
+__unn'/sette__ *V -satte, -satt* relieve, rescue.
+__unn'/si__ *V -sa, -sagt lit.* 1 denounce, reject. 2 threaten: **u- på livet** t- sby's life.
+__unn'/sigelse__ *-n lit.* 1 denunciation. 2 threat.
unn'/skylde *V +-te/*-a* 1 excuse, pardon; apologize for: **ha en u-t** excuse one, let one be excused; **jeg ber Dem u-** I am sorry, I apologize; **unnskyld** (when one doesn't hear) I beg your pardon, pardon me; (before a question, when leaving, etc.) excuse me, pardon me; I'm sorry; **nei unnskyld** no, really now; **være u-t for (fra) å komme** be unavoidably detained. 2 excuse, justify; serve as an excuse: **det u-er ikke hans oppførsel** this does not justify his conduct. 3 *(refl.)* **u- seg** excuse oneself; apologize (for): **u- seg med** plead as an excuse. (See also **unnskyldende.**)
+__unnskyl'delig__ *A* - excusable, forgivable, pardonable.
+__unn'/skyldende__ *A* - 1 apologetic. 2 extenuating: **det ligger noe u- i ordet "dikter"** there is something e- in the word "poet" (Ibsen).
unn'/skyldning *+-en/*-a* apology, excuse; pardon: **be en om u-** beg one's pardon, forgiveness; apologize; **gjøre u-** make an apology (**for** for); **til ens u-** as, by way of an excuse for one.
+__unn'/slippe__ *V -slapp, -sloppet* escape (**fra** from): **ingen detalj u-er ham** he misses no detail, nothing e-s him.
+__unn'/slo__ *pt of* **-slå**
+__unn'/sloppet__ [/sloppet] *pp of* **-slippe**
+__unn'/slå__ *V -slo, -slått*: **u- seg** decline, refuse; excuse oneself; **u- seg for** decline, refuse (sth, to do sth).
+__unn'/så__ *pt of* **-se**
*__unn'/såg__ *pt of* **-sjå**
unnt.=**unntatt**
+__unn'/ta__ *V -tok, -tatt* except: **når u-s** except for, except that. (See also **unntatt.**)
+__unn'/tagelse__ [also -ta'-] *-n* cf **/tak**
+__unn'tagelses/tilfelle__ *-t, pl -/+-r* cf **unntaks/**
+__unn'tagelses/tilstand__ *-en* cf **unntaks/**
+__unnta'gelses/vis__ *Av* cf **unntaks/**
+__unnta'gen__ *P* cf **unn/tatt**
unn'/tak *-et* (=**unna/**) exception (**fra** to): **med u- av** except for, with the e- of; **uten u-** without e-; bar none.

+unn'/takelse *-n* cf **/tak**

+unn'takelses/menneske *-t* exceptional person, genius, superman.

unn'taks/laus *A* (=+**/løs**) absolute, invariable, without exception.

unn'taks/tilfelle *-t, pl -/+-r* exceptional case, circumstance.

unn'taks/tilstand *-en/*-et* state of emergency; *mil.* martial law.

unn'taks/vis *Av* exceptionally, for once: **ganske u-** as a rare exception.

+unn'/tatt *P* (=+**unntagen**) excepted; (usu. *prep.*) except (for).

+unn'/tok *pt of* **-ta**

+unn'/vek *pt of* **-vike**

***unn'/vere** *V -verer, -var, -vore/-i* cf **/være**

+unn'/vike *V -vek, -veket* 1 escape, flee, run away: **en u-veket fange** an escapee. 2 avoid, evade.

+unn'/vikende *A* - elusive, evasive.

+unn'/være *V -te* be, do, go, manage without; dispense with; spare: **jeg kan ikke u- min formiddagskaffe** I can't do without my morning coffee.

u'/normal *A* abnormal; anomalous.

u'/norsk *A* - un-Norwegian: **U- og norsk** U- and Norwegian (book by Knud Knudsen, 1881, proposing native substitutes for many words of foreign origin).

u'/note *-n* (usu. *pl*) bad habit; quirk: **det er med båter som med hester og kvinnfolk, de har sine u-r og luner** boats are like horses and women, they have their quirks and their moods (Bojer).

un'se *+en/*ei* ounce.

+un'te *pt of* **unne, une²**

u'/nytte *en/*ei* 1: **til u-(s)** to no purpose, uselessly. 2 *dial.* harm; useless thing.

u'/nyttig *A* - 1 useless; needless: **alt u-** everything u-. 2 futile, in vain (e.g. resistance): **det u-e i** the futility of.

u'/nødig *A* - 1 superfluous, undue, unnecessary. 2 needless, senseless, wanton.

u'/nødven'dig *A* - cf **/nødig**

u'/nøyak'tig *A* - careless, inaccurate, inexact.

+u'nøyaktig/het *-en* carelessness, inaccuracy, inexactness.

***u'/nøydd** *A -/-nøydt* unconstrained, voluntary.

***unøy'teleg** *A* - unusable, useless.

u'/nåde *-n* disfavor, disgrace: **falle i u- hos en** fall out of sby's favor, get in bad with sby; **på nåde og u-** unconditionally.

u'/nådig *A* - ungracious; angry, unfavorable: **ta noe u- opp** take sth in bad part; be infuriated by sth.

u'/offisiell' *A -elt, pl -e* unofficial; informal, off the record.

uomgjeng'elig *A* - 1 unavoidable: **u- nødvendig** absolutely necessary. 2 hard to get along with, unsociable.

+uomstø'telig *A* - incontrovertible, irrefutable.

+u'/omtalt *A* - unmentioned: **la noe u-** pass sth over in silence.

+uomtvis'telig *A* - incontestible, incontrovertible, indisputable.

***u'/opna** [/å'pna] *A* - cf **/åpnet**

+u'/oppdra'gen *A -ent, pl -ne* badly behaved (children); ill-bred, uncultivated (adults); impolite, rude (behavior, remarks).

+u'oppdragen/het *-en* bad manners; ill breeding, rudeness; crude, impolite behavior.

+u'/oppfinn'som [/-såmm] *A -t, pl -me* unimaginative, uninventive; lacking in ingenuity.

+u'/oppfordret *A* - of one's own accord, unasked, without being told; on one's own initiative.

uoppfyl'lelig *A* - impossible, unrealizable.

u'/oppfylt *A* - unfulfilled, ungratified, unrealized.

+u'/oppgjor't *A* - (=***/oppgjord**) 1 *merc.* unsettled; outstanding (account): **ha noe u- med en** have sth o- with sby, have a bone to pick with sby. 2 *naut.* unreadied.

+uopphol'delig *A* - *lit.* immediate; *(adv.)* forthwith, without delay.

+uopphø'rlig *A* - continual; incessant, perpetual, unceasing; (*adv.*, also:) without stopping.

u'/oppklart *A* - unexplained, unsolved (murder, mystery).

u'/opplagt *A* - 1 disinclined, not disposed, not in the mood (**til** to). 2 (of athletes) not in form, off one's game. 3 depressed, in the dump,s indisposed.

+u'opplagt/het *-en* disinclination; being out of form; depression, indisposition.

u'/opplyst *A* - 1 unlighted, unlit. 2 ignorant, uneducated, uninformed.

+uopplø'selig *A* - 1 indissoluble. 2 *chem.* insoluble.

+u'/oppmerksom [/-såmm] *A -t, pl -me* inattentive, unaware, unobservant: **ikke u- på at** not unaware that.

+u'oppmerksom/het *-en* inattentiveness, unawareness.

uoppnå'elig *A* - unattainable: **u- for en** (also) out of one's reach.

+u'/oppredd *A* - (of bed) unmade.

+uoppret'telig *A* - irremediable, irreparable, irretrievable.

+uoppset'telig *A* - impossible to postpone, pressing, urgent.

+uoppsi'gelig *A* - (=***/oppseieleg**) 1 irrevocable (e.g. contract, treaty). 2 *merc.* unredeemable; irredeemable. 3 (of employee) irremovable; having tenure.

+u'/oppskåret *A -, pl -ne* uncut.

+uoppsli'telig *A* - 1 imperishable, indestructible (material). 2 boundless (energy), inexhaustible, unfailing (good humor); perennial (joke).

u'/orden *-en* 1 confusion; disorder, mess, shambles: **i u-** out of order; (of nerves) frayed. 2 disorder, tumult.

+uordentlig [/år'ntli, also u'-] *A* - disorderly, irregular, messy; careless, disheveled, untidy; improper.

+uordentlig/het *-en* disorderliness, irregularity; messiness; untidiness.

uorg.=**uorganisk**

u'/organise'rt *A* - 1 unorganized; spontaneous. 2 non-union (workers).

u'/orga'nisk *A* - unorganic; *chem.* inorganic.

u'/ortodok's *A* unorthodox.

+u'/overensstemmelse [/åver-] *-n* 1 discrepancy, divergence, incongruity (**mellom** between): **være i u- med** clash with. 2 disagreement, dissension.

+uoverkom'melig [u-åver-] *A* - impossible; insuperable (e.g. task); prohibitive (e.g. price).

u'/overlagt [/åver-] *A* - 1 ill-considered, rash. 2 unpremeditated.

+uoverset'telig [u-åver-] *A* - untranslatable.

+uoversku'elig [u-åver-] *A* - 1 boundless, enormous, vast. 2 immeasurable, incalculable. 3 unforeseeable, unpredictable: **i en u- framtid** for an indeterminate period.

uoversti'gelig [u-åver-] *A* - impassable, insuperable, insurmountable.

+uovertref'felig [u-åver-] *A* - unrivalled, unsurpassable.

+u'/overtruffen [/åvertroffen] *A -et, pl -overtrufne* unequalled, unsurpassed.

+u'/overveid [/åver-] *A* - rash, unpremeditated.

uovervin'nelig [u-åver-] *A* - impregnable (fort, virtue); insuperable, insurmountable (obstacle); invincible, unconquerable (army).

+uovervin'nelig/het [u-åver-] *-en* insuperability, invincibility.

u'/par *A* - mismatched, odd.

u'/para *A* - (=+**-et**) 1 mismatched, odd. 2 *bot., zool.* unmated, unpaired.

u'/parlamenta'risk *A* - 1 *pol.* unparliamentary (form of government). 2 undiplomatic; impolite, rude.

u'/partisk *A* - detached, disinterested, impartial; non-partisan, unbiased, unprejudiced.

+u'partisk/het *-en* disinterest, impartiality, lack of bias (or prejudice).

+upas'selig *A* - indisposed, unwell.

u'/passende *A* - improper, unbecoming, unseemly: **oppføre seg u-** be improper, misbehave.

u'/perso'nlig *A* - impersonal (also *gram.*); objective.

u'/plasse'rt *A* - 1 *merc.* uninvested. 2 (of sports entry) unplaced.

+u'/pleid *A* - 1 ungroomed, unkempt. 2 (of speech) uncultivated.

+u'/plettet *A* - spotless, unsoiled; immaculate, unblemished.

u'/pole'rt *A* - unpolished.

u'/polit'isk *A* - non-partisan, non-political.

u'/populæ'r *A* unpopular.

***upp'** *Av* cf **opp**

***up'pe** *Av* cf **oppe¹**

upper/cut [øp'per/køtt] *-en* uppercut (in boxing).

Upp'/sala *Pln* city, university in Sweden.

u'/praktisk *A* - 1 impractical, un practical; theoretical. 2 clumsy; inconvenient.

u'/presi's *A* 1 imprecise, inaccurate, inexact. 2 unpunctual.

u'/priorite'rt *A* - *merc.* unsecured (e.g. creditors); unencumbered (e.g. property).

u'/pris *-en* outrageous price.

u'/produktiv *A* unproductive.

u'/prøvd *A -/*-prøvt* unproven, untested, untried; inexperienced.

+u'/påaktet *A* - (=***/påakta**) unheeded, unnoticed; disregarded.

+upåkla'gelig *A* - entirely satisfactory; impeccable, irreproachable, unimpeachable.

+u'/påkrevd *A* - (=***/påkravd**) superfluous, uncalled-for, unnecessary.

upåli'telig *A* - undependable, unreliable.

+upåli'telig/het *-en* undependability, unreliability.

upåpas'selig *A* - careless, heedless, remiss.

u'/påtalt *A* - (=***/påtala**) unchallenged: **la noe gå u-** let sth pass, overlook sth (an offense).

+upåvir'kelig *A* - (=***-verkeleg**) 1 immovable, resolute, unalterable. 2 impassive, insensible; unaffected (**av** by).

u'r¹ *-a* rock-strewn slope, scree, talus (the debris of boulders resulting from cracking and erosion of a cliff or mountain).

***u'r²** *-en* 1 *meteor.* mock sun, parhelion. 2 rainclouds over the mountains or on the horizon.

u'r³ *-et* 1 clock; (pocket, wrist) watch. 2: **frøken Ur** *fam.* female voice which gives the time on the telephone.

UR⁴=**Undervisningsrådet**

ur- *Pf* 1 primeval, primordial (forest, man, etc.); primitive (Christianity, instinct, etc.); proto- (Germanic, type, zoon, etc.); first, original (performance, showing, etc.). 2 exceedingly (comical, old, etc.).

u'/raka *A* - (=+**/rakt**) unshaven.

ura'n *-et chem.* uranium.

ura'n/mile *-a* uranium pile.

uransa'kelig *A* - inscrutable.

+uransa'kelig/het *-en* inscrutability.

+u'r/avstem'ning *-en* poll; plebiscite, referendum (among members of an organization).

+ Bokmål; * Nynorsk; ° Dialect.
After letter: ' stress (Acc. 1); ` tone, stress (Acc. 2); · length.
Below letter: . not pronounced.

urba'n *A* urbane.
urbanite't *-en* urbanity.
+**u'r/befol'kning** *-en* aborigines, autochthonous population.
u'rd[1] *-a* cf **ur[1]**
***u'rd[2]** *pp of* **yrje[2]**
Ur'd *Prn* one of three Norns (goddesses of fate) in Norse mythology.
***u'rde** *pt of* **yrje[2]**
u'/redd[1] *A* - 1 brave, courageous. 2 easy (in one's mind), unafraid: **det kan vi være u-e for** *lit.* we can feel at ease about that.
+**u'/redd[2]** *A* - cf **/reidd**
+**u'/rede** *-n* confusion, disorder; tangle: **i u-** confused, disordered, tangled; in a mess.
+**ure'delig** *A* - dishonest, false, fraudulent.
+**ure'delig/het** *-en* dishonesty, falseness, fraudulence.
+**u'/redt** *A* - cf **/reidd**
u'/reell' *A -elt* unreal, unsubstantial; airy; unrealistic.
+**u'/regelmes'sig** *A* - 1 irregular. 2 improper; erratic. 3 *bot.* asymmetric, zygomorphic.
+**uregelmes'sig/het** *-en* 1 irregularity. 2 impropriety: **u-er i skattevesenet** improprieties (=dishonest acts) in the revenue service. 3 unsymmetric structure.
u'/regelrett *A* irregular, not according to the rules.
+**uregje'rlig** *A* - 1 uncontrollable, unmanageable, unruly: **bli u-** get out of hand. 2 *naut.* hard to handle, to maneuver in (or on).
u'/reglemente'rt *A* - (esp. *mil.*, sports) against the rules, irregular, non-regulation: **u- støt** foul.
u'/reidd *A* - (=**/redd[2]**) 1 (of bed) unmade. 2 (of hair) uncombed, unkempt.
u'/rein *A* 1 unclean (animal, food); impure (blood, style, thoughts, water, etc.); dirty (e.g. color). 2 *naut.* foul (bottom, waters). 3 *mus.* false, muddy, out of tune. 4 *pol.*: **u- valgliste** printed ballot which has been altered (according to specific rules) by the voter with e.g. a write-in candidate.
***u'rein/skap** *-en* filth; uncleanliness.
u'/reinslig *A* - 1 dirty, filthy; unclean; uncleanly, unsanitary. 2 *fig.* dishonest, dishonorable, underhanded.
***urek'neleg** *A* - countless, incalculable.
+**u'ren/het** *-en* 1 uncleanliness. 2 dirt, filth. 3 *(bibl.)* sinfulness, uncleanness. 4 impurity.
+**ure'nslig** *A* - cf **/reinslig**
+**ure'nslig/het** *-en* 1 filth; uncleanliness. 2 *fig.* dishonesty, dishonorableness.
u'ret(e) *A* - (of terrain) covered with rock-strewn slopes, stony.
u'/rett[1] *-en* wrong; injustice, unfairness (**mot to**): **gjøre noen u-** do sby an i-, wrong sby; **gjøre en skjelm u-** (see **skjelm**); **ha u-** be w-, in the w-; **med u-e** unjustly, wrongly.
u'/rett[2] *A* - wrong (factually; morally): **handle u-** act unjustly, wrongly.
***u'/rettferd** [/-fær] *-a* cf **urettferdighet**
u'/rettfer'dig [also -fær'-] *A* - unfair, unjust (**mot to**); (esp. *bibl.*) iniquitous, unrighteous: **de u-e** the unrighteous.
+**urettfer'dig/het** *-en* injustice, unfairness; (esp. *bibl.*) iniquity, unrighteousness.
+**u'/rettmes'sig** *A* - illegal.
u'/rettvi's *A (*archaic)* unjust.
***u'/rettvi'se** *-a* injustice, unfairness; (esp. *bibl.*) iniquity, unrighteousness.
u'r/fjell *-et geol.* Archean rock.
+**u'r/fjær** *-a* (=***/fjør**) mainspring of a watch.
u'r/folk *-et* aborigines; primitive people.
u'r/gammal *A -t, pl -gamle* (=+**/gammel**) prehistoric; ancient.
u'r/germa'nsk *A* - 1 ancient Teutonic. 2 *gram.* Proto-Germanic.
u'r/histo'rie *-a/+-en* protohistory.
U'rian *Prn*: **min herr U-, mester U-** *archaic, derog.* my good man, my fine fellow, Mr. so-and-so.
u'rias/post *-en* dangerous, exposed post.
***u'/rikkande** *A* - cf **urokkelig**
***urik'keleg** *A* - cf **urokkelig**
u'/riktig *A* - 1 incorrect; false, untrue. 2 wrong; improper.
uri'melig *A* - 1 absurd, preposterous; unreasonable (behavior, demand, person, price, etc.); excessive, exorbitant. 2 *(adv.)* unreasonably; amazingly, especially.
+**uri'melig/het** *-en* 1 absurdity, preposterousness, unreasonableness. 2 excessiveness, exorbitance.
uri'n *-en* urine.
urina'l *-et* urinal.
urine're *V -te* urinate.
uri'n/prøve *-a/+-en* 1 *med.* uroscopy. 2 specimen of urine.
uri'n/rør *-et/*-a anat.* urethra.
u'r/jøde *-n* Jewish watch-seller.
u'r/kapsel *-elen, pl -ler* watch-case.
u'r/kasse *-a/-en* clock-case.
+**u'r/kirke** *-n* early church.
u'r/kjede [*/kjee] *+-en/+-et/*-a* watch chain.
u'r/kraft *-a/+-en* primitive force, strength.
u'r/kristendom [+/-dåmm] *-men/*-en* early (primitive) Christianity.
°**u'r/liten** *A f -lita, nt -lite, pl -smd* cf **ør/**
u'r/lomme *-a* watch pocket.
+**u'r/maker** *-en, pl -e* (=***-ar**) watchmaker.
u'r/menneske *-t* aborigine, primitive man.
u'r/natu'r *-en* primitive nature.
u'rne *-a/+-en* urn (vase; ballot box): **gå til u-ne** go to the polls.
u'rne/hall *+-en/*-a* columbarium.
u'rne/lokk *-et* cover of an urn.
u'r/nordisk [/nordisk] *A* - Early Scandinavian, Proto-Scandinavian (by some called Primitive Norse).
u'/ro *-a/+-en* 1 restlessness, unrest; disquiet, uneasiness; alarm, anxiety, worry (**over** about): **i u-** restlessly. 2 (political) unrest; commotion, disturbance, excitement; bustle, noise, stir. 3 balance (in a watch). 4: **u-a** *dial.* restless person, wiggleworm; (paper, straw) mobile.
u'/roe *V -a/+-et/+-dde* 1 bother, disturb; disquiet, trouble. 2: **u- seg** worry; *dial.* move, stir (with a faint noise).
u'ro/elemen't *-et, pl -/+-er* disturbing element, factor.
+**urok'kelig** *A* - immovable, unshakable; steadfast, unwavering; firm, inflexible, solid.
+**u'/rokket** *A* - unmoved, unshaken; firm, solid, steadfast.
u'ro/kråke *-a* fidgety, restless person.
u'r/okse *-n zool.* aurochs (Bos primigenius).
uro'lig *A* - 1 (of person) fidgety, restless; troubled, uneasy (**over** about); anxious (**for** about, for); disturbed, nervous, worried. 2 rough, stormy, turbulent (meeting, sea, etc.); agitated, unsettled. 3 noisy, unquiet: **u- avdeling** violent ward (of asylum); **en u- klasse** an undisciplined class. 4 disharmonious, jarring, restless (colors, lines, etc.).
+**uro'lig/het** *-en* 1 fidgeting, restlessness; uneasiness; anxiety; agitation. 2 roughness, turbulence; commotion. 3 noise, noisiness; disturbance (esp. in *pl*): **u-er** riots, (street) demonstrations.
u'/roman'tisk *A* - unromantic.
+**u'r/oppførelse** *-n* premiere (performance).
u'ros/kråke *-a* cf **uro/**
+**u'ro/stifter** *-en, pl -e* (=***-ar**) agitator, trouble-maker.
+**u'ro/vekkende** *A* - (=***/vekkjande**) alarming, disquieting, disturbing.
u'r/premiere [/premiæ're] *-n* (original) premiere (performance); first showing (of film).
u'r/skive *-a* clock (watch) face.
u'r/skog *-en* virgin forest; jungle.
ur't *-a/+-en* 1 herb. 2 *archaic* plant.
+**ur'te/aktig** *A* - herbaceous.
+**ur'te/gå'rd** *-en archaic* garden.
ur'te/hage *-n* garden of herbs.
+**ur'te/samler** *-en, pl -e* (=***-ar**) herb gatherer.
u'r/tid [*/ti] *-a/+-en* (hoary) antiquity, the beginning of time, the earliest time: **fra u-en** from time immemorial.
***u'/rudd** *A -/-rudt* cf **u/rydda**
***urug'geleg** *A* - cf **uryggelig**
ur'ven *A +-ent, pl -ne dial.* indisposed, not quite up to par, under the weather.
u'r/verk *-et* clockwork; movement (of watch or clock).
u'/rydda *A* - (=+**-et**, ***/rudd**) 1 (of land) uncleared. 2 (of room) littered.
u'/ryddig *A* - 1 littered, messy, untidy. 2 *fig.* confused, disordered (e.g. ideas).
+**uryg'gelig** *A* - immovable, unshakeable, unwavering; immutable.
urø'rlig *A* - 1 immovable, stationary; (of property) real. 2 motionless, still. 3 untouchable; cold, unsympathetic. 4 (of capital) tied up, untouchable.
u'/rø'rt *A* - 1 untouched; virgin(al) (e.g. forest, woman); intact. 2 unaffected, unmoved (**av** by).
***u'/røynd** *A -røynt* inexperienced, untested.
u'/råd [*/rå] *-a/+-en/+-et* 1 difficulty, trouble: **ane u-** smell a rat; **ha råd for u-** be resourceful, have a way out. 2 impossibility: **det er u- å selge** it is impossible to sell.
urå'delig *A* - inadvisable, unwise.
USA=United States of America
+**u'/sagt** *A* - (=***/sagd**) unsaid, unspoken: **om det er sant skal være u-** no comment.
u'/sakkyn'dig** *A* - (=/sakkunnig**) incompetent, not expert; layman.
u'/sa'klig *A* - non-factual, unobjective, unscientific; biased, colored, slanted; indulging in personalities, showing prejudice: **u- kritikk** personal attack.
u'/salig *A* - 1 hapless, unfortunate; miserable, unhappy. 2 dangerous, unhealthy; accursed, fatal. 3 *(archaic, bibl.)* unsaved.
***u'/samd** *A* - in disagreement (**med** with; **om** over).
+**u'/sammenheng'ende** *A* - (=***/samanhangande**) disconnected, disjointed, incoherent.
+**u'/sammensatt'** *A* - (=***/samansett**) 1 simple; in one piece, solid. 2 *gram.* simplex.
u'/sams *A* - disagreed (**med** with; **om** over): **bli u-** fall out.
u'/sann *A -sant* false, untrue, untruthful; not true to reality; insincere: **tale u-t** tell a lie.
u'/sannfer'dig [also -fær'-] *A* - 1 untruthful. 2 false, untrue.
+**usannfer'dig/het** *-en* 1 mendacity, untruthfulness. 2 falseness, insincerity.
+**u'sann/het** *-en* 1 falsehood, untruth. 2 falseness, untruthfulness.
***u'/sanning** *-a* falsehood, lie, untruth.
u'/sannsy'nlig [also -sy'n-] *A* - improbable, unbelievable, unlikely; *(adv.)* incredibly: **u- kjedelig** unbelievably boring.
u'/sans *-en* folly, nonsense.
u'/sanselig *A* - ethereal, immaterial, incorporeal.
u'/sed *-en (+archaic)* immorality, iniquity, vice.
***u'/sedd** *A -/-sett* cf **/sett**
use'delig *A* - immoral.
+**use'delig/het** *-en* immorality.

***u`/sedug** *A* - cf **usedelig**

***u`sedug/skap** *-en* cf **usedelig/het**

usedva'nlig *A* - rare, unusual; exceptional, outstanding, extraordinary.

***u`/seiande** *A* - ineffable, inexpressible, unutterable.

***usei'eleg** *A* - cf **usigelig**

+u`/seier *-en* (=***u/siger**) *archaic* defeat.

+usel'gelig *A* - (=***useljeleg**) unsalable.

***u`/seljande** *A* - cf **uselgelig**

***usel'jeleg** *A* - cf **uselgelig**

uselska'pelig *A* - unsociable.

+u`/selvisk *A* - unselfish.

+u`/selvsten·dig *A* - cf **/sjølvstendig**

+u`selvstendig/het [also -sten'-] *-en* 1 dependence, dependency, subordinate position. 2 lack of independent thinking, of originality.

***u`/semje** *-a* disagreement, discord.

+u`/sett *A* - (=***/sedd**) 1 unseen: **kjøpe u-** buy sight u-. 2 unnoticed: **slippe u- bort** escape u-.

+usi'gelig *A* - (=***useieleg**) *lit.* 1 indescribable, too (awful, happy, wonderful, etc.) for words. 2 *(adv.)* immensely, inexpressibly, very.

***u`/siger** *-eren, pl -rar* cf **u/seier**

u`/signert [/singne·rt] *A* - unsigned.

u`/sikker *A -t, pl -sikre* 1 doubtful, uncertain (**om** whether; **på** of); insecure, unsure; precarious, risky, unsafe. 2 faltering, shaky, unsteady; (esp. of light) flickering, wavering; erratic (driving); diffident, hesitant, vacillating.

+u`sikker/het *-en* 1 doubt, uncertainty; insecurity, unsureness; precariousness. 2 shakiness, unsteadiness; flicker; diffidence, hesitation, vacillation.

u`/sikta *A* - (=**+-et**) unsifted.

+u`/siktbar *A* unclear; having poor visibility.

u`/sjene·rt *A* - 1 undisturbed; unhindered, without interruptions. 2 unembarrassed, unrestrained; bold, free and easy, off-hand.

***u`/sjølvsten·de** *-t* 1 dependence, dependency; subordinate position. 2 lack of originality.

u`/sjølvsten·dig *A* - 1 dependent; subordinate. 2 lacking in originality; unoriginal.

***u`/sjåleg** *A* - inconspicuous; unimpressive.

u`/skadd *A -/* skadt* undamaged, unharmed, uninjured; intact, safe, unscathed.

uska'delig *A* - harmless (**for** to); innocuous, inoffensive; out of commission.

+uska'delig/gjøre *V -gjorde, -gjort* neutralize, render harmless; disable, knock out; disarm, put out of commission.

***u`/skap** *-et* bad figure; ugly shape.

***u`/ska·pleg** *A* - 1 formless, shapeless; amorphous; bulky. 2 improper, indecent.

+u`/skarp *A* blurred, dim.

u`/skifta *A* - (=**+-et**) *jur.* (of inherited property) undivided (among the heirs): **sitte i u- bo** retain u- possession of an estate.

u`/skikk *-en* (social) abuse, bad custom, objectionable practice: **det er en vemmelig u- med disse drikkepengene** this tipping is an infernal nuisance (Heiberg).

u`/skikka *A* - (=**+-et**) unfit, unqualified, unsuited (**til** for): **gjøre en u-** disqualify one.

uskik'kelig *A* - naughty, not nice.

***u`/skil** *-et* insult; injustice.

***u`/skipa** *A* - disturbed, out of order, upset.

***u`/skipla** *A* - unaltered, undisturbed, unharmed.

u`/skjedd *A* - not happened, undone: **ingenting i mitt liv ønsker jeg u-** there is nothing in my life I would wish u- (Egge).

***u`/skjønande** *A* - incomprehensible.

***uskjø'neleg** *A* - incomprehensible.

+u`/skjønn *A -skjønt* ugly; unesthetic, ungracious.

+u`/skjønnsom [/-såmm] *A -t, pl -me* (=***/skjønsam**) harsh, ungracious; uncomprehending; ungrateful.

u`/skodd [/skodd] *A -/*-skott* unshod.

u`/skole·rt *A* - unschooled, untrained.

+u`/skreven *A -et, pl -ne* (=***/skriven**) unwritten (books, laws, letters): **u-ne kjelder** oral sources.

u`/skrømta *A* - (=**+-et**) genuine, sincere, unfeigned.

***u`/skuld** *-a* cf **/skyld**[1]

***u`/skuldig** *A* - cf **uskyldig**

u`/skyld[1] *+-en/*-a* innocence; naiveté; chastity.

***u`/skyld**[2] *A* unrelated.

uskyl'dig *A* - 1 guiltless, innocent, not guilty. 2 harmless, inoffensive; guileless, naive, simple. 3 chaste, pure.

+uskyl'dig/het *-en* 1 guiltlessness, innocence. 2 harmlessness, inoffensiveness; guilelessness, naiveté, simplicity. 3 chastity, purity.

+uskyl'dighets/stand *-en* state of innocence (ref. to bibl. story of Adam and Eve in garden of Eden).

u`skylds/kvit *A* - (=**+/hvit**) lily-white; with the whiteness of innocence, of purity.

***u`skylds/tilstand** *-en/** cf **uskyldighets/stand**

us`le *pl of* **ussel**

***u`/slegen** *A -e/-i, pl -ne* cf **/slått**

+u`/slepen *A -ent/-et, pl -ne* 1 rough, uncut; unground, unpolished. 2 *fig.* inelegant, rude, unrefined.

us`ling *-en* coward, wretch; scoundrel.

usli'telig *A* - (=***u/slitande**) eternal, everlasting, indestructible; long-wearing.

+u`/slitt *A* - (=***/sliten**) not worn, unworn; fresh, new.

+uslokkelig [uslok'keli] *A* - (=***u/-sløkkjande**) inextinguishable; insatiable, unquenchable.

***u`/sløkkjande** *A* - cf **uslokkelig**

uslå'elig *A* - unbeatable.

+u`/slått *A* - 1 unmown (e.g. hay). 2 unbeaten, undefeated.

u`/smak *-en* 1 bad taste. 2 *fig.* lack of taste, poor taste.

usma'kelig *A* - (=***u/smakleg**) in bad taste, offensive, unsavory.

u`/smidig *A* - 1 rigid, stiff; inflexible. 2 unadaptable, unaccommodating.

u`/sminka *A* - (=**+-et**) 1 without make-up. 2 (of talk, etc.) plain, straight, unvarnished.

u`/snakka *A* - (=**+-et**) unsaid: **ha ingenting u- med (en)** have nothing to say to, have no desire (reason) to meet (sby); **ha litt u- med en** have a bone to pick with sby, a score to settle.

u`/snobbet(e) *A* - unsnobbish; democratic, informal.

u/soignert [/soanje·rt] *A* - poorly groomed, sloppy, untidy.

u`/sorte·rt *A* - unsorted.

u`/spa·rt *A* - unspared: **ikke la noe bli u-** spare nothing.

+uspi'selig *A* - inedible.

+uspo'rlig *A* - intraceable; imperceptible.

+u`/spu·rt *A* - (=***/spurd**) 1 unasked; not consulted. 2 uncalled (for); uninvited.

***us`se**[1] *-a* muddle, tangle.

***us`se**[2] *V -a* 1 complicate, entangle (sth); waste. 2 prattle.

us`sel *A -elt, pl -le* 1 miserable, pitiful, wretched; paltry (amount, wages, etc.). 2 base, despicable, low. 3 *fam.* ailing, sickly.

us`sel/dom [+/dåmm] *-men/*-en* 1 misery, wretchedness; penury. 2 baseness, meanness: **mot u-men, sviket . . . står samlet hele riket** the whole country stands united against baseness, treachery (Øverland).

us`selig *A* - 1 miserable, wretched; paltry; shabby, base. *2 confused; messy, tangled.

u`/stadig [also -sta'-] *A* - inconstant; unstable; changeable, erratic, fluctuating; capricious, fickle, flighty; flickering, unsteady.

+u`stadig/het [also -sta'-] *-en* inconstancy, instability; changeability, variability; capriciousness, fickleness, flightiness; unsteadiness.

u`/stand *N*: **i u-** out of order.

ustan'selig *A* - ceaseless, constant, incessant; continual, steady.

u`/stell *-et* 1 disorder, mess; confusion. 2 *dial.* damage: **gjøre u-** do harm.

u`/stelt *A* - messy, unkempt; neglected.

u`/stempla *A* - (=**+-et**) unstamped (document); uncanceled (stamp).

+u`/stemt *A* - (=***/stemd**) 1 *mus.* untuned. 2 *gram.* unvoiced.

u`/straffa *A* - (=**+-et**) 1 unpunished: **han er tidligere u-** he has no previous record. 2 with impunity: **et folk kan ikke u- leve over evne** a people cannot live beyond its means with impunity.

u`/stude·rt *A* - uneducated, without a college education.

***ustur'teleg** *A* - cf **ustyrtelig**

ustyg'gelig *A* - dreadful, horrible: **noe u- stygt** sth horribly ugly (Ibsen).

u`/styr *-et archaic, dial.* 1 chaotic disorder. 2 riot; tumult, uproar.

u`/styren *A +-ent, pl -ne* uncontrollable, wild.

usty'rlig *A* - unmanageable, unruly; violent, wild; ecstatic: **u- glad** e-ally happy.

ustyr'telig *A* - (=***usturteleg**) incredible, tremendous: **u- mange blomster** an i- number of flowers; **u- med penger** loads of money.

u`/stø *A -tt* 1 unstable, unsteady; tottering; quavering, shaky; **u- på hånden** with unsteady hand; **u- i matematikk** shaky in math. 2 irregular, undependable; intermittent.

+u`stø/het *-en* 1 instability, unsteadiness; uncertainty. 2 irregularity, variability; undependability, unreliability.

u`/sunn *A -sunt, pl -e* unhealthy (e.g. skin color); unwholesome (e.g. air; reading).

+u`sunn/het *-en* unhealthiness; unwholesomeness.

usurpa'tor *-en* usurper.

usurpe're *V -te* usurp.

u'sus *en* practice, usage.

+u`/svekket *A* - unabated (interest, zeal), undiminished (energy), unimpaired (vision).

usvi'kelig *A* - 1 unfailing; unerring; sure. 2 undeviating, unswerving; unfaltering.

***u`/svip** *-en* unfortunate appearance; disagreeable manner.

u`/sympa'tisk *A* - unattractive, uncongenial, unpleasant.

usy'nlig *A* - invisible (assets, power, ray, stitch, etc.), unseen; imperceptible (**for** to).

+usy'nlighets/hatt *-en folk.* hat which makes the wearer invisible.

***u`/synt** *A* - not clear; having poor visibility.

u`/syra *A* - (=**+-et**) unleavened.

u`/systema'tisk *A* - unsystematic.

u`/sæl *A lit.* miserable, unhappy, wretched.

***u`/sæle** *-a* misery, unhappiness.

***u`/sætande** *A* - undependable, unreliable.

***u`/sømd** *-a* impropriety, indecency, unseemliness.

+ Bokmål; * Nynorsk; ° Dialect.
After letter: ' stress (Acc. 1); ` tone, stress (Acc. 2); · length.
Below letter: . not pronounced.

usøm'melig *A* - (=*/**sømeleg**) improper, indecent, unseemly.
+**u'/sådd** *A* -/*-*sått* unsown.
uså'rlig *A* - invulnerable; immune, unassailable.
uså'rlig/het *-en* invulnerability.
ut' *Av* 1 (go, move, peek, rent, sing, throw, etc.) out (expressing direction): **beint, like, rent ut** pointblank, right out; **han måtte ut med det** he had to come out with it, had to say it; **han ville ikke ut med det** he wouldn't admit (say) it; **jeg vet verken ut eller inn** I'm at my wit's end, I don't know which way to turn; **ut fra det synspunkt** from that viewpoint; **(kjenne) ut og inn** (know) from A to Z, inside out. 2 (with time) along, on, up: **en mann ut i årene** a man (well) up in years; **ut på høsten** late (later) in the fall. 3 through, to the end: **drikke ut** drink up; **fullt, helt ut** completely; **lese ut** finish reading, read to the end; **tømme ut** empty out; **uken ut** to the end of the week.
*-**ut** *A* - cf **-et(e)**
ut'a- *Pf* also cf **uten-** 1 outside of, on the outside of, e.g. **u-bords, u-bygds.** 2 (with *prep.*) **u-for, u-til.**
ut'a/bo·ks *A* - *(dial., adv.)* by heart, from memory.
ut'a/bo·rds *A* - *naut.* outboard; *(adv.)* on the outside of the ship.
ut'a/bygds *A* - non-local; *(adv.)* outside the local community, the district; **u- fra** from another district.
ut'a/bys *Av* (=+**uten/**) non-local; non-resident; *(adv.)* outside the city (town): **en u- avis** a newspaper from another city; **reise u-** leave town.
+**u't/ad** *Av* out; outward(s); on, to the outside; externally.
+**u'tad/til·** *Av* externally, on the outside, outwardly.
+**u'tad/vendt** *A* - 1 extrovert, outgoing (person). 2 superficial (idea).
+**u'tadvendt/het** *-en* 1 extroversion. 2 superficiality.
ut'a/dø·rs *A* - (=+**uten/**) outdoor; *(adv.)* outdoors, out-of-doors, outside: **holde lensmannen u-** keep the sheriff from the door (Falkberget).
ut'a/for· *P* (=+**uten/**) 1 beyond, out of (reach, sight, town, etc.); outside (of) (one's circle, the house, a room, etc.); off (the coast): **u- all sammenheng** apropos of nothing; **u- døra skal hesten stande** outside the door the horse shall stand (folk song). 2 *(adv.)* outside: **føle seg u-** feel left out, on the outside; **holde en u-** keep one out of it (in the dark); keep one from being involved; **være u-** stay out of it; be out of it, not know what's going on.
ut'a/frå *P* cf **ute/fra**
***ut'a/hyses** *A* - outdoor, *(adv.)* outside the house.
u'/takk *-a/+-en* ingratitude, thanklessness: **u- er verdens lønn** ingratitude is the world's reward (saying; title of folktale by Asbjørnsen).
+**u'/takknem·lig** [also -nem'-] *A* - 1 ungrateful (**mot** to; **for** for). 2 thankless, unrewarding (job; part).
+**utakknem'lig/het** *-en* 1 ingratitude. 2 thanklessness.
***u'/takksam** *A* 1 ungrateful. 2 thankless.
u'/takt *N* 1: **i u-** out of rhythm, step, time; off beat. 2 lack of accord.
u'/tal *-et* (=+/**tall**) countless number, myriad (**av** of): **et u- av** (=**utallige**).
ut'a/lands *A* - (=+**uten/**) foreign; *(adv.)* abroad, in foreign parts, outside the country.
ut'a/landsk *A* - (=+**uten/**) foreign: **på u-** *hum.* in a f- language; **snakke u-** talk a f- language.
***u't/aldra** *A* - antiquated, obsolete, out of date.
utal'lig *A* - countless, innumerable; no end of, untold.
+**u'/ta·lt**[1] *A* - unsaid, unspoken: **jeg har ikke noe u- med henne** I have nothing to say to her; **ønske noe u-** wish sth unsaid.
+**u'/ta·lt**[2] *A* - uncounted.
***ut'a/med** *P* 1 outside. 2 *(adv.)* around about, outside.
***u'tan** *P* cf **uten**
***u'tan-** *Pf* cf **uta-**
u'/tange *-n* *dial.* brawler; squaller, yowling brat.
***u'tan/om·** *P* cf **uten/**
***u'tan/riks** *A* - cf **uten/**
***u'tan/verk** *-et* cf **uten/**
***u'tan/åt** *Av* cf **uten/at**
uta'pelig *A* - sure, which cannot be lost.
ut'a/på *P* (=+**uten/**) 1 on the outside of; on top of, over (e.g. an article of clothing): **se (noe) u- en** see (sth) by one's outward appearance. 2 *(adv.)* on the outside: **adressen står u-** the address is on the o- (of the letter).
ut'apå/skrift *-a* address on an envelope; sth printed, written on the outside.
***u'tar** *Av, sp* *-st* farther out; nearer the exit, the outlet.
u't/arbei·de [*/arbei·e] *V* *-de/+-et* work out, work up; prepare; **u- et foredrag** p- a lecture.
+**u't/arbei·delse** *-n* preparation (**av** of).
u't/arma *A* - (=+**-et**) impoverished.
u't/arming *-a/+-en* impoverishment.
***u'tarst** *A* *sp of* **utar**
+**u't/arte** *V* *-a/-et* degenerate, deteriorate; develop, turn (**til** into).
u't/asa *A* - exhausted, worn out; *(pop.)* beat, dog-tired.
+**ut'a/skjæ·rs** *A* - (=*/**skjers**) beyond the skerries, on the open sea: **u-seilas** open-sea sailing.
+**u't/a·st** *A* - cf /**asa**
ut'a/til· *Av* on the outside; from the outside.
u't/av *P* usu. *dial., lit.* from, out of: **u- gull** (made) out of gold; **u- mor** (received) f- mother; **u- seg** beside oneself.
+**u't/bad** *pt of* **-be**
u't/basune·re *V* *-te* trumpet out; proclaim to the world.
+**u't/be** *V* *-bad, -bedt*: **u- seg** ask (for), request; **svar u-s** please reply, RSVP.
+**u't/bedre** *V* *-et* repair; improve.
+**u't/beta·le** *V* *-te* pay; disburse, pay out; cash (e.g. a check).
+**u't/beta·ling** *-en* disbursement, payment.
u't/bløytt *A* - (=+/**bløtt**) softened by soaking.
***u't/bod** [/bå] *-et* cf /**bud**
+**u't/brakte** *pt of* **-bringe**
+**u't/bre** *V* *-dde/-dte* 1 spread (out); unfold. 2 circulate, disseminate, spread abroad. 3 *(refl.)*: **u- seg** spread (out), unfold; **u- seg om (over)** enlarge, expatiate on (upon).
+**u't/bredelse** *-n* 1 spread; spreading (**av** of). 2 circulation (of a newspaper); dissemination (of news, of an idea, of a plant); diffusion, propagation (of a doctrine); distribution (of a plant etc.): **den har en stor geografisk u-** it is widespread, has a wide d-.
+**u't/bredt** *A* - (=*/**breidd**) 1 (of wings) outspread, spread out; (of a map) unfolded. 2 widespread; widely circulated, disseminated, distributed: **en u- avis** a widely read newspaper.
***u't/brei·ing** *-a* cf /**bredelse**
***u't/breisle** *-a* cf /**bredelse**
+**u't/bringe** *V* *-brakte, -brakt* 1 deliver, distribute (e.g. mail). 2 bring (in), yield. 3 propose (e.g. a toast); call for, lead (e.g. a cheer).
+**u't/brode·re** *V* *-te* embroider (upon) (e.g. a story).
u't/brott *-et* (=*/**brot**, +/**brudd**) 1 breaking out, escape; *mil.* breakout; breaking away; bursting forth. 2 burst, outburst; cry, exclamation. 3 eruption, explosion: **være i u-** erupt. 4 outbreak (e.g. of measles): **krigens u-** the o- of war.
u't/brukt *A* - worn out; spent.
+**u't/bryte** *V* *-brøt, -brutt* break out; cry, exclaim.
+**u't/bryter** *-en, pl -e* (=*-**ar**) 1 dissenter, rebel. 2 prison-breaker; escape artist.
+**u't/brøt** *pt of* **-bryte**
+**u't/bud** *-et* (=*/**bod**) 1 *hist.* calling up; call to arms. 2 *merc.* offer(ing) for sale (**av** of).
+**u't/buet** *A* - bowed, bulging, convex.
u't/bu·rd *-en* *folk.* 1 apparition, ghost of a dead child (illegitimate, murdered, or unbaptized). 2 supernatural being that arises from afterbirth that is not burned, and tries to do away with the mother and child.
+**u't/by** *V* *infl as* **by**[2] 1 offer for sale (esp. stocks and bonds). 2: **utbudt** *hist.* called up (for military service). 3: **utbuden, utbudt** invited out.
u't/bygd *-a* 1 coastal district, outer district. 2 outpost, out-of-the-way place.
u't/bygg *-et* addition, annex; bay, projection (on building).
+**u't/bygge** *V* *-bygde, -bygd* 1 develop (e.g. waterpower, by building electric power stations). 2 enlarge, expand, extend (e.g. the road system). 3 build, build up (defences; an organization); organize, work out.
u't/bygging *-a/+-en* development; enlargement, expansion, extension; organization (**av** of).
+**u't/bytning** *-en* 1 exchange, switch, trade; replacement. 2 exploitation; utilization.
+**u't/bytte**[1] *-t* (=*/**byte**) 1 proceeds; profit, return, yield (**på** of); *merc.* dividend. 2 advantage, benefit (**av** from): **med u-** advantageously, profitably.
+**u't/bytte**[2] *V* *-a/-et* 1 exchange, switch, trade; replace. 2 exploit.
+**u'tbytte/deling** *-a/-en* profit sharing.
+**u't/bytter** *-en, pl -e* exploiter.
+**u'tbytte/rik** *A* (=***utbyte/**) profitable.
u't/danne *V* *-a/+-et* (=*/**dane**) educate, train (**i** in); cultivate, develop (one's talents): **u-et til** qualified as, trained as; **godt u-et** well educated, trained; **u- seg for (til)** be trained for, study for; **u- seg i** qualify oneself in, study (e.g. languages, typewriting).
+**u't/dannelse** *-n* cf /**danning**
u't/danning *-a* (=*/**daning**, +/**dannelse**) education, instruction, training (**til** as).
u't/debatte·re *V* *-te* exhaust (e.g. a subject), thrash out (e.g. a problem).
+**u't/dele** *V* *-te* 1 apportion, distribute, pass out; issue (rations). 2 give (orders); award (a prize); administer (a sacrament).
u't/drag *-et* excerpt, extract, selection; abstract, summary (**av** of).
+**u't/drivelse** *-n* *(lit., bibl.)* expulsion (from Paradise); exorcising (of devils).
***u't/dry(g)ing** *-a* dragging out (esp. of time).
u't/dunsting *-a/+-en* (=+**-ning**) emanation, exhalation, vapor.
+**u't/dype** *V* *-a/-et* 1 deepen, dredge. 2 *fig.* deepen, give depth to; amplify, expand on, go into deeply: **u- sine kunnskaper** extend one's knowledge.
+**u't/dø** *V* *-(d)de, -dd* die off, out; become extinct.
+**u't/dødd** *A* - (=*/**døydd**) 1 extinct; dead. 2 abandoned, deserted, ghost (e.g. town, street).

u`te *Av* 1 out (referring to location); outdoors, outside; abroad: **langt u-** far off, out; (in relationship) distantly; **sauene går u- hele året** the sheep are outdoors all year; **u- av seg** beside oneself; desperate; *fam.* unhappy; **u- og hjemme** at home and abroad; **være u- og ...** be out ....ing (**jeg er u- og leter etter noe** I'm (out) looking for sth). 2 at an end, finished, over, up: **det er u- med ham** he's done for; **hans makt er u-** his power is gone; **så er den historien u-** so that's the end of that (story); **tiden er u-** (the) time is up. 3 later: **u- i måltidet** later in the meal. 4 (with *prep.*): **u- etter** looking for, out for (sby); **politiet er u- etter ham** the police are after him; **han er u- etter meg** he's got it in for me; **u- for** exposed to, come across, run into; **jeg var u- for noe aldeles forferdelig** I had a perfectly awful experience.

u`te/arbeid [*/arbei] *-et* outdoor work.

+**u`te/bli** *V* *-ble/-blei, -blitt* 1 not attend, stay away; *jur.* default, fail to appear (in court). 2 not come off; fail to materialize, occur.

+**u`te/blivelse** *-n* 1 absence, failure to appear; *jur.* default (**av** of). 2 non-occurrence.

+**u`te/fra** *P* 1 from out (in): **stemmer høres u- hagen** voices are heard from out in the garden. 2 *(adv.)* from outside; from abroad.

+**u`te/gang** *-en* (=***/gonge**) (of animals) grazing outdoors (in winter).

+**u`te/glemme** *V* *-te* (inadvertently) leave out, omit.

***u`te/gonge** *-a* cf **/gang**

u`te/jente *-a* hired girl (who works in the outbuildings on a farm).

u'/tekk *A* *-tekt dial.* disagreeable, offensive.

utek'kelig *A* - disagreeable, improper; offensive.

u't/eksamine're *V* *-te* graduate (sby): **bli u-t** g- (**fra** from).

u't/eksperimente're *V* *-te* develop (by experiments).

+**u`te/late** *V* *-lot, -latt* leave out, omit; cut, delete.

+**u`te/latelse** *-n* omission; cut, deletion (**av** of).

***u`te/lege** *-a* lying outside, in the open.

+**u`te/ligger** *-en, pl -e* (=***-jar**) homeless person who sleeps outdoors; bum, hobo, vagrant.

u`te/liv *-et* outdoor life; camping.

***u'/teljande** *A* - countless, innumerable.

+**u`te/lot** *pt of* **-late**

+**u`te/lukke** [/lokke] *V* *-a/-et* debar, shut out; exclude, preclude, rule out.

+**u`te/lukkelse** [/lokkelse] *-n* exclusion (**av** of; **fra** from).

+**u`te/lukkende** [/lokkene] *Av* exclusively, only.

+**u`te/lukket** [/lokket] *A* - 1 impossible, out of the question. 2 debarred, shut out; excluded.

+**utem'melig** *A* - (=***/temjande**) untamable; uncontrollable.

+**u`ten** *P* (=***utan**) 1 without: **u- ham ville vi vært fortapt** but for him we would have been lost; **u- videre** w- further ado; as a matter of course; straight away, then and there; **u- å vite det** w- knowing it. 2 but, except; but for, except for: **ingen u- deg** nobody b- you (in older usage only **du** when it is the subject). 3 *(conj.)* without; except, unless: **ingenting ble bestemt, u- at de skulle fortsette** nothing was decided e- that they would continue.

+**u`ten-** *Pf* cf **uta-**

+**u`ten/at** *Av* (=***utan/åt**) by heart: **kunne u-** know by heart; **lære u-** memorize.

+**u`tenat/lekse** *-a/-en* memory work.

+**u`tenat/læ·rt** *A* - learned by rote; memorized.

+**u`ten/bo·ks** *A* - cf **uta/**

+**u`ten/bo·rds** *A* - cf **uta/**

+**u`ten/bygds** *A* - cf **uta/**

+**u`ten/bys** *A* - cf **uta/**

+**u`ten/dø·rs** *A* - cf **uta/**

+**u`ten/for·** *P* cf **uta/**

+**u`tenfor/liggende** *A* - external, irrelevant, non-essential.

+**u`tenfor/stående** *A* - (usu. as noun) outsider.

+**u`ten/fra** *Av* cf **ute/**

+**uten'kelig** *A* - (=***utenkjeleg, *u/tenkjande**) inconceivable, unthinkable.

+**u`ten/lands** *A* - cf **uta/**

+**u`ten/landsk** *A* - cf **uta/**

+**u`tenlands/reise** *-a/-en* journey, trip abroad.

+**u`ten/om·** *P* 1 around: **det er ingen vei u- dette spørsmålet** there's no way around this question, no way to avoid this question. 2 outside (and around); outside of; in addition to: **u- all tvil** beyond all doubt; **u- det vanlige** out of the ordinary; **u- ekteskapet** extramarital(ly). 3 *(adv.)* around; outside, without; in addition, on the side: **"Gå u-", sa bøygen** "Go roundabout," said the Boyg (Ibsen); **komme u-** avoid, evade; get around (sth); **verden u-** the outside world, the world outside.

+**u`tenom/snakk** *-et* beating around the bush, circumlocution, irrelevant talk.

+**u`ten/på** *P* cf **uta/**

+**u`tenpåklistret** *A* pasted on, stuck on.

+**u`tenpå/skrift** *-a/-en* cf **utapå/**

+**u`ten/riks** *A* - foreign: **i u- fart** (engaged) in foreign trade, shipping abroad.

+**U`tenriks/departementet** [/-mang·e] *df* (=***Utan-**) the Ministry of Foreign Affairs (=U.S. Department of State).

+**u`tenriks/eta·t** *-en admin.* foreign service staff.

u`tenriks/handel *-en* foreign trade.

+**u`ten/riksk** *A* - *pol.* foreign.

+**u`tenriks/minis·ter** *-eren, pl -rer/+-ere* (=***utan-**) Minister of Foreign Affairs (=U.S. Secretary of State).

+**u`tenriks/politikk·** *-en* 1 foreign policy. 2 international affairs, situation.

+**u`tenriks/polit·isk** *A* - 1 relating to foreign affairs: **Norges u-e stilling** Norway's position in f- a-. 2 international; concerning international affairs.

+**u`tenriks/tjeneste** *-n admin.* foreign service.

+**utensi'lier** *pl* (=***utensil, -el**) *lit.* tools, utensils.

+**u`ten/skjæ·rs** *A* - cf **uta/**

+**u`ten/verk** *-et, pl -er* (=***utan/**) 1 *mil.* outwork(s) (outer fortification). 2 externality.

+**ute'rlig** *A* - *archaic* indecent, lewd, obscene.

+**u't/eske** *V* *-a/-et* challenge, provoke: **u-ende** provocative.

+**u`te/stengt** *A* - (=***/stengd**) excluded; locked out; shut off, out.

u`te/stående *A* - 1 outstanding: **u- fordringer** accounts o-. 2: **ha noe u- med en** have a score to settle with sby.

u'/tett *A* - leaky, not tight; *fam.* unable to keep a secret; not housebroken.

u't/etter *P* 1 along, through. 2 *(adv.)* out, outwards; out from land; away.

+**u'tett/het** *-en* leakiness; crack, leak; *fam.* inability to keep a secret.

***u't/falding** *-a* cf **/foldelse**

u't/fall *-et* 1 outcome, result, upshot (**av** of). 2 attack (**mot** on), denunciation (**mot** of), diatribe (**mot** against). 3 *mil.* sortie. 4 (in fencing) forward lunge. 5 outflow (of a river); outfall. 6 (in boatbuilding) outward pitch or slope (of each length of planking on ship's side).

u'tfalls/port [/port] *-en* 1 *mil.* sally port. 2 gateway (e.g. to the world).

+**u't/fart** *-en* 1 *lit.* excursion; outward journey; emigration. 2 exodus: **u-en fra Oslo i påsken** the Easter e- from Oslo.

+**u'tfarts/sted** *-et* (popular) excursion spot; resort.

u't/fattig *A* - extremely poor, impoverished; poor as a churchmouse.

u't/felling *-a/+-en chem.* 1 precipitation. 2 deposit, precipitate.

u't/ferd [*/fær] *-a/+-en lit.* leaving home, going abroad; emigration; (viking) expedition.

+**u't/ferdige** *V* *-et admin.* draw up, make out (a document, report).

+**u't/ferdigelse** *-n admin.* drawing up, preparation (**av** of).

***utferds/hug** [u'tfæ·rs/] *-en lit.* desire to travel (esp. abroad).

+**u'tferds/trang** *-en* (=***/trong**) *lit.* desire to travel (esp. abroad).

u't/fiska *A* - (=**+-et**) fished out.

u't/flod *+-en/*-a* 1 *med.* discharge, flux; flow. 2 mouth of a river.

+**u't/flukt** *-en* 1 excursion, jaunt, outing; picnic. 2 alibi, excuse, evasion.

u't/flytende *A* - 1 blurred, indefinite, indistinct. 2 discursive, rambling (style). 3 blurred, indeterminate, without character.

+**u't/flytter** *-en, pl -e* (=***-ar**) emigrant.

u't/flytting *-a* 1 moving out. 2 emigration.

u'tflyttings/attes·t *-en* certificate of change of residence.

u't/folde *V* *-a/+-et* 1 display, put forth, show (activity, courage, energy, etc.). 2 *lit.* spread, unfold, unfurl (a flag, leaves, wings, etc.); unveil (a plan). 3 *(refl.)*: **u- seg** blossom out, develop, expand; open, spread out, unfurl; be displayed, be shown, become visible.

+**u't/foldelse** *-n* display; development; unfolding (**av** of): **føle at de beste muligheter i en selv aldri skulle få komme til u-** feel that one's best talents would never get a chance to develop (Undset).

u't/for·¹ *N* downhill (skiing contest).

u't/for·² *P* 1 out over, over, (over and) down (a cliff, edge, pier, etc.). 2 beyond, out in front of, outside of. 3 *(adv.)* down, over (the edge of sth): **sette (stå) u-** set off down (the hill).

utfor/bakke *-n* down slope (skiing).

u't/fordre *V* *-a/+-et* challenge (**til** to), defy; lay oneself open to, tempt (danger, fate, etc.): **u- en til duell** c- sby to a duel; **u- skjebnen** tempt fate.

u't/fordrende *A* - 1 aggressive, challenging, defiant. 2 (sexually) provocative.

+**u't/fordrer** *-en, pl -e* (=***-ar**) challenger.

u't/fordring *-a/+-en* challenge.

utfor/kjøring [u'tfårr/] *-a/+-en* (=***/køyring**) downhill run (skiing).

utfor/løype *-a* downhill tracks (skiing).

+**u't/forme** *V* *-a/-et* formulate, shape, work out; amplify, develop.

u't/forming *-a/+-en* formulation; amplification, development.

utfor/renn [u'tfårr/] *-et* downhill race (skiing).

+**u't/forske** *V* *-a/-et* examine, investigate, study; inquire, search into; find out (about).

+**u't/fri** *V* *-dde* liberate, set free; deliver, release, rescue (**av** from).

+ Bokmål; * Nynorsk; ° Dialect.
After letter: ' stress (Acc. 1); ` tone, stress (Acc. 2); · length.
Below letter: . not pronounced.

u't/friing *-a* liberation; deliverance, release (**av** from; **av** by).
+u't/fritte *V -a/-et* pump, question closely; cross-examine.
+u't/fylle *V -fylte* fill (a gap, need, pause, post, etc.), supply; fill in, out (a form, questionnaire, etc.); fill in, up (a hole, will, etc.); complement, supplement: **u- hverandre** s- each other; **u-ende** supplementary.
u't/fylling *-a/+-en* 1 filling in, out, up; supplementing; complementing. 2 filler.
u't/føre *V -te* 1 export. 2 carry out, execute (an experiment, instructions, a plan, threat, etc.); perform (a duty, task, trick, etc.); draw, make (a woodcut); do, discharge, fulfill (etc.): **godt u-t arbeid** well-done piece of work.
u't/føring *-a* (=**+-else**) 1 carrying out, execution, performance; fulfilment (**av** of). 2 workmanship.
utfø'rlig *-A* - comprehensive, detailed; *(adv.)* at length, fully, in detail.
u't/førsel *-elen, pl -ler* export (**av** of); exports, export trade: **ta på u-** carry with one from the country (thus avoiding duty).
u'tførsels/artik'kel *-elen, pl -artikler* article for export.
***u't/førsle** *-a* cf **/førsel**
utg. = **+utgave/*utgåve, utgitt/*utgjeve(n)**
u't/gammal *A -t, pl -gamle* (=**+/gammel**) aged, ancient, hoary.
u't/gang *-en* 1 departure, egress, exit; (esp. *bibl.*) going out: **spille til u-** *eccl.* play a postlude while congregation is leaving the church. 2 exit (=place of exit; stage direction). 3 end (**av** of) (a month, year); conclusion, ending (of a book, play, etc.): **lykkelig u-** happy ending; **mannlig, kvinnelig u- på verslinje** masculine, feminine verse ending. 4 outcome, result. 5 *typog.* break (for paragraphing). 6 (in bridge) game.
+u't/ganger *-en, pl -e* (=***-ar**) domesticated animal kept outdoors in winter.
+u'tgangs/bønn *-a/-en* (=***/bøn**) *eccl.* closing prayer.
u'tgangs/dør *-a* exit (door).
u'tgangs/punkt [/pongt] *-et* 1 point of departure, starting point. 2 basis, origin (**for** of).
+u'tgangs/stilling *-a/-en* (=***/stode**) 1 initial, starting position. 2 basic position (in an argument).
+u't/gav *pt of* **-gi**
+u't/gave *-a/-en* (=***/gåve**) edition (**av** of); version (e.g. of a story): **annen u-** the second edition; **en mindre u- av sin far** a smaller copy of his father; **av nyeste u-** the latest model.
+u't/gi *V -gav, -gitt* 1 publish (book, newspaper etc.). 2: **u- for** tell around that (of sth untrue); palm off as; **u- seg for** pass oneself off as.
u't/gift *+-en/*-a* expense; disbursement, expenditure, outlay (**til** for).
***u'tgifts/auke** *-n* increase in expenditures.
u'tgifts/post *-en* item of expenditure.
+u't/giing *-a/-en* cf **/giving**
+u't/gikk *pt of* **-gå**
+u't/givelse *-n* publication (**av** of).
+u't/giver *-en, pl -e* (=***-ar**) publisher (**av** of).
u't/giving *-a/+-en* (=**+/giing**) publication (**av** of).
***u't/gjevar** *-en* cf **/giver**
***u't/gjeving** *-a* cf **/giving**
+u't/gjo'rde *pt of* **-gjøre**
+u't/gjort [/jort] *A* - (=***/gjord**) accursed, hexed: **det er (som) u-** it is just my luck; **det er rent u- med fluer i år** the flies are a regular curse this year (Kinck).
+u't/gjøre *V -gjorde, -gjort* 1 compose, constitute, form, make (up). 2 amount to, come to, total.
+u't/gjøt *pt of* **-gyte**
u't/glatting *-a/+-en* evening out, leveling off; *fig.* ironing out, smoothing (over).
+u't/gli'dning *-a/-en* (=***/gli(d)ing**) 1 landslide. 2 *fig.* slipping; backsliding; *(pl)* abuses: **moralsk u-** moral deterioration.
u't/graving *-a/+-en* 1 digging out, dredging, excavation: **u- av Tyskebryggen** e- of the Hanseatic wharf (in Bergen). 2 hole, pit, trench; *(pl)* excavations.
u't/greiing *-a/+-en* 1 clarification, straightening out, untangling. 2 *admin.* account, explanation, report.
u't/grunn *A -grunt* shallow offshore, shoaly.
+u't/grunne *V -a/-et* fathom; figure out.
+u't/gyte *V -gjøt, -gytt* 1 shed (blood, tears); pour out, vent (one's anger). 2 *(refl.)*: **u- seg** express oneself, pour out one's feelings. 3: **u-t** (of fish that have spawned) spent.
+u't/gytelse *-n* 1 gush(ing), outpouring, shedding (**av** of). 2 effusion, harangue.
+u't/gå *V -gikk, -gått* 1 come, emanate, issue (**fra** from); originate (**fra** from, with); radiate; be issued, sent out. 2: **u-ende** outgoing (mail, order, etc.); outward-bound (streetcar, train, etc.); **u-ende vindu** window opening outwards. 3: **u-tt** *merc.* out of stock; tired out; extinguished; worn out (e.g. shoes).
+u't/gående *N*: **for u-** outward-bound; on the way out.
***u't/gåve** *-a* cf **/gave**
u't/hage *-n* outlying pasture.
***u't/hald** *-et* cf **utholden/het**
+u't/haler *-en, pl -e* (=***-ar**) 1 *naut.* outhaul(er). 2 libertine, roué.
u't/hamn *-a* (=**+/havn**) harbor near the open sea; outport; port of refuge.
+u'thengs/skap *-et* display case, showcase, esp. for posting latest edition of a newspaper.
u't/heve *V -a/+-et* 1 emphasize, point up, stress. 2 *typog.* italicize: **u-et av meg** the italics are mine.
+u't/hevelse *-n* 1 emphasis, stress. 2 italicizing; italics.
u't/hogd *A* - (=***/hoggen**) 1 carved, hewn, sculptured. 2 (of forest) thinned out; cut down.
u't/hogst *-en* (=***/hogster**) cutting, felling (of trees); destruction (of a forest, by logging).
***u't/hola** [/håla] *A* - hollow(ed); undermined.
+u't/holde *V -holdt, -holdt* 1 *lit.* endure, sustain; persevere: **u-te toner** s-ed notes. 2 suffer, undergo. 3 bear, endure, stand: **jeg kan ikke u- ham** I detest him, can't stand him.
+uthol'delig *A* - bearable, endurable.
+u't/holdende *A* - dogged, persevering, persistent; tireless: **være u-** persevere, persist.
+u'tholden/het *-en* endurance, stamina; perseverance, tenaciousness.
+u't/hule *V -te* gouge, hollow (out) *fig.* undermine.
+u't/hungret *A* - famished, starved.
u't/hus *-et* farm building, outbuilding, outhouse (barn, stable etc.).
u'thus/bygning *-en* cf **uthus**
+u't/hvi'lt *A* - cf **/kvilt**
u't/i *P* 1 (out) into; (out) in: **hoppe u- elva** jump (out) into the river. 2 in: **u- januar** (along) in January. 3 *(adv.)* in; (out) into: **han sprang u-** he jumped in (out into sth); **har du vært u-** have you been in (swimming).
u'/tid [*/ti] *-a/+-en*: **i u-e** at the wrong time, out of season; **i tide og u-** in season and out, i.e. all the time.
u'/tidig [also -ti'-] *A* - 1 untimely; unseasonable; misplaced. 2 unpleasant; unreasonable; naughty, undisciplined.
+u'tidig/het [also -ti'-] *-en* (=***/skap**) 1 untimeliness; unseasonableness. 2 unreasonableness; lack of discipline.
***u't/ifrå'** *A* - (=**+/ifra**) 1 excellent. 2 *(adv.)* exceedingly, extraordinarily. 3 *(adv.)* from outside.
u't/igjen'nom *P* out through (a door, gate, etc.); throughout (e.g. the years).
u'/tilbø'rlig [also -bø'r-] *A* - improper, undue, unwarranted.
+utilbøy'elig *A* - averse, disinclined, indisposed: **ikke u- til å tro at** inclined to think that.
u'/tilfreds *A* - discontented, dissatisfied (**med** with).
+u'tilfreds/het *-en* discontent, dissatisfaction.
u'/tilfredsstillende *A* - unsatisfactory.
u'/tilfredsstilt *A* - ungratified, unsatisfied.
+utilgi'velig *A* - inexcusable, unforgivable, unpardonable.
utilgjeng'elig *A* - inaccessible; unapproachable.
u'/tilhogd *A* - rough, uncut (timber).
+u'/tilhyl(le)t *A* - open, unveiled; unconcealed.
utilitaris'me *-n* utilitarianism.
utilitaris't *-en* utilitarian.
utilitaris'tisk *A* - utilitarian.
utilla'telig *A* - 1 forbidden, not permissible; illicit. 2 disgraceful, outrageous (behavior); flagrant, gross, unforgivable (error).
utilnær'melig *A* - distant, standoffish, unapproachable.
+utilnær'melig/het *-en* reserve, standoffishness, unapproachability.
+u'/tilpass *A* - indisposed: **føle seg u-** not feel well.
+utilregnelig [utilrei'neli] *A* - not responsible; insane, of unsound mind.
utilrå'delig *A* - inadvisable.
u'/tilslørt [/-slø'rt] *A* - not veiled, open; barefaced, unblushing; overt, unconcealed.
+utilste'delig *A* - *lit.* not permissible, outrageous.
utilstrek'kelig *A* - inadequate, insufficient.
+utilstrek'kelig/het *-en* inadequacy, insufficiency.
u'/tilta'lende *A* - unattractive, unpleasant, unpleasing (appearance, behavior, etc.).
u'/ting *-en* absurdity; monstrosity; monstrous thing: **det er en u- å oversette svenske, danske og norske bøker innen Skandinavia** it is an unfortunate practice to translate Swedish, Danish, and Norwegian books within Scandinavia (Dagbladet).
u't/jamning *-a* 1 evening up, smoothing out. 2 adjustment, equalization; harmonization.
+utje'nlig *A* - unserviceable, useless.
+u't/jevne *V -a/-et* 1 even up, smooth out. 2 adjust, equalize; harmonize: **u- motsetninger** h- (mediate) contrasts; **u-ende** appeasingly, conciliatingly.
+u't/jevning *-a/-en* cf **/jamning**
+u't/kalle *V -kalte* call up, mobilize.
u't/kalling *-a/+-en* calling up, mobilization (**av** of).
u't/kant *-en* (outer) edge; fringe(s), outskirts; outer reaches: **i u-en av** in the outskirts of.
u'tkant/gate *-a* street on the outskirts of a town; suburban street.
u't/kast *-et* 1 (rough) draft, design, sketch (**til** for, of); rough cast (of a bust, etc.). 2 *mil.* ejection (of empty cartridge or shell).
+u't/kaste *V -et* throw out; toss off (an idea): **u-et** ejected, evicted.
+u't/kastelse *-n* 1 ejection, expulsion. 2 *jur.* dispossession, eviction (**av** of).
+u't/kaster *-en, pl -e* (=***-ar**) 1 bouncer (in a café). 2 ejector arms (on a reaper). 3 ejector (on a rifle).
u't/kik[1] *-en* (=**/kikk**) 1 *naut.* lookout, watch (person). 2 lookout place, post; crow's nest.

u't/kik² *-et* (=/**kikk**) esp. *naut.* lookout, watch: **holde u-** be on w-, keep a l- (**etter** for).
u'tkiks/mann *-en, pl -menn/*-menner* (=-**kikks/**) *naut.* lookout; sentry, spy.
u'tkiks/post *-en* (=-**kikks/**) ɪ lookout post. 2 lookout, sentry.
u'tkiks/tønne *-a* (=-**kikks/**) *naut.* crow's nest.
u'tkiks/tå·rn *-et* observation tower, watch tower.
+**u't/kjempe** *V -et* fight out, through.
u't/kjørsel *-la/+-elen, pl -ler* (=*/**kjørsle**) ɪ carting, trucking out. 2 gateway, vehicle exit; drive, driveway.
u't/kjø·rt *A* ɪ carted, trucked out. 2 exhausted, worn out.
+**u't/klare·re** *V -te* clear (through customs).
u't/kledd *A -/*-kledt* ɪ decked out, dressed up, rigged out (usu. in a costume). 2 (of inside walls) coated, covered, lined.
+**u't/klekke** *V -et/-klekte, -et/-klekt* hatch (chicks, ideas, plot, etc.): **ekspeditionschefen (hadde) u-et en ypperlig plan** the department head had concocted a superb plan (Elster d.y.).
u'tklekkings/anstalt *-en* (=+**utklekkings/**) fish hatchery; *hum.* breeding place (of an educational institution).
u't/klipp *-et* (newspaper) clipping, *(Brit.)* cutting.
u'tklipps/bok *-a, pl -bøker* book of clippings, scrapbook.
***u't/kome** *-a* cf /**komme**¹
+**u't/kommande·re** *V -te* call up, mobilize; call out.
u't/komme¹ *+-t/*-a* (=*/**kome**) ɪ *lit.* opportunity, possibility; means, way: **det er ikke noe u- med ham** there's no dealing with him. 2 income, livelihood, subsistence.
+**u't/komme**² *V -kom, -kommet* (of a book, etc.) appear, be published, come out.
+**u't/konkurrere** [/kongkurre're] *V -te* outdo, outstrip; crowd out, displace.
***u't/kropen** [/kråpen] *A -e/-i, pl -ne* cf /**krøpet**
+**u't/krystallise·re** *V -te* crystallize (out).
+**u't/krøpet** *A -et, pl -ne* (=*/**kropen**) crafty, wily.
+**u't/kvi·lt** *A -* (=*/**kvild**) rested (up).
***u't/køyrd** *A -køyrt* cf /**kjørt**
***u't/køyrsel** *-køyrsla* cf /**kjørsel**
***u't/køyrsle** *-a* cf /**kjørsel**
+**u't/kåre** *V -a/-et* choose, pick out: **den u-ne** the chosen one (e.g. bride- or bridegroom-elect).
+**u't/la** *pt of* **-legge**
+**u't/lade** *V -de/-et phys.* discharge.
u't/la·dning *+-en/*-a* (=*/**lading**) ɪ *phys.* discharge. 2 blowing off, explosion (of feelings, words).
+**u't/lagt** *pp of* **-legge**
u't/land *-et*: **u-et** foreign countries, the outside world; **fra u-et** from abroad; **i u-et** abroad; **(reise) til u-et** (go) abroad (other Scandinavian countries are often excluded from the term).
+**u't/late** *V -lot, -latt* ɪ: **u-t** let out. 2: **u- seg med** give out, let it be known; **u- seg om noe** expatiate, express an opinion on sth.
***u't/laup** *-et* cf /**løp**
***u't/laupar** *-en* cf /**løper**
+**u't/lede** *V -et* ɪ derive, trace the descent (**fra** from). 2 ascribe, attribute (**av** to); conclude, infer (**av** from).
+**u't/leg** *A -* (=*/**læg**) *hist.* outlaw(ed); outcast: **gjøre (lyse) u-** outlaw.
u't/legd *-a hist.* banishment, exile; outlawry.
u't/legg *-et* ɪ disbursement, expense, outlay: **godtgjøre en hans u-** reimburse sby for his o-. 2 *jur.* distress: **gjøre, ta u-** distrain, levy a distress (**i** on).
+**u't/legge** *V -la, -lagt* ɪ lay out, place, put out (food, poison; a document, list for signing, etc.). 2 plot out; set off (esp. land) (**til** as, for); **utlagt til park** plotted as a park. 3 let out (e.g. clothing). 4 *jur.* distrain. 5 *jur.*: **u- en som barnefar** name one as the (alleged) father of one's child. 6 (esp. *bibl., lit.*) explain, interpret, construe (e.g. a text).
+**u't/legning** *-en* ɪ exegesis, interpretation (esp. of the Bible). 2 any of the actions listed above under **utlegge.**
+**u't/leie** *-a/-en* rental, renting (**av** of).
+**u'tlendig/het** *-en* exile, expatriation; stay abroad: **leve i u-** expatriate oneself.
u't/lending *-en* ɪ foreigner; alien, outlander. 2 *(bibl.)* pilgrim (Heb. 11, 13).
u't/lengsel *-elen, pl -ler* (=*/**lengsle**) longing to leave one's home, esp. to go abroad (opp. of **heim/l-**).
***u't/lengst** *A -* farthest out.
***u't/lengt** *-en* cf /**lengsel**
u't/levd *A -/*-levt* ɪ decrepit, spent, wasted (by riotous living). 2 decadent, effete. 3 outlived, superannuated.
+**u't/leve·re** *V -te* ɪ deliver, hand out, hand over; give up, surrender; hand back, restore, yield. 2 give away, reveal (a secret); leave to the mercy (**til** of) (e.g. criticism, gossip, etc.). 3 *(refl.)*: **u- seg** give oneself away; compromise oneself.
+**u't/ligger** *-en, pl -e* ɪ *tech.* boom, jib (of a crane, derrick, etc.). 2 crossarm, traverse (e.g. on a power pole). 3 *naut.* outrigger. 4 *hist.* traveling merchant (esp. in Nordland, from Trondheim).
'**u't/ligne** [/lingne] *V -a/-et* ɪ balance, offset; equalize, neutralize: **u- motsetningene** n- the contrasts. 2 *admin.* make a pro-rata assessment of (**på** on) (e.g. members of a society; taxpayers of a district): **u- skatten** make a tax assessment. 3 *typog.* equalize (a line of type). 4 (sports) tie (the score).
u't/likning *-a* (=+/**ligning**) ɪ equalization, neutralization; balance, tie. 2 *admin.* assessment.
'**u't/lodning** *-en* (=*/**lodding**) ɪ lottery: **et bordteppe til u-** a tablecloth to be sold at a lottery. 2 distribution, parcelling out.
***u't/loge** [/låge] *-a* expense, fee, outlay.
u't/lossing *-a/+-en* landing, unloading (of cargo, freight).
+**u't/lot** *pt of* **-late**
+**u't/love** [/låve] *V -a/-et/-de/-te* promise (as a reward): **finnelønn u-es** (in ads) reward.
u't/lufting *-a/+-en* ɪ airing (out), ventilation. 2 cleaning up (of an unhealthy, immoral situation).
***u't/luting** *-a* cf /**lodning**
u't/lyd *-en gram.* final sound; final position: **i u-** finally.
+**u't/ly·sning** *-a/-en* (=*/**lysing**) announcement (of an opening).
***u't/læg** *A* cf /**leg**
+**u't/læ·rt** *A -* (=*/**lærd**) (fully) qualified, trained (**i** in).
u't/løe *-a* small, isolated (hay) barn.
+**u't/løp** *-et* (=*/**laup**) ɪ discharge, outflow. 2 mouth, opening, outlet (of river, canal, etc.); discharge pipe. 3 *fig.* outlet (**for** for) (energies, etc.). 4 end, expiration (of time period): **ved u-et av mars** at the end of March.
+**u't/løpe** *V -løp, -løp(e)t* ɪ expire, run out: **tiden var u-et** the time was up (had e-d). 2 *typog.*: **u-ende toner** fadeaway tones.
+**u't/løper** *-en, pl -e* ɪ *bot.* runner, sucker. 2 branch, offshoot, spur; ramification.
+**u'tløps/renne** *-a* drain; sewer (outlet); waterspout.
+**u'tløps/tid** *-a/-en* expiration date.
+**u't/løse** *V -te* ɪ *phys.* release (e.g. a parachute; energy, heat); set off (e.g. an explosion). 2 bail out (e.g. a prisoner); redeem (e.g. property); buy out (e.g. a partner). 3 bring (forth), provoke, start; liberate, release: **u- formelige latterhyl** p- howls of laughter.
+**u't/lø·sning** *-en* (=*/**løysing**) ɪ release; setting off (e.g. of an explosion). 2 bail, ransom; redemption; getting out of hock. 3 release, relief (of tensions, etc.); orgasm: **få u- for** find expression for, a release from.
u't/lån *-et* ɪ lending; loan (**av** of). 2 loan desk.
u'tlåns/rente *-a/+-en* interest (on loans).
u't/magra *A -* (=+-**et**) emaciated, wasted.
+**u't/maie** *V -a/-et derog.* bedeck, bedizen, dress up (**med** with); *(pop.)* doll up, rig out.
'**u't/male** *V -te* depict, describe (in detail); embroider upon, paint (a verbal picture); picture (in one's mind).
u't/mark *-a* ɪ isolated (or outlying) field. 2 isolated (desolate) area, wilderness.
u't/marsj *-en* ɪ marching out (from a fort or camp). 2 marching practice, maneuvers (outside a camp, etc.).
u't/matta *A -* (=+-**et**) exhausted, weary, worn (out).
+**u't/matte** *V -a/-et* exhaust, tire out.
+**u't/mattelse** *-n* ɪ exhaustion, weariness. 2 *tech.* fatigue.
u't/med *P* out along, (out) by; alongside, beside: ***mellom bakkar og berg u- havet** mid hills and cliffs by the sea (poem, Aasen).
u't/melding *-a/+-en* (—+/**meldelse**) resignation, withdrawal.
+**u't/merke** *V -a/-et/-te* (=*/**merkje**) ɪ characterize, distinguish, mark (sby); be characterized (etc.) by. 2 *(refl.)*: **u- seg** distinguish oneself, excel, stand out (**ved** by, **i** in); be characterized (by), be remarkable (for).
+**u't/merkelse** *-n* (=*/**merking**) distinction; honors: **ta eksamen med u** graduate with highest honors (summa cum laude).
+**u't/merket** *A -* (=*/**merkt**) ɪ excellent; outstanding, splendid; fine: **u- godt** *educ.* excellent. 2 *(adv.)* excellently, splendidly: **det passer u-** that suits me just fine; that fits very well.
***u't/merking** *-a* cf /**merkelse**
***u't/mødd** *A -/*-mødt* exhausted, worn (out).
+**u't/måle** *V -te* ɪ measure, mete out; assess, gauge. 2 survey (for mining, etc.).
+**u't/navn** *-et* (=*/**namn**, */**nemne**¹) nickname.
***u't/nemne**¹ *-t* cf /**navn**
***u't/nemne**² *V -de* cf /**nevne**
***u't/nemning** *-a* cf /**nevnelse**
***u'tnemnings/brev** *-et* (letter of) appointment.
u't/nes *-et* outermost headland, point (jutting into the sea).
+**u't/nevne** *V -te* ɪ appoint, name, nominate (**til** as). 2 *hum.* dub, label: **u- til geni** label as a genius.
+**u't/nevnelse** *-n* appointment, nomination (**til** as).
+**u't/nytte** *V -a/-et* ɪ exploit, make the most of, utilize (resources; talents; possibilities). 2 *derog.* exploit (na-

tives, workers), manipulate; take unfair advantage of; cash in on: **u- sine venner** e- one's friends.
u't/nytting *-a* (=⁺**-else**) **1** development, exploitation, utilization (**av** of). **2** *derog.* exploitation; manipulation, taking advantage.
***u'/to** *-et* bad character.
***u'/toen** *A -e/-i, pl -(e)ne* **1** coarse, piggish, vulgar. **2** depressed, downhearted.
***u'/tokke** *-n* disfavor, displeasure; unpleasant feeling.
***u'/tol** [/tål] *-et* cf **/tål**
***u'/tolig** [/tålig] *A* - cf **/tålig**
u't/om· *P* **1** out past, outside (of). **2** *(adv.)* usu. *dial.* around about; outside; in addition, on the side.
utopi' *-en* Utopia.
uto'pisk *A* - Utopian.
u't/or** *P* (=ut or**) out from, out of.
u't/over [/åver] *P* (=**ut over**) **1** (out) over; about, (all) around (e.g. the room); across, throughout (Europe, the country, etc.): **kua falt u- taket** the cow fell over the edge of the roof (Asbjørnsen); **slå vann u- en** throw water (all) over one; **se u- forsamlingen** survey the audience. **2** down, out (the bay, fjord, etc.); out (along) (the path, road, etc.): **bilen kom kjørende u- Drammensveien** the car came driving out D-. **3** well into (the day, evening, summer, etc.); throughout: **hele sommeren u- t-** the whole summer; **u- våren** well into the spring. **4** beyond, past (a boundary, present circumstances, etc.). **5** *(adv.)* out, over; outward; *naut.* off, seaward; beyond, farther out: **et sted hvor bjørk hang u-** a place with overhanging birch trees; **i bakgrunnen sees fjorden og øyene u-** the fjord and the islands beyond are seen in the background (Ibsen); (with time) on: **en tid u-** for a time to come, for a length of time; **fra august og u-** from August on.
⁺**utover/hengende** *A* - (=***/hangande**) overhanging.
u't/pakking *-a/⁺-en* unpacking.
⁺**u't/pante** *V -a/-et jur.* distrain upon, levy a distress on; seize in payment of a debt; foreclose on.
⁺**u't/parselle're** *V -te* lay out in lots, plot (e.g. a subdivision).
⁺**u't/peke** *V -te* **1** point out, single out. **2** designate, name, nominate (**til** as).
u't/pensla *A* - (=⁺**-et**) detailed, elaborate(d), worked out minutely; labored.
u't/pi·nt *A* - suffering, tortured; exhausted (soil); ragged, tattered (nerves).
u't/plukk [/plokk] *-et* excerpts, extracts, selections (**av** from); *derog.* rehash (**av** of).
⁺**u't/plyndre** *V -a/-et* plunder, rob; fleece, skin; loot, sack.
u't/plyndring *-a/⁺-en* plundering, robbing; fleecing, skinning; looting, sacking.
u't/post *-en mil., geog.* outpost: **skogens siste u-er** the last o-s of the forest (Undset).
u't/prega *A* - (=⁺**-et**) **1** distinct, marked, pronounced; distinctive (e.g. personality). **2** typical: **et u- industriområde** a t-ly industrial district. **3** *(adv.)* distinctly, strongly, to a high degree; typically: **u- praktisk anlagt** having a distinctly practical turn of mind.
⁺**u't/prege** *V -et* mint, stamp.
⁺**u't/presning** *-en* cf **/pressing**
⁺**u't/presser** *-en, pl -e* (=***-ar**) blackmailer, extortionist.
u't/pressing *-a/⁺-en* blackmail, extortion.
⁺**u't/prøve** *V -de tech.* test, try out.
⁺**u't/pønse** *V -et* (=**/pønske**) devise, think up (a plan); figure out; concoct (a story).
u't/på *P* (=***ut på**) **1** out on: **de gikk u- isen** they were walking around on the ice; **katten ligger u- hellen** the cat is lying out on the doorstep. **2** later (on) in; well into (the night, the wee hours, winter, etc.): **u- dagen** later in the day; **u- morgensiden** toward morning. **3** *(adv.)* out (at, in, or to a certain area, place, etc.): **folk, som hadde vært u- i styggvær før** people who had been out (at sea) in bad weather before; *dial.* **gå u-** go courting on Saturday night, go bundling.
u't/rangere [/rangsje·re] *V -te* **1** cast off, discard, scrap. **2** sidetrack (a train).
***u't/rap** *-et* landslide.
u't/rast *-a dial.* outlying parts (of a farm).
⁺**u't/rede** *V -et* **1** clear up, disentangle, straighten out. **2** *admin.* elucidate (a problem). **3** defray, meet, pay (expenses).
⁺**u't/redelse** *-n* payment (**av** of).
⁺**u't/reder** *-en, pl -e* (=***/reiar**) **1** *hist.* outfitter, supplier (of fishermen). **2** contractor (for horses to the army).
⁺**u't/re·dning** *-en* (=***/reiing**) **1** account, elucidation, explanation (**over** of); (committee) report. **2** defrayal, payment (**av** of).
⁺**u't/re·dsel** *-clen/-la, pl -ler* (=***/reisle**) *hist.* contribution, duty, tax.
⁺**u't/regning** [/reining] *-en* cf **/rekning**
***u't/reiar** *-en* cf **/reder**
***u't/reiing** *-a* cf **/redelse, /redning**
u't/reise *-a/⁺-en* departure, outward voyage: **på u-** outward bound.
⁺**u'treise/tilla·telse** *-n admin.* exit permit.
***u't/reisle** *-a* cf **/redsel**
u't/rekning *-a* (=⁺**/regning**) calculation, computation, reckoning (**av** of).
u'/trengsmål *-et*: **i u-** needlessly.
⁺**u't/rense** *V -et* cf **/renske**
⁺**u't/renske** *V -a/-et* usu. *pol.* clean out, do away with, purge; cleanse, purify.
⁺**u't/rensking** *-a/-en* cleaning out, purging; cleansing, purification.
⁺**u't/rette** *V -a/-et* carry out, do, perform; accomplish, achieve: **ikke kunne u- noe** be helpless, powerless.
⁺**utret'telig** *A* - cf **utrøttelig**
⁺**u't/rigger** *-en, pl -e* (=***-ar**) outrigger.
u't/ringa *A* (=⁺**-et**) (of neckline etc.) cut out, rounded; low-cut, revealing; décolleté.
utri'velig *A* - **1** unattractive, unpleasant; depressing, irritating; peevish, unsociable. **2** sickly; not thriving.
***u'/trivnad** *-en* **1** dwarfing, stunting; stagnation. **2** dissatisfaction, unhappiness.
⁺**u'/tro** *A* - cf **/tru**
⁺**utro'lig** *A* - cf **utrulig**
u't/rop *-et* sudden cry, shout; ejaculation, exclamation.
⁺**u't/rope** *V -te* **1** proclaim: **u- til konge** p- king. **2** cry, shout; hawk.
⁺**u't/roper** *-en, pl -e* (=***-ar**) **1** barker, peddler (who hawks his wares). **2** herald, town crier.
⁺**u'trops/tegn** [/tein] *-et* (=***/teikn**) exclamation point.
u't/ror *-en* rowing out to sea, to the fishing grounds.
⁺**u'tro/skap** *-en* cf **utru/**
u'/tru *A ⁺-/*-tt* (=⁺**u/tro**) **1** unfaithful (husband, wife). **2** disloyal, untrue (e.g. servant): **Tro og U-** True and U- (folktale by Asbjørnsen).
⁺**u't/ru·gning** *-en* hatching; incubation.
utru'lig *A* - (=⁺**utrolig**) **1** incredible, unbelievable; amazing, fantastic: **gjøre det u-e** do wonders; **de u-ste historier** the most a- tales. **2** *(adv.)* incredibly, unbelievably, etc.: **han kom seg u- fort** he recovered surprisingly fast (Sverdrup).
u'tru/skap *-en* **1** adultery, infidelity, unfaithfulness. **2** disloyalty, faithlessness.
⁺**u't/ruste** *V -a/-et* **1** equip, supply; furnish, provide (**til** for; **med** with). **2** *mil.* arm, equip, outfit. **3** bestow, endow (**med** with): **godt u-et** gifted, well endowed. **4**: **u- seg** equip oneself, prepare (**til** for).
u't/rusting *-a* (=⁺**/rustning**) **1** equipping, outfitting. **2** equipment, outfit. **3** *fig.* endowments, gifts.
⁺**u't/rydde** *V -a/-et* eliminate, eradicate, obliterate; do away with, wipe out; exterminate, kill off.
⁺**u't/ryddelse** *-n* cf **/rydding**
⁺**u'tryddelses/krig** *-en* war of extermination (**mot** against).
u't/rydding *-a* (=⁺**/ryddelse,** ⁺**rydning,** ***/rydjing**) elimination, eradication, obliteration; doing away with, wiping out; extermination (**av** of).
u'/trygg *A -trygt, pl -e* **1** dangerous, unsafe (bridge, ice, place, etc.). **2** insecure, uncertain (feeling, person); changeable (weather); precarious (existence): **u- på en (noe)** unsure of sby (sth); **leve u-t** live insecurely.
⁺**u'trygg/het** *-en* insecurity, precariousness, uncertainty: **tidens u-** the i- of the times.
⁺**u'trygghets/følelse** *-n* feeling of insecurity.
u't/rykking *-a* (=⁺**/rykning**) **1** plucking, pulling out (**av** of). **2** *mil.* sally, sortie; (of fire engine) call, trip; (of police) muster, turn-out.
⁺**u'tryknings/ordre** *-n mil.* orders to make a sally; (of fire engine) a call; (of police) order to turn out (in force).
⁺**u'trynings/vogn** [/vångn] *-a* emergency vehicle (ambulance, fire engine, police car, wrecking car, etc.).
u'/trykt *A* - unprinted, unpublished; in manuscript.
u't/røn *A dial.* westerly.
utrøs'telig *A* - inconsolable (**over** at): **være u-** (also:) refuse to be comforted.
⁺**utrøt'telig** *A* - **1** indefatigable, tireless, untiring (person). **2** endless, incessant (labor); unflagging (zeal).
***utrøy'steleg** *A* - cf **utrøstelig**
⁺**u't/sa** *pt of* **-si**
⁺**u't/sagn** [/sangn] *-et* assertion, statement; *jur.* testimony: **etter hans u-** (also:) according to what he says.
⁺**u't/salg** *-et* (=***/sal**) **1** sale, selling. **2** (clearance) sale. **3** sales outlet, store.
⁺**u'tsalgs/pris** *-en* (=***-sals/**) retail price.
⁺**u'tsalgs/vare** *-a/-en* (=***-sals/**) sale item.
⁺**u't/satt** *A* - **1** exposed (**for** to) (danger, bad weather, etc.); liable, open, susceptible (**for** to). **2** postponed, put off (**til** until). **3** *mus.* arranged (**ved** by). **4** *mil.* posted.
⁺**u't/satte** *pt of* **-sette**
⁺**u'tsatt/het** *-en* exposed position, exposure, vulnerability.
⁺**u't/se** *V -så, -sett* **1** choose, pick out, select; designate (**til** as); earmark (**til** for). **2**: **u-ende** (bad, nice) looking.
⁺**u't/seende** *-t* appearance, looks: **godt u-** good l-; **kjenne en av u-** know sby at sight; **gi det u- av at** make it appear as if; give the impression.
***u't/segn** [/sengn] *-a* cf **/sagn**
⁺**u't/seiling** *-a/-en* **1** departure (**from** a harbor). **2** entrance, exit (**of** a harbor).
⁺**u't/sende** *V -te* dispatch, send out; emit; transmit: **u-t korrespondent** special correspondent.
⁺**u't/sendelse** *-n* cf **/sending¹**
u't/sending¹ *-a/⁺-en* **1** dispatch, sending out. **2** broadcasting, (radio) transmission. **3** broadcast, telecast. **4** *phys.* emission (of electrons etc.).
u't/sending² *-en* **1** delegate, emissary,

envoy; ambassador. 2 missionary. 3 *folk.* curse; sickness brought on by magic; supernatural being.

***u't/sett** *A* - cf **/satt**

+**u't/sette** *V -satte, -satt* 1 expose, subject (**for** to). 2 postpone, put off. 3 post, station (e.g. a watch). 4 *mus.* arrange. 5: **ha noe å u- på noe, noen** find fault with sth, sby. 6 *(refl.)* **u- seg** expose oneself (**for** to), run the risk (**for** of).

+**u't/settelse** *-n* (=***/setting**) 1 delay, postponement. 2 *archaic* infant exposure. 3 putting, setting out: **u- av yngel** stocking with fingerlings. 4 *mus.* arrangement (**av** of).

+**u't/si** *V -sa, -sagt* 1 declare, express, say. 2 *archaic, dial.* discharge; evict.

u't/side [*/sie] *-a*/+*-en* outside; outer edge, side.

u't/sig *-et* 1 leakage, seepage, trickle. 2 slow outward flow, movement; outward course (of fish, fleet). 3 point of seepage; leak; outlet.

u't/sikt +*-en*/**-a* 1 view, vista (**over** of, over); lookout point, prospect. 2 chance, outlook, prospect (**til** for, of): **det har lange u-er** that may not be (happen) for a long time yet; **stille en noe i u-** hold out a prospect of sth to sby. 3 (of weather) forecast, outlook.

u'tsikts/plass *-en* lookout point.

u'tsikts/punkt *-et* 1 lookout point. 2 *fig.* perspective, viewpoint.

u'tsikts/tå'rn *-et* lookout tower.

U't/sira *Pln* twp, Rogaland.

u't/sjalting *-a*/+*-en* 1 *elec.* shunting, switching off. 2 replacement, substitution.

***u't/sjånaḍ** *-en* cf **/sende**

+**u't/skeielse** *-n* 1 debauchery, dissipation, profligacy. 2: **u-r** excesses.

+**u't/skeienḍe** *A* - dissipated, dissolute.

+**u't/skifte** *V -a/-et* replace; supplant (**med** by); change (a tire).

u't/skifting *-a* (=+**/skiftning**) 1 replacement; changing, switching (**av** of). 2 apportionment, division (of an inheritance, etc.). 3 reapportionment of farmlands (to consolidate strips into single holdings).

+**u't/skille** *V -skilte, -skilt* 1 isolate, separate (out), set off (**fra** from); sort out. 2 eliminate, remove (e.g. undesirable elements). 3 *chem.* liberate, set free; precipitate. 4 *biol.* excrete, secrete. 5: **u- seg** break away, separate (**fra** from); *chem.* precipitate.

+**u't/skipe** *V -a/-et* export (by ship), ship out.

u't/skjelling *-a*/+*-en* dressing down; scolding.

u't/skjemt *A* - (=***/skjemd,** *nt* **/skjemt**) spoiled (food; child; object); (of a woman) ruined.

+**u't/skjær** *-et* (=***/skjer**) outer reef, remote skerry.

+**u't/skjæring** *-a/-en* (=***/skjering**) 1 carving, cutting out. 2 sth carved, cut out; cut, opening.

***u't/skoren** [/skåren] *A -e/-i, pl -ne* cf **/skåret**

u't/skott *-et* (=***/skot**) 1 projection; projecting part of a house. 2 sth rejected, e.g. fish thrown back in water.

u't/skra'pning *-a*/+*-en med.* curettage, scraping.

u't/skrift *-a*/+*-en* copy, transcript (**av** of).

+**u't/skrive** *V infl as* **skrive** 1 conscript, recruit: **u- til hæren** draft into the army. 2 discharge, dismiss: **u- en fra hospitalet** let sby out of the hospital. 3 impose, levy (taxes). 4 copy, transcribe, write out. 5: **utskrevet** (of notebook) filled; (of author) finished, written out.

u't/skriving *-a*/+*-en* conscription; levy (**av** of).

+**u't/skudd** *-et* 1 reject. 2 (of people) dregs, riffraff, trash.

+**u't/skyte** *V infl as* **skyte** 1 postpone. 2 launch, shoot. 3 reject. 4 send forth (e.g. flowers). 5: **u-ende** projecting. 6: **utskutt** emptied (e.g. a gun, an area); rejected; launched.

u't/skyting *-a*/+*-en* (=+**/skytning**) 1 postponement (**av** of). 2 firing, launching, shooting. 3 rejection. 4 sending forth, out. 5 projection. 6 *typog.* imposition.

u'tskytings/rampe *-n* launching ramp.

+**u't/skåret** *A* -, *pl -ne* (=***/skoren**) 1 carved. 2 cut out; low-cut.

u't/slag *-et* 1 movement, swing, turn; deflection (of an indicator, e.g. on a scale); fluctuation: **gjøre u-et** be the decisive factor, turn (tip) the scales; clinch it. 2 effect, outcome, result; manifestation, reflection, symptom (**av** of); *med.* reaction (e.g. from vaccination): **gi seg u-** manifest itself; result. 3 pouring, throwing out (e.g. of water). 4 sink (for receiving dirty water). 5 quartering (of a hunting dog). 6 *tech.* efflorescence.

+**u't/slagen** *A -ent, pl -ne* 1 outspread, outstretched. 2 whole: **den (hele) u-ne dag** the livelong day, the whole day through.

u'tslags/bo'rḍ *-et* 1 wall-hung table. 2 drop-leaf table.

u'tslags/givenḍe *A* - (=***/gjevande**) decisive, determining.

u'tslags/vask *-en* utility sink.

u't/slett *-et med.* rash.

+**u't/slette** *V -et* annihilate, efface, obliterate; delete.

+**u't/slettelse** *-n* effacement, erasure, obliteration; annihilation, destruction; eradication.

+**u't/slitt** *A* - (=***/sliten**) tired (out); worn (out; away).

+**u't/slynge** *V -et/-te* sling, throw out; toss off (e.g. curses).

u't/slått[1] *-en* outer, outlying meadow.

u't/slått[2] *A* - 1 beaten, knocked out: **få tennene u-** get one's teeth k- out. 2 beaten, defeated, worsted: **en u- rival** a d- rival. 3 (of hair) down, flowing, hanging loose; (of arms, wings) outspread, outstretched. (See **slå, utslagen.**)

+**u't/smykke** *V -et/-smykte* decorate, embellish; *fig.* embroider.

+**u't/smykning** *-en* decoration, embellishment (**av** of).

+**u't/snakket** *A* - talked out; talked over.

+**u't/snitt** *-et* 1 excerpt, extract, section (**av** of). 2 *math.* segment (of a population).

+**u't/solgt** *A* - sold out: **u- fra forlaget** out of print; **u- hus** full house.

+**u't/sondre** *V -a/-et physiol.* secrete; excrete.

+**u't/sone** *V -a/-te lit.* atone for, expiate; **u- seg med** be reconciled with.

u't/soning *-a*/+*-en* 1 *eccl.* atonement. 2 reconciliation.

+**u't/sorte're** *V -te* sort out.

+**u't/sovet** [/såvet] *A* - (=***/soven**) slept out, thoroughly rested.

+**u't/speide** *V -a/-et* spy on (a person etc.); spy out (secrets, etc.).

u't/spekule'rt *A* - crafty, scheming, wily.

u't/spent *A* - extended, outstretched, stretched.

+**u't/spill** *-et* (=***/spel**) lead (in card playing): **ha u-et** *fig.* have the initiative.

+**u't/spille** *V -spilte* 1: **handlingen u-es** the action takes place. 2: **u-t** finished; played out; **stykket er u-t** the play is no longer running.

+**u't/spi'lt** *A* - bloated, dilated, distended.

+**u't/spione're** *V -te* spy on (a person etc.); spy out (secrets etc.).

u't/spjåka *A* - (=+**-et**) *derog.* bedizened, dolled up, rigged out.

u't/sprang *-et* jump, leap (as from airplane).

+**u't/spre** *V -dde/-dte* spread (e.g. rumors): **u-dt** spread around, out.

+**u't/spredelse** *-n* spreading (**av** of) (e.g. rumors).

+**u't/spring** *-et* 1 fountainhead, source, wellspring; point of origin. 2 projection (e.g. on building).

u't/sprungen [/sprongen] *A* +*-et, pl -ne* (of flowers) full-blown, in bloom, open; (of trees) leafed out.

+**u't/spørre** *V -spurte, -spurt* question closely.

+**u't/spørring** *-a/-en* (=***/spørjing**) interrogation, questioning (**av** of).

+**u't/staffere** *V -te* decorate, trim; bedeck, bedizen; dress up, rig up, trick out.

+**u't/stede** *V -te* draw (up), issue.

+**u't/stedelse** *-n* issuance, issue (**av** of).

+**u't/steder** *-en, pl -e* drawer, issuer (**av** of).

***u't/stelling** *-a* cf **/stilling**

+**u't/stikker** *-en, pl -e* (=***-ar**) projecting pier, wharf.

+**u'tstikker/kai** *-a/-en* (=***-ar/**) projecting pier, wharf.

+**u't/stille** *V -stilte, -stilt* 1 display, exhibit, show. 2: **u-t** posted; set out.

+**u't/stiller** *-en, pl -e* exhibitor.

u't/stilling *-a*/+*-en* 1 display; exhibit, exhibition, exposition; show, showing (**av** of). 2 posting (of sentries).

+**u'tstillings/gjenstanḍ** *-en* object for, on display; exhibit.

u'tstillings/loka'le *-t, pl* +**-r**/***-** display room, exhibition hall, showroom.

+**u'tstillings/vindu** *-et* display, show window.

+**u't/stilte** *pt of* **-stille**

+**u't/stoḍ** *pt of* **-stå**

u't/stoppa *A* - (=+**-et**) stuffed; padded.

u't/stopping *-a*/+*-en* 1 stuffing, taxidermy. 2 padding (**av** of).

u't/strakt *A* - 1 outstretched, stretched out: **ligge u-** lie full-length. 2 extended, extensive; sprawling; wide; far-flung; comprehensive, far-reaching: **finne u- anvendelse** be extensively applied.

+**u't/strekke** *V infl as* **strekke**[1] extend, stretch (out).

+**u't/strekning** *-en* 1 extending, extension, stretching out. 2 area, dimensions, size: **et punkt har ingen u-** a point has no area. 3 degree, extent: **i stor u-** to a great e-.

***u't/strekt** *A* - cf **/strakt**

u't/stridd *A -/*-stridt*: **han har u-** his struggles are at an end, he is at peace.

u't/stryking *-a*/+*-en* (=+**/strykning**) crossing out, deletion (**av** of).

+**u't/strømning** *-en* 1 flow(ing), issuing forth, streaming out. 2 flow, emanation, stream.

+**u't/stråle** *V -te* radiate (heat, light); emit.

u't/stråling *-a*/+*-en* radiation (**av** of); emanation, emission.

u't/stude'rt *A* - mannered, studied.

u't/stykking *-a*/+*-en* (=+**/stykning**) parcelling out; division (into lots, etc.).

u't/styr *-et* 1 equipment; outfit; appointments, furnishings; fittings, trappings; décor, (stage) properties. 2 trousseau. 3 format, getup (e.g. of a book), makeup (of a newspaper article, person, etc.).

u't/styre *V -te* 1 equip, fit out, furnish; provide, supply; endow (with e.g. talent): **sparsomt u-t** sparsely furnished. 2 decorate; get up, make up (a newspaper article, book, etc.).

u'tstyrs/forret'ning *-a*/+*-en* store selling household linens, draperies.

u'tstyrs/stykke *-t, pl* +**-r**/***-** play with elegant settings.

+ Bokmål; * Nynorsk; ° Dialect.
After letter: ' stress (Acc. 1); ` tone, stress (Acc. 2); · length.
Below letter: . not pronounced.

+**u't/støte** *V -te lit.* 1 push out; expel. 2 eject, emit. 3 utter, let out (e.g. an oath).

+**u't/stå** *V -stod, -stått* 1 bear, endure; suffer, undergo: **jeg kan ikke u-** I can't stand, I loathe. 2 be postponed, wait.

+**u't/stående** *A* - prominent, protruding: **med u- øyne** popeyed.

+**u't/suge** *V -de/-et/-saug, -d/-et* squeeze, suck dry; bleed white, grind down.

+**u't/suger** *-en, pl -e* (=*-**ar**) bloodsucker, extortionist.

+**u't/sulte** *V -a/-et* starve.

+**u't/sunget** [/songet] *A* - *archaic* sung (to the end).

+**u't/svevelse** *-n* (usu. *pl*) debauchery, dissipation; riotous, wild living; fast life.

+**u't/svevende** *A* - debauched, dissolute, riotous.

+**u't/sydd** *A* - embroidered (**med** with).

u't/syn *-et/*-a* 1 perspective, view. 2 view (of the outside), vista. 3 lookout (point), overlook.

***u't/synning** *-en* southwesterly wind.

+**u't/sæd** *-en* (=*/**sæde**) 1 planting, seeding, sowing. 2 (sown) seed.

u't/søkt *A* - 1 choice, picked, select; exquisite; studied: **en u- fornærmelse** a studied insult; **med u- høflighet** with elaborate courtesy; **med u- smak** with exquisite taste. 2 *(adv.)* highly: **et u- spotsk smil** a highly scornful smile (Boo).

+**u't/så** *pt of* **-se**

utt. =**uttalt**

+**u't/ta** *V -tok, -tatt* 1 select: **u- til** s- for (e.g. Olympic games). 2: **u- patent** take out a patent. 3: **u-tt** removed, taken out, withdrawn.

u't/tak *-et* 1 removal, withdrawal (**av** of) (of money from bank); drain, drawing (upon). 2 departure point; start. 3 selection (**av** of).

u't/taking *-a/+-en* selection (**av** of).

u'ttakings/komité· *-en* selecting committee (for sports events).

u'ttakings/renn *-et* ski trial(s).

u't/tale[1] *-n/*-a* pronunciation (**av** of).

u't/tale[2] *V -a/-te* 1 articulate, pronounce; declare, express, state. 2 *(refl.)* **u- seg** express oneself, express one's opinion; advocate, speak (**for** in favor of, **imot** against).

+**u't/talelse** *-n* comment, expression of opinion, remark; declaration, pronouncement, statement (**om** about).

+**u't/ta·lt** *A* - marked, pronounced; express(ed): **med den u-te hensikt** with the express purpose.

+**u't/telling** *-a/-en* disbursement.

u't/tenkt *A* - 1 conceived; thought out, up. 2 contrived, invented.

u't/tilbei·ns *A* - (=+/**bens**): **gå u-** walk with toes pointed out.

+**u't/tje·nt** *A* - 1 (of military duty) completed, served. 2 worn-out.

u't/tog [/tåg] *-et* excerpt, extract.

+**u't/tok** *pt of* **-ta**

+**u't/tredelse** *-n* 1 retirement, withdrawal. 2 *med.* extravasation (of blood).

u't/trekk *-et* 1 drawing out; extension. 2 (organ) stop. 3 (trombone) slide. 4 (sliding) section (of spyglass). 5 *chem.* extract; distillate.

u'ttrekks/seng *-a* (children's) extension bed.

u't/trykk *-et* expression (**for** of) (contempt, nationalism, satisfaction, etc.); look; term, phrase (**for** for): **et merkelig u- i ansiktet** a strange l- on one's face; **gi seg u-** show itself; find expression (**i** in); **kan De si meg u-et for "thank you" på norsk** can you tell me the e- for "t- y-" in Norwegian.

+**u't/trykke** *V -trykte* (=*-**je**) 1 express, give expression to, voice (a feeling, relationship, thought, etc.). 2 *(refl.)* **u- seg** express oneself.

+**uttryk'kelig** *A* - (=***uttrykkjeleg**) clear, express; definite, explicit: **nevne u-** mention by name, explicitly, expressly.

***u't/trykkje** *V -trykte* cf /**trykke**

u'ttrykks/full *A* expressive: **et u-t ansikt** (also) a sensitive face; **lese u-t** read with expression.

u'ttrykks/laus *A* (=+/**løs**) blank, expressionless, unexpressive.

u'ttrykks/middel *-elet/-midlet, pl +-midler/*-el* means of expression.

u'ttrykks/måte *-n* phraseology, style, way of speaking; delivery, diction.

u't/trykt *A* - express, explicit: **sin fars u-e bilde** a spitting image of his father.

u't/trøndsk *A* - from outer (i.e. southern) Trøndelag.

u't/trådt *A* - 1 well-worn, worn (down, out). 2 hackneyed, trite. 3 *med.* extravasated (of blood).

u't/tun *-et* outer farmyard, around which storehouses, barns are located.

+**u't/tvære** *V -a/-et* draw out, spin out: **u-ende, u-et** prolix, verbose.

u't/tynning *-a/+-en* thinning out (of hair, trees, etc.); watering down (of wine etc.).

u't/tæ·rt *A* - emaciated, wasted.

u't/tømmende *A* - exhaustive, thorough: **behandle u-** exhaust, treat e-ly.

+**u't/tømt** *A* - (=*/**tømd**) drained, empty; depleted, exhausted, used up: **mine krefter er u-** my forces are spent.

u't/tørka *A* - (=+-**et**) dried out, up; desiccated, drained dry, run dry; (of marsh) reclaimed; (of branch, part of body) withered.

+**u't/tørret** *A* - cf /**tørka**

u'/tukt *+-en/*-a* fornication, prostitution: **u- mot mindreårige** sexual abuse of minors.

u'/tuktig *A* - immoral, lewd, obscene.

u'/tur *-en* bad luck.

***u'/turvande** *A* - needless, unnecessary.

***u't/vakt** *A* - exhausted from lack of sleep, from keeping watch.

***u't/vald** *A -valt* cf /**valgt**

+**u't/valg** *-et* (=*/**val**) 1 choice, selection (**av** of): **det naturlige u-** natural s-; **ha stort u- i stoffer** have a large choice of textiles. 2 collection, selected works; anthology. 3 committee; board, commission.

+**u't/valgt** *A* - chosen, selected; choice, hand-picked, select: (esp. *bibl.*) **de u-e** the elect; **ens u-e** one's chosen mate.

+**u't/valgte** *pt of* **-velge**

+**u't/vandre** *V -a/-et* emigrate (**fra** from; **til** to).

+**u't/vandrer** *-en, pl -e* (=*-**ar**) emigrant.

u't/vandring *-a/+-en* emigration.

+**u't/vanne** *V -et* 1 freshen (soak in water, e.g. salted food, to remove salt). 2 dilute, water down (also *fig.*): **u-et aksjekapital** watered stock; **u-ing av prinsipper** watering down of principles.

+**u't/vant** *pt of* **-vinne**

+**u't/ve** *-en* longing to leave home; yearning for adventure.

u't/ved *P* out by; on the outer side of.

u't/veg *-en* (=+/**vei**) 1 exit, way out: **møte en på u-** meet sby on his way out. 2 possibility (**til** of), remedy (**til** for), way out; recourse, resort, solution: **det kunne bli u- til kjole og motorsykkel** it might be a way of getting a dress and a motorcycle (Grieg); **prøve alle u-er** try every means.

u't/veksle *V -a/-et* exchange, trade: **u- studenter** e- students.

u't/veksling *-a* 1 exchange (**av** of). 2 *tech.* gear; transmission.

u't/vekst *-en* 1 (abnormal) growth, protuberance; cancer. 2 *fig.* excrescence, growth (**på** on).

+**u't/velge** *V -valgte* choose, pick out, select. (See also **utvalgt**.)

+**u't/velgelse** *-n* (=*/**veljing**) 1 choice, selection (**av** of): **naturlig u-** natural s-. 2 *(bibl.)* election, predestination.

***u't/vendes** *Av* on the outside.

u't/vendig *A* - 1 exterior, external, outside: **til u- bruk** for e- use. 2 *fig.* external, outward, superficial: **u- teater** s- acting, drama.

+**u'tvendig/het** *-en* superficiality.

***u't/verke** *V -a* cf /**virke**

***u't/vertes** *Av* cf /**vortes**

u'/tvetydig *A* - clear, unambiguous, unequivocal.

u't/vide [*/vie] *V -a/+-et* 1 enlarge, expand, extend; dilate, stretch, widen: **u- stemmeretten** extend the vote. 2 *math.* raise: **u- en brøk** r- a fraction. 3 *(refl.)* **u- seg** enlarge, expand.

+**u't/videlse** *-n* (=*/**viding**) 1 enlargement, expansion, extension (**av** of). 2 area of expansion; addition.

u't/vikle *V -a/+-et* 1 develop (ability, muscles, technique, theory, etc.); bring forth, encourage, foster. 2 elaborate (on), set forth, unfold (an idea, plan, etc.). 3 emit, give off (a gas, heat, etc.); generate (power, steam, etc.). 4 *mil.* deploy. 5 *(refl.)*: **u- seg** develop; evolve (**til** into); form; *mil.* deploy.

u't/vikling *-a/+-en* 1 development; advancement, growth; esp. *biol.* evolution. 2 exposition, expounding. 3 emission, liberation (e.g. of gas); generation (e.g. of heat). 4 *mil.* deployment.

u'tviklings/gang *-en* development, process of development; evolution.

u'tviklings/histo·rie *-a/+-en* history of (sth's) development.

u'tviklings/land *-et* developing country.

u'tviklings/lære *-a/+-en* (doctrine of) Evolution.

+**u'tviklings/trinn** *-et* stage of development, evolution.

+**utvi'lsom** [-såmm] *A -t, pl -me* (=*-**sam**) 1 clear, obvious; indubitable, undoubted. 2: **u-t** *(adv.)* without a doubt; undoubtedly.

+**u't/vinne** *V -vant, -vunnet* extract, obtain, recover: **u- salt av sjøvann** o- salt from sea water.

u't/vinning *-a/+-en* extraction, reduction (**av** of).

+**u't/virke** *V -a/-et* (=*/**verke**) bring (it) about; obtain, procure (through persuasion, prayers, etc.).

+**u't/vise** *V -te* 1 send out; eject, evict, expel; banish, deport, exile (**fra** from). 2 display, point out, show; evince, make evident, manifest: **u- stor forsiktighet** show great care. 3 point out (trees for felling).

+**u't/visket** *A* - blurred, dim, indistinct; smudged; *fig.* (also) washed out.

+**u'tvi·snings/ordre** *-n* deportation order.

+**u't/vokst** *A* - full-grown, grown (up).

u't/vortes *A* - 1 exterior, external; outer, outward. 2 *fig.* external, superficial. 3 (as noun) appearance, exterior.

u'/tvungen [/tvongen] *A +-ent, pl -ne* free (and easy), unconstrained; spontaneous, unforced; natural, unaffected.

+**utvungen/het** *-en* absence of restraint, ease (of manner); naturalness, spontaneity.

+**u't/vunnet** *pp of* **-vinne**

u't/vær *-et* outer (coastal) fishing stations, villages.

***u'/ty** *-et* cf /**tøy**[1]

***u'/tyd** *A* difficult, severe, unfriendly (person).

uty'delig *A* - indistinct, unclear, vague; dim, faint: **snakke u-** mumble.

***u'/tyrst** *A* - cf /**tørst**

***u'/tyske** *-t* 1 ugly, dangerous person or animal; brute, monster, rogue. 2 ogre, troll.

***utø'meleg** *A* - bottomless, inexhaustible.

u'/tørst *A* -: **drikke seg u-** drink one's fill; quench one's thirst.

+u't/øse *V -te* pour (out, forth), shower, vent (e.g. one's anger); (of blood) shed, spill.
+u't/øve *V -de* 1 exercise; practice. 2 exert (e.g. influence). 3 perform (e.g. great deeds).
u't/øvende *A* - 1: **u- kunstner** practicing artist; **u- musiker** performing musician. 2 *pol.* executive (authority): **den u- makt er hos Kongen** the e- power rests with the King (Norw. Constitution).
+u'/tøy[1] *-et* (=***/ty**) vermin (e.g. lice, plant lice, termites, mice, rats, etc.).
u't/øy[2] *-a* outer(most) island.
+u'/tøylet *A* - unbridled, unreined; undisciplined, unharnessed: **en u- fantasi** an unchecked imagination.
***u'/tål** *-et* impatience.
utå'lelig *A* - intolerable, unbearable (heat, pain, thought, etc.); insufferable (arrogance, insolence, person).
u'/tålig *A* - (=***/tolig**) *dial.* 1 intolerable, unbearable; sensitive. 2 impatient (**med** with).
u/tålmo'dig [also u'/] *A* - impatient (**etter** for, **over** at).
+utålmo'dig/het *-en* impatience.
u'/tålsam** *A* (=/tolsam**) cf **utålsom**
+utå'lsom· *A* 1 impatient, restless. 2 intolerant, unforbearing.
+u't/ånde *V -et* die, expire.
***u'/tått** *-en* inclination, tendency to evil; vice.
uunngå'elig *A* - inescapable, inevitable, unavoidable: **finne seg i det u-e** bow to necessity, resign oneself to the inevitable.
uunnskyl'delig *A* - inexcusable, unforgivable, unpardonable.
+uunnvæ'rlig *A* - (=***-verleg**) indispensable; essential.
u'/utforska *A* - (=**+-et**) unexplored.
+uutgrun'nelig *A* - (=***-grundeleg**) 1 inscrutable, unfathomable; impenetrable. 2 strange, unaccountable; mysterious.
+uuthol'delig *A* - intolerable, unbearable, unendurable (**for** for).
+uutsi'gelig *A* - (=***u(ut)seieleg**) inexpressible, unspeakable, unutterable: **hva ei med ord kan nevnes i det rikeste sprog, det u-e, skal diktet røbe dog** what words cannot express, even in the richest language, the inexpressible, shall yet be revealed in poetry (Welhaven).
uutslet'telig *A* - indelible (e.g. impression).
uutsli'telig *A* - imperishable, indestructible; indefatigable, tireless; perennial.
+uutslokkelig [-slok'keli] *A* - 1 inextinguishable. 2 unquenchable (enthusiasm, hate, thirst, etc.).
+uuttøm'melig *A* - (=***u(ut)tømeleg**) inexhaustible (subject, supply); unfailing.
u'/utvikla *A* - (=**+-et**) 1 backward, undeveloped (country, industry, society); embryonic; rudimentary. 2 (of a person) immature; undeveloped.
***u'/van** *A* cf **/vant**
***u'/vand** *A* 1 not fussy, not particular. 2 plain, simple: **u- mat** plain food. 3 easy, not difficult, simple.
u'/vane *-n* bad habit: **han har den u- å snakke for lavt** he has the b- h- of talking too softly.
uva'nlig *A* - unusual; extraordinary, uncommon: **en u- stor og vakker mann** an unusually large and handsome man (Snorre).
+u'/vant *A* - (=***/van**) 1 unaccustomed, unused (**med, til** to). 2 new, unfamiliar, unknown: **det u-e** the unknown.
u'/varig *A* - brief, fleeting, not lasting.
***u'/varleg** *A* - incautious, unwary; careless.
u'/vaska *A* - (=**+-et**) unwashed.
U'v/dal *Pln* twp, Buskerud.
+u'/vederhef·tig [also -hef'-] *A* - irresponsible, unreliable, untrustworthy.
+uvederhef'tig/het *-en* irresponsibility, unreliability, untrustworthiness.
u'/vedkommende *A* - (=***/vedkomande**) 1 extraneous, irrelevant: **det er saken u-** that's beside the point. 2 (of a person) unauthorized; (as noun) interloper, intruder: **u- forbys adgang** unauthorized persons keep out.
+uve'gerlig *A* - 1 *lit., obs.* inescapable, unavoidable. 2 *(adv.)* inevitably, of necessity; unfailingly.
***u'/veges** *Av* astray, off the path.
+u'/veisom [/-såmm] *A -t, pl -me* impassable, rough (terrain).
+u'/vel· *Av* 1 ill, indisposed, unwell: **føle seg u-** feel unwell. 2 ill-at-ease, uncomfortable.
u'/velkom·men *A +-ent, pl -velkomne* (=***/velkomen**) unwelcome.
u'/venn *-en* (=***/ven**) enemy (person with whom one is on bad terms): **bli u-er** fall out, quarrel (**med** with); **være u-er** be on bad terms, be unfriendly, not be friends (**med** with).
u'/vennlig [also -venn'-] *A* - (=***/venleg**) unfriendly; ungracious, unkind.
+uvenn'lig/het *-en* unfriendliness; ungraciousness, unkindness.
u'venn/skap *-en* 1 enmity, hostility (**mellom** between; **mot** to). 2 discord, friction, strife; quarrel.
u'/venta *A* - (=**+-et**) unexpected; unforeseen, unlooked for.
***u'/ver** *-et* cf **/vær**[1]
u'/verdig *A* - 1 unworthy (**til** of); humble, insignificant. 2 disgraceful, shameful.
u'/verje *-a* (=**u/verge**) *dial.* sth used as a weapon (not intended to be so used); improper or dangerous weapon (e.g. a stone).
***u'/verkeleg** *A* - cf **/virkelig**
***u'/verksam** *A* cf **/virksom**
***u'vers/bolk** *-en* period of bad weather, stormy season.
***u'vers/ri** *-a* cf **uværs/**
+u'/vesen *-et* bad practice, offensive, scandalous behavior.
u'/vesentlig [also -ve'-] *A* - immaterial, unessential, unimportant (**for** for); inconsiderable, insignificant.
***u'/vete** *V -a* cf **/vite**
u'/vett *-et* 1 folly, foolishness, unwisdom. 2 faint, swoon, unconsciousness: **falle i u-** faint. 3 delirium, raving: **tale u-** rave.
***u'/vette** *-t folk.* evil spirit.
u'/vettug *A* - (=**+/vettig**) foolish, senseless, stupid; crazy, mad.
+uvi'den/het *-en* cf **uviten/**
u'/vigd *A -/*-vigt* unconsecrated.
u'/viktig *A* unimportant: **ikke u-** not negligible.
u'/vildig *A - jur.* impartial, unbiassed, unprejudiced.
***u'/vilja** *A* - cf **/viljande**
***u'/viljande** *A* - involuntary, unintentional.
u'/vilje *-n* 1 reluctance, unwillingness (**til** to). 2 ill will; antipathy, aversion, dislike: **ha (føle, nære) u- mot** have (feel, nourish) antipathy to.
***u'/viljug** *A* - cf **/villig**[1]
uvilkå'rlig [also u'/] *A* - 1 involuntary, spontaneous. 2 *(adv.)* involuntarily; inevitably, invariably: **høyere lønninger må u- føre til høyere priser** higher wages unfailingly lead to higher prices; **jeg måtte u- smile** I couldn't help smiling.
u'/villig[1] *A* - 1 grudging, reluctant, unwilling (**til** to). 2 sulky, sullen; brusque, ungracious.
+u'/villig[2] *A* - cf **/vildig**
+u/vir'kelig *A* - unreal; intangible, vague.
+u'/virksom [-såmm] *A -t, pl -me* idle, inactive, passive.
+u'virksom/het [also -vir'k-] *-en* idleness, inactivity, passivity.
uvis'nelig *A* - imperishable, unfading; eternal, undying.
u'/viss *A* 1 doubtful, dubious, uncertain; hesitating: **på det u-e** hanging in the air, indefinite; haphazardly, at random. 2 *(adv.)*: **u-t hvorfor** for some unknown reason.
***u'/visse** *-a* cf **uviss/het**
+u'viss/het *-en* uncertainty; doubtfulness: **holde en i u-** keep sby in suspense.
***u'/vit** *-et* cf **/vett**
u'/vite** *V -a* (=/vete**) faint, swoon.
uvi'tende *A* - 1 ignorant, uninformed (**om** of). 2 uneducated.
+uvi'ten/het *-en* ignorance: **leve (sveve) i lykkelig u- om** be blissfully ignorant of.
+u'/vitenska·pelig *A* - (=**/vitskaplig**) unscientific; unscholarly.
***u'/vitug** *A* - cf **/vettug**
***u'v/led** *-en* wrist.
u/vurde'rlig *A* - inestimable, invaluable, priceless: **av u- betydning** of inestimable significance.
***u'/vy·rde** *-a* cf **/vørde**
***u'/vyrden** [/vøren] *A -e/-i, pl -ne* cf **/vørden**
u'/væ·pna *A* - (=**+-et**) unarmed.
+u'/vær[1] *-et* (=***/ver**) bad (heavy, rough) weather; squall, storm (also *fig.*): **det trekker opp til u- a** storm is brewing.
***u'/vær**[2] *A* dissatisfied.
+u'værs/fugl *-en* 1 bird flying in a storm; *fig.* ship or person out in a storm. 2 *folk.* bird which heralds a storm; *lit.* prophet of doom.
+u'værs/himmel *-en* stormy (threatening) sky.
+u'værs/ri *-a* 1 short, sudden storm. 2 short period of bad weather.
+u'værs/svanger *A -ert, pl -re* (of sky, weather) lowering, threatening.
+u'værs/tegn [/tein] *-et* sign of a storm.
u'/vø·rde *-a* (=**+/vøre**) *dial.* 1 carelessness, negligence; slovenliness. 2 careless, heedless person; daredevil.
u'/vø·rden *A +-ent, pl -ne* (=**+/vøren**) 1 careless, heedless, reckless; slapdash; rough (in speech). *2 contemptuous: **der fer liksom noko u-e over Viv a** c- expression passed over V-'s face (Vesaas).
+u'/ærbø·dig *A* - disrespectful, irreverent (**mot** to).
***u'ærleg/dom** *-(m)en* crookedness, dishonesty.
u'/ærlig [also -æ'r-] *A* - 1 crooked, dishonest. 2 *archaic* ignominious, without honor.
***u'/ærug** *A* - discourteous, impolite.
u'/økono·misk *A* - 1 unprofitable, unremunerative. 2 uneconomical, wasteful.
+u'/ønsket *A* - unwanted, unwished for (e.g. child); undesirable (e.g. person).
u'/øvd *A -/*-øvt* unpracticed, untrained; awkward, inexperienced.
+u'/øvet *A* - cf **/øvd**
u'/ånd **-a/+-en* evil spirit; lack of spirit, poor spirit.
+u'/å·pnet *A* - unopened.
u'/år *-et* bad year (for crops), crop failure, famine.

+ Bokmål; * Nynorsk; ° Dialect.
After letter: ' stress (Acc. 1); ` tone, stress (Acc. 2); · length.
Below letter: . not pronounced.

V

v [ve'] -*en* (letter) V, v.
V=venstre; vest
v.=veg(en); venstre; verbum; vest; von.
v/=ved[2]
va'[1] -*et cf* **vad**[3]
va'[2] *V -dde* (=**vade**) ford, wade: **v- i den hvite snøen** w- through the white snow; **v- i penger** be rolling in money.
vab'be *V -a/+-et* plod, slog, trudge; slop, splash about (in mud, swamp, etc.).
+**va'/bein** -*et* cf **vad/**
vab'le[1] *+-n/*-a* blister: **slå v-r** blister.
vab'le[2] *V -a/+-et* blister.
vab'let(e) *A* - blistered.
va'd[1] *-et/+-en dial.* fishline.
va'd[2] *-et/+-en* seine.
va'd[3] -*et* ford, fording place; shallows.
va'd/bein -*et* saddle-shaped spool fastened to gunwale (to let the fishing line run over).
va'de [*va'e] *V -de* cf **va**[2]
va'de/fot [*va'e/] -*en, pl +-føtter/*-føter* foot of a wading bird.
va'de/fugl [*va'e/] -*en* wading bird.
+**va'der** -*en, pl -e* (=***-ar**) **1** wading bird. **2** *(pl)* waders.
+**va'de/sted** -*et* ford, fording place.
va'de/støvel -*elen, pl -ler* wading boot.
va'd/ho'rn -*et dial.* **1**=**vadbein. 2** (cow) horn to blow on.
+**vad'/mel** -*et* cf **/mål**
+**vad'mels/klær** *pl* clothes of homespun.
vad'mels/kufte -*a* homespun coat.
vad'/mål -*et* frieze, homespun (cloth).
***vad're** *V -a* **1** wander aimlessly: **v- rundt** stumble around. **2** *(refl.)*: **v- seg bort, vekk** get lost, lose one's way.
vad'/sekk -*en, pl *-er* carpetbag, traveling bag, valise.
Vad's/ø *Pln* seaport, Finnmark.
vaf'fel -*elen, pl vafler* **1** waffle. **2** *fam.* box on the ear.
+**vaf'fel/hjerte** -*t* (=***/hjarte**) heart-shaped waffle (usu. one section of a whole w-).
vaf'fel/jern [/jæ'rn] -*et* waffle iron.
vaf'fel/kake -*a dial.* waffle.
+**vaf'fel/søm'** -*men* (=***/saum**) smocking.
vaf'le *V -a/+-et* box, cuff.
vaf'se *V -a/+-et fam. plod*, wade.
va'g *A* vague; dim, hazy, indefinite; (of sound) muted, subdued: **en v- uro** a vague uneasiness.
vagabon'd -*en* hobo, tramp, vagabond.
vagabonde're *V -te* bum, knock around: **v-ende strøm** *elec.* stray current.
+**vagg'** -*en* dump car (on a RR train).
vag'ge[1] -*a* **1** =**vagg. 2** short sled for hauling timber.
vag'ge[2] *V -a/+-et* rock, sway from side to side; (of flowers) wave; roll, walk with a rolling gait: **v- i hoftene** swing one's hips.
vag'ge/stein -*en* rocking, tippy boulder.
+**va'g/het** -*en* vagueness; dimness, haziness.
vagi'na -*en anat.* vagina.
vag'l -*en/-et* (=**vagle**[1]) perch, roost.
vag'le[1] *-n/-t* cf **vagl**
vag'le[2] *V -a/+-et*: **v- seg** roost, go to roost.
vagn [vang'n] -*en zool., dial.* killer whale (Orcinus orca).
+**va'/ho'rn** -*et* cf **vad/**
vai'd -*en* **1** *bot.* woad (Isatis tinctoria). **2** wood (dye).
vai'e *V -a/+-et/+-de* (of flag etc.) **fly; flutter, wave; float, sway.**
vai'er -*eren, pl +-ere/+-rer* (=**wire**) cable, wire.
vai'sen/hus -*et* orphanage.
va'k[1] -*et* **1** (of fish) jump, surfacing. **2**: **ligge på v-** keep watch.
va'k[2] *A dial.* **1** awake; sleeping lightly, wakeful. **2** sharp, wary, wide-awake.
vakanse [vakang'se] -*n* vacancy (of a position).
vakan't *A* - vacant (of a position).
va'ke[1] *V -te/+-a* (of fish) jump, surface; (of boat) float, stay afloat.
va'ke[2] *V -te/+-a* (=+**våke**) **1** be, lie awake. **2** (keep) watch (**over on,** over); be watchful.
va'ke/kone [*/kåne] -*a* (woman) night watcher (either over a patient or at a wake).
va'ken *A +-ent, pl -ne* (=+**våken**) **1** awake, wakeful, wide-awake. **2** alert, vigilant. **3** bright, wide-awake (person).
va'ke/natt -*a*/-en, *pl -netter* vigil, wake.
va'ker -*en, pl +-e* **1** *aeronaut., naut.* vane, windsock. **2** float (on a fishing net).
+**vakk'** *pt of* **vekke**[2]
vak'ker *A -ert, pl vakre* **1** attractive, handsome (person, place, position, sum, thing, etc.); comely, pretty: **en v- dag** one fine day, one of these days. **2** good, nice (behavior, manner, person, weather, etc.); commendable, laudable (action, behavior, intention, etc.): **be v-t** ask nicely, beg; (ironic) **det skulle være v-t** that would be a fine kettle of fish; **vel og v-t** safe and sound. **3** *(adv.)*: **fare v-t** be careful (**med** with), treat carefully.
vak'ker/hand -*a dial.* right hand.
vak'le *V -a/+-et* **1** (of a building, empire, person, etc.) reel, totter; stagger, sway, wobble: **v-ende** shaky (belief, theory, etc.). **2** hesitate, vacillate, waver; shilly-shally.
vak'le/voren [also +/vårren, */våren] *A -ent, pl -ne* **1** rickety, tottery, wobbly. **2** shilly-shallying, vacillating.
vak'ne *V -a/+-et* (=+**våkne**) wake; awake, awaken, waken: **v- opp** wake up; **en v-ende interesse** a growing interest.
***vak'se** *pp of* **vekse**
***vak'sen** *A -e/-i, pl -ne* cf **voksen**
***vak'si** *pp of* **vekse**
vaksinasjo'n -*en* vaccination.
vaksinasjo'ns/attes't -*en* vaccination certificate.
vaksi'ne -*n* vaccine.
vaksine're *V -te* vaccinate.
***vak'ster** -*en* insomnia, vigil, wakefulness.
vak't[1] *-a/+-en* **1** guard, watch (also *mil., naut.*); (watch) duty (e.g. in an emergency ward); vigil: **femten (seksten) mil i v-a** *fam.* really making steam, under full steam; **gå v-** make the rounds on a watch; **holde v-** keep watch; **slutte, slå v-** form a guard, set up a watch (**om** around). **2** sentinel, sentry, watchman; person on duty. **3** guardhouse, place of watch.
vak't[2] *A - eccl.* converted.
***vak'tar** -*en* cf **vokter**
vak't/arres't -*en mil., naut.* imprisonment (in guardhouse, or brig).
+**vak't/avlø'sning** -*en* changing of the guard; relief of the guard, the watch.
vak'te[1] *V -a/+-et* cf **vokte**
+**vak'te**[2] *pt of* **vekke**[2]
vak'tel -*elen, pl -ler zool.* **quail (Coturnix coturnix).**
vak't/havende *A* - on duty, on watch: **v- offiser** *naut.* officer of the watch.
+**vak't/hold** -*et* (=***/hald**) guard, watch: **ha v-** have the w-, stand w-.
vak't/hund -*en* watchdog.
vak't/kommandø'r -*en mil.* commander, officer of the watch.
vak't/mann -*en, pl -menn/*-menner* guard, watchman.
+**vak't/mester** -*en, pl -e* (=***/meister**) **1** caretaker; (in a museum) attendant. **2** *hist.* commander of a watch.
vak't/post -*en* guard, sentry.
vak't/skifte -*t, pl +-r/*-* changing of the guard, the watch.
+**vak't/som'** *A -t, pl -me* vigilant, watchful; alert, observant.
+**vaktsom/het** -*en* vigilance, watchfulness.
vak't/stue -*a* (=**/stove**) guardroom.
+**vak't/tjeneste** -*n* (=***/teneste**) *naut.* duty, watch; *mil.* guard duty.
vak't/tå'rn -*et* watch tower.
va'kuum -*et* vacuum.
va'kuum/bremse *-a/+-en* (=+**/brems**) air brake.
va'kuum/meter -*eret, pl -er/+-re* vacuum gauge.
va'kuum/pakka *A* - (=+**-et**) vacuum packed.
va'l[1] -*en* **1** *myth., poet.* fallen warriors; warriors dedicated to death on the battlefield. **2** *poet.* field of battle: **så samles vi på v-en** we'll gather on the battlefield (Internationale).
***va'l**[2] -*en dial.* underwater ridge **or** shoreline, dry at low tide.
***va'l**[3] -*et* cf **valg**
val.=valuta
Va'l/berg *Pln* twp, Nordland.
va'l/bjørk -*a* birch with twisted grain and irregular rings, used for furniture.
***va'l/bolk** -*en* period between elections, term of office.
Val'/borg *Prn (f)*
va'l/bygg -*et hist.* two-rowed barley.
val'd[1] -*et* hunting preserve.
***val'd**[2] -*et* **1** dominion, power: **ha v- over** have d- over; **i mitt v-** in my p-. **2** (area of) dominion, possessions, territory. **3** brutality, force, tyranny (=**vold**).
***val'de**[1] *V -a* have dominion over, possess, rule.
***val'de**[2] *V -a* cf **volde**
***val'de**[3] *pt of* **velje**
Val'dres *Pln* region, southwest part of Oppland.
val'dris -*en* person from Valdres.
***val'ds/ferd** [/fær] -*a* cf **volds/**
***val'ds/mann** -*en, pl -menn(er)* cf **volds/**
***val'ds/styre** -*t* tyrannical government.
***val'ds/verk** -*et* act of violence.
***val'd/ta(ke)** *V infl as* **ta** cf **vold/**
***val'd/tekt** -*a* cf **vold/**
va'len *A +-ent, pl -ne* **1** numb. **2** feeble, halfhearted, lukewarm: **et v-t smil** a feeble smile.
valen's -*en chem.* valence.
valen't *A - chem.* valent.
valeria'na -*en bot.* garden heliotrope, valerian (Valeriana officinalis).
Va'le/strand *Pln* twp, Hordaland.
val'/fart -*en* pilgrimage (**til** to).
val'/farte *V -a/+-et* make a pilgrimage (**til** to); flock.
+**val'farts/sted** -*et* (=***/stad**) place of pilgrimage, shrine.
***va'l/fri** *A -tt* cf **valg/**
***va'l/før** *A* eligible for office.
+**val'g** -*et* (=***val**[3]) **1** choice (**mellom** between), selection: **etter eget v-** according to choice; **fritt v-** take your pick; **ikke ha noe v-** have no choice. **2** election: **holde v-** have

an e-; **ta imot v-** accept e-.
+val'g/agitasjo'n -en electioneering, political campaigning.
+val'g/agn [/angn] -et election bait.
+val'g/bar A eligible for office.
+val'g/beret'tiget A - *lit.* eligible for office.
+val'g/dag -en election day.
+val'g/delta'kelse -n voter participation.
+val'g/distrik't -et constituency, election district.
+val'g/flesk -et *derog.* election promise.
+val'g/fri A -tt 1 elective, optional: **v-e former** o- (language) forms (permitted in textbooks etc.). 2 *lit.* having freedom of choice.
+val'g/frihet -en freedom of choice.
+val'g/fusk -et election fraud.
+val'g/handling -en election, polling, voting.
+val'g/kamp -en election campaign, electioneering.
+val'g/kampan'je -n election campaign.
+val'g/kandida't -en candidate for election.
+val'g/kongedømme -t elective monarchy.
+val'g/krets -en constituency, election district.
+val'g/liste -a slate (of candidates).
+val'g/loka'le -t polling place.
+val'g/lov [/låv] -en election law.
+val'g/mann -en, pl -menn elector.
+val'gmanns/valg -et election of electoral college.
+val'g/møte -t meeting to elect officials.
+val'g/protokoll' -en pollbook (to record votes).
+val'g/rett -en franchise, right to vote, suffrage.
+val'g/rike -t elective monarchy.
+val'g/sogn [/sångn] -et election district (other than in a city).
+val'g/språk -et motto, slogan.
+val'g/styre -t election board, election committee.
+val'g/tale -n campaign speech.
+val'gte pt of **velge**
+val'g/u'rne -a/-en ballot box.
Va'l/hall *Pln myth.* Valhalla.
va'l/hendt A - fumbling, unsure.
vali'd A - *psych.* valid.
validite't -en *psych.* validity.
+vali'ser -en, pl -e (=*-ar) Welshman.
vali'sisk A - Welsh.
val'k -en rat, roll padding (for hair, clothing, etc.); roll of fat.
val'ke V -a/+-et full (a felting process used on woolen cloth).
***va'l/krins** -en cf **valg/krets**
valkyr'je -a/+-en *myth.* Valkyrie.
***vall'** pt of **velle**[1]
val'lak -en gelding.
Val'/land *Pln* Old Norse name for France (and Italy).
val'le -n whey.
Val'le *Pln* twp, Aust-Agder.
val'le/slette -a *dial.* slush.
vallo'n -en Walloon.
vallo'nsk A - Walloon.
***va'l/mann** -en, pl -menn(er) cf **valg/**
val'mue -n *bot.* poppy (Papaver).
***va'l/møte** -t cf **valg/**
va'lne V -a/+-et become numb; numb.
va'l/nøtt -a *bot.* English walnut (Juglans regia).
***va'l/o'rd** -et motto, slogan.
+val'p -en (=***kvelp**) puppy.
+val'pe V -a/-et (=***kvelpe**) whelp.
+val'pe/sjuke -n (=***kvelpe/**) distemper.
+val'pet(e) A - puppyish.
va'l/plass -en battlefield, battleground.
val's[1] -en waltz.
val's[2] -en (=+**valse**[1]) barrel, cylinder, drum; (steam) roller; platen (on a typewriter); *typog.* ink roller.
+val'se[1] -n cf **vals**[2]
val'se[2] V -a/+-et waltz: **v- opp med en** *fam.* give sby a dressing down.
val'se[3] V -a/+-et mill, roll (e.g. metal).
val'se/jern [/jæ'rn] -et rolled iron.
val'se/konge -n waltz king.
val'se/mølle -a flour mill (using rollers).
val'se/takt -a/+-en waltz time.
val'se/verk -et rolling mill.
+va'l/slynge -a/-en catapult.
***va'l/styre** -t cf **valg/**
Val'søy/fjo'rd *Pln* twp, Møre og Romsdal.
val't pt of **velte**[2]
val'te[1] V -a/+-et: **skalte og v- med noe** dispose over sth, do as one likes with sth.
+val'te[2] pt of **velge**
val't/ho'rn -et 1 French horn. 2 hunting horn.
***val'tre** V -a cf **vralte**
va'l/urt -a/+-en *bot.* comfrey (Symphytum officinale).
valut'a -en 1 *merc.* value (in cash, in goods received, etc.); worth: **få v- for pengene** get one's money's worth. 2 *merc.* currency; foreign currency; exchange: **fremmed v-** foreign e- (funds).
valut'a/balanse [/balang'se] -n foreign currency balance.
+valut'a/begren'sning -en currency (exchange) restrictions.
+valut'a/behol'dning -en foreign exchange reserves.
valut'a/kurs -en rate of exchange (of foreign money).
valut'a/note'ring -a/+-en foreign exchange quotation.
valute'rings/dag -en *merc.* date when interest begins.
valø'r -en 1 *merc.* value. 2 validity. 3 (color) nuance, shade; poetic nuance.
vam'mel A -elt, pl *vamle* nauseating, sickly sweet; (also *fig.*): **vamle fraser** cloying (sentimental) phrases.
vam'p -en (of a woman) vamp.
vam'pe[1] -n *dial.* jacket.
vam'pe[2] V -a/+-et vamp.
vampy'r -en 1 *folk.* vampire. 2 vampire bat. 3 bloodsucker; vamp.
vam's -en doublet; jacket.
va'n[1] -en, pl *-er *myth.* Wane, one of the Norse fertility gods (esp. Njord, Frey, Freya).
***va'n**[2] A cf **vant**[4]
vana'dium -iet *chem.* vanadium.
van'/akte V -a/+-et despise, have contempt for, scorn.
van'/arta A - (=+-et) delinquent, neglected (esp. of children); depraved (of adults).
van'd[1] A *dial.* 1 difficult: **det er v-t å vite** it is hard to know. 2 finicky, hard to please.
***van'd**[2] A *vant* cf **vant**[4]
***van'd**[3] pp of **venje**
vanda'l -en Vandal; vandal.
vandalise're V -te vandalize.
vandalis'me -n vandalism.
***van'de**[1] -n difficulty.
***van'de**[2] V -a/+-et pick and choose; disdain, reject.
***van'de**[3] pt of **venje**
van'del[1] -en behavior, conduct: **handel og v-** everyday dealings; **moralsk v-** moral c-.
+van'del[2] -elen, pl -ler cf **vondel**
***van'de/laus** A not difficult, simple.
van'dels/attes't -en certificate of good conduct (given by police, esp. after World War II to non-collaborators with Nazis).
+van'dig A - soggy, watery.
van'dle[1] V -a/+-et: **handle og v-** buy and sell.
+van'dle[2] V -a/-et cf **vondle**
van'dre V -a/+-et 1 roam, rove, wander; tramp, trudge, walk; *(bibl.)* walk (e.g. in the way of the Lord): **v- heden, herfra** *(bibl.)* pass away. 2 (esp. of animals, geol. features) migrate.
van'dre/bibliote'k -et, pl -/+-er traveling library.
van'dre/eventyr -et migratory tale (folktale which has passed from country to country).
+van'dre/hjerte -t *med.* abnormally moveable heart (cor mobile).
van'dre/lyst -a/+-en wanderlust.
van'dre/poka'l -en 1 traveling trophy. 2 *hum.* shopworn girl.
van'dre/premie -n traveling trophy.
+van'drer -en, pl -e (=*-ar) nomad, wanderer: **En v- spiller med sordin** A Wanderer Plays on Muted Strings (novel by Hamsun).
+van'dre/sagn [/sangn] -et migratory legend.
van'dre/stav -en *lit.* pilgrim's staff.
van'dre/utstilling -a/+-en traveling exhibition.
+van'/drevet A -, pl -ne mismanaged.
van'dre/år -et year(s) of traveling.
van'dring -a/+-en 1 hike, ramble, walk. 2 moving from place to place; migration, wandering. 3 journey, trail: **jordens v- rundt solen** the earth's j- around the sun.
van'drings/mann -en, pl -menn/ *-menner *lit.* wanderer, wayfarer.
+van'd/skjær -en/-et (=*/**skjer**) *zool., dial.* shrew (Sorex).
+van'dt pt of **vinde**[1]
va'ne[1] -n custom, habit: **av v-** by h-; **ha for v-** be used to, be in the habit of; **komme i v- med** get in the h- of.
vane[2] -n cf **van**[1]
+va'ne/dranker -en, pl -e (=*/**drikkar**) habitual drunkard; alcoholic.
va'ne/dyr -et creature of habit.
+va'ne/forbry'ter -en, pl -e (=*-ar) habitual criminal.
+va'ne/gjenger -en, pl -e creature of habit.
+va'ne/gjengeri' -et acting, thinking in customary or habitual ways; being in a rut.
va'ne/kristendom [+/-dåmm] -men/ *-en *eccl.* routine Christianity (not inspired by active faith).
va'ne/menneske -t, pl +-r/*- slave of habit.
+va'ne/messig A - habitual, perfunctory, routine; *(adv.)* perfunctorily, routinely.
+va'nemessig/het -en perfunctoriness; routine.
va'ne/sak -a/+-en matter of habit: **det er bare en v-** it's just a m-.
va'ne/tenking -a/+-en (=+/**tenkning**) conventional thinking.
***van'/faren** A -e/-i, pl -ne poorly served (**med** by) sth.
van'/før A crippled, disabled: **de v-e** the handicapped.
***van'/føre** -t cf **vanførhet**
van'føre/heim -en (=+/**hjem**) home for the disabled, handicapped.
+van'før/het -en disability, infirmity.
vang' -en field, grassy spot, meadow; area adjacent to *seter* buildings.
Vang' *Pln* 1 twp, Hedmark. 2 twp, Oppland (in Valdres).
vang'e -n 1 *tech., naut.* cheek (on mast, pulley; gun, carriage). 2 *arch.* string (board) (on stairway). 3 bed (of lathe). 4 sidewall (of corner fireplace). 5 side member (of chassis).
***van'/gjerd** [/jær] -a error, mistake, oversight.
***vang'le** V -a rove, wander; be undependable.
***van'/greie** -a disorder, lack of order.
***vang'sne** -n plowshare.
***van'/halde** V *infl as* **halde** break, violate (the law).
+van'/heder -en (=*/**heider**) *lit.* dishonor.
+van'/hedre V -a/-et (=*/**heidre**) *lit.* bring shame upon, dishonor.
***van'/heilag** A - cf /**hellig**
van'/helge V -a/+-et desecrate, profane.

+ Bokmål; * Nynorsk; ° Dialect.
After letter: ' stress (Acc. 1); ` tone, stress (Acc. 2); · length.
Below letter: . not pronounced.

+van'/hell -et bad luck, misfortune.

+van'/hellig A - (=*/heilag) blasphemous, profane, unholy.

+van'/hellige V -et cf /helge

+van'/helligelse -n desecration, profanation (av of).

van'/helse -a archaic, dial. bad health, sickness.

*van'/heppe -a bad luck, misfortune.

van'/hjelpen A -e/-i, pl -ne (=/hjelpt) cf +/hjulpen

+van'/hjulpen A -ent/-et, pl -ne badly served (med by).

*van'/høve -t disparity, disproportion.

vanil'je -n 1 vanilla. 2 bot. vanilla (plant) (Vanilla planifolia).

+vanil'je/stang -a (=*/stong) vanilla bean.

vanil'je/sukker -et powdered vanilla bean mixed with sugar (used in cooking).

*van'k -et blemish, (physical) disability.

van'/kant -en wane (round edge of board due to curve of log).

van'ke V -a/+-et 1 ramble, roam, rove (om about). 2 frequent, go often, visit often (hos at, with). 3: det v-er one will get, there will be (det v-er ris you (he, she, etc.) will really catch it; det v-er kaker cakes are being served).

+van'kel/modig A - changeable, fickle, vacillating.

+van'kelmodig/het -en changeableness, fickleness, vacillation.

+van'/kundig A - (=*/kunnig) ignorant.

+vankun'dig/het -en (=*van/kunne) ignorance.

van'/kunne -a cf vankundig/het

*van'/kunnig A - cf /kundig

vanl. =vanlig

*van'/lage V -a deform, make wrong, misshape.

*van'/la'gnad -en ill fortune, tragedy.

va'nlig A - customary, usual: som v- as u-; til v- usually.

+va'nlig/vis Av usually.

*van'/lykke -a misfortune.

van'/makt -a/+-en impotence, lack of power, weakness.

van'/mektig A - impotent, powerless.

+vann'[1] -et cf vatn[1]

+vann'[2] -et cf vatn[2]

*vann'[3] pt of vinne[2]

vann'[4] Av cf dann[2]

+vann- Pf cf vass-

+vann'/aktig A - watery; chem. aqueous.

+vann'/avkjø'ling -a/-en water-cooling.

+vann'/avkjø'lt A - water-cooled.

+vann'/avstøtende A - water-repellent.

+vann'/bad -et 1 bathing in water. 2 chem. water bath. 3 cooking in double boiler: stekes i v- bake in pan of hot water.

+vann'/bakkels(e) -(e)n cream puff.

+vann'/basseng' -et pool, reservoir.

+vann'/blemme -a cf vass/

+vann'/blå A -tt pale blue.

+vann'/boring -a/-en drilling for water.

+vann'/brokk -en/-et med hydrocele.

+vann'/bøtte -a cf vass/

+vann'/damp -en cf vass/

+vann'/dråpe -n cf vass/

+van'ne[1] -t 1 waters: klart, åpent v- ice-free waters. 2 water level; tide, water: holde seg oven v- keep afloat, fig. keep one's head above w-; høyt v- hight tide, high water.

van'ne[2] V -a/-et cf vatne

+vann'/fall -et cf vass/

+vann'/farge -n cf vass/

+vann'/fat -et cf vass/

+vann'/flate -a/-en cf vass/

+vann'/fordam'per -en, pl -e evaporator.

+vann'/forsy'ning -a/-en water supply.

+vann'/førende A - water-bearing.

+vann'/gang -en 1 flow, passage, seepage of water. 2 (on ship) waterline.

+vann'/glass -et 1 glass, tumbler. 2 water gauge. 3 chem. water glass (solution of sodium or potassium silicate).

+vann'/grav -a 1 water jump. 2 moat.

+vann'/hode -t med. hydrocephalus.

+vann'/holdig A - damp, moist; geol. water-bearing.

+van'ning -a/-en cf vatning

+vann'/innta'k -et cf vass/

+vann'/kant -en shoreline, waterline, water's edge.

+vann'/karaf'fel -en, pl -karafler water carafe.

+vann'/karse -n water cress.

+vann'/kikkert -en water glass (for examining things under water).

+vann'/kjemme V kjemte cf vass/

+vann'/klar A limpid, transparent.

+vann'/klosett' -et cf vass/

+vann'/kopper pl chicken pox.

+vann'/kraft -a/-en cf vass/

+vann'/kran -a cf vass/

vann'/krukke [/krokke] -a water jug.

+vann'/kur -en med. hydrotherapy, water cure.

+vann'/lating -a/-en urination.

+vann'/le'dning -en cf vass/

+vann'/lilje -a/-en bot. water lily (Nymphaeaceae).

+vann'/linje -a/-en 1 waterline. 2 naut. load line, watermark.

+vann'/lås -en trap, esp. P trap (in sinks etc.).

+vann'/mangel -en cf vass/

+vann'/mann -en, pl -menn 1 water bearer; water seller; water witcher. 2: V-en astron. Aquarius. 3 naut. ordinary seaman who assists man in charge of cargo and ship's water supply.

+vann'/masse -n mass, volume of water.

+vann'/melo'n -en bot. watermelon (Citrullus vulgaris).

+vann'/merke -t watermark.

+vann'/orgel -elet, pl -ler hydraulic organ.

+vann'/pest -en bot. water thyme, waterweed (Elodea canadensis).

+vann'/pipe -a water pipe (hookah, nargileh).

+vann'/pisto'l -en squirt gun, water pistol.

+vann'/plante -a/-en aquatic plant.

+vann'/polo -en water polo.

+vann'/post -en (town) pump: Konene ved v-en The Women at the Pump (novel, Hamsun).

+vann'/renne -a cf vass/

+vann'/rett[1] -en cf vass/

+vann'/rett[2] A - cf vass/

+vann'/rotte -a zool. vole, water rat (Arvicola amphibius).

+vann'/rør -et cf vass/

+vann'/skade -n water damage.

+vann'/ski -a, pl -/-er water ski.

+vann'/skille -t cf vass/

+vann'/skorpe -a cf vass/

+vann'/skrekk -en 1 fear of the water: ha v- be afraid of the water. 2 hydrophobia; rabies.

+vann'/slange -n cf vass/

+vann'/spring -en (water) faucet, tap.

+vann'/stand -en water level.

+vann'/stoff -et hydrogen.

+vann'stoff/bombe -a/-en hydrogen bomb.

+vann'stoff/hyperoksy'd -et pharm. hydrogen peroxide.

+vann'/stråle -n jet of water.

+vann'/sykkel -elen, pl -sykler water cycle.

+vann'/tett A - cf vass/

+vann'/tønne -a cf vass/

+vann'/vei -en cf vass/veg

+vann'/verk -et cf vass/

+vann'/vesen -et 1 water commission, waterworks. 2 water sprite.

+vann'/vogn [/vångn] -a 1 water truck. 2 street sprinkler.

+vann'/øse -a cf vass/ause

van'/ry -et discredit, disrepute, ill repute: komme i v- come to shame, ruin one's reputation.

van'/rykte -t discredit, disrepute, ill repute: få noen i v- bring sby into disrepute.

van'/røkt -a/+-en mismanagement, neglect.

van'/røkte V -a/+-et mismanage, neglect.

van'/råd -a/+-en dial. 1 poor supply, poverty. 2 improvidence, lack of foresight.

*van'se V -a flit, roam, rove around.

*van'/seda A - bad mannered, rude, uncivilized.

+van'/sire V -te disfigure: med sitt v-ede ansikt ble hun snytt for sin vår with her d-d face she was cheated out of her youth (Hamsun).

van'/ska'pning -en 1 deformed creature, freak, monstrosity. 2 deformity, malformation.

van'/skapt A - deformed, misshapen.

van'ske -n 1 difficulty, problem, trouble. *2 fault, mistake.

van'skelig A - 1 difficult (language, person, problem, task, times, etc.), hard (å to): falle v- be d-; ha v- have difficulty (for in); være v- stillet be in straitened circumstances. 2 (adv.) hardly, scarcely: det kan v- skje this can hardly (not very well) be done.

+van'skelig/gjøre V -gjorde, -gjort hamper, impede, make difficult.

+van'skelig/het -en difficulty (med about, over, with, ved in): gjøre v-er cause difficulties, raise objections; komme i v-er get into straitened circumstances; get into trouble.

+van'skelighets/grad -en degree of difficulty.

*van'/skipa A - 1 disordered, mistaken. 2 angry, upset.

*van'/ski'pnad -en confusion, disorder.

+van'/skje'bne -n misfortune, unhappy fate.

+van'/skjøtsel -en mismanagement, neglect.

+van'/skjøtte V -a/-et (=*/skøyte) neglect: et v-et barn a n-ed child.

van'/slekte V -a/+-et degenerate; disgrace the family name: det er en som v-er i hver ætt there's a black sheep in every family; v- på sine foreldre disgrace one's parents.

+van'/smekte V -et lit. thirst; languish; feel faint.

van'/stell -et poor care, poorly done work (housekeeping, farming, etc.); mismanagement, sloppiness.

van'/stelle V -stelte, -stelt give poor care, mismanage, run badly: hvem har styrt og v-t verden så den er blitt slik den er blitt who has ruled and misruled the world so it has become what it is (Scott).

*van'/stode [/ståe] -a difficult situation.

van'/styre[1] -t mismanagement, misrule.

van'/styre[2] V -te misgovern, misrule, rule badly.

*van't[1] -en lack, want (på of).

van't[2] -et 1 naut. shroud (rope in ship's tackle). 2 cushion (on billiard table). 3 side boards (on ice hockey rink).

+van't[3] pt of vinne[2]

+van't[4] A - (=*van[2], *vand[2]) 1 accustomed, used, wont (til to); bli v- med (til) get used to; de arbeidet v- they worked in an experienced way (Evensmo); være godt v- be used to living well. 2 customary, usual (pattern, place, way, etc.): han løp til sitt v-e tog he ran to his u- train (Bang-Hansen).

van'/takk -a/+-en ingratitude, poor thanks.

van'te[1] -n glove (diff. from hanske by not being made of leather).

van'te[2] V -a/+-et dial. 1 be wanting, want for; lack, need. 2 be lacking, be short (på of): det er alltid noe som v-er sth is always lacking. 3 be wrong with sby: *Viv ser kva som v-ar honom V- sees what ails him (Vesaas).

+van'/treven A -ent, pl -ne (=*/triven) deformed, dwarfed, stunted.

*van'/trivast *V -treivst, -est/-ist* cf /trives

+van'/trives *V -des, -(e)s* (=*-ast) 1 (of person) be dissatisfied, be unhappy, not enjoy oneself. 2 (of animal, plant) become dwarfed, stunted; not do well, not thrive.

van'/tri·vning *-en* stunted person, plant, or animal.

van'/trivsel *-en* 1 dissatisfaction, unhappiness. 2 dwarfing, stunting; stagnation.

van'/tru[1] *-a* (=+/tro) 1 disbelief (**overfor** in); mistrust, skepticism. 2 unbelief: **jeg tror, hjelp min v-** Lord, I believe; help thou mine u- (Mark 9,24). 3 paganism.

+van'/tru[2] *A -tt* (=+/tro) 1 doubting, mistrustful, skeptical; **den v- Thomas** the doubting T-. 2 unbelieving, unconverted. 3 infidel, pagan.

*van'/truen *A -e/-i, pl -ne* cf /tru[2]

van'/vare *N*: **av v-** by accident, inadvertently.

*van'/vares *Av* accidentally, inadvertently.

*van'/vett *A* cf /vidd

+van'/vidd *-et* (=*/vett, */vit) insanity, madness: **det glade v-, det skjæreste v-** sheer m-; **elske en til v-** love sby madly; **på v-ets rand** on the brink of i-.

+vanvit'tig *A* - (=*-vettug, *-vitug) 1 demented, deranged, insane. 2 *(adv.)* crazily, insanely, madly: **v-forelsket** madly in love.

van'/vø'rde *V -vørte/*-e* (=+/være) *dial.* 1 disdain, scorn, show contempt for. 2 neglect, treat carelessly.

van'/vø'rdnad *-en* (=+/vørnad) contempt, disdain, scorn.

*van'/vø'rdsleg *A* - contemptuous, scornful.

Van'/ylven *Pln* twp, Møre og Romsdal.

van'/ære[1] *-a* disgrace, dishonor, infamy.

van'/ære[2] *V -a/+-et* bring shame upon, disgrace, dishonor.

va'r[1] *+-en/*-et* matter, pus; "sand" (in one's eyes after sleep), "sleep".

va'r[2] *-et* pillowcase; featherbed cover.

va'r[3] *pt of* **vere**[3], **være**[2]

va'r[4] *A* 1 alert, aware, sharp: **bli v-** become aware of, notice; **være v-** be sensitive (**for** to). 2 careful, cautious, wary (**med** with): **bedre føre v- enn etter snar** a stitch in time saves nine. 3 gentle, soft, tender: **snakke v-t** speak softly. 4 reticent, sensitive, shy.

var. =**variant**

va'ra/formann *-en, pl -menn/*-menner* vice-chairman, vice-president.

+va'r/aktig *A* - *lit.* enduring, persevering, persistent.

Va'ralds/øy *Pln* twp, Hordaland.

va'ra/mann *-en, pl -menn/*-menner* deputy, substitute.

*va'rande *A* - 1 admonishing, warning. 2 constant, continual.

*va'ra/von *-a* means, way out (in reserve).

*va'r/band *-et* cf **vare/bind**

va'r/belg *-en hist.* follower of Skule Bårdsson who led uprising against Håkon Håkonsson in 1239.

Va'r/dal *Pln* twp, Oppland.

var'de[1] [*va're] *-n* beacon; cairn, marker of stones; lookout, place to keep a watch; signal fire (on mountain top).

var'de[2] [*va're] *V -a/+-et* set up markers: **v- opp vei** mark a road.

*va'rde[3] *V -a* 1 guard, protect. 2: **v- til** be concerned with, be related to.

*va'rde[4] *pt of* **verje**[5]

var'de/vakt *-a/+-en* watch duty at a cairn or lookout station.

*va'r/dyvle *-t* cf **var/døger**

Var'd/ø *Pln* seaport, Finnmark.

var'/døger [also va'r/] *-eret/-ret* (=*var/dyvle) *folk.* 1 genius, tutelary spirit. 2 premonitory sound (or sight) of person shortly before he arrives.

va're[1] *-a/+-en* article; *(pl)* goods, merchandise, wares: **ekte v-** the real thing; **en sjelden v-** a rare sight; **sterke v-r** alcoholic beverages, liquor.

va're[2] *-n*: **ta seg i v-** look out, watch out (**for** for); keep from; **ta v- på** attend to, take care of.

va're[3] *V -a/+-te dial., lit.* 1 warn: ***v- åt** (the same). 2 be careful with mind, watch. 3 *(refl.)*: **v- seg** beware, take care; watch out, (**for** for).

va're[4] *V -te/*-a* go on, last; (of time) be: **det v-te lenge før vi så ham igjen** it was a long time before we saw him again; **v- ved** continue, keep on; **det v-te og det rakk** more and more time passed (Asbjørnsen).

*va're/band *-et* cf /bind

+va're/behol·dning *-en* inventory, stock on hand.

va're/bil *-en* delivery truck.

va're/bind *-et* dust jacket, wrapper.

+va're/bytte *-t* (=*/byte) exchange of goods, exchange in kind; barter.

va're/heis *-en* freight elevator.

va're/hus *-et* 1 department store. 2 warehouse.

va're/kunnskap *-en merc.* commodity study; knowledge of commodities.

va're/lager *-eret, pl -er/+-re* stock of goods.

va're/magasi'n *-et, pl -/+-er* department store.

+va're/marked *-et* (=*/marknad) *merc.* commodity market, produce market.

va're/merke *-t, pl +-r/*-* trademark.

va're/messe *-a/+-en merc.* exhibit, fair.

*va're/mur *-en* cf **var/**

+va're/opptelling *-en* (=*/oppteljing) *merc.* inventory.

va're/parti' *-et, pl +-er/*- merc.* consignment, lot.

va're/prøve *-a/+-en merc.* sample.

va're/skur *-et* warehouse.

va're/sort *-en* line, type of goods.

va're/sykkel *-elen, pl -sykler* bicycle built for deliveries.

+va're/ta *V -tok, -tatt* attend to, take care of, watch out for.

va're/taking *-a/+-en* (=+/tagelse, +/takelse) care (**av** of); attention (to orders), conduct (of affairs).

va're/tekt *-a/+-en* 1 care, charge; guardianship, (safe)keeping. 2 custody, imprisonment.

va'retekts/arres't *-en* 1 custody. 2 house of detention.

+va're/tok *pt of* **-ta**

va're/trekk *-et* (cloth) covering, protector; dust jacket (on book); slip cover (on furniture).

va're/vogn [/vångn] *-a* delivery truck, pickup truck.

var'g *-en* 1 wolf. 2: **v- i veum** outlaw; *fig.* persona non grata.

Va'r/haug *Pln* twp, Rogaland.

varia'bel *A -elt, pl -le* changeable, variable.

varian't *-en* variant.

variasjo'n *-en* variation.

varie're *V -te* vary; change, fluctuate: **v- med** *math.* v- as; **v- en melodi** *mus.* make variations on a melody.

varieté *-en* cabaret (variety) show; cabaret, variety theater.

varieté/stjerne *-a/+-en* cabaret performer, variety star.

variete't *-en* variety (e.g. of plant).

va'rig *A* - durable, lasting, permanent; enduring (fame), fast (color): **v- svekkede sjelsevner** (cf **sjelsevner**).

+va'rig/het *-en* durability, permanence; duration, life: **av kort v-** brief, fleeting.

*va'ring *-a* cf **varig/het**

va'rlig *A* - 1 careful, cautious. 2 delicate, gentle; gingerly.

+va'rlig/het *-en* 1 care, caution, cautiousness. 2 gentleness.

*va'r/læte *-a/-et* 1 care, caution, cautiousness. 2 delicacy, gentleness.

*va'r/låten *A -e/-i, pl -ne* 1 careful, cautious. 2 bashful, shy.

var'm *A* warm (blanket, feeling, friendship, room, etc.); hot (argument, bath, coffee, compress, stove, water, weather, etc.); ardent, fervent (admirer, desire, love, etc.): **det går v-t for seg** things are getting hot, violent; **holde en sak v-** keep an issue alive; **holde stolen v- for en** hold a position for one while he is engaged in sth else, pinch-hit; **v- som ei glo** warm as toast; **v-e pølser** hot dogs, wieners.

var'm/blodig *A* - 1 (of animals) warm-blooded. 2 *fig.* hot-blooded, passionate.

var'mblods/hest *-en vet.* hot-blooded horse (of Arab or thoroughbred ancestry).

var'me[1] *-n* 1 heat, warmth (also *fig.*); heating; ardor, fervor: **holde v-n** keep warm; **sette på v-n** turn on the heat (in furnace or cookstove); **ti graders v-** ten degrees above zero (Centigrade), ab. 50° F. 2 fire: **gjøre opp v-** light, start a f-; **sette v- på noe** set f- to sth; **ta v-** catch f- (**det tar v- i noe** sth catches f-).

var'me[2] *V -a/+-et* (=*verme) 1 heat, warm; heat up, warm up: **v- en om hjertet** warm the cockles of one's heart; **v- opp** w- up (engine, food, etc.), warm over (food). 2 give off heat.

var'me/appara't *-et, pl -/+-er* heater.

var'me/belte *-t, pl +-r/*- meteor.* belt of warm air.

*var'me/bolk *-en* warm period.

var'me/bølgje *-a* (=+/bølge) heat wave.

var'me/dirrende *A* - shimmering with heat.

var'me/dis *-en* heat haze.

var'me/dunk [/donk] *-en* hot water bottle.

var'me/effek't *-en* thermal power.

var'me/elemen't *-et, pl -/+-er* heating element.

+var'me/enhet *-en* unit of heat (esp. calorie).

var'me/flaske *-a* hot water bottle.

var'me/grad *-a/-en* degree above freezing.

*var'me/gust *-en* warm wind.

var'me/isolasjo'n *-en* heat insulation (in a building).

var'me/kjelde *-a* (=+/kilde) heat source.

+var'me/leder *-en, pl -e* (=*/leiar) heat conductor.

var'me/omn *-en* (=+/ovn) electric (room) heater.

var'me/plate *-a/+-en* hot plate.

var'me/pose [*/påse] *-n* hot water bottle.

var'me/pute *-a* heating pad.

var'me/stråle *-n* heat ray.

var'me/stue *-a* 1 shelter house, warming house. 2 shelter for the homeless.

var'me/utvikling *-a/+-en* generation of heat.

+var'm/hjertet *A* - (=*/hjarta) warmhearted.

*var'm/hug *-en* kindheartedness, warmheartedness.

*var'm/huga *A* - kindhearted, warmhearted.

var'm/jomfru *-a/+-en* (in restaurant) woman supervising the preparation of hot dishes.

var'm/luft *-a* warm air.

var'm/rett *-en* hot dish.

+var'mtvanns/behol·der *-en, pl -e* hot water heater (mounted on wall).

+var'mtvanns/bere·der *-en, pl -e* hot water heater (in cellar).

+ Bokmål; * Nynorsk; ° Dialect.
After letter: ' stress (Acc. 1); ` tone, stress (Acc. 2); · length.
Below letter: . not pronounced.

var'mt/vatn -et (=+/vann) hot water.

***va'r/mur** -en (=*vare/) retaining wall.

***var'm/vatn** -et cf varmt/

va'r/nagle -n pin (in an axle etc.).

***va'rne** V -a cf verne

***va'r/o'rdig** A - closemouthed, reserved.

var'p[1] -et 1 naut. warp, warping line. 2 warp (in weaving). 3 cast of a seine net; sudden jerk: **gjøre et v-** make a coup, a killing. 4 seine net.

var'p[2] pt of **verpe[2]**

var'p/anker -et naut. stream anchor.

var'pe V -a/+-et 1 dial. cast a seine net, fish with a seine net. 2 dial. (in weaving) warp. 3 naut. kedge, warp. 4 transport timber over water by warping. 5 fam. ease, move (sth) along a little at a time. 6 fam., naut. heave, throw.

***va'r/sam** A cf /som

var'sel -elet/-let, pl -el/+-ler 1 warning: **en måneds v-** a month's notice; **uten v-** without w-. 2 omen: **et godt v-** a good o-; **ta v- av** divine, read (the signs, to predict weather, fishing, etc.).

var'sel/skilt -et danger sign, warning sign.

var'sel/skott -et (=*/skot, +/skudd) warning shot.

var'sels/rop -et shout of warning.

***va'r/semd** -a cf **varsom/het**

***va'r/simle** -a doe that mounts guard for a herd of reindeer.

***va'r/skie** -a frame (to contain a load).

+var'sko [also var'-] -et cf **varsku[1]**

var'sku[1] -et warning: **rope et v-** sound a w-; **v- her** (interj.) look out (esp. for blasting operations).

var'sku[2] V -dde, -dd 1 alert, warn (**om** about). 2 inform, notify: **jeg dro hjemmefra uten å v-** I left home without leaving word (Undset).

var'sle V -a/+-et 1 alert, warn (**om** about). 2 inform, notify; announce. 3 be an omen of; augur, bode, forebode.

+var'sler -en, pl -e (=*-ar) zool. butcher-bird, shrike (Lanius excubitor).

var'sling -a/-en alert, warning; (weather) forecast.

+va'r/som· A -t, pl -me (=*/sam) 1 careful, cautious, wary (**med** about, with). 2 careful, delicate, gentle: **fare v-t med** treat with care; **et v-t kyss** a g- kiss.

+varsom/het -en care, caution; gentleness, tenderness: **med v-** carefully.

var't[1] pt of **bli[1], verte**

***var't[2]** pp of **verje[4]**

Var't/dal Pln twp, Møre og Romsdal.

var'te V -a/+-et: **v- opp** serve, wait on table; **v- opp med** serve, treat (sby); relate, retail (e.g. stories).

Va'r/teig Pln twp, Østfold.

+var't/penger pl (=*-ar) admin. allowance, interim pay (given to a temporarily unemployed official).

***va'r/trekk** -et cf vare/

***va'rug** A - cf **varig**

va'r/ulv -en werewolf.

***va'r/veitsle[1]** -a care, custody, guard.

***va'r/veitsle[2]** V -a guard, take care of, watch.

va's -et 1 foolishness, nonsense, rubbish. 2 confused, tangled mass, jumble.

vasall' -en vassal.

vasall'/stat -en satellite country, vassal state.

Va'sa/orden -en The Vasa Order (Swedish order of knighthood started in 1772).

va'se[1] -n vase: **blomster i v-** flowers in a v-.

va'se[2] -n 1 bunch, jumble, tangled mass: **komme i v-** become utterly confused. 2 dial. fascine; heap of twigs, branches, etc. placed in water to lure fish.

va'se[3] V -a/+-te 1 tangle, twist; jumble: **v- tråden sammen (i hop)** tangle the thread. 2 talk nonsense, twaddle. 3 mill, wander confusedly; trudge, wade. 4 dial. poke, root around. 5 (refl.): **v- seg** become jumbled, tangled; **v- seg bort** get confused, lost; **v- seg fast** get stuck.

va'se/kopp -en pop. chatterbox, fool, (pop.) gasbag.

vaseli'n -en vaseline.

va'set(e) A - 1 tangled. 2 fam. crazy, foolish, silly.

vas'k[1] -en 1 wash, washing (**av** of) (a car, clothes, one's body, etc.): **kjemisk v-** dry cleaning. 2 laundry, washing: **henge opp v-en** hang out the wash. 3 sink, washbasin: **gå i v-en** come to nothing, fall through, go down the drain.

vas'k[2] -et splashing, wash, washing; *(=**vask[1]** 1).

***vas'kar/klut** -en cf **vaske/**

vas'ke V -a/+-et 1 wash (car, clothes, gold, hands, ore, etc.): **bølgene v-er mot stranden** the waves w- against the shore; **v- opp** do the dishes; **v- opp med en** fam. have it out with one. 2 shuffle (cards). 3 naut. (of a boat) roll, splash (in waves); be awash, ship water. 4 (refl.): **v- seg** wash (oneself); **som har v-a seg** fam. out of the ordinary; **det er gutt (jente) som har v-a seg** he's (she's) quite a guy (gal).

vas'ke/balje +-a/-en laundry tub, washtub.

vas'ke/bjø'rn -en zool. raccoon (Procyon lotor).

vas'ke/brett -et washboard; washboard road surface.

vas'ke/dag -en washday.

vas'ke/ekte A - 1 colorfast, washable. 2 dyed-in-the-wool, staunch. 3 genuine, real.

vas'ke/fat -et (portable) wash basin.

vas'ke/fille -a dishcloth, washrag.

vas'ke/hall +-en/*-a room for washing cars (in a filling station).

vas'ke/hanske -n bath mitt.

+vas'ke/kjeller -en, pl -e (=*-ar) laundry room.

vas'ke/kjerring -a charwoman, washwoman.

vas'ke/klut -en 1 washcloth; cleaning rag; dishcloth: **jeg føler meg som en v-** I feel like a wet dishrag. 2 fam. weak-willed, wishy-washy person.

vas'ke/kone [/kåne] -a charwoman, washerwoman.

***vas'k/ekte** A - cf **vaske/**

vas'ke/maski'n -en washing machine.

vas'ke/middel -elet/-midlet, pl +-midler/*-el detergent.

vas'ke/plass -en 1 washing place (e.g. by a river). 2 place for washing cars outside a gas station.

vas'ke/pulver -et detergent (powder).

vaskeri' -et, pl +-er/*- laundry.

vas'ke/rom [/romm] -met laundry room; wash room.

+vas'ke/seddel -elen, pl -sedler 1 laundry list. 2 (book) blurb.

vas'ke/servan't -en washstand.

vas'ke/skinn -et chamois.

+vas'ke/tøy -et laundry, washing.

+vas'kevanns/bolle -n (=*-vass/) wash basin.

+vas'kevanns/fat -et (=*-vass/) wash basin.

vas'ke/vatn -et (=+/vann) bathwater, wash water; slop water: **helle barnet ut med v-et** throw the baby out with the b-.

***vas'last** V -ast (of eyes) water.

***vas'le** V -a bother, putter (**med** with).

+vas'ne pl of **vassen**

vass'- Pf (=+vann-) water-.

vass'/arv -en (=*/arve) bot. common chickweed (Stellaria media).

vass'/ause -a (=+vann/øse) water dipper, ladle: **Marit v-** hist. July 20.

***vass'/bein** A horizontal.

vass'/blande -a dial. watery, watered-out liquid, solution.

vass'/blemme -a (=+vann/) water blister.

vass'/bløyte -a dial. soggy ground.

vass'/blå A -tt (=+vann/) pale (watery) blue.

+vass'/bøtte -a (=*/bytte) bucket, pail.

vass'/dam· -men (=+vann/) water puddle.

vass'/damp -en (=+vann/) aqueous vapor.

vass'/dele -t, pl +-r/*- geog. divide.

vass'/drag -et watercourse.

vass'/dråpe -n (=+vann/dråpe, *vass/drope) drop of water.

vas'se V -a/+-et wade; slog, trudge.

vas'sen A +-ent, pl vasne watery (color, eyes, food, land, etc.), weak sloppy, slushy.

vass'/ende -n (inlet) end of a lake.

vass'/fall -et (=+vann/) waterfall.

vass'/far -et course of a river, brook, etc.

vass'/farge -n (=+vann/) watercolor.

vass'/fat -et (=+vann/) basin (of water, usu. for washing; naut. also for drinking).

vass'/flate -a/+-en (=+vann/) surface of the water.

***vass'/fly(ge)** V infl as **fly(ge[1])** (=+vann/) (of eyes) water.

vass'/føring -a/+-en (=+vann/) flow of water.

vass'/gov [/gåv] -et dial. shower, spray; steam.

vass'/gras -et (=+vann/gress) bot. water starwort (Callitriche).

vass'/graut -en (usu. barley) gruel, porridge cooked with water.

vass'/hjul -et (=+vann/) water wheel.

vass'/hol [/hål] -et (=+vann/hull) water hole, puddle.

vass'/innta·k -et (=+vann/) water intake.

vass'/kald A dial. cold and damp (weather).

vass'/kalv -en 1 zool. water beetle (Dytiscidae). 2 vet. placenta (around calf or foal).

vass'/kjel -en (=+vann/) teakettle.

vass'/kjemme V +-kjemte/*-kjemde (=+vann/) comb with water, slick down (hair).

vass'/klosett· -et (=+vann/) stool, toilet.

vass'/kraft -a/+-en (=+vann/) water power.

vass'/kran -a (water) faucet, tap.

vass'/laus A (=+vann/løs) arid, dry: **v- elv** dried-up river.

+vass'/le·dning -en (=*/leidning) conduit, water pipe; aqueduct: **den sylviske v-** anat. aqueduct of Sylvius.

vass'/lendt A - marshy, soggy.

vass'/løyse -a dial. lack of water.

vass'/mangel -en (=+vann/) water shortage.

vass'/mål -et dial 1 water surface. 2 water level.

vass'/pytt -en (=+vann/) (water) puddle.

vass'/renne -a (=+vann/) canal, conduit, irrigation ditch; roof gutter.

vass'/rett[1] -en (=+vann/) water rights.

vass'/rett[2] A - (=+vann/) horizontal, level; (in crossword puzzle) across.

vass'/rør -et/*-a (=+vann/rør, *vass/røyr) 1 water pipe. 2 bot. (common) reed (Phragmites communis).

vass'/sele -n yoke for carrying water buckets.

vass'/sjuk A (=+vann/syk) 1 (of soil) acid, sour. 2 (of plants) waterlogged.

vass'/skille -t (=+vann/skille, *vass/skil) geog. divide, watershed.

vass'/skorpe -a (=+vann/) surface of (the) water.

vass'/slange -n (=+vann/) 1 (water) hose. 2 zool. water snake (Natrix). 3 astron. Hydra.

vass'/sprut -en (=+vann/) spurt of water.

vass'/stråle *-n* (=⁺**vann/**) jet of water.
vass'/sur *A* (of soil) acid, sour.
vass'/tett *A* - (=⁺**vann/**) watertight.
vass'/tre *-et dial.* yoke for carrying water buckets.
vass'/tro *-a, pl -trør* water trough.
⁺**vass'/trukken** [/trokken] *A -ent/-et, pl -trukne* (=⁺**vann/**) waterlogged; sopping wet.
vass'/tønne *-a* (=⁺**vann/tønne,** ***vass/tynne**) water barrel.
***vass'/varmar** *-en* hot water tank, water heater.
vass'/veg *-en* (=⁺**vann/**) water route, waterway: **ha lang v-** have to fetch water from a long way off.
vass'/velling *⁺-a/-en* watery gruel.
vass'/verk *-et* (=⁺**vann/**) waterworks.
vas't *I* 1 *naut.* avast. 2 *dial.* **v- litt** hold on, stop, wait a minute.
va'/støvel *-elen, pl -ler* cf **vade/**
va'ter *N*: **ligge, være i v-** be level.
va'ter/bo'rḍ *-et naut.* waterway (heavy beam around outer edge of ship's deck).
va'ter/pass *-et* spirit level.
⁺**va'ter/sott** *-a/-en* cf **vatter/**
va'ter/stag *-et naut.* bobstay.
vatika'n *-et* Vatican.
vat'n[1] *-et* (=⁺**vann**[1]) 1 water: **av reneste v-** of the first rank, first w-; **få v- på mølla** get grist for one's mill; **gå i v-et** be fooled, be taken in, bite (on); **hans tenner (munn) løper i v-** his mouth is watering; **late v-et** urinate; **sette (båt) på v-et** launch (a boat); **ta seg v- over hodet** bite off more than one can chew. 2 lotion, tonic, -wash, etc. (e.g. **barbér/v-, hår/v-, munn/v-, rosen/v-**).
vat'n[2] *-et* (=⁺**vann**[2]) (freshwater) lake.
***vat'nast** *V -ast* be filled with water.
vat'ne *V -a/⁺-et* (=⁺**vanne**[2]) 1 water (an animal, a plant, etc.): sprinkle (the lawn, street, etc.); irrigate: **v- ut** soak. 2 (esp. babytalk) urinate. 3 land on the water.
Vat'ne *Pln* twp, Møre og Romsdal.
va'tre[1] *V -a/⁺-et* level, make level.
vat're[2] *V -a/⁺-et* 1 moiré, water (fabric, silk, etc.). 2: **v-et** moiré, watered; (of snow, water surface, etc.) rippled, wavy. 3: **v-et papegøye** budgerigar, shell parakeet.
Vat's *Pln* twp, Rogaland.
vatt'[1] *-et/⁺-en* 1 batting, cotton wool; padding. 2 *fig.* insulation, packing; soft talk: **legge i vatt** treat with kid gloves.
***vatt'**[2] *pt of* **vinde**[2]
vatt'/dott *-en* wad of cotton.
vatte're *V -te* pad, quilt: **v-te talemåter** circumlocutions.
vat'ter/sott *-a/⁺-en med.* dropsy.
vat'ter/sottig *A* - dropsical.
vatt'/plate *-a/⁺-en* layer of batting.
vatt'/teppe *-t, pl ⁺-r/*-* comforter, quilt.
vaudeville [vådevil'le] *-n hist.* vaudeville (a type of musical comedy popular in 19th century).
***vav'de** *pt of* **vevje**
vav'l *-et* babble, babbling.
vav'le *V -a/⁺-et* babble.
vav're *V -a/⁺-et* waver, weave.
***vav't** *pp of* **vevje**
ve'[1] *-en, pl -er* pain, suffering; woe; *(pl)* (birth) pangs: **ve og vel** weal and woe, welfare.
ve'[2] *-et hist.* sacred place (in Old Norse religion).
ve'[3] *I* alas, woe: **v- den som** woe to him who; **v- meg** ah, me; woe is me.
ve'ḍ[1] *-en* wood; firewood.
ve'ḍ[2] *P* 1 at, by, near; on, to: **bli, stå v- sitt** stick to one's claim, opinion, etc.; **de sitter v- bordet** they are sitting at the table; **professor v- et universitet** professor at a university; **rødme v- ens ord** blush at one's words; **skulder v- skulder** shoulder to shoulder; **stolen står v- vinduet** the chair is by (near) the window; **v- meg der kleber ingen plet** to me there clings no blot (Ibsen); **v- siden av hverandre** side by side. 2 about, with: **det er ikke noe v- ham** there's nothing special a- him; **det var det gode v- det** that was the good thing a- it; **det var noe rart v- hennes øyne** there was sth strange a- her eyes; **jeg kunne ikke gjøre (noe) v- det** I couldn't do anything a- that. 3 (with time) at; about, around; on, upon: **v- flere tilfelle** on several occasions; **v- soloppgang** at sunrise; **v- tolvtiden** around 12 o'clock; **være like, nær v- å** be just about to, on the point of. 4 by, by means of; through: **lede noen v- hånden** lead sby by the hand; **omkomme v- sverd** perish by (the) sword; **v- navn** by name. 5 *(adv.)* by: **like, nær, tett v-** close, near by; almost, on the brink; **(bli, være) ille ved** dismayed, upset. (For uses with verbs, e.g. **bli, holde, komme, ta, være,** see these.)
ve'da *-en* Veda.
⁺**ve'ḍ/aktig** *A* - woody.
ve'ḍ/band *-et dial.* timber line.
⁺**ve'd/bend(e)** *-(e)n lit.* ivy.
⁺**ve'd/bli** *V -ble/-blei, -blitt* continue, go on, keep on: **v- å gjøre noe** c- (go on) doing sth, persist.
⁺**ve'd/blivende** *A* - 1 continued. 2 *(adv.)* still.
***vedd'** *-et* 1 bet, wager: **slå v-** make a b-. 2 mortgage: **sette garden i v-** mortgage the farm.
ved'de[1] *-n* cf **vær**[1]
ved'de[2] *V -a/⁺-et* bet, wager (**om** on); make a b- (**med** with).
⁺**ved'de/kamp** *-en* competition.
⁺**ved'de/løp** *-et* racing; race.
⁺**ved'deløps/bane** *-n* racetrack.
⁺**ved'deløps/fart** *-en* racing speed: **komme med v-** come at breakneck speed, come racing.
⁺**ved'deløps/hest** *-en* racehorse.
ved'de/mål *-et* bet, wager: **inngå (tape) et v-** make (lose) a b-.
⁺**ved'der** *-en, pl vedrer* 1 battering ram; *naut.* ram; *tech.* hydraulic ram. 2 *lit., zool.* ram. 3 *zool.* moth such as burnet or forester moth (Zygaenidae).
***ve'ḍe** *V -a* gather wood.
⁺**ve'der/fares** *V -fores, -fares* (=***/farast**) *lit.* befall: **la sausen v- all rettferdighet** do full justice to the gravy (Boo).
⁺**ve'der/heftig** [also -hef'-] *A - lit.* dependable, reliable, responsible; honest, solid, without frills.
⁺**vederhef'tig/het** *-en lit.* dependability, responsibility; honesty, solidity.
⁺**ve'der/kvege** *V -et lit.* refresh, restore: **en dyp og v-ende søvn** a deep and r-ing sleep (Falkberget).
⁺**ve'der/kvegelse** *-n lit.* comfort, refreshment, restoration; comfort, happiness, relief.
ve'der/lag *-et* 1 compensation, recompense. 2 *arch.* abutment, pier.
ve'derlags/fri *A -tt* free, gratis; *(adv.)* **v-tt** free of charge.
⁺**vederstyg'gelig** *A* - abominable, detestable: **v- kaldt** abominably cold; **den v-e gikta** that confounded rheumatism.
⁺**vederstyg'gelig/het** *-en* abomination.
ve'ḍ/famn *-en* (=⁺**/favn**) measure of wood, 6×6 feet, with varying length (less than a cord).
ve'ḍ/fang *-et* (=⁺**/fange,** ***/fangan**) 1 armload of wood. 2 woodgathering. 3 twigs and brush for burning.
⁺**ve'ḍ/favn** *-en* cf **/famn**
⁺**ve'd/føye** *V -de* affix, annex, attach; append: **til v-de priser** as marked.
ve'd/gå *V infl as* **gå**[1] admit, acknowledge, confess.
ve'd/gåing *-a/⁺-en* (=⁺**-else**) admission, acknowledgment, confession (**av** of).
⁺**ve'd/hefte** *V -et* attach.
ve'd/heng *-et* esp. *anat., bot., zool.* appendage, appendix; attached item.
ve'd/henging *-a* (=⁺**/hengning**) adherence, attachment (**ved** to).
⁺**ve'ḍ/hogger** *-en, pl -e* (=***-ar**) 1 person who cuts firewood, woodcutter. 2 motor-driven wood saw.
ve'ḍ/hogst *-en* (=***-er**) woodcutting.
⁺**ve'd/holdende** *A* - continual, incessant (e.g. rain); persevering, persistent (person, stare; effort, etc.).
⁺**ve'dholden/het** *-en* perseverance, persistence.
⁺**ve'ḍ/hugger** *-en* cf **/hogger**
ve'disk *A* - Vedic.
vedk. =⁺**vedkommende/*****-komande**
ve'ḍ/kasse *-a/-en* woodbox.
ve'd/kjenne *V ⁺-kjente/*-kjende*: **v- seg** acknowledge, admit, recognize.
***vedkjø'meleg** *A* - melancholy, sad, touching.
ve'd/komme *V infl as* **komme**[2] concern: **det v-er ikke deg** it is none of your business; **hva meg v-er** as far as I'm concerned. (See also **v-ende**[1,2]).
⁺**ve'd/kommende**[1] *N* (=***/komande**) 1 party, person concerned: **rette v-** appropriate, proper authorities. 2 *(et)*: **for (mitt) v-** as far as (I) am concerned, for (my) part.
ve'd/kommende[2] *A* - (=***/komande**) 1 concerned, in question: **v- hefte** the issue in question. 2 concerning, relating to: **papirer v- saken** papers r- to this matter.
ve'ḍ/korg *-a* basket for carrying wood.
vedl. =⁺**vedlagt/*****vedlagd**
⁺**ve'd/la** *pt of* **-legge**
ve'ḍ/lad *-et* wood pile.
⁺**ve'd/lagt** *A* - (=***/lagd**) accompanying, attached, enclosed: **v- sendes Dem** e- please find; **etter v-e liste** as per list e-.
ve'ḍ/lass *-et* load of wood.
ve'd/legg *-et* enclosure.
⁺**ve'd/legge** *V -la, -lagt* attach, enclose (with a letter, papers, etc.).
vedli'ke *Av* cf **like**[2], **vedlike/holde**
⁺**vedli'ke/hold** *-et* (=***/hald**) maintenance, upkeep.
⁺**vedli'ke/holde** *V -holdt, -holdt* keep up, maintain.
ve'ḍ/pinne *-n* stick of wood.
⁺**ve'd/røre** *V -te* affect, concern; be relevant: **det v-er ikke saken** it has no bearing on the case.
⁺**ve'd/rørende** *P* concerning; apropos, pertaining to.
ve'ḍ/sag *-a* wood saw.
ve'ḍ/sjau *-en* laying up wood (wood chopping, hauling, and piling).
ve'ḍ/skie *-a* stick of wood.
***ve'd/skifte** *-t* association, connection, dealings.
⁺**ve'ḍ/skjul** *-et* (=***/skjol**) woodshed.
⁺**ve'ḍ/skog** *-en* woods from which firewood is cut.
ve'ḍ/skur *-et* woodshed.
ve'ḍ/skåle *-n* woodshed.
ve'ḍ/stabel *-elen, pl -ler* woodpile.
⁺**ve'd/stå** *V -stod, -stått* acknowledge, admit, stand by (one's convictions): **v- seg** (the same).
ve'd/ta *V infl as* **ta**[1] 1 accept (an offer, a fine). 2 adopt, carry, pass (a motion, resolution, etc.); vote (an appropriation, etc.). 3: **v-tt** accepted, adopted; conventional, traditional.
ve'd/tagelse *-n* cf **/takelse**
ve'd/tak *-et* 1 adoption, passage. 2 decision, resolution.
***ve'd/take** *V infl as* **take** cf **/ta**
⁺**ve'd/takelse** *-n* 1 acceptance (**av** of). 2 esp. *admin.* adoption, passage (**av** of).

+ Bokmål; * Nynorsk; ° Dialect.
After letter: ' stress (Acc. 1); ` tone, stress (Acc. 2); · length.
Below letter: . not pronounced.

ve'dtaks/før *A* having a quorum.
ve'd/tekt *-a/+-en* 1 by-law, ordinance, rule. 2 convention, custom.
+**ve'dtekts/messig** *A* - 1 according to regulations, regular, regulation. 2 conventional, customary.
ve'd/tok *pt of* **-ta**
ve'd/tre *-et, pl -/+-trær* stick of wood.
*__vedun'der__ *-et* cf **vidunder**
*__vedun'derleg__ *A* - cf **vidunderlig**
+**ve'd/vare** *V -te* continue, last, persist.
ve'd/varende *A* - continual, lasting, *persistent.*
*__ve'd/vendel__ *-elen, pl -ler* cf **vi/**
ve'd/øks *-a* (woodcutter's) axe.
Vef'sn *Pln* twp, Nordland.
vef't *-en* weft, woof.
vef'te *V -a/+-et* weft: **være v-et med** have a weft of.
vef'ting *-a* 1 weaving. 2 weft.
ve'g *-en* (=+**vei**) 1 road; way: **av v-en** out of the w-; **det ville ikke være (var ikke) av v-en** it wouldn't be amiss; **fare av v-en** *dial.* have a miscarriage; **gå av v-en for noe, noen** avoid, shun sth, sby; **gjøre v- i noe** make an opening in sth; **gjøre v- i vellinga** *fam.* get things done, make headway; **i v-** away, off; along (**gå i v-** start in (**med** with), start off; **hun satt der og snakket i v-** she sat there talking away (Undset)); **i v-en** in the way (**for** of); the matter, wrong (**med** with); **hva er det i v-en** what's the matter; **kommer ingen v-** gets nowhere; **på god v-** well on the way; **på v- (v-en)** *fam.* along (in pregnancy); **v-en til Trondheim** the road to T-. 2 *anat.* (usu. in compounds) canal, duct.
Ve'ga *Pln* twp, Nordland.
ve'g/anlegg *-et* road construction.
ve'g/arbeid [*/arbei] *-et* road construction, work; (on a sign) road under repair.
Ve'/ga'rd *Prn (m)*
°**ve'ga/skille** *-t* cf **vege/skill**
ve'g/bane *-n* road, road surface, roadway.
ve'g/bom [/bomm] *-men* road barrier, toll bar.
ve'g/dekke *-t* road surface, surfacing.
ve'g/direktø'r *-en* Commissioner of Highways.
ve'ge[1] *V vog, +-d/*-e/*-i* (=+**veie**[1]) 1 weigh; *fig.* consider, ponder: **v- opp** w- out (e.g. flour); **v- opp (for)** equal, make up (for). 2 be of import or weight; count. *3 rock, teeter, tilt. *4 lift up, pry.
*__ve'ge__[2] *V -a* make a road, make one's way.
+**ve'gel/sinnet** *A* - *lit.* capricious, fickle: **Den v-e** The Fickle Woman (play, Holberg).
*__ve'ge/mot__ *-et* crossroads.
*__-ve'ges__ *Av* cf **-veies**
*__ve'ge/skil__ *-et* cf **veg/skill**
vegetabi'lsk *A* - vegetable.
vegeta'r *-en* vegetarian.
+**vegetaria'ner** *-en, pl -e* (=*__-ar__) vegetarian.
vegeta'risk *A* - vegetarian.
vegeta'r/kost -en vegetarian food.
vegetasjo'n *-en* 1 vegetation. 2 *med.* swollen tissue (as in adenoids).
ve'getativ *A* vegetative: **det v-e nervesystem** the autonomic nervous system.
vegete're *V -te* vegetate.
ve'g/farende *A* - traveling, wayfaring: **en v-** a traveler.
vegg' *-en, pl *-er* 1 wall (of a cell, cliff, heart, house, room, tent, etc.): **bort i alle v-er, bort i v-ene** harebrained, ridiculous, senseless; **innen fire v-er** indoors; **på vid v-** wide open; **sette en til v-s** drive one into a corner; floor, nail one; **spansk v-** folding screen; **v- i v-** wall to wall; next door. 2 *anat., biol.* partition, septum, wall.
veg'ge/dyr *-et* bedbug (see **/lus**).
veg'ge/lus *-a zool.* bedbug (Cimex lectularius).
veg'ge/mellom *Av* cf **vegg/imellom**
veg'ge/pryd *-en* wall decoration; *fig.* (of girl) wallflower.
vegg'/far *-et* crevice between logs in a log house.
vegg'/fast *A* - 1 attached to the wall, built-in, permanent. 2 *lit.* solid as a wall.
vegg'/felt *-et, pl -/+-er* wall panel.
vegg'/flate *-a/+-en* wall surface.
vegg'/imel'lom *Av* from wall to wall.
vegg'/kart *-et* wall map.
vegg'/pane'l *-et, pl -/+-er* (cellulose) wallboard.
ve'g/grøft *-a* roadside ditch.
vegg'/smed *-en zool.* death watch beetle (Anobium).
vegg'/tavle *-a* blackboard.
vegg'/teppe *-t, pl +-r/*-* tapestry.
vegg'/ur *-et* wall clock.
*__ve'g/hittar__ *-en* pathfinder.
ve'g/høvel *-elen, pl -ler* road grader.
ve'g/kant *-en* edge of the road, roadside, shoulder.
ve'g/kart *-et* road map.
ve'g/kryss *-et* (=*__/kross__) 1 crossroads. 2 (railroad) crossing. 3 *fig.* parting of the ways.
ve'g/laus *A* 1 roadless, without (access) roads. 2 *lit.* aimless, without plan.
*__ve'g/lei__ *-a* direction.
ve'g/lengd *-a* distance; stretch of road.
*__vegn__ [veng'n] *-a* fishing equipment.
+**vegne** [vei'ne] *N* (=*__veg'ner__) 1 behalf: **på v- av** on b- of; **på mine (dine, hans, farens) v-** on my (your, his, the father's) b-. 2: **alle v-** everyplace, everywhere; **alle vide v-** *dial.* (the same).
ve'g/nett *-et* network of roads.
ve'g/oppsynsmann *-en, pl -menn/*-menner* road maintenance man.
ve'g/overgang [/åver-] *-en* bridge, crossing, overpass.
ve'gre *V -a/+-et*: **v- seg** refuse; **han har v-et seg for å yte keiseren skatt** he has refused to render tribute to the emperor (Ibsen).
ve'g/rett *-en* right of way (over another's property, or right to use a road).
ve'gring *-a/+-en* denial, refusal.
ve'g/side [*/sie] *-a/+-en* roadside.
+**ve'g/skill** *-et* (=*__/skil__, +**veiskille**) crossroads, fork (in the road): **stå ved et v-** stand at a c-, at a parting of the ways.
ve'g/skilt *-et* road sign.
+**ve'g/skraper** *-en, pl -e* (=*__-ar__) road grader.
ve'g/sperring *-a* 1 closing off of a road. 2 barrier across a road, roadblock.
ve'g/stell *-et* 1 care of roads. *2 road commission.
*__ve'g/synt__ *A* - allowing a clear view of the road.
ve'g/undergang *-en* (road) underpass.
Ve'gus/dal *Pln* twp, Aust-Agder.
ve'g/vals(e) *-(e)n* (=+**/valse**) steamroller.
ve'g/vill *A -vilt* lost, stray; confused, disoriented.
+**ve'g/viser** *-en, pl -e* (=*__-ar__) 1 guidepost, roadsign; landmark. 2 guide. 3 city guide, map; directory. 4 *naut.* fairlead(er).
+**ve'g/vokter** *-en, pl -e* (=*__/vaktar__) road maintenance man.
Ve'gårs/hei *Pln* twp, Aust-Agder.
vehik'kel *-elet/vehiklet, pl +vehikler/*-el archaic* vehicle.
+**vei'** *-en* cf **veg**
+**vei'/anlegg** *-et* cf **veg/**
+**vei'/arbeid** *-et* cf **veg/**
+**vei'/bane** *-n* cf **veg/**
+**vei'/bom** [/bomm] *-men* cf **veg/**
vei'de *V -de/+-et* 1 *lit.* hunt, go hunting; follow, track. 2 clean out, gut.
vei'de/hår *-et* (animal) whisker, vibrissa.
+**vei'/dekke** *-t* cf **veg/**
vei'de/mann *-en, pl -menn/*-menner* *dial., archeol.* hunter.
+**vei'/direktø'r** *-en* cf **veg/**
*__vei'dn__ *-a* hunting; hunting gear.
*__vei'e__[1] *-a* fluid, juice.
+**vei'e**[2] *N*: **skaffe til v-** provide.
+**vei'e**[3] *V -de* cf **vege**[1]
°**vei'es** *N*: **du store v-** good grief, good heavens, of all things.
+**-vei'es** *Av* cf **-veges**
+**vei'/farende** *A* - cf **veg/**
+**vei'/forbin'delse** *-n* (connecting) road, road connection: **er det v-?** is there a road?
*__vei'fte__ *V -a* cf **vifte**[2]
+**vei'/grøft** *-a* cf **veg/**
+**vei'/høvel** *-elen, pl -ler* cf **veg/**
*__vei'k__[1] *-en, pl -er* cf **veike**
vei'k[2] *pt of* **vike**[2]
vei'k[3] *A* weak (ice, muscles, person, etc.); flexible, pliant: **han ble v- i knærne** his knees buckled.
+**vei'/kant** *-en* cf **veg/**
+**vei'/kart** *-et* cf **veg/**
vei'ke *-n* (=*__veik__[1], +**veke**[2]) wick.
vei'k/helsa *A* - in poor health.
*__vei'king__[1] *-a* reduction, weakening.
vei'king[2] *-en* weakling.
*__vei'kje__[1] *-a* (=*__vækje__) girl.
*__vei'kje__[2] *V -te* slacken, weaken.
vei'kling *-en* weakling.
vei'k/liv *-et dial.* abdomen.
vei'kne *V -a/+-et* become weak, weaken.
+**vei'/kors** *-et* cf **veg/kryss**
vei'k/rygg *-en* 1 small of the back. 2 *fig.* spineless person.
+**vei'/kryss** *-et* cf **veg/**
vei'k/skap *-en* weakness.
*__vei'k/år(e)__ *-a* vein.
*__vei'last__ *V -ast* break apart, crack, separate.
vei'le *-a* break, crack, fault; drawback, flaw.
+**vei'/lede** *V -et* guide, instruct.
+**vei'/ledende** *A* - guiding, instructive: **v- pris** suggested (retail) price (est. by government price control).
+**vei'/leder** *-en, pl -e* guide, instructor; marker, trail sign.
+**vei'/le'dning** *-en* 1 direction, guidance, instruction (**i** in): **under hennes v-** under her g-. 2 directions, guide, handbook.
+**vei'/legeme** *-t* roadbed.
+**vei'/løs** *A* cf **veg/laus**
+**vei'/mann** *-en, pl -menn* road supervisor.
+**vei'/nett** *-et* cf **veg/**
+**vei'/oppsynsmann** *-en, pl -menn* cf **veg/**
+**vei'/overgang** [/åver-] *-en* cf **veg/**
+**vei'r** *-et* cf **vær**[2]
+**vei'/rett** *-en* cf **veg/**
+**-veis** *Av* cf **-veges**
+**vei'/side** *-a/-en* cf **veg/**
+**vei'/skille** *-t* cf **veg/skill**
+**vei'/skilt** *-et* cf **veg/**
+**vei'/skjell** *-et* cf **vege/skill**
+**vei'/skraper** *-en, pl -e* cf **veg/**
+**vei'/sperring** *-a/-en* cf **veg/**
vei't[1] *-a* (=*__veite__[1]) 1 ditch. 2 alley, narrow passage or street.
vei't[2] *pr of* **vite, vete**[2]
*__vei'te__[1] *-a* cf **veit**[1]
vei'te[2] *V -a/+-et/*-te* ditch, drain by ditching.
vei'te/kant *-en* edge of a ditch.
vei'tsle *-a* 1 *archaic* feast. 2 *hist.* king's right, while traveling, to demand food and lodging from his vassals. 3 *hist.* enfeoffment of royal property.
*__veitt'__ *-et* flyblow, fly egg.
+**vei'/undergang** *-en* cf **veg/**
vei'v *-a* 1 crank. 2 *dial.* rotation, swing, turn.
vei'v/aksel *-elen, pl -ler* crank axle, crankshaft.
+**vei'/vals(e)** *-(e)n* cf **veg/**
vei've *V -a/-de/+-et* 1 swing, wave: **v- med armene** w- one's arms. 2 crank, turn, wind: **v- på symaskin** t- a sewing machine. 3 rock, sway, swing.
+**vei'/vesen** *-et* road commission, highway department.
vei'v/hus *-et* crank case.
+**vei'/viser** *-en, pl -e* cf **veg/**

+vei'/vokter -en, pl -e cf veg/
+vei'v/spill -et (=*/spel) hand organ.
+vei'v/stang -a, pl -stenger (=*/stong) connecting rod.
vei'v/tapp -en crank pin.
*ve'k[1] -et bend (in road); deviation; nuance, shade.
+ve'k[2] pt of vike[2]
+ve'k[3] A cf veik[3]
ve'ke[1] -a (=+uke) week: **første dag i veka/uken** first day of the w-; **til veka/uken** next w-.
+ve'ke[2] -n cf veike
ve'ke/blad -et (=+uke/) weekly (magazine, newspaper).
ve'ke/dag -en (=+uke/) day of the week; weekday.
ve'ke/gammal A -t, pl -gamle (=+uke/-gammel) week-old.
ve'ke/kort -et (=+uke/) pass good for a week.
ve'ke/lang A (=+uke/) week-long, week's.
ve'ke/lønn -a/+-en (=+uke/, */løn) week's pay.
+ve'ke/penger pl (=+uke/, *-ar) weekly allowance.
ve'ke/presse -a/+-en (=+uke/) weekly press; the weeklies.
+ve'ket pp of vike[2]
ve'ke/vis Av (=+uke/) for weeks: **i u-** (the same).
+ve'k/het -en cf veik/skap
vekk' Av (=vekke[5]) 1 away, off: **v- fra** a- from. 2 absent, away, gone: **v- i en** crazy about sby. 3 lost, missing: **komme v-** get lost. 4 (as *imper.*) go away, *(pop.)* scram: **v- med deg** (the same); **v- med fingrene** hands off, let go. 5: **i ett v-** incessantly; **fort v-, stadig v-** constantly.
+vek'ke[1] -a (=*vekkje[1]) small bell (e.g. for cow or on horse harness).
+vek'ke[2] V vakk, vekket cf kvekke[1]
+vek'ke[3] V vekte/vakte (=*vekkje[2]) 1 awaken, wake, wake up (sby). 2 *fig.* arouse, call forth, inspire: **v- til live** call forth, revive (e.g. a memory). 3 *eccl.* convert (e.g. Christians to true faith): **de vakte** the pious, the true believers.
+vek'ke[4] V vekte (=*vekkje[3]) 1 open a vein: **v- blod** draw blood. 2 chop open a passage through ice.
vek'ke[5] Av cf vekk
+vek'ke/klokke -a cf vekker/
+vek'kelse -n (=*-ing) 1 awakening, stirring. 2 (religious) revival; conversion.
+vek'kelses/møte -t (=*-ings/) revival meeting.
+vek'kelses/predikan't -en revival preacher.
+vek'ker -en, pl -e (=*vekkjar) 1 awakener (sby, sth that awakens one). 2 eye-opener, rousing or warning experience.
+vek'ker/klokke -a (= *vekkjar/) alarm clock.
+vek'ker/ur -et (=*vekkjar/) alarm clock.
*vekkj'e[1] -a cf vekke[1]
*vekkj'e[2] V vekte, vakt/vekt cf vekke[3]
*vekkj'e[3] V vekte cf vekke[4]
*vek'se V voks, vakse/-i cf vokse[2]
vek'sel -elen, pl -ler 1 *merc.* bill of exchange: **egen/v-** promissory note. 2 *arch.* trimmer. 3 (on railroad track) switch. 4 change, shift (e.g. of fashion).
vek'sel/aksep't -en acceptance of a bill of exchange.
vek'sel/bruk -et rotation of crops.
vek'sel/drift -a/+-en rotation of crops.
veksele'r -en *merc.* broker, money changer.
+vek'sel/falsk N forgery.
vek'sel/obligasjo'n -en promissory note for (short term) secured loan.
+vek'sel/rytter -en, pl -e (=*-ar) *merc.* kite flier (one who makes use of accommodation bills, or "kites").
+vek'sel/rytteri' -et *merc.* kite flying, kiting (see preceding word).
+vek'sel/sang -en (=*/song) antiphony; antiphonal singing.
vek'sel/spenning -a/+-en *elec.* voltage of alternating current.
+vek'sel/spill -et (=*/spel) alternation, interaction, interplay (**mellom** between): **det evige v- mellom forskning og praktisk arbeid** the unending interplay between research and practical work (Aftenposten).
+vek'sel/strøm' -men (=*/straum) alternating current.
+vek'sel/virkning -en (=*/verknad) interaction, reciprocal influence.
vek'sel/vis Av alternately, changing off.
vek'sle V -a/+-et 1 exchange (blows, letters, greeting, etc.): **v- noen ord med en** e- a few words with sby. 2 change (money); (of facial expression, weather, etc.) change, shift, vary; alternate (**med** with).
vek'sle/appara't -et changemaker, money changer.
+vek'sle/penger pl (=*-ar) change.
vek'sler pl of veksel
vek'slings/side [*/sie] -a side (of ice-skating track) where speedskaters change lanes.
vek'st -en (=vokster) 1 growth: **i sterk v-** in rapid g-; **stanse i v-en** stop in its development, stunt its g-. 2 size, stature: **liten av v-** small of stature. 3 plant(s), vegetation: **nyttige v-er** useful plants.
vek'st/benk -en hotbed.
+vek'st/beting'else -n condition of, prerequisite to growth.
+vek'sterlig A - cf voksterlig
+vek'st/fremmende A - (=*/fremjande) growth-promoting.
vek'st/hormo'n -et, pl +-er/*- growth hormone.
vek'st/hus -et greenhouse.
*vek'string -en 1 adolescent, youth. 2 sapling.
vek'st/vilkår -et conditions of growth.
vek't[1] -a/+-en weight (of an argument, a load, responsibility, stone, etc.); stress: **legge v- på** attach importance to, lay stress on.
vek't[2] -a balance, scales: **V-en** *astron.* the Balance, Libra.
vek't/arm -en arm of a lever.
+vek't/bespa'relse -n saving of weight.
vek'te pt of vekke[3,4] vekkje[2,3]
+vek't/enhet -en unit of weight.
+vek'ter -en, pl -e (=*-ar) *hist.* watchman, night watch.
+vek'ter/vers -et (=*-ar/) watchman's song (or cry), to mark the hours.
vek'tig A - heavy, weighty; grave (objection), strong (argument).
vek't/klasse -a/-en weight class.
vek't/laus A (=+/løs) weightless.
vek't/lodd -et counterweight, weight.
+vek't/løfter -en, pl -e (=*/lyftar) weight lifter.
+vek't/løs A cf /laus
vek'tor -en, pl -torer 1 *phys.* vector. 2 *med.* carrier (of a disease).
vek'tor/analy'se -n *phys.* vector analysis.
vek't/skål -a (scale) pan.
+vek't/stang -a, pl -stenger (=*/stong) lever; arm of a scale.
vek't/tap -et loss of weight.
vel'[1] +-let/*-et 1 good, well-being, welfare: **jeg vil ditt v-** I wish this for your own good. 2 welfare organization, society; league (of citizens living in a certain urban area).
*ve'l[2] pr of velje
vel'[3] [*ve'l] A - 1 well (=good; healthy): **alt v-** all well; **gid det var så v-** if only that were true; **jo det var v-** yes indeed; **som v- er** which is lucky (for us); **v- den som kunne glemme** happy the man who could forget (Ibsen). 2 *(adv.)* well (see also **godt**): **både v- og lenge** a good, long time; **det går ham v-** he is doing w-; **føle seg v-** feel fine; **komme v- med** be a great help; **komme seg v- hjem** get home all right (safe and sound); **lev v-** goodbye, best wishes; **så v- som** as w- as; **v- hjem** (farewell to one's guests, expressing wish for their safe return home); **v- likt** w-liked; **v- møtt** welcome back; see you (next time); **v- talt** w- spoken. 3 *(adv.)* happily, successfully; as soon as: **da han v- hadde gjort sitt toilette** as soon as he had finished dressing (Sverdrup); **v- nede snudde han seg** safely down, he turned around (Elster d. y.).
vel'[4] Av (stressed) 1 (usu. initially) indeed; of course; to be sure: **v- er han ung, men ....** of course he is young (yes, he *is* young), but . . . ; **ja v- er han dikter** certainly he is a poet (Ibsen). 2 (with *adj.*, *adv.*) rather, (a little) too: **bilen er v- liten** the car is on the small side; **talen ble v- lang** the speech got rather lengthy. 3 (with nouns, *pron.*) fully; every bit; and then some (often with **så**): **en mann på v- 30 år** a man of thirty-odd years; **v- så viktig** at least as (every bit as) important; **klokka er (godt og) v- åtte** it's just past 8 o'clock.
vel'[5] Av (unstressed, either following verb or finally, where it may also be stressed; often preceded by **da** or **nå**): 1 (question, often requiring repetition of verb): **du skrøner v-** you're lying, aren't you? **du skulle v- ikke vite hans adresse** you don't happen to know his address, do you? 2 (supposition) I suppose, may be, probably: **ja, vi må v- det** yes, I suppose we have to; **det kunne v- være** that might well be. 3 (hope) I hope, I trust; no doubt, surely: **han har v- fått brevet mitt** I trust he's gotten my letter; **du har v- hørt om ham** surely you've heard about him; **han vil da v- ikke gjøre det?** I trust he won't do that? 4 (surprise) really, surely: **hvem skulle v- ha trodd det?** who would have believed it? **De tenker da v- aldri på å** you surely aren't thinking of. 5 (impatience) of course: **ned til hotellet, v-** down to the hotel, of course. 6 (emphasis) certainly, really: **han er v- vemmelig** he's really repulsive (Sfinx).
vel'[6] I 1 (expectantly) well (in that case), well then; all right, O.K.; **nå v-** (the same); **v- v-** (the same). 2 (compliantly): **ja (jo) v-** yes, indeed; yes, of course; to be sure; well, yes; I see; O.K.; **nei v-** (after negative statement) no, indeed; no, of course not; well, no. 3 (obediently) yes (madam, sir); certainly: **ja v-** (the same); **nei v-** no (madam, sir).
+vel'/aktet A-*archaic* highly regarded, respected; (in letter writing) esteemed.
+velan' I all right, well, well then.
+vel'/ansten'dig A - *lit.* decent, proper, respectable.
+velansten'dig/het -en *lit.* decency, propriety, respectability.
vela'r[1] -en velar.
vela'r[2] A velar.
vel'/assorte'rt [*ve'l/] A - well-assorted, well-stocked.
+vel'/befin'nende -t comfort, health, well-being.
+vel'/beføy'd A - appropriate, just, legitimate.
+vel'/begrun'net A - well-founded; soundly based.
+vel'/beha'g -et 1 delight, relish, zest: **med vitende og v-** deliberately, with full knowledge (of the consequences). 2 *eccl.* (God's) pleasure: **i mennesker hans v-** good will toward men (Luke 2,14).
+velbeha'gelig A - pleasing, satisfying;

+ Bokmål; * Nynorsk; ° Dialect.
After letter: ' stress (Acc. 1); ` tone, stress (Acc. 2); · length.
Below letter: . not pronounced.

(adv.) luxuriously: **hun lå v- tilbakelenet i sin seng** she leaned back l- in her bed (Boo).

+vel'/beholden *A -ent, pl -ne* in safety, safe and sound.

vel'/berga [*ve'l/] *A* - (=+-et) 1 safe, safe and sound: **v- i hus** (of grain) into the barn in good condition. 2 well-supplied (**med** with); well-fixed, well-off.

+vel'/berådd' *A* -: **med v- hu** deliberately, purposely.

+vel'/beten'kt *A* - judicious, well-advised.

***ve'l/boren** [/båren] *A -e/-i, pl -ne* cf **/båren**

***ve'l/budd** *A -/-butt* well-equipped.

vel'/bygd [*ve'l/] *A -/*-bygt* well-built, well-constructed, well-proportioned.

+vel'/byrdig *A archaic* highborn, wellborn.

+vel'byrdig/het *-en*: **Deres v-** *archaic* your Honor, your Worship.

+vel'/båren *A -ent, pl -ne* (=*/**boren**) *archaic* highborn, wellborn.

+velbå'ren/het *-en*: **Deres v-** *archaic* your Grace, your Worship.

+vel'de[1] *en* majesty; might, power; monumentality: **i all sin v-** in all its (awesome) majesty; **en v- av hår** a mass of hair.

vel'de[2] *-t* 1 dominion, rule; authority, command. *2 (=velde[1]).

+velde'dig *A* - benevolent, charitable.

+velde'dig/het *-en* benevolence, charity.

+vel'/dekket *A* - well-laden (table).

***ve'lder** *pl* tools; gear, tackle.

vel'dig *A* - 1 enormous, huge, tremendous, (etc.). 2 *(bibl., lit.)* mighty, powerful. 3 *(adv.)* extremely, tremendously, very: **han var v- kjekk og gråt ikke** he was very brave and didn't cry (Hoel); **v- hyggelig** *(pop.)* awfully nice.

+vel'/dreven *A -et, pl -ne* (=*/**driven**) 1 well-run. 2 (of dogs) well-trained.

***ve'le**[1] *-a* cunning; trick, wile.

***ve'le**[2] *-t* tail (of a bird).

***ve'le**[3] *V -a* 1 lure; set traps; fool. 2 bustle, fuss.

ve'le[4] *V -te* cf **vøle**[4]

+vel'/egnet [/einet] *A* - well-suited (**til å** to).

***ve'lende** *-t* gullet.

***ve'l/far** *-et* departure, farewell.

vel'/ferd [*ve'l/fær] *-a/+-en* 1 well-being, welfare: **til v- for** for the benefit of. 2 social service, welfare (provided through official agencies).

vel'ferds/konto'r *-et, pl -/+-er* office which provides welfare services (e.g. entertainment, recreational activities, social benefits, etc.) to sailors, soldiers, employees, etc.

vel'ferds/sak *-a/+-en* matter of sby's welfare.

vel'ferds/stat *-en* welfare state (in ref. to social services provided by official agencies).

Vel'/fjo'rd *Pln* twp, Nordland.

vel'/forma [*ve'l/] *A* - (=+-et) well-formed, well-shaped, well-turned.

+vel'/fortje'nt *A* - richly deserved, well-earned, well-merited.

vel'/funde'rt [*ve'l/] *A* - sound, well-founded.

vel'/fødd [*ve'l/] *A -/*-født* well-fed.

vel'/gang *-en archaic, dial.* good health, prosperity, well-being.

+vel'ge *V valgte, valgt* (=***velje**) 1 choose, select (**til** as): **v- seg ut** pick, select; **jeg v-er meg april** I choose April for my own (Bjørnson). 2 elect (**til** as); hold an election, vote: **v- en inn** elect as member (**i** of).

+vel'ger *-en, pl -e* (=***veljar**) 1 elector, voter; constituent. 2 (on automatic telephone switchboard) selector switch.

+vel'ger/masse *-n* electorate, (the) voters.

***ve'l/gjerande** *A* - cf **/gjørende**

***ve'l/gjerar** *-en* cf **/gjører**

***ve'l/gjerd** [/jær] *-a* beneficence, charity, good deed.

vel'/gjerning [/jæ'rning, *ve'l/] *-a/+-en* beneficence, good deed.

***ve'l/gjeten** *A -e/-i, pl -ne* well-reputed, well spoken of.

+vel'/gjort [/jort] *A* - (=*/**gjord**) well done.

+vel'/gjørende *A* - (=*/**gjerande**) 1 benevolent, charitable. 2 beneficial; blessed, pleasant, refreshing: **en v- motsetning** a r- contrast.

+vel'gjøren/het *-en* beneficence, good deed; kindness (**mot** to); charity.

+vel'/gjører *-en, pl -e* (=*/**gjerar**) benefactor.

+velgå'ende *N*: **i beste v-** the best of health.

***ve'l/halden** *A -e/-i, pl -ne* cf **/holden**

+vel'/havende *A* - well-off, well-to-do: **en v- mann** (also:) a man of means.

+vel'/holden *A -ent, pl -ne* prosperous, well-off, well situated.

+vel'/holdt *A* - in good condition, well-kept, well-preserved.

+ve'lig *A* - *archaic* lively, spirited.

velin [veleng'] *-et* 1 parchment, vellum. 2 vellum paper.

velin/papi'r *-et* vellum paper.

***vel'je** *V vel, valde, valt* cf **velge**

+vel'/kjent *A* - (=*/**kjend**) familiar, well-known.

vel'/klang [*ve'l/] *-en* euphony, harmony, melodiousness.

vel'/kledd [ve'l/] *A -/*-kledt* well-dressed.

vel'/klingende [*ve'l/] *A* - euphonious, harmonious, melodious.

***ve'l/kome** [/kåme] *-a* cf **/komst**

***ve'l/komen** [/kåmen] *A -e/-i, pl -ne* cf **-kommen**[2]

***ve'l/komme** *-a* cf **/komst**

+velkom'men[1] *et lit.* welcome.

velkom'men[2] *A +-ent, pl -komne* (=*/**komen**) welcome (gift, guest, letter, etc.): **by (hilse, ønske) en v-** bid (wish) sby welcome, welcome sby.

vel'/komst [*ve'l/] *-en* reception, welcome: **til v-** by way of welcome.

vell'[1] *-et* fount, spring; flood, torrent, wealth; abundance, profusion: **et v- av lys** a flood of light.

+vell'[2] *-et* cf **vel**[1]

vel'/laga [*ve'l/] *A* - (=+-et) well-prepared (food).

vel'/lagra [*ve'l/] *A* - (=+-et) matured, seasoned.

***vel'le**[1] *V vall, volle/-i* cf **velle**[2]

+vel'le[2] *V +-et/+velte* (=***velle**[1]) gush, issue, well (**fram, ut** forth, out).

+vel'/levnet *et* (=*/**livnad**) high living, luxury, luxurious living.

vel'ling *-a/-en* 1 gruel: **som katten om v-en** (treat sth) with extreme caution (as if afraid of getting burned). 2 mire, mush. 3 *fig.* mixture, potpourri.

***ve'l/livnad** *-en* cf **/levnet**

***ve'l/lukka** *A* - cf **/lykket**

vel'/lukt [/lokt] *-a/+-en* fragrance, perfume, scent.

vel'/luktende [/loktene] *A* - fragrant; perfumed, scented.

vel'/lyd [*ve'l/] *-en* euphony, harmony, melodiousness.

+vel'/lykket *A* - (=+/**lykt**, */**lukka**) successful (occasion, vacation, etc.).

vel'/lyst [*ve'l/] *-a/+-en lit.* 1 delight, rapture, thrill. 2 lust, sensuality; sexual desire, pleasure.

vel'/lystig [*ve'l/] *A* - *lit.* sensual, voluptuous; lascivious, lustful.

vel'/lysting [*ve'l/] *-en* libertine.

vel'/lærd [*ve'l/] *A* - learned.

vel'/læte [*ve'l/] *-t* commendation, praise.

vel'/makt [*ve'l/] *-a/+-en* strength, vigor; prosperity, wealth: **i sin v-** in his prime; in his palmy days.

+vel'makts/dager *pl* (=*-**ar**) days of prosperity; palmy days, prime.

+vel'/menende *A* - well-intentioned, well-meaning (person).

+vel'/me'nt *A* - (=*/**meint**) well-meant: **et v- råd** a w- piece of advice.

+vel'/næ'rt *A* - well-fed, well-nourished.

+velnært/het *-en* plumpness, sleekness.

vel'/nøgd [*ve'l/] *A -/*-nøgt* (=+/**nøyd**) (well-)satisfied (**med** with).

***ve'l/nøye** *-t* satisfaction.

+vel'/oppdra'gen *A -ent, pl -ne* well-behaved, well-bred.

vel'/ordna [*ve'l/] *A* - (=+-et) orderly, well-arranged.

velosipe'd *-en* ordinary, velocipede (an old-fashioned bicycle).

+vel'/overveid [/åver-] *A* - considered, deliberate, well thought-out: **mindre v-** ill-advised, not advisable, rash.

+vel'/pleid *A* - well-cared-for, well-groomed; neat, trim.

vel'/proporsjone'rt [*ve'l] *A* - well-proportioned.

vel'/renomme'rt [*ve'l/] *A* - reputable, well-reputed.

vel'/retta [*ve'l/] *A* - (=+-et) well-aimed, well-directed.

***ve'l/rådd** *A -/*-rådt* cf **/berådd**

***ve'l/seda** *A* - well-behaved, well-brought-up.

velsigne [velsing'ne] *V -a/+-et* 1 bless: **Herren v- deg og bevare deg** the Lord b- thee and keep thee. 2: **v-et** blessed; glorious; *fam.* confounded (**den v-ede villanden** that c- wild duck (Ibsen)). 3: **v-et** *(adv.)* gloriously, wonderfully: **hun hadde så v-et gode og trauste hender** she had such w- good, firm hands (Falkberget).

+velsignelse [velsing'nelse] *-n* cf **velsigning**

+velsignelses/rik *A* beneficent, beneficial; richly blessed.

velsigning [velsing'ning] *-a/+-en* (=+-**else**) blessing; *eccl.* benediction: **det er en guds v- at han ikke kom** it's a blessing he didn't come; **en (guds) v-** *fam.* an abundance, any amount, no end (**av** of); **med min v-** with my blessing, consent.

+vel'/sittende *A* - well-fitting.

+vel'/situe'rt *A* - well-off, well-to-do.

ve'lsk *A* - 1 *archaic* French, Gallic. 2 Welsh.

vel'/skapt [*ve'l/] *A* - shapely, well-formed, well-shaped.

+vel'skapt/het *-en* shapeliness.

vel'sk/bind *-et* half leather binding.

vel'/skikka [*ve'l/] *A* - (=+-et) well-suited (**til** for).

+vel'/skreven *A -et, pl -ne* (=*/**skriven**) well-written.

***ve'l/skyldig** *A* - ingratiating.

vel'/smak [*ve'l/] *-en* good flavor, tastiness.

vel'/smakende [*ve'l/] *A* - flavorful, palatable, tasty.

vel'/spekka [*ve'l/] *A* - (=+-et) fat, well-filled (e.g. purse).

vel'/stand [*ve'l/] *-en/*-et* affluence, prosperity, wealth: **sitte i v-** be affluent.

velstands/mann *-en, pl -menn/*-menner* affluent man.

vel'/stelt [*ve'l/] *A* - well-cared-for, taken care of; neat, trim, well-groomed.

vel'/stilt [*ve'l/] *A* - prosperous, well-situated (economically).

vel'/sty'rt [*ve'l/] *A* - well-administered, governed.

vel'/stående [*ve'l/] *A* - prosperous, well-off, well-to-do.

vel't *-en* 1 overturn(ing), roll(ing), tumble: **v- i v-** end over end. 2 *archaic, dial.* trump: **av v-en** of the finest sort, highest class; **være i v-en** be highly popular, be in fashion; (of a person) be lionized, be the man, woman of the moment. 3 *agr., dial.* roller (to break up and smooth the soil).

vel'/talende [*ve'l/] *A* - eloquent.

+velta'len/het *-en* eloquence.

vel'te[1] *-a* 1 heap, pile; confused mass, welter. 2 *forest.* pile, stack of logs

(for further transport or to be dumped down a slide); place where logs are gathered (for further transport, etc.). 3 *agr.*, *dial.* roller (to break up and smooth the soil). 4 *agr.*, *dial.* furrow; furrow slice. 5 *dial.* tipped over or upset position.
vel'te[2] *V valt*, +*-et*/**volte*/**-i* 1 overturn, upset; fall, tip, topple over; tumble. 2 crowd, pour, stream; roll, surge: **så v-et forbannelsene løs** then the curses poured forth (Evensmo).
vel'te[3] *V -a*/+*-et*/**-e* 1 roll (over); thrust: **v- ansvaret over på en** shove (shift) the responsibility onto one; *(pop.)* pass the buck. 2 overturn, tip over, upset; overthrow, topple: **v- over ende** tip over. 3 *(refl.)*: **v- seg** roll, toss; wallow (i in); **v- seg inn på en** intrude on sby.
vel'te/fjøl *-a* (on a plow) moldboard.
***ve'l/te'nt** *A* - cf /**tjent**
vel'/tilfred's [*ve'l/] *A* - contented, satisfied, well pleased.
+vel'/tjent *A* - (of person) deserving, that has served well.
+vel'/truffet [/troffet] *A* -, *pl -trufne* striking, well-drawn (e.g. portrait).
ve'lum *-et*, *pl vela* soft palate, velum.
+vel'/underrettet *A* - well-informed.
***ve'l/unnar** *-en* cf /**ynder**
velu'r *-en*/*-et* velour(s).
+vel'/valgt *A* - (=*/**vald**) well-chosen.
+vel'/valt *A* - cf /**valgt**
vel'/vilje [*ve'l/] *-n* benevolence, friendliness, good will; favor, kindness.
vel'/villig *A* - (=*/**viljug**) agreeable, friendly, well-disposed: **sjåføren gryntet v-** the chauffeur grunted obligingly (Evensmo).
+vel'villig/het *-en* benevolence, friendliness, goodwill.
vel'/vis [*ve'l/] *A archaic* (ironic) sage, wise.
+vel'/voksen *A -ent*, *pl -ne* (=*/**vaksen**) fine, good-sized, strapping; well-proportioned, well-shaped; able-bodied, adult.
vel/være [*ve'l/] *-t* comfort, well-being.
+vel'/ynder *-en*, *pl -e* benefactor, patron.
+velærver'dig/het *-en lit.*, *hum.* reverence: **hans v-** his Reverence.
vel'/øvd [*ve'l/] *A* -/**-øvt* (=+/**øvet**) practiced, well-trained.
***vem'ber** *pl of* **vomb**
***vem'jast** *V vemst*, *vemdest*, *vemst* cf **vemmes**
vem'melig *A* - disgusting, nasty, repulsive; foul, vile; annoying, unpleasant.
+vem'melse *-n* disgust, loathing, repulsion (**for** for).
***vem'mer** *pl of* **vom**
+vem'mes *V vemtes*, *vemmes* (=***vemjast**) be disgusted, repelled (**over, ved** by, at).
ve'mod *-et* melancholy, sadness.
vemo'dig *A* - melancholy, mournful; plaintive, sad; wistful.
ve'mods/full *A lit.* melancholy, mournful, sad.
***vem'st** *pr*, *pp of* **vemjast**
+vem'tes *pt of* **vemmes**
Ve'mund/vik *Pln* twp, Nord-Trøndelag.
***ve'n[1]** *-en*, *pl -er* cf **venn**
***ve'n[2]** *pr of* **venje**
ve'n[3] *A* 1 *dial.*, *poet.* comely, fair, pretty. 2 *dial.* agreeable, nice; (esp. of animals) gentle, goodnatured: **kjære v-e** (in requesting, persuading, etc.) please; **men kjære v-e deg** (as expression of mild surprise) but my dear man, woman.
***ven'd** *-a* 1 run, trip, turn (to a place and back). 2 line of verse or song. 3 twill pattern (on cloth). 4 face, right side (of cloth).
+ven'd/bar *A* reversible.
ven'de[1] [*ven'de] *-a dial.* 1 run, trip, turn (to a place and back); turn (at end of a row of plowing or sowing). 2 time: ***denne v-a var verre enn nokosinne før** this t- was worse than ever before.
***ven'de[2]** *-t* change, turn (of events).
ven'de[3] [*ven'de] *V* +*-te*/**-e* 1 turn (a collar, one's head, a page, etc.): **v- nesen hjemover** head for home; **v- om** turn around, turn back; reverse; **v- opp (og) ned på noe** turn sth upside down; **v- på skillingen** be tight, pinch pennies; **v- ryggen til en, v- en ryggen** turn one's back on sby; **v- tilbake** return; turn back; **vite å v- sine ord** know how to put things, how to choose one's words. 2 face, look out (**mot** on): **huset v-er (ut) mot havet** the house faces the sea. 3 *naut.* put about, veer. 4 *(refl.)*: **v- seg** turn (**mot** toward; against; **til** to); turn over; (of wind, a stream, etc.) change, shift direction; **v- seg til det beste** turn out for the best; **det v-er seg i meg** I feel nauseated, my stomach is churning; **hvor man (så) v-er seg (hen)** everywhere, on all sides, wherever one turns.
ven'de/hake *-n* cant hook.
ven'de/hals [*ven'de/] *-en zool.* wryneck (Jynx torquilla).
+ven'de/krets *-en* (=*/**krins**) *astron.*, *geog.* tropic: **den nordlige v-** the Tropic of Cancer; **den sydlige v-** the Tropic of Capricorn.
ven'de/kåpe [*ven'de/] *-a* turncoat; opportunist.
ven'del/rot *-a bot.* valerian (Valeriana officinalis).
ven'de/punkt [*ven'de/] *-et* 1 crisis, turning point. 2 *math.* inflection point. 3 *astron.* apsis.
+ven'der[1] *-en*, *pl -e* (=***-ar**) turner; tedder.
+ven'der[2] *en*, *pl *-*/+*-e hist.* Wend.
ven'de/reis [*ven'de/] *-a*/+*-en* putting back, return (without accomplishing one's object): **gjøre v-** put, turn back.
ven'de/sirkel [*ven'de/] *-elen*, *pl -ler geog.* tropic (see /**krets**).
vendet'ta *-en* vendetta.
ven'ding [*ven'ding] *-a*/+*-en* 1 turn, turning (of a dress, hay, one's head, etc.); reversal; movement: **en v- til høyre** a turn to the right; **en v- til det verre** a turn for the worse; **i en snever v-** in a pinch, in an emergency; **rask (fort, kvikk, lett) i v-en** quick, quick moving; quick-witted, quick on the uptake; **sein (seig, tung) i v-en** slow, slow moving; slow-witted, etc. 2 phrase, turn of speech: **stående v-** stock (set) p-. 3 trip, turn: **hun gjorde en v- bort i fjøset** she made a trip to the barn (there and back). 4 *naut.* tacking, wearing. 5 *med.* version.
ven'disk *A* - Wendic, Wendish.
***ven'dsle** *-a* sale, turnover (of goods).
ve'ne *-n* vein.
venerasjo'n *-en* veneration.
vene'risk *A* - venereal.
***ve'ne/tenest(e)** *-a* cf **venne/tjeneste**
venetiansk [venetsia'nsk] *A* - Venetian.
Venezia [vene'tsia] *Pln* Venice.
+venezuela'ner *-en*, *pl -e* (=***-ar, venezuelan**) Venezuelan.
venezuela'nsk *A* - Venezuelan.
veng' *-en*, *pl *-er* (=+**vinge**) 1 wing (of airplane, bird, insect, etc.) (also *fig.*): **få luft under v-ene** get a chance to show what one can do; **(gå, komme, være) på v-ene** fly, (get, be) on the w-; **under ens v-er** under sby's w-. 2 (winglike objects): blade, vane (on mill wheel, turbine, etc.); side of nostril; *dial.* outrigger (on dugout boat); cuddy, (small) cabin aft on main deck.
veng'e/bo'rd *-et* cf **vinge/**
veng'e/fang *-et* cf **vinge/**
***veng'e/skoten** [/skåten] *A -e*/*-i*, *pl -ne* cf **vinge/skutt**
veng'e/slag *-et* cf **vinge/**
***veng'je** *-a* cf **veng**
***veng'le** *V -a* fly unsteadily (like certain insects).
+venin'de *-n* cf **venninne**
***venin'ne** *-a* cf **venninne**
***ven'je** *V ven*, *vande*, *vant* cf **venne**
***ve'nleg** *A* - cf **vennlig**
***ve'n/leik** *-en* beauty, prettiness.
venn' *-en*, *pl *-er* (=***ven**) friend (**av** of); *fam.* boyfriend; connoisseur, lover (e.g. of food, wine): **bli v-er** make f-s; make up; **en v- av meg** a f- of mine; **gjøre seg til v-s** make f-s (**med** with); **v-en min** my friend; darling, my dear.
+ven'ne *V vente* (=***venje**) 1 accustom, get used (**til** to). 2: **v- av** break (a habit), disaccustom; **v- av et barn** wean a child; **v- en av med noe** break one of sth; **v- fra** wean (also fig.). 3 *(refl.)*: **v- seg** accustom oneself, get used (**til** to); **v- seg av med noe** break oneself of sth, get rid of some habit; **v- seg på noe** *dial.*, *fam.* get used to using (or enjoying) sth.
ven'ne/flokk *-en* circle of friends.
+ven'ne/gave *-a*/*-en* (=*/**gåve**) gift from (to) a friend (friends).
ven'ne/hand *-a*, *pl -hender* hand of friendship.
+ven'ne/hilsen *-en* (=/**helsing**) friendly greeting.
+ven'ne/hånd *-a*/*-en*, *pl -hender* cf /**hand**
ven'ne/kjær *A* friendly.
+ven'ne/krets *-en* circle of friends.
ven'ne/lag *-et* friendly get-together, party of friends; **i godt v-** among good friends.
ven'ne/laus *A* (=+/**løs**) friendless.
ven'ne/råd *-et* friendly advice.
Ven'nesla *Pln* twp, Vest-Agder.
ven'ne/sæl *A archaic* 1 (of people) friendly, popular, well-liked. 2 (of advice, thoughts, etc.) benevolent, friendly, kindly.
+ven'ne/tjeneste *-n* (=*/**teneste**) act of friendship, friendly deed.
vennin'ne *-a*/+*-en* (=***veninne**) (female) friend; girl friend.
venn'lig *A* - (=***venleg**) 1 friendly, kind, nice (**mot** to): **ville De være så v- å flytte Dem** would you please move, would you mind moving. 2 cheerful, inviting, pleasant (cabin, grove, room, etc.). 3 (as suffix) pro-, -phile. 4 *(sup.)* **v-st** please; if you please.
+venn'lig/het *-en* 1 friendliness; kindness. 2 friendly turn, service; act of kindness: **vil De gjøre meg den v- å** will you kindly. 3 cheerfulness, pleasantness (e.g. of landscape).
+venn'lig/sinnet *A* - (=***ven(n)leg/sinna**) friendly, kindly disposed.
venn'/skap *-en*/+*-et* (=***ven/**) friendship.
vennska'pelig *A* - (=***venskapeleg**) amicable, friendly: **en v- atmosfære** a friendly atmosphere: **stå på en v- fot med** be on f- terms with.
+vennska'pelig/het *-en* friendliness: **i all v-** amicably; as a friend.
ven'stre *A* - 1 left: **til v-** to the l-; **på v- hånd** on the l- side; **v- om** *mil.* l- face. 2 *pol.* left, leftist, radical: V- (a Norw. pol. party, ab. = the Liberal Party in England); **v- fløy** av the radical wing of.
ven'stre/hand *-a* left hand.
ven'stre/hendt *A* - left-handed.
+ven'stre/kjøring *-a*/*-en* (=*/**køyring**) left-hand driving.
ven'stre/mann *-en*, *pl -menn*/**-menner pol.* members of a *Venstre* party (in Norway = a liberal).
ven'stre/oriente'rt *A* - left-wing.
ven'stre/parti' *-et pol.* leftist party; (in Norway) the Liberal Party.

+ Bokmål; * Nynorsk; ° Dialect.
After letter: ' stress (Acc. 1); ` tone, stress (Acc. 2); · length.
Below letter: . not pronounced.

***ve'n/sæl** -t cf venne/
ven't -en lit. expectancy, wait, waiting: først den deilige v-, så selve den kjæres komme first the delicious wait, and then the coming of the beloved herself (Kinck).
ven'te1 N: i v- in prospect, in store; ahead, coming: er her ikke et uvær i v- isn't a storm gathering, a storm in prospect (Ibsen); ha et barn i v- have a child on the way; skuffelser i v- disappointments ahead.
ven'te2 V -a/+-et 1 anticipate, expect (av from, of); await, wait (på for): la v- på seg be long in coming; v- med noe delay, put off sth; vi v-er ham til middag we are expecting him to (for) dinner. 2 (refl.): v- seg expect; fam. be expecting (a baby).
ven'telig A - 1 likely, probable, to be expected: som v- var as was (to be) e-. 2 (adv.) most likely, probably.
ven'te/liste -a waiting list.
ven'tende A 1 expectant, waiting. 2 (fam. also v-s) coming, (to be) expected.
+ven'te/penger pl (=*-ar) allowance, interim pay (to an official, during unemployment).
ven'te/rom [/romm] -met waiting room.
ven'te/sal -en (large) waiting room.
ven'te/tid [*/ti] -a/+-en wait, waiting period.
+ven'te/værelse -t waiting room.
venti'l -en 1 vent, ventilator. 2 naut. porthole. 3 (air, auto, gas, horn, organ pipe) valve. 4 fig. outlet, safety valve.
ventilasjo'n -en 1 airing, ventilation (of opinion, a room, etc.). 2 ventilating system.
venti'l/basu'n -en valve trombone.
ventile're V -te 1 air, ventilate. 2 debate, discuss, ventilate (a question; an opinion).
venti'l/gummi -en valve rubber (inside air valve on tire).
ventrik'kel -elen, pl ventrikler anat. 1 (brain, heart) ventricle. 2 stomach.
ve'nus/hår -et bot. maidenhair, Venushair (Adiantum capillus-veneris).
ve'nus/mål -et measurements of the Venus de Milo, an ideal of female beauty.
vep's -en (=*kvefs) wasp.
vep'se/bol -et 1 wasp's nest. 2 fig. hornet's nest.
vep'se/stikk -et wasp sting.
***ve'r1** -en cf vær1
***ve'r2** -et cf vær2
***ver-** [væ'r-] Pf cf vær-
veran'da -en, pl *-er porch, veranda.
***verande** [væ'rande] A - cf værende
***ve'rast** V -ast (of weather) clear up, get nice.
ver'b -et, pl -/+-er (=+verbum) verb.
verba'l A verbal (conjugation, function; agreement, expression, etc.).
verba'l/note -n verbal note (unsigned diplomatic memo).
***ve'r/biten** A -e/-i, pl -ne cf vær/bitt
***Ve'r/brauta** Prn cf vinter/
***ver/bror** [væ'r/] -en, pl -brør cf vær/
+ver'bum -umet, pl -er cf verb
***ve'r/byte** -t change in the weather.
verd1 [væ'r] -a cf verden
***verd2** [væ'r] -en meal.
ver'd3 [*væ'r] -et lit. value, worth: la noe stå ved sitt v- let sth go for what it is worth.
ver'd4 [+vær't] A (+usu. v-t) worth, worth-while; deserving, worthy: den ene tjeneste er den annen v- one good turn deserves another; det er ikke v-t (you) had better not, it's not worth it; er det v-t? is it worth it?; mindre v-t of less value; (after noun:) all ære v- praiseworthy; et forsøk v-t worth trying; svar v- worthy of an answer; umaken v- worth the trouble.
Ver/dal [væ'r/] Pln twp, Nord-Trøndelag.
ver'd/auke [*væ'r/] -n admin., merc. appreciation, increase in value.
ver'dauke/skatt [*væ'rauke/] -en admin., merc. tax on unearned increment.
***verde** [væ're] -t cf verd3
+ver'den en (=verd1) (the) world: bringe, få ut av v- get out of the way, get rid of; du store v- good heavens, great Scott; En V- One World; gå gjennom v- go through life; hva i all v- what in the w-; ingen v-s ting not a thing, nothing at all; komme til v- be born; v- rundt the w- over; v-s gang the way of the w- (also name of an Oslo newspaper: V-s Gang).
+ver'dens/alt -et lit. universe.
+ver'dens/ansku'else -n world view.
+ver'dens/ba'rn -et eccl. worldling, worldly person; unconverted person.
+ver'dens/berøm't A - world famous.
+ver'densberømt/het -en 1 worldwide fame. 2 world-famous person or thing; celebrity.
+ver'dens/borger -en, pl -e citizen of the world.
+ver'dens/by -en cosmopolitan city, great metropolis; cosmopolis, modern Babylon.
+ver'dens/dame -n sophisticated lady, woman of the world.
+ver'dens/del -en 1 part of the world. 2 continent: Antarktis er en hel v- the Antarctic is a whole c-.
+ver'dens/erfa'ren A -ent, pl -ne experienced, worldly wise.
+ver'dens/erfa'ring -a/-en experience; knowledge of the world.
+ver'dens/fjern [/fjæ'rn] A 1 impractical, starry-eyed, unworldly; academic, impracticable. 2 isolated, remote, secluded.
+ver'dens/forak't -en contempt for the world.
+ver'dens/fred -en world peace.
+ver'dens/hav -et ocean: på v-et on the high seas; de syv v- the seven seas (e.g. Atlantic, Pacific, etc.).
+ver'dens/herredømme -t mastery of the world, world dominion.
+ver'dens/histo'rie -a/-en world history.
+ver'dens/histo'risk A - historic (e.g. significance); in the history of the world: v-e begivenheter events of world importance.
+ver'dens/hjø'rne -t corner of the world, quarter of the globe.
+ver'dens/kart -et map of the world.
+ver'dens/kjent A - world famous.
+ver'dens/klok A worldly-wise.
+ver'dens/klokskap -en wordly wisdom.
+ver'dens/krig -en world war: første v- World War I.
+ver'dens/litteratu'r -en world literature.
+ver'dens/makt -a/-en world power.
+ver'dens/mann -en, pl -menn man of the world.
+ver'densmanns/messig A - like a man of the world; suave, wordly-wise; sophisticated.
+ver'dens/marked -et world market.
+ver'dens/mester -eren, pl -ere/-rer world champion.
+ver'densmester/skap -et world championship.
+ver'dens/omseiling -en circumnavigation of the globe.
+ver'dens/omspennende A - global, world-encompassing, world-wide.
+ver'dens/rekor'd -en world record.
+ver'dens/rike -t empire: det romerske v- the Roman E-.
+ver'dens/rom -met (outer) space.
+ver'dens/ry -et world fame, world reputation.
+ver'dens/situasjo'n -en world situation.
+ver'dens/språk -et world language; universal language.
+ver'dens/trett A - world weary, world worn.
+ver'dens/utstilling -a/-en international exhibition.
***verd/full** [væ'r/] A cf verdi/
verdi' -en 1 value (also gram., math., mus.), worth (av of): evige v-er eternal v-s; uten v- of no v-, worthless. 2 (often pl) assets, securities; sums (of money).
+verdi'/angi'velse -n statement of value.
+verdi'/ansett'else -n assessment, estimate, valuation.
verdi'/brev -et registered letter.
+verdi'/forring'else -n depreciation.
verdi'/full A valuable; worthy.
ver'dig A - 1 deserving, worthy (til of): ikke v- til å løse ens skorem not worthy to unloose the latchet of one's shoes (Luke 3,16). 2 dignified: sette opp et v- ansikt put on a d- expression. 3 (as a suffix) -valued, -worthy, e.g. in mindre/v-, ros/v-, se/v-.
+ver'dige V -et condescend to give, grant, vouchsafe: jeg v-et ham ikke et svar I did not deign to answer him (Boo).
+ver'dig/het -en 1 dignity: bære med v- bear (endure) with d-. 2 position, rank: under ens v- beneath one (one's dignity); komme til ære og v- win honor and esteem. 3 worth.
+verdi'/gjenstand -en article of value, valuable (object).
verdi'/laus A valueless, without value, worthless.
+verdi'/måler -en, pl -e (=*-ar) measure, standard of value.
verdi'/papi'r -et, pl -/+-er security (as bonds or stocks).
verdi'/post -en insured mail.
verdi'/sak -a/+-en article of value, valuable (item).
verdi'/sti'gning *-a/+-en appreciation, increase in value.
***verd/laus** [væ'r/] A cf verdi/
***ver/dotter** [væ'r/] -a, pl -døtrer cf vær/datter
ver'dsens N (=+verdens): ingen v- ting not a thing, nothing at all.
***verd/setjing** [væ'r/] -a cf /settelse
+ver'd/sette V -satte, -satt (=*/setje) 1 assess, evaluate (til at). 2 appreciate.
+ver'd/settelse -n 1 assessment, evaluation (av of). 2 appreciation.
***verds/histo'rie** [væ'rs/] -a cf verdens/
***verds/histo'risk** A - cf verdens/
***verds/krig** -en cf verdens/
ver'dslig A - mundane, worldly; profane, secular, temporal: en v- tanke a w- thought.
+ver'dslig/het -en worldliness; wordly things.
+ver'dslig/sinnet A - wordly (-minded).
***verds/meister** [væ'rs/] -eren, pl -rar cf verdens/mester
***verds/rekor'd** -en cf verdens/
***verds/rom** [/romm] -met cf verdens/
+ver'dt A - cf verd
***vere1** [væ're] -a residence, sojourn, stay.
***vere2** [væ're] -n vet. warble; maggot of warble fly.
***vere3** [væ're] V er, var, vore/-i cf være2
***ve're4** V -a cf være3
***vere/stad** [væ're/] -en abode, residence.
***ve'r/eten** A -e/-i, pl -ne weather-beaten, worn.
***ver/far** [væ'r/] -en, pl -fedrar cf vær/
ver'ft -et, pl -/+-er (=verv1) shipyard.
+ver'ge1 -n cf verje3
+ver'ge2 -t cf verje1
+ver'ge3 -t cf verje3
+ver'ge4 V -a/-et cf verje4
+ver'ge/løs A cf verje/laus
+ver'ge/mål -et cf verje/
+ver'ge/råd -et cf verje/
***ve'r/hår** -et cf vær/
verifikasjo'n -en verification.
verifise're V -te 1 attest to, certify. 2 verify.
verita'bel A -elt, pl -le real, regular, veritable.

ver'je[1] -a (=+**verge**[2]) *hist.* weapon.
ver'je[2] +-n/*-a (=+**verge**[1]) *jur.* guardian.
ver'je[3] +-t/*-a (=+**verge**[3]) 1 defense; protection (**mot** against). 2 charge, trust; custody: **i sitt v-** in his charge (custody), under his protection.
ver'je[4] *V* -a/+-et (=+**verge**[4]) defend, protect (**mot** from); shield (**mot** against): **v- om** look out for.
***ver'je**[5] *V ver, varde, vart* cf **verje**[4]
ver'je/laus *A* defenseless; weaponless; undefended.
***ver'je/let(t)** -en *zool.* mimicry; protective coloration.
ver'je/mål -et *jur.* guardianship.
ver'je/råd -et child welfare council (since 1954 called **barnevernsnemnd**).
ver'k[1] -en, *pl* *-er 1 ache, pain. 2 inflammation; matter, pus; swelling.
ver'k[2] -et, *pl* -/+-er 1 work: **gå, skride til v-et** go to work, set about, start in; **gå strengt til v-s mot en** deal severely with one; **sette i v-** bring about, effect, realize. 2 act, deed, doing: **et kongelig v-** *archaic* a royal deed. 3 creation, product, work (**av** of) (e.g. artistic, literary, musical w-). 4 mill, plant, works; mine; *mil.* fortification, work(s). 5 (public) department, institution, service (see e.g. **post/v-, telegraf/v-**). 6 works (=mechanism, movement).
+**ver'k/brudden** *A* -ent, *pl* -brudne (=*/**broten**) *lit., bibl.* 1 palsied, paralytic. 2 decrepit.
+**ver'ke**[1] *V* -a/-et (=*-**je**) 1 ache, pain: **det v-er i ryggen** (my) back a-s. 2: **gå og v- med noe** *fig.* have sth on one's mind; **v- etter noe** hanker for sth. 3 *med.* be infected: **v- ut** suppurate.
***ver'ke**[2] *V* -a cf **virke**[2]
ver'ke/finger -eren, *pl* -rer (=**verk/**) infected, swollen finger.
***ver'keleg** *A* - cf **virkelig**
***ver'keleg/gjere** *V* -gjorde, gjort cf **virkelig/gjøre**
ver'ken[1] -et linsey-woolsey; cotton and wool twill.
ver'ken[2] *C* neither: **v- .... eller** n- .... nor.
ver'kens/kjole -n dress of linsey-woolsey, of cotton and wool tweed.
ver'k/finger -en, *pl* -rer cf **verke/**
***ver'kje** *V* -te cf **verke**[1]
***ver'k/laus** *A* free of pain, painless.
***ver'knad** -en, *pl* -er cf **virkning**
***ver'k/sam** *A* cf **virk/som**
+**ver'ks/eier** -en, *pl* -e (=*/**eigar**) mill owner, mine owner.
***ver'k/semd** -a 1 activity. 2 (industrial) concern.
***ver'ksetjings/makt** -a executive power.
+**ver'ks/mester** -eren, *pl* -ere/-re (=*/**meister**) 1 plant manager. 2 *jur.* contractor.
+**ver'k/sted** -et, *pl* -er (=*/**stad**) repair shop, workshop; garage: **mekanisk v-** machine shop.
+**ver'ksted/formann** -en, *pl* -formenn shop foreman.
+**ver'ksted/klubb** -en shop union.
+**ver'k/tøy** -et (=*/**ty**) implement, tool; equipment, tools.
+**ver'ktøy/kasse** -a/-en tool box.
+**ver'ktøy/maski'n** -en machine tool (such as metal-working lathe).
+**ver'ktøy/skap** -et tool cabinet.
***ve'r/kunne** -a meteorology.
***ve'r/kåpe** -a opportunist, turncoat.
***ve'r/lys** -et (=*/**lyse**) northern lights.
***ver'me** *V* -de cf **varme**[2]
***ve'r/melding** -a cf **vær/**
***ver/mor** [væ'r/] -a, *pl* -mødrer cf **vær/**
ver'mut -en vermouth.
vern [væ'rn] -et 1 defense, protection; bulwark, shelter (**for** for; **mot** against). 2 corps, organization (for defense), usu. in *cpds.*, e.g. **barne/v-, heime/v-, land/v-.**
verne [væ'rne] *V* -a/+-et (=***varne**) defend, protect, shelter: **v- om** stand guard over; cherish, safeguard.
***verne/bu** *V* -dde prepare defenses.
verne/helgen -en patron saint.
verne/idrett -en physical training (in the armed forces).
verne/lag -et welfare council (esp. for young people).
verne/plikt -a/+-en compulsory military service, conscription; *fig.* compulsory service: **avtjene sin v-** serve one's term in the armed forces.
verne/pliktig *A* - liable to be drafted: **i v- alder** of draft age; **v- befal** reserve officers; **v- soldat** conscript, draftee, enlisted man.
vernepliktts/bok -a handbook or folder, issued to person of draft age, which contains his registration, information on military service, etc.
verne/skatt -en 1 tax levied for defense purposes. 2 *hist.* tax levied on man exempted from military duty.
verne/skog -en forest reserve (protected by law against cutting).
verne/skole -n school for retarded children.
verne/ting -et *jur.* venue.
verne/toll -en protective tariff.
vernissa'sje -n opening day (of art exhibition), varnishing day.
+**vern/løs** [væ'rn/] *A* unarmed, weaponless; defenseless.
+**vern/sko'g** [væ'rn/] -en cf **verne/**
verona'l -en/-et barbital.
vero'nika -en *bot.* veronica.
ver'p -et 1 egglaying. 2 *dial., folk.* pile of stones or twigs (accumulated by passers-by, orig. as propitiation).
ver'pe[1] -t staging on shore from which salmon net is let out.
ver'pe[2] *V* *varp*, +-et/*vorpe/*-t (=+**verpe**[3]) lay eggs: **egget vil lære høna å v-** (said of or to a young person who corrects his elders).
+**ver'pe**[3] *V* -a/-et/-te cf **verpe**[2]
ver'pe/høne -a laying hen.
ver'pe/moden *A* +-ent, *pl* -ne of laying age, mature.
+**ver'per** -en, *pl* -e (=*-**ar**) (egg) layer.
ver'pe/sjuk *A* (=+/**syk**) 1 about to lay an egg. 2 *fam.* anxious to talk.
Ver'ran *Pln* twp, Nord-Trøndelag.
***ver'rast** *V* -ast worsen.
ver're *cp*, *sp verst* 1 worse: **hva v- er** what is worse; **til det v- for the** w-. 2 (without *comp.* sense) bad; (*adv.*) awfully: **han bar seg v-** he complained loudly. 3 (*sup.*) worst: **det v-ste er** the w- of it is; **i v-ste fall if** w- comes to w-; **ikke v-st, ikke så v-st** not bad, not so bad, not bad at all; (as *adv.*) not very: **det var ikke så v-st mørkt** it was not so very dark (Undset); **det blir v-st for ham selv** that will be his tough luck; **på det v-e** at its worst.
ver's -et verse (=line, poem, poetry, stanza): **disse v- er ville vekster i en sommer drysset hen** these v-s are wild blossoms strewn about in summertime (Wildenvey).
versa'l -en *typog.* capital letter.
ver'se/fot -en, *pl* +-føtter/*-føter (metrical) foot.
ver'se/kunst -en cf **vers/**
+**ver'se/maker** -en, *pl* -e (=*-**ar**) rhymester, versifier.
ver'se/mål -et (poetic) meter.
verse're *V* -te 1 (of rumor, story, etc.) be abroad, circulate, be traveling around. 2 *jur.* pending.
***ver's/fot** -en cf **verse/**
versifikato'risk *A* - versifying; verse.
versifise're *V* -te put into verse, versify.
versjo'n -en version (**av** of).
***ve'r/sjuk** *A* cf **vær/**
***ver/skap** [væ'r/] -en relationship by marriage.
***ve'r/skifte** -t change in the weather.
ver's/kunst -en (art of) versification; poetic arts.
***ver/skyld** [væ'r/] *A* related by marriage.
ver'sne *V* -a/+-et become worse, worsen.
***ver/son** [væ'r/] -en, *pl* -søner cf **vær/sønn**
ver'st[1] -en verst (Russian unit of distance=1066.77 meters, ab. 3/5 mile).
ver'st[2] *sp of* **verre**
***ver/syster** [væ'r/] -era, *pl* -rer cf **vær/søster**
ver't[1] -en 1 host (also *zool.*): **gjøre regning uten v-** fail to take sth into consideration. 2 (hotel) proprietor; innkeeper. 3 landlord.
***ver't**[2] *pr of* **verte**
***ver'te** *V vart, vorte/-i* 1 become; be (in the future): **det er uvisst når det vert** it's uncertain when it will be; **han vart erving til godset** he became heir to the estate. 2 remain, stay: **han vart ikkje lenge der** he didn't stay there long. 3 be (with perf. part. to form a passive): **han vart dømd** he was sentenced. 4 (with *adv., prep.*): **v- av** become of, turn out (**det vart inkje av** nothing came of it); **v- av med** get rid of; **v- etter** remain (behind); **v- for** be exposed to; perceive; **v- opp i** change to; **v- til** come into being; **v- (ille) ved** feel (badly); be alarmed, repelled.
vertika'l *A* vertical.
vertin'ne -a/+-en 1 hostess. 2 hotel proprietress; innkeeper's wife. 3 landlady. 4 stewardess (on plane).
ver'ts/dyr -et *zool.* host animal.
ver'ts/folk [also vær'ts/] -et 1 hosts; host and hostess. 2 landlord and landlady.
ver'ts/hus -et pub, tavern; *hist.* inn.
ver't/skap -et 1 (the) hosts. 2 position of host or hostess: **påta seg v-et** act as host, host.
ver'ts/plikter *pl* duties as a host (or hostess).
ver'v[1] -en cf **verft**
+**ver'v**[2] -et assignment, mission, task: **betro (gi, pålegge) en et v-** entrust (assign, give) sby with a task.
***ve'r/varsling** -a cf **vær/**
verve[1] [vær'v] en life, spirit, verve.
ver've[2] *V* -a/+-et recruit.
+**ver'ver** -en, *pl* -e (=*-**ar**) recruiter.
***ve'r/åtte** -a scent in the air.
ve'sal *A* 1 weak; scrawny. 2 *fig.* miserable.
ve'sal/dom -men/*-en 1 weakness; scrawniness. 2 *fig.* misery, wretchedness.
ve'sal/mann -en, *pl* -menn/*-menner poor wretch.
ve'sel -elen, *pl* -ler *zool.* ermine, weasel (Mustela erminea).
ve'sen -et, *pl* -/+-er 1 being, essence, substance; nature. 2 being, creature (also *derog.*), thing. 3 bearing, manner, way(s). 4 fuss, to-do: **gjøre v- av** make a f- about, over. 5 board, department office; service, system (see e.g. **fyr/v-, skole/v-**).
+**ve'sens/beslek'tet** *A* - closely akin, having an affinity (for each other); similar in nature.
+**ve'sens/forskjell** -en essential difference.
+**ve'sens/forskjel'lig** *A* - essentially different (**fra** from).
ve'sentlig *A* - 1 essential (difference, meaning, point, etc.): **i alt v-** in all essentials. 2 appreciable, considerable, substantial: **ikke v- større** not a- larger. 3 chief, main, principal; (*adv.*) chiefly.
vesi'r -en vizier.
ves'ke -a 1 briefcase, portfolio. 2 (ladies') handbag, purse.
ves'la *df* little girl (term of endearment): **V-** (used as proper name, developed from nickname).
ves'le *df of* **liten**

+ Bokmål; * Nynorsk; ° Dialect.
After letter: ' stress (Acc. 1); ` tone, stress (Acc. 2); · length.
Below letter: . not pronounced.

ves'le/finger *-eren, pl -rer* (the) little finger.
+ves'le/gutt *-en* **(=*/gut)** little boy (usu. term of endearment).
ves'le/jente *-a dial.* little girl.
ves'le/mor *N* little girl (term of endearment to child or young girl): **V-** (used as proper name, developed from nickname).
+ve'sler *pl of* **vesel**
+ves'le/voksen *A -ent, pl -ne* **(=*/vaksen)** (of child) grown-up (acting).
ves'ling *-en dial.* weakling.
ves'per *-en* vespers.
+ves'per/gudstjeneste *-n* vesper service.
ves'per/tid *-a/+-en* vespertime.
***ves'se** *V veste* absorb water, get sopped.
***vesser** *pl of* **voss**
ves't[1] *-en* vest, *(Brit.)* waistcoat.
ves't[2] *Av* west: **v- for** w- of; **i v-** in the w-; **mot v-** to the w-; **i øst og v-** in all directions; everywhere (cf **Vesten**).
ves'ta *Av* from the west, westerly.
ves'ta/fjells *Av* west of the mountain(s) (i.e. the central North-South mountain range of Norway; ab.= **vestlandsk**).
ves'ta/fjelsk *A* - west of the mountain(s) (cf preceding entry).
ves'ta/for' *P* (to the) west of: **Slottet østafor sol og v- måne** The Castle East of the Sun and West of the Moon (folktale, Asbjørnsen).
***ves'ta/frå** *P* cf **vest/fra**
Ves't-Agder *Pln* county in southern Norway.
vestalin'ne *-a/+-en* vestal virgin.
***ves'tan-** *Pf* also cf **vesta-**
***ves'tan/etter** *P* from the west, westerly.
***ves'tan/om'** *P* cf **vesten/**
ves'ta/til' *Av* in, to the west.
***ves'ta/ver** *-et* cf **/vær**
ves'ta/vind *-en* west wind.
+ves'ta/vær *-et* storm from the west.
Ves't/by *Pln* twp, Akershus.
ves'te/knapp *-en* vest button.
ves'te/lomme [/lomme] *-a* vest pocket.
+Ves'ten *Pln* the West (e.g. when speaking of the western world, western civilization, the western United States, etc.): **det ville V-** the Wild West.
+ves'ten/ *Pf* cf **vesta/**
+ves'ten/for' *P* cf **vesta/**
+ves'ten/fra *P* cf **vest/**
+ves'ten/om' *P* (around) to the west (of).
+Ves'ter/havet *Pln poet.* Atlantic Ocean.
+ves'ter/landene *pl* **(=*/landa)** *lit.* the Occident, the West (in contrast to the Orient).
ves'ter/landsk *A* - occidental, western.
ves'ter/veg *N*: **fare i v-** (see next word).
ves'ter/viking *N*: **fare i v-** *hist.* make a viking foray) to the west (usu. Great Britain and Ireland).
ves't/etter *P* 1 westward across (along, on). 2 *(adv.)* to the west, westward.
ves't/europe'isk *A* - West European.
Vestf. =**Vestfold**
Ves't/fold *Pln* county in southern Norway.
ves't/folding *-en* person from Vestfold.
ves't/foldsk *A* - (of) Vestfold.
+ves't/fra *Av* **(=*/frå)** from the west.
ves't/gående *A* - west-bound.
vestiby'le *-n* lobby, vestibule.
Vestin'dia [also ves't/] *Pln* (the) West Indies.
ves't/kant *-en* west side: **Oslo v-** w- of Oslo (usu. considered more elegant than the east side).
Ves't/landet *Pln* West Norway (west of north-south range), including esp. districts of Rogaland, Hordaland, Sogn og Fjordane and Sunnmøre (occ. also Romsdal and Vest-Agder).
ves't/landsk *A* - of, pertaining to **Vestlandet.**
ves't/lending *-en* person from **Vestlandet.**
ves'tlig *A* - western; westerly: **v-lengd/+lengde** (longitude) west.
ves't/makter *pl* Western Powers.
Ves't/nes' *Pln* twp, Møre og Romsdal.
Ves't-Norge *Pln* West Norway (cf **Vestlandet**).
ves't/norsk *A* - West Norwegian.
ves't/over [/åver] *Av* westward; in, to the west.
ves't/på *Av* 1 in the west, in the western part of. 2 west, westward.
ves'tre *A* - west, western.
Ves'tre Gau'sdal *Pln* twp, Oppland.
Ves'tre Mo'land *Pln* twp, Aust-Agder.
Ves'tre Sli'dre *Pln* twp, Oppland.
Ves'tre To'ten *Pln* twp, Oppland.
***ves't/røn** *A* western, westerly.
+ves't/vendt *A* - **(=*/vend)** facing west, west, western; oriented to the west.
+ve't *pr of* **vite**
ve'te[1] *-n hist.* beacon (wood laid ready for a signal fire, at regular distances along mountain tops).
***ve'te[2]** *V veit, visste, visst* cf **vite**
vetera'n *-en* veteran (**fra** of).
veterinæ'r *-en* veterinarian, veterinary.
+veterinæ'r/høyskole *-n* college of veterinary science.
ve'to *-et* veto.
ve'to/rett *-en* (right to) veto.
ve'to/strid *-a/-en* veto controversy (esp. conflict between the Norwegian *Storting* and the Swedish king in the 1870's and 1880's over the latter's right to veto constitutional amendments).
***vet'rung** *-en* yearling.
vett' *-et* **(=*vit)** intelligence, sense(s), wits: **det er vondt når v-et vanter** it's hard to manage without brains (proverb); **fly v-et av seg** *pop.* run one's legs off; **gå fra v-et** lose one's wits; **ha v- på noe** have an understanding of sth; **ta til (*åt) v-et** come to one's senses; **være fra v-et** be out of one's head, one's mind.
vet'te *-t/+-n folk., myth.* spirit, sprite.
+vet'tig *A* - cf **vettug**
vett'/laus *A* 1 foolish, stupid, witless. 2 senseless, unreasonable: **v-e flyginger** senseless flights. 3 frantic, wild (with fear, rage, etc.).
vett'/løyse *-a* 1 senselessness, unreason. 2 folly, foolishness, stupidity.
+vett'/skremme *V -skremte* **(=*/skræme)** scare (sby) out of his wits.
vet'tug *A* - **(=+vettig, *vitug)** *dial.* sensible; bright, intelligent: **er du ikke v-?** aren't you in your right mind?
ve'um *N lit.* sacred places: **varg i v-** (see **varg**).
ve'v[1] *-en, pl *-er* 1 weave, weaving; web, woven piece. 2 loom. 3 cobweb. 4 *fig.* network, tangle, web(bing).
ve'v[2] *-et/*-en* 1 *anat.* tissue. 2 *fam.* maundering, prattling; nonsense, twaddle: **det er bare v- it's** just talk.
***ve'v[3]** *pr of* **vevje**
ve've *V vov/+-de, +-d/*vove/*-i* 1 weave: **v- vadmel** children's game (imitating the motions of weaving). 2 *fam.* maunder, prattle, talk nonsense. 3 *fam.* walk unsteadily; meander, ramble. 4 *(refl.)*: **v- seg bort i noe** get oneself entangled in (with) sth.
Ve'vel/stad *Pln* twp, Nordland.
+ve'ver[1] *-en, pl -e* **(=*-ar)** 1 weaver. 2 *zool.* daddy longlegs, harvest man (Phalangida). 3 *zool.* weaverbird (Ploceidae).
+ve'ver[2] *A -ert, pl -re* active, agile, nimble; lively, quick, sprightly; fragile, graceful, slight.
veveri' *-et, pl +-er/*-* textile factory.
+ve'verske *-n* (woman) weaver.
ve'v/gogn [/gångn] *-a dial.* loom.
ve'v/greie *-a dial.* loom.
***vev'je** *V vev, vavde, vavt* wind, wrap around.
ve'v/kjerring *-a, pl *-ar zool.* daddy longlegs, harvest-man (Phalangida).
ve'v/knute *-n* **(=*/knut)** weaver's knot.
vev'le *V -a/+-et dial.* 1 mangle (clothes). 2 babble, talk nonsense. 3 meander, wander around confusedly. 4 wrap around. 5 *naut.* rattle (down) (=furnish shrouds with ratlines).
vev'ling *-en* 1 *naut.* ratline. 2 *dial.* wristwarmer.
ve'vnad *-en, pl *-er dial., lit.* 1 weaving; weave. 2 tapestry; woven piece.
ve'v/reie *-n* loom and equipment.
Vev'ring *Pln* twp, Sogn og Fjordane.
ve'v/skei *-a* reed (on a loom).
ve'v/stol *-en* (hand-operated) loom.
Ve'/øy *Pln* twp, Møre og Romsdal.
v. f. =**vest for**
V G =**Verdens Gang**
vi' *pn, ob oss* we: (also editorial and royal) **vi (er) alle** all of us (are); **alle vi som** all of us who; **vi alene vide** *hum., archaic* we alone know (quot. attr. to King Frederik VI of Denmark, now used e.g. to characterize overbearing bureaucrats).
+vi'- *Pf* cf **vid-**
vi'a *P* via.
viaduk't *-en* overpass, viaduct.
+vi'be *-n* cf **vipe**
vibrafo'n *-en mus.* vibraphone.
vibrasjo'n *-en* vibration.
vibra'tor *-en* vibrator.
vibre're *V -te* vibrate; quiver, twitch; pulsate, tremble.
vi'ce ver'sa vice versa.
vi'ce- *Pf* cf **vise-**
vichy/vatn [visj'i/] *-et* **(=+/vann)** Vichy water.
vicomte [vikång't] *-n* viscount.
vi'd *A* 1 extensive, spacious, wide (opening, plain, sea, world, etc.); broad (definition, interests, outlook, etc.): **på v- vegg, på v-t gap** w-open; **hva i all v-e verden** what in the wide world. 2 ample, full, loose (esp. clothing). 3 *(adv.)* far, wide(ly): **det går for v-t** that's going too f-; **for så v-t** for that matter, in a sense; in that respect; as far as that goes; **for så v-t som** in so far as; **så v-t** so far, to the degree; to such a degree; (just) barely; **det var så v-t jeg kunne gå** I could barely walk; **det var så v-t hun ikke la på røret** she came close to hanging up on me (Hoel); **v-t og bredt** far and wide.
***vi'da** *Av* cf **vide[2]**
Vi'dar *Prn (m)*
***vi'dare** *A* - cf **videre**
+vi'd/bremmet *A* - **(=-a)** broad-brimmed.
vidd'[1] *-a* cf **vidde**
vidd'[2] *-et* 1 wit, wittiness. +2 *obs.* wits.
vid'de *-a* **(=vidd[1])** 1 width (**på** of); fullness, looseness; (on RR track) gauge. 2 *fig.* breadth, outlook, range. 3 open country, wide expanses, esp. the mountain plateau (above the treeline): **ta sin ferie på v-a** take one's vacation in the mountains; **På V-ene** On the Heights (poem by Ibsen); **komme på v-ene** stray from one's subject.
vi'de[1] *V -a/+-et* broaden, widen: **v- seg (ut)** become wider, spread out, widen (out); **v- ut** stretch (sth).
vi'de[2] *Av* far and wide.
+vi'den[1] *-en* cf **viten**
+vi'den[2] *Av poet.* far and wide (esp. in phrase): **v- om** (the same).
+vi'dende *-t* cf **vitende**
+vi'den/skap *-en* cf **vit/**
+vi'dere *A* - **(=*vidare)** 1 ampler, looser, wider (see **vid**). 2 additional, further (attempt, delay, informa-

tion, etc.); more: **hva så v-** what m-, what then; **uten v-** without f-ado. 3 very much (in neg. expressions): **ikke v-** none too, not overly, not very (pleased, polite, rich, etc.); **ikke noe v-** not (nothing) much; not worth while; **han hadde ikke noe v- menneskekunnskap** he didn't have much knowledge of human nature (Hoel). 4 *(adv.)* farther, further, on: **enn v-** besides, in addition; **inntil v-** for the present, for a time; **kjøre v-** drive f-; drive on; **med v-** and so forth; **og så v- (osv.)** and so forth, et cetera; **(gå, les) v-** read on; **sende v-** pass on.

+**vi'dere/befor·dring** *-a/-en*: **til v-** to be forwarded.

+**vi'dere/føre** *V -te* carry on, continue, pursue.

vi'dere/gående *A* - 1 further, more extensive; more extreme (e.g. demands). 2 higher, more advanced.

+**vi'dere/kommen** *A -ent, pl -komne* advanced: **for begynnere og v-komne** for beginners and advanced students.

+**vi'dere/sende** *V -te* forward, send on, transmit; reship, transship (**til** to).

+**viderver'dig** *A - lit.* unpleasant; boring; annoying, troublesome.

+**viderver'dig/het** *-en lit.* annoyance; tribulation, trouble.

***vi'd/farande** *A* - widely traveled.

vi'd/faren *A +-ent, pl -ne* widely traveled.

***vi'd/femnande** *A* - comprehensive, far-ranging, inclusive.

***vi'd/fløygd** *A -/-fløygt* far flown.

vi'd/gjeten *A +-ent, pl -ne* famous, renowned.

vidime're *V -te* certify.

vidis'se *-n* certified copy.

vid'je *-a* 1 *bot.* willow (Salix). 2 (birch) wand, withy (used for fastening).

vid'je/band -et (=+**/bånd**) withy band.

vid'je/spenning *-en* withy binding.

***vid'ke** *V -a* dilate, enlarge, expand; broaden, widen.

+**vi'd/kjent** *A* - (=***/kjend**) widely known.

vidløf'tig *A* - 1 lengthy, prolix, prolonged; circumstantial, copious, detailed; complicated. 2 *fam.* dissipated, dissolute; wild.

+**vidløf'tig/het** *-en* 1 copiousness, lengthiness; complexity. 2 dissipation, dissoluteness; escapade, prank.

+**vid'ne**[1] *-t* cf **vitne**[1]

+**vid'ne**[2] *V -et* cf **vitne**[2]

***vi'dne**[3] *V -a* become wider.

+**vid'nes/byrd** *-et* cf **vitnes/**

***vi'd/open** [/åpen] *A -e/-i, pl -ne* cf **/åpen**

+**vi'd/otte** [/otte] *-a* cf **/åtte**

+**vi'd/spu·rt** *A* (=***/spurd**) famous, renowned, widely known.

vi'd/strakt [*vi'/] *A* - extensive, far-reaching; far-flung, vast: **vårt v-e land** our far-flung country: **v- lesning** extensive reading.

vi'd/syn [*vi'/] *-et/*-a* breadth, vision; tolerance.

vi'd/sy·nt [*vi'/] *A* - far sighted, tolerant.

vidt' *nt of* **vid**

+**vidt'/bekjen·t** *A - lit.* renowned.

+**vidt'/berei·st** *A - lit.* far-traveled.

+**vidt'/berøm·t** *A - lit.* far-famed.

+**vidt'/forgre·n(e)t** *A* - (greatly) ramified, widely-branching.

+**vidt'/gående** *A* - extreme, radical.

+**vidtløf'tig** *A* - cf **vidløftig**

+**vidt'/rekkende** *A* - far-reaching.

+**vidt'/skuende** *A* - far-sighted: **en v-ånd** a man of vision.

+**vidt'/spennende** *A* - comprehensive, wide; far-reaching; wide-ranging.

+**vidun'der** *-eret/-ret, pl -er/-ere/-re* (=***vedunder**) miracle; (of person) marvel, prodigy, wonder: **et v- av fullkommenhet** a miracle of perfection.

+**vidun'der/ba·rn** *-et* child prodigy, wonder child.

+**vidun'derlig** *A* - (=***vedunderleg**) marvelous, miraculous, wonderful: **for en v- morgen** what a w- morning; **det v-e** the miracle, the miraculous.

vi'd/vank *-en* (=**/vanke**) (long) journey, wandering: **komme på v-** go on the road; usu. *fig.* go astray, get lost; **være (gå) på v-** (of thoughts) roam, wander freely.

+**vi'd/åpen** *A -ent, pl -ne* (=***/open**) 1 wide open (**for** to). *2 (lie) flat on one's back.

vi'd/åtte *-a*: **på v-a** astray, lost; in the wilderness; **streife på v-a** roam afar.

vi'e *V -gde/+-et* 1 consecrate, ordain (**til** as); dedicate, devote (**til** to). 2 (of the marrying official) marry; *poet.* join together, unite: **v-es** be wed. 3 *(refl.)*: **v- seg** devote oneself (**til** to); **v- seg musikken** devote oneself (fully) to music.

+**vi'else** *-n* cf **vigsel**

+**vi'elses/attes·t** *-en* cf **vigsel/**

+**vi'elses/ring** *-en* wedding ring.

vi'er *-en dial.* (=**vidje**).

vi'er/kjerr *-et* willow thicket.

Vietna'm *Pln* Vietnam.

vietname'sisk *A* - Vietnamese.

+**vi'e/vann** *-et* holy water.

+**vi'evanns/kar·** *-et* aspersorium, vessel for holy water.

+**vif't**[1] *en*: **på v-** (of a girl) out for a good time.

vif't[2] *-et* 1 breath, puff, whiff (**av** of). 2 flutter; waft, wave.

vif'te[1] *-a* fan; blower.

vif'te[2] *V -a/+-et* 1 flutter, wag, wave; flash, flaunt: **v- med noe** wag, wave sth; flaunt sth; **hunden v-er med halen** the dog is wagging its tail. 2 fan; blow gently, waft. 3 *(refl.)*: **v- seg** fan oneself.

vif'te/forma *A* - (=+**-et**) fan-shaped.

vif'te/reim *-a* fan belt.

+**vi'g** *A lit.* lean, tough; limber, lithe, willowy.

vig'de *pt of* **vie**

***vig'ge** *-a* mountain field above the tree line.

vigi'lie *-a eccl.* vigil.

+**vig'le** *V -a/-et*: **v- opp** agitate, stir up.

Vi'gmo/stad *Pln* twp, Vest-Agder.

vignett [vinjett'] *-en* vignette.

Vi'gra *Pln* twp, Møre og Romsdal.

vig'sel *-elen, pl -ler* (=+**vielse**) 1 consecration. 2 wedding.

vig'sel/attes·t *-en* (=+**vielses/**) marriage license.

vig'sel/mann *-en, pl -menn/*-menner admin.* one who can perform (civil) marriage ceremony (=justice of the peace).

***vig'sle**[1] *-a* cf **vigsel**

vig'sle[2] *V -a/+-et* consecrate, dedicate, devote (**til** to): **på v-et grunn** on sacred ground.

***vig'sle/vatn** *-et* cf **vie/vann**

vigø'r *-en* vigor: **i (full) v-** in fine fettle, in great form.

vi'k *-a* 1 (small) bay, cove, inlet: **Vika** harbor district in Oslo (=**Pipervika**). 2 corner of the mouth.

Vi'k *Pln* twp, Sogn og Fjordane.

vika'r *-en* substitute (for a clergyman, doctor, teacher, etc.); *(Brit.)* locum tenens; deputy (**for** for).

vikaria't *-et* 1 position as a substitute. 2 period during which one substitutes.

vikarie're *V -te* (act as) substitute (**for** for).

***vi'ke**[1] *-a* cf **veke**[1]

vi'ke[2] *V veik/+vek, +veket/*vike/*-i* 1 give way, yield (**for** to); recede, retreat; depart, go away, leave (**fra** from); look away, waver; turn aside: **v- av veien** get out of the way, off the road; **v- bort** (esp. *bibl.*) depart, get thee hence; **vik fra meg, Satan** get thee hence, S- (Matt. 4,10); **v- tilbake** draw back; flinch, recoil (**for** from); hesitate to; **v- til side** draw to the side; **v- unna** fall back; turn aside; **v-ende** evasive, shifty (answer, eyes, etc.); declining, falling (market, prices, etc.); **på v-ende front** in retreat. 2 *lit.* give up, waive: **v- plassen** yield one's place (**for** to), stand aside, step down; **v- tronen** renounce the throne.

+**vi'ke**[3] *V -te* (=***-je**) 1 rein aside, turn (a horse). 2 set (the teeth on a saw).

Vi'ke/bygd *Pln* twp, Hordaland.

Vi'ke/dal *Pln* twp, Rogaland.

Vi'ken *Pln hist.* district around the Oslofjord.

vi'ke/plikt *-a/+-en* duty to yield to other traffic.

+**vi'ke/spor** *-et* sidetrack, siding.

***vi'ki** *pp of* **vike**[2]

vi'king *-en* 1 Viking. 2: **i v-** on Viking expeditions.

vi'king/ferd [*/fær] *-a/+-en* Viking expedition, raid.

vi'king/tid [*/ti] *-a/+-en* Viking Period (ab. 750—1050 A.D.).

vi'king/tog [-tåg] -et Viking expedition, raid.

***vi'kje** *V -te* cf **vike**[3]

***vi'kje/spor** *-et* cf **vike/**

vik'ke[1] *-a bot.* vetch (Vicia).

+**vik'ke**[2] *V -a/-et/vikte* 1 *dial.* extend, stretch (metal). 2: **v- en sag** set a saw.

vik'le *V -a/+-et* 1 coil; twist, wind, wrap (**om** around); **v- inn** entangle, tangle up (**i** in); wrap up (**i** in); decoy, draw in, trick; **v- opp** twist, wind up; **v- ut** disentangle, untwist, unwind; unfold, unwrap. 2 *(refl.)*: **v- seg** wind, etc. itself (**om** around); **v- seg sammen** get tangled (up); **v- seg ut** disentangle, extricate oneself (**av** from).

+**vik'ler** *-en, pl -e* (=***-ar**) 1 *tech.* winder. 2 *zool.* leaf roller moth (Tortricid).

vik'ling *-a/+-en* 1 binding, wrapping. 2 *elec.* winding.

Vik'na *Pln* twp, Nord-Trøndelag.

vik'se *V -a/+-et archaic* wax (a mustache).

vi'ksk *A - hist.* pertaining to Viken (land around Oslofjord).

vik'te *V -a/+-et*: **v- seg** act important, put on airs: **kjerringene skal ikke gå og v- seg** the women mustn't put on airs (Sandemose).

vik'tig *A* - 1 important (**for** to). 2 self-important, snooty, stuck-up; impertinent: **han svogeren min er blitt så v- som bare det** that brother-in-law of mine has gotten so damn snooty (Sandemose).

+**vik'tig/het** *-en* 1 importance: **av v- for** of i- to. 2 arrogance, self-importance.

+**vik'tig/makeri** *-et* acting important, snobbery, snobbishness.

vik'tig/per *-en* conceited fellow.

vik'tig/propp *-en* conceited fellow.

viktoria'nsk *A* - Victorian.

+**viktua'lier** *pl* (=***viktualia**) provisions, victuals.

vi'k/væring *-en hist.* person from Viken.

vi'k/væ·rsk *A - hist.* pertaining to sth, sby from Viken.

vil' *pr of* **vil'je**[2], **vil'le**[2]

+**vil'den** [also vil'-] *A* - cf **villen**

vil'der *-en dial.*: **komme på v-** go astray, get lost.

vil'dre *V -a/+-et* 1 wander aimlessly or confusedly; *dial.* wander in delirium. 2 (esp. of thoughts) cause to wander, lead astray. 3: **v- seg (bort, vekk)** *(refl.)* get lost, go astray.

vil'dren *A +-ent, pl -ene* confused, lost.

Vil'/helm *Prn (m)*

+ Bokmål; * Nynorsk; ° Dialect.
After letter: ' stress (Acc. 1); ` tone, stress (Acc. 2); · length.
Below letter: . not pronounced.

*vil'ja pp of vilje[2]

vil'je[1] -n volition, will; desire, wish; intention; determination: få sin v- get one's way; gjøre, være en til v- (dial. v-s) do as one wishes, yield to one; hans siste v- his last will and testament; jeg har ikke med min beste v- kunnet forhindre ham try as I might, I haven't been able to stop him (Ibsen); med v- intentionally, on purpose; med god v- with mutual good will; med eller mot sin v- willy-nilly; sette sin v- igjennom impose, work one's will.

*vil'je[2] V vil, ville, vilja cf ville[2]

vil'je/fast A - determined, firm-willed, strong-willed.

vil'je/kraft -a/+-en 1 willpower. 2 strong-willed person.

vil'je/kraftig A - strong-willed.

vil'je/laus A (=+/løs) weak, weak-willed; docile, passive.

vil'je/sak -a/+-en matter of will.

vil'jes/akt -a/-en act of volition, will.

vil'je/sterk A strong-willed.

vil'je/styrke -n strength of will, will power.

vil'je/svak A weak-willed.

vil'jes/ytring -a/+-en expression of (one's) will.

*vil'jug A - cf villig

vil'/kår -et 1 condition, term: ikke på noe v- in no case, under no circumstances. 2 (esp. pl) circumstances, conditions. 3 dial. pension paid by new owner of estate or farm to former owner (esp. by son to father).

vilkå'rlig A - 1 arbitrary (=despotic, high-handed, overbearing). 2 arbitrary (=haphazard, random; capricious): et v- valgt tall a randomly selected number. 3 biol., psych. voluntary (movement).

+vilkå'rlig/het -en arbitrariness; capriciousness.

*vil'kårs/dom -(m)en jur. suspended sentence.

*vil'kårs/folk pl farm couple that has retired and is supported by present operator.

*vil'kårs/laus A absolute, categorical, unconditional.

*vil'kårs/setning -a, pl -ar conditional clause.

vill' A vilt 1 wild (animal, enthusiasm, flower; rumor, scheme, etc.); savage, uncivilized; ferocious, fierce; unruly (child, horse, etc.); frantic, frenzied: være v- etter noe be crazy for sth. 2 astray, lost: gå seg v- go a-, lose one's way; lede v- lead a-.

vil'la -en (private) house (in residential district); villa.

vil'la/klausul -en zoning ordinance restricting area to one-family dwellings.

vil'la/kvarte'r -et residential district (of one-family dwellings).

*vil'lan A cf villen

vill'/and -a, pl -ender wild duck.

*vil'lar/korn [/kånn] -et folk. magic charm which causes one to go astray or lose one's memory.

vil'la/strøk -et residential district (of one-family dwellings).

vill'/basse -n wild, unruly boy.

vill'/dyr -et wild animal, beast.

vil'le[1] -a dial. 1 confusion. 2 delusion, fallacy. 3 gaiety, wildness.

+vil'le[2] V vil, ville, -et (=*vilje[2]) 1 (as an expression of volition) want to, will; would, would like: vil du være så snill å would you please; jeg vil (ville) gjerne I want, would like very much; jeg vil hjem (bort, til Norge, osv.) I want to go home (away, to Norway, etc.); hva er det du vil? what do you want?; som du vil as you like, wish; gjør hva du vil do what you like; man kan hva man vil where there's a will there's a way; han vil ikke vite av det he won't hear of it; dog ikke som jeg vil, men som du vil nevertheless not as I will, but as thou wilt (Math. 26,39); om Gud vil God willing; jeg v- ønske at I wish that; uten å v- det unintentionally; for hjelp ei gavner denne mann som ikke vil hva ei han kan for help is wasted on this man who does not want to do that which he is not able to do (Ibsen). 2 (as expression of the future) shall, will; should, would; is (was) going to: han vil snart være her he'll be here soon; han vil komme til å forstå en gang some day he'll understand; jeg vil verge mitt land, jeg vil bygge mitt land I will defend my country, I will build my country (Bjørnson); det er jo det vidunderlige som nu vil skje it is the miracle that is now going to happen (Ibsen); det v- glede meg hvis I would (should) be happy if; bare han v- komme if he would only come; bilen v- ikke gå the car wouldn't start. 3 (other idioms): (following statements) vil jeg tro I guess, I imagine; det vil gjerne gå slik it usually turns out like that; det vil si (dvs.) that is; det får gå som det vil, la komme hva der vil come what may; han vil ha det til at he insists that; vet du hva det vil si å do you know what it means (what the implications are) to; (with omitted infinitive) hvor vil du hen what are you driving at?; jeg trodde de v- hit I thought they were headed this way; han v- til å gå he was about to go, started to go.

vil'le[3] V -a/+-et/*ville dial. 1 confuse, lead astray, mislead. 2 stray; be footloose, a wanderer. 3 (refl.): v- seg get lost, go astray.

*vil'le[4] pt of vilje[2], ville[2]

*vil'leg A - voluntary.

+vil'lelse -n delirium: tale i v- be delirious, rave, wander.

+vil'len [also vil'-] A - (=+vilden): i v- sky at the top of one's lungs; wildly.

vill'/ender pl of -and

+vill'/farelse -n 1 delusion; error (esp. eccl.), fallacy, mistake: sveve i en v- labor under a d- (misapprehension). 2 jur. ignorance of the law.

vill'/faren A +-ent, pl -ne lit. 1 gone astray, lost, stray; off the path, the route. 2 erring, straying, wayward; eccl. heretic.

vill'/farende A - cf /faren

+vill'/fremmed A - (=*/framand) 1 completely strange: et v- menneske a complete stranger; v-e strangers (to each other).

+vill'/føre V -te mislead; lead astray.

+vill'/het -en 1 savageness, uncouthness, wildness. 2 ferocity, rage, violence. 3 unruliness, uproar.

vil'lig A - (=*viljug) 1 ready, willing (til å to); (e.g. of an instrument) responsive; (e.g. of a plant) easily cultivable. 2 (adv.), naut. apace, briskly, roundly. 3: v- vekk (adv.), fam. incessantly, steadily.

+vil'lig/het -en 1 willingness. 2 favor, good turn.

vil'ling[1] -en dial. 1 wild one, wild person. 2 zool. whiting (Gadus merlangus).

°vil'ling[2] -en cf velling

vill'/katt -en zool. wildcat (Felis silvestris); (also fig., of young girl).

+vill'/lede V -et (=*/leie) 1 lead astray. 2 mislead; deceive.

vill'/mann -en, pl -menn/*-menner barbarian, savage, wild man.

*vill'mann/skap -en barbarism, barbarity, savagery.

vill'manns/liv -et barbarian life, life of a savage; life in the wilderness, life of adventure.

vill'/mark -a wilderness, wilds: Der v-en suser Where the Wilderness Soughs (book, Fønhus).

+vill'/nis -et 1 tangle of trees, shrubs; thicket; dense undergrowth, jungle (av of). 2 fig. chaos, mass, tangle.

+vill'/rede en/et bewildered, confused, perplexed (om about); i fullkommen v- completely b- .

vill'/rein -en wild reindeer.

vill'/rot -a dial., bot. henbane (Hyoscyamus niger).

*vill'/råd -a bewilderment, confusion, perplexity.

vill'/rådig A - bewildered, confused, perplexed.

vill'/skap -en 1 savagery, violence, wildness; fury, passion: anfall av v- fit of passion. 2 fam. madness, nonsense.

vill'/skott -et (=*/skot, +/skudd) 1 bot. sucker. 2 fig. aberration, deviation, excrescence.

+vill'/som' A -t, pl -me 1 lit., poet. aimless (wanderer, wandering, etc.); confused, faltering (glance, movement, etc.); incoherent, wandering (speech, thought, etc.). 2 desolate, wild (path, terrain, way); wild and wandering (animal, bird, wind, etc.): vandre den v-me sti tread the trackless path (Wildenvey).

vill'/spor -et: på v- on the wrong track, off the track; astray, lost; bringe (føre) en på v- throw sby off; lead sby astray.

+vill'/sti -en (=*/stig): på v- astray, on the wrong path.

vill'/strå -et 1 bot. matgrass ((Nardus stricta). 2: (komme) på v- (get) lost.

vill'/styr -et dial.: gå, være på v- go, be wild, untended.

vill'/styring -en wild, undisciplined person: han hadde vært en v- he had been pretty wild in his younger days (Undset).

vill'/svin -et zool. wild boar (Sus scrofa).

vill'/vin -en bot. Virginia creeper (Parthenocissus vitacea).

+vil're V -et cf vildre

vil'ske -a 1 dial. wildness; fury, passion: *rape av stad på v-a rush off wildly. 2: i v- in delirium, out of one's head.

vil't[1] -et game (animal); prey, quarry.

vil't[2] nt of vill

vil't/bestan'd -en amount of game, game population.

vil'ter A -ert, pl -re boisterous, spirited, wild; (of a girl) tomboyish; frisky, madcap; playful, tousled (e.g. hair).

+vil'ter/het -en boisterousness, friskiness, wildness.

+vil't/handler -en, pl -e (=*-ar) one who sells (wild) game.

vil't/saus -en sauce (made with sour cream) served with game.

+vil't/voksende A - 1 (of plant) growing wild. 2 unruly, untrained: et v- talent an undisciplined talent.

*vi'm -et notion, whim.

*vi'me[1] -a confused state, daze.

*vi'me[2] V -a/+-et talk or act confusedly; wander around in a daze.

*vi'men A +-ent, pl -ne (=vimet(e)) confused, flustered, in a dither.

*vim'le[1] -n nausea, queasiness.

*vim'le[2] V -a/+-et feel nauseated, queasy.

*vim'len A +-ent, pl -ene nauseated, queasy.

vim'pel -elen, pl +-ler pennant; banner, ensign.

vim're V -a/+-et 1 stray, wander: v- om, omkring w- around. 2 flicker, quiver, tremble.

vim's[1] -en flighty, restless person, scatterbrain; fussbudget.

vim's[2] A 1 erratic, fluttery. 2 confused, unthinking.

vim'se[1] -a flibbertigibbet, scatterbrain (woman).

vim'se[2] V -a/+-et fidget, flutter, fuss; bustle, dart, scurry: v- omkring s- around.

vim'se/kopp -en flibbertigibbet, scatterbrain.

vim'set(e) A - fidgety, fluttery;

flighty, frivolous, scatterbrained.

vi'n *-en* 1 wine: **piker, vin og sang** wine, women, and song. 2 vine: **russisk v-** *bot.* kangaroo vine (Cissus antarctica); **høste v-** harvest grapes; **Når den ny v- blomstrer** When the New Wine Blooms (play, Bjørnson).

vi'n/berg *-et* vineyard (on mountain or hillside).

vin'ḍ[1] *-en* wind; flatulence, (body) gas: **slippe en v-** break w-; **snakke om v- og vær** chit-chat, pass the time of day; **spre for alle v-er** scatter to the four w-s; **være i v-en** be popular, much sought after.

vin'ḍ[2] *A dial.* warped.

***vin'dal** *A* blustery, stormy, windy.

***vin'ḍ/auga** *df -, pl -augo* cf **vindu**

***vin'ḍ/auge** *-t* cf **vindu**

***vin'daugs/rute** *-a* cf **vindus/**

+**vin'ḍ/bar** *A* - bleak, exposed to the wind.

vin'ḍ/blaff *-et* puff of wind, small gust.

+**vin'ḍ/bøytel** *-elen, pl -ler* 1 *fig.* gasbag, windbag. 2 *fam.* creampuff.

vin'ḍ/drag *-et* breeze, gust; current of air.

vin'de[1] *-a* winch, windlass; reel (for fishpole, selfbinder, yarn winder); spindle, spool.

vin'de[2] *V* +*vandt*/**vatt*, +*vundet*/**vunde*/*-*i* 1 reel, wind; hoist (up). 2 (*refl.*): **v- seg** curl, twist, wind.

vin'de/bom [/bomm] *-men* road barrier which can be raised or lowered by a winch.

vin'de/bru *-a* (=+/**bro**) drawbridge.

vin'ḍ/egg *-et* 1 wind egg (lacking a shell, or unfertilized). 2 *fig.* worthless plan or idea.

vin'del *-elen, pl -ler* 1 *dial.* twisted strand. *2 curl, lock. 3 *bot.* bindweed (Convolvulus). 4 (in horology) fusee.

vin'del/trapp *-a* (=***vinde/**) spiral staircase, winding stairs.

vin'ḍ/fall *-et* tree(s) blown down by a storm, windfall.

vin'ḍ/fang *-et* 1 *naut.* sails, spread of canvas; part of ship's hull which holds the wind. 2 (small) entry porch serving as protection from wind.

vin'ḍ/flage *-a* passing wind.

+**vin'dig** *A* - wind-blown, windy.

vindikasjo'n *-en jur.* vindication.

vin'ḍing *-a*/+*-en* 1 winding, wrapping. 2 turn, twist; convolution.

vindise're *V -te jur.* vindicate.

vin'ḍ/jakke *-a* windbreaker (jacket).

vin'ḍ/kast *-et* (sudden) gust (of wind).

vin'ḍ/kule *-a* blast of wind, strong gust; squall.

***vin'ḍ/lyse** *-t* northern lights.

vin'ḍ/mølle *-a* windmill: **kjempe mot v-r** fight with w-s (like Don Quixote).

vin'ḍ/pust *-et* puff of wind.

vin'ḍ/pølse *-a meteor.* wind cone, wind sock.

vin'ḍ/retning *-a*/+*-en* wind direction.

vin'ḍ/rose *-a*/+*-en* 1 *meteor.* wind rose. 2 *naut., obs.* compass chart.

vi'n/drue *-a*/+*-en* grape.

vin'dsel *-elet/-let, pl* +*-ler*/**-el* card, reel (of thread or yarn, esp. silk).

vin'ḍ/skala *-en meteor.* wind scale.

vin'ḍ/skeiv [/sjeiv] *A* 1 crooked, warped; wry. 2 *math.* skew.

+**vin'ḍ/ski** *-a* (=*/**skie**) gableboard (facing board fastened to edge of roof gable, sometimes with projecting, carved ends).

vin'ḍ/skjerm *-en* 1 windshield. 2 windbreak (wall or screen).

+**vin'ḍ/skjev** *A* cf **/skeiv**

vin'ḍ/stille *-a* calm: **ligge i v-a** lie becalmed.

vin'ḍ/styrke *-n* force of the wind (esp. as measured on the Beaufort scale): **v- 12** hurricane.

+**vin'ḍ/støt** *-et* (=*/**støyt**) sudden gust of wind.

vin'ḍ/tett *A* - windproof.

vin'ḍ/tunnel *-en* wind tunnel.

vin'ḍ/tørke *V -a*/+*-et* air-dry, dry in the wind.

+**vin'ḍ/tøy** *-et* (=*/**ty**) weather-proof material.

+**vin'du** *-et, pl -er* (=***vind/auga,** ***vind/auge**) 1 window; windowpane. 2 *anat.* fenestra.

+**vin'dus/blomst** *-en* potted plant to keep in the window.

+**vin'dus/dekoratø'r** *-en* window decorator (dresser, trimmer).

+**vin'dus/glass** *-et* window glass, windowpane.

+**vin'dus/haspe** *-n* hook (on a casement window).

+**vin'dus/karm** *-en* 1 window frame. 2 windowsill.

+**vin'dus/krok** *-en* brace, hook attached to window to hold it open.

+**vin'dus/nisje** *-n* window niche.

+**vin'dus/plass** *-en* seat near or by the window.

+**vin'dus/post** *-en* 1 windowsill. 2 mullion.

+**vin'dus/pusser** *-en, pl -e* 1 window washer. 2 windshield wiper.

+**vin'dus/rute** *-a/-en* windowpane.

+**vin'dus/utstilling** *-en* window display.

+**vin'ḍ/øyd** *A* - (=*/**øygd**) squinteyed.

°**vin'ḍ/øye** *-t* cf **vindu**

vi'n/fat *-et* wine cask.

ving'[1] *-en* 1 wing (in football). 2 wing (unit of military airplanes).

ving'[2] *-en* cf **veng**

vi'n/ga'rḍ *-en* (=+/**gård**) vineyard.

+**ving'e** *-n* cf **veng**

+**ving'e/bein** *-et* wing bone: **ta en ved v-et** admonish sby, set sby straight.

+**ving'e/bo'rḍ** *-et* drop-leaf table.

+**ving'e/brutt** *A* - broken-winged: *fig.* with one's wings clipped.

+**ving'e/fang** *-et* 1 wingspan, wing sweep. 2 *fig.* power, scope.

+**ving'e/fjør** *-a* wing feather.

+**ving'e/hest** *-en* Pegasus, the winged horse.

ving'el[1] *-elen, pl -lar* indecisive person.

ving'el[2] *-et*/+*-en* indecision, shilly-shallying.

+**ving'e/mutter** *-en, pl -e/-mutrer* wing nut.

Ving'er *Pln* twp, Hedmark.

+**ving'e/skrue** *-n* wing screw.

+**ving'e/skutt** *A* - winged (i.e. shot through the wing); *fig* without the will to live.

+**ving'e/slag** *-et* beat, stroke (of a bird's wings); *poet.* beating of wings, wingbeat.

+**ving'e/spenn** *-et* wingspan, wingspread.

+**ving'e/sus** *-et* whirring of wings.

+**ving'et** *A* - winged.

vi'n/gjær *-en* wine yeast.

vi'n/glas *-et* (=+/**glass**) wine glass.

ving'le *V -a*/+*-et* 1 dart, flit here and there; walk uncertainly. 2 act indecisively, vacillate.

ving'le/pave *-n* shilly-shally(er), vacillating person.

ving'let(e) *A* - shifty, unpredictable; unsteady, unsure; fickle.

vi'n/gud *-en* god of wine.

+**vi'n/gå'rḍ** *-en* cf **/gard**

+**vingårds/mann** *-en, pl -menn* wine grower; *bibl.* husbandman (Matt. 21,33).

vi'n/handel *-elen, pl -ler* wine shop.

+**vi'n/høst** *-en* (=*/**haust**) grape harvest; vintage.

Vin'je *Pln* 1 twp, Telemark. 2 twp, Sør-Trøndelag.

vin'k *-et* hint, sign, tip; signal (e.g. by a gesture of the body or hand): **gi et v-** drop a hint, make a sign; **oppfatte v-et** take the hint.

vi'n/karaf'fel *-elen, pl /karafler* wine carafe.

vi'n/kart *-et* wine list.

vin'ke *V -a*/+*-et* 1 beckon, signal, wave (e.g. the hand): **v- av w-** off. 2 (of light) blink, twinkle.

vin'kel *-elen, pl* +*-ler* 1 angle; corner. 2 (try) square, triangle. 3 *mil.* chevron, stripe. 4 angle iron. 5 (on pipe) elbow, knee.

vin'kel/bein *-et* leg of an angle.

+**vin'kel/dannet** *A* - angled, forming an angle.

vin'kel/hake *-n* 1 square, try square (used in drawing). 2 *typog.* composing stick.

vin'kel/jern [/jæ'rn] *-et* (=*/**jarn**) angle iron.

vin'kel/rett *A* - perpendicular, square, at right angles (**på** to).

+**vin'kel/skriver** *-en, pl -e* (=***-ar**) 1 pettifogger, small-time lawyer, shyster. 2 inferior writer.

vin'kel/spiss *-en* vertex.

+**vi'n/kjeller** *-en, pl -e* (=***-ar**) wine cellar.

+**vi'n/kjenner** *-en, pl -e* (=***-ar**) wine connoisseur.

-vin'kla *A* - (=+**-et**) -angled.

vin'kle *V -a*/+*-et* angle, form an angle, turn at an angle; **v- seg** zigzag; make a sharp turn.

Vi'n/lanḍ *Pln* Vinland (name given to a part of the North American east coast by Norse explorers ab. 1000 A.D).

vi'n/lauv *-et* (=+**løv**) grape leaf, vine leaf: **v- i håret** vine leaves in the hair (allusion from Ibsen's Hedda Gabler to the bacchantic revels of the ancient Greeks).

vi'n/legging *-a*/+*-en* wine making.

+**vi'n/løv** *-et* cf **/lauv**

vi'n/monopo'l *-et* 1 state liquor monopoly. 2 state liquor store.

vinn' *N*: **legge v- på** attach great importance to, make a point of.

vin'ne[1] *-a dial.* season's work (on a farm).

vin'ne[2] *V* +*vant*/**vann*, +*vunnet*/**vunne*/*-*i* 1 win (approval, contest, favor, friends, a lawsuit, etc.); gain (altitude, reputation, time, etc.): **hvo (den som) intet vâger, han intet v-er** nothing ventured, nothing g-ed; **v- for seg** w- over (to one's side); **v- fram** advance, g- ground; **v- fram til noe** attain, reach sth; **v- inn på en** g- on sby; **v- over, på** beat, defeat; **v- seg venner** win friends. 2 improve, make a better impression; grow on one: **v- ved nærmere bekjentskap** i- upon closer acquaintance. 3 be able, manage (**å** to): **v- med** keep up; **han vant ikke mer** it was all he could do (Egge); **han vant til dørs** he m-ed (to get to) the door (Ibsen); **det forteste han vant** as fast as he could (Falkberget). 4: **v-, v- ut** *tech.* extract (e.g. oil, ore). (See **vinnende**).

vin'ne/folk *-et* seasonal workers (on a farm).

vin'ne/kjær *A* - covetous, grasping, greedy.

***vin'neleg** *A* - feasible.

vin'ne/lyst *-a*/+*-en* avarice, greed.

vin'nenḍe *A* attractive, engaging, winning.

+**vin'ner** *-en, pl -e* (=***-ar**) 1 winner (i in). 2 winning card.

vin'ne/sjuke *-n* (=+/**syke,** */**sykje**) avarice, greed.

vin'ning *-a*/+*-en* 1 gain, profit (**ved** on): **v-a går opp i spinninga** one just about breaks even (lit. the gain is lost in the getting). 2 advantage, improvement: **til v- for perspektivet** to improve the perspective (Ibsen).

+**vin'nings/forbry'telse** *-n jur.* crime for profit.

+**vinnski'pelig** *A* - diligent, industrious.

vi'n/perse *-a* winepress.

vi'n/ranke *-*a*/+*-en* grapevine.

+**vi'n/røḍ** *A* (=*/**raud**) 1 wine red. 2 wine-colored: **det v-e hav** the w- sea (Homer).

vin'sj *-en* winch: **det skrek i v-ene** the w-es screeched (Evensmo).

+ Bokmål; * Nynorsk; ° Dialect.
After letter: ' stress (Acc. 1); ' tone, stress (Acc. 2); · length.
Below letter: . not pronounced.

vin'st -en lit. 1 advantage, gain, profit. 2 prize, winnings.
vi'n/stokk -en grapevine.
Vin'stra Pln river, village, in Gudbrandsdalen.
*vin'stre A - cf venstre
+vi'n/tapper -en, pl -e (=*-ar) 1 wine bottler. 2 obs. barman, tapster: "Hver sin smak", sa v-en, han drakk mens de andre sloss. "Each to his taste", as the tapster said; he drank while the others fought (proverb).
vin'ter -eren, pl -rer winter: i fjor v- last w- (w- of last year); i v- this (present) w-, the w- just past, last w- (of the present year); om v-en during, in the w-; til v-en next w-; v-en over throughout the w-.
*Vin'ter/brauta Prn the Milky Way.
vin'ter/dag -en 1 winter day: v-s dial. in the winter. 2 first day of winter (October 14).
vin'ter/drakt -a/+-en 1 (woman's) winter suit. 2 fig. winter dress (of snow covering). 3 zool. winter plumage.
vin'ter/dvale -n winter dormancy, winter resting period (e.g. for plants); winter sleep.
vin'ter/frakk -en (man's) winter coat.
vin'ter/føre -t winter driving conditions, sleighing, snow covering.
Vin'ter/gata Prn the Milky Way.
vin'ter/grøn -en (=+/grønn) bot. wintergreen (Pyrola).
vin'ter/kledd A -/*-kledt dressed for winter.
+vin'ter/klær pl (=*/klede) winter clothes.
vin'ter/kåpe -a (woman's)winter coat.
vin'ter/landskap -et pl -/+-er winter landscape, scene.
vin'terlig A - winter, wintery; cold.
vin'ter/natt -a, pl -netter 1 winter (winter's) night. 2: v-nettene period around October 14, when winter begins.
vin'ter/opplag -et winter storage: i v- laid up for the winter.
vin'ter/rug -en winter rye.
+vin'ter/sol(h)verv -et (=*/solkverv) winter solstice.
vin'ter/sport -en winter sport.
vin'ters/tid [*/ti] Av in winter(time).
vin'ter/søvn -en hibernation, winter sleep.
+vin'ter/tøy -et winter clothes.
vin'ter/veg -en (=+/vei) 1 road usable (only) in winter, winter road; road kept open in winter. 2: vise en v-n send sby about his business, send sby packing; reject (a suitor).
*vin'trast V -ast become winter.
vin'tre V -a/+-et 1: v- over winter (over). 2: det v-es it's getting towards winter.
+vin'trer pl of vinter
violoncell [fiolångsell'] -en cf fiolonsell
vi'pe -a zool. lapwing, pewit (Vanellus vanellus).
vipp' -en/+-et 1 bob; flip, jerk, whip; fam. flexibility, give, whip (e.g. of a fishing rod). 2 pol. balance in number of representatives of two parties: stå på v-en hang in the balance. 3 eyelash; head, spike (on grain). 4: slå v- play tipcat.
vip'pe[1] -a 1 (well) sweep. 2 seesaw, teeter-totter. 3 elec. current limiter.
vip'pe[2] V -a/+-et 1 (of birds' tails); bob, wag; dart, flit. 2 seesaw, totter; rock, sway, swing (back and forth). 3 tilt, tip; knock over; fling: v- avgjørelsen tip the balance in favor of a decision; v- en av pinnen knock sby off his (high) perch; v- noe i været fling sth into the air; v- regjeringen oust the cabinet. 4 elec. (of current, light) blink (because circuit is overloaded).
vip'pe/brett -et seesaw, teeter-totter.
+vip'pe/måler -en, pl -e (=*-ar) fam. electric meter (which measures current used above a minimum amount).
vip's I pop, presto, zip.
vi'rak -en 1 frankincense. 2 lit., fam. praise.
virgi'nia/tobakk' -en bot. Virginia tobacco (Nicotiana tabacum).
virgi'nsk A - Virginia, Virginian.
viri'l A virile.
virilite't -en virility.
vir'ke[1] -t 1 activity, work; calling, profession. 2 lumber, raw material.
+vir'ke[2] V -a/-et (=*verke[2]) 1 have an effect, influence, make an impression (på on, upon); appear, look, seem: det v-et sterkt på ham it had a great influence on him; it made a strong impression on him; han v-et høy he s-ed tall, gave the impression of being tall; medisinen v-et ikke the medicine had no e- (did not work); v- som en rød klut be like waving a red flag in front of a bull. 2 effect, bring about, work: hadde et menneske tro nok, så kunne det v- mirakler if a person had faith enough, he could w- miracles (Undset). 3 (of machinery, etc.) function, work. 4 lit. work (esp. at sewing, weaving, etc.); produce, make: v- fisk dial. prepare fish for salting; v- for en sak w- for a cause; v- opp hoven clean and prepare a hoof for shoeing.
+vir'ke/dag -en weekday, workday.
+vir'ke/evne -a/-en ability to work, capability.
vir'ke/felt -et field of action, province, sphere.
+vir'ke/kraft -a/-en capacity, efficacy, strength.
+vir'ke/kraftig A - effectual, efficacious.
+vir'ke/krets -en (=*/krins) field of activity, province, sphere.
+vir'kelig A - (=*verkeleg) actual, real, veritable; bonafide, genuine, true; (adv.) really, truly.
+vir'kelig/gjøre V -gjorde, -gjort carry out, execute, realize; fulfill, implement.
+vir'kelig/gjørelse -n fulfillment, realization (av of).
+vir'kelig/het -en reality: bli til v- become a r-; (often in def. form) flykte fra v-en flee from r-; i v-en in r-; actually, as a matter of fact.
+vir'kelighets/fjern [/fjæ'rn] A - divorced from reality, impractical, unrealistic; academic.
+vir'kelighets/flukt -a/-en escape from reality.
+vir'kelighets/nær A - in touch with reality, realistic.
+vir'kelighets/sans -en realism, sense of reality.
+vir'kelighets/tro A - faithful to reality, realistic.
+vir'ke/lyst -a/-en active spirit, drive, energy.
+vir'ke/lysten A -ent, pl -ne active, dynamic, energetic.
+vir'ke/middel -elet/-midlet, pl -midler agent, means, remedy; instrument: komiske v-r comic effects.
+vir'ke/måte -n manner of operation.
+vir'kning -en (=*verknad) effect; consequence, result.
+vir'knings/full A - effective, effectual.
+vir'knings/grad -en efficiency (of a motor).
+vir'knings/løs A ineffective, ineffectual; futile, in vain, useless; inoperative.
+vir'k/som' A -t, pl -me (=*verk/sam) 1 active, energetic. 2 effective: et v-t middel an e- remedy.
+vir'ksom/het -en activity; operations, undertaking, work: i v- active, at work; i travel v- busily at work.
vir're[1] -n millinery wire.
vir're[2] V -a/+-et 1 lit. twist, wind (om around). 2 circle, move in a circle; whirl; ramble, rove (omkring around). 3 rock back and forth (esp. one's body); quiver, shake; (esp. of color, light) shimmer: v- med (på) hodet shake, toss one's head from side to side (in despair, doubt, etc.). 4: v-seg (refl.) coil, curl up.
virtuell' A -elt potential, virtual: v-t bilde phys. virtual image.
virtuo's[1] -en virtuoso; master.
virtuo's[2] A brilliant, masterly (esp. in technique).
virtuosite't -en virtuosity.
+virtuo's/messig A - brilliant, masterly (esp. in technique).
vi'rus -en/+-et virus.
vir'var -et confusion, jumble, mess; chaos, tangle, welter.
+vir'vel[1] -elen, pl -ler (=*kvervel) 1 eddy, swirl, whirl; tumult. 2 cowlick, whorl; (on violin) scroll; (on drums) roll.
vir'vel[2] -elen, pl -ler anat. vertebra.
vir'vel/dyr -et vertebrate.
vir'vel/søyle -a/+-en spinal column.
vir'vel/vind -en whirlwind.
+vir'vle V -a/-et (=*kvervle) 1 spin, swirl, whirl; eddy: v-s churn; v- opp stir up; v- opp støv raise the dust; v- seg i dansen swirl around the floor.
vi's[1] -a/-en/-et, pl - fashion, manner, way(s): når det er på den v-en (det viset) if that's the way it is; på et v- in a way; på en eller annen v- in one way or another; på annet v- in some other way; på lovlig v- lawfully; på sin v- in (his, her, its) way, in a way.
vi's[2] A wise: de v-es stein the philosophers' stone; bli v- på dial. learn about.
vi'sa pl of visum
*vi'sar/gut -en cf viser/gutt
vis-à-vis [visavi'] face-to-face, opposite, vis-à-vis.
vi's/dom' -men/*-en wisdom; doctrine, teaching.
vi'sdoms/o'rd -et wise saying, word of wisdom.
vi'se[1] -a/+-en ballad, ditty, song: den gamle v-a the same old story (refrain, song); det er enden på v-n that's the end of that, that's the end of the matter; forstå en halvkvedet v- take a hint.
*vi'se[2] -n tip, top (of a plant); head, tassel (on grain).
vi'se[3] V -te 1 show; display, exhibit; demonstrate, evince: v- farge show one's colors; v-es be visible. 2 indicate, point to, show; register: termometeret v-te 12 kuldegrader the thermometer r-ed 12 below. 3 naut. pass, reeve (a line); (of a cable) grow, lead. 4 (with prep., adv.): v- bort turn away; v- fram display, exhibit, show; v- fra seg reject, turn away; v- igjen (dial. att) folk. tell (by magic) where stolen or lost things can be found; klokka v-er 11 the clock shows 11; v- en (hen) til noe, noen direct, refer sby to sth, sby. 5 (refl.): v- seg appear, make an appearance; show oneself; show off; become apparent, prove, turn out (to be); det vil v- seg we shall see, it remains to be seen; det v-te seg å være riktig it turned out to be correct; v- seg nødvendig be found (turn out to be) necessary; v- seg situasjonen voksen be equal to, rise to the occasion.
vi'se- Pf 1 deputy, vice-. 2 ballad, song.
vi'se/bok -a, pl -bøker songbook.
vi'se/formann -en, pl -menn/*-menner vice-chairman.
vi'se/konge -n regent, viceroy.
+vi'selig Av (=*visleg) wisely.
*vi'sen A -e/-i, pl -ne cf vissen
vi'se/president -en vice-president.
+vi'ser -en, pl -e (=*-ar) hand (on a clock), pointer.
vise're V -te 1 visa; check and stamp a document. 2 sight (a gun, etc.).
+vi'ser/gutt -en (=*visar/gut) errand boy.
+vi'ser/pike -a/-en errand girl.
vi'se/stubb -en snatch of (a) song.

vi'se/stump [/stomp] *-en* snatch of (a) song.

visi'bel *A -elt, pl -le* in sight, to be seen, visible.

visi'r *-et, pl -/+-er* visor (of helmet).

visita's *-en eccl.* (bishop's) visitation (for purposes of inspection and examination).

visitasjo'n *-en* 1 *eccl.* visitation; visitation trip. 2 examination, search; check (**av** of).

visite're *V -te* examine, inspect, search; check.

visitt' *-en* 1 call, visit: **avlegge v-** make a call; **gå, komme på v-** call (**til** on); **på v-** visiting. 2 *fam.* visitor: **ikke hjemme for v-er** not at home to v-s. 3 doctor and assistants as they make hospital rounds.

visitt'/kort *-et* calling card.

visjo'n *-en* vision.

visjonæ'r *A* clairvoyant, mystical, visionary.

vis'k *-en* 1 bundle, wisp (of hay). 2 whisk, whiskbroom. 3 *dial.* jumble, tangle.

vis'ke *V -a/+-et* rub, wipe (**av** off); *mil.* clean (a gun barrel): **v- ut** blot out; erase, rub out; **v- seg om munnen** wipe one's mouth.

+**vis'ke/lær** [also vis'-] *-et* (=***/ler**) eraser.

+**vis'kelærs/ball** *-en* rubber ball.

+**vis'ker** *-en, pl -e* (=***-ar**) 1 swab (for cleaning cannon); cleaning rod (for gun). 2 windshield wiper. 3 ramrod.

visko's *A chem.* viscous.

visko'se *-n chem.* viscose.

viskosite't *-en phys.* viscosity.

+**vis'le** *V -a/-et* 1 speak with defective s's. 2 hiss; rustle, sizzle, whistle.

***vi'sleg** *A* - sensible, thoughtful.

+**vis'le/lyd** *-en* 1 hissing sound. 2 *gram.* sibilant.

vi's/mann [also vi's/] *-en, pl -menn/ *-menner* wise man: **vismenn fra Østerland** w- men from the east (Matthew 2,1).

vis'mut *-en chem.* bismuth.

***vis'n** *-a* sign, trace.

vis'ne[1] *V -a/+-et* fade away, wither; wilt.

vis'ne[2] *pl of* **vissen**

vis'p *-en* beater, whisk.

vis'pe *V -a/+-et* beat, whip (food): **v- med halen** wag (its) tail.

+**vis'pe/snekker** *-en, pl -e pop.* fumbling person; clumsy ox.

viss'[1] *A* certain, sure (**på** of); inevitable: **den v-e død** c- death; **det er både sant og v-t** that's a fact, that's for sure; **en v- mann** a c- man; the devil; **gå på et v-t sted** go to the toilet; **på en v- måte** in a way; **v- i sin sak** c- (of what one is doing, saying, etc.); **det er v-t mellom dem** *dial.* they are engaged. (See also **visse**[2], **visst**[3].)

***viss'**[2] *C* cf **hvis**[1]

***vis'sa** *Av* surely, to be sure.

***vis'se**[1] *-a* assurance, certainty: **få v- for** get a- of; **i v-a** anyway, at any rate; **til v-a** certainly, to be sure.

vis'se[2] *N*: **til v-** certainly, to be sure.

vis'selig *Av* certainly, surely.

vis'sen *A -ent, pl visne* (=***visen**) dried up, wizened; wilted, withered.

vis'sen/brun *A* brown as dried leaves.

vis'sen/pinn *-en fam.* weakling, weak person; Caspar Milquetoast.

viss'/hendt *A - dial.* sure-handed.

+**viss'/het** *-en* assurance, certainty: **v- om at** the c- that; **få v- (for)** know for certain; know the worst; learn the truth; **gi v- for** prove; **ha v- for** be sure, know for sure; **si med v-** say with confidence; **skaffe seg v- (om)** make sure (of); learn for certain; **vite med v-** know for certain.

***viss'/høv** *A* accurately aimed; having a good aim.

***viss'/mon(n)** *-en, pl -er* affirmation, confirmation.

***viss'/o'rdig** *A* - able to find the right word.

viss't[1] *pp of* **vite**

viss't[2] *nt of* **viss**[1]

viss't[3] *Av* 1 certainly, surely; indeed, of course, to be sure: **ganske v-** to be sure; **ja v-** yes indeed; certainly; **jo v-** certainly, of course; (ironic) indeed; **nei v-** no indeed; **så v-** certainly; **v- er han sterk men** of course he's strong but. 2 I believe, I think: **vi har v- truffet hverandre før** we have met before, I b-. 3: **se v- på en** look fixedly, meaningfully at sby.

viss'te *pt of* **vite**

viss't/nok' *Av* 1 no doubt, to be sure (. . . but): **v- var vi ikke mange, men vi strakk dog til** we were few in number, to be sure, but we were sufficient (poem, Bjørnson). 2 (parenthetically, as reservation) I believe, I think: **hun er v- bra igjen** she is recovered now, I believe.

***vis't** *-a* (place of) residence; trace, track.

vis'ta cf **a vista**

vis'tra *-en/+-et* 1 trade name for a cellulose fiber. 2 a rayon and wool material.

visuell' *A -elt* visual.

vi'sum *-umet, pl -a* visa.

vis'vas *-et* nonsense; (as *interj.*) baloney, fiddlesticks, tommyrot.

***vi't** *-et* cf **vett**

vi'ta *-et* life, life story; vita.

vita'l *A* vital (appearance, forces, principles, etc.): **en v- personlighet** (also) a dynamic personality.

+**vita'lie/brødre** *pl* (=***/brør**) *hist.* band of pirates that harried the northern sea routes (late 14th, early 15th cent.).

vitalite't *-en* vitality.

vitami'n *-et, pl +-er/*-* vitamin.

vitami'n/fattig *A* - low in vitamins.

vitaminise're *V -te* add vitamins.

vitami'n/mangel *-en* lack of vitamins, vitamin deficiency.

vi'te *V veit/+vet, visste, visst* (=***vete**[2]) 1 know (**av** from, **om** about); be aware, have knowledge (**av** of): **det er ikke godt å v- når han kommer** it's hard to know when he will come; **en kan aldri v-** you never know; **få v-** hear, learn (of); be informed of; **vet du hva** not at all, what nonsense; (do) you know what; **v- beskjed** be in the know, (really) know; **v-ende** knowing; **være v-ende om** be informed about. 2 (with *prep., adv.*): **vi vil ikke v- av at du sager veden vores** we won't hear of your sawing our wood (Hamsun); **før han visste ordet av det** before he knew it, before he could say Jack Robinson; **han ville ikke v- av henne** he wouldn't have anything to do with her; **v- av seg** be aware of, know what one is doing, saying, etc.; **v- med seg selv** know inwardly, be inwardly convinced; **v- verken ut eller inn** be at a loss, not know which way to turn; **v- seg sikker** feel secure.

+**vi'te/begjæ'r** *-et* curiosity, inquisitiveness; eagerness to learn, thirst for knowledge.

+**vi'te/begjæ'rlig** *A* - inquisitive; eager to learn.

***vi'te/hug** *-en* cf **/begjær**

+**vi'te/kjær** *A* cf **/begjærlig**

vi'te/lyst *-a/+-en* curiosity; thirst for knowledge.

vi'te/lysten *A +-ent, pl -ne* inquisitive; eager to learn.

+**vi'ten** *en* knowledge, learning: **konflikten mellom tro og v-** the conflict between religion and science; **omfattende v-** extensive (wide) knowledge.

vi'tende *et* consent, knowledge: **med (uten) mitt v-** with (without) my c-; **med v- og vilje** deliberately; **mot (mitt) bedre v-** against (my) better judgment.

+**vi'ten/skap** *-en* cf **vit/**

+**vitenska'pelig** *A* - (=***vitskapleg**) scientific; (in humanistic studies) scholarly.

+**vi'tenskaps/akademi'** *-et* academy of science: **V-et i Oslo** The Oslo A- of S-.

+**vi'tenskaps/mann** *-en, pl -menn* cf **vitskaps/**

+**vi'tenskaps/selskap** *-et* scientific academy, society.

***vit'je**[1] *-a* check, inspection (esp. of nets, snares, etc.).

***vit'je**[2] *V -a* 1 visit. 2 check over, inspect.

***vi't/laus** *A* cf **vett/**

***vi't/løyse** *-a* cf **vett/**

vit'ne[1] *-t, pl +-r/*-* 1 witness (**for** for, **til** to); eyewitness; *jur.* deponent: **ha v- på noe** have a w- to sth; **være v- til** observe, witness. 2 evidence: **bære v- om** bear witness to, give e- of.

vit'ne[2] *V -a/+-et* give evidence (**om** of); bear witness, testify (**om** to): **v- for, mot** t- for, against.

+**vit'ne/avhøring** *-en* examination of witnesses.

vit'ne/boks *-en* witness stand.

vit'ne/fast *A* - attested (by witnesses).

vit'ne/forkla'ring *-a/+-en* deposition, sworn testimony.

vit'ne/før *A* eligible to testify.

vit'ne/førsel *-en jur.* 1 calling of witnesses. 2 testimony.

vit'ne/mål *-et* 1 testimony. 2 (school) report.

vit'ne/prov *-et* deposition, testimony.

vit'nes/byrd *-et* 1 testimony, witness: **du skal ikke si falskt v- mot din neste** thou shalt not bear false w- against thy neighbor. (Ex. 20, 16). 2 evidence, proof (**om** of). 3 *educ.* certificate, diploma, report (card). 4 testimonial; letter of recommendation.

+**vit'ne/utsagn** [/utsangn] *-et* (=***/utsegn**) testimony.

***vit'rast** *V -ast* become wiser, get a better understanding.

***vit're** *V -a* inform, warn: **v- om** call attention to.

vitrio'l *-en chem.* vitriol: **blå v-** copper sulphate; **grønn v-** ferrous sulphate; **hvit v-** zinc sulphate.

vit's *-en* 1 joke, witticism: **slå v-er** crack jokes. 2 point (of a joke, of an action); purpose, sense: **hva er v-en ved det hele** what's the point of it all; **det er ingen v- i å ta saken opp** there's no sense in taking up the matter.

vit'se *V -a/+-et* crack jokes, joke.

vi't/skap *-en* (=+**viten/**) (natural, social) science, branch of science; (in the humanities) scholarship (often disting. as **ånds/v-**); (a) discipline: **sosiologien er en ung v-** sociology is a young science (discipline); **Det kongelige norske Videnskabers Selskab** The Royal Norwegian Scientific Society (in Trondheim).

***vi'tskapleg** *A* - cf **vitenskapelig**

vi'tskaps/mann *-en, pl -menn/*-menner* (=+**viten/**) scientist; (in the humanities) scholar.

***vi't/skræme** *V -de* cf **vett/skremme**

+**vit's/maker** [also vit's/] *-en, pl -e* (=***-ar**) joker, wit.

+**vit'terlig** *A* - known (**for** to), notorious, obvious; (*adv.*) actually, as is well known, notoriously.

+**vit'terlig/het** *-en*: **til v-** *jur.* as witness, witnessed by.

vit'tig *A* - witty: **en v- hund** a wag, a wit.

+**vit'tig/het** *-en* 1 wit, wittiness: **et typisk uttrykk for norsk ubarbert v-** a typical expression of unbarbered Norwegian w- (Wildenvey). 2 witticism, witty remark; crack, gag: **saftige v-er** broad witticisms (Undset).

+ Bokmål; * Nynorsk; ° Dialect.
After letter: ' stress (Acc. 1); ' tone, stress (Acc. 2); · length.
Below letter: . not pronounced.

+vit'tighets/blad -*et* humor magazine.
+vit'tighets/tegning [/teining] -*en* cartoon.
***vi'tug** *A* - cf **vettug**
vi'v -*et*/+-*en archaic, hum.* wife; woman.
+vi'/vank -*en* cf **vid/**
vivasite't -*en lit.* vitality, vivacity.
vi'vat *et* cheer, viva (**for** for).
vi'vat/rop -*et* cheer, viva.
+vi'/vendel -*elen, pl* -*ler* (=***ved/**) *bot.* woodbine (honeysuckle) (Lonicera periclymenum).
viviseke're *V* -*te* vivisect
viviseksjo'n -*en* vivisection.
v. l. = **vestlig +lengde/*lengd**
VM=**verdensmesterskap(et)**
vn.=**vegen/+veien; vestnordisk.**
vod'ka -*en* vodka.
***vod've** -*n* muscle.
voffe [vof'fe] *V* -*a*/+-*et fam.* bark.
vo'g *pt of* **vege[1]**
vog'ge[1] -*a* cradle (also *fig.*) birthplace: **det var ikke sunget ved hans v- at** no one could have dreamed of him that; **fra v-a av** from earliest infancy.
vog'ge[2] *V* -*a*/+-*et* **1** rock: **v- et barn i søvn** r- a baby to sleep. **2** rock, sway: **v- i hoftene** sway, swing one's hips; **gå hjem og vogg** *pop.* go and have your head examined.
vog'ge/ba'rn -*et* baby.
+vog'ge/gave -*a*/-*en* (=***/gåve**): **få i v-** be endowed (by a good fairy) with the gift of.
vog'ge/mei -*en* rocker on a cradle.
vogn [vång'n] -*a* **1** wagon; carriage, coach; chariot: **han er ikke tapt bak en v-** he's no fool, he knows what's what. **2** baby carriage; handcart, pushcart (with four wheels). **3** railway car; streetcar, trolley (car): **siste v- går kl. 24** the last t- leaves at midnight. **4** vehicle (such as a motor car, truck, van, etc.); automobile, car. **5** (machine) carriage (e.g. on a typewriter).
vogn/borg [vång'n/] -*a*/+-*en hist.* circle of chariots.
+vogn/fører -*en, pl* -*e* (=***-ar**) driver, motorman.
vogn/hall +-*en*/*-*a* car barn.
vogn/ladning -*en* carload.
vogn/lass -*et* load, truckload.
vogn/mann -*en, pl* -*menn*/*-*menner* drayman (cab owner, trucker using horsedrawn vehicles).
vogn/park -*en* fleet (of busses, cars, etc.); rolling stock (of railroad); total number of cars (in a country).
+vogn/skjul -*et* (=***/skjol**) buggy shed, wagon shed.
vogn/smu'rning -*en* axle grease.
voile [voa'l] -*n* voile.
***vok** [vå'k] -*a* cf **våk[1]**
vokabula'r -*et, pl* -/+-*er* glossary, vocabulary, word list.
voka'l[1] -*en gram.* vowel: **norsk har ni lange og ni korte v-er** there are nine long and nine short vowels in Norwegian.
voka'l[2] *A mus.* vocal.
voka'l/harmoni' -*en gram.* vowel harmony.
vokalise're *V* -*te gram.* vocalize.
voka'lisk *A* - *gram.* vocalic.
vokalis't -*en mus.* vocalist.
voka'l/musikk' -*en* vocal music.
vokativ [vok'ativ] -*en gram.* vocative.
***voke** [vå'ke] -*a* night watch, vigil.
***voke/natt** [vå'ke/] -*a, pl* -*netter* cf **våke/**
vok's[1] -*et* wax: **som v- mellom hendene på en** like wax (soft clay) in sby's hands.
***vok's[2]** *pt of* **vekse**
vok's/bleik *A* - pale, waxy white.
vok's/bønne -*a* wax bean.
vok's/duk -*en* oil cloth.
vok'se[1] *V* -*a*/+-*et* wax (e.g. skis).
+vok'se[2] *V* -*te* (=***vekse**) **1** grow (**opp** up); increase, rise, wax: **v- av seg** outgrow (e.g. a childhood ailment, bad habits, etc.); **v- en over hodet** outgrow sby; *fig.* become too much for sby, get out of hand; **v- fra sine klær** outgrow one's clothes; **tiden har v-et fra jer** the times have passed you by (Ibsen); **v- fram** grow (up), spring forth (up); **v- med oppgaven** rise to the occasion; **v- til** become big, grow (up); **v- til med noe** be, become overgrown with sth. 2 *(refl.)*: **v- seg (skjev, stor, vakker osv.)** grow crooked, large, pretty, etc.).
+vok'sen *A* -*ent, pl* -*ne* (=***vaksen**) **1** adult, grown, grown-up; mature: **være sin oppgave v-** prove equal to the task. **2** full-sized, hefty, large: **en voksen dram** a man's size drink.
+vok'se/sted -*et* habitat, place of growth; place to grow up in.
vok's/farga *A* - (=+**-et**) wax-colored.
vok's/figu'r -*en* wax figure.
vok's/kabinett' -*et* waxworks.
vok's/lys -*et* (=***/ljos**) wax candle, taper.
vok's/papi'r -*et* wax paper.
vok's/tavle -*a* wax tablet.
vok'ster -*eren, pl* *-*rar* cf **vekst**
vok'sterlig *A* - (=**+veksterlig**) luxuriant, thriving.
***vok'ster/vilkår** -*et* cf **vekst/**
+vok'te *V* -*a*/-*et* (=***vakte[1]**) **1** guard, watch, watch over; herd, tend: **v- på noe, noen** keep a watch on sth, sby, watch sth, sby. **2: v- seg** *(refl.)* be careful, beware (**for** of), watch out (**for** for); **de v-et seg for å røpe språket** they took good care not to reveal their language (Evensmo).
+vok'ter -*en, pl* -*e* (=***vaktar**) guard, keeper, watchman; herdsman: **fredens v-e** guardians of peace.
vol [vå'l] -*en dial.* round stick or pole, esp. tiller on a rudder.
vol.=**volum**
volang' -*en* flounce, ruffle, ruffling.
vo'lapyk -*en* Volapük (an international auxiliary language).
+vol'd -*en* (=***vald[2]**) **1** force, violence; *jur.* assault and battery: **bruke v-** apply f-; **gjøre, øve v- på noe, noen** do v- to sth, sby; **med v- og makt** with brute force; at all costs, by hook or by crook; **ta med v-** rape, ravish. **2** power: **i hans v-** in his p-; **dra fanden i v-** go to hell; **gi seg Gud i v-** commend oneself to God.
Vol'da *Pln* twp, Møre og Romsdal.
+vol'de *V* -*te* (=***valde[2]**) be the cause of, cause, occasion.
+vol'delig *A* - forcible, violent; *(adv.)* by force.
+vol'd/gift -*en jur.* arbitration.
+vol'dgifts/dom' -*men* award, decision by arbitration.
+vol'dgifts/domstol -*en* arbitration tribunal (esp. of World Court); court of arbitration.
+vol'dgifts/kjennelse -*n jur.* award (decision of arbitrators).
+vol'ds- *Pf* violence.
+vol'ds/dåd -*en* deed of violence.
+vol'ds/ferd -*en* violence.
+vol'ds/forbry'telse -*n* crime of violence.
+vol'ds/forbry'ter -*en, pl* -*e* violent criminal.
+vol'ds/handling -*a*/-*en* act of violence, brutality.
+vol'ds/herredømme -*t* despotism, tyranny; rule by force.
+vol'ds/mann -*en, pl* -*menn* assailant, assaulter; perpetrator of violence; bully, gangster, tough.
+vol'd/som' *A* -*t, pl* -*me* **1** vehement, violent; harsh, intense, severe: **v- motstand** violent resistance. **2** tremendous; terrible, terrific: **en v- appetitt** a tremendous appetite; **v-t sulten** terribly hungry.
+vol'dsom/het -*en* vehemence, violence; intensity, severity: **v-er** violent actions, deeds.
+vol'd/ta *V* -*tok*, -*tatt* **1** assault, rape. **2** *fig.* seize forcibly; overpower.
+vol'd/tekt -*a*/-*en* **1** assault, rape (**av** of). **2** *fig.* act of violence.
voll'[1] -*en* (grassy) field, meadow; (piece of) grassland, turf: **danse på v-en** dance in the meadow.
voll'[2] -*en* **1** breastwork, rampart. **2** bank, embankment.
Voll' *Pln* twp, Møre og Romsdal.
***vol'le** *pp of* **velle[1]**
volley [vål'li] -*en* volley.
voll'/grav -*a*/+-*en* moat.
voll'/høy -*et* good quality hay cut from grassy meadow.
***vol'li** *pp of* **velle[1]**
volontø'r -*en* **1** apprentice, unpaid trainee. **2** *mil., archaic* volunteer who served without pay.
vol't -*en, pl* - *phys.* volt.
vol'te[1] +-*n*/*-*a* **1** (in fencing, horsemanship) volt. **2** esp. *gymn.* somersault (in the air). **3** (in card tricks) pass. **4** change of front, volte-face.
vol'te[2]** *pp of* **velte[2]** (=volti**)
vol't/spenning -*a*/+-*en* voltage.
volu'm -*et* esp. *phys., mus.* volume.
voluminø's *A* voluminous; full, large.
Volund [vå'lunn] *Prn myth.* Volund, a master smith in a Germanic legend retold in the Poetic Edda.
Volu/spå [vå'lu/] *Prn* poem about the gods and creation, from the Poetic Edda.
vol've -*a*/+-*en myth.* prophetess, sibyl (woman thought to be able to confer with the gods through magic and to foretell the future).
vom' -*ma, pl* -*mer*/**vemmer* **1** belly; *vet.* rumen: **fylle v-a** fill one's b-. **2** paunch, pot.
***vom'b** -*a, pl vember* cf **vom**
vo'n[1] -*a* **1** expectation, hope (**om** of): ***det gjekk etter v-a** things turned out as expected; **på v-a** in the hope; **på v- og våge** on a chance. **2** likelihood, possibility (**om** of): **det var v-det, mente gutten** that's likely, thought the boy (Asbjørnsen); **ut av v- og vett** absolutely impossible. **3** *dial.* good hunting area, spot.
***vo'n[2]** *A* -: **eg mår det ikkje v-** I can't do without that.
***vo'n/broten** [/bråten] *A* -*e*/-*i, pl* -*ne* disappointed.
vo'n/brott -*et* (=***/brot**) *lit.* disappointment.
von'd [von'] *A* (=**+ond**) **1** difficult, hard: **det var v-t å gå** it was hard walking; **jeg har v-t (for) å tro it** is difficult for me to believe; **gammel vane er v- å vende** you can't teach an old dog new tricks; **være v-t om (bli v-t for)** be scarce, be hard to find. **2** bad, unpleasant: **en v- lukt** a bad smell; **v- mat** unsavory food; **han har v- samvittighet** he has a bad conscience; **gjøre v-t verre** make bad worse; **sette v-t blod mellom** stir up trouble between; **smake v-t** taste unpleasant. **3** miserable, unfortunate: **ha (få) det v-t** be (become) miserable, unhappy; **lide v-t** suffer; **så lang som et v-t år** as long as a month of Sundays. **4** harmful; painful, sorrowful: **en v- finger** an aching finger; **en v- tanke** a painful thought; **gjøre v-t** hurt; **ha v-t av en** feel sorry for, pity sby; **han har ikke v-t av det** it won't do him any harm; **jeg har v-t i hodet** my head aches, hurts; **ha v-t i halsen** have a sore throat; **ønske v-t over en** wish sby ill. **5** evil; malicious, spiteful: **den v-e** the devil; **v-t ment** intended maliciously; **gi v-t fra (av) seg** speak spitefully, complain; **snakke v-t om en** slander sby; **ville en v-t** menace, threaten. **6** angry: **være (bli) v- på** be (get) angry at; **gi v-t fra seg** speak angrily.
+von'del -*elen, pl* -*ler* (=**+vandel[2], *vondul**) bundle (of hay, straw, used as fodder).
***von'd/kyndt** [von'/] *A* - bad-tempered, cross.
von'dle *V* -*a*/+-*et* gather, prepare, bundle(s) of hay (for feeding).

vond/lynt [von'/] *A* - (=***-lyndt**) hotheaded, ill-tempered.
vond/o'rd [von'/] *-et* abuse, rebuke; sarcasm, taunt.
vond/skap [von'/] *-en* evil; evil act.
***vondske** [von'ske] *-a* discomfort, indisposition.
***vondsleg** [von'sleg] *A* - (rather) bad; angry.
***vond/tenkt** [von'/] *A* - suspicious.
***von'dul** *-en, pl vondlar* cf **vondel**
vo'ne *V -a/+-te dial.* expect, hope.
***vo'n/laus** *A* hopeless.
***vo'nleg** *A* - likely, probable.
***vo'n/løyse** *-a* hopelessness.
vo'nom(s) *Av dial.* 1 (often before a comparative) than expected: **vi har gått v- langt i dag** we have walked pretty far today (Asbjørnsen). 2 most likely, probably.
***vo'n/vere** [/være] *V only inf* do without.
vor [vå'r] *-en* (=+**vorr**) *dial.* 1 bank of stones, moraine; row of stones on each side of a boat landing (where boats can be pulled ashore). 2 wake (of a boat, fish). 3 distance a boat moves forward by each pull of the oars.
***vo'rd** *-en* guardian angel, watchman.
+**vor'de** *V -er, pp -et (no pt) archaic, poet.* be, become, grow: **helliget vditt navn** hallowed be thy name (Luke 11,2); **kong Agilulfs hår er v-et hvitt** King A-'s hair has turned white (Kinck).
+**vor'den** *en* genesis, nascence: **i sin v-** in the making; embryonic.
+**vor'dende** *A* - coming, future, prospective: **en v- mor** an expectant mother.
***vore** [vå're] *pp of* **vere**[3]
-vo'ren [also +-vårren, *-vå'ren] *A +-ent, pl -ne* -ative, -ish, -y (inclined, tending to be), e.g. **små/v-, vakle/v-.**
***vori** [vå'ri] *pp of* **vere**[3]
+**vor'ned/skap** *-et hist.* serfdom.
vor'pe** *pp of* **verpe**[2] (=vorpi**)
+**vorr'** *-en* cf **vor**
vorte[1] [vor'te] *-a* 1 wart. 2 nipple.
***vor'te**[2] *pp of* **verte**
vorte/mjølk [vor'te/] *-a bot.* spurge (Euphorbia).
vorte/svin [vor'te/] *-et zool.* warthog (Phacochoerus).
vortet(e) [vor'tet(e)] *A* - wart-covered, warty.
***vor'ti** *pp of* **verte**
***voss'** *-en, pl vesser* person from Voss.
Voss' *Pln* twp, Hordaland.
vos'se/rull *-en* waltzlike folk dance (or music) from Voss.
Vos'se/strand *Pln* twp, Hordaland.
vos'sing *-en* person from Voss.
vote're *V -te* vote (usu. by a jury of parliament).
vote'rings/tema *-et* question to be voted upon.
voti'v/tavle *-a/+-en* votive tablet.
vott' *-en* 1 mitten. 2 *fam.* spineless creature, weakling; softie.
vo'tum *-et, pl vota* vote (usu. with written opinion expressing one's reasons).
vo'v *pt of* **veve**
+**vove**[1] [vå've] *-n poet.* billow, wave.
***vove**[2] [vå've] *pp of* **veve**
+**vovet** [vå'vet] *A* - dangerous, risky; bold, daring.
***vovi** [vå'vi] *pp of* **veve**
VP=**Venstres Pressekontor**
vra'k *-et* 1 driftwood, flotsam, wreckage; ruin, wreck: **et v- av en mann** a human wreck. 2: **kaste (slå) v- på** refuse, reject.
vra'ke *V -a/+-et/+-te* 1 refuse, reject; cast off, discard, throw out: **velge og v-** pick and choose. 2 (of fish etc.) sort. 3 *dial.* gather debris.
+**vra'ker** *-en, pl -e* (=***-ar**) grader, sorter (esp. of fish).
vra'k/gods [/gots] *-et* wreckage; waste.
vra'k/stump [/stomp] *-en* piece of wreckage; driftwood, flotsam: **blandt v-ene** in the wreckage.
vral'te *V -a/+-et* (=***valtre**) waddle.
vrang' *A* (=***rang**[2]) 1 wrong (side); inside out; reversed: **ta strømpene v-t på** put on the stockings inside out; (in knitting) **v- maske** purl; **strikke v-t** purl. 2 contrary, difficult, troublesome: **glemme det v-e og skakke** forget what troubles us (Ibsen); **slå seg v-(t)** cause trouble, turn out bad; be obstinate, refuse to budge; **en v- og vrien person** a cross and contrary person. 3 *archaic, dial.* erroneous, incorrect, wrong; unjust, (morally) wrong: ***i r-e enden** on the wrong end; ***ein r- dom** an unjust sentence; ***ein r-eid** a false oath.
vrang'/bord *-en* ribbing (edge on mittens, socks, sweaters).
vrang'e *-a/+-en* (=***range**[1]) 1 reverse, wrong side; bad side. 2 "wrong throat", windpipe: **få noe i v-en** choke on sth, get sth down the wrong way; **stick** in one's craw.
+**vrang'/forestilling** [/fåre-] *-en* delusion; misconception.
vrang'/lære *-a/+-en* false teaching; heresy; aberration, deviation.
+**vrang'/lærer** *-en, pl -e* (=***-ar**) heretic, teacher of heresy.
vrang'lås *N*: **gå i v-** (of locks) get stuck; (of situation) go wrong; reach an impasse; (of person) become obstinate, refuse to budge.
vrang'/side [*/sie] *-a/+-en* bad side, wrong side; seamy side.
vrang'/strupe *-n* "wrong throat", windpipe: **få noe i v-n** choke on sth; *fig.* get a strong aversion for sth; **komme i v-en for en** *fig.* stick in one's craw.
vrang'/vilje *-n* contrariness, obstinacy, perversity; ill will.
vrang'/villig *A* - (=***/viljug**) contrary, obstinate, perverse.
+**vrang'villig/het** *-en* cf **/vilje**
+**vran'ten** *A -ent, pl -ne* crabby, ornery, sour; grumpy, peevish.
+**vre'd**[1] *A* (=***vreid**[1]) angry, irate, wrathful (**over** about; **på** at).
+**vre'd**[2] *pt of* **vri**[2]
+**vre'de** *-n* (=***vreide**) *lit.* anger, wrath: **Herrens v-** the wrath of the Lord; **V-ns Dag** Day of W- (Latin hymn); **V-ns Druer** Grapes of W- (novel, Steinbeck); **øse sin v- ut over** pour out one's w- on.
+**vre'des** *V -edes, -es lit.* become angry, wroth: **v- ikke** be not wrathful.
+**vre'd/laten** *A -ent, pl -ne lit.* bad-tempered, quick to anger; wrathful.
+**vrei** *pt of* **vri**
***vrei'd**[1] *A* cf **vred**[1]
***vrei'd**[2] *pt of* **vride**
***vrei'dast** *V vreiddest, vreidst* become angry.
***vrei'de** *-n* cf **vrede**
°**vre'l** *-et* cf **vræl**
+**vreng'e** *V -te* (=***rengje**) 1 twist, wring (esp. one's lips, mouth, etc.); grimace, make faces; jeer, sneer: **v- etter** jeer at, mock, ridicule; **v- på** distort, pervert, twist (sby's words). 2 invert, reverse, turn inside out; **v- av seg** strip, throw off; **v- med øynene** show, turn up the whites of one's eyes. 3 *(refl.)*: **v- seg** twist; *fam.* vomit; **v- seg om** change, turn (**til** into).
+**vreng'e/bilde** *-t* caricature, mockery, travesty (**av** of).
+**vri'**[1] *-en/-et* (=***vrid**) 1 twist. 2 sprain, wrench.
vri'[2] *V -r, vrei/+-dde/+vred, -dd* (=***vride**) 1 twist, wrench, wring (**av** off); turn (esp. a key): **hvordan en v-r og vender på det** no matter how you look at it, how you slice it; **v- halsen om på en** wring one's neck; **v- nøkkelen om** turn the key in a lock; **v- opp vasken** wring out the wash. 2 *(refl.)*: **v- seg** squirm, twist; writhe; **v- seg fra, unna** wriggle away from, out of; **v- seg fra å gjøre noe** shrink from doing sth; **v- seg fram** wriggle one's way ahead.
***vri'd** *-en* cf **vri**[1]
***vridar** *-e'n* cf **vrier**
+**vrid'de** *pp of* **vri**[2]
***vri'de** *V vreid, -e/-i* cf **vri**[2]
***vri'den** *A -e/-i, pl -ne* cf **vrien**
***vri'ding** *-a* cf **vridning**
***vri'dnad** *-en* cf **vridning**
+**vri'dning** *-en* (=***vriding**) 1 twist, twisting; wringing. 2 *phys.* torsion. 3 contortion; squirming.
vri'en *A +-ent, pl vri(d)ne/+-ene* (=***vriden**) 1 contorted, twisted. 2 difficult, hard, intricate: **v-e variasjoner over Händel** i- variation on Händel. 3 difficult, obstinate, uncooperative (person).
+**vri'er** *-en, pl -e* (=***vridar**) doorknob; latch handle.
vrikk' *-et* 1 turn, twist, yank; flip. 2 sprain, wrench.
vrik'ke *V -a/+-et* 1 sprain, wrench. 2 turn, twist; wag, wiggle, wriggle; work (sth) back and forth or side to side. 3 *naut.* scull.
+**vrik'le** *V -a/-et* (=***rikle**) *dial.* wiggle, work (sth) back and forth or side to side.
vri'/maski'n *-en* wringer.
vri'mle *V -a/+-et* abound; crawl, swarm, teem (**av** with): **en v-ende masse** a t-ing multitude; **det v-er av katter** the place s-s with cats, *(pop.)* is lousy with cats.
vrim'mel *-elen, pl vrimler* crowd, mass, mob; multitude, myriad, swarm (**av** of): **kaste seg ut i v-elen** plunge into the crowd; **livets v-** the tumult of life.
***vring'el**[1] *-elen, pl -lar* hair-splitter, quibbler; difficult person.
vring'el[2] *-elet/-let* 1 hair-splitting, quibbling. 2 tortuousness, twisting.
vring'le *V -a/+-et* cavil, quibble: **v- seg bort** wiggle out of sth.
vring'let(e) *A* - 1 complicated, confusing. 2 (of a person) caviling, quibbling.
vrin'sk *-et* neigh, whinny.
vrin'ske *V -a/-et/+-te* neigh, whinny.
vri'om/peis *-en fam.* hairsplitter, quibbler; ornery person, stubborn coot.
+**vris't** *-a* cf **rist**[1]
+**vris'te** *V -a/-et* wrench, wrest, wring: **v- noe fra en** wrest sth from sby; **v- seg løs** wrench oneself loose.
vræ'l *-et* howl, roar, yowl; (of pigs) squeal.
vræ'le *V -te/*-a* howl, roar, yowl; (of pigs) squeal.
vrøv'l *-et* 1 drivel, nonsense, twaddle: **stykket var noe forferdelig v-** the play was pure d-. 2 fuss, to-do, trouble: **gjøre v-** make trouble; **vi skal ikke ha noe v-** stop that nonsense.
vrøv'le *V -a/+-et* 1 jabber, prate, talk nonsense. 2 make a hodge-podge of, muddle.
+**vrøv'le/bøtte** *-a* jabbering fool, muddler; jackass.
+**vrøv'le/hode** *-t* bird brain, fuzzy-minded person, silly fool.
vrøv'let(e) *A* - drivelling, muddle-headed, nonsensical.
+**vrå'** *-en archaic* 1 corner, nook; cranny. 2 hideaway, secluded spot.
Vrå'l *Prn(m)*
v.s.a.=**ved sida av**
+**V-tegn** [ve'-tein] *-et* victory sign, V-sign.
+**vug'ge**[1] *-n* cf **vogge**[1]
+**vug'ge**[2] *V -et* cf **vogge**[2]
+**vug'ge/gave** *-n* cf **vogge/**
vulgarise're *V -te* vulgarize.
vulgaris'me *-n* vulgarism.

+ Bokmål; * Nynorsk; ° Dialect.
After letter: ' stress (Acc. 1); ' tone, stress (Acc. 2); · length.
Below letter: . not pronounced.

Vulga'ta *-en eccl.* Vulgate.
vulgæ'r *A* common, low, vulgar.
vulgæ'r/lati'n *-en* Vulgar Latin.
vulka'n *-en* volcano.
vulkanise're *V -te* vulcanize.
vulka'nsk *A* - volcanic.
vulka'n/utbrott *-et* (=***/utbrot, +/utbrudd**) volcanic eruption.
vul'ke *V -a/+-et pop.* vulcanize.
vul'st *-en* 1 ridge, roll; bead, rim. 2 *arch.* torus.
***vun'de** *pp of* **vinde**[2]
+**vun'det** *pp of* **vinde**[2]
***vun'di** *pp of* **vinde**[1]
vun'ne** *pp of* **vinne**[2] (=vunni**)
+**vun'net** *pp of* **vinne**[2]
vurde're *V -te* 1 appraise, assess, evaluate (**til** at); estimate, judge. 2 appreciate, value.
vurde'rings/sak *-a/+-en* matter of judgment.
+**vur'm** *-en* fixed idea.
v.v.=**vice versa**
vy' *-en lit.* view, vista.
***vyrde** [vø're] *V -e* cf **vørde**
***vyr'deleg** *A* - cf **vørdeleg**
***vyrd/laus** [vø'r/] *A* cf **vørd/**
***vyrdnad** [vø'rna] *-en* cf **vørdnad**
***vyrd/sam** [vø'r/] *A* cf **vørd/**
***vyr'dsle**[1] *-a* cf **vørdsle**[1]
***vyr'dsle**[2] *V -a* cf **vørdsle**[2]
***vyr'k** *A* 1 careful; solicitous (**for** of). 2 work (day, time, etc.): **både v-t og heilagt** both work days and holidays.
***vyr'ke**[1] *-t* material, stuff.
***vyr'ke**[2] *-a* cf **yrke**[1]
***vyr'ke/dag** *-en* weekday, workday.
+**væ'bne** *V -et* cf **væpne**
***væ'gen** *A -e/-i, pl -ne* accommodating, agreeable, compliant; yielding.
***væ'gje**[1] *-t* accommodation, acquiescence, compliance.
***væ'gje**[2] *V -de* agree, give in, yield: **han lyt v- som vitet har** the one who has some sense will have to give in.
***væ'kje** *-a* cf **veikje**[1]
°**væ'l** *-a* cf **verden**
***væ'le** *V -te* pile wood (for burning).
væ'pne *V -a/+-et* arm (**med** with; **mot** against): **v- seg** arm (oneself).
+**væ'pner** *-en, pl -e* (=***-ar**) armor-bearer, squire.
+**væ'r**[1] *-en* (=***ver**[1]) 1 battering ram. 2 *zool.* male sheep, ram. 3 *astron.* Ram.
+**væ'r**[2] *-et* (=***ver**[2]) 1 weather: *fig.* **be om godt v-** ask to be forgiven; **snakke, tale om v- og vind** make small talk; **være ute i, komme ut i hardt v-** have a rough time of it. 2 storm, (strong) wind: *naut.* **legge på v-et** heave to; **ligge på v-et** be hove to; lie by. 3 air; atmosphere, aura: **det var et v- av freidighet over henne** there was an a- of confidence about her; **(bort) i v- og vind** carelessly, haphazardly; at random; **grått i v-et** a gray day; **i v-et** into the air; high up; *naut.* aloft; **snakke, tale bort (hen) i v-et** talk irrelevantly, ramblingly; **til v-s** into the air; up. 4 scent, wind (of an animal, a person): **komme under v- med noe** get w- of sth. 5 breath, wind: **dra v-et** draw b-; **Åse gisper etter v-et** Å- gasps for b- (Ibsen); **ta v-et fra en** take sby's b- away.
væ'r[3] *-et* 1 fishing grounds; fishing station. 2 nesting place, rookery.
+**væ'r-** *Pf* (=***ver-**)
-vær[1] *-en* -ing, -ite (of person, indicating home district), e.g. **lom/v-**.
*-**vær**[2] *A* having the quality given in first part of the word, e.g. **blid/v-, glad/v-**.
+**væ'r/bitt** *A* - weather-beaten, weathered: **furet, v- over vannet** furrowed, weathered o'er the sea (national anthem, Bjørnson).
+**væ'r/brent** *A* - (of skin) tanned; (of hair) bleached by the sun.
+**væ'r/bror** *-en, pl -brødre* (=***ver/**) brother-in-law.
+**væ'r/datter** *-a/-en, pl -døtre(r)* (=***ver/dotter**) daughter-in-law.
+**væ'r/drag** *-et* breeze.
***væ're**[1] *-t* 1 being, existence, e.g. in **nær/v-, sam/v-**. 2 lodgings, residence, e.g. in **hus/v-**.
+**væ're**[2] *V er, var, vært* (=***vere**[2]) 1 be, exist: **dersom han ikke var** if he didn't exist, if he weren't alive; **det var det** that's that; that's the question, that's it, that's the thing (**hva skal jeg gjøre? Ja, det var det da** what shall I do? Yes, that's the question); **det var (er) riktig** that's right; **det var så det, sa reven** that's true enough, said the fox (Asbjørnsen); **er det sant? Ja, det er det** is that true? Yes, it is; **i høst som var** *pop.* last fall; **v- enig** agree, be agreed; **det får v-** it will have to be, let it go. 2: **vær så god** please; (when offering sby sth) please help yourself; (when calling sby to the table) please come and eat, please come to the table; (when inviting sby to go first, do sth first) after you, please; (when handing sby sth) here (there) you are; (when answering, expressing assent, replying to thanks, etc.) by all means, certainly, (yes) do, you're quite welcome; (when answering the phone) =hello; (**vær så god og sett Dem** please have a seat, please sit down); **vær så snill** please (**vær så snill å sende meg sukkeret** please pass me the sugar). 3 (as auxiliary, with perf. part. esp. of verbs of movement and changing condition, inst. of the usual **ha** in the perfect) **han er gått for dagen** he is gone for the day; **av jord er du kommet** from earth art thou come, **han er blitt ganske tykk i det senere** he has become quite fat lately. 4 (as auxiliary, with perf. part. of trans. verbs inst. of the **bli** of the passive): **nå var det gjort** now it was done; **vi er budne bort** we are invited out. 5 (with *prep., adv.*): **v- fra seg** be beside oneself; **v- innom** drop in (only in past and perf.: **jeg var innom hos Olsen** I dropped in at O-'s); **v- med** accompany, come along (**får jeg v- med** can I come along); **v- med i (på)** have, lend a hand in; take part in; **v- om seg** be on one's toes, be sharp; look out for one's interests; **v- oppe i** be mixed up in; **v- over en** be upon one (**vinteren var over oss** winter was upon us); **v- sammen** be together (**med** with, **om** in); go steady (**med** with) (**de var sammen om forbrytelsen** they were together in the crime); **v- til** be, exist; be for; be good for (**hva skal det v- til** what's that for; what's the good of that); **v- ute for en ulykke** be in an accident; **v- ved** admit. 6 (*refl.*): **det v- seg i England eller i Amerika** whether in E- or in A-; **v- seg noe bevisst** be alive to, be conscious of sth.
+**væ're**[3] *V -a/-et* (=***vere**[4]) 1 smell, sniff. 2 scent, smell; detect, sense: **v- bort** blow away.
+**væ'relse** -t room: **dele v-** be roommates, share (one's) room(s); **fireværelses leilighet** four-room apartment; **to v-r og kjøkken** two r-s and kitchen.
+**væ'relses/pike** *-n* hotel maid.
+**væ'relses/temperatu'r** *-en* room temperature.
+**væ're/måte** *-n* bearing, behavior, manner.
+**væ'rende** *A* - (=***verande**) 1 fit to be in, live in: **her er ikke v-(s)** this is no fit place to be in, live in; one can't stay here. 2: **bli v-** remain, stay (at a place); **et v- sted** a place to remain, a permanent place.
+**væ'r/far** *-en, pl -fedre* (=***ver/**) father-in-law.
+**væ'r/fast** *A* - storm-bound, weather-bound.
+**væ'r/foran'dring** *-a/-en* change in the weather.
+**væ'r/gud** *-en* weather god.
+**væ'r/hane** *-n* weather vane.
+**væ'r/ha'rd** *A* exposed to the weather, harsh, weather-beaten.
væ'r/hatt *-en* chimney hood.
+**væ'r/hår** *-et zool.* whisker.
væ'ring *-en* Viking mercenary for Russian and Byzantine rulers.
-væring *-en* -ian, -ing, -ite (of person, indicating home district).
+**væ'r/lag** *-et* climate, weather conditions; *fig.* atmosphere.
+**væ'r/melding** *-a/-en* weather report, forecast.
+**væ'r/mor** *-a/-en, pl -mødre(r)* (=***ver/**) mother-in-law.
+**væ'r/omslag** *-et* change of weather.
+**væ'r/profe't** *-en* weather prophet.
+**værsgo'(d)** *I* cf **være**[2]
+**væ'r/sjuk** *A* - sick or in bad humor because of the weather.
+**væ'r/slitt** *A* -weathered, weatherworn.
+**væ'r/slått** *A* - hard-hit (by storm), storm-battered, storm-driven.
+**væ'r/sønn** *-en* (=***ver/**) son-in-law.
+**væ'r/søster** *-a/-en, pl -søstre(r)* (=***ver/**) sister-in-law.
+**vær'/sågo'd** *I* cf **være**[2]
+**vær't** *pp of* **være**[2]
+**væ'r/varsel** *-elet/-let, pl -el/-ler* 1 weather forecast, prediction. 2 sign (of coming weather).
+**væ'r/varsling** *-a/-en* 1 weather forecast, prediction. 2 weather bureau: **dette er v-a for Vestlandet** this is the w- for West Norway (radio Bergen).
+**væ'rvarslings/stasjo'n** *-en* weather station.
Væ'r/øy *Pln* 1 twp, Nordland. 2 island in Sunnfjord.
væs'ke[1] *-a/+-en* 1 fluid, liquid: **desinfiserende v-** disinfectant. 2 juice, sap; *archaic* humor. 3 discharge, matter, pus.
væs'ke[2] *V -a/+-et* 1 secrete fluid; ooze, run, weep; *med.* suppurate. 2 *lit.*: **v-ende sår** bitterness, open wound.
væs'ke/form *en* liquid form, state.
væ'te[1] *-a/+-en* humidity, moisture, wetness; rain, water.
væ'te[2] *V -te* dampen, moisten, wet: **v- seg** wet oneself; **øynene v-er** *dial.* (my) eyes are watering.
***vø'le**[1] *-a* heap, mass, pile (**med** of).
***vø'le**[2] *-a* fixing, repair.
vø'le[3] *-t* 1 *naut.* float, marker. 2 *dial.* bird's tail.
vø'le[4] *V -te* fix, repair: **v- om** fix up; **v- på** be fixing up.
°**vø'le**[5] *V -te* cf **vørde**
***vø'nast** *V -test, vønst* cf **vone**
***vø'ne** *V -te* cf **vone**
vø'rde *V +-te/*-e* (=+**vøre**) 1 esteem, respect, value. 2 pay attention to; bother about: **du skal bare ikke v-** just don't bother (Hamsun). 3: **tvi vøre** for shame, pfui to you.
***vø'rdeleg** *A* - 1 respectable. 2 impressive, notable, worthy. 3 solemn.
***vø'rd/laus** *A* 1 heedless, inconsiderate; reckless. 2 careless, indifferent; slovenly.
vø'rdnad *-en* (=+**vørnad**) *dial.* 1 consideration, esteem, respect: **vise v- for** show respect for. 2 dignity, solemnity. 3 care, orderliness.
vø'rd/sam' *A -t, pl +-me dial.* 1 polite, respectful. 2 careful, orderly.
vør'ds/laus *A* 1 heedless, inconsiderate; reckless (**med** with). 2 careless, indifferent; slovenly.
***vør'dsle**[1] *-a* care, cleanliness, orderliness.
***vør'dsle**[2] *V -a* keep in order, take care of.
+**vø're** *V -te* cf **vørde**
°**vø'ri** *V pp of* **være**[2]
°**vør'k(j)e** *-t* cf **vyrke**[1]
+**vø'rnad** *-en* cf **vørdnad**
+**vø'r/sam'** *A -t, pl -me* cf **vørd/**
+**vør's/løs** *A* cf **vørds/laus**
vør'ter *-et/+-en* brewer's wort (fermenting infusion of malt).

vør'ter/kake -a special sweet, round bread (containing brewer's wort).
vør'ter/øl -et unfermented drink of malt and hops.
+**vå'** -a *dial.* 1 injury, misfortune. 2 anxiety, doubt.
+**vå'ben** -et cf **våpen**
+**vå'/bønn** -a/-en (=*/**bøn**) *archaic, dial.* curse.
vå'd -a *dial.* piece of weaving; fishnet.
vå'de [*vå'e] -n accident, misfortune: **i, ved v-** by a-; *danger, distress.
*__vå'deleg__ A - dangerous.
vå'de/skott -et (=+/**skudd**, */**skot**) accidental shot.
vå'de/verk [*vå'e/] -et *archaic, dial.* accident; reckless act.
+**vådevil'le** -n cf **vaudeville**
vå'e -n *dial.* hard-luck Joe, unlucky man; daredevil, reckless person.
vå'g[1] -a 1 pole to pry with, crowbar. 2 arm of a scale. 3 weight (used to balance scales). 4 old unit of weight (=ab. 39.5 lbs.).
vå'g[2] -a *dial., archaic* billow, wave.
vå'g[3] -en bay, fjord, harbor; inlet: **Bergens v-** Bergen h-.
vå'g[4] -en *dial.* matter, pus.
*__vå'g__[5] -et daring trick, foolhardy act, risk.
vå'gal A reckless, risky: **v- kar** daredevil, foolhardy fellow.
Vå'gan *Pln* twp, Nordland.
*__vå'ge__[1] N chance, risk: **det får stå sin v-** we'll have to risk it; **på von og v-** at random, by chance.
vå'ge[2] V -a/-de/+-et 1 hazard, risk, venture; dare: **du kan bare v-** just you d-; **v- spranget** take the plunge. 2 bet, stake, wager: **v- for, på** (the same); **jeg skal v- på at De kan ikke utgrunne det** I'll b- that you can't figure it out (Hamsun). 3 *(refl.)*: **v- seg** venture (**på** on, upon); dare: **det får v- seg** one will have to take the chance; we'll have to risk it.
vå'ge/hals -en daring, foolhardy person.
vå'gelig A - bold, dangerous, risky.
vå'ge/mot -et boldness, daring.
+**vå'ge/spill** -et (=+/**spell**, */**spel**) audacious deed, daring venture, risky business: **det var litt av et v-** it was sth of a gamble.
vå'ge/stykke -t, *pl* +-r/*- daring deed, risky thing; feat.
+**vå'g/hals** -en cf **våge/**
vå'g/mat -en *dial.* support for crowbar (acting as fulcrum).
vå'g/mor -a core of a boil.
vå'gnad -en 1 *jur.* risk. 2 *dial.* risking, venturing. 3 *dial.* risky undertaking.
+**vå'g/som'** A -t, *pl* -me (=*/**sam**) 1 bold, daring, venturesome. 2 dangerous, risky.
Vå'gå *Pln* twp, Oppland.
+**vå'k**[1] -a (=***vok**) hole, open course in ice (on river, lake, or sea).
vå'k[2] -en *zool.* buzzard hawk (Buteo): **fjellvåk** rough-legged buzzard.
*__vå'k__[3] -en child (esp. boy).
*__vå'k__[4] A poorly, weak.
+**vå'ke** V -te cf **vake**[2]
+**vå'ken** A -ent, *pl* -ne cf **vaken**
+**vå'ke/natt** -a/-en, *pl* -netter 1 night of insomnia, wakefulness. 2 night of watching over a sick person; wake. 3 vigil.
+**våk'ne** V -a/-et cf **vakne**
vå'l[1] -en *dial.* heap of twigs, branches; pile of tree stumps, roots, etc. on burned-over land.
vå'l[2] -et/*-en *dial.* bawl(ing), scream(ing), squall(ing).
vå'le V -a/+-te *dial.* bawl, scream, squall.
Vå'le *Pln* twp, Vestfold.
*__vå'leg__ A - dangerous.
Vå'ler *Pln* 1 twp, Hedmark. 2 twp, Østfold.
*__vå'me__ V -a walk stumblingly, as though blind.
vån'd[1] -en *zool.* European vole, water rat (Arvicola amphibius).
vån'd[2] -en *archaic, lit.* flexible, slender branch or stem; wand: **høy og smekker som en v-** tall and slender as a w- (Undset).
+**vån'de**[1] -n *lit.* anguish, distress, pain: **i ve og v-** in a- and woe.
+**vån'de**[2] V -et *lit.*: **v- seg** groan, moan; writhe.
+**vån'de/full** A anguished, painful.
vå'ning -en *lit.* dwelling, home.
vå'nings/hus -et farmhouse.
vå'pen -enet, *pl* -en 1 weapon; *(pl)* arms: **til v-** to arms; **Ned med våpnene** Down with Weapons (novel, Suttner). 2 coat of arms, escutcheon. 3 arm, branch (of a milit. service), e.g. **fly/v-**.
vå'pen/art -a/-en 1 kind of weapon. 2 arm, branch (of a milit. service).
+**vå'pen/byrd** -en *archaic* bearing arms.
vå'pen/djerv A - *archaic* valiant, valorous.
+**vå'pen/drager** -en *hist.* armorbearer, squire.
vå'pen/felle -n comrade-in-arms.
+**vå'pen/ferdighet** -en skill at arms.
vå'pen/før A able to bear arms, able-bodied, fit for military service.
vå'pen/gny -et/*-en clamor of weapons, of battle.
vå'pen/hus -et *archaic* church vestibule (where weapons were left before entering church).
+**vå'pen/hvile** -n cf **/kvile**
vå'pen/kjole -n military tunic.
vå'pen/kvile -a (=*/**kvild**) armistice, cease-fire, truce.
vå'pen/lykke -a/+-en fortunes of war, success in arms.
vå'pen/makt -a/+-en armed force, force of arms.
vå'pen/skjold -et coat-of-arms, escutcheon.
vå'pen/stillstand -en/*-et armistice, cease-fire, truce.
vå'pen/øving -a/+-en (=+-**else**) military drill, training.
vå'r[1] -en spring, springtime: **i livets v-** in the s- of life; **i fjor v-** last spring (s- of last year); **i v-** this (present) spring, the s- just past, last s- (of the present year); **om v-en** during, in the s-; **til v-en** in (the next) s-; **i v-es** last spring.
vå'r[2] *pn* -t, *pl* -e our, ours: **barna v-e** our children; **denne v- venn** *lit.* this friend of ours; **landet er v-t** the country is ours (Øverland); **vi fikk reddet v-t** we were able to save ours (our things); **v- alles far** *lit.* the father of us all; **her går vi hver v- vei** our paths part here; **vi skiltes fra v-e sydpå** we parted from our people in the south (Grieg).
*__vå'rast__ V -ast cf **våres**
vå'r/bløyte -a spring thaw.
vå'r/bær A: **v- ku** cow that freshens in the spring.
*__vå'r/bære__ -a cow that freshens in the spring.
+**vå'res** V -edes, -es (=***vårast**) become spring: **det v-** its turning into s-, s- is coming.
+**vå'r/flom'** -men (=*/**flaum**) spring flood.
vå'r/frakk -en (man's) spring coat, light topcoat.
+**Vårfru'e** *Prn* our Lady (Virgin Mary).
vå'rfru/mess(e) *en eccl.* Annunciation Day, March 21 or 25.
Vårher're *Prn* Our Lord; (in exclamations and oaths) Lord: **ikke et av V-s beste barn** no better than he should be, no Sunday school teacher; **V- skal vite, V- vet** Lord knows.
*__vå'r/hæse__ -a spring drought.
vå'r/jamdøgn -et (=+/**jevndøgn**) spring equinox.
vå'r/knipe -a shortage of feed in the spring.
*__vå'r/kunn__ -a comfort, consolation, sympathy.
*__vå'r/kunne__ V -a comfort, console, sympathize with.
vå'rlig A - spring, springlike, springy: **v- luft** spring air.
+**vå'r/lø'sning** -en (=*/**løysing**) spring break-up, thaw.
vå'r/onn -a spring work (on a farm, esp. plowing and sowing).
vå'r/parten *df*: **på v-** in the spring of the year.
+**vå'r/rengjø'ring** -a/-en spring cleaning.
°**vår's** *ob of* **vi**
vå'r/semes'ter -eret/-ret, *pl* -er/+-re spring semester.
vå'r/sild -a *zool.* alewife, spring herring (Pomolobus pseudoharengus).
vå'r/vinne -a *dial.* spring work (on a farm).
°**vår'å** V *if* cf **være**[2]
vå's -et chatter(ing), jabber(ing), nonsense.
*__vå'sal__ A difficult, toilsome.
vå'se[1] V -a/+-te chatter, jabber, talk nonsense.
*__vå'se__[2] V -a struggle, toil, work hard.
vå'se/kopp -en chatterbox, person who talks nonsense.
vå'set(e) A - nonsensical, silly.
*__vå's/klede__ *pl* clothes for bad weather, work clothes.
vå't A wet; damp, moist, soaked: **en v- båt** *naut.* boat which easily ships water; **gjøre seg v-** wet one's pants; **uten å smake v-t eller tørt** without food or drink; **v-e varer** liquor, spirits; *(pop.)* booze.
vå't/hatt N: **Jakob v-** *folk.* old name for July 25; if it rained on this day, it meant a wet fall.
vå't/lendt A - marshy, wet.
*__vå'tne__ V -a get wet.
vå't/salta A - (=+-**et**) green-salted (hides, salted without tanning).
*__vå't/sam'__ A damp, moist.
+**vå't/vær** -et (=*/**ver**) rainy weather.

W

w [dåb'belt/ve] -en (letter) W, w (not used in assimilated words).
wagon [vag'gån, vagång'] -en (train) car.
wann' *Av* cf **dann**[2]
Warszawa [varsja'va] *Pln* Warsaw.
water [vå'ter] -et toilet, (water) closet.
watt' -en, *pl* - *phys.* watt.
W. C. [ve' se'] -et toilet (water

+ Bokmål; * Nynorsk; ° Dialect.
After letter: ' stress (Acc. 1); ` tone, stress (Acc. 2); · length.
Below letter: . not pronounced.

closet); lavatory, restroom (in hotels usu. not containing bath or shower); **gå på w.c.** visit the john.
weasel [vi'sel] *-elen, pl -ler* weasel (vehicle for use on snow).
weasel/bil *-en* weasel.
week-end [vi'k/enn] *-en* weekend (trip, vacation): **dra på w-** take a w- trip; **være på w-** be on a w- trip.
week-end/tur *-en* weekend trip.
wel'ter/vekt *N* welterweight.
Wenche [veng'ke] *Prn (f)*
wes't/fa'lsk *A* - Westphalian.
whig [vigg'] *+-gen/*-en, pl whigs/*-ger* Whig.
whisky [vis'ki] *-en* whisky (usu. Scotch).
whist [vis't] *-en* whist.
Wi'en *Pln* Vienna.
+**wiener** [vi'ner] *-en, pl -e* (=***-ar**) 1 Viennese (man). 2 *fam.* Viennese waltz.
wiener/brød *-et* Danish pastry: **da skal de fattige ha w-** then the fat will be in the fire, the jig will be up.
+**wienerin'ne** *-a/+-en* (=***-ar-**) Viennese (woman).
wiener/vals *-en* Viennese waltz.
wiener/wurst [vi'ner/vurst] *-en* Vienna sausage.
wiensk [vi'nsk] *A* - Viennese.
wire [vai'er] *-n* cf **vaier**
wol'fram *-et chem.* tungsten.
wol'fram/lampe *-a/-en* tungsten lamp.
worcester/saus [vu'ster/saus] *-en* Worcestershire sauce.

x [ek's] *-en* (letter) X, x (not used in assimilated words).
x-akse [ek's-] *-n math.* x-axis.
xantippe [santip'pe] *en* shrew, termagant (name of Socrates' wife).
x-e [ek'se] *V -a/+-et:* **x-e ut** x out, cross out.
x-kromoso'm [ek's-] *-et biol.* x chromosome.
x-stråle [ek's-] *-n phys.* x-ray.
xylofon [sylofo'n] *-en mus.* xylophone.

y'[1] *-en* (letter) Y, y.
y'[2] *V -dde* cf **yre**[2]
yacht [jått'] *-en* yacht.
yacht/klubb *-en* yacht club.
y'-akse *-n math.* y-axis.
yale/lås [jei'l/] *-en/-et* yale lock.
yankee [jæng'ki] *-en* Yankee.
***yd'de**[1] *V -a/-e* sprout.
***yd'de**[2] pt of **y**[2]
+**y'de** *V -et* cf **yte**[2]
+**y'derlig** *Av* cf **ytterlig**
+**y'd/myk** *A* (=***aud/mjuk**) humble, meek: **y-st** most humbly.
+**y'd/myke** *V -et/-te* humble, humiliate: **y- seg** humble oneself.
+**y'd/mykelse** *-n* humiliation; indignity: **Marshallhjelpen har vært følt (av britene) som en sviende y-** the Marshall Plan was no doubt felt (by the British) as a bitter h- (Arbeiderbladet 1951).
+**y'd/mykende** *A* - humbling, humiliating (**for** to).
+**y'dmyk/het** *-en* humility, meekness.
yen [jenn'] *-en* yen (Japanese coin).
Ygg'/drasil *Prn myth.* tree of the universe.
y'-kromoso'm *-et biol.* y chromosome.
y'l[1] *-et/*-en* howl.
°**y'l**[2] *-en* cf **øl**[1]
***y'l**[3] *pr of* **ylje**
y'le *V -te* howl.
***yl'je** *V yl, ulde, ult* 1 swarm, teem. 2 warm up; give off warmth; steam.
***yl'last** *V yltest, ylst* become shaggy, woolly.
***yl'mast** *V -dest, -st* become furious; fume.
***yl'men** *A -e/-i, pl -ne* exasperated, incensed; fierce, grim.
***y'm** *-en* 1 weak sound. 2 dim feeling.
y'mis *A -t, pl ymse* changeable, different, various; unlike: **y-t** miscellaneous, various (things); miscellany; **jentehugen er så y-** girls' minds are so c-; **det er så y-t med det** that may or may not be true; it's up and down; **i ymse høve** on various occasions; in some instances. (See also **ymse**.)
***y'misleg** *A* - changing, different.
***ym'se**[1] *V -a* alternate, change, exchange.
+**ym'se**[2] *A* - different, various; unlike: **det er så y- med det** it's only so-so, it's up and down; **så y-** one thing and another, this and that; **folk er så y-** people are different. (See also **ymis**.)
ym'se[3] *pl of* **ymis**
***ym'se/sidig** *A* - mutual, reciprocal.
ym't *-en/+-et* hint, inkling, whispered rumor (**om** about).
ym'te *V -a/+-et* hint (**om at**): **det y-es om at** it is rumored that.
yn'de[1] *+-n/*-t* charm, grace: **barndommens y-** the g- of childhood.
+**yn'de**[2] *V -et* be fond of, favor, have a taste for: **y-et** favored (**av** by), favorite; **en y-t figur** a favorite figure.
yn'de/full *A* graceful, lovely.
***yn'deleg** *A* - graceful.
+**yn'der** *-en, pl -e* admirer, lover, patron (**av** of): **han var ingen y- av** he was no l- of.
+**yn'dest** *-en lit.* favor, good graces: **i y- hos en** in sby's g-; **komme i y-** rise into f-; **sette seg i y- hos** ingratiate oneself.
yn'dig *A* - charming, graceful, lovely; delightful, gracious, sweet; *(pop.)* cute, ducky.
+**yn'dig/het** *-en:* (usu. *pl*) **y-er** (physical) charms, graces.
yn'dling *-en* darling, favorite, pet: **gudenes y-** favored by fortune; **publikums y-** the audience favorite.
+**yn'dlings/beskjef'tigelse** *-n* favorite activity, hobby.
+**yn'dlings/hustru** *-en* favorite wife.
yn'dlings/rett *-en* favorite dish.
***yng'd** *-a* youth: **i y-a** in y-.
***yng'dest** *pt of* **yngjast**
+**yng'e** *V -a/-et/-te* (=***yngje**): **y- opp** rejuvenate; **y-s** feel younger.
yng'el *-en* 1 fry, spawn, young: **slippe ut y- i elva** stock the river with fish. 2 *lit.* brood, offspring, progeny.
***yng'jast** *V -dest, yngst* look, seem younger.
***yng'je** *V -de* 1: **y- seg opp att** be rejuvenated. 2 produce young (spawn, litter, etc.).
yng'le *V -a/+-et* produce young (propagate, spawn, etc.).
yng'le/plass *-en* breeding place, spawning ground.
yng'ling *-en lit., hum.* young man, youth: **de lysssky y-er ute på trappen** the bashful youths out on the steps (Boo).
yng're *cp of* **ung**
***yng'st**[1] *pp of* **yngjast**
yng'st[2] *sp of* **ung**
yng'ste/ba'rn *-et* baby of the family, youngest child.
yng'ste/mann *-en* youngest man (in a class, office, etc.); (the) junior.
Yng'/var *Prn (m)*
Yng've *Prn (m)*
yn'k *-en* 1 moan(ing). 2 pity: **det var en y- å se** it was a p- to see; **hun gråt så det var en y-** she cried pitifully.
***yn'kast** *V -ast* cf **ynkes**
yn'ke *V -a/+-et* 1 feel sorry for, pity: **y-s over** (the same). 2 *(refl.)*: **y- seg** groan, moan; complain, whine.
yn'kelig *A* - 1 pitiable, pitiful; miserable, sorry, wretched. 2 abject, cowardly, spineless.
+**yn'kelig/het** *-en* 1 misery, wretchedness. 2 abjectness, cowardice, spinelessness.
+**yn'kes** *V ynktes, ynkes* (=***ynkast**): **y- over** feel sorry for, pity.
+**ynkver'dig** *A* - miserable, pitiable, pitiful.
***ynske** [yn'sje] *-t* cf **ønske**[1]
***ynske/liste** *-a* cf **ønske/**
***ynske/mål** *-et* cf **ønske/**
***yn'skjande** *A* - desirable.
***yn'skje** *V -te* cf **ønske**[2]
***yn'skjeleg** *A* - cf **ønskelig**
***yn'skje/mål** *-et* cf **ønske/**
yoga [jo'ga] *-en* Yoga.
yogi [jo'gi] *-en* Yogi.
yp'pal *A dial.* aggressive, quarrelsome.
***yp'pare** *A* - better, more excellent.
***yp'parleg** *A* - cf **ypperlig**
***yp'parst** *sp of* **yppare** cf **ypperst**
yp'pe *V -a/+-et* 1 incite, instigate, stir up (fight, quarrel, etc.): **y- innpå** *fam.* pick a quarrel, start a fight. 2 *(refl.)*: **y- seg** act aggressively, show off; pick a quarrel.
+**yp'perlig** *A* - (=***ypparleg**) excellent, superb, superior; choice, first-class, first-rate.
+**yp'perst** *sp of* **yppare** (=***-arst**) best, most excellent; most highly placed.
+**yp'perste prest** *-en* (=***ypparste/**) high priest.

yp'pig *A* - 1 lush, luxuriant (foliage, vegetation, etc.); fertile, rich (e.g. soil); lavish, luxurious. 2 (of a woman, a woman's figure) voluptuous; ample, buxom.
+yp'pig/het *-en* 1 lushness, luxuriance; richness (esp. of vegetation). 2 voluptuousness; buxomness.
y'r[1] *-et* 1 drizzle, mist. 2 multitude, swarm, teeming mass. 3 glint, twinkle: **et yr i øyekroken** a glint in the corner of his eye (Evensmo).
***y'r[2]** *pr of* **y[2], yrje[1]**
y'r[3] *A* 1 elated, giddy, intoxicated (**av** from, with e.g. happiness); ecstatic; uninhibited; frolicsome, lively (person, wind, etc.). 2 *fig.* (of nature, the seasons, etc.) full of creative forces, full of life, reawakening; (of the air) effervescent, sparkling. 3 befogged, dazed.
y're[1] *V -te* 1 drizzle, mist. 2 snow (finely and densely). 3 prickle, tingle: **spenningen y-te i meg** the excitement tingled through me (Evensmo); ***det y-er i kroppen** I feel a prickling through my body (Aasen).
y're[2] *V -te* (=***yrje[2]**) mill, swarm, teem: **y- av** abound with, be swarming with; **y-ende fullt** packed (**av** with).
y'ren *A +-ent, pl -ne* drizzly, misty; snowy.
y're/regn [+/rein] *-et* cf **yr/**
***yr'je[1]** *-a* 1 host, mass, swarm. 2 foggy, windy weather.
***yr'je[2]** *V yr, urde, urt* cf **yre[2]**
yr'ke[1] *-a* (=***vyrke[2]**) *dial.* weekday, workday.
yr'ke[2] *-t* craft, profession, trade; job, occupation, work.
yr'ke/dag *-en* weekday.
***yr'ke/laus** *A* cf **ørkes/løs**
yr'kes/bror *-en, pl +-brødre/*-brør* colleague.
yr'kes/gruppe *-a/+-en* occupational group.
yr'kes/kvinne *-a/+-en* career woman, working woman.
***yr'kes/laus** *A* cf **ørkes/løs**
+yr'kes/messig *A* - occupational; professional.
yr'kes/myalgi *-en med.* myalgia (muscle cramps).
yr'kes/nevro'se *-n med.* occupational neurosis.
yr'kes/rettleiing *-a* vocational guidance.
yr'kes/sjukdom *-men/*-en* occupational disease.
yr'kes/skole *-n* vocational school.
+yr'kes/sykdom [-dåmm] *-men* cf **/sjukdom**
+yr'kes/veileder *-en, pl -e* vocational guidance counselor.
+yr'kes/veiledning *-en* vocational guidance.
***yr'kje** *V -te* make, prepare.
y'r/regn [+/rein] *-et* (=**yre/**) drizzle.
+y'r/våken *A -ent, pl -ne* (=***ør/vaken**) unable to sleep, wide awake (e.g. after a night of watching).
***ys'me** *-a* haziness.
***ys'men** *A -e/-i, pl -ne* hazy.
ys'te *V -a/+-et/*-e* make cheese (by warming milk so that it curdles).
***ys'tel** *-en* fresh curd.
+ys'ter *-en, pl -e* (=***-ar**) cheesemaker.
ysteri' *-et, pl +-er/*-* cheese factory.
***ys'te/verk** *-et* cheese factory.
***y't** *-en* push, shove.
y'te[1] *-a* 1 outer layer (of wood in tree). *2 exterior, surface.
y'te[2] *V -te/+-et* 1 contribute, render (support, tax, etc.); bestow, give (praise, recognition, etc.), extend (help); offer (e.g. resistance). 2 (of animals, soil, etc.) produce, render, yield.
***y'te[3]** *V -te* move away, set to the side; push, shove; dispose of.
+y'te/dyktig *A* - fertile, productive; (of machine) efficient.
y'te/evne *-a/+-en* ability to contribute, pay, produce; efficiency, performance; productivity, yield.
+y'telse *-n* (=***-ing**) contribution, rendition; output, performance, production; payment.
+y'ter *-en, pl -e* (=***-ar**) contributor, payer, e.g. in **skatte/y-** taxpayer.
***y'ting** *-a* cf **ytelse**
***y'tleg** *A* - shallow, superficial.
+yt're[1] *et* external appearance: **ens y-** one's appearance.
+yt're[2] *V -a/-et* 1 express, say, utter: **y- seg** e- oneself. 2 reveal, show: **y- tegn til** show signs of; **y- seg** appear (**som** as).
yt're[3] *A* - 1 outer (door, harbor, side, etc.), external (appearance, cause, circumstance, events, etc.); exterior, outward: **det y-** the exterior, the surface; **i det y-** externally, on the face of it, outwardly. 2 (*sup.*): **ytterst** farthest out, most outlying, outermost, remotest; extreme, utmost; last (**den y-e dag** the day of judgment, the l- day; **ligge på sitt y-e** be at death's door); (*adv.*) at the extremity, farthest out; exceedingly, extremely, highly: **y- få** very few; **y- pinlig** most embarrassing.
Yt're Re'ndal *Pln* twp, Hedmark.
Yt're San'dsvær *Pln* twp, Buskerud.
yt'ring *-a/+-en* 1 expression; remark, utterance. 2 manifestation, revelation (**av** of).
+yt'rings/frihet *-en* freedom of speech, of the press.
yts't *sp of* **ytre[3]** (=**+ytterst, *yttarst, *utarst**)
yt'ter/dør *-a* front door, main entrance.
yt'ter/frakk *-en* overcoat, topcoat.
yt'ter/grense *-a/+-en* border, boundary, (extreme) limit: **y-n av hans tålmodighet** the end of his patience.
yt'ter/kant *-en* 1 (of an area) edge, fringe, outskirts. 2: **i y-** at the limit.
yt'terlig *A - lit.* 1 extreme, inordinate. 2 (*adv.*) far out, near the edge (end, tip), outlying; exceedingly, extremely, highly. 3 (*comp.*): **y-ere** further; additional, still more.
yt'terlig/gående *A* - extreme.
+yt'terlig/het *-en* extreme; extremity: **fra den ene y- til den annen** from one e- to another; **gå til y-er** go to extremes.
yt'ter/plagg *-et* outer garment, outside clothes.
yt'ter/punkt [/pongt] *-et* extreme; point of extremity.
yt'ter/side [*/sie] *-a/+-en* exterior, outer side; outside; *fig.* surface.
+yt'terst *sp of* **ytre[3]**
+yt'ter/såle *-n* (outer) sole.
+yt'ter/tøy *-et* outer clothes, outside clothes: **ta av deg y-et** take off your wraps.
yt'ter/vegg *-en, pl *-er* outer wall, outside wall.
Yt'ter/øy *Pln* twp, Nord-Trøndelag.
***y'vast** *V -dest, yvst* dread, shudder at.
y've *V -de dial.* (of hair etc.) bristle, stand out; grow, swell: **y- seg** puff up, swell up; strut.
y'ven *A -e/-i, pl -ne dial.* 1 bristling, distended, swollen; chubby, plump. 2 arrogant, puffed up, strutting.
+y'ver[1] *-et* cf **jur**
***y'ver[2]** *P* cf **over**
***yv'st** *pp of* **yvast**

Z

z [sett'] *-en* (letter) Z, z (not used in assimilated words).
zebu [se'bu] *-en zool.* zebu (Bos indicus).
+zeppeliner [sep'peliner] *-en, pl -e* (=***-ar**) zeppelin.
+zir [si'r] *-en* cf **sir**
zodiakal/lys [sodiaka'l/] *-et* (=***/ljos**) *astron.* zodiacal light.
zool.=**zoologisk**
zoolog [soolå'g] *-en* zoologist.
zoologi [soologi'] *-en* zoology.
zoologisk [soolå'gisk] *A* - zoological: **z- hage** zoo.
zootomi [sootomi'] *-en* zootomy.
zulu [su'lu] *-en* Zulu.
zulu/kaffer *-en, pl +-e* Zulu (Kaffir).
zweck [svekk'] *+-en/*-et* point, purpose, sense.
+zwinglianer [svinglia'ner] *-en, pl -e* (=***-ar**) Zwinglian.
zygote [sygo't] *-n biol.* zygote.

Æ

æ'[1] *-en* (letter) Æ, æ.
æ'[2] *I* 1 (to express spite) ha ha, nyaa nyaa: **æ bæ** (the same). 2 (to express surprise, hesitation) er, uh.
Æ'ge *Prn myth.* Aegir, god of the sea.
***æ'le** *V -te* send forth shoot(s), sprout.
æ'r[1] *-a zool.* eider duck (Somateria mollissima).
***æ'r[2]** *-et* scar.
æ'ra *-en* era.
+æ'r/bar *A lit.* (of women) respect-

+ Bokmål; * Nynorsk; ° Dialect.
After letter: ' stress (Acc. 1); ` tone, stress (Acc. 2); · length.
Below letter: . not pronounced.

able, virtuous; chaste, decent, modest.
+æ'rbar/het -en *lit.* respectability, virtue; decency, modesty: **i all æ-** in all d-.
+ærbø'dig *A* - respectful; deferential: **Deres æ-e, æ-st** (ending to business letter, formal letter) r-ly yours, most r-ly.
+ærbø'dig/het -en respect: **med (i) æ-** respectfully; **vise æ-** show deference, respect, reverence (**for** for).
æ'r/dun -a/-et eiderdown.
æ're[1] -a/+-en honor; glory; credit, praise: **all æ- verd** commendable, praiseworthy; **gjøre en den æ- å** do sby the h- to; **gjøre en æ-** do one c-; **gjøre æ- på** do c- to; do justice to; **gå ens æ- for nær** *fig.* step on one's toes; **holde i æ-** honor, venerate; **komme til æ-** come into favor; **sette sin æ- i** pride oneself on, take pride in; **æ- være Gud** g- to God.
æ're[2] *V* -a/+-et honor, respect; revere, venerate: **æ-es den som æ-es bør** give credit where credit is due; **ærede** h-ed (in polite formulas, e.g. **ærede forsamling** ladies and gentlemen; **Deres ærede brev** your esteemed letter; **min ærede kollega** my honorable colleague).
*æ're[3] *V* -te: **æ- godt** (of crop, field) look as though it will be productive, be a good year.
*æ're/doktor -en cf **æres/**
æ're/frykt +-en/*-a awe; veneration.
æ're/full *A* creditable, honorable; full of honor, glorious: **et æ-t verv** a great honor.
+æ're/gjerrig *A* - cf **ærgjerrig**
*æ're/gjerug *A* - cf **ærgjerrig**
*æ're/kjensle -a sense of honor.
*æ're/kjær *A* high-spirited, proud.
æ're/krenke *V* -a/-et/-te (=*-je) defame, libel, slander: **æ-ende** defamatory, libellous.
+æ're/krenkelse -n (=-ing) *jur.* defamation, libel, slander.
*æ're/krenkjar -en one who defames, libels; slanderer.
*æ're/krenkje *V* -te cf **/krenke**
æ're/laus *A* (=+/løs) 1 (of person) dishonored, without honor: **en æ- død** an ignominious death. 2 (of action or person) dishonorable, dishonest: **et æ-t menneske** a d- person.
*æ're/mink -en discredit, disparagement.
æ'rend -et errand, mission: **éns æ-** for one thing only; on purpose; **gjøre, utrette et æ-** (*fam.* also:) urinate; **gjøre, lage seg (et) æ- hen til bordet** find a pretext for going over to the table; **gå ens æ-** act in sby's interest; play one's game; **gå æ-** do, run e-s; **i æ-** on an e-; **han hadde vært et æ- i byen** he had gone to town on an e-.
+æ'rends/gutt -en (=*/gut) errand boy, messenger boy.
*æ'rends/laus *A* 1 having failed one's errand. 2 having no errand: **æ-e har ikkje tilgjenge** no admittance for unauthorized persons.
+æ'rends/svenn -en (=ærend/svein) *archaic* errand boy, messenger.
æ're/rik *A* - glorious, honorable, of honor.
+æ're/rørig *A* - *lit.* defamatory, libelous, slanderous: **æ- omtale** defamation.
+æ'res/begre'p -et concept of honor, sense of honor; *(pl)* **æ-er** code of honor.
+æ'res/bevi'sning -en honor (accorded, bestowed upon sby); salute.
+æ'res/bolig -en honorary residence.
+æ'res/doktor -en honorary doctor.
+æ'res/følelse -n sense of honor.
+æ'res/gave -a/-en gift in honor of one's service, etc., presentation.
+æ'res/gjeld -a/-en debt of honor.
+æ'res/gjest -en guest of honor.
æ're/sjuk *A* (=+/syk) inordinately ambitious.
æ're/skjelle *V* -skjelte abuse (verbally).
+æ'res/legio'n -en legion of honor.
+æ'res/lønn -a/-en 1 honorary annuity, pension, salary. 2 *lit.* reward.
+æ'res/medlem [/me'dlemm] -met honorary member.
+æ'res/opprei'sning -en redress, satisfaction; damages, restitution.
+æ'res/o'rd -et word of honor: **gi sitt æ-** give one's w-; **på mitt æ-** on my w-.
+æ'res/premie -n special prize.
+æ'res/runde -n tour de triomphe, triumphal swing around the track.
+æ'res/sak -a/-en matter of honor, sacred obligation.
+æ'res/salutt' -en salute of honor (21 guns).
+æ'res/tittel -elen, pl -titler honorary title, title of honor.
*æ'ret(e) *A* - pockmarked, scarred.
æ'r/fugl -en *zool.* eider duck (Somateria mollissima).
ærgjer'rig *A* - (=*-gjerug, *ære-) ambitious.
+ærgjer'rig/het -en 1 ambition (**etter å** to); pride. 2 *derog.* ambitious person.
*æ'rleg/dom -(m)en cf **ærlig/het**
*æ'rleg/skap -en cf **ærlig/het**
æ'rlig *A* - honest; frank, sincere, straightforward; honorable, upright: **det har du æ- og redelig fortjent** you have really and truly earned it; **æ- talt** honestly, to tell the truth; **det er den æ- verd** it's easily (well) worth that.
+æ'rlig/het -en honesty; frankness, sincerity; integrity, uprightness: **æ-en selv** the soul of h-; **æ- varer lengst** h- is the best policy.
æ'r/stegg -en, pl *-er eider drake.
*æ'rug *A* - 1 courteous, polite. 2 honorable, noble.
*æ'rug/skap -en 1 courtesy, politeness. 2 honorableness, nobility.
ærver'dig *A* - august, venerable.
+ærver'dig/het -en augustness, venerability.
æsch' *I* cf **æsj**
*æ'se[1] *V* -te fit beams into position.
*æ'se[2] *V* -te cf **ese**
æ'ser *pl of* **ås[2]**
*æ'sing -a/-en cf **esing**
æsj' *I* (expression of distaste, repulsion) ugh; pfui; ick, icky.
æt'ling -en *lit.* descendant, heir, scion (**av** of); *fig.* offspring.
ætt' -a/+-en *lit.* 1 clan, (extended) family, kin. 2 descent, extraction; line, lineage: **av høy æ-** highborn.
æt'ta *A* - (=+-et) of (good, bad) family, extraction.
*æt'tar/lag -et family characteristic, trait.
*æt'tar/minne -t family tradition.
*æt'tast *V* -ast be descended, come, stem (**frå** from).
+ætt'/båren *A* -ent, pl -ne (=*/boren) *archaic* 1 (by virtue of one's family) born, heir: **æ- til Norges kongestol** b- to Norway's throne. 2 of good family.
æt'te *V* -a/+-et *archaic* be descended, come, stem (**fra** from).
æt'te/ga'rd -en ancestral estate, family farm.
æt'te/gransking -a genealogy; genealogical investigation.
æt'te/kjensle -a *lit.* family pride.
æt'te/saga +-en/*ei (=*/soge) family saga (esp. the Sagas of Icelanders, written in the 13th Century ab. Icelandic and Norwegian family feuds of the 9th and 10th Centuries).
*æt'te/svip -en family resemblance.
æt'te/tavle -a family tree, genealogical table, genealogy.
ætt'/far -en, pl +-fedrer/*-fedrar *archaic* ancestor, founder (of a family), progenitor.
ætt'/grein -a/+-en branch of a family.
*æt'ting[1] -a descent, (family) extraction.
*æt'ting[2] -en relative; descendant, heir.
ætt'/led -en (=+/ledd) *lit.* generation.
+ætt'/lede *V* -et *hist.* adopt (usu. one's illegitimate child).
ætt'/legg -en *hist.* 1 family line. 2 genealogy. 3 generation.
*ætt'/leie *V* -dde cf **/lede**
ætt'/stor *A* - *hist.* high-born, noble.
ætt'/vill *A* -vilt *dial.* disoriented, lost.
*æ've -a 1 long time; eternity: **i all æ-** for all time; **om alder og æ-** in time and eternity. 2 lifetime: **i mi æ-** in my l-; **det veit ingen si æ-** no one knows his own life span.
*æ've/heim -en eternity, the hereafter.
*æ'veleg *A* - 1 continual, lasting, unceasing. 2 eternal.
*æ've/lengd -a endlessness, interminability; eternity.
*æ'v/o'rd -et beginning of time, most distant past.
*æ'vord(s)leg *A* - everlasting, infinite, unending.

ø'[1] -en (letter) Ø, ø.
+ø'[2] -en cf **øy**
+Ø=øst
ø.=øre[2]
+ø'de[1] -t desert, desolate area, wasteland; emptiness, nothingness: **det store, svarte ødet** the great black n- (Evensmo).
+ø'de[2] *V* -te cf **øyde[1]**
+ø'de[3] *A* -/ødt (=+øyde[2]) deserted, lonely; desolate; bare, denuded, empty: **legge ø-** lay waste, ruin.
+ø'de/la *pt of* **-legge**
+ø'de/land -en spendthrift, wastrel.
+ø'de/legge *V* -la, -lagt cf **øyde/**
+ø'de/leggelse -n cf **øyde/legging**
+ø'deleggelses/lyst -a/-en destructiveness, destructive urge.
+ø'de/legging -a/-en cf **øyde/**
øde'm -et *med.* edema.
+ø'de/mark -a cf **øyde/**
ø'dipus/komplek's -et Oedipus complex.
*ød'le -a cf **øgle**
+ød'sel [also: øs'sel] *A* -elt, pl -le 1 extravagant, prodigal, wasteful. 2 lavish, profuse, unstinted.
+ødsel/het -en 1 extravagance, prodigality, wastefulness. 2 lavishness, profuseness, profusion.
+ød'sle [also: øs'le] *V* -a/-et 1 be extravagant (**med** with), prodigal (of), wasteful; squander, waste:

ø- bort, vekk (the same). **2** be lavish (**med** with); lavish (**på** upon).
+**ødsʹlig** *A* - (=***audsleg**) (of a place) deserted, desolate; lonely, lonesome, sad.
+**ødtʹ** *A nt of* **øde**[2]
+**ø. f.**=**øst for**
+**øgʹle** *-a/-en* (=***ødle**) **1** *zool.* lizard (Lacertilia).
+**øgʹle/yngel** *-en derog.* offspring of vipers.
øhʹ *I* oh (groaning; contempt).
+**øʹk** *-et* (old) horse, nag, plug.
+**øʹke** *V -et/-te* cf **auke**[2]
+**øʹke/navn** *-et* nickname.
+**øʹkning** *-en* growth, increase (**av** of).
økologi [-giʹ] *-en* ecology.
økologisk [økolåʹg-] *A* - ecological.
økon.=**økonomi, økonomisk**
økonoʹm *-en* **1** (good) manager, thrifty person. **2** economist.
økonomiʹ *-en* **1** economy; finances: **ha god ø-** be in good financial condition. **2** *educ.* economics.
økonomikkʹ *-en* economics.
økonomiseʹre *V -te* economize: **ø- med** be sparing with.
økonoʹmisk *A* - **1** economical, thrifty (housewife, method, etc.). **2** economic, financial (policy, problems, etc.).
økʹs *-a, pl* ***-ar** axe; hatchet.
økʹse *V -a/+-et* **1** chop, hew: **ø- til** hew, shape (e.g. beams). **2** *dial.* jaw, scold (**på** at).
økʹse/blad *-et* axeblade.
økʹs/egg *-a/+-en* axe bit, edge.
økʹse/hammar *-en, pl -hamrer* **1** butt of the axe. **2** *archeol.* hammer axe.
+**økʹse/hode** *-t* axe head.
økʹse/hogg *-et* blow of an axe.
***økʹsel** *-elet/-let* **1** enlargement, increase (in number); propagation. **2** young (animals); brood, offspring, etc. **3** excrescence, growth.
økʹs/emne *-t, pl +-r/*-* material suitable for axe handle; amount of iron needed for axe head.
økʹsen *A +-ent, pl -ne* (of female animal) in heat.
økʹse/skaft *-et* **1** axe handle. **2**: **god dag mann-økseskaft** (said of a reply which is totally irrelevant to question it is supposed to answer, in allusion to folktale by Asbjørnsen).
***økʹsle** *V -a/+-et* increase, multiply, propagate: **ø- seg** breed.
***økʹsle/før** *A* capable of propagating, mature.
***økʹsle/sam** *A* productive, prolific.
***økʹslings/evne** *-a/+-en* reproductive ability.
***økʹslings/lære** *-a/+-en* study of reproduction, propagation.
Økʹs/nes *Pln* twp, Nordland.
økʹt *-a dial.* **1** between-meal period; work done during this period. **2** afternoon coffee time (around 3 or 4).
***økʹte** *V -a* have afternoon coffee (and food), rest.
økumeʹnisk *A* - *eccl.* ecumenical.
øʹl[1] *-en dial.* **1** (mild) warmth (in house or outside). **2** heat haze.
ølʹ[2] *-et* **1** beer; ale: **lære, vise en hvor David kjøpte ø-et** give, teach sby a lesson, teach sby some manners. **2**: **en øl** (*pl* - or *-er*) bottle of beer; (in restaurant, also glass or stein): **en øl, takk** a b-, please; **kjøpe to øl** buy two b-.
+**ø. l.**=**østlig lengde**
ølʹ/anker *-eret, pl -er/+-ere/+-re* beer barrel, keg.
ølʹ/bass *-en* coarse bass voice (due to beer-drinking).
ølʹ/bolle *-n* (wooden) ale bowl (usu. hand-painted).
ølʹ/brikke *-a/+-en* (beer) coaster.
øʹle[1] *V -a/+-et* drink beer.
***øʹle**[2] *V -te* **1** excite, inflame: **ø- opp** stir up. **2** flatter: **ø-ast med nokon** talk sby into sth.
ølʹe/brød *-et* beer soup with raisins and toasted bread cubes.
Øʹlen *Pln* twp, Hordaland.

ølʹet(e) *A* - beery.
ølʹ/gang *-en* brewer's yeast.
ølʹ/glas *-et* (=+/**glass**) beer glass.
***ølʹje** *V -a* heat; give off heat, warmth.
ølʹ/kagge *-en/+-a* (=+/**kagg**) beer keg.
ølʹ/kveis *-a* hangover.
+**ølʹle** *V -et* cf **øle**[1]
+**ølʹle/brød** *-et* cf **øle/**
ølʹ/mage *-n* beer belly.
***øʹlnast** *V -ast* grow warm, warm up.
ølʹ/ost *-en* beverage of 2 parts milk and 1 part beer boiled separately and combined.
øʹl/røyk *-en* (heat) haze.
ølʹ/sjapp *-a* **1** (in ref. to older or foreign conditions) beer joint, saloon, tavern. **2** (small) store which sells bottled beer.
+**ølʹ/tapper** *-en, pl -e* (=***-ar**) *hist.* innkeeper; tapster.
ølʹ/tung [/tong] *A* - beer-sodden, drunk.
ølʹ/tønne *-a* (=*/**tynne**) beer barrel.
ømʹ *A -t, pl -me* **1** sensitive, sore, tender. **2** affectionate, loving, tender (**mot** towards). **3** gentle, sentimental, soft (e.g. air; music).
+**ømfinʹtlig** *A* - **1** sensitive, tender; thin-skinned, touchy: **ø- for** anxious, concerned about; **en ø- mikrofon** a s- microphone. **2** delicate, fragile.
+**ømfinʹtlig/het** *-en* **1** sensitiveness, tenderness; sensitivity; touchiness. **2** delicate nature, fragility.
+**ømʹ/het** *-en* **1** sensitiveness, soreness, tenderness. **2** affection, love, tenderness (**for** for). **3** gentleness, sentimentality, softness.
+**ømʹ/hjertet** *A* - tender-hearted.
+**ømʹme** *V -a/-et*: **ø- seg** complain, groan, whimper.
ømʹ/skinna *A* - (=+**-et**) sensitive, thin-skinned. **en ø-et hæl gjør ingen mann til Akilleus** a s- heel makes no man an Achilles (Ibsen).
ømtåʹlig *A* - **1** sensitive (**for** to), thin-skinned. **2** delicate: **et ø- emne** a d- topic.
+**ømtåʹlig/het** *-en* sensitiveness.
***øʹne** *V -te* **1** (of animal) snort, stare wildly around (in fear). **2** fool, jest.
+**øʹnen** *A -e/-i, pl øne* crazy, senseless.
ønʹske[1] *-t* (=***ynske**) desire, wish (**om** for); request: **de beste ø-r** best w-es; **hennes høyeste ønske** her greatest wish.
+**ønʹske**[2] *V -a/-et/-te* (=***-je, *ynskje**) **1** desire, wish (for): **la mye tilbake å ø-** leave much to be d-ed; **ø- en alt godt** w- one the best of everything; **ø- en til lykke** congratulate one; **ø- velkommen** (bid, w-) welcome. **2** (*refl.*): **ø- seg** wish for (oneself) wish to have; **ø- seg langt bort** wish one were far away.
+**ønʹske/hus** *-et* dream house.
+**ønʹske/konserʹt** *-en* request program.
+**ønʹske/kvist** *-en* divining rod, witching stick.
+**ønʹskelig** *A* - (=***ynskjeleg, *ønskjeleg**) desirable, to be desired: **med all ø- tydelighet** in no uncertain manner.
+**ønʹskelig/het** *-en* desirability.
+**ønʹske/liste** *-a* list of desiderata; want list.
+**ønʹske/mål** *-et* goal, hope, wish; desideratum.
+**ønʹske/oppgaʹve** *-a/-en* ideal assignment.
+**ønʹske/stilling** *-a/-en* ideal job, position.
+**ønʹske/tenkning** *-en* wishful thinking.
+**ønʹske/vær** *-et* perfect weather.
***ønʹskje** *V -te* cf **ønske**[2]
+**ønskverʹdig** [also ønʹsk/] *A* - desirable: **ikke ø-e personer** undesirable people.
øʹr[1] *-a, pl *-ar* (=**øyr**) delta, sandbank, sand point (usu. at a river mouth); sandbar: **han drev en landhandel ute på øra** he ran a country store out by the mouth of the river.
***øʹr**[2] *-et* (attack of) dizziness.

øʹr[3] *A* - **1** dizzy, giddy: **ør i hodet** confused, unclear. **2** ecstatic, wild: **ør av fryd** wild with joy.
øʹr- *Pf* tiny.
+**-øra** *A* - cf **-øret**
***øʹrande** *A* - cf **ørende**
***øʹre**[1] *-a* confusion, doze, muddle.
øʹre[2] *-n, pl* - **1** *øre* (coin)=1/100 *krone*, ab. $.0014: **ikke en ø-** not a red cent; **ikke fem ø- verd** not worth a (plugged) nickel; **han er ikke syk for to ø-** he's not the least bit sick; **på ø-n** to the penny. **2** *hist.* (weight) 1/8 *mark*, or ab. 1 ounce (used esp. for precious metals and coins).
+**øʹre**[3] *-t* (=***øyra, *øyre**) **1** ear: **en skal høre mye før ø-ne faller av** (also) I can hardly believe my own ears; **forelsket oppover ø-ne** head over heels in love; **ha lange ø-r** listen (for sth one is not supposed to hear); **ha noe bak ø-t** have sth up one's sleeve; **ha ø-ne med seg** keep one's ears open; **henge med ø-ne** hang one's head, mope; **holde en i ø-ne** keep sby in line, make sby toe the mark; **holde ø-ne stive** listen attentively; keep one's wits about one; **komme en for ø-** reach one's e-; **skrive seg noe bak ø-t** make a mental note of sth. **2** ear, handle (e.g. on kettle); lug (esp. plate on each side of ski to which bindings are fastened): **små gryter har også ø-r** little pitchers have big ears.
øʹre[4] *V -te* be dizzy; doze; be dazed, delirious.
Øʹre *Pln* twp, Møre og Romsdal.
+**øʹre/bein** *-et* bone in the ear.
+**øʹre/betenʹnelse** *-n med.* inflammation of the ear, otitis.
+**øʹre/blad** *-et* (visible) ear.
+**øʹre/dask** *-en/-et* box on the ears, cuff.
+**øʹre/dobbe** *-a/-en* (=+/**dobb**) eardrop, earring.
+**øʹre/døvende** *A* - deafening, earsplitting.
+**øʹre/fik** *-en* box, cuff on the ear.
+**øʹre/flipp** *-en* earlobe.
+**øʹre/gang** *-en anat.* auditory canal, a- meatus.
+**øʹre/klips** *-en* earclip.
+**øʹre/kyte** *-a zool.* a small carp (Phoxinus aphya), minnow.
+**øʹre/lapp** *-en* **1** earflap. **2** earlobe.
+**øʹrelapp/stol** *-en* wing chair.
+**øʹre/lege** *-en* ear specialist.
+**øʹre/merke**[1] *-t* earmark, notch (=brand, on animals).
+**øʹre/merke**[2] *V -et* earmark, notch animal's ear (to show ownership); *fig.* earmark (e.g. public funds).
+**øʹren**[1] *pl of* **øre**[3]
øʹren[2] *A -e/-i, pl -ne dial.* dazed, dizzy; confused.
øʹrende *Av*: **ø- liten** tiny; **ø- stille** still as a mouse.
+**øʹrens/lyʹd** *en*: **det er ikke ø- å få** one can't hear oneself think; one can't make oneself heard (above the din).
Øʹre/sund *Pln* The Sound (betw. Denmark and Sweden).
+**øʹre/sus** *-en/-et* ringing in one's ears.
+**øʹre/sønderrivende** *A* - *lit.* earsplitting.
+**-øret** *A* - (=+**-øra, *-øyra, *-øyrd**) -eared; *bot.* auriculate.
øʹret(e)** *A* - (=øyret(e)**) full of sandbanks.
+**øʹre/telefoʹn** *-en* earphone.
+**øʹre/trompeʹt** *-en anat.* Eustachian tube.
+**øʹre/tuter** *-en, pl -e (bibl., lit.)* **1** backbiter, gossip, slanderer. **2** flatterer.

+ Bokmål; * Nynorsk; ° Dialect.
After letter: ʹ stress (Acc. 1); ʹ tone, stress (Acc. 2); · length.
Below letter: . not pronounced.

+**ø're/tvist** *-en zool.* earwig (Forficula auricularis).
+**ø're/varmer** *-en, pl -e* 1 earmuff, earwarmer. 2 cuff (on the ear).
+**ø're/verk** *-en* earache.
+**ø're/vitne** *-t* earwitness (**til** to).
+**ø're/voks** *-et* earwax.
ø'r/fin *A* very fine, soft, tiny; infinitesimal, nearly inaudible, etc.
-øring *-en* coin of so many *øre*: **to/ø-** two *øre* piece.
+**ør'k**[1] *-en* cf **ørken**
°**ør'k**[2] *A* cf **vyrk**
°**ør'ke/dag** *-en* cf **yrke/**
ør'ken *-enen, pl -ner/+-ener* desert; wasteland, wilderness: **som en røst i ø-en** like a voice in the wilderness (Matthew 3,3).
+**ør'ken/aktig** *A -* desert-like.
ør'ken/romantikk' *-en* romance of the desert.
ør'ken/sand *-en* desert sand.
ør'ken/vandring *-a/+-en* desert journey, wandering in the wilderness; *fig.* unrewarding, wearying task (e.g. the making of dictionaries).
+**ør'kes/løs** *A* idle; aimless, futile, useless.
Ø'r/land *Pln* twp, Sør-Trøndelag.
ø'r/liten *A f -a/+-en, nt -e, pl -små* 1 tiny, wee little; infinitesimal: ***dette ørvesle ver som det blir kring ein fager skapning** this tiny aura which a beautiful person creates around herself. 2 (as a noun) little bit, mighty little: **ørlite konjakk** a drop of brandy.
ø'rn *-a/-en, pl *-ar* 1 *zool.* eagle (Aquila). 2 *astron.* Eagle.
+**ø'rne/aktig** *A -* eagle-like.
ø'rne/blikk *-et* eagle eye.
ø'rne/klo *-a, pl -klør* eagle's talon.
+**ø'rne/nese** *-a/-en* (=***/nase**) *anat.* aquiline nose, hawk nose.
ø'rne/reir *-et* eagle's nest.
+**ø'rne/øye** *-t* (=***/auga**) 1 eagle eye. 2 *bot.* hawk's-beard (Crepis paludosa).
ø'rn/unge [/onge] *-n* eaglet.
+**ør'ret** *-en* cf **aure**[1]
ør'sk *A* befuddled, confused, dazed.
ør'ske[1] *-a* confusion, daze, fog: **i ø-** half asleep; **snakke i ø-** be delirious.
ør'ske[2] *V -a/+-et* talk fuzzily, without making sense; be delirious, incoherent.
ør'sken *A +-ent, pl -ne* befuddled, confused, dazed.
Ø'r/skog *Pln* twp, Møre og Romsdal.
ø'r/små *pl of* **-liten**
Ør'sta *Pln* twp, Møre og Romsdal.
ør'tug *-en hist.* monetary or weight unit (=1/3 *øre*).
***ø'r/vaken** *A -e/-i, pl -ne* cf **yr/våken**
ø'r/vesle *A df of* **-liten**
***ø'r/vill** *A -vilt* senseless.
***ø'r/vænast** *V -test, -st* despair, fear (the outcome).
***ø'r/væne** *-a* 1 despair, hopelessness. 2 sth hopeless.
***ø's**[1] *-en* excitement, flare-up.
+**ø's**[2] *-et* violent downpour (of rain).
+**ø's**[3] *Av*: **ø- pøs regn** pouring rain.
+**ø'se**[1] *-a* cf **ause**[1]
***ø'se**[2] *-a* excitement, flare-up.
+**ø'se**[3] *V -te* cf **ause**[2]
***ø'se**[4] *V -te* excite, goad, infuriate.
+**ø'se/kar** *-et* cf **ause/**
***ø'sen** *A +-ent, pl -ne* angry, choleric.
øskj'e *-a* (small) bentwood box (often decorated; for carrying butter, cheese, etc.).
***øs'le**[1] *-a* nonsense, tomfoolery.
***øs'le**[2] *V -a* banter, fool, fool around.
+**ø's/regn** [/rein] *-et* violent downpour, shower.
+**ø's/regne** [/reine] *V -a/-et/-te* pour, rain violently.
+**øs't** *Av* cf **aust**
+**øs'ta-** *Pf* cf **austa-**
+**øs'ta/drag** *-et* easterly breeze (from the east).
+**øs'ta/fjells** *Av* cf **austa/**
+**øs'ta/fjelsk** *A -* cf **austa/**
+**øs'ta/for'** *P* cf **austa/**
+**øs'ta/vind** *-en* cf **austa/**
+**øs'ta/vær** *-et* cf **austa/**
+**Øs't/banen** *Pln* East Railway Station (in Oslo; short for **Østbanestasjonen**): **ta Ø-** take a train from the Ø. station.
+**øs't/blokk** *-en* cf **aust/**
+**Øs'ten** *Pln* the East, the Orient.
+**øs'ten/for'** *P* cf **austa/**
+**øs'ten/om'** *P* east of.
+**øs'ter-** *Pf* (=***auster-**) east-.
Øs'ter/dalen *Pln* Glomma river valley (down to Elverum) and tributary districts.
øs'ter/døl *-en* person from Østerdal.
+**Øs'ter/land** *Pln lit., poet.* (the) East, (the) Orient.
+**øs'ter/landsk** *A -* eastern, oriental.
+**øs'ter/på** *Av* cf **aust/**
+**Øs'ter/rike** *Pln* Austria.
+**øs'ter/riker** *-en, pl -e* Austrian.
+**øs'ter/riksk** *A -* Austrian.
øs'ters *-en* (=***ostre**) 1 *zool.* oyster (Ostreidae): **stum som en ø-** silent as a clam. 2 *fam.* dummox, fool.
+**Øs'ter/sjøen** *Pln* the Baltic.
+**øs'tersjø/land** *-et* Baltic country.
øs'ters/skal *-et* (=+**/skall**) oyster shell.
+**øs't/etter** *P* 1 eastward along, through. 2 *(adv.)* east, eastward.
+**øs't/europe'isk** [/au-] *A -* cf **aust/**
Østf.=**Østfold**
Øs't/fold *Pln* (=***Aust/**) county on east side of Oslofjord.
øs't/folding *-en* (=***aust/**) person from Østfold.
øs't/foldsk *A -* (=***aust/**) pertaining to Østfold.
+**øs't/fra** *P* cf **aust/frå**
+**øs't/gående** *A -* cf **aust/**
+**øs't/kant** *-en* eastern edge, part: **ø-en** the East Side (of Oslo).
+**Øs't/landet** *Pln* (=***Aust/**) East Norway (esp. the more level parts of the Southeast).
+**øs't/landsk** *A -* (=***aust/**) pertaining to Østlandet.
+**øs't/lending** *-en* (=***aust/**) person from Østlandet.
+**øs'tlig** *A -* cf **austlig**
+**øs't/mann** *-en, pl -menn* cf **aust/**
+**Øs't-Norge** *Pln* cf **Aust-**
+**øs't/norsk** *A -* cf **aust/**
+**øs't/over** [/åver] *P* cf **aust/**
+**øs't/på** *Av* cf **aust/**
+**øs'tre** *A -* cf **austre**
+**Øs'tre Gau'sdal** *Pln* twp, Oppland.
+**Øs'tre Mo'land** *Pln* twp, Aust-Agder.
+**Øs'tre Sli'dre** *Pln* twp, Oppland.
+**Øs'tre To'ten** *Pln* twp, Oppland.
øv'd *A -/*øvt* (=+**øvet**) experienced, practiced, trained; expert, handy, skilled (**i** in).
ø've *V -de* 1 commit, perform; exercise, exert: **ø- (en) bedrift** p- an exploit; **ø- vold** do violence (**mot** to), use violence. 2 practice: **ø- opp** train. 3 *(refl.)*: **ø- seg (i noe)** practice (sth, e.g. dancing, music, etc.); **ø- seg på pianoet** practice (on) the piano.
+**ø'velse** *-n* cf **øving**
Ø'ver/bygd *Pln* twp, Troms.
***ø'ver/heit** *-a* cf **øvrig/het**
+**ø'verst** *sp of* **øvre**
+**ø'verst/befa'lende** *A -* commander-in-chief.
+**ø'verst/kommande'rende** *en* commander-in-chief.
+**ø'vet** *A -* cf **øvd**
ø'ving *-a/+-en* (=+**øvelse**) 1 practice (**i** in): **komme ut av ø-** get out of p-; **ø- gjør mester** p- makes perfect. 2 exercise; training (often *pl*): **holde seg i ø-** keep in t-; **holde ø-er i** conduct e-s in. 3 *mil.* drill, maneuvers, training.
+**ø'vings/lærer** *-en, pl -e* (=***-ar**) practice teacher.
ø'vings/skole *-n* training school (where practice teaching is done).
ø'vings/tid *-a* practice time; exercise, training period.
ø'vre *A - sp øvst/+øverst* 1 higher, upper: **den ø- av Heiegardene** the u- Heie farm; **den ø- del av byen** the h- section of the city. 2 *(sup.)*: **ø-st** upper; highest, uppermost; top; **ø-ste klasse** *educ.* graduating class, top class; **den (det, de) ø-ste** the chief one(s), the one(s) h- in rank; **ø-ste dekk** *naut.* the upper deck; **fra ø-st til nederst** from top to bottom. 3 *(adv., sup.)* at the top, on top: **ø-st på bakken** at the top of the hill; **ø-st ved bordet** at the head of the table.
Ø'vre/bø *Pln* twp, Vest-Agder.
Ø'vre Ei'ker *Pln* twp, Buskerud.
ø'vre/lippe** *-a* (=/leppe**) upper lip.
***ø'vre/munn** *-en* upper part of mouth.
Ø'vre Re'ndal *Pln* twp, Hedmark.
Ø'vre San'dsvær *Pln* twp, Buskerud.
+**ø'vrig** *A -* other, remaining, rest (of): **de ø-e** the others; the rest; **det ø-e** the remainder; **for ø-** besides; for that matter; **huset for ø-** the rest of the house.
+**ø'vrig/het** *-en* (=***/heit**) 1 authority, government: **ø-en** the authorities. 2 (an) authority, official.
+**ø'vrighets/perso'n** *-en* (an) authority, official.
øv'st *sp of* **øvre**
***øv'ste/prest** *-en* high priest.
øy' *-a, pl *-ar* island: **på øya** in, on the i-.
øy'/bu *-en* (=***/bue**) islander.
+**-øyd** *A -* (=***-øygd**) -eyed.
+**-øydd** *A -* cf **-øyd**
øy'de[1] *V -de* (=+**øde**[2]) 1 destroy, lay waste, ruin. 2 dissipate, squander, waste: **jeg har ødt mitt gods med sang og vin** I have w-d my goods on song and wine (Øverland).
+**øy'de**[2] *A -* cf **øde**[3]
øy'de/ga'rd *-en* deserted farm (often used to name such a farm even after it has been put to use again).
+**øy'de/legge** *V -la, -lagt* (=***-je**, +**øde/**) destroy, lay waste; ruin, spoil.
øy'de/legging *-a* destruction, ruination.
***øy'de/leggje** *V infl as* **leggje** cf **/legge**
øy'de/mark *-a* (=+**øde/**) wasteland, wilderness.
***øy'den** *A -e/-i, pl -ne* 1 desolate. 2 wasteful; lavish.
***øy'd/sam** *A* 1 wasteful. 2 lavish.
***øy'dsle** *-a* squandering, wastefulness.
***øy'dsle/sam** *A* 1 wasteful. 2 lavish.
+**øy'e**[1] *-t, pl øyne/øyer* (=***auge**, ***auga**) 1 eye: **få ø- på** catch sight of; notice, see; **ha et godt ø- til** have an eye on; be in love with; be down on; **ha for ø-** have in view, in mind; **ha øynene med seg** have one's e-s peeled, look sharp; **holde ø- med** keep an e- on, watch; **kaste sine øyne på en (noe)** take a fancy to sby (sth); **med store øyne** wide-eyed; **se en like i øynene** look one straight in the face, look right into one's e-s; **se noe i øynene** face sth; **si en noe like i øynene** say sth right to one's face; **under fire øyne** confidentially, in private; **ute av ø-, ute av sinn** out of sight, out of mind. 2 eye (of a butterfly wing, cyclone, millstone, needle, potato, etc.); eyelet; pip, spot (on cards, dice, dominoes, etc.); dab, fleck (of butter, fat, etc., in or on sth).
***øy'e**[2] *V -a*: **ø- seg** moan, whimper.
+**øy'e/blikk** *-et* instant, moment: **et ø-** (e.g. on telephone) one m-, just a m-; **for et ø- siden** a m- ago; **for ø-et** at present, at the m-; **han kan komme hvert ø-** he can come at any m-; **i dette ø-** at this m-, just now; **om et ø-** in a m-; **på ø-et** immediately, this minute.
+**øyeblik'kelig** *A -* 1 immediate (danger, departure, etc.). 2 momentary (excitement, misunderstanding). 3 instantaneous, sudden. 4 *(adv.)* at once, immediately, instantly.
+**øy'eblikks/bilde** *-t* snapshot.
+**øy'e/bolt** *-en* eyebolt.

+øy'e/bryn -et brow, eyebrow: **rynke ø-ene** frown.
+øy'e/eple -t eyeball.
+øy'e/glass -et eye bath, eyecup.
+øy'e/hule -n *anat.* orbit (eye socket).
+øy'e/høyde -n eye level.
+øy'e/hår -et eyelash.
+øy'e/kast -et glance, look: **(kjærlighet) ved første ø-** (love) at first sight; **sende en et ø-** give sby a (meaningful) look; **veksle ø-** exchange glances.
+øy'e/krok -en *anat.* canthus, corner of the eye; (also *fig.*, *lit.*): **et glimt i ø-en** a twinkle in the corner of (his, her) eye.
***øy'eleg** *A* - frightful, terrible.
+øy'e/lege -n eye specialist.
+øy'e/linse -a/-en *anat.* crystalline lens (of the eye).
+øy'e/lokk -et eyelid.
+øy'e/med et 1 aim, goal, object: **i det ø- å** with the aim of. 2 cause, purpose: **et velgjørende ø-** a worthy cause.
+øy'e/merke -t: **ta ø- i** fix one's sight on, use as a landmark.
+øy'e/mål -et measurement by eye: **etter, på ø-** by eye; **sikkert ø-** sure eye.
***øy'en** *A* -e/-i, *pl* -ne dreadful, horrible, terrible.
+øyen- *Pf* cf **øye-**
+øy'e/nerve -n *anat.* optic nerve.
+øy'en/lokk -et cf **øye/**
+øy'ens/lyst -en 1 thing of beauty, visual delight. 2 lusts of the eye.
+øyensy'nlig *A* - (usu. *adv.*) clearly, evidently, obviously.
+øy'en/tjener -en, *pl* -e *lit.* timeserver.
+øy'en/trøst -en *bot.* common eyebright (Euphrasia officinalis).
+øy'en/vidne -t cf **øye/vitne**
+øy'er *pl of* **øy, øye[1]**
Øy'er *Pln* twp, Oppland.
+øy'e/skrue -n eye screw, screw eye.
Øy'e/stad *Pln* twp, Aust-Agder.
+øy'este *A* -: **på ø- blikket** *fam.* this very instant.
+øy'e/stein -en 1 eye; eyeball. 2 *fig.* apple of (one's) eye.
+øy'e/stikker -en, *pl* -e *zool.* dragonfly (Odonata).
+øy'e/sverte -a kohl, mascara.
+øy'e/syn -et sight, vision: **få i ø-** catch sight of, get to see; **ta i ø-** examine closely, look at searchingly; **så langt ø-et rakk** as far as the eye could see (Normann).
+øy'e/tann -a, *pl* -tenner eyetooth.
+øy'e/vippe -a eyelash.
+øy'e/vitne -t eyewitness.
øy'/folk -et island people, islanders.
øy'/ga'rd[1] -en skerries (group of islands offshore which serve as a breakwater and protect the inner passage for shipping).
+øy'/ga'rd[2] -en cf **øyde/**
***-øygd** *A* -/-øygt cf **-øyd**
øy'gne** *V* -a (=augne**) catch sight of.
øy'/gruppe -a/+-en archipelago, group of islands.
øy'k -en, *pl* *-er (old) horse, plug, nag.
***øy'ke/for** -et fodder (for a horse).
øy'/klima -et island climate.
***øy'ks/emne** -t foal.
Øy'/mark *Pln* twp, Østfold.
+øy'ne[1] *pl of* **øye[1]**
+øy'ne[2] *V* -a/-et catch sight of; glimpse, perceive: **ø- igjennom** glance through; **ø- ingen utvei** see no way out; **ø-er du dybden** do you penetrate the mystery (Ibsen).
Øy'/olf *Prn (m)*
øy'r -a, *pl* *-ar cf **ør[1]**
***øy'ra** *eit, df* -, *pl* øyro cf **øre[3]**
***-øyra** *A* - cf **-øret**
***-øyrd** *A* -øyrt cf **-øret**
***øy're[1]** -n goods, property, e.g. **laus/ø-.**
***øy're[2]** -t cf **øre[3]**
***øy're[3]** *V* -te (of sand on river bottom) shift; form sandbanks: **øyrast ned** become buried under sand.
***øy're/fik** -en cf **øre/**
***øy're/hinne** -a *anat.* ear drum, tympanic membrane.
***øy'ret(e)** *A* - cf **øret(e)**
***øy're/verk** -en cf **øre/**
***øy're/vitne** -t cf **øre/**
øy'/rike -t island kingdom.
Øy'sle/bø *Pln* twp, Vest-Agder.
Øy'/stein *Prn (m)*
***øy'stre** -a large dipper or bowl.
Øy'/vind *Prn (m)*
***øy'/væring** -en 1 islander. 2 person from Øyer.

å'[1] -en (letter) **Å, å.**
å'[2] -a creek, (small) river, stream: **mange bekker små gjør en stor å** every little helps.
°å'[3] *Av* cf **hvor[1]**
å'[4] *I* ah, o, oh; oh well; **å ja** oh yes; well, yes; yes and no; **å, jeg ber** don't mention it, not at all, that's all right; **å nei** oh no; I suppose not; **å pytt** bah, pooh.
å[5] *infinitive marker*: **begynne å lese** begin to read, begin reading: **de holdt opp å snakke** they stopped talking; **det er sunnere, det å gå** it's healthier, walking (Ibsen); **etter å ha skrevet** after having written; **kunsten å bygge** the art of building; **redd for å være alene** afraid of being alone; **ved å gi lekser** by giving lessons; **å lide er å leve, å leve er å lide** to suffer is to live, to live is to suffer (Garborg).
å'[6] *P dial.* on, upon: **att å bak** on one's back.
°å'[7] *Pn* cf **hva**
Å' *Pln* fishing village on Moskenesøya in Lofoten Islands.
å'/band -et *dial.* crossband on a pack saddle.
å'/bit -en *dial.* breakfast.
å'bits/leite -t *dial.* breakfast time.
å/bor [å'bår, åb'bår] -en *zool.* perch (Perca fluviatilis).
å'/bot -a/+-en *jur.* compensation, damages (to be paid by tenant for not keeping house in repair).
***å'/breisle** -a (bed) covers.
***å'/brengen** *A* -e/-i, *pl* -ne insistent; demanding, importunate.
***å'/brengje** -a importunate person, pest.
***å'/bruig** *A* - cf **/bryen**
***å'/bry[1]** -et jealousy.
***å'/bry[2]** *V* -dde be jealous of, plague with jealousy.
***å'/bryen** *A* -e/-i, *pl* -ne jealous.
***å'bry/skap** -en jealousy.
***å'/bu** -a obligation (of tenant) to keep house in repair.
***å'/bu'rd** -en 1 crop(s), production, yield. 2 land anchor.
***å'/byrgjast** *V* -dest, -byrgst guarantee.
***å'/byrgsle[1]** -a guarantee.
***å'/byrgsle[2]** *V* -a guarantee.
***å'byrgsle/laus** *A* free of responsibility.
å'/bøle -t *hist.* residence.
å'/bøter *pl of* **-bot**
Å'/dal *Pln* twp, Buskerud.
***å'/fall** -et current, flow, stream (e.g. of water in a mill).
***å'/fengen** *A* -e/-i, *pl* -ne (of drink) intoxicating, strong.
°åf'fer *Av* cf **hvor/for**
Å'/fjo'rd *Pln* twp, Sør-Trøndelag.
***å'/fløy(e)** -a small flat-bottomed boat.
***å'/fløygen** *A* -e/-i, *pl* -ne eager, impetuous, violent.
***å'/fått** *A* - out of order, wrong: **det er alltid noko å-** there's always sth to complain about.
***å'/gang** -en flood (of water), rush, streaming in; *fig.* flood of visitors; encroachment; invasion.
Å'ge *Prn (m)*
å'ger -en/+-et usury: **drive å-** practice u-.
å'ger/kar -en usurer.
+å'ger/karl -en cf **/kar**
å'ger/pris -en exorbitant price.
å'ger/rente -a/+-en exorbitant interest.
***å'/gjengen** *A* -e/-i, *pl* -ne demanding, obtrusive.
Ågot [å'gåt] *Prn(f)*
å'gre *V* -a/+-et practice usury: **å- med sitt pund** exploit, make the most of one's talents.
***å'/gøye** -a captious, faultfinding person.
å'h *I* oh.
***å'/hende** *V* -a/-e grasp, understand.
***å'/hug** -en devotion.
***å'/høyrar** -en hearer, listener.
åhå' *I* ah, aha, ahoy.
+åja' *I* cf **å[4]**
+åjo' *I* cf **å[4]**
å'k -et 1 yoke (also on electromagnet): **bøye seg under å-et** bow one's neck to, submit to the y-; **spenne i å-et** yoke, put to the y-. 2 *tech.* pier, pilework (to support wooden bridge).
***å'/kall** -en river sprite.
***å'/kave** -n bustle, rush, uproar.
***å'/kavt** *Av* impetuous, vehement.
Å'ke *Prn (m)*
å'ker -eren, *pl* -rer 1 (cultivated) field. 2: **gå i å-en** (of boat) go aground, be cast ashore.
å'ker/bruk -et agriculture, farming.
+å'ker/bruker -en, *pl* -e (=***-ar**) farmer.
å'ker/bær -et *bot.* arctic raspberry (Rubus arcticus).
+å'ker/dyrker -en, *pl* -e (=***-ar**) farmer.
å'ker/flekk -en patch, small field.
å'ker/høne -a *zool.* 1 *dial.* corncrake, land rail (Crex crex). 2 partridge (Perdix perdix).
å'ker/jo'rd -a arable soil.
å'ker/kål -en 1 field turnip (Brassica campestris). 2 *dial.* cf **/sennep.**
å'ker/land -et arable land, plough land.
å'ker/lapp -en tilled patch, small field.
å'ker/lende -t arable land.
å'ker/reddik -en *bot.* jointed charlock (Raphanus raphanistrum).
å'ker/rein -a balk, ridge or strip of unplowed land between fields.
å'ker/rikse -a *zool.* corncrake, land rail (Crex crex).
å'ker/sennep -en *bot.* charlock, wild mustard (Brassica kaber).

+ Bokmål; * Nynorsk; ° Dialect.
After letter: ' stress (Acc. 1); ` tone, stress (Acc. 2); · length.
Below letter: . not pronounced.

å'ker/snelle -*a bot.* equisetum, horsetail (Equisetum arvense).
å'/kle -*kleet, pl -klær* (=*/**klede**) 1 hand-woven tapestry used as wall hangings in old Norwegian homes. 2 coverlet.
***å'/korn** [/kånn] -*et* acorn.
***å'/kost(e)** -*a* thickening for soup.
Å'kra *Pln* twp, Rogaland.
+**å'krer** *pl of* **åker**
å'l[1] -*en* 1 *zool.* eel (Anguilla): **glatt, smidig som en ål** slippery, smooth as an eel. 2 fold in stockings.
å'l[2] -*en* 1 dorsal stripe. 2 channel (in river bottom); groove (in ski). 3 *dial.* shoot, spear, sprout. 4 *typog.* bodkin.
Å'l *Pln* twp, Buskerud.
***ål-** *Pf* all, completely, e.g. **ålvåt.**
***å'/lag** -*et* assigned task, assignment.
***å'/laup** -*et* attack, siege.
å'le[1] *V* -*a*/+-*et*/-*te* 1 crawl, wriggle; wind in and out: **å- seg** snake one's way (forward, up, etc.). 2 sag: **strømpene dine å-er seg** your stockings are sagging.
***å'le**[2] *V* -*a* sprout.
å'le/glatt *A* - slippery as an eel.
å'le/gras -*et bot.* eelgrass (Zostera marina).
***ålei'ne** *A* - cf **aleine**
***å'/leite** *V* -*a* hang over (sby), plague, torment.
***å'/leiten** *A* -*e*/-*i*, *pl* -*ne* oppressive, troublesome.
å'le/kiste -*a* eel trap.
å'le/kone -*a zool.* eelpout, viviparous blenny (Zoarces viviparus).
Å'len *Pln* twp, Sør-Trøndelag.
å'le/slank *A* slender, svelte.
Å'le/sund *Pln* city, Møre og Romsdal.
***å'l/etar** -*en* glutton.
å'let(e) *A* - 1 (of animal) striped down the back. 2 eel-like, slippery.
å'le/teine -*a* eelpot.
***å'l/eten** *A* -*e*/-*i*, *pl* -*ne* gluttonous, greedy.
***å'l/gjengd** *A* -/-*gjengt* 1 much frequented, popular. 2 common, prevalent.
***å'l/huga** *A* - 1 decided, determined. 2 avid, eager.
***å'l/kjend** *A* -*kjent* notorious, well-known.
***å'lmanna/møte** -*t* cf **allmanna/**
***å'lmann/veg** -*en* cf **allmann/**
***å'l/menn** *A* -*ment* cf **all/**
***å'lmenn/daning** -*a* cf **allmenn/dannelse**
***å'lmenn/hug** -*en* public spirit.
***å'l/menning** -*a* cf **all/**
***å'l/mente** -*a* (the) public.
***å'l/muge** -*n* cf **all/**
***å'/loge** [/låge] -*a* assigned task, assignment.
Å/lov [å'/låv] *Prn (f)*
+**ål'rei't** *A* - cf **all right**
***å'l/vaken** *A* -*e*/-*i*, *pl* -*ne* (=*/**vak**) wide-awake.
***å'l/velt** *A* - with all four feet in the air.
***å'l/velte** -*a* upside-down position: **liggje i å** animal) lie on (its) back.
***å'l/veltes** *Av* on its back.
***å'l/våt** *A* -*vått* soaked through.
å'l/yngel -*en* elvers (=young eels).
***å'l/æt** *A* cf **/eten**
***å'l/æte** -*a* glutton, greedy person.
å'me -*a* caterpillar, grub, larva.
Å'm/li *Pln* twp, Aust-Agder.
***å'/mol** -*a* pebbles in a river.
å'/mot -*et* confluence of two rivers.
Å'/mot *Pln* 1 twp, Hedmark. 2 town, Modum twp, Buskerud.
Å'/mund *Prn (m)*
+**å'/møte** -*t* cf **/mot**
***å'/måle** *V* -*a* broach, mention.
Åna-Si'ra *Pln* fishing village, Rogaland and Vest-Agder.
ån'd +-*en*/*-*a* 1 spirit; genius, intellect, mind: **lovens å-** the s- of the law; **språkets å-** the g- of language; **store å-er** great i-s, great m-s; **å-en er villig** the s- is willing; **å-en fra 1814** the s- of 1814; **å-en og materien** m- and matter. 2 spirit (=ghost); genius: **hans gode å-** his good genius; **den hellige å-** the Holy S- (Ghost); **gi opp å-en** give up the ghost; **mane å-er** conjure s-s.
Ån'dals/nes *Pln* port town, Møre og Romsdal.
+**ån'de**[1] -*n* (=***ande**[1]) 1 breath; breathing: **dra å-** breathe, draw b-; **holde en i å-** keep sby busy, on the alert; hold sby's interest; **komme i å-** warm to one's work, get into one's stride. 2 *lit., fig.* breath of wind, breeze.
ån'de[2] *V* -*a*/+-*et* (=***ande**[2]) 1 breathe, draw one's breath, respire: **å- for** live (and breathe) for; **å- fram** b- out, whisper (e.g. words); **å- inn** inhale; **å- liv i** bring back to life; **å- på** blow on; **å- ut** exhale; b- a sigh of relief; die. 2 *lit., fig.* blow gently, lightly. 3 *lit.* express, reveal: **hvert åsyn å-et glede** each countenance shone with joy (Ibsen).
+**ån'de/aktig** *A* - ghostly, spectral, spooky.
+**ån'de/drag** -*et* 1 breathing; respiration: **havets å-** the b- of the sea. 2 breath: **i samme å-** in the same b-; **til hans siste å-** to his last b-.
+**ån'de/drett** -*et* cf **/drag**
+**ån'dedretts/orga'n** -*et* respiratory organ.
+**ån'de/hull** -*et* 1 breathing hole. 2 *zool.* spiracle, stigma; lung opening in a land snail.
+**ån'de/lett** *A* - light as air.
ån'delig *A* - spiritual (father, life, love, meditation, movement, sense, etc.); intellectual, mental (effort, food, interests, etc.); moral (decay, force, values, etc.).
+**ån'de/løs** *A* breathless.
+**ån'de/maner** -*en, pl* -*e* (=*-**ar**) conjurer, necromancer; *hum.* spiritualist.
+**ån'de/nød** *en* choking, difficulty in breathing.
+**ån'der** *åndra* (=***onder**) short right ski for climbing (used with long left one and usually having reindeer hide on the underside).
+**ån'de/verden** -*en* (=*/**verd**) spirit world, world of spirits (ghosts).
ån'd/full *A* brilliant, inspired, witty.
+**ån'dfull/het** -*en* brilliance, wit.
ån'dig *A* - *obs.* spiritual.
ån'd/laus *A* dull, plodding, uninspired; inane, insipid.
ån'd/løyse -*a* dullness, inanity.
ån'd/rik *A* brilliant, witty.
ån'ds/arbeid [*/arbei] -*et* creative (artistic, intellectual) work; cultural pursuit.
+**ån'ds/arbei'der** -*en, pl* -*e* (=*-**ar**) cultural (creative) worker (esp. authors, artists, and scientists).
ån'ds/aristokra't -*en* intellectual aristocrat.
ån'ds/aristokrati' -*et* intellectual aristocracy.
+**ån'ds/beslek'tet** *A* - congenial; kindred (souls).
+**ån'ds/dannelse** -*n* (=*/**danning**) culture.
ån'ds/evne -*a*/+-*en* (in *pl*) intellectual talents, mental ability.
ån'ds/fattig *A* - dull, retarded.
ån'ds/felle -*n* kindred soul.
+**ån'ds/forlatt'** *A* - dull, boring, uninspired.
+**ån'ds/fravæ'relse** -*n* absent-mindedness, preoccupation.
+**ån'ds/fravæ'rende** *A* - absent-minded, preoccupied.
ån'ds/frende -*n* congenial soul, kindred spirit.
+**ån'ds/frihet** -*en* (=*/**fridom**) intellectual freedom.
ån'ds/frisk *A* alert, of sound mind.
ån'ds/føde [*/føe] -*a*/+-*en* food for the mind.
+**ån'ds/gaver** *pl* mental ability, intellectual endowment.
***ån'ds/heim** -*en* cultural world, world of the spirit.
ån'ds/høvding -*en* cultural leader.
ån'ds/kraft -*a*/+-*en, pl* -*krefter*/*-*er* mental power; strength of mind; spirit.
ån'ds/liv -*et* 1 cultural life, culture. 2: **å-et** *hum.* the cultural leaders.
+**ån'ds/nærvæ'relse** -*n* presence of mind, resourcefulness; composure.
+**ån'ds/nærvæ'rende** *A* - having presence of mind, resourceful; composed.
ån'ds/retning -*a*/+-*en* school of thought; line of thinking, trend of thought; orientation.
ån'ds/rett -*en jur.* ownership rights to anything intellectually produced (incl. copyrights, patents, trademarks, etc.).
ån'ds/slektskap +-*et*/*-*en* intellectual, spiritual affinity or kinship.
ån'ds/sløv *A* - dull-witted, stupid.
ån'ds/snobb -*en* intellectual snob.
ån'ds/svak *A* 1 feebleminded, mentally retarded. 2 idiotic, imbecilic.
ån'ds/verk -*et* creative work (book, painting, play, etc.).
+**ån'ds/virksomhe't** -*en* cultural, intellectual activity.
Å'nund *Prn (m)*
+**å'pen** *A* -*ent, pl* -*ne* (=***open**) open (conduct, contempt, letter, question, sea, vowel, window, etc.); exposed; candid, frank (admission, expression, etc.); blank (line, space, etc.); vacant (e.g. position): **den åpne dørs politikk** the o- door policy; **for åpne dører** in public, publicly; **ha å-t øye for** have a keen eye for; **mangen vei står meg å-** many a road (path) is o- to me (Ibsen); **på å- gate** in the street; **under å- himmel** in the o- (air).
+**å'pen/bar** *A* clear, evident, obvious.
+**å'pen/bare** *V* -*te* disclose, divulge; manifest, reveal: **å- seg** appear, be evident, reveal oneself; **å-t religion** r-ed religion.
+**å'pen/barelse** -*n lit.* revelation.
+**å'pen/baring** [also -ba'r-] -*a*/-*en* revelation (**for** to): **Johannes Å-** *(bibl.)* Revelations.
+**å'pen/het** -*en* 1 openness, receptivity (**for** to). 2 candor, frankness, ingenuousness.
+**å'pen/hjertig** *A* - candid, frank, openhearted: **å-e tilståelser** c- confessions.
+**å'penhjertig/het** -*en* candor, frankness, open-heartedness.
+**å'pen/lys** *A* obvious, open, undisguised: **fattigfolk gikk å-t til henne** poor people sought her out openly (Undset).
+**å'pen/munnet** *A* - 1 open-mouthed. 2 indiscreet, loose-tongued.
+**å'penmunnet/het** -*en* lack of discretion.
+**å'pne** *V* -*a*/-*et* (=***opne**) 1 open (an account, a door, a letter, a meeting, negotiations, etc.); begin, launch (a campaign, an offensive, etc.); dedicate: **å- ens øyne for noe** o- one's eyes to sth; **å- igjen** reopen. 2 *(refl.)*: **å- seg** open (up); **å- seg for en** o- one's heart to sby.
+**å'pner** -*en, pl* -*e* (=***opnar**) opener.
+**å'pning** -*en* (=***opning**) opening (**av** of): **en å- i veggen** an o- in the wall.
+**å'pnings/høyti'delighet** -*en* inauguration, opening ceremony.
+**å'pnings/tale** -*n* inaugural, opening address.
+**å'pnings/tid** -*a*/-*en* (business, office) hours.
***å'r**[1] -*a, pl* -*ar* cf **åre**[1]
å'r[2] -*a, pl* *-*ar* cf **åre**[2]
å'r[3] -*et* year: **denne årsens tid** *dial.* this time of y-; **dette år** this year; **et barn på seks år** a child of six; **fylle 20 år** reach (the age of) 20; **gjennom årene** in the course of time, through the y-s; **et godt år** (also:) a good year for crops; **i de siste årene** during recent y-s; **i det**

herrens år in the year of grace; **i to år** for two y-s; **i år** this y-; **om et år** in a y- (from now); **om året** annually, per y-; **samme år** in the same year; **tidlig på året** early in the y-; **til års** advanced in y-s, (relatively) old; *dial.* next (the coming) y-; **trekke på årene** be getting old, on in y-s; **år for år** y- by y-; **år og dag** ages, a long time.

***å'rast** *V -ast*: **det å- godt** things are thriving, it's a good year (for crops).

å'r/bok *-a, pl -bøker* annual, year book.

Å'r/dal *Pln* 1 twp, Sogn og Fjordane. 2 twp, Rogaland.

å're[1] *-a* (=***år**[1]) 1 *anat.* blood vessel; artery, vein. 2 *fig.* artery, vein: **byens å-r** the city's (traffic) arteries; **marmor med å-r** veined marble. 3 (creative) ability, streak, vein: **en poetisk å-** a poetic vein.

å're[2] *-a* (=***år**[2]) oar: **holde på å-ne** rest (on the) o-s; **legge seg i å-ne** lay into the o-s; *fig.* put out great effort; **legge å-ne inn (opp)** unship the o-s; *fig.* retire, stop working; **legge å-ne ut** ship the o-s; **reise å-ne** toss o-s.

å're[3] *-n hist.* open hearth (in middle of floor).

å're/betennelse *-n med.* phlebitis.

å're/blad *et* blade of oar.

å're/forkal'kning *-en* (=***/forkalking**) *med.* arteriosclerosis.

å're/helle *-a hist.* hearth stone (in front or placed vertically at end of open hearth to protect adjacent beds from sparks).

å're/hinne *-a anat.* 1 chorion (around embryo). 2 choroid membrane (in eye). 3 pia mater.

å're/knute *-n med.* varicose vein, varix.

å're/lang *A* lasting for years, of several years duration: **ved å-t arbeid** by y-s of toil.

å're/late *V infl as* **late**[1] *med.* bleed (sby).

+**å're/mål** *-et* (=***år/**) term (of years): **på å-** for a term of years; **forpaktning på langt å-** a long lease.

+**å'remåls/dag** *-en* (=***årmåls/**) anniversary, jubilee (of a person, firm etc.).

å're/slag *-et* stroke (of an oar).

å're/stein *-en* hearthstone.

å're/stue *-a* (=**/stove**) *hist.* log house with open hearth in center of room and a smoke vent in the roof.

å're/tak *-et* stroke (of an oar).

å'ret(e) *A* - grained, striped, veined.

å're/toll(e) *-(e)n naut.* oarlock, thole.

***å'/rette** *V -a* fasten by driving a wedge in (as head on a hammer).

å're/vis *Av*: **i å-** for years (and years).

+**å'r/fugl** *-en* cf **orr/**

årg. =**årgang**

å'r/gang *-en* 1 course of a year, year: **i sin tredje å-** in its third year; **å-s vann** water the year round. 2 (annual) volume (of a magazine): **å-en 1955 av Bonytt** B- for 1955. 3 vintage; *fig., hum.* age group: **å-en 1947 av Chateau Haut Brion** vintage 1947 of C-; **de yngre å-er** the younger age group.

***å'r/gjengd** *A -/-gjengt* year-round.

+**årh.** =**århundre**

***å'r/hag(e)** *-(e)n* year's crop, production: **god å-** good year.

+**å'r/hane** *-n* cf **orr/**

***å'r/helle** *-a* cf **åre/**

+**århun'dre** [also å'r/] *-t* century.

århun'dre/gammal *A -alt, pl -gamle* 1 100 years old. 2 centuries old.

+**århun'dre/skifte** *-t* turn of the century.

+**å'r/høne** *-n* cf **orr/**

-årig *A* - year(s), year old: **den sju/å-e gutten** the seven-year old boy; **en fem/å- krig** a five-year war; **på sitt 50-å-e jubileum** on his 50th anniversary.

å'ring[1] *-en* yearling.

å'ring[2] *-en* (crop) year; harvest.

-åring *-en* -year-old, e.g. **fem/å-** five-year-old.

å'rle *Av archaic* early.

å'rlig *A* - annual, yearly; *(adv.)* annually, per annum.

+**å'rlig/å'rs** *Av* annually, every year.

å'r/mann *-en, pl -menn/*-menner hist.* representative of the king, steward.

***å'r/mål** *et* cf **åre/**

***å'rmåls/dag** *-en* cf **åremåls/**

+**å'r/rekke** *-a/-en* (=***/rekkje**) series of years: **i en lang å-** for many years.

å'r/ring *-en* annual ring (on trees).

-å'rs *A* - -year: **100-å- jubileum** centennial; **på sin 70-å- dag** on one's 70th birthday.

å'r/sak *-a/+-en* cause, reason, occasion (**til** for): **av den å-** for that r-; **det har sine å-er** there are r-s for it; **ingen å-** don't mention it, not at all, you're welcome; **være å- i** be the c- of.

+**å'rsaks/begre'p** *-et* concept of causation.

å'rsaks/forhold *-et* causal relationship, causality.

+**å'rsaks/sammenheng** *-en* causal relationship, causality.

å'rsaks/setning *+-en/*-a, pl *-ar* 1 *philos.* law of causation. 2 *gram.* causal clause.

å'rs/balanse [/balang'se] *-n merc.* annual balance sheet.

+**å'rs/beret'ning** *-en* annual report.

å'rs/dag *-en* anniversary (date).

+**å'rsens** *po of* **år**[1]

å'rs/fest *-en* annual celebration.

å'rs/gammal *A -t, pl -gamle* (=+**/gammel**) one year old.

å'rs/inntekt *-a/+-en* yearly, year's income.

å'rs/klasse *-a/-en* 1 class (of a certain year). 2 generation; age group, people of the same age.

å'rs/kull *-et* (of students etc.) class, year.

å'rs/lønn *-a/+-en* (=***/løn**) annual salary, year's wages.

å'rs/melding *-a/+-en* annual report.

***å'rs/mot** *-et* anniversary date.

å'rs/møte *-t, pl +-r/*-* annual meeting.

+**å'rs/oppgjør** *-et* (=***/oppgjer**) annual account, settlement (of debts, pay, etc.).

å'rs/oversikt [/åver-] *+-en/*-a* annual survey, summary of the year's activities.

+**å'rs/penger** *pl* (=***-ar**) annual subscription; annual appropriation.

+**å'rs/regnskap** [/rein-] *-et* (=***/rekneskap**) year's accounts; account books, records for the year.

å'rs/skifte *-t* turn of the year; **ved å-t** at New Year's.

å'rs/skrift *-et/*-a* annual; yearly publication.

å'rs/tal *-et* (=+**/tall**) date (of the year), year: **hvilket å-** what year; **lære å-** learn dates.

å'rs/tid *-a/+-en* season (of the year): **på denne å-** at this time of year; **de fire å-er** the four s-s.

å'r/støtt *Av* annually, yearly; occurring every year.

å'rs/vekst *-en* crops, harvest.

***å'rs/vokster** *-en* cf **/vekst**

***å'rs/von** *-a* harvest prospects.

+**å'r/tier** *pl* decades.

+**årtu'sen** *-et, pl -er* millenium, thousand years.

å'r/vak *A* vigilant, watchful, wide-awake.

å'r/veg *-en* (=+**/vei**) crops, harvest.

å'r/viss *A* annual, yearly; certain, regular.

+**å'r/våken** *A -ent, pl -ne* alert; vigilant, watchful, wide-awake.

+**å'rvåken/het** *-en* alertness, vigilance, watchfulness.

å's[1] *-en* 1 (long, narrow) hill, ridge. 2 *geol.* esker.

å's[2] *-en, pl æser myth.* Old Norse god.

å's[3] *-en* 1 beam, roof beam. 2 axle. 3 plow beam. 4 upright from runner to bed of sleigh.

Å's *Pln* twp, Akershus.

å'sa/lære *-a/+-en* (Norse) mythology.

Å'sane *Pln* twp, Hordaland.

Å'sa-Tor *Prn myth.* (name of) Thor, the thunder god.

å's/drag *-et* (stretch of) ridge.

Å'se *Prn(f)*

Å'sen *Pln* twp, Nord-Trøndelag.

Å'seral *Pln* twp, Vest-Agder.

å'/sete *-t* dwelling place, estate, property.

å'setes/rett *-en jur.* immediate heir's right to retain possession of paternal farm, upon payment of a reasonable price; primogeniture.

Å's/ga'rd *Pln myth.* dwelling place of the gods.

+**å'sgårds/rei** *-en* cf **osko/**

Å'sgård/strand *Pln* village, Vestfold

***å'/sikt** *-a* intent, purpose, view.

å's/kam' *-men* crest of a ridge.

***å'/skode** [/skåe] *V -a* perceive, regard.

***å'/skodeleg** [/skåeleg] *A* - clear, lucid; graphic.

***å'/skoding** [/skåing] *-a* opinion, view.

***å's/leies** *Av* by the ridge (or mountain) route.

å's/mark *-a* hilly terrain.

Å's/mund *Prn(m)*

Å's/nes *Pln* twp, Hedmark.

å's/rygg *-en, pl *-er* crest, ridge of a hill.

+**ås'sen** *Av* cf **hvordan, hvorledes**

Å's/ska'rd *Pln* twp, Møre og Romsdal.

Ås'ta [also ås'-] *Prn(f)*

***å'/stad** *-en* cf **/sted**

***å'stad/gang** *-en jur.* inspection, visit to the locus, scene (of the crime, etc.).

***å'stad/sak** *-a* case involving local inquest.

+**å'/sted** *-et lit., jur.* locus; place in question, scene (of the crime), spot.

+**å'steds/befa'ring** *-a/-en jur.* inspection, visit to the locus, scene (of the crime etc.).

å'/syn *-et/*-a archaic* 1 countenance, face: **Herren løfte sitt å- på deg** the Lord lift up his c- on thee. 2 sight: **bort fra mitt å-** out of my s-.

å'synje *-a/+-en myth.* goddess.

***å'/synleg** *A* - clear, lucid; graphic.

å'/sæte *-t* cf **/sete**

å't[1] *-et* 1 bait (for predatory animals); brit, plankton (for fish, whales etc.). 2 carcass, carrion. 3 *dial.* chewing, eating. 4 *dial.* biting, stinging insects; beggars, parasites. 5 *dial.* dirt, sand (for melting snow).

***å't**[2] *P* 1 at, to; for: **flire åt ein** giggle at sby; **gi rom åt'n du Ola** you make room for him, O- (Østgaard). 2 over to, towards, up to: **setje stolen åt bordet** set the chair up to the table. 3 (other idioms): **gå åt ein** be wrong with one, come over one; **komme åt ein** get in a blow at sby; **være åt ein** ask sby, go to sby (**om** for); be after sby (**om** to). 4 *(adv.)*: **bere seg åt** act, behave; **bere åt** go wrong, go to hell; **gjere åt** cure, heal by magic; practice magic, witchcraft; **gå åt** die; **hjelpast åt** help one another.

åt- *Pf* cf **at-, ad-**

å'/tak *-et dial.* 1 attack: **gå til å-** charge. 2 case, attack (of sickness). 3 effort, exertion.

***å'/takar** *-en* assailant, attacker.

***å'/take** *V infl as* **take**: **å- seg** exert oneself, make a great effort.

***å'taks/hær** *-en* attacking (offensive) forces.

+ Bokmål; * Nynorsk; ° Dialect.
After letter: ' stress (Acc. 1); ' tone, stress (Acc. 2); · length.
Below letter: . not pronounced.

***å'/tale** *-n* **(=*/tal)** blame, censure, complaint.

***å't/bu'rḍ** *-en* method, procedure.

å'te *-a* cf **åt**[1]

å't/ferd [/fær] *-a* **(=+at/)** behavior.

åtferds/mønster [å'tfærs/] *-mønstret* **(=+at-)** *psych.* behavior pattern.

***å't/finning** *-a* blame, censure, criticism.

***å'tfinn/sam** *A* overly critical.

***å't/gang** *-en* 1 access, admittance. 2 opportunity.

***å't/gaum** *-en* attention, attentiveness.

å't/gjerd [/jær] *-a* 1 measures, step; arrangement, preparation: **treffe å-er** take steps. 2 *folk.* magic formula, remedy. 3 mending, repair.

***å't/gjersle** *-a* 1 mending, repair. 2 healing by magic, sorcery. 3 means, way to put sth in order; magic means by which to cure, heal.

***å't/gå** *V -dde* notice, observe.

***å't/halden** *A -e/-i, pl -ne* close, parsimonious; strict.

***å't/hug** *-en* attention; reflection.

***å't/huge** *V -a* give attention to, notice.

***å't/kome** *-a* 1 access. 2 claim, right, title.

***å't/løye** *-t* 1 laughter. 2 sth funny, sth to laugh at.

***å't/nøye** *V -nøgde, -nøgd/-nøgt* satisfy.

***å't/renne** *-t* noose, slip knot.

***å't/ror** *-en* access by boat.

åt'sel *-elet, pl +-ler/*-el* carcass, carrion.

+åt'sel/eter *-en, pl -e* **(=*-ar)** carrion-eater.

***å't/skild** *A -skilt* apart, distinct, separate.

***å't/skiljing** *-a* parting, separation (**frå** from): **til å- frå** in contrast to.

+åt'sler *pl of* **åtsel**

***å't/søken** *A -e/-i, pl -ne* demanding, importunate, insistent.

***å't/sø'knaḍ** *-en* 1 attack. 2 demand, request.

åtť *pp of* **eie**[2]

åt'te[1] *pt of* **eie**[2]

åt'te[2] *Num* eight: **om å- dager** in a week.

åt'te/dags *A -* eight-day; (a) week's.

åt'te/del *-en* eighth (part): **å-s note** *mus.* e- note; **å-s pause** e- rest.

åt'te/kanta *A -* **(=+-et)** octagonal.

åt'tenḍe *Num* eighth: **hver å- dag** once a week.

åt'tenḍe/del *-en* cf **åtte/**

+åt'ter *-en, pl -e* **(=*-ar)** 1 figure 8. 2 (an) 8 (in a suit). 3 eight-oared boat (with eight rowers).

åt'te/tal *-et* **(=+/tall)** figure 8.

åt'ti *Num* eighty.

åt'ti/del *-en* eightieth (part).

åt'tienḍe *Num* eightieth.

åt'ting *-en* **(=*åttung)** 1 keg containing ab. 4 gallons (1/8 barrel). 2 *hist.* area making up 1/8 of a *fylke.*

åt'ti/åra *pl df* **(=+-ene)** the eighties.

åt'ti/åring *-en* octogenarian.

åt'tring *-en* boat with 4 pairs of oars; esp. in Nordland, an old type of boat with five pairs of oars, or with four and space for cargo in the middle.

***åt'tung** *-en* cf **åtting**

åtť/æring *-en* cf **åttring**

å't/vare *V -a/+-te* **(=+ad/)** warn.

å't/varing *-a* warning; notice.

***å't/vik** *-et* help.

+å'/vekst *-en archaic* 1 growth. 2 production, yield, profit.

å'/velte *-a dial.*: **i å-** helter skelter.

å'/verk *-et* 1 *jur.* harm (to property). 2 *dial.* difficult achievement, work. 3 *dial.* prodigy, rare phenomenon.

***å'/verke**[1] *-t* cf **/virke**

***å'/verke**[2] *V -a* cf **/virke**[2]

å'/virke[1] *-t* logging, tree cutting.

+å'/virke[2] *V -a/-et* cut (trees), log.

***å'/vokster** *-en, pl -rar* cf **/vekst**

ADDITIONS AND CORRECTIONS

Entries in parentheses refer to the main body of the Dictionary, as does the abbreviation "cf," unless the words "above" or "below" are added.

°a[4] *Av* **(=da**[1] **2): morn a, morna** goodbye.

(age[1]**)**: 1 awe. 2: where there is no discipline *replaces* where there is no order.

(akkord 3): greie akkorden meet the quota; fulfill the contract.

akkor'd/forhan'dling *-a/+-en jur.* negotiations with creditor(s) (to avoid lawsuit or get postponement of payments).

***ak'sje/husvære** *-t* = **+/leilighet**

+ak'sje/innby'delse *-n* announcement of stock issue.

(+akterut/seile): outdistance.

al'ḍring *-a/+-en* ageing (of people), growing old.

algorit'me *-n math.* algorithm.

+all'menn/fa'rlig *A -* **(=*-leg)** dangerous to the public (esp. of crimes, e.g. arson, sabotage).

***an'dre/grads-** cf **annengrads-**

antikva'r/handel *-en* second-hand trade, trade in antiques.

+arbei'ḍer/vern [/væ'rn] *-et* **(=*-ar/)** *jur.* safety regulations (at work sites).

+ar'beiḍs/leder *-en* **(=*/leiar)** foreman, supervisor.

(arbeids/lyst): jeg har ingen a- I have no ambition.

(arbeids/måte): working method(s).

(arbeids/nemnd): arbeids- og tiltaksnemnd employment council (appointed for each county, to stimulate employment opportunities).

+ar'beids/tilla'telse *-n* **(=*/løyve)** work permit.

artiums/oppgave *-n* = **/stil**

ar've/a'vgift *-a/+-en* inheritance tax.

ar've/merke *-t jur.* hereditary feature (e.g. in paternity cases).

att'/føring *-a/+-en* rehabilitation.

att'førings/hjelp *-a/+-en* rehabilitation aid.

***at'tåt/arbeiḍ** *-et* extra work (as source of income).

a'vbeta'lings/kjøp *-et* instalment buying.

avde'lings/sjef *-en* floor manager (of department store); section head.

(*av/døyvd): muted.

a'v/trappe *V -a/+-et* de-escalate, reduce by steps.

+bagatell'/salg *-et* **(=*-sal)** sale (esp. from kiosk) of small articles (e.g. postcards, stamps, souvenirs).

(+baker): for smed å rette b- *replaces* **rette b- for smed.**

+ba'k/streversk *A* **(=*-arsk)** reactionary.

(ball[1]**): b- i hatt** (game).

(ballast: han mangler b-): he lacks experience (background).

(ballong): 2 (large) flask (for wine or acids).

(bane[3]**): b- seg vei** force one's way, make one's way.

bank[4] *-en* crossbeam (on timber sledge or trailer).

+ban'k/innskudd *-et* **(=*/innskot(t))** bank deposit.

ban'k/inspeksjo'n *-en* banking commission.

(+bark[2]**)**: 2 *med.* cortex **(hjerne-, nyre-).**

basunis't *-en* trombone player, trombonist.

(be 1): be seg fri for ask to be excused from.

(+be/arbeiḍe 2): revise.

(bedøve 2): drug.

+bekjen't/gjørelse *-n* announcement.

+belas'tnings/sykdom *-men* debilitating illness (esp. due to physical or mental stress).

(+benåde): reprieve: **b-et** favored, graced.

(berg/frue): pyramidal saxifrage.

+beskyt'telses/likhet *-en biol.* mimicry.

(+bestemmelse): 3 provision, regulation.

bestre'belse *-n* effort, endeavor.

besø'ks/rett *-en jur.* visiting rights (e.g. of divorced person, to visit children).

(+betenkelig): 4 doubtful, dubious.

(+betenkelig/het): qualms.

bevi's/oppta'k *-et jur.* collection of evidence.

(+bilde 1): komme inn i b-t enter into the picture, be(come) relevant.

+bil'led/skjerm *-en* **(=*bilet/)** TV screen.

bil'lig/bok *-a* **(=*billeg/)** paperback.

bi'l/rute[1] *-a/+-en* car window, windshield.

bi'l/rute[2] *-a/+-en* (bus, truck) route, schedule.

(bil/veg): road passable by motor cars.

(binde 1: b- en en skrøne på ermet): put one over on sby *replaces* lie to sby.

bi'nyre/bark *-en* adrenal cortex.

bis'pedømme/råd *-et* diocesan council (of bishop, one minister, three laymen, to promote church activity).

(bite[3] **1: b- en av)**: cut (sby) short, silence *replaces* silence, interrupt sby.

(blank 4): zero: **førtien b-** 41.0, forty-one even.

(bli[1] **1): b- gående og (gruble)** go around (brooding), also with the verbs **liggende, sittende, stående.**

(*bok/heim): world of letters.

+bo'lig/byggelag *-et* housing cooperative.

+bo'lig/formid'ling *-en* housing council, housing authority.

+bo'lig/sektor *-en* area (field) of housing.

bonde/praktika *en* farmer's almanac.

+bor'ger/væpning [/ve·pning] *-en* **(=*-ar)** militia.

(botn 1): det er ingen b- i ham he has an unlimited appetite.

brann'/byll *-en* carbuncle.

brann'/syn *-et* fire inspection.
brann'/takst *-en* assessment of fire insurance.
bren'nevins/a'vgift *-a/+-en* liquor tax.
(brusk): gristle.
(+brynde): lust, desire *replaces* sexual desire.
(+brytning): 5 (optical) refraction.
bu'rs/dag *-en pop.* birthday (cf **geburtsdag).**
(bygg/herre): proprietor (of a house under construction) *replaces* builder (=owner of home).
(bygnings/ingeniør): construction (structural) engineer.
(bølgje/slag): lapping of waves; groundswell *replaces* wash of waves.
+bø'rn *pl obs. of* barn.
(+daddel/løs): irreproachable.
+da'gbrudds/drift *-a/+-en* open mining, strip mining.
+da'glig/vare *-a/-en* **(=*dagleg/)** household article.
damm'/brett *-et* checkerboard.
(daske 3: d- med): sleep with *replaces* flirt with.
da'ta/behan'dling *-a/+-en* (electronic) data processing.
da'ta/maski'n *-en* computer.
(dels): in part, some.
(+den/gang 2: "d- ei" sa Tordenskjold): you failed *replaces* I caught you.
(diplom/ingeniør): College of Engineering [Technical University] *replaces* Norwegian Technical College.
(doning^1): 3 timber sledge.
(+dra 3): d- på dør rush out; leave (exit) in a hurry.
(drag): 9 *fam.* **ha d- på (jentene)** have a way with (the girls).
(dragning 2): yearning.
drif'ts/fond *-et* operating funds.
drif'ts/kreditt' *-en* credit for operation (of an enterprise).
dri'v/stoff *-et* fuel.
(dryg 5): drøye 50 meter all of . . ., well over . . . **(han hoppet . . .).**
du'gnads/arbeid *-et* labor service (e.g. of soldiers assigned to help harvest).
(dusin): tretten *replaces* **tolv.**
dy're/park *-en* animal park, (small) zoo.
død's/lysing *-a/+-en* **(=/melding)** death notice, obituary.
+død's/å'rsak *-en* cause of death.
(dør): sette (dra) på d- *replaces* **sette på d-.**
EDB =elektronisk databehandling (cf **databehandling,** above).
(ei: "den gang ei," sa Tordenskjold): failed *replaces* didn't succeed.
ei'dsvolls/mann *-en, pl -menn/*-menner* member of constitutional convention at Eidsvoll (1814).
***ei'n/lye** *-dde* listen intently.
ek'teskaps/lysing-*a/+-en* **(=+-ning)** notice of marriage (in *Norsk Lysingsblad*).
+em'bets/forse'else *-n* misdemeanor by public official.
(ende^1 4: gjøre e- på): finish off *replaces* (also = destroy, kill).
(+engang 2): finally: **jeg ble da e- ferdig** I f- got through.
(epigon): derivative (artist, thinker).
(+erkjennelse 2: komme til e- (av)): gain insight in(to).
et'ter/byrd *-en* afterbirth, placenta.
et'ter/forsking *-a/+-en* **(=+-ning)** criminal investigation.
et'ter/utdanning *-a/-en* adult education, refresher course.
fabrikk'/tilsyn *-et* (office of) safety inspection (for factories).
+fa'g/lærer *-en, pl -e* **(=*-ar)** *educ.* special teacher (for a particular subject).
fa'gning *-a* delight, joy, pleasure; cordial welcome.
fa'g/prøve *-a/+-en* apprenticeship examination (for skilled workers and craftsmen).
(falle 5): f- sammen med be identical with.
+fami'lie/forhold *pl.* family circumstances.
fang'st/felt *-et* fishing (sealing) grounds.
(fat 1): forlange ens hode på et f- call for sby's scalp (cf Matt. 14,8).
***fat'tast** *V -ast* cf **fattes,** below.
+fat'tes *V -edes, -es* **(=*fattast)** be lacking: **ett f- deg** *bibl.* one thing thou lackest (Mark 10,21).
+fav'n(e)/ved *-en* cf **famn/**
fei'l/vurde'ring *-a/-en* error in judgment.
+fel'les/marked *-et* **(=*/marknad** *-en*) common market: **Det (*Den) europeiske f-** the European C- M-.
fel'les/reise *-n* excursion, group travel.
feng'slig *A* -: **ta i f- forvaring** commit to prison.
feng'sling *-a/+-en* imprisonment.
Fen're *Prn(m) myth.* Fenrir (also called **Fenresulven;** a monster wolf in Norse myths).
fer'dsels/rett-*en jur.* right of access.
+fer'skvanns/fisk *-en* **(*-vass/)** freshwater fish.
(+fiendtlig): inimical.
fi'n/høvle *V -a/+-et* plane, smooth.
fiskeri'/grense *-a/+-en* (off-shore) fishing limits.
fit'te *-a pop.* cunt, pussy (female sex organs).
+fjell'/vant *A* - **(=*van^3, *vand^2)** used to (traveling in) the mountains.
fjer'n/melding *-a/+-en* telecommunication.
+fjer'n/valg *-et* **(=*/val)** long-distance dialing.
(flukt): *fig.* loftiness, sublimity.
+fly'/angre'p *-et* air raid.
(flyge/blad): broadside.
+fly'/mekler *-en* **(=*-ar)** air freight broker.
+fogderi' *-et* bailiff's district, bailiwick.
+fol'de/dør *-a* **(*falde/)** accordion door, folding door.
fol'ke/bo'ksamling *-a/+-en* public library.
fol'ke/mord *-et* genocide.
fol'keretts/stridig *A* - contrary to, violating international law.
fol'ke/tannrøkt *-a/+-en* **(=+/tannpleie)** socialized dental care.
+fon'ds/mekler *-en, pl -e* **(=*-ar)** investment broker.
(+forargelse): i f-ns tegn a cause of offense.
forde'ler *-en, pl -e elec.* distributor; collector.
(+foregangs/mann): leader.
(+fore/teelse): occurrence *replaces* p- (Boo).
+forfat'ter/rett *-en* **(=*-ar/)** copyright; copyright law.
(+forgudelse): adulation.
+forgyl'ler *-en* **(=*-ar)** gilder.
+for'hånds/stemme *-n* absentee ballot.
+for'hånds/stemme *V -te* cast an absentee ballot, vote in absentia.
+for'hånds/trekk *-et* withholding tax.
for'/knappet *A* - buttoned in front.
forleg'ning *-en* (military) camp.
for'liks/mann *-en jur.* arbitrator, mediator.
for'liks/mekling *-a/+-en jur.* arbitration, mediation.
for'må'ls/løs *A* - aimless, purposeless.
for'n/minne *-t* antiquity, historical relic (find, site).
fornor'sking *-a/+-en* Norwegianization.
for'nyrdis/lag *-et* an Old Norse meter ("Old-Lore Meter").
(+forplantnings/lære): sex education *replaces* genetics.
forret'nings/bank *-en* commercial bank, merchants bank.
forsik'rings/teknisk *A* - actuarial, (pertaining to) insurance.
(+forskrudd): crazy, mad, twisted.
for'sorgs/vesen *-et* (poor) relief administration.
+for'svars/gren *-en* (branch of) the armed service(s), the military.
for'svars/messig *A* - (pertaining to) defense.
forsy'nings/nemnd *-a* rationing board.
***forsy'tar** *-en* breadwinner, provider, support.
For'søks/rådet *df educ.* Council for Experimental Programs.
(+forut/setning): 1 presupposition. **3** *pl* background.
+for'ut/tinging *-a/-en* advance booking, advance order.
fos'ter/ba'rn [fos'ter/] *-et* foster child.
(fot 2): vinne fast f- gain a firm foothold (footing, foundation).
fo't/tøy *-et* footwear.
(fred/lyse: et f-t sted): a hallowed (inviolate, sacred) spot *replaces* a hallowed spot.
+frem'med/lov *-a/-en* alien law.
fri'/brev *-et* passport; privilege.
+fri'/gjører *-en, pl -e* emancipator, liberator.
+fri'/havn *-a/-en* cf **frihamn**
+fri'hets/berø'velse *-n jur.* deprivation of freedom, imprisonment.
fri'/lager *-et* restricted area where goods may be held without custom duties.
fri'lufts/nemnd *-a* recreation council.
+fris'k/het *-en* freshness.
fri'/språkig *A* - outspoken.
fron't/linje *-a/-en* front (line).
+fullbyr'delse (also **full'/**) *-n* completion, execution (e.g. of a sentence); consummation.
funksjo'ns/hemmet *A* - handicapped.
fyl'kes/kommu'ne *-n jur.* county as administrative unit.
fø'de/varer *pl* (articles of) food, foodstuffs, victuals.
fød'sels/begren'sning *-en* birth control.
(føre^2): 1 pilot (a plane); navigate, steer (a ship): **f-e en i ulykke** get sby into trouble; **f- i pennen** compose, put on paper. **6: f- i seg** ingest, take in.
ga' *pt of* **gi, gje** (unofficial form).
(galei): på g-en on a binge, on the loose.
(gammal 1): de gamle (*also*) the ancients.
gang'/felt *-et* pedestrian crossing.
ga'p/skratt *-en* guffaw.

+ Bokmål; * Nynorsk; ° Dialect.
After letter: ' stress (Acc. 1); ` tone, stress (Acc. 2); ' length.
Below letter: . not pronounced.

(gard/vord): guardian spirit.
gass'/bluss *-et* gas jet, gas light.
+gav'n *-et* cf **gagn**
+gav'nlig *A* - cf **gagnlig**
(general/forsamling 2): annual *replaces* board.
gi'v *-en* deal (in cards): **en ny g- i boligsaken** a new initiative in the housing problem.
+gjen'/finne *V -fant -funnet* find again, recover, retrieve.
+gjen'/finning *-en* recovery, retrieval.
+gjen`nom/gåelse *-n* scrutiny, survey.
gjen`nom/isnet *A* - chilled, frozen.
(gjennom/trekk): 2 movement, turnover: **det er stor g- av folk i firmaet** there is a rapid t- of employees in that firm.
(gjerning): *pl* ***-ar 1** (life)work.
gjo'rde^{3} *-t* cf **gjo'rd^{1}**
(gjø^{3}): fertilize, manure.
gla'ning *-en* (*pop.*) mug, kisser: **gi 'n en midt i g-en** paste 'im one on the kisser.
(glans/tid): golden age.
+glass'/perle *-n* glass bead.
***glo'/hug** *-en* ardor, enthusiasm, zeal.
(+gnist): 4 "Sparks," radio operator (on ship).
(god 1): g-e tider prosperity.
gra'ds/adver·b *-et* adverb of degree.
gratisteri' *-et* (attitude of) expecting handouts, (*pop.*) freeloading, mooching.
***gren`da/hus** *-et* (= ***grende/**) community center.
gren`se/gang *-en* (= **/oppgang**) surveying of boundaries; delimitation.
+gress'/gang *-en* meadow, pasture.
(grev^{1} 1): pick.
(grunn^{1} 2: gå til g-e): perish, go to pot *replaces* go to rack and ruin.
grun`ne^{5} *V -a/+-et* ground (paint).
grunn'/takst *-en* basic rate (e.g. for telephone).
grøn'lands/sel *-en* harp seal (Phoca groenlandica).
grøn't/anlegg *-et* (small) planted area (in town).
gu'l/aktig *A* - yellowish.
gu'l/brun *A* yellow-brown.
gyl'len/tal *-et* (= **+/tall**) golden number.
Gymna's/rådet *Prn* the Council on Gymnasiums.
(gå^{1} 1): gå og (with another verb) be doing (sth), cf **ligge 6, sitte 5, stå 8.**
gå'/gate *-a* pedestrian street.
+hai`ker *-en, pl -e* (= ***-ar**) hitchhiker.
hallusinato'risk *A* - hallucinatory.
hal's/beten·nelse *-n* throat infection.
(hammar 5): cliff.
(ham/skifte): metamorphosis, transformation, transmutation.
han'dels/mora·l *-en* business ethics.
han'dels/næring *-a/+-en* business, commerce, trade.
***hand'/laus** *A* helpless, inert.
ha`ne/bein *-et* (= **+/ben**) rooster's leg: **gjøre h- til en** *hum.* (of man) court sby, make up to sby, seek sby's favors.
ha`ne/kam *-men* cock's comb.
(harselas): ridicule, sarcasm *replaces* teasing; **(drive h- med en)** ridicule sby *replaces* tease sby.
hasj'(isj) *-en* hash(ish), marijuana, pot.
hau`g/bue *-n* = **haugebonde**
hav`ne/vesen *-et* port authority.
+he'ders/tegn *-et* decoration, medal, order.
hei`me/bakeri· *-et* (= **+hjemme/**) home bakery (specializing in "home-made" goods).
hei`me/yrke *-t* home industry (arts and crafts).
(+hekke/løp): hurdle race *replaces* hurdles (race).
+hel'breds/hensyn *-et* reasons of health: **trekke seg tilbake av h-** retire for r-.
(helle/ristning): petroglyph.
hel'se/messig *A* - (pertaining to) health: **av h-e grunner** for reasons of health.
hel'se/sport *-en* health-building sports (e.g. for handicapped persons).
hel'se/vern [/væ·rn] *-et* health care: **psykisk h-** psychiatric treatment.
(helst 1): mostly, usually.
(+henge^{3} 1): h- ut hold up to scorn.
+hen'/rive *V -rev, -revet* carry away, charm, enchant.
(+hen/sovet): departed.
+her'/i *Av* herein, in this.
+her'/på *Av* hereupon, on this.
her'/under *Av* under this; included in this.
(heste/blomst): coltsfoot (Tussilago farfara).
***hev^{4}** *pr of* **ha^{1}** (older form).
hjel`pe/korps *-et* aid corps, emergency service.
hjer`te/god *A* kindhearted.
H-mjølk *-a* (= **+-melk**) homogenized milk.
hob'by/forret·ning *-a/+-en* hobby shop.
(+holde^{2} 4): h- (en knapp) på bet (a small sum) on; **h- sammen** stick together; **h- ut** bear up, endure.
hornis't *-en* horn player.
+ho'ved/forhan·dling *-en* main bargaining session (on wage agreements).
+ho'ved/strøm *-men* mainstream.
ho'ved/verk *-et* chief work, masterpiece.
hu'd/sår *A* sensitive, thin-skinned.
***hu'g/skremt** *A* - frightened, terrified, terror-stricken.
hun`dreårs/skifte *-t* turn of the century.
hun'/dyr *-et* cf **hunn/**
hu's/tukt *-en* home discipline; parental authority.
hæ'r/rop *-et* battle cry, war cry.
hæ'r/tokt *-et* *lit.* foray, raid.
hø'g/tysk *-en* High German.
(+høk): h- og due tag (game).
hø`re/appara·t *-et* hearing aid.
høs't/fag *-et* trade (profession) negotiating wage agreements in autumn (cf **vårfag**, below).
+høy'/tysk *-en* cf **høg/**, above.
hån`dverks/brev *-et* diploma, certificate of proficiency (in craft or trade).
(i^{2} 6): henge i en tråd hang by a thread.
idio't/sikker *A* foolproof.
+ik`ke- *Pf* non-.
+il'ds/fare *-n* (= **elds/**) danger of fire, fire hazard.
(ille 2): i- ute in a bad way, injured.
informasjo'ns/retable·ring *-a/+-en* information retrieval.
(+inn/bitt): determined, irrepressible *replaces* repressed, stifled (anger).
inn'/kjøring *-a/+-en* (= ***/køyring**) testing, test run, trial run.
inn'/snø·rt *A* - laced in, tightlaced; constricted, hidebound, narrow.
inn`tekts/skatt *-en* income tax.
(ja^{2} 1): ja da yes indeed; all right.
(jenke): j- sammen fit together; adjust.
(jorde^{1}): på j-t *pop.* off base, mistaken.
jung'el/telegra·fen *slang* the grapevine.
kaf'fe/rast *-en* coffee break.
kam'p/glede *-n* fighting spirit.
kanselli'/råd *-en* *obs.* counsellor.
kas`te/maskin [-masji·n] *-en* catapult.
(kjenne/merke): criterion, feature.
kjer`ne/full *A* hearty, pithy, vigorous.
klang'/laus *A* (= **+/løs**) dull, toneless; lifeless, monotonous.
(kleiv^{1}): *pl* ***-ar**
(klirre): tinkle.
(klore^{1}): k- seg fast dig in, cling.
knul`le *V -a/+-et* *pop.* fuck, have intercourse with.
+kong`e/tro *A* - (= ***/tru**) loyal to the king; royalist.
kontak't/flate *-n* contact surface, interface.
kor't/tids- *Pf* short time (e.g. **-parkering** parking).
kraf't/forsy·ning *-a/+-en* power supply.
+kras'ser *-en, pl -e* scraper, (pipe bowl) cleaner.
kremasjo'ns/byrå· *-et* funeral parlor (for cremations).
+krig's/forbry·telse *-n* war crime.
+krig's/forbry·ter *-en, pl -e* war criminal.
kritikk'/løs (***/laus**) *A* uncritical.
kro'n/vitne *-t* *jur.* state's evidence.
ku'k *-en* *pop.* cock (male member).
+kun'st/dyrker *-en, pl -e* (= ***-ar**) art lover, connoisseur.
ku`se *-n* *pop.* cunt, pussy (female sex organs).
(kvinne/sak): women's rights.
kø'/nummer [/nommer] *-et* queue number, serial number (in store, waiting room, etc.).
kå'l/rulett· *-en* stuffed cabbage leaf.
(lag^{2}): 1 (on tires) ply. **8: midt i l-et** average, medium, middling.
(land^{1} 1): komme i l- med pull off, carry through.
lan'dbruks/høgskole *-n* college of agriculture.
lan'd/måling *-a/-en* surveying.
(leve^{2}): l- seg inn i familiarize oneself with; enter into the spirit of.
(leve/måte 1): livelihood; life style *replaces* mode of living.
li`ke/verdig *A* equal.
(likning): *3 parable, simile (= **+liknelse).**
***lit^{3}** *-en, pl -er* cf **lett^{1}**
liv's/krav *-et* crucial demand, vital need.
liv's/lede *-n* depression, spleen, tedium.
liv's/mot *-et* courage (to face life), spirit(s).
lo's/vesen *-et* pilot service.
+lov/bunden *A -et* regular.
lo'v/utkas·t *-et* *pol.* bill, proposed law.
luf'tpu·te/båt *-en* hovercraft.
lun`ne/drag *-et* haulage.
+ly's/tåke *-n* nebula; shimmer of light.
+læ`rer/råd *-et* (= ***-ar/**) teachers' council.
lønn's/nemnd *-a* labor mediation board, wage board.
lå`ne/konto·r *-et* pawnshop.
(malm): 6 ring, resonance.
mari`ne/olje *-a/-en* marine oil.
+mar'keds/undersø·kelse *-n* market poll.
(mar/svin): 2 porpoise (Phocaena phocaena).
(maskinist): engineer.
mas'se/medium *-mediet, pl -media*

mass medium.

mau'r/syre *-a* formic acid.

(⁺meinings/felle): fellow partisan, one who shares (one's) views.

mel'lom/fag *-et educ.* minor subject (for university degree), cf **grunn/, hoved/.**

me'nighets/fakulte·t *-et:* **M-et** a private divinity school (founded 1907 in opposition to the University of Oslo theological faculty; since 1913 entitled to confer degrees).

(⁺merke[2] 1): brand, imprint, put one's stamp on (sby, sth).

(⁺mester): 3 master, proprietor (of shop) (opp. of **svenn).**

mik'kels/bær *-et* type of blueberry (Vaccinium uliginosum).

miljø'/skadd *A -dd/*-dt* handicapped (harmed) by (early) environment.

miljø'/skapende *A* - : **m- faktorer** factors conducive to creating a given environment.

miljø'/vern *-et* protection of environment; ecology.

mje'le *-n* sandy soil.

moms *-en* (=**merverdiomsetningsavgift, merverdiavgift)** value-added tax.

(mor/eld): phosphorescence (esp. of plankton in sea).

mo'se/tak *-et* gathering of lichen (as fodder).

(⁺motor/drevet): power (e.g. mower).

(mottakelig): impressionable, receptive.

(myr/snipe): snipe (cf **snipe).**

mø'dre/heim *-en* (= ⁺**/hjem)** home for unmarried mothers.

mør'tel/verk *-et* plant for producing mortar.

⁺**må'neds/kort** *-et* commuter's ticket (valid for one month).

må'ne/sonde *-n* lunar space probe (spaceship).

(napp[2]): (ha) n- i en pokal (have) a leg on a trophy.

nasjona'l/produk·t *-et* national product.

(natt-og-dag): Viola *replaces* Vida.

⁺**natu'r/forekomst** *-en* natural deposit (of ore, gas etc.).

natu'r/foruren·sning *-a/⁺-en* pollution.

natu'r/skade *-n* damage from natural catastrophe.

(null[1] 2): n- i fattigkommisjonen nonentity.

⁺**ny'/tegning** *-en* new issue of shares.

nyt'te/last *-a/-en* payload.

næ'rings/fattig *A* - not nutritious, low in food value, poor (of food, soil, etc.).

(nærings/liv): economic life, economy.

nøt'te/skal *-et* (= ⁺**/skall)** nutshell: **det er saken i et n-** that's the whole thing in a n-.

***nå'men** *A* numb.

⁺**objek't/glass** *-et* (= ***/glas)** microscopic slide.

o'mega *et* omega: **alfa og o-** the beginning and the end; the basic principle; the indispensable person.

(⁺omfatte): 2 consider, regard **(med** with): **o- med interesse** take an interest in.

om's *-en* = **omsetningsvagift**

⁺**om'sirklings/hastighe·t** *-en* orbital velocity.

(⁺opp/gjør 1): accounting.

(⁺opp/mykning): 2 easing, softening up.

(⁺opprinnelig 2): primitive.

(opp/rop): 3 call to arms; manifesto, proclamation.

(⁺oppsetsig): disobedient, rebellious *replaces* stubborn.

(⁺oppsetsig/het): rebelliousness, recalcitrance *replaces* stubbornness.

(⁺opp/si 1): discharge.

(⁺opp/stille 2): construct (a theory).

opp'/tining *-a/⁺en* thawing out.

opp'/trappe *V -a/⁺et* escalate, increase by steps.

o'rd/tilfang· *-et* vocabulary (**i** of).

(⁺oven: o- i kjøpet): furthermore.

ovenikjøpet cf **oven**

over- [å'ver] *Pf* chief; super-; over-.

overlyds- *Pf* supersonic (e.g. **-fart, -fly).**

over/trykk *-et* 1 overprint, surcharge; transfer. 2 excess pressure; *phys.* positive pressure.

⁺**over/våking** *-en* surveillance (e.g. of potentially subversive activity).

⁺**o'vervå·kings/politi·** *-et* security police.

(paradis 2): hvor lenge var Adam i p-? How long could it last?

(parodisk): caricatured, parodical *replaces* ludicrous.

pasien't/venn *-en* hospital volunteer; Gray Lady.

paten't/band *-et* (= ⁺**/bånd)** steel band for packing crates.

ped'dig/rør *-et* (= ***/røyr)** reed or cane used in basket work.

(pendle): commute.

⁺**pen'dler** *-en, pl -e* commuter.

(penteri): (=pentry) *replaces* **(= pentri).**

(pepre): pepper, spray (with bullets).

(⁺pille[3] 1: p- med): pick at, tinker with.

pi'p *-en fam.* breath: **sette p-en til** choke; be completely exhausted; **ta p-en fra en** dumbfound, overwhelm sby.

pitt' *-en pop.* cock (male member).

(plan[2]): bed, floor (of truck).

plan'ke/kjøring *-a/⁺-en* (= ***/køyring) 1** *hist.* horse-drawn transport of lumber. **2** *fam.:* **det er p-** it's plain sailing, dead easy.

'**pla'n/lø·sning** *-en* (= ***/løysing)** planned solution.

plan'te/vern [/væ'rn] *-et* conservation activities (for protection of vegetation).

(plass 9): site.

(*plunder/sam): (of job) tricky, requiring skill and patience.

poeng'/jag *-et* (deplorable) struggle for grades (to secure admission to the university).

po'ker/sjanse [/sjangse] *-n:* **ta en p-** take a long shot.

politi'/ve·dtekt *-a/⁺-en* police regulation.

pos't/vesen *-et* postal service.

(prange): 1 scintillate, shine. 2 dazzle, be ostentatious *replaces* 1 *and* 2 *in text.*

(press *-et* **1):** crease (in trousers).

prestasjo'ns/lønn *-a/⁺-en* incentive wages.

(prinsipal[2]): p-t as first alternative.

propa'n *-en* propane (gas).

(proprietær): squire.

⁺**protokoll'/fører** *-en, pl -e* recorder, secretary.

prø've/forele·sning *-en* (academic) lecture given by candidate for degree of dr. phil. or a professorship.

pu'le *V -a/⁺-et pop.* fuck, have intercourse with.

(pågangs/mot): drive.

⁺**på'/gripelse** *-n* apprehension, arrest.

på'/hengt, *A* - added, hung on.

ra'dio/amatø·r *-en* amateur radio operator, ham.

(rakke[3]: r- ned på): abuse, run down, vilify *replaces* make derogatory remarks about, run down.

ras'te/plass *-en* picnic ground, roadside park.

red'nings/korps *-et* emergency service.

(regjering 1): administration.

(rekning 1): gjøre r- med count on.

ret'nings/givende *A* - guiding, giving guidance (directives).

ret'nings/nummer [-nom-] *-et* area code.

⁺**ret'tighets/tap** *-et* loss of civil rights.

***rikleg** *A* - cf **rikelig**

(rive[3] 8): r- bort snatch; buy up.

***rjupe** *-a* cf **rype**

***rom'/tenkt** *A* - broadminded, generous.

ron'ke *V -a/⁺et pop.* jack (jerk) off, masturbate.

rus'se/handel *-en* pre-World War I trade between Russian "peasant skippers" and North Norwegian fishermen (cf **pomor/).**

rus'se/norsk *-en* Russo-Norwegian pidgin used in the **russehandel.**

rus't/behan·dle *V -a/⁺-et* coat (car body) against corrosion.

(⁺røver: halvstudert r-): cf **halvstudert** *replaces* ignoramus.

(røy): 2 *slang* girl.

(rå[3] 2): command, dispose over, possess *replaces* predominate, prevail.

rå'/fisk *-en* unprocessed fish.

sa'ga/øya *df* the Saga Island, i.e. Iceland.

⁺**sa'ks/behan·dler** *-en, pl -e admin.* person who prepares incoming cases for treatment by superiors.

sal't/rett *-en* course consisting of cold meat cuts, sausages, etc.

sam'bands/satellitt· *-en* communications satellite.

(samfunns/kunnskap): civics.

(samfunns/lære): sociology.

sam'funns/rekning *-a educ.* applied (practical) arithmetic.

sam'le/perm *-en* portfolio.

sam'le/verk *-et* anthology, compilation.

('sammen/bitt): tight-lipped.

⁺**sammenlign/bar** *A* comparable; commensurable.

(⁺sam/vær): companionship.

san'd/bakkels *-en* = **sandkake 1**

san'd/blåse *V -te* sandblast.

(⁺sanitets/forening 1): society concerned with public health: **Norske kvinners s-** The Norwegian Women's Public Health Association *replaces* the Gray Ladies (. . . hospital).

(sans: ha s- for): have a flair for.

satellitt'/samband *-et* satellite communication.

sel'la *A,* **sel'lende** *Av* chock full, teeming (of fruit tree).

sel'skaps/serve·ring *-en* catering.

(⁺selvgod/het): smugness.

(⁺sette[1]): 1 s- alt inn på (noe) stake everything on (sth); do one's level best (to). **5 (s- seg inn i):** enter into.

+ Bokmål; * Nynorsk; ° Dialect.
After letter: ' stress (Acc. 1); ' tone, stress (Acc. 2); · length.
Below letter: . not pronounced.

si'de/hogg *-et* jab, poke, thrust.
sik'rings/mosjo·n *-en* therapeutic exercise.
(sissel/rot): a fern.
sivi'l/status *-en* marital status.
(sjuke/heim): nursing home.
***Sju'/stjerna** *df* cf **Syvstjernen,** below.
ska'de/virkning *-a/-en* harm, harmful effect, injury.
+skakende *A* - appalling, shocking.
+skif'te/forval·ter *-en, pl -e* administrator (of estates), probate judge.
(skitten/ferdig): uncleanly; dirty, filthy.
sko'le/skulk *-en* truancy.
(skor/fast 2): trapped.
(skorpe): scab (on a wound).
(skott³): *3 movement, progress: **det kom s- i arbeidet** the work began to pick up speed.
skra'p/handel *-en* junk shop.
skrubb'/sår *-et* abrasion, scratch, scraping.
skrø'n *-et* fib.
sku'rings/stripe *-a/+-en* glacial striation.
+skyss'/godtgjø·relse *-n* (= ***/godtgjersle**) refund for travel expenses.
(slag/ord): aphorism.
slam'me *V -a/+-et* prime (with a thin coating of mortar).
(slepp 1: gi- s- på): renounce.
+sli'ter *-en, pl -e* (= ***-ar**) (hard) worker, toiler; drudge, grind.
sli'tning *-a/+-en* struggle; tension.
(slå² 8): s- ut beat, defeat.
(+smeike): cajole, flatter.
små'/kupe·rt *A* - (slightly) hilly, rolling.
+sna'rere *Av* rather (cf **snart³ 4**).
(snau 3): s-e 50 meter a bare 50 meters.
snø'/søte *-n* type of gentian (Gentiana nivalis).
so'ne/tal *-et* (= **+/tall**) zone (exchange) number (in long-distance dialing).
(sosial): s-e utgifter welfare expenses (e.g. employer's share in pension fund).
sosia'l/arbei·der *-en, pl -e* (= ***-ar**) social worker.
sosiono'm *-en* social worker.
spal't/bar *A* fissionable.
(spalte¹): 4 groove.
spa'ning² *-a/+-en* (police) surveillance; cruising.
spesia'l/prepara·t *-et* proprietary drug (medicine).
spesia'l/skole *-n* school for handicapped or retarded children.
(spile¹): 3 picket (in fence).
(+spill¹ 3): slå s-et over ende throw up the game; break off (negotiations).
spo'n/plate *-a/+-en* pressed wallboard.
stikk'/flue *-n* biting fly, stable fly (Stomoxys calcitrans).
stilett'/hæl [/he'l] *-en* spike heel.
sto'r/magasi·n *-et* (big) department store, emporium.
stor'm/ta *V -tok, +-tatt/*-teke/*-i* captivate, overwhelm.
(stor/sinna): great-souled, high-minded *replaces* large-minded, liberal.
(stor/tenkt 2): great-minded *replaces* large-minded.
+straf'fe/fullbyr·delse *-n jur.* execution of sentence.
straf'fe/regis·ter *-et* **1** police blotter. **2** police record.
strid's/bror *-en, pl -brødre/*-brør* companion at arms; fellow fighter.
stry'ke/fri *A -tt* **1** (of garment) drip-dry, not to be ironed. **2** *educ.* without failing grade: **s- artium** (proposed) examination certificate showing only subject grades, without any overall pass or fail judgment.
+strøm'/deler *-en, pl -e* (= ***straum/delar**) *elec.* (current) distributor.
+stu'die/veile·der *-en* (***/vegleiar**) student adviser.
(+styrer): *4 (chief) editor (cf **blad/**).
styr't/hjelm *-en* crash helmet.
støt'te/blad *-et bot.* bract.
(støyt 1: gi s-et til noe): trigger.
(stå²): 10 ha mye å s- i have one's hands (more than) full; **s- inn** (or **innover**) (e.g. **mot land**) head in (for shore). **11 (s- seg (godt)):** be well preserved.
svar't/sladd *-en* censor's blot.
(sverme 2: s- for): be enthusiastic about; be fond of *replaces* be crazy about, be passionately fond of.
+svøm'me/tur *-en* swim.
+svøm'ning *-en* swimming.
(synde/register): roster (of one's sins).
+Sy'v/stjernen *df* the Pleiades.
sæ'r/drag *-et* characteristic (peculiar) feature (trait).
ta'le/pedagog [-gå·g] *-en* speech therapist.
+tal'te² *pt of* **telle²**
(tangere): t- rekorden equal (previous) record.
+tan'ke/kors (***/kross** *-en*) *-et* crux, enigma, mystery, puzzle.
+tan'ke/krets *-en* conceptual world.
ta're/vase *-n* sea tangle, sea wrack.
(tarm/slyng): intestinal obstruction.
+tegne/serie [tei'ne/] *-n* comic strip.
(tid¹ 1): før t-a before its time, premature(ly); **gode t-er** boom, prosperity; **med t-a** in time.
+ti'e/løfte *-t* pledge of (professional) secrecy.
+ti'e/plikt *-en* obligation of (professional) secrecy.
(til¹): 2 t- så lenge for a time, for the time being. **7: t- gagns** cf **gagn; t- sjøs** at sea.
tjom'mi *-en pop.* **1** chum, companion. **2** fellow, guy.
(+toll/frihet): tariff exemption.
(+tone/angivende): leading.
to'ne/føring *-a/+-en* modulation.
Tordenskjold: T-s soldater the same people reappearing in various public roles (based on a historical episode in Admiral T's career).
trafikk'/avvik·ling *-a/+-en* flow of traffic.
tre'nings/institutt· *-et* gymnastic institute, health center.
(tunge/tale): glossolalia.
(tupere): tease.
turis't/sjef *-en* head of tourist office.
tverr'- *Pf* cross-, inter- (e.g. **t-/faglig** interdisciplinary).
tve'/tulle *-n* hermaphrodite.
ty'pe/kasse **-n** typecase.
tys'klands/fange *-n* political prisoner from concentration camp in Germany (World War II).
(u/blid): 4 angry, displeased.
u'/formet *A* - unformed, unshaped.
u'/formid·let *A* - abrupt, unprepared, unintegrated.
ugri'pelig *A* - impalpable, intangible.
(+uimotsigelig): (= ***umotseieleg**)
***umotsei'eleg** cf **uimotsigelig**
Un'der/huset *n df* the House of Commons (cf **overhus**).
un'der/løpen *A pl -ne* bloodshot (cf **blod-**).
(+under/spist: være u-): *omit* (or drunk).
ung'doms/patrul·je *-n* youth patrol (for protection in special areas).
universite'ts/lektor *-en* university instructor (lecturer, assistant professor).
+u'/oversik·tlig *A* - impenetrable; with poor visibility; unclear.
+us'sel/het *-en* cf **/dom**
u't/brent *A* - (***/brend**) **1** burned out, extinguished; (of volcano) extinct. **2** *fig.* faded, pale.
u't/mål *-et* (land) claim, stake.
u't/nørding *-en* northwest wind.
(utskytings/rampe): launching (launch) pad (stand).
(ut/tynning): militær u- partial troop withdrawal.
(ut/veg 2: det kunne bli u- til kjole og motorsykkel): means could be found *replaces* it might be a way.
(ut/vekst 2): blemish.
***u/varande** cf **uforvarende**
vak't/sel·skap *-et* night watchman service.
van'/kle *-dde* fit (sby) badly; be unseemly (for sby).
(varg 2: v- i veum): outcast, pariah.
(vegg 1): se i femte v-en look into space, stare vacantly.
+vek't/tall *-et educ.* weight, weighting (assigned to subject when calculating final standing).
(velsigne 2): i v-ede omstendigheter pregnant.
veng'e/båt cf **vinge/**
***ver'ne/buing** *-a* military preparedness.
(verne/skole): vocational training school (for juvenile delinquents).
Ves'ter/heimen *Pln poet.* the United States (as a home of Norwegian immigrants).
Ves't/isen *Pln* the Jan Mayen section of the Greenland Sea.
Ves't-Tyskland *Pln* West Germany (the German Federal Republic).
ve'v/stue *-a* (= **/stove**) workshop for textiles.
+vil'let *A* - deliberate, intentional.
(vind¹): ha v- i seilene have a favoring wind, ride the wave, be successful.
ving'e/båt *-en* hydrofoil boat.
vog'ge/sang (**/vise**) *-en* lullaby.
+vok'sen² *en pl voksne* (= ***vaksen**) adult, (a) grown-up.
+vok'sen/opplæ·ring *-a/+-en* adult education.
(vørds/laus 1): ruthless.
vå'r/fag *-et* trade (profession) negotiating wage agreements in spring (cf **høstfag,** above).
yr'kes/retta *A* - (= **+-et**) *educ.* professionally oriented (as distinct from **allmenndannende**).
yr'kes/skade *-n* work accident.
æ're/skjenne *V* **-skjente** abuse, libel.
æ'res/krenkelse *-n* (= ***/krenking**) libel.
(+øgle): 2 *archeol.* saurian, brontosaurus, dinosaur. **3** *arch.* gargoyle.
øk'se/komité· *-en* budget-slashing committee (lit. "axe commitee").
øy'en/bryn *-et* cf **øye/**
(år³): med årene as the years pass, in time; **på år og dag** for ages, for a long time, in many a year.
å'rs/beste *N* (of athlete) record for the year: **hans å- på 500 meter var 41.0** his record for the year in the 500 meter race was 41.0.
å'rs/verk *-et* man-year.
(*åt² 2): of (possession): **son åt presten** the pastor's son.

TABLE OF ABBREVIATIONS

A	adjective
ab.	about
adj.	adjectival
admin.	administrative
adv.	adverbial
agr.	agricultural
anat.	anatomical
anthro.	anthropological
approx.	approximately
arch.	architectural
archeol.	archeological
Art	article
astron.	astronomical
Av	adverb
bibl.	biblical
biol.	biological
Bm	Bokmål
bot.	botanical
Brit.	British (English)
C	conjunction
carp.	carpentry
cf	see
chem.	chemical
comp.	comparative
conj.	conjunctional
cp	comparative
cpd.	compound
def.	definite
derog.	derogatory
df	definite
dial.	dialectal
dipl.	diplomatic
eccl.	ecclesiastical
econ.	economic
educ.	educational
elec.	electrical
eng.	engineering
esp.	especially
f	feminine
fam.	familiar
fem.	feminine
fig.	figurative
folk.	folklore
forest.	forestry
geog.	geographical
geol.	geological
gram.	grammatical
gymn.	gymnastics
hist.	historical
hort.	horticultural
hum.	humorous
I	interjection
if	indefinite
imp	imperative
indef.	indefinite
inf.	infinitive
ip	imperative
IPA	International Phonetic Alphabet
journ.	journalistic
jur.	legal
lit.	literally
lit.	literary
m	masculine
masc.	masculine
math.	mathematical
med.	medical
merc.	mercantile
meteor.	meteorological
mil.	military
mus.	musical
myth.	mythological
N	noun
naut.	nautical
neg.	negative
Nn	Nynorsk
nt	neuter
Num	numeral
ob	objective (case)
obs.	obsolete
odont.	odontological
ON	Old Norse (Norwegian)
opp.	opposite
P	preposition
p.	page
pers.	personal
Pf	prefix
pharm.	pharmacological
philos.	philosophical
photog.	photographic
phys.	physics
physiol.	physiological
pl	plural
Pln	place name
Pn	pronoun
po	possessive (case)
poet.	poetic
pol.	political
pop.	popular (folkelig)
(pop.)	slang (American)
pos	positive
poss.	possessive
pp	perfect participle
pr	present (tense)
prep.	preposition
Prn	proper name
pron.	pronoun
prp	present participle
psych.	psychological, psychiatric
pt	past, preterite
pv	passive
refl.	reflexive
sb	subjective (case)
sby	somebody
sg	singular
sp	superlative
SP	standard pronunciation
sth	something
sup.	superlative
tech.	technological
teleg.	telegraphy
theo.	theological
twp	township
typog.	typographical
usu.	usually
V	verb
vet.	veterinary
wk	weak
zool.	zoological

Note: for technical reasons some words are abbreviated differently in the italicized grammatical identifications after the entry than they are in the rest of the text.